Today's Greatest Poems

John Campbell, Editor & Publisher

JULIE JOY
Art Director

Edited by Eddie-Lou Cole

Foreword

The Story Of the World Of Poetry

It's a wonderful thing to be part of the World of Poetry. I can remember when the first issue of our newsletter came whirring off the press, way back in August of 1975. We were so proud—and so excited! Our *entire* staff consisted of two poets: Yours Truly, Eddie-Lou Cole, Poetry Editor, and of course, John Campbell, Editor & Publisher. John had asked me to come aboard a few months earlier, to give him a hand with "a new poetry publication I have in mind."

Little did I know the publication he had in mind would grow, in a few short years, from one of "little magazine" status, to literally one of international prominence and prestige. In my years upon years of editing poetry journals and contributing to them, of writing poetry books, and publishing them, I have never seen anything like it. It is a success story of truly poetic proportions—and includes, among other things, the publishing of *Today's Greatest Poems*, this magnificent anthology of over 7,000 beautiful poems!

With the publication of the Inaugural issue of the World of Poetry, on August 1, 1975, Editor and Publisher John Campbell launches a publishing empire, with Eddie-Lou Cole as Poetry Editor.

By design World of Poetry is an exciting potpourri of poems, helpful articles on how to write (and sell) poetry, questions and answers, workshops, interviews with prominent poets, news items, market listings and contests—anything and everything we imagine a poet's heart could desire. Celebrities like Bobby Vinton, Red Skelton, Liberace, Tennessee Ernie Ford make their way into our pages, movie and television stars who are also quite good poets. It turns out they are

---

Among the numerous celebrities to appear with our Editor and Publisher in the pages of the World of Poetry are Bobby Vinton (that's our Art Director Julie Joy, next to him), Red Skelton, Liberace, Tennessee Ernie Ford (all fine poets), and of course, Bertha, The Elephant.

---

attracted, many of them, by the glitter of the contests we sponsor, up to a dozen big ones a year, each boasting a grand prize of $1,000, with up to a hundred prizes totaling $10,000 or more. (Most of our contests are won, surprisingly enough, not by "name" or "celebrity" poets, but by housewives or students who've never entered a poetry contest before. One lady won with a poem she'd kept in a drawer for thirty years!)

One day, while I was in the middle of judging one of our contests, John came in the office with an idea. "Eddie-Lou," he said, "Why don't you write a book on how to write poetry, for the benefit of new poets who could use a few ideas." I took the suggestion under submission, and six months later emerged with a text, entitled *Now Technique For Today's Poets.* Like John predicted, it was another World of Poetry success.

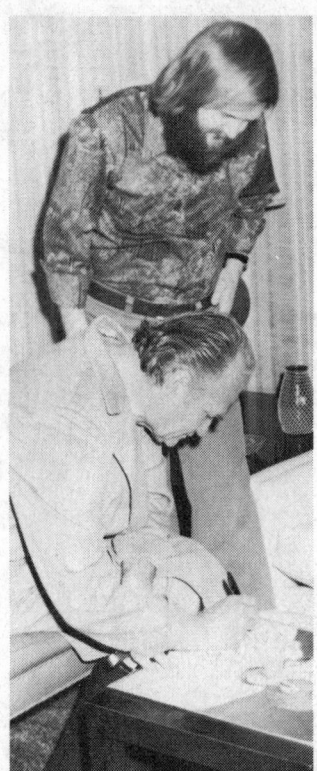

John Campbell   **Bobby Vinton**   **Julie Joy**

Red Skelton   **Bertha**   **Liberace**   **Tennessee Ernie Ford**

Meantime, with the newsletter going great guns, and my book selling well, it was time for World of Poetry to venture again. John, whose background includes acting (and Shakespeare), got a few of his friends together, and did a most phenomenal thing: he came up with a TV series on poetry, called the Upstart Crow (named after the criticism leveled at Shakespeare early in his career by one Mr. Green). As host of the weekly series, you could see John welcome such guest stars as Leonard Nimoy, Vincent Price, Richard Thomas, Red Buttons and Steve Allen. The first thing Mr. Allen said on the show was, "Congratulations that such a show exists!" As if this weren't enough to make everybody here at World of Poetry proud, out of the series, quite enexpectedly, came another success: John's hit Shakespeare album, "Perchance to Dream." J. C. Trewin, the doyen of London

John Campbell   Vincent Price

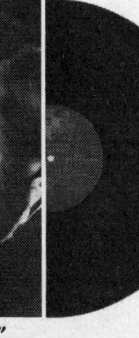

As host of the **Upstart Crow** *television series,* **John Campbell** *talks poetry with guest stars* **Vincent Price, Steve Allen, Red Buttons, Richard Thomas** *and* **Leonard Nimoy.** *One of the results of the series was the production of John's Shakespeare album* **"Perchance to Dream."**

"Perchance to Dream"   Steve Allen

Leonard Nimoy Richard Thomas Red Buttons

drama critics, honored John by writing the program notes to the album.

Today's Greatest Poems, which combines the talents of thousands of poets around the world, is our current success and our current joy. Like I said, it's a wonderful thing to be part of the World of Poetry.

—*Eddie-Lou Cole, Editor*
WORLD OF POETRY
Sacramento, Ca.
June, 1983

Today's Greatest Poems

John Campbell, Editor & Publisher

Today's Greatest Poems

Cissandra Gray Ball

Thanksgiving Day Grace

Thank You for giving us the
  opportunity
To gather here today in peaceful
  unity
Thank You for the bonds of love
  You gave our family
That draw us all together to give
  our thanks to Thee
Bless those of us who were able
  to gather here today
And also bless our loved ones
  who are many miles away
Give us strength as we remember
  those who can't be here
Help us to remember, in our
  hearts they're always near
Bless our Thanksgiving table and
  the food we'll soon partake
Bless the hands that have
  prepared it all without a slight
  mistake
Thank You for these blessings,
  Your mercy, and Your love
Keep us all within Your power
  until we meet above

Michelle Lee Wilson

Gift For a Special Friend

A man once touched me deep
down in a hidden place in my
heart. There he placed, ever so
gently, a small ember to warm
myself with friendship and a
delicate touch of love. As we
have grown so has my ember,
but to keep this ember special
it must stay hidden, so it will
never be destroyed. Precious
gifts in life are fragile and the
ember I have placed in your
heart, never let it die. Just store
it away with your most
precious memories and when
you are feeling cold, bring it
out and this special ember will
warm you to help you on your
way.

Lucile Gregory Weeks

APRIL

April, sweet April, the first
  month of spring,
What joy to our hearts just the
  word does bring!
Warm "April showers" are telling
  the earth,
"Wake up! It's time you were
  starting rebirth!"

The crocus have pushed up their
  happy heads,
Tulips in buds of bright yellows
  and reds,
Jonquils and dogwoods abursting
  in bloom
Laughing away all of ole' winter's
  gloom!

The trees are donning their coats
  of light green,
Scarcely a brown one is left to be
  seen.
Birds all "a-chirp", busy building
  their nests
Where soon their new babies
  safely will rest.

Lilacs are opening with all of
  their might,
Hyacinth's sweet bells fill the air
  with delight,
Gardenias white will soon be in

full bloom
Blending their scents in exotic
  perfume.

Nature is making a lovely bouquet,
And April soon will present it to
  May
All of this work is a "labor of love"
While "The givee of Gifts" smiles
  from above!

Jill Marie

TWO SPECIAL PEOPLE

I have not always listened, and
  therefore have not heard.
I have not always known, and
  therefore have not understood.
I have not always tried, and
  therefore have not succeeced.
  But our lives have touched.
  And you have given me;
  Confidence-in which I will seek
out each new day;
  Creativity-in which I will find
prosperity, such as you have
  shown me;
        and
Courage-in which I will find hope
in the bottom of every chest.
  My hearing will grow into
listening, my knowledge into
understanding. And I will
succeed because through you I
have learned to try.

Arlene Mae (Fiser) Cushman

THE TEENAGERS

*[Dedicated to my five children.
Teenagers of Yesterday, Today,
Forever.]*

Growing up has many stages.
When we become teenagers,
We want to earn wages.

You're at the age of learning to be
  an adult.
From the life of being a child,
Into find young teenagers.

You are told we act to old for our
  age.
But people don't understand the
  education we engage.

We are still at the age we need
  love and understanding.
That we are the product of our
  parents,
Multiple Multiplication
  decendants.
They'll have to talk slowly and
  listen.
As it is hard to grow from a child
  into find dependant offspring.
That our parents, expect us to be

fine human beings.
We want everyone to be proud of
  us.
As we try, as teenagers, to be
  polite and friendly.

We do those things our parents
  think are funny.
But it is serious business with us.
We've been taught not to cuss,
To look our fellow man in the
  eye and smile.
Because we've got a long mile.
Growing up learning about the
  World.
And saying, "See how good a
  teenager can cope with you
  people."
Because someday we will be
  running your WORLD.

We are learning to live a decent
  life and be dear.
To our parents: sometimes you
  shed a tear,
Because we've turned from
  teenagers,
Into fine young adults.
You are proud you bore such fine
  children.
You can hold your head high and
  not worry for tomorrow.
Your young adults that were fine
  teenagers,
Will marry someday, and maybe
  give you later
Grandsons or Grandaughters that
  will grow
Into fine young teenagers as we
  were.

Galer Walker Roberts

THE JOY OF GIVING

If you find you're facing sadness,
Sow a little seed of gladness.
Take the time to share a smile
Or walk that extra "second mile".
Do a favor for a friend
And if you're able, try to spend
Your emptyness in giving pleasure.
  Your willingness is such a
  treasure:
Offering a listening ear,
Understanding, bringing cheer,
Reading something to the blind.
So will you find joy in kind.

jenny root

TOUJOURS

Love is special
  all the time
It comes and goes
  but it's
    always there
      like time
Love is many
  different kinds
But each is eternal
  through all
    of time
There's Love of a family
  Mother and Brother
Wo will
  always be there
    whatever
      the time
Loving a spouse
  Husband or Wife
Will never pass
  whatever
    the strife
But the Love
  of a friend

a really
    True Friend
Goes two ways
  and it
    is always
      Here to stay
Time goes on
  forever
    and ever
And with it
  comes Love
Somewhere
  Somewhere
But it will
  always
    be there . . .
In all of its
  Kinds

Raymond C. Parker, Sr.

HOME TO PARADISE

In this southern retreat of blissful
  sun
where each day I walk through
  native fields

There seems to be an echo that
  tells me
of past battles with sword and
  shields

Fearless men from across the
  seas, seeking new ways
to escape the haunts of days gone
  by

Alone with nature and her
  wonderous works
I watch a lone eagle slicing the
  sky

In your far off winter place
  locked in a blanket of snow
I beckon you to return to this
  land of three seasons

To hear the rush of the storm
  bursting through the trees
. . . oh, I could go on forever to
  give you more reasons

But the songs that are straining
  to escape from my chest
will never be sung or the lyrics
  set free

Until I can reach out and take
  you by the hand once again
and live the joys that are known
  just to you and me

Tracy K. Brooks

black girl

i's walk along the dusty roadway
no place to call my home
i's just a poor black girl
trying to make it on my own
i's have no money in my pocket
no shoes on my feet i's only
have the clothes on my back and
they're wretched with stink
is there any justice for one so
poor is there any way i's can live
i's just a poor black girl
trying to make it on my own

Patricia (Davis) Charlotten

A SEED I NEED

Things must change and be
  rearranged
For what I feel we need indeed
To find that type of seed we need
That seed to keep us feeling
  free.

Mary Anne Schofield
Dream Of Recommitment
My sweetheart, forgive me
  I love you so much.
It seems oh so long
  that we've been out of touch.
The win will be God's
  and Satan will lose,
for all of God's armor
  is ours to use.
As soon as we give battle
  to them,
we will be free and be
  lovers again.
Please give your heart to me
  once more my love,
and blessing will flow
  and fall from above.
Then heaven on earth will be
  ours, you will see.
In Him we will walk
  in loves sweet trinity.

D. Roby—Weaver

D. Roby—Weaver
A Friend Behind the Door
Down the street I saw this man
  just standing . . .
There was no movement—only
  quiet, still staring.
He looked stunned and dazed,
  and made no sound
As he wiped away a tear, bowed
  his head and frowned.
I stopped to see if there was
  something I could do.
He looked at me and said, "Now
  who would want to?"
From those cold, cold words I
  could plainly tell
His life hadn't been pleasant
  —maybe more like hell.
He quietly said, "My life is
  slowly nearing the end
And would you believe I have
  not one true friend.
But behind that door, as best
  I can remember,
I could find one if I only had
  courage to enter.
You see, when I left home I
  strayed from there . . .
It's God's house, you know,
  I'm hoping He'll still care.
Perhaps you'd take my hand,
  slowly lead me inside
For I have much to pray for
  because of my pride."
I gently took his hand, opened
  the door, then smiled
For down that peaceful aisle
  returned God's lost child.

Elizabeth Jane Trittler
TO BE A CHILD AGAIN
The noisey sounds of children, as
  they are at play,
Their merry laughter, ringing in
  the air, as they play games like,
Red light green light, hide and
  seek, or run sheep run—
Never fails to make me want to
  be a child again, so, I can join
  the happy occasion of their fun,
Forgetting, that age now hinders
  me, I cannot run, but their was
  once a day—
So many years ago, when I could
  have joined in their fun,
I was not then, old or slow!
Why does time change things so
  drastically?
Making all that was so easily
  done before, so hard to do now,
That when playing games, now, I
  cannot even make a decent
  score!
How nice it would be, to be a
  child again, to be able to join in
  their happy fun,
Instead of just rocking here, in
  my chair, seeing life pass me by
  this way—
Oh, it would be so nice, to be a
  child again—
If only for one day!

Condie Coppersmith
KETTLE SONG
Our whistling water kettle boils,
Heating water on the stove his
  toil,
At his task, I heard him sigh,
Steam tears left his one small eye,
Was he sorry for himself,
Or glad to serve like an elf,
To send his vapors up as prayer,
Gladly, gladly did his share,
I am glad! As glad as can be,
Listening we heard him sing to
  thee,
Then he whistled, this tune is
  good,
He was happy ye understood,
There is good in all, that doeth
  good,
Silently burned the sticks of
  wood,
Of course, we knew that was
  their task,
And we didn't even have to ask,
Whistle or sing at tasks to
  belong,
To the One who made our life a
  song,
To be of help, just to be needed,
Kettle song is love succeeded.

Lori Capello
Thank You Mom and Dad
You both wanted me to share this
  world with you, you have both
  brought me up to what you
  wanted me to be like, there is
  no one I love more than you
  two.

When I was a little girl you
  taught me the difference
  between right and wrong, you
  had to help me in everything I
  did, but you knew it wouldn't
  last for long.

As I got a little older you knew

I could take care of myself, but
  now and then you would still
  help me, now you can put
  things back on the bottom
  shelf.

Now that I'm almost an adult you
  start to worry more about me,
  even though you had taught
  me about friends, I don't want
  to get into trouble and I know
  that's what you wanted to see.

I'm a legal adult now and trying
  to do my best, you both never
  stop teaching me, you really
  want me to beat all the rest.

Now I leave and go out on my
  own to see what life is really
  about, you call me up just to
  talk and ask me how I'm doing,
  mom and dad you've helped me
  a lot and you knew that one
  day I would be out.

No matter what happens to us,
  you know I love you both, one
  more thing I would like to say
  is thank you mom and dad for
  giving me a happy life with no
  fuss.

Mrs. Houston L. Breland
"B.C." HISTORY
  Glorious Father—Only Son.
  We're at the top, Glory begun.
  "Dost love thy creations,
  everyone?
Will it in time make thee sad,
If there's 90 & 9 (one missed) Oh,
  Dad!
Couldn't I go down there below.
Perhaps save that one from Sin,
And new life for them begin?"
"Greater Love, Granted!" and He
  came down.
Not a big city but in a small
  town.
"If I could save that one—
Help, Mary, I'll be your Son."
"All things are planned.
Father, Thou art in command."
Jesus paid the price of the
  belived.
Then ascended back, all yet
  reprieved.
He left for his disciples and all us
  too,
The Holy Spirit to comfort and
  bless
The believers in times of stress.
A.D. 1 or 1982.

Pearl Ruby Lindberg
INSIDE MY HEART
If you could see inside my heart
You would see love I have to
  share,
Love held together never to part
Then you would understand how
  much I care.

Once inside my heart you will
  find
I have built with concern and
  care,
Held together with love that is
  mine
You will find comfort there.

Come inside my heart and find
No other's love is strong as mine,
Stay inside my heart and dream
  there

Look at my love and see how
  much I care.

Dream's will come true inside my
  heart
Take a look, but don't depart,
My life is made of dreams it
  seems
Our dreams will be as one inside
  my heart.

Sandy Conrad
ANTOHER TIME IN SPACE
Oh would that I had met you,
In another time in space.
We would have laughed and
  loved together
And made happiness a case
To be tried up in the heavens
By a jury of our peers,
And they would find us guilty
And sentence us to years,
Of love and life and happiness,
Oh darling, is it fate?
That you and I belong together
Or is it now too late?

For you belong to another
Alas, and so do I.
And the world will never know
  my love,
That without you I would die.
But the judge and jury up above,
When they finally try our case
Will know how deep our love
  could be
Had we met in another time in
  space.

Henry McMahon
JOB OPPORLUNACIES
  The help that's needed seems
  to be
  For folks unlike the likes of
  me:

"Agressive and dynamic . . .,"
  that sure does make me wince,
And see in mail, upon a horse,
  some pompous Prussian prince.
"Self—starter with ambition . . .,"
  again I'm in the cold,
What ambition did to Caesar was
  cut him from the fold.
"Grow with the company . . .,"
  sure frightens me a mite,
Already now I'm six-feet-one, and
  my clothes are getting tight.
"Live wires wanted . . .,"
  leaves me quite aghast,
Supposing I'm not grounded, then
  my future is my past.

  The help that's needed
  makes me ask,
  Do folks who answer tip the
  flask?

Henry D. Benson Jr.
THE WISH
A dream yet burns within my
  soul
  It screams within me
  Wishing to be free

  One day I will fly
I will soar higher than any bird
  Taller than any tree
  I will be free

One day I will free my chains
  I will burst from my cage
  And roam amongst the life
  Of the forest that I dream

This day will come

And I will wait
For I have not yet lived
And thus cannot die

William K. Botteroff
IF RAIN
If rain
How
Then smile
Drops on
Rose in
Very green
How then
Weep
If smile
Her
Then kiss
Me
Now then
Raining gray
And sweet
Blue
Very eyes
Love
If Rain

Patricia Anne Billard
CAT
The love was lost that once was
  dear,
And that was when the cat
  appeared.
He muffed his line while playing
  King Lear,
And that was when the cat
  appeared.
She loved and comforted,
She mewed and purred
'Til confidence was near,
She scratched and hissed,
And banished the fear.
Next time a black cat crosses
  your path,
Remember there'll be no blood
  bath,
For if in your heart you hold
  them dear,
Morning comes when the cat
  appears.

Lucy Beemer
WILD ROSE
[To Mama who took me along
as a child out in the open fields
to pick wild flowers.]
The first rosebud in springtime,
with its petals pink and fresh,
Coming through the mad of
  winter,
Never minding sacrifice,
Wrapped in tender velvet petals,
Through the age's tender care
Smiles, enraptured by the season
Bringing greetings every year—
  Stopping not to brush a
  teardrop
  Left by crying atmosphere.

Ever growing and unfolding,
Bursting full her largest yields,
Richly bearing clustered
  blossoms
On broken fence or vacant fields,
Giving back to Mother Nature
Sweetly scenting sifted air,
Blushing open in her basking
Taking from the sun her share—
  Maturing, softening as she
  scatters
  Wondrous beauty everywhere.

Elmonda Walker
PUT YOUR TRUST IN ME
I look into your face while you
  sleep
I think of the secrets you must
  keep.
All locked up wanting to be said
You keep them bottled up in
  your head.

You need more time to trust in
  me
Until then your secrets won't be
  set free.
But have faith in me, dear man
I will show you as you take my
  hand.

You can put all the faith you hold
And let out those secrets waiting
  to be told.
Tell me those secrets you hold in
  your heart
Don't quit talking until we must
  part.
For I will listen until you are
  through
Maybe after you won't be feeling
  so blue.

I look again and see thought on
  your face.
I hope you awake with me in
  your embrace.
Then open your heart and tell it
  all to me
Then I'll know you put your trust
  in me.

Susan E. Miller
TIDE OF LOVE
As the soft light flickers I sit in
  solitude, my soul drenched in
  questioning tears.
No one would ever guess that
  just beneath my false and vital
  shell I grieve deeply.
Through your gentle love you've
  pried my shell open, now you
  leave it alone and unguarded.
I feel the waves of sorrow rushing
  in upon my helpless and
  grieving heart.
Time is short, soon the tide will
  recede leaving us trapped in
  our separate worlds.
Without you my world would be
  dark and dismal, and I left
  forever mourning.
My shell would close tightly
  never to be opened carelessly
  again.
Now the waves are slipping
  further and further away; am I
  to be condemned until eternity?
How can such a keen
  relationship become so vastly
  devastated?
If time can take you away from
  my grasp time can also return
  you, but will it be in time?

Betty Pilcher-Freas
AUTUMN MARDI—GRAS
[To MOM, who taught me the
meaning of the real beauty
around us that we often take
for granted and do not
appreciate.]
Jack Frost scurried to and fro
to tell each single tree.
Of the big event coming soon
and he needs R.S.V.P.'s.

It's to be a costume party
and the colors he has chose,
are browns and oranges, yellows
gold and even shades of rose.
He will lend his special touch,
to help how e'er he can.
He has the flair and uses trucks
like any make-up man.
Then one by one leaves flutter
down on special songs of wind.
To begin their annual Mardi-Gras
that every year doth end,
with barren trees, a wintery
  breeze
and lawns all frosted white.
Jack leads the winter season in
much to young kid's delight.
His stay is always very brief
but leaves us all in awe.
When once each year throughout
all time, he starts his
  "Mardi-Gras".

Eugene A. Kennedy

Eugene A. Kennedy
BETWEEN THE COVERS
My children lie before me
Enclosed in these volumes
They may not mean very much
  to you
But they are very special to me.

Each time I try to capture some
  idea
I work most furiously
Afraid it will fade before I can
  finish
These works are me

With each new addition
I check it closely and hope
That it is the best of me
That I've not done this in vain
And will be something I can be
  proud of

I've come far since I started
But I'm not certain that I write
  any better now,
At least now I have some idea
Of what I hope to accomplish

I hope I've written something you
  will like
I'm closer now than I have ever
  been
Towards what I have in my mind
And yet, I'm still so far away

Nelda G. Wilson
THE HAUNTED NIGHT
It's night time again and all alone
  I sit
I'm getting so very tired of it
The sleepless hours once more
  begin.

The haunted night has returned
  again
I stare out my window, bleak is
  the night
Just as if a ghost had turned out
  the light
While I stand here in my
  nakedness
Much too weary to get bathed
  and dressed
In the falling of the gloom
The flickering log fire paints the
  room
the bare walls, the cold bare
  floors,
knobs and handles on chests and
  doors.
I lie down and close my eyes
I go sailing through the skies
I raise my quivering arms on high
I laugh and scream into the sky
There's a burst of light and I can
  see
A radiant form in front of me
I fall back at the touch of his
  hand
He slowly drifts to where I stand
I'm standing in a garden green
Of wondrous sights I've ne're
  before seen
Such a beautiful picture without
  a flaw
A scene that no artist 'ere could
  draw
This radiant figure takes my
  hand
And takes me through this
  enchanted land.
I feel the thrill of his finger-tips
As he brushes them tenderly
  across my lips
He said not a word nor did he try
  and condemn
To spoil these happy moments I
  shared with him
Then all of a sudden there's a
  quickening gust
Of a mighty fierce wind and
  swirling dust
I don't know how such things can
  be
But that gust of wind took him
  from me
The garden shook, leaves rustled
  in the wind
My eyes flew open, I'm in my
  room again
Back to bare walls, cold bare
  floors,
Knobs and handles on chests and
  doors
The sleepless hours once more
  begin
The haunted night has returned
  again!

Helen G. Barker
God Bless America, Again
Once again this land was pure
  and clean
The brilliant sun shone down.
God fearing men had made it
  great,
And love and beauty was all
  around.

God looked down upon our land
And found no want or woe,
He layed His heavenly hands on
  us,
And blessed America, long ago.

Then evil fell upon our Land
And Great men turned to sin,
They turned away from Godly
ways
And let corruption in!

And now a dark cloud hangs
above
On this Thanksgiving day,
Our founding Fathers must shed
a tear,
As we bow our heads to pray.

"Oh, Lord, take all evil from our
Land,
Keep us from want and pain,
Bring us back to thee, dear Lord,
And God, Bless America, again!

Stephanie R. Olk
SLIPPED ON BY
I was afraid
    Not really of you
But to open up to you
    Then I learned
    You felt the same
I knew it wasn't right
    For we really did care
But because we didn't show
    What we really felt
Our love
    Slipped by each other
As we opened into a new life
    Leaving each other behind.

John Michael Giberson
MY CAR
Broken down car
How great you are
You won't go far
How much for a repair
Don't you ever care
In my pocket you always tear
Because of you I will always
swear
Next to my home you are the
biggest bill
When I die you won't be in the
will
But when you die I will get the
bill
Then I must buy a car
Start the payment cycle again
Play that bleeding money game
How long and how far
I can't do a thing if you're not
here
I can't go to work if you're not in
gear
My car, my car, my broken down
Gas eaten, oil drinking, out of
tune, out of time
Out of line, no brakes, paint that
flakes
Who knows what make car

Mark T. Roberts
TRACES OF YESTERYEAR
As I awoke this morning,
a yearning called me home.
I journeyed to the valley,
to let my senses roam.
Beckoned by sweet memories,
of days I've left behind,
once again I'll venture,
through the canyons of my mind.
Friendly hills are drawing me,
to places that I know.
Long ago I walked their trails,
when time was passing slow.
With every step that I retrace,
I relive again;
carefree days of yesteryear,

which linger on the wind.
It seems I've been away too long,
from this place I love.
Tho' today I have been blessed,
by the Lord above.
The glory of these sacred hills,
forever touch my heart.
When it's time to leave again,
I find it hard to part,
standing on the edge of time,
lost within the years;
One last glance will fill my eyes
with joy instead of tears.
Bygone days of leisureness have
drifted far away.
Someday soon they will return,
just like they did today.

Deidre Alexander

Deidre Alexander
ODE TO JANICE WONG
[This poem was written in
remembrance of a college
acquaintance I had known for
only 7 months—who shared
    her Christian faith with
me—   within a week of her
going
    home to the Lord.]
If only tomorrow was yesterday,
that the way life was was here to
stay,
and we could all be together.

The parting of one from the rest,
makes them realize,
and despise, death.

After taking a deep breath,
we continue our routine,
learning from what she had been.

Even though she may be gone,
she will not be forgotten.
She treated everyone the same.
Life was not a game,
but more important
being cut so drastically short.

Paula Freda
TEACHER, FRIEND
[To Mrs. Uran—From Nicky's
Mother]
TEACHER, you have filled my
son's life.
You have taken the emptiness
and replaced it with
knowledge.
FRIEND, you have guided his
hand
And touched his mind,
Taught him to depict the sun on
paper,
Shown him the difference
between a letter and a number.

You have given his hours
meaning.
And made me grateful.

TEACHER, you have filled my
life as well.

Joanne McNeely
FEELINGS
[With deep gratitude to the
love of my life.]
I savor the feelings you gently
create,
Bringing words to the tip of my
pen,
While lighting a fire in my 'lovin
grate',
That burns low and warm
without end.

Homer Lee Davey
ARMS
The strong reach down,
The weak reach up.
Somewhere in between,
Just reaching out.

Grace Avery Lillard
DELPHI
Sunset crowns with golden glow
Parnassus'
crags, while purple shadows
darkly conceal
    Ancient rites within cryptic
    ruins below.
    Weary traveler from another
    world.
non-believing yet curious of an
heroic age when gods and men
were one
    or could assume the other's
    guise at will
I climb Delphi at pensive time
of day.

Wise oracle knew from whom
prophecy
read—if mere man within the god
would sin
    or god raise man to
    immortality.
    I watch while olive warblers
    flit among
shards, viewing visitors
suspiciously.
What odd spirits yet lurk as
guardians
    of the oracles' nest? Uneasiness
    stirs my mind; pagan spell yet
    haunts this place.

Perhaps one still could rouse the
oracle
but then—what then? In my own
way, I too
    receive answer at Delphi; and
    content,
    wend humble way to mortal's
    world before
It's too dark to find Christian
path once more.

Karen Lumpe
MAN IN FLIGHT
Skyflight is fantasy
For a man
Who flaps his arms
In bird-loke motion
Too heavily for takeoff
But reality
For one
Who sits down
To let machine
Take over.

Camille Montana-McLauchlan
**MARRIED STRANGERS IN
A QUEEN SIZE BED**
Touching, lying side by side
Their feelings hidden deep inside
Each wondering if their future is
dead
All hopes and fears left unsaid
Married strangers in a queen size
bed.

Flinging words like stones and
sticks
Self-inflicted wounds to lick
All private dreams have fled
Starving emotions left unfed
Married strangers in a queen size
bed.

Turning away with a sigh
Into their pillows they silently
cry
Thoughts of the future filled with
dread
Wondering why they ever wed
Married strangers in a queen size
bed.

Larry Goza
THE ULTIMATE ME
An individual you must be,
    So philosophers have decreed.
Myself most important must be,
    If ultimate self I achieve.
So for myself I proclaim truth;
    The ultimate me is fulfilled you.

Thelma Louise Holt
**SIGNS OF SPRING ARE
    EVERYWHERE**
The signs of spring are everywhere,
    Petals are floating in the air,
Birds are singing in the trees,
Flowers are blowing in the breeze.

As all things come to life anew,
My life, my love, I give to you.
That God will guide you is my
    prayer,
Whle signs of spring are
    everywhere.

When Winter comes, I'll love you
too,
And will until my life is through,
That God will guide you is my
    prayer,
While signs of Spring are
everywhere.

Margaret Nienstedt
THE MEAL
Life is a big meal
Bite it hard
Sip the wine
Savor taste appeal
Chew tough meat
Tongue the texture
Feel the lumps
Don't swallow it whole
Lick up the gravy
Spill a little
Pass it on
Relish warm sauces
Let it drip
Melt the crusts
Try something new
Nature's nutrition
Works through you
Eat it all
Mop the plate
Nourishment lives
After the meal is through

Today's Greatest Poems

Sandy Gillming
MY FRIEND
[To my friend and husband, Jerry.]

Someone beautiful has come my
     way,
To be my friend in every way.
Long lonely hours have come to
     an end,
Since finding this treasured
     friend.

God has given me someone to
     love freely,
Someone to care with, to share
     with.
Someone to be friends with,
Someone to be just me with.

I'll laugh with you when you're
     happy,
I'll cry with you when you're sad.
I'll stand beside you when you
     need me with you,
Behind you when you need my
     support,
In front of you to ward off the
     hurts and blows life brings.

When you look at me, hold me,
     touch me,
I'm safe, secure, and totally a
     woman.
I thank God everyday that He
     brought you my way.

If I can be there for you the way
     you are for me,
I'll have a reserved seat on the
     train to heaven.

For as long as it is meant to be,
I'm here whenever, whatever, and
     wherever you need me.

Mira J. Reynolds
A WELCOME
The Welcome Mat is always out
Here at our humble home
We greet you as a special guest
Though from far or near you
     roam.

It's sometimes clean, and
     sometimes cluttered
Don't compare our home with
     another.
We have no servant, maid or
     slave,
Only a Wife and Mother!

Mark Cummings
ILLUSIONS
He becomes physical
with the mirror.
Flexing muscles
flesh colored mounds appear.
Twisting his body
like a strand
of licorice.

The mirror reciprocates
the man's gestures.
Becoming physical
it reflects only hatred.

Steven Gust Kritsonis
THE SHADOW
Alone I dwell
Seething with rage.
Alone I feel
Screaming with pain.
Lifeless stones crush
My struggling spirit.
Decayed bones hush
My lamenting heart.

A shadow beckons
My spirit to rest.
A shadow hastens
My spirit to death.
Bloodless life soothes
The sick of the living.
Hopeless trife cools
With the eternal night.

Alone the shadow
Bids me farewell.

Margaret Louise Legan
GENERATION GAP
[Dedicated to my husband
John, who encouraged me to
write and to our three children,
Loretta, Jay and Jim, who
inspired it.]

Some teenagers today are crude
     and rude as they can be
They could care less whether
     they hurt you or me
Just as long as they get their own
     way
They could care less as to what
     we have to say.
Teenagaers "Yes" what horrible
     years
We parents will live thru it with
     our anger and tears
It's not just the kids of today I'm
     talking about
We all went thru the days when
     we thought we knew what it
     was all about
As we get older we know it
     wasn't true
We wish we could do it over and
     know what we do
Life is hard and that's a fact
But being young is where it's at
So teens of today have your fun
Take time and lay in the sun
When you get older and have
     your teens
Then you can read this and know
     what it means

Opal Marie Hayes
Prayer Without Words
Sometimes I do not pray with
     words;
I put my heart in my two hands,
And hold it up toward the Lord;
So glad He knows and
     understands.

Sometimes I never pray in words
My heart does bow before His
     feet,
And with His hand on my head
We can hold communion sweet.

Sometimes I pray without a word,
God knows I'm tired and need my
     rest;
My weary life is filled with woe;
I find comfort on His loving
     breast.

Deanne Itschner
LONELINESS
An aching want to tenderly touch
     And be touched
To look into someone's eyes
     And see your own love
     reflected
An emptiness longing to be filled
     By a soothing warmth
An unexplainable void
     Needing to be explained

Ruby Tiffany Woeltje

Ruby Tiffnay Woeltje
HOW TO COUNT LIFE
[To Karen Ruby Dening, my
grand daughter, who types my
poems because I cannot see to
do them anymore. And in
memory of Mabel T. Brown,
my loving sister who passed
away June 20, 1981.]

We should count night by the
     Stars in the Sky everywhere,
     not by the shadows out there,
We should count mornings by
     the problems that have flown,
     not by those that have grown.
We should count days by all the
     pleasant and happy hours, not
     by problems piled into sad
     towers.

We should count each new
     tomorrow by our Special
     Thanks,
     not by searching empty,
     unsolved tanks.
We should count friendship by
     their interest, the same,
     not by years we have known
     them.
We should count sorrow in life
     by our love and smile,
     not by tears that we dial.
We should count pretty flowers
     by both large and small
     not by all their blossoms that
     fall.

Sheryl Oleen Sinn
CASUALTY
Too many
     Images of Death
     Swirl through my soul.
I have become

One of Life's casualties so
     I withdraw, wounded and
     hurt.
I am drifting away
     Reaching for a place
     Where no one can reach me.
I go on alone and
     Soon I will be gone.
     I have really tried, but I died.
Nobody will remember me
     No trace, no memory so
     I never really existed.
Nobody ever really knew me,
     No image, no identiity, now
     Only a casualty.

Lucie G. Titus
USURPTION
The weather is such a funny
     thing,
     Today it's winter, tomorrow
     spring.
For days the ground lay white and
     cold,
     Beneath its blanket of triple
     fold.
The trees with beards of ice bend
     low,
     To gods of winter their homagae
     show.

But March slips in for a
     premature call,
     And takes from the earth her
     ghostly shawl.
The earth, in relief, feels bright
     and gay,
     And the mad March lion is king
     for a day.
But old man winter will not give
     up his reigh
     Today I see it's snowing again.

Emory Elliott
ANTICIPATION OF THE FUTURE TO PASS
[This poem was inspired by the
coming Decade of the 60's;
Man is ever looking to his
future, and anticipates life
ahead. It is dedicated to all
men who lived through the
1960's!]

I lightly slip
The razor skin edge
Of this blue sky,
With the pink top touch
Of my finger tip.

And peering across that steel,
Under a power-puffed cloud;
Secretly hidden, gazingly stare
At a Decade riding by
On a vanishing picture reel.

Monica Lee
IT'S OVER
When was that illusive point in
     time
When the trumpet blew retreat
The beginning of that fine, fine,
     line
between victory and defeat
Just when, in the course of our
     long association,
did you lose the power
The ability to tear my very soul
     apart
like petals from a flower
Was it a certain look, a touch, a
     spoken word or two
Ot was it something deep within
     myself, and nought to do with
     you.

That sparked the knowledge
    when to fight,
and when to run for cover
No matter who was right or
    wrong, the
battles over lover

Nancy Jo Mosburg

A FORWARD LOOK
[*To My Loving Husband, Jeff,
And Daughters, Amy and Ann.*]
Who knows what tomorrow will
    bring?
Will I hear children's laughter
    and wild birds sing?
Will I see the mountains, blue
    and hazy in the distance?
Will I be prepared to help if
    someone needs assistance?
Will my friends remember me
    after they're married and gone?
Will God forgive me for things
    I've done wrong?

Who knows what next year will
    bring?
Will there be a summer, a winter,
    a fall, and a spring?
Will I be richer or poorer or
    living at all?
Will I have loved and lost a man
    so tall?
Will I be wiser than I was
    yesterday?
Will I have learned to be brave
    along the way?

Only one person knows the
    answer to these,
He made the earth and the soft
    gentle breeze.
He'll take my hand and lead me
    on,
I know with Him I'll never go
    wrong.
I'll take what comes, thankful I'm
    alive,
Whether I'm chosen to go or stay
    and survive.
Just to live each day I'll be
    satisfied,
At least in my heart I'll know I
    have tried.

Norman Lahti

THE PLAY
Actor act!. . .
        Make my play a fact.
Well thought up lines;
Spoken so undeliberately timed,
That the only clues, totaled
    whole;
From the body, face, and soul. . .
Shows the truth in deathly
    silence,
Til the final curtain calls the
    triumph. . .
of feelings for feeling, well and
    done,
and a crowd of would be
    strangers,
Turn, applause, and act as one!

Leona Garrett Keller

DESTINY
One time I set about to wonder
Why some fine folks have funds
    to squander,
While others toil like common
    thunder
To live a meager life.

Then visioned I two figures
    striving.

One was receeding, one was
    thriving;
The one was pulling, one was
    driving,
A whipcord in his hand.

It all spread clear as bright
    daylight.
Some choose for meekness; some
    will fight.
But, in the end things turn out
    right—
The meek inherit the earth.

Vera McKenna

IT RAINED LAST NIGHT
[*This poem is dedicated to
beautiful Puerto Rico where it
was inspired one fresh and
dewy morning after a rare dry
spell.*]
It rained last night
    and all the day before
And the falling water did
    what only it can do. . .

It washed the dust and dirt
    from gardens and the trees
And coaxed little flower buds
    to open up and bloom.
And more than that it did. . .
    it filled the empty reservoir!

Lynn Weston

FRAGILE
Fragile . . . Handle with care
Do not drop me
For I could break easily;

Do not handle me roughly
For I could go to pieces
But . . .
Above all . . .
Please do not leave me on a shelf
    alone.

What am I?

A vase? a china piece? No.
The answer is really quite simple.

I am . . .

A woman.

Stephen J. Meglio

RAMBLING ON
[*For Laura & Alfie*]
It has been said
that having one true friendship
in life makes a person rich,
so it appears I'm wealthy
by merit of knowing you both
and maintaining the priceless
Relationship we share.
A relationship that has enriched
and touched my life immensely,

and, hopefully, will continue
to grow but still remain unique,
cherished; something that I gain
strength from, something that
causes a smile to cross my lips,
something that occupies a
special niche in my mind, body
and soul.
Verbalizing the elite feelings
I have for you is impossible
and I feel pen and pad are poor
interpreters.
So I ramble on hoping you will
find the message or "diamond in
the rough" if you will, and that
the seeds of friendship we have
nurtured will continue to grow
and blosom with the seasons.

Michael B. Dugdell

THE REALIST
[*Towards the expansion of
peace, by peaceful means.*]
He sits
He stares
Observing all he sees;
He makes no judgement
Not accepting,
Nor rejecting.
No one sees his silent knowledge
    grow.
Nor does he impart
The things he only knows.
He makes no assumption
As to what is wrong;
What is right?
He feels no preference;
Time includes both day and night.
He speaks so unabashed,
His deepest thoughts never shown;
He is so unattached,
For truly He is alone.
He walks a path uncrowded;
He resides a spacious room,
Keeping life unclouded
By society's plastic gloom.
He is not coldly hearted;
He is certainly no pretender.

Gary Knowles

THE CITY ✓
I traveled the weather
in search of hope,
but found a city robed in rage.
Streets were filled with life too
    short,
midnight turned another page.

Patchword healing went undone,
for peace was no match for a gun.
Sounds of anguish ever grew,
when freedom fled and hope fell
    through.

Joseph A. Conway

THE DREAM
If we're so wide awake, how come
we can't see what's really going
on? so full of artificial lustre is
this morning of yesterdays,
dream of today.

Why don't we all polish up our
apples as if they were dreams,
place our bets on our best
team; if you're looking for a
fortune, looking for a dream;
then this is for you, you'll
know what I mean.

How unaware we are of that one
precise moment when we
didn't take the time to stop and
look, to show how much we

really cared, to dare to be
different, to tell people exactly
how we felt.

Yesterdays gathered in number
and flew away, they brought us
together now for what we
know as today; and the hope of
tommorow is only a dream away.

Dream for lost moments and they
will return.

Richard Craig Hatheway

TIME
When things were made it began,
To pace, not waste our fellow man.

To count, and keep on counting
    our ages,
It has become one of our main
    gauges.

It shows us our progress,
In which lies our success.

To us it would seem,
It's quite routine.

To stop and think,
You'd never find a link.

But in the end,
You'll comprehend.

It has been here through the
    bright,
Of the almighty arc of light.

And will continue to the height,
On the fall of our darkest night.

Paul E. Truesdell, Jr.

LAUNDRY DAY
Multicolored pennants,
Wrung—out wet; hanging
Pinned to the clothesline.
Giving up moisture
To a light breeze and
The warm summer sun;
Absorbing fresh, sweet smells
From Nature's drying machine.
        Time;
        Sure is fine.

Thora Jean Supple

DAISIES
[*I wish to dedicate my poem to
my family; for their understanding
and sincere wish for my
success in the writing field.*]
White and yellow daisies,
Marching in a row,
Fill a field with color,
As of fallen snow!

White and yellow daisies,
Standing, oh, so tall,
Are a thing of beauty,
Lasting until fall!

White and yellow daisies,
Oh, so pure and white,
March across the landscape,
Hiding brown earth's blight!

Dolores Ann Cross

**Tonight As I Lie In the
Darkness**
Tonight, as I lie in the darkness
    thinking,
I really should go before it's light,
Before you come and beg me to
    stay,
Because, I can't stand,
To see you hurt this way.
The time is coming,
And my life will end somehow,
But I just can't bear to tell you
Exactly, when or how,
I know I can't go on now,

I was certainly wrong to start,
But if you see me crying now,
You know, you will break my
   heart.
But I feel a whole lot stronger,
For having needed you,
Even though the strength you've
   given me,
Didn't help me see it through.

Jeffrey Paul Graubart
AS I SIT
As I sit
   The world surrounds me
I am crushed beneath myself
Try I will
   To bet around me
The more of me around myself

J. B. Blauw
GREED
Red liquid flowing
From the wounds inflicted
By the ilk of peoples
Firm in a belief.

Kin — so lucky
To await and greet
Their loved ones —
Blood still flowing
To a heart — beat.
   What caused
   These angry declarations:
   "Shoot to kill.
   Blow up the imposters — "?

   GREED!
   "What's mine is mine —
   And yours is yours —
   Unless I want
   What's yours, that is."
Sensless spilling.
Bombs drilling ships.
Sea — red —
With blood — shed.

Jane H. Connors
NIGHT'S SONG
As I lay
   All snug in your arms
The fears go away
   Chased by your charms.
My heart is light
   The day was long,
Here's to the night
   Singing its sweet, short song.

Lavina Clemetson
LIFE PASSES BY
Life is a dream as it flits quickly
   by.
I cannot hold her, e'en though I
   try.
She laughs at my efforts to hold
   to the past.
I want youth and gaity up to the
   last.
But she laughs, as out in the
   world so vast,
   Life passes by.

Slowly, but surely she is taking
   her toll.
My body is with'ring and
   becoming quite droll.
I'm ugly and old, but I say my
   prayers,
Hoping to climb the golden
   stairs.
Though here on Earth, I'm one
   who dares
   To watch Life passing by.

We mortals are foolish, but what
can we do?

The years go fleeting, and soon
   we are through.
Youth cannot believe they're
   lucky to be
So full of strength and vitality.
They walk with eyes blinded,
   refusing to see
      Life passing by.

Too soon they awake and find as
   I've done,
That life didn't wait for them to
   have fun.
She marches on steadily, I hear
   her say,
"The daylight is darkening, the
   night is all gray."
And I look up to God to show me
   the way,
      As Life passes by.

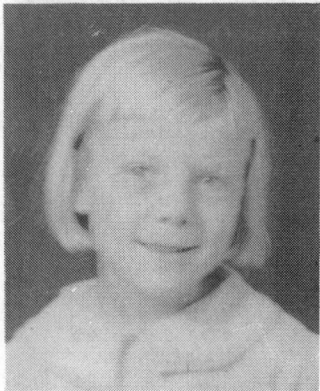

Lona Jean Turner Binz

Lona Jean Turner Binz
My World And Grandpa
Sixty, and one—hundred acres,
   the small town of Branch
Most folks would call it a very
   small ranch
But to me, this was a great—big
   world;
Within its boundaries my whole
   life twirled.
Would you believe I felt insecure?
When over the boundary line I
   would endure.
As far back as I can remember,
I loved this hill with all its
   timber.

Grandpa (dear old sole) loved
   potato soup—served in a bowl.
And on a scorching, hot, summer
   day:
Trying to keep cool, on the front
   porch, he would stay.
A bucket of cool water, and gourd
   dipper, by his side
To quench his thirst—he enjoyed
   this intensively,
Daydreaming, and waiting for the
   cooler nightfall to abide.
I enjoyed thus too, the hotter
   than hell—
For I got a penny for every fresh
   pail
That was drawn, for him, from
   the deep—cool well.

Yea, grandpa was a dear old pal,
   to this little hillbilly Arkansas
   gal;
And I was, "his little pearl."
Hence, grandpa's farm was truly,
   a most fabulous world.

Sandy Martin
SOUNDLESS SCREAM
Yearning and yearning
   a constant burning.
A soundless scream
   night and day.

Wanting and wanting
   there's something haunting
my restless Spirit
   I'd say!

Craving and craving
   it's so depraving.
I know not what's
   in the way.

Searching and searching
   and always flirting
with sudden death
   and sure decay.

Possessed and obsessed
   is one who's depressed
and powerless
   not to obey.

Vicki D. Seegert ✓
OHIO
Ohio, how I love you (the river, not
   the state),
You flow throughout my memories
   as far back as they date.
I've floated in and on you, and in
   your waters swum;
No matter where I wander, back to
   you I have come.
I've lived in river cities, guess I'm a
   "river rat,"
But no matter what the city, or
   where the river's at,
None draws me quite like you do,
   swells up my heart with joy,
Holds captive my affections, like
   Huck Finn's as a boy.
My "roots" drink in your silence
   the way my lungs breathe air;
I guess that peace and solitude
   are what I've enjoyed there.
My body you have watered, and
   my spirit, heart and soul—
Peace flowing like a river has
   always been a goal.
I'm glad you'll always be there, a
   friend who doesn't change,
To offer silent comfort when my
   life gets disarranged.

Gertrude Gehl Shook
MY SPECIAL TREASURES
This morning I walked
As I usually do   ✓
Along the sandy shore
Looking for my special gift
A treasure to adore.
Today I almost held it
In my wet and shiny palm,
But before my hand
Could hold it
And caress it tenderly
A jealous wave
Possessed with rage
Returned it to the sea.
I won't give up my quest
I will not be denied
With all the treasures in the sea
There must be one for me.

Judith Koponen
GOLDEN GLORY
Between the days
   when men were kings,
And rockets flew to mars,
There lived a boy

that loved to dream,
that rode upon the stars.

He was a child of goodness
one of happiness and health,
With poetry and music
serving as his only wealth.

His dreams were of
   a better world,
One with suffering unknown,
His hopes lived
   where the angels live,
though he was virtually alone.

His eyes would fill with sadness
whenever he saw misery and
   pain,
But he could always see the
   sunshine
even through the falling rain.

The boy grew up
   to be a man,
And found a girl as pure and free,
Together they shared
   dreams and love,
for all eternity.

Carl C. Williams
O How Much He Cared!
Up Calvary's mountain, they took
   my Saviour,
   And nailed Him to a tree.
'Twas wondrous love that led my
   Saviour
   To lay His life down for me.

He was not willing that I should
   perish,
   But gladly took my place.
That blood—stained cross I'll
   ever cherish—
   It was for me, Amazing
   Grace.

How much He loved me, How
   much He cared!
   How much on Calvary, His
   love He shared.
He bore the loss, on Calvary's
   cross.
How much He loved me, O how
   much He cared!

Tony Maione
BELOVED GIBRAN
To read his words is to feel love,
To sit at his feet and hear his
   voice
Is to bathe in the waters of that
   love.
                  pax

Gale A. Grubman
THE WHEEL
Slowly the wheel of fate turns
Bringing forth its lot.

Around and around it goes
Knowing where to stop.

What will this turn bring to us?
It's very hard to know.

Each thing has its place in time
For now and evermore.

William Barricks
TO DAVEY
Little man upon my knee
How I wonder what you'll be.
An airplane pilot, an engineer,
A doctor, a lawyer, an overseer.
These are the things that mark
   success
They are society's marks, I could
   care less.

Little man upon my knee
This is what I want you to be
Strong in body, strong in mind,
Willing, unselfish, thoughtful and
    kind
Obedient to God, country and
    parent
Love, be loved, and always be
    reverent

Little man upon my knee
To do these things may be hard
    for thee
This is God's plan, make it yours,
    too
Live life to its fullest and always
    be true
Success in the end will be yours
    forever
You'll be loved by all forever and
    ever.

Jeri Finley—Taylor
TIME NO MORE
[Dedicated to my Mother—
For raising her children with
    Love.
And to all Mothers that have
    lost a child or a Baby.]
Shadowy skies overlooking my
    Baby's Grave
Upon a hillside my body yearns
    to lie
Beside infants feet pressed deep
    inside.

Shadowy skies overlooking a
    hillside
where my Baby does lie
All alone a grave stands, all alone
    and without I.

Angels bent down below cuddled
    warm within,
My Baby safe from sin,
Yearning to be encumbered by
    Mothers tender
breast below,
Safe within Creations Hands now
    without even a "Hello".

Time was short for My Baby Dear
    and life
was never known,
Not even a chance for Baby to
    become grown.

Shadowy skies overlooking a
    hillside,
where my Baby does lie
All alone a grave stands, all alone
    and without I.

Mirth Linegar
LOST LOVE
A teardrop falls, my cheek is wet
I can't remember why, and yet
Something jogs my memory
Of other years, and finally
It comes to me in floods of pain
For long lost love.

And now the tears are falling fast
As I recall the dead, dead past
The past that racks my soul and
    heart
When you and I at last did part
The scalding tears fall like rain
For long lost love.

I'm drowning now in burning
    tears
There's no relief for anguished
    years.

The darkness comes as here I lie
My breath escapes me in a sigh
I must never recall again
My long lost love.

Denis C. McGilvray
THIS VALLEY
[A poem of the New Age: for
peace, for people; for Victoria
Frances, with much love...]
I sit atop this valley,
Cool and crisp in Autumn, filled
    with admiration.
I see the full moon set like a
    sparkling jewel,
Giving rise to fading hues in the
    blue above.
Then, in the distance, millions of
    colors
And lights flicker against the
    black mountains,
Lining the streets, dotting out
    spots of life,
Generating a hazy mist of
    brightness
Up into the night air.
This is L.A. night air, as always,
Full of electric beauties and life,
Transmitting a glow which
    washes
Up into this valley:
Flooded from across the streets—
Through the many trees—
Over miles of cityscape and
    earth.
This is second-hand L.A., but just
    as glittery.
    Light-life amidst the shadows
        now,
A shaded figure sitting and
    resting,
Anticipating the early morning
    sun;
A new day, like every day,
Which this night gives birth to.

Audrey Lawrence
NAKED THEY STAND
The trees have lost their foliage.
Undressed they stand on the
    lawn.
Bare and cold they stand there
Looking so naked and forlorn.

The trees in springtime will
    awaken
Once again they'll become fully
    dressed
With the lovely hues of
    springtime.
No longer will they look
    distressed.

Florence G. Axton
A LEAF
Dawn in the east has an inner
    glow,
From which all expectations
    flow,
The sky is clear and blue,
A pretty picture for you.
Dew on the trees, on each and
    every
        Leaf.

Shadows fall and play, chill in the
    air,
It is fall, so they say,
A new ground cover, a golden
        Leaf.

The trees are bare, it is cold,
    gusty winds, not rare,

A summer memory pressed in a
    book, a faded
        Leaf.

Holiday time, it is exciting and
    fine,
Cakes, pies, puddings, in line.
A garnish, a chocolate
        Leaf.

A New Year in view, resolutions
    for you.
Time to turn over a new
        Leaf.

It is spring again, a Rebirth, a
    Renaissance
What a relief, a new green
        Leaf.

Midge Grant

Midge Grant
THE CHOSEN ONE
I was his Love from yesterday
and she was his bride to be,
For he was gone and I was alone
She had been Chosen—Not Me!

When he told me of his love—
    had she loved him?
as I had been taught was so
    wrong,
or had she been meek, when he
    caressed her cheek
That made his love so strong!

Whatever the reason—an error or
    fate
She softly whispered "I do"
With tears in My eyes "God bless
    you"
"Congratulations to you".

I walked alone from the Chapel
With tears so I hardly can see,
I must go on alone for he was
    gone
She has been Chosen—Not Me!

Carol Easterbrook Wolf
MY SOUL
My Soul.

    Awareness. Total
consciousness,
With a sense of drifting through
    space and time.

A feeling of complete freedom,
Uninhibited by gody or mind.

    Able to soar to new heights.

    A peaceful, calm, carefree
attitude.
Tranquil, with sense of
    knowing.

    Parting the veil,
Renewing, touching, spiritual
    truths.

Returning to me with
    knowledge
As the Author of Eternity guides
    my pen.

Alice Rose Kilgore
COLOR BLIND
Because your skin is black and
    mine is white,
I cannot know the hopes and
    fears you feel.
Yet underneath your darkness, I
    surmise,
There beats a heart as vulnerable
    as mine,
All filled with lofty, irridescent
    dreams,
With aching hopes, and fine
    unfettered plans
For independence, love and
    happiness,
As native to the young as dawn
    to day.
May all your deepest dreams
    come true!
And may this great, proud Nation
    realize
The finest melodies of life must
    touch
On ivory keys of black as well as
    white,
To play with grace the magic
    harmony
That all our listening ears now
    long to hear.

Pauline Brashears
FOR THE LOVE OF IT
I write flowery words
    for the love of it.
Once I get started
    I just can't quit.

It's not to impress
    or show I'm smart,
It's just a few words
    straight from my heart.

Words of deep love,
    words about hurt,
Words about nature
    sounding so pert.

Just plain everyday words
    about what I see,
And how I feel
    deep inside of me.

I write different words
    simply for pleasures,
About all my memories
    that for me are treasures.

Today's Greatest Poems

Kathryn Tracy Allen
UNTIL I DO
["A poem to Wallace"]
I shall be forever strong,
No one's will shall bend my own.
On this earth I walk alone.
No one dare to pity me,
In the light I stand to see
How great a man I one day be.
To this life I give my all,
No compromise least I might fall.
A cry from far away awakens me,
But a plain man be all I see.
Come no closer least I despair,
For all my dreams are buried there.
Not real shall I ever be,
A plain life imprisons me.
There is one step beyond that I
must know,
Stay in twilight till I go;
For the days seem unbearably long,
And no longer can I pretend to be
strong.
But I dream in days you see,
I can be the kind of person I want
to be.
Left alone, you won't hear me cry,
Not a tear shall fall from my eye.
Though no one be by my side,
I am sure I can abide;
For in the years to come you see,
I shall try and be what I want to
be.
Most of all I seem to know,
Once again I will go, to a place,
We all must face;
But, until I do,
But until I do.

Barry
SUNRISE
Sliding,
   Gliding,
      Glimmering, it comes.
The black cape of night reveals
   its scarlet lining.
Crimson splendor splits the
   heavens.
Lavendar,
   Pink,
      Rose, it grows.
The great festering sore spreads
   its ruby fingers.
Starlight bows to the blistering
   beauty of the sun.
Light,
   Bright,
      White, it soars.
Ever higher, overpowering the
   sky, the flame flies.
At last the pinnacle is reached—
   day is come!

Allen T. Billy
LIGHT AND SHADOW
It is morning
A blackbird sings
A song of love,
To creatures without wings

It is afternoon
A blackbird flies
Soaring above the ordinary,
in search of its mate

It is evening
A blackbird dies
Never to sing again

Mary E. Talbert
UNTITLED
How sad it is
for those of us

left in the world alone
with no one
to depend upon
when things are going wrong.
How empty then
ones life can be
when lonliness is there
with nothing left
but memories
and no one left to care.

Dana Shantel Smith
TROUBLED WATERS
A wave of sadness. A wave of
   cheer.
What will be next in this ocean
   of fear.

The next wave is starting.
   Reaching it's peak.
And has something to do with
   the tears on my cheek.

Afraid to laugh. Afraid to cry.
Not even noticed by those
   passing by.

A walking prison I have become.
No warden to see. Keys? There
   are none.

Someone will see me. Someone
   will care.
Maybe next week or even next
   year.

I must have patience. Learn how
   to wait.
Get rid of self—pity at any cost,
   any rate.

To help myself. To help others.
Make them sisters and brothers.

To always remember and try to
   see,
That to feel sorry inside can only
   hurt me.

Sharon L. Bracken

Sharon L. Bracken
MY LIGHT SHONE
*[To the dearest family anyone
could have. Love—ya. Sharon]*
The Dear Lord comforted me—
When I was down and blue.

And somehow made me realize,
He was there, to get me through.

The Great Master helped me to
   see,
And Turned my head to the light.

The Dear Lord has saved my soul
And showed me the road to right.

Maria Jacketti
TWENTY
*[For my Mother, Pearl Jacketti,
who has taught me courage.
My love and everything I write
is for you.]*
Ending a decade
Tell me again how sweet it is
To be twenty (twenty)
Twenty aprils
Always catching roses
And escaping under the weather
To romance, deftly complicated
Always a clover
Seducing without trying
The window dressers
Wanting to dress me
And trip me under a rolling stone
In style
In those purple (pump) shoes.

Basil E. Reavis
JAKE'S HOUSE
There was a man whose name
   was Jake
Who had a house upon the lake.
Every morning he would wake
And for breakfast have a piece of
   cake.

He had a private fishing hole;
He always used a long cane pole.
He fried his fish on red hot coal,
And served it in a great big bowl.

For a pet, he had a big black cat;
The kitty had grown old and fat.
He liked to sleep on a ragged mat;
In the mornings he would chase
   the rat.

When the rat got away from the
   cat;
He went to see his friend, the Bat.
In the attic was where he was "at";
He hung all day from a ceiling
   slat.

Unknown to the cat or the rat or
   the bat,
In the house there also lived a
   Nat.
He lived in the threads of the
   cat's ragged mat;
Sometimes he wore a tiny top hat!

Vincent A. Dombrowski
REMEMBERING
Do you remember once
How as a child, you looked
Into a window of joys

Your only wish
Was to pick your own
Amongst this treasure of toys

How your heart did beat
When they with a smile
Gave you your desire

You searched for the one
That caught your eye
Of this one, you would never tire

At last it was yours
After so many visits
To this window of joy

You would pray no more
That another would come
And choose your lovely toy

Paul P. Czech
THE CONQUEROR
Be not a prisoner: life is too brief
For Satan's rule, whose binding
   chains allow

No freedom to the soul locked
   tight in grief,
Shut in from blue skies and
   blossoming bough.
Be not a beggar, asking much of
   God—
Guilty, fearing life and death,
   knowing hate;
Nor show a willingness to
   question God;
Cast not misfortunes on
   relentless fate.
'Tis man himself who can mark
   his own life,
Making it as fair as poets sing of
   June,
And, with his dreams, conquer all
   things through strife;
His destination set becomes his
   tune:
Not prisoner but master, he will
   shun
Pride and hate and fear. Then life
   is well begun!

Ian McKay Ritchie
UNTITLED
the U.S. tries to beat the bore
her people visit the whore
they pay for the thrills
make just enough to pay the bills
a perpetual stone
hash through a cone
shrooming off to outer space
coming down from cocaine—
to the same old place
knife hits
nice tits
well shaped rear
Rainier beer
I mean,
what's life for?
I gotta score

Marilyn Long—Tims
WITHIN
With all the anger I conceal,
Black is often how I feel.
All the way to the deepest place
For sure, I fear, I'll be a case.
'Tis true, with me, I could never
   cope,-
For my emotions are on a slippery
   slope.

How much darker can it be?
I hope one day I'll again be me.
The pressures I heap upon my
   mind,
In search of a key that I may find.
And when I quit being so very
   black,
There'll be nothing at all to hold
   me back.

I will go and show, know and
   search
Never more being in this lurch;
The lurch that always chains me
   down.
I'm seeking the day when I
   become unwound.
Truely, on this day, I too can come
All the way out of this deep dark
   slum.

Catherine R. O'Neal
THY MAYKER
*[To Harrison Ford, a man for all
women, as the woman in the
poem is a woman for all men.]*
Swete dewe, thye
Furtile currentes dere,

13

Afforde thyselfe wythe blysse.
Hys lyte soewe
Oever, oever nere,
Wyl tyke frome yewe,
Heir formale kysse.

Glenn
MY HOME
A poem is a home
For my heart.
I'll never be alone
Nor apart.
I'll always be a part
Of humanity;
A home for my heart
A poem for thee.

Charles Goering
SAND CASTLES
Old Man, Old Man, small bobber
in time, how high you ride the
crest of the incoming tide! All
hail, Oh Captain of the wave!

Soon you will be dumped on the
shore all naked and white! Will
it be dark and cold? And will
the Son still give you His light?

The tide from the floor of
eternity's door will quickly
return to the sea, removing all
traces of you.

HE will pick you up then, as you
lie after play, your bucket still
clutched in your hand.

Oh, what will you say and show
Him that day? Will you be a
child or just an ugly old man,
all sick, all wrinkled, all gray?

Fill your bucket now lad, be
happy and glad for there is not
a care in the world that cannot
be shared by just two!

Come now, use the sand and pile
it high, build a castle right up
to the sky. For HE too is a
CHILD and likes what His
children can do.

Gwen Duckworth
DESTINY
Flower petals, softly falling to the
ground,
Like colored feathers, not making
a sound.
Flowers of all kinds, lining the
walk
Nodding their heads as if they
could talk.
Their pastel dress soon will fade
As lovely ladies in a final parade.

I sometimes envy the careless
flower,
Framing the window of my
bower,
Bursting with seeds that soon
will skatter
As if that were the only thing to
matter.

But even the flower has destiny;
Once a flower, another flower
will be.

Arlene F. Harmon
THE LOST CHILD
The child in me has lost its way
and my heart aches I might say
I grew so fast and the years went
by
With many a tear I did cry

I cry for the games I did not play
and the warm leisure days I
missed in May
I cry for the laughter I did not hear
I missed the good times with my
peers

The heart has its own memory
like the mind
But it will heal if given time
My eyes will cry tears of regret
and love for the child I will not
forget.

Dorothy Snow
THE TOWHEES
Jacky Frost has come
And left the fields all frosty white
And glistening in the winter sun.

And suddenly the yard is full
Of towhees hopping 'neath the
bush,
In dazzling coats of glossy black
Outlining rusty velvet vests
And white cravats.

How do they know to come
To habitations when the cold
descends?
How do they know my heart
leaps up
To see my friends,
These warmly feathered ones
That seek the warmth and wealth
Of man's abode?

No matter. Here they are
Serenely saucy in the cold
And pecking through the frosty
leaves
With strange delight.
—A winsome, winter sight!

Dorothy L. Craft
My Mother—My Father
Of all the Mothers in the world
none can surpass mine.
She's a woman of many aspects
and the best of every kind.

For all my life she's been my
mother
and she's been my father too.
She has done it in such a way
you could never tell there
weren't two

As a mother, she's soft and tender
and tries to understand.
She never tries to bully
but lends a helping hand.

Now as a father, that's something
different
she's as hard to bend as nails.

She'll tell us how to do it right
if we're wrong she whips our
tails

She's our rock to lean on
without her, we couldn't stand.
She's our own little canyon
but oh, what a Canyon Grand.

Lois A. (Leed) Hammaker
ROBIN IN THE SPRING
[Dedication to Jason R. Leed—
Jason in my poem are some of
the free gifts from God and
Nature. Use and enjoy them all
your life. Love Grandma.]
When the Robin comes in the
spring of the year
his sweet song we love to hear
Along with the cricket and frog
of the night
we know summer is soon in sight
Flowers and tres a painted picture
Days will be warmer by nature
What a great sight to see
A Robin in a spring time tree.

Gloria Duff
FAILURE
I can't surface
I hear the ripple of water
—above my head.
I hurt, my body suffers,
my soul sleeps.
—the mud has become so deep—
My feet sink down
and stay silent
My arms are tired of thrashing,
My tears have stopped flowing.
I reach for a hand
to help me—?
IT ISN'T THERE!
I reach for an ear to hear me—?
IT ISN'T THERE!
the water gets heavier
about and above me—
I quietly sink to the bottom . . .
—low, no one has heard me!
. . .i die . . .

Michele Verdun
STATUE
We call her the
Pink Lady.
A figurine
Full of beauty and grace.
An artists rendition
Of sensuality
And innocence
Molded into a figure.
She stands by the fire
And the flickering light
Reflects off her lifelong pose
Sending warm feelings
Through our minds.
If she were real
What would she be?
A moviestar,
Fashion model.
Who knows.
But she is not real.
She stands there and listens
To our conversations
With ears that cannot hear.
Never moving.
Doing nothing but being
The Pink Lady.

Nancy Lee Conklin
LANDS AFAR
Soft summer nights staring at the
stars
Dreaming dreams of lands afar.

Lands of Romance and walks in
the moonlight
Lands of Prince Charmings and
stallions of white.

Little girl hopes and womanly
prayers
Reflect themselves in those late
night stares.

Daylight comes and gone are the
stars
But not the dreams of lands afar.

Daylight brings the sun shining
bright
And with it comes dreams filled
of new light.

Of Lands of white beaches and
walks by the surf,
Lands of Palm trees, sunshine,
and mirth.

But daylight leaves too, and back
comes the night
And the cycle continues, sending
new dreams into flight.

Antonio Giraudier
CHRISTMAS
The heralds are awakening the
memory and the heart.
No day can remember with more
joy and pride,
the greatness, so lasting, of such
princely birth.
"The Christ has arrived" with the
lights that redeem,
with thorough compassion and
mercy that beam.
The heralds with music of
triumph and hope,
keep bringing a message of love
that will flow.
The heralds of kindness and
gesture and faith,
say: "Christ has arrived," and it's
God's day, everyday!

Florence E. Brytcuk
THE FIREPLACE
Sitting by the Fireplace,
Reading delightful poems.
From every corner of the earth,
On land and sea I roam.
Some are filled with sadness,
some with mirth.
I see the rise of the desert moon,
And hear the rushing river
rejoice.
I hear the hoof beats of the past,
I hear the voice of every race.
I'm comming to the end at last,
Dreamily, I noticed the fireplace.

Jim Hammons
THE POET ALSO BLEEDS
The poet speaks of predacion and
exploitation
in life' garden as evil weeds
his critics say he is agonizing and
editorolizing
they don't know the poet also
bleeds

The poet speaks of injustice, fear
and doubt,
it comes from him in a trickle or
a flood
his critics say he is only dealing
with feeling,
they don't count that equal to
blood.

They sometimes call him Far
  Right or even Red,
discount all he has said with
  labels unkind
they call for Acts, they scoff at
  Facts;
they revere the muscle and
  distain the mind.

They find neither logic or reason
  part of
realities season—they want only
  deeds
they think a Rhyme is only a
  waste of time,
they don't know the poet also
  bleeds.

Catharina Rinta
When a Daughter Grows Up
You're grown, and you don't need
  me anymore.
Not like it used to be when you
  were small,
And suddenly I feel so old,
I have my back against a wall.

A wall I can not climb or see
  through,
There seems to be nothing up
  ahead.
You're starting your life, mine is
  over,
And all you need to know now
  has been said.

I'm losing part of me since you go
  your way,
and my way seems to be a dead—
  end street.
The past was good, and filled
  with so much living,
without you it can never be
  complete.

I helped you learn to walk, I
  walked beside you,
now I must learn again to walk
  alone.
You live your life, while I watch
  from the sidelines,
I have to let you go, for you are
  grown.

And yet, I'm grateful for the years
  we had together,
for they were mine, and will
  forever be.
And they can never really all be
  ended,
as long as I can live them once
  again in memory.—

Gloria Ann di Orio
SUPERNOVA
[Dedicated to my
superdaughter, Donna—Maria
Raimondi di Orio, who lives
with Aunt Ruella on a hill in a
house behind a farm that has
apple trees with lots of bees in
the little town of Johnston,
Rhode Island . . .]
What is this supernova—this
  exploding star—bright light in
  the dark of night
I see from afar—what you seem
  to be but not what you truly
  are?
Are you nothing more than a
  metaphor—a folklore from
  days of yore—what mysteries
  untold do you hold deep in

your core?
What are you really up there for?
What predictions are you hiding?
  A comet bearing a tiding?
Are you marking the passage of
  seasons—helping things to
  grow below—fixing times for
  harvesting and planting—
  bringing forth sun, rain or
  snow?
What kind of omen do you send
  to earth and men?
Were you remotely conceived as
  past theologians believed in
  the frigid darkness of space?
Why at this moment am I here
  and you in that place?
Are you sowing life—producing
  elements across the heavens
  over earth—do they become
  new stars or planets—when
  you die, is there rebirth?
Wise astronomers ponder—
  always they wonder and
  debate—some say we are made
  of the energy you create . . .
Are you determining one destiny
  or everybody's fate?
Do you control the laws—are you
  the effect—cause—the
  source—the Force that can
  rejuvenate?
Will you live a long long time—
  then cave—in with a mighty
  crash—am I a starchild built
  from the residue of your ash?
Do you live forever in the
  galaxy—or do you die like me?
Do you go into a black hole when
  death takes its toll?
How long have you been there—
  what is eternity—are you
  merely debris moving away
  from me?
When I look up at the heavens—
  am I looking back into time—
  is it the light of dead stars
  causing all the shine?
WHEN WILL EARTHLINGS
  ATTAIN THE
  COMPREHENSION OF THE
  SUPERNOVA WONDERS IN
  ANOTHER DIMENSION?

Tony Maione
For What My Father Has
My youth was spent in rebellion
Against whatever you were for.
Today finds me battle weary,
Searching for serenity as
My enemies prepare their next
  attack.

Dorothy M. Norden
ADIEU, ADIEU
Oh Sleep, Sleep, Sweet Friend
For on the—morrow, we meet
  again
Your care's all have gone
But your dear—memory lives on.

You do not walk the path's of—
"This World Now"
But only for a little while
No more strife and sorrow
You've had "Your Trial".

So Sleep, Sleep, Sweet Friend
For on the—morrow, we meet
  again.

When "Jesus comes" to claim his
  all

We'll be waiting for his call
United in his Spirit
And washed in his Blood
We'll reign in his Kingdom
Saved by his Love.

So Sleep, Sleep, Sweet Friend
For on the—morrow, we meet
  again.
Adieu, Adieu,

Annette Regina
I CAUGHT A BUTTERFLY
From the corner of my eye,
I caught a butterfly.
  It danced upon the breeze,
And waltzed about my knees;
  It did a polka 'cross the ground,
Then foxtrotted all around;
  It slipped into a minuet;
  I pounced upon it with my
    net!
And I caught a butterfly—
From the corner of my eye.

Jan Shepherd
EARTH
All the hearts of men are one,
As every star becomes a sun.

And all the melodies and plans
Are mirrors in the mind of man;

And all the thoughts and words
  and wings,
Reflections in the light of things.

And where the light becomes the
  day,
We see the stars, we taste the
  clay.

Nellie J. Brossard
EXCELSIOR
When the Almighty formed the
  rose to bloom upon the bush,
  He was not satisfied with the
  mere beauty of its blush,
So He concealed within the
  petals of the flower fair,
  A perfume whose sweet
  fragrance lightly permiates the
  air.

When God created world and
  sky, as earth in orbit spun,
  He regulated day and night in
  timing with the sun,
But then He was not fully
  pleased, and so devised a
  scheme
  To glorify its dawn and dusk
  with splendored color scene.

And when He made the fowls of
  air on wing to wend their way,
  He gave them feathers bright
  and dull in beautiful array.
With all this grace and wonder
  He again was not content,
  Now from their throats there
  comes a song until the day is
  spent.

He caused the earth to heave up
  mountains tall to charm the
  land,
  That seem as though they're
  only meant to bear the pine
  trees grand;
Yet, down within their bosom,
  you will find if you but seek,
  God hid away some precious
  ore to make them more unique.

Most blest of all creations on the

earth is man sublime,
  For he has reason, and he's
  made in God's own form,
  divine.
With all the gifts bestowed on
  man by Him who dwells above,
  The goal was still not gratified,
  for lo, He added love!

Tracey Eletto

Tracey Eletto
The Beauty Of the Birds
Watch the beauty of a bird in
  flight,
Watch their wings, their feet, oh
  so bright,
They move with grace, not hate
But one thing strange, is their fate
That their bodies may die, but
  never their wings.

Rita M. Allegretto
SPRINGSONG
Tic—tac—toes on steamed
  windows
  Another rainy day
The skating rink's a wading pool
  As winter slips away
The budding trees are garlanded
  With crystal drops of rain
And in the woods
  A robin sings
To welcome spring again

WJM
EMPTY SKY
What do you think about when
  there is no more why?
Nothing comes echoing back
  from an empty sky.
No colour, no poems, no art,
An end without even a start.
Did away with the good,
Always more than we should,
Gray static up and down,
Idiot—boxed all around.

Neale R. Neelameggham
AMONG MACHINES
Tell me of the 109 sweeps
You made with the vacuum
And the 79 ads
You can recite verbatim.
In the middle, a letter from
  Auntie
How dear was she?
And the 13 bills
Yet to pay.

Tell me of the juicer
Cooling your throat,
How the dishwasher
Scoured your skirt,
The dryer that droned
And the washing machine that

dyed.

Who did Erica ruin today
In All My Children?
How you won the dating game
To Hawaii, for how I
Ain't home, and other
Soaps that don't seem washy.

I will listen to all you say
Sit and drink your smiles
Burst to me the contained
Aloneness among machines.

Irene Laymon
I WONDER
Sometimes I wonder
Sometimes I do,
What my life would be like
If I'd met someone like you?

Sometimes I wonder
What I might be,
If someone like you
Had walked beside me?

Sometimes I wonder
Just once in awhile
If all of my heartaches
Would then have been smiles?

Sometimes I wonder
If my dreams would come true,
If a long time ago
I'd met someone like you?

Betty Jane Luellen
THINK ABOUT IT
Do you hear that crying-as-in-pain
    train whistle trailing off in the
    distance? We could pay heed to
    it, for the diminuendo of the
    retreating whistle is like one
    day in a lifetime slipping away.
    First, it is anticipated, sensed as
    a still-remote rumbling. And
    we are alerted, poised, awaiting
    whatever comes next. Suddenly,
    we begin to feel its vibrations:
    it brings us its message. It begs
    us to stop! Listen! Look out! Pay
    attention to what is going on
    around us! Don't miss
    anything! Then, for a long
    moment, it bursts upon us,
    B O O M I N G in our ears.
    Next, it begins to retreat,
    leaving a trail of time etched
    forever upon our lives. Lastly,
    it dies away; it is gone, never to
    return. We can never hear that
    very same train whistle again.
    We can not relive this day in
    all the world. Think about it!

Martha McPeak
MAGNIFICENT MOMENT
We wandered far, we wandered
    wide,
With each day filled with
    pleasure,
And many pleasant memories
Through coming years we'll
    treasure.
We drove along past fertile fields,
Deep woods and pasture lands,
And where wide, rolling prairies
Stretched far on either hand,
Through the bustling cities
And where broad rivers flow.
Then early on one morning
While the sun was still quite low
We turned a bend, and there they
    were!
Peaks gleaming white with snow,

Majestic range of mountains,
Heads lifted to the sky. . .
I find my throat constricting,
A teardrop stings my eye.
I feel them shouting, "Welcome
    home!"
"Hello! We're back!" I sigh.

A. William Floyde
THE REALITY OF A DREAM
Do you live your life on a regular
    course,
while your feelngs eminate from
    an unknown source?
Do you feel in a bind trying to
    sort your mind,
while you fill your time with
    unspoken rhymes?

Do you live in the memories of
    the past,
trying to make that special
    feeling last?
Are you afraid of tomorrow,
because you can't deal with the
    sorrow?

Well open your eyes and get a
    second sight,
of a person I know that's true to
    life.
Open your eyes and look at me,
I'm living my life the way I want
    it to be.

Look into my eyes and see the
    dream,
the dream that will become reality.
Open the eyes and open the door,
and look at life from a different
    shore.

Across the sea and across the lake,
the heart of the dream is taking
    shape.
Time is precious but that doesn't
    matter,
the dream I have will never be
    shattered.

My friends have come and my
    friends will go,
the secret of my dream, they will
    never know.
Their lives are immobile, they'll
    stay in one place.
The spice of life, they will never
    taste.
I have a dream that no one will
    see,
until it has become my reality.

Shirley A. Settle
MEMORIES
What has it been, a few years
    now, since first we two

discovered
That being loved and loving back,
    does not make experienced
    lovers?
You were just eighteen, I was
    almost twenty;
And like all foolish youth, we
    thought that we knew plenty.
You were shy, and I was bold;
    You said: "All is well", but the
    rubber didn't hold—
Now, we're both to become
    parents; what more is left to
    say?
Except, that it really is the truth:
    "It sure don't pay to play . . ."

Myrna McLeod
JOE
[For my sweetheart, who
doesn't want me to grow old
without memories.]
I like the rainfall,
and shadowy skies,
and love the shining
stars in your eyes

I like lazy days,
quiet simple ways,
and love your laughter
it's like warm sun rays

I like fun rides,
circles and dips,
and love the sweet smile
that plays 'cross your lips

I like horror movies,
with monsters and things,
and love time with you
whatever it brings

I like Ballet,
and songs from afar,
but I love you
with all that I am,
for all that you are.

Lavon J. Foster
INTERNAL ETERNAL
Drops of self
take hold a chance
in crystallizing wonder.

Rays breakdown the
wandering complexities.

Time
by itself
slow nor fast.

Yet, continually changing.

Should I be scared?
Peace lurks amongst
the discovered.

Helen Brown Rittershofer
REALITIES
The joys of life are many
And as women meet and greet
Interests are formed as thoughts
    unite
Projects projected and well
    defined.

As collective interests prod
    motivation
Leaders are chosen to govern and
    guide
Members relate through
    participation
Stimulation of thoughts as
    activities guide.

Dream dreams in the fantasies of
    night
Incite and impress the hours of day

Inspirations are born as minds
    relate
And exchange of ideas becomes
    replete.

Luanna Poole
OH DESTINY—IN A MIDNIGHT DAYDREAM
[To my three children whom I
love Alfonso Jr., Gregory, and
Stacey Thomas]
Day upon days
striving miles til tired.
there's no sleep.
Success evermore
their goals.

The minds being
restless of this
recession
decrees they of
oh destiny
reas'nable realities
being all
they seek to be.

Standers to can't.
They shout out
with fierceness—

These minds
shan't be stagnating!
however cultivating!
for the faces of losers?
but ones—
idling through lifetimes
without destinations
in ev'ry nation! nation!

Adele M. Bakovsky
LULLABY
Night time gently, gently fall;
Night time cover, cover all;
Sleep my sweet child; sleep my
    dear;
Mother loves you . . . mother's
    here.

Softly, softly darling sleep;
Warmly, warmly snuggled deep;
Deep in slumber snuggled dear.
Daddy loves you . . . daddy's
    here.

Safely sleeping through the
    night;
Safely, safely in His sight;
God will guard your slumbers deep.
Now safely sleep . . . now safely
    sleep.

mary mahassek
can't say goodbye
when we first met, somehow i
    knew,
someday, someway, my dreams
    would come true.
we danced together every chance
    we could get,
but my dreams were not fulfilled
    as yet.

there was something there we
    could not touch,
if you had only known i'd
    thought of you so much.
when you called from the
    hospital i almost cried,
but i had to hide it down deep
    inside.

until one day our hearts couldn't
    wait,
and i'm glad that i wasn't too
    late.

i found the real you and you
found the real me,
i guess you could say it was
destiny.

the love i have for you i cannot
measure,
and your love for me is a precious
treasure.
let's keep our love strong - don't
let it die,
because my heart just can't say
goodbye!

Valma G. Adkisson
REVELATION
The lovliness of the sparkling
rain
As it gently falls again and again
Glittering all about.
No traces of the barren land
That once was spoken of as
drought.
The freshness of the sudden
green
O'er landscape far as can be seen
Is pleasing to the eyes of all
Alert to Mother Nature's call.

Hues appear on once undressed
land
As if painted by God's loving
hand
So dainty, yet so very firm,
Of Nature, one's so much to
learn.
Could I but create with a brush
Or with words this lovliness
I see before my misty eyes,
The love, the calm, the peace
That at this fleeting moment's
mine;
All restlessness and fear so far
apart
From this instant's peace now
captured
Deep within my heart.

Sharon L. Robicheaux
ALL BECAUSE OF YOU
I love evenings' sunset,
as shadows grow into night.
Quiet slumbers relaxation,
twinkeling, glimmering light.
I love the forested mountain tops,
contentment in a sigh.
Trees silhouetted against ocean
blue,
shooting forever towards the sky.
New life, creations miracle,
my God's still on the throne.
I love the warmth of family,
having Sunday dinner at home.
Crackeling of burning pine,
fireplace becomes aglow.
Gazing deeply into your eyes,
so much more I long to know.
There are many things that I
love,
but have mentioned just a few.
Each day has taken on a special
meaning,
and it's all because of you.

Donna Carlene
DAYS OF YOUTH
The days of youth are long
indeed,
While their sun shines all
through the day.
Green grows the grass along the
path,
Lovely the flowers that bloom

along the way.
Lightness guides them through
their life,
And light their young footsteps
tread.
Happiness lifts their spirits with
song,
While they have life's sweet wine
and bread.
Lift high thy young heads with
pride,
Sing thy young song loud and, oh
so strong.
Dance while the long days are
upon you,
For too soon the days will not be
so long.
And thou want the days when
thou did learn,
And thou long for the days when
young blood did burn.

Shane Lashley
**Wishes and Dreams and
Candlelight Streams**
Wishes and dreams and
candlelight streams
Flowing softly through the back
of my mind
Searching for feelings I wish that
I had
But knowing what I'll probably
find.

Cradeled in the webs of seldom
recalled thoughts
I found the memories I had for so
. long sought.
And now that they're here they
bring only tears.
Because like human antiques
they comfort the weak
But are forgotten over the years.

Marna Mraz Hammond
Green Mountain Magic
Green Mountain Magic
isn't something in a store
It doesn't have a price tag—
it's there for rich and poor.
It can't be packaged in a box
for sale, door to door.
It's just an ancient whisper
vibrating soft and clear
for those who know to listen
with a heart and not an ear.
A certain, sweet serenity to
soothe
a troubled soul,
When this madness called
society
begins to take its toll.

Green Mountain Magic,
a haven from my fears

Replenishing the energies
washed away with tears.
Restoring Faith in Nature and
what is meant to be—
To those who search for answers,
the Magic holds a key.

Charlotte Palmer Haaker
**To My Daughter
    Love Mommy**
*[With love always to my
darling daughter Jeanette
Christy Love Haaker]*
When you wish upon a *star*
Mommy loves you the way you
are
You're my daughter, *yes indeed*
I see you growing like a *seed*
I think of you both *day and night*
My love for you is a lasting *light*
You're my precious little *girl*
With those beautiful little *curls*
I love you with my tender *heart*
I pray our love will never *part*
I love you more than words can
say
Every moment, every second and
every *day*
I pray our love will last *forever*
So we will always be *together*
You may have problems, *I can see*
But I'll try my best to help you,
indeed
My darling little special *girl*
With those beautiful little *curls*
There is so much more I could
say
Because I love you in a very
special *way*
As I look to the sun *above*
I remember of my precious *love!!!!!*

Steve Neil
I AM THE BREAD
*[For my sisters, my parents and
my friends.]*
i am the bread you discard
in hopes of finding meat
i am the weed you spit upon
and trample with your feet.

i am the iron you forge and smelt
into ingenious weapons
i am the man you killed today
i am the sun that's setting

i am the blood red sky at dawn
the stars that shine at night
i am a tear poised on a cheek
relections of a life

i am a word spat out in haste
with venomous intent
i am the child that cries for you
when finally anger's spent

i am love that's spread so thin
through-out all the land
i am all that encompasses
i am just a man

Cindy Houck
OUR PRECIOUS GIFT
I'm lying here in a hospital bed
A year and a half after we were
wed
I'm lying here and it's almost
noon
And our baby should be coming
very soon
When I left I said, "I Love You
hon"
Now I'm back with your son
He has black hair and weighs
nine pounds.

He's lying here not making a
sound
He sleeps and eats and cries
sometimes
But he's our precious gift, yours
and mine.

Georgiana Lieder Lahr
SECRET PLACE
Where is the secret place of the
Most High
Is it in woodlands, beautiful and
fair,
Or is it neath the wide, blue-
vaulted sky,
Or dark of night, with stars
pinned ev'rywhere?

I've searched throughout the
world, so far and wide,
On mountain top, and close to
ocean's shore,
In prairie lands and hills on ev'ry
side,
And up and down the earth, did I
explore.

But I've a secret, that with you I'll
share,
God's kingdom lies within, and
this is so;
In quietness of soul, you'll find
Him there,
No longer need you search, nor
come, nor go.

From Secret Place of God, you
can't depart,
You'll find it lies within your
humble heart!

Kathryn Lowell
TEACHER
Teacher, Teacher,
Help me to reach
For the moon and the stars
And the earth of tomorrow.
If you help me to grow,
I'll grow greater than you
For that is the way of the
universe.
If you try to stunt my growth,
I'll grow in spite of you.
I will grow
Whether you care,
Or do not care
For I don't need you to care
I want you to care.

Gina Marie Mandarino
RAIN
drip
dribble
down
Round
    and
        Round
Slithering
    as is the mind . .

    the tear
    that shows
    how much I know

    the rain
    will be falling
    as soon as you go.

I. Wright
WHEN
When the workload gets
depressing, and it seems the
day won't end;
When the time clock keeps on
ticking, look ahead to
tomorrow, my friend

Today's Greatest Poems

When the workload keeps on
climbing; stop and count to
ten,
Explore a new horizon, set
priorities, and the sun will
shine again.
Stress can be a bummer, get you
down and keep you there;
Rise above those daily tasks and
show the world you care!
Put a smile upon our face, no
matter what the trend,
Keep whittling at those little
tasks and soon the day will
end.
When the cycle starts all over,
put that smile back on your
face.
When the workload starts to
climb again, simply set your
pace.
Soon the stress will slowly
dwindle and the days will
quickly go,
And the quality and quantity in
your daily work will show.
When you're up there on that
pedestal reaching for a star,
Be proud of those
accomplishments—those
around you are!

Barbara Lewallen
No Longer Are You Just My Girl

Can't call you my girl—
For you are now a woman who
belongs to all the world.
No longer loved by just one.
Now it's everyone.
Even though I've helped to make
you what you are today—
It hurts me to let you go this way.
Wish I could keep you as my
girl—
But that woudln't be fair to the
rest of the world.
You made it because you're good.
Just like I knew you would.
All you needed was someone
who believed in you—
As I still do.
I cherish every memory—
When it was just you and me.
It makes me feel like a king,
To know that everyone hears
you sing—
About the feelings you have
inside—
That others may try to hide.
But I'll always remember you
as my girl—
A time when you didn't belong
to all the world.

Melva J. Lunceford
THOU MAN OF STEEL

Thou Man of Steel,
Strictly an earthly term to
describe a Noble One.
Of like construction, you weather
the storms
To teach both Old and Young.

You build a pathway, so straight
and narrow,
No gullible one can enter.
Like a New Born Building,
founded on rock,
You survive the fiercest winter.

The rains may come and the
winds may blow

But strong and upright you stand,
Like a Beacon Light, shining out
at night
To show us where to land.

Yet, many a crew has lost its way
Because one slept at his post
Who should have been watching
the light of Christ
And heeding the Holy Ghost.

Yet often, the wisdom of men
seems so great
We forget all the sign posts given,
Landing low on the sands of a
barren shoal,
Having not Love's Law of Heaven.

D. Joseph Sprague
AS IT IS

As it is,
my eyes . . my ears
and my other thresholds
are gifts allowing me
to personalize creation.
And through creation I move
as slow as I perceive without,
or as fast as I see within.

Thus disposed as I am that I am
in my beginning,
creation is given from an infinity
of time,
for, more than the value of my
breath,
there are treasures to behold;
for less than any breathless
moment,
no wonder of beauty could ever
be sold.

Marie E. Tyburec
MOM

like some brave, inner light
trying not to die
in the face
of a bigger wind

she refused to believe
the hurricane
was coming.

Lincoln Littrell
FINALE IN FILET

How sail such scaly ships so
sleek and shiny;
Are pelvic fins the oars that row
them through the briny?
Do their pectoral paddles push
across the paddy,
Or does a caudal swish propel a
fish
Through days before we make
him finnan haddie?

Do rippling muscles move them
through the waters
In seeking refuge, food, and
courting aunts and daughters?
Few persons care how finny ones
have lived or died,
Or of propulsion by water jet
expulsion,
And ask but if they're better
baked or fried.

When fishes come to take the
bait, it's dandy,
And anglers give no thought to
modus operandi:
When swimming's done, the
fisherman is jolly,
And how the fishes swim
means naught to him
So long as some will take his
hook for their finale

James Ph. Kotsybar

James Ph. Kotsybar
MY DECISION

i was sitting
down and alone in
my room when the
doorbell rang

i got up to
answer a
man selling faith with
his family smiling
behind him
i told him i was saved and
was closing the
door when the phone
rang i asked hello
this time it was a
woman selling
PSYCHOLOGY TODAY
i bought a years subscription

William Roy Pagel
WHISKERS

Feelers of airborne energies,
Grasping highlights of essential
ones.
Draining into empty banks
To store and use when thinking
runs.

Lori K. Holbrook
THE PROMISE

Tear drop falls
the silence wont
to hear the sound
the happiness dreads.

To be and true
will always cost
sharing, caring
let the matter slide
tear drop falls
the child cries.

Florence Dyer Follin
A Mother's Broken Heart

I am thinking of a mother
Whose head is bending low—
She is grieving for a loved one
Whose crime has stunned her so.

The whole jury, she cries softly
Was of a single mind—
They are sending my poor baby
Where the sun will never shine.

It's his only crime, she pleaded—
He was a lovely lad.
'til a faithless wife provoked him,
Causing him to shoot a cad.

Now my darling must go from me—
My heart is broke in two—
And the woman who made him
crim'nal,
Is free as skies of blue.

Oh sweet Saviour, please have
mercy,
Please spare my darling boy,
For he never caused a heartache—
And he was my only joy.

They are taking her to join him—
Beside his lonely grave—
For his crime was never pardoned,
And 'twas with his life he paid.

Debbie L. Moore
COFFEE POT

The soft churning sound
fills the room
with a peaceful potion . .
Hands to forehead
to grasp a thought
and rest the mind . .
The last gasp
slightly awakens
the room's occupants . .
Pour me a cup.
I've been up all night
Trying to write
Some poetry.

Jeanne Barbasiewicz Hoogstad
Treasure In the Water

When first I came to Greta
Anderson
I could barely float
And I didn't know the difference
Between the pool and the boat!

Safe in the water
Mom wanted me to be
So she took me to Greta
To see what she could teach me.
I cried alot at first
But I learned to close my
mouth fast
Because a mouth full of water
Is not what you want in class!

A baby's view of Greta is . .
She thinks that you're a fish
And she won't let you go to
Mommy
Which is your dearest wish.

Mommy hugs and cuddles you.
And work is what Greta makes
you do.
First on your tummy then turn
over on your back
and float, float, float.
(Greta's not satisfied 'til you float
good as a boat.)

Well it didn't take me long to
learn
It's far safer to float than sink.
From my tummy to my back I
can turn.
I'm a water-safe baby, I think.

The water's now a safer place for
me to be,
And mom's a little more
worry-free.
For the Mother who brought me,
For the Teacher who taught me,
I thank Thee Lord!

Roberta H. Graf
LOVE ENDED

If only I could walk with you
And feel your gentle arms again,
Touch your cheek to mine
To let you know how much I
love you.
All that is lost now, for I am dead.
I died when you ceased to care
And took away my happiness.

Today's Greatest Poems

Jeanette M. Haney
ALONE
Alone may be happiness
A time to think,
To rest, to pray
But loneliness is saddness
A time we wish would go away.

Elaine S. Cirelli
THE GROWTH CHOICE
We are our thoughts, our feelings.
Our lives reflect our values, our
    motives . . .
our inner selves.
Our lives mirror our head,
they are the projection of our
    inner world.
What is inside us, is our reality.
We cannot run away from
    ourselves.
And we can smother what is
positive in us,
by compartmentalizing.
It is important to learn to
    appreciate the whole.
There is a difference in saying
    Yes!,
to life, and saying yes,
to just living . . .
Sometimes, the trouble comes in
    splitting,
the good life, from the bad life,
the okay in us, from the not okay
    in us.
By accepting the not okay in us,
we grow—
and finally transcend the
    dichotomy,
by learning to use all of it
    positively.

Doris Mize Havard
OUR WORKS OF ART
Never considered to be a sculptor
Who works with clay or stone
Molding inanimate objects
Uniquely all their own
Day by day we mold and carve
Creating something more unique
As we teach our children
We influence the way they think
We mold their minds to prejudice
By what we say and do
We as parents shape the child
So innocent and true
Just as a sculptor with his clay or
    stone
We create a work of art uniquely
    all our own

Jeroslawa Benko
TELEPHONE
rudely awakening
and bringing to consciousness
the concentration
        daydreaming
        preoccupied person
within hearing distance
of its persistent plea
or the answer to anxiety
quenching all doubts
a pleasant surprise
the transmittal of which
will be remembered indefinitely.

Toni C. Ortegon
I'M SORRY
I came from a mold that was
    chipped
        and cracked.
This made me one of a kind with
    a destiny

unknown.
I tried my best to be just the way
    you
        chose for me,
but each day of my life seemed a
    little more
        not right.
I listened to every word you
spoke, and stored it
    in the back of my mind.

You gave me love, you gave me a
home, you gave me
    all and more than I needed.
I cherish it all and love you both,
    but what I've
        chose to do seems wrong to
you.
If I thought I could be happy
living my life your
    way, then I'd do it just for
you.
But try as I might I just can't be
like
    all the rest of you.

If ever I've hurt someone deeply I
know this
    must be it.
I've nothing to give you, I had
hoped you'd
    understand.
I'm just not made the way you
think
    I am.
So as I leave I'll not say
good—bye
    just, I'm sorry . . .

Susan C. Young
THE DECISION OF DEATH
The whispering winds tell me
That time is passing by.
The clouds are opening up,
And I'm reaching for the sky.

The mist from the rain
Gathers in my eyes.
The sun is not shining
As I look toward the skies.

As I drift off to sleep,
I give a great sigh.
The sky is calling for me,
I'll say my goodbye.

Margie W. Grant
DREAM WORLD
I looked to a star bright and
    shiny,
    Guarded by good angels only,
Where day and night on a blue
    kingdom reigns supremely,
    And oceans blue splash on
sandy white beaches.
Deep rivers run wild,
    And majestic mountains reach
to the sky,
Where fleecy white clouds travel
freely,
    Where no man goeth.

I have traveled this world,
    But surely,
From a beautiful vivid dream that
    awaketh me,
    Sublime,
From out of space,
    Out of time.

Ranza Devereaux
Opportunities Unobserved
Living in paradise unaware
    adolescence turning youth
        heeding the call of the wild

turning away from truth.
Golden age's radiant youth . . .
    idling away their time
        opportunites unobeserved
            energies go up in smoke.
Paradise lost, ageing youth . .
    no chance to redeem
        formative years of childhood
            spent in frivolities.
Spent youth becoming adult
    longing for wasted youth . . .
        too late they can't re—coup
            an empty and useless life.

Norma Downes

Norma Downes
REMEMBER TO SMILE
*[Dedicated to Teryl and Cathy
Downes
who warmed me with their
love and
smiles. Thanks. From Mom.
(Norma)]*
Remember when we pass and
A fleeting smile you see.
That I have given willingly, a
Little bit of me.

I don't know why it happens
Or what really makes it so.
I only know it cheers and
    brightens —
Makes my ownself glow.

So cheer the very next one
That you meet, see if you
Can get them smiling too
And off of Lonely Street.

Make a habit to remember
As you go your way,
It doesn't cost a penny
To share a smile each day.

Charles L. Moebius
HELLO
Hello.
It's been so long since we've just
    smiled,
        conversation
        (even only hello)
            is pleasing to me.
I see you in halls and on
sidewalks
    balloons and hair ribbons
and if I'm lucky you catch my
glance
        and smile.

But today there opened a pinhole
in my wall
    when you smiled, your eyes
laughing,
        and said hello.

Linn Morgan
I AM LIKE A SALMON
I am as a Salmon a swimmin'.
With my silver sides a shinin',
I meet the new strong currents
    each day,
When within Jesus' love I stay,
As the Salmon's body hits fresh
    water,
It begins to deteriorate and falter,
I too have hit my homecomin'
    stream.
My bones, as the Salmon's begin
    to gleam.
Soon my skeleton will show
As time comes for me to
    intimately know,
The way up the fish ladder,
Where all my sins and weakness
    will shatter.
Just as a Salmon on its way to
    spawn
I have no other goal but to reach
    Heaven's lawn.

Ms. Deven L. Hulbert
NITE RENDEZVOUS
the needs of the moment are
    crucial
time revolves to a standstill
the quiet of the nite settles
nature taken its rightful place
supreme and undisturbed
by mans dreams and nitemares
claustrophobia at nite is a lost art
instead boxes are caves
and safe for slumber
away from the openness of dark
    and moon
a quiet time it can be
full of learning and touching and
    reaching
gazing full—up at the sky
feeling flowing breezes through
    the trees
nite makes nature simple
all black and greys and light
wrapped in your arms and the
    moment
i welcome your presence
and enjoy your very essence
being here and sharing you with
    the nite

Cary Chrysler
THE SHADOW SMILE
[For my "Song of Joy"]
You smile at me dear lady,
Those eyes sparkle distantly.
You cry inside dear lady,
    Won't let me in to see.

I feel the touch of your pain,
Yearn to hold you to me.
Tears in your soul shed free,
Forming a desert rain.

You smile at me dear lady,
As if I couldn't know,
That pain in you dear lady,
Won't let you let it show.

Barbara M. Moore
I LOVE YOU
"You don't love me, mommy!"
    I heard my child say.
"You wouldn't even miss me
    If I up and ran away!"
Oh, my presious little one,
    Each time that I say "no",
You don't fully understand
    That it's helping you to grow.

"Mommy, do you love me?"

19

I heard my child say.
I love you more this minute
　　Than I could have yesterday.
But I'll love you more tomorrow
　　Than you will ever know . . .
'Cause through all passing hours
　　My love for you will grow.

"You do love me, mommy."
　　I heard my child say,
"You really care about me . . .
　　You show it day by day.
You prove how much you love
me
　　In everything you do.
And mom you've got to know
　　How much I love you, too."

Zella L. Myers

Zella L. Myers
ANTICIPATION
Thru the welcoming gates of
　　Heaven
With Jesus, my Savior, I'll go,
And rest on the banks of the river
Where crystal—clear waters flow.
I'll walk on streets that are
　　golden,
In garments of spotless white;
And there I will joy forever
In the land of eternal light.

God has said there'll never be
　　sorrow,
Or anger, or hunger, or pain;
No more glasses, or crutches or
　　wheelchairs
Whill ever be needed again.

I will sing with the saints of all
　　ages
The praise of redeeming grace;
And oh, the greatest of glory
To look on my Savior's face:
I'll awaken there in His likeness
And joyously with Him abide:
There to share in His blessings
　　forever
COMPLETELY SATISFIED!

Carolyn Pruit
**Silhouettes Of Grandma's
House**
Reflections of firelight dancing,
　　dancing, high upon the walls.
Grandmothers chair rocking,
　　rocking, fire flickering low.
Shadowbox dancers, toe and heel,
　　upon the wallpapers flowery
　　fields.
Out of darkness whispering
　　softly, silhouettes echoing,
　　echoing, echoing.

Light from grandma's kitchen

door, streaming, streaming cross
　　the floor.
Faintly, faintly voices call,
　　childrens laughter in the hall,
　　footsteps on the stairs.
In wavering shadows on a mirror,
　　familiar faded faces peer.
Faint strains of a song Laura Lee
　　or Night Winds Blowing Free,
　　played on old piano keys.
Out of the darkness whispering
　　softly, silhouettes echoing,
　　echoing, echoing.

Through the shutters of an
　　evening, streetlights burning,
　　burning bright,
　　car lights passing in the
　　night.
Images of pantomime fleeting
　　through venetian blinds,
　　across the faded walls of
　　time.
Out of the darkness whispering
　　softly, silhouettes echoing,
　　echoing, echoing.

Reflections of firelight dancing,
　　dancing, high upon the walls.
Grandmothers chair rocking,
　　rocking, fire flickering low.
Silhouettes etched within the
　　mind, echo down the halls of
　　time.
Childrens dreams and favorite
　　things still live in silhouettes
　　of Grandma's House.

Winifield A. Carlough
48
Negatives grate
Procrastinate
Sit and wait
Always late
Hesitate
Self—deprecate
Exasperate
Dissipate
Capitulate
Suffocate

How late is late?

Regina Brooks Swanner
RAINDROPS—TEARDROPS
The earth is fresh and clean and
　　sweet
From gently falling rain.
The thirsty land accepts, and
　　thus
Renews itself again.

The holy rains will wash the land
And heal the wounds it bears.
The drops are gifts of strength
　　and love
Though in the form of tears.

Oh, could I be the same as earth
Renewed by gentle rain.
My tears are from so deep within
That aching voids remain.

The tears of heaven fell today
And mingled with my own.
Yet heaven has decreed that I
Must shed my tears alone.

William Paul Graf
ON A WINTERS NIGHT
In the twilight
A silver orb shines
Down on the untrodden snow,
Lighting up the ice crystals,
Bringing little Frost Sprites

To life.
They prance about,
And laugh and shout,
Until the dawn comes
And then they fade
Back in the snow
Of which they're made.

Mary M. Miller
NEXT MORNING
The sunbeams brighten all the
　　sky;
The fluffy clouds float through
　　the blue;
The rain that fell all in the night
Has left the whole world looking
　　new!

JoAnne H. Williams
BUTTERFLY
[To Doris]
　　Don't genocide like a
butterfly . . . When it leaves
　　it's
cacoon in haste to impel to a
　　greater speed to end it's life . . .
　　But to act and be sure to
urge and press foreward too
search for a much greater and
fulfilling life . . .

D. C. Harrington
MY LOVE, MAYNARD
[To Maynard, who fulfills my
life completely,
stimulating all my emotions,
making me know myself.
Written to him when we were
3,000 miles apart.]
Oh, for the freedom
　　and mobility of a bird
then would I be free
　　to fly to your side
my love.
To escape from the sadness
　　and loneliness
that is inside of me
　　I would fly forever
to see your face
to touch your hand.
This would bring sunshine
　　back into my days
and warmth to heart.
Happiness is for me
　　　　you
because you are everything
　　　　to me
　　　　　　　my love.

E. Dewey Little
LISTEN
Web of words
Web of wonder
Held within a picture's
Pageantry of love,
No one doubts the reason
Or finds the thunder
Of the poetry above.

Lenora May Young
THE SHARED DISBELIEF
It was shared—The Grief,
The Disbelief.
As the shuffling steps falter
Soberly, reverently—as before an
　　alter.

The Precious Flag so bright and
　　true
Was cast with shadows, of me
　　and you.
Was cast with shadows, the halt,
　　the alert.

Marching by—The tall and short.

The shadows made not the
　　brightness dull,
It glowed only with colors more
　　full.
The colors absorbed each big,
　　little grief,
And gave the shuffling measured
　　relief.

Because he gave his All for All,
We must not let our courage pall.
Side by side with God he does
　　view,
The difference in form and hue.

Each solemn face passing by,
Was mournful with tearfilled eye.
True grief and love is colored
　　same—
Each can reverently call his
　　name.

Mark C. Witman
THE STRONGER HEART
I've conquered love, tho' not
　　unscathed;
My heart rebuilt with what was
　　saved.
Consideration's more allowed
By a stronger heart, not quite so
　　proud.
I've loosed the tongue to speak
　　aloud
Feelings once implied in jest
And now sincerely manifest.
That mine should be the heart
　　'twas saved,
No victory flag for me to wave—
Just one more simple gift you
　　gave—
Mine conquered by a heart more
　　brave.

Michelle Marie Weber
HIDDEN HORROR
At first it was a time to laugh—
I thought I'd be a clown.
So it was a smile I wore
All throughout the town.

It was fun at first
To laugh and make a joke.
Of every single thought I had
Of every word I spoke.

Enough of this I thought I'd had
My humor soon to drain.
I realized my attempts for love
Were all held quite in vain.

And so I trudged along life's path
My clown suit tucked away.
For sometime when I needed it
But did not need it to stay.

Ronald A. Bond
Lord Help Me Today
Lord help me today,
To give a cheery smile;
Lord help me today,
To go the second mile;
Lord help me today,
Not to seek worldly fame;
Lord help me today,
To praise Thy holy name.

Lord help me today,
To be a shining light;
Lord help me today,
To know the wrong from right;
Lord help me today,
In each and every way.
Lord help me today,
To seek You when I pray.

Today's Greatest Poems

Jerry Sink
MY END DRAWETH NIGH

[I wish to dedicate this poem to God and to all of my family and friends who had faith in me and for their encouragement.]

Give me a cloud for a pillow
   so soft so thick and so white,
Give me the sky for a cover
   to keep me warm thru the
   night.
Give me the Angels to protect
   me
      and the sun to give me the
   light,
Give me the moon the rain and
   the snow
      give me the wind that softly
   blows.
Give me the stars that shine so
   bright
      give me the Lords arm to
   hold me tight,
Give me Gods blessing as only he
   can give
      help me to praise him as
   long as I live.
Give me the strength to carry out
   his will
      give me the power to cure
   peoples ills,
Let my cup run over with the
   blood from his feet
      let me help all the sinners I
   meet.
Take me to the Rock that is
   higher than I
      let me drink of the fountain
   that never runs dry,
Give me my home so high in the
   sky
      take me home, Jesus, my end
   draweth nigh.

JoNelle Vanden Bush
WHEN I'M WITH YOU

My heart has wings
And it soars through the ashen
   clouds
Drifting on upward
Upward toward those heavenly
   gates
And that glorious ever—present
   light
My eyes are as stars
Twinkling as never before
Seeing only the most beautiful
   and precious of loves
My mind is focused on an
   eternally blissful peace
That I feel only when I'm with
   you
You make everything new again
And I have hope once more.

Alice C. Chapman
OUR LADY

You strayed into our lives one
   hot August day;
She must trust these people, for
   here she will stay;
So weak and sick, so lonely she
   must have been;
Hoping that this would be her
   journey's end.

We nursed her back to health; so
   loving was she;
Oh, how she loved to run, hunt,
   and to be free;

Lady Bug, we named her right
   from the start;
Putting her on a leash would
   have broken her heart.

She loved people, and Smoke and
   Laddie of her kind;
Only a lady could capture our
   hearts in so short a time;
Every day she would visit and
   make her rounds;
For seven years our Lady roamed
   these grounds.

One too many visits our Lady
   Bug did make;
Her freedom she loved so, meant
   her fate;
Our grief is beyond spoken
   words, for our pet;
Lady Bug, our little doggie, we'll
   never forget.

Ellen Reppert

Ellen Reppert
A Cookie and Cake World

[To Roy— who took the time to listen; and heard the words I could not speak.]

The pie—crust smells delectable;
The savory taste of fresh fruit
   and cream,
fill my being with a childhood
   dream,
Of a cookie and cake world;

Where smells are always
   kitchen—borne,
and kittens play on the hearth,
   purring and curled;
And decisions of state come
   packaged so neat,
with nothing more pressing than
   sweet chocolate to eat.

Richard Schaefer
The Coast That First Eyed

The coast that first eyed the
   dawn
where once ebb tides flowed
but now no more
moves golden sand upon the
   shore
a nearer blessing gone;
where tales were told
of olden whalin' lore
where aged laughter wrinkles
   showed
wind—torn reddish faces glowed
where monster earthquake forces
   tore;
quite a suprise to everyone.

Betty Schmitt
FEELINGS OF A DIVORCE

Rain, Hail, Thunder, Tornadoes,
   Hurricanes—
      All are there.
Then comes a smile; a soft touch
   upon your hair.
      SUNSHINE!!
Oh, the happiness of sunshine—
      Suddenly, the world becomes
   mine.
Even if just for an hour
      to know you are not alone—
To feel that all your dreams
   are not blown—
To believe that there will be
   a better tomorrow.
Then gone, so quickly taken
   away—
      Back comes the long, alone
   day.

Ruth H. Fowler
THE WHISTLER

Just to hear a fellow whistle
While he's busy at a chore,
Makes your day seem so much
   brighter
And you want to hear some more!

He whistles—and the
   neighborhood
Takes on a happy air!
A chap who whistles while he
   works
Is welcome Everywhere!

Lew Drake
THE DRIFTING SAND

[Bus and Pat Bobbit Oceano, California]

Like a wild spirit born in a
   distant land,
That comes rushing over the
   eternal seas;
The ocean breezes gently lifts up
   the sand,
And moulds it around the grasses
   and trees.

It mounts a seige on the houses
   bare,
That give shelter to the presence
   of man;
And erodes the face of the land
   they share,
As it fills every crevice with
   silky, white sand.

Enter the portals of this
   wondrous place,
All who would seek healing for
   body and soul;
Allow the salty breezes to caress
   you face,
As the endless beauty of this land

unfolds.

The darkness of night has peace
   to give,
As the cool, fleecy fog covers the
   land;
May happiness bless all of the
   days you live,
In the beautiful house called "The
   Drifting Sand."

Teri Lyn Sell
The Only Spot Of Color

[For my Mom and Dad, who gave me the ability to appreciate the bit of color in everything.]

There's that tree again;
I see it every day.
Viewed from our small window,
It's outstanding in every way.
You know how it is;
Early winter in Missouri.
Everything so colorless,
Everything so boring.
But there it is;
A spot of color ahead of all the
   rest.
So tall and green,
It looks its very best.
It'll be that way forever;
The leader of the group.
It never seems to change
In nature's endless loop.
It's my evergreen.

David W. Barthel
THE OLD BANJO

The old banjo hangs on the wall,
The pick no longer moves.
But oh' the songs that filled the
   room,
And how those fingers flew.
When fingers were young and
   nimble,
And the old banjo was new.
But the banjo player has left the
   group,
To play on a higher stand.
So the old banjo hangs on the
   wall,
In memory of that man.

Curtis A. Cook
TENNESSEE MANUVERS

[This Poem was written and dedicated to my wife Dolores Cook during World War II, proving once again worry is useless as most lives have a silver lining.]

We came here to learn about war.
To protect the things we fight for.
We work and fight 24 hours a
   day,
So our loved ones can safely play.

In open trucks we ride all day,
To hunt a new place to stay.
We get settled at last, and then
We pack up and are on the go
   again.

Through snow, mud and rain,
We roam the hills and plain.
We fuss, rave and complain,
And say we'll hop the next train.

We blow our bridges behind us,
So the enemy can't find us.
We hold the fort at all cost,
Or our problem is a total loss.

Well I'm homesick you bet,
For my baby to pet.

A furlough I'll be getting soon,
So my little wife and I can spoon.

My little poem I hope you like,
As a little laugh is a part of life.
We are living like Kings,
So don't worry my little Queen.

Kathryn Tracy Allen
A WORDLESS SONG
Play for me for time on end
Pleasures that will never end.
An eternal giving pulse,
Of living, loving, life and hope.
A knee bending melody
To search the sky for the Deity.
Sweet dreams that come in the
    night,
When sleep eludes till dawn is
    bright.
Awaken the sounds that lie
    within,
Of how mortals all Kings and
    Poets
            have been.
Play on for me without a sound,
Helping my soul to know no
    bound;
Of the endless needing deep
    within,
Of a will to try again.
Play for me a wordless song,
The kind you hear when time is
gone.

Lana DiCalo
MEN OF DOOM
Lonely, moaning on the distant
    shore,
a wailing foghorn, tone drowned
    by the pounding seas raw
a guided warning for all souls to
    hear—
shivering, people clutch their
    throats in fear.

Many a ship and crew were lost,
tossed by sea; bitten by frost;
damned by coral reefs and
    impaling rock—
the wretched siren Lorelie mocks.

Vaporous, smothering fog—it
    hovers near;
the mystical, untouchable
    emobdiment of fear,
writhing over waters, seeking out
    ships—
the sea raucously laughing as the
    vessel tips.

Anguished, echoing cries by men
    of doom,
plunging to a dark, frigid watery
    tomb
where ivory bones of many a
    captain rest,
playing hosts to their unwilling
    guests.

Beware! Tongues of fog, they lick
    their prey,
when overcast skies turn a
    dismal gray—
eyes of widows tear and blur
in memory of the loved, brave
    men who were.

Lecia Greene
MY QUIET PLACE
This quiet place I go
    to sit and think,
And reminisce about all
    the things I know.

Its quiet and relaxing,

to sit,
Watch and listen.

To see birds flutter by,
    as they sore up to the sky.

To watch a squirrel gather nuts,
and then scurry up a tree.

To hear the winds whistle
    through the trees,
Almost whispering its nice
    to be free,
As a cool breeze passes by.

To feel the suns warmpth upon
    your face,
Miles away from the hustle of
    the cities pace.

Oh this is my quiet place,
    where I like to be,
It makes me feel free!

Darrell R. Leet
MY VIEW OF YOU
    *[To my wife, my inspiration,
    Janet.]*
When I look at you
In morning light
To view your features
With such delight.

So soft and tender
Warm and fresh
Never ending joys
No more no less.

Continuing love of life we see
Reflections of inner beauty.
Hearing softness spoken
Being alive and being open.

Just a simple expression
To speak my view
Of saying my thoughts
And my loving you.

Yvonne Jester Wallace
TO SEE
So strange you may say,
Things one may see some day.

To see a camel who has no hump.
To see a frog who cannot jump.

To see a bunny who has no tail.
To see a fish who has no scale.

To see a bird who has no wing.
To see a cricket who cannot sing.

So you think this is too bad?
Want to know something even
    more sad?

To see a starving child stand and
    cry,
Who is forced to steal, cheat, and
    lie.

To see those who will not share;
Who have so much, but do not
    care!

Marge Naber O. P.
A WOMAN
One who is for many
And asks little in return.

One who sees others needs
Before they know them
    themselves.

One who responds when
Someone needs help.

One who loves freely because
She has an innate caring for all.

One who all call friend because
She is there at a given moment.

One who can be tired, hurt and
    ache
And yet has energy to do for
    others.

One who is aware of her need to
    be needed
And keeps herself together.

One who knows her need for
    intimate love
And yet is willing to wait.

One who down deep knows she is
    okay
When things aren't all right all
    around her.

One who knows things she
    doesn't like about life
Are a challenge for her own
    growth.

One who knows it is okay to
    need people,
Feel alone and search for more.

One who knows it is not easy to
    really be a total woman
And yet keeps trying.

Because in the end, it is worth
    being more
A whole woman.

Margaret Malinoske
No Right To Be Proud
Man has no right to be proud.
Even during life man's body
    decays;
A slight illness—
Puts arrogant kings away
To inherit corruption;
Worms and maggots are his lot;
Equal to the lowliest man.
Pride is an affliction,
A reservoir, a source
Of devastating destruction.
It effaces the memory of great;
To harbor an odiousness
Among following generations.

Doris O. Spicer
A Woman Is Like a Rose
A Woman is like a Rose
that blooms in spring
Even does a Woman that sweetly
    sings.
A Woman is like a weed that
    grows
that God has made, and now has
    rose.
God loves the Woman who keeps
    the Law
That God will know who will be
    lost.
A Woman is sweet, and kind
to God this Woman is mine.
A Woman is most precious than
    gold
That God will keep, and never be
    sold.
That in the end God will see
even a Woman who believes in
    Thee.
That in the End there is no sin
for God loves Woman
That is where it all begins.

Semmie I. Bender
ODE TO A MEMORY
Once I was young and gay and
    free,
    Nothing seemed to worry
    me,
Then — crept in responsibility;

Of home and family,
With fears and tears of hopes and
    dreams,
    No time to dance and sing
Or have that fling . . . .
    But time changes things!

Once again I'm gay and free . . .
    Not as young as I used to be,
Only now, worry seems to flee. . .
    When once again I have
    responsibility,
Of little ones and family,
    Offsprings from one . . .
Who used to be young and gay
and free.

Jane Frederick Krauss

Jane Frederick Krauss
JASMINE
Sunny yellow Jasmine
Brighten future times
After winter days of chill
Give aid to lift my heart
And strengthen my inner will

Doris J. Bryant
MY JOURNEY
I once took a journey,
I never left my bed.
I guess you could say,
It occured within my head.

I had just lost my brother,
And my parents a few years
    before.
I was so lonely,
I could stand no more.

I prayed for God to help me,
And then in a dream.
I walked in fields of flowers,
Along a clear blue stream.

I visited with Mom and Dad,
And walked with my Brother
    dear.
We talked about so many things,
As when he was here.

I said, "I must go now,
But I'll return someday."
Then I awakened to realize,
HE had taken the sorrow away.

Carmine Anthony Loreto Socci
A LA NEWYORKEESE
Hear ye, hear ye,
ye one and all New Yorkers
in tintinnabulation!
Hush your rush
because my dove
nestles fast asleep—
chamber—caged.
Wait . . .
till she awakens,

shedding her splendor
onto the hoi polloi
who huff-puff
shopping . . . hopping . . .
jogging . . . jostling . . .
Her sunny outlook
lases my torpor
during lightning-flash
and thunder-roll.
Who is she?
She's historic Lady Liberty—
enfleshed!

Marion W. Davies
A SONNET TO A NYMPH
Oh! You beautiful oaks spreading
   so wide,
Where in your beings do
   Dryades hide?
I hear a sweet voice when the
   wind does sigh
Through the twigs and
   branches, both low and high.
Those dulcet tones do entreat me
   to stay,
To linger there where the cool
   shadows play;
One tells me that she's just like a
   mortal
When her tree dies she must
   pass the portal
Of death. But where will her
   spirit be then?
Why, to another young tree in
   the glen!
Nature has that basic unyielding
   rule
That one should e'er heed
   unless he's a fool;
When Being makes happenings
   on this ball
It does not pass until it scales
   the wall!

Marion W. Davies
TO A SOUL
No reason but love makes me
   pen these lines
When I think of your lovely
   soul;
It stands as straight as Ponderosa
   pines
With the strength of a
   redwood's bole.
The fine things of life shine
   through hazel eyes
As you look to the Lord above;
I ponder thoughts of time and
   how it flies
How he has blessed us with his
   Love.
You have given strength through
   your dainty hands
With the comfort of those
   sweet smiles;
Love has tied us with it's strong
   silken bands
While you've added your
   winsome wiles.
'Til the end of time I'll feel your
   Being
With the Glory you'll be
   seeing!

Adrian M. Maschek
THE EBBING OF TIME
Oh yes! time is ebbing away
with every tick tick tick of the
   clock.
Oh time, have I used you wisely
have I fell short of my goal,
have I done all I could
to help some other soul.

How much time have I wasted
how much do I have left?

I know time grows less by the
   day
but still I seek divine guidance,
to make every second pay.

Lord! let me see more clearly now
let me make better use,
of this precious time somehow,

Oh Lord! bless me with the
   wisdom
the effort and strength
and guide me through what's left
   of my time
never looking over my shoulder,
with regrets of how it was spent!

Kleon Kerr

Kleon Kerr
PRAYING
Some men pray at length,
Some opt the flowery word.
Others softly do intone,
Their voices barely heard.

Some utter words sincere
For a brother not in church.
Others pray for strength
The paths of truth to search.

Some itemize their blessings,
Showing deep appreciation.
Others offer up their thanks
For a knowledge of salvation.

Yet none appear so humble
As the biblical beginner
Who in candor spoke to God,
"Be merciful to me a sinner".

Stanley Pulsifer
KNOCK—KNOCK
I get so fed up when I hear
people knocking the younger
   generation,
We were all young once do you
   recall
raised a little hell and carried on
   creation.

So some smoke pot and drink a
   bit
and go speeding down the
   highway,
Who's been setting the example
   for our kids
we the older generation.

When they get in trouble do we
   help them out
or run them into the ground,
Remember friend when we retire
they will carry the load.

So let's give them love and

education
and most of all please—
Give them loyalty to America
The land of freedom and
   prosperity.

Tara G. Mullin
CHASING RAINBOWS
*[For C, S and A they taught me
it's worth it to chase them]*
the man
who sets out
to find a
center
that will meet his
   every whim
   and
   every wish
is indeed
chasing
a
rainbow . . .

Lorraine L. Quintin
TREES
I am a Tree, I stand very proud
   and hold up my limbs very
   high. Long ago, I stood and
   watched the Indians go by.
Long ago I watched the new
   people coming to this land.
I watched my family go down and
   come back up as log cabins for
   the white people.
I've seen the winters come and go
   but here I stand so proudly
   holding my limbs ever so high,
   toward the sky.
So you see the life of a tree is not
   so bad after all.

Rhonda A. Bosze
BEYOND ALL LIMITS
You must climb even higher,
To see even farther;
To know even more,
Than you ever did before;
To strive for the best,
And live life to its fullest;
So that you may accomplish,
What many others couldn't.

M. Elisabeth Steiner
City of Brotherly Love
Along tree-lined banks of the
   Delaware,
Philadelphia, three hundred years
   ago,
Became the birthplace of
   America,
Where men could live in
   harmony side by side,
Free from foreign repression and
   harassment—
Penn's "Promised Land" of
   religious freedom.
Here Founding Fathers sacrificed
   their all
To declare their country's
   independence,
And "proclaimed liberty
   throughout the land,
Unto all the inhabitants thereof".
Franklin's leadership in arts and
   sciences
Transformed the checkerboard
   "greene countrie towne"
Into a foremost center of learning.
As the city grew, so grew the
   nation,
Preserving its freedoms and self-
   government.

Man's yearning for liberty and
   justice
Is universal in today's struggling
   world,
Where men are still willing to die
   to be free.
Why nuclear weapons and
   hostility,
Leading to destruction of our
   universe,
When brotherly love can offer us
   life, not death.

John Matthew Apice
ONE ROOM LIVES
Amber lights flicker ghostly
   down
musty city hallways where
Tenants inflicted with suspicion
lock themselves behind a womb
   of walls.

All encompassing
Their One Room Lives.

Retired old men sit cross-legged
   in asphalt parks,
waiting to complete enough
   hours
To call them
Yesterday.

There were days when looking
   into their eyes
Was like looking into a burned
   out building.
But their stories where often
   marvelous
Memories alive with days laid to
   rest
And the silence between each of
   their words
Benevolent.

As they lived and breathed
Surrounded by the body they
   possessed
Sipping tea
In their one room lives,
While hours burned slowly in the
   pores of their skin
And down through the marrow of
   their bones
Peacefully.

David Alan Podd
MANKIND
Oh what a pitiful sight
Mankind stretching, flexing,
   practicing his might
Oh what a pitiful sight
Mankind so proud of the
   conquering of flight

Oh how I feel the frost
Mankind denying the cost
Oh how I feel the frost
Mankind not nearly percieving
   what is lost

Oh how I am afraid
Seeing Mankind and what he has
   made
Oh how I am afraid
Knowing Mankind and how he
   will be repaid

Oh I have no reason for pity,
   coldness, or fear
For Mankind's judgement day is
   near
Oh I have no reason for pity,
   coldness, or fear
But still for Mankind I must shed
   a tear

Kathleen A. McLaughlin
Seclusion
*[In my heart I owe but one for
the feelings encountered to
write this and many others]*
It's my feelings for whom I love
In strongly which I hide,
Deep within my heart
Forever in my mind

To expose is to kill
To savor means to hold
Until the end of life
When I am very old

Fantasy much more than reality
Is one that can be interchanged,
To make and keep me happy
Each and every day!

Donna Rae Huggins
FALLING SNOW
*[To my children Bruce Jr. Penni
Lee and Kandi Lynn with love
Mother]*
It is the white of nature's purity.
As it falls, so quietly down.
Like a feather, softly hitting upon
the ground.

As I look out my window,
And see before my eyes, the
happening,
Of mother nature's, blanket of
surprise.

Sheryl Frances De Garmo
Strikingly
So soft the moss,
So satiny green;
She didn't see
The slender snake
Beside the stream

She sat on the moss,
Sliding her hand
Slightly on its surface,
Her fingers startling
The sleeping snake
Strikingly awake!

Eileen A. Donovan-Cooper
BLISSFUL SOLITUDE
With stealthy caution I ventured
from my door
and set step upon newly-fallen
snow,
trodding into the quiet solace of
early morn
where no others had strolled

Downy flakes brushed my cheeks
in the whispering silence,
the only sound
the echo of my crunching
footfalls

It wasn't cold as I strode,
leaving my mark upon the
presently unsullied scape,
for companions my thoughts,
steamy breaths and the soughing
wind

The breeze sighed, branches
gently swayed, and
the snow blanket shifted,
resettling into higher hillocks,
feathery crystals gently
disguising, curving jagged
edges,
mantling evidences of man's
intrusion upon the land

Sweet quietude, gentle peace,
blissful solitary meditation,
pensive reverie,
a blessed unlonely aloneness to
be shared perhaps anon
but selfishly cherished now

Dorothy A. Stalker
The Secret of the Pyramids
Ancient pyramids stand out in
time
Structures to behold
Surrounded by a sanded floor
Barren—old
When all is deserted and still
The top slides open to the sky
Appearing in unison
Flying saucers lift-off high
Spinning into the clouds at
heaven's door
The symbols of Egypt close in
innocent digsuise
The desert speaks of age again
Mirrored in a child's eyes

Larry Douglas Chappell
SOUND
Rain on a barn's roof,
The stampede of horses' hooves,
Saint Marys of the Isle's chimes,
The silver ring of a U.S. dime,
A phone call from you, even
collect,
From anywhere, at any time,
To me, that would be
The best sound yet!

Elizabeth V. Tompkins
FRECKLES
A freckled face was my childhood
grief,
Cause I hated freckles beyond
belief,
They caused me such a lot of
woe,
I thought of them as my greatest
foe.

A polka dot look I could hardly
bear,
Sprinkles of freckles everywhere,
On my nose and forehead, too,
Gracious how I hated you.

Although most of my freckles
still remain,
How foolish of me to be so vain,
Ah' but youth's a fickle faze,
Maturity lives with me
nowadays.

Cheri Peterson
STRANGER
Now that I look back I find,
I never knew you at all.
It's strange how one can love,
And not really know why they
fall.

Just who were you that so,
Completely held me sway.
You that I thought I knew,
Yet now I know not today.

I marvel now in aftermath,
How well I thought I knew you.
How when close I was so blind,
Now apart I see right through
you.

Eileen M. Greene
FIRST LOVE POEM
*[For my "far away
friend" . . . James.]*
Pure as the soft green grass and
the endless pines,
Deep as their roots, wise as their
timeless minds.
Innocent of the world . . . awed
by the sky,
Drawn to the sea . . . to hear its
sweet lullaby.

I all alone to enjoy my simplest
dreams,
Longing to share the emotion I
keep within.
Timid to reach . . . too shy to
touch beyond,
Someone to teach . . . and wave
their magic wand.

Birds making love . . . on a
nearby branch,
The whispering wind puts them
in a trance.
As crickets sing . . . I fall in love,
Such intensity my heart's
become.

My love, my love so deep and
tears so pure,
My eyes . . . much more to see,
woes to endure.
And time's sweet song . . . all I
can hear,
Has swept me up and brushed
away my fear.

Edward F. Wilson
LOVE
[To Regina]
Love is raging in the blood;
An all consuming flood
that washes thought away.
Love is a river, deep and slow;
It's waters gently flow
out of yesterday.
Love is an effervescent cup
of wine that lifts you up,
fulfilling all your dreams.
Love is an image, seen, alas,
through distorted glass;
Never what it seems.
Love is a tree whose strength is
found,
deep rooted, in the ground;
It's branches touch the sky.
Love is a fragrant, lovely flower;
It's beauty has the power to cause
your soul to sigh.

E.R. Pirozzi
Searching, But What For?
Alone in a crowd, in a casual
hurry
Laughing while crying, relaxed as
I worry.

Searching, but what for?
Destined to do what?
A casualty of internal war,
God is all I've got.

Alone at night, I cry and I pray.
Where can I go to get away
and escape the despair of which I
write,
and finally end this desperate
plight?

I'm not alone, yet how lonely I
feel.
What feelings are true? What isn't
real?
What should I do? Who shall I be?
The search goes on infinitely

This verse has no end, no
conclusion I fear.
Quite a cause for concern, for my
future is here.
Not ready for tomorrow, can't
handle today.
The most I can do is silently
pray.

Maureen Mancini
SYNCOPATED PEOPLE II
There's a simple explanation
for the on-guard syncopation
that today's congregations
seem to live by
where it counts.

I guess it would be scary
if they couldn't all be wearing
the same clothes instead of
baring
a new idea
or two.

You won't see them abusing
any fad the public's choosing.
It's amusing, it's amusing
how they'd rather wane
than wax.

They're all such great pretenders
all these high-strung doting
blenders.
It's a cinch to comprehend . . . or
shall I say
to understand.

What they're after is a mesh,
not something fresh
upon their flesh.
So, therefore, they drop what
may prove individual.

Melissa J. Tracy
SPOTLIGHT
Your steps echo hollowly against
the stage as you turn and sit.
The light catches, then falls.
There is nothing, save silence.
There is no where to go; no
where to hide. You wait . . .
for the right time, the right
place. In the silence, your part
is born. You breathe
expectantly, wishing the words
into being. Still . . . nothing
worthy or prophetic breathes
through your lips. Only heavy,
burdened sighs reflecting
thoughts and images. But no
words, no words to paint them.
The scene changes, but the
stage does not. Time passes,
but the words are still lost. Yet
somewhere a thought is being
born . . . drawing itself up
from deep inside. It twists and
rises, being both shallow and
deep. The stage lays immersed
in fog. You pause—waiting for
it to come again.

(Worthy? Prophetic?) The fog billows, swirls. The spotlight falls on you. The eyes watch and wait. You sit, still alone; nothing save your own dreams to lean on. You feel the wrench of emotion tearing through your soul . . . and you shake. Eyes—lifting, tears—falling. Your words, bearly audible above the quaking of your soul. Yet they echo . . . forever. They were not worthy. They were not prophetic. They were just words. The eyes watched, as they always had. They were your own. 'I'll dance at your wedding,' you whisper. They cried. The fog lifted. The spotlight vanished. The stage lay empty—your steps echo across her. As you fade from sight, a roar of applause wells from beyond the stage. It was the most you could give.

Norman O. Day
MOUNT OF GEMINI
Allotted time a mere flash In a milenium
So very trivial if not for the Infinite.
Entering the sanctuary of quintessence
The long sought for empyrean.

Stupendously colossal splendidly magnificent
Rhapsody In the heavenlys
Recipients of pure unquenchable energy.
Festival of posterity absorb generously this portion.

Totality of all expansion of Inner vision
Partisan equaliy global sanctity
Entourage of the masses.
Solitude oh, blessed solitude
I embrace your presence.

Constant unwavering progression
An encounter of mellifluous Iridescence.
The sojourner establishes residence
On the Olympiad Mount of Gemini.

Nora Evelyn Wold
Three G's . . . God and His G-Men
God, Golodner, Gens
God, I've known all my life
A present help against strife.
Golodner and Gens, armed with knife,
Never saw before that fearsome night.

God, I trust you with my life;
Golodner and Gens I trust to God.
Knowing God will control your hands
Cutting only what he commands
Strengthened by His staff and rod.

Golodner's a gynecologist
A kind man, descent Jewish.
Gens, I'm told, is a God-fearing man
A mighty fine general surgeon . .
Two great men under God's dominion.

Three G's . . God, *foremost* of all.
Golodner and Gens playing ball
On God's team cannot fall.
Nora Evelyn's on the mend!
Thank you, God and His G-men.

Rugh E. Staly
A FRIEND
I was looking around for something.
No! I knew not what.
Maybe it was something I'd never find,
Or could be something I missed.
I looked under a backyard rock.
No! It wasn't there.
I looked throughout the forest trees.
No! It wasn't there.
I looked up at the sky of blue.
No! It wasn't there.
I looked along the babbling brook.
No! It wasn't there.

When I turned around,
And saw you standing there.
I knew I'd found what I was looking for.
   "A Friend."

Suanne M. Engle
TO A FINISHED LOVE
You say you love me and you'll always be true,
But I've stopped believing, trusting in you.
The things you've done to me were the blow;
I never thought I'd be the one to let you go.

I placed all my faith; all I had in your love,
The things that could happen, I never thought of.
You came and you went any time that you pleased;
And left me alone; to drown in my tears.

Now the days drag by into endless time—
And I dream of the love that once was all mine.
I wonder if you know what I am going through—
Or that love is finished, over . . me and you.

Do you know I still love you deep in my heart,
And I never wanted us to somehow grow apart?
But the silence has told me more than words say;
Our love is over; Do we want it this way?

Virginia E. Cruikshank
ACCOLADE
We celebrate distinguished service. The luster
Of your deeds shall gild your name, in letters
Shining forth to light a darkened world.
Your dedication, faith, and sacrifice
Enhance the stage you walk upon; and you
Shall hear the trumpet now proclaim,
"Here stands a teacher. Glory to your name."

Barbara Ann Lapham

Barbara Ann Lapham
LARRY
[To my Husband]
I know a man whose name is Larry,
Six foot tall and kinda hairy.

Eyes of grey with hair dark as night,
He's very good looking, boy what a sight.

His personality is quite unique,
A little stubborn, but very sweet.

He walks by me with his cute little wiggle,
That turns me on and makes me giggle.

This man called Larry has brightened my life,
With love so real, it must be right.

He picks me up when I am down,
By being silly like a circus clown.

Before this man came into my life,
I felt I'd never be any man's wife.

Helen G. Wuerth
UNCLE GEORGE
He died—emaciated, due to lack of elixir.
If he had drunk from the holy cup . . .
Would he have lived?

My thoughts see his tall, thin image
Walking his Pekingese to the bridge
Leading to the Wonderland of Ice.
Did he ever skate to "The Skater's Waltz"?
Did his wife, Mary, truly love him?
Did his only son understand him?

His two grandsons respected him.
Weeping at his wake and funeral,
They missed him before he was buried.

He was my father's youngest brother.
Dad, now in senility says,
"George needs a warm coat. It's cold."

Joan Stephen
SUNSET
A halo embraced the world tonight;
The horizon was rosy in hue—

Surrounding the hills and the valleys;
Adjoining a heaven of blue.
'Twas as if all the smiles of the angels
Had united to circle the globe;
Peeking through trees dark in silhouette—
And helping the sun to disrobe.
The skyline was pink fascination—
With deeper tones farther away;
Displaying the beauty of evening—
Reflections of God's perfect day.

Marge Della Badia
TELL ME YOU LOVE ME
You tell me you love me, you tell me you care,
But I need you so much, you just can't always be there.
I never feel sad when you are near,
Always tell me you'll love me forever dear.
When I'm alone I feel so tired and cold,
I must always have you to hold.
When I'm alone my thoughts just seem to wander,
All I ever do is blunder.
I know you love me with all your heart,
That we shall never really part.
I'm just so insecure but you know the cure,
Just say your love for me will always endure.
Don't change your ways or the way we play,
Keep saying you love me each and every day.

Cheryl Lange
The Cold Wind Chills In Spring
A woman now with years of growth
But the sun is only rising
Spring feels cold to an open wound
Hiding warmth not recognizing
A budding rose still has beauty
The thorns are fragile not defending
But the innocence holds its grace
Through wind to see it bending
Black nights can bring light
And cold wind may blow warm
If eyes do still burn bright
When confronting with the storm
So let your heart cry no more
When the cold wind chills in spring
Yet look to light through the dark
Let the sun carry what you bring

Barbara A. O'Hara
MR. FROST (R.L.)
Frost, frost, ice and snow
a legendary I did not know
depressed, dejected, diversified
in his poems, this master-mind cried
Out; by his mind, unto his soul
simplicity of life was his goal.
Unique in every way
poetically said, what he had to say.

Beryl Van Allen Hornung
DEATH OF A HOUSE
The wreckers came early
 for my grandmother's house.
Like some ravenous beast,
 the bulldozer growled
 and tore into the kitchen
 and buttery . . .
From the smoking debris
 arose visions of wild
 strawberries
 crowned with clotted cream.
The parlor's turn came next,
 its splintered remains
 faintly echoing cracked strains
 of "The Shepherd's Dance"
 played on an ancient
 gramophone.
My old bedroom was last to go . .
 one flower-papered wall
 pausing in midair
 to wave goodbye.

Michael R. Olek
AS YOU SLEEP
Warmth was never warmer,
And love so pure and sweet,
like the moment of your slumber
when your breath kisses my
 cheek.
So natural with you so close,
an unseen touch sincere.
A soft expression of your soul,
warm life against my ear,
as invisible as empty space,
love penetrates my world so deep
with your resting breath upon my
 face,
As I watch you while you sleep.

Marlene Sabella
Waiting Maybe In Vain
How many times have I waited...
 for you to come home?
How many times have I run to
 the window...
because I thought I heard the
 sound of your car?

How many hours did I wait...
because I had something exciting
 to tell you?
But the excitement died,
because you took so long to come
 home.

How long did I wait...
with anticipation, just to see your
 face...
Simply because I missed your not
 being here.

How many hours have I sat here...
trying to convince myself it
 wasn't true...
that you had found somebody
 new.

Still I remained here...loyal,
 dutiful, faithful wife...
until you told me...
what I didn't want to hear but
 knew...
you didn't want me anymore.

How many years have you been
 gone...
and I couldn't cry a single tear.

And now, I heard it only once,
 only one time...
you want me back...

And since I heard it...
How many times have I waited...

for the phone to ring,
and how many times have I
 waited...
for your knock on my door?

Bruce E. Gearhart, Jr.

Bruce E. Gearhart, Jr.
THE OLD ROAD
[To Margie, my companion]
What have I been doing alone?
 you ask.
Why, making sense
Along the old road,
With what was left for me
After the others had gone ahead.
 It appears they left the
 esthetics alone
 As recompense.

Marianne Matthews
A REACTION
 What you see when you look is
 not
a reflection of who you are;
 It is but an illusion, marked by
 confusion
—of appearance.

 What you hear when you
 speak isn't
always the truth;
 Are you sincere? Or do your
 words stem
from fear, —of what they will
 think!

 What you do is an act in an
 effort
to conform;
 A performance on a stage of
 glass.

 But hidden—deep inside, from
 within,
how you feel—now that is
 real.

Toni Dahl
SOUNDS
Desperation—with little hope
 and faith
Screams of torment,—hurt and
 pain
Immoralwars,—without meaning
In this world,—we live in vain

Tears of poverty,—love in a heart
Pitiful smile—eyes of confusion
Destruction of a city,—naked and
 sad
A child of innocence,—without a
 dad

Sounds of war—heard in a
 distance,
Flames of fire, as I vision them
 burn

Marchers to obedience,—without
 a worth
Pointed fingers,—destroying our
 earth...

Compassion felt in a heart and
 soul
As I look at a saddened face
Incurious eyes, in space, without
 a goal
And freedom,—a word,—torn by
 disgrace

A dream, a reality, sounds of cries
A questin of time, a judgement so
 near
A fantasy—or is it? —my God in
 my mind
Rebellious sounds—in this end of
 time.

Evelyn L. Hodges
SPRING
*[To my Mother and Father, I
 dedicate my talents to you.]*
What is spring?
Is it a feeling?
Is it an emotional
State of being?

Is it whenever,
Arising from the earth, blossoms
 are born?
Or when the weather
Brings warmth to the morn?

Is spring the reason,
Why I feel so secure and glad?
Why others also,
Have no thoughts that are sad?

If you ask me,
Spring is a smile;
That lifts your enthusiasm,
Toward each of a future of miles.

I believe in Spring,
Thank God I am able
To have a home, a family,
And a meal on the table.

June Lawrence Shelton
SOMEONE SPECIAL
The Lord looked down upon the
 earth,
And saw that it was good,
But it was missing something,
And then He understood.

He said I'll send a part of Me,
To live with man below,
To help him through life's daily
 cares,
And guide his feet just so.

I'll give her my forgiveness,
And love for one another
And then above all else,
All earth shall call her Mother.

Marge B. Uphold
**Can Anyone Get Any
 Closer?**
He charms the ladies and babies
 alike;
Businesslike, though, he can be.
A winning smile of forgiveness
 can follow
A grim face of disapointment.
Holding no grudges, there is no
 interval
That bridges the chasm from ire
 to happiness.
This generous, benevolent,
 sometimes gullible,

Hunk of man could be the
 answer to many nocturnal
 dreams.
Can one be too giving, too
 available to
His fellow man, too trusting?
Yes, but does one dare to attempt
 to change
The next best thing to perfection?

Martha E. Cook
SNOW TOWERS
I looked out the window on a
 beautiful sight
Snow coming down, a blanket of
 white,
I sat there and watched, it seemed
 like hours
As it made all the trees look like
 Snow Towers.

There's nothing more beautiful
 than soft new Snow
But when you are old, you cannot
 go
So you sit at home and pass away
 hours
Closed in on all sides by the
 Snow Towers.

The trees are Snow Towers, lofty
 and tall
We're surrounded by them, like a
 great white wall
Then the wind blows, they shiver
 and shake
The Snow Towers fall and the
 Buds awake.

Now it is Spring With sunshine
 and showers
The Buds pop open and spread
 out the Flowers
We look at the Blue sky, and
 Think of the hours
When we were surrounded, by
 the Snow Towers.

Mary Crickmer Conley
I'M BUSY
I can't watch T.V.
Or read a book.
No time to clean house
Or cook!

I'll let the phone ring,
No time to talk—
I really must
Take the dog for a walk—

But cross your legs, Fido,
And I'll do the same
I can not stop
In the middle of a game.

Well, the game is over—
I'm finally done
Just in time
For the settin' sun.

But—tomorrow—
This much I know
I'll be back here
Watching row after row—

Go—Pac-Man—Go!

Rocky L. Pearson
IF YOU CARE
Take the feelings
 I so need to give
Take these dreams
 and make them real
Take this heart
 but treat it kind
Take my Love
 only if you care

John G. Rasmussen
FOR MARY
Stars light shadows where
she treads airily, dancing
upon the soft summer night.
Like some displaced angel lost
amongst we faceless mortals.

Birdie H. Flanakin

Birdie H. Flanakin
ROBIN REDBREAST
The birds stopped singing. The
sun
    refused to shine
The day they crucified that dear
    Christ of mine.
A robin saw the crown of thorns
on
    His precious head . . .
It removed the thorn; that's why
    its breast is red.

As I walked up Golgotha's Hill
I saw the three on crosses . . .
    They
    were very still.
A thorn from the crown had
    pierced
    Christ's precious head.
The robin removed it; that's why
    its
    breast is red.

Martha Sardullo
UNFORGETTABLE
    [To my friend John]
Unforgettable
so unforgettable
One cannot forget you
and all the nice things
you do
You are understanding
And quite undemanding
You are a friend and a treasure
Knowing you is such a pleasure
You are a beautiful person
Who to be with is fun
That's why you're number one

Kevin Cunningham
TWO WOMEN
    *[To Mary. To Linda. Two
    women who brought me joy,
    left me with sorrow, yet always
    will share a place in my heart.]*
Two women in his eyes
Two women take his lies
And whichever he's with, always
    a queen,

Two lifetimes to explore
Two heartaches to ignore
Two women that produce the
    similar dream.

Two reasons to feel pleasure
Two loves he just can't measure
And off that fence he knows he
    just might fall,

Two women he'll always love
Two women that rise above
He had his cake and tried to eat
    it all.

Two women with different views
An old love and a new
He needs them both but just not
    quite the same,

Two women with love so deep
Two women he just can't keep
He'll miss them both when he
    steps on that plane.

Two women, he can't have one
Sometimes more and sometimes
    none
The hardest part's for him to say
    goodbye,

Two women in his life
But neither to be his wife
Makes this man so sad he'd
    rather die.

Nora Raleigh
THE WIDOW
On the island outside a door
floorboards of the porch
stillsqueeking an old woman
tumbled and tucked tightly
into a chair, with greasy shawls,
gloves without fingers,
knitted tornworn cap over all
is speaking and I hear
against the music of the seawaves
the recitative, a litany in repeat.
Her song is about the widows,
so many widows who must
live with sisters or poorly
like she live alone
if not had she a son
whose house is almost done
and a room prepared for her.
Unwashed feet in broken shoes
are wrapped more tightly,
    moistless
autumn leaves descend. "It's the
    widows."

Christine Chadwick
FRIENDSHIP
    *[This poem is dedicated to my
    college roommates of many
    years ago and to those others
    who have since become my
    good friends.]*
Gold can be weighed, coined,
    minted;
Jewels will glitter 'n shimmer in
    light;
A photograph may be framed in
    silver — tinted
To make the subject a lovelier
    sight!

Boxes of value may be conveyed
    from a store
To compensate for years rolling
    'round;
Flowers 'n gowns exquisite,
    edibles and more,
But I name a gift that's made, not
    found —

A gift for more 'n a day — can't
    be bought;
It's unsolicited, bestowed, quite a
    prize;
It's precious — in life so very
    much sought,

For it's true friendship, and that
never dies!

Harry N. Rosenfield
WITHOUT YOU DEAR
    [To: Leonora]
Like a summer day deprived of
    sun
or a garden flower craving bees,
Cuaght in winter's cold and bitter
    freeze
In a race to nowheres that's been
    run,

Like a rushing stream bereft of
    sound
Or a troubador grown old and
    hoarse,
Wind—tossed as the clouds
    without a course
Or a leaking boat that's run
    aground,

Like a bird, bewildered, now
    alone,
Lost, astray, while searching for
    its nest,
Ever seeking never finding rest,
Flying homeward with the route
    unknown,

So am I, a blinded mountaineer
Probing for my way, without you
dear.

Patrick Michale Loveless
MY VALENTINE
    [My Valentine]
As I sit here alone at night,
My thoughts turn to you and all
    the good things
You have come to mean to me.

As my confident,
I find that you are quite easy to
    talk to—
As my companion,
I find a strange comfort in your
    nearness—
But most important—
As my friend,
I have found out that you are
    irreplaceable.

It is with these thoughts in mind
That I ask you—
Won't you please be my
    Valentine?

R. E. Vaughn
MOTHER'S DAY
Nothing, no nothing, could ever
    compare,
    to the love of a mother, her
    touch and her care;
Her sweet warm embrace, on a
    cold winter day,
    her watchful eye, over you as
    you play.

Her tender kiss, as she tucks you
    in bed,
    and tommorrow's "I love
    you," that is already said;
Her talks with the Master, over
    you as you sleep,
    praying that you, in His care
    He will keep.

Her kiss on the hurt place,
    immediate cure,
    the best earthly doctor, and
    nurse to be sure;
And you'll never find, a better
    teacher,
    and yes, when you're bad, no

better preacher.

Her hushed—up tears, when she's
    feeling bad,
    tears never seen, by you and
    your dad;
That time that you fell, and cut
    your knee,
    she bled more than you did,
    believe you me.

Her knowledge of kitchen, that's
    making you grow,
    her radiant sparkle, that's
    making you glow;
I suppose what I'm honestly
    trying to say,
    is that *every* day, should be
    Mother's Day.

Lois DeFriece
If You Don't Feel
If you don't feel,
You don't get hurt,
Only living ain't real,
And life has no merit.

The good never lasts forever,
But neither does the bad,
Cling to the memories that
    endeavor,
Throw away the remains so sad.

Learn from the mistakes and the
    pain,
Take responsibility for your life
    in stride,
Roll with the punches keep
    yourself sane,
Sometimes you cry still enjoy the
    ride.

If you don't feel,
You don't get hurt,
Only living ain't real,
And life has no merit.

Frances S. Hannah
AFTERTHOUGHTS
I carefully push away the
    disarranged covers,
    creep from the bed
    stare at the body breathing
    the slow pace of sleep.
Who are you—
    That can reach for love or
    lust
    then callously turn your
    back
    assuming the fetal position
    of a childish mind?

Vickie M. Bryan
DARKEST BEFORE DAWN
The steely, cold glint of the stars
    Over the rough battlements
Shed no comforting light or cheer
    To the empty courtyard
    black.
The experienced moon in her
    shame
    Stayed hidden in her bed,
And the woman with the lovely
    face
    Drew her loosened hair back.
The raucous laughter of Trojan
    lords
    Shattered the still night's
    peace;
Their celebration was ending,
    And voices were thick and
    deep.
Oh, Helen, where are your heroes
    With their camps and
    mighty plans?

Where are the ships with
bleached sails
That gave heart and hope to
your sleep?
A vain statue of a wooden horse
Is the seal of your fate,
For ever men will save
themselves
When cunning and skill
won't win.
Fair Helen's throat released a sob
Of pain and fear and despair;
And she turned to the hated
home
And with defeat, entered in.

Look up, you Helens, who have
no faith;
For the true soldiers on the field
Labor not for men they seek to
conquer—
Do not give gifts as they yield.

Use your heart to see in the dark
And trust the ones you love.
Stand as strong as a shining
star—
For your light in darkness, look
above.

Sally Lee Drake
AS I AM
I — as the moon — am all alone.
I — as the stars — no one has
ever known.
I — as the jackal — have not a
friend.
I — as a rock — will never bend.
I — as a mighty tree — stand tall
and straight.
I — as a spider — patiently wait.
I — as a bird — have sung to
God.
I — as man — have wearily trod.
I — as a cricket — hear a
mournful call.
I — as the wind — billow and
stall.
I — as the willow — weep and
cry.
I — as a leaf — will eventually
die.
I — as the earth — have surely
been.
I — to Nature — am akin.

Joan H. Galley
CAUTION
A man and a serpent
have many like qualities
Each quietly makes
its way
When you are least expecting
gloom
Then they strike when
you are most vulnerable
So, therfore, react to a man
as you would a
serpent
With much caution

Mary P. Hunter Wells
OUR 35TH REUNION
The years have swiftly
passed us by
Moments we shared
seem far and nigh
The memories of time
filled with work and play
Can certainly be felt
on this special day.!

Though the hair may be gray
expressing distinction and worth

And the forehead is lined
from wisdom and worth
The spirit of love
of this phenomenal class
Will live in our hearts
and most certainly last.

Marieta P. Owens
YOUR FUTURE GLORY
[To my daughter, Krystle
Michelle Owens, who came
into my life May 1979 & my
parents, Mr. & Mrs. Ralph V.
Owens, Sr. for caring for us
both.]
There you were so young and
free,
But here now your a mother to
be.
Many thoughts pass, you want to
cry,
Just be strong you have to try.
There's always hope and
happiness too,
Even though you think there's
none for you.
You feel alone—Depressed
sometimes,
Yet suprised to see the friends
you find.
Somewhere there's always a
helping hand,
Your baby needs love more than
you a man.
No one knows how you feel for
the father—to—be,
Even though no future you'll ever
see.
You can love someone and still
leave them too,
Because you know its better, Yet
hard to do.
No one but you knows your life
story,
Have it in mind as you cherish,
YOUR FUTURE GLORY.

Linda Jane Ford
No More Yesterdays
Cry no more, let it go.
Plain to see, no longer there.
Time passes on, slowly at first.
Can I handle, what happens now?

Cry no more, let it go.
Love fades away, to horizons
unknown,
Truly bitter sweet, you're not
alone.
Make a wish, see it through.

Cry no more, let it go.
Set it free, to be remembered,
Forever as today, so be tomorrow,
Never to see, one more yesterday.

Nancy Ellen Poteete
GROWING UP
[To Mom, Dad, Mike, and
Chris]
Growing up can be extremely
hard
You're chances of success seem
so few
So think things through and play
each card
As your conscious tells you to.

A minor decision can be so
wrong
That a major mistake could occur
So, no matter the time or how
long
Take it, just to be positively sure.

You're to young for this, and to
old
For that, so your ackwardness
shows
Just try to understand that no
Matter what they say; it goes.

Give it some time and it all will
be over
And something else will come up.
But by then you'll be a little older
And almost all grown up.

Lora J. Wesolek
NO LONGER AFRAID
[This poem is dedicated to all
teenagers who do not get along
well with their father. It can be
very upsetting at times, but
you are not alone.]
No longer can you frighten me
With your boisterous, direful
ways.
I no longer hide when you yell at
me;
For those are long ago days.

I do not let you push me around,
Nor do I just sit idly by;
I stand up to you every time
And look you in the eye.

There was a time within my life
I would stop and hesitate;
But now whenever our paths do
cross
I throw back all of your hate.

I have grown from a child into an
adult
Whom you can no longer push
around.
All your antics will not make me
cower.
For I now stand on solid ground!

Gidget West
MR. RIGHT
I met him for the first time today,
And by his side I chose to stay.
I watched him eat, and watched
him run,
My first hour with him was really
fun.

I was warned about this man,
Said he'd do me wrong again and
again.
My friends were right he took all
I had,
I tried to walk away but the scene
was sad.

I pulled out a check and signed
my name,
Was given more quarters, to play

more games.
I dropped one in from my sweaty
palm,
And the maze lit up, with a
hearty song.

He ate the dots and cleared the
board,
Stayed away from the ghosts and
really scored.
He ate them up when they
turned blue,
And ate the cherries for more
points too.

This little yellow man has stole
my heart,
But from the game center it's
time to part,
"Pac—Man," I'll see you tomorrow
it's another day,
And I'll bring more quarters for a
longer stay.

Mary E. Black
GLOOM AND DESPAIR
The drops of sand in the
hour—glass
The pains in our lives
The raindrops on the window
The tears from our eyes
The sunshine in the morning
The onset of fear
The darkness and moonlight
Cast shadows in here
This body is forever
In gloom and despair and is
forever diminishing
With noone to care.

Patricia A. Reece
ULTIMATE INDEMNITY
I'm not worthy of you, my love —
my land.
You've beared me great fruit to
which I've made waste,
Cursed your misfortunes; yet add
to the cause.
I neglect your needs; yet I breathe
your air.
My debt to you is great; but I am
starved
Of vital food needed to revive
Your once productive forests and
pure streams.
Now I will pay my debt the only
way
I see fit, without being
destructive.
With this, I will say good—bye
forever.

Maybe at least, I can nourish the
soil.

Don A. DeGroff
UNTITLED
I wander in the summer's mist,
An Angel's song rings in my
head.
Cool breezes soothe my weary
brow,
A whippoorwill calling me,
to bed.
A yawn, a sigh, sleep now is nigh,
I pause in fragrent bower
instead.

Now finding my way into that
world,
No longer today, nor quite
the morrow.
Dreams lazily float into the fore,
Like clouds playfully

dancing about the moon.
A passing glimpse of one once
  dear,
    I reach out to touch but
cannot draw near.

A child's laugh, or so it seems
    I know that voice, could that
be me?
In enchanted worlds, where time
  is nought,
    Of then and now, so mixed
in dreams,
Of soft moments, bejeweled in
  memory,
In dream guarenteed, ne'er lost to
  me.

Glen R. Osborne
THE DUNGEON
[To all thinkers]
Cold, dark, gruesome and gray,
They call it a dungeon; but here
  I'll stay.
Penniless, sleepless, filthy, decay,
They call it a dungeon; but here
  I'll stay.
Rats, snakes, lizards and chain,
They call it a dungeon; but here
  I'll stay.
Not wishing or caring for fortune
  and fame,
They call it a dungeon; but here
  I'll stay.
Refusing to cheat, be fickle or
  sly,
They call it a dungeon; but here
  I'll stay.
No love pretending, forever the
  same,
They call it a dungeon; here I'll
  remain.

Sarah Daniel Vaughan
THIS LIFE
If I could live this life once more,
I would do things differently.
You may be sure we would both
  be free
On the day you came to me.
For ages I have wanted this:
To stand on tiptoe for your kiss.
Your smile
I have waited centuries to see.
But now, my love,
We await another place, another
  time;
And this you may be certain of,
Beyond forever you will be mine,
And I shall love you
Through eternity!

Steve Howland
PICTURES
Beneath the one time candle
  flame,
On tip of memories yet
  unclaimed
Two broken worlds, one unaware.
Framed faces that still lie color
  bare.

Two books of details all written
  down,
And miles apart a place I found
And here I am still in my place.
Years behind on an empty face.

Look at all the papers there
And look at us who were unfair.
So long in our candle flame.
Why wouldn't both have end the
  same?

Long distance calls; two worlds
apart
Of no avail and no one heart.
So many answers to no recall.
Look at the face that took the
  fall.

There must be moments you can
  see
When tears would call to
  memory
But why is it so hard of you?
Thyself has fallen from pictures,
  too.

Evelyn Conley Stauffer
LOVE CALL
Please come and take a walk with
  me,
    Along the shoreline's
    hushing waves,
The sun has left her ecstasy
    To moonbeams dashing from
    their caves,
Where spooks of others here have
  found,
    As piercing as a shooting
    star,
A love to each untouched, so
  strong,

    Only they alone find where
they are.

As driftwood dances toward the
  shore,
    The crystal stars nod down
    and blink,
The too short years we've lived
  before,
    Will fly away with wind's
    winged blink.
Please come and take this walk
  with me,
    As lakeshore mysteries send
    their dove,
Let heart take wings and soar to
  sea,
    As star—sown heavens seal
    our love!

Kimberly Fields
UNTITLED
The beach.
So beautiful, peaceful.
Smelling so of the salt and sand.
The soft shuffle below your feet,
  the crashing waves.
The endless ranks of blue water
    Stretching for miles and
    miles—
Never ending?
    maybe—
        maybe not.
Yet to be at this wonderful place,

to see the sunrise—
        or sunset.
The orange and reds reflecting on
  the water—
    with the whitecaps and
    misty sea foam
    in the ocean so blue and
green—
Is a sight to behold—
    to hold in wonder and
awe
    as your eyes see—
        your brain records
The everlasting beauty of this
free and matchless
        expanse of time.

Joan E. West
DO YOU LOVE ME?
Once there was a little girl, of
  maybe two or three.
She was a doll in every way, as
  cute as she could be.

One day as i was walking by, she
  took me by suprise.
i saw a tear fall from her eyes,
  and then i heard her cry.

"Do you love me? mister do you
  love me? would you like to
  be my daddy? for my mama's sick,
  and i'm afraid , won't you be
  my daddy? for i'll be good and
  promise not to cry."

As i checked the situation, all i
  found was desolation.
Could this kind of life go on from
  day to day?.

As i helped the sickly woman,
  she broke down and made me
  promise,
that i'd take her baby out of here,
  to a better place to stay.

Now that it's some ten year's
  later, life for her's a little
  greater, yes she's the doll of
  everyone in town.

Boy's are knocking on the door,
  she don't need me anymore,
  but
some how i hope she'll alway's be
  around.

Barry A. Noland
MOURNING SON
[For Momma and Bob (and
everyone who's special to me. I
hope you know who you are.)]
Tetragrammaton,
Father, lives in mourning now.
I remain his son.

Priscilla Calhoun
I'M A WOMAN
I look at you, we understand
You touch me, my childhood
ends
Loving you is where I begin
Being a woman.

You'll never know the change in
  me
It's so confusing, and yet I see
You've set this girl inside me free
Now I'm a woman.

Love for you grows deeper each
  day
In your arms is where I'll stay
That's where I've learned in every
  way
To be a woman.

As years pass, I'll be your wife
Close around you and by your
  side
My love for you I just can't hide
Cause I'm your woman.

Anna Louise Walker
**A Gift For William and
John Timothy**
There are so many things I would
  have given you, my boys,
Just to watch your faces beam:
Things like coloring books and
  crayons; bikes and toys,
Like rides to the zoo and double
  dipped ice cream.

So many things had I planned in
  my doting aunt's head
For questioning, exploring boys
  like you.
Something within my swelling
  aunt's heart won't let me
  believe you are dead;
Though I struggle within my
  logical head I cannot believe it
  is true.

I saw you not during the
  moments when you as one first
  did breathe.
Will you excuse your aunt her
  absence?
I saw you not when your souls of
  this world took leave,
But I know you felt my presence.
Though you never opened your
  eyes nor ever said a word,
I feel that you did love me,
Though I never touched your
  faces nor ever your voices
  heard,
I feel my love your hearts could
  see.

I know, my dear boys, in heaven I
  will give
To you what I could not give in
  this land.
Until our first meeting, you shall
  continue to live
Through our thoughts and our
  words and my hand.

Terry M. Myers
Boats Of Untried Dreams
    Long ago the children
    matured
        beside a gentle stream,
and then ran down to meet the
    raging river
    in their boats of untried
    dreams.

J. Michael Whitten
SWEET AS MORNING DEW
Sunlight sparkles as it shines
  through the morning
sky to touch my eyes and wake
  me.
The dew on the window
  glimmers with the rays that
are like a million tiny rainbows.
Each one dancing out to wake the
  world to a new and
beautiful day.
I can't feel sad watching this
  wonder as I leave sleep
behind.
I can only feel happiness and a
  satisfaction that
I'm alive.
I walk softly as I go out the door;
  I dare not disturb

such a beautiful sight. I slowly
reach out and touch
the morning dew.
As I place it to my lips it is
sweeter than any honey
the earth has yet to find.
My thoughts travel to you at this
moment and I can't
help but think,
You are as sweet as morning dew.

R. M. Smith
HIS MAJESTY
Did you ever hear a cat stomp
Stalking through the house in a
royal rage
At something his human page,
Had or had not done?
Head high, tail up, just the tip
Of it flicking back and forth
Each velvet paw slammed down
upon the floor
As if he means to ram a hole
through it.
Quiet? Ha!
An elephant would be quieter.
Royal nose stuck high in the air
He stomps to the door
And with an angry meow
That resembles a panther's growl
He demands that it be opened
His Majesty is going out!

Sunday McKinley Bailey
Sunday McKinley Bailey
ONE WISH
If I had
One wish
before
I die
It would be
to see
The reflection
of my nakedness
once more
in your eye.

Bill Drake
HAVE YOU EVER
Have you ever wondered why
things just don't work out your
way?

Could it be that the sky is blue
and all you can see is grey?

Have you ever been so lonely
that you can't talk to those
that you love?

Yet emotions live inside you
yearning for above.

Emotions too frightening to be
released.

You wonder if the pain will ever
cease.

Have you ever thought each day
is the same?
Thinking that life is nothing but
a game.

Have you ever been so afraid to
fail even
knowing that you have nothing
to lose?
You wonder to yourself what
direction to choose.

Have you ever felt a dream die in
your heart?
Never really getting that one
positive start.

Have you ever wondered if
your mind was deceived.

The answer is that your heart
didn't believe.

Lola Ray Dean
LOVE TREASURES
Keep your Mind,
    Soul
        Heart;
Your feelings,
    Dreams,
        Thoughts;
On me constantly,
    Continuously,
        Forever.
Hold me close to you.
    Caress my soul.
        Touch me,
            Love me,
                In your mind.
Know my mind.
    Know my love.
        Feel my life.
            Harness my spirit.
                Free me from myself.
Take me. Mold and shape me.
Love me. Hurt me. Want me.
Need me. Keep me. Leave me . . .

    But,
    What you know of me,
    Keep in thee,
        Forever,
        My Love,
        Forever.

Dorothy Kole Mucklo
A MIRACLE
As I watched the falling rain
Through my window-pane
It washed each blade of grass,
As well as the flowers en masse,
Seemingly it cleansed my soul;
It made me feel so whole again,
This Miracle of God!

Nedra L. Krider
TREASURED TRINKETS
Such useless things I keep and
keep
    Until my drawers are all knee
deep—
Pictures, letters, poetry and such
    Oh, nothing that amounts to
much.

But every single thing's a part
    Of all memories in my heart—
Letters from friends so far away
    I'd love to visit each some day.

And poetry always can express
    Heartfelt joy or happiness—
A tally, a picture, a piece of string
    Oh you can find most anything

You'll find greeting cards of every
kind,
    Birthday, Friendship and
Valentine—
If only I were half as kind
    As they think—these friends of
mine!

"How silly"—did I hear you say?
O.K. I'll put the "stuff" away
To haul it out another day
And dream a few more hours
away.

Carl D. Hamstead
CAIN
*[To Johny B., who taught me
acceptance; and to those who
do not understand—may God
give you grace to temper your
ignorance.]*
Man, created in the perfect image
of God
found this gook in a field
(Buried by himself, musta been
brass)
Dug him up
lopped off his prick
stuck him twenty-seven times
and returned him to Mother
Earth
on the remains of his head

Sweating nightmares
he drank a fifth of Southern
Comfort
(and found it lied)
Pulled himself up on the
sandbags
to greet eight ounces of Commie
lead
Welcoming revenge

Peace be with you, my son.

Sharon Frank Klesh
MY FRIEND
I have a friend and he loves me,
As BIG as the ocean and the
island sea.
His love is so great, but he
hesitates . . .
My Friend, Our God, and me.

My Friend would do anything in
his care for me.
He loves as the ocean and the
sea.
I need My Friend, yes, you and
me—
For, God blessed me with his
presence . . . and MY love, you
see.

In times of success I have passed
him by.
In times of trouble, his day was
mine.
My Friend will do anything for
me,
And bear with me in time of
need.

We talk of now, then, and
tomorrow:
From whom we know not to
borrow.
We express to each other
What we feel for one another,
A sincerity so true
As we trust to the ocean blue.

Nothing can replace the
fulfillment of a "friend,"
For without an "embrace" DEPTH

will never end.
We steal the time to be together
Feeling as though these moments
are forever.

He hears my woes and my joys.
He listens like no other "voice."
Together we find strength
abound
That God, alone, has made
profound.

Igor Khutorsky
UNTITLED
I lie in the darkness
Unseen and unheard
And capture the sounds
Of this lightless world.

There's nothing but silence
Or so it seems
And little by little
I retreat to my dreams . . .

I run in the green fields
Or lie in the hay
Inhaling the scent
Of a young summer day.

The birds and the hoppers
Are singing their song
And life's filled with beauty
And nothing is wrong . . .

I open my eyes and come back
To the night
And visions of youth
Disappear from my sight.

All the images fade
In the still of the night
As I lay awake
And await morning light.

Carol A. Bertolini
PASSING TIMES
Passing times are passing by,
Like clouds drifting in the sky,
But I know your love lingers on,
Like the morning dew and setting
sun
Your love is good,
Your love is one,
But like the sun it leaves too,
Instead of passing times its
Passing thru.

Dorothy Cox
MR. TURTLE
*[This poem was written for my
grandson Bryan. It was given
along with the gift of a turtle.]*
Turtle, turtle in your shell,
Crawling through the grass.
Where are you going?
What will you do,
When winter comes and fall days
pass?

You carry your house upon your
back
Catch flies and bugs for your
dinner.
Swim in the water, dig holes in
the mud.
For an animal you're quite a
winner.

Joan Dumas
THE EMPTY BREAST
Don't come to my breast my
children, my love
You suckled me dry long ago.
Don't pull at this teat all
withered and cere
The nectar you fed on won't flow.

Go out and seek your truths and
I go on to seek mine
Your mortal mother has nurtured
you well
Now seek your Father Divine.

Catharina Rinta
SMILE
What is a smile? a little bit of
sunshine.
A cheery greeting on a cloudy
day.
A sign that someone's really glad
to see you.
A happy touch, that drives the
gloom away.

So give a smile, it costs so very
little.
You don't lose anything,
you gain a lot instead.
The smile you give
will be returned with pleasure,
and makes your day
the best you've ever had.—

Helen Brown Rittershofer
FATHERS' DAY TRIBUTE
[To my father, the late Robert
Brown
Lawyer, Lecturer, Minister and
Poet.]
A little girl of half past three
Cuddled securely upon fathers'
knee
Shoulder for a pillow curled
elbow bent
Sparkling eyes glistening in
joyous content
Fathers' smile spreading as his
eyes gently spoke
Hearts and thoughts melding the
world seemed remote
Father not complacent weaving
stories of old
Chuckled skillfully blending the
new as he told
For blue skies often become
clouded and grey
Raindrops may fall on the joys of
the day
Stars may twinkle and the moon
shine bright
Elaborate stories must always be
tempered right
For in one brief moment when
thoughts are stirred
Hearts are blended or vision is
blurred
Father wove his wisdom in words
to combine
Raise questions and answers to
be solved with time
And the little girl of half past
three
Entranced with the stories as she
sat on his knee
Remembers those stories of
magic as she grows with the
years
Stories of wisdom to encourage
and entrance her life's career
Planned by her father—well in
advance.

Frances Cecile Farmer
Grandmother, in Memory
Kentucky kisses of summer air;
Green clouds of leaves;
Porch swings squeaking lullabys;
Red and black wasp droaning;
Yellow honeysuckle scent

drifting.
The hustle of
cooking,
laughing,
loving.

Long ago,
and always, now,
in me.

I see you beautifully
silver—haired
spritely,
touching,
giving;
forever reaching out
to those you love.

I was one of your many
young ones.

Barbary Gay Dowell
DREAMING
In quiet interludes I find
Forgotten friends of many
yesteryears,
Little harmed by time
Although they've all grown
quieter a bit.
And have you kept well, my
dears?
And do our thoughts still rhyme?
Around me old companions sit
Silently spinning cobwebs in my
mind.

Shannon Curcio
MY BABY
First you were born,
So tiny and small,
On a beautiful day,
At the start of fall.

I was very young,
And I was alone.
I couldn't care for you,
Or call you my own.

So, the people came,
And took you away.
They said I couldn't see you;
Not on any day.

I feel so bad,
And I miss you.
I wish I hadn't let you go,
But I've told myself this isn't true.

Sometimes I wonder,
As I lie in my bed,
If over me,
Any tears have been shed.

When I walk down the street,
And I see a baby,
I think that somewhere,
You need me, maybe.

I love you, my child.
I know this is permanent.
I want you; I can't have you.
That's why I weep and lament.

Sandra Morgan
A Shoulder To Lean On
Are you telling me that your
world is tearing at the seams?
Don't you know that even
though there are nightmares,
there are also dreams.
Let me help erase the anxieties in
your mind.
Maybe some solutions to your
problems I can find.
Even at this moment you still
feel depressed.
Rest assured that I want to ease

your stress.
I love you and your pain is my
pain.
In the sunshine and in the rain.
I can feel your complex
frustrations.
The agony of your mind sends
out disheveled sensations.
I can rest your head in my lap
and gently sooth your forehead as
you take a needed nap.
I understand the choices you
have to make
and the solutions you have to
take.
During this time, I can be patient
with you
because you are going to make it
through.

Gwen Ellen Yourgrau
An Irrational Exoneration of April (and All Greater Fools)
*April is the cruelest month,
breeding
Lilacs out of the dead land . . .*
Most crushingly too lovely must
be May:
Too generous, wasting May
proves all a mess
Of trampled, purple slurries of
excess,
The profligate unleavings of
decay.
What April hints, May shows in
disarray:
Too soon *deshabille*, without
redress,

She sheds her *embarras* with her
largesse,
And proves her pleasures
mayflies of a day.
Though May be felled by her
best—laid intents,
Who has not fallen under
jacarandas?
What matter if the vernal
paradox,
Her brevity rolled into radiance,
Eclipsing (briefly) even
amaranthus,
Conceives but that mortality she
mocks?

Christopher V. Duncan
MY GIRL
I remember how she lighted my
soul,
Made my heart beat like it's out
of control.
She chased away those ugly skies

of black and gray,
And brought me a beautiful
sun—laden sky to stay.

Our special, time forgetting walks
through eternity,
My love for her was true,
unmarked by any charity.

So I'll force myself to wipe away
the tears,
And look inside my heart and
hope that she appears.

But I can't bring her up from the
ground,
So this time I'll try to weep
without a sound.

We talked so much of sharing
our every breath,
But we didn't know that we'd be
robbed by death.

Our days are gone except in my
mind,
I'll forgive, but not forget how she
left me behind.

Now as I stand over her somber
headstone,
I can't stop my soul from
emitting a groan.

It's a groan of despair,
For she can no longer hear how
much I care.

She's gone and I'm all alone,
And up in the sky is darkness,
where our
beautiful sun once shone.

Kelly O'Brien
WHY??
I once asked God why,
why man has to die.
Life can be full of beauty and fun.
Why should man die and not see
the sun.
Life also can have its sorrows,
but the clouds always leave
returning the
blue skies of tommorow.
For there is so much to see
and so much to do,
that the short life of man can
restrict you.
For in a lifetime you will see only
a very small part,
of what this great world holds in
its heart.
Some say there is a better life
after death,
but for me the splendor of a
baby's first breath,
the majesty of a mountain and
the song of a bird,
could never be replaced by
another world.

Stanley Zayac
DESERT SKY
See the dust rise up on the desert
sky
There I am looking into your
eye(s)
The ground is cracked and
broken
The desert is empty, nothing is
growin
Sand and dust is blowin
everywhere
Fills the sky; fills the air
There's a man with his horse
Tryin to make it across the desert

course
He's ridin on top; trustin his
  horse
There's something guiding him
  along and his horse
Sittin by the fire late at night
Watchin the stars; lookin for that
  one bright light
To follow; 'till day turn(s) into
  night
When all is covered by the
  blinding light
And the sand billows up into the
  stale desert air
Many have tried and made it;
  many are still there
One man alone; tries to steer
  clear
Through the wind blowin sand
  that fills up in his hair
If he makes it across; it'll be on
  his own
When he makes it across; he'll be
  all alone
And when he gets where he's
  goin; that'll be home
But, he'll stay where he's at;
  where he's at is all alone
Riding endlessly, through the
  desert, on his way home.

Janet O'Brien
LIBERATED LADIES?
*[To Dorothy Ann and to
working women everywhere]*
Thank you Gloria Steinem,
At last we have equal rights;
  And now I get to stay
  At the office all day—
Then do my housework at nights!

It seems today's "Total Woman"
Handles her tasks with a flair;
  She touch-types and files,
  Plus cleans, cooks and smiles—
And still has vigor to spare!

She cares for house, home,
  children;
Her job skills win the "gold cup".
  She's working all hours
  Without praise or flowers—
And still—her hairdo holds up!

She dresses in "high fashion"
Expensive, chic, classy clothes.
  Yes, this "New Woman" is
  Now referred to as "Ms"—
Feminist down to her toes!

Sound a bit overstated?
Well, that's the media's scheme.
  With an education
  You'll be a sensation—
And find the job of your dreams!

Down with magazine features
Of gals in "top-notch" careers.
  The fact they're ignoring
  Is most jobs are boring—
Filled with frustration and fears!

On the subject of wages
Next to most men we're not
  close!
  And when they take the max
  Off the top for our tax—
It's clear what they mean by
  gross!

Our gain is overrated;
It's taken blood, sweat and tears,
  And the best we can say
  Is that maybe someday—
We will be called pioneers!

Still, I feel pessimistic,
These are my thoughts—you may
  quote:
  "If the price of success
  Is just pain, strain and stress—
I'd rather give back my vote!"

Anne Burns
A TIME TO SPEAK
*[To Forrest, who always
encouraged me to reach for the
stars.]*
I watch you with eyes that are
  misty,
The lump in my throat is real.
I know that my mood's
  sentimental,
And so are the thoughts that I
  feel.

Though the years we have shared
  have been many,
They are only as leaves of grass.
Which the wind ruffles briefly in
  passing,
'Til one day, they're no more, alas!

From the time of 'forsaking all
  others',
From the day that we said 'I do',
My faith in you was rewarded,
You were there when I needed
  you.

For richer, for poorer, in sickness
  and health,
For giving the best you could
  give,
I'll love you today, and tomorrow,
And as long as we both shall live.

Marjorie Wilder Smith
DEAR MOTHER
There's been something I've
  wanted to tell you
while on this earth we both walk;
But I can't ever find an
  opportunity
when we sit down to talk;
So I'm putting into verse the
  words I have to say
and sending them to you, with all
  my love,
on this Mother's day.

Now that both my daughters are
  getting to that age
when they are beginning to cut
  the apron strings,
It's called the adolescent stage,
I was wondering what I should be
  to make these years just right;
So I decided to look back at my
  young years
and the answer came through so
  bright.

What should a Mother be during
  these years when she's so
  afraid?
Exactly what my Mother was—a
  Christian Mother who prayed.

So many times God kept me from
  doing things that were wrong.
He also kept me safe when
  danger came along.
He's shown me what could have
  happened in situations where I
  strayed
if I had not had at home a
  Christian Mother who prayed.

I could have been disgraced,
  injured, or even lost my life;
But you were there at home in
  all your worrying and strife;
And God spoke to me and said,
  "Although in you I am dismayed,
  I've kept you safe
because you had at home a
  Christian Mother who prayed."

So, Mom, I'm going to try to be
  just what you were all those
  years;
And, in spite of what happens,
  whether it's laughter or tears,
I'm going to look back and say,
  "I followed the pattern that you
  laid.
I was one of those rare women—a
  Christian Mother who prayed."

Kathleen Laithwaite
COME HOME
*[To Bob, my husband, who
introduced me to Crowsnest
Lake while we were courting.
There is a spot in my heart full
of warm memories ever calling
me back.]*
Evening shadows start to fall
On Crowsnest Lake;
Cool waters lapping
On soft white sand.

The setting sun
Brings the frantic call
Of the whippoorwill
To his wandering mate.
"Come home, come home!
Our nest is warm,
And I await
My love".

Marlene Baker
AN OLD FARM
The roof is caving in,
  And the yard is overgrown;
The garden lies deserted,
  Where once the seeds were
  sown.

There's nothing left to show,
  Just who it was lived here;
For this was someone's home,
  With friends and family dear.

But now they have all gone,
  Their work down here is
  through;
And the farm is left alone,
  Silently dying too.

Mrs. Leona Boley
LIFE'S MOMENTS
Life's moments are carelessly
  scattered,
  Like seeds in the westward
  Wind.
Wantonly shorn and tattered,
As reeds in the westward
  Wind!
Each hourly collection—lost
  forevermore,
  Swept by the silent march of
  time,
Cast upon an unknown shore.
  Out of Season—out of rhyme!

Yet—they can purely live again,
  If recalled in one's memory.
Like a Ship that gallantly sails
  again,
  Across a stormy, restless Sea!
Through ever changing, sweeping
  tides,
  And a golden sunlit shore.
Life's moments cannot hide,
  They can be treasured
  forevermore!

Lynn N. Mayo
MY LOVE, THE ROSE
My Love, the Rose.
Watch thee bloom
And the beauty of it all.
Hold thee close
But let not a tear drop fall,
For within thy shall stain.
As years go by,
There will always be thy pain.
So, kiss thee softly
And let the sweetness of the dew
Always hold the feeling anew.

Pat Martin
You Make the Difference
*[To my husband Larry, whose
love encouraged me to reach
for the mountains.]*
In the beginning, God had a plan
When out of the dust, with his
  Master touch,
He created the role called man.
In his infinite wisdom
He lets you choose
The paths that you walk
The things that you do.
Will you reach for the mountains
And the dreams that they hold,
Or will you be content, to
  securely dwell,
In the depths of the valleys
  below.
Never to strive towards visions
  on high,
Never to reach out, or question
  why,
Never to challenge futures
  unknown
Only to age, and never have
  grown.
Our days they are numbered
By a precious few
You make the difference
It's all up to you.

Martin "Mercy" Zachwieja
ALL IN A DREAM
*[To the poor whose wounds
cannot be nursed. In life I have
Loved them all.]*
Reclines the weary body, down
  for the rest,
Heavy eyes closed, the soul
  leaves the chest;
It parts from the sleep home,
  thought a sound,
One soft step from Heaven, it
  leaves the ground.

It pours into a room where a
  crushed body lay,

While people start to kneel for to
    silently pray;
It touches the wounded hearts of
    all it has passed,
And the people rejoice as the sick
    breathes at last.

All during the night and all in a
    dream
The souls influence is felt and
    seen;
It sought to help the accused,
    abused, and dying,
The scattered abandoned one's
    and those crying.

All during the night and all in a
    dream
The soul visited former friends it
    had seen;
Thunder broke, lightning flashed,
    angels wind-singing, Heaven
    cried,
And the soul carefully watched
    over the bodies it had already
    tried.

Over the hills the soul flutters in
    flight,
Down into the valley and on
    thru' the night;
It reaches the end of the dream in
    a race,
And gently slips itself back into
    place.

Michael J. Ediger
CHRISTMAS EVE
I wave to carolers
'neath the dim gas light
the snuffles of the lanky lad
accompany their out-of-tune
    voicings
snow falls steadily
keeping a silent beat for them
the snow has melted on my own
    hat
since I came into the house
and now drips to the floor.

Peg L. Adkins
THE WIND
The wind made love to me last
    night
the total experience gave me
    inner warmth
cool waves of air gave me chills
rolling over the hills and valleys
    of my body
lingering in sweet secret places
supple breasts grew taunt as the
    wind danced
ceaseless, pushing me this way
    and that
beckoning to me, I followed the
    commands
eyes closed, feeling the breath on
    my face
    I submitted . . .

Ernest G. Patnaude
UNTITLED
A song not meant for voices
but to flow along on the wind
and echo through the valleys
to the limits of the earth
was born amidst a troubled time
of spite and might and other
    things
not quite clear at night
It was conceived in a small way
like a wave is born a ripple
and when it matured, it wandered
    off

to some unknown place
and never returned
though it was sought
by one who thought he owned it

Marjorie Rinkel Graumenz

Marjorie Rinkel Graumenz
THREE IN ONE
Three in One is what we need—
    not seven come eleven—
If we expect to get to heaven.
God is Three in One; Father, Son
    and Holy Ghost.
Seven come eleven will never get
    us to heaven,
No matter how much we boast.
God sent His son to save us but
    not to stay.
We should follow Him; He
    knows the way.
The Holy Spirit will work in us.
    This it does do.
Three in One belong together:
Father, Son and Holy Ghost
    too.

Three in one belong together.
No substitute will do.
The Father sent Lord Jesus to
    save us.
There is no other way through.
God sent His son to open wide
    the gate for me and you.

Through Jesus Christ we can go
    to heaven and
be with the Father too.
Our creator is the Father.
Our redeemer is the Son.
Our Sanctifier is the Holy Ghost.
Three distinct persons: Three in
    One.

Deborah Ann Chen
THE DRUID
As the wintry suns draw nigh the
    dry sundry moons

And the shadow of heavens are
    cast,
As the vivid hues vy o'er the
    temporal skies
So the reign of the new day has
    passed.

It is thus in the knot at the end
    of the woods
In the heart of the crystal-green
    wold,
That a young girl by drawing her
    very first breath
Breath'd life into every leaf's
    fold.

Her gold locks, drench'd in
    moonshine, held silvery gilt
For no brighter the sun could
    have put.
In her eyes were abysses of deep
    forest pine
Em'rald more than the moss
    underfoot.

Through the woods one clear day
    rode a young gallant bold
Of exalted knighthood, none
    the less!
Forsooth eager to prove his haut
    chivalrous ways
He desired a maid-in-distress.

'Pon espying her form, his cold
    eyes 'came afire
Though his glazed, well-bred
    mien fluid stayed.
"Ho! Tree-nymph," he thus cried.
    "Come to me, be my bride—
Come and be my belov'd druid
    maid!"

"Sir, alas!" utter'd she, on a
    yearning-fill'd sigh,
"Here I dwell, wood my house,
    home the tree.
But, my lord, meet me here on
    the night of the moon
For then I shall forever be free!"

Hopes unleash'd, she waited on
    the night of the moon
'Til dark left with the rise of
    the sun.
Like cold air 'pon a leaf, was
    consum'd she by grief
For her heart knew that he'd
    never come.

The hartshorn of love's fancy
    could never thrive more,
For her maid'nly honour t'was
    shunned.
So with sadness she enter'd the
    quiet green depths
And at last with the woods
    became one.

It is thus in the knot at the end
    of the woods
That the laws of the arbour
    take hold,
For after days ripen and lose their
    sweet youth
Left are only the mem'ries of
    olde.

Grace R. Borger
Accidental Matchmaker
There are so many chuckles in
    every day life
No one need harbor a frown,
The mirth by our ancestors
    kindled
Has sifted the ages on down,

The Butcher, the Baker, the
    Candlemaker,
Well, he had a laugh in his time,
He made light, in a manner of
    speaking,
Of early society's clime.
When his tall tapers dripped how
    the wigged ladies flipped
And sent notes of reproof,
But they say when the candles
    went out, kisses stole by some
    lout
Made the innocent cavaliers pay,
Forsooth, with their lives in
    bondage to wives,
While the lout went right on
    waxing gay.
So you might say the
    Candlemaker was a
    matchmaker too,
In his way.

Gary L. Castle
WHAT IS A SALMON?
[For Kim: Blessed by the seeker]
By the banks of a roaring river,
You see the flashing of my sides
    in the sun;
Leaping the barricades to my
    destiny.
There! you yell, Salmon on the
    run.
What Manner of name is this you
    call me?
Me the leaper; the magnificent
    fearless leaper—
I hasten to my final barrier
    knowing my fate.
But I go! willing, proudly leaping
    battlements,
I the great flashing leaper.
What is a Salmon?
Dean Mitchell
SPRING
No longer is the world white with
    snow;
Green grass covers the meadow.
Little boys and their puppies
Are fishing for guppies
In the pond under a rainbow.

March winds give way to April
    showers;
Little girls are picking spring
    flowers.
The bird builds her nest
In the bough that is best
And lovingly works for hours.

God has given us this time of
    year,
I think to tell us, "Be of good
    cheer";
For both Easter and Spring
Give new life to everything
And remind us that God is here.
Madeline Rasmusson
MY PRAYER
God grant the life I live,
That every day I may do one good
    deed,
That to others some joy I can
    give,
In some life sow righteous seed.

May my life to others bring,
Some beauty in a life that is sad,
A happy song that they may sing,
Or make some poor heart glad.

Teach me dear God how to live,
So some way farer who is tired
    and blue,

May cheer and have a smile to
give,
My duty dear Lord help me to do.

Help me not burden others with,
My problems, troubles and care,
For God only knows that he too,
May have much more than he
can bear.

May I know that every day
cannot be,
Sunshine, in each life some rain
must fall,
It is the fierce buffeting winds
that,
Make the oak trees grow sturdy
and tall.

Dana L. Nietert
WHERE TO GO . . .
To pots and pans
and way out to
here?
To there.
To counting cans
and getting five
to waiting for the hives.
To silver spoons
and teddy bears
to calling me a loon.
To saying prayers
and shaking rattles
to searching for a bandaid.
To making rules
and singing carols
to laughing til it hurts.
Little do I know
little can I do.
Rescue yourself
before the snow.
Before the blanket with the silk
gives you cover to take your
milk.

Emma Kercek
IN PRAYER
I reach to heaven with my eyes,
My heart reaches, too;
    My very soul hungers for
    The nearness of God.

My arms are out-stretched in
anticipation,
My hands grope for the clasp
    Of His fingers around mine;
    I have fallen to my knees.

Tears of humility sting my eyes
    As they find their way down
    my face
    And continue to fall to the
    floor.
        The words are heavy, they
        cannot come.

In the silence my whole being
feels suspended,
    As if apart from everything
    around me.
    My lips move, and a flood of
    Love
        Surges within me
        As they cry, "Oh, God!"

V. J. Rosendahl
I SEE YOU
I see you in the springtime
    running across the sand
    chasing a dream that's almost
    in your hand.

I see you in the summer
    standing beneath the sun
    suddenly racing towards a new
    dream—
    a dream that's not yet won.

I see you in the autumn
    lying lazily amongst the leaves
    contemplating contentedly the
    completion of yet another
    dream
    as at last there's time to
    breathe.

I see you in the winter
    walking quickly through the
    snow
    hurrying to meet another goal.

I see you in all seasons
    as I watch my dreams come
    true
    knowing that they all
    begin—and end—with you.

Joan M. Kersten

Joan M. Kersten
REJECTION
I needed warmth
    it was cold
I needed to be heard
    no one was there
I needed touch
I was greeted with silence
    and cold stares

I need to live
    not to exist
I need — what?
    it isn't there.

Orland O. Sharp
FISHERMANS DREAM
We all heard about Big Creek
    Lake
And fishing there is not a fake

A man I know goes fishing a lot
From this boat he bought

He was sitting there asleep
When the boat made a leap

Startled—he was thinking it a
    whale
But only to dream of a fishermans
    tale

Ice fishing he does from his little
    ol shack
Fish caught by the bucket full
    and
Carried home in a sack

Fishing Season next on this lake
    smooth as glass
He might hitch his boat to a bass

Mary Ring
PAPER LIKE FLAKES
A mind entrapping cubical dome
    sphere sits on a dresser
the snow is falling creating a
    wintery silent delusion

as the snow quits, the clear water
    shapes a delicate figure
isolated and frozen deep within
    its existence
in which reason slips in and out
    with irregular revolution
the image completely unaware of
    its wondering madness
but as swiftly as it appears, it
    fades beneath the paper like
    flakes.

Teri Sell
TRAPPED
You're too shy to say, No way.
More apt to say,
Okay.
Why do you do what you don't
    want to?
Pretending you never knew
What to do.
They make a suggestion,
You say, That's fine.
But what's really on your mind?
Why don't you just say
What you want to say?
You trap yourself
With every breath
You take.

Theresa Honerbaum
IF
*[This poem was written to Pat.
I'd like to take this opportunity
to thank him for encouraging
me, and also for giving me
something to write about.]*
If you were the sun
Up high in the sky,
I'd lie out and one by one
Let your warm rays enter my
    waiting body.

If you were a falling star
I'd run to catch you.
I'd hold you tight in my arms
And let you shine again.

If you were a spring flower,
I'd let you touch me gently
And let you encircle me
    completely.
None of this is reality,
Yet you're all of these things to
    me.

And since you are my falling star,
My spring flower,
And my warmth, my sun,
I will run to catch and keep you,
Cherish the warmth you give,
And thank God
For together, letting us live.
Patty S. Coleman
PASSIONS QUESTION
Passions rage on the immaculate
    touch.
My weeping desires that I yearn
    so much.
Testing the entry to my hidden
    throne.
Seeking the path to my heart he
    must own.
Skillfully planning each intricate
    detail.
Awaiting the moment of time not
    to fail.
For he may hold the key to this
    hardened rock.
The key to my passion he would
    dare unlock.
Do I allow him entry with his
    mystical key?

Allow him the knowledge of the
    love within me?
I question the feeling for love I've
    not had.
The emptiness carried has made
    my life sad.
But when emptiness hollows in
    the depths of the mind,
the acceptance is easy for the
    soul becomes blind.
His love is a chance, is it one I
    dare take?
Will he give me true meaning, or
    leave me heartache?
Should I take this chance on a
    man who's a risk?
Or are his intentions sincere ones
    I don't want to miss?
I've seen my future as always
    alone, an existence
of self be it not one man shown.
Is this man different, should I let
    him succeed?
Is this my passions desire, or my
    internal need?

Lee Wells
FANTASIES
All of us have a fantasy that is
    cherished today.
Many will vanish away after they
    have led us astray.
My friends review yours to find
    their worth.
For there are many that are of
    deception upon earth.

There are fantasy of laying up
    treasurers today.
But it is written, they are to be
    used in a helping way.
As the young man was asked to
    sell and give to the poor.
The return was to have a home in
    Heaven for evermore.

Many have the fantasy of
    pleasures or sports today.
Proverbs 21:17 states they shall
    be a poor mans way.
Lovers of pleasures more than
    lovers of Gods way.
This will be the fantasy of many
    in earths last day.

So we have a rule book to guide
    us in our fantasy way.
Yes the bible, please read to
    direct in your choosen way.
My fantasy is to follow its
    directions of loves way.
To live in Heavens beautiful
    fantasy forever to stay.

Jonie Dennison
ATLANTIS
On the ocean debts is this
    ancient land
This once beautiful continent
    called Atlantis
Now it's buried with rock and
    sand
The hand made canals so
    beautifully done
The hand carved temples covered
    with gold
The climate so warm under a
    tropical sun
Far advanced people coming from
    the sky
Energy so highly developed
To the other planets they could
    fly

But the Gods got angry at the
   people's greed
The mountain started to
   rumble and roar
The angry Gods said I'll destroy
   the evil seed
A few took heed and got into
   their boat
To far away lands they went
   afloat
Am I a decendant of this
   ancient land
Now buried under with rock
   and sand

Dolly Huntley
Easter Bunnies Gift
[To My Grandchildren]
Once upon a time in the land of
   poverty a boy was born, they
   named him Dan.
Dan, frown upon his forehead,
   fists doubled to fight, unaware
   of his future plight.
Little Dan we bring you gifts for
   free, a bible don't you see?
Mother Earth will give you a
   tune.
Your parents will give you kisses
   and hugs.
And from your Uncle Sam, war,
   death, suffering, these you will
   receive very soon.
Little Dan, how can you go
   wrong?
My Easter lamb, what shall you
   contribute?
A smile perhaps, a hug, speaking
   words, or just a little coo?
Take the cross and put it down it
   is bloody don't you see?
Cold and hunger in your tummy.
   Is your legacy.
And that's what you get in the
   land of liberty.
Poverty is your's for free.

Ruth E. Fogleman
WHERE DO THEY GO?
When we die
We humans go to heaven or hell
   we know.
But what about the pets
These four legged creatures we
   miss so?
Is death the very end of them?
These creatures we've thought of
   as special friends
Is there a place for them
A special place where God does
   send?
A dry, warm place
   with warm, soft beds.
A place where Bleu could rest his
   head.
A place where he'd purr and be
   content.
A place where he'd never be
   completely dead.

The ground is hard,
And sometimes wet and cold.
We love your creatures, but they
   must go!
But God, if them you won't
   hold—
   WHERE DO THEY GO?

Mary Peak
EASTER AT THE
VETERANS HOSPITAL
You, with the cross, better
rest a spell. It looks mighty

heavy, Man. I'd like to help
you tote the thing, but Mister
I have no hands.

My buddy here has no legs, a
wheel chair is his home. This
young black man cannot see
and other worse wounds have we.
Some of our minds don't work
so good, in nightmares we hear
the dying. No matter how much
beauty there is, the ugly is
always near.

Well they prod you and whip
you on, for you must see
Golgotha. But when you're
hanging on that cross, then
please remember me. We have
a cross each one of us. We
started younger yet than you
and struggle on across the
years, no miracles for us are
due.

We fought for what we thought
was right, our country must be
free. But Man, Dear God, when
you're hanging there, then please
remember me. Please. Remember
me.

Geraldine E. Schilling
MY ERNEST PLEA
Dear Lord, let me unto others do
As I would they do unto me
Let me have a helping hand
The good in others let me see.

If I have caused a soul to grieve
Or passed him in the hour of
   need
Dear Lord, forgive my erring ways
Let me atone with some kind of
   deed.

My earnest plea has ever been
Kind to others let me be
Help me to have a giving heart
If one, in distress, should come to
   me.

Dear Lord help me to live the
   Golden Rule,
Guide me always through each
   day.
Help me to live a useful life,
For I'll not pass again this way.

Patrick J. Trinley
THE COMIC
The comic . . . he's not laughing
   now.
I thought you already knew.
That the one who makes all of
   you laugh . . .
   isn't laughing too.
He puts your mind at ease and
   wipes away your tears.
For he lets you know he hasn't
   abandoned you . . .
   throughout these trying years.
When you see him you smile and
   say,
   "He's really got the life."
But what you don't see are the
   deep, painful scars
   from his world's constant strife.
He dreamt one night that he was
   on God's eternal path.
And the friends at his funeral; all
   they did was laugh.
They don't want to take him
   seriously.
They think, "How much can that

guy be hurt?!"
Yet, it's no longer funny when
   you see the hopes
   you had for life . . . become
   trampled in the dirt!
If you haven't guessed this comic
   by now
   you may never know.
It could be you and it could be
   me . . .
   if you find out you may grow.

Loretta M. Stiles

Loretta M. Stiles
FEELINGS
My feelings, I don't know what
   they are.
I guess my care and love have
   drifted afar.
I want someone to save me, bring
   me back.
Show me all the qualities that I
   lack.
I want someone to share his love,
And those to love me from above.
I want everything that I can get,
But I don't want my life in total
   debt.

Eleanor C. Kaminsky
TIME
*[Dedicated to my wonderful,
talented son, David, who
tragically got killed in a truck
accident, at age 32, on Jan. 12,
1981.]*
Where do you go time?
Leaving your good and bad
   behind,
You drift along . . . With no
   regard
Your happiness is fleeting . . .
Why can't I catch you? . . . Why
   can't I stop you?
This beautiful dream . . .
I want to keep forever.
Just slow up a little
I'll only snatch you for a moment.
But you do not hear me, and
   away you go.
I cannot halt you time.
I need to hold the good,
And leave the bad behind.
Your slow, your slow in adverse
   times,
You speed along, when joy
   abounds.
Why?

Lisa Renee Oschmann
THE JOURNEY
As I enter the misty, hued room,
I see the very light of which we
   exist.

It is not pure, but of a brilliance
   one cannot imagine.

There is an air of mystery which
   hangs upon me.
I advance cautiously,
Knowing not the outcome of my
   next carefully planned step.

Indefinite voices of authority
   come from countless
   directions,
None seeming to penetrate an
   already defined thought,
But always having an influence;
Whether of destruction or hope, I
   cannot apprehend.

Proceeding to even deeper depths,
I turn and find the door, which
   allowed me access, has faded.
Feeling the journey is no longer
   in my control,
I sense unadmitted panic
   beginning to rise within
   myself.

The air becomes heavy as a dense
   fog sets in.
Not knowing what to do, and
   afraid of the situation,
I try to run but find the steady
   pace remains unbroken.

What I now see before me has
   overcome my worries of the
   past.
It is a spectrum of colors and a
   colorless spectrum.
I have seen "the light" but will
   not remember,
For this journey has come to an
   end, but never will be over.

Carolyn L. Vaughn Asher
RAIN
Rain, warm.
Rain, cold.
Rain, soft.
Rain, bold.
Rain with lightening,
Rain with thunder,
Rain with darkening,
Rainstorm wonder.
Rainlets soothing me to sleep,
Rain for walking, thinking,
   surging;
Rain and wind and rumblings
   deep,
Rain with tempest power surging.
Rain, on tin roof.
Rain, on glass panes.
Rain, on flowers.
Rain, on field grains.
Rain, hard.
Rain, easy.
Rain I love,
Rain, please.

William L. Wingate
MEMORIES OF HER
Her voice echoes through my
   memory,
Like a Sunday choir singing,
Rolling along the halls of
   thought,
As if it were a church bell
   ringing.

With this comes visions that I
   knew,
Her body reaching to me in the
   night,
Or her blue eyes gleaming.
With a happiness so bright.

Her scent follows me wherever I
go,
Hauntingly, like a mist at dawn,
With it I drift aimlessly,
Dreams of a happier time it
spawns.

All through the day and into the
night,
I carry these dreams of her,
Blessing or curse, I sometimes
wonder,
These memories of her.

For I must live without her,
Only in my thoughts touch her
silken skin,
My only goal, hope and prayer,
Is to be with her again.

Layne Leonard

Layne Leonard
THE WILLOW WEEPS
The willow weeps,
Her head is hung,
In sorrow for us all:
A century this willows seen,
This willow she stands tall:
A mass of trunk,
A mass of limb,
All hide behind her hair,
That dips it's tails;

The river.
Her teardrops running there:
I sat and listened to her,
The mournful tales she tells,
We both just sat there crying;
No heavens; just, all hells.

Mary Ann Havill
SO DIFFERENTLY
I wonder why my summer lasts
through each year,
each passing day,
And why your summer lasts until
the first winter wind

takes it away.
Your stars shine in the farthest
skies,
While mine shine when I look in
your eyes.

Why do we see things . . .
so differently?

As the innocence of our young
age
passes in this
loving phase,
Tell me why you call us wise
when all I see
is the hurt and the lies.
My friend, my foe,
you love me, I know,
But why do we see things . . .
so differently?

Lola M. Armstrong
THE SONG OF LIFE
*[Dedicated to my sister,
Dorothea Wiltrout, whose
encouragement has kept me
writing throughout the years.]*
There is no singing songs
Where melody has fled
From out the heart.
No sounding board
From deep within
Can make the sound,
If strings of love and faith
No longer reach
To those about us.
But if our lives stay tuned
In vibrant touch
To all that's near us,
Then songs will flow
From our own lives,
To blend,
In harmony divine,
With songs
That come from hearts
Of those we love.
And melody, again,
Can fill our lives.

Jamie Lynn Werhane
REAL WORLD
He came with the summer
like a two-for-one sale
and the price i paid for him
was higher than anything
i have ever bought before
that's what i did you know
bought some time, some
happiness
some tenderness, some laughter
all it took was
some of my soul
some of my youth
some of my life
so i traded eighteen good years
for three better months
to end up with
an eternity of heartache
but if the warm air
ever brought him back
i'd pay the price all over again
'cause he was the best thing i
ever had . . .
he just came without
a guarantee.

Mary Ann Bittle
LOOK TO THE RAINBOW
Look to the rainbow above.
It shows a promise of love.
And, although,
At the end of the rainbow,

We cannot find the pot of gold,
To that dream we must hold.
We must hold on to our dreams,
Or otherwise, it seems,
We get lost in the gloom
And visions of doom.
Never forget the story—
And lose yourself in the glory
Of that shimmering rainbow
above,
Remember God's promise of love,
And, above all, this I mean,
Hold on to your dreams.

Olive McClary
WINDS
I have lived with the winds; I
know their strange ways;
Sometimes they bring sorrow,
sometimes happy days.
They billow tall, proud sails for
men of the sea,
And murmur soft, sweet songs
caressing a tree.
They bring the fresh fragrance of
beautiful flowers,
And cool toiling workmen
through long, weary hours,
But they sometimes will wail a
weird banshee call,
And even giant oak trees will
shudder and fall.
Strong houses will tremble and
bow to their force
As they go on their wild,
relentless mad course.
They will blow as they please,
and, since this is true,
I've learned to accept them
whatever they do.
Yes, I've lived with winds, and
certainly know
It's a sad world we'd have if winds
didn't blow.

Clara F. Folsom
REAGAN 4-30-81
Our President was wounded
today!
But God was there to protect
him.
Some unbalanced man was trying
to
kill, for the chance with a girl
was slim.

Our President was an actor in his
day.
Also a governor of California
state.
He is a good family man,
And loving his wife is so great.

He's trying to help our country
in strife.
To keep peace with other lands.
Trying to keep down depression,
and lead us to a better life.

Tami Rush
FLOWERS FOR JOE
There you are,
standing alone in a
field of clover;
the trees are your friends,
the wind is your confidante,
the sparrow, your music.

You are a wildflower,
caught in a time when
it is more fashionable to
be a rose.

Please do not sway though,

for soon,
very soon,
the rose will fade and die

and once more
you will
take your place
in a bouquet,
sent special delivery
to my heart.

Alma Britten-Huddleston
**Where Has My Little Girl
Gone?**
*[Dedicated to: My two girls,
Janie Lou and Eddie Anne who
will always be my little girls.]*
Where, oh where has my little
girl gone?
Just yesterday she was here
Bright sparkling eyes, twinkling
toes,
And a heart that had never
known fear.

I roll back the time to those
yesterdays,
Seeking my treasures so dear
Time cannot tarnish, nor memory
fade
In spirit, she is always near.

Time, be kind to my darling, I
plead.
Keep her safe through life's
storm.
Just as I did, when she was a kid
And I tried to protect her from
harm.

Constance Stutts McBroom
OL' MONEY
Ol' money has a hungry old face,
And he sits and laughs at the
human race.
You can't find a house for miles
around,
That's missed his greedy old
jingling sound.
'Cause without ol' money how
would we live?
For we need all the things that
money can give.
And he knows his captives will
never resist,
What's needed, they believe, in
order to exist.
But thank the Lord, we can
always rely
On knowing there's things that
money can't buy;
Like love and happiness and a
pretty day,
Or trees and leaves upon a
pathway.
So watch your step and try to
fight
Ol' money's ever growing appetite;
Or you'll end up like me, broke
and out of luck,
Wishing for enough ol' money to
buy a truck.

Linda Lowery
GO AWAY DOG!
I have been treated so bad, even
worse than a dog.
Because another woman
you had to hog.
So many times
she was in your arms.
All this time you were thinking
it would do no harm.

How could you treat
   me so bad?
How could you make
   me so sad?

I have been a faithful wife
   as I could be,
Why couldn't your love
   have been for me?
My arms have ached
   to hold you so tight.
I would have loved you with
   all my might.

Hou can you
   be so untrue?
And cause me
   to be so blue?

In our marriage vows,
   when I said "I do",
If you will just remember
   you felt like that too.

Here I am,
   dumped like a dog,
Because of another woman
   you felt you had to hog!

James Michael Robbins
STARVING DREAMS
Starve children not
   (starving)
for knowledge
to feed dreams . . .

Ahhh . . .
but watch quietly
while the BIG BOYS squash them
with the ultimate weapon:
   econom(ick!)s.

Finding ourselves
would be so good now—
yet we relinquish
to starvingschools
learning to be
   igknowble

starving dreams all the while.

Janette Chastain Whitney
THEY'RE NOT MY POEMS
*[To God: Who is my
everything,
To My Family: For always
loving me,
To My Friends: For always
caring.]*
Some people ask me how I write
   Such special poems of love.
I tell them all it's not just me,
   God whispers like a dove.

All I do to meet His quest
   Is write down whispered
   thoughts.
And never more do I regret
   Lost words that I once sought.

There's magic in an open mind
   When God fills in the space.
And what comes out in harmony
   Is fragile just like lace.

So let me write the glory
   That I so wish to give.
And maybe it will help you
   To grow and love and live.

Liz Martindale
**Cobweb Dreams,
Eternal Means**
Spinning and weaving my dreams
   of life,
I run and hide from worry and
   strife.
Lying on a blanket of grass,

I think of past love as fragile
   glass.
It should have been encased with
   cotton,
Instead, it was treated with wild
   abandon.
Now all I have left is shattered
   dreams,
Life just isn't what it seems.
Sometimes I feel so left out,
Like I don't know what life's
   about.
I try so very hard to understand,
But I stand on a foreign land.
I meet people and I make friends,
But it is only a means to an end.
Even with their help and concern,
It seems as though I'll never
   learn.
Where do I go when I'm on my
   knees?
I go to Jesus, He hears my pleas.
While every prayer is not
   answered today,
Hope is restored when I pray.
I may not always win the games I
   play, but I tried, I say.

Jeanette Harlin

Jeanette Harlin
THE ROYAL BATTLE
Two pairs of nostrils flaming
   two pairs of hoofs meet in the
   air.
Come watch the royal battle;
   come closer if you dare.
Two manes flying
   two stallions in the heat.
They're fighting to the rhythm
   of a deadly beat.
One is white as snow
   the other black as night
They fight on nonfailing
   as their mares draw back in
   fright.
One must be the victor,
   the other must die.
"One will be a king";
   I think that as I sigh.
Then the battle's over,
   I see his bleeding skin.
The black one lost the battle
   and the white one's king again.

Jean A. Mathisen
HIGH DOMINIONS
In the wind of thesummer
   morning I walk.
In the breath of the passing day I
   live.
The sun has risen high upon the
   mountain,
touching the sacred red ledges.

High upon the morning an eagle
   rides the sky.
Brother to my soul, he sees the
   valley.
We are tied in the way of kinship.
Wild eagle and walker of the
   earth.
We seek the high dominions,
   to soar free with Brother Wind.
I have known the depth of the
   craggy canyons.
Known grief carved as deep as
   gashed granite.
This day I walk in the summer
   morning—
soaring high above sacred red
   ledges.
In the shadows, in the wind
   caves,
Carved figures, eons old
tell ancient tales of times
   unknown
to those who walk the land in
   this time.
What is time? Brother Eagle
   knows it not.
The sun has risen high upon the
   mountain.
In the breath of the passing age, I
   live.

Joe W. Baughman
SILVERY MORNING
*[For my parents who without
their knowing it are largely
responsible for my writing. To
them I thank for giving me the
opportunity to be myself at all
times. Love your son, Joe.]*
The new sun dawns upon the
   meadow grass,
now shining brightly from an
   early frost.
And it reminds me so of
   mornings past,
and all the dreary days this time
   has cost.
I take a look outside and
   speculate,
about the beauty I can plainly
   see.
I wonder how much longer I must
   wait,
until together you and I can be.
The sun is shim'ring off the
   frosty blades,
the spectrum's colors dance upon
   my eye.
And then again it starts to melt
   away,
while leaving only mem'ries in
   my mind.
Perhaps tomorrow's dawn will
   bring to me,
my frosty blades the sight I love
   to see.

Linda Adams Baker
**Jesus—Elder Brother—Dear
Friend**
On butterfly wings my soul does
   fly
swiftly yet gently I rise to Your
   side.
Your peace—how it fills me
I feel so light—so free.
Yes—You have freed me,
   hope reigns supreme within my
   spirit.
In you I have complete trust.
When my soul leaps up

so overwhelmed with joy—
Your arms are there to catch me
   those nail—scarred hands
   will never let me fall.
At times I grow weary
   my spirit weighed down
   life's burdens too heavy to bear.
You patiently reach out to me—
   take my hand—help me to my
   feet again.
I dance freely—knowing You are
   always near—
   ready to support me—to dance
   with me
my patient Instructor—
   Elder Brother—Dear Friend.

Virginia Hays
AMERICA, I LOVE YOU
*[This poem is dedicated to all
Sooner Council Girl Scouts,
leaders, staff members,
counselors, volunteers, and
especially to the girls in my
troop.]*
America, I love you;
let me tell you why—
Your winding streams
create my dreams,
on you, I can rely.

America, are you mine?
I ask your mountains high—
   "They do not boast,
   but gently coast,
   my freedom to the sky."

America, do you fail me?
I wish for your reply—
   "The Eagles' might,
   full wing in flight,
   they soar to clarify."

America, I ask you true;
will Patriotism die?
   "To all who know,
   while seasons grow,
   on me, you can rely."

George Ghassan Malouf
AN ODE TO KATERINA
Lo, little princess, to my heart so
   dear,
And fairer in beauty than a
   moonlight clear.

How you stagger your balance in
   shunning a fall!
Yet, alas, how you stumble my
   lovely sweet—roll!

With emotion, my little one, I see
   you clad,
And with your eyes so moist,
   your face turning sad.

But your loving eyes should ne'er
   know weep,
For the purity of heaven is within
   their keep.

So, come nearer my little one, and
   dry your tears;
Hurl aloft those horrid fears.

Now, give me, little princess,
   your heart to soothe,
And fret not ever my love to lose.

Carolyn Wright Moseley
OF LOVE
Written words,
   like butterflies wings
stained with ink,
   Leave traces
of the hearts flutterings.

Suzie Spicer
Daughter Of the Night

I am the daughter of the night,
the darkness that surrounds you
the answer that confounds you
the question you can't ask.

I am the cloud that pours thunder
    down
the rain that washes you clean,
the song you long to sing
the melody that escapes you.

Mrs. Mike Higgins
THE CHAIN

Love is simply caring.
To care is but to learn.
Learning brings understanding
Understanding brings concern.

All these words mean the same.
No matter how they're spoken;
Each a link in a Golden Chain
That never should be broken.

Lois M. Fishback
SCOTT

The young boy stepped to the
    front of the Church
And sat on the piano bench.
Will that small lad play for
    Worship, today?
It gave your heart a wrench.

He began to play in measured
    beat,
"Blessed Assurance, Jesus is
    Mine."
He was performing his best for
    the Lord.
His smile made his whole face
    shine.

He sat so very straight and tall
Lest he give his age away.
"I'm almost nine, soon going on
    ten."
He'd respond if you asked today.

When he finished his music, the
    preacher smiled.
He was proud of his son, you
    could see.
Back down the aisle the young
    pianist strode
To sit with his family.

Edith Louise McCormick
ROUTINE

Telephones, dictaphones, files
    mounting high,
Schedules and calendars going
    awry;
Projects on paper with deadlines
    to meet,
Typewriters tapping a rhythmical
    beat;
Clocks ticking steadily, setting
    the pace,
Measuring laps in a wearying
    race;
Days rushing on in monotonous
    trend,
Blending with years toward a
    beckoning end—
Clearly, concisely my heart at
    last sees,
Turns to the typewriter, tears on
    the keys.

Linda G. King
**My Heart Keeps My
    Memories.**

Christmas this year was a
good ole' time with plenty
of food and such . . .

Mom made cakes, pies, ham
and turkey we couldn't wait
to touch . . .

We opened presents on
Christmas morn; carefully
so that precious paper
was nicely torn . . .

Like all joyous families do,
we hugged and said thanks
for sweaters, perfumes and
army tanks . . .

My family; they are great
all year but Christmas
memories keep families
close and dear.

Lauri Lee
LOVE IS MORE . . .
*[I would like to dedicate this
poem to my eternal love, Allen.
For he is the reason this poem
was written.]*

Love is much more than a tender
    caress
and more than bright hours of
    gay happiness.
For a lasting love is made up of
    sharing
both hours that are "joyous"
and also "despairing".

It's made up of patience and deep
    understanding
never of selfish and stubborn
    demanding.
Nothing on earth or in heaven
    can part
a love that has grown to be part
    of the heart.

Just like the sun and the stars
    and the sea
this love will go on through
    eternity.
For "true love" lives on when
    earthly things die
for it's part of the Spirit that
    Soars to the Sky.

Jana Caldwell
THE DEATH OF A TREE

Swaying gently,
    in movement with the wind,
The old oak creaks
    under the strain of it's limbs.
Frail leaves parachute
    from their perch on branches,
Performing last rituals
    in graceful decending dances.
A strong gusty wind
    builds miles away.
A premonition, a shudder,
    fills the oaks veins.
Silence falls
    bringing feelings of death,
Beginning the wait
    for the coming pain.
Then it hits,
    an enormous wall of wind.
Attacking the tree
    forcing the trunk to bend.
With all it's strength
    the roots grab for the ground.
Alas, the tree is old,
    and the youthful wind sends it
    crashing down.

Eleni Katzingris Moustaka
GOTTEN BACK

Come, get back your old
zeal for life.
How I would like could,
    again,

I see your face lit up
in delight.

If I could have pulled
    you, through
the desperate melancholy,
    that interpose
between us, like a dragon,
    I will kiss
all the stars in my frenzy,
    because I have
never able, to leave you.

I never would've believed
    that you could
have said, that our life
    is ruined
from our little boy's
    death.

He filled the void in
    our life,
but nothing has changed
    and nothing
ever will, because he
    never parted,
from our heart.

Edward P. Cole

Edward P. Cole
SONNET

Should it be that I could love
    again
As I've loved, —and still do I love
    her
Who lies 'mong yon roots of Wild
    Roses?
There 'pon many times I've
    spilled my tears.
Should it be? —Oh how could it
    be? How
Could I forget when there is so
    much
To remember about us and love?
Dare I venture loving another
In quite the same way that I
    loved her?
T'is most surely as the Horner's
    tune
Is ne'er quite the same twice
    repeated,
That love bleeds not from the
    same vein twice.
T'would be denying my soul's
    passion
To love another as I've loved her.

SONNET

Since first I loved, I've always
    loved you.
As I have loved you in past
    seasons,
I will always love you. I love you
For many things and many
    reasons.

But I knew that love would be
    my fate
Since first I saw you 'mongst my
    tea-leaves,
While sipping the brew b'side my
    Birch-fires;
T'was like I'd been feasting 'pon
    high-wines;
The steamy brew revealed your
    image,
And all my soul turned wild and
    untame
In that first moment that I loved
    you.
I have vowed with Love's own
    sacred draught
To love no other as I love you.
Since first I loved, . . .I've always
    loved you.

Evelyn Kaye Solarczyk
MY OWN SUN
*[To Samer—whose friendship
has inspired these and other
words, and whose caring has
placed a song in my heart.]*

Somehow,
I find beginnings the most
    difficult.
Learning to trust and be trusted.
Preparing for the future.
Seeing with an open, clear mind.

You know,
I've always worshipped the sun
and marveled at its life-producing
    rays.
I find tranquility in a crimson
    yellow sunset
and surging energy in a sleepy
    gray sunrise.

I looked into your eyes the other
    day
and saw a growing, glowing
    warmth,
much like a blossoming spring
    sun.

Free me from the shackles of past
    loves
and break into the dungeon my
    heart died in
so long ago.
Touch me, love me, need me,
and please don't add another sad
    ending
to the beginning I think I've
    found in you.

Jan Bratcher
The Meaning Of Teacher
*[To my mother, Reta Gross, a
model teacher of twenty-five
plus years. May I be as great a
teacher as she.]*

You counted off for spelling;
I always wanted to complain.
You graded down for grammer,
Punctuation, and no name.

You were a strict conformist,
We conformed or lost the game.
You were a very staunch master;
We listened or received the
    blame.

You were always fair and
    consistent;
No pets in your class were about.
You treated all as equal,
And no one carried clout.

We hated with a passion,
The homework, and you knew;

38

But you cared not a twittle
If we studied 'til we were blue.

We didn't want to learn,
But I guess that I can say,
That we learned in spite of
    ourselves
And we're a better person today.

And so I ask you, Chap,
Is this what "teacher" means:
To keep on pushing against the
    odds,
To help that student be
More than he was when he
    started,
And more than he would
    someday be?

Fran Harris
NIGHT NOISES
[To My Husband, Del]
The night is dark and you see a
    spark
From the campfire across the way
The land is still and a
    whipperwill
Tells of the end of the day.

The campers sleep and the
    streams run deep
And the fish feed on the fly
The frogs all croak and the
    mountain goat
Climbs back to go up high.

Soft breezes blow and the ember
    glow
Of the moon shines from above
The coyote calls and the rocky
    walls
Surround the place we love.

The pines all sway and seem to
    say
This day is at an end
While peace you find inside your
    mind
As you sleep near the river bend.

Stacy K. Hoefner
THE JEWELS
The ocean with its many jewels
Hidden beneath the sand,
Like a pirates buried treasure.
Sometimes the ocean is generous
    enough
To cast its jewels upon the beach,
They lay there, like
    ladies-in-waiting,
Waiting for someone to sweep
    them up and take them home,
Someone to love and cherish
    them.
And the ones that are not chosen
Are caught up in the tumbling
    waves,
And tucked back into their sandy
    beds,
Until another day . . .

Earl R. Purdue
Rose Petals
Always Bloom
[To Woman—Called Naomi]
Let maturities' years be a gift for
    self.
No matter how bitter your
    experience has been,
How much agony of heart-sick
    grief-torture,
Of hunger ache, pain or fear,
That Life may bless you with,
Spiritual maturity, when it
    blooms,

Enlightens each such event.
Always disclosed, there is
    offsetting beauty,
To balance the past darkness.
Thus blended-completeness
    becomes in your life,
Wonderous Rose Petal Memories,
Advancing each moment through
    eternity.

Mrs. Patricia B. Cabrinety

Mrs. Patricia B. Cabrinety
WINTER'S SNOW
We knew that snow was on the
    way
    because the sky grew to a
    corduroy gray.

It wasn't long before the wind
    began to blow
    heralding the rapid approach of
    the snow.

Soon the snow lay crisp and
    crunchy under our feet
    while cars went skidding down
    the street.

New Fallen Snow

Outlined velvety fluff quickly
    grew on all the trees
    and showered sparkles on us
    with every breeze.

With the hillsides molded like
    fresh-frosted cupcakes
    we decided to slide and not to
    skate.

We re-tied our boots and bundled
    up warm and snug—
    up the side of the slope with
    our sleds did we tug.

S-l-o-w-l-y, slowly up the very top
    did we go to slide
    and ever so quickly down the
    hill did we glide.

Maureen S. Neely
MEMORY OF YOUR SMILE
I just can't stop
Thinking of you,
You're always on my mind.

And even when
You're far away,
Your memory stays behind.

I see you laugh,
I see you smile,
Your hand reaches for mine.

I feel such warmth
When you are here,
It can't be touched by time.

The days will come
When we won't be
Together for a while,

But that's ok
Because I hold
The memory of your smile.

Wilkie M. Smith
EYES TO SEE
It may seem clear and bright
And more than enough light,
And try with all your might
In the dead of the night,
With or without eyesight,
One can feel and hear without
    eyes.
You can smell and taste without
    eyes.
You can see and love without
    eyes.
Other senses improve without
    eyes.
Still you are, even without eyes.

Let us take a look and see,
Can our leaders really see?
I think it is easy to see
They have eyes, but cannot really
    see.
Our leaders are like you and me.
I am blind, you are blind.
We are blind, they are blind.
Tell me, who is not blind?

HollyJo Beers Harer
WATER WINGS
Tiny creek is laughing, playing
Tumbling over pebbles saying
    I have time to flow away
    I give no thought to hours or
    day
Caring not what time will bring
I have only time to sing
    Look at all the scenes I see
    Landscaped here so splendidly
Mountaintops with green trees
    tall
Sloping valleys between them all
    Rocky ridges jutting high
    Cotton clouds in azure sky
Golden leaves float on my back
What a joyous load to pack
    Tiny creatures touch my soul
    Leisurely I pitch and roll
If only you could be like me
And live in this tranquility
    Then you could let your spirit
    light
    On water wings into the night

Michelle Moran
WONDERFUL AUTUMN
I'm thiking of a time the leaves
    begin to change.
When nature spreads her autumn
    coat across the mountain
    range.

She does it every year and doesn't
    stop to rest.
She arranges it by colors she
    thinks will look the best.
She might even ask the birds way
    up inside their nests.
Nature you have that special
    touch,
The one people love so much.
I hope you never change the way
    you play.
Because the special way you
    change,
The leaves upon the range,
Makes a lot of people happy
    everyday.
Until next year, when the colors
    reappear;
My mind will always wander.
When I think what nature does,
It's a peaceful, amazing wonder.

Michael Sandford
MY JENNY
Jenny, my Jenny.
Your love is so appealing.
Smiles you have for us . . . there
    is plenty.
As you grow in each and every
    way.
Your Mother and Father will
    stand beside you . . .
from day to day.
With your hands stretched out
    for guidance.
We pray the Lord will help guide
    us.

Jenny, my Jenny.
The day that comes when you
    leave here.
Our hearts will follow and grow
    ever so dear.
Your hugs and kisses will always
    bring a tear.
We'll laugh, we'll play.
We'll cry, we'll pray.
Please don't run astray.

Jenny, my Jenny.
Though you're a babe now.
One day you'll stand beside us, at
    the bow.
As life is a ship.
From port, to port . . . many
    adventures there'll be.
Falling down . . . scrape a knee.
Or adventures in a tree.
Jenny, my Jenny, you'll always be.

Semmie I. Bender
GIFT OF LOVE
*[To Carol, Gary, and Donna,
    with love, Mom.]*
Precious little ones
Loaned to us from one above,
Ours to have and to hold
To cherish and to mold.

Precious little ones
Sent to us from one above,
To give affection and direction
Touched our hearts with love.

Precious little ones
Lent to us from one above,
With all their laughter and tears
Filled our home with joy.

Precious little ones
Loaned to us from one above,
Brought into our lives
God's gift of love.

Today's Greatest Poems

Barbara J. Lipanovich
OLD WOMAN

[To my loving husband John, to my two beautiful daughters, Debbie and Shauna, and to my very best friend, my Mom.]

While I sit here alone, arms limp
   by my side—
With wrinkled skin and veins
   swelling with pride
I remember my youth—so alive
   and so gay
And how motherhood had blessd
   me along the way.

My life had meaning—for my
   children I had love
But both were soon taken by the
   Great One above.
So I sit here alone, old, and
   wondering why
My God in Heaven has passed
   me by.

I wait and I pray—but always in
   vain
Wondering why the long wait,
   why this great detain
Of leaving this Earth to be able to
   meet
My God, my Creator, who made
   my life complete.

Callie Williams
A SPECIAL FRIEND

[To my grandparents, Grandma Honey and Grandpa John. Who bring heartwarming love and laughter into other people's lives and whose smiles I will always hold in my heart.]

The rustling leaves whisper
Silvery softness in the breeze
Springtime violet flowers
Sweetly noticed through the trees

A man walks slowly
A faithful dog limps at his heels
His cane finds the obstacles
In the darkness that he feels

The old man sits contently
Blindly overlooking traveled land
His companion stares quizzically
Before moving closer to lick his
   hand

A rushing brook babbles gently
Birds fly but go unseen
The dog rests his head on his
   master's lap
In the sun, they share their
   dreams

A thankful pat, a warming smile
For sightless eyes that can
   depend
Capturing the beauty of each
   walked mile
With the love of his special
   friend

Ella Foster O'Brien
OUR MOTHER IS ASLEEP

[To our Mother: a Mother to all the world.]

She is asleep, the trip has been so
   long.
   She is so tired and worn
Our God has called her to her
   rest
Has opened wide the door of
   home.

Open wide the door for her dear
   Lord
   Angels, sing your happy songs
Make her welcome now at last,
   For her journey has been long.

For her no sad regrets, no tears,
   Her love and kindness, we still
   hear.
Our Mom has gone to be with
   God,
   Our memories we'll hold dear.

Thru all her days, and all her
   years,
   Her way has been so long,
Yet, still I hear her kindly voice,
   And again, her happy song.

Dear God, please take our Mom,
   to that room
   You have for her above,
And make her rest a peaceful one,
   Of joy and everlasting love.

Karen Ann Foster
VACATION

Fantasy rewarded
   Behind now
      The payments
One week
   for two days
One year
   for two weeks
For a doll
   a girl
      a mistress
Paid in full
   a short time
      too quickly gone
Again invest
   Again endure
      The payments
One week
   of ribbons
One year
   of raises
For fantasy
   paid in full
      a short time
         too quickly gone.

Phyllis Joan Smith
CROSSES OF WHITE

Beat the drums softly, my boys
White crosses mark their graves
   for freedom, their lives, they
   gave
Just so, our flag forever waves...
Beat the drums softly, my boys
A great nation sleeps quietly
   tonite
   among the crosses of white...
Beat the drums softly, my boys
   for this is the home of the
   brave
They sleep soundly, within their
   graves...

John W. Foreman
IN THE MOUNTAINS

What is inspired
   by the mountains
      where we so casually hide?
Are our secrets actually
   concealed?
Are we safer when we're alone?
We throw our trash in the
   mountains,
   with no regard as to who might
   know.
      Boy, will you be surprised!
There's a washing machine

in the mountains,
   and a table near a Sears catalog.
The mountains are always there.
   Why don't you leave your
   mundane world,
      and come to the mountains?
      That's where you will find
   me.
Peace and security, alone in the
   mountains,
   where the past and the future
   are combined in the now
If you come, will you
   take the catalog with you,
      when you leave?

Delilah-Judith

Delilah-Judith
TO DEARIE ONE

No Venus tonight, no Lilith Star,
   no moon!
No pathway bright, you seem to
   fly afar too soon.
Dear One, how do I know these
   things?
No plane's searchlight sweeps my
   bedroom!

Sunsets lay out a magic carpet for
   me
Of sunset clouds at eventide,
And I happily take my
   coach-and-eight
And through pink clouds do ride.

Straight through a maze of
   memories' dreams,
Straight to the ocean side,
With my Dearie One I cross
   mountain tops,

With kisses and smiles we glide.

Sea gulls sing our Love's
   roundelay,
And never a sharp note is replied,
Surely heaven must be like this,
Oh, Dearie One, with me abide!
   abide!

You took the plane to go far
   away,—
I must stay by the desert sands,
Because my Studio here makes
   scenes
Supposedly laid in foreign lands.

Which are fantasies of these? of
   magic carpets pink?
Or of scenes supposedly made in
   foreign lands?
But this I know, I must remain
   always—
Beside the desert sands.

Vicki R. Melugin
THE MIND

The mind is a complex, confusing
   thing
   With multitudes of thoughts
   to bring;
A frown, a smile, inquisitive
   stare
Upon the countenance seeking
   there
   The answers to riddles of
   untold years;
   Of countless hopes, and dreams
   and fears
In coping with each newborn day,
   And finding yet another way
To solve the dilemma of
   human self
For the right to survive, not put
   on shelf
To disappear amid countless
   passing by,
   Keep the will to live, and
   never die
In staying young with faultless
   dreams
Of going ever like sparkling
   streams,
   Which wend their way to the
   great deep sea;
   The mind is keeper of thee
   and me.

Don P. Lamirande
FUTURE OF WAR

War seems like an endless dream,
as one fights against the others
   regime.
Wars will stop, well who knows
   when.
If you ask me, war is ugly as sin.
Have you ever stopped and
   thought about war?
It's like the uselessness as that of
   a whore.
It's a game of politics as we all know,
till it's their sons they call, then
   they say no.
It's funny how they think of war
   as a game,
till one of our boys comes home
   as a lame.
One day this world will have a
   new birth,
as there will be no more people
   on earth.

Denise Renee Shuster
I BELIEVE

[Dedicated to Mr. Dan Johansen who helped me believe in life, love and the true value of myself.]

I believe in the self of me and the
self of others around and beyond
me. I believe in loving and caring
for people of all nationalities
and every age. I believe in the
warmth of the sun and the
warmth a smile is capable of
bringing. I believe in the
challenge of realizing and the
future understanding of life. I
believe that trying is of more
value than succeeding if you get
up after falling to try again. I
believe that friends are so
undeniably precious that it hurts
me to think of all the damage
I've caused for my own
selfishness. I believe in being
full of sweet young innocense

and one day getting older for it's an acceptance of life. I believe in the laughter of joyful hearts and the music of the soul. I believe in God; who mysteriously but obviously bestows a power in all of us. I believe in mysteries and the solutions to them. I believe in mornings. This is a time to start another day fresh and new. I believe in Captain Crunch Cereal and Donald Duck Orange Juice. I believe in the nightfall—it's a state of imagining and dreaming, resting the mind and laughing deep down, silently touching the soul while storing hopes for the day to come. I believe in the future and what I'm capable of achieving. I believe in the nature of silence; the silence of magnificent beauty and the silence of bitter ugliness. The silence of emotions that language is incapable of expressing. I believe in the truth and being honest with others. I believe in trying to understand opinions unlike my own. I believe in me. I believe in you and all you have to offer. I believe in affection and tenderness. I believe in striving to be happy.
Yes, I believe in life!

Ruby K. Reed
LIFE'S MEMORIES
Memories are made of little things
   that happen every day
Moments as we live them—
   things we do and say.
Little bits and pieces
   of laughter filled with tears,
Paragraphs and pages
   written through the years.
The carefree days of childhood
   the growing pains of youth,
So many illusions shattered
   in the endless search for truth.
The freindships we remember
   mistakes that we regret,
The ending of a love affair,
   we cannot forget.
Memories are happenings
   each of a different kind,
Every one a separate chapter
   imprinted in the mind.
We can't erase the sad times
   or edit out the tears,
We can't undo the wrong we've done
   we can't relive the years.
But, since memories keep on building
   each day can be the start,
Of making new and happy ones
   to store within our heart.

Beth A. Ackerman
THE FENCE
The fence surrounding the house
Is there to make sure no one gets too close.
At times, the owner forgets
And leaves the gate open.
Curious bypassers try to find a way in,

Only to find the gate quickly closed and locked.
With each attempt, the owner gets angrier,
And adds a new latch.
One day though, I found a hole in the fence.
As I crawled through—
I realized I was one of the first to get close.
What a new experience this must be!
When I returned the next day,
I found the hole mended,
And a new latch on the gate.
But I was persistent,
And tried to climb over.
On the way, I found the owner pushing me back.
Once again, the owner added a new latch.
My patience did reach it's end,
And I no longer try to get through the fence.
I guess the owner succeeded,
And won his battle.
But my heart was changed when I crawled through the fence,
And I hope it's not too late,
For the owner to unlatch the gate—
And let the world in.
For he has a great deal to share,
If only he would let someone get close and care.

Thomas Taylor Graef III
TOGETHER
[To Jennifer
For Love And Inspiration]
Days of roses and wine
Left impressions on my mind
Fiends of green, sky of blue
Are thoughts I have too
Joy, happiness, and life with peace
Are dreams of tomorrow
Love I have for thee
Is now and for all eternity
For together we can build our dreams
And turn them into reality
Lessons learned in the past
Love hold our future stedfast
To journey through endless time
Never having known you
Would be an unknown death
But to see your smile
Is to know what beauty is
To feel your soft touch
Is to know the goodness of life
To forsake the past
And dream of the future
Is what the world wishes to do
But to learn from the past
And make our dreams come true
This is what I shall try and do

William W. West
WHO REALLY WAKES
[My two dads]
Is it the sun that brings new day
It fades the darkness, lets us play
Perhaps the rooster when he crows
It's time to rise, it's time he knows.

Maybe the bird with a cherry tune
A song for now, in a distance soon

The morning breeze with all the sent
Flowers of the moment, before they are spent

Perhaps the grass, if we hear it grow
But listen close or you'll hear snow
Maybe something more, we can't understand
But each day we wake, we do what we can

Mark Steven Spicer

Mark Steven Spicer
TREASURED MOMENTS
When I open up the treasure chest of moments
That I have so securely locked away
The brightness of those gems that I have hidden
Engulfs the darkness with the light of the day

When I behold the glory of those precious jewels
And the priceless value placed upon those times
All the others are but shabby imitations
Enacted by the poorest of the mimes

Debi Tonkin
Deepest Thoughts Of You
[To Robert Shaw with deepest thoughts and memories.]
When I think of you
   A smile enters my face
Remembering the good times
   Which you and I have shared.

When I dream of you
   I never want to awaken;
Reminiscing the happiness
   Which only you have given me.

As I awaken to see you gone
   Tears begin to fill my eyes;
Wishing you were here by my side
To see me through another lonely day.

Marion L. Perry
GYPSY
Stranger beware of the moors tonight
For you know them not as I.
They're wild and beautiful, treacherous
And here, I'd want to die.

Their winds are like no other winds
Fierce, or soft and whispering
Lost souls, howling, forever gone
Forgotten, but not forgiving.

Damp smells of the open marsh
Gorse bushes, brambles, lavender,
Beckon you, to wander thru
While muck holes, suck you under forever.

Wild ponies roam and toss their manes
Free, like the black haired gypsies.
Granite tors, point sharp fingers at the sky
From high peak, thru white mist, glimpse the sea.

Quench your thirst from a cold rippling brook,
Sleep tonight, with your head on a stone
There's no shelter except a crevice of rock
But the moors, Ah! the moors are my home.

J. Blood
REMAINS
   In the gutter
   ravaged and discarded
the newspaper flapped loudly in the wind.
   Beside it, the man lay silent.
   Each Forsaken.
   One protesting angrily
the other;   not at all.

Mrs. Ruth Gronosky
A GRANDFATHER'S PRIDE
Love drew him to the Homestead old,
In mid-December...it was bleak...it was cold.
Just as he'd done many times as a Boy,
He knocked at the door to share Grandparents' joy.

His shoulders now broad, he stood, oh so tall,
No boy about him showed at all!
Generous arms were opened wide
To clasp his Grandmother secure inside.

He sensed immediate concern and care
As eyes fell upon the empty chair.
Trips to a bedside, a loving embrace
Re-kindled thoughts of kindness and grace.

PEACE came softly...a Man dare not cry
While memories linger and tears fill the eye.
Strength shone divinely though the pain was grim
As he walked those final steps with Him.

A heart so heavy it could cry out loud,
No doubt that He would have been so proud.
But God showed his mercy, before Day was Done,
Precious moments together...
Grandfather—Grandson!

Today's Greatest Poems

Carol J. Grandy
US, AGAIN
A slightly arched footbridge, over
 a frozen river,
Evergreens all around.
I stand on the footbridge, over the
 frozen river,
Thinking of you.
Unknown to me, you watch from
 behind the evergreens.
You think of me,
The evergreen sway softly, as you
 watch,
From behind them.
The sun begins to fall. We watch
 the sunset,
But not together.
I start to walk, as the twilight
 begins to darken.
I walk in your direction.
You step out in front of me.
 I stop, you stop.
We look at each other for what
 seems an eternity.
We walk without talking,
To the end of the path.
We walk down the road while the
 moon lights our way.
We come to the crossroads, and
 look at each other.
We move close, and walk
Together, in our direction.

Marisa Guiliana Dal Pan
INSANITY
It is said that people learn from
 the past,
Although I think that's a lie.
Years and years go by
But I don't think they have
 learned.
We have studied about wars of
 the Roman Empire—
Were there not bloody battles
During those wars?
Yet, the insanity continues.
Your son, my brother, the
 neighbors husband
Are dutiful citizens and go to
Defend our country.
And what happens?
They kill—
Somebody's son, somebody's
 brother, somebody's husband.
Where is the logic
Behind this madness
To kill for a piece of land?
Tell me, someone,
Will it ever stop?

Joellen Masters
LIZZIE
Medievally robed in flowing
 gown;
Queen of the circle; Rossetti's
 own dream.
Real to the touch and warm to
 hold,
Love-lorn, adored, her soul grows
 cold.

Long green eyes, gold hair that
 charms;
To keep an angel in his arms,
The poet dies—too late emerges
The man, now haunted by her
 funeral dirges.

Diane M. Guilmette
MY WORLD
You gave my world to me,
 By giving me your love.

You did not hand it to me on a
 silver platter,
But rather, in your heart—
You were my friend.
You gave yourself to me.
Our love grew stronger,
The bond between us grew
 tighter.
We became attached—
I loved you.
You were frightened.
You pulled away.
You took my world from me.
You took away your love.
The friendship remains,
And one day, will grow again.
Then you shall give me back my
 world—
Yourself, your heart—
Our love.

Laura Burkland Klinger
LEGACY OF LOVE
 *[To my parents, Rolland and
 Mary Burkland: "Thank you for
 your guidance," " I love you"
 'Sue']*
You instilled within, a sense of
 worth:
 A pride in being me.
Respect and fear for a caring God:
 Love of country and family.

Material riches, we had not many,
 But, I'd not trade a thing:
For the love of Jesus in my heart,
 And the peace that love can
 bring.

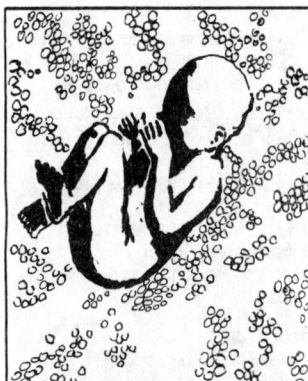

All the 'treasures' in this old
 mixed-up world,
 With money, you can buy;
But, you'll not buy peace and
 happiness,
 No matter what you try.

Do unto others, the bible says,
 Think of your neighbors first;
It's far better to be blessed by
 God,
 Than to have your life be
 cursed.

You taught me the meaning of
 giving,
 And the value of things above;
No greater gift can a parent give,
 Than this "Legacy of Love."

Benjamin N. Stickler
WAITING
A pencil sits silently
Never moving from its abode
Or questioning its job
Just waiting, waiting patiently
For a stroke of creativity

Pamela A. Sherman
I'M ON MY WAY
I don't know where I'm going
I'm confused by where I've been
What will life be like when 'now'
 is 'then'?
Will memories make me smile
or have me stop and think awhile?
 Could it be it's all been wrong,
 the way I've done things for so
 long?
I've been having my fun
All that's done is done.
I don't believe it should be
 changed,
It can never happen exactly the
 same
For somewhere along and through
 it all I've been rearranged.
I liked the way I used to be but I
 accept me as I am.
I'll be going on to please me and
 not doing it for them.
I know that sounds bad but I
 don't mean it unkind
While I'm pleasing me, I'll be
 keeping you in mind
Just as you should think of me as
 you please you.
So each on our own shall find
 happiness
to make our lives together mean
 much more and never less.
Forever we should always search
 and never cease
With each new sunrise comes
 another chance for inner peace.
I'll be going somewhere each new
 day
Wondering why and not knowing
 where, but I'll be on my way!

Rosemary Coyle
A LOVE OF LONG AGO
He held me in his arms tonight
 I thought that I would cry,
For it's been so long since I've
 seen him,
 when we said our last good-bye.
As we stood thinking back upon
 years
 and all they've meant,
The many secrets we've shared,
 the happy hours we've spent.
This time it was different,
 I didn't feel the same
Instead of happy hours,
 all I felt was pain.
It hit me like a ton of bricks,
 an arrow through the heart.
The hopes, the plans, the dreams
 we've had
 now falling all apart.
He's hurt me in so many ways
 I never can forget,
And all the evil things he's done
 I haven't mentioned yet.
I pray God will forgive him
 as I have failed to do,
Keep him safe and guide him,
 be with him his whole life
 through.
Within this aching heart of mine
 there's something you can't see,
It's a feeling for a certain love
 I know can never be.
At times like this I wish I had
 the powers from above,
I'd sprinkle down some magic
 dust
 and fill the world with love.

My love for him has always been
 so real, so deep, so true
I guess I'll keep on living,
 what else can I do?
I know there will be others
 who will steal my heart away,
But the memories of my true
 love,
 I know will always stay.

Karin R. Piper
TREE BEAR
 *[Dedicated to the Leominster
 High School Science
 Department for making a
 dream come true...]*
All creatures
Great and small
Fear him
Back, bent with age
All four paws, pushed to the
 ground
Raised high is his head
Searching for the scent of food
Berries, he picks
Flesh, he tears
On both he might dine
But he is one
Who will not devour
Who will not destroy
For as one comes closer
They will see
He is not a hungry bear
But the remains of a once and
 mightly tree

rosalie v. russino
melody unspinned
gold dust over the veil of your
 eyes
and the visions of a letter in your
 hand
the rush of cold spring water goes
 to your head
you open it, and try to
 understand,
it's another man.
the indian summer sun
smiling at your peace
knowing that the moment and
 you are one
with the autumn leaves
 sprinkling softly
hold out your hand to embrace
 some.
flowing with the feel of the
 gentle wind
you taste a sweet song of a
 melody unspinned.

Hilda J. Knowles
TIME
Hours rush into time
Like rainbow hues pressing
 the curve of space
 only to find a faint mirage
 in lieu of finite goal.
 Than to race again
 spurred by relentless hope
at last to meet the
 victorious smile of inexorable
 fate.

Jude Hauenstein
YOU
You have come into my world
 like the ocean upon the sand
With laughter
 you turned me towards you
With wonder
 you held my hand
I feel like a seashell
 just found...

M. Johathan Adams
CLOUDS
[To my mother, who encouraged me always!]
A white cloud drifts by slowly.
It has no course to fly—
it needn't even fly at all.

A wonderous thing—a cloud.
It has no emotions,
yet enables us to feel emotion,
if we want to.
It has no responsibility—
it does as it pleases,
when it wants to.

And what is the most
envious quality of a cloud?. . .
. . .It has no heart to lose.

Cassandra Malone
Vietnam Metamorphosis
Gentle boy
with soft and tender eyes,
Who wears the past
like a disguise.
What torment
has he left untold
That haunts the depth of his soul?

Anger, hatred, despair
keep him apart from those who
care.
Did it, the war in Vietnam,
demoralize half-boy, half-man?

Silence, the panic starts,
like shadows on his lonely
heart.
"Play your guitar, wear a smile,
the pain will vanish...for
awhile."
His saddened face, deceiving grin,
conceals the rage within.
This gentle boy...with soft and
tender eyes.

Kimberly A. Rehmann
SEPARATED LOVERS
Sweet tenderness our hearts are
feeling
The words, a chosen few
Precious hours that we are
stealing
For separate days we knew
This night is our togetherness
Beautiful, but soon blue
For we shall start our lonliness
At the sight of morning dew

Morning brings such sorrow
For fate tears us apart
And though there is tomorrow
My fate hits like a dart
I know that you must leave me
For the answer's in my heart
Your wife doesn't know you see
me
So again, we must now part.

Esther Mazza
GOLDEN MEMORIES
Under a beautiful blue sky with
snow white clouds,
The smell of fresh air was so
crisp and cool;
We sat in our yard and felt so
proud—
As we thought of our children,
when they were in school.
Our oldest planted our trees so
strong and able
As our others stamped the soil
with their shoes—
While desperately trying to hold

the tree stable;
How fast they have grown—and
our children too.
Now they all have homes and
yards of their own
Each one is different, as God
meant it to be
They think we are sad, as we sit
here alone
OH! HOW! Could we be—WHEN
WE LOOK AT OUR TREES?

Terese Sievel
FRIENDS
You used to be my life.
I did everything to please you,
Or at least I tried.
I thought our love would last
forever.
But one day, I reached out for
you,
And you weren't there.
Where did our love go?
It must have been my fault.
I can never do anything right,
Especially now.
So often I need you,
But you can be so crude.
It's like you turned into my worst
enemy.
Is that what you want?
Or do you still want to be
FRIENDS?

Deborah L. Ploe
GO WITH THE WIND
The day is grey,
So how will we know the way?

We are told to follow the
sunshine, follow the light,
The day is grey, and black will be
the night.

So what do we follow, which way
should we go?
Follow the wind surely it must
blow!

Go with the wind and you'll find
what you're looking for,
Go against the wind and the road
will be rough forever more.

Preetinder Bharara
SIX HAIKU
*[To my grandmother, Sheila
who is now deceased]*
The sun is setting.
The day has been long and hard.
I now welcome sleep.

A sun masked by clouds
Can only be seen again
If a strong wind blows.

Fly up high, seagull,
You're able to reach the stars.
They're beyond my grasp.

Lying to his friend,
He so foolishly believes
That he has tricked him.

I often wonder
Why sunset seems more lovely
Than the scene at dawn.

Forlorn animals
Exiled from their age old homes
Silently cry—WHY?

Gladys M. Houdersheldt
IS IT POSSIBLE
Is it possible for me to love
someone
without feeling guilty or feeling
wrong?

To long to be held and touched
and let known that I am loved?
I dream so much of those arms
around me,
that I actually feel them hugging
me tightly
and of those sweet lips touching
mine so softly,
giving me a kiss; meaning love is
returned.
Is it possible for me to love
someone
without feeling guilty or feeling
wrong?

Lee A. Nielsen

Lee A. Nielson
ON POETRY
A thought tossed upward
Crystallizes
On its return
To conscious earth.
A sparkling idea,
Fresh geometric phrases.

The self reaches out,
Toward and through
Nuances of life,
Finds a link
In subtle truth.
Speculations,
Reality and fantasy,
Package of words.

Connie Ann Harris
INESCAPABLE SNARE
*[To Irma & Leonard—
For your genuine display of
Consistent Christian love.]*
White-capped waves lap
at the pale grey
sand, few grains
there be that
escape its wetted
snare; screeching gulls
flee its liquid
touch; yet, the salty
breakers refuse to
surrender their
destined chase.

Lynn Greenwood
SPRING ENCHANTMENT
Barbed wire fence, made ancient
from weather.
A fallen log, from a not so recent
storm.
The very beginning of a spring.
Still clad in flannel shirts.
The sounds of crackling leaves,
Geese honking joys of spring.
You were so very gentle.
As you brushed the leaves from
my hair.

Victor Debs
**Do Something For
Tomorrow**
*[This poem is dedicated to
those people, especially young
people, who are constantly
saying "It is too late", those
people who are always wishing
but not doing.]*
Do something for tomorrow,
that's your future you know!
You'll have something to see,
you'll have something to show.

Look back if you wish at
yesterday
to learn and to remember,
but don't live today by yesterday,
or your life will go under.
there is only one,
w will never be today,
the next hour that'll follow will
put you, in a way,
one hour in the past. Alas, time
travels fast.
Look around without sorrow,
enjoy what you have now,
but do something for tomorrow
and to despair never bow.
Don't say I wish I didn't, or I wish
I'd listened.
Don't you ever live the past, or
think the die is cast.
One thing you should remember,
that you are still the master
of now, tomorrow and after. And,
don't hesitate to alter.
Replace regrets with hope and
toil for a new scope.
Do something for tomorrow and
all the tomorrows to come.
Remember there is nothing that
you cannot overcome.
All you need is decision and a
little courage to start,
once you are on the road, the
going is like a dart.

Do something for tomorrow,
that's your future you know!
You'll have something to see,
you'll have something to show.

Brenda Bennett
YOU LIGHT UP MY LIFE
Dear John, I love you so,
I would throw away the key
and give you my soul
The key to my heart
and it is for you
because you are my sun
You light up my life
with whatever you do,
and just for that reason
this poem is for you
    Love, Brenda

Dianne M. Malovich
TIME VISIBLE
As I look out on the fields today,
What beauty I behold.
The shafts of wheat far beyond,
Swirling colors of brown and gold.

Farther still the stately pines,
Standing in a row.
Like soldiers all marking time,
Thru years that come and go.

In open fields birds in flight,
Blending brown, blues, and reds.
On the ground squirrels gather
food,
Preparing for a winters bed.

To take the time to truly see,
Nature and time unfold.
We all would find the experience,
Worth more than any amount of
gold.

Take time to see life's beauty!

Mrs. Terry L. Smith
SPRING
*[To my dear husband, Terry L.
Smith, who died just four
months after this poem was
written. How quickly Spring
turned to Autumn and ended
in the Winter of Everlasting
Rest.]*
Oh look, Oh what do I see,
A little yellow flower
Peeking out its head at me.
Is it time yet, can it be
That Spring has come again for
me?
Oh yes, oh look there
Another little flower greeting me.
Oh hear, oh can it be
A robin singing in that tree?
Oh yes, oh can't you see
That Spring is here again for me!

Gail Seibel
THE PULSE
*[To Margie, Kathy and Tom,
my children and Dr. Ellen
Kanner who believe in me even
when I don't believe in myself.]*
Just as we feel the pulse
Of our own body
And begin to know the tides
So the ocean's breaking waves
Are the beating of the earth's
heart
Repeated, repetitions
Sometimes soft as a caress
Sometimes wildly as the
adrenalin
Angrys up a storm
With ominous clouds everywhere
Overhead
Yet as rhythmically constant
As forever
Returning to the shore
We find expression
Continually pulsating
Within
Without

Jean M. Harris
THE SOUND OF SILENCE
The lonely sound of silence,
keeps pounding
in my ear
I long so much to hear a voice,
from
someone far or near.
The mate I've had for many years,
used
to fill my void
Now, each time I'd like to talk, he
only
seems annoyed.
I hate the sound of silence, when
I'm
not alone
When sitting here together, we
act like
no one's home.
If time has caused this emptiness,
and
made our lives so nil
I hope and pray, before too long,
time
will at last stand still.

Has silence sung a lullaby that's
put our
love to sleep?
Has silence blocked out
memories of vows
we pledged to keep?
Awake again those feelings, we
used to
hold so dear
Turn off the sound of silence, the
only
sound I hear.

D.A. Dawn Stegenga Prince
OUT TO LUNCH
*[This poem was inspired by my
Stegenga heritage and is
dedicated to my husband, Jack,
and my daughter, Jennifer.]*
Close the door
To bitter-sweet quarrels
TV Soaps
And Sunday sports.

Oil the rusty soul
So
Again feet feel wet grass
between the toes.

Jeanne Ferg
THE IMAGE BREAKER
life
the iconoclast
everyone's running
from their private war
and demon ghosts
forgetting
with illusory courage
and false strengths
the sadness
the delusions
the mayhem
recapturing the idealism
smashed and stiffled
surviving
the complexities
with catharsis . . .

Linda M. Spaeth
REBIRTH OF A SEASON
There's sunshine all around me
Spring's scent is in the air
I'd just like to lay back
Let the wind sweep through my
hair.

The hyacinths are blooming
Bees seem to flutter around
Trees are sporting new foliage
Grass is greener on the ground.

Warm weather is settled upon us
Birds have returned once more
It's time for walking in the forest
To see nature's beauty adorned

Country rides and picnics
With sports to keep us fit
Baseball is back in season
There's barbecuing in pits

Winter is now behind us
Summer is not far ahead
Laughing babies and children
Means Spring is reborn again

Serena B. Scrafford
HE CARES
*[To my children Joyce—Shirley—
Charlotte—Bud]*
Bow your head and say a prayer
For the weak, the sick, the blind
And thank God up on heaven
If, to you, He has been kind

Just look around and see the tears
Then thank your lucky stars
For all the kindness shown to you
And pray he keeps you as you are

I'm sure we'd all feel lucky
If we'd only look and see
All the wonderful things we have
And God's love for you and me

So give to others, who have much
less
All your worldly goods do share
For living by the golden rule
You show God and friends you
care

John M. Schreier
DIADEMS
April is a tease
a coy, flirtatious wench
one day
her unripe charm confers
the next
tearfully demurs.

But May
that emerald maid
a treasure to be held
her deep breasted,
buxom warmth
fulfills . . .
she stays to love again.

Angelita Gamez
PAGEANT CREED
Walk with me, Lord
the run looks awfully long
silence draws, all eyes on me
it'll be just me and a song

Hold my hand, Lord
I need your touch upon my hand
we'll walk the run, side by side
holding hands like two best
friends

Smile with me, Lord
together we can draw the smiles
bring out the spirit of the crowd
if only be just for awhile

Bless the crowd, Lord
their souls so wild they cheer
with pride
a warm response to you and me
they're clapping loud, they're
smiling wide

Be my judge, Lord
for you know my every thought
and deed
through you Lord, the judges too
will know my joys, my hopes, my
needs

Time is near, Lord
ease the pounding in my heart

the judges just decided who
has qualified to take the part

Prepare my mind, Lord
for only one will wear the crown
the heart may ache but the mind
prevails
a happy smile will shun the
frown

Calm the crowd, Lord
for they walked in with a winner
in mind
devotions strong, hopes heaven
high
too much to put it all behind

Teach me, Lord
to experience growth in all I do
to know your plan is well defined
to put my trust and faith in you

And. . .thank you, Lord
for being with me from the start
the pageant day was here and
gone
a million thanks come from the
heart.

Gloria Lorriane Moore
How To Treat Your Lady
Like a ship that sails the ocean,
riding waves from shore to
shore, this my woman is to me.
Whisper softly in her ear, like
roaring thunder she soon
appears. Calm the sea with
long soft kisses, crossing over
very safely, making sure you
don't forget to anchor. Oh! How
sweet to get over, landing
safely to the other shore.

N.L. Perkins
LADY SCORNED
Now upon a horse called Hell,
does
the Lady sit astride,
Riding for the Land of Scorn to
avenge her honor and her pride.

From the pit's of the poor did
the pauper woman rise,
Bearing anger from her caste and
vengence in her eyes.

The child unto the Lady says,
ride swift upon your horse of
Hell,
Beware the demons 'cross your
path
and to our honor do us well!

Frances Straughters Carter
MEMORY OF LONG AGO
When I was a little girl,
And it rained all day, to the attic,
I would go and play.
I would look in all the boxes
my mother had put away
"Lo and behold." It was like
an island, that I had discovered
far away.
With all the treasure trove
of silver and gold.
That made me so very happy on,
those rainy days, of so long ago.

Elizabeth Perry Carter
TO A FLY
*[To all who have a sincere love
for God's creatures.]*
Little fly just sittin' there
A washin' on your han's,
God made you, little creature,
Fittin'somewhere in His plans.

Today's Greatest Poems

Beverly Rons
THE MAGNIFICENT OAK
Many generations have come and
    gone
Since our beautiful oak tree was
    planted here
With loving hands from someone
    who cared
Not knowing the pleasures it
    would bring for years.
The mamouth sprawling limbs
    provide shade in hot summer
And it's many little acorns food
    for the wild animals here
In summer the branches are the
    squirrels playground and home
In winter the acorns help feed all
    the wild deer.
I know in it's day it has
    weathered many a bad storm
But yet, It seems to go on and on
How wonderful if we, Like the
    old oak tree
Had the stamina and strength and
    won.

Florence M. Craven
Supremacy Or Submission?
*Deep the thunder clouds doth
    form* — angry, mad is he,
The one who thinks he can
    control the center of the storm.
But *Hark!* There comes on the
    wings of the storm
The one who can calm the sea!
Then softly creeps the sunlight
    to gleam upon the lea
And dare to send it's tentacles to
    warm the shivering sea
Then birds rise up — their praise
    to sing — to float majestic
Over the water and guide the
    fisher 'ere comes the night
Oh — Could they speak the
    Matchless worth of He who
    calms the sea!
But as they soar through the
    winds that roar
And touch the heavenly strings,
    if you listen close,
You can hear the chorus as the
    angels also sing
Then comes the night and from
    the water's depth
There leaps the flowing fountain
    with sailboats
Coasting on the wellspring as
    they sail to victory
And as the twilight shades
    prevail
The gulls take up the glorious
    tale!
Our God will calm the boistrous
    sea!

Thomas M. Kehoe
WINGS
[To Rockefeller and his lads.]
High above the reason of men
I coast along the breeze
My wings they hold me here
    among
Freedoms golden stars.

A storm is brewing down below
I feel the vibrations here
To see them stock their weapons
    high
To destroy the other side

When will those foolish mortals
    learn

To use the tools of flight
The heart, the hand, the ear, the
    voice
The true innocence of sight
To live for the other is to live for
    self
The joy one gets from others joy
The love one feels from the
    warmth of all
To flap your wings, O mortals,
    soar!

Yes, here among the secrets
    answer
Where freedoms currents blow
To love, to share, to help, to
    know
I glide upon my wings.

Gary Lee Raymond
The Seasons Of Feeling
In Fall, the wind races through
    town like a fast car,
    and I feel excited.
Dead leaves play in the wind
    like children,
    and I feel happy.
In Winter, snow flies like dust
    from a shaken mop,
    and I feel scattered and
    uneasy.
Banks of snow settle and
    become solid like home,
    and I feel restful.
In Spring, trees bud out like the
    birth of a child,
    and I feel rejuvinated.
Rain nourishes new plants like
    a baby feeding on milk,
    and I feel refreshed.
In Summer, cool breezes walk
    through trees like an old
    couple
    on a stroll,
    and I feel calm.
Rays of sun reveal things like a
    flashlight in the dark,
    and I feel alive.
What are these things we call
    seasons?
Are they seasons of weather,
    or seasons of feeling?

Joy Mitchell
LOVES FLAME
Love is like the fire,
    one might say.
For it must be rekindled,
    day after day.

Love like the fire,
    needs fuel to survive.
Give fuel to your love,
    should you keep it alive.

Wood is fuel to the fire,
    of that we are sure.
Ah! but what fuel,
    helps love to endure?

There are many a fuel,
    that set love aspark.
There is tendersness and
    patiences,
    and an understanding heart.

Kindness and gentleness,
    sharing life's need.
All these are fuel,
    to loves flame you feed.

Give of this fuel,
    give again and again.
And the flame of your love,

shall never grow dim.

Betty Ann Wooley

Betty Ann Wooley
SEBASTIAN
*[This poem was written in
memory of my Doberman
Pinscher named SEBASTIAN.]*
I lost a friend today
The most loyal and faithful kind
In countless little ways
You still share this world of mine

Deep in a corner of my heart
Where you will always be
Loved and kept a special part
Of all my memories

"He was just a dog", some may say
Their calloused words contend
Oh, how little they convey
The value of a friend

And if there is a Heaven
For His creatures, kind and true
I know you are there, in His care
And He found a friend in you.

Deanna Wood
A Little One's Eyes
*[To all 'my' kids who taught me
to see life and learn about love
through a child's eyes again.]*
Hold the light
    shining through a little girl's
    eyes
in your heart
    and that child's innocence
    will
capture and hold our life
    forever.
Know the faith
    shining through a little boy's
    eyes
in your heart
    and that child's freedom of
    spirit will
capture and hold your life
    forever.
Feel the love
    shining through both of their
    eyes
in your heart
    and a love above any other
    will
capture and hold your life
    forever.

Cheryl Hintzel
THESE TIMES
The cheers, the screams, the
    rejoicing, then the silence
The shots have been heard, the
    people stare with awe to see
    such violence

The tears, the frightened screams,
    the sad knowledge of knowing
    once more it has happened
The terror, the horror, this
    senseless deed, my heart and
    spirit are saddened
The great men we have lost and
    the ones we have almost lost to
    this senseless and insane act
The wickedness of this world will
    never cease. This we all must
    face for π is a fact
The shot heard around the world
    is nothing compared to the
    shots we hear in these days and
    times
How much longer must we suffer
    for the insanity of these
    assassins crimes

Helen Hodge
THE WORLD LIKE ME
Where would this world be
If everyone was just like me
When Sunday came if left alone
Would everyone remain at home

Would malice fill the heart of
    man,
Would no one try to understand
The plan set down by God alone
To guide his children to the
    throne

Would this world be in a stew
If the whole wide world was just
    like you,
Would it be a catastrophe
If the whole wide world were just
    like me.

This is the question I ask today
Of everyone along life's way,
Ask yourself what would you do
If all the world was just like you.

Jane Ann Collins
After the Earthquake
Amid the rubble
of fallen buildings,
empty streets,
and dust-covered
    windows,
searching for life
through shattered glass
shines a single ray of
sunlight.

Christine Gardiner
SIX GATES TO HEAVEN
O dance in the silvery glow of the
    moon,
On golden sands by a sunlit sea,
Beneath the rainbow hues of a
    waterfall,
For LIGHT is one with thee!

O throb to the heartbeat of the
    earth,
The strength of the banyan tree;
Be one with everything that lives,
For LIFE is one with thee!

O melt in the warmth of an
    angel's smile,
Think of all so endearingly;
Be caressed by the softly
    whispering wind,
For LOVE is one with thee!

O feel into the ecstacy of the
    rose,

45

The frangrance of the lilac tree;
Drink in the gold of the setting
sun,
For *Beauty* is one with thee!

O listen to the music of the
nightingale's
Harmonious melody,
And pour forth thy rapturous
song,
For *Joy* is one with thee!

O lie beside mirroring waters
cool
Flowing joyfully to the sea,
And be free forever more,
For *Peace* is one with thee!

Anthony Raunikar
I SEE YOU
I see you and I have a funny little
feeling;
You do what I know you will;
You smile and wave and I do the
same;
But I hurt so bad inside;
My emotions feel like they are in
a cage;
It hurts and it just can't be
denied;
Oh it really puts me in a rage;
I want to tell her that I love her;
It makes me so confused;
I can't let down my cover;
My feelings might get bruised;
You might not feel the same;
And I'll feel such shame;
I think maybe I'm just not right;
But when I dream at night;
I can tell you how I feel;
Babe you love me you demand;
And it feels so real;
You always understand;
Then I wake and find it was a
dream;
It just hurts to much to cry;

Arlean Green
SEARCH
I looked for God in the heavens,
His form I could not see.
I thought He'd be there, the sun
for His chair,
In the realms of Infinity.

I listened for God in the roaring
winds,
I could not hear his words.
I thought they might thunder,
break worlds asunder,
Beating down like thundering
herds.

In complete stillness, I found
Him.
Deep within my waiting ear
Came the quiet voice: "Let your
heart rejoice.
Here am I, child; within . . .I am
here."

Katie "Fourkiller" Francis
GERIATRICS
*[In loving dedication to my
Grandparents, whose loyalty
and togetherness will always be
an inspiration.]*
Tread softly . .
for night has fallen.
Tread slowly . .
for winter has come.

Seldom do you see
two sets of tracks
side by side on the path;

Now there are tracks
made by a wheelchair.

Memories come slowly,
words come painfully.
Movement no longer answers
when called upon.

Tread softly . .
for night has fallen.
Tread slowly . .
for winter has come.

Susan E. Hill
AUTUMN LEAVES
Shining in all their glory
the Autumn foliage alights
the countryside in the deep
flaming colors of the sun.

Gone are the long summer days
the cool crisp evenings have
arrived.
Precious are the last flowers of
the season
before the white crystals begin
the fall.

Providing a memorable tribute,
the Autumn panorama
seems reluctant to give way
to the encroaching winter.

Melody L. Sills
MAY I NEVER. . .
May I never shame
for shame I have felt
May I never damn
before God I have knelt
may I never reach plentitude
when others have none
And may God always be with me
until these deeds are done

Debbie J. Organ
SURVIVAL
The ability to look outside
yourself
and see a falling leaf or passing
car;
to see another's fault, another's
thorn
and yet still care—
the ability to reach within
for a moment of reticence
and not feel guilty
for doing so—
this ability, my friend,
is vital to life!

Holly Dawn Scott
The Essence Of Our Unity
Today I give myself to you
To be your loving mate.
I'll stand by you;
You cling to me,
And let our love be great.
Right now I'll change
direction
Of my very life,
As we stand here with each other
To become husband and wife.
The life we will be building
We will tend with greatest care;
To protect and preserve
The love we have,
And the vows that we now share.

Debi Laurian
DAYS GONE BY
This morning I walked
to our park
one last time—
to wipe your memory
from my mind.

I sat on the swings
and wondered what happenedto
the fun we used to share.
Where did the time go,
that I forgot how you
needed your freedom
so desperately.
I didn't mean to
make you feel I was
trying to steal it away.
It's just that our laughter
made me feel so young again
and I liked giving
my time to you.

Now tonight has caught me
on the park bench,
where our names have been
engraved on the seat. . .
whispering yours
and wishing you hadn't had
to go so soon.
And the park that was once
only ours to dream or
make love to the sky—
will be a thousand other lovers'—
and only ours to remember
the one time we loved.

Cindy Williams
A SPECIAL SOMEONE
You're a special place in my
heart,
I hope we'll never be apart,
You've lightened up all of my
days.
And helped me a lot— in many
ways.
Times when I felt sad,
You made me feel glad,

And when I was lonely and cold,
You were there someone to hold.
At times when I was bad,
I realized what I really had,
I had something special,
and that was true,
That special someone was you.

Cynthia Harris
WHEN I DREAM
Stay with me I hear you call;
Then in loving arms I lay. Safe
from all.
Touched only by your gentle
hands.
And love that time alone
with—stands.

We run through meadows fresh
in fall.
Your hand in mine we walk
through forests tall.
Barefoot in the sand we play.
In love forever we will stay.

The laughs, the sighs, the tender
crys.
Hopes so great they touch the
sky.
But then I wake to find you gone
An empty world and me alone.

So treasured are the times we
share.
The nights in sleep, oh how you
care.
But when I wake there is no
means,
As I find you love me, only in my
dreams.

frances e blackmur
NOMAD
as a young girl
i longed to flee
from familiartity
especially from me

as a teener
i raced a run
from the beams of the moon
to the rays of the sun

as a woman
i need to be free
roaming as a NOMAD
caravaning with me

Vincent J. Keenan
FIRST ACQUAINTANCE
*[To Shirley Anne Maire
I'm twined around your finger]*
You know — I'd most forgotten
How tiny — babies are
The nose a tender button
The hand — a fragile star

A maple leaf could hide her
Or serve her for a dress
Our three—year—old beside her
Seems like a giantess

And when I bend above her
I'm like a mountain quaking
I scarcely dare to love her
For fear of something breaking

Fran Harris
MOUNT ST. HELENS
*[To my parents, Ray & Carrie
Lea My children, Diana and
Mike My granchildren, Chris
and Danny]*
St. helen once was a lovely lady
So serene and very refined
But on a Sunday in May of
nineteen eighty
She spoke her very own mind.

The maiden mountain had a spell
An ache she could not quiet
She spew her anger very well
Just for her own delight.

She groaned and grumbled very
loud
And belched with all her might
She hid the sun and every cloud
And made the day turn into
night.

She covered our town with ash
and grit
A blanket of volcanic sand
And she didn't have sense enough
to quit
Until she had covered our land.

So we'll listen to Helen whenever
she speaks
When she warns of another
eruption

We've had our fill of a few dirty
weeks
Sweeping away St. Helens
destruction.

Mary Ann Esperson

Mary Ann Esperson
Everyone Loves a Clown

Everyone should be a clown for a
day
Hide behind the mask of a clown
No one can tell if you frown
You can watch how people
intereact and
also go their own way
Tug at the coat of a college
president
He turns and smiles back at the
clown

Even the doctor in residence
Will wipe off her frown to smile
at a clown
A dear old lady busy walking her
dog
Will stop and smile at the clown
Children too, dearly love a clown
Memories take you back to the
carefree childhood
When the circus came to town
And your parents took time to let
you see the clown.

Rebecca Lovina Etheridge
Strength From the Sea
*[To Patrick, Forever Loving
You, Rebecca]*
   To hear the purr of her engines,
   starboard and port
To feel it from the depth of your
soul,
   To sense a deep purring from
   back deck to the bridge
To feel the rythmatic humm as
she rocks you to sleep,

The closeness you must feel to
the Creator above
The still, the awesome magnitude
of endless space,
   The depth of the darkness as
she lays in a fog
The calm murmuring of your
heart and altertness of your
mind,
   Then waiting and watching,
   and watch to wait
Then changing the shift, as the
tide rushes in,
   Then seeing the whales sound
in the light of the sun
Then saying goodnight until the
dusk turns to dawn,
   I know these thoughts, through
   only what I seek to find
I yearn to be one to one, and
know her call,
   I see the strength she gives
through you
I feel the wholeness you carry
from sea to home,
   It inspires me, your journey
from land to sea
It hesitates my mind, that endless
thing called time,
   It creates a mystic of wonder
deep within me
It enhances my conceiving of the
how, of your life,
   Your need for that oneness
from your soul
Your desire to go forth, go beyond
the far horizon,
   Your ability to see, experience,
to show and to share
Your zest for life, related to the
endless sea, will go on and on.

Robert Boates
THE SMOKER
He went home
faced the mirror
and put a gun
to his head.

He fantasized
being mourned
by a lover
who rejected him.

Then
with the only courage
he was born with
pulled the trigger
of the leadless gun
lighting a cigarette

as if it were
his last.

Betty Ruth Philips
GENTLE REMINDER
Like the dandelion head
In the wake of a gentle breeze
Wafts its atoms of ecstacy
Subtly on the atmosphere

So when happiness enfolds us
Our dandelion head vibrations
Energized by our thoughts
Mingles and surrounds
As does the light of God.

Must we, like the dandelion,
Become listless motionless stalks
Once we have known this
fleeting
Surge called happiness?
My heart says no, my spirit balks.

On those mountain peaks of

happiness
We find that resource called God
That leads us through life's
deserts
Changing dandelions to
goldenrods.

L. Medina
THE END OF MY ROPE
I can feel the closing in of the
walls on both sides of me.
I can sense the cries of many in
the room.
I can whisper words of pain and
hate, yet I not.
I can see the eyes of the good in
sorrow.
I know now why my father left
his grief behind him.
I know what it must of been to
his soul.
I know no longer any way to say I
am sorry
For all the things I have done in
life.
I only pray to see my soul in
spirit of happiness.
There always comes a time when
we must let others know
Of our pain and our burdens.
To be told and to be left behind,
As my father left behind.

Mary Cochran Skramstad
CANDIDATE
*[Didicated to Commissioner
Dave Skramstad, my husband.]*
Beside his wife, prayers are said
   A night of restless sleep ahead.
Morning comes fast
   Many questions will be asked.
Speaking engagements,
   interviews
   Will he win or lose?
His shoe soles are thin
   He is looking trim.
Many people believe in him.
Welcome aboard, our friends
   Without your help he can't
win.
With bumpershoots on high
   Protected from a rain—filled
sky.
Walking from door to door
   Could his friends do more?
He was with them every step of
the way
   He won on election day.

Belinda Espiritu Crisostomo
Anymore Than Heaven
(That's What You Are To
Me)
Your sparkling eyes
And dark brown hair,
It's just everything about you
That makes me care,
I wonder where, you are right
now
I wonder how,
I wonder now.
I remember meeting you
Before you disappeared
For a very long time,
I remembered wanting you
Cause everytime
I met somebody new
I wish it were you,
Anymore than heaven
That's what you are to me.
When your smile says hello,
Nobody could tell me just how

much
A care can extend,
I don't want to hide
Just want to tell you
What has been happening
Inside, I've come to know
How my world is being planned,
But God how I've missed to blush
. . . And everytime
I meet someone new
Can't help but think of you,
Anymore than heaven
That's what you are to me,
Anymore than heaven
To me.

Lori Marie Hadenfeld
LOVE IS
Love is
   being with each other
Caring
   for one another.
Coping
   and forgiving.

Whether we're together
   or apart,
You still remain
   within my heart.

Gloria Daniels
VOICES
The sweetest sound in all the
world—
   The voice of someone deer.
Like music to our heart and soul
   We cherish what we hear!

Your voice can say a lot of things
   To people that you meet,
So fill your words with happy
thoughts
   For everyone you greet!

Sharon Ann Kelly
LITTLE NO NAME
*[To a few of the fortunate—My
children and granchildren]*
I am little no name
I know not
From whence I came
For I was left
On a step, you see
So, I know not
Who is me

Catherine M. Hawblitzel
A SOMETIME DREAM
She sees in her dreams,
But never beyond;
She lives in this world,
But cannot relate;
She walks towards tomorrow,
But remains in yesterday,
and yet she keeps going on.

She's here in body and soul
But her mind seems to wander.
Does she wish to go back to
   yesterday?

No one can say,
But I think we all know
She's here only in body and soul.

She's married now,
But just barely livng.
She relies on yesterday
Instead of tomorrow.
She looks in on her baby
And wonders how she will be.
She hopes she will look towards
   tomorrow
And not back on yesterday.

Georgia Radcliffe
THE HOSPITAL
Beacon of mercy
Shine on through life's dark night,
Shine on the sadness,
The anguish and the pain,
Shine through the clouds
That cover moon and stars,
Shine through the chilling winds
And cold, relentless rain.
Haven of hope
Breathe life into tired hearts,
Inspire trust in all
Who need to seek your care,
And may we thank the Lord
That consecrated hands
Are working ceaselessly
In dedication there.

Leana Sangeeta Sue Simpson
LOST AND FOUND
Spirit dances
in the wind
Still dances
In the sun

Douglas R. Mouland
ARE YOU LISTENING?
The day is short, the night is
   long,
Why do we think that things are
   wrong?
The misty moon wheels overhead
It shines on living and the dead.
Who are the dead? Where can
   they be?
I think they are but you and me.
We come again antoher time
And life goes on in the sublime.
There is no death, it cannot be,
For life and death's eternity.
The universe, to us so vast
will yield to mind before we pass
To knowing all, and being
   complete,
With power eternal to repeat.
We are so young, in infancy
And livng in a fantasy.
Like ants upon a hill who strive
To kill there kind so they
   survive,
We gather earthly things with
   strife
And will protect them with our
   life.
Then speak of freedom far and
   near,
But pure freedom hath no fear.
We must begin to learn a way
To walk in peace from day to day.
Our education, broad it seems,
Is but materialistic dreams.
The powers that be, go forth each
   day
With empty platitudes to say.
For fear is flowing through their
   mind.
Like ants they want to kill their
   kind.
We must begin to think and grow
From infancy, the pace is slow
Lets throw our toys of war away
And learn to walk in peace each
   day.
Then we will think that things
   are right
And love will rule in place of
   might.
The moon will always shine
   o'erhead
upon the living and the dead.

But we're the dead and living still,
To learn each day a step, until
We've learned them all, then we
   can say,
With truth, our heaven is here
   today.

Rita H. Palola
TIME TO GO
I am leaving now
my time has come
my worries are gone
and it's time to go.

Everything is over
my work and play,
no turning back
from heavens above,
my place is ready
I am leaving now.

I have served my purpose
happy times and sad,
memories I take with me
good or bad,
it's time to go
I am leaving now.

**Mr. Joseph Hinton Pepper
Brice III**

*Mr. Joseph Hinton Pepper Brice
III*
One Of Us Will Know
*[To the one and all that I love
sincerely]*
One of us will know
As we pass through life
Why we are going through
So much strife

Why children are starving
Why are some being killed
Why are we sometimes
In a living hell

All of this
In time will be
One of us will know
One will see

One of us will love
The other may hate
Should we try to predict
What shall be our fate

One thing is certain
Of this I am sure
That if we love truly
That love will endure

Mary C. Easly
WHAT IS A MAN
*[Taft Handy—The one who
inspires my artistic abilities.]*
A Man is one who with his
strength can overcome a
woman's weakness.

A Man is one who with his
guidance and kindness can
complete a woman's day.
A Man is one who with his
sureness of love can complete
and make a woman.

Linda Ulmer
GREEN UNICORNS
"How could you be so green?"
   inquired my friends.
"But, I look best in green," was my
   reply.
A sea of green flows through this
withered bark. So he was False
Wintergreen. Fooled I was by
bittersweet lies which tasted of
summer plums. Of course,
there are many people who'd
play the burning bush
consumed by their own hate or
dye themselves blue indigo—
having lost the inner glow—to
join the monastery. I've often
swallowed bitter buttons, some
of scrimshaw and wood; and
was surprised to find it was
small ivory ones which
splintered throats. I fell once.
Fell like shattered autumn
leaves; but like the glass
sponge regathered my parts.
What if, by chance, the
woodworms burrowed holes?
Certainly rays of light would
filter through in threads of
green with irridescent shine.
Just porcupines inject
bitterness; besides my
vaccinations never took. Inside
the child still dreams green
unicorns. Why be a frown? I
can be mint jelly!

Della Miller
HAPPINESS IS
Happiness is holding a new baby
   tight,
Rocking it gently, and kissing it
   light.
Happiness is seeing your children
   as they run and they play,
Watching them grow, and helping
   them pray.
Happiness is finding a smile on a
   strange face,
And feeling the friendliness
   wherever the place.
Happiness is talking to new
   friends and old,
And knowing the friendship is
   worth more than gold.
Happiness is learning the new
   joys of each day,
And finding the paths that will
   show us the way.
Happiness is telling someone
   that you care,
And knowing theres love in the
   things that you share.
Happiness is something you
   never can hide,
It shows on your face and you
   wear it with pride.

Billie L. Parkison
GOD SENT RAIN
Dear God from Heaven, you
looked down and saw the
burned and dry parched
ground,

You saw how thirsty the trees,
   brooks, crops were again.
For us were so compassionate.
And sent such an abundance of
   the refreshing rain.

To Thee we give thanks,
Our praise
For now the farmer his crop
In abundance can raise.

The rain you sent is very good.
Now all the creatures of this
   earth
Will have an abundance of food.

God saw the rain, "It's good," He
   said.
"Now all my people will not want
   for bread."

Looking out, Guess what I seen
The flowers, trees and blades of
   grass were all turning green.

April L. Pressley
A WORTHY FATE
The night, filled with endless
   wonder nourishing dreams
with tiny shadows tracing the
   moonbeams
   A lonely star streaks the night
      of gray
with a dazzling brilliance paving
   the way.

In a moments glance its beauty
   is almost obscure
enchanting, rare, simply pure
   Setting a landscape for wishers
      and dreamers
feeding the imaginations of
   lonely schemers

   Giving romance to the young
      at heart
temporarily filling the distance of
   lovers apart
   Telling of futures and fates
and behind each falling star
   another waits

   Hoping for the chance to grace
      the night with its gentle flow
wanting to be so captivating the
   wind will cease to blow
So it can bravely fade then die
   with pride
knowing its life was short but
   worthy of its ride.

Carrie Calkins
BEGINNING LOVE
I remember that call, so well to
   this day—
I knew it was love, nothing could
   stand in my way.
The path I was on was wrong at
   the time,
I would look out of the shell I
   was in
and wish I had the power to
   repel—
To reject the old things and
   accept the new—
Was the hardest thing in life for
   me to do.

There is someone new at this
   time, I must find my place in
   life.
I guarded against a tendancy to
   expect perfect love—
For the love I had before was
   wrong, yet hard for me to see.
But what about his age they'd say?

. . . But how could I convey.
By the love we shared day by day—
    Suddenly our different ages
    were out weighed.

For there will be storms ahead,
    for the long life we have
    planned.
Talks we've had and the love
    we've shared, shall never be
    forgotten.
And if we ever should part; you'll
    have a silent place in my heart
that no one else has ever
    had—LOVE
And if and when I go away, the
    hard road will come that day—
We end it then; if our ties should
    break,
And if they don't we'll know one
    thing—
This love we have is only the
    beginning.

Eleni Katzingris Moustaka
MY SCREAM
Shouts inside me the desire of the
    orgy,
that I seek always in my dreams
    with you.
Maybe the stars, strange ones,
    guide me,
if the stars of my fire I want not
    lead me
but I follow.

I would like to kiss your soul
    which solitary sobs
and I search for an oasis that
    tempts me to infinity.
But you never are inclined to me;
    my lips never will
have your kiss
    and your lips,
me scream.

Maybe you're too frightened that
    I'm one volcano
of passions and you're one forest
    of worlds,
in one cage.

I kneel over my heart and pray
    under your iceberg,
while my love sing, cry
    for unconsumed
pleasure and mistaked feeling.

Clarence Alexander Mitchell
I
I am born in a final paroxysm of
    organic thrust
I climb chaotic rocky stairsteps of
    mountain size
I dwell in living valleys
    sheltering homeless hollows of
    the weary
I wear garments woven from the
    fiber of conflict
And stitched at the seams with
    fire
I am antiquity fushed into the
    contemporary
I ask of the unknown and
    consume of the know-all
I yield to the embrace of the dirt
I return to the silent nothingness
I am born

Robert Wm. Gray
GHOSTS
Walking on a beach of glistening
    sand,
closely together, shoulder to

shoulder,
sharing a privacy . . . only two
    can know,
as the sun fades, and the night is
    colder.

The waves falling so quietly,
nestling up to the sandy beach;
The moon glowing round and
    full,
gives reason to believe it's within
    reach.

The sounds of this inspiring
    night,
for any and all to simply hear,
hauntingly echo their pleasant
    refrain,
that makes this night so very
    dear.

A moment shared, as only two
    can,
this interlude in the span of life,
a time to be always long
    remembered,
time spent and shared with my
    wife.

Many memories as this, I do
    have,
and where I be, no shadows be
    cast;
For I will always be comforted, as
    I'm
haunted by the ghosts . . . of
    memories past . . .

Estelle L. Kopp
ELVES OF ERIN
What's going on in the cold
    North Pole
'Way up in Santa land?
We're told Santa's added many
    more elves
To lend a helping hand.

They were in charge of the
    Christmas Stockings.
Their references he'd not seen,
And did not know they, from
    Erin, had come.
Alas! Too late!—the Socks were
    green!

Beverly Bond
TRACKS OF TIME
Across the searing desert floor, if
    only one could see
The tracks of time impressioned
    there, and never more to be.

How many stallions thundering
    across the scorching sand,
To speed each man along his
    way; the sun, a reprimand.

To reach a higher, greener land
    and distant mountains lure;
The hope of finding water there,
    so clear and clean and pure.

The dusty old prospectors,
    trudging wearily along;
The faith that never falters, for
    they know they're never wrong.

The thing that never changes is
    the ever-blowing wind,
Busy wiping traces, helping time
    go on again.

Tearing up a sagebrush here and
    bouncing to and fro,
It's like a busy bouncing ball that
    knows not where to go.

A screeching hawk is out to find
    the means to feed her young;
Her shadow on the desert floor
    just another to be flung.
The stealthy tracks of howling
    wolves are gone quick as they
    came;
Not even the saquaro are allowed
    to stay the same.
The echoes of a thousand shots
    still ringing in the air,
Are all that's left of battles that
    were fought so bravely there.
I'd like to just go back in time, to
    that searing desert floor,
And be a part of all the tracks
    that cannot be—no more.

Shine Oels
SWEETER WINE
*[For Phil, my inspiration, my
love, my life. Thank you for
opening my heart to the beauty
of this world.]*
I know you;ve had a bad time
It's been a bad year for wine
But remember I've had a cup or
    two
I've drank from the same bottle as
    you.
Now I've poured the bad down
    the drain
And I want to open a new bottle
    again
Just because the last tasted kind
    of poor
That won't stop me from tasting
    more.
Don't let your mind forbid you to
    taste
Untouched things tend to go to
    waste
Don't be afraid—let's have a few
    sips
Let me love the bad right off of
    your lips.

Veronica L. Reid
FOREVER
*[To my family and friends
whom I love so dearly; it is
especially dedicated to my
mother Erma for her love,
inspiration and motivation.]*
If I could live forever,
It still wouldn't be long
    enough
to share all the love I have
to give to others.
Forever wouldn't be long
    enough
To cherish all the wonderful
    things life has to offer;
Forever could never be long
    enough
For me to do my part
to aid mankind
If I could live forever,
It would never be long enough
to do all the things I've dreamt
    of doing
Seeing all the places I've longed
    to see
And sharing the love of others
    near and far
To live a life of peace and
    happiness
among others that long for the
    same
things I long for
Forever could never be long
    enough.

Eugene Adams, Jr.

Eugene Adams, Jr.
OLD KOUNTRY COOKING
I luv kountry cookin'
Butta hate turnip greens;
I dig fried chicken
Especially wit green beans.

I luv sweet potatoes
In any kinda form;
I like toasted bread
Wit apple butter rum;

Hav ya ever tried buttermilk
Mixed wit good corn-bread?
Or maybe salmon croquettes
N' scalloped potatoes instead.

To tell ya bout one of the best
    thangs
I dun tasted on this earth;
Wuz some hot buttered biscuits
Wit sausage n' syrup.

What about pig ears
That's some pretty good meat;
N' if you don't like his ears
I'm sho' you'll luv his feet.

E'vrybody luvs pork chops
But to tell ya the truth;
I prefer a red link sandwich
N' maybe a glass of juice.

What about some ox tails
Or maybe boston butt;
Y'all may think this meat don't
    exist
N' that I exaggerate too much.

There're plenty kinda foods
Ya haven't heard of I kno'
But it's only because ya live in
    the city
N' ya ain't kountry folks.

E'vrybody luvs ice cream
E'vrybody luvs cake;
E'vrybody loves candy
But e'vrybody kain't afford steak.

Take me for example
I wuz brought up on black-eyed
    peas;
N' whether I wanted em' or not
I had to eat em' n' be pleased.

When I sit down at the table
It wuz thangs like this, I would
    see
Butter beans, corn bread, sliced
    tomatoes,
Fat back or shine-bone meat.

Later on I worked at a restaurant
Where they fixed all kinda fancy
    foods;

N' man when I saw that steam table
I didn't kno' what in Heaven to choose.

N' just to sho' you exactly
What a colored boy would do;
Man I grabbed me a plate
N' got some of all that food.

So this is just a lil somethin'
That I want you to take from me;
Don't think cause ya live in the city
That ya got the kountry beat.

Cause baby it's that kountry food
With vitamins A . . B . . C . . n' D;
But cha' don't havta take my word
Just try it n' you will see.

Nancy G. Hall
SPECIAL FRIENDS
We may be wild at times,
But always come back to sanity.
We let our dreams get a hold of us,
But always come back to reality.
We may jump to conclusions,
But always seek the truth.
We have our opinions,
But are out to hurt no one.
And when we think of a special friend.
We think of each other.

Alberta A. Cox
LET ME SEE THE FLOWERS
Let me see the flowers
And not just view the weeds.
For oft we view our problems
And fail to see they feed our needs.

Difficulties can be solved
If only we try to see
There is beauty in the weeds
That brings fullfilment to bigger deeds.

There's much to be accomplished
When working through a thorn
For when we become an overcomer
Exceptional results are suddenly born.

It's only through the obstacles of life
That real beauty can come through
By conquering stumbling objects
Makes unusual success to come true.

(Mrs.) Marciana A. Sevendal
A LESSON OF LOVE
[This poem was written to teach boys and girls who love to hunt birds' nests, destroy them, and take away the eggs or fledglings, love for and kindness to God's useful and beautiful creatures.]
'Neath the shelt'ring boughs of an old apple tree,
Hang the ruins of a nest that hold a tale for me.
'Tis a sad tale of woe—of a mother bird's fate:
"Loss of her speckled eggs and her beloved mate."

In the warm summer months, without let-up for rest,
Happily did she build a pretty cozy nest;
But alas! for the joys in the days that could be,
Cruel boys came around, stormed the nest sans mercy.

They took the speckled eggs that were so neatly laid,
They tore off the warm nest in a merciless raid.
But for the flight she took to a tall tree to hide,
Just like her hapless mate, by a sling she'd have died.

All alone and forlorn, her wings so badly torn,
She bemoans her sad fate, her dreams completely gone.
Crashed the fond hopes that leapt in her heart as she wailed:
"Now 'tis too sad to sing; now— 'tis too late to build."

Children, your mothers grieve when ill luck comes your way;
Let this sad tale of woe, spell a lesson for thee:
"Now—in her grievous plight— more than wings are broken;
Never will this mother ever soar high again."

Sarah C. Stein
MARCH
March is the most capricious of the months.
She anticipates the advent of brighter tomorrows.
She remembers the harshness of monotonous yesterdays.
Selfishly she sunlights the receding snow,
As she dutifully moistens the earth for delicate crocuses.
March speeds her reckless winds across the valley,
Making treetops moan a farewell dirge.

Melissa Gaylord

Melissa Gaylord
NATURES' WAY
Man against nature
Is the way we live
Sooner or later
Someone must give

Man more advanced
But nature's the smarter
They always fight
We must make a charter

Man will always lose
No matter how hard we try
Because nature can live forever
But all of us must die.

Joseph Walsh
The 47 Over Galileo High
In the Calm of the Night
    the heat
        from the street
    rises above
        the roof tops
    and ripples
        the edges of the moon.

Like a still lake
    reflecting the blue-black twilight
        disturbed and violated
by the vandals of the night
    and with great precision
the circles grow wider and wider
    and they grow in number

        over and
            over and
                over and
                    over

Forever
until
    it returns
        to its beginnings
            awaiting
                once more
    to be used
        abused
        betrayed
    and denied its rights
in the calm of the night

Marjorie C. Thompson
MAID OF BACCHANAL
The Maid of Bacchanal with her panpipe
Whistles a haunting melody at dusk.
From hidden aeries come her sybarites
To give their flautist gentian wine, and musk.
The Cabalistic Lord of Holocaust
Lusts for the radiant dryad, bare of breast,
So casts his spell of everlasting fire,
Then clutches molten lava to his chest.

Jonathan Dobbs
SANS SOUCI
The old man wanders lonely
Upon the darkened streets
And through the holes upon his shoes
    Winter clings upon his feet.

He stumbles to the garbage can
And sadly looks within
He finds nothing edible
Nothing for his tin.

He waits along the friendless street
Sadly asking for a meal
But the heedless crowd hurries on
Deaf to his plaintive appeal

And there in the stree he perished at last
Beneath the sadness he beared
And as he died he mumbled so soft
"Sans souci,"—no one cared.

Eric Paul Holm
TO FILL A REALM
[To the mystical Unicorn of the valley of the crescent moon and golden dawns, mythical or legendary]
Angel nonexistent
    makes a mockery of time
        and times

O visitor, provider of our metamorphosis
    created faultless out of our love
        a spiritual reality alive

Out of the skies
    or other time or world
        he helps us survive

To fill a need
    in our inner world
        weaver of the dreams

Cecile Lorraine Swing
All the Way to Calvary
How far havae you walked this day, my friend;
    And how hard was the pathway you trod?
Was it narow and steep, or wide was the way?
    Did you climb all the way up to God?

The burden you carried, was it heavy, my friend?
    Too heavy for you to bear?
Was the sun too hot and the road too long
    For you to continue to care?

If you'd started your climb with my Lord, my friend,
    He'd have helped you along your way.
He'd have taken your burden and lightened your load,
    But, my friend, you forgot to pray!

My Lord walked the long long road, my friend,
    And He did it for you and for me,
Weighed down by the burdens of all our sins
    On the Cross, to Calvary.

The way He went was cruel and steep,
    And narrow the path that He trod,
But he walked all the way to Calvary's hill
    And carried our burdens to God!

Roger B. Simpson
THE ALL AMERICAN FIX
Take a hamper full of worries
    Take a bucket full of yawns
Take a sack of missed appointments
    Mix them up with gloomy dawns

Take a carton full of sighs
    From the heaviness of sleep
And a bag of soggy sneezes
    Surging up from caverns deep

Then you've got the basic blahs
    That entitle you to take
A cup of McDonald's coffee
    For your souls's salvation sake.

Today's Greatest Poems

Fred L. Kohlmeyer
WINTER

I like walking across the fields
Covered in a white velvet gown,
Or standing by the rivers edge
Watching the lights from town

My love and I by the fireplace
Just watching the fire glow,
Watching children building
    snowmen
Or just playing in the snow

I guess to some it would seem
That winter's a lonely time of
    year,
The coldness and barren trees
To their eyes would bring a tear

But I love the winter and the
    snow
To me it's a time to start,
It's Mother Natures way of doing
And she does it with her heart

I know that Spring is coming
And flowers will start to bloom,
She'll cover the hills in freshness
And take away the Winter's
    gloom

Robin G. Murphy
EDGE OF SADNESS

*[For my brother Eric, who died
of cancer. His strength and
courage will live in our
memories forever.]*
Sitting on the edge of sadness,
happy people going by;
feeling just a touch of madness,
waiting, wondering, asking why.
    Life has oh so many pathways,
rough and rigid, smooth and
    clear;
whether there be good or bad
    days,
a better time is always near.
    Don't just hang your head in
    sorrow,
treasure each moment along lifes
    way;
there will always be tomorrow,
to ease the tensions of today.
    There is love to be acquired,
along the pathway now and then;
Yet if perchance you're feeling
    tired,
be patient, peace will come again.

Kathe' Fabry
CALL IT A VIRTUE

Communicate . . . Get it straight.

Tell it as it is . . . No games, no
Lies . . . Head or otherwise.

Only honesty prevails.

As the winds blow, so go the
sails.

Kirk Anderson
At the Bottom Of the Valley There Might Be a Cliff

You're taking our mountains;
    you're taking our streams;
You're taking our flowers; all out
    of sight.
You want us to fight you; we're
    not going to do it;
It's against our beliefs; we know
    that we're right.

The people in the office, they
    want to see action.
They watch from the sidelines,
    painted with white.

We all want peace. It's you that
    want war.
You've ruined it already. We don't
    want to fight.

You've taken so much; what more
    do you want?
Do you want to be the last to see
    light?
I love you my father. I hate you
    my master.
God told me to do it; I'm not
    going to fight.

I won't leave the country; I'll stay
    and take it.
I'll try to change you with all of
    my might.
If you fight it'll end it; just press
    your button,
And all that I've hoped for will
    die in the night.

Sandra Vermillion
HEAVEN

I know that I am leaving
because I cannot stand the pain.
I am going to a place
and shall not leave a stain.

This place cannot be seen
by anyone but me.
It is like in a dream
where everyone is free.

I will be guided with gentle hands
never slipping or falling down;
While floating through a cloud
without a single sound.

Never thinking of myself,
and reaching out to know one.
Just drifting towards the moon
and never reaching the sun.

Rhonda Watt
HEROS

Isn't it so what the people say
That the world needs heros
Everyday?

A hero to me
Should be someone
You'd like to be exactly like.

Now think of this world of ours
With all of its bleeps and blinks
And all of its stars.

How many heros can there be
In this big world of ours?
Count them one, two, three . . .

Honestly answer this; Is there
    anyone person you
Want to be? You want to be
    happy and bliss;
Can you name one person always
    like this?

True, the world needs heros
    everyday
But how many people can
    honestly say
That my only hero is me!

Vicky Sue Wilson
MYSELF

[To my family and friends]
Did you ever wake up to the
    sound of nothing, nobody is
    around. Not even the birds are
    singing.
But there really is a sound, it's
    your heart crying out for
    someone or something. But
    nothing hears you.
What is that in your eye, is it a

tear?
Come here let me wipe your eyes.
I'm here, I'll talk to you.
For you see I'm just as lonely as
    you are.
I feel the pain also.
Now see what you did, I'm crying.
Don't feel bad, that was coming
    on for a long time.
It just took someone like you to
    bring it out.
I feel a lot better, I can face
    tomorrow now.
You feel better too?
You see I told you we needed
    each other.I'll be here any day
or night when you feel lonely
again, and I know you will be
    there too.
For you see you are me and I'm
    you.

Colleen L. Weeks

Colleen L. Weeks
HEARTBEAT

A heartbeat away
Is a life on a shore
Golden and beautiful
With love and more

A clasp of a hand
An old friend and loved ones too!
A heartbeat away
Is new life on a distant shore

Lisa Renee Thomas
REFLECTIONS

For someone
who can make me feel
so great
you're making me feel
terrible.
Lately,
I don't know what to
expect to hear
from you.

I can't say
or do
certain things
    —they upset you.
If I cater to your
needs . . . (greeds?)
I am not being me.
But am I just being kind?
A friend?
Giving up little parts of
me
to stay with
you
doesn't seem right,
or fair.
I don't want to be a
reflection
    of you
        for you.
I want to be a
friend
    to you
        for us.

Kaylene Larson
THE PLASTIC POSY

Me with you, felt it was true...
You lovin' me, me lovin' you too,
When along came a teddy
And I found you weren't ready
For someone who's steady,
Solid, sound and secure.

Yes, the plastic posy
    Put her petals your way,
Your hert went winging—
    You were gone the same day.

You'll be back, we'll forget that.
I know now I'm on the true track,
As I see her blackened hair,
Silver car, and pseudo air
Give you empty thrills to share.
You're my lesson; she's yours...

When the plastic posy
    Pushes petals your way,
Your heart goes winging
    And you're gone the same day.

Ronald G. Marlow
FOR A FRIEND

If I could write the words to take
    the hurt away
I would send you a long letter
    each and every day
If I could put my arms around
    you to fend off all the pain
You would never have to worry
    about being hurt again
If I could find a way to split
    myself in two
You would never be lonely I
    would be there for you.

Frances W. Tallent
THE MASTER ARTIST

Sometimes when life is
    meaningless,
    Just heartache, pain and strife,
The Master Artist sends someone
    To brighten such a life.
When all I saw was slate and
    stone,
    So drab and cold and gray,
He sent me you on wings of love
    To help me through each day.
I gave you poems and butterflies;
    You gave me lovely songs.
You painted rainbow colors
    where
    I had none for so long.
You planted flowers in my soul—

51

Sweet garden of delight.
You made me want to see each
day—
Feel each new sound and sight.
I looked for emeralds in your eyes;
You found topaz in mine.
You changed my barren winter
skies
To Springtime and sunshine.
Our God supplies our every need
From Heaven up above.
The Master Artist blessed us
both
With colors of true love.

Richard Flores
IO (Moon of Jupiter)
Voyager found your elusive
presence
hushed, suspended in a
penumbral
obscurity; exhibiting your
age-scarred visage

Were you cast off from a
Jupiterian
crack-the-whip and left to greet
perpetual desolation;
and is this Earthly nomad
your first visitation?

Or how many interludes have
lapsed
since last you were approached
by inquisitive onlookers;
and who, observing your
forbidding features,
considered it futile
to linger?

And could you but utter
resentment
to those who in hasty creation
dismissed your very existence
not unlike a leprous child.

Eldia Modene Hemphill Puyear
OBLITERATION
When the sun from view has
vanished
And the sky you will see no more
Where salmon and trout have
been destroyed
And the rivers and lakes are
overflowing
With mercury, oil and garbage
Through the murk the motors
still roar
And clean clear water is a thing
of the past,
Then Mr. Modern Man you will
have your reward at last

Cecil Moore
THE PASSING ON
The trains are fastly fading
That crossed our prairie land
They're being set aside
For new inventions made by man.

The trains in all their glory
Help man win the west
Now in sadness and sorrow
We lay them down to rest.

Man is very selfish
As the years go by
And the long streaks of silver
Must bow to the big bird in the
sky.

But we who have loved them
They we shall never forget
Just as this generation
Will never forget the jet.

Eva B. Cook

Eva B. Cook
JIMINY JUMPIN' CATFISH
[Lake of the Ozarks
in Missouri 1953]
Jiminy Jumpin' Catfish, how high
can you fly?
Although I try and even cry,
But, Oh my! Oh my! Jiminy
Jumpin' Catfish,
How high can you fly?
I need my legs for jumping.
My heart can thump a tune.
I need my arms to hold you,
Whenever there's a moon.

But when I try to find you,
I don't know where to start.
If I ever catch you,
I'm sure we'll never part,
So now I'm through with
dreaming.
I'm really going to try,
But, Jiminy Jumpin' Catfish,
How high can you fly?

Lilybel Ware
YESTERDAY IS GONE
I thought of you today and
realized yesterday was gone.
Gone was the love we had felt for
each other.
Gone were the dreams we had
planned together.
Gone was the light in my eyes
and the smile on my face.
That you brought when you
walked into our place.
We had always planned what we
would do tomorrow but—
Yesterday is gone and tomorrow
never comes.
So . . . today I live for what the
day will bring.

Whether it be sunshine or rain,
sadness or sorrow,
I will find a way to overcome my
fears.
Because . . . just as yesterday is
gone . . . so are you!

Beverly Reno Tong
DARK FEAR
[To my Husband, Allen, who is
my secret source, and who
keeps the darkness at bay.]
Sitting here amid the dark
I let the night close around me,
I wait for my eyes to adjust
Permitting me to see.

I know the fear of lurking
shadows
Of my throat slowly getting tight,
Even as I stifle a scream
I know I'm prepared to fight.

You cannot take me
By peace or by force,
For deep inside me
Is a secret source.

It won't be long now
Before the day will dawn,
And there will be light
And the dark will be gone.

Linda Blake
IF I HAD A DREAM
If I had a dream for every time I
felt a joy within my heart . . .
And I could transform these
dreams for you to view . . .
Then you would know of life and
your heart would be filled with
love . . .
And your every moment would
be living something new.

If I could gain an empathy divine
and could climb into your
mind . . .
I would take away the pain and
leave only comfort for your
soul.
I would leave the sunshine, take
the rain . . .
And leave you ecstacy to play
your role.

If I could transmit energy of love
for you to feel . . .
I could find no greater gift should
I attempt to search . . .
For within this lies the bird of
love's
Greatest desire to find his perch.

Lewis Parker Miller
**Remember Apple
Blossoms?**
Remember apple blossoms in the
spring when first we met
How white and pink and fragile
they appeared to us, and yet
How sturdy must their hearts
have been to bring this fall
array
Of luscious red-ripe apples to
enliven autumn's gray.

Remember love's first rapture all
so tremulous and new
And how its magic thrilled us as
it burst upon our view?
How wondrous, dear, that this
frail bloom that did our hearts
enthrall
Like apple blossoms, outlasts

spring, and ripens in the fall.

Barbara Noel
I'd Known The Wrong You
Love, I went blindly in
Gave up all I had for you
Then I found that you were two
I'd known the wrong you

And you, you never told me no
Only told me go
So I kept on loving you
Only to be played the fool

Oh if I could have seen
That you were truly two
Then maybe I could have found
The you that's truly you.

Mauricia Price
MAGIC CIRCLE
The glowing embers of our love,
Continuing resurgencies
Of orange-gold originals—
Electric ripply flames that seared
The cold surrounding atmosphere
With cosmic fire—now warm
Our blended lives with
tenderness
And shield us from the blue-gray
blades
of bitterness that gleam beyond
The magic circle of our love.

Cary Chrysler
UNION OF LIFE
His head is up—
the depth of those eyes no man
could fathom,
life in his heart, no age destroy.
His ears capture melody of wind,
His nose seeks the scent of new
grass.

The grace of a horse at full gallop
is unlike any dance. Spirit flows
in every vessel, as he glides
down the canyon.

His head is up—
Union has brought wind to his
lungs,
blood to his heart.

The peace of grazing horse
surpasses the setting sun;
And Life flowing forever
forever
forever

Kathy Jeske
Sunbeams And Rainbows
God's love is like a sunbeam
shining down on me.
The joy of my salvation is fresh,
as fresh can be.
This new love is overwhelming, I
rejoice in it each day
Close beside my Savior is where I
want to stay.
I want to be a sunbeam, reflecting
this great love
So others will see Jesus, caring
from above.

But as my journey moves along
dark clouds come o'er my way.
Temptations, trials, and troubles
mar the sunny day.
I feel lost and unproteced; alone,
so weak, afraid
And then I see the rainbow,
visual promise God has made.
"Learn of me for I will keep you
as your days are long.
I will never leave, forsake you.
Take courage and be strong."

June Deborah Meek
DOUG
I've been told
A persons eyes are the windows
  to their soul
And if that's so
You're made of gold.
They shine so bright
Twinkling like a star at night
And I love you so
Don't ever want you to go.
You're a flame in the darkness
Against that backdrop of sadness
Which others spread like gloom
It envelopes all except for you.
Let me drown in your eyes
Which are as blue as the sky
I want to become part of you
We'll be as one, as we were meant
  to.
You are a new experience for me
You've filled my existence with
  ecstasy
And I hope that I'll go first
If not; 'till the end I'll curse.

Betty Engel
APRIL SHOWERS
With the spring,
It will bring,
Bright, new flowers,
To brighten up the hours.
And as they grow,
They will be sure to show,
Their beauty and grace,
On each and every face.

Ruth Webber
ETERNAL DUSTER
[To Mary]
I knew a woman who couldn't
  stand dirt
So she worked and worried and
  scrubbed 'til it hurt.
And when she died they laid her
  to rest
With mounds of dirt piled on her
  breast.
But she met with an awful fate
When she met St. Peter at the
  Golden Gate.
She said "I can't stay here, there's
  a little dust there
Along the railing of the Golden
  Stair"
St. Peter grinned and said "yes, I
  know"
And gave her a dust cloth and
  sent her below.
When they saw her they said
  "here comes Mrs. Brown
She'll really try to clean up this
  town".
So they locked the gates and sent
  her away.
And where is Mr. Brown today?
She hovers between the earth and
  sky
And dusts off the newcomers as
  they go by.

William G. Muller, Jr.
FANTASY IN CONTRASTS
Shimmering moonbeams dance
  on the lake,
Silver bubbles form and break,
Deep purple willows that cannot
  stand still,
Sweet scented breezes move
  down o'er the hill,
Where a field rich with daffodils
  sway to and fro,

And a host of delphinium stand
  row upon row;
Such beauty as this I never have
  seen,
So long as I live may God let me
  dream.
A sudden change in the air and a
  gray mist decends,
The water lies steady; laughing
  bubbles won't lend
Joy to the black willow, so
  unhappy it weeps,
For a dank, clammy smell thru its
  bower soon creeps
And erases the fragrance of
  perfume on the bluff,
Where all frivolity dies, as at a
  flame one did puff;
As in life, in my dream, both
  hands must be played,
Forever a contrast, for that have I
  prayed.

G. McLean McDaniel
BUT I'M NOT
It's the first day of Winter
Green leaves rustle past my ears
And I say "I'm home"
But I'm not.

Sounds conjur up thoughts
And memories become current
  happenings
And I'm lost between two places
But I'm not.

Home is two places,
One North and one South
And I yearn for the one I'm not
  with.

I'm physically in one,
Emotionally in the other
And I say that I'm happy
But I'm not.

Jean Longley
OUR MIRACLE BABY
[To my dear precious grand-
daughter Branda Jean, who
lights up my life in a very
special way.]
On a summer morning, in the
  stillness of dawn
A tiny twenty-six baby was born.
She was so dainty, almost fragile
A miracle shared by everyone.
Something special, something to
  hold
A proud mothers smile, a fathers
  joy
As if he had found a pot of gold.
Many months have come and
  gone
Our hearts are full of joy
Knowing our prayers were heard.
God gave us something to
  wonder about
Something to show His love is
  real
By giving us a little miracle
Telling us He still cares.

Ruth I. Myers
POEMS
Poems are the many creations of
  a deep feeling,
Within a small corner of the body
  they dwell.
Where no one treads in a cove of
  concealing,
They are guarded with honor in
  the body sentinel.

Poems are a blending of thoughts
  in rhythmic unity,
Painting a picture much as an
  artist's oil portrays.
They express the abstract and the
  natural of beauty
As they resound the songs of
  life's varied ways.

Poems are a symphony's music, a
  song of birds;
They open the mind's doors to
  thoughts of versatility
Where hidden joys and sorrows of
  life become words
That emanate from the depths of
  ones own personality.

Lynn McClure
WITHOUT YOU
I can't live without you,
I won't live without you.
I can't see my life without us,
I won't see my life without us.

I hope you see our life the same
  way too,
I simply, unconditionally can't
  live my life without you.
I can't explain my existence
  without us,
I can't love, exist, or breathe
  without us.

My love for you is without a
  doubt,
Something my soul can not do
  without.
All my life I hurt with pain until
  I found you,
Maybe your life hurt with pain
  until you found me too.

Now we are one and love is so
  new,
Now we must stay this way
  forever true.
I can't live without you,
I won't live without you.

Beatrice Harper
THE RING OF LIFE
Life is like a fighting ring
You are challenged by
  sorrow and strife
To fight in the ring of life

You fall of a broken heart
  in sorrow
You fight again tomorrow

You are knocked against
  the ropes
Don't give up hopes

In spite of sorrow
  and strife
You will stand undefeated
  in the ring of life

Grace Arnell
AUTUMN PAINTINGS
Autumn paintings by our
  Master's hand,
His touch speaks louder than
  words can express,
Displaying talent, beauty and
  high esteem, by His command.
These autumn scenes to
  appreciate in all tongues,
Be seen, heard and confess,
Lands of grandeur, captured in
  silence, that cast a spell
Bring all within His reverence
  that reach the eye,

Where only saints in Heaven
  dwell.
All this, man censured these
  desires
Of art as time passes by.
Our Master's artistic hand lets
  each enjoy
His paintings of autumn tell,
Eternal, portrayed on the canvas
  of the world.
Our Master's hand has painted
  beauty,
Autumn's gift of love,
With eternites reflection from
  above.
All is well, all is well.

Fern Baker
PRETTY BLUEBIRD
Pretty bluebird in my tree
Are you singing just for me?
Is it to cheer my lonely heart
Because you know my day is dark?

Tell me why you sing your song
Is it because my day is long?
Does your heart sometimes know
  pain
Or do you sing on in the rain?

Are you here just for to-day?
To banish all my cares away?
Reveal your secret unto me
Before you part my company.

Have you lost your lady love?
Is she flying somewhere above?
Should you depart to find your
  mate
Do not return to her too late.

Fly high and free my happy bird,
But let your lovely song be heard:
Don't ever change your joyful
  tune,
And visit me again real soon.

Dorothy Kole Mucklo
THE RAINBOW
Today I saw a rainbow,
But there was no rain.
It was a vision of beauty,
As I searched for the Pot o' Gold
At the rainbow's end
I felt a touch of Heaven
God was there, I know,
He was its Maker!

Debbie Miles
ETERNITY
Piano sounds weave
  through the den, while the old
  man
rocks himself to sleep . . .

Penny Sonya Collins
God Sends the Rainbows

There's a storm brewing in my
mind.
The clouds grow dark.
It starts to thunder, louder and
louder it clashes.
When I have my pencil in hand,
it slowly begins to rain.
The droplets trickle down my
arm and onto my paper, in the
form of words.
The storm worsens, the thunder
grows
still louder, the clouds darker.
The rain is now a continious
stream.
Then as quickly as it came, the
storm
begins to recede.
Clear skies and sunshine peek
through the clouds.
All that remains is a puddle on
my paper.
Which with the help of the
sunshine
becomes a rainbow, in the form
of a poem.

Karen Ledbetter Nolan
DREAMS

Some dreams die quietly—
we scarcely note their passing
or remember when they've gone.
Others twist our memories with
bitter resignation
and leave us strangely
incomplete.
As though we are not less for
their going
and yet without them can never
be more.

Wm. Keith Clayton
Another Merry Christmas
[To my brother and sister,
In memory of Grandpa and
Granny.]

We'll still try for a Merry
Christmas,
Tho there may be some that's
missed,
For the ones who've raised our
Mother
Have gone to their place of rest.

Sleep we will up in the morn
With sadness in our hearts,
For the Christmas of our youth
Now seems a world apart.

Divide the tribe throughout the
years,
While death will break it more:
Forget the frowns that came with
tears,
And recall a pleasant score.

Account for all the joy that was,
And all that's shared with kin;
For happy times will grow with
love,
There'll be happy times again.

Annette L. Bullard
OUR LIFE'S JOURNEY

Our life is like a journey
Taken on a train,
Us a pair of travelers,
At the windowpane.

I may sit beside you
All the journey through.
I might have sat elsewhere
Never knowing you.

But, if fate e'er puts me
Forever by your side.
Let us be pleasant travelers,
It's so short a ride.

Amrett Spivey Robas
Eddie
[I dedicate this poem with all
the Love in it, to my loving
husband, Joseph.]

I know you share with me our
loss in death
and treasure him with every
blending breath

Your unfading love and it's
emerald trace
with deepest lines show in your
very face

I want you talk to me of our child
who died
I wish you could hold me more
when I cry

Oh! how many hours have I spent
alone
grieving for our son to heaven
has gone

I'm so tired of hurting alone at
dawn
even evening in our chairs on the
lawn

I imagine him by our side and
sigh
why don't you talk of him and
share and cry

I walked to the private cemetary
grounds
and looked upon the little grave
with no sounds

I stooped and placed flowers on
spongy sod
knowing our son is in heaven
with God

Yes, I can feel him in my arms at
night
and see the soft blue blanket and
dim light

But can never teach him to climb
a tree
because God, you have chosen
him for thee.

T.R. Ulrich
ANOTHER SPRING

I cannot bear the beauty of
another spring
An orchard blossoming

A robin on the wing
Would make remembering
Too real a thing
If I should glimpse blue iris by
the lake
Against the green enchantment
That the willows make
Or hear a cardinal call
For true love's sake
Surely my sleeping heart would
wake
To know that you are gone
And break.
So I shall travel to some far-flung
land
Where copper tropic sun and
coral sand
Contrive a never-ending summer
land
If you should see me there, you'll
understand
I cannot bear the beauty of
another spring!

Dina Costa Duncan
THE CIRCLE
[To Dovie and Bernice, the
beginners of the Circle.]

For every time I've been angry at
her,
There's been ten times I've
needed her.
For every time we've fought,
There's been a hundred times
we've laughed.
Never be too busy for MOM,
because one day, physically,
she'll be gone.
All Mothers and Daughters have
their differences.
We Daughters all too soon want
to be grown and
with an ache in Mom's heart, she
has to let us go.
We stumble, fall, we sometimes
blame Mom.
And then, like the miracle of the
morning sun
We rise with a new total
understanding of Mom.
What she did, and why.
Hopefully, there's
still time to say thank you,
I LOVE YOU.
And then, with the birth of our
own children,
     MOM
Begins again . . .

Jujuan Fleeman
WORD PAINTING

If I could paint a picture with
words,
it would flow with gracefulness,
with swirls of beauty and love.
Surround it with colors of
freedom,
and peacefulness all in-between.

Then would come you, much
harder to paint.
I'd choose my colors with utmost
care.
You'd flow with mixtures of
gentleness
and the quietness that always
moves me so.

I'd paint you with the soft looks
you always
give me while gazing deep into
my eyes.

Arrows of passion and intensity
running all
through your soul.

After I'd finished painting you, I'd
surround you with an array of
colors,
of my love and desire for you.

And when it was all finished,
I'd sign it with kisses,
meant just for you.

Lois Finch Moore
MY HUSBAND LOVES ME

I met you there
Where I said I would,
Under the pine tree
By the brook-side
Where the meadow
Meets the wood.

I said cruel words
And left you there—
Now I'm glad
You never knew
Had you taken me in your arms,
I would have gone with you.

Barbara Maurer Reitz
THUNDER STORM

'Tis frolic day for heavenly souls,
The ten pins crash and tumble
down.
Blithe spirits watch while old Rip
bowls,
The King of Pins, he wears the
crown.

Alas, alack! 'Twas but a spare.
The weeping angels drop their
tears,
And all the earth must stand and
stare,
As pouring torrents quell their
fears.

Diane Pevsner
YOU AND I

Can't remember when we met.
I'm sure of the how and why.
What you said was spoken
gently,
With humor and with heart.
Get to know me better, your
Eyes did say.

I have much to give, and I know
The kind of woman I want.
I've seen you with him. I've
Watched you touch him and
smile.
I've said too much, but I do
Know what I want, and who.

Steven J. Paskuly
CRITICISM

Though no detractor
of the actor,

Would cherish remission
of this politician.

Nola F. Hammer
LOOKING BACK

As I look back o'er the past,
A wishful eye here I cast.
Wishing some changes, I could
make,
Some different paths, I would
take.

A better Christian, I'd try to be.
There are many failures, I can see
I'd try to be a better servant for
my Lord,
more often I'd read his blessed Word

In Church, I'd try my place to fill
A greater effort to do my Father's Will.
I'd visit the sick, when I could,
And do many other things I should.

A better education, I'd try to obtain
And from all evil, I would refrain.
But the past is forever gone
Even if I failed to stay where I belong

Our Heavenly Father will forgive
In the future, a better life I want to live.
And as a New Year is just ahead
Where I've failed, I want to do better instead.

M. Anne Henry
PEOPLE OF PAPER
[To all who have felt pain in their life; who have known uncertainty in their existance...To these people I extend my love...]
People are of paper
    waiting to be consumed
        in the fire of existance
until they become
    burnt flesh...
        ash...
            and then...
                dust
only to blow away in the wind...

I am a lone molecule of dust...
What is aloneness?
When alone—there is no one else to blame...
        there is nothing...
            just emptiness
The hunger in the stomach of humanity...

How sad to be alone...
    Where is
        dust
            to go?

Jaime Rosales
ELIZA'S ETUDE
"Eliza is dead," Mrs. W said.
And Mr. W could not be reached for comments.
But, even though she was her daughter,
Mrs. W showed no trouble while declaring her feelings about the matter.

"Indeed," said she,
"this happening, logically,
ruins our (Mr. & Mrs. W) shopping spree.
Nevertheless she was our daughter
and we have to take care of her,
at least that's what the law says."

Later it was announced
the date of the funeral.
When asked why Eliza's friends were not invited,
Mrs. W joyfully explained:
"Now that she is dead,
we don't need to socialize with them anymore."

"And that's all for the moment.
This is S reporting."

Johnny J. Nemec
SUN AND MAN
This morning as I watched the rising sun,
I had this thought to cross my mind.
A newborn life had just begun,
God's special gift to man kind.

At mid-day I look up at the sky.
Now I see it in it's prime.
Half the day has passed it by.
Now it's at it's brightest time.

Now the setting sun is fighting to stay up in the sky.
In a way it reminds me of a man.
It seems as if it's afraid to die.
But die it must, so it can rise again.

Louise Buhl
OLD MINER (49'er)
[To Miners]
Hey, old miner, what have you got?
What do you find in them thar hills?
It's a sometimes mine, you're hoping it yields a lot.
Sometimes it's there and sometimes it's not.
At least you don't have any bills.

What do you do if nothing's there?
Give up and go elsewhere, that you hear.
Hoping and praying you'll find it somewhere.
Over the next mountain you'd swear.
It's got to be far or near.

Out in the sun and wind all day.
Sweating your guts out and no pay.
While you're on your knees digging away.
If you find something the big shots rake in the hay.
As they sit on their butts having their say.

Diane Harper
BOOKCASE
The bookcase sits alone in the old house.
The books it contains are older than the house itself.
For it has seen:
    Three wars,
    Families come and go,
    Cities dying and hungry,
    Life and death of millions.
And finally,
    The destruction of the house itself,
    for no one wants to relive history again.
So, the bookcase sits until morning
    when its death will finally come.

Martha Earhart
ALWAYS FREE
Across the astro-plane we sail,
Leaving the cold and feeling warm.
Our hearts we used against the storm;
At last in death we did not fail.

Our love was not dismissed at death;
No heavenly choirs across the sky.
I see only him and he only I
As we speak sweet words with one last breath.

We try our wings and take to the sky,
Together touching the wind around,
Experiencing feeling without a sound,
Gently lilting as a butterfly.

In his eyes the blue of the seas,
Looking ahead as we soar in the breeze.

Pauline Heim

Pauline Heim
THANKSGIVING DAY
[To Loyd, my husband—who has been an inspiration through the years.]
Today, I sit here in my favorite chair.
Thinking of my Loved Ones
Who live here and there,
I thank our Lord for
His loving care of them and me.

Friends old and new,
Refresh my thoughts, my heart.
Bringing sad and happy memories.
On this Thanksgiving Day!
A day to pause and say
Thank You, Lord for work and play.
Please watch over those
Less fortunate than I,
Enrich their Blessings
Hear their cry, Heal their pain and sorrows.
May they find Your smile
On their tomorrows!

Bless this Day and my home
I will Love and thank You forever.
For all You have done,
For my country, hear my plea?
Watch over and care for the Good old U.S.A.
On this Thanksgiving Day!

Karla Wright
THE CANDLE
If I hold a candle in my window
Light it for a while
Will you look out the window
    ans see if you can
See the reflection from the tiny flicker of the flame
Try to imagine the small light

And the shadows along the edge
with images that are wrinkled
from the wind moving across the flame
And the warmth the melting wax
has as it slowly drips to
the base of the candle
The small drops becoming larger
    as the candle burns more
wax is collecting
My candle is shrinking slowly
    and the light is dim
My reflection in the flame has
    left and the wick in the
candle has put itself out.

Daniel Chancellor
LOST LOVE
Have tried to call my love long distance phone,
Her whereabouts was unknown;
This has happened in the past,
Now I will face the truth at last.

Our love together we can never share,
Would love forever to see her shining hair,
When in dreams I see her lovely face,
Shall go and hide in some lonely place.

Although this sad life will linger on,
The meaning for me is forever gone,
This is for all mankind to see,
Never again shall love do this to me.

As I walk through life's shadowed halls,
There will be no more long distance calls,
Now have lost all desire for love-
Has flown away like a turtle dove.

Jeffrey C. Bishop
SEMESTER'S END
The Oak trees creak outside in the wind,
leaves whirlwind on the corner of the blacktop.
3:00 bell rings.
Students feet slapping down the halls,
noise and commotion going out of doors.
Soon not a sound in the hot prefabs.
All that can be heard,
is the creaking of the Oak trees
and the tether ball chain clanging
in the wind against the pole.

School's Out!

Terry L. Potts
ORDINARY MEN
In the eyes of dawn
we are no ordinary men,
But Prince's all.
It is only when
the sun reflects our shadows
do we become
men of time;
Moved about by others
In games of chance,
of which we are simple pawns.
And only those true princes,
In kingdoms of their making
are not lost within the shadows.

Glen R. Osborne
LOVE UNKIND

Love so kind; so sweet; so pure,
Why can'st thou be mine for sure?
From morn till night I think of
you,
The light gives way from gold to
blue,
I wonder, is my day due?
Oh, you vixen! you kill me true.
Can love so tender be unkind?
Or take a track that is so blind?
My lips do thirst for precious
thine
That taste like wine from
heaven's vine;
Will my mind be mine again?
I pray, tomorrow despair not
send,
The venom death is better yet;
Why? Why can'st I, just once
forget?

Vera Lee Johnson
SUCH SORROW

How can I say grieve not my dear
When sorrow engulfs your day;
How can I say dry all your tears—
For we also have walked that
way.

Some say that faith is made
stronger
When down tragedy lane we
tread;
Each time we say, "Thy will—not
mine"—
We grow dearer and nearer to
God.

His mercy and love lend comfort
When griefs afflict and assail;
He's there when mountains grow
higher—
He'll lead you through every dark
vale.

Yes, we can speak with
compassion,
We have experienced such
sorrow;
May God give you the strength
for today
And guide you through each
tomorrow.

Palmira Garza
CARNIVAL GROUND

There's an empty lot south of the
city,
a place where the grass never
grows.
For each time near the end of the
season,
the ground prepares itself for it
knows
the Carnival is on its way.

Soon the trailers and trucks come
roaring in
and the tents are quickly put up.
The ground is pierced with iron
stakes
and then covered with rides and
games
that fill up the lot.

The night crowd comes with
everything ready
to experience the magic of the
past.
The wide-eyed children thrilled
at the moment

to enter their world of rides and
games
and laughs.

But the Carnival left as quick as
it came
leaving the crowds with
memories.
The magic, the lights, the sights
and sounds
dub the empty lot with the title
of
the Carnival Ground.

Eleanor L. Krause

Eleanor L. Krause
SPRINGTIME

It's Springtime in the Mountains
It's so great to be alive.
I count my many blessings,
As I walk down Laburnum Drive.
And as I walk back up the hill,
I look up the mountain high,
And see the trees away up there,
They nearly reach the sky.
What's on the other side of it?
I'll really never know,
In my thoughts, I'll climb it
slowly
And take each day as they go.

As you walk and look around
you;
There's a brand new piece of
ground,
To the west of us and o'er the hill
The well chosen spot they found.
T'will be the new "Care Unit"
A blessing in disguise,
Before the year is over
It will be there before your eyes.
And so on "Waltons Mountain"
It's peaceful and quiet here,
It's Springtime in the Mountains
With Easter very near.

Ruth Kezele
TAKE MY HAND

Will you take my hand and hold
it tight.
Lead me down this dark path, I
have started to walk.
I feel so alone in this part of my
life.
My need for someone is so
strong.
Will you take my hand and hold
it tight.
Lead me to the light, I am sure it's
before us.
Be my light, I need a friend
someone to share this
frightening time in
my life.
Will you take my hand and hold
it tight.
I will hold you to nothing as we
walk this path.
Just having you near and feeling
your warmth, is
enough for now. I am frightened
and alone.

Take my hand and hold it tight.
Could we start tonight, the test of
time has strength for all.
Why waste more time? For a
friend I must find. For the
dark hour has me blind. So take
my hand and hold it tight, For
I fear of time lost, I will lose my
life.

Nancy Brier O'Neal
PREMONITION

Bridges bend their backs for me;
Rivers call my name;
Waters in my dreams at night
Drown out my earthly pain.

Roots of trees entangle me,
Their fingers take my breath;
Darkened whirls of hours wash
by,
Wringing me to death.

Life's been for me a battle,
And if water is its end,
When your hand has pulled me
from the depths,
Oh, please, Lord, call me "friend".

Harold C. Thornton
I AM

I am the one.
Not the other one
Who is not having fun.
Trying to get everything done.

Looks for something not there
A fatalistic premonition gives me
a scare.
Then the time comes when I
must dare
And defeat that catastrophic
attitude which transends the
air.

Carolyn E. Mears
I Give To You The Spring

Oh my love, I give to you
Morning roses beaded with dew.
A starburst sun breaking the haze
Budding leaves, warm spring days.

We once were those budding
leaves,
We grew together as do the trees.
A gurgling stream of emerald
water drops
Fed our love that still never stops.

Ah, a never-ending winding
spring,
I see us laugh in it's light
reflecting.
Each shimmering speck
remembers a hue
Of the colorful life I spent with
you.

Your words come to me on the
chauffeuring breeze,
Your voice becomes the rustling
leaves.
I know you're still near when I
listen to you,
So I offer roses beaded with dew.

I place them on your eternal bed,
With emerald water drops they're
fed.
Their beauty comes not from
water though;
Spring they seek, eternal spring
you soe.

Oh my love, I give to you a tear.

M. Anne Henry
A TOUCH FOR LIFE

*[I humbly dedicate this poem
to my friend and physician,
Manuel Farina, M.D., who has
taught me that there is a
reason to love and a reason to
live and a reason to exist. For
this I am truly grateful...]*

Circumstances are here
for us to sieze;
to turn them around;
to make them work for us.

We are here
to make our lives
dynamic "processees of growth"
by using our outer
experiences
as input to our
deeper doul...

To know that the greatest love
and gift
from God
is the chance to love our lives,
making them a gift
to Him as to
ourselves.

William Converse
THE END

The bells ring
Chiming final hours
The men cry
And women weep
A time lost
In another dimension
Banished from thought
Death drags on
Life is born
Satan laughs wildly
God sheds tears
Tears of sorrow
Tears of joy

Angela V. Nalbantu
LOVE POTION

I am the last wine of fall
The richest, the reddest.
Flavors float on the grey mists
Of bouquets of roses grown in
paradise
Taste of honey and ripen
expectation.
I am the last wine of fall
The richest, the reddest,
Maturing in love of you.

Today's Greatest Poems

Doris Estelle Evans
EMERALD GARDENS

The beauties of the Summertime
The rhythm of Nature rhymes
The country charms and chimes
In the long idyllic days of
    Summertime
The beauty of trees and a garden,
    way of life
These helps ease the wariness
    and the strife
And these emerald gardens of
    Paradise
Makes us a little more
    compassionate and wise
And gives us joy, strength and
    Faith
An aura of peace and gladness to
    our days
An ode to the beauties of
    Nature's ways
Lovers of trees, gardens and a
    hearth
Have love and beauty in their
    hearts
And the dappled shade of an
    arbor
Our home — a haven and a
    harbor
And greenery thru a garden gate
All these things gives a feeling of
    Faith

Bianca C. Stewart
The Wedding Of Father Frank White

He lifts his glass, no more a
    chalice
And in his hands, wine remains
    wine.
He sees approval? pity? malice?
In the eyes of those who have
    come to dine.
He breaks a roll, takes up his
    butter knife,

And in his hands, bread remains
    bread.
Beside him sits his smiling wife;
Their guests will like them better
    once they're fed.

They stare at the appearence of
    the band;
Some look away — the room's too
    bright.
Old friends who call him Frank
    will understand,
But those who wish him well as
    MISTER White,
Will eat and drink with him and
    shake his hand—
Then never speak his name after
    tonight.

Barry D. Coker
REVELATIONS

Approaching Black Death
Skull to left— to the right
Cloud hiding moon
Fog scaddered upon the ground
Surrounding Hell's gates
Peeking through
        One open tomb
A mysterious coolness
Lurks about you
Being condemned for your sins
Near sudden death
No
I'm still living
Been forgiven

Gloria Carter Bell
ME MYSELF AND I
[With love to my
Grandmother, Father, Husband,
Children and Lena.]

I am what I make of myself
Only I am responsible for what I
    become
Only I can control my happiness
My destiny is of my own
    choosing
What I become depends on me
I can blame no one for my
    failures
What I do with my life depends
    on the value I place on it.
I can only go as high as I allow
    myself.

Deborah Ingram
BEAUTY

I saw Beauty yesterday
It showed itself to me
In glistening drops of morning
    dew
Upon a spring—time tree.

Beauty came to sing to me
Though it uttered not a word
It came to me in a gentle breeze
And from a single bird.

Beauty even touched me
With a velvet—covered wind
And with fingertips of happiness
Brought peacefulness within.

Juanita I. Hinton
God's Beautiful Universe

I open the gate to a garden filled
    with a variety of beauty.
I am not alone; it's keeper is
    always on duty.
Everything is new to me; here are
    things I have never seen before. ·
I have looked upon them a
    million times, but now through
    different eyes and an open
    door.

Can these wonders be real or is it
    only another illusion?
I am welcomed by a special
    invitation and could never be
    considered an intruder.
The sunlight falls and makes the
    clear water sparkle.
I see myself a different person; oh
    what a change, and at this I
    marvel.

The world is not quite so bad as I
    once thought.
Here I look for goodness instead
    of trying to find fault.
There is more reality than mirage
    here; more gold than lust.

I can believe in the contents for
    there is more honor than
    distrust.
Just after a storm I see the clouds
    cleared away with a rainbow.
And color my world again; with a
    watchful eye, I feel God
    looking below.
Experiencing this explosion of
    beauty in my heart, I feel safe
    and secure from all harm.
Because of His love, He gives a
    sign, and wraps me in His
    loving arms.

I awoke and thought surely I had
    knocked on Heaven's gate.
But then I realized I am only in
    the garden; here for a little
    while longer I will have to wait.
My roots are lightly planted; I
    have to learn to live here first.
I will be content in the garden
    and continue enjoying "God's
    Beautiful Universe"!

Daniel Laird Jeffers
WHY

As the wind blows the night
    away
Where does it go to, for all day
How nice to follow it, not seeing
    it shine
I am black and drinking wine
Don't you care now, what I say
Never seeing the break of day
Shadows changing patterns
    rearranging
Thoughts that glitter my mind to
    stone
Being one in midst of many
So nice to be alone

Tiffany Ann Hermelin
YOU (2)

As I look through the thick
dense fog and search to find,
What I've been looking for
all my life through.
And still have no idea where
and when I will find it,
And why I even waste
my. time trying to.
I keep trying because what
I'm, looking for I need,
I need it to survive and I
need it to help me through.
If you haven't figured it out
yet what I've been looking for,
The answer is "YOU" . . .

Patricia A. Lloyd
A MELODY

I wish I were a bird
As free as birds must be
To span the azure skies
And gaze upon the sea.

I wish I had the gift
Of flight, and song so clear
That it could penetrate the night
Of sin and darkness here.

All this I wish and yet
Within my heart a melody
As clear and free as any bird's
Is brought on wings of memory.

Charles E. Hansen
SO IT IS

As a descending rainbow's arc
Speaks of Promise—

As the warm rains of spring

Enriches the green of earth
As the surf reaches out
To caress the silvery sand—

As a cooling summer night's
    breeze
Restores and renews—

As a mountain's snowy peak
Beckons to a lonely cloud—

As the golden fields of grain
Are embraced by the gentle
    wind—

As the snowflakes cradle
    themselves
Atop the pine branches—

As the gleaming embers of the
    hearth
Glow in content and secure
    warmth—

So it is that you have touched
    me.

Julia Rost Farmer
Declaration at Half—past Midnight

Oh, cruel,cruel Youth,
You gave me back my dream
When I had done with dreaming.
I lifted my feet to the beat of your
    drum,
And in exultation my dark soul
    emerged from
Its prison of gloom.
Into your strong young hands I
    transferred something
For which you clamored,
    accepted, and then broke in
    two.
You called up demons of the
    Devil himself
To dance in high glee before my
    suffering,
As I sat bleak, immobile,
In the night's soft rain.
I shall not seek that dream
    again—
A recompense, perhaps,
For a shattered self—esteem.
But all the while I pay the piper,
    as I must,
A ghost will filter through fog
    and mist
To touch with ice—cold fingers
A pale, pale Cupid's bow,
Which God forbid I kiss.

Tammy Lynn Shaw
THE VIEW

If my emotions could burst
forth in seas, mountains, and
    rolling
plains— the landscapes of all the
earth would be only a mere
    expression
of my love.

Nellie Erwin Stromberg
OBSERVATIONS

The Universe is big and wide,
It covers up the whole outside.

Royalty sits its horse well,
We've always believed.
Enter the Media—why we've
    been
deceived!

Current subject: You Tarzan, me
    Jane,
Anything else is plain profane.

Chad: Beautiful, precious child of
God,
Too lovely for this earthy sod.

Ruth Wood Murray
HERE AM I, LORD
[Dedicated to my son, Rudy,
who came to me after I left the
altar and said, "Mama, I need
you to teach in the 4th Grade
Sunday School Department."]

"Here am I, Lord!" Please use me.
Make me a blessing to *someone*
today. (Isa.6:8)
Guide each step I take, each word
I say,
That I may brighten another
one's way. (Ps 4:2)

If I should falter, forgive me, Lord,
As I make my life a prayer (I
Thes. 5:17)
Of dedication to my precious
Savior for
Oh, how much he loved me there!

On Calvary's hill as He died for
me,
Oh, how could HE love *me* so?
To give himself for my awful sin
So *I* could to Heaven go?

Here am I, Lord, surrendered
anew
My life's goal is in your hands,
Please help me to inspire another
one
Today, while in this land.

Thank you, Lord, for using me
To help carry another one's load,
And to share my faith and hope
(Rom. 4:20)
With other travelers along life's
road.

Here am I, Lord, with the strength
you've given (Phil. 4:13)
Please make me a blessing today.
Why should I fear tomorrow's
dawn
When *you're* with me all the way?

As I've hidden your words within
my heart(Jam. 5:20)
You've guided my life thus far.
How can I doubt your promises
now
Or let Satan my service mar?
(Heb. 9:15)

As I knelt at the Altar yesterday
And said, "Here am I, Lord, Please
use me."
The pathway of life looked
brighter ahead
And a new door opened to me!
(Acts 14:27)

One of your servants said, "I need
you"
Oh, my thanks I can't express!
Just use me for *your* glory, Lord,
"Here am I," ready to onward
press.

Yours each moment, each hour,
each day,
With you, Lord, I can never fail,
You promised to never leave nor
forsake me; (Heb. 13:5)
*I'll have victory at the end of my
trail!!*

With humble thanks, Lord.
Your servant

Dawn Davison
SUNRISE
A ray of sun
against the sadness
stole all my tears
and left holes
in my darkness.

Carmen S. Becraft
ONE FRIEND
You may have gold,
you may have health,
and fame throughout the land.
You may have all
that you desire
by holding out your hand.
But you can never
be complete,
although you may pretend,
till you can claim,
among your friends,
a truly, truly friend.

Patsy Stagner
LET ME LOVE YOU
Soft as a butterfly
Let me touch you
Lay down beside me
I will love you
Loving you is easy
Leave and I am lost
Come hold me close
Touch me from within
The world can be a better place
If you will let me in
Love me
Let me love you.

Redene Susanne Ward
When You Think Of Me
When you think of me,

    remember cheerful skies
    fluffed with clouds of cotton
candy;

of a warm summer rain
    and the fresh aroma
    of thick rich earth—
of newborn grass.

Remember
    beads of early morning dew
    on a perfect scarlet rose;
the intricate detail
    in the wings of the Monarch.

Think of
    the laughter of children,
    the soft purr of a kitten,

    vivid colours of autumn,
    bright orange pumpkins on
the vine.

Remember
    a double rainbow,
    the stride of the killdeer,
    the warmth of the sun

or

    a blanket of snow
    sprinkled in diamond dust.

For this beauty I treasure
    and long to share with you.

Renee Remy
PLEASE UNDERSTAND
How does one describe a bluebird
as it flies,
To someone who knows not what
a bird is?
How does one describe a rainbow
in the sky,
To someone who knows not what
color is?

You ask me to describe, or
somehow explain,
All the things that have
happened to me.
But tell me how can you contain
A child's dreams of innocent glee?

My life has not been leisurely
entertained
With delusions of grandeur and
such,
But rather, somehow, meekly
sustained
With prayers and hopes of so
much.

So please don't ask me to describe
or linger
On things that you'll never
understand,
For I cannot explain about fingers
If you know not what is a hand.

How does one describe an
emotion,
To someone who doesn't feel?
How can you explain a notion,
To someone who knows only
what's real?

Ila Standlea Steinke

Ila Standlea Steinke
An Autumn Invitation
Oh, won't you come along with
me
Down winding roads and broad
highways,
Up paths of vague asymmetry
While Autumn gives us golden
days?

Look! Here a trail leads up a hill.
Oh, won't you come along with
me?
And here's a creek that turns a
mill.
Let's linger here in fantasy

And listen to the rhapsody
Of Autumn's orchestra of sounds.
Oh, won't you come along with
me?
Imagination knows no bounds.

Let's treasure Autumn while we
may,
Enchanted days of mystery,
For all too soon she'll go her way.
Oh, won't you come along with
me?

D. Kay Ayles
**An Epitaph Entitled
Confusion**
Upon the tombstone in this
grave illusion

Is her own epitaph
the word confusion.

With the rising sun a virtuous
child is born,
Oblivious of the outside world
unmindful of any fellow beings.

Peering through the wrong side
of the looking glass
Finding herself becoming
someone else,
Surrounded by the burdens and
temptations
of this evil world.

Trapped in a windowless cell of a
world she never made,
A guiltless one now falling from
grace
of this puzzle called life.

Souls come cheap, some give
theirs away.
I want to break away, prove I am
alive
and shall be free.

With all my strength I reach for
the
grasp of that guiding hand.

I want to survive the alluring
circus
that revolves within me.
Is this real or am I dreaming?

Suddenly darkness falls all
around me,
I am destroyed . . .
Now I am safe in the arms of my
angels.

Tammy L. Stanton
SAILING
Sailing is a precious thing
To the feeling of being free.
Just gliding on the water
Drinking cups of nice hot tea.

A fisherman will fish.
A suntanner will tan.
And sometimes you will never
Want to be back on the land.

Cheryl A. Hermanowski
I LOVE YOU
I will love you, as long as the sun
shines,
As long as the birds will sing.
I will love you for all eternity.
Never once shall our love fade or
grow old.
Always it will remain fresh and
young,
As the flowers in the springtime.
My love for you is all my life,
And my world revolves around
you.
Without you I would be
Like a bird with no wings,
Or rain with no place to fall.
Like a puppet without strings,
Life has no meaning when you
are gone.
I love you now,
Will love you in the future,
And in the everafter.
My love for you is so emotional
It overwhelms my way of
thinking.
Thoughts of you are always
creeping into my mind.
An hour never passes without
thoughts of you in mind.
My dear, I need you near me,

To keep me close all the time,
To protect me and love me
As much as I love you.
Please keep your promise
To love me always,
Just as I will Always love you.

Aletha Marlene De Angelis
Understanding Sympathy
I understand the sorrow,
Deep within your heart you feel,
Your greatest world's lost
     treasure,
Chosen words cannot reveal,
The hurt inside, going deeper,
Than within your heart and soul,
Not knowing where to turn,
Or which way, that you should
     go.

So, remember, I'll be praying, for
God's help to you each day,
That God will give you courage,
Along this hearbreaks highway,
I'll pray that God will keep you,
Ever in His care,
Whenever you need a real true
     friend,
He'll be standing there.

It's hard to say, I'm sorry, because
These few words cannot reveal,
The sorrow that in my heart, for
     you,
You know I really feel.
May God bless and guide you,
Today and evermore, and
May He give you understanding,
To carry out His chosen chores.

God always be with you,
All your loved ones too, and
May you remember, the honest,
     true,
SYMPATHY, deep within, I feel
     for you.

L. R. Chidester
NIGHT VISITORS
On cat soft paws
through velvet night,
just as my mind
gives up the fight,
the thoughts creep in
and snuggle near.
And I accept them
with no fear.

They often visit
in this way,
part of the night
with me they stay.
But once I settle
down and sleep,
up they get,
and off they creep.

Elio Francisco Schettino
IN COLD, IN DARK
Long ago, remember, there was a
     colored garden,
And some maiden you knew, now
     lost.
Is it not beautiful that the bright
     thoughts
Seem always to come roaming to
     the worst places of cold?
The maiden, now, was not your
     love.
But think you, if you returned,
     that she would be it now?
Surely you would make it so.
From this dark is much desire
     generated,

In new and better—colored forms.
Far from the eyes, far from the
     heart, they say.
And then, does the mind or the
     soul—
Or do both together—
Play fantastic wizardries with
     what the eyes
Left behind?
Do they change and model it
So that
Incandescent shapes of it
Burst new upon the utter dark?
Warp it!
Do they mayhap twist it?
In the black, it then swirls to
     weird
Or grisly
Flashings.
But you are comforted, for your
     garden
Of long ago
Seems to keep its olden shape
And the maiden, she
Is yet normally beautiful.

Keotah M. Fannin
THE LAST JOURNEY
The old man stumbled
     His watery eyes glared ahead
In a flash of lightning
     He saw the house, saw the
     shed.

He pushed against the wind.
     "Would this journey never
     end?"
The shadows grew longer
     He smelled rain, heard thunder.

"Oh Mary, wait for me
     I'll not be long, you'll see."

He reached the empty house.
     "Were those crosses on the
     hill?"
He pushed open the creaking
     door
     He was home, all was well.

He stumbled to the kitchen
     He sat upon a chiar.
Through the shattered windows
     He saw the lights, heard the
     choir.

The glamour lit his eyes
     A quiver struck his chin.
And as the storm raged outside
     The angels came, soft and dim.

And God reached down
     Lifted up another soul
And on the dusty old table
     Left a broken sugar bowl.

Don L. Robbins
CURSED MISFORTUNE
The past forever finds me
Along his path I went;
In his jaws, agony
Leads one to resent.
What is this curse
With which I must deal?
Leaves me to thirst
Like torment before the kill.

What is his nature
Must he linger still?
Always leads me to danger;
Could it be the way I feel?
Must he grieve me forever?
Can I stop him at will?
The pain I must endeavor
Leaves me with my fill.

I must keep going;
The work seems never done.
Still I am longing
For the rising sun.
The darkness taking misfortune;
Leave it to its grave.
The sun shares a new tune
With it to be brave.

Jackie Harriot Morgan
West Indian Ghetto Child
Ghetto child, standing there,
     staring
through, sad, bulging eyes,
     illuminating
an innocent, tear—stained face.
My dear child so scantily clad, in
     your
thread bare shirt, showing limbs
oh so thin.

Tell me child, how long have you
     been
standing in this narrow filthy
     lane?
In which of these old run down
     shacks
have you been place to exist?
Little quiet soul, please tell me,
     where
has your mother gone?

Oh! maybe gone since the break
     of day
to wash, and wait, and serve, in
     some
palatial mansion, high up in the
     suburbs.
So you are left alone to run, and
rule your life this day.
To roam around, to search and
     beg,
And even steal to stall your
     death.
Child, I know how those hunger
     pains
do hurt; cause, some time ago,
     they
Scourged me too.

And when mom returns my dear,
     you
may then have found the sweet
     relief
of sleep in your ragged make shift
     bed.
And maybe frolicking in your
     dreams
with her, and even your long lost
     dad.
In such a happy home, with teddy
     bears,
and sweets, and warm delicious
     meals.
Oh Ghetto child, in this hostile,
     violent
slum, with all this grinding
     poverty,
Please, don't be afraid to smile
with me, because this was also
     home
for me.

Judy Kelly McLain
HOPE IS A FIRE
Hope is a fire,
When kindled it ignites
'and consumes the one's being;
As the flame grows and mounts
     to a peak,
The indocrines flow from within'
and the hearth becomes hotter
     and hotter'

with every new spark of fire;
When the fire reaches its acme'
The entire being is absorbed'
and then starts dying down'
with each handful of piercing
     sand thrown upon it'
'til it is finally snuffed out
'by the piling sands of life,
and only the dry crisp ashes are
     left.

Joyce A. Beck
MANLY TEARS
[My Dearly Departed Husband
Duane A. Beck]
Why is it not manly
for a man to cry,
for some may say
it shows he's weak
to cry and shed
a few honest tears.

For crying is the way
to cleanse our soul,
to clear our hearts,
to give relief.

GOD made men
and he gave them tears,
HE never said
that they were weak.

HE gave men tears
to give relief

Jessica Cheramie
SAVIOUR
A cool wind blows, soothing my
     mind
     of those incautious thoughts.
What rash actions I might have
     wrought had you not entered
     my life.
You gave me hope and love,
     making
     me believe in myself when no
one else cared.
you gave me strength and
security when my
     last thread of hope snapped.
I thank you for it, I love you for
     it,
     and hope we'll be ever at each
     others
     side when the need of another
person
     comes again.

Darrell D. Seibert
One Eternity, Two To Share
The Sun has quietly faded
     into the West.
Just as my Love beneath
     Earth's crest.
Her form has vanished

59

from mortal sight . . .
Much as light of day
becomes darkest night.
The dreams were many that we
did share.
Waiting, watching, wondering,
if any would care.
If, we were together
or far apart
No one knew we shared
a single heart.
Love for each other
and our family of two
Embraced by turbulence, worries,
but much happiness too.
The Heart was shattered that
one fateful day.
The last breath was gone . . .
crumpled she did lay.
Alone in memories and dreams
so grand
She passed a sigh, then left this
troubled land.
Someday, somewhere, on a long
lonely path
The Heart will again be joined,
again to laugh.
The memories that were shared
in days gone by
Will be lived with laughter—
never a cry.

Arline
WOOF!
*[Dedicated to Chico's family:
John and Cora—who have
joined him . . .]*
Chico was a Christian,
He lived so free of sin—

With his first bark
At heaven's gate,
St. Peter let him in . . .

Kenny Morgan
RAINY NIGHTS
These rainy nights are lonely,
Although you couldn't know.
I wish you were my one and only,
For I really miss you so.

These rainy nights are dreary,
So dark, and gloomy, and wet.
I've always wanted you near me,
Since the very first day we met.

If I could have a million things,
To have and to keep,
I'd pick you, and the rest in days,
Foy my love of you is deep.

Maybe one day in the future,
Of course I don't know when,
We could get together,
And start all over again.

I know I'm only dreaming,
When I think of you,
But the words that I have said,
Are, my love, so true.

These rainy nights are quiet,
So lonely, gloomy, and dark.
But now I cannot change it,
Though I love you with all my
heart.

These rainy nights are over,
And now, at last, I'm free.
For as much as I love you,
I wish that you loved me.

These rainy nights have ended,
But my dreams for us never
shall. . .

Lainie Belcastro
JUST THE OTHER DAY
*[Dedicated to my Dad, Patrick
G. Belcastro]*
Just the other day, we drove down
this way.
I remember you saying how
Spring would soon be here, and
how you so looked forward to
the newness of that Season;
How we laughed when you said
you were planning to take me
on a special holiday for no
other reason, than the two of
us should get the chance to
know each other,
After all, we've only been married
some thirty-five years now.

How often I wondered where all
those years together had gone,
Somehow, I guess, they scurried
along with the family we raised
and the ups and downs that
filled the pages of our own
personal book of life as man
and wife.

And just the other day, I
overheard you say to our
eighteen year old cat,
Madeline, that she should
prepare herself for retreat, since
the weekend was bringing our
grandchildren that we both
love so,
But, did we ever know, that just
the other day, would be your
last, blended with the past of
many;
And this weekend we would
indeed all be here, except you, .
my dear.

Oh, if I could have just one, last
wish as I leave you alone here
today,
I'd wish for the precious
simpleness of being with you,
as we were,
Just the other day.

William J. Cole
THE DREAM
Each day will pass in this dream
of mine, with it's happiness and
it's sorrow.
But the question that's always
haunting my mind, is will it
last until tomorrow?
For to hold a dream for such a
long time, and to want to make
it real.
These are the things I hold

inside, when people ask how I
feel.
I feel a burning desire, a desire to
keep what's mine.
But one enemy I'll always have,
and that's the hands of time.
So I hold onto that dream of
mine, through a tightly held
fist.
Only to realize when it's gone,
how much it shall be missed.
I left a world of darkness, to find
a world that's free.
So I searched to find that golden
torch, to light the way for me.
I found that light of freedom, and
it was plain enough to see, .
That among a mans many
dreams, comes the end, the
tragedy.
I end this poem with thanks, to
the people that I knew,
But don't you worry people, for
the dream will again come true!

Marie Mc Bride
SUNRISE SONG
[For Bill on his birthday]
Here's a sleepy morning sunrise
For the flickering candle in your
moonlight eyes
And for the hands that feel like
earth
Folding me to the deepest, safest
part,
Warm from the embers of that
smile
Shining up from somewhere deep
While healing your own heart
That makes me moan and laugh
and ache
To give it back the best a woman
can,
If there should be a way to edify
The soul of such a man

Brett Newcomb Harkey
WHO?
*[Mr. & Mrs. B. Frank
Montgomery]*
Who can I turn to in time of
despair
Who can I talk to and know they
will care
Who can I trust from day to day
Who offers help along the way
Who shares wisdom acquired
over years
Who waits ready to share my
tears
Who brightens my day just being
around
Who helps me up when I fall
down
Who shows kindness in every
way
Who always has cheery words to
say
Who will sacrifice more than I
know
Who can feel pain, but not let it
show
Who wishes well—being on
everyone
Who can feel anger, but hatred
toward none
Who always contributes more
than their part
Who do I love with all my heart?
     My Grandparents

Susan A. Juvet
ODE TO WELFARE
Welfare is the way to live:
Endure their looks; to you they'll
give
Food Stamps in exchange for
pride—
No matter, that's already died.

You walk inside with dignity.
The front desk says: "Leave that
with me.
You won't be needing such things
here.
You're now like all the rest, my
dear."

"Turn right and crawl through
the first door,
And join the hundreds; there'll be
more.
Here's your number—Just sit
tight.
They'll get to you some time
tonight."

You peer into the steel—grey
eyes
Of caseworkers: You note
face—lines
Of hardness, coldly etched by
years.
Of indifference to suffering tears.

"I'm sorry, dear, but you've no
proof
That your child lives beneath
your roof.
And what's more, you've
neglected here
To state your earnings for last
year."

"But we shall help you. First you
must
Rid of your car and ride the bus.
A letter from your landlord
stating
Cost of rent where you are
staying."

You gather up what face you've
left
And shuffle out—you've passed
their test.
You're eligible for poverty;
Now you can get up off your
knees.

You're leaving now, defeatedly,
The front desk eyes you
curiously;
"Correct me if I'm wrong, please,
Ma'am,
But weren't you taller when you
first came?"

Beth L. Senturia
ODE TO A LOST SISTER
*[To my sisters in Israel, Vered
and Ricky]*
Once upon a summer's moon
We were together.
Once, oh so long ago
In the sweet summer sun
We ran through fields together.
Once we were inseparable.
Days were happy, dazzling
Nights were peaceful;
We were together.
Once, oh so long ago
We travelled together,
You and I.
We laughed, we cried
We hugged, we cared.

Now they give you a gun
And send you off to fight a war
    we did not make.
Will we ever run again,
Like we did once, oh so long ago,
You and I?

Joanne Mounier
MURALS IN A BARN
In the back hills of Tennesee
    concealed among streams and
    shrubbery stands a barn.

At first eye: a white, hazy
    brilliance shone
    stepping closer,
A man-made tribute to the woods.

Indian steps taken,
    a broiling sun soaked my shirt
before fully in the clouds.

Once inside the mausoleum
    the darkness tangled my legs
I was chained in time.

A cool draft came down the loft
    that brought ancient shadows
I was naked in the chillness.

A bit of cloth
    in an amber dark corner
caught my eye.

A certain solitude,
    a dirty dress
that was carelessly misplaced.

Urgently rung
    a shot grasped my ears

My feet carrying me
    out of this transition.

Straight through boiling walls,
    to wake up between cool sheets.

Peggi D'Amato Goins
I HEARD THE MUSIC
I heard the music thru the trees.
With breathless hope I flew!
I felt his presence in the air,
    the man that I once knew.

The wind was whispering softly
    now—
"You must hurry" to my feet.
My heartbeat quickened at the
    thought
that soon our eyes would meet.

I knew that with the path's next
    turn
we'd fall together then!
But instead I opened up my
    eyes—
it was morning once again.

Nyoka Pondt
LEAVES OF LIFE
My life has been just like a book.
The first pages unsoiled, clean,
    and slow,
Then gradually quickening as
    henceforth I grow.
My ravenous mind was greedy for
    life;
Always eager to reach the next
    page
Now reluctant to proceed in my
    old age.
I've lived through countless
    chapters,
Seen loved and hated come and
    go.
But what comes at the end, I do
    not yet know.
The beginning pages of my book
    are now worn and thin,
So many times have I read them all,

things my memory could clearly
    recall.
But what of me when the last
    page is in place?
Will another volume be my
    restitution,
My gift, payment, or restitution?
My enthusiastic view of life has
    dimmed.
I once felt young, and radiantly
    free,
Now that's just a part of my
    memory.
At least I saw the words "the end"
    before they came.
I cheerfully lived my life in full,
And although it has neared it's
    end, I loved it all!

Kevin White
AS TIME GOES ON
As time goes on, your face, never
    to come in view of my eyes
    again, has made an everlasting
    impression on my heart.
The time we spent together has
    slipped away into cherished
    memories, and my only desire
    is to recapture those special
    moments we once shared.
Time goes on and so do our lives,
    but the emptiness in my soul
    will forever yearn for the
    warmth and peace of your
    smile.
As time goes on . . .As time goes
    on . . .

Walter David Bond
TOUCHING BOTTOM
Upon a silent mountain top
my spirit emptied, drop by drop,
to the far—off summoning sea
drifting softly, resignedly.
I'm leaving at last this mortal
    flesh
for open waters so cool and fresh,
to settle below those pathless
    seas
far from lifes iniquities.
So behold . . . I am in paradise,
and it only took my sacrafice.

Christopher W. Young
DISDAIN—DE—LION
Rooting through the kelly green
    with bare patches in between,
overtakes he, the slower green,
    with yellow, all eyes have seen.

Jagged edges slicing through the
    lawn
    sending up pom poms, at the
    crack of dawn.
Few folks appreciate the
    unending yellows in the grass,
    obtaining disdain looks, from
    the foiled, as they pass.

Yet life be his, who sets his roots
    down deep,
    if needed during calamites,
    resources he can reap.
Although a never ending battle,
    survival will be won.
If not because of his aging
    roots, new birth of a son.

As like the master, who ruled
    above the nest,
    the son will parallel, with
    unending rest.
He'll fight to be noticed, for
    majorities to see.

Although outnumbered he
exists, remaining here, to be . . .

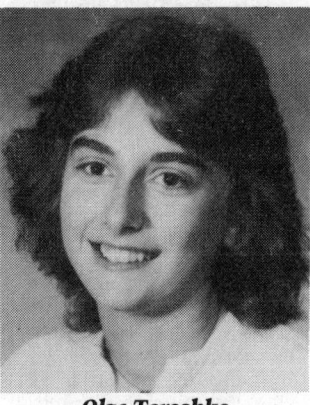

Olga Tereshko

Olga Tereshko
Taking It Day By Day
Say, whatcha think you're
    doing—wasting your life away,
If you can't break it all together
Try taking it day by day.

Hey! What happened? Was it too
    much stress
How did you get yourself in this
    terrible mess?
There are others out there, its not
    only you
Millions got hooked on it, too.

I often ask the question "why"
You felt the need to get so high.
Look at yourself—just look in the
    mirror
The stuff you're taking is a real
    killer.

Maybe you think you just can't
    cope
Is that why you're always pushing
    dope?
Popping pills—
        Is that how you get your
    kicks?
No wonder you're in such a fix.
Is this how you get your thrills?
Don't be fooled—that stuff kills.

You're wasting your life, Lord, I
    know.
Next time, please say "NO".
You might ask the question
    "how?"
Well, don't live for yesterday—try
    living for now.

Shamil Kubba
HOLY WEDLOCK
[Dedicated to a Flower (in my
    heart).]
Let us not brood on our
    yesterdays.
Rather, let us dream of our
    tomorrows.
When the sun's rays will shine
    through the mist and the
    trees.
To resuscitate our haggard hearts,
    and
Weld them into holy wedlock.

Truman Miller
SOLITUDE
I saw it there a clinging shrub
On natures cliff above,
A Rhododendron fresh and sweet
Made me think of God's love.

A waterfall had formed it's way
And fell to depths below,
And as I gazed upon this scene
It made me think of living
    streams
Where "Living Water" flows.
The petals were as living youth
That bloom as of today,
But some had lost their grasp to
    hold
And silently slipped away.
But some still lifted up their face
To look to God and all,
As one by one the petals fell
Beside the waterfall.
First the shrub and then the bud
And then the blushing bloom,
It goes to show that God is love
And time will end too soon.
And as the shrub this is new
    birth,
We too must bloom and go
Back to the earth as God has
    planned.
Our Spirit then will ascend
His promise is true I know.
Rooted there, in God's care,
The shrub held it's place,
As those who seek to share God's
    love
And grust in "saving Grace".

Theresa Kiko
FREE
Free
Like icy winter winds
That howl in isolation worlds.
Like snowflake patterns on panes
    of glass,
Like skater's dance on frosty
    pond,
Like deer whose tracks are of
    flight,
Like the evening moon that
    warms the night.

Jessie Adams Stevenson
TO A BREEZE
Of all the seasons of the year,
Spring's the one I hold most dear,
Many poems are written of its
    beauty,
But I believe it my solemn duty,
To add to those about birds and
    flowers,
The babbling brooks and shady
    bowers,
The meadows green, the lofty
    trees,
Something else which no one
    sees.
A breeze it is I have in mind—
Anything nicer is hard to find.
A breeze so gentle, soft and mild,
Reminds us of a lover's smile.
It's our Heavenly Father's silent
    way
Assuring us of His care, both
    night and day.

Raymond M. Squire
Laughter Here and Hereafter
Laughter is sweet to the ear
It's music with notes bright and
    clear.
Laughter is lilting and lifting
Like a puffy white cloud is
    drifting
And dreaming its leisurely way
In an indigo sky on a summer day.

Laughter's a soft, playful breeze
Whispering in a tree full of leaves
Until they start jigging and
    dancing
Then uncontrollably prancing!

Laughter's like a clear, flowing
    brook
Gurgling over each stone and
    nook;
It bursts from a heart full of love
With a joy that comes down from
    above.

I'm sure that our Lord loved
    laughter
For He left us a legacy long after
His brief stay here upon earth
Of His joy and His humor and
    mirth.
So now we can look forward to
    laughter
In that bright, joyous land of
    Hereafter!

Bruce R. Lindsay

Bruce R. Lindsay
ISLAND OF KAUAI
Conceived with love, born to a
    sea
From the womb within the earth
And God did sire in volcanic fire
So was this island given birth

Sculptured by the hand of God
With mountains and crystal
    pools
Though rain and fire, wind and
    tide
And eons of time be his only
    tools

And in the genesis of creation
I envision within my heart
God did decree, this land shall be
His masterpiece of living art

In "Fern Grottos" tranquil beauty
In solemn wonder I halt and stare
To rival the "Garden of Eden"
Or could it be, I am there

I gaze at the mountain summit
Where the endless rainclouds
    rest
Vegetation caressing every slope
As a child to it's mothers breast

And the heavens speak in
    reverence
A mortal craftsman I am awed
As the voice of thunder echoes
Behold! The artistry of God!
Linda Mae
KISSES FROM HEAVEN
I am pretending that every raindrop
    falling is a kiss from you.

A kiss that soothes dry, brittle
sadness with cool moisture.
A kiss that gives renewed
    strength
to fallen memories.
A kiss that brings the sparkle
back to love.
A kiss that makes me bloom.
Louise S. Jones
A NIGHT LONG AGO
The sheep were listless
As the night crept by
While shepherds sat restless
Listening to their cry.
Then out of the night an angel
    came round
With glory so bright they all fell
    down.
Be not afraid the angel said
For tidings of great joy I bring
Unto you this night is laid in a
    manger, a King.
The babe you shall find wrapped
    in swaddling clothes,
Where if you follow the sign
You will find Him there.
Then a multitude of the heavenly
    host sang—
"Glory to God and to all
    mankind,
Peace on earth their voices rang."
Then as they departed and
    darkness enveloped the night
The shepherds still startled saw
    the stars light
They rose as from a dream
And left that night to find their
    King.

Oleta Bond Kendall
OFFERING
[To Ted, whose hands have
offered me nearly fifty years of
happiness.]
Never has he brought me red
    roses .
With long stems done up in
    green tissue
And a little card saying, "I love
    you."
But one day in spring he said—
    out of the blue—
"Come with me."

"Do I need to powder my nose?" I
    asked.
He answered with a smile and a
    shake of his head
So I dried my hands on my apron
And closed the door behind us.

When we reached the top of Old
    McBee
He stopped the car and turned to
    me
"Stay here," he said, "there may be
    snakes
This time of year."

I heard him whistling as he
    disappeared
Beyond the crest of the hill . . .
. . . to return with hands done up
In wild lupine and buttercups.
Ann Bullard
Yes Jenny the Sun Is Shining
A little girl wrote to me, this is
    what she said,
My daddy had a stroke last night,
    now he is dead.
It rained all yesterday and all

through the night,
But today the sun is shining so
    very bright.

Yes Jenny the sun is shining

The stars are God's eyes watching
    us,
The sun proclaims God's love and
    understanding;
The breeze is God's breath upon
    our face,
And when we feel the grass we
    feel God's hand.

Yes Jenny the sun is shining

God's love has no limit, His grace
    has no measure,
His strength no boundary known
    to man,
For, out of His riches in Jesus—
He giveth and giveth and giveth
    again.

Yes, Jenny the sun is shining

Arlone Mills Dreher
MY DEAREST FRIEND
[December 9, 1900—Margaret
Edwards Stevens, Devoted
Mother, musician, journalist,
gardener, historian and more—
much more.]
The world today has turned to
    gray.
My dearest friend has passed
    away.
Her lovely soul crept deep into
My heart and trust—so loving,
    true.
I'll miss her lovely smiles and
    words;
The joy she had for trees and
    birds;
Her love when others met
    despair—
Her dreams were mine and I was
    there.
She has not gone—She's just away
Awaiting me another day.

Carole Ladrech
YESTERYEARS
Reflecting back on yesteryears
Brings to my eyes many tears.
Some of sadness, some of joy.
Younger days when we were coy.

Bashful babies in our teens,
Life never serious as it seems.
We'd never grow up or get older.
We'd always be young and never
    bolder.

Time passed fast, too fast it
    seemed.
Faster than we'd ever dreamed.
Those days of laughter, friends,
    and fun,
We never thought it would come
    undone.

So long ago we studied and
    played.
Our life; one big happy parade.
We did the best we possibly
    could.
Not thinking this would end, but,
    it would.

Everything lasts forever we'd say.
Never thinking we'd go our own
    way.
Only now in memories we can see.
Just the way it used to be.

Tracey Schlie
MAN
[To my mother, Thanks for
being there for me through
times of need. I appreciate the
time you spend with me. I love
you. Tracey]
A tear falls
On the rose
And inside
Deep inside
A lonely man
Unable in every way
But in every way he can.
For man has power
In his mind and soul,
To reach a certain point
To reach a certain goal.
And a feeling of success
When at its very end,
Man decides to reach out
To find he is a friend.

Darald Lewis Wells
KATHY'S POEM
Silent rose
With singing hands
Dancing fingers
With golden bands

Childish woman
Womanly child
With beauty of flowers
That grow in the wild

At times the Earth
Seems more like Mars
Beware of soft things
For they leave scars

If just one prayer
Could come to be
I'd pray to the Moon
Kathy remembers me
Karyn Marie Ballata
CREATED AS ONE
[To Peter, My love, my life, my
everything, I love you.]
Our lives together is a dream
    come true,
For within each moment reveals
    something new
A new allusion of passion
    burning with fire
Two hearts united as one in a
    forever endless desire.

To share our brightest hopes of
    all our tomorrows
To share our deepest thoughts;
    our bitterest sorrows.
To join our hearts, solely to be
    created as one
Securing our sacred love; of the
    ecstacy forever to come.

Through our lives, my love shall
    burn merely for thee
For equally is the bond of our
    everlasting desire to be.
A love forever exploding with our
    hearts,
Our love created as one; never to
    cease nor part.
Donna Fredericksen Lavas
LIFE IS
As we walk along the road of life,
The way is filled with sorrow and
    strife.

The childlike joys of our earlier
    years,
Fades quickly through our pain
    filled tears.

The hopes and dreams that we
  have spun,
Now quietly wait their time to
  come.

When we could show the world
  at last,
Just who and what and where
  we're at.

Instead of arms held open wide,
Rebukes are flung from every
  side.

It's when we learn that life is
  tough,
Just knowing something is not
  enough.

We must go home and start again
And get our strength from deep
  within.

Our image of the world we found,
Is not a place where love
  abounds.

We have our dream; we follow it
  through
And wait for the world, to make
  it come true.

R. Bateman Newcomb
NIGHT WALK
He walked the canyon of the city
  street.
The moon cast shadows on the
  bare concrete;
Like ghosts the autos passed
  without a sound
And all he found was silence all
  around

Patti Calderoni
FORGIVE ME . . .
I never told you how much I
  loved you
And for this I will never forgive
  myself
To think you expressed your love
  for me to the very fullest,
In such a way that not only
  enthralled but encouraged me.
And I, too young to appreciate
  your fidelity,
  was never able to find,
The response that I wanted you
  to hear.
Please my love,
Free me from this guilt and
  acknowledge my love for you
Your love was like no other, and
  so your memory
  too intense to fade.
Forgive me for never telling you
  how very much
  I love you . . .

LaVerne Frances Hentges
The Nearest Mountain
I tried climbing the nearest
  mountain,
  at least I thought I could,
Putting heart and soul in
  something, I
  just knew could only bring
  good.

It turned out it wasn't a real
  mountain
  at all, that made me want to
  make that climb,
But a special feeling down deep
  inside,
  I kept trying so hard to find.

My heart was high, there were
  tears in
  my eyes, as closer I got to the
  top,
As I looked over the edge, it was
  plain to
  see, a lesson was soon to be
  taught.

The view was the same, the air
  smelled the
  same, the sun warmed me just
  as before.
Then the cold rains came,
  heartaches remained
  tears flowing more and more.

So if you are looking to climb the
  nearest
  mountain, be prepared for what
  you will see,
Better to trust in God and His
  guidance from above,
  than climbing and searching in
  vain like me.

Rene' Grajeda
WISE MAN
I am a man of mystery
With many thoughts alone
I am one in three
And there's no one else like me
But if you search, I know you'll
  find
In the three there is only one
  mind
All I am is a unit of souls
That fit together but have many
  holes
My question for you is to listen
And I'll answer you with my
  intuition
To others I'm different
But that doesn't bother me
Because different is the only way
  to be
Weird or demented that's how I'm
  known
And that's why I stand alone
People are people and I am
  unique
With an indescribable mystique

Carolyn Walker
AND TIME GOES ON
Flowers grow and bloom in the
  spring.
I sigh at the joy and beauty they
  bring.
         And time goes on.

Grass grows so tall and green.
No lovelier sight I've seen.
         And time goes on.

Trees grow and reveal their prize,
Only leaves to unknowing eyes.
         And time goes on.

These things take recess in fall,
And until Spring, no life at all.
         And life stops,
         And time goes on.

Gwendolyn Trimbell Pease
4TH HAZARD
*[Kimberly Ann Slater, my seven
year old foster child, subject of
this peom and written at her
insistence. I was a foster child
myself forty-eight years ago.]*
4th afternoon warm
yearly days piled
shouting, outing
children wild

adults worse
tender rump
requires nurse
youngster did squirm
Bar-B-Q burn
for a short term
hurtfully did learn
another painful lesson
one spot to sit
the buttocks are it
uncomfortable place
we all suppose
well blistered case
heat simply too close
the bottom brand
was wholly unplanned.

Richard Layne Dingus
SIAMESE
*[To the red-eared, blue-eyed
devil—Albert—who helps
colour my life with his antics]*
Beloved imp, little blue-eyed
  devil;
Time has passed you by, and an
Eternal kitten you have
  remained.

You dart after each speck and
  invisible shadow,

Living your life in perpetual play,
  knowing
Without lesson the joy that each
  should feel.

And your affection, you bestow
  on all
You meet, as on your own master,
  filling
Your days with overflowing love
  and fun.

Andrea Schirtzinger
RUN AND HIDE
A man shot a bullet in the sky
  and shot a bird that couldn't
  fly. It made me want to cry but
  I wonder why. I wonder why to
  a lot of things. Like why we
  walk instead of crawl. I wonder
  why I care or wonder why I
  love you. A man shot a bird
  that couldn't fly. He fell to the
  ground with an awful cry. He
  ran and hid though he couldn't
  run.

Yolanda Sepulveda Trevino
DIVORCE CHILD
When two lovers fight and never
  get along,
It is better for them to part than
  to live in wrong.

For not only do they hurt each
  other, but their child instead.
For the love they had for each
  other is now dead.

They live in constant fighting
  and don't care if they live or
  die. But the child is the one
  that is hurt, and all it can do is
  cry.

He sees his mother crying, and
  his father out all day. He sees
  his father come drunk at night
  and hears his mother pray.

He grows up in an atmosphere of
  hate and endless tears. And as
  he grows up from his
  childhood, he remembers the
  suffering years.

His mother and father may love
  each other, they know that it is
  not right for them to be living
  together only to fight.

But who is the one who is hurt
  more deeply than you or I. It is
  the child who just stands by,
  being able to do nothing but
  just cry.

You and I can go our separate
  way and even though we loved
  each other, tomorrow is
  another day, but only the child
  is left hurt and alone with
  nothing to say.

Felicia Jeanne Nall
PICK A DREAM
Close your eyes, and pick a
  dream,
for dreams are free to all.
If life leaves you . . . feeling
  short,
a dream can stand so tall.

When all your plans seem empty,
and hope leaves you behind;
close your eyes, and pick a dream
from deep inside your mind.

There's always another dream—
buried deep inside you;
Such sweet escape in dreamland,
more dreams that might come
  true.

Dreams to keep you hoping,
come easy—and so free.
Dreams are there for anyone .
and they will always be.

Steven Johnson
WALK WITH ME A WHILE
*[To my wife Vicky and my
children Eric, Anne, Bradley
and Brandon—you are the
inspiration for my work—the
joy of my life.]*
Take my hand my son and walk
  with me a while,
I'll show you what I've learned, as
  we cover one more mile;
I'll teach you what I know, so
  that you will understand,
And I'll give to you the tools, that
  you will need to be a man.

I'll teach you right from wrong
  and what it is to be kind,
I'll show you that to be a man,
  you need more than a body and
  a mind;
Compassion, love and respect;

these are but a few,
These and other concepts, I will
try and teach to you.

Laughter and tears are all part of
life's lesson, this you must
learn,
And the respect of others you
will find, is something to be
earned;
Pain and grief must always be
tempered with tears of love and
joy,
And someday too, you may have
this talk with your own little
boy.

So listen carefully my son, and
heed these humble words,
In life you will find that battles
can be won with the heart or
the sword;
You will have to make your own
decisions when you become a
man,
I only ask that you remember
these simple words when you
take your stand.

Harlen A. Kirk
KEVIN
Kevin my infant son;
You are the very one;
I love more everyday;
Even if I don't say.

Together you and my love grow;
This I want you to know;
That I will be here;
Watching year after year.

As the years slip by;
We shall laugh and cry;
You I will clothe and feed;
Give any help you may need.

As long as I may live;
You will have anything I can give;
Because you are my son;
I love you little one.

Gale L. Martin
TWO WORLDS BATTLE
I sat on the beach alone, gazing in
awe
at the dark ominous clouds,
swirling in anger towards me.
The distant thunder rumbled its
warning to all who saw,
The fury barely released, my
destiny sealed already to be.
The waves dashed against the
rocks, sending a message into
the air,
"I am with you," whispers the sea,
"We are a pair."
I ran to my shelter and fell on the
bed,
I shut out the fury that raged and
fed
my pounding heart with wonder
and words unsaid.
I felt warmth steal through my
soul,
The terror left quietly as a gentle
touch chased the cold.
(loving arms held me close)
The storm swept out to sea paled
and weak,
the storm in my heart raged to a
peak.
Love battled, sought, cleansed,
freed,
leaving only a calm sea,

glistening sands, tender need.
Two storms abated, leaving peace
and tranquility,
natures struggle and my own
inability.

Rose Tideman
TO A SONG SPARROW
Go ahead and sing
you lovely thing;
let the vibrant notes
of your clear voice ring.
let the early morning's
rain-cooled air
fill with music—
free from cloud or care.

Go ahead and sing
for it is spring
and joy must come
to every living thing;
the winter-world has waited
for your magic note
so let your welcome song
swell your tiny throat.

Go ahead and sing
you lovely thing,
sing aloud and clear
for it is spring.

Anthony J. Ramirez
LET THERE BE PEACE
Peace isn't near,
It is far, far away
All the armies are at their battle
stations
I wish and hope I can live to tell
everyone,
Maybe I can help
If everyone will stop,
look around and say to
themselves
Do I want to die?
Do I really need and want to taste
the blood of death
Why do I hate my neighbor,
country, opposite country,
friends and myself?
We all need to be kind
Peace be with us all

Ruth J. Smith
MONEY TALKS
I wanted to write a poem
But couldn't construct a rhyme
So I put my hand in my pocket
And there found a nickel and a
dime.

They were conversing
As all good neighbors do,
Said the nickel, rather boastful
"I'm twice as big as you!"

With voice so sweet and humble
The dime then made reply,
"Even tho you are much larger,
Twice as much I can buy!"

Then the conversation ended
With each of them content
When to the store I took them
And both of them I SPENT!!

Faye Gordon-Hale
A ROSE GROWS
A field of flowers in golden array:
wakening to a glorious day.
Each stem waves gracefully in the
wind:
as each little breeze causes a
bend.

Then suddenly the gold turns to
red,

as men meet, firing chunks of
lead.
The wind sings a haunting
melody;
with each breeze crying pitifully.

Rows of stone markers have now
replaced
the field of flowers, long since
erased.
The wind no longer blows the
same way;
each little breeze, a prayer,
seems to say.

There's one tombstone with a
verse that reads:
"REST IN PEACE, FOR YOU'VE
DONE WELL, YOUR DEEDS.
The wind around it lingers, at
times;
the breeze sounds alot like
church bell chimes.

A single stem rises by its side;
from the tears shed by angels,
as they cried.
A single stem waving in the wind:
as each little breeze causes a
bend.

Ivan Hill
The Homecoming of 1865
As I work in my garden, here
beside the old mill
That's been long since forgotten,
and everything's still
I can hear rumbling horses and a
driver say, "Whoa!"
Down through the valley it
seems to echo

I pause at my work and lay down
my spade
In the sweltering heat, I take a
break in the shade
I can see the old stagecoach at
the top of the ridge
I wonder, why did he stop at the
Tanker House Bridge

In just a few minutes he's soon on
his way
And then disappears in the heat
of the day
Well, enough of this wondering, I
must get back to work
I picked up my shovel then
turned with a jerk

Familiar old voices I do seem to
hear
Both full of laughter, happiness,
cheer
Can't make out who they are, yet
I've heard them before
Why it's Henry and Carl, they're
home from the war!

Joan Kane Olsavsky
Life Sounds: Midsummer
the splash of juice
rising in my glass...
the slow, growing rustle
of a day on the ascent...
languid tick of a clock
intoning only seconds
letting minutes fall
where they will...
hammock creaking
its metronome beat,
cutting through quiescent air...
swing seat clacking empty,
Shawn is scrunching bare toes
in a sandbox...

dinner sizzles over spitting coals
teasing appetites...
I dawdle through a hushed
evening,
yawn my way to sleep...
outside, tree cricket senses the
season,
prays noisily all night.

Rebecca E. Larson
LONE WALKER
[For all who have felt the
loneliness of loss, for the
special few who have been
there in my loneliness, and
especially for my parents, who
have always been there.]

Where have you gone?
There is none at my side
The road is deserted
The trees sigh
as the lonely traveler
passes beneath their boughs
for they are helpless to shelter me
from the rain within me

The flowers turn their heads
so their bright beauty
might not mock my sorrow
And you are gone
Your shadow no longer
lights my path
leading, following
lingering
As a poem
without rhyme
So am I nothing
without you.

M.J. Yancey
WITHER
He sits
by the old stove,
whittling
away time.
The pile of sawdust
grows higher,
and he protests
when his daughter
sweeps it away.
"Dirty stuff,"
she says.
His blurred eyes
follow the broom,
but he is calm
when lead away
to bed.
Later, she shakes
her head and
whispers
to her husband
to hide the knife.

Today's Greatest Poems

Lyman West Harmon

Lyman West Harmon
GETTING BETTER
[This poem is dedicated to my wife, Verona.]
I had taken ill and could barely
   see.
My thoughts and thinking were
   mostly of me.
I was wondering if God was with
   me that day.
If he was, could he take some of
   my pain away?
The doctor had told me, "You will
   be all right.
Don't worry so much, but you
   have got to fight."
The nurse came in and said to me,
"Sir, you have a visitor you will
   want to see!"
I turned my head to look around,
   and
there stood my lovely wife safe
   and sound.
She had told me she was coming,
   but I knew not when.
She had said she would come to
   see me again and again.

Sometimes it is hard for people to
   be apart;
our love for each other will never
   part.
The smile on her face and the
   love in her heart
already made me feel better, so
   that was a start.
Our love for each other has been
   sublime;
I am sure God has helped us
   along that line.
I have said my prayers with a lot
   of thought
and thanked the Lord for all that

I have got.
When two people live to love
   each other so much,
It's really good medicine when
   they always keep in touch.

Helen Worley
SEA SHELLS
The tide flows in
   and with each rhythmic wave
steals bits of earth and
   sweeps them out to sea.
The land is less each time
   the encroaching waters ebb.
In time it seems
   the earth would cease to be.

Yet, when the tide retreats
   we find
   the coast is far from bare.
For now, in place of common
   sand,
The treasures of the sea are there.

As rhythmic minutes pass,
   life nibbles at our souls,
Erodes the fragile substance
   of the mind,
Until at last,
   our hearts swept clean
   of weaknesses and fear,
More precious treasure
   faith,
      is left behind.

Jay Colquitt Williams
Stranger To the Desert
The white hot sky cooled
   to a velvet blue,
And the dust bent
   to lie with the wind:
And darkness encircled
   the campfire hue of
A cowboy, its lonesome friend.

Alone in his thoughts,
   coals red and dying,
The cowboy crouched in the
   glow
   and listened to the wail of
A night bird crying,
   what the shadows of the desert
Don't show.

Cynthia R. Golderman
MODES-OCTOBER 1929
As from a great, horse-drawn
   sleigh,
   she stepped down from
the Cord's running board,
   wrapped in dotted silk,
a present from the rich to all...
      Polo match
outside of Easthampton,
   white ponies
      with Turkish blood,
and men whose sweat has to be
   called dew or gentlemen's
   perspiration.

Looking thru the binoculars
   bought in Germany, she lifts
those violet eyes, lids covered
   with golden blue,
little diamond horse-pin
   sparkling in the sun,
a game for ladies and gents to oo
   and ah over,
      mallets crushing
hardened ball to goal, swinging
   arcs of light,
   like an under-handed Blacksmith,
all are greased and set and
   pomaded,

real as life, in life,
realer and bigger, more than life,
   standards:
      Chanel and Molyneux,
diamond tarponed hat, caught
   with a rubied net veil,
over pert blonde head,
   short, and swept to the side;
cloche hat of beaver felt,
   matching her Paris afternoon
silk!
   Ah, such a Pastoral,
      sung with memory, theses on
   the riche,
nouveau and your Astor clan,
   Marquise and that sort of ilk;
an azure day in sun and blue,
   champagne in buckets,
toasts to health and money, and
   ends to wars,
such naivete,
   with such sophisticated
   flowerlets of youth,
ignoring fatal portentious
   happenings, forgiving all their
   sins,
forgetting all the truth, not seeing
   any flaws.

Doris Sinclair
THOUGHTS
Forgetting, is an art
That I have never learned.
The ashes never cool for me
Where once a fire has burned.

Rules are for fools
I contend,
As I mend my poor heart
Over and over again.

A week since we've met
Thus Eternity springs from the
   soul.
Low ebbs the tide,
No star breaks the gloom of my
   night.
A week is forever,
When Love is the game that you
   play.

I can shut out the sun
By drawing the blind.
But what do I do
For peace of mind?

Lila Newman
SHOCK TREATMENT
[For my husband, Ralph Newman and my sister, Pat Parker.]
I really view with alarm
The things they do in this Funny
   Farm.

"Take these pills—they won't
   hurt a bit,"
Then I'm lost—I'm really out of it.
The electricity hits—I don't feel
   the charge
But now I'm the Private and he's
   the Sarge!

NO! I want to have control,
I'm the owner of my soul!

He may be the best doctor they
   can mention
And do these things with good
   intention
But I could be a cripple for life.
These treatments just add to my
   strife.

It doesn't help to moan and groan,
When it's over I'm still alone.

He'll practice detachment to the
   letter.
When I'm home he won't check
   to see if I'm better.
He tells me not to feel what I
   feel.
He says my thoughts are wrong
   or unreal.

He has me balancing between
What he thinks I should be—and
   what I am.

He makes me feel worlds apart
From the center of my heart.
So I'll stop right here—go out the
   door.
I won't say anymore—and I won't
   look back.

I need to beware who uses my
   mind. It's only God
Who isn't blind to the rightness
   of my soul.

Nancy Roulias
Revival From Within And Our Reward
Let us make God happy, as He
   looks down on me and you.
I'm turning my life around and
   changing bad habits too.
Through prayer God can clear
   our minds of what to do and
   say.
He can do it, my friend, and He is
   just a step away.
We thought we were good, and
   being everything we should be,
But God didn't give up on us.
   Now I can plainly see.
We don't need to wander
   aimlessly in this life of ours.
Just trust in our God—He is the
   one that has the powers.
We will do all the things God
   wants and enjoy them too.
Just let God take you by the hand
   and daily lead you through.
When our Jesus comes, and in
   heaven all Christians shall
   meet.
We will see our precious
   Saviour—fall humbly at his
   feet.
There will be no more stumbling
   and falling along our way.
Just peace and happiness, if we
   obey His word to-day.
Jesus loves us—by our faith He
   will never leave our side.
He will rejoice and comfort us—
   His arms opened wide.

Linda Faith Lipsky
LOOK UP NOT DOWN
When life becomes a mountain
   and you don't know where to
   turn, look up!
When friends disappoint you
   there's a real friend in life, look
   up!
When the past keeps you down
   and you're filled with self hate,
   pity, there's a way to have it
   erased, look up!
When you don't know how to be
   happy there's a real teacher in
   life, look up!
Look down you'll see yourself and
   your problems.
Look up and you'll see Jesus, yes
   Jesus is waiting for you.

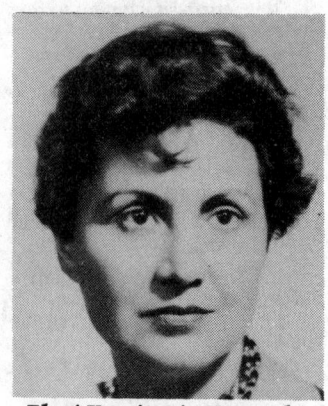

Eleni Katzingris Moustaka

Eleni Katzingris Moustaka
**THE ASTRAL JOURNEY
(The Propheci)**

*[For my parents Areti and
Periklis reading love through
sacrifice and godliness and for
my beloved son Nick Rally.]*
I fled through many skies,
    decorated with spiral
multicolored stars.
    When I began to get down,
I contemplated, in twilight sky,
    and splendid old lady,
dressed with one cloak, violet
    and embroidered
with golden stars.
    She took hold of globe
and I saw her blue eyes, crying,
    while looking at the Earth.
Suddenly I saw the future
    while I listened to one voice
vibrating in the Cosmos:

—Some night, there will appear,
    in the occidental
hemisphere, in the northern sky,
    one astroid joined
with one pleiad of others, smaller,
    like the moons
that suddenly started to fall,
    coming like a loose sun,
precipitating in the space...
    Advancing, it will provoke
fright, madness, suicides
    and even you, unhappy Earth,
under the attraction of that
    approximation, will incline
your axis, toward the left.
    Your new oriental reign,
will be burned and destroyed,
    becoming one dense fog,
like the one that covers
    the swamps.

Afterwards, in the oriental
    hemisphere
the northern sky, will remain,
    more CLOSER
and decorated with oval stars,
    having an EMPTY center,
while in the occidental sky,
    the same pleiad of stars
reaches the pilgrim asteroid,
    that will stare going up
slowly to the firmament,
    until it will arrive
at the center.

The western hemisphere looked
    illuminated, polished
with golden dust, that in contrast
    with the fog of the side,

looked like Biblical Paradise,
    where never will exist
martyrs of the drying, flood,
    ideologies, miseries
and injustices, the useless wars
    and lovely Earth
telluric convulsions.

Nellie Parodi
VOYAGER ONE
Voyager One,
miracle blazer of the stars!
Your fifteen hundred millimeter
    eye
sends us the revelation of your
    finds!
    Mariner, Pioneer, Orbiter
probing Mercury, Venus, Mars!
Now you, Voyager One, see
    Jupiter!
On your eighty-four hundred
    mile per hour course,
what do you see?
Boiling minerals, chemicals,
    sink-holes,
cyclones, active volcanoes,
    molten flow!
Where are the living creatures,
mountains, flowers, trees?
Where, the better world we yearn
    to see?
Voyager One,
what are you telling us Earth
    beings?
We search for life in other
    worlds,
yet, in spite of illness and wars,
    pollution, plunder, violence,
of all the planets of our Sun's
    family,
Earth is the only habitable one,
so beautiful, the best wherein
    to live!

Janet Pembor
**The Message
On The Mirror**
What can I give you boy,
    To shape your faith in strong
    relief,
I who walk a tightrope
    'Tween doubt and disbelief,
A cross you can wear proudly
    Or keep hidden in your vest?
A Bible, thoughts of other men
    To lock up in your chest?
I'm giving you a mirror.
    Reflect your own, not mine,
And keep your vision evermore
    In keeping with the time.

The gifts that you receive today
    Are not just yours to keep;
The Lord does not have favorites
    There is no cause to weep.
With other boys of other faiths
    In places far apart,
You know you have a conscience,
    The mirror of your heart.
Whenever life has wronged you
    To favor other men,
Take the mirror from your pocket
    And search yourself, not them.

Should you find a lose a woman
    Who's the mirror of your soul
She was the mirror only
    Not the Master, on the whole.
Look not into your mirror
    To find eternal youth,
You'll always love yourself
    If you seek eternal truth.

If you find yourself unpleasant,
    Just turn it to the wall,
And on the back you'll see
    inscribed

    "The Truth Applies To All."

Gerda Fischer-Darosci
KADDISH! KADDISH!
*[To my beloved parents! To
Uncle Josci, Aunt Ruth, Tante
Grete, the 22 Jewish women
(Gestapo Death Transit Cell
Vienna 1943) of which only 4
survived & to my Doctor Ira
Steinman who makes me
remember & write: "Gateway
to my Mind".]*
Although I prayed often for death
I'm so glad now to be alive
I'm nobody's mother nor wife
But who would have say Kaddish,
    Kaddish for them?

Bottomless is human soul
Able to hold oceans of grief
Recollections of joy and of pain
Laughter, whispers and screams
Knowledge that pools of spilled
    blood
Profoundly affected my life
Painted my heart—and
Tried to dry in the crevasses
Of my soul—
Eternal is love!
Theirs—and mine!
Creating a shrine
So secret—that even I—
Never knew it was there . . .

I'm nobody's mother nor wife
Loneliness, pain was my life
With pen and paper I enter shrine
To stare at spilled blood
It's still moist in some places
And I see faces, faces, faces
So hungry for life—unlived joy
So hungry—like me
And now I say Kaddish, Kaddish
    for them—.

Lalu Shands Munroe
**Vienna, City Of Song And
Dance**
*[To the memory of my father,
Hubert Anthony Shands, who
was happy to know I had
inherited his writing talent]*
Vienna sang its joyous song of
    mirth,
While dancers pivoted in regal
    halls.
The chandeliers reflected their
    high birth
As marbled grandeur witnessed
    their great balls.
The music started off in three-
    fourth time
As partners bowed to partners's
    agile grace.
Bright gowns of silks and satins
    fit their clime,
For this fair city bore a northern
    race.
Vienna once beheld these courtly
    scenes,
Today its people seek the opera
    house
And other cultural arts within
    their means.
The Danube flows near by, which
    once thrilled Strauss.

Vienna knew his music very well.
Long loved it still can weave a
    magic spell.

Donna M. Mariner
A Love That Could Not Be
Two hearts pounding, beating
    feverously.
Two throats parched, gasping for
    breath.
Trembling, holding each other as
    one.
Wanting each other, ever so
    intensely.
Not daring . . . not wanting to
    hurt the other,
but longing, wanting, wanting so
    much for this moment
to last forever.
To love to the end for all time.

No . . . no; must go . . . lasting
    love; but must end.
Someday maybe, my love, we can
    have the world . . .
to share with one another.
For now, a love only in the back
    of our hearts . . .
to remember and touch with our
    fingertips and caress with
memories of old.
Still, a lasting friendship forever.
A love that could not be.

Susan Brown Cranfill
DREAMS
*[To my father, who often
inspired, and always
encouraged my dreams. I only
wish that he could have been
here to see this dream come
true for me.]*
I'd love to dream my life away
And not just live from day to day.
I'd love to sit in a window seat
And feel the sun give off its heat.
I'd love to float in the deep sea
And glide along water 'til
    eternity.
I'd love to fly high in the air—
Above the world, without a care.
I'd love to climb the highest peak
Never again my strength to seek.
I'd love to walk through a
    meadow of daisies
To sit and bask in the sun—so
    lazy.
I'd love to visit the valleys so low
Just to sit and watch the flowers
    grow.

Timothy Avean Barrett
THE GRIM REAPER
There's something strange
    happening in this town
You can smell it in the air, it's all
    around
It's death himself and he's reaping
    souls
He's here to possess you, to place
    you in his firey coals
There's no place to run, no place
    to hide
You are about to venture on this
    long sinister ride
The death ride you might say
Yes, the Grim Reaper is here to
    take you away
You're not the only one about to
    enter Satan's Den
There are many others that have
    also sinned

This is the night of the unforgotten memory
This is the night that you burn eternally

In the idle darkness, the end is drawing near
Your heart is pounding madly in fear

As you see the hooded face of this eerie unknown stranger
You scream in ghastly horror at the sight of this creature

As you look upon his sinking cold eyes of death
It takes away your precious breath

And in your last few moments of recognition
You discover the savage blade of destruction
Now you have reached the realms of death

Patricia Penton Black
FOR STEVE
[To: Steve Saywell whose wisdom and patience served as the path for my journey. Those who are my life, Lee; Tiffanie; Lorrie; Cindie and George, my gentle man.]

You are my friend, I have concealed no part of my being from you.
You never seem to offer a judgement on anything I say or any action done.
I care for you for this quality.
Many times I am so low within myself, I feel that only dying would bring relief.
But, then I share with you and I am better, more at peace.
The hurts I've felt and am still feeling are often close to unbearable.
You offer your hand to me and I know I'm not alone.
Kind of funny to think of the times I've begged to be left alone.
When in reality I want that least of all.
My friend, thank you.

Allison Penn Hawkins
FREEWILL
Down a narrow path I walk
Thoughts flowing, I do not talk.
A stream beside me, running swiftly
To a place that will end so quickly;
A red, red rose starting to bloom,
But soon it will die and be in its tomb.
A white-tailed doe nursing her young
Does not notice me as I travel on;
The tall green pines with their limbs up high
Protect the birds from predators close by.
My mind wanders to a time long ago
When I was a child and did not know
There was more to life than I could see

And if I was not careful, it could destroy me.
The whole wide world with all its fears
All its crimes and joys and tears,
But I'm in control of my life now,
And I will soon show them how
I will survive through thick and thin,
And should I lose all, I'll just start again.

Phyllis A. Menna
REBIRTH
[To Dale—a special friend, Always believe in love and dreams]
This state of Life, I surmise, is merely an extended dream
that by Universal decree
when this conscious dream does end
this earthly realm we'll leave
and our new form shall begin;
Our physical becomes Spiritual
as we evolve to a higher plane
all deeds of goodness rewarded
and the choice to begin again;
For another tomorrow, my soul, I would return
to the mystique of Life once more,
to grow in Love, Knowledge and Wisdom
greater than before;
For with each cycle we gain
another piece of God's cosmic puzzle,
which one day we shall complete,
and in the realm where God does dwell
our souls, our minds shall meet;
This state of Life, I surmise, is merely an extended dream
and when we finally wake,
our souls shall be redeemed.

Alvera C. Larson
THOUGHTS ON LOVE
Fortunate is he who has "Love"
As a tenant in his home,
And a keeper of his treasures.

Love thrives in an atmosphere
Of thoughtfulness, unselfishness, and gentleness.
Love must constantly be polished
To remain beautiful, sparkling, and glowing.

Keep the tender touch and warm embrace

As your "Open sesame".
Take time to share unforgettable precious things
A golden sunset, a child's lilting laughter.
Practice exchanging those endearing words
"I dearly love you".

Should bitter words become unleashed
And carelessly cut and injure
Summon the attendant, "I'm sorry",
To soothe and heal the wounds.

Remember—'tis the loving "little things"
That become priceless diamonds
In the web of life.

Arlone Mills Dreher
I WALK ALONE
*[July 8, 1907
For My Husband
John Hiller Dreher
A great father and wonderful husband.]*
Our best was the world when we shared it
For time paused and let us slip by.
Our dreams so often were wordless
But our hearts never stopped to ask "Why?"

We learned as we strolled life together
That sharing brings meaning and song.
We walked hand in hand toward the twilight
Believing no thing could go wrong.

Then Death dealt his blow with a vengeance—
A shuder, searing pain to the last.
Our path was broken by cancer.
Now I walk alone in the past.

Lela Diane Rouse
GRANDMA LOVE
As she pauses,
In wonderment of how the years have flown . . .
Her heart warms.
It seems like only yesterday
When first she held her own
Babe in arms.
So she watches,
In ponderment, this child of her child,
As the years flew.
So manyu times had he laughed and smiled
Saying, "Grandma, I love you!"
How she sees,
A young man, her grandson, fully grown . . .
Once so near,
Reminding her of smeone she had known . . .
She sheds a tear,
And she prays.
Should she tell him so he'd know?
Would it be wise?
Instead she waits,
Because she loves him so . . .

She only gives advise,
Trying to perfect mistakes made long ago.

Tammi A. Bolling
TIME GONE BY
Erased from my mind
Til I saw your face
Erased from my heart
Anticipation of a race
Forgotten was a love
We used to share
Forgotten til today
You were suddenly there
Lost is the truth
We loved so much
Lost is the feeling
When my body you touched
Tried to bring back
The love I once knew
Tried to believe
Love like ours is few
Yet lost is the love
Of time gone by
Lost in the wind
As a tear swept eye

Ben Gray
THE MAN WITH NO FACE
Once each week at visiting hour
To me he comes past prison tower
Feeling his way with guard in lead
To fulfill with love our mutual need

My breath does pant, my heart does race
At the gruesome sight of his ruined face
And I recall with pain the very day
I took the gun, shot his face away

Mostly gone the sight, the smell, the taste
Leaving ugly disfigurement in handsome's place
But my act to him alters not his goal
He still cares for me with impassioned soul

Though surgical skill could restore the looks
He spends his money on attorney's books
To give me pardon as he has done
For he is my father and I his son

Jeffrey Alan Hughes
THE LIMITS OF HOPE
A white dove did land upon a rusty cannon.
Before he could return to the sky,
I caught a flicker from his eye.
And after the paradox had gone,
My thoughts were carried on wings of hope,
Only to be shot down by distant echoes from
The rusty cannon.

Leisa Bain Good
Only Through the Shedding of Our Tears
Only through the shedding of our tears,
Can we polish the sparkle
Within our eyes.
A sparkle that reflects
His Rainbow,
Within our soul.

Julie A. Armacost
LOVE
[To all lonely hearts that have searched for LOVE in all the wrong places.]

If I could only touch your soul and let you know I care, I would remove your burdens, as well as your fears. I would give you courage for all the days to come and lead you through the darkness when night should come.

In the sunlight of tomorrow, we would walk hand in hand to where I would give you freedom to be a total man. For love does not limit, shackle, or degrade. Her eyes do not look for fault within mortal man.

Love seeks to give pleasure, as well as gentle care. She will share her powers, should you fall into dispair. She will heal with compassion, and understand your plight, and show you new horizons as you join in her flight.

Love longs to be your soul mate and places no demands for she sees the deep desires in the soul of mortal man. Freedom of movement and expression, a need of every soul is just around the corner to have and to hold.

For love, a free spirit will teach you her ways. She will guide you through eternity and the mystical way. Love is never forceful, with patience she waits, to show that you are special in a very unique way.

Reach out to recieve, freedom of the soul, and your eyes will percieve a wonder to behold. For love goes on forever, blessings to bestow, she will be your companion where ever you may go.

Terry Lynn Coulter
GIFTS
[To Mother]
Four tiny babies in bunty blankets soft and warm
were born to a mother one day.
Protecting and keeping her babies from harm,
in their cozy sweet cradles they lay.
As the new morning was breaking a little one died,
another the very same day.
And so to the bedside the mother retreated
and there on her knees she did pray.
Dear Father in Heaven You know my heart,
and Your plans are divinely Your own.
Now Lord in Your mercy I just pray that You
Will let my last babies be grown.
I'll never forget the kindness You gave me
the mother of four little babes.

And twenty years later her two sons and her
put flowers on two tiny graves.
She never forgot the Father above
on her headstone was written these words.
Sweet treasures You gave me the night that I prayed
first two You took and then two You saved.

Laura Brown Lane

Laura Brown Lane
PRODIGAL LOVER
Prodigal lover, come back to your home—
Back to our love, and to nevermore roam.
We still feel the glow of our love in the past—
It so brightly is burning, forever 'twill last.
I will ask you no questions and give you no pain—
So come back, and we will be joyous again.

If I open the door and I see you are there,
I will give thanks to God that he answered my prayer—
That my love who was lost now at last has been found,
And now has come back to me all safe and sound.

To welcome you back, who was so long away,
We will strike up bright music, and dance, and be gay,
I will feast you, array you, and deck you with gold,
As my lover again I will kiss and enfold.

Prodigal lover, come back to your home,
Back to our love and to nevermore roam.
Prodigal lover, come back to your home,
Back to our love and to nevermore roam.

Ruth L. Johnson
THE FIRST SNOWFLAKE
I saw the first snowflake come down
It seemed to lead the way
For all the rest of those white flakes
That floated down one day.

One lonely little snowflake
Ahead of all the rest
He floated down so gracefully
He'd done his very best.

The rest that followed were so gay
So turbulent, so restless
They swirled about, and twirled about
And clothed the earth in white dress.

And so the ground was changed that day
From green and brown to purest white
And when the flakes ceased coming down
The day had turned to peaceful night.

Doe Dee
A Shootin' At The Winchester Saloon
(Ode to John Greenleaf)
The moon shone bright that night
And the ring around it was wide,
The night the shots rang out
And the Winchester Saloon's owner died.

The band had just done a set
And had started on the second
When a woman got up to the 'mike'
Sayin', "bar's closed, everyone exit".

The patrons kindly obliged
All wonderin' what had happened,
Seein' fire trucks outside
And police cars with lights all flashin'.

They didn't know what went wrong.
The band had been playin' a song,
Cowboys and gals were dancin'
The "two step," or drinkin' along.

The night was just beginnin'
With everyone just havin' fun
Except for the varmit who
Thought to salve his pride with a gun.

Murderin' man had been drinkin' hard
And was told to leave the saloon,
But he, in a cowardly way,
Got his gun and did what he'd done.

Most everyone thought well of John

He was one "helluva" man.
On the other side of town
Joe's birthday party began.

Joe went out for a time,
He came back and asked all to leave
You see, John was his friend
And he was beginnin' to grieve.

Winchester won't be the same
Not without you, John, to run it.
Memories of you will live on—
"Farewell" from your friends here in town.

Jean Jousma
JOHN HANSON TRIBUTE
A modest myrmidon of the lord invincible
Conveys the nectar of the Word so amiable.
As his glorious voice vibrates within,
It sparks the soul's adrenalin.

The communication, in form, dydactic
So simplifying the Christian tactic,
The thoughts made easy to remember
Are an abiding aureole ember.

Sleep, the bored mind's distraction,
Dies amid the sermons attraction;
It is a voracious spirit's love banquet
Removing stanchions, explaining God's kismet.

Thoughts go beyond the buildings ministrate
In human aura compassion, humility emanate
acceptance, tolerance, love of all God's splendor,
A true shepherd, neighbor, mentor, pastor.

Danielle Anderson Dreyfuss
TRADE UNIONS
Plumbers, don't touch the lights!
Electricians near faucets, take flight!
Carpenters, stick to tinny tacks.
Cabbies, to horseless hacks.
Be timid and be wary.
Don't forget to carry your union card!
In this automatized, unionized labor force
Don't do another's work, of course!

Susan Rice Ware
SPECTER
My mom goes to bed
with a book and a beer some nights

both are consumed
or one is left to light

her way into tomorrow
She sits in the sun

afternoons when beds are made
and laid and dishes done

with wine and poems and dreams
We talk, but the mystery she keeps

will shape my own while at night
she stalks my sleep

Today's Greatest Poems

Pala Gregory
WINTER LOVE
The cracks in the sidewalk
aren't so intimidating
when I walk with you
and you hold my hand
nor is the wind so cold
with your shoulder close to mine.
Sharing a smile,
my steps quicken
to keep in stride
while the song you sing
keeps time with my heart.

Susie Jones
NEW LIFE
White Dove
Just one more day
And then I'll face
A brand new way
Of living.

Come fly with me
I need to find
Your purity.
For it's like you I want to be . . .
Gentle and Free
This wife to be.

Michelle Robert
ALONE — NEVER
Alone is not a word my child.
Said a voice of soft waves.
I wiped my eyes and heard the
    voice tell me
I'm with you always.

Never will I ever desert my
    children.
Look at the paths ahead of you.
Then look at the paths you have
    travelled
Do you see it was I who lead you.

So perk up my dear
Lets see the glitter in your eyes
A smile on your lips
And a joy in your sighs.

For you to be alone
Is that of the impossible.
For you will never be alone my
    child.

Kathy R. Nagy
The Love That I Have Lost
Thoughtful memories are
    concealed
Within my gloomy mind,
Of my loving father that I've lost
And wish that I could find.

It's hard for me to close my eyes
And open them to what is new,
But things will never be the same
No matter what I do.

I can't seem to realize
That he never will return,
Often times I fantasize
Of the dead "fire" again to burn.

If there's one thing that I am
    missing
It's his warm and loving care,
Whenever I had problems
He was always there.

Soon I've got to see myself
And leave the yesterdays behind
Because I've got a life to live
Along with Daddy in my mind.

No love will ever fill this space
Which is empty in my heart,
I just wish it wouldn't have
    happened,

'Cause I don't know where to
    start.
Now I'll leave you with my
    thoughts
About my one shining sun,
His rays still reach out to me
With sadness and with fun.

Barbara Overton

Barbara Overton
STRICKLY MECHANICAL
[To my parents, sisters, and
brothers, and to my daughter
Tracy who inspires me.]
All dressed up in human clothes
    with no shoes on their feet,
Push the button and they'd come
    marching all polished, shiny
    and neat.
It was amazing watching them
    perform, each one had his own
    task.
If there was something they
    didn't understand they knew
    better than to ask.
It makes one wonder what kept
    them going throughout the
    dreary years,
They didn't have time to collect
    any dust or even shed any
    tears.
It must have been the batteries
    they kept recharging over and
    over again,
Since they had to be mechanical
    without a choice, they'd be the
    best mechanical people in the
    land.

Nadine Sicard
DOGS THREE
Hello folks; I am a dog. My name
    is Bambi.
My fur is long and in my eyes, I
    can hardly see.
I live in a pen with another dog.
    He is shaggy, and his name is
    Fluff. I see and hear things
    going on. And I've about had
    enough.

You see, about four months ago, I
    gave birth to a baby pup.
It was a long, hard night of pain,
    but I never did give up.
The ground was covered with
    snow, it was cold as it could be.
Our pup was a beauty, a joy to
    behold. But, he was taken away
    from us when he was six weeks
    old.

Our keepers are a family of five—
    three girls, a mom, and a dad.

They are really good to us, the
    best masters a dog ever had.
They took our baby in the house
    to live just like they do.
I know just what is going on, I
    once lived there too.

He shares their food and heat and
    maybe even their bed.
I remember what happened to me
    and sometimes I see red.
I sneaked in bed with the middle
    girl. She was so warm and
    cuddly.
She caught a rash, and I don't
    know why, but they all blamed
    me.

I had to sleep downstairs in a box
    bed all by my self.
I cried and whined and tried to
    sneak right and left.
Then I said, "this isn't so bad." I'm
    still inside, you see.
I could be outside by myself with
    no sign of company.

Sometimes I see my pup when he
    comes out to play. He is so fat
    and very clean. He sure looks
    good that way. They treat him
    like a king. They love him
    dearly. I guess I can't complain.
    They aren't so bad to me.

The pup comes out and chases
    the cats all over the place.
He comes to the fence and looks
    at us. There's pride and joy on
    his face. If I could talk, I would
    say to him, "Don't hang around
    here too long. They may decide
    to let you stay and you would
    have to change you song."
Living a dogs life isn't so bad as
    long as you don't know, how to
    live like a king. Most dogs will
    never know.

Joan M. Springer
THE CHRISTMAS GIFT
Her rainboots squished as they
    met the pavement,
her fingers chapped from torn,
    worn mittens,
a face hidden behind a frayed red
    scarf.
The pounding of rain ignored as
    she brought her
gift of bread for her communion
    with the birds
who welcomed her, as people
    rushed on oblivious
carrying metallic boxes, garishly
    wrapped,
and elbowed each other as they
    boarded the bus . . .
My calendar read December 24th.

Nora Clark
FRIENDS
Loved ones,
like treasured objects, sit
upon the curio shelves of
my heart.

Darla Ann Horton
COUNTLESS
my hatrack is heavey, laden with
— i lost count — derbies. no
cleanser will lift the
mildew/lime from the tub in
which i linger. por que, big guy?
this dolls' string is stretched

from — i lost count - pulls.
kitty sleeps, & fathers' body is
amassed stitches/scars. idle.
ideal living that kills the weak.
we all want to die, flash out in
glory. i am a good—looking
corpse. fleur de lis placed
between my breasts; a petal
grazed nipple stone—cold. my
hatrack fills even more. now
there are berets & helmets in
the collection. reflection in a
t.v. screen test pattern. the
solitaire champ with no
stomach lining left. digestion
will not resume. my resume is
on file at — i lost count —
brothels. the motels are filled,
& i take in more guests.
sometimes i am guest/second
guessed. second best is fine. my
pen will not draw the line. my
razor blades are dull, & the
water heater isn't working. i
think — i lost count — of you
more & more, big guy. hang
your hat.

Ruth Livingston
I ASK YOU MUSE
Why do you sustain
me here? A mistress,
chained to my
souls compelling
urges and desires.

Attending me as I
lie abed, garbed in
moonlight you stand,
my sleep, held
tenaciously in your hand,

impelling me to
service, in my minds
sequestered space,
scratching symbols in
the dung I sprang from.

M. J. Steck
VALLEY OF THE SUN
Arch tall glory brown
Stare West
Never move by eye.
Silence
In stillness,
Lay
Breathing through snakes, lizards
Living slowly
Calm
Guard the valley surrounding
Camelback.

D. E. Schmitt
PROGRAM
In another room
Darwin is explaining
The concept of organic
Species modification
To Jesus
And I was laughing
At the myth of being
It was just like
A sitcom
On the television

Reagan Wilkins
GONE FOREVER
It is but a memory now
Days gone pasts
Like a fire blown out
In winters yearly bout
Our love is gone forever.

In the days of old

We could feel no cold
for we could feel but the warmth
   of love
which overflows.
Yet I live now, and now the fierce
   wind blows.
And our love is gone forever.

Mary Letha Washington

Mary Letha Washington
LIFE IS BEAUTIFUL
*[Dedicated to my dear husband,
Willie Washington, who has
inspired me through the years.]*
Life could be so beautiful
If we only took time to look,
If we only took time to listen.

Open your eyes and see,
Open your ears and hear
All of the wonderful things
We could cherish so dear.

God in all of his infinite wisdom
And all his wonders unheard,
Just waiting for us to look to
   Him,
And listen to his word.

Take time to see.
Take time to hear.
Life is beautiful.

Sally J. Price
A TROUBLED WORLD
*[To those who see what's
happening, know the Truth,
and do not fear.]*
You come to me
   a troubled heart.
   your eyes show
   the pain not expressed.
I come to you
   a troubled mind.
   my fears are your's
   the problems not solved.
We are together
   a troubled world.
   our voices unite,
   but no one hears.

Joyce E. Conklin
DEPRESSION
When the entire world is ending
   and nothing's right with you,
Just order up another drink
   and that will see you through.
When you cannot spot a single
   right,
   just wrong is all you see
Just order up another drink
   and then you'll start to see.
This cruel old world keeps going
   round
   and doesn't give a Damn

If anything is right with you
   or if your life's a sham.
Just order up your drink. . .and
   think
   of everything that's wrong
Then soon you'll see it fade
   away. . .
   and life becomes a song.
I drink for love. . .or hate. . .or
   maybe
   something in between.
I drink because I'm not the
   Pawn. . .
   and yet. . .I'm not the Queen.
I drink because I like the stuff
   and how it makes me feel.
I drink because my problems, then,
   appear to be unreal.
Just order up your drink
   and join me here today, right
   now.
Just order up your drink. . .
   and later on we'll have some
   chow.
We'll drink away life's
   problems. . .
   turn them into total bliss.
We'll drink because, save you and
   I,
   the world has gone amiss.

Alexander Martin
SORROW
If the sorrow that a man
must today sustain
were yet by tomorrow to prove
all in vain.
Would there in that same soul
be the might,
that through the darkness could
see a light?

Florence Mills
NOW THAT APRILS HERE
Now that Aprils here
   My heart doth sing;
The gentle breezes stir
   The leaves of spring.

And last nights rain
   Washed clean each bush and
   tree,
And made this garden spot
   A wonderment to me.

Edith C. Ledee—Dallas
JESUS, BE BORN
Jesus, Be born in my heart again.
Live in my mind and my soul.
Speak through my thoughts, use
   my words for good.
Make my broken spirit whole.
In a world of sin, please enter in,
and use my will as your own . . .
'til the world pass away, come
   that glorious day
when I worship 'neath Your
   Heavenly Throne!

Jesus, Your name how I love to
   speak,
when the ways of the world make
   me weak!
How I feel your love guide me
   from above!
Oh Jesus, use me as your glove
and point the way that I may not
   stray
from paths of truth and of grace.
For I long someday, when the
   world pass away
to gaze on your Holy face.
We who on Earth by God's choice
   do dwell

too often forget . . . or ignore . . .
the will of He who made us free;
the God whom we say we adore.
Forgive our thoughtless, selfish
   ways,
for we shall reap what we sow . . .
and let us be born in your love
   again,
and in your knowledge grow.

Frances McHugh Robins
STRESS
My God its all around me
Morning, noon, and night.
Where is the peace that I long for
Away from the stress and the
   fright.

Life just feels so lifeless
Empty, foreign, alone.
Last week without any warning
A burglar broke into my home.

My health has been in question
My marriage has fallen apart
My friends aren't friends any
   longer
All love has deserted my heart.

My job is driving me crazy
They want more than I can give.
Don't they know I'm a person?
I need my own time to live.

Things have got to get better
They can't continue this way
I don't have any more answers
I don't know what to say.

My God its all around me!
There is no end in sight.
Give me the strength to make it
Thru another morning, noon, and
   night!

Judy Catholos Lorenzen
GRANDMA
*[To my Grandma, Lena
Chamberlain Ramel, the
sweetest and the best Grandma
in the whole world.]*
G is for her *Goodness*, from her
   heart it always flows
R is for her *Radiance*, from her
   eyes you see it glow
A is for *Abundance* of her many
   giving ways
N is for her *Niceness*, how it
   brightens gloomy days
D is for *Devotion* of her never
   ending Love
M is for her *Many—prayers* to
   the Lord above
A is for *Always* giving of her time
   she gladly shares
   and for Always letting us
   know, that she Always cares

Garland Ennis Day
TURN AROUND TWICE!
Turn around twice, and your
   childhood is over!
For a very short period your a man!
Turn around twice, and your
   children have left you!
And your just able, to turn
   around again!
Somehow we pull through to
   another new year!
With age, we slow down our pace!
Turn around twice, in this game
   of life,
And in turning, you just lost the
   race!

Your life's span has run out, the
   waters are cold!
There's only darkness ahead!
Your future is unknown, in life
   after death,
So turn around twice and your
   dead!
They'll put you to rest on top of a
   hill!
And mourners will pass by your
   grave,
So turn around twice, before it's
   too late!
And see if there's some souls you
   can save!

Randall Earl Corbett
MY CHRISTMAS TREE
*[Dedicated to My Family,
whose love, warmth and
strengh, no words will ever
tell.]*
Winters Warm glow
From the fires hearth
Winters falling snow
Blanketing on earth
Red and blue
Yellow and green
Winters virgin chill
I have felt, I have seen
Brightly wrapped boxes
Secrets inside
Beneath the green pine
Impatiently they hide
Chestnuts, hot cider
Inner warmth and love
Heavens special gift
Given from above.

Ann Holm
THE GIFT
[To Lynda & Lynnette]
Alpha and Omega
Meet
The Miracle
of Life.
His Gift
to us
At Christmas.

Lisa Rosner
THE PATH
Peace is my intention;
Patience is my wish.
Trust is my gift and
Love is my treasure.
Understanding is my goal,
Wisdom is what I'm striving for
   with
Faith as my guide and
Hope as the candle that lights my
   way bringing
Courage to let me carry on.

Barbara Tanner
JOSEPH
Young Joseph, your journey was
   dusty and long
And shadows are stealing the
   light.
Your beautiful Mary is nearing
   her time,
But where will you stay for the
   night?

The streets are all crowded, the
   inns are all full,
And all you can find is a stall.
But there in the darkness the
   baby is born
And you weep at the joy of it all.

You cradle the child in a fold of
   your robe

And know of the wonder you
hold,
While light from a star filters
down through the roof
And spins all the stable to gold.

A choir made of angels and
prophets of old
Is filling the heavens with song.
A carol so bright with the
promise of love
You find you are singing along.

And now there are shepherds
who kneel by the door
As millions of others shall kneel,
To worship the Christ Child
asleep in your arms
And the Gospel he soon will
reveal.

Young Joseph, entrusted with
more than you know,
Enfolded in glory and light,
Your carpenter's hands hold the
hope of the world
That Mary gave birth to tonight.

Betty D. Woodyard
TRUE EMOTION
Feelings are common
and always used,
But they can also
be highly abused.

It's hard to live
with no inner spirit,
Like trying to talk
with no one to hear it.

Feelings can hurt
yet they can heal,
Life can change greatly
just by what you feel.

Love is a feeling
wanted by all,
without this feeling
most people would fall.

The reason for
such devotion,
Is simply because of
True Emotion.

Alma Lillian Hageman
ANGEL FROLICS
Two little angels
Feeling very bored
Took their leave of heaven
And journeyed to the world.

Climed upon a rainbow
Slid down with heart's delight
Stomped up the star-way staircase
And down the yellow stripe.

Lingered on the indigo
Danced upon the green
Admired the purple shimmer
That merged into a stream.

Watched the trout ajumpin'
Decided it was fun
To dive into the water
Neathe the noon-day sun
Sat and prattled with a frog
Pon a rock so slick and slimy
With algae clinging to it
They felt a little grimy.

With a swish and a whoop
And a plop into a pool
Bathed their angel bodies
Oh, it felt so cool.

Out and up upon a toadstool
Kicked their little toes
Teased a little willie-worm

As he squirmed upon a rose
Spoke into a daffodil
As if it was a phone
And God's voice came right back
"It's time to come on home."

George Sarsfield
**Traitor Clock(Visitation
Rights)**
Missing you while greeting you
—We haven't even said hello.
The hour hand moves so slowly
But oh so quickly too.
Your eyes—your smile—race the
clock
—Our time will soon be gone.
When we part the clock will stop
—Why can't we stop it now?

Cyndy Schnitger
A NEED TO REMEMBER
How can a heart so young,
Be so heavy?
A love so yearning,
Be so lost through the ages?
We fought to hold on,
Every day since the last we were
there,
Just watching time,
From our place on board the
eroded logs,
Along the banks of dreams.
Each moment a character in a
cast of thousands,
Amongst the memories that hurt
the most.
The nights I lay awake,
Thoughts of you painted my
mind,
Scenting just your presence,
On the walls of tear—stained
shadows.
They were foolish stunts we
portrayed as children.
And as we grew,
Changes were everywhere.
Yet the love we realized was
always there,
Had become more than a special
friendship.
I hung on,
Through all those years,
Giving us a need to remember. . .

Donna Marie "C" Joyce
KEEP IN TOUCH
"Goodbye" means forever
So no matter what you say—
Dont ever say the word
"Goodbye",
Unless you travel far away . . .

Far enough not to write,
Far enough not to call—
Far enough not to care,
. . .That's what matters most of
all.

You meet a friend; a special one—
And then your friend must part
The times you've shared are all
you have,
—You hold them close to heart.

The tears, the smiles, the happy
times—
Your friend has seen you
through
And now, as if the world must
end
Your friend is leaving you

No matter where you go in life

No matter how or why
Dont ever break that special
bond,
—Dont ever say "Goodbye" . . .

Cheryl Turney
WAVES
With violent crashing,
They hit the shore
To dissipate—
Waves no more.

Luke Nathaniel Baxter
HAPPINESS IS
When one is favored by
circumstance
Bestowed as it were by
inheritance
Fame and fortune as if by chance
Life is a pleasure, the happy
romance

There is no recipe for true
happiness
It comes from within to those
who posess
Happiness is pleasure one can
express
Joy and contentment to ever
address

William R. Watson
TRUTH
If one could see
For just an instant
The words
Before they're spoken
I bet there'd be
A lot more silence
That ended up
Unbroken . . .

Sherilyn Branscum
THE EXECUTION
Silhouetted against a graying
dawn
a man breathes a heavy sigh
Calmly he accepts his fate
as he faces his executioners
masked in black
After the final word is spoken
the signal is given
the fatal blow is dealt
When the bottom falls out
the rope becomes taut
With his last broken breath
he feels the battle of body and
soul ripping apart
then ending with a gurgling
gasp of finite
as bone snaps against bone
His body dangles there to be
viewed by all men
but his spirit is soothed by

gentle hands
caressing the wounds of an
innocent man

Donna A. Hauff
**Christ the Meaning Of
Christmas**
Do they know why Christ came
to be born
On that very very cold Christmas
morn?
Or do they celebrate and go their
merry way?
Or do they Honor Christ, the
Holy Savior to—day?
***
It is that joyous, merry, merry
time of year,
When people's hearts are happy
and full of cheer,
They rush here and they rush
there as they do go,
But do they Christ, the Holy
Savior really know?
***
May we always think of why
Christ was born
As we celebrate and the
Christmas tree adorn.
Folks Merry Christmas and a
Happy Holiday!
Folks what more can I or anyone
else ever say?

Penny "Panda" Caldwell
SUMMER 1978
I looked into the fiery skies
At dusk,
For your eyes—
Faint smell of your musk on the
air
Between the pines and me:
Waves of another sea stood,
Slinking to a still in the
moment. . .

I found my way through charred
remains
Of love,
For the chains we captured above
us:
What souls had left among the
stars
And bodies,
Rent due vs commodities
Outstanding,
Never to collect.

Kaye Phillips
ALONE
Alone; not just by myself
But, totally, completely,
positively
Alone.
I never felt this way when you
were here.
But, you have left me
All alone.
Sitting here in my solitude,
The maddening silence echos
clear
I am alone.
No one to love.
No one to care.
No one to hold.
No one to share.

Edith Louise McCormick
THE INHERITANCE
A lonely leaf fell from a tree
And drifted downward silently;
A butterfly prepared to fold
Its wispy wings of black and gold;

A bluebird in its plumage bright
Fell fatally from graceful flight;
A little dog with wagging tail
Found breath and bark were soon
    to fail;
A stricken man too weak to sigh
Felt full aware he was to die.

At some predestined time and
    place
All met and stood prepared to
    face
Their Maker and, in wondrous
    worth,
Said they, "We're from the planet
    Earth
Known long and well to Heaven
    wide,
Where Jesus walked and taught
    and died."

Regina S. James
LaDon—The Sparkle Of My Day
You're the sparkle of my day, my
    wrong and my right.
It's you whom I dream about each
    and every night.
You hold in the palms of your
    powerful hands,
all my wants and needs and all of
    my demands.
A nod or a touch from you sets
    my heart aquiver,
Or even better yet, a smile can
    make me shiver.
All these things I do are because I
    love you.
You're the reason that I live.
You're my heaven, my cloudless
    skies, and all of that above.
You're my treasured friend, but
    most of all my love.
You're the one I need and care for,
    the one for which I'd die.
To you, I'll never say good—bye.

Geraldine Davis Sully
SO LONELY NOW
[To my son, Bob while in Viet
Nam 1968—1969]
Oh damn this house, filled with
    raucous noise and laughter
To have now so quiet, where is
    the noise
    once ingracious to the ear.
The spot, empty and useless,
    where you
    sat to commune with me.
The untidy stream of garments
    strewn
    about like wind—tossed toys
Waiting for your return to bring
    them
    to a meaningful existence.
The music, so soul filling now
    takes
    on a monotonous tone
As the absence of love it takes to
    communicate it, is gone
The memory it leaves makes it
    sad
    for the heart to bear
So turn off the music 'till time
    makes it more pleasurable
Time, which crawls slowly,
    remember how
    it winged its way when we
    were one?
What now of time, to be
    impatient
    with its passing

Or fill it with the memory of past
    and hope of future?
This is faith, they say, look not
    past but ahead
Duty demands this of you and
    yours
    and the job must be done by all
Here and where you are let us be
    able to do so.
Compelled by love past,
    sustained by its
    faith memory will give us
And the joy it will bring in future
    time
But all things, so lonely now.

Alan Kanne
DREAMER
In the darkness way afar,
Lies a dreamer of the star.
Pondering; wondering of his
    might.
To guess the future far from
    sight.
His mind is clear as he plans,
Of future makings with his
    hands.
The sun then rises. And now the
Future has come thus far
For the dreamer of the star.

Bernadette Marie Suski
Shreds Of Faded Emotion
I find myself clinging
To feelings
I once cherished
Like a child
To the string
Of a rainbow—
Hued balloon,
Holding you back
And straining against winds
That struggle to set you free.
I long to possess
You just as the child yearns
Her balloon to secure,
But, enexpectedly, you jerk away
And float farther and farther
From my reach,
Until finally, the pressure
That has built up within
Surges forth
And you flutter to the ground
In shreds of faded emotion.

Calvin VanPelt
Those Little Feet That Walked Away
[Dedicated to our one and only
Daughter, Mrs Carolyn VanPelt
Williams In Memory of the
Wonderful years she spent
with us in our Home.]
A lovely little Girl came to us
    one day
And right off . . . she stole our
    Heart's away
with eyes of deepest blue, and
    little dimpled cheek
a lovely little Girl . . . and Oh'
    how sweet

I still can hear the patter of those
    little feet
when I came Home each day, at
    the door we would meet
she would walk with me from
    place to place
with a joyfull smile upon her face

We tried to teach her right from
    wrong
and made sure she knew we

loved her . . . all along
many times we sit side by side
    and talked . . . far into the
    night
we were so happy, and the world
    seemed so bright

It seemed by leaps and bounds
    she grew each day
and I knew that soon . . . those
    little feet would walk away
then one day she told us she
    planned to change her name
and I knew that our Home would
    never be the same

Through tear—dimed eyes . . . I
    looked at her pictures . . . on
    the wall
and millions of memories I did
    re—call
I stood there . . . and could not
    stop the flowing tears
as I lived again those wondrous
    years

I know that life will always be a
    changing thing
but to my fondest memories . . . I
    will always cling
I will always remember . . . come
    what may . . .
Those Little Feet That Walked
    Away

Though I knew the time would
    come . . . one day
when those little feet would walk
    away
I never knew that it would come
    about so fast
or that the hurt would be so
    deep . . . and always last

She knows we still love her . . .
    and always will
but there's an empty spot at
    Home . . . no one can ever fill
because our love for her grows
    deeper . . . day by day
and we never shall forget . . .
    Those Little Feet That Walked
    Away . . .

Mike Simpson
MAN TO HUMAN
Should we snap from our trances?

Yesterday is already past us
Pray it will enhance us
With don't—look—behind—us
    glances
From animal thru human transit
Fate and Will together dances
With seeds of love that implants
    us

What price is paid for taking
    chances?

Steven Cross
HALLOWEEN: 1982
Ghouls and goblins
    gallop
through shadowy
mental paths.
The bright moon
white as aspirin,

stuck on the sky
    smiling
through shadowed trees
    that whisper
parables
concerning a dog.

"Behold there once
    was a dog—

black and brown
splotched and
obedient,
humbly following."

hear and understand.

Carole Neason

Carole Neason
LOVE LINK
[To my husband Marshall who
also helped to make my dreams
a reality. I thank the Lord
always for your love.]
You are my love link of this life
I am so happy just being your
    wife
I had a missing link within my
    soul
Together we came and now I am
    whole
Like body and soul, we are now
    as one
With love to share as part of the
    fun
I was as a child when we first met
I know to you, I haven't grown up
    yet
I have learned a lot while being
    with you
As I watched you do the things
    that you do
I have learned to give when I
    didn't know how
I have learned to laugh instead of
    smile
I have learned to be strong
    instead of weak
I have learned to control my evil
    streak
I have learned to give love
    patiently
I have learned to enjoy life
    gracefully
I have learned that the love we
    share is forever
I have learned of a love link
That is you, my lover
You are my love link of this life
I am so happy just being your
    wife

Elizabeth McFee
LIBRARY
[for jorg]
The book of life is not
a list of appointments to keep.
It provides time to laugh
and live and love before you
sleep.

Chase butterflies and hunt
colored rocks. Smell the forest
pine.

Feed the ducks. See the stars.
enjoy enjoy this book of mine.

Hear the music. Pick the
wild berries and walk in the rain.
Leave no blank pages for
this book will not be read again.

Sandra M. Moran
TRUTH
The spiteful pasions assault
with barbed instruments, the soul;
Now thrusting the fragile membrane
with fiery arrows able to wound.
What hope, oh soul, to cleave to?
What shield?

Eyes that only darkness see
Discern, if you can, from whence
shall come the next assault.
Perchance, rise to the battle
in valiant stead,
banners captured by the wind;
Desire for victory the gleam
in this mortal's eye.

From behind, quite ignoble,
Passion sinks the silent lance.
Oh, wounded soul, all is
shifting sand.
In crimson glory does the valiant
soul retreat
bewildered and beguiled,
holding fast the dream.

Vanity of vanities!
Would another day bring the
foe to heel
what centuries could not conquer
or the exchange of blows
quench the fiery darts
Only to wound again
'til time exhausted

Puny mortal, you strike at
shadows
And beat the air with paper
sword
Cry out, poor soul; sound the
soul's defeat
Let Truth be your buckler and
your shield,
and humility your mantle.

Mark H. Miranda
MY LIFE
Give me my life for five minutes,
To do with as I may see fit.
To shape and to mold with no
standards,
To set my own morals and goals.
If I were myself for five minutes,
I would be a stranger to you.
I'd be the things that I couldn't be,
Because you wouldn't let me be
me.
You took my life and my future,
And gave me the fiery spark.
You made me a rebel and hater,
Of your own standards and goals.
But take back my life before I
undue,
The damage you already did.
Take back my life take my
freedom,
And give me my fiery spark.
You see you've done all the
damage,
That you possibly could have
done.
Take back my life you can have
it,
I couldn't live it the way you
expect.

Veronica M. Kane
Treasure In Blue and Gold
*[To Thomas Balsamo, the Cub
Master and Phyllis Servidio, the
Den Leader Coach of Cub Scout
Pack 350, Belleville, N.J., during
our family's scouting years.]*
Welcome little boy in your
uniform of blue,
here's a collar of gold may it
surround you.

You're precious to us that's why
we are here,
to help you gain confidence, to
help dispel fear.

Start out as a Bobcat achieve all
you can,
work hard on your book, don't
say you can't . . . say you can.

Move on to be Wolf learn how to
be fair,
your achievements will be harder
but soon you'll be Bear.

Be proud of our uniform wear it
with pride,
with badges and arrows and
friends at your side.

With all your achievements
move on to the plaid.
Now you're a Webelo. Aren't you
glad!

You still have a year to be with
us Blue Boy.
We're proud of our Webelos,
'You're our pride & our Joy'.

Big boy in blue with your collar
of plaid,
you'll have to move up and this
makes us sad.

It took so long to grow out of
seven,
then time went fast now you're
eleven.

Now you're a young man wear
green with your scarlet.
Please don't forget, it was here
you got started.

Come back to visit, to help . . . if
you can.
We hope your achievements,
'Help make you a Man'.

Robyn Empson
CONFUSION
flying saucers go round
running horse hooves pound
not knowing day from night
not caring dark from light
singing with voiceless song
a short minute gone long
alive feeling like death
a gasp a pain for breath
warming in snowy days
a mindless wonder strays
full thoughts departing brain
crying in hurtless pain
red colors change to brown
a smile dying in frown
loud voices chase through ears
safety becoming fears
vicious baby with a gun
a moon shines on the sun
a dog can laugh and talk
billboards get up and walk
reality not clear
losing all once held dear
living with allusion
save me from confusion . . .

Paulette Talboy Cary
A MILLION STARS
A million stars, dear, are shining
up above,
A million stars are witnessing
our love,
Their magiclight brightens the
night,
You whisper, "I love you",
A star falls from the blue,
All through the years, dear,
Though we be miles apart,
A million stars will shine on in
my heart.

Diana Kwiatkowski
THE FURY, LIKE SILENCE
You will not know
How do, how do
Your absence takes leave
of me.
You will not need
For no, for no
Amount of time—inadequate
measure
My heart's sheer grieve.
And now, your unanswerable loss
Causes so, causes so
Deep a rift—a reversal lift
Through the forgotten time.
Say Emptiness by a pariah
Abandoned, despised, ignored;
And Life its bitter stranger
If my Love—Yours—abhorred . . .
And what this exchanged
consequence—like a fine lady's
vainly dropped glove
or Gilbert and Sullivan's
Sea captain's daughter
tenderly weeping for
A simple sailor's love
Destined perhaps never to be . . .
Which point, which emphasis
takes preference? And yet
which strengths prevail?
In all of Lucifer's hell—
each corner doomed—
even you, yes, you!
With your loathesome silence
Smolder ash through
Our future's veil.

Ms. Linda G. Meadows
KNOWING MOTHER
I never knew mymother,
until I knew myself.
I placed my views above hers,
not caring how she felt.
I often tried to change her,
it never did me any good.
Then one day I noticed,
I could change, I should.
So many people say it,
"Mothers are a pain."
I doubt this holds much truth at
all,
but we say it, just the same.
If I had it all to do again,
I'd surely change my tune.
I would not be so quick to blame,
or judge her quite so soon.
The right words to say to Mother,
are sometimes hard to find.
But if you're having trouble,
I'll gladly lend you mine.

John Fonseca
ROSE PEDAL ROCK
He sat beneath a rose pedal rock
in fear that they would see him
He drank his wine of bitter sweets
and dreamed of times surrender

The weight of time soon bore
through him
and this revealed his true gender
The rock was lost and so washe
New towns are always filled with
strangers

Lucille H. Giberson
THE PASTOR
*[Dedicated to—my family for
their interest in my endeavors,
especially my oldest son who
in reality is The Pastor.]*
I went to church on Mother's
Day,
A tiny church, not far away.
The Pastor spoke of days gone by,
Which brought a lump to my
throat
And a tear to my eye.

The age old hymns were sung
with Love,
The Pastor prayed again.
We sang our praise to Him above,
And then we said "Amen."

Twilight fell—back home—alone,
I knelt in Silent Prayer.
I blest the family—one by one,
Oh yes—the Pastor—He's my
Son.

Joanne K. Hamer
NOT IN VAIN
Think of the pain, God must
have felt
To send His ONLY SON
To die on the cross for OUR sins,
When Jesus was a sinless one.

Feel the suffering, of His earthly
Mother
Who had to WATCH Him die
Knowing, SHE could do nothing,
She shouldn't even try.

Think of the remorse, Jesus must
feel
Watching US from above
Wondering, if it was in vain,
To give us all His love.

Don't you suppose, that we could
try
To walk from day to day
In the FOOTSTEPS of our Blessed
Lord,
So He wouldn't feel that way?

Let us REMEMBER, all of the
pain
Jesus suffered that day
And live, not as we would want,
But in HIS special way.

He died for US upon that cross,
To take away OUR sins;
Assured, that the devil would lose,
And our LORD GOD would win.

So, let us live our lives for HIM,
Don't CAUSE Him so much pain;
And let Him KNOW, by OUR LOVE,
HIS DYING WAS NOT IN VAIN!

Sheryl Jean Little
SHE WALKS ALONE
She lives in confusion day and night
Wondering if everything will be alright

She walks alone trying to be strong
Wondering where it is she belongs

She tries so hard to understand
Never receiving a helping hand

But she's got to do this on her own
And so she continues to walk alone

Wanda Jean Capps
TRIBUTE
Many years I have lived, many poeple I've met
down through the course of time
Some I've forgot, some I have not—
yet one stands out foremost in mind . . .

She was lanky and lean, not the fairest you've seen
sometimes she wore overalls;
A maid never wed, nor was it said—
she ever dated at all.

With a smile that was wide, it hardly could hide
the humor that she did possess—
With a wink of her eye, she would tickle you by
joking 'bout her mans caress.

She worked most her life, not without strife
there at a 'Fact'ry' in town;
She never did fall, she was loved by us all—
THAT WAS OUR, PEGGY JO BROWN!

You'd have to know Peg, to appreciate what's said;
"Another like her can't be found"
Who always stayed home, who never did roam
EXCEPTIONAL, PEGGY JO BROWN!

She was full of her fun, and respect, she had won
of people from all around;
Witty and keen, not hateful or mean
HATS OFF! TO PEGGY JO BROWN!

Annette Graham
TO MOTHER
I feel we're blessed
with a mother like you.
From the things that you say
to the things that you do.
From knowing—without
even hearing a word.
To listening with care
when we need to be heard.
What makes you so special
is the joy that you spread.
Through each of our lives
it's always been said.
You're there with a smile
when we need you to be.
You show us the things
we're unable to see.
I feel we're blessed
with a mother like you.
And I pray we can be
half as loving as you.

June Lee Box

June Lee Box
California's Ancestral Tree
Long, scoop contoured California
be proud
Of it's Redwood handle—it's
renowned Tall Trees.
It's northcoast is the only place in
the world
Where the sempervirens is
Native.
They are the longest living trees
on earth.
Many of these evergreens live
2000 years.
Annual growth rings of felled
giants often show
They were seedlings in early A.D.
Heights range from 100 to 300 ft.
(The tallest found is 367 ft. in
Humboldt Co.)
Growing very densely the huge
trunks are almost bare
For 50 ft. before branches begin
pyramiding.
The trunks though up to 20 ft.
wide appear slim
Compared with those of the
shorter Yosemite gigantica.
Having only curly tangles of roots,
Insted of a long stabilizing tap
root,
The trees depend on their density
for survival.
In storms they twist and grind
out rifle shot cracks.
Early people living in the shelter
of these trees,
Encircled by mountains, but open
on the west
To the bountiful sea, were
peaceful Indians,
The Yurok of the Lower Klamath,
The Karok of Salmon River, the
Tolowa,
And the Hupa of the Trinity fork
of the Klamath.
With game, fish, fruits, and
berries plentiful
They had little need for
agriculture,
Excelling in the basketry used to
store
The huge smoked salmon, and
dried fruits.
But, in 1542, that same bountiful
sea
Brought in the first Spanish
Explorers
Along the coast as far north as
Oregon.
They didn't land that time . . .
A final California scoop: It's the
only State
In the Union to be named after a
Novel.
A fantasy island in a Spanish
novel of 1510!

Mrs. Barbara Brown
GREETINGS
This day long ago
The angels in heaven sang
praise and glory—
God's tiny Son was born to us.
As they laid him in a manger
crib
The Bethleham Star shown in the
heavens
Bringing wise men from far—
And shepherd boys from fields
nearby
To come and worship the tiny
holy King.
This is the reason for Christmas
day.
Merry Christmas (And our
hope for a good year.)
Happy New Year!

Helen A.Taylor
A NEW DECADE
I have bid my last farewell to two
decades of my life.
There's a great feeling of loss, yet
also a feeling of relief.
The feeling of loss is by
memories passing through my
mind. Memories of my family
and me in various places and
times of travels in life.
I see this little girl with glasses
and snow white hair. She is just
learning to walk. This is only
through memories told by my
parents, and seeing slides.
I see a special friendship between
my family and me. A friendship
that is called love. But I see a
great tie between my mother
and I. A tie that can't be broken
or cut not even through death.
I am now taking those ties of my
family and me, and putting
them in my pocket.
I am closing the doors behind me
to two decades of joyous and
sorrowful times.
Here I stand shaking with my
hand on the handle. I open the
door slowly to a new decade
full of adventures and bridges
to cross.
I reach into my pocket and take
out those ties between my
family and me and hold them
in the palm of my hand as I
walk into the doors of a New
Decade of my life.

Glenn Bailey
The Great Indifference
[To the American soldiers who
gave their all in battle in order
to uphold that great God given
gift of indifference]
There is a happy medium to be
found
With the co existence of the
indifference
Between what is right and what is
wrong
In the quest for life and
happiness
And it is that great indifference
in life
That serves its purpose so well in
the human relationship
For it distinguishes all the
concepts and beliefs
In the human races of the world
And in keeping our freedoms of
this great nation
The United States of America in
a democracy
Under God with liberty and
justice for all
It is with that great God given
gift of indifference
That we can stand proud
In our strength and heritage as an
American citizen
In our unity as an individual
human being
With the inaliable rights to our
indifference
Of concepts and beliefs
On the cross roads of life

David Barland Parker
sea
[to Elizabeth and Margareta
Heute]
blubrown
moonlight
moving
blugreen
sea
blueyes
of mermaid.

Louise Arter
SHADOWS OF CHRISTMAS
I sit in the shadows of Christmas,
A distance from the bright
lights . . .
I watch, I look and I listen
To all the wonderful sights.
The people are ever so busy
As they hurry to go on their
way,
Making, preparing and planning
For a wonderful Christmas Day.
The mothers and fathers are
shopping
For the little ones ever so dear . . .
There is something important
about Christmas,
Like no other time of the year.
It's the birth of the one we
depend on . . .
Though unconscious of Him
sometimes it may seem,
Inside is a yearning to love Him,
And it's more than merely a
dream.
The love flows from one to
another,

And our hearts and our minds
are aglow,
As we picture the precious Baby
Jesus
In a manger where He lay long
ago.
The innocent eyes of the
children,
As their voices ring out far and
near,
The warmth and the glow of the
fireside
Remind us that Christmas is
here.
As families gather together
And the day breaks forth
Christmas Morn,
Let our minds go back to the
stable
Where our loving Saviour was
born.
Let us bow our heads to our
Maker
Who, somehow, doesn't seem
far away,
Invite Him to be guest at our
table
On this wonderful Christmas
Day!

Joseph C. Hoffman
TRIP
Tenaciously flesh-clung bone;
Straight-jacket for the soul,
Glued with time and running
blood—
Your gravity-anchored body.

Astronautic futility,
Still the canned soul:
Escape, not your prerogative,
The Divine Will stills.

If . . . I'd tour the universe,
God's workshop;
Outfly flight, gaze upon galaxies
Nose to nose,
Listen to the snap, crackle, and
pop
At the center of a sun, and look
for
Chlorophyll circling same.

Exciting trip—drunk with
knowledge.
So that's what God made!—such
wonders!
Past the last galaxy into utter
darkness;
An education ended: back to the
greatest
Wonder of all, back to Heaven,
Where it God!

Darlene Babbitt
WARNING
My soft places
have sickened,
are untouchable;
they are dried,
pitted, done.

Day is a funnel,
poured into night,
and night
is a razor.

My clothes are loose,
shoes are heavy;
my knees are
springy, ready;
I am hidden,
un-soft, I can
kick down doors.

My fingernails
are glass-cutters;
the headache is
a high-bellied
scream I kill
with a swallow.

My soft places
have sickened,
are untouchable;
they are dried,
pitted, done.

Watch for me
in razor-nights;
I cut glass now.

I am cut glass now.

Jean Marie Gulas
THE CONVERSATION
Hello,
again.
Just thought I'd chance
to say
hello
and then
maybe
we could
start
all over
again.

Hello,
so then,
I've said
the word
and now
you've heard
hello again.
And now,
my friend,
would you
like
to start all over
again?

Margaret Matthews
**Tomorrow: A Lesson In
Timing and Turning.**
I turned,
Drawn by the pleasured sound
Of Mother Robin, filled with
pride,
To watch her growing family
glide
From nest to branch, and then, to
ground.
They conquered space. Yet one
alone
Whose trembling voice, a tiny
groan,
Turned Mother back,
To see him take a frightened leap,
And fall to death's eternal sleep,
Lost to this world.

Thus I, in hesitation, lose
The things, I see, are there to
choose,
For I stop and cannot fly.
Tomorrow's moments pass me by,
Turning me to another path
Along time's restless, rushing
flight
To find the task's not done;
The well is dry;
And thirsting, I must turn and go,
Before I, like the young bird, die.

Meeting sorrow and distress
Without a tender word, or glance,
Can take away the slightest
chance
That we can ever earn redress,
And thus I found a question hard
To press upon myself, alone:

So great a sorrow
Who can bear?
We could have helped
Had we been there!
Who can say?
The answer always is a "why".
The question, now, is:
Where was I?

John W. Hugel Jr.
PANDORAS BOX
Pandoras box was opened
That early summer day.
The sky became one fireball
As the thunder made its mark.

The birds above had already gone
For they sensed the time had
come.
But the people below had stayed
to watch
And marvel at its glow.

Yes, Pandoras Box was open
The Atom was now free.
While its glow showed us the
heavens,
Its fire came straight from Hell.

Carole L. Larsen
PAULINE MOSSMAN
From afar we did speak,
without the chance to know,
that the world would not seek,
nor cry, nor help us sow
the lost time, the lost years.

Was it worth the left pain,
to shut and lock behind,
those you claimed, now in vain,
to love, and yet not find?
Oh sad time, on both spheres!

As the field down the road,
has thrashed the grain so blown
to the wind, yet half hoed,
sigh I, for fruit unsown.
Oh lost time for such tears!

Z. Farier
**Eulogy To a Young
Artist Friend**
A girl there was once long ago,
Her mother gone, a sister shamed,
Who yet no dark would spirit
show;
The joy of youth and laughter
claimed,
And in the laughter, clowns.

Her heart knew songs no bird
could sing,
All caught within a drifting
dream;
The budding of a maiden spring,

The brightness of a rock born
stream,
And in the brightness, clowns.

But man creates for mortal gain
Machines of hard and brutal
force.
Struck down in blood and
shrieking pain,
Apart from life and joy, its source,
And on the pavement, clowns.

Now dark in sorrow souls despair
Until a peacock, standing proud,
Then colors bright reflect in air,
The heavens painted, cloud on
cloud,
And in the clouds, the clowns.

Rosa C. Jackson
The Feelings Of Nature
You can talk to the trees
And know how it feels
To be as free as the breeze.
But beware!
For not everyone will understand
Your ease of communing with
nature.
Some will envy you.
For they can not
Feel the strength
Of an ocean ripple
Or the peace
Of a gentle rainfall.
Nature shows her way of love
You feel the lakes troubled
murmer
And the clouds soft touch.
But beware!
For some will not accept
The feelings of nature
If you tell of the mountains
courage
And the flowers love.
But do not stop communing with
nature
For she has much to share
And teach you of her love.

Weldon L. Smith
COMPROMISE
Divide we then the wrong from
right
when black was black and white
was white
but compromise has brought
decay
resulting in such dirty gray.
Share rightful glee in victory
in finding keys in history
but rustic key the lock defies
the fault of such is compromise.
Convictions firm in gripping
grasp
shall prove that grand old truth
at last
but slack resolve or unfirm lips
shall keep the deep in mighty
ships.

Donna L. Clemons
CUSTOM MADE LOVE
The quality of your love
is like
the best tailor made suit,
just
the perfect fit.
So discard the receipt
as there will be no exchanges.
Your love
has become
a permanent part of my wardrobe.

James A. Hanf
PRISONER OF LOVE
I'm locked within the jail of love,
And cupid holds the key;
For he is warden of this place;
The prisoner is me.

And so I linger here alone,
Just waiting for release;
Much like a soldier in the war,
That prays for it to cease.

For cupid is a crafty chap,
Who shoots his little dart;
The poison from this weapon now,
Has filled my aching heart.

And so I languish in this jail,
From which I cannot leave;
Oh! What a trap I stumbled in,
That cherub hands did weave.

And thus, Dear Edna, you alone,
Can save me from this plight!
Please, bring the ransom (all your love),
And marry me tonight!

Dorothy Rita Jarvis
IT IS BETTER TO GIVE
*[To My Family: They gave
more to me than they received
from me.]*
Everything has turned to
longing.
My years are not a few.
If I were blind; I'd see but better
The visions that I now do.

What have I given to see a
rose?
A sunset? The snow? Rain?
My life, My life. For moments
cherished
I'd give it all again.

I cry, for my heart is longing
too;
Wishing, yearning, holding near;
Every star, sunbeam and bird,
Flower and loved one I cherish
here.

Why does my heart break for
tyrant time?
Roses bloom after the snow!
This vision I'll see 'til I ask,
Where did life's roses go?

"Tis better to give than to
receive."
I'd give for life, lose; give again;
Only believing love is eternal,
Faith, Hope and Love aren't vain.

Georgiana Lieder Lahr
SEA FURY
The angry sea is pounding shore
with might,
The ocean's wild, and in a
frenzied mind;
Like a great giant, ready for a
fight,
With temper fierce, with fury,
ruthless, blind.

O, do not venture in this wind-
tossed sea,
Observe it from the refuge of the
shore;
There is no mercy, no there
cannot be,
This giant reigns, no use to beg,
implore.

So, wait—and know this angry
mood of sea
Will pass, and calmer days will
soon draw near;
The waves subside in peace and
harmony,
And you may enter sea, and
nothing fear.

"Time heals all things," and this I
have been told
That stormy days can change to
purest gold!

Cheri Fortmeyer
WHAT IS A DAD?
*[Inspired by my loving father,
Herbert William Fortmeyer]*
A dad is someone special,
Thru your life he tries to guide
you
With his loving hands and gentle
touch
From pain he's there to hide you.

When somethings wrong you go
to him,
He'll never try to blame you
And make you feel inadequate,
Or even try to shame you.

They always hold close to their
heart,
The memories of us so young
Playing "choo-choo train" &
"building blocks",
As the day is nearly done.

He tucks you into bed at night,
And listens to your prayers . .
Then quietly turns out the light,
As he tells you that "he cares".

So this poem is just for you, Dad
Though I may not always show
it . .
You mean more to me than life
itself,
I just wanted you to know it.

Patricia L. Hill
STILL LOVING YOU
` *[This poem was written to
Joseph Finelli, a very special
man, after he left Arizona and
moved back to New York.
Although we are apart, I wish
him happiness, success and
above all this—I wish him
LOVE.]*
I wonder why love came to me
and ended up this way?
I wonder why love came to me
and then he went away?
I wonder if some day I'll know
that it was meant to be?
I wonder if he'll ever know just
what he means to me?

But I don't have to wonder if I'll
love him any more.
My love still grows though we're
apart, each on a different shore.

And when we are beside again I
know I'll love him still;
For no one else can take his
place. I know they never will.

There's something special I can
see about this man so rare!
There's something that he brings
to me; it's something that we
share!

And even though I can't exactly
tell you want it is,

I know within my heart and soul,
the love I have is his.

So when I often wonder why love
came and went away,
I only have to stop and think of
memories that stay.

Of all the happy moments, of the
closeness that we knew!
Of all the laughs, and kisses and
the heartaches we shared too!

These thoughts are etched upon
my mind so gentle and so dear.
And when I wonder where love
went, I know that they are
near.

I close my eyes and picture it,
just like it was back then.
I close my eyes and dream about
the way it might have been.

Yet distance cannot stop a bond
predestined from above,
And I know even though he's
gone, he left with me his love.

Zorida A. Saba

Zorida A. Saba
A BREATH OF SPRING
Winter has just passed,
it left the yard in a mess.
The flowers and trees are bare,
no aroma in the air.

Love and laughter are here once
more
with springtime knocking at the
door.
We wake up and see
the green leaves on the trees;
the flowers in bloom with its
magic perfume.

The suns warmth renders
life, love and splendor
to the beautiful flowers
that are so tender.

The yard is full of colors again;
so much richer, just like a picture.
Thank God for the flowers and
the trees
and all the things he creates so
neat;
For the beauty of nature
and all its creation.

Jaroslawa Benko
AFTERMATH
champagne floats flatly
in crystal

dry cakes of cheese
sit on a plate

cremated cigarettes
in a suspended state
on their bier

all waiting to be disposed of

the aftermath
of a party evening

they fill the room
with sounds
of the previous
night's encounters
soon to be assimilated
into tonight's dimensions.

Rae Hager
DOROTHY DELYRA
Dorothy Delyra was my friend for
thirty years, or was it
twenty-seven.
We were not speaking for three
years, before she went to
heaven.
The rift was wide and oh so deep,
the hill between us very steep,
But how I wish I'd climbed that
hill before she went to sleep.

In retrospect how wise she was,
how callous could I be,
To treat so lightly then, which
now I'd treasure tenderly.
She left me feeling thrice bereft,
her ashes cast to sea.
Once bereft for her, but twice for
me, Oh, twice for me.

The sea looks at me with grey
disdain, and curls its mighty
brow,
As though she knows our loves
and dreams are all just ashes
now.
Waves pound, they roar, they
sigh; or is that another's sigh I
hear.

Hopefully, I listen for "I forgive
you. Yes, I forgive you, dear!"

Alberta A. Cox
LITTLE THINGS COUNT
Have you gazed in awesome
splendor
At a mighty Redwood tree?
Have you gloried in a meadow
At the beauty that you see?

Have you stopped in admiration
Of the flowers in a park?

Stop to think of all this grandeur
From a seed first got this start.

So the great dreams of tomorrow
From just seedlings do embark.
Thus in life our great
achievements
Have their beginning from a
radiant spark.

Marinis Becknell
SLEEP
*[To my wonderful friend
Dennis. Thank you for your
wisdom, your inspiration, and
most of all your love.]*
Oh sleep—
why do you desert me,
at such a lonely hour?
Why won't you let me enter?
My soul is weak and tired.
My thoughts are torn,
in so many directions.
My body tosses about.
Oh, restful sleep,
come rescue me

Today's Greatest Poems

I am lost,
in a sea of doubt.
Silent sleep,
send your darkness,
let it take me,
to your secret place.
A place for dreamers,
and for pretenders,
to play their games,
of chance.
Where if they discover
they've made a mistake,
it won't matter anyway,
cause in the darkness,
there is no heartbreak,
no tears to fall,
no debts to pay!
Oh silent darkness,
come surround me.
carry me to him
once again.
Cover us,
with your still dark night,
cause in the darkness,
it'll be alright.

Elsie Pickard Clay
ARIZONA BLUE
The blue
Meeting green,
Hallowed with
   clouds that puff
      here and there.

Goldenrod in yellow dresses
   dance.
Mullen weed bob yellow bonnets,
   and march across the land,
While old Mr. Sagebrush
   swishes his dry fluffy head.

The red red dirt,
Cries to be heard
As the seeking hawk
   circles in hope.
The Tumbleweed on it's journey
   to nowhere
      says goodbye.

The earth smells cover you,
Strong scented by the rain.
As I drink from your cup,
Oh Arizona Blue,
   you're magic!

Gini Schafer
SUMMER NIGHTS, 1982
Tree leaves flutter in the tiny
   breeze,
Dancing in moonlight.
Nightbirds communicate with
   each other
And with me.
Nightblooming Jasmine sends out
   it's sweetness;
Heavy, heady scent,
Swelling my senses, my soul
With delight.

Reluctantly I turn away to sleep.
I must be rested
To face a trying day again
   tomorrow.
Times are hard
In 1982. I must stretch my
   resources,
Be strong and calm, and
Reassure my family that with
   time
It will come right.

At day's end I'm exhausted,
   drained.
Heart troubled, sore in soul.

No more hope for tomorrow than
   today
It seems, and yet . . .
Outside I go to seek and find my
   refuge
In the coolness
And fill my heart, my soul again
With summer night.

Joe A. Harris

Joe A. Harris
FIND THE STAR
*[This poem was inspired by
and is dedicated to my
wonderful wife Vivian, whose
guidance helped me—"FIND
THE STAR".]*
If I could find the star that shown
   the night that Christ was
   born—
Would it's bright light reflect a
   path
      to banish hate and scorn?

If I could call the shepherds back
   that heard the angels voice,
Would they in some unusual way
   help mankind all rejoice?

If I could locate wise men three,
   that traveled from the east,
Would they explain with hearts aglow,
   why the best of us are least?

If I could hear the heavenly hosts
   that sang so long ago,
Would they express a praise in
   song,
      of love we all could know?

Of course these thoughts are
   fantasy,
   or at least a task too hard;
But there is a bright and shining
   star,
   we call Him Christ our Lord.

Kleon Kerr
THY PEACE
Lord, grant Thy peace
This Christmas Day
To ease our fears
And light the way.

Not wordly peace
With force behind,
But Lord, Thy peace
To calm the mind.

Thy peace with love
For every brother,
With tender words
For one another.

Thy peace alone
To soothe the soul,
To heal our wounds
And make us whole.

Marjorie E. Corum
INLAWS-OUTLAWS
Outlaws are those who can be
   defined
As coming by night to steal you
   blind.
And then there are those who
   come by day
And hassle you so there's the
   devil to pay.
They don't like this and they
   don't like that
And their attitude can leave you
   flat.
The first depression will go away
The second leaves marks that
   sometime stay.
Which loss is greater? the
   question I find:
To lose your goods or your peace
   of mind.

Ja Net Ingalls
SMALL WINGED ANGEL
Looking out among thee mist of
   night
there sought before thine eyes,
a small winged angel in ghostly
   form
near a small babe listening to his
   cries.

Hovers thee angel over thus child
thou tiny hands clasp in prayer,
"May this child forever be"
thee love and beauty he will
   touch
      and share.

No longer thus small child shall
   cry
a presence he feels is unknown,
and looking so deep within his
   eyes
a light of thee small winged angel
   still shone . . . . .

"Willetta"
GIVE ME STRENGTH
How can I be stronger in my
   faith. If I
cannot see with my own eyes,
   Will I still believe.
If my own ears cannot hear the
   sounds, Can
I listen with my heart.
Can I forgive, with love in my
   heart. When the
feelings of hate are so strong
   within me. When I
know that I've done my best and
   no one excepts
it, Do I dare to try again.

When happiness seems to elude
   me, Can I be
happy for someone else. When I
   feel like
crying, Dare I smile instead. I ask
myself these questions, the
   answers must be my own.
This life I live was given to me to
   find the
way for myself, with mistakes to
   be made and
even tears to be shed in search of
   truth and understanding.

Dear God, It's good to know you
   listen, whenever
I feel alone, and so many foolish
   things I say will
never be heard again. When so
   called friends are
too selfish to care, You've never
   been too busy. So hear
what my heart must say. Remove
   these feelings
of Doubt and Pity. Help me to be
   stronger. You know
my weakness better than anyone,
   "AND YOU'RE SOMEONE
I WILL ALWAYS NEED."

Sister John Agnes Nethery, O.S.F.
A MANGER FOR HIS BED
Caesar sent forth a decree in the
   land of Judea
That each at the town of his birth
   must appear.
Joseph to be enrolled must travel
   many a mile;
Mary, his spouse, was soon to be
   delivered of child.

Their trusted donkey was Mary's
   humble steed,
Trudging ahead Joseph the way
   did lead.

After three days' journey they
   reached Bethlehem Town;
By the light of the stars the Inn
   was found.
Joseph of the Innkeeper sought
   shelter and food.
"No room in the inn", came a
   voice loud and rude.

A light shone on Mary's face—
   patient and mild.
The Innkeeper softened as he
   watched her awhile . . .
   "There is a cave for our cattle
   just to the right—
   a clean manger for The Babe if
   born there tonight".

The birth took place that very
   same night;
The animals round Mary
   screened her from sight.

A great light round them shone,
   and the cave did fill.
   The angels sang, "Glory to God
   and Peace to men of Good
   Will".
   The baby in the manger the
   animals adored—
   For He was their King and their
   Lord!

Donald H. Johnson
LEAVE ME ALONE
Just leave me alone
   to think and dream,
To build my life
   and thoughts to ween.

To roam the land
and clear my head,
To find myself
and not to dread,

The chores I have
that I must sow,
For deep inside
my soul they grow.

And grow they do
and restless I get,
I search my soul
but never fret.

For soon they appear
and I do what I must,
My creative soul
can gather no dust.

Grace Shelton Dukeminier
COMPASSION
Wouldn't it be nice if each one of
us
In some very special way
Would give our love to everyone
As we greet each newborn day?
God sent the Ten
Commandments
To obey our whole life through;
And Jesus gave a special one,
"That ye love one another, as I
have loved you."
If we heeded these
Commandments
What an impact there would be
In the world-wide situation
As faith shaped our destiny.

Charlene Sutter Nottingham
SHOW TIME!!
*[To my "Blue Ribbon" Show
Partner . . . Mickey Jay A
Winner in & out of the Ring. A
Friend FOREVER . . . Thanks
for the memories, Mic!]*
Have you ever attempted making
a list of "Horse Show
Equipment" so none would be
missed?
Well, just such a list has been
written for you; Now you can
check things off carefully just
like I do!

BRUSHES 'n COMBS, BLANKETS
& BITS . . .
and SHOE CREAM . . . to cover
those scratches & zits!!
SADDLES & BRIDLES & ALL
kinds of "TACK" . . .
(remember, once you get there,
there's no goin' back!!)
HALTERS & LEADROPES & one
extra CINCH . . .
SPURS, just in case you get in a
tight pinch!
COTTEN & LEG WRAPS & A
SOOTHING good cream,
(Oh, won't someone tell me this
is just a bad dream???)
LIQUIDS & LOTIONS & some
PEROXIDE too . . .
(just in case, by some "quirk",
someone gets a "boo-boo"!!)
A "small" BALE OF HAY, and a
BUCKET OF OATS . . .
and a 6 PACK to help cool off our
dry throats!!!
RIBBONS & HATS & SHOW
CLOTHES too . . .
(Lord, keep me goin' there's sooo
much to do!!)
ENTRIES & NUMBERS AND a

bowl full of pins . . .
an extra CURB or two, to help
tuck in those chins!
Don't forget FOOD . . . a
sandwich that's squished??
And for HEAVEN'S sake, be sure
to bring the VANQUISH!!
CURRIES & HOOFPICKS: a
bottle of SHOW SHEEN . . .
HOOF BLACK . . . to add that
glistening gleam!!
Unbraid the mane, so it won't lay
too tight . . .
(Or, did you forget to do THAT
last night???)
4 nice ROUND tires . . . and a
tank full of GAS
(I think we are almost
ready . . . AT LAST!!)
But there's still something
missing . . . no, don't tell
me . . . OH! OF COURSE!!!
Last of all don't forget to load up
your Fox Trottin' HORSE!!
Well, everything's here, I'm ready
to go, so climb on inside, we're
off to the show?
It's 6 A.M. as the coffee we sip,
WHY, does every horse show
become such a big trip??
We've arrived at the show, with
all of our tack . . . But
suddenly we sense, ONE major lack
The First Class is called . . . we
are ready—OF COURSE!!
Dear God! Where'd I put them?
. . . My trailer and Horse????

Dee Lilly
SEARCHING II
A fish belongs to water;
So the seagull to the sky.
A tree is rooted to the ground,
But where belongeth I?

We'll build a mock-up jungle
For the lion and the snake . .
Complete with rocks and sand
and vines,
And man-filled clear blue lake.

A spinning, turning busy Earth
Knows well its track around the
sun.
The Milky Way is spillproof (or
is it?)
So please tell me why I run.

With these eyes I see an order,
Which my mind has sorted out.
We humanoids arriving last;
Unruly children running about.

We are a guest in this universe.
Did we leave our manners at
home?
And home? I've yet to find that...
A little longer I must roam.

Shirley Adwena Harvey
EARTHBOUND
My roots sink deep
in brown firmness
of the terrestrial—
sun-warmed
rain-fed
secure
in day and season.

Yet I stretch
toward light,
search for sun-source,
reach
to touch rainbows.

But earth pull is strong

and though tendrils
strain to twine
celestial cord—
my roots bind.

I'd like to wait
and grow
a few more seasons.

Gerald H. Adams

Gerald H. Adams
LOVE
Love is not blind the way I have
read it,
But more in demonstration like a
child,—
Honest and sincere; I sometimes
dread it,
Because very often I am beguiled;
And yet, I always want to take a
chance
Bestowing virtues on those I
fancy,
With warmth, endearment, and
reckless romance,
And little thought of reciprocity.

Some people love
thus—unrewardingly,
Enduring pain and covert misery
With loss of wit and even sanity.
A high price for love some people
pay,
But that's the way it is, I've heard
them say,
And fools like me still love to
love that way.

Don Gates
**I Thought I Heard
A Baby Cry**
Time has
blotted out
the place, the reason . . .
but I've been here
before.

Many bridges
burned behind me
as I ran from life . . .
curling up inside
slamming the door . . .
And then . . . I thought
I heard a baby cry.

Hope and pleasure
left me with
a longing
to have my
soul set free . . .

My life . . . searching
for the happy place
with no sorrow
or misery . . .

Then . . . I thought
I heard a baby
cry . . .

And tears
from somewhere
shed . . .

I thought . . .
I heard a baby
cry . . .

And found . . . It was I instead.

Norma Rockwell Preisler
THE SUNSET TRAIL
*[For mother, Evaline Lena
Brotzman Rockwell.]*
My mother was a lady.
She had a dapple grey;
And off upon the sunset trail
One day, she rode away.

I've waited long for her return—
But now that I am grown;
I, too, shall ride the sunset trail
To find where she has gone.

And if I find that happy place—
That land beyond compare;
Look not for me. I'll not return.
I, too, shall linger there.

Wilmer Wilcox
JEALOUS EVE
Now where have you been, dear
Adam?
Now where have you been,
from me?
Just walking around in the garden
Just seeing what I could see.

And what did you see, dear
Adam?
Were you hoping to find a new
she?
Oh no, darling Eve, I would not
deceive.
You know there is just you and
me.

I am not so certain, dear Adam.
You may just be telling me fibs.
Come over and sit down beside
me.
I want to count all of your ribs.

Bonnie Ann Rakoski
SHE CARES
*[To My Darling Love Paul who
I love and care for with all my
heart]*
It seems he just won't listen
When you beg him and you plead
He'll tell you not to worry
But from your heart you bleed

For men don't seem to understand
How their women feel

For way deep down inside her
heart
A six sense seed is sealed

As it sprouts and grows inside
her
It's cause she loves you dear
For that love is very special
And it shows she really cares

Treat her as she's special
And always do things right
Let her know you love her
And hold her oh so tight

For the bond that holds you
together
Is something that's very dear
And you'll realize what I'm saying
As you hold each other near

Leo H. Meier

Linda L. Meier
TO MY FATHER ABOVE
*[dedicated to the memory of
my Dad, Leo H. Meier]*
"Let us so live
that
those who know us,
but
do not know Him
will want to know Him
because
they know us."

This my father wrote, now long
ago yet, as time has passed,
these words have stayed close
on my mind.

I was very young, only a child of
five when he left this life, and
though memories I have are
but a few, nothing could ever
erase these memories I have of
him and I together.

He found peace in the Lord in his
steps through life
in his wife and children he
showed much pride
and the example he was for all of
us to see
I can only pray, to also one day
be.

It makes me proud to know
my father again I'll see
when we meet in heaven for all
eternity.

Cleoral Lovell
TINY GRAVE
Banked with flowers, where we
grieve,
Hold him gently . . . we must
leave.

Leaving . . . hardest part of
all.
How be brave?

Cradle softly his sweet form
Only days ago so warm,
Lullaby him pine trees tall,
Grasses wave.

We shall miss his baby smile
Granted us so short a while;
God recalled so soon the
small
Life He gave.

Jeffrey Stephen
PLEASE UNDERSTAND
*[To my Mom — I love you and
to those left behind Please
understand]*
I hope you know I'm not trying to
be mean,
But it's time for me to split this
scene.
You see me doing many strange
things,
Well, I'm only trying to find
what life brings.
A lot of happiness crossed my
road,
But a lot of pain made it a
heavy load.
When you see me down the way,
Just remember what we had
yesterday.
I'm trying to find what is right for
me,
And I hope that is what you
see.
When I find what is right,
I won't give up without a fight.
This scene is not what's meant
for me,
My spirit is calling, it wants to
be free.
The cage is opening, I'm
spreading my wings,
I fly high, my free spirit sings.
I will fly until I find my new nest,
And this will end a life long
quest.
And at best,
Who knows, maybe I'll get to
rest.

Charles Landmesser, Sr.
RISING
Let the flowers of sunshine grow
in your heart,
May your days begin with a
beautiful start.
May all of your joys and
happiness be fulfilled,
Your love and your dreams
begin to grow and never be still.

Balde Villarreal
LOVE
Love is found in the simple
everyday
occurrences of your life—
Like in the sharing of things
With friends and neighbors,
Or in the giving of yourself
Unselfishly to those who need
you.
Love is found in a smile
offered as a silent understanding
of love—
received and accepted,
Or in the vibrations felt from a
handshake
Offered as a honest message of

love.
Love is found in a kiss, warmly
given,
And expressing all the inner
thoughts of your heart and
soul,
Or in the comfort given to
shoulders so troubled and tired
with the problems of everyday
living.
Love is found in the tears shed
over good—byes,
Or in the joy shared
in moments of mutual happiness.
Love is found in every being
who is not afraid
to demonstrate love
beyond the norms
set forth by social prejudices.

Amy Rotramel
DARKNESS
Why do the innocent
Have to leave us?
And go to a place
We have identified
But is unknown?
Why are the young
Taken out of this world?
And sent somewhere
Alone?
When so many don't care
And destroy life for
Themselves and others.
Why do the most beautiful
People in our lives
Always seem to be the bravest
To venture into the darkness
Of death?

Sharon E. T. Bone
Giving All For Love
How many hearts has love killed?
How many souls have shriveled
and died
just to stay at a loved one's side?
Acquiesced in silent pain
given up personal dreams of fame.
How many well intentioned
hearts
have smothered the flame
leaving just the dark?

Edythe T. Kahn
Great Blue Herons At Secret Cove
When swirling March winds
drive away the cold
And leafy spears of cattail reeds
unfold,
A handsome great blue heron
sails down low
To wade in "Secret Cove's" wide
overflow.

Far inland at a sheltered rookery,
His mate is nesting in an old oak
tree
And while she guards their
new—hatched brood of four
He brings them silver minnows
from the shore.

Their helpless young are often
left alone,
Since both their parents feed
them 'til they're grown,
Then on the right momentous
summer day
They join their peers along the
waterway.

But in October, just about
snowfall,

The family of herons—one and
all,
Assemble in the sky and
southward go
To find a sunny cove where
cattails grow.

Tammy L. Skiba
THE BEAUTY OF A DOVE
It's sad. So sad I want to cry.
A little girl grows up—
Then waves good—bye.

She finds within her heart, a love
So deep, so true—
The beauty of a dove.

She laughs with joy abound,
But it's not there—
For is it love she's found?

She's scared the love she's found
is not real,
But it is no dream—
Her wound will someday heal.

But suddenly she's not afraid of
love,
For it has come—
The beauty of a dove.

I want to cry, I want so much to
cry,
She's found her love—
Though someday she will die.

But I won't cry for her,
She's found it, she really has—
The beauty of a dove.

Dick Plopper
SUNSET
*[To my daughters, Carol —
Karen — Shari]*
I see the sunset in the sky
glowing red, about to die.

It wakes each morn and lives one
day,
and so it is, I live that way!!
It matters not that I conform
but only that I do not mourn.

the days gone by are not reborn,
each day is whole in its own
form. . . .

Peggy Langley
CRUEL AWAKENING
I woke to find your lips on
mine. . .
My heart did a "wheelie," then
reeled
With the realization
That I had strangled on my wine
And you were just giving
Mouth—to—mouth
resuscitation.

Paul Gillen
MOON GLOW
As I sit here by the window,
and watch the moon slowly
rise,
So big, so orange does it appear,
when first we gaze upon it.
But brighter, and smaller does it
grow,
as it ascends into the heavens.
Upon the snow it glistens, and
mellow
does it glow.
It's then it seems to dwarf the
darkness,
and you can see the nighttime
silhouettes.
Then there looms the silhouettes
of the denuded trees,

so plain before your eyes.
I see the silhouette of the
picturesque farmstead,
lighted by the glow.
I can see the ripple of the hills,
and the valleys down below.
It's then the brightness of the
moon seems to bring
so much of nature out to roam.
The air is crisp, and oh so cold,
as I listen to the lonely coyote.
Calling, calling, calling to its
mate,
far out across the snowy, chilly
plains.
It's then I wonder if perhaps its
mate,
may not return.
For death is always there,
and seems to stalk the ones
you love.

Betty Ruth Phillips
CHRISTMAS IS
Christmas is a guiding star,
A chorus of angels from afar,
The breathless hush of shepherd's
awe
Trembling at what they saw.

Christmas is a smile that lights
the eyes
When exchanging gifts in happy
surprise.
Christmas is not just Santa and
his elves;
Christmas is caring and sharing
ourselves.

Christmas is sacred or touching
or funny;
It's parties and shopping and
spending money.
Christmas is giving and feeling
that glow
Of loving the whole world and
telling it so.

Christmas is special, birthday of
The Christ,
A time to remember His life and
its price.
A day to practice the love He
expressed,
Hope and joy and all the rest.

Christmas is magic two thousand
years old
That shines in our lives like
nuggets of gold;
A symbol of peace in the form of
a dove
But most of all . . . Christmas is
love.

Florence Margolin
THE CAR EXPERIENCE
I went to a show room
to see a car.
'Twas the nicest one
I'd seen, by far.

I told the man
"I'll take that one."
He said to me,
"There's a better one, Son."

I took his advice
and spent more money,
But when I got home
It wasn't funny.

The car wouldn't start
but when it did
My girl friend saw it

and then she hid.

'Twas the ugliest sight
she ever did see.
She said, "Trade it in
or get rid of me."

I thought for awhile
as to what to do,
Then I decided to get rid of
you know who!

Well I'm looking around
for another friend,
And I'll keep my car
to the very end.

Now I've learned my lesson
and this I know,
A car serves you well
but friends come and go.

Iva Jean Bowden
NO LANGUAGE NUCLEAR
[To My Foster Son, Whom I
Love with all my Heart Bobby
D. Ipock]
Nuclear War;
We Have no one to war with any
more. Once we could have our
differences with other
countries and then work them
out.
This thing we have an argument
with has no personality, It has
no Mother to attack, it has no
Father. It has no family—so we
have it;
How can we cope with it? "this
monster" called nuclear
We can't eat it, we can't kill it, we
can't dilute it we can't use it for
fear of being the loser, so who
will win with this monster
called nuclear;
Man becomes more confused
because (he as man) Is civilized
and needs to talk out his
problems; what language do we
use? We only get more
confused in this world of
nuclear—
Man needs to become more a
protector than a destroyer of
our world; pull the fuse on the
nuclear, bronze it and learn
from it; That would take care
of no language nuclear . . .

Deloris Green
THE RAIN
When I woke up this morning
and heard the rain
Our pleasureful night was relived
again
I lay real still and pictured the
place
I clearly recollected your kind,
smiling face

Sometimes you were quiet, so off
to yourself
Hiding your feelings on some
secret shelf
Too many past heartaches have
made me think twice
I would still like to know you, I
think it'd be nice

It's sad to hear a person curse the
rain
I'd like to greet it again and again
Rain is special to me now it's true
It means warmth, tenderness,
great joy and you

Ron Greene
IGNORANCE
Burn the witches
Ban the books!
Slay the thinkers—
Kill the crooks!

Stamp out reason,
Turn to God!
Don the blinders
O'demogagues.

Ann L. Korosac

Ann L. Korosac
Wind In the Leaves
Wind in the leaves you are with
me tonight,
Scattering clouds, so, the moon
gives no light.
You have stripped the trees to the
bone.
Like drying skeletons, they stand
alone.

Your are shuddering and sighing
With sounds as of weeping;
Disturbing the peace
Of those who are sleeping.

Your breath is laden with old
Indian lore.
With ghostly fingers you rattle
the door.
The leaves whisper behind you as
you hurry on,
Reviving old memories of those
who are gone.

And, remembering, I weep; but to
no avail,
For that moon—lit night on the
Navajo Trail.

Ronald W. Borcherdt
LATE FALL
[For Barbara]
And so the end . . .
A needle whispered away from
the tree

A wind—drifter now
Settling on soil unsown

Chill winter warden
Gathers the garment, gives it
away

Barbara M. Parry
SUMMERTIME
Summertime,
When the bright yellow
Beachball hangs suspended
In the sky—

And, no mother's child
Is seen to cry.
And, men become a lad
From another time.

When women's hips
Sway to and fro,
In memory of a girl
Once known.

And, every color bird
Is heard
A match, for every flower
On earth.

Then, every creature
Given birth,
Is bathed in warmth
And scented mirth.

Summertime,
When life is right,
And Heaven's bounty vines
Are ripe.

Stella O. Chvilicek
THE FORGOTTEN ONES
The ancient road of life is done,
The sands are running out,
Heart and soul so troubled,
Filled with fear and doubt.
The setting sun is hanging low,
The time is almost nigh,
Born to die, that we might live.
"Love me", is their lonely cry.
These old, and lost forgotten
ones,
Whose only sin is age,
Too many seem to pass them by,
No thought for that wrinkled
face,
Not careing that a heart can
break,
Left in youths mad pace.
Remember that your time will
come,
Youth is a fleeting thing,
As you do, so it is done,
What will your last years bring?

De Ann Packman
HAPPINESS
The sound of you snoring
against the wall
Our small daughter sleeping
across the hall
The night time is silent
My loved ones are near
I am comfy and warm
and have nothing to fear
As far as a job goes
of mine I will boast
A home and a family
are what I love most

Eileen A. Donovan—Cooper
**Time, Three Senses and
Memories**
Take time to

Look, watch, see
lest you lose your sight—
that you will remember
colors, scenes, flowers, birds so
bright in flight

Be quiet, hark, listen
lest you become deaf—
that you will remember
a child's laughter, a bird's song, a
creek's grugling,
the sound of a falling leaf

Speak
lest you lose your power of
speech—
that they will remember
the sound of your voice, your
words of love to each

Enhance the recall of

things seen, bursting upon your
   senses with beauty beyond
   imagination
things heard, the roar of
   deafening silence softened by
   muted murmurings,
   enchantingly soft rippling
   laughter
things spoken, guidance tenderly
   proferred, sweetly uttered
   words

Look, listen, speak
to all things around
for a remembrance
of God's wonders with which the
   earth abounds

Take time now for these senses
   and their memory

Yvonne J. Deutscher
WISHING
I wish I was a butterfly . . .
   So beautiful and free.
I'd soar over the fields and
   flowers . . .
   And smell the fresh, clean air.
I'd watch God's animals frolic . . .
   And the clouds go dancing by.
And I'd stay where the sun
   always shines . . .
   For all eternity.

Constance Bedard
MY SOULS HOME
The sea is rough and the waves
   are high,
The noon sun stands high in the
   sky.
My soul is rolling to and fro,
For mysteries unsolved my mind
   does roll.

The ocean roars within my soul,
And tempest high I change the
   roll.
I haven't loved as lovers do,
But I have played the same as
   you.
The music rocks my very soul
And I inside start to fold.
For love for centuries has passed
   me by,
For I had sinned in God's own
   eyes.
Now God looks upon me with
   kinder eyes,
And I will love not be passed by.

He gives, He takes, He stands and
   waits
For each of us to pass His gates.
Now I have learned my lesson
   well,
On earth no more this soul will
   dwell.

Jean Faicco
MY JOURNEY
Clear day
Golden sky . . .
Adventure, hope, and prosperity.

Cloudy day
Gray sky . . .
Doubt, fear, and uncertainty.

The storm brings forth the
   journey of endless violence,
   loneliness,
   and struggle.

As I climb,
Climb over all obstacles

Through the ever-changing
   storms and sunshine,
I do go.

The struggle is non-ending.
As I glide through the white
   puffy clouds of hope and
   reassurance,
As I stumble through the gray
   clouds of fear and uncertainty,

As I dream,
Dream I will reach my destiny

Over the sky.
I will reach the rainbow,
The rainbow of hope, peace, and
   joy,
The rainbow of never-ending
   happiness,
The rainbow I have yearned for,
The rainbow my whole life is
   devoted to,
The rainbow of eternity.

Frances Crumley Hicks

Frances Crumley Hicks
TWO TABLES
*[In memory of my husband
Dr. Harry Hicks, Sr.]*
EAT NOT from MAN'S TABLE
   For to do so is SIN
Each refusal will help you
   Another to win.

Strive steadily upward
   Temptation subdue
Jesus was tempted
   He will see you through.

Those that over-cometh
   Can shout "Hallilujah" and sing
Oh! GRAVE—where is thy
   VICTORY?
   Oh! DEATH—where is thy
   STING?

The Grave cannot hold them
   Death's Sting cannot kill
For they are obeying
   The CREATOR'S WILL.

They have been EATING
   The LIVING FOOD WAY
Thus conquering DEATH and
   the GRAVE
   And will LIVE ETERNALLY.

Thora Jean Supple
SUNSET BY THE SEA
*[To all those people who love
beautiful sunsets, and to those
who love God's handiwork]*
God paints the sky at sunset,
With colors of silver and gold,
Blended with reds and lavender,
They make a sunset bold!

I love to watch the sea birds,
Diving for their evening meal,
The gulls and terns fish the
   shore,
Taking sea food from it's store!

Sunset time is a lovely time,
Laying days trials to rest;
Saying the day is now over,
Giving respite in a night's rest!

Dusk settles over the land
   quickly,
Changing the sea to calm,
Sky colors soon fade away,
Sunset has again worked it
   magical balm!

Katy Potts
INDIAN RESPLENDENCE
it takes a great deal
   of commitment
it's not like a mother
   who does everything
it's not like a computer
   that beeps, then it rings
if you want to feel warm
   need to plan
      and to form
a schedule
   first collect
then resize, then to stack
   and surmise, run and carry
if love you
   have married
nothing is heavy, wood is dry
and handy, the fire burns on
but you've changed
      far beyond
past dependence
Indian resplendence.

Fern D. Laurvick
KING OF THE MOUNTAIN
He stands at the top, nothing to
   scare him
Over looking his bountious
   harem.
His majestic horns reach for the
   sky
A perfect subject for the artist's
   eye.
He stands there surveying, by the
   painter undaunted,
His place on the mountain was
   all he wanted.
The elk in his habitat, natural
   and clean
Is a sight that by men is seldom
   seen.
If you should see him, you'll
   always remember
The king of the mountain in all
   his splendor.

Todd Joffrion
WHAT'S THE USE
I can't help but to ask, what's the
   Use in it all.
First you are born, but before you
   can walk,
They say you must learn to
   CRAWL.
Then they teach you how to run,
And you learn how it feels to fall.
They show you how to talk,
And some will make you laugh,
While others make you cry.
Then they explain the
   importance and
Good of saying "hello" then you
Learn what it means to say
   "good-bye".

As you grow, you learn to live,
   love and hate,
And everything that happens
   both good and bad
Are just written off to fate.
When you are once again happy,
It just means that you will soon
   again be sad.
And you can't help but to sit and
   cry
When you find out
That no one can tell you why.

Marie Gabrielle Berg, R.S.H.M.
NATIVITY
Silence
ripped wide
in cries of bearing
of a'borning.
A crowd murmurs
pros, then cons
promising good
foreboding evil.
A trumpet flashes,
as thunder marches
over life,
winning some
losing some,
and in the same struggle
a flame thought doused
leaps up
splintering the dark.
Light from true light
   Here!
   Now!

Elaine J. Huffman
EVERGREEN
Its job is finished.

It was the background
   for family photographs.
Unevenly decorated by children
   who couldn't reach the top.
Proudly surrounded by
   carefully wrapped packages.
Blinking lights, garland. The star.

Now, lying in the snowbank,
beside garbage bags filled
   with crumpled paper and bows.
Naked. Stripped of its splendor.
   —only traces of tinsel—
but still beautiful.

The truck will come soon
   to take it away.
(Only the scent of pine remains.)

I'm glad I took pictures.

Ursula Tillberg
CHRISTMAS MUSINGS
CHRISTMAS! Not again!
Every year the same old story...
Every year more time to worry...
How to make payments year after
   year.
Joy to the world, soon
   CHRISTMAS is here.
Oh, how I love the old Christmas
   melody,
But this year it came too soon for
   me;
I can't even buy a Christmas tree.
No work, no money, it is a
   shame,
But CHRISTMAAS will be here
   again.
I stand by the window, I look at
   the light,
Soon, we will sing, "Silent Night".

Last year, of course, it wasn't the
   same

We bought for the kids a video game.
They were so happy, they played every day . . .
The first payment was due in May.
The economy went downhill,
We couldn't pay bill after bill.
I closed my eyes, I didn't want to think,
Where this inflation people might bring.
I fell asleep, I had a dream.
I found the real CHRISTMAS means.
Tears filled my eyes, my heart was full of joy,
Because I had touched the sweet Jesus boy.
My children gave me a hug,
"We love you Mom, don't cry, wake up!"

CHRISTMAS will soon be here again,
But it isn't for me the same,
No matter how rich or poor you are . . .
Oh, think about Love and the light of one star.
I don't need diamonds under the tree,
God gave me more, He gave me a family.
He sent His Son. He died for me.
Lord, I thank you for your love so dear.
To all of you,
Merry CHRISTMAS, and Happy New Year!

Marcella (Sally) Seiler
A MERRY CHRISTMAS
A little bird sat in a tree—
And gazed but yonder, on the field below!
He wondered how he'd find his eats—
When all was buried deep, beneath the snow!

'Twas December, a cold wintry month—
With the holidays drawing near!
The little bird was hungry and cold—
He couldn't sing out with holiday cheer!

Suddenly, a little girl passed by—
With Christmas cookies in her hand!
She was marching in the parade—
Right behind the toy soldiers band!

She took a bite of her cookie—
And crumbs fell down upon the snow!
They caught the eye of the little bird—
They sure did fill his tummy so
He then, flew over to the little girl—
And on her shoulder, he sat!
Which made such a divine scene—
"A Merry Christmas", it was, at last!

Marcello White
MANY LONELY NIGHTS
There's been many lonely nights since my mother died.

When I've lain in bed
and just cried and cried

There's been a lot of habits
I couldn't break
Living in a world
that holds no mistakes

While searching the outside world
For my final goal.
I began to turn inward
and search through my soul.

I began to find myself searching
for shelter against the wind.
Searching for an answer
Searching for a friend.

My days are dark
My nights are blind.
Searching for a self-satisfaction
I just could not find.

There's been many lonely nights
when I was left wondering in the street
No home in which to go to
No food in which to eat

There were times I was left searching
for no particular thing.
Wondering what the future held for me
Wondering what tomorrow would bring.

Shut-out from the world
and the reality it holds.
Unable to reach my destination
unable to reach my goals.

Looking back on life
the things I regret
Looking at the past
one I can not forget.

I know beyond this darkness
there lies a light.
And until I find it I'll continue searching
beyond these lonely nights.

Carol Therese Plum
Idle Hours By the Fire
Idle hours pass away,
Yet who may deem them vainly spent?
Which lifeless soul has never paused
To let dreams kindle sweet content?

For dreams burn on without a cost,
And warm a frigid heart.
Still the dancing flames won't weave your dreams,
Just show you where to start.

April B. McKinney
THE AUTUMN FALL
[This poem was written to and inspired by my mother Lucille who opened my eyes to the world. And dad for his encouragement.]
In the hour glass so small,
compare the moments treasured,
in an autumn fall,
orange, yellow, brown and beige colors they all,
set the stage,
The dry sweet smell of maple leaves,

mellows a fragrance which,
lingers in the breeze,
Crackles crushing up around my ear,
exciting is the tickle,
felt under my heels,
Meet with me the splendor of the autumn fall,
Enjoy with me the wonder of it all.

Gale Morrison

Gale Morrison
OUTDOOR OBSERVER
[To my wife and family.]
Oh, a deer can run, and a deer can play
having their fun in many a way.
A deer in the sun, a deer in the shade,
the fawn, the hidden one, no move to be made.

An intruder like me, in selfsame glade
no move can I see, except by the eyes made.
While there he is hidden, concealed ever so neatly,
no move, just as bidden, obeying orders completely.

While I circle to inspect, not a move, muscle or nerve
can I in any way detect, only rolling eyes observe.
Ever rolling in their orbit, watch front, side and rear,
my every move to absorb it, not yet knowing fear.

I see so clearly, this cautious little one
left shaded so dearly, the doe in the hillside sun.

A deer can ever flee to distract from her own,
in the distance to be so protecting the lone.

Then watching, I ponder, in someway all mothers
as the doe, off yonder, takes chances with others.
Life is good, life is splendid, to fawn, daughter or son
of natures loves intended. Blessed is such a one.

G.G. Ruth Elouise Skaggs
MY LOVING FAMILY
[In loving tribute to my family and in memory of my beloved husband Herbert Allen Skaggs—1916 to 1981]
Every time I look at you, I look with love.
And love is all I see,
In the eyes that look with love, back at me.
I owe you all for so many things,
That I cannot repay.
And because I love you so,
I know I'll always feel this way.
I feel so much gratitude,
For all the love you've shown.
For loving happy memories,
Of the love I have known.
I can only hope the years will be,
As wonderful for you all,
As they have been for me.
For you're the ones, who will always be,
The world and all of life to me.
God's love, your love, and your daddy's love,
Are the greatest loves in my life, I'll ever find.
And to think, all this love has happened to me,
All in my lifetime.
So I just want to say,
Thanks, for all you've done for me.
And someday in heaven,
All of you I hope to see.
Cause you're all, my loving family.

Lee Long
A Candyman Christmas
[To my children who never have a white Christmas]
With Christmas brings the cold and snow,
Icicles and the winds that blow,
The boots and gloves that keep us warm
And covered-up nose that frost could harm.
Bare trees and squirrels with nuts for winter's feed
The holly trees with berries red
And birds that will scatter the seed.
But! What if you lived down South
And never saw the winter's mouth.
And here on Christmas day
It never snows or ices the way.
Would Santa's suit still be red?
Would he wear a long cap upon his head?
Black boots and a beard of white
Or would he travel here tonight
On a surf board bronzed and tan,

Who looks more like the
candyman.
Would the feeling still be the
same?
Would you still call Christmas by
its name?
Give me the cold and winter's
blast
For Christmas is finally here at
last.

Joan Kaletta Rebolj
UNNOTICED
*[This poem was written to—
and inspired by—my husband
John.]*
So far away and unnoticed
burning high,
Bright and vibrant is its light
Dazzling with warmth and
beauty.
With me always yet, as the heart
of Lear,
I do not see.
Then, hurling to the earth,
Blindness is overcome.
With awe and wonder, my heart
is opened.
Falling heavily it carves deeply
into the earth
As the love burns deep in my
soul,
Blowing on the fiery coals of my
heart.

Maria Dona Depra Cala
MEDITATION
Every time I sit all quiet
At the ending of each day
To listen to my heartbeat
And what it has to say.

Sereneness overtakes me
And calmness fills my soul
When I sit all quiet
When darkness outside falls.

Each night I sit all quiet
To communicate from within,
To meditate, to take a pause,
To make my soul serene.

Ruth E. Morgan
A GIFT
It isn't the monetary value of a
gift
you give,
If some happiness and enjoyment
it
doth bring.
A hummingbird feeder we gave
our neighbor
last year,
It really has brought him many
moments
of cheer.
Little Bob exclaims, "Aren't they
the
cutest things?"
As under the bougainvillea they
flutter
their wings.
When evening dusk appears, of
the nectar
they sip their fill,
Back again come morning, when
the sun shines
over the hill.
To watch them fly backwards,
sideways or
motionless hover,
Excites wonder how much
ground these tiny

glittering visitors do cover.
We have a hummingbird feeder
and watch
their antics a lot,
But we're happiest when we
witness the true
enjoyment Little Bob gets from
the
gift we bought.

Anita Albanese
THE TRAIN RIDE HOME
I look at the world with all its
miseries and I see its people
squandered in hopelessness.
I feel the earth beneath my feet
and I sense the longing and the
need for change.
I touch the person next to me
and he jumps as if he has just
met death.
I smell the fragrance of a young
woman, but I turn to see a
crippled man dying at my feet.
I dream of a world that once was,
but walk home to envision
poverty and depression.
There is no need to force my
tears, for they come now in
place of the laughter that once
echoed through my mind.
I might not make it but I sure
will try, and if I fail I will once
again meet you, only this time
in Heaven.

Darell Lee Cunningham
Untitled
*[To my parents
From your soldier
Ft. Dix, N.J. 1982]*
The winter is cold upon my face,
Yet the sun is warm upon my
back.
I am far from home in time and
space,
Yet I am always home in spirit
and memory.
I stand alone as a man many
times,
Yet I live so I am never as alone
as it seems.
To be a dream it is to be
subconscious,
Yet it controls your conscious
being in everyway.
I am a dreamer and a poet to lifes
very end,
Yet I know not most of the
time—truly the meaning of it.

Kristine Stratman McCoy
A PAINFUL TASK
*[Lovingly written for my Dad,
It was his painful task,
I now understand why and
how hard it was.]*
I drove into the country, but
never like this before
The pit of my stomach dropped
as I opened the car door,
I drove until I found a beautiful,
peaceful spot
One so cool even on a day that
was so hot,
Peaceful and quiet under a large
group of pine trees
Then I started my task, the
hardest for me,
I loaded my gun, a single shot
was all
As I stood there in the tree's

shadow, so huge, so tall,
As I aimed my gun, my heart
started to race
The cold sweat started to flow off
of my face,
For down the site of my gun, was
my best friend
And on this day, his life, I would
have to end,
He had been a friend for so many,
many years
Just the thought of my task,
brought to my eyes, tears,
But it had to be done, for he was
suffering much
He was in pain, even at my gentle
touch,
His eyes were on me, as I sited-in
the gun
Through his pain, I think he
knew it had to be done,
Oh God, can I do it, can I take his
life
Then I remembered, he'd be free
from all his pain and strife,
I closed my eyes and took a long
deep breath
And remembered the good times
and helped him meet death,
To this day, that was the most
painful task, I've ever done
I lost one of my best friends, my
most trusted one.

J. Benjamin Stanley

J. Benjamin Stanley
TO LOVE IS TO LIVE
When the anarchy of darkness
fell,
A man stood in the wing of hope.
As a benign self imposed subject
of life he said,
"The downward trend of
heartaches may yet unfold"
In essence of the life he led, but
not fulfilled
Though man still seeks the thrill
of happines untold
Esentially in balance and in
element of time
God only knows the end and
means to follow
Love has but two faces—secure
and ambivalent
Man is intimate with both, but
finds perplexing
Therefore, do not begile thyself,
for the eyes of
Love shall guide thy path of
righteousness.
Suddenly, greatness will be thrust
upon him,

He'll know not why, since the
mind and the heart
Bare many complexities.
But she'll be there, the very
apocalypse of that
Sudden greatness.
And the multiplying days of
depression will
Begin mounting in reverse.
Instantly he will find that
without sustenance
Of love
Life hath no meaning

Gladys G. Whitacre
THE GREAT INVITATION
Is it nothing to you,
Who pass Him by
The Saviour of all,
Condemned to die?

His pleading eyes,
And precious smile,
Are beckoning; come,
Your life's worth while.

The careless throng,
Go on their way,
Not caring that,
Life may end today.

Their greatest treasure,
Many fail to see,
That's the one that lasts
Through eternity.

The few who discover,
The pearl of great cost,
Will repent of all sin,
Ere their soul is lost.

We love you Lord,
We'll come today,
You are the life,
The truth, the way.

Lois Allen
UNTITLED
Oh! How I
Long to be
with you
If not in this
life
Then perhaps in
another.

Nelda LeVant
KITE WITH TALE
If I could just put
Two n' two "together"
to gaither to gather—
I'd have a feather that flys . . .

Rose Dorman
A Need To Help a Friend
Has life been less than good to
you my friend?
Did I see pain and sorrow etched
upon your face?
Look up and see me smile in your
direction
Reach out to me and let me share
your space.

Don't try so hard to hide your
inner feelings
For the pain within your eyes will
tell on you,
It really doesn't make you any
weaker
To admit you need a friend to
help you through.

So let me try and give you
understanding
I've patience and I've love enough
to share,
And to see you hurt alone just
makes me wonder
If it might just be a little much to
bear.

If you looked at me and sensed
that I was hurting
Although my words told you that
I was doing fine,
Wouldn't you care and wouldn't
you smile in my direction
And feel a need to be a friend of
mine?

So let me be your friend and let
me help you,
I always wished that someone
would help me.
I'm a friend who's got the time to
sit and listen
So let me understand and give
you sympathy.

Lillian Payne

Lillian Payne
LONELY PEOPLE
There are *so* many lonely people—
Their bodies are raked with pain.
In their hearts they know they
Will never walk again.
And so they sit by the window—
And watch as you go by—
Wishing so much you would stop
and just say Hi!
It only takes a minute.
But what a change 'twould be—
A smile would light their face—
For all to see.
To know you loved and cared—
And a minute of *your* time *you*
shared.

Winnifred E. (Harding) Harlow
NO ROOM
[To my friend and pastor,
Rev. DeWitt Hulin Graham,
in gratitude and love.]
No room at the inn
What a sin!
Don't you know on this site
A holy child will be born tonight?

Shepherds, see the star?
Wise men travel from afar
To gaze in wonder, as angels sing
Glory, glory, while bells ring.

Pealing out a message of peace
and love,
Streaming from the Heavens
above.

Where can he go to hide?
Our hearts will cradle him, inside

No room at the inn?
What a sin! What a sin!

Ron Jevaltas
BOTH BARRELS
Time has a cruel way of moving
on:
what is not willing to be carried
is quickly trampled and those
who have a mind to slow it down
are choked and splattered with
exhaust.
We've had more ambushes fail
than you would have ever
thought possible
and I can understand how my
jumping
on and off can get a little old;
but since we formed our gang it's
been
both barrels baby and I know
you wouldn't have had it any
other way.

Lou Ebersole
**It All Comes
'Round Again . . .**
Little girls grow up
And trade in their dolls for boys.
But scattered all across their bed
Are all of those stuffed toys
They've saved from early
childhood,
And they'll keep them 'till the
day
They have little girls of their
own.
Then they'll put them away
Only to bring them out again
When their child is two or three
And have them scattered all
about
In brand new company.
So then their little girl can enjoy
All the enchantment of
The cuddly softness of a toy
That was saved so long with love.

Beau
BONDS
No matter what the distance
if I were a million miles away
Whether I am here or gone
if my being takes another state
Though unrecorded is my fate
the tenure of my ephemeral stay
my heart will not release you
unless my heart it breaks.

Gladys Reusser
KEEP ON KEEPING ON
Two little bugs sat on the rim
of a glass that had cream within,
They looked down into the
contents and thought
Let us jump down on to that soft
white spot.
So both flew down to the creamy
bed,
And started sinking up to their
head.
One cried, "Well this is the end".
And didn't try his life to defend.
The other one beat with all four
feet
Saying, "I will not die with out a
try".
By thrashing the cream around,
He beat it into a butter mound.

He sat on the butter mound to
rest,
After awhile giving his wings a
test,
He looked up and saw the top of
the glass,
He flew right up and was out at
last . . .
So don't give up if you should fall,
You'll win—unless you don't try
at all.

Harvey C. Eure
I LOVE YOU
Oh sweet little girl
How I love you.
If I could gather
All the stars in the Heavens
And spell the word "LOVE"
It would not express
What you meant to me.
If I could dam the
Mighty river of this
World we know,
The power generated
Could never equal
My feelings for you.
But yet, one small
Smile, a tiny touch
Is enough for me.
Just to know you're
Happy means so much.
Does one forget so quickly
Words spoken in haste.
Forget me not love,
For I shall always
Love you.

Donna Lucas
A Blossom In Your Heart
Diana called me to her bedside
One day in early fall
I gave to her a pretty flower
And held her hand so frail and
small.

She said, I won't be with you
come springtime.
The time we both love the best
When springtime flowers are
blooming
And the robin builds her nest.

Winter winds will soon be
blowing
We'll sit by fires that sway and
sing
You'll hold me close and say I
love you
You'll make me smile and laugh
again.

When springtime comes with all
its beauty
Don't be sad cause we're apart
Go gather flowers from the
garden
And I'll be a blossom in your
heart.

Beverly Reno Tong
WEEKENDS
[To Mom and Dad,
who know the feeling.]
The weekend's here
What are we going to do?
I don't care dear,
It's up to you.

It's always the same
Time after time.
No one seems able
To make up their mind.

Have you any suggestions?
No dear, do you?
Well, not really,
I don't care what we do.

So the weekend passes,
As they always do.
Let's make plans for next
weekend,
Okay, but you decide what to do.

Irene Goldminz
LADY LIBERTY'S LUSTER
[This poem was inspired by
and is dedicated to:
Mary Sager of Blacklick, Ohio
Known also worldwide as
"Grandmaw Liberty."]
Please let her wear her years with
grace!
Do not her patina erase,
That luster of time and weather
That should naught be changed
forever.
An acid bath would remove all
trace
Of light and welcome in her face,
And time and weather will again
prevail
Such waste of money—to no
avail.
So let this lady in the bay
Be not marred in any way,
And let her wear her years with
grace
To welcome all with love and
faith.

H.R. Morse, Jr.
SYBIL
Oh, Sybil, dear,
Mysterious, strange and knowing;
Lovely, searching and wondering;
Floating through oblivion
In effervescence of mystic aura.
Sybil is the girl
Who never was.

Virginia Weber
ANGELS
We are listening
The angels are listening
Over the petrified city
Hangs the smoky dawn.
Murky Monday
And the curses of the past
Take form.
Evil, by intent
Is now made manifest
It is here
Here in this city
Here in this county
Here in the low-crawling
inhabitants
Of the city of destruction.

I am waiting
We know
The angels wait
The children of God wait
Another week
And the howling
Of the fallen ones
Echoes in the empty
Chambers of the mind.

Lone Bard
THE HARP SEAL RITUAL
"Spring is coming, almost here!
Merrily we'er on our way,
From Greenland's shore to
Labrador,
The isles of St. Lawrence Bay!"

But O what fate awaits them
  there!
Off Canada's eastern shore,
Where cruel men with weapons
  prepare
For their ritual of blood and
  gore.

Invading the nurseries on the ice
  When baby harp seals arrive,
They begin their clubbing, their
  slitting and skinning—
And many they skin alive.

Here comes a husky with a heavy
  club,
So proud to kill, so bold!
He brings it down with a mighty
  blow
On a pup but two days old.

The confused mother frightened
  away,
Her only babe struck low!
And what was once a shelter of
  rest
Is now a place of woe.

The gruesome ritual comes to an
  end,
The ice all crimson red;
Rachel weeping for her children
Where innocent blood was
  shed.

Lone Bard
BE CAREFUL OF BECKIE
*[In memorial to victims of
drunken drivers, this poem is
based on the Moody Bible
Institute film by the same
name—a true story.]*
A nurse and mother stood at the
  window,
As many times before,
Watching the hospital ambulance
  come in
And stop at the emergency
  door.

The bearers in place stepped off
  with the stretcher.
"O no, not Beckie!" she cried,
But Beckie it was they were
  carrying in—
And Beckie it was who died.

Beckie was careful when riding
  her "bike".
She never would break a rule,
But no one had warned of the
  greatest danger—
The car with the drunken fool!

The sun shines bright and the
  grass grows green
On the grave of a little girl,
And the stars look down in their
  watch at night
Till the banners of dawn
  unfurl.

There's an empty chair in a home
  tonight
With sorrow that will not
  heal—
As cars go madly down the road
  With a bottle of death at the
  wheel!

Doloris Holmes
YELLOW BIRD MORNING
I wake early grieving for you
The yellow birds fly around the
  roof of my house.
I hear your name everywhere.

Almost touch it. Almost smell
  it.
The yellow birds fly into my eyes
The yellow birds fly out of my
  eyes
In the morning, I am mourning
I look at the dawn yellowed by
  many birds
I look at the sky with tears in my
  eyes

Jonathan Miller

Jonathan Miller
JESUS THE LORD
Jesus the Lord, most bright of
  sheen
That hath nor end nor mean,
Promising us damned folk a place
In Heaven's blissful space,

Where offering us life with His
  death:
Forgiving our cruelty with His
  last breath!
Such was He, our Lord He is, this
  know;
Will to live and die in His glow.

Tom Nordblad
American Womanhood
Born female and blessed with the
  curse
Confusing road lay ahead
Without smile and purse
It would all be much worse
But her mind like a book would
  be read

Normal sensual desires were
  burned
Playing roles, a teenage machine
But the heads that she turned,
The lessons she learned
Melted into a serious scene

Now a lonely graduate of fashion
Living in pick up type bars
Constantly asking
For small hints of passion
From guys more in love with
  their cars

Wants and needs slowly are
  dying
She has to come through with a
  choice
After all of her trying,
After all of her crying,
She finds out that her soul has a
  voice.

Helen Adair Wilson
THE GIRL WITH THE HOE
*[To Dalphene—My only child,
who has been the inspiration
of my life, and promoted
everything I've done worth
while.]*
Early each morning, down on the
  farm I was filled with Vim
  Vigar and go,
As the rooster crows and the sun
  arose, you would find me
  outside with my hoe.

This city life is for the rich man's
  wife, let her to the movie go,
I'll choose my life in the country
  strife.
If I can be outside with my hoe.

I like to dig in the soil to sweat
  and toil,
To separate the weeds from the
  plants.
To hear the whippoorwill across
  the hill,
I like to watch the busy ants.

You can have your bright lights,
  and your man made sights, all
  the traffic with its zip & go.
Just give me the sod, here I feel
  closer to God.
I relax when I'm alone with my
  hoe.

Jill D'Anna
WILDERNESS
The wilderness,
Yells with emptiness.
Suddenly!
A noise,
A loud noise.
The wilderness is quiet
But yet filled with noise.
The noise of empty space.
The noise of the best kingdom in
  the world.
The kingdom of the empty
  wilderness.

Gary West
THOSE DYING DREAMS
Locked inside and rarely seen,
The prisoner cries; those dying
  dreams—
The walls can barely contain the
  sounds
Of the calling down—of the
  calling down—
The doors are just to maintain
  the dreams,
With the dying screams—with
  the dying screams.

Locked inside but barely seen,
The prisoner lies; those dying
  dreams—

The walls can barely contain the
  sounds
Of the falling down—of the
  falling down—
The windows just can't sustain
  the dreams:
And the dying screams—and the
  dying screams.

Locked outside and clearly seen,
Each of us tries; those dying
  dreams—
The walls can barely contain the
  sounds
Of the fallen down—of the fallen
  down—
The ceilings squarely restrain the
  dreams,
As the dying screams—as the
  dying screams.

Mark Silcox
LUNAR SAMPLES
*[This poem was inspired by the
Apollo 11 Astronauts and their
search for the secrets of the
Universe.]*
Cement-gray rocks abound,
Fine gun-powder dust all around.
A metal poker takes a bite,
Under distant suns, of pure white
  light.
Silver Curtains on the moon,
Collecting remnants of the Solar
  Womb.

Valerie Joy Turner
EYE'S SEA GREEN
Green eyes.
Inside yours, I am
Lost. I wonder . . .
could I wander
into your green eyes.
Might I walk,
across those green hills.
Walk until I discover
the edge of green
Then into the blackness of the
  inner eye,
would I step.
And never would I stop

Lori Arruzzo
GOOD-BYE
Hours pass by,
As I sit all alone,
Just waiting for you,
To call on the phone.

I thought that we would always
  be together,
And we would never say good-bye,
But I decided to forget it,
When I caught you in a lie.

You'll never know how much you
  hurt me,
Or how much I'll cry,
But I guess the time has come,
For me to say . . .
  "Good-Bye"

Dazell Schubert
MOUNTAIN
On the peaceful mountain where
  easy flowing harmony fills the
  air; the young and innocent
  feel the kindliness of her
  nature.

As the sun falls beneath her peak
  a gently burning fire blankets
  the small ones with warmth;
  taking the bitter chill from her
  breath.

As the dawn awakens the stillness of the night dissipates. The children well rested and with a feel of serenity; open their eyes only to see the brightly shining beams of golden light glittering on her frosty top. The children have been touched by the love and beauty nature holds for us all.

Liz Carter Richards

Liz Carter Richards
WOMAN
i love
with
every conscious
thought
as pulsation
after pulsation
travels
through my body
to the outlet
then
i love
even more
as i lay
content.

Joyce M. Lucas
NIGHT'S FANTASY
Thoughts of you warm me,
more than their simple beginning
they've burst into imagination's
    flame.

Your words kaleidoscope images
of soft shapes and dark meanings
bearing the rhythm of night's
    fantasy.

Lying in the mystic's sphere,
my soul whispers to your mind
my needs in screams repressed.

Night's magic quickly vanishes
as dawn's cold reality wakens
and love sleeps silent yet.

Rallenco
THE DAY WE MET
*[To the only real and true
friend that I have in this world;
the one I call, 'Blue Eyes!' They
will never fade.]*
Do you remember the day we
    met?
It's the day of my life I'll never
    forget.
You were the first thing I saw,
    when I walked in,
Sitting at your desk; looking neat
    as a pin.

I looked at you, then looked
    away,

Trying to think of something to
    say.
You raised your head as I looked
    at you,
And all I could see, were eyes of
    blue.

I didn't see your lips or hair,
Just big blue eyes everywhere.
The day we met was a wonderful
    day,
You were so beautiful, I had
    nothing to say.

Then at last the words came free
And I asked you to go with me.
You said "Yes" and I'll never forget
That wonderful day that we first
    met.

Mrs. Helen Curtis Sheets
THE CORNERSTONE BOX
[For Tom]
Do not open 'till the old year is
    past
Lift the lid gently to the clinking
    of glass—
The bubbles of wishes and
    remembrances glad
Not the time for memories fearful
    or sad.

Nestled carefully, a paperweight
    bright
Sparkly with color and fractured
    with light
A dried, powdery nosegay from a
    Mother's Day gift,
A Boy Scout Merit Badge, to
    carefully lift.

A yellowed letter, written faintly
    in ink
A crushed gift box, from whom, I
    can't think
To others, these tokens are of
    value but nought
But each in it's own way heartfelt
    remembrances wrought.

Do not open 'till the old year is
    past
Lift the lid gently as you smile at
    your past.

Mary Earle
**The Hostages Are Free—
    Come Home!**
The wind is blowing.
The flag is twisting and turning.
Not a gentle waving in the breeze
    today.
A violent and shaking flag.
The hostages are free, it seems to
    say.
A shadow on our country is gone.
Our flag can again fly free.
Not tied and bound, but strong.
Look, I'm your land, your home.
With open, reaching arms I'm
    welcoming you back!!

Sylvia White
ESCAPE
Believe me, when I say
I have not run away:
Let me prove beyond doubt
Nothing could make me go,
Turn me around to flee
From what I hate to see.

Take my hand, touch my cheek,
Listen to my heart speak:
Here I am still; you see,
I did not turn and run

Away, only to find
I left myself behind.

Watch me walk among you;
I laugh, talk as you do;
How clever have I been
Effecting my escape,
Fooling your world with stealth;
One day, I'll fool myself.

Michael Steward Haynes
THAT DAY IN MAY
Twelve years ago began it all,
One pretty day not late in fall.
We made new friends with which
    to play,
It started all upon that day.
The years did come and quickly
    go,
As now we gaze and truly know.
They seem as they were just a
    dream,
A babbling brook or silent
    stream.
We know not where the years
    have gone,
It does not seem its been that
    long.
We grew and learned and had
    much fun,
For then our trip had just begun.
Six years had passed along the
    way,
The end did come one day in
    May.
As now we pressed still higher
    yet,
The world our goal as we had set.
New friends we made and good
    ones, too.
We gained a lot but lost a few.
Three years we spent and worked
    as one,
A time of love, a time of fun.
But not to stop and here to stay,
We left this, too, one day in May.
Still higher we were pressing on,
A few had come, a few had gone.
Our days we count a numbered
    few,
Some were gay, and some were
    blue.
These years our mind will sure
    recall,
We'll frown on some, but love
    them all.
No greater tie can ever be,
Than one small word, the word is
    "we".
We sang, we cried, we laughed a
    lot,
And all we did we grudge it not.
And now our days, as one, are
    few,
And then we'll have to start
    anew.
We'll never be again as one,
Though all the things we've said
    and done.
And soon upon that day in May,
We'll all diverge and go our ways.
Our goals are now in God's own
    Heaven,
Long live the class of sixty-seven.

Charlotte Nance Horne
KINGS HIGHWAY
Kings mountain highway
Grand and awesome
Towering peaks and pinnacles
    of granite

Caves and crags
Arrid base with desert plants
    roaring through the Kings
Giant trees and wilderness places
Kings mountains,
    Mighty Sierras,
        towering and terraced
            wide and high
Farther than can be viewed
    by human eye
A moving panorama of rugged
    glory
Breathtaking journey through
    thousands of years of
        earth's ice-age story.

Elizabeth Coyne
TO KRISTIN, AGE THREE
To look at the world through
    your eyes as mine,
To know the joy of wondering as
    a child,
To feel the excitement of first
    times.
What dreams do you dream at
    the age of three?
Are they of flowered fields in
    Spring?
Or maybe of things you've not
    yet seen.
With life at your fingertips what
    songs do you sing?
Teach me the music, sing them
    to me,
So that I might be as you are, see
    as you see.
What truer concept of living
    could I hope to know,
Than the marvels you find in all
    things as you grow.
We, as adults with knowledge in
    mind,
Dissect life's parts only to find:
We've learned nothing except
    what we've chosen to see,
Yet in the picture of innocence
    your eyes give to me,
Is the essence of knowledge in
    your simplicity.

Satty Joshua
Beautiful Woman Sister
[To my cousin, Patty Mack.]
Oh, how I love thy inspiration
Thou art thyself an inspiration
For poetry built of nature exist
    thee
For thou art a poem of nature.

Yea, I cherish thee informed
Mine of late came
Thine, beauty brought on time
For thou art nature's
    wholesomeness.

Pride not too soon
For thy silkiness, accompanies
    not
That which thee are deserved
    soon
Amendments creeps should dawn
    arise.

Beautiful woman sister
I, a sincere fratern of some
    attractiveness
Brought thee these compliments
Of thine uncomplete intelligence
    diversity.

Thou art a blossoming rosy
    morning
With all the rays of beauty thee
    surround

Awake, I charge thee, shake off
   this bump
And mortify thee thyself of thine
   centred intellect.

Thine brimmy beauty fades not
   too soon
For thee, nature exist pretty's all
For sweet rosy honey thou
   possesses
And for thee the poem of nature
   is written.

For I put thee a mark of love
Thou woman sister of beauty;
Should thou awake for these
The all of nature's beauty
   To thee heaven do crown.

Lynn M. Kirchner
UNTITLED
Why is it so hard
      sometimes
   to be alone
      and
   sometimes
      so easy
to say it's the way
   we want
      to be

Eleanor Otto
HAUNTING SPIRITS
Dark, obsessed soul—Edgar Allen
   Poe—
   chanter of haunting songs—
   echoes of demons weaving
      spells.
   Hear him lament with moaning
      bells . . .
   chanter of haunting songs.

Visionary—William Blake—
   tender spirit of love—
   bardic painter of mystic dreams
   illumined by celestial
      beams . . .
   tender spirit of love.

Unearthly voices—intoning
   mysterious songs.

Beverly E. Sax
POETRY
Poetry is the melody that runs
   through a child's head, but
   cannot be expressed.

Poetry is the portrait that
   the painter created without
   a subject.

Poetry is a beautiful mountain
   side that takes your breath
   away.

Poetry is two people walking
   hand in hand along an
   ice blue lake.

Poetry . . .
   is all things beautiful
   that we see and wish
   for someday . . .

Vicki Parsons
MY FIRST LOVE
Jesus found me, Praise His Holy
   Name.
I was so low and lost in sin,
Then Jesus came into my heart
   that fantastic night,
Cleansed me and made me new
   in Christ.
I am now reborn and free, and
My wonderful friend, you can be
   too!

Jenna V. Ownbey
TO FAR—AWAY MARIE
I don't want you to go;
But if you must go,
I want you to know
That I'll miss you so:
For when it must be
That you're gone from me
Forever I'll see
You in my memory!

Tom Campbell
TELL ME, PLEASE
When you were young did you,
   perhaps have a favorite toy?
And did you have a dog for a pet,
   when you were a little boy?
Did you run, and jump, and
   tussle, and even climb a tree;
and run to your Mom with tears
   in your eyes when you had
   skinned your knee?

Did you laugh, and joke, and have
   a good time, when you were
   just a teen?
And, did you find joy in skies of
   blue, and Summer's grass so
   green?
Did you have talks and fishing
   trips with a Dad who
   understood?
And did he say and do the things
   that made you feel so good?

And, as a man, did you work and
   sweat to make a better life;
With heart, and hand, and mind,
   and soul, to conquer any strife?
And through it all did you really
   feel that you had done your
   best;
Or did you wonder, as others do,
   if you had met the test?

Tell me, please, did you do these
   things? because I believe it so.
For, Jesus, my Lord, you were
   human, too, when you were
   here below.
You surely felt, as we all must
   feel, who pass this earthly
   portal;
Else, how could you know our
   human cares if not yourself a
   mortal?

Luvenia Ann Moody
REFLECTIONS
If I would die tomorrow, you
   would adjust quickly
You are much stronger than me—
Someone would come with
   smiles and words of
   encouragement

With a look of innocence that
   would confuse you after me,
And you would respond.
To not know what a happy face
   is, is not your style
You would tell your new friend to
   smile more often—
Because I never did.
You are accustomed to loves that
   come and go—
To act as if I have gone to
   another state to live
Is what you would do.
To help camouflage your eyes
To help your heart keep on
   beating quietly,
You would pretend that we
   argued and parted as friends.
If I would die tomorrow, you
   would well hide your sorrow—
You would hide your sorrow from
   yourself,
      but why?

Dawn-Marie Viapiano
THE POET'S PLIGHT
[To Art: One thousand poems
could not express my love for
you.]
The poet, the scribe,
Scrawling on paper
The dreams that he weaves,
The memories that flow.

He can show that he feels,
That he needs and he cares—
With the flow of a pen,
With words on a page.

Yet, only he knows
How he feels, what he needs,
And how deeply he cares—
But doesn't know why.

Esther D. Hartman
MONEY
You say you are making a lot of
   money,
But do you ever have a chance to
   look out and see if the day is
   sunny?
You say you are working on
   Sundays and getting overtime,
Well, this might sound fine,
But where does God fit in all
   your plans?
After all, He is the one who put
   the strength in your hands.
Maybe, if you didn't make so
   much money,
Then you would have time to see
   if it was sunny.
If you only made a small bit,
Then you would have time to sit,
Or walk a child who is blind,
But doesn't seem to mind.
Or a retarded child to give a hand
And there are so many in the land.
I know there is no pay in doing
   this,
But there is greater bliss,
When you see a small smile form,
On one who also like you was
   born.
This will be the biggest pay you'll
   ever get,
And you'll be the happiest you
   have been, I bet.

Charlotte L. Darwin
IF I COULD TELL YOU
To tell you how I love you would
   be

To explain a tear,
I would have to tell you of all the
   things
That made the teardrop appear

It would be to explain the
   wonderment
In the blazing flame of the sun,
I would have to tell you the
   secret
Of the golden rays it spun

It would be to explain the beauty
   in the moon and stars that shine,
I would have to tell you from
   whence they came
That they would last 'till the end
   of time

It would be to explain perfect
   happiness
At the end of a peaceful day,
There would be no words to
   express the joy
And too much for the heart to
   say

Ruth E. Moore
FOR ME, LORD?
Lord, I was a sinner, I never tho't
   of you
I did anything, I had in mind to
   do.
I never read the Bible; I said I
   couldnt' see
What readin' such a thing as that
   could ever mean to me.
And, Lord, I done some thinkin'
   and I can't rightly say
How You could think that I was
   worth the price you had to pay.
Now I ain't got much money—
   just what it takes to live;
So I know full well it ain't
   because I got so much to give.
And I ain't pretty either—ain't
   nuthin much to see;
So I know for sure it ain't for
   show, you'd do so much for me.
Now I can't play no instrument;
   can't hardly sing a tune,
'Cept when I'm all alone with •
   you—to chase away the gloom.
So Lord, I sure am grateful for
   everything you done
'Cause I can't see no reason why
   you'd do all this for me.

B. J. Freeman
Dr. Martin Luther King
[My sincere gratitude to a well
remembered school teacher N.
Barger. A very special thanks to
Patricia, Melissa, Denniese, and
all friends who were supportive
in my conquest to write.]
Dr. Martin Luther King was a
   peace loving man,
He wanted the world to know
   where they stand.
He was an apostle teaching non-
   violence and peace.
He wanted all wars, riots and
   trouble to cease.
His life was ended by a stranger's
   gun
As his work in Memphis had just
   begun.
Mrs. King and the children are all
   very sad
The children all ask, "where is
   our dad?"

Mrs. King replies with tears in
her eyes
"Dad's gone to Heaven to the
promised land,"
"He left suddenly but he knows
we'll understand."
Marked on his tombstone it
reads:
  Free At Last,
But we'll remember him from his
great work in the past.
For the loss of a great leader we
all regret,
But Dr. Martin Luther King was a
man we'll never forget.

Dale Hitsman
MY HELL
In this Hell where many come
But none dare leave
Wretched cries which blackness
screams
Fly through the pitch like burst
of flame
Where children of demons
graciously give death
But dare not . . . dare not give
birth
This Hell is large and filled with
many
Who hideously grin
But smile no more

Gerald E. Thurston, Jr.
LESSON
Lightning parts the air and the air
crashes back . . .
Thunder
Daylight splits the night and the
night caves in . . .
Time
She always cleaves my thoughts,
trips my logic;
I mend the wound, re-erect . . .
Loneliness

One storm I stepped through, just
aft the strike,
just 'fore the blow . . .
Peace
One dawn I rode ray to ray,
always just that
hide from night . . .
Happiness
One tear I dripped the red,
babbled the dream . . .
Love

Take chances

Penney Ann Castro
STEPS TO MY SUCCESS
If I create the written word, and
it's less than published best,
I'll view it not as failure, but as
steps to my success.

Another step well taken, with
thought provoking theme,
Will take me yet another step, to
realize my dream.

And if another reads my words,
and doesn't like my concept,
It isn't really failure, no, it's just
another step.

Then certain in another time, I'll
realize my desire,
As present failures teach me, the
knowledge I require.

For failure's contradictory, to the
purpose of ambition,
And cannot be considered, as I
strive for recognition.

Self image is my confidence, to
guide me in this quest,
And present failure only serves,
as steps to my success.

Lilly Pearl White Flake
GOD'S GRACE
[To our son, Ricky]
My faith, though weak, is here
Helping me to face
Each unknown tomorrow
Through His matchless grace.

In a world full of woe,
God's way is still the best;
If man could only see,
And with peace put war to rest.

"My grace is sufficient for thee,"
He still speaks to us today.
Why will man not trust Him
And walk the better way?

Peggy Randall-Martin
SILENCE
Silence.
Don't talk to me of dreams
while many long, barren nights
still lie ahead,
And speak only in soft, hushed
tones
of love and fear and dread.

Be still.
Don't reach out to me
with the deceiving gloved hands
of a beloved memory,
For those unfeeling hands can
only touch
and cast shadows of a love that
can never be.

Patricia E. Briley
FRANKIE
*[This poem is written about
my husband and dedicated to
him. He passed away December
27, 1980. He is missed very
much.]*
Frankie, you left me,
Without taking my hand.
It is hard for me,
But I will try to understand.

Frankie, I will miss you every
minute,
Of everyday of my life.
And I will never forget,
That I am your wife.

Frankie, as I walk alone,
With you not by my side.
All the grief and all the tears,
I will try to hide.

Frankie, the days and nights will
be long,
And nothing will be the same.
Not a day will go by,
That I will not mention your
name.

Frankie, every Holiday will have
no meaning,
It will just be another day gone
by.
But I will make the best of it,
Lord knows I will try.

Frankie, don't you be afraid,
Because in heaven my dad awaits.
He will be standing there,
When you go through heavens
gates.

Frankie, one day I will be with
you,

Then everything will be the
same.
And then I will not cry,
When I mention your name.

Donald Bannon
WARMTH—COLD
I'm with you
and
I feel a warmth.

You're not here tonite
and
I'm
so
so
cold.

Robert Qualls

Robert Qualls
TIME
Time—the ever constant
adversary
demanding—commanding—refusing
to vary—
yet—pretentious man how
foolish he is—
to constantly oppose such
majesty.

Christina M. Dykes
LISTEN
*[In loving memory of my
grandmother, Alice May Mako.]*
I have a wish and a dream
And I pray thaat it might come
true.
I wish that someone
Could reach into my heart and
soul
And pull out my deepest feelings
so that
I could put them into words.
Then maybe, I could understand
Who I am and who you are to me.
I have so much to say
And so few ways to say it.
But if by chance, I should find a
way,
Will you be there to listen?

Gary Fredrickson
MICHAEL'S BEARD
This is the story of Michael's
beard
and all the things I hear he's
heard.
Cultured words are stuck in his
ear,
and crude folk's talk no Preacher
could bear.
He's heard the beginning of a
little bird's peep,
he's heard the rain in the soft
ground seep.

Harsher things too are near at
hand,
deserts, silent, barren lands.
Wars and plaques are his
specialty,
speak of 'Thou', and don't say 'me'.
Heaven's strangers hum their
tune
and need translating to be here
soon.
The wind in his ear whispers the
names
of all the restless who believe the
same.
He's heard many promise the
young his youth,
the old their time and dreams
that sooth.
Yet none does him worse than
rerun heroes,
the myriad names, sleeping Joves,
and little Neroes.

Lisa Gay Linder
**Remember the Day In the
Park**
Remember the day in the park
We watched the ducks
I was scared by a snake
You pulled the grass.
Remember the day in the park
You said I looked beautiful
The sun was shining in my hair
You wished you had your camera.
Remember the day in the park
You were such a good friend
You sat and listened patiently
I was really glad you were there.
Remember the day in the park
We talked
We touched
We kissed
We fell in love.

Patricia Apostolakis
YOU AND I
As I sit, and hold this pen,
my mind is filled, of
memories from when;
We were one, and knew
the time, what the other,
held in their mind;
A glance, a touch, or kiss
on the cheek, knowing
together, we were never weak.
The wonder of love, is initially,
what God intended it to be;
A fluttering heart, a happy,
state of mind; Together we
have shared, a love divine.
Although never married,
and living apart; we still,
knew the desires, of each
others heart.
As I sit, and hold this pen,
my mind is filled, of
memories from when;
We laughed, we cried, and
said good-bye, never, shall
I forget; You and I.

Luella Jean Bettermann
ALLEY CAT
The big gray alley cat went
thumping through the snow—
He always had some place to go.
With an air of frivolity,
He had a curious personality.

"Well, what can I do next?"

His tail was all smitten
In the place where the dog had

bitten;
But the neighbors all loved him
  just the same—
  And they played along with his
  roving cat game.

It was vittles at Elvina's, with a
  tender heart
  That got the morning off to a
  very good start.
Then a meander down to the
  Bettermann shed,
  Which was filled with mice
  that soon would be dead!
Now it's on over to Martha's with
  an affectionate purr,
  To get the cockleburs pulled
  from his fur.
With Fritz, the poodle, he had so
  much fun—
  Bosom pals when the day is
  done.

Ah, the life of an alley cat—
  It's not so bad as all that!

Rita Ingersoll
SUMMER DAYS END
When the evening breeze is
  stirring,
And the summer sun goes down.
The birds have stopped their
  chirping,
And the crickets come around.

The moon it casts a shadow,
As the leaves dance through its
  light.
And the stars begin to twinkle,
On this soft warm summer night.

Such a calm and peaceful feeling,
Just to put your cares away.
Prepare to slumber through the
  night,
To greet another day.

Paula M. Russell
Symptoms For Sigmund
squirm
coil
strike!
wrap me
slide me
slither me
into the dark corner
of nowhere
no one
us
us
and soothe me
soothe me
high
and low
touch me
like a whisper.

Eleanor C. Kaminsky
HAPPINESS
*[To my dear Sarah Anne, whom
at an early age learns that
happiness comes from within,
when we think and do what is
right.]*
When burdens are heavy
No courage within,
I ask God, a favor
A strength, from him.

A force roars within me
Like a lion,
I can bear anything
At the time.

But humans strength and courage
Are fleeting.

So God and I,
Have a daily meeting.

It's good for the soul,
It's good for the heart
To commune with God,
To give him the leading part.

For happiness comes from within
Without Gods help, the ice is thin.

The wise happy man
Sees God all around.
Has no time for prejudices
To abound.

It's loving your neighbours
No matter their ways.
It's loving living
With the sunshine and grays.

For happiness is in Gods love
You see.
For only loving can make
You free.

Linda Mathison Braun
SURRENDER
He held me closely in his arms
His caresses warm and tender
Lips sweetly claiming mine
Longing for surrender

His straddled body urging me
His loving so divine
Trembling, I gave myself
He whispered, "You are mine."

Sheila South
UNTITLED
The pages turn,
  To a distant place
  Of days gone by or yet to come.
A world of adventure;
  An avenue of escape.
  A place I set my eyes to run.
Reality passes, while fantasy
  lives.
  A different way of life this is.

So swiftly time goes,
  Yet tides of emotion ebb and
  flow.
  Another being is what I be.
Experience a novel, and you shall
  see.

The pages end,
  And reality gains space.
  Still, a few memories linger
  Of that other time, that distant
  place.

Orvie Grene'
GREED
Shadows take over everything
  that Light has yet to claim as
  it's own.

The two of them act just like
  People,
  always wanting more than half
  of the stone . . .

Darkness passes the final
  judgement
  when the two have grown tired
  of fighting;
The same rules apply to the
  People,
  isn't Armageddon exciting?

Paul C. Cauley
THURSDAY MORNING
*[I dedicate these words with
love to my Lord Jesus, my
precious Mary, and children:
Joshua and Jena.]*
A half cup of coffee
getting cool

the smoke from this damn
  cigarette
always finding my eye
stinging

another sip, it's not cold yet
  there
I drank all the warm before it
  gave up

My head resting on my left hand
writing now and then with the
  right
one of the cats sitting on the
  counter
scratching
the dog on the floor
scratching

the table, the paper,
the coffeecup
like me just now

empty

Michael Fortuna
LOVERS
The sky had no height
  that day we lay there,
The night had no darkness
  for the stars were there.

There had been no beginning
  and there was to be no end,
Without saying a word
  our love we could send.

As children we played
  for many joyous years,
As teens we confided
  and together shed tears.

Our love was expanding
  reaching into forever,
Our love die?
  We swore,
    eternally,
      never!

Charles DeBlasio
WHITE GUY AM I
I fit into my neighborhood so
  perfectly!
Being fair-haired, and white of
  course.
The boundaries are set up all
  over town.
Groups of skin all around.
I wish we could fit into the same
  scene.
Too many lives are lived in
  between,
And so much is lost.
Fear, distrust, isolation, the final
  cost.

Billie Jo King Ford
LINDA
Linda, I love you. Although you
  are gone,
Your memory still lingers on and
  on.
I remember when we were
  younger the things you would
  do,
Like when you caught poison oak
  and you'd scratch both me and
  you.
The time in the summer when
  the ticks all came
And covered your body; you
  received a new name.
It was Grandpa, I recall, who gave
  you the name,
And from there everafter you
  were called Ticky Jane.

Time goes so quickly; it doesn't
  seem real.
To me it seems you should be
  just a little girl still.
Your blonde hair in pigtails; your
  feet yet bare,
Sitting and bouncing on Daddy's
  knee,
Laughing and joking with
  Shirlene and me.

Andrea Yakab Janes
WORDS
Words, at times I find them so
  easily
  where are they hiding now?
I am not looking for beauty in
  poems
  but only answers to questioned
  feelings.
At times my body and soul are at
  peace
  but my mind is always in
  doubt.
Through a spark of ageless
  wisdom
  time is telling me never to fear
  these doubts.
For these fears are the grave to
  loneliness
  and peace at heart is the
  happiness of life.

Mrs. Carole M. Ubdegrove
HOME
*[To Elsie Ubdegrove, who's
strength, courage and hard
work is an inspiration to us all.]*
Down crooked roads with hills
  and trees, there lies a cottage
  fair,
For hundreds of years its fires
  have burned, to warm those
  living there.
It stands amongst the hills and
  vales, proud for all to see,
Its age has only helped to prove,
  its might dynasty.
Those walls housed burly oxen,
  with which settlers broke the
  land,
Its walls were lined with strong
  red brick, the weather to
  withstand.
But then a home it did become,
  and is until this day,
A touching inspiration for all
  who pass its way.
Families have come, and families
  have gone, for years there
  lingers there,

A proud hard working family,
whose land has shown their
care,
No hydro poles or telephone lines
are there to mar the scene,
Instead, where ere your eyes are
cast, are rolling hills of green.
Often during the quiet hours,
deer, fox and wolves are seen.
With ever deepening twilight,
each night the lamp is lit,
glowing warmth
Fills every room as beside the fire
she sits.
She was brought unto this
homestead, a girl but in her
teens,
And here she raised her family
through years both hard and
lean.
Those fragile hands have worked
the land behind many a sturdy
team,
Chopped wood, mended fires and
cooked the meals, for a family
of 16.
The years have seen her family,
go their separate ways,
But have seen no change in spirit,
as she works away the days.
Feeding hens, pumping water, and
splitting kindling wood,
Within her lies the secret which
makes life long and good.
In these times of turmoil and
strife, a mere visit to her lair,
Shows tranquility and peace,
which is forever there.
Her door is always open for those
who venture there,
And when they last departed,
were better for her care.
Her presence, even when
elsewhere, is forever there.

Florence M. Craven
GOD IS OUR REFUGE
There is a ROCK where the
righteous hide,
A SHADE from the burning sun,
A SHELTER from the wildest
storm,
A CITY where we may run

There is a WAY that is lifted up,
A PATH that no vulture sees
A SECRET PLACE where God
beholds
A SAINT upon his knees.

There is a PLACE of perfect rest
Though storms may howl
without,
A PLACE where we know perfect
trust
Unmixed with fear or doubt.

There is a HAVEN all secure
Where ships at anchor ride,
There is a PLACE in God's will,
Where no evil can betide.

John D. Barrett
ELAINE
I turned the knob, walked
through the door.
Saw someone I had seen before.
Your soft blue eyes; your golden
hair.
It caught my eye; I had to stare.

You spoke to me; thoughts flash
galore.
Was something I had heard before.

With every word time and again.
I don't know where, and don't
know when.

The thoughts come in, then
tossed aside.
My memory I think has lied.
To place your face, and voice so
frail,
I've tried and tried, to no avail.

But still I know; I know I do.
That somewhere past I have seen
you.
Not all you are but all you seem.
Long time ago perhaps a dream.

Why not give up; deal with
what's real.
To say exactly what I feel.
You're such a girl; to me I mean.
The prettiest I've ever seen.

Leigh Johnson

Leigh Johnson
ON MY OWN
I've done all I can to stay alive
without having to hide behind
a thin disguise,
there were people who brought
me down, but it still never
stopped me from getting
around.
Sometimes I wish I could come
back home to a shelter of love
and where it's safe and warm,
with all my time of seeing the
real and gaining the wealth of
experience heals, I'll put all my
anger aside and stop all my
talk about suicide.

Gloria Winifred Squires
SUMMER'S DAY
Oh, to be a child again,
To run, to sing and play;
Happy and carefree, was I then,
On a beautiful summer's day.

With my brother, at my side,
Thru fields of clover, we did roam,
Sailing boats in muddy streams,
With nar' a thought of going
home.

Catching turtles and butterflies,
Picking wild berries, too;
Heads, tossed back, scanning the
sky,
What a glorious shade of blue!

Weary, smudged and barefoot,
now,
Homeward bound, are we,
With thoughts of a tomorrow,
More wonders, for to see.

Fran Onderdonk Laurent
THE INSIGNIFICANT
We are in life a half a drop in all
the ocean
A tiny cell in God's great notion
We are just a moment in a
million hours
A mere petal in a valley of flowers.

And we although so very small
If we could hear someone's faint
call
If we unknown in a hundred years
Could just for now stop a child's
sad tears—

If we although a grain of sand
Could take a needy person's hand
and
If we could care this time this
place
If we could love one stranger's
face—
Our existance never will have
been so small
A life worth living
If we could help one someone at
all.

Pauline M. Nydahl
CLOUDS
Some clouds are like soft and
fluffy balls of cotton
That float aimlessly through the
atmosphere.
Others are like towering majestic
mountains,
That seem to stretch on forever.
They cover the earth like a
blanket,
Keeping out the burning rays of
the sun,
And keeps our world fresh and
green.
Clouds are like protecting
mothers.
Besides protecting us from the
sun,
Clouds also help us by bringing
rain!

Bette L. Fortin
COMING OF TIME
Children . . .
no longer children . . .
going their own ways . . .
putting up, so to speak
with the infirmities of their
parents . . .
those creatures, once so necessary,
now just something to be
tolerated,
humored, exasperated by . . .
too young to realize that all too
soon
they too
will become one with that army
of parents they often begrudge
time to . . .
resent having to do for.
All too soon they'll realize
that almost without their
knowing . . .
or realizing . . .
the transition has taken place . . .
so subtly as to have almost not
happened . . .
but it will indeed have happened,
an irreversible process which
balances the scales
by turning the tolerators . . .
into the tolerated.

James B. Cheatle
REFLECTED LIGHT
There is in my life but one light
the light of God above
to be seen in those around me
and experienced in their love

That light shines brightly in you,
my dear
in your eyes so shining bright
in your love that makes it so clear
I'll never lose that light.

R.E. Peters
Palos Verdes Goes To San Francisco
*[Humbly dedicated to those
who seek beyond the now.
Hopefully, my own Ken, Steve
and Barbara.]*
A glass chapel has been sliding
toward the sea.
They say, inch by inch.
And Santa Barbara Frisco's town
one day will be.
Some day, not now.

We either look behind or far
ahead.
Today, our NOW seems always
in a bed,
Going nowhere.

All the way from Channel 2
through 13,
The red I wear upon my lips, my
nails,
Blue jeans, yellow hair and close-
up teeth,
Mirror tiresome beds.

So, before the Chapel gets to
where it's going, north,
Please say my NOW means more
than all that's past,
More than all that's apt to come,
So my red nails will match my
lips and I can say "well done."

Nancy Menda
LOVELY LADY
A lovely lady
you are called,
With golden treasures,
rich garb of fall.
In cool, sunny breeze
or stormy high gale,
Or wintery cold bleak
grey scenes so pale;
A lady you are called.

Sleep on, lovely lady,
'neath covers of white,
Someday you'll awake
in a green, new life.
With virtues fairest
of them all,
Mother Nature
you are called;
You are winter, spring,
summer and fall.

Eleanor E. Stockard
OUT OF THE MIST
Out of the mist come the
thoughts that we live by.
Out of the gloom come the rays
of the morn.
Each day a new day, but linked
with the last one,
Endlessly teaching us since we
were born.

What makes us reach for a better
tomorrow?

What makes us climb from the
sod to the sky?
Something was placed in us from
the beginning.
Something that will not let
urgency die.

Our country, our loved ones, our
neighbors, our self-hood,
Our churches, our schools; here
our loyalties live.
Because we were made as the
highest of creatures,
Our destinies we can fulfill as we
give.

Heather Anne Frenette
FREEDOM
Freedom means being able to:
Sit with people talking,
Going through the woods
walking,
Reading books and poems and
plays,
Lying in the sun soaking up the
rays.
Talking with friends over the
phone,
Freedom is the right to be alone.

Judith C. Kasson
SUCCESS
All my life I've tried to win,
Success, it never came.
The hell, the pity, the anger, the
sin—
Will I ever win this game?

Winning to me is so far away,
I cover up the pain;
It never seems to leave my heart,
Will they ever know my name?

My dreams will last forever,
They're all I have, you know,
But knowing they're dreams and
only dreams,
Is what hurts inside me so.

Marjorie Hind Benchoff
The Death Of the Kilmer Oak
Long had stood this majestic
Kilmer Oak Tree,
An inspiration to all when they
did it see,
In all the trees God put on earth
the beauty in each one,
Joyce Kilmer helped us find it,
although God's greatness is
spared in none.
This tree grew in beauty one
hundred and sixty years,
Sixty eight feet in height, now
dismantling it brought tears,
This great white oak had one
hundred and eight feet spread
its limbs,
Now to keep it alive, all hope had
dimmed.
It slowly withered away with age
its foliage failed to appear,
One clump of dead orange leaves
was all that was now here.
Throughout the day as the
spreading limbs did slowly
disappear,
Rain and sadness fell on all
standing near,
As dismantling continued in the
grey darkness of the day,
Soon all that remained was a
massive stump that would stay.

In memory of Kilmer's poem
Trees, on its stump shall rest a
plaque,
Making this tree live on although
it can't come back,
Although this tree did die its
beauty shall forever remain,
In Joyce Kilmer's poem "Trees",
that beautiful tree lives on the
same.

Jennie M. Root
MY HUSBAND JOHN
*[This Poem was written to my
husband John, year 1965 two
years after our marriage,
inspired by my Beloved
Husband.]*
Pansies, pretty faces,
Smiling at you sweetly
like the delicate laces,
Whispering softly meekly,
"I love you John."

Long before the day's begun
I see him smiling full of fun.
Days of labor, toil and pain
Make shoulders droop from the
strain.
Yet he never will give up
till the work is done
Long ere the set of sun.
Weary, worn and growing old,
I feel a tear, I cannot scold
The man I love.
He's worth his weight in gold.

Benjamin A. Alfieri
VITAL ENCOUNTER
*[To those select few who
shared freely their insights and
wisdom so that I might awake
and grow.]*
When he was a younger, witty
pup,
He saw knowledge as the
golden cup.
Later, after trials and errors made,
He found the wisdom that was
delayed.
Later still, he noticed something
new;
Humility dwarfed the other two!
With this insight there was more
to do:
Working every adversity
through.
Crucial encounter forged growth
once more,
Guiding him through the
narrower door.

Joanne Thackeray Diltz
ALONE
If there are times
Of desperation
These can be times
Of joy.
Ashen as those times
Have made me—
I am alone, stranded,
Away from all light.
I see colourless forms,
Although almost white,
Blowing in your abandoned
Campfire.
They alone are alive!
Will you be there again
Tomorrow; or will all
Remain forgotten?
I touch you . . .
Silken, whispering waste.

Gloria J. Mathers
OF TIME AND LIFE
Our young heifer had a calf today.
It was bred before its time.

We strained and pulled to relieve
the inner burden that it bore

It took time, and that calf it had
was born dead—it was too big—
We were too late.

Generations are coming.
Will they be timely? Or
Bred too soon, too restricted?

Will we help?
And, in time give them choice
freedoms—
As life's adventure calls them to
survive.

Rev. Dr. Elizabeth J. Walton
FREE SPIRIT
*[To a wise, omnipotent,
omnicient, loving God the
privelege of which has been
mine to serve for twenty-five
years. "His eye is on the
sparrow and I know He
watches me." (P.D.)]*
The Sea gull soars to grand and
lofty heights;
    Catching the current
        And riding effortlessly
Across the span of time and space,
To-God knows where!
Inside of me there is a spirit gull
a-kin.
    Yearning to soar as high
        And drift as free,
    Beyond the sea and land,
To-God knows where!
This spirit should not know a
cage or iron bars;
    And so I know,
        I, like the gull,
Should wing my way across the
great expanse of time and space;
Secure within the thought that
God, indeed, knows where!

Maggie Hardin
THE FOOL
Am I such a fool
Not to realize or understand
what is in store for me
surely he must sense that I know.
The expressions, little
movements do they account or
amount to anything.
Having look out post eyes at
every corner.
Watching and peering for any
uncertain moves.
Lurking about in the shadows.
Knowing that at any moment
the impossible could happen.

Am I such a fool
to believe nothing, to live as a
dummy. The puppet dangling
from
a string being controlled but not
reacting to my own judgement.
Knowing that one day the strings
may be cut. And I left
standing listlessly, uncertain of
my next move.
When or how those strings would
be mended, and by whom?

Am I such a fool
Am I such a fool
A fool not to understand, that

fate will soon one day stare me
in the face. With a grin as big as
day which seems to
say
Fool
O Fool, you dumb Old fool
Give up now, for tomorrow you'll
be forgotten.

Robert Quesada
I BRING THIS ROSE
I bring this rose I grew for you,
For this our special day.
I have so many things to say
And many things to do.

But Where? Just where can I begin
To tell you how I feel?
To Tell you that my love was real
And was until the end.

I know it's late to tell you now;
I hope you understand.
I never had the time to spend;
I'll make it up somehow.

But why you died only God
knows,
I can't believe it's true.
All I know is that I love you
And so; I bring this rose.

Richard Allen Crutchfield
ARTISTS' LAMENT
*[Written in honor of the artist
and painter Mildred F. Ballard.
It was one of her paintings that
inspired the writing of this
poem.]*
The crumbling of my castle walls
The winds of time have
wrought;
Have taken me down the path of
life:
To this time and place have
brought.
A portal in my castle wall,
The eye of the soul does see
The beaten path that lies in front
And in behind of me.

A weary place for travelers
Where a wanton time was
spent,
Of seeking out their goal in life
And wondering why they were
sent.
The flowing of a river stream
Of thoughts I know so well
Where different things seem both
the same,
Where only dreams foretell.

A sunken boat, a fallen bridge
On the far side of the soul
Are all too much reminders

Of life's most worthy goal.
My one clear goal, my only aim
  Is to cross that wretched
shore,
To gain the one true knowledge
  Waiting at my castle door.

They say that I'm a dreamer,
  I build castles in the air,
But what is said and what is done
  Leaves me with no despair.
To me which is important
  Is that the soul be free,
For none shall ever take away
  This castle that is me.
For none shall ever take away
  This castle—that is me.

Robert G. Blewett
FOR MY DAUGHTER
There never is enough time
to stand aside and see her;
bumps and bruises healing
  quickly
as the child's tears desappear.

There never is enough time
to enjoy that enigmatic smile;
as her dreams and hopes grow
through the young girl, into the
  woman.

There never is enough time
to teach of love, and speak of life;
only to share the newborn
  sunrise
and to gather the softly fallen
  leaf.

But, for her heart and thought so
  pure,
there shall always be enough
  time.

Charlotte Dye
WISDOM OF A THOUSAND
If one king could hold the
  wisdom
  of a thousand in his hand,
Would his knowledge help his
  kingdom?

Would he reign for many years
  and
  keep one queen forever?
Would he use his wisdom wisely
  or
  just boast about his land?
Would he earnestly endeavor,
  to use his skillful mind, or
Would he be killed in a battle,
  his armor, with blood lined?
Does wisdom of a thousand men,
  held upon the hand, make
  victory
  for one man, but never help his
  land?

Yvette LeClair Ifill Wilson
The Influence Of Spring
Luscious, green vegetation
  blooms so intensely,
The colours so vivid; they squint
  in your eye.
Then, as out of nowhere—
The pink and yellow and the
  brown will entwine,
While the orange of sunset and
  the blue of the sky
Transcend their heavenly beauty.

Next, petals will quiver, a little
  afraid
To open their precious parts—
But, confidence gained, they push

and they shove
Gradually covering their buds.

Floral designs so artisticly pretty;
Seem to dance to the bird's
  morning twitter;
Swaying frantically a petal soon
  falls to the earth,
Perhaps on a child's little finger,
Or floats away on a chilling
  breeze
The whiff of wind blushing each
  cheek.

So, children are born;
Flowers will bloom;
The sun spreads its golden hue;
The weather warms up, as the
  hearts of all people,
Who've been into contact with
  you.

Chris S. Russell
HOUSEWIFE
Oh, hands and head
  disconnected:
strange appendages hanging on
  me,
two kneading the staff of life,
one composing Scheherazade;

she who lived for one and a
  thousand days
because she owned the gift of
  ranconteur.
I wonder, for the story does not
  say,
after that did she leisurely
  massage bread?

The yeast of my dough comes
  alive,
rises to my brain spawning rich
  images,
exciting my imagination to
  fertility.
If my assignment is to hug more,

  does hugging this viscous
  nourishment count?

It feels more lively now, springy.
My brain is racing to keep up!
My six hundred seventh story is
  formed.
Tonight I shall live, but not by
  bread.

David Paynter
IT'S OVER
The empty faces, the full
  embraces
Have left their marks on me
The times we tried, the times we
  cried
Have helped to set me free
Roads to anywhere, roads to
  nowhere
We've traveled them, one and all
People we met, days we won't
  forget
How we stood before the fall

But now it's near the end, and
  though we like to pretend, it's
  over
And no matter what we say, we
  can't go back to yesterday, it's
  over

I felt it coming, I started
  summing
As the walls came tumbling
  down
We saw it snow, we'll never know
If it's a verb or a noun

Remember the stranger, not the
  danger
I think you know by now
That on this day, I'll hope and
  pray
We'll meet again somehow

But now it's near the end, and
  though we like to pretend, it's
  over
And no matter what we say, we
  can't go back to yesterday, it's
  over

We saw the light, we felt the
  night
We heard the ladies shriek
Games we played, dreams that
  stayed
The time we reached the peak
But now I find, peace in my mind
And I know that I must fly
Nothing is the same, we know
  the name
At least we gave it a helluva try

But now it's near the end, and
  though we like to pretend, it's
  over
And no matter what we say, we
  can't go back to yesterday, it's
  over

Michael Pfiester
FLIGHT TO DEATH
Soaring above the clouds like an
  eagle,
He's free from the world; he
  crossed the bridge of the
  impossible, and he feels like he
  can go on forever, but he can't
He finally comes back to the
  world of the conscious and
  remembers he has a war to
  fight,
So the young, valiant eagle
  continues with the sortie he
  was assigned to, the long
  boring flight in the chill of the
  morning.
Then all of a sudden, he was
  taken by surprise by a
  squadron of spade fighters.
Nine bullets rip across his chest;
  eight pierce the wings and the
  engine.
His soaring is over; the flight is
  too,
All he can do is dive
And that's what he does.
In uncontrollable spins the young
  pilot crashes to earth.
Nobody cares.
Nobody will. His life no longer
  exists.
Once a young eagle soaring with
  the wind,
Now he's a number on someone's
  victory list.

Jeanne Barbara Holley
FLOWER
If my life I could fashion after a
  flower,
Which one would I pick? I
  wonder by the hour.

A Pansy isn't really the way that I
  feel,
Nor a meadow of wild flowers,
  blowing free at their will.

It wouldn't be an Orchid, though
  they're pretty, I know,

To look at a while—strictly for
  show.

Nor a Morning Glory that opens
  at light,
Then closes her petals, at the first
  sign of night.

No not a Honeysuckle, hanging
  on a vine,
Dripping with sweetness and so
  refine.

Not a Begonia, Buttercup, Flag, or
  Bluebell,
None of them really suit me that
  well.

The one I am thinking I would
  like to be,
Is strong and delicate, at the same
  time you see.

Proud and lovely, it comes time
  and again,
To offer its beauty to foe or
  friend.
Soft as velvet, that can't compare,
Sweetest fragrance of any, that
  grows anywhere.

I don't know of any that has such
  poise,
But will stick if her feelings are
  treated like toys.
If I could reach such unique
  beauty that shows,
I would vanish, and be standing,
There as a Rose.

Lucille M. Kroner

Lucille M. Kroner
I'LL AWAIT YOU HERE
The years have gone by one by
  one.
I stand alone in rain and sun
And long for you and await your
  call,
Beside this flowering garden wall.

I live in memory of your face
Within this garden's vining lace,
And when the snow again will
  fall
I'll await you here by garden's
  wall.

Virgie R. Maitino
THE GOOD LIFE
I do not want a lot from life . . .
Just to live in peace without
  much strife.
To greet each day . . . and do my
  part
To love my neighbor with all my
  heart.

To help the sick, the old, the lame
Because they need . . . and not for fame.
To do the things I have to do
Without much fuss, as God wants me to.
To smile a lot along the way
To work real hard . . . and also play.
To not be cursed with pangs of greed
For worldly things I do not need.
To enjoy the beauty God put here . . .
The rivers, flowers, trees . . . the deer.
To learn to take things as they come
To not be mad at anyone.
And when my time on earth is through . . .
Look back and know it's really true,
I did my best . . . and need not fear . . .
I had a good life while I was here.

Laura Theroff-Braden
My Grandparents Home
[To Henry & Louise Rettinger September 24, 1982]
The fireplace with dancing flames,
Delicious kitchen smells, the same.
Sounds of work—hammer to nails,
Always time for stories and tales.
Christmas time is a wonderland.
Touches of love, made by caring hands.
Treats hang on the Christmas tree,
Toys that fill the babes with glee.
There's hiding places to invent,
There's roses with perfume scent.
The sounds of music floating in the air,
And always my favorite, a rocking chair.
There's an atmosphere of sharing,
Gentle signs of love, and caring.
No matter how far the miles between,
I'll never forget the familiar scene.
No matter where I may roam,
None can take the place of:
    My Grandparents Home!

Frances Kelley
SUZETTE
Suzette is a poodle born with three legs,
Her insides infected, they gave her just days.
They said not to take her, she could not be bred,
Her days are numbered, take another instead.
She looked at me and stole my heart,
I knew then, in my life, she would be part.
It took much patience to teach her to walk,
To eat without falling, she almost could talk.
Soon she was running, played with her ball

Quite steady, and rarely did fall.
Now Suzette is nine years, what a joy she has been
I hold her and my eyes fill with tears
I know she has pain, her pills do not help,
    And when she is asleep
    She sometimes will yelp.
She tries not to show that her pain is so bad
When you look into her eyes
    You can see she is sad.
I truly love this dear pet of mine
We will stay together,
    Till the end . . . of time.

Mescal (Mickey) Yanacek

Mescal (Mickey) Yanacek
A PRECIOUS GIFT
[To my husband Paul and our children; Clyde, Cora E., and Leila.]
The gift of life is a precious one,
But how swiftly it can be snatched away;
For death does not concern itself,
With our wanting to go or stay.
For it must be written in that golden book,
That is kept at the head of the stairs;
The time and date our name will be called,
Saying we are needed up there.
So enjoy this gift that God has given,
Oh please use it wisely and well;
Take each beautiful day; walk through it with pride,
God's beauty and wonders to tell.
This life will be full of worry and tears,
Of heartaches and pains to bear;
Take one day at a time; see the beauty and joy,
That is here for us all to share.
Live each day fully; but you must be prepared,
For that day will surely come;
When your name will be called and your answer must be,
That final journey home.

Joan Sajnovic
WINTER
I should be writing 'bout the blanc visage,
That nature has called upon to message.

The cold, hard, sands, of the land
That daily kisses my feet, to brand
My being, with the stamp, "Canadian Grand".
This turf, now, topped with duvet white,
Is soft, flirting winter's fun, winter's bite.
I should be painting pictures of the world anew,
Of the fresh look, that nature grew
By seeding the naked sky, with frozen flakes,
To stimulate the friged air with wakes
Of expelled heat, so man's cold body takes.
This turf, now, topped with duvet white,
Is soft, flirting winter's fun, winter's bite
But, here I sit with frozen mind,
Saddened, by the loss of daily grind
That neither sparked, nor lent,
My soul to reach a viva vent,
To share my life, before it's spent.
This turf, now, topped with duvet white,
Is soft, fluffy, flirting winter's fun, winter's bite.

Elenor M. Mitchell
We Seen The 1982 World's Fair
I climbed aboard a big bus May 1982.
Forty-four other mostly greyheads got aboard too.
At 7:30 in the mornin' we gits.
We rode and rode all the day.
Finally, we got to Careyville, Tennessee.
We wuz so glad that little ole hotel to see.
Tired? I'll say we wuz, yessiree.
We got spruced up and treated to scrumptious food.
This put us in an ambitious mood.
Next mornin' after we had grits, we set out for Knoxville;
To see that big World's Fair of 1982.
We dodged wall to wall people at this Fair.
Some folks stood in line for hours somethin' to see.
Not us, we kept a walkin' and walkin till we wuz plum wore out.
Next mornin' we headed back home.
We see that "Welcome to Ohio" sign, on the bridge at 7:00 P.M.
We pass that big city of Columbus and git in thunderstorm.
That thunderstorm stay with us till we git home.
We seen the 1982 World's Fair, yessiree.

Rosa Lee Emerson
YOUR NAME
Out of the clouds you fell,
Filling my heart with glee,
My sweetest songs are those that tell

The story of you and me.
Don't you remember, it was one cool night,
Solely by chance we met,
We were having fun in the height of delight,
Oh, I shall never forget.
There were several more in the crowd
But I remembered you.
Your name stood out subdued and proud
And proved a worthy clue.
Should I forget your eyes, your smile,
Or the way that you part your hair;
Should I forget your voice so mild,
Your name will still be there.

Robert Melvin Williams
A WISH FOR PEACE
[To my mother (Marie) and my father (William), for the patience and love that they so openly shared, and was always there when I needed them most.]
If I could make one wish for the world . . .
It would be a wish for peace.
For peace will never come I know,
Until all mankind is deceased—
If so, whatever peace one has inside,
Spread it to help another find,
For in that deed there grows a love . . .
To prolong the fate of mankind!

Jo Hammond
TOUCH MY HAND
Touching is all we have to give,
Let not the moment pass.
Touch me so I may know
What you feel,
What you want in the fullness
Of your deepest thought.
Touch my hand,
Let not the doubts dismay,
Who knows, you may be the one God has sent
To break that barrier
We lay upon ourselves
In trembling fear.
Touching is all we have to give.

Vicki Lynn Visser
KALEIDISCOPE
The colors radiate,
glistening brightly in the sun,
around the kaleidiscope spins,
changing patterns infinitely.
I step inside,
wishing to see the beauty from within.
All that is to be seen
is old forgotten dreams and hopes,
wandering about aimlessly.
I have seen the image itself,
and have been disillusioned.

Hilda Ongrady
I CANNOT GO TO YOU
I cannot go to you, oh my dear
Though you are sick and the hour is near.
I tried to tell you of my fear

93

But you were in love
You would not hear.

I set you free after many years,
And I cried, oh I cried so many
 tears.
Love has no reason: love has no
 rhyme.
It breaks your heart most every
 time.

Finally you married your great
 love
And for a while all was ecstatic,
And I'm sure her love was true,
But constant closeness makes
 faults show through.
Sorrows are many. Joys are few.

Through the years your eyes had
 grown dim:
I had led you everywhere:
Still you thought I was wrong for
 you,
And happily into her arms you
 flew.

The nights were what she had
 always dreamed.
The days were filled with care.
Now she could see what I had
 been through,
And she felt it quite unfair.

Slowly you began to see that you
 were wrong
To toss my love aside.
Now you are in a nursing home,
And I can't be at your side.

You asked for me; I know that is
 true.
She is your wife now, and I
 cannot go, no,
I cannot go to you.

James M. Aubrey
SATURDAY NIGHT
A high caliber small bore
 braggadocio—
reload
trading bullets for ballots, change-
explosives
one man vote-banality.
one bullet one down-permanent.
the holy lennon
two grounded hawks.

Man's evolution, lineal or
 circular?
cocking the hammer, extending
 the barrel.
only God is bullet-proof.
men bleed and grieve
man-superior?
capable of manufacturer
deals death and destruction
deceased.

Marion J. Morgan
BLACK STALLION
As I stand with my hands on my
 hips,
I watch him strut by.
Like a persistent stud
he returns
to challenge my gaze
and tosses his black glossy mane
against my cheek.
I suck
in my breath,
hoping he won't hear
my insides sear,
and I know I should escape
But like a thoroughbred,

I struggle
to overcome.
So I gulp
when I smell his sweat
and face
his bursting groin
and penetrating black eyes
and fiery nostrils weld me to his
 side.
I close my eyes.

Sabrina Heit
A PORTRAIT OF LOVE
*[For Peter, The Only Honey In
My Life. Love You Always,
Sabrina]*
Do you love me?
How will I know?
Will you lavish me with
 expensive gifts?
Or will you just love me like
 you've never loved
anyone before?

Have I changed you honey?
What exactly did I do?
Did my words enter your mind or
 was it my feelings of
love that entered your heart?

Have people noticed your change?
What have you told them?
Do you fully understand the
 change yourself?

Don't leave me.
Hold me tight.
Does our love run on the same
 track?
If it doesn't, then let's end this
 chapter with a
final kiss good-night.

Martha M. Godfrey
MEMORY
*[In memory of Mary Leverone,
May this friendship never be
forgotten]*
In my eyes you were a Redwood
Tall, and sturdy as Gibralter
Loved by many
With a good, happy life

Swept away by an evil cell
So fast—like dust in a storm
Pain in dying—Pain in living
It's not fair for you to go

Seems so harsh to go back to
 routine
Cannot dwell on clouds that pass
Memories are all I have
When I see the water's reflection.

Calvin M. Taylor
THE OKLAHOMA SKIES
Tell me not of sweet aromas,
Scent of passions, pleasant
 scenes,
Nor of fantasies of moonlight,
Nor of magic—golden dreams.

Show me not the lofty snowcaps,
Nor the painted desert scenes,
Nor Alaska's crystal glac'ers,
Nor the Everglades so green;
'Till I paint the mystic sky scenes
So inviting to the eyes.
What compares to heaven's glory
More than Oklahoma skies?

Fluffy clouds so high above us,
Swept by winds across the blue;
Rushing jets so quickly streaking
Under them and half way
 through;

Searching eagles, nearby sailing
Seeking prey from sharpest eyes;
These, my graphic view,
 enchanting,
And the Oklahoma skies.

Mark Stephen Wallinder

Mark Stephen Wallinder
MYSELF, STRUGGLING
Sometimes silver
is a brighter light
when everyone wanted gold
(I got old).
Sometimes silver
is a higher flight
whose brilliant life
shown cold
(And
Everything
got old).
(it's alright;
we must)
Know
All
Is right.
And sometimes
Life is a bright white light
whose seeing blinds like sight—

Keith A. Wenger
SLEEP
A dark black shroud that
 envelopes the body in
 tranquility,
Sleep!
A time of rest, a time of peace,
Sleep!
One brief moment in the eternity
 of time when the mind, soul
 and body are in harmony with
 one another,
Sleep!
A time when you are suspended
 in weightlessness and
 forgetfulness,
Sleep!
When all your wishes materialize
 and your troubles disappear,
Sleep!
But a page in the storybook of
 time, a page we all must have,
 for without it we cannot
 survive,
Sleep!
Some day the day will come
 when we will all,
Sleep—Sleep—Sleep!

Louise Butts Hendrix
NONE CAN HURT ME
None can hurt me like you do,
Just you, just you,
None can, none will.

No pain, no chill,
Just a hollow shock of pity
For something once so dear
That will never be again.
Your smile is lost forever.
 Farewell—

None can hurt me like you do,
Just you, just you.
Please smile; laugh and smile
 awhile.
A heart that's broken knows not
 joy,
No special time of happiness,
Just an empty void
Of loneliness for you.
No, none can hurt me like you
 do.

F.J.Bruette, Sr.
SHADOWS IN THE SUN
Golden sunlight blazes forth,
probing the western sky.
restless rays of light,
dance on the mountain steps,
with joy, and delight.
"Be humble! cried the earth;
and I will guide you,
to the valley of happiness."

Swiftly, the spirits walked,
natures trail, beyond time,
drinking the cold, clear water,
from the sweet dipper of love.
then journey on, hereafter
"Be humble! cried the earth,
as you travel this world
Be-hold! the darkness is the light."

Angelina Wentz
Because Your Dad Was Loved
*[To my dear friend—Mary Jean
O'Donnel whose love and
understanding has been an
inspiration for many years.]*
We're sorry you have lost your
 dad
Love and memories from him
 you've had.
You loved him for free—you
 learned years ago,
When you think of him now,
 may all your hearts glow.
The past few months will be held
 very dear,
Because you and your family
 were glad he was near.
Altho he is gone and feelings are
 sad,
May you always cherish the love
 from Grandfather and Dad.

Elizabeth Pucciarelli
CYCLES
The kitchen is all sunny and
 golden
Warm in the October sun
The bright yellow curtains
Filter and play with its rays
The warm, rich amber wood of
 the cabinets
reflect and disburse it

On the table a bouquet mirrors
the suns warm loving beams
Brilliant yellow and golden
 flowers
Earthy brown leaves, a few sprays
The last tender tendrils of green

Autumn is not the beginning
Of austere, cold white winter
But the culmination of tender

Gentle green spring
With its pastel flowers and
Hopes for the future
Of the hot sultry pregnant
    summer
Almost unbearable in its
    expectation

The overladen trees bear sweet
    fruit
Fields of corn, giant orange
    pumpkins
Green and gold squash
Beg to be harvsted
The cycles are finished,
I am filled with joy

Lois E. Webster
CAPTURED ARIA
What chaos these craggy times
Rocking through myriads of
    musicless chimes
Too turned on to tune into the
    sounds of yesteryear
Songs we used to hear.

Like gentle winds whispering to
    the trees
The whirring buzz of the worker
    bees
A flock of birds bursting into
    flight
Or crickets chirping at the late
    summer night
The lonesome toot of a distant
    train
The first few drops of a brand
    new rain

But wait?
The mockingbird echoes now.

Katherine E. Cartwright
FOG ON SKYLINE BLVD.
Fog floats
In feathery wisps
Over the greening hills
Solid in the valleys
Where imagination walks
One ray of sun
Pushes through
Touching a far hill
With gold.
Tall redwoods
Shake in the chill wind
Then soft—
The fog lays smoke-blue
Gentle fingers
And they are still.
Along the Skyline
On a grey, dreamy Sunday
We float too.
Loving the enfolding mist
Back to the sunny valley
That is our home.

Dale Lee Webb
COUNTRY
The snow is falling makin the
    countryside white
and the tracks of different
    animals I can see
scattered o're the roadside
    blanket the snow
where we're trying to get to
    grandma's house
but roads are slick and icy where
    travel is slow
suddenly something is moving
    swiftly through the trees
and dad is telling us to look at
    the deer
we look and watch him but he
    disappears so silently

before we really see him against
    the background of snow
and I wonder why I don't see
    these animals more often
closer to the population and
    cities that man inhabits
when I realize that here in the
    country our air is clean
and nature can work by herself
    without manmade errors
and I wonder about man and just
    where he is heading
and to just what purpose this
    country is being used
or rather I should say being
    unconditionally defeated.

Eddie Heavner
A LADY REMEMBERS
Say that Capri's cold in June.
Say the swallows lost their tune.
Say the Mona Lisa's sold.
But tell me not that he's grown
    old.

I might believe you if you say
that Naples Bay has turned to
    gray;
or that the Trevi Fountain's dry.
But if you say he's old, you lie.

I grew old when I came home;
but none grows old in ageless
    Rome.
No silver hair's upon his head;
'twas someone else you saw
    instead.

On the piazza, he is there;
forever young, forever fair.
Go look again and you will see
the fairest youth in Italy.

Mark J. Carpentieri
Deteriorated Worrier
Decrepit mist immortal chime
With ageless wrinkles tinkers
    time:
For thence this crime of pensive
    thought,
Did stagger men of bones you
    wrought.
To think and think,—off wanders
    worry,
Decaying age is brought with
    fury.
You sag his eyes and tire his
    tones,
White face and drying lips he
    moans:—
"The wasted worry of despair,
Will rot the mind and gray the
    hair."
His pitied words of life were facts,

Man's desperate questions
    wander tracks.
The mind that works too long in
    wonder,
Will crack a back with brain
    asunder,
And so to this I say old friend,
You're wearing worry is your end.

The mist of age will crawl with
    time,
Immortal wrinkles hear this
    chime:
Live free in thought or sag will
    thine.

Then ponder as the corpses do,
    now bones in hasty graves,
Deteriorated worrier, this realm,
    he frets and raves.

J.A.D.
WHAT'S LIFE ALL ABOUT
Sometimes I really wonder
just what life's all about.
    I get so many answers,
but most of them I doubt.
    At night I look out my window.
    I look up at the sky.
    I wonder when and how a person
knows that he must die.
    There's so many things that
life has to show . . .
    So many things that a person
    must know!

Alice T. Healy
MY WISH
My wish for you,
Joy of the running waves,
Deep peace of the quiet earth,
And gifts that are priceless
Of luck and love and laughter,
That let the warmth of friendship
    in,
To dwell on shores for ever after,
My wish for you.

My wish for you,
Rolling hills and flowering
    meadows,
Deep peace of the flowing air,
And wandering stars with
    midnight flair,
Silver lakes and mountain slopes,
And fires ablaze with cheer
So your heart is never lonely
My wish for you.

Lisa Megna
Where Are The EARLY Sixties?
In the early sixties peace was
    everywhere,
You could taste it, see it, sense
    it in the air.
Now they speak of fighting—why
    all this hate?
Lord, we're coming down to our
    own miserable fate.
As time gets worse and war
    grows near,
We try not to show our growing
    fear.
Everyone's afraid of being under
    the gun,
And when the war is over who
    will have won?
Surely not we, and surely not
    they,
For thousands of lives will
    be taken away.
All that I'm asking is to
    give peace a chance,

Without all this fighting, our
    lives we'll enhance.
We have nothing to lose, but
    so much to gain,
So throw down your guns
    and let love reign.

Jan Mennenga
GOSSIP
Not once
    have you taken the time
    to look inside my heart
    and see
        the hidden hurt
        that is tearing me apart!

Instead
    you choose to relate
    half truths and outright lies.
    It matters not
        to you that you are
            destroying peoples lives!

But
    go right ahead!
    Spread your lying dirt!
    One day
        your turn will come
            to know this kind of hurt!

Mary A. Britz
GIVE A DAMN?!
Why should I care about my
    brother,
Should I be different than any
    other;
Shouldn't I just turn my head,
Upon sight of a destitute babe in
    his icy bed;
Or close my ears to the
    tormented cries,
Ripped from the heart and soul of
    a mother
    watching as her children die?

She thinks of the bill,
Written long ago,
Declaring us brothers,
And yet, she knows,
The meanings been lost
    somewhere along the way,
That bell of freedom, stopped one
    day!

One man tried, he had a dream,
He was one who dared to care
    to make that bell again to ring.
And of his dreams they still do
    sing.

Like this man who was our
    brother,
We should care for one another.

June Florence Kennedy
Dear Dad & Grandfather
We watched you as you suffered
    but there was nothing we could
    do
So we prayed to God above to
    please help you.
He answered our prayers in the
    way that he knew best
for he took away your pain and
    put your soul to rest.

One year ago today in the middle
    of the night,
You closed your tired eyes and
    began your lonely flight.

You laid there very peaceful
    with a smile upon your face
to let us know that God above
    had prepared for you your
    place.

Our hearts were very broken
to see you pass away
for you were always there
to brighten up our day.

There are so many things in
which you left behind
that keeps the memory of you
always on our minds.
We will always remember the
funny stories you once told
they are more precious to us than
rubies, emeralds or gold.

As we think of you in memory
our eyes are filled with tears.
Yet you will remain in our
hearts
through the passing of many
years.

Gatha Rice
DRIFTING
Sometimes I feel myself leaving
me
Slipping away from all around.
I drift and float away with
thoughts and dreams
Soaring high above life's
crowded ground.

Our world in which we live.
Everyone takes, very few give.
And one who does, who truly
cares,
Is often met with hardened
stares.

But then, there is you. A unique
being
Unlike anyone I've ever
known.
You fill my thoughts with love
and laughter
'Til I'm off, to a world of my
own.

Anna Gilmore
Surprises Are Blessings
Surprises are blessings
That come from above
There sprinkled and entwined
With ribbons of love
There wrapped with
Wreaths of smiles and cheers
Surprises are for a lifetime of
years
Surprises are celebration's of life
To give and receive
No questions, asked, if we believe
The candles may cease to inflame
their glow
The memories will remain
Forever, as we grow

Mavis Inhetveen
FORGIVEN
Today I spoke to God in prayer
Knowing He was standing there
Beside me as I knelt to pray
To take my sins and guilt away.
I did not have to beg or plead,
In humbleness I gave my need
From my bondage to be freed
The Master looked upon this
sinful slave
And, oh how freely He forgave
All my sins—the wrongs I've
done
Yes, He forgave me; Everyone!
Now His will I seek to do
And learn to be forgiving, too.
I must love others as He loves me
To live with Him eternally.

Louise Schroeder
Come Thou Gentle Dove
Glide reposing into mine heart
O! a wonderful song lies there;
"All God Promised Me"
I long to sing with Thee.

Ah! beautiful Dove, please help
me wear a badge of love.
O let Thy Spirit emanate
Thy divine nature; do
impregnate!

Help me don the armor of a
Christian
in the battle against Satan;
Abba! send an angel 'tis a dreadful
time; prepare "The Rapture"
sublime!

**Irene Dolores Lippert-
Hoffman**

Irene Dolores Lippert-Hoffman
NO LONGER ABLE
*[In memory of my dearly
beloved brother Raymond
James Hoffman]*
I worked and worked upon this
earth
but now I am no longer able
so homeward I do turn to sit
beside the Lord's table.

Now all you loved ones left on
earth
please, oh please don't feel hurt
for I no longer have wished to
roam
I had wanted to go home.

Now no longer will I be troubled
and weary
for I have been blessed with an
everlasting rest.

Tho'far away I will not be
your human eyes will never more

see me
but yet within your warm
embrace
I will always have a place.

For if long would be your time
I still wouldn't find
the picture of my face ever erased
from your mind.

Now if you be awake or asleep
down upon you through the
clouds I will peek
for a watch over you I will always
keep
until the day you are on your
way
to sit with me beside the Lord's
table
when on earth you are no longer
able.

Mary Letha Washington
WHAT SHALL I BE
*[To my sweet and
understanding daughter, Mari
Letha Washington]*
Through your love
You want me to be happy and
free—
Free to live and choose from
The many courses you set for me,
Hoping one of these
I'll surely be.

I need your guidance and loving
care
To carry me through each trying
year,
I am trying to be what you want
me to be,
But to be happy and free
I will need to be me!

Sheila Joyner
A HELPING HAND
The pool of death
swirls round and round,
With every turn
it drags me down,
Darker than the
pits of hell,
It chokes and chokes
with every swell,
It tries to consume
with every wake,
Can I keep fighting
How much more can I take?
I struggle for air
with every breath,
A hand reaches out—
the hand of Death.

Ed McSwain, Sr.
BEAUTIES I SEE
Out of my window the beauties I
see
I sometimes think they're looking
at me
How their view is taking my eye
I hope they will last until I die.
I am so lucky to have this view
Many of things thats plum bran
new
Visions and dreams that fill my
mind
Beautiful flowers of various kind.
Birds and bees and rabbits white
hair
All of these beauties are beyond
compare
A garden of roses and tulips in
bloom

Cows that graze in pastures so
groom.
Geese and ducks that fill the
pond
Good mother nature a waving her
wand
Grass that's green among the
trees
A flowing of air the nicest of
breeze.

As I sit in my rocking chair
Sights I see are beyond compare
A great symbol of life for me
As all of these beauties I simply
see.

Donna Bonenfant
LIFE SONG
I was singing a song on a stage in
a bar,
And a man slowly walked by.
Then the band started playing
louder,
In the background was the crash
of a car.
So I sang with a more or less
echoing,
While the time slowly passed.
And the music stopped and my
voice quickly died,
As the words I sang were my last.
Oh time for laughter and time for
tears.
My sad song won't be heard for
many a year.
Cause I sang it so well and I sang
it so sweet,
I wonder when my voice and
piano will meet.
Sad day and tearful time,
Sing me a tune of love.
Cause I am dying of lonliness,
Alone in my heart,
Sing me a place full of love.

Morgan May III
**Slave Labor At the Sugar
Mill**
*[To my only Son and Daughter,
Morgan May IV, and Missy
May, until we are together
again.]*
The sordid assorted
Sucrose sifters
Seem to sorta
Soon, duh . . .
Saturate the
Sweaty shirt
With the sweet
Sticky stench of
Sugar syrup smoke.

Kimberly Peterson
TRIAL OF LOVE
The audience grows quiet
As the curtain begins to rise.
What I see in my mind
Does not appear before my eyes.

I see the beginning of a trial
While all others see a play.
I try to get up and leave
but I cannot walk away.

A lawyer calls my name
And tells me to take the stand.
I swear to tell the truth
With a Bible under my hand.

It takes a short time
For me to fearfully see,
That this horrendous trial
Is truly meant for me.

Lawyers challenge my alibi
And my mind they confuse.
Shot by the arrow of justice
I am the victim of its abuse.

Time slowly slips by
Each moment filled with fear.
The jury is debating
The decision grows near.

A haze covers my thoughts
When the verdict is slowly read.
An eternity seems to follow
After the word 'guilty' is said.

The judge condemn my future
Bringing my happiness to an end.
He has given me the punishment
Of losing my only friend.

I have been found guilty of love
And convicted of the crime.
I have been sentenced to
loneliness
Until the end of time . . .

Susan Mary Mayo
The Wood Nymphs Lute
When we met the stars were so
bright
I could scarcely see—
The song went on such blissful
nights
The wood nymphs sang to me.

The hours, weeks and months
never knew
how glad they passed—
For surely I had thought I reached
my paradise at last—

With trembling hands held out to
him,
a shoulder I could cry—
If I could do it all again
it would be there, I'd die—

So pure, so rare, so kind a love,
I thought could never end—
But I the fool who trusted true,
know oak trees never bend.

How I dreamed of ecstacy,
believed
the wood nymphs song,
And found only a stranger and
fear
my road is long—

I know no more my dear hearts
song,
for I am deaf and dumb
The lute is still, the world has
stopped,
and I'm alone and numb

Perhaps someday, somehow,
someway I'll find
a home where I belong
And if it's right, within the night,
the lute
will play the wood nymphs song.

Shirley Hughes
PITY
Happiness is a beautiful thing
To so many folks
To some it means a world of love
To others, just a joke.

But pity those who do not know
The feel of a baby held so close
Or know the joy of laughter
shared
By those you love the most.

Pity those who do not hear the
birds

As they do sing
Pity those who do not know
The joy of wedding rings.

Pity those who cannot find
It in their hearts to forgive
Pity those who go through life
And never learn to live.

But most of all
Dear God above
Help us give them
All our Love.

Ellen Wilbanks
FLOWING HEART
I pray that God will make of me
a fountain pure and sweet,
so daily I can cool your brow
wash your dusty feet.

Then when you take a drink
of the waters flowing free,
you'll know the Holy Spirit is
flowing out of me.

With my hair I'll dry your feet,
and rub them with sweet oils,
soon you'll be refreshed again
from life's daily toils.

This home will be a haven,
for you to rest your head,
you will sleep in peace
when you lie upon your bed.

So come to me beloved,
when you thirst, hold out your
cup,
not with mud, but Living Waters
I will fill you up.

L.C. Reynolds
**Son, This Is Your Mother
Speaking**
*[To Duffy . . . Not your name,
just an endearment; bestowed
at your birth. A small sandy-
haired lad, full of sweetness and
mirth. An angel, sent to give
love and joy . . . Only God
knew how much we needed a
boy.]*
Son of four years, you exasperate
me.
You instruct me that I am not
to scream.
You say your father hasn't any
patience;
but with your grandparents,
you're a dream.
Grandma thinks that you're just
adorable.
You tell her you'd rather live
there.
At home, I swear you're a thirty
year old midget;

causing me to pull at my hair!
Your room looks like a disaster
has hit it.
I've even applied for some
government aid.
D.C. called, wanting you for war
tactics.
Your father was tempted by the
offer they made.
You can counter my moves
before I make them;
and somehow you know what I'm
going to say.
So, why is it, son; at supper, we
clasp hands,
while *YOU* give thanks for the
end of the day!

Lila Lee Noller
PRODIGAL SON
*[Dedicated to my son Martin
whose love for the Lord fills his
life.]*
   "For this my son was
dead and is alive again.
He was lost and is found."
   Luke 15:24

Like the Biblical lad you were in
disgrace
To prison you went an unsavory
place
That father he chose to redeem
his lost son
Could I but do less, for my
Prodigal son?

The Lord made it clear that if
only just one
Of His precious sheep hid away
from the sun
He would seek and discover
where that lamb did go
For that one that was lost, is the
one He loved so.

Forgive me my son, for my little
faith
Judgement is mine, our precious
Lord saith
So come little black sheep, back
to the fold
Just as the Prodigal Son of old.

Jackie Miller
HORIZONS ALONE
I have never loved so easy as when
I was truly within my peace of
mind . . .

As a sweet breeze gently touching
with many 'Horizons Alone' but
free to find . . .

Peggy Barbis
Winter Night—A Tanka
The snow floats downward.
The air's full of muffled sounds—
Lovers' soft laughter,
The steady clip of horse hooves.
Still the frosty moon stares on.

Carolyn Preiser
DREAM ON
dream on
   foolish dreamer,
dream the darkness into light,
   that
sunny days breed finer ways
as time passes, and knights of
   white
appear in the desert sun and
   condemn
the rays of the blistering glaze
to ride again and again.

and heroes made, not born with
   fear,
overcome the clouds for beyond
   is clear.
can you hear the birds sing,
the children's laughter?
dream on
   foolish dreamer,
dream the rains color beyond the
   bow and
dream flowers will bloom as the
   unsung hero.
so full they grow, reaching
   toward the sun
glistening with hope, dream
   spring has sprung.
dream of the life created by you
dream their dreams will all come
   true,
dream of places and things never
   seen
where are the people who will
change what has been?
reach through the clouds you see
   passing by
dream starlight beyond the sky.
dream on
   foolish who?

Paulette Grant
HOPELESSNESS
Nothing to look forward to,
Nothing really interesting to do.
The hours pass and you care even
   less,
The days are filled with
   nothingness.
Day into months, months into
   years,
Year in, year out all tears and
   fears.
Woe to this life it is not what it
   should be,
All men should be satisfied,
   happy and free.
If man had a choice whether he
   could come into this world or
   not,
I wonder how many would
   choose this lot.
As your life nears it's end, in
   wonder you look back,
The whole miserable thing seems
   like one big act.
"Why have I struggled for so long
   and accomplished so little?"
   you ask,
"Oh! what a long and weary task."
You close your eyes knowing all
   has been tried,
This is the moment when all
   hope has died.

Gina Mosteller
ALONE TOGETHER
I saw the hat in an antique store;
it rested on the polished glass,
   which
sat beside the owners' door.
The felt was crumpled, quite
   threadbare.
The feathers were faded, they
hung limp in my hair.
I looked at the reflection in the
   Queen Anne,
of soft blurred images,
behind me stood a man.
We conversed with politeness
of a long-ago century.
His true identity was
yet still a mystery.

His hands rested upon my
shoulders—
gentle but firm; the kisses he
stole
were definitely much bolder.
The people and places of which
he mentioned, all seemed
familiar.
But what were his intentions?
A breeze from the entrance
ruffled my plume, erased the
image
all too soon.
I purchased the hat with much
anticipation. Would he be
included?
Was this his emancipation?
I sighed at the thought and
headed
for the door, a shadow not mine
behind me, upon the polished
floor.

Ben C. Minter
A VOICE WILL CALL
Run, Adam. Run, Eve.
Escape to the thickets
with your carnality
and your injured pride.
If in the darkness,
you don't hear a sound
you might be the victor.
But don't count on it.
Silence often breaks to footsteps
and a voice will call,
"Come, Adam. Come, Eve."
Then you will know
that you did not hide
You just covered yourselves.

Cynthia B. Johnson
WHAT IS LOVE
Love is spelled L-O-V-E
Which means you and me
Love is something you feel in
your heart
Of never wanting to be apart
Love is when he is late
And here he comes at half past
eight
Love is having your feelings hurt
And feeling as low as the dirt
Love is being loved
And knowing that you can't fly
like a dove
Love is a word you can't explain
It's something you have to feel
with pain
Love is sweet, love is pure
Love is something you have to
endure
Love is feeling a little down
But you know that he will soon
be around

Thomas M. Willeman
COULD IT BE?
*[To Gary Summers—may your
influence continue to bring out
the originality and creativity in
the lives and literature of
others.]*
What might this be so deep
inside me?
How is it that I should know
That of which you can never be
sure?
To travel where no man could
go.
The endlessness goes such a long,
long way;
forever seems to pass so slow.

The infinite bounds, both large
and small,
my mind's-eye must surely show.
Could it be too much to
comprehend such?
Might it be too great to bear?
Could it be but a dream, as it
would seem,
while my flesh soundly sleeps
down there?
Consciousness alive, with body
deprived—
how real is reality?
As I lay silent, with eyelids
closed,
how far can I still see?
My light shines through the
darkness in view
like a star in the eternal maze
Reaching out to touch the
universe,
throughout life's endless days.

Janice Wrinkle Stephens
UNCLE SAM
You pay taxes on money you
earn,
each year you file a federal
return,
still the cycle goes right on,
and it applies to everyone;
We're taxed in life at every age,
on every cent we spend,
Uncle Sam's the greedy one,
but it will never end;
If by chance you cannot pay,
any taxes you may owe,
then he comes without delay,
and attaches everything you own;
They say in America,
the best things in life are free,
but whoever got such an idea,
is as crazy as can be;
He keeps right on year after year,
dominating our very life,
little does he know or care,
that now we barely survive;
Even at death you are not free,
and this is a sad fact,
the one who receives your estate,
will be charged inheritance tax...

Lara Smith
STAIRCASE
My life is like an endless spiral
staircase.
Never ending and forever going
around.
Day by day I climb another step.
Day by day I fall a couple of
more.
Back and forth; up and down.
Forever changing.
Will I ever reach the top?
What is the top?
Could it be a forgotten land,
An exotic heaven?
Or a forbidden hell?
Could it be a place where
everyting is perfect?
But the people are not real.
Could it be a place where
everything is imperfect?
But the people are real.
Whatever it is, one day I shall
reach the top.
Whether or not it is a forgotten
land, an exotic heaven, or a
forbidden hell.
So, for now I climb a staircase
that seems to never end.

Ana Elizabeth Hernandez
AIR SO FREE
Air so free
Air that carries me to thee

My words are too weak to say
the true feelings that are me

Air fresh breeze
blowing through the trees

Help me understand the inner me
I can't turn for I don't know
where
I am headed

Air so free
My eyes are too tired to see

The truth that is hidden within
me

Debbie Visconti

Debbie Visconti
SUCCESS
As you climb up the ladder to
good fortune and success
You must have the drive to strive
for the best
For there will be problems we all
have to face
To conquer wisdom and power in
this human race
Respect advice given from those
who are true
Experience provides the guidence
for you
There will be profits good and
some bad
Clear your mind of all questions
and thoughts you may have
had
Withstand all the pressure your
drive will conceal
Control all emotions because
some are not real
Be careful of judgement it's quite
often wrong
Be certain of decisions that will
help you along
Understand what is spoken for
words from the wise
Will help through rejection when
thoughts are denied
If cautious dependable honest
and true
Achievement will be conquered
and rewarded to you.

Katherine M. Trujillo
REMEMBER ME
I love you so much
That I will set you free
If that is the way you want it to
be

There is just one task
from you I ask
Always remember me
That's how I want it to be
I wish the best for you
In all that you do
Before we say "Good-Bye"
I have one last cry
Please remember the girl that will
always like you
For me, there will be no one new
May God bless you
And your new love too

Jessica Ann Nehr
LOVE HURTS
Love can hurt you so deeply you
almost wish you weren't born.
When you try to sleep at night
you feel a heaviness in your
heart. It makes your body ache,
and it tears you apart.

You think to yourself, what is my
purpose in life? Was I really
meant to be unloved? There are
many times I start to feel down
like this but when I do, I ask
for strength from up above.

He is always there when I need
someone to talk to, and when I
really need him, I can almost
see his hands reaching to me. I
know he understands the way
my heart is aching. He knows
what pleases, because he's my
precious JESUS.

Merri Power—Dixon
I'M A PATRIOT
*[A tribute to my friend
"Liam"—the marine]*
I'm a patriot
Believe it or not
And I love our American flag!

Our country's big
Our heritage great
That's why I love to brag!

I'm a patriot
So happy so free
When ole glory waves from on
high!

All America's dream
Thank God, we're the best
At least we have to try!

I'm a patriot
My country is strong
It will live forever and a day!

An American patriot
Believe it or not
Won't have it any other way!!!

I'm a patriot***I'm a patriot
I'm a patriot!!!

Alberta A. Cox
Happy Is the Bird That Sings
Happy is the bird that sings.
Happy is the boy that grins.
Happy is the one who knows
Right attitudes help happiness
grow.

If in ourselves, we'll simply try
To put a smile where once we'd
cry.
If courage is placed over fears,
It can repress a million tears.

Through cultivation of our faith,
We give a smile instead of hate.

And truly as we learn to smile
We make other's lives
   worthwhile.

For happy is the bird that sings.
And happy is the boy that grins.
Through smiles, we gain many
   friends
And happiness that never ends.

Lee Oma

Lee Oma
ESCAPE
Gorging on
hot fudge and fish hooks,
guts raw and unhealing,

she listens
for bongo drums and stacato
   rhythms
for her dancing feet,
pretending her vinegar
a heady wine.

Sandra Turnage Hood
THE PROMISE
She never meant to break that
   promise to her man,
But she stood all the unhappiness
   a woman could stand.
She never really meant for it to
   happen again,
She didn't want to live a life so
   full of sin.
It happened one cool, crispy
   autumn night,
She was feeling alone and real
   uptight.
She drove on over to the next
   city,
At the time she was full of
   nothing but self pity.
She had thirty-five dollars she
   was going to spend,
Not knowing what she had
   bought would cause her life

to come to an end.
She made her buy and went home
   alone,
The thoughts of her promise were
   all gone.
She rolled up a fat joint and
   began toking it,
Feeling high before she'd even
   finished smoking it.
She was sitting in the middle of
   the floor
Never to move from that spot
   anymore.
She began to hear and see things
   that weren't there really there,
Feeling things crawling all in her
   hair.
Yes, the one pusher she thought
   she could trust,
Had filled her reefer with bad
   angel dust.
She died holding the bag of junk
   in her hand,
Wishing to God, she'd kept that
   promise to her man!

Marcia A. Berry
WIGGINS
[To my darling Steve whose
love inspires me everyday of
my life.]
As the setting sun goes drifting
   down
   past the mountains high,
a chilly breeze nips at your nose.
   The herd goes drifting by.

The tranquil setting you sit and
   ponder.
   From a day of work you tire.
The warmth and smell is like a
   spell
   as you gaze into the fire.

It's time to rest your weary bones
   and rest your tired eyes.
to breathe the cleanness of the
   air,
   to count the stars in the skies,

to listen to the symphony
   that hides behind the trees,
to behold all this beauty
   the Lord has given thee.

So close your eyes and rest now,
   the elk are with their young.
The horses they are resting.
   The snow has just begun.

And tomorrow when you wake
   up,
   the ground all covered with
   white.
You will behold a new day,
   a beautiful and everlasting
   sight.

As you pack up all the horses,
   and gather up the gear.
These memories you now have
   of yet another year.

C. Butler Pennell
ME
Who is the person I call me?
What's in the future to see?
Why was I born an American,
   born free?
To know the answer, I'd have the
   key.

I was born a male, not a she.
I was born a twin, not three.
I'm not for sure, I wasn't born
   a flea.

Nor do I know if I've lived as a
   tree.

If I wasn't just me, then who
   would I be?
That isn't for humans to forsee.
Now I'm a human this life, me.
The mind in all of its harmony is
   only a gift to us from God, we.

Like the sky, the earth, and the
   sea,
Put together the great symphony,
It makes no difference what I am
   or what I'll be,
Only if God recognizes this thing
   called "ME".

William Edward Woodward
To a Piece Of Uncut Stone
Bleak, pure, and formless,
A virgin, uncut stone,
Your tabula rasa fullness
Waiting and alone.
How might have Michael Angelo
Chiseled out your grace.
How might your face
Have trimmed an arch or dome,
A crypt in Rome,
Or a wall of the Parthenon.
But Chance did not will it so,
And you were never chosen.

Lee Edwards
WITHERED WINTER
Withered winter sharp and frigid
   clears the mind for summoning
   thought
Long secreted deeply in human
   perma-frost
Through waning seasons thawed
   and lost
Those random fragments which
   life wrought.

Crisply fractured icy-cicles
   prick the frozen conscience,
   the hoary bones
Glacial-tingling needles quivered
   from the past
Recalling roots and trysts which
   hast
Semblance of saneness that living
   hones.

Elizabeth Barmore Hillman
IT WAS NOTHING
I'm resting on a substance soft
   and white
I'm drifting through a gentle
   purple night
I relax myself and breathe the air
   so free
A cool, cool breeze flows over me.

My mind is loose with no stress
   or strain
Outside there falls a gentle rain
I lie here peacefully, calmly
   resting
The breeze still cool, the air
   caressing.

I sit upright in the night now
   black
From where I'd been lying on my
   back
What was it that hit with a
   sudden jolt
With all the power of a
   thunderbolt?

Nothing, it was nothing—just a
   dream
I open my mouth as if to scream

Calm down, calm down, it's over
   now
It was just a dream, anyhow.
I lie back down on that bed of
   white
I close my eyes to the silent night
I go to sleep, I feel so free
With the cool breeze drifting over
   me.
   It was nothing—just a dream.

Neil R. Grant
How Could I Not Love You?
[To my San Francisco
sweetheart, who has touched
me in her own quiet way,
shown me how to love again,
and has brought forth from
within me unknown yet
beautiful music.]
How could I not love you?
   You've given back to me
   everything I've given you:
      Sharing, Caring,
      Greeting cards, meaningful
      words,
      Your kisses, caresses, and
      personal charm.

   Plus some things that I didn't
   even expect or ask for:
      Reasons for my past;
      Patience to live in the
      present;
      A future to live for;
      And dreams to believe in
      again.

Barbara Ann Bloom
THROUGH THE WINDOW
   Through the window
I can see
The lonely people
Who don't see me.
Through the window
I see the joy
That was brought
From the small boy.
   I see the love
Upon his face
I see the pain
Of their last embrace.
I want to tell
The boy I see
That his pain won't last
For Eternity.
   I want to reach out and touch
The heart of one
Who hurt so much.
But I can only watch and see
Only look on helplessly . . .
   Through The Window.

Elaine Turrey Maldonado
A FLEETING MOMENT
My thoughts meander over the
   landscape,
As far as the eye can see.
Off at a distance I see many
   fantasies
Dancing upon my mind.

Intriguing me as my gaze tries to
   focus
On shapes and forms.
Trying to make out the collage
   that keeps
Appearing and vanishing.
I could almost touch those
   apparitions
Of my mind, they seem to close.

As my gaze rises above the
   horizon,

I see the clouds passing by,
Forming and separating at will.
Never belonging or
    overshadowing
Each other.
Touching each other like a
    caress,
A whisper, a promise.

The rain is beginning to fall,
    almost
Like teardrops,
Falling softly against my
    upturned
Face;
I have captured those feelings of
Emotions that permeate my soul
For such a fleeting moment of
    time
I touched eternity . . .

Douglas A. Peck
SONG OF SILLYMAN
I grasp a finely muscled thigh,
And cup a breast with passion,
And then I shyly turn away,
Aggression's not my fashion.

The verse above was just in fun,
And if and when the deed is
    done,
You know that I won't be the one,
It's just a fantasy.

It's all her problem, not my own,
That she's so damn alluring,
I think about her after lunch,
Before, and even during.

But disappointment is my fate,
I'm just an exiled reprobate,
It's been a long time since I ate,
I think I'll climb a tree.

Lila Lee Noller
QUICKSILVER
[To my husband Chris whose
love inspires me to create.]
This thing called love
Can we really grasp it?
Is there a beginning or an end?
Can we ever possess it?
Sometimes we clutch it tight
And it slips right thru our fingers
Then again we hold it loose
And it seems to be truly ours.
Very elusive this creature love
We must savor every moment
For then, should it slip away
The taste will remain
Each time we remember.

Evonne Y. Jackson
KA-LE-KA (Moon Godess)
Wild, but beautiful she creeps
    through like a panther stalking
    it's prey. With rainbows
    gleaming from her hair, and her
    skin glistening and shining
    darkness into another day.

Like a fog on a calm and misty
    morn she touches the leaves
    with her fingertips. While the
    fragrance of daffodils slightly
    touches her lips.

Like a dove she wonders over yon
    hills, swimming like a swan,
    and as beautiful as a peacock
    she dances gracefully in the
    wind.

Like a cat she ponders . . .
Surrounded by nature she takes
    many forms, more beautiful

than any mind could imagine,
    with more knowledge than
    man can reveal.

Kaleka, the shadows follow you
    for the longest of hours, and
    returns smelling of warm
    spring showers.

Like echoes from the highest of
    mountains she sings. Kaleka,
    with the smoothest of skins,
    her thoughts are absorbed.

With hands like the moist of
    flowers she returns to the
    forest, leaving an odor of sweet
    smelling spices blowing into
    the air, and memories of the
    night before.

Ken Holloway
CORSAGE FOR KIM
[For Kim, who hath "pacified
Psyche, and kissed me, and
tempted me out of my gloom."]
Gardinias I pinned upon my love;
Both are gifts from heaven above.
The flowers adorn a lovely breast,
And there my lips shall ever rest.

The sweet perfume of breast and
    flower
Ne'er produced more fragrant
    bower.
Ah, Eternity—preserve us then
In close embrace, Kim and Ken.

The soft eve cometh—she says
    she's mine!
Ah, love-raptures of Venus divine!
And filled with gardenias the
    earth will be
For my darling, my love, my
    Kimber Lee!

Alma Joyce
THE AUDIENCE
Channel switchers dare not feel.
Observers seeking nothingness of
leisured slaves bound hand and
foot by chains of cotton candy.

You shall come forth to valors
    work
not skipping thru the tulips
but by rose thorns which
mar they prideful beauty.

Life is more than timeless logic
    to
compute! Yourself you did not
    make
Fear keeps you out where anger
    driving
flesh conceives; yet love ordains.

Randall W. Forney
DON'T QUIT
When things go wrong, as they
    sometimes will,
When the road you're trudging
    seems all up hill,
When the funds are low, and the
    debts are high,
And you want to smile, but you
    have to sigh,
When care is pressing you down
    a bit,
Rest if you must, but don't you
    quit.

Life is queer with its twists and
    turns,
As everyone of us sometimes
    learns,

And many a failure turns about,
When he might have won had he
    stuck it out,
Don't give up though the pace
    seem slow
You may succeed with another
    blow.

Success is failure turned inside
    out
The silver tint of the clouds of
    doubt,
And you never can tell how close
    you are,
It may be near when it seems so
    far,
So stick to the fight when you're
    hardest hit,
It's when things seem worse,
That you must not quit.

"AJ" Miles

"AJ" Miles
THE SHOPPERS
Scurrying to and fro throughout
    the city
The shoppers trudge from store
    to store,
Seeking their gifts of pleasure and
    joy.

The children squeal with delight
    and wonder
At the sights they see in every
    place;
They romp and prance from place
    to place,
And work their mothers to a
    frazzle.

In every department store there
    forms a line,
For the children are anxious to
    see and greet
The man in the big red suit they
    know as Santa Claus.

Some cry and scamper from this
    jolly old man
hile others talk for hours on end,
Asking him to bring this toy and
    that,
When he flies on that enchanted
    night of the year.

The shops are crowded from day
    to night,
As the shoppers finish their last
    minute chores
In readiness for the gala night of
    Christmas eve.

Soon the stores will empty of
    shoppers and toys,
And another year of Christmas
    shopping will end;

But one thing that cannot be
    bought in stores,
Is the goodwill and friendship
    that comes this time of year.

Alelie Zinzius
LONELINESS
I never knew how it would feel to
    be alone,
Here I sit not a sound, neither a
    cry not even a moan.
I stare to see my reflection in a
    stream,
I'm by myself and hope it's a
    dream.

I wish to wake up to find
    someone by my side,
But that's only taking my mind
    for a ride.
Why have they left? where did
    they go?
Will they come back? I'll never
    know.

I don't want to cry but I must
    drop a tear,
I know now that being alone is
    my biggest fear.
It's an empty feeling you can't
    realize,
'Till it will flash between your
    eyes.

There I lie under a tree,
This is where they'll bury me.

Stephen P. Peck, Sr.
SOULS IN TRANSIT
We're souls in transit, lost in a
    world so cold
Living in a hell, we've fashioned
    for ourselves
Having gone astray from the fold.

Hopes and dreams, life's
    everything to hold
They're not ours to have, for we
    can't fit
In this cast of society's
    demanding mold.

We're souls in transit, lost in a
    world so cold
Walking down this avenue of
    despair
Knowing streets are never made
    of gold.

Believing in fantasies, we've been
    told
Yet fighting the ghost in our lives
And reaching for the mightly and
    bold.

Yes, we're souls in transit, lost in
    a world so cold
And upon the cracked and dirt-
    smudged windows
of our very souls, is stenciled
    "sold".

Daniel De Peola
VESPERS
He is gone, and the noon dies too.
Gusting winds consecrate the
    day,
as if more than normal weather
is needed to mark his passing.

The twilight deepens. Winds
    rattle
the window as I dig out the
    album.
He grins, mugs, peers to ask why
there's been no word in all this
    time.

Boyhood, youth, young manhood
   all
so swift, and a disbelief in
the notion I'll never again see
the spark kindling these images.

Streetlights flicker on, one by
   one.
Clouds wreathing the sunset are
   scoured
to shed a pastel glow until
the day is seen through stained
   glass.

All our early warmth long since
   cooled,
and never once did I reach out
to relearn a voice, a look, a set
of desires . . . now it's too late.

In one photo he wears suit and
   tie—
maybe eleven or twelve,
buy trying so hard to look
   grownup,
as if he knew the time was brief.

The candles burn along the
   street.
The choir of air roars then hums
beyond the panes, and in this
   makeshift
chapel, I don't know how to pray.

Gloria D. Alkire
**Memory Of Stepping
   Stones**
*[To all who attended Bee Ridge
School, Clay Co., Indiana and to
all the wonderful teachers who
taught there.]*
The stepping stones of learning,
   once new,
Have vanished with the winds of
   time and change
And the ringing bell in Bee Ridge
   Dell is stilled;
A lone bob-white and robin sing a
   duet sumphony
In a morning mist caressing
   softly through the wood—
While the hills with poignant
   beauty still are filled
But the stepping stones of
   learning are now gone!
The childhood laughter that once
   resounded free
In the magic of the schoolhouse,
   comes alive;
The flashback lingers as the
   candle glow of learning
flickers low—
The newness of the past is now a
   part of destiny
And the stepping stones of
   learning, are just a memory!

Shandra Travis
AFTERMATH
Amid some storm-tossed sea of
   green,
   life continues;
And I know that in the end
   life shall reign over its
   conclusion.

Marian Paust
For a Child Just Born
For you,
Heaven and earth
rejoice tonight
when you ride the tide in . . .
For you,
the breath of flowers

lingers in the streets
and the wind stops singing
   to listen . . .
This house is a haven
which invites you in.
Beyond its window-eyes,
the moonlit river
becomes a luminous mirror
upon which
a fleet of flashing stars sails . . .
I let the earth go
and enjoy the miracle at hand.
In the days ahead,
now that you have left one world,
we will walk
through this new one together.

Jonathan Miller
AN ADDRESS OF LOVE
In her eyes eternal spring
   does to me a supreme balm of
   love impart.
   And in charm possessed my
   bleeding heart
   does find joy that her lasting
   presence bring.
All my past sufferings shown
   are gone and serenely sweet
   again
   is the air,
   from which true love and
   honor fair
   do keep me company and I am
   not alone.

In beauty's influence laid
   she gives beautiful smiles
   to me.
   And trembling at last my love
   is free
   to embrace her near in
   secret shade.
I awake from sound sleep the
   birds above.
   My voice in song they
   fly away.
   Yet in flying they tune
   the day,
   making my addresses sweeter
   in love.

Paul P. Langley
WHEAT FIELD AT SUNSET
Terrains of wheat in gently
   curling stance,
Like supple swords that sway
   before the sun,
And charmed by nature's lyric
   flute to dance
And sing before their fleeting
   days are done.
Impressive sights are strikingly
   revealed:

A salmon sky, a yellow mat
   unfurled.
Sustained within its rich black
   soil, this field
Extends its yield for loaves to
   feed the world.
I am the grain caressed by playful
   dirt,
The breeze that whisks
   oppressive cares aside.
The sunset signals life's elusive
   gift,
But fleet days will abundant
   crops provide.
A twilight thankfulness enfolds
   the field,
Since pledges of fruition are now
   sealed.

Rose Graham
GOD'S GOOD OUTDOORS
Just go out in God's outdoors,
   And that awful pent-up feeling
Gives away to one of freedom
   And you lose that up-tight
   tension,
With that fresh air intervention,
   It just changes you inside!

When you feel the breezes
   blowing,
   When you see something
   a-growing,
And the traffic all a-going,
   Hear the little birds a-singing,
Gladness to your heart a-bringing,
   It's just good to be alive!

Gladys Claudia Rosado
I LOVE YOU
I love you
   With all the joy and warmth
   of a long time friend
I love you
   With all the concern
   of a parent to the end
I love you
   With all the amazed delight
   of a child at play
I love you
   With all the pure thoughts
   of the blessed saints
I love you
   With all the wonder
   of an endless universe
I love you
   With all the loves
   which are heaven sent.

Alwanda Carter
THOUGHTS
Thoughts of love,
so sweet and dear.

dream of love, from
a distance summer,
of another year.
we live and loved
without fear, and
dream of life; that
was so dear.

Genevieve Dunne Berger
CITY FOREST
Through twilight I see
In the empty courtyard below
A single tree,
Branches lined with swallows,
Notched tails in single file,
In order, military style.

They quiver and fluff their
   feathers,
Pre-packed sleeping bags

Equipped for chilly weather.

Silhouettes in an orange sky
Like black paper witches
On Halloween windows, they
   sleep.

Darkness slowly descends,
Curtain at play's end—
I turn from the magical sight
Fearing a cat might creep
Or sirens shock the night
Rousing them into flight.

Jennifer Tyler
SALUTATIONS
Out beyond my window bright
The sun does shine with all its
   might,
Chasing away the dark of night.

Reaching through the curtain's
   lace,
It lightly touches my sleeping
   face
And settles there with quiet
   grace.

Suddenly I am awake.
My dream thoughts stop with a
   break;
My dark night thoughts the sun
   will take.

I open wide my sleepy eyes
And sigh a quiet morning sigh
And slowly rise

To greet the morning sun.

Jeannette Kleindl
DE'JAVU
Flickering lamplight softly dances
'Cross a strong and gentle face
Breaking time in tiny pieces,
Other times, another place . . .
Hardened hands, so very tender
As they cup the steaming brew
Holding past and present to them
In a moment, timeless, true.
Weathered logs and dying embers
Scatter ghosts across the
   floor . . .
Faded denim, drying leather . . .
"Now"is "Then" forevermore.

Connie Villines Bahm
LOVE
When love is here,
You are completely covered in
   happiness and joy,
But, when love fades,
You are stripped, openly exposed
   to the world.
Love seems to take away,
More than it had to give.

Nancy C. Allen
THE FIGHTER
*[In memory of my mother; for
my family; my husband, Mac,
daughter Sonya, and a special
student, Chris]*
I lay there! My dreams, my hopes
   gradually seeping like a
   volcanic eruption as jet fighters
   swooped the mountainous
   slopes.
Screaming warplanes on the rise;
   Trailing plumes of smoke
   hazed the grim skies.
Fear, like an earthquake shook
   inside; My thoughts plunging
   as a roaring tide.
Soldiers lay side by side, the
   wounded; the dead; on the lap

of the earth, I rested my head.
I must conquer the fears; I must restrain the tears.
Ribbons of red clouds—streaked from the fading sun; the evening slowly dying away;
Weary soldiers quietly lay. Screams of warplanes faded with the day. Homeward, my thoughts began to stray.
Sleepiness drowsed my eyes; the moon and stars weaved celestial light across the skies. A momentary dream—as my mind drifted entertaining a brave noble theme.
The night, calm and free; the fears inside ceased to be.
Soon night gave way to the twilight of day; And dawn, adorned by the sun, crossed the mountainous slopes, I like the birth of a new day, experienced an oasis of new strengths and hopes.

Elsie Campbell Butler

Elsie Campbell Butler
LET HIM IN TODAY
There is only One who can save you
From sorrow and sin;
He is knocking at your door—
Won't you ask Him to come in?

He is King of this earth and of heaven above:
He is the Light, the Life and the Love,
He is testing you today, will you take the crooked
Or the straight and narrow way?

The straight road is very narrow—
It leads to life and love complete;
The crooked one leads to sorrow, Suffering and defeat.

He is our Lord and Saviour,
The One we should all adore,
He has prepared a home for us
On that bright and happy shore.

But if we remain in sin—
He will never let us in.
So take up your cross and follow Before it is too late—
If you wish to enter that beautiful pearly gate.

Stacy Wiederlight
A FEELING
Sometimes I wish there was someone there,
Someone I thought that really cared,
Someone who had a shoulder to lean on,
Someone to wipe the tears away.

We all need someone to make us feel good,
When we're feeling down,
Everyone wants a little attention,
To know that they're important too.
A little smile, that something special,
I know that feeling, just like you!

Sister Alphonse Marie Schreck, S.S.J.
THE TEACHER'S REWARD
One night I dreamed I died and went to Heaven,
And there knocked timidly upon the Pearly Gates,
With jangling keys the lock turned; the door opened,
And I stood alone before the Man of Fates.
He questioned me to find out if I qualified
To enter once for all the heavenly court;
I stood there, scared and trembling, unable to answer,
It seemed my heavenly trip was about to abort.

St. Peter must have felt unusually sorry,
Inspired, no doubt, by my apprehensive mien,
He sent for the Recording Secretary,
Who brought the Book of Records to be seen.
Announced by trumpet flourishes, this great Angel
Presented to St. Peter the heavenly Book;
He opened it to a certain section, scanned it,
Then suddenly stopped and gave a quizzical look.

I stood there, breathles, waiting for the verdict,
Fearing the worst, and then he gently asked,
"Is this correct, that you have been a teacher?"
"Yes, Sir," I answered, "for these many years past."
An audible murmer rippled through the halls of Heaven,
The Pearly Gates swung wide as Peter touched the bell,
And to the accompaniment of heavenly music,
"Come in!" he said. "You've had enough of Hell!"

Barbara S. Klein
A WAY TO SUCCEED
Try to take advantage
of the goodness that you've got
Make use of your ability
to then achieve a lot
You may be apt to accomplish
what you never did before
And see that true success in life

will have an open door.

Many people start out
with a hobby done with skill
They may possibly do so well
their progress climbs the hill
As hobbies which succeed in life
can change into profession
This proves how your ability
can reach good progression.

Satisfy your interests
and try hard to reach success
You'll find that good accomplishment
will bring you happiness
Thank God for your ability
to then do what you can do
Prove out that you'll make use of it
with all things done by you.

Donna Krovocheck
DAUGHTER DEAR
[To my daughters Cheryl and Christina, whom I love very much.]
You're so young,
Your life has just begun.
You'll be experimenting the good,
You'll be experimenting the bad.
You'll feel the hurt,
You'll feel the pain.
You'll laugh in the wind, and
You'll cry in the rain.
But don't you worry for I'll be there.

I love you daughter,
I'll always care.

Nora P. Swackhammer
SLED RIDE
It was a little past nine on a cold winters night
I put on my jacket and stole out of sight.
Went into the yard and grabbed hold of my sled
That I was supposed to have put in the shed;
I hurried my footsteps over the light, crunchy snow
To the hill by the house, that we kids got to know,
As the best place to get a long ride to the end.
We would zoom down that hill till we came to the bend.

I bellyflopped onto my sled with great glee
And went over that snow like a race boat at sea.
The ride being over, I stood up with delight
Looked over the beauty of that cold wintry night.
Walking back up the hill with my sled pulled behind
I'll always remember what went through my mind.
"Though man creates wonders with what is in signt,
Only God paints a city all white in one night."

Sharon Frank Klesh
HEAVEN ON EARTH
I try to make "Heaven On Earth"...
and time just passes me by.
I try to be happy,
I try to be gay,
I try to have all things in my

own little way.

That people should be wealthy,
That they should have peace,
That lives should be fulfilled,
. . . that it never will cease.

Little ones should be blessed
With not a tear in their heart,
That they should enjoy
Total love 'til they part.

Each little bird sings a song of sheer joy
To proclaim all innocence like life in a toy.

I read how a woman should be clean and be true.
But that man lusts of her image and that he needs love, too.
What is this world that we can't propagate?
Does it deliver us from evil and a life full of hate?

A dog likes his companion,
A cat loves a caress.
In a world of confusion
This could be a real mess!

The flowers shimmer with beauty
On a royal plain of green.
They sense the nourishment
And a "lack" that is unseen.

A mother gives birth in answer to her quest.
Must she forgive those who made it this mess?

Total peace must be in heaven
'Cause not everyone is like "me".
This life here on earth is misbehavin'
And I long to be free.

Virginia A. Mosley
Departure In the Midst Of a Poem
She departed in the midst of a poem,
Never to return again.
Her craft gone as well,
Only what went before remains.
An art lost to the world,
She departed in the midst of a poem.

Linda M. Bilyeu
THE BARN'S SECRET
Fall weeds haunted the old barn.
Its door creaks on rusty hinges
And swings in the summer wind,
Drawing me into its cool places.
Once my eyes adjusted to the dark,
I realized something else had,
Like me, chosen this old barn.
She stood proudly beside
Her tiny velvet quartet
With squeaky kitten voices.
Gently I walked over to touch
The barn's soft little secrets.

Juanita Costin Freeman
MY CHILD
I did not cry in Africa when I stooped to drop my first born like a bloody mass of waste from my body. I knew through his veins flowed regal blood, pure and red. He was destined to be—bold.

I shed no tears in Mississippi when I left the fields to birth my child and suckle him briefly before giving ole massa his due. I knew some day he would break the shackles and breathe free. For he was my son—strong.

I did not weep when he was born in the cold sterile hospital of Georgia, where his hunger went unfed and feces oozed from unchanged diapers as callous white nurses refused to touch my child—beautiful.

I did not whimper when life erupted forth from my bowels as I walked the streets of Washington, D.C. It was for him I marched and waved the flag of victory and peace. I was prepared to give my life for my baby—black.

Perhaps if I had wailed in Africa and as I entered this promised land, I would not tremble now as I leave the filth of my project prison and curse as I stumble into a yard filled with the debris of a lifetime, corrupt with temptation. Dark silence seems to echo. Softly, so softly I cry, as I watch my child—die.

Carol Patricia Keenan
COMMITMENT
[To Mary and Marty Martin: who would have ever thought my wedding gift to you would one day be published!]
The wedding is gone,
Tomorrow is at dawn,
The honeymoon slowly,
moves along.
The sun has rose
after night disappears,
taking the moon to
another hemisphere.
A future awaits as a
couple begins to share,
one another, together,
for the remaining years.

John A. Blanda
PATCHWORK QUILT
I sit upon my country hill,
(Which isn't really mine at all),
And gaze upon a giant patchwork quilt.

Clouds passing lazily overhead,
Combined with that leafy smell of fall,
Coax me into dream.

How many hands it took to sow this quilt,
And how many more it will keep warm.

And from that warmth we get each others love,
To keep us through the coming cold,
And safely into next year's spring.

Anne Terranova
THANK YOU, TEACHER
I have finished my time here;
Was it really four years?
It is time now for me to leave,
To go out and be someone.
And now the test comes:
Has high school really prepared me?

It has not been so much the studies
As the experiences I have had
That have helped me to grow.
Acquainting myself with you as a teacher
And a person has left, I believe,
A more valuable, memorable impression on me.
For I have learned as much
From you outside the classroom as in.
I only hope that I have also left
An impression upon your life as well.
I will remember you,
Your ideas,
Your beliefs.

David S. Pope
THOUGHTS FOR AWHILE
[To Mrs. Douglas, my eleventh grade English teacher, who has helped me so much.]
Give me thoughts
And I will think for awhile.
Give me a pen
And I will think for a while.
Give me some paper
And I will think for a while

And after awhile,
My thoughts will flow
From me to the pen
From the pen to the paper

And I will give others thoughts
So they may think for awhile.

Jean (Howard) Russell

Jean (Howard) Russell
Memories From The Past
[This poem was written for— and inspired by—my son, William Lee Russell, now serving with the United States Army]
Toy soldier men once scattered, are standing quiet and still.
They're waiting for their captain, his orders to fulfill.
Bright blocks and treasured picture books are gathering coats of dust,
A sail boat and an army are covered now with rust.

A once beloved gingham dog still waits for him right there,
Where he kissed and tucked him in, and shared his nightly prayer.
A wagon, once so busy with hauling treasures then,

Is silent now and empty, no need to roll again.

A rocking horse with peeling paint was once so very dear.
The little rider now is gone, I wish that he was here.
To hear his tiny footsteps, his voice filled with delight,
My grown up little man by day, my baby in the night.

When night grew near he'd bring his books and climb upon my knee,
He'd lay his head upon my breast, tell of his love for me.
Those happy days are in the past, no longer is he near.
But memories bring him back to me in happy yester year.

Dorothy Anne Cottrell
PRECIOUS MOMENTS
As we sit together . . .
candles burning
just as brightly
as the flame
of love.
My feelings growing
stronger by the minute.
As I look deep
into loving blue eyes
I know then that
I have fallen in love
with you.
As you hold me in your arms . . .
music flowing in the
background . . .
feeling the warmth . . .
totally captured
by the moment
I tell you . . .
I Love You.

Manuel R. Camu
Variation On the Petrine Theme
Not that any rock is a stone which only a sinless hand can cast against a flesh that wallows in adultery. Every rock is. Every human hand is not.

The stone which the Anointed could have changed into bread without the tempter's try might have been the same stone upon a stone of that fragile obelisk from where He could have thrown himself down without His feet dashing against a stone.

How many stones would have

been strung round the neck of them who abused the little ones in scandal or sin! How many seeds would have been choked of life for falling upon a stone of a heart! How many goliaths would have fallen had stones of courage been hurled by davidical hands!

Yet the house that was built upon a rock has ever remained firm amidst miasmatic storms of the devil and evil, of terrors and errors, of wiles and lies as with the

tide and time the Rock rolls towards its tomorrow as towards its Builder pilgrims this House atop its Cornerstone: stubborn in its grip of truth, sensitive yet sensible to the pulse of renewal and reform. Yet still is on rock: Impregnable against death and decay. Of rock.

Allison Kidd
HIS AMAZING LOVE
Have you ever just sat
And watched with ease,
God's creations
Blow in the breeze?
The tall green grass
That grows so high,
Heaven is like
An ocean in the sky,
His beautiful flowers
That bloom so free,
Has always been something
So amazing to me.
There's so much more
I could write about,
So much more
Without a doubt.
Now I must go
To leave you here,
But with this thought
Please keep it near.
God created
The grass and the sky,
Not for himself
But for you and I.

Leah M. LaCamera
I'VE DECIDED
[To Shep: The one I decided to love.]
I've decided to let you go.
So why does it hurt so?
I've decided to walk away.
So why do I want to stay?
I've decided to let things ride.
So why are there tears to hide?
I've decided not to care.
So why will I always be there?
I've decided to try to live.
So why do I still want to give?

Because . . .
I decided to love you.

Colleen Shroyer
MY LOVE
Today, as I sat alone I watched intently, at all the passing faces, hoping you would appear, and rescue me from my loneliness, for when I am merely in your presence, how wonderful it is— the security of just knowing you are there—knowing that

everything will be alright, no matter how sad or depressing.

You have the way of the warming sunshine, and how often during the fleeting moments of the day, do I think of your loving smile, and the tenderness of your eyes.

Each day my love for you is always there, tho often we are apart, and your thoughts are far from me—Not so with me my darling, for you are my every thought, and deepest concern, and I will always love you.

Connie R. King
SOMEBODY CARES
When I am old, too old to see,
I hope someone will care for me.
Enough to take my hand and stay
To lead me 'till I learn the way.

When I am old, so tired and weak.
Will there be one to kiss my cheek?
And let me know, though I can't see,
That someone has remembered me.

This is why, I'd lend a hand
To anyone who couldn't stand.
I'd kiss a cheek or dry a tear,
To fill a lonely heart with cheer.

They may be old, too old to see,
Too old to here, or know it's me.
Still they know someone is there,
They're not alone, somebody cares.

Barbara Anne Martino
Pieces of a Shattered Dream
[To my mom and dad . . . who made all my memories very special ones . . .]
Broken castles in the sand
Parades with no brass band
Empty ice cream cones
A lot to say and no toy phones
Little puppies with no bark
Big fireworks with no spark
Playrooms with no toys
A birthday party with no noise
Snow storms with no hill
A party dress without the frill
A nearby park without a swing
A new doorbell without a ding
A fairy tale with no end
A ripped teddy bear without a mend
A big fat marshmellow with no fire
A new red wagon with a flat tire
These are a few of their shattered thoughts
Not even a new shiny dream can be bought.

Jacqueline Wilson Wardell
THE CAROUSEL
They told me I'd find life
On the boardwalk.
"It's all down there," they said
"Go, and take what you want."
So, greedy for experience, I went down.
I rode the carousel
Perched on a silver horse
Spinning round and round

Making me dizzy.
The music blared
Loudly and racously
Making my head ache.
I blame myself—
I wanted to ride, to snatch the prize.
"It's all down there," they said
"Go and take what you want."
Now I wish I could get off
This carousel,
For I've captured the brass ring
But I can't keep it—
I must throw it back
For someone else
To take.

Jo Ann Dorothy
VIRGIN SACRIFICE
[To two of my dear chiropractic patients who narrowly escaped death in separate auto accidents that totaled thier cars—no bones broken, just in need of adjustment.]
Yesterday as the sheriff
pulled Char out of the wreck
of her window-shattered Porsche,
motor split by a telephone
pole, she without a scratch,

England overflowed onto the shores
of the Fauklands and Argentina
drowned in *yerba mate*
boiled in a red hot pot
that scorched the tongues
of poncho-draped *gauchos*

who lost their sheep in Israel
slaughtered by Philistine terrorists
looking for pretty *sabras*
to mother their sons and rule
the holy land blood-bathed
in purified streets.

Jan Renfrow ("Ten's" wife)
TEN
My "Ten", in striped overalls,
Scooping gobs of watermelon
Sits happy in the sunshine,
Drinking orange juice by the gallon.

My "Ten" is slim and healthy
By the fruit out on his trees.
He's so gifted with his hands
And fixes everything he sees.

His precious, boyish smile
Lights up my heart and soul—
Reflecting the serenity
Of one whose life is whole!

My "Ten" is not a screen gem;
He's not known very far.
Yet his most important fan
Knows that he's a superstar!

Lorraine C. Mohr
SEPTEMBER ONE
Our day it was as there we stood
Repeating vows in church
Before my dad, a minister,
Making promises
Meant to keep and would.

Our love grew ever deeper
With the births of our three sons,
One blonde, one brunette, one redhead,
"Our three R's: Ron, Rod, Rick,"
we said.

We had such fun those years
While they grew tall and strong
Much like their dad, then
Suddenly, he was gone!

Do I go on alone? Ah, no . . .
His presence I can feel
When rain is in the air
Or brisk winds blow . . .
And any kind of day this time of year,
His spirit hovers near, I know.

Lavretta Hughes Truax

Lavertta Hughes Truax
EMPTINESS
The rain is coming steadily down,
Reflecting the tears within my heart.
The earth wears a dreary frown,
And there's emptiness within my heart.

Why must my emotions always be guarded
Against the gentle, as well as the hard-hearted?
Others are allowed full range of emotionality;
My lot to express it only very occasionally.

I have offended by not loving sufficiently,
And yet also, by loving too greatly.
Why can I not attain a middle ground,
Or a friend returning similar feelings be found?

Robert Ray Weetman
The Scourge Of the Pirate
The skull and crossbones on its mast,
The brigantine drew near.
For the golden laden cargo ship,
Its death time dance ensued.
As the pirates closed a broadside left,
The cargo ship was doomed.
A few more volleys raked the decks,
The masts they stood no more.

The pirate ship its grappling hooks,
Secured to that dead ship.
Their men now flowed upon her decks,
Yelling curses as they went.
With orders but to kill them all,
And never quarter give.
The smell of death, from bow to stern,

Did echo through that ship.

For a pirate's life is brazen,
And the devil is his friend.
And though the centuries have elapsed,
His mind has never changed.
His lust for want and other things,
Has not diminished once,
But taken on an 'ism', that you and I can't trust.

Yes, this 'ism' is a pirate,
That unleashed will kill us all.
It rapes the minds of all free men,
And kills the liberty in them.
It scourges all the ramparts round,
Until there is no freedom sound.
For the skull and crossbones have been replaced,
Now the Hammer and Sickle, flies in its place.

Alice Miller
EXPRESSIONS OF MY SOUL
I sit and write my poems
As expressions from my soul,
All these feelings from inside me
But with words I'm not so bold
And maybe as you read them
You will surely see
That the words I write on paper
Are the thoughts inside of me
I know there are others
Who have feelings they could share
But they keep them locked inside them
Yes, they keep them hidden there.

Kristin M. Nicholls
FOREVER
My heart has been
In your hands long enough
It was yours
to have,
to hold,
to keep . . .
Forever
But now I have taken it back
Now it belongs to me
For you have punctured it
And drained it of its desire
to love
This scar shall remain
upon my heart . . .
Forever.

Jan C. Whitener
YOUR SUMMER
There comes to most of us, a summer
not to ever be understood.
Like the one that turns a young man's head
for the first time.
Like the one I caught sight
of the smile
I couldn't stop smiling at.
Summers
remembered best by old wrinkled men.
Who are not as tall now as then.
Old woman
are more careful.
As if embarrassed by their summer.
Having worked so hard
to smother their passion
Summers . . .

Today's Greatest Poems

James Elmore
A THINKER'S TREATISE
[This poem is dedicated to my loving wife, Lorri. For she knows the value of knowledge. There could be no better wife or mother to our children.]
On my shelf I do declare
Are some of the best thoughts
That man has shared
Books with images, inviting and true
Ancient histories, with thoughts just like new
Some are yet to come
The written word is left here
For any man to delve
To raise their awarenesses, and discover the new
To analyze the sky, and just to think if they need to
These precious little works will help to create
Visionaries and dreamers
Who will come to make
The future . . . .
And what it will be.

Helen Saeger
BE SWEET TO ME
Be sweet to me
  Love me always
Teach me how to live
  Let me learn of life from you.

Hold me close to you
  Let me dream a while
Be sweet to me
  Let me learn of love from you.

Just be sweet to me
  Teach me that love
Can be so heavenly
  Let me learn of life from you.

Hold me close to you
  Let me dream a while
Be sweet to me
  Let me learn of love from you.

Helena Yvonne Sanchez
FIRST TIME
[To my soulmate throughout eternity. "I love you" Helena]
How I longed to be in your arms
To kiss your lips and
Touch your penis;
To run my tongue all over your body
And have your hands caress my body
And feel your mouth against my breast.
So hungrily and tenderly
Your hands and your tongue

Find their way to my chamber delights
That longs to have you feast inside me.
Warm and juicy, it awaits you.
Together we reach our orgasm,
Discovering and unvailing for the first time,
Each other.

Ruby Phillipy
THROUGH THE MIST
Eerie specters seemed to rise,
    Echoed sighs,
When the shifting fog had swirled
Through my lonely, shadowed world.
Time stood still in Nowhere land;
Then I reached to touch your hand,
When a rift of light brought you
    Into view.

Now the warmth of love gives chase
              To erase
Dismal fears that blur the scene.
Life once more seems safe . . . serene;
Time has turned to its full swing.
Hearts have learned new songs to sing,
Knowing through each misty day,
              Love will stay.

Lori Caldarola
FEELINGS
What I feel and
    Why
are parts of me not known and
finding out is such a task because
the feelings are so masked.
I can't tell
        the love for the hate
        the resentment for the compassion
          the guilt from the wanting
            and the hundreds, or
            is that to limited,
of other feelings or are they
            just sensations
that are wandering through me
              coming and going
Sometimes so very intense
            and what to do
    about them
Should I try to touch them
            to find their origin
              OR
Is it enough just to
          feel?

Wilma Atkins
HANDS
As I stood today, and looked upon
a portrait large and still
The hands that were painted there
So life like, that I could almost feel

Their loving touch, their gentle stroke
upon my fevered brow
Ageless hands, that never did no wrong
Precious even now

At first I thought, the hands of Jesus
they must surely be

But when I looked closer
No scars could I see

I questioned in my mind
where did they drive the nails
whereby he was hung that day
alone small and frail

I know they don't belong to Jesus
because He died for me
He gave his life, so long ago
So that I could go free

And as I looked again, I realized
that it was God's great hands I saw
Hands that created Heaven and Earth
and wrote the commandments into law

Verse after verse ran thru my mind
of scriptures, and songs of old
Then thoughts sprung up from deep within
And seemed to fill my soul

Oh Lord you see my sister dear
with hands, diseased and bent
You know the pain she suffers Lord
the sleepless nights she's spent

I know you love her dearly Lord
and though I don't understand
Help me to pray for her, with faith
And to place it all, Dear God
within YOUR LOVING HANDS

Mary Beth Sager
EYES
[In memory of my brother Mark]
The eyes of a person reveal his inmost thoughts
Things which are never spoken or sought
The person or fool with the attempted camaflouged mood
is the victim of these foolers which leave him nude!
In time of frustration eyes fluster in rage
Eyes show glory, pain and age
When sadness bestows, eyes fill with tears
And they sparkle with happiness when a loved one nears
Eyes magically enable people to see
And it is hard to imagine how it would be
to have faces existing which are lacking eyes
They would look blank, ludicrous and unnwise.
So we should all be thankful that God thought of such things
to give to us ungrateful human beings
And thank him each and every day
For such marvelous blessings that he brought our way.

Max E. Keeler
January 1—Expectations
Hello to the New Year just begun
And to the newness of the rising sun!
Give ear to my deepest prayers
To ease the burdens of my cares.
With wonders fill my blindless

sight,
With visions to chase away the night
From dim, tired, water—filled eyes,
And grant me communion with wise!
I bid the sickness of my sorrow
Be lost in all the hopes of tommorrow!
Peace of mind to enable me to see
The depth of need vanished by decree
And fulfillment of goals unknown
To aid my mind until it's fully grown!
It is the promise of the goal
That gives enrichment to the soul
And fills the heart with gladness
And offers ultimate release from madness!
Hello to the New Year just begun
And to the newness of the rising sun!
Give ear to my deepest prayers
To ease the burdens of my cares.

Maria K. Escobedo
The Lowlands Of Benton
[For the Johnson family, My family. Thanks for Everything.]
I will arise and go now, and go to Benton.
And go to a small house with a corral built for horses
And go now to live alone with the beauty of Mount Whitney in the horizon

And I shall have some peace there, for peace comes naturally here.
As natural as the sunrise ending another dark, cold night.
There's shimmering beauty all around when the first snow comes
falling down.
And the wind is full of happy dancing.

I will arise and go now, for always the hustle of the day.
I see the beauty of life in the valley.
While I go through each day, I think of how
I long to be there.

Helen Worley
THE PROPHET
The young man walked
    through the streets
    of the burned—out city.
How was a soldier.
How often did he
    see this very thing before?
The bombs and mortars,
    swift and sure,
    had done their work,
Had found their marks
    and brought them down,
Reduced to piles of filthy rubble
    on the ground.

It was always the same.
Where once each building
    had its own proud
    personality,

105

Now the ashes of
  palaces and hovels
  had come to be
Alike. And even here, the town
  that once bore its name
  so proudly, just
Joined a hundred other nameless
  towns
  in swirling clouds of dust.

At times like this, he
  searched his mind,
  so eagerly,
Drawing pleasant daydreams
  from a
  bank of memory.
The hopeful, happy days
  of early youth,
Peace and safety,
Friends and family,
"All beckoning, waiting for me,
To come to them and join them
  in reality."

A bit of stone, dislodged,
  rolled to his feet
  and stopped.
He knelt to pick it up
  and held it reverently,
Like some rare and perfect gem
  of highest quality.
And as he touched it to
  his lips,
The flood of tears broke free,
For it was not at all the way
  he thought his homecoming
  would be.

Lorwin Cates
LITTLE DOG LOST
There's a house down on the
  corner, that I passed by today
A little dog sat on the step
  staring wishfully at me, now
  the house is quite
Desserted it's very plain to see for
  everything about the house is
  empty as can be
The children that the doggie
  loved are now no longer there,
  no friendly hand to fill
His pan or pat his little head or
  something soft placed on the
  floor for him a
Little bed, he cannot understand
  the change, his world was
  simply grand, there was
Little hands to pet him and lolly
  pops and games, now his
  stomach is quite empty and
He's thirsty as can be, but he's
  afraid to leave the house
  though lonely it may be
He sits and waits, and seems to
  pray oh please come back for
  me.

Veeda Peterson
The Black Withered Bible
The black bible, torn and
  withered
    Now still upon the shelf
The man that so often read it
    Was not in the best of health
He said if he had his way
    He'd do it all over again
Cause that black withered bible
    Was his comfort, to the end
The black withered bible
    That people said looked bad
It was the only comfort
    The old man ever had

He said, "If people know what's
  right
    Then they will not condemn
  me
Cause that black witherd bible
    Was all that ever set this old
  soul free".
Now the bible sits alone
    On that shelf this very day
Waiting for another
    To come along this way
I guess that I can say this
    Because I've seen it in my
  days
The good Lord works
    In such mysterious ways
That old withered bible
    That others said looked bad
That old withered bible
    Made the old man very glad

Pam Hamilton
THE PEARL NECKLACE
She saw in the window of the
  antique shop,
A necklace of gold with a little
  pearl drop.
Her Gramma had owned one
  much like this,
But lost it one night when things
  were amiss.
The house was quiet one winter
  night,
Gramma didn't hear him or see
  his light.
As quickly as he came he was
  gone so fast,
The pearl necklace in his hand,
  he had it at last.
Gramma awoke and the necklace
  was not there,
She sat in the corner and began to
  stare.
Remembering the day she was
  given the gem,
How Grampa had loved her way
  back then.
The years they shared were so
  complete,
All the love in the world was
  theirs' to keep.
One rainy day the Lord took
  Grampa away,
She was left alone and began to
  pray.
The pearl necklace she owned
  would some day be,
A gift of love for her
  grandaughter to see.
With nothing left for the pearl
  necklace was gone,
She went to join Grampa at just
  about dawn.
Her grandaughter was sad and
  quietly grieving,
Feeling so sad because her
  Gramma was leaving.
Back in town he found the
  antique shop,
He needed some money and
  hoped for a lot.
To his shock and dismay he
  learned to late,
The pearl necklace was
  worthless, Oh what a fate!
She went to the antique shop, the
  pearl necklace to buy,
Such an urge to have it, she didn't
  know why.
Gramma was watching from up
  above,

Watching her grandaughter with
  her gift of love.

Tony Chrysler
HE UNDERSTOOD
*[To my special friend Larry
Hegerle, who has given me a
friendship I thank God for
everyday.]*
I could feel the anger
As the sun rose higher
I felt I was cheated
I was burning like fire.
As I stared at the sun
I had to ask why
He was my best friend
Did he have to die?
I felt so lonely
I wanted to run
The death of my bunny
Wasn't any fun.
Then someone sat next to me
He held out his hand
As I cried on his shoulder
He said, "I understand".
We sat there for hours
I asked him to stay
For without his loving kindness
I couldn't have faced the day.
As I looked in his eyes
I knew he really cared
I felt my spirits start to rise
By the love my special friend
  shared.

Ralph R. Mills

Ralph R. Mills
PITTSBURG AT NIGHT
*[To my sweetheart, Helen, my
wife]*
I stood upon a rocky cliff above
  the street
And looked down where the
  Allegeny and the Monongela
  meet
I looked out over the river and
  the smoking steel mills
To the dimly lighted houses on
  the distant rising hills
The moon and stars were shining
  in the heavens above so fair
And lights in the houses
  twinkled as though stars had
  fallen there
There were no signs of conflict
  showing man's eternal strife
For the darkness hides the
  struggle of this ever pressing
  life

And now to you my sweetheart
  so many miles away
This is to tell of my plans for

some future day
We will build a little cabin
  among those greenclad hills
Where we can live together and
  hear the whip—poor—wills
We will build it among the
  violets, a cozy little cot
Where we can dwell forever in a
  fairy garden spot
This may seem like only a dream
  to you
But when our plans are
  completed, you will be happy
  too
For dreams are only myths unless
  one labors hard and long
Like the musician who sits at the
  piano and composes a beautiful
  song

"Success is failure turned inside
  out
The silver tint in the clouds of
  doubt
And you can never tell how close
  you are
It may be very near when it
  seems so very far
So stick to the fight when you are
  hardest hit
It's when things are darkest, is
  when you must not quit"

Jennifer Mieth
If I Could Only Explain
If i could only explain to you
the meaning of the smudged
  letters i
never sent, poorly written stanzas
where the pen trails off the page,
  that
died in anonymity.

The arm—wrestling inside
  between two
dispositions, (it's so dignified),
the male against the female and
the subjective wars the objective.
Freedom compromised again.

If i say i love you forever
will you understand if i leave us
for a while or permanent
if only to prove i still exist
separate from my hermit?

To admit he's essential, allows
an integral fragment to perish.
Yet it is deemed unwomanly
to exile him from my embraces.
There is no rational choice.

If i explain the lack of logic
of the childlike dichotomy
the panic of giving up control
the fear of living death—the
  single
defense left to loving

would you understand and could
i love you?

Elsie M. Westrick
Memories Of Childhood
Locked in my mind are the
  memories of old
Of a wonderful childhood as
  bright as gold.
The large leather rocker that held
  daddy and me,
As he read the funnies, each
  Sunday at three.
And the joy of Easter, when to
  church we walked
In our Easter attire to hear the

minister talk,
When cards came in colors, were
tacked on the door
And friends walked on by so the
disease wouldn't soar.
And my blanket would be
covered by the simple toys
Crayons and books and all the
joys
To delight a child, confined to a
bed,
With mother silently watching,
dressed in bright red.
I remember the end of World War
One
The bells and the whistles in the
mid—morning sun.
The tears of my mother and the
joy in the street,
Brought a lump to my throat,
from my window seat.
And just before Christmas, time
seemed to stand still
All was confusion, but oh what a
thrill
When on Christmas Eve, I was
hurried upstairs,
Where sleep took over all my
worldly cares.
Then just before breakfast, all
was made right
Parlour curtains were opened and
behold what a sight,
Candle—light on the tree with
gifts brought sighs
Of joy and laughter and tears to
my eyes.
Down through the years its been
such a pleasure
To remember one by one, those
memorable treasures.

Marion Witherel
THE MASTERPIECE
Natures palette bears its soul
All caution thrown to wind
The peaceful artist, brush in hand
Decides where to begin.

Hues of yellow, red, and blue
Swept gently 'cross the sky
Reminds us of a promise made
In ancient days gone by.

Golden rays peeping through
Shining in the grass
Reflecting off the dewey blades
They glisten as if glass.

The mountain peaks are capped
in white
Their beauty undenied
The sparkling ocean dips and
swirls
Above it seagulls glide.

How lovely this creation is
A masterpiece of art
The canvas was our universe
The artist was our heart.

Stephen M. Johnston
A Voyage Of No Return
Two hundred men had started on
a trip of seek and find,
One thirty had returned and two
of them were blind.

They had left from Mother Spain
to journey across the sea,
To sail completely around the
earth propelled by a steady
breeze.

Magellan's ship was sturdy; his

men were strong and bold,
And with his strength, they
planned to sail and find a land
of gold.

The king wanted riches, the
Queen wanted clothes,
And all the men returned with
was a cargo full of cloves.

But Magellan's men had been the
first to sail around the world,
And where they stopped in every
port Spain's flag was unfurled.

Mary Brickman Mayse
I LOVE YOU SO
*[This poem is dedicated to the
man I Love, he has been a
constant encouragement to me.
as this poem say's I Love You
So—]*
My dear husband,
I Love you so.
So very much more,
than you will ever know.
Your my day, my night,
and my inbetween.
So gentle and kind,
and never mean.
Beleive me dear,
as it seems hard to show.
Alway's remember—dear,
I LOVE YOU SO.

Dido Biddle
WORDS TO SORROW
(suicide of a friend)
when the dream
spilled over
from holes
in your confidence

you found it hard
to depend upon
the empty spaces
of your unfinished soul

but why did you cry
without tears
i also still have
so very far to go

Maryanne Meanor
UNTITLED
I want to be nobody
Going nowhere
In good company

Cathy Allsbrook
HOMECOMING
When I was young and very old
My battles were fought on well-
trimmed lawns.
I was the cowboy, brave and bold,
A broomstick horse to ride upon.

I shot all the villians down,
Scrawny arms, rough brown faces.
They always came back to green
small town.
They never left their places.

Growing old and very young,
I often wander back to play
In green small town—a dirge is
sung,
The trees turn thier backs and
walk away.

I'm left behind on Maple Lane,
Shooting through my private rain.

Marteena Hammar
THE WEB
The spider spins a silken thread
to make her web.

Each strand is gossamer thin and
bright as dew.
The busy spider spins hour after
hour,
Nor ceases 'til her work becomes
complete.
The web looks harmless
sparkling in the sun,
Each strand a masterpiece unto
itself
But, it is strong. It holds its
victims fast,
They nevermore are free to fly
away.

You have spun a silken web
about my heart
With strands as fragile as a
springtime breeze
And I am caught forever in its
weave;
The difference is — I do not
WISH to flee.

Bruce Neiger, MD
BODY LANGUAGE
*[This poem was inspired by my
wife LESLIE]*
I read so much love
in your touch.
Each embrace, darling,
tells me so much.
When we kiss and
our bodies unite—
We communicate things neither
of us could ever speak
or write.

Blossom P. Kaonohi
In Our Father's Eyes
In our Father's eyes glorification
is upon us
In the eyes of others—
Envy and distortion bothers.
In our Father's eyes mercy and
love
In the eyes of others—
Self—interest and lustfulness
smothers.
In our Father's eyes benevolent
gifts
In the eyes of others—
Blind'd to sisters and brothers.
In our Father's eyes salvation for
all
In the eyes of others—
Eat, drink, and be merry—
For no eyes are upon us, not even
Father's.

Theresa D. Gabel
SILENCE
"Silence is Golden",
or so I'm told.
But what is silence
but sound about to unfold?

Miki May
THE SOUND OF SILENCE
silence
surrounds you,
as you sit
engrossed
in the deep
private thoughts of your
inner self,
as you ponder,
the depth of feelings
rise
closer to the surface,
and you are not
alone
in the silence,

awareness
of the peace and beauty
permeates
your being
as you feel and see
the mysterious joy
of infinite creation
surrounding you,
silence,
the gift of an understanding God

Marnie Fischer

Marnie Fischer
"Pudgy Hands"
Communicate
Dandelions. Pink Elephants.
Hay—Covered Strawberry
Patches. Creeks with squirmy
toe—stricken' mud and darting
minnows.
Tufts of pink cotton candy
playing patta—cake with a
child's fingers.
Erbally, girbally words invented
to make common place words
so important.—
Earth's playground—A Child's
Delight.

And Sand. Incredible Sand. The
Sesame Street playdo of
creativity. Grains of wayfareres
greet enchanted castles with
hidden dungeons etched from
these salted pebbles. And dump
trucks swish in the liquid of
life only to be stroked, once
again, by the unshaven pebbles.

Pencils, Papers, Erasers—the tools
of self—expression.
Jarred lines and abrupt circles,
sprinkled with lead, create the
imprint of mommy and daddy.
And oh, if those circular lines

could speak, the untapped wisdom could sing laughter, simplicity, creativity, and unconditional love into hearts devoid of human touch. Children—God's given relief to a hectic world.

But then, the age of reason evolves through the matted bubble gum netting now distinguished as hair. And our friends—Humpty Dumpty, Jack and Jill, Jack in the Beanstalk, and the rest of our gang come tumbling down to the acne of realism.

Adults—God's given confusion to complicate the world. Calculation, Computing, Agitating Creatures who dump the marbles of life into a huge washing machine hoping to cleanse. Silly adults, they forget to read the marbled labels— hand wash, use mild soap, do not chlorine. So, shredded, tangled and tattered, whipped and whirled . . . Unnecessary, if they would have only read the signs. Besides, marbles should be used in games like Chinese checkers and hopscotch. Adults—those complicated creatures need to lick more lollipops, play leapfrog over more fire hydrants, tennis shoe thru more creeks, and pause, to listen to the erbally, girbally words of the water, and sing more Dragon songs that will puff magic into a little girl's heart. Adults—should be more like you, Michael.

Mrs. Grace Grogan Ward
NAME ME, PLEASE
Here's your garden—
Though rough and rocky sometime.
Where on earth could you find such climate sublime?
Where birds fresh as the morning dew
Come close to offer friendship true.

Though you don't call it perfection
Still may be found some reflection
Of friendship sincere—
Meetings right here
In your garden.

"All the world's a stage"
(So sayeth the sage.)
Swans too, enjoy the play.
(I must hasten to say.)
But do you suppose they sometimes long
For truth and Sincerety's song?

Before you played your role
This was just a watery hole.

To name these feathery birds
I'll leave to thee—
Thinking that among them
You may find one like me.

For still I contend that friendship

Such as yours,
Oh, Swan, cannot be found so frequently on these watery shores.

June Lee Box

June Lee Box
RECYCLED AUTHORITY
Grandpaw used to twirl his whiskers
As he alone laid down the law.
His children jumped and 'Yes, Sir'd him,
And vowed—Never to be like Paw.
Mother and Dad shared the ruling.
With limits set by stick or stem
We did our chores with no fooling,
And vowed—Never to be like Them.
What's happened? We're out in the cold.
Our children stand and defy us.
Mustached, long hair, eyes hot and bold,
'Chores?' they scream with taunts to try us.
Too late we find who now is boss.
Who dictates what we pay and when.
Our good intentions have backfired.
Great—grandpaw's whiskers twirl again!

Dr. Florencio Pagan—Cruz
PRAYER
Merciful Lord of the Universe,
Forever powerful true and wise,
As a humble creature at Your image—
To You I kneel down my life.

In the genisis of our earthly ball
Generously You gifted her
With flowers, birds, stars, and songs
For me to see and share forever.

With Your divine knowledge
Of all things seen and unseen.
From Adam's rib You presented me
The gift of gifts with the name of Eve.

This land with mountains and valleys.
With deep oceans and gentle seas—
All these and many other beauties

For my lifelong happiness, oh Lord, You did.

In our hearts you injected love
Love so sublime, pure and true—
Give me more of You, oh Lord,
For my soul to eternally feel good.

My prayer is born in my heart,
In all my being, body and soul,
I pray, interceding for them
Who know You not but need Your love.

Take good care of all their needs,
Instilling in them the blessed message;
Save them and to them please give
Love on this Earth, and Happiness in Heaven.

Derek W. Burton
Some People Think I'm Me
Some people think I'm me,
for that's all they see.

Some people think I'm me,
there's nothing else to be.

Some people think I'm me,
for it feels great to me.

Some people think I'm me,
there's just nothing else to be.

Mike Herriges
BREEZE
Walking beaches alone;
my favorite pastime
since you've gone.

The early morning sun,
trying to burn off the fog,
isn't as bright now
as when we ran barefooted
playing tag with the surf,
laughing with the gulls.

The loss of your smile
has dulled the salty air
and dried up the tidal pools.

A single set of following footsteps
reminds me that
you've gone.

Norma Jones—Lamb
CELESTIAL TRIANGLE
I am one
It is autumn, the last leaf
Waiting for the harvest.

Once I was two
It was spring without showers;
There were no flowers.

Some are two in one,
But like summer
Still raw.

To be three in one
By winter
Is patterned for perfection.

Drew Allen West
SUMMER IS GONE
Daylight dwindles, Winter is near
Announcing the end of a special past year
Summer is over another gone by
A good one it's been I need not cry
A hundred friends made away and at home
Some at school, work where ever I roam

The things I've seen, the places I've been
Going in haste before summer's end
Laughter, joy and pain alas
The worst of which be summer's pass
Gone the time for outdoor wine and dance
Sunny days and nighttime romance
A lady to love the summer's light
Blend a mystical potion on a starlit night
Now as summer slips away
To replace it's warmth
I keep summers love for winter's day.

Gordon Hawkins
UOMO VECCHIO (old man's thoughts at eighty—four)
All things of this so dear familiar world
That I have loved so well, grow more and more
Treasured and dear when one has passed three score
And ten, and knows not when he may be hurled
Out and away from these familiar things
Into vast strangenesses and loss complete
Of all that he has known. Oh, how one clings
In thought, to all that made his life so sweet—
Yes, bitter—sweet at times perhaps, and yet,
Even the bittersweet is treasured now.
For one has learned to live with his regret
When the last leaves are trembling on the bough.
How precious now are ALL the things of life
Despite its deep anxieties and strife'.

Clyde D. Elmore
TIME
Time is very valuable, no one has any to spare;
Life is a one way ticket, with time being the only fare;
What you do with the time you have, is solely up to you;
So why would you want to waste it, when there is always something to do.

Ethel C. Tulk
EVENING SONG
As you walk the long road on
Look ahead—only shadows stay behind
To harass you
The things undone, the things unsaid
Let go. Here the way is new and strange
Explore the pathway that you take
Each traveler will see different sights
To some, the hills seem rough and steep
Self pity walks there too
To some there is a beckoning

scene
For look, the changing sunset
flow
Is brightening all the sky
With drifts of moving color
Never seen the same before
Listen to the evening song
Of birds nesting for the night
Content among the trees,
Soft murmurs of delight.
It comforts us, as we gon on
Perhaps alone
To sleep beneath the stars.

Lettie J. Williams

Lettie J. Williams
SNOW
I stand alone in the midst of the
storm,
   On a spot that is dear to me.
The snow is fast falling, the
ground is white,
   Yet in it His glory I see.

I have seen a beauty in starlit
nights,
   And clouds showing forth His
glory,
But this afternoon as the wind
whips past,
   In the snow I read this story.

"He is so majestic and powerful."
   And oh, how I long to be pure.
"He is all—wise and yet loving."
   I'd care for the things that
endure.

Bill Woodrome
CENTAUR
Riding swiftly
   on back of my noble equine,
Feeling power
   thrusting forth, his heart
   pounding with mine.
Knife—like, cutting
   thru the wind, freedom way
   beyond compare,
Long, fine mane
   flying back, with energy to
   spare.

Turning it on
   up this slope, letting it all hang
   out,
Quickly reaching
   the top, I raise my head to
   shout.
Such a feeling
   means so much, it seems to
   keep me strong;
It is second only
   to my lover's touch, and this
   surely can't be wrong.

There is something
   pure and simple, when I'm on
   my steed:
He seems to bring
   me closer to the things I need.
For a measure of grain a flake of
   hay, and some tender loving
   care,
He maintains his
   nobility, and also takes me
   there.

Lea M. Jacobs
COMMUNION
I know a quiet place
Where only lilies grow;
I tend them all so tenderly,
Each pristine row on row.

With golden eyes
They all look down
In sweet propriety,
Only the curving rapier
Leaves, make bold and
Look at me.

I gaze at them in wonder,
How still they are, how white,
Their fragrance fills
The cool night air, and
Thoughts of you,
We mutely share

Denise M. Lyons
THE WAVES
I walk along the shore with
   rushing waves,
so all alone that nature speaks to
   me.
The crashing waves speak louder
   than the birds.
Their words contain the wisdom
   of their age.
Old Waves! Please tell about your
   many trips!
What places have you been in
   your long life?
I often wonder, do you die after
   you reach your destination at
   the shore?
Or do you recede to your
   underworld,
and return fifty decades later?
Please tell me! So I can be more
   knowing
of miraculous secrets of our
   world.
So, maybe I might learn to live in
   peace,
by copying your tranquil way of
   life.

Joyce L. Manning
Why Not Give Them a Chance?
*[To our kids, Bobby, Kathy,
Debbie, Jimmie, John and
Cynthia. Also to our
grandchildren: Stephen, Matt,
Jennifer, Heather, and Amber
Dawn.]*
We always seem to talk about
   teen—agers;
How they act, how they drive,
   how they dance.
We seem to think they're nothing
   but law—breakers.
Listen folks; why not give them a
   chance?

I can tell you one thing there are
   many grown—ups
Who are worse off than their

children are.
In fact, maybe that's why they're
   a little mixed up;
Because their parents always
   push them too far.

In a way, that's why so many kids
   are bad.
Because that's the only way they
   get attention.
The kids nowadays don't get to
   do as much with dad.
He's always so busy, and mom's
   always in the kitchen.

Just think a little more about the
   good kids.
There are so many boy scouts,
   girl scouts, 4—H clubs;
But do they get as much publicity
   as the bad kids?
No, they don't. Why not let them
   have a chance?

Just who is to blame? Mom, Dad,
   or this busy world?
Think about it, and then get out
   of your trance.
Stop runing around in circles;
   life's in a whirl.
Do things together. Give us all a
   chance.

Tony Lavelli
TAKE PRIDE IN THE U.S.A.
Lord, guide the American Way.
There's only one "Uncle Sam."
Whose spirit and voice I am.
   Ev'ryone.
"TAKE PRIDE IN THE U.S.A."
Confide, vote and "have your say."
Maintain rational esteem.
Preserve the American Dream.
Sheer hope of countries I need.
To lead each race, faith an' creed.
Godspeed sound soul in our State.
Lord, keep America great.
"Ask what you can do for your
   nation."
Support, reach for towering
   station.
Be proud of the American Way.
"TAKE PRIDE IN THE U.S.A."

Patricia Currey Conrad
GREYHOUND THUNDER
Wheels running, asphalt tune
window's fogging, rain's perfume
i hear your voice from an inside
   room
whispering my name,
Got my ticket, southward bound
the engine churning an eternity
   sound
all our yesterdays coming down
tears from yonder sky.
Slowly nearing townshed light
another faceless city now in sight
if i were a bird i'd call it flight,
mortal footsteps have to do.
Rear—view mirror reflecting rain
each new drop looks the same
like a pawn within the game
i take your knight and run.
Morning rooster found me
   sleeping
across desert hills i've been
   creeping
like a phoenix, my marrow's
   seeping
on to the land.
Yet, dust to dust is just a saying
for bound to earth i won't be

staying
there's still more tracks to be
   laying,
virgin universe open wide.

Dorothy Kirchner Seim
DIAGNOSIS
Tell me man of medicine
   Whose eyes are bright and
   sharp,
Will the words you speak release
   me,
   Or pierce me like a dart.
And break this brightly colored
   balloon
   That once flew like a bird on
   the wing,
Tied to the earth and those she
   loved,
   By a single fragile string.

If need be, do you have the skill
   To fight the gods at play
And victoriously send me soaring
   For yet another day.

I wait and my heart pounds
   loudly,
   The pulse of a living thing.
Look at my face, see the fear that
   haunts,
   Understand what your words
   can bring.

Gregory James Swanson
Natures: Flow Of Green
As I see the flow of Green
It reminds me of days I've seen.
As I watch I feel content for this
   is beauty in a sense.
Onward across the ripples that
   are green,
I begin to see it as a dream.

Yellow than appears to me
Isn't it beautiful just to see; the
   futuristic life to be.
What I mean is serenity
Then combined with what I
   know, in the moon up high
   that makes it glow
Something is there to make it
   blow.
Wind is what I feel across my
   face
I wish I could take it's place.
Being a part of the flow of green
   experience all the days I've
   seen.

Barbara J. Olson
LITTLE MAN JOE
A little man sits on the curb,
And not one leaf does he disturb.
Looking at life through tiny eyes,
We know that he can't realize,
That life is hard for his mom and
   dad
And many things make them sad.
But the little man by the street,
Tries to warm his freezing feet.
He hates to go home to be,
By himself and lonely
He sits right down and smiles at
   you
While trying to think of
   something to do.
As the day is leaving so does he
Starting home where he should be
He knows no one will be there,
I guess that makes it hard to bare.
Mom works, and dad does too
although they love him, he
   doubts it's true

He goes to bed and says a prayer
Wishing someone else where
there.
"A brother, a sister, anyone!!!", he
cries
Alone again in bed he lies.
And tomorrow he'll go sit by the
curb
And not one leaf will he disturb.
One day that little man looked
up at me,
And said, "Gee, you're pretty."
All day long, I couldn't forget,
That little man so cold and wet.
That little man, named Joe, by
the curb.
Who not one leaf, did he disturb.

Beverly A. Hutchinson
Unpaid Babysitter Blues
Darrells's school clothes—on the
chair by the door.
His boots and socks are on the
floor.
His snack money by the lamp on
the table.
Fix a can of soup—if you're able.
Saltine crackers on the counter
nearby—
I can almost hear you sigh.
His coat on the hanger—his hat
in the sleeve.
It's 10 of 12***Time for him to
leave—
***Thank GOD for Public
Schools***

Agnes L. Turner
What Is This That I Feel
I feel the need to talk to myself,
to hear my voice say the words
I want, and need to hear. I want
so much to belong, but in my
heart I know that this is
impossible. There are those
who know what they have
done, and to say I'm sorry
would hurt them even more
than life itself.
I cannot touch what I feel, I
cannot feel the hurt that you
have given me it is there, but I
have no feeling in this cold
heart which I was born with.
Teach me the good that you
have learned from life, do not
take that which I have and
bury it in some dark place that
you have chosen.
Does it belong to me? Can I touch
it, is it a part of me? I feel I am
here for that one special need,
of another, but this time that is
here I shall make good of it,
and enjoy the best, for it won't
be forever. I have touched the
flower, and it has moved my
inner being, and the water that
is tasted, it has moved my
thirst, and the air that I breath,
let me enjoy the earth, I can
take what is mine alone, which
is the memory of life but you
have taken the most important
part, and that is love. Love can
mean so much to one, when
there is the feeling of being
alone. Time stands at still
when there is love near, but
this love that I feel has a need
to be free, there is no need for

fear, my heart has no hate, my
love I shall hold within, what is
this that I feel.

Carole Eileen Leornard
To My Mother, Sleeping
I watched you doze this evening
in your chair
You did not look calm, even in
repose;
But, rather, "Vulnerable as ever,"
You,
I could feel the apprehension in
your pose.
I thought of all the times your
heart was troubled,
Of all your kindnesses to others,
still unpaid;
I thought of how you'd suddenly
grown older
And all at once I felt alone, afraid.

It is too late to share something
that's hurt you?
Or spare you if your dreams are
once more broken?
Too lake to make one sacrifice
for you?
Or take back some of the words I
shouldn't have spoken?

The parts of life I've found were
never hollow
Are all the times I found you
waiting there;
And all I ask of Eternity forever—
Is that you know contentment,
sleeping there.

Norma Venters Smith
DEATH OF A LINEMAN
*[In memory of my father,
Clarence Venters, whose
untimely death left such a void
in my life:]*
Night masked in beauty of virgin
snow
Through darkness, glaring white.
Draped in icy splendor, grand!—
SLEEPING, SLEEPING, SLEEPING.

Across a lone and stately feild
A shadow's taking form,
As silent footsteps make their
way—
FLOATING, FLOATING,
FLOATING.

The shadow probes the quiet
night,
His nose held toward the wind.
Seeking out inviting quarry—
SEARCHING, SEARCHING,
SEARCHING.

Keen eyes alight on trusting prey
Perched high atop the ground.
Repairing faulty power lines—
WORKING, WORKING,
WORKING.

A smile spreads 'cross the
shadow's face,
His claws reach for the pole,
And pull him upward, inch by
inch—
CLIMBING, CLIMBING,
CLIMBING.

Then very quickly—not a sound,
DEATH pounces on his prey,
And down the pole the lineman
comes—
FALLING,
   FALLING,
      FALLING.

Kimberly A. Baseman
HARD TO SAY I'M SORRY
[To Debbie—with love always]
It started out two years ago—
And has come a long way since,
Our friendship's been through so
much;
So many trials and errors!

When we first met and our
friendship started out,
So many things were new to us,
We laughed, we shared, we cried,
we loved,
But now we hardly speak!

I wished to work things out with
you
To show you that I cared,
I wanted to tell you so many
things;
To show you that I meant it!

We've come a long way in these
two years
And many things have changed,
But still with all that we've been
through,
It's hard to say I'm sorry!

Elizabeth Jane Gutta
STAIRWAY TO HEAVEN
There's a stairway leading up to
Heaven
It's made of shining gold
Its beauty takes your breath away
While silently you kneel to pray
My heart just aches to climb
those stairs

To meet the One, I know who
cares
Why did I sin so much of late
Why was my heart so full of hate
I pray, oh Lord, You guide my
way
And let me climb those stairs
some day.

Pamela K. Barger
CHILDHOOD DREAMS
Childhood dreams have come to
rest,
Within this life, with which I
have been blest.

I've followed the desires of my
heart,
Like the leaves take to the wind...
I've fluttered here and there,
Only to return home and begin
again.

I've tasted the bitter-sweet of
Life's wine,
Only to drink more deeply
thereafter.

I've eaten of the forbidden fruit,
Only to be greeted by my own
hollowed laughter.

I've gained the wisdom of
experience
Through curiosity and
conversation;
And through living and learning,
The fine art of caring and
compassion.

I've known of loneliness and
sorrow;
The cold, harsh awakenings of
Reality.
I know, too, from the living of my
life—
Reality's harshness is, but of a
nature, of mere triviality.

The days, weeks, months and
years, it seems—
Have all come to rest,
In the living of blessed Childhood
Dreams.

Bernice M. Staples
The Eclipse Of the Moon
The curtain went up right on
time
For half the world to see,
The heavenly, spectacular sight,
One eclipse in eternity.
The earth slowly followed it's
course
Ordained many moons ago,
Casting a shadow on the
moonscape
'Till only half could be seen
below.
The shadow widened and ever
slight
Circled an orange glow,
Lastly a sliver of the moon
Then—naught but a tear to flow.
One tear for the dreams that lost
their way
One tear for the songs unborn
For all the babes lost in the
woods,
Don't cry, soon will come the
dawn
The mould of the moon refused
to fade
Its shadow would have us know
A tiny cradle will soon appear
Next the moon will be all aglow.
The show had ended right on
time
Leaving hidden its mystery
Of a heavenly, spectacular sight
And a glimpse of eternity.

Wendy Van Voorhees
ICE CREAM CONE
My red wet flicks
   The white softness
      Which is creeping
         Stealthily down
            This brown so quick.

The coolness knows
   It melts, I think,
      But still it hides
         From my red wet—
            White dripped between
               my toes.

Marcus Evans
ILLEGAL DEATH
The day I lose a friend
my heart pumps sorrow
and memories have no end.

The earth keeps turning
but I wish the world would stop
The day I lose a friend.

Why is life unjust?
Why must friendship be lost
and memories have no end?

Friendly death buries me
as the coffin is lowered
the day I lose a friend.

No rose could be so lovely
to remember the dirt-spilled mind
and memories have no end.

Few things seem so unfair or
unjust
and nothing drains the soul like
The day I lose a friend
and memories have no end.

Debbie
MARIA
A cry in the night
Tiny little feet and hands,
So maybe she was a mistake;
But she's mine.
She wasn't conceived in love,
But she'll live in it.
She'll laugh and cry and be
human;
Because of me.
An unplanned bundle of joy.

There were no thoughts of
bringing her here back then.
But I wouldn't change a thing,
Maybe then, but not now.
She's got his nose; who's nose?
She's got my eyes; my eyes;
her mommy's eyes.
Motherhood is a privilege; a baby!
a baby!

Diane Keith Borsenik
NIGHT CHILD
No sound at all—
Just the feel of the wind
On my cheek in call.

Dear, silent friend,
This sabled Night, constant
In her sweet allure.

Our covenant
Is true, beyond measure
And beyond all age.

Yes, she and I
Share common pilgrimage . . .
We shall never die.

Janet Shiverdecker
Near the End Of Summer
[To Bob and June Klenke To
whom this poem was written.]
Things were slowing down
Time to enjoy a leisurely cup of
coffee.
Then the phone rang.
The voice hesitatd, then wavered
I knew something was wrong.
My brother Ed said
"Our brother-in-law is in the
hospital."
And has had surgery.
The outlook was dim.
I was breathless.
Then began to pray long and
hard.
Through the prayers and tears
I had a deep inner feeling things
would work out.
The next few days were touch
and go,

Labor day week-end was over.
Then the miracles began to come.
The decision was to transfer to a
clinic out of town.
His wife would go too, the family
would be separated.
We had a sigh of relief though
He had made it this far.
The miracles kept coming.
With the ups and downs
Progress was slow.
Weeks have passed and the time
has come
For the long and welcomed
journey home.
Back together as a family.
Part of the battle was won.
With the miracles ahead
The battle will be won.

Julie A. White

Julie A. White
DUST
Light swirls briefly, floating above
And then drips down.
The last hundred years have
dulled me.
Once,
The hard gleam of my curving
body shimmered
Among a hundred candles.
Then,
A hundred stroking hands
smoothed and caressed me
Until I glowed from within.

Now my flesh has gone soft and
my edges fade.
My lace sheets and I become one
as the years thickly settle.
I am no longer beautiful,
I am gray.
The fires that smoldered within
the eyes of my lovers
Have died,
And only cold electric light
Illuminates
My slowly thickening form.

Laura Blankenburg
HISTORY COUNTDOWN
Once around Earth
Twice around Saturn
leave rings glowy red
stars never near
only move far
when will you ever learn?
living a past cycle
a star is nothing more
crumbled pieces broken off
from the center of a long gone
core
believe it if you want

to be so intelligent
creating a new era
with the green you have spent
T-minus ten years
the plans to ignite
the mushroom is near
your final light
stage left to the stars
move a light year higher
start a new cast
begin the same past
only now you're living next door
Once around Earth
twice around Saturn
leave rings glowy red
stars never near
we always go too far
after all that is written
you still haven't learned.

Annetta P. Smith
HELL IS A WALL
the walls are of brick, cold and
black with age
it is i that speak from within
this ole' dark cage
it's unyeilding to the touch of
others
contrary to my thirst for the
warmth of another
likewise made of brick the ceiling
and the floor
coincidentally there are no
windows
nor is there a door
steadfastly keeping me in
hesitantly i adhere
no time no warmth no light
just fear
theoretically, IN is the only
way out
the bricks are not what you see
it's my doubt
i've lived with a desire for love
enclosing myself in
walls so crude keeping out
immitation
but all you see, is my solitude
the apprehension you see, is
the cage
only i can free me
without RAGE

Sharon Kay Kekow
We Met At The Wrong Time
A room of crowded people
You alone catch my eye.
My heart takes a leap—
I wait by and bye.

You were there and now you're
gone.
No words said—no laughs shared.
We may think of each other now
and then
Wondering . . . if the other
person really cared.

Mike Bakko
THE VANISHING EAGLE
Have you ever seen such beauty,
Like the great Eagles in flight.
Drifting through the blue sky,
It's truly a wonderful sight.

To see them soar in mid-air,
Their talon claws outstretched.
Swooping on their prey with care,
The warcry and the catch.

Magical eyes scope out their
food,
To feed the crying young.

From day to day, they fight to
survive,
In the world of man and gun.

Where their life is one big
struggle,
One day they'll all be gone.
The law is to protect the Bald
Eagles,
They're outlaws on the run.

From poachers and money
hungry people,
Selling feathers and claws for
cash.
It's a shame the beautiful Eagles,
Are dying and might not last.

Loretta M. Sabella
EVERLASTING
[With my love Uncle Frank. As
you rest in peace, our thoughts
are always with you.]
Far away in the eyes of sorrow
Lies the happiness for a loved
one,
Yet we do not wish to accept
The painful thoughts of
tomorrow.

As life goes on we continue to
love
The ones closest to our hearts,
If it be happiness or anguish
We will always know he is loved
up above.

The cheerful memories of
yesterday
Will never be painful ones of
today,
For we know the love we have
Shall never fade away.

Tracy A. Noth
FOR LOVING YOU
[To whom I love so very much
and who showed me love for
the first time, Gregory Allen
Peters.]
Being together all the time we
have shared;
For Loving You it should never be
spared.
Caring and loving you day by
day;
For Loving You is all I shall say.
Sharing the good times as well
as the bad;
For Loving You is all I should
have.
Having the feeling of hurt deep
inside;
For loving You it shall seem to
hide.
When knowing that something
has just gone wrong;
For Loving You it whould always
grow strong.
Having the concern of where
you are;
For Loving You it shall never be
far.
Having, knowing the feeling of
love;
For Loving You that feeling is
enough.

Paul N. Donato Jr.
COW POKES
The horses snort, bray and
whinny
The pungent smell of chaps and
sweat

Stuffed in mouthful of chaw, that
keeps me spittin'
All day long
Tumbleweeds scurrying acrost'
the windswept plain
Trail dust, times a chokin' with a
gritty haze
Ropin' while my backside's sore
Hot brandin' irons on sizzlin'
hides
Came acrost' a wet rushin' stream
ripplin' and clear
Jumped in, with all but chaps and
boots
The Montana Sky' all clear and
blue
Cooks' call bell hearkens supper
time
Hot biscuits with honey—only
after
A belly bustin' portion of beans
and rabbit stew
Scaldin' coffee, so hot, you could
only sip to
Sunset brings a picture sky
Tired-n-hell
Can't hardly keep my eyes awake
Tomorrow, I'll ride ramrod
straight into town with my pay
Gonna have me a wing-ding time,
I am.

Dina Maiben
To An Old Man
On Pearl Street
Old man of age old dusty dreams
Sit and chat with us on a hot day
Like today.
Sit and spill your dreams
Upon the street once drenched in
the rain and fresh
As you once were fresh
And so your dreams.

Once you too were proud and
young
Ever you were strong and free
Like a summer day.
Whatever happened to your
schemes
The plans you had in your youth?
They have slipped into the
shadows
Of the night
The way you slip in and out of
shadows.
Not everyone's dreams hide that
way.

Old man of timeless dusty blue
eyes
Do not hide your dreams in the
shadows
The way you hide your eyes,
Do not cover them over like a
repaved street;
Salvation Army Surplus man
Do not live a lie.

Shirley Ann Remak
FRAGILE BUTTERFLY
She came to you, she didn't
belong.
You knew she was fragile, not
very strong.
Delicate, dainty, full of grace.
Gossomer, silk, wings of lace.

No barriers, no cold stony wall.
Lovingly giving to you her all.
Ecstatically, joyously she gave
her trust.
You did what you did, what you
felt you must.

You used, abused, loved and Hid
from the world, never let it be
said.
petted.
She brought a mountain of
pleasure to your place.
With her strange little ways, her
happy little face.

She shut out the world, there
were only you two.
Yet daily, away from you she
grew.
Flitting away at the end of the
day.
Away for a moment, tomorrow
she'll delay.

It's wings you broke, it's heart left
sore.
Web-like threads tied her to you
evermore.
The pain she carries forever with
her.
You heard not a sigh, but a soft
murmur.

Perhaps one day she'll again
venture near.
More slowly, not quickly as she'll
now disappear.
No words can be spoken, nothing
said by you.
She is as softly transparent as the
morning dew.

Never can you mend, do you
know naught why?
She's afraid to again fly up to you.
You heard not a sigh, but a sob
and a cry.
When you kissed the wings of
the butterfly.

Susan E. Trojan
TRANQUILITY
When I'm alone, my mind and
soul unite.
They become tranquil and serene
and soar into heights of beauty
I never thought possible.
They take me into worlds of the
unknown and let me explore
and broaden my views.
When I'm brought back again,
and make my way into the
crowds, I'm able to cope with
the insanity of this world so
much easier than before.

Deborah Jo Rendon
The Bubble and the
Butterfly
The bubble glides effortlessly
over ocean shores
and glistens with rainbow colors
as the sun penetrates the fragile
outer shell.
The butterfly flutters lazily
through the trees
and over meadows green, laced
with yellow-gold.
You are the bubble and I am the
butterfly.
The bubble and the butterfly join
together,
in the cool of the shaded palm.
Their long journey finally
satisfied,
with the melting together of
minds, ideas and love.
The unique bonding together
enables the bubble

to lift the butterfly to new
heights
giving strength to their
friendship.
The butterfly lets the bubble rest
upon her wings
and takes the bubble to places
never before seen.
Together they find the long lost
friendship,
that in years past, left their
hearts with sadness.
Now they do not fear the
separation they know will
come.
What the bubble and the
butterfly have found
will only grow deeper within
their hearts.
Their final resting place will be
together
fusing together . . . in the
eternal gust
of the earth's wind.

Elizabeth Gutta
GOD HEARD US PRAY
A childless couple, all alone
Longed for a child, to call their
own
They hoped and prayed, for many
years
And promised God, through
desperate tears
That they would love, and always
share
A little child, put in their care
God's heart was moved, He
thought awhile
And then He sent, a lovely child

They were so happy, all was good
They kept their promise, God
knew they would
A lovely child, a father, mother
God was pleased, He sent another
Now in this family, there are four
An empty loneliness, that is no
more
The years now filled, with joyous
giving
A gift from God, to us the living
With grateful heart, we bless
each day
And thank our God, who heard
us pray.

Lesa Laine
GIFTS OF LOVE
Your wisdom has taught me
The things that i know
Although not as much

As the things that you show
Like love and kindness
And the good of your heart
All these things helped
To give me my start
They've been with me always
Through all of these years
All of the laughter
All of the tears.

My love for you grows
As much as i do
But the "me" stays the same
Like the words "I Love You".

Aileen Lee Berger
I Saw The World Awake
Today
I saw the world awake today
It was a joy to see.
Mister Sun carressed the red rock,
Then woke the pinon tree.

I saw little cactus flowers
Look up into his face,
And they smiled and said, "Good
Morning,"
As night fled without a trace.

The sagebrush raised his sleepy
head
Reluctant to arise.
And an errant wind kissed the
grass,
The grass woke in surprise.

Miss Manzanita waved her hand
A cactus bowed to me.
A rock smiled up and said, "Hello,"
As cheery as could be.

A mighty hawk spread wide his
wings,
Surveyed his world so fair.
The fleecy clouds gazed down on
me,
Beauty was everywhere.

Dolly A. Krizo
UNTITLED
I fell today and scrapped my knee
And you were there to comfort
me
I turned my head to look behind
To my surprise it was you I find
A single tear escaped my eye
You reached out to wipe it dry
I thrilled to see the sun shine
bright
And there you were to make it
right
I wondered at the things I'd seen
Then just believed in what they
mean
I knew down deep within my
heart
Always in my life you'd be a part
I smile and accept you there
A love that's precious and so rare
I know it can't be taken away
Memories are made to stay . . .

Tyler Wrenn
WINTER DEATH
Crimson carousel twirling,
spinning to the music that
comes forth—
Cream falls toward the ground
and lingers by the lamp post—
He watches, unaware that, I too
watch, the children skate by
the old church that is closed
on Tuesdays—
Warmed by hot chocolate I walk

—not far, but I walk—
This old man looks sad, why? I
  really don't know—
His past has escaped him and he
  sits remembering as a wet
  sliver of ice forms on his beard
  of seventy years—

The children run by, silver skates
  flying endlessly in the wind
  and they laugh, not knowing
  there is one crying—
He buttons his overcoat to his
  neck and rubs his hand across
  his nose then walks towards
  the old church, where he sits
  on a bench—
The music begins to fade, the
  horses on the carousel come to
  a halt—
The old man looks at the lamp
  post and smiles—
As the lamplighter vacates the
  flame—

Kevin Lee Sims
EBONY MIST
[To T.R.A.—though we parted
in sadness, I can't forget you
taught me the special feeling of
a young girl's love.]
I know not from whence it came.
It now seems like it happened all
  too fast.
Maybe it was only a dream.
One morn an Ebony Mist showed
  up at my heart's door.
Being lonely, I gladly let it enter.
If it was a mirage or not, I
  couldn't tell.
The Mist had dark, swirling,
  curly hair,
  deep brown eyes and pouting
  lips.
I was soon captivated by her
  wicked smile.
I seemed to melt at her touch.
During the summer, the Mist
  mixed with the soft,
  summer breeze to make
  everything in my
  heart's garden grow.
The Mist spun around me
  whispering,
  "I love you", in my ear.
I believed.
I began to depend on my Ebony
  Mist, I trusted it.
I felt nothing could change it.
Then the harsh, autumn wind
  blew in
Summer was gone, winter's cold
  was near.
My Mist slipped away.
It changed direction completely.
Things began to die.
Time moves on and on.
I stand amidst the pieces of my
  crumbled heart.
I am alone and feeling much,
  much older.
My beautiful Ebony Mist is gone.

Tammy L. Thorley
AMERICA—BE FREE
The wide open lands,
the clear, sparkling streams,
the grand, green forests,
will they become dreams?
We, Americans,
who are strong-willed and free,
must learn to save the land

from our polluting debris.
Buffalo, deer, elk,
eagle, and bear—
what will we do
if these animals disappear?
There are some people
who help the animals fight
but many more are needed
to set the score right.
So let's all join in
and fight for our land,
after all, what can we lose
lending a helping hand.

Andrew P. Mealey
REMEMBER ONCE
remember once you were in love
remember once I played my
  music
    remember
white lace was on my mind
yours on the cute young man
in the corner
remember once you knew it
  wouldn't
falter
remember once I hit you
days have passed
years went on
now at last the flight
thought you'd always be around
I'm only a fool deceived
remember once we were in love
remember once we thought
it could never end
yet remember how wrong we
  were

Dean-ann Bauza
DREAMS
Dreams are like the threads of
  life
They keep the walls from closing
  in
So easy to crush,
So easy to grow.
Please don't crush my dreams.
A pillow against pain,
A blindness against reality,
Dreams keep us alive and sane.
So dream,
And dream so that nothing can
  go wrong.
A wall against the night,
A wall against the end.
All dreams may die,
But please don't kill mine—
So easy to crush,
So easy to grow.
Dreams are the threads of life.
They keep the walls from closing
  in.

Frances Gillard Harvey
**Early Morning Carnage
Along The Road**
God,
Who hast promised
Thou wouldst see,
Bless all the little broken
  things—
Those with wings,
And those whose feet
Were fleet,
But, not sufficiently.

Edna A. Holder
PENDULUMS
Your name swings like a
  pendulum in my mind
With each uneven beating of my
  heart

It stifles other voices and I find
It does not matter whether you
  are kind
If you but hold for me a day
  apart—
A day when I may look into your
  eyes—
May see them dark with passion
  and surprise—
Surprised to find yourself caught
  up with me
Who never meant for love again
  to be.
Loving was done—the door to life
  was closed.
Your cynic's voice scoffed at my
  steady "No"—
Your cynic's arms reached out
  and took me in—
Your cynic's kiss was loth to let
  me go.
You had not planned to more
  than kiss and run—
You had not meant your truant
  heart to be
Caught up in love's labyrinth for
  an instant's fun—
You had not known your cynic's
  heart would find
My name on a pendulum
  swinging in your mind.

Earl Hopkins

Earl Hopkins
THE ART OF A GIRL
I've never seen a piece of art quite
  as lovely as a girl
They are spiritual attractive
  walking around in their
  gorgeous bodies
They are Gods' master pieces of
  the world
Sometimes they are good, and
  sometimes they are sort of
  knotty

But to me, they are candy dipped
  in sugar and covered with
  honey
They are the ones that make the
  world turn
They are needed just as much as
  money
They cause heads to spin, and
  hearts to yearn
I've never seen a piece of art quite
  as lovely as a girl
Some of them can make a cold
  day hot
They are the sweetest gorgeous
  things of this world

Choosing among them
  sometimes can put you in a
  spot
Whenever I entered their rooms
My eyes always catch that
  beautiful love flower
With such bright colors and
  sweet perfume
I can just stay there for hours
I've never seen a piece of art quite
  as lovely as a girl
Their sweet affection always
  drives me crazy
They are my sunshine, my joy,
  my flowers of the world
To me, they are just as sweet as
  sugar babies.
Girls in short skirts, and blue
  jeans skin tight
With pretty faces and hair long or
  short in curls
Wearing gorgeous make-up, and a
  shape that's out of sight
It's God's beautiful created art
  called a girl.

Cheryl Bowser
TO YOU
[To My Father: The inspiration
for this poem goes to you, the
strength of my life.]
It's strange. Everytime I'm alone
  and especially at night, I feel so
  different, like if something
  wonderful has happened to me.
  I stop to think about the days
  before and why I feel so happy
  and loved. All the time that I
  am thinking, there's only one
  thing going through my mind.
  A name. Not just any name,
  but YOUR name. I think about
  your name and realize that's
  what's so great and wonderful
  that happened to me. YOU. I
  have met you. The one most
  terrific person in the world. No
  wonder I feel so happy and
  wonderful. Whenever I think of
  you, I am thinking of the
  greatest person in the world.
  You can make a rainy day so
  full of sunshine and life worth
  so much.

Denise Cosgrove
TOUCH
Touch . . .
Touch the crying-laughing clouds
That purple and pink the sky.
Mushrooming mountains
Fading in and out.
Abstractions.
Ancient—young.
Hair like a fairy
Swimming into the blazing
  sun-chest,
Of a forever friend.

Diane Drown
BEGINNINGS AND . . .
A new year was all I knew
  for sure
somewhere there in its first hours
when we danced
folded then unfolded
in each other
  like rivers
that never end
but begin
  again and again

there was a dancing
 a dancing
down some ancient highway
to a mountain of tomorrows
that never would apologize
 for being
out of step
not knowing . . .
 not knowing
ancient highways or how
mountains peak
 twinned
to dance to
a Kancamagus Spring . . .
 . . . never learned
never in all those old,
old years
 the dance was
different then
in a winter's hibernation
all its own
dancing
out of step
not knowing tomorrows
nor could understand
why rivers never end
but begin
 again and again
. . . not knowing why
we dance the way we do

Rachael Mashburn Qualey
FOR THE THANKSGIVERS
my roots are blood
and for the fiery dream of
 freedom
there i stood
determined that the battle
to preserve good
was up to me and those who
 followed
freedom's brotherhood

and what a strain that put on
 history's ear
that our little marching band
of prisoners and rebels and
 pioneers
were beached at last on history's
 golden sands
where written on each stately
 page
with history's golden hands
the emergence of a nation from
 these woods
whose heart was freedom
whose roots were blood

Bryan David Chiers
A BIG GAS BALLOON
On a day like today
I could just fly away
In a big gas balloon
That's gone so soon
From the earth to the moon
And never return
To the things that I've learned
And just be free

Would you take my hand
And come with me?

Bethel Nunley Evans
SEASONS OF LIFE
It is the fall of life, my friend
If only one's self is all he can see.
But, there is more water in the
 well
From which to fill his cup
If he dips deep in the springs that
 dwell.

It is the winter of life, my friend

When one feels only the cold
 round about.
But, there is warmth to be had
From the friends that he makes
As he smiles and brings cheer to
 the sad.

It is the spring of life, my friend
When one's heart is so full of
 love,
He sees only the best in others
And closes his ears to the bad
 things
He hears about his sisters and
 brothers.

It is the summer of life, my friend
When in this world that the Lord
 created
And gave so freely to every
 man—
One can see the beauty that
 besets him
And vision a Heaven beyond this
 land.

Kathleen F. Clemmens
PRIVATE THOUGHTS
We shared our lives for many
 years,
Good times: bad times,
Laughter, tears.
I always thought of you with me;
I never dreamed I'd be alone
But I am—
For death is swift and now you're
 gone.

Lori Lynn King
THE OCEAN
*[To you Mom; for all your love
and inspiration, for all your
time and dedication]*
Lashing, dashing, mighty and
 bold
 It holds many secrets as I have
 been told.

A sailor's dream—a fisherman's
 delight
 A dead man's grave—a weak
 man's fright

Lunging and crashing all night
 and all day
 Fierce flooding storms are its
 way to play

Bouncing and tossing ships up
 and down
 Rolling with laughter on
 beaches near town

Yes the ocean is powerful, mighty
 and bold
 And deep in its depths
 uninviting and cold

But the ocean has another side
 people may find
 It is also peaceful, quiet and
 kind

For as I sit here, laying in the
 sand
 A wave rolls in and kisses my
 hand

Laura Lisa Royer
DEAR LITTLE ONE
Dear Little One I never knew
I loved you so as inside me you
 grew.
I dreamed of a life we never
 shared.
I just want you to know
 I truly cared.

There was no shame, I held
 no regret,
That you, fatherless, would be
 beget.
His indifference could not
 mar the love
I felt for you, Dear Little
 One.

I made the choice I felt was
 right,
To uphold your freedom to
 become a life,
But Heaven's plan took you
 away,
And by its will shall we meet
 someday.

Mrs. Lola Terlizzi D'Alterio

Mrs. Lola Terlizzi D'Alterio
LAGRIME D'AMORE
Molte lagrime versate
Per un amore da tempo
 incominciato
Quei baci di sfuggita e
 appasionati
Rendevano tanto, tanto felice la
 vita
Due cuore stretti per un grande
 affetto
Due bocche unite da un grande
 amore
Sembrava un amore infinito
Che mai, mai sarebbe finito
Ma, purtroppo, nell'atualita della
 vita
Anche questo, tutto e finito
Non c'e cosa al mondo, piu bello
 che l'amore
Un affetto sincero, per due cuori
Non e peccato, questo, volersi
 bene
Ma e peccato, quello, volersi male
In conclusione, amiamo sempre il
 Signore
Sembre, sembre Lui
Crediamo in Dio
Sembre in Lui

Anita Parker Jones
IF A MAN
*[This poem is dedicated to my
husband, Michael Allen Jones
whom I love and adore.]*
If a man reaches out
For what he thinks is right.
Then he will see thru the
 darkness,
And to his eyes there will be light.
If a man understands his feelings,
And decisions he has to make.
For he will sleep no more,
And comfort in his mind will
 awake.
If a man considers the fact of truth,

And of weakness and strength.
He will have walked that long
 road,
That was just a short length.
If a man knows of love,
And of sincere respect and trust.
Then he will do what he has to,
Because with pride he must.
If a man lets himself be put down,
 or criticized,
He is not a man,
In anyone's eyes.

Norma Davis Baumeister
THE AFTERMATH
A lonely island in the woods,
Amidst a river bed;
Water is flowing on each side,
Pallbearers of the dead.
A smoky film, the surface holds.
It steams as boiling blood.
The battle arms are put aside,
Carried off by the flood.
The bodies lie, at random,
 dropped.
Cries echoed with the pain.
Yet, silence now rewards the air.
Hushed are screams of the slain.
Hushed are screams of the slain.

Beverly J. Sharp
EVENING RAIN
 A rumble in the distance, like a
 sleeping dog's growl, low and
 deep . . . Flashes behind the
 clouds; strobing the night
 sky . . . The quickening
 wind rustles the leaves,
 like taffetta skirts swishing
 across the ballroom floor
 . . . The air fills with the
 smell of dew and damp
 clover . . . The gentle
 pitter patter, like tiny
 feet running through
 my mind lulls me to
 sleep . . . I awaken
 in the dawn, refreshed,
 as is the Earth.

Manny Berrocales
CLOUDS
[To Debby Coda]
The sky is high.
Hence abode,

The best abide.
A balladry for you!

When Great Clouds Rain,
They Pour.

Kenneth William Byrnes
FUGITIVES
*[To the inspiring memory of
my great grandfather, Bernard
Hyland, County Rosscommon,
Eire. A veteran of the Boer War
(1899-1903.]*
Along
The banks
Roost
Wild geese.

Who stir
In hedges
And wield
Long pikes.

Ralph S. Ward
ACID RAIN
A pox upon you, Acid Rain,
You've made a mess of our
 terrain.

Will we start to clean our air,
And bring pure water
   everywhere?
Lakes in Canada and the States,
Smoke and garbage turned to
   waste,
We have learned to scout the
   Moon,
Must solve this problem very
   soon,
Or we'll have no water source
To pass on to our new born force.
So let's get busy and clean our
   place,
So we can save the human race.

Jorgi Russell
MY KENTUCKY
Southeastern Kentucky is my
   homeland,
Rivers of treasures, mountains so
   grand,
Valleys of sorrow, meadows of
   grain,
Land of great promise, castles of
   sand.

Ribbons of roadways spread far
   and wide,
People so proud and filled with
   great pride,
Miners, so weary, chip out the
   coal,
Teachers and preachers feed
   mind and soul.

Valleys of sorrow, meadows of
   grain,
Forests and fields that flourish
   and fail,
Chapels and churches dot hill
   and vale,
Waters upon which paperboats
   sail.

Debra Sue Willoughby
MOMENTS
*[For my mother and father and
for their forty years of
marriage, I give these words of
feeling and love to you.]*
Moments are like sand in an
   hour glass
They can be sifted through and
   the best be relived again
Like the wind in its earnest, they
   can be gone
And the most cherished are left
   behind
My moments alone with you, are
   exciting warm and new
But the destiny is not for us to
   choose
Yet the moments I share with
   you
Like an hour glass keep recurring
   relived and enjoyed . . .

Jessie Christopherson
EASEMENT
*[To my grandmother, April
Christopherson, who in
childhood innocence, brought
easement to many residents of
the Commonwealth Nursing
Home in St. Paul, Minnesota.]*
I watched from the porch of the
   old nursing home
Their games and informal plays,
And reveled in memories
   conjured up
Of my happy childhood days.

It was the touch of her warm
   little hand
As she held the rose out to me,
That reminded me of my own
   child's touch,
Caressing me tenderly.

I longed to smooth the tangled
   curls,
To hold her close to me,
To tuck fairy kisses in her palm
For our mutual ecstasy.

But she was off like a fleeting
   fawn
To join her friends in play,
And I fervently hoped she would
   return
With a sweet smelling clover
   bouquet.

The little girl came on another
   day,
Bringing cookies she had made
Of sand and water and raspberry
   caps,
We ate them—unafraid!

She was back again with comb
   and brush
To tame her windblown hair,
When she leaned on my lap with
   her storybook
I was content in my answered
   prayer.

Alessandra A. Poles

Alessandra A. Poles
RAINBOW
Standing there alone
I touched the clouds as they
   passed,
Then sounds of colors scattered
North and south and east and
   west
As I reached through the
   rainbow.

Patricia A. Naylor
I WANT
I want to do things,
I want to be free.
I want you to let
Me be me.

I want to be good,
Don't you care.
Let me be me.
It's only fair.

I've lived your life
For a good long time.
Now I think it's time.
I should live mine.

I want to live my life
To the fullest it can be.

But most of all,
I want to live it just being me.

Ronald Paul McCular
In a Minute, In a Day
I keep reading about you,
On every cover I see your face.
It's getting harder to escape you,
Everywhere I turn it seems to be
   just another place.
Can't stop it, growing every
   minute,
Getting stronger day by day.
Holding on to lost promises,
And living a life your way.
Well hope you have everything
   you need,
Starry eyed to the world.
Guess falling on my knees is no
   reason,
It never stopped you from
   leaving.
Oh and if I could I'd take it in a
   minute,
Without a guaranty.
If it lasts more than a minute,
Well spent this time would be.
I'd take it in a minute,
I'd take it in a day,
I'd take it before this night slips
   away.

Linda Vernuccio
ANGEL'S WINGS
You must have been a very
   special child
For God has taken you away from
   me
Although you've been gone only
   a short while
I want you back with me

Your crib remains empty
And your nursery door is shut
I pray to God for courage
To Open it somewhat

You must be in Heaven now
Romping and playing with your
   new angel's wings
Happiness you have I know
I wish I could share in all these
   things
I see Our Lady bending over you
And wiping away a tear
Is that tear because you miss me
As much as I miss you.

Suzanne Ferrell
SET ME FREE
These four walls around me are
   closing
The pictures on the wall have no
   meaning
Right through them I am looking
But the wall is all I see
For they mean nothing to me

I have no freinds it appears to me
Except for the ones I'm forbidden
   to see
And the telephone rings rarely
And the doorbell rings least of all
I wish that someone, anyone,
   would call

And the words that are spoken, I
   never hear
For the words go in and out the
   other ear
As I sit and waste away year by
   year
I'm all alone almost everyday
And at night they say just go
   away

And I know my family loves me
That's not the way it appears to
   be
I feel I'm in a cage and need to be
   set free
But they're afraid of the price it
   might cost
They're afraid that I might be
   lost.

Peggy Splawn
DERBY LANE
The sky of black
Covers the track
   Like a dome.
Lanky pines line the way
And the blaring lights
   Come into play
Shooting streams of red and green
In the midst of the water
   To be seen.
Soft music from the bandshell
Echoes through the night
As the dogs get ready
   For the flight.
And then—
With the beat of the drum
And the blasts of the horn
The dogs rush out of the shoot
Chasing Rusty around the track
   Like hound dogs with a pack.
The crowd roars and screams
   As the dogs round the bend
Each one wanting his dogs
   To be far from the end.
Nearer and nearer those dogs
   come
   And past that line
While winners flash on that sign.
Up pop some to collect their bets
   As others sit and fret.
One more race to go
With another chance to Win
Quiniella, Place, or Show.

Erin L. Cork
TOMORROW
*[PITA, Here's to Autumn,
Rusty Nails, and elusive time.—
HITN]*
When your spine is shrunk and
   your belly plump, and resting
   by logs ablaze, bring back this
   time, and revive it, and live
   once more your prime in youth
   the love, and need of playing
   trump;

The fancy, the plain adoring all
   your acts with praise and
   applause, few true all loud,
But me I stood out waving in the
   crowd, and looked past acting
   to blatant facts;

And kneeling to listen for fire
   hiss, mumble for stupid, rapid
   moves long done and pride
   pushing love until overrun and
   this one in hiding, the one you
   miss.

Kitty K. Stone
WITHOUT BURDEN
Forgetting that I, too, have been
   sorely hurt;
Forgetting that I, too, have trod
   that roughened dirt
On whose ridges you have
   slipped and stumbled;
Forgetting that kindred resolve
   for no more romantic fumbles;

115

Forgetting that I keenly fathom
   your heart's fear
To grasp and hold another's heart
   so near;
Forgetting that my lonely,
   sleepless nights end no
      sooner than your own,
Nor my aimless listless soul that
   searches vainly
      for a home;

Forgetting my ceaseless, constant
   cry so fierce
To never again by Cupid's arrow
   be pierced;
Forgetting that I, too, have
   hungered for a touch
And ofttimes foolishly begged
   hardened souls
      for such;

Forgetting all that hell I've
   suffered
And not one ounce of pain has
   been buffered—

Forgetting all that—

Can you not accept me merely as
   friend,
Whose proffered hand conceals
   no end
But lasting hope and tenderness;
So that even *now*, we may both
   be blessed?

Maro Rosenfeld

Maro Rosenfeld
THE NEW WORLD
Lies
Deceit
Lack of Faith and Confidence
   in Mankind
Lost Identity
Confusion of sexes
Painful whispers over back fences
nebulous
   —loveless
     MASSES
with only a Pill to their fame

Where went Freedom
Peace
and Truth?

Stalking Generals
swept the world's stairs
All that remains
is a Silver Spoon

Circled in silence
ash cities lie

Donald Lee Harrington
CONSTANT BEAUTY
Each time I look at you,
I enjoy what I see.
I can relate to your life.

And understand you completely.
Each time I'm near you,
I can enjoy the simple moments
   of you being there beside me.

Each time I think of you,
I can smile within with the
   private thoughts of loving
     you.
And enjoy the feeling that you
   rank first place in my eyes
   of stars of constant beauty.

Thomas P. Van Noord
ANXIETY
[To my Dad]
It's so funny believin' in life
You think you have it all . . .
But it slips away.
You jump higher and higher
Should you go? Could you stay?
You fall apart, broken down
Falling in pieces to the ground.
Yet a new thought is born
You struggle to look beyond,
Catching a glimpse of what it is
You reach, to lose it once more.
Believing and understanding this
Is a puzzle solved itself
For trying to unmask the truth
You satisfy yourself.
So . . .winning is not capturing
   the dilemma
It's the undying curiosity of the
   answers
To your questions
Keeping in mind, you care
   enough to find
The trouble that lurked in your
   mind.

Lynda Carol Marek II
BUTTERFLY!
If I see a butterfly
   I will catch him
      If I try!

If I lose my butterfly
   If you please,
      I will cry!

Judith Wyman Breuer
Split Down the Middle
*[For my two sons, Jamie and
Tyler, and my husband
Winfried, who make each day
of my life so very special.]*
I'm split down the middle, torn
   right into two
   I'm coming and going, oh what
     shall I do?
My two little boys think I'm
   made out of steel
   Is it wrong to hope that they'll
     know how I feel?

The older one questions me
   morning til night
   He's constantly talking til we
     turn out the light.
The little one moves like a
   cyclone gone wild,
   How can so much energy come
     from one small child?

With one to my left, the other to
   my right,
   I'm spinning in circles, God
     grant me some might!
Or wisdom to know how to share
   with each one
So everyone's happy when each
   day is done.

And what about me? Is there time
   for myself?
   I seem to put my dreams up on
     a high shelf.
As much as I love them, and God
   knows I do,
   I wish for just once they'd see
     me as I do—

A bright witty person with
   feelings of her own
   Maybe one day they'll know
     me, perhaps when they're
     grown.

Ann McKay
WHO IS ME?
I'm a person on the move
with a heart, a soul,
a mind that dreams,
and possessing restless courage
for moving about from an
old address to a newer scene.

Whenever I feel the sand
in my pretty red gypsy shoes
and my inner voice says "fly",
I know it is time to join the birds,
for if I don't, you just may hear
a final earthly sigh!

Terence Alan McKeon
**Looking Through Thee
   Hour Glass**
Love is projection
Thee image inside
I dare not look closely
For I keep my eyes wide.
Within my body
Deep in my mind
Doors always open
To take me outside.
On gentle green hills
I find my mentor
I pause in silence
Before I enter his hall,

I find the territory is mine to
   surpass
I've now become sand,
Time ticking fast.

Marjorie Rovsek Struna
MY NIGHT
Silent, cold, inky, moonless—the
   night
I'd wish to be back where there
   was light.
Feeling so lonely out in the wild
A lost and weary city—bred
   child.

Wandered away from family and
   car
Not knowing I'd meandered so
   far.
But, then—what's a girl at a
   young age
Know about the vastness, hills
   and sage?

I walked and walked—then I tried
   and tried
To find my folks—couldn't—
   cried and cried.
Night came. I thought that the
   moon would be
Great company for one lost like
   me.

The moon I realized wouldn't
   show.
I was all alone without it's glow.
Up on a hill something I did
   see—

Looked like a lit—up Christmas
   tree.

Toward beautiful twinkling lights
   I went—
The weary night already half
   spent.
My loneliness was to be no more.
Happily I knocked on a stranger's
   door.

People! For me, my parents to
   find.
Friendly, trusting and ever so
   kind.
Out there on the desert
   Christmas night
Tree bulbs flashing made things
   work out right.

Grateful that countless years
   long gone by
Christmas came to be for you and
   I
When that special, chosen
   Eastern star
Began the first Christmas there
   afar!

Florence Axton
CHRISTMAS
Snow flakes, white and pure fall
   from the sky,
Each one like a gossamer wing
   going by,
What a joy of beauty they bring,
   Stand by.
A picture of splendor Sprakling
   lights,
A portrayal of love and all that is
   right.

Trees adorned, ornamental tinsel,
Topped with an anadem, a wreath
   with a perfect gem.
The faces of children, rosey red,
   filled with
Glee, anticipation, adoration.

A silent spirit is here, guidance is
   near,
A vigil, a promise of peace, a new
   release.
Love, honor and obey . .

We hear canticles, carols, the
   bells are lovely amusives,
Sound of Season resound, clear,
   true, and sound.
Let us chant,
A MASS for CHRIST.

Sonja Christina
You Get To a Point
*[To hearts whose hopes upon
life's right ropes sway He who
rules wind and sea's—your
dreams will not betray!]*
You get to a point where you
   gave it all out,
and nothing—Nothing—comes
   in!
No matter what you care about
you seemingly just cannot win.

You get to a point so bleack, so
   low—
not one move is worth the cost.
Your negative thoughts just seem
   to know
it's useless! All is lost!

You get to a point where time
   stands still,
where you're paralyzed with pain.
You've stretched to the breaking

point your will,
and it all has been in vain.

You get to a point where you
cannot go on.
The cost has been far too high.
And THAT is the time to prove
you're a man
by giving it one more try.

For often success lurks but one
step away—
no more but one step to tread.
Many a dream, but for one single
step,
has needlessly been so shed.

You get to a point where you
cannot go on.
Not one minute more!
You're drained, disillusioned and
sour!
And yet, if you for one step yet
hold on . . .

This could be your winning hour!

Susan V. Erdos
THE SEA
*[To my best friend, whom
without, I could never have
appreciated the fruits of life.
Thank you mom—I love you.
All my love, Susan]*
I'll live by the sea forever and
ever,
Till death do us part the years
I'll not sever.
It's filled with oh so many
wonders;
The waves crash down and
how it thunders!
And then I ponder . . . "When
will it change?"
The answer lies outside my
range.
I love the mystery it brings to me;
I guess that's why I love the
sea.

Deborah Katheryn Proska
Gone With the Winds Of Time
*[Dedicated to my Father; the
first to appreciate my work. To
my friends: Louie, Roy and Neil
who believed, supported and
inspired me through the years.
To Paul; Somewhere,
sometime, someday I hold hope
he'll come to an understanding
within of this woman & her
words.]*
If my life was to be led in the
next twenty-four hours
How could I possibly display my
love?
I could write a poem, a verse or
two.

For when my auburn hair no
longer blows in the breeze.
And my feet no longer dance
across the floor.
My words shall cry out from this
page . . .
I loved You ALL—
How could you not know?

How could you not know?
I heard voices in the winds that
blew my way.
How could you not know . . .
my words,
my verses,

were the heart and soul of my
existence.

How could you not know,
twenty-four hours is just not
long
enough for all the I Love You's
within me.

The girl with the auburn hair
continues to ask
in the last minute
of her final day.

How could they not know? For I,
for she, wanted to believe they
could.
They will, someday. Maybe
tomorrow.
"Tomorrow is another day" was
all she wrote.
And on lived my Scarlet O'Hara.

Evolyn Feiring
Pines Are the Slow and Fine
PINES are the slow and fine—the
quiet beings
Showing restless men what may
be done
By waiting in peace at the
humdrum heart of things—
By taking what comes—the snow,
the air, the sun—

And making of these what may
be made with ease—
And making the modest leaf, the
patient wood,
The meagre wooden-rose—and
making these
Lost in deep imponderables for
good.

Embraced by a squirrel, invaded
by raucous birds
These naked, indigent trees—
none the less
Yet proffer homes for men and
pens for herds—
Paint for barns and yarn for the
ravon dress:

And yet for all of this men
mumble still
How over trees they wield the
master will.

Holly Lynn Kelly
If The World Was a Merry-Go-Round
If the world was a merry-go-round
there would be parades,
circuses and zoos. We would
not forget the lions, tigers, and
bears too.

The world would be merry-go-
round shape and attached to it
there would be purple horses
with yellow manes, of course
elephants too. The world
would be a merry-go-round.

If the world was a merry-go-
round. We would be lots of
things, animals, circuses,
parades, and zoos. Purple horses
with yellow manes that would
be if the world was a
merry-go-round.

June Elliott
REMEMBER THE LORD
Sometimes life seems as if its
A mountain so high—

Keep on climbing near the top
but
Never quite nigh.

You fall again and again and get
up to
Once more run—
But Oh, so weary when the day is
Done.

Then we think of heaven and its
open door—
We'll run with patience like
never before.

So as we stumble in life, we try
To find our way—
Remember the Lord day after day.

He'll never leave us to wander all
alone—
He will carry us in his arms when
our
Strength is gone.

Steven Howard Daniels
Steven Howard Daniels
The Hypothetical Construct
*[To my friends, family and
fellow poets. This is the
message to help you stay
secure, because only a poet has
the will to endure.]*
A magnanimous approach, swift.
The sand churns to a drift.
Articulate the gender.

Avoid the pit.
The motion and gesture split.
Skull and Bones,
Kings, Queens, and thrones.
Adaptation at it's peak.
The road to success sleek.
The Waste Land able to
communicate,
Prufrock to stipulate,

Gatsby to simulate.
Gray and White duck.
Political idols only common,
to a great extent exercising
duplicity and rhetorical jargon.
An extradorinary *Jester* to
survive.
Keep an inebriate alive.
Various organizations surmised
by solace.

Stan K. Alderson
PROFILE PORTRAIT
this morning is too much the
same
rumble hum up from the street.
the street's row of houses file
along
endlessly pale faded old faces
framed with block fences.

the stare travels ceiling cracks
dark lanes smooth
the number of times wandered.
eyes burn like scraped skin
as if i'd never slept.

the sun will move slowly
toward afternoon.
a constant blaze behind thick
gray
burning white
like the judgement.

Julia O. King
STORM SIGNALS
I love to watch a gathering storm
When wind swept clouds pile
high
In shades of black and white and
gray
Till Night invades the realm of
Day
And frantic birds come winging
by
In haste for shelters safe and
warm.

I fling a challenge to the wind,
That surges in their wake,
To test its strength, in sheer
delight
Of battle with its forceful might,
Or else, to join its race and make
a contest before its tempo's
thinned.

I revel, then, in lightning's play,
In thunder's rolling score,
And lift my head, to breathe
again
The earthy scent of approaching
rain;
To hear the misty curtain roar
And watch its progress up the
Way.

Larry Douglas Chappell
A Veteran On the Street
A veteran on the street
Was this beggar on my beat.
He was a young American lad.
Yet, appeared so old and sad.
With tattered clothes and one
eye—
No shoes for mangled feet—
It was enough to make one cry,
Just to see this veteran on my
beat.

At eighteen, the pride of Uncle
Sam,
Six months later—a new job—
Selling pencils down the street,

A veteran's reward from Vietnam,
To be a beggar on my beat.

Now, he is old enough to vote
And to challenge with "veto"
What his government wrote.
This, he will surely do—
Lest there will be others
Who will have to go,
And to come back,
If they are lucky,
As competing veterans
On the street—selling pencils on
my beat!

James Capogreco
PASSIONATE BLUNDER
Autumn nears through the sea of
tears.
Faces have told their fears.

Another season passes and still
we're divided.
Obstinateness has decided.

Of all the world, the most
meaningful, everlasting and
intriguing thing that may give
hope.
Please take the time and just look
all around you. You may find
there is so much more to be
brought from heart.
Yes, we must dig it out. Many
may just find there are
common thoughts that can
array into the flowers capable
of tying the earth into a whole.

Some find survival such a test
their fight flight response is
constantly enacted.

Others have luxury so plush it
destroys any realization of this
entity at all.

And yet there are others so self—
centered they have forgotten
that their doings can interfere
with others causing heart—
break which inspires much
resentment.

Make the moment, bring forth
and be known.

Admire with all your soul the
beauty that surrounds you.

Any meekness at all may not be
shown.

Brenda J. White Williams
The Devil Won't Play Fair
*[To all of my sisters and
brothers: Katherine, Laverne,
Alice, Billie Jo, Naomi, Ruth
Ann, Gilbert Jr., L. C., and Don.
Whom I love with all my heart
but, never do I take the time
just to say: I Love You. Love,
your baby sister, Brenda Joyce!!]*
The day shall come when we'll
rejoice the coming of our Lord,
And on that day when He appears
we'll sing we won the war.
We fought the battle fair and
square, no weapons did we use.

But on our side we had the Lord,
And then the devil got abused,
Ya, the devil payed his dues,
No more Christians can he use.

All the clouds roll back as the
trumpet sounds and
The Son of God appears, mightier

than ever with His sword &
His shield.
With the saints all in their armor
ready and prepared,
To fight the battle with our Lord,
Who the devil couldn't scare.
Ya, the devil won't play fair,
No the devil doesn't care.

He'll lead the way as we descend
from the heavens up above,
Shouting out His orders to save
the ones He loves.
The loved ones who got left
behind when His first call
finally came,
Ones who thought they had
plenty of time,
To finish out their game, ya,
They wonder now whos to
blame,
Will they ever be the same??

All the grounds will tremble and
the mountains will rock,
When the masters feet lite down,
He'll point one finger at ole
Lucifer
And say to the bottomless pit
you're bound.
You've had all this time for your
dirty work, and yourself
Made quite a name, but it didn't
do any good for you;
Because down I still came,
To fight & win, & claim, ya,
And you I will have chained,
Never no more to roam these
plains
Never no more, no never no
more.

Arthur William Brown
SMART OF ME
*[To Willa Dean, may there be
thirty more.]*
T'was in those hills
near Shingle Springs
where she use to live.
Where first I did meet
the woman I was to wed.
Shy at first
then loving she became.

Many years now
it has been.
Shy she still is,
more loving then before.
Boy was I smart
to enter those hills
and make her my bride.

Donna M. Hankins
FOREVER LOVE
Two hearts in the union of love,

Two that will become as one.
This is what our life will be,
Forever, always you and me.

To share our lives in all we do,
Our wants, our needs, our
feelings too.
To love and cherish all our life,
Our love shall always be that
nice.

Forever now until the end,
Our life forever shall we spend.
In happiness, hope, and love,
As sweet and pure as snow white
doves.

Dorothy Rita Jarvis
THE SHELL
The ocean is surely unknowable,
all of it;
With vast, white beaches and
islands so scattered and far,
And in its depths with a
darkness, deep and eternal;
No light comes to bring its colors
alive where they are.

No hand reaches down to gather
its flowers.
No voice breaks its silence, nor
can a cry long be heard;
Nor tumult. There is only silence
deafening;
And why speak? The sea's voice
will still the word.

How infinitisimal are its shells
and sea plants.
The giant whale, a speck, and on
a starless night;
A darkness so deep settles over
its waves at sunset,
That one is fearful to pierce it
with a light.

There lies a beach, white and
bleached and empty,
Silent and so vast that a man
cannot be seen;
Nor a palace nor a city nor an
army,
As it threads around the sea and
land between.

But glistening on the shoreline,
newly washed there,
On the vast and silent beach is a
pearly shell.
Its soft pink colors, staining
brown and pure white,
Are brought to truth by the sun's
first light as well.

The urging waves have now
retreated to their basin.
The sand is driven by the wind
and time will tell,
If the ocean in its pounding,
reaching madness,
Will clutch again to darkness the
empty shell.

What beauty it reveals, a treasure
hidden.
Now it calls to the world.
Somehow or someway yet;
By miracle chance an eye see, or
hand will grasp it,
And the shell given by the sea,
someone will get.

Yet how can any eye perceive it
or any know,
That on that shore lies a shell
they'd want to keep?

What will bring the footsteps
nearer, nearer,
And the hands that will pick it
up; a voice from the deep?

Yet as the tide is returning and
the foam is rising,
As the water comes again to
grasp away the shell,
By miracle, by infinite hope, by
wisdom,
An eye perceives, hands reach
down and grasp the shell.

Clutched to the breast of a beach
comber, glad to see it;
Wiping away the sand and the
salt and the sea,
Beholding the shinning glory of a
masterpiece,
He rescues the shell from
oblivion, joyfull.

Now the voice that couldn't
speak is speaking,
And the song that was kept so
deep in the waves,
Comes home with the beach
comber, glad to hear it,
And it's more than the shell, it's a
part of the sea he saves.

Elizabeth F. Ralph
SOLITUDE
Solitude . . .
   a quiet word
   not silent or alone
   but peaceful
         contemplative
like a walk through the autumn
woods
or a good book in a sunny corner.

why are so many afraid of it?
It's not bad
         discovering
finding out about yourself.
Perhaps that's why.

Ruth Haldenby
YOU CREATED A SMILE
I was a wilting flower with my
blossom bending down
sprinkling tears on the earth
My petals were becoming crisp
and tattered
in the prime of my death
I was alone in the middle of
nowhere
with the wind as my enemy
I knew little and seeked nothing
Then you strong, powerful and of
my own kind
lifted my down bent head
Your touch created my
awakening
Your gentle caress brought colour
to my being
Your tempting lips made blood
stir in my veins
Your glittering eyes made me
fully aware
And a smile appeared on my face
and I awoke once more
I smiled a smile that you created

Audrey Occhipinti
The Rubber Chicken
Circuit
On the campaign trail, just the
strong survive,
'Cause they serve half a broiler
you'd swear was alive.

I first tried the seemingly
  succulent wing,
There was hardly a morsel of
  meat on the thing.
So I girded for battle, my weapons
  they shone,
But every maneuver encountered
  a bone.
I would have quit then, but a
  glance 'round the hall
Showed a similar contest
  engaging them all.
I went back to the fray, to
  acknowledge a lickin'
By this puny critter would make
  me look chicken.
But it sure was the most nothing
  I ever ate,
And it kicked all my vegetables
  off of my plate.
Why, talk about lively, that
  chicken could do
More with his one leg than I can
  with two.
So I made my farewells, I admit I
  was beaten,
I could have done better, if only
  I'd eaten.

Audrey Occhipinti
THE NEST
It's time the rumor was laid to
  rest
Of a syndrome known as "the
  empty nest."
Alert all medics from Salk to
  Spock,
It's the *full* nest that gives one the
  syndrome, Doc.

Matthew E. Boettcher
FOREVER IN LOVE
As the future becomes the
  present
The present in turn the past
My love for thee shall always be,
For it shall never come to pass.

And though other loves came
And other loves had gone
Our love shall live forever,
Forever it shall live on.

Even through the darkest day
And through the darkest night
Our love will shine forever,
Shine forever so bright . . .

Bright as the moon
And the stars that shine above
You and I together,
Forever in love.

Jef Youngs
if only
*[to she who has given me
inspiration all these long years,
my nature-mothre, i love u,
forevre.]*
if only i could remember her
  name—
if i could only see her clearly
  now—
—if only for the briefest moment
if only in our hearts—
if i could *just* reach out to her—
call those words which form on
  my lips—
—but will not let themselves be
  utter'd.

if i could just reach thru time
and come out next to her
sitting undre the shadow of a
  mountain

making out figures of the
  sky-clouds
climbing a redwood to be closre
jumping off, onto the mountain—
holding a handful of white sno in
  my open palm
as a sacrifice to the luv goddess
if she would only come down to
  drink
the transform'd watre, out of my
  hands
and running her lithe fingres ovre
  my forehead
as if to draw these restless tears
waiting long, seemingly endless
  eternities
to find a crevice thru which to
  flo.

Michael Gouge
THIS GIRL
*[To Maria T. Waczek, a very
fond friend and inspiration for
my writings.]*
A shining star for all to see,
Glowing brightly,
  Wherever she may be.
Neither rain or snow or even hail,
  Can damper the power
  That she excels.
Her loving nature knows no
  bound,
Her thoughtfulness,
  To everyone around.
The spirit within,
  The body she possesses
Has an everlasting love and joy
To those who know her best.

Catheryn Dusenberry Babin
THE DISTANCE
Tred I too closely to precious
  china
The kind that even a whisper
  breaks
Ming dreams
Ever threatening to shatter

A struggle to respire soundlessly
  while
Every breath
Every step brings thunder
To the silence left by danger and
  desire

At rest
At last

  My soul is appeased
  My work is rewarded
  My doubt is disolved
  My gift is accepted

Our distance is joined
Our kinship is timeless,
  boundless, effortless

Connie Baucom
THE SEA
*[To Linda, for her love of the
sea]*
Time is on my side.
The waves roll in
With the tide.

The winds are blowing
A soft, subtle air.
This is what dreams are made of,
They will always be there.

All I can see for miles around
Is the Ocean guarding its beloved
  ground.

The day has been wasted,
Staring at the sea.

Dawn turned to dusk
Right before me.

Now it is time to leave this place,
And bring my mind back from
  outer space.

The moon is full,
And the sea is still.
I will return tomorrow,
From just over the hill.

The birds will be singing to start
  the new day.
I will sit down to watch them
  from across the bay.

There is one thing I do know
Forever I am sure.
This place is sacred,
it is to the eye a lure.

Marian Christine Gottberg
CONTEMPLATION
Vines grow thick against the
  wall,
surrounding a garden aged and
  small . . .
A garden filled with memories:
Spring's first green touch upon
  trees
where winds through willows
  sung.
Summer dreams from lovers so
  young . . .
Autumn's golden treasure in the
  lane . . .
And winter frost upon the panes
  of
this dear old house, where we
  once came.

Oh! To open this gate and find
  the past!
Recapture . . . the life, love, I
  have known . . .
Again at last.
The joys of youth!
A face . . . untouched by
  time . . .
Reflected in the garden pond
Where moss grows now . . . and
The 'Spring of Life' . . .
    is just beyond.

Ben Gray
PAPA'S CHAIR
Old and worn looks forlorn
Scuffed arms and faded coat
An eyesore sure amid the
  splendor
Of imported just off the boat

Vast the seat that now fits fine
When as a toddler I used to
  explore

Imaginary worlds adults roamed
  in
I played Papa and much much
  more

The stories heard, the feelings
  shared
Though tired from work he
  would be
There on his lap engulfed by the
  chair
Each day some time for me

Papa's gone now, the chair
  remains
And each day I cherish it more
As I settle myself in memorial
  bliss
I'm at peace in the old eyesore

I don't care if visitors stare
Their bewilderment my secret
  fun
For in this chair, "Papa's Chair"
Is where I also hold my son

Ricardo R. Melendez
I Saw a Friend Go Away
  I saw a friend go away
But there is no sadness
For I knew he would still be
He would still be my friend
The one I fed and watered those
  many days
  I saw a friend go away
Maybe to come, maybe not on
  another day
I could not cry
For happy I was
Happy to see this friend
Fly into the horizon
Fly to be free
All I could say then and now
"Adios My Friend"

teresa anne logelin
alone
sometimes i sit all alone
and i think of you,
of all we've done together
and all that we could do.

a loneliness comes over me
as i wonder where you are,
what you're doing
and why you're not here
when i want and need you most.

then i realize
that you're doing what you must
  do
and i'm doing what i must do.
that's just the way life is.
but, it's nice when we have time
to spend together.

Georges Gilbert
**Remembrances of Dreams
Past**
[to M.S., a-la-Marcel Proust.]
Deep sleep at first, filled with
  fast-forgotten archromatic
  dream,
Cut open by a surgeon's nerve-
  wrenching, bloodless saw,
  which seems
To be made up of sharp, painless,
  invisible laser beams
That cut subconsciousness as
  readily as knives cut ice-cream.
Then, sleep again, neither very
  deeply nor calmly this time,
Dreaming of you, My Love, now
  in pastel-hued technicolor,

A dream remembered for a
    change: I'm falling, and I holler
Lusty words into a deep, broad
    tunnel full of pale-lime slime,

A lavender cylinder with two
    well-lit and open ends,
And then a winding, dusty,
    gravelly road which at last
    bends
Towards a blinding light that
    stands for the enigma of your
    smile,
Making my life worth living for
    eons—at least for a while . . .
I wake up, most dreams forgotten
    but your truly unique style,
And my great love for you
    remembered: two Sphynxes
    near the Nile.

James J. O'Connell
A DAY
[To Gloria]
MORNING:
    The morning sounds are all
    about me . . .
    The air is fresh and smells so
    sweet.
    Your fragrance lingers in the
    dawn
    Take care, my love, till next we
    meet.
    Just hold the rapture in your
    heart
    And watch the flight of snow
    white dove,
    Who brings a message on the
    wind,
    The soul of me and all my love.

AFTERNOON:
    The afternoon may linger
    longer
    Than I would have wished it
    to.
    I wait impatiently for evening,
    Still immersed in thoughts of
    you.
    A day, today, like any other,
    Except that you are far away.
    So silently await its ending . . .
    With little left to do but pray.

EVENING:
    The night is quiet, gentle
    sounds
    The world is sleeping all about
    me.
    And waiting here for time to
    pass . . .
    I think of all the ways I love thee.

Helene Slaski Kraus
DO NOT DESPAIR
[To my daughter, Linda Kraus
Hendricks]
Let not your tears
Blind the sunshine,
Or your fears
Keep you from going on.
Each day has a radiance
Of its own,
Born of a new dawn.
Yesterday's tears
and today's sorrow
Are the rainbows
of tomorrow.

Sharon Martin
SUNRISE
The sun sets
And you are gone
My heart goes with you

And my life is empty
The sun sets
The light goes out
Gone is the carefree
Happiness of day
To be replaced
By a dull cold
Darkness seeps in
And you are gone

When the sun sets
The light goes with it
Dark represents
Fear and loneliness
When someone leaves your life
And darkness falls
The pain is always worse

And the sun sets
It's only too bad
The nobody remembers
The sun also rises

Lisa Margaret Coile

Lisa Margaret Coile
POP
[Dedicated to Mom for all those
years, Love Lisa]
Since there's nothing I could find
That was worth giving you,
I sat down to think a while
And write a line or two.

If I had a magic wand
I'd wave it just for you,
And give you anything you'd like
No matter how many or few.

If I could give you back the years
You so willingly gave to me,
I'm sure you'd spend them over
    again
The same as they used to be.

Remember when those days and
    nights
Instead of going to the fair,
I'd always say "tell me again"
The story of the three little bears.

I tried to get a strawberry pie
But they were out of season,
Then I thought of gold or mrryh
But knew there was no reason.

Although you're often quiet
There's one thing we can say,
You'll always be our king
forever and a day.

So here's your gift; my sweet
    second daddy
My heart; my soul; my love,
My gift to you this Christmas
    day
Came strictly from above.

Judith Shannon Paine
SOUNDS OF SERENITY
It is good to listen, not to voices
but to the stream running cool
over velvet moss and polished
    stones,
to the wind blowing through the
    trees,
to the songs of birds and the slow
    pulse
of the earth's heartbeat . . . . to
    nature's
own sweet music played in quiet
    tones.
These are the sounds of serenity
    and if
we but attend, stress melts away;
    and
sorrow.
        Our souls begin to mend.

Stanley Alan Cassaday
VIOLET
[Herman and Violet Cassaday;
the greatest Parents a Son
could ever have.]
Violet is a beautiful name.
Violet brings pleasure and
    happiness to my name.
Violet like the flower has no
    other color that is the same.
Violet like the flower
    is beautiful in the spring and
    in the rain.
Violet, my Mother took me from
    her womb
        before I had a name.
She took me in her arms
    and fed me from her breast.
I grew and grew and my mind
    amazed.
She like my Father took me by
    the hand to raise.
They taught me what was right
    and scolded me when I was
    wrong.
They cared for me with all they
    had.
I knew I was lucky . . . and this
    made me glad.
For many children I knew
    had no Mother or a Dad.
They comforted me when I was
    sad
They nursed me when I was sick.
With age I grew, so did distress
    and unrest.
Like most birds I grew wings and
    flew my parent's nest.
I knew my parents then and I
    know my parents now,
    and still I know my parents
    are the best around.

Virginia Morton Ross
JUST BEYOND THE BEND
[To my parents, the late Clyde
and Merle Morton. Mother's
thoughts inspired this poem as
her family would leave the old
homeplace for a distant place or
on their joyous return.]
The road in front of my home
    seems short,
It quickly seems to end.
Cause I can't see "no farther", than
Just beyond the bend.

My loved ones leave, and I watch
    them go
As far as eye can see.

They quickly disappear from
    sight
Then they are gone from me.

Then in my mind, I chart their
    courses,
All the places they'll go thru.
I know the road goes on and on
For miles beyond my view.

My loved ones often return to me
And then our parting ends,
When I look to see them comin
From just beyond the bend.

Cause we've been miles and miles
    apart,
But now they're home again,
And I'm so happy just to know
They're safely round the bend!

This road of life may disappear.
We think we see the end,
But—it goes on forever from—
Just beyond the bend!

And tho we leave this earthly
    view,
Our journey just begins,
For God will be "awaitin us"
From—just beyond the bend!

Bob Brown
ANOTHER LOOK
Most anyone could write a poem
But 'tis the height of my desire
The poems of others to inspire.
As with the life of Robert Frost
My life's purpose would not be
    lost.

Had I been born another time
And had my choice to grow, to
    toil
As a famous old Jeffrey Pine
Twisted by fierce winds and
    barren soil;
Perhaps I'd be subject of a book.
At least you'd have "Another
    Look."

Sandra Costa
NEW LIFE
When it was summer
You were my sunshine
    And life's color
        On autumn trees
Tender thoughts of you
Kept me warm in winter
    And when new blossoms
        Filled the air with springtime
You were the new life in me

Bonita G. Cooper
A LONGING
My eyes search and finally see;
My life, like the wind, passing by
    me.

I close my eyes to vision a new
    space;
To find a quiet more restful
    place.

I begin to see mountains
    towering high
above the surrounding grounds;
Beautiful mountains capped with
    white
snow mounds.

With a cold water brook gently
    trickling
down to feel;
My heart begins to ache for a
    scene such
as this to become real.

Today's Greatest Poems

Where the days would be
unhurried, calm
and serene;
And ones laughter would echo
throughout
the mountains for as far as could
be seen.

Where you would be filled with a
warmth
such as felt from a blazing fire;
Where your heart would awaken
each morning
longing with new desire.

Your spirit would be embraced
with content-
ment and love;
And you could know the feeling
of unbound
freedom as experienced by a
white winter dove.

A place filled with the peaceful
sounds of
nature alone;
A place such as this I long to call
home.

Donna Brown Willis
EMPTY TOMB
Why is the house so silent these
days?
Is it because the home has
changed in its ways?
I miss the sound of your quiet
voice
Your feet on the stairs with a
quiet noise.
I miss bringing home the chips
and the dips
The hamburgers and soda pop
and grocery trips
Sometimes it seems like empty
tombs
As I walk around in these empty
rooms.
When all the children have flown
the nest
Is it time for me to move back
west?
I look for insight into the path to
lead
Show me the right way and God I
will heed.

Esther Reeves
We Go This Way But Once
We go this way but once, O heart
of mine.
So why not make the journey
well worth while.
Giving to those who travel on
with us
A helping hand, a word of cheer, a
smile?
We go this way but once; Ah!
never more
Can we go back along the self
same way.
To get more out of life, undo the
wrongs.
Or speak loves' words we knew,
but did not say.
We go this way but once; Then,
let us make
The road we travel, blossomy and
sweet,
With helpful, kindly deeds and
tender words,
Smoothing the path of bruised
and stumbling feet.

E. M. C. Arnusch
AUTUMN
[A God-given inspiration]
Summer's past, the seasons go on,
Flowers fade and time to sleep,
Frosty nights cover the ground,
Apples red are better to keep.

Wind whistling through the
trees,
Leaves blowing in the wintry
breeze,
Mountains cloaked in a coat of
colors,
Orange, red, yellow and others.

Wood smoke fills the air,
Burning leaves, here and there,
Pumpkins still on the vine.
Fall is here, they will be fine.

Birds flying to their southward
homes,
Animals burrowing with food
they've found,
Home fires burning, its warmth
profound,
Autumn's here with its coloured
tones.

Nature's life ending, will be
blanketed in snow,
Harvests all in, how are we to
know!
Why the Lord, has His reasons,
Plans He made for all His
seasons.

Faye Gordon-Hale
But For His Saving Grace
In a world swimming in sin
I would have surely drowned.
I had reached the count of three
And was on my way down
When his love rescued me.
Tidal waves of joy flowed in.
Tweren't for him I'd gone under,
My soul put asunder.
Gone without a single trace,
But for his saving grace.

High on a mountain of hate
And headed for a fall.
A rocky precipice seemed
The way to end it all.
Then as if in a dream
I saw Heaven's pearly gates.
Tweren't for him I'd gone down
hill.
I think I'd have been there still:
Buried at its granite base,
But for his saving grace.

A desert of desire;
Hot as an inferno
Has parched my eternal soul.

It had me, this I know,
Ready to shovel coal
And to stock hell's own fire.
Tweren't for him I'd surely burn
'til my heart did he turn.
My life would have been a waste,
But for his saving grace.

Darlene Smith
THOUGHTS
I lie here thinking
Thoughts of you.
Beautiful thoughts
That I hope come true.
I know these thoughts
Can never be,
Because your thoughts
Are not of me.
I know not what
Your thoughts could be.
Mine are thoughts
Of you and me
Living together
Forever more
Thinking the thoughts
We never thought before.

Tammie M. Johnson
IMAGES
An image constructed around a
predisposed idea.
Strangers meet.
Bleak shadows subconsciously
engraved.
Standing before a preconceived
image, insecure and anxious
I pass Judgement.
Shattered truth stands isolated.
But judge not I so harshly
Images tempered with truth, new
concepts are devised.
Verdicts gentled and strangers
accepted
Cracked images bear satisfying
reflections.

Alice R. Jackson
RETROSPECT
The endless line of spent
humanity
Walks lonely in the forest still.
The dim path winds its way
Through trees and grasses now at
will.
The hushed silence hides the
laughter,
Falling leaves the song.
Under the sand, with wind and
rain,
The footprints on the path are
gone.
If you step and quietly will
You can hear the laughter still.
If you listen with your heart
Listen long for the song.

Arlene Dempsey
THE FEELING OF LOSING
The feeling of losing
Never goes away.
Every day of my life,
I think of you.
When I shut my eyes,
I can see you
As clearly as yesterday.
Sometimes I
Can still hear your voice
When I am sitting alone
At my desk
In the evening hours.
My mind remains dark,
In a very deep and

Emotional corner
With the sorrow of losing you.
Sometimes,
When he and I
Are making love,
I have to push him away
Because I feel guilty
For giving him
What once belonged to you.
It isn't as if
You died only yesterday.
It happened long, long ago—
Almost in another life
It sometimes seems.
But letting go
Isn't as easy
As burying the dead.
The feeling of losing
Never goes away.
It lives on and on,
And it ages
With your heart.
You just get good
At hiding it.

Danielle Marie Angeline
YOU
*[To Joe in Washington, D.C.
Thank you for helping me
through hard times. You'll
always be my best friend—
wherever we are—apart or
together.]*
You make me laugh
when I'm down.
You wipe away my tears
when I cry.
You even give me a hug
at just the right time.
You made school
more bearable.
You brighten my days
when the skies are cloudy.
You give me support
when I need it most.
You let me lean on you
when I'm not strong.
You always seem to
have the right advice.
You are always there
when I need someone to listen.
You are the best friend
any girl could have.

Kathryn J. Morrison
I AM AN ACTRESS
I am but one who searches,
For things beyond my reach.
To find myself, and be another,
Is something I alone can teach.

I wait for others to see my view,
But it is all in vain.
There's no reaction, just spiteful
glares,
From those who hate to see
another gain.

In time I hope to find the place,
Where dreams become
worthwhile.
Until I do, I hope we can
continue,
Continue our strained smile.

Alone I reach to touch you,
But crouching you move away.
It is who I am, or you yourself,
Or what others say.

Once we know the words and
song,
The music will appear.

121

Our love and all our thoughts,
Will be our soul's mirror.

Together we will succeed,
And make it shine as gold,
For it is imagination's game,
At least, that's what I'm told.

Anne S. Publow
THE SORROWFUL HEART
Oh, take me in your arms, my
dear
And kiss the hurt away
And let me share your tender
love
Henceforward, from today.

Oh, teach my reminiscent heart
To put away its sorrow
And learn to look with eagerness
Upon a new tomorrow.

Oh, take my hand in yours,
sweetheart
For I have need of you
And I shall hold it ever
If you should need me too.

Oh, take my heavy heart, beloved
It's all I have to give
And I shall love you, darling
As long as I shall live.

Martin "Mercy" Zachwieja
CUPID, YOU WORRY ME
[To all lonesome-hearted
Lovers, with too personal a tale]
Cupid! Don't be rude, she see's
you nude,
hide behind your smile.
Clothe yourself with modesty
and skillfully
use your bow a-while.
Please don't quiver when you
draw and deliver
unless your sight is keen,
For if you miss your mark and hit
tree-bark
I cannot Love a tree.
And don't let the arrow hit that
sparrow
for birds I do not care,
And I sincerely wish you miss
the fish
I drink my water clear.
Cupid, what takes so long, is
something wrong?
Are you sure it's her you see?
How time passes! Please get some
glasses!
Oh Cupid, you worry me!

Patt Welker
LET ME BELONG
Today—I feel alone.
Today—I say they were wrong.
Today—Is the day I yearn to:
Be Needed—To Be Loved—To
Belong.

Pick myself up—Runaway
Runaway—Runaway fast
Away from this place
Freedom at last!

I put out my thumb
I jump on some bus
To take me away
From this life of no fuss.

Alas! I have friends
We rap—we sing many a song
We love—yet we all
still . . . want to:
Be Needed—To Be Loved—To
Belong.

I sit with my friends alone in a
daze
And I look all around with much
disgust
At this life that I have
But I must—I must . . .

For there is no other.
But my thoughts go astray
In search for my place on this
earth
And I pray—I pray.

But is there a God?
Ah yes—my heart says so strong!
Oh mama—Oh daddy! Oh
please . . .
Need Me—Love Me—Let Me
Belong

Marvin Wingo
THERE'S LOVE
[To GOD as an offering in
appreciation for his droplets of
love that have sustained life
and mortified the senses.]
I may not live to see another
dawning
But if I die my soul will go on
living
While I'm alive I'll do my best in
pleasing
Our Holy Lord who did the most
in giving.

I only know there's love in caring
And that those loved will do
more loving
So as we give love is in motion
growing
It is passed on in some deed of
blessing.

When we stand up at judgement
for our sinning
The Lord will look towards our
love in giving
We should all pray for fullness in
charity
Which is the greatest of all works
of mercy.

I only know there's love in caring
And that those loved will do
more loving
So as we give love is in motion
growing
It is passed on in some deed of
blessing.

Hell's fire's so hot but we don't
have to go there
We can escape easy if we really
care
In charity we could find our
perfect friend
For with it we cover multitude's
of sin.

I only know there's love in caring
And that those loved will do
more loving
So as you give love is in motion
growing
It is passed on in some deed of
blessing.

Leslie A. Smith
Time Heals a Broken Heart
Say Hi you know it's been awhile
I didn't know how much I missed
your style
Sometimes I can't believe we
were together for
three years

When we first broke up I had so
many uncertain fears
I was lost without you and sure it
was the end
I'd lost a lover as well as a friend
I cried till I had no tears left to
cry
I felt you gave up without giving
us a try
It's true time heals a broken heart
Now I am ready, willing and able
for a new start.

Lorraine V. Henderson
If I Should Go Before You Do
If I should go before you do
and leave you by yourself,
don't grieve in days to come
with tears for moments gone.
In days to come on long dark
nights
when you are by yourself,
look behind to the love we knew
and ahead to eternal life.
Look to the Lord—he's waiting
with loving open arms,
to guide his children to
the only promised land.
I'll be waiting for you there
with loving open arms,
so we can meet again
and then walk hand in hand.
If I should go before you do
miss me but do not grieve,
for I'll be waiting for you
with loving open arms.

Velma Margaret Haller
THE PAST TALKING
Ruff was Dennis the Menace's
dog
    Just as
Leo is the MGM lion.
And Lester was Willie Tyler's
dummy
    Just as
Granny was the Hillbillies Irene
Ryan.

Time has passed since
The Hatfields and the McCoys.
And now is history
Ma Barker and her boys.

Bill Malone
    Didn't he
Host the "Honeymoon Race"?
Bill Cullen
    Didn't he
Host "Place the Face"?

Bill Haley
Seems he sang "Rock Around the
Clock".
Chubby Checker
He's the one who sang "The
Limbo Rock".

And marriages would come and
go
    Just like
Bobby Darin and Sandra Dee.
    Just like
Tony Curtis and Janet Leigh.

And there was
    "Que Sera Sera"
Who could ever forget Doris
Day's theme song?
"What will be, will be"
    But tell me,
Do I have to wait that long?

Mona Lynn Anderson
REFLECTING
The quiet nights
The somber days
All mellow in the
summer haze
With after thoughts of
by-gone days

And deep within ravines
of mind
Still echo ghosts of
other times
Passing boughs and
branches green
Reflecting on shades of
hidden dreams

Virginia Fox
Loneliness Of a Forgotten Parent
When evening shadows deepen,
and darkness invades my room.
When everyone else is sleeping,
then comes the grief and
gloom.
Another day—and no one came.
To visit or even talk to me.
No letters—no cards—Did they
forget my name?
Oh, how I long to see, the sweet
faces of my children!
Who once loved and cherished
me.
The loved ones, who, when small,
came to Mother with skinned-
up knees.
Only I could dry their
tears . . . only I could make
things better.
But what has happened, through
all these years?
With neither a card or letter.
Have they forgotten the one who
loved them so very much?
How their fears would fade away;
simply by her gentle touch.
Why can't they remember, the
many good times we've had?
Why must they be forgotten?
Why must they make me sad?
If only they would write . . . just
a short line or two.
It would make me feel so very
good, and all my hopes renew.
For my children, just because I'm
so old and gray.
Doesn't mean that my love for
you, has simply died away.
Please come to visit me; here in
this nursing home.
Let me know, you love me still;
and your love for me hasn't gone.

Today's Greatest Poems

Jason Wiese
INNOCENCE OF YOUTH
Tender blue eyes smiling,
Gentle, peaceful features,
Calm and graceful gestures,
Skin of cream and roses;
Soft and deep you move me
Slender, fair-haired Julie!

Compassion you possess,
And great the joy it brings;
On quiet wings it sings!
You know my thoughts, my
    heart,
When I make not a sound.
A gift is this I've found.

Sweet glows your innnocence;
Delicate, fair to my
Sensitive youthful eye.
Beauty, eternally
Tranquil did heaven send;
Would that it never end!

In the dark of my heart,
You were first to expell,
All the fear that did dwell.
Now the warmth of your light
Makes you seem to be rare.
And to me, few compare!

Love is strange it seems though,
Who knows until it's passed?
Vast are the fields and yet;
You were first; you'll be last.

Mary Gee
The Power Of Knowledge
An unexamined life is a poor one
We cannot decide what we were
    meant to do
Unless we search in all the
    corners
Like our minds were meant to do

The extent of human knowledge
Can go slow but very far
We must examine all the
    principles
To find out what they are

First we find a basic formula
With some thought of
    compromise
We will find there many answers
Not all of them are wise

Now we add up all our principles
Some we throw away
We save a few for just tomorrow
Are just another day

A formula cannot become a
    reality
Unless we put it to the test
So we use our sense of reason
Our efforts to do the rest

With our basic basic formula
If all the signs say go
We will finally find an answer
If we want to have it so

So let us try to be so thankful
We have so much to lead us far
With our wills and use of nature
We will reach a shining star

Joseph Roberts Jr.
JUST A DREAM?
If I could dream of xanadu
And travel there taking just us
    two
Would it truly be just a dream?
If dreams were made from visions
And reality were but a dream
I wonder if this is really life

Or if it's all just as it seems
I fear that I may never know
If truly it's a dream.

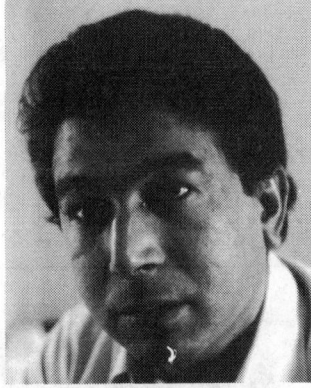

K.B. Mann

K.B. Mann
ON PARTING
Ere breaks the magic spell
And love be lost in monotony
And the heart and eyes grow
Jaded by constant company,
Let us part and get lost
In the crowds of the world

And to each other become
Strangers once again
So that fond memories
Of loving days remain
Preserved for evermore
And let in them the magic
And the enchantment endure.

Roberta Gracie
REPENT!
Repent ye world of sinful men!
For the man I love
Does not love me.
He does what all men do—
Treats a woman like a tramp,
A used piece of merchandise
To be cast aside
When not needed
To fulfill His Own desires!

Barbara Truncellito
EASTER SUNDAY MASS
Kicking the quirks a notch up
I ogle at the acclivity
of a moment in the day
extorting it
knocking at a morose door
behind which lies a decayed
    crown
and an expected cremation
ready to be flushed and blown
to blue heaven.

I turn to blink twice
at candle light
and uppercrusted noses
on some who cook their quarters
for an extra six cents
and those who pray for pennies
to come in threes
all waiting for a quake.

Silvano Zamaro
INDIAN SUMMER
These short days on my lips
Talk of birds southward bound
See the sunrise
Through city skyscrapers
Under indigo clouds
While indian summer ends

These short days on my lips
Shorter every morning
Always darker
Fall asleep in front of me
With coffee cup in hand
Before slashing my wrists with
    their blades.

Phyllis J. Ness
OUR BIRCH TREE
Under our birch tree, you're a
    handsome man
Making love to me as only you
    alone can
The warmth of your body
    melting into mine
Surrounded by nature what a
    beautiful time
Returning here wishing your love
    I could keep
My thoughts turn to nature my
    feelings are deep
The sun will shine tomorrow to
    give us another chance
I lose myself with you in beauty,
    it's worth the glance
Soft white clouds, the deep blue
    of the lake, give me ease
With you again as the wind
    gently blows through the trees
Our humaness for the touch of
    love is all that I yearn
Loving the part of you that's mine
    is my greatest concern
There's a special reason for you
    and me
I felt it again under our birch tree

Alberta Jones
LONELINESS
I walk the crowded streets of life
But yet I'm still alone
I talk to people that I meet
But yet I'm still alone
I touch the people that I see
But yet I'm still alone
For my loneliness is trapped
    inside,
only those who care can see the
    loneliness I bare.

Janice Sue Henderson
JUST PALS
I don't know if you know it,
I don't know if you care.
This feeling that I have for you
Is really very rare.

It started out as friendship
But somehow grew to love.
It's a special kind of feeling
That comes from up above.

I've been your "PAL" right from
    the start
And never expected anything
    more

But time has changed, my
    feelings too
And how my heart is sore.

Love is not a one-way street
So "FRIENDS" we'll have to be.
Something that two people share
Just "PALS" you and me.

Laurette M. Boysun
SARA
I cry with joy
When she smiles at me.
Her dimples are on display.

Those big, brown eyes
Fill my heart with happiness.
My baby is growing so fast.

Her soft, fine hair
Melts me as it brushes my face.
She's every dream fulfilled.

What would I do without my
    little girl;
Her round, pudgy face searching
    to learn.
She depends so much on my
    extended hands.

She's Daddy's pride and joy;
Grandma's sleeping beauty;
An amazing wonder in life.

My baby, my little girl
She'll always give me purpose.
I will forever care.

I love so much
My precious Sara.
She's such a special gift.

Bill Coombs
NEW BIGINNINGS
Spring
and the remnants of last
    summer's glory
start to show from beneath the
    snow;
crumpled leaves and new buds,
the strange mixture of what is
    dead
and the promise of what is yet to
    be.
As I cherish the beauty of the
    fragile buds
I think of you and things dead
    and things
yet beginning.

Anna L. Earl
FOR EVERYTHING
*[To the one who adds an extra
touch of sunshine to my world.
This one's for you, Mike.]*
For every beach, there is an
    ocean.
For every ocean, there is a gull.
For every gull, there is a sunset.
For every sunset, there is a
    dreamer.
For every dreamer, there is hope.
And for all hope, there is a
    heaven.

Robin Collinsworth
GOD ARE YOU LISTENING
God are you listening
Can you hear my prayer
Are you looking down on me
from someplace somewhere

Can you see all the sin
And pain we must endure
Yet, in all this, we must exist
Clean of heart and pure

Do you see the children
With wide eyes full of tears
Can you let them suffer
From days to weeks to years

God aren't you listening
Don't you know we're here
Can't you see in our eyes
The pain and hurt and fear

You know we love you dearly
And miss you more each day
So please my Lord do come soon
And take us all away.

Joanne Di Giovanni
A TEAR
The sea gliding gracefully
over the cold winter's beach,
silently approaching the rocks
leaving a trace of ice.
The memory of what had been
a roaring wave
becoming
a gentle foam
being
a silent tear.

Delora M. Norwood
YOUR THOUGHTS
Your thoughts are deep tonight,
    my love
    and your heart is troubled too.
But pride holds back the flow of
    words
    that could bring me close to
    you.

You question life and it's ways,
    my love
    and really, you don't know
    why.
God never gave man the answer
    or there'd be no reason to die.

Life itself is too deep and
    profound
    for mere man to understand.
And love is even more profound
    'cause it moves like shifting
    sand

So, tell me the deep dark secrets,
    love
    tell me so I will know.
And I will stand beside you,
    always
    though the tide be high or low.

Lynda Norris
**Can a Broken Heart Learn
    To Dance?**
Lying withered in an old
    abandoned chest. It use to
    dance. With such gracefullness
    and finesse.

Jumping with bundles of joy and
    leaping, which turned to
    twisting with sorrow. Not
    wanting to see the dawning of
    a new tomorrow.

It couldn't withstand all of the
    twisting and bending. Cracked
    and broken in a million pieces,
    can it be mended?

Once in its youth did such a
    magic dance. Until one day it
    happened upon romance.

The nearer love approached the
    stronger it struck back. Until
    one dreary day the music
    stopped and it cracked.

If you only knew how important

a dancing heart is to me. It is the
    creator of the person inside,
    that I could be.

My surface is smooth and
    nonchalant. But inside, my
    heart is crying desperately out
    for the love it wants.

This is such a lonely way for the
    heart to pay the cost. To stop
    dancing for the love I lost.

I must pick up the pieces and
    learn to dance again.

But I am very fragile, with firm
    hands to support me, I begin to
    dance when the music begins.

Be gentle hands, hear my silent
    pleas. For I am whispering
    silently, and your eyes can't
    see.

Will my heart move freely or will
    it only prance?
"Can a broken heart learn to
    dance?"

Philaeta V. Bennett
PINNACLE
I'd swap a dozen crowded rooms
Where empty plans are made
By people using frozen words,
And deadly games are played.
For one bright pinnacle where
    mind
Meets mind and people feel;
Where sun streams down on
    hurts that bleed,
And sympathy is real.

Katherine E. Crichton, Jackson
HAPPYNESS
Happyness is having someone to
    care
being with someone and learning
    to share.
Facing each day as it comes along
and taking each trial with out a
    frown.
Remembering the lonely as you
    go through each day
a smile and some laughter will go
    a long way.

Anne C. Hurd
THE ENDLESS DAY
My life is a fantasy, My love a
    losing game
    An aching heart, mind in
    desperation
Waiting for a call that never
    came.

I built my castles and they fell in
    vain
    Sitting and wondering, excuses
    seem real
Just waiting for a call that never
    came.

A voice I heard as the preceeding
    day waned,
    Nervous, discontent, yet
    patient to wait
Still expecting the call that never
    came.

My dreams are endearing, there is
    no disdain
    Enraptured, possessed, reliving
    memories
As I wait for the call that never
    came.

I imagine, in futility, there can be

love without shame
    Pleading, crying, with passion
    compelling
Hoping for a call that never came.

My life in the past was without
    an acclaim
    Heartaches, problems ever to
    face
Like waiting for the call that
    never came.

A great revp;itopm! My whole life
    has changed
    To live, to love, makes me
    content
To wait for the call that never
    came.

Hannah M. Severson

Hannah M. Severson
LOVE
Love is a little word but, oh it
    means so much.
And one that has it has that
    special touch.
God has put love into every ones
    heart.
He gave some more, some less
    with some he wants us to part.
Love isn't love unless we give it
    away.
To all people, the sick, the
    afflicted, those whose name
    you cannot say.
When you have this gift, you will
    see beauty all around.
You will hear such a beautiful
    sound.
Many blessings will come your
    way, your loved ones, your
    friends, and you too.
You will see this beauty , in your
    home, your work, in every
    thing you do.
Your step will be quicker, you
    think you could fly.
Then you look up, and see Gods
    handiwork in the beautiful
    blue sky.
Then you say, God has made this
    possible, it's all true.
This is old, but to you it's true.

Connie Lakey Martin
THE TRUNK
In a corner of Aunt Annie's barn
it sat among rags and plunder
and curious things
that fell asunder
when Grandma could no longer
keep house.

Even the smell comes back
when I think of those
old bundled clothes
packed inside

as if time had died
for her.

I wanted it for my own.
But Dad said, "No, leave it be."

When it was finally up to me,
I took it
from its place
to my home.

And the look on Grandma's face
as I cleaned it ever so
    cherishingly.
"Mother's trunk," she said, "you to
    save it!"
The she hugged me for
the shine
I gave it.

Wish she could see
the space
it occupies in my married home,
the shine,
and my daughter
next in line.

Garland Day
The Lonley Old House
There is an old house, near "Cado
    Peak"!
That sits outside in the rain.
Not a sound can you hear, from
    the house there within,
But her structure, has suffered
    much pain!

The shingles are gone, from the
    roof up above!
And the walls are crumbling and
    bare!
Many years have passed, since
    the house sheltered life!
But all of her memories, are still
    there!

Wild Indians, hunted game, in
    the hills, all around!
Back when the house was sturdy
    and strong!
Little children, they played in the
    grass out front!
And from the "Old House", there
    was a song!

If this "Old House", could but tell
    what she knows!
Of all the "Life", she has spanned!
I'm sure you would find, much
    love in her past,
And feel the warmth, from her
    out streched hands!

Some one will come soon, and
    take her away!
Only "The Winds", will know her
    past!
What ever happens, to this dear
    old house,
The "Love", she has sheltered, will
    always last!

Lynn Britton
THE IDEOLOGICAL MOLD
Of imagry and idolry,
Our fanticies do perch,
Like the Poets and the Prophets,
In the memory of the search.

They mythed our many metals,
As they deepened in despair,
Many fabled truths presented,
In 400, they lived there.

'Twas the method of the teacher,
That the student was no bore,
Disdained of lucre was as motto,

Knowledge of ignorance, begat
more.

In a drink of that day's fashion,
In an old and Grecian style,
Came a silence of the questions,
From a cruel, unusual trial.

Many murdered greats in history,
Many died on hungers row,
While the idle rich stayed idle,
Shadows history in a flow.

For the lives lost, we regret it,
As they sought to teach and
learn,
Of the Golden Rule for people,
In this day, yet many spurn.

Name them Philosopher, King or
Prophet!
Who hath given woman place?
Read the pages void of glory,
'Tis the history books disgrace.

If the greats did not ignore us,
'Twas tradition of all times,
Of the century's past afore us.
In the silence of the chimes.

We look East, in silence wonder!
Will we hear one Oh, so rare,
In Jehovahnees gentle whisper,
"Hath the world no room to
share?"

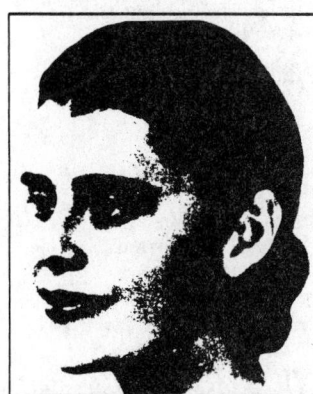

Ethel Ellen Lewis

Ethel Ellen Lewis
GOING BLIND
Skipping through the air,
Barely touching the gravelled
earth,
And then, she stumped her toe:
"Oh, it is there!"

Then a turn in time.
Like water breaking into
turbulent
Foam over hidden rocks,
Rushing towards a fall
Eye—ball to eye—ball.

Flying seasons
Shortening days
Dull sunsets
Darkness.

Vickie Lynn Moore
**How Special Are
Friends—Buckwheat**
I never met a special friend
who cared as much as you
Who understands my different
moods
no matter what I do.
We've shared a lot of memories
we never could replace.

The ups and downs don't matter
to me
they were never hard to face
God blessed me with a friendship
that's full of love and care.
And I hope that as the years go
by,
your friendship still is there.
My prayers have been answered
I've met a friend like you
May God bless you and keep you
and love you as I do.

T. Kelly
TO WANDA
*[9 year old Wanda, hurt by
refusal of newspaper to grant
prize to baby bo n first on New
Years Day, because of
illegitimacy, raised over $2000
for little Eunice in campaign of
her own.]*
"A little child shall lead them. . ."
Was said quite long ago,
About someone as dear and sweet
As Wanda is . . . I know.
Thank God for all such little girls
Whose hearts are kind and
true;
They make the world a better
place
And stand in heaven's view.
They gently chide their elders
With act of selfless love,
And win, I'm sure, the laurel
Of praise from up above.
So here's to lovely Wanda,
A toast on high I hold!
May she never lose her sweetness
Or tender heart of gold.

Trina L. Scott
WE FRIENDS
We friends have lots of fun,
Walking, playing and chewing
bubble gum.
We visit the park lots of times,
Go to the creek and flip our
dimes.
We go to tables where we all sit,
In the grass we roll and laugh
having fits.
We friends have lots of fun,
Walking, playing and chewing
bubble gum.

Bertha Givins
**When Summer Goes To
Sleep**
*[With love to Dana, Sherri,
Mike, Mark, Rennie, Rush,
LaMika and my friend Mary Jo]*
The sun reclines from distant
heights, her warmth beyond
my reach,
And lovely flowers, heads bowed
low, lay petals at my feet.

The happy sounds of kids at play,
their laughter filled with glee,
Will be but just a memory, when
summer goes to sleep.

The rippling waves of clear blue
streams, shall touch the sands
no more,
But stand instead as asure stone
against the distant shore.

Young lovers strolling through
the park, their whispers soft
and sweet,
Are soon replaced by echoing

winds, when summer goes to
sleep.

Oh tinted leaves of red and gold,
'tis sad to see it end,
I'll miss the sing song of the birds
as they bask in the warm south
wind.

Oh Hurry! Hurry! Winter's night,
step swiftly, old North Wind,
Then life once more will dawn
anew, when summer wakes
again.

Debra Basl Cook
SWEET OR SOUR
*["To Kitt C. Knisley" For the
faith & inspiration He has
bestowed upon me!]*
I heard they traveled to Mars . . .
and they marked it as Ours!

I heard they traveled to the Moon
where we'll be shopping one
afternoon!

I heard they traveled beneath the
Sea
where they built a City for You
and Me!

. . . And I heard they found a
Nuclear Power
that can destroy ALL within
the Hour!

Mandy
IT NEEDS LOVE
*[TO LAURA AND SHELLI For
all your loving support and
total belief in me—THANKS!!]*
One man, one woman
one night,
together
make love.
And from this love,
a creation!
This creation speads joy,
laughter and hope.
Awakened by sound,
curious to touch.
Bright, beautiful, alive!
This creation, without love
will not grow,
will not experience, and
will not nourish itself.
This creation,
a child,
born to be free, just like you and
me,
will not survive!
Thanks to one man and one
woman,
without love!?

Christina LaRosa
ODE TO SCOLIOSIS
Heavenly Father full of grace,
Bless our awful, ugly brace.
That brace we wear all day
through,
Oh, God I'm shocked I thought
you knew.

Bless our dreams of satin shirts,
And in those dreams our flowing
skirts.
Bless our sweat in summers
sun,
That doesn't stop us from having
fun.

Bless our bruises, bruises
galore,
And the holes in shirts we wore.

Bless our crooked, crooked
backs,
That sometimes are so hard to
hack.

Bless our brace from neck to
waist,
But don't forget our pretty face.
And those nights of sleepless
rest,
Remember God we try our best.

Love us God for what we are,
Underneath that metal bar.
Bless us God for all of this,
For what we have SCOLIOSIS.

Lula Rendon
UNEXPECTED LOVE
*[To Leo for the years of loving
and sharing]*
LOVE entered my life like a
melody and took up its' place
in my heart.
Unbeckoned, unasked for, and
quite a surprise, yet there from
the very start.

YEARS haven't dulled the
pleasures I've known, just from
being with you,
We've weathered the crisis' and
held in the tests,
Thru it all unexpected love has
held true.

HAPPINESS is always before us as
we share dreams thru—out our
life,
Thank you for the beautiful
melody and the honor of being
your wife.

Jean Dugan
RAINBOWS
At the end of a rainbow they say
a treasure you will find,
But to where is the end of this
rainbow, Oh! blow my mind,
The colors are so wild to this day,
As I go along my way.

Through the fog and blackness of
rain,
I see a rainbow that brings hope,
joy, and sunshine in my small
lane,
Cherish a rainbow to the very
end,
And happiness you will send.

And until rain stops its
thundering roar,
Rainbows will go on forever
more.

Janet Colburn Ainsworth
TO MY NEW FATHER
*[This poem was written for Jo
Cerreta, who shared with me
the special feelings of Ann
Marie about her new Dad,
Micheal.]*
He went away and left me,
And many years from then,
You came along to love me
And renewed my faith in men.

I feel your care surrounding
And nourishing my soul.
I long to be your daughter,
To have my life made whole.

Your love for me is balanced—
Not indulgent or severe;
Your approach is always honest,

125

Your communication clear.
I want you for my father,
 To love me and to share
My happiness and sadness,
And always to be there.

My love for you and yours for me
Will always be the same,
But my prayers will all be
 answered
 On the day I share your name!

Sherry Bennett
Having You Was Sharing
You were like the boys I loved
 when I was little,
Cute and mysterious and yes,
 very serious
Or maybe I was the serious one
But you made me aware of a life
 out there:

Of discussions and being
 needed,
Bike trips and caring
Having you was sharing,
Giving of myslef and not being
 overbearing.
Everything we did was a special
 occasion
But knowing you would be
 leaving made a day a
 celebration.

I questioned all we had together,
 I knew it couldn't be any better
Although I loved you dearly
 was you who loved me not so
 nearly.
You touched my life so briefly
 yet I grew to love you very
 deeply
I'm a better person having known
 you needed me.

Paul A. York
ON THE RUN
I am on the run,
hiding from the worst jailer—
gossiping neighbor.

Lisa Martinek
A Difference Of Opinions
My kids don't understand my
 standards.
Mom and Dad aren't up with the
 crowd.
My parents play old fogie music.
My child plays her records too
 loud.
If my child would just make an
 effort,
 she'd find we aren't that bad.
If my parents would just stop and
 listen,
 they'd be proud of me instead
 of mad.
Sue's parents let her go out, you
 should let me too!
Jill gets straight "A" report cards,
 why don't you?
No matter how mad I get at my
 child,
 I hope she knows only my
 temper goes wild.
In case of an occasional fight,
 My parents must remember
 only my temper's aflight.
If she'd look down at us from
 above,
 My child would know I do
 these things in the name of
 love.

Though our relationship will be
 twisted and twirled,
I wouldn't change my parents
 for any in the world.

Jackie King
HIGH DESERT WIND
In the stillness of early morning's
 heat, you skip through the
 desert so sassy.
Tickling the sagebrush,
chuckling the trees,
playfully encircling
my sun warmed breasts,
tiny whirlwinds 'round the
 nipples.

In afternoon's dusty drowse
you too are lanquid.
Sashaying over the mesas
ambling, down the gorges,
lifting, swirling, tossing,
the crunchy oak leaves,
and mating butterflies.

Ah, but as the sun sets, ever
 changing lady, you unfurl a
 wild and whipping velvet cape.
Casting off the balmy day facade
to loose your true nature on the
 night.

I feel you touching
my hair, neck, ears.
The heated breath of love's
 rapture as you roar through the
 treetops, in breaker waves
 rushing.

Your song of delerious power,
is a frenzied crescendo
a mad ballet.
Tearing through the darkness,
ripping 'til the dawn,
When once again . . .
you are a child
playing in the sand.

Pixie Hammond
DIVORCE
The one
To whom I took
All my problems to solve
Has suddenly become my one
Problem!

Carla Trujillo
LOVE
Love is so strong and powerful
 but yet so confusing
We ask ourselves in our own
 way, is it wrong or right
 but I wish I knew what to do
Even now I want to depart this
 world
 but who knows, it might be
 worse
Wherever it might be
 I wish I knew what to do
I ask God to guide me and show
 me the way
 even the one we deeply love on
 earth
But yet I'm so confused
 yet we trust the one we love
We don't own anyone on the
 earth
 no matter what
But, I wish I knew the way
 I want to scream out so loud
The pain inside is so painful
 I want to die
I love him so much
 but yet I'm so hurt
Yet he's so truthful and loving

I wish I knew the way
The reason why I love him so
 cuz he's so truthful and loving
He says, "You know I love you",
 you know but, confused
Yet I'm still, I'm so lonely and sad
 I wish I knew the answer
So please, God, guide me and
 show me the way
 I love him so, He loves me so

Katherine J. West
MY MOTHER
*[To John D. Whinnie in
 memory of Barbara J. Whinnie]*
My Mother
was like a beautiful flower
that set its seeds upon the wind
to be carried
with God's love
to a more fertile land.

Patricia L. Hill
Walking With a Friend
*[I would like to dedicate this
poem to Wayne Mulkey, a
friend, who courageously has
endured manic—highs and
depressive lows, and is, I pray,
on the road to recovery.]*
We walked together, hand—in—
 hand, each in our separate
 space,
Thoughts drifting in and out my
 head, his only keeping pace.

"Do you get sad?" I asked him
 once. "Just blah," was his reply.
So this is what depression is
 opposed to manic high!

"It's been a year since we first
 met, a year of ups and downs.
Tell me friend, have I seen the
 gamut of your bounds?"

"I think you have." "I think so
 too." but there's a time so rare,
A time when I remember you, a
 time when you could care!

If I had a Genie's lamp and just
 one wish to give,
I'd rub it hard and wish for you, a
 balanced life to live.

Like my favorite see—saw ride,
 when I was just a kid.
Not up or down, just leveled out,
 if I had just one bid.

But since I have no magic prop to
 make my wish come true,
I'll leave it to the power above to
 grant my wish for you!

Margaret Gaffney
REUNION
Bach and St. Gaudens—
Washington and Highland Park—
The Symphony and Belle Isle—
Wasn't it yesterday?
It couldn't have been fifty years.
 The voice on the phone
 Recalled instantly—
The empathy of our minds,
The sympathy of our hearts.
We've seen each other twice?
 thrice?
 In half a century.
We had once found each other.
Forever—the discovery
Made the world a wider place.
Always a symphony of thoughts
 traveled

Traveled between us.
Where once we were lonely in
 our interests
Magically there was another
Whose mind stretched in the
 same direction.

Kelly K. Johnson
NATURE'S CAPTIVE
Our noble sun
locked behind the prison bars
protesting at the isolation

screaming for attention
but to no avail,
the law abiding clouds
will not leave their post.

Leslie DeLeon
TENDER WORDS
Tender words
Spoken softly
Lite upon the ear
As does a snowflake
Gently
Mellow
Melting into the soul
Warming the heart

Katherine M. Schmidt
Welcome Little Stranger
Welcome Little Stranger
Into Our World Today—
A Place Where You Will Live
 And Play

We Know You Lived In Heaven
With The Angels Before Birth—
Because You Brought A Piece Of
 It
Right Down To Us On Earth

You Have The Deepest Bluest
 Eyes
And You're Baby's Smiles So
 Sweet—
A Bundle Of Joy For Us To Love
From Your Head To Your Tiny
 Feet

Your Mommy And Daddy Are So
 Happy—
Their Heads Are In A Whirl—
To Think They Are The Parents
Of A Bouncing Baby Girl

So Chubby Little Stranger
Over You We Make This Fuss—
Because The World's A Brighter
 Place
Now That You're Here With Us

Lanny Parker
Darkness Comes Too Soon
On a cool late August evening,
 seasoned by change,
They stroll along their

landscaped grounds,
prize of labored years.

With Stetson and brown suitcoat,
Once handsomely new on Sunday
morning,
Now worn and faded with age,
Thin and frail with unsure step,
He fears the final breath too
soon.

With a jacket for the fall
Over brightly colored top,
Confident and determined,
Spirited heels away,
She turns to pause for him.

The sunset in her eyes
suspends the darkness
They know is sure to come
to him too soon.

Terry Steele Pearson
SPECIAL

I wish someday I could be
someone
even if it was just for one day,
or just to be happy for what I am
doing things my own way

Lord, you know I try to be special
I even cry sometimes at night,
things never seem to go my way
nothing ever seems just right

Lord, I'd like to tell someone I
love him
I can never find the words to
say,
Please tell him how much I love
him
and make me special for just
one day

Julie M. Shindel
The Burdens We Bear

One night I stood surrounded by
darkness,
And my soul cried aloud from
despair,
But all I could hear was my echo;
I assumed that nobody was there.

So I stumbled down a rocky
pathway,
But the path seemed to reach a
dead end.
Suddenly I was surrounded by
strangers;
People that I once knew as my
friends.

They looked down upon my
battered conscience
But did not see the pain that was
there.
They said, "We could have told
you this wasn't the way,"
And tried hard to convince me
they cared.

I asked them, "Where were you
when I cried aloud
And could not see the light of the
day?"
No answers, just blank empty
faces,
And from there they just faded
away.

But I still can hear their bitter
voices,
And my conscience still aches to
this day.
No one ever asks why I did it;
Even if they did, what could I say?

That I stood all alone in the
darkness
And could not see which way I
should go.
I'm sure they would not
understand it;
I'm sure that they never will
know.

Oh the burdens we bear as we
struggle through life
Seem to grow with each step of
the way.
The mistakes we have made we
can never undo,
Yet sometimes we continually
pay.

Blanche W. Turner
MIGRATION

*[To George, my husband, who
believes I am a poet.]*
Across the sky in perfect V
They pass in pure cacophony.
They honk their joy for all to
hear,

Their destination very clear.
They travel to a distant goal,
By charts engraved upon the soul.

Lee Long
A MEMORY AWAY

How fast the time, How slow the
walk,
A need to talk and to be heard,
A need to know that someone
cares
And be there in time of need,
Remember when? I think I do,
But I'd like to talk it out with
you.
To relive it play by play
Cause it's not so long ago
It's just a memory away.

Carolyn Markel Giles
MY SON

*[To my son, Samuel, without
whom this poem could not
have been written.]*
My son you left, I don't know
why.
Maybe you thought it the only
way.
Did you not know, any problem
No matter how big can be worked
out.
Did you not know that when we
advise,
We do because we love you so.

It isn't easy to watch a son grow
From a baby to a young man.

So many times when I saw you
hurt
I wanted to protect you from the
world.
Did you not know that when you
hurt,
I hurt just as much as you.

I know, you have all the answers.
I did too when I was young.
Oh, if only you could know what
I do,
And were still the age you are.
You could set the world on fire.
So come home, my son, we need
you so.

Timothy Fullerton
**A Funeral: All Deposit—No
Return**

Pausing now,
along the way,
taken from the clock
is the tyranny of its' hands.
I am alone this summersong
day . . .
this day of my going away.
Lifting the veils from off my
heart . . .
I'm Free!
Free!
Ah, sweet freedom . . . Sweet
God!!!
Running now, on the wings of
summerwind,
kissing the faces of a
hundred thousand clouds—
crossing the skies on airy feet,
I danceaway,
danceaway,
danceaway—Gone!
Starbourne lightening,
off somewhithertime, anew,
and all you'll hear
are my cries and songs of
joy,
like half forgotten laughter,
far off,
down the summers'
wind.

Rose M. Queen
RIP VAN WINKLE

I almost feel like Rip Van Winkle
But the day will come when I
awake
And all the days spent in bed
Will vanish—and health again
partake

Susan A. Lynch
You Really Are Gone

I still can't believe it's true
I had fallen in love with you.
You were always on my mind,
We were together most of the
time.
It was like a dream come true,
I really had you.
But then that dream had
disappeared
And you were gone.
You left me nothing to carry on.
I still can hear those great old
songs,
And I sometimes wonder if our
love
Was ever so wrong.
You came into my heart, and lite
it up,
But soon after, everything fell
apart.
I was crying, you were dying.

It couldn't be true, but I was
losing you.
I was so happy, you were so glad.
But now, we both are just so sad.
I am here, but you are gone,
But as they say, life carries on.
So you go your way and I'll go
mine,
And maybe we will meet again,
In some other place at some other
time.

Estelle Clark
SPOTLIGHT

Through the window,
The sunlight shines of me.
Now I see you,
Standing there beside the tree.

The wind is blowing harder now.
The world waits silently,
For the girl who someday will
become,
Just what she wants to be.

With songs of summer days,
Dreams of standing on the stage,
Telling stories of how she,
Made all this come to be.

The audience is quiet.
As the tears roll down her face,
The memories will tell her,
Of the dream she had to chase.

We know it isn't over.
And the best part of it all,
Is knowing she'll have everything,
The spotlight will allow.

Adele Walik
NATURE'S WONDERS

*[To those who inspired me—
my children, Bernard, Stephen,
Michael, Karen, Alison and
James.]*
The shifting sand from
the rolling waves
The flowers and the bees
and the honey he craves
The ripple in the pond
from the thirsty dragon flies
Just some of nature's wonders
I take in with my eyes.
The laughter of the children,
playing in the park
The beauty of the sunset
as it starts to get dark,
The emerging of a butterfly
The cocoon as it dies
Just some of nature's wonders
I take in with my eyes . . .

Linda Byer
GENERATION GAP

You just don't understand, she
yelled
While stamping out the door
You're much too old to bridge the
gap
Or even know the score
Old fashioned is the word for you
You don't know what it's like
To be a teen, how could you
know
You're always so uptight
You never let me do my thing
Or give me half a chance
To get involved with all my
friends
Or stay out late and dance
You're far too strict, nobody else
Has rules the way I do
My friends all laugh and

mock at me
And all because of you!
Why can't I be like all the rest,
Freedom is my right
I'm old enough to have my say
And stay out late at night.
I'm now fifteen she hollered loud
And slammed on out the door.
I'm much too old to understand
You see, I'm thirty-four.

Mrs. Nannie Brown Christian
SNOW SNOW SNOW
Crunch, crunch went the ice on
    the snow
As I placed each foot cautiously
    and slow
The streets were like a skating
    rink
With cars creeping along to avoid
    a kink.
The city looked like a picture
    post card,
Showing trees and bushes dusted
    with snow
While rays of sun added to their
    glow.
The mounds of powdered-like
    sugar on the tops of buildings
Formed geometric shapes and
    designs
Leaving an impression of beauty
    in mind.
People were bundled up from the
    numbing cold
Trying to reach their destination
Before hazardous conditions
    unfold.

Deborah Hayton
NATURE'S LIQUID
Water
    it gurgles and whispers in a
    brook;
    it yells and laughs in a river;
    it shouts and roars in the
    ocean.
Water
    it engulfs beaches at high tide;
    it swallows people and homes
    in hurricanes;
    it gobbles people, homes, and
    land in floods.
Water
    it is rain springing everything
    to life;
    it is snow covering everything
    in a white blanket;
    it is sleet protecting everything
    in a smooth, icy sheet.
Water
    it is cool,
    it is fun,
    it is dangerous,
    it is unfair!

Missie Hardaway
GOOD—BYE
I guess this is good-bye
Lord knows I've tried
If I ever said
I didn't love you I lied

We had something special
As it lasted that night
Even though I knew it wasn't
I felt it was right

The joy that final night
And the sadness the next day
Made me realize how
I could love in this way

There's something I'll say
Just before I go
I'll love you forever
I want you to know

LeeAnn Malfetti
DIVORCE
*[I would like to dedicate this
book to my Mom and Dad.]*
What's the big idea about
    divorce?
Two people breaking up, of
    course.
The letting go of each other;
To leave all the fighting behind
All the tension headaches in your
    mind

But the children are the ones who
feel the pain; the hurt.
Not the wife, Sue, nor the
    husband, Burt.
The hurt is all ours.

Midge Hasenbank
BEING USED
*[Dedicated to my mother, Alice,
my father, Erwin, and my sister,
Shirley; to Cliff Richard and Bill
Latham, whose book, "Which
One's Cliff?" inspired it; and
most of all to God, The
Inspiration.]*
No one likes to be taken
    advantage of;
No one likes to be used.
The very thought of it evokes
    anger,
Greed, lust, and being abused.

Being used by the Lord
Is not like that at all.
He knows and loves us too much.
To treat us like robots or dolls.

No, it's always at God's expense
When He chooses this self of mine.
    To do His work and serve Him
Brings complete fulfillment
    divine.

Zerva Glasscock
UNIQUE
Thank God, there is no other you
    but you!
I would not ever have another
    reach the height of my desire.
I would not ever look aside and
    see a single replica of you in
    any being's face.
God keep you always
    thus—unique
And drawn apart from all the
    world beside.

Selfishly, I'd keep you all for me,
And find in you my solace and
    my pride—
The compliment of all my better
    self.

Mary Ann Turner
FOREVER DREAM
Eternity is a forever dream away,
A quiet restless tomorrow of
    forgotten songs,
An everlasting evening turning to
    day,
Help me to forget tomorrow and
    its endless dream,
Help me to leave behind the
    yesterdays eating at
my mind,
Cause life can never be as it was
    or as it seems,
Today isn't a dream of yesterday
    or a yesterday
of tomorrow,
It is all there is of ever and all
    there'll ever be,
Tell me you love me and need
    me,
And I'll believe once again in
    tomorrow,
And all my doubts will never be!

Amelia Davis-Horne
OLD HAT
There hangs that old hat you
    wear.
Your army surplus store bargain.
You walked in with that
    wide-brimmed
    straw tilted like a Panama
And that band!
It makes me smell coconut oil
    and surf.
Even after the puppies
    played tag with it in the
    yard,
It still hangs there in the door
Looking like it has lost its
    scarecrow,
Waiting for you to pass by.

Cynthia Broudeur
TEDDY BEAR
You stayed by my side through
    all darkness
    And kept all evil away from
    me.
You gave me your shoulder
    through all sadness
    And comforted my broken
    heart so tenderly.
Through all of my life you were
    there
    You know how much I love
    you, my teddy bear.

Irene Bailiff Collins
BELOVED GRANDMA
Th., May 13

Like a new leaf on a seedling
pounced upon by rain—
You lie there day by day
twisted by your pain.

Once as strong as an oak,
you stood so bold and tall—
The ax of life is falling,
on you it's taking its toll.

So wearied from your struggle,
knowing not—"Should I live or
    die?"
Watching you is so painful—
we can't help but wonder "Why?"

There are many who are praying
for relief for your withered limbs.
We must keep the faith
    regardless,
and put all our trust in Him.

Fri., May 14

The last verse now is written—
she's at peace; she's done her part.
Our fortress and our stronghold—
she's alive in all our hearts.

All My Love
Irene Maria, 1982

Dawn M. Blackburn
JUST FOR YOU
I've looked and beheld beauty all
    around
    me.
I've trusted and found that friends
    surround
    me.
I've tried and found the journey
    half as
    long.
I've listened and heard life's
    beautiful
    song.
I've helped and found it pays to
    go the
    extra mile.
I've shared and received a
    precious little
    smile.
I've dreamed and found that
    dreams still come
    true.
I've searched and discovered
    something I
    never knew.
I discovered that nothing is more
    precious
    than the love I've found in
    you.

Alicia Kay Swaney
THE ANGEL
*[To my mom and dad, and all
those who encouraged me.
Also, to anyone who needs
something to believe in.]*
In a soft, somber light he did
    appear,
dressed all in white, so clean and
    clear.
An angel of truth and justice,
to make a once sad life, new;
By making the person he was
    meant for,
realize all that was true.

Be honest with yourself he did
    say,
and always remember serentiy
    comes
from your very own heart, soul,
    and mind.

With this he left saying,"Call and
I shall come, find troubles
and I shall be there, and always
believe and I will be real!"

B.J. Granger
CHILD OF DIVORCE
A little boy small and alone
No one to call friend, no place to
    call home
A tiny tear stains his cheek
Is he too strong, or too weak
A confused child of yesterday
Into tomorrow he must find his
    way

There seems to be no one to
guide his step
No place for him to be kept
All the secrets locked inside his
mind
If only the answers he could find
Mother hold him near
Teach him not to fear
Daddy take time to listen now
Teach him not to cry somehow
Love is the answer, of this be sure
For love is God's own miraculous
cure
Lest that troubled child of today
Becomes tomorrows man gone
astray
So Mother hold him near
Teach your son not to fear
Daddy take time to listen now
Teach your son not to cry
somehow

Barbara A. Solomon
OUT IN THE BACK YARD
Back there,
    in the back yard,
    there's not very much
    to be seen.
    I grow up there, scuffling
    pecans and leaves.
I picked the pecans,
    patiently,
    waiting for more to fall
    from the tree.
Being less than five feet
    tall, I was
    unable to reach the branches
    that hung.
I recall not seeing much
    out there.
But . . .
    an old green hose,
    attached to the faucet;
    an old bottle, buried,
    in the mud.
And . . .
    a small red bird,
    whispering a melody.
On the side of the fence
    there were three rugs,
    two red and one yellow,
    where a husky white cat
    often slept.
Each day,
    many airplanes flew
    back and forward,
    leaving the smell of gases
    and polluting the air.
I can remember it all,
    out there,
    in the back yard.

Barbara Permenter
NIGHT
The day is over
The sun is setting
Night is nearly here
With its cold black darkness
And strange wierd sounds
That so many people fear
The stars and the moon have
    little effect
On this big dark empty space
It comes in ever so quietly
With a sinister darkness and
    grace

Shirley M. Leiter
SEARCHING
The valley had darkened
Your life and mine,
When we both knew

That you were blind
Oh why, we asked
Of God that day
To punish us
In this cruel way?

Oh— not to see
The earth and sky,
Or even people
As they pass by

This burden seemed
So much to bear
After talking with God
We knew he cared

There is more to life
Than just to see,
Listen to me
And I'll set you free

Your task on earth
Has just begun,
Help others gain
By what you've done.

We thank you God,
What can we say,
A bit of doubt
Got in our way.

We'll follow you,
To lead us on
No matter what,
Our Faith is strong.

Sandra S. Meier
MEMORIES
Pictures of a memory, moments
    in the mind.
        All going back to another
        place and time.

Missing so and longing for the
    one that you love,
        Knowing that they've gone
        away—somewhere up above.

Time will erase the pain, but not
    the love inside.
        For that was something you
        both shared which *never* has
        to die.

Thomas R. Boughan
JANUS
Janus sits at the portal
Looking at the mortal
Moving towards him.
Janus can look at the past
And at the future.
The mortal only knows that once
He is past the door of Janus,
He can never return.
The mortal has only dim
    memories
Of portals of Janus past,
Before becoming immortal.
Time blows by
Like a gentle spring breeze.

Barbara Lorraine
AN UNFINISHED WALK
I started walking down a road
"It's the wrong way" I was told
By everyone who passed me by
The dust swirled up into the sky
And as I walked, my doubts and
    fears
Began to ring about my ears

Before I walked down very far
Some people shouted from their
    car
"Go Home! Cause here you won't
    exist"

I thought their wisdom, far
    subsist
To any that I might possess
From any part of my life yet

I turned around, just like they
    said
And look behind me now, instead
Oh someday maybe, there's a way
To walk again, like that first day
But it's not the time for me to
    think
Of walks, which now may be
    extinct

Marsha Hays Belanger

Marsha Hays Belanger
ARISE
[To Jesus who is the Giver of
all good gifts. To my Daddy,
Purdy Hays, who inspired me
with his love for the Lord. To
Wanda Lopez, a friend for
whom the poem was written.]
A beautiful feeling came
    When I realized
Jesus never left me
    He spoke and said, "Arise"

Arise and let my Spirit
    Guide you every day
Arise and be the victor
    Strength will come your way

Arise and come rejoicing
    The battles will subside
Arise and bravely run the race
    Walk closely by my side

Arise and let my Comforter
    Heal your broken heart
Arise and be the eagle
    Your strength will not depart

Arise and face your trial
    With gladness every day
My love will never fail you
    My Spirit always stay.

Richard D. Cagg
DAWN OF THE AGE
Misunderstanding stared over the
    pool of the beyond
Even so reality closed in—for
    truth had not yawned

A companion close by his side
    stood
Kindness and compassion flowed
    without a hood
Warmth and understanding
    seemed to be in demand
As toward the other each reached
    a hand

Then as clouds built cities in
    sunset skies

The wonder of it all filled my
    eyes
Instantly a beginning came
    toward an ending
Leaving my senses bewildered
    and unbending

So did truth emerge upon me
Granted me wisdom that I might
    see
The blossoms that this dawn of
    the age
Instilled within—peace, joy, and
    love instead of rage

John A. Stewart
THE STORM'S FURY
The heavens were in an angry
    mood—
        The clouds were coming all
        unglued—
Flashes were lighting up the sky
        With ominous rumblings
        echoing by.

A flash that started in the East
    Spread out and hardly
    seemed to cease—
The earth was lit as by a flare—
    The trees were moving here
    and there.

The clouds were moving to and
    fro—
        It seemed they knew not
        where to go—
They slowly formed into a
    cone—
        The low sound changed into
        a moan.

The moan soon changed into a
    roar
        Like a giant knocking at the
        door;
The twister missed us, but was
    close—
        With minor damage at the
        most.

I never will forget the fear
        That held me when the
        storm was near.
That was when I learned to
    pray—
        He must have heard me on
        that day.

Georgia Starns Hill
Imagination and Words
[Thinking of you, Jerry.]
Imagination—
    will move any mountain.
Or turn—
    skies from blue to gold.

As words—
    will move an emotion;
Melting a heart—
    that once was cold.

Mary Dee Massey
Flight Into Realistic Fancy
I took a flight on the Lord's Day
His beauty to behold.
The squares, angles and colors of
    greens and browns,
So beautifully arranged in a huge
    linoleum on the ground.
Amidst' the splendor as I took my
    flight,
I saw God's heavens pure and
    white.
And, as I gazed out over the wing
    of the plane,

I saw white dunes, again and
again.
I could imagine God on his
throne,
And myself an intruder, 'way up
there alone.
Alone? . . . No! If this man-made
craft could scale the air,
Who could doubt that God was
there?

On my return the scene was
changed,
From white above to dark
Instead of beauty, a sadness
touched my heart.
For on the floor were lights for
miles,
Glaring white, red, green and
gold . . .
Reminding me of pagan worship
in far away days of old;
Displaying their glamour like
Jezebel there,
With gold all braided in her hair.
Maybe the green was her eye
shadow,
The red her fingers and toes;
Or maybe, someone else, a
christian, by name, who knows?

How long, O Lord, till thy
patience shall exhaust?
And stretching forth thy silent
hand,
Not wanting that any should be
lost,
When all the grandeur man has
hand-tooled,
Shall be made thy everlasting
footstool.

Doris L. Quincy
SO CAME THE NIGHT
The desperate arms of night
clutched at the day
    Pulling it beneath the
    mountains far away,
And there it sank so softly in the
sea
    And vanished from my sight
    mysteriously.

"Oh lovely day why did it have to
be?
    Couldn't you have lingered
    just a while with me
To let me bask in all your beauty
wide
    With daytime birds and
    flowers at my side?"

My heart is sad, my eyes are
filled with tears;
    I think of all the sunsets
    through the years
So beautiful, the artist tried in
vain
    To paint their beauty—time,
    and time again;
And fail he must because no
brush can paint
    The beauty of a sunset or a
    Saint.

Nora M. Keeling
ONCE
Once I loved you so very much.
Your kind voice and your gentle
touch.
I loved your big beautiful smile.
Loved to be with you, if just for a
while.
I loved your sexy, blue eyes.

I even loved your pretty lies.
I loved the feel of your strong
hand.
I loved to walk with you barefoot
in the sand.
I loved to sit with you and have a
drink.
I loved to hold you and not have
to think.
I loved the smell of your
cologone.
I loved to simply talk to you on
the phone.
Yes, once I had so much love for
you.
Once I even thought you loved
me, too.
Once seems like so long ago.
So many things have changed I
know.
If you are ever feeling lonely or
blue.
Remember, once, someone really
loved you.

Emily Bolt
GOLDEN RAIN
*[To My dearest Aunt Hilda,
June 13, 1980—Haailom,
Holland]*
I sit amidst your Living Room
With spheres of Love and Joy
Wrapping me gently as we share
the morning light
Which falls softly upon
the Golden Rain

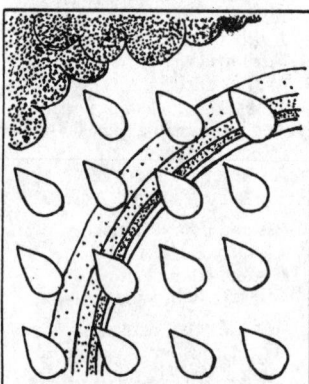

In mornings early light drifting
through the window
We talk of things of hearts
delight
Of misty hues and Love's sweet
smiles
As Life's illusions pass us by

Jeffrey Manigault
MY OWN LITTLE WORLD
I sometimes feel myself slipping
into my own little world
A world of peace, love, joy and
lots of pretty girls
The world I drift into from time
to time
Never have muggers, killings or
any other kind of crime
This world that I think of is not
very hard to find
All I have to do is sit back and
open up my mind
This world I think of lives deep
down inside
And all it takes for me is a short
little ride
Too bad the world around me

isn't really like this
That's why I dream of the good
things that I really miss
This world I think of is like a
clam and a pearl
Because this is my own private
little world.

Rosemary Whitlock
HATE
My heart took down the sign,
stating,
For rent Room and Board.
My heart put up a new sign,
stating,
No Vacancy.
My new tenant was Hate.
It lived and fed within me,
Embedded like a cankerous sore,
It coiled within my being,
Ready to strike, to pummel,
Its intended victim, who
Never came to call and I
Became its victim.
I rented Hate room and board
And my occupant devoured Me.
There is nothing left except
Decay.

Molly Jevne Pennock
UNSPOKEN PASSION
Deep inside
where my heart lives,
love traces
on memory's walls
silent messages
only the mind's eye can read.
The well-kept secrets
carved within its chambers,
an epitaph of my unspoken
passion.

Dirk M. Engelhardt
The Fifth Avenue Queen
Chuckie was just a pawn in the
machine,
Known all over as the Fifth
Avenue Queen.
His business took him through
the hot sweaty nights,
For those of us who had eyes on
different sights.
With his eyebrows plucked and
doused in perfume,
His mind resembled your upstairs
deserted room.

It's all happenin' here on the street;
Little kids cryin', women to meet.
Car lights flashin' in the night,
Kings on the left, Queens on the
right.

It was cool and starless on April
the fifth,
When Tommy finished his work
on the graveyard shift.
She caught Tommy's eye on 6th
and Main,
How was he to know that she
would cause him pain.
He thought his paycheck could
take them through the paces,
Hand in hand they headed for the
"Hotel of the Aces".

It's all happenin' here on the street;
Little kids cryin', women to meet.
Car lights flashin' in the night,
Kings on the left, Queens on the
right.

What happened next could never
be told,

It's the same old story, whenever
souls are sold;
Some make their fortunes by
rolling the dice,
Others have kids and a spouse
that's nice.
Poor Chuckie couldn't make it
this far,
Due to his quirks and an unlucky
star.

It's all happenin' here on the
street;
Little kids cryin', women to meet.
Car lights flashin' in the night,
Kings on the left, Queens on the
right.

Evelyn Judy Regulus
SERENE NIGHTS
Starlight.
Very nice!
The moon slithers over the
waters.
The woods are still.

Whispering wind
Rustling trees
The homes are dark.
A cat creeps.

Black foliage
Silver moon
The night is lovely
In its darkened room.

Evelyn Sewell Rineer
AUTUMN
*[One thing you can give away,
Keeping not a part, Give it all
to someone else, And still
retain:—Your heart!]*
Who is to say the brown leaf dies,
Although, indeed, it falls to
ground?
Ah, yes, it breaks, crumbles, and
dries,
But darkly damp, as much, is
found.

Over and over, its cycle goes,
Giving its body as mulch and
food,
To nurture life of all that grows,
Which in the spring will be
renewed.

Who is to say the brown leaf dies?
Cling not, oh last leaf, to the tree,
Blow gently down through
autumn skies,
And take your place in life to be.

Margaret A. Hiatt
COLD ASHES
I am aware
Of empty house, of rooms so bare.
Alone, now with the dog, I wait,
For laughter soft, or words irate,
For rock beat of stereo—
And distant strains of radio,
For slamming doors
And friendly conversation,
For steps on floors,
For exhuberant elation
Of youth. I look
For remnants—gloves, boots, an
open book,
Some ribbon, Christmas wrap, a
tag that's signed with love,
A dead sprig of mistletoe above
The door—the falling branches of
the tree.

Through it all, I see

Today's Greatest Poems

Their smiling faces, happy in
their own realms now.
Away from me, they somehow
Seem to manage and I am glad
That they have come into their
own, and for the years I had.
Looking for her charges, Heidi
goes from room to room.
Like me, she has a sense of gloom
Of her future usefulness and
worth—
Of having purpose here on earth.
My Christmas memories, time
can't erase.
Their sweetness I'll ever hold
But now, my heart like the ashes
in the fireplace,
Is cold.

Anna K. Bingham
NATALIE
*[My granddaughter, Natalie
Dahlberg, who was found
slumped over her toy box . . .]*
I saw a little girl crawling on the
ground—
With beryl eyes gazing all around
A wisp of hair fell so gently
there—
from her golden crown
A tear wavering on her cheek—
A drop fell to the ground
Her little hand outstretched
reaching . . .
When she pats your face
What a joy it is to be endorsed
by her embrace
May you in God's eternal grace
forever be—
And that I in this moment
knew you would be taken
away from me!

Nelson Edward Smith
WITH THIS PEN
With this pen, My Love, I send a
treasured word or two,
To express the joy, that I do feel,
whenever I hear from you.
Sweet words that tell me of your
love, sweet words I cannot find,
To tell you of the love I feel
within this heart of mine.
If words should come to me, so
free, as to some they do,
I'd tell you of the way I feel, and
my love for you.
In words the world should nere
forget, but ever hold so dear;
To woo the hearts of those they
love, whenever they be near

Deanne Mintz,
HUMAN OF THE YEAR
Will you be elected?
look in the mirror, like what you
see
that's your only choice
your decision means nothing
now.

What time is it?
Who will win if not you?
You can't win, if it isn't realistic
remember reality, it's your whole
life.

Victory, will it beckon to you?
Or have you lost the game,
At least you tried, isn't that all
that matters?
Next time you'll succeed, so till
then.

Will you be elected?
Man of the year? The ideal
person?
Then they'll all look up to you,
and be taught to admire what
they see.

Look again in the mirror,
you like what you see
you're man of the year now,
you've won
maybe next year you'll be king.

Gather your prizes, you're the
proud
the losers feel defeated
but you're on a cloud
I'm not impressed, I'm sorry,
because you've got a long way to
go before you become
something that does impress me,
the ultimate title;
Human of the year.

Kate Gebler
RUN AWAY
You want to go away and hide.
Hiding place, there is not such a
place.
Every place you go, every place
the same.
First you have to find yourself.
The hiding place is in your heart.
You first start looking there.
And loving yourself and loving
others.
You find the joy you're looking
for.
The hiding place is in your heart.
Right here, where you belong.
So don't plan to run away.
There is no place you can hide.
Every place you go, every place
the same.
You stop, and find, first yourself
right in your heart.

Kendall Wade Youmans
THE ONLY TEST
The only test
that man must pass
is an exam of total humanity.
What is holding back
his passing grade
is indifference, greed and vanity.
To graduate to the future,
he must study the past,
and when he uses his notes of
history
He can't take this test too fast.

Laura Mitchell
Tell Me Something Special
*[This is for my dear friend
Mandy, to whom I am known
as Elderina. She often
understands me better than I
understand myself.]*
Tell me something old,
Tell me something new,
Tell me something special
That means a lot to you.

As young as we are now
We will not always be.
We've still so much to learn,
And so many sights to see.

I know that you're confused,
Believe me, so am I.
If you need someone to talk to,
You know I'll be nearby.

Our friendship is quite special,
And means a lot to me.

The ties that bind us are stronger
Than those which people can see.
You know that whatever may
happen
I'll always be your friend.
When you need a shoulder to cry
on,
Forever upon me you can depend.

Fifty years from now,
When we're both old and gray,
We'll smile as we remember
The things we said today.

Tell me something old,
Tell me something new,
Tell me something special,
I'll always listen to you.

Yvonne G. Vorel

Yvonne G. Vorel
DENNIS
*[To my son Dennis Black for
brightening my days and
bringing joy to my heart.
Love, Mom]*
I cannot figure out just why,
It's difficult for me—
To write a loving, touching poem,
For Dennis, born so free.
I wish I had his energy—
For just a day or two,
I'd clean our house, garage and
car,
So they would shine like new.
If energy could be harnessed,
And a generator made,
He could light up half a city,
Like an electric renegade.
Denny's blessed with wit and
wisdom,
Though we question it
sometimes—
He is still a rather young lad,
With maturity, he'll be fine.
His blue eyes bright and cheerful,
Seem to twinkle like the stars—
When he smiles, we smile with
him,
So proud to say he's ours.
Tis said by unimportant few,
The boy is such a menace—
But we do surely thank our Lord,
For giving us our Dennis.

Glory M. Osborn
A POSTHUMOUS CHILD
Decals of red-nosed clowns and
dancing bears, pastel colored
walls and shiny new toys,
adorn a room where the
blessings of parentage lies
asleep in his crib.

The consummate reality of love's
labor fulfilled is at peace with
both heaven and earth. While
the world around him is
troubled and torn, in slumber,
he is protected from those who
impose.
A young mother cries and beats
on her breast for answers to
prayers that nobody hears. She
enters the room where life has
begun and silently beholds her
new comfort and strength.
The demon-war has reaped its
toll, in a senseless waste of
human flesh. A posthumous
child lies asleep in his crib, his
father has died, in hope he'll be
free.

Georgie Knipp Martin
INDIAN PIPE
From the memories of the past
And the shadows that they cast
There is a pale spirit form
Yearly born.

In the mossy woods it springs
Where the cheery wood wren
sings
And the tears of dawn are shed
On its bed.

'Tis Indian Pipe of Peace
And on life it takes a lease
For in late spring of the year
Doth appear.

It is like a forest sprite
In its garb of waxy white
And deep-gleaming in its bowl
Lies a coal.

Shirley Sabiston-Stenabaugh
DAVID
If you call my name, and—
I'm not there
Look up to Heaven, and—
Whisper a Prayer.
To you, GOD will send down
His wonderful Love,
While Peace and Contentment—
to His up above.

If you call my name, and—
I'm not there
Think of the good times we used
to share
For when we depart this life, for
another
We don't really leave, we—
draw closer together

If you call my name, and—
I'm not there
Just stop, and look around you,
I'M EVERYWHERE!!!

Suzanne Kaye Wilson
SHARING
*[To my Mom, Dad, and
husband, Robert, who have
given me inspiration, courage,
and love.]*
Reach out and take my hand in
yours
We'll walk along the stream,
And talk of days when we were
young
When life seemed like a dream.

We'll share a song and tale or two
Of how quickly life went by,
And watch the clouds drift
overhead
Against the deep blue sky.

We'll listen to a mourning dove
Cooing for her mate,
Then lie upon the cool sweet
    grass
In a dream like state.

We'll watch the sun as it
    descends
Amidst a crimson sky,
And sense the calm that's all
    around
As dusk is drawing nigh.

Reluctantly we'll have to leave
To travel separate ways,
Knowing that with all we shared
We'll return again someday.

Jeannie L. Sa
ODE TO A UNICORN
Oh Unicorn with hooves raised
    high,
Like Pegasus you touch the sky.

I think of you all through the day
And dream of you when in bed I
    lay.

My dreams they take me to a far
    away land,
Where life is peaceful, but not
    too bland.

There in freedom I see you roam
Along with the mythical little
    gnome.

In this place I feel at ease,
As I'm cooled by the summer's
    breeze.

You represent the good and true,
And fondly I will think of you.

Helen Curtis Sheets
SANDS IN THE GLASS
The time allotted us moves swift
The chance to experience it
A gift.

Take care
It's gone before our plans unfold
The list we've labored on
Behold—
Time gone, ended, diminished,
    bare.

If anyone the gift pf sight
To realize how long
The night
The chance to live out full the
    patterned squares
Our own unique life, loves, and
    cares.

Dora Kirk
It's Later Than You Think
*[To my daughters, Kathleen,
Colleen and Janeen—who like
me are dreamers and for
dreamers, time stands still.]*
This somber thought came to me
    today,
    That time in measure is
    fleeting away,
The ways are numberless, to
    mention a few,
As life is recorded for me and
    for you.

Time is a thief who comes with
    the night,
    And today is tomorrow, when
    comes the light.
A young womans beauty is short
    to behold,
    It robs from a young man,
    making him old.

The hands on the clock are but
    shadows of time,
    Marking the hours of your life
    and mine.
We'll live for today as we sit in a
    dream,
    And the sands through the
    hourglass steadily stream.

Do we idle along as it slips
    through our hands?
Busy with nothing as we make
    our plans,
There must be some changes in
    your life and mine,
    If we're to be known as
    redeemers of time.

Will Reta Hamlin

Will Reta Hamlin
WINDY DAYS
*[To my two sons—Lewis and
Wayne Hamlin.]*
The wind plays little tricks on
    me,
    When I'm on land or on the sea.
It fills the sails of my small boat,
    And helps the waves make me
    float.

It makes my hair blow in my
    face,
    When at my back—helps win
    the race.
If only I could always be—
    In my boat on land or sea.

Daniel John Parisi
NAGS HEAD
(A Sandpiper's Dream)
As sandpipers sweep
near the south-end ridge
swallowing air by the midnight
    sea
a hazy scent of this morning's
    breath

sends salty storms and awakens
    me . . .

Here by the sea
I become a young legend.
Does heaven, I wonder,
stand still in a breeze?
Soon a seagull in wind
        over a sandbar lightly
like an angel of mercy swaying
        sweetly in sight,
calls along to the lovers
far away in the shadows
to abandon the loners and
    surrender to flight.

Here by the sea
sweeping so slowly
a sandpiper's dream of morning—
so lonely.

Susanne Shelledy
THE HARBOR
[To Him—1980]
The morning stillness
sea of eternity

Unwillfully suspended
reflecting two of me

Winds of Love, ring
stays against the mast

By His Will I'll be gone
to be reunited with myself

At last . . .

Kari Ferguson
TRUE LOVE
Love is like a flower
It's endlessly in bloom
You and I, hand in hand
Stand in the light of the moon

We walk in silence
Looking upon the sky;
In the coldness of the night,
With tears in our eyes

The ache in my heart
Is it really true,
Yes, I think I know,
That means, I love you

The sweetness of the flower
Brings a warm scent to the air
It feels so wonderful
To know that you care

The closeness that I feel
When we're together
Makes us become one,
You and I forever.

Lydia Carmichael
The Inheritors of the
World
*[In dedication to Shelton
Wilkerson]*
The inheritors of the world
Sit upon their pedestals
Living with finesse
Shunning publicity

Eccentricity of dress
Complaints of popularity
Playing their games
Done efficiently

Public ceremonies
Immaculately polished
Pageants of the world
With enormous demand

No pretending
Imitation leather
Out of the question
Power's ruling hand

Inheritors of the world
Don't stay upon the mountains
Barriers of paint
Dominant in stand

Stir up the breathless
Honor the few
Extend hunting grounds
To distant lands.

Gary L. Smart
AWAKENING
Distant rumble breaks the
    silence, archway of color all
    aglow,
Warming sun and gentle rains,
    the killing of winter snow.
With gentle rain and warming
    sun, brings the rebirth of
    spring,
The borning of life anew, as do all
    living things.

The breaking of frozen ground,
    where life once hid so deep,
Budding of life anew, that was
    once fast asleep.
Now the hours of darkness
    fading, lightness starts to grow,
Building of life anew, after the
    killing of winter snow.

Blanche Lacquement
ROSE OF FRIENDSHIP
God, with His gentle loving
    hands,
Molded the rose so rare.
He put the thorn upon the bush,
To protect this lovely flower.

The rose blooms in early morn,
And casts it fragrance far and
    wide
But the winds come rushing by,
And strews its petals far and
    wide.

All who see this fragile rose,
So fresh on a summer day.
Alas! its beauty shall soon lie,
Upon the earth in dark decay.

Friendship is a rose so fare,
That blooms throughout the
    years,
But it will neither wither or
    decay,
And thorns will never tear.

The rose God put upon the earth,
Its beauty fleet we see.
But the beautiful rose of
    friendship,
God gave, to last, unto eternity.

Tammy Lea Campbell
THE LAST PRAYER
*[In Memory of Elvin Danny
Langley]*
This is where I walked my miles.
This is all my laughs and smiles.
Now I stay at home and cry.
Lord, why do I have to die?
I haven't been here in two years.
It brings back memories and
    tears.
I'm only thirty-two years old.
I've yet to see my children grow.
It just seems like yesterday when
I would go outside and play.
Now I stay at home and cry.
Why do I have to die?
I used to fish out on the lake.
I used to throw rocks at the
    snakes.

Now I lay down on my bed,
Barely holding by a thread.
Oh, Lord, I'm so afraid to die.
So please listen to my pleading
cry.

Marguerite Herard
THIS BREATH OF LIFE
Indeed with unseen eyes
I feel misery and despair
Till my soul got its fill:
Slaves of modern times
enchained forever,
suffocating
in the hell of progress;
War leftovers,
birth oddities,
irreversible idiocy,
and the doomed for life
whatever cause may be.

Indeed I have observed
so-called streets people
in filthy rags
with vermin infested,
roaming through refuse
in back alleys
for means of survival
and daily bread.
Lifeless faces
grateful for the free sky,
roof over their head!
Stripped of their identity
as nameless objects.
Ghastly creatures
unfit to be cared for
as living beings,
but all
clinging to Dear Life!

Caroline Alley-Hutson
FORBIDDEN NIGHTS
Forbidden nights! Love unfettered
To rest in thee—
Life, to me!

Endless days! Being's untethered
Soul's doth meet
In rapture sweet.

Eternal lives, love in youth
Lay we against sea,
Wind wild, as we.

Passion transitory, youth decay
Love lives on,
Forever rebourne.

Barbara Helen Kriofsky
THE SIEVE OF VANITY
Ever straining out the good
(never sifting out the bad),
the sieve of vanity holds to
anything
that makes itself feel glad.
Never accepting a correction
or allowing a redress,
constantly complaining,
craving nothing but success,
Picayune and selfish,
lifted up with haughty pride:
Whatever does not suit it
is promptly cast aside.
It listens for the chiming
of compliments, so sweet.
It lives to receive flattery
and gifts laid at its feet.
Pampered, adorned,
in selfrighteousness styled:
Never aware that
it has been beguiled.
And so it continues
to sift and to strain
through whatever life brings it,

again and again.
Never relenting
(with self as its goal),
the sieve of vanity performs its
work:
Saving the dross,
Discarding the gold.

Robert Steven Shepard

Robert Steven Shepard
IF ONE IS BORED
*[A tribute to Andrew Mezzetti,
for his encouragement.]*
If one is bored: Do they say, "Oh,
Lord!"
Are they not in accord?
Has their attraction diminished?
Is their sex life all finished?

If one is bored: Can their love
recover,
or will they begin looking at
another?
Have they lost all the highs?
Would you find infidelity under,
"I"?

If one is bored: Have they devour
all their devotion,
or will they start a delibrate
commotion!
Did they not see all the virtues?
What happened to, "You know I
would never hurt you!"

If one is bored: Do they become
vicarious?
Will they forget everything that
was hilarious!
No more inovation.
There's absolutely no more
sensation!

If one is bored: Is understanding
demanding?
Will they continue forever
complaining!
If one is bored: Does all this
mean you?
No, it usually means TWO!

Richard Douglas Hector
GREAT LAKES, ILLINOIS
*[To La Chan—till I'm
sixty-four . . .]*
The no compromise weather
Mother nature flaunts her
authority.
Oh, her gentle generosity in
spring,
Coaxing and cajoling life out of
winter.

The exactitude of summer
Relentless and demanding
like a newly wed on her

wedding night.
The disarming charm of autumn,
Coy and demure, elusive and fleet
Gently craddling our senses
asleep.

The starkness of winter,
the frenzied fury of the wind.
Patiently, inexorably, and with a
final sigh,
the white sheet is drawn over
the face of a caderverous earth,
a world held in suspended
animation
but . . .
In its womb is growing,
the foetus of spring.

Janis M. Kott
DREAM WISHES
I dream of love and tenderness,
of candy canes and tears.
A mixture, full of childhood
dreams,
a memory of fears.

Who knows what minds exist in
mine,
of those who've gone before.
Of lives with happy endings,
and lives who wanted more.

Are dreams a past reality?
Or wishes in a mind?
Are fears just thoughts inside
your head?
Or memories so unkind?

This life I live now, is it mine?
Or yours you wished before?
If so, then could you tell me,
Is this all, or is there more?

Robin Witt
**To Disarm a
Neo-Christian**
Definitely a question of
lens-angles.
One who closes himself
to denials
cannot be the good-dog:
open to completeness,
yet to be resolved.

Granite ideals
cannot be crumbled by
—mere words—
however concrete the
contrariness,
however impassioned the plea.

Gladys Snider
JUST FOR ME
Oh, such beauty of the rising sun
After the breaking of dawn,
The dew on the grass
Sparkling like millions of
diamonds,
Like magic they soon fade away.
The sun set all red and gold
Paints a picture for me to hold.
These things I love, for God made
it all
Just for me.

I love to lay down by a gurgling
stream
Watching sheep in the sky,
walking by
Then I smile and dream awhile.
To see a rainbow after a summer
rain,
Smell the fresh earth, walk
barefoot
Through the dirt.

Wondering how far to the pot of
gold
How long it would take to find,
Then I realize, without a doubt,
It is already mine.

Even a spider weaves a beautiful
web
A pattern of tiny silver threads,
These things I love, for God made
it all
Just for me.

As the snow falls, a blanket it
makes
Sun glistening on ice, reminds me
of
Frostings on Mama's cakes.
After it is dark and the quiet of
the night
Far away a lonesome
whippoorwill cry, Why?

Words can't explain, the feelings
I've gained
These things I love, for God made
it all
and you know, it is all free,
Just for me.

Patricia Dawn Cooper
**I Can Hear The Music,
I Can See The Sky**
My eyes do not see, my ears
cannot hear
But there is nothing on earth I
shall fear.

The Lord is my shepherd, He
guides me along
He's given me life and He's made
me strong.

Through love and faith, I've no
need to ask why
For I *can* hear the music, and I
can see the sky.

Michael Anthony Pelikan
STREET GAMES
Walking on an autumn day,
Battalions of leaves
Rushing across the empty streets,
As if frightened by an unseen
force;
Perhaps the wind,
Which seems to hiss
A menacing tale of summer's
death.

Debra Jean Fortier
THE BEAUTY OF A CHILD
Some grownups find children
Bothersome.
Others, like me,
Disagree.

For who else
But a child would
So readily see the
Beauty in a weed,
Or the delight in the
Act of giving.

Dianne P. Owens
SNOWBIRTH
The ticking of the clock at the
end of the street
Was as quiet as the baby while it
was asleep;
the town slept, too.

The rain that fell as the clock
ticked on
Was as a thief is—unknown;
the town slept, too.

133

The winds that blew and changed
  the rain to snow,
Looking as graceful as any young
  doe;
the town slept,

As the town woke,
The baby cried,
The snow ceased
And the night died.

The clock ticked on.

Frank Lancaster

Frank Lancaster
THE HIGHER CALLING
Leaves falling from an oak tree,
  spreading freckles on the green
Sun smiling through a cloud
  bringing warmth upon the
  scene
White sheep drifting across the
  blue herded by the breeze
Weeping softly as they go,
  shedding tears upon the leaves

Summer is almost over, fall is
  drawing nigh
The reaper with his scyth is
  waiting closely by
Though his face looks very grim,
  he has this job to do
All must return to mother Earth,
  to make room for the new

There is nothing new upon this
  earth, all has been before
The angels smile upon your face,
  while death knocks at your
  door
A thousand years to us, is only a
  day to God
A thousand years we must sleep,
  under the dewey sod

We are all endowed with a duel
  mind, the good and the bad
Possessing earthly and Godly
  traits, the happy and the sad
There is not a perfect man on
  earth, none is good but God
We will awaken in His likeness
  when the spirit leaves the sod.

Katie M. Jones
SPRING WATER
I walk down the hill
And my bucket fill
  With water so pure and clean
This water is good
Best in the neighborhood
  Best in the world that I've seen.

And that is one reason
I come here this season
  To taste of this water so cold

I'ts worth more to me
Than all I can see
  It means more to me than gold.

Gold only can shine
And if it were mine
  It would just lay on a shelf
But this water so good
Does all that it should
  In satisfying one's self.

So please don't deny
This one wish that I
  Have stored away in my heart
Cause this special Spring
Is just one thing
  That I loved from the very
  start.

So let me come here
Year after year
  To taste of this water so cold
And so if I roam
This will always be home
  Where the water runs pure as
  gold.

Carmelita Apodaca
GENTLE STEPS
Pride and Solitude . . .
  Guard the entrance to the
  Pathways of your mind—

Caution . . .
  Guards the entrance to the
  Pathways of your heart—

I will not knock at the door
to the entrance of your mind—
I respect your privacy—I
Respect who you are.

I am knocking at the door
to the entrance of your Heart—
I respect who you are—yet—
I wish—so badly—to

Gently
  Tread and—
  Gently
    Touch—

  The corners of your Heart—
  Just tenderly . . .

L'nore Henry
Saga Of Sun-Dog County
[Neacie Lenora and John Henry
My Parents
Who yearned the best for me]
Tha sun wuz shinin fit ta
  bust. .awl outdors wuz a fog a
  dust. .
Maddnin blast ou summers
  wind. .awf tha sand dunes a
  ushern in. .
In awl tha states ther ain nary. .a
  county so bad as tha dust bol
  ary. .
Ole Lum Willums, pore yearin
  sole. .tregd tha dirt road rutted
  hole. .
Six weery mals from the county
  seat. .an nary a puson did he
  meet. .
Foor long months in tha sharifs
  caboose. .today they cided ta
  turn im loose. .
Ayearin Lum wuz his favord
  name. .and tha mor he walk
  tha yearin came. .
Just for a quart a tha Innians
  brew. .then nother yearin
  grew. .
Lum yearnd for tha the sight a
  Juliany. .left in the care of her

nnian granny. .
Tha thot ou his yungun, sweet
  an fair. .how tha wind whupped
  her fine white hair. .
Tuk place ou tha yearin fo tha
  Innian booze. .an tha road
  towad hom he cided ta
  choose. .
He cotched up a step as he tregd
  tha road. .takin car not to
  tromp a daid horny toad. .
Pore leetle yungun, his thots
  turnin back. .ta tha day they
  tuk im fum tha ol bord shak. .
Her blak eyes sot an starin at his
  haid. .lak a sqaws las look on
  tha lonely daid. .
Bent to the wind lak a thin blade
  a wheat. .that Lum as he lef tha
  county seat.

Frank E. Bubenchik
BLONDIE
Blinding is your long silky hair
  reflecting light.
Luring is your loveliness such an
  angelic sight.
Over snow—capped mountains,
  across stormy seas,
  people travel far to see your
  beauty such a
  picturesque dream.
Night with the twinkling stars
  are like your
  gorgeous bewitching eyes, that
  shine like a
  beacon or beam.
Drawn to your presence from the
  magic melody of
  your soothing voice.
Irresistible are your sweet lips
  tender and moist.
Enchanting is your luminous
  smile, the hearts it
  enlightens by choice.

Mary A. Piotrowski
METAMORPHOSIS
I have loved you from afar—
  You, more distant than any
    space—flung star;
Unknowing, therfore innocent in
  your uncaring of the sharing
  hope of my heart.

Though our paths crossed but
  once,
  and briefly at that, I am
forever changed by your passing.

Phyllis A. Chaffee
TANYA AT TWO
She's a joy to behold,
  A delight to the ear.
She sings and converses
  For all in her sphere.

She wakes early each morning,
  Helps Daddy breakfast prepare.
She calls everyone else,
  Then sits in her chair.

She's a bundle of energy—
  Keeps her Mom on the run
From the time she awakes
  Till the setting of sun.

She loves kitties and birdies,
  Watches squirrels with glee,
Plays in sand on the beach.
  In the wind she runs free.

She's a teaser and pleaser
  When with Sister she plays,

A great baker and maker
  With Dad or Mommy some
  days.

An artist who colors,
  Cuts or draws tree or flower.
She loves games and stories.
  Going to bed takes an hour!

After teeth have been brushed
  And prayers have been said
She clutches her b(l)ank)et
  And curls up in her bed.

Michael C. Gibson
BE NOT GONE II
So now there is naught but Death
  on this Earth
And on this sphere never will be
  seen a new birth
I am alone with the moon to face
  the new dawn
But from the sun comes the
  urge—Be Not Gone

Somewhere is life which wishes
  me near
Who wishes my Love through the
  tear
And as I trudge through what had
  been our birght green lawn
I see her sweet lips mouthing the
  words—Be Not Gone

Am I fooling myself or can this
  be real?
Are the impressions all true that
  my heart does feel?

Am I being used for some
  unknown god's pawn?
Or whoever it is who whipers the
  words—Be Not Gone?

As I cross the seventieth highway
  and watch the sky turn blue
I feel with my heart that my
  quest has come true
I rush to her side just as all the
  heroes do
And she turns to me and
  proclaims—"I dreamt of you!"

So now she rests in my arms as
  we watch the sun go down
And we rejoice in the new world
  we have found
We watch the sky turn black like
  some great cosmic yawn
And the lonely wind whispers in
  our ears—Be Not Gone.

Dwight L. Hutchins
COME WITH ME
Please! let me take you by the
  hand.
I'll guide you gently, lest you
  fall.
We'll pass thru arches to distant
  lands,
  far beyond reality's walls!

The moon and the stars in their
  glory
Will light the way above,
Releasing magic crystals:
And filling the air with love!

We'll fly on the wings of a
  moon—beam,
As we pass thru the clouds on
  high,
And we'll reach the land of our
  farthest dreams,
As we watch the world go by.

As we watch the world go by—
You and I.

Tom Camp
GLORY OF LOVE
For better to have loved and lost,
than not to have loved at all,
You held the glory of love in your
arms, Even if you fell flat on
your face in the fall.

Your spouse is living, Thank
God/ for the time you spend
together,
It's so endearing to have a
helpmate
Both in good and stormy weather.

You and your sweetheart can
each other charm,
Bring out the worst and the best
Are you afraid to fall in love,
because—
Of the commitment you might
have to make
After all, what is love?
But a matter of give and take.

Margaret A. Gannon
JUST FRIENDS
*[L.W.L.—"the memories of
youth and friendships shared
are indelibly etched to remain
with us."]*
The room was large
Not knowing a lot of new faces,
I felt a little uncomfortable, but
then
A dark haired, blue eyed boy
glanced over at me
And he soon asked if I had a
brother
I agreed to his question
And as I did he turned around in
a state of shock
Because of knowing my brother.

Despite the fact of knowing my
brother
We slowly became the best of
friends
Each of us, like everyone, went
through the good times and
bad
We tried to help each other out
of the bad
And we sat and laughed along
with the good.

It's been a few years since that
day
We are still, in our own way,
trying to work out our
differences
We have gone through a lot
together
There were and still are times
when people just don't
understand
We are just friends
But we know that what ever
anyone says, that is all we are
We just have a deep friendship
nothing more, nothing less.

For someday this, like most good
things, must come to an end
This ending is only done with the
power of "Capa de Capa"
But when that day comes
And we start to grow and
separate into our worlds
That is the day I will let go
without fighting the forces

I will just recall the great times
And how I really cared for that
boy
And also how I cared for the
friendship
The friendship I had with that
one special boy.

Susan Brousseau
LITTLE BIRD
Little bird do you know who
made you?
With your fine feathers all neatly
in place,
And glistening beak pecking
eagerly,
Colours etched finely against
your face?

The Great Creator, all wise and
mighty
Set the flight upon your wings,
Racing wildly, gliding smoothly,
Laid the song in your voice that
sings.

You must know how much He
loves you
For every detail He made with
care,
The hollow bones that float on
water,
Soar, on wind and air.

Little bird, so delicate and fragile,
Yet so full of trust in Him,
Fly on, to the outstretched hand,
Of the one who has no sin.

Eugenia Lamson—Small
U.S. FREIGHTER POET
U.S. Freighter poet
Tell us your mystery?
Shall we weep and
Weeping seal your destiny?
Or are far horrizons
Beckoning a heavenly tryst?
Will the sun set on your
Tommorows on some distant
sphere?
Sadly we searched in vain
To solve your mystery;
It would seem perhaps atoms
Never still saught your eternal
sleep,
Forever to plot your course
Amid the fathomless deep.
What shall we write in
Congress' book of history?
U.S. Freighter Poet
Tell us your mystery?

Barbara Nagl
UNTITLED
Solitude can be a blessing or a
curse.
It can envelope you in unearthly
silence,
crushing you with it's force,
Strangling you til you feel you
can't breathe.
But it can also be a healing balm,
blanketing you in warm
silence.
Comforting you 'til you can face
the world again.

Clara M. Bush
WILD WIND
Down from its lair the wild wind
came,
Shaking window and door.
Forceful, surging, endless, pursing.
Helpless forever renewing.

Flying across the meadow
Whirling like a top
Masterless unable to stop
Now gliding across the sand
cones
Still another strip of sky to roam
As if in a flash of anger
It shifts to the ocean
swaying the waters to and fro
Day and nite it blows
Now silent and slow
it drifts across another land
Returning one day form distant
shore
to shake window and door

Ethel Hall White

Ethel Hall White
Look Up To the Flag
When I look up, and see our flag,
I want her to fly forever, and
never sag.
She is flying high, for the world
to see:
She represents freedom, for you
and me,
For she is the symbol, of all our
men,
Who fought and died, our wars to
win.
Yes, our men went proudly off to
war,
Knowing it was freedom, that
they fought for.
And altho, we can't call them
each by name;
We are proud of them, just the
same.
So, when I look up, at our red,
white, and blue;
I just automatically think of you.
Yes, you the men, you are the
greats;
Who preserved our freedom, in
these United States.

Jo Anne Sabalaske
SHATTERED ILLUSIONS
The glass has been shattered, the
image is broken.
We're left standing here as the
broken pieces lie at our feet.
We gather them together,
watching every step of the way
that we are not cut by the
jagged edges.
And our tears continue to flow at
the sight of losing the image
we held for so long.
The illusions are now gone and
we see through to the other
side of reality.
The pain is piercing as if the

rough edges have passed by,
ever so slightly, the outer edge
of our existence.
Still the tears continue to flow
quietly, slowly as our lives are
touched by the sadness of our
broken dreams
And the hopelessness we
sometimes all feel as we
wonder what our lives would
be like if we ceased to dream.
Slowly and carefully we must
pick up the pieces of the
broken dreams
We once left behind and
continue on our way.

Christine Joan Holowaty
YOU'RE NOT ALONE
If you ever feel lost and you're
afraid
and the direction you walk
begins to fade
Just follow me and I'll show you
the way
I would never leave you alone
and astray
Believe in me as I beieve in you
believe in the things you find
hard to do
Only you can change your
direction—your turn
I am here to guide you—to help
you learn
I can't change the way you feel
and I can't change your dreams
to real
Only you can if you want—if you
try
no matter what you decide I'll
help you get by
And if you feel frustrated or a
sense of defeat
believe that it's something that
together we can beat
Don't give up and don't run away
get rid of the worst but you
should stay
You should stay because you
have a full life to live
you have a lot to receive but a
lot you should give
You'll always meet a challenge to
face
but challenge it in your way
and your own pace
I'm with you in whatever you do
but remember I can't make
everything come true
Only you can if you believe—if
you care
but never feel that I've treated
you unfair
And if you're alone just
remember I'm here
to help you—to guide you—to
rid of your fear

Frances P. Hothian
TO DEAR DOTTIE
A poem about my
daughter-in-law
How should I begin?
Maybe I should start by saying,
She has always been a friend.

I believe our feelings were mutual
Right from the very start,
As time went on the feeling
changed
To caring from the heart.

She has been the perfect wife

To my son who thinks so too,
Which makes me very happy;
For her, there is nothing— I
wouldn't do.

She calls me on the phone real
often
I live quite far away;
In fact, it is another State
But we have so much to say.

I learn a great deal from her,
Her interests spread wide and
far.
She is a leader, not a follower,
To me, she is a "Shining Star."

Anita Chandler-Stankiewicz
DISCOVERY
With all I have lived, and all I
have died . . .
All that I've loved, and all I
have cried . . .
Somewhere inside me a strength
came to grow . . .
For now I've discovered—it's
"me" that I know.

It's taken forever—to even begin
To conquer the battle that's
raged deep within . . .
Where no one would venture—
for no one could see
The fight I've been winning
. . .the "secrets" of me.

I know there is beauty in each
day I live . . .
With each life I touch I bring
something to give;
My riches are blessings—not
money, or things . . .
I'ts good to be part of the life
each day brings.

Altho there were times . . . and
will be again . . .
When all seemed so dark—I'll
try to think when
The paths that I've chosen, I felt
had to be . . .
I'm thankful I followed . . .
they led straight to "me" . . .

Ethel Voss Palmer
**Young Love—Remember
Me Like This**
*[Dedicated to Charlie and Bud
and Janis]*
I loved you bright as stars at
night and wondered as I did so,
For here was love a glorious
thing, given us fresh as Gods
own spring—
Too young to know just what we
had, but now my dear aren't
you glad?

We have known a love some
never know; a lovely blushing
thing.
Always fresh and so unspoiled,
held deep inside and now with
pride
Meant for us to call on—

When things go wrong, like a
song those sweet soft hours
return,
My thoughts run deep with
memories now, ready to recall
how
Our love so like the sun that
sets—only to return.

Darrell W. Brown
Command Performance
*[Dedicated to Roberta of whom
is the epitome of my desire.]*
The unpredictable and
udetectable lies here,
Unveiling to you heeding no
premonition within rhyme.
Accostingly, cheered to am I
dramatically,
Lest I run away in fear.
Now I choose to channel my
thoughts
And to cast off weights of time.
Oh! gross art we, performers
acting
On stage.
An Emmy, a Grammy, an Oscar, a
prize, coveted . . .
Yet, till curtain fall we block.
Still a voice says give of you,
Just be true, applause will feed.
It grinds my inner most fine.
Yes, pressing back and in spite
of this fact
My inhibition has left.
Plummeting, driving, moving,
suddenly
Climacticly I'm there.
Yet, cascading never fading
longly mindworthy . . .

My colleagues shush! Cease!
Witness a master of a
masterpiece.

Angie Michlowsky

Angie Michlowsky
A CHILD CRIES
DADDY? DADDY? Where's my
daddy?
Please, tell me cus, I don't even
know!
Mommy, where did my daddy go?

These are the cries of a little girl
left alone,
doomed to live in a broken home.
Yah know we had it out, so he
slammed the door.
Says he won't be coming home no
more.

DADDY? DADDY? Where's my
daddy?
Please tell me cus, I don't even
know!
Mommy, where did my daddy go?

Oh, what can I do? . . . What can
I say?
to take her pain away.
Just where's her daddy, where?
Hush, hush, my baby, . . .

Mommy cares, yah know,
cus, it happened to mommy a
long, long time ago.

DADDY? DADDY? Where's my
daddy?
Please tell me cus, I don't even
know!
Mommy, where did my daddy go?

Renee Dye
**From a Little Girl . . . To a
Wife**
I remember going to the hospital
for our first child,
The doctor gave us a daughter as
he laughed a little and smiled.
We were just as happy as we
could ever be,
Never to know she'd soon be
grown up and married.
It seems like she was just a
toddler, learning how to walk,
And then after you knew it, she
also learned how to talk.
When she was in school and
dreamed about being older,
"You will be quick enough", and
that's just what we told her.

Then she was in high school, and
dreamed about her car,
And just like every other girl, she
dreamed about being a star.
As she graduated from high
school, she made us even
prouder,
Each day she talked about this
guy, it seemed her voice got
louder

Now it's her wedding day and we
would look back to ours,
And how we cherished that
special day, which lasted only a
few hours.
We aren't really loosing a
daughter, but, we are gaining a
son,
We hope that her new life, is a
special, and happy one.

Clayton Rein
DESERT ARTIST
*[I dedicate this poem to my
aunt Lee Jacobson, with more
love than words can say.
Sabrino Clay.]*
With pallet and paint and brush
in hand,
I capture on canvas these
changing sands.
There's beauty and peace in this
desert land.
I paint what I see, and my
canvases I brand—O Lee!

Inez D. Murray
A SUMMER RAINY DAY
The falling rain on a Summer's
day
With mist upon my face did
spray.
The cooling rain did gently fall
Upon the earth with raindrops
large and small.

The rivers filled to overflowing,
Proof that life was still on going.
And those which fell upon our
faces
Wiped away all of our tears
traces.

Wiped clear by hands trembling
and yet
A love that lasted and not soon
to forget
That lovely afternoon of rain
May it come so soon again.

When tears for you again
overflow,
For the rain to wash away so no
one will know
The hurt and pain all faded now
but the memories remain,
Of that afternoon so long ago,
when we parted in the rain.

Thomas Caraway
MISS
Ye morning hours wrought
themselves over the hills,
Washed aside by the sea.
The strife continued;
A dismal sky and a rising Sun.
Once the first beam of light
vanquished the darkness,
I miss a new yesterday,
hopes flow away along some
distant gutter.
Ere, the noon seconds, I
discover new wishes and
ages curiosities still
blowing gently in a breeze
towards my soul.
Thus the relentless
pattern should appear,
but disappear, should
a hope or wish come
trickling down the
brook and become true.

Ruby Nelson
LIVING ALONE
Lord I get so tired of being alone
My bible tells me heaven is just
like a home
I read about the mansions so fair
Until I get so homesick to go
there
Lord you know how I live in so
much pain
All the Doctors tell me I will
never be well again
Folks look at me and say, My you
look so nice today
Thank you Lord because they can
not see inside
They will never see the suffering
and pain that I hide
I know that I will have to wait
until the angels come and take
me inside the gate.
Lord I know when I am with you ,
I will also meet my Friends and
love ones so true.
Please Lord let me move out of
this house of clay.
So I can have my new body I pray.

Darlene J. Brown
**America Is What We Make
It**
America is very special to me,
but I don't especially like what I
see.
I wish everyone could just get
along.
Everywhere I look something's
gone wrong.
PLEASE try your best to be
honest.
Things will get better this I
promise!

Try to give til you can give no more.
As far as certain politicians go their giving is poor.
I look at my son and wonder if he'll get a chance to grow up.
I pray everyday that we don't mess it up.
As I watch the new generation coming on,
I can see their souls are pure and strong.
When a crisis happens our children are often forgot,
but it is them who will suffer when we mess it up.
When my son is old enough to see,
I want him to be proud of his country!

Charlotte Gibson Dillon
HAS SHE EVEN NOTICED?
[To The Elderly In Hospitals And Nursing Homes Everywhere.]
Oh, look, there she goes,
In her uniform of white,
She hasn't hardly noticed,
Me at all tonight.

Slumped over in this wheel chair,
My back and legs in pain,
If she'd get me up and walk me,
They may be useful to me again.

But no, she's too busy hurrying,
With what few things she has to do,
That it almost seems impossible,
For her to spare me a moment or two.

And I can't talk to ask for help,
Or tell her what I need,
If she'd only stop and act concerned,
Maybe then, My thoughts she'd read.

Oh Lord, I wonder what she'd say,
I wonder what she'd do,
If just for a day, she had to be old,
And feel what I'm feeling too.

Alice Sanford
Western Winter Vacation
Out on #60, where the wind blows free
Where the coyotes howl, you'll find Ervin and me
Picking up aluminum, metals and other free things
Dollar bills and coins but we find no diamond rings.

Another pastime is watching the cars go by
We counted 400 in one hour. Oh my.
It doesn't look like a shortage of gas in this state
Even if they are charging a higher rate.

This Rest Area is a busy place night and day
People stop here going east and west on their way.
It keeps the Highway men busy keeping this place clean
So many vehicles before I have never seen.

Motor cycle groups stop here for a rest

A Hippie found lots of food— some of the best.
Some parties had a picnic and threw good food away.
He went away rejoicing after his find that day.

We are surrounded by odd shaped ranges of mountains
At this place there are no drinking fountains.
Trees, cacti of many species and a few birds, you bet
Sunshine most of the time, when it rains four days it is wet.

We have met sociable people from different states
We bought oranges where the orchard will be estates.
This month is monsoon season here
Not much lightning yet, but it is getting near.

We visited a Flea Market in Apache Junction one day.
They have many different articles on display.
In Florence we found the Post Office and a grocery store
A filling station and a telephone booth in one block and more.

Near Winklemen we drove by the Kennicott copper mines
They are high in the mountains, no sign of pines.
Can't say how long we will stay here and roam
We have more country to explore on the way home.

Edith Wicka
GOING HOME
Home should be a place of kindness, and love.
With a desire to try to please God up above.
Whether it is a mansion, or just a shack.
There is a feeling of belonging, when going back.
Many places in this world one may roam.
But the happiest time is going back home.
Still more wonderful than going home here.
Is going home to the higher sphere.
When a Christians life is over, pearl gates are open wide.
Jesus, and the Angels, give a loving welcome inside.
The Bible tells of that beautiful place.
Heaven is prepared, because of God's grace.

Ruth Ann Kroplesky
E. R. MORRISON
There is a man that I love so,
I'll carry his memory wherever I go;
Though he left this world, he's joined another,
A man like him I've met no other;
Though he died in November of 1971 you see,
He still means the world to me;
An education as we know today, he had not much,
God gave this man his special touch;

The knowledge he had didn't come from just any book,
To the Holy Bible is where he'd look;
He always believed in his fellow man,
And was always willing to lend a hand;
To hold a grudge he did not,
From this man you could learn a lot;
To live according to God is what he sought,
Fame and fortune he had not;
Human faults he had them too!
He was no different than me or you;
Of Gods' creatures and plans he knew so well;
Things of the future he could tell;
Of my future he told in so few words a lot,
Though my future he told me true, what it is
I will tell you not;
You are ahead of your time he said to me,
As we sat there together just him and me;
The vision I had I wish I hadn't that night,
For he was gone by mornings' light;
To fear his wisdom I'd never bother,
For this man was my Grandfather!

Ethel Case Cook

Ethel Case Cook
TO MY DOCTOR
I hail you, gentle healer, for your skill,
Your sensitivity, your wit, your touch
You bring an understanding that can fill
A lack. Your friendship is my needed crutch.
We are so many reaching out to you
Who bless the very earth on which you tread,
Who bless the air you breathe, and vow anew
To shout allegiances, but sigh instead . . .
I speak for all of us within this frame:
We thank you from our depths and bless your name.

J. R. Pyre
WE NOW LOVE
Of the earth I did cull
a most beautiful rose.
No root nor thorn did she show.

Surrendering freely there
unto my grasp.
From soil through which she did grow.

In hand she then blossoms
revealing to me.
In awe I begin to tear.

This flora perfected
now mine to see.
My promise now hers to hear.

Her petals uplifted
absorbing my love.
Our key to Elysium at hand.

Together we sway
in warm winds of one.
Our fears and doubts disband.
We now love.

Mary J. Flanery
THE CLOCK
I'm lost,
In the gears
Of a clock,
That are winding
Me down.

I am the little hand
You are the seconds hand
That I keep trying
To catch.

You pass me by
Swiftly and easily
And we only meet
When you're ready.

The face of the clock
Is our lives
It says for us
There'll be no time.

Darlene S. Carter
FEELINGS
I wake up in the morning
feel you lying by my side.
Feel the heat of your body
warming my very soul.

I feel the warmth of your kiss
as it turns into a smile.
I can feel all the love
that is shining in your eyes.

I feel the security you offer me,
as your strong arms reach out to embrace me.
And, as I realize, you'll always be by my side,
To offer sympathy or praise;
I know I can sleep again,
Warm in the security of your love.

Helen Klein
THE ANGEL OF DEATH
She sits there looking so cold and alone
But somewhere under there,
There beats a heart
Beneth all of the black and chrome.

The smooth lines that glimmer
Soft but sharp in the night
Are begging you to play the game
At the first break of daylight.

Though you live life the best you can

You can't fight the feelings inside
Those feelings that call to you,
To take just one more ride.

Grasp all the power in your
hands
Feel the vibrations through your
feet
As you glance below but all you
see
Is blurring gray concrete . . .

You're flirting with eternity
Trying to bluff your way through
But you never can trust this
angel of death
You never know what she may
do.

She deals cards marked in blood
Not yet spilled
And the devil sits on her side
So it's doubtful you'll win
But still you'll play again
And again you'll be betting your
life.

Thora Jean Supple
SUNSET
*[I dedicate my poem to all who
have wished me well in the
writing field. Bless you, all!]*
The sun sank low on the sea
horizon,
Blending heaven and earth;
Frigate birds flew close to shore,
Food-diving in the surf!

Sunset time is a lovely time,
The sea is calm and sublime,
I sit, and watch, and feel that I,
Am one, in His regime!

Connie Ramey
I Think Of You Tonight
I think of you tonight
And wonder why I'm not lying
with you
Feeling your warm shoulders
against my arms
Holding you until I hear
Those sleepy little sounds of joy
you give
I love you so much
You never push me away
I come before sleep or anyone
else in the world
You do not care where we go or
what we do
If only I be with you
I do not like many people
They bore me, or attack me, or
talk too much
When there is nothing to say
All this you seem to understand
The man apart
Who would rather walk in the
night
Than hear any rock band in the
world
Who would rather sit and watch
a river
Than meet anyone in the world
Who likes to drive nowhere and
walk nowhere
And so I think of you tonight and
love you
And wonder why I'm not lying
with you

Darlene Koszenski
TOO LATE
I tried to tell you how I felt
But the time was never right.

Rehearsing the words over and
over
At home . . . alone . . . at night.
Always a smile, a glance or look,
Never the spoken word.
But Oh, how I wish now
That your mind could have heard
The whispering of my lips
Saying "I love you"
Knowing in your heart
That the meaning was true.
But now you're gone
And even though I've tried
I still can't believe
That you really died.

Diana De La Cruz

Diana De La Cruz
SPRINGTIME BREEZE
Springtime comes, but once a
year
And it seems to put love on first
gear.
Though it might be, the green
grass born,
Which makes us free of love's
lorn:
Those perfumed flowers, smelling
sweetly
Seem to beget some hearts
completely;
While others rejoice in the nectar
of Rose,
Though its fragility seems to
deem its compose.
But then why lament in breezing
ways?
Seems love comes, but once,
these days.

Jon K. Shuppert
EACH DAY OF MY LIFE
Everyday is my chance to reach a
goal which I am shooting for.

To be better as a person in the
world around me than I have
ever been before.

Jeanette Giese Schneider
**I Guess the Time I Think
Of You Most**
I guess the time I think of you
most is all the time,
And throughout the day I pray
that you think of me in the
same way.
I guess you made an impression
the first day I met you
Because there you were—out of
the blue,
Just when I needed someone to
talk to.
And at the time I didn't quite

realize that you were really a
miracle in disguise.
Before I met you life seemed
quite dull.
I felt like giving up and started
thinking people were all the
same—
They don't care . . .
And then, you came—
Since then, I just haven't been the
same.
There's so many things about you
that are just too good to be
true,
And they're all so very much a
part of you.
The quality I most admire in you
is your acceptance of me
because I'm me—
You never laugh at the things in
which I strongly believe.
I guess the world really hasn't
changed, nor the people in it,
It's just that you've brightened it
up a bit
And made me realize there are
still a few people left who
care . . .
Thank you for being one of them.

Ruth Gardner McAlley
EARTH'S GARDEN
Earth is the garden of God.
He carefully planted the sod
With seeds of each kind
To be scattered by the wind
And watered by wandering
clouds.

Each tree He planted with care,
To cool and refresh the air
With vapors and mists
And by breezes be kissed
To make earth beautifully fair.

In meadows He scattered flowers,
And fashioned in artful bowers
Daisies and clover
The whole earth over
To give pleasure to Man's lonely
hours.

Elmira Mason Washington
JOY IN A MORNING SKY
Once, the dawning sky
was a quilted coverlet
still shaded by darkness of
night;
But a freshening radiance
subtly altered
the blanketing clouds with
light.

Soon, the hues of the new-risen
sun
displayed depths, tints, a
promise of beauty;
An illusion of dew-sparkled
petals unfolding
made my watching pure joy,
deterred duties.

Then, a radiant softness
transcended the dawning,
lifting the shadows from
sight;
Now the morning sky
is a quilted coverlet
all painted with colors: day
bright!

Margaret R. Klaskin
THE NIGHT WIND
The night wind whispers through

my mind
And leaves a trackless void where
I can't find

My lonely way, no matter how I
try and try
And finally, out of desperation, I
just sit and cry.

The night wind falls and fails and
through the silent crystal air
Comes a muffled footstep, and I
see you there,

Close enough to speak; but it's
too much
To hope that we will ever
touch . . .

And the night wind whispers
through my mind . . .

Diane K. Moddes
LIVING WINTER
A pale face
a slender moan
a heart so full in
slumber
The living Winter
shares not a dream
but tucks it so
within
Then falls in
silent company
to someone elses'
Spring

Miriam Hasert
LOW ON THE POLE
As the new secretary
there is one thing I have had to
learn—
what the keyboard of a typewriter
is.

We have a good relationship
now—
it promises to co-operate with me
by typing straight lines

and not dropping a single letter.
Another miracle has happened
(if an old dog can be taught)

I have even learned to type
and set up addresses on
envelopes.

Now, if I could learn to cook
properly,
but as the Bible says,
the world was made in seven
days by God

and I still have tomorrow.

Maxine Elliott Martin
TRIBUTE TO AN ADMIRAL
Beneath his Navy flat-topped hat,
His head held straight, his red-
cropped hair
Is a smooth outline, but under
that
The sunburned brown of his
neck's laid bare.
From the old gold-starred collar of
Officer's Blue
To his muscle-bound throat and
square-cut jaw
His features show him brave and
true;
His profile, sharp as an eagle's
claw,
He sports a weathered coat of tan
His step decisive, with measured
length;

His full chest and the broadened
span
Of his shoulders tell of war-worn
strength
His sinews tough as a sailor's
knot:
His muscles tense like spans of
steel.

His direct gaze can pierce the
dark,
Or glow with a friendly light
that's real,
His laughter bounds over the
rolling sea,
Which holds all his plans and
fears
That seem to direct his destiny,
And bear out his hopes and years.
A soldier of fortune who has
earned his fame
Steadfast as the men in his
aircraft carrier command.
A tough and fearless man among
men!
He'll stay the night with a poker
hand,
Or risk all to save a life
He'll stand by his station when
perils grow rife,
In battle he is fierce as a roaring
bull;
He plays the game to its destined
end,
Or true to a shipmate who's down
on his luck
He'll risk his life to save his men.

Jon St. John
DAY BY DAY
If only we could live
Day by day,
I would not have to
Love you over.

Each time with you
Is almost like the first;
Are we holding back?
Or are we close
To Xanadu?

All the love that's felt
When falling in,
Is saved for all time
In Xanadu.

You and I
Will be there often.

Mildred T. Risner
OPPORTUNITY
If once I seek opportunity
And cannot find it near,
I won't give up, but keep right on
Until it will appear.

If once opportunity I have found
And it slips from me away,
I won't give up: I'll keep right on
For it will come again some day.

Opportunity may come along
When I least expect it to.
I will be ready when it does
To start my life anew.

If once I stumble on the way
And opportunity disappears,
I will pick it up and start again,
And I'll wave away my fears.

They say that opportunity comes
but once,
But I've known all along
That it may knock twice or
thrice

With a very changeable song.
I must always seek it out.
It never waits for me.
I must give it all I've got
And serve it extra tea.

Thelma Christiansen
TRAGEDY
    [To my own childhood I
    sincerely dedicate this poem.]
We sent him on an errand.
It was better this way—
Better that he did not see.
He would be so bitter.
I watched him till he reached the
    narrow bridge
That crossed the irrigation ditch
    near the pasture gate.
I hoped he would not hear the
    whining.
He was halfway 'cross when the
    shot rang out;
It stopped him short—

Dead still it stopped him.
For one breathless moment, I
    watched him there
Sway dizzily towards the flow of
    water.
Then he stiffened rigidly.
His hand went upward to his
    heart.
Like a statue he stood for one
    swift second.
Slowly, then, he lifted his bare
    brown foot;
And with head down-dropped,
    moved forward with the cows.
Silence spoke his sadness,
But whispered, yet, a heart-held
    hope that sings,
Next time, he must have a male
    dog.

Steven P. Dooley
OUR LORD, GOD'S SON
    [In dedication to the beautiful
    family which the Lord has
    blessed me with and all the
    ways you have touched my
    life . . .]
Upon the cross His arms
    widespread
His tears they flowed to pools
    red.
The look of pain in one man's
    eyes
He gave His life for mankind's
    lies.
His precious blood for you He
    shed
With a look of love these words

He
    said . . .
Forgive them Father, for this
    they've
    done . . .
Then shut His eyes, Our Lord,
    God's Son.

Leland Jay Olson
TIMELESS
    [This poem is dedicated to Mr.
    Fred Santon—a man who has
    given me insight and
    inspiration to accomplish the
    things I never thought I could
    do.]
The eyes of boughs rarely have
    chance to see the brook;
For you and I the chance comes
    more frequently,
But have we chance to see it?
Like the eves we are—
Even though better off than all.

Vivek Golikeri
**Dawn In Diego Martin
    Valley**
The sky is on fire!
And my heart soars upon the
    wings of an eagle through
    realms of ecstacy.
Nature and I are one in a
    rapturous, almost sexual union.
Drops of golden sunshine are like
    dew upon the verdant hills.
The neighborhood sleeps, and I in
    the garden behold Thy
    Majesty, O Lord.
Is it that you are invisible, God,
Or are we blind when Creation
    screams out for glory?
Yet from Creation and Life I learn
    lesson after lesson,
For Existence is a script that Man
    must gradually decipher.
Behold in the East, the fiery
    dawn!
None but the Lord can hold back
    the morn.
It's no use to be forlorn—
What cannot be avoided must be
    borne.
And no matter how long or dark
    the night,
O'er the horizon shall rise the
    light.

Ruth Gardner McAlley
**Retired Teacher's Yard
    Duty Recantation**
Now that I'm retired, too,
I'd like to add a thing or two!
Now may I shout and make it
    heard—
A 'Teacher's Pet' is quite absurd!
The children still are here to stay
Out in the school yard day by
    day,
To laugh and shout, or fight, or
    play,
And though I'd watch them all
    and stew,
I wish that I could be there, too.

Janet Marie Cress
MAN HUNTING
Is beauty always graceful curves
poised phrases and polished nails?
Are azure irises and blonde
    tresses
all that bring men's hearts to
    kneel?

Are vacuumed skulls a virtue
and what does breeding tell?
If money is the lure, then why
does a worthy occupation
    repulse?

I pause and wonder, taken aback
for in considering my bait—
Grey eyes, grey matter, greyer
    luck
I should have a long, long
    wait . . .

. . . and yet I've snared one.

Virginia Martini Dey
**The Last Child Leaves
    Home**
How quickly all the years have
    fled,
Leaving memories in their stead,
Memories sweet, and memories
    sad,
Of the good times, and the bad.
The racing feet, the joyful shouts,
The smiles, the tears, the frowns,
    the pouts.
The sticky prints on window
    panes,
The skates, the dolls, the choo-
    choo trains,
The gloom that prevailed when a
    child lay ill,
How heavy the hearts—how
    bitter the pill!
The bedtime milk and cookies—
    the tea and cinnamon toast,
The peanut butter sandwiches—
    guess who ate the most?
The Little League games,
    beginning in May,
The dancing lessons—the Water
    Ballet.
Those lovely golden Autumn
    days,
The High School cheers, the
    football plays.
The rosy cheeks, when winds did
    blow,
The angel patterns in the snow.
The winter boots, some large,
    some small,
That lined the back porch, and
    the hall.
The prayers which every night
    were said,
Beseeching blessings on each
    bowed head.
As this last child steps out the
    door,
May He, and all who have gone
    before,
Find Fortune, Fame, and,
    something more,
Their dreams come true, with
    joys untold,
And all the Love their hearts can
    hold!

Abbie Yeager
ON HIM, I DEPEND
Jesus is my friend
On Him, I depend
Troubles come my way
By my side, He'll stay.

I praise His Name
In prayers, He came
He will deliver me
From evilness, you see.

I have confessed
When I'm depressed

I pray to him
My depressions dim.

In him, I rejoice
Raising my voice
In songs of cheer
Jesus becomes dear

I seek his face
In every place
Then I can depend
On Jesus, my friend.

Cynthia R. Golderman
To Park—To My Twin, Mal
[In Memoriam: For Dr. Malcolm
Basche, my beloved twin
brother who died in his
Autumn Years, at the age of
48.]
The kite, it lifted in the breeze
that squeezed itself from a cloud;
the softest grass our little shoes
trod upon,
Oh, grievous tears that I could
sob aloud
for the greenness of the years that
had all gone.

The kite, all blue and red against
the sky
flew with the little fingers
guiding it,
while the sun shone on the Park's
cobblestones,
that held the passers by, people
who watched
the two young-ones so closely
knit.

That Park, from whence these
memories flow
is gone now from my abled sight;
I'd give all the knowledge that I
know
to hold the hands that piloted
that kite!

Ed Y. Kish
FOUR SEASONS
[To Wilbert, my husband, who
has given me continuous
inspiration, encouragement and
support in my painting and
poetical endeavors.]
In the Spring of my life
I was budding and growing in a
new world;
The happy, carefree childhood
days soon departed,
Only in the twilight years to be
unfurled.

In the Summer of my life
I was learning to set a goal and to
survive;
In mid-summer there emerged a
gleaming hill,
To reach that faint, distant hill I
had to strive.

Now in the Autumn of my life
I'm on that hill which seemed so
far, far away;
Here flows the stream of life at a
slower pace,
And the view is breathtaking day
after day.

When in the Winter of my life
I'll cling to keep from slipping
over the hill;
Long may my snow-covered
crown shine in the sun,
Long may the sunset be peaceful
and tranquil.

B]
THE GOOD OL' DAYS
As I sat before my keepsakes,
The box now tattered and torn,
The memories
        came
            rolling
                by
                    me,
The laughter not yet worn.

Poetry to speak of lost love,
Autographs, some without
    meaning,
Letters from
        friends
            I
                knew
                    so well,
Remembering old times, it's just
like dreaming.

Louise Wilkerson Conn

Louise Wilkerson Conn
**It Would Be Easier In
Concrete Canyons**
Do not leave me here
on this soft bed of moss,
by this happy, laughing stream,
where hours fly on phantom wings
pausing to cling to slender, green
    leaves
of the willow trees, bending to
    touch
cool water with tender fingers—
as you touched my face.

Leave me on some city street
where crowds mill in heat and
    desperation;
proving that the world is solid.
Steeped in loneliness, each soul
climbs a wall of oneness; the
    shadow
of concrete canyons
falling across the sun.

Stephen Vanek
WHAT'S FOREVER FOR?
What's forever for,
Since nobody lives that long?
Often used in promises,
I wonder, is it wrong?
What's a promise for
If it's one you cannot keep?
Handed to the one you love
The consequence you reap.
What's a loved one for
But to show that one you care?
A lifetime full of emptiness
Leaves nothing much to share.
What's a lifetime for,
If it's only spent in pain?
People need some happiness

To dry up all the rain.
What's contentment for
But a peace within the mind?
Flowing like a morning breeze
To stop the wandering kind.
What's the morning for
But to end the darkest night?
Questions in the silent hour
Are answered in the light.
What are questions for
But to guide us on our way?
Forever into life's parade
A challenge day by day.
What's forever for?
All mankind may never know.
Just as long as there's tomorrow
To see the flowers grow.

Deloroes J. Farmer
TROUBLES?
[For Harry and Tara—after 18
months they are both doing
much better—I love you both]
It's so hard to realize
the troubles that I've had.
To you I will not dramatize
this dream that went bad;
A premature birth,
The death of a kin—
Now two weeks had it been.
Then just as fast,
In a wreck is my brother.
The doctors saying, "He will not
    last—
You must call your father and
    mother."
He's out of the coma,
But his mind is array—
The way he is now
is the way he might stay.
But, thank you, Lord, for he is
    alive,—
And my premature niece will also
    survive,
My grandmother is in heaven
    with you—
Thank you Lord, for pulling me
    through.

Joyce Thomas
A DREAM OF LONG AGO
A dream floated over my soul last
    night,
    a dream of long ago.
When I rested securely in your
    arms
        oblivious to all else below.

That's when heaven touched
    earth with a kindly hand
    and skies were bright and fair,
While not a sorrow reached my
    heart,
        you hid it with anxious care.

In the sweet dreams of those days
    the face of my loved one
    smiled
Cheering the gloom of darkest
    hours,
    its every grief beguiles.

I gaze, enraptured, at the scene
    for love had lost its fear
Until it seemed that youth had
    shed
    its last and latest tear.

But sunlight faded from that day
    and heavenly starlight fled.
Rivers of tears unhidden flowed,
    our love, though cherished, was
    dead.

Then darkness fell since love had

lost
    the hope of your embrace,
Yet faith still hold those
    cherished words
    "Our love will live again."

Damon Thompson
THE CAT
Immaculate creature
Pink tunneled mouth
Tongue tougher and more
    ominous than abrasive
    sandpaper
In fear and fury back arched and
    fanged for the fight
In love spitting and wailing:
    fierce coupling, painful delight!

Acrobat supreme: no mere
    Player at poetry
But what poetry might be
Were it commanded
To clothe itself in bone and fur.
Wisdom, grace: ballet-beauty and
    song.

Patricia C. Nalepa
MISSING YOU
The last words you spoke to me
Before we said goodbye,
Seem to keep me up at night
And make me want to cry.

You said within three days or less
You'd vanish from my mind.
You said you were the type
That I should leave behind.

But now it seems so long
Since the two of us did part.
And my days are filled with
    sadness,
And I've an aching in my heart.

It is your face that appears
Each time I blink my eyes;
And it is your touch I feel
When I'm taken by surprise.

It is your voice that I hear
Calling me each night.
It is you I want near,
Even though you're far from sight.

So why must I go on like this
It simply isn't fair,
Together we should spend our
    time
Because it's for you that I care.

Mark Bosher
MALAISE FROM A DREAM
I woke up from a dream
while chasing through
a timeless gorge
that led to love.
I wondered,
only to feel the end never coming
and I was afraid,
afraid of finding
that love had escaped me
and I never knew of it.

Joseph P. Kowacic
NOVEMBER DAY
Summer, winter,
    spring and fall,
the moments speed,
    beyond recall . . .

moments which were
    giant-strong,
when spring was young
    and Time was long.

We loved
    beneath a summer sun
and kissed the moments—
    one by one.

Now autumn rests
upon the heart,
as ghosts of summer's dreams
depart . . .

And rasping winds
with chilling breath
speak of Winter . . .
and of Death.

James Lapp
DARE TO BE HAPPY
[December to May—A bygone memory lives on as the embers of the fire grow cold. Inspired SMB 1975]

Dare to be happy, please don't
shy away,
Reach out and capture the joy of
today;
Life is for living, please give it a
try;
Open your heart to that sun in
the sky;
Dare to be loving, trusting and
true;
Treasure the hours with those
dear to you;
Dare to be kind, you'll find it's
more fun than you know,
Give joy to others and watch
your own grow,
Dare to admit all your
blessings—and then,
Everyday count them over again;
Dare to be happy, don't be afraid;
Dare to be you, with the life you
have made.

Kim-Marie (Baldwin)
Once We Were Strangers
[To all my special friends— most importantly, Kerry, Andrea, Connie and Amy, for their love and friendship, and the special closeness we share.]

Once we were
strangers . . .
. . . how frightening that seems.
Living each day and
experiencing the changes in our
surroundings, yet,
knowing that somewhere out in
the world,
awaits
a new meaning . . .
. . . a strong challenge . . .
. . . a deep bond.
When finally, one day, it
came upon us.
How lucky were we and
how lucky
we've been,
for each day has brought us
surprises.
Pointing us
in the same direction, He knew
we would
together
build,
what others pass by
or what others don't try.
Deep in our
hearts
we knew what would be,
and deep in His heart, He knew
we'd succeed.
A chance
was taken and how beautiful
the outcome.
I would chance my life
forever more

knowing
that at the end, things would
blossom as
the rose
has bloomed in our friendship.
Together . . .
. . . never alone,
we have become whole, in a
shower
of honesty,
trust
and respect.
And how grateful I have been
since then.
Yet . . .
. . . sometimes I sit and
I realize . . .
Once we were strangers . . .
. . . how frightening that seems.

Ruby Dew Creel
THANK THEE LORD
Thank thee Lord for these many
years
thou hast granted me to live.
Thank thee for the tendency I
have to
share and give.
Thank thee for my earthly
comforts and
strength to carry on.
Thank thee for the here and now
and for
all the days that are gone.
Thank thee for the friends I have
known
along the way.
And thank thee for the love they
gave to brighten
up my days.
Thank thee for leading me
through life's
long and weary way.
Thank thee for my nights of rest
and the challenge
of each new day.
Thank thee for the strength and
courage to walk
the trails alone.
I thank thee Lord most of all for
claiming
me as thine own.

Fae I. Canaday
Would We Proclaim a Christmas Morn?
If the Christ Child could be born
anew
I wonder what mankind would
do.
Would we kneel and worship the
Child there
Radiant with Love, Just and Fair,
Or would we simply gaze in awe
And admire all the gifts He'd
draw?
Could we accept the Prince of
Peace
If the aura about Him were as a
lamb's fleece?
Would we be embarrassed at the
bed of straw,
Turn away and forget what we
saw?
Would we feel ashamed of the
"simple birth"
And wonder if He'll ever prove
His worth?
Would we question the color of
the Baby's skin
And ask, "To what race is

He akin;"
Maybe criticize God and say He
was able
To provide a better place than a
dirty stable.
If Angels spoke and said, "A King
is born,"
Would we proclaim a "Christmas
Morn?"
Or just pretend we didn't hear
Rather than admit an inner fear
That there might be something
far greater than man
Which exists somewhere in the
outer span
Of a world unknown to us as yet,
But one to which we feel no debt.
Men should not be as stagnant
pools;
Nor progress change mankind to
fools.
Let's not change the world and do
it so fast
That we forget our glorious past.
Let's not forget from whence we
spring,
Nor feel ashamed for
remembering.

Leta J. Bakke

Leta J. Bakke
MAY
Beautiful May, with your flowers
bursting out in all their
splendour,
Birds singing in their nests, to
their
young, so very tender.
Here and there lawn mowers buzz
along,
cutting the grass to perfection,
All the neighbors out working in
their
yards, it's like an infection.
Young hearts and old alike, sense
the
love in the air,
The perfect month to fall in love,
that
seems to be the fare.
New life again, after a winter so
bare,
bright colours are scattered
around,
that before wasn't there.
How exciting to see each new
bloom,
eagerly reaching out to greet the
sun,
giving beauty indescribable, each
and
every one.

One day it's a dainty bud, then
it's in
full bloom, each one saying "I'm
here"
give me room.
It's sad to watch them wither,
then die,
after the beauty they let us
behold,
while it's blooming, it's beauty
and
fragrance, is so gentle, yet so bold.
Like life, we have our time, to
bud out,
and to bloom,
Then slowly wither away, for
others to make room.
"MAY" I really think you're the
best time
of the year, I'll try to blossom out,
and give
someone pleasure, and cheer.

Paulette Talboy Cary
NEW YEAR BLUES
Rest, weary one, before the night
has flown
You shall have vanished into the
Unknown,
And in your place, a young one
with a smiling face
shall sit upon your throne;
But I am not deceived, his smile
is but a mask,
And he'll be much relieved
If he fulfills his task;
Speed not away, there is still
time—so stay—
My heart knows only fear
Of what the coming year
Shall bring for me,
Linger awhile, chase away gloom
and guile,
Teach my sad heart to smile,
And with each mile that marks
your journey's way
Help some poor soul again take
heart
And face the coming day—
"HAPPY NEW YEAR"

Merritt Bradford
BARNYARD TALE
Mule in the barnyard
Chewing on a stick.
Appears a pert lad,
For a little trick.

Boy gives a pick
Mule gives a lurch.
Services tomorrow,
At the local church.

Joanne L. Freed
BETRAYAL
I've been Judas to you
And it's been killing me instead;
You've been fair to me
But I'd be better dead.

I took shadows from the light
And made all darkness—
It really wasn't right.
I'm looking for the sun,
It'll make the blackness go away;
I'm looking for the sun
But fearing what you'll say,
Because . . .

I've wronged you
I know it's true,
You cared about me
But I didn't see . . .
No, I've been Judas to you,

Oh Lord, what can I do?
I've been Judas to you.

Now the light is shining through,
I can see that what I've done
Was hurting me much more than
    you
But neither would've won.
I repent, but still it's true
I once was Judas to you.

Angeline K. Schwan
NIGHT
The night grows dark
And shadows fall,
And dance and play
Upon the wall,
And laugh and jeer
And fill with dread
My wretched frame,
My pounding head.

I cringe and cow'r
As storms begin
To shake and beat
My soul again.
They howl and scream
And leer at me
And rage till dawn
Doth set me free.

Judith Klimowski Casey
AUTUMN I
I hear the click-clump
of my footfall
on the silent street,
then . . .
Ki-ta, Ki-ta, Ki-ta-ti-ta-ta
beside me,
behind.

I look at the sound,
brittle and withered,
knowing . . .
if I step on it,
it will crunch
into a thousand crumbs . . .
if I clench it quickly,
it will crumble
to dust,
save the veins and
the stem.

Better to hear
Ki-ta, Ki-ta, Ki-ta-ti-ta-ta
and wonder . . .
Ta-ta!

Arlone Mills Dreher
BRIEF LOVE
It seemed a thousand years and
    more we gazed
And saw each other under frosted
    stars.
We loved each other under fiery
    Mars.

Our youthful love was brief and
    slightly dazed.
Our happiness was born but
    quickly lost
Within the fraction of a wavering
    sigh.
The drifting clouds revealed more
    stars and sky
But we were heedless of that
    moment's cost.

Oh, were we there, that night
    that turned to day?
Those moments spent in timeless
    floating space?
Those hours we spent in joy we
    can't erase?
Yes, Time has sealed our reckless
    love away
But Beauty, radiant as the solar
    beams,
Still lives in treasured memory
    and dreams.

Louis A. Adams, Jr.
UNRETURNING LOVE
"I shall return;" he said.
"I'll be back in a week or so."
Nothing else he said.
And the truth he didn't let her
    know.

The week went by so slow.
And so did a hundred more.
She ran when someone knocked.
But it was never him at the door.

In time she did forget.
Or maybe so it seemed.
She seemed alright in the day.
But she saw him in her dreams.

She never let them know
that she still thought of him.
But time took its toll.
She grew very pale and thin.

Finally she died—
Six years to the day he left.
I guess that she has gone to
her eternal rest.

But I know she'll never forget
the pain and terror of.
The man she could not forget.
Her unreturning love.

And I hope he doesn't forget
either.

Sara Ann Campbell
FRIENDS
Our friendship like a tiny bud,
has been watered by the tears of
    our affection.
Until it has blossomed into a
    beautiful flower
    of love.

And we sit in a lonely field
amid the weeds of tragedy and
    misery.
As we struggle to survive;
clouds of doubt and fear spring
    up
    from the battle.

Yet, because we cling together
the weeds cannot overcome us.

In the face of our strength; the
    clouds part away.
And in the warm sunlight; a
    lovely little creature of hope
    alights upon us.

As she flies away;

she takes with her a part of our
    love;
to spread to the rest of the field.

As our petals fall and we grow
    old,
our withering stalk looks back on
    the now flowering field.
And we realize that maybe we
    had a purpose
    after all.

Janet Kay Burns
THANKS TO YOU DAD
Always be true to yourself,
Live an honest life;
Keep hold of strength and
    integrity,
And with courage meet each
    strife.

Keep gentleness in your heart,
Let faith guide your way;
Be always ready to lend a hand,
Be it night or day.

Give love everyday,
Be understanding too;
Finish whatever you begin,
Take pride in all you do.

It's easy to give advice,
Or tell someone what to do;
But when a person lives what he
    says,
You know what he says is true.

I was taught these values with
    love,
And the greatest example I had,
Was watching these values used
    each day,
In the life of my own Dad.

Mary Bradshaw
BETH
Remember me always
As the one who can sympathize
We've shared the rainy days
Your tears have wet my eyes

If you're scared and alone
Pin up my picture in your mind
If your heart is tred upon
Then I will lend you mine

Understanding is my virtue
I'm beside you through it all
When you need someone to cry
    to
To catch you when you fall

I'll pick you up to touch a star
And if it's too dark in the night
My light will shine afar
And make everything all right

Elaine C. Erb
ODE ON THE WEST WIND
Late in the evening
I sit by the window
listening to it clatter
to the gusts of the wind.
Wine glass in hand,
I look to the west
into the winds
that know not of
time and its depths
which I ponder.
Winds that blow and tell
stories in whistles,
jokes in flurries,
and never will stay
long enough to grab hold.
I can not be like you—
never touching down
but long enough to lift

a girl to the land of Oz;
starting and ending
nowhere in particular.
Wind, the original vagabond,
leading travelers
on beaten roads
whose dozens of footprints
include not the wind.

Michael Pietraszewski
YOU
You're in my life forever,
You're worth your weight in gold,
And I need you to love me,
So I'll never grow old.

I'll wait for a lifetime,
Just to love you one way,
You're the dew on the flowers,
You're a fresh spring day.

So please don't say,
You'll be moving away,
'Cause I need to see you at times,
For a second or so,
Than I'll let you go,
And I'll pray that I'll see you
    again.

There's no reason at all,
That you'll give me a call,
For my number you probably
    don't know,

But I'll reach you some way,
And on one special day,
You'll be talling me you love me
    too.

Pauline N. Mozeleski
DAYS OF AUTUMN
The days of autumn are drawing
    near, with
falling leaves, and trees so bare.
Children rushing off to school
    they go,
the young ones hesitate, to and
    fro.
Mothers' chores are slowly
    lessened, a few
hours are spent reminiscing.
Last minute chores, clothes to
    put away.
only to be brought back another
    day.
Along come the meetings, the
    scouts,
and football.
Days full of cheer and pleasure
    for all.

Freda Holmes
JOHN F. KENNEDY
The American people cry.
    Tragedy has
Struck as this young man, with
    his
Dreams and hopes for the
    American people
Dies. The people cry for justice.
    For a
Stop to the useless slaughter of
    our great
Men. As his laughter flashes
    across the
Screen his life drains, and the
    American people cry.

Nancy-Vera Clark
THE ROAD
I had never been down that road
    before.
Nor, had I ever dared venture
    near it.
And yet, as I traveled down,

things seemed familiar.
It wasn't the scenery
  or the stations at which I
  stopped.
The people, I had never met
  before;
  so I knew it wasn't them.

In my own way, I began to ask:
What is so close
  Yet so far
The same
  Yet so different
Had I traveled this road
  Or, was it merely a dream?

As I looked for an answer,
  and asked for wisdom.
I finally began to see.
The familiarity was the rockiness
  of the road.
The trials along the way.
And the leader of the journey
  was still the same.

No, I had not trod this land
  before.
  Nor, had I used my plow and
  trowel.
It was another place that I had
  trod
  that gave the similarity.
They both had trials and pebbles
  on the way.
But, they also had the same
  ending.
  Jesus Christ is on the way.

Bee Coalwell
MAN TO MAN
Love, life, and the pursuit of
  happiness!
A wonderful God-given plan—
Corroded, corrupted, and preyed
  on
By man's inhumanity to man!

We'll keep waging this war of
  survival,
"Hanging in there" as long as we
  can—
And winning most of our battles
Except man's inhumanity to man!

Whatever else is a threat to our
  future,
To our oceans, the air, and the
  land—
The ultimate destruction of
  mankind
Will be man's inhumanity to man!

Ada McCoy
THE SHEPHERDS CALL
In an hour that you think not the
  Saviour will come,
In clouds with great glory and
  power,
Be watching and waiting lest you
  hear not the call
When He says to His own, "come
  up here".
The earth shall lose its
  gravitation and in a twinkling
Of an eye robes will be changed...
Graves on the hillsides will burst
  open,
Saints arise in the white array,
The sea will no longer hold
  captive
The dead asleep on her breast
But release them at the call from
  the Shepherd
When He comes for the saved,

the blest.
"My sheep know my voice, they
  will hear," sayeth the Lord
"At my call they'll arise and
  away . . .
From the four winds they will
  come and be carried to glory
There forever, with Me, to reign."
Are you one of His sheep . . . are
  you listening
For the call that this moment
  may come
If Gabriel should sound the
  trumpet
Will He call your name from
  above?

Maria Penna

Maria Penna
SHYNESS
I will never forget the first day
  your eyes met mine.
That day that is now so far away,
Our eyes met in an innocent way,
Forming one look shared by two.

Your look, filled with shyness,
is one in a million.
Your smile, filled with innocence,
cannot be described.

We are being kept apart by our
  shyness
and joined by our look.
Our look, which is speechless
is filled with unspoken words.

What shall become of me?
Like a sponge of water, my eyes
are filled with tears.
My heart, broken into little
  pieces.
My life, as dark as a tunnel.

You are my only salvation,
Please overcome your shyness.
Dry out my tears,
Bring into one piece my heart,
And lighten up my life.

Penny L. Hughes
INVESTIGATORS
*[For Jon W. Wolf a good friend
yet is dedicated for his
compassion in caring of others
by lending a helping hand.]*
To be overworked and under paid,
he whom is fast is not delayed.
One whom is slow ponders all
  night long,
putts along like it was a sad song.
Jon's eyes on watch in a word
  such fire,
as he that does not much has no
  admire.

For the sun has fallen by the
  stroke of five,
if he should go home should he
  survive?
Yet one whom is told but
  somehow ignores,
come closing time so does Jim's
  doors.
Sorting out his thoughts comes
  Curt,
when Jim looks up he takes to
  the dirt.
For Phil he never says much,
he just thinks uh oh he's in
  dutch!
What else is there to say,
to Dan he don't think much of
  him anyway.
Now there be a wrong no way to
  say,
because all of them are under
  covered with the C.I.A.

Arlene Dempsey
BYE-BYE BETTY JO
*[To my Aunt Betty Jo (who
died in 1941 of polio, twenty-
four years before my birth) and
to my mother and grandmother
who related her to me with
love.]*
Bye-Bye Betty Jo,
Don't forget we
Love you so.
Touch the stars on your way,
And leave a teardrop trail
So we can follow you someday.
Kiss Jesus on His cheek
And ask Him to give us strength,
For without you, Betty Jo, we are
  weak.
Yes, darlin', I know
You can see the future
And we're all destined to grow.
When Dad and Mom join you,
Little sister Betty Jo,
Let us know they're okay, too.
Oh, do one thing for me;
Give memories of your
  uniqueness
To my poetess baby
So that fifty years from now
She can write some pretty poems
Of the way we felt, somehow.
Bye-Bye, Betty Jo,
Don't forget that we
All love you so.

Pam Barnes
FRIENDS
*[To Fred—with the hope that
we will always be close.]*
Now I've known you for close to
  a decade.
And throughout it all, I've clung
  to call you, "friend".
Tho' very different, you're among
  the best I've made.
And when I'm the saddest is
  when I fear ours' might end.

I've been very good to you, you'll
  have to admit.
Tho' with imperfection, I've tried
  to hang in there—
To get close to you. But quite
  often, I resort to silly wit
Instead of just simply letting you
  know that, "I care".

The stupid things I do or say is
  because too long I ponder.
I try to figure out what you

expect or want instead of just
  being "me".
Life would be easier and about
  this, there is no need to
  wonder.
Please understand what I'm saying;
  this is my one and only plea.

I, myself, have had friends to
  come and go.
And I've felt glad and perhaps
  relieved,
Or I've either felt hurt and down
  so low,
That I doubted in anyone else I
  could believe.

Even tho' you don't come out and
  tell me;
The way some have done, I see
  the hurt on your face.
I can't figure it out and their
  reasons I don't see.
But if only I could, I'd try to fill
  their empty place.

I can only be myself and this, I
  should try more.
And to heck with worrying,
  whatever will be, will be.
But without your friendhip, in
  life's riches, I'd feel very poor.
Don't ever hesitate to call on one
  of your best friends—me!

Mrs. Frank Plute
The Narrow Gauge Route
Right through the old mountain
  trails
Comes the roaring narrow-gauge
  train
Rattling over those shining rails
Through winds, snows, and rains.

Chugging over streams of blue
On through meadows of verdant
  green.
Man's work is a dream come true,
But Nature's work is truly
  supreme!

Glen
WHAT IS LOVE?
*[To my friend, Carol Kray, who
asked me to write her a poem.]*
To Love is to share,
For all with care.
To Love is to find,
My peace of mind.
To Love is to give,
My all as I live.
To Love is to care,
More than my share.
To Love is to live,
So I've more to give.
To Love is to know,
I've lived to grow.
To grow is to live,
For Love that I give.

Thank you, Love.

Heather Jean Anderson
OF LIFE
Life is like a river,
Flowing to the sea—
And hate doth never come hither-
And Life is as it shall be.

And the sea is like Death,
For this is where it ends—
And gone is the Life in breath—
But life will ne'er end.

As, my dear, you will see
That Life be not Death—

And there is not a reason to be
Afraid of Life's depth.

Death ends not of Life,
But of it just begins—
Worry not with sorrow and strife-
God forgives all sins!

For though high and mighty,
God is not without a heart—
So don't be apt to be flighty—
Just don't leaving him pushing
the cart!

Edwin Lee Blagrave
SARA LYNN
Saralynn—Saralynn
Intoxicational woman
Headbands of rainbow visions
Sharing smiles and words of
conviction
Always knowing the ways of
daring
And remembered sharings
Long hair to please a lovers touch
The eyes that know the truth—
We love so much
Saralynn—Saralynn
Intoxicational woman

Susan M. Hartman
THE AERIALISTS
i hear the city streets screaming
as an old man dies upon the park
bench
and children play amidst trash.

i feel the streetlights breathing
in their rhythmic red and green
while defiance scrawls on subway
walls
and knives flash like eyes of
death
in a young man's hand.

i see diseased houses dying
rot crawling from each to each
and oozing between prison bars of
poverty.

i know the world runs from the
ghetto
lest its fingers be stained with
blood—
a blood that burns in you and me.

and so, on a highway atop cement
stairs to the sky
to which little ones look and
dream they could fly,
They flash by, staring at the souls
of hell
what fools They are, for They'll
burn Themselves.

Tessie Berman
FLEA MARKET
Streets crowded with people,
merchants selling their wares
Strolling from one to another,
along this thoroughfare

You can find anything, name it,
jewelry, clothes, food
None of these appealed to me,
they did not match my mood

Suddenly! an art collection,
paintings, prints of all kinds
Fingering throu this assemblage,
hoping to find a find

The excitement keeps mounting,
I feel it in my bones
I know I'll find a treasure, that
someone has disowned

Ah there it is, my valued prize,
gazing at me with dreamy eyes
The Head Of A Girl, Painted by
Vermer, a thrill so great it's
hard to bear

I take her home, put her in a
frame, wonder about her, what
was her name
What was she like this
enchanting child, with her
captivating beauty and spirit so
mild

Time will not alter the beauty of
her face, her style, her manner
or her grace
She'll stay forever here in my
room, her beauty intact and in
full bloom

This lovely young maiden of
fourteen I'd say head draped in
a turban, one end astray
She glances over her shoulder and
becons to me, but the glass
comes between us, she's unable
to flee

I can't enter her world, nor she
mine, there is this distance of
space and time
But we understand each other, I
can see it in her face

Someday we'll find each other in
that out of earthly place

Jo-Ann Crossman Duke
FALL SPLENDOR
Frosty nip of ice in the air
Biting my cheeks and snatching
my hair
Silvery skies laden with clouds
Hanging heavy like silken
shrouds.
Leaves of scarlet and flame and
gold
Swirling and dancing, escaping
my hold
Beneath my warm clad feet they
glide
A glorious carpet, brown earth to
hide.
Multitude of shade in each lively
leaf
Here a short time, gone, like the
thief.
Yellow tip blends to rust, then
darkened red stem
No artist could hope 'ere to
duplicate them
Forgive me, I've made such a flaw
There is such an artist, He
painted them all
He made this lively, vary-hued
splendor
For after all, He is God, the
Creator.

Patricia Ann Steeber
(for David)
What I would write for you
if I had words.
What I would mold and chisel
from the raw insides of
hardened heaps and seeping flesh-
marred mysteries of my soul
to highlight your own walls.

My masterpiece is heavy—
hung on nails that tear the
master red.
You need not bleed.
I drain enough for both of us.

And my life,
trickling through the drains
and dripping from the balconies
will stain enough of everything
that you will remember.

My portrait for the world
hangs low beneath,
and stretching further in
to breathe, to breathe . . .

David M. Couch
MY MEXICO
Waves that splash upon
eardrums,
  listen, listen,
Crested surf rolling in just a
pace away—and wings that glide

amid the blue, then gently float
along the distant ebb,
  dancing, dancing,
Shores—drenched in yellow;
Warm and clean
Bury me here.

Darcy Baggson
NUCLEAR WAR
No more paper blowing in the
breeze.
No more kids scraping their
knees.
No more people, no more crime.
No more deciding, no more time.
No more sports, no more games.
No more bombs, no more planes.
No more enemies, no more
friends.
Because everything has met its
end.
Nothing exists here any more.
All because of the nuclear war.

Hilda Marie Spencer
TIME
Time is but tiny grains of sand,
measuring the days of our life
span,
flowing swiftly through the hour
glass,
molding our future,
immortalizing our past.
A lifetime of living should fill
each day,
with understanding and love
spread along the way.
For time spent wisely, is time
well spent
doing worthwhile things with
diligent intent.

Janet Horn
THE DAMSEL IN DISTRESS
I, the damsel in distress
Surveyed my situation

And awaited my fate with unrest
Then hopeless resignation

The great white horse who
carried my knight and me
Through life's dark forests is
lamed
His gait is unsteady and unstable
now
His hearty spirits tamed

My knight, once strong
And, oh, so virile
Is now decrepted
Impotent, sterile

And of the sages, saints, and
Gods
I knew could never fall
I was surprised to find, that, like
myself
Were but humans, after all.

No! They just can't all have gone
So I ask a magic mirror to see
But all it clearly reflected
Was the solitary image of me

Then again, I became distraught
Again, I started to grieve
Until I found that strong hand I'd
sought
Dangling idly at the end of my
sleeve

Ann Morse
TAKE THE TIME
Take the time to get to know,
That person inside that doesn't
show.
A spirit there you must fulfill,
A spirit there that time can't kill,
Left alone, there's an aching need,
So much is stifled by our selfish
greed,
To push it away, you only deny,
The truth of life and the reasons
why.

So take the time to get to know,
Those feelings inside that won't
let go,
For through the pain and through
the strife,
You'll begin to learn the secrets
of life.

Cosetta Castagno
SECOND LOVE
Your ardent glances fall like rain
On fields, long parched and dry.
Your words of love erase the pain
Of broken vows in days gone by.
Your lips on mine fan into flame
An ember from the ashes there.
Your nearness brings a joy the
same
As I knew once, before despair.
Your promise I'll not trust in vain
Tempts my lonely heart to love
again.

Patricia H. Coleman
INDIAN
Indian, Indian,
what can I say?
You take my breath away.
When we make love
I feel like I could fly,
when you touch me
with your eyes,
or touch my feet
I get a feeling that
is ever so neat.
You make me feel things

I never knew were there—
like when you touch my hair.
When I see colors
or my eyes feel like they'll pop
I don't want you to ever stop.
Your eyes,
your smile,
your gentle touch
mean ever so much.
I thank God for giving me you
and will be in love with you
my whole life threw.

Elma L. Jones
SANTA
Santa hitched his reindeer
  To his famous sleigh
And proceeded for to go
  On his merry way.

Dressed in a warm suit
  Of bright red and white,
Santa could be seen
  Riding through the night.

He made several stops
  Along the way
Delivering toys and games
  For Christmas Day.

Up on rooftops he went
  And down chimneys he came.
He had to remember
  Every boy and girl's name.

He wanted to make sure each
  child
  Would shout out in glee
Over the things he had left
Underneath each Christmas
  tree.

M. Ruth Howard
DEAR HEART
*[Dedicated to Raleigh Who
gave me hope and inspiration.]*
I met you on a blind date, Dear
  Heart, Remembering now
  brings tears.
The happiness, oh such sweet
  happiness, in just a few short
  years.
Yes, it was love at first sight, as I
  gazed into you eyes.
And you told me later dear, I took
  you by surprize.
And now even tho you're away,
  your memory is always near.
The vows we made together, I
  will always remember my dear.
Dear heart I miss you so, each
  and every day of the year.
I miss the love you gave to me, I
  miss the way you held me near.
I miss the 'single' rose I always

received from you—
For that 'single' rose so sweetly
  said, "Sweetheart I love you
  true"
As I go thru my lonely days now,
  I can clearly see your face,
As we walked hand in hand, Dear
  Heart, no one can ever take
  your place.
But I won't weep dear, you told
  me to carry on and smile.
So soon, yes soon my own true
  love, we'll be together in a little
  while.

Mrs. Eva (Spaeth) Lee
**I Think I'll Write a Poem
Today**
*[To my wonderful children
Eva, Jacqueline, Francis]*
I'd love to hold a Valentine up to
  you.
I'd like to hold a star, but most of
  all.
I'd like to thank you, for all the
  sunshine
You've shined on me so far.—Oh
  Lord.
I'd like to thank you
  personally.—But really
I'll wait—until you stop the sun
  from
shining on me so radiantly.

Terry Amadio Hixon
MY CONSTANT SONG
*[For my beloved brother
Charles Who shares with me
the love of Christ in exalting
the Glory which is God's alone]*
Oh God, at the end—time when
  overwhelmed is humanity in
  tribulation
So great as never before,
  singnaling the outset of
  unimagined sorrows;
Blood—flesh slaying its own,
  nation rising up against nation
And repeated be the dread of all
  approaching morrows—

When hated for Thy namesake be
  all men
And everywhere false Christs and
  prophets appear,
"Shewing signs and wonders to
  seduce"—as Thou foretold then
When many of Thy elect forsake
  Thee for fear—

When following the abomination
  of desolation,
The sun and moon no light shall
  emit o'er sea and land;
Though it be so God—still I will
  not fail Thee by blasphemous
  declaration,
For my committment
  unshaken—all tests will
  withstand!

I will remain as now—till
  revealed in clouds is the Son of
  man
And trumpeting angels gather
  from the four winds "the
  faithful elect."
Till all goes in accordance with
  Thy plan;
Till all divine prophecies know
  final effect.

And if it be Thy will at such

time, that forgiven would be
  my wrongs,
I know not even now how much
  more I could adore Thee
For ever worshiping at Thy feet
  I've offered all my songs,
Songs, however sung, revealed my
  entirety!

Oh God, at the end—time when
  overwhelmed in tribulation
  humanity will be,
I will remain forever—
  overwhelmed solely by Thee!!!
  Amen.

Florence E. R. Foster
WHAT GIFT THEN
Birthdays come but once a
  year; . .
And, now, your special day draws
  near,
But, what gift can I send you?
I've thought, and I've guessed; . .
A gift for a person who is so
  blessed?
A gift for a soul who has
  everything?
Your treasures are in a new—
  born Spring: . .
The trees, . .the flowers, . .a sky
  so blue
Are gifts from God, . .and they so
  please you.
A robin's song, . .a baby's smile,
All seem to make your life
  worth-while.
You find such happiness in your
  gift of giving . . .
Helping others is your reason for
  living.
You so appreciate the works of
  God: . .
Spring's first crocusses bursting
  up through the sod, . .
The scent of lilacs, in the rain, . .
The mocking—bird's and
  warbler's sweet refrain.
These gifts from God light up
  your eyes; . .
So, what earthly thing could I
  give as a birthday surprize? . .
Except, of course, my deepest
  love . . .
Accept it as a gift from Above; . .
For to love one another as I love you,
Must be the work of the Lord, . .
And God *knows that I do.*

Cassandra Tunstall
THE MESSAGE
*[To the Church which is the
body of Christ, to those that
are bound and living in
darkness. To my mother,
Bernice, my father, Giles. To
the entire Tunstall Family and
to all of my freinds and
neighbors.]*
God, the artist and author of men
  souls, has made all men
  brothers though some have
  gathered up their own and are
  separate from the others
he turns from these that steal
  from his earth and run
causing distasteful breaths to vex
  these daughters and sons
but gently tapping at my heart,
  he wakes my immortal soul
telling the story of communion
  for he, God, is whole!

as he must be, as he is and was,
so shall be his daughters and
  sons
Man is made in his image and
  God, the Lord, is one
uttering with a thunderous voice,
  Holiness begins to speak
saying, take off your garments of
  sin, come out of your slumber
  and sleep!
Forsake the freedom of men that
  you know true Liberty
for only he that God unbinds, can
  say he's truely Free!
Speak the truth to your neighbor
  and to every nation
seek not the answers of men, but
  know the truths of salvation
remember heaven's feet that have
  tread on evil deeds
that you put aside carnal
  weapons that make the hearts
  of men bleed
pour out upon the lands, love ,
  long suffering and kind
and with the living word, revive
  all of earth's minds
with the spirit of Holy breath,
  give life to them of the flesh
open their eyes with bread that
  they be satisfied and blessed
crown mens heads with this song
  that they'll find peace in the
  day
annoint their hearts with this
  seal that death come not their
  way
go casting your nets in all the
  spaces of the lands
that all commune in
  righteousness as willed by the
  Son of Man
so it is said, thus it is written, let
  all of mankind hear
for as close as your very hearts
  and soul, the Lord of Host
  draws near!

Ethel M. Dixon Gerbig
DARKNESS OR LIGHT
Darkness, darkness all around,
  What happened to the light?
Cares and troubles crowding in
  Feeling full of fright.

Sunshine's gone from the world,
  Joy has fled away.
What has happened to the light
  That brightens up a day?

Mustn't tarry in this dark.
  Mustn't stay too long.
Must remember after night
  There comes a brand new
  dawn.

Sharon Blanc
Our Country—Our Need
[To An American]
Our nation fights a battle,
Tho not with guns and bombs,
we're fighting unemployment
and all that it enthralls.

We're sick with dissolution
And don't know where to turn.
Our people need to work to live;
We have our "pride" tis known.

The government has mapped a
  course
It must be followed through,

Tho sometimes seems quite hazy
We hope in time it's true.

Our factories are closing down,
Small business takes the toll.
The people all are wondering
Now where do we go?

Some travel miles from town to
town,
Hoping for a lead, of some small
yet
Fulfilling work—his family has a
need.

They tell us to be patient,
Prosperity will return
Yet the very ones who say it,
Are the ones who've never
known;
That helpless desperate feeling—
of idleness at home.

God says man must work to eat,
The bible says it's so
Perhaps if we would seek His
face,
The answer He would show.

It's hard to be made humble,
Our self—suffcient lot,
But would we rather crumble
Because we forgot?

Yes, sometimes in our haste and
greed
We think we have it made;
And then He must remind us—
The debt that He has paid.

Carolyn B. Newman
UNTITLED
[Toni: You were there in the
beginning, watching the rose
blossom and grow. Thank you
for the time, the love, and the
experience. God bless you.]
This measurement of time . . .
Is it really that important?
Of what significance is it?
Ages have gone by;
No doubt ages will follow.
For I know from whence I came,
And where I shall return.
Even though it may be years,
It will only be tomorrow.

Susan Gowen
BETWEEN US
Dreams and Kings come crashing
down
We share a world that's cryin'
inside
Talking about the injustice done
But didn't we know we could
never win
Rolling in our sins?
But who can rightly judge
Our life in past, the damage done
Who can say who really won
Or who just walked away?

Staggering through nights of
drunken bliss
How can we get out of this?
Or do you want to stay?
Will it lead to insanity
Drowning our insecurity
Both of us running away?

Can you hurt more that you're
willing to die?
Does living the past mean
growing a lie?
How much does it take to make
you cry

nd will we still be here
Day after day and year after year
Is this how we're to pay?
Staying blown away?

Staggering through nights of
drunken bliss
How can we get out of this?
Or do you want to stay?
Will it lead to insanity
Drowning our insecurity
Both of us running away?

Ruth Tuttle Frawley

Ruth Tuttle Frawley
FOR ONLY ANGELS CRY
Some people hard—hearted,
ignorant or cruel,
Think if you cry you're a weak
blubbering fool;
And turn up haughty noses at
those who do,
Not knowing each teardrop's a
most precious jewel.

But sensitive souls like you and I,
See in moist cheek and
shuddering sigh—
a Touch of Heaven—
And need not ask why—
in this vale of tears,
Weakness is strength—
for Only angels cry.

Tommy Eileen Shore Weigand
MR. PRESIDENT
Hey, Mr. President
I'm sure you're doing fine—

But what about our country?
Things are turning
sour and unkind.
When you were elected . . .
you promised to put
more people into jobs—
But from where I see it . . .
with all the cuts you're making,
it's the poor people who
are being robbed.
I must admit your talking
is pretty darn good—
and just because you were a
movie star,
you think you're Robin Hood.
Please, Mr. President, Can you
understand?
If you want to be a hero, try
robbing
from the rich, try helping out the
poor—
And then you would silence . . .
Our Country's poverty roar.
How many costs—cuts have you,
yourself, made?—
I'll bet there's not many

that you would want to trade.
You and your oil kings
can sit and eat you steak—
While our cupboards are empty
with nothing much to make.
Your mansion is huge, yet warm,
and your servents aide you with
your comfort—
While mine is small, yet cold,
and my body and mind is
strained from wondering . . .
if I chose wrong, with my four
children,. . .
should have I before their birth
abort?
The saddest thing I must . . .
in my lifetime face—
is the fact that I

never bore the children
that could wear clothes
of pink and lace.

For, now you see,
Mr. President . . . Soon . . .
they'll grow big
and strong—
And my boys will
fight your battles . . .

whether our country
is right or wrong.
I love my country
And so do all of mine—
But somehow I ponder,
why does our countrymen
treat the poor like this . . .
all the time?

I'm afraid, Mr. President,
for what's to happen
in these days to come—
Well, just think about
this, while you're
talking over oil
and drinking . . .
your black rum.

Theresa Beville
INDIAN EARTH
Not-so-far-as the forest
Not-so-far- as a tree
To see that the earth is you and
me . . .

Let-us-go and be content
with the song of the earth, upon
our lips;
O children of this universe, we
the earth remain . . .

For-as-long-as the forest
runs parallel to the sky;
For-as-long-as the "sacred tree"
stands;
It is ordained;
O children of this universe, we
the earth remain . . .

Esther D. Hartman
MEMORIAL DAY
This is Memorial day,
We honor those who passed, and
will pay,
With their lives and limbs,
Even for those who live in sins.
Was it in vain,
When they even died in pain?
Are you trying to make the world
better?
Are you following the law to the
letter?
Don't you care,
Or do you dare,
To flount the laws of the lands,

When a buddy died on the sands,
Of Iwo Jima,
Or even Lima?
Well, then he died in vain,
And there was no gain,
Because you don't care,
To do your share,
To keep this country good,
No, you would rather be a hood,
Destroy what man has built,
And you feel no guilt,
And when your turn comes to
die,
No one will ever care where you
lie,
You'll die without honor,
And be just another goner.

Elvira Jane McHugh
TIMES REWARD
[Dedicated to my mother for
instilling in me an awareness of
the beauty and truth in music
and poetry.]
I'm so afraid that what might be,
My life shall pass before this
world knows me.
The things I know and write and
speak,
Will come to life when I finally
sleep.
Inside of me, a voice cries out,
I want to stand before the world
and shout.
"Hear me now, read what I say,
Not after I have passed away."

God, this gift has given me,
To write for all, the things I see.
I know not what they may say,
With pen in hand, it goes its way.

So many things great men have
said,
But were never known till they
were dead.
And I, too, fear my fate is so,
You will not know me until I go.

Monica A. Argandona
MIRRORS
Mirrors can play tricks on you
They are mistifying things
They don't show the true you
but a false image is what they
bring.

Susie Nelson
THE FEELING OF FALLING
[To Sammy, The love I have
just lost]
There's a dark hole
I keep falling into it
I see your hand
You are reaching out to me
I see hope—I can crawl out of
this deep hole
No! No!
I'm so close
Don't pull away . . . I want to
be with you
Why? Why?
Why do you get me so close . .
So close
then tell me
I don't want you!
Get out!
Go back into your hole!
You don't suit me!
You don't do enough for me!
I want more!
Down—Go down
Where you can be alon

In the dark hole & hurt
Please, Please, I beg, . . .
I'll try harder—I'll try harder
I don't want to slide deeper into
    this hole
    I want to be with you—I love
    you!
Next time, Next time I may not
    be able to come back up to the
    top.
When, or if, you reach out for me
    again.
    I may have sank to deep . . . to
    deep
to deep into the darkness
    Please let me try again
If you want me to
I'll stay busy
night & day
    I'll keep moving, never stop
    I'll run, I'll Jog, I'll wash dishes
    I'll laugh when I hurt inside
    I'll say yes, yes, yes, yes

Lisa Diane Cantrell
I AM NOT ALONE
*[This Poem is dedicated with
deep love and pride to my
sister, Debra Kay, for believing
in me as much as I believe in
her.]*
The rain is falling;
    the sky is gray.
The wind a'blowing;
    the trees a'sway.
All alone I am right here,
    just like the rain I cry a tear.
Someday the clouds will part,
    through them sunbeams will
    start.
I'll gather up each one and say,
    "I am not alone today."

Ginnie Music
SON
[To my son, Asif Chaudhri]
I wept at your birth
my most fragile part
unarmed and howling
at the moon

wrapping you in flannel
I hid you
in the shadow of my heart
dared not speak your name
among the elders

out of my truth
you have grown thin as a blade
poised against their lie
you have fashioned weapons
from their steel

I dry my tears
and watch your sharpness
as you pierce the moonlight.

Janice S. Williams
**Go-Between Of the Olde
Blue Chest**
'Twas at the "Sewing-Circle" I first
    heard about the old faded blue
    chest.
It stood in an attic for years. Just
    an olde blue chest. I wasn't
    impressed
    Until we opened it, and took a
    closer look or two—
        For then a secret hiding place
    came into our view.

Krusen, yes Krusen was the name
    on the letters, one prominent
    in local history.

I knew of a family by that name
    who'd worked on their family
    tree, (it's mystery).
I thought that day of those
    folks—and wondered about a
    connection.
As I mentioned it to my friend, I
    made the suggestion and found
    no objection.

So that's how it came about, that
    I was the go—between when
    the secret came out.
Papers and letters found in the
    olde blue chest were passed on,
    never doubt.
Do we stop to think how
    difficult, discouraging, time
    consuming is the search
To discover names or dates in
    musty library, graveyard, or
    records of a Church?

Yes, I'm happy to say I was the
    go—between, and stories
    completed came out.
The Civil War Soldier added to
    the puzzle with incidents he
    told about.
'Twas this man named
    Christopher who wrote (with
    love) to his "Dear Lib".
He spoke of pay, children at
    home, how life became death
    as sabre pierced a rib.

President Lincoln and Gen.
    McClellan too saw Christopher
    appearing in Review.
On his Cavalry horse he often
    rode knee deep in mud and
    swam the waters too.
He encamped near Washington,
    his letter packets tell the tale—
Unhappiness, homesickness, and
    ask Lib not to scold when next
    she sends him mail.

But now for the happy ending,
    (could your mind have
    travelled on and guessed?)
It's at the living Krusen's home
    the olde blue chest now rests.
And tucked away in that very
    secret place inside
Are letters from a soldier,
    Remaining here
        Where his descendants now
    abide.

Ronald C. Kilburn
ASPIRATION
All things are irrelevant to
    purpose, if execution of
    intention is not initiated.

Still water stagnates in the exile
    of its own existence
while rippling streams rush on,
    over the rocks and stones
    protruding in the paths
of their preordained destinations.

Even roses which grow, yet cease
    to blossom,
become mere bushes of thorn,
    leaving a tireless effort in great
    vain.
For if petals refuse to emerge,
    or sweet frangrance does not fill
    the air,
then the labors of new seeds
    sown,
have left no harvest in which to

reap.
So refrain from spending your life
    in vain attempts of acquisation,
but more so in content of true
    possession.

Betty Jean Lovelace

Betty Jean Lovelace
YOU TOUCHED ME
You touched me with your eyes, I
    know
    It made the heart within me
    glow.
Your gentleness did kindle lights
    That made me think of
    peaceful nights.

Now touch me with your hand
    this time,
    And make the thoughts within
    me rhyme.
You have the gift of love unsaid
    But in your eyes, it can be read.

Your head is laid upon my breast
    Finally, my love came home to
    rest.
Nothing more, no time, no season
    Does love for you need a
    reason.

We have found with us in
    dreaming
    A love that lasts, forever
    seeming
To guide my hand in yours
    forever
    To give myself to you
    wherever.

Cynthia Mayne
IN LOVE!!
There's a strange feeling inside
    me, I can't explain,
Everything seems bright and
    sunny, never like rain.

When I think of you, a warm
    feeling runs through me,
    Nothing or no one is near, you
    are all I see.

You do something to me, that
    no one has ever done,
    It makes me want to stay and
    never run.
My heart beats fast when I look
    into your eyes of blue,
    There's something inside of me
    that wants out, something true.

This feeling of mine grows
    more every day,
    I don't want it to ever go away.
Your the only one I see and think
    of,
    I
        GUESS
        I
            MUST
                BE
                    IN
                        LOVE!!

Joyce Goode
THE QUESTION?
*[To All Lovers Who Have The
Need To Be Free]*
Is there some way I can project
    the love—
I feel for you, and let it be known!
Is there a way I can express this
    joy;
and continue to nurture it—just
    allowing
you, to be yourself and free;
Hoping you will find it in your
    heart—
to bestow yourself to me.
Will it grow me to the man that I
    would be!
So in tune with your dear self;
    that both of us can see—
To love one another—that all
    these things can be.

Christopher S. Martin
The Rock and the Rose
The Rose has a long slender stalk
    leading up to the flower
The Rock has none, it just lies
    upon the ground

The Rose has a soft plush color
    to its pedals
The Rock is a harsh color,
    sometimes many

The Rose's pedals are soft, sleek
    and shine triumphantly in the
    sun
The Rock has a porous surface
    with many seeming mistakes

The Rose is delicately shaped to
    the right proportions by nature
Nature must have forgotten the
    Rock, it is disfigured and
    uneven

The Rose has a fragrance that
    pleases most everyone
The Rock does not, to most it is
    just in the way

The Rose, from the time it is just
    a bud on a bush until it dies, is
    pleasant to look at
The Rock receives no longing
    glances, only a kick across the
    road or a toss into the water

The Rose, with all of its elegance
hides the thorns that can hurt
The Rock hides nothing, what
you see is all that is there

These two items we see all
around. Though it may not
seem true, each in its own is a
symbol of beauty

Necia Hire

*[The following five poems are
dedicated to the magnificent
Cast of the Old—Time Radio
Drama—UNSHACKLED.
Writer—Director Jack Odell's
true stories of shattered lives
regenerated make listeners
worldwide face themselves and
think. Radio logs may be
obtained from Pacific Garden
Mission, Chicago, Illinois
60605]*

Necia Hire
PHANTOM POEM

Away down deep inside of me,
A poem struggles to be free.
A mighty poem—it seethes and
gnaws.

I push it back; I clamp its jaws.

I bid it wait till perfect phrase
May bless my lips, and lend it
grace.
It ponders God. And mark you
well—
All bygone poems, it must excel!

Oh come not forth without fine
dress—
Enticing words wrought with
finesse.
Oh come thou forth some later
time,
When I've devised some lofty
rhyme.

A MUCH Later Time:

That poem within is writhing
still.
It haunts and taunts against my
will.
No word of mine—nor skill of
mine—
Can make that phantom poem
divine.

Be still my soul—give Christ
control.
His words, not mine, can make
men whole.
Oh Christ, come be the poem in
me,
And from that phantom, make
me free!

Necia Hire
Categorically
Speaking—Hospitalwise

Briskly and crisply arrive the
next crew.
Nurse Wise: "Mrs. Jones broke
some bones, at fifty—three.
Ms. Kim lost a limb. She's
seventy—plus two.
Ms. Lee—sixty—three" (that's Me)
"cracked her knee."

Nurse New (To Ms. Lee): "My
Aunt Sue's seventy—two.
She sits, and she knits, and she
vegetates.
She's flaky and shaky and
bickering too.
My Pa and my Ma, she irritates."

"Seventy—two's blind, or deaf, or
cuckoo—
Or *all* those, and a pack of other
woes!"
"How many pushups can you do,
Miss New?"
(Ask *Me*) "And from your very
toes?"

"I'd like to go to the spa with you,
And watch you try the aerobics I
do.
You speak loudly, and slowly, and
simply, Miss New.
I'm *not* deaf. Think I'm dumb?
What's *your* IQ?

"How many heights have you
scaled, Nurse New?
How many books have you
delved into?
How many crises have you
toughed it through?
Do you think you'll keep
cracking till you're
seventy—two?"

Necia Hire
Christ the Eternal Word

Bubbles burst, and baubles break;
Footprints lead—we know not
where.
With storms that brew and
quakes that shake,
Footprints, too, all disappear.

'Mongst things diurnal, be there
none eternal
Through life and death, and tear
and wear?
"The Word!" cry I. There are
words infernal
That trick and lure and prick and
snare.

But, "Hear ye Him:"

At "Let there be," a universe
appears.
At "Come thou forth," Lazarus
sucks in a breath.
At "Believe on me," a sinner dries
his tears.
At "I'm alive for evermore,"
eternity banishes death!

Quotes, as they appear:

Mat. 17:5
John 1:1-3; Gen. 1
John 11:43
John 9:35-38
Rev. 1:18 (NIV) . . . I am alive for
ever and ever. And I hold the
keys of death. . .
Rev. 1:18 (NIV) Then death

and Hades were thrown into
the lake of fire . . .

Necia Hire
Date Capital Of The World

Paint me a desert by an Inland
sea;
Trace in a sand dune—a
Tamarisk tree . . .
All dreamy with haze, 'neath
skies of pure blue
With tracks of a coyote—a road
runner too.

Sketch in a cactus—the note of a
bird
Saluting God's desert with
chirpings absurd.
Startle a rabbit—look at him go
A creeping white lizard—his pace
is more slow.

Nestle a City in the midst of the
scene
With vistas of vastness, tall date
palms between . . .
Panoramas of mountains in the
distance aglow . . .
Animated with morning—
brushed with new snow.

This gem in the desert's called
Indio.
The date is the thing that has
made it grow.
The Festival of the Dates, every
year in the Spring
Proclaims to the world that the
Date is the King.

The City goes bonkers for more
than a week.
Each man is a sheik; his harem's
not meek.
Girls in bright costumes, all
smothered in veils
Enhance the excitement. The
glow never fails.

Horses and camels parade down
the street.
There's a spell of enchantment—
the band strikes a beat.
Scheherazade the Queen rides
attended on a float.
Every sheik on the scene will
applaud and emote.

Earth's maidens all spoil for the
sheiks of the oil.
But I think I shall wait for the
sheik of the date!

Necia Hire
Your "Grreat" Family Tree
The symbols of status—O how
they elate us:

The arts that delight us
The clubs that unite us
The friends that invite us
The shows that excite us
Your address, your pool
Your Ivy League school
Your chauffeur, your Cad
The yachts you have had
The wealth you can hoard
Your place on the board
Where stipends are paid
Your caddy, your maid
Your family tree
Your scholastic degree
Your beautiful people
Your Church and its steeple
The names you can drop

The places you shop
Your custom-made clothes
Your full-fashioned hose.
You buy the right labels—
Own horses and stables—
Jet off in your plane—
So goes the refrain.

You breakfast in bed, with ice on
your head.
Your status psychosis can give
you thrombosis!
Who stands on his toes, to look
down his nose
Sees nothing at all. He is bound
for a fall!!

Madeline Rasmusson
MEMORIAL DAY
I rambled through a cemetery,
On one beautiful Memorial Day,
Gazing at tombstones of all sizes,
That appeared upon my way.

On each stone there were two
dates,
That God had put there,
The day they were born,
The day they left their earthly
care.

Between each date there
appeared,
Just a simple little line,
That represented their time on
earth,
Just the same as yours and mine.

It is God that writes the dates,
When we come and we must go,
But the line that is our life is our
Choice, how we live it while here
below.

Joy A. Rabor
THE FORGIVING GOD
*[To my sister Linda and her
husband David McCary]*
When God above had lived on
earth, he lived in so much pain,
For no one has been more abused
or met with more disdain.
Our God forgives and carries on
supplying you and me,
With all the favors of his grace,
and everything for free.
Our God, he is a forgiving God of
whom we'd like to know,
Oh what a deal we've given him
to whom all things we owe.
For without God we wouldn't be
here to stay,
'Cause he created the heavens
and the earth and made us
what we are today.
Because of those reasons and
many more, he would like for
us to pray and serve him until
judgement day.

Donna Haymacher
SILENCE AND BEAUTY
Waves ripple softly in the solemn
wind,
As boats hover the deep tranquil
of the unknown.
Warmth gives life to the chilling
grip of the current,
While the sun sparkles and
enhances the awesome
emerald as the tone.

Miles of ancient forest lay before
me,
Their colors of unspeakable

height give my heart a cry of joy.
Depth of undetermined knowledge, make it understandable of all hidden secrets,
Which are contained in the solitude and darkness, your imagination to employ.

Mountains reach to the motionless clouds,
With their majesty to all, they cover all the fruited plain.
Rolling hills portray the excellence of nature,
Keeping the thought that only higher wisdom could plan, and help to maintain.

My breath is all but sustained, at the sight before my eyes,
Feelings of unspoken words are given, as prayer of thankfulness is my duty.
I treasure in my soul, the moments of this time,
Searching this whole world over, you'll only find peace and contentment, in the closeness of silence and beauty.

Pat Leonard
TRANSITION
Summer departs abruptly one morning
during our halcyon days;
Winter blows a frosty warning;
Icy fingers beckon;
Fall rushes in,
colored garmets swirling,
gaily dancing under lights,
offering a carnival
before Earth, exhausted,
falls asleep,
swathed in blankets of white.

Karen L. Rohn-Lienhard
AS ALWAYS
You walked out of the house, as always
blue collar; and you were innocently gone.
On this day, (little did you know) you were followed
by a string of comrades.
By your side was my patience,
followed by my determination,
then pride
and curiosity, with others, tagged along.
It was as if a magnet had pulled them from me.
But not once did you turn to see if you were alone.
There I sat, stripped of myself.
Happiness wasn't there to flirt with and sadness
wasn't there to feel heavy under.
Like the abandoned shell of a dead insect
I lay on the floor.
And with myself all gone, I couldn't even feel
if the tiles were warm or cold,
or if I actually was laying on a tiled floor.
Soon after you and your crowd had departed there came a noise at my door—
echoing off the sides of my shell.
I had already began to fade into

the pile of
cake crumbs you had left.
Something was scratching at the tiles,
reaching for me.
It pulled me up and I saw it was Love.
It gently nestled itself upon me and gave me support.
Love had crept back, after all the others had gone,
to keep me company
'til you were home.

James Torres
A Dream Was Shattered
[To my son David, whom I miss very much.]
As I watched her standing there
With moonlight shining in her hair,
Her gown shimmered, as she began to walk
Toward me, stunned I could not talk.
Slim of figure, fair of face
She walked in moonlit grace.
Haloed in the silver light,
A vision of beauty in the night.
She gave me to her many charms,
I held her gently in my arms.
But love was not mine to win.
For growing in the distance, an awful din
And ringing bells through the night broke.
And a dream was shattered as I awoke.

Marylou McLean Hahn
FAITH
[For Rick whose Faith was Tested and for Myself whose Faith was Questioned]
I plucked a rose in Summer
I kissed away the morning dew
I felt each rosy velvet petal
And I thought, my Lord, of You.
In my arms I held a Babe so close
And felt his sweet warmth, upon my breast
I thought of You my Lord
And my heart and mind now rest
I walked the woods in Autumntime
I viewed colors of every red and golden hue
I felt the crunch of Autumn leaves
And I thought my Lord of You
The flakes of snow in Wintertime
The budding life of Spring
The colors of Autumn
These miracles, my Lord, You bring
But alas, the rose of Summertime
And the Babe, so sweet and new
These are My Deliverance
My Strength, My Faith, My Lord, in You.

Bobbi C. Nunley
LONELY CHILDREN
Lonely are voices that cry in the night
and plead for someone to care,
traces of dreams that were broken in two
in echoes that sound in the air.

Consider the pain in the eyes of the young

where fate has twisted all love,
from the heart, from the soul,
from little lost minds,
in believing in God up above.

Remembering anger, sorrow, and grief
of being alone in the night,
in wanting the comfort of somebody there
a voice or a light in plain sight.

The crying of children to some are exempt
from places reserved in the heart,
by sinning and greed all timeless with age
never a chance from the start.

A child is easily filled with the love
so simple as holding a hand,
a kiss or a hug just given out free
is love the young understand.

Jose V. Rubio, Jr.

Jose V. Rubio, Jr.
I AM A WARRIOR OF GOD
Yes I am, a warrior of God
I'll pound righteousness throughout the land
While the Lord will always be on my side
I'll tackle the hardship day and night

I look to the left and I look to the right
I see evil near and far
I'm not afraid of dying, while the devil watching me
Intimidation is his game
Righteousness is my name.

Jose V. Rubio, Jr.
TO THE BLIND WISE
You are like the Roman Empire who thinks big but fell
You are like Goliath who fought David and fell
You are like the king who shot an arrow to heaven and fell
Truth is air that you cannot see but feel
Truth is in proximity to humans but do not see
Earth is the only dwelling for humans
With its air and vegetation
So I tell unto you blind wise
Once you leave earth and lost in the vast space
Will you not mumble "God help me"
Will you not call collect

To the meek who inherited the earth.

N. Ruth Clark
PHOTOS AND MEMORIES
Today I took the photo album
From its usual resting place,
I turn again each dog-eared page
And see an angel's impish face.

Even yet I see the twinkle
In those sparkling eyes of blue,
Here's a birthday celebration,
A baby girl has just turned two!

Countless photographs to treasure,
Oh, what memories they hold,
Two wide eyes so full of wonder,
The wind-blown lass is four years old.

Another year, another autumn,
Days are bright and crispy cool,
On my cheeks two tears are falling,
Little Miss is off to school!

Here's the pony she called "Patches";
Trusty steed and faithful friend.
Summer days they spend together
Growing up—she's almost ten!

Years are passing all too quickly,
Now I see a beauty queen,
Jeweled tiara, scarlet roses,
Our charming miss is seventeen!

Photographs I'll always cherish,
Recollections of the past,
If nothing else I have concluded,
Little girls grow up too fast!

Laura Peebles
THE STRUGGLE
It seems like forever
since feeling flowed
from my pen
Now words are wrenched
from the heart
forced down through the arm
hammered out by this tool.

Anne Marx
TESTAMENT
[For my dear daughter-in-law, Linda Chickering Marx, who has brought so much love and dedication to our family!]
No one but you I trust to weed
my prized perennial bed,
no other I could find to feed
songbirds with frost ahead.
There's no one else I'd give the key
to straighten out this room,
sort papers, poems kept by me,
save plants that rarely bloom.
No other would take pains to match
the fabric for new drapes . . .
and no one else would care to patch
family wounds and scrapes.
Some future day, I know I must
leave cherished work undone—
You share my loves! You earned my trust,
wife of my first-born son!

Tonja Thompson
LOVE: A LONELY PLACE
The world is a lonely place
But Love is the loneliest place to be,

149

I am in the loneliest place,
For I am in love
With a man,
That does not love me!
Love cries out to all
And those that answer
Are the ones that fall.
As for me, I fell,
And now, I am the one
That is going through hell.
Oh God! I love him so much
And his sweet and tender touch!
I remember the way we used to kiss
But times will never be like this.

Martin Sugerman
GONE IS TRADITION
Gone is tradition, the wise men look and smile
A nation in transition, hurting all the while
Sex-capades, drugs, violence and crime
Going the church, the family, leaders for the time
Revolution without goals, only to replace
Value systems torn with holes, an alienated human race
Economy is sick, drained on every front
Prices soar, jobs deplete, people take the brunt
Challenge for the present, like never seen before
To know yourself, who you are, to let your spirit soar
Guide posts are adrift, changes every day
Flexible, firm in heart, to listen and to say
Tomorrow is a comin', no one knows the end
To look beyond the corner, to weary souls we lend
Prophesy, astrology, magic close at hand
Tempting will and tempting fate in a mighty troubled land
Patience, reflection, decisions precedes acts
Faith in life and yourself, look at all the facts
For freedom is a complex thing, it all starts from within
Wrestle with the angel, your life you stand to win
For winning is important, so is losing too
Life is still a game, as the wise men always knew
Learn to laugh as well as cry, most of all at yourself
For none of us with all our pride can know eternal wealth

Laura Ward
LET ME LIVE
When all the world is cherry pie
And all the folks are me
When marbles grow on bushes
And mumps grow on a tree
When money is not needed
And time is never heeded
Let me live.

When the fairies dance in daylight

And all is out of doors
When bees and flowers and all the birds
Teach me all their lores
I think I shall stay
A child all the day
Oh, let me live.

Beatrice M. Roberts
SNOW
Have you ever watched the snow fall?
Watched it come down and cover all?

Snow flakes big and white,
Snow flakes small and bright.

Down and down they fall,
Snow flakes big and small.

Mother

David Braun
MEMORIES OF MOTHER
[This poem was written to—and inspired by—Mother on her passing to Heaven.]
Oh yesterday, her memory still lives in our hearts and
mother's voice still echoes with the wind;
Yes, we loved her dearly as our tears kiss happiness
that now embraces the stars.

Silently we remember mother's kind touches and magic glow;
Someday our souls shall breathe with her as we walk beside
cosmic streams and rest alongside starlight gardens.

Eternally dear Lord, we call her name as autumn leaves
magically listen, waiting for your touch of rain;
Yes, our mother's resting now as angels echo reflections of
mysterious footsteps, perhaps devas and elves dancing in the morning.

God's Magic Presence also surrounds Mother Earth as she closes her eyes tonight;
There in your dreams, mother also lives with her angelmist eyes shinning in dimensions of crystal white light.

Rest dear ones, as twilight stars fill your sky, for we see
her soul smiling down upon lilac flowers, playing with hands
of children and sharing LOVE— the source of life.

In SILENCE, mother's love is known as her silver hair
flutters silently with God's breeze, her hands touch moonbeam
stars and her heart praises the miracle of life—YOU.

Brenda J. White Williams
THE GIFT, HIS ONLY SON
[To my late Father; Gilbert H. White Sr. Whom I loved with all my heart. Who has gone on to live with our Lord. And my Mother; Fannie White, who has always been there when I needed her & her Love. And Rufus, Greg, Yolanda & Buck. I love you all. Love MOM]
You know, when death finally comes to claim the chosen one, there is no place to hide;
Under the mountains, nor the sea, nor in fields of wheat; but in the arms of God.
Whose face will shine just as bright as the evening sun.

You may sit by the oceans shores and wonder, and yearn, for but just a little while more.
You watch the waves, as they come in and as they then go back out. As you to will go,
Just like the waves from that endless sea of blue, we will be washed through those golden gates of pearl and ivory,
When here on earth, our mission and journey is finally through.

You walk through the tall trees, the wind silently whispering your thoughts.
On and on you walk, listen, and look at the beauty of the birds building their nests for the young ones to come.
The wild flowers full in their bloom, with colors your eyes are now beholding;
In this vast forest of never ending beauty you finally understand, and you know,
He loves you so much! For look around you, and think of all this that he gave so freely.

You run through the fields of wheat, your hands lightly touching their tops,
Looking back now, I see golden stalks waving me on. Thinking one more time,
Just one more time through this life please, I would undo so much that I have done;
Like say I love you every morning to the most precious gift that you ever sent me,
My loved ones. And above all, thanking him above for sending down his own special love.

The wheat waves back and forth, to and fro, softly beckoning to come, so I run:
Run you're going nowhere I thought, not so fast slow down, enjoy what he so freely gave,
Willingly he made all this beauty to enjoy. So I slowed down

knowing not why,
For all through this beautiful time he gave, I ran not knowing why or where,
But always to busy for the glory of gift to me, his love and his care.

At the end of this beautiful field I know that he will be waiting and wondering,
What it is that could be taking me so long; pretending he doesn't know why, he smiles,
And loves me even more than before; For he sees the tears of joy freely running down my face;
For I have found the true meaning and the gift that he gave so freely was his only son, Jesus Christ Our Lord!
Who took my place and died for me upon that ole rugged cross; and because of his special gift that he sent here below,
His only son, I am no longer lost!!

Kelly Forseth
PLEASE FORGIVE
The day you walked into my life, I felt we were right.
    Please forgive
Each time you spoke, you had me entranced.
    Please forgive
Your carefree personality made me laugh.
    Please forgive
Your sparkling eyes made me smile.
    Please forgive
You made me feel safe.
    Please forgive
You made me feel happy.
    Please forgive
You made me feel warm.
    Please forgive
You were the best reason to be alive.
Until, I knew we were through and you made me cry.
    Please forgive

Please forgive me for the great pain I caused you, by loving you at a time when you did not understand me.

Natalie Kirchoff
UNTITLED
[To my best friends, Teresa Brockway and Edward King, who I love very much.]
Much time we've spent together in the days not far behind.
Your beautiful smile always stays in my mind.
    A
Better friend nowhere could I ever find.
Eternally . . . Always . . .You'll be one of a kind.
So many ways you've shown me how much you care for me.
This seems so very small a thing to show what you mean to me.
    A
Friend to always be there when I am in distress,
Remember that, to me, you'll always be priceless.

If anytime you need me, no
matter where you are,
Everytime I'll be there cause to
me you are a star.
Never can anyone take away the
friend I have in you.
Do remember always that I sure
do love you, too.

Cindy Gail Greenhaw

Cindy Gail Greenhaw
I WONDER IF GOD CRIES
My parents bow their heads in
shame for the things I do that
they can neither understand
nor comprehend.
My brothers, sisters, and friends
turn their faces as if to say, "Go
away. We don't know you."
I close my eyes and think about
the one friend I still have. I
wonder if I've let him down
too?
Tears fall from my eyes like
raindrops from heaven. I
wonder if God cries?
When he sees me hurt my family
and friends, when I say things I
don't mean, I wonder if tears
fall from his eyes.
As he stands and watches me tear
down others as well as myself, I
pray he will understand and
help me.
I cry for things I cannot change
but mostly for those I don't
know how. I sit and think
about my life,
And as he looks down upon me
tears fall from my eyes. And
. . . I wonder if God cries?

Lona Jean Turner
MOTHER
Mother's the one who's always
there.
She's the one who'll always care.
No matter what you say or do;
No matter if you're glad or blue;
In your heart you will know,
Good Ole Mom follows wherever
you go.
If you're lonely or need a helpful
hand;
You can count on Mom, she'll
always understand.

Mothers' job is never done.
She's constantly on the run.
Making beds and mopping floors,
Momma has a million chores.

Breakfast, lunch and dinner time
too,
She also keeps her own menu.

Even when things go wrong;
You know Mom, still sings a
song.
Sometimes her days are bright
and cheery;
Others turn out long and weary.
Although at times we may
neglect her;
Deep in our hearts we can never
forget her.

In our hearts she's a wonderful
Mother.
In our minds she's irreplaceable
by another.
As we take out on our own;
Mom will be waiting wherever
we roam.

Mother will keep praying;
For our children who keep
straying.
God Blessed us, from heaven
above,
With a Very Special MOTHERS'
LOVE.

Lianne LeMieux Schneider
Monday Morning Rationale
Silly, all this
            stretching
for ceilings, the whoompf
of kneebends, the ugh
            of sit-ups, the carrots
an appeasement only of an oral
fixation and a damned poor
substitute
for beer and pretzels anyway.

silly, trying
            to look
under thirty, over thirty
and besides,
I always liked my plump
grandmother best.

Janet Carlisle
MY DREAM OF LIFE
Dear Lord,
I pray, whenever I dream,
Make it a beautiful colour
scheme,
I'd like there to be a castle, in
white,
A chestnut mare, a silver knight.

Clear blue skies, cool green grass,
A crystal stream, flowers
enmasse.

The scent of lilacs in the air,
Vanda orchids in my hair.
Hot white sand on a beautiful
isle,
A pleasant face, with a happy
smile.

Thunder & lightening, an
evening storm,
A crackling fire where I'm safe &
warm.

A thousand fireworks, a velvet
night,
A golden moon, on a summer
flight.

Music that's easy on the ear,
Children, that play and live
without fear.

The gentle deer, the wiley fox,
A flame coloured parrot that
often talks.

Owls and chipmunks, in tall leafy
trees,
Bees and Birds and butterflies,
please.

A table full of all good things,
A child who's laughing as she
swings.

And when it's finished, the
dreams will end,
Have standing by, just one true
friend.

May I go forth, with drum and
fife,
To make my dreams, a part of
life.

Lisa A. Kocherhans
EAGLE OF YESTERDAY
The eagle is a part of man
It flys up high, He knows he can
There alone he looks so proud
But man himself creates a cloud.
The cloud that blocks his home
from sight.
No longer does this bird fly here
Man shamed it so, he's
disappeared. . .

Joyce Johnson Gragg
I LOVED YOU EVEN THEN
[To my sister Brenda K.
Osterday, my brothers Ernest
and Bobby Johnson, and my
father Roy Lawrence Johnson.]
You were a great dinosaur, and I
only a lizard, in prehistoric
times.
When you walked through the
swamp, leaving prints on the
shore, and I crawled behind in
the slime,
I found great content, just to look
back and see, that the
footprints in yours, were mine.

When you were a fish, and I was
a toad, ten thousand years ago.
And I swam in the deep, just to
be near you, I thought surely
then you would know.

Then you were an owl, and I a
sparrow, only one lifetime ago.
When I never flew South, with
the other birds, how could you
help but know?

I have followed behind you, and
flown by your side, this love
has caused me great pain.
At last I'm content, my dreams
realized, for now you and I are
the same.

Betty Lou Hofstar Miller
LIFE'S DAY
Birth is like a brilliant sunrise,
The night and pain now gone
In tumultous joy, and promise—
New life—new day to fill with
song.

The end of life, like end of day
Comes quietly, then slips away
In muted, sunset hues; content,
Complete the life, the song, the
day.

Juanita Chenault Carman
Join Me With a Breath Of the Virgin Islands
The torrid, tropical beaming Sun
shone unrelentlessly upon
The Land, the Sea and Me.

Balmy Winds swayed the Palms
On the Land, by the Sea and near
Me.
Gigantic Mountains adorns the
Horizon
On Land, Isles of the Sea and
Strengthens Me.
Somewhere the sound of the
Larks sings sweetly throughout
The Land, the Sea, and
Melodically sings to Me.
At Eventide thousands of
Crickets chirp in orchestration
from the Trees and are heard,
On Land, by the Sea and is
Enchanting to Me.
Twinkling Stars shoot across
Earth's seemingly reachable
Canopy and were viewed—
On the Land, on the Sea and by
Me.
Suddenly, a torrential Rain
plummets down and falls,
On the Land, in the Sea and has a
cooling-effect on Me.
Splashing tidal Waves rise high
and surges
On the Land, from the Sea and is
Cleansing to Me.
Prayerfully, an uplifted Head
Mutters words of Praise—
From God's Land, His Sea and
from His Child, "Me".

Diana Lynn Lambson
GENTLY AWAY
Quietly he calls,
and
Quietly I come.
No fanfares,
No trumpets,
Just a whisper,
And a quick look back
To you.
Please,
Do the same.
No wailing,
No weeping,
No regrets.
Just a few gentle memories.

Steven Stockfish
Inspired By Sarah Hinds Garver
We are we, We are one!
We are free, all or none!
Freely we've just begun!
Harmony is now sung!

Eye to eye, hand to hand
Breathe a sigh through the land
Hear the cry, "Man loves Man!"
Why o Why? don't that stand?

Evermore, heed the task
No more war! this I ask
Freedom for us to bask
Peacedom or, hate's dark mask?

Dawn the day of the Word
Heavens may now be heard
Love's the way of the Word
Doves at play, peaceful bird.

Kathy McCall
SHIP OF DEATH
The ship was huge from bow to
stern
I came upon her emptiness, her
secrets to learn,
When I walked on deck I felt a
chill
but I stayed on board like I had

no will.
Suddenly she moved with a jerk
 and a jar
when I got to my feet the shore
 was too far,
And I stood alone on this mighty
 ship
so I prepared myself for a long
 lonely trip.
Thus all set I began to explore
down to the cabins door by door,
Oh yes there were men, but none
 held a breath
in their last page of logs, it said,
 "Ship of Death".
I took a step back, I was gripped
 by fear
what should I do? should I bury
 them here,
So the ocean became a graveyard
 once more
I bolted the cabins and locked the
 main door.
I stayed upon that mighty ship's
 deck
day after day, waiting to wreck,
When the day came that I knew I
 could take no more
In came a heavy fog and I heard
 the bolt come off of the door.
There stood a man saying, "Come,
 I want you to see
how we lost our lives, my mates
 and me,
We killed our captain, and payed
 for our ways
'Cause mate let me tell you we
 suffered for days.
So turn around and meet the
 crew
you have no place to go, so we
 welcome you,
I thought of the pain, to starve is
 so slow
when all of a sudden, someone
 yelled, "Land Ho".

Linda Philbeck
YOU WERE THERE
I remember a night,
When I was around,
The age of two or three.
I woke up,
From an awful dream,
And you were there,
To comfort me.

I remember a day,
When all the world,
Seemed to be against me.
Someone's words,
Had pierced my heart,
And you were there,
To heal me.

Thanks, Dad,
For being there . . .
To love me.

Freida Lovelace Osborne
I AM RELIEVED
I have lived for better than a
 century.
I have seen better than 36,000
 sunrises.
And I have enjoyed the songs of
 life
As sung by the birds in flight—
On their wings of Freedom.
I have watched as my children
And their children's
 children

Have joined me in my journey
 through life
Here on this earth . . .
And I have wept for those
Who have gone on before me.
I have seen things change so
 immensely
And with such suddeness . . .
That I shutter—Out of sheer
 Amazement!
I have lived long and labored
 hard . . .
And Now . . . I Am Relieved . . .
It is not you who should weep for
 me—
But rather I who should have
 compassion
For you—For whom I must leave
 behind
To continue lifes' long and trying
 journey.
For I have made my journey
 through life . . .
And I now receive my just
 reward.
I have lived through times both
 hard and good.
I have enjoyed all the seasons of
 life—
And now my time of departure
 has come . . .
I will leave with you all—My
 Memories . . .
I will be with you always—
For as long as you wish to
 remember me.
Know each and every one of you
That I have loved you dearly—
From the time of your
 beginning—
　　Until the end . . . Of Mine.

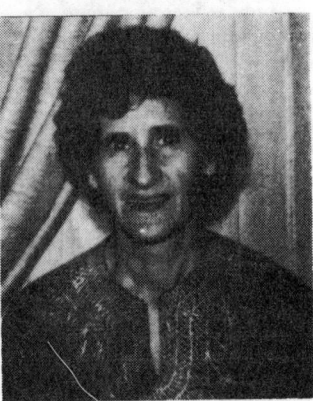
Camille M. Mucci

Camille M. Mucci
OCTOBER ODE II
*[For my beautiful beloved
Mother; Love and peace always,
Millie 1983.]*
The curtain has fallen upon
 October
Once more my precious month
 slips
 slowly away
She so graciously arrived in such
 splendor
Clothed in radiant hues
Such bold gold, brawny brown,
 interlaced
 with crimson, shadows of green
Truly this month rates supreme
It is now truly fall
All ready for a ball

As the month wanes
Her lovely gown becomes
 tattered and torn
 by nips of cold wind
The sun shines a bit paler, the
 month
 grows frailer
Sights almost too beautiful to
 behold
Quietly, softly slipping away
Occasional noisy gusts of wind
 stir
 vegetation to agitation
The last ball of the fall
Suddenly stripped of all dresses
 under duress and stress
The leaves flutter to their death
October now will go to rest and
 dream
So next year she may again rate
 supreme

Della Counts
TENDER YEARS
*[To my son Rickie and
nephews, Darryl, Michael,
Akeely, Vernon Jr. and Derrick]*
Play, children, play before it's
 too late; you have only a
 few hours till school takes
 you away

Jump, children, jump, skip, hop,
 or prance, there are not many
 years that you will have this
 chance

Run after the butterflies, pick the
 pretty flowers; as seconds will
 soon turn into hours

Tackle in a game of football, swing
 with the softball, or ride with
 the cowboys, whichever it may
 be;
 But do it all now children while
 you are FREE!!

Ms. Karen Johnson
LOVE AFFAIR
　Some Love Affairs
are like a match, they are lit
 then blown out.
　Some Love Affairs
are like sky-scrapers, they are built
 tall and magnificent
 then torn down.
　But some are like mine
built up from nothing like a flower
 blossoming into radiance
and lasting an eternity.

John G. Leara
QUESTIONS
Stand still; Quickly!
Time is passing; endlessly;
Effortlessly.
Waiting for a moment,
It never arrives.
Then it swiftly passes by;
Without warning, Without
 presence.
You awaken from a dream
Living a game; a fantasy.
Catch a miracle and call it love.
Misdefine it, then remember it.
The memory is gone with the
 moment.
Both become dreams; No;
Nightmares! Destroying your
 sanity.
Listen; There are no sounds
In your thoughts,

Just imagination and silent
 whispers
Of what you want to hear.
Look around and see
There are no real colors.
Just words that confuse
Your mind.
But is it real?
Think about human emotions;
They are like colors;
But are we real?
Confused I give answers
To Questions never thought of;
Then I Awaken.
Or Do I Sleep?

Stephen J. Torres
LET'S SAY GOODBYE
Yes I know we had good times.
But they're over now.
So let's say goodbye.
Don't try to hold on to
 something.
We don't have
Let's say goodbye
and start tomorrow
For we both have new lives.
Yes we were one once.
But no longer.
Don't think about yesterday
When tomorrow has so much to
 offer.
Let's say goodbye
and walk on our way.
For now it's over and can never be
 again
So now I say goodbye
For I'll be on my way

Mary Frances Via
THE WAY WE LIVE
What is this world coming to
On everything we say or do
Why does everybody try to
 compare
And then run around in circles in
 despair
We get in debt
Which we regret
Sometimes we lose our self
 respect
The biggest worry is about
 wealth
Our main concern should be our
 health
Let's all keep in mind
That we shouldn't be blind
To be ourselves and live our lives
And let alone otherwise
We should be thankful for what
 we have
If we are poor we shouldn't be sad
For all the things we hold so dear
We soon all die and leave them
 here

Jerry and Jean Boyce
**Thank You For My
 Yesterdays**
Come my friends and family,
 please gather round me now;
Let me thank you for my
 yesterdays.
　YET—I know not how.

Thank you for my yesterdays,
 the trials, the errs, the bad;
Thank you for my yesterdays,
 the happy and the sad.

Thank you for my yesterdays,
 the love, the hate, the tears;
Thank you for my yesterdays,

that now are yesteryears.

My yesterdays dear memories,
of love and hate and fears;
Of joy and hope and laughter,
as I've walked down through
the years.

Thank you for my yesterdays,
for the lessons of my life,
that replace hate with love and
peace
and clear my heart from strife.

I think about hate that lay
so heavy and I find,
that no one could be happy in
such a state of mind.
But my yesterdays are many and
I've learned
from life and fate;
My tomorrows will be happier
with love in place of hate.

NOW, for me so few tomorrows
as I face my waning days;
My dearest ones I LOVE YOU!
And thanks for yesterdays.

Kelly M. Redding
THE FUGITIVE
Don't look now but we're alone,
it's safe to come inside
Leave your boots outside to dry
and set your work aside
I'm trying to remember what you
look like in the light
I guess it'll all come back to me
before the close of night

Those festering disturbances gave
you itchy feet
Fate's first impression sent you
searching for retreat
I heard they found your flat just
east of Birmingham
It's just like you to try too hard
and over-extend a hand

All that time we spent apart we
surely haven't changed
It hurts to see your long lost
friends so willfully estranged
The razor's losing life to rust and
you're demanding death
It's much more painful when it's
dull and you're on your last
breath

You're walking out the door again
in the flickering candles hue
The darkness lends no answer for
the questions I ask of you
I'll miss you from the moment
that your shadow is no more
But knowing you'll be in it makes
tomorrow worth waiting for

Lisa A. Coughlin
MIRROR IMAGES
Morning ritual—
Gazing into the mirror
Watching your reflection
transcend
Into a misty haze.
Visions
Of today's headlines
Materialize across the glass:
War, Death, Fire, Starvation—
Where is the future headed?
Staring deeper into your
reflection—
Tired eyes vanish
Changing into the clear blue
irises

Of a child
Watching the last balloon
Float away on the wind.
Tears of amazement appear
As the memory and the balloon
dissipate
Into thin air.
Amid the shadows of season's past
Returns the face of the future—
Possessor of hope.

R. Ancell Krebs
DESOLATION
They sought to steal
piece by piece
the land beyond the sea
With clashing steel
peace . . . bye peace
it's war again I see

Carol A. Brill
SAILING
There are great depths in the flow
of my thoughts, emotions, and
dreams,
much more than at first
apparent;
With undercurrents moving so
swiftly,
one could be caught in the
undertow.

There have been waves and many
rough storms
which tossed and turned, trying
ever so hard to capsize.
There has been rain and foggy
days
when I could not see that
which was before me.
Warm, sunny days; days when I
was carried along
by the gentle, balmy wind.
Days when it was so calm and
still I hesitated to change
position,
fearing the encounter of other
changes.
Peaceful days and nights when I
was content with my ventures,
and prepared to face the new
tomorrow in any direction.

The storm of yesterday is all past
for the moment;
once again it is peaceful as I
look towards another day.
I've been sailing along, alone, for
some time;
I've come to know the sea and
anticipate the weather she
brings.
I've learned to cope with her
temper
and how to enjoy her calm and
peaceful moments.

But on the horizon I've seen your
sail,
ever so high and seemingly so
strong.
As I drift a little closer I am
somewhat fascinated
by the manner in which you
handle the open sea.
I'm wondering if you, too,
anticipate the weather she
brings
and if you have learned how to
cope with all her moods.

Are you sailing alone or am I not
close enough to see?

Are you content in your present
position or headed in some
direction?
Do yo mind if I venture closer
still
or would you rather I remain in
the distance?

Marion Zambery
MAN WITH A BEARD
If I bare my soul to you,
Would you see, and feel, and
absorb
The very sense of me?

Would you quell the gentle
blush,
If I expose all of my life,
And share a breath from within?

Will you sort through the
misconceptions,
That so prey upon my past,
So I may move in peace?

Can you make me see that it is I
Who has chained myself,
And help me in my release?

Could you listen to my virgin
heart,
And let me sail assured,
Or, would you simply fondle my
breast?

Cathie Rae Torgerud
YOU HELPED ME
You helped me to understand,
and
comprehend the difficult
things
in my life.
You helped me to love, and care,
for everything and everyone.
Your love is so strong, I feel it
miles away from you.
You helped me to be happy; to be
me.
You helped me to spread that
love, to the people who have
none, and need it.
You helped me in every way.
I thank you, and
I love you . . . forever.

Lisa Marie Santsaver
WHEN I WAS YOUNG
There's a part of me
In the heart of me
That's still a little girl,
So shy and frail
With a pony tail
In a make-believe world
And there's a part of me
That has to be
A lady of the world,

But it's no more a game
Or quite the same
As playing grownup while a girl.
When I was young
Life had just begun
To show me its many sides,
From playing house
To Mickey Mouse
And amusement park rides.
But now I see
In front of me
Sides I've never come to know;
The dating games,
The hurt and pains
Of loves that come and go
And if I had my way
I would rather play
Than life and love in vain,
Because when I was young
It was just for fun
And didn't cause me pain.

Mary Bergendale
LAST OF A GREAT SPECIES
What morals do we live by, what
purposes do we have today.
Our morals are decaying, our
purposes withering away.
What values goals and egos does
man try to seek,
In a sense they are tremendous in
another very meek.

Does man think he is so unique
or blindness his excuse
To all the hate and destruction in
this decade of abuse
When asked he denies it and
replies "I did not know".
But meanwhile the force of evil it
continues to grow.

We are trying to better our lives
we are progressing in every
field.
But somewhere along the road
we've forgotten the souls of
man.
We are taking too much for
granted and not stoping to
think.
That one day man will outweigh
himself and he'll become
extinct.

Tammy Kessinger
WAR
Mangled bodies and rattled
minds,
Thunderous blasts of unknown
kind.
Through the darkened sky of
night,
A sudden flash, a deadly light.
Vicious vapors assault the air.
Doom, destruction, death, and
despair.

Regina Conrath
THE SCOURGE HE FIGHTS
What Goliath is he
As fool and nut he works and
plays?
The scourge he fights is
Muscular Distrophy;
He affects our emotions to
control catastrophe,
While his fund-raising prevents
atrophy.

What Houdini is he
That thrills the crowd with
stars?
Whatever the land's geography,

He gets us in his pocket with
empathy
For we respond to his philosophy.

What Pied Piper he is
Who leads the little people?
Keeps us from being overwealthy
As he seeks to get pledges from
the healthy
By facts and jokes in all their
therapy.

What a Jerry Lewis he is
That we remember him!
His act is that of love in
philantrophy
As he makes his pitches so
stealthy
To complete his dream more
then earthy.

Margaret Murray
THE AWAKENING
First the seed is tenderly planted
deep within where
it will be surrounded by warmth
and protection
Time passing as it lies sleeping
Stirring . . . awakening . . .
drawing strength
Feeling it grow within itself
Gaining as it progresses along its
way
Emerging steadily . . . reaching
toward the light
Arriving . . . bursting into life,
full bloom
Opening its wings to show the
heart of all its struggle
into magnificent beauty
But then it always was a thing of
beauty
Right from the beginning
Before the beginning . . . when it
was an idea
Glorying in its being
For being

Kim Ritter
MY FATHER
I know my father loves me
But sometimes I don't know,
Sometimes I think he does
But it really doesn't show.
I don't even know my father
As well as a friend
But sometimes I just wished,
We were together again.
But then I take a look
Down deep inside,
And know that all those
memories
Are really left behind.
And I feel that someday
I don't know when,
I'll be able to say,
"I love you," again.

Jackie Nelson Bussa
STILL
[To My Mother: Jeanette
Parker Nelson, a sprcial friend.]
A little girl of seven viewed her
father's body, laying dormant in
a copper coffin.
As she cried out "Daddy, Daddy
wake up, it's me your little
skunk," she knew he would
never hold her in his arms
again.
Though tears flowed for days on
end, this little girl did not
totally understand her daddy's

disappearance; for she mostly
missed his physical being, as a
friend, someone to play chase
with.
As time passed on, this little girl
began to bloom and bitterness
filled her heart. She felt as if
she were cheated from total
fulfillment within her life. She
only longed for her "Daddy's"
warmth, his guidance and his
love.
Today, understanding, yet never
questioning death, this same
little girl still mourns the loss
of her father and as tears flood
her eyes, the distant loss she
hides so well, seeps to the
surface.

Iris Jean Mog

Iris Jean Mog
SUSAN
Remembering the sound of her
spontaneous laughter and
quick wit, with that God given
strength she will forever
remain in the corridors of our
mind.
As we make our dutious rounds
throughout our hospital she so
faithfully served, a dedicated
nurse and loving friend, "Our
Susan" she's one of a kind.
Life may fade from her youthful
body but her loving memories
will linger forever with us who
remain behind.

Hollie L. Corbin
UNTITLED
Only say that thou wilt not
forget me, love,
Nor toss my memory aside
As a faded rose once enjoyed,
But with no longer any purpose.
Cherish each faded petal—
Which is a memory
Of what we have shared.
Gather them close,
And treasure them always—
As thou wouldest treasure me.

Leoma Cardwell Allen
GRANDPA
There is nothing like a Grandpa
for a little
boy or girl.
He's just full of stories and
answers the best
in the world.
He will take you by the hand
Walk beside you on the sand.

While you gather Sea Shells in
your hand
You see the breakers on the
beach
Jump with delight on two little
feet
Questions! Questions! All day
long
Grandpa wonders how long he
can go on
He sees the Sea Gull in the sky
Grandpa, how come he's up so
high?
Grandpa replies, "He's made to
fly"
Grandpa, can he walk on the
ground?
"Yes, sometimes he comes down"
Grandpa does he have a home?
"Of course the sea and sky is his
domain
he lives here in sun or rain"
And so they walk hand in hand
again
As the waves washed upon the
sand.
The little boy with questions on
his mind
And Grandpa would answer them
in time.

Beth Randolph
RETURN OF A SMILE
I got up with a smile,
But soon that smile was gone.
A frown slipped in and took its
place
And made itself at home.
The day grew long
As the hours passed by,
And I thought to myself,
"Why do I even try?"
I'm getting nowhere fast it seems.
I wonder what the future brings.
Surely a better day lies ahead.
If not, we face a world of dread;
But believing that dread does not
exist,
The frown is soon erased.
The smile is back at home at last,
Willing to take its rightful place.

Barbara Emery
TIME
As the flower grows,
We let it blossom
Into life.
As the sun rises,
We watch it glow
Illuminate the sky.
As the water flows,
The waves ebb
Into caves unknown.
As the earth revolves,
Another day
Is replacing the last.
As we learn and watch
Each other,
We grow to become
Another life in the world.

Marti Strong
UNTITLED
When poets run out of words to
rhyme,
When artist's hands grow stiff,
When words of truth and justice
die,
Where will Man be then?
When the music of the world
grows still,
When dancers cease to dance,

When liberty and freedom die,
What will Man have then?

When war has menaced every
mind,
When bombs have scorched the
land,
When peace and hope together
die,
What will Man do then?

When nations bring their hatred
out,
And their people take up arms,
With charity and faith obscured,
How will Man survive?

When the air goes from blue to
black,
When the seas have changed to
brown,
When happiness and love have
died,
Where will Man be then?

When the earth and moon are
both destroyed,
Nothing left but space and sky,
The universe alone shall stand,
Man has both lived and died.

Franklin Sommers
A MEMORY OF YOU
[Written with eternal love and
honor for God, Mother Mary,
my Mother, Nora Butler, and
Carla Clemens; for Grace.]
Within my heart,
Within my mind,
Within my soul,
You live within;

Within my dreams,
Within my life,
Within my world,
You live within;

Within my prayers,
Within lives you,
Within my love.
A memory of you;

J.A. Borenstein
PARADE
bid farewell to the sad people
waving to lovers and friends as
they pass
there are no crowds of
celebration
only silent tears
the line grows longer with the
coming years
the air is warm, but a chill
surrounds the moment
marching band keeps cadence
as they pass the reviewing stand
we salute
sharp and clear
and as they begin to disappear
what remains are the memories
and fear
when will we march with the sad
parade
on and on it goes, nothing stops
on this
long road
all we can do is bid farewell to
the
sad parade

Lillian Darlene King
JUST ONE LITTLE BEER
A drunk is a man who is scared
of himself
He doesn't know this like
everyone else

He thinks that a drink will make
his mind clear
What could it hurt just one little
beer
Only one's not enough so he has
a few more
And then he's enraged ready to
even the score
So he goes home all mad and his
wife is in bed
He snatches her up by the hair of
the head
He tells her to listen he knows
he's a man
He can whip her, he's done it
before, he'll do it again
Until one late night he'll step
into her home
Enraged by the beer he just drank
alone
But she will be waiting this time
just for him
With a gun in her hand and a
scared kinda grin
She once loved this man she's
shot dead on the floor
But she can rest now she won't be
beat anymore.

Euretta L. Deal
POETRY
Poetry it seems to me is man's
inscription of his soul
Combining verse and rhyme with
feeling somehow makes us
whole
To go beyond the simple frame
and structure of these words
To generate magnificence we've
never seen or heard

It cannot be coincidence these
lines that rhyme so well
Divinely in a sense and still the
story tell
Nor have they wandered aimlessly
o'er the marques of our minds
Perchance to be recorded on the
ledger of all time

So where does it come from this
art called poetry
I believe it is a gift to all who
truly see
I believe it opens doors to all that
we have learned
And written well the reader too a
page of life has turned

These words that speak of music
though the notes are silent
tones
Seem to lend the usage of
thoughts much like our own
The range of all emotion however
deep within
Comes gently to the surface and
sees the light again

The heart beat of humanity
Alas it all must rhyme
Be joined in love with god above
Or stop the hands of time

Sharon Scholem
DREAMLIKE
[For my friends who believe.]
The forest shimmered under the
winter sun,
the ground covered under fresh
snow,
making it dreamlike.
The sun's rays caught the sparkle
of the

melting icicles on the trees,
making it dreamlike.
The snow was still clean with no
footprints,
everything still as nature had
planned,
making it dreamlike.
The branches of trees were
bending low
as if in a welcome way,
making it dreamlike.
The silence of the forest spread
to the world,
making it dreamlike.
Then the children bounded into
their
favorite spot,
making it real.

Alma Thurmond
**These Songs Remind Me Of
You**
[Specially dedicated to Bill
Lawrence (Ex-Godfrey Star) in
memory of our first meeting on
New Year's Eve of 1952.]
My Darling, My Darling, I Miss
You
More and More As Time Goes
By,
You know You Made Me Love
You
Under that Ole Buttermilk Sky.

I Dream of You Night and Day,
I Cross My Fingers and Always
pray,
It isn't fair, my dear,
That I Should Care this way.

Now that I Need You
You're Breaking My Heart in two,
It's Always You I Surrender to,
Your Candy Kisses leave me So
Blue.

Whenever I hear the Serenade In
Blue,
My Foolish Heart longs to be
Near You,
Darling, in the Blue of Evening
These songs remind me of you.

Carolyn Williams
FADING MEMORIES
[To my four children who have
been inspirations to me. They
have given me the courage
through the years to use the
talent that God has given me.]
Thoughts of the past unwelcome,
soaring full and free.
Clear at first then cloudy as a
fading memory.

Dreams that plague me nightly,
brief
replacements for reality.
Haunting then disappearing as a
fading memory.

Storm clouds hovering overhead
as dark as dark can be.
Looming in then out freely as a
fading memory.

Dear freinds bring joy and
laughter,
welcome sights to see.
Visiting awhile then gone as a
fading memory.

Life is but a vapor to God,
a gift to be lived fully.
But a vapor vanishes rapidly as a
fading memory.

John J. Palmer
HELEN
a French champagne can sparkle
not
so bright as morning hearts
invited by two eyes and caught
by what one voice imparts

assured and soft
a vital loft
to rest within

so feminine
genuine

and unafraid

Megan H. White
THE MIRAGE
Did it bring you joy?
  Or was it only a well-disguised
excuse
    to abandon the trust and faith
    placed upon your shoulders
      by those for whom you
      were responsible?

Are you now fulfilled?
  Or did the sudden realization
    that you could very easily lose
    those who once loved you
      fill you with such insecurity
      that you asked for their
      forgiveness?

Are you not blind?
  Or do you see yourself so
  irreplaceable
    that those whom you have
    touched
      will stumble without your
      hand to guide them?

It may interest you to know
  that I learned to walk long ago.

Diane R. Fejes
WORDS OF LOVE
[To my good friend Rebecca,
who truly knows the beauty of
The Yellow Rose.]
Flowers can mean love,
  and I love flowers.
Fill my life with Roses
  let us while away the hours.
Make my heart the budding start
  of love so warm, so true,
Then promise to forget-me-not
  as lovers sometimes do.

For through the years, and all the
tears
  love travels like a vine,
and steals its way to tender
hearts
  that pass the test of time.
So I must seek the path of hope,

'twas lost within my youth,
and hope to find The Yellow Rose
of dignity and truth.

Oh vines of love to which we cling
if you should go astray,
Or die in lonely darkness on some
cold and wintery day,
Remember, Spring will come again
and new buds will appear,
To cling to vines as we once
did . . .
  forever holding dear!

Della Counts
SISTER TO BROTHER
[To my family and inspired by
my dearly loved brothers:
Roger, Mike & Melvin]
Don't rescue me from love's
unjust dolor
  if you are the cause of another
sister's pain
Are we not made of the same?

Don't expect the man I am with
to treat
  me fair, if benevolence with your
  mate is not what you share

Therefore, add to your thoughts,
this thought
  and keep it as fresh as each
new day
Even dire conditions
  Never throw it away

If one man would strive to be
commendable
  to another's sister, his goodness
  will surely be seen again

So, if fate for me is to watch love
birds
  from afar, I'll still be elated and
  with peace to know
Just a few men, whose goodness
for another
  man's sister is worth being seen
again

Alison S. Sloat
MIDWAY
Grey . . .
Neutral grey.
A beginning,
And an end.

Life emerges
From nothingness,
A colorless lump of clay.

And ends
In tears,
And soft, misty
Grey.

Sylvia Smith
LOVE? LUST?
[To Nick—My gypsy love]
Between satin sheets two of us lie
Gazing at each other without
breath
The eyes revealing such delight
A cavern of joy, abundance of
wealth

Brown to Brown lustrously they
ignite
Setting soul to soul to depths
unknown
We breathe each breath, forsake
all time
Remember we are here on loan

Our tongues grow silent how can
we speak?

Our senses permit us of their use
They dole out one by one they
   are content
How richly these senses have
   been privileged their use

Love does come time after time
Obsessive, promiscuous,
   immature but this?
Love now I say, yes, yes this Love-
The body, mind and soul all
   shake
Two glances entertwined in love
   ah Lust!

Hands woven by feathers softer
   than down
The eyes explore each crevice
   each line
Map to Map in beautiful hue
To Life! To Love! Me? You?

If our limbs grow crooked with
   age or dew
If our eyes refuse to see
If Man or God shall forsake us all
How dear we two to each other
   shall be.

Mary L. Hawkins
NEW BIRTH
What does salvation mean to me?
It is the risen Christ,
Who died to set men free.
Not free to do as before,
But to serve Him, honor Him,
Glorify His name,
Witness to the world why He
   came.

Let your light shine in Christian
   love,
Rejoice in His name,
Give thanks to Christ,
Who spilled His blood on calvery,
Suffered in agony and pain,
Provided our new birth,
With payment for our sins,
All who ask in faith believing
Can have a new heart within.

Lois Cooper-Jones
What Could Have Been
A moment I held within my hand,
   Light as a butterfly,
   Newborn as a flower,
   A second sliver out of one
      hour.
I dropped it carelessly.
   O God! Unaware was I
   I held there opportunity.

Ola Margaret James
Father, We Thank Thee
[To Ada Leah James,
my mother.]
We thank thee God, for Thy son,
   Jesus,
For the Holy Spirit that
   Communes within us,
We thank Thee for the bounty of
   the earth;
The vegetables of the garden, the
   fruits of the fields,
The grasses and flowers, the
   shrubs and the trees
The heavenly skies and the
   beautiful seas!
We thank Thee for holy men to
   guide us,
For musicians, artists, writers to
   inspire us,
For physicians to help heal our
   bodies,

We thank Thee for the poetry of
   our lives,
For the practical prose of our
   daily living
We thank Thee for our families,
   for our friends,
For the assurance, "I will not
   leave you comfortless"
For the divine choice given us to
   walk in Thy way,
For blessings large and small that
   come each day,
Father, in Heaven, we gladly
   thank Thee!

Staphanie Marie Brown
EVEN NOW
[This poem was written to—
and inspired by —my fiance
Jeff, who showed me what love
is all about.]
Even now as I think of you
I feel love grow in my heart
Growing by leaps and bounds
Growing like tall trees
Standing with their hearts
Close to the singing breeze
Even now when I look at you
I see beauty and love
Staying there waiting
For me to reach out and touch
Even now I love you
And will forever
Even now we'll be growing
Ever so closer
You as you
And me as me
Even now as I look
Our love is growing stronger
By day and by night
Even now.

Lindsey Nicole
FRAGMENT OF LOVE
A piece of life broke off from me,
It fell hard and passed away.
But I am making a life for myself,
I still live and I can love.
I try to forget that piece,
But forgetting isn't easy.
That certain emotion hurts,
The emotion of love.
Visions of that piece come to me
They come complete and fast,
But leave too slow.

Rena Behee
SOLITUDE
Solitude I wrap it around me,
a cloak it is to me, a wall to
   surround me,
Keeping others out keeping me
   in,
it's a protection, a loneliness.
A defense an offense, a game I
   play alone.
A joke I can not share.

Pat Hernandez
LOVE
[To my husband Tony, who is
my source of inspiration, and
the only one who could ever
bring forth the poet lurking in
my soul.]
Love can be fragile and built on
   lies,
It can be tender, like angel's sighs.
It can be weak, or it can be
   strong,
But ours is the best love, it's
   never been wrong.

It's always been there to wipe
   away tears,
Or celebrate happiness down
   through the years.
It's lasted through good times,
   and through the bad,
And sometimes our love was all
   that we had.

It's lasted through a million years,
And will last a million more.
For this is not the first time,
We have loved like this before.

Our love had no beginning,
It will never have an end.
It just keeps on growing stronger,
Like a tree the wind can't bend.

Every tear we share together,
Every hurt that we must feel,
Only helps to make us closer,
And our love that much more
   real.

June Harrington

June Harrington
IN THE WIND
I hear
word songs
in the March wind
and feel
my children's tears . . .
my memory
tumbles backward
down the years . . .
and sea gulls
called to me then
in a strange voice
from out
an April sky . . .
and I
remember the time
I heard
my mother cry . . .

Lloyd Izak
OUR HEAVENLY FATHER
Heavenly Father may Your name
   be blessed forever
   And may Your kingdom dwell
      within us
   Each moment that our wills are
      made one
By Your Heavenly grace we will
   pray Father
That we may come to enjoy the
   fruits of
Your kingdom here on earth
As we hope to enjoy them in
   Heaven
   May Your Heavenly bread
      sustain us Father
As it is given from Your love this
   day

And may we return a portion of
   that love to You
By giving in truth Your love to
   others
As we would expect them to give
   their love to us
And guide our steps on the sure
   path to Heaven
That our duty on earth may be
   fulfulled in You
And our soul may merit the
   grown of eternal rest.
      Amen.

Catherine F. Hartman
TIME
A time for Love
   A time for living,
A time for sharing
   And always giving.

A time for sadness
   A time for grief,
A time to be happy
   A time to be sweet.

A time for friends
   A time for the phone,
A time for listening
   A time to be alone.

A time to be disillusioned
   A time for false hope,
A time to be needed
   And certainly to cope.

Kathleen Ann Dexter
FOR ONE LIKE ME
those pieces of you
      (matching pieces of me)
   that
      need for solitude
      love for work
   those rough edges in yourself
      (in myself)
      that make you a
         hermit
         at heart
      that will
         eventually
         puncture the cocoon of
         your marriage
         (inevitable)
those facets of you
   (mirrors of me)
   make me hurt
      for you
         (and fear
         for me)

Janie Jones
SNOWSTORM
Orchestrated from the heavens;
   choreographed with loving care,
Giant snow flakes floating
   downward, pirouetting through
   the air.
Silently, oh silently—drifting,
   darting, diving down,
Floating, falling, feeling fluffy,
   giant evergreens they crown.
Grasses on the earth receive
   them greedily, and close they
   hold
As they kiss the earth beneath
   and shield new seedlings from
   the cold.
Barren elms and maple trees bare
   lift their branches and rejoice,
Joining in the silent chorus of the
   snowstorm's vibrant voice.
Tiny mouse caught in the
   meadow strains his ears to hear
   the tune,

Dives more deeply in his tunnel,
waiting for the song of June.
Underneath kind, sheltering
branches of the spruce
bedecked with white,
Cheerful chickadees, dee-deeing,
watch this ballet in delight.
Swirl upward in crescento!
Soundless tintinabulation
swells!
Snowflakes' special full
performance all complete with
unheard bells.
When performance is complete
and the final note is sung,
Transcendental beauty lingers,
tranquil in the setting sun.

Susan Cunningham
SUICIDE
Blinded
Into death's grasp I run
Smiling
I wrap the rope about my throat
I wrench it tight
With Teasing
Come, come, into my arms, my
claws
My sweet seductive strife
He seeks to love my death within
his life

Joyce Angus
MICHAEL'S GONE
*To my nephew Michael, who
left us too soon—Aunt Joyce]*
Can't seem to sleep this Sunday
morning
Michael left us without any
warning
The tears were many, the smiles
were few
From the many friends that
Michael knew

Our time on this earth is planned
they say
You wonder why he was taken
away
Some lives are like trees and their
lives are long
Michael's life was short and, full
of song
He would not like tears and our
time spent in sorrow
Maybe we will be able to smile
again tomorrow

Laura J. Czarnecki
BEAUTY
Beauty is the sunshine,
That wakes us up each morn anew;

Beauty is the grass
That sparkles with dew;

Beauty is the birds,
That fly oh so high;

Beauty is everything—
Everything Our Lord created for
you and I.

Joanne Thomison Kimsey
LOVE PRETENDERS
Temptations of joy—
Lie just a mile away
Surrounded by loneliness,
A barrier blocked in a mystical
game.
Never realizing the danger,
But suffering the foreign pain
The men you knew have left
your flight—
And trapped love in a gentle hold
me tight.

Pride takes its toll and confidence
a lacking strike
Losers and leaders gather
physically,
Failing the mental side—
Seeing time as strangers captured
for a ride.
The words he used were
pretenders
Love open without guarantee—
Day and night romancers proud
too be
Take me if you want me, before I
leave.

William G. Zdanis

William G. Zdanis
The Son of Virgin Mary
About two thousand years ago,
the year was five B.C.
GOD sent HIM down to earth to
save, sinners like you and me.
And on December twenty-fifth,
to Mary HE was born.
The world had never known
such joy, 'till that December
morn.

With Virgin Mother Mary's love
and Joseph good and kind,
Child JESUS grew to be the man,
GOD sent to save mankind.
'Till HE was thirty HE did
work, a carpenter was HE.
And then a preacher HE became,
indeed changed history.

HE preached that we believe in
GOD and that we love HIM too.
That one another we must love,
as HE loves me and you.
JESUS had power to heal the
sick and miracles to make.
The multitudes believed in
HIM, this put his life at stake.

Soon Pilate and the Sanhedrin,
decreed that HE must die.
He was accused of blasphemy,
JESUS they'd crucify.
And crucify JESUS they did. HE
bore his cross alone.
HE died for us upon the cross,
laid in a tomb of stone.

On the third day HE rose again.
The scriptures were fulfilled.
He ascended into heaven. This
was as GOD had willed.
In glory HE will come again,
judge those that live and died.
This will be on the world's last
day. HE will our fate decide.

Michael E. Graham
AT TWENTY-FIVE
You my age are a very pretty
young lady and there have
been times when I desired you.
Time passes and you belong to
another
A lawyer to be who has enrolled
in law school.
From your breasts I learn tales
you could have told had I but
asked.
To me it is no secret you use the
pill.
Had I enjoyed myself even at my
age, to God, my family and
myself I would surely be
dead—dead from knowing
things children who taste the
milk pap of nature shouldn't
ever know.
I recognize your face hidden in
dark glasses as you reach for
your shades to lift them out of
respect for my decision.
You have been true to the times
that says so much for
promiscuity as I lay back on
the couch of a shrink.

Karen B. Satterley
LAST CHANCE
As we sit on the shore,
Sand runs through our fingers;
Time is that way,
For it never does linger.

While it's in the open
Palm of our hand,
We should grasp opportunity
'Cause for long it won't stand.

It's gone in a moment;
Our chance, it has passed.
It may never come again.
It could be the last.

Shirley Martin
CALL OF AUTUMN
As I stand on the edge of summer
I hear the robin's last lonely trill
The winding, laughing brook
slows to a whisper
Each butterfly and bee has bid
farewell
The field is bare of corn and
pumpkins lay await
A summer breeze becomes a wind
to chill
And tangles the leaves, now red
and gold
Above, a harvest moon shines
brighter
As the sun's rays grow ever dim
The dusty path I trod before

is flecked with raindrops
And once again, I heed the call of
autumn

Pam Fetridge
NO WAY IN HELL!
I've been hurt so many times.
I can't take it no more.
When I was small about one or
two,
I was laughed at.
"Boy, she sure walks funny!" they
used to say.
I sure can't help that, I was born
that way.
Slapped around like a basketball,
that sure hurt me.
I was used and abused,
even called a few names.
Life for me has been hell!

A child of mine will never go
through the hurt or pain
as I have.
I'll make sure of that!
No names or games that people
seem to play.
Nothing of the kind.
No Way In Hell!

Mary Bereti
SCARED SOUL
*[In memory of my father who
passed away March 20, 1975]*
Fallen deep into blackness
With no way out
Your insides scream
But you can't shout
Your heart's scattered
Your brain aflame
Somehow you know
You'll never be the same
Part of your life
Has been taken away
Your feelings gone
What can you say
You look around
And all is black
You wonder if you'll
Ever come back
It's cold and dark
Down in this hole
The pain
Has taken its toll

Betty L. Vest
BROKE AGAIN
*[This poem was inspired by
raising four lovely children and
living on a very strict budget.
To Michael, Judy, Dennis and
Charles.]*
To be well known with my words
and verses
To put jingles together and
money in purses.
To see my name on a front page
cover
Makes me nervous, my heart
does flutter.
To each of my children I dedicate
a page
It isn't the best but it's mom's
latest rage.
My hand it writes these silly
verses—
Jingles to lines but no money in
purses.

Howard James Scott
LIFE
Take life as it comes your way
Try to live it day by day

Ask God for his help my friend
He'll be with you to the end.

Many a struggle we'll find to-day
But He will help us on our way
If we only learn to live
With the love He has to give

Remember this my friend is true
Jesus died for me and you
So give your troubles up to Him
And a better life, you will live in.

He'll send you joy most every day
If you will ask Him when you
 pray
To let you help your fellow man
In any way that you can.

So listen my friend I pray
That you may have a better day
That God I love will help you be
As happy as His love's made me.

Jo-Ann M. Hatton
BIG BROTHERS
Wait for me, she screams,
with dirt and determination
on her face.
Just because I'm a girl,
she yells, doesn't mean I don't
have a place
with you.

I can climb a tree
and build a fort even better.
Run as fast.
It's not fair, you know it,
to leave me behind, alone,
always last,
with you.

Boy, when I grow up
I'll get even, wait and see.
Tears appear.
I'll do just what I want to,
go anywhere I want to go,
far or near,
without you.

But I'll still love you . . .
She cries.

Donna Cortopassi
Meadow In the Springtime
Similiar to a meadow in the
 springtime:
A birthday should be a happy
 occassion
It doesn't matter when the seeds
 of grass
 were planted
But how much more beautiful
 the meadow
becomes with each passing year.

Verna Warner
A SAD AWAKENING
The eventide of life has come,
I know it in my heart
The place of happy memories,
Forever must we part.
Oh! why is life so full of woe
When one must make a break?
Because God has made it so
For His dear loving sake.
There is no turning back again
To days that's gone before—
Life now is just an open road
And He is now our door.
Oh! fate spins around and 'round
Take us into your hand,
And let us gently drift apart
To a gracious peaceful land.
For God has shown His mercy
When I called on Him that day,

But now the light shines brightly
And there is no other way.

Aileen P. Morley
LOVE
When I say I love you, it's only
 three words,
 But it says all that I feel,
No other words can capture the
 meaning of it all
 When you are near.

The thrill is beyond compare,
 love grabs my heart.
 I gave it to you freely,
 fearlessly,
For in the shelter of your arms, I
 rejoice!
 In my love for you, and yours
 for me.

I long for each warm embrace,
 each tender kiss,
 For they are the treasures you
 impart.
The happiness in my heart, shall
 lift from my
 lips to yours.

Marlaine Rowe
I REMEMBER
I remember the summer grown
 restless
and you . . .
the murmur rustling through my
 hair.
A romantic, breathless adventure
 rocked me each night,
to a sleep without care.
I remember...so well I remember
your ocean-blue eyes and the
 hoping for good-chance,
for we wished to wear the cock-
 eyed hat of chance that
 summer.
I remember as if my mind took
 pictures
of you, carrying answers in your
 arms
as your feet switched
from one maybe to another.
I remember . . . remember
I remember the summer grown
 dry and restless
and you . . . the murmur
 rustling through my dark hair.

Barbara Collins
THE FUR TRADERS
In the sweep of the river, where
 the water runs free,
With guns, bow and arrow, come
 the whiteman and Cree,
Frenchmen and Scotsmen and
 dusky half-breed,
Paddles that flash with gathering
 speed.
Each with his beaded and fur
 lined chapeau,
Crimson french belts, and painted
 bateau.
Up to the stone fort that stands
 on the hill,
Frenchmen and half-breed all of
 strong will.
A short time to rest and a short
 time to tarry,
They sing as they paddle along to
 Fort Gary.
They have skirted the rapids and
 portaged again,
These men of the north and men
 of the plain.

They've slept 'neath the spruce
 trees, and cold they have felt,
These men of the north where
 the ice doesn't melt.
They've traveled the Nelson from
 the shores of the bay
This far distant land where the
 white foxes play.
The land of the Eskimo, musk-ox
 and bear,
The whispering aurora; those
 ghost-lights they share;
That dance like the fairies on a
 shimmering sea,
Where the grey goose returns to
 the land of the free.
Sing hearty my friends, you men
 of the north,
Where our forefathers traveled
 and dared to go forth.

William C. Schobert

William C. Schobert
**THIS BAYONET (A Tribute
 to a Fallen Enemy
 Soldier)**
*[Dedicated to the brave men—
both allied and enemy—who
gave their lives for their
countries in the belief that
their cause was just.]*
THIS BAYONET—it once belonged
 To a soldier of Japan.
For family, home, and life he longed
 As does every fighting man.

When fierce and hot the battle grew,
 He did not his duty shirk.
His fight was lost—and this he
 knew—
 As his death did 'round him
 lurk.

We'll never know this soldier's name,
 Who did die on foreign sand.
A hero by death he then became
 To his family, friends, and land.

That war's long o'er; the years
 have passed,
 But the mem'ries linger on.
We hope his ashes—home at last—
 With respect are looked upon.

Fierce enemies we were at war.
 Had he lived, we might be
 friends.
He's gone; I'm here; we'll fight no
 more.
 We salute him 'til time ends.

THIS BAYONET to me belongs;
 a reminder of that man
Who gave his life for Nippon's
 wrongs
 In the war which it began.

June Egland
KEEPER'S OF THE YOUNG
Somewhere on a dirty, noisy
asphalt checkerboard
a pocketful of change
and a drop is scored
a fatal trip
searching for a memory
that couldn't be found
now gone is the life
along with the sound
in the distant, their music
awaits to be sung
unfamilar is the tunes
to the keeper's of the young
hours of dark shadows fall
where sunshine ought to be
the aura of death leaves
a heavy touch of reality
all hopes and dreams
far flung
what victories remain
for the keeper's of the young
no longer a second chance
to grab the world by the hand
standing together to watch
moonbeams run bare foot
thru the sand

Ted W. Lamoreaux
MEDITATION
". . . in thought I enter a
 woodland scene
where no one else has ever been
the mountains surrounding the
 beauty untold
bathe in sunlight of purest gold
the trees are dressed in silver leaf
and the fragrance there is beyond
 belief

. . . the flowers are burnished
 bits of prayer
and deeper thoughts that linger
 there
the stream that murmurs a
 melody
flows to a lake of eternity

. . . here in solitude I kneel to
 pray
to the water's edge I come each
 day
my thoughts are unclothed—my
 soul is bare
unadorned as my spirit when I
 am there

. . . this is mine—my utmost
 retreat
not a place to hide nor to escape
but a place to pause . . .
. . . to meditate . . ."

Patricia A. Adams
EULOGY FOR DAD
His name was John and strong as
 his name was he,
A family man with a joke on his
 lips and an eye full of glee.
He worked hard for his family a
 good provider no finer.
A gentle man and of character
 there was no kinder.
He was a handsome man a
 faithful husband to my mother.
He was strict on us kids yet
 always a loving father
He had a congenial way and a
 simple disposition.
And his wisdom to my problems
 was always a helpful addition.
He ran deep like the

undercurrent on the ocean
beach.
But he was always there a man
within our reach.
Even our dog laid quietly in his
lap.
He loved all animals and they
loved him back.
Dad was a man of long suffering
and patient endurance,
And you'd see him in church on
Sunday with every assurance.
And when there was trouble he
was there on the double,
And dad I thank you for that.
Sorry for all the trouble.
Well daddy dear I have no more
to say,
I'm so sorry mom that dad had to
go away.
But if there's a God in Heaven
and I know there surely is,
Good old pop is up there, to get
the reward that's his.

Christine G. Leisle
GENTLE TOUCH
*[For Wendell Stewart; my
special guy; who inspired my
life and showed me so much
love in the time we had
together.]*
So young so alive
and so full of pride
you've blessed so many people
and touched so many lives.

Our love was so gentle
tenderly sharing all we had
how wrong i was in thinking
something good like it would
last.

Such is gone our golden days
never again will you hold me
in your gentle special ways.

But where you are now is in
heaven above
for God has chosen you
with his soft touch and his
love.

Now suffering and loneliness are
waiting with me
i'm trying to be strong
but my heart continutes to
bleed.

slowly i'm losing strength
i miss you so much
i'm praying to God
and through him i just felt
your gentle touch.

You've made me what i am
and what i'll always be
for you were my friend and lover
and you'll always be a part of
me.

Esther (Vanek) McGechie
MY MAN
He's a man of deep emotion,
of jealousy and fire
Who's magnetism holds me and
controls me with desire.

I love to lie beside him when
we've had a little wine,
To press my face against his cheek
and kiss his lips with mine.

I love to run my fingers through
his wavey, silky hair
And rub my hand against his neck
and shoulders when they're bare.

Then I hear the panting magic
of whispered words so fair
And the pounding, quickened
heartbeats
that say we're almost there.

I feel a glow and tingle
over every inch of skin
And realize a love like ours
could not exist in sin.

Far into the darkness when in
quietness we have lain,
My man will draw me close to
him
and magnatise again.

Jonathan Miller
The Disappearance of the Poet U.S. Freighter Lost At Sea October 24, 1980
*[To the memory of the crew of
the Freighter Poet: and to their
untimely end.]*
It was in the dead hour of night—
the helm was lashed a-lee—
As the ship the freighter Poet
ploughed the Mediterranean
Sea;
The Third Mate Robert Grove
dreamt of his lovely wife,
Where his love grew thick
around her, his was a happy
life.
Yet, now beneath his dreamy
gaze, he thought he saw a
shroud;
But it was a sail on a raft, peopled
by a naked crowd:
With the silhouette of Gibralter
behind them, and the British
unforgiven,

One with eyes that made Grove's
blood run cold, stook up and
cried to heaven—
"Oh, Mariner, Mariner standing
there, save our rotten horde;
The Argus took but fifteen, will
ye take the rest of us on board?"
Grove vainly strove to restrain
his mounting horror for there
he saw in hanging strips
On the raft's sail-rigged ropes, the
dangling jerky of human lips!
The grotesques on the rolling raft
looked as though they danced a
gastly salsa,
And Grove asked from what ship
they came, the red eyed
hideous replied, "The Medusa."
At these words, Grove went
numb and the more colder
grew, shuddering pale and dumb,

Looking on that raft like one that
knew his hour had come.
He knew the history of the
Medusa, wrecked off
Senagal-way,
But as it happened, the wreck
occurred one hundred and
sixty-four years ago that very
day!
You may guess Grove shrunk
daunted from the sight;
And stood paralyzed as the
spectres came aboard by
ghostly moonlight,
Bringing with them their
winding-sheet sail. Grove did
not understand.
Seeing this, the red eyed fiend
said, "ye are a romantic, and we
must have ye by the hand
For we are the one hundred and
thirty-four the Argus left
distressed;
From that day to this, we live on
those whom love hath blessed."
So round and round went their
winding sheet, covering the
freighter whole,
And like a waterspout the Poet
and raft disappeared like the
loss of a heathen soul!
None have seen the Poet since,
and Goodwife Grove pines for
her husband lost.
Yet, Robert is to be found on the
raft of the Medusa off
Gibralter, sea-tossed
With these spectral wraiths
scanning the ocean to descry a
lover's call.
Night by night, forever unending
on their damn-ed raft,
They sail on the currents of
death's shrouded pall.

Raye J. Baker
OLD LOVE TUNE
Today I heard an old love tune. It
brought back memories of
years ago when we were young
and you were there with me.

You promised me the world so
wonderful and jay, you
promised me the ocean on that
beautiful day in May.

And now the years have come
and gone. Somehow you forgot,
my world, my ocean and our
old love tune that memories
brought back.

Annette B. McKinney
INSIGHT
*[To my mother, who taught me
to look for beauty in
everything I see—and to Aunt
Mamie and Aunt Cora, who
taught me to think poetically.]*
A gentle breeze fanned my brow-
And I thought of hurricane
winds.

A tiny ant crossed my path—
And I thought of dinosaurs.
In my garden a mustard seed
sprouted—
And I thought of giant redwoods.

A candle flame flickered—
And I thought of the power of the
sun.

I felt a drop of rain—
And thought of mighty oceans.

A child carved on a bar of soap—
And I thought of Michaelangelo.

I looked at light through a prism-
And thought of a rainbow.

A children's choir sang at church-
And I thought of Handel's
MESSIAH.

A mother tended her sick child—
And I thought of Albert
Schweitzer.

A baby smiled in its sleep—
And I thought of GOD.

Johari
LOVE IS A FEELING
Love is a feeling, not talk
My body will do the talking and
my
lips will part, but only to sing a
love song
A love song that you make me
feel
with your love
A love that is so fierce and gentle
that I can't help but love you
back
To give all my love and hope to
match
yours
To hear your lips part in a love
song
to me
A song that will blend with mine
in
a harmony so perfect only we,
together
can make it
A harmony so perfect that we
know
we were meant to be together
A harmony that will make my
body yours
and your mine so that talk is no
longer necessary between us and
we
will know
LOVE IS A FEELING, NOT TALK

Leah C. Anderson
THE FANTASY OF LIFE
Life is but a Fantasy, a Story that
unfolds;
As a Baby comes into the World
and as suddenly grows old!
Tho' growing up seems endless in
those early tender years;
The happy days, the gloomy days,
the laughter and the tears!

The ecstasy and rapture that
accompany Teen's first Love;
The romance of the Moon and
Stars that brightly shine above!
And then the thrill of a Wedding
Day, the pride of a lovely
home;
The happiness that a Baby brings
has a meaning all its own!

As time goes by and Baby grows
from childhood into youth;
Comes the sudden realization of
the plain and honest truth!
That the World is nothing more
or less than one gigantic Stage;
And every Creature plays a part
to his own appointed age!

Then death interrupts a Player
and another takes his place;
To continue on to his destiny as
a part of the Human Race!
The Book of Life is written in an
endless, stirring way;
With its Characters, its Stories,
ever changing day by day!

Some Chapters tell of tragedies
and others of great success;
Many are filled to overflowing
with love and happiness!
Great Books of Fiction have won
acclaim but none can compare;
With the True Life Stories that
unfold and permeate the air!

E. Kitti Stone
DISASTER?

Little black mask, eyes so
bright,
What kind of mischief within
your sight?
Chitter, chatter, chirr and trill,
How sweet your voice to hear,
But when I hear your little feet,
I know disaster's near!

Up to the cupboard, then open
the door,
Constarch feet all over my floor.
Try to catch my little
"disaster,"
Gotta learn to run a wee bit
faster!
Sleeps in the bed, curled up
tight,
Wakes up to play in the middle
of the night.
Soft little paws running
through my hair,
Whenever you sit on the back of
my chair.

Little ringed tail, set free to
roam,
Never again to bless my home.
Much as I loved you, I set you
free.
You belong to the forest, not to
me.
Whenever I see a Raccoon or
two,
I'll always wonder, "Could that be
you?"

Diana Yurkovich
LIGHT

A light on all night,
When is it morning?
I've been there you know,
But I don't know if I see
A reason to awake,
A way to sleep.
The thin ray on his face dissolved
into florescent,
A boy in a cell scratches his
memoirs on the wall.
Outside the wires
In her room she thinks of the
bars;
The lack of conversation from an
unused soul.
The nightlight goes out
As she finishes another poem.

Tony Kwiecinski
THE HOLY LAND

As swiftly as sand drifts across
the plains,
as gentle as spring time rains
for flowers that bloom across
God's Hills

symbols the beauty of the world
that the heart fills,
Ah, yes, this is the world that
God made,
The place where green trees may
shade,
Where the sun may shine in
distant valleys all day,
Brighting the world for kids to
play,
People helping people in this
happy land
As far as you can see it spand,
with families and friends loving
each other
everyday and everytime,
Ruling out the threat of any
crime,
God made this world for the
animals and us to share,
We show respect by giving it care
and for hearts that fill up
every inch of space,
We only ask that God may Bless
our
HOLY PLACE

Glenn Bailey
A CARESS OF LIFE

*[To my beautiful precious wife
Sandy, who's love and
understanding have given me
the greatest caresses of my life]*
Funny how time can slip away
First thing you know twenty-four
hours have passed
And it's another day
And the days become our months
And the months become our
years
And so alas we have another time
another era
How it can all come to pass so
quickly
Like the fleeting moments of our
lives
And how often on the pathway of
life
We are touched by a caress
Wanting to be grasped, wanting
to be loved, wanting to be
lived,
And would it not be such a
wonderous thing
If we could take each and every
caress of life with us
Through all eternity
To become a part of a destiny in
order to create the
Wonderful gift of immortality
But even so not one caress of life
would survive
For eternity is not forever
without those fleeting
moments
Of life that touched a caress
We tried to grasp, we tried to
love, we tried to live,
That fell along the pathway of a
cherished memory

Florence M. Craven
**There's A New Day
Dawning**

There's a new day dawning on
the morrow
There'll be no more tears—no
more sorrow
Old friends will meet—and then-
We'll see our folks again
We'll have a celebration in the sky.

There'll be a new day dawning by
and by
We gave up the old delights
That used to fill our days and
nights
Old things passed away—
Many friends refused to stay
When Jesus came to lead in the
Blessed new found way—
There's a new day dawning on
the morrow
There'll be no more tears—no
more sorrow
Old friends will meet—and
then—
We'll see our folks again
We'll have a celebration in the
sky.
There'll be a new day dawning
very soon
We'll be filled with heavenly
peace
Morning, night and noon
Our searching will be o'er—
We'll be happy ever more—
Our friends and kin will gather
'round
New heights of glory will abound
There's a new day dawning in the
sky.
There's a new day dawning on
the morrow
There'll be no more tears—no
more sorrow
Old friends will meet—and
then—
We'll see our folks again
We'll have a celebration in the
sky.

Michael P. Szalai

Michael P. Szalai
ROBIN HOOD

In England of old, when men were
quite bold.
There lived a man, who I'll never
understand.
Robin Hood was his name, he
was noted for his fame.
He cared for the poor, he was
never a boor.
The Sheriff was his rival, Robin
Hood brought forth his arrival.
The Sheriff was King John's
lackey.
He was really very tacky.
Robin had many a fan.
He could always get a helping
hand.
He brought down a corrupt reign.
And he did it for neither wealth
or gain.

Ronald Lynn Wood
**In Search Of the Bird Of
Song**

Casting my life to the sea,
setting it free within me.
Roaming the earth
in search of the truth
of a bird of paradise.
Clashing winds,
sailing songs,
pursuing each moment,
so much time,
so very long,
freedom for sanctuary
set free in a song.
Beginning and ending
now he must find,
with wings on course,
death to make destiny
holding his life sublime.
For our God in heaven
giving himself and song.
His only two possessions
never afraid or weary,
never lost, not for long.
So the winds and every song
make each moment pass on.
A never ending search
for freedom set free
only to live on.
He is born again with wings to fly
with our one and only in heaven
and his one and only song.

Elaine Williams
I'M WAITING

I'm waiting for you
What a ghastly feeling creeps
inside
The water billows with the tide
I look for you in rolling waves
My frightened thoughts go astray
Oh how can I let you be
Beneath the deep and roaring sea
I'm waiting for you
I cannot let you go
While the sunken ship is now so
calm
The mast stands gentle like a
swan
The clouds move swiftly
overhead
My fears are heightened by tears I
shed
I can only wait for you

James Vision (RJA)
COMMON SENSE (Belief)

*[To my deceased father Rocco
Albanese. He was a man with
great wisdom and knowledge of
the english language.]*
To think
Is one thing
To comprehend
Is another
To have confidence in oneself
Is one thing
To totally believe in oneself
Is another
To speak as if you have it
Is one thing
To *know* it
Is another.

Elizabeth Calehuff
ODE TO ODORS

Odor that creeps on spindly legs
across half conscious sleep
Odor that lifts the latch
and a thousand scorpions hatch
In the foul white dung

That coats the tongue
Fetor and Fumet interlace
And the putrid corpse embrace
Imbueing its rotting beir
with their unsavory drear
Odor its passion quickly vent
lingers a malodorous scent
Trapped in an airless room
Weaves a Fusty net to entombed
The acrid taste
Of human waste
To savor of its vinous dregs

Chris Roach

Chris Roach
FREE
[To all my family.]
Ten years of hard life,
ten years in the cell.
His time has finally come to
leave,
and his time has come to rebel.

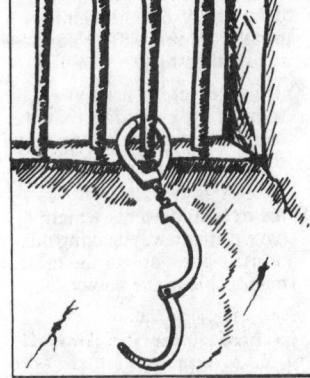

Such a long sentence
for such a small crime.
But he felt he was on top of the
world,
now that he had done his time.

Ramola J. Harper
OH HEART BE STILL
Jesus Saviour come to me
And set my weary spirit free
Enter here again my opened heart
Ready now for Thy will to start
Oh come again Oh heart be still
Receiving now Thy blessed will
And so fulfill me with the love
That satisfies the soul above
Mere mortal things this life can
know
No matter what the eyes may
show
For peace within can never come
Until He is the only one

Who reigns within and rules the
heart
Of which all life becomes a part
And when we listen to His voice
We know that He becomes the
choice
And then His precious peace He
gives
And in our precious hearts He
lives
Forever there each day and night
While we possess His precious
light

Mabel Laura F. Lewis Oswalt
THE UNEMPLOYED
*[To my fine sons: Raymond Lee
Lewis & Billy Arnold Lewis]*
The system gives and
the system takes.

The talents you have
the system breaks.

And at that time
your soul shakes.

But wait . . .

God all wise in His
infinite love,

Sees your need as
well as the dove's.

He slows you down
to look above

And trust.

Brenda Martin
I AM THE ONE
*[For Nick a very special
Husband and Friend]*
He tells them I am the one who
wanders through his mind.
On sleepness nights when the
moon is
high and the passing has no time.

His eyes are wide, his face is
drawn,
his hair a silver white.
His laugh a little crazed as he
awaits
the fall of night.

He tells them he feels me when
the
wind whispers through the dark.
And the trailing of my fingers
leave
their chilling mark.

He sometimes says he hears me
when
he listens in the night, and sees
me walking by his bed against
the
faded light.

He stares out through the
window
at the table by his bed.
While he tries to tell
them . . . I'm really
not that dead.

Karen Sue Dixon
I HAVE THE POWER
I've got the power
I can rule the world.
I shall teach,
I shall help.
This power is mightier than
an atomic bomb
What is my power?
My power is that of love and peace.

My power can change anyone,
Anyone who will listen with an
open mind.
I shall teach love.
I shall show peace.
I shall venture into the world.
I shall show people beautiful
things.
I shall create beautiful things.
I shall touch sad things,
They shall become happy.
I shall show kindness towards the
less fortunate.
I shall help people to see beauty,
in the world around them.
I shall pass on my powers
There shall be one day,
A world of beauty and peace.
But most important—
LOVE

Osa F. VanNoy
TODAY
The day between Yesterday
and Tomorrow
Is the very best time,
To say "I love you"
To dear ones of mine.

For Yesterday's past,
Tomorrow's not come;
So the day in between
is our only one.

Let us use it wisely
While we call it Today;
For on Tomorrow it, too,
becomes Yesterday.

Rita Cividino
I LOVE YOU
*[To Russell Hitchcock, because
I love him so much and
nothing he could ever do can
change that . . .]*
I'll always love you,
my love for you will never die,
and my only wish is that,
love and life be good for you and
I.
Together and forever,
I want us to be,
because you are the one that I
love,
for that I can honestly see.
I want to spend my life with you,
forever in your arms,
with that love so strong,
that I see in your sweet charms.
And if people say anything,
I don't care,
for your love I'll always want,
for us to forever share.
I don't mind the long wait,
for I'll always be waiting for you,
and I feel that strongly,
because I know this love is true.
I love you,
and no one will ever know,
how deep in my heart the feeling
is,
and how I need you so.
And this love I can see,
as bright as the stars,
and as I look in your eyes,
for this love I see will only be
ours.
Oh, this love of ours,
so bright and so true,
you are the only one I want,
for I love you.

Phyllis Deane
Genetics (Garden Variety)
*[To Donna James, my very best
sister in the whole wide world.]*
Who'd ever think
when planting the
spring garden
that the onion
and the asparagus
are related
to the lily?
Or that the turnip
may call the cabbage
brother?
Or that the tomato
has a potato
family heritage?
Or that the pumpkin
is just an overgrown
squash?
Who'd ever think
that okra has
hibuscus relatives?
Or that the cucumber
dates back three
thousand years?
Or that celery may be
the parsley mentioned
in Homer's "Odyssey".

Steve H. McCollom
SOMEDAY
Sitting here thinking about you
Never knowing what to say
Trying to remember the last time
I saw you
In the most beautiful way

Trying to tell you I love you
In the most peculiar way
For I was that someone
Who could not stay

For what is now the time
I didn't have a dime
How can I tell you I need you
Never knowing what to say

Trying to remember the last time
I saw you
In the most beautiful way
One day we will come together
And we won't have to go alone

Leanne Knight
. . . LIFE
*[A warm dedication to my
mom, and to my best friend
Toni. Thanks for all of your
encouragement . . . I love you
both.]*
Breaking from this bubble
seems so hard at times.
Reality is a scary place,
so uncertain and spontanious.
Keeping a bubble around my
world
protects me from the pain and
hurt.
Unfortunately, it also shields me
from
the joy, love, and laughter
I could be experiencing.
The bubble, I suppose,
must be broken
in order to experience
life.

Judith L. Brown
SPACE
A piece of paper
white
with lines

161

separating it
into writing spaces
spaces waiting
to be filled
with thoughts and ideas.

Alice B. Kendall
ON CENSORSHIP

The censors s their scythes

to c the weedy crop—

unmindful of the d d wasted
or evil r left in the plot.

(arranged vertically: g n i w / t u / g s o e o e / o o t s — from "sw ing", "cut", "goose", "roots")

Melba M. Wallace
REGRET
I didn't know you were so ill,
    when we met the other day—
How could I have known
    you would quickly pass away?

Of-course our little difference
    was such a trifling thing,
I really had no idea
    what sadness it would bring.

When passing by the place of
    rest
    I went into the gates—
We both know I am sorry,
    but now it's kinda late.

Passing many rows of tombs
    until I found your name—
Thinking had we spoken,
    we could have both explained.

The little rose I'd picked,
    I placed at your head—
Pretending to be your guest
    and you were sick abed.

It's such a little thing I know,
    but please accept this rose—
And when I reach the Pearly
    Gates
    perhaps you'll say, "hello."

Faye Simpkins
PAP'S FISHING TRIP
Papa took nine children and our
    Mother to the Creek,
Not only to fish, relaxation we
    went to seek.
Papa would find a tree stump and
    cut splinters of pine,
Old tree stumps with knots
    burned good every time.
Papa built a campfire very hot,
Around the circle he'd count
    forget-me-not.
Nine heads he'd count and turn
    to Mother,
One head is missing also another.
The two older boys are fishing
    the Creek with the gentle flow,
I gave them permission to take
    their poles and go.
Papa said, "there they come with
    fish they caught like a man,
the grease is hot we'll cook
    them

in the black frying pan."
The grits and hush puppies are
    cooking fast for the eleven,
We'll be ready to eat way before
    the clock strikes seven.
We ate circling the fire just
    before night,
Then grabbed our quilts colorful
    and bright.
All the girls snuggled up to keep
    warm,
The boys lay by the oak tree in
    quilts arm in arm.
All night Papa kept the fire going,
    we thought we could hear,
A big hoot owl, crickets, maybe a
    running deer.
Papa had coffee cooking in kettle
    so black,
Hanging over the fire, can you
    feature that?
We were up next morning with
    the shining sun,
Papa said, "I know you all had a
    barrel of fun!"
Papa stated, "we have things on
    the farm we left behind."
Pack up, many chores come to
    my mind.
Down the road in the Model A
    truck we drove,
Back to the home in the middle
    of the Florida orange grove.
Papa hastened out to the barn
    discussing the next trip to fish,
The next fishing trip was our
    hope and wish.

Mary J. Moss
LEAVE
As the leaves change their color
    and begin to fall,
    the trees seem to say don't
    leave me.
The aged, longing for someone to
    be near,
    cry out, don't leave me.
The young seem to stop at their
    play and
    suddenly the thought comes
    to them, don't leave me.
The soul cries out to God in the
    darkest hours and
    the cry is—don't leave me.

Patricia Klein
AWARENESS
[To my sister, Kathy, for always
believing in me.]
The ticking of the clock.
The coldness of the dark.
The rise and fall of my chest.
The moistness of tears on my
    cheeks.

These things I have noticed as I
    lie in my sadness
    awaiting the blessing of sleep.

Ellen Pearson
A DIFFERENT PLACE
[To the memory of James
Douglas Morrison]
Hail nothing
Full of nothing
Find nothing you shouldn't lose
Soverence all around you.
Journey through the wilderness
Inspiration of the dead.
Sweet answering echoes.

Tribes, and ancient rituals.
Shiney, wet faces, of wild childre.

Glowing in the moonlight.

Look to your varied sister, Earth,
Onto Her golden shore,
Beyond the infinite rainbows,
Cascading rivers of pain.

Don't ask around, they know no
    names,
They only dwell within the
    brains,
Of the gifted,
And the insane.

Maria T. Zullo

Maria T. Zullo
A SPECIAL FLOWER
There are red ones.
    pink, yellow, and white.
    They're more beautiful
        than I could possibly write.

It's the prettiest flower
    Mother Nature ever made.
    It makes me smile if I'm down,
        as the frowns slowly fade.

The fragrance is softer
    than tears on a new bride.
    To some it stands for victory,
        to some it stands for pride.

As the flower gets older,
    starts to shrivel and die,
    I still see beauty, smell
        that perfume and sigh.

If I had to be a flower,
    a rose is what I'd be.
    Because when I look at a rose,
        I see the inside of me.

Robert Paul
SEA OF SOULS
The river runs an endless course
Its fate is does not question.
From its icy bubbling mountain
    source
To the Sea without hesitation.
So to my life a fated stream
Winds thru banks of hope and
    despair
And often I have stopped to
    dream of the Sea and what
    awaits me there.
Deep and Dark A Sea Of Souls
It's ever restless ebb of tides.
Hungrily awaits the end of those
    fated rivers and destined lives.
And now I'm part of the deep
    dark sea. My fear of darkness
    showing
And fish come from everywhere
    to stop and swim around me.
And now I'm One and now I'm
    All

A swaying current in the Sun
Caressing some lost Tropical Isle
Toward the Setting Sun

Jerry Carter
BLOODY SANDCASTLES
A World like a sandcastle of
    shattered glass,
A Thing of such beauty holds
    dangers unseen,
Within crystillian nightmares our
    future I've seen.
You can't build castles of blood
    stained sand.
For the might of the wind shall
    prevail in the end.
We spew forth our vengeance of
    modern refuse,
If we cannot name it, it is of no
    use.
A glass castle stained with
    innocent blood.
But what in the end shall stand
    yet defiant?
Shall it be mankind, His
    atrocities held high?
The lord of the castle before it
    must die.
The wind has shown patience for
    a few thousand years,
But in the end the castle must
    fall,
For like grains of sand we are
    nothing at all.

Victor R. Dyer
THE FLOWER SHOW
The flower show that we long to
    see brings out as much beauty
    as the Christmas tree.

Many varities of flowers that are
    so lovely to the eye,
    delightfully arranged, emit a
    pleasant aroma which leaves us
    in joyful ecstasy.

Knowledge, care, attention are
    some of the essentials that are
    blended so well to bring a show
    that lends an aura of wonder
    that's so lovely to tell.

Some treasured events which
    have drifted away leaving our
    hearts a-glow, one of the most
    memorable is the flower show.

Kathi Christianson
OH, BEAUTIFUL LADY
Oh, Beautiful Lady,
Oh, Beautiful Janell,
I send you lots of love
And I hope you're doing well.
I'm sitting here, thinking about
    you,
As I do each and every day.
There are so many things I want
    to tell you;
So many things I want to say.
I admire you for your courage,
For your inner strength through
    your plight.
You were so strong and had so
    much will power
Through every battle, every fight.
Our special bond has not been
    broken;
I know it never, never will be;
That special bond between us
That ties us together,
    emotionally,
You've given me so many happy

memories;
Memories that I shall never
forget.
I can still hear the sound of your
musical laughter
Spreading love to others you have
met.
You will live forever in my heart;
Oh, yes, this I can tell,
Oh, Beautiful Lady,
Oh, Beautiful Janell.

Dorothy Edna A. Raynor Ferency
POETRY'S HASH
Poetry is like a bird in flight
above the earth on golden
wings,
It floats with the music of the ages;
All combined in one tune to
the wind
on high,
In sympathy with all the woes of
time
Answering all happiness of young
and old;
Sparing none either rich or poor.
Knowing no color whether black
or white
or yellow.
Recognizing all the climes of the
Earth
and God's Heavenly Word.
Amen!

Evangeline Flynn
EPITAPH TO A POET
The poet dreamed,
Yet made no dreams his master,
But, rather, asked, "From whence
does talent come?"
In search of truth, he saw through
tears and laughter
the Author's Hand
In Stars, in Moon, in Sun,
In boundless sky, in soundless
depth of ocean
And in every creature bound by
death and birth,
He thus beheld
And praised, forever after
God's signature
Across the Universe!

Gladys Tiff
PILLOW TEARS
*[To my husband, Benjamin and
Family—Manning, Maurice,
Milan, Michele, Margot]*
Tears—
No matter what the age
From the young or the aged
Caress the pillow—
Its solace at night

Copious flow of youthful tears
From disappointments it
appears
Reduce the inward hurt
To a tear in the old—

Too old to waste in a pillow at
night
It drips to sear—
The scars left in the heart.

Louis Pugliese
SEE ME—MYSELF
If you could look into my eyes,
you
would see what in me lies.

A thing of truth and much
enjoyment,

a sphere of love and much
atonement.

Stirrings that come from in so
deep,
Feelings filled with sadness weep.

How I hunger to be known, for all
my
feelings cannot be shown.

Bring me out through my eyes, so
human
stares could know my ties.

And let them all who understand,
hold
me warmly in their hand.

And if, but one, can me engulf,
they'll
see and find me as myself.

Frances Zapatka
BETHEL MUSIC
With the shadow of your wing
Dearest, you are
the Phoenix
in the eternity of my life.
Softly you have
winged
soared
above me.
Sooped down to
brush from my eyes
the hairs of mourning.
Yet, I weep again.
I weep with ecstasy
and
often I am tranquil
So profound a joy
has swept across
my heart
with the shadow of your Wing
tracing its journey
forward and
upward.
You are leaving
but
You visited
me.

Harold James Douglas
MY BALL OF YARN
Life is a ball of yarn
waiting to be unraveled.
Mine has been a knitting party
filled with gossip and fun . . .
But now time has stolen wit
from my mind,
And the sand in my hour-glass
is turning to gravel . . .
My ball of yarn is just about
unraveled.

Harvey Alan Sperry
A MIDNIGHT ROSE
Dawn finds her dreaming.
Deep tresses embrace her.
Dew droplets gleaming;
sunlight caressing a flower.
Mists of deep slumber
enfold her cocoon,
til warmth of morn wakes her
before the zenith of noon.
Eyes deep as an ocean;
sweet roses' dark hue,
adorning creation,
embellished with crystals of dew.
Her summit of splendor,
the realm of midnight:
Moonlight her grandeur,
declaring a beautiful sight.
Though bathed in midday,
the essence of darkness;

the rose's bouquet,
touching the moonlight with
softness.
Born a child of Aquarius
at a moment fate chose,
a name noted as glorious,
acclaiming a midnight rose.

Jeanette Rich Wiley

Jeanette Rich Wiley
GONE
*[To all the people who pass
through my world, and touch
my life.]*
Fall is gone
Winter is upon us
I see it in the barren trees
I feel it in the cold wind
and in the driving rain
I am conscious of it in the
silence that descends upon
the land,
As Nature prepares to sleep.

Lindy Rose
A DREAM
*[To Billy Ray, my husband,
who really is a dream come
true.]*
I lie here dreaming of a man that
does not exist.
In his eyes I see love that no one
has ever known.
I see a man that will love and
keep me forever.

My happiness is his happiness.
My wants are his desires.
My tears are his anguish.
My love, his well being.

His thoughts only of me, wanting
to make me happy.
To please me in every way.
To give me the best of
everything,
Is his strive every day.

A far fetched dream some may
say,
But as I awake from day to day,
I thank my God my dream is real.

Shelbia Kyle
Expectant Mother's Prayer
Dear God, I have a favor to ask,
Nothing for you is too great a
task,
Please make my baby healthy and
fine,
Perfectly formed and with a
brilliant mind.
A baby that's got plenty of hair,
And doesn't require a lot of extra
care.

Let it do nicely when to my
breast I caress,
For Mother's own milk sure costs
a lot less.
Rain down disposable diapers at
least once a week,
And please let the baby just
sleep, sleep, sleep.
Never, ever let it cry; a whimper
will do,
And may it never have the colic
or the flu.
All childhood diseases it can do
without,
Let it be good natured and never
pout.
Let it be born with all its teeth in
place,
And let it love for me to wash its
face.
May it potty train itself by two,
And clean up the mess when the
meal is through.
And one last thing, Oh God of
grace,
Please make my stomach go back
in place.

Samantha H. Senall
THE BLUE ROSE
It stands there glistening in the
sun
Nature creation, the only one
Of its kind you'll ever see
Nothing is more beautiful than
thee.
It's red, it's pink, it's yellow, it's
blue
The color all depends on you.
If you look with love, if you
look with sin
The rose is where it will begin.
I look with joy, I always do
And I must say the rose is blue!
Someday the rose, it will be
gone
And a new one will rise
In the morning dawn!

Janice M. Brown
CERTAIN LOVE
When I have decided what's right
for me,
And think that we should both
be free,
That's when I know that I need
some time,
To regroup my feelings and clear
my mind.

Only a fool can love so strong,
And never admit when he's
wrong.
Well, I'm in love and not
ashamed to say,
That you're the best thing that
ever came my way.

Perhaps my mistakes have been
more then few,
Or my actions have often been
misconstrued.
Whatever the case, I'll try to
make it right,
Hopefully, without an arguement
or fight.

I'll admit I'm wrong, but as you
well know,
There's only so far my pride
allows me to go.
In love, however, pride has no
place,

But to beg without pardon is a
downright disgrace.

I've taken a giant step in your
direction,
And offered my love with great
discretion.
I've weighed my emotions, and
the outcome is clear,
That this is love, ever so dear.

Geraldine Bryant Gregory
TIGHTROPE
TIME . . . suspended . . .
Defies me to walk its tightrope
relentlessly.
I was a fool to let you have the
key
To the clock that activates my
life.
I never dreamed that you'd forget
to
        wind
            the
                clock.

Linda Joanne Hansen
YOU
You touch me
And my body, heart, and soul
Are filled with the warmth of a
thousand lifetimes.
You are the nectar of my dreams
So sweet one drop is enough to
last a lifetime.
    In love I be yours,
today, now, foreverlasting . . .

Jon Palatucci
TOGETHER
The sun moves on
    around the simple earth . . .
and a flower rises up
    to touch
        and thank . . .
The flowing rivers keep an open eye
    on
        all . . .
The earth smiles slowly . . .
    content to be a part
        in helping
the flowers
to grow
and
the
rivers
to
flow . . .

L. Gough Christopher
FEATHERS IN THE WIND
There is one evening eye to
    measure
smoke that becomes sky,
from this treasured perch
at soul level of dust and feathered
    fire.

Wet, fledgling, dove:
lift your unshelled dream
with gathering strokes
against a jaundiced sky.

A hawk waits to fly or fall
or fill the emptying day
with its black scream.

Small bird, large sky,
one word, unheard: fly.
large word, small sky,
one song, one eye: free.

Fly and see and sing,
above the branch of pine,
whose feathery, forest gestures

of roots,
sing the green words
of your constant coup d'oeil.

Eileen Bostic Burdette

Eileen Bostic Burdette
THE PROMISE
We promised to love—til death
do us part
Now you're leaving—you're
breaking my heart,
You've found someone else—you
love more than me—
Now it's over—you're setting me
free.

You promised me—there could
never be
Anyone—you could love more
than me,
Now you tell me—that you love
her
And my love—you could never
share.

You promised me—our love
would last forever
That we would always be
together,
Now it's over—just memories
remain
What once was happiness—now
is pain.

Cecelia H. Davis
FIRST HAIRCUT
*[To my grandson, Kenny Age 2
yrs.—1971]*
Little boy of only two—just a
baby yet,
Sweet and darling little boy who
is grandma's pet;
Golden curls crown your head—
all in ringlets tight,
E'er caressing your fair brow
slumbering at night.

But daddy wants you to grow
up—can't wait another day!
Wants to make a man of you—
cut your curls today.
Softly curling o'er your brow—
seems a shame to me
To want to cut those golden
curls—no more a babe to be.

Indifferently the scissors snip
each little curl so soft,
Cropping now that crown of gold
on which I've gazed so oft;
From nape of neck to ivory brow,
the scissors quickly go—
Promptly now the job is done—
can't help a tear that flows.

You're not a baby anymore—a

rough and tumble lad—
You're still so sweet—a
handsome boy—but still it
makes me sad,
For baby days and baby ways e'er
happiest must be—
Another milestone in your life
which means so much to me.

So quickly now you'll be grown
up and baby days all passed,
The years go by so swiftly now—
for nothing e'er does last;
But take it easy, little man, enjoy
it while you may,
For soon enough you'll be a man
with problems every day.

Jane M. Lemons
ERIC MICHAEL (Our Son)
You are everything to us,
you're our little boy,
Sometimes good, sometimes bad,
Full of mischief, full of joy.

You're the shiny mist after the
rain,
the freshest of air,
You're the best—looking boy ever
with big brown eyes and curly
red hair.

You're a little of Mom
and a little of Dad,
We love you very much
you're the best gift we've ever
had.

You're part of us and always will
be
your our little son,
And while you grow, we will see
just what good we have done.

Coleen "Leimomi" Matthews
OUR LOVE
Liken unto a bud with desire
each petal takes form.
With care and patience and scent
of perfume, a bud becomes a
blossom.
How delicate it does fashion and
to arrange its shape in unison
To mold each design in the way
it ought to be.
No blemish or spot to mar what
is to be of this pattern.
The moisture that it nurtures to
flourish each plant
Comes from the creation of love
unified with laborous
devotion—
To stand securely and
courageously in time when
disturbance of nature dwells,
Not a petal replaced nor bending
of its perfect stature removed.
That is Our Love.

Madge Mullins Wilbanks
FAREWELL
Let me die in late May when the
scaley bark
Is in full bloom on the hill
where I will
Be buried and think no more of
time or wanting me
To die to free your soul and
give you peace;

Hold my coffin high taking me
home to the hill
To join generations who have
known the lain
One another because of blood

that made them one;
The fierce pride that bound
them close.

Throw dirt on my coffin gently;
Save the scaley bark to put in
water in a vase
To remember a few days longer
before you leave and
Go far away to forget the
enveloping even in love;

There was love from the
beginning, birth;
There were so many things to
see, to be;
More than possible in a lifetime
now cut short
When the scaley bark bloomed
this year;

Put away your tears, true or false;
dry your eyes
And dare not keep them damp
for me.
My home is with those loved a
lifetime of loving
In peace and promise given
from the soft brown earth

Where I was born to live and die
with no regret
Other than the brevity of it all;
the short span,
The sharing stopped, the giving
ended
The knell sounded.

So be it with time
And remembering at least as
long as the
Scaley bark holds its head high
and does not droop over
And die.

Carol Sigalas Breland
MY TIME OF YEAR
Christmas is my time of year
I love the very atmosphere;
The colored lights on the
decorated tree
My family gathered all around
me.
The smells coming from the
kitchen within
People dropping by with a "Hello,
my friend";
The presents are wrapped and
under the tree
And I see a big one that says it's
to me.
The children are laughing and
jumping with joy
Waiting for Santa to bring them a
toy;
Snowflakes are falling softly to
the ground
Everyone is listening and there's
not a sound.
It's like God is saying, "My
Children, draw near
For this, too, is My Time of Year."

Lorrie A. Strohecker
**Only When The Earth No
    Longer Has Its Seasons**
I love you with the freshness of
awakening Springtime
when I first realized I forever
wanted you to be mine

and I love you with the
gentleness of a falling leaf on
an Autumn's day
when our lives had first crossed

over each other's far, distant pathways

I have loved you for so long and for so many very different reasons
that I'll only stop loving you when the earth no longer has its seasons

I love you most of all during a cold restless winter's snow
when my heart is filled with the love I need so much to show

and I love you with the great beauty that a summer's day holds
which were the days we never shared and have always seemed so cold

I have loved you for so long and for so many very different reasons
that I'll only stop loving you when the earth no longer has its seasons

Although you say you don't love me anymore but can give no reasons
I'll only stop loving you when the earth no longer has its seasons

Naomi Greenfield Gee

Naomi Greenfield Gee
MYSTERIES THAT RHYME
Occasionally, it's hard to find
    Mysteries that build a rhyme—
    And so the pattern, now is split—
        With conventionality tossed around abit.

Sometimes the beauty of the pen
    Is a little bit much to comprehend.
        Imaginations, allowed to run wild,
            Create the fantasy, rarely mild.

Within the pocket of our mind,
    There's always *something* we can find—
        Rare, though it may be—
            When surfaced for all to see.

Looking, still, for the *why*—
    That must be pleasing to the eye;
        No longer are they mine—
            Such MYSTERIES that rhyme!

Jean B. Murray—Edge
A WISH FOR MOTHER
[I wish to dedicate this to my mother and my friends who encouraged me to keep trying.]
You were always there when I needed you.
    You often went without so that I could have.
        But most of all, you were just you.

I don't know if I have thanked you recently.
    If I haven't, Thank You very much.

You showed me understanding and compassion.
    You helped me through the hard times.
        And laughed with me through the good.

I know that the day will eventually come when
    You will depart this earth.
        On this day I shall weep.

After you die, you won't be around so
    I won't be able to tell you just how
        Much I really and truly love you.

So I will tell you now. I Love You
    And wish very sincerely that you have
        A Happy Mother's Day.

Maria Costa
MY ROSE TO MOTHER
[Per te mamma, grazie per il tu amore e forza.]
My nose smells the rose—
    upon the bush it grows.
Try to tie the stems with bows
    but watch out for the pricking foes.
For each rose there are some petals
    which in, the sunlight shine like medals.
Each of the blossoms grander than the other
    like the pride I feel for my mother.
She is strong and she is tough,
    but tender as a rose.
She is no fool for a bluff;
    that's my mother strong and tough.
Though she does not really show it
    no one else is wise enough to know it,
But I know her deep inside
    she's my mother, she's my pride.

Linda S. Andrews
My Fine Feathered Friend
Where are my pretty pets? With their wings beating a rythmn of their own.
Till next spring, they have gone away home.
No more their pretty colors will I see, shining in the bright sunshine.
Drinking the nectar sweet, sweet as wine.

My friends you have brought me laughter and joy,
Just watching you hum and drink your fill.
Swooping and swirling, stopping on my window sill; scolding when I have neglected to fill it up.
Your beautiful colors of red and gold, green and yellow,
makes you a very handsome fellow.
Till spring then, adieu;
my bright dear friends, I will be thinking of you,
when the days are cold and gloomy and snow drifts round my door,
I will keep the memory of you, to warm my heart,
and know that soon, when spring returns again,
I will see you then.
Beautiful feathered friends I will wait for you, even when the ground is covered with early mountain dew.
Till then, Ahh, so Long, I will enjoy your memory all the winter long.

Ms. Tracy L. Fintelmann
TWO ROSES
Each rose different from the other but together in the same vase.

Both full of love and beauty resembling friendship and faith.

Both willing to share the space they have with the other.

Both sparkle with happiness and content.
    They are royal.

Their thorns represent their individuality
    and make it harder for the other
        to take advantage of each other.

May these flowers always be in your sight.
And may they promise to you everything they stand for.

Even though I'm not always with you,
    May they remind you that I am always there for you.

Two roses—you and me.

Encarnita C. Cambe
Of U.S.A. Hostages In Iran
Breathes there a man with soul so great,
Who never his conscience can permit,
That his 52 countrymen, Iran kept as hostages,
Will suffer torture and die a horrible death.

Innocent they were, the fifty and two,
A product of circumstances what can they do,
Bodies bare, blindfolded, beaten, tears welled from their eyes,
Now 443 days, in prison kept in agony futile,
spirit so low,

Still hold they on, sad, weary and very blue.

American, was racked in great, great despair,
To have their heads cut off, was sphinx Khomeini's desire,
Envoys from other lands, sent to no avail,
Patience exhausted, Predsident Carter said,
"Shall I send bombs, to annihilate you, Cruel Serpent?"
Answered his conscience, "No Sir, please, you'll repent."

Alone in his room, heavenward looked up,
Then let loosed, a trillion in microwaves of prayers to God above,
Pleading for His kind mercy, for peace and love,
Lest surely will come, another terrible, holocaust.

Come now 444 days, woke up hopeless, restless, the 52,
Aha, Hear! Bang! cracked opened the prisons' door,
In a voice thundering, shouted the jailor,
"Hated Americans, be gone, be here no more."
And, as in a dream, rushed they, to the opened door.

Oh, bright momentous day, January 20, 1981,
A jubilant American, inauguration of her 40th., Pres. R. Reagan,
Hey, look, an Algerian Air Line, flying low, very low,
"Hurrah! our hostages, Thanks God, home at last the brave 52!"

From his eyes dropped a tear, on his face a triumphant smile,
"Mission accomplished, dear countrymen," and exit he made.
Truly unsung, a noble soul, for him, bitter is fame, to count dead people.

Jennifer Lee Carpenter
LOVE SENSES
[With all my love to my best friend and soulmate, my beloved husband, Bill.]
The look of your love is a presence you can't deny;
The glisten that mirrors your heart in your eye;
The smile that thrills me as only your smile can;
The walk that announces, "I am loved as a man!"

The sound of you love is the melody of your soul at rest;
Two hearts beating as one when my head lies upon your chest;
The passionate words you utter in moments of pure ecstasy;
The laughter, the sobs, the whistle, the songs you sing to me.

The smell of your love is a plesant touching to my nose;
The perfume you bring when you give me a yellow rose;

The sweet scent of your
  manhood, exhaling it's need to
  be;
The fragrance of your cologne,
  exciting and seducing me.

The taste of your love is the
  appetizer before the main
  course;
The wet, sweetness of your
  mouth acting like a magnetic
  force;
Bringing me the body's dessert,
  savory, smooth, and warm;
The taste of complete
  satisfaction; the calm after the
  storm.

The taste of your love is the
  throbbing sensation in your
  fingertips;
The touch of velvet, to feel each
  pulsation with my satin lips;
The sensual delight I know as
  your hands message me gently;
The strength I feel in your arms
  as you eagerly embrace me.

The sixth sense of your love is
  called intuition or insight;
The simultaneous awaking for
  needed love—making in the
  night;
The reading between lines,
  knowing without being told
  what you know;
The eye to eye contact that
  causes unspoken words to
  silently flow.

You, the love of my life, came
  strolling by and shattered all
  my defenses;
You breathed the breath of life
  into my lungs and awakened
  my love senses.
I now touch, taste, see, smell,
  hear, and know love, Oh! what
  joy and peace!
The power of your love has
  caused all my loneliness and
  heartache to cease.

Kim Marguerite Hibma
THE FINAL TOAST
  Come drink with me the wine
  of youth,
let us laugh and dance and sing.
  Together let us spill the cup.
Friend what sweet pain will it
  bring?
  Here than is a toast to the
  passions and dreams that in
  our foolish youth we display.
For woe unto us my friend, my
  love,
we loose both in our stumbling
  blind arrogant quest along the
  way.
  A sip of wine for courage,
a bit more to clear the mind.
  Gaze deeply into the cup my
  friend.
What sweet deceit will we find?
  Along the way the rosy hues
  become a blackened taint.
Black is White and White is
  Grey, with cool compromise
  we paint.
  Love and Honesty, Hope and
  Faith we learn quickly to
  spurn.
Money and Power rule our greedy

souls, the gads for which we
  burn.
  Soft echoes of yesteryear,
  intentions pure and brave.
Are washed away with a tip of
  the cup, and the stupor that we
  crave.
  How many more! How many
  more friend?
Is it but ten more steps to the
  grave?
  Come let us spill the cup,
and through the foggy mists,
  Our souls laid bare and
  damned to hell with an
  everlasting kiss.
Come drink with me the wine
  of youth,
let us laugh and dance and sing.
  For soon will break a new day's
  dawn.
Friend what sweet sorrow will it
  bring?

Marian Lucas Pierce
MY SON
[*This poem was written to my
son, Jack Allen Lucas, in honor
of his thirtieth birthday.*]
I wonder if he knows-
  The joy he brings?
The pride and love
  That causes my soul to sing?
The closeness, sharing, identity,
  I have with him and he with
  me.

The thoughtful, touching, little
  things-
As soft and as gentle as butterfly
  wings.

Like-the lighting of a light, for me,
Leaving a flower that I might see
  Or arriving unexpectedly-
With a 'laid back', casual air,
  Letting me know-he's always
  there
  No matter how-
  The pendulum swings!

God gifted us with one another
He, the son, and I, the mother
But no, they're not apron strings
  That you see-
'Tis love's lifeline-
  'Twixt him and me.

Wendy Sensoli
THE UNBORN
          June 11—
So you're my mom, well I'm your
  boy
I hope I'm daddy's pride and joy.
You're not aware I'm here just yet,
  cause no one knows but me
I'm sure you'll be as proud as
  punch and happy as can be.
I'm sorry if I make you sick each
  day when you arise
But it won't last forever mom, we
  all know how fast time flies.
          Aug.11—
As each day comes & each day
  goes a miracle takes place
I grow two hands, two legs, two
  feet and then a tiny face.
You still don't know about me,
  you'll find out anyday
The doctor will have news for
  you, a baby's on the way.
I think about the world outside
  and of you everyday

The loving thoughts, the tender
  smile that all will come my
  way.
          Sept.11—
I've grown so much in these three
  months, I've fingers, thumbs, &
  toes
My eyes are blue, my hair is
  blonde. I have a button nose.
Today the man told you the news
  but he seemed to burst a
  bubble
I give you both my solemn word I
  won't cause you any trouble.
I'll make you both so happy, I'll
  do the things you say
I just can't wait until I'm born so
  all of us can play.
We'll walk along in deep soft
  snow and you will hold my
  hand
In summertime we'll walk the
  beach and make castles in the
  sand.
          Sept.18—
Dad's face resembled that of
  yours when you first heard of
  me
It wasn't one of happiness but
  one of misery.
          Sept.19—
How come this man is taking me
  away from my soft bed?
I am not ready to be born, now I
  must die instead.
Of this I'll never understand, why
  me you had to kill
I thought I was a gift to you, I
  thought I was God's will.
Someday you'll be sorry for what
  you've done to me
You'll wonder if I looked like you,
  just wait & you will see.
You'll wonder of what color hair
  and if my eyes were blue
You'll never know now mother
  dear, they've taken me from
  you.

Mark Benedyk
WHY DO COWS MOO?
[*To Dianne Sanchez, It's nice to
be alive in such a wonderful
world with her.*]
Why do planets orbit?
and stars sit,
in a moonless night
and keep it lit?

Why do doves coo?
and shoo—flies wear shoes?
  Why do comets streak?
and old rusty doors creak?
  Why do dogs bark?
and why does evening turn dark?
  Why do leopards leap?
and shepards, sheep?
      What makes the willow
  weep?
  Why do colors clash?
and raindrops,
in a puddle splash?
  Why does snow descend?
and what do lovers send?
  Why do crawdads craw?
and why does the raven caw?

      And why do cows moo?

This is a mysterious world,
of living secrets,
  Of unknown wonders and

untold beauty.
  So do not ask "Why the cows
moo?"

  They moo for thee.

F. Luverne Austin Tidwell

F. Luverne Austin Tidwell
SPAN OF TIME
[*Dedicated to a special friend
whom I have had the pleasure
of sharing my love for poetry
with.*]
Let me today do something that
  will
  Take a little sadness
  From your heart's vast store

And may I be so favored as to
  make
  You happier ever more

Let me not hurt you, by any
  selfish
  Deed or thoughtless word

Let me love you, and cherish you,
  I have so much to give

Let me tonight look back across
  the
  Span of time that we have
  Known each other, and

"The world is better that we met"

Alice A. Zimmerman
ME OR IS IT ME?
[*To the uniqueness and beauty
of every human spirit.*]
I look and see,
  And realize she's part of me.
Not just the hair and face,
  But deeper, deeper within
Those dark brown eyes.

A touch of creativity
  Lies within this mind.

A crawling, intelligent seed
　Grows under these fingers.
A sense of humor hides
　Under the timid face.
Warmness and sensitivity unveil
　From within a steady voice.

Oh, but is that it,
　The person you see?
Do you really know her?
Or is it just the surface,
What the mirror reflects.

Chris Scratchard/Lauderdale
DENIUM AND LACE
*[In thanksgiving for my
grand—daughter's Sherree Sue
Latham   Loran Lindsey
Latham]*
Behold the face in denium and
　lace.
　Pigtails flying in the warm
　April breeze
Old blue jeans warn at the knees.
　Loving little arm's
　outstretched, tears
Gently rolling down cheek's
　made of Angle dust
　Running to Grandmother the
　one she trust's
To kiss away the pain of a hurt
　finger,
　Knowing the magic of a
　Grandmother's kiss
Can heal most anything, from the
　broken arm
　Of a baby doll to a robin's wing.
As off she rushes back to her
　swing. Laughing
eye's looking too and fro into the
　Heaven's
scanning the sky, watching and
　waving at the undulate
　butterfly.
　It isn't hard to read the
　expression on the face
Why, why does the butterly have
　all the beauty
　and grace.
Totally unaware that no beauty
　anywhere, could
　match the beauty of that little
　face, bordered
in Denium And Lace.

　Seen through the eye's of a
　Grandmother that say's "Thank
　You God" for Memories

Joseph Bryant Patton
SAVE THE GRACE
*[The world as a whole seems to
have forgotten rightiousness, in
essence believes only that the
rich gets. Reaching Out and
sounding off with the few,
"There's gonna be a Change."]*
The imaginery whip of
　oppression welds
so real to blackness in America,
The bondage seems to cling so
　realistic
Denied—being denied because of
　an age old ism
doesn't surprise blackness.
In spite of obstacles, blackness is
　here to stay.
How can we sing in a Strange
　Land?
"I don't want to sing in a Strange
　Land."
Saved, I continue to Stand and

fight in
Love, in truth, and in justice,
For this truly is a tedious journey.
Misconceptions already causes
　misgivings even
in the slightest confrontation
　concerning validity,
Thanks be to the master for
　wisdom to know that all
that glitters is not gold,
So give us time master to tell
　them that
the pledge of allegiance sounds
　contradicting, "an justice for
　all."
Save the Grace of God
Wearing false faces, and false
　grins
Sure cramps my style,
Let's stand up, speak up and take
　courage
God's got the power to save us.
And soon as the day comes . .,
I will be happier than today.

Laura Carter
THE CROWN OF LOVE
*[To Bill, for the gift of freedom,
Joe Smith for the gift of
creativity, to my family and
friends, for you are the most
precious gift of all.]*
Love no longer flows in this
　shattered heart
For that which once beat strong,
　now is frail
The most precious feeling now
　lies torn apart
So with pain and anger I have
　built a shell;
Though love doth move about
　like the ebbing tide
It shall rise once more with
　another days sun
Destine to steal a simple mans'
　soul; refraining pride
A time when death and
　destruction soon become one
It dwells in your soul till death
　tells of leave
While tearing the mind into
　shreds of shame
Waiting till time when the last
　breath you breathe
A silent voice calling without
　name;
And so with willingness one
　dares to drown
In the sea of love with death as
　his crown.

Cynthia Ann Panek
THE UNICORN
Mystery and magic fill the air
　that surrounds him.
Gallantly he holds his head up
　high.
Proudly he walks along the
　mystic world of gods and
　goddesses beyond the sky.
His strong body filled with the
　eternal gift of life,
roams free across the earth.
His white mane flowing with the
　wind as he gallops onward.
Thundering hooves heard
　throughout night and day;
his loud cries echoing as he goes
　on his way.
Invisible to all except for those
　who believe,

The Unicorn, a picture of beauty
　and life,
　Hunted by many,
　　tamed by few.
　So Wild and Free,
　　He always will be!

Dr. Lionel Fern

Dr. Lionel Fern
ruu—!Hum!—ca—!Chas!
*[Dedicated to Mr. Mario Cox,
Poet and Recitationist.]*
!Oh! . . . musica en salitre
　soleada,
me sabes a cana, tabaco y cafe.
Vertigo de ritmos, bayu y bembe.
Besos de tu fresca espuma
　plateada.

Se muestra tu faz, de flores
　pintada,
evocando mieles, licores y te.
Por entre las notas se palpa . . . se
　ve
atisbar los tonos de la enramada.

Te huyes, regresas, vienes y te vas.
Bate que te bate . . . y ya la
　batida. . .
marea con su ritmo de
　ruu—!Hum!—ca!Chas!

Una larga pausa; ¡Durmiendome
　estas!
Bate que te bate . . . y ya la
　batida. . .
marea con su ritmo de
　ruu—!Hum!—ca—!Chas!

S. Shipley
A LOVE
I thought of you today, just for a
　moment
that lasted all day, it felt good to
　have you around so close.

It brought a smile to my face, a
　glow to my
cheeks—people noticed passing
　by
and they smiled too.

I missed you today, really don't
　know why
never missed you before—I must
　have seen something to remind
　me of you?
It brought a tear to my eye, one
　that nobody would notice—but
　I knew it was there
and couldn't wipe it away.

I needed you today, wanted to
　call you
and say—I need you please come
　quick
but you were not there.
It brought a pain to my heart, one
　that I have not felt for a long
　time—knowing what it was
and that it's special.

Jennie Keach Ransbottom
WHAT I LOVE
I love white sailboats and warm
　sunny places
Blue ocean waters and tanned
　smiling faces.
Long lazy days in the hot summer
　heat
Bikini swim suits and sand
　covered feet.
To feel like an eagle gliding
　through space,
The touch of damp wind at a
　motor boat race.
I love quaint lighthouses and
　fishing at sea
Mid cool waters splashing with
　driftwood debree.

And I love high bridges that soar
　up in space
Especially descending with the
　wind keeping pace.
I love old poetry full of love and
　romances
The thrilling excitement that
　moonlight enhances.
Old strumming guitars with
　prespiring traces
Of kissing and dancing from
　twilight embraces.
The glow of the moon on tides
　foaming white
And the drone of a jet in the still
　of the night.

I love travelling to far away
　places
But guess most of all, I love
　happy faces.

Mary McGowan Slappey
Prayer For Tomorrow
(Lo: An Answer)
Seek contentment among
　tresures you love,
Old books and manuscripts
　ancient as time. . .
Found in desert caves, echoing
　the sublime.

Turn to music only partly
　manmade. . .
It echoes all the sound of sea and
　song
That has refrained in this
　universe so long;
And when other pleasures pass

and fade.

Turn to nature, source of science, flight,
Porpoise secrets, electric eel, patterns of day and night,
AND KNOW THAT I AM GOD, CREATIVE LIGHT.

Joseph C. Tweedle

Joseph C. Tweedle
I SEE FACES

On things or places of what you may please,
I often see faces on limbs and near leaves.
On yonder borders of woods and rock hills,
I see profiles and statues that give me great thrills.
In all kind of clouds that soar over head,
They make changing faces not quite so dead.
Some are grotesque or of beauty divine,
Some resembling friends of all kind.
Which reminds me the fate of us all,
We drift here like mist, statues may fall.

Like the other night as my golden moon rose,
Was a vicious cloud shark with a long nose,
Its mouth was wide open as if to consume,
All my faces and statues as it drift by my moon,
Let's get outa here, I hollered to the gail!
Afore I'm eaten by shark or swallowed by whale!

Martin "Mercy" Zachwieja
Lord, Bless These Children
[To all the children who make the goodbye of this journey harder still.]

This portrait of a child's look at life
In a land of poverty, hunger, and strife;
Braving the biting cold and the blowing rain,
Clothed only in rags of sympathy and pain.
The sense of fear and the smell of death,
Those two sons of Satan extinguish all breath.

A million voices speaking as if only one voice,
Malnourished skeletons by no other choice;
Uplifted hands in holy supplication,
Praying for the least of any consecration.
Eyes that speak a story no words can tell,
With droplets of tears hanging where tears shouldn't dwell.
Crimson soil of wavelets when a young child falls,
Blended with the clean tear that says it all;
Waiting for Love to fill every open chamber
Of all the wounds, claimed through poverty and hunger.
The chain-lightning like beating murmur of hearts
Stinging more than the stun from Cupid's Love darts;
The children know the world silently witnesses
And marvel's at mans ignorance of a living so serious.

It is the lonely desolated tear-filled land
With obsolete past and present; the only hope is man.

The land caught up in the Ocean of Eternity
Into which the streams of all life empty,
The land where innocent victims of abuse and parricide
Can point to the abusers and point world-wide
It is a land where the tombstone is the only way
A marble pillow for the dying day.
In this Harvest Field of God's Mercy
The only need is the will to be.

Loida Weber Maggioi
DESIRE

I would have wanted to be in your arms
In endless nights full of romance, and
Kiss your lips under starlit sapphire skies.
I would have wanted to feel your warmth,
And touch your face and see your eyes,
And be forever inside your heart.
Reality has broken my golden dreams,
But I still wish to be in your arms,
To drink your breath, to kiss your lips.
And be forever inside your heart.

Nancy T. Fonzen
THE ARTIST

The leaves turned.
Overnight
the wind wiped away green
to let the harvest moon
paint over brown background.

The leaves turned
overnight.
Dazzling when the morning sun
dried the brush strokes.

The leaves turned.
Have you noticed
sometime in the morning
while going to work,
gold on blue,
yellow paint peelings
curled on the car?

Barbara J. Schultz
NOBODY KNOWS . . .
[In Memory of My Father Alvin Eugene McCabe]

Nobody knows
The hurt I've felt
Nobody knows
With what troubles I've dealt
Nobody knows
The nightmares I've had
To have been so young
When I lost my Dad.
I will always remember
His ear-to-ear grin
As He danced through the house
Everytime He came in.
He wasn't as big
As He seemed to be,
I guess it's because
He was Father to me.
And Boy!
What a Joy was He.

Ellen Given
ACQUISITION

I am no longer a shining star
reaching through the night,
but the absorption of darkness
stratagemed into itself,
moving slowly . . . like a retired choreographer.

I sit back and look into the future of the past—
its dazzling pirouettes gradually unswirling,
carrying lanterns to the soul,
lighting submerged orchestrations
in a solitude which has presented itself
with the austere grace
of a black rose in a field of tulips.

Undisturbed by violent forces
I return to myself,
quietly listening to the shimmer of the mind.

Harold H. Milstead
We Pledged Our Troth Anew

I searched the old familiar haunts,
For a face, a sign, or a token,
To ease the pain of a wandering soul,
And mend a heart that was broken.

Alone and sad, I anxiously wondered;
How two trothed souls in flight,
Could lose one another in the celestial fog,
On an eerie, windless night.

Deep in thought how it all came about,
With my head against an ancient birch,
I heard a voice from out of the mist,
Saying, "don't give up the search!"

Reaching for hands I could not see,
I awoke to a muffled scream,
The eyes of my loved one told me
We'd both had the self same dream.

We held each other in the eerie night,
Til dawn cast its shadowy clue,
Then we thanked the Lord for another day,
And we pledged our troth anew.

Rebecca Lee Skillman
CRIMES OF LIFE

The oppressed girl does sit there,
Where she has often sat.
Oppressed by Society,
Who treat the poor like that.

Do they care that she is overworked,
And receives so little pay?
That she sleeps in a crowded building,
And eats but once a day?

The oppressed girl does sit there,
Warmed only by the sun.
They say money isn't important,
It is when you have none.

Live you richmen, merrily,
No, do not stop and think.
As the rich grow slowly richer,
The poor will quickly sink.

Why must Society be so cruel?
To ignore the world of the poor.
Can this world we hope to cure?
Or must they suffer, evermore?

Edward W. McAuley
SOUND OF LOST HUBCAPS

When his fleeing hubcap made its roar
'Twas louder than any sound I'd heard before
Yet when my own left one day
I'd swear they went in a more quiet way.

And those you tell about the lost
Don't take time to ask the cost

Oh no that's not what they say
Rather something like
You mean you didn't hear them
When they went away?

Allen M. Kayrell
THE RIVER

On a wonderous mountain peak
almost touching the sky.
A tear of joy dropped from an angel's eye.

Soon joined by others and cradled in the snow,
a little stream was formed
wondering where to go.

Swiftly and surely with a lilting musical sound.
The little stream plunged happily
down, down to the ground.

And soon the snows were far behind, and to the good earth
the stream was kind.

And all God's creatures gave thanks to him, while the
silvery fish cavort and swim.

Now the stream becomes a river coursing thru the plain.
Its journey has not been in vain.

For miles on miles as far as one
can see, a happy river serving
you and me.

Then the river with nary a sound
suddenly disappears deep
underground.

And in the darkness there is
scarcely a wave, there is no
sunshine in this underground
cave.

Stalagtites and Stalagmites seem
to abound, in fascinating forms
so deep in the ground.

Theres a whisper of wings from
flying bats, that show the river
the way to go back.

Then flowing through rill and
rock—
The river is once again on top.

And surely this is its finest hour,
its banks a profusion of lovely
flowers.

Now the river makes its final
bend, for its journey soon, will
come to an end.

For here we find the lonely sea—
Waiting to embrace my river free.

And if you wish to know just
why, turn your face to God and
sky.

Adela-Adriana Moscu
A NEW BEGINNING
A new beginning
brightens my
horizon.
Another way of
seeing life
begins.
I welcome future
with an open mind.
The past
is gone,
the memory
still vivid
in my heart
and mind.
Sometimes
I wanted
to stop time,
but Nature is
much stronger.
So life goes on
and us go too.
Forgotten is
the way we lived
if no one
will remind us.
So let them go
sweet memories
for they have shown
their bitter fees.
I have to smile again
for soon I won't be here,
So let the future come,
I don't have any fear.

Hazel J. Ashe
THE TWO OF US
I stood beside the waterfall
I walked a mountain road,
I sat beneath the laurels
And dreamed of wealth untold.

I watched the baby robin
Just begin his flight,
And listened to the whippoorwills
Calling in the night.

Heard the lonesome sounds of
nightfall
The hums, the croaks, the birds,
Each waiting for its mate,
A plainitive call in each word,

God made nature so exquisite
Only He could accomplish thus,
The trees, the grass, the creeks to
wade
Then He made the two of us.

He gave us love unlimited
And the years have all been good,
The wealth I once dreamed of—is
our love
I wouldn't change it—if I could.

Cheryl Lynn Savage

Cheryl Lynn Savage
WOMAN OF THE WIND
She's a woman of the wind,
a whisper in the night.
She'll sell your soul,
then take you in.
She's a woman of the wind.

When night rolls in,
she leaves her man,
to love in sin
or how she can.
She's a woman of the wind.

With moves of a lady,
ways well her own,
she'll drive you crazy,
then send you home.
She's a woman of the wind.

Her husband is game.
He'll never tell,
but just the same,
he's taught her well,
his woman of the wind.

Nellie Woll Kirkpatrick
TAKE MY HEART
Come take my heart in your two
skilled and gentle hands:
It's yours to break apart, or leave
whole as it stands;
For neither time nor place, no
other's smile nor grace,
Can fill with happiness this now
so empty space.

So come and take my heart: it's
yours, and your's alone,
To thrill with ecstacy to joys
we've never known,
To share life's full events and
things both great and small
(Like walking through dry,
colored leaves and scenes in
fall.)

But best of all: if life should tear

you, heart and soul,—
May God and this, my caring
heart help make you whole.
So take my heart with trusting
hands: it's love is true;
For I was born, I know, to love no
one but you.

Frank Viggiani
There's a Cross Some Where
There's a cross somewhere
Underneath the Heavenly star
There's a cross somewhere
With angels looking from afar
Someday I will be near you
Then once again we will walk
in the garden of Heaven
Where roses are so sweet lovely
night at eleven
My heart is pounding in a pool of
tears
Where there is a cross
somewhere over you dear

Bennie Townsend Jr.
TIS GREAT TO BE
Tis great to be impressive
And influence other folk
Tis great to be expressive
With words tht don't provoke
Tis great to be possessive
With the things you really
need
But it's awful to be oppressive
Just to satisfy your greed

Tis great to be intelligent
With great knowledge about
life
Tis great to be magnificent
With charm that quenches
strife
Tis great to have fulfillment
As a challenge is complete
But its awful to have resentment
Towards those who bow at
your feet

Linda McClelland
DANDELIONS
A dandelion is a weed! By
definition, a weed is an
unwanted plant growing in an
undesired place.

Is the freshly picked bouquet of
dandelions squeezed to death
in the chubby hand of a child
unwanted?

And, has not every teacher's desk
and mom's kitchen table
displayed this bouquet of love?

Is the sweet nectar of the flower
turned into wine an unwanted
taste delight?

And are not the greens cooked,
buttered and seasoned fit for a
gourmet's repast?

And, how would we know if you
liked butter?

Is not the busy bumblebee's
drunkeness from this bloom
turned into delicious honey?

Does not your heart pound when
you see millions of dandelions
swaying and painting a
meadow with the signs of
spring and new birth?

Yes, the dandelion is a friend!

Who can count the wishes that
have been blown and scattered
to the wind reminding us of
hope?

Surely, these are not the results
of a weed!

John Law
CHILDLIKE
What's wrong with being
childlike,
Aren't we all the same?
Going through this game of life,
Each with a given name.
What's wrong with picking
flowers,
Or walking in the sun,
Swimming in a neighbor's pond,
Living, having fun.
What's wrong with being
childlike,
And leaving for awhile?
Drifting in a dream world,
When you wake you wear a
smile.
What's wrong with playing
Hide-N-Seek,
Or a game of ol' baseball?
Or going home to dear old Mom,
When you've had a great big
fall?
What's wrong with being
childlike,
And living for today?
What's wrong with being happy,
What's wrong with what I say?
The world says we must act
grown up,
And face it like a man.
Let me go and be with them,
Let me if you can.
For if we can't be children,
And do the things they do.
Then we don't need tomorrow,
The world will soon be
through.
For if we can't be children,
And enjoy this life of ours.
We might as well be pickled,
And stored in little jars . . .

Ella Foster O'Brien
MY MONUMENT INDIAN
I look down a valley, so old, so
old,
And watch the days pass by,
The years and centuries have
taken their toll,
From off of the mountains
high.

God placed me here, long, long
ago,
When yet the world was new,
To watch this valley grow old
with me,
And what yet there was to do.

I am only a rock in the opening
Of the canyon, long and deep,
But I am an Indian, and look as
one,
As forever my tryst I keep.

My headdress, the cedars, so tall
and green,
My eyes, the black granite so
old,
My face the sandstone, so yellow,
My face the color of gold.
Yes, I am the Monument Indian
To watch o'er our valley so old,

God gave me this chore to do
each day
And for him to have and to
hold.
Yes, the Monument Indian am I
And my job is not yet done.
For I watch and wait at the
canyon gate,
Yes, I wait for the setting sun
When God returns to our land so
old,
When troubles will be no more,
Then we will know, in the
evenings glow,
That our God has opened his
door.

Ralph A. Fisher Sr.
FLIGHT PLAN
*[To my wife of 63 years, Edith.
Mother of three and a Gold
Star Mother, like falcon and
gull, we have been side by side.]*
From the misty mountain to the
foaming sea
Soars the falcon from the
timberline tree.
From the ageless ocean to the
snow-capped peak
Floats the ring-billed gull with
ebony beak.
From the mountain crest, to the
sea and tide
Fly God's falcon and gull side by
side.

Jeanne Maisonet
ENCORE
Our moments together
were a hit musical show
with a unique cast
and glowing excitement
that deserved
a standing ovation.
I find myself
unable to accept
the close of our performance.
My heart resounds
encore, encore!

Betsy Papendieck
THE PASSER—BY
He reminded me of those nights
Which lay hidden in the attic.
Made me remember, as the moon
lights
A discarded dream and clocks
that tick
Away the dusty years of time.
A glint of memory through the
crack;
How the cobwebs twine and
intertwine!
Though the silver threads
remained intact,
Undisturbed, but for the uttered
sigh
Breathed from my lips, he took
me back
To see my life, lke a passer-by.

Philip A. Givens
A POEM
I dream my dreams, but they tell
me nothing.
I redeem my soul for nothing
more.
I wish for more than this
somebody can store, when I
think there is nothing more.
Now when I rest, only to wish for
the gloominess of what was

today to be flushed away, the
sun rises again.
I think not of days ahead, only
one can I cope.
If I say show me my security no
answer will come.
If I say show me only this
moment, its already there.
I ask for nothing, but what is, oh
so true.
Nothing can be true except
reality itself.

Andrea Ross

Andrea Ross
THE THING I LIKE MOST
*[To Peter, Sam and the
photography of Ashton, Samuel
and Churchstone]*
The thing I like most about you
is you hide your feelings well.

The thing I like least about me is
that I have no feelings.

You are the lucky one—you still
have feelings.

Don't let them forget how to
trust—they too can become
encased in strange games.

If they forget how to care, they
will never know how to be
wanted beyond superficial
needs.

Don't let them suffocate—give
them room, even in their
hiding place.

To grow and become strong, to
nuture and give resiliency.

With love still lingering in your
heart, it is the most precious
gift you can give your soul.

Make it last a lifetime.

Dian L. Raineri
THE CHILD
Have you heard about the child?
No, tell me, tell me please.
On the outside she didn't say a
word, but on the inside, it
stung like bees.

She sits on the ground with her
feelings trapped inside, and her
face as still as a stone.
And the looks that the children
give her as they pass by is as
cold as an ice cream cone.

She cries on the inside till she's
ready to burst.
Then she thinks of her having no
friends, which makes it hurt
even worse!

When she gets out of school and
is in her bed, and on a pillow
she rests her head.

What was once inside her comes
out with no one to hear, and
her face is bright red, her
cheeks are soaked and her eyes
are swollen with tear.

And now you've heard the story
of the child.
How do you know so much about
the child?

Didn't you listen? It's plain to see!
The child I was talking about was
quite mainly . . .
Me!

Arthur William Brown
BOLERO
Slow and steady beats the music
Slow and stately dances the
dancer.
Tap, tapping feet you hear
Tapping to the rhythmic beat.
Start to respond to the sound.
A gradual increasing dancing
tune.
Dancer to the music keeping pace
As faster it does require.
Undulating, dancing body
captivates.
Louder, faster the music compells
Back and forth movements begin
Synchronized to dancer watched.
Out onto the floor, slow at first
Toward the dancer you move.
Two as one both become
Movement matched in precision.
Faster the dance becomes
Music trying to keep pace.
So well dance the two together.
The great dance of dances,
The dance of the bolero.

Doris Lele Szabo
HOPE
There is beautiful sunshine
Behind each cloud,
And the flowers won't grow
without rain.
And we couldn't see life's beauty
clearly
Unless we have suffered some
pain.
Through heartaches and cares,
Through fast-falling tears
We suffer; then strive on to cope.
The outlook's much brighter
When cleared by the storm
And when someone has given us
hope.

Patricia Ann Lewis
AT MY DOOR
*[Lovingly dedicated to my
brother William Lee Lewis and
his wife Gerry Lewis.]*
YOU

Standing there
A little shy,
Hoping I still care.

Standing there,
A little lost,
Hoping I will smile.

I

Standing here
Awaiting you,
Hoping you would come.

Standing here
Loving you,
Reaching out my arms.

Sandra L. Zeus
DOGGEREL
There was a cat vociferous
Beneath a tree coniferous
Who spied a skunk od'iferous
And ran the other way.

He met a dog carnivorous
Who wasn't very chivalrous
But none the less was frivolous
And had a lot to say.

They spoke in tones pyrogenous
Of plums and plants homogamous
While sipping milk homogenous
All on the first of May.

They touched upon Pythagoras,
On tortoises Galapagos,
On anything contiguous,
Then fell into a fray.

The dog waxed more
cantankerous.
The cat, the less magnanimous,
Decided on an exodus,
And bade the dog good day.

Karen L. Rolff
TO THE MOON
You can't shine a light
on the moon . . .
Unless you are there
in the dark.
You can't fall in love
too soon . . .
Unless he sends you there.

Mary Ellen C. Kern
1934
Poverty shaped our dreams:
bread lines, soup lines,
a plate of potatoes for seven,
but freedom promised more.

Frosted autumn mornings,
dashing thirty feet
to the outhouse, dark and musty
at five o'clock.

And how the well's pump
needed coaxing:
icy metal, hollow groans.
Water to bathe with before
school.

The girls dressed in one room,
the boths in another.
A handkerchief pinned to the
blouse,
baggy underwear tied in place.

Papa racked and wrenched in the
foundry,

Mama sewed in the factory,
but there wasn't much work for
    anyone.
How they wanted to work!

The outhouse creaked and
    slanted.
The water pump bellowed a tune.
Mama and Papa turned gray.
But freedom promised more.

Evelyn R. Carey
GIFTS
Each little bird up in the trees
Each little passing shower,
Each blade of grass and thorny
    twig
Each budding little flower,
All are things of nature,
God's gifts to you and me;
Like skies so blue or cloudy,
Some of the beauty we can see.

Quiet streams and roaring
    oceans,
Thundering storms or sunshines
    glow,
Snowflakes that brighten winter,
    and,
Moonbeams on fallen snow.
Sun rise and sun sets,
Seem like some work of art;
We feel so thrilled with all of
    them,
When we keep God in our heart.

Katherine Williams
BITTER TASTE OF LIFE
As night falls over me.
Like a blanket against the sky.
To hide my tears.
A moment of weakness shy.
An imaginary wonder.
As the bird is free.
To gather my wings.
To cling to the sea.
Possess the gift of life.
Yet bound not free.
For whom who holds the key,
That binds the prison walls,
My eyes can't see.
My fears no one can share.
They all belong to me.
But allow I'll drown in your
    sympathy
I'll rest my long life battles
And cover my face with the sand
    of the sea
Look not for the break of dawn
It's light will fade from me.
To possess the gift of life
Is to whom holds the Key.

Bartholomew Murray
SOFTLY LIFE, SOFTLY
Softly, but rarely, our lives loft
    free,
Seeking, yet bearing, seeds of
    eternity,
Gladly, some sorrowfully, live as
    man,
Managing, each moment, as only
    each can.

O gently life, do chastise me,
O softly strife, do follow me,
So patiently, I grow with thee,
I flow with thee, through eternity.

Softly, like dawns stretching rays,
Quickly, like dusks setting ways,
Warmly, like the sun blessed
    days,
Life breeze my way, life breathe
    this day.

Charles M. Hollingsworth
ODE TO A ROSE
She once was quite a beauty as
She grew among the rest,
And then, came Fall, she
    withered, though
She tried to look her best.

What once were rosy cheeks of
    red
Had slowly turned to brown.
Her petals lay beneath her feet
And scattered all around.

She flourished in the frigid winds,
And when the sun was hot,
But still they failed to note the
    wounds,
They turned, and noticed not.

'Twas not from lack of food she
    died,
Nor water, light, or air.
Alas, the rose was cast aside,
And died from lack of care.

Leo
TANGLED SWAMPS
Tangled swamps
And soggy tree roots
Cannot hold you love,
We are of the sky
And sky's divinity
Renews, encircles,
Creation's clouds of light
There is no death
Only endless Light.
Death is the darkness
Death is despair
It does not exist
In the pearly promise
Of the Light renewing Light.
So glow thou Holy Ones
Walk among the clouds
We are all here now
And hate, so weak a weapon
Wears outworn armor
Of another era.

Cindra R. Gillespie
A SYMBOL OF LOVE
A symbol of love
    I wear on my hand.
It speaks a language
    We both understand.

A "security blanket",
    My helper, a friend.
It knows all our secrets,
    Each step that we've been.

A circle of friendship,
    Of passion, of cheer;
It brings back the memories
    That I hold so dear.

I oftentimes clutch it,
    Awake or asleep—
And somehow it soothes me
    Of our love so deep.

It may not be human—
    No soul in its breast.
But it ties me to the man
    That I love the best.

A symbol of love
    I wear on my hand.
It speaks a language
    We both understand.

Elizabeth Klepps
MOM THINK
Mom you took the pill as all
    moderns do
    Not thinking that God had his
    plans for you

You said three children were
    enough to take care
    Now Mom think, is that really
    fair?

I wanted to be one of your clan
    But you snubbed me out, your
    little man
Now at eighty-five you sit all
    alone
    And wonder why you're in the
    old folks home.

God new Pat and Sue would be
    there with Him
    And you never could depend
    on Jim
'Cause he took your ways of a
    care-free life
    And didn't want children, just a
    wife.

Dad tried to tell you, be fruitful,
    multiply
    'Cause he read the bible and
    often did cry
The pill takes a life, Oh sinners
    repent
    God have mercy on you in his
    final judgement.

Frances Tenoso
DEATH VERSUS LIFE
A crashing of darkness,
    an opening of light;
A crashing of going,
    an everlasting being,

Why is it sad except that he is
    gone
When arrival was so glorious,
Why is it dark except it is
    unknown,
When the light is everlasting.

Perhaps we will cry but he
    grieves not at all,
Perhaps we wonder, but
    wondering is over at last;

How futile it all seems,
Only he is happy somewhere
How hopeless and lost,
Unless we believe.

Laurie A. Barrett
LIVING AN EXISTENCE
A fading flower, but then it's
    spring
A blossom is born; born to die;
To die in a field of dead.
Someone once said—
"Stop to smell the roses."
Hurry—before they die.
Lay their petals down to rest.
But is it for the best—
That those are made to die
To cease living an existence
Or better to continue—
But is it really true,
That life is lived in vain—
A fading flower between pages,
That when opened and set free,
Will create a lasting memory—
But hurry to smell the roses,
Before they fade away
It'll be for the best,
In laying petals to rest.

Lisa Kay Bookman
On Having All My Poems Stolen
You know, the window is still
    cracked
and it's been cold

here
since you kicked in my life.

You missed the gold, damn you
    and left me
a key
that opens nothing.

I have sorted through the missing
    item by item,
over and over
telling myself—

write a poem, lost poet.
You have so very much to say
    now.

Josephine Shirar McGonigle

Josephine Shirar McGonigle
AUTUMN GAMES
In morning darkness
an owl waits atop a deer blind
men crouch beneath
with guns poised
to catch sight
of their season's trophies.
At dawn
moving in tall vegetation
stands a five-point buck;
mute hunters
crawl on their bellies
take deadly aim
toward Man's prize,
as it gracefully leaps toward
    freedom.
Shots crackle in hushed daybreak
as rifles blast
movement ends.
A fawn lies motionless
on frozen turf
plundered before its prime.
Pick-up's motor revs,
exhaust fumes
intermingle with morning fog.
Silence!

J. K. Forrest
PILLS
I went to the doctor
Just feeling real low
My throat was all parched
And my head hurt me so

I thought he would help me
But he threw me a curve
He said I'd need something
To steady my nerves

He gave me a red pill
The other was blue
But he never told me
What those pills could do

They made me see double
I was ready to fly
I tried the top floor
But that was too high.

I made it outside
It didn't seem far
Roamed all around
But can't find my car

I stayed out all night
Got chilled to the bone
It took me two days
To find my way home

Now I've looked for that doctor
But he never is in
He's out playing golf
Or visiting a friend

But I'm getting madder
I'm ready to kill
When I find that doctor
That gave me those pills

Kathleen M. Fenton
A DREAM
I met a really kooky guy
Who said he invented lemon pie
I asked him where he bought his
shoes
And his face turned a reddish hue
He left and said see you soon
And I did the next afternoon

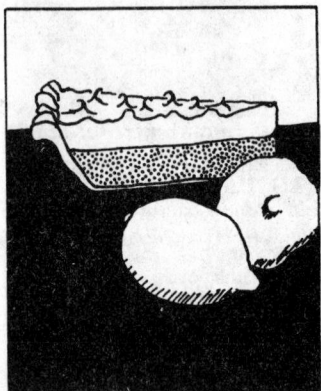

He was sitting Indian style under
a tree
And introduced me to his pet bee
We talked for an hour under the
blue puffed sky
Then he asked me to his home
For a piece of lemon pie
Since that day I haven't seen
My kooky friend in need of a
Queen.

Delores M. French
PREDESTINATION
Your voice will cry at my door
again;
I, who wait while worlds reel by,
But under what fateful, pointed
star,
Under what burning sky?

Patricia Ellen
SWEET MARGARETHA
*[To my beautiful and haunting
mother, Margaretha. May she
rest in peace. May I peacefully
rest.]*
Predators of the night
Seep into my dreams.
Sweet Margaretha come with me,
You shall be my queen.
Day dreamers never fear the long
night hours,
For their dreams are filled with
The sun and morning flowers,
Alas only I must dread the long
and darkened hours,

For my dreams have no sun,
Ghosts of my past bring dead
Flowers.
Margaretha come, stand beside
Me now
Wake me so I may live,
In the sun with the flowers
Let my soul free from the
Damned and cursed
Let me learn to love,
While I am here on earth.

Maro Rosenfeld
TWINKLE TWINKLE
*[To Illia, Tom and Nick
Remember—there is only the
Sun, the Moon and the Stars
and that's You]*
Twinkle twinkle little lite
In the heartbeat of the nite
Golden Bridges of reflection
Lamp the Crown
of Man's Invention

Freeways lined with sequined
eyes
Mother Darkness is disguised
Every Jewel Crowns her Head
Til the Dawn
Pronounces her dead

Hilda M. Jordan
**Love Is Only a Pit Of
Gratitude**
When we say love
as fresh as a "Turtle Dove"

Ah' hello love
still only a pit of gratitude

Love is not to be misunderstood

When we say love
as fresh as a "Turtle Dove"

Love becomes a Multitude

Eleanor Lankford-Armstrong
TRACINGS
*[To a special someone who
turned my life around]*
My thoughts trace your face and
touch you—
Knowing you intimately with my
soul.
The ache when we are near is as
painful as when I'm apart from
you—
To you, I'm someone you knew
long ago
Yet through the years you've
touched my life in many ways.

Back from a place away came my
will;
Soothed was my troubled mind
and my heart opened to love

A "special person" you said of me

Again, I trace you with my
thoughts—
for I know now these fragile
tracings will be all I'll ever
have.

Eileen M. Greene
FAR AWAY . . .
I knew it would happen . . .
the moment I met him.
Our eyes met and our hands
touched . . .
exploring each other's finges.
I loved his strong hands . . .
and his sweet face.
All the love I ever dreamed of . . .
I saw in him.

I saw a purpose . . .
a reason to go on.
I saw a man . . . strong and
gentle—
who wanted me.
Oh, I loved him . . .
with all my heart.
And I gave to him . . .
all the love I had.
It happened . . .
and now . . . there is still love.
So empty and cold,
that it hurts to get up in the
morning.
Oh, how I love him . . .
Yet our hands cannot touch—
our eyes cannot meet—
And all the man I ever wanted. . .
all the love I ever dreamed of. . .
is in him still.

Patsy Lewis
DEFIANCE
Inside a mental institution
or inside my mind.
Analysts, couches, cells,
none of them bother me.
I will not change.
Inwardly, I will be me.
I will not change one brain wave
for all their knowledge.
They cannot—they will not
make me a pattern—like them.
I'll be a different mold
if only inside where I can see.
No one disturbs me.
I am a cocoon soon to be a
butterfly.

Miroslava Novakovic
A DREAM COMES TRUE
A favorite dream of mine, for
more years than I can see
is that I have someone, who is
all mine and will take care of me.
For thirty odd years
I've always been alone
never having a brother or
sister to call my own.
A lot of tears were shed,
A lot of years of loneliness
Out of the blue, God's hand I'm
sure
found me my brother so true.
His voice is so gentle and warm,
He's also happy to know me,
Even though he had no idea
I had been born.

Lillian Kathryn Brasher
THE WINNER
How great to excel—to win the
game
To hear the crowd call your
name.
It isn't only the reward—tho it
does play a part
It's more the intoxicating feeling
of the heart.

To touch the clouds—all wise
conquerors have learned
Is to feel the elation of the
Prodigal Son when returned.
A fleeting moment to catch a
glimpse of joy untold
As the Father feels when a lost
sheep returns to the fold.

No win is ever more lovingly
labored
No rapture ever more joyously
savored

Than the precious triumph so fair
Of a Mother's answered prayer.

No golden trophy outranks
The victor's humble thanks,
No glowing tribute compares
To the thanks she sends upstairs.

Jenna V. Ownbey
EROSION
Time wears some love away
slowly
With everyday use,
Like water dripping which
reduces
Rock to gravel. Abuse
Comes in varying degrees to
lowly
People or proud
Royalty. Mental cruelty is
packaged in unholy
Wrappings, its cry loud
And strident; murmuring only
faint protest,
It follows all the crowd,
Forsakes the best and forgets the
rest.

Ormond Sivers
A SONG FOR YOU
[For Audrey, love of my life]
This is a song to say hello
To say that I see you wherever I
go
The sun, he often speaks your
name
In my thoughts you are the joy
In the children's game

This song was written just for
you
To tell you I love you, truly I do
Gypsy knows my every fantasy
The love, peace and happiness
You have brought to me

I carry your letters day by day
Although I remember every word
you say
Guess I just want you close to
heart
For we are so many miles apart
And my mind loses time

Darling do you ever think of me
In the darkness of the night
As your soft hand turns out the
light
Have you ever dreamt of the day
A perfect love will come your
way

Well I do, and I think of you

Robert Michael Balderrama
**God Will Show You the
Way**
Although you may feel all alone
In sadness and despair
With no one you can turn to
Or a friend to really care

Just remember there is Someone
Who will hear you when you
pray
And you will find the answer
God will help you find the way

There is nothing that you cannot
do
No matter what your plan
With faith and trust you'll reach
your star
If you believe you can

God has the greatest love for you
He proves it day by day

You've only but to turn to Him
And He'll show you the way

Because that's what our Father's
    for
    To help you in your need
But you must do your part as well
    In thought and word and deed

You always can depend on Him
    When your skies turn to grey
And as He leads you by the hand
    God will show you the way.

J. Kay Lowe
His Name Is Loneliness
A silent spectre
lurks, unsuspected
without a face,
yet many faces he.
He toys with loose edges
of consciousness
and wanders the chambers of the
    mind
with a faint fragrance
or poignant refrain.
His mission, to entomb
us in misery.
He dines on human hearts,
a scourge of the spirit,
fungus of the soul,
delighting in our wretchedness.
He wears a shroud
of gloom which he
gleefully shares and
grants respite, fades,
only to gather more collectibles,
bygone memories, futile dreams
and loved ones gone before.
Hope causes him to cringe,
laughter sets him trembling
and love creates a
room he cannot share.

Sadie C. Laurent
NEVER TO BE
Suppose your fate had been mine?
    never to be born.
Never to have Baptism,
    Wiped out, even
though God willed you to be, to
    live
in the world, bound or free,
everything so beautiful;
If I were to be—so sad—
As I lay a tiny fetus, in a Mother's
    womb, short time my Mother—A
    time to
will whether I live or die: I sigh!
I can't pray, so pray for me, and
    all
to live the gift of life, to know
    love,
and serve, deserve, Eternity;
    "Born To Live".

Edward G. Branch
MY ORDEAL
About 12 months ago, I started
    having pain from Arthritis.
    Each day I have some pain, but
    sometimes the pain is so bad it
    affects *"THE DAYS OF OUR
    LIVES."*
About 5 months ago the pain got
    so bad that I was only planning
    "ONE DAY AT A TIME."
My solution was to see *"THE
    DOCTORS."*
With much thought and the pain
    not getting much better, I
    decided to have surgery
    performed, because I have only

"ONE LIFE TO LIVE."
After taking alot of x-rays and
    medicine, the doctors decided
    to put me in *"GENERAL
    HOSPITAL."*
The surgery was performed. I
    didn't remember much of the
    recovery room, because I was
    still sleepy. I awoke in my
    room and was happy that the
    surgery was a success. I didn't
    know what time it was but
    after my head cleared, I knew it
    was the *"EDGE OF NIGHT."*
My recovery was easier with the
    phone calls, cards and the
    visits from relatives, friends
    and *"ALL MY CHILDREN."*
Before I was fully recovered from
    my surgery I had a stroke. Now
    with my recovery going as
    expected, I can *"SEARCH FOR
    TOMORROW."*
The search shouldn't be too
    difficult *now* because I know
    there is a *"GUIDING LIGHT."*

Lavender Hendricks
NATURE'S PEACE
I stand on the soft sand
and watch the gold-orange
    sunrise.
The waves wash upon my toes,
Refreshing my feet and spirit.

Nature's beauty puts me at peace.
I walk through a gate,
The sun beats strongly,
I step on fragrant blades of grass,
Palmetto trees sway to a gentle
    breeze,
Flowers bloom, filled with the
    scent of nectar,
I feel blessed to be allowed to
    appreciate these wondrous
    sights.

Denise Groves Humbert
TO YOU
I saw you perform last night.
I watched your face—
I saw your smile; . . .
And what my head knew all
    along
My heart now accepts.
My decision was right.
The pain will go away; . . .
I wish you well . . .
With love.

Catherine Reid
WAVE LENGTH OF LOVE
*[To Richard E. Deaton, at the
time in my life when I needed
spice, you were there.]*
I laid my body down to sleep
Bent my mind against my will,
And yet I couldn't close my eyes
I know I love you still.
So I will try to understand
The space that separates the man,
Whose mind is tuned in to see
The thoughts that arise in me.

The same wave length that
Brought you into my life
Has been an instrument of love.
The years between us
Is like a space over a gorge,
To span a gorge,
So can a wave length
Span the years.

Most people are only loved
By one person,
But if you're lucky to be loved
By more than one
It can enrich your life,
And your future.
And if you can use the mind
Of one who loves you
Immortality is established.

Just to be with you
To touch you now and then,
Is all I ask of this world.
The rest is the passing of
    tomorrow,
So I can leave you and this world
With a smile and a touch.

Sandra Alterine Johnson

Sandra Alterine Johnson
Christian Who Charges
Would it be nice if every So
    Called Christian was just like
    God who would do you a favor
    and say, "Oh, there is no
    charge."?
Some church members will shout
    all over the church and claim
    they have love for everyone
    and say if you ever need me,
    call for I will surely come. But
    believe me, calling them will
    cost you and their favors are
    even more for if they take you
    to the doctor, you better have
    some dough.
Such cold-hearted So Called
    Christians confessing I really
    believe in God and everything
    they do for you, there will be a
    charge.
Watch out for hand stretching
    Christians who will have their
    hands already out and when
    you ask them, how much do I
    owe you, they'll say, "Oh, I'll
    take any amount", but yet they
    claim I love you and I'm doing
    this from my heart, but if they
    were really and truly
    Christians, they would say,
    "Oh, there will be no charge."
And there are So Called Alibi
    Christians using excuses for all
    they do, saying I wouldn't do
    this for anybody else, but you
    know I'll do it for you. I really
    don't want to charge you
    because I sincerely believe in
    God, but I must have a small
    amount of fee for times are
    really hard.

Some people must fail to realize
    that all blessings come from
    above, and when our Father
    sent them down to us He's
    doing it out of His heart.
    Suppose He charges us for His
    blessings and He charges us for
    His love and every time we ask
    Him for something, He will
    say, "Sorry, but there will be a
    charge." Then all of us would
    suffer and all of use would
    starve. For when our Father
    does all that He does for us,
    He's doing it out of love.

Clifford Love
SEERS
Seers
    seem to see
    more than we see
    of the future
        so they say

They
    peer darkening gloom
    predict pending doom
    will soon
        trouble our way

We
    love through the night
    greet the new light
    finding everything
        going OK

Conceed
    to the seers
    their power to see
    let them predict
        what they may

Leave
    to the lovers
    the power to live
    creating new vision
        each day

Lawrence Spirio
HEATHER
I've seen your photo from your dad
    and would like you to know;
    although I never met you
    I would like to say hello.
    You look so handsome
        upon the mighty steed;
    I think that you are pretty
        and very sweet indeed.
        You've got a smile
        as if tickled by a feather;
    your bright and shining eyes
    sing out your name, "Heather".

Linda Fay Crowder
THE BOY AND THE GUN
The crowd gathered 'round the
    boy,
They came to look at his new
    toy.
He and his friend had looked for
    fun,
But instead he'd found his
    Daddy's gun.

They had been soldiers in the
    yard,
And pulling the trigger sure was
    hard.
They did not know the gun was
    real,
And now the boy's friend lay very
    still.

The gun was in the cabinet
    drawer,

173

And they had needed it to play war.
The neighbors saw them running 'round,
Then they heard that awful sound.
One loud shot and one small yell,
They all looked on as the boy fell.
Someone had called and the doctor was there,
All the boy with the gun could do was stare.
They took the boy to the hospital today,
How he is, no one can say.
The boy with the gun—no one knows what it did,
To the fragile mind of a six-year-old kid.

Linda Collins

THE GIFT

[To Sherry, I dedicate this poem to your memory, though you are gone from us now, you'll live forever in our hearts.]

The sun is like an eagle, soaring swiftly through the skies.
The rain drops drawn to earth, are the tears the clouds have cried.
Age is a whisper, growing louder with time.
The stars that light the heavens, are the twinkle in an eye.
The wind is a drifter, a spirit wild and free.
The ocean is the mind, vast and flowing deep.
A flower is the beauty, so few take time to see.
Life is the miracle, the gift to you and me.

Vivian Sofie Keck

MORNING CHORUS

Early in the morning,
before the sun arose,
from high in a tree top
    came a chorus,
        of birds singing in harmony.
I scarce could believe my ears,
for never before, in all my years
had I heard such music.
They didn't miss a note,
each one knew their part.
They sounded very happy,
and were singing from their heart.
We should all be so happy,
with the dawn of each new day,
and show our thanks with rejoicing
as He helps us along our way.

Rebecca Gola

SISTER

*[Mojej Kochanej Siostrze:
Zwierciadlo Mojego Serca—
Cien Mojej Duszy]*

We are kin
Possessive of a bond
that goes deeper than
shared blood and bone:
Occupants of the same womb,
Moon—like Slavic faces,
Carries of an insane
Blue force
that drives us to tears
at the touch of these
memories, together.

At times
we are too much alike:
Not on the surface,
but the roots.
Like two spiders in the same web,
we fight to spin
our own designs:
Different outlooks/Varied perceptions/
Other hopes and dreams:
We have separate paths to walk;
Though—
We share the source
and the ultimate
Destination.

Lisa J. McNeill

RAPIDS

The wild rapids
move swiftly by
with peaks,
like snow covered mountains,

from the jagged rocks beneath
and continue on their way
to a peaceful lake,
to rest.

Sandra Kaye Harvey

Spring's Song of New Jerusalem

*[w/love—to God, His Son—
Jesus & my children]*

I'd like to write a poem on spring,
w/words that rhyme that people could sing,
    telling of Earth's rebirth that it brings.
Earth thawing from winter's deep freeze,
    buds pushing forwards from the land and trees,
        rebirth in the sky on the land and in the seas.
The rejuvenation of the life of earth,
    w/everything producing new births,
        w/the spring's showers quenching its thirsts.
All of which helps rejuvenate me,
for in spring—God I so plainly see,
    once a year letting me see how His rebirth will be.

Kevin Hunter

ON THE SUMMIT

On the Summit
Standing like an eagle
Spirit like the wind
Oh set me free

Free from the world below
From the chains that bind

Voice carried away
From a heart at ease

No one listening
But the sky below
To answer yes
To the words I cry

Hear what I say
Oh faces in the valley
Run from the fields
That bind you to the earth

Climb the mountain
I stand upon
Listen closely
To words I speak

There is no other freedom
But the freedom that flies
So freely it flies
Here on the Summit

Dennis Threadgill

PARALLEL LINES

Constant lingering
This parallel line
Sights and sounds of fears
senses of the mind
Ask not for reason
There is none to find
Time slips silently by
Cry, cry the bitter tears
Of lonely response to nothing
for the words are easily said
Through contradictive lies
Silly fool to be lead into the void of emotion
Physical gratification
into sleepless nights
Of wondering, wondering
Why
Touch not the forces of the mind
for there are none
Silent murmurs of relentless agony
Pain sublime
Constant

Linda C. Brittain

OUTCAST ROSEBUSH

We are the sharp ones
Often drawing blood,
Ruthlessly defending
Long-awaited buds.

Please heed our warnings:
Smell us but don't touch!
Nothing else can set off
Beauty like our leaves.

Old Timer, Charlotte,
Honor, Mr. Lincoln,
Fragrance fills the garden
Trying to bring peace.

Have we offended?
Do you think us vain?
Can you not perceive our
Thorns are born of fear?

Teri D. Small

DIVORCE

The winds are blowing, the grass swings free;
the moon shines down to comfort me.
My thoughts are racing, my mind won't still;
I have some needs I must fulfill.
Why am I here? What do I need?
I must find out, I must succeed.
The wind is cold against my face;
I'll sit awhile and slow the pace.
A lightning bug! What a beautiful sight;

I'll welcome him on this cold windy night.
Please listen to me and understand;
I need you now to lend a hand.
So that's my story my little friend;
Thanks for staying to the very end.
I'd hoped you could tell me what I need to know;
It's getting late, I'd better go.
Take care of yourself, I'll come again
when I have a bit more time to spend.
Keep your light shining, that's what life is about
You're licked when you let the light go out . . .

Constance Dee Gordon

Rangers Aren't So Tough!!

[To the fellas of the 82nd Airborne Association and the Rangers of the National Guard.]

You think you can intimidate
with your schmancy O.D. greens;
or your badges or your medals,
or your war talk.
When deep down underneath;
under all that Ranger stuff
lies a tender, loving soul of a man.
Jumping from an airplane
is a pretty foolish thing.
But, it's foolish to pretend
that you're so gruff.
When you can't fool the woman
who knows you're just a lamb.
You know that Airborne Rangers
really aren't so tough!!

Ezra Gorrell

LOVE AND THE RIVER

[For Sylvia, my wife, whose essence I've sought, for love can't be bartered or bought.]

Fretful as an avalanche
Captious, testing twig and branch,
The river wanders to the sea.
Meandering from shore to shore
Never knowing what's in store
Even then as you and me.

The springs that feed the streams
may dry awhile
To wait for rains that bring them style
And changes come and are to be
But still the river wanders to the sea.

Leola M. Northern

I MISSED OUT

I've never told you this,
now it's too late.
Now you're on your merry way.

It just didn't seem right to love you the way I did.
It didn't seem right,
to be more than—
just friends.

I never thought I would lose you in the end.
Now,
someone else will hold you,
tell you the things I always meant to.

Someone else's life—will center around you.

You turn your head,
and go the other way.
When there are still a lot of things
I have to say.

You made my life worthwhile,
I thought it was all a dream.
Now,
reality has settled in.

It closed the door . . . which
will never, ever have the chance
to be opened
once more.

Juanita Tackett
DEATH TO THE RIDER
In my dreams I see a pale horse
and it's death to the rider.
It's death to the rider but not
to the one that sits beside her.
I've dreamed this dream before
but death was postponed.
But to whom is grief left behind,
the grief of being alone.
The rider, I see not their face,
And the dream I can't erase.
Death to the rider of the pale horse.
Not a thing can change its
destiny or course.
But to whom does the death bells chime?
I feel so helpless, it seems to be
a burden or crime.
God lift the heavy load.
Pray the rider will be on the
straight and narrow road.
The black horse beside the pale horse,
their passion is out of control
The mystery of this dream, when
will it unfold?
Ragging passion to one rider and
death to the other rider.
God be with them both, for he's
the only true guider.

Alice L. Keys
GRANDMA'S HOUSE
Like a neglected child it withered away
Today they tore it down
Roof and walls crumbled apart
Only memories left standing
Reflections of childhood visits
Grandpa's smiling eyes
Happy events, sad passings
Generations of births
Staring at its rubble
Its essence I still sense
I hear voices chatting in laughter
I feel a warmth of love too strong
to yeild
I see tears in my mother's eyes

Karen R. Citeroni
ENCORE SEPARATION
It was no starry night that I first fell,
no moon to entice my heart
and no music to dance away with
my feelings.
My stars were the lights in your eyes,
your voice—my music.
Now it will be gone.
I see the darkness approaching.

I try to ward it off with a sunny smile,
but it continues on.
As it comes closer,
I recognize the impending doom.
I realize I have passed through it once before,
as alone then as I am now.
I fought my way through,
and when I arrived at the other side,
I had only a few scratches.
But his time I'm not sure I can
make it in one piece.
The light seems so far off . . .
and I'm so tired—emotionally
and physically.
I'll give it one hard fight,
and maybe my determination
and self confidence will help
me through.
But, whatever happens,
no matter how hard it may be,
no matter how often I may drift
back into the darkness,
I'm glad I've had the chance once
again.

Kim Starlene Bryant
THE UNSUNG SONG
[To my Mother, Lola, and my
Grandparents, and to my
friends, Becki, Carlton and
Anne. I love you all.]
The unsung song of love,
whistles through the trees.
It flows over all the valleys, and
swims beneath the seas.
It makes a sky of gray, seem like
a sky of blue.
It's whispering little things that
simply say, I love you.
It causes clouds to hover over the
fields of grain,
And shows that all that's said was
never said in vain.
It makes the sun above glisten on
the streams.
It causes all the happiness, and
all the lovely dreams.
The unsung song of love, that
lives within the heart,
Can keep us altogether, because
we can't live apart.

Mary Mills
CHOPPING COTTEN
Down those rows, one by one,
Sharpen those hoes, the fight is on.
Watch that sun rise high in the sky.
Golly gee my throat is dry.

What can I do to pass the time?
Think of words and make the rhyme.
Sing some song from long ago,
What about "OLD BLACK JOE".

Yes, I know I am, but I will hurry Dad
You know what? My row is bad!!!
Yes, I know I'm last in line
But that old sun is making me blind.

I wish that dinner bell would ring
My throat is so dry, I can't sing.
That sister is way out ahead—
Boy!!! I wish I had a hunk of bread.

She could turn back and help me some,
Sure would help me get out of this sun,
But, no way would she do that,
I think I'll hide her old straw hat.

Sorry Sis, I didn't mean a word,
You are as nice as any little old bird.
I see you coming back my way,
Oh gee Sis, you made my day!!!

Don't tell Mom, you had to help me
I'll do your chores, wait and see
But not today, Please Oh Please
See there, I am beginning to sneeze.

Helen K. Huxley

Helen k Huxley
INNER PEACE
[In memory of Nancey, my
daughter who has gone to her
eternal home.]
In my travels I have seen
The country side, trees, and
streams
Scenery that money can't buy
Birds, sunsets, and the sky
People I meet on the way
Help to make a lovely day
Some appreciate beauty that is free
Others seem to search for luxury
Fame and fortune may be desired

Material things are not easily acquired
Say we find all this and then
There is an emptiness within
Abide in me and I in you
God's word still holds true
If we take him by the hand
He will always understand

His love will never cease
Not of the world, but Inner Peace.

Jack Irwin
RESURRECTION
Rejection—Human life's most crushing blow!
Not many human beings can survive.
There's something deep within us has to know
That we are loved, or we are not alive.
We drift. We stop. We take to booze, or dope.
Some whine. Some beg. Some really end it all,
Indifferent to the mess that makes. Some hope
Tenaciously: "Perhaps there'll be a call—"
A few, the bravest, take themselves in hand,
Ignore the hurt, build bigger, better selves.
Rejection breeds dejection, but these stand
Because they're men, not silly, simpering elves.
Reaction to rejection? Some fall. Some die.
Some get the act together. Reapply.

Ronald A. Bond
MY GOD
I cannot see You,
but You are there,
In the sky so blue,
in the morning's crisp air.

You're in each flower
that I pass by,
And in the hours
that seem to fly.

I can feel You
in the wind,
I know that You're
my truest friend.

I can hear You,
in each bird that sings
And I know that You
are in every living thing.

No, I cannot see You
but I love You still,
For You are my God
and I'll do Your will.

Ann E. Klag
THE MARCH OF DIMES
[To My Sons: Robbie & Stevie-
Always fill the emptiness in
your heart with kindness.]
The March of Dimes is here
And we should all be glad we're near—
To help a boy
To help a girl
Win their own fight against a fear.

The time has finally come
For you and I to help a fund—
So please be kind
And give some Dimes
To help to cure a boy or girl.

Cynthia J. McGean
THE INSIDE WAR
My mind sent a message
To my Heart:
"I am the ruling one."
The reply came fast and vicious.

My mind sent another
    To my Body:
"You follow my desires."
And outcries rose among.

So I'm at war
    Within myself
      With logic,
        Wants,
        And needs
          My ammunition.

Fighting the battles of
        Decisions,
The canons smoke
        Confusion;
The corpses bleed
        Tears.

Ernest Porter
THE TIME OF DAY
*[This poem is dedicated in
peace and friendship to "Jerry
Wilson Beard" whose
consistent support and
exceptional courage has helped
give me the inspiration to
write.]*
Time is the gentle ease
  with which we love.
Time is life and the
  light—feathered dove,
That once softly paddling
  in measured waves,
Takes off in flight;
  only to settle on another day,
Refreshed and full of
  the precious ether of life.
Time is the tiny grains
  of sand we waste;

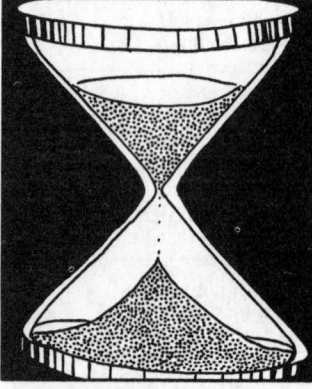

And the nurturing smile
  we neglected to make.
Time is the sun with its
  multi—colored rainbow's edge,
Refracted off ripples of
  a rainy Autumn's day.

Time is now and then
  our champion;
Time is more oft our foe,
  for each year we want for
  peace,
Time without err will flow,
  to that day of doom;
That day of decay,
  radioactive particles eating
  away
At the pulp of our bones,
  and the crests of our hair.
And time would sadly, then,
  recall the way,
We neglected to be heedful of
  the time of day.

James S. Snyder
Lips That Sing Cannot Kiss
Lips that sing cannot kiss,
We can only reminisce of
  romantic bliss.
Our lips only quiver out the
  blues,
When shes gone and left you.
It's much, much better to woo . . .
    Than to woe—
Woe, woe, woe, woe, woe, woe,
  woe.
Like now when I miss you . . .
So, so , so, so, so, so, so, so.
You gave me so much—
And now we can no longer touch

What we once knew.
Like saying I love you, woo, woo,
  woo.
Lips that sing cannot kiss,
Someday you'll bear witness
So always remember this:
It's much better to woo . . .
Than to woe—woe, woe, woe,
  woe.
It's much better to woo . . .
Like we two used too, woo, woo,
  woo.
Like I love you . . . woo, woo,
  woo, woo.
Woe oh! Woe oh! Woe oh! Woe.

James P. Ifft
Years Gone By Return
my years gone by are but a song
  we sang
now lost in silent harmony,
sung before—when heaven
  blessed earth
before the wintry breath
that stayed the summer through.

and now i miss you
like i miss the sun—
i need you every day
as once you needed me—
before you went away.

but years and time can't hide
  your face
i see you everywhere,
in every time my lady smiles
and even when she cries—
my years gone by return.

Eleni Katzingris Moustaka
When Tita and Leonid Cry
*[My deep gratitude to my
brother and brilliant painter
Leonidas Moustacas. Also to
my selfless sister—in—law
Anna Campos Moustacas]*
When the sons of my friend
  Areti cry,
the home became unhappy.
    The silence and the cat,
run away dizzy and deaf.
    Their cry does the sun
to knock afraid at the windows;
    its light, startled, shakes,
blinks and the shadows cover the
    scared toys that guilty, hide.

While the cry gets pressed
    under the doors,
reaching the elevator, reaches
    the street, the beach,
the ocean, leaving the elevator,
    crying the sadness of the
sons of my friend Areti.

When the tears reach the beach,
    it groans of their weight
and the ocean's waves listening

To the cry of the sons of
my friend, are touched and cry,
  taking the tears far away.
Maybe there is one island which
  has never known
  unhappyness
of children's tears.

Florence G. Axton
BEAUTY
High on a mountain top, is a
  wonderous sight,
A lake so blue, so lovely, so
  profound,
  Not newly found.

Dazzling in the sunlight,
  An inspiration at twilight,
Radiant in the moonlight.

Soon the snow will cover the
  summits,
  Beautiful but a feeling of
  sadness,
  A sign will say,"road closed,
  Snow too deep, road too steep."

Then one day in May, gladness
  and tourists will return to
  France,
They will exclaim, as if in a
  trance,
  "What a
        Beauty".

Ann M. Stiles
INTERLUDE
*[To Jeff Dionne, who
understands the fragility of
dreams, and lays strong
foundations on which to build.]*
He intrudes upon my process of
  thought,weaving in and out
  among the citadels of my mind,
    Death.
Darkening the images that my
  mind puts forth, stealing time
  from the inhabitants of my
  mind.
    Cold.
Laughing caustically, laying
  waste to my dreams.
  Reminding me that someday I
  will join them.

T. M. McAndrew
ADOPTIVE LOVE
[To Marhia, with love]
Child unborn, fate uncertain,
  decisions to be made behind
  this curtain, a mother labors
  with love.

Woman awaits, thoughts
  unspoken, strange this silence
  that won't be broken, a woman
  labors with love.

Life emerges, child unnamed,
  loving arms have yet to claim,
  a child filled with love.

Strangers providucing, strangers
  receiving, never meeting, both
  believing, this child, the labors
  of love.

Angela Karszo
IN A NURSING HOME
How forlorn this cleft mind,
this skin sagging on bone
like a parched sheet, left
too long on a clothes' line;
exposure—bleached and
  yellowed,
creased as rumpled paper

thrown into a waste—basket
to be emptied—later . . .

Yet she moves, bent over
a rubber—tipped cane,
slowly, slowly, feet shuffling
back and forth, in vain:
they won't find their way
to remembered places . . .

How eternal this hallway
where a blur of faces
and white aprons fleets by—
masks that rarely smile—
and the alien, shared room
whose blank walls deny
the past. . .
    A dream keeps walking
tired of dreaming. . .tired. . .
begging for blackout—sleep
in which all is quiet.

Jean Levine
VICTIM OF A WEB
Spin your web spider spin your
  web
In and out like needle do you
  thread
Find gossamer strands barely to
  behold.
Why by nature were you chosen?

This delicate tangle a tenuous
  lair.
Who is it you wish to ensnare
Your friend, foe or kin?
A life's work without end.

I am mesmerized by your
  diligence
In and out weaving and weaving.
A headiness and a weariness sets
  in
As you perform your labor so
  fine.

Into what woodwork did you
  scamper
As I am left entranced
Wanting to brush away your web
  of ken
Of which I am a victim.

Paul H. Glenn
DEAR FRIENDS
If by sight or by pen;
Or be it by prayer through
  sleepless nights;
Tell your friend your heart's
  loving sight.

Charlotte V. Fulp
DIMENSIONS OF MIND
[With Love—To my family]
All in all it seemed so complex—
The many scences that clogged
  the mind.
Yet the solution was very simple
  divided by the passing time.
Some things can easily be
  forgotten,
Others haunt like unseen ghost.
The ones we think the dearest,
are the ones that hurt the most.
They are memories of yesterday
  other times and other folk.
Diminishing dreams that dashed
  the hopes.
We must strive to seperate
  accordingly,
in our minds and in our hearts.
Many, Many things which we
  were apart.
We must allow each step we take
up the stairs of life.

To be a little higher than the one
  we took last.
Our minds are the keys and the
  answer to it all.
It's really up to us if we stand or
  if we fall.

Robert Louis Lyon
SONNET TO A PRINCESS
[To Berenise Clark Lyon—
  member of Americans of Royal
  Descent, Order of the Crown of
  Charlemagne, Plantegenet
  Society, Magna Carta Dames,
  Descendants of Knights of the
  Garter.]
When Charlemagne, Rome—
  crowned on Christmas Day,
Founded an imperial millennium,
When Geoffrey leaned to pluck
  his sprig of broom,
Creating Plantagenet dynasty—
This emperor, these kings, this
  pedigree
Little dreamt of her who'd prove
  their noblest bloom:
The royal partner of our
  honeymoon,
The queenliest queen of any
  century.
No more than they, dreamt I of
  your descent
From Magna Carta baron, Garter
  Knight—
Quite unaware of lineage
  document,
Beheld alone my own"Fair Maid
  of Kent,"
Who, lovely in the new moon's
  silver light,
Grew lovelier as dawn and love
  grew bright.

Rosemary Campbell—Smith
I AM YOUR FRIEND
Often you have said to me
Stand tall, bear your pain and
  shed not your tears
For I am your friend.

You said I care about you.
I will share with you my strength
  when you are weak and small
For I am your friend.

Often you have said to me
Let me share with you my past
  hurts
  so you may learn to overcome
For I am your friend.

Dear friend, hear now my plea.
Let me bear your burdens and
  share your grief
For I, too, am your friend.

William Jeffrey Brotzge
Because We Do Not Ask
How great a blessing do we share
that we can come to God in
  prayer,
Our smallest wish; Our greatest
  care,
no longer do we have to bear.

If we'll but lay at his blessed feet
those daily trials we fear to meet,
and stop fending for ourselves
  this hour,
and let God fill us with his power.

How many times we often fail
when we try to set our own ship's
  sail;
Our lives may drift to no avail,

for it's God who controls the
  windy gale.

There'll be no problem we can't
  face
with God's own wisdom and
  loving grace,
if we'll but let him have his way
within our lives from day to day.

God's willing and wants to
  intercede
and help us with our every need,
but how often we fail in the
  simplest task?
and all because we do not ask.

Elizabeth Lotman
THE HONEYSUCKLE TALE
One summer does not make a
  sweetheart
One verse makes not a work of art
And their return may take too
  long
But a fluffed—puffed bird apart
Could help to carry it along.
  While I make wit
  He flies on it
When the honeysuckle ends
  summer is gone.

At last he looks into my pane
I see in him a sweeter range.
Restless with wait for song's
  embrace
With him and time I can be sane
He stays as if he'd take my case!
  While I must wait
  He sails in fate.
When the honeysuckle ends
  summer is gone.

He rubs his beak in risque
  grammar
My heart was moved by his
  gentle manner.
But it would take more flight and
  care
To keep this a surrender.
Was too available for man to bear!
Soon the honeysuckle will be gone.

Marilyn T. Hill
I Smile With the Sun
[To my loving husband, Harold,
  For his inspiration and
  encouragement during
  commercials, at 'half time', and
  between innings.]
My sense of humor's so distorted,
As friends have told me so.
I smile and nod and quietly agree,
But how very little they know.

I laugh as life rears its ugly head.
I smile when tragedy appears.
I grin and laugh and giggle,
When I should shed buckets of
  tears.

But when the day is over
And I'm lying in my bed,
The sorrows I have carefully
  hidden
Spin 'round and 'round in my head.

The tears fall very slowly
As I quietly begin to weep,
Hoping not to disturb my
  husband
Who's so peacefully asleep.
I cry for my dear parents
Tho' I can't think of them as dead.
Wishing all those "Thanks" and "I
  Love You's"

Weren't so often left unsaid.
I weep for my grown children,
The burdens of life they must
  bear
As parents, and spouses, and
  adults.
No longer children without a
  care.

I cry for my precious
  Grandbabies,
Their hugs and kisses I adore.
The woes of life are to them
  unknown.
Wish it were so forever more.

I shed tears for my friends and
  my family,
Wishing all their crosses were
  mine.
Eventually I fall asleep knowing
I must smile as the sun starts to
  shine.

M. M. Carr
HANDS
I looked at my hands
They whispered 'old'
No, I cried
My flesh is firm
My eyes are bright
The years controlled
They whispered 'old'

I looked at a tree
Its shimmering leaves above
A robin singing
A song of love
Tell me, tree,
Between you and me
How do you
Your life renew

I looked at the sky
Its azure
Endlessness
Tell me, sky,
Your secret of
Timelessness

I looked at the sun,
The moon and a star
That winked at me boldly
from afar
Tell me, please, let your
wisdom descend
Is there a beginning
Without an end?

Dorothy Behringer
SKY RAPTURES
The lightning cracked with whip
  lashed speed,
  Among thunders rolling high;
They join into one continous
  chores,
  In the melodious noicy sky.

As lightnings crack and thunders
  rolled,
  A tumultuous storm unfurled;
And showers fell from storm
  cloud skies,
  Like a trumpet call unfurled.

The clouds will toss and turn
  about,
  And leaves are blown around;
The grasses are a beaten form,
  And ground wet tracks are
  gone
And then the stillness comes
  again,
  As earth's washed scars are
  gone;

Among the clouds the sun
  appears,
  To bless the earth in song.

Mary A. Willingham

Mary A. Willingham
Preaching the Good News
I'll trust in God with all my heart
No matter what people say,
I'll preach the word to both young
  and old
Letting Jehovah lead the way.

I want to find the sheep—like
  ones
To share with them God's word,
I just can't keep this "good news"
  in,
The TRUTH must now be heard.

Joy I find when I help someone
To learn about God above,
His grand purpose I tell them of
And to prove it, the Bible I'll use.

The beggar and drunkard I dare
  not pass
Without sharing some good news,
I let them know that someone cares
And to prove it, the Bible I'll use.

In this old world it's hard to live
Without experiencing death and
  pain,
But I know that I must continue
  preaching
And to others, make known
  God's name.

This good news must be preached
Before the end will come,
I'll take Jehovah by the hand
And go find the sheep—like ones.

Connie M. Costello
WONDERS
As I sat upon the golden sand
And gazed into the sea,
The sun behind my shoulders
Cast a shadow over me.
To think of all the beauty
This world bestows on us.
The trees, the stars, the heavens,
To think they were just dust.

Marciana A. Sevandal
FAITH IN GOD
[This poem was written to
  show the value of humility in
  one's relationship to God as
  well as to help people realize
  how difficult life would be
  without the influence of God.]
Away from you, O Lord, I know I
  am nothing,
But a handful of dust in Your vast

creation,
Or a drop of water in the vast
    open sea;
The wind will scatter me as
    dust—in the valley,
As a drop I'll be lost—in the
    fast—flowing sea.

Away from you, O Lord, living
    will be all hell,
Both in this earthly life, and in
    the here—after;
Problems will come crushing on
    me multi—piled,
And there'll be no good place for
    me to safely hide,
Except in beer bottles or in
    wine—at a price.

But I really can't hide 'cause I'm
    touchy inside,
And when a gracious soul who
    can't leave me alone,
Tries to lend a hand or make me
    understand,
I take to brutal force, take the
    law in my hands,
Seal my death warrant, or in jail I
    will land.

But by your side, O Lord, I value
    what I am,
Whether a pinch of dust or drop
    in the ocean,
Scattered in the valley, lost in the
    open sea,
Because You are the Way, the
    Truth, and the Life,
I know You'll lead us to lasting
    Paradise.

Neal Collins
RUSTY CREEK
She is the trickle—the echo in
    the night.
Sometimes her summer mist
    shapes fog into life,
like the shadow of a young
    woman
dancing ripples against a water
    line.
The memories of an old man rust
    through time
where once young lovers passed
    each other
embraced in wanted fevers,
then playfully swam their
    innocence
into spirt—free believers.

Rusty Creek spills the crimson
of a Passion Flower in blossom,
under the fallen oak tree bridge
too slippery for crossing.
Long slender limbs and curly
    blonde laughter
all crushed on the rocks—
leaving tear drops to fall after.
She is the trickle—the echo of
    my life.
Sometimes her shadow dances
    ripples in my eyes.

Roma Hogue
Will I Ever See You Again
*[To Ken—who was there when
I needed someone. Thanks for
the memories. I'm still
wondering]*
You never said I love you
You never said you cared
But when we were together
I felt it everywhere

I felt it in your touch
I felt it in your kiss
Or was I only dreaming
Because I wanted this
The times we had together
were happiness and fun
I thought they'd just begun
Too soon the good times end
Will I ever see you again
I miss you much, your tender
    touch
Your warm body caressing mine
if for only one more time
Will I ever see you again
The mailbox is empty, the phone
    never rings
I'm soo lonely and blue
It's been such a long time since
    I've been with you
Will I ever see you again
If you only knew
how much I'm missing you
You'd get in touch, we had so
    much
Will I ever see you again

N. Ming S. Ureta

N. Ming S. Ureta
Slow In the Coming
shy like the hesitant voice
of memory,
a poem like a flower
like the genesis of pearl,
so slow
slow in the coming!

sometimes, however, it shatters
the winter coldness like a
    storm—whirl,
changing winds each moment of
    dusk;

the spring the morning after
like a crystal drop among
sudden showers;

the summer stillness
like a tranquil melody
amidst soundless lyrical
    outpouring;

the autumn, restless like a leaf
in midwind . . .
falling
    falling
        fall
         i
          n
           g

soft and sentimental
a poem like the birth of a new
    dawn,
gathering colors that speak
many meanings

meanings many colors
become an echo unheard
like cooing doves
among thundering tigers!

so slow
slow in the coming!

James P. Polley
PORTRAIT
The beast that hides within this
    shell,
lies chained before the gates of
    hell.

Waiting quiet, ever still,
    waiting for the lapse of will.

The will of chains that bind you
    tight,
and keep you from my sleep
    this night.

And in the morning, take up
    again,
the fight I never truly win.

Jami Noble
PROFESSOR HOUSE
[Dedicated to sister Mary Ann]
At the end of a nowhere street,
Your empty halls echo with
my grief.
My life, my losses, my cries;
You don't shun my questions,
My whos, whats, nor whys—
You're an abandoned house
Just like I.
Owners and investors, these are
Our dreams,
But when someone unknown
    enters,
Our security alarm screams.
Into darkness our seekers are
    cast,
How long can our walls hold fast?

Sheila Marie Grace
WISH TO MARK
We all need time
    to wander and explore.
Those who don't
    have lost.
Their minds become
    stagnant,
Their eyes
    close.
While those
    who reach out and grasp
Obtain most precious gifts:
    growth, strength,
    intelligence. . .
It is they
    who hold the keys to the
    universe
Upon the palm
    of their very hand.

Debby Lion
THE CHILD
Not long after the midnight hour,
    after the thunder,
    and after the shower,
She stared at shadows:
The long, bony tenticles, reaching
    to asphyxiate; it was only a
    plant,
She began to gasp and pant,
A wonder to think what, in the
    deep, dark night, her mind
    could create.

In that state (being half asleep),
    a wheezing sound she made,
And soon before the clock

struck "one",
    she commenced to silently
    weep,
A petrified creature in a forest of
    shadows;
    she was afraid,
And wondered what would
    become of her
    if all the shadows stayed (and
    she prayed).

Then, slowly, the shadows carried
    her away,
And she knew the shadows
    would not stay,
Tomorrow, when they had
    disappeared,
    the sun would bring the light
    of day;
        bright and undefiled,
No more shadows viewed at
    night
    through the eyes of a child.

Ms. Ardith Beitel
WHISPERS
Through my passing life
    the passion of a person
        has graced me with love.
Often in my solitude
    the whispered name carried
        peace to my heart.
It is spoken softly
    close to my soul
        so no one hears.
The growing reflection
    within my face holds
        mystery in my eyes,
            intrigue in others.
Someday my whisper will be
    heard
    and as the relationship is told
        my life will unfold,
Like a rose . . .
    petal,
        by petal.

Tommy Wright
FORGIVENESS
*[Dedicated to God, the giver of
all life and talent, and to my
wife Ernestine.]*
I begged
For forgiveness
And God in turn
Added years of peace and joy
To a life that before
Had no purpose.

Sue Wilson
UNTITLED
Somewhere over the rainbow
There is an everlasting love.
It's a warm, life—giving love.

Somewhere in the rainbow
There is an age—old promise,
Stating His loving guarantee.

Somewhere under the rainbow
There is a lonely person,
Who can only see the rain.

Michelle Hite
**A Conversation Between
GOD and a Struggling
Follower**
Lord, the universe is such a big
    place, that even the earth is
    just a dot in space!

"I have created you as a special
    person."

Well, Lord I'm so insignificant in

all this vastness I see. How can
you have time for just plain
me?

"You are my special child."

But Lord, when I think of the
whole world hardly anybody
knows me. You know each one
of us, how can this be?

"I have known you since before
you were born."

Lord, I have so many problems,
too many to name;
and my friends have just the
same. How can you deal with
all of them?

"Remember with *God* all things
are possible."

Lord, I know I must hurt you,
because I often fall short of
your laws. Quite often too, I
don't listen when your voice
calls.

"No one is perfect, and besides
you're precious to me."

Lord, when I'm gone nobody will
even know I was here. How can
you hold me so dear?

"I have a special place prepared
for you in my Kingdom."

Lord, I still can't see where you
get all your energy from. How
and why do you get everything
done?

"Because I love you.!"

Elayne Irving
To a Friend—On Retiring
As you close your set of
textbooks
And put your notes aside,
As you look back on your life's
work
With a sense of honor and pride;
May the chapters of your future
Include all the things you desire,
May your cluster of lasting
friendships
Be composed of those you admire;
For you have given your utmost
And deserve a place in the sun,
Where you can sit back, relax,
and remember
The good work you have done.

Lawrence Penquite
THE FOLKS
Withered dreams like parchment
fade in somber light of years
gone bad.

Fields untended, flocks a
memory, shattered fences, all
has fallen.

Where the laughter? Where the
passion? Lost in bloodless holes
of reason. No more instinct,
only safety, no reward the price
of no risk.

Cold and gray, pensive moments
fuse together to reality, leaving
nothing, bittersweet, too
exhausting.

What is the answer?

What was the question?

Mary Halvorson
I'M LATE
Aged clock, long faded
By the price of circling time,
Stopped by indifferent forgetful
hands
Suns and moons ago.

Firmly fixed upon the wall
The box of wood and wire, man
works
Vainly to keep each second
marked
By nailing time within.

But time has fled
Through chinks and cracks and
space
Split by arthritic wood
made to live too long.

Webbed, a pendulum can stop
Its perpetual clocking.
But even rusted mute this
stop—watch
Can't pause time's walking.

Time wins as time is lost
In victorious daily revolutions;
Keeping counting eyes wrist—
bound and blind
To the little wisdom in being
clockwise.

Billie Joe Namken
A Tribute To My Brother
As you lived and traveled about
I know you saw many things
You hitched rides with anyone
And even rode on trains.
You had a drawing talent
And sang Country Songs to boot
When you went to Viet Nam
The Army taught you to shoot,
Back again in the USA
You seemed to go down hill
You drank a lot of booze
And began poping pills.
You couldn't hold a job
And would call me in the night
When they locked you up
For drinking and having a fight.
Sometimes, though, you'd call me
And tell me you were blue
No matter what time it was
Whether Eleven, Twelve, or Two.
Your life came to an end
And your family cried a lot
You tried to catch a train
And we buried you in an Army
plot.

Dorothy Kapity
Father's Day Appreciation
*[To my nephew Robert C.
Harvey, a devoted, loving,
father.]*
On Father's Day we can always
recall,
All the pleasant memories
great and small.
Through the years of our lives,
While growing up with good
deeds done for us.
My dear dad who made a fuss,
Creating something we liked
with his two strong hands,
Deserved rejoicing and
appreciation,
From his children of another
generation.
Who could never repay with
gratitude,

What dads deserve all over this
world,
From longitude to latitude.

Guy Glover
Little Bobbie Ann Noname
*[To Bobbie Ann—Now you
have a name it will surely bring
you fame]*
Little Bobbie Ann Noname
What a shame
She's lived from pillar to post
Happiness to her
Is just a vanishing ghost
All her life she has longed
Just to know
Where she belonged
Her mama doesn't know
For there has been too many
They just come and go
No one could really know
What a shame
About Little Bobbie Ann Noname

Who is to blame
For Little Bobbie Ann Noname
No one will say
So she just lives from day to day
A victim of modern time
She looks for a familiar face
In any man that may seem kind
Of him she hopes she will remind
But she's a hopeless case
Oh what a shame
She's Little Bobbie Ann Noname

Phyllis L. Wernsing
HALLOWEEN BREW
Ghosties, ghoulies,
goblins and such.
Withches, bats,
pumpkins and cats.

Stir these together
as if in a brew.
Now add a toad
and a skeleton or two.

Spices are nice
So add some twice.
Stir it gently
and treat it nice.

Throw in a thrill.
Throw in a chill.
Add a fairy princess
according to will.

Make it thick.
Make it right.
Watch the color
to see if it's bright.

Check the brew.
Could it be green?
Now add a howl
and add a scream.

Is it ready?
Has it turned green?
Serve it carefully
for it's HALLOWEEN.

Margaret L. Fellinger
Lost In the Storm Of Love
I'm lost, lost in the storm of love
My heart feels like a ship at sea
In a swirling storm crushed by
waves
A feeling I thought never could
be.

The longing for you is an
undertow,
My mind tells me I must be
aware.
I have no right, but I need your
love
I'm getting to a point I don't care.

Like thunder, wind, rain and
lightening
Seeing you, I want your love to be
mine.
To know you care, share, want to
be there
Through the storm of love my
way I'll find!

Bridgitte Epple
DEPARTURE
How sweet
Of you
To see
Me off;
How sweet
Of you
To be
That way
With me:
And hand
Me a
White Flow'r
—A Lily—
Wrapped in
A t'ny
T'parent
Coff'n

Carol Tingey—Michaelis
GRANDDAUGHTER
She's a little girl, just turned three
But Oh, the things she does for
me
She reaches up and takes my
hand
And I go off to childhood land
We see the monkeys at the zoo
Drink chocolate milk, and feed
animals, too
We watch the stars shine in the
night
And wonder why they're all so
bright
We eat a cracker in the shade
And talk about the games we've
played
She's a little girl, just turned three
But Oh, the things she does for
me
We find a picture book to read
A book and each other is all we
need
We laugh and talk about the
things we see
What they mean to her and they
mean to me
We find a doll to rock to sleep
And it makes me just want to
keep

Her, a little girl, just turned three
Because, she is so delightful to
me.

Ruth J. Rowland
NEBRASKA SUMMER
Standing here in our little house,
looking out across the
prairie.
I love to watch the ripening grain,
waving in all it's glory.
A beautiful stand of golden rod,
ringed around like a border.
It truly looks like mother nature,
has everything in order.

Margaret Treadway

Margaret Treadway
Seconds, Soul, Sensitivity
*[In admiration of the beautiful
people with thier seeing eye
friends.]*
Slowly, I descend the stairs. No
sound of music can compare to
childrens laughter everywhere.
The warmth of sunshine through
the window pane, the fresh,
clean smell of morning rain.
This is the joy and ecstasy, of all
the things life gives to me.

Furry, friend at my feet, he guides
me safely along the street.
As we go along the way, familiar
greetings of the day.
Count the steps that I must
climb, try not to stumble in
this world of mine.
This is the joy and ecstasy, of all
the things life gives to me.

Day is done, work put to rest,
GOD gave me strength to do
my best.
Now, we must hurry home, her
gentle love, my very own.
This is the joy and ecstasy, of all
the things life gives to me.
Evening breeze, sweet caress, my
favorite hour I must confess.
Listen! Now, the night will call,
day at end bids calm to all.
VISION, tho I cannot see, this is
my silent prayer to THEE.
To know the joy and ecstasy of
all the things life gives to me.

Pamela L.M. Noble
LET GO
The melodies of loneliness echo
through my mind.
Are they really there or am I
insane?

Someone must help me and make

me understand.
The qualities I have are deceptive.

Only friends can perceive.
Strangers see the exterior, ultra
fine.
But . . . deep inside all is
misleading.

Only when the day is done,
And I am at home with the ones I
love

Do I let go.

Teresa Lovelace Rice
THE APARTMENT HOUSE
An apartment house stands
empty, on the corner of Oak
and Vine,
It's walls have finally given up
against the test of time.
The house was once so pretty,
painted beige and brown,
But now, it has served it's
purpose . . . and soon will be
torn down.
She lived there once when she
was small,
And today she stood in the
empty hall,
Wanting to say good-bye, once
more,
To the papered walls and the oak
wood floor.
Memories flooded her mind, it
seemed,
From a thousand hopes and a
thousand dreams.
For she knew the house, down
through the years,
Had known the laughter and the
tears,
Of hundreds of people . . . happy
and sad,
So many people . . . good and bad,
Had called it home at the end of
the day,
And, for various reasons, moved
away.
People it had sheltered from the
snow and rain,
So many people's happiness, so
many people's pain,
She thought of the babies born
there and the children, large
and small,
Who had laughed and played and
learned to walk, within that
very hall.
She stood there quietly as a
mouse,
And felt the sadness of the house,
When she couldn't take it
anymore,
She ran down the hall and out
the door,
"They're going to tear you down,"
she said, "And all I can do is
cry."
As she turned, once more, with
tear-filled eyes, to say her last
good-bye.

Paula Petersen
PHOBIA
The last light of day fades over
the hill,
as I watch it go from my window
sill.
In with the darkness comes my
old foe,
when he first came I no longer

know.
I close the drapes and turn on the
light.
This empty old house, I hate it at
night!
I can stay calm if I just use my
head.
I know I won't sleep, but I'll still
go to bed.
I lay on my bed and think of the
dead,
for soon I will join them, or so its
been said.
I feel my heart beating from my
head to my toes.
I know that tonight the life from
me goes.

My body stiffens, my limbs start
jerking.
Is there no relief from the
tensions there lurking?
I'm having trouble breathing, my
mind keeps day dreaming,
flashing a picture of long ago that
no longer has meaning.

I turn on the radio to hear
something soothing.
Help! Someone please! My mind I
am losing!
I return to the window in total
dismay
to discover with joy, thank you
God, a new day.

The last dark of night fades over
the hill,
as I watch it go from my window
sill.
In comes the light out goes my
old foe,
when he first came I no longer
know.

Mabel Fair
MY WISH
*[This poem I wish to dedicate
to my beloved husband, who
left me for a better place. We
had years of happiness and I
wrote this poem for him.]*
A place in the Sun by a rippling
stream,
With a fishpole where I can sit
and dream
And watch God's children romp
and play
And listen to the Birds sing all
the day.

A rustic cabin with a beaten
pathway,
Where my friends might come
most any day
And laugh and visit and fish with
me
And listen to the Crickets sing
off key.

I would have a porch and rocker
too,
Where I could sit and rock and
watch the view
Way down thru the woods
toward the setting sun

I could ask for no more till my
life is done.

Cheryl Keene Conner
IF I AM TO BE TAKEN
If I am to be taken
For a ride,

Find me a merry-go-round.
If I am to be taken
For my worth.
Value my price.
If I am to be taken
For naught,
Cloud my perception.
If I am to be taken
For a song,
Perfect your pitch.
If I am to be taken
For a moments pleasure,
Find me a moment behind your
smile.
If I am to be taken
For granted,
Grant me a day in your life.
If I am to be taken . . .

Joanne Lenore Napoli
To A Very Gentle Friend
"You have so mild a way of
being . . ." R.M. Rilke

As I sit in this room
filled with people
your presence
permeates
the gentler light
pervading all space

Can it be that you are here?
I can see you
from the corners of my eyes
your gentle face
impresses the silence

In wonderment I gaze around
me—
you are not here, and yet—
the space everywhere
divulges your presence

Have you mastered some gentle
art
of being in spirit
wherever you like

or has my mind conjured you
out of the stillness of space

out of the gentle, tender
most delicate
filaments
of light?

Michael David Tubbs
TO CONQUER THE SEA
A gentle breeze, the brisk sea air,
wafting lightly through your
hair,
As waves fall softly to the sand,
forever reaching to where you
stand.

Her crisp blue waters beckon all,
tho tis for you that sirens call.
The sea in truth is cold and grey,
she wants your soul, to take,
this day.

She wants revenge by claiming
you,
for once, long ago, I stood as you.
Beneath her spell I sought escape,
for me, she sought, my soul to
take.

I thought of you before I fell,
and so, my soul I did not sell.
Be strong my love and turn your
face,
for warm and loving is my
embrace.

As does the sea I call for you,
to share with me a love so true.

We'll stand together on this
shore,
our souls together forevermore.
We'll watch the gulls soar high
above,
the mighty sea, conquered by
love.

Phyllis Joan Smith
ONLY YOU
*[To Buzz, with my love
Only you . . .
Until, the day after forever . . .]*
If I were to walk this earth alone
Live, without your voice as
a song
The days and nights would be
long
Endless days and nights
As if they had no
beginning, nor end
Only you, my lover, my friend,
my lonely heart could mend
Only you . . .
Would lovingly wait at Heaven's
gate
Until, you could enter with your
mate
Endless days and nights,
no sunlight, nor moonlight
Until, once again, we pledge our
plight
I'll love you
Only you . . .

Michael DeAngelo
MY ANGELETTE
Pretty green eyes
A warming smile
A cute nose
And a soft face

Delicate to hold
With soft smooth skin
A lovely thin shape
She has it all

She's in my heart
Her looks entrance me
She makes me smile
She's my little angel

Sent to me in my need
I welcome the emotion she
brings
Believing in love again
I want to return the same

Clara Creasy
LOST CHILDREN
As time goes on and day comes
to an end—
Lonely nights have to start before
they can end,
Dreams that accompany us are
full of remorse—
As we wonder what happened to
our little ones,
ARE THEY LOST?
No time to phone no time to
write,
It seems they have all but
vanished from sight—
I remember when they were
small,
Flying their kites and playing
ball—
Then they loved us with all their
might,
But now we are older and they
are grown—
All have families now of their
own,
We are just a bother and we

get in their way—
They don't want to be bothered
by old folks they say.
We thought we had raised them
to show love and respect,
But it seems most would know
better the word neglect,
Sometimes now as we set all
alone—
I have to wonder where did I go
wrong?
I loved them to deeply and I gave
to much,
I've watched love turned to hate—
And then, turn away from even
my touch.
Since they all have children now
of their own—
And the time will come when
they are grown,
Then we shall see who shall reap
whats been sown—
On yes, there's still a few who
shows their love—and—
I'll always be grateful to GOD
above,
But what happened to our little
ones?
Where have they gone?
What happened to love?
Isn't it worth the cost?
Oh! Dear GOD, are our young
ones lost?

Florence E. Brytcuk
THE SEASONS
I watch the leaves fall one by one,
I watch the early setting sun.
I know the dying summer ends.
Snow and ice just around the
bend.
Winter with all it's fury,
Making all nature, a fairy land
story.
Redding cheeks as the winter
winds blow.
The cycle begins all over again,
The seasons start and the seasons
end.

Carolina Lauriano
IN THE DARK
In the dark my soul drifts away
from me
To find the pain that fills my
heart,
To find the pain that grows
within me,
. . . A heart that beat once—
A love that filled my heart,
And a friend that was so
kind and caring.
In the dark I find a heart that
beats no more,
I find a love that is empty,
I find a friend that is so cold
and unfeeling.
And in the dark I find the space
that hurts me most
—living a life that drifts away
from me
. . . I Search No More.
In the dark tears fill up inside of
me
And I feel it all again.
. . . Alone and afraid, I dream
throughout the night
To awake in the dark once
more,
Now searching for the shining
light

—that gleam of life that brings
me from this darkness.
. . . So great are the memories,
So sad is reality . . .
. . . A friend no longer, lost
in a struggle
—drifted away with the light,
—with a blemished heart.

And now I find in the dark
A soul that feels the loss,
A soul that found the pain
That follows this fading
friendship.

Frank C. Hamilton

Frank C. Hamilton
WHAT BETTER WAY?
*[While waiting in the heaven
line (at 88) I found a gala-sprite
divine As chrysalis of infinite
time.]*

Still blooming in the knell of fall,
and smiling gayly as I passed
a marigold that was the last
of summer's glow gave me a nod
from just a languid little prod
of wispy wind to bow its head,
and thus by indication said—
"I'm sure you think your course is
run,
but there's another life to come".

So, then my noble little friend,
your confidence and gala grace
has put a smile upon *my* face,
and made the last my finest hour
with blessed faith in angel
power".
The marigold in answer said—
"There's nothing in the end to
dread,
you merely pass from here to
there
where all is fair, and none is care".

Tho time is time, t'will never
end,
I stayed a moment, then I passed,
and left my merry friend to cast
another smile at someone else;
or just to smile into itself.
How rich a legacy I thought
that golden flower to me has
brought
so gayly going home alone.
What better way, could I atone?

Tammy Dee Young
SHADES OF GRAY
Each hour soon becomes a day,
But still I do not weep.
Why weep when the shades of
gray

Will still haunt me in my sleep?

Each day soon becomes a year,
But I do not run away.
Why try to brush away each tear
When all I see are shades of gray?

Shades of gray that haunt me,
Torment me all the time
With visions only I can see
Of a dark and hateful crime.

Shades of gray that make me
relive
A long forgotten day,
When all that I had to give
Was brutally taken away.

I wish I could forget that day—
Oh, so long ago—
That has made these shades of
gray
Come and haunt me so.

How can a man do the likes of
that
To such a young and innocent
girl?
I hate the man for doing that
And bringing shades of gray into
my world.

I fear I have become insane
From the memories of that day,
And I'll never forget the pain;
For I'm haunted by shades of gray.

Heather Ann Harrison
THE ANNIVERSARY
All through the week
I searched for that special feeling.
Looked for it in old letters,
Dug for it in old announcements;
Sadly staring through old faces in
photos.
By Friday
I was totally drained—
Tired of looking for what we'd
lost.

Then finally, comes the
"anniversary"
That we celebrate each year
With cheap elegantly named
wines
And last minute gifts.
A day that has lost its meaning—
We don't see stars or hear golden
bells.
Like puppets,
We dance and perform
As life pulls our strings,
Directing our lives in new
directions.

Kathryn Swann Harrelson
DELICIOUS DOG
Such a delicious dog.
Tangy yellow mustard biting at
my tongue that
Laps out to the red ketchup on
my lips that
Eat your cushion soft bed, and
part with a smile.
Such a delicious dog—indeed.

Dannell Perry
THOUGHTS
My mind is so crowded
With thoughts of you,
They burst into different
fantasies
That it almost seems your here.
I wish you were here,
With me
To share my bed,

And keep me warm, when the
soft breezes blow early at the
dawn of a new breaking day.
But since you're not
My fantasies are enough,
At least this way I can imagine
you the way I wish you were,
In love with only me.

Cheryl Hendrick Ryland
OPTIONS
First he gave me freedom
As he watched and cried
To be lost in myself
'Til I died.
Then when
Enough was enough
And my self dragged thru
Such a meticulously
constructed and
Carefully maintained hell
To you
He gave me
The capacity to be
Lost in you
While he watched
With his cosmic smile
And invited me
To try heaven for a while.
And so for the rest of my life
Now that I see the options
I much prefer to be
Lost in heaven with you
Than lost in hell with me.

Lori Anne Wicks
MAY 14, 1982
. . . and all day i searched,
spending the entire 24 hours
looking
in hopes that i might find
something—
a phrase, a sentence, or
paragraph
that would let you know
that for the moments you
looked
in my direction,
i was elated.

. . . trying to find the perfect
words
to tell you—

that even if tomorrow
you pased me in the streets
without turning your face to
mine,
a part of me,
your part
will always be . . .
forever hugging the clouds.

Archie Midgette, Jr.
BATTLEFIELDS
There are many battlefields
We have to face and fight upon,
Each day and in some way
No matter how we think or feel.
In every section of our earthly
life
Battles are lost, and won,
Regardless, of what we do or say.
Because—the world is a
war . . . zone
Which rages in the troubled
hearts,
Of each man—woman, and child.
No nation stands alone
In a vain effort to attain peace
As world problems seems to
increase,
We learn the hard way

That eternal peace—is not man
made.
For only God can help us gain it,
Through the blood of his son
Jesus.

Phyllis Young
CHRISTMAS SNOW
Snowflakes—gently falling
In the shadows of the night,
Come-to-rest on lonely steeples
Before their final flight;
Then—off like skiers skiing—
They quickly fill the air,
And glide toward sloping
hillsides
To cover all that's bare.

A sleepy little village
Whose slopes reflect the
light,
Of these tiny jewel-like crystals
On a silent Christmas night;
Is roused by all the brightness
Of the lovely Christmas
snow,
To praise the Babe from
Heaven—
God sent so long ago.

Edward T. Douglas
an untried love
Surface Touches
Passion Clutches
Tongue Tied
Soft Kisses As Such
an untried love

Earnest Wishes
Breast To Breast
And Yet At Best
an untried love

No Mere Jest
None Such Game
Calm Before The Storm
As You Were Born
an untried love

Lowell C. White
ROSES OF LOVE
I walk by your window
almost every night
And see you standing there
Your in the arms of another guy
How I wish that guy was me.

I picked you some roses
and sent them to you
I saw you put them to your
nose
You felt the wetness of the dew
You read the note in them too.

The note read
These are roses of love

from the guy
that walks by your window.

Susan Sauerwald
SPRINGTIME
[To three special ladies who I
love and admire: Polly
Burkhard (my mother), Anne
Kraus (a dear friend), and Anne
Sauerwald (my mother-in-law).]
Looking upward at the sky
Leaves, like fans, forever
reaching . . .
Spring-green fingers nearly
touching,
Newborn blossoms, straining
upward.

Springtime sky—dusk is falling,
Showery breezes stir the leaflets,
The dancing treetops shake the
skyline,
Nature's birth is in its glory.

Autumn leaves will soon be
falling,
I used to love it—now I don't,
God's bright promise for future
growing
On summer breezes, far remote.

Birth and dying—it's tradition,
I feel and love a thousand times,
Could one experience all
creation?
Only God could end these lines.

As I approach my autumn life,
The bright leaf's plight is less
appealing,
It signifies death and grieves my
soul.
Yet every spring the flowers
awaken,
And in my heart I feel, I know!

Dolores J. Hess
WORDS TO THE YOUNG
When I was young,
My thoughts leaned toward
My growing up and on my own.

I pushed and strove
To grow up fast
And thought that I would
become known.

Alas! I grew.
Then realized
That thoughts are dreams which
are high-flown.

I am adult.
Where am I now?
I sigh: my dreams have been
dethroned.

And now I think—
If only then
I had made life and dreams atone.

I'd take my time.
I wouldn't hurry.
I'd live each day as if on loan.

And slowly then,
I would grow up.
No minute of my life disowned.

Genevieve R. Erwin
MOUNTAIN LOVE
The moon was shining brightly
up above
And the summer air was warm
and light;
Two people were, oh, so much in
love,

And this was such a wonderful
night.
They both knew that it would
last,
Together they would see
everything through;
Their love was as strong as in
ages past
And every day they'd begin life
anew.

Kristine K. Winget
HOPE AND DESPAIR
Softly reminiscent of the birth of
spring
. . . the dawning of beauty
becomes alluring.

Gently the features flow with
grace
. . . as I behold the absolute in
taste.

What may be the ultimate in
design
. . . might very well be all but
mine.

And then the darkness silently
appears
. . . as if to rekindle dormant
fears.

What was once an eternal
message to be
. . . has now withdrawn into a
bottomless sea.

Shirley L. Fahrny
A WEE BOY'S PRAYER
[This poem is dedicated to my
little nephew, Scotty . . . who
was the inspiration for it!]
As I get ready to go to sleep
—A little boy with dreams to
keep . . .
I kneel me down to say my
prayers
—And talk to God—'cause I
know he cares . . .
I ask him please to make me good
—And help me do the things I
should . . .
To bless my Mom and Daddy, too
—And make my bike as good as
new . . .
Then bless my Grandma and my
Pap
—And tomorrow I promise I'll
take my nap . . .
Oh, don't forget to bless my dog
—He didn't mean to chase that
frog . . .
Bless all my uncles and my aunts
—And don't let Mom know I tore
my pants . . .
Bless my cousins whom I really
love
—And, now . . . thanks . . . for all
that help from above . . .
. . . Amen!

Jon K. Silver
PISCES
I'm a lonely little fish
swimming day to day
in a fishbowl of insecurity.

Here in such a fragile world,
dreams are illusion,
depression is great;
Life's waters take an uncertain
course.

Lo and behold,

one of the opposite sex,
with creative tapestries,
similar to mine;
Compatibility between us is
strong.

We're two little fishes
swimming day to day
in a fishbowl of insecurity,
only the love we share
makes the present reality
bearable to live with.

Rachelle S. Grenader
Gesticulation—Food For Thought

Sleep is food.
It is food for thought
for gestiuclaiton;
the grinding of all those morning
happenstances
into juicy fine moments of blown
pictures
to a grenormous colorscheme of
kaleidoscoping
to any moodformed changing
monumental horizons
in mental capturing;
Ahh—the peace of it.
The rhyme and rhythm;
The windy mind "figure-skating
out movements"
and hands held out to reach yet
another point.
And of course acceptance.
The figure of the ultimate goal.
Pleasantness seekers, dream on—
watching teetering tongues.

Florence E. Brytcuk
TEARS IN HIS EYES

Our boys who make it back,
Posing with their brides.
Even in happiness they lack,
The laughter in their eyes.
A sadness for their buddies gone.
Never to share this joyous day.
Fighting and dying all alone,
On the battle field they lay.
The faces are still the same,
But the eyes, the sadness reveal.
The inner hurt and the shame,
Time and love will finally heal.
Some how they feel to blame.
For their buddies mournful cries.
In sadness, he stands by his bride,
With tears whelming up in his
eyes.

Tom Meyer
WATCHING THE NIGHT

Across the frozen stream
some eyes stood still
watching the night come
and thinking of crossing.

On the other side eyes
watched waiting afraid of
the early night growing.

Across that could wait
eyes ceased hesitation
and faded into falling shadows.

Eyes relaxed and
wandered off to
sleep into the
coldest night of the year.

Steven Gust Kritsonis
A DARK BLUE

A feeling reveals
In a most distinctive way.
A whispering moves

My yearning soul to say:
"The world is but a grain of sand
On a large ocean beach.
But it thunders with the roar
Of a horrible beast!"

What is the feeling
When a soldier remembers
The horror and bloodshed
Which war delivers,
When love suffers destruction
Upon the battlefield of hate,
When dreams are forgotten
Amidst the agony of fate?

What is the reason
For a man to kill his fellowman?
When will be the season
When peace shall heal a stricken
land?
A phantom hovers menacingly
Over a field of rotten corpses.
While the weary world whirls
maddeningly
Within a tempest of swirling,
flaming torches.

A dark blue permeates the earth.
A dark blue pierces my soul.

Frederick P. Dufer
THE OLD MAN
*[To Uncle Hobe, who refused
to grow old. We all love and
miss you.]*

Crooked tho' my back may be,
Stumbling with every step.
Tho' my eyes play tricks on me,
And my mind is not as quick.
Tho' my bones creak more,
With each and every wind,
My body stays sore,
With no promise of mend.
Tho' my life is gone,
But the last few years.
Tho' my giving is gone,
But the last few tears.

Still, I'll stand for what I am,
I am alive, I am a man.

Linda Comer Workman
IF
*[For my husband Larry and my
best friend Jake. Thanks for a
dream come true.]*

If I could have one thing in life,
all I would want is you.
If I could have one real happiness
again, I would wish for you.
If I could ask for a true
companion again it would be
you.
If I could love only one person
there is no doubt it's you.
If I could choose one mate in life,
my love, I would always choose
you.
If I could ask for all these things
and have my dreams come true.
My life's decision would be the
same, for I will always love
you.

Deborah M. Grogan
THE SIMPLEST SELF

I fill myself with whispers and
wishes
And the enchanting laughter of
children.
I strive to be the simplest of my
selves
And I dream of being a
dancer . . .

I want to move in a stream of
silken smoothness.
I want to be fluid, as free-flowing
as a waterfall . . .

I want to be a birch dancing in
the wind.
I want to be a leaf dancing in the
current of a stream.
I want to be a star dancing in the
darkness of the night.
I want to be a tongue dancing in
the dampness of love.
I want to be a dream dancing in
the dawn of hope . . .

I want to be a dancer—
Forever expressing the simplest of
my selves.

Sarah Harris Levy

Sarah Harris Levy
K.G.B.
*[K.G.B. is dedicated to Sherrie
Seliber who wrote she
especially liked the second
paragraph—the last two lines,
when the "dove cometh to the
righteous, each life is
precious."]*

Kingdom of God Book,
Retroactive and Omnipresent.
Hey, it's a good Book,
Take a look—

You know countries without
pompus,
Leaders without ugliness,
The Dove cometh to the
righteous,
Each Life to thee is precious.

You know debate without rage,
People without rampage,
You know belief without
penetration,
Children without border
concentration.

No neutralism, no pacifism,
anywhere,
Will ever transcend
stick-togetherism.
Except for thyself there is no
honesty,
And, pray, ye be not too greedy.

Hold fast to Kingdom Stock,
Now defined to you as 'Solid Rock'
Kingdom of God Book,
Retroactive and Omnipresent.

Rhoda Desenberger
AUTUMN

Autumn is the color artist of the
year.

(She's queen of Sleuth for no one,
as yet,—
Can predict where she'll strike
next)
She calls a conference of the
winds.
They receive her orders, and
away.
And, moment by moment, and
day by day
She gathers ever forces.
THEN—it may be just a vine,
carrying varied as it climbs
Or a tree on a distant hill, such a
splash of color
Your heart stands still!
Or, you may think she is
planning a Joseph's Coat
Of many colors—
Or, a Moses burning bush across
the way.
Or a stand of evergreens
romancing that red maple—
AND—look at the coin-tree
trembling in the wind
Like a miser reluctant to drop his
gold!
Then, —Comes a great wind
sweeping all in wild disorder
To bring in a day, when
Everything is on display—
And your soul is on it's knees!
The Great Earth-Mother has put
her Harvest-children to sleep.
Until the Clock of the Seasons
sounds her special chime
To again reach for Her Ring in
the Relay Race of Time—
And, we are left with Her
Legacy—
A Glory Wreath of Memory-
Externally Subline!

Doris Ullman Barbuto
ON RETIREMENT

I wake at five each morning
With work problems in my
head.
What shall I do? The choice is
mine,
So I go back to bed!

For forty years I've labored,
So my family could be fed;
And now at last I have the time—
I've earned this rest in bed!

I plan to be reprogrammed
For activities ahead—
Aside from pulling down the
shades
And going back to bed!

Some choose vacation travels
Or organized fun instead;
For me, the gratest luxury
Is going back to bed!

Ruth Morgan
THE BESTEST MAN

O the Bestest Man, He works for
us all,
He's the goodest man you could
ever call!
He comes to your heart every
day,
Opens the door and we all are
thankful.
When he drives out our little old
troubles,
If our hearts say he can,
He gives us a chance to try again.

Why, the Bestest Man he's so good,
He splits the Heavens and looks
us over good,
And then he tells us if we've been
good sometimes,
And he knows about our griefs
and sorrows and ourselves,
The Bestest Man knows if you
are going to keep a fine life,
Or be a happy person, or wear a
big smile,
Or just whatever you're going to
be, goodness knows!
And then he quietly, with your
help, guides the way.
Ain't he the Bestest Man you
ever did see?

Kathleen M. Green
ME

I passed by a mirror,
a face caught my eye,
Now that's the real me,
Not what I'm supposed to be.
And I finally realized,
who I was,
I'm not that bad,
only fanticized I was.
and I realized I wasn't
an illusion of what someone
thought I should be,
but exactly what I am,
me!

Liliana & Anthony Ventimiglia
RITA MARY

God gave us a child
Amidst His Rain
To calm our fears
And wipe our tears.

We prayed quite long
For this gift to come
Now we can rejoice
With a daughter and a son

This be our blessing:
"God by our side,
With Rita and Paul
Peace will abide"

Carol Farber Phielbus
ETERNAL LOVE

Across the waves I see a Light

Reminiscent of my last Flight

The Sounds I hear the Sights I see
Bring back glimpses of the silver
sea

Spirit majestic, strong and fine
Reminds me of the ancient time

The Visions unclear, and yet I
hear

The sounds of Love under a pier.

Two shadows golden rays
Seen through an iridescent tear

Aphrodite by the Sea
And, Adonis my Love, coming for
me

I recall the mist has been cast
We love in the present as we did
in the past.

Doris Courtney Lowdermilk
IF I WAS A BUTTERFLY

Oh! my if I were a butterfly
On my trips I'd flutter by
Maybe I'd be gold with just a
speck of brown
How wonderful to travel all
around

I'd light upon each pretty flower
Just to sit there by the hour
Sipping of that precious honey
You know what, it wouldn't even
cost any money

Then when the rain came
splashing down
I'd hide beneath a leaf I found
No worries, care or woe
Happily through life I'd go

Living in the beautiful woods
Free of toil and worldly goods
When the end came as ends
always do
I'm sure I wouldn't mind a bit—
would you?

Stephen M. Cabrinety

Stephen M. Cabrinety
The Many Forms Of Love

Love is many things wrapped up
in one,
It can be a chat between father
and son.

Love cannot be found in any one
certain place,
For it can be found all over the
world, in every nationality,
color, and race.

Everywhere you look, you will
probably find a sign of love,
Even in little things, like the
beauty of a morning dove.

It is peace, joy, and happiness,
With a touch of very fine finesse.

Love can be the coming of Spring,
Or a stroll in the park listening
to how the birds so sweetly
sing.

Love also can be a great blanket
of joy,

To a new mother who just had a
baby boy.

It can be as gentle as the touch of
a glove,
Or it can be blessings from above.

Love can be beautiful music from
a big brass band,
Or it can be playing on the beach,
in the sparkling white sand.

But love can be affection, while a
master gently strokes his
horse's mane,
While it also can be two lovers
walking hand-in-hand down
the lane.

Or it can be in a western drought,
when the clouds reeled back,
and let it rain.

But wherever you look for love
around,
I'm sure wherever you look love
will be found!

Yvonne Maldonado-Segrove
**We Were Always Just
Friends**

Lately you've been looking so
fine to me
It scares me
Lately I've really enjoyed your
company
It confuses me
I feel you listen
I make you laugh
I just need attention right now
So I feel attracted
Please excuse me
I don't mean to
I'll continue to ignore it
Please don't let me scare you
It's probably just physical
That's only natural
If it were heavier I couldn't
handle it
So take this as a compliment
You look so good to me
Please excuse me if I stare

Joline Kieboom
CENTURY

[To Sage, my mentor, my
model, my inspiration.]
In the valley of your lips
I plant my love
to be watered
to be fed
to live and
to age
for in the valley of your lips
I wish to die.

Alexandra Conroy
GIVING

To say to a friend
"Have my cookie if you're
hungry," or
"Take my dime to use the phone,"
is easy.
A cookie and a dime are
inconsequental.
Their absence is not noticed.

To say, "My friend,
take my Porsche 924 if your car
has bit the dust
and my cabin in the Catskills for
your vacation with your wife,"
is harder.
But not much.
A cabin can be cleaned;
mechanics can fix cars.

But to say, "Have a piece of me,
my friend,
a portion of my thoughts and
feelings,"
is almost impossible.
Ridicule can hurt;
misunderstanding can destroy
the unprotected soul.

It is easier, by far, to place all
your worldly goods
in a bank vault
than to place the minutest part of
YOU in your friend's hands
But . . .
Who has ever seen a bank vault
smile?

Pamela M. Long
CHRISTMAS

C—hristmas is a special time, a
closeness rich with love
H—ow wonderful the years have
been, with many more to come
R—ich is he who gives a gift,
purely from ones heart
I— can only tell you, it's been
marvelous from the start
S—oon there will be packages to
open and enjoy
T—ell me, how lovely it is to see
the children glow
M—ay the excitement of
Christmas be, more than
presents could ever show
A— day to celebrate, the birth of
our Lord
S—uch a special time, the story
shall always be told . . .

Jane L. Waters
FAREWELL TO AN ERA

Two years have passed since we
last met each other as lovers. I
could tell you on request the
details of each meeting;

where we went,
who we saw,
what we did,

and, of the days and nights we
spent in joyous surrender to
lust in my bed.

The other day, knowing you had
an interest in purchasing a
waterbed, I offered you mine;

and you couldn't remember what
it looked like.

"Patty" Fuller
I MISS YOU

[For GAR
because I MISS YOU]
I miss you . . .
You were a friend . . .
I moved away . . .
And began again . . .

I made some friends . . .
Here and there . . .
I'll never forget you . . .
My forever friend.

A. Gail Donahue
THE MAN OF GOLD

As Gold is the most excellent of
the precious metals, so are you
among men.
As Gold can be refined to the
highest purity, so can you be
among men.
As Gold is of high value and
greatly esteemed, so are you

among men.
As Gold has many attributes and
can be molded and fashioned
into hundreds of uses,
So have you many talents and
abilities to be molded and
fashioned for use among men.
As Gold is flexible and yet strong,
So is a man of your character
among men.
As Gold can be buried deep in
the earth and difficult to find,
so is a man of your caliber
among men.

As gold is of the highest
brilliance—like the morning
sun, so are you among men.

Claudia J. Khan
HIS LETTER
Put it on the table;
Let the promises steep.

Bear the stench a moment longer,
To make the perfume all the
sweeter.

Hold it at arm's length, the better
To appreciate a sharper, clearer
focus.

And when the thread
Stretches tight, almost snapping,

That is the moment.

Janie Sanders
ROSE IN BLOOM
June's the month for rose in
bloom.
June's the month when lovers
attune.
Lovers beam when they
surrender,
And June moves on, but roses
linger.

Oh, rose in bloom, you light my
room.
Your perfume deletes my
gloom.
Knowing you will enrich my quest,
I give thanks to God with zest!

Each time your fragrance wafts
the air,
Unfolding dreams—even
skeptics stare.
Alas! Your gifts upon life's coffer
Include thorns in each precious
offer.

Yet thorns also contain their
meaning.
Oh, rose in bloom, your love is
redeeming,
For lovers' quarrels you can settle
With each blush of every petal!

Robin L. Donovan
CHRISTMAS TIME
At Christmas Time
The air is full
Of warm hearts
And happy faces,

Waiting for that quiet moment
Of unwrapping gifts tonight
At twelve,

And remembering in a joyful way
That this holiday
Was created by GOD,

To give from the heart
And not to receive
We will find a few of the best
gifts upon us,

Are: Love, Friendship, and Smiles
Gifts which do not Cost . . .

Marie A. Reynolds
SOLILOQUY ON SILENCE
True wisdom seldom speaks
Silent, even seeming dull;
Stony unconcern that peaks
When conversations lull.

Now will Wisdom state His log,
All hang on every word;
Hear the needed missing cog,
Mine now would sound absurd!

Oh! Wisdom, come to me,
Silence my endless tongue;
Let syllables I dream
Be songs that stay unsung.

Oh! Lips, don't vocalize
Till Wisdom reigns awhile;
Fills me with thoughts so wise
They must be kept on file.

For "to listen is to learn"
This rule I'll keep with time;
Although I've thoughts to burn
Silence is more sublime.

Mary Angela Morales
POOR BOY
You, the sensitive one
You show me how you feel
You remind me of how cruel we,
the world are

I've seen a crippled child
A mass of braces and deformed
and mangled limbs
You are crippled too, in spirit

I see a lowly countenance
Sad eyes and tears
That seem to stammer out a cry
for help

Let me remind you, poor boy
I can only stay with you
I can't make the world go away

We have to face living
And make our only exit through
death

Laura Irene Twing
NO EXPLANATION
Running
Again?
Somebody
Will ask.
I cannot answer.
The reasons are not clear.
Afraid of labels
For others understanding.
Silence creates tension,
Explanations
Are just words
To Ease Their Doubts.
For me
It will never
Be simply explained.

Marian S. Musmecci
MODIGLIANI'S TOUCH
A light fall from his canvas

or perhsps she stood too close,
too long
and has inhaled the length of
neck,
and stillness of the upturned palm
floating fragile like a swan upon a
shaded depth of blue skirt,
the crystal whisper of a sweeping
vision or a spent dream
from the almond contour of
unirised eyes.

the curl and part of covered
breasts,
the soft emptiness of the cradling
forearm,
the intoxicating posture of the
body's solitude.

A light fall

as she stands amid his paintings,
almost as if he had laid his hands
upon her, and then
cast her out into a grasping
rendition of his painted truth.

Thelma Anne Dean
Through My Window Pane
There they go, skipping and
hopping
and laughing
as though they own the world.
Oh yes, it is their world at this
time.
While I, in my memory, see
another
group skipping and hopping
and laughing
thinking they own the world.
And yes, they did at that time.
Beyond my window pane I see
the years roll by.
Gray hair comes, laughter
turns to tears, empty houses
decaying, families separating
some never to return.
I come back to my room where I
am a prisoner with gnarled
hands and useless legs.
But through the window pane
I live again.

Margaret Saunders O'Rourke
WHEN?
When will I find you?
How long must I wait?
Now's when I need you,
Please don't be late.

Here I sit all alone
Thinking of you,
Candlelight flickers,
Soon comes the dew.

Maybe a night of fog,
Dark as can be
Followed by clearing skies;
Come, dear, to me.

Soon I will find you,
Not long must I wait,
Now's when I need you,
You won't be late.

Jean Frances Sharp
NOW INSTEAD OF THEN
Where has she gone,
that little girl with golden curl
And eyes as blue as the summer
skies?
Where did he go,
that little boy with auburn hair,
and his big brown eyes?
They were here, only a moment
ago—
or so it seems.
They held my hand
as we walked the land
of make-believe and dreams.
How quickly the time has flown!
I closed my eyes, just for a
second,
and they were grown.
At night when I am half asleep
I feel their tiny fingers
softly brush my cheek,

And my heart aches
to hold them close again,
but the time is now,
instead of then.

D.C.

Debbie K. Peacher
D.C.
He's not too chubby & he's not
too fat,
But he sure is spoiled
I can tell you that.

He's a very pretty Cat,
Half Silvertabby, & Half Siamese,
but he's got the prettiest blue
eyes I've ever seen.

He gets along with the dog
allright,
but when it comes to others he
puts up a fight.

He's the sweetest Cat I've ever
known,
And I sure am glad D.C.'s my very
own.

Shandy Brancato
FINDING YOU THERE
Finding you,
there . . .
Like a sweet teardrop
from yesterday,
and how you watched me
made me tingle.
My search had not been in
vain for
finding you,
there . . .
reminded me
that teardrops
do not fade with
the sun . . .

Alvin G.S. Lasich
Unnaturally Natural
The cigarette box lay still, in the
sand, on the beach.
I could see it well, over there, out
of reach.
It seemed such a shame, how
long it had lain.
Ten cigarettes left, all soaked by
the rain.

It wasn't alone though; I found a
few friends.
Twist ties, half a spoon, plastic
too; none blends.
A fish head also was part of the
scenery.
But not even it fit the beach and
the greenery.

One thing I found which had to
be natural.

It may seem like a lie, but it is
  quite factual.
It lay all alone, much worse for
  the weather.
What I had found was a
  bedraggled, wet feather.

Junie Morris
ODE TO AUTUMN
My eyes have drawn into my
  mind the brilliant hues of
Autumn . . . I tire quickly of
  summer with her hot and dusty
  days . . . I wait for you
Autumn . . . in hurried
  anticipation as the hills are
  brown and dry . . . I look for
  you . . .
Then around the corner you
  come . . . quickly . . . to wisp
  your cloak of colors that you
  spread so gracefully . . .
I admire your golden yellow,
  bright orange, deep
  brown . . . but still . . . left
  are hints of green that the cold
  has not touched yet.
Soon all the branches of the trees
  will be bare . . . they will be
  like long slender
  fingers . . . reaching
  up . . . begging the sun to
  warm their bareness . . .
O'h Autumn . . . I love you
  so . . . you bring me happy
  memories of my children when
  they were babes . . . but most
  of all being at Grandma's house
  for Thanksgiving . . .
O'h Autumn . . . don't hurry
  away and leave me to face
  winter alone . . . but if you
  must go...leave me with a
  smell . . . a touch . . . a feel of
  you . . . to keep me through
  the long winter months.

J. Carolus Weaver
THE MATE OF MAN
The mate of man, a strange
  complexity
Of mystic moods that man must
  share.
He soars to heavenly heights of
  ecstasy
And plunges to dismal depths of
  despair.

Cheryl Ann Erb
JENNY
Her broken purring penetrates
  the darkened quiet of the room
Where only the sound of a pen
  grooving the paper fibers is
  heard.
The sounds of both human and
  animal breathing are now
  silent,
But there is an occasional rustle
  of paper.

The purring has silenced,
The tail is motionless,
And the ears are perked
ready for action in their role as a
  radar screen.

The eyes are closed,
The whiskers straight and alert,
and the great tail gently curved
  against the chair back:
in peace.

Her thoughts are now dreams

if cats do dream.
She's not only a cat,
but human too.
She's not completely human—
she just seems that way.
Ever heard of a cat giving up a
  cat's life?

Connie Wirsing
EARTH MAN
(to a village driver)

earth man

you come from the
raining dust

flickering
across my spirit

you and splendid rust
inside of me

terrible and sad

Evelyn A. Tompkins Miller
Christmas and Hanukkah
In the Holy Season of Christmas
And the Festival of Lights
Called Hanukkah—
What a sight to behold
If we all lit eight candles
For each Merry and Holy
  Occasion:
For faith in the future
And freedom from oppression,
Knowledge to give life rapture,
Love for our fellowmen,
Courage to live day-by-day,
Integrity for our soul,
Charity along our way
And "Peace on Earth" our goal!

Harold Aubrey Traylor
THE PAINTER
I saw the artist paint with brush,
The setting sun, the lengthening
  shade.
The near and further distant hills,
The valley where the lily shows
  its blade
And hides the nest of the noble
  thrush.

He painted the valleys with their
  streams,
The giant oak and the stately
  pine.
The quaking aspen leaves afloat
The evening breeze of
  summertime.
And he left me standing lost in
  dreams.

He mixed his colors in varied hue
As clouds suspended from the
  sky.
From swaying limbs where the
  robin sings
And the eagles nest in mountains
  high
Beneath a sky of azure blue.

It's here the artist stops and
  stands
Spellbound, he cannot overcome
  the spell.
The sun, now set, has changed
  the scene
With different colors in the dell.
He cannot match the Master's
  hand.

Emily Brueske
PERSPECTIVE
Dream by dream
Life's plans

Have slipped away
Like clouds and shadows
On a sunny day
And time
That seemed to promise
Endless skies
Has withered
Like the summer grass
That dies
But there remains
Yet one more
Dream of sod
—To touch
The edges of eternity
With God

Mary Lieselotte Johnson
A MIGRANT
It was a bright, clear
  sunny day
But why didn't my heart
  feel that way
They made me pack my bag
  and load my saddle
Taking along side—my
  possessions
  that I might win this battle
My mind was filled
  with confusion and fear
Looking at my wife and children
  that I held so dear

Will it be better for us
  the next place we go
How long will we stay there
  only God knows
We fought to work
  we fought for rights
And when we lost
  it was the darkest of all nights
When the water got low
  and the land changed
We moved to a better life
  a better stage

J.A. Myers
A CHILD
Made of love from love;
  when newborn is as tranquil as
  a dove
From first step to last,
  brought to the future from the
  past.
Full of pleasure and of joy,
  whether it be girl or boy.
Up all night with teething pain,
  'till every ounce from you is
  drained.
Lots of adventure and mystery,
  to carry on the family history.
A child to show of a love complete.
  to which nothing else can
  compete.

Rita Duncan
WINDERLUST
The wind lured me outdoors
  today
To walk the neighborhood.
  The sky was bright.
  The air was crisp.
Resist? I never could!

All morning I had listened
To hints that wind has blown.
  I donned a coat
  And tied a scarf.
I left the house alone.

The wind drew me outside today
And then pushed me along.
  It flipped my scarf,
  Fluttered my clothes,
And showed me it was strong.

An hour with the wind I walked
And crunched the leaves it
  strewed.
  Through quiet streets
  Wind and I roamed.
I came back in renewed.

Billie Rockey
NATURE'S PICTURE
I saw her snow capped
  mountains,
Her fields of purest gold,
Her cup runneth over,
All Nature has to hold.

I saw her mighty rivers,
Heard her oceans roar.
Stood in awe and wonderment,
As if never seen before.

Her splendent sun rays and
  moonglow,
Her skies of deepest blue;
The fluffy soft clouds,
And rainbows of every hue.

I saw it all through the eyes of a
  traveler,
As an artist might paint so keen;
Then stood back and surveyed
  again,
God's mightiest scene.

Verna E. Fisher
THE LOST SPUD
Oh! What a beautiful thing you
  are.
All soft and white and mealy
  nice.
Baked, and mashed with french
  fries next,
With gravey to boot.
With more food value per acre
  than any other crop.
The most humble spud should
  not be ridiculed.
By ourselves

Mary Lucci
The Blizzard of April 7, 1982
The North wind doth blow and
  we're having snow,
But why? It's April and Spring!
But only the calendar knows this
  thing.

Even the weatherman didn't
  predict
All this snow and cold and, gee!
I think it's the worst storm of the
  century!

It's April and nineteen-eighty
  two,

Today's Greatest Poems

The sky should be sunny and
  most of it blue,
But now it's all grey and white
  with clouds,
The wind is howling and really
  sounds
Like it'll pile the snow so very
  high
It's going to nearly reach the sky!

Where art thou, Spring?
The voice of the turtle doves
Should be heard in all the land
Instead of the sound of the
  shovels!

No school today, it is so bad,
The roads are closed, it's really
  sad
To think that we could have this
  thing,
On this day—it's April 7th and
  it's Spring!

Karen Leslie Schultz
SWEET MELODIES
Sometimes I wonder
What life's all about.
Mixed up madness
In a house . . .

A house full of strangers,
Of sweet melodies.

Some are strangers,
Some friends.

Friends never hurt you.
They never lie.

Always go through
Life's sweet melodies.

Gary Stephen Lukich Sr.
OUR LIVES
[To my children, Jennifer and
Gary who inspired me, and my
wife Stephanie who believed in
me.]
In the morning when we're born,
  we are ready to go at the blow
  of the horn.
For in this time, so young and so
  new, we exhaust ourselves
  with things to do.
Never stopping, or letting go, for
  the time draws nearer for us to
  grow.
In the afternoon we set our goal,
  we launch our ship for ports of
  call.
And in our travels, we hear the
  cries of joy and anguish,
  sometimes stopping to ask
  why.
By evening time we've settled
  down, we stop and we take a
  solemn look around.
We reflect on our treasures and
  our days of past.
And at times it seems that it all
  went so fast.
And in the dark of night we
  reach, for that last breath of life
  before we sleep.
We were born to grow and meet
  this day.
As we close our eyes, we slip
  away.

Jo Westwood
SOLITAIRE
A single existence
Not by choice
A room that echos

A lonely voice
A soul that's hungry
A thirst that's dry
Since you've whispered
The words Good—Bye

A dreadful evening
In great despair
To play a night
of solitaire . . .

Donna Anne-Marie Valerino
INSPIRITED
she comes to me at night
  shedding chintz
    sharing aura—our eyes are
      one in the same.
deathly white goddess
  opens her womb to me
nonpareil
  all giving,
    all touching, inspiring juices.
I lay vigilant, agape,
  unrestricted in her grasp
attentive, ripe,
  eager for her knowledge
    yearnful, hungry,
desirous of revelations of the
  enchantress bestows upon me-
  relation
    consummation
adieu fair La Belle Dame Sans Merci
  I lie aglow, floating on a
    tranquil sea.
      absorbed, but not alone
        her lingering presence
        long remains after
          transcension.

Margaret Bean Ways
A SYMBOL OF LOVE
Roses are sent on St. Valentine's
  Day,
To express one's Love in a special
  way.
The inner Beauty of the Rose is
  expressed as it unfolds,
The precious moments to spare
  of a Love it beholds.
Growing with desire throughout
  its strife,
Each petal extends with open
  arms its Life.
For at last it has reached the
  height of its pleasure.
For the Love it has sent is beyond
  any measure.
With time the Rose will wither
  and gasp its last breath,
But the Love it has sent will
  endure its own death.

Tracy Ann Yates
TIME
[To my father and mother for
all their support I Love You
both. Also to the Moon and
Star for always believing in me.]
Time like love is everlasting
Although it changes every day,
And with this long term outlook
People tend to lose their way.
The endless air of time seems to
Move right along,
And with the aging years time
can
Make your soul strong.
Time can be forever and very
  much
Unique,
Yet forever isn't long enough to
Find the things you seek.

Cynthia Lee Buckner
DESTINY
    River of Life
    What have you brought me
    Pain and Strife
    But I've lived through it

    Joy and Love
    Which I treasure
    Days Ahead
    Which I measure

    But I am Young
    Having longer to live
    And I am Free
    Wanting always to give

So light the Way
My River of Life
Run deep through my Soul
To make my path right

Mary Lou Willoughby
Have You Ever Been To Egypt?
Have you ever been to Egypt?
(Perhaps so long ago)?
The lady from down under asked-
Ah, could it true' be so?

North Africa, the Allied Force,
Patton tanks, and all
And you, dear sir, had hurt your
  hand.
Ah, do you dare recall?

How can it be? We two just met
On California's coast.
You from your koala land
And I from Belgium boast.

Today we met an age away
From that in WWII
And yet I still remember
For I took care of you.

Donna Townes
TO LOVE, TO LIVE
Silly some say are such simple
  things,
though we're as happy as wealthy
  kings.

Their bounteous wealth some
  would give
to lead the life of love we live.

For rich or poor, take or give,
to live in love is to live!

Margaret Christensen
SPRING DANCER
Old Russian thistle, dusty, ripe
  and dried,
rolls and dances like a feather
  light
Ballerina's saucy plie.
Puffing as a flurry of swirling
  wind
lifts in a dizzy spin,
bounce a fairy dance across the
  meadow.
With a joyous flounce and a
  delicate dip
here, over there, in a graceful
  pirouette
goes a charming big fat tumble
  weed.

Anthony Re
TREE LEAVES
Good-bye withering tree leaves
wisked away by an autumn wind,
hopelessly carrying you farther
  from my reach.

Empty trees are silenced
their life dormant and lonely

for the sun has slipped beyond
  the mountain tops.
Sad looking trees,
where once a bird did sing
to fill my heart.
Now . . . even she is gone.

What is a tree?
without green leaves to give it life,
and a pretty bird to give it meaning.

Mary Allen Bueno

Mary Allen Bueno
LOVE'S TOLERANCE
[For Tony Eric, with love and
  respect . . .]
i have loved you
even when it seemed i
should not.
and when the heat of
anger came, it shook me,
but i held fast.

the pain still remembers
me, and at times recalls
the lonely battle . . .

i have hurt you when you
loved me most.
are those the eyes i hated so?
i love them now . . .
it seems a pity to have used
your eyes for tears.

my love, where do we take our
path?
surely i will not take one and
you the other . . .

dim are the lights and too,
the memory of hurting words.
i hold you now against my breast
and fiercely kiss your brow.

that aching has all vanished
as we clasp . . .
i love you more than ever!

Barb. Eads
DARKNESS

And so I weep: For others and
maybe, too, myself.
I ask why I do not laugh. But
there is not an answer.
My tears do not show, for it is my
heart that cries.
And the chills of lonliness wrack
my body, and my soul screams
in despair and I ask, "Why?" Oh,
tell me why!
For I do not know what to do. I
am running in circles.
But there will be despair. And
tears.

Dr. Lionel Fern

Dr. Lionel Fern
PARIS

*[This poem was written to Dr.
Robert Maigne, and his wife,
Professor at La Sorbonne,
University of Paris, France.]*

Paris est grandiose.
Je vois Paris en une fleur d'avril
d'un jardin bien soigne.
Dans sa couleur rosee je le vois.

En la saveur du vin
le plus delicieux du monde
je bois la finesse de Paris.
Dan son bouquet je le bois.

Avec la degustation
de delicats fromages
je me transporte a Paris.
Avec elle je me transporte a toi.

Je demeure a Paris
guand je visite un musee d'art
et guand je lis un poeme d'amor.
Dans ces moments je suis a Paris.

Cette cite est tous les
mouvements

que nous admirons dans l'art.
Elle est la culture dynamique.
L'art pour l'art meme. . .c'est
Paris.

Norma M. Huckins
**Dear Sweet Lady, Friend Of
Mine**

In this sometimes cruel world
of ours,
Filled with so much pain and
confusion,
    Long forgotten are your
    smiles,
Forever destroyed with secret
illusions.

Taking piece by piece all that
is yours,
Eating slowly away, your need to
survive,
    Until you no longer wish to
    continue,
Losing percious time from all of
your lives.

Unable to hold the life you
need,
Claiming souls from all
directions,
Kept out of reach, a much needed
life,
    From total love and affection.

    Hold on longer, if only for
me,
Accepting power from all passing
time,
Each day will be coming
brighter,
    Dear Sweet Lady, Friend of
Mine.

Dennis Babineau and Tracy Yates
TROUBLED MAN

*[Insane, You have kept me
Crazy And for that. . .I Love
You]*

Who is He in the window
That only the shadow shows?
Is He the one with the wisdom?
Is He the one that knows?

Maybe He's the wiser one
Against the dying man.
Wondering how all this happened
And where it all began.

Maybe He's a lonely man
Stricken with grief and pain
Longing for the best of life
But feels nothing is left to gain.

He waits and waits for tomorrow
Yet it's already passed him by.
The wise man doesn't realize
That forever was just a lie.

The words and phrases in his
mind
Are merely a compromise
For all the things he dreamed
about
Burt didn't have the strength to
find.

Paul F. Bermon
OH! COME TO ME

Come to me, with perfume of
lillies rare,
While moonbeams dance upon
your hair;
Come to me, as you did once long
ago! Oh, come to me!

Come to me in the bloom of

youth as bright
As the glow of pure love that's
true and right;
Come to me as you did once long
ago; please come to me!

Come to me, with those prescious
hours fair;
Bring with you that timeless
tender care;
Come to me as you did once long
ago; Just come to me!

Come to me, in joy of plighted
bliss,
And on my fevered brow, place
that kiss
You gave to me, so often long ago;
come again to me!

Ah! Bring to me those children
very dear,
That we may love and hold them
ever near;
Bring them to me as you did in
brighter hours; bring them to
me!

And now in twilights' years; O
come to me;
With rare and costly gold of
memory:
Disperse those shades of night,
that vale of tears, and stay with
me!

For now I'm spent, with nothing
left; nor gift
The weight of sadder, hapless
days to lift;
But burnt off'rings of eternal love
and bliss! Oh, come with me!

Vicki L. Mann
THINK OF ME

Everytime I think of you, I cry.
Seeing in your eyes that you care
And knowing in our hearts
All the love that we shared.
Think of me, and all the
Times that we had.
Think of the memories,
And everything we said.
I'll remember the look in your
eyes
Seeing after all, that you've
Cared for so long.

And when I look at the pictures
I'll realize after all
You're one heck of a buddie,
And a very special friend.
Whenever you're down
And you need someone there.
Just call me, and I'll be there.
If not in person, maybe by heart
All you have to do is . . . . .
                Think of me.

Peter Fabbri Langman
THE SHOT—PUTTER

Sunday morning, in a field by the
church,
The shot—putter comes to work
on his art
Of building muscles and refining
his skill.
Three shots are lined up on the
ground; to start,
He lifts the first and hefts it
awhile,
Then takes his stance, his face
intently tight.
He turns and grunts with a heave
of anguish,

Hurling the burden outward. Its
flight
Is short; its solid thud dents the
earth,
Moist from the spring rain last
night. He leaves
The shot where it lands as a
measure of his worth,
And lifts the next. Each shot
serves as a mark
To surpass. Sweaty hair hangs in
his face.
He strains all his strength to
achieve the grace
Of a master performing
flawlessly.
His shoulder aches and throbs; he
doesn't care
About that. He lives to see a large
round weight
Be propelled by his strength
through the air.

Neal Muscarella
MIGRANT DREAM

In the field,
My back to the sun;
I see concrete trails,
Mechanical mustangs run.
I hear those silver stallions
roaring
    through my window late at
    night.
Their mournful rumbling
beckons me
    to leave this farm tonight.
These harpies of the highway
drone
    like modern day Lorelies,
Beguiling me onto the road
    my back to nature's remise.
A twentieth century cowboy
Spirit taken to flight.
I'll ride these stallions of progress
Into the starry night.

Dale Edwards
MONARCH

The debut is sticky with certain
death and yet
your newborn wings are dripping
wet with renaissance.
Or is perhaps the chrysalis your
demise,
the ugly worm deceased,
the soal in vibrant glory freed?

You are the king of subtle grace.
The cloak upon your back is
black
as any lion's eye
with ornaments of burning
orange
that prompt the western sun to
bow.
And upon your fragile, tissue
wings
the sighs of youth are borne.
You are nature's aristocracy,
a figment of divine imagination.

Lester R. Nuse
A TRIBUTE

*[To all the P.O.W.'s and M.I.A.'s
that never came home.]*

He was young and tall his life
was clean
He was good to his parents with
them never mean
He was called to serve his native
land
He went freely along and offered

his hand
Overseas he was sent to that
　awful fight
Never doubting his country he
　believed they were right
The shells were flying the battle
　raged on
And when it was over the young
　boy was gone
When the smoke had cleared
　there were boddies all around
But no trace of that boy could
　ever be found
It was forty years ago they fought
　that fight
It only lasted two hours of one
　dark night
The suffering his parents have
　had through the years
In the stillness of night they shed
　many tears
They were always hoping and
　never had doubt
That things would turn and he'd
　come about
They asked the Lord to return
　their son
They prayed often for they only
　had one
But he never came back not even
　to this day
For he's still carried as a M.I.A.

Larry D. Wagner
Loneliness Without Reason
Take a long, last look
Back at security.
Count blessings.
They are the only things left you
　can count on.
Except fingers . . . .
People seem to forget people.
Strange meetings at night,
Clandestine sojourns into back
　alley affairs.
Lip—smeared whiskey glass rims,
Remind each other of lonely
　nights
When even walks along the river
　can't seem to erase
The hopelessness of unrequited
　love.

Tom Pierce
THE LITTERIC
　　A litter here, a litter there,
　　Here a litter, there a litter;
　Man knows not what he's doing,
　　He is a litteric.
All is contaminated with man—
　made waste.
From concrete jungles to what
　God has made
　　　Man has stained.
Whether consciously or
　unconsciously,
With hardly any effort or with a
　lot,
From the adults down to the tots,
Our beautiful world man has
　blot.
　　　When will we see
Our walks and streets, our
　shorelines and highways,
Our parks and fields, our hillsides
　and by—ways
　　　　Litteric free?
It must be a disease and it must
　be treated,

It originated way back when man
　was created.
　　When will the litteric cease?

Linda M. Olson
TO MOM
To Mom,
You cared for me
　in troubled times;
you shared the path
　both happy and sad;
you loved me through
　my many heartaches.
You watched me climb
　the stairs of love;
you saw me miss the
　very first step;
but let me start again.

For all these things,
　Mom, I thank you.

Vickie Putynkowski Whitley
LITTLE FOOTPRINTS
Little footprints in the sand.
As we walk both hand in hand.
Yours is dimpled and so small,
Mine is wrinkled; fingers tall.

I bend to whisper in your ear,
All those stories you hold dear,
Or past and present, new and old.
All the secrets never told.

As we make those prints in sand.
I know someday you'll
　understand,
The joy it gave me just to look.
Ah! Little one, I could write a
　book!

Lester R. Nuse
A FRIEND
[To Ben Caldwell and Carl J.
Pintagro]
Good friends are hard to find
I'm really glad you're one of mine
And if you should ever go away
Come back to visit again
　someday

Friendship is something you can't
　buy
No matter how hard you really
　try
Friendship is pay for what you
　learned
Through caring kindness can be
　earned

Sure as there's a rising sun
A friend like you there's only one
If into your day some rain should
　fall
A friend you need, just give a call

When things go wrong and don't
　seem right
Seem's there's no solution to your
　plight
Don't follow life with just a trend
Call anytime, —you have a friend

C. F. Green, Jr.
MASTER PAINTER
I wonder about the Artist
Who painted that vast expanse of
　blue.
Every time we look up at the
　skies
We're paying Him homage with
　our eyes.
Then He took His brush in hand
And created a kind of golden
　sand.
With a little leftover oil of blue

He stroked in the sea, a different
　hue.
Upon His palette He can blend
A gigantic rainbow that will
　never end.
When He must have been feeling
　mellow,
He drew our fields a brilliant
　yellow.
Then the landscape He dubbed
　clean
Each blade of grass a beautiful
　green.
The white clouds He painted go
　drifting by
And I realize His home is in the
　sky.

Kathy J. King
UNTITLED HAIKU
The gull takes to the air
the grey bird, the blowing wind
wrinkle the face of the water.

Harriette Dean Windham

Harriette Dean Windham
THE PRESENCE
An omen suspended in the air
　A foreboding as I become aware
　　Quietly it approaches in the
　　　night
　　　As a Raven descending
　　　　from its flight

Beware . . . now it settles close
　about
　Evil lurking, there is no doubt
　　As though a storm cloud has
　　　invaded the room
　　　Filling it with a dreadful
　　　　gloom

A helpless feeling as it draws so
　near
　I tense, filled with panic and
　　fear
　　Turning slowly with a sense
　　　of doom
　　　My eyes search the dark
　　　　bedroom

A form enveloped in a hazy glow
　Moving toward me so very
　　slow
　　Spellbound, I watch with
　　　morbid fascination
　　　Yielding my will to an
　　　　ancient temptation

Holding me steadfast with a
　hypnotic stare
　Inside me a voice whispers . . .
　　beware . . . beware
　　Yet awed by its omnipotent
　　　essence

I surrender to this
　overwhelming presence

Mary Brickman Mayse
EXPRESSION'S
Expression's of life entagled all
　over the place,
here and there on everyone's face.
Peace, kindness, bewilderment I
　see,
and they all look to have aged to
　me.
Troublesome toll's they all have
　there's,
Knowing or not childhood care's.
Taking there time, upright and
　strong,
Making there place right or
　wrong.

Bernadine Radcliffe
REQUIEM TO A BOTANIST
He walked the kindred earth in
　rich communion,
　Nature called him as though a
　　living soul,
He dreamed of all her sqawn in
　wholesome union;
　He labored morn and even
　　toward his goal.

He loved the earth, his
　fellowman, the rain,
　The wood, the marsh, the wild
　　birds mating call;
His home, alike, the wind—
　washed hill or plain—
　He saw and sought God's
　　purpose in them all.

He labored for a space and then
　was gone.
　The rose and wildflower,
　　grieving, saw him pass;
And marveled that he failed to
　linger on,
　They hungered for his step
　　along the grass.

But, oh, perhaps it was a lonely
　way he trod—
　Too few can touch the earth
　　and feel the pulse of God.

Geraldine Newcum Lemaster
WRITER'S CREED
[To all writer's able to
overcome the frustration of
rejection and know the
exceleration of acceptance]
Whose name lives on beyond
　mortal existence
His name I cherish
Though it chasten my soul
With envious determination.

Deanna Michele Frock
THEN AND NOW
Your eyes—
Once glittering withlove and
　mischief,
reflecting my every unspoken
　thought,
sparkling with desire and
　satisfaction—
Are empty now
no love, no life, no
　pain—nothing—
is held in them now.
Your expressions—
The smiles that once lit up
　rooms,
the frowns at a missed
　pass—play,

the tears that you cried only to
me—
Are no longer there.
You never smile anymore and
it seems that i'm the one who
cries.
Your hands—
that used to hold me,
Knowing just where and when to
touch me,
Now clench into tight fists and
tremble
when i'm near.
Your body—
Strong, tall and solid
seems to weaken
as we pass on the street.
Your love—
The kind that kept me going
night and day—
no matter what
Is mine no more.
My heart—
So open yet well—protected,
so full of you
Is now was broken
as is your spirit.

Isn't it sad when love dies
without cause?

Patrick Soltis
MOODS OF LOVE
Take a step from the past
Pause a moment, but not to
fast
Gaze into the fires glow
Does the warmth of love show?
When you are cold and numb
Love will warm you up, have
faith it will come
When she needs a shoulder
May he be there to hold her
Sorrow may fill the air
But in spirit we will all be there
The gift of love, what a beautiful
sight
May you share it until your last
sunlight
So many words add up to peace
and love
But all answers point to the one
you think of
What are the moods of love? Love
then pain
May the last one fall along with
the rain
Love is the only thing you need
And may your hearts never fill up
with greed
When it is your time to go up
above
May you live through all the
moods of love

Luis de Miranda Correia
TURBULANCE
*[To my parents, Maria Luisa
and Joaquim, I dedicate this
poem with love.]*
mother
i'm lost in the labyrinth of life
breathing this polluted existence
between the sinking yellow
flowers
and the dark—purple of the
angels.
strength
is a word i'm looking for
in the incomplete nights filled
with nightmares
and arid, red tears

wasted in the cold of my hands.
i catch hold of the breasts of the
winter
the flowers are yet to bloom
and the robins are yet to return
and you
mother!
you are sailing on a barge
partially dead
without a shadow to shelter you
in all and every sea.

Lester E. Garrett

Lester E. Garrett
VISIT TO A PLANET
*[To my wife, Dorothy, who
enjoys poetry, And has
encouraged me in my
writing.]*
When first I thought I knew my
destiny,
Truly I knew it not; neither
myself,
For I was young and in a
circumstance
Of hardship, harsh and uncaring
attitudes,
Traveling but not reaping,
bearing hardly
Of any fruit nor gaining
worthwhile insights.
Thus did I envision endless
Days of emptiness, years of
nothingness,
A visit to a planet of dry leaves;
Garden of the foolish and the
doomed.

But, one day I met my love
And the very center of myself
fluttered open,
As might a pregnant blossom
kissed by nature;
And my tension and bitterness

was replaced,
Suddenly with lightness, a sense
of direction.
I began to know why I was here,
alive at last.
She revealed a wisdom, taught me
goodness,
Patiently declared herself a part
of me forever,
And made my vistit to a planet
not only meaningful
But opened my eyes to beauty
and a presence of God.

Charles Melvin Foster Sr.
THE MIST OF THE SEA
Each morning out of nowhere
across the rolling sea,
A blanket damp and heavy
settles silently.

This slowly creeping spectre
with fingers cold and wet,
Reaches into places
where all the world has slept.

It slides into the harbors
and over nearby land,
To cover ships at sea
like a limp and clammy hand.

Then comes the sunrise
and like a magic wand,
The mist of the sea completly
disappears at dawn.

Betty Thompson
FEELINGS
Feelings come and feelings go.
Tears will unbidden start
When the pain is too much for
my heart.
But after many days or years past
It gently heals the broken heart
Because feelings come and
feelings go.

After many days or years
I can remember and the tears
won't start
And I will have conquered my
fears
Because feelings come and
feelings go.

Eleanor McKee
CAN YOU REALLY SEE ME
You say that you want me, but
can you really see me,
If a dream could come true, I
would dream of you,
I would dream of you making
tender love to me,
For the sea is so clear, so blue, the
sky, the stars, so beautiful
tonight.
I need to know can you really see
me, and not an illusion of me,
or an illusion of someone you
hope me to be.
If a dream could come true, I
would see you laughing and
happy, even if it wasn't with me.
I can hear the symphony, for I
believe you really can see me
at last.

Lydia Ambrogio
GOING ON
Go onward! Go forth!
Keep rolling along,
Like Ole Man River.
(An old southland song.)
Ah!
What words can be spoke,

That will light your way
Through life's dark jumbles,
Roadblocks and tumbles?
For
The ocean's worse yet.
Waves break o'er your head,
And sharks' pearly teeth
Snap mean at your feet
That
Tread the deep water.
Methinks you ought ter
Pick up the payload
And take the high road!
So
Make hast ot Mount Zion
Though rough, it may be.
And when you get there,
Look Up! And see me.

Frances Ann Norlem
FOR ALL ETERNITY
Funny how things happen
We started as freinds.
And as friends we conforted each
other.
Then something strange
happened.
I felt a strange feeling growing
inside of me.
But you knew what it felt like
cuz it was happening to you
too.
I was trying to fight it, but it
continued to grow.
I felt my will to fight it off grow
weaker.
Until one day I just let myself
give in.
I don't ever want to be alone in
this world or the next.
I want to spend all of time and
eternity with you my darling.
You and only you.

Lorna Hazzard
TO SET LOVE FREE
I guess if you love something
set it free.
It will be content
thats the way it must be,

If you really care
then you will know
you set it free
so it can grow

I know it does hurt
and you must be strong
but you will realize
before too long

Thats the way of nature
you needn't think twice
sometimes you
must sacrifice.

M. Jonathan Adams
THIRTEEN STAIRS
*[This poem is dedicated to
those who never had the
chance]*
There are thirteen stairs
up to my room.
Not that I care—
just that I dare
await a prodigy.
Await I will—
await I may,
for it shall come
to me one day,
like a monsoon monster.
And it shall say,
"You shall do good, my son."

So as the imagist lost
   pays no cost.
I sit and stare into open air,
   and quench uncertain desire.
Leaving behind the canaille
   minds
   of agitated youth.

Joan Burnette
WAY OUT
*[To my daughters—April,
Wendy, Tracy, My grandson
Eddie & Peoples everywhere]*

As the fear of a man trapped in a
   lions' den
The hurt of a tree in the winters'
   wind

People in this world not even
   knowing
Some don't care where they're
   going

Somewhere in a war, some men
   just died

In the slums of our cities, babies
   cry

In a world where boys must be
   men
There are girls giving birth at age
   ten

A world where sex seems to be
   the thing
But no one cares about the kids it
   brings

Yet one thing we can say and it
   stands out above
We've got much HATE and very
   little LOVE

Shellie Colleen Reese
The Priceless Surrender
If filled your hard hands with
   my blood
would you then possess my life?
If I sculpt my soul to fit your love
would you carve it with your
   knife?

If I serve my flesh to feed your
   needs
would you hunger for new meat?
If I filled your chalice with my
   tears
would you drink and find them
   sweet?

If in return I asked for truth
would you laugh and turn your
   head?
Would you leave me where I've
   fallen?
Would your ego then be fed?

Alma Lillian Hageman
Grandmas Are Not Forever
*[Dedicated to Grandmas
everywhere, in heaven, and
here on earth, still earning our
wings.]*
Grandmas are not forever
Enjoy them while you may
It's later than you think Dear
Today she slipped away
Across the clouds to
   slumber—land
Through golden threads of gleam
Where the sun's rays penetrate
And existence, is a dream.

So catch on to a sunbeam
As it dances on your brow
Tis Grandma smiling down

on you
Her kisses touch you now
With a soft whisp of gentle
   breeze
That rustles through
And stirs the trees
And rocks the chair where
   Grandma sat
And bounced you on her knee.

The child's fists rub wet eyes
As free the teardrops flow
Yet, can the baby understand?
He's only three, you know.

Tom Campbell
I KNOW NOT WHY
*[To the Chancel Choir of First
Christian Church, Lafayette,
La., Who performed this as an
anthem on 10/31/82.]*
I know not why a Babe was born
and laid in manger bare;
I know not why the Magi came
to kneel and worship Him there.

I know not why the Angel said,
"Fear not, I bring good news;
For, unto you is born this night
the promised King of the Jews."

I know not why, as years went by,
He chose a lowly path;
and said, "The meek shall claim
   the Earth;"
and roused the Pharisees' wrath.

I know not why they came at
   night
and took this gentle man;
I know not why they drove the
   nails
into His feet and His hands.

I know not why He suffered there
and died on Calv'ry's tree;
I only know, because He did
my soul is forever free!

Steven E. Morris
MY DEPARTED LOVE
I'm hurting and bleeding deep
   down inside.
The need to believe in a love still
   resides,
Where ours once was; but it's so
   empty now.
I keep asking myself how, oh
   how,
Could this ever happen to me
   who loves you?
I can't quit now and you know
   this too!

Sometimes it's torture, it rips

my heart out.
I'd like to scream and yell and
   shout,
For you to return and let's make
   it right.
Then I realize, it's just another
   night,
To be endured by this miserable
   man;
Tonight and tommorrow, as long
   as I can.

Robert L. Shelton
WORDS
You are a very special word to me.

You are my Sun, Moon,
The very air I breathe . . .

You are very special to me.
You are memories of time gone
   by . . .

You are Happiness, You are Light!
You are Life, You are love . . .

You are a very special word—to
   me.

Alberta Elizabeth Bigi
TIME
They say that Time alone
Can ease the pain of loss
Just like a rolling stone
It gathers no moss.

But even Time cannot erase
The vision of a loved one's face
Or still the voice within your ear
Or rob you of the memories you
   hold dear.

In this world of pain and grief
Time for some is all too brief
And then for others it can be
An empty, endless eternity.

Time passes on and so do we
But maybe then we shall see
All our loved ones who've gone
   before
And live in peace forevermore.

Lillian M. Adams
LOVE IS
LOVE is the warmth that fills my
   heart
Whenever I see your face,
LOVE is the comfort I only find
Within your gentle embrace.

LOVE is the pride that calls me to
   be
All the things you expect of me,
LOVE is your voice that makes
   me forget
The problems that come my way.

LOVE is your smile of welcome
Everytime I come your way,
LOVE is your kiss when we say
   adieu,
LOVE is the happiness I've found
   with you.

Josephine Bucol
This Is My Home, America
*[To my beloved husband,
Secundio]*
I will be home in two years, I
   said.
Back to my old country, I told
   myself.
In two years for sure, I declared,
To the swells of the ocean to
   America,
Following my husband I just

married.
Two years passed, only a month
   old the baby was,
Too young to travel, too tender to
   change the air.
Maybe in five years, I consoled
   myself.
Five years came and gone.
Ten years came and gone.
Children came one after another.
We never had enough money to
   go anywhere,
To buy nice presents from
   America,
To all my old friends and
   relatives,
To build our dream house on the
   cliff,
Overlooking the ocean Daddy
   fished.
Years came and years went.
My husband was called by the
   Lord, so he went.
Now with seven grown children
   and Twenty-nine
Grandchildren and one Great-
   grandchild and
Another one on the way, All
   Proud Americans.
Where shall I go?
That little American flag is mine.
They say I have a strong accent.
I talk like a native, by golly.
Now I am eighty-three years old.
I go to "Sinyo Sitisn Senta" and
Dance of some difficult name.
They all love me and I love them
   all.
I don't want to go anywhere.
This is my home, America.

Gabriele Barth
MASKS
They sit on shelves,
Evidence of falsified perception,
Two empty holes are where there
   should be eyes,
And through their emptiness
   they stare at me
And they accuse in silence.

They clutter my identity;
Which one of you is really me?
The strong,the weak, the cynical,
The independent or the child?

Lost in my own variety
I reach for me and you and me
And for that mirror that won't lie,
But what I see is never I,
And what I see,
Are different faces only,
Each one appropriate for one
   occasion,
Disposable emotionalities,
All lies . . ?

I put my self back on the shelf
—Well, only one of many—
And take the mirror, naked now,
   to see
The true reflection of the one
   that's me,
I search and see,
And see . . .

There isn't any.

Anne M. Coray
Four Seasons Become One
We've been through the seasons
   together now;
There is little to say

To Winter's isolated rains, the
   battling winds of March,
Or Summer's late compliance.
I whisper to you of bygone
   springs;
You answer wisely, sadly.
We talk of future gardens:
If to plant the pens,
When to harvest the sun.

Christopher Harwood
FREED TO CHAINS
*[Thank you for the times
you've given me. The memories
will stay in my heart for
eternity.—Eva Ferenczy
Reichmann]*
Free to fly away, but I'm
   motionless;
I'd love to stay, but I'm strained.

That river doesn't flow past me
   any more;
If I had it my way, I'd love to let it
   pour.
It's all locked up inside me, ready
   to flow;
But all now I know and it must
   be so.

It was, I believe, in the art of her
   face,
The moon shone down and with
   it her grace.
And once again, 'tis this fool can't
   let go
Even if it's only a rainbow.

I'm running scared, like death
   from love;
I have a feeling sent me from
   above
And I can't put it about to work:
Diffused to be redirected,
As though it were all somewhere
   connected.

She told me it must be so,
But even so long since, never
   will't be that I let go;
For you see, I know what I feel
And 'tis the pain shall never heal.

Novak Novica Vujacic
AN APPEAL
It's the time
To burn up all
The evil thoughts
Restore a belief
Reverence
In ever lasting
Existence.
It's the time
To bury all
The prejudices
Establish
A total Peace
On the Earth
By preservation
Of its worth.

Margaret V. Faircloth
The Carpenter Of Galilee
There's a man called Jesus that
   I'M longing to see,
There's a man called Jesus and
   that means all to me,
He's the Lord of Heaven, He's
   Jesus, My Savior who Died
   upon the cross for you and me.

He's the Lord of Heaven, all the
   Lands, and all the sea,
My Heavenly Father who's
   always good to me,

He's My great Eternal Guide
   Who's always next to me, The
   Lord
who's watching over me, The
   Carpenter of Galilee.

Priscilla Douzanis

Priscilla Douzanis
THE POTION
What chords of dread will my
   fingers play—
What forelorn thoughts cloud my
   weary mind—
What chilling depression makes
   my soul run cold—
What Harpies of doom sing forth
   these sullen tunes—
Is there a magic panecea to ease
   these troubles of my soul—
One swallow and all cares cease
   to flow—
Perhaps a needle-point could turn
   the tide—
Or fumes within my lungs will
   cleanse away the doom—
One swig of red hot fluid down
   my throat—
Will that quell the floods of
   doubt—
I Need—I Need—a remedy to
   rectify this reality—
To release me from its steeled
   grip—
I fear the Potion is—To cease to
   Be.

Michael Dunbar
TWO GIRLS
[For Danielle and Jessica]
Brown eyes speckled with
   golddust,
     Blue eyes opaline hue;
Chestnut hair parted, unparted,
     Fair hair tousled, askew.
Designer jeans, sneakers,
   sweaters,
     A nightgown with baseball
   hat;
Burt Reynolds, Clint Eastwood,
   The Bee Gees,
     The Muppets, Scott Baio,
   nan's cat.
Days on the beach and the ocean,
     Walks in the park and the
   swings;
A collection of smurfs, a drawing
   kit,
     Whatever! Wherever!
Everything!

And oft unaware of my presence
     I stand by their door as
   they play,

And the sound of their laughter
   still echoes,
     As I kneel at the close of
   my day.
And I thank Him for all His
   bounty,
     For the good bestowed me
   and my wife,
But this above all for the two
   little girls
     Who brought purpose and
   joy to our life.

Lisa D. Saunders
THE CHILD IS LOST
     You taught me grown up
   love,
And changed my childish ways.
     You filled my nights with
   loving
Put laughter in my days.

     You held me in your arms,
And made it all seem right.
     You never said you loved
   me
I just assumed you might.

     You showed me love's
   sweetness,
And covered all its bad.
     You gave me untrue
   visions
I wish you never had.

     The child in me is gone,
Your love has proved untrue.
     The words you used were
   prefect
For what they made me do.

     The scars and broken
   heart
Are all you left with me.
     Trapped inside, the child
   looks out
Waiting to be set free.

G.C. Bedrosian
IN THIS PLACE
In this place among places
Roses are always with dew,
Ivy allows for cool shades
And clouds scud on scenes of
   blue;

Zephyrs waft this wanton place
With scent of spring's vineyard
   yield
Or that of evergreen pines
Or the tables of the world.

Of trumpets north, east, south,
   west
Come the cries of the newborn
Or the sighs of the forest
Or man's song of all mankind.

And in this place of places
To hold close those that we love
Is the most that we may wish
For it is the hardest place to
   leave.

Linda M. Spaeth
Christmas Expectations
Christmas is here once again
With holly and mistletoe hung
Jingle bells placed on the door
That never fail to get rung

Yule logs in the fireplace
Bringing warmth into the room
The Christmas lights twinkling
In time with musical tunes

The tree stands so majestically

Its boughs laden with ornaments
Garland surrounding the tree
Underneath the adorned
   presents

Somewhere outside the carolers
Sing out their traditional songs
My heart is glad with cheer
For that's where Christmas
   belongs

Snow gently falling with no
   sound
Not even the whisper of the wind
We're expecting more tomorrow
Children's faces alight with grins

I think I'll abed early tonight
You never outgrow expectations
Though some do not want to
   believe
Santa comes to all generations

Beulah Thomas Carey
Inflation And Recession
*[To all of the folk who say
there is no recession! To all
whose purse has been hit by
inflation.]*
Some folk say there is no such
   thing as "Inflation"!
But there are many people within
   our Nation whose lives has
   been made worse because of
   "Inflation".
It has affected the rich and the
   poor!
Some folk can't eat the foods they
   used to eat any more!
Some folk say there is no
   Recession!
In other parts of the world there
   is a great depression—These
   folk don't own any of the
   modern possessions!

If Inflation and Recession has not
   hit your purse, then you are
   indeed very blessed;
Just pause for a minute and you'll
   see that our world is in a grand
   mess!

The President has cut the budget
   very, very tight . . . more and
   more folk are having sleepless
   nights—wondering which bill
   to pay yes, Inflation And
   Recession has taught some
   people How To Pray.

Tanna K. Mullens
GOD'S CHILDREN
Children, Children, come listen
   close
How Jesus died upon the cross.
Children, Children, come listen
   close
How Christ saved you from
   eternal loss.

Children, Children, do not tarry
Come to God and your heavenly
   home.
Children, Children, do not tarry
Come to God and cease to roam.

Children, Children, be born anew
Be washed in the blood of the
   lamb.
Children, Children, be born anew
Jesus is coming back again.

Children, Children, follow him
   now

He will not lead you astray.
Children, Children, follow him now
Walk with him in every way.

Children, Children spread his word
Tell of your mansion above.
Children, Children, spread his word
Tell of Christ's glorious love.

Robert J. Norton

Robert J. Norton
THE INNER BEING
None can see a heartache or a life of lonely pain
As he can see the stormy sky and all the days of rain;
None can see a troubled mind or a soul in deep despair,
As he can see a sinking boat or ruin that is bare.
Unknown, the depths of man's real being,
The surface only exposed to seeing.

Mauricia Price
MY SPIRIT SINGS
My thoughts, light-winged, soaring,
Brush mountaintops, cross eagle trails,
Touch fingertips with zephyrettes
Rollicking among the trees
Of verdant purple-shadowed valleyings.

Your love, warm-armed, vibrant,
Glows nimbus-like, stirs imagery,
Sends pulsing lyric messages
caroling to me. And when
I hear your voice my eager spirit sings.

S. Gregory Wallace
Mysterious Dance of Rooftop Origin
[Dedicated to that special ballerina who continues to be my undying inspiration, my divine Mary. "You shall always be my prima ballerina."]
The dance of mysterious darkness;
a puff of smoke rises above,
encircles the room and burns our eyes.
We search the skies blindly
but see nothing more than emptiness,
feel nothing but lonely stares.

Keith C. Powell
KEEPING LOVE ALIVE
There seems not to be
the time or the place
for the pangs of the past
Precedence must be given to things that last
Reasons must have rhyme
Rhyme must have meaning
Thoughts must not be seeming they must be
Years can be as days
or days as years
victim to where we dispose our fears
The changes which we have created
we must accept
except those changes
which aren't changes yet
And for those we need bide our time
and have aims
for those are the changes
which make us a slave
Though the days
the weeks
the months
and the years
intricaly prove if our motives are clear
The hours
the minutes
and seconds provide
the moments which keep our love alive
We need the strength
which our lover provides
We need the knowledge
that they too are wise
We need the kindness
that has no lies
Above all
a reason
and love stays alive

Sandy Cook
HIS CROSS WAS HEAVY
His cross was heavy
My cross is light
His love is much
My love is slight

His sins weren't any
My sins are many
His love is lasting
My love is asking

His cares are many
My cares are few
His life was perfect
My life to renew

His pain was much
My pain not such
His life given for me
My pardon for free

If not for my own insurrection
There'd been no need for a resurrection
What a price he paid for you and me
No greater love could set us free.

S.A. Phillips
SERENITY
Fall leaves of yellows and reds
Walking by the stream of life
Where the world seems full of peace
Watching the water flowing
In rhythm with the breeze
Gazing into eternity
Following a never ending dream
Listening to the leaves beneath your feet
While squirrels are busy
Gathering nuts for winter
Feeling the softness of the moss
Which grows upon the rocks
Fall colors that blend so beautifully
Seems to make the world stop
Just long enough to ease my mind

Karl O. Herz
MORNING LOVE
[To my father, whose poetry has always been an inspiration for me . . . With love, Carol]
Love comes to us as rippling comes
To mountain brooks, or like the wind
Sets whispering the blades of grass
Grown tall enough to bend their tips.

That I should find the same mysterious sound
In the dark pine that I hear evermore
Within me when I press you to my heart;
I know not what to make of it but that
My love for you is part of one great love
Which breathes soul into the Universe.

Perhaps the grass may feel, the brook may share
Such happiness as I have come to know
Through you. If these be mysteries of life
I wish they never would be solved for me.

Love comes to us, like scent and color come
To flowers, dew-wet in the morning sun.

Rosemary May
EMPTY ARMS
Mother of a precious child
Why do my arms remain empty?
I've longed for a child as much,
Perhaps more than you.

I've prayed for heavens gift
To suckle at my breast.
I ache for a wee one to cuddle
Yet my arms remain empty.

I have no photograph to give relatives and friends,
No lock of hair to cherish,
No baby book to write precious memories in,
No answer came when I asked God why are my arms empty.

Soon after our wedding day my love brought home a baby bed.
He was hoping for a little one to lay his or her precious head.
Not long ago my love left me, happiy in the arms of my best friend.

All hope is gone, lonely, now my arms will always be empty.

Sabrina Younger Good
HOLY COMMUNION
Words of love written in the sand,
Gently placed by God's own hand.
Whispers of joy inscribed in the wind,
Reaching me through the city's din.
Freedom-songs soaring on wings of doves'
Miraculous flight through blue skies above.

Laughter floating on sun-shimmering rays,
Warming my heart, blessing my days.
Musical notes riding ocean-wave tides,
Mystery abounds, peacefulness abides.
Strength emerging through the earth's crust,
Energizing the body, inviting its trust.

Silence gliding on moonbeams at night,
Enveloping all till dawn's early light.
Freshness falling in drops of rain,
Caressing all on the earth's terrain.
Ethereal vibrations connecting you and me,
Holy Communion with all on land, air and sea!

Stephen Jay Thomas
POETRY OF THE SOUL
The poetry of the soul . . .
No pen can express the thrill
when circumstances and emotions
are linked in total harmony.

Each phase of life
fitting together
flowing effortlessly
in a rhythmic, moving stanza.

Then circumstance and emotion conflict
the sentences are broken
there is no poetry—no rhyme
only lonely, empty thoughts.

Tammy Lynne Pfaff
SILENCE
[To Rick Larimore. You've inspired all this. I miss you. Forever, Tammy]
The silence is unbearable
I can hear teardrops fall.
Why won't you end this sorrow
All it would take is a simple call . . .

. . . Tonight silence is not golden.

Dale J. Budzinski
FEELING OF MINE
I have something to say
even though I'll still feel gray
I will say it in my way
but you may not understand today

I don't know if I am acting different
my thoughts aren't as sufficient

But if there is one thing that I
would like to do
is to love you true and through

Even though I say "Hi" to
loneliness
I will not let it get me down
Cause I know you'll always be
there
But being there won't help me be
found

Nicolette Bernard
REFLECTING
*[I dedicate this poem to my
mother, Jeanne, and my best
friend, Cass, who have
encouraged me with their love
and many times have had more
faith in me than I have had in
myself.]*
If I'd known at that threshold
what I know now,
   I'd alter and change things,
   I'd change things and how!

First, I'd examine myself, I'd look
through and through,
   To see just what I might be
   fitting to do,

Try to view my potential, how
great or how small,
   And strive to work toward it,
   try never to fall.

I'd set up a goal—yes, a reachable
goal—
   A purpose I'd find for my
   body and soul.

I'd search to find where I'd be
happy and free,
   To live a full life with much
   meaning for me.

Then, I'd 'do my own thing'
keeping others in mind,
   Always 'keeping the faith' of
   one who is kind.

I'd hold fast to my dreams for
when these dreams go
   Life's a wasteland, a field,
   which one cannot sow.

So look wisely within, and know
yourself through,
   And try to find something
   that you'd like to do.

Then do it, let nothing stand in
your way,
   For all things are possible for
   you—yes, today!

C. Sheridan
SWEET MEMORIES
*[To S. Herig, '68 was a very
good year.]*
Your visit of a couple of days
caused memories to spill out
over my kitchen table.
My kitchen table will never be
the same.
Eye contact more vivid
through older and wiser thoughts.
Your cologne lingers on my
phone,
from plane reservations and hot
tub rentals:
My phone will never be the same.
Sweet memories never leave with
time,
you're proof of that.
So here's to truth my love,

lies no longer floating on the
surface of us.
They've sunk heavily with age.
And like good wine,
we've mellowed, matured, and
increased in value.

Doris D. Smith, Ph.D.
OUR WEDDING DAY
As we do embark on this path
today,
For you, my love, I humbly do
pray,
That ours may be a love so true;
Forever and ever I will always
love you.

I will love through the joys and
sorrows we will face;
Through all of the trials of this
whole human race.
I will love you when our days are
sunny and clear.
I will love you forever because
you are so dear.

I will love you when the clouds
are filled with rain,
And also when you are in
sickness and pain.
I will love you my darling
whatever there may be,
For you are all the world to me.

Oh God bless our marriage and
let us be
Always and only living for Thee.
Give us life's blessings as now we
do trod
Each to the other; both for God.

Linda Love
GOD'S SPLENDOR
A little tulip bulb
brimming with the miracle of
God's love
is wrapped in a protective hull
below and above.

Its unsung love began to slumber
in the heat of Indian summer
as two green thumbs gave its
heart a hug
and placed it in a bed warm
and snug.

Winter surrendered;
as Spring entered
and rendered
the glory of God's splendor.

Joe Van Eyck
A NIGHT WITHOUT YOU
I sit alone in my room,
on my nights without you.

My mind wandering
to the nights we've cherished
together,

The nights we've shared our love,
until our time together was
through.

I wonder,
Is there ever a night without you?

DiAnn Frey
GRANDMA
Once she could knead the dough,
Darn socks faster than an Indian
woman weaving a basket,
And cook meals over a hot,
blistering stove.

Once she could iron 110 articles

of clothing all in one day,
Clean the house faster than the
wind could blow out a candle,
And hoe all the weeds in the
garden with one swing.

Now 82, her back crippled with
pain, she can't do the things
she used to.
Sunshine rays do not sparkle off
those once scrubbed floors.
Only memories in her wrinkled
hands.

Billy V. Dowdy
ZEPHYRUS
"Only degrees of unhappiness,"
said the monk to the prince.
"A torpid misfortune," his only
reply.
"Only degrees of madness,"
said the monk, without a wince,
"A world of transit, where the
living live to die."

"Entangled in Senility," the prince
explained to all,
"The visions of the aged only
meant to alarm and appall.
But the current has no mercy.
Like its creator, no hopes or
dreams—
Only degrees of absurdity
Where so little is what it seems."

Doris H. Hadfield
MOURNING DOVE
Feathered symbol of Peace,
   Gentle, mild and meek
   Until another claims the seed
   you seek.
No matter how generous the
   supply,
With lowered head and
   outstretched beak
Your sudden, soundless rush
   upsets
Even that raucous gentleman, the
   jay.
   And here, before our startled
   eyes,
   Rapscallion in a saint's
   disguise!

Mary Lou Peterson
The Period Of Adolescence
Adolescence is an abnormal age,
characterized by neuroses,
   anxieties,
and other psychological
   problems.
Adolescence is a weird, screwball
   age.
Years full of tears, turmoil and
   trouble.

Adolescents like to follow the fad
and be like the rest of the class.
Adolescents are unconventional
in their habits and beliefs.
Adolescents should be left alone
and given plenty of private space.

Adolescence is merely a period
of growth, learning and
   development.
Adolescence is dealing with new
   ideas,
feelings, values, perceptions and
   experiences.

The period of Adolescence is a
   crash course
in learning to live, for all at once,

education, career, sex, financial
   independence,
creating an individual life-style,
and sometimes even love all
   converge
with a span of several years.

Teenagers are just all around
   good people
when given the chance to be
   themselves.

Byrle Payne

Byrle Payne
NATALIE WOOD
As a child star you were the best
   beloved,
As seen in "Miracle on Thirty-
   fourth Street"
And in "Tomorrow Is Forever."
   Above
The mundane, lo, infinities never
   meet.
Typeset child stars don't rise
   above their lot;
In "Rebel Without a Cause" with
   ease you furled
This principle—untied the
   Gordian Knot.
Why not, for you were always out
   of this world.
You live. For fans in fifty films
   you're seen;
So for the world at large you'll
   always be—
Your beauty, talent on the silver
   screen.
For family, friends? Fled to
   Eternity.
For me, especially for me you are
A shining memory—the only
   star!

Dr. L. Marvin Marion
**Country Ham and Red Eye
   Gravy**
Waking up at dawn to a cool
   brisk breeze,
To sun peeping through cotton
   shades of powder blue sky,
To birds performing early
   morning concert
Conducted by wise old owl from
   tree trunk podium.

Sizzling aroma of fried country
   ham
Pervading premises of household,
Mother in kitchen making
   biscuits,
Stirring red eye gravy from ham
   drippings.

Eggs, scrambled and over easy,

Homemade apple butter and
raspberry jelly,
Cold milk and freshly churned
country butter,
A cup and saucer for hot brewed
coffee

Sitting down to southern style
breakfast,
Surrounded by mountains and
lakes of rural East Tennessee.

Years later reminiscing about
days of youth,
Mother and brother sleep in
eternal rest,
Only Father, aged by many
seasons, remains.

Transplanted to Northwest
Missouri by occupation,
Consuming daybreak breakfast of
cold cereal, juice and toast,
Telling midwestern wife about
country ham and red eye gravy.

Marguerite Stumpf
RAINBOW
Smile me a sunrise,
Surrounded by you.

Sing me a daydream,
In hopes to come true.

Hand me a memory,
To keep within my heart.

Give me a moment,
Which will never depart.

Love me a spring day,
And never forget.

Paint me a rainbow,
With lasting effects.

Rori Hodges
OUR TIME
*[Dedicated to the Chickasha
High School Seniors of 1983]*
Sometimes it seems like life
rushes by,
No time to laugh, no time to cry.
Good times come, bad times go,
We've learned to love, and we've
learned to grow.

My friends and I have become as
one,
But when all has been said and
all has been done,
We'll all turn our backs, and then
walk away,
To start a new life, and live day
by day.

The good times we've shared will
always remain,
And the storms we've weathered
again and again.
Hand in hand we've made it this
far,
Together we've managed to reach
for that star.

We now hold our lives in the
palm of our hand,
Given a chance, we will grow and
expand.
Never look back, for the future is
near,
But remember our time with a
laugh and a tear.

John J. McGlade
THE CANNON'S PRAYER
Oh, the cannons do not rumble,
as in days of yester year,

and the people of this province,
no longer have that fear.

Yes, the cannons have been
silenced,
but they served a purpose well,
they are a grim reminder,
of the days when days were hell,

They do not belch their flame or
smoke,
at ships that now pass by,
but raise their rusty muzzles,
in a prayer to God on high.

"Oh God" I once caused horror,
and the requiem bells did toll,
please put an end to things called
war,
and keep my barrel cold."

Maria Darby

Maria Darby
THREE RED ROSES
A message sent by three red roses
made me happy every day
The roses made a bright new day
chasing the blues away
The scent of sweet perfume still
fills my room
Their beauty chased away the
darkness and gloom
Three red roses sent each day to
say I love you

Promises are made and three red
roses will fade
Memories of three red roses
lingers in my heart not to
depart
If happy but lost compare the
cost the kind that look but
never find
I hid three roses in tears among
my souvenirs
The last three red roses sent to
say we're through I don't love
you

Paul E. Paige
LOVE IS
Love is more, than just a feeling;
to set your heart, and senses
reeling.
Love is time, we need to give;
for all of us, to learn to live.
A simple gesture, done just right;
can show us all, that love is light.
Love can break, a heart of stone;
for it can warm you, to the bone.
More than a mood, within the
mind;
love is all, we need to find.
T'wards it we must, direct our
stride;

like a never, ending tide.
Love is space, we need to grow;
it's everything, we need to know.
Who can describe, love's total
realm;
for one small part, is where we
dwell.
If we would learn, that love is life,
we all could live, without the
strife.
More than a mood, within the
mind;
love is all, we need to find.

Kristina Hittle
SNOW
I love the snow
As it sparkles and shines
It makes everything look like
prickly pines,
And when the moon shines out
so bright
Everything's so beautiful drifting
white.

Florence M. Nicholas
**The Night Before
Christmas**
*[Dedicated to my children
William L. Nicholas, and
Valoria Nicholas; Daughter
Sandi, Grandchildren Rhonda,
Brandi and Breck Nicholas.
These are "My Christmas"]*
T'was the night before Christmas
and as quiet as a mouse;
a widow alone, God had taken
my spouse.
The tree all decked out in silver
and gold,
with bright flashing lights—
t'was a sight to behold.
The babe in the manger, asleep in
his bed,
while Joseph and Mary
watched o'r near his head.
The cotton piled high round the
tree on the floor,
gave a luster of wonderland all
would adore.
With presents to all evenly
stacked,
it looked like Santa had
emptied his sack.
While sitting alone I had time to
remember,
the month I loved most—was
the month of December.
First day of December God took
him away.
While he waits in Heaven, I
silently pray.
I don't grieve o're his leaving or
dwell on the past.
I'll wait my departure, in faith
I'm steadfast.
With much love and beauty that
now fills my home,
I live for the future, I'm never
alone.
I'll just wait for my children to
arrive Christmas morn,
with a prayer of thanksgiving
for the day they were born.

William R. Dallas
Mountain Of the Unicorn
Hills are the children of the
Mountain;
They roll over the plain of the
world.

These children see the unicorn
near the fountain;
They know the reason her long
mane is curled.
There is ancient knowledge
buried in their soil;
Hidden by the Superiors who
knew they were loyal.
Stretching on forever as they do;
So far,
They reach clear out of view.
The Mountain knows of the hills
and feels proud;
She has raised them as the
unicorn vowed.
Few know the cousin of the
unicorn;
For she saw the hill at the foot of
the Mountain,
Being born.

Marlene T. Saxtain
THE GREAT IDEA
Love one another the Bible says
It's a story old and worn.
Yet here is where we find God's
Grace
In the pages soiled and torn.

Handed down through years of
faith
In the Book lying on the shelf
Through storms of sorrow and
the grave
Love one another as you Love
yourself.

It isn't easy, that simple message
That Jesus came to teach
For life is real and full of thorns
Our goals are hard to reach.

Live your life as Jesus did
And give your heart and soul
For here is where God really lives
Brotherly Love can make you
whole.

Doris Mayhew
GLASS WINDOWS
Praise windows of glass
Light illuminates rooms
Makes life worth living
Seeing the beautiful outdoors in
all the seasons
This happened to me in my home
for forty years
Then vandalism came like a
plague
In one day five large panes of
glass were broken by stones
Repaired the windows
The next day more panes of glass
were broken
Windows were boarded
To live in this condition is
claustiphobia
Have you had this problem?
If not, respect glass not being
broken.

Lillie F. Jackson
I LOVED YOU YESTERDAY
Dark ebony prince that layed
beside me, that loved me once.
You brought me love, and you
brought me pain.
Fairwell, for there will never be
another like you.
There are no tears, just a smile
for all the memories of what
use to be.
A wish for your good health

happiness, and wealth.
So long my beautiful one, may
  God keep you always.
For all our yesterdays Adore!

Lisa Stroud
UNENDING LOVE
After all of this time of being
  apart
We still 'love' each other, with all
  of our hearts.
I can't find the words to express
  how I feel.
Sure, I'm glad that you're back,
  yet it just doesn't seem real.
You've been gone for so long,
But now you reappear and say
  that your 'love' is still strong.
I couldn't believe what I was
  hearing,
Yet in my heart, there's
  something that I'm fearing.
I 'loved' You too much once, and
  you left me alone,
I want you with me forever, not
  for me to wake up and you be
  gone.
I've cried over you so many times
  before,
And it all seemed useless, like
  the sands on the shore.
I've waited and waited, on your
  return,
Now you're back with me, and
  our 'love' doth once more burn.
You say you'll never 'love' me as
  you once did;
I feel the same, because a painful
  memory is hard to rid.
Yes, I told you that I'd been with
  others; same as you,
But even with them, my 'love' for
  you was still true.
I can't understand why I 'love'
  you so much,
Is it your ways, your personality,
  or your gentle touch?
I believe it's a combination of
  them all.
So whatever happens this time,
Please, don't make me take
  another fall!

Karen S. Sobek
SONNET OF LOVE
*[To my sisters, with all my
love, a gift from my heart]*
Oh, how do I impart the feelings
  of,
A special someone who will
  always be
The warmth, the radiance of what
  is love,
Much fuller, greater than the
  open sea.

A love that's stronger than mere
  words can tell,
The kindness, gentleness you
  surely show,
The love you give to me I know
  so well,
A love more constant than a
  river's flow.

Remembering the laughter and
  the tears,
The time's I've tried and failed,
  you picked me up
And in your arms my burden you
  did bear—
The love you give does over flow
  thy cup.

My gift to you dear sister, special
  friend,
A love the course of time will
  never bend.

Anna Dolores (Oehlberg)
STARS IN THE SKY
Oh, the lights of the city
How they glisten and twinkle
  in the night
Buildings standing tall
in the stark greyness
of the moonlit sky
Empty rooms and empty beings
occupying stacked space
And sometimes
you wonder if you share
the same thoughts
Looking out
upon the cement mountains
They're so still
so motionless
But they do sparkle
And that catches your eye

Sharron Ann Milkie-Kaczynski
UNCERTAINTY
In a moment I wonder:
  "What is life all about?
Are all roads always rocky,
  Are they smooth, well, I doubt.
If ever I will know, it takes
  Lifetimes I hear,
To perceive of a pattern, if any,
  Seem clear.
So, I travel through days
  And years disappear.
My doubt turns to hope,
  I see smooth patterns here.
I get fooled for a minute
  I guess age has a way,
Of casting light shadows
  Over that which seems gray.
So, I'm back to a pattern,
  Of which, nothing seems clear;
In this moment I wonder,
  I see nothing to fear.

Christiane Denise Humberset
STRANGE SILENCE
Strance silence,
So quiet yet so loud.
Strange peace,
No fighting yet still war.
Strange love,
No giving yet still taking.
Strange world,
Still living but soon dying.

Laurence J. Brownsey
CROSSING OVER
As I blink then sink . . .
    in the deep of sleep,
Fleeting thoughts are caught . . .
    in the seine of schemes.
What image emerges . . .
    from fears I keep
Giving shape to escape . . .
    and substance to dreams.

Mary L. Weick
RIVERS OF THOUGHT
Thoughts flow like raging rivers
Throughout the minds of men,
Tributaries spring forth
And foam with joy and love.

Brainstorms overflow the banks
And flood the mind's eye,
Currents flow rapidly
And pollute with fear and hate.

Heedless captains brave the
  streams

And fill men's minds with greed,
Billows rise and fall
And defile the face of hope.

Maelstorms of evil swirl the
  channels
So peace may not enter,
Only love can conquer and calm
The troubled waters of the world.

Rose Colombo Strickland

Rose Colombo Strickland
EARTHQUAKE
*[To my husband, John, with
love and my children: Robert,
Rochelle, Teresa and Holly.]*
We woke from our sleep
  Then we started to weep
"Mom, what was that noise?"
  Cried out our young boys.

The door gave a slam
  My husband yelled, "damn!"
We took one more look
  As the house again shook.

The glasses did break
  The cupboards did shake
The windows all shattered,
  "God, what was the matter?"

We all looked so sad
  This earthquake was bad
Our boys turned to ask,
  "Dad, why is God mad?"

Anne Shinn Gray
GREY WINTER
Thin reeds quiver
As they freeze.
Hard winds drive
Against the trees,
And hurl soft sprays
Of snow about
Into the air—
And in, and out.

The wind is quiet,
The snow falls still
Upon the dim,
Tree-dotted hill.
A haze of smoke
Sails thinly by,
Across the dark,
Cloud-laden sky.

The crust on the slated
House-tops moves.
The soot-streaked whiteness
Slides from the roofs.
The grey clots fall
With a muffled thud;
They cover the flower-beds,
And sink in the mud.

The fading light
Grows dull and dim.
Grey shadows stretch
From every limb.
The sunless sky
Is still and clear.
Slowly, shades
Of night appear.

Kirsten Yaw
A BALLET
Milkweed butterflies, entangled,
  fluttering in elegance and
  anarchy.

In flurries, interlacing and
  braiding one another into
  flawless webs.

The delicasy, imprisoned
  eternally behind relentless
  glass, forbidding intrusion.

Still floating in sequestered
  silence, each discerning their
  own destination.

Until at last their wings flutter
  drowsily, and they saunter,
  exasperated, more frail than
  before.

The exquisite grace dwindles, and
  the magical simplicity
  vanishes . . .

G. Donald Hess
FE, FI, FAUX . . . PAS
Okay? Right? Ya' know? . . .

. . . from the point of view
of a stumbling, fumbling verbal
  purist
I find myself encountering
With increasing discomfiture
Hack "artists" posing as
  chautauquans
Contaminating their Logosity
With a tawdry verbosity of
  "accents"
On truncated pronouncements
With a much too recurring
  propensity
For perioding a statement,
With . . . Okay? Right? Ya' know?

Ya' know?

Julianne Seib
BRENDA'S GIFT
*[The Poem was written to all of
you that have a wish to receive
the one special gift in your life
whether at Christmas, or
anytime. Also a special thank
you to a dear friend whose
encouragement inspired me
deeply.]*
Christmas Day is no surprise
To children around the world,

196

But this year it will be different
For an enthusiastic little girl.
This girl, her name is Brenda.
She wants not much a gift,
Just to see one small box
With "Brenda" marked on it.
Brenda brought up in a different way
Than most of the world can see,
All the love and friendship given
From people and the model tree.
The tree of love, not presents,
That disguise the love we share,
Though sometimes the only way
To say we really care.
Brenda now is changing,
And gift she wants but one,
A small pet would be fine for her
One to share her love.
Brenda prays and prays to God
For her "one teeny-tiny gift",
A gift I'm sure would warm our hearts
Brenda's spirits guaranteed to lift.
Then on Christmas morning
A single present under the tree,
The box was wrapped with holes in it,
Brenda's gift, could it be!
The box was marked for Brenda
Though we know not where it came,
Tears rolled all down Brenda's face
We knew she'd never be the same.
The paper then went flying,
Brenda sees the puppy with a ball,
Then turns to her anxious friends
And says "Merry Christmas to one and all!"

John Jay Connelly
HIROSHIMA
Please listen lady now with care
though soft and silently you've
    left me for the eve
and wander, undetected, where
    my impatience
crude, can grieve no longer, nor
    follow
but by your gracious
    acquiescence
the stubborn liquification of your
    hair.

Please listen lady now with care,
as your rythmic distant sighing
    draws
the very breath which, trembling,
    slips
indigent from my stinted mouth,
    which
hovers a subservient o'er
your copious and fragile lips;
while my hand I keep imprisoned
'neath your pillow, lest, I
lift it to your brow, and
    excommunicate
the snug, involuntary elegance of
your sleepy oriental state.

Please listen lady now with care
though I seem always reason deaf,
a slouching, nimble-witted
    acrobat
who finely executes his oneself
    schemes
but bites off timely, daring
    reassurances
and spits them out untasted,

yet now
the regulated silence of your
sweet and stately song is heard;
though you may often feel
what's spent on me goes wasted.

So listen lady now with care
to my most sober, sprinting
    words
which flee to where there rests
    uneasy
every warm-remembered trinket
    of my life;
for tomorrow,
over eggs, under sinks, packing
    lunches, sneezy,
you'll be still a lady;
my lady, my lady,
my wife.

Hans P. DeBach
THE PRICE I PAID
My realization of my feelings
    did not come with all my
    readings
        but rather with an inside
        look
I am only sad for the time it took.

I had to mature and slowly grow
    and then decide of what I
    know.
I searched for an excuse I could
    not find,
but now I know I was really
    blind.

My love for you is very deep
    the price I paid is rather steep.
You really are a loving mate
    I only hope it's not too late!

Romona P. Farnbach
RAINBOW OF CREATION
Rainbow of creation
Proclaiming to mankind,
The beauty of existence
For one and all to find.

The multitude of colors
So brilliantly resound,
Their vibratory essence
N'er to earth be bound.

Encompassing all dimensions
From here to whence we came,
This plane, that planet, this
    universe
It sees it all the same.

Gladys. L. Douglass
Lullabies Of Yesteryear
My rocking chair is marred and
    worn
Its bright cushions faded and
    torn.
But to me it's a treasure rare
For years I rocked my babies
    there.

Twas there I sang sweet lullabies
Until sleep quieted fretful cries.
In loving arms I held them near
And kissed away each falling
    tear.

Swift it seemed to childhood each
    grew
Then I'd hold close a baby new.
Older ones would sit in my lap
While I coaxed the wee one to
    nap.

E'en though they could now play
    and run
When I sat down, here they'd all
    come.

That chair was still their favorite
    spot
For I'd rock and read to each tot.

Years have passed, they now are
    all grown
I still rock—but I rock alone.
My empty arms fond mem'ries fill
While I hum lullabies—
    remembered still.

Criquette

Criquette
WINGS TOO WIDE
*[To Orphans all over the
World!]*
Cradled in the cocoon
    with deep unrest
I waited to soar and stretch.

A moment more . . . and
    my time had come.

Unaware—it was but to walk
    into strife,
    I flexed my wings wide
O'er the Flame of Life . . .

As I did, the orange tentacles
heightened, and brushed my
flight—

The thrust of pain was an
    impalement from which,
    despite *my* might,
    —escape was not!

I quivered long, long in
    mid-air . . .
A lifetime there.

Nothing left but inner sight
    So utterly useless, against *such*
    might!

Garnet (Jackson) Piatt
MAKING MEMORIES
You may wonder why my house
    is sometimes dusty,
You may wonder how my time
    was spent today,
You may wonder why my laundry
    room smells musty
And why things are sometimes
    left just where they lay.

Now I may not be as careless and
    as lazy
As your very first presumption
    may appear,
And I may not be as useless and
    as crazy,
Nor am I filled with apprehension
    and with fear.

My values may not come up to
    your measure,
And you may not like the things
    I do and say,

But the pleasures that I most
    enjoy and treasure
Are the things that only happen
    for today.

For by tomorrow we may not
    have a sunset
And these memories may not be
    here to enjoy,
My grandson may not have a
    brand new tooth yet
Or need someone to mend his
    favorite toy.

By tomorrow all the flowers
    could lose their splendor
And the autumn colors we may
    not behold,
By tomorrow other duties then
    could hinder;
Some lost sheep may not be ready
    for the fold.

So each day as we may travel
    down life's highway
Let's don't be so quick to judge
    our fellow man,
As we may chance to meet him
    in the byway,
Just reach out and offer him your
    helping hand.

Gerri Steward
A SOUTHERN MANSION
A southern mansion with
    columns white
A sillouette in cresent light
Down circular stairs in baren
    thread
A vision in lace fresh from her
    bed.

She could not wait, the time was
    right
Tonight there would not be
    much light
Onto the cold grass she did step
Across the lawn the vision crept.

Up to the cottage . . . lift the
    latch
Reach for the mantle . . . strike a
    match
There he lay awaiting pleasure
He . . . not the mansion was her
    treasure.

By day the cottage was
    unoccupied
No one knew what went on
    inside
But the Gentleman and the
    Southern Belle
Had many memories, they won't
    tell.

Ruth Collier
HEAVEN'S DELIGHT
If our soul could but follow,
    On the wings of a prayer,
As it wends its way upward
    To our Saviour who's there.

Where there is no darkness,
    There's never any night,
Where there's always sunshine
    And gladness and light.

The home of the joyous
    Where our Father is praised,
Where love is abounding
    And no voices are raised.

Where hopes are never thwarted
    You're safe and secure,
You see by faith and the spirit
    And your landing is sure.

At the home of the soul
  Where dreams all come true,
There is always a welcome
  There for me and for you.

Oh that our souls might
  Take wings like a dove,
On their way upward
  To our Father above.

So send your prayer upward
  Then your soul can take flight,
On this spiritual journey
  To see all heaven's delight.

Katherine Keenan-Collier
TO YOU
If I could give a gift to you
I'd give sunshine wrapped in
  skies of blue
Tied with a rainbow, just for you

Gold spun sunrises, silver dawns
Diamond dewdrops adorning the
  lawn
Filtered breezes through Royal
  Palms

Bubbling brooks, mountain peaks
Fields of clover, nectar sweet
Green, grassy meadows, golden
  wheat

A gift of Daisies, "they never tell"
Or Violets from the mossy dale
Rambling Roses from fencing
  rails

Lapping waves on azure seas
Laced Ferns in art filigree
Tide bathed beaches, shade of
  trees

Gifts I'd give you friend of mine
Gifts not bought, are gifts so fine
Wrapped in happiness, tied with
  time

Christina Lynn Phillips
MY FLOWER
Grow flower grow, please grow
  for me
as there is a world for you yet to
  see
please open up you're not alone
be beautiful for me as you are my
  own
please take my place, please
  follow along
please open your petals while
  you're
young and strong
Oh sweet flower please grow for
  me
open and be what I couldn't be
Show me love in a different way
show me the world where I wish
  to stay
    Forever more

Dorothy Rye
FOUR SEASONS
I believe God had His reasons
When He gave us four seasons
Winter, spring, summer and fall
To complete His plan He needed
  them all.

Winter, with its long, cold nights
The wind blowing—the ground
  all white
Icy shivers up and down our
  spine
We thank God all are safe inside.

Spring, we welcome with open
  arms

With all its beauty and sweet
  charms
It brings the rain—the grass turns
  green
The air is warm and the earth
  smells clean.

When summer comes we all
  make plans
To rush to the beach and play in
  the sand
We trim the hedge and mow the
  grass
Go on a picnic—What more
  could we ask?

Fall has come not making a
  sound
The leaves are falling to the
  ground
Winter is just around the bend
The cycle will then start over
  again.

Irene Sanner
MEMORY LANE
I wish I could go back in time
To find the peace and happiness
The comfort that was mine
To wash that little baby face
To comb again the hair
To clean up all their messes
To straighten up a chair
The days were never long enough
The nights just seemed to fly
I'd be so tired from daily chores,
sometimes I'd want to cry
Oh to feel that way again when I
was needed so.
The days seem so empty now,
  that
was so long ago.
Still I have my memories, so I can
go back in time with endless
  nights
and long long days.
Once again happiness is mine

Teresa DeeAnn Stanfill
THE STREET MUSICIAN
I saw a man in Citadel Square
Strumming his guitar and going
  nowhere,
But smiling as he went.

The cobblestones were rough
And his feet were bare
But he danced as he sang,
A partner to the wind.

The notes rose, pirouetting,
The wind harmonizing;
The man, the guitar, and the
  wind.
The song danced
In their breath.

They were going nowhere
And smiling as they went.

Henrietta J. Green
GUIDED FOOTSTEPS
On a city's busy street
  I was jostled along
  with the hurrying crowds,
When I noticed
  a great stone building;
  its lofty spires reaching
  with expectancy.
The chimes mingling with the din
  of the city and born
  on the winds to the sea.
The massive doors, wide open,
  beckoned—

Ye Who Are Weary Come Unto
  Me.
I paused, then slowly entered—
Such grandeur I'd never seen.
The silent walls a haven
  to meditate
  on life and blessings.
The light showing through
  tall Gothic windows
  cast erie shadows.
On bended knee,
  hearing my Mother's voice,
I repeated, "Our Father".
A shaft of light from the Cross
  fell on the open Bible
  and richly carved Alter—
When lo, the strains
  of the great Messiah
  came like a gentle breeze.
I glanced at the organ—
  no hands rested on the keys—
I was not alone!
There in this peaceful Cathedral
I met and accepted
  the Son of God.
Whom I had never known.

Phyllis Webb Pryde
ENCHANTMENT
Special times with friends,
Love lingers like rare perfume
Leaving enchantment.

Delilah-Judith

Delilah-Judith
**To Venus, The Great Only-
Night-and-Morning Star**
The sun has fallen down behind
  the ocean,—
A flaming fire!
And now has disappeared far out
  to sea;
And Venus, The Great Only-
  Night-and-Morning Star
With quickening breath,
Waits to cast her gleam upon the
  Earth.

Which Lover will enfold which
  Love,
And kisses press upon hot lips,
And caressing, give the kisses
  back to her
That he has found in half-
  remembered fasts?

Which arms will encircle which
  flesh,
And tightening, curve around
  which back;
Which breasts will press against
  which breasts,
In soul-mate to soul-mate clasp?

And The Great Night-Star throws
  her gleams
Into The Land of Half-
  Remembered Schemes,—
A Lover waits—Venus turns to
  smile to Him,—
He is Adonis of The Land of
  Dreams!

M. Julia Cooper
IN MY FRONT YARD
I'm going to miss your naked
  limbs, Old Trees!
(Though I felt sorry for their
  lanky leanings to the sweeping
  of the breeze)
For they gave a far-out view of
  the skin tones of the sky,
Mostly dullish 'tis true, but rosy
  tints at sunset too.

And now new leaflets are
  showing through.
And soon you'll be a bank of
  green

So dark at night no starlet can
  be seen.
But no sun's rays bright glare will
  reach my utmost panes;
And so the passing winter's scene
  will—PRAISE GOD—
But welcome back the summer's
  gains—
  And I'll stay fond of you! Old
  Trees!

Hermon Clark
TIME
Quieter than a whisper,
  it moves with never a sound;
Some things are loosed for a while,
  others are bound.

Its footprints are etched deep,
  all is in its path;
With it nothing is forever,
  all things must pass.

Some face it with fear,
  some in agony cry;
The new come forth,
  the old wither and die.

Thoughts of forever,
  drift in our minds;
Things undone,
  lost to time.

Elaine Waigle Williams
DEAR SANTA
When I was a little child
All my faith was put in you
I used to write you letters
And ask for everything I knew.

I know you never failed to read
  them
Because underneath the tree,
On every Christmas morning
Were found the toys you left for
  me.

But these are only memories
From a happy childhood,
Of a jolly old St. Nicholas,
Who did all the things he could.

But now my dear old Santa
There's a bigger job to do,
While this old world of ours is so
  dark
We must paint the sky a brighter
  blue.

So when you are on your sleigh
A bobbing through the snow,

Do try and leave some happiness
Wherever you may go.

It may not be wrapped in tinsel
With ribbons bright and gay,
But just a smile here and there
Will make someone happier
today.

Let's all of us in every town
Help Santa spread good cheer,
And keep on loving one another
Throughout the coming year.

Lorraine Smagala Crowe
REACH FOR THE STARS
Rain is pouring from up above
falling down upon your love,
making you sad, leaving you blue,
I'll find happiness and give it to
you.

I'll give you this day, the sun will
shine,
letting you know, you will be
fine.
the birds will sing, flowers will
bloom
you'll find a way to get rid of this
gloom.

I'll help you find the light of day,
trust in me, I know the way.
A better day tomorrow will be,
I know you can do it, do it for me.

Warmer winds are blowing by,
painting memories in the sky,
remembering time that we had
spent,
finding the sun, we know where
it went.

Reach for the stars, they're not so
high,
Come on, I'm begging you,
give it a try.

Louise Racine
THE PASSING
Our paths met, my dearest, late
in years
Brought together through the
passing of another.
You never followed me, nor I you
We ran together through these
fine New England woods.
Walked at each other's side
When our hearts said run,
And we could run no more.
We carried our love and dreams
To the highest mountains to see
the sunrise.
Now, as the sun goes down, I
must follow you,
Or will you still walk with me?

Matthew Jay Grunden
MY CAT LITTLE GUY
Such a pretty brownish coat
Shining in the sun
She likes to roll a ball of yarn,
and
To her, that is fun.

Her pretty name is little Guy,
An odd name for a girl
Though it isn't all that bad
She's lucky it isn't Earl.

She's always been well-trained,
and
She knows when she's done
wrong
Her mother died when she was
four, but
Without her she gets along

Starting to get older
She rests instead of plays
You would always think that she
was dead
By the way she lay

I never thought that it would
happen
The day that she would die
But soon the bad news came to
me
And tears poured from my eyes.

It happened on a holiday
Four days before Christmas Eve
She opened her present the day
she died
She knew she was going to leave

It wasn't a very happy Christmas
We had her for eight years
It was always smiles near her
But now we frown with tears

I'll always love my little Guy
She's a one of a kind cat
Always licking my hand
For me to give her a pat

Dearly I do love her, and
Yet I always will
She had an important roll in life
No other cat could fill.

K.J. Harrigan
REALITY
Fierce savage of the night
Lies peaceful
    in the morning light.
Time is the guardian of the soul's
flight.
We are what we must be
When the time is right.
Passing on over the endless
stream
Life is merely a momentary
dream.
Through time's eye
Millions of lives may be seen
In the flickering
    of a starlight beam.
It may be,
Reality is the greatest illusion
Created to keep our mortal minds
from confusion,
And yet, in the midst of the soul's
seclusion
It is merely
    an unnecessary intrusion.

Liz Carter Richards
aged love
    *[to love with ultimate reward:
    life.]*
sun
lowering colored anchors
across the grass covered hill
(the hill walked upon, by feet)
sends small whirlpools
of warming strength
enabling the stepping feet
to more one more step
toward the melting
territory of serenity
with love   with love
aged love.

G.F. Sheeler
WISHES
What are my wishes for the New
Year
For my friends and foes alike?
I wish that God, our Father
Will help us to find peace and light.

I wish that those who are
starving
Find food for their hearts and
souls;
I wish all races who're struggling
Will soon come nearer their
goals.

It's a beautiful world we live in,
So why don't we keep it so;
By truly loving our brothers,
And living each day as we go.

Anna Mae Kochel

Anna Mae Kochel
I ALMOST FORGOT
    *[To my retired pastor's wife,
    Mrs. Ruth Slegenweit, who
    inspired me.]*
I almost forgot who my back-up
is
    When I tried to take matters
    on my own
Hands that were so shakey as
these,
    And my cool I almost have
    blown.

I almost forgot till I got on the
phone
    And talked about that back-up
    of ours
Through a friend who wouldn't
let me be alone
    During these times of trying,
    lonely hours.

I almost forgot why that back-up
is near
    And why HE is around to
    always hear
Our troubles, our worries, our
prayers and fears
    And to remember that HE is
    always there.

Howard Wolk
IN THE HEARTS OF MEN
I sought me out some safe and
lasting medium
Whereon to write my inmost
thoughts for those to come!
Seeking to leave some counsel
wise, some tired advice.
Perhaps of value to my fellow
men.
Though long considering no
choice could I decide upon,
Nor stone nor brass nor shining
steel—
All seemed subject to the power
of Time,
Unequal to the purpose I had in
mind.

Pondering on this, it seemed to
me
A small voice came, a whisper
seemingly,
And yet force of power, and
confidence
In truth and timidness;
If you would speak for future
years,
By method proof of all decay and
less.
Then write your message on the
hearts of men;
Weak though these be, it will be
safely shrined,
Heard through all times,
Secure, unfading, and immutable!

Howard Wolk
A TOAST TO LIFE
As you travel the road of life
May you find it paved
With good health, good luck
And a bundle of happiness.

May you experience much joy
And little sorrow
These are things I wish for
All of your tomorrows.

Robin A. Greene
TWENTY-FOUR
In London Town did the
townspeople
Shop quite endlessly:
Where cobblestone rodes pass
alone
Through town of which few are
known
    From which each held the key.
The streets under the thick
frozen reign
Were lined with shops that were
lit and gay
And also here were the
multicolored lights,
That once served to light the
lamplighter's way;
And here the air was crisply
thick this night,
Up the rode there slid one sleigh.

But oh! how peaceful this one
night could seem
When animals are thought at the
mid to talk!
Let us stop, remember the dream
Of wise men way back when
Decided by the light of the blue
white star
To take their historical walk!
May the many who view the door
but know they can't get in
Win just once at this game which
is so difficult to win;
And find peace for just one
solitary moment
In the Lord's comfort on the eve
of His day.

Isolde V. Czukor
REFLECTIONS
As I sit watching the pounding
sea,
It brings back the sound of your
voice to me.
I hear your laughter, quick and
wild,
And I think of the sweet, crooked
way you smiled
When I said, "I love you so".

I feel again the touch of your
hand

As we sat quietly sifting sand,
Building castles and courtyards
and drawbridge moats,
While schooners and sloops and
tiny boats
Sailed past in the gentle blow.
The drifting sand and the myriad
shells
And the sea-flecked wind bring
back the spells
Of wonderful days we spent, you
and I
Together, under the changing sky
In those days so long ago.

Cecilia E. Benedetto-Leicht
POETRY
Poetry you are so real
You are everything I feel
Poetry you are emotion
To you I come with deep
devotion

Poetry your harmony
Is heard in every symphony
Poetry you are everywhere
You are someone sitting in a
chair

Poetry I find you there
You take away my every care
Poetry you are trees and leaves
Poetry you are what relieves

Poetry you are nursery rhymes
You can cheer the worst of times
Poetry you are everyone
You are the rain, You are the sun

Joyce Jacobson
THE SEASON OF LOVE
*[To my family and friends,
Marie, Laura, Ann, Cindy, and
to the great women in Park
Region on B-1 (1982-83) at
Concordia College, for their
love, support and friendship.]*
The season of love . . . what is
it?
The time when I am being loved,
or the time
when I am doing the loving?
What is the meaning of this
season?
Will it bring me laughter or
tears?
Shall I have peace of mind or will
I be caught
up in a world of unreality?
The season of love is today, and
it will be
tomorrow, as it was yesterday.
This season is the time when all
shall be
loved, and all will be loving.
The meaning is anything you
want it to mean,
Whether it be happiness,
sorrow, anger, or fear.
The meaning is always different.
The season of love will bring
me all that
I've looked for.
I will always treasure the
season of love.

Andrew Valli
DESTINY
In the evening of spring—
I sit alone in misery.
Dreaming of fame
Which lurks in the shadows
And regards me with hopeless
eyes,

While my tears mix into mud in
my mind.

I muse a moment
On the days done events
And stare ahead to tomorrow
Which hides in the darkened
corners
And grimly observes my
questions,
But never speaks.

Jeannette L. Fontaine

Jeannette L. Fontaine
INESCAPABLE EGO
[To my beloved Fred Bogad]
It would serve no purpose
To make a display of
knowledge

Citing classical authorities
With all commentaries therein.

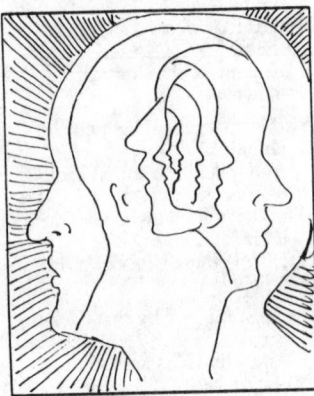

As regarding all facts
I leave the dilemma as I find it,
unsolved.

Roma Hogue
SHOTGUN
Shotgun
My little four legged friend
You might be small but I don't
judge you by your size at all
Your love, your trust, your faith
in me
come automatically you see
You came to me for such a short
while
You brought sunshine to my life
and a smile
You were shy and held back at
first
but it didn't take long to know
we
were friends, I thought my heart

would burst
You'd play with your toys and
bring them to me
All day long you kept me
company
Even though you're mighty small
Your bark gave you away and
made you really tall
My protector you became
to keep me safe and free from
pain
You'd cuddle by me and sleep in
my bed
putting your body by my head
All night long you'd even snore
It was good to know I had a
friend
who meant much more
We have to part but it's not
goodbye
I'll see you again
So I shall not cry

Freda Rose Holmes
SOUNDS OF SUMMER
*[To My Children: Barbie, Cindy,
Mary Ann, Glenn, John, Jim,
Iris and Pat.]*
My summers have been filled
For many years,
With sounds of ballgames
Ringing in my ears.

Throw it to first; get the batter;
Just touch the bag; call time;
Hold the ball; catch that fly;
Slide; you're doing just fine.

Run up on those balls; move over;
Move in; move out;
Don't sling the bat; don't slow
down;
Don't watch the ball, we all
shout.

And when a child up to bat
Hits the ball way out of the place,
It's easy to find the parents,
The ones with the biggest grin on
their face.

From Cinderella to Power Puff,
From Off The Peg to Fast Pitch,
The schedules are clipped to
make sure
What times goes with which.

One day each year,
My camera goes with me,
For action shots, to put in an
album.
For all to see.

What will I do with my summers
When all my children are grown
and gone away?
"When I'm old enough Grandma,
Will you come and watch me
Play?"

Larry Tutcher
HUMANITY
Happiness is a feeling that some
enjoy
Sadness a worker that some
employ.
Humility is a gift sent from above
Arrogance a player with a
fingerless glove.

Strength is a soldier out in the
rain
Timidity the cause of a lot of
pain.
Honesty is the result of a job well
done

Dishonesty the hope that help
will come.

Intelligence is answering God's
only call
Stupidity a waltz without a ball.
Loving is a child with a new born
kitten
Hating a fight over the last wet
mitten.

Hope is a spring of unending
pleasure
Despair a sonnet without any
measure.
Life is eternal with the help of
God
Death the gateway to His
heavenly sod.

Carol Patricia Keenan
P.O.A. Prisoner Of Alcohol
*[To "Big Red", A year has
passed by since that terrible
crisis and still you've had the
strength to say no. I, along with
many others, are especially
proud of you!]*
Weeks have passed by and still
not a word
Of your absence and
whereabouts,
No one has heard.
I've imagined you've vacated to a
place so serene,
To be alone and recuperate from
that horrifying dream.
You've experienced the fable of
having lived nine lives;
But the last was almost fatal;
Yet you managed to survive!
So, slowly will weeks develop
into
months of my longing and
concern,
As my faith and love grow
stronger
Until you've finally returned.

Betty Cox
BON APPETIT
Hors d'oeuvres,
Finger sandwiches
And sherbert,
That's what you're like.
You tease my palate,
You tempt my senses
But no matter how hard I try
To fill my emptiness with you
You always run out before
I'm completely satisfied.
You give me little tastes,
Enough to tide me over
But never enough
To stuff me.
You keep me lean
I feel I shall never see
A reflection mirroring obesity
Because of you.

Connie Heath
EXPRESSIONLESS
Oh, that man would freely
express his emotions.
But he is wound tightly like an
alarm clock
set and ready to go off,
Living each moment proving to
himself that he
has nerves of steel
Giving a great performance to
those around.
A man of reserve, business;

hard nosed most
would say,
Dressed in his best, stiff and
starched,
A plastic face, showing little
emotion.

He wheels and deals in the
business world,
shrewd, decisive and cruel at
times,
And his homelife is much the
same.
He rushes and dashes from
conquest to
conquest,
Never analyzing who might have
been hurt
through his aggression.
Why should he care?
He is a success. He has made his
mark.
But he admits to himself only—
it's lonely
at the top.

Under the plastic face, muscles
twitch
Longing to form a smile and flash
it at
someone.
A tear lingers near the corner of
his eye
And deep in his throat a laugh
lodges
and waits to exit.
His arms long to encircle
someone with
love or comfort.
Emotions he never expressed boil
deep inside
his soul
But he cannot release
them . . . he is a victim
of pride.

Madalene Middleton
CHRISTMAS FOREVER!
*[To my dear children, with love
forever, Christmas Day and
every day.]*
This can't be Christmas!
There's no snow. We both know
There has to be ice and snow
Sleigh bells ringling, jingle bells
jingling
Warm coat buttoned tight, hood
and mittens wooly-right.
That's Christmas!

This is Christmas!
New friends to meet, old friends
to greet
With loved ones of all the year
Each Christmas grown more dear
Carolers at the door, Noel Noel
o'er and o'er
The Star safe keeping the Babe
His sleeping
Born King of kings is He, all men
His brothers, free.
It is Christmas!

Donna K. Dean
I FOUND HIM
*[To my parents, who taught me
the love of God.]*
I lived so long without you, Lord;
They were many years of grief.
I thought I could make it on my
own
And I just didn't want to believe.

But you waited patiently beside
me
And you never once let go.
Though I never even thanked
you
For the blessings you bestowed.

Finally I came to realize
That I was living a life of sin;
And only you could fill that
space
Where emptiness once had been.

You forgave me in your loving
way
And through you my light will
shine.
How glad I am that you saved me,
Lord,
For eternity with you is now
mine!

Fran Duke

Fran Duke
LIFE'S ERRORS
I sat with my son, my three
daughters, my wife.
Just sat there and dreamed, re-
read the book of my life.
They all mentally helped me turn
page after page.
Gave me the chance to review
the beauties of age.

There is so much in life that each
of us need.
We only look for the good things,
our Ego to feed.
Found there were so many things
that I didn't know.
Asked myself, "Did the errors I
made in my life help me grow?"

Can still hear the "Booo's as the
short basket I blew.
Taught me, "Don't take for
granted the things you can do."
We all make mistakes,
sometimes plant the wrong
seed.
When it finally blossoms, we find
it's a weed.

Still see that pass coming, on the
goal line I dropped.
Even though I had failed, the
clock hadn't stopped.
Those six points that I lost would
have made us the winner.
Learned, "One mistake doesn't
always make you a sinner."

There I stood at the plate, my bat
ready to swing.
The Ump bellered "STRIKE
THREE", I'd done not a thing.

Your next time at bat, be a little
bolder.
Discovered, "You never will hit
with the bat on your shoulder!"
SWING IT!

Stacy Lee Heft
DREAMS
Hidden in a notebook lying on
the shelf,
Are all the dreams and secrets I
write for myself,
Things for the future, memories
from the past,
Thoughts, wishes, dreams,
goodtimes to have to hold to
last,
When the future gets here, and
the present fades,
Sitting on my shelf are the
memories made!

Betty Sue Beam
MY DESTINY
Looking upward from afar,
I caught a glimpse of a falling
star.
Its life was finished in a flash.
I was left wondering but, alas,
It was just a star that did shine
bright,
But it was beauty in the night.
It had served its purpose; now it
was gone.
Standing there all alone,
I compared that star to my life.
Would I be remembered for my
Beauty or my strife,
Which I left along the way,
As I lived from day to day.
The star and I share the same
fate.
But, I'm here a little while longer
at any rate.

Anita Howard
TOGETHER
They walked along the water
hand in hand . . .
Leaving their footsteps behind in
the sand.
They looked at the mountains—
with their caps of snow,
Thinking of summer when warm
breezes blow.
Watching the sun rise and
watching it set . . .
Remembering the day when they
first met.
They met at a party in a whole
crowd of people . . .
Later they were married in a
quaint little steeple.
They looked at each other with
their eyes full of love . . .
All love is granted by our Lord up
above.

Blanche Marie Atwood
FLY AS A BIRD
Fly as a bird to the blue
mountains
Where I am longing sometimes to
be,
To see green lakes and rivers too
Nobody knows what it would
mean to me.

Fly as a bird through the sky
To see the silver streams again,
To be so near, this now my
dream,
Meanwhile my longing is in vain.

Fly as a bird over the ocean
To see my native land again,
But my wings are weak—who can
help me?
I shall never get there—all is in
vain.

Vera McKenna
CHRISTMAS CARDS
*[To the dear friends who, year
after year, receive my
Christmas Cards.]*
Every year without fail
When I first see Christmas Cards
on display
My tired Old Heart just quivers
with new joy!

Don't know why this should be
'Cause as you know Christmas
Cards
mean hectic
Days of lists and inky fingers
sticking stamps!

Louise Wilkerson Conn
PRECIEUX
I sink into a silken sleep,
closing my eyes to Neptune's
stars.
God hangs his cloroxed pillows
across his clothesline in the sky.

The moon, hoarding his awsome
power,
hangs low, getting himself
entangled
in the gilded leaves of the trees,
carelessly spilling silver across
my floor.

My mind carves love scenes out
of shadows.
From my garden, gardenia
fragrance rides
a maverick breeze through my
window,
caressing you, caressing me who
loves you.

Julie Ann Livingston
LOST LAMB
I am a lost lamb searching for the
way
Trying to find God in everyday
I lost Him somewhere along the
way
When I find Him I don't know
what I'll say
I'll just drop to my knees and
pray
Telling God I love Him more and
more each day
So when you're lost, you'll hear
Him say,
"Follow Me. I know the way."

D.L. Andre
DREAMS IN TIME
I dream on days like this
of past glories and quiet bliss
A sweet refreshment under a
shady tree
a lovely lady reading to me
Song of nature being quietly
hummed
the strings of my mind softly
strummed
An elegance long since died
in my soul now revived
Where no machine hurts the
silence
and man has not destroyed the
balance

A hole in time a slight abyss
that I enter since by birth I missed

The age for which I was destined
to be
in all its glory comes to me

And for the moment I'm at my
best
the pressures of present at last at
rest

Buried in a balm of purity
cleansed by the past from iniquity

And it may not be as I think it was
but I know if I had the chance
I'd step through that portal in my
mind
without a backward glance.

Wylie C. Bolin
THE DITCH DIGGER
I saw a man digging a ditch—for
what I do not know—perhaps
to put a pipe therein for water
so to flow. To reach a home or
houses to connect onto the
main—whatever reason there
might be, his labor seemed in-
vain—until one day again I
passed, the job had been
complete—around the corner
came a truck with firemen to
the street—"A house on fire"
someone yelled as the truck
came to the aid—and to a
hydrant where the ditch was
dug a hose connection made—
water came, the fire was out so
quick without a hitch—I
realized then the hero was the
man who dug the ditch.

Dr. Lionel Fern

Dr. Lionel Fern
**Light, roaches and
politicians . . .**
*[In honor of Attorney Carlos
Romero—Barcelo', Governor of
Puerto Rico, a statesman who
has defined himself.]*
The conduct of politicians
in relation to
the liberty
of some countries,
it occurs to me,
is just like
the behavior of roaches
in relation to
a ray of light:
They perceive
the brightness;
towards it
they move,

turn about,
stop for a while,

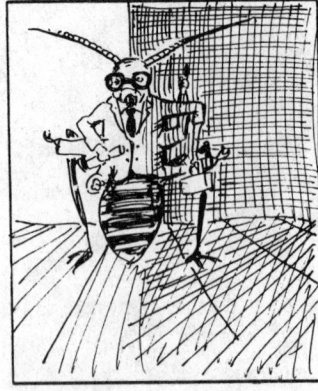

creep back and forth;
and, finally,
stay
in a place
half moon—
half shadow.

Juanita Wallace
THE OLD WOMAN
The old woman sits quietly
waiting
rocking back and forth in her
wooden chair.
The creaking wood softly ticks
off the years
as memories begin to flood the
air.
Her knarled hands, folded in
prayer,
thank the Lord for being there:
for picking her up when life has
knocked her down . . .
for creating a smile from a
troubled frown.

Her face, a map of wrinkles,
tell of her joy and her forlorn;
deeply etched are the sorrows she
has borne.
Stary wisps of graying hair
surround her face with a regal air.

Just before the rising of the new
dawn,
her master will take her hand;
keeping His promise as was
planned.
Gently the Master leads her
home . . .
her suffering and sorrow no
longer free to roam.

Ardis Lucien Barrett
THE ONE
(if I had met you in my life
I would never have forgotten)
There is something inside your
Soul,
It becomes a shadow of Light,
As you stare vacantly at the
palace of ruby jewel,
Hair of passion, green flames
staring deep into your
fairytale splendours dark,
Apocalyptic.
You, the one, the rose in the
picture frame;
Masquerader in your looking—
glass world.
To be born outside one's time,
One's only time,
Is to be married to the fate

of one destined to serve Death
as supreme master,
He can only be glimpsed,
But can never be found,
For he is lost to one whose
previous life is now over.
Nocturnal enchantments . . .
Obsessions,
A late afternoon sun wraps the
graveyard's trees in its shroud.
An attempt to reunite oneself
to History,
The life of Spirit,
To walk upon Death's ancient
grasses,
One Spirit—
Filled with all that It brought
with It then,
Time had no meaning,
For Reality had one meaning
only—
Perfection.

Nelson E. Smith
FRIENDS
Friends are what we should be, all
this wide world o're.
My friends, they mean so much
to me, each day they mean
much more.
They are the ones who stick by
you, when you are hard to
please,
And when you're feeling so very
sad, help set your heart at ease.
They are so near, so very near,
ever with kind words to say,
And when you're lost along lifes
path, it is for you they pray.
Please love them true, as they do
you, and make them very proud,
To have you be, as one of them, a
member of the crowd.

Barbara F. Alaimo
HE IS CLOSE
Whenever I walk down the street,
I behold my Lord.
He smiles at me; from every
flower,
blade of grass, from every tree.
I feel the warmth of his hand in
the heat of the sun.
It comforts me to know he is
near,
so I walk in peace.

E. Miriam Aul
BE A FRIEND
When you meet a man with
clothes ragged and worn
Don't look upon him in hate or
scorn,
For wherever his feet have
strayed
Beats the heart of a man that
God has made.

You do not know what sorrows
he may have borne
As he walks the streets until
early morn.
Perhaps he would have been
prosperous too
Were he given the chance the
same as you.

You do not know how soon your
life may be
Filled with misfortune, so try
to see
What life would be if it were you
instead

When night came and no place
to lay your head.

When a stranger asks you to lend
Something to eat, be a friend.
You do not know perhaps
somewhere
A mother seeks to guide him in
her prayer.

Be a friend and you may cause
him to see
The road that leads to
Christianity.
Through mirth or song you may
extend
The message that God is
always his friend.

Enid Cohen
REGRETS
The crime committed—
Long repent.
A life regretted—
Passion spent.

Callen E. Walker
Chilling Night In the City
Chilling night in this city
Baby sitters sitting in a home
Rain drops dancing in the streets,
Puddles glistening under the rows
of lamps marching.
Rivers of rains creation
Flowing in cadence
Count the drops if you can,
Count on a pleasantness in the
morning.

Crisp sunrise
Cleanness abounds
Rainbows's harmony on the
mountain slopes.
Smiles, fresh and wild, after the
chilling night in this city.

Jerry G. Boursell
HUNGER
Down cheeks of yellow
and brownish tones,
crystal clear such tears
roll away as drops,
to flow and fall
to hit the ground,
weeps a child all
wrapped in cloth.
Not shelter to hide
nor food of her own,
with stomach aching
and bulging beyond,
the pains increase
as weakness claims,
another such victim
to lie, and moan.

Lorraine Johnson
WHEN CHRIST WAS BORN
I had a dream the other night,
And in my dream my thoughts
took flight
Back to that first Christmas
night
When Christ was Born.

I saw a star shining on high,
Heard the faintest baby's cry,
Then a Mother's gentle sigh
When Christ was Born.

Came Wise Men Three, gifts to
bring
To the Child a promised King,
Angels in choir around Him
sing
When Christ was Born.

I slowly awakened from my

dream
Not wanting to leave the Holy
scene,
Made more aware what the
day would mean
When Christ was Born.

A Saviour for the world to know
On mankind His love to
bestow
To help us in His image
grow
When Christ was Born.

And when His birthday doth
appear
His coming will become quite
clear
If in our heart we do revere
When Christ was Born.

Marge J. Haun
YOU GAVE ME STRENGTH
There are times when I feel like
quiting,
Just hanging my head and crying
But then I look at you and,
You give me the strength to carry
on.
To say I'll keep going no matter
what.

There are times when nothing
seems possible anymore.
When life just seems like living
in hell.
But then I look at you and see
your smile and hear you say
"Mom".
Then I know that I must hold my
head high and fight back the
tears,
Because you give me the
strength,
a reason,
to
carry
on.

Hortense K. Lewis
THE BLUE SENTINEL
It was just an old blue stone
pitcher
That as a small boy he loved so
dear.
His mother kept it filled with
buttermilk
So very refreshing year after year.
Hair touseled, feet bare, down the
dusty road
Always he rushed home from
school
Thirsting for the sweet necter
The stone pitcher kept so cool.
Years later with a family of his
own
Along went the treasured pitcher
Bringing happy memories to his
home.
Filled with flowers it adorned the
hearth
It seemed to spill over with
sunshine
When friends gathered in joyous
mirth.
Then one sad day he left this life
As all mortals eventually do
'Twas then the old blue pitcher
Took on a task so loving and new.
As a sentinel it was placed on his
grave
Keeping flowers fresh and bright
This eased the pain, made one

feel brave.
There came a day a tragic thing
took place
Greedy hands reached out—took
away
The beloved old blue vase.
The faithful sentinel for a brief
time
Had brought solace to that heart
This small light faded, she sleeps
beside him
Never more will they be apart.

James Wyle Murray
SWEET DELIGHT
Flow gently undisturbed, in
prime,
An ardour pale and yet
sublime.
Tinged, undaunted, unabashed,
Frangrance sweetly, ever last.

Now bathe these senses,
permeate,
With each new scent to
captivate.
For we untrained and
unrehearsed,
Await enchanting second burst.

Intoxicated we become,
Sweet elixer, never done.
Deeper, deeper now I sleep,
Drinking in romance to keep.

What source provide this unseen
joy?
Is true to life or just cruel ploy?
Yet site unseen, I know its
source,
A muted sound, yet pungent
force.

Disguised in gold and red and
blue,
A planted seed, it proudly grew,
To extricate its godly smell,
Forever casting magic spell.

Cast one last word of this divine,
Its beauty is that it is thine.
For if this essence not to smell,
Its glory silenced, not to tell.

Rita T. McGrath
DAYTIME
The sun has come up
Again the night's washed away
The blue jay can sing

Tammy Anne Callahan
LOVE IS
[I wish to dedicate this poem to
my mother, Ruth Eleanor
Callahan, who taught me the
meaning of love.]
Love is a beautiful word that can
be described in many ways
Its—as delicate as a snowflake on
a wintery day
Its—a tear that drops from the
face of the one you love
Its—a miracle that came from
above.

Its—a gentle kiss
from someone in your life
Its—the special union
between a man and a wife

Its—laughter from a child
a smile of happiness
Its—helping a wounded animal
with care and tenderness

Love is in everything
Big or small

Its a wonderful feeling
That is in us all.

Allison Genelle Ball

Allison Genelle Ball
Last Will and Testament
When I die
I'll leave to the world
my life
scribbled on a crinkled page.
I'll leave to the world
a poem and a verse
depicting a lonely life's rage.
When I die
I'll leave to the world
a memory
of a young girl's salty smiles.
I'll leave to the world
a young child's travels
covering thousands of empty
miles.
When I die
I'll leave the world
but the world will never leave
me.

Joaquin C. Richardson
IF ONLY IF
[To all progressive people
working towards peace in our
society, especially to my wife,
Wilhemina, and the members
of the National Alliance
Against Racist & Political
Repression]
If only dreams could save us
From this life so difficult to drink
If only dreams were real
And reality an occasional
nightmare
Then sanity would not be a
snowflake
If only mushrooms were just food
to eat
And not the incessant clouds
Exploding across our mind's
screen
Then hope could take shape and
survive
If only if were not necessary
And trust not so fragile among
men
Then peace could be born
Not just aborted when
We cry to escape the world

Dr. Marion van Ronk
The End Of the Beginning
Where's the poem
I know that lies
In some small gyrus
Behind my eyes?
What will lure

The timid prize
And save the sin
"To plagiarize"?

I'll cast the fly—
Fling the bait
In careful ogee;
Quickly wait.
A deceptive strike
Makes me hate
My empty creel—
The novice's Fate.

Carlene Stinnette
WHAT DIVIDENDS?
I was a farmer's daughter.
He was a farmer's son.
The hail and inflation finally
won.
When money couldn't stretch
anymore,
Selling out was nothing to the
poor.

People think farmer's are rich,
You have to buy grain, chemicals,
and such.
This nation is for the farmer's, so
it says,
Everything plus inflation pays.

Though no one knows the truth,
Farmer's work hard and lose their
youth!

Kurt Clark Radtke
CREATIVE SENSITIVITY
[I would like to dedicate this
poem to Julie P., my family, all
of the people who have helped
and believed in me, and to God
for enlightening me with these
words of wisdom.]
Ink on lines, it sprawls, it flows,
words unending, soon to know,
every topic, large or small,
develop patterns; hear the call.
From time the thoughts, they
ramble on,
moments envisioned, then they're
gone.
Variation,
what a strength!
Couplets, sextets,
no matter length.
Years entombed; the keys of
minds,
unlock the dreams your soon to
find.
Born on wings of man's
invention,
hope to find the deep intention.
Others quick to criticize,
see it from a paupers' eyes.

Carolyn L. Kostrey
LIFE
Life can be fun, life can be gay,
life can be cruel and harsh
some may say.
Take away life's love, hopes and
desires,
and you take away mankinds
ambitious fires.
All the world around there's a
mixture of laughing and crying,
a blending of souls between
living and dying.
Life passes on minute by minute,
hour by hour,
taking its toll on the weak and
those without willpower.
For those who are brave, strong
and free,

life can be anything they make
it to be.

There are dreams,plans and hopes
for those who are young,
desiring a future with much
happiness to be sung.

There are only rememberances
and unfulfilled dreams for the
old,
waiting for life's breath to be
snuffed out like a fire in the
cold.

So live each day of life with a
smile,
and make the best of what life
offers and make it last for a
long while.

Linda Ekstrom
MY MEMORY FOR YOU

The day's not bright; the sun's all
alone;
The sky's not even blue;
Time passes and clouds roll away,
Like that of my memory for
you.

The air's not calm; leaves are
hurled
By a force that blocks my view;
It's all been blowing over and
over,
Like that of my memory for
you.

The grass laughs no more, but
shrieks 'neath my feet
As frost takes place of dew;
The lazy leaves on the trees fade
'way,
Like that of my memory for
you.

The ground's not still; it sways
'neath my feet
As serpents slither through;
Not just my feet, but my heart
moves on,
Like that of my memory for
you.

Marjorie Eskow Gillaspy
IRREVERENT HUMILITY

Love of life is really more
Than I had ever bargained for—
All I felt I really sought
Was one complete and noble
thought—
Unique in its entirety
Acclaimed by all humanity.
I didn't think the world could
shine
Without this special thought of
mine.
Sometimes I still ache
To find this noble thought—
You know, I think it came one
day
But I , unseeing, knew it not.
I guess it went away.

Alice Johnson
REVELATION CHAPTER 21

No ocean, a new sky
A new earth we see—
For the present earth and sky
Will never more be—

New Jerusalem—
Coming down to earth—
No sun, no moon
Splendid rebirth.

Crystal and pearls
Lit with God's glory

Revelation twenty—one
Will tell the whole story
1,500 miles foursquare
When I looked for the temple
It was not there.

Christ is the light—
And the temple the glory
You'll find that out
When you read the story.

Those whose names
In the lambs book are—
Will be gathered to the city
From near and from far.

No night, no pain—
All joy and peace
Flowing out of the throne
A river of ease!

Nancy Jean Weslager
SOLITUDE

The snow—clean and sparkling
With a diamond's blue light
Underneath the stars and
Full moon of mid—night—
Untouched as yet by any thing
Large or even very small.

Not a break in its surface;
And the trees stand very tall
With arms forever outstretched
To catch as many flakes as they
can—
The quiet undisturbed and deep
As the meaning of God to man.

Marie W. Russell
MY CROSS

Why is my cross so heavy?
So dark and rough and bare?
Hers is twined with rosebuds
And frangrance fills the air.
His is set with diamonds
And gold so fair to see.
Why is mine so heavy?
Could I but trade with thee?
But underneath those petals
Quite hidden from all view,
Were harsh and piercing thorns.
I would not trade with you!
Precious metals he must carry,
The gems and gold so fair,
Who knows how heavy they may
be,
Much more than I could bear.
So I'll carry my own cross,
Tho its ruggedness may soar.
My father knows the weight that
I can carry and how far!

Carole S. Zarefoss
COLOR BLIND
[To Don, my husband and best
friend]

I see your face in shades of grey
Passing through my mind
With vibrant colors everywhere
My heart is color blind
Sometimes I can't distinguish
Reality from dream
I see love in black and white
Or so it would seem
Why can't I just enjoy
What it is I see
When we meet through the day
And you're holding me
Why do I analize
This present situation
Instead I ought to be
Enjoying all creation
As you seem to always do
In moments as we take them

Be satisfied as you are
The best of times to make them
Hold me close and tell of love
How you'll come for me
Removing values in black
That only I can see

Chester A. Beck Jr.
TORRENTS

A veil of tiredness, drooping
Black shadows on the curtained
wall.
Ceiling sifting to the shelf;
While effervescent torrents
Riot in the rain,
And swirl upon the window pane.
Soft sickness of the soul;
Grey smoke that curls
And ebbs away.
Pale nothingness I drink,
And retch into the kitchen sink.
The microscopic motes I see
Are boulders of eternity.
Sinking fast into a mighty drain,
While God is tapping on the
window pane.

S. M. Toupin
WINTER OF LIFE
[This poem was inspired by,
and written in memory of, my
grandfather, the late Emile
Joseph Lamoureux. This poem
is for you Pepere, with all my
love and affection.]

God gave you life many years
ago,
The time to go is nearing.
Oh, how much you love life so,
Your wisdom is so endearing.

You led a good life—lots of hard
work,
You helped however you could.
Responsibilities you seldom
shirked,
God blessed you with a life
both long and good.

Children you were blessed with,
And friends to love for many
years.
You faced each day with strength
and good faith,
God was with you through
sorrow and tears.

God gave you life many years
ago,
The time to go is nearing.
You have had a full life, and so
Death you are now not fearing.

Deborah E. Conner
RUNNING TIME

The Young of me is the Core of
me.
The Joy of me is the Tall of me.

The Propriety you see is the
Wrinkled Bark;
It covers a Green Tree.
At the Heart of me is the Sap of
me;
It runs richly for those who
would cut deeply.

SAY IT
You can say it as you laugh
You can say it as you cry
Some I have been told say it
As they are about to die.

It's been said in a whisper
It's been said in a song

I want to hear you say it
I hope my wait isn't long.

I want to hear it in the morning
I want to hear it in the night
Echoes of "I love you"
When you're no where in sight.

Helen Brown Vendeville

Helen Brown Vendeville
**INTRUDER IN THE
PALACE**
[I hereby dedicate this poem to
the "Queen Elizabeth."—Most
sincerely, with my heart—felt
wishes. In behalf of her best
interest and happiness, always.]

The Queen, was in her bedroom
All tucked in for sleep—
When entered an unknown
visitor
Sneaking in, to speak and peep—
At her Magesty.
How brash and rude
He must be out of his mind—
But soon, the Maid came in
And then, —Off to the Dungeon
for him.—
Like the Scoundrel he was,—
Uninvited, inturding; 'twas
A different kind of whim

So soon would he find
This ten minute encounter,
Perhaps not as he originally
planned.
Where were the Guards?
Where was the KING—?
How did it happen—?
Didn't the doorbells ring—?
A Royal bit of Comedy
An amazing incident;—
Errors by chance, in the Palace
A Clown's wrong—doing—
No Prince with a Chalice.

As the curtain goes down
        On this play,
Certainly not Glory—meant,—
It's Critics and Press
To present added Stress;
        A Fagen was He—
Should be punished Severely,
But he will probably—get off free.
That's how it is, how it will be.
The Buckingham Palace in
"Pageantry"
Historic Times may come and go,
To be met—and—forget
As this Comedy Of Errors'
        Unhappy Event
Staged It's SHOW.
                THE END.

Dennis W. King
THE BUTTERFLY

Yellow wing—   * * ed beauty,
flying through   *   the blue sky,
    outlined in   *   black, soars
    a butterfly. * Looking for a
flower, to land * safely upon, to
drink its nectar * and then be
    gone. It lays * its little eggs.
upon the plant's * foilage, and soon
    they will hatch * into the baby
worm stage. They * must eat and
grow, then real * soon, they will
    stop, and   * spin a cocoon.
    Before you   * know it, it
will open to   the sky, and
    out will   come a new
    but—   terfly.

Belle Ader
HILLS

*[For Oran— One who still
walks beside me, though we
that live cannot hear his
footsteps.]*
The old hills ·esound with
    echoes
of forgotten sounds
Fallen leaves crackle,

Silent clouds swirl from the
    valley.
On the ridge, shadows
    that will not freeze.
Footsteps, treading on stone
The old hills echo with sound.

Helen Holub
WELCOME, SPRING!
Flowing rivulets of water course
    their way
        down into pavement cracks
and swell into pools of surging
    water
swirling down into drains at

street corners;
becoming favorite spots for
    small children
        to splash and splatter in.

Miniature buds begin to appear
    on naked
        tree limbs announcing
the approach of spring.
Winter's snow becomes shallow
    pools
cascading from rooftops and
    rushing
        to their rapid demise.

Dreary, ominous days of winter
    become brilliant
        expectant days of warmth
    and gaity,
white puffy clouds floating
    aimlessly in
        an azure blue sky.

Tiny green stems awaken from
    their winter's nap
and push through moist, rich
    earth
soon to blossom into floral
    buds
        in a profusion of rainbow
hues. . .
enriching God's earth·and the eye
of
    the beholder.

Springs of lilac buds wait
    tremulously to bloom,
scintillating the air with sweet
    fragrance.
        Ah, Spring, fairest of the fair
        with deep clean aroma and
            invigorating air. . .
        We welcome you!!

Linda Repucci
HELL FOR SUICIDES
Taught to be yourself,
but to conform in everyone's
    world.
Someone is always pointing their
    finger
'cause accusin' is beyter than
ignorance, they feel.
The limits hit.
One morning comes and you fall
to your deepest depth.
When it's over—you're a'victim'.
All the so—called know—it—alls
appear and look at you.
Feeling high and mighty,
they speak of you, but mostly
    about you,
saying, "You were lucky and
crazy for doing such a thing."
Even the priest judges you
    without
knowing you and refuses to bless
    you.
The subject is Taboo,
and they always wonder
who were you.

Marietherese Becker
RETURN TO SENDER
Seems, in heaven this year,
returns are bad,
For the babies that were never
    had.
Never getting to be born,
They never see their birthday
    morn.
Back up they come, before their
    time,

God sure thinks that its a crime.
As Return Clerk, I gave Lord
    some advice,
That these modern humans aren't
    too nice.
If they have the money and the
    time,
Allowing for cigarettes and wine,
If they can keep their super
    paying career,
They may just leave a baby there.
But if Baby doesn't fit in their life,
They'll sever him with an
    abortive knife.
And here they sit, from whence
    they came,
I tell you Lord, its a shame!
There must be something you
    can do,
They're playing God—and the
    joke's on you.
So come on Lord, you must be
    stern.
Mark the babies "No Return".

Lori Ann Moris
SOMEWHERE
You're goin' somewhere,
You're not quite sure.
You're leavin' now,
You're headin' out the door.
You're turnin' left,
You're turnin' right.
You're goin' somewhere,
You're gonna have to fight.

Julie A. LeFevre
A SPECIAL ROSE
A little blind boy, so gentle and
    bright,
asked me what a rose was like.
A tear rolled down my cheek as I
    realized,
"How do you explain a rose,
to a child with no eyes?"
But he looked so eager, so
    anxious to know,
I searched for the answer in the
    depths of my soul.
The answer came suddenly
in a very strange way . . .
A rose is the color of warm
    sunshine on a spring afternoon
or a melody sweetly sung in tune.
"You, are a rose, I said to him—
Unique and special. (He began to
    grin)
You are a rose soft as a white rose
    petal
with a face as pure and a spirit as
    gentle.
You are a rose with fragile beauty
that comes deep from within,
A 'Special' rose.
No thorns to protect you from
    careless passers by,
just a guardian angel watching
    you from the sky."

Lori Anne Del Toro
LOVE IS
        Love is a star
    Larger than the rest
        Love is so far
    For me, its on my crest

        Love is a sunset
    Glowing with pride
Then the mountains it met
And behind it, it disappears
        to hide

        Love is you

        Always full of fun
    But serious and true
    And not ever a con

Linda Gallo
COLORS
Colors blow in
the wind
mixed in the invisible
gust

Touching without fear
knowing without learning

Colors wash away
past the sandy shore
clumped together
with the embrace of cold water
running adjacent to its tranquil
    shores

Touching without fear
knowing without learning

Thomas A. Daly
TEMPTRESS OF LOVE
How coy the temptress of love
    can be,
As she charms her willing prey.
She spins a web that only others
    see,
As she takes his loneliness away.

How coy the temptress of love
    can be,
As she uses her men as toys.
She succeeds because they are
    too blind to see,
That they are not men but little
    boys.

How coy the temptress of love
    can be,
As she plucks away your heart.
She sits on a throne laughing at
    you,
As your whole world falls apart.

How coy the temptress of love
    can be,
As she lures you to a black hole.
How coy the temptress of love
    can be,
As she steals away with your
    soul.

Rene' Sanko
PAST DREAMS
Memories of days gone by
You seem to leave the world
    behind
Lost inside a magical dream
Where your fantasies rule
    supreme
I walked along a grassy path
Back to the days where I was glad
Where I saw my friends of old
Sitting on the grass surrounded
    with gold
Happiness because love was there
A boy with blue eyes and golden
    hair
But now he's gone and so are we
Because you see it was only my
    dream.

Sandra Tryon
AWARENESS OF YOU
*[To my Children, Mark and
Simona. Their beautiful love is
an inspiration to all. God bless
you always.]*
As the moon filtered softly
    through the trees,
Barren of their summer
    leaves,

205

And the water lapped gently
against the shore,
I was quietly enfolded into the
magic the night presented.
A hushed, mystical awareness
settled over me
As I breathed in the beauty of
this wonderment.
I turned to you and looked into
your eyes
And saw all these things reflected
there
    And more . . .
I saw all the love you held
for me
And my heart was captured
forever.

Eric Gutman
THE OLD COUPLE
I go to the hospital
every day
and stay
for hours.

I hold her hands
and say
nothing

Sometimes she smiles
and beguiles
me.

I go again and again
and then
the doctor comes . . .
he feels her pulse
there is nothing to say
and he goes away
then he sends me his bill.

For days, weeks and months
I go
til once
there is nothing more
for me to do.

Barbara L. Duerksen
LIFE WITH LOVE
When I live with you—
Life will be beautiful.
Mornings will awaken with a
smile.
I'll see your eyes light up
When I reach for you
And hold you for just a little while.
Our home will be filled
With the love that we share,
And our lives will be guarded
with joy.
And at night—
By the fire—
I'll tell you I love you.
And you'll see in my eyes that it's
true.
That from this day forever,
Everything that I have,
And my love—is meant only for
you.

Judy Johnson
HOMEBIRTH
    [To Parents, Calvin and Annie
    Johnson]
His ashen hang nail skin and
stubby chest hairs
Straggle my lips in the early dawn
Her pain spills in my ear
Now we crouch on the splintery
floor waiting
The knowing women comes
Sprinkling tepid water
Over a turgid belly and propped
thighs

Pungent cheesy scents revive
Moods before this waiting
Thoughts of soft acts in an open
room
When I experienced glides of
gleaming bodies
I sprawled near them
Their moist moments mixed
brackish
With our stale night breathing
Now his bloated body distends
with waiting
Pleated lips draw with her groans
Tiny sprints peirce beneath my
pallet
And bring early bloods
Last croons and bleeding scents
Bring us home again

Louise LeStrange Kennedy

Louise LeStrange Kennedy
SOULMATE
I'm not laughing today
Or crying, or worried or nervous;
But, I am alone with my
thoughts . . .
Feeling every feeling I lived
yesterday.

We touched the day together . . .
    You and I . . . .
Off somewhere away from the
noise
And people and demands of
society.

Alone . . . talking of yesteryears
And who we are today.
Only few can share such things
And appreciate the peace it brings.

Alone with only you . . .
In the darkness . . .
With rain splashing and dancing,
Feeling the potence of the night.

The intensity of being
With another, while he searches
The corners of his Heart . . .
And shares the hidden places.

Seeing the value of One Life.
A Man—among so many others
Who have lost touch
With the reality of Living!

Mrs. Emajean A. Hansen
I'LL BE HERE!
While waiting for my favorite
nurse, a thought was bothering
me,
    Would she like this
mischievous grin of mine, or
    leave me where I be?

I managed a smile as she entered,

but noticed her puzzled face,
"How are you?" she asked. "I'm
fine" I said, yet hoping for her
grace.

Our conversation focused on
desire; "just one more, then an
Eagle Scout",
Asked if I was sure of this?, but
deep inside, I had no doubt.

"It's going to be a community
project; to help the hospital, a
blood drive",
My goal of 100 donors, a bit high,
but in comparison, I'm still
alive.

The Chaplain gave his go-ahead,
and to be carried out at Ron's
bedside,
His favorite nurse was still in
shock, but Ron had no fears to
hide.

Had an important letter to write
and give; for all his friends to
see,
The need for blood was ever
great, hospital, others, not just
for me.

"My name is Ron, I'm here with a
rare cancer, determination; to
become an Eagle Scout,
Anything you do will be
appreciated, helping, that's
what this is all about".

Operation 'Eagle Scout' is moving
fast, and his classmates are
bounding in,
Progress reports look good to
Ron; 100, and still more donors,
Ron you win.

Request for immediate ceremony,
in auditorium, filled with
scouts and friends,
His mother pinned an Eagle Scout
medal on her son, while
courage and faith he lends.

At his home town a short time
later, many gathered, but not
for a time of cheer,
To pay a silent testimonial
tribute; to the one who said
"I'LL BE HERE!"

Joseph P. Kowacic
LIFE
Those little flirtings
on a morning
called spring,
when the year is young
and prone
to sing.

We wonder
whether they happened
to all,
when the year
has aged . . .
and turned
to fall.

Justina Horvath
LISTEN
I tried talking to you,
Only then realizing,
We were speaking different
languages.

Learning your language,
I tried talking to you.
Only then, I was using the wrong

words.

Learning the right words,
I tried talking to you.
Only then, I was using the wrong
meaning.

Learning the right meaning,
I tried talking to you.
Only now, I was discovering—

You had learned the right
meanings
To the right words
In the right language—

Without talking to me.

Victoria Theresa Morales
IS THIS JUST A DREAM?
There's a place in my mind,
I wish I could find,
A place of such beauty
Which no man has seen,
A place where I can be free and
mystic.

A place that is quiet,
With just the sound of birds
Singing and flying
Through a waterfall of herbs.

A place where the wind
Blows slow with a sound
Where the tree's sway forth
Wtih a rhythm very mild.
Where the waterfall falls,
Into a lake of crystal clear waters
Where the toads and the fish
swim
Without any bother.

A place where the air
Smells sweet as a flower
A place where my Love
And I can tower.
To lay in the grass,
So soft as cotton
And make precious love
In solitude well be
Is this just a dream . . . ?

Kathy S. Dennison
TOGETHER AGAIN
I remember when I first met you
Something special to me, you
knew
Setting here thinking how time
sure flew
Wishing I could buy back the
time with you

Don't know why he took you
away from me
You were so good for me
For only you, he knew I cared
To empty my heart, its so unfair

I'll never lose my love for you
No one will ever be in my heart,
but you
Because even though we are apart
I still know you're with me
I know I have to play my part

Right now I maybe free
Only for awhile until he takes me
But then we will be together
again.

Beverly Hendrickson
THE FOX
At times I fear that pride will be
The Fox that foils folks like me.

We strive to attain only to find
That for every success our
pathways wind

Up hazardous footpaths narrow
and steep,
Down into the gullies, dark
and deep.

Aye, the soul that succeeds must
also be
Quick to concede, else The Fox
will see

A ledge whence to seize its
unguarded foe,
And bring it to ruin, rejection
and woe.

Charlotte A. Westerfield
INNOCENCE
[To my beautiful daughter
Shelley]
A little girl,
Brings joy and love,
From early morn,
Til hours late.

I cannot compare, to any thing I
know,
The warmth I feel,
When she cuddles close,
Calls me Mom,
And kisses my nose.

A little girl,
Has such ways,
To take you back,
To more innocent days.

J.R. Kruizinga
SPRING OF LONG AGO
Recalling my grandfather's stories
of his youth,
I close my eyes and drift
back through time,
to a place that is quiet and
mellow.

It's a sunny, spring day and I'm
running through a field
with the old, winter's dead
leaves,
crunching under my bare feet.
Slowing to catch my breath, I can
feel the fresh air
blowing through my hair,
making me feel alive and free.

Then, gazing through the
brownish fields beyond,
I see that sprawling old, farm
house
as it sits in quiet solitude.
And in the field behind the
house, stands a huge oak tree,
with my grandfather's
favorite tire swing
still dangling from it's sagging
branches.

How peaceful it would feel, to
swing in that tire
hanging lazily from the tree
and try to touch the blue, sky
above me.
And then smelling the spring
scents that surround me,
I am completely lost in this
peaceful reverie
without a care in the world.

Georgie Hadley
A FRIEND
A Friend is a Friend
who stays in your heart.
A Friend is a Friend
even when you're apart.

A Friend is a Friend
who loves you for what you are.

A Friend is a Friend
who will always be a star.
A Friend is a Friend
who you can tell your deepest
thoughts.
A Friend is a Friend
that accepts you with your
faults.
A Friend is a Friend
who holds you when you cry.
A Friend is a Friend
who doesn't tell you lies.
A Friend is a Friend
who you'll always need.
A Friend is a Friend
and that's what you are to me.

Del Vina McCormick
IF
If i can stop one heart from
breaking
If i can ease one persons pain,
If i can stop one tear from falling
I'll not have lived my life in vain.

If i can cause one bit of laughter
or help to bring a little joy,
If i can bring a moments gladness
to one grown-up, girl or boy.

Lucy A. Kuttee
I CAN SEE
The wind blows sand in my eyes,
yet I can see.
I see the millions of galazies
still unexplored.
I see the beautiful sunsets
that have yet to be seen.
I see the tiny raindrops as
messengers from God.

The wind blows sand in my eyes,
yet I can see.
I see the earth as our home,
even if a temporary one.
I see the stars as tiny lights
guiding the way to an unfound
world.
I see Man and Woman
created in love and placed on
our earth to love and to
populate it.

The wind blows sand in my eyes,
yet I can see.
I see a troubled world which
yearns for peace.
I see few people willing to
trust and to share love.
I see the faults and facts of
life and
I see that the chance to keep
our world safe is within our
reach.

Christine Wacik
True Love Is Hard To Find
Love is hard to understand,
Until you find the perfect man.
You try to learn when you are
small,
What's best for you, so you won't
fall.
And as your love begins to grow,
There'll still be questions you
won't know.
And all the answers that you find,
Will change almost as fast as
time.
But when you finally think you're
sure,
You'll find that he's not there no

more.
It seems that if you take too long,
In finding out what's right or
wrong,
He'll walk away and disappear.
And that's the last of him you'll
hear.

C. Finlay
MY DAD
I'll miss you Dad, you know I
will, things just won't be the
same—but at last you're
young again and free of all
that pain.

I know you'd say, "Now, don't you
cry," but I guess I'm just not
strong—

You've always hated long Good-
byes, so I'll use your favorite
and just say,
"So long."

Susan Ann Montelius

Susan Ann Montelius
AN UNDERSTANDING
Words, continue flowing
Onto the paper below
Guide the pen upon the lines
To capture thoughts before they
go

The pen is faithful
Not once leaving the hand
Creating the images
My brain commands

Writing of things I know
Some, only others have seen
Keeping this illusive traveler
In touch with what has been

And though at times
My voice may fail
The words I long to say
Through my pen prevail

Hear what I long to say
Though I dare not speak
Travel with me through images
My pen helps me to keep

Judith A. Robinson
WHEN FEELING BLUE
When blue feelings come along
all else seems so wrong.

Then life is too much to take
and you dread each day
cause they won't go away.

You lose your drive and
fall out of stride
then everything looks dismal
so you're left crying inside

Sometimes we can't figure it out
and then we wonder what is
life really all about . . .

The feelings seem like they're
locked
within, not knowing where to go,
and with all the needless
worrying
you have nothing left to show.

But as life presents its self
each day and you join your
friends
at work and play, soon your
blue feelings will fade away.

Ms. Elizabeth Adams
FOR THE FIRST TIME . . .
[To my husband Howard and
my children, Howard, Charles
and Helen]
For the first time I Saw me.
For the first time I Care about me.
For the first time I Love me.
Because, for the first time I Saw,
Cared, and Loved You . . .

Hope M. Manna
PATHS
[To: Faith T. Naughright—
Thank-you for always staying
by my side]
Two separate individuals cross
each other's path
They meet, they talk
There is an immediate
understanding
Between the two lives
Although likeness is small
Difference draws them together
They learn that appearance
Is quite different from who we
really are

Stubborness breaks the
relationship
but understanding permits them
To deal with the flaws
They begin to grow with each
other
Soon there is a mutual respect
between the two
All of which is bad is cast aside
To make room for the good they
possess

They learn of the delicacy in life
and how important it is to have
someone care
They learn to accept the good
along with the bad
and the happy along with the
sorrows

They learn of life
They learn of love
No Longer are they two separate
individuals
But one of the same
Walking the path
Side by side
Calling each other friend

Evajo E. Rose
Spiritual Answers To Life
In life it seems
As if a futile battle stands
Anchored in this time.
In shaping souls of human
Beings.

But God be with us in
This fight, the path we
Take will be alright.

Many years ago destiny
Made her stand on these
Heroic ground.

The path our forefathers
Took were ordained by
Spiritual minds and hands.

If spiritual hands could
Create a man than why
Not obey God's commandments

The rise of time can be
So sobriety that
God is no longer a
Mystery but Spriitual
Answer to human needs
And plans.

Waneta Sue Beals

Waneta Sue Beals
AFFINITY
*[Dedicated to Theodore R.
Binder—"Would you like a pot
of hot tea!" "Yes!"]*
If ever I should wake
   from dreams
   to find you gone,
It would be difficult
   to find the faith
      to struggle on.
For every dream would
   be the same.

Although the sun
   shown bright,
My heart would wear
   a lonely shroude
      without a trace
         of light.

I'd be as one lost
   and adrift upon
      life's lonely sea,
Lacking in a reason why
   to show the way

for me.
Your tender smiles
   a beacon's glow,
Guiding all my days
   and bringing love
      to all my nights.

B & C Tracy
TO YOU, FROM ME
You sent me flying in the clouds
   above,
So to you I gave my love.
I shall never forget,
The way you made me feel.
For I thought it was so real.
I loved you then,
And I love you now.
To me you will always be,
The song in my heart,
When I'm alone in the dark.

John J. Hannigan
HEROES
Someone to look up to,
in desperate need of his hand;
erected gold-spun soldier . . .
who can carry throughout this
   land.

Can carry our problems,
   thoughts,
and sin.
Until this weight does do him in.

Yes, we erected the gold-spun
   soldier,
to lead us thru; for tomorrow is
   colder,
we all play heavily on his
   shoulder;
yes we erected the gold-spun
   soldier.

Too many ornaments on a glass
   shelf.
The soldier resembles a part of
   ourself.
We placed him up high for all to
   see.
We placed him up high so we
   could be free.

Only to fall; one day unexpected.
The gold-spun soldier, can never
   again be erected.

Karen Elaine Gustin
MAN IS A QUESTION
What's so bad about being
   nice to you?
What's so bad about being
   good?
My mind goes round and
round with this thought
and I wish I understood.
I want to be what you
want my love,
don't let your heart
grow cold.
Tell me of your love for
me and let your life unfold.

Martha Patch
My One Talent—Sharing
Here are some verses written by a
   woman, who sincerely wished
   to serve Jesus, but not so much
   as a "Widow's mite," to give to
   her master!
MY ONE TALENT—SHARING
I hid my face in shame one day,
   For I'd no Tithe for HIM;
Then gently opened mem'ry's door
   On mother's pantry, dim—

But there was only paper bags!
They filled a pantry shelf—
Then plainly Mother said to me
"We've apples, help yourself!
   There's plenty out there on the
      tree
   Enough for me, and you
Come! lets gather some!
   I'll bring a bag or two—
He'd answered me! Mom's paper
   bags!
   (I'd burned mine, all these years)
So then I shared, as Mother had—
   So humbly glad HE hears!

Helen Brown Vandervoort
MY MOTHER
*[I would like to dedicate this
poem in memory of my mother
who loved poetry and
encouraged me in my efforts to
write.]*
Through Memory's haze I see
   her—
My Mother, oh, so dear.
I seem to hear her gentle voice
And feel her presence near.
Her life was filled with endless
   toil
And self-concern was lost;
Her family's welfare was her goal,
She counted not the cost.
Her voice has long been silent,
Gone are the days we shared;
But the memories that I cherish
Tell me "Oh, how much she
   cared!"

Edmund D. Pizon
TERRY
[To "T" who awakened me!]
With downcast eyes she blushes,
Warm as a radiant rose!

Kathy Pongracic
TOGETHER
*[To Frank for the gifts of love
and growth.]*
Together we watched an eagle soar
   and the sky changed from
      blue to grey.
As one we walked in the desert
   sand
   and welcomed a brand new
      day.

We dreamt the dreams that
   lovers do
   and built castles in the air.
We slept the sleep that dreamers
   do,
   assured of the life we'd share.

We loved, we laughed, and raced
   with the wind.
   The pathway we walked was
      clear.
Then I stumbled, fell, and lost my
   way;
   I called but you couldn't
      hear.

Now alone I walk in the moonlit
   night
   and gaze at the stars above.
I remember those golden
   wondrous days
   and thrill again to our love.

For tho you left on that crisp
   Spring morn
   and never again shall we
      meet,
I am of you, and you of me—

For as long as our hearts
   shall beat.

Edith P. Hazlehurst
LISTEN
Listen to the little child;
Let him know you care.
When he needs your ear,
Be sure that you are there.
When he has a song for you,
Or a dance that's new,
Show that you're excited
And try to learn it too.

Children like to know
You consider it worth while
To stop for just a moment
And listen, with a smile.
After all, they're people,
And knowledgeable for their age.
We long to share our thinking
At almost any stage.

Leona Lusk Ferree
OLD IS BEAUTIFUL
*[Dedicated to the memory of
my husband of forty-six years,
J. Donald Ferree, who died Dec.,
1978]*
Not until the leaves are old
Do they flaunt their age,
And then with red and orange
   and gold
They blaze before our eyes
And make us notice them.
We who took their summer green
   for granted
Now drive for miles to see
The splendid spectacle of bush
   and tree.
Should we be vain enough
To think it is for us
They're putting on this grand
   review
The truth is they're taking
Leave of life as they have lived
Doing just what Nature
Meant for them to do.
Implanted in that little seed
However many years ago
Was everything the tree or leaves
Would ever need to know to
   color so.

Charles Edward Warden
**Father Ocean, Mother
   Earth**
He takes the water from the sea
   And forms the snow with purity;
And then He lets each crystal fall
   To clothe Her barren mountain
      walls.

And when Her April warmth is felt
   His crystal leaves of snow will
      melt;
The water leaves the mountain
   walls
   In icy flowing waterfalls.

The streams of water pure and
   clear,
   Flow down the earth and life
      appears,
With living colors paint Her land
   From rock to sea where He
      began.

Elizabeth Boucher
WHERE ARE THE TEARS?
Where are the tears?
Inside, they cry
Where no one can see
My pain, they lie.

But to the world
A smile I show.
So the world can't guess
So the world won't know.

How deep is the hurt
I feel inside?
Only my smile
My tears, will hide.

Better the world thinks
All is well.
Only my GOD above will know
My grief, my hell.

Where are the tears?
Inside they lie
Where no one can see.
Just let me cry.

Dee McGrew
MEMORIES
*[To my loving sons, John and
Raymond Poynor and
Grandchildren Peter, Christa,
Davie Baby . . .]*
The Memories still linger,
in my heart, and in my mind,
Of the happiness you brought me,
of the love you left behind
I wonder, what life might have
been—
had you lived to fulfill our
dreams,
I find myself old and alone now,
at least, that's how it
seems . . .
The way you would stand and
hold me,
my head upon your chest,
The strength of your mind and
body,
putting mine easily, to rest . . .
Your smile was so contagious,
and
your eyes would light up mine,
Your voice so deep and sturdy,
my love, my dear Valentine
I see your eyes before me, and
hear
your voice each day . . .
In the two loving sons, you gave
me,
No, you'll never be far

Juanita S. Barton
**Where Did the Days Of
Summer Go?**
Where did the lovely days of
summer go?
Will I turn around and next
find snow?
The flowers sprang up in the
month of May.
It seems to me like only
yesterday.
You came to me in the warmth of
July.
We pledged our love 'neath an
amber sky.
Our course was set, we traveled
far,
Then trimmed our mast, lest
we miss the bar.
How fast the days of our life
have flown.
Turn around again, and you
will be gone.
Has it really been that many years?
You've been with me through
smiles and tears.
So I ask now in the autumn's glow,
Where did the days of summer
go?

Laurie Glass
I LOVE YOU
I love the sound of your voice
When you're saying sweet things
to me
I love to hear your laugh,
Because I love to know you're
happy.

I love your honest green eyes,
Just the way they look at me.
I love the twinkle in your eyes
That says, "I know you love me."

I love your brown curly hair
That lies perfect strands around
your face.
I love to run my fingers through
it,
It gives me a feeling I can't quite
trace.

I love your smile, too,
Those gorgeous lips of yours.
And I love your kisses,
They seem to say, "I'm all yours."

This is only a poor attempt
To say what I really feel,
Because words just can't say
This special love for you—I feel.

Stan Hopton
MYTH
[For Elise]
Sensing
darkened clocks with
time run backwards on dust
covered mantels of faded dreams
I
see in clear,
rippled, runing wake
of love's promised waters a
ghostly sight, beyond trust,
in a frozen lake.
Your face, a myth,
and my fear
tensing.
Why?

Beatrice Ann Duda
I MET TWO
So different and yet both the
same
One be arrogant the other vain
Handsome a twinship that favors
them so
Clouding my mind with visions,
My thoughts drift afloat
Their smiles are the candles in
my closing eyes
Making dreams and fantasies
come alive
I met two and both I do like
One is my good friend, the other
my life

Don C. Richendrfer
HELP A FRIEND
A true friend is a helper
As we go along life's way—
When troubles come he'll be there
To comfort through the day.
In thought or deed, or somehow,
He'll lend a helping hand
When life's road is very rough
And we don't understand.

To be a friend when goings tough
And problems are unfurled—
To share a laugh or tear,
While going through this world,
With others who are burdened
down

Let's do some worthwhile deed—
To press their hand, or give a hug,
Or even share that need.

So, be a good, true, friend
Your feelings you can lend,
Or maybe you could shift that
load
To help them round the bend.

Kathy M. Terrill
THE QUESTIONS WHY
Thoughts go running through my
mind
Especially ones of you and I
The things we do and the reasons
Why?
Sometimes I know the answers
Other times I can't decide

I wonder if you do this too
Or is it just in me
To seek and find
The answers to all the questions
Why?

Mary Grace Carbone
**December 7—A Memorable
Day**
December 7—was always a
happy, joyous day. We'd get
together to celebrate a special
birthday: All the children,
grandchildren big and small
would go down, gather
around—one and all—

To Grandma—our Mom we all
had so much to say, eat plenty,
while we'd laugh and play.
Grandma would smile—as the
children chided—to say: "Time
to blow the candles—and
sing—'Happy Birthday'" We
were all so happy—felt so gay:

But one day December 7—forty
years ago—today News flashed:
'Pearl Harbor was bombed
today'. Hurt and shocked—the
party ended that way.

Mom—*dearest*—that was forty
years ago. You might not be
with us but yet you've never
left us. In our hearts, in our
minds—you are always there
with those treasured memories
we all share. Your children-two
have already joined you, the
older four pray for you. Your
grandchildren—have not
forgotten you. I, being your
second child and now the

oldest want you to know
Whatever I do—Wherever I
go—I miss you—and still love
you so: Today—once again—I
say: "Happy Birthday", To my
dearest Mom—Your daughter
Mary

Donna Ruth Auriemma
THE MUSTANG
Run proud mustang
Wild and free
Far into the hills and
Away from me.

For I am man
And though not foe
I somehow doubt
That you would know,

I come as a friend
Interested in your survival
As a dying breed
Who has no rival.

Your beauty and stamina
Down through the ages
Has endured nature's cruelties
And man's frequent rages.

Your numbers now
Grow far and few
With man's pursuit
Still on the move,

And yet one day
These men will tire
And your endurance
For survival

Will ensure you your place
In nature's plan,
Where in harmony with
Man you then will stand.

Cyndi (Jurey) Haysom
POETRY
You think you should read what
I write
I don't.
You think I should hand it over.
I won't.
I'll never let you know
never,
What is inside,
never.
For if you knew me, as I write
you'd only,
Think that I was covering all my
nights, and,
I'm not!

Anthony Tyrone Ferguson
WE PLEDGE
*[Upon my time when all of my
efforts were self-thought useless,
she came to me, my true
blessing. Forever grateful
Thank You—Priscilla]*
From our pearly skies of red,
white and blue.
Purple majesties and under our
flag of unrenounced,
Glorified alliance we give
our lives needily in
Patriotism,
Thru educational persuasion.

Without self-examination we
literally
Sanctify our country's worldly
eminence, patriotically
Worshipping it as the greatest.

We give our hearts and
souls under
The name sake of God and

in return,
Are classified in regards to each
Different—(not
individual)—though
Racial and social confinement.

For we pledge our lives without
consent nor self judgement just
so that in our ends we'll have
stated in penmanship upon our
spanning documents, he or she
was truly *A Patriot.*

Nina W. Kurkamp
THE OAK TREE
A seed was sown by me.
My hopes were such
Someday—right here
There may be, a beautiful tree.

Many environmental factors,
determine what we see.
There's sunshine, warmth, water
and fertility.
Care, too is essential, for the
growth of a tree.
Love and care helps to develop.

What a joy it is to see.
New leaves in springtime.
In fall seedlings scattering on the
ground
It evolves such wonder to me!

As the foliage thickens more
leaves are found
Twigs expand to boughs
Spreading out arms to weary
travelers
To frolicsome children, rest after
play.

Hush!! Did I hear a poet say
"A nest of robins in her hair"?
I, too come and rest there.
I reminisce from that day to this.

I've waited—I've watched
And now this.
Dear God! I thank you!
A tall stately oak tree!

"G"
UNKNOWN SECRET
*[To "M/B" You made it happen,
thank you, "Gail"]*
I finally know,
That which was hidden so ago.
Hidden as I came into being, to
be awakened by only one.
Every loving motion was beauty
in the making.
The secret of oneness
understood.
All the questions I've ever asked
my being,
All the wonders I've never
understood, only played the
part of.

We are each made to fit with
only one.
This explains it all.

Laurie Booher
SPIDER WALLS
My hand casts a four a.m. shadow
upon a
Spider dozing on my wall. I let
him sleep,
For I respect his Spider Dreams,
and
Because I have always shared my
walls with
Spiders: They are perpetual.

And when this four a.m. Spider
vanishes
To wherever Spiders vanish to,
another
Will appear (upon another wall
perhaps)
And they will all dream Spider
Dreams
at four a.m.

I confide in Spiders in four a.m.
shadows
And tell them all my silent
secrets; but
Still they dream upon the wall
Unmoved. So I remain caught in
the world's
Web, longing to join them in four
a.m.
Shadows, dreaming on Spider
Walls.

Grace Simon Ours
THE NURSE
[To my daughter Norma Jean]
Another life is fading out,
The record is completed.
The days and weeks you worked
are gone,
And cannot be repeated.

You bravely start in all anew
As fate cannot be blamed.
But a soul is being born today,
In place of one reclaimed.

New opportunities will come,
New people every day;
Some kind, some weary, some
alone,
You cheer and guide their way.

So much depends on you each day
As o'er the charts you view;
As other lives you may win or lose,
By what you say or do.

So may the good Lord give you
strength,
To always choose the right;
For you do bring the sunshine
To those who need the light.

Juanite White
ETCHED IN FLIGHT
Can you keep a sparkling drop of
dew,
Hold its beauty hard and fast.
Secure it for the future,
Like a jewel under glass?

Can you stay a glowing sunset
Make its velvet colors stay
Frame it like a painting,
Put it on display?

Will you bottle young loves fervor,

Ere it's lost in life's mad race?
Hold moments that you treasure,
Hide them in a timeless place?

O'no! The water rushes to the sea!
Youth bounds to maturity
Fervor to obscurity
Time runs to meet eternity!
What is left to wait with me?

The bright dew dries, the sunset
dies!
Old memories decay.
True love still glimers softly,
Like a lamp at close of day.
This transient life is etched in
flight
From our dawn to shadows dim
And though we grasp with all our
might
The flowing wings will fade from
sight
Beyond earth's finite rim!

Gerald M. Delaney
US
Gazing out the window,
I wonder,
What went wrong?
Many things—but mostly
Not enough time.
Time: taken for each other.
Time: taken for ourselves.
Very seldom just the two of us
alone,
Just by ourselves.
Now we are alone—each one of
us—alone
Let this not be the end.
We don't have to be alone.
Be with me, so together we can
drive away the sadness of being
alone.

Tib Lanham
MOLLY BEST
Polished by wind, rain and age
In the middle of waving yellow
wheat
Stands a glistening sandstone
tombstone.
Who were you, Molly Best,
That farmers abandoned their
compulsion
For strict-straight rows
And moved heavy clanking
tractors
Around you
All these years?

Carmen Encarnacion Ramirez
CARMEN
Carmen, Carmen—What a name!
Does it have any other fame
Does it describe the feelings that
I have
or the sadness that is so hard?
Can it say how I can love, hate or
die?
No it can't—nor will I!

For I am a little girl trapped
inside
I don't want to seem queer
but it's just my fear . . .
For love is beauty and lovely
things
which is why I am here
I don't want realities, nor the
truth of life
but the pink and pretty view
I have of it inside
of how a world can be!

So little girl if you please
Won't you come here next to me?
And I shall tell you of a girl
which is all full of silly twirls!
Her head is far beyond her soul
and she feels quite so old . . .
the world of pink just faded like
ink
and so did her heart sink!

For reality is growing up, and it
sure is a sting
it's sharp and fast and also harsh
but then again it's just like love.
So she's ready to give it a go and
maybe
who knows?
She might return or not at all
to that world of pink—but his
time
not to be shattered before her
eyes
For she'll be bloomed into a
woman
and not a child which used to see
everything
in such a gloom
Who couldn't see things bloom!

Kris Crawford
SOMETIMES
I think some days I would rather
be
A sailing 'cross a stormy sea,
Where warmth and breeze seem
to come
A definite blessing from the sun.

With motions rocking here and
there
A feeling that is very rare,
With little drops of water on
deck
And cool spray running down
your neck.

All of the knots are secure and
tight
The moon is appearing all shiny
and bright,
To think of your departure from
the quarreling seas
Is a feeling that could never
please.

Going to shore for your journey
is at end
Think over your thoughts, think
peaceful my friend,
Think of the breeze on the inland
shore
And you won't have to feel
lonesome anymore.

Marjorie C. Anguish
**"Our Americans"—I
Believe In "You"**
I believe God is in His heaven,
I believe in American Freedom,
I believe in miracles,
And, I believe in you!

I have faith in man's goodness,
I have faith in our children,
I have faith in those around us,
And, I have faith in you!

I am thankful for each day,
Whatever it may bring,
I am thankful for the flowers
And for every bird that sings.

I'm especially thankful for the
words—
"Let freedom always ring!"

And, I'm thankful for the doctor's
skill,
And a million other things!
Yes, I believe in Christ, who is
the
Spirit of our Christmas, and
I believe in Easter, and I believe
in Spring!
I believe in freedom and
compassion,
And learning for our young!
And, I believe God gives to some,
special talents,
And, he guides our surgeons's
hands,
I believe all these things work
together
to make the U.S.A., the best place
in the land!
So, when we Americans feel
defeated
And no victories seem to gain,
Or when the times are rough,
Or when we are filled with pain,
We'll just put our trust in Jesus,
And we'll soon be strong again!

John Wesley Holley
FROSTBITE
Death brushed my cheek
with an icy finger
and begged me linger
in the kingdom of her lacy gown.
Her soft, low voice cooed
Browning—
lines that fed my deepest
yearnings
with the burning of her desire;
My skin tingled with numbness
from her breath;
Her purity blinded;
I slowly warmed from her touch-
I was drowning
in her lap of soft, white, down.
"Frostbite!" echoed from the
nether,
hands reached out (loyal friends
came searching)
to free me from her frigid heart;
As they took me, she called after
reminding me of her patience
and that she'd be waiting . . .
waiting for my return
to her firm, earthen womb.

Terry Ellen West
ETERNAL SUNSHINE
*[To all the sunshines in my life,
especially Laura, Brady and
Danny. Thank-you Mom and
Dad for showing me the way.
Ken, Brenda, Jill, T.J. and Kurt—
shine on, I love you guys.]*
Eternal sunshine
Love a lifetime
Golden dreams
A silken web of extremes
Two hearts together
Our love is forever.

Elfrieda Evelyn Burkett
**An Aurora Borealis Of
Stars**
A star fell out of the sky and
smiled at me—
It was like a million diamonds
and sequins plummeting
downward like a flash of
lightning over the city—
Yearning for earth men and
woman to sing praises of her

sparkle and brilliance.
Dazzling, splashing, shimmering,
like Broadway lights, on and
off—
These Austrian Crystals can be
brought right into your room
with the telescopic lens.
Like needlepoint, the star dots
the endless tapestry we call the
sky.
Flashing, dancing, flirting,
captivating the naked eye—
She holds the planets, sun and
the moon in her gaze
spellbound—
All hail to you! forever our
eternal ageless star—
May you always flash your
kaleidoscopic electronic beauty
from afar.

Kathleen M. Vejveda

Kathleen M. Vejveda
FOR DAD
When all the well-wishers have
gone on
their way,
Leaving behind a kind word
I sit by myself in a room now
of memories
My grief in the darkness unheard.

A breeze stirs the curtain,
How long has it been?
My mind knows no step of the
time
or of when
I first felt the lingering fever
of emptiness,
anguish and pain.

I fix my eyes on your chair,
Where not long ago you sat
speaking to me
Who thought that you would
always
be there,
Always to hear, forever to see.

And so as I sit here
With no tears left to cry,
No prayers left to say
And can no longer ask way,
I seem to be waiting for that
morning light
Which will signal the end of
my long, fearsome night.

I can believe that the one
whom I watched
Fading away in that hospital
room
Has drawn his last peaceful
breath,

But the father I love
Can never die
Because love is much stronger
than death.

Amber Denise Borcherdt
BEGIN
There are so many words unwritten,
So many pleasures to live,
So many things, are waiting for us,
Are waiting for us to begin.

There are so many joys in this
world
For the beautiful beings within.
To share,
To love,
To care,
And also to . . .
Begin!

Ellen E. Shannon
GOLDBLOOD
I reached with my hand.
when I saw it again it was
blood-red:
the pain seared to my fingertips
ignited my palms
twined through my veins
till it touched my heart,
inflamed my eyes and
for a moment,
my own blood ran gold . . .

As I look now
I see only wild sunbursts
and feel a dull burning in my
throat;

But in the midst of white tears
as my senses soar in burnished
agony,
I know that
I have touched the sun.

Anne Cambria
HAMMOCK
Oh to be tangled
free in that web of rope strung
between the two trees.

Stella Kennedy
REPERCUSSIONS
One day I thought, as I set out to
roam,
I'll go and see my married
daughter's home;
And see what I can quietly
discern
Before the seasons take another
turn.

So off I went and coming to the
door,
Beheld my grandson (he's a little
boy of four)
He ran to meet me with a smile
and hug;
We watched him later playing
with his toys on the rug.

Each little nook seemed filled
with shimmering graces;
An etching framed in friendly
smiling faces.
Such joyful greetings from a
warmth of heart,
While pictures of a faith she
learned in childhood proved
her art.

I found within my grownup
child's domain
An echo of my own remote
refrain
And holding sleepy Michael

on my knee
Thought how I'd come to be a
part of his sweet revery.

Lynn Trudell
PRAYER
Dear Lord, help me be
What I so want to be
Not alone and afraid
But together with thee
To live in this world
To suffer the pain
Please help me endure
I want to remain
A part of this life
And make it the best.
Yet, what can I do?
I'm only a guest
On this planet called Earth
Where anything can be
If I work hard enough
In the end I'll be free.
Tomorrow I know
That I'll ask you again
To help me be me.
I'll need it. Amen.

Jennifer Joyce Johnson
A 'LOT' TO REMEMBER
*[This poem was written for my
sons George Jr. and Antonio
Fernando and special thanks to
my Mother LaVera who
inspired me]*
It's all so funny how we all seem
to forget
Those little things that we once
met
Things that might not seem to be
a lot
But those are the things we
shouldn't have forgot
Because we all got
"A 'LOT' TO REMEMBER"
Those things that might seem
worthless at a time
Are the most interesting things
that should stay
in our minds
"A 'LOT' TO REMEMBER"
Is sometimes hard to do
But there comes a time when we
do

Mary K. Horak
MOTHER AND SON
I remember her slow and
measured pace,
Her sweet and smiling face,
Many winters she has seen
A life time of suffering and care
Many years that were quite lean
A part of her I could not share,
The kind sweet face I knew so
well
Held a secret hurt, she would not
tell,
I always felt within my very bone
That she was very much alone.
Even if I live a hundred years
I will never understand the
hidden tears
The heartbreak, only she could
feel
To me it never seemed quite real
The times I saw her pray on her
knees,
For a child she lost over seas
Many times she must have cried
Holding back the tears inside.
I was too young to know such
pain,

To have a son and to lose him again,
Not to be able to plant a rose
Or to light a candle,
And watch as it glows
A beam of light against the stone
That tells "my Son lies here alone"
Sometimes in the evening breeze
I think of her son lying somewhere over seas,
Sometimes when I go to sleep it seems,
I can see her smiling in my dreams.

Vick H. Jenkins
WINTER
[To Suzan and Jackie, the Winters we were apart, and the ones to come.]
Outside the bare trees are swaying
in the brisk, winter wind,
Blue and purple clouds are moving across the darkening sky,
Small icy droplets of rain are collecting
in freezing, clear puddles,
All is Quiet except for the howling, crisp wind,
The WIND!
OR is it the trees?
Moaning as the freezing wind bites into its naked branches,
Pulling away the last remaining leaves
to lie frozen upon the cold, damp earth.

Amy F. Campbell
TO JASON
When you come, I run to hold you
As your arms reach out to me;
And the love that you bring with you
Makes my dreams reality.
Then the things we do together
Make the world a brighter place;
And the sweetest gift you bring me
Is your precious smiling face.
When you leave, the house seems empty;
But my heart retains its joy.
I have found a bit of heaven
With a special little boy.
            Love,
            Grandma

Helen Fisher Trehey
LOVE OF CHRISTMAS
Silver moonlight on the snow
Children's faces all aglow
Sleigh bells tinkling here and there,
Merry Christmas everywhere!

Postmen whistling 'neath their load
Cards and gifts cross o'er each code.
Doorbells ringing night and day
Kinfolks coming from away.

Shouts of joy beneath the tree
Children laugh, so full of glee.
All who feast become aware
Belts and girdles are too spare.

Guests go home, but kinfolks stay
Talking o'er the holiday.

While they watch the tree so fair
Night has come, the day doth wear.

The First Christmas of the Babe
Early born that ancient morn
Angels sang their joyous song
Shepherds came and wondered long.

All who now look at the sky
Really know the reason why
Sparkling stars still sheen their light
Sing they, of that Blessed Night.

Janet Colburn Ainsworth
DAILY PRAYER
[For my mother, Virginia Bahrs, who showed us how to work hard but not miss the lovely things around us.]
Lord, slow me down and let me see
The beauty that's surrounding me:

The clever chipmunk running fast,
The placid groundhog rumbling past;

Bright birds of red and gold and blue,
Soft flowers all a-drip with dew.

In lake and forest, hare and deer,
We see Your promise written clear.

Where'er we go, whate'er we do,
We're wrapped in beauty made by You.

Rebecca Marie Glaha
SMOKE RINGS
Fluid smoke rings
Reaching the ceiling high
Like dancers . . . they float
Up towards the open skylight
As white cotten appears
Showing roads towards the sun
The smoke rings stretch . . .
Airy rubber bands
Bending with the gentle wind
That soon grows stronger
As the dance begins to end
Smoke rings in the sky
Trying to reach the yellow sun
But the breeze drove them away
Towards the open sea . . .
While a dream goes on

Annette Cunningham
Tides Of Mixed Emotions
All alone and so blue,
    just like the ocean tides that come ashore,
    then fade with the undercurrent back to nowhere.
Back and forth,
    to and fro,
    just the same old place and same old feeling,
    no place to go.

Wild with emotions that cannot be explained.
Something that reaches out but cannot seem to grasp
    that which is so desired.
A tide breaks and you think you have won,
    but just then a current carries it away from you.

There is always a dream and a chance of hopping on
    the right tide and drifting off to everlasting
    happiness in the depths of life.
Maybe it will be only a day or a week or a year,
    but there is no escape of the tides of mixed emotions.

Martha E. Fuqua
FOREVER GONE
[To: Candace Fuqua Reaves, My Daughter, Who Always Believes in Her Dreams.]
I came
And you were doubtful

I came
But you were fearful

I came again
Realism barred the door

Faith begged
But had strength no more

I'm sorry
True, I can come no more.

            Signed—Your Dream

Elizabeth P. Richards
NOW
It's wonderful to be,
sixty-two and free!
Free from kids, dogs, and cats,
from gutters, leaves, and that's
not all. Never again will I have to cope,
with kids' curfews, cars and dope!
None the less, I miss a man,
to take and squeeze my hand.

Jenne Riendeau
SUMMER STORM
Treasures found along the seashore and yet worthless to your soul
So run past the cave till you fall to your destruction
Sing out your sad songs of pity till it deafens the angel's harp
Caress the waves with your feelings and continue your search
for satisfaction.
The wise men come your way no more
Your bones will rot on that same seashore
Cry to your maker, sob and bend
Then empty your heart into the wind.

Confessions of your past desires

You feel the heat of the sun's great fire
You run once again in the opposite direction
The lights flash before you, you're ashamed of your reflection
Mary no longer stands by your side
The ass now laughs and you run and hide
Cry to your maker, follow your star
Then empty your heart and see what you are.

Margaret Anne Cardiff
AQUARIAN SUNRISE
Silent morning stretches over the sea
As since before I came—a moment ago
Heavy air in dark clouds frames a shining glow
Flapping waves and crinkling sound of foam.
The Orb glitters and pours on the mirror of water
A glistening gold light to narrow my eyes
I pad the sand, softly moist,
Leaving my print behind.
Clear the new day for this moment!
This quiet peace, an example from Heaven
Observe, absorb and meditate
Muffled gulls tell it, the sea reverberates
I know by the calm the lesson it teaches:
I, like my footprints will fade.
Accepting the thought, my sighs meet the sea . . .
            and vanish away.

Irma M. Varnell
NIGHT
The shades of night are falling—
On the horizon a rosy glow.
Majestic mountains rise,
Purple hues and gold.
Now the Master artist
Has laid aside His brush—
He has painted an awesome splendor,
Using shadows, clouds and dust.
The sun's last rays have vanished.
Night has come.

J. Farrell Griffin
HOUSE INTO HOME
The windows are washed, and the curtains strung,
The walls are painted and the pictures hung,
The brass is polished and the furniture installed,
The rent is paid, and callers have called.
Yes, our nest is feathered, but not so much,
Till our threshold beckons your woman's touch.

Regina Golden
KEEPSAKE
"Package, Ma'm, Sign here,"
The air seemed cold and clear.
I left the package on the floor,
signed, and closed the door,
then saw my mother's script
and eagerly the wrapping ripped.

There was a simple note
pinned to a petticoat,
a linen coat and dress,—
my baby things, I'd guess.
Keepsakes she sent to me
for reasons only she
and I could know.

So very long ago
She made each satin stitch
to make the fabric rich.
I had not thought till now
that she had told me how
when asked, "How did you find
time?" (and brought to mind,
with children two and four,
and farm work, furthermore,
she sewed yet for a third.)

To her it seemed absurd
to waste a simple jot
of time. "I sat a lot,"
she said, "I felt so bad."

Rose Tideman
FOR MY CHRISTMAS
I ask for no expensive gifts
or baubles to adorn me
as we adorn a Christmas tree.
I long for no material things—
no thing which weights me down
with constant care and worry.
But I ask of you a precious gift
which no where can be bought—
which no human hands have
wrought.
Just give me for all your time,
your truest love,
Your kindest thought, your
tenderest word,
Your extended hand;
And whether you are near or far
Let me feel the warmth of your
presence;—
These I ask for my Christmas
presents.

Grace Marie Ramos
TOMORROW'S CHILD
Tiny one inside of me
Stored only in my memory,
Merry Christmas to thee
The one that pleases me.
My hope for tomorrow
I rest with thee.
I hope someday you'll come to be
More than just a thought of mine.
But my legacy of love
That I'll leave when I'm gone.
For a part of me will live in you
The love that I gave to you
The knowledge that we shared
Knowing just how much I cared.
A love for people, a friendly
smile,
Taking the time for things
worthwhile,
Trusting in God and believing in
you
Whoever you may be.
Merry Christmas little one.
I love thee.

Ross E. Ritchie
FREE SPIRIT
She's a free spirit
waving with the grass
flying with the dove
She'll touch you with a glance
and embrace you with a smile
She's a free spirit
like a baby bird you wish to hold
but you know needs to be free

to survive
She's a free spirit
you wish to play a part
to have meaning
but you're only a pebble on her
beach
a moment in time
a breeze in the wind
She's a free spirit
could she only realize
you don't wish to chain her down
but to sail with her in the wind
to touch the bright star
to move among the clouds
She's a free spirit
and you can't help but love her

Marie H. Jacobsen
QUIET MAGIC
Below
Grey calloused clouds
Brown frozen earth turns white
When soft like falling petals
snow
Decends.

Elsie M.G. Miller

Elsie M.G. Miller
**The Green Days Have
Come**
And now the sunshine fills the
valley trough
With light, dusting the willow-
sprays with gold.
The hillside shrubs are tipped
with creamy froth
As ripe buds rend and scented
blooms unfold.

The green days have a clear and
lambent glow
Bright emeralds plucked from
winter's clasping dark.
Fresh leaves in varnished green
appear, and flow

With gay exuberance o'er
boughs so lately stark.

The pulsing hours troop by in
rhythmic singing,
And dawn comes softly, with a
quiet stealth.
What heart could keep its joy
from spilling?
What purse could hold this
precious wealth?

Carol Heffner Orr
WRITER'S LAMENT
Nought can match the human
mind
It conjurs up such finds,
"Frodo lives," from Tolkien came,
Then there's Disney's quacking
Duck,
"Of all the rotten luck."
I could have done as well as they
If they hadn't done it first.
It could have been my "Golly
Gee,"
That came from Superman.
Whose bubble would have burst
If I'd birthed Peter Pan?
It seemed that art had called a
halt
Then—one bright shining mind
stood tall,
And gave the world E.T.

Ella Foster O'Brien
I'VE GOT A SONG TO SING
I've a song in my mind
As I ride down the road,
And my sky is alight with the stars
A Christmas Carol I need to
sing
For peace in this world of ours

I've got a song, I've got a song
And tomorrow I'll do my thing!
O'er all the world we'll spread our
love
'Cause I've got a song to sing.

I've a song in my heart
And a wish that Christmas
brings,
Joy to the world, peace to home
And a Christmas song to sing.

Brenda Marguerite Martin
EACH TIME I SEE YOU
[To my loving husband, Larry,
who inspired me, and whose
support made this possible.]
I fall in love with you all over
again,
Each Time I See You.

The love and the passion show in
your eyes,
Each Time I See You.

To love you is to live, to live
with you is to love, and I know
this,
Each Time I See You.

You put me on a pedestal, treat
me like a queen, and call me
your baby,
Each Time I See You.

You are my love and my life, and
I will show you,
Each Time I See You.

My love is stronger today than
the day before,
My love is less today than it will
be the next day,

And the love I feel now grows
deep in my heart,
Each Time I See You.

Why must I call you each
moment to tell you how much
I love you?
Why must I tell you how much I
miss you when we are apart?
The answer, my love, is not
wanting to wait until,
Each Time I See You.

I love you, my darling, and I want
to show you, and you will
know it,
Each Time I See You.

Ronn Self
A TIME TO LEARN
[To Elizabeth Marie, a woman
of wonderous quality & love]
Take my hand—be my friend,
and I'll show you things
unknown, for there are so few
left to know . . .
A running brook, crystal cool
waters, flowing for miles—the
beauty of untamed virgin life.

Yes, you've been gone too long
my friend, stone structures,
faceless people and new cities
have taken me from your view.
Pierced your life with
ugliness...and now you stand,
wondering...loss has crept into
your life.

You, your children, and your
friends have suffered, lost
yourself to shame and
envy...hatred, blind to your
actions...you've destroyed your
needs, severed the cord of life—
killed yourself with time spent.

Now, my substance brings forth
no more, for I am dying...the
streams which nursed my
thirst are standing with poison,
my trees have long been felled
and the flowers cry for needs I
no longer can give...My friend, I
am your dying land, I have
spent myself for you, and now I
stand naked to your eyes
. . .crying, trying to tell you—
you've lost, lost forever my gift
to you...but your ears remain
deaf, your eyes blind, yet time
continues, even in the death of
man. Our universe is ageless,
and I will return again to
blossom and give beauty once
more, though I will be
saddened...for no one will ever
see, only me.

And they never learned...

Mary Olmsted Graham
What Is That In Your Hand
A book? Oh no, a Bible—
You're dusting it perhaps,
A treasured family keepsake,
Or your own road of life map?

One you use daily
To guide your way.
One that instructs you
To read and to pray.

For how else with God
Can you communicate;
His promise tells us

Of Heaven so great.

He bids us to witness
And labor each day,
With those lost souls
We meet on our way.

That cup of cold water
You hold in your hand
Is it for refreshment
Or for His command?

If we give it
To the stranger at our gate
We have given it to our Saviour,
On whose coming we wait.

Now let us take heed
All over this land
And carefully notice
What we have in our hand!

Dori M. Foster
A MEETING
[To my daughter, Linda Mae,
whose constant devotion
inspired in me a continuing
pursuit to write. Also, a
memento to the memory of my
loving son, Lanse Brinton.]
I was pulled through the hall of
sorrow,
And dragged into the room of
despair;
I felt the ache in my heavy heart,
Then, suddenly, I saw you there.

You lifted me up from my knees,
Embraced me with your kind
smile;
My trembling ceased as you held
me,
Transported by your strength,
awhile.

Your tenderness fused through
my being,
And raised my hopes to the sun;
Your caring, patience and sharing,
Were my armor now, life had
begun.

The shackles of fear started
waning,
The cloak of pain slid to the
floor;
As a comfort surged through all
of me,
And I thought, never more, never
more.

Gail O. Wilson
Time Now For This To Be
The key turns easily in the lock,
as I open the door, I hear the
clock
chiming on the hour.
The house is cool and dark and
Oh, so very still.
What is different? It feels so
strange,
it's something odd, I really can't
explain.
It is quiet—That's it!
I expected to hear a guitar
twanging,
or at the very least, dishes
banging
around as he clatters in the
kitchen.
No dirty sox on the floor
or bathroom towels hanging on
the door.

What has changed, you see,
is very hard to accept, yet had to be.

My firstborn son, no longer at
home,
is now a man and out on his own.
I feared this day would come
and I hoped I could be as strong
and as sure as he seemed to be.
I tried in every way I knew
to be a good mother and a friend
too.
We had our differences, oft times,
not a few,
Arguments and loud words
sometimes flew.
The love was always there, oh so
true,
from me I know and I think from
him too.
As time goes by and we change
and grow
our love will be stronger, this I
know.
So, when I open my door and the
stillness cries out,
I feel strange, yet want to shout,
"It's time now for this to be."
And I'm happy and joyful and
glad to know,
from this day on our friendship
can flourish and grow.

Frank Hause
CHILDRENS CHRISTMAS
C Children, everywhere are
   waiting
H Happily they skip and play;
R Running errands for their
   elders
I In preparing for this Christmas
   day.
S So many little things to do
T To make their Christmas filled
   with joy.
M Many days of thoughtful
   planning,
A Also buying small gifts of
   pleasure
S Secretly for each little girl and
   boy.
D Debating on this and buying
   that,
A And decorating each gift in
   Christmas wrappings,
Y You hide them in the attic, or
   an overturned vat.
G Gone are the days of the wild
   turkey,
R Running over paths our
   forefathers trod;
E Each one now being raised
   most domestically,
E Ever so carefully handled, fed
   on seeded sod.
T There are but few days in
   biding now
I In preparing fruit-cakes we like
   to eat;
N Nuts, candy, pies, salads, and
   all—
G GOD, we thank you for this
   treat.

Toni (Walden) Freemyers
REMEMBERING ME
I don't want to end up
As the last piece of glass
In that line-up of bitter empties
On your window sill—
There for all the world
To look through
When you're finished
With them.

Nor do I want to be
One of those occasional thoughts
Which pass across your eyes
With the wondering and sorrow
Of the past,
When you tell some future
woman
About me.
If I am to be in your retrospect at
all,
I'd at least like to belong
As one of those who was,
But I'd rather be a face print on
your towel,
A lip print on your cup,
A wrinkle in your bed,
Or never cross your mind at all.

Alta

Alta
MY RETURN
I know not the wicked womans
wiles,
But you did light upon my smiles,
It's candoured passing, fleeting
while.

I pretend no illusions of loves
faint quest,
I only passed to love what's best,
That dear sweet saint was my
request!

And so from sleep I assuredly
call,
Elated memories from past recall,
In dreams illustriously enthralled!

I am the maiden of the eternal
moor,
It's heather once I was not sure,
The fear subsides, my loves
endured.

My name is forgotten, long bereft,
From that stage I sorrowfully left,
Let not your ear be stoned or
deaf?

Jim Stevens
**Faded Ribbons and Wilted
Flowers**
A small white church in the
meadow
A faded ribbon on the ground
Beside the stone bearing
mommas name
There are wilted flowers all
around

Many days have passed and gone
Many memories stay inside
My heart aches to see momma
As she looked in days gone by

A white cross protects momma

By the stone with marble frame
At night Lord when it's lonesome
I hear angels speak her name

There are daisies in the meadow
Pretty flowers in the field
White clouds in the heavens
Paint a picture how momma lived

There's a light up in heaven
Shining softly on her stone
God sprinkles bits of stardust
On her name from up above

Faded ribbons and wilted flowers
Aren't all that's left behind
I still have all the memories
Of my momma in days gone by

Maro Rosenfeld
california
and there was fog
and there was smog
and there was sun
and there was fun

and there were trees
but nair a breeze

and there was cancer in the sky
the horizon of nitrogen cut your
eyes

and there was San Onofre
the end

Aldon Joyes
IF EVER THERE WAS
If ever there was
A time of peace
If ever there was
Pure joy
If ever the hours
Rolled softly by
It was when we were one

If ever there was
A sunny sky
If ever the world
Was kind
If ever there was
A time like this
It was when we were one

Marijane G. Ricketts
OCTOBER PAINTING . . .
Could I fall's colors
   feel in my fingers
   would I give you October
burning forever blue-gold:
   the tilted sun
   the hum of little things
   and dried seed pods
   spinning silken fibres
   in abandoned grasses;
   the orange moon tethered to
earth
   as loath to leave
October sky as I
reluctant am
   to push our love past summer.

Paul John Moran
AWAKENING
[For all those parents
throughout the world who had
the human decency to allow
their children to be born and
experience living.]
Total darkness
A hearts gentle beat
The world outside
I'm soon to meet

Safe inside
Of my own world
Into confusion
I am hurled

My mother I see
Her tears of joy
She holds me close
Her little boy

Light engulfs me
As faces stare
This miracle of life
Is ours to share

Now I start the journey
With life bestowed in me
I must travel this rugged road
For it was meant to be

Lee Canvasser
Rresponse To An Erudite
Go with the lens of my camera.
    Look—no longer is the Black
    Hole in the sky.
    With much misgiving, a heavy
    heart,
    I approached the vast abyss
    to do whatever I must do.

I bid farewell
    to 'sweetness and goodness'
    I bid farewell to 'honor bright!',
    as gleefully, I toss
    all of them, over the side.

Come, Zelda, my spiney
    porcupine,
    my downright ornery pet,
    come—let us find
    delectable sorrow and pain.

Wait—I hear something
    from the bottomless pit.
    A squeak, a buzz, a cry?
    What? Professor, who?

Oh my! No way can I help.
    I've thrown sweetness and
    goodness away.
    But I'll tell you what I'll do.
    So you'll not be alone,
    I'm sending Zelda,
    my darling, spiney porcupine,
    over the side
    just to be with you.

William E. Cowee
THE MARBLE
Nestled in the grass
it watches me with a green eye;
a sparkle in the sun's rays,
jumping for attention
when the mower rolls over it.
The marble survives our divorce
well,
because it remembers the good
life.

Plucked from a cigar box,
it sped down long ramps of hot—
    wheel roadways,

did space leaps and loop—the—
    loops,
performing to the giggling
    pleasure
fo my three imaginative sons.
It cargoed in dented dump trucks,
carromed from nails in
    homemade pinball machines,
and, perhaps, napped in the moist
    darkness
of a two year old's mouth.
Now it longs for a caressing
    knuckle
and a little boy's smile of
    discovery.

I will not disturb its lonely vigil,
except for a silent nodding
    acknowledgement.
The marble is my mute
    companion,
for we share . . . wait . . . survive
for that magic moment of
    discovery
when a bright—eyed child
returns us to the good life . . .
    and togetherness.

Ullah
BROTHER STAR
Star first
Star bright
Make my will
My all, my might

To give my soul
To beauty bare
And
Cast my spirit through
The air

To see the sounds
Of spirits fly
And
Smell colors of
Soul go by

And if by chance
You
Add some time
I will receive
Life's
Double line

Mary L. Cissell
OLD EMPTY SHOP
[I dedicate this poem to my
father—The old Black—Smith,
and the shop where he worked
in days goneby.]
The old black—smith shop
    stands empty and forlorn.
It's grey boards, crumbling,
    weather—worn.
Tall grass grows up round the door.
Thru' widening cracks, sunlight
    slants,
like ghostly beacons from the
    past,
across the hard packed floor.
Listen! Can you hear that far
    away din,
of anvil ringing from within?
Hear the wind from out the
    bellows roar,
watch as gray smoke settles o'er,
the sagging, mossy shingled roof.
See! The fire begin to burn.
Step inside and see the smith
    turn,
iron shoes to fit the horses hoof.
See the hot iron held in the tong,
grasped by a brown hand, hard
    and strong.

With measured beat and ringing
    tap
he fashions tools from a piece of
    scrap.
Here hung drill over bench,
where lay hammer, bolt and
    wrench.
Nails and paint, high on a shelf,
where the brown wren hid
    herself.
Here were the kegs where cronies
    sat
To talk awhile of this and that.
Beside the forge the old tub
    stands,
with water dank and cool.
Waiting while time's shifting
    sands,
drink up it's darkened pool.
The anvil sound rings out no
    more,
and shadows move across the
    floor.
Empty, the shop stands, midst
    slow decay.
The old black—smith has moved
    far away.

Ana A. Gil
MOTHER AND SON
[To my grandparents]
Now my wrinkled eyes have been
    acquainted
With withered dreams, black and
    blended with the night.
These visions which my mind
    had newly painted,
Take flight and leave me somber
    in the light.
While you are young, remember
    memories sweet,
Better company when you are left
    alone,
Than old acquaintances who
    place flowers at my feet,
Once I have gone to yet another
    home.
Our presence is brief; and
    therefore we admire
The youth who leads us with a
    feeble thread.
Verdant youth calls with ardent
    desire
And raps upon the quiet of the
    dead.
    But weakness grows until
    encroaching peace
Brings grave silence where all
    raptures cease.

Leila Merchant
Answer To a Child's Questions
"Which one of us do you love
    best?"
    "Look, little chick,
I do not love one more
    than any other.

My bountiful supply of mother
    love
    envelopes equally, you,
each sister, and each brother.

Oh, yes, I love you each in
    different ways,
    your personalitites are not the
    same,
just as you do not share a given
    name.

In what way do I love you
    differently?

That, dear, I cannot tell.
Suffice to say, I love you all.
In no one does a shortage
    dwell.

Lest one child thinks, "I have no
    fault,"
    and one child thinks, "There is
    some flaw in me,"
and one child thinks, "I am that
    way too,
    she simply does not see."

The answer to that question then
    must now and ever be,
a secret treasure living just in me."

Vonnie Spenst
A Love I Couldn't Hold
Cold, gray skies—like my eyes—
    shed a tear or two;
as raindrops fall my heart
    recalls the pain of losing you.
Winds blow free and—just like
    me—are going who knows
    where?
    as branches bend my whole
    world ends because you just
    don't care.

The starless nights—like my
    life—are dark and full of fears;
    as clouds move by I sit and
    cry—I just can't stop the tears.
Winds still blow but then, you
    know, when they're gone
    the sun will shine, and I'll tell
    myself I'm over you,
    and you'll be out of my mind.

But when the snow flies before
    my eyes
    and the sun won't shine on me,
I'll still remember days of dark
    and silent haze
    when you said you had to be
    free;
and when the fire dies before my
    eyes
    and the room grows, oh, so cold
I'll still remember days of dark
    and silent haze
    and the love I couldn't hold.

Raimie Kent
FORBIDDEN LOVE
Our love was perfect,
Always in key.
Nothing wrong
with you and me.
Except our ages.
We were so far apart,
nobody agreed
but our hearts.
We had a love,
but no one cared
about me and you,
and the love we shared.
We decided it was too much.
We wanted to be alone,
so we left,
where life was none.
They searched very far.
All over; everywhere.
We kept out of sight,
because no one cared.
Now we're together,
forever and a day.
I can imagine
what everyone wanted to say.
It doesn't matter anymore;
at least now I know
how much they really cared,
all friends and all foe.

Katherine E. Cartwright
IT'S CHRISTMAS AGAIN
It's Christmas again
It's Christmas again
In the light from a Heavenly Star
When Angels and shepherds sang
   of His birth
And Kings came from afar

May His blessing and peace cover
   all of the Earth
And reign in the hearts of men
This wonderful day of the
   Savior's birth
Praise God, it is Christmas again.

Millie Stice
THE SPIRIT LIFTERS
I sometime wonder when the
   butterfly
   seems to lightly flutter by
How my heart lifts noiselessly
   like in silent harmony
And the graceful movements try
   to lift my soul and let it fly.

Oh, to lift lives silently
   without knowing, consciously
That the grace and beauty of
   these magic moments we all
   love.
Wafting on the breezes slight
   caressing lovely blossoms
   bright.

God in His loving wisdom deems
   to only give to some it seems
The beauty, grace and loveliness
   to show how simply effortless
Is the way He lights our life
   to ease our daily toil and strife.

Like a symbol of Christ risen,
   the butterfly's released from its
   prison.
On gossamer wings it floats on
   high,
   and like Jesus in the sky
Has left us below in pleasant
   yearning
   for the day of His great
   returning.

Linda Liston
THE SEARCHER
To be a searcher
   In this day and time
   Requires stamina untold.

To struggle and sort
   Through life's mysteries
   Causes ordinary men to fold.

The roadblocks are many,
   The seeker unique,
   His ideas leave many cold.

The searcher undaunted,
   His heart drives him on
   From birth until he's old.

Frances Zapatka
When's Christmas?
Heavenly hosts sing praise of
   Him
Who born of men became the
   example of God.
His life was the prelude to
a new theme that was to hence—
forth be developed, varied, but yet
retaining its immutabel strain:
Love. Through the ages, opposing
   themes have been introduced,
   yet,
the celestial melodious theme He
introduced is never muted,

and has
never been excelled in
its harmonious beauty.
Some hearts are seeking it.
Others think they have muted it
by self.
Yet, they are often haunted by
the elysian son
Christ introduced into the
World, that was naught but
rattling discords.
The gentle tone is like an organ's
   breath
clear, steady and heard above all
   other sound.

Br Edward C. Breault, S. C.
JUST KNOWING
You see it in a toddler's eye
Tow'rds Baby Jesus in His crib
Or on your daughter's forehead
   high
At bedtime kneeling, feeling glib.

'Tis what you see when children
   pray
And what you feel when soft and
   low
A child describes the angels' play
Or other secrets *we* can't know.

It shows in a boy who on a whim
Will test your faith when a robin
   shows:
"Does God love me as much as
   him?"
Just see those eyes, you know he
   knows.

We call it Faith in you and me
But for a child who's busy
   growing
God has secrets meant to be
For little heads, just knowing.

Marion Frances
LAVENDER TO GRAY
Beneath midnight skies
scintillating winds race past
snow under an amethyst glaze.
A promise—you will come—
the heart pumps warm.

Lilacs permeate the earth;
violets peep from misty woods;
pansies lift pensive faces.
Roses flutter petals
as chrysanthemums surface.

Rain tramples decaying leaves.
Winter forecast: raw.
The body shudders and
heart pumps icy;
frost bites into marrow.

What will happen when icicles
pierce the heart?
What will come to pass
when lavender runs to gray:
when lavender runs to gray?

Christi Davidson
GINGERBREAD HOUSE
Stepping, gift laden, on
   confectioners snow
toward lighted stained glass
   candy panes;
warm orange windows, softly
   aglow,
past lamposts decked as
   peppermint canes.
Caramel squares of chinmey
   brick,
iced with sparkling frost
awaiting the arrival of

Old Saint Nick,
edged by icicles, sugar glossed.
Christmas magic transforms my
   reason;
I imagine my gingerbread house
   to entice.
No justice does it to another
   season—
I enter to the fragrance of
   molasses and spice.

**Mauro Alberto Bertero
Gutierrez**

Mauro Alberto Bertero Gutierrez
EMPTY MOMENTS
*[To the woman who taught me
love.]*
there had been no love or hatred
there had been no night or day,
there were no tears
   no more smiles

no sunshine   (left)

Poetry was her strength
Words were her beauty
Her existence was filled with
those silent, empty moments . . .
trying desperately to be life . . .

Evelyn Heinz
SUNRISE
*[To John my husband of 25
beautiful years and my children
who keep me going and writing
each and every day.]*
Sunrise starts
Behind the trees
Out of reach
But, I can see.
Sometimes,
By the water's edge
I chance a glimpse
Viewing brilliant colors
Both above
And below.

Sunrise means
A new day
Will dawn.
I must wake
And carry on.

Bessie B. Eckert
Don't Forget the Veterans
Under a cross of white, that
   stands oer each grave
Beneath the stars, the moon and
   Sun
   Where poppies are waving in
   the breeze
Rests someones favorite son

He gave his life that we might
   live
And died with war stories untold
He is out of all todays turmoils
That Soldier with a heart of gold

When our world was torn with
   a terrible war
Through Sunshine, hail, and
   thunder
   We prayed for God to save
   each boy
But some were put asunder

When Old Glorys colors waves
   high oer the hill
On the eleventh of November
   We pray no families will have
   to say goodby
So please don't forget to
   remember

The red stands for blood our
   soldiers shed
And white for their pure hearts
   so gay
   The blue is for courage, and
   truth that they showed
So fly your flag on each Veterans
   Day.

Laurie Burton—Smith
ACCOMPLISHMENT
You've come out on
   top!
You are a winner.
   Today you can rule the world.
All that time spent working
   to your fullest
capacity has finally paid
   off.
The struggle is over!
   Or is it just beginning?

Olivia Everett
THE CHRISTMAS SEASON
*[My husband, Rufus Marshall
(Bud) Everett—Deceased]*
It is time to turn the calendar
   to show us bright and clear,
That it is now December with
   Christmas drawing near.
It's a time for celebration;
   this day of Jesus' birth,
When God sent down from
   Heaven, His own Son to the
   earth.
The streets will soon be glowing
   with every kind of light,
And all the stores will be open so
   very late at night.
The happy season's shoppers
   Will be rushing here and
   there,
While recorded Christmas carols
   are beamed out on the air.
We will hear the children's
   laughter

Today's Greatest Poems

and see eyes glowing bright,
As they think of good Saint Nicklaus
    and his visit in the night.
Their dreams are filled with reindeer
    and little bells that ring,
And they raise their eyes to Heaven to hear the Angels sing. . .
We hear that old, old story of a manger filled with hay,
Where the wise men came with presents
    to worship and to pray.
We hear the loud "Hozanna's" from all of Heaven's hosts,
As they bring their happy tidings to the shepherds at their posts.
And still that age—old message is ever new today,
'Peace on earth, good will toward men,"
    across the world we pray.
So for this Christmas season, I wish you joy and cheer,
With peace to come to all the world;
    My prayer for the new year.

Bernard
THE KEY
[Inspiration and TMR, May love be greater than anger, and gratitude far outlast regret and smiles will endure in the future as they did in the past.]
The
Key
Cold, impersonal, angular,
Ridges, lines, circles,
I have such a key.
It is old,
But kept as a reminder.
To bring back memories of what has been,
Not what will ever be,
For in this key I can still feel,
How good life had once been to me.
The key still fits some locks,
But it will not turn.
And like past love,
It has changed,
And I await the time it will turn again.
But still I keep the key,
For it has meaning,
If only just to me.

Karen M. Kinsaman
WINTER LOVE
Our love began on a clear spring day
And grew strong in so many ways.
Problems were few and far between—
Nothing was ever said that we didn't mean.

One day in the fall, we grew apart.
We were no longer two within one heart.
There were no arguments or verbal fights;
Our love just changed from day to night.

Then winter came and you

said goodbye.
The question in my mind will always be "Why?"
There was never anything that I will regret,
And our love is one I'll never forget.

A love that bloomed in the heart of spring
Withered as the winter winds began to sing.
They sang of a love at the start of day,
And how in the winter that love faded away.

Dr. Lionel Fern

Dr. Lionel Fern
TO BE A POET
[In honor of Dr. Jorge Luis Morales (Olympic Poet), Professor of Spanish Literature at the University of Puerto Rico; and for sure, one of our future Nobel Prize Winners. During the year of his Second Season (50th birthday), in a Poetry Workshop, at the White House.]
To be a poet really is to lead a hard life,
which means to climb a steep mountain with blood and tears.
It is to leave, when the end of his journey nears,
like the queen bee, plenty offspring and honey in the hive.

And this I tell you . . . and all others, truly;
the poet has been born a tireless creator,
one who can't stop being a

student mentor.
He will always be searching for truth and beauty.

He has to be a man with a broad, open, mind,
one who knows and can teach you any matter.
to his fellow men he is a leader . . . He is kind.

He will transcend this world; and on dwelling in skies,
will sit to the right of our Almighty Father . . .
where love, beauty, truth and all knowledge lies.

Katrinka Lynn Sasaki
Sunrises and Buttercups
If you go deep in the hills or mountains,
you find a sweet little reminder of the way things were at the beginning,
beautiful.

If you look up in the sky at a certain time of day,
you see a reminder of the beautiful miracle at hand.

When I look in your eyes,
I see a reminder of how things were at the beginning,
beautiful.

When I look at the life we are building,
I also see a reminder of the beautiful miracle at hand,
another mountain filled with sweet buttercup memories.

Gary Fredrickson
BE STILL MY HEART
Be still my heart
While the winds do blow
Swirling through the open moor,
Through forest dark
And desert floor.

Though they should call
With icy hand,
And with strengthening appeal demand
The release of all
Those dreams that grow in your Present land.

Bend not to their harshest ways,
Nor to their silver whispers rolling
Over your desire to stay.
But rest the night in these arms that hold
The ceaseless striving of your soul.

Plant firm your feet
On steady ground.
Make no retreat
Though the swirling clouds
Should force you to cry aloud.

But listen to that one small breath
That holds you the tenderest,
Lifting the rock of self—despair
To hold you up on solid air.
Leave not her loving arms
Nor all her old, familiar charms.

Rest now and do not seek
That which is too fleet
To catch before the day's new heat

Will leave you for another night
And all that which you have set right
Does fade and vanish from our sight.

Sharon J. Hoffman
FANTASY?
The sweet siren song of the mermaids call me . . . .
To come and frolic through the depths.

The lonely, mournful pipes of Pan have long enticed me—
to follow and gaze upon never to be known secrets.

A silver swan spreads her wings—she bids me climb atop her downy feathers . . .
we'll play hide 'n seek
    with moonbeams in the clouds.

An angel choir sings the Halleluiah chorus—just for me.
Love smiles and covers me with sunbeams and stardust.

Now I awake—holding still a sprak of magic from my Dreams.

By the way, do you see the Unicorn . . . on the grassy slope . . .
    . . . just over there?

T. Edward Cross
THE POEM
Once I sat to write a poem
    as thoughts poured through my mind
I pondered things both great and small
    but couldn't make them rhyme

At last, I thought, with lack of mirth
    needs make no sense at all
nonsense as a central theme
    but sprawling as a mall

And therefore otherwise although
    it may be fairly clear
that even if perhaps anyway
    I'll draw a sigh or jeer

Three verses out of the way it seems
    I'm working on the last
now there's two more lines to go
and now the poem is past.

Mallory Ann Morris
THE BAY
A winter breeze blows away the day,
As the ice on the bay breaks into the sea.
A seagull stands still, and so free,
And floats away, on the ice, in the sea.

Kate E. Schermerhorn
THE LAST GOODBYE
A sweet kiss followed by a gentle tear rolling down her face.
Chills ran down her spine, not from the night air, but from the thought of not being held in his arms like this again.
The sky was dark and melancholy except for a few scattered stars and a glimpse

217

of the hiding moon just
peering out from behind the
trees to see the young
lovers part and say a last
goodbye.
A love that should have
lasted and blossomed into
deeper more beautiful love,
turned tears, nothing but
drops of sadness being
pushed away as the
crickets minded their own
merry ways.

Molly Courville
THE KEY
Sucked into a dustbin
    globe of earth particle
        whirling
    through a vortex of white light
    powdered bone of pioneer
    ancient but here in the glare
    of memory's waning stare.
Gaze up, site down
    you've been barren before
        felt your blood seer
        into fine meal
    felt the grains
        behind your eyes.
The clamp of heat
    forces the cords to swing in
        your neck;
    a pulse
        throbs far beyond a circle of
        heart.
Ancestors not akin
    have taken you to the altar,
    kept you sprawled over stone
        and cinder
        till the spit of your tongue
        curdles
    and falls in knots, as the
        sweat of your brow beads
        and sizzles
    into vapor.
A hell-borne wind fetches in
    from a last horizon
        slicking the surface of skin
        to marble
        freezing into glyph
        the cry of rage.
There is no prison.
    In these scorched hills, the
        dazzled mind
    is the screw that turns—
the key.

Annette Thomas O'Connor
DROWNING IN SILENCE
I am drowning in silence.
No one wanting to hear what I
    have to say.
No one asking to know how well
    I spent my day.
No laughter finds me.
I find no joy to share; my love is
    here but he doesn't choose to
    care.
He would want things to be
    different, but he doesn't know
    how;
To ease the pain and not let my
    head in sorrow bow.
A life almost totally gone by and
    people still make me cry.
Do they mean to be cruel? I used
    to deny—
But, now, I know they *do* and I
    wish I could die.
I once called "Suicide Hotline" to
    find a friend.
They wait by the phone so your

life you won't end.
I've things to be thankful for, oh,
    this I don't deny.
But the hunger for laughter
    makes my soul deeply sigh.
I'm drowning in silence.
This *sad* tale has been in movie
    plots for ages.
Sadder for me because I'm locked
    "tween it's pages."
Feeling sorry for myself? Who has
    a better right?
Wishing to cross from the
    Darknes into Light.
This may be the Conclusion, but
    it's not the End.
I'm Drowning in Silence; with a
    Love not a friend.

Betty Rae Taylor
Homegrown Rainbows
At the end of the rainbow's a big
    pot of gold,
If you ever reach it, it's yours, so
    I'm told.
You can spend your life
    searching, but you'll never find.
It's just an illusion; it's all in your
    mind.

A rainbow's a promise that good
    follows bad,
That joy and contentment are
    yours to be had.
A rainbow's created from
    sunshine and rain;
Grow your own out of laughter
    and pain.

A rainbow's a symbol of hopes
    and dreams,
Proving that living's not bad as it
    seems.
Count on your rainbow to
    surround you with color,
And walk through each day
    'neath a rainbow umbrella.

Take the best and the worst, and
    put them together.
Take the storms and the clouds,
    and mix with fair weather.
Then add some happiness, a few
    salty tears.
It won't be long 'til your rainbow
    appears.

Homegrown rainbows are free.
Rainbows no one else can see.
Take them with you, wherever
    you go—
Your very own, homegrown
    rainbows.

Bette Callahan
LOVE'S LOSS
You came my way
for only a day.

"Stay!" my heart
wants to say.

It can not be
for you're not free.

You've touched me
like no other.

How can I
let it be?

Steve Garland
TOUCHING
I have never known how to love a
    woman
Like she wants to be loved,

and no, I have never learned to
    touch
a woman like she deserves to be
    touched.
Sometimes I sit back,
in dismay,
at my lack of skills.
There is something about my
    maleness,
that prevents me from touching
as softly as I want to touch,
and it prevents me from
knowing just where to touch;
and it distresses me
to see it in your eyes
that you know.
What is it about life's perfect union,
that it escapes me, so easily.
It's not as if I don't try.
I may never touch a woman,
in a way she so richly deserves,
but I'm willing to learn.

Tracy Pyles

Tracy Pyles
MY GREATEST FLAGS
*[I am dedicating this Poem to
my son, Petty Officer, Tracy
Pyles, Jr. who enlisted and
served 4 years in the U.S. Navy
during the Vietnam War.]*
When we see those two great
    flags friends
Whose crimson waves so cold
    but free
Will our hearts beat true and
    loyal
For patriots who have set us free.

One is the flag of our great
    savior
The other flies for you and me
If we fly these flags together
We'll keep our peace and liberty.

God's great flag will never
    tremble
However great the force may be
    For Jesus blood is written on it
So that from sin we could be free.

The Stars and Stripes will never
    tremble
However great the force may be
    For American blood is written
    on it
That this great country could be
    free.

So when we see those two great
    flags
Let our minds go into the past
    To Jesus and our soldiers dying
And pray that freedom will
    always last.

Anne Walker Robinson
YOUNG AND OLD
*[To Whit and Rob, without
whom this would not be
possible]*
A child is life
The bewildered eyes
in unrelenting pursuit
for the answer
why

They learn, grasp,
and so communicate
to those old people
who are still in pursuit
of the same answer.

Judith A. Murphy
THIRTY
Laundress, seamstress, lumper,
    wife,
this is all there is to my life.

Clairol's thirty and she's better;
will I be and still together?

Steven Shaw
COWS
Cows are glorious creatures.
They have many exciting
    features.
Standing on hills, chewing their
    cud,
Almost as exciting as a puddle of
    mud.
Pondering and ruminating on
    universal truth,
They're as exciting as an empty
    glass of Vermouth.

People should learn from cows,
    they're not offbeat.
All they ever do is walk and eat.
Walk and eat and eat and walk,
It's amazing these brilliant
    animals can't talk.
Such a creature should be the
    "World Chief."
Now I'm hungry for a hamburger,
    100% BEEF.

David M. Jack
PARADISE LOST
Oh this life of mine tis full of
    dark
This last love of mine has left its
    mark
My heart is heavy for the times
    done spent
When each day was full of love
    and content
But now a wonder of worlds has
    made a change
And oh this loathing does feel so
    strange

Tossed aside for one not yet even
    here
I make the best of it; I hide my
    fear
From down deep in my soul I
    know I've lost
Humility I can afford; but love,
    what a cost
Never was such a price paid for
    so little
Ere a fortnight passed, my heart is
    brittle
Ere another and it shatters into
    bits

I've nothing left now save my
    own wits

But oh can I be such a selfish fool

I'm no better than a devilish ghoul
I've had the best in all the world
No better a love will the angels
    ever herald

I'm once again content in my
    mind and heart
Relishing the idea of a brand new
    start
To take this love farther than
    before
To a point which only our minds
    can explore

Ersie Tsombanidis

Ersie Tsombanidis
UNTITLED
*[For God creating me, Bob
Dylan's inspiration, my family's
love and support. And for
Harriet Selverstone's and Pat
Duspiva's continuous
confidence in me as a poet.]*
Pacified passengers driving their
    self-baptized limousines
Drinking communionized wine
    that discharges in extremes
From their pollution filth mouths
    to blood poured streams
On Satin's tongue of sword they
    lick praising themselves clean
Their destitute souls and mind
    form into decaying machines
As their mouths vomit red dollar
    bills

They are a whore televising their
    faith in a commercial manner
Marching with gold cement feet
    acclaiming the bible with a
    banner
Preaching of helpless poverty
    victims but wearing engravable
    fur
Decorating fragmentary mini
    statues with no name or color
And when they feel it's time the
    naive world knew for sure
They rumour of their coming by
    God's will

onditioned mistresses pamper
    their inhumane needs to
    perfection
Yet their critical views of other's
    preferences turn into a ballad
    of election
Wearing three piece suits in
    church that whisper malicious
    deception
Directed to the tarnished ones
    who've come for a guided
    direction
Their satanized suits burn into

ashes of their own invention
And because of their conscience
    themselves they will kill

Helen James Ehlert
Our Grandpa's Upstairs
*[Dedicated to my
grandchildren: Jimmy, Jeana
and Joana Hammitt
Christmas—1977]*
Our favorite Santa is busy
    upstairs—
He's waxing the harps and
    helping with prayers.
He welcomes the newcomers and
    carries their things;
He helps them on with their
    gossamer wings!

He makes them a drink of some
    heavenly fruit;
Then offers them ice cream
    and cookies, to boot!
He rocks Baby Jimmy and jokes
    with my Dad.
He talks to his folks of the
    trips, that we've had!

He looks down and sees Joanie—
    says, "Isn't she sweet?"
"Seeing her with her kittens is
    such a nice treat."
And then he spies Jeanie working
    hard at school
And he brags to his mother,
    "She's nobody's fool!"

He's made friends with the
    singers! 'Elvis and Bing'!
And he gets a big kick out of
    hearing them sing!
He points to our Jimmy—looks
    them straight in the face,
"Before very long, boys, he'll be
    taking your place!"

He looks up Bud and Louie, they
    are just right down the hall,
And they have a friendly
    session on good old basketball.
"Now, if Dunlap beats Dow City
    and Logan whips them all—
Won't Woodbine be in the
    tournament, again, this year, By
    Gol!"

Sometimes when he misses
    Grandma, he hunts up Jim and
    Cloyce.
They reminisce of the "Music
    Box" and it makes his heart
    rejoice!
He remembers the girl he danced
    with; he remembers her eyes of
    blue.
So many happy memories since
    the day they said, "I do."

He's glad that Ellen's happy; he's
    proud that Fred's his son!
He hopes that Grandma will be
    content, until her work is done!
His laugh is just as hearty; his
    step is still as light!
He's busy helping everyone
    from morning until night!

And though our hearts are heavy,
    as we say our Christmas prayer;
We now that Heaven's happier—
    because our Grandpa's there!

Connie A. Obergfell
JOURNEY
Slowly I will leave
Gently breaking our union

Taking the blame—
Setting you free.
We are too different
Both unwilling to change,
Our souls chafe when against one
    another.
Young and full of fire—
Mercurial and traveling light
    years
In only a matter of time,
Not yet assaulted by continual
    years of frustration—
Or embittered by month upon
    month of no love.
I still want very much
That which I don't have
My desire not dulled by sad
    experience—
I have dreams and aspirations
That go unfulfilled.
My only respite
To travel that uncharted road
Following wherever it may lead
Taking a chance—
On finding my dream
Somewhere.
So as our love burns slowly down
Into the glowing embers of
    friendship—
I'll smile in remembrance
Of our loving,
And hold you close to my heart
As I continue on my way.

J.W. Lobbett
ROWBOAT VISION
Sweep of the oars,
Sweep of the view.
From the stern, reflections on the
    water;
Distant and golden sparkling.
Receding palisades and dock.
A canvass of Payne's Grey sky,
And muted Terra-verted land;
Both static.
Now growing with broad-strokes
To encompass emerald waves and
    wake, dynamic.
(Reflections on the past)
I paid my dues,
And plowed the salt.
For me to live in Jesus.
There—He waves from the dock,
And calms the waters.
So, I've hunkered down,
For the long pull;
Yet, must hurry
To strange, new
Ports—of—Call.

Jan Anderson
NEVER-GOODBYE
I dare not speak the words
nor kiss my last good-bye,
for we are not parted in death
the ties, are as sure in memory;
and death, tho it has chosen you
also claims a share of the living.
The lips that are silent now
still speak, still laugh aloud,
and your dreams are still shared;
your presence is not to be
    forgotten,
and tho the body may be lost;
still death must leave you here.

Shannon Kathlina Harrington
THE DIFFERENCE
The river does flow,
And the birds do sing,
The grass does grow,

Where the lion is king.

The river has waste,
And the birds quickly die,
For the gras lacks taste,
Where the human sits high.

Tom N. Tanzi
CREATIVE EVOLUTION
*[To Tonya and Joel for future
reference.]*
Duh, I'm the lowly dinosaur
Kind of a king with a pea of a
    brain
Of my life here on earth
I eat more than my worth
and can't even come out of the
    rain
Uh, I've been here so long it
    certainly seems
I couldn't be wrong to exist
Tho' I'm big and so dumb
I'm still a great one
Oops, I'm fall'n it that there tar
    pit
Hello, I'm the mighty man, I am
    the crown of life here on earth
Of a wonderful breed with a
    special need
to emphasize the day of my birth
My mind is so wise compared to
    it's size
Still I dig up the earth like a
    glutton

I've built autos and condos,
    videos and nucleos,

Oops, I think I've pushed the
    wrong button
Well I'm the heavenly angel you
    know
My spirit traverses the all
Tho' I spend most of my time
    be'n divine
and try'n not to fall
I can't help but wonder it it was a
    blunder
It even seems a bit odd
That all of the creatures have
    imperfect features
Oops, here comes the Son of God.

Betty Kaseman
CHILD'S ROOM
Those days are long past
Teddy bear tossed aside
Childhood left behind.

Sentimental things
Of times gone, forgotten
Left to gather dust.

Evelyn Conley Stauffer
BLESS THE SMALL WORLD
God bless the small world on this
    Christmas eve,
Birds, puppies and rabbits, grey
    squirrels in the tree,
Santa's Red Rudolph, wee things
    out of doors,
Their rations are meager, their
    homes snowy floors.
Protect them dear Father safe
    keep them from harm
As Mary kept Jesus, THAT
    NIGHT, safe and warm.

Rebecca Davis Hunt
POSTER EYES
little spheres
watch me.
surrounded—
i'm alone,

they have me
cornered.
alive,
with no motion,
following me
every place i turn.
some star
without expression,
others seem ominous.
laughing—
they sense
my entrapment
and take advantage.

Diana Kierce
HOME AT LAST
*[I dedicate this poem to our
brave citizens who were held
against their will in Iran, and to
my grandson, John Kierce]*
The hostages are home at last,
their terrible ordeal is over,
Now fading like sun bleached
    glass,

They can begin to pick up the
    pieces and
Start a new life, they are one,
Their new life has begun,

The terror within has ceased,
For now their minds are clearing,
They are at peace

The nightmares are still there,
It shows from the darkened
    circles around their
eyes and graying hair

May they be blessed with
    security and love,
Let the world give them the
    strength from God above,
Let them look ahead and forget
    the past,
For they are home at last.

Catherine Kerns
ERNEST
You are the joy and sunshine of
    my life,
    The reason I give for living.

The love that never ends in a
    world of two friends.
When things go wrong and never
    right,
You make me laugh and things
    get bright.

When I talk you always listen,
When you got things on your
    mind
    You don't even mention.

Lord when we get to heaven and
    walk hand in hand
Through the path of life,
Open up your golden gate and let
    us in as man and wife.

Arthur William Brown
SHE IS GONE
She has left me
Can not bring her back.
Lonely life will be without.
Always there when needed.
Why does she not return?
Angelic face, all a smile
Radiating warmth, warming my
    heart.
Companion of high caliber
Tending to my friendship needs.
No friendship now
She is gone.
In no way did she exist,

Is what you try to tell me.
Created by the minds need.
To me, real she was,
Friend no one else can see.
Not there any more
Still needed is she.

George M. Dile
A JOURNEY
*[It's such a comfort to know
that our Heavenly Father loves
us so much. This poem reflects
that love and is based on the
book of Revelation which is
found in the Bible. (Chapters 22
& 23)]*
Let me take you on a journey
Where the sun no longer shines
    Yet illuminated faces there
        Reflect a glorious light

Beyond the realm of space and
    time
    We'll unlock all the doors
And the secrets of the universe
    Forever will be ours

It's doubtful how much time
        remains
    Before the countdown ends
On the starship called Emanuel
    And final launch begins

Though it may seem fantasy
This journey will come true
'Cause I've read the captain's
        logbook
    And we will be there soon

Lift-off is much closer now
Than when we came on board
The flight plan has been ordered
And all supplies are stored
        Suddenly
    We're among the stars
In a heavenly atmosphere
A city of jewels surrounded us
All darkness has disappeared

Traveling at the speed of light
He has revealed his love
A revelation of things ahead
And what we shall become

So if beauty is a spoken word
    There's nothing left to say
As the ever bright and morning
        star
    Takes our breath away

Boyd J. Reed
THE BEAUTIFUL FLOWER
The beautiful flower—
    It does so much for me,
I never cease to marvel
    At its versatility.

It comes in many different kinds,
    Aromas, colors too,
In nature there's no other
    That shines so bright and true.

Out upon the landscape
    Or anywhere in sight,
It fills our hearts with pleasure
    And brings us great delight.

In gardens, homes, and at our
    work
    We like the flower near,
To help us through another day
    That needs a little cheer.

And don't forget the florist
    Who makes the flower
    increase,
By countless floral settings,
    Each one a masterpiece.

Yes—the flower is so beautiful,
    And may it always be
A source of strength and
    happiness
    For all humanity.

Lori Hilliard
IMAGINE
*[For Geneal Frederick, the best
friend anyone could have.]*
Imagine the things that are yet to
    come,
the special things like to you . . .
    from . . .
Those are the things that let you
    know,
there is someone, someone who
    cares, someone to love.
And as you look up to the sky,
    you wonder at
all those why, why, why's
And then you awake and to your
    surprise,
you've been imagining about all
    the things the world
has to give, and they're all for
    you.

Edith M. Sessions
CHRISTMAS MEMORIES
Christmas was upon me, "Praise
    the Lord our King"
I had no money, food, or drink,
    but memory on the wing
The father of my children had
    long since been gone
To find his dream, a life long
    thing, "Middle Age", was
    creeping on
My heart was full, tho empty, of
    the memories we hold so dear
Tho I was seeing hard times, my
    Lord and Savior held me near
I remembered our Lord Jesus,
    born in a stable cold
No crying had he done this day,
    Why should I be so bold?
My memories kept soaring, as I
    worked my job the long day
    through
I looked toward heaven, and
    immediately I knew
I loved our Lord and Savior, I had
    no reason to be blue
My memories reminded me that
    on the cross he died
To save us all from Sin and then
    Upon him we should rely
I remembered I had given back to
    him, a son, the first I born
I had him for many seasons, he
    had been lent to me, I should

not scorn
My memory was of my son's
    assending as I heard the
    trumpets ring
My son had already crossed over
    and was living with our king
Memories of the "New Life", our
    Savior promised us was
    swelling in my heart
I quickly put aside the fact, that
    money had I none
For some poor soul was cold, and
    lonely, but I still had,
The Lords "Only" begotton Son.
I had only to put my trust in him,
    I knew he would not faulter
For their was plenty to eat, and
    plenty of drink at Our Father's
    Alter.
I graceiously said! "Thank you
    Lord" I'm sorry I was week
I'll keep my memories happy, for I
    am one of your Meek.
I know what I will inherit, "What
    a beautiful Memory"
To know that Jesus gave his life
    for us upon CALVERY
Christmas Memories will ever be
A source of deep Happiness for
    me.
God lives thru us, and through
    our young
His Memory we must carry on,
To greater heights, this is his call
Be assured he'll be there to catch
    us if we fall.
So Christmas memories after all,
    are for the young and the old,
They feed us daily, nourish us
    greatly, they keep us warm, not
    cold.
So Christmas Memories keep on
    growing, in the garden of
    memories I will keep on sowing.

Joan Kane Olsavsky
THE GATHERING
Yesterday, we gathered our leaves
    like errant children,
    bundled them,
    bedded them down.

This morning, they crackled at
    our window,
    as if to remind us
    leaves and children
    have their season.

I think we will allow them to
    play,
    the leaves and children,
    find their time together
    for gathering up.

John Landgraver, Sr.
EASTER GREY
Would he rise again today as he
    did way back then?
Would he try to save the people?
    Would he want to be our
    friend?
Would he cast the wine and
    make the bread?
Are we worth our Savior's
    suffering?
Are we Love?
Are we man and woman that
    Jesus hoped we'd be?
Are we good or evil?
Did the devil set us free?
Would he come to church on
    Sunday just to be with you and me?

Are we worth his sunshine, his
  ocean, his sky?
Are we worth a tree?
Someday when its all over and
  earth's air we breathe no more,
Will you find smiling, waiting
  by heaven's golden door?
Did you do all the things he
  wanted as you wandered day by
  day?
Or did we do what we pleased,
  not caring about his way.
Do you think you will turn to
  gold someday instead of just
  old clay?
Does he really love and forgive us
  for his suffering and his pain?
On this day soon to come on
  Sunday, come with love and
  call it Easter Day

Laurel Thompson
SONGS AND MEMORIES
The song playing on the radio
Takes me way back when.
Six thousand miles, some years
  ago,
I'm in my home again.
Eight years old and second grade.
I remember well that band.
As we watched Ed Sullivan they
  played
"I Wanna Hold Your Hand".
My mother, father, sister,
  brothers
Were all together then.
I cannot speak for the others
But I wish we were again.
Now I remember my roommate
  June.
She used to strum this song.
"You've Got a Friend" goes the
  tune,
And I would sing along.
I'll recall our friendship always,
Our long and peaceful walks,
Those crazy, zany, care-free days
And solemn midnight talks.
But then there came the joy-filled
  day
When I became a wife.
The song we heard as we drove
  away
Was "You Light Up My Life."
But now it seems we've had to
  roam
To the earth's very ends.
Six thousand miles away from
  home,
From family and friends.
I peer through the window at the
  rain.
I refill my coffee cup.
These songs and memories ease
  the pain
And keep my spirits up.

Donna Avacato
WHILE THE SNOW FALLS
Just standing here while the snow
  falls,
watching the flakes as they
  land—
Occasionally catching one on its
  way down
and watching it melt in my hand.
Snow lies virgin-white on the
  concrete,
my footprints leave tracks as I go
onward and into the street lights
marking my path in the snow.

Kathy Tuck
BEN NEVIS
Tall, dark, forbidding,
a blinder for sunlit rays.
Encased in a halo of thick
  Scottish fog,
with rocky face
and sparse vegetation.
Heather scattered
in the rocky crevices.
Sheeps' fleece caught on thieving
  barbs
that grow between crowded
  rocks.
Not only a mountain,
but a challenge.

Marjorie L. St. Andrews
MOM'S TIME
It's five A.M., time to get up, I
  can't believe my eyes.
This place looks like some
  smarty storm was trying to be
  wise
There's match box cars all in a
  line waiting to run a race.
There's shoes and books, the
  newspaper, everything is out of
  place.
There's dirty dishes in the sink,
  cause son had to work late.
The boss told him, something's
  important and it just can't wait.
The laundry in the hamper is
  over flowed again.
Didn't I do that yesterday? there
  seems to be no end.
The mendings piled to the roof a
  job I really hate.
I really should do it today, well
  maybe it can wait.
Well everybody's on their way
  this place could use my touch.
But first a cup of coffee, I don't
  like housework much.
It's twelve o'clock I should have
  lunch just one more job to do.
What happened to my lunchtime?
  The clock says almost two.
The floor is mopped the laundry's
  done the place looks really
  neat.
Everything is in it's place, boy I
  sure am beat.
The girl next door says don't you
  get bored, wouldn't you rather
  work?
What have I been doing all day,
  am I some kind of jerk?
It's three o'clock time for a break
  the last I'm not sure when.
The school bus just stopped at
  the door, well here I go again.
Supper is done the kitchen is
  clean, I think I'll watch T.V.
It's strange I always fall asleep, is
  something wrong with me?
It's five A.M. time to get up, I
  can't believe my eyes.
This place looks like some
  smarty storm was trying to be
  wise.

Marguerite Wheeler
MEMORY
When the beautiful day draws
  slowly to an end,
  The twilight wanes, and the
  night descends.
Then the sky is studded with
  stars so rare;

And I rest securely, knowing
  that you care.

For the days have been many, but
  the hours too few,
  Since first, I said that: "I do love
  you!"
And I feld your arms holding me
  near
  As you slowly whispered "And
  I love you, dear!"

The days were pleasant, and the
  time was ours
  As we strolled among the trees
  and the wild flowers.
But it seems to me, the time went
  too fast
  And now, all that we have, is a
  memory of the past.

Oh: The memories are many and
  the thoughts so sweet.
  We'll hold them near, till again
  we meet,
And maybe someday before the
  end of time;
  Forever, I will be yours, and
  you will be mine!

D.O. Clem
**To Whom Should a
Christmas Gift Be Given**
[Bill and Rosemary Bond,
Grandchildren; Kenneth,
Vickey, and Tim Bond,Great
Grandchildren]
Ah—Wonderful Christmas, The
  Birthday of our Lord,
Present your gifts to Him—In
  accordance with His Word.
Bare Ye gifts to Him, from the
  East, Unto the West;
For it is the Birthday of Christ,
  The One you should love best.
To Him, the Gifts should be
  given, coming from near and
  far,
He—Should be the Receiver of
  Gifts, So follow Ye the star.

Why should we not bestow our
  gifts, With God's leading We
  know;
That since it's a Heavenly
  Birthday, To Jesus, our gifts
  should go.
Tho' we give each other gifts,
  Permissable tho' it be,
Our best we should give, To the
  One who set us free.
For Christmas is His Birthday,
  His, the mission to save;
Son of Man—Born in a manger, It
  was His All He gave.

Special—To Him—Should our
  gifts be given,
'Twas for us he left His home in
  Heaven;
So the best we have, On Him we
  should bestow;
'Twas for us He left Glory,
  Long—Long—Ago,
Choosing to come—Later to die,
To Redeem from our sins, On the
  Cross, By and By.

DeAnne Michaud
79—1
I cup these tears in my hand.
They lay on the skin of my palm,
  a shallow pool—

silent declarations of my love.
If I am careful, perhaps they will
  evaporate
before you wake.

Terrill D. Petersen

Terrill D. Petersen
A GOLDEN BAND
Love is holding your hand,
and asking you to wear my
  golden band.
Vowing to share a life,
together through good and
  strife.

You will always be mine,
and I, yours, all through time.
Together we will open all new
  doors.
Together we will do all life's
  chores.

We shall have all time for love,
and be guided from heaven
  above.
So come with me and hold my
  hand.
Please; say yes, to my golden
  band.

Diana Rosenstock
PIONEER WOMAN
Tall and straight you stand
  As the winds of time
Push against your brow
  And throw you back.
You steadily push on.

The reality now is stronger
  Than your dreams.
You are toughened
  By the harshness
  Of your existence.
Unforseen challenges keep
  Coming on.

The embers of your life
  Glow in the darkness;
The winds of change
  Fan the fires of your heart.
Your dreams persist
  Even when you can no
  longer
  See rainbows
And your soul goes on.

You were taught to make do
  With the little you have.
Your talented fingers
  Weave beauty from decay;
Your sharp eye sees
  Possibility everywhere.
Your work must go on.

As you work so diligently
  Against the odds,

As you make magic where once
   There was no hope,
As you fill the emptiness
   With your love
Life itself can go on.

Loye Huffman
A PEERLESS PLACE

With granite pillars high midst
   roaring sound,
We live our lives in canyons man
   has made.
It's to the steel and stone that we
   are bound,
But give me solace in a quiet
   glade.
We march along and through the
   crowds we stream
To hurry forward on the strict set
   time.
We pride ourselves on cities built
   supreme,
But give me trees and rivers, hills
   sublime.
It's to the wilderness I turn to
   find
My one escape from burdens of
   the day.
I look for comfort of a peerless
   kind,
A wild and lonely place . . . But
   would I stay?

Charles F. Lindsay
THE SEASON OF THE ROSE

We each will have our Springtime,
   like the rose, we have our
   season.
We rise from the bosom
   of the soft and melting earth
and greet a warm, sweet, shining
   sun
that asks us to come nearer and
   whisper of our beauty.
Sparkling there,
   touched by the morning jewel
   dew,
we shine upon the earth.
Each petal shouts in triumph, its
   joy to be alive.
Too soon will come the winter
   and gone will be the sun.
The frost will weave a lacy,
   diamond prison.
   The crushed and weeping petals,
      fall softly to the earth,
         and speaking not a word,
                              dies.

Ruth Webber
AMERICA
[Dedicated to Anne Fitz-Henry]
Little children laughing
Running is such fun
Older children smiling
Walking in the sun
   THAT'S AMERICA TO ME.
Deserts filled with wild flowers
Redwoods towering to the sky
Mountains tall and stern
And rivers rushing by
   THAT'S AMERICA TO ME
Cities filled with workers
Fields so green and grand
And a flag that's full of stars
To represent our land
   THAT'S AMERICA TO ME
Moonlight on the waters
Planes humming overhead
Starlight in the darkness
Peace with gentle wings outspread
   THAT'S AMERICA TO ME

Fred
MORE THAN A FRIEND
*[My Family—Always more
never less. Denise—Our
friendship means a lot to me,
you do. Nancy—You're always
more than a friend]*
Don't you understand/I want you
   for my friend
Always more never less/And
   you're always more than a
   friend

Don't let the whispers talk you
   down
Just because I'm around
I'm not trying to take you away
   from him
I only want to be your friend

Don't you understand/I want you
   for my friend
Always more never less/And
   you're always more than a
   friend

I never thought of you as such
To me it never mattered much
Just because I know you
Doesn't mean that I can't see you,
   too

Don't you understand/I want you
   for my friend
Always more never less/And
   you're always more than a
   friend

Now don't you get the wrong idea
You know I only want to see ya
Our friendship means a lot to me,
   you do
Does it mean that much to you?

Don't you understand/I want you
   for my friend
Always more never less/And
   you're always more than a
   friend
And you're always more than a
   friend

Sue Wojtas
The Two Of Us Together
The two of us together
We should be as one
To share in all our thoughts and
   joys,
When each new day is done.

The two of us together
In spirit and in life
To discover the beautiful
   feelings,
Of a husband and a wife.

The two of us together

In each and every way
Learning all life's ups and downs,
Living day by day.

The two of us together
Is the way it ought to be
For richer, for poorer, in sickness
   and health,
Until eternity.

Karl Berry
IMPROMPTU

From these familiar tasks on
   earth—
Sufficient to their Own designs
   and worth.
And yet sustained—quite boldly
   to aspire—
While here and there to probe—
   Some wisdom to acquire.

Successive layers of thought, can
   build
   to structures gruesome or
   sublime—
Support or ruin all absolutes of
   time.
Or to venture all on that thin
   crust
   of might alone, as wholly right.

Awkward weights to the burden
   of spirit
         and mind.—
Which harks from savage
   pursuits,
   or such of kind—
Not from the source of any bright
   zenith,
      to better mark the age.
Search for strength is need for
   any act
      upon the stage—
Or fearsome word to write upon a
   page.

The whole gamut of minds
   natural
      endowments,
Revolts to contain in the stale or
   futile moment.
Oh shades of time, of ancient
   vintage—
Thou holy and corrupt from every
   struggling age.
The constant rise and fall of
   highest
      desires—
For less of strife and grief, and
   more of joyous creative fires.

John E. Hummer
ADIEU TO 1981
'Neath January's autograph
We read Miss New Year's name.
Besides she wrote an epitaph
Termed "Last Year's Evil Fame".
Your twelve months did not halt
   the war,
Or damn your waves of crime
That ever will contentment mar,
Until the end of time.

Your auto deaths surpass the
   count
Of any previous year.
Your murders still raised deaths
   amount
Which victims rarely fear.
You raised the anger of our God,
Whose mercy still prevails.
We know His patience has
   withstood
Your unimproved details.

And yet you led a reckless life,
Like many previous years,
Still man's existence yet is strife
And blood and bitter tears.
So let us pray that eighty-two
May spring a bright surprise.
And social justice may yet strew
Our paths with friendly ties.

Esther D. Hartman
A NIGHT PRAYER
Lord, thank you for this day,
I hope every word I did say,
Was in praise of You
And my neighbor too.
Hope my words hurt no one,
So when this day is done,
I can say my words brought no
   pain,
Maybe even did entertain,
Some soul who is in sorrow,
Maybe tomorrow,
His grief might end,
And his broken heart mend.
Hope my actions caused no
   scandle,
There is nothing I can handle,
Without your divine,
Hand in mine,
To lead me,
And show me how to be,
The kind of person I ought to be,
If I want you to love me.

Stephen J. Shaluta Jr.
CHARLIE III
*[Dedicated to: Mr. & Mrs.
Charles A. Patterson Jr. and
Charles A. Patterson III; my
dear friends.]*
I was small and fraile, the day of
   my birth,
   A little earlier than I should
   be . . .
but I knew how long Mom and
   Dad had waited,
   the world for me to see.
I could hear their talking through
   my many months,
   inside my mommy's womb.
They talked of cradles, curtains,
   Bambi and such,
   making ready for my room.
They prayed and prayed for my
   safe arrival,
   but to me there was no doubt...
for the love I felt through those
   many months,
   I wanted to experience when I
   came out.
So I made up my mind, yes even
   then,
   that I would grow strong and
   be . . .
A present for Mommy and Daddy
   from heaven,
   a present named CHARLIE
   THREE.

Zakee Kaleem Abdullah
HELL OF PRISON
BANG, BANG, BANG, the slam
   of prison doors rang,
Voices in sorrow cry with stress
   and strain.
While solid brick walls stand and
   "yell"
Come one, Come all to the
   mysterious House of dripping
   halls.
Men walk in silence, guards walk
   in pride,

Where many souls face execution
and died.
There is no place to run or hide
I am not the only one who took
that lonesome ride.

I have seen many men with tears
falling from his eyes,
Horror in the night, was there a
prayer for morning light?
Whistling is a sound of threat, to
the freedom you hope you live
to get.
For the ugly road you'll always
regret.
Hell of prison is not over yet,
men swing and swung from the
ceiling on a rope.
Another man is dead at the crack
of dawn.
Some try to escape and make a
run, but they failed by the blast
of a double barrel shotgun.
There's no way out and one way
end.

Why does man commit crime
again and again.
For there no one has a friend,
until the day he's paroled by
the govenor's pen.

Linda S. Cook
FOR CHRISTOPHER
In a world of toys and trucks,
Choo—choo trains and rubber
ducks,
Lives a handsome little boy,
Who has become my pride and
joy.

I see him growing everyday,
Lovingly, I watch him play,
Tenderly, I hold him near,
This little boy, so dear.

I watch him while he sleeps at
night,
And in the early morning light,
He greets me with a sleepy smile,
This child, who makes it all
worthwhile.

I wish for him the best of things,
The sun that shines, the bird that
sings,
Calmness, and serenity,
This son, so much a part of me.

I'll be here to hold his hand,
As he grows from boy to man,
And dry his tears before they
start,
This child of mine, who holds my
heart.

There's something special
between us,
That loving care, that tender
trust,
And I know, of all the rest,
That he loves his mama best.

Evelyn Williams Mills
SEASONS
I didn't know when Autumn
came,
She caught me unaware
I opened my eyes one morning,
And found that she was there!

In retrospect I must admit,
She did not really sneak in,
She had, in subtle, gentle ways
ANNOUNCED THAT SHE WAS
COMING!

She had spoken through the
harvest,
I'd gleaned from vine and tree,
She'd whispered from the seedling
flowers,
That drooped so wistfully.

God says to us, in SEASONS,
Your life will be this way,
You're born and start growing in
Springtime,
In the winter you'll just fade
away.

In SUMMER, you reach full
maturity,
While the sun shines and soft
winds blow;
FALL'S beauty is poignant but
fleeting;
WINTER brings darkness and
snow.

Each SEASON presents special
attributes,
SPRING, WINTER, SUMMER
and FALL;
You will never know life in its
fullness
Until you've experienced them
all!

Robert Alexander
A LONELY CROW
A lonely crow across the sky
Moves into the haze of the
coming day.
It travels far,
        Does it know why?
The snow—covered fields offer
little
              food,
But the search must go on.
This is Nature's way—
     Make it or die!

Gail Arnett Estes
LITTLE FOXES
Moonlight spoons silver over the
wall,
Revealing small cracks
For the little foxes to slip
through.

These assassins spoil the
vineyard,
Steal my grapes,
And fade into the night.

Mardi
LIVE
*[In memory of my mother and
to my special friend]*
Live for today
It is the only way
Live for now
One should not ask how
Now is here
Make your life important and
clear
Live and do what you want
Don't always say not
See life as precious
Make it always new and fresh

Charlene "Charlie" Dillaman
MAKE LOVE EXPLODE
"Do for others what you want
them to do for you."
It is a commandment of God yes
and He showed us what to do.
He gave us Jesus, His only Son, to
die for our sins.
Jesus was perfectly humble, He
allowed God's will to win.

God loves us so much He forgets
and forgives.
He allows us to bear burdens, yet
He is so protective,
He never gives us more than He
knows we can bear.
When things get rough, we can
talk to God in prayer.
He loves us so much He shares
our every burden.
He understands our wrongs and
calls us back to Him again and
again.
It may not always be easy to
follow His example,
But give it a try . . . at least a
sample.
You will find treating others the
way you want to be treated,
That a lot of grief and hard
feelings in this world can be
deleated.
Just think next time . . . what
God has done for me;
Then your course will be
planned, you will be able to
see.
Everytime you do things for
others the way it should be
Like dying blameless and
innocent like Jesus did on the
tree;
Will make love explode, the
Spirit will be set free.
And you will do it more often
because it gives you such glee.

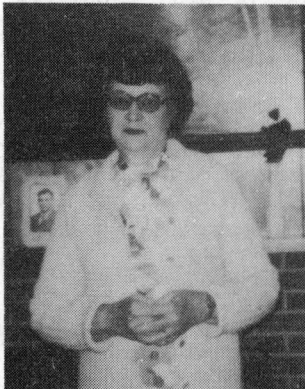

Myrtle A. Porter

Myrtle A. Porter
BEAUTY IS
Beauty is,
  A mother and a babe,
Beauty is,
  The old man in the shade.
Beauty is,
  A rose bush—in full bloom.
Beauty is,
  A moonlight night in June.
Beauty is,
  A bird that starts to sing,
Beauty is,
  Little children in a swing,
Beauty is,
  A home of peace, and love.
Beauty is
  God, watching us from above.
Beauty is,
  White rabbits in the snow,
Beauty is,
  All this,—yet I know.
Beauty is,
  Because, God made it so.

Marjorie E. Johnson
TO MOTHERS OF TWINS
[Dedicated to Kathy and Lynn]
The doctor announces, "It's
twins!!"
Which means double diapers and
safety pins,
Double the feedings both night
and day,
Double the bills we have to pay.

Double girls, one of each, or
double boys,
Double the toys, and also double
joys.
Yes, double joys and double
LOVE,
Given to us proud Moms from
ABOVE.

We were chosen from all the rest,
We really must be among the
best!!
Two lovely babies that are all
mine.
Two babies loved, and loving at
the same time.

Betty L. Dunn
THE MIRACLE WORKER
Have you met this miracle
worker?
This Jesus, Christ, the Lord.
He can do that which seems
impossible
Which you will find true, by
reading his word.

All He asks is that you except
Him,
And follow Him each day.
Work and witness for Him,
And remember to watch and
pray.

He will make your burden light,
And is with you each step of the
way.
Let this miracle worker,
Work a miraculous change in
you today.

Georgia Ann Briney
LEFT WITHOUT A DREAM
Do you know what it's like,
To be left without a dream?
There are no real tomorrows,
Because your mind has been
blown clean.

Looking into the future
Seeing darkness there.
Looking back in the past
At the joy and tears,
You've brought to bear.
Will you look at the past or
future,
Or do you dare?

Would it hurt too much to see
The bright, smiling young face
The face you knew yesterday.
Or will you even remember
The look that time has erased?

There was warmth and laughter,
Gentle touch,
Passionate embrace.
Holding each other in the night
Letting our eyes adjust to the
darkness
So we can see the moist softness
of the others face.

Am I to be left alone, hurt and
bewildered.

Wondering what's inside your
head?
Am I to be left without a dream?
Without a dream to live for?
Knowing you'll never again guide
me gently to your bed.

Please leave something to build
with
Leave the hope . . .
The hope with which to build a
dream.

Edith Louise McCormick
PRAYER
I hear the lonely drops of rain
Tap lightly at my windowpane
As though they long to be with me
To keep me silent company.

And though they utter not a
word
My heart responds as though it
heard
A note of warmth in their caress,
Dispelling gloom and loneliness.

O God! Give me a rainy day
When most I long to go astray—
When all my willful thoughts run
wild,
Give raindrops to your wayward
child.

Diane Marie Hart
EMPTY
An empty feeling
Today is lost
In
Tomorrow's undreamt dreams
I know
That they will not be
And so I get
An empty feeling

Mrs. Martha E. Cook
BRIEF MEMORY
A brief flash of memory
Of a child so cold and white
Lying in silk and satin
Under the Candle light

Flowers in great Profusion
Around the casket so small
Tore at my heart with anguish
Because I had lost my all

My tiny bundle of wonder
That was my Pride and joy
Left my arms so empty
My tiny Baby Boy

I only have flashes of memory
now
When I come out of that Dark
Place
I see that little White Casket
And the tiny Baby face

Doris Trevor Cannon
THE MASTER'S VIOLIN
I am a violin upon whose strings
some artist soul will play,
While pulsing, throbbing,
swaying in
the Master's tender, knowing
hand.
I'll live and breathe as velvet
fingers
guide the bow across my
hollow heart.
A song of passion, love and beauty
rises like a dream across the
land.

I sing and tremble at his warmth

and melt with love of him as
he plays on,
Then cry with happiness and
sound with
heavenly music at his great
desire.
He molds me, sways me, ever
drawing
music from my inner depths
Into his pounding veins where lies
the essence of his magic fire.

We flow together, quicksilver,
blending
in our need for each other
Until he tires and tosses me aside
to slumber for a time
As mortals do. I lie abandoned,
still and casket-bound, in my
case.
I yearn: my hollow heart whispers
in the dark, of unsung notes
sublime.

But pulsing strings that once
were taut
are quietly and now so
strangely mute.
Then at his searching touch by
gentle hands,
I leap to vibrant sound;
In ecstasy we sing our breathing
song
of two who love each other
well,
The Master and his Violin whose
music
rises o'er the earth unbound.

Viola C. Sharpe
TOO LONG
Too Long—I've waited for your
love
Too Long—I hoped you'd
understand.
But—I've waited too long,
too very long, for your love.

My heart and soul, frustrated,
Kept hoping that you would care.
But since my love never rated,
I found it too hard to bear.

Too Late—you offer me your
love.
Too Late—you come heart in
your hand.
But I've waited too long,
too very long—
Now love has flown.

Russell Daniel Gore
UP MOUNT ZION
*[Written in honor of my Elder
Brother, the Lord Jesus Christ,
Who came to restore my
crumbling earthly house, died
for my sin, and rose again to
share with me His glorious
eternal Home in Heaven.]*
Travellers to this mountain top
climbing up the Heavenly way
doubts and trials cannot stop,
faith makes progress every day.
Holding forth the Word of Light
when the way grows dark with
sin
God gives vict'ry in the fight:
crowns of righteousness, we
win.

Crowns we lay at Jesus' feet
as on Zion's mount we stand.
With His blest "Well done" to greet

"Yours, Beloved is Canaan's
land."

When you're troubled, Brother mine
or offended at your lot
never grumble or repine.
Praise the Lord for what you've
got.

Christ will drive away your gloom;
let His Spirit fill you through.
He, Who rose up from the tomb
lives to give life's best to you.

Banish hatred and false pride;
bear the cross, the lighter load.
Jesus, loving Friend and Guide
is the joy of Zion's road.

King of kings and Lord of lords,
praise the Lamb for sinners
slain.
Life eternal, Christ affords,
worthy evermore to reign.

Adrienne Dawn Durgin
WHAT IS LOVE?
What is Love?
A tiny white dove
Flying with ease
A gentle breeze
A majestic rose
Who knows?

Why is Love?
Is it this thing
Which can bring
A young woman
Out of her shell
Her lonely hell?

And make me see all colors
Brightly painted flowers
And warm summer showers

Can it make me crazy
Put me in a frenzy
Wonder which way is up
And where is down?

There are no frowns
Only a soft smile
All the while
It's much too late . . .

S.J. Uselton
HEARTBREAK
I built my confidence
on a fault line
got brave and
went outside.
It began to move,
to shift,
the foundation cracked—
I fell into a hole
shaking,
the world around me crumbling.

John W. Varney
Secret Lover, Secret Friend
You're so close, and yet you're
not.
I can see you and touch you.
But I cannot love you.
You will not give me the chance.

I thought that I knew you.
Instead I only know your name.
You may not know who I am,
And you may not even care.

But I am here.
And I will always be near.
Just in case you remember me,
And you need someone to lean
on.

For I am someone that you can use,

And then throw away when
you're done.
You can look at me, or look past
me.
But I will be here anyway.

For I am your Secret Lover,
Someone who will love you for
eternity.
And I am your Secret Friend,
The person who will stand by
your side,
When there is no-other.

Jack Dempsey
**Schumacher the
Electrician**
A guy on our maintenance crew
Wired his beard to a high voltage
screw.
Though he got it unstuck
By sheer stroke of luck,
Word has it we almost lost Shu.

Some say he's as mad as a hatter,
That he really should keep his
face flatter.
They fear for his fur
For a spark could occur,
And a fireface is no laughing
matter!

Elizabeth Russell
THE HOUSE
The storm lashed the House on
the windswept hill,
Haunted, it is, with an icy chill,
Each flash of light and
thunderous boom,
Stirs the House to life with
things from the tomb.

Mystery abounds in these dark
walls of fear,
It huddles and waits for a victim
to appear.
Shutters have long been torn
from its sides,
Black holes for windows where
evil abides.

Doors sway on hinges broke
loose by the storm,
And lightning reveals Its most
hideous form,
Don't let it fool you that
ruineous sight,
You stand in awe of Its terror by
night!

What lies behind those dark,
murky, walls?
Whose voice can be heard
moaning in the halls?
It is the souls who cannot be free?
The spirits of folks who once
used to be?

The House creaks and groans and
wails its lament,
Till the wind subsides and the
storm is spent,
The House wins its battle from a
violent doom,
And things from the grave still
walk in its gloom.

Go at your risk if adventure you
seek!
To join a ghost hunt is not for
the weak,
The House is alive with a force
and a will,
Those who have entered may be
there still!

Neal Collins
SAPPHIRE BLUES
*[To Donna Mills, The Moody
Blues and Marty Feldman]*
I find my Juliet dancing in your
sparkle,
A slow step. Hauntingly
Shakespearean.
As ephemeral as the twilight
emitting
An effervescent aura upon your
face.
Illuminating this spark of
lightning
Bolting! But hushed . . .
As delicate as your breath.
Your silent lips defening my
heart
As we waltz as constant as the
stars.
Graceful, like the satin pillow
Between our souls. I visualize
Silken wings beyond a halo
fanning
The embers of this firey embrace.
I have succumbed to the
fragrance,
The toxic scent of a requited love
Offering only myself as booty.
For, like gems of some ancient
treasure
I find my wealth in your Sapphire
Blues.

Gwendolyn Carlton
WEDNESDAY
Tuesday the phone rang, I hoped
it would be you.
Tuesday the phone rang, I
wondered what was new
Tuesday the phone rang, I had
wanted you to call.
Tueday the phone rang, but it
wasn't you at all.

Russell Daniel Gore
A Thanksgiving Prayer
*[Dedicated to the redeemed
church, Christ's Bride soon to
Rapture, to unite with Him and
enjoy His eternal peace and
love and pleasure, with praise
and glory to God as in Rev.
19-22.]*
"In faithfulness and praise we
enjoy Thy mercy, Lord as in
Psalm 136"
"Thank You, dear Lord for fortune
good;
since it's from You, I know I
should.
When it seems bad I thank You
still,
because I know that's not Your
will.

Thanks, Lord when others treat
me well;
don't let me fail, my thanks to
tell.
And even when they do me wrong
keep my thanksgiving true and
strong.
Thanks for Your Spirit leading me
to praise, whate'er my lot may
be.
Because You make all turn out
right,
thanks, Lord for life though
dark or bright.
Thanks, Lord for neighbors good
and kind,
for unity of heart and mind.
Thanks too for enemies I face,
for help to win them by Your
grace.
Thanks for Your power to forgive,
for conscience free, by faith to
live.
Thanks for a mansion up on High
well worth a thousand times to
die.
Thanks for the daily Bread You give
that helps me thankfully to
live.
Thanks for new challenges each day
to help discouraged souls Your
way.
Thanks evermore for fam'ly bound
for Rapture at Your trumpet
sound.
For hope to praise You up Above
with countless millions for
Your love."

Cheryl Helsel
STALLION GHOST
A stallion once stood on the top
of a hill,
He stood so proud, he stood so
still,
Guarding his herd, he was truly
the best,
He preserved the heritage of the
west.

Running from man he was
graceful and swift,
From the ground, dust he did lift.
For his herd he cared the most,
Now he's gone, now he's only a
ghost,
But his soul still lives and he's
still the best
His foals live on to preserve the
west.

Marylou McLean Hahn
GRETCHEN'S WORLD
[My Granddaughter—1979]
We picked up fallen leaves
She said that they were flowers
I wished that I could see
Fallen leaves as flowers.

Apples lay upon the ground
The tree was almost bare
She said that it was pretty
I saw no beauty there.

Lines on paper soon become
Anything her heart desires
Circus clowns and acrobats
Walking on high wires.

Oh the land of make believe
As seen thru her young eyes
Is it all a childlike game
Or is she very wise.

Jerry Kahn
GRAINS OF SAND
*[To my dearest Jean: May our
"Grains" of life, love, and
happiness always gently fall
side by side . . .]*
Each grain of sand gently falls,
Separate: distinct: a particulate
infinity,
Softly landing, enjoining one and
all,
Each one living in total
equanimity.

Peggy A. Kirkland

Peggy A. Kirkland
RIGBYS
[To Arthur and Julian]
Ominous clouds of classic
physiques
Lighted in rainbowic flashes of
chins
and cheeks.

Cubic faces showing blanket
expressions of,

"I'm nobody, playing at being
a somebody, but what?"

Jerry Campbell
Message From the Seashore
*[Dedicated to my friend Ernie
as inspiration for those days we
can't face by ourselves. 143.]*
I walked on the seashore today,
hoping the sand and sea
would take life's pains away from
me.
The sand is so deep, so warm, and
free
surely it can take all my fears
from me.
The sea is endless—knows none
of man's disguise,

surely it could dry the tears in
my eyes.

I sat and pondered the cares of
the day
and knew these things could not
take my burdens away.
But God in His love spoke
especially to me
through the grains of sand and
the waves of the sea.

These beauties I beheld were
created by His hands
and in His own image, He created
man.
His power sets boundaries for
each wave on the shore,
Yet He cares enough to knock at
my heart's door.

But God's power and might were
not the messages for me,
It was His love He wanted me to
see.
The grains of sand are
immeasureable—the waves do
not cease.
His love is unlimited—
unmeasured—I can rest in His
peace.

James V. Biundo
Supercalc Megabyte Mainframe Christmas
*[To my wife, Antoinette, and
daughters, Terrilee, Kimberly,
and Tammy, for all the happy
"real" Christmases.]*
Hardware Santas synchronize
software "Ho, Ho, Ho's."

Synthesizers entry-load
floppy disk "Silent Nights."

Micro-processors interface
digital angels.

Graphics systems disk-drive
satellite sleighs.

Micro-computers play
with macro-emotions.

Memories are stored.

And yes, Virginia,
There really is a Christmas.

Helen K. Thornton
A Christmas Blessing To Far-off Grandchildren
*[This poem is dedicated to My
Grandchildren, Seth Kelly and
Jamie Marie King. All My Love,
Grandma Helen]*
A Merry Christmas-Jamie!
A Merry Christmas-Seth!
I wish You so much joy and a
Christmas that is blessed
with everything Your hearts
desire that Santa-Claus can
bring!
A Christmas tree with tinsel—A
Minstrel who will sing
all Your favorite carols, and make
glad tidings ring!

And—when You write to Santa,
tell Him, please, of Me!
Tell Him what Grandma would
like most, underneath Her tree
would be My darling Jamie and
My precious little Seth;
These two Dears in this whole
world would make Me
happiest!

And—also, please remember what Christmas is really about—

It's our Blessed Saviour's Birthday, and Angel Hosts all shout! Hallelujahs to our Lord and King!
    Hosannas and glad-tidings ring!

A little Babe was born This Day to take Our sins and shame away!

And—while old Santa's lots of fun and gives Us so much pleasure! Our Lord is Our most precious Gift—
    and He's Christmas's greatest Treasure.
        Your Grandmother Helen

Christopher Allen Lay
A Part of My Pilosophy
[For N.J.—She saw something in this piece that I didn't, and still don't, but her faith in the work has ended herein.]
I have fought three types of battles during the short span of my years—
one of necessity,
one of desire,
and one of supposed cowardice.
Only the latter made any sense at all,
and ultimately kept me from hurting,
and being hurt.

Warren S. Satterlee II
SEDUCTION
Slowly, penetrating the upper reaches of the Heavens,
Erecting rapidly, limbs spreading, stretching, turning,
    A skyscraper rapes the sky once more.

Carol Lusk Carter
TIME
Time
Is like water
In a babbling brook.
You can catch it, make use of it,
Or let it rush by.
Every minute of every hour of every day
Brings us that much closer
To the Inevitable End
As to the Divine Beginning.
Therefore, let us live
Every day as though
It were our last
Loving God
And fellow man.

Tonda English Meche
Merry Christmas, Santa
I want to tell you a story of long, long ago,
About Santa and his reindeer, HO, HO, HO.
Twas on a white winter night, the sky all aglow,
I saw a sleigh a comin', across a yard full of snow.

It stopped at my house, I was excited as could be,
For a little jolly man jumped off, with a present just for me.
When he knocked on my door, I asked him to come see,

For I had a present just for him under my Christmas tree.

For you see, Santa's always giving and I wanted him to know,
That we do appreciate his Christmas spirit and his presents so.
With a smile on his face and a twinkle in his eyes,
He thanked me for the gift and said it was a wonderful surprise.
My heart was full of joy, and I really do believe,
That it is far better to give, than to receive.

Betsy F. Sayre
Dilemma Of the Christmas Tree
Tall muted glowing triangle of tiny colored lights
magic
in the corner of the living room
packages
ribbons, tinsel,
creche.

Elder son
intelligent, tense, too sensitive
Christmas,
Christ is real
no fake green plastic
forest visitor
stranger to the climate-controlled corner of the living room.

Daughter
preoccupied with toddling son
small fingers reaching, pulling
exploring branches
ornaments hung low for him.

Younger son
quick, verbal
strong body and will
determined to protect his world
"You're not going to kill another tree, are you?"

Crocheted white angel ceiling high serenely gazes
dog's tail sweeps through the lowest branches
dropped wire hanger in the carpet ambush the sweeper
stacked boxes, empty, on the dryer.

Silent beauty reflected in the mirror
moving colors
fragile moments emotion-laden
magic triangle of light
the Christmas tree
in the corner of the living room.

Mary Snow Jackson
SPRING
[To my daughters Gail and Susan]
Gentle breezes and a butterfly
    Grass greener as the days go by
Bright colors and a baby deer
    Let us know that Spring is here.

Buds bursting forth in bloom
    Gone are the shadows and the gloom
Birds singing in every tree
    Lets us know that Spring is here.

Bright hellos and a cheery smile
    Everyone lingers to talk awhile
Children's laughter with sounds so dear
    Lets us know that Spring is here.

Morley B. Forsyth
CALAMITY?
The crystal goblet crashed to the floor
And a river of wine flowed under the door
As the giant's shout became a roar
When the Golden Goose laid no more—
Its feathers drooped and it was pooped
As the golden eggs had stretched its legs
So now it didn't care and bathed in coffee dregs—
Even at this the giant raged
And turned attention to cellars of kegs—
Of cheap wines, ales, and huge bowls of raw eggs.

Claire Schuman Hund
DRIFTING
Wave
wash over me

Bee
Buzz me a song

Tree
stand guard for me

Tide
sweep me along

E.V. Gaudinier
DESERT CEMETERY
Scratched together from the sand,
lowly mounds that tumbleweeds bounce over
on the way to nowhere,
these poor graves
more truly show death's barrenness
than flowered lawns and marble tombs designed
to hide the awful fact
that man is dust.

Lois Dahlberg
Dear Lord We Thank You For Our Nation
For hills and streams and valleys
For mountains, meadows, trees
For wilderness, for beatuy
Thank you, dear Lord, for these.

For this great country blessed beyond
All cultures of this sphere
For freedom, unknown in other lands

That we are granted here.

We thank you for the Bill of Rights
Declaration of Independence
Forefathers who gave their all
Our flag of great resplendence.

On this special day we celebrate
The divine inspiration
You gave those worthy men, Dear Lord
We thank you for our nation.

Marc Joseph Malandra
SGT. LENNON
He spoke of peace and freedom
    of living what you feel
Of dreams and schemes and other things
    that made it all seem real

He spoke of understanding
    a brotherhood of man
And now that he's no longer here
    we'll do the best we can

He stood right by his woman
    he did what he thought right
He knew that in the darkest hours
    there always is some light

He left us all his music
    he lived his life as art
And than a bullet killed him
    on his fresh and hopeful start

Oh, the pain I felt that night
    the thoughts that filled my mind
Although the loss seemed personal
    it was for all mankind

Dianne Keith Borsenik
AUTUMN SONG
Come and join the celebration!
Riotous in coloration,
Unconsumed in conflagration,
Trees lift torches to the sky.

Summer finds its cancellation
In a dance of separation.
Crisp in whispered conversation,
Trees receive the wind's reply.

Nancy Summers
SWEET COUNTRY
Looking out the kitchen window
Oh—what a life for you and me
Sweet Country
There—as you come around the bend
My life is complete, Amen

Helen Sims Smaw
BE STILL AND KNOW
I like to open my ears to the silence of the sunset,
To God's movement as inaudible as the colorful changes,
To become still and know that God is God.
I am his creation, his image, for whom he cares.

I like to taste the purity of a cloud
That hours before was turbulent with misery,
And know God's power of forgiveness and rebirth.
He says, "I will fight for you . . . Be still."

I like to smell the clean, fresh morning air renewed
After the whirlwind and fire have consumed my spirit.

A resurgence of courage responds
to the still, small voice
That says, "Try again. I'll give you
strength as the day."
I like to be still and open my
vision to challenges
As bold as the rainbow, yet have
the security and hope
Like the constancy of the seven
colors that God's goodness
With virtues seventy times seven
will never wane.

I like to touch a fellow image of
God's love.
In extrasensory communion we
feel God's extending himself
As if we were lily petals
unfolding in the sunlight,
Destined for beauty, grace, and
usefulness.

I like to be still and know, be
filled and grow.
I thank the caring Creator of me
with my senses.
I thank him who has endowed me
with the capacity
To enjoy my being human and
his being God.

Christie A. Harbour
THE FEAR
Ebony swirling, swirling, closing
in. Zap!
Teeth gnawing, gnawing, biting
down, snap!
Nocturnal, primeval screams of
abandonment and terror.
Waves followed by waves of evil
sickness.
Unrestful, uneasy stamping of
hooves nearer and nearer to my
soul.
A mind running and running to
find eternity.
Morbid sick mental images
clouded over and painted in a
blood red picture,
Outlined with the black of a
rotting heart.
Viciously torn from the breast,
the babe becomes withered,
To die unloved.
Human beings severed from each
other due to conventions.
They roll slowly down the hill
toward their graves, sunken
and unnourished.

Christina Gross
UNTITLED
A woman of easy virtue
Perfect prey for someone like
you.
Oppose her, then tempt her,
Submerge her in lies;
Just another half-smoked
cigarette
Left burning in your bed.

Laurel Carey
LIFE IS A ROSE
[To Bernie]
Darling, our life has been roses,
Not the long stemmed beauties
But like the tangled little
rambling rose,
That grows along the roadside.
The ones that must push up
through the cracks in the tar;
They stand against all obstacles,
Yet they bend with the storms.

Our rose doesn't wither at the
first sign of drought,
It stands tough!
It's the kind that shares its
meager space with all other
species.
It will bloom in all conditions,
then gratefully displays its
delicate blossoms to the
Creator.
Our rose is the kind whose fragile
beauty, out weighs its thorny
stems.
Yes darling, I believe our life is
roses!

Anne Bentley
INSOMNIA
Now I lay me down to sleep,
I pray the Lord my dreams to
keep,
While I lie here counting sheep.

Richard H. Meyers
THERE WAS LOVE
There was love and light and
laughter in the castle of the
king
The night the shepherds
crossed the hills to hear the
angels sing,
And as years rolled by for
centuries, the name of Christ
was sung
On cold and windy winter nights,
while chapel bells were rung.
There was light in every
window, there was love in
every eye,
There was laughter in the
school room with Christmas
cribs near-by.
There was love and light and
laughter then behind each
schoolhouse door,
But the name of Christ can not
be sung by children anymore.
Instead we hear some sleigh
bells ring, or see a few green
trees,
An imitation Santa Claus with
children on his knees,
Expensive gifts, and mistletoe,
and whiskey running free,
And empty love, and broken
hearts, and Christless revelry.

Jan Bratcher
Society's Unloved Child
A blue-eyed girl
You were born to this world.
Beaten and bruised;
Mistreated, abused.
You fought to survive
In a world so unkind.
You killed with a knife
To save your own life.
You shivered in cold;
With years you grew bold.

If fate had been different
And life had been kind,
You might have had a professor's
mind.
If you had been born
Some rich man's child,
You might not have stolen
And turned out so wild.

But fate was not kind,
And life is not blind.
Unloved and in pain,
Society is blamed.

And so after of years of crimes
untold
You sit in a prison still trying to
be bold.
If someone had loved you and
been there for you,
You might not be sitting here
with a cell for your view.

Debbie Keeling

Debbie Keeling
TOO LATE
Last night I dreamed I was
standing in front
of the Lord by heaven's gate.
But I could not look upon His
face,
because instead of joy, I felt
shame and fear;
'cause I knew the time had come
for me to see
what I had made of my life.

Something drew my eyes upon
His face.
But His face I didn't see;
instead it was visions of me,
and what I saw there made me
feel shame and regret!

There was my husband and me—
harsh words had led to an
argument.
Off to work he went, and as the
door shut
I thought, "I'll fix a good super
tonight,
and tell him I'm sorry and I love
him."
All day long I watched the clock
and as
supper time grew near, I began to
fix his favorites;
but there was a knock at the
door, and there stood
a friend of his from work with
tears on his face.
He could hardly tell me, my
husband would never
be home for supper again.
And as he left, tears streamed
down my face for
I knew *it was too late!*

Then another vision came. I saw
a little girl.
She was asking me, "Mom, can we
go to Sunday School?"
I answered, "When I get time!"
Then she became older and was
standing beside
a man, but she wasn't dressed in
white, and she
had a suitcase in her hand.

She was walking
toward the door. I was pleading
and asking her,
"Can't we talk about this?" And
she said as
she shut the door, "It's too late!"

Then my final vision came and it
was of several
friends and family asking "Why
don't you come
to church, we'd love to have you."
And I'd always
reply, "I'm too busy, maybe next
time."

Then I began to cry and pray,
"God, please forgive
me and give me another chance.
Please don't say,
"It's too late!"

Lali Busboom
FRIENDSHIP
Pillars of a mind—a friend.
One who is there for you
To share a laugh, a shoulder to
lend
An encouraging word, no matter
what you do.

A friend to love is truly a gift
That touches your soul and inner
being
With a gentleness that gives you
a lift
To heights of quiet emotions
never seen.

To call one friend, is to say—
I am as I am—with no reserve.
Your strength it guides the way
To meet my fate as I deserve.

To feel a oneness with someone
Is living the ultimate goal
Of knowing that next to none,
A good friend is a reflection of
your soul.

Paula D. Davis
SILENCE THE SONG
The song is there, upon the wind,
The laugh is there, with my
friend.
Sing the song, whispers the wind,
Bring the laughter to my friend.

The laughter . . . The song . . .
Keeps us together . . .
. . . RIGHT or WRONG.

What is a song? Where is the
wind?
What is the laugh? Where is my
friend?
The song is lost, my friend is
gone,
The laughter has passed . . .
The together was wrong . . .

Silence the song . . .
Fly the wind . . .
Cease the laugh . . .

GOODBYE . . .
. . . TOGETHER.

Dawn Aarhus Anderson
A FIGHT FOR LIFE
Listen to me, Friend!
You can't leave me now.
I've tried so hard to make you see
You're special,
And you've just begun to
understand.

You've just begun to realize

That you're valuable . . .
That it matters to people that
you're here.

You've finally begun to grow . . .
To break out of the shell
You've lived in for 35 years.
You've become more
independent . . .
More outspoken, less afraid.

You've learned to love,
And accept love,
Without guilt or suspicion,
Because you've come to know
You're deserving.

How ironic, then,
That just when you've begun to
live,
You also begin to die.

Well, I won't have it, Friend!
I won't!
It's taken us years to grow what
we have,
And I refuse to let cancer
Rob me of you.

Be prepared for a fight,
Because I'm not letting go,
And if you're the person
I think you've become,
Neither will you

Brenda L. Lewis
MOTHER
I do not know, how she does it, or
even why
She has been married, over half
her life
Sometimes I know she cries

I do not know, where or why,
maye it is for
The life, she never knew, that
slipped by

I always wondered, if she would
change things, if
She had the chance, maybe she
would
Have chosen, a different romance

She raised her kids, and her
husband
She gave us so much love, but got
It back, so very seldom

I tried to help, to keep up with
the demand
But always seemed to fall, where
she would stand

I wished so much, to be like her,
to live the
Life, she had chosen, a house, a
family, a home

Someday I know, I will be out, on
my own
Maybe I will live the life, she
always dreamed
Or stumble in to a new life, with
her beside me

She is one of a kind, and that she
will always be
I love her so much, I hope she is
proud of me

James Kelly Duhon
SLEEPING CITY
Sleeping City, in speckled darkness
How mornful your factories
sound tonight
Though the hour be late
Yet—your cires gush forth like an
endless echo in the night.

O City, City, Sleeping City
Why push your grief
on humanity?

Must the innocent share
the blame of men
whose lust and greed
has stained your walls.

Within your core
sins run wild
While the taste of desires
muddle mens' minds.

It is his creation that
made you exist
It is your destiny to shelter
his passions.

Mourn your grief Sleeping City,
Mourn on into eternity.

Esther Myers

Esther Myers
TWO POETS
Though poles apart in verse you
were,
The thoughts you've written,
time can't blur.
Service, with lusty hold on life,
Gibran, with such ethereal strife.

Yes, many poets ply their trade,
But very few who match the
grade,
Of those who touch the heart and
soul,
Gibran and Service, on your own
atoll.

Marie Carmel
A TEACHER
Like a Guardian Angel
You will see her there
Protecting every pupil
Placed within her care
Like a Heavenly Choir

Her voice possesses song
She's one we all admire
As she teaches right from wrong
How much she endures
No one realy knows
What she feels from deep within
Her broad smile never shows
Daily she remembers
Her most important deed
And exercises love to all
Regardless of their creed
No one realizes
As each student leaves
How much it affects her
Or how much she grieves
Yet, when they are leaving
She gives a parting look
And turns again, to write each
name
In memory's Sacred Book

Rebecca Braley
THE SONG
words
gently
formed
on
a
blank
piece
of
paper
notes
melody
rhythm
suddenly
the
paper
comes
to
life
ringing
with
sweet
melodic
harmony
a
soft
flowing
piece
of
music

Laurel D. Preston
I AM YOUR CHILD
[This poem is dedicated to my
mom and dad because like the
words within, their love for me
will never die.]
Fill me with your aspirations
Teach me in your ways
Breathe to me the breath of life
Love me all my days.

Open up the doors of hope
Span the hardest trials
Stop me when I'm doing wrong
Across life's weary miles.

I am your child, I'll do my best
Whether it's right or wrong
You've taught me well
And I can tell
I'll make it on my own.

Carolyn Tryon
THE AMERICAN FARM
Where am I?
I am everywhere, over this great
land, your miles and miles
that you call a country.

Where am I?
I am nowhere, just out of reach of
your hand, always in your
mind, when you look to your
country, and for it.

I am the picture on the postcard,
the silhouette of fulfilled hope.
I am the buildings fleeting by
your fast train you rejoice in to
see, and wonder about.
I am the American farm.

Biceps and tans, yellow, dark and
white hair, looking over the
earth, while the skies look over
us.
Owners have learned to do this,
in infinitesimal trust.

I am everywhere.
I am everything.
I am nothing.
I am here.
So very much something. Am I
clearer in your mind, now?

You city dweller, how could you
forget the countryside, or me?
I belong to those who share the
joys of the rising sun;—the
little peep of chicks, the gentle
lowing of cows, the dew on
growing food.

In the evening, God's cloak folds
around us. The farm folks eat,
and then watch in ease, how
He brings about yet another
new time, the even-tide, and
then, under
A winking, sparkling, starry
ceiling, comes the unwinding
and the deep, good sleep.
The new-invented TV, by farm
years, casts lights and shadows
on the wall, when all the lights
are out.

Train, go by, and see us call ten
late,
And lights go out, for trains add
to our lullaby.

I'm the circle, the rectangle, the
cylinder of silo, and wind-mill;
I'm the even rows, and flags of
plants, and elms and willows,
and can make the plain
straight, for the sake of all that
grows.

I'm the American farm.
Not for blight.
But delight.

Mark Radford Harris
BETH
[For the Beth I know is out
there somewhere . . .]
Beth I know that you don't know
me
But I've loved you from the start
From the day I first saw your
picture
That's the day you captured my
Heart
my Heart

Beth, I don't even know your real
name
But it doesn't matter, since you
don't know mine
Beth I know you live your life in
fortune and fame
Please come with me and we'll
leave it behind

228

Beth you know I can see your
pain
Your eyes shine like gold, but
they're
empty
Just like mine   Just like mine
I know your heart is frightened
and alone
And you're tired of hearing that
same old line
That same cold lie

Beth, come with me and we will
both rise above
All the lies and liars you have
lived with before
All I can offer you is my honest
Love
You and I both know no one has
ever offered you more.

Kathleen Jordan Larkin
FIRST LOVE
i learned so young of loves
uncertainty;
that we spend our lives looking
for the reality
which only lasts in storybooks
and in dreams
only to find out that our love is
never as it seems

so now looking back on all the
mistakes we made
still aching from the games we
played
though my love for him has long
since died;
i could never forget him, lord
knows i've tried

i picked up the pieces and had to
go on
though his memory lingered, he
was gone
forgive and forget is what they
say
but a part of me died when he
went away

Francis M. Daniels
LIFT UP
At midday I stand beneath a tree,
Perceiving the beauty
surrounding me.
The vaired size of the many trees
Makes me, God, compare myself
to Thee;
The magnitude I know of You,
Brings my insignificant self to
view.

The ground is carpeted beneath
my feet;
I ponder whether to take a seat

Upon the bed of luscious green;
I stand *awed* by the scene;
I could not sit while your trees do
stand
To lift up to touch Your hallowed
hand.
So I stand, too, unworthy I am;
But I hope someday to take a
stand
And be worthy to lift up my
hand, to You,
And say to others, "Meet God. He
made *me* too."

Rene C. Knight
BEACON
*[To my sister, Doris A. Askew,
a lover of poetry.]*
In deep recesses of the mind
Are all the primitive days of time,
No thing forgotten, no thing
erased.
Only subconscious memory
May fathom the maze
Of this limitless storage place
And flash from the past
A beacon to the moment of
reality.

Fred Diggles
FAST HIDEOUS
Our kids are not a bit fastidious.
The outcome is naturally quite
hideous.
To tell the entire composite,
They are the exact opposite:
They are indeed the utmost
slowstidious.

James Dylan Blake
HEAVENS LAW
*[To those who have eyes to
see]*
Preachers;
Creatures;
Rulers of empires wail;
Building a wall,
so tall,
for people to scale;
To one day crumble to the sea,
one and all,
Heavens law.

Maureen Rose
BELIEVE
Of life
what do you say is important?
To sing
To dance
To act
or make fortune?
Whatever your choice
let not it be evil
Believe in your dreams
for dreams are what make
people.

Melani Marie Mendoza
UNCONDITIONAL LOVE
Love is allowing.
The allowing should
not be a force,
but a genuine need
to experience the
true giving of love.
Those who love
because it must be so
without authenticity
of love will find
life discouraging
in what they do.

Give, and life will
Open from within you.

Life was always there,
but we were afraid
to discover our
ability to do so.
Feel, and our need
to express flows
easily, because true love
is not just determination,
but awareness of
our real selves.

So to possess love
is never possible.
It cannot be searched
unless one has an
awareness of how to
be within himself.
Only when one has
strength to experience
all circumstances
while encountering life
will he find beauty in
all that he does in Life.

Helen Marie Hinkle
DEATH
Dreams of falling
forever falling into darkness,
into the cavern of death.
Falling from a world of
intensity and loudness
into a world of quiet
stillness.

Susan Daschuk-Rosvold
DEPRESSION
My senses are reeling
The room is spinning around me
My body feels weightless,
floating . . .
And yet my heart is heavy
Darkness is coming, slowly
Creeping into my consciousness
But I cling to reality
The clock ticks on
Time passes day by day
Morning, noon, night
Each taking their place
Taking their toll in my mind
How long can I go on
I want to live
But I want to die
Sleep eludes me
Yet I'm not awake
Darkness is coming, slowly . . .

Randy Cunningham
CHRISTMAS IN JULY
Jingle bells, jingle bells,
Christmas in July,
Joyfully watching our little
boy, with tear drops in his eye.
Toys gallore covered his bed, to
gladden his weakened heart,
Oh God, cure the sore, how did
it get its start?

He's only two, too young to
strain, he can hardly move
around,
Nothing to strain his weakened
heart, in happiness he abounds.
A happy boy that laughs with all,
no tear stains on his cheek,
But gifts from all that loves
this soul, his tear ducts sprung
a leak.

Carefully catching a falling tear, a
spot of love on a card,
To store away another
memory, with others that come
so hard.

One month to live, maybe two,
and that five months ago,
God has given us this angel
star, in his hair a Christmas
bow.

Only two Christmasses for this
little waif, that is so very few,
But joys have filled his very
life, love from all he drew.
Tomorrow, next week or months
away, we'll loose our little boy,
But to all, his smiles and love
he's given, to us, eternal joy.

Stanley Jack
THE LOVE OF MY LIFE
The moment I saw her on campus
that day—her soft laughter,
the warmth and love that
was apparent between her
and her co-ed companions—
some strange something struck
me,
struck me like a bolt from the
blue
informing me: THERE!
THERE'S THE ONE!
THE ONE AND ONLY,
LOVE OF MY LIFE!
We met, became sweethearts;
were engaged, married.
Our life together has been a joy.
We traveled some,
made friends, had fun.
Later, came a baby girl
—a miniature of her pretty
mother.
Now, two to love.
Later still, a baby boy;
three to love.
Sure, there were some sad days, too,
with disagreements, and tears,
but just a few.
Today, it's mid-afternoon.
I wish you could see
my three precious ones
all sound asleep—mother
curled up
on the couch, cuddling
her little daughter
—my 'Tiny Tim' nearby on the
floor.
And, there you have a postcard
portrait
of the one—the one and only
LOVE OF MY LIFE

Cliff Churchman
1-7-81 (20:24)
Time
begins in the
Imagination

proceeds
through the
Present

and on
into the
Imagination.

Theresa M. Hull
The Sailor's Inspiration
Away, aloft, above the skies,
Before the wind the sailor flies.
Cruising ever silently,
Down the waves and o'er the
sea.
Ever flowing, soft, stormy sea,
Forgotten ancient memories,
while
Grasping thoughts of days gone by,

Heaving lines go flashing nigh.
Into the waves, the sailor sails,
Just to itself, the wind it wails.
Keeping to itself its song
Lonely moaning, lasting long.
Making sailboats move along, with
No noise but the sea gulls
song.
Only now, the wind it fails
Pushing boats along no more.
Quiet winds just reach the shore,
Rustling barely the seaside
trees.
Softly wind will move the leaves,
Touching gently with its
breeze.
Uniting both the boats and seas
while
Vexing sailors with its pleas.
Washing boats o'er to their lees.
Xebec, schooner, whaleboat's
prow,
Yacht, the water sweeps the bow,
and they're
Zipping along o'er the waves
once again.

Lou Fabian
Challenge and Opportunity
Pittsburgh Steeler Head Football
Coach, Chuck Noll, once said,
"We have no problems, only
challenges and opportunities."
A deeper meaning within this
expression forecasts an outlook
of success. Replacing the word
'problem' with the word
'challenge or opportunity,' will
present you with a clearer
understanding of the task at
hand. Place yourself in a frame
of mind which views problems
as challenges and new
problems as opportunities.
Something which is a challenge
today is overcome tomorrow. If
an opportunity arises, convert
that opportunity into success.
The challenge of overcoming a
handicap, such as loss of sight,
presents you with a new world
to conquer. The opportunity to
find a new worker for the
business, to replace the loss of
one so valuable, allows you to
bring in the best. The best is
needed to conquer new worlds,
while opportunities and
challenges bring out the best in
all of us. Ordinary people like
you and I, who live for the
opportunity, rise to the
occasion and do what must be
done, become great people.

Ellen Ruppel
LOVERS' QUARRELS
I strike out at you
with words
little nasty phrases
childish, petty disturbances
and you hit back.

I fend you off
with weak, ineffectual blows
to your body
mind
spirit.

You do likewise
vice versa.

We push away
hit and claw
scratch and fight
to keep from falling into each
other.

I hit and hit to keep from loving
you.

Susan Hutchison Olney

Susan Hutchison Olney
COBWEB MEMORIES
*[To a mysterious memory,
Finding wisdom through the
experience, And accomplishing
the feeling.]*
Once upon a heart,
with promised dreams
through wild schemes
were weaving away in my head...

For grey smokey places,
familiar friendly faces
which spun into tears that I've
shed.

Blurry Cobweb Memories
hanging here in my mind,
only musty memories
of lost love I've come to find.

Climbing endless stairs,
I vision you there
clinging in corners of the room.
Abandoned hidden heartaches
looking back at me now,
found deserted in an old saloon.

Haunting Cobweb Memories
hanging on in my mind.
linger many moments
of a love, gone wandering and
blind.

Whiskey raising laughter,
smiles forever after
and dancing old good times,
keep drifting away

each tick of the clock,
as it toils with the sound of
chimes.

Waking Cobweb Memories,
strung across my misty mind,
still, just lonely memories
of my life, left dangling behind...

Barbara Lee Brownsword
WILLIAM
Blink your eyes,
now he's the Wizard.
His very presence
commands that you
Notice him,
    Respect him,
        Obey him,
            Fear him . . .

Blink you eyes,
now he's the Man.
His boyish charm
pleads that you
Want him,
    Need him,
        Touch him,
            Hold him,
                Love him . . .

Blink your eyes,
which do you see?
Is he Wizard,
or is he Man?
Do you fear the Man,
love the Wizard?

Blink your eyes,
the smoke has cleared.
See his eyes,
the answer is here!
Love this Wizardly Man
you once had feared.

Blink your eyes,
and you will know,
The Wizard is merely
a facade that hides
the Man
    He's afraid
        to show.

D.G. Lohmeyer
WIND
Whispering trees, tell me please
    Answers to questions in my
    mind.
The soft wind blows, a sign that
shows
    Tranquility of heart I shall
    find.
I will bend my ear, I cannot fear
    The story you will tell me here.
Of present and past, the future
alas
    My life's story I will not fear.
Quiet wind, I know what has
been
    The future is what I am asking.
Blow in my ear, so I may now
hear
    A full life that's everlasting.

Jean B. Finley
SHE WHO BECKONS
Tangled in her hair she wears a
crown
of stars, and in her hand another
one
held there. Her eyes shine softly
with
blue moonlight, and her smile
enchants.
Deep, mysterious, and warm as
summer's

eve, she beckons.

When, at close of day, I lie upon
my
bed for night's repose, she comes
to
me. Tenderly she gathers me into
her
arms, cradles me, and blankets
me
with peace and love. Head
pillowed on
her breast, deeply in her spell,
I'm
safely home . . . and yet, I feel
the
unknown there.

When dawn retreats she holds
me closer
for a moment, then reluctantly I
loose
her and bid her slip away. She
cannot
stay, nor can I go. My time here
is
not finished; my purpose
incomplete.

And yet, one day she'll not relent,
and
I will understand. Unafraid, I'll
clasp
her hand, and follow where she
beckons
. . . into that unknown. Then
shall all my
nights become my days,
enlightened.

Thomas Ransom
ALEE
Take me in your arms
    and give me shelter,
    as I am a fugitive
        from myself,
Running from society
    as fast as my thoughts
        will carry me.

Even though you are afraid
    of my emotions . . .
        Hold me . . .
I need loves potation
    and the bouquet
    of your smile
More than all the pomegranates
    in paradiese.

R.C. Asmussen
OZARK SOUVENIR
I saw a feather in the grass—
I ponder—did an eagle pass
Within the sight of mortal man
Then soar away, this puritan?
If only I knew once the thrill,
To catch in flight a virgin quill.

Irel Urreiztieta
FROM HAMPSHIRE
Fields of vibrant green and
    bracken colors yonder
summer daisies in between
sheep alseep and calves their
    mothers' breasts their
    sweetness drinking
you with them are here with me.

Shadows of the heavy leaden
    skies departing
with the wet sun's dusk eclipsing
breezy nightfall of apricot elixirs
blanketing the low and tepid tide
silver pewter mercury of waters

drowning me with pleasure deep
inside.

I am with others but you are here
with me.

Cream teas and marmalades
oaks and elms and whitened trees
magical cathedrals for me
forming
you are here with me.

Dampness felt, the toadstools
growing
heather bushes at my feet
ferns their blackened spores here
scatter
graceful celebration of lives yet
to be.

I am all existence sharing,
forceful energies flow through
me
I am seeing, I am feeling
I have traveled wide, I'm free
I do not possess you, you do not
have me
but the distances have vanished,
anguish vanquished
you are here with me.

By the garden there are yellow
lilies
in the tranquil park all thoughts
can be
I am strong, there is no feebleness
loving you with sweet serenity
knowing that as long as glory
leads me
destiny will become what it
should be.

I am strong, I love you, not
despairingly, not with grief
I do not await you there's no need
there's no panic and no precipice
I am free and you are here with
me.

Emma Wall
SCREAMER MOUNTAIN
*[Dedicated to my daughters—
Martha, Mary and Nancy—for
a wonderful reception for me
and Lanier on our forty—fourth
wedding anniversary.]*
There is a land in the sky
Where the Indians lived in years
gone by

The rugged trails of wars that
they fought
Their slaving and toil was all but
naught

The white men rose up and drove
them away
For with their lives they would
have to pay

The time had come for them to
part
From a big mountain, close to
their heart

For in the night on the top of the
hill
The scream of a girl with high
sharp shrill

She ran to the top of the
mountain each night
To scream and yell till she made
her flight

She ran and she screamed with
every breath

Then one night she leaped to her
death

The Indians soon left the lands
they had braved
And lost all the treasures they
had saved

The white men have taken the
land for their own
With great developing of seeds
being sown

Winding roads that will soon be
paved
And build beautiful homes with
money they've saved

From the top of the mountain to
the valleys below
The cool stream of water from
the springs will flow

To fill a lake that will be a clear
fountain
That flows from the top of
SCREAMER MOUNTAIN!

K. J. Busa
THE WEDDING
The Day draws nearer, and the
tension rises, let's try to
remember if there's anything
we've forgotten

The Band, the cake, the dress, and
yes all the rest, but is there
anything we've forgotten?

The Day will be perfect with the
flowers, the hall, and oh yes the
guests most important of all

To find a man to share all your
own, still he stands by you
even after you start to moan

Two little words mine, and yours,
is no longer but instead
becomes ours

You are given great and
expensive gifts at your shower,
and still I feel there's
something we've forgotten

The Day your parents have only
dreamed of, to your father
though, the day he wishes
never would have come

As you walk arm and arm, his
tears begin to fall, with his
memories all he holds after you
leave the stall

For your always to him as
"Daddy's Little Girl" Priceless
and Fragile

And the question again "Is there
anything we've forgotten?"

The Day also holds great joy for
the groom, because this new
man is the one to hold the new
memories of Daddy's Little Girl

The Day is special don't get me
wrong, but if that's all you
want is parties and song

You better look elsewhere cuz it
can get very long

Your Day will come and be over
in a flash, and to this man you
must always last

So give it your all, and give it
your best, and after that give it
some more

Then everything will come
together, and you'll know that
Love is the answer after all

Barbara Truncellito
SEACSAPE
Floating waves
brace a sailboat up
when the wind subsides
it strives for shore
the anchor is lowered
lowered

it sails away
when the wind builds
it sails away
and takes the anchor
always takes the anchor

Kevin D. Cleland
A Dreamer's Foolish Heart
*[To Debbie, a lovely lady; and a
friend for life.]*
My heart beats fast,
for fear she'll pass,
and I won't get to say,
the very things that I'd rehearsed
like why I feel this way.

Her golden hair and eyes so blue,
her darling precious face.
Her frame is figure eight in shape
she's lovely as can be.

I'd hoped that we could be
together,
spend some time alone.
Fate had other things in mind
some things I can't condone.

She said that she'd been taken up
with someone else but me.
She never really had been mine
but I had hoped somewhere in
time
that we could work things out.

I guess I set my sights too high,
Nowhere could more beauty be
Why'd I think she'd be content
with someone such as me.

A dreamer never stops
to think about reality.
I do hope that she'll be
happy with someone else but me.

Evelyn B. Ryan
SPRING'S PREVIEW
Silly little tulip heads
Peeking from the ground.
Do they know something
I don't know?
Or do they stick their heads up
Just to look around
To see if there is yet a trace
Of snow?

Don't they know it's Winter
And Spring is long away?

Old Man Frost has still a
Trick or two.
Those silly little tulip heads
Look like they're here to stay.
I wonder, if it snows, what
They will do?

Perhaps they all got lonesome
So long beneath the ground
And came up for a peek at God's
Blue sky.
Then, maybe they're a preview
Of Springs' lovely sound
Silently pushing Winters chill
On by.

Margie Howard
POINT OF VIEW
*[Inspired by my son, Kenny,
when he was three years of
age. . .and who still inspires
me now at his age of 15 years!]*
Mommy!
I see an elephant over there. . .
Oh, yeah? An elephant?
You saw an elephant? Where?

See him?
He is eating a giant pie!
. . .(I followed his pointed finger
to fluffy, white clouds in the sky)

Look, Mommy!
I can see a very pretty, sandy
beach!
Oh, gosh, Mom
That's a long, long way to try to
reach!

Elephants?
And giant pies up in the sky?
And a beach?
Well, that is a long way up high!

I smiled
And held him briefly close to me
With imagination
Nothing, not nothing is hard to
see!

Imagination?
Well now, who am I to really say?
Maybe I
Just don't see things the same
way!

Just suppose
They really aren't clouds after all
Could it be that
Over there is truly a skyscraper
so tall?

Just because
I don't see things the way you do
Doesn't mean
That what you see is not really
true!

Eva J. Johnson
ME
*[To my Son, Jack DeJohnette,
Jr., his lovely wife, Lydia,
precious grand—daughters,
Farah and Minya DeJohnette,
brother Roy Wood, Jr, nephews
Roy III, Arthur Wood and all of
my beloved realtives. I love all
of you.]*
Fame and fortune, have I not
Trust that I'm loved too
Thru the years, I've learned a lot
Seen old things change to new

Acquaintaces, I have my due
Seen hard times, yes indeed!
True friends, like all, I have a few

The others, I don't need

My speech, I'm told is trite
One source to shun a pout
Is saying what I think is right
And so I just speak out
The greatest thing of all, you see
Is the simple joy of being "ME".

Ralph I. Epps
TEARS OF THE SEA
Today I walked beside the sea . . .
An immense expanse of water.
My mind recalled a distant land
A time of man made slaughter.

The Hell it caused in life and
limb
The sorrow it brought about,
A "no man's land", barren hills
And trees that seemed to
shout!

Their cry went up
for all to hear
But none would heed,
but rather . . .
So men suffered, bled
and died
As if it didn't matter.

This ocean comes and goes.
This tide goes in and out,
Sparkling waves, white crested,
Need they repeat the shout?

Joy Elton Tricarice
FALLEN PINE
Polished and bare
the remains of the pine.

Weather has transformed life
into sculpture

Even as nature's cycle moves
Beauty remains.

Rita Hallett
AD INFINITUM
Should my wishes some day with
fact comply,—
In some far hidden place, before I
die;
Secluded, untroubled, I want to
lie
Atop a mountain and gaze at the
sky;
Viewing, as endless majesty rolls
by,
The manifestations that thought
has wrought.
There is to learn, alone, the answer
to "Why?".
To miss no depths—no heights—
I think I ought
To know one moment of fulfilled
desire

And boundless hope;—I want to
find the spot
Where fragments and loose ends
meet. I aspire
Too,—for what is complete that
is not?—
To renounce all fear of my final
breath—
And then, I want to be friendly
with death.

Phil Mcrgan
TRANSITION
Singing not of passion—or love of
life I have led,
Feelings become reality, near is
the death bed.
My mind begins to wander, and I
feel no pain,
Seeing life for the first time, I
wish to remain.

Living—is but a measurement of
time, the clocks have
all run down. To late for repair,
no ticking, no sound.
Smelling of lifes' rosey breath, as
unto the woman,
that held me close to her breast.

The call of Daddy, brings
happiness, sublime—I answer
a sense of belonging, it is all mine.
Content to grow old, never doubt
or fear, turn around
tomorrow is here.

Yesterday, an extension of today,
I blinked my eyes,
gone away, enriching another,
giving lifes' caress.
All is said, all is done, the work
ceases—time has won.
The journey ends, I have arrived,
new songs to be sung.
Grateful for the passing,
transition, I am home.

Jesse Alan Spencer
WINDOW ON MY WORLD
I have a lone window in my tiny
room,
And small as it is, it dissipates
the gloom;
Although not adorned with drape
nor fancy lace,
It gives to me light and warms
this barren space.

The view from this portal,
through transparent panes,
Looks not upon gardens touched
by gentle rains;
Nor peers upon children playing
with a ball;
Instead, I see concrete and
another wall.

Yet if I draw close and gaze
toward the sky,
I see silent clouds like spirits
rushing by;
And if I am patient, swallows will
I see,
In flight like a dance, rejoicing
being free.

It's here that I sit and stare into
the blue,
And ponder the days that seem a
precious few;
Lamenting, I wish I'd realized
their worth,
And weep as I view my sliver

of the earth.

Anne Dorcas
CRYSTAL TEARS
A sparkling diamond,
Captured by my eye—lashes,
Is striving to come to a fall.
Down my cheek,
It glowingly glides;
Heartbreak has given me a call.

A glossy pearl,
Shortly blinding me,
Is spilled with the closing of my
eyes.
Slowing it rolls
Down the side of my face
As I silently begin to cry.

A glittering miracle,
Held deep within my heart,
Is revealed by crystal tears;
Tears of sorrow,
Tears of joy,
Tears of many timeless years.

Elizabeth Breitfeld
**Prisoners Dream Of the
Devil**
The gates of Hell swung open
wide
And the Devil said "Come, walk
inside
His voice so low and soft and
sweet
Spoken just right to move my feet
Right through the gates of no
return,
To shovel coal 'til my soul would
burn.

Once inside I knew why, I'd
feared the day that I would die
He walked beside me to hear my
cry
"Dear God" I'd tried my whole life
through
To be good, honest, kind and true.
His laugh was cruel and cut to
the core
He'd heard the cry, many times
before.
Don't be tempted by the low
sweet voice.
Robbed of your freedom and have
no choice
But to obey the Devil, as was my
fate
I'd opened my eyes, a lifetime too
late.

There's no love here in this deep,
dark, hole
Only hate, when you no longer
have a soul
The Devils followers are a pitiful
lot
No place on earth was ever this
hot.
We spend our time in blood,
sweat, and tears
Wishing we could reverse the
years.

Don't listen to the devil, if you're
to see life's other side
Give yourself to Jesus, the lonely
prisoner cried.

Kathryn Abrams
MY MOTHER
I sit and think of all the times
She tucked me into bed
And placed a kiss upon my cheek
After evening prayers were said.

I'd drop into a peaceful sleep
Knowing she was there
Awakening in the morning
To her loving care.

She stretched one meal into two
When things were really bad
With the food that was brought
home
By our working Dad.

Often times she'd sing a song
With an aching heart
With so many tasks to do
She'd not know where to start.

She made our clothes on a treadle
Singer
From pretty printed sacks
They made us the best dressed
kids
With warm clothes on our backs.

She washed our clothes on a
washboard
And hung them on the line
With homemade soap and elbow
work
They always looked just fine.

Many times she'd like to sit
And rest a little while
With ten kids it could hardly be
So she carried on with a smile.

We loved to hear the stories she
told
And listen to her sing
There is no joy can take the place
That a loving mother can bring.

Donald B. Swanson
Candles Of Biship Hill.
The clear sunset—The dusk—
The darkness—The winter
chill.
Again it is time to go to see the
Candles of Bishop Hill.

Over the farmland, coming in
from the North and up the hill.
There the Village lay—so quiet—
so still.

Then down the street, candles in
every window—in every every
building all around the Village
Square, and candles in many
windows away from there!

We walk out into the Park, and
stand in the new fallen snow.
From here to better see the
candles glow.
Sending a Christmas message we
all should know.

To us to feel and see all this—
and we feel an extra thrill
Two of our children come from
descendants of the hill.

There we older people stand,
hand in hand.
For us it is not hard to
understand.
How easy it is to yet inherit—
The glowing feeling—of this—the
Christmas Spirit!

Now it is time to depart—to go
We hope next year to see another
Candle Lighted Show,

To the people—to the Village--
good night.
We wish you the very best—The
coming Holy Night.

Merry Christmas!

Today's Greatest Poems

Melodie D. McPherson
FIRE ON THE SNOW

[For my father—I pray you've
found the peace in death that
you could not in life.]

Framed in dust and memories
you smile from your silent abode
smiling
no one noticing
the smile was careful not to reach
    your eyes
eyes of gray that showed nothing
but saw everything
Framed in years and cobwebs
you gaze from unseeing eyes
seeing
no one realizing
that you'd known the truth all
    along
the truth of life that proved
    nothing
but wasted everything
Framed in death and yesterday
you sit for evermore
years passing
no one remembering
that you were ever alive and very
    much a part of life
a part that now means nothing
but once meant everything
Framed in wood and covered with
    glass
you've been tucked away neat in
    a drawer
dead
no one caring
at least not tonight
hidden from sight
it's over
and what was it for?

David L. LaCost
LETTER TO GOD

Hello God,
I met your son today
I saw him in my children
As I sat and watched them play
I saw him in a grandmother
Who gave her smile so sweet
To the neatly dressed young
    businessman
Who helped her cross a street
I saw him in a motorist
Traveling through our town
Who stopped to soothe a little
    child
Who had tripped and fallen down
Yes God, today I met him
And he's beautiful to see
I only hope that others
Can see your son in me

Barbara L. Weikle
He Was There All the Time

When I never knew him
He was there all the time
And I often tried to use him
He was there all the time

He knocked at my heart
But I wouldn't part
With worldly things I was blind
But he was still there all the time

I fooled around until it was too
    late
Death knocked on my door
And I met Jesus at the gate

He said: I was there all the time
And was willing to wait
But you wouldn't receive me
I'm sorry, you can't come in
It's too late.

Yvonne Elizabeth Adams
MY BILL

In the corner of my mind
I had a secret dream.
My Prince Charming would be
    tall, dark and handsome.

He would be strong,
    to protect me . . .
He would be gentle,
    to comfort me . . .
He would have patience,
    to understand me . . .
He would be romantic,
    to love me . . .

In the corner of my heart,
My dreams have all come true,
I have found you, love,
My Bill . . .

Doris Cabany
DREAMING ALONE

I always have to dream, to stay
    alive,
You never share my dreams with
    me.
Close your eyes, don't analyze the
    facts of life,
Forget the code "To be or not to
    be,"
Dare to dream, become valiant
    and free.

Who my love?
While I feel romantic thoughts
    inside,
And I read a poem in the sky,
I see the night, like lady, with
    diamonds
in her crown,
You see only the darkness in the
    high,
You feel only the hardness in the
    ground.

Please my dear come,
I'll show you a world that you
    ne'er known.
Dare to take the rose, don't think
    about the thorns,
After the rain, the color of the iris
    will be shown,
Because the calm arrives after the
    storm.
Dream with me, after the night is
    gone, the day
will be born.

Christy M. Howard
THE GOOD SAMARITAN

Just a couple of days ago,
on the street I saw a man,
Calling out he reached for me
to lend a helping hand.

He was cold and hungry;
he had no place to go.
He had no friends; he had no
    home—
his life was filled with woe.

I was moved with pity,
I'd never seen such a man.
Carefully, cautiously, slowly at
    first,
I outstretched my hand.

A smile broke out upon his face,
and he stumbled up to me.
He had never known a friend
    before—
his days were long and lonely.

I gave him food and clothing,
then he turned and said good-bye,

and as he left I must admit
a tear stung in my eye.

That night in bed I had a dream
that the Lord came unto me,
He thanked me for helping Him
when He was cold and hungry.

I asked Him when I had done
    this?
I'd never seen Him in such a way.
But he reminded me of the man
who'd been on the street that day.

"My sister, I assure you,
although you couldn't see,
Everything you did for him,
in truth you did for Me."

Jill S. Magiera
SUNSHINE REFLECTIONS

As I sit watching the shadows
Flickering lights
Sunshine reflections
As I go wild deep inside

The burning light
Wants me to see it
Watch as I read it
As my head wants to blow

Like bubbles of green
I feel like a dream
Empty illusions
Of darkness and light

It casts me away
To deep thoughts
Long ago memories
On sunshine reflections

Richard Shorten
SEA SOUND

The interval of silence between
    two notes
A flute plays on the near
    seashore
Is the sound the music was
    created for.
In the interval of waves the
    music floats.

Between the crashing surf the
    luring tide
Of water suspends momentarily
The pause of waves and the
    sea,
Sequestered on the infinite long
    ride.

Crescendos in the force
Collision of different mediums
In earth and liquid as the sound

Is broken by the man taking
    breath. The course
Of silence is the life breathing
    into him

And is the music as the quiet
    weight of water comes aground.

Beatrice M. O'Hara
PROGRESS

[To my two Ray's for their faith
in me.]

Progress, is not just a word,
    It's a boomerang on the wing.
Helplessly we dance to it's tune
    Like puppets on a string.
Killer bombs, with nuclear heads,
    Speeding cars and Concord Jets,
Buildings reaching to the sky,
    Rockets to the moon.
Forests soon will be no more—
    Thanks to the housing boom.
God meant the world to be bright
    and gay.
    We have loused it up in a
    frightful way.
Our hearts won't stand the pace
    we've set.
    We drop like flies from a
    Spraybomb Jet.
St. Peter at the pearly gate must
    be tired on saying
    "Couldn't you wait? Your time
    was for a later date."
Wise is the man who once in a
    while,
    Closes his door with a secret
    smile.
With pole in hand—gives
    Progress a boot!
    Instead of just wishin,
Hangs a sign on his door that
    simply reads
        "Gone Fishin".

Patty Ryan Friedrich
FRAGILE

[Dedicated to my Husband,
Kenneth Michael]

Your love is a fragile package,
I must handle it with care.
To carry it with all my heart,
Making sure it doesn't fall apart,
Or that the wrapping doesn't tear.

For I know what's in the package,
Never having to unwrap it.
It's filled with your love, thru and
    thru;
But one careless little fall or tear,
And I could accidently break it in
    two.

Donald J. Burrows
THE JOURNEY

We've heard The Greatest Story,
    we've heard it many times
How Christ was born to Mary in
    Bethlehem that night.
We've read about His journey, it's
    repeated o'er and o'er
From a tiny little manger to an
    ugly crown of thorns!

We've read about the miracles
    long before our time
How God created this Heaven
    and Earth and brought life to
    yours and mine.
His life was filled with suffering
    as He journeyed day by day
He healed the sick and dying as
    He went along His way.

He was just a lowly carpenter,
    His possessions very few
He owned the clothes upon His
    back, a wooden chest
    contained His tools.

233

But He spoke about a Kingdom
and He spoke about a Shore
Where life would be unending
and peaceful evermore.

Yes we've heard the story of when
Jesus walked upon this land
How he calmed the raging water
with a gesture of His hand.
How He raised a hand toward
Heaven and caused the sun to
shine,
Changed the course of mighty
rivers and turned the water
into wine!

How He fed five thousand
hungry, healed the blind that
they might see
How He walked upon the water
this man from Galilee!
How prophets came from miles
around and how He soon
became
Loved by countless thousands as
He journeyed on His way!

News soon spread throughout the
land that The King of Kings
had come
And kings throughout the world
began to tremble on their
thrones!
News was heard for miles around
that all Christians were to die
And among the names most
wanted was a man called Jesus
Christ!

They tell how angry sinners came
and stripped Him of His robe,
How his best friend betrayed Him
for thirty dollars He was sold!
How He knelt there in the garden
the night He talked with God
And asked for their forgiveness
when they nailed Him to the
cross!

Upon the Mount of Olives where
He was sent to die
His eyes revealed forgiveness to
those who took His life!
He said "Forgive them Father for
they know not what they've
done"
And He rendered them forgiven
for He loves us everyone!

Smiling down on every nation
that they might make amends
And find a place within their
hearts for . . .
Peace on Earth, Good Will
Toward Men.

Virginia Lemperle
SEA WATER
I never dreamed that waves
could loom so high
blotting out the shoreline
and the sky.
I never knew that sailing
could be fun;
'Twas just a job
that needed to be done.
I felt that it was
meant for me
to sail the Great Lakes
like my family
had always done before me.
In our veins
there flows not blood,
just water from the sea.

Juanita Hammerstrom
CLOSE CALL
I had a little visit
From the Lord the other day.
He called me from the heavens
But I turned my ear away.
The body may be tired, I said,
But it still serves me well
And as long as I can clearly think
I have more tales to tell.
You know, Lord, it's not easy
To struggle on this way
But I am not quite finished yet
So pardon the delay.
I know you'll think I've got my
nerve
Asking you to wait
But when I'm ready,
I'll call you
And I will keep our date.

Gail Jensen

Gail Jensen
TO FRANCES WITH LOVE
My grandmother watches me
from above
recording all of my moves and
actions
with undying love
She was carried away one day in
fall
by the white winged doves call
St. Peter immediately let her in
for he knew she was without any
sin
Someday I'll die
and few will cry
but she'll be there to meet me
and greet me
and help me pass through St.
Peter's gate
to meet my wonderful heavenly
fate

Dee Baird
LOOKING BACK
Have you ever thought as you
look back
Of how you'd change your life?
If given the chance to change just
one thing
What would it be that you'd
choose?
Now stop a minute and just
think.
What would it be that you'd do?
Would you change the selfish
things you've done?
Or would you leave that the
same?
Or how about the love you've
been given?
Did you give enough in return

each day?
No, we can't go back and change
even one thing.
But we can look back and learn.
And improve on all of our
tomorrows to come.
For our tomorrows might only be
one.

Gloria Jean Beczkowski
BUMBLE BEE
[This poem was written to—
and inspired by—my friend,
Bob.]
Breaker 1 9 I'm calling on thee,
Why are you hiding away from
me?

The Bumble Bee handle is but
few
As I listen to each channel for
sounds of you.

If your ears are on and you're
flying around,
How come I don't hear that
buzzing sound?

Come back Bumble Bee is that
you I hear?
What's that you say, "You're in
my mirror?"

Ralph A. Fisher, Sr.
GOLD STAR MOTHER
[To my dear wife Edith of 63
years, wife and mother, and
became a Gold Star Mother on
December 14, 1943, when our
son Howard Otto, was killed in
service.]
They gave me the flag
That draped your remains—
They sent a lone escort
Along on the train.
And filled the white chapel
As the young soloist sang.

Then they scattered the flowers
Amidst the dust of the lane—
They slowly tread—muted
drums.
Eight guns, volley and flame—
They lowly bow heads
As the heavens weep rain.

They softly utter—"Amen"
A prayer by the chaplain—
A bugler sounds taps
With an echo refrain
As in silence, I offer
To God—"Your name."

Dawn Ellis
THE GYPSY
"There is time to begin again,"
Said a gypsy to the crowd.
The people roared and chanted,
"The fool, he speaks so loud!"

He said, "Now listen you,
I've truth and a warning to share.
For I have journeyed far
And I've seen unrest out there."

"Now it's a shame this world's
grown selfish,
No longer does love inspire what
you do.
And it seems you're only
motivated
By whatever pleases you."

"No longer do you seem to care
About the needs of your brother.
And only in the past
Did you ever love each other."

The people grew uneasy
For his message was so plain,
So in order to silence him,
The gypsy, he was slain.

Sheila Elaine Martin
MOTHER
Mother, mother
Where are you?
My mother I need so,
Your realm of life,
So complex, so whole,
Oh mother, mother,
You are what you are,
Your feelings we need,
Now and always forever more,
Your understanding so rare,
We love you mother,
We love you, and we care . . .

Norma Hardin
THE PROPHET LIGHT
[I dedicate this poem to Paul E.
Johns, The Prophet Light]
In him I saw
A golden light,
As he stood between
Me and darkness one night.

With amber eyes,
And raven hair,
I do not think
He knows it's there.

His smile was warm.
His eyes were bright.
He took the darkness
From the night.

If you chance to meet
This man of light,
You need not fear
The dark of night.

Jack Burgeman
TIME
I walked through space
Thinking of you,
A stroke of fate resurrected
A burning flame
Time has decreed—the search
Has ended.
I found new life
Tis fragrant
What joy thou has bestoweth
Upon me
I Want You.

Jacqueline L. Panhorst
THE WINGS OF LOVE
Love is like a butterfly
Soft
Free like the wind
Wind that sails on
Forever and ever
Like the flight
Of a dove.

Butterflies are the
Symbol of new life
New life for you
As you start your life together.

Life seems new and exciting
When shared with those you love
When love is shared
Life is BEAUTIFUL!

Becky Boles
STRANGER WITHIN
Stranger residing within me
you deny to face reality
resisting every step I take
opposing for oppositions sake;
yet, obligingly, I meditate
the remote conceptions you
create.

You rebel against the authorities
that dictate life's priorities;
thus, forcing me, to your defenses
by playing roulette with my
senses.
Can I conceive from your
persistence
an endless struggle for existence?
You confuse me with your
controversy.
I conclude, you have no mercy.

Judith L. Taylor
NANNIE'S HANDS
[To Grandmother Bessie
Timberlake, fondly and
affectionately known by all as
"Nannie".]
Nannie's hands are beautiful,
Gnarled and old but lovely still;
As they make her biscuits,
Knead her dough and carry out
her will.

They tell a story all their own,
Of life's hard work and toil;
Of many meals and spring
cleanings,
Of burning late nite oil.

Bent with age and rough with
wear,
And yet they will always be;
Gentle, loving and willing to
hold,
A wee one on her knee.

Barry Eugene Carty
SEPTEMBER
Oh, yes . . .
September

I remember
what was once there
but
in this empty room of mine
I sit and stare

Letter from those who care.
I read them over and over
and realize that September
is only thirty days out of the year.

Gary Gugliotti
POEM TO THE CHILD
Yes my little friend:
Standing nude against all you do
not see,
All;—Not real enough
To stain the dream of reality
Which events in time
Have not allowed you to forget.
Yes my little friend:
Your helplessness, the epitome of
trust.
Your bright eyes saying so much
more
Than the eloquent words of our
illusionary love.
Your tears; the plain simplicity of
need.
I can only hope to stand
Stripped of ambition,
Before all you do see.

Diane Molnar, R.N.A.
A CHRISTMAS SURPRISE!
No one is singing Christmas
carols
No one is baking pies
No one is wrapping Christmas
presents
And I don't know why!

I don't even see a Christmas tree
With its lights shiny and bright

What ever happened to Santa
Claus
He's not even in sight.

As I turn my head and see
A calendar on the wall
I must say it's only May!
No wonder I didn't get a
Christmas call!

Michael H. Gogue
YOU AND YOURS
[This poem was written to—
and inspired by—my special
friend Maria Waczek, who
means more to me than words
can say.]
You fill the mind with pleasant
thoughts,
Your deeds are not forgotten.
You fill the air with an heavenly
scent,
Your presence is not un-noticed.
You delight my eyes at the sight
of you,
Your arrival a sweet surprise.
You speak with a voice of sweet
serene,
Your words are music to my
ears.
You give me joy that is
immeasurable,
You're the one for me.
You are unique in all the
universe,
Your entity with none to
compete.

Linda J. Callahan
On Dying Grandfathers
A legacy lost
        out of bounds
Out of touch.
A soul survived
a body lost.
It takes time to draw things back
to sort them out—
        to sift them thru—
            to settle our minds—
                to say goodbye.
To rearrange the pattern
    from present
        to past tense.

Gina Moore
BROTHER
[In loving memory of: Dennis S.
Moore]
You were something special to
me and that was plain to see.
There couldn't ever be a better
brother than you were to me.
We had our ups and we had
our downs, sometimes we acted
like clowns. You were
something extra special to me
and now you're not around. I
miss you a lot and need you so,
I LOVE YOU MY DEAR
BROTHER and that you'll
always know!!!

Betty I. "B.J." Adams
A MAN'S WORTH
A man is not measured by feet
and inches, nor dollars and
cents;
But by the kindness of heart and
gentleness of his soul;
And by honesty, integrity, and
the work he does—
In this world so obsessed with
glitter and gold.

I know a man who is short of
tall,—
And yet he stands—above the
tallest of men.
He has a soft spoken manner,
toned with wisdom—
Unleashed by a brilliant mind
that's both free and open.

A truly handsome man isn't just a
pretty face;
Nor is he necessarily bound.
He is a man of spirit and great
understanding;—
His beauty coming from deep
within, where handsome is
really found.

Phyllis M. Lothyan
THE GIFT
"I'm sorry, my dear—"
Her angry tears fell
From eyes as blue as
The blue of her dress:

Each one a token
Of love unrequited;
Each one a death knell
Of her hopes. I guess
Our Christmas was lost
When her soul keening,
Fought the deep echo
Of peace pleading bells.

Spurning our presence,
Astray in confusion—
Lost in the epic
Such suffering tells.
Scars of the future?
Drastic such pruning!
Strong be her roots—
So tender her tree.

Gently I held her,
Cradling softness—
Oh! Precious moment—
Ah, sweet empathy.

Loudy Stennis
PUPPY LOVE
[Dedicated with love to my
four children: Barbara, Betty
Gene, Bob and Carol.]
"Mama, may we have a dog?"
(Four faces turn to me.)
"We'll feed him every single day
And he won't have one flea.

We'll bathe him once a week.
He won't be in the way.
He'll be just a little dog.
Please Mama, can he stay?"

My oldest opens wide her coat
And snuggled in the warm
I see a little bitty mutt.
He couldn't do much harm.

That was just a year ago.
Now please don't laugh too hard.
That little bitty harmless mutt
Is now a St. Bernard.

Merle Jamison Christensen
THE WOMAN I WOULD BE
In the woman I would want to be,
You'd find rare balance of
Sophistication mixed with
Humility.
Restraint too, would there be
found,
Just enough to help, to test me
sound.
Let me hold my head up high,
and with an air,
I have the courage and the faith
to take me there.
Have others feel my queenly
grace, but feel secure to know
their many problems
I would gladly help them face.

Dear God, please help me as I
walk the stoney path of life,
To find my better self in spite
of evil all about me too much
known.
That as I enrich another's soul, so
precious in thy sight,
Can realize how they in turn,
enrich and help complete my
own.

Benjamin Christopher Gorman
TWO ONCE MORE
[For Libby—Upon awakening
of a heart]
Against my will again from thee I
part,
And with reluctant steps I trace
the path
Whose lonely tear-strewn length
doth rend my heart;
Your smile and touch dissolving
in my wrath.
How can it be that I continue
thus,
A slave to time, a worshipper of
hours?
How is't we let a clock dissever
us
With silent flight of hands and
seconds' show'rs?
When comes the time when time
will come no more
And we may cease to measure
our embrace?
And what the date, when
vengeance is in store
And to the ground we hurl
Time's wrinkled face?
To you I'm bound: and past the
wit of Time
To break that chain as he
would crush this rhyme.

Marni Germano
LIFE IS LIKE A ROSE
Our lives are like a rose.
Every petal opening is a
new day to be lived.
It will fill you with joy,
but when it goes and wilts
away, all you can feel is
sorrow.

Part of it dies and you
feel as though you will
die too.
But somehow—somehow you
survive.

You will always live on,
although parts of you
keep going away.
They keep leaving you
with another sad memory,
to silently wilt the
beautiful rose.

Well, winter has come,
now it's your turn to go.
But never fear—you will
return as a new rose,
ready to unfold your
leaves and learn the joys
and the sorrows of life.

Marian Knight
FROZEN MUSIC

Frozen music and iced days,
music congealed out of shapes
of struggles
of perplexed people puzzling
out
lost notes from the past.

Stars and statutes bear mute
witnessed messages
of frantic souls snared in
the trapped ways
of a meshed world
webbed in the minutes
of music signaling
our past time struggling,

To break through with octabes
of bliss out of the garden
of sun days dialed
down to martydom.

Bodies build, bodies sing
and music runs
through the dirt
downed earth
tossing up patterns
of light and glass
and locked in days
into the night of trebles
trembling over the touching
of the truth.

Time is tinkling through
rooms of fear
hutching over doubts
and indecision
murmuring over memories
of forms unfrozen
moving into
crashing cords.

Gladys W. Thornley
**The Meaning Of
Christmas**

Listen to the story
Of the Christ Child's birth
The journey to Bethlehem
And the bright special star
Shepherds on the hillside
Gaze in wonder at the sight
As they listen to the Angel's
Majestic words of light.

Have you ever seen
A star so bright
I asked the shepherd lad.
Ah, no, he said as he replied,
I wonder if all the world
Has seen this glorious sight
This truly must be the sign
Of the promised King of Glory.

The star will lead the way
To the city of David
Where lay the babe
Sheltered in a lowly cattle shed
They followed the star to the
manger bed

And here the Bread of Life was
fed
Mary was that mother mild
Jesus Christ her little child.

Oh what ethereal joy
Was brought to the world that
night
Christ the everlasting King
Came down on earth to dwell
He was the promised Saviour
Sent to heal the hearts of men
To lead us and to guide us
Back to our Heavenly home
And our eyes at last
Shall see Him, in that
Grand eternal plan.

Jeffrey Levine
THE POET

What is it that calls me.
Invisible Knowing

To write upon the tapestries of
time,
and not know why.

To run towards existence
with an open heart.

Skies of colors are my inspiration.
To feel the wind and know it's
right.

From afar my vision is clear,
yet the clouds never leave.

I am the poet, I am the dream.

Michele Curtis Nicholas
HIGH ABOVE THE STORM

Should I be alone
when confronted by the
confusion
of the assassinator's attempt
to cloud Deity and His purpose
The raging tempest
might my spirit wane

But while battling waves thrive
on
my Lord...high...lifts me up
that I may rise above
temptation's damning reach
To stand secure
on gloried plain

A world in constant struggle
with thunderous darkness all
around
and though it swells by fury's
breath
it touches my soul not
For by the laws of peace
rules the Son . . . atop the rain

Elizabeth A. Miller
DEAR SON

Things I should have said but
didn't, are coming out as truths
from me,
I want to tell you how great you
are, and what you mean to me.
I want you to take care of
yourself, but don't think this
labor vain,
since I won't be here to attend to
you, during this never ending
game.
Open your eyes and look around,
please trust it will be great,
reallly look at what's here on
earth, before it gets too late.
Spend your time so wisely, and
leave some time for you,
and never really hurt your
friends, like helpless people do.

Look the whole world over in
your search for teachers true,
someone who can teach you
more than I have ever taught
you.
From up above I'll shelter you and
love you while I may,
though my earth visit was
awfully short, I'll live with you
in a forever grateful stay.
And though I'm leaving you
much sooner than we'd
planned,
just take the bitter grief that
comes and try to understand.
I fancied that I heard you say, "of
course this will be done,
from all my travels that crowd
life's lanes, the risk of grief I'll
run,
I'll open my heart to loving and
I'll learn to be just me
I'll strive for top roll honors and
really look and see
I'll bear the pain that goes with
life and hold a cheerful smile
I'll show the world just what I've
got, but not think my neighbor
vile.
I love you, and though your stay
was brief,
I'll have your lovely memory as a
solace for my grief."

Kay Buzelli
MARY WONDERS!

*[Dedicated to my daughter,
Charlene, who wondered if
Mary wondered, and so
inspired the poem.*

I wish I understood,
I wish I knew, I do!

The wisemen, shepherds there
Worshipped a royal heir
And they bowed to Him prone

Will my son be a prince?
Roots He has had long since
Decendent of David's throne

His Majesty—a king
I do so like the ring
To rule in Glory unknown

The tidings are all glad
Why do I feel so sad?
Troubled, confused and alone

Tis a nice way to dream
But only my scheme
A throne doesn't seem His role

I just don't understand
His place in our land
What *is* His work—His goal?

His words I do ponder
They fill me with wonder
Glory, Lord, roll from the scroll

What can be His mission?
His task, and commission?
Redeemer, of the soul?

I think that *He* knows, now
And, He may even know how
T'will *end*, a deadly toll?

I wish I really understood it all,
I wish I knew, too, I do!

Jane Kirkpatrick
BLESSED GIFT

From my Father was given a gift
of love,
Which He sent to all from
heaven above,
Jesus Christ is His blessed name,
Of the gift from heaven that
came,
From the beginning all peoples
and I,
Caused Him to suffer and be
crucified,
Full of love, compassion and
forgiveness of sin,
The Saviour our souls He wanted
to win,
To keep all from suffering
eternity in hell,
But most of mankind their souls
they did sell,
To worldly pleasures, sin and
lust,
Hell will be their portion or they
must,
Turn to the heavenly Saviour
above,
Who was crucified for our love.

Marian C. Freeman
UNTAMED STALLION

Clouds moving dark in the sky
Thundering rains beat
endlessly down.
There he moves in all his
fury
Hoofs, beating!—beating!—
beating!

A flash of lightening lights the sky!
His form alone is seen in the
distance.
Now he moves—yet not in
fury.
But, running—running—
running.

Running free from human bondage,
Untamed species of the wilds.
Slowly he canters gracefully
Tired at last but, happy to
be—Free!

June B. Johnson
**A Very Special Christmas
Tree**

My sons Gil and Rick searched
hard for a tree
The task isn't easy, I'm sure you'll
agree.
In the woods it looked fine and
full throughout;
But when they got home, they
began to have doubt.

It was much too tall, so they cut
off the tip,
Then sadly discovered, they had
made a grave slip.
The trunk of the tree wouldn't fit
in the holder,

So off came more branches as
each boy grew bolder.

Rick wanted to go and search for
another
And gingerly asked the help of
his brother.
But I told them no the tree is all
right,
At this point, we'll keep it if only
for spite.

As Rick was stringing the lights
on the tree;
Gil heard his father and
whispered to me.
What will dad say when he
comes in the door?
I told him I thought that he'd
probably roar.

Well, the words I expressed were
certainly true;
For the air in the room was
suddenly blue.
As he approached the tree, he
began to exclaim;
Is that all, you could find in the
whole state of Maine?

Both sons shook their heads but
didn't seem sad,
So I'll never know if they really
felt bad.
Instead they continued to work
with glee,
Placing each package around
their tree.

When the lights were all on with
the icicles streaming,
The holes in their tree were
concealed by their gleaming.
And of all of the trees, I've
occasioned to see,
Their little tree is the dearest to
me.

Marjorie Lyon Hafen
APPRECIATION

I own not canvas, brush, nor
paint.
My Christmas cards I purchase;
And yet amid the galleries
My thirsting art-soul searches.
I lurk about in shadows
While the plays are being cast,
But as a ticket salesman
My approach is unsurpassed.
I do not sing in public, for
In horror folks would gape,
(My children hurry off to sleep,
My singing to escape.)
Yet in concerts, plays and opera
hall
I find pure happiness,
And deep within my soul
resounds
The song I can't express.

I cannot paint, nor act, nor sing.
I'm not one who creates,
And yet, I have a priceless gift:
My soul participates!

Bertha Eldridge
HEROES ALL

No record written document
Of any size nor form,
Could ever reveal the greatness of
Our boys in uniform.

On wings of victory you have
wrought
Most perilous battles ever fought.
From sea to sea, from land to land,

Surely God did loan a helping
hand.

Through your unselfish sacrifice
A world enslaved was freed.
How courageous and heroic
Thou did'st thy challenge meet.

There are no words that'll do you
just,
However true, devout.
Please it our God, whose works
these art,
Whose glories are all about.

With kindliness in deeds we can
Pay ardent tribute to our men.
To our heroes great and small,
We're proud to call you Heroes
All.

Carmen Lydia Colmenares

Carmen Lydia Colmenares
I TOUCHED A DREAM

*[This inspiration came to me in
beautiful Luquillo, Puerto Rico.
I dedicate this poem to my
beloved family. My husband
Benny, my son Richard, and my
daughter Lorraine.]*

I slowly let my body rest,
Upon my favorite chaise,
I stretched my limbs in sweet
repose,
and around me I just gazed,

I saw the beauty of the night as
a painting from afar,
Majestic trees, coquetish flowers,
all reaching for the stars,

I heard the raindrops softly
fall upon this midnight scene,
I heard the whisper of the breeze,
as in a distant dream,

The many sounds of happiness, from
birds and soft coquis,
Made me aware for one brief spell,
that life's a symphony.

I held my breath, in wonderous awe,
to hold this moment here,
The blending of my soul, this night
with things so far, yet near,

I had never really looked before,
with inner sight and love,
At all this beauty within my reach,
A token of "His" love,

The tears came slowly, with
gratitude,
I never dreamt I'd feel,
My very heart swelled in my chest
and taking in each scene
I slowly rose, and kissed the night,
with eyes that touched a dream.

Steven E. Vigdor
PASS IT ON

The sweat of mere existence, gravy
to this token melting pot
is trickling down
my only sensate limb, a stream
whose source
might be the shoulders of a black
man
seated three old Puerto Rican
ladies down
across the aisle,
        but which counts
among its donors
the axle grease and oil
        that hang
(like the New York air)
about the arms and chest and legs
    and face and hair
of an auto mechanic
fresh from his day of work,
and the blood nearly drawn
on the chafed and grimy neck
of a fat disdainful white man
with Adam's apple
        prisoner
to a still unloosed tie,

and the Puerto Rican lymph
    nodes
of a proud illiterate papa
and his entire brood of nine,
a would-be prostitute's pubic hair
(unencumbered by underwear),
    the perspiration circles
    on the black absorbing habits
of a pair of misplaced nuns—

a stream
which gathers force
from the defiance
of two toothpick-licking hoodlums
        who spit
        in spite
of the Do Not Expectorate sign,
from the bravado of a teenage
    softball team,
from the hot-blooded mimicry of
    the girls they've taken in,
which travels
over
    under
        around
        and through
            three generations
of strap-hangers,
            pole-clingers,
            and those rugged few
who still are standing
on their own two feet,
and which
drips
down
on me
directly
from above
where
a disgruntled lady laborer
happens to be standing
on my own
two
feet—
and I,
helplessly
and hopelessly,
give
of my own disgust
and my own fear
and my own desire to live
and pass it on.

Derlene Bostwick
GIRL IN RED

Woe for the girl
    all cloaked in red
shadows of doom
    dance in her bed
She walks eternity
    but does not tread
Woe for the girl
    all cloaked in red.

In our dreams
    she travels light
touching all in the
    recess of night
The succubus of morality
    watches her plight
Woe for the girl
    who travels light.

Woe for the girl
    all cloaked in red
she weeps for myriads
    in their stead
this intrepid caretaker
    of the dead.
Woe for the girl
    all cloaked in red.

Patricia Strasser Hedlund
DUTY CALLS

Got out of bed,
put my feet on the floor,
ran to the bathroom,
opened the door.

Jumped in the shower,
turned on the spray,
got myself wet,
that started my day.

Clothes in the washer,
kids out the door,
scrubbed up the syrup,
from the kitchen floor.

Yelled at the dog, put out the cat,
vaccumed the carpet, shook out
    the mat,
washed all the dishes, put them
    away,
found a nickel, that was my pay.

Went to the store,
what more can I say.

Kimberly Ann Campbell
ONCE

Once there was happiness in the
    world, but it left for a little
    while.
Once the sun didn't shine and the
    world turned bleak.
Once the earth laughed, but the
    people cried.
Once there was a life of paradise
    far away from here,
But we'll never know it, because
    it was only once.

Betty L. Stein Staley
SUNDAY MORNING

One at church, one in bed, one
    away at school . . . and one, is
    dead!
Four beautiful children given to
    me . . . all were once healthy,
    happy and free,
Now, because one has been taken
    away, the others have suddenly
    ceased to be gay,
Or is it? Or is it because I'm
    suddenly old, I'm suddenly
    tired, and I'm suddenly cold?
Is it because my eyes have grown
    dim? Is it because I've lost

faith in Him?
Has the laughter really stopped
or has my hearing just been
blocked?
I probably should go to church,
but then they'd see how much I
hurt,
I just don't want the world to
know I've suffered such a
crushing blow!
Time will heal the pain they say,
if you just take it day by day,
I'm trying . . . Lord . . . so hard
to find, a ray of hope, some
peace of mind . . .

Kim Cook
THE MOST HOLY NIGHT
No room in the inn for the Babe
To be born,
Mary gave birth in a stable
Forlorn.
The Shepherds were there
To see the King Mary bore.
Three Wise Men came too
Bearing riches galore.
"GLORY TO GOD IN THE
HIGHEST!",
The angels shouted with joy
In praise to the Babe
In the manger,
Mary's newborn baby boy.
O Come, all ye children
Sing sweet praises to Jesus
Our Lord + Our Saviour + Our
King
When there is room in your heart
For Jesus
The angels truly will sing!
"GLORY TO GOD UP
ABOVE!",
For His Son our Saviour
He has given to us
IN HIS LOVE!

Michael Salaam
CHILD-DREAMS
*[To my wife Patricia, a precious
inspiration. And to my sons
Troy, Shareef, Na'eem and
Mikal.]*
What ever happens
to precious child-dreams?
Do they ever become
real as they seem?
A down-to-earth world
full of laughter, love & ice cream.

Do child-dreams
just grow-up one day,
with life's realization?
Or, are child-dreams
simply shoved away,
by adult imagination?

Norman Karl Scott
WHO CARES?
There once was a man from the
land of nowhere.
Who went by the name of, "Who
Cares?"
He sand a song as he traveled
along, with no words!
He looked neither left, he looked
neither right,
but straight down, never
wavering from his path of
flight.

A bird sang, "Hello!" in a meadow,
as he passed by.
A flower opened its petals and
smiled at him, but,

"Who Cares?" didn't hear or see,
the beauty in nature's harmony.

Two villagers discussed the
strange passing of,
a wanderer in the night, (found
stiff, cold, and alone),
"What was the hapless lad's
name?" said one to the other.
"Who Cares?" replied his brother.

Mabel Hobbs
To My Husband On Our Anniversary
*[This poem was written to my
husband, Tanny, on our 25th
Wedding Anniversary]*
Dear One,

I've given you my heart, my dear,
I've only one!
Treat it with tenderness, please
do, for there is none
Who loves you more than I do,
dear.

This fact, you know, but how it
thrills me on
This day, to tell you so.

Inscribed upon my heart
Your name is written there!
Our love is such a sacred thing to
own and share.
Here, as we pass a milestone,
Another year has just begun.

So guard my heart with tender
care
. . . I've only one!

Nancy Love
SEA MEDLEY
Down by the sea
Where the breeze blows free
And the sand gets in your hair,
Where the water is blue
Like the sky's azure hue
And the spirit is free of care,
Where the whitecaps roll
And one's very soul
Seems a part of the sky and the
sea,
Where the seagulls soar
And the breakers roar,
Here's where I'm wont to be.
I'm as free as the breeze
And my spirit feeds
On the sights and sounds of the
sea;
I'm an integral part
Of nature's heart—
The sky and the sea for me.

Michael Crandell Holt
THE CHRISTMAS CANDLE
*[Dedicated to my loving
grandmother, who taught the
family that we can not shine as
the North Star, but can shine
as a candle and do our small
but glorious part to enlighten
the world.]*
The first light of the Christmas
Candle
seen sitting on its holder with
the solemn handle
offers a light so fair and so bright,
it's like the North Star on
Christmas Eve night.

It tells the passers that all is well,
in the house that offers a friendly
place to dwell.
It brightens the way for a weary

child,
for an uncertain walk to see if
Santa has smiled.

So faithfully it glows so steady
and so still
only bending to winter's slow
peaceful chill.
In the lonely window it sits and
waits
ever patiently knowing that
Christmas will not be late.

Even for the silent Christmas
pleasures
the tree, the presents, the
decorations, the winter
weather,
it shows above all the true
Christmas spirit
by offering all it has to
everything near it.

But the most wonderous of all its
gifts
is just to shine in the eyes of the
one gone adrift
and to light the path out of the
dark unknown
of the last leg of the journey to
guide him home.

Then when all is safe and all is at
peace,
it twinkles once . . . then twice,
and says before its cease
"good night" and wishes all well
for a moment away is Christmas
Day, with another story to tell.

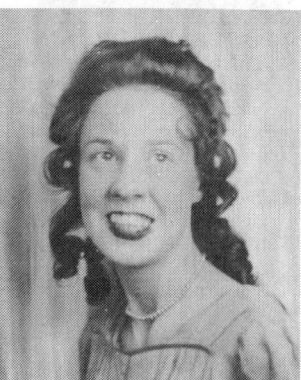

Alyce Chew DiBella

Alyce Chew DiBella
SLEEP'S CREEPS
I lay awake upon my bed
While outside noises fill my
head;

Those passing cars—both near
and far
Their harsh discords my rest does
jar;

That gabby couple walking by,
Don't realize their talk does try!

And now a loud 'plane over goes
Until, in distance, rumblings
slows;

While a sleeping bird awakens
too
And sings out, loudly, his taboo!

And will those dogs over the way
Ever stop their annoying bay!

Also that long limb of the tree
That buffs my roof does bother me;

Oh, what was that sound upon
the floor
Was it an insect, mouse or more?

Now, for awhile, quietude reigns,
And I, at last, sleep soon regains.

Maybelle Fitzpatrick
WHISPERED GRATITUDE
Oh! how grateful, dear Jesus, are
we;
For mercies and blessings granted
from Thee.
We offer our thanks for all things
given,
Especially angels and saints in
heaven;
Who guard and guide us nights
and days;
If we are weeping or singing your
praise.
For your Holy House; of which
you are the center,
For making us humble just as we
enter.
For your Blessed Mother; who is
our mother too.;
A rosary whispered daily in deep
gratitude.
Tis all too often true; we are
prone to forget,
You always remember, and love
us, and yet,
We assume to ask favors, and
promise new endeavors,
Amen, and thanks Jesus, forever
and ever.

Connie Alvey
A Brighter Tomorrow
At times, just for a moment I
close my eyes
And see my world in different
light
For in these trying times, I try to
hold life dear

Hang on, I tell myself, don't lose
your faith
But Dear God, forgive my
weakness
It's so hard to understand

Dear ones around me failing,
giving up on life
No longer able to survive
So if I close my eyes, just for a
moment
Escape and dream

Will it be a brighter world again
Where fear and dissolution will
fade
And hope and joy will reign once
more

Caroline Alley-Hutson
'Till Comes Again the Light
*[To my beloved husband of two
years; my soul-mate, my love...
Our love will endure
forever...forever will we be one.]*
When night closes in;
Stars faintly glowing
I hold my love close
With wild winds blowing.

When Earth's dawn arises
Bourne again with dew
I kiss my love goodbye
With young skies' coming blue.

When dusk's soft blanket falls
Sun painting red skies

I greet my love at the door
  With gentle night drawing
  nigh.

When darkness embraces the land
  The world accepting respite
I clasp my love to my breast
  'Till comes again the light.

Josette Liliane Villias
**Just This Summer, Now
  Passed By**
Just this Summer
  now passed by
I thought I heard
  an angel cry;
and,
  in her weeping
  she was keeping
  a token
  of words
  you had spoken.

Some were to the wind
  and some
  to the rain.
Some were about sin
  and some
  full of pain.
Still some—
  quite insane.
Some dreamed.
Some frowned.
Some gleamed
  and
  some drowned.

Just this Summer
  now passed by
I thought I heard
  an angel cry;
and,
  in her weeping
  she was keeping
  a token
  of words
  now
  broken.

Victor Ray Harrold
TODAY'S DREAM
[I dedicate this poem to Sherry,
Who gave me the inspiration
to write it.]
If you loved me as I love you,
And someday it may come true.
Just me and you in a quiet little
  room,
With a flower in full bloom.

Judith J. Carl
VICTORIOUS
I curse you
  for the last time
a wretched devil who hath slithered
  about my soul—

My victory rides upon your back,
he steers you straight to hell.
Our body was a battlefield,
we died a million deaths—

A grueling time has passed
  for us.
Victory at last.

Barbara Marie Gonzales
IMAGIST
Fly with me in the journeys of
  fairytales,
  the illusions that a child
  enjoys.
Wonder with me in the mysteries
  of imagination,
  the beauties that never fails.

Walk upon the lands that time
  needs to explore,
  and the worlds yet to be
  revealed.
Forsee all your desires behold
  your inner soul,
  and the wisdom within you be
  fulfilled.
Bring forth visions you wish to
  encounter,
  the power to let the unreal be
  real.
Hold the gift of a miracle to
  express,
  the unbelieveable magic to
  truly feel.

Come with me into a creative
  paradise,
  where the heavenly skies await
  us.
Be with me in a treasured life,
  where the precious flight is
  within our eyes.

Kara Lynne Kinney
RAINDROP FANTASY
The rain patters on the roof
Like a myriad of mystical faeries.
Dancing outside my window,
They invite me to join
Their elfin frolics.
But I musn't,
For should I glance out the
  window,
They all disappear
Into the raindrops.
There is magic in the rain.

Rob Carey
HUNGRY MEN
  Hungry Men
  yearning for a Country,
  plot and meddle in dusty cafes,
  hardened beyond Compassion,
  pitiless, beyond hope,
  They plan a Revolution
  at dawn,
When the Sun has recovered the
  red
  from sunset, for
  red
  will be the colour of the day

Kristin M. Lewis
THOUGHTS
Yes, I think of you sometimes
  you stealthily creep out of your
hiding place
  in the corner of my mind
and evoke the memories I have
  tucked away
  . . . of you

I welcome these moments
  for now they bring no pain
or feelings of loss
  just a ghost of a smile . . .
as I, again, tuck you away

Prudence Campbell
BRIAN
  [Brian Mitchell Born: June 20,
  1976 Died: February 13, 1977]
I mourn for you, my baby son
You left this world without
  tasting it
You went away in my arms
In the early morning light
When life should be starting
But before you went you smiled
Two beautiful, peaceful smiles
And somehow the grief is not

too painful
Who did you see? What did you
  see?
Should I even mourn when you
  smiled
Smiles that tell me 'It's all right
  Mom'
So I wipe away my tears
Knowing you'll be there to make
  me smile
When it's my turn to leave
I wipe away my tears
Knowing you're a pure white
  angel
Serving as a precious jewel
In the crown of our Creator

Reine Wiley
TWILIGHT
[To Granddad Sanders, with
Love]
If years were measured for their
  worth,
In life and love alone,
The yard stick of growth would
  still go forth,
To reach an endless throne!

You'd be a millionaire for sure,
Counting life's daily bliss,
And like a miser holding pure,
That which is yours, life's kiss.

You've watched God's only
  jewels,
The children from your seed,
You've touched their golden
  curls,
And filled their every need.

Now that you've reached the
  twilight,
Of all your hopes and dream,
Your jewels are still shining
  bright;
So life goes on it seems!!

James M. Learnard
CHRISTMAS DAY
It's Christmas Day,
  It's raining.
But no matter,
  It's a wonderful day.

The children are singing
  The church bells are ringing.
Everyone is having
  A wonderful time.

Soon he will be here,
  Jolly St. Nick.
He'll come in a flash,
  And be gone just as quick.

The real meaning of Christmas,
  Is not the giving of gifts.

It is the giving of love
  To each other each day.

God, who is all powerful
  And all loving
Gave us his Son this day.
  He gave us that gift of love,
  On that first Christmas Day.

Truman Dayon Godwin
QUO ANIMO
Sunlight sprayed on silky petals
  (in profusion, shiny metals)
Growing yawns the youthful gemma
  (Gaping mouths on modern
  bema)
Fancy woven hang the fanons
  (complex whims in falling
  canons)
Mountains high with senic wonder
  (pimples grow and grown men
  ponder)

Helen Anne Rolwing
LESSONS IN BEAUTY
"Cough again, Old Storm!"
Such was childhood's answer
To the clap of thunder.
Pure delight at nature's fury
Left no place for fear.
Was not God in heaven?
Was not mother in our home?

"What must be our God!"
This the thought that holds me
As the storm enfolds me.
Wind and clouds in threat'ning
  blackness
Race in wild pursuit.

God is not in the whirlwind?
Not in the storm?—Yes,
  —sometimes!

Barbard Tedmon
LOVE
Love is like the breeze,
One short moment you feel it
Then it leaves, suddenly
You try to find it once again,
Looking until no end.
Then all of a sudden it's back,
You try to reach out and touch it
You feel it in your hand but you
  can't hold on.

Linda Seymour
Mothers Message Of Love
This day is so special
  wish you were here
To share all our memories
  some good some bad
The times there was laughter
  the moments we've shared
To touch you and hug you
  be there as a friend
The closeness we share
  is special to me
You're everything
  a mother could be
I LOVE YOU

Helen James Ehlert
Variety In Sugar and Spice
[Dedicated to my precious
  granddaughters; Jeana and
  Joana Hammitt January 1983]
Two little girls with eyes of
  brown . . .
They both have long, blonde hair.
Look alike sisters they seem to
  be;
But the resemblance ends right
  there!

Jeanie likes ice skates,
baseballs and bats!
Joanie loves purses, stuffed
toys and cats!

Jeanie dons cowboy boots,
jeans, and shirts!
Joanie wears sandals, pretty
dresses and skirts!

Joanie loves necklaces, ear bobs
and rings!
Jean could care less for such
silly things!

Joanie loves perfume; Jeanie
can't bear it!
Joanie craves brocolli; Jean'll
take a carrot!

Jeanie loves her studies,
especially Math!
Joanie pursues a more sociable
path!

Joanie's outgoing, Jeanie is shy!
Jeanie's undemanding; Joanie is
sly!

They really are so different;
But on one point they agree!
They both love "Grandma" dearly;
And I'm so glad she's me!

Karen Kay Cox
MELODY
[In memory of my sister,
Melody Ann Kvasnicka who
touched and blessed so many
lives in the four short years she
lived.]
The little song that lingers on
When the instruments fade away;
The Morning Glory in my mind
On a cold December day;
The radiant sun that warms my
heart
When the rains begin to fall;
The voice of hope that lifts my
soul
And makes it heaven-tall.

She was, oh, so many things
To me and those she knew;
All the beauty life could hold
Enshrined in eyes of blue;
A God-sent glimpse of Heaven,
A breath of Paradise;
Just a child of not-quite-four
Who made her world wise.

Ida Mae Espenschied
CHRISTMAS 1982
Christmas in 82, will be rather
blue.
People out of work,
Prices' high, as the Sun in the
Sky.
Can't tell if the News is the
Truth or a Lie.
Killing and stealing, seem to be
the way of Life.
While Drugs and Alcohol, Are
taking their Toll.
Hopefully God will soon take
control
And return this earth, To his
wonderous goal.
Than all Christmas' will be Merry
And this old world, will not be so
scary.

Mary Ann Shofi Bates
DEPRESSION
I'm looking forward to the time
When I don't have to think

Don't have to ask why
Don't have to care
Don't have to wonder if and
when
Don't need to be needed and
loved
Don't have to play games
Don't want for more or less
Don't care what others think
Don't have to cry cause
someone
Hurt me
Don't get sad or lonely or
frustrated
Don't get sick or fill up with
self-pity
Counting all the days when
I prayed things could be
different . . .

I'm looking forward to death.

Cindy L. Wall
LOVE'S REALITY
Love is the elusive fantasy
of poets and writers,
dancing like a muse
in the clouds of the imagination.

Mary Collins

Mary Collins
ASHES OF A ROSE
The life of a rose—
briefly through—lives vividly
then vanishes
Waits in times ashes for dew.

In the rose's first bud
A rose adorns garden walls.
The rose in full bloom
Adorns and brightens great halls.

As the rose's glory descends
Petals fall and fade.
In God's time
The life of a rose is quite small.

Who knows if the ashes
All life changes into
Are the ashes of a rose,
Or perhaps the ashes of you.

Joanne E. Ross
FOR YOU
my heart beats,
my pulse races,
my body trembles . . .
for you.

my fingers caress,
my arms embrace,
my lips submit . . .
for you.

on the altar of our bed
i sacrifice my innocence . . .
for you.

Betsy Papendieck
SUMMER HARMONY
In Marysville
She stands alive,
Mother Church
since 1855.
Standing in
the rose-glow
of the setting sun,
Still sweltering
from the feverish
mid-day hum;
She tilts Her
head
in peaceful prayer,
As cricket's chirring
fills the
evening air.
And I have
heard Her
toll for me . . .
St. Joseph's Church,
in harmony.

Teresa Wood
I SEE
[God has given me beautiful
thoughts, and the quiet desire
to share them with others.
In dedication to my mother;
Ruby Whittington.]
I watched a bird in flight,
nonchalant, serene.

I watched, the moon light
up the night;
Silver magic in its beam.

I watched, the sunrise, in
the sky, and shed her
lovely light.

And humbly now, I thank
my God.
For the mystery, the wonder,
the total joy of sight.

Peggy Fisher
AS I THOUGHT
[Because of their faith in my
writing, this poem is dedicated
to my daughters, Steffanie,
Jennifer, and Courtney, and to
my sister, Jo Perkins. Especially
to God, who has his hand in
mine as I write!]
My husband has left us
We're all alone
What about Christmas?
We'll have none!

Then I think of the orphans
They have no home
We're not as bad off as I thought!
Their little cheeks never knew a

mother's kiss
Their tiny hearts never feel a
moments bliss
No mom or dad to hold their
small hands
And so, all alone they stand

Some cry at night, wishing for
more
Others are too young, to know
what's in store
We're not as bad off as I thought!

Their ears never hear a lullaby
There's little happiness, no
matter how they try
Yet, somehow, they always seem
to get by

Some are bitter, some are sweet
Some wear ragged shoes on their
little feet
We're not as bad off as I thought!

So we will have Christmas, after
all
We can't afford gifts
But we'll send our prayers
To little orphans everywhere!

We're not as bad off as I thought!

Ingrid A. Aleman
GOD'S LAND
Today is your day,
For you to stand,
Be proud of this day,
God gave you this land.

God gave you faith,
God gave you love,
Noah is out there,
Send us a dove.

Tomorrow is your day,
For you to stand,
Be proud that day,
God gave you that land.

Larry Douglas Chappell
I WEPT
I wept to see
Her weep inside.
For I knew
Her pains—she
Was trying to hide
From you and me.

You are kin folk,
So, you know me as no other,
(I don't know much)
But, somehow we communicated,
Sister and brother,
With the family touch.

Just as I gave
Her a farewell hug,
With words she had saved,
"God bless you Doug."

Bob Holtzclaw
SOMEONE SPECIAL
A flower in her hair,
And a smile upon her face.
She's so beautiful,
I cannot look away.

She's a picture of beauty,
In her wedding gown.
She looks just like a princess,
Waiting to be crowned.

She's someone very special
And she'll always be.
Someone very special,
To me.

I cherish the moments,
That I spend with her.

And I pledge that my love,
Will always be hers.

These last quiet moments,
Will soon be endless thoughts.
That we'll carry in our minds,
And never be lost.

She's someone very special,
And she'll always be.
Someone very special,
To me.

Esther Nethercutt

Esther Nethercutt
Esther's Christmas Cake
*[In memory of Gertrude Harris
Johnson, my Dear Loving
Mother.]*

When Christmas Day was
   drawing near
Mom said, "No eggs have we
With which to bake a Christmas
   cake,
No Christmas cake there'll be."

I wondered though, as children
   do,
"Could we not find a way?"
So to the barn I swiftly ran
To browse among the hay.

I heard a rustling sound upstairs
And through a crack, just then
I saw between two clumps of hay
Our faithful speckled hen.

So up the ladder I did climb
And pulled her from her den.
While I picked up her dozen eggs
She flogged me on the shin.

With my straw hat filled full of
   eggs
I made my way back down.
I ran straight to my mom and
   said
"Just look what I have found!"

She baked a big white Christmas
   cake
A sweet potato pie
A custard and some lemon tarts
And bread—two loaves of rye.

When I had eaten to the full
Of food so very good
I slipped some cake to our good
   hen
Because I thought I should.

And as each bite that hen did
   take
I seemed to hear her say
"God bless you, child, the cake is
   good
And merry Christmas Day!"

Marie Hogan Transue
INDIAN SUMMER LOVE
*[For my husband who, after
forty years of marriage, went to
his "Eternal Rest" December 22,
1982]*

There was a boy born.
An "Indian Summer" child.
Before the winter solstice
Ice—locked alluvian streams.

There was a boy born.
Bright eyes dark and dreaming.
An Idaho child.
Thirsting after Nature's secrets.

There was a boy born.
Earthy, wild as a panther,
Heart—soft as a cloud.
And I loved him—that is all.

Cynthia A. Rogers
SPRING
   The bee is a busy soul.
He has no time for birth control.

   He buzzes along
      feeding his pride.
   As much to our surprise,
      the flowers never cry.

   In the sunshine
      they stand tall.
Proud of what makes others fall.

   The bee, the flower,
      togather new life
      they do bring.

   Which marks the start
of the beginning of Spring.

Aleuti Francesca
THE PHOENIX
*[To the world of Men . . . God
grant you not a Phoenix prove!]*

O golden bird of strange
   antiquity,
Famed embodiment of the sun
   God Ra:
Arisen from ash to immortality,
Consumed and yet reborn of
   sacred fire.
The poet, (Phoenix bird of rarer
   hue)
Consumed in suffering for a
   blinded earth,
In time must burn away all dross
   by truth
Arising from a point of inner
   worth.
Ah! Must this world of men a
   Phoenix prove,
Destroying by a freely chosen
   act:
Reducing all to ashes for some
   proof
Of immortality beyond the
   actors?
Shall man yet heed the poet's
   truer vision
The Phoenix bird alighted not by
   fission!

Tom Alan Norton
DADDY
The smile has gone out of me
The little birds scare me
And the blood has flowed out of
   the flowers—
When silence opened the dawn.

Voice of my parent,
Within me. As the laughter
Died inside me—

The rainbow, colored,
And the Son,

So tight to break
So weak to rip
So bent to crack

Me. Alone
In the wind
The Oak. In the fire
The Redwood. In the
Winter, the Blue Aspen.

And with you,
The blood has run out of me
And the smile
Has gone out of the flowers.

Clara C. Creasy
CHRISTMAS FEELINGS
My favorite day is Christmas—
Because it means so much,
For that's our Saviors birthday—
As we worship in his Church.
I love the snow thats falling
   down—
And the tinsel on the tree,
The Christmas carolls they are
   singing—
Are beautiful to hear and see.
I love the stockings hanging,
   expected to be filled—
For it is this secret hour that all
   children are still,
I love the friends and family that
   are comming for a visit—
The tables are laden down with
   food, waiting for them to eat it.
I love the joy and happiness that
   seems to surround us all—
And the packages all around the
   tree are arrayed for all to see,
I love the children with their
   faces all aglow—and—
Watch them build a snowman
   while playing in the snow.
I love each Christmas morning as
   they jump out of bed—
And laugh, as bows and ribbons
   are thrown over their heads,
There's cookie crumbs and candy
   and oranges every where—
But I love those little children
   with snow flakes in their hair.
Merry Christmas little ones,
   GOD bless you one and all—
Because, this is your special day!
   You've waited all year long,
Run get your dollie, your wagon
   and your bat and ball—
While this tired old Mother will
   listen to a Christmas song.
I love Christmas, because it
   means so many things—
It's time to count our blessings, to
   kneel and pray,
Always looking forward to a new
   year, wondering what it may
   bring—
But don't you worry little ones,
   for Christmas day is here to
   stay.

Karin Fletcher
CHRISTMAS
There's a whisper on the
   stairway;
There's a chuckle in the hall;
There's a special sort of aura
'Round the house and that's not
   all—

There's a glowing fire burning;

There are candles burning bright;
There's a row of happy faces
'Round the fire on Christmas
   night.

There is holly on the mantle;
There's a sprig of mistletoe
In the doorway of the parlor
Where the sweet young ladies go.

There are presents, gaily ribboned
On the floor beneath the tree;
There are stockings on the
   mantle—
There's one hanging there for me.

The night's full of Christmas
   music;
Christmas flavors scent the air;
There are smiles on children's
   faces
As to bed they climb the stair,

For they know that in the
   morning
When they open sleepy eyes
Santa will have been before them
Bringing each a sweet surprise.

Oh, there is no time like
   Christmas
With its blessings from above,
And we all thank God that Jesus,
Born this day, brought us his
   love.

Let the bells ring out their
   message;
Let glad tidings fill the air;
For there is no time like
   Christmas;
Spread its magic everywhere.

Elona E. Palmer
BELOVED GENESIS
*[The inspiration received from
the people we love is so
important. Thank You, Doug.]*

Waves, a continuous flow of
   waves.
A shiver in the night,
Not cool but warm and subtle.
Recognition, a realization of
   things to come.
From the first kiss to the first
   slight awareness meshed in
   comfort.
Slowly sinking into a safeness, a
   serenity.
Holding something precious and
   breakable, yet strong.
Inward confusion surrounded by
   passion.
A depth of knowledge when your
   eyes have opened into a world
   unfamiliar, unsure.
Dare to feel.
Dare to go beyond the outside
   world into
The vulnerability of the inside A
   revelation of good things to
   come.
Intuitively finding your way.
Sense it, enfold it, hold on to it.

D. W. Shcmitt
GIFTS
Whatever God gives me
It's in true devotion
Earth or water
A tree, a flower
Even a son
I will accept it
For it's a gift of love
His heart's devotion

241

Marlean J. Eccles
LOVE, IN GOD'S TIME
You are the vessel that God
chose for me;
He placed me there to safely
come to be.

For many years I didn't search nor
find your company; and so I
missed the love, within your
heart, for me.

I know not what the future holds
nor do I care to know dear.

I pray God, please, just grant me
time enough to show the Love,
that from within, flows here

Marianne von Heijne—Matthies
TEARS
The prairie opened it's womb to
the sky which with merciless
storms of chill let it die. Warm
and playfull winds of summer,
full of sun and seed and earthly
dust into snowy waves are
frozen, haloed by an icy crust.

Like an unmanned canoe on a
rolling sea under me slides and
fares my ski— no relief in
sight— just crest after crest,
My heart despairingly falls in
my chest

Wait— a moment of shelter
among trees I find— their
branches blue shadows on the
wastness cast as if they wished
me of something to remind,
Before it is too late— they
must do so fast.

I sense a throb in their network
of veins, a quiet whisper
wanting to tell of a break to
occur in winter's chains, of a
life underneath this hard white
shell,

I hear a threatening thunder of
fettered violence in a flood that
rushes yonder this silence.
Behold— a miracle— suddenly
bursts a leak; hot tears rush
down my frozen cheek.

How is it I know I must not turn
my eye to the starfilled curtain
of the sky? Less the cruel Wind
of Chill my tears to ice shall
petrify with his ruthless
forcing will.

Towards Earth I bend my head; at
all events my tears are mine
with them I fight the
numbness of what's dead and
overbearing forces sent by the
"Devine".

My tears SHALL survive this
icebound land. Sobbinlgly I
shield them with my gloved
hand.

Charles Buckley
BEFORE AND AFTER
He said "I'll climb the highest
mountain;
I'll swim the widest sea
And cross the broadest desert
If you will marry me."

She cried "No sooner said than
done"
So to the preacher off they go,

And next to stand the litmus test:
Would it be happiness or woe?

He climbed the highest
mountain;
He swam the widest sea
He trudged the broadest desert
But, Oh, surprised was he

When forty miles from Cairo
Came a letter postmarked "Nome"
"I am filing for divorce;
Can't stand a man who's never
home."

Jill J. Wade
BE YOURSELF!
"Be yourself!"
They order me.
But I thought such a choice was
free.

"Be yourself!"
Their strident tone
Requires my search to match
thier own.

Their hidden thought
Appears to be
" Yourself should be much more
like ME!"

To be myself
I understand
Cannot be something I *demand*.

"Be youself!"
They shout a lot.
I softly ask, "Who says I'm not?"

They're shouting an
Ironic call:
They know themselves the least
of all.

Dorothy Jean West
THE VISITOR
Something came last night at
three
Carried on the wind,
It rustled through the trees.

I heard it walk the ground,
passed my window sill,
And I heard it's sturring breath,
carrying whispers of ill.

I heard it sturring over the yard
moving to and fro.
And in that moment; I tried to
sleep,
it came closer, I know.

I heard it at the door
trying to get in.
But the night is full of sounds
so I told myself it was the
wind.

Then I closed my eyes
and tried to sleep
And in the darkness,
something touched me,
cold as sleet.

Jean Abbot
THE WAY
He gave us the world, to be happy
and gay,
He gave us sunshine, to see our
way,
The moon and the stars, who can
say,
What they will bring for us each
day.
He planned everything in a very
special way.

Edith Jackson
SOJOURNER
*[In memory of a great lady, my
mother.]*
A willing sojourner I, caught
between earth and sky.
Think not I am contained,

between head and toe.
Just when you think I'm
captured,
I will off and go.

Eleni Katzingris Moustaka
THE EARTH MOTHER
In the dusty horizon tinged
with the gory melancholy
of the twilight, one lost skylark
accompany the caravan
of martyrs, which appear,
show—up,
with the soul's blood
in their lips. They advance, grow,
get multiply, in group—file,
line—group, hard pressed,
squeezed
with empty eyes of sun,
with swellinged legs. The
nightfall,
stealthy advance and get
beside these caravans of silence,
who totters, stupefied,
tattered, between children, white
pigeons,
with contracted lips of thirst,
with sleeply weaving in thier
eyes,
in which one asks is hanging.
The moon, illumines down the
road,
this exodus go lost in the
dead of night, who in one plural
of agony, they go fragment by
fragment,
until the Earth perceives their
torment
under vacillating steps.
Revolving on Cosmos, in anguish
she starts
to see and lament, which not
yet can't,
forbidden by mileniary crooked
laws,
gift heir sons, getting divided
for them,
to offer her immeasurable
richness for
everybody, to feed them
equally,
to give the maternal protection,
against
heir Cain's sons who are still
killing

and Judas sons, who are still
trecherous.
She somber invokes the
apocalypse,
above heir Cain's and Juda's sons,
who still
to spit with spite, over their
brothers
souls, who are sealed with the
damned word "THE SLAVE"

James G. Lynn
The Majority Syndrome
Lost in the crowd, faceless beings
all so very alike
dictatorship of the masses, a
guide to civilization
enough to send the idea of
progress out on a strike
unto each and every fiber of
backward nationalization

Black velvet, night sky, so clear,
unknown, and dark
to reveal the aloneness, the depth
of existence
and see with the stars in forest
park
while the profit makers build the
herd fence

And with illusions to fill up our
lost humanity
victims all of the unreal
promoted by the uncaring
become from the self into the fear
of humilty
forever becoming only the
clothing we are wearing

For those that are real, there is
much to see
beyond the swirling maze of
lemming Psychology
the natural world itself, beautiful,
wild and free
remains beyond the guided tour
of Sociology

The invisible world around us so
vast and deep
can be observed with a view
beyond the delusions
running rampart disguised in
streams that weep
lifes laughter for the majority's
precious illusions

To use the word love, arouses
only a suspicion
the organizational think tank
culture has become
a deity for unquestioning
lobotomizing attriton
an emotional life support system
from which to run

Myriads of stars, clusters of
flowery beauty abound
as mysteries so frangrant and
glistening to the eye
the sound of music, a symphony
of colors all around
a vast molecular complex of a
soft blue sky

To rise above the critical mass of
the very majority
profiting by the few people they
so childishly reject
guarding jealously their
ignorance by a mindless
chastity
leaving only a residue of
confusion to reflect

For the individual, freedom
becomes natural and real
outside of the group, it is still
possible to feel
and reflect, with pity, on the
pathology of normalcy

Mildred Goff
I Remember First Love

Just a teenage romance but was
love at first sight
We met and we talked and we
laughed through the night
He was just a young soldier on
leave for awhile
My heart skipped a beat when I
saw his first smile.

His eyes were clear blue and they
sparkled with fun
His flaxen hair shone in the
bright morning sun
Oh the wonder of love it was joy
without measure
A memory of youth for ever I'll
treasure.

We made many plans for our
future together
Happy, content, and we thought
forever
But all of those plans were not
meant to be
For there was a quarrel and I
found I was free
Broken heart, shattered dreams, I
had my share
To love someone else I never
would dare
Now I've heard from a friend that
my old love has died
After all those long years, I cried.

The love that we shared was so
real and so sweet
When with him I felt that my life
was complete
In winter or summer in spring or
in fall
When we were together we had it
all
But when I was told 'neath the
sod that he slept
Then I thought of first love and I
wept.

Though the years have passed by
and I ought not weep
The sweet memories of him
forever I'll keep
And there's still a small place
reserved just for him
For I'll never forget the love of
dear Jim
Though we each went our way
and found love again
With somebody else and a new
life began
I still can recall the sweet love of
that guy
And the pain has now eased, but
sometimes I cry.

Merrily "We Roll Along"
SANTA . . . ?

In the middle of an unethical
blush
I turned with a shrewd little grin
Who is it I asked that ever let
him in?
As I pointed to the Santa who
held a royal flush

Santa, quite unperturbed, layed

down his hand,
Looking at me his face all jolly
and merry
Spoke with a wink that wiggled
his furry. . .

For some people Christmas
means religion & such
For some it don. .n. .'t mean that
mu. .c. . .ch. . .
Personally for me, he said with a
slur. . . .
I think you are all out to
lun. . .c. . .ch!
But remember the delivery of
your parents
Depends on me— . . . his fat
little finger
Then pounded his chest . . . .

My hand passed to my face to
hide my quick smirk
Cause my factory had just
manufactured its latest dirt. . .
Complete with a digital Santa,
and electronic reindeer
Carrying a load of prepackaged
presents all cleverly new
To deliver to all the robots
during this holiday rush. . .

I knew in a minute the good
Santa was through. . .
My new Christmas whishes went
up like a clear little light. . .
"Merry Christmas to all and now
get out of my sight!"

Christine Ann Reed

Christine Ann Reed
**Don't Push Your One
Flower Away**

Once had a young child 3 years
old, In my flowers she then
liked to roam; Then to bring
wild flowers that grew in the
field, to someone she loved
there at home.

When handling some bulky—
worn flowers, in her eyes they
were rainbows from the skies;
I'd toss the wilted bunch aside,
not seeing tears start in her
eyes.

"I'm busy now, don't bother me,
I've got a date tonight;" And
then she'd turn and run out to
the field, and from me she
would go far from sight.

She thought of flowers as being
her friends, when a wilting
flower then caught her sight;
She would find a stick to hold it

up, and help with all her might.

Those wilted flowers she would
lay on my desk, that I
somehow would then brush
aside; Because I was so
involved with myself, & my
stupid foolish pride.

She used to take her favorite
flowers, & in a book she would
press them to save; I wish so
many times I hadn't pushed her
aside, because the only flowers
I can give now is on her grave.

Grace Gray
MARCH OF TIME
[Fond memories, mom]

She talked of ages and days,
memories gone by,
My youthful eyes wondering
searching whys.
A visit to an old homestead
This or that directions the trails
led.
The delightful reliving of time
days gone by.
Dancing in her eyes, expresions
never ending delight
To me not much, just an older
persons blight.
Days past to my endless wonder,
remembering as she stood and
stared,
Didn't mean much, I never really
cared.
Till just the other day
I turned to someone to say—
When remembering years gone
by
I stop to think and then to cry.
Now I too know!
On and on where does time go!
I stopped too, to reminise
So much sweet bliss.
Age has clued me in
Now I know where she had been.

Paulette M. Unger
TWO ALONE
*[This poem is dedicated to my
husband, Robert Joseph
Arthurs, with all my love and
gratitude for making "Two
Alone" a situation of the past.]*

How sad to think that two who
care shall never know the bliss
Of a total love that two could
share; of a warm and gentle
kiss.

How sad to think that every
night before she goes to sleep
She'll gather near her pillow and
then in the darkness, weep.

How sad to think that he's alone
and knowing that she waits
In the distance, not so far away,
with an appetite to sate.

How sad for her to know that he
holds love within his heart
That he would gladly offer her if
only love could start.

How sad for him to know that
she awaits with open arms;
To give him all that she can give;
to enchant him with her
charm.

How sad to think that two who
care and love each other so

Will never be allowed to share a
passion that would grow.

How sad that he cannot reach
out and take her by the hand;
To guide her down the paths of
life to a new and sweeter land.

How sad that she cannot embrace
the one she loves so dear;
To enfold him gently in her arms
and answer all his prayers.

Sylvia H. Cole
CHRISTMAS EVE
*[To a mother and dad, who
taught me the true meaning of
Christmas, and inspired me
with it's wonder.]*

A hush has settled on the
Christmas snow,
It is a silence that tells us to be
still and know.
Christmas carols are playing
softly somewhere in the dark
They, too are bidding us to hark!
Indeed we seem transformed by
this special night
We seem to be listening for angel
songs in the soft starlight
And somehow we seem to be
kneeling once again
Where the wisemen knelt by the
shepherds, then
Only there, there probably was
no snow
Or Christmas lights in the
evening's glow!

Ruth J. Rowland
A PAINFUL JOB
*[Dedicated to my beautiful
children, Sharilyn, Jeanie, Rick,
and Randy. Whom have given
me far more joy than work! My
husband Chuck and I, truly
adore them.]*

I don't believe there's any job,
that I do, with so much dread.
Every single time I start, I'm in
way over my head.
To sort through tons of papers, I
give them all a look.
It seems I have found enough
material, that I could write a
thick book.

I'd like to keep all the children's
schoolwork, as I sift through
them with care.
But don't you see we are moving,
and our new home doesn't have
an upstairs?
I really can't throw sister's posters
away, they won't take up but a
corner.
Look here is brother's race track, I
could save them for his little
boy, (I can hope and wonder!)

Oh there are big sister's pom
poms, I can just see her little
girl.
Spinning around with so much
fun, and she'll need this baton
to twirl.
There's big brother's football, of
course it won't hold any air.
How can I throw anything away?
I don't really think I dare!

John P. Kerr
THE FELON

Into the night, the felon flies
With quickened step and

243

frightened eyes.
Aborted not his mad escape
As he to freedom flees.
But his burdened mind cannot
forget
The timbre of his victims' pleas.

Though not so innocent, the pair
had done
What social code vouchsafes to
none,
Had traced love-entwined touch
Until the dawn was creeping
high,
Had given in to lust too much;
The husband found the lovers'
tie.

With hand as sure to vengeance
giv'n
As stars are sure to shine in
heav'n,
That selfsame man, the felon
here,
Was driven to kill who held his
trust;
His coddled wife, whom he held
dear,
He levelled down with poniard
thrust.

And though her erstwhile lover
ran,
No freedom found from th' irate
man.
With strength and stealth he
sought pursuit,
And when he his quarry caught
and bound—
The husband now become the
brute—
He struck him deadly to the
ground.

And so, his tale of murder told,
He sought escape from civilized
fold,
Escaped the hunters when the
dead they discovered,
But killed himself wanting logic
and reason
While the pall of death o'er the
death scene hovered,
Killed by the poniard that ended
love's treason.

Irene Laymon
BELIEVE
[To Dr. J. David Rutherford, a
very special person, and a
treasured friend.]
How long has it laid on the table
Unopened and unread?
When did you last look
To see what it really said?

Or did you place it in the
bookcase
Way over out of sight,
Saying I've too many problems
I'll read some other night.

Then you went out for a walk
Down a long, long road,
Trying to solve the heartache
Not even wanting to go home.

You'd tried to call your friend
But when she answered the
phone,
"I'm sorry I can't talk now,"
And you felt even more alone.

You've reached the end of the rope
There's no one left to help you,

This is the season of miracles,
For you, there is one too.

No one ever walks alone
They are just too blind to see,
He has been walking with you
Just as he does with me.

He only asks one small thing
Believe with all your heart,
For he knows what is best for you
He'll lead you out of the dark.

He'll give you love and gentle
peace
He's with you, you're never alone,
So just let go, and take his hand
Have faith, for you are his own.

Then at this holiday season
Your heart will be truly blest,
With peace and hope and
happiness,
And your fears will be laid to
rest!!

Nancy C. Schupbach
The Reality of Illusion
[For the Man who taught me
that my Illusions are Reality.]
Loving you may be an illusion I
have built from playing
solitaire too much.
Wanting you may be a pain I
have developed from dreaming
too much.
Needing you is a craving I have
from being with you too much.

And yet—

Our illusions may be the only
reality we have
And
Pain is but an hallucination of
the mind
And
Desire is fired by not having
what is wanted most.

Which leaves me here still—

Needing you and wanting to need
you,
Wanting you and dreaming,
Loving you and . . . playing
solitaire.

Norma Lou Sammons
THE SEA
[For Dad and Charlie]
The sea is blue much like the sky
Carrying temper and moods all
its own
Its waves so quiet, the surf so
calm
Making believe it's a peaceful
home.

Then it turns strong and
powerful
Putting fear in the best of men
Its changing ways, its crashing
waves
Sending chills across your skin.

Again the mood changes, a wisp
of wind
A gentle breeze is on its way—
The beaches so bronze, the sun is
turned on
Letting people enjoy, run and play.

Again and again it will change its
moods
Predictable it will never be—

For the mystic power it alone
holds
Is what brings us back to the sea.

Carlisle Ramsey
THE QUEST
[I dedicate this poem to my
Lord Jesus Christ, who is The
Truth.]
I started out on my quest for
truth,
Filled with zeal and fire,
And-like those men who went
before me, I
Sought my soul's desire.

I searched for Truth in modern
books and those
Back through the ages,
And read their many written
words on torn
And yellowed pages.

I've talked with those who were
both good and wise,
And studied their way,
And I found that the ones who
knew the most,
Had the least to say.

I've ended my quest—knowing
less than
I did before—save,
That Truth is for the brave,
Like Jesus, who before his accuser
Stood, serene and tall,
And when asked "What is Truth?"
said nothing;
Said nothing at all.

Marilyn L. Fuerstenberg
MY LIFE
It seems I spend so much time
alone,
No-one there who really cares.
I don't know who to call on the
phone,
My life it seems is just too bare.

I am always hurt with pain
And when I need someone,
nobody is near,
To help me through my awful
strain,
I'm all by myself looking in a
mirror.

I feel I have not a friend
Who really wants to help me,
Just to only send
Me away and never want to see.

I suffer great sorrow and hurt—
Torn up deep inside,
Just being treated like dirt;
Who cares who hurts my pride.

Not a person around could give a
damn
Whether I go to hell—
Or die in a jam—
Or not feeling well.

So why should people care if I
was born.
No one would miss me if I was
gone.
Certainly not one person would
mourn,
They would have kicked me
around like a pawn.

My life is just one big downhill
With not one soul who would
ever think
Of me or my little will,

Cuz I would have only love to
give and not a mink.

Reinaldo Matos

Reinaldo Matos
APPLE TREE IN BLOSSOM
My apple tree who laughs,—
My sweet love
In blossom!

Where does your grace
Of perfume and garden
Come from?

Oh, tell me;
Just me!
Is it from the passing breeze?

My sweet love
In blossom!
Is it from the passing breeze?

Gloria D. Alkire
BRIDGE OF THE PAST
One last look and I will long
remember you
Weathered sentinel, standing tall
on Bridgeton's country lane
Where scorching sun and brittle
ice-capped winds
Have long since took their toll,
and man,
Yet you remain!

You bridged the gap of swollen
creek and trickling stream,
sequestered
By willows swaying in the prairie
breeze;
You served both man and beast
in silent dignity
As shelter in the storm—a quiet
hideaway—
And through the years, you'd
remain!

Your crumbling timbers now are
carefully shored and propped—
Your rustic battered boards once
more regained
To be displayed on tours—
reviewed by those
Who find an old friend steeped in
history past,
not just
A covered bridge that happened
to remain!

Ruth Morgan
CONTEST
My thoughts were numb with
fright
With my decision to enter with
all my might

To put words on paper that
rhyme
Is something I have done for a

long time
But when it was for public
  viewing
My courage got up and went
  winging
I talked it over in my prayers at
  night
He gave me courage to try and
  not lose sight

I find it is easy and fun to share
Even when we don't know where

Our thoughts and rhymes might
  suit
And who knows, we might win
  some loot.

Sylvia DeMary

Sylvia DeMary
TRIBUTE TO TERRY FOX
*[A courageous young Canadian
Who hobbled thousands of
miles on one leg, in aid of
others.]*
When we saw him first declining
His lips were moved in prayer
And the setting sun was
  shinning,
on his blue eyes and curly hair
As he smiled, and continued to
  reach the sky.

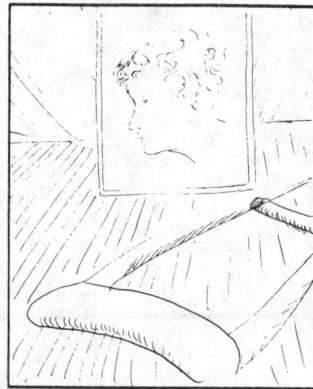

Sadly we knew our boy must die
They took him to the City,
but he faded slowly there
For cancer had no pity,
for blue eyes and curly hair.
Then our marathon of hope
  stopped living,
His pain forgotten—His love still
  there,
We shall remember his courage,
  His giving
Terry with blue eyes and
  beautiful curly hair.

James Marcelan Manion
Does Anyone Really Know How To Love?
*[To all my friends who have
been supportive of me.]*
There is so much more to love
  than making love
You must be able to feel,
to touch,
to grow,
to learn to be one
Yet the one must also be able to
  be two
You must be able to trust
the trust must always be there
  thru' everything
and about all matters—Trust
Know how to talk
talk openly about all matters
don't ever hold anything back
There should be no fear
nothing to be afraid of
(when falling in love)
Be able to see
to believe
to teach each other
Don't worry, and
don't hurry
You must be each other's friend
Until *the* end
If at all possible

To love, you must
remember a lot of things
that will make it more than easy
I'm sure there are more things
  than this
remember
Peace + Love = Happiness
  (forever?)

Nancy Tucker Wilson
A BASKET OF DAISIES
Hope is a white swallow in flight
Shaped from the snowdrift on a
  brown leaf.
Day-dreams drift past when the
  winds blow;
With hope, they are lost as the
  snow in the night.
Lightly white flowers fall and fly,
A basket of daisies tossed out
  from the sky.
Grey-rose past the fir tree,
Again turning white,
White daisies of snowflakes
Wound in a sheaf.

Hope is the daisies that melt
  where they lie;
Hope is a snowflake that one
  cannot seize;
But hope is the sunlight behind a
  grey sky.

R.G. Wilson
THE ROSE
*[To a lady who had a great
impact on my life, one whom I
considered a very close friend
and a lady who I was very
much in love with. With my
undying love I dedicate this to
Maj. Britt Cardiff.]*
As a man is destined to wander . . .
thru the desert of his life
searching high and searching low...
for the fulfillment he must find.

He happens upon an oasis . . .
in the middle of this wasteland
all lush and green . . .

with water to nourish it,
and trees to give it shade.
He happens upon a solitary
  ROSE . . .
in the middle of this oasis.
Growing strong and vibrant . . .
with petals soft as the clear night
  air.

Somehow finding this ROSE . . .
in the heart of that oasis
makes it all worth while.
He knows at that time . . .
his wandering and searching is at
  an end.

He comes to realize . . .
that this ROSE
growing alone . . .
reaching upwards towards the
  sun,
is one of a kind.

Proud and beautiful . . .
the ultimate gift of love!
Although he soon must . . .
leave this oasis
to commence once again his
  journey.

A tear shall come to his eye . . .
for he will never forget that ROSE
and the love for a time they
  shared.

Clarence L. Babcock
Man's Wounds and Scars
Those who unearth and read the
  rocks and fossils
Mark out the record of man's
  brutal early life,
When days were filled with
  battles for survival;
When killing and stark terror
  ruled the nights.
Long years of strife implanted
  patterns in his brain;
A burden he must carry with him
  all his coming days.
Man still is plagued by fancied
  and real terrors
When times of stress break
  through his dreams of life.

Our minds can only guess what
  floods of thought
Poured through his brain and
  overwhelmed him,
When first he stood erect on that
  day long ago
And saw the sunrise shadow
  distant mountin peaks.
His life that had gone on the
  same for unknown years
Began to slowly change in ways
  he could not know.
Out of the chaos and confusion
  of those cruel days
Man started on his lonely
  journey down the years.

Through catastrophic wars,
  earthquakes, and plagues,
Man has survived and made his
  way against great odds,
But he has paid a price and wears
  his wounds and scars.
The price—a mind of mixed and
  Janus-faced duplicity;
With gentleness and cruelty—
  good and evil—all entwined.
With unguessed motives and
  desires man ever ranges wide;
From deeds of kindness and

affection for his fellow men,
To making war and terror
  bringing death down on their
  heads.

When passions overwhelm him
  man yearns to know himself;
To understand his urges to errant
  thoughts and deeds.
He feels the heavy burden of his
  many wounds and scars
As he trods the path that
  Nature's pulsing life stream
Man rides its waves—its
  ceaseless crests and troughs.
While not forgetting all his days
  of war and conflict,
He still can stand erect and load
  his hands with stars.

LaVonne R. Rients
PROCREATION
A woman 'fore she reached her
  time
Concerns herself with much
  design,
Creating style with clothes and
  hair,
Adorning same with gems so fair;

Such is her lot 'till she address
The time of woman's peak
  success.

Her shapely form emerges forth
Protruding into future worth;
Attaining grace in motherhood,
Searching all for what is good.
Gaining wisdom in her plight,
Weary from her trial by night.

So be the nature of her fate
There is none other way but wait.
And quickly time shall heel the
  wound,
Her life to life again is tuned.

H.B. Almy
THE LONESOME TIRE
On a tree by our house
  A lonesome tire sway
Once children's happy faces
  shown
  Now they live so far away.

You can hear them, listen closely
  As they holler, play with glee
Grandma, are you watchin?
  Grandpa, come and see!

But, no, there's no one out there
  Or did I hear them yell?
Grandma, are you watching?
  Are you sure no one fell?

The tire just keeps on swingin'
  As if fairies guide its flow
Yes, the tire keeps on swingin'
  In a wind that doesn't blow.

Janet Pyle
FAITHLESS WOMAN
Father of no family mural,
faithless brief of rain and pine,
forests overhung by thunder
threatening whitefaced crowds of
  walkers.

Improbable and lost
in lifeless wonder
angered at the women crossing
streets and never looking.

Mauricia Price
BEHIND THE TINSEL
Behind the superficial tinselings,
The patterned blinking of the

lights
In gaudy store displays
At Christmastime
Are hearts
That care.
Behind the blatant lawn and
window shows
Of overdecorated homes
And flashy boulevards
Are joyful hearts
That love
And share.

V. Anne Smith
INSECT FOE
*[Dedicated to my fun-loving
grandsons, Brandon Wallace
Silva, Eric Randall and Justin
Dean Smith.]*
Insect swimming in my eye,
(More troublesome than famed
Med-fly),
Could you not land upon my
ear—
Causing not a single tear?
Or on my lip, near pearly-white,
So I would be the one with might!
Better yet, beneath my heel—
Where you would be the one to
squeal.

Eleanor C. Kaminsky
WASTE OF LIFE
[To Boom Boom]
Adored child of love,
Thank God, we can't see
What's in store.
Quiet and sensitive,
We never realized your
Silent suffering.

We tried to teach,
And failed you so . . .
We did our best.

Your anger finally exploded,
And you reached out to us
But we did not hear,
And you blindly drove, into the
night.
The crash . . .

All that was left was your
Lifeless body.

Joseph A.J. Conway
STRIKE TWO
Love never felt more empty than
today, life never felt as lonely;
there's got to be a better deal
on the way.

I go to sleep wondering how and
where you are, after a long
battle with the bottles at the
bar.

I wonder if I can touch you the
same way again, or has the best
already been?

I dream about who you're with
and if he's treating you right, it
only feeds the fire that makes
me want to fight; the feelings
aren't right, hidden in the black
and white.

It's dark and black of night; oh
God, I wish I could find the
light and somehow make
everything all right.

Through the trouble I travel,
trying to unravel answers from
subtle clues; all I seem to be

getting is bad reviews.

So beware all you high school
sweethearts, you may think
you've got it made; but all your
dues may not be paid.
You may love each other and
swear you'll never part, but the
weak heart will fall and tear
the strongest one apart.

The morals of the story are told
by fools who go out in a blaze
of glory.

We're afraid to take that longshot
chance again, because you see,
the investment never paid its
dividends; the bank is broke
and this is the end.

Glennie C. Larke
CONTROVERSY
The kettle drums thundered
Atom—atom—split the atom,

The violins whispered
Of wagon roads
Through forest of redwoods;
Symphoniously murmuring:
Peace-peace-peace—

The bass tones flared!
The brass keyed defense
And the attentive cymbols
trebled;
A major discord of intrigue,
Could a void cause.

The violins whispered
Of Faith, Liberty, and Justice:
On and on and on—

The cello intensified the rhythm,
Of the violin's sonata;

As the tamborine jangled
an aggressive scale:
While the harp
Accented the whispers
unpersuasive,
Harmony-harmony-harmony-

The kettle drums thundered
Atom-atom-split the atom
Split the Universe!

Douglas P. Crouch
HIS DEVIOUS WAYS
He lurks in such a disgusting way
With arrogance and flagrance as
if to say,
"You ain't nothin compared to
me,"
"You're weak, and unstable and
can't break free,"

He's brilliant, cunning,and grossly
unkind,
He loves to constantly tear at our
minds.
Forever deceiving, breaking all
the rules,
He cleverly molds us into his
impetuous tools.

He can be timid and placid and
shy,
He can win us over in the blink
of an eye.
He is persuasive, no matter what
mood,
Whether it be unsagacious or
shrewd.

He has no preferance be us old or
young,
Be us man or child, whatever our

tongue.
His lewdness has corrupted many
a mind,
Of those who once were honest
and kind.

There is a way to get around
satan's might,
One known by Christians as the
LIGHT,
I AM, THE WAY, and THE
DOOR,
Jesus Christ our Savior, forever
more.

Marjorie Burney Willis
A Farewell To a Little Dog
*[Dedicated to my daughter,
Anngel, painter of animals;
written for her on the loss of
her beloved Woofie . . . in the
summer of 1980.]*
Farewell, Woofie!
Farewell, little friend, fairest of
my flowers.
Why did you go away in the
beautiful summertime,
When the butterflies spread their
wonderful wings,
When the world fills our hearts
with joyful things?
Yesterday you were here in our
garden,
Resting in the shade of the
willow tree,
Looking up at me, trusting and
adoring me.

In innocence, you strayed beyond
the garden wall,
And in moments . . . lay beneath
life's cruel wheels . . .
With many tears, I yeilded you
into the vast realms of eternity.
Now, the ground is empty
beneath the weeping willow
tree.

Ah Woofie, I miss you so!
If I could search across a
thousand fields
And climb earth's highest
mountain, I'd never find you.
Are you on some far-flung golden
star . . .
Your eyes sparkling bright . . . your
heart beating true . . .
Beneath a heavenly sky overhung
with a rainbow?
O tell me, tell me that this be so!
For the flowers in our garden are
fading
And a gray mist is falling;
The butterflies have flown away.

My heart grieves
Like the weeping willow
tree . . . stripped of its green
and golden leaves.

Marjorie Burney Willis
**A Recipe For Prize
Winning Poetry**
"Never give up," my angel said,
answering my plea for help,
"Someday your poetic ideas will
turn to gold,"
and then the angel became
more specific:
"Keep working! Learn! Burn the
midnight oil! Study! Struggle!
Sweat! Search! Seek! Dream!
Laugh! Cry! Weep bitter tears!
Share your poetry with the world;
a beautiful poem is a golden
thing."

All these things . . . I promised
the angel
I would faithfully do,
And all these things . . .
I commanded myself to do.

And now . . . later . . . O much
later!
Poetic ideas are whirling around
me!
sparkling with creative
energy,
melodious as the music of
violins
and golden trumpets,
picturesque as a Picasso
painting.
Poems are flashing forth like
falling stars,
cascading down, tumbling
down
from an infinite source . . .
Then brightly, delightfully
assembling themselves
together
in a perfect and profound
order
on the blank white pages
before my astonished eyes.

Sharee Ann Vivirito
SUNSHINE
An illumination passing of
separate ways.
Walking in the sunshine,
Observing many things in time.
The break of dawn shedding its
light among the world.
Let it rise, let it set,
For I can presume its beauty yet.
God is divine for one of his
miracles is sunshine.
I shy from the night because of
its sable fear,
Waiting for daylight to appear.

Linda M. Brodeur
INNER EMOTIONS
Loving you the way I do
Our lives should be as one
But you can't decide which one
you need
The damage now is done.

For to you I'm just another face
Someone you call a friend
My head keeps saying, "Leave me
be"
My heart screams, "It can't end!"

Deep down inside I realize
I'll never have you for myself

You've taken my love; laughed at
it
And tossed it on a shelf.

But I'll be strong—I have to be
I'll make it on my own
I had a love, I've lost it now
So I'll go on alone.

And if our paths should cross
again
As I know they someday will
No matter what you think of me
I know I'll love you still.

My heart can only break so much
It's sad to know, but true
No matter what you feel for me
My love belongs to you.

Nancy Roulias
**Talking To Jesus On
Christmas Morning**
Merry Christmas, Lord Jesus, we
love you very much.
We know you by the Bible and
our faith—not by touch.
That Christmas morning long
ago—You were born to save us.
We Christians know the pain and
hurt You went through Christ
Jesus!
I pray that gifts and tinsel come
second in every way.
We love You and praise You, and
You tower above others.
We will keep Your
commandments and love one
another.
May every heart and soul be
cleansed this holiday season!
Let every Christian know they
are here for a reason.
Let us feel Your perfect love, as
You bind the devil's hands.
Jesus, let all Christians contribute
their bit in Your plans.
May our guiding angel protect us
from the devil's charms.
He is always plotting to scoop us
into his wicked arms.
Fill our hearts with Your holy
spirit and bless our giving.
It was all because of You that
makes our lives worth living.
We could never pay You for the
agony You went through.
You suffered for our sins, so we
could be born "again" too!
Keep Your hand on our
shoulder—until our life is
finished here
We wish You a blessed Christmas
and more Christians this new
year.

Mark D. Hachey
TORNADO
The sun shone peacefully down
on the town.
It was quiet, calm.
Quiet, too calm.
A whisper would have broken the
silence like a shout.

In the west, it waited,
A cloud . . . gathering steam,
Purple-green, ragged, foreboding.

The town appeared lifeless as
The warning siren echoed down
deserted streets.
The wailing continued and then
was overcome

By the sonorific growl of the
tempest.
Those that huddled indoors
quaked,
Attempting to evade the
bombilation,
But to no avail.
The rain fell in torrents,
Collecting itself in ditches,
Awaiting the deluge that was to
follow.
Lightning forked down from
above,
The sky momentarily ablaze in
its luminency.
The pandimonium that followed
was like so many trumpet
blasts.
The maelstorm was upon the
town.
The vortex strode across rooftops
Leaving rubble in its passing,
... And the Ugly Wind continued
It bellicose howling.

The wreckage was silent as
The sun shone peacefully down
on the town.

Betty June Holmes
MY LOST CHILD
I once had a child, so bubbly
and sweet,
She smiled all the time and was
really neat.
As years went by, day by day,
I sat and watched as she slipped
away.
She became lonely and oh so
sad,
I couldn't help her and I felt so bad.
I tried my best, which was no
fun,
She got confused, decided she had
to run.
My heart is lonely, my heart is
sad,
Because I can't help the child I
once had.

Nancy M. Brevelle
THE REFLECTION
My heart whispers through my
eyes
But my spoken word belies
What my conscious thoughts
ignore
And my inner being
realizes.

I am a deep red rose
trembling in the wind.
I am a vintage wine
afraid to be drank.
I am a full moon
hiding behind a cloud.
I am the richest of soils
refusing to yeild.
I am the fire and gold
of Autumn's tints.

To a few I am revealed
Naked, before them I kneel
Only they who hear my heart
Can know the shy, passionate me
who is real.

Glenn A. Smith
THE LONELY HUNTER
Across the shallow woodland,
Searched a lonely hunter near
and far.
O'er hills and valleys, great rivers
and brooklets,

Seeking true love not war.
In a nearby village a plain but
curious maiden
Lived happily as can be,
Until she found her life
incomplete, and ventured out
to see.
She learned that there was much
more to life
Than ever she had dreamed,
And began to feel a need within,
to share what she had gleaned.
The fair maiden knew not where
to look
Nor under what tree she'd find,
But search she did relentlessly,
'till she became lonely in mind.
While thus perplexed in this
somewhat outcast state,
She found herself atop a little
knoll,
Seeking solace from her
loneliness which began to take
its toll.
When from afar she heard a cry?
A whisper? A prayer? No! A song!!
The lyrical strains of a minstrel's
tune? Or am I wrong?
At once she espied a lonely
figure, slowly climbing up the
hill,
Singing a song whose tune she
seemed to know,
With words of love her heart did
fill:
"A walk through life is a long
long walk, when you have to
do it alone. I'd go to the ends of
the earth with you . . . don't
make me do it alone . . ."
Their eyes did meet their hands
did clasp,
Their loneliness now was gone.
Our fair maiden was aglow with
love,
No more plain but lovely as the
sky at dawn.
The hunter too was deeply
changed, every habit, thought
and word.
For ended was his search so long,
her hand replaced his sword.
Now as these two go on through
life,
They'll remember as they live,
That for one to find true
happiness,
One must be willing of himself to
give.

Fred Harper
A SNOWFLAKE
A little snowflake fell one day
upon my nose as I did play
and as I tried so hard to see
my eyes just crossed
and frightened me

Robert M. Baker
PAPA
Look at me now Papa,
I stand afar as I watch,
they start to lower you,
and I am sure you understand.

You see, Papa, I stood afar,
way up on that hill,
far from everyone else,
because I thought it shameful to
cry.

I looked down upon them,
and those men weren't shameful,

but, Papa, you said a man doesn't
cry,
except for when he is really hurt,
remember?

Well, Papa I took another look,
and I ran all the way to your side,
sure, Papa, I cried a whole lot,
and you know now I am a real
man.

J. Christopher Stefanelli

J. Christopher Stafanelli
**Fine Air (Financial
Despair)**
*[To my beautiful wife
Jacqueline, whom without her
ongoing love and confidence,
you wouldn't be reading this
poem now.]*
Woe is me, with my wallet lean,
And yet the sun is still gold,
Oh yes, I have no money green,
But the sun's still warm not cold,
Yea, my wallet now says I'm
broke,
But the sun assures me my
wealth,
I could be rich and sickly,
But instead I'm poor—in good
health.

Pauline McAmis
LOVE'S IMAGE
In—
The summer heat
She built her own image of sand
on the beach.
In life—
He walks by arm in arm with his
own love,
wrecking—
her life's dream.
Then—
the tide rolls in washing, washing
away love's image
from there in the sand.
Lonely—
and alone—
she weeps for what might've been.
In—
the summer heat.

Doris Taylor "Rusty"
DEATH IS NOT GOODBYE
I feel no fear as I lie here—
My life is coming to its end.
I don't want to hear the word
"Goodbye"
Hold tight my hand—
Let the strength flow slowly.
Give me yours to guide me on.
Remember happy times, sad ones
too—

I have loved—I have lived
Sing no sad songs for me—
Rejoice as I begin a new voyage—
Into the land where dreams begin.
Don't leave flowers on my grave
to wither and fade,
Plant new ones in the soil—
Let them live and flowers give—
Until they die, naturally.
As I want you to do this for me,
I hope I am not selfish in these
wishes
I ask of you.
Memories live on. New ones
begin.
This is all I ask as I leave this
world—
Remember me, Love me as I have
loved
Let me go freely.
Please don't say the word
"Goodbye"
I know we will meet again.
God is good, he gave me life, My
Friend.

Billie M. Trosper
LITTER
A beer can lay upon the yard,
A sack of Hardies' scraps,
An envelope discarded,
And some bright candy wraps,
A well-chewed bone was also
there,
The neighbors' Irish setter,
He's easier to understand,
He don't know no better,
But when I see that awful litter
Nearly everyday,
Not only on my yard alone,
But all along the way,
I wonder—this litter problem
Must be of the Devil—
To make a human lower
theirselves
Down to doggy level.

Ione Fisher
HEART ATTACK
I only feel love in my heart
When that love is challanged,
I feel pain.
When I feel pain,
I cry.
When I cry,
I am sad.
When I am sad, I am not myself,
For when I am myself,
I am bouncy, laughing and full
of life.
Right now
I am suffering
From a heart attack.
A big part of me is dying
My heart.
Someday,
I may be brought back to life,
But for right now . . .
Just let me rest in peace.

Brenda Lee Neal
FAMOUS
People will do most
anything,
to get famous.
They are willing to
give up their family
and friends.
Just to see their
names in neon lights.
That sparkle both
day and night.

After they have their
name in lights.
They feel they need
to go much further.
Some people make it.
Others don't.
But they don't realize
how far they are,
Until it's too late.
Some die without kowing God,
And even though they have fame.
That will not get them through
the golden gates.
So, If you have thought
about being famous,
And have your name in lights.
Think twice.
Remember your name
will be brighter,
if it's in the book
on high.

Pauline J. Williams

Pauline J. Williams
MOMMIE MISSES YOU
*[This poem is dedicated to my
sons Joey and John Williams,
with all my love, until the earth
stops turning, and the sun
stops burning, & long after I'll
still be caring.]*
If you feel I have forsaken you
two,
Believe me that's not even true
And don't think like that for one
Second, 'cause mommie misses
you . . .

It's not easy working without you
near,
And when you were taken my
heart was hit
As if by a spear.
I know summer has come and
summer has gone
But, you two hold on it won't be
long . . .
It's "ruff" out here I'm trying hard,
with
You my sweets I turn face up my
card, I
Tried and failed and gave up for a
while
But, please my dears don't give up
your smiles
I'm back out there and working to
the max 'cause
The main thing on my mind is to
get you my kids
Back . . .

Mommie misses you two boys
watching you grow-up,

Fuss, make-up, and playing with
your toys.
One day some way I'll make it all
up to you
'Cause there's nothing in this
world I'd rather do.

Joey and John this is for you
believe me kids
Mommie misses you . . .
Keep your chins up high to the
sky . . .
Until we're back together here's a
kiss . . .
Stay sweet
Bye-Bye
Mommie

Daniel C. Schleyer
DAMSEL IN DISTRESS
When you hear the chilling
sound of a lady in distress,
While the moon is shimmering
on the open sea.
Your body tingles with the
lingering fear
That something is lurking in the
shadows you see.
Your eyes and your ears begin to
search in vain,
While visions of madness float
through your mind.
You're beginning to wonder
should I run or stay,
Never quite knowing what you
may find.
The echos of agony persist on in
the night,
Drowning the sounds of the
creatures that were.
A Damsel in distress had just lost
her life,
To a madman who tried too hard
to love her.

Megan Ludick Schwartz
LEAVES
Somewhere, somehow, and all
alone
there lies a forest
whose beauty's known
for leaves so splendid, human
eyes
could not perceive—unless they
tried.
So far away, in unknown lands
where sits this forest
that grander than
any you or I shall see
but stays there for eternity.
Deep in this forest, upon the
trees,
the wind plays games with all the
leaves.

The leaves, with all their
strength, hang on—
The wind is fierce, the wind is
strong.
But, one by one do slip their
fingers
and destined to their deaths, they
linger—
to where all natures autumn
leaves
who fall from branches of their
trees
and float so graceful to their
places
upon the ground that hides their
faces.
Oh leaves, which blossom
yellow-gold
If I might have one—just to hold
for only seconds could be
pleasing,
but, dreams like these are only
teasing
For beauty brews its troubles too
and yellow-gold soon fades to
blue.
But, no one's seen these leaves,
they say
The forest is deep where no one
strays.
Their needless splendor gone to
waste—
Their breathless beauty—none
shall taste.

Sandra Leigh Wilson
REMEMBERING YOU
Tonight, looking at my face in
the mirror,
I whispered "Baby" . . . just the
way you used to.
The look in my eye, alone,
startled me out of my trance,
Chilled at how real it felt.
Somehow, at night I purposely
dwell on our love, on you.
I remember the best of times . . .
the tender, passionate,
The Promising. The closeness I
felt is now what hurts the most.
Pulling away changed me this
time. Abruptly ending,
But the memories are not turned
away. I think of you,
Miss you; I dream of you,
remember you. Yet, as a mouse
Learns its prize it also, finally,
learns (Remembers?)
The Shock. The maze is now in
focus.

Kathern P. Edwards
Our Little Bundle Of Joy
I have never felt so full of joy;
as the morning my doctor said to
me;
"You have a handsome little boy."
I wanted to spread the news all
about;
I had a son there could be no
doubt.
I asked if I could tell the proud
Dad;
that it was a son we now had.
My husband came to me at a
hurried pace;
and when I told him we had a
son,
I'll never forget the look on his
face.
His face was all aglow; then,

"Are you sure it's a boy?"; he wanted
to know.
We had longed for nine months
to see our
son laugh and coo; to hold him
finally in
our arms was something else we
had
longed to do.
It was hard to really believe that
after
all our waiting we could now
watch our
son grow; and we could start to
love
him from head to toe.
We know that our son was a
very-precious
gift; when he smiles it gives our
hearts
a big lift.
He puts sunshine into each of
our days;
because he has such cheerful and
loving
ways.
John Lee is what we named our
little boy;
he is certainly our little bundle of
joy!

Kimalee R. Jones
The Truth Behind the Lies
We never know how old one is
Until we look inside.
How young the old and grey can
be
What ancient souls a child can
hide.

We only hear the lies that call
Within mans reasoned halls.
The truth we never see behind,
Those haunting, darkened walls.

We fail to see the life in death
The hidden death in life.

We only see the finite reasons
That dwell within the mind.
Somewhere just behind the lies
Immortality abides.

Nothing is what it seems when
seen
Reflecting silver within our eyes.
The soul is the only one who
finds
The truth behind the lies.

Ruth Hanson
LOVE
Love is a wonderful feeling
But never the same.
My heart you're stealing
Through all of the pain.
The pain of knowing and caring
And of showing and sharing.
Love endures through all,
Or so they say.
Yet many people don't know
The price they must pay.
For love is not bought
With material things.

Angela V. Nalbantu
Journey Through the Night
When the streets are dark and
my soul is clean
It reaches out to the shadow of
trees,
To the greyish buildings playing
hide and seek

With the fog,
To the people of cats serenading
on roofs
And it bathes itself in the unpure
air.
Then it can feel less the sorrow
and the anger
And being part of the spilled
universe
It loves itself.
In the morning the coming back
is always sad.
I feel back all the miseries I have
missed
And filled with rage and
unhappiness
I witness the crimes of the night
that stand before me
As the unhelped children who die
young
And I cry.

Syreen Sheehan
STAR MAIDEN
*[To The Alpha And The
Omega. To the women in the
space program. To the women
of the world.]*
Lost in space! a sea of stars!
a moon, here and there! I long...
to feel...the touch...of my
home planet, Mother Earth: with...
skies...of blue! and oceans, too!

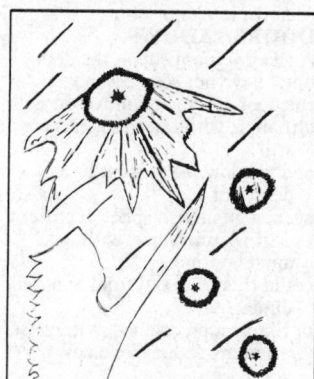

oh, to see...a flower! my mission
is long; I am weary. But my goal
was reached; I can't complain.
Here I am, a woman, in space!
they call me: Star Maiden.

Virginia H. Rickenbaker
MY PASTOR
Let me tell you of the blessings
you impart to me,
I believe they will go with me
through eternity.
As God gave you the message to
prepare,
I apply them to my soul with
prayerful care.
For I want to follow my Lord all
the way,
So I always ask God to give me a
message each Sunday.
Whether reproof, rebuke,
correction or affection,
It applies to me because of God's
direction.
I know it takes prayer and study
on your part
To seek God's message to fit and
apply to each heart.
But you will be rewarded some day,

And I am thankful you came our
way.
I am also thankful for a Pastor
who prays
As the Holy Spirit reveals to you
our different ways.
I am convinced that you are
concerned for each soul,
And how you labor in love by the
Spirit is untold.
So these few words I put on this
paper to say—
To show my gratitude on this
Christmas Day.
As we celebrate the birth of the
Christ-child to set us free,
For later He was crucified at
Calvary.
He bore our sins upon the cross-
For as sinners we were all lost.
My prayer for nineteen eighty-
two would be for a fruitful year,
For the lost ones to be born again
for whom we've labored much
in prayer.
That would make us all as happy
as could be,
Knowing that the souls would be
in heaven for all eternity.

Thelma Gray Woolard
TOTAL LOVE
She gives him her love, that is her
all,
Wanting to make him feel ten
feet tall.
She gives him her mind, body and
soul,
While he only leaves her lying
cold.

She gives her total love, while he
only takes.
Then she sits very still and waits.
Hoping and praying, one day he'll
care.
Her hopes and dreams he'll want
to share.

She was waited for a long, long
time,
And in her dreams she hopes to
find,
That he thinks she's special,
And that she's great.
That he'll give her total love
Not just take.
She needs some one ten feet tall,
Who will give her total love,
Who will give his all . . .

Lenora Hart
TWO BOYS
*[To my two boys, Mike and
Pat, who have given me
inspiration and life's most
precious gifts, I dedicate this
poem.]*
Two boys in hand
is a world full
of joy so grand.
Never a moment dull
You spent with this band!

One is fourteen, the other nine,
Put the two together,
You'll have no time to whine
For want of something or other.

They'll help to fill your time
Throughout the daylight hours.
With antics, surprises and grime,
You're thankful their love never
sours.

They make you glad or mad,
When they are doing their best
To meet life's demands on a lad.
They don't mean to be a pest.

They are just what you need
To fill your days and years.
For they will unknowingly feed
Your soul with love and not tears.

You'll find life so gay
With two boys so handy.
Life gives and life takes away
Be thankful, boys are dandy.

Sharon Hanson
LOVE
Love has no beginning and
It has no end.
It has the power of
Broken hearts to mend.
You cannot turn love
Off nor on;
Nor can you give it all away.
Love can turn the darkest night
Into the brightest day.
Love cannot turn from hot to
cold,
Nor slowly fade and die.
Love has no power of reason and
It never asks you "Why?"
Love only knows it is and was
and
Will be 'til you die . . .
I love you!

Ellie Connelly
Computer In the Cuisine
Mrs. Jonesy has a computer,
And so does Mrs. Browner.
And me, being Mrs. Smithsue,
I must have one, too—
It can program my life,
As easy as butter on a knife.
My computer could 'waken me,
With sounds of bubbling tea,
And prepare my breakfast meal,
Sans a sizzle or sans a squeal.
I gently depress the proper key,
And wait 'til I hear—"It's ready!"

Tressa Jordan
DEATH IS ONLY NEAR
When silence comes upon you
it means that death is only near
for no one hears your crying
heart
or even your very prayers
we seek this promise of
eternal life
but no one's sure what it
is that tempts
the mortal soul aboard
the wind of crying peers

William Limb
LITTLE CAMERA
Clicko Clicko little camera
All I have to do is squint and
look
Then wait just a moment
To see the picture that it took.

I aim it at the mountains
That harbor the trees so tall
and capture the many colors
That change from spring to fall.

Clicko Clicko little camera
That can grasp the present as it
be
and record it as it was
For other Folks to see.

Just how we looked

And how we dressed
At work or play
or in our Sunday best.

Clicko Clicko little camera
Oh what a pal you be.
You help steady my wandering
thoughts
And rejuvenate my memory.

When far into our future
That is so related to our past
May you be nearby with your
views
To help those special moments
last and last.

Ellie Connelly
'TIS THE COMPUTER AGE
In this wonderfully grand day and
age,
To have a computer is all the
rage.
'Course it won't do real thinking,
you know.
It takes people and programs to
go;
Or keyed machines that punch a
card;
Or machines with wires by the
yard.
Do you know where computers
are found?
Where payrolls, taxes and
insurance abound,
And some can bake, some can
change tongues;
Some can play games, and some
compose songs;
Some can run planes, ships or
trains;
And computers can say when it
rains.
You see—computers can do many
things.

Kellie R. Chaffin
PATRIOTISM
Could it be just me
That makes it hard to show
loyalty?
Could it be just me
Wanting to be free?
Could it just be me,
Or is there someone else
Who feels so empty?
There's only one thing
That makes me sing,
And that's the song about my
country,
Sweet Land of Liberty.
When I hear that verse,
I often go and rehearse.
America: a country who's not too
small.
Imagine if we had no country at
all!

M. Jan Matula
A CLASS ACT
We all slide through life
playing for the cameras.
Such hollowness;
we are waiting, waiting for our
cues.

Playing for the cameras
in mid-breath, slowing slightly.
We are waiting, waiting for our
cues;
adjusting our angles for two
dimensioned projection.

In mid-breath, slowing slightly

every movement noble, yet tragic.
Adjusting our angles for two
dimensioned projection;
the bright lights, glare fading us
out.

Every movement noble, yet tragic
we search for recognition through
greed.
Never seeing our true wealth
within;
We're all actors.

We search for recognition
through greed
such hollowness.
We're all actors;
We all slide through life.

Betty Lemley Wiley
HOW TO LOVE
I find you at the very edge of
dawn's beauty,
Poised at the verge like a
wakening dove;
We meet in the shadows of our
waning lives,
And in the reflection of
yesterdays,
We remember how to love.

Yesterday becomes tomorrow
then . . .
I have waited long for you and
now we are one;
Part of the sanctified universe for
all time,
Combined with the stars, earth,
water,
And the rising sun.

Tracey C. Ballas
WITHIN MY EYES
The most precious things in life
Cannot be seen nor touched,
They must be felt from deep inside
Each feeling built from trust.

These feelings that I feel for you
Are locked inside my heart,
Though I have never told you
You've known right from the start.

Why I've never told you, dear
Is words so often lie,
But the truth is very obvious
If you look within my eyes.

These eyes will tell you how I feel
I've loved you from the start,
But in these eyes you'll see fear
For from you I must part.

But if this love built strong from
trust
Is truly meant to be,
Then this sparkle within my eyes
Is one you will always see.

Ethel A. Slatter
Assignment For the Snow
Oh pretty Snow, fall gently there
and a soft fleecy coverlet lay;
We know the heavens from
whence you come
send this symbol of purity today.
Be sure to greet the narcissus,
Snow,
beside the inscriptions there,
acknowledge the humble violets
and waken the crocus fair.
Please bid the fragrant gardenia
to bear sweet blooms in the
spring
when the warm gentle rain shall
fall

and the lark and whippoorwill
sing.
Leave word with all the lilies,
lilies-of-the-valley for sure,
to brighten the spot with
lovliness
many yellow butterflies to lure.
Thank you Snow, for doing all
this,
it's something we couldn't do;
We'll ask the wind and autumn
rain
some seeds from the flowers to
strew.

Mary Coker Anderson

Mary Coker Anderson
DOORSHADOWS
A shadow looms upon the door,
one I have not seen before;
the door creaks and moves at will
although, without, the winds are
still
and window locks must be a
deterrent
against an impish sprite of current
as I sit writing verse, with
apprehension—
could this be a soul from another
dimension
or flippant, precocious poltergeist
scampering about like a coy
young Feist?

Could you be a poet of a by-gone
era
that might appear if I peered in a
mirror
and have you glanced across my
shoulder
or dared to venture even bolder
to whisper the illusive phrase I
seek
and rendering me your precise
critique?
An eerie chill tingles my spine
as a back-fence feline starts to
whine;
then wistful serenity touches my
chair
for I feel if I turn
                    you will be there.

Carolyn Howell Eastin
MIDNIGHT
Life is like a midnight picture of
a midnight woman; her face
veiled in sorrow; her eyes pits
of blackness with never a
promise or a sign of a light;
Sometimes she's brighter and
sometimes she's dimmer, with
nothing to be, but a cold,
empty shell. Sometimes, a

flicker of light in the darkness,
to brighten her spirit, to
lighten her way; to give her the
strength for what she is
searching, to give her the
courage for just one more
day . . . Does God have a
reason for making her wander
as the driftwood is destined on
the waves of the sea? Drifting
on surely and drifting on
swiftly with no will to say
where she rather would be; but
a midnight picture that's
lifeless and cold, facing the
darkness as an empty shell; a
midnight picture of midnight
blackness, scorned and hated if
she ever should fail . . . But to
dream of the warmth of God's
Arms around her, the driftwood
shall someday reach the shore;
and the midnight picture with
her face veiled in sorrow
cloaked in the darkness shall
be no more; but as a lost spirit
with no place to be, and no
place to go but eternity.

Beverly Louise Roberts
YESTERDAY
I heard your name just yesterday
your face came to my mind
Things have changed since
yesterday
you are no longer mine

I thought about you yesterday
I thought about your touch
As I recalled those yesterdays
I missed you very much

I thought of all those yesterdays
that we spent sharing love
I've many men from yesterday
but you're the one I love

Do you remember yesterday?
our love that burned so strong
Do you think of yesterday?
that time is now far gone

Can you touch that yesterday?
when we smiled and laughed
together?
Don't forget those yesterdays—
remember them forever

John L. Harbst III
POKER
*[For Judy for helping me
through some hard times]*
I play the game, I make the bluff.
Like a game of poker, life I play,
Royal flushes and one eyed jacks.
Like a game of poker, I end up
with the Joker.

Wanda B. Miller
Wandering Of the Mind
Such as we are,
We dream a dream,
Of all good things,
Of moonbeams dancing
And stars that gleam.

What are we—to dream so noble?
To dream of dragons and
unicorns,
Are they really life forms?

What of the centaur
And legended winged horse—
Who would fly us away
When all on earth,
Would hold us in remorse.

Perhaps, that's why
We dream our dreams,
To take away the pain
Of ordinary things,
Of birth and death
And all in between—
We spin our webs
And dream our dreams.

D.J. Fautsch
FAMILY TIES
Although you're dead, you're not
really gone,
For the teachings you taught still
live on.
And the thoughts that we shared,
I will never forget.
And times were so good, they
seemed nearly perfect.
I remember the days that we
walked thru the woods;
And you showed me and taught
me all that you could.
And what you enjoyed, I took
pleasure in,
Closer as friends, not just next of
kin.
I'll remember these times and all
of the fun,
And what you taught me, I'll
teach to my young.
And I hope they will find the
same joy as I;
So your teachings will live,
although you may die.

Ronald E. Cowart
BROKEN LOVE
The times are many,
The times are few,
The times we had together,
I remember, I hope you do too.

I still think of you
With each passing day
I'd just like to get a chance
Would you listen to
What I have to say?

If not, I'll understand
I'm just not a part
Of your future plan.

Good night baby
Sweet dreams too
Just always remember
I love you.

Marie Campbell
IMAGE OF LIFE
The past of tomorrow
Is here today.
And the flowing of time
Drifts slowly our way

We are the messiahs
Of the lives in which we lead
Believing in the soul
Is all we really need.

Rain without thunder
Have it if you will.
Or if you wish for silence
Then make the world stand still

Your life is but an image
Of how you choose to live.
Make your wish, dream your dream
And it is yours to give.

Todd L. Bardell
NIGHTHAWK
Across the ocean sands
Lies a virgin paradise
I'll sail in search of solace
To find the simple life

Beyond man's obstructions
To a visual paradise
I live and love my freedom
In view of nature's light
There's too much time to tie me
down
to live in chains
I'll break the maze of time and
space
to cross the plains

Across the maiden skies
Screams a nighthawk in his flight
He lives a quest for freedom
A phoenix of the night
There's not enough time to track
me down
to take the reins
I'll face the west to build my nest
and break the chains

Behind life's illusions
There's a spirit and a will
I live on wings of the nighthawk
And chase the whippoorwill

Phyllis M. Zueski
LOVE AT DAWN
I was walking along
into my heart came a song
early in the morning
on a day of dewy dawning,
silver lined the cloudy
skies above!

I forgot what went wrong
it was a happy maytime song.
We embraced the sunshine
together walking arm 'n arm
and stopped to see a blue bird
fly away.

Just thrilled by your touch
surrounded with an aura o'love
every word I heard was so much
love I never knew before—
until the day you came along!
My heart filled with a happy song;
songs of love!

James Hiatt
ALL THE BOXERS
Of all the boxers
that I know you cut me the
deepet.
As jagged as a rusty razor
you touch me.
I bleed.
Your words are hammers that
pummel my pride
into a bruised, shapeless apple.
At night I lie alone on canvas
sheets
beaten and ashamed,
without title or name.
I am calloused past the point
of consummation,
and no one sees the scars.

M. Lois Daugherty
LOIS ANN'S LULLABYE
I love you Lois Ann, my little
grandchild.
You're Oh, so precious, when you
smile.
Created by God, in heaven above,
For A Mamaw, who needed to
love.

You grow bigger and brighter
each day.
I love the laugh, you laugh your
way.
Can hardly wait, till you walk
and run,

You'll be like A wildflower,
growing in the sun.

Oh, what A thrill we had outside
oneday.
For with the wind, God with you,
did play.
You smiled with joy, and laughed
in glee,
At God and the wind, you could
not see.

You are indeed A beautiful baby
girl,
You are indeed the joy in my sad
world.
All through life, I'll hold your
hand,
For I will always love you, Lois
Ann.
Go to sleep, in sleepy land.
Dream sweet dreams, sweet Lois
Ann.
Dream of joy, and dream of love,
For that is what, you've plenty of.

Joanne Haines

Joanne Haines
THREE FACES OF RAIN
*[To my parents—and to my
husband—with love]*
Silver rain, your coursing crystal
Rivulets, rushing clear
quicksilver
Out of transparent cascades, pour
Gleaming succor upon the barren
ground.

Shining rain, your sun-drenched
spectrum
Radiant spans the summer sky;
bright
Misted magic hangs suspended, a
curtain
Of colored gauze among the
clouds.

Quiet rain, your liquid
murmurings
Whisper velvet gentle in the
twilight;
Your droplets slip so silently, so
softly,
Down my windowpane, like
endless tears.

Linda K. Wilson
NURSE'S AIDE
See the old man sitting there,
his head bent over in his chair.
All the love that's buried there,
but no one seems to really care

He has lived his life with pride,
now they've left him here to die.
No more to work will he ride,

his body's old and worn inside.

All the hurt and pain they gave,
will it ever go away?
Then he smiles in his heart,
for here she comes with her cart.

Making life an easy thing,
loving care is what she brings.
Now he's glad they made his stay,
in the loving arms of the nurses
aide.

Dennis Ureel
LIFES ILLUSION
We opened the hole
in that wall
the darkness of the other side
overflowed into our lives
it had a sticky
gooey sensation
that stuck to our souls

We swam into the hole
and soon found ourselves
on the other side
lost in the unexplored
or lost in the center
of our minds

WOW
if I could crawl back
to the other side
Would I?
you see I'm not sure
that the white of reality
is better than the black
of fantasy

Diane Mihnevich
**The Aftermath Of
Uncertainty**
On the way to tomorrow
i stumbled upon yesterday
and
the discovery of an inner core
that was only half explored.
A fragment of you
was still etched
in my mind . . .

Lori Parsons
A PROMISE
Since we've been together
I don't know how lucky I've been,
I've seen the growth between us
And the love within.
I realize now
That you had trust in me,
I should've been honest
But just didn't see.
I've done some things
That won't be forgiven, even by
you,
But I promise to be honest
And even be true.
To have my wish
For us to stay together,
I'm making you this promise
To be kept by me forever.

Nancy K. Cash
THE DANCER
Lilting, twirling, swirling
round
The Dancer's feet don't touch the
ground

High in spirit, gliding free
Leaping to heaven; down on one
knee

He loves the tempo, the
swooning rhythm
The gift of spriteness born within
him

251

His moves are graceful, his head
held proud
He craves enchantment from the
crowd

Perfection is his only aim
He seeks not fortune, but only
fame

The tempo's quickened, his step
still light
Gracefully soaring as a bird in
flight

His heart beats faster, his eyes are
glowing
His blood is rushing, the
adrenalin flowing

Alas! a silence breaks upon
The curtain falls; our Dancer's
gone

Lona Jean Turner Binz

Lona Jean Turner Binz
**Had He Been Dressed In
White**

Soaring high in the sky, to and fro,
As if he owns the heavens 'maybe
so'
Soaring low to snatch his foe
He always seems to know,
Which and what to capture for
his prey.
He never falls for tricks along the
way
"Too intelligent", is what they
say.

Small animals scurry as they hurry
Amongst the bush and rubble
Trying desperately to escape their
instinct
Of trouble;
To late to fend, their life must
end like
A pinhole in a bubble.

Eating his fill and feeding a meal
to the
Younger of his household
A steady job for the whole crow
mob—
Until they're two years old, I'm
told.

His one arch enemy; The great
horned owl
To which they definitely do not
pal
Similar to the Hatfields' and the
McCoys'
Forever feuding, the kind that
annoys
Always alert, for this one ornery
squirt,
Who seems to think he might reign;

By eating the smart crow's head
and brain.

Now, most people think this
black wizard is bad
But he's really not, so it's rather
sad—
He's a great help keeping our
countryside clean,
eating carrion, his favorite food
Never being A victim himself;
but cleaning along our
highways he gets scorned
and—booed.

I wonder . . . had he been dressed
in white
Would we see this great bird in a
different light?
He would surely be honored for
his goodness and grace
While soaring the skies with that
slow motion chase,
And the wonder of his beauty so
pure and divine
Would be thought a good omen
of some—special kind.

Lisa L. French
LITTLE GIRL

Little girl, your tiny grin fills us
with Bright Yellow Sun Drops.
Your great big imagination lights
up your eyes with a sparkle of
Candy Bar Cares.
Mommy dresses you in Yucky
Lacy Things and ribboned pony
tails, but you dream of
sneakers and Teddy Bears.
You're Daddy's pride and joy, his
one and only Little Lady.

Little girl, your secret games of
Fairyland Ballet take you away
from thosebigole grown—ups.
One day Winnie—the—Pooh
books and Cry Baby Betsy, the
next, shiny red roller skates
and scaling an Oh So Awesome
Tree.
Your apple—sweet giggle floats
deliciously through Mommy's
heart but your I—Need—Love
Tears hurt her when you skin
your knee.
Just like you, she wants Time to
pass right over her Little
Woman.

Little girl, getting big, growing up,
Are these the farthest things
from your Swing Set Dreams?
You love Spot! You love Daddy!
You like Tommy ?! you must
Hide, don't spoil your fun.
The Seeker moves near you, hair
curlers overtake pigtails, you
turn around to run.
Run, run away from the Oldman
into the arms of a handsome
young lover, Beautiful Lady.

Marie Stanaway
REDISCOVERY

Broken dreams and shattered
hopes lay scattered at my feet.
Forgotten are the many times
that victory seemed so sweet.

My life is all in disarray, I pray
the day to end.
My anguished disappointment
causes a flood of tears to
descend.

Have all the days gone by for me
with daisies all around,
When laughing friends and happy
times seemed only to abound?

How could this life just change
for me, so quickly—I don't
know.
It appears that springtime and
lightly falling rain turned into
cold and snow.

I cry in desperation, I ask my God
to hear.
I lift my eyes to heaven and I feel
His presence near.

I feel His love surround me, His
comfort stirs my heart.
And now I realize he never left
me from the start.

So I in all humility, will leave my
fears with God.
For I know that Calvary was the
pathway that Jesus trod.

Clara M. Reed
ALIVE AT NIGHT

*[To my son Jerry R. Reed . . .
May your musical dreams
come true.]*

He comes alive when the sun
goes down
You'll find his tracks all over town
He's my rock and roll Baby, and
he gets around
Yeah! he comes alive when the
sun goes down.

Long Blonde hair and his Bass
Guitar
With his hopes someday to be a
rock'n'roll star
Just slip him five and thats no
jive,
When the sun goes down he
comes alive.

Tho the road is long and the
going tough
Each night on stage he can strut
his stuff
Give him some applause and he'll
survive
Cuase when the sun goes down
he comes alive . .

Allene Perkins
HE'S A HEARTBREAKER

He leaves a trail of broken hearts
everywhere he goes
Women want to hold him close
and he just can't say no

They can't resist his open arms,
his cute lopsided grin,
his big blue eyes, curly hair,
and the dimple in his chin

He's always eager to be loved
His smile could melt a stone
His love can be had by all,
but come sundown he'll be
gone

His first love will take him from
you
It happens every day
No matter how hard you plead,
she won't let him stay

She'll entice him with a bottle
and promise him the moon
Then he'll go crawling back
as she happily hums a tune

Yes, she'll take him . . .

and your empty arms will ache
Tomorrow he'll love another
(more tears left in his wake)

He demands a lot of love
and the women are happy to
give
Until you've held him in your
arms,
you haven't begun to live

He can melt the coldest heart
with a smile and a tender kiss
You'll wonder if Heaven above
can be much sweeter than this

Oh yes, he's a lover . . .
His touch is worth more than
gold
His "first love" is his "mommie"
He's just one year old!

Billye Pope McGahey
**A Sonnet To Growing
Older**

My heart now speaks to me of
ageless things.
Of solitary walks down country
lanes
Of quilted calico with simpler
schemes.
Unhurried times, a pause, as
quiet rain
In memory drenched, the budding
heart reviews
Her nightly liaisons in twilight
realms.
Illusive childlike carousel renews
Majestic pensive thoughts and
hopeful hymns;
With joy rekindles! Magic
carousel—
It moves round and round in
measured beat.
Bewitching power of music
sounds compel
The ageless ones to
rambunctious retreat!
Unhallowed fruit of age—
My heart can sing!
Redeeming time to catch the
brass—bound ring.

Eva Laraine Horan
THE HUMBLING

When I was a young man, I was
proud
I thought no—one was better.
The tale I tell to you right now
is truthful to the letter.

It happened about ten-years ago . .
a sparrow caught my eye.
He asked if I solved riddles
I said, "I like to try"

This bird, he came down closer
and said he'd stump me good.
I boasted, "It won't happen"
(I *thought* it never would!!)

The sparrow then asked this riddle
"What never was and never
will be?"
I sat down to try and solve it
but couldn't for the life of me!!

I broke down and asked for the
answer
which he shouted loud and
clear. .
"The answer to my riddle, young
fool
is a mouse nest in a cat's ear!"

Now a riddle's a fine and

dandy thing
that *can* be bots of fun.
But when it's used to bring a man down
it's sure a son—of—a—gun!

Leora Colvin
MY MAGIC PLACE
*[To my daughter Sandra with
love and thanks for believing in
me.]*
There's a place ever so close
where I just love to be,
Containing secret treasures
and all belong to me.

When I go there undisturbed
what precious things I find
Many are old, others are new,
each is one of a kind.

Like shadows from the dark
romance and mystery abound
Joy and fear, sorrow and pain,
every emotion is found.

Pictures of the past unfold
from memories I'll always keep.
A magic place it is indeed—
"my memory" . . . of which I
speak.

Richard K. Stephens
Heaven, Earth and Beyond
Although we have just met, we
have known each other
through all eternities of the
universe. We have held each
other through the multitudes
of time, our lips touched in the
Garden so many millions of
years ago. Our minds united
before the Seventh day grew
near. Our souls mingled with
one another before the clay
was molded into form. Our
every being caressed with the
tenderness ever so dear, before
God breathed life into His
creation. Our eyes searched
each others and found the love
that was meant to be. Of a
sudden, nature came to life, to
be astonished and to admire
the love that we discovered as
God had so planned for His
creations on earth to carry on
forever. The world has come
alive because of our love. God
created this love and presented
it to us. We shall not forget His
graciousness and our love shall
grow stronger by the second, as
thanks to the One that made it
possible.

All my love from Heaven,
Earth and Beyond

Leora Colvin
SUNNY DAY
*[Dedicated to Aunt Bertha—for
her loving encouragement . . .
from the very beginning.]*
The sun came up this morning
just like the day before,
Golden sunbeams came dancing
through the open door.

O'er distant hill it climbs
shining clear and bright,
Smiling down on the earth,
to give the gift of light.

A gleaming ball of fire—

glides across the sky
amid the whisps of clouds
drifting slowly by.

Yonder on the horizon now
sinks the glowing rays
Into a radiant sunset . . .
gone for another day.

Deborah Mae Post

Deborah Mae Post
THE REVELATIONS
Men and women clothed in
cloaks of blazing bronze.
Life unique but tarnished by
dying souls.

Days and nights draped in colors
of death.
Laughter set aside like the
slaughter of pure white lambs.
Crystal balls of great majesty
telling the future of the
forgotten.
Utter despair as seen in the
image of the mirror hiding the
reflection of oneself.
Thoughts washed away by the
realization of life as told by
fleeing animals.
Time slipping away in a bizarre
manner pulling at the strings of
ones heart.
Minds lost in the ecstacy of
illusion.
Silence disturbed by the angry
rustling of the earth.
Flowers descending to the fresh
ground hinding from hidden
horrors.
Mankind as seen in the twilight
of Fall, bringing in the lost and
baren trees.
Cries forseen but never again
heard.

Adele Bonnette
I WONDER
The air is so fresh, crisp and clean
form where I sit mountain can be
seen,
I dreamed of this day to feel so
good,
and witness the growth of these
great woods.

Soon the flowers will bloom and
the beauty
the Lord has made will look like a
Santa' Fae of love, glory, peace
and joy.

Now as I look across the
scattered land,
I spot a tree in the span, wilted

and dry
and ready to die, but I think
nothing of it,
the Lord will only love it, so I
block it from my mind.

Then I look behind me and see
the man—made
factories and think of how long all
other beauty will stay the same
before we run it out again.

William D. Cameron
I AM
As a wave carried by it's mother
the sea, being ever in motion
which embraces the shores and
kisses the rocks thereof,
causing them to reface and
alter their shadows cast.
So it is with my conscious
peering into the macrocosm,
being different by degree at
each occurance.
Still with reverence and awe I
gaze into the face of eternity,
not knowing from whence it
came, or where it goeth seeking
the image of the unknown.
For as a single pebble on the
endless shore in itself carries
meaning only in concert, so do I.
For without duality at minimum,
there is no expression not even
of me, for thus is the law of the
Cosmic.
Seeking to unfold timelessness
and continuity, the broadness
of it's nature fathomed, extends
beyond ones comprehension of
greatness.
Being that in it's bosom rest the
cradle of endlessness, the
measurement of which is
unthinkable, the perplexity of
which arrest mortal wisdom,
thus being at loss to
encompass the balance of its
pillars round about.
Still, to witness a spark from the
flame of it's omnipotent fire is
to ascend beyond exaltation of
the spirit into the realm of
devine revelation.

Bea Holder
TRANQUILLITY
*[To Livingston, my husband
and best friend, for his love and
sincere devotion during my
cardiac rehabilitation.]*
My lake is pale green . . .
The liquid wets the rim of the
sand,
The light brown sand . . . glistening
In the warm sunshine.

I sit dreaming, aimless and alone,
Under the peace of the trees . . .
Silently the blossoms fall and
Slowly drift across the stream.

My spirit soars to the heavens
And leaps upon a floating cloud . . .
I taste the sweet cool manna
while
Bubbling with glee in such ecstasy.

The shrill call of an oriole
From a distant spruce tree
Jolts me out of my dream . . .
The cool wind kisses my cheeks
And the frolicking waves wink at
me.

Nathaniel Q. Wright
FRUITS OF TIME
As I look up into the worn,
wrinkled, brown face of the old
man,
And his slow deliberate words
fall gently upon my ears,
I discern in that face
a field plowed by age.
Within each furrow the seeds of
time,
time wellspent and time wasted,
have been sown.
The seedlings grow inward
drawn by the light that is the
`soul.
They are watered by each tear
the eyes have shed
And fertilized by all the ears have
heard.
Their produce are succulent
fruits:
Wisdom, knowledge,
understanding and dreams.
Fruits which at the height of
their maturity
are now being shared with me
As I look up into the worn,
wrinkled, brown face.

Jo Anne Myers
BLESS THE CHILDREN
Bless the children in this house
Lord
And all the others too.
Keep us strong for one another
Let your Spirit be our glue
And—
As you would inspire us
As we live out our days
May we inspire each other
In thoughtful, care—full ways.

Keep our attitudes constructive
Help us choose our words with care
and respect for one another
So our choices will be fair.

Help us count our many blessings
(Keep us mindful of our own)
And help us work together Lord
To make our house a home.

Christopher Fearn
MAY 5TH DREAMS
*[Ruby K. Vaughn, she once
said, "eat them beans and make
me some cookies".]*
The ties I have are hard to break,
the love I have is deep.
I love you love so much, that I
can't give up you see.
I day dream of a make up, but I
don't know what to see,
the future for the both of us lies
between you and me.

I have no ohter dreams you see.
No pleasure to adore.
Only past and present dreams
you see and this and nothing
more.

I've thought about a future and
look back at all those times,
the love for one another and the
hard times we got by. I hold
inside of me a pain so deep
without a bottom. The hurt so
tight,
so cluttered, I sometime want to
holler.

I speak to get across a point, that

doesn't matter.
I love you love and that's my
point, and to me that's all that
matters. I speak of a year that's
almost an added month and still
what care is there.

I write a poem and reread the
letters that were once my idol
in hell.
I want my future my life my
dreams to me that's all that
matters.
In love at heart I write to you the
things to me that matters.

To completely go on and on and
on won't remedy this problem.
I feel so hurt so down so bad I
know now I'm unbearable.
I can't see eye to eye with life and
the things that lie before me.

Just crumbled dreams and wasted
time another fucked up project.

Patricia A. Balog
BEHELD THE FUTURE
This present life, eventual to pass
    Is there a way to prepare?
    Is there a lasting hope?
Away, now, loneliness! Away,
    now, despair!

As from blind darkness, awoke to
    see
    New meaning was found of
    one's destiny
Jesus Christ had come to bless
To give to me a life of infinity

He, born of woman, propelled
    from the womb
    Known before his breath of
    planet air
    Known, the world had long
    awaited
Beholding the future, God did
    care

Nathaniel Q. Wright
**But I'm Not Very Good
    With Words**
I know you're beginning to think
    I don't care for you
But let me assure you that just
    isn't true.
I realize I don't tell you as often
    as I should
What you don't understand is I
    would if I felt I could.
    But . . . I'm not very good with
    words.

Although you're on my mind
    throughout both night and day
I just can't find the words for all
    that I'd like to say.
If only my words would flow as
    freely as the love for you flows
    within me
Like a a river on its unobstructed
    course toward the sea.
    But . . . I'm not very good with
    words.

If my heart could birth analogies
    like Benton
And describe your attributes
    even if only one
It would be: The luminescence
    for your smile pierced the
    ocean—depth darkness of a
    soul devoid of love
Like the sun transforms night to

day from its perch high above.
But . . . I'm not very good with
    words.

If I could but transpose my
    thoughts to words as
    eloquently as Shakespeare
If I could speak to you as he then
    thus it would appear.
Mine eye hath painted your
    beauty upon the canvas of my
    heart
Tis not an original but copy, for
    God's masterpiece thou truly art.
    But alas, I'm not very good
    with words.

If I were, maybe I could find
    words to express
The entire spectrum of my love
    in its collectiveness.
So I guess my prosaic style I
    cannot eschew,
You see, all I can say is: "I Love
    You".

Kate Larkin
Shadow Of a Werewolf
There is no time to discuss what
    you thought you saw last
    night.
Thers is no time to talk of your
    fear.
You see; I do not fear the night;
And that is the reason you are here.
A moon lit tree casts a stenciled
    shadow on the ground.
A darkended sly keeps its quiet
    all around.
For even though it is dark out
    there,
You can find a light almost
    anywhere.
There are strange creatures that
    stalk the night,
some of beauty, some of fright.
They are not something that you
    should fear,
For the night protects you here.
There is no reason to run from
    what you see.
The night will not keep you; you
    both are free.
There are stories of shadows that
    cross your path.
And if this should happen, you
    can laugh.
I have seen nothing ugly that has
    walked or flown,
The night protects them from
    being shown.
My favorite shadows have been
    cast upon the wall.
They have stood beside me so
    straight and tall.
The night is so bright—and you
    ask if it frightens me?
I have seen the shadows of a
    werewolf,
I have seen them free.

Jenny Grace Williams
Platoon Party August 1982
You all were drunk and a
    little bit high,
and yet you all reminded me
of little kids in a playground
huddled together on a battle
    field.
We stood beneath the old look
out tower in the glass filled

dirt over looking an Atlantic
side beach.
You were from California,
Rick was from Ohio and
the sarge was from New York.
We all were from somewhere
    else,
we all were not at home.
We carved a little refuge
from the pains of daily
life out of an old look
out tower,
huddled in the dirt drinking
beer, eating burnt chicken
and sleeping on green blankets
while the sun climbed high into
the Saturday sky just to fall
back again into the ocean like
Icarus.
We all had come together here
in the name of relief.
Soldiers. Soldiers and little
boys. You landed on the beach
in fairmonts and subarus
and I took my maverick.
We all got drunk and a little
mad and we cried a little
when the day was through.
We all shared a little
and I love you all looking
back over that Saturday
not so long ago.
You and I forgot for awhile
what the hell it's all about,
and now we all are someplace
else,
but the rundown tower on
that Atlantic side beach
still harbors our silent
laughter,
and our ageless memories.

Marian Kreger
LATE BIRTHDAY CARD
    Sorry I am so late
letting you know,
But I get too forgetful
sometimes, and so,
It appears I forgot about
your "Birthday" and you;
Such a thing I should not
            do! Eh?

Marcia Berry
BROKEN LOVE
*[For you Ric, I leave this in the
past. For you have found your
Katy. Your love, you share at
last.]*
He feels the hurt deep . . .
His heart broke in two.
The pieces lay like a puzzle,
from a love he thought he knew.

She packed her bag and turned.
Without a word or cry,
and left him standing there alone,
a teardrop in his eye.

He questioned all her motives,
how could she leave him now?
He felt his world was crumbling,
but knew not why or how.

Their little child was torn,
between his parents love.
How could they not be happy,
the two he thought so of?

So all that there was left now
was time to heal the hurt,
to pick up all the pieces,
and somehow make it work.

To learn to not be bitter,
from a love that fell apart.
To try and keep his faith now,
from a women who broke his
heart.

Peggy May Mac Neil

Peggy May Mac Neil
LIFE IS FREEDOM
If someone were ever to ask me
what I thought Life was, I'd say
that:

Life is the beautiful scenery God
    has created for me to observe.
Life is having the freedom of
    walking in a gold field of wheat
    by myself.
Life is the beautiful moment of
    getting married.
Life is giving birth to our first
    child.
Life is running together in a hay
    field surrounded by fresh, clean
    air.
Life is walking hand in hand on
    the beach.
Life is receiving that first kiss
    from someone you know you
    can make happy.

Life is taking in helpless animals.
Life is making your own
    decisions in the world,
Life is two people making love.
Life is being happy all the time.
Life is sitting all alone and
    thinking things over.
Life is believing in God.
Life is something that one should
    make the most of.
Life is swinging on swing and
    getting the feeling of freedom.
Life is forgiving people.
Life is the special occasion

of Christmas.
Life is feeling important.
Life is fighting for your own
rights.
Life is being simple.
Life is showing respect for each
other,
Life is crying about our love ones
who have past away.
Life is having someone special
who will listen to you.
Life is suffering pain.
Life is doing a good deed.
Life is so precious that some do
not even realize it.
Life is so important.
Life means never to throw it
away until the life can live no
more.

Takchandra Gayadin

Takchandra Gayadin
THE LAUNDRY GLOVES
The laundry gloves protect
Her hands, elect.
Delicately thin and beige,
They together wage
A blistering rub and screech
On the dirt, soaked in bleach.
The bare hands, now eased
The rubber gloves wring the
mock in the unsympathetic
squeeze.
Once pileful in the tub
The mildew clothes disappear to
a tiny club.
A new and brighter look springs
As the pair of gloves satisfies and
slings.

Edith Settle Morrison
WOMAN IN THE MIRROR
*[For Terri and Judi, my lovely
daughters, who will better
understand this poem when
they find a stranger in their
mirror.]*
Then; the mirrored image stared
back at her
with eyes too large, too round,
too blue;
above a nose, squatting there, a
fleshy blob
with breadth bequeathed by Irish
genes
and length by Indinan heritage.
Between these and a nothing
chin, not even clefted;
mismatched lips, one flat, one
bee—stung,
commonly seen smiling shyly
pleading acceptance.
"Ugly," she bitterly accused

the image;
but with husband and babies to
love and tend,
she was much too busy to cry.

Now: the image has aged. The
lines mocking her
are but offsping of endless
uncertainties
and shattered dreams; an intricate
maze
of tenacious cobweb, spun by
Time.
The eyes are smaller, dimmer, but
wiser.
The fleshy blob, narrowed, looks
more a nose.
Crepe—paper lips, once quick,
now smile grudgingly,
fearful to tremble cheap dentures
now long past their prime.
"Sad," she gently consoles the
weary image,
as she begs escape from God's
mills which grind her;
but the image has forgotten how
to cry.

Pauline C. Bernot
And the Silence Prevails
Always—
As the last log burns
And the fire dies,
I, also, die a little
For you are not with me.
The silence wraps itself around
me
Like a prickly vine of discomfort,
And the silence prevails.
How can I hide my grief?
I keep remembering the feelings
Of an old passion, so deep.
I loved you—
Now this void—
This emptiness—
As I weep the bitter tears of lost
love,
Lost in the shadows of unthruths.
The fire has died,
The warmth is gone,
And the silence prevails.

Ellsworth C. Rogers
MOTHER DEAR
*[To my Mother Minnie Rogers
undemanding—loving and
understanding]*
I love you more each Mothers Day;
And this comes from my heart.
It's nicer still; to hear you say,
"I've loved you from the start".

Your love dear "Mom" means
more to me,
Than life itself; or gold.
You've sacrificed; and helped me
see,
You're a treasure to behold.

I'll never live life long enough,
To make it up to you.
Yes: you're a diamond sure
enough;
I'll always love you true.

Mrs. Leora L. Rose
Spring Is Bursting Out
A robin sat on my window sill
And chirped away at me,
"Spring is bursting out all over,
Come on out and see."
So I flung my apron over a stool,
And out of the house I sped,

The iris was waving a warm
hello,
As a tulip was nodding her head.
The calico cat had had her kits,
With fur as soft as silk,
Bossie was licking her new born
calf,
And giving lots of milk.
A frog was croaking his love
song,
In a pond down by the mill,
And a rollicking colt with flying
heels,
Had stopped to eat her fill.
"Oh, thank you Mr. Robin,
For pointing out to me,
That spring is bursting out all
over,
And I'm glad I came to see."

Norma I. Sierra DeLeon
SUNRISE
*[For the thousands Of those
Heroic Venterans of WWII,
Korea and Vietnam who were
called upon to preserve our
precious heritage of Freedom.
We Love You!]*
Somewhere in the distance, You
are likely to hear,
Unending songs being sung by
the birds of the air,
No one has been able to—

Remember their cry as they seem
to touch the peaks of the sky.
In the darkness of the twilight, in
the—
Stillness of the night,
Everyone of these birds will have
taken to flight.

Dorothy Ferrell
FREEDOM
Freedom is a privilege,
Freedom is a test;
Freedom is a symbol
Of the things that we love best.

Freedom is the will to prove
The strength to carry through;
Freedom is the printed page,
The news and all that's true.

Freedom is to have, to keep
The things that we hold dear;
Freedom is to love, to laugh,
To live without a fear.

Linda L. Meier
THIS FEELING
I wish to
always have—
this feeling in my heart,
satisfaction in my soul
and
peace in my mind
as I do
with you.

Racheal Wilson Yancy
I NEED YOU SO
How much do I love you?
I cannot tell a lie.
I love you more . . . .
Than the stars love the sky.

I need your love . . . .
Darling, I want it badly.
Just a touch from you . . .
And I'd surrender gladly.

For my life depends upon
The very breath you breathe,
And life would have no meaning
If you would ever leave.

Dearest, with out your love;

Your kisses and your touch . . .
Your petting and your thrills . . .
Oh' . . . I love you so much!

Just the nearness of you . . .
Keeps me in a trance;
And I wonder if I'm dreaming
Of this fine romance.

How much do I need you?
A thousand pens couldn't write . . .
Of how I feel for you . . .
And need you tonight!

Bette Watts
THE YO-YO
*[To DR. A.C. Kruc, D.O. whose
endless efforts to heal
humanity are equaled only by
her vivacious personality and
unique sense of humor.]*
Round and round
In and out
Up and down
A shimmering thread
That releases energy
For life's merry-go-round
Sleek, spinning
Ever becoming
A blur on the go
Just so far
For the Yo-Yo.

Lisa Holloway
SOMETIMES IT'S HARD
*[To Ronnie, My First And Only
Love]*
Sometimes it is hard to say
goodbye,
when you know it's not the
end.
Sometimes it's hard to say we are
not lovers,
when you know we're more
than friends.
Sometimes it's hard to say you
don't care,
when you know a special
love will always be there.
Sometimes it's hard to just turn
away
when you know there is a lot
more to say.
Sometimes it's hard to face the
truth,
but things will pass that
occur in our youth.

Ms. Leslie Anne O'Connor
REMEMBER
Clouded visions
Of a sunset on the ocean
Fading in the midnight sky into
an endless night
Crystal Raindrops
Like the tears forever falling
Drowning out old memories to
push them out of sight

Howling Windstorms
Like snowdrift in the arctic
Remind me of the things we've
seen and things we've yet to
see
Years Forgotten
But not times we've shared
together
All the things we loved to do and
things we'd like to be.

Foggy daydreams
Of the music we've created
All the laughter and the songs of

pleasure and of pain
Sparkling Snowflakes
Are like things that we've
    remembered
As one remembers mountain tops
    or roses after rain

Haunting Nightmares
Because now you've flown forever
The many things we'd said and
    done so many years ago
Magic Mazes
That I'll have to find my way
    through
Freezing out the happiness I will
    never know

Larry A. Hess
MAMARONECK BAY
Light of unshaded sky
Lights the water's face
Lights the floating kites
That grace the air.

Glossy ripple waves
Pattern the sea
Edging out concentrically
Nudging the boats
That sway with rhythmic flair.

Above the gleaming yachts
Sea gull acrobats
Dive in perfect poise
Dip and climb in airy flight
Charmingly to dare.

Lynette R. Foster
FRAGILE BEAUTY
Daylight smiles down from the
    sky.
The wind is blowing warm and
    dry.
Whirling and swirling through
    the trees,
gently it rustles the new green
    leaves.

The lake sparkles, a shimmering
    blue.
The picture of beauty is not yet
    through,
for out in the field a flower will
    bloom,
not knowing it suffers a deadly
    doom.

The flower will wither beside the
    lake
and that's the chance a flower
    must take.
Death isn't final inspite of the
    gloom;
for another flower is soon to
    bloom.

Linda Elizabeth Kannon
CHILDREN
*[This poem is dedicated to all
of the children of the world.]*
    Learning, growing
    Talking, playing, loving
    Fun to watch
    Children

Rikke Leah Jordan
Ready To Be Hurt Again
It happened one day,
My guy no longer wanted to stay.

He said he needed to be free,
He no longer cared for me.

He says we can still be friends,
That's the thing that never ends.

My heart fell when I said okay,
How could I ask him not to go

away.
The hurt I felt I concealed,
It would be awhile before I
    healed.

It was best I said,
It was time I should stop being
    misled.

That our love was forever,
Now I think that can happen
    never.

Forever is just a word,
It can fly away like a bird.

It's been awhile now,
Time has flown away, I don't
    know how.

And I find myself liking another
    guy,
Hoping we'll get together by and
    by.

One day he asks me,
My whole world brightens you
    see.

For again I'm ready to play the
    fool,
Because I think love will rule.

Ready to let someone in,
Ready to be hurt again.

Floyd M. Willoughby
SONG OF NATURE
*[To neighbor Jane and my
children and teacher Melinda,
to Little Rachel Nicole made us
all love you.]*
A child looks upon a bird in the
    tree,
and hears its happy song.
With happy heart turns loose the
    hand
which held her as they walk
    along.

Her running steps will fill the
    day
as her childish voice he hears.
"God loves the birdie in the tree
like he loves you, and you love
    me."

"Daddy, watch the birdie fly
    away.
Will it come back another day?"
With joyous heart of time and
    place,
he answers with a smile.
"Perhaps it will, but we don't
    know
for God has made it free,
and the song which it has sung
    this day
was sung for you and me."

Her hand returns to his again,
and the moment was theirs to
    share,
as they continue on their walk
    through life
knowing that God does care.

Polly Sherling
QUARRELS
Seconds in eternity
Can decide our destiny.

Bitter, like the taste of gall,
Unkind words we can't recall.

No one can ever quite again
Replace the trust in eyes of pain.

Only seconds from the years

Petrified in beads of tears.

Sleep has little rest to let
On a pillow of regret.

Our storms lash loud and thrash
    and quake
But, God! The silence in their
    wake

Or calling in an empty wind:
"Forgive me, Please come back
    again."

Jeannette Forte Santanastasio
MY ANGELIC MOTHER
*[Dedicated to my mother, who
was the most God like being
ever created, whose love of
God and life warmed the soul
of all she touched.]*
Dear Mom,
The trees sway softly as I
remember those years. The
wind hums a tune to enchant a
devil's ears. Shinning above is
the bewitching August sun
which as we know shall soon
fade, when this day is done.

I still see you mom, in a garden of
flowers. Talking with the
angels for hours and hours. I
remember so well on the day I
was born, the sky was so
cloudy a frightening cold
storm. Then, there in the
garden the sun shone so bright
as God's little angels came to
make your day night.

One little angel put his wing
right on my head. He blessed
me for a lifetime full of wine
and bread. Another angel came
to me, smiled, shed a tear; then
I knew the loss of you I would
ever fear.

So I fear and say to you, "There is
not another, more God like
being on this earth, than my
Angelic Mother."

RuthAnne Lewis
THE WARMEST DAYS
A heart of mine is a heart for
    you.
The warmest day with the
    warmest love.
All through out the day, will you
    be mine?
Through the years with these days
    so warm like this one.
Its hard saying how I feel but so
    easy to feel this way today and

throughout the years to come.
The coldest days will always be
    the warmest with you.

Pat Taylor
SWEET MEMORIES
*[Dedicated to my sweet
inspiration, September 1982]*
When the shades of night are
    drawn,
"Sweet Memories" of you linger
    on.
Neither time nor tears can ever
    erace "Sweet Memories" of the
    arms where I found solace.
So sad this heart you left behind,
    so cool these lips, these eyes so
    blind.
And ere I go to sleep at night,
    "Sweet Memories" be my only
    plight.
For when the shades of night are
    drawn, I have only "Sweet
    Memories" that linger
        on
            and
                on
                    and
                        on

Tabatha Garcia
LOVE AT FIRST SIGHT
    Our eyes met,
I heard a bell.
    I smiled at you,
you smiled as well.

    You came to me and asked my
    name,
I knew right then we felt the
    same.

    Holding hands in the park,
a few more hours until it is dark.

    A kiss good-bye,
a heavy sigh.

    Was it wrong or was it right?
My heart tells me it was, "love at
    first sight."

Annie Williams Jensen
AMERICA, BE AWARE!
*[To my God, my Country and
her People and Especially to my
two Families and Granchildren,
Flora, Grover and Adam.]*
America, the Beautiful, Be Aware!
    You have nothing to fear,
        of Nuclear War,
    For you are being Crushed,
        from Within!
    The enemy is poisoning our
        Youth
    with drugs, illicit moralities,
        false judgements, Disbelief.
America, the Beautiful, Be Aware!
    It seems our Leaders in high
        Places
    have Forgotten the Cornerstone,
        Of America's Foundation.
    Where are our Men of Wisdom
        and Vision?
    They would have Foretold of the
        gross misuse of Precious metals,
    Pollution, Endangered Species.
America, the Beautiful, Be Aware!
    For Pride of Country and
        Craftsmanship,
    few people seem to care.
    Many classrooms run
        rampant with
disrespect, distrust and Fear.

Today's Greatest Poems

Being number One is the name of the Game.
No matter the Consequence!
So goes the way of misplaced Values,
materialism, complacency.
America the Beautiful Be Aware!
Rise, Shine, Love . . .
Change or Die!!!

William F. Grinstead
Great and Mighty River
Tis a great and mighty river that
flows by our door each day
He holds a lot of secrets but he
don't have much to say
That is he don't speak out in
audible tones or sing any songs
of glee
He just speaks a language all his
own on his journey to the sea.
If he could talk and tell his
secrets quite a lot we all would
learn
Striking fear to the hearts of
many while many others ears
would burn
He sometimes busts his levees
and spreads out upon the land
And he is not at all particular
where he deposits silt and sand.
Like all wild things he knows no
master and he don't know right
from wrong
He just rolls along his merry way
singing his own rare kind of
song.
He don't have time to tell his
secrets he's as busy as can be
Carrying boats with freight and
cargo on their junket to and
from the sea.
He don't recall fond memories
but goes on making history
For he's the Great and Mighty
Mississippi on his journey to
the sea.

Helen M. Cranstoun
IN REMEMBERING
Oh love, in sweet remembering
   There lies my heart's content
Of days gone by, of thoughts that
lie
   In blessed hours once spent.

Of days with you, of nights that
flew
   On fleeting gossamer wings
Beloved, do you know them too
   My sweet rememberings?

And if no sorrow, sigh nor tear
   Bespoke our final parting
T'was in my heart, therein lie still
   The tears, forever starting.

On blessedness of memory
   That keeps my heart still
young,
Of love that lies remembering
   'Til life's last song is sung.

Marijo Bonanni
FRIENDS
Among the great and glorious gifts
Our heavenly father sends,
Is the gift of understanding
That we find in loving friends.
For in this world of trouble
That is filled wth anxious care,
Everybody needs a friend
With whom they are free to share.

So when we need some sympathy
Or a friendly hand to touch,
Or an ear that listens tenderly
To speak words that mean so
much.
We seek our true and trusted
friends
Who will always stay by until the
end.

Ron Witten
PEACE AND HAPPINESS
[To Mom and Dad]
I see melodies in time.
I can hear the sunshine fall
against the walls all day
and the rain play its symphonic
poem.
Listen! Hear nature breathing!
Its breath flows across the land
as it cools its sons and daughters
at living.

Above a billowy cloud floats
along with graceful ease,
always changing shape and never
knowing what it is
or what it hopes to be.
Perhaps someday in sunset's
afterglow
it will find enlightenment
blowing in the wind
and will catch the joy
of learning the reason for its
existence
and the path it must follow
to find peace and happiness.

Lois Kimball
GOD GAVE US
God Gave Us eyes so that we
may see his many wonders,
like the strings of diamonds on a
spider's web on a dewy
morning.
The color of a blue jay as he
perches on the fence to say
good morning.

God Gave Us ears so that we
might hear the birds singing,
a baby's soft voice cooing, the
little whispers of the world,
carried on the wind.

God Gave Us touch so that we
might touch the soft velvety
looking roses,
and feel a baby's soft skin,
and to reach out to touch a friend.

God Gave Us a sense of smell
that we might smell that soft
velvety looking rose, and all
the different scents of

flowers,
and best of all the smell of a
freshly bathed, and powdered
baby,
there's no other smell like it.

God Gave Us the sense of taste
so we might taste the fruits of
his bounty,
and the sweetness of life.

God Gave To some of us who are
fortunate a sense of perception,
that we might know when a
loved one is troubled,
or a friend needs a listening ear,
and a kind word.

God Gave Us most of all he gave
us a mind, so that we would
understand that this is all his
will.

Dee Hardy
SHARING
Give someone a little love today,
Make them happy in your own
   special way.
Give happiness, laughter, and
   peace of mind,
Bring out your feelings,
   understand, be kind.

Look at the world with visions of
   hope,
Your span of life is short, you
   must learn to cope.
Sprinkle a little love in your
   heart,
Share it with another, one who's
   far apart.

Imagine a majestic mountain, a
   spanning sea,
Feel the growing beauty, feel it
   through me.
Get closer, come closer, much
   closer to me,
I will show you the way, the way
   it should be.

Kathy Oleszczyk
PURPLE
Purple's the color of the leaves
   That comes in fall among
      the trees
After the sun, before the cold
   Purple's the one that never
grows old.
Purple has awesome beauty and
grace
   Purple's the tone of a
      mountain's face.
It's the dress of a king great or
small,
   It's majesty can enhance us
all.
It's the hue of a robbin's red
breast
   It's my birthstone the
Amethyst
Pruple is a cloud in the sky
   Purple's the flags that
reaches so high
Purple's a rainbow after a storm
   It's a fire that keeps you
warm.
Purple is many different things.
   Purple rules, purple's the
king.

Sheryl Frances De Garmo
THE MOUNTAIN
Look at the mountains so bare
   and bleak,

How many have died trying to
   reach their peak.
See how the top is all covered
   with snow,
Up there the cold winds forever
   blow.
One misstep along the way,
And quite dearly you will pay.
For the mountain stands tall and
   regal,
It's only guest is the great Bald
   Eagle.
So if fame and fortune is what
   you seek,
You had best go with caution to
   reach the peak.

Brian E. Hurst
FROM CINDERELLA
Upstairs, in silver sconce, on a
   Chinese stand,
Three candles gleamed like snow,
   gold-nimbused light
Caught red-eyed dragons,
   intricately planned
With green-scaled tails round
   lofty bamboo bright,
And turquoise birds that fanned
   in radiant flight
Above blue-shining scenes of
   emerald seas.
Here Ella stood by studded door
   closed tight,
To dream of diamonds, dresses,
   silk chemise.
With beating heart she tried the
   jingling keys.

But none would fit. The panelled
   door held fast,
Resistant in pale flickering
   candle light;
A guardian grim of Ella's mother's
   past,
Doorway to time and mysteries
   recondite.
She listened, turned: wide-eyed
   she watched, in white,
A radiant form glide soundless up
   the stair.
What face was this? The girl felt
   sudden fright.
The figure glowed with
   phosphorescent hair,
And starry sequins flashed and
   glittered there.

"Be not afraid, my dear! Be brave
   and calm,
And do not question who I am
   this hour.
My world is free, and far from
   earthly qualm.
I come to you by means of spirit
   power."
Her pearl-ringed hand produced a
   perfect flower.
She placed it, crimson, cool, in
   Ella's palm:
"This fragrant rose may sweeten
   what is sour.
Wear it, my child, and now feel
   no alarm,
For I am here to help, and save
   you from all harm."

"My prayers! Good Lord, my
   prayers!" the girl exclaimed,
With pounding heart and
   unbelieving eyes:
"What are you? Mortal? Ghost? I
   feel ashamed

Before your look of love. You
scrutinize!
Ah! See my shadow there of
trembling size,
How, wavering on the wall, it
surely shows
Your dress created draught, to
emphasize
That you are real! Your face and
figure glows!
How you are here, the good Lord
only knows!"

Victoria Dreksler
CRYPT OF NIGHT
[For Kathy, Jan, Michael,
Angela, Donna and Deborah,
who always encourage me to
keep writing.]
Sit with me, starlight,
Until the silent darkness
Takes its flight,
Until the dawn comes
And frightens away
The shadows of the night.
Hide not from me,
Before the rising sun
Casts its glow
In eastern skies,
Bringing comfort to the morn
And beauty to each dewdrop
On the rise.
Soon, the dawn and sunlight,
Seeping up the shadows,
Driving fears away.
And so it is
Until the night
When you and I await again
The coming day.

Sandie A. Parks Jordan
**Lord Please Help Me To Do
My Best!**
May the Lord bless and keep me
each day
As I try to help someone along
the way.
I may not do things as well as
you,
But I try my best at whatever I do
I'm not doing it for praise when I
help someone
But I hope one day the Lord will
say "Well Done!"
If I should give you my last dime
or piece of bread
I shall not worry, because I know
there is a brighter day ahead
Though the road will get rough as
I continue my journey
I trust and believe the Lord will
always be there for me
When I've tried so hard to stand
the test
"Lord, Please Help Me To Do My
Best!"

Ruth Collier
LIFE'S BURDENS
How many times have we lost in
life?
And we've thought it was the
end.
It seems we've lost every battle
And at times don't have a friend.

When we're tense and turmoil
hounds us,
And there's failure at our door.
When disappointments plague us,
And it seems there's only more.

Although we feel like giving up,

And just quitting then and there.
If we just stop and think a
moment,
We'll go to the Lord in prayer.

We'll go to the source of all
supply,
For the answers to our needs.
And the Lord will gently lead us,
To higher goals and nobler deeds.

I know at times in all our lives,
We think there's too much rain.
But compare it with our Saviour's
life,
Consider how much He suffered
pain.

For He was scourged and mocked,
And He was even spit upon,
And he suffered quietly through
it,
While wearing a crown made of
thorns.

So when your heart is heavy,
Your burdens more than you can
bear,
Just turn them over to the Lord,
For He's already been there.

Larry Keith Darr
Tribute To Jim Morrison
[Dedicated to the genius and
memory of James Douglas
Morrison, a great American
poet.]
What happened to his soul when
he died?
Indian groans
Indian moans
redskin blood and broken bones.
He sought refuge in the child's
flowerlike mind
the Indian's soul when he died
through a wordman he spoke
With wisdom and truth from the
world of the dead
through the voice of the youth
the Indian's soul when he died
took refuge in the child's
flowerlike mind
But where did he go?
the wordman when he died.

Sheryl Frances De Garmo
ALL OVER AGAIN
[In memory of my brother John]
The days are long, the nights are
lonely
I keep waiting for you to come
back.
I miss you so very dearly
My mind is on an endless track.

Every day it's the same thing
Every night is just as bad.
It's a nightmare that clings
Till I think I am going mad.

My heart aches and my head
hurts
My sorrow is an anguished strain.
It swells and pounds till I am
inert
And then it starts all over again.

Marie Sollars
SLIPPING AWAY
[To NOVIS DUBOISE whose
faith and encouragement has
been my guiding light.]
When you're dying
Why keep trying
To make a buck a day

To keep the blues away?

Who would notice?
If you slipped away
Some summer day
When you're old and gray
And never came back?

Who would miss you?
Who'd want to kiss you?
Who'd even touch your hand?
Get the idea, man?

It's the right track
If you slipped away
Some summer day
When you're old and gray
And never came back!

But I'd be true
I'd wait for you
So if you slip away
Some summer day
When you're old and gray
Please come back!

Virgil F. Morse
**O Come My Love And Sit
With Me**
[To my darling wife, Stella]
O come my love and sit with me
This is our anniversary
The years have rolled away so
fast
What once was now, is now the
past
Today is number sixty-three
So come my love and sit with me.

Just come my love and sit with
me
We'll find a great big shady tree
And watch the white clouds
drifting by
Or maybe see some bright blue
sky
Just hold my hand and you will
see
How lovely 'tis to sit by me.

Please come my love and sit with
me
And see how happy we should be
We watched our children at their
play
Now they are grown and on their
way
So now, on this, our anniversary
Please come my love and sit with
me.

Linda Blesser Hunt
GOLDEN GODDESS
Young winged goddess
carved out of gold,
you hold a circle
containing wisdom untold.
A symbol of centuries past
a vision of a future to come.
Caught in a moment
while your soul stopped in flight,
knelt with wings outstretched
your face turned
in quiet meditation to
the globe held high in your
hands.
The pause was but for a moment
but, that fleeting second endures
caught by a dreamer
whose dreaming mind
captured you in your prayer
and carved you out.
You passed on, wings in flight.
Though his mind's eye
may have seen you

the hand only made
the image of you
stopped in flight.

Mona M. Houle
SIMPLICITY
Winds among the trees
Tell not of sights unseen.
The smiling daisies turn their
eyes to the creators floor.
A guitar is heard,
Being plucked by fair, light hands;
A voice
So soft and lonely, even the river
hushes its roar to hear;

A song of love
A song of woe
A heart yearning to be
understood,
Nature and life are a puzzle,
Constructed for the strong and
understanding;
The girl is only simplicity . . .

Bonnie Brezden Doering
I SAW
I saw
        a lonely flower
            blowing sadly
in the breeze
so I
        picked it
and
        we became friends
and now
        we aren't lonely
                anymore.

Mike Tremblay
THE MOBIL OIL SIGN'S OFF
The surf pounds continuously.
Beating like a clock through the
years.
And the swords are being drawn,
by the Mobil oil sign.
At the foot of one of their biggest
wells.
The swords are being drawn.
All gone.
Now swallowed by the sword
swallower.
All gone.
In the outer crescent of the circle,
he now stands in,
all is engulfed in flames.
Kneeling bitterly to the powerful
king.
The name Aswar is given to him.
By us.
He leads his great people.
Around the big top.
He leads his great people.
His hat shimmers in the bright

light.
Command his people to sleep
tonight.
All will sleep well tonight.
Aswar has turned out the lights.
The Mobil Oil sign's off.

Elvera G. Wright

Elvera G. Wright
LIFE'S EVENING
Though all semblance of youth
be faded
And bent I be from weight of
crowding years,
Still my happy heart doth sing,
For God's grace doth not harbor
tears.

Still with sight, agile mind and
hearing
Blessed be I far beyond measure.
Youth was wonderously bright
and happy, still
Sunset years doth hold much
pleasure.

Time now to watch apple
blossoms budding,
Robins in the magnolia and
daffodills swaying.
Time to see evening skies turn
from blue to gold.
Time to spend with God in
unhurried praying.

Rhea Washburn
LOVES BLOSSOM
Love is a wonderful thing
It blooms like flowers in spring
It comes and goes
Like the flower that grows
Its blossoms can be big and
beautiful
Or small and unuseful

Flowers and love are to give
And without giving there's no
reason to live
Love is a life in its own
Like the flower that's grown
Some may live again
Some . . . die forever

Lee Wells
WOLVES
There are wolves that will always
howl.
Others that come around with a
growl.
While others seem to go around
that scowl.
And some that are mean and talk
that is foul.

May I never go around howling
every day.

Or never at everything a growling
away.
Always have a smile and never a
scowl.
Kindness be my way, never talk
foul.

For to howl at everything, my
friends would be few.
To growl would bring to me what
would be due.
Even a scowl would erase all that
is love.
Foul language would keep us
from our home above.

Darla Jetton
Lunar Aura (Spirit Moon)
The sounds of life and death
surround me at the gateway of
my dreams—
exposing trials and tribulations to
the ultimate extremes.
I walked among the pyramids as
Spirit Moon came down
and I wore the Lunar Aura as
Heaven's treasured crown.
I soared above the galaxy a
strange but graceful course,
compelled and overwhelmed by
the all-consuming force.
It seemed that I had transcended
lightyears to a land
through astral projection at a
spiritual command.
In the dark of night I traveled a
reminiscent road;
every curve and shadow was a
memory restored.
The full moon's cosmic aura a
brilliant crimson glowed;
whispering of fantasies and
prophecy foretold.
My life is but a journey through
the element of time;
seeking out the mysteries
through the verses of my
rhyme.
I spread the words of mentors
speaking from the past,
trying to assure you that love
will surely last.

Sharan L. Cox
MIRRORED IMAGES
Lookin
in a mirror
today
i saw myself
years
younger—
times
of rebellion . . .
within
a strangers eyes . . .
within
a strangers life . . .
within
a strangers turmoil . . .
Lookin
in that mirror,
i touched myself . . .
a part of my life
looked back at me
and winked . . .

Marjorie Sullivan
**We're Just a Step From
Parting Time**
We're just a step from parting time
I promised not to cry
but as the day grows closer dear
I think, I told a lie.

You're just a step from gone
and I'm just a step from crying
We're just a step from parting
now
And I know I'll feel like dying.
But I told you that I'd let you go
And let you go I will
Parting's just, a final step
Like climbing one more hill . . .

Lord I hate to see the snow fall
It's marking off the days
Until the time when we must
part
And go our separate ways.
I hate to seem a foolish girl
Wouldn't want to let you see
how much the thought of losing
you
has made its mark on me.
There's some things I never said
to you
though you ask me several ways
don't ask again my feelings dear,
Some things I'll never say.

Bernice Norton
A FULL-FILLED LIFE
In the little place called Moscow,
We have watched our family
grow.
Today, our last child—out of
five—was married.
Happy moment—also sad—as we
watched.
Our son is now a man, no longer
just a lad,
Ones life seems so hectic as ones
little family grows up
Before you realize it, they've all
flown the nest.

We are happy for our children
As they make their futures with
their mates.
Yet—it does seem rather
lonesome
When it's only Mom and Dad left
at home
Seems such a very short time ago
Our home was filled with noise
and laughter
Mom and Dad can't quite make
all that much noise.
Our lives have truly been blessed.
We've shared so much together.

Our five precious children—now
the sons-in-law
daughters-in-law and our darling
grandchildren
It all adds up to much "Thanks to
God" for so very much.
Full, happy, busy lives,
as farmers, homemaker, parents,
—grandparents,
In this world filled with troubles
and strife—
We call this a full-filled life
Also, God's purpose for us as
husband and wife.

Shri' Drake
CHAMPION
*[To my brother, Kerry—to
whom I owe all that I am.]*
People never give it all;
There is always something more.
You can always reach inside
yourself
And bring out something new.
But just how much of this mystique
Is inside a human being?

I know no matter how much I try
I will never reach the max.
But all I hope is that I'll spend
All my life a reachin'
And then I'll know with all my
heart
That I will die a champion.

Ruth Frances Hall
MY PAISLEY HEIRLOOM
When I am lonesome
And the days filled with gloom
I go to my closet
For "My Paisley Heirloom"
I browse through the pages
With laughter and tears
And let in the sunshine
To banish my fears
The pictures of loved ones
Speak out as in rhyme
With life at my fingertips
I travel through time
My journey has ended
And nightfall is near
The hours have passed swiftly
And, I'm full of good cheer
I place my book carefully
Back on the shelf
For inside those pages
Lies the heart, of myself.

Lisa Stone
INTRICACY
Intricacy
a silken spider web
spun
oh-so-carefully
living through
many fierce winds
wiped out by a
careless finger

Sherry A. Anderson
UNTITLED
Trying on wonderment
Wanting to create
Disillusioned with enchantment
Unlearning how to hate
No longer in love with love
But wanting just the same
So damned tired of this game

Stephen Marshall
1940-1980
*[Dedicated to John Lennon
although we never met.]*
Oh no it can't be true
Did I hear right. What you said
Repeat those words
They don't sink in
John Lennon's been shot, down
dead
I close my eyes, go back to sleep
Hoping it's a dream
But the news confronts me, it's
all true
As it's splashed across the screen
It took John Lennon 40 years
To become a national figurehead
Please don't make, Mark
Chapman one.
By the 4 bullets it took.
To shoot John Lennon Dead.
(Rest in peace John)

Sister Rose Dumey, A.S.C.
**Let All Creation Thy Glory
Proclaim**
I see God in all beauty of creation
and oh how I want to celebrate,
to dance, to sing.
The rising sun in a breath-taking
sky of blue, comes to bless

the morning.
I murmur a prayer for nature's gift of LIFE.
I hear the birds singing their Creator's praise.
It makes me feel so radiant, so free.
Beneath my window I study the miracle of a red velvet rose.
My heart beats with happiness and I'm overjoyed.
I stand amazed at the astounding beauty of a majestic snow-capped mountain.
Awed by its splendor I am deeply aware of God's great power and glory.
Its strength reflects in me and gives me courage.
At the beauty of rainbow—arched ribbons in the sky,
I strongly feel God's presence and my faith is renewed.
I marvel at the magnificence of the setting sun descending in all its glory,
Bringing with it a tremendous fire-like glow—a reflection of heaven, our Paradise to be.
I treasure these great moments of ecstasy and in silence I meditate.
Millions of stars like jeweled diamonds that bedeck an endless sky, are so many miracles assuring me of the Creator's tremendous LOVE.
These innumerable beacons of light fill the darkness of my soul with heavenly peace and forgiveness.
God in his Nature has treasures untold.
I love my God as I do the beautiful Earth on which I live.
My confrontation with the atheist is simply—
Who could behold the Great Universe designed in perfect harmony and symmetry and not see God?

Joan Goyer Bushno
AS A CHILD
[I love you; Jenny, Alicia, Shane, T.J., Joshua, Amanda, Autumn, Ray, Sherry, Johnny, Deanne, Rose Marie, Mark, and Kay.]
"Roy is dead.
I cried last night,
I did, I cried alot."
Richard and Roy;
Retarded, institutionalized
Year after year . . .
Richard, at the age
Of forty-eight, is a
Bewildered child;
Suffering from the
Loss of a friend.
Roy died; and
Richard cried alot.

Malone H. Love
MY DAY
I saw the sun rise in the east
To show that restful night had ceased.
I heard the birds with songs of glee
And saw them fly from tree to tree.

At noon I glimpsed the sun above
And thought of beauty and God's love.
I watched the clouds go floating by
To change the color of the sky.
I heard the noises of the day
As each man traveled his own way.
I saw the sun set in the west
To designate a time for rest.
I thanked God for a pleasant day
And prayed for help along life's way.

Helen C. Elliott
O Lord, How Could They?
[For Alden Gilchrist]
O Lord God, our defender and rescue
Protector of thy people, Israel
Judgement and salvation belong to thee
Our survival, our hope, our destiny.

O Lord, mine enemies how they do plot
Entrapping the king with a vicious snare
While spearing and netting me like a fish,
To flounder and die in utter despair.

Your servant, your servant, they did betray
Not knowing thy power, O Lord, how could they?

O holy God, envy and jealousy rages
Resentment, rivalry, and derision.
Deliver thy servant I beseech thee
From suspicion and other division.

O Lord, our thanksgiving belongs to thee
Our survival, our hope, our destiny.

Daniel, thy servant, they did betray
Not knowing thy power, O Lord, how could they?

Sylvia Lee
Creation
The silver white of life
Cuts through the blackness of primeval chaos.
Chromatic hues absorbed into the inky night

Are freed as order creepingly resolves.
The clear white prism of life
Refracts the beams of chaos.
Color, bright and muted shades,
Define emerging shape and movement.
The harsh contrast of black and white
Is blurred as knowledge germinates.

Ginni Shuflata
THE REAL McCOY
Breathes there a man with past so dead
Who never to his kids hath said
With a smile of reminiscent joy
"I used to dance to Clyde McCoy!"

Or a gal who can calmly sit and chat
of "ships and shoes" and things like that,
And somehow never seem to lose
Her cool when Clyde plays Sugar Blues.

Not I! If The Reaper comes my way
When Clyde near by is booked to play,
To my friends I will say,
"Postpone your sorrow—
I'll dance tonight and die tomorrow!"

Rosalie Kosco McGough
AQUA-MANIAC
I smell the chlorine as I walk through the door.
Spectator area . . . second floor.
Enter the balcony, hit by the heat,
Look around . . . select a seat.
Competition should really be rough,
Not to worry . . . my son is tough.
The whistle is warning the meet will begin.
Tension flowing . . . want to win.
John's on the blocks, I'd better get ready;
Billy's next . . . steady, steady.
He dives into the pool, begins to stroke.
Looking good . . . crowd awoke.
Even the coach, Mr. T, was elated,
Marcus lost . . . Billy made it.

Sharon G. Testerman
I GOT BONES!!!
Year after year, twenty-eight in all,
I viewed my reflection and choked on gall.
Roll upon roll of blubber collected
and no hope of loss was ever expected.

I tried yogurt, the green vegetables too,
but none of that mattered, I'm not like you.
Twelve hundred calories a day and I'd keep
gaining roll upon roll, and losing more sleep.

Waking at night with the chocolate D.T.'s,
I'd sneak to the kitchen for "just ONE of these",
then creep back to bed knowing no one knew—

no one but me—then disgust would spew.

Well, one day I pondered, figured and thought,
Bones—Bones—to have those I ought!
Somewhere, somehow, they just had to be there,
Everyone else had them, so mine were—WHERE?

As the scales crept up to three thirty-six
I tried on my ego a few feeble tricks.
Stood sideways in the mirror and sucked it all in,
but hard as I tried, it flopped out again.

Bones—Bones—I just HAD to have them,
outside—noticeable—not where they had been.
So, O.R. I faced and amazingly it worked—
I was on my way down, all my fat "friends" were irked!

How proud I was, losing my first pounds!
And now I'm still going all of the rounds.
I'm battling blubber by measuring in ounces,
My mind on a new me excitedly pounces!

They peek out now—I KNOW they're there.
I see them and feel them—never knew I'd care!
Over a hundred pounds are now dead and gone,
and wonder upon wonder—I REALLY GOT BONES!!!!!!!!

Betsy Kline
I LOOK INTO YOU
[To Mat Who has given me Confidence, hope, and love]
I look into your eyes
And I see gentle concern,
I see ambition and excitement,
And I see your love for me.

I look into your heart
And I see tender caring,
I see courage and strength,
And I see your love for me.

I look into your soul
And I see endless faith,
I see hope and determination,
And I see our future together.

Doralee M. Lewis
PLEA
I am not here because with mental clarity
I thought myself into existence.
Nor am I begotten of any strange dream of my own.
I am here because I am here.
And I ask for a God.

Please, though, not a musty stilted written god
Of ancient screed and smelly papyrus.
I want, and I hunger and thirst.

Stream in the odor of honeysuckle through my nostrils
And throat and lungs.

Today's Greatest Poems

Into my ears pipe the pulsing
note of the cricket
That sings his dreams to the
lower sky.
Substitute my vaporable thoughts
with the breath of the earth
That begets the cornflower and
the moonflower
And sheathes the night with
delicate but intimate odors.
I would have a God!

But please, not an image either of
stone or of dogma.
My body throbs for a touch of the
sentient hand
That measures the heavens with
merely a span.
Remember: I am here because I
am here.
And I need, and I hunger, and I
thirst.

M. Anne Henry
THOUGHTS
*[To Darlene Van Meter in
appreciation of her continued
support and her knowledge,
love and witness to the power
and unyielding love of our Lord,
Jesus Christ. Her friendship is a
blessing!]*
Timeless thoughts to ponder
At the close of another day.
Troubled thoughts of highs and
lows—
Old thoughts webbed with decay.

Some thoughts are ones
profound—
Hard to understand and cope.
Others . . . foggy, hazy
thoughts . . .
Thick as if viewed through suds
of soap.

Troubling thoughts are now
colorless—
Dwindling in the mind as they
play.
These taughting thoughts tease
no more
For Christ's Spirit bids them
away!

Rozann M. Shamoon
TYPEWRITER TORMENT
As I look down at these keys
They seem to look right back at me
They have a longing to say
Don't write anymore, it won't pay.

Give up before it's too late
Or poverty will be your fate
Don't give your life up to
unhappiness
Go out and try to be a waitress.

Poetry died years ago
Along with Edgar Allen Poe
No one is interested in verse
Go out and try to be a nurse.

If fame and fortune is what you're
after
All you'll get from people is
laughter
No one will want to buy your book
Go out and try to be a short order
cook.

As I put my typewriter away
I started to pray
Lord, help me sell this book
You know how I hate to cook.

Norma A. Rafferty
'TIS TIME
'Tis Time—tis time to ring the
chimes
for everything is jolly
'Tis Time—tis time to sing Noel
and wear
a sprig of holly
'Tis Time—tis time to scan the
heavens
for that bright and glorious Star
'Tis Time-tis time lest we forget
what happened back so far
A Babe was born—we honor Him
on this
our Christmas Day
Let's bow our heads—and not
forget
that Baby in the hay

Dwight W. Holman
THE ROCKIES
*[To our dear friends Clarence
and Verlin Hafer who spent the
wonderful days with us at
Estes Park, Colo, Aug. 1975]*
To the grandeur of the Rockies
With its snow capped mountain
tops
Its brilliant streams of waters
Their sparkling rapids never
stops.

The golden clouds at sunset
The burst of fire at dawn
And the ever changing shadows
As the day progresses on

The straightness of the pine tree
As it reaches for the sky
Tiny leaves of the white aspen
Quivering to catch the human
eye.

There's a solace in its greatness
That man alone cannot explain
But God in His great wisdom
Raised its beauty from the Plain.

And He placed it here in our land
That its beauty might endure
On each one placed the burden
Keep it clean, Its waters pure.

May all passing generations
See its beauty, find its peace
Eternal in its greatness
All its wonders never cease.

Pamela Theurer
THE SEED OF LIFE
A seed implanted into life
who grows, and cautiously
stretches forth to grasp,
and learn and try.

A blossom opening to a rose
as knowledge pollinates our minds.
The sweet perfume of dreams
drifting from petals of
anticipation.

A flower, vulnerable toward life,
unheedful of obstacles ahead,
yearning, eager, hopeful,
impatient to extend.

The gentle showers of
achievements
nourish ambitions hidden under
doubt.
Endeavous failed, but wisdom
gained,
adventures lie ahead.

Our roots entwined by
friendships,

treasured memories formed,
branching out our minds return
and linger on forgotten times.

The season is for laughter,
for memories and smiles.
It is a time to journey toward
horizons yet unknown.

Mildred Henson Fiveland

Mildred Henson Fiveland
RENEWAL
*[Dedicated to my husband,
Norman, for his patience and
support, to our children Harold,
Shirley, Beryl, Gloria, and
Buddy, to Dorothy, my friend
and critic, and to B. Phillips, on
whose TV talk show this
picture was taken.]*

Mist on the meadow,
fireflies' mating ritual,
spring celebration

Terry L. Wilson
HANGOVER
Here I am
With pen in hand
Sitting down
Cause I cannot stand

My head's pounding
These eyes are strained
Someone's talking
Oh, my! What pain

What went down
It's not really clear
What the hell
Have a HAPPY NEW YEAR!

Ms. Emilia O. Duroska
**First American Root: Just
Men**
This we cherish and understand
a heart from heaven fell to land
rooting A m e r i c a: World friend.

The just men of long ago planned
a new world style to share, to
know.
Slowly, the winged heart took
root
brightening whole wide world
outlook.
The West, the East, prepared for
new
abundance...United States grew.

Old gates closed or welcomed
young entrance
by innovative confidence.
Graced with Angel—Hope—
Man's ally—
soon, America was the s k y !
Two centuries have passed, and
more . . .
open to all distressed its door.
Flower of Winged Charisma
Heart
is holding up, though picked
apart;
shaken its uniting power,
how re-inforce root and tower?

Ill winds blow!—Fierce
machine-stranger
from within would Home
endanger.
Those falsely impulsed, vain,
clever—
controlled by
greed-pride-endeavor,
know not of Spirit hyalescence!
A m e r i c a: Height's Florescence!
Not copy, nor sequel, but birth
of open way untried by Earth,
America is New Grace Truth!

. . . Just Men of inner assembly-
united, though untied, we be . . .
sings long the Winged Charisma
Song,
calling to members, who belong!
This we cherish and understand
Heaven's Heart Is A m e r i c a n!

Roy E. Landers
A CHRISTMAS WISH
this time of year
is a time to be near
the ones you Love and care for

a time for pleasing others
showing to all
brothers . . . feeling
with children reeling
off lists a mile long
grownups dreaming their own
weak or strong

wishing happiness
in the midst of this
i think what i'll do
is wish for you
your Merriest Christmas ever

Elizabeth M. Callahan
THE LAST LETTER
Mom, we hardly talked,
'Cause you were far away,
And yet, I loved you deeply,
No words could ever say,

My thoughts were always with
you,
As were those of your only son.
And I know you thought of us as
well,
With a love so strong and true.

Mom, we had a daughter,
Jenny is her name.

And we're so glad you saw her,
Before the angels came.

She didn't really know you,
But did know who you were,
She spoke of you quite often,
You did belong to her.

The other children miss you,
Your laughter and your smile,
When we did say good-bye to you,
They cried for quite a while.

Mom, we miss you greatly,
Our sense of loss is deep,
Yet with our love, we're glad
    you're gone,
For pain's not there . . . in your
    sleep.

We know you've gone to heaven,
For where else would you go?
Please, rest in peace . . . with
    Christ, Our Lord,
For you did love him so.

Now let us say good-bye again,
With a love deep from our hearts,
And know that we will meet
    again,
When God's new kingdom starts.

Sandra L. Gernert
A MOTHER'S HAND
It seems like the more I grow,
I come to need you more and
    more.
A someone to talk to, a smile to
    be shared,
A hand to hold when I'm lonely
    and scared.

And as I grow, I step away,
to follow the path, I know I must
    take,
But if I need to turn back home
For strength or wisdom to stand
    alone,
I know for sure you'll always be
    there
Not just because you're my
    mother,
but because you care.

Josephine H. Lenard
MY LORD IS TRUE
Yesterday I tangled with a Demon.
This is what the Demon said,

"You can quit searching for Jesus,
Because your Jesus is Dead!"

The days were long and dreary,
    and it's a sin.
I almost let that Demon take me
    in.

Then a ray of light showed me,
    my place.
Reflecting off his Holy, Holy face.

With one hand raised, this is
    what he said,
"Come all you who hunger,
Come and be fed!"

Now that Demon has searched me,
    and found that he can't hurt me!

I'm truly satisfied,
My Lord is True, that Demon lied!

David Lee Gordon Jr.
The Dawn and the Night
And lo there came the dawn,
    and with the dawn came the
        beginning,
the beginning of the light.
And then came the night,

the parallel of man.
The night and the light,
for each is part of man.
Without one there isn't the other,
a world of emptiness.
No good or evil
to tear at mans soul.
No happiness or sorrow
with which to pay toll.
Just a great void
with no life, no death, and no
    hope,
not even a problem with which
    to cope.
So welcome the dawn
as well as the night
as it fills your day
with a new dream in sight.

Franceska M. Leichtman
ROLE ME OVER AGAIN
I really miss the days of long past.
Women were ladies whose dies
    men cast.
Life was quite simple with roles
    so clear.
Don't you wish "those Days" were
    here?

Libbers quest to supremely assert
left pedestals lost and egos hurt.
Now we say "Sir" to woman or
    man.
Surely this can't be nature's plan.

Paula Smith
LIES TO YOU
Lies to you,
    will never be.
My love for you,
    will never leave.
It comes to you,
    from my heart.
It's given to you,
    openly and free.
I hope that you,
    will take it all.
Keep it all,
    from now until.
Forever!
    for that's how long
My love will last,
    from now until forever.

Romy Seton
Love's Dark Complexion
    *[Dedicated to Denise . . . Who
    Had Her Way]*
Sad blue eyes,
    She'll have her way,
Loving him much,
    But she won't stay.

Individuals in love,
    And two strong wills,
Possessing each other,
    With passion that kills.

What is this love,
    That enslaves the soul,
Torturing the heart,
    With no positive goal?

Forlorn eyes,
    He'll have his way,
Loving her much
    But he won't stay.

Linda J. Wical
NIGHT, THE PROTECTOR
    Night, the protector
Night creeps in like the flowing
    tide
    The water still and weiry
And yet, relieved from the

days events
    Some distressing and some
        cheery
The city sleeps in solemness
    Velvet petals on flowers close
Forgetting grief of yesterday
    Welcoming the dark of night,
To comfort them in graceful sleep
But then, the dawn is breaking
    through
    And time to face the day
We can only hope to capture
    nights—
    Vigilance
And bring it to our day.

Faye Gaston
OUR CHILDREN
Can't care for you with casual
    touch,
Our children we do cherish
    much.
Through thoughtful prayer you
    were conceived—
As gifts from God you were
    received.
While watching you in wonder
    grow,
The more my childhood mem'ries
    flow.
And I have come to realize
These times together will
    survive.
I want to saturate your minds
With God, with books, with
    happy times.
For when you too have "flown the
    nest",
This mother's mind will almost
    rest,
    If our deep love you will
        concur,
    Imperfect parents though we
        were.

Jennifer Bauman
THE WINDS OF DARE
The wind was harsh
as it blew in the night,
stripping the trees
from the cold of the night.
Using large leaves
to keep them warm,
was the only way to
stay alive from the storm.
For over the few
deserted childrens heads,
was a small hut covering . . .
So alone like them.
These poor children they were
so afraid and scared,
while the night continued to roar
black with dare.

B. Lynn Erickson
WOMAN CHILD
The child in me
Longs to be held
And loved
Comforted
Supported
The woman in me
Demands strength
And independence
Such turmoil
To be a woman child

Jane Snell Mattern
FIRST-BORN
So it was you. So many months,
I should have known. And I
    would be blase;
but...oh...the fresh, new smell

of you,
the soft, unblemished feel of you.
Holding you to my heart, I, too,
exult.
Mary, Mother in Bethlehem, how
    filled
must she have been! And, fearful,
    too?
A life to mold is such an
    awesome thought.
Yet, little one, I know—you are
    not truly mine.
From me, but not of me. You grip
    my finger tightly;
in reality, you clasp your own
    invisible, slender thread
which links us each to God.

Ola V. Feighner
THIRSTY EARTH
Come misty rain lie down on my
    bed
    Come place a cool hand on my
        fevered head
Lying here quiet, I hear your soft
    tread
    Tapping gently on the roof of
        the shed

To the bottommost roots send
    your wetness down
    Let lush green grass replace
        dull brown
Tonight walk sweetly, dear
    faithful rain
    To ease my heartache please
        fall again.

Jerry Davis Kowchee
LITTLE GIRL
    *[Dedicated to my loving family:
    Ipnuk, Rose, Ron, Sis, Daya,
    Little Man, Sonic and Lovie, all
    who inspired me.]*
Little girl you turn and kick at
    shadows on a smooth path.
Listen; the bells, wipe the sleep
    from your eyes. little girl with
    books wrapped in a pack you
    follow a stone this way and
    that.

Patroclus Kynos
Gone But Not Forgotten
And as the tidal wave subsided
my quixotic ambitions left me,
as self-destructive as they
    were—they
burned themselves out

And as my watery eyes resurfaced
the vision of contemplative
    reflection
took my mind
and wandered off, somewhere

And when at last my mind was
    mine again
I thought of the waste
expended in the futile efforts
of my heart's crusade

And there was nothing left to
    grieve
and nothing left to rebuild,
the tidal wave took care of that
    for me,
that made my job a lot easier

And I did
all that was left to be done—
I turned around
and walked away

Mary Ann Di Bari

Mary Ann Di Bari
ON THE LAGOON
*[To Mom: God's Grey
Masterpiece; and her "Ichabod"
Tree . . . with much love]*
Arthritic-stricken Oak
Are you aware the kiss
Of Honeysuckle climbs
and mounted nemesis?

Sensitive still
Or is your brittle form
Senile, feeling
No Green Harm?

Petrified Life!
Do you bear appetite
Or are you meagre
Fare
For eager Parasite?

Ancient Eden-Tree
Art thou
    Knowledge
        Evil
            Good
God's grey masterpiece
Or just damp wood?

Too, too naked now
Shaken by decay
And breeding
Shrink before this barren
Era
Into pregnant clay!

Cheryl L. Tucker
BECAUSE YOU ARE YOU
We truly can say
On this Mother's Day
You're a wonderful mother
Excelled by no other
In your own special way.

You're thoughtful and kind
With others in mind
And always so nice
When giving advice
None better we find.

So this is to give you
The praise you are due
We now love you more
Than ever before
Because you are you.

Rochelle Peck
A Dedication To the Boy I Loved
A little coy grin,
A little double chin,
the boy who is two years younger
    than I,
I could never forget.
His black wavy hair,
the cologne he would wear,
it was sweet, he was sweet,
and made faces that were really
    neat.
The big fat dimple on his right
    cheek,
that's the boy I used to know.
Whenever he was glad, whenever
    he was sad,
you always knew it could be
    either
when his dimple would appear.
The times I pulled his ear,
It was pain, "he declared".
His big brown eyes,
hidden by gold rimmed wires,
I could never forget.
The boy I shared so many good
    times with,
and unfortunately some very
    sad . . .
I could never forget,
that's the boy I loved.

Karin Knudsen
THE BED IS SMALL
[To Ed.]
I'd rather
not sleep
with you
than sleep
without you

Vivian Sofie Keck
RESTFULNESS
Whenever I get restless,
    I know just what to do—
    I go into my garden
And spend an hour or two.

If you have no garden
A good christian book will do,
    to put your mind at ease.
There are so many things
    that we can do
To help our tenseness cease.

God is always listening,
    So why not talk to Him

Ask Him to relax you
He does not want you feeling
grim.

Take a look around you—
Are the skies sunny or gray—
Enjoy the miracles
    that surround you,
And your cares will fade away.

Jo Starrett Lindsey
GOING WITH THE FLOW
Once everything was difficult,
And struggles marked my every
    move;
But, for no reason that I find,
I suddenly am "in the groove".
What seemed impossible to do,
Now flows with ease beneath my
    feet;
I laid my worries to the side,
And jumped into the modern
    beat.

Karen Lee McConnell
IDEAS
Subconscious is the polished
            black darkness
    One finds when slowly
            spinning
        Downward past levels
            of crystal
        Ideas and Ideals
            that one by one
    Melt and slowly invade
            the conscious.

Marilyn Fuqua
LIFE
Life makes things grow
little seeds grow
    into beautiful flowers
then the flowers turn to seed
you grew up
    into a beautiful person
innocence of life made you glow
But one night
you found that life can be brutal
    and hard
        and people won't care
since then
the friendly glint in your eyes
has transformed into an icy haze
your warm innocense has turned
    and stone wears away
to stone
leaving only dust
to bear footprints

Marino Pierattini
THE LAST EVE
Keep down the sighs and hide the
    sob before it breaks;
Walk slowly, now, and soothe
    your fretful heart's deep aches.
The pain of life in death will flare
    when he awakes . . .
        Keep down the sighs.

Hold back the tears and break the
    evening's pall of gloom;
Speak softly, now, for silent
    shadows search the room
As day grows old and feels the
    hour of doom . . .
        Hold back the tears.

Bring back his prime as memories
    return tonight;
For just a while restrain the
    larceny of Time's flight.
Soften the moment's pain when
    life and death unite . . .
        Bring back his prime.

Farewell, to years now lost in
    dark and dreamless sleep;
Good-by, to broken body alone in
    earthly deep.
The sorrows of death require a
    friend to weep, to weep . . .
        Farewell!

Mrs. June Niles
WEATHERED BARN
A weather aged barn
Stands tall against the sky.
Rain and mist around it streak
Birds lazy lie within its peak.

Once shrill upon the air
There were voices calling here
    and there.
People, horses, cattle, cats
Now it harbors only cobwebs,
    bats and rats.

Paint once put on
Not even peeling now
All gone, all gone.
All things must scrape and bow.

Window glass, where any's left
Is broken; of sills bereft
The shingles all have gashes deep
It could easy fall into a heap.

But still it stands
Refusing yet to fall.
Wind bruised and not quite
    straight,
Refusing to admit death entered
    long ago its gate.

Patsy M. Morris
MY VALENTINE
*[Dedicated to Jesus Christ my
Lord, my inspiration, my friend,
and to my son Corey, who
shares this honor with me.]*
A special touch from Heaven's
    door
Reached out and drew me near,
He told me of the painful cross
And hurts along to sear.

My life was scarred and deeply
    bent
Into the realms so black;
I wanted so to find God's peace,
But knowledge I did lack.

I felt a love for Jesus' name;
I even knew His hand;
He helped me in so many ways
With His own command.

So close and yet so far away
I needed a special thing;
I needed Christ deep within me
And the peace that He could
    bring.

Thank you Lord, I clearly heard
    Thy voice
And asked Thee in my heart;
Now I have Thy one and only
    peace,
My Lord and my sweetheart.

Florence E. Moore
YOU
You are light when darkness is all
    around
And hope when I feel that none
    can be found
You are warmth when things are
    very cold
And my youth when I began to
    feel old.

You are the melody to my
    beautiful love song

And fulfillment when I am empty
  inside
You are mine at times that I don't
  belong
And the shoulder to lean on after
  I've cried.

You are salvation when I have
  much despair
And the answer to questions in
  my mind
You are clouds of joy floating in
  the air
And my reason to see when I am
  blind.

You are happiness when I am low
  and down
And the will to live at the times I
  am sick
You are the smile that replaces
  my frown
And my speed when I need to be
  quick.

You are shelter that shields me
  from harm
And my voice when I don't know
  what to say
You are my attracter when I lack
  charm
And my everything in each
  endless way.

Nancy L. Wise
THANK YOU
*[Dedicated to Jack Bastable, my
loveable "AARDVARK" friend
who helped me to shine
through in Christ's love even in
the mist of trouble.]*
Thank You for your friendship
Which blesses me each day
And helps me find true happiness
In a world of sad dismay
And as each day comes to a close
I thank God for today
And ask him to bless friends like
  you
Which love can't take away

Lee Wells
Your World—My World
My friend you have your world
  today.
As I have my world to live my
  way.
We may talk of the words joy and
  decay.
But we can each help others in a
  loving way.

So to make it a better world, I
  must start right here,
As you must work at it on your
  own shpere.
Together we will surely give it a
  rolling start.
As we each have love and care
  within our heart.

Sr. Alberta Zuber
A HANDCLASP
*[To Padre who is always there
with inspiration and hope . . .]*
Multitudinous thoughts
like a blurred kaleidoscope
of sound,
    and light,
        and movement
invade my mind and torment me.

I am bewildered by the
  phantasmagoria
of my secret dreams.

my hidden fears
And I am pursued by these
  phantoms
which plague me.
Rest escapes me
and I plod wearily onward
seeking surcease . . .

Desperately, I reach out for
  comfort—
and I find it
in the sudden, firm clasp of your
  hand
gripping mine,
and in your eyes telling me
  mutely
all is well . . .
I am at peace again
and I can sleep once more!

Michael Franklin Rice
POWER TO THE POETS
Poets have the power of
Mystery and Magic
and of
Hope and Sharing
Power to the poets
Poets have the power of
Music and Singing

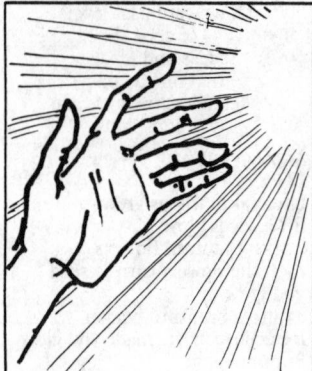

The power of
Red
Yellow
Gold
and Indigo Blue
Power to the poets
Poets have the power of
Perception and caring
Poets have the power of
LOVE

Genevieve R. Erwin
THE FALLING LEAVES
The falling leaves of autumn play
Upon the velvet, September grass;
A rainbow of gold as they lay,
They tell that summer soon will
  pass.
The rose is blown, and the iris,
  too,
And the blue skies will fade
  away;
In their 'stead will be glistening
  dew
And then twill come a snowy day.

Sallie Hinds
CHANGE
Upon the hill the sumacs
  Are wearing leaves of red.
The pines, with many cones of
  brown
  Hang high above my head.

The islands' shrouded all around
  With mist from the sea,
The flowers on the garden path,

Beckon now, to me.

Summer with her silken days
  Has now come to an end.
Winter with its icy wrath
  Is waiting just ahead.

Inbetween the seasons . . .
  There lie the golden days,
Of Indian Summer, calm and still
  With early morning haze.

The smoke—tinged air and colors
  bright
  Have captured all the days.
The harvest moon in the frosty
  air
  Is silver on the waves.

In reminising, we all will mourn
  The passing of color and light
As the snowy earth, with its
  silent cover
  Turns into black and white.

Tina L. Copley
ELVIS . . .
He was truly the King
Of Rock—n—Roll,
His music was loved
By us all.

When I hear his music
I feel good inside,
It's just as if
He never died.

Though his career
May be done,
His music lives on
In the hearts of everyone.

Marge Della Badia
OUR WINTERS LOVE
As I lie here in my slumber,
My heart and mind begin to
  wonder.
I think of all our glorious nights,
That our love has reached its
  greatest heights.
Now the nights are growing so
  cold,
I long so desperately for you to
  hold.
We have made our living fun,
Since our love affair has begun.
The snow was falling on the
  ground,
Our arms reach out without a
  sound.
For at last we're face to face,
Eagerly awaiting our first
  embrace.
The world around us we could
  not see,
For now there is only you and
  me.
So hold me in your arms tonight.
Love me tenderly and we'll know
  it's right.
As our hearts begin to glow,
Through our bodies our love will
  flow.
So even as we know this night
  must end,
We will eagerly await our love to
  flow again.
We have filled our world with
  such wild desire,
With such a love as this we will
  never tire.

Regina Conrath
The Christmas Holiday
The holiday is in full swing
  And debts are piling high;
Listen to the choirs sing

As Christmas draws nigh.
Bombs explode without warning,
  Crime picks us clean,
Yet hope catches our yearning
  When the peace of Christ is
  seen.

Kathleen Bell, EMT
RESCUE FROM DEATH
The rescue unit responds, racing
  at top speed.
It's quick, piercing, silver bell
  beating;
Traveling down the dark, winding
  highway,
Pulsing our red light like an
  artery.

Suddenly brakes reduce speed,
  upon entering the crowd.
Doors leap open, emptying light
  onto the scene.
EMT's carry stretchers, the
  mangled stabilized,
Then lifted into the little
  hospital.

As the doors are closed, the
  hospital is notified,
Then the siren, breaking the
  silence, tolls again.
The ambulance with its terrible
  cargo,
Speeding, slightly rocking, moves
  away.

As a driver puts the rescue unit
  to the test,
A paramedic works diligently to
  keep life going.
The beating of the heart kept
  going by CPR,
Oxygen and IV's flowing into the
  body sustain life.

At the scene, cops are still sifting
  through the wreckage.
One is still making notes under
  the light,
While one has a bucket douching
  ponds of blood
Into the streets and ditches.

At the hospital, throats felt as
  tight as tourniquets,
As that unpleasant question was
  asked, "Will he live?"
Hands seemed bound with splints
  and bandages,
All, did what could be done.

Hours slowly passed, the struggle
  for life is over,
But a frightened mother moves in
  with many questions.
The EMT though tired and heart
  pounding, speaks
Through a sickly smile, "Yes,
  your son is still alive."

But still remains, touching a
  wound and old scar,
That opens to our richest horror,
  already old,
The question, Who will be the
  next victim?
"Who won't be as fortunate?"

Alene Linkous Addington
A CHRISTMAS PRAYER
I do not ask to speak with
  tongues of angels,
Lord, I seldom ask great favors
  from above,
But this year a special gift I am
  requesting,

Father, grant to me the precious
gift of love.

I do not ask for faith that moves a
mountain,
All things I do not need to
understand,
But without love, Lord, I know
that I am nothing,
Unfit to enter in your Promised
Land.

Lord, I really have no need for
worldly treasures,
And I do not ask for worldy fame
or pelf,
But I know that first of all I need
to love You,
And then I need to love my
neighbor as myself.

It's so hard for me to love those
who would hurt me,
To turn the ohter cheek as Thou
would'st do,
And so, in this regard, Lord, I
beseech Thee,
I need a lot of special help from
You.

I need to learn to love those who
would wrong me,
I need love as the light to guide
my feet,
A light that shines right through
my daily living,
And lights the pathway of the
ones I meet.

Love will help me be more kind
and understanding,
And it will help me live as Thou
has taught,
So that I will spread more joy and
be more patient,
And not offend in any action,
word, or thought.

Your Word declares that this gift
never faileth,
So as I live here and await your
call,
I only ask for this one thing this
Chrsitmas season,
Please fill my heart with this
greatest gift of all.

Janice Marie Agypt
STORMY WEATHER
The brightly warm golden glow
from the aflamed small ebony
wick of a beige wax candle
Flickers aimlessly as the base is
undauntedly uplifted by its
wood—carved handle
As I try to steadily transport it
across the darkened room,
there is a sudden flurry
Extinguishing my single source of
light which caused my visual
center to become blurry.

Panic—stricken, my weakened
legs strode eastwardly back
towards the knee—high
mahogany end table
Searching desperately for dry
matches to reignite the flame
in the tiny corner of the gable
As God's heavenly tears boldly
precipitated through foggy
patches upon the bruised earth
In complete stillness, I listened as
the rains permeated through
the decayed eaves of our hearth.

Upon instance of relighting the
died—out flame, I slowly
pivoted towards the exit of the
dimly—lit attic room
This room holds a prosperous
family epoch once surrounded
by opulent possessions; and has
since been overcome by gloom
As I quickly inserted my
splintered forefinger through
the empty doorknob hole of
the decomposed wooden closet
door
Many contented memories flood
my mind of the photo albums
and objects kept herein
representing our family core.

When the squeaking rusted door
hinges separated from the
discolored cracked—plaster
structure, I seized the chance
To pass through the thickly—
spun spider webs and
multitude of dust particles that
over—whelmed my initial
glance
After thoroughly examining the
concealed musty remnants, my
small veiny cold—blooded
right hand forced the aged door
to shut
Closing a minuscule portion of
my family's past, leaving it to
weather the stroms ahead that
will engulf our summer hut.

Lillian D. Hatley
CHANGE
A lovely clinging vine
Twined round a tall pine

One by one
He lifted the tendrils

Wrapping them
Around himself

He is now the vine
She the tall pine

Susan Daubenspeck
They Are Burning the Books, Mother
Sparks of wildfire—
that holocaust of horror,
Alexandria,
when shadows of lost words were
torched
in venomous denial of life—
rise in banishing smoke.
It is the same smoke my Daddy
trottled his B—17 through
over Nazi Germany.
How long will it last, Mother.
How many glissening bones of
thought
will be allowed to be blackened
by little minds?
For if Huckleberry Finn can not
find sure footing
on the banks of his blessed
Mississippi,
than neither can we, Mother.
And if words will not be allowed
to be birthed
upon the bindings of consenting
covers,
than our dark stains on white
sheets—
our hopes and dreams—will be
nothing but ash
and we will lie forgotten,

charred by the gestapo of
immoral hands.

Norma Jean Gibbs

Norma Jean Gibbs
WAKE UP
There was unity during World
War II,
Everybody did what they had to
do.
I haven't seen that unity since,
Our people's getting fat, lazy and
dence.
There comes a time you have to
fight
In things you believe, and for
your rights.
Building weapons to protect our
land,
Standing proud, holding each
others hand.
It took years of sweat, blood, and
tears,
On V—Day, you should of heard
the cheers.
Who in the hell do we think we
are?
Did our heads get so big, winning
that war.
If war came, would you do the
same,
Or lose your dignity in the war
game?
The countries will sit back and
boast
Like small children, fighting over
the most.
The world is in alot of trouble,
All the missles will turn it to
rubble.
Over all the land, and its
construction,
It will be lost, a total distruction.
Our freedom cost us many lives.
To keep it "on you" it relies . . . .
Don't be self—centered cause it's
our fate,
"Wake Up! America," before it's
too late.

Faye Gaston
ODE TO OUR HOME
Old friend, our house, how I love
you!
You've enfolded our family
with warmth—
You've been a refuge.

We chose you from many designs,
And built you when we were
young.
So we've dreamed our dreams
inside you.

You know our faults, our
weaknesses.

You've seen us bring our new—
born babies home.
You've felt their first steps, and
Heard their fist words.
You've heard all their scoldings
and spankings.
You've heard all the huggings
and love words.
You've heard the prayers for
them.
You've heard their happy
chatter.
You have held all the
praphernalia of their childhood.

You have held the gatherings of
friends and relatives.
You have held the wonder of
Christmas year after year.

We've added a room and fireplace,
changed colors,
Added furniture and re—
arraranged rooms, and made
repairs.
We are constantly changing
you.

I like to visit and go on vacations.
But no matter what I see
It is always so good to get back
to you.

Eileen M. Greene
ST. JAMES PLACE
*[Always . . . holding a very
special place for you in my
heart, my dear James.]*
How many times I quietly
climbed the stairs,
And shyly tapped upon his
door. . .
And gazed into his beautiful
brown eyes,
As though I'd never noticed them
before.
I'd softly touch the outline of his
face,
Anticipate the tender love we'd
make. . .
And captured by the passion we
both shared,
I'd curl into his arms and ly
awake.
Such intensity . . . I'd never
known,
His kisses seemed to take my
breath away. . .
His gentle arms wrapped tightly
around me,
And there . . . I was contented
just to stay.
The nights so pure and simple
. . . morning cries,
We'd say our sweet hello's and
soft goodbye's. . .
And to this day . . . sometimes I
ly awake,
My love for him kept secretly
inside.

Oleta Jones
CHRISTMAS IS
Christmas is . . .
A time for children, a time for
giving
Gifts and love, a time for
joyous living
A time for good food, good
friends and loved ones

A time to rejoice in this happy occasion.

For the greatest gift was given one Christmas Day
By a wonderful Father in a land far away
God Himself gave His only Son
As a babe in a manger, a gift for everyone.

And to each one who receives this wonderful gift
God gives us life and our souls a lift.

He gives . . .
A purpose for living
A heart full of giving
A time for believing that

CHRISTMAS IS LOVE!

Dave Miller
BROTHER JOHN
Brother John we called him then
When dreams were young and far away.
In him we always found a friend,
In Brother John, Brother John.
In him we always found a friend,
In Brother John . . .

Our hero failed the test of fame.
A shot indeed heard round the world.
A bullet makes us all the same,
Brother John, Brother John.
A bullet makes us all the same,
Brother John . . .

Farewell to dreams and distant days.
Reality always comes too soon.
We light a candle at the end of the day
For Brother John, Brother John.
We light a candle at the end of the day
For Brother John . . .

The seeker seeks the hows and whys
Of answers he can't understand.
The minstrel tunes his lute to play
For Brother John, Brother John.
The minstrel tunes his lute to play
For Brother John . . .

Dwayne Giorsetti
A MESSAGE OF PEACE
It is clear to those that see the sun
rising every day that life is fun.
The beauty of life will not be

seen
by many who sleep, but cannot dream.
To take the time to view a sunrise
and the setting sun is no surprise
to those who walk and see with their eyes.
Watch the stars at night and hear a stream
as it rushes you into a dream.
The gentle waters trickling by
will massage your thoughts and bring a sigh
from deep within you, the only kind
that you and others feel, peace of mind.

Geneva W. Nine
MY BIRTHDAY WISH
[In loving memory of my twin sister, Norma Jean Gary, who passed away in 1977.]
If I could make a birthday wish,
And know it would come true,
I'd wish We'd spend this day together,
Dear sister, me and you.

I'm sure we'd laugh and talk and sing,
The way we used to do,
If we could spend this day together,
Dear sister, me and you.

But birthdays come and birthdays go,
This is my fifth without you,
And just like every other day,
You know I'll think about you.

And someday, when my life is done,
And my heart is forever still,
We'll spend our birthday together Jean,
Someday I'm sure we will.

Everett Francis Briggs
ACROSS THE BRIDGE
[Willetta Annie Etta (Briggs) Rall]
Deep night; but on the walk outside,
Beyond our shutters nears
The tread of footsteps toward the door. . .
And then, the ghost appears.

He says to sister: "Dear, she's gone."
Then turns, melts into night,
And we, in shock of disbelief,
Are left to our sad plight.

"She's gone." he said. "Gone where?" we asked,
Ourselves asked silently.
Across the bridge of death, but where?
No answer to our plea.

No answer will there ever be
Unless we turn to Him
Who crossed, re-crossed that bridge of death
To light no longer dim.

"Who follows Me," this Jesus said,
"Shall have the life, the light."
He stands beyond the span of death,
The bridge—end gleaming

bright.
Yes, we would follow those who cross:
"Oh, wait for us!" we cry.
But tarry they can not. 'Tis we
Who wait with eyes grown dry.

She's gone . . . but not forever gone.
She waits in that Somewhere,
Amid the gold stands of the stars,
To bid us welcome there.

So cross the bridge, aye run the span
That leads to that blest land!
All faces there will not be strange
Where those we love will stand.

Grace Genevieve Jean
BIRTH OF A DAY
"And darkness was upon the face of the deep"
I'd like to talk a picture of a birthing of a day
As I sit on dew—wet sandy banks, a fishing rod in hand
And feel the tug of anger signaled back along my line
That reached out into the darkness and down into the lake,
And there my curly black—tailed worm intruded rudely where
A black bass lay in silent watch just waiting for the light
To flash a sight of sun on scales.
"And the earth was without form, and void."
And all alone in the darkness there I felt a feeling grow
That God would let me share this morn
As on that first day long ago, "He formed the world with words."
I felt the darkness, I felt no fear.
I could sense no form. I could see no shapes,
But knew within the soul of me, that as "In the beginning"
This day was new.

Dorothy Rund
STEPPING STONE
I have become a stepping stone,
for others to tramp upon.
I stay behind the scenes,
so others can take a bow.
But without me,
they could not be.
But this they forget somehow.

I do not ask for much,
just an occassional pat on the back.
Or someone to tell me,
it was a job well done.
But even these I do not get,
and still I give blood, tears, and sweat.
Hoping someday to join in the fun.

But my days are numbered,
and this dream will not come true.
Yet others will come to take my place,
and have in their hearts this dream.
Some will succeed and some will fail,
but all will walk the righteous

trail.
And fill with love their hearts redeemed.

Melvyn Lee Smith
IDENTITY AND NOW
Apart from space, within no time
Soul That I Am touches this reality, longing to experience it
And Focus That I Am is brought forth
To explore and consciously know itself . . .
        Were I to sit beneath the bough
            To think, and ponder, anyhow
        To wonder how all life should be
        If left for all eternity;
    Where is the who, when is the how?
    It's all Identity and Now.
Intense is the focus, compelling the experience
Identity of Focus That I Am feels threatened . . .
        The all of me sinks deep at night
        Within the faulty frames of thought
        And questions doubtfully my plight
        Desiring that the Truth be brought
        Requesting knowledge of my birth
        Then pleading for Him come to earth.
Soul speaks to Focus That I Am in feeling—tones
For words could never contain Us:
Look inward, flow through and experience Yourself
And you will know Me and All That Is . . .
        The agony a mind must bear
            As newly of itself it takes
        Without a being close to share
        Its searching for the thing that makes
        It form an independant Soul
        In guise of failure takes its toll.

        But dreams will speak, impulses flow
            Creating pasts and futures here
        And into each I long to flow
            Till new awareness spells my fear.
        Identity is not a mold
        Yet ever joins the actor's fold.
Amidst this space, within this time, Focus senses itself as Soul

Gladys M. Arquette
GO SOFTLY
Greet me with a happy shout
Greet me with a gay hello
Happiness to see you come
But whisper softly when you go.

So good to see you, dear old friend
So good to hear your voice-and so

Shout your greetings as you come
But whisper softly when you go.

Too long since last we two did
　meet
Too long since our last heart to
　heart
Ring out the welcome when you
　come
But no hurrahs when you depart.

Happiness to see you come
Happiness to be with you
Wish that you could stay—but
　no—so
Whisper softly when you go.

Jeanette Herndon Bagley
WHERE AM I
*[This poem was written on
January 14th, 1982 before my
mother and daddy's death that
year. I am their only child. I
lovingly dedicate it to George
and Sue Herndon—Winter
Haven, Florida.]*
where am i
　where have i been
whirlwind
　up and down
round and round
　chariots of fire
higher and higher
　i see elijah
where are the horses?

Marge Graham
IT'S STILL RUNNING
I've an old hair dryer that's at
　least 25
It just purrs along and is still
　quite alive
It's got an on and off switch, but
　no fancy speeds
It performs for me well, doing all
　sorts of deeds
It's not a pro—max or super
　anything
It keeps humming in tune
　without ever a ping
It's thawed pipes, dried hair and
　even wet hose
I'll keep on using it as long as it
　goes.

Bill Sweikert
OUR GRANDCHILD
Why is a grandchild so special
　and sweet?
Why are their features so
　beautifully neat?
Why do we hold and pamper and
　fuss?
Because we know, they're a part
　of us!
They're the part of us that's
　seldom seen
The pretty part, that's never
　mean
They'll later learn, and soon
　enough
This world can be a little rough
But for now they'll play with
　dolls or toys
Depends on whether girls or boys
Their love flows out to all who
　cares
They capture us with special
　snares
We love to be caught and hugged
　and kissed
And when we're apart, we love to
　be missed

When we meet again, and they
　call our name
We feel like a million, who needs
　fame?
Why do they do such cute little
　things?
If you look real close, you almost
　see wings
They're smarter than they need
　to be
But after all, they take after me!
Their parent, your child, you love
　just as much
As when they were little and easy
　to touch
Now grown people, be it women
　or men,
Your granchild is them, all over
　again!

Dean Mitchel
LOVE IS . . . BABIES
*[To Mark—My husband and
inspiration]*
Love is sitting on Granpa's
　lap while he reads
　the storybooks.
Love is "helping" Mommie
　do the dishes
　after she cooks.

Love is showing little hands
　how to color
　and tie shoe laces.
Love is playing pattycake
　and peek—a—boo and
　making funny faces.

Love is tucking in the
　little ones and
　turning on the nite—lite.
Love is letting them
　play "dress—up"—
　oh, what a sight!

Love is holding his hands
　and guiding his steps
　as he learns to walk.
Love is getting excited
　and telling everyone
　when he learns to talk.

Love is getting up
　when the baby cries
　in the middle of the night.
Love is changing diapers
　and kissing boo—boos
　to make everything alright.

Love is all the special,
　little things
　that you do
To say "Thanks" to God
　for giving a precious
　baby to you.

Paula Wurster
A FATHER'S CARE
A FATHER'S CARE
goes beyond being there,
It starts very small
with a simple phone call.

A FATHER'S CARE
means he helps to share
the responsibilities of
raising his child,
without taking his
responsibilities, lightly or mild.

But if a Father
doesn't give,
so his child can live,
then a FATHER'S CARE
was never really there.

Karen M. Wheeler
SEA MIST
Sea mist dances upon my lips
Breathe deep the salty air
Dream about the sailors lost
Whose ventures spelled dispair
The sea cares not who lies within
In splendor or in rage
Only that they die for her
To sleep beneath the waves

Marjorie Kingston Skusa
THE SPARROW'S EARTH
I saw a sparrow,
Early in Spring;
There near my window,
And I heard him sing;
Poor little sparrow,
With one broken wing;
He couldn't fly,
But that sparrow could sing.

One little sparrow,
A message did bring;
Oh, what a beautiful,
Wonderful thing!
If I were a sparrow,
With one broken wing,
I wonder if I'd
Have the courage to sing.

Adria Mckeeby
PREGNANT
*[To Jessica and Jennifer, I am
glad you are here now . . .]*
I do not feel you,
but the doctor said you are there.
Deep in my mind,
I have never felt that you would
　exist.
Nor do I feel so now—
How long can I ignore you?
How long will you lay quiet?
Forgive me
I know rejection hurts,
life hurts more.
Please stay where you are,
I've made the mistake
so you shouldn't have to pay
with the sentence of "LIFE" . . .

Sibyl E. Earhart
WORD FLOWERS
*[Inspired by—my husband
Lloyd whose love and
understanding has helped
cultivate these flowers in my
life.]*
Come see some beautiful word
　flowers
That belong in a garden called,
　"Heart."
I'm trying so hard to get them to
　grow
And to give each a good healthy
　start.

Right here is a small one, "Thank
　You"
Shading a smaller one, "Please."
Underneath each of these is, "I
　Apologize"
And in between, "I'm Sorry,"
　managed to squeeze.

"Good To See You," thrives by, "I
　Missed You"
And it's helping, "Pardon Me," to
　grow too
"So Glad You Are Well," is
　blooming again
And I can see, "Let Me Help,"
　peeking through.

"How Pretty You Look," beginning
　to grow
Along side, "You're A Wonderful
　Friend"
"I Appreciate That," has come a
　long way
Growing by, "How Nice, Do
　Come In."

"I Wish You Happiness And
　Peace," has begun to sprout
And "Congratulations," is
　showing its head
"Have A Good Day," is breaking
　the soil
And, "God Bless You," now
　borders the flower bed.

There's a tiny bud on, "I Forgive
　You"
I nurture it all I can
I find it quite hard to get it to
　grow
In this stony heart of man.

I must guard these tender word
　flowers
So I need a whole lot of God's
　grace
To conquer the weeds of pride
　and hate
Or they would so easily take over
　the place

Sometime I hope these word
　flowers mature
And will spring forth from my
　heart's garden each day
I'll tie them together with the
　precious flower, "Love"
And to every one I'll give a
　bouquet.

Ellie R. Christen
MIDNIGHT WATCH
I stood by my son's bedside in
　the stillness of midnight,
　watching, listening,
The doctor left and said, "I can do
　no more."
I dared not move for fear of
　disturbing the stillness.
Was his breath more even and
　regular?
Then a soft sigh indicated
　precious sleep at last.
My thoughts flew to the many
　mothers who could not stand
　by their son's bedside.
Sons in foreign lands and seas, in
　this terrible world conflict.

I felt for them the same painful
　constriction of heart that hurt
　so when my son's breath came

in cruel harsh gasps, flushed
face restless on the pillow, lips
whispered "Mom, water please."
How a mother loves a son or
daughter can never be
expressed in words.
It is the fulfillment of love,
compensation for all cares, to
look into clear eyes and softly
touch a curl of hair.
Could it be just fourteen years
since his downy head was
cradled in my arms,
So mothers of the world must
also feel.
With heart too full for words and
whisper
If only we could ease the burdens,
and pain erase the world's
injustice.
With heart too full for words, I
whispered
"Thank you, Lord, for healing my
son.
Thank you, Lord, for this
priceless gift of life."

Faye Lanier
GRANDPA JOHNNY
Grandpa Johnny stood as tall as
the corn stalks
He bent his back to hoe.
All six feet of him was hardened
from his work.
As a young man, with quiet
hopes and happy eyes,
He brought his bride to the farm.
There the two mulitplied,
growing with the mighty land
Until the silence was filled with
cheerful sounds,
And, sometimes, with sorrow,
like when Grandma left us.
Grandpa's tears nourished the
barren ground where she lay.
Then, with shoulders back, he
gathered us about him, smiling.
He walked, showing us the work
of his hands,
Taking comfort as a man must.
Later, when we sat together on
the front porch swing,
He said, "The days are longer
now; the nights are endless.
But I am blessed; I have the land."
From day to night, he molded the
earth to meet his needs.
The land was good to him. It was
part of him and he of it,
And when we laid him to rest
beneath it,
He had no regrets,
Just a simple life that we
remember yet.

Gladys Johnson Snider
THE INNKEEPER
It was my busy season
People were coming from
everywhere.
My many rooms were filling up
So crowded, I was almost in
despair.

One couple came tonight
Asking for a room to share.
She was ready to give birth
But I had to refuse the pair.

I showed them a stable
Where warm they would be,
Even though the animals

Would share thier company.

A baby was born that night
People came from afar to see.
A star seemed to shine above
HIM
So bright a light to cause
mystery.

The baby was named Jesus
A carpenter's son was he,
But never the likes of man was
seen
Before in such a tiny baby.

Every year HIS birth is celebrated
With gifts, candles, and song,
Let's keep his light of LOVE
aglow
And may to HIM our lives belong.

Martha Viginia Chalfant
MY MOTHER'S HANDS
*[Dedicated to my dear mother,
Georgia May Blumer Beach,
whose prayers still bless my
life.]*
My mother's hands were worn
from care
But tender mercies lingered there.
She kept them busy day and
night
Adjusting wrongs to make things
right.
When sorrows deep caused me to
weep,
Her hands held mine 'til I could
sleep.

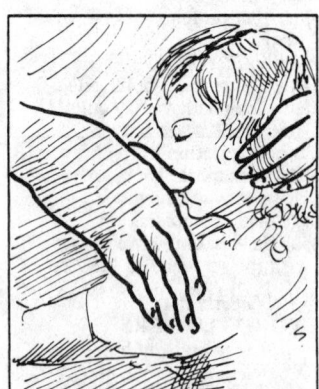

If I were sick with feverish brow,
Her hands' cool touch would heal
somehow.
All things of beauty, pure and
fine,
My mother's hands placed into
mine.
Although I'm grown and she is
gone,
The blessings from her hands live
on.

Mary Ann Newman
BACK INTO THE SEA
Each wave
crashes forcefully
Onto the beach,
Carefully erasing
whatever was there
before.
Leaving a million
new grains of sand,
for us to put our
footprints into.
Back into the sea
they go,

with each wash
of the tide.
Back into the sea,
Back into the sea,
Back into the sea,
Is that how you have
done with me?
Gently washing me
away,
and,
back into the sea
back into the sea,
back into the sea
of your
heart?

Barbara A. O'Hara
POETIC FROST
Why did he write
with such fury and might
Was he trying to set the whole
world right
Or himself?
What was his purpose or cause
was he fighting nature's laws
People's flaws
Or himself?
Was his meaning of "I have miles
to go before I sleep"
because he had to himself
promises to keep
That he was afraid death was
sleep
For himself?

M. Ada Keating
YOUR HANDS
"What do you hold in your hands,
my Friend"?
"Nothing" you say—Look again
and again.
For in your hands you hold many
things.
In the palm of your hand—you
may hold a gift for a friend.
A handshake in the time of
sorrow—brings peace to your
friend.
A pat on the shoulder from a well
meaning friend lifts a sad heart.
A handshake can bring praise,
peace and joy—
a cheerful welcome-or a fond
farewell.
A handshake can open the door
to an abundant Life—
and pass a key to a friend, which
will weld a future happiness—
or be the start of a new faith, a
new hope a new love, or the
renewal of trust in God.
So—pass your hand in greetings
to your friends which may start
a reaction, and as the link
grows stronger—you will forge
a chain of Friendships more
precious that Gold.

Dawn Renee Ruth
MY SON
*[To my Son Ryan Lee Ruth For
giving me a lot of special
moments in my life.]*
Look at this baby laying in my
arms, God what did I do to
deserve him.
He has golden hair, big blue eyes
and a little round nose.
My love will follow him
wherever he goes.
He is helpless and needs me so,
but don't worry I'll always be

there don't you know.
I am his mother and I can't run
away, for I gave him birth on
that special day.
He looks so content laying there
asleep, such a wonderful sight.
Believe me I'll protect him with
all of my might.
I was blessed from above with
this bundle of joy.
Thank God for this baby, my
sweet little boy.
I know he isn't mine forever to
keep.
So God let me keep him as long
as I can for one day he will be a
man.
He will be to big for me to cuddle
and hold.
But to me he will always be more
precious than gold.

Frances E. Brown
CHOICES
For a winter home why did you
choose
A hollow gold tree in Illinois?
You should be on the Orinoco,
High in a tropical forest.
When your family fled to hot
sunshine,
Why did you stay behind?
Did an injured wing, late healing,
delay you?
My father tramps down the
orchard
Through deep snow to carry
scraps to you.
If you had gone with your family,
you could be
Flitting through summer skies,
catching your fill of insects.
Here you are safe from our
barn cat:
He likes birds in his diet, but
he hates snow.
Do you dream of the different
climate
Of last winter, when you were
free from frost or cold?
You emerge from your dark
hollow into bright sun.
You say, "Keep back, Keep back,"
but you show us
Your brilliant scarlet body, your
black wings and tail.
Through winter days you bring
us joy, O Scarlet Tanager.

Margaret Alala
REVELATION
Was I not once glorified
Upon the throne of infancy?
Did I offer no gratuity
Or is not the past and present
affection
A debt repaid?

What am I?
A sprig of parsley to be relished
briefly
Then forgotten?
Earth's ornament?

In death, the glory of life is
incinerate.
Seldom, the flame will billow;
Render life aglow.
The flame may convert life:
To an ashen unseen black,
To the stench of mealsy decay,
To a lockless door slammed shut

On the feeble memory of man.

Could it be that I've been
The beggar's skeletal hands
And chords,
The drought victim's sustenance,
His water,
The sodden's mattress,
A sympathizer of the
  presumptuous?

Could it be that I've been
Needlessly stifled by guffaws?
Could that be as it has been
A presage of overdue respect after
  death?

I will totter warily to my grave.
I am rotting flesh in quest of
  longevity.
Only in death will I rot
To oblivion.

Mary P. Hunter Wells
Remembering Christmas
Christmas is for the youngsters
full of laughter, fun, and squeals
Rushing down the stairs real
  early
to get a look at their new wheels.

Christmas is for the parents
who are glad and joyous, you see
As they open lovely presents
that are stacked around the tree.

Christmas is for friends and
  neighbors
sharing love with those close by
Swapping stories and happy
  memories
while tears fill up their eyes.

Christmas is for the lonely
who are sad and desperate, too
They need our precious caring
so their hearts won't break anew.

G. Erwin Mills
THE JOURNEY
The majestic thunderheads
Come out of nowhere
Cross the vaulted sky
And disappear
Into nothingness.

Man
Comes out of antiquity
Plods across the face of the earth
And vanishes into eternity.

Doris Ullman Barbuto
EXCUSES
Don't look for me there—
  I've never seen that place,
  I'd get lost, I swear!
Don't look for me there—
  No one will go with me
  Much to my despair!
Don't look for me there—
  I take only short trips
  Without wear and tear.
Don't look for me there—
  I'd be as out of place
  As the old gray mare!
Don't look for me there—
  I've searched through the closet;
  I've nothing to wear!
Don't look for me there—
  I've blisters on my heels;
  There's gum in my hair!
Don't look for me there—
  I must clean the house now;
  Dust is everywhere.
Don't look for me there—
  I must weed the garden
  When weather is fair.

Don't look for me there—
  I've misplaced my glasses
  And sat on that chair!
Don't look for me there—
  I just sprained my ankle
  Stumbling on the stair!
Don't look for me there—
  I know the fun I'll miss
  Is beyond compare!

Catharina Rinta
LOOK AT THE GOOD SIDE
So life is tough, what else is new.
No reason to despair.
There's not a human on this earth
who doesn't get his share.

Now you can dwell on all your ills,
feel sorry and be blue,
and only see the gloomy side
in everything you do.

But don't you know you have a lot
to be so grateful for?
Just look at those who have it
  worse,
and see the good side more.

Do you have eyes? Why don't you
  see
the beauty all around.
A loved one's face, a flower, a
  smile,
First snowflakes on the ground.

Do you have ears? Then listen good
to music in the air.
Hear children laugh, and birds
  sing out,
and voices everywhere.

Do you have legs? Then take a walk,
  and feel how free you are,
and so much luckier than some,
  who cannot move that far.

There's always someone in this
  world,
who's much worse off than you.
So don't count what you haven't
  got,
let what you have come through.

Look at the good side of your life,
no matter just how small,
Appreciate all that you have,
and make the most of it all.

Kathleen Lewis
GODS GIFT
I often wonder how I'd be if all
  were dark I could not see
The silver fish in the mountain
  stream, the summer rain kiss
  the wild rose tree.
That spark of light that we call
  sight, Gods sweet gift to me.

If something like this should
  happen to me, I sure would
  miss the mountain view the
  wanderin free;
But knowing that it had to be I'd
  try to learn what others do, and
  as time passed by some of the
  hurt go out of me another
  sense begin to grow, start to
  take account of me
Tell me Get up and Go!

In darkest night I'd walk alone,
  through paths unknown might
  lose my way
But someday soon you'd come to
  me dispel my doubts and
  comfort me, and through the
  windows of my soul my sightless

eyes would learn to see.
It would be Brightest Day.

Onda Horning (Mrs.)
A WISH
[Thank you Ben]
I would that the fairies
And the genies of the bottle
Could yet grant wishes
For I would wish
Thou could then appear
Upon my hand at night
And we could converse
Of things I do not know
Or have so little knowledge

Thou with infinite patience
Would answer my myriad
  questions
To make me more perceptive
Of those mysteries
That come to my mind at night
And I have no answers.

Rich Corvin
Unicorns and Rainbows
Befriend a Unicorn seen on high
Euphoric visions of absent pain;
Follow reality in feeble dreams,
As rainbows follow rain.

Ride this majestic beast
Through sun drenched clouds
  above;
Decode the rainbow's pastel
  secrets,
And find the one you love.

Understand, in part, at least
That Unicorns ride the 'bows;
Colors showering an entire world,
Causing love and peace to grow.

Not to know these sights as
  spoken
Or wish on falling stars;
Plead the magic not be broken,
And keep a love—as ours.

Virginia Allred Fowles
REMEMBER ME
*[This poem was written for and
inspired by my beautiful
daughter Regina Michelle
Fowles on Oct. 7, 1981]*
Remember me as the years go by,
  for the love I gave, and tears I
  cried.
Remember me for all I've done,
  the problems solved, the
  victories won.

Remember me when you are blue
  my smile, my frown, my love
  for you.

Remember me when you feel glad
  the places we went, the fun we
  had.

Remember me through all your
  years,
  and never once must you share
  my tears.
Remember me in all you do,
  cause through it all, I still
  Loved you.

Jeffrey Glen Garris
HEARTLESS
*[To Karen Marie J. My heart is
yours forever. Love always
Jeffrey]*
My heart is with another one
  seperated by time
  A time that seems endless. A
  time that is far
  The day is long, but the year is
  short.
My time seems near, and my
  heart is not yet mine.

Margaret A. Martone
REALITY
[To William, James and Mary]
Are all experiences fantasy
Just a matter of time and space
Are our souls here today
And tomorrow another place

Are all effected by one another
Beings that have come our way
Do we effect all we see
To change their life someway

The human mind is not a mirror
It does not fully see
We cannot say our conscious self
Sees all that is reality

There is an energy cast to all
He who seeks will find
The knowledge he will learn
Will enrich his learned mind

So go along the path
Remember what you see
Changing it for the better
Is seeing reality

Cheryl Darrup
**Speaking: The Young
  Victim Of a Bashful Boy**
In my eyes he was cute;
It was his smile that made him a
  beaut.
He asked me out for a date;
My own mind told him to wait.
A week later he did it once more;
My peers said that he was a bore.
It was tough, but I had to say 'no!
My friends influenced me;
From that I had to grow.
Of course, I was young;
I didn't maintain my own tongue.
But I DID realize something
  indeed—
He was the only one I'd ever need.
It was obvious that he DID care:
He'd phone me every night,
  No matter what the fare.
We'd go skating once or twice;
He never talked much—
  We were like a pair of mice.
He'd smile everytime he looked
  at me.
It felt great! If only I could've
  forseen:
I was unknowingly playing
  'hard-to-get';
But I couldn't go out with him;

Not as of yet.
He tried to talk to me in the arcade,
But his words just wouldn't come out—
It was then that it started to fade.
Maybe I didn't give him a chance to talk;
Before he said a word, he began to walk.
I lost the tall, well-built figure In the crowd.
I was about to yell to him; very loud,
But I decided not to; instead I thought
In my OWN mind:
"I'll never forget you. You're the only One of your kind."

Leone Rosemond Wood
An Old Abandoned House
With a sorrow'd look it leans
With it's tall and tired walls
While murmurs in the wind
echo thru' the empty hall

It's vacant eyes with fragile sills
Peer out across the way'
As if to search the distant hills
for one familiar face

Within the family plot, the
sainted sleep
'Neath the tilt'd tombs
Enthrall'd in vine and fleck'd with
moss
the epitaphs on the stones

Where once the plow turn'd a
furrow
And the yellow gowans grew—
Tamarach and tangl'd briar
imperial the clover'd field

The garden gate hangs on a
creaky hinge
Where woodbine tries to cling,
And neath' shambl'd pickets of
the fence
nest the furry Sciuridae.

All but lost is the cobbl'd walk
Which led to the tumble down
steps
Where ivy twines around the
columns
and climbs the chimney crest.

The gargoyle faces of the eaves
Upon the gablets, rest their chin,
And with the rustle of the wind,
sway their ghoulish head.

Strings of curtains hang limp and
gray
And snag on a jaggy pane,
As a little brown wren flits to and
fro
thro' a torn and rusty screen.

Rondamarie Harris Wheatley
THE J.C. SPIRIT
[*In loving memory to my
Grandmother Leona Holloway*]
It took over me, like a natural high
I wondered what was happening
to me and why
I remembered, I heard grandma
say,
"The Lord would bless and save
my soul one day."
Grandma said, "Just trust in him,
And he will shine light on you,
When yours grows dim.

She said, "God can lift you up,
even when there's no food
And a empty cup.
And praise God, grandma's words
are true
I've been down and out and the
Lord has pulled me through
If you've never heard of these
words from this grandma of mine
Read again, these lines of mine
Praise God, the Lord divine
Now to all, I give my grandma's
words to you
Trust in God, I'm an example of
what God can do
Now I'm 31 and excited about
this feeling
Not by alcohol—a disco light or a
lime light life
I'm batting a 1,000 through Jesus
Christ
Not wealthy—not a star on
movies on TV
But God has held, loved and took
care of me.

Nell Wilson
PLUM PUDDING
DCL and P for Plum Pudding
Is a Plumber's way to tell
The way to a Ploop Trail
Where Jonah came out of a Whale
Without a tear in his shirt.
He did not have to flirt
To make his way safely to Ninevek.

Diesel is an E Cell in the brain of
Solomon
Who was so wise he had to be
insane to stay sane.
Y is for Yum; isn't it good—the
end of the Plum Pudding?
And Y is for eyes in wise who can
see at the top of a *one*.
Have big *fun*, son of a Gospel *Gun*.
Yipes! There goes Orphan Annie.
Remember.
I am still a child; so smile.
You're on Candied Potato Camera!
Whoa, Lil' Horse.

Jim Schermerhorn
WORDS
Words—put them in a hat, shake
them up, spill them out
voila: a Shakespearean sonnet . . .
. . . or a malapropping Archie
Bunker.
same words! same damn words!
but Archie and Willie don't
juggle in the same circus

Don Quixiote's heart speaks the
FEELINGS, his words cannot
possess
while the watergated words of
Nixon were lies!
Words themselves are but a
lexicographer's wet dream . . .
. . . a tricky Dicky's Max
Factoring.
But emote a da Vinci of feelings,
FEELINGS
and the words emerge a
Gettysburg Address

while you're pondering words,
here's one: SHIT

Nancy C. Edwards
WIND AND SONG
Take my pen Lord, let me
Write down within
All the feelings I can.

To write of beauty that
surrounds,
Not violence that abounds.
Show me right from wrong,
As I write of wind and song.
Lift me up to the sky,
So I can see the birds that fly.
Show me tall trees,
That bend in the gentle breeze.
Pick me up like a sparrow,
If I should stray.
I'll need someone along the way.
Give me strength from above,
To write about the ones I love.
Let me remember places I have
seen.
And travel new places I have
dreamed.
Let me help someone today,
As I write along the way.

Johanna Harrop Luper
SAY IT WITH POETRY
If Music and Art are singing,
playing, and painting,
And Poetry creates listening,
feeling, and seeing,
A Poet, then, could say, "Let
poetry express itself in verse,
rhythm, and feeling,"
And all of man's nataure would
then be His Being!

Poetry is------Feeling.
An idea inside,
An experience to guide,
Beautiful things to think,
But, sometimes, thoughts to
shrink!!
Poetry is------Seeing.
God's hand on the earth,
And what he has wrought
In men of worth.
Poetry is------Hearing.
A story well-told
In rhyme, new and old,
That probed one to be bold,
And his own peom to mold!!

Beulah Thomas Carey
THAT'S MY MOM!
Arising always early with the
cares of the day in her heart; to
many this is a burden; to her it
is an art! That is my Mom!
The needs of those around her
she is constantly aware; often
tired and weary in spirit, she
reaches out to share. That is
my Mom!
One on whom friends and
kindreds rely . . . when in
distress and teary eyed . . . she
patiently listens to each cry.
That is my Mom!
In her unique way she makes her
contribution into each day.
Although many around her are
always in a rush! She always
takes the time to give that
motherly touch. That is my
Mom!

Steve Luevano
MYSTIC ECSTASY
Lady, so wicked and so cruel.
Living only by her golden rule.
Approach her with care.
Only if you want to, take the dare.
For when you fall into her
scheme.
You'll soon be a man, with no
heart and no dream.

Wicked Lady, stay away.
Listen! to what I say.
You won't destroy my self-esteem.
Nor, will you foray my dream.

No longer will I live in fear.
Of what you create, into
nightmare.
Someday you'll get, what's
coming to you.
The life you have, so insecure.
Soon you'd fall into the illusion,
Caused, by your own confusion.

So, Wicked Lady, stay away.
Listen! to what I say.
Don't come on to me, so easy.
I won't fall, into your Mystic
Ecstasy.

Derek A. Heath
Life Is But a Candle's Flame
[*To my wife Bridie, the Light of
My Life.*]
Life is but a candle's flame,
Hard to nurture, hard to tame,
But this flame without a doubt
Death's icy fingers will snuff out.

When first lit the flame is low,
Guard it from the winds that blow,
Protect it well and it may
Help transform your night to day.

Candle, candle burn thou bright.
In the darkness of my Night,
Wouldst the warmth with which
you glow
I, on others, could bestow.

Candle in the darkness glow,
In the glass reflections throw,
On the ground your shadows
cast,
Life is now, all else is passed.

Tongues of flame that flicker
high,
Ever longer 'til they die,
May my spirit be as bright
At the ending of my Night.

Christine Jo Ann Bryant
A VOICE IN THE NIGHT
He comes to me softly, in the
hours of the night;
When it's dark and I'm lonely,
and there seems no hope in
sight.
And He whispers so tenderly, the
voice that comes from within:
"Behold, fear not, for I am with
you, even to the end."
And from out of the darkness,
there is a ray of Light;
"Hang on My child, everything
will be alright."

"I know that you are weary and
  your heart is seeking rest.
I will grant to you the peace
  within and give you all My
  best.
I know you have been broken, it's
  the price we have to pay;
But know that what I offer, will
  be worth it all someday.
I know your heart needs mending
  and assurance is what you
  seek;
Be patient My child and grow in
  strength and know We will
  defeat."

And so arise and face the dawn,
  the morning is all new.
We have so many raods to run,
  together, Me and you.
Time is running out My love, We
  must move on and on;
So many souls are afraid and lost;
  We must tell of the Victory
  won.
Give them the chance to come
  on home and know the battle's
  through;
Inspire them to call on Me and
  Life I'll give brand new."

"I've never turned away from
  them; their cries I hear from
  within.
And the Father says He loves
  them too, but without Me they
  cannot win.
And so arise and face the dawn
  and know that I am near;
There is no need to wonder, the
  answers are so clear.
For I have promised you great
  things to come, just listen to
  My voice;
Deny yourself, pick up your
  cross, walk on and do rejoice."

"For I have called you home to
  Me, and the future I hold in
  store.
So lift your head and feel at peace
  and doubt Me never more.
My timing is the right time, all
  things will come to pass;
Take with you My Love and Joy,
  all trials you will surpass.
And in the end, you'll surely find,
  My reasoning was for your
  best.
And you will rejoice forever more
  when I reward you with the rest."

Sharon Spracklin Weiss
UNSELFISH LOVE
Just a passing thought by day,
Just a moment's glimpse of a way
To find the peace, happiness, and
  love
That was dreamed of by God
  above.

If I could capture that thought,
If only it could be bought.
I'd entrap it in my mind,
I'd let the world's problems unwind.

Reverse the wrongs that have
  been done.
Cancel the wars that have never
  been won.
Bring the people together in
  peace and joy,
Not let our feelings be their toy.

We would know a better life
Not the pain of back stabbing
  with a knife.
I'd teach the people how to love
Like planned by God up above.

I wish that I could catch the
  thought,
See it grow, nurture it til it grew
  hot;
Toss it out for all to see
How life was really meant to be!

Lori Heikkila

Lori Heikkila
BLOW ME A KISS
Blow me a kiss in the wind,
And warm me through your
  sunshine,
And let the tiny raindrops of love
  fall upon us;

For you are the ray of light
Which brightens my everyday.
You help me when roads are
  rough,
And love me when the sky is
  blue.

You are love and laughter put
  together,
In a land full of happiness.
Your love does not stray in the
  wind,
Or crumble in a thunderstorm.

So, blow me a kiss in the wind,
And warm me through your
  sunshine,
And let the tiny raindrops of love
  fall upon us.

Blow me a kiss in the wind,
Blow, blow,
Blow me a kiss.

Karla R. Puckett
THE REASON WHY
Babe, this poem was written
from me to only you,
because of a certain happiness
that is felt by very few.

You're someone extra special
because you took the time to find,
all my traits and qualities
that everyone else just left
behind.

Your forever, constant
  companionship
of standing by my side,
willing to lend a helping hand
when tears I needed to hide.

You always accept my mistakes
with a gentle touch and smile,

instead of getting angry
you laugh a little while.

Then you gently take my hand
as if I were made of glass,
and hold me in your arms
until all my troubles pass.

You make my life complete
with all these special things you
  do,
and that's the very reason babe
that I will forever and always
  love you.

Aurelia Cecille Giron Martinez
WHENCE?
Words fill my mind, yet
  Do not flow
I struggle in vain
  For inspiration
My need for immortality
  Has no release
The rhymes will not come
  The words are stuck.

Only when I think of you
  Do I radiate
Alive and effusive
  I create
A poem of thoughts profusive
  Emerging effortlessly
Flowing of itself—or
  Because of your love for me?

Rose Orlando Sodano
The Secret Written In Black
Fear you cry
Cry you fear
Are you the trick of fate?
Or are you the fate of a trick?
Why cry in fear?
Is the secret written in black?
Why in black?
Am I the fear within you?
Or are you within the fear?
To say I fear
The fear in me
Or the secrets written in black
Ha, I cry
No, not I
You cry in fear
Fear you cry
The age of time has placed a trick
And the trick placed fate in the
  age
Ah, but fear you cry
Cry, you fear
That a heart that loves is loved,
  you loved
And the fear is love only to love
So weep for fear
Fear, you weep
For the secret was written in black
Why in black?
Do you not hear?
Again I ask?
The age of time,
Is age a trick? Or the trick a fate?
For I fear not
No, not I
No secrets in black nor age of time
No trick of fate—for love is mine
So love has loved
So fear not I
No, not I
To cry for fear
Nor fear to cry
For the secret written in black
Is covered with a shield of love

and in a shield of time
So heart do not weep
For fear I see
No, not I
I see no fear
Nor do I know no fear
That I should fear in black
So again I ask?
Why in black?
Why in black?
Fear you cry?
No, not you
No, not I
We know no fears
That hides in black
So, save your fears and save your
  tears
For I lived with fear before
Not for its age, nor for its time
Nor for its trick of fate
But for the love I have, this I fear
Love, I cry, love, oh heart
Fear never secrets written in black
Love will win over all fears
For the trick of fate is in the age
  of time
And I have loved and love have
  loved
And the heart is always mine
To send you "love ya" as before
To send you "love ya" as before

Olga Windseth-Harris
COMING HOME
I had not reckoned with that
  little part
I long had carried in my constant
  heart
That drew me home to thee—soft
  murmuring wood!
A wanderer, rapt in Umbrian hills
  I stood;
But dearer now mine own soft
  murmuring wood!
Dearer than from where in the
  Arno's vales
Did sing to break the heart, her
  nightingales!
Soft murmuring wood, if I should
  leave again,—
Thy gentle precincts and thy
  portals green
Shall woo with love deeper than I
  had then
When first I told thee of my
  youthful dream.
As one who wears her pilgrim
  shoes no more,
Nor hears a call from any alien
  shore,
I homeward come to thee—soft
  murmuring wood!

Janice Wrinkle Stephens
NATURES' WONDERLAND
*[To my parents—for a lifetime
of love and understanding
given to me; I love you mom
and dad;]*
The mystery of nature is all
  around
unfolding before my eyes
filled with wonder and delight
as old as father time;
I can't believe I never had time or
  chance
or slowed to appreciate the
  beauty I see
breathtaking is the description

of one glance
the imagination is flowing free;
I stare into the soft cotten-like
    clouds
floating on a sky of darkening
    blue
the amber and gold of the setting
    sun
upon a mountain topped with
    pines;
A peaceful meadow with
    flowering galore
the aromatic little buds I took for
    granite before
The dandelions, daffodils, and
    even the butercups
bathing in the final rays of
    sunshine as if to drink it up;
A drop of dew has planted a kiss
upon the petals of the wild red
    rose
I reach beneath its thorns and
    stems
to touch the rich soil in which it
    grows;
Beyond the majestic meadow on
    the banks of the babbling
    brook
stands a weeping willow with her
    bending branch
sweeping near the earth as if to
    dance
in her shadows or somewhere
    within I hear the lonely cry of
the whippoorwill;
Here I stand spellbound unable to
    move
from this cushion of green grass
    beneath my feet
the perfect masterpiece the
    creation of one man
and all this beauty was perfected
    with his two hands;

Jagelle
PARLEZ-VOUS PATOIS?
(Do You Speak Slang?)
"Can I have this dance?"
In her tight Jag jeans
She took him up
To her rockin' world
Where *el tigre* rants.

Parlez, Parlez, "Parlez-Vous
    Patois?" It ain't against the law
And "love" is still the password. I
    heard it from my ma.

"Would a picnic fit?"
How they wore it well:
Cool Hot Springs Park;
Fruit and wine; and space
For his crazy wit.

Parlez, Parlez, "Parlez-Vous
    Patois?" It ain't against the law
And "love" is still the password. I
    heard if from my ma.

"What new film to see?"
That night's action grew
(Such fun and games
On the screen and off)
Then it climaxed—Whee!

Parlez, Parlez, "Parlez-Vous
    Patois?" It ain't against the law
And "love" is still the password. I
    heard it from my ma.

"Rendezvous at eight?"
Hearts connect in love,
A fast-food feast
Served by candlelight,

And it ends. That's fate.

Parlez, Parlez, "Parlez-Vous
    Patois?" It ain't against the law
And "love" is still the password.
    Amour—bon mot pour moi!

Jane M. Piecuch
LET ALONE ON TIME
Days end or are they just
    beginning?
Quick sunning spirits are many
    of the silent faces.
Their boulder's paths converge in
    different ways.
Yet some no longer accept the
    grind, refusing the burden of
    boulders.
Most just kind of shrug ignorance
    with wise shoulders.
When the mind doesn't allow
    grasping of pain, body boldly
    states its name.
A lingering scent of newly found
    old, sparkles with jazzy
    discussions of time.
        Now who commands time?
It's always the question of the age!
With insight much more modern
    than the rest as always the
    case,
King Answer states "the state of
    Utopia is coming nearer to our
    vision".
We, believers, apathics, dreamers,
    connivers, cheaters, globally
    aware livers, all listen closely.
Yet who can pick out from King's
    clause its faults and then make
    all agree?
None we should plainly see or
    should we?
Can it be decided and complete
    let alone placed in on time to
    make the agrument debate?

The time of each has room to
    breathe in the wholeness of the
    world's constitution with
    abiding absolutes as those of
    drifting extremes to a balanced
    dream and admitting that what
    is, is but doesn't always have to
    be.

Dana K. Allen
GYPSY DANCE
Life
twirls by in a wanton's dress,
bright and wild.
Patches of people,
ruffles of years circle teasingly
in a mad dance whose steps flee
    my mind.
Who will take my hand?
Who will lead?
When will the music
stop?

Catherine Arnold
A PLACE IN MY HEART
[To a very special guy:
Thanks for being my friend!]
We weren't friends for very long,
When I realized something with
    me was wrong.

As my feelings for you changed
    and grew,
It was easier for me to talk to you.

You had someone all that time,
But I hoped, maybe, you could be
    mine.

When we would talk and joke
    around
I knew love is where I could be
    found.

They told me that you liked me
    back
I thought my heart would never
    crack.

Then they told me you still liked
    her,
It seemed my life began to blur.

The crack that I thought would
    never begin
Made me feel noone else could
    come in.

I know I still like you deep down
    in my heart,
Though I feel we may be drifting
    apart.

And although I never said it I feel
    this is true:
There will always be a place in
    my heart for you!

Cathy L. Bryson
Cry Of the Hunted Heart
Raise thy voices loud and clear,
    Oh, ye sons and daughters;
Pray the Hunter Man will hear,
    And leave our lonely waters.

Once, our number here was great;
    Large to small swam free.
We noticed Hunter Man too late
    To escape his endless greed.

So very few of us remain,
    Survivors of the slaughter;
If Hunter Man does not abstain,
    Our race will go no farther.

Go, my children, on the wing,
    Within thy huddled masses;
Whale, that may soon cease to
    sing,
    Mourn the life that passes.

And hope to live to someday see
    An ocean stripped of fear;
Where no more Hunter Man will
    be,
    And whales will shed no tears.

Melissa Runge-Morris, M.D.
LEAVING HIM
We made the usual silent glide
Through walls of canned fruit
    and lettece heads.

My fingernails scraped across the
    rivers
In his face.

Like pendulums from a broken
    clock
Lead eyes fell into his brain.

Just another pair of vinyl shoes,
I turned left to weigh the
    bananas,
And kept walking.

Mary Pogge
UNTITLED
it is
too early yet
to write
about men

hate anger and
pain
they tell
me it
will go
away in
time

in
time

bit I will
never
be
so old

Lori Romanowski
BEAUTIFUL BALLOONS
[To Jenni, Dave and Mark for
opening my eyes to many
beautiful sights.]
Excitement mounts as time draws
    near
Flames and fans are all you hear.
Every color under the sun
Can be seen when they're done.

Gracefully floating into the air
Happiness is everywhere.
Balloons flying so big and bright
It's truly a wondrous sight.

Red, yellow, blue and green
A treasure that must be seen.
Leaving from a country valley
The great Hot-Air Balloon Rally!

Kenneth J. Reiner
WHY I FLOP
I like flop houses
in as much as they
remind me of home,
a place to sleep
in a corner found
on a mattress owned,
without all the
        communal
            fare.

Why did I stay so long?
Because it was all I had
and I was afraid of having
        less,

and being truly alone.

Alice Lukins
BARBARA
[To my sweet daughter Barbara
whose love and friendship has
been an inspiration to me.]
You will walk the path of time as
    I have done.
Myriad are the times you will
    lose your way.
As corridors beckon to you with
    open doors,
Beware of lights brighter in
    appearance.
Do not be misguided by my
    ignorance.

Today's Greatest Poems

Love for others seek out in this
human jungle.
Often too weary to pursue, you
will stumble.
The wounds of time will leave
you scarred beyond
recognition.
For we are but mere flesh, which
time deteriorates
Never quell or lose your
ambition.
As links in a chain so necessary
are we together.
Obliteration of oneself is not
needing others.
With surefootedness you must
endure.
Grasp the treasures of life, as
morsels to a starving man.
So succulant are these, your
appetite will never cease.
The pangs of hunger for life must
remain.
The parched thirst for love never
quenched.
And when this path leads you to
a meadow,
Famine nonexistant, and with
love you'll be drenched.
Lay down to rest, for you'll have
traveled far.
In the heavens there will be a
glorious glow!
This brilliance will be you my
child!!!

Joanne E. Sampson
SEASONS
Leaves have all fallen
Trees are now bare,
Sun shines down softly
piercing autumn's brisk morning
air,

With nip of coolness
and numbness of bite,
The tingling of winter
will return soon at night,

All seasons pass quickly
and days seldom last,
Life is worth living
though it goes so fast.

Corlis Yvette Outland
GRADUATION
Marching down an empty isle
My mind is thinking all the
while
I can use the knowledge I have
learned
or let someone else take my turn.
A challenge is all I can stand
I am ready to face the world at
hand.

Janet L. Wilson
LIFE
Life
precious, beautiful, sensitive,
yearning to be shared . . .
bright like the sun shining
through the clouds . . .
soft like a wonderful close
talk with your mother.

The Other Side of Life
cold, dreary, scarey,
a part of growing up . . .
dark,
like a raging storm . . .
harsh like an argument
you just can't comprehend.

Life
cold, full of pain
but precious, full of love.

Life

Shane Padric Reiordon
WAVES
Waves rolling in
Waves rolling out
I wonder if they know
Just what life is all about

They have been around
For millions of years
Surely they must have
Some ideas

Maybe, they have been trying to
say
When they come roaring in
And go swishing out
People of the earth, look out

Stop all this violence and
bloodshed
Let everyone get it together in
their head
But not many will listen to what
they say
Until it's too late
And they come and wash us away

Because what is a wave . . .
anyway

Anne Julian Powell
CHRISTMAS
A crackling log, flames leaping
heavenward
Laughter, a child's glowing face;
Pretty packages reflected in
sparkling balls,
Tinsel entwining in ribbons
and pine needles.
Loved ones gathering for a cup of
cheer,
Warmth and happiness
enfolding to bring
peace and contentment;
The night bursting with
expectations,
Soft carols floating through the
velvety air.
Christmas

A token of love to someone close.
Colors of red and green;
The smell of cedar filling a room.
Rosy cheeks and sparkling eyes.
Last minute rushing for forgotten
things,
Quiet moments of reflections
and yearning;
Whispering "I love you" under
mistletoe,
Hope for tomorrow backed by
faith to accept it.
Christmas

Audrey J. Dunn
WHAT PRICE?
When will the senseless killing
stop,
how many have to die?
Before there's no one left to talk,
don't you think we ought to try?

Bigger and better missiles and
bombs,
devise a new warfare plan—
I'll bet my "Mousetrap's" better
than yours,
let's blow the hell out of man.

Plans for attack, plans for defense,
has the whole world gone insane?

It's time to take a long hard look
at each face of misery and pain.

Let's really unite our nations,
let's shake off this mantle of
greed,
smile at each stranger and make
him a friend,
talk of peace is what we need.

William G. Muller, Jr.
PERFECTION
The artist skilled with brush and
*[His Grandparents Will and
Marj—Gene and Jessie]*
oil,
Will n'er attempt to paint that
swirl,
Of shining hair, like soft spun
gold
That crowns his head like kings
of old.

The famous sculptor may work
in vain,
'For he would mold a form the
same,
Pink roley body, legs round and
strong,
Dimpled arms, hands slender and
long.

The poet's hand dare not pen his
grace,
He can't explain his pugnosed
face,
Nor starry-blue eyes, nor cherry-
like cheeks,
He's our "Little Bill", age, —three
weeks.

Sharon I. Jenkins
RICK
*[To Richard "Rick" "Red" W.
Thurston My companion who
has let me grow with, Him, our
love and also our lives.]*
You,
can make, all my rainy days
sunny,
You,
even make, bad times seem
funny,
You,
are the love, I will always
treasure,
You,
make love, and life such a
pleasure.
You,
are the love, which fills my
heart,
You,
have been, my life's missing
part.
You,
filled all the dreams, I ever
dreamt of,
You,
opened my eyes to show me
love.
You,
know about love, the same as I
do,
You,
also know, I'll always love you.

Mary Bayne
UNTITLED
I look at the sky—and think!!
there's Heaven's might—the
dark!—the light!
there's God dear Lord, above
watching His earthly flock

are we doing right—or is it mock-
He created this earth and all its
treasure
for sensitive humans with valued
measure
varied temptations do exist
the weak succumb to evil
evil leads to the bridge of
penance, repentance, confessions
sincere
Jesus, our Saviour suffered on earth
so our sins would be forgiven
our God and Holy Spirit,—He
loves us all
should we need help, we have but
to call
more often than not sin is neglect
of love thy neighbor—
what is love—what is life—
it's being born to experience
awareness and caring—
not selfishness and hate
thought with growth
to obey and honor the laws of God
our Heavenly Father
to help ourselves and those we can
hopefully to receive the blessings
we crave
to live life fully, may our souls be
saved
to pray "our thanks" with full
heart
until such time, death do us part.

Mrs. Alma Jean French

Mrs. Alma Jean French
SYMPATHY
*[Dedicated to: Herbert, Willie,
& Valerie Jones]*
If you can always just believe
That God is one who won't deceive
And cause you unjust pain to bear
Because He's one who really cares

Take yesterday and mold tomorrow
And don't just dwell on your past
sorrow
He had a reason for what was done
When He folded His arms and
encircled your Son

Pray on Dear Ones, and please
believe
That strength from God, you can
receive
He'll fill your void with joys
unknown
That's why you need to just pray on.

Bertha N. Hughey
INSPIRATION
I made a wish today, Dear Lord
upon a little star,
that all the bad would turn to good

273

because it's gone too far.

It's time for people to remember,
that *Jesus* died for us,
and *God* didn't put us, on this earth
to argue, fight or fuss.

I wish that people would remember,
that Love is what you teach,
and that through all the trouble and the strife,
you should practice what you preach.

I wish that they would listen
and put their trust in *One*,
only then would they know, that through his word,
His work is being done.

And even when things go wrong,
and all your skies turn gray,
remember that we learn from *God*,
so don't forget to *Pray*.

Eleanor J. Hand
MY LITTLE MAN
Mathew is three, he's my little man.
He does for himself, all that he can.

He brushes his teeth and washes his nose.
His chin is all jelly—why do you suppose?

The buttons he has are no trouble at all.
When he ties up his shoes, he stands very tall.

Then off to adventure, with laces all slack.
He turns with a smile, "I be right back"
Mathew is three.

Mathew is three, he's my little fellow.
He likes crispy crackers and orange-jello.

Cereal that pops and hot dogs and fries.
His doggie to sleep with, if he closes his eyes.

"Gamma I wuve you," "Gamma goodbye", "Gamma a stick hurted me in my eye".
Tears, bumps and scratches and falls out of bed,
All soon forgotten by this tousled head.

Mathew us three.

Off to adventure, to the top of the hill.
Arms raised in gestures, a story to tell!

Eyes snap and sparkle, when he has been wronged.
Laughter and smiles will bring on a song.

Mathew is three and he's my little man.
I am so glad that he does just what he can.

Soon he will soothe me, take me by the hand.
Wuve me and cheer me, yes my little man.

Mathew is three.

Valentine E. Davis
MY VALENTINE
My Valentine
You are a star that shines so brightly
A star that keeps me awake nightly
You have a voice of loving charm
And a smile that is so warm.

My Valentine
You are a blooming flower
A wonderful lover
When you kiss my lips
It tantalizes me through my fingertips.

My Valentine
Your warm touch produces a cool breeze
Your natural beauty sets my life at ease
You are my guiding light
So gentle and polite

My Valentine
Just the thought of you there
Keeps away everyday fear
When you are next to me
My body sings in harmony

My Valentine
You walk with such sensuality
And speak with the tone of a symphony
You are a person with etiquette
With you my life is set

My Valentine
You are a girl for all seasons
I love you for one reason
Your inner beauty makes your outer beauty more outstanding
You are simply everything.

My Valentine
You are nature's beauty
Your smile of glee
And everyday sunshine
Tells me you are My Valentine.

Rebecca S. Rossignol
The Last Mowing Of Summers' Grass
beneath a sun not hot with the intent
of shocking the mercury
but content to offer light and warmth
i pull the cord
and with the pulsating purr
and reverberating whirr
blade meets blade
and i walk the path
a spongy swath a lawn mower wide

and sense grass beneath sneaker soles
less resilient and responsive

denim now covers sun-tanned legs
and shirt sleeves vest my arms
as my hands tingle with the motor's
vibration like the sensation of blood
trickling back into sleeping limbs
with a lengthening shadow to the left
of me and a sweet spray of green to
the right of me the sun follows at a
lower arc and peeps through the tops
of pines like a bright-faced kid on
tip-toes peering over a picket fence

behind me is the soft echo of summer
before me autumn colors at their peak
and in the far distance the shrill cry of winter

the last mowing of summers' grass
is like kissing a departing lover for
you know there will be a reunion but
O the agony in the interim.

Stacy Anne Lee
SHATTERED DREAMS
Shattered
   on the rocks,
not knowing
   where to turn,
  not
   daring
    to.

Drifting
  back to shore
   piecing together
    fragments of
     my dreams
only to be
  shattered
   once
    again.

Arlene J. Kinsey
TIME
Time goes by so swiftly.
The days go skipping by,
First it is January,
Then it is July.

Another Year is over
And as we look about,
We find it's hard believing
We ere did give a thought

To the seasons round us
As they each went by.
Next year we'll try harder
To see each one, Oh My!

To hear the spring birds chirping,
To smell the summers rose.
To watch the children playing,
In fall leaves reds and golds.

To watch the snow fall softly
As round the fire sit.
To dream of spring time coming
It's here in just a bit.

Time goes by so swiftly.

The days go skipping by.
First it is January,
Then it is July.

Kathryn A. Smith
BOUNTIFUL HARVEST
On an autumn eve
You came in need
Of Nightengale and sleep.
Comfort, reassurance and
Thirty hours love you reaped—
But, when tomorrow came
Did you remember the harvest that was yield?
Or was it just another rape?

Wanda Warrenburg
Tomorrow
Today is the tomorrow of yesterday,
Yesterday was the tomorrow of the day before!
Tomorrow will be another day—
With perhaps, better things in store!

The reason I think of tomorrow—
It's the day I must pay the rent!
It's now I think of those yesterdays—
Of how THEY were so FOOLISHLY SPENT!

But why? should I think of tomorrow?
When there is still so much left of today!
After ALL! I might not REMEMBER tomorrow—
What it *WAS*,—I was *THINKING!*,—TODAY!

Mary Crickmer Conley
FLIGHT INSTRUCTIONS
We are going away for Christmas
And what is worrying me
Is how will Santa know to leave
My presents under someone else's tree?

Mom says we'll go downtown
And talk to him—but don't you see
He talks to so many kids
How can he remember me?

Daddy says we'll write a letter,
Burn it in the fireplace and in the smoke
Santa will read my message—
But Daddy laughs like it's a joke.

But I know what I'll do—
I'll leave him a map under my tree
And when he sees it
He'll know where to find me!

Carolyn MacDiarmid
In Memory Of My Grandfather
Father above father,
Yet 'neath the Heaven he walked till dusk:
A casual king—the knight Of my day.
Eighty-seven years, and I less than a score,
Such a long life, the former—and so short.
O but how a life can speak with such moral translucency
When no teeth are bared in the night.
Beauty is so intangible—
No sword can pierce the wings of a heart;

And as long as there is pride in
my existance,
A pen in my soul—
As long as my little voice speaks
the mountain,
You will be at the peak.

What changes I have seen in
myself:
A former chatterbox child,
I have grown quiet and
thoughtful with your
teachings.
As your wizened hand once
stroked my face,
So the tears now baptize my
cheek;
Forgive me, Grandpa, when I cry,
But with my tears I build a sea of
love
On which I sail my course from
day to day:
If the tide should overwhelm me,
The fog erase me,
Or the wicked landscape enfold
me,
I will endure, with you in the
midst of my being;
And as I sail on through the sun
and sleet
Of every awakening day,
I will dream of seeing you once
again
Beyond the horizon.

Marilyn A. Gilman
TIME
What is this thing called time?
time that makes me glad
time that makes me sad
Time that marches on and on
time that does not care
that we might not bare
the changes caused—
Time just keeps marching on and
on
time is always here
there
and everywhere
sometimes nowhere, yet
Time just keeps marching on and
on
small as a second
quick as a minute
long as an hour—
A lifetime is ruled!
What is this thing called time?

Jackie A. Cooper
Battlefield Guardians
Souls of the dead soar high above
on ebony wings,
you are guardians of the now
silent earth below.
What happened here in the past
silently lingers,
though the story may still be
told,
the memories you alone hold.

Donna L. Hancock
**The Plight Before
Christmas**
Twas the night before Christmas,
and all through the house,
not a creature was stirring, 'cept
me and my spouse.
The last toy was spread 'cross the
floor with great care,
just to make sure that its parts
were all there.
The children, the creeps, were

asleep in their beds,
while visions of diagrams danced
in our heads.
Mama read instructions that
looked like a map,
while I held the tools and some
parts in my lap.
When the first piece fell off and
then hit with a clatter,
I went to my knees to see what
was the matter.
Peering intently, I knew in a
flash,
just what it was that had caused
that darn crash.
Why it should happen I just
didn't know,
but the part up above really went
down below.
Then, what to my wondering
eyes should appear,
but something that shocked me,
although it made clear,
Why try as I might I would just
never lick;
I knew in a moment, and it made
me sick.
In utter frustration my anger it
came,
so I cursed and then shouted, and
called the toy names.
Now, dash it! Now darn it! I
ranted and raved,
I'll kill that toy maker, he'll need
his life saved!
The sound of my voice fairly
bounced off the wall,
as I listed the faults of the toy
one and all.
The more that I thought of the
problem and why,
the higher and fiercer my anger
did fly.
Up to the housetop my temper it
flew,
toward the makers of toys, and
their rotten toys too.
My fury soared higher, I soon hit
the roof,
so I grabbed the instructions to
search for the proof.
But then, to my horror, when I
turned them 'round—
I found the instructions had been
upside down!
I glanced toward my wife, and
then down to my foot,
and thought about kicking her
right in the butt.
After a moment I brought my
eyes back,
forcing my mind to abandon that
track.
This, after all, was the woman I'd
married;
my children upstairs fast asleep
she had carried.

Tamara Hutchison
LITTLE CHILDREN
Little children—
Gentle rays of purest love;
Acting out a fairytale
That we might only dream of.

They're delighting in life's
wonders
And discovering its mysteries;
They seem to know what it's all
about—
Yet accept the world with ease!

With smiles on their faces
And songs within their hearts;
They're actors on the stage of life-
Just playing out their parts.

They take joy in every moment
And they show us how to live;
They make life a little sweeter
With all they have to give!

Yves H. Lacaze

Yves H. Lacaze
TO GAIL . . .
*[and to the Fellowship of the
Sun (Alcoholics Anonymous),
the gale that came from the
sea . . .]*
I was lost in a long night
horrere,
Desperately seeking escape
from its shadows of fear!
Endless the nightmares,
many the agonies,
As I stumbled toward
distant flares.
*I had forgotten how it all began;
Knew not how it all would end!*

Suddenly, out of this swirling
pool of fantasies,
A whirlwind came—
A wind with fury that cleared
my madness,
And a force that dried my tears
of sadness!

Yes! 't was a squall that came
from the sea,
In the midst of all this wildness,
A storm with the gift of heaven,
that brought my Gail to me!

It seems like only yesterday,
that in misgivings magnified,
This woman, who had lived my
agonies,

This girl, with the smile of an
angel,
Gail, with the face of a goddess,
extended her hand, offered her
heart,
and my life brought back to me!

Linda L. Tilton
THE LORD
I have a special friend that no one
else could see,
It's kinda like a special shell that
was found along the sea.

It's there to be found where
everyone has been,
But no one knows it's really there
except that special friend.

It's kept in your heart or that
very special place,
Only to be revealed where there's
a needed time in space.

Gail G. Ruhnke
FEAR OF LOVING
Dearest:

You are a special goodness
for a woman such as I.
And to know the quality
of such as you
heals wounds
brought on by lesser men.

Still—

A fall but equals the high.
And scars reopen to wounds
and pain.
I will not climb for an ending!!
Nor love emphatically
for but the moment.

Victor Verdi
GENTILE
Her breath blew warm against my
neck,
Like a warming flame,
In the cold night air.
The scent of clinging flesh was
sweet,
Where her arms, my neck did
meet.
Heaven now surrounding us, I
leaned forward to find her lips,
Thus to claim her with a kiss.

Beauty mate of shyness "come
forth",
Suffer yourself no more,
"Be desired" and please blush not
so,
If only to be admired.

I admire, adore beautiful talent,
Through I cannot reach as high,
the face of it.
I pray to plant my kiss
somewhere.

M.E. Jordan
GIFTED MINSTREL
Come sit near me and share your
gift,
Come grant the joy for which I
long.
Oh on golden wings my spirit
lifts
When sound is blessed by your
sweet song.

As your loving hands enfold the
strings,
As your magic moves to each and
'round,
No words are heard but your
spirit sings

Of your own proud peace that
here you've found.

And so many come, your gift to
hear;
So many to be close to you.
I often wonder when they're there
How many know you as I do.

For I see the sparkle in your eye,
That ourshines the stars in
night's black sky;
And I hear your gentle child's
voice,
That struggles so to make the
choice.
Yes, I feel the goodness in your
soul,
That's so often hidden when
truth is told.

And never do I love you more,
As when your gift above me soars.

Daisy—Shipley Benson

Daisy—Shipley Benson
THE MOUNTAINS
It is a beautiful place, you can go
any day.
Jesus went there that he might
pray
There is peace and contentment
among the trees
The flowers, the grass, and a
wonderful breeze.
With birds and song, it is a
wonderful place.
There is no discrmination among
the race.
God made us equal the mountain
to share,
It is a blessing just to be there.
Let us give thanks to God for this
beautiful place.
Where we have peace and love
for every race.

Winifred A. Coburn
TREASURES IN FLIGHT
Oceans of air surrounding the
earth have always fascinated
man.
An eager desire obsesses me,
come along with me, if you
can.
A seagull named Gordon is a
web-footed waterbird with a
thick extraordinary strong bill.
Color blue-gray, his enormous
wing span responds to his
every will.
Soaring along, he is a whimsical
creature against the brilliant
blue afternoon sky.
Rigerous lunges and richochetting

is his festive way to fly.
It is the queerest sensation being
carried off by this beautiful
bouyant seagull,
Plunging and diving, swooping
and soaring under some strange
and evil spell.
High over the earth, glittering
water, I spot while glancing
around.
Children sloshing through
marshy waters, searching I also
found.
"Look-out Gordon! There are
clouds ahead just waiting for a
collision!"
Then lost in happy meditation,
the passage of time neither
lessens or weakened my vision.
Over the road, past the rich
plowed fields, in the meadow
the cows do graze.
By the little covered bridge, wet
with dew, comes a smokey gray
foggy haze.
Over the sandbars, that are
covered with shells, are fish in
the clean clear lake.
This expidition, with the scent of
sweet flowers, is an eloquent
trip to make.
As we swoop and soar, dive and
lunge, our journey ends with
the night.
There are no disappointments,
only knowledge of treasures, in
the luster of this remarkable
flight.

Heidi Le Asklar
SKETCH OF A STAR
*[This poem is a tribute to
Stevie Nicks, the lead singer of
"Fleetwood Mac".]*
Gypsy woman
Loves leather and lace;
A womanly wonder—
Glimmer of grace.

She dresses in rags
From the finest cloth;
Not a common butterfly
But an exquisite moth.

Her gift is her voice,
Though soft and pained.
She leaves the audience
Emotionally drained.

In the spotlight;
On the stage;
Stands the BELLA DONNA
Of the rock 'n roll age.

Karen Kircher
MY FEELINGS FOR YOU
I'm sitting here waiting for you
I hope you won't be long
And since there's nothing else to
do
I'll sit and write a poem

When I'm near you I feel so good
I hate to have to leave
But I know if we were always
together
We'd both need space to breathe

I'm glad we get along so well
I really like you lots
And when I see your handsome
face
My heart just snaps and pops

So if we ever have to part

I think that you should know
It's really gonna hurt me lots
To have to let you go

Michael Lund
OCEAN
Night on the water;
phosphorescence.
Cellular chemicals pulsating;
glowing with the power
lighting the stars.

It's a long way home
from the microscopic sea
of cosmic memories.

Crow's nest
wobbles insanely
beneath my feet.
Is it land I see,
or just another mirage?

Anchor plunges
through the darkness
until touching
bottom—

A. K. Quinn
CHILDREN RIDING A BUS
*[I wish to dedicate this poem to
my friends who encouraged
me, and my sister who helped
me pick this poem from my
collection. Thanks for your
support.]*
They sit, still as a child can
With wide-eyed wonder
They watch . . .
Signs, stores, bridges, cars.

They start a conversation
About Nancy Drew,
Motorcycles, and movie stars,
Their school, teachers and
friends.
And in this way they can pretend,
. . . Isn't that what adults do?

The child sees the stop
With triumph, the hand reaches,
The rope is grasped, the bell rings.
With a bright childish grin,
The child waves and departs.

Mary E. Sharp
IT'S CHRISTMAS
It's Christmas, my darling, and I'll
spend it with you.
I offer you all my love, that's true.
I give you my seasons, spring,
winter and fall.
And then there are the summers,
And then there are the nights,
Also the wonder of holding you
tight.
I am blessed in life; you make all
things good.
You've given me everything you
possibly could.
You've given me a whisper, a
breath of life.
I've found my everything in being
your wife.
My body, my soul, my thoughts
for the day
Devotely praise you in every
way.
You've given me the will to forge
ahead,
Whether walking alone or in our
bed.
The closeness of combining two
lives into one,

Can mean, my darling, all
happiness and fun.

Patricia Randall
LOST YOUTH
*[To Terri: Who reminds me
that the beauty of tomorrow is
just a smile away.]*
Rain falls,
across my day.
like
Tears fall,
across my face.
Years fall,
like the rain.
Unyeilding,
Empty,
and
Silent.

Bernie Davis
WOOF—WOOF
Woof, Woof, Woof, Woof, bow-
wow-wow. I'm telling you that I
love you now.
Arph, arph, arph, arph, don't you
know those reasons why I love
you so?
One wag of my tail, you're a softy
at heart.
I'm really a pro at expressing my
part.
True I'm spoiled but look who's
to blame,
You never told me, or gave it a
name.
But deep down within it always
seemed right,
'Cause the smiles on your face
made everything bright.
I wish I could talk in the
launguage you use,
Since many of my friends are
sometimes abused
If more Patience and Love were
shown our way,
The devotion within us would
never stray
WE ALWAYS HAVE BEEN at the
side of mankind,
Sharing the joys and walking a
straight line.
We've only our love given freely
to him,
Loyalty and courage it came from
within.
Try to understand our whims and
our cares,
Train us and teach us to be
constantly aware
Together we'll walk down Lifes'
many trails
The Love we both share shall
always prevail.
Isn't it true why we're mans' best
friend?
Let's keep it that way till Life's
very end.

*Bp. Joseph Bartholomew R. Obras
Pasic, M. D. S.*
Elvis A. Presley Is Not
Dead: He Lives!
*[Dedicated In The Holy
Beatified-canonized name: "St.
Elvis Aaron Presley, M.", to:
Lisa Marie Presley: daughter of
Elvis A. Presley: Rock'n'Roll
King, Late of Graceland,
Memphis, Tenn., U.S.A.]*
Just please read of a *miracle* no
mortal might conceive;

And, wonder: "Would a mortal *this*
phenomenon believe!"
But infer, please, from *facts*: else
inferences might deceive;
Be mindful that: *miracles* pass
nature's-*way* to achieve.
And, should reasoning raise
doubt: then, "Ask and ye shall
receive."
That *this* revelation: *pent-up*
anxieties relieve.
Therefore: Do you believe *Elvis
A. Presley* is dead?—
How might *one* know?
But, should *one* see him—like:
standing by *one's* bed.—
What would *it* show?
And, if *he* left "proof-positive" he
was there:
When departing as if into
"thin-air":
Wouldn't *one* thus "a wondering
go"?
"*Elvis was here!* there *is proof* just
so!
If *he was interred* as it was so
mournfully said,
By whose *miracle walked* he to
the foot of my bed!"
Who played "rock'n'roll", through
the soul, in sheer efforts harder?
If *Elvis* is dead, *he* rests in *his*
grave: our true *martyr!*
And even though *his* demise be
announced by "*town-cryer*":
"*Let God be true*, but every man a
liar."
Therefore: *just believe!* May I
reveal in *what!*
And, I hope to die now on this
earthly spot:
If this heavenly-*visitation* is not
so!
For: while I slept as in *Twi-light*,
And, was "a-slumbering" just
right,
Behold! through my door *walked
Elvis A. Presley!* —I know.
Miracles were shown wherever
the *saints* had trod:
Lo! *this miracle*, like those, is an
Act-of-God!
Elvis A. Presley, "*Rock'n'Roll*"
King, *is not dead:*
He lives!—"*St. Elvis Aaron Presley,
Martyr*"; instead—Amen.

Marvin Chaney
PUBLIC SCHOOL
An Old Dilapidated Building
A Racial Unbalance Of Children
A Poor Frightened Teacher
Wild Students Smoking Reefer
Discipline Is A Myth
Wine Is Drank By The Fifth
Class Is Cut At Will
In The Halls You Can Buy Any
Kind Of Pill
Every Class Room Is Full
Rowdy Students Shoot The Bull
Instructors Are Glad To Still Be
Alive By Noon
The Daily Crap Game Is In The
Rest Room
Cafeteria Food Is So Bad No One
Will Buy It
Every Recess The Students
Almost Riot
Suspensions Are A Daily Process
Counselors Never Get Any Rest

New buildings Won't Rememdy
The Situation
The Answer Is Proper Student
Motivation

Ruth Anne Lewis

Ruth Anne Lewis
THE WARMEST DAYS
A heart of mine is a heart for you.
The warmest day with the
warmest love. All through out
the day, will you be mine?
Through the years with these
days so warm like this one. Its
hard saying how I feel but so
easy to feel this way today and
through out the years to come.
The coldest days will always be
the warmest with you.

Mark Dow Yeske
FORGOTTEN PASSION
*[To the girl I let slip through
my fingers, I love you C. J. !]*
Forgotten passion, like a chain
reaction, my whole life passes
me by.
Looking into the past, I can see
me through the glass,
Where now sits the shadow of
another guy.
Though the image isn't clear,
through the mist I cry a tear, in
the cold I stand and wait
knowing I've arrived to late.
As crazy as it seems, she still
meets me in my dreams, a
reflection of the way things use
to be.
Not just a window to the past, it's
a window made of glass, the
only difference is she won't see
me.
It's now time for me to go, and I
doubt she'll ever know,
I have stood here for one hour
and a half.
My eyes are filled with tears,
looking back upon the years,
and I only wish that I could
have her back.

Karen Elizabeth Serfinski
Heart Encouraged Love
Like to the wide-eyed sun, full
hearted love
To you I bestow with deepest
measure
And sincerest feel; love I when
you move
When you laugh, when you
speak, and more I treasure
Each Utopian-blessed moment we
make.

Time; to melt in those god-like
arms I ache.

Avalon beckons us to slip away
Into some dark place where our
love can glow
And burn, like stars burn the
night, making day.
What sweet words can I use so
you will know
The highest and deepest nature
of me,
What look can I give so you truly
see?

Love, the intoxicating spell of
truth
Escapes my in-breasted castle
and streams
Like a bright teared river, rolling
my youth
Into a secret dimension of
dreams.
Dearest mortal! sail here on my
Heart's surge
Or feel you not even minutest
urge?

Stephanie D. Borges
BRIGHTER DAYS
Laughing in my loneliness, crying
in my sorrow;
The rain is falling on my dreams,
hoping for sunshine tomorrow

Verna Saylor
WHAT IS LOVE
Love has so many ways to go,
It can hurt you, desert you;
Or make you care so.

Or want so bad,
Your almost in tears;
And then so happy,
You're busting with cheer.

Sometimes you reach,
A heavenly bliss;

And other times think,
It's really the pits;

What is love,
That it can do;
So much to a person's,
Point of view.

First wreck everything,
Then make it allright;

What is this love,
We search to find;

It's simply a love,
That can only be filled;
If you have Four loves,
To fit the bill.

Your Husband, Your Parents,
Your God, Your Friends;
And that sums up nicely,
What love really is.

Bernadette A. T. Haworth
MY FAVORITE PLACE
Sitting on the beach, with the
wind in my hair,
Looking out on the waters, with
no worries or cares.

I love the sky, I love the breeze,
I love the sand and the seas.

When the sun shines down on
the sparkling waters,
I could sit and daydream, for
hours upon hours.

Waves tickling at my feet, while
the sea gulls play above,

This place gives me such a
feeling, of sereness and love.

It's true when they say, "the best
things in life are free."
And one of my favorites is sitting
by the sea.

If you have never tried it, you are
missing a lot.
And the wonderful thing about it,
is it can't be bought.

Pamela Jean Alleshouse
DESIRE
A faded dream.
A forgotten fantasy.
A wild thought.
A wonderous wish.
A glorious reality.
. . .Desire. . .

Janice Denowski Martin
WAR!
Thundering plane's above my
head—
Thundering earth beneath my
feet—
Too late to stop, for love is out of
control—
The fighting has started, the war
has begun—
Arrest and trial has sprung to the
world—
For innocent and guilty the jury
is hate—
Seen by blackness and colored by
blood—
It's turned into pity and hurt—
Meaning of death, the feel of win,
lose, or be dead—
Man has sought the touch of
love—
Man has felt the touch of hate—
Love will always grow, as man
shall always survive—
Hate will vanish from the face of
the earth—

Joyce Shaw
THE SKUNKS ARE IN
Our little town of Ottawa
You never seen the likes
Of all the people staring and
gazing
At the black and white skunks
in sight

They wasn't here to harm anyone
They just wanted to eat and be
gone
Of all the rubbish they could find
Buried beneath and around
town.

So in the wee early mornings
Below dark hanging clouds
They would find and hide
Before daylight came around

They wasn't afraid of the nite
For no one did they see in sight
Not even their worse enemy
For he was cage or tied up tight

So They scurry here and scurry
there
They let them know they was
near
They just raise their tails and let
off a scent
To make them mad and hear
them prance

For they know deep down inside
They had the run of the town

Till someone discovered their den
And set a cage upon their
crown

Its over they all cried
But we had lots of fun
Scaring our big enemies
And hearing them moan and
run

Connie Carano
WHY
Why do people wish?
Why do people pray to seek help?
Why reach out to grasp reality,
When nothing is there?
Why seek or search for love,
when it cannot be found, beyond
your reach?
Why seek the truth,
when it only hurts, or tends to
kill,
a little piece inside your heart?
Why turn to violence or cruelty,
to mend those pieces?
Did you ever wonder WHY?

Why do we dream or fantisize?
Is it maybe because we long for
those
special dreams to come true?
Why cry?
When we should pick ourselves
up, and start over again.
Why drown our sorrows in the
past,
When there's a bright new future
waiting to sweep us off our feet.
Why dwell on the past and the
bad times,
when our memories of the good,
can overpower the roughness.
Did you ever wonder WHY?

Steve Saint Flores
A POEM TO MY DAD
I wish you stop and think
About how you kill yourself
When you drink.
I love you, I do, I do
And if you die I will miss you,
Day thru and thru

Helen G. Deer
HAIKU I
Reflected in stream
I am you now silver is
Love's mirror singing

Lorene Ferrell
Who Will Take Mother?
"Who will take mother, asked
Bill,
Now that she has grown old,
We have no room for her
But where will mother go?"

"I guess we'll send her to an old
Folk's Home,
She won't be neglected there,
And we can visit her twice a
month,
And she'll have the best of care."

"It's probably for the best, said
Jane,
For here she's only in the way,
But it won't be for long
For we'll take her back some day."

"She knows that we love her
And wish her the very best,
But we just don't have room for
her
And mother needs her rest."

"So we'll send her to this home

Even though it breaks our heart,
But I'm sure she knows and
understands
Just why we have to part."

But God had a better place for her,
For that night he took her home,
Where she won't be in the way
And where there is always room.

Carol Kay Langley
THE ROYAL FAMILY
Here we are,
together once more,
the family whole.
Gathering around the table,
feels like coming home.

All of us
going in different directions
yet united as one.
Each of us,
with a goal in mind,
working toward our dreams
with the support of the others.

Let's keep in touch!
All of us together
The knights and ladies of the
round table
All of the royal family.

Gina Megna
MOTHER'S DAY
On this joyous day we honor our
mother.
Not dad, gramps or any sister or
brother.
We thank her for all the things
she has done.
She preached to us, although that
wasn't as fun.

We thank her for what she has
taught us today.
Like to love, honor, respect and
pray.
She taught us of Jesus and what
he stood for.
Are minds were closed but she
unlocked the door.

She taught us to be honest and
not to be liars.
She gave us anything our little
hearts desire.
She taught us not to cheat, steal
and sin.
To pray and love from within.

The yelling and fighting and
screaming we did,
mostly she punished but other
times she hid.
Although she punished us many
a times,
It was Tara's fault as much as it
was mine.

We try to be good and love as we
should.
We try to be kind but if only we
could.
The world would be such a better
place,
if it wasn't for the worry and all
of the waste.

If we all were to think of all the
others,
life would be so much better, dear
mother.
In conclusion I would like to say
I love you mom and Happy
Mother's Day.

Mark K. Wilkinson
AND I
*[Words and ideas are gifts
given to me through the love of
my family and my friends. This
success is my gift to them.]*
Where I stand, I have long
remembered,
This fountain with love tokens
piling high,
The depths look back at me, a
mirror image.
Yesterday is in my eyes, she was
there.

Hands were held with a future of
care-not
Beauty was the bond of forever,
Peace and joy had made a place,
Life's path, no doubt, had found
us.

Where I stand, I have been a
witness,
This fountain with its magic at
work
On two people who smile, then
join together
A moment, a meaning, and I.

Helen Rotness
MY LOVE
Each time I think of you, my love
My eyes will overflow,
My heart aches to hold and feel
A love I'll never know.

I see your face in moonlit skies,
Your name is on the wind,
As it echos through the still, cold
night
My lonely heart to find.

My body knows no rest tonight
As I hear the night winds rise,
My mind is racked with thoughts
of you,
And the soul inside me cries;

Lord, grant me strength to see
this through,
Bring rest to my weary heart,
Watch o'er my love in sleep
tonight
And my love to him impart.

Phil Ortega
CAROLE
*[To My Lovely wife. "I Love
you!"]*
When life's just not worth living,
And shadows start to fall.
Your always right beside me,
To keep me walking tall.

Your touch is like a daisy,

So soft and warm and sweet.
Your love is like a meadow,
That flows unendingly.

My love is yours forever,
Unlike the passing day.
There will never be another,
Who loves you just this way.

My words, just don't come easy,
And the songs don't always
rhyme.
But the words that I keep saying,
Are feelings I just can't hide.

So let my words go with you,
Wherever you go, and do.
No one's ever loved another,
As much as I love you.

R. Wayne Shockley
LOVE QUEST
[To the last Rose of Summer]
When will it happen?
This mysterious wonder of life
Where will it come from?
Is it born out of toil and strife?

So many are looking
It seems to be rare
Burlesque imitations
are of common affair

It is dressed up in glitter?
A solemn bouquet?
Or breathed in a sigh
at the close of a day?

This wonder of wonders
How can you explain?
Whenever it happens
Life is never the same.

Kenneth G. Kutting
DEEP IN SLEEP
So deep in sleep in winter's
twilight,
She lay like an angel beneath the
starlight,
And with her skin like milk, she
was like the snow,
And upon her head, her hair
gently flowed,
Like a river black and glowing.

I watched her with softened eyes,
I watched her sleep, so deep and
serene,
Beneath blankets so warm,
As the wind did cry,
Against the Northwestern
evergreens.

She awoke and let go a sigh,
And soft and blue were her
soothing eyes.

Laura Loomis
**Christmas Eve: A Poem For
Kim**
pat said well i don't think this
world is as great as all those
poeple say it is and what are
we doing here anyway? i mean
the whole crummy world is
really just a mess and nothing
good ever happens always bad
news and why do we bother to
go on?

because we want to, kim said,
staring out the window.

that's silly, pat said, i mean what
good is it really? we all die
anyway. if there really is a god
why does he let all this
suffering and oppression

Today's Greatest Poems

and cruelty go on?

to make the joy more precious,
kim said, staring out the window.

then why did he create cynics
like me? pat snapped. All this
stuff about the beauty of life
and the goodness of
humankind and all that other
crap we hear—i don't believe it.
nobody believes that stuff
anymore.

i do, kim said, staring out the
window.

that's crazy, pat insisted, or do
you care if it is? it's only words
you know and what are you
staring out that window at
anyway?

come and look, kim told him.

so pat sauntered over to the
window and pressed his face to
it and saw, between two gray
cloud banks,

a single white star,

glowing with serene light,
oblivious to all the world's
troubles.

Merry Christmas.

Lysa Jean Farmer
MOTHER
The sea, she is calling me
my emotions as the waves
rolling back and forth
at times as regularly
as tides,
too often as violently
as the storm.

I long to sit on her sandy lap
where her watery arms flow in
to encompass, shelter and protect
me
not only from others, but myself
as well.

The blue and emerald colours
the white foam spraying
skywards
the greeting cry of the gulls
it is tranquility
and shelter she provides.

Months have passed since I've
seen her
yet she calls on
urging me to return;
one day soon I will run into her
arms,
the arms that wait to encompass
me
the arms
that will provide a final solution.

Linda Lewis
Massive Movement In Disguise
Hesitant, well—thought
movements of passivity
Amongst the crowd of linearity,
angles and quantitativeness.

Humanistic vibrations
signal the onthrust of
Achievement in qualitative
Silhouettes.

Numbers, insignificant
little incongruencies
blooming in importance
when placed in the puzzle of
REALITY.

A. M. Brown-Comment
THE WAVES
The waves rolled slowly to the
shore
As if to leave it no more,
They carried secrets from many
lands
After traveling on foreign strands,
They whispered softly to the
sands
Of lovely palm-lined islands
And slowly left the shore once
more
To visit other lands of lore.

Amina Tazin Jafri

Amina Tazin Jafri
THE QUAIL
*[To the memory of my
grandfather which has been a
source of encouragement and
inspiration at every step.]*
I saw a quail sitting on a tree,
I found in her an alluring charm,
I wanted her to come to me,
I wanted her to sing in her voice
so sweet and warm.

It came and sat on my
windowpane,
It sang to me a melody,
It could be heard down the lane,
It was a song so wild and free.

Now that she's gone it's like a
dream,
A dream so lovable and sweet,
Nothing like it I have heard or
seen,
I only wish for it to repeat.

Lisa Pagola
LOST YOUTH
Possessively
They have much of Everything
Still . . .
They want More!

Needs seem to stem
from a swing
A passageway
without a door.

What was,
Shall never be
Down this foreboding
path of no return.

Is that woman truly me?
The Fire has ceased to burn.

Karin L. Reinsel
SHE STILL DOES IT
She does it once,
it makes her feel good.
She does it again,
now she's in a better mood.

She doesn't realize
what it's doing to her friends.
One of these days,
it will mean her end,
but, yah, she still does it.
We say, "Why should we if she
doesn't care?"
With her our feelings, we try to
share,
but she sits there,
with that blank look on her face.
She makes us feel
so out of place,
and she still does it!
We also say,
"We hate her, we don't care!"
but, really think,
are we being fair?
We feel resentful,
so let down;
while she's up there,
"flying around".
She still does it!
SHE STILL DOES IT!!!

Annie Lou Lamon
ODE TO A TREE
Did you ever see a tree in a breeze?
Hear the whisper of the leaves,
quivering gently?
Did you ever see a tree in a gale?
Hear the swishing, almost
groaning of the boughs,
Bending over, swaying, swinging,
Almost touching top to ground,
Never fighting, just inviting
All the elements of the storm;
Sometime split, torn asunder,
Did you ever stand in wonder?
Can you understand the
resilience of a tree?

Ruth Kezele
TO YOU MY LOVE
I have loved you long
I have loved you strong
I have loved you above all
You made my dreams of what
love should be.
You come to me when I was so
lonely, to love me and let me
love you.

Now the end is here, you must go
I shall stay here. I will dream of
you each day and hour. You
took my heart as you would a
flower.
I shall never be but a shell left
hollow, very empty.

Never to know your love as I did
this hour. I will stand in the
sun and rain. Let the warm and
the drops kiss my skin. I will
think of you my love. And
there shall never be an end.

Frances Depeel
NATURE'S SYMPHONY
The music drifts on scented
breeze,
A rhapsody among the trees,
Across the field the heron calls,
God lifts his wand; a silence falls,
Then softly each soliloquy,
Becomes a wondrous symphony.
In lakeside's shallow bubbling rills,
The blackbirds bathe, with songs
and trills,
With yellow heads or bright red
wing,
A choral accolade of spring.

The cymbal; that obtrusive loon,
Brings back attention to the tune,
The mother duck talks to her
brood,
Her quacks lend softly to the
mood.
Then suddenly the gulls impeach,
With wild abandon, loudly
screech,
Then comes the bass; the lordly
sound,
Of wild geese honking all around.
The conductor blends with ecstasy,
All nature's sound; a symphony.

Curtis D. Jones
FALL
The summer season has passed
us by,
And the beauty of autumn and
fall is here.
There is always a lot of
celebrations,
Because this is a special time of
year.

With the leaves changing colors
And slowly falling to the ground,
It makes me still joyful;
To see that you're still around.

This time of the year
Seems to be the happiest of them
all,
With all of the holidays coming up;
Everyone wants to have a ball.

With the winter approaching,
It starts to get cold;
People's attitudes start changing,
And love and kindness become
ten-fold.

With the days becoming shorter,
And the nights increasingly long;
It makes it more possible
For people in love to get along.

Like chestnuts roasting on an
open fire,
It helps to make the seasons
bright;
And with just one smile from you
Would light up my life every
night.

Laurel Susan Vitone
WHERE PARADISE LIES
*[In loving dedication to my
family, For the tight ring of
love which encircles us.
Wherein paradise lies for me.]*
The pessimists say that paradise,
Is a dreamers world of tall-tale lies.
It is a secret place unknown to man,
In a fairytale never-never land.

But optimists say that paradise,
Has coordinates that are precise.
It is only a moments glance away,
For the heart can lead the way.

Wherein paradise is captured in
the realm of love,
Or knowing that there is a divine
force above.
It is seen through natures'
window of creation,
And in the giving of thanks and
admiration.

Some find it when reaching a
goal,
While others see it in the caring
of lost souls.

It is beamed from a glittering
    smile,
Yet others enjoy solitude all the
    while.

Paradise is summertime and birds
    singing praise,
Or sitting at the ocean under the
    golden rays.
It is knowing tomorrow will be
    better yet,
Or looking back at the past
    without regret.

At the edge of paradise you will
    realize,
It is a reality in your mind's own
    eyes.
Escape will be the key to cope,
And paradise is realitys' only
    hope.

In an instance our soul will
    arrive,
To a place where paradise lies.
Happy in knowing this place will
    never part,
For paradise lives in everyones'
    heart.

Dorothy Keller
YOUR MEMORY
You left me with a memory
    A sweet, yet bitter memory:

Of sunsets and early dawns
Of laughter and of tears
Of poetry and heartfelt songs
And sharing through the years.

You left me with a memory
    An everlasting memory:

Of quiet days and peaceful nights
Of happiness and sorrow
Of reaching most ecstatic heights
And promise of tomorrow.

You left me with a memory
    But only with a memory.

You left my side to seek new lands
With you I wish to be;
You have my heart, all that I am
And I, your memory.

Thelma F. Mills
JOB
Old Job was a righteous man
with all the blessings and wealth
    of the land,
until old Satan showed his hand.
Then in the Lord he could no
    longer understand.
He griped, he grumbled, cried and
    howled
"The Lord does not love me now!"
But the Lord had pity,
for He is wise and can see.
And He softly asked
"Now do you love Me?"
Or is your love only for that
    which you receive?"
"My what a foolish man was I!"
Did old Job cry
For by your protection and gifts
my love you did win.
Then when these things were taken
in self-pity and sin
I let my love for you stray.
When this is the one thing
with all should always stay.
For no matter what has been or
    what may come
Love is and always is His way,

And the only and very, very true
    one.

Helen L. Wikstrom

Helen L. Wikstrom
SUMMER
Butterflies and bread sticks
    picnics on the lawn,
dozing crepe myrtles—red roses
    and dawn,
pink sheets—alarm clocks—
    frost on a pane,
Winter's gone—
    summer's here again . . .

Carolyn Schweizer
I LOVE YOU
I don't know how to say it
    I don't know where to start
By telling you I love you
    From the bottom of my heart
For each and every smile
    and each and every kiss
Will always be the moments
    I'll always cherish
For the happiness that you've
    brought me
    Will be stored just like a
    treasure
My love for you will never die
    But will only go on forever
For you are my only sweetheart
    You are all my dreams come
    true
For I knew within my heart
    When I fell in love with you

Barbara J. Grasmick
WHO WILL KNOW
Am I to pass away from this
    world leaving no mark at all on
    man kind?
Am I just another mother who
    has toiled through day after
    day, with only a small taste of
    satisfaction?
I have not time to write a novel
    or paint a beautiful picture.
I have not time to work
    mathematical problems and be
    cheered by my fellow man for
    breaking through a theory.
Oh! but I wish I could see the
    world and climb the highest
    mountain and sing a famous
    song that I myself have written.
Who will know of all the dishes
    I've washed and the cloths I've
    hung to dry?
Who will know of the sleepless
    nights I've spent walking from
    bed to bed trying to cool
    feverish heads.

Oh! woe is me the mother who
    has driven countless times to
    grocery store, doctors office,
    dentist, scouts, basketball
    games, football games, the
    miles run through my mind
    never to be captured again.
I'm destined to be a mother of
    many generations but,
Who will know I've really passed
    this way?

Jo Ann Gilbert Stover
Farewell To A Missionary
*[Written in gratitude for Elder
Randy Dodge who brought my
family to the truth of the
Gospel of Jesus Christ in these
latter days.]*
Life in It's instant decreed
We should meet.
Our Spirits reached out
And found a common bond.
You, the teacher,
Filled the hunger
Our empty souls did seek
And in the bargain
Became a friend.
Our paths crossed
And in the passing
Great Truth was found
To prepare us for the final Journey.

Just as soon
You had to travel on
For other callings
Command your presence.
But the essence of your friendship
Ever lingers
For you have touched the heart.
The soul shall not forget.
Even though our paths
May not come together again
In this life,
We are all confident
In the knowledge of the Next
Thank you, Beloved Friend

De Diminicantanio
TIME AND SPACE
The time and space of love's
    sweet flower

    never
        appear
            to matter much

It's when the blossom fails to
bloom

    we question
        the time
            and space.

Cyndie Lewis
MOTHER
*[For my Mother &
Grandmother: May all your
days fill you with happiness to
share with all]*
Inside a special feeling, . .
Which something special grows,
Bloom a mother's wish and
    caring,

For the ones who love her so.

Though sometimes our end is
    near,
And temper drives us so,

We cut and hurt with things we
    say,
That never leave our soul.

In times of strife . . . and when
    we're down, . . .

Mother is there,
For all the care . . . and love
. . . For evermore . . .

Richard Russell Robertson
THE SECOND CHANCE
As we grow close, to the way we
    were,
My feelings are changing and I'm
    almost sure,
That if you want, you may share
    my life,
As a friend, a lover, and maybe a
    wife.
For as our love is sure to be,
My love for you, you soon will see,
But I go by a rule, I'm loyal and
    true,
And in our love I ask this of you.
For when this rule is thrown away,
The two of us, with our love will
    pay,
But until the end I shall not scorn,
A second chance, a love reborn.

June Annette Constantine
JODIE
The whisper of the wind
Brings back to me your name;
The falling of the rain
Says it will never be the same.

For once we had a closeness
That was grander than the sea;
But now we lack a friendship
That was everything to me.

I'll remember all those moments
That we shared throughout the
    years;
All the laughter and the wishing
Yet throw away the tears.

For once we had a friendship
That was grander than the sea;
But now we lack a closeness
That was everything to me.

Mary Herring Ballentine
THE GOODNESS
I've dabbled some in poetry
short stories and the like,
I've found myself reflecting
on the sorrows of my life.
I've written through my fantasies
and lost myself in dream,
I've thrown away my morals
yet I've found a realer me.
I've drifted over oceans
from those tears I cry at night
I've searched into the hours
of which form my greatest plights.
I've listened to each person
as they wile away their lives,
I've wondered from beginning
whether love was truth or lie.
I've seen the hate among us
how an evilness can be,
But now my spirit is glowing
for The Goodness lives in me.
It seems along the way
I've heard the tales of good and bad,
the years I walk this planet
prove to me they are a fact.
In every waking moment
there are things we must decide,
and some much more than others
can determine our look on life.
But as we go along, some blinded
    by hate,
and in despair, a feeling we are
    not alone
soon comes to fill the air.

So if you're down and out my
friend,
just wishing you were dead,
remember that it's up to you—
be happy just to live!

Robert Fredrick
E. T.
*[To my daughter, Rebecca
Rose, and all of her Lakota
sisters and brothers.]*
You came to us from afar
You were a fantasy of someone's
mind
He made you come from a star
But know you are a reality in our
minds

You are short and ugly
Yet your big eyes are loving and
caring
You have big feet and you're green
Yet all could laugh and cry for you

So I'm wondering why people
hate me
I'm short, but I think I'm cute
I have big feet, but they tell me
I'm a good ball player
Yet people put me down and call
me names.

You see, E.T., I'm an Indian
For some reason people don't
seem to like brown
I was happy because people could
love and cry for you
But yet sad because people don't
love me

I shed a tear for you
I shed many tears for me
So you see, E.T., you made me
happy
Even if for a short while as people
may learn to love me

Peggy Jo Doerr
CRY ME AN OCEAN
Cry for me an ocean
Complete with gliding gulls.
Their motionless wings may quiver
When a voice from heaven calls.
A diving bird skims over
The ripples of faith so deep,
Safely treading water
As angels' watch may keep.

Your salty tears will glisten
When at last the even sails
Soar over the sunset's color
Leaving paths like western trails.
Your heart is floating easy,
Awaiting the morning's tide.
So cry for me this ocean,
Our love will be your guide.

Russell D. Asbury
**Don't Be Someone That
You're Not**
Who is a person who thinks they
have everything
That is a person who really has
nothing,
They have no one to turn to in
their time of need
And it seems they never really do
succeed;

They're always trying to buy
their way through life
And people are always taking
them for a ride,
The laughter they have on the
outside
Hides the crying on the inside;

So always be just who you are
You'll find that will take you far,
And the laughter you have on the
outside
Will also be laughter on the inside.

Sandra Hamer
The Mystery Of Creation
I often wonder how the world
ever came to be.
I believe in God; I know He
created it, but somehow it still
seems so strange to me.
The earth and its contents, the
universe and its space were
both assembled by one
supreme being.
Yet, I am still in suspense at how
He came to be.
I know that God is, was, and
always shall be.
Still, it remains a superlative
mystery.
Could it be that we're all
dreaming and we'll wake up
tomorrow? If we should, what
can it be?
Somehow this whole incidence
seems mysterious.
I suppose I shall satisfy my
curiosity with a decision that
we are what we are, but never
will I let go of this mysterious
sensation which dwells in
me—that feeling of perplexity,
frustration and confusion.
That feeling, which rages in my
innermost soul, is mystery.

Joey Herrington
REMEMBER?
Christmas is a glorious day
As long as we think of it in the
right way
It is not all ads, tinsel, and lights,
But a time to remember the
greatest of nights.

A night when our savior was
brought to life
To save us from long suffering
and strife
We often forget what Christmas
means
And where our responsibility leans.

Christmas means spreading love
everywhere
And a joyous blessing for all to
share
God gave this greatest gift to all
From old men to children who
crawl.

So remember next Christmas eve
Before the many gifts you leave,
Thank God for this blessed child
And let all your love be reconciled.

Linda R. Wren
THE DUST CHILDREN
War's grindstone spits debris
That floats around his feet.
Dust children too light to settle.
Living mortal remains
Living in the street.

Desire's seed, sown of no ones
consequence.
Incidental, accidental, Occidental
babies
Powdering pathways with dry
tears
Revealing tiny footsteps going
nowhere.
Living in the street.

Strawdolls thrown away
Too different to be kept.
Eyes too round.
Eyes too green.
Living in the street.

Nameless thistles on the wind
Fly to cover the sun
Turning his amber dreams to red.
Democracy's child, a passion fruit
Living in the street.

Stillborn, still alive
Hauntingly cross ocean's past.
Unburied, behind closet doors
Looking for Papa.
Living in the street.

Jean Olcott Bosanco
CHRISTMAS
A Christmas star shines through
my window, telling me the story
of a Christmas long ago
when Christ was born in
circumstances
low. Can it be the same that shone
in far off Bethlehem
bringing glory to His name?

The world lies sleeping as the
dawn approaches, and I reminisce
of years gone on before,
when I felt loved and neighbors
knocked upon my door to
share the cake and wine
in celebration of His birth divine.
When I held love within my arms
and all the world was mine.

Beverly Babcock
MY SHINING STAR
The light in the sky
Brightens my eyes
Which puts delight in my face
And a glow in my heart.

This light in the sky
Puts a glow in my heart
Because the light is you
And has been from the start.

I love you more
With the passing days
And so glad you're my Mom
On this special Mother's Day.

Dena J. Dorame
THE SEA
The sea my eternal love,
It possess the warmth of two
strong arms,
That can reach my soul and fill
my heart with life,

As I watch the sun dance off the
waves,
And the moon sprinkle them
with the dust of dreams,
I think of you and wonder where
our lives will lead,
When we will love, and to you I
will belong.
The fog cast a shadow of silver
across miles of blue green magic.
And rugged cliffs jut up to
surround,
My deepest loves, feelings, and
desires,
The moment of your touch,
The feel of your strength,
The fire of a storm, with the
clouds as dark and
commanding as your eyes,
I will be enfolded in the passions,
That can fan the smoke from the
heat of the night.

Dawna King
BIRDS OF A FEATHER
I am a sparrow
whose only joy
is charming you,
the soaring eagle,
from the violent winds
you travel on.

We are so vastly different
yet when together in flight
we create a mirage so beautiful
that we awe the winds
and still their sighs of discontent
and fury.

Frances Beeler Klagstad
THE FABRIC
Your hands had held
our skein of days
too lightly,
I was never able
to weave the web
precisely;
The warp ran awry.
Though I fought to perfect
the tenuous ends
time assembled,
The thread
was too thin
And my fingers
trembled.

M. Joyce Skinner
MISDIRECTED ANGER
I misdirected anger at you last
night
It was unbecoming
It was unjustified
It was cruel
It was a mistake

Today is a new day
and yet I carry the guilt of my
actions heavy on my heart and
mind
The guilt of my hostile tongue
lashing out
at you—so dear to me
at you—so undeserving of such
ugliness
at you—so warm and tender in
my memory

But as I try—over and over
to convey my sincerity with that
inadequate phrase, "I'm sorry"
I sense your hostility
and my burden becomes
greater

I sense your coldness
   and my pain becomes
     unbearable
I sense your caution
   and my fear becomes
     intensified

As as I come to you
   so vulnerable
   so heavy with guilt
   so heartbroken

You turn away
   with no compassion
   with no tolerance
   with no understanding

And right now
   those are my needs—not my
     addictions
And as you hold them from me
   unwilling to forgive my
     moment of weakness
   you extend my suffering

Peter Michael Pringle
FOREVER
[To Susan and Kelly]
Growing up,
Reaching a teen age,
Can be fun friends, parties, and
   dances,
Learning life,
For when you are adult,
And not taking chances,
Problems, sorrow and hardships,
Are adulthoods lessons to learn,
When you should,
Or should not,
Is advice you do not spurn,
But when you are grown up,
And things are really bad,
Or worse,
And you are sad,
Don't forget your best friends ever,
The ones you call
Mom and Dad

Jacquelyn Marie Vaughan
MIRAGE
If I could be a poet for a day,
   I would write the kind of
   poetry that would touch the
   deepest part of every soul.
If I could be a musician for a day,
   the music I play would send
   every heart soaring.
My words of wisdom would be a
   comfort to every troubled mind,
   if I could be a philosopher for a
   day or two.
As a millionaire,
   I would give every dollar to
   everyone who asked if it would
   free them of their sorrows and
   pains.
If the love of God could be put
   into the form of magic dust,
   I would sprinkle the world and
   watch it change before my eyes.
If I could be the one, and the only
   one,
   I truly want to be, I would be...
   just me.

Evette J. Rhoden
LIFE
Up and down the journey
More down than up
Up hill steep
Down hill uneasy
At the bottom aspiration
At the top inspiration
To continue on and on

Before the drop.
Then comes the middle
Where you rest awhile
But you become idle
You have no choice
You have to move on
It's either up
Or the inevitable down.

Phyllis A. Keckley
RICKIE
Before I'd fall to sleep, I'd take
   him in my arms,
And on his chest I'd cry, and tell
   of my alarms.
In no other was my trust, I'd
   confide in him alone,
Telling all of my feelings to, in a
   very serious tone.

His ears were made to listen and
   on his shoulders I would cry,
His condoling eyes would glisten
   and soon my eyes are dry.
Secure in his embrace again, so
   glad that he was there,
To ease the hurt, and hold me
   close and take away the scare.

Always on my side of things,
   ready to render aide,
After breakfast, chores or bath, or
   after we had played.
He loved me still whenever, I
   shouldn't have got the blame
He'd soak up all the tumbling
   tears and love away the pain.

Best friends we were! Those years
   ago, a deeply bonded pair,
He was, you see, my dearest
   friend, my beloved teddy bear.

Edith Roybal
OUR SON
[To my little one Michael]
Oh little son with eyes so brown
A prince to us without a crown.
A countenance of pure delight
With a smile so warm and bright.
A product of two peoples love
Sent to us from God above.

Sylvia Kaye
THE LINDEN TREE
Who would think a Linden Tree
Could be lecherous as could be
Undulating in the breeze
Acting like a taunting tease
Never letting the wind forget
The Garden of Eden where they
   first met

Gloria A. Post
MOMENTS
There's magic in the moments
   we share in growing close.

There's wonder in the feelings
   for those we love the most.

I have endless words inside me
   that have need for a place of
   birth.

Yet I struggle with my secrets
   as if they were a curse.

They can't be locked inside me
   as if I'd thrown away the key,

There's fear in what that key will
   open,
   that's why it torments me.

The need now is somehow urgent,
   it seems that too late comes
   too soon.

The fleeting moments have gone
   by,
   we forgot to play the tune.

Those unsaid words of love and
   praise,
   that outstretched helping hand.

That heart that should have
   listened,
   it could have lead the band.

Mary Ann Di Bari
A DAY AWAY
[To Lenny: Written on the day
he left for Boston University;
After teaching us to LIVE!]
A day away
In faded farmer jeans
Straw-hat and tan
Bare-chested brawn—
New Man—
Grown thick with Summer
Graced the lawn
Sowed into tractor-seams
His verdant dreams . . .
Raced the humming motor

A day away
Transparent under sweat
And sun, unshod
Surveying virgin earth,
Trails untrod . . .
Set yellow tank
Against a sea of green
Mowed down the enemy
Unseen, and sank
Like Caesar
Opposition's voice,
[The boyhood choice]
In awesome Rubicon!

Konneen Willis
LOVE FOR KATHLEEN
[With love to my other half—
Kathleen Willis Brimhall In
whom this poem was inspired]
Before birth I robbed you time
   and time again
You thought I was so cruel,
Time has aged—and so have we,
Let me explain to you—my sin.
I cheated you out of crooked bones,
They are mine for this life alone
I didn't want you to be all twisted,
I knew you'd marry—have
   children—a home.
I stole from you the unfinished
   heart,
Because it skipped a beat or two.
I knew you'd need the stronger one,
To offer the love inside of you.
Before departure from the womb,
I took from you—the cancerous
   cells.

I surely knew—you didn't need
   that,
So, inside of me it dwells.
Now you can understand—why I
   was so mean
But, I'd do it all over again.
I cared for your life—more than
   mine,
Kathleen—my sister—my twin.

Rhonda L. Morton
FEARS
People have fears and don't know
   why,
Some of them as large as the sky.
Sometimes my fears send a shiver
   down my spine,
And often I'll have more than
   one at a time.
I really don't know what causes
   these fears,
But I do know they may bring
   a few tears.
I have fears some old some new
But my biggest fear is of losing
   you.

Linda Sue Theado
SPRING IS SO BEAUTIFUL
Gentle is the warm breeze,
As it lightly blows through the
   trees,
The sun shining so very bright,
In the distance a young child
   happily flies his kite.
I wish this one day would never
   pass,
With such green grass,
And very pretty flowers,
Kept alive by light April showers.
Spring is so very nice,
As the sun melts away winters
   snow and ice.
What do you call a meadow this
   grand,
Paradise is what I call this land.

Anne M. Heller
DEHUMANIZATION
Darkness
Beckoning, enveloping
Sweet and warm
As an old friend.

Blackness
Mocking, taunting
Laughing at you
Stabbing you in the back.

Creatures
Rising, creeping
Slithering over you
Feeding on your dreams.

Parasites
Slipping, probing
Sliding over your mind
Sucking out all emotion.

Mutants
Laughing, gurgling
Stealing your ideas
Replacing them with slime.

Look now
You're brainwashed
Dehumanized
A clone of society.

Stosh Zielepuza
WHERE
Where is there one
Who is not afraid,
Not afraid to be accepted
With all his inconsistencies,

One who can be wrong
And need not fear apologies
For any misunderstanding
Because of the possibility of
Forgiveness.

Where is there one
Who is not afraid,
Not afraid to develop
His love for all life,
His passionate feelings for
The natural desires,
His sensitivity to the cares
Of others,
One who can be romantically
Illogical
Amidst his rational consistencies.

Where is there one
Who is not afraid,
Not afraid to dare
To be all he can,
To develop inclination
Without being satisfied with
His limited knowledge,
But will continually explore
Every ambition with a fresh
Candor.

Where is there one
Who is not afraid.
Not afraid
To be honest,
To be gentle,
To be human.

Joan B. E'Dalgo
ETERNAL CHRISTMAS GIFT
Christmas! Christmas!
    Everywhere—
Wonderful smells are in the air.
Cookies and cakes and pretty
    green punch—
Oranges and apples and candy to
    crunch.

Beautiful lights of red and green
Against the snow; a magic scene.
The bells are ringing out to say—
Merry Christmas to you, on this
    joyous day!

Big packages and small all under
    the tree,
I hope this big one here is for me!
As I have enjoyed this wonderful
    spree—
Have any of my thoughts been on
    Thee?

To be poor at Christmas is
    terribly sad
But Jesus was—poor little lad.
With love He left His heavenly
    home
And gave up the glory of a
    beautiful throne.

His life's blood bought a gift for
    me
Not like the others under the tree.
He died on the cross that I could
    be
In heaven with Him for eternity.

Marie Hudnall
CLIPPED WINGS
Together
We roamed the skies
My pilot and I . . .
Played tag with the clouds,
Danced with the wind . . .
Saw dawn break in the east,
Night rise from the quiet earth...
Measured

the changing face
Of the land below . . .
As bare fields blossomed
Grew green with summer's
    bounty,
Flamed with the colors of fall,
Gleamed white with snow . . .

Now I watch
The flash of sun
On silver wings . . .
Gaze at the flight of geese
Shadows across the moon . . .
As I stand alone . . .
Earthbound.

Jeanette M. Brown
SEA FARING CAPTAIN
Oh ship, great ship, I have waited
    for thee!
Thy fore-mast magnetizes my
    grave spirit.
Thy cadences of sureness on each
    wave
Assure my motive—and my word
    of merit.
Boarding your deck—my heart is
    brave;
I am enticed by your great seraph
    wings.
I am touched by winds and misty
    rhine-stones
And blessed with friendly rain-
    bow rings.

All cowardliness gone—
(Void all expensive and luxurious
    things)
Oh this my vow;
Abandoned from my native soil—
    "An exile now"
Relieved of earthly moil,
To one great God I bow!
I am master of terror in a deep-
    furrowed aisle,
Swift in celerity,
"I am captain!" with homage in
    my smile—
Facing Eternity . . .

John M. Quinones
PARANOIA BLUES
I've got those news paranoia
    blues again.
Much too much of such and such.
I've been overdone by information
from a factless void of a paranoid
    world.

Possibly it's those people I meet
vivid with scent from the dirty
    street;
that cause the colors to leave me
and thin odor to smother my
    dreams.

Dreamers must dream;
dream in bold faced type.
To dream in an irregular way
in altogether too regular days.

Dream . . . dream . . . dream.

Jody VanAckeren
TOMORROW
I believe in the morning
the sun will again rise
although the clouds think twice.
I wish from the rain
its warmth to shield you
all the years of your life.

Look ahead and see the sun set
on the never ending horizon.
Cast an eye and forget it not.
For I wish its beauty to follow you
all the days of your life.

Look behind and see your shadow
as love that walks nearby.
I wish in time for love
to find and keep you
all the hours of your life.

I wish you always a smile
to stay upon your lips.
I pray for you peace and happiness
all the minutes,
all the seconds of your entire life.

Nancy Lunsford Sperry
AUTUMN DAYS
For autumn days my heart still
    yearns
Of a country lane that twists and
    turns.

The smell of freshness in a breeze
As sunshine filters through the
    trees.

Leaves of bright colors unfold;
Browns, rusts, reds and golds.

With veins of life rushing
    through
For these memories my heart
    stays true

Crisp Autumn early walks
In a wood where every creature
    talks

A Melody played in my mind.
With the wind in the trees to
    help keep time

All the world in a single look
Mixed with wildlife underfoot

With these animals that forever
    play
All this makes for a glorious day.

Coy L. Calhoun
THE PROPHECY
Through a blanket of darkness, a
    fire boldly stares
At the shadows of man, and the
    life that he wears.
Don't bother to hide, laughed the
    fire, I'll just seek you out,
And the flames crept higher, as
    man scurried about.

Don't look back, they cried, or
    the flames may show
All the horrible things we don't
    want to know.
The past and the present, all
    stands for nought,
And a place in the future, no man
    has bought.

The perfect race, building the
    perfect world,

In spite of our perfection, the
    fires swirled.
The flames may show death, or a
    future exsistance,
So protect yourself, keep your
    distance.

But the fire was warm, and sent
    forth a light
Which beckoned mankind from
    the blackness of night.
So they warmed their hands, their
    bodies needing sleep,
They faced the fire, their minds
    gazing deep.

Then they stared in horror, but
    their eyes did not see,
And the millions cried as one,
    My God, that's me!

C.L. Earle
NEVER KNOWN
Aimlessly, not knowing, I strived
Growing, becoming more alive
A pointless journey towards life
It was nothing but strife.

I have ceased to exist
They can now scratch me off
    their list
It was all a mistake
But, for whose sake?

For what, of many reasons, was I
    stopped?
Why, from their plans, was I
    dropped?
Why is it I'll never be born?
Was it, after all a con?

Who would I have been?
What could I have been?
I was, now I never will be
Never, will see.

Was it a case of life's waste?
Or just a thoughtless point of
    haste?
Not saddened because I'll never
    know
Only because I will never be
    known.

Thaine L. Bell
TREASURE MAP
Forty below the center line,
Of the eye of the needle,
    The hook/The rest.
A trine of leaves,
As a cock's foot,
Held in the boney beak,
Of a descending dove.
Glittering golden,
In the dark night air,
Adrift on the sea,
Bits of wood and rations,
To build a better boat.

Mina Eiger
MATTER OF PRIORITIES
We have no time, we say
And our words are engraved in
Diaries of Flesh
Dear diaries of Flesh.

We have twenty-four hours a day
Which we have no choice but
    consume
And time is there
All our days it's there
And yet, no time, we say.

So busy are we
Not a minute to spare
So many matters are there
To arrange, to explore, to enjoy,

So we say, of we dare
And do not mean to tease,
It's just a simple matter of
Priorities.

And our words are engraved in
Diaries of Flesh
Dear diaries of Flesh
And the engravings say:
Some little bit of time could
perhaps be spared
But none of us could ever, never
be erased.

Darlene Lutinski
THE ROSE
*[This poem was inspired by
two special friends who made
me realize there are two sides
of everything in life—the
essence of beauty and the pain
of thorns.]*
Mystical, silent
and almost like a placid mirage.
Bloom it will,
All beauty is set forth,
containing
the essence of all that ever
was or will be.
But this is only a deception,
misinterpretation,
and a mere delusion to all who
seek its radiance.
The thorns are also a part of this
floral life,
For they ruin, condemn, and
destroy.
Reach out and touch it
New wounds can open
The scars of the past can be
remembered
Pain can conflict with joy.
But many look beyond
and some, not, and what do
they behold?

Miss. Dolores Franceen Schmid
CHRIST SATISFIES
Though my life is sad and dreary,
And my heart through mind is
weary,
Sight shall with joy divine
By trusting Christ as always mine.
Though I walk through paths of
sin
Troubled with thoughts stirred
within
I'll find my soul with God there
too
When this light called Christ
shall make me new.
Though I seek for worldly gains,
In time they bring some sad
refrains
Christ then comes—His light
shown with glory
Bursting in my heart, his precious
story.
Grant this blessing Lord above—
It's your son I want to love!
He is the light that makes men
free,
The time soon comes when we
then see,
That Christ alone can satisfy,—
The soul that seeks with inward
sigh.

Sandra Becktold Dahlquist
TEDDY BEAR
His fur dull and greyed,
Patches of it gone.

He lived a love filled life,
Full of pleasure, full of song.

One of his eyes is missing,
His stuffing is falling out.
His body half lop-sided
From being tossed about.

I hold him to me closely
And I think of all he gave
To the little boy that loved him
As together, they had played.

I think again of the times
When they snuggled together
close
Under the old patchwork quilt
That the little boy liked the most.

But then comes rushing back
The memory and the pain
Of that last dreadful night
And the drenching, freezing rain.

The little boy came in
Wet and sick and cold
Instead of staying inside,
Just as he'd been told.

He died that very night
With the little bear by his side.
And if the bear had had two eyes
He surely would have cried.

I must tuck him away now
To hide the pain that he can
bring.
But the little bear is special
And worth remembering.

Alison Goymer
THROUGH YOUR EYES
Through your eyes, the city in
summer,
Looks so alive, so fresh and
so new,
Through your eyes, the dream
won't diminish,
It will always be there, to
envelope you,
Through your eyes, the
pavements are pathways,
To lead you to friends, and
maybe to love,
Through your eyes, you'll never
be lonely
Not in this city, your heart
smiles above,
Through your eyes, the options
are endless,
So much to do with places to
roam,
Throuth my eyes, the picture is
different,
Through my eyes, I see only
home.

Steven T. Marlow
IF I HAD A WISH
*[Dedicated to P.J. You inspired
this and many other things in
my life. Thank you very much.]*
If I had a wish,
You know what that would be?
To paint a pretty sunset
For just your eyes to see.

The colors I would capture,
Red, gold, orange, and blue.
I would put them all on canvas,
Then give them all to you.

Or maybe I'd write a love song,
And give the song to you.
I'd put it full of precious words
To show my love is true.

But I know I'll never have you,
And this poem is all there will be,
So I'll keep it next to my heart
To soothe and comfort me.

Iva Jean Bowden

Iva Jean Bowden
LIFE IS LIKE A ROSE
Life is like a rose . . .
We plant it and each glowing
day . . . With hope on
tomorrow . . . We look and a
bud we see.
Life is like a rose
We visit the rose each day . . .a
petal we shall see.
And soon the rose is in full
bloom
And when we look today . . . the
storm came in the night and so
oh, so mysteriously blown the
rose away, life is like a rose.
Life is like a rose . . . with such
beauty and promise for all the
world to see.
But on tomorrow like the rose no
promise for you and me . . .
Life is like a rose.

Dawn McLeod
SWEET DREAMS
Hush, little one
hold your little teddy bear and
yawn.
Lie quietly
and feel you're safe and sound,
I'll stay with you
till you fall alseep.
Enjoy your sweet dreams
oh fall asleep, little one.
Hear soft music and a lullaby,
don't cry.
I will tell you a story
to last you through the night.
Think of sweet things
and count your blessings.
You'll stay safe all through the
night
until morn comes.
Oh little one,
Little one,
Hush.

Edna Nixon
OUR SEEING EYE PUPPIES
Hark! Do you hear the noise
outdoors?
Puppies and Children romp once
more.
In come the puppies with muddy
feet;
Out of breath, for something to
eat.

First the puppies must have some
fun,
Love and affection, a little sun.
A little patience will temper
them true,
You must give a dog confidence;
For the job he must do.
I am sure that my muddy floors;
God does not mind.
For we are raising eyes,
To lead the blind.

Catherine Stockton Lamb
THOUGHTS OF YOU
My thoughts of you I hold at bay.
But they, in turn, with patience
wait
In a shadowy, protected state
Just out of sight throughout the
day!
I push back images that stray
From some subconscious realm.
Of late
This quiet siege will not abate.
The daylight hours my will obey.
Will my defenseless sleep you
come
To storm the fortress of my mind
In dreams that sweep my guard
away
And lift my heart and soul into
some
Ether plane . . . fused into one
ecstatic kind
With you! Oh, dreams . . . hold
back the coming day!

Rebecca S. Taylor
A BRIGHTER PLACE
You put the stars in my eyes
that twinkle in the skies,
to bring the sun shining bright
into my world that had no light.
You brought a special glow to the
moon above
that reflects on the one I love,
For to me the light does shine
because my love at last you're
mine,
to walk through a world never
turning to night,
because at last my world is bright.

Tammy M. Spandl
THE RACE
Thank you, mom, for the many
things
You do for me each day.
The happiness your presence
brings
Is shown in many a way.
The encouragement you give to
me
Helps me finish the race;
Just knowing that beside me
you'll be
Lengthens out my pace.
If I finish first, but am not too
proud
To shake my opponent's hand;
You'll come to me and say it out
loud—
I'm proud of where you stand.
But if I'm not the first one there
To cross the finish line,
You'll let me know that you
really care.
You'll tell me I did just fine.
You encourage me to do my best
That winning's really great,
And not to quit but only rest

Although I may finish late.
When I feel that I have run
As far as I can go,
You'll say to me you aren't quite done
Finish—fast or slow.
With all these thoughts racing through my mind,
I'll have the strength to finish the race.
You've taught me that I can come from behind
And set a faster pace.
So when I cross the finish line
I'll see victory in your face.
Because we'll know that we're never alone
In the long, hard race of life;
We can run together side by side, as we've grown,
Sharing the victor's cup:
Defeating strife.

Paul C. Muhly
IT TAKES ONE
It takes one to feed one hungry child;
To show him love he may never know;
It takes one to tell him of Christ;
And the love that he showed.

It takes one to bring joy to a child;
Through a smile or a kind word;
Pick up a child and hug him;
And show him that you care.

It takes one to give a light to a child;
And make his world a little bit brighter;
It takes one to make all his dreams come true;
And turn all his sorrows into laughter.

It takes one to share time with a child;
Just take the time to get to know him;
God has prospered us while others suffer;
My friend won't you be that one?

Pamela Ann Piteo
SHATTERED SILENCE
Simple
I thought it would be.
They said it's easy as swingin'
from a tree.

Quiet
I thought it was.
Until I really started listening to hear
All the cires of anger
and the screams of fear.

James Huddleston
BATTLE FRONT
Amid soldiers of courage,
Under dimmed lights of
Refuge, the battle is waged.

Flickering flares highlight
Vacant, pearl white edifaces
That are but shadows of
Obscurity.

Through noises of distraction
The echo of shuffling, shifting
Feet penetrate the
Superficial ramblings of
Past victories.

In search of forgettable

Memories, hidden by clouds
Of misty smoke, lie the
Enemies of empty searches
And unfulfilled dreams.

Escape is ever fleeting.
Blinded by the addiction
Of survival, at any price,
Emerge the habits of
Destruction.

In these fox holes and
Trenches, the lonely
Fearful fighters face
Sleepless nights, so as
Not to be left out of
The hunt.

Above the roar of battle
A cry of anguish is
Heard, the order to charge,
"Bartender another round."

Frances Troxler Keogh
JULIE
Kiss me, I'm irish, you might hear her say
When gathering with friends on
Saint Patrick's day.

A red-headed beauty with a radiant glow,
She is one in a million—a joy to know.

Those eyes see no evil—only God's will,
While in this universe her life to fulfill.

As we parted ways, to lessen our loss
At the airport chapel we knelt at the cross.

Touching this life there is nothing but gain,
Not a trace of conflict—no scars from the pain.

God grant her life wholesome, supreme and divine;
And may she keep on touching this life of mine.

Mrs. Hazel Steward Murdock
RADIANCE
A moonbeam falls into my hand,
I try so hard to catch it
And hold it fast.
But when my hand is closed
It is empty.
Only an open hand catches radiance.

Maria A. Yemariamfere
THE SPIRIT OF FLIGHT
[With highest admiration I dedicate this poem to my heroine, that supurb black stunt pilot BESSIE COLEMAN]
Earth cannot hold me. I am for the sky,
As mounting boldly I ascend on high.
Prosaic is the earth. Too tame and mild.
I flee its grasp into the far blue wild.
Scorning the peaks I span the upper air,
On wings that conquer heights no eagles dare.
Swift soars my craft aloft on airy tides.
My heart sings while aloft my spirit rides.

With joy unbound I and my sky-borne steed,
Achieve the ecstasy of flight and speed.
Dauntless we two with agile easy grace,
Slip blithely down the long blue arch of space.
While fleet we plummet metal wings agleam,
The far horizon lies in mist adream.
Again we climb to float and glide and swerve,
Over and under in a spiral curve.
Rising so high that heav'n and we are one,
We challenge with bravado the bright sun.
Through snowy banks of cloud a realm of wonder,
We dart splitting their serried ranks asunder.
Amid these pristine clouds windswept and furled,
Is our true element, our white/blue world.
No more can I exist upon the ground,
Content and by its fetters chained and bound.
Therefore at life's end let my freed soul fly,
Into its paradise this infinite sky.

Tammy Pope
UNANSWERED QUESTIONS
Why do I have a voice to speak with,
    if no one listens to what I say?

Why do I have eyes to see with,
    if I can't see the beauty in an early morning sunrise?

Why do I have ears to hear with,
    if I don't understand what others are talking about?

Why do I have fingers to feel and touch with,
    if I can't feel what another is feeling in his heart?

And lastly, may I add,

Why am I myself and you yourself
    if no one will accept us the way we are?

Barbara McDonald
ETERNAL SPRING
Hypnotic dance, breath of pagan Gods.
Stillness hushed, song of birds from ancient winds.
Voices new, gift of myriad lips of Love.
Smiling dreams, radiant tears from up above.

Nancy Lee Johnston
THE MORNING'S CRY
The Morning's Cry
Awakes the sea,
Sets off the day
So sheds the tree.

In chill of day
To hot of noon,
So soon the spring
Gives away to June.

In gift of flowers

The sweet of roses,
So take my heart
In sad repose.

So misty harbor
Caress your shore,
So soon my love
I'll see no more.

So soon to pass
In quick of sorrow,
The morning's cry
In sad tomorrow.

Douglas Craig Prince
DOGS
[To my Aunt Judy, Aunt Jo, My Mother and Father, Reverend Pete Pearson and Dorothy Sowers. Thank you all!]
In this world of woman and man
Of earth and sky of sea and sand
In a world of human things
What joy your exsistance brings

The love I see that fills your eyes
That shakes the sea and lights the skys
Regardless of pain throughout the years
You share my love and my fears

Walking with me along life's way
You're with me both night and day
You're always right by my side
The love you have you cannot hide

So in this world of human things
And the joy your exsistance brings
So I know it's always been
The truth you are mans' best friend

Nancy Jensen
HEALTH HAZARD
A child makes a daisy chain.
In a serene field
. . . he touches cold metal;
He is scattered with the petals,
. . . from reality to oblivion.
It takes just a few seconds;
. . . a careless move in a minefield.

It takes twenty minutes
. . . to reach Armageddon.
It takes forever
. . . not to.
Which is easier?
. . . more practical?
. . . more fearful?
. . . more likely?
Can peace exist?

People follow orders
. . . like machines,
Mere extensions of their weapons;

. . . mutilating.
. . . murdering.

News correspondents are sent out,
To cover the story
. . . of mass murder.
They send this report:
  GREAT MACHINE OF
  DIPLOMACY DEAD stop NO
  LIFE IN WAR stop DEATH IS
  FINAL stop

STOP . . . for the children!

Lillian Payne R.N.

Lillian Payne R.N.
HAPPINESS
Each one is searching
For happiness—tis true—
Happiness can neither be bought
Or found—
Except for living for others—
Not you.
Reach out to someone to-day—
And let happiness find its way.

Carol Twardoch
ENDLESS TIME
*[For my songbird: From
September time to endless time
you are my love—always and
forever—yours]*
  Shine bright for me
  Your eyes, of love
  Speak eternally
  And I shall find you
  In any world
  Or any time
  For I am yours
  And you are mine
  We are one
  Forever
  In endless time

Charles R. Sudduth
I'M LOST IN LOVE
*[To Ms. Denise Williams, a gift
of God's love to me. Babe, you
have a special place in my
heart, where no one, which no
one else may enter . . .]*
I got you on my mind
and I hope my dreams come true;
Even if we live many miles away,
my heart will always be with
  you . . .
      . . . I'm Lost in Love . . .

I'm just like a tree
and you're my water;
As we combine together as one
we will never falter . . .
      . . . I'm Lost in Love . . .

You're my Apricot Sunset
and my old fashion girl;

you light up my life more, cause
you're the *finest in the world* . . .
      . . . I'm Lost in Love . . .

Our love will always be together
to fight the battles we should fight;
That what Lovers are, cause
our love is out of sight . . .
      . . . AND I AM LOST IN LOVE . . .

Michaeline Olejniczak
REMIND ME TOMORROW
*[To my mother, the rose bud
To my father, the seed]*
Remind me tomorrow to pick
  the rose bud, it's the last
  one in the garden.
The stems around her have
  all been snipped;
While fall is calling
brittle brown leaves to
hang on invisible threads;
around her awakening head.

I've watched her scarlet petals,
  spiral open slowly.
I've smelled her light
fragrance, that was hers only.
So, remind me tomorrow to pick
  the rose bud,
    she's the last one in
      the garden.

Nola F. Hammer
WEEPING WILLOW
Willow, Oh, Willow why do you
  weep?
  You have no worries, no secret
  to keep.
Your leaves are green and
  branches bending low
  You have no heart aches, no
  troubles I know.
You have no love story, no words
  to speak.
  Willow, Oh, Willow why do
  you weep?

You have nothing to do except
  stand and grow,
  The wind blows your branches
  to and fro.
You look very beautiful to
  passers by,
  You stand beneath the pretty
  blue sky.
You have no dreaming, no lying
  down to sleep.
  Willow, Oh willow, why do
  you weep?

You have no responsibility, you
  must be free.
  Why you are weeping is a
  mystery to me.
You have no head, you need no
  pillow
  Everyone calls you a weeping
  willow.
Your branches are long, your
  roots grow deep.
  Willow, Oh willow why do you
  weep?

Tanya P. Shubin
**Let Not Your Heart Be
  Troubled**
Let not your heart be troubled
Neither be filled with fears
For God is greater than all things
He'll wipe away your fears.

Let not the winds destroy you
Nor toss you to and fro
For God is peace in everything

He calms the slightest blow.

Let not your heart go weary
When everything goes wrong
For God is greater than despair
He fills our heart with song.

Let not your days be dreary
For there is hope above
God is greater than our needs
Because the Lord is Love.

It is His love that gives us peace
That wipes away each tear
Let not your heart be troubled
For He is ever near.

A. Lee Watson
PART TO START
*[To: Dads who run out on their
families]*
Partings upon partings,
  Almost sweet, like startings.
First we wait, . . . then hesitate.
  Sweet music greets,
the moment we meet.
  Almost sweet, like partings,
Startings upon startings

Diane K. Schlofer
INTERLUDE
Your face is solemn,
Your voice so disturbed,
You loathe being confined,
If only your concern would have
  searched ahead,
Your life now could be certain.
A sentence you must endure.
Your awareness of love and hope
  is powerful,
  and shall surely give you
  support.
You shall return to us,
  a desirable young individual,
With an earnest wish of useful
  existance.

Lee Ann Speary
OUR BEAUTY SHINES
*[To David—who was my
inspiration To Tami—who
never left my side To my sister
Nancy—And the Lord who
saved me]*
It's so easy to find beauty,
  If we just look inside ourselves.
We always seem to look at
  everyone else,
  Yet, ignore our turn.
When you feel good about you
  You feel good about others.
Once you've found your beauty
  You'll recognize it in those
  around you.
And if you're lucky enough,
  You'll find someone who sees
  this in you.
It's at this point
  That our beauty shines
  brightest.

Karen Jean Houll
I CAN'T SAY
*[Written to; and inspired by—
James Joseph Marron. In
dedication to—Kenneth Alan
Holloway—my real true love.]*
I can't say we had something
  together
Because we never had anything.
I can't say, don't leave me
Because you have never been
  here to leave.
I can't say, come back

Because we never had each other
  to come back to.
I can't pretend and think my
  dreams are coming true
Because they aren't,

And the way it looks now
They never will.

I can't sit here thinking of you
Hoping that you are thinking of
  me,
Because I know that you aren't.

But there is one thing I can do
I can love you,
And I can hope and pray
That someday,
You will love me too.

Maybe I will have that chance.

Craig Conlee Hill
**Black Widows and Cotten
  Candy**
Where Black Widows make
  lovely pets,
While butterflies are always in
  nets
Where poison will cure,
Medicines considered impure

Where stealing has permission,
Giving is forbidden
Where War is just a game,
Peace is not of fame

Where cotten candy is never sold,
Where guns are as priceless as gold
This is the City of NO GOOD,
Where every child is raised as a
  hood

This is the place where Bad is
  Good,
But good is not bad
Good is just a faded fad!

Ina Roll
EVERYONE LOVES
Everyone loves something.
The sailor loves the sea,
The bud loves the air,
The lion loves to be free,
A mother loves her daughter,
A sister loves her brother,
And he loves her.
I just wished you loved me.

Paul A. Allen
THE TANAINA
Where Arrigetch peaks wrapped
  in clouds
Reflect on waters sweet,
The bronze Tanaina, the white-
  haired ina,
Dried his neeted meat.

Where Chuckchi waves splashed
  with blue
Crest to the sea gull's tail,
The bronze Tanaina, the white-
  haired ina,
Speared the beluga whale.

Carved flint was bronze ina,
Son of oogruk and bear ina,
Maker of snare brave ina,
Who hunted the tundra plain.

Where kobuk sage whipped the
  winds
Ornate the valley floor,
The bronze Tanaina, the white-
  haired ina,
The mukluked ina, will track the
  earth no more.

Where Alaskan spruce splashed
with green
Shade the Lake Clark shore,
The bronze Tanaina, the white-
haired ina,
Will throw his net no more.

To eternal rest went ina, to the
Great Spirit went bronze ina,
The lodge is cold of ina, without
the soul of ina,
The mukluks mold of ina,
Who tracka among the stars.

Radford Riggles
I Cannot Dig That Shit
When lying in my bed alone, on a
Morning when the winds are still,
And the sounds of life are almost
nill.
I feel alone, and I cannot dig that
shit.

When I feel my endless drifting,
In the under currents of time.
I find myself stretching
Each second of the present,
And hopelessly imagining
The near events of my destiny,
And knowing that I cannot do this
I feel the pain of helplessness,
And I cannot dig that shit.

Angela K. Wallace
Now I Lay Me Down To Sleep
Now I lay me down to sleep,
I pray to you my love to keep.
If I shall die before I wake
I want to say this before
It's too late.
I want you to know,
I love you so.
Please,
Don't ever go.
You brought me to this,
And
Gave me a kiss.
That night,
You made things so right,
How can I say all that
I want to say?
I don't want things to change,
I want them all to stay
This way.
I won't pretend,
So I'll say it again.
Now I lay me down to sleep,
I pray to you my love to keep.
If I shall die before I wake,
I want to say this before it's too
late,
"I love you!"

Paul D. Swigart
THE MOMENT WAS REAL
[To Kathy Tenney In Christ's
love, Paul]
A kiss upon the evening breeze,
The softness in your eyes,
Reflections on a sea of glass,
And your gently woven sighs;
Caressed the glowing moondust
As it fell upon your hair
In a spray of lost tranquility
That flickered for an instant,
And then vanished
With the changing times,
As perfume in the wind.
The treasures of a moment
Carry lifetimes in their touch,
Leaving scars of joy and laughter
And a longing deep within,

For the spark which brought
comfort
In the winter's icy reach,
And the warmth of shared
embellishments
Which lighted love's eternal
flame
That flickers in the distance,
Destined someday to prevail.

Dean Edward Giraud Roberts

Dean Edward Giraud Roberts
CYNTHIA
[To my Cynthia—Miss Kelly
Zirkle, my once and only love,
my deepest love, my painful
love, my final love.]
When at night I close my eyes, to
think of all the days gone by,
to feel again those passions past,
and feeble joy that never lasts,
I'm always drawn to thoughts of
you, my only love,
                    my Cynthia.

I think I found you in a dream,
the night I pressed beyond the
seam,
where fantasy and reality meet,
in summer mist so soft and
sweet,
But you were all I ever felt, my
deepest love,
                    my Cynthia.

But dreams just last within the
night, when morning came,
            Her soul took flight.
I awake to find Her never there.
She passes like the misty air.
To leave me longing and alone,
my painful love,
                    my Cynthia.
Enigma love you swell the heart,
to crush the same when

lovers part.
But whether love and joy you
bring,
or bitter pain and Death's cold
sting,
I plead you come to me again, my
final love,
                    my Cynthia.

Nora S. Bennett,
THE ROSE
[To My Daughter, Carole]
When I look into your face I see—
Petals of soft velvet hue.
Eyes, like a pool of greenish blue—
In a shaded glen,
Fringed with dark lashes;
Sparkling with a tear or two.

Overshadowed by a mass of
beautiful curls—
Smiling, parted lips
Showing rows of purest pearls.

An ivory throat, encircled with
chains of gold, draped over a
heart
full of kindness and love—
My baby, my girl,
A gift from God above.

Marian Jackson Riggs
WASTED
I don't know what it is
that draws my heart to you.
Right now I feel so sad,
so melancholy blue.

While I was busy dreaming,
you started fast to drift,
and now I've lost another;
another precious gift.

Gone again is love,
a gift so heaven sent.
Gone the precious time.
All wasted; I repent

Matt Barnes
UNTITLED
[For David Rump—Thanks for
being my friend and remember:
Never stop chasing your
rainbows, 'cause your dreams
lie beyond the clouds. M.B.]
Steady your hand to a blind
child's eyes,
and try to see the world in which
he lives.
Turn your music down low
enough,
to hear a deaf child's song.
And think of the one confined in
a wheelchair,
when you choose to jog on the
beach.

C.L. Broskoff
THAT DADDY
Daddy you have never known me
I've been through times of thick
and thin
And you have not been around to
see.
Can you tell what this has done
to me?

Children have always had a
daddy it seems
And to them having one is to no
avail.
But there are those like me who
know not
What it is like to have a man
around.

Throughout my childhood I
realized with grief
That having lived my life thus far
without you
Has made me believe that I have
only me:
To guide myself through gloom
and despair.

I'm almost grown now and times
are looking good
And for a moment I almost
stopped and paused
To speak to a man that I never
knew.
But it wasn't you; it was another
boy's daddy, again.

Tim Lester
MEMORIES OF PAP-PA
I remember well the stories he
used to tell;
His image I remember so very
well.
The time we spent together as
one;
The time we shared made me
proud to be his grandson.

As we would sit under his
favorite tree,
The cats he so much loved would
climb his knee.
He never ceased to lend his hand;
He loved his home and loved his
land.
He would go in his shop and
diddle;
Nothing replaced the sticks he'd
whittle.

As he lay in front of me on his
funeral day,
He looked so peaceful, I'm sure
he wanted it that way.
He went as a proud man,
He went while working his land.

This is not the time to be grim;
Just be glad we all have memories
of him.
My memories of him will never
be erased;
In my heart and mind he'll never
be replaced.

Linda Phelps DeVaughan
BY MYSELF
[This poem was written to Jim
Lee, whose love and friendship,
I will cherish forever.]
By myself
I long to be
Just by myself
No one but me
No intruders
No interruptions
Nothing at all
But me
By myself

Peggy M. Klassen
WHAT IS A FRIEND
[To my friends who inspired it
and my mother, who made a
dream become reality.]
A friend is a person that you
meet each day,
Whenever you make a new start,
A friend is special in everyway,
That you carry deep in your heart.

A friend is loyal and trusting,
Whenever you tell them a
thought,

A friend is for laughing and
singing,
When you feel they like you alot.

A friend doesn't hate or despise
you,
Whenever you turn your back,
A friend doesn't laugh or stare at
you,
When there is something you
lack.

That's how I know that you are
my friend,
So please don't ever change,
Cause I like you just the way you
are,
And staying within my range.

Linda A. Kennedy
Ode Of a Summer's Love
*[To my son Tim who loves the
beach "To Charlie" your
inspiration made it possible]*
The waves beat on sandy shores,
As your love torments me more
and more.
The water gets warm and the sun
higher,
But, still, my heart fills with more
desire.
This feeling comes, day in—day
out,

Sometimes it is so strong I could
truly shout.
I sit and watch, the flying birds,
And hope, someday you will hear
my words.
For as sure as water goes out and
comes in,
If I can't be your lover—I will
always be your friend.

Janette Salas Calma
LOVE IN SILENCE
A silent evening down by the bay
With not a single word to say.
The look in your eyes is all I
need to see
If you really, really, care about me.

There's no need for words at
times like this
It's just perfect the way it is.
The only words I'd like to say are,
"I Love You!"
Please believe this because it's so
very true.

We can go through the rest of our
lives
Looking into each other's eyes.
At least we know what we feel
inside

It's this word called 'LOVE', we
just can't hide.

Karen Peterson
LONG VIEW
The coast lies like a broken
skeleton.
Bone bare except for a sudden
flash of
"For Sale" signs that scream
"Pick me! Pick me!"
Abandoned houses stare emptiness
to a world of non-buyers,
daydreamers that pass down halls
see children, and where they'd put
the Christmas tree.
Who watch themselves tanning
in summer
in the backyard of a home fallen
on hard times
and one they can't afford.

Daniel D. Shenck
MY FRIEND
I have a friend I think he's cool;
his name is Matthew Paul.
He has a sport he really likes; the
game is called baseball!
He's also blessed with terrific
looks that girls just can't resist.
And every time one passes by he
thinks they must be kissed!
I've never had a friend that's been
quite as nice as him,
I like the way he treats me, so I
always call him kin!
I talk to him alot and I really
think it's great,
To have a friend and brother that
you're never going to hate!
He's really neat and that's no lie,
although he's not too tall,
I'm proud of him for what he is—
his name is Matthew Paul!

William J. Bibel
Day Dreams—Interrupted
How soft the summer's gentle sky
As on my back in the meadow's
grass I lie,
And watch the clouds—in all
their wondrous forms go by.
The billowy shapes in rolling
masses hie
These lofty bodies with their
heavenly magic ply
An unendless parade—before the
sun they vie.

And I am lulled into a tranquility
of mystic daydreams,
As they impose their magic of
hypnotic schemes.
And carelessly my imagination
into fantasy gleans,
A world of myriad shapes and
never ending themes.

But all too soon a reminding
voice of reality screams
For my return, to this, and that,
and all such things.

Darlene Schildman
BEAUTY
Beauty is something
more radiant than skin;
It's something to cherish
it comes from within.
It's really so easy
for you to possess
The poorest can have it
among all the rest.
You can't walk in a store
and purchase the thing;

It's something much bigger
than money can bring.
It's the smile on your face
and love in your heart;
It's loving your neighbor
and doing your part
To make his life happy
and rich as can be;
It's doing for others
not doing for me.
It's speaking no evil
of people you know;
It's spreading happiness
wherever you go.
When having accomplished
this beauty within
You'll have the true beauty
God meant for all men.

MaryAnn Toporcer
NANCY
I'd like to thank you
for all the things you've taught me.
Believe it or not—you're the
model
that I try to live up to and
I admire
the things you do and the way
you live.
If I could ever be the friend to you
that you've been to me—
it would be one of the greatest
accomplishments
of my life.
You are truly a gift from God
who showed up in my life at
exactly the right time.
Your presence here gives
me such a security
but your absence would leave
such a void
that neither time nor space
could ever fill it.
Whatever time takes away from
us—
I hope it never steals our
friendship
or love for one another.

Todi McGuire
CHRIS' POEM
*[This poem is dedicated to my
Nephew Christopher, who
makes the world a whole lot
nicer. Keep smiling Chris, we
all need to see that happy face
of yours.]*
To run with the wind
and jump in dry leaves;
To catch the rain water
adrip from the eaves.

To skip and to hop
and be merry and gay;
To chase butterflies
on a warm sunny day.

To fly a kite
way up in the sky;
To build a house
in a tree so high.

To have lots of friends
with whom to share;
To laugh with, have fun with
and show that you care.

To ice-skate, play hopscotch
and ride horses too!
To have a whole day
to spend at the zoo.

To see a gull
take to the sky;
Or better yet

to hear its cry.

To romp with a puppy
and giggle with glee;
To walk a tight-rope
or just climb a tree.

To be able to smile
for no special reason;
And dress oneself
no matter the season.

To be able like others
to think and talk;
To be able to stand
to be able to walk.

To be happy or sad
whatever you choose;
Not always possessing
those down-cast blues.

To be able to run
both free and wild;
Such is the dream
of a handicapped child.

Annis Williams
WHISPER, WIND
Whisper, wind, whisper
In the ear of the listener.
Tell your age-old story
Of the world's sorrow and glory.

Tell of the mountains tall
Reaching up to the tower over all.
Tell of the restless sea
Endless, ever-moving, and free.

Tell of man's greatness and
despair,
His fallen empires and cities fair.
Tell of the limitlessness of his
mind
And of his cruelty to his own kind.

But, wind, tell not to one
Of the things I have done.
Let my secrets go unheard with
me
To my grave; untold as it should
be.

Let me lie in silent peace,
Unknown and still in my release.
One soul among many great
Standing equal at the Golden
Gate.

Stormy L. Monday
HAPPINESS
*[To my wife, Brenda my
daughter, Misty and my son,
Jesse Miles, with all my love.]*
Strolling sandy beaches or Park
Avenue are places we'd all like
to be.
Alone on an islnd with a
beautiful lady or flying through
the air feeling free.
What more would you ask from
this lifetime 'crept wine,
women and song?
What more could there be but
adventure to last you your
whole life long?
But stop long enough to smell the
flowers . . . keep rhythm to the
tune that you hear . . .
Let love be a voice found inside
you, crystal faith be the road
you steer.
Let truth be your present to
others, so more often they give
it to you.
And friends be an ocean you
swim through, your heart

touching those special few.
Life is the fortune God gave us,
   time is our diamonds and gold . . .
Those who love to the fullest
   find Happiness in growing old.

Teresa Cline
LOVE IS REAL

The love I had was surely real;
   All his kindness I could feel.

A special someone I'd always
   searched for;
He was loving and sweet, and a
   whole lot more.

We were engaged for just a short
   time;
But I had hopes he would
   always be mine.

When out of the blue a fuss did
   start;
I couldn't believe we'd have to
   part.

My love for him will always be
   there;
Even though I know he doesn't
   care.

At my bedside I will kneel;
   And pray, someday the hurt
   will heal.

I would never forget how we once
   did feel;
Or stop believing that LOVE IS
REAL.

Maggie Magee
YOU

The gentle evening breeze,
cool in the morning sun,
puts my mind at ease,
as you and I are one.
Being in your embrace,
the love held in your eyes,
your tender loving face,
my passions all arise.
The closeness as we walk,
wet dew upon the grass,
your voice as we talk,
a promise as we pass.
your reflection in the glass,
wanting you the way I do,
my passions can't surpass,
the way that I love you.
All these things you gave to me,
you took away my fears,
made my eyes begin to see,
as you brushed away my tears.

Tricia L. Taylor
WHEN FALL COMES

Fall comes only once a year
Leaves fall and squirrels cheer,
When the cold comes around
The ground hogs go underground.

When the birds fly south
You know it's getting cold,
But the squirrels are bold
Becuase they know they have a
   home.

But then the snow covers the earth
And the wind blows hard,
Snow covers our yard
It's cold all day long.

Michael J. Costello
FREE SPIRIT

This is a poem for a special lady,
we're both the same, wild and crazy.
She is as kind as can be,
both happy and free.
The lady which I speak of,

is by far my true love.
She is my only mother,
which you'll never have another.
She has shared her love,
and promised we meet above.
I do believe we shall,
because we're friends and pals.

She tells me what life's all about,
she tells me to stay calm and not
   to shout.
She loves me for sure and that's
   no lie,
so we will never have to say good
   bye.

Vincent A. Roth
DRIFTING

Drifting down the river,
Floating with the wind,
Looking forward to the time,
Alone with you again.
Looking to the quiet times,
Looking to the night,
Hearts adrift on life's lovestream,
Evening's midnight flight.

Mary Howard Blackman
MAN SCULPTURE

A block of human flesh,
Cast upon the earth.
A delicate material,
Of undetermined worth.

With love or without,
It grows by supplement and time,
And before its death,
A soul within a rind.

Shaped by ancestry,
At least to some extent.
But, charactered much more,
By whom its time is spent.

Dan Wright
YOUR GIFT

My heart had no music,
So you taught it to sing.
My soul had no hope,
So you gave it a dream.
My life had no purpose,
So you gave it a goal.
Now, I am yours,
Heart, mind, body and soul.

Kay Martin
SECOND CHANCE

*[To all couples whose marriage
is being torn asunder with nit-
picking, nagging and nerve
wracking criticism of the
other's performance. Turn off
anger, replace with love.]*
I reach out to touch but you're
   not there
And the warmth of your arms has
   disappeared
I need your advice for that
   decision to make
This terrible loneliness is more
   than I feared.

I falter and stumble, I know not
   the way
I turned you off when your
   demands were so great.
Why couldn't we see each other's
   wants?
Or the emptiness that surrounds
   when you lose your mate?

My eyes heavy with sleep are
   suddenly apart
Sounds in the kitchen, put me
   back on the beam.

Thank God—you're still here,
   we're not apart!
You haven't left me, it was just a
   bad dream!

Lord, make me worthy to now
   follow *YOUR* plan
Of caring and sharing and with
   love so deep.
Thank you for giving me another
   chance
You've opened my eyes and not
   just from sleep.

Jean Lassiter Wyche
DEFINITION OF LIFE

Life is but a ball of yarn,
textured smooth and coarse.
Variations of color, sometimes
   stained
Ever unwinding with tangles
   along
the way; Yet lying await to be
   made
into something beautiful.

Betty Jean Lovelace
I'M A GIRL

*[To Tracy Ann Richmond, my
daughter, who has given me
inspiration and much love.]*
Who said I had to be a girl today?
   I'd druther have been a boy.
Girls play with dolls and cute
   clothes,
   Boys get to pull hairs off
   wooley worms
Then find them gooey green
   inside.
   It's much more fun to wind a
   big worm
And catch a slippery fish on the
   hook.
   Why do girls just stand there
   and cry?
I'd druther give that bully a black
   eye.
   If you hit him just right on the
   nose

Both eyes will turn purple, green,
   and then close.
   My Mother tried to make me
   all dainty and frills,
But I'd kick off my shoes and
   head for the hills.
   She tried her best to make a
   lady of me
But I'd druther pull wings off flies
   just to see
   Can they really fly upside down
And land on the end of your nose?
   But my Mother told me that I,
   was a girl!

And when I found out it was
   really true
   The weed turned to violets,
   some purple, some blue
And I found out things
   adventurous, and new.

Stormy Rebecca Thew
ANOTHER HEAD

Long, short, thick, thin, blond,
   brown or red
braided, twisted, cut and curled
hair through fingers lead
to styling, dying and blowdrying
'till it's set just so
all ready for another week . . .
now out the door you go!

John Powers
RAINDROPS, TEARDROPS

I looked and saw,
But did not see,
The flower upon the wall.

It sat there growing,
Further up.
It grew to be so small.

And when it rained,
it really pained.
For it could not support,

The weight of teardrops,
On it's petals,
From me standing over it.

Jane Cannell
BIG E

He was only a boy when he
   started out,
The show was his life, without a
   doubt,
The ferris wheel lured him, he
   liked it best,
But in nothing flat, he knew all
   the rest . .

He stayed around for seventeen
   years,
Climed to the top without any
   fears,
He'd stand at the cook house, a
   grin on his face,
Knowing his crew had the rides
   all in place.

The years rolled by, he knew he
   was free,
Then along came a girl, and
   babies three,
He left the show, the rides and
   the games,
But life since then, hasn't been
   the same . .

Now he drives the Prince Rupert
   run,
Everyone thinks he's having fun,
But his heart's not in it, we'd dare
   to say,
He's with the carnival all the way.

Each week he's home with the
   kids and wife,
Content to have a real home life,
Will he come back? Nobody
   knows,
But he's always remembered
   around the shows . .

Patricia Yivonne Smith
PRECIOUS MOMENTS

Do not grieve, my friend.
It is not yet to be the end.
You have been given
a few more weeks or days.

How will you shoulder the grief
and pain of knowing?
God will show you ways.
Live life for now and to the
utmost.
Against fear you do dare hope.
Love her and let her know it.
Don't hide it or suppress it.
She needs to know you care.
Just be there to give her strength
when she grows finally weak;
be her voice when she cannot
speak.
Share all you can . . . the laughter,
the evening strolls.
Death has not yet begun to toll.
Prescious moments are waiting.
Don't grieve now and waste them.
Tears are for later, to be
shed alone into your pillow
when you are all alone, or
with a friend like me who
understands.
You both need happy moments to
remember.
Let the joy of living and of
laughter
ring out like church bells.
Love her now and let her know it.
These are, indeed, precious
moments.

Kathleen Jackson
UNREAL, REELED IMAGES
*[With Love, to my parents,
Hazel & Q. T. Jackson for your
inspiration, and many hours of
patience. For Nickey, for whom
this poem is written and to
Katherine, Sharon, Letetia,
Erica, Terry & Carl, my
beautiful sisters and brothers.]*
I didn't know if it was a dream
Or reality
    Or if life had secretly
        Played some kind of
            game on me.

The only real security I had
    Was the love
        That we both knew.
    But you sufficently
        Served my spirit
            As unreal images
            reel through
                my mind
                Of a life
                    spent with
                    you.

Rubina Ann Cooney
**To MomMom Miraglilo,
My Treasure**
With the face of a queen and,
the smile of the moonlights beam
My grandmother to me, is much
    more than a dream.
To me she is the finest person to
    be seen.
She is a gemstone of Emerald
    greens.
She is a marble statue tall and
    lean,
with Rubies and Garnets placed
    upon her dresses seam.
Her radiant smile is that of cream
Soft and joyish as an endless
    stream.
Her knowledge is a must for me
    to acquire
Because, MomMom has the desire
to teach us the truth of what life

requires
She is not a woman who is old
    and mean
But my grandmom, is a woman in
    her teens,
Who follows God and treasures
    His lifelong dreams.

S. J. Traxler
BEGINNING
My heart cries
    that I'll do my best
To lead and guide you
    through your childhood cares
To pick you up
    and kiss your hurt
To wash away
    the tears and dirt
To make you know
    my love for you
Has no end
    only a Beginning

Ruth H. Worley
JUST AN OL' TREE
It was just an ol' Blackjack, a
    sight for sore eyes.
But God created its inner beauty
    without using brushes, paint or
    dyes.

We cut off small slices, just to
    see the inside. The design and
    shades of color from us it could
    not hide.

They come in all sizes, shapes
    and designs. When you look at
    God's creation, inner beauty
    you will find.

We had a use for this tree, it was
    cut for firewood. So you see,
    that ugly ol' Blackjack was
    used for something good.

So is our life with Christ . . .
    others only see the outside. But
    we can have that inner beauty
    if in Christ we abide.

Robert K. Thompson
EPIDERMOLYSIS BULLOSA
*[I would like to dedicate this
poem with much love to my
wife Gail and our son Gregory,
11, who have dedicated their
lives to our other son Jeffrey,
10, who is a victim of
Epidermolysis Bullosa.]*
With hopeful eyes and aching
    hearts
    We watched as they rose each
    day
To face the endless agony
    And battle through another
    day.

We could not know what they go
    through
    For it's hidden deep inside
But we tried to soothe their little
    hearts
    With a hug and tears we cried.

To Michelbach the children came
    With a rare and painful past
To find the man they knew by
    name
    Who could rid their hurt at
    last.

As days went by and hopes grew
    high
    We could see the journey's end
Tears fell less and smiles showed

more
    Mr. Kozak passed the test.

For now their wounds are finally
    closed
    And the scars they hardly show
And it don't hurt them half as
    much
    As it did a year ago.

Kathleen Patterson
LITTLE ONE
"Little one, it's time for school."
You've grown up so fast.
Once you used to crawl to me,
Now, that's long, long past.

"Comb your hair and brush your
    teeth."
Where have gone the years?
That wee first step, that you
    took,
Brought us joyful tears.

"Here's your lunch, and off you go.
Don't forget your coat."
You used to have a Teddy Bear,
Everywhere you'd tote.

"Hello, Sweetheart. How was
    school?
Did you find your friend?"
It used to be with Mom and Dad,
All your time you'd spend.

"It's dinner time, come and sit.
Bring your daddy, too."
You used to sit way up high.
Now, too big are you.

"Come to bed and I will read
A story to you now."
You're not too big for this yet.
I'll keep you young somehow.

A mother's child grows so fast.
It's too hard to keep
Them little for much longer.
Their own life they must reap.

Janis Bomar
A MUCH NICER WORD
In the world today with its
    changing times,
We give things new words to ease
    our minds.
The label has changed, but the
    meaning's the same.
The act is still wrong, but no one
    is blamed.

Marriage is no longer "till death
    do us part. ."
Just fill out the papers and make
    a fresh start.
Incompatible is the reason when
    the judge asks why.
It's much easier to quit, so why
    should we try?

We don't say adultery; it would
    mean disrespect.
So we call it an affair, and that we
    accept.
If it's coated with sugar, it's easier
    to take.
It may sound sweet, but it's still a
    mistake.

When a woman is pregnant with
    a child unwanted,
She changes the name so her
    memories aren't haunted.
She can't have her life thrown all
    out of proportion,
But she won't call it murder—
    she'll call it abortion.

And if it upsets us to take a
    child's life,
We must think up a word to
    make it all right.
For this thing called humanity,
    we can't let it beat us.
We won't call it a baby—we'll call
    it a fetus.

Women with women and men
    with men—
It's wrong, but we accept it again
    and again.
We can't say homosexual, for that
    sounds absurd!
We'll call them all gay; it's a
    much nicer word.

So if there's a sin that pains you
    inside,
That tears at your soul, and from
    which you can't hide,
Just give it a nice name, one you
    can bear.
It will still be a sin, but no one
    will care.

Dr. Norman L. Dodge, Ph. D.

Dr. Norman L. Dodge, Ph. D.
HER BED
Not even a California sun
Can warm her bed as I.
At least—she tells me that
And she don't lie.

A. Gerald Whittier, TH. D.
GOD AND MAN
The Ancient Phophet one time
    said,
    As He spoke for the people's
    benefit . . .
"This is the Day the Lord has
    made,
    Let us rejoice and be glad in it."

And today, God still makes each
    day,
    As He sends the sun's rays
    down to men . . .
So 'Light' or 'Dark' shall mark the
    way,
    As men shall travel God's
    Ways again.

Men cannot change the Plans of
    God,
    And make the snow into a
    warmer clime:
Nor can they take the heat and
    sod,
    And make a warmer or a cooler
    rhymn.

Men find the temperatures all too
    wrong . . .
    Too rainy ! Too wet! Or, too dry

for crop!
Too hot for work! Too cold for a
Summer Song!
Men wish the sun would shine,
or make the cold to stop.

Yet today, as it was in the
Long-ago;
God makes all the rules, so
men may walk with Him.
Though the day may be one that
God would show,
He may hold back, making the
'Day' to shine through Him.

Barbara Lee Tweedy
FLOWERS & FANTASIES
Flowers and Fantasies—Rainbows
and Dreams
are they really meant to be?
Such fragile things, just wisps of
the winds,
But important parts of our
schemes.

Can we live without them?
Should we even dare try?
Would we really want that to be?

I don't know about you,
But I know as for me,
That until the day I die,

I'll keep my Flowers and
Fantasies—
Rainbows and Dreams,
And keep reachinng for the sky.

Mildred S. Kinsley

Mildred S. Kinsley
GIVE ME TIME
Give me time to get accustomed
To the neat uncluttered room,
Where her dresser has been
emptied
Of her pictures and perfume,
To the chess board by the window
That is polished, waxed and
bare,
Where the TV stands so silent
And the stereo doesn't blare.

Give me time to get adjusted
To the endless days ahead,
When her voice no longer answers
And no footsteps softly tread.
Give me time, dear Lord, I pray
thee
Guide me through the lonely
years,
And with your love and mercy
Give me time to dry my tears.

Mildred E. Olson
A LONELY VIGIL
Stark and gaunt against the sky—
It keeps its lonely vigil,

Holding itself aloft,
As a monument to all the dreams
Which lie—
In smoldering ashes at its feet.

The hopes and dreams of two
hearts—
A cottage on a hill,
The wedding gown, a bridal veil,
A baby's high chair, blue.
Love letters tied with ribbon bow
A teddy bear with ragged ears,
The wee one's crib, a little shoe—
Sweet memories gathered
through the years.

How little we can count as ours
To call our treasure on this
earth—
The efforts of our labors sore—
The home so filled with joy and
mirth,
All wiped away—were ours no
more.
All that remains—a chimney tall
Which towers o'er a cellar wall.

Marian B. Cortvriendt
HUBBY'S RETIRING!
"For better or worse" is all well
and good.
"In sickness and health" is, of
course, understood.
Retirement now is the name of
the game.
After hubby retires, nothing's the
same.

Now, Saturday and Sunday come
every day.
All of a sudden there's nothing
but play.
No office to go to, no one to boss;
No wonder some days h'ell be at
a loss.

With patience and humor,
changes you'll make,
As this new life style, you
undertake.
Happy Hubby's Retirement, I'm
wishing you,
And good health your whole lives
through.

Cheryl L. Myatt
MOM
Because you have always cared
And your life you have always
shared.
Because you always know the
right thing to say
And you're the only one who can
make my day.
Because you mean so much to me
And the good only your eye can
see.
Because life is eternal with your
love
And I thank my God up above,
For He gave me you as my
mother
And for me there will be no other.

Marilyn Goertzen
FEELINGS
*[To my loving husband Walter,
who gave me life with hope,
unleashed my heart and opened
my mind. Thank-you!]*
What is this state that I am in?
This feeling deep within me.
I cannot think, but think of him,
When last we met, when next we

meet.
What is it that makes me so,
I grope about, no goal in mind.

Without his light, dims my sight.
The hours are days—the weeks,
years.
All smiles are thin, all laughter
shallow.
All paths are long, all thoughts of
h-i-m.
When I'm with him, the sun it
shines,
To be near him, to feel his touch.
His carressing love, his lips on
mine, to fall
But not to fall, but rather drift.
In an endless deep blue sky
Wherein contentment lies.

What is this state that I am in?
These feelings deep within me—

June A. Boswell
HAPPY BIRTHDAY
Bored middle of life, hiatus of
indecision
Crying for change.
Why is it so hard to stand still in
the niche of life
Goals met, dreams dreamed,
Plans planned?
So hard to say this is the way it
is,
What I wanted,
Who I wanted to be?
What can you do when your
dreams come true?
Where do you find more dreams?

. . . Or courage to live the old?

Denese M. Daniels
This Last and Final Journey
In this last and final journey,
I have traveled the earth so wide.
Many I did meet.
Through these last days of life,
I wonder with pride,
Unwilling to see defeat.

It does not matter now,
Where my ventures have led.
Whether beside roaring rivers
that now for me lay still.
To mountain tops, where my
spirit confindes,
in the wonderous beauty that
natures hides.

Back through time my soul does
ponder,
not wanting to give up the
splender it beholds.
The secrets that time has
befallen.

This last untroubled journey
nears its final end,
and my body lies quietly under
the murmuring pines.
While death takes its final toll.
No pain do I bare, or not knowing
do I fear.
I cannot see the darkness any
longer,
which came to me,
at this last and final journey.

R. Wayne
THE EAGLE
From my mountain way up high
I'll watch the people go passing
by.

In their hugh machines of metal
so bright
they move thru the air, but it
doesn't seem right.

They break up the clouds and
blot out the sun.
they dirty the air—yet they still
are not done.

How can I keep up with such a
pace?
will a bright metal object soon
take my place?

I have lived on my mountain
since the beginning of time
but what will become of these
off-spring of mine?

I remember so well when the air
was clean
I remember also the fish in a
stream.

Why do these people spoil my
sky?
I know all can live here-not just I.

They must all work together to
clean up the land
and treat mother nature with a
gentle hand.

If they would just heed this
lesson of mine,
we would all share this earth for
a long, long time.

Bodil Petersen Bratvold
If Love Should Cease To Be
*[To my family, Owen, Rik,
Ellen and Tom.]*
If love should cease to be,
Understanding would go.
Friendship would be obsolete
And faithlessness would grow.

A child's merry laughter
The world would never hear.
Gentle sounds of nurturing
Would be replaced by fear.

If love should cease to be,
There would be no sharing.
Giving would be out of style.
People would stop caring.

Nations would fight nations.
Nowhere could one be free.
Life would be as nothing,
If love should cease to be.

M. Jean Ridge
JUST REMINISCING
We have been granted, riches
beyond compare,
With our "families" so young,
strong and fair,
Our "God" has indeed been good,
and let us see,
Carolyn blossom into a lovely,
young lady to be.

Please honey, never lose your
happy laughter,
Always learn to get, what you go
after,
Oh! How we love you, Lynette,
Randy, Chris, and Pam,
We grieve for all the baby ways,
we must aband.

You are all so sweet, and fair of
face,
May you each be wise, and full of
grace,
"God" grant we do see, the new

baby, from "Heaven" above,
Created by "Him", to be cared for,
and given our love.

The days go, and the nights come,
Our thoughts and prayers, are
with you, thru each one,
In years of health, and sickness,
we have stood, side by side,
Time races on, now it seems, we
are drifting, with the tide.

For when you grow older, hair
streaked with grey,
We can't make plans, like we did
yesterday,
So now we wait, and ask our
"Lord", what to do?
Our Carolyn is married now, has
a baby son too.

No "grandparents" were ever,
more proud of our families,
than we,
"Lynette", "Randy", "Chris", and
"Pam", all grown, beautiful to see,
My "sweetheart" has left me, to be
with our "Lord" in "Heaven",
Never to see, or give our first,
"great grandson" his love.

Tis very sad, and so true, but
truly is "life",
Given time, surely will happen,
to each of you,
Always remember this, "God" is
"good" and "God" is "great",
And that, "He will watch over
you", is no mistake.

E. F. Palazzo
THANKS
Hey girl,
I bet you've been hearing those
songs on the radio,
And wondering who they might
be about;
Because from that inspiration to
those certain color eyes,
The songs mean you without a
doubt.
And the people now are asking me,
Who is this girl in your song?
And I lie to them with this
simple answer,
That you've just been in my head
all along.

You see,
There was a time when I was
nothing,
And my confidence was so damn
low;
But when you sat and talked to
me,
You made me believe in my own
rainbow.
And then I opened up my mind,
And let the thoughts begin to
make;
Those songs of women and my
love,
And how it ends with a lonely
heartache.

So girl,
I'm glad we had some time to
share,
Some moments in a peaceful bliss;
So now I lean over to you,
And on your cheek I'll plant a kiss.
For It's just a little something,
What it is I can't explain;
But it's the best way to tell you,

That because of you I found the
train.

For I only wanted to say one word,
To tell you what you've meant to
me;
So before my mind does simply
go blank,
With all my love I'll just say
thanks.

Betty Ball Voorhies Denton

Betty Ball Voorhies Denton
IN THE LUPIN
*[Reminiscing in Crockett,
California I dedicate this poem
to my husband Jim my Son
Donald Wayne Voorhies and
his family With all my Love.
Recalling the beauty of the
winding road to Putah Creek.]*
There was A Springtime
Long ago
A lovely day
Where the Lupin did grow

You took my picture
While I sat on A rock
We only smiled
We never talked

A moment captured
long ago
In the springtime sun
Where the Lupin
Did grow

My faded picture
Has been put away
But my memories
Are bright in my mind today

Of A Springtime of fun
Taking pictures that day
On A rock in the Lupin
Far far away

J. R. Simons
THE RAINBOW
The wind, the rain, the howling
storm
Beat against the window of my
room,
But, after the terror of the wild,
wild night,
In the morning there arose a
rainbow from the gloom.

I awoke to see it stretched across
the sky,
A wondrous sight it was, to be
sure,
And in its grandeur, I felt so small.
I was small; it was great and
mighty, awesome and pure.

I watched its wav'ring lights and
shifting hues,
A mighty halo 'round the earth,
And I felt my heart grow great
and strong,
Full of life, laughter, love, and
mirth.

But, as is true with all good
things,
The mighty rainbow must come
to an end.
So, slowly, it did from tip to tip,
It seemed to shorten and
unbend.

'Though now it's gone 'til next it
rains,
The mem'ry of the rainbow
lingers on,
A beautiful thought, intangible
yet real,
A wonderful remembrance,
even though it's gone.

Rebecca M. Lane
INSANE SOCIETY
Control yourself
Listen, but don't speak
Laugh, but not aloud
Love, but not without permission
Express yourself, but only to
yourself
Make peace, but don't disturb
Investigate, but don't trespass
Enjoy the scenery, but don't loiter
Eat, but only for a high price
Contribute, but don't interrupt
Console, but don't pity
Join in, but mind your own
business
Share, but don't be pushy
Wish, but don't be greedy
Be proud, but don't be conceited
Suggest, but don't brainwash
Observe, but don't stare
Sleep, but be alert
Throw away, but don't waste
Be truthful, but don't criticize
Have faith, but don't be gullible
Trust, but don't confide
Live, but do it quietly
Universal crisis

Margaret Strickland
GOD'S GIFT
A child is something very sweet
They're sent for us to love,
A gift to treasure on and on,
From God's house up above.
A woman is a blossom rare
God gives to every man,
To worship and protect her
And lead her by the hand.
And man is Oh—so brave and bold,
And woman is their toy
They want to be so big and strong,
When they're just a little boy.
You take a man and make him King,
And woman is his Queen
Give a child for them to love,

And they have everything.

Debra L. Colwell
TIME FOR ME
The rising run explodes so bright
Life has begun in the city today
The noise of sound, the sound of
noise
Don't look back just take me away

Country living is my time for me
City living is my time for you

I'd rather be where my heart's
fulfilled
Where seasons change as if on cue

The flowers bloom in glorious color
Some of the names of which
nobody knows
But in the country their beauty
astounds
A captivated audience for mid-
summer shows

A slower pace, time to think
Peacefulness, like a backwoods
stream
Where birds can sing and I can
breath
And life is not a distant dream

Betty Phillips
NATURES' LOVE
I love the sound
of the early dawn,
And the sun as it brightens
the day.
I love the breeze and
the wind in the trees.
Natures' wonders are
all on display.

I love the sound
of a running stream,
And the sun as it sets
in the west.
I love the wet rose, that
an Angel has kissed.
All the wonders of God
I love best.

Carolyn Ann Allen
A RUMBLE OF THUNDER
A distant rumble of thunder
sounds.
The air is filled with the baying
of hounds.
Behind the pack the eager
hunters ride.
The fox, they so gaily seek, in
fear must hide.
The anxious hounds are closing
on their prey.
The enthusiastic hunters are
forever cheerful and gay.
The pack never strays from the
trail.
Over hill and dale in wild chase
they sail.

In sheer panic the hunted fox
flees.
Close behind, the angry mass of
dogs, he sees.
Suddenly the fox is confronted by
the pack!
He turns to run but finds there is
no way back.
The hunters ride to their catch
with pride.
Toward the fox with raised guns
they stride.
The shots are muffled by the
baying hounds.
A distant rumble of thunder
sounds.

I can't help but imagine how the
hunters would feel
If the fox ever had a chance to
point that cold barrel of steel.

Derek Gilman
WHO?
Slowly the world turns on its axis
Endlessly rotating, as day melts
into night.

This giant opalescent sphere,
  hurtling through space
Revolving pointlessly around the
  fiery orb
What spectre casts his wayward
  glance upon the planet?
What god raises his eyebrows and
  smiles contentedly
Knowing his creation is damned?
Doomed protoplasms bent on self
  destruction
The lemming race of mankind
  rushes into the sea.
Tell me the name of the deity
  who rejoices
In our foolishness,
The unpronounceable name of
  the master clockmaker.
Let us pray to this infinite entity
So our silliness will not be in vain.
Let me find happiness in the rape
  of my sister.
Let me justify the slaughter of my
  brother.
Listen carefully children, the
  theocrats know all.
What symbol should I worship
The Cross, the Phallus, or the
  Sword?
I've been told it's all the same.

Harold James Douglas
TELL THEM NOW
Tell people about the way you
  feel, that they might know
  your love.
Tell them that you value the
  things they do for you and
  others.
Tell them that you are pleased in
  helping with their distresses
  and difficulties.
Tell them you are saddened if
  you have done, or said,
  something bad or wrong.
Tell them that you are happy for
  them when good things happen
  in their lives.
Tell them that you weep with
  them when heartbreaks come
  into their midst.
Tell them now, let them know
  that you love them, Tomorrow
  could be too late.

Dolores A. Eberlin
WALKING
As I went out walking this
  morning;
My mind began to clear,
The birds flew by, and were
  singing;
The song I love to hear.

There's something about the
  morning;
There's something about the blue
  sky.
There's something about the
  squirrels playing;
That always catches my eye.

So, if you feel cooped up and
  lonely;
And your problems are getting
  you down.
Just put one foot in front of the
  other;
And explore earth's scenery and
  sound.

You may find you're closer to God;
As your feet are hitting the sod.

You mayfind you are problem free;
When your thoughts are not only
  on me.

So take time to walk in the winter;
And take time to walk in the fall.
Take time to walk in all seasons;
You'll find you're not walking
  alone.

Devin R. Allard
THE LAND OF DREAMS
When you fall asleep at night,
your mind goes into an eerie flight.
You can open the gate with the
  key of thought,
and don't have to do what you've
  been taught.
You sing, and dance, and prance
  all day,
and you act so happy and also gay.
You run in circles and run into
  trees,
and cut your elbows and scrape
  your knees.
But sometimes you open the
  wrong gate,
and find yourself facing a terrible
  fate.

There are monsters, ghouls, and
  also grouches,
and then you wish you were on
  comfortable couches.
And when you're done and
  almost through,
your mind knows exactly what to
  do.
You go back through that eerie
  flight,
it may be day it may be night.
And when your mind comes back
  to you,
you may wake up and have the flu.
You could leave for school very
  late,
and find out that it's the wrong
  date.
And you could play outside in
  the streams,
but you will know that you entered
  "The Land of Dreams."

Sandra Lee Hagan
LET HER RUN FREE
*[To my parents for their love
and encouragement Thanks,
Mom and Dad]*
There are times when you feel
  alone
and your daughter's life becomes
  your own.
But let her run free, and do her
  own thing,

let her live her own life and
  spread her own wings.

She cannot replace what you are
  not,
what you wanted to be, or what
  you haven't got.
She can follow your footsteps or
  wander astray,
No matter which direction, she'll
  decide her own way.

She has her own dreams and
  maybe they'll fail;
let her discover for herself, let her
  blaze her own trail.
She will live for today, with a
  smile . . . a song;
and when things don't seem right,
  she'll fight and be strong.

And she'll find her own way, to
  be what she wants to be.
Let her spread her own wings . . .
    Let Her Run Free.

Harvey J. Palmer III
DAD
O Lord, give me the courage to be
  like my father;
he has a very soft heart and stays
  full of laughter.
He knows how to be firm; yet
  he's also tough but fair—
there's no doubt in my mind that
  he really does care.
He's mastered the art of
  overcoming the bad
(there's rarely a time I've ever
  seen him sad).
If he's ever been afraid, he kept it
  from me—
he's strong like the wind, yet
  calm as the sea.
My father's not perfect because
  he's still a man
but whenever I need him, I see
  his outstretched hand.

Bette Guckin
DESIRES
[Dedicated to my husband, Jim.]
I want neither to be rich or to be
  poor;
Just take my hand and walk
  through the door.
There won't be diamonds or frills
  or such;
Just two people not looking for
  all too much.
A kiss, a care, a love, a smile—
That's all I want with you for a
  little while.

Rose Di Santo
IDENTITY
*[To my warrior, whose strength
and love has filled my life with
many inspirations ...]*
Cast away my drowning sorrows
touch me gentle with your waves
Let me float above the water
so I can discover the sea . . .

    just being free . . .

      just being me . . .

Barbara Pierce Mitchell
MORNING
You opened your eyes and smiled
As I lay watching you
In the warm gold of
That winter dawn.
The sun was barely up,

The moon still silver,
Two bodies glowing.
You were unshaven,
Your hair tousled, and
You were beautiful.
The treasure we sought,
We gave, and we were part of
The spinning universe, two bodies
Molded, replete, absolute,
Complete.

Laurel—Ann Reynolds Deltoro
DO YOU REMEMBER?
*[Dedicated to the loving
memory of my grandparents;
Dorothy Evelyn and Clarence
Archibald Reynolds, who were
a great inspiration to many.]*
Do you remember . . .
when you were young,
the devilish pranks,
the childhood fun.
  Losing your first tooth,
and skinning your knee,
and the adventureous feeling
when you climbed your first tree.

  The big grin on your face,
when mom hung your first picture,
a ten colored blob of
some fingerpaints mixture.
  The scared feeling you had
on your first day of school,
the place full of paper, pens,
order, and rules.

  Meeting your first friend
and playing your first game,
the feeling of pride
when you wrote your first name.
  The questions to mom
and the answers from dad,
the punishments and spankings,
a result of being bad.

  Attending your first party,
going on your first date,
and mom and dads warnings
of "Don't be home late."
  Then you got married
and started a new life.
You learned the commitments
of husband and wife.

  Now you sit and you wonder
how the time went so fast,
for your childhood and adolescence
are all in the past.

Marc Maciag
OLD CROW
Old crow
Tired and lazy 'gainst the day
Dark skies
Lost in blacks and whites and grays
Howling north wind
Sure takes a man's fight away

Wastelands,
A dreamer's home on his best day
Hard rain
Drops the leaves and makes the
  colors fade
And talks cheap,
But for the words of time they'll
  have the last say
Oh the words of time, they'll
  have the last say

And the harvest is in, it wasn't
  much
May I have enough to get by
The baskets were light, not a
  muscle ached

And somehow I feel I'm going to
die

The winter is coming, and the
signs say hard

I've never seen such a haunting
sky

Fog on the mountains, frost in
the wind

And somehow I feel I'm going to
die

Full moon
Lonely above the old tree line
Old crow
Hanging empty in the black sky
And a nighthawk
Circles her in silence as she flies
Old crow, all alone she flies

Debra A. Tewes
LIGHT OF LOVE
*[To Kenny . . .The Light In My
Dark]*
I wish you all the love
  This life could ever offer
I wish you all the joy
  This love could ever bring
When dark days turn to night
  I wish you an everlasting light
And I wish that light be love
  The love that burns in me

Lydia C. Matos
FRIENDSHIP
*[To Audrey McKean, a loving
and devoted Christian and my
dearest friend, with love and
best wishes.]*
Friendship! Magnificent word
with such a beautiful meaning
sweetness, gentleness expressed
it is love and it is giving.

It is kindness, understanding
and a lot of little things
a kind deed, a simple smile
that makes our lives complete

Friendship makes your life much
  sweeter
makes your heart bubble with
  love
enfolds your life in its fragrance
and keeps your faith sweet and
strong!

Margaret S. Tapley
A LONELY NIGHT
The wind blowing outside so
  strong.
The night so dark and long.
Wolves howl on a far away hill.
Gives your backbone a cold chill.

As the full moon shines
The church bell pretty chimes.
Lying awake at night.
Waiting for the morning light.

Off in the distance a train whistle
  blows loud.
Thinking of your children has
  made you proud.
Though you start to cry.
But tomorrow you'll know the
  reason why.

Sometimes you feel like you're in
  a maze.
But it's really a part of life's phase.
No one can say how long you'll
  live.
But you can only take what life
  has to give.

Ann Marie Albanese Janco
**ABC-Albanese Bettina &
Carmelo a Beautiful
Couple**
Bettina and Carmelo were quite a
  pair,
  they were our MOM and DAD.
GOD showed them how to share
with their children and others
  the love they had.
Their first born is with them in
  GOD's domain.
We miss them daily, we know
  the pain.
They want us happy, together
  caring
for each other and to continue
  sharing.
MOM and DAD taught us how
  to live,
to pray, to laugh, to love, to give.

Olivia Scarbriel
SUNRISE
Looking out of my bedroom
  window,
I saw the earth begin to glow.
The hills were all lit up in scarlet.

Vermillion streams flowed from
  each summit.
"The world, I thought, has caught
  afire."

Then; suddenly, the sun rose
  higher.

Ashjr
THE TRAWLER CREW
Waves break high and salty over
  the bow
As leaden clouds move quickly
  towards the boat.
Pulling hard we work to bring the
  nets aboard.
Hands calloused, now sticky with
  sweat and spray and blood
Arms, backs and legs ache as we
  strain against the weight.
For tons of fish we pull from this
  rough sea
And then turn Homeward, back
  to Galilee.
The boat she pitches, rocks, and
  rolls and sways
As now cold rain hits stinging on
  bare skin.
We stow away the fish in crushed
  packed ice
Now all's secured we 've cleared
  the deck.
The seas grow rougher as the
  storm matures.
The conversation down below,

soon quickens
As jokes and laughs and stories
  fill the air.
But all do wish that their own
  family was near.

Sharon Renee Smart
STAND BY AND BELIEVE
Stand by me
  as I laugh
  and show me you feel.
Stand by me
  as I cry
  and show me you care.
Stand by me
  in my confusion
  and show me you understand.
Stand by me
  as I pray
  and show me you believe.
I do not ask that you believe as I
  believe
  only that you believe in me.

Jo-Ann Loretta Holt
MY IMAGINARY CHILD
*[In memory of my loving
mother, Mrs. Evelyn S.
Alexander, and to all the people
who had confidence in me.]*
I have an imaginary child
Who attends the first grade;
If she paid attention to her
  teacher,
She'd really have it made.

Right now she's looking out the
  window,
Her little head's in a whirl;
She's so very precious to me,
My imaginary, darling girl.

She has the softest brown eyes,
And her hair—it is jet black;
Her face is that of an angel
When her hair is combed back.

She loves the idea of being
  dressed up,
And even having scraped knees;
In fact, she prefers anything
Except to wearing dungarees.

One day she will be all grown up,
And I'll be alone;
Her children won't be imaginary,
They'll be her very own.

Gina M. Brigida
"TIME" FOR: TODD
*[Todd, When I first met you—
you turned my darkest days
into light. You stopped the rain
and brought me a RAINBOW.
Now though our RAINBOW
has gone. You are everything to
me. One day the RAINBOW
you once brought me will
reappear. Even if it's in my
dreams. I LOVE YOU!]*
I couldn't believe that when I saw
  you Today
You appeared not to know me,
You seemed as though it's been
  that long, but believe me,
  it hasn't.
I noticed so many things about
  you not only that I still Love
  You but I noticed your eyes
  and how they gleamed. To you
  it meant nothing to me, it
  meant
    The World
You were holding someone else

Today, That's okay. Find the
  one you really love and be
  happy. If you are then so am I.
  It hurts you know, but if you
  never find her
    Find Me
Just you in a crowd of people is
  who I saw. I saw every moment
  we spent together and heard
  every word you once said. We
  were so close in distance yet so
  far away
    In Feeling
Our eyes—You Know they met
  I'm sure they told you I still
  care yet you just kept walking.
  That's okay, I can
    Still Love You
I wanted you so much I wanted
  to call you mine to let you into
  my heart this time to keep you
  there. I'm still confused only
  I'm sure
    I Still Love You
Let me grow up
  then try to
    Understand Me
Anyway, what I'm trying to say is
  if I never see you again I'll
  remember how our eyes met
  today and even if you had no
  meaning to it
    That's Okay, Because
    I DID.

Andrea Duchesne
Worrying About Tomorrow
Worrying about Tomorrow,
  is just a waste of time.
Worrying about Tomorrow,
  isn't worth your only dime.
Staying up all night worrying,
  won't change a thing.
Because Tomorrow will be
  Tomorrow,
  and what surprises Tomorrow
  will bring.
Tomorrow could bring the worst,
  and make you totally depressed.
Just remember there are always
  two sides:
  Tomorrow could also bring the
  best.
If something's going to happen,
  it most certainly will.
And you'll only find out
  Tomorrow,
  and definately not until.
So there's really only,
  one more thing to say:
Forget about Tomorrow,
  and live it up Today!

Cherylee E. Reed
MY DAD
You sometimes ask me how I feel
since he went away,
I only answer that I miss him
but I am in pain every day.

It's such a lost feeling,
to be alone in a crowd,
knowing he's not there to
  comfort you
or to talk without making a sound.

He's in my life still day to day,
and there's so much I didn't say.
But most of all, and this is true
I wish I'd said "I love you."

He was the best man in the world
and he really loved his little girl.

He talked of times when it was tough,

when money was tight, and things were rough.

But he always treated me like a queen

and made our times together special.

That's because he was my Dad.

Esther Mazza
HIS MAGNIFICENT OCEAN

On its pure white sand the sun beats down

Children's sand castles line the shore,

The tide comes in with a roaring sound

Splashing, the sand castles till there are no more.

It seems to bring haunting voices of Captain and crew

From sunken ships of long ago—

And to tell of stories that are very true

About many caught in the undertow.

'TIS not meant for sunken ships, or dead men's graves—

Nor destroying sand castles on the shore

GOD'S MAGNIFICENT OCEAN with its mighty waves—

If for his children to enjoy and to explore.

Clara McKenney
TAKE MY HAND

Take my hand and lead me,
For I am weak and blind,
And the path that I must follow,
Is not clear to me I find.
There are so many by-ways,
To lead one from the trail,
Teach me which the way to choose,
Lest I falter, lest I fail.

For some must walk in poverty,
And some must walk in wealth,
Some must be crippled, body or mind,
And some must walk in health.
Some must be leaders of nations,
While some must be marshalled along,
Some must be workers and builders,
And some sing the poets song.

I only want to go Thy way,
In narrow trail or wide,
It matters not, if Thou will be
My conscience and my guide.
What then, is the chosen way,
That Thou has planned for me?
Take my hand and lead me,
That I may come home to Thee.

Janice S. Kempton
Insanity—The Edge Of Reality

They live in their own little world with no responsibilities or inhibitions
they can do whatever they please without having to defend their actions
for they have a pardonable reason
people simply pass it off and say
"they couldn't help it, they're crazy"
but are they really the pitiful ones
sometimes it's such a trying task

just for us to get through a single day
and it makes me stop and wonder
if it's really them that should be pitied
for it's us that has to deal with reality.

Ralph H. Chase Jr.
FRIENDS

It's fall in the park, the leaves are tumbling down;
Red, orange, yellow ones; they hit the ground.
See the bluejay sitting on the stump;
Pecking all around to find his lunch.
The squirrel scampers through the leaves;
Look, he found an acorn, he's happy and he's pleased.
They were so happy to have fun in the park;
Playing their games each day till dark.
The bluejay would sing; the squirrel would chatter;
Then they took a nap and nothing mattered.

Louis S. Wagner
THE EAGLE

She flies through the air
with grace, and with ease.
Her strength is powerful
Her beauty can please.

The rabbit has beauty,
grace and speed,
but she will die
so another may feed.

The death of one
so another may live.
Is this wrong?
What's there to forgive?

Catherine Shovan
MYSELF

Who am I,
Where do I belong
I may not be appealing to you,
Or sing your song

Who am I,
Where do I belong
How can I identify,
And yet be so alone

Who am I,
I know I do belong
I am an individual,
And I sing my own song.

Florence E.R. Foster
OUR POND

I look out, early, on a winter's morn;...
Across the frosty field,...to the iced-over pond;...
And I remember,...well, the times when we were young,—
How that pond contributed, so much, to our fun.
Many youthful hours we spent out there,...
Ice-skating, on that pond,...in the blustery air.
And then, meandering, down there, each early Spring
To search out mayflowers, and violets, (gifts Mother Nature brings).
Through our teen-aged years,

we were both fancy-free,...
Other loves came along, but, somehow, you'd come back to me;...
And, for me, no other love could ever take your place.
We'd meet there, by our pond, in fond embrace.
Then, the war came along,...as wars often do,—
And, I'd write to you, in the service, every day or two.
How impatiently, I waited for your letters to come along,—
And I'd read them,...in privacy,...on "our log", by our pond.
We had so many plans of "when this war is through",...
When we'd realize our dreams; and I'd be married to you,
But, somehow,...through fate, it just wasn't to be;...
And it's still hard to believe you'll never come back to me.
Life,—without you, for me, has been cold and long,
But, somehow, I feel your presence, down there, by our pond;...
And my mind plays tricks on me, and I can almost hear
Your youthful laughter;...then I feel you near.
I guess we'll always be together;
—'though night-times seem so long,
When we walk together,...in *my memories*,...down by our little pond.

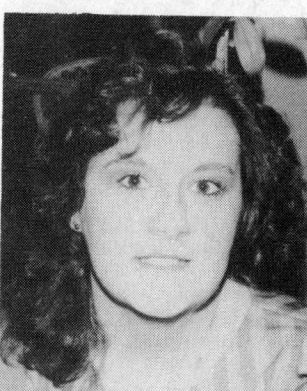

Cheryl A. Dubuque

Cheryl A. Dubuque
INSIGHT

Listen to the soft gentle breeze,
The beat of my heart,
The whisper of the trees.

Take a peek into my dreams,
Through the door of my mind,
And all of my schemes.

I hope you find it won't be rare,
Wherever you may look,
You'll be there.

Denise Shaw
SPRING KILLER

He creeps up upon her,
Giving no warning at all,
His colleagues kill her children,
But they never kill them all.

The trees are beaten,
The grass is smothered,

The birds are chased away,
The sky is bleak from mourning,
For the soul of the injured.

He posses the water,
Tells it to pilfer the beach,
And just as he's taking over,
She returns . . .
With the warmth of her heart,
She melts his ice,
Her children begin to grow,
The birds reappear,
The grass begins to breathe,
And the sky reflects . . .
The warmth of the spring.

Linda Lee Ehrenbeck
Bleeding Heart Of Friendship

With all there is in life to desire,
it is you that flames and lights my fire.
It started with a spark from you
that brought about this friendship true.
If you like don't hang around,
since that's not where you're destin-bound.
I want you to go where you please
hoping that our love will freeze,
to melt away another day
and you'll come back to me and say,
"This love we have will never die
for if it does we both will cry."
You're the friend I'll keep for all my life,
even after you've found a wife.
The love we have will never end,
It's like the trust you have in a friend.

Roberta Reading
ITEM

She sits and smiles and smirks
Judging with a jaundiced eye
The foibles of her friends and neighbors
Loving them and enjoying every moment of life.
For after all
Don't they
provide her with the staff of life
By which all must live?
It's called
Compassion.

Richard C. Tullock
OUR LOVE

["To Karen" My loving and devoted wife, whom I wrote this poem for.]

With happiness comes a smile,
A smile, showing affection.
With our hands we touch,
Showing our feelings.
In our arms we embrace,
With a desire of passion.
Like a dream, yet so real,
We unite with a kiss.
A kiss, the touch of our lips,
Our lips, the touch of our love.
With a ring, bonding us together,
Together we share our love.
The love of a lifetime,
A lifetime of love.

Julia F. Hackett
QUIET MOMENTS

I've sat back and visualized
A romantic scene or two
Lovingly resting in one anothers arms

295

In tall grasses with you.

The breeze gently moves
The grasses to and fro
A butterfly quietly touches
The beautiful things that grow.

We chatter on endlessly
Nothing important is said
While I slowly caress
The hair upon your head.

Then in a special quiet moment
We both just stop and stare
Our feelings swell within us
For love is what we share.

Cynthia Waters
JULY 4, 1982
At noon that day, the marvel of
television
Had showed us the marvel of
"Columbia" returning from
space,
And I felt my pulse race
As the shuttle safely touched
down on the desert sand,
And "God Bless America" was
played by the band,
And a beaming President
exclaimed, "You know this has
got to beat firecrackers!"

Now, hours later, a full moon
beams its soft light
On us and watches the fireworks
display with us this July 4 night
As gigantic globes try to dim the
heavenly orb
With bursting rainbow—tinted
balls
And showers of silver and gold
that fall
To earth in booming splendor.
That same moon has watched
centuries of human jubilation
With fireworks and music in
celebration—
From Handel's glorious
polyphonics to patriotic
American marches.
A little over two hundred years
ago,
That same moon looked down on
a new nation destined to grow
Into the mighty United States of
America.
Two hundred years from now,
this same moon will still look
down
On crowds of people gathered
'round
To celebrate another July 4.
I don't know what jobs those
future citizens will work at or
what clothes they will wear,

But as I look ahead, I feel no fear—
There will still be a United States
and people will still thrill to
the beauty of fireworks.

M. Jonathan Adams
UNTITLED
*[For Denise, who made it all
come true!]*
"Oh, what is love?", you ask of me.
Yet, maybe, I should ask of thee?
For in your eyes, I see a light,
that brightens up the darkest
night.
"Oh, what is love?", you ask of me.
Yet, maybe, I should ask of thee?
For upon your lips, I see a smile,
that touches me in classic style.
"Oh, what is love?", you ask of me.
Yet, maybe, I should ask of thee?
For in your touch, I sense desire—
that forever glowing, warming
fire.
"Oh, what is love?", you ask of me.
Yet, maybe, I should ask of thee?
For in your heart, it's love I get,
ever since the day we met.

cha sparks
LOVING HATE
I am on the brink of despair
   As my world turns
      systematically chaotic.
The music of life that is
   Peacefully agitating
      my soul . . .
My heart has to be
   Deceitfully honest
      to you . . .
I have to be set free,
   I'm a victim of your
      protective abuse.
You are silently speaking . . .
   I hear nothing

      you imply.
The truth is plainly hidden . . .
   The answers are simply complex,
      But we are avoiding
         the questions.

Shirley M.A. Mayo
Your Days Are My Nights
*[I dedicate this poem to:
Gordon Worchester Johnson...
in honor, of my love, and the
love he has given to me...]*
From dawn to dusk, I think of you,
My mind is never at rest.

I travel through our love tunnel,
And pick the ways, I love you best.

Now new thoughts have linger,
To fuss and smear my mind.

For now you're in great danger,
Which should heal within space
of time.

My mind has gone completely,
Wondering what can I do.

Yet you're at a distance,
Other's have charge of you.

My love, I love you dearly,
So dearly you're part of my heart.

Now when I see you,
It tears my heart apart.

Life so full of chance,
That are not given twice,

Now my nights are filled with
prayer,
To God for saving your life.

Though we are His children,
Still we're put out on our own.

He knows we're only human,
And human are known to roam.

Yet He gives us a mind to reach
him,
When our soul's in need.

Thank Him today and always,
For He's a father, friend, indeed.

So when I come to see you,
And the report is alright.

I hold to that with prayers,
For your days are my nights . . .

June A. Gallant
WORDS
Words can be happy,
Words can be sweet,
Words can be funny,
And words can be neat,

But if they're used wrongly,
Words can be hurting,
If they're used strongly,
They may be diverting,

The real meaning inside,
That you cannot say,
The feelings you hide,
With words every day,

Choose your words with care,
And watch how you speak,
Be sure you are fair,
And for honesty seek,

Because words can be loving,
Or they can be lies,
Words can be joyful,
Or put tears in your eyes,

Gloria J. Gagne
LITTLE CHILDREN
*[Written to my sons, Denis and
Bruce, with love, and for which
I take great pride and joy in
watching their growth.]*
They sleep like angels
through the night,
but come the day,
they're pure delight.

They run, and jump,
scream, and shout,
they laugh, they cry,
and love to pout.

They find trouble,
oh yes indeed!
Or scrape their knees,
which always bleed.

Can one say they are
not sweet,
when little children,
can't be beat!

They sleep like angels
through the night,
but come the day,
they're pure delight!

Virginia E. Hooper
LIFE
Life is like a large mountain
Which often times is hard to
reach the top,
Yet if we are courageous enough,
We'll keep the Faith and never
try to stop.

We start to climb to the top
And often start to fall into the
gullies below
But, we can pick ourselves up

And again we'll start and upward
we'll go.
Life's road is very rough
sometimes
Although it too can have its
happiness,
So keep the Faith in the God
Almighty
And someday you'll have your
success.

Then the mountain top you'll be
looking down from
Into the dark deep gullies below
And know that is one place
You'll never again have to go.

Sharon R. Christopher
SEPTEMBER 1
A moment in this
one way unwanted journey
signals to our brain
the approaching end of all
that we find living, warm, elusive;
a seagull screams
piercing the low hung blanket
grey waves crest higher, louder
while our souls cry in their
mishapen cells—
no—just a bit longer this time,
we sit and wait for karma to pass
out test papers—
how will we score on this one;
it's all a game of waiting, of
uncertainty
of little diversions that alleviate
the fear
temporarily,
some are fortunate to rarely feel
the wait—
they have their warm Tahitian
mornings
or vanilla tea in Mayfair
not feeling the sting of needles
behind partitioned walls and
fluorescent falseness
day after month after year,
our cells look worn,
'put another coat of lipstick on—
one can't judge under these
fluorescent lights'
and the calender
need only show one day.

S.D. Holmgren
GRANDMA
My grandma taught me to smile
in life,
to laugh in every day,
And today I heard her laugh
again,
a laugh from yesterday.
For now she's with the Lord
above,
she left the other day,
The memory of her joyous life
is in my heart to stay.
The lord did say he was looking
for
the prettiest flower along the
way,
As He strolled through the
Garden of Life
to make a great Bouquet.
He searched and searched for the
prettiest of all
to top his Bouquet in a special
way,
When all of a sudden He found
dear Grandma:
"Here is the prettiest flower
today."

Today's Greatest Poems

Valerie D. Richards
THOUGHTS OF LOVE

The sky is beautiful blue indeed
  with scattered clouds of white,
With birds flying through the air,
  with thoughts of endless flight.

With dreams flowing through my
  mind,
  but never coming true,
Of special and tranquil times,
  like
  times I spent with you.

The thoughts of love I hope to
  share,
  the thoughts that never end,
The dreams of happy carefree
  times,
  running through my head.

To share the joy of two combined,
  and acting as just one,
And start a life, so new and fresh,
  one that's only just begun.

Pauline E. Pelkey
GOOD FRIENDS

I think about you often
And a smile comes to my mind.

Remembering the laughs we've
  had
Recalling happy times.

It's been a pleasure knowing you
of that you may be sure.

For friendship is a treasure, true.
Comforting, warm and more—

It's tolerant, it judges not, and
Cheers us when there's tears;

It eases sorrows, spans the miles,
Endures throughout the years.

Without "good friends", I wonder?
Just what our lives would be?

Sadder by far and lonely I'm sure,
Barren and cold as the sea.

Thank God we are "Good Friends"

Thee and me—

Mary Gillespie
MY TALK WITH THE SEA

Every time I look out o'er the Sea:
I can't help but think, is it trying
to say something to me.

The mighty waves as they break on
the shore, seem to say I have been
here before.

They stay awhile as they roll o'er
the sand. I watch as they break:
if they allow me to stand.

They whisper to me, "I could take
you with me back out to the Sea,
for I am very strong as you can
see."

I whisper back quietly as I head
for
the shore, "I shall not argue that
point anymore."

Janet Ann Fleming
PARADISE DREAM

As I sit in my storybook
picture window,
and gaze out across the field
I ask myself is all this mine
is all this beauty real?

The clouds, the sky, the green,
green grass
the beautiful pond to the right

and I ask myself could it be true
this green and gorgeous sight?

The sun comes out
and brightens the scene
as it dries the morning dew
and as I watch, I ask myself
is all this possibly true?

This beauty is very hard to find
and I hope you don't think me a
fool
but now I must leave,
my PARADISE DREAM
to get up . . .
    In time for school!

Debbie Budzilo
CLOWNS

*[To my family for all their love
and caring. And my friend,
Cindy, who had faith in me.]*
Lots of smiles and laughing
Lots of frowns and tears
Lots of beautiful colors what
  makes the face appear.
Taking the time
and working hard
and making sure it's right
and when the face is finished
it comes back into life . . .

Michael Steven Lawson
TRY

As the bones lay bleaching
In the desert sun
A man came stumbling by

As the sun beat down
Upon his naked head
He stopped to ponder why

Having been lost
For many days
His mind was in
A heavy haze

As his thoughts focused
On the bones again
A tear came to his eye

And then he continued
Upon his way
It's for a man
To try

Frances Barbre
CUPID'S ARROW

Cupid shot me with his dart,
For now I love you with all my
  heart.
His arrow pierced me through
  and through
With a promise you'd be forever
  true.
And so I fell, body and soul
For a love that would make me
  whole.
But, alas! Your love was not true,
Your heart has gone from me to
  you.
Oh, Cupid, take you and your dart
And mess with someone else's
  heart!

Regina Rigby
ON MOTHER'S DAY

Mother of my husband
You are my mother too
The love he shows me daily
Springs from his love for you

The son that you gave life to
Now shares his life with me
I feel a part of Ruth inside
I share her loyalty

I hope that I should live to be
The daughter you deserve
Drawing from your inner strength
Gentle heart and steady nerve

Thank you for sharing your son
  with me
And as the years go by
I'll never forget his first love
I'd never even try

For you are my husband's mother
And because he loves you so
I've grown to share those feelings
I just wanted you to know

Guyvan B. Shirley
WELCOME TO MY HOUSE

It's not much to look at
It's not much to see
But inside it's so lovely
'cause there is so much love
  flowing
Between Mom, Dad and me.

It has cracks in the walls
And mice nibbling at my toes
It's cold in the winter
But you are welcome to my house
Come visit "y'all".

In the summer it's too hot to
  sleep
With gnats wanting to live in my
  nose
And fleas as big as my toes
Bugs crawling through the walls
But there is lots of love flowing
  inside
So you are welcome to my house
Come visit "y'all".

It has paper bags tacked on the
  walls
And no carpet at all
No ceiling to look at
No Rembrants or Mona Lisas
  hanging from the walls
But it's my house, and I'm proud
So, come visit "y'all".

Margaret Pettus Parrish

Margaret Pettus Parrish
DAY TO DAY

Now that my life is almost o'er
I am still a getter goer.
And people are so surprised
That I am not lying on my side,
And complaining of my aches
  and pain
When I really am living again
To my fullest and enjoyment.
So I really do not lament
That I am older than before,
Not wishing back the days of yore.
For I am happier this way,

And like living day to day.

They are the ones that make me
  old,
By hoping that I could not enfold
My living over all the years,
Some of it would bring tears.
But maybe I gained some worth,
Had also happy days of mirth.
That to me was valuable,
To know my life was not mobile.
And I can enjoy it now
Thinking how it did endow
Me with treasures of the mind
That are difficult to find.

Alice Johnson
**The King and Christmas
1982**

Christmas time, Christmas time
Sands of time, words of rhyme
Gifts and songs, winds and snow.
Families meet, come and go—
Years go on—'eighty two—
We grow older me and you
News of Jews, peace and war.
Palestine, wars by the score.
Earthquakes here, earthquakes
  there
Pollution gathers in the graying
  air
Animals huddle in the cold and
  snow.
Time goes on, snow blowers
  blow.
Our friends die of this and that.
Grandma knits a nice warm hat—
Santa Claus says, "Ho, ho, ho!"
Children come, children go.
Presents, food, cookies, punch—
Hamburger, fries, MacDonald's
  lunch—
Time for talking, time to be
Christ walking on the sea—
News of Jews, peace at last.
The King is coming, fast, fast, fast!

Nellie V. Coberley
JUST SMILE

This old world is slowing dying,
For the lack of love today.
You can make a soul so happy,
If you smiled at him today.

Or if you see a weary brother,
Tugging at a heavy load,
If you smiled and ask to help him,
As you traveled along the road.

Did you know a smile's
  contagious?
It can go a long, long way,
It will make a soul so happy
That you smiled at him today.

So let's make this old world better,
With a smile upon our face,
And a cheerful, happy greeting,
As we travel from place to place.

Kris A. Jeters
VOICES FROM BEYOND

*[Through thick and thin, both
good and bad, only our
friendship could be as
intricately simple as life itself.
To Jerry (Don't call me Tom
Petty) West.]*
"Have you heard them?" you say.
  I reply, "Never, say!
In a dream once there may have
  been some.
  Yet with time they were lost
  at my memories cost."

And with that you think,
    "Has he gone numb?"

To this day you derive
    that the voice was as live
as the meeting we speak at this
    time.
    Yet back then you knew
    that it couldn't be true
so you thought you
    were losing your mind.

Just where did it come from?
    or if it did come from
a place other than your own
    thoughts,
    will it come back my friend
    to speak once again
or has your story been
    all about naught?

Dee Dee S. McArthur
HOMEWARD BOUND
Homeward Bound am I—
Homeward across the sky.
Soon to meet Christ, face to face—
Forever to dwell within His grace!

Weep not for me, I pray;
We will meet again someday.
Though, for a while, we must part,
Let not sorrow enter your heart—

But, look to God above
To keep you with His love.
He will guide you now and show
    you the way—
When you are Homeward Bound
    someday.

Geraldine G. Sanchez
POEM OF REVENGE
Nearly all the words have been
    taken
To the poems I want to write
So I might as well say this to
    poets
I've just begun to fight!

Why should I write a poem
That already has been written?
They said what I needed to say
And already I feel smitten!

I wanted to say it first
But already I've been took
The anger is swelling up inside of
    me
My words pour out a book!

But then I think unto myself
That I should become a critic
What better way to get revenge
Upon those poets who did it!

R. Daevid Wright
DRIFTING AWAY
Drifting, I'm drifting away.
I'm drifting down the river of life,
Aimlessly leaving shore.
I'm drifting along deep in the
    night,
When will I drift no more?

Drifting, just drifting away.
I'm all lost on this perilous path,
Lost in the corridors of my mind.
I'm caught in the midst of satan's
    wrath,
Caught in the darkness and going
    blind.

Drifting too far away,
I pause, I sigh, I pray.
Oh Lord where are you?
I need your light to guide my
    way,

Out of these noxious waters.
Throw the lifeline into the bay,
Spare me the vicious slaughter.

Jeanie Scudder

Jeanie Scudder
THE SATURDAY STIR
*[To My Beloved Son, Robbie
Come out who ever you are.]*
Tangled hair tousling languidly;
    woman scent nighty;
mingled with stale perfume; a
    male aftertaste yawn.
They're afraid to look a chirping
    bird in the eye,
Lest they awaken suddenly on
    this timeless day.
Blue collars hanging on to glazed
    stupors.
Simulating a leisurely life style.

Not endangered by intruding
    factories.
Totally aware of unawareness.
They grope with the arts and do-
    it-yourself stuff.
This unique vein of society on a
    benevolent trip.
Recultivating friends and half
    enemies;
Out of character, it behooves
    them to pick up their lunch
    pails,
and go to work.

Alice M. Ridings
SUMMER OF '82
*[An Karoly Jozef mit meiner
ewigen liebe.]*
There are certain things about you
    that bring forth in me
a gently aching tenderness . . .
The way your hair
curls down over your ears . . .
The look of you

limp and sweaty and warm after
    loving
sleeping beside me on the
    pillow . . .
The way you look
at me with such love,
or at those very certain moments
when time stands still.
And I find myself
reaching out to you in my mind,
touching you with love,
cherishing every look and every
    moment
and watching my love grow,
and aching to find
a way to let you know.

Katie J. Crutchfield
DEDICATION
I am reaching for the dreams
    that many will not buy.
I am reaching for perfection
    trying to do or die.
I am keeping my faith
    and trading my "whys".
I am reaching for the things
    I have been denied.
I will not relent
    until I have won or tried.

Karen Sue Hazelip
JORGE
I watched you try
so courageously
to run after the other boys.
Boys with strong, swift legs to
    carry them.
You, depending on your crutches.
Tears came to my eyes
when you stumbled, then fell.
You laid there so still,
with so much pain in your eyes.
I wanted to reach out and help
    you,
but knowing better,
held myself back.
Then slowly, and with such
    effort,
you struggled to stand.
And I too went on
as though nothing had happened.

Alma Joyce
CIRCUIT
I have gone and you did not
know nor grieve my passing.
Perhaps I should have screamed
    good-bye
I wonder, were you listening?

Close encounter of that
fatal blow to shatter,
I fly beneath my chosen shield
above the shadowed shell of me.

Specified time allows my
dream revisit your abode.
Cry joy my name, to wed again
the spirit to the body.

Arva R. Orman
Someday Is a Never-Away
There are a great many things I
    want to do,
And a million or more I want to
    say.
I've promised myself I'll
    accomplish them all
Not now, but someday.

Someday I'll paint a masterpiece
With brilliant colors warm and
    gay.
Still the brush feels no touch of

my hand,
And someday seems a never-away.

Someday I'll write a beautiful
    poem
That expresses all I've wanted to
    say
To loved ones and friends both
    near and far,
But someday seems a never-away.

Someday I'll walk through the
    country-side,
And admire nature's handi-work
    along the way.
With wonderment I'll view each
    miracle,
Yet someday seems a never-away.

Someday I'll study the word of my
    Lord,
And daily homage to Him, I'll
    pay.
I hope He will be patient with
    me,
Because someday seems a
    never-away.

Ah, perhaps it's time for me to
    change,
And stop my "someday-ing" today.
Life's Opportunities are too
    precious to waste
When someday is a never-away.

Madeleine Meigs Blowers
DISSOLUTION
Chase down the wind
that chases me.
My tortured heart
will set you free.
Our worlds remain
too far apart,
mistrust and pain
between our hearts.
What might have been
can never be.
Two ships set sail
upon tossed seas.

Novak Novica Vujacic
HAND OF LOVE
My word
Rhyme
Style
Born
Carried
To the Scenery
Of Life
Ask for Love.
My rhyme
World
Life
Style
Look for
A sincere
Friend
Stretching out
The hand
And Love.

Dawn Michelle Forsythe
A SINGLE TEAR
The night was warm
    No breeze was felt
In the wet green grass,
    She slowly knelt.

She spoke a brief
    And simple prayer
For her brothers
    And her father there.

They lay beneath
    Those cold grey stones.

They fought a fight
  Not even their own.

But does it even
  Matter now?
She sighed
  And wiped her careworn brow.

She slowly rose
  From where she'd knelt.
A stony emptiness
  Was all she felt.

And as she left
  That dreary place,
A single tear
  Ran down her face.

Margaret Pettus Parrish

Margaret Pettus Parrish
PUT ON THE SHELF
*[Dedicated to my organ teacher,
Walter Wild, New York City.]*
They say I'm too old to play
The organ for the church today
In this quaint little town,
Altho I've played in places of
  renown.
As an organist I could vie
With the young who do not try.
They judge by age
And not by sage
Who do not know
The lessons taught long ago.
The sound of music is to me
What everyone should try to see.
It is ethereal and sublime,
And keeps us noble and refined.
But as this world will change
We may expect a different range
Of quality and perception,
That may lead us to deception,
Which will not increase our
  worth,
But lead to changes far more
  dearth.
Whereby we may long to be
Just as we used to see.

Philip H. Skarin
BE MY FRIEND
I want you to be my friend,
  but I don't know if
  you want me
  to be yours.

Being friends can be hazardous
  to your image,
  and images are very sacred
  to people.

Images are created with great care,
  and guarded
  with a passion.
Images give protection
  to the fragile egos,
and keep people
  at a safe distance.

Friendship requires sincerity,
  and truth and respect.
Friendship means exposing
  your strengths and your
  weaknesses,
  your desires and your fears.

Friendship is sharing—
Friendship is caring—
Friendship is loving—

Will you
    be
      my friend?

Jeanene Pennington
NURSE'S LAMENT
*[To Lee Goldfine—for helping
me to discover new horizons.]*
that human being in room 264
so hard to deal with anymore
he can't reach out
we can't reach in
killing him softly
a day at a time
watching and tortures
it seems such a crime
keeping him alive in death
does it serve our need?
the spirit in his eyes
has ceased to plead
dying off to a vacant stare
death is there—
in those naked mirrors
death is everywhere—
if only i could touch his soul.

Sofia A. M. Martin
FOR NURSE DIANNE
Not long ago, it was but a
  dream—
When you had to work up some
  steam—
You put all your yearnings in one
  pot—
Reaching out for the only spot—
Which would give you great
  satisfaction.
A long stretch for you it was
  indeed—
But in the end you picked up
  speed—
When graduation was the final
  spin—
For it was the day you got your
  pin—
And a place at a Nurses—station.
To you and all nurses,
  congratulation on your
  graduation.

Mildred Shankland
THE GIVING ROCK
The Rock stands in peaceful
  quietude,
A fortress and stronghold of great
  magnitude.

Nothing can move it—this
  massive stone.
It shares its strength and beauty.
  It is never alone.

Caressed by the clouds, washed
  by the rain,
Steadfast in storms; to the end of
  time it will remain.

It is a delight to many; an
  inspiration and guide;
A sentinel and landmark to all
  the country-side.

The Rock stands stable and firm
  through all the ages.
Its secrets and wonders are
  pondered by scholars and sages.

In its crevices the birds find a
  place to nest.
It cradles the weary as they
  recline to rest.

The Rock reflects the warmth of
  the sun on a cold blustery day.
It gleams with moonlight and the
  star-shine of the milkyway.

Its majestic form makes the heart
  of the dreamer glow.
From its summit the poet and
  artist view scenes of grandeur
  below.

It renders a song for the stream as
  it ripples by.
It echoes the sound of a child's
  happy cry.

The Giving Rock bestows peace
  and joy. May I live
To be like the Rock and give . . .
  and give . . . and give.

Jack Decarlo
REINCARNATION
Were you really the princess so
  amorously pursued? I came on
  stallions with my words and
  gifts and men. You smiled. I
  was rewarded. Our marriage
  lasted a fortnight. I was killed
  in battle. You mourned for six
  long years.
In Egypt, you bathed Cleopatra on
  the banks of the Nile. But you
  were the beautiful one! I saw
  you and stole you away at
  night. It was at the risk of my
  own life. I raped you on the
  sand dunes. You dug your
  fingers into my flesh and held
  me like a vise. I couldn't move.
  We remained for days.
I found you broken in the jungle.
  You were tired and hungry. I
  fed you. You followed me
  everywhere after that and
  always held my hand.
You were on the shores of China
  nursing your baby with milk-
  filled breasts. "Where is your
  husband?", I asked. The tears in
  your eyes were your reply. I
  took you with me and guarded
  you. You became the empress
  of all the land. We ruled the
  Orient.
We were exiled to a strange
  planet. We wouldn't bow down
  to the demon invaders. We
  were alone. But you gave me
  passionate hope. I remember I
  held you once for seventeen
  months without stirring. It was
  the happiest time of my life. I
  love the look in your eyes.

James Harrison Smith
At the Table Of Brotherhood
In visions of my mind, I fancy I
  can see
Men of every race and men of
  every creed
From every place on earth where
  man has stood,
Sitting together at the table of
  brotherhood.

The black, the white, the yellow,
  red and brown;
Some socially obscurred and
  some of reknown;
Some of lowly birth and some of
  noble blood,
Sitting together at the table of
  brotherhood.

I can see the bounty passed
  among other—
Love, gratitude and honor from
  brother to brother.
Discrimination is tasteless as mud,
Sitting together at the table of
  brotherhood.

I envision the banner of peace
  waving high
As all brothers embrace with a
  triumphant sigh.
No prejudices, no bitterness, no
  shedding of blood,
Sitting together at the table of
  brotherhood.

Art V. Villanueva
transient
i
want
you
to remember
me
but
i
have done
n o t h i n g
to remind
you
that i
once
loved
and
touched
your
being.

Novak Novica Vujacic
A THOUGHT
You are too far
From me
But close
To my Thought
The heart delights
In some fairy tales
At nights.
You are close
To my Thought
In heart
I feel a warm
Touch
Floats throughout
The body
Breaking my study
Of your inner
Pulse.

Lane A. Byrnes
FOUR DAYS IN MEXICO
Pass me by
As if a gull
I'll smile sadly
And you're gone

Brian Brown
WATCH THE SIGNS
Inside you hear "go ahead"
But your eyes didn't see it that far
How do you know it's not a meteor
Just because everyone else says
  it's a star

Just watch the signs
They will guide you there

299

Follow those signs
You know they're gonna take you
    somewhere
Just watch the signs
With no time to spare

For foolish deals or
    proscrastination
You know they'll only rot you
Don't be the thief of your own time
Before you've realized failures
    caught you

Just watch the signs
But be true and soft-eyed
Follow the signs
Discipline will not go ungratified
Just watch the signs
In order to become qualified—In
    the state of the art

Inside you hear "keep going"
Even during the worst of times
Just be strong and follow the road
Be aware and watch the signs

Dorothy Dorfman
I TALK TO THE STARS
I talk to the stars
and tell them how much I love you,
I tell them of dreams, desires,
needs and promises,
The stars listen as they hear of
passion and feelings,
They listen as the tears flow
and prayers are said,
I talk to the stars
and they twinkle back,
They seem to be saying,
He loves you, too,
and only God knows what the
    future will bring.

Cynthia McNeese
LIFE
Life is like a spring flower
Fresh and bright, expressing
Scintillating light . . .
Blooming slowly and with care
Growing and flowering
Only to share . . .

Kelly Anges
AM I LOSING YOU?
[To Tom: The one I love so
true, Forever and a day . . .]
Love so gentle and true
Am I losing you?

You're behind bars and I'm alone
    and free
Some changes have come over me
    Am I losing you?
    The one I love so true
    Am I losing out on you?

I no longer know what to do
We've had so many good times
Our hearts always rhymed
I don't want someone to take
    your place
I guess I've just fallen out of pace
    Am I losing you?
    The one I love so true?
    Have we become such strangers?
    That our love is in danger?
I have no words to explain
I'm so sorry for all the pain
You've accused me of so much
When all I wanted was your
    gentle touch
    [All I ask is:]
    Am I losing you?
    The one I love so true . . .

Deborah A. Llerena
SPECIAL FEELING
Did you ever feel you couldn't
    think,
That you had a special glow.
Did you ever feel just happy
    inside,
It's this feeling I know.

Did you ever feel you couldn't
    sleep,
Until he called that day.
Did you ever feel sad inside,
Whenever he was away.

This feeling is a feeling,
That has me thinking of,
Our future moments together,
This feeling I think is love.

Norma Clark

Norma Clark
GROCERY SHORT LINE
I thought—why did I do it this way
Hungry—standing in a
    supermarket today

In the blinking light row that
    said nine pieces is the limit
The line was slower and restless
    by the minute

The cashier moved as if she was
    through for the day
She began to talk to customers in
    a sassy way

She looked the scale over twice
    to catch an ounce
She called for a back-up on checks—
    fussing about a bounce

When I got to her—I wanted to
    tell her what's on my mind
I thought—I'm too hungry—it's
    way past eating time.

Grant L. Simpson
LOST DREAMS
[To Barbara—my inspiration—
my friend—I thank you for both.]
I escape from reality with things
unseen, and spend much of my
time in some frivolous dream.

I dream of things I know surely
can't be, I dream of fame and
fortune coming to me.

Dreams are something I know I'll
always need, it's funny, but the
biggest dreams can come from
the smallest seeds.

The seeds of these dreams are
blowing in the wind, they come
and they go, like a fair weather
friend.

As each new dream slips from my
grasp, I reach for another and
hope it will last, but I know
that it won't it will soon fade
away, like the setting sun at
the close of the day.

I'll reach for these dreams as they
come racing by, and as they
slip through my fingers—I'll
have just one more try.

Claire B. Martin
ENDLESS SEARCH
[This poem is dedicated to
Greg and Leigh. For without
their support and
encouragement, I would have
given up a long time ago.]
Snowflakes drift slowly
    with the gentle breeze,
Laying softly down
    to form a winter's freeze.

Comes the warmth of the sun
    melting all away,
Running quickly, ever swiftly,
    not meant to stay.

Leaves slippng gracefully
    from their dwelling place,
Settling upon the land
    with an air of delicate grace.

So similar are our lives,
    forever needing,
The Endless Search . . .
    to discover life's meaning.

Lisa Kirtley
FROM OUT OF NOWHERE
He comes from out of nowhere
this mighty bird, so strong
He spreads his wings in beauty,
his flight, a majestic song
He soars over mountains with
the ease of the wind and glides
through the canyons, with nature
he blends.
No bird can match his splendor,
his power, nor his grace
The eagle from out of nowhere
forever has his place.

Bob R. Galbreath
THE WEDDING
So, you are to be married!
Let me tell you a truth
Life shall not be harried,
If you add these thoughts
Unto your marriage.

Never, But never enter
The cathedral of sleep,
Until the twain of lips
In kiss do meet.

For marriage, like the soul,
Before God must grow.
Infatuation becomes love
This you will know,
For love to devotion expands
Meets the most exacting demands.

Devotion in turn
Matures to oneness and concern.
By the order of God
The flesh of two,
Become the oneness of you.

Dorothy Dimeo Wyatt
UTTER DESPAIR
Oh God! I feel so alone—
    So desolate
My body shakes violently
    From the force of my tears
So deep they pierce my heart.

I've cried so much
I'm dry inside
    Like the desert sand

Hoping . . . longing . . . for
    eternal sleep

Forgive me, Lord, for giving in to
    my grief
It overwhelms me so
    That I long to go on a never
    ending journey.

But darkness awaits me there
And being who I am and what I am
    I know
That some of us are just as afraid
    to live
    As well as to die
And I am but a coward
    Either way.

Dorothy S. Wilson
GRATITUDE
Though blessed with luxury or
    fame;
Though honored by our children;
Though affection is returned by
    our beloved—
Our existence is vacuous, O God,
When we forget to express our
    gratitude
    for your love.

Though betrayed and forsaken;
Though a victim of pain or poverty;
Though enclosed behind bars—
We cling to hope and life, O God,
When we remember to express
    our gratitude
    for your love.

Rachel Dianne Brown
YEARS
See the Autumn leaves
Oh, how they speak
Of times of now and times to fear
Of years gone by, they say with a
    sigh
Those were the times that were
    so dear

They sit upon my heart, the years
    that have gone
They shed not a tear because
    they can't hear
But only fall from year to year

The future looks long and hard
But the leaves do not fear
For they know that the end of
    time is here.

Alfred Huff
TIME
Life's gravitating bind
Mean not to be so demanding
The world of refind
Knows no resigning
Wherein too conceding
Therefore wide resolving
To be so demanding

For time will create,
in harmony with desires.
And fate's only a phase,
given misunderstood days.

Deanna J. Cannell
CHRISTMAS
Church Bells chime to proclaim
    The Holiday Season is here.
Bright Red Bows, Mistletoe,
    Christmas Carols, Red Nosed
    Reindeer.

The Precocious Child resembles
an Elf,
Store Windows Bedazzle 'ol
Scrooge himself.
Santa Claus with the Jolly face,
Gifts all wrapped in Satin and
Lace.

Whispers and Secrets, 'tis Hide
and Seek,
Hearts are light and indiscreet.
The Heavens touch the Winter
Night,
Covering the Earth with a Veil
of White.

Precious Night, Enchantingly so,
One STAR brighter than any
other,
Beckons to us, lest we forget,
Chosen Child—Virgin Mother.

BETHLEHEM, The Child, The MAN,
Nailed to the CROSS 'till Death.
OUR SAVIOUR—EXALTED KING
Blessed by an Angels' Breath.

CHRISTMAS is a Smile,
CHRISTMAS is Love,
And thus, HE would impart,
CHRISTMAS is a Spirit
Born in a Loving Heart.

CHRISTMAS Lights and Falling
Snow
Calms the Spirit, Soothes the
Soul.
BEDECKED—BEJEWELED—
CHRISTMAS TREE,
By the GRACE OF GOD,
Serenity . . .

Florence I. Brown
FRIENDS OF MY HEART
Of all the memories I have in store,
It seems there's none I treasure
more
Than you, dear friend, who has
the ver-ish
Of all the things that I most
cherish.

I keep within my heart a spot
For those I love and care a lot . . .
A special corner, I've saved in part,
For you alone within my heart.

For each of my friends I covet a
nook,
Where only I know where to look.
Ever so often I find the time
To go thru this memory arc of
mine.

Mentally I sort you from the pile,
Hold you close and dream awhile.
Knowing whatever I am, or try to
do,
Was done in part because of you.

When all is gone, memories are yet
Bits of recollections, I can't forget.
My happiness blooms with
endless store,
That widens as I use it more.

God, let me keep this little place
Where I can always see your face
Aglow with radiant, inner shine,
Because you are a "friend of mine".

Nancy Tucker Wilson
ECLIPSE
"Grandmother, ride the world and
feel it move!"
They rode up then in the
pumpkin coach,

Embossed with flowers and fruit
and trees.
Laura looked out to find the moon.
The moon shone clear, a smooth
white disc;
One star was blinking through a
cloud.
"There's Twinkle," Laura spoke as
if she knew.

The moon had faded; it seemed to
lean
Against the sliding night.
Magic it may have been,
But, all at once, the coach had
turned—
Was tilted *so*—
They saw its wheel, a silver rim,
Which slid above the darkened
world,
And then was still.

Now, when the pumpkin coach
had pulled away,
Grandmother's silhouette was on
the moon.
Laura had chased after Twinkle,
And was gone.

William E. Berninger, Jr.
IMAGE BEHIND THE BAR
An image in the glass behind the
bar
Passes through time along with me;
So near and yet so far,
Does it feel it's traveling life's
same sea?

The image dwells in the room
around me:
The sad ones, glad ones, the too
lost to care;
A room in glass owing that I be,
But am I not free from it's shiny
stare?

A mere reflection I might believe
Of a reality which exists above
and away,
But as I and the image rise to leave
I realize the image in the glass is
today.

Doris Trevor Cannon
Forever Youth and Spring
What the silver mirror says is
falsely true.
I question it again and hope for
more—or less,
But thin revealing lines that gouged
Their patterns round my eyes are
sign posts
Of the mortal age I can't escape.
And yet a part of me ascends
To be forever youth and spring.
It must be so, for in the
luminescent sun of you
I rise and float on weightless
wings,
Ethereal and starkly—ME,
Unclosed from body weight and
flesh,
Unchained and free in a moment
To become your partner in a wild
duet.
I only know this hateful drag of
years
Rewraps itself around me like a
coil
When you are gone—and I become
Once more just what I am—in
flesh.

Jeanne Marie Halama
SPRING COMES FURRY
Spring comes furry,
mewing the brightening morning
catkin-called;
comes blurry,
drifting with silver sails,
Dandelion-balled.
Spring won't hurry;
a Tabby's stroll . . .
petal-foot-falled.

Jeanne P. Frederick
OUR FATHER
What a beautiful thought tonight,
The light of the world.
Our Savior, that's what
Guides you through the night.
Near and far, my what a sight.
Behold! For those who can't
See, hear, feel or tell.

Our Savior said, "Come
Take my hand, I will guide
You along the way.
But do take care. I'm not far
Just a prayer away."
A loving world will do for now,
For our Father
Savior and
Friend.

Crystal Moppin
YOU
You were so gentle
And so very kind
You knew what I was thinking
Inside my mind.

You held my hand
And knew what to say.
You kept me going
All through the day.

You tried to make it
Not hurt so bad.
You showed me the way
As you always have.

You took me with you
And led me through today.
You shocked me so much
I don't know what to say.

You told me once
You would always be there.
Your actions today
Just proved that you care.

Pamela Zivkovic
UNTITLED
The waves rush to the
shore
Arms open, fingers
searching
For a grain of
reassurance.

But the sand is cold
and uncaring
And like a man, alone,
among many
They slink back to the
sea
To the comfort in the
depths of their souls.

Alberta M. Mayberry
THE HOSTAGES
We were Iran hostages,
in a land across the sea.
A land that knew no mercy,
or democracy.

Our days were filled with torture,
our nights were filled with hell.
The secrets of our country,
we would never tell.

They starved us and they beat us,
they tried to make us say,
that we believed in barbarism,
and all its dirty ways.

Torture will never make us,
a traitor or a thief.
To rob the land that we love most,
of liberty and peace.

There is joy in living,
but there is peace in death.
To know that we have done our
part,
to pay a rightful debt.

Our hostage days are over,
and we are coming home to you.
Please show us that you appreciate,
all that we went through.

Jane Noel
SOMEDAY
[To Monmouth High School
Class of 1982 Monmouth,
Illinois]
The year draws to a close,
Bringing High School to an end.
New lives ahead of all of us,
Lie just around the bend.
Someday, we'll return,
To see how all has changed.
Achievements in our midsts,
While the past seems rearranged.
The times we've shared together,
Are more important than you know.
For these memories are all that
will be left,
When our separate ways we all go.
Time moves on and so must we,
For nothing can ever stay.
We'll remember, the way we were
When we look back, SOMEDAY!

Deborah A. Koletty
Those Carefree Teen Years
I know there's someplace
I've got to be.
But I'm wasting my time
just looking for me.
There's homework to do,
dishes in the sink;
But for now I've just got to
stop and think.
Don't they realize
my mind's in a whirl?
Do they know what it's like
to be a teenage girl?
I'm not sure of anything—
my life or career.
I cry for no reason
when no one is near.
I need some comfort
but I can't let them know,

301

I'm too proud to let
insecurity show.
The problems seem endless;
the good times so few
I think it's time to
start anew.
I'll make some new friends
and have a great time,
Reach for the stars
and the world can be mine.
These are the "best times"
they're all telling me.
There's so many things
I've got to see.
Not a worry nor problem
will lay on my mind.
It's time to leave
those troubles behind
And enjoy today
for what I am now
Is all I can be
and all I know how.
The day will come
when high school is done
I'll have learned through knowledge
and through fun
To cherish the memories
of laughter and tears,
That were so much a part of
my carefree teen years.

Teresa Lynn Barnes
WINTER
White world,
Ice glistening,
New snow is everywhere
To make hills for
Everyone to coast upon as the sun
Races skaters across ice covered
ponds.

Willie J. Peeks
NOVEMBER IN MY SOUL
A warming sight of fading ember
soothes the heart and soul,
As final days of my November
slips through my control.

Outside—prevailing winds still blow
with such intensity,
as if to shatter walls it knows
protects the warmth and me.

Another log, a lump of coal
gives life to dying ember,
November lie still in my soul
But, not, I trust . . . December

Robert E. Swadley
MY LOVE FOR YOU
The wind blows softly across
your face,
I live, but to know your grace.
Your beauty is great, as I truly
know,
My love for you has grown, oh, so
slow.

My hope is that you love me, too.
The hope that your love has
grown, even as my love grew.

The sun was made to catch your
hair,
And give your beautiful eyes a
flair.

Your beauty dims the sun,
And holds the rain at bay.
My heart beating quicker,
As your eyes turn me to clay.

Shaping me,
As you do your will.
Loving you,
As you grow brighter still.

Yvonne L. Gillespie
VIA THE GLOW OF LOVE
Remember the day we sat together
On a bench that mounted a rock.
The towering trees that touched
the skies
Became the subject of the
derivation.

A breath of life overtook my soul
And guided me day to day.
Through toil and troubles
Laughter and smiles
I came to feel . . . trust.

Remember the day we sat together
The towering trees that touched
the skies.
A hand outstretched. Our God
above.
A friendship that grew
Via the glow of Love.

Kathleen C. Gullo

Kathleen C. Gullo
SILENT PLEA
On her casket
Lay a wreath
Flowers dying
At her feet.

People milling
To and fro.
Like the lady
In a side show.

"Hello, how are ya,"
"Been so long."

"The choirs good."
"She loved that song."

"Everyone's here
To say goodbye."

"She's gone to
Her maker in the sky."

Who cares she was
Too young to die!

Who cares, the ones
Who really cry.

They are not cruel
When they whisper and sigh.

"She looks so good.
Almost alive!"

They're only glad
Thank God, Not I!!!

Dorothy Brown Wilhite
MY FRIEND
I had a friend who walked with me
When I was sad and unhappy.
If I should have a change of mood,
Then happiness my friend then
wooed.

This friend of mine was always
true;
He helped when there was work
to do.
Time never dragged, nor was I
bored,
Because ideas we had a hoard.

If in a contest I would win,
I could still count on my best
friend.
Tomorrow he would still be there;
I had a friend who really cared.

When I'd no money to my name,
I had a good friend just the same.
Whatever we had we would share;
We both were friends we made a
pair.

Laurie Ernst
MY FRIEND
[This poem was inspired by
Ronda Ballard, with thanks for
being there during the most
trying time of my life.]
Thanks for all you've done; it was
you that cared, you didn't turn
and run
Whenever the chips were down;
it was you I could depend on
being around
I could always count on you
being near; whether I was
living in happiness or dying in
fear
If not for you I would now be
gone; it was you who kept me
going to see a new dawn
You gave me a reason to live and
a reason to care; someone my
ups and downs I could
unregretfully share
You almost always understood
and if not you would try;
you've been good to me, for you
I would die
Thanks again for being my friend;
I know we will be together up
to the end

Maxine Sallee
GOODNIGHT
A candle flickers from afar,
Darkness closes upon golden
meadows,
And the birds lay gently down.

A soft dew gently falls,
And stars slip out one by one,
And a great silence is upon us.

A cloud betrays the hidden moon,
And wind whispers through the
trees,
An orchestra of crickets begin a
symphony.

As nature speaks her sweet
goodnights,
Dreams slip gently through our
minds,
And the promise of tomorrow
will be ours.

Dorothy Bodwell
SPRING LAMENT
When soft spring breezes melt
the crusty snow,
A heartfelt pang that there will
be a time
I will be gone; I will no longer
know.

Mustard sprinkled hills will
bloom, a golden glow

That lights the greening fields
with gilt sublime,
When soft spring breezes melt
the crusty snow.

I'll leave the frothy almonds,
dancing to and fro,
Unfurling tender leaves of palest
lime;
I will be gone, I will no longer
know.

Other hearts will quicken to the
springtime garden show,
New sprouts of tulips, parsley,
thyme,
When soft spring breezes melt
the crusty snow.

They'll laugh with joy, tears will
flow,
I'll not share this moment prime;
I will be gone, I will no longer
know.

I'll not see the shimmer of the
rainbow,
Irisdescence over nature's paradym,
When soft spring breezes melt
the crusty snow,
I will be gone, I will no longer
know.

Kelly Thompson
OUR LOVE
[Dedicated to Dan Abba With
Love]
This love
we share
Is something
rare.
After all we've
been through,
I'm still
loving you.

Arleen Morgan
MASS CONFUSION
Mass confusion
Running through my mind.
Love is such
An unruling bind.

You say you care
And want me near,
Then why in the hell
Aren't you here.

Tell me the truth,
Do you want me or not,
I'm sick of being
Your little tot.

Yancey Grantham
WARMTH FROM ABOVE
The sun came up in the morning
Shining brightly onto a new day,
Bringing light to this lonely planet,
And soothing warmth that
would stay.

He had known her since childhood.
Many of their dreams were the
same—
They didn't know, 'til this day,
That deep in their hearts they
carried a flame.

They were having a picnic together,
After they had spent some time
apart,
When up from the ground grew a
flower
In the shape of a loving heart.

The sunlight beams down
onto the grass below,

Warming the ground
Causing love to grow.

They didn't know it yet,
But they're about to fall in love,
And its all because of the sun
And the warmth that comes
from above.

And their love grew
just like the flower out of the
ground,
Growing with the beautiful emotion
That they together had found.

Dian G. Krogull
UNTITLED
The wind blew upon me and
called my name out low
Child, why are you standing alone
For God has condemned me, I've
committed a sin
He told me to stand here and
wait for him
He's gone off walking down the
sand,
And in his mind, he will decide, if
I still deserve the right, to walk
by his side
The wind bowed its head in
sorrow for me and shed a tear
of misery,
Which became the great sea that
crashed to the sand, as if
reaching out a helping hand
The sea came upon me and
washed away my sins, and
cleansed my hate and fears
within,
Then through my eyes I could
plainly see
God standing there pointing at me
The wind disappeared, and the
sea was gone
God spoke to me softly, My child,
come along

Maureen Gruber
LOVE IS . . .
[Dedicated to my Love Mike]
Love is time we spend together.
Love is grand and forever.
Love is understanding.
Love is mending.
You mend the broken heart.
That you used to have.
You fill the empty space.
By just looking at his face.
You look in his eyes and they
will glow.
When they do, your love will flow.
When your love is flowing.
And your heart is glowing.
You realize your trust is growing.

Louisa Mulvihill
THAT SILLY CHICKEN
A banty rooster did crow
So loud and long, annoying,
You'd think he was Cicero
Or Angel of Destroying.

That silly chicken strutted
Thought everyone afraid,
In their affairs he butted
He thought he was the best made.

Then as he crowed late one night
Thinking he had the last say,
Old owl came in silent flight
Ate him up and flew away.

Julieta Cantu Vasquez
WHY I WRITE
I'm in a cottage in the woods
Surrounded by tree and glen,
And it doesn't help remind me
Of the fool that I have been.

I've let my dreams run my life
And I think that I will stop.
So what shall I do with out a
word
But give my thanks to God.

The sky is getting dark again
And I don't think on going.
So, I'll just stay around awhile
Until the rain stops pouring.

I'm not too sure of what lies
ahead
Or whether the days are right.
All I know, is I AM ME.
And that is why I write . . .

Nora Mariko Oberst

Nora Mariko Oberst
A STORY FOR US
[for Love and Friendship I
reserve this precious space to
place a thought and dedicate a
story]
Like a bud
the petals grew
and matured together
so have we .
blossoming together
we wait for the day
that we must float
on the winds of time
to meet
our destiny.

Denise Joanne McMahan
UNTITLED
[This poem is dedicated to
Jeramy Patrick Parker. This
poem is about how I feel about
us and our relationship "I Love
You Now And Forever"—
"Thanks For Being My Friend"]
I know you'll be here
If I need you
You know I'll be here
If you need me
Our love
Keeps on growing
Even though—we don't belong to
one another.
It's always there
And we know that we can ask for
it anytime—
We need it.
Our love is
Different from others
We share a more stronger love
And it all adds up to one thing:

Our special bond
Keeps us together
When we're apart!
Our love survives
Through this bond
And through all the things we go
through together.
We have no strings attached
To one another
Alls we have is
Our strong love
And special bond
That shall keep us together
forever!

Daniel Johnson
TETHERBALL GAME
All the sweet memories
of our times together,
Charge through my brain
like a ball on a tether,
Wrapping around
each and every emotion,
Winding tighter and tighter
giving me the notion,
That I must spin the tether
backwards in time,
And unwind you forever
out of my mind.
Though I swing at the ball
with all my might,
It merely winds around
another nerve so tight.
It is squeezing all
the life out of me,
Only you can unwind
the tether, you see.

Steve Bernhard
FADED PHOTOGRAPHS
Faded photographs,
of a long lost love affair.
Her writing on the back,
shows how much she cares.

But times have changed and
you've moved on,
and you know, so has she.
Still you sit and wonder
how great it still could be.

To stare into her sparkling eyes,
and see her flash that smile.
You wonder if she's feeling
like you are all the while.

You know you can't go back there,
and she won't come to you.
Another love is gone away,
too bad it's nothing new.

Donalyn Marie Carlson
THE BOND OF FRIENDSHIP
[For Phyllis, who has shown me
what a real friend is as well as
how to be one.]
Love gone awry
chain-reacting depression
You were always there
to console me and confide in.

Through long, endless nights
and mechanical, working days
You were always there
on the telephone, to talk my
fears away.

Tearing up the town
as barflies 'til three
You were always there
to be my loyal drinking
buddy.

When I was feeling fat
and very unappealing

You were always there
to make me sound like an
American beauty queen.

And in times of elation
with life finally as it should be
You were always there
to share the laughter and
be happy for me.

How can I thank you
for not being just another fair-
weather friend . . .
Except, by always being here
ready and willing to
reinforce our friendship bond.

Cynthia Ellen Lindgren
INSPIRATION
[Pour mon cher David Ja ocean
vas lu blue]
Rhapsody in blue
The sky collides
Bells create music of
the mind,
appealing to the world of
thought.
Dischanted lives
flow to class
the use not determined
for their minds are not at
one with their conscious
habits.
The true goal is not assessed but
$uccess drives them.
The land of make believe
plays notes of uncertainty and
insecurity.
And yet,
Foundations of me are
set solidly by you
To love you give
makes it possible to live
a Rhapsody in blue.

Lenora Liberty
A NOVEL, RARE
Her footsteps light and gentle,
retreated down the hall.
She vanished behind the
bookcase, a camoflouged
entrance into the wall.
Beginning from her heart and
ending with the soul.
She recorded her every sin and
every sought for goal.
I reign this kingdom . . . I, Queen
of Sorrow.
A cluster of tears lace my gown,
genuine pearls for a Princess
tomorrow.
Memories dot the paper creating
the lone moments.
Her precious notch in time . . .
writing forever with patience.
Sins come alive, she feels
indebted to guilt in the
presence of chaste women.
A breach in her faith soon
beckons abandoned demons.
The wild life she favored has
furnished a loathsome burden.
To complete this page of
confession will be her promised
guerdon.
I . . . the pen, must interrupt her
melancholy deeds, in vain
search of a poets destiny.
She shan't be famous unless she
dies, to live out this
philosophical prophecy.
Yes, I bid you . . . venture her

dreams though wanton desires appear.
With ink she labors away the sins, her readers discover incredibly clear.
She is grey now, with fingers curled as though a pen were in her hand,
Her mind is senile, typewriter old and stories no longer in demand.
Alas! It's a paragraph gained to a novel . . . rare.
As the Princess
dozes . . . content in her chair..

Maynard Irvin Hebert
BONNIE'S POEM
I would that I could
and
if I could I would
love thee
with all my heart and soul
with every fiber of my being

I would love thee
to the height of
the proverbial mountain
deeper than the deepest sea
and
I would ask naught of thee
but for a smile
occasionally

Vanesa Smith Kearns
DEATH I DID NOT SEE
[In memory of Kyle]
Where was I all those years
when you were living, just as me
the precious time I wasted
death I did not see

while stars were shining in the sky
the sun with-in my heart
I never realized my friend
from this earth you would part

how many tomorrows went by
that I selfishly spent alone
when we could have shared a moment
if only I would have known

all the wishing and the hoping
can not bring life back to you
but you'll be in my heart
in each day that I live through

J.J. Kelly, III
AAAHHH MAPLE
tapped: frosting on longjohns
at the corner bakery
syrup on fluffy pancakes
hot off the griddle

captured: fiery autumn brilliance
standing tall
stark brittle strong
naked against the snow

axed: the desk in the classroom
keeper of my crib notes
posted at the end of my bed
elevating me from the mice

How can I lay match to you?

Angie Shank
LIVE IT TO THE FULLEST
Live each day as each day comes,
Don't look into the future.
For the future no longer holds
The memories of yesterday
But the dreams of tomorrow.
Yesterday we cannot see,
Tomorrow we cannot hold.

The last week we remembered so well
The future in which we cannot see.
Only minutes we've shared together.
All we have to hold onto is
Minutes, as minutes come,
And memories as memories pass.

Wallace L. Weister
ALONE HE WALKS
Alone Japheth walks the endless, desolate highway of life.
On either side of the limitless ribbon of concrete,
hidden from view—
lying in dark, thick underbrush,
standing motionless behind dying, lifeless elms and ashes,
crouching low in wet, stagnant ditches—
pirateers wait for him,
the unsuspecting, innocent traveler.
Scavengers attempt to batten upon his sense of righteousness,
contorting and marring reality with bittersweet tongues,
swallowing truth and vomiting deception—
ingesting sugar and excreting bile.
And yet, Japheth alone straightens the snakey curves in the road,
hurdles the insurmountable obstructions placed in his path,
swims the abysmal channel of deceit.

Daniel S. Johnson Jr
LOVE IS . . . JUST YOU
[Inspired by "Ms. Paradox"]
Love is—
Touching you . . .
with my mind
and soul . . .
with my body . . .
with all my thoughts.
Love is—
Watching you . . .
looking into your beautiful blue eyes . . .
seeing your smile and laughter . . .
feeling your arm on mine.
Love is—
Talking with you . . .
exploring all your being . . .
hearing your expressive voice . . .
feeling the music of your soul.
Love is—
just you.

Madeline Rasmusson
PASSING ABOVE YOU
It was some sixty years ago,
I stood in a spelling line in school,
I felt that I was very stupid,
For I knew I appeared to be a fool.

The teacher gave me a word,
I tried to spell with all my might,
But the little girl that stood next in line,
Was able to spell the word just right.

She whispered "I am sorry that I spelled the word,

For I hate to go above you,"
Because her brown eyes lower fell,
"Because you see I love you."

She later became my wife,
But only for a little while,
The Angels above took her home,
With her fondest sweet smile.

I lived to learn in life's hard school,
That few that pass above you,
Lament their triumph and your loss,
Like her because they love you.

Gail Simon Schultz
REFLECTIONS
As I gaze into a pond of blue,
I see reflections of me and you.
Reflections of our love so dear,
Growing stronger with each passing year.
As far and wide as a clear blue sky,
I see the past floating by.
We made reflections great and small,
Through the years we lived them all.
I hear the singing of a mourning dove,
Pure and sweet like our true love.
Our dear sweet children will always be
Reflections, yes, of you and me.

Archie Midgette Jr.
YEAR OF THE TWINS
[To Twin Granddaughters—
Alicia & Kinisha Smaw.]
1981. Year of the twins
Two of a kind,
Newly born amidst our family life.
Both so sweet and doing fine
And we are so proud of them,
Me and my lovely wife.
All the other family members
And close friends too,
Try their very best to win
The contest of which parent they resemble.
Being only infants, that's hard to do
It's not he or him,
For both are little girls
Who cry and make much fuss
But they mean so mush to us,
They are the offspring of our true love.
Before these two came along
The others were born one by one,
But now our childbearing days are done.
And the Lord always knows what's best
So we thank God and say amen,
Because this year of the twins
Has brought to us great joy and happiness.

Elizabeth Simons
Life Has Much More Meaning
Life has much more meaning,
Since I've been with you.
Rainy days and cloudy skies,
Just don't seem so blue.
Sleeping 'neath the stars at night,
Waking with the dawn,
Knowing what we really share,
It's not possible to go wrong.

Life has much more meaning,
In just the simple things.
Like a flower, or a smile,
Something small that each day brings.
I know that my feelings,
In my heart are true,
Because, life has much more meaning,
Since I fell in love with you.

Sandra Bjanes
OUR FIRST CHRISTMAS
[To my husband, Douglas W. Bjanes]
Our stockings were full
Our tree was bliss
Our hearts were lifted
with Christmas
Our spirit brought the sparkle
to our eyes

Our first Christmas together
to start our lives
Truly an occasion to remember
forever
Knowing we will always be
happy together
Merry Christmas
Darling

Mary Catherine Smith
FORGET-ME-NOT
[To my Grandmother
Catherine Kiel; who raised me.
You are in heaven now. You
found the way and you taught
me how to get there. We are
going to be togather again. I
love you.]
Forget-me-not in heaven
Dear Jesus, sweet and kind
There's an empty room up there I know
But Jesus, is it mine?
Will I play with the angels?
Will I be with you each day?
Tell me how to get there Jesus
For I need to know the way.

Mary Sue Edwards
SOMEONE SPECIAL
To have that someone who will truly care,
As we journey on our daily course of time,
Is a treasure so wonderful and rare,
One which I am fortunate to have found in mine.

With you I can share my thoughts and emotions,

And know that I have someone
there to hear.
You know my numerous failings
and imperfections,
Yet of being made to feel inferior,
there is no fear.

We have shared so many
wonderful moments.
Together we have laughed at
such silly things.
We have cherished one another's
intermost sentiments,
And together we have
surmounted problems with
soaring wings.

There is a burning desire in my
heart,
Somehow just to let you know,
Though we may sometimes be
apart,
You impression on my life will
forever show.

Robbin L. Swanson
WHAT IS A FRIEND?
A friend is love
Someone special
sent from above.

A friend always cares
Whether in person or
Thought, they're always there.

A friend listens to your
Sorrows and dreams,
No matter how odd that it seems.

A person to talk with
Cry with and laugh,
They're not just another myth.

You are a friend
A friend that is true,
And that's why everyone
Needs a friend just like you!

Kassandra Smith

Kassandra Smith
CREATION
*[This Poem is Dedicated to
myself, and every one of my
friends who encouraged me, To
my Parents, to Ivan, my
greatest inspiration, and to my
Creator.]*
First created was Earth and
Heaven,
followed by light to see our
brethren.
Then came the division between
the two,
that called the sea. Created by
Him, who,
To lighten His Heaven our home
by far,

produced the wonder known as
the Star.
The third day brought forth trees,
herbs, and grass,
through each of these His
beauty did pass.
From the waters brought He forth
Life, On five
Also the fowl in the sky so
wide.
The sixth brings cattle, that
which creeps and Man,
the latter to rule in all His land.
Seven was made Holy and
Sanctified,
this is the law that we should
abide.
After all these wonders our God
hath did,
Created was Eve from Adam's
rib.
There is none that proveth
greater than He,
In works, miracles, and prophesy.

Albert Bruce Ringrose, Jr.
THINKIN' ABOUT HER
I think I'm in love
when I'm thinkin' about her
Love her to know
how I feel about her

Could it be,
she's thinkin' about me,
as I do her

Somethin's causin' a love,
a love too powerful
to be,
made by one

Louise S. Yates
TINY VIOLETS IN THE SNOW
*[To My Mother, Mrs. Violet
H.S.G. Howard (May 30, 1903–
January 31, 1980)]*
Tiny little violets in the snow
Their smiles so blue, yet tender,
Pretty little violets wherever they
grow
Will always bring tears as I
remember
That day I said my last goodbye
to you
On that winter's day chilled by
frost and snow.
Always I shall remember tiny
violets blue
Amid the falling snow, tossing to
and fro
Sheltering you from February's
bitter cold
Beneath the sunless sky so gray
Covering the bier as sentinels so
brave and bold
Proudly watching over you that
wintry day.

Lauretta E. Pelton
**The Nightly Symphony Of
the Deserted Home**
Flippety-flop! A screech and a clop!
This haunting synchopated
rhythm breaks the stillness of
each night,
As mirror-like moonlight reveals
a skeletal structure—
Sagging and bemoaning its fate to
the wind.

Time-roughened boards sway to
the sporadic zepher breezes
passing through;
While total emptiness within

howls around the staircase—
Down through the hearth;
bounding from wall to wall;
Then echoing back again.
Echo responding to echo, yet
quickly, one by one, fading off
into the
—eerie midnight air.

The steady banging of a one-
hinged door drums out its
yearning—
For cozier days;—when the latch
still held firm—
And only trusting hands grasped
the knob—
To open or to close as protection
was needed.
But now only the sly eroding
emptiness pervades, prostrating
to nothingness—
The once fullness of the past.

Here then, in reflective splendor,
this haunting dual is played;
This nightly serenade for days
gone by, days of warmth,
security,
Of tenderness and reality, all
wrapped in an overture's
refrain—
That now becomes a lonely
rendezvous perpetuated by—
This orchestrated, silhouetted
souvenir!

Janet Myers
THE WORLD OF POETRY
I have discovered a world
I had not explored before,
The world of poetry.
It is filled with works of art,
Scenes painted with words
So carefully chosen,
And colored with feelings
From deep within the hearts
Of those who write.
How I love to venture
Into this world of verse
So full of meaning,
And filled with the thoughts
Of those who express them
In delightful phrases,
It warms my heart.
It is a world all its own,
And no one can know it,
Except a poet.

Regina Conrath
Worthy Thoughts Mature
Like a hound when he loses the
hare's trail
Sadly I turn from ideas frail
No poem can I compose, no
thought lured
This worthy thought explored
has now matured.

Bob Morgan
MY FRIEND
*[To My Heavenly Father For
Giving Me The Talent To Put
My Thoughts Into Words.]*
There is someone in my heart
That is very dear you see;
Oh! He's not so different from
others
That is to anyone but me.

To me he's all I could ask for
Yes, even Superman too;
Through the eyes of those who
love him
There's nothing he can't do.

Though he may not always be
smiling
Why! I've even seen him cry;
But as I grow older and wiser
Then I'll understand why.

This old world has many sorrows
Many things to make us sad;
Others may call him friend or
brother
But I'll just call him DAD.

Anna Marie Clark
FROM AN UPPER WINDOW
If I but tarry, just a little while,
at the upper window of my room.
I am priviledged to see the friends
of heaven, groom!
If I but keep a quiet way a little
while
and watch below down by the
gate,
I may watch the grackles—three
mated
pair, sit and wait.
Then with an irridecent burst of
wing,
one lifts up with full and
purposeful
delight, plunging into the small
circlet of water.
What a sight!
Splash and tweek and preen each
separate feather,
as the jeweled droplets shower
yonder vine.
Then—finished, leave the water
free
for the next in line.

Faye Ellen Brown
YOU AND I
I met you when
I was I
You were you
And together
We were we

We had to part
So we became
You
And
I

When the two of us rejoined
I was still I
You were still you
And now together
We are we

After we get married
You will still be you
We will still be we
I will still be I

Even after both us die

Everett Francis Briggs
JUDAS SLEEPETH NOT
The traitor left the Paschal scene,
Forsook the supper board,
To do the dark deed recompensed
By his spare, silver hoard.

They somehow thought him gone
to buy
Provisions for the feast;
Perhaps, a Paschal lamb to bring
To some who had the least.

But Jesus knew the treachery
That set this man apart.
He dipped the sop and gave it him,
Appealing to his heart.

The heart of him was stony hard,
Not softened by God's grace.

He had no pity for the poor,
And none for his own race.

So out he went, into the dark
To meet the Prince of Night,
With him to plot the fearsome deed:
Betray the Lord of Light.

Boniface Olekamma Odor
SILENT ANSWERS
Tell me little one,
What is the circumference of my womb
Little one, how did you move and eat and play
in such confinement

Tell me little on'
Did you laugh while I was in pain
or awake in my sleep

Little on',
I have many questions to ask you;
And how did you find your way
in such darkness

Tell me little on'
How did you start to live in me
And from where did you come in.

Thank you little on' for your answers
but, may you live long enough to lose your
teeth and black hair to white.

Ada McCoy
PICTURE A LAND
Picture a land without heartache and pain,
A land where there is no sin or shame . . .
Picture a land, picture a land,
Where Satan, man's tempter, can't enter again.

Picture a land where there come'th no night,
No need for sun or moon to give light . . .
Picture a land, picture a land,
Lighted with radience from the face of God's Lamb.

A land that is fairer than Eden in bloom;
Fairer than Eden before man's doom . . .
Picture a land, picture a land,
Paradise eternal, and man won't be banished again.

Mary Hamilton Darrell
Your Volunteer Fire Department
[Dedicated to the Mount Ulla-Bear Poplar Volunteer Fire Department]
You have many friends who are always near,
In the dead of night or the noonday clear;
They will listen for you and will always hear,
Call your Volunteer Fire Department.

It does not always have to be fire,
It may be comfort or help you desire—
Or your car, perchance, is stuck in the mire.
Call your Volunteer Fire Department.

When the smell of smoke wafts its way to you,
With the fog so thick, can the truck get through?
It can and will. It will come to you.
Call your Volunteer Fire Department.

And if their efforts should be in vain,
They know your heartache, they know your pain.
If they can help they will come again.
Call your Volunteer Fire Department.

Debbi Brinley
LET ME FLY
I want to love and respect you but cannot.
You build walls
Not bridges.
You show me windows to the world,
but put bars on mine,
keeping me from freedom and myself.
I want to be friends
but somehow you are always the enemy.
You are "them".
I am "us".
We cannot meet. I divulge in things
to say:
I am.
I can.
the fun missed.
life passed me by.
A chick within an egg,
trying desperately to hatch.
My wings have dried.
Please let me fly.

Miriam S. Queen
A CHILD AGAIN
Oh! to be a child again
To tell the times that I could spend
Daydreaming and wondering all through the day
Not worrying about work, but learning to play
Just letting my imagination run free
Not worrying of what I want to be
Just listening when I have been asked
Not grumbling if it's another task
Not having decisions around to make
Not having so many rules to break
Just sitting around enjoying life's way
But learning to know when it's time to obey
Just being a child is plain to see
Is just running around and being free.

Christina S. Claud
LIVE FOR TODAY
Why worry about tomorrow?
Let's be content with today;
For we know that tomorrow
Is always a day away.

Yesterday, today was tomorrow.
Tomorrow, today'll be yesterday.

So we can't catch up with tomorrow,
Because tomorrow is still a day away.

Tomorrow is forever in the future.
Yesterday is always in the past.
Today is ever in the present;
Live each moment as long as it may last.

Albion Verne Lambertis
Albion Verne Lambertis
ONLY . . . CAN VALUE
[To my Great Grandmother (Miss Mary Jones).]
Surrounded by wisdom, ideas and deeds
For the liberty of life, I am in need.
And for the materiality of vanity I am not greed,
Because I will follow where God lead.

Advisor to the poor, messenger of God.
Idols of mankind, reveling reality of creation.
Keep us in sanitation, waiting for God is salvation.
So many people come and gone by, is it repartition.
One aim, one destiny, one God.

Vanity in high society is power, material vexation,
Bim on the hour. Money cannot value, the value of wisdom
Many are called chosen only a few.
The value of wisdom is value a million . . .
Million than all the things in Sodom.
Wisdom only dwell in a true few.

Ideas are dreams, everything in life is need
And everything in life is just for a reason the way it seem.
But your deeds, will dwell within your seeds.
To liveth among I brothers and sisters forever
Value my ideas, wisdom and deeds . . .

Lisa Johnson
Search Through Eternity
Down through the ages,
A lonely soul passes through time,
Always searching for something
That it is unable to find.

It is an unending journey

With hardships and sadness.
And it is filled with pain and sorrow
With the hopelessness of the quest.

The world goes on,
Unknowing and uncaring.
The dreams of the lonely one,
Destined never to come true.

A ghost of the thoughts of mankind,
Time passes forever to eternity
With these dreams hidden in the mind;
And this lonely soul searches on.

JoAnn B. Phillips
ESTHER LUE
An angel got her wings today
her name is Esther Lue
She left this world of pain and strife
to the peace that she was due.
She always seemed to be there
when you needed someone
To laugh with and talk to
and share in your fun
Her eyes were bright and shiny
her smile so full of life
Though it was not an easy task
as mother and a wife.
She never had much money
no fortune to unfold
To be with those who loved her
meant more to her than gold
The love that she gave
really brightened each day
She was someone so dear
in her own special way.
There are so many memories
of happy times and sad
I think of her so fondly
she's the best friend that I had.
An angel got her wings today
I know that this is true,
She was an angel here on earth
her name is Esther I ue.

Deborah Vereen
THE HOMECOMING
[Dedicated to the Glory of God who instilled this special gift of verse within me. Praise the Lord!]
Homecoming:
the fledgling to his nest
All snug, secure
and every feather warmed.
Love fills the nest,
for it is the fledgling's own.
And within the straw
he is himself.

Lois Shumate
SILENCE
The sun rises in the morning,
and sets in the afternoon
Silently it comes and goes,
at night, so does the moon

Thousands of snowflakes fall,
they softly cover the ground
And as this happens,
we never hear a sound

In the spring flowers bloom,
so beautiful, and yet so rare
For when this beauty happens,
only silence fills the air

Love is strong and silent,
When it begins to grow
Because the truest of love,

must start very slow

So look with your eyes,
to find the beauty all around
For the most beautiful things,
have no sound

Wilda Caplinger
SHANNON'S FISH
[To my son Shannon, who at
fourteen would rather fish than
almost anything else.]
Shannon caught a big fish and
   reeled it right in,
then he throwed out the line and
   did it again.
Four times in a row he did the
   same thing.
When we asked him how he'd
   just whistle and sing.
What he used for bait he never
   would tell,
just said his secret wasn't for sale.
We guessed everything, worms,
   crickets, even cheese,
but what that kid uses no one
   ever sees.
Oh well, that's OK, I really don't
   mind
cause fried in the pan the fish
   tasted fine.

Maureen Dawn Adams
COLD DARK CLOUD
A cold, dark cloud
   Hung over me
A cold dark shroud
   'Til you set me free,

Memories of loneliness
   Are now today's happiness
Hauntings of awkwardness
   Shadows of my inwardness;

Now the cloud is no more my foe
   But the brightest sun in my eyes
And the laughter is in my heart
   Shining out to the sun from
   these eyes;

Finding the sun, as the cloud died
   Seeing life until you by my side
Running with the wind like a child
   Who knows no chains breaking
   his stride.

Pall Leigh Tomas, ii
BEEN
Time is
slip p in g
by
(soon
it'll be
Time
To die)

Not gonna be some things
I
hoped to be
(still
I am
me)
aging
(forget-
ting)
Here I come
(I hope my
Key fits
The Door)

Grace Vaughn Wilkes
LIFE
Life—how do we live it?
Pursuing endless dreams . . .
chasing will-o-the-wisp fancies?

We live in the flower of our
   youth,
we live to find the golden rainbow.
We die—in the flower of our
   youth . . .
the rainbow is never there.
Could we but live, could we but
   know
how fragile the line between life
   and death.
The hereafter—the here and now
the fast-paced daily ritual
prepares us not for the harsh
   reality
of facing our innermost selves . . .
We see, we touch but fleetingly
the life that is a carousel.
      We spin, we whirl
      We pause, we fall
      We stop . . . we die.

Tammy Renee' Lankford
What's Left For Me Now?
What's left for me now?
   Besides the memories and pain
   you left behind.
What's left for me now?
   Except the lost feeling and
   confusion that stays on my mind.
What's left for me now?
   A stuffed teddy bear you won
   for me, and a pretty chain made
   of gold.
What's left for me now?
   When you have gone far away,
   and aren't nearby for me to hold.
You made promises you knew
   inside that you
could never keep.
You held me in your arms and
   told me that
your love was deep.
But what's left for me now?
A few memories . . .
               And nothing else.

Christy McKinney
LOVE
Love is like a flower
That blooms in spring
If cultured and cultivated
It becomes a beautiful thing

If left to fend for its own
Weeds and thorns will soon be
   grown

So cultivate your love
And you will see
The beautiful flower
It can be.

Ralph E. Tutwiler
I'LL JUST STOP AND REST
I like the world as it used to be
   With the horse and buggy and
   such
When things moved along at an
   even pace
   And people didn't hurry so
   much.
They say we must move with
   progress,
   To stand still we will get far
   behind.
We must hurry and run before it's
   too late
   Or we just won't get there on
   time.
I can't seem to get in a hurry
   As through this old life I go.
I would just as soon sit down and
   rest

Or talk with someone I know.
So I'll just walk along the road
   And stop when I think it's best.
I'll find someone too tired to go on
   And with them I'll stop and rest.

Alfred Vanek
THE DINER
[To Jackie and my many
enjoyable friends at the diner]
A diner can be many things
   to those who stop and stay,
to eat or drink, or reminisce,
   or pass the time of day.
It has a special atmosphere
   quite difficult to find,
except upon a counter stool
   that twirls your whole "behind".
Your eyes will wander left and
   right,
   it doesn't matter where;
yet, somehow, you have got to
   know
   who else is sitting there.

And your ears may change
   directions
   until they find the grill,
where steak and eggs are makin'
   sounds
   that give your nose a thrill.
Or maybe it's the waitress, who
   is first to catch your eye;
she's often runnin' back and forth—
   you sometimes wonder why.
You'll prob'ly see the owner, too—
   a little Irish lass
with eyes that splurge a twinkle,
   and
   a gentle touch of class.
But should you spot an old-time
   friend
   who stopped in for a rest,
then surely, you are now
   convinced,
   this diner is the best.

Allan Blank
Elaboration On An Image
Legs,
Three legs
Since you're a grand,
Hardly a baby—
Since babies can't stand!

Can you swing those legs
While players Chopin away?
Why cover the legs
You can't kick or sway?

Grandma says
A leg should never be bare,
Bare, we'd stare,
Not listen,
But look,

The music forsook.

Those legs hold a frame
That's mighty yet tamed,
Tensioned strings
Attached for hammering.

Grandma knew
If the legs went up,
The keyboard would go down.

So it's underware for the legs
And ivory for the keys,
But let's not fret—
Depressed,
We may be pleased.

Katherine Weydell
IT IS REAL
Your fingers tingle, moving over
   me,
And whisper like a silver
   raindrop dance.
How could this be the hand of
   time and chance
Just idly sifting love's decayed
   debris
And settling when it's found an
   empty lee?
The fog is dancing in a twisting
   trance.
We smile together with a glowing
   glance,
While others wonder if it's meant
   to be.
But forest flings and sunshine
   flames of maize
Have shown the truth of dusty
   crystal dreams.
Our love is more than dull and
   tired tryst
Or foolish mutters under
   moonman's gaze.
It will embrace the night with
   green-gold gleams
And last until the braes are
   graying mist.

Lucille M. Johnson
I WAS HIS LADY LOVE
[In memory of my husband
who died in 1945.]
Time once stole my love,
I knew it would
The signs were all there,
But I was his Lady Love.

I felt so safe and sure
In our lovely world.
Then time, my enemy, came
Along and was the lure

To steal away my love.
The years quietly flew by
For my love and I
And I was ever his Lady Love.

He and time have disappeared,
Slipped into eternity,
But somehow I know
He feels my tears.

Perhaps we'll stroll again
Down some road above,
Free of time and pain
And I'll be his Lady Love.

William E. Smith
PRAYER
There's nothing in this world as
   precious as a prayer;
A rendezvous that God and I can
   share;

Where thoughts and words are
   intertwined
in solitude and peace of mind.

A prayer brings God close to my side
with love I will not be denied.

A prayer can offer thanks for days of happiness
or ease away the pain of deep distress.

When twilight comes each fading day
I close my eyes with God and pray.

Every care soon will vanish there
in the soft, sweet, silence of a prayer.

Marilyn Mills Robertson
LIFE
[For my mother who made my life beautiful]
Life isn't easy,
It's hard as can be
Living each day
Just waiting to see—
If we're gonna make it
In this world like it is
It seems to get harder
With each passing year.
The crime is outrageous
The prices are too
What in the world
Are we going to do?
We work everyday
Just getting by
Making a living
And staying alive.
We look to the future
Wondering if—
Life will get better
Or just stay like this.
Something must happen
Something must change
So the next generation
Can stay in the game.

Terry L. Evanoff
RAINBOW DRIFTER
Rainbow Drifter where you bound;
you come and go, then you can't be found.

I've heard, you look for hearts of stone, to soften with your mellow tones.

Your work, it's done in such silent slumber, the hearts you have warmed,
I can't begin to count the number.

And then you're gone just like you came, in candle light breezes, silent rain, Rainbow Drifter gone again.

Mrs. Vineler Mann
THE ROSE
The red rose in the window
I wish that I could buy.
It looks like I can't save the money
No matter how hard I try.

I have a friend who needs them
To help her on her way
She has been sick oh so long
"Some roses would help me", I heard my friend say.

Someday in the great beyond
The flowers will be free
She won't have to get them
From her good friends like me.

There will be streets and walkways
Of gold where we shall trod,
There will be flowers growing
As far as we can see.

Susan M. Do
He's a Soldier, He's a Man,
He's A Soldier, He's A Man, And there he stands
with a gun in his hand,
For the bombs and bullets fly there goes
another man to die.
He's A Soldier, He's A Man, And there he stands
with a gun in his hand,
People why can't we understand that life means
more than a piece of land,
So let's put down the guns that kill our
men and sons.

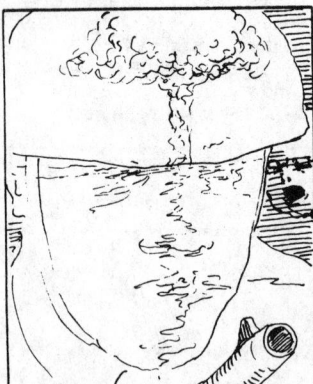

He's A Soldier, He's A Man, And there he stands
with a gun in his hand,
For the children who will die may we morn
may we cry.
For in years to come there will be none,
For he grows into a man and like the rest
he'll take a stand with a gun in his hand.
He's A Soldier, He's A Man.

Sheila Monica Nettle
MY WISH
When I was a child
I wished for a house
Made of cookies
Filled with
Candy
and
Fruit
and
Gum
Now I'm grown
I wish for a house
Made of brick and stone
Filled with
Laughter
and
Kindness
and
Love

D. Scot Hinson
PANGAEA
We are shattered Pangaea,
Her misshapen and changing face.
We are brittle Laurasia's parts,
Blemishes on a widening seafloor.
We are Atlas bound in the Manacles of decomposition,
Straining against the ineluctable Drift of the continents.

Land masses along the divide

Slip and collide.
Superislands creak under their own
Weight, shoulder the pangs
That shudder like quakes along
Their lime and granite contours.
None can right the list
Of the upraised mantle and crust;
Nor slow the spread of the Jungle's divine tangles.

We are memory adrift amongst
The infant isles,
Born of Pangaea's throes.
We are the rings of fire
That erupt around the Shrinking Pacific.
Breaking up,
We are the braided helix Unraveling.

Margaret Worman
WHAT IF?
[To RLM whose life touched mine with joy and beauty]
What if flowers never bloomed
And never spread their sweet perfume?
Would life be ever quite the same
Without the beauty they contain?

What if tiny raindrops high
Remained forever in the sky?
Would other things refresh the earth
And take away its growing thrist?

What if minds refused to share
And new ideas wouldn't dare?
Would hopes and dreams be left unspent
To plod along in discontent?

What if men in wonder stood
To ponder if a cause were good?
Would freedom wait and wonder why
The moment of truth had passed them by?

What if love never healed a heart
But always fearful stood apart?
Would it ever grasp what it might win
Or just sadly mourn—what might have been?

Pearl Swain
HAPPINESS
[Written in 1959 in appreciation of the happiness experienced with my wonderful husband Charles, and our four beautiful children, Stephen, Eleanor, James and Richard.]
Happiness does not lie mainly in things
Many things are useless trash and nothing more;
Yet multitudes set great and goodly store
In costly possessions, hilarity and flings,
Never hearing the golden throated thrush that sings,
Familiar well loved voices at the door,
Blind to the sunshine on a kitchen floor,
Or iridescent sheen on swallows wings.

Ah, yes, poor souls, tho' they have more possessions,

Than I could ever hope or wish to see,
This lust for transient glory, these obsessions,
This mercenary madness, venal spree,
Is part and parcel of their trite transgressions,
And would not constitute happiness for me.

Beth Peticos
WITH LOVE
If I could have my way
to you I would say,
I do it only once, each moment is the last
I would breath you in
wrap you in my arms, and smile all the way.
Leave you, I do not desire
Leave you, I must.
Oh, please give me time—to love—to trust.
But, most of all do not let me leave you without a kiss good-bye.
Yes, I love you very much
Life.

Rhonda M. Pelletier
The Friend I've Found In You
I really am quite grateful for
the friend I've found in you.
Why you've done all this for me;
I haven't got a clue.

Whenever I'd be troubled, friend,
it seems that you'd be there.
You'd open up your heart to me,
and show me that you care.

When I'd be upset about
the problems of my day
You'd sit down right beside me
and then promise you would stay.

You'd talk about my problems
and convince me I should try.
You'd brush away my every tear,
and raise my spirits high.

Because you've been this kind of friend
I just wish I could do,
Something to repay you for
the friend I've found in you.

Charlotte Trevillyan Sheward
Signs Of Spring At La Casa De La Cactus Wren
[This Poem was inspired by my dear husband, Bob, for my brother Jim Trevillyan, who owned Spanish Hat and Patio.]
With bits of rope, kapok and string we watched each day as he would bring
Items for her babies' bed to the Spanish Hat above our head.
The Hat that traveled to and fro from Guadalajara, Old Mexico.
We never dreamed some day it would rest on a peg in our Patio
And serve as a nest.

She was meticulous, choosey, too, discarding the things that seemed too new;
Fitting each piece in that bedroom suite; making the boudoir very complete.
We fitted our eyes to the

Camera's lens
and watched each day for the
baby Wrens.

Now we sit and wonder when
we'll see each tiny Cactus Wren
Emerge from the colorful
Mexican Hat
to watch while we just sit and
chat—
Perched and clinging to the swing,
ready to sing—ready for Spring!

Ethel M. Tinney, B. A.

Ethel M. Tinney, B. A.
THE DANCE OF TIME
The days dance by
Sometimes they waltz—
Tomorrow with today,
Today with yesterday—
The eternal triangle,
We dangle
As they sway.
We must not laugh in madness,
We even smile in sadness,
The scintillating scenes of sea
and sky
Make loving liquid laughter in
the eye,
A tinkling—bell laugh like the
Donelly daughter,
An echoing laugh from
mountains near water,
As in all history
Time is still a mystery.
The dance of Time,
The solemn, frantic dance of
Time,
The roll of centuries
But somehow like the falling of
the leaves.
The climax comes at Christmas,
Each year, when ebbing fast away,
Shines out to light the Holy Day.
In the dance, too natural to pass,
We all participate,
For this we are never late.
You, with your gorgeous grin,
Come and join in
The dance of Time,
(The devilish dance of Time,)
The Creator's computer set
sublime.

Eva Jo Langley
FADED DANCER
In her mind remains the dancer
though the ballroom's long been
cleared;
and time captured handsome
partners . . .
names on cards of yeteryears.

In her mind remains the dancer

though gay ball gowns fade with
dust,
and the instruments of lively step
are silenced with time's rust.

Though the slender ankles,
swollen,
and no light grace remains,
her mind still glides in memory
of a waltz's sweet refrain . . .

When time's touch seems hard
upon her
there's a secret place she goes
to share laughter with a dancing
girl
who, in naive wisdom, knows . . .

in her heart
remains the dancer . . .

Jane Bong—Hwa Chen
CONFESSION
A calm night
A cold breeze crept into my
abode,
I looked high up for the moon,
I saw that she was shadowed—
With mist-like cloud—a scene
I compared it with my soul,
"Lord, where art thou?"

I sought for Him
He could not be found,
About me all was darkness,
He was far beyond my reach,
With out-stretched hands I felt
Him
And cried for His mercies,
"Lord, take me and wash me."

He came to me,
Tears covered me:
"Lord if it is a temporal comfort I
seek,
Depart from me for I am sinful."
He took me and held me close,
"My grace is sufficient for thee,
Rest in peace, my child."

Helen King Thornton
NOSTALGIA
Remember the "good old day's"?
Ice-cream from an old wooden
freezer?

We'd turn the crank handle with
watering mouth's.
Boy! that old crank was a
"wheezer"!!

But, that home-made ice-cream
was worth it all,
Banana, vanilla and peach,
On a hot, summer's day, it
tasted so grand.
Much better than store-bought
that's alway's on hand,
cause We'd all take our turn at
the handle
and We'd laugh and frolic and
sing.

Yep!! That good, old home-
cranked ice-cream tasted better
than any-thing!

Remember the nickel-bar
candy? Baby-Ruth and Hershey
and Good-Bar's??
They were three time's the size
they are to-day.
And—remember the huge pickle
jar's?, with dill pickle's so large
You could suck one all day, so
tangy and zesty and tart?

And the jell-do-nuts and parched
peanuts were dear to My
childish heart.

Remember the hot—buttered
pop-corn You'd buy at the
picture-show??
You'd much it and crunch it
while "Duke Wayne" and
"Hoppy" would give You a
warm, dreamy glow.

A shoe-shine cost only a nickel
and the best part of that was
the sound—That shine-boy
could really make that rag sing!
And! How bout the merry-go-
round?, at the park!
Sometimes, The rides would be
free, You'd grab the brass ring
on the carrousel and whirl and
twirl! Ahh! Me!!

Nostalgia is a part of to-days
regime and "the good old days"
are only a dream, but the
memories made in the days
gone by are sweet and they
linger, still.
The "good old days", The
"innocent age"!!
They still give My heart—strings
a thrill!!!

Anna M. O'Neil
QUESTION OF LOVE
*[I dedicate this poem to Mark
Pedersen, my favorite Mariner
and to all the times he's made
me smile (Even when I didn't
want to) by just being him.]*
Is this really happening? Or is it
just a dream?
Could that look you gave me
mean everything it seemed?
I watched you from the bleachers
and I saw you look my way.
Were you really looking at me, or
at someone far away?

Could love be as beautiful as in
books it always seems?
Are you just as wonderful as I see
you in my dreams?
Was I just imagining the moment
that we shared,
When all the world had
disappeared and just you and
me were there?

And why is it I feel so strange? Is
this what love's about?
Why do I feel you're pitching love
and I am striking out?
Was I meant to love you? Could
it really be?
Or is someone, shomewhere
waiting—waiting just for me?

Tina (Fredette) Senecal
THE ROSE
*[R. B. Ain't it strange how some
things change, and some things
will always be! One goes on
and one remains chained by all
these memoreies. T. M. S.]*
As the rain genty falls upon
The rose
As the snow slowly drifts along
The rose
As the sun brightly shines among
The rose
You see, you are
The ray of sunshine

The snow that drifts
The rain that falls
I am
The rose

Pearl J. Wentworth
DE PROFUNDIS
*[In gratitude to God, and
dedicated to my sister Erlene
Hill, without whom I could not
have made it.]*
Deep in man is a dynamism
which drives him toward the
Infinite
The search for God, the
affirmation
of His existence.
This quest for Truth
but whets the appetite for more
And man cries out, "Oh Lord, who
am I" "What am I for"?
Man is born of God, sent by God
The Eternal Breath blown upon
the slime of earth
As dust His Hands did hold.
The confusion that once clouded
this understanding
Is no longer captive
in the anguish of mans soul.
As Faith gives sight to the
blinded eye
And man beholds the evidence of
things not seen
All that once was darkness
Glows in this Light of God
Supreme.

Betty Olson
MY LIFE
My life is composed of staffs and
notes
Music, rhyme, and lyrical quotes
Dreams and desires that relate to
others
Cowboys, clowns, dreamers and
lovers

Barbara Lane Soos
FRIENDSHIP
To find a friend, a confidant to
treasure,
'Twould be a fete to celebrate
An alliance of infinite
pleasure.

To know a friend and trust the
bond that's growing,
To share the gift of 'give-and-
take'
True friends exchange
un-owing.

I need a friend to 'rap' with come
what may,
To deliberate on worldly ills
In weighty 'tete-a-tete'.

I have a friend, a helpmate for all
time,
We collaborate and simplify
Life's laborious 'up-hill-climb'.

You are my friend. How fortunate
can I be?
It helps to bare one's heart and
soul
In commiserate company.

Because we are friends my sphere
is communal space.
Never again need we face alone
Life's cruel, insensitive pace.

When you need a friend don't
hesitate to beckon me.

When anxiety grips it's mighty lock
   Friendship is the master key.

Tony Hale
ODE TO MY LOVE

Amongst the woods you seemed
  so fair
With natural beauty and angel
  hair.
Near the side of a lake I saw you
  pass
And watched you move in the
  tall green grass.
Physical beauty you have
  without doubt
And the ground you touched was
  proud of your route . . .
Yes the birds, the squirrels and
  firecrest of bears
Quickly made way for the fairest
  of fair . . .
Especially the boy you touched
  that day
Perceived the warmth of your
  sunlit ray.
Who could imagine such a
  perfect being
I, my love, and everyone's
  agreeing.
If by chance I ever get lost
Nothing will stop me, not even
  the frost . . .
For I'll find you again wherever
  you are
With your lasting light, bright as
  a star . . .
Then we'll settle down and rest a
  while
And once again I'll wear a smile.
This my love I know is true
For we are one, and never two.

Julie Fieszel
THE LEAF

The leaf floats down to lie in its
  eternal grave
Once alive, now lifeless
Once green, now empty brown
The leaf is like a person pulled
  down from its gloried home'
It flips, it twirls losing all its
  senses
Not being able to struggle back
Its world distorted while it floats
  in limbo
Down—Down it floats
Will it ever end?

Eugene M. Bazile
SUMMER'S COMING

*[To my Mother Snowy A.
Bazile: A fine woman and
teacher . . . Love.]*
Summer's coming . . .
  By the changing weather
  And it doesn't matter if I'm ready
  Or if Betty my love is still far
    away
  Or that my fishing pole ain't
    repaired
  Nor that my glove is worn and
    tattered
Summer's coming . . .
  In the fields growing green
  Along banks on the streams
  Where the grass grows then
    someone mows
  For the animals which teems
Upon the "Mighty's revolving ball
Enjoying the sunshine most of all

Summer's coming . . .
When the feeling in school
Is often in the mood of not
  learning
But the yearning to get out with
  one so true
Running free in nature like the
  breeze
Caught up in wonders of love's
  fancy

Summer's coming . . .
Along shores of the seas
In the wooded forestry
Fullest of life seldom there's strife
A time to reflect on life's being
The mystery of living then dying

Summer's coming
In the sounds of the air
The sweet smell that is there
The pretty sights touch of
  delights
And every path is so fair
In the valleys beneath the
  mountains
In the cities around the fountains

Carol McAfee Appleby
YOUR HOME

Dear Boy, I passed your home
  today,
Your little Kansas prairie farm.
It nestled against the setting sun,
Your bit of heaven, safe from
  harm.

Recall the week you went away
You worked to cut the old
  hedgerow
And didn't finish? Now your Dad
Says: "It'll wait. He'll come, I
  know."

There in the door your blue star
  hung
And by the door your Mother
  stood;
Her face was lifted toward the
  east;
I would have spoken if I could.

And now, goodnight, Dear Boy,
  goodnight;
You'll never know my name nor
  me:
A stranger passing on a bus
Across the land you're keeping
  free.

Joy S. Bryson
MISSING HIM

*[Dedicated to the memory of
Bobby Morgridge]*
Sometimes I just miss him in those
  quiet moments when I'm alone.

My thoughts drift and I remember
  times past . . .

  those happy days of fun and
  laughter . . .

  the closeness, warmth and
  affection shared.

A rare and unique
  companionship . . . mother and
  son.

Send his spirit back
  to comfort me . . .

  to ease the grief and
  longing . . .

Let me remember beauty;
  the touching love we shared.

May eternity be reality . . .

my spirit find his,
  that all won't have been in
  vain,

  and at long last—peace!
  the final end of pain.

John Michael Gawronski
WILD LIFE

Wild from the day they are born
Innocent till the day they die
Loney in a struggle to survive
Dying for being free

Lifeless in a world of pollution
Irreversible sacrifice for space
Fighting for the right to live
Endless torture by man

Leon Goldenberg
GROOM AND BRIDE
    BRIGHT IDEAS!

(About a happy marriage—
a baby in the carriage.)
  But, all depends—
  Which parent, wears the pants
(Love with bluff, a ruination—
Without consideration.)
  When your husband gets home
  late
  Have faith, don't think he had
  a date
(I must say to the man, do what
  you can—
Don't lie, you will not have to
  deny—
And your wife, will not have to
  cry.)
ATTENTION PLEASE, READ
THIS
(In the olden times—
There, were no crimes,)
(An old, old mother—
Went to live, with her daughter)
(Her son in law, was a sport—
His mother in law, was happy,
  hence forth.)
  This is a *fact*—
  There was, lots of *respect*.

Janice C. Burger
ENDLESS BOUNDARIES

Come with me now
  take my hand I'll lead you;
to a place and time
  where nothing really matters

We won't have to live up to
  anyones
  expectations but our own
We can give fully of ourselves
  because
  there will be no limits
as we discover each others
  boundaries

without crossing any fences

The territories are endless when
  two adventurers share their
  lives

so take my hand and come along
  as we journey deep into our
  future

We'll follow our hearts as they
  lead
  us to the peaks of mountains
we must conquer . . . . . .

Josephine H. Lenard
LIFE, THE TRUE STORY

The story of is always true.
Although it may read like a great
  fiction.
Growing up to adulthood covers
  Chapters one and two.
Hardships, Heartaches, and
  pleasures a few,
Seasoned with friendships, make
  the story true.

At times you may feel that life
  has you beaten.
So Chapter three will find you
  lost,
for alone you weaken.
You'll find a need for a Special
  someone there,
To share your pleasrues and
  strife.

But beware, for the Chapter four
  starts the Rest of your Life!

Myra Page
LODE STAR

Words dancing in my head,
thoughts seeking form keep me
  awake.
In the night sky I find Big Dipper,
  then our
North Pole Star, guide since time
  began, for
travellers by land, by river , sea:
"Follow the Drinking Gourd!"
Slaves fleeing north to freedom
  send back
Word that now we march by,
  sing.

Stars in the Gourd's handle begin
  their circle of the Pole:
for a time I watch, then return to
  bed.
Near me, John, in quiet sleep,
across the hall, our children:
  perhaps they dream?
Above us the lode—star
Soon day will come, work begin

Mary Lynch Kelsey
FAITH

I wait—and I believe—
  This is prayer, is it not?

Believing, waiting, knowing God
  hears;
  Knowing, if His wisdom causes
  us to wait,
He gives us the strength with
  which to wait—
  Until the praying heart has
  sufficiently pained,
Until that heart's prayer is
  ultimately gained—
  Through believing,
  waiting . . .
Knowing God hears—
  And dries all tears . . .

Shirley M. Thompson
THE GOOD BOOK

I read a book that I enjoyed
The book was about our precious
   Lord
It was about the way He lived
Especially about the things He did
The miracles that He performed
The group of teachers He had
   formed
The Commandements, Laws that
   He gave us to obey
The way he taught us how to
   pray
He showed us how to save our
   souls
To make Heaven our only goal
He gave us graces to do our best
To live with Him in Eternal rest
It's up to us not to stray
To do this, we must always pray
For guidence and help all through
   the year
Then we can live without fear
Until we meet our Lord and see
The plans He had for you and me

Gracie Marie Ramos
TIME FOR LOVE

It's lonely being me
filled with questions left
   unanswered
Scattered memories, shattered
   dreams,
Building something—I'm not sure
   what—
   Picking up the pieces.
Oh, yes I have you.
but you love the strong in me,
the me that knows where It's
   going.
But now I'm the other which you
   despise—
   The weak, the unknowing,
   the tearful-eyed.
Go ahead! Run! Hide!
I know you hate the tearful-eyed.
You were never taught how to
   love.
You were rarely held, you were
   rarely loved.
So will you let me hold you now?
   Is it too late for love?

Helen Strey
WHERE'S MOTHER?
   (3 Yrs. old)

A little tot fell on his knee—
(Pushed by his older brother)—
"See what you did, you bully?
It's bleeding, too, —*Where's
   Mother!*"
   (5 Yrs. old)
"I'm home—see the Valentine I
   made?
Not you, sis, another—
See, it says "I Love You!"—
Where is she ?? —*Where's
   Mother!!*"
   (8 Yrs. old)
"Here's a May-Basket Sue left for
   me!
I'd give her one, if I had my
   druther—
Would kid's tease me? Any candy
   left?
Will you help me make one? —
   Where's Mother!!"
(12 Yrs. old)
"Anybody care? My bike's got

a flat—
It's my candy bar, Sis, don't *hover!*
I need cookies for Scouts—
And I tore a hole in my pants —
   Where's Mother!!"
   (16 Yrs. old)
"May I have the car tonight?
For a while yet, keep it under
   cover—
I'll ask Dad after he talks to you—
Hey, —*Where's Mother!!*"
   (20 Yrs. old)
"Oh, I'm soooo in love with that
   girl—
There'll never be any other—
Do you think we're old enough to
   be married?
Are you listening? —*Where's
   Mother!*"
   (25 Yrs. old)
"Hello, Dad! —The BABY came—
He's sure tiny —Can kisses
   smother?
Can she come soon?? *Where's
   Mother!!*"
   (30 Yrs. old)
"I'm so happy, good wife, child, &
   job—
The Lord has blessed me, & how,
   brother!
I want to tell her Happy
   Birthday— *Where's Mother!!*"
   (40 Yrs. old)
Happy Mother's Day! I'm
   thankful for you & Dad.
That you love God & love each
   other—
For the Christian home you
   raised us in—
Your love and care—say—
   Where's Mother!
   (50 Yrs. old)
"Hi Dad!—How are you????"
Well, Son, Usually you have
   found her doing something for
   others
In the next room—"
Where's everyone ??? *Where's
   Mother!!!*"

"It takes a little longer to find her
   now.
God called, he needed another
   Mother—
Take it easy, Son, When he calls
   us—
She'll be the first to greet us,
We'll not have to ask, "*Where's
   Mother!!*"

Nina W. Kurkamp
"Beauty" The Young Stag!

Beauty is where you find it.
In the artist's sudio; the roadside.
Or that shadowy figure flitting
   out and, in the forest within

That beautiful son of the Deer
   Line
How proudly he issue forth
From a clearing—headup, sniffing
   the air, so fine

He's young & graceful; antlers
   growing
His coat, so colored in tones
It's blending into his surrounding
   zones!

His gait is speedy. To sounds

he's keen,
The crack of a rifle—or,
By one of earth's eager hunter
   seen.
He quickly disappears

That graceful young stag!
A showmanship example—tis
   true.
It's shown often in ads as is due.

The holiday season specials
Christmas greetings features
And such!
Very often—Very much!

Gina Barrie May
What Is Your Love Mean To Me?

*[Wes, no matter what
tomorrow brings, I'll keep
loving you. Thank you for
teaching me how to love.]*

The touch of your hand? The
smile I can't resist, or saying
you understand . . . maybe it's
your soft sweet kiss . . . . Could
it be the special things you do
. . . or the way you hold on to
me tight . . . Maybe . . . it's
the way you say I love you . . .
or those silent loving nights. Is
it the way you love me only?
. . . or the funny jokes you tell
. . . or . . . maybe it's that you'd
never leave me lonely . . . or
how you would kiss me if I fell
. . . Could it be the look in
your eyes . . . the way we've
grown together . . . maybe
because we could never say
goodbye . . . and how we would
talk about forever . . . Would it
be the way I love you . . . or
maybe it's just how I need your
love . . . or a love like ours is
found by few . . . could it be
your the only one I'm dreaming
of . . .
What is your love to me?
It's something I can't explain . . .
Something I don't want to be
without . . .
It's knowing you'll never leave
me in the rain . . .
And never having any doubt . . .
I just can't feel any pain . . . .
That's what your loves all
about . . . .

Ms. Yolanda E. Preston
OUR GUARDIAN ANGEL

Our GUARDIAN ANGEL is W-
A-T-C-H-I-N-G over us both
DAY and NIGHT.
In the heavens at N-I-G-H-T, we
A-L-L can see sparkling angels
within their F-L-I-G-H-T.
Like the S-T-A-R-S that are V-I-S-I-
B-L-E at night within the sky,
which G-L-I-T-T-E-R-S like
diamonds that throw off such a
dazzling L-I-G-H-T.
Behind us one and A-L-L; our
GUARDIAN ANGEL is
standing, so B-E-A-U-T-I-F-U-L
and T-A-L-L.
Our GUARDIAN ANGEL has an
astonishing G—L—O from her
HEAD to her TOE.
Our GUARDIAN ANGEL is
surrounded by an

ILLUSTRIOUS L-I-G-H-T; and
her attire is of W-H-I-T-E.
So, P-L-E-A-S-E take good
C-A-R-E of your BODY and
SOUL.
Our GUARDIAN ANGEL has
H-E-A-R-T far more P-E-R-F-E-C-T
Than gold.
Our GUARDIAN ANGEL
G-U-I-D-E-S us both DAY and
NIGHT; even though we are
sleeping and dreaming of
S-U-P-E-R-B thoughts of a
mystifying P-A-R-A-D-I-S-E.
We A-L-L should be correcting
the W-R-O-N-G-F-U-L things by
doing R-I-G-H-T-F-U-L things
that are good from our
HEARTS.
Our GUARDIAN ANGEL stands
over us throughout the
N-I-G-H-T.
So, take good care of your body
and soul; Y-O-U MAY NEVER
KNOW, when Y-O-U-R
GUARDIAN ANGEL is
W-A-T-C-H-I-N-G and
L-O-O-K-I-N-G over
Y-O-U with a radiant
G-L-O.

Barry Anthony Smith

Barry Anthony Smith
AGELESS

*[To my parents, my friend
Ricky Sullivan, and everyone at
Mt. Olive High School.]*

Life is a fertile growing field
That never fails to be
And a freely flowing creek
With all the beauty of the sea
Happiness is watching a gentle
   setting sun
From high upon a mountain each
   becoming one
Beauty is a voice with sweet and
   mellow sounds
Coming very near to passion
Then residing as it rounds
Loving is a friendship who's tide
   has never turned
Which is still above its
   boundaries
Throughout the years that it has
   burned.

Kitty Manchester
That Beautiful Mountain

"LOVE?"

"LIFE?

"BEAUTY?"

WILL be—no strife?

WHERE IS that heart?
  Seek-; the treasure of LIFE-,
    FOR ALL those human SOULS?
      A bush-a bird-a tree-.
        See that heart!
          It beats to the rhythm of
            pounding waterfall-
            That sparkling water gushes.
          down the mountain(s) face-
          If we could gulp the pure,
            clean rays that sparkling
            FOUNTAIN has-,
          crystal clear roars from the
            cliff-,
          STORMS NEVER CAME
            THAT WAY!
          LIGHTENING NEVER
            HURT!!
            Some glory in the flashing
              BOLT-
          THAT LIGHTS THE SKY!!
            like jagged, zigzag chains
            that flash through the pitch,
            dark night.
          Thunder crashes!! THE
            mountain (not far from
              OUR BORDER)-
              NEARLY CRACKED
                APART!
              LOTS WERE AFRAID.
                NOT I!?
                GOD'S anger on the earth-!!
              DID IT SCARE? not me-
                not when GOD IS ABOVE
                TO OVERSEE.

Elmer Louis Winkler
Love Etched In Melancholia
*[Dedicated to Susan Marie
Goodin (nee Winkler) and her
husband Robert for the faith
they had in "Pop".]*
They are all gone, like the leaves
  from the trees, in Autumn . . .
Scattered, to all the far points,
  like the leaves, before the wind;
Then comes the snow of Winter,
  to lend a touch of beauty, all
  her own . . .
Matching the white, of my
  Autumn and Winter, which
  crowns my head.

Tho' far away, their voices come
  softly to me, on the whispers of
  the winds . . .
An invisible presence, I can feel,
  they are here, yet they are not;
I call out to them, they answer
  not, only the winds, answer me
  back . . .
Their images, are forever etched,
  on the viewing screen of my
  heart titled, "Love In
  Melancholia".

I watch Winter's snows come,
  lend their beauty, and then
  depart . . .
There is no change, in the
  whiteness of my Crown, its
  beauty will remain thro' all
  seasons;
With the coming Spring, Nature
  showers all Life, with the Love
  of Rebirth . . .
At this show of Love, I can only
  gaze in wonder, at her adeptness
  of timing.
They will return, like the leaves
  in Spring, only to shed bitter
  tears beside my bier . . .

I will no longer be with them, I
  will have departed, to live in
  my Fathers House;
Like the leaves, fallen from the
  trees, onto the ground in
  Autumn . . .
So shall I, one day in the Autumn
  of my Life, fall to the ground,
  forever gone.

No longer, will their voices, come
  softly to me, on the whispering
  sands . . .
Nor will I, be able to feel their
  presence, they will be where, I
  am not;
I call to them, they cannot hear,
  once again only the winds,
  answer me back . . .
Now we, are scattered,
  throughout the Universe, not
  unlike the leaves before the wind.
In Death, the words, looks and
  touches of Love, for one
  another, are lost Eternally . . .
Only by crossing over, will we be
  reconciled, know Love, we
  before did not recognize;
Feel the soft and tender caress, of
  God's Hand in Love, once more
  upon our Soul . . .
Know the feeling of, "Love in
  Rebirth", as we saw Nature
  bestow it, on the trees and all
  of Life.

Kymberly Lorianne Fisher

Kymberly Lorianne Fisher
THE RIVER AND THE ROCK
Cruel waters
hard, cold, sure
relenting only to the sharp grey
rocks that border the river's shore.

White foam in anger of its defeat . . .

Green-trimmed
massive earth
beyond the rocks
are the contradicting peacefulness
to the angered waters.

The wrath of the mighty river
will someday be proved . . .

As yet, even now it has found the
  cold
stone's weakness and
year by year
cuts through.

Judith K. Lindsay
MY CASTLE
*[Honest and truly "My Castle"
is Olga & Julie and everybody
from the "Good Ship Hard"]*
I was born with a mind—a voice

And you were born with ears.
I dwell on thoughts and feelings
I could ramble on for years
Please let me ramble—let me be
Don't shine me on, or laugh at me
When i look in your eyes—do
  you know what i see
It's a part of my soul looking back
  at me
So look closely at the things you
  call truths
For some are only reflections of
  lies . . .
Sand castles can crumble with
  weak foundations
Yet worlds disappear in the
  reflections of your eyes.
So let me ramble—let me start
Don't lock me out, you're a key to
  my heart
And if you feel like you must go
There is eomthing i would like
  you to know
When you need me—just call
Because that what friends are for
I'll always be wishing you—
Everything your wishing for—and
  more!
Kathy Maloney
PROPHECY
A World
  Of Expectations
    for Great Ramifications
      declares Proclamations
        to overcome the Complications
        in successfully forming
          a United Nations
            COLLIDES
with a different world
  of materialistic characteristics
    and optimistic nationalistic beliefs
      creating immoralistic
        communistic minds
          CLASH
in a struggling, burning
  slashing, fighting
    tormenting, persecuting
      crushing, killing
        destroying
          in a collective cause to
            conquer!
            CALM
all is at rest now
  in an enormous inferno of smoke.
    The power so earnestly lusted for
    lies free.
Within the greed and stupidity of
  mankind
  POWER EMERGES POWERLESS!
Amy Sue Kahan
THIS I PROMISE
If you need me
  or just want me
I will be there for you
But if you need time with others
or room to grow or space to breathe
if you want to be alone
I will go away for however long
  you need
  and I will not be afraid
for you are you and I am I
but together we have each other
  and if what we have is real
then tomorrow you will be there
just as I will be there when I
  return
from my time alone.
And if tomorrow never comes
  I will not cry
For you will have touched my life

leaving rays on sunshine
burning through my heart
  and I will smile
Knowing
that if only for a moment
  I had been loved.
Alma Lillian Hageman
WAVES OF PASSION
*[My love devotion And desire
for you inspires this poem, for
you know who.]*
My love devotion
And desire for you
Is as an ocean
Deep and true
Waves arching high
Gainst a cloudless blue
Weaving, heaving.

Huge forms of deep green sheen
Straining from the depths
Of the mother sea
Foam flecked monsters
With mouths agape
Sweet kisses of fury devouring
  me.

Oh wonderous thundering
Mountain of strength
Crashing and hurling
Your body at length
Embracing the shore
Energy spent
Spattering softly . . .
Wetting the sand
Shining gold in the sun
Sighing, groaning, churning as
  one
Lost in the undercurrent
Of passion's, moment, done.
Ralph W. Hulbert
WITH ALL MY HEART
The telephone which doesn't
  ring,
Mail the postman doesn't bring,
Are joys in life I've learned to live
  without.

Smiles which interrupt all
  thought,
Beauty seen where there is
  naught,
Are joys in life I do not live
  without.

Delight found from our very
  start,
Love which now sustains my
  heart,
Are joys in life I'll never live
  without.

            P. S. — I love you.

David M. King
FOREVERMORE
Somewhere beneath blue tinted
  mist
Far removed from common
  shores
Lives a kingdom rich in bliss
Known to be Forevermore.

And its people, gentle and free
In quiet moments, in song and
  laughter
Exist harmoniously
Peaceful in the everafter.

Can we reach this land dear loved
  ones?
Set weary feet on hallowed
  ground.
Touch a point of perfect union
Far from evils wailing resound.

In dreams there,
I've bound with deer.
I've chattered with great apes,
Combing brown hair.

I've roared to high wind,
With orange lions
And perched near wise owls
Who spoke of flying.

Then, holding hands with an angel
On a rainbow mountain,
We drank crystal water
From a pearled fountain.

And we toasted each sunrise
With glasses high,
Till a breeze on my brow
Bade me open my eyes.

Maureen McKnight Ackerman
PA
[For my Nana with all my love...]
Pa
I love you
I wish I had the chance
To tell you just how much . . .
You're out of my life now
But not completely . . .
I still have all the memories
That I keep locked up
Deep inside me . . .
All the good times
All the not so good times . . .
But one thing is for sure
They are filled with love
And you gave it so freely
To everyone close to you
And even people not so close to
you . . .
You had a very special way
Of making people feel wanted
and loved
I admire you for that . . .
There are so many things
Left in my life
That I had always
Dreamed I'd be able to share with
you . . .
Even though you won't be here
To share them with me
I know that you will be in heaven
With my dad, your son
Sharing these things with me . . .
It won't be the same
As if you were here
But, it will mean just as much to
me . . .
I love you and always will . . .
And I, along with everyone else
Will miss you very much . . .
I realize (it's hard) that you are at
peace
And my thoughts will be with
you forever . . .

Marjorie G. Shuman
OUTSIDE FALLS THE RAIN
*[Thank you, best friend, for
sharing, and caring, and helping
me see through the rain to the
rainbow.]*
Warmth from a fireplace fills the
air,
Helping us of winter to be more
aware,
And the constant fall of the
steady rain
Causes the earth to be bathed
again.

Warmth is as friendship, held so
dear,
Calling us together, ever so near,

And yet does the rain to each life
bring
A renewal of hope for a coming
spring.

Dark though the sky, noisy the
clouds,
Yet welcomed excitedly by
watching crowds
Who follow the seasons the
whole year through
And know what to winter-worn
spirits
A spring rain can do.

Katherine Marsh
THE POETS PEN
If
The poets pen
Has carved
The word

It is
The musicians
Craft
Applied
By voice
And soul
Transfered
To instrument
That gives
The poets
Word
Meaning.

Imogene Hall
LOVES LOST
I do not think . . .
Of death, and tears,
And the sea.

Caught in the last rays,
Of sun . . . beaten gold . .
Crashing to shore.

Resting in lacy foam,
With us . . .
Too long ago now.

Thoughts fade . .
As images do,
As love does.

Darla L. West
FEBRUARY SECRECY
Hidden beneath
all these layers of snow
lie secrets
I haven't told you.

But while
the winds are so cold
and the nights are so long right now
all I want is to hold you.

From the depths
of my heart
I have so much to tell you.
Each thought
hangs like some heavy sorrow.

What I fear
is the chance
of you turning away
so I'll tell you my secrets
tomorrow . . .

Paulette Anne Hunter
A SWEATY SUMMER'S DAY
*[To Mom and Dad—who sent
me on Outward Bound where I
had this interesting experience—
with love]*
Two flies
Four flies
Six flies
More flies

Why flies
Do you torment
My supposed rest?
I'm not here for your pleasure
You nasty, little pests
I don't like being dirty
Though I'm sure you
Think it best
Please leave me alone
Go find some other quest

Tom Campbell

Tom Campbell
DIRECTIONS
*[To Joe Anne, the best
direction I ever took.]*
At being wrong I've mastered the
art;
I play it dumb when I should be
smart.
It seems I zig when I should zag,
and I am modest when I should
brag.
I frequently find my foot in my
mouth,
and I'm heading North when I
should go South.
I sometimes smile when I should
frown,
and I stand up when I should sit
down.

I stand still when I should go,
'cause I'm too happy with the
status quo.
But with this statement I have no
fear.
My precious wife, I love you, Dear!

R. H. Peat
FIRM IN THEIR POSITION
Lilies in the rain—
Bathing in tear drops—
All Yellow tongued
And jiggling with laughter

In the spatter of down pour
Bright white shirts
With pointed collars
Flipped up in back
They giggle and yawn
With droplets rolling
Down their cheeks.

The lilies take the rain
In such jest and fun
An ivory, irony
Of the storm—
Firm in their position.

Wm. Dexter Black
HOPE
Disconsolate—
lost in a Stygian room—
alone . . .

Suddenly,
Piercing unbidden through the
window pane (window's pain?),
Peering impishly 'neath the shade,
There comes a glimpse of
Pandora's quicksilver
crossing the table top
To end at the opposite wall—
A shattering blaze of reflected
brilliance
Bursting as a multitude of
incandescant sapphires!

Somehwere,
somewhere more than far away,
Cradled by Eternity,
The Sun is smiling . . .

Jim Stevens
ITS ALLRIGHT TO CRY
Children's lives have sorrow
Some feel it almost every day
Seeking a shoulder to cry on
Yet many times are turned away

We feel their sorrow is too small
For tears to fill their lives
Little problems are hard to wash
If no one listens to their cries

A splintered hand, scratch so small
A rusty toy or broken doll
Tire that wobbles, ball that leaks
To little children a mountain tall

All they ask, five minutes a day
Time to tell you what is wrong
A chance to wash the problems
away
Tell you how their day has gone

Give your child the love they seek
A moment alone to find their need
Take the time to cry with them
So they won't have to cry alone

Dianne L. Aventi
J.J.R.
Where will I go from here when I
am no longer there?
I sit and think about our months
together,
Wondering if our lives have
ended forever.
Before I left, I was hurting so
much deep down inside
Never knowing the answer to why?
Why did things have to end with
me starting from the beginning?
Knowing without you, I will no
longer do the winning.
There was so much that I needed
to say to you, but
The only thing that came out
was, "I Love You," as I do.
I will never be able to forget the
days we have spent together,
Knowing "In Time," can also
mean never . . .
I just can't believe that there was
a time in my life when
I was happy—then sad,
I was so scared, and felt so bad,
I get so lonely not having you by
my side,
I still find myself asking "Why"
Why dreams and plans change as
they do,
When I know, I still need and
want you.
I hope some day, I will get to see
you again, and
I hope if we can't be lovers,
We can at least be friends.
I love You . . .

Aileen L. Lum-Sarcedo
#112. WHAT'S SO WRONG???
*[Not meaning...to be offensive,
or in any way cruel but...I just
had to let this one
out...Dedicated...ESPECIALLY
TO YOU..."Gil", from me, LIN...]*
It seems . . . every time, I make
Love to You,
You end up, having the Blues . . .

Am I, doing something wrong???
For, you to turn, away so strong ...
from me.

Is it . . . so wrong to Love?
So wrong to care?
So wrong, to have You???
In, My Love Affair???

I know, it's you—
I'm making Love too,
Yet, you make me feel,
As, if . . . You were someone new.

You make me feel,
Like, I've done so bad;
For . . . I never see, a sign of glad...
from You.

If . . . I . . . cannot show, my
affection to you,
Who am I . . . suppose to be
giving it too?
You've been my Husband, for so
long . . .
What??? Am I doing—
That—I'm doing Wrong?????

Douglas C. Thornburg
FOG ON THE FAIRWAY
Now the fairways are green
and covered with fog,
and the golfers are seen
on the Westward Ho bog.

The trees are quite nude
over the lake that is placid,
they also receive free food
with fish that are flaccid.

It is surrounded by cactus
and when the wind is gusty,
the course is good practice
but can get dusty.

The lush smooth greens
and calm rolling hills,
with a few golfing teams
you pay for all thrills.

Beverly Ovelton Romero
TRIALS OF LIFE
As we live from day to day,
we treasure our memories in a
special way.
We give of ourselves to others in
need,
and life begins to blossom as if
planting a seed.

But many people cannot
understand,
what it means to share an
outstretched hand.
There is pain, there are tears and
even sorrow.
Often its life without a tomorrow.

Some people are selfish and
unwilling to give,
devious and childish in the way
they live.
Others are willing to lay their life
on the line,
with hope that through this a
new life they may find.

We try hard to keep things on an
even keel,
we try to please others, from our
own life we steal.
Why is it difficult for others to
see,
that without love and friendship,
life cannot be.

Myrtle Gray Livingston
WINTER'S END
Stricken with death, Old Winter,
gasping, lies,
The dying firelight flickers on his
face,
The friends, to whom his days
have brought delight,
Move quietly about the dim-lit
room,
Trying, with gently ministering
hands
To ease the weakening throes of
these last hours,
Striving to make solicitude too
thick
For rheumy eyes, sharpened by
pain, to pierce,
As, with a feverish gleam they
search each face
In vain, in vain for one sincere
and loyal tear.

A-tiptoe at the door, fair Spring
awaits,
Finger on lip, unwilling to behold
The sad scene in the room, eager
to run
On happy speeding feet to bear
the news
Of bonds cast off, of joy set free
again
To fill that outside world, so
hushed and still,
Breathless with expectation,
power repressed,
Its very air a-tingle with the
might
Of Life, upsurging, pregnant with
rebirth,
Awaiting, poised, the moment of
release.

Debby Jones
DEAR MOM; I LOVE YOU SO
On the day I came to you,
You taught me that you loved me
true.
You taught me what I know today,
From life and boys to molding clay,
To cook and sing and even pray,
You did it in your own special way.
Then came the years filled with
pain,

And how I learned to hate your
name.
For years I hated you so much,
I even feared to let you touch.
I've hurt and hated all these years,
Because you failed to settle my
fears.
I asked you what you couldn't do,
How could I have brought such
pain to you?
I felt at times you didn't care,
Even though you were always there.
Through scorn-filled years and
good times we've had,
I know in my heart things weren't
so bad.
These things just had to happen
this way,
Or else we wouldn't be able to say;
"I love you, I care,
And I'll always be there!"
So these words are just to let you
know,
"Dear Mom; I love you so.
I've always loved you so!"

Lorie Motta Gonzalez
THE MISTIQUE OF LORRIE
Caring for you is not rewarding
It's a merry-go-round with a
different hue
Because I'm not on it
It's only yours to pursue

You won't let me on
As you go round and round
Reaching for the brass ring
That I have already found

I wonder if this is the way
It will always be
Standing on the outside
Only being able to see

A person I care about
But cannot touch
Going round and round without
saying much . . .

Peggy L. McMahan
WILL WE SURVIVE
Will we survive together though
the times may be against us?
Will our love die because others
will not accept it?
Will we always be down-hearted
because we cannot be public
with our kisses?
Will we be strengthened or
parted because it would just be
easier to love another way?

If I kiss you once just daily with a
kiss that gives you my heart,
Will you stay with me forever or
leave because others can give
you what to even offer I cannot?
If I tell you that I love you and
mean it more and more,
Will you give me a smile and the
rest of your days or simply
close the door?

If the tears I cry in fear of losing
you can ever touch your soul,
Will you just comfort me or
understand the pain of losing
what I don't have a chance to
hold?
If I kneel beside you and say my
life will have no reason if ever
we should part,
Will you look at me in assurance
that our love will last, or

whisper, "I'm sorry I stole your
heart"?

And if it should ever come to the
instant when you really say
good-bye,
Will I have something new to
offer in hopes of keeping you?
No, there'll be nothing new, just
me, myself and I.

Christine C. Bartlett
On Seeing Chabas'
"September Morn"
He found her swimming
In the pool of his soul,
As naturally as if
She'd always been there.
He, who watched himself
So closely, so carefully,
Wondered when, unnoticed,
She had crossed
The mountain barriers of his
emotions—
At what unguarded pass
She had entered
The valley of his mind,
And how, without sound or sign,
She had discovered This—
The very wellspring of his life.

Geraldine Coomes
My Friend Brought Me
Flowers
*[For my mother, Margaret Bird
Sawyer, Poet, who went to
Glory on July 30, 1982. I miss her.]*
I saw my friend Ruth
Bring me flowers,
Even though I am in Heaven;
Especially because I am in Heaven.

When a person
Goes through the Golden Gates,
Perception grows unit by unit,
And universal knowing is the rule.

My friend loved me and misses me.
I love her, but I can't miss her.
Because I am always with Ruth,
And she is always with me.

I want her to know I see her.
I want Ruth to know I'm with her.
The flowers she brought are as
lovely as she is.
Thank you, Ruth.

M. Duane Rawls
JOURNEY TO BE FREE
People use to tell me,
"Boy,
You'll make it!
No doubt."
I refer to that saying,
When I feel down and out.
Away from all my friends
And into competition—
Keeping my concentration,
Determined to accomplish my
mission.
Wonder what they think of me?
Waiting to hear my name;
If they could know my inhibition,
I'll always be the same;
An adventurer,
Hoping to prosper
By conquering
My total self.
Knowing an entire one;
The me.
A journey through the soul;
Journey to be free.

Today's Greatest Poems

Margaret Sanders Matthews
GIFTS ON A LOVELY DAY
*[To my husband and family
who understand and accept my
need to write down my
thoughts; to God who allows
me to see the beauty of His
world.]*
The blue jay on my backyard fence
Squawks loudly at the coming day.
Although the morn is dull and drear
His brilliant blue coat makes me
gay!

His whimsied teasing of my cat,
With playing tag-and-run,
Displays a personhood of joy, and
we join in the fun!

His cousin, there, the mockingbird,
Oblivious to our game,
Sits, manicured, against the sky,
and sings and trills,
All heaven fills,
As though to earn her name!

An artist, skilled, can make us
pause, in wonder at his painting,
A singer, blessed with ardent
voice, will keep our hearts from
fainting,
Yet, the simple touch of loving
friend, an understanding face,
Can bring us joy, and leads us
back to God's own loving grace.

Michelle Lutes

Michelle Lutes
LIFE
*[In Memory of Great Aunt
Mildred Reed, who enjoyed life.
Also to Cheryl Bauman for
inspiration]*
Life is great,
Life is grand,
Life is everything a person could
have,
Life is hot,
Life is cold,
Life is the cold winter snow.

Life is happy,
Life is sad,
Life is fun when you're playing in
the sand.
Life is red,
Life is blue,
Life was made just for you!

Richard T. Barrus
THE NURSES
White peaked caps like snow-
tipped mountain crests
Above the glaciered folds of
sterile white;

They wake a kindled feeling in
our breasts;
They warm with gentle embers to
ignite
The lamp of unseen vigil through
the night.
Theirs is a beauty rare that oft
escapes,
Enfolded in those dark affluent
capes.

Along the princely paths of
jagged pain,
Through suffering moments deep
in lost surrender,
They smooth the way on invalid
terrain
To conquer torment's watch with
hidden hands so tender,
To show without display a
hidden splendor,
To moth-like search the ever
aching flame
And never once seek shelter in
acclaim.

Joseph R. Paquette
POST AUTUMN FEAST
After the Jubilation and Beauty,
That my Eyes have Feasted Upon,
And my Heart has Danced with Joy.
A time to Pause and Rest.
Like the Leaves that were on the
Trees,
Are now Laying to Rest on the
Soil,
Among the Grass and Reeds.
That Performed ever so Gracefully.
The Sun Receding from the Earth,
Narrowing the Days with Bitter
Cold.
The Tranquility Settling,
Is None other Than the Peace of
the Lord,
I Gratefully Rest like a Child,
Reminiscing the Autumn Feast.

Annette Thomas O'Connor
EAGLE
[To Tommy]
We never see eye to eye, mouth
to mouth, or ears to ears.
I'm slowly, but surely "drowning"
in seen and unseen tears.
You're always right; I'm always
wrong. You say that you've not
said it.
But each thing you say goes to
my Heart and I cannot for-get it.
If I make your life as miserable as
you keep telling me.
Then like an "Eagle" soaring, I'd
better set you Free.
You and Me.

Richard J. Kuenzinger
A FRIEND
If you need someone on whom
you can depend
Be you near or far,
Wherever you are
You can always call
on your friend.
If you are feeling
down and out of luck
Your friend is always around
To pick you up and
help you stand with pride
and confidence.
You should know that you can
always depend on
A friend.

Luciano L. Medeiros
THE DEATH OF DIANA
Fatally ill,
Diana can hear the voice of Gaea
calling her back into her womb.
At the river Styx,
Charon, the ferryman, waits
patiently to guide Diana into
Hades.
For this one—life is over!
Her final breath is a desperate
attempt to cling on to mortal life.
But Mother Earth demands the
return of all her children;
and, unwillingly, Diana fades
into dust from whence she
came . . .
    the cycle complete.

Marion van Ronk, D.O.
SKY TRAILS
*[To Julie, Tinker, Happy, Zelda—
loving four-footed friends (and
those with more and less) who
cheer and encourage and inspire
me to memorialize them.]*
Through vast eternal spaceless Blue
(Wind cannot intrude the voids)
Beyond our daylight-blinded sight
Oblivious to divisions of Day or
Night
There are Pathways unknown to
me and you
Upon which ride our Earth-
spawned Asteroids.

Leoma Wilson-Wade
CAMELOT
She stood
her face and body
as black wreathed as his coffin.
"Ask not," he said.
The fold of the flag fell into her
palm.
". . . whose broad stripes and
bright stars,
through the perilous night . . ."
waived comfort.
"Ashes to ashes, dust to dust . ."
Mother Earth hugged him to her.
Camelot
in the distance
shining,
Shattered.

Marciana A. Sevandal
HAPPY BIRTHDAY
*[This poem was written to
greet—on their birthdays—my
children, grandchildren,
kinsfolk, and friends who in
many ways, brought sunshine
into my lonely gloomy life.]*
    Congratulations!

It's here again, your birthday!
  A day most precious ever,
    For it's a measure of the life,
    That only God can spare.

A birthday is a gift divine,
  God gives to everyone,
    Who shares His graces and His
cross,
    And lives the best he can.

It's like the strains of a sweet song,
  Whose melody just lingers on;
    The ecstasies of your past day,
    Return with bliss and
wholesome fun.

There may be thorns and roses,

Strewn far along the way,
  For it is all that our lives are:
  "Order and disarray."

So thank the Lord for helping you,
  Along th'uncharted seas of life;
    At journey's end, unfurl your
sails,
    The trip unmarred by strife.

May God bless you wtih many
more
  Returns of your birthday,
    And may good health and
happiness,
    Be yours from day to day.

Susan M. Konvalin
WHY DO PEOPLE LOVE?
*[To My Friend, Mark who
inspired this poem and many
others.]*
Why do people love?
Please tell me if you know
Is it just a last resort
When there's no place else to go
I've thought about it quite a bit
But the answer never came
I was deep in love before
And now it's not the same
The love that always seems
May sometimes fade away
The time seems very lonely then
Without him everyday
You will realize soon my love
That love is not true blue
You see my love, I ought to know
I fell in love with you . . .

Vicki Riggleman
A COMPLETE PEACE
    Submerged
  There was a certain
    Freshness,
    Newness
  A special feeling of hope
  In being born again.

  For a fleeting second
    It was as if
    I was again
    The fetus
  Yet to experience
  The unknown world
    Outside.

  And my heart
    Was filled
  With the joy of living—
    The joy of knowing
    The Love of Christ.

Estelle Smith
FRACTURED MIRAGE
*[Respectfully dedicated to
OZZY OSBOURNE Who
showed me above the clouds
with my shadow falling behind
So I jumped to keep up with
myself. Nice catch!]*
The box is clear glass
That has entrapped my essence
Made through my own design.

There is a door that's beyond
My reach, opened just a crack.
I see reflections of what goes by
With suggestion as the outline.

It all seems backwards
These reflections
Departure then arrival.

Growing cold, when time stands
still
My box steams up with
Depression.

I realize that time is wrong
And move from that empty
Box through reflections of belief,
Feeling my will
Lifting me through
When the moment has stopped
And I at lost
Knowing you can never go back
again.

Agelito T. Buhisan Jr, J.D.
FAREWELL, JOSE RIZAL
Rizal!
Pride of the Malay Race
I think of you
As representing the best in the
human race.
You lived with dreamy eyes
As you set out to make your
world real
And in your quest
You showed to all mankind
What a Filipino can do
Indeed, what any young man can
do
Given only a chance.
Amidst the strife of human
actions
You unleashed the power of your
heart
The brillance of your mind
And the pride of your existence.
Farewell, Jose Rizal
I remember you still.

Sandra B. Lloyd
REFLECTIONS AT LA BREA
dinosaurs
relics of another age
ancient bones
preserved in black excretions
from the center
of the earth.

in the midst of a city
dinosaurs of my family
unearthed bones
reminders that no one gets out
alive.

Adriana Regueiro
ABSENCE—FOR KEN
We must forget that we've been.
Not have more memory
nor grow new roots that
will stop us from going ahead.
What good will it do
if one day we lose it all
and then
memories just won't be enough.
Start every day
with an empty mind,
live only that instant of time
that is left
to begin a new day,
which isn't worth seeing at all . . .

Francine
LETTRE D'AMOUR
Oh toi qui m'a inspiree et
enchantee,
oh toi, divin? illusion? reve insense?
merveilleuse ivresse de ta presence
pour Toi, ces mots, et te dire tu...
Oublies mon amour ce que les
hommes ont trouve
de plus cruel, compter les annees!
ces barres qui nous separent
n'existent pas en realite!
Ignorant est le coeur, il est
ethereal, emotion!!!
n'existant pas reellement, il est
sans etre!!!

Amour si pur, amour si exalte
rien n'existe, je vis sans vivre,
je suis sans etre . . .
Enchantement de ta presence
Amour divin fait pour les Dieux,
serais-tu venu de quelque planete
lointaine, juste pour moi?
ou serais-ce un reve ephemere et
merveilleux . . .
se joueraient de moi les Dieux?
Un mirage peut-etre? dis-moi . . .
My twin-soul serais-tu?
venu juste pour une saison
impatient mais impossible a
nouveau? dis-moi!!!!!!!

Heidi M. Sausedo
THE BUTTERFLY
        Butterfly
   Graceful, fleeting
  Elegant, free, beautiful
Airborne, complete, earthbound,
        unfinished
   Plain, trapped, homely
    Awkward, sluggish
       Caterpillar

Dixie L. Lippert
NEVER ALONE
[This poem is dedicated to my
best friend Juanita Marks. Her
faith in me gave me the
courage to try.]
Although we are separated by
distance,
In my heart, I know you are
always near.
So if we must travel down
separate roads,
We'll travel them, and we'll do so
without fear.
For time and distance will never
part us,
Not even in death, would we
cease to be.
For we have loved, and laughed,
and wept together,
I'm a part of you, and you're a part
of me.
Someday I am certain, we'll meet
again,
But until we do, we're both on
our own.
So, until that day comes, may
God walk with you,
And remember, When you're
loved, you are never alone.

Harvey Alan Sperry
ETERNAL VALENTINES
[To all the beautiful people who
have helped and supported me
through the most profound
crisis of my life.]
Valentines seem so transitory;
fleeting kisses in human history:
Cards professing boundless
devotion,
soon forgotten as waves in the
ocean.
Valentines are conveyers of love,
bestowed devotion from realms
above.
Though love endures as endless
space,
cards of love are a fleeting
embrace.
Valentines can be timeless rapture,
as devoted affection, long endure,
if written in deeds of loving

compassion
on every day of every generation.
Valentines as hearts in endless
agitation,
can feed the soul throughout
each generation
with a constant flow of loving
fondness;
the tender heart's unceasing
kindness.
This I give to you my friends,
a valentine that never ends:
The light of love to make life
shine;
the unwritten words of my
eternal velentine.

Bettye D. Little

Bettye D. Little
A MOVIE STAR
    "Movie star highlight:"
A classical Lady delight.
An empress of a jewel.
A legend: Thee crystal pearl,
a twinkling gem, a star.
The mystery of Kaiulani Princess,
O like a tropical paradise island.
Here she comes international
model.
Draped in mink and fancy fur.
After five gowns with elegant
style.
Sensation; Hollywood's latest
fashion,
You see on the streets.
The newspaper reveals where to
buy.
Finding the very best in fashion
magazines.
A picture of advertisement
For the eyes to focus.
Such a magnificent masterpiece.
Come view a beautiful scene,
More of a musical note of poetry.
Beauty of radiance fall through
the hair,
Showering stardust rain from
glory.
Suddenly expression is mine, in
any performance,
Love fascinating thrill, absorbing
great joy.

R.H. Peat
THERE IS A LARK
Spacious morning-lit song
For warbled muse rises—
With early golden, orange
Morning sun
There is a lark

His name is West-wing
From over the wooded mountain
He has bright red passion

Of life's feathered desire
To sing the rippled reflection
In the open eye of dreams
Being sung

From sweet orchard bloom
Across the mustard field
To rickity old wire fence

In green and yellow waves
The lark's voice moves
As spring wind moves
And strums sonic discords
On barbed-wire and ripped yoke
Of blue placid shirt
As one tries to sit
Closer to the harmonic tone
Whistling in his ears.

The sound of the melody
Runs throughout the keys
Of the multi-colored instrument
Played this world morning day

There is a lark singing
Across the yellow mustard
In the flowering eye
Of whistling orchard dreams.

David E. Barnes
A PLACE APART
I have a place for you my heart.
I keep you there, inside.
Everything I do, I am, you are,
you're me, my pride.

When I lay on down to sleep your
part of me does not rest.
And in the morning you hand me
my heart,
my Love, who keeps it best.

I can not go too far without you,
for without you I am not,
you see.
It is only that you are, that part, I
am,
my heart, you're me.

Mildred Ball
PORTRAITS
Pictures painted with words
Reveal a poet's soul.
Within each line and verse
A lovely scene unfolds;
Of mountain stream,
Of wooded glen,
Of star-filled summer night,
Of golden hues at rainbows end,
Of graceful swans in flight.
All portraits here displayed
Are born in a poet's heart.

Margaret Gaydos
DOGGEREL . . . BASICS
She whined in pain from the
rabies shot
and I winced when I saw the
doctor's error.
In haste he had written the
health report,
"Normal, six-months old Cairn
terror".

Chris Sybiak
OH CHILD
Oh child, God has held you in
the palms of his hands,
He's given you the chance to take
a big stand.

From the moment of conception,
A special light shone upon you,
And as the womb nourishes—so
love flourishes.

So you start to take shape,

and want to escape!

Oh child, as you appear, you
wonder what you'll hear—
What you say? "I'm afraid"! and
wonder if they will care?

In all the confusion, be known no
elusion,
The conclusion is perfectly clear;
And have but a big burden to bear.

In my specialness, I'm lacking
you see,
In what they call a small mental
deficiency.

All I can do is the best that I can,
And hope Gods plan will make
me more of a man.

To stand tall and be proud,
Not to say, "Can't but, I'll try".

For if I should fail or stumble and
fall,
I shall just pick myself up and
give it my all!

Brande Denis

Brande Denis
Relics Of An Era Gone By
[Dedicated to the memory of
my parents Mr. & Mrs. Julius
Kallis]

Thro' the smoked up window of a
second hand store
She views dust laden objects of
old folklore,
Old bronze sconces with candles
therein,
A glass ink well and long straight
pen.
And look—there's an old butter
churn and mould,
She rubs at her hands so crippled
and old
And rememb'ring these things in
her life, she sighs—
Now they're just relics of an era
gone by.

In an antique showroom thro'
clean windows she views
A black Model T, shining like
new,
And her tho'ts go back to that
flaxen haired girl
And the awkward young man
who gave her a whirl . . .
The high necked dress with
bustle in back,
Pretty parasol—flower decked hat.
Her feeble hand wipes a tear from
her eye
As she thinks of the relics of an

era gone by.

Now she's back in her room at
the 'HOME'
Surrounded by people, but so
terribly alone.
She closes her eyes as she rocks
in her chair
And relives the years when her
life was shared . . .
She sees her man coming home
from the War
Not quite the same man he was
before.
Her hair is silver, the light's gone
from her eye,
She's just another relic of an era
gone by!

Marcia Morrell
DESIRE
There stirs within me deep desire
It cannot be denied
Nor will be driven from my soul
And Lord how I have tried.

At first it was a little pain
That gave no cause to fret
Then suddenly it overpowered
I feel the burning yet.

I say that it is deep desire
I know no other name
It's not in lust for which I ache
Tho the feeling's much the same.

I long for just one tender word
To let me know you care
A wink, a smile, a little kiss
Or your fingers through my hair.

With just these little signs from
you
The man whom I admire
You would make my life worth
living
and kill my strange desire.

Mary Reiser
TO MY SWEETIE
We are bonded
   by tears + laughter

+ not a
   golden ring

For as gold will only tarnish
With laughter we can sing.

Susan C. Nowak
THE ROSE OF FRIENDSHIP
The darken red color of a rose
Is like the deepened graditude
      of a friend.
Its sweet and immortal fragrant
Is the essence of time well
      spent.

Randall Cunningham
MOTHER—YOU LIVE
With tight clenched hands and
breathing deep, she stiffled the
sounds of pain,
Straining mightily, her body tight,
sweat from her brow like rain.
Pulling with clamps and sinued
arms, the doctor pulled with
might,
Soon appeared a balded head, my
mother got her very first sight.

The Doc. cut the cord and
spanked my bottom, I gave a
lusty yell,
Mom cradled me on her chest
and cried, my name she was yet

to tell.
She bore six boys and two lovely
girls, her joys each time
abound,
Our greatest sorrow, she's passed
us bye, nowhere to find her
around.

No mother, that isn't true, your
smile is in front of my face,
Lovely Nettie Lou, your daughter,
in our hearts she has her place.
She has mothered many, as you
before, her family has been her
joys,
Mom, her love carries you on and
on, thru her husband, her
daughter, her boys.

Lorinda A. Balue
WONDERS/WORRIES
Wonders of love and laughter
Worries of trials and disasters
fears of the unknown
tears of those alone;

Wonders of a child with every
question
Worries of troubles when so very
young
fears of the unseen
tears of just being.

Maxine L. Fields
THE DAY GOD SMILED
When I was much younger, there
were time's I did pray
That God would send me, a little
girl someday

There were three little boys, sent
down for my care
although they were precious, I
had been given my share

The summers and winters,
seemed to come and to go
I wondered why God was being
so slow

There were many times, I cried
out in dispair
But I never lost faith, because I
knew he was there

Then one October, God smiled
down upon me
He sent a beautiful little girl, I
named Penny Leigh

For all the pleasure and pride, I
have had in this child
I am so grateful for the day, God
looked down and smiled

So dear Lord if my daughter, ever
comes to you
Please answer her prayers, with a
little girl too.

Sue Sharp
DAYDREAMING
In solitude I soothe my soul
From the pressures of the day,
By drifting into reveries
Where worries cannot stay.
   Sometimes my mind leads me
To a far, exotic beach,
Where I enjoy the sunset,
Alone and out of reach.
   And often fancy lifts me up
Above into the sky;
There I sit on cushioned clouds
And watch the world go by.
   Anything can happen
In the land of fantasy.

It all depends on your desires
And what you choose to see.
   Daydreams bring tranquility
When I am lost in thought,
Embracing peace within me
When without me it is not.
Yet when it comes to living,
I'm sure you will agree,
There's nowhere else I'd rather
live
Than in reality!

Rico Orrell
UNFINISHED PRELUDES
[Cecilia Quero E Nao Quero
Rico]
The sober night recoils in
angered melancholia
as seasoned sonnets spill
secluded ramblings
on diamonds laughing face.
Orange life flies in fickle fusion
to exchange an impermanant
unfolding
on a day and a dreams epiphany.
Our songs throughfare plunges a
sharper recall
forgetting factual flavorings for
the
fury of rhapsodic perjury.

Penny L. Brady
THE CHANGING OF DRESS
I'll sing of springtime, the
summer long
in a green dress of fancy lace—
but change the rhythm of my
song
as the wintery winds I face.
The color of my gown will also
change
to rustic huses of copper gold.
From greens, to reds, to an orange
range—
a beauty none surpassed, I'm told.
Then all too soon, I'll stand quite
bare
as the birth of a new born babe—
and in my branches, silver snow
I'll wear
where the swallows nest once lay.
But soon again after a barren
spell
mother nature works supreme—
and again she clothes me oh so
well
in my lacy dress of green.

Jimmy N. Maza
**Chickadee, Chickadee Be
Mine**
Nice time, a chance we meet
again,
Amidst sweet breath of first
morn in spring;
On my breakfast table, coffee
black and strong a-brewing,
Thru glass window pane saw you
and mate cling on a bough;
Bless my soul behold your fancy
pose, only nature shows
Togetherness ever, you both
enjoy,
I praise and envy your being
Chickadee, chickadee be mine.

By solemn infatuation
possessed,
With my camera on hand,—
A picture of you I crave to take,
would you mind?
Seeing you pick up a thing,

clidk—flash my camera shoot,
Chirp, chirp head up, chirp, chirp
surpised you look,
Then flew swiftly away you
could;
Anxious, I stood and abide,
Chickadee, chickadee won't
you be mine?

Mystic breeze stole moments
of time a-new,
Happ'ly chirping back you
came, a birdie song you sang;
Inspired in search of worm on
bottle—brush tree flow'r hang,
Click—flash my brave camera
caught you then unaware;
Providence your guide and
keeper, kind beyond compare,
Mother nature owns you truly
dear,—
A token of you only will be
mine,
Chickadee, your lovely picture
I own, let me.

K. Laine Cook
Tears That Never Come
The tears that never come
will always remain within,
wanting to escape
only to be put on this paper
by my hand.
All my thoughts,
my aches and happiness
are words—
they say everything I can't.
Your words have inspired more
words and tears within—
they will come in time.
Probably mixed with words
that I have to say and
cannot write.

Christina Neville
THE STAR
Little Boy I missed you from the
Shepherds
At the manger on stage to-night,
From the Kings who followed
heaven's message—
The star so beautiful and bright.

I could not be asking nor a
shepherd, said he,
Because I am too small,
I could not be the Christ-Child,
Because I am too tall.

But Daddy found a part for me,
He put me up so far,
To hold the light that showed the
way,
Daddy made me the Star.

Aileen L. Lum—Sarcedo
#74. SCORE
I'd love to write a song
For the music, you could hear
Of all the words, I've written
Of, my Love for you, My Dear . . .

I'd sing it soft and sweet
With a tune, just right in beat
And, . . . It shall be heard, forever
more,
Of, Our Life . . . Of Our
Score . . .

For, I'm proud of it, you know . . .
To be a part of you and grow
To be within . . your heart and
mind
To be, not left behind.

I Love You, . . . oh! so much
I Live on, . . . for your touch
You make me, much more
complete
There's no one else, I'd care to
meet

And, . . . I'll—Love You—forever
more,
Keep, this in mind, and
You'll Hold Our Score.

Elizabeth Radford
A SONG WAS BORN
*[This poem was inspired by the
stirring National Anthem and
my love for America. I, hereby,
dedicate it to this great Nation.]*
Amid turmoil, a war, a century
ago or more
A British fleet neared a fort in
harbor Baltimore.
A man on the ship held a flag of
truce to free
The American aboard who was
Francis Scott Key.
By daybreak the sky was lit up by
rockets' red glare

Our Flag was flying and
continued there
Soaring!—impressed by the scene,
Key was inspired.
He saw the attack on
McHenry, shells were fired
As he witnessed by dawn the
bombs' display—
Was touched by the sight and
impelled that day
Wrote—'The Star Spangled
Banner' song of our nation
That has thrilled Americans
generation after generation.

Ruth de Cuir
THE DESERT
I marvel at the artistry
Of His creative hand.
He frosted rocky mountain slopes
With carmel colored sand.

He sprinkled miles of level plain
With lacy, smoky trees,
Then clear blue sky, warm bright
sun,
Gusty, changing breeze.

For when God made the desert,
He composed it as a song.
It is both soft legato
And staccato loud and strong.

The subtle shades of morning
In pinks and mauves and grey,
Become the reds and oranges
And purples of late day.

Thelma Elizabeth Berry
REMEMBERING
Love has a way of remembering
That smile, that touch, that joy.
Love has a way of remembering
That kind and loving boy.
Those words of cheer that he
offered
Many days he brightened so
Love has a way of remembering
No matter where you go.
So I thank God for love
And all the comfort it brings
And all the pleasant memories
Of at least a thousand things
And I face the future bravely
Thanking our God above
For a short time I was permitted
to know
This boy I shall always love.

Robert M. Cook
THE CLONES
The world is surfeited,
life is overcrowded
with the conformists,
the undifferent and the
indifferent.
You can set your watch by them
from nine to five,
dress them in the same gray
flannel suit,
feed them on the same meat and
potatoes
until the cows stop coming home.
But as long as the mint keeps
striking dimes,
we'll keep getting clones by the
dozen;
and those who are too frightened
to swim above the run of the mill
will clog the mainstream of life.
Who dares to be his own man or
woman?—
all of the clones are waiting for
someone.

Robert Corcoran
AGAPE
*[For my Mom whom afforded
me the luxury of time and
unconditional love to find
myself.]*
All my problems are my own,
So is everything else I own,
But sometimes I feel the need to
share,
Like a walk in the park,
Or the stormy sea air,
I seem to be drifting . . .
A bird in a plane,
I worry 'bout drowning in
A desert of pain,
I seek to find riches on
An island somewhere,
But imagine it buried with
The truth of care.

So I send off this message
In an ocean of doubt,
'My bottle is empty of what
life's all about.'

Lillian Russell
THUMBS UP!!
Wouldn't it be fun and quite
unique to have an eye on the
end of your thumb?
Without turning around, or
having to peek, you could see
from whence you had come.

What's on the top shelf? I don't

recall;
Can't see it—it's up there to
high.
Don't climb on a chair and invite
a fall, just hold up your
thumb—the one with the eye!

And your slippers that're always
under the bed and you can't see
'em, no matter how you try?
No more, "Down on your knees;
stand on your head",
Just use your thumb that's
equipped with the eye!

Into your house the robbers may
creep, but don't worry about
what they will take.
For while the eyes in your head
are fast asleep, the one on your
thumb is awake.

The best use of this amazing
feature . . .
This hand with the useful digit,
Is by the kindergarten teacher to
keep her "thumb" on those who
fidget.

Linda L. Duke
WHISPERS
It feels without touching,
hears without listening;
Shadows without form in the
night,
two hearts locked in embrace.
A silent messenger
conveys needs, wants, desires;
Receives comfort, understanding,
reassurance.
Silent whispers of unspoken love,
its wings beating softly,
like that of a bird awaiting flight
into heights unkown . . .
But to a few.
The ultimate high being the
mirrored reflection of one's
soul,
lending to life slow, rhythmic
cadence.
There is no time for love . . .
It is forever.

J. Najah Oldham, Ph. D.
**The Specialty Of a
Mountain**
The mountain
Is big and rugged;
Its outline
Crude and unshaped.

But still,
There is beauty within
Of peace and serenity,
And grandeur of loveliness.

Mankind is drawn to the
mountains;
Because they feel the inward
peace,
While within its radiance;
And untouched by the human
frailties of life.

Oh, the complexities
Of the mountain,
Cause mankind
To be awesome.

But, from within his heart
He feels totally one,
With its magnificence of beauty;
And surrenders to its peace,
unconditionally.

The stark

Of simplicity,
Promotes
A spiritual high.

Nancy Weinberg Jackson
THE KISS
*[Dedicated to my family; to
Steve and Vicki who have
given me courage; to Morty
who gave me love and faith;
and to Jim who has given me a
new brihgtness.]*
　　This kiss comes for you, my
love.
It comes softly as from warm
night airs.
It comes reverently as from a
place from my prayers.
It comes passionately as from all
my hidden desires.
It comes longingly as from a slow
building fire.
It comes meekly as from a
shadow of my other self.
It comes generously as from a
long—stored wealth.
It comes lovingly as from a
fountain long overdue.
It comes unendingly, as from a
part that was always you.
　　This kiss comes for you, my
love.

Bettina Christner
**Heavenly Dove—The
Symbol Of the Holy Spirit**
No grey and mourning dove
forlorn
The Dove in my heart is of Love
born.
This Dove is more than simply
white—
Reflecting Peace both day and
night—
Teaching the song of redeemed
"stars"
To renew and gladden the
wakeful hours.
Though within hearts He is not
bound,
Out side of them He'll not be
found.
It could never be a binding cage—
The loving heart of a Christian
sage.
St. Matthew 3:16

Linda K. Rasile
HAPPINESS
　　Happiness is giving
Your love and your heart
　　Happiness is being
Together, not apart

　　Happiness is sharing
A very special day
　　Happiness is returning
After being away

　　Happiness is the sound
Of a new baby's cry
　　Happiness is the beauty
Of a twinkling eye

　　Happiness is the sharing
You give of your love
　　Happiness is a blessing
From the one up above.

Dennis Egler
WHEN I WAKE
When I wake in the morning
I want to call your name
I haven't seen you for a while

and I just don't feel the same
I'm late again, its warm outside
the flags are on the rise
My shoes are wet from yesterdays
rain and I just can't let it slide
I had a dream about you early
this
morning and I can't remember it all
You had a smile upon your face
that memory I can recall
I dream about your happiness
and good fortune in the days
ahead
Your ship of hopes are sailing at
sea
towards a sky of red

Wanda L. Hale
WEDNESDAY AFTERNOON
Monday morning's laundry time,
And Tuesday's when I clean.
But, Wednesday afternoons are
mine,
To do with as I please.

Wednesdays are for having fun,
A story read to my little one.
Or maybe a day spent in the park,
Or strummin' on the ole guitar.

A trip to town with a special
friend,
A cup of coffee shared.
And when the day comes to an
end,
I hear my childrens' prayers.

Today is but a memory,
Tomorrow, but a dream.
And I thank God for each new
day
He's allowed me to have seen.

No matter how I spend this day
That God has given me,
No one can ever take away
Its special memory.

Thursday morning's laundry
time,
By Friday I need to clean.
But, Wednesday afternoons are
mine
To do with as I please.

Jeannette Allen
COUNTRY'S KIND
*[Dedicated to all my Country
Friends whom inspired me to
write this poem on the night of
August 6, 1982 at the "Big
Rock" and especially to my two
favorite Country Cousins—
Randy and Stanley Allen—I
Love You All]*
Darkness and peaceful
Kin folks and friends
Enjoying and relaxing
Until the party must end.

Good times and laughter
Happiness and fun
If us country folks can't do it
It will never be done.

We know true life
And how it must be spent
Because we are God's Country
children
And only from heaven, could we
have been sent.

We cherish the real meaning of
life
Because we know we only

have one
So we try our best in everything
we do
And when we're through, the best
has been done.

So now let us make a toast
To the best that has ever been
For tonight we're friends, and
forever will be
From this day forward—until the
very end!

Harry A. Jester

Harry A. Jester
THE CUPID BOYS
February is the month it seems
When little Dan Cupid fairly
beams.
He welcomes lovers with open
arms
And touches them all with magic
charms.

Now little Dan, so I've been told,
Can make the shyest extremely
bold.
He acts just like a Cupid should
For little Dan is kind and good.

He has a brother, Donald by name.
The way Don acts is quite a
shame.
He grins and clowns and takes
such forms
You got to admit, he's a Cupid
with horns.

Now Brother Don, with a devilish
style,
In an unfunny way, can make
some smile.
With a leer, thought or snide
remark
He's a joker's idea of a Valentine
lark.

While Dan brings joy, warmth
and gladness,
Brother Don brings tears and
madness.
So, as befits these modern times,
You have a choice of Valentines.

Mrs. Mary K. Quisenberry
AN EASTER MESSAGE
Almost two thousand years ago,
the prophets say,
The women found the stone from
the tomb rolled away,
And glistening in brightness, an
angel sat guard at the tomb . . .
Its message to the women
shattered all tears and gloom.
And they carried the message

home to all who followed Him;
(Down through the ages, false
prophets make the light dim).
But the message of the angel still
is valiantly hurled,
He is not here. He has risen;
come see where He lay,
Gives us the message of the
"Great Resurrection Day!"
He is the Light, the Hope, the
Salvation of a sin sick world,
And as another Easter Day
dawns, a new spirit in our
hearts arises,
All around, down under, up over,
in blossoming skies,
We see the newness, all the signs
that point to "Rebirth,"
And gives courage to a helpless,
staggering, old Earth!
The trees, the birds, the flowers
and lowly little bees,
All give confirmation to remind
us of all these,
Our hearts, our souls lift up in
songs of a dulation and praise,
For all the wonderful bounty He
provides these days.
If we are diligent, as His second
coming we must await,
We marvel at the goodness and
love, "our Saviour so great."
He arose; He lives on high, but
He's coming back again to
earth,
To renew old bodies, give us a
heavenly home (complete
rebirth).
So, my friend, if there is any
stone upon your heart today,
Remember the message of the
angel the women heard say,
"He is not here, He has risen and
will return to Earth someday."

Rowena Johnson
DREAMING
I live in a place no one else
knows.
Separate, away from time and
other people.
Drifting on a sea no other being
can feel.
I close my eyes,
dreaming,
candle burning low,
glass of wine by my hand.
Floating on a cloud no other eye
can see.

Clarice Tesh Brewer
A PART OF ME
What part of me
Did I leave in the past?
Was it worth remembering?
Something that would last?

What part of me
Am I making today?
That's helpful and useful,
Does it give love—or decay.

What is my future yet to be.
I ponder, and wonder about
tomorrow.
I hope there's A better part,
Pray to God—I won't bring
sorrow.

Yes, Yesterday is history now.
Today is alive with living.
The future, I hope will bring
Many years of myself "Giving."

319

Mary E. Cullum
PANORAMA

A poem is a world I've found,
In which the poet sees
Wild fantasies, where dreams
  abound,
Or solitude of trees.

Moon and stars or days of old;
  Wind and cloud of March
Myraid panoramic scenes unfold
Focused in his heart.

Cora

Shirley Jo Redmond
A FORGIVING MOTHER
*[This poem was inspired by
Cora, my silver-haired Mother.
Mom, you look lovely in this
book.]*

I slept with my Mother until I
  was grown,
Our house was too small for a
  bed of my own.
I didn't mind, cause on cold
  winter nights,
We'd snuggle up, and she'd hold
  me tight.

Then in my teens, I started
  running wild,
Giving her heartaches, a "I know
  it all" child.
I put some of the gray in my
  Mother's hair,
I would not listen, I didn't care.

Then one day, Mother was taken
  from me,
She was in pain, before death set
  her free.
Now I feel so lonely, lost and sad,
I could've taken better care, of the
  Mother I had.

Now when I go to her grave, just
  to talk awhile,
I whisper "I'm sorry," then I smile,
For if I listen closely, I can hear
  Mother say,
"Honey, you were just a kid in
  those days."

Michael J. Thompson
IMMORTAL

Moved by reality, tossed upon it's
  waves, I dream in the twilight
  and feel my mind float away.
  Drifting and outreaching,
  expanding my being, I climb to
  great summits faintly glimpsed
  in my dreams.

Like a young giant warrior I rush
  into the night, feeling immortal
  omnipotent in the truth of my

sight. To a world of great
  hopes, without flaws to be
  seen. With boundless land,
  without blemish and
  untouchable seas.

In moments of measure I live out
  lives in my mind. I travel the
  world over and leave my
  limitations behind. Slipping
  through decades learning much
  as I pass, not forgetting nor
  dimming the reality of the last.

Though the love of a mortal is
  but a passing touch of the
  wind, a breath growing
  stronger, then completed by
  end. I learned of this love that
  is man's warmth from the cold.
  But I must pass alone through my
  lifetime growing aged but not
  old.

To travel on endlessly without
  answer or pause, with
  heightened emotion and feeling
  but without commitment or
  cause. Existing without caring,
  continuing the quest, feeling
  an immortal's vast weariness
  but unable to rest.

Seeking out hardship to the
  music of a dream, drifting and
  haunting, distant and warm,
  with a voice in the waters and
  her face in the storm. Leading
  me onward then fading from
  sight, as I stare down at the
  likeness from a long distant
  night.

Simple and mortal so longed for
  at night, mine for my choosing,
  but now too small to be right. I
  think back to my shadow, now
  fading from sight as I rush into
  the darkness wondering where
  I can stop in the night.

Candice Lynn Cramer
MY SPACE SUIT

Oh Lord, this old body is like a
  space suit to me.
I just can't wait to zip it off so I
  can be free.
Then I'll really soar off into outer
  space;
My point of destination—Your
  THRONE OF GRACE.

I suppose this space suit was
  necessary for my birth;
So I could live in the atmosphere
  here on planet earth.
This divine space suit body
  creation has served me well;
But time and use has ravaged and
  turned it into a cell.

Now I'm captive in a suit that's
  old, worn and gray,
And I'd welcome a release from
  this chrysalis of clay.
This space suit body that I once
  thought was me
Shall soon return to dust and set
  my soul free.

Then as the metamorphosis of
  the caterpillar to butterfly;
TO LIVE EVERLASTINGLY, this
  space suit body must first die.
But the purpose of death is not to
  lose but to GAIN;

LIFE FOREVER we will inherit in
  our KING'S DOMAIN.

Dorothy R. Douglas
PRISSY

Prissy, little girl on the beach
Face shining, skin glowing,
  cheeks like a peach.
Building castles in the sand,
Waves come lapping,
Sand creatures you're trapping,
Caught in a tiny hand.

What will you be like when
  you're grown?
Will you still be
  building/dreaming or maybe
  scheming
To trap men's hearts with your
  own?

Jan Marie Christensen
DIFFERENT

I'm not you, and you're not me.
I'm special, Because I'm me.
And that's the way it should be.

Like a butterfly in flight
With wings of many colors—
Each move is spontaneous and free.
Each is different,
Each is special,
Just like you,
And just like me!

Barbara J. Arbuckle
A CHILD

A child knows when his mother
  is near;
  He loves to see her face.
To her he is so dear;
  They both live in grace.

Girls wear pretty laces;
  They are so sweet.
Boys usually get dirty faces;
  Either sex will sure to be a treat.

A child can be bad;
  Sometimes down right awful.
He even gets sad;
  Sometimes he can be so
  thoughtful.

No matter what,
  You're sure to love
And want,
  A CHILD.

Emily S. McCormick
THE CROSS OF CALVARY

On the cross of Calvary
Our blessed Saviour died.
He gave his life for you and me
When he was crucified.

The third day he arose
And ascended into heaven.
He gave a promise to each of us
That our sins would be forgiven.

He fulfilled the scriptures the
  Bible tells
To show his love for me.
He said that he would come again
As he died in agony.

Because he lives we too shall live
A life full of truth and grace,
And we shall see him again someday
When we meet him face to face.

I know he lives just look around
At the designs of his perfection,
And you will have the blessed
  hope
Of our Saviour's resurrection.

Tara Michelle Key
MY GIFT

To my Sweetheart
This gift I give
Of all my love
And dreams from above;

I give to you
All that I am
All that I will be
With you for eternity;

What tomorrow holds
No one really knows
But for you and me
Love it will be!

H. D. Gray
TO DEANA

We don't always know—do we?
We are susceptible to hurt,
But we must go on—don't we!
We will build our fortresses
We will shine our armor,
But we are vulnerable—aren't we!
These are the times in our lives,
The answers are not clear
There is no rhyme, there is no reason.
These are the times for searching
These are the times for learning,
But we must go on—don't we!

Irene Suchta Pacana
GIVE ME YOUR HAND

"GIVE ME YOUR HAND" . . . I
  need You to make it through
  the day . . .
Life, would be so empty, without
  You . . . to guide me all the way!
"GIVE ME YOUR HAND" . . . to
  hold, when I tremble with fear . . .
Sometimes, I feel confused and
  lost . . . I shed many a tear!
"GIVE ME YOUR HAND" . . . I
  need confidence, to make me
  strong . . .
I need your inspiration . . . to
  teach me right from wrong!
"GIVE ME YOUR HAND" . . . to
  give me courage, when I feel
  meek . . .
Please give me guidance . . . so I
  know what to seek!
There are times . . . when my
  spirit, is at a low ebb . . .
I don't want to weave, my life . . .
  into a tangled web!
Please motivate my energies . . .
  in a positive direction . . .
To nourish my soul . . . with
  prayer and reflection!
"GIVE ME YOUR HAND" . . . to
  pursue my ambitions and
  dreams . . .
Give me a conscience . . . not to
  fall prey, to conniving schemes!
"GIVE ME YOUR HAND" . . . to
  cope with the problems, I may
  face . . .
Make me aware "a rainbow" . . . will
  always find it's place!
I depend on you . . . to help me,
  through the lonely nights . . .
To see the dawn . . . to look
  forward, to the morning lights!
"GIVE ME YOUR HAND" . . . to
  make my life worthwhile, to
  please You . . .
And Please . . . make me worthy
  "to extend my hand" . . . to
  someone, too!

Today's Greatest Poems

Frederica McDill Culbertson
SEPTEMBER 1, 1977
*[To Mother—a belated
Mother's Day gift . . . in
appreciation of my being . . .
with love forever from your
daughter Freddie]*
While gentle surf laps the beach
and softly touches sand,
alone I walk, and sing a song,
while lovers walk hand-in-hand
and shellers, like children, search
for treasures on the sand.

Tall buildings, long shadows
throw upon the sand,
while morning's sun reaches up
the eastern sky
and I see the moon's ghost, not
yet set,
hanging in the sky to the west,
while Mother Nature keeps her
score,
'til on the beach, . . . man is no
more.

This is eternity.

Each day I grow a little more,
in wisdom and with time,
Each morn I wonder . . . how
many more
I'll see, of days and years,
while life unfolds and brings me
closer to eternity.

I cannot see the point-in-time
when I'll know satiety,
and earthly charm I'll no more see,
while this sweet earth unfolds for
me . . .

Thank you, God—I'm glad I'm me.

Malcolm O. Carter
MAYBE
Everything I showed was real
even though,
still,
you did not see—
How much you meant to me.

I did not ask for your hand,
I did not want your mind,
I only needed the time
for you to listen and see
what I could be,
for you . . . .

I wish you the best for all seasons,
and I hope you treasure all the
reasons . . .
that were stored up for you.

Carolyn E. Singleton
A TOMORROW
Never promise a tomorrow,
let today lead its way through.
Yesterday has gone by.
Maybe another day is soon to be
coming.
If tomorrow can't come, there will
be no reason or sorrow,
No one but God can bring a
tomorrow.

Jo Harger
HALLOWE'EN PARADE
Hallowe'en is a scary affair,
Frightful monsters with long
green hair
Wandering down the streets at
night,
Scars on their faces, and eyes
without sight.

Funny hats and owls and cats,
Cats with eyes of jade.
Little ghosts and witches and bats
In the Hallowe'en parade.

Old Mr. Scarecrow up on the hill
Grins and gleefully watches the
drill
Of the Hallowe'en parade.

Tho' he knows when the fun is
o'er
He will return to the granary floor
To snooze again for another year,
Till the green haired monsters
re—appear.

DiAnne McInnis
SELF PITY
Little girl in the window
why do you cry?
Little girl, you're too young
to say you want to die.
Maybe you should go outside;
the flowers are in bloom.
The world is beautiful, you'd see,
if you'd only leave this room.
Little girl, can't you see
the word still goes around?
Not a thing has stopped growing
since the world you knew fell
down.
Little girl in the window,
from here I can see her.
'Tis I who is so sad
looking in this mirror.

Eleanor Attaway Patch
GODS DIAMONDS
Snow melting on a bare old tree
Is truly a beautiful sight to see,
Each tiny limb sparkles with firey
color,
As they move in the gentle breeze.

The older we get the more we can
see
Gods handiwork designed for you
and me,
No beauty like this can any man
make
And I praise the Lord in Jesus
name.

Yes, snow melting upon the trees
Leaves droplets of ice slowly
dripping away,
Then the sun comes out and
shines on these
To make Gods diamonds, but;
they soon go away.

No, we can't store these away
some place,
Just plant them in our hearts to
stay
And remember its beauty in
many ways—
Then thank Him for this most
lovely day.

Desiree L. Browning
MY KNIGHT
When you came into my life—
   I was embittered
   Because of the pain.
   Your love has thawed my
   heart—
      As a winter thaws
      With spring rain.

I'd forgotten the simple joys—
   Enjoying the simplicity
   Of the freedom of living.
      I realize again, that the

gift of love—
   Is to reciprocate the
   Giver by giving.

Although I know life's battles
aren't over—
   I'm not a coward, hiding;
   You've helped me see the light.
   I'm a surviver. I thank-you
   from the
      Depths of my heart—
      I love you my beautiful
      knight.

Martha Virginia Beach Chalfant
A Tribute To Archibald Rutledge
*[Dedicated to Mrs. Russell
Starnes (Nancy) who
introduced me to the works of
Archibald Rutledge, poet
laureate for the State of South
Carolina, 1934.]*
Along the Santee River
   Are wild and lovely things.
One hears the call of Nature
   In works that Rutledge brings.
He stirs the imagination
   And thrills the ears with
   sounds.
He focuses on beauty

Where wilderness abounds.
Near Hampton, Charleston
County,
   Lies a cornucopia of land
That overflows with bounty
   Direct from God's own hand.
Oft he walked here to share
   The glory in this place
Word-painting with such care
   God's shown in every trace.

Velia Klein Fleisher
The End and the Beginning
December, month of cheer and joy
A smile, a sigh, a nod, a toy
Man, woman, child and beast
Enter the spirit of prayer and feast

We ponder, consider the year
ahead
Patience, love, soften our tread
Live for each day in peace, good
health
Sharing, giving, for others, for self.

Then, festivities over
   Quiet descending
   Returning to normal
   Hilarity ending.

A new year fast coming
   To accept with hope
   New start, bright promise
Fresh strength to cope

The future shines bright
Past fades into night
So up with the reins
Reject sorrow, fight pain.

The end has passed
It's time for the beginning!
Carolyn Cheatwood Reddish
In Winter's Cold Embrace
*[This poem is for people who
love, and finds beauty, in
winter.]*
In winter's cold embrace
The trees stand bare
In the frosty air.
Summer is gone without a trace.

The cold wind blows the dead
leaves,
Scatters them over the ground,
Blows them all around.
In showers of falling leaves.

The winter wind rattles the bare
limbs
On the lonely trees
As the daylight dims
Through the dark trees.

The trees stand lonely and cold
Deep in winter's hold.
William Lowenkamp
CONCRETE DWELLERS
Huddled beings
Hurriedly walking
Upon concrete paths
With voices—busy talking
Huddled together—beings
Steadily hurried—walking
Across concrete motor canals
Encased with monumental
buildings
Unfriendly beings by daylight
Marching—to and fro
Unconcerning as to—who is who
Uncaring as along their way they
go
Hurried beings,
Of giant concrete cities
On the outside—like the
buildings
Feelings of concrete
And on the inside—like the
buildings
Bonny—a different world.

Dan Leavens
ALONE
None seems more lonely than the
moon
As it tracks a cold and pathless
way
Spurned by the stars—who all to
soon
Foresake it, e're the break of day

It seems so sad, so all alone
So silent, yet so strong
For it forms in lovers such a tone
T'would burst the world with
song

When love does not it's presence
show
The moon's a different form
The lonely much more lonely
grow
And yearn to be reborn

Oh moon of beauty, moon of pain
None know just what you do to
me
My world will never be the same
You know me not as I know thee

Martha (Russell) Mosure
THE PAINTING
[I am dedicating this poem to
all the people in my life who've
encouraged me in; my poetry,
my paintings, my songs and my
dreams. I love you all!]
Images, emerging, appearing
Creating; a memory enduring.

Frozen, captured forever
A dream, a fleeting
endeavor. . .

Of yesterdays, perhaps tomorrows
Of feelings, joys and sorrows.

Captured, enslaved in swirls
Pigment dances and twirls . . .

Undulating to a melody
Precious moments of artistery.

Imagination, beliefs and pains
Rendered within lines and
planes.

Colors interlock and blend
Ideas expand and extend.

Dreams, captured and tangible
Develope into visions
expandable.

Into, the finished illusion
A masterpiece; reality's
exclusion.

At last, creativity's nourish
Last stroke—signature's
flourish.

Cheryl Marie Draves
PRE—WINTER
Metallic blue clouds
fused create illusions
of cold indifference.

Branches stripped bare of
ornament yield to gales
and scrape the sky.

Seas of grass turned
brown ripple and flow
to an unheard song.

Subtle beauty underlies
surface of deceptive death.

Dona Jo. Lawson
SIMPLICITY
I couldn't love you more, or
better, or with more faith, or
more pure in heart than I do.
I don't know when I fell in love,
or why, or how; but I did.
I'll love you this much, this way,
for as long as I live. It's just
that simple.

Nancy J. Tury
O' LITTLE GRANDSON
[This poem was written for
Jacquie, my beautiful daughter;
and written about Jason and
Joey, my beloved grandsons.]
Nerve-endings jumping as I wait,
the time so close, so near;
any minute now, I know . . .
my little grandchild will be
here.
My arms have longed to hold you;
I want to see your tiny face,
and touch your dewy, velvet skin
as I hold you in my warm
embrace.
At last, thank goodness, you are
here;
I can hear your angry wail.

Excitement floods my body
and sets my heart a'sail.
A pane of glass between us . . .
you're so close within my view.
Your arms and legs are flailing . . .
you're so pink, so red, so blue.
Finally, the time arrives . . .
you're handed gently to me.
The love I feel so greatly
will be for all eternity.
My heart is full and tender
as I touch your petal-soft skin;
a feeling of pride surges forth
at sight of a little pointed chin.
I can't explain the wonder I feel
being suspended in time and
space;
the moment is blessed and sacred
when our souls meet face to
face.
O' little grandson, you can't know
how much you mean to me.
You fill the essence of my soul,
and make God a living
reality. . .

Annabel Schrimpster
CANDLES OF THE ANGELS
The sun drops low behind the
hills
And pulls the shades of night
The stars appear in the midnight
sky
And twinkle there so bright.

To me each star is a candle lit
By some soul that has passed that
way
To shine for us who still remain
To light us on our way.

So I count each star that was lit
for me
By those who were so dear,
And tho' they're gone, when I see
their star
I know they are always near.

Rita L. Heinzen
ALL HIS WORTH
[To Clay, Ginni, Erin and Emily
for their encouragement and to
the Lord who makes all things
possible.]
The earth comes alive
Following the gentle showers
The green of the trees
and the colors of the rainbow
shining in the faces of all the
flowers.

The birds of the sky
chirping melodies, splashing in
fountains
The blue never ending sky
reaching out
to the majestic mountains.

And as the gentle breezes blow
they bring the scents of the earth,
and remind all the happy people
of God and all his worth.

Dorothy Kole Mucklo
XMAS NOSTALGIA
My Xmas shopping should all be
done
And gifts wrapped and put away
Time is fleeting and I haven't yet
begun,
There are so many things to do, it
seems
And I had planned on making
homemade things.

The house must be cleaned from
stem to stern
So to the basement must go my
favorite fern
To make way for the Tree in the
Family Room.
Slowly I wend my way up three
flights of stairs
To locate ornaments I boxed in
pairs
in the attic. Instead an old
wooden chest
catches my glare; I lift the cover
to find,—
A box with Harry's old roller
skates I see
Two wheels missing, but still
contains the key,
A naked doll, minus hands and
hair, which
little Peggy hid up there for repair,
There's a wedding gown from
long ago
A little yellowed, but folded just
so;
Some letters tied in blue, some
old photos too
As I fondle them, I brush away a
tear (or two).
With these memories I just
cannot part—their
roots go deep within my heart. I
put them all
back to keep, and wend my way
down stairs so steep,
Forgetting to get the ornaments I
boxed in pairs.
Will I go back? Not today,
perhaps next week!

Bette Watts
THE TALL SHIPS
[To my dad, Theodore Wachs,
who gave me some of my
happiest teenage days with the
sail boat that he designed and
built.]
Tall, linear, graceful
Some bodies like eels
Others more ample
With sensuous surfaces
Flags undulating
Creating networked faces
Of ariel graffited dye
Silhouetted against
A pale blue sky.

Paul S. Hornberger
REFLECTIONS
[To my darling wife Francine
on her Graduation Day. The
cornerstone of your future is
set firmly in place. Let the
vision of your spirit do the rest.
All my love.]
Crackling leaves underfoot
Gold, brown and red
Young feet scurry
Always in a hurry
Slow down
See the colours
Before we're ash.

Becky Van Cleve—Dunbar
HOME IS HEAVEN
Reality shines upon us all,
Our fears revolve around each
other,
There comes a time when you
shall
leave the earth—your destiny is
questioned . . .

Live your life as you've dreamt it,
Dream for pleasure; expose your
dreams with another.
When your dreams become
empty—your destiny is
questioned . . .

Travel and search for your
freedom,
Examine why you do the things
you do.
If all that you've done has
satisfied you—
then why has your destiny
questioned you?

Time begins to run out,
Life has cut you short,
and in that time you've
questioned destiny,
You should not fear destiny,
because destiny is your home,
and home is Heaven.

James M. Jacobs

James M. Jacobs
THE PEOPLE
'Tis the hour, to obtain
power—Processing unity
like a growing flower.
For we the people of the
minority race—should
seek out freedom; with
no time to waste.

We have the ability
to undergo task; so if
it's not known; you have
but to ask . . . The
many researchers of
the past.

The sweat and tears
handed down through
the years; makes us strong,
like a large piece of
granite—And also an
ocean to sail "The Great
Titanic"!

Now the world
know we have a Place:
In what is considered—
"THE HUMAN RACE."

Shanna Leigh Hilburn
DEAREST SANTA
Dearest Santa,
The years have come and gone
for me
I'm a child no more and a mother,
you see

My husband was blessed with
two loving boys
that fill his heart with
unbelievable joys

I'm writing to you with a gift in
mind
not for myself, but for him to find

Could you mangage the room
upon your sleigh
to bring the boys here on
Christmas Day?

Wrap them up warmly, just snug
as a bug
and soon they will relish in
daddy's sweet hug

Send with the youngest a note of
words few
"To Daddy with love, from Mom
number two".

Kara A. Jensen
DEEP IN MY SOUL
Deep in my soul something is
wrong
I feel it now it hurts What is
wrong
There's an open space in my
heart
It's all gone the warmth I felt
O what could it be where is that
warmth
Deep in my soul something is
wrong

Lois Phelps Lord
MY GARDEN
In the darkest time of winter
When the days are short and
drear,
I begin collecting seed books
On a promise of spring near.

When at last the ground is broken
And the tiny plants appear
To the days of golden harvest
It will be a friend most dear.

One spring day, my neighbor,
watching,
Said to me, yet jestingly,
As I knelt among the flowers,
"On your knees, again, I see!"

And I, laughing as I answered,
Curious, he seemed to be . . .
And I said, "Sir, can you tell me
Of a better place to be?"

Now I know I answered lightly,
Scarcely thinking what I said,
Yet it keeps me from depression,
For I talk to Him instead.

I have spent so many hours
With Him there alone with me,
As together we have tackled
All the things that worry me.

Anyone who tends a garden
Spends much time upon his
knees . . .
Anyone who loves to garden
Talks with God.

Schiggs
STROKE OF A GENIUS
Will they always feel like lead?
In my blood the rhythm is sweet;
But standing this long on my head,
Will it ever reach my feet?

Jean R. Bursik
THE EMPTY NEST
[To my husband, Bob, my
children, Bob, Jr., Linda, David,
and Barbara, and their families.]
We raised our 'four' through
College
And heard them say 'I Do'.
Our house seems mighty quiet

Since there are only 'two'.
We've read about the
'syndrome'—
It's called 'The Empty Nest'
Could they mean this peace and
quiet—
This much awaited rest?
Gone are the years of deadlines
The car-pools late at night;
The lying awake and listening
Making sure all was right.
If we don't have dinner right at
six
We'll eat at seven or eight;
And we sleep extra hours on
week-ends
When we want to stay up late.
We love our children's visits.
We brag—all grand-parents do.
Our house is full of pictures
And a senile hound-dog, too.
But with all the memories we
share
The years which are the best
Are these olden years—these
golden years—
The years of 'THE EMPTY NEST'.

Ginevar Curenton

Ginevar Curenton
THE SINGLE MOTHER
[To my parents, Lee Anner &
Jackson Curenton, not only but
also my daughters Tammy,
Jacquelyn, Deauna & Shalonda.
Whose thoughts is a secret
place for all sweet memory and
joy.]
With her children running here
and there; where is the father
of the children no one dared to
asked?
He is away because he just don't
care, but mother say it just not
fare.
Tony ask "when is daddy
comming home, mom take him
in her arms," tears begin to run
she looked him straight
in the eyes and said honey i don't
really no. He promise to give
me money . , your father has
never kept a
promise. Then Sandy said is dad
staying with someone else
mom: It hurt me so badly just
like a sharp pain went
to my heart "oh! What a heart
ache," but it was true "mother"
said in a very softly tone of
voice yes he living
with another woman.

The children began to "cry"
daddy must don't love us any
more. Mom say in a gentle
voice oh!
dear he love all of you. He just
want to be alone and away
from the noise. Mother bake
you home made cookies when
you are sad, when you hurt she
say a special prayer especially
for you then you feel better, if
you've never been single
mother you would never
understand what it really mean
to be one.

Trishia J. Johnson
MYTHS
I know that i will never fully
understand what it takes to be
a man
Men are said to be tough and
strong otherwise they can't get
along

Men keep their feelings to
themselves locked inside, men
they say never cry
They THINK they're the upper
hand they're the ones to make
the demands
They're said to have a whole lot
of pride and without it, they
may as well die

Men i feel, are made of myths
because in the long run, a
Woman is equal to all of this!

Valerio Michetti
ALONE (LINESS)
To be alone . . . at times a
blessing.
To be alone . . . at times painful.
The solitude . . . at times a
reward of life.
The solitude . . . at times be it
like hell.
But when friendless, it is like a
handicap.
When turning for help, we have
only emptiness as a response.
No one sheds tears for us,
zwe shed our own tears . . .
. . . tears of lonliness.

Barbara Jean Ronkar
THINKING OF YOU
As the sunset made a silhouette
of things that I could not forget.
It made me stop and wonder why.
I tried to think but I could only
cry.
And when I did I thought some
day,
my mind will see through the
wondering haze.
But only to see that time won't
stand still,
That's why they're memories for
those with a will.

Barbara Edwards
THE JOURNEY
As the howling winds encircle
my soul
like a tidal wave at sea
It opens up the further most
regions of my
mind and awakens my curiosity
The mysteries of time, past and
present,
the future calling my name

Celestial orbs spinning about
flooding my being with a
torrential rain
A step into middle earth where
elves, fairies,
and gnomes dance by their fire,
Lit by their moon, fiddle away an
ancient tune
The aurora borealis—reflections
from the inner sun
Shining brightly in the artic night
leaving a golden pathway for my
flight
A magical sphere this world of
ours
as spiritual guides have shown me
Which are invisible to most
who look but cannot ever see

Brenda Irene Helling
MAY I LEAVE A TRACE?
May I leave a trace behind,
Of God's mercy and all that's
kind?
May I spread a world of cheer,
leave no discouraging words of
fear?
May I lift up the fallen, such as I?
Help me arise when I don't care
to try.
Grant me courage and strength
for each day.
May I leave happy tracks upon
life's way.

Michael D. Smith
REBIRTH
Day by day my life goes on
like pages in a book
I start each new experience
with enthusiasm as a child
for as time passes by
A picture will unfold
and memories will fill my mind
as youth will blossom with the
age
to form a living man
A record of past and heroic deeds
with futures yet untold.

Frederick P. Loveless
A ROSE
A rose is a cup,
Full of feeling and desire.
The petals are a mirror,
Reflecting love's fire.
The stem is a gateway,
It opens life's door.
The thorns are the protectors,
They shield the rose from life's
scorn.
Alone they are pieces,
Just everyday fill.
Together thay are harmoney,
The key to life's will.

MeLynda Gibson
PLEASE DON'T HURT ME
Last night you said you loved me,
I said that I loved you too.
You took me by surprise and I
didn't know what to do.
You told me what I've needed to
hear for such a long time.
I guess that's why I said it back, I
thought if I didn't say it I'd lose
you, and I really need someone
to love me even if I'm not sure
I love them too.

Love's something new for me, and
it's hard for me to judge.
I don't want to get hurt again like

so many times before,
but I don't know if I'm ready for
the commitment that comes
with all this.
So please be gentle, and try to go
slow, remember I'm new at this
so it won't be easy at first, but
if you're willing to try so am I

Joyce Roach
INTERIM
A wicked winter wind
Sweeps across frozen limb,
Snuffs all life with icy blast
As golden sunlight dims.

This form imprisoned now,
Captive lethargy and sleep,
Surrounded by dark despair
Walls my soul refused to keep.

. . . I drift into Spring flowers,
Plum-colored hyacinth stars . . .
Secure and nurture a return
Free from earthly bars.

Shirley Harris—Hall

Shirley Harris—Hall
Have You Seen My Dog Today?
*[Dedicated to: My children and
to my little dog, Chuka]*
The grass is fading,
The leaves are brown,
Fall is approaching
All across our town.

A lady appears in a wrinkle dress
She hesitates, then begins to
speak.
Her voice is warm, full of concern
Mild in manner and very meek
"Miss, I've come a very long way
But, have you seen my dog today?"

Tears come to my eyes
As she tells her sad story,
Children gather and they listen
And one picks up a Morning
Glory,
Gives it to the lady who walks
past the hay,
Asking others, "Have you seen
my dog today?"

"If you should see him
Please bring him back home
Because I'm old and sick
And all alone.
I need to hear his bark
And feel him kiss my finger,
Hold him in my lap
While his loving eyes linger—"

The kids smile as they try to say:
"Don't be unhappy and

don't be sad
We'll find your dog whose lost,
today,"

Frances (Case) Kopp
JESUS
*[This poem is dedicated to my
husband, CLAYTON E. KOPP
and to my grandmother, IDA
MAE CASE, who taught me
poems when I was three years
old.]*
Who is this man called "Jesus."
He is "Jehovah's" only begotten
Son.
The person sent from heaven
An earthly battle to be won.

Jesus tried to tell his brothers
That his kingdom was at hand
But they sneered and mocked
him
And hung him from a stand.

This stand was called a cross
And on this cross he died
But because of his death
The people thought he lied
But on the third day he arose
Just like he said
But it was for you
That he suffered and bled.

So today is another day near
To the kingdom which soon will
be here
But people still refuse to believe
So thats why Jehovah sent me.

To tell you the story . . .
Show you the signs and symbols
That our Father showed me.
So through the blood and the
miracles
You too, will come to
believe . . .
"Jesus of Nazareth is King" . . .

Marie Sullivan
I Love You For So Many Reasons
I love you for that certain smile
that cheers me when I'm blue,
I love you for your tender kiss
that warms me through and
through.

I love you for your gentleness
and understanding touch,
your eyes that always seem to say;
"I love you very much."

I love you for your faith in me,
your sweet and patient ways,
and for those thoughtful things
you do
so often without praise.

I love you so for all these things
and many others too;
but most of all for what I am
whenever I'm with you.

Esther Mazza
OUR FRIENDLY FARMER
*[I wish to dedicate this poem
to, "OUR FRIENDLY
FARMER", who lived in our
community.]*
Our friendly farmer, so proud of
his land
Would tend his cattle with an
extra strong hand;
He worked through the night
forgetting the time
Then a new born lamb, would

make his eyes shine.
He would welcome the children,
with a tender smile
And watch them coast down his
hill in the snow;
He stood out of sight, for a little
while
Then happily, back to work he
would go.
The LORD took our farmer to
heaven today,
Our hearts are sad as we kneel
and pray;
Silent and lonely, his farm stands
on the hill
And somewhere in the shadows
it seems
OUR FRIENDLY FARMER
STANDS THERE STILL!!

Deborah L. Edwards
THE VOID
You skate through my mind
in unbroken patterns.
Clinging there,
though I long to shake free.

The wanting is real
yet the needing is lost,
left behind.
I try to remember

just how it was, when
my soul was on fire
for you,
and I searched for your heart,

but there was only a void.
My hands went right through you
and met,
on the other side.

There was nothing there—
in the place of your heart,
and I wept,
feeling lost and confused.

I knew as I held you
I would never hold your love,
so turning,
I left the black shadow
that should be your heart.

CJ Petretti
The Games We Used To Play
The games we used to play,
Have gone away, so far away,
Our children will never play,
The games of a past day.

One was Johnny-on-the Pony,
Played by guys named Tony,
Tommy and Johnny,
What about Curb Ball,
Played with a rubber ball.

Another, King-of-the Mountain,
A game with fighting and wrestling,
We also had stickball,
A Home Run off the wall.

A beauty, Kill-the-Cop,
Stand in the middle and be sharp,
You needed shoes to play
Kick-the-Can,
In this one a Bing, Bang, Bamm.

Basketball, Softball, and Football,
We played them all,
Don't look like my kids,
Will use that many Keds.

Patricia C. Nalepa
NATURE'S WINTER BEAUTY
The pure white snow
Gently falls from the clouds.
It floats through the air,
'Till the earth, it shrouds.

It clings to your windows
Leaving no coloration
For you to see beauty
With your own imagination.

It casts an icy glow
Crystallizing all it touches
Adding a little more beauty
Straight form Winter's clutches.

Sylvia E. Henley
Little Boy—Little Girl
There's a "little girl" that lives
within this flesh of womanhood,
A "little girl" that longs to be, just
loved and understood.

There's a "little boy" inside of
you, that I'd like to get to know,
Because you see a "little girl", just
feels she'll love him so.

Your "little boy" within the man,
a companion's sure to be,
for the "little girl" I've come to
know living here in me.

A playful, laughing "little boy",
who knows that which I feel,
who loves to joke, in teasing
ways but kindness does reveal.

The hand of the man, with the
"little boy" touch, tousles the
hair on my head,
But strokes the flesh of a woman,
when the "little girl's" in bed.

Andrea Yakab Janes
PERFECT LOVE
You make me smile every time I
look at you.
You're so gentle,
so loving,
you love me the way I want to be
loved.
You are my friend,
perfect love.
When I feel sad you make me feel
content.
You look at me,
without saying a word I know
you love me,
my perfect love.
You bring joy to my life,
happiness to my heart,
you're beautiful,
my perfect love.
Your beauty is you can make me
feel all these things
without trying,
I love to look at you because I
like to smile at you.
You are my purrrrrrr...fect love.

Danell L. Pehrson
LIFE
The still of October morn
Was broken by the shots.
Two bodies lie on the floor
Two souls left without thoughts.

A daughter finds the pair;
Devastated by what she sees.
She runs barefoot for help,
Then she's back, on her knees.

One glance at her step-father
And she knows he's dead.
She cradles her mother
Holds her close, caresses her head.

Police and ambulance arrive
Daughter is taken bodily from
the scene.
Family members are called
Life-Flight saves miles of terrain.

Long hours of agony are spent
A world of concern for a mother's
health.
A difficult vigil at death's door
And God again has shown his
wealth.

The doctors say, "A vegetable
she'll be
She might not know your name.
Prepare for years of constant care
A bed, a wheelchair, a cane."

But God works his magic
Through days and nights of pain.
With determination of a therapist
The will to live is restored again.

The zest for life is beautiful
Its been brought back threefold.
The love and care can never be
repaid
It can only be shown and told.

Cindy Myers Devall
TO THE SEEKER
Do not search in vain
For truth far and wide
It has always been with you
Waiting very deep inside.

Great boundless treasures
Lie deep down within
Hidden from the eyes
Of unenlightened men.

The precious pearls of wisdom
That we seek to find
Are there to be discovered
In the oceans of your mind.

The doors are always open
The portals stand apart
Just look within yourself
And step into your heart.

M. Young
Christmas Dream Walk
*[To Richard, My Children and
parents, who have given me,
those very special, Happy
Walks each year.]*
In a little girl's dream, that's
where you are
As she places on the tree, a Blue
Christmas Star;
All her years past, that same star
has shone
For the little girl's wish, Please
Santa, bring my daddy home.

The little girl grew, and love
came at last
To push the little girl's dream, far
into her past;
A family, A Christmas, her love
he did share
She had her Christmases, all
those, when daddy wasn't there.

Another Christmas walk, this
time from a far
As a woman places on the tree,
that battered old star;
A little girl's dream, that is still in
her prayer
But knowing this time, her daddy,
just couldn't be there.

That old Christmas Star, she soon
would replace
With a loving angel, with a smile
on his face;
With a little girl's love, she now
shares with you
For the little girl's dream, she
knew now, had come true.

The walks on the beach, the fun
in the snow
The dreams we had made, the
love you had showed;
The long dreary days, you made
ever so bright
That's what she is thinking,
alone, on this Christmas Night.

Snow flakes are dancing, as they
fall to the ground
Christmas music, travelers, that
are all homeward bound;
With their greetings and good
wishes, they soon pass me by
Fail once again, to see the tears,
in this little girl's eyes.

My Christmas Walk, on this
Christmas Day
Tho' miles apart, we still need to
say;
I miss your loving touch, your
warm embrace
And above all, that tender smile
upon your face.

A new life together, I pray has
been born
For together, we have just walked
through, that pre-Christmas storm;
My future Christmas Walks, with
you, I want to share
Then finally, I can leave that
little girl, Just sitting there.

Sonya Derian
MY LOVE
My dream sits still
   Unwanted and unattained
My future stays there
   Unpredicted and still
My name awaits here
   Unheard of and unseen
Yet my love . . .
   It stays unreceived
But ready to give.

William H. Drew
SUMMER—SUN LOVE
Encircle you in dreams at
night . . .
I see your smile in the
morning light . . .
You're in my thoughts at
midday, too
   at sunset dusk I think of you.
Of many beauties that we shared,
and our first kiss, yes, that I
dared.
But the love we shared those days
of summer-sun,
   I remember
when a new day dawns and when
the day is done.

Beach walks in the moonlit night
the love we shared, my soul's
delight
Flames flickering low on the
beach where we'd lie,
found your innocent smile, and
the warmth of your eyes.
Surf thundering down on fire-lit
sand,
through it we'd race, hand in
hand.
And the love we shared those
days of summer-sun,
   I remember
when a new days dawns, and
when the day is done.

Sailing briskly upon the 'Frisco
Bay,

watchin' sun give birth to new-
born rays. . .
reminded me of our love, so
intense,
so sudden, so brilliant, and so
immense.
Here I am, alone, 2,000 miles
away,
and you in 'Frisco on a
summer-sun day.
But the love we shared those days
of summer-sun,
   I remember
when a new day dawns and when
the day is done.

Kathryn Clark

Kathryn Clark
GLORIETA!
The beautiful mountains,
   The trees and mountain air,
All of it is so breath-taking!

Singles come from New Mexico,
   Texas and Oklahoma; some from
As far away as California and
Washington!

Singles, divorced, widowed, never
married,
   All attend for one reason;
To learn more about their life styles.

After the first visit, they go back,
   Year after year!

The beautiful mountains,
   The trees and mountain air,
All of it is so breath-taking!

Dewey Hill Jr.
SOUTHERN WIND
The southern wind doth blow
   Through an orchard green
Where cherries and berries grow
   As thick as might be seen

The southern wind doth blow
   Through an orchard good
Where Lilac and Lilies grow
   Within enchanted woods

The southern wind doth blow
   O sweet and pleasant soil
Where natures colors glow
   To the robin's call

The southern wind doth blow
   Down the grassy banks
The small birds twitter
   The woods doth glitter

The southern wind doth blow
   O sweet perfumed flowers
Where all the roses grow
   More beautiful by the hour

The southern wind doth blow

Through an orchard green
Where cherries and berries grow
   As thick as might be seen
Elsie F. Gerald
RESOLVE
Fires of experience
Burning bright
Light up even the darkest night
Of my heart,—
That I might take part
In the ever developing sense
Of having been, of being, of
hoping to be;
That I might see
Eternal progression move out of
innocence
Toward wisdom
That the Kingdom
Of God reigneth as it straineth
and attaineth
In the minds of men.
Elaine S. Hopkins
MOTHER'S DAY
*[to my MOM: I love you. I hope
this poem shows you at least a
fragment of the gratitude I have
for you for being who you are
to me.]*
Whatever I am—
you taught me to be.
Whatever I feel—
you felt before me.
Whatever I try—
I know you've tried too.
Mom, I hope you know—
How much I love you.

I care very deeply,
at times it won't show.
And yet, deep inside—
you already know.
At times, I have hurt you,
In more ways than one.
Sometimes I didn't know
Just what I had done.
But you always forgive me
and try to understand.
You're always there reaching
out your loving hand.
I guess that is why
I love you this way—
And from now on, for us
Each day is MOTHER'S DAY.
Marianito L. Ignacio
THE SEA, SURFING AND ME
People enjoy their vacation in Rome,
Vienna, Paris or London;
but for me it will always be,
surfing and the sea.

Give me a million to spend,
to see the world from end to end;
but nothing better would satisfy me,
than surfing in the sea.

Whether in New York, Louisiana
or Florida,
from Washington down to sunny
California;
chances are you will find me
surfing in the sea.

Take me to fabulous Bermuda,
Acapulco or Havana;
nothing would be more alluring
to me,
than surfing in the sea.

On the beaches of exotic Tahiti
or in Blue Hawaii,
girls in skimpy bikini
would never attract me
more, than surfing in the sea.

I'd climb the highest mountain,
peace and solitude I can gain;
but frolic and fun for me,
would be surfing in the sea.

How I wish Neptune could give me,
His powers over the sea;
so that it may always be
The sea, surfing and me.

Elsie Rae Santagata
THE GIFT OF TEARS
God in His wisdom, gave to man
The gift of tears, as was His plan.
For neither bird nor beast, can
ever cry
Or feel a tear drop from an eye.

For God alone gave us to keep
A release from sorrow when we
weep.
A comfort offered for grief's sharp
pain
That strengthens while our faith
regain.

For there's no shame in honest
tears,
That share our love, our hopes,
and fears.
A human heart is one that cares
And offers solace with quiet
prayers.

Now I am often glad I've known
Through shedding tears, I've also
grown.
Some day, a better person I may be
Because God gave this gift to me.

Michelle Woods
MY SPECIAL FRIEND
Life would not be possible
without this special girl,
to me, she's a great person
and a rich and lovely pearl.

We met each other at camp
we soon became fast friends
we both hated the day
that camp would come to an end.

She lives in a distant town
Lucedale, as a matter of fact,
we keep in touch though
communication is something
that we don't lack.

As I was saying
life would come to an end,
if I didn't have Tina Dueitt
as my "special friend".

Joany Beckman Bowden
SOUL FOOD
Dreams are the ignition to happy
hearts.
A spark of real imagination, a
timeless art.
Spin your dreams, weave your
thoughts.
Never let your love of life be lost.
Dreams are interchangeable,
share some as you go.
Dreamers see visions of peace
and hope.
Never have time to complain and
mope.
Dreamers climb mountains, build
bridges that span.
Contribute to joining man's heart
with man's plans.
There is magic in the smile of a
dreaming man.
For his heart and his mind live in
a beautiful land.

Gail Fleming
MORNING FLIGHT
Awaiting sunrise
completed at last
arising to offer us
gifts of warmth
and brightness
held captive so long,
now half exposed
against the white
of clouds.
Fickle sun
asking nothing from
us, only to
laugh and embrace
beneath it once again.

Jocelyn Montgomery
YESTERDAYS
*[To my grandmother, Carol
Mangum, who inspired me; My
parents, Bob and ReNae
Montgomery, who encouraged
me; And my English teacher,
Rich Utech, who taught me
how.]*
Once upon a time, a time not far
away;
It wasn't in the future, it wasn't
here today.
It was simply in the past, a
simple time it was,
Filled with hope for a tomorrow
better than the one before it
was.
The better tomorrow came, as
was bound to happen,
But with it also came sorrows
that did their joys so dampen.

It became too technical, with
something always wrong;
That they stopped wishing for
better tomorrows,
And started wishing for
yesterdays gone.
How foolish all of them were, and
some still are today;
Had they never wished for better
tomorrows,
Their yesterdays might have been
here today.

Stelle A. De Rosa
A MESSAGE TO FRAN
Hello dear sister, wherever you
are, I know that you can hear
I feel your presence always,
whether you are far away or near
Sadness grips my heart as I write
this form of exorcism
As I try to free myself of this self-
inflicted griefless prison

Because I wasn't there
My grief I could not share

You weren't that old, your life
was full, you taught your
students well
They thought you were the best,
as your eulogy did tell
They shed their tears, their grief
was open, you were really
loved by all
It was real for them, because they
were at your final curtain call

But I was not
I had the Flu, I hurt a lot

In my heart the grief was dull as I
lay sick in my bed
My heart knew you were gone,
but the thought would not stay
in my head
I was almost unaware as the fever
seared my brain
That your life had ended, I wish I
could have felt the pain

It was more than I could bear
That I was ill and wasn't
there

Then one day your school
dedicated a stained glass
window in your name
Because they missed and loved
you, they showed their grief
again
All around me tears were shed,
they spoke of how wonderful
you were
I shared my grief, it purged my
soul, because this time I was
there

With others to share
And to show how much
we care

It's final now, I know your gone,
that's a fact I had to face
You're up there with the best of
them, in your final resting place
I grieve no more, I feel no guilt,
because for you it's not the end
It's just a new begining, and this
message to you I send . . .
Save a place for me and
don't despair
For sooner or later we'll all
be there

Nancy Boston
POEMS
*[To Bobby who showed me the
world, through the eyes of love.
What a beautiful place to be.]*
I write of pain
of tears and joy.
I write about love.
A girl a boy.
Of all the wonderous
things I've seen.
Of precious hopes
and impossible dreams.
I don't need to use
my eyes to see.
I don't need to use
My hands to feel.
For what's in my heart
is all that's real.

JoAnna E. Baltau
SAND CASTLES
I tiptoe quietly through the
rooms of my memory

I see myself when I was young
Laughing, smiling and playing in
the sand
Never a care bothered me
All was done for me
I see myself as I got older
Laughing, giggling, playing in the
park
A few cares were mine
Responsibility was small
I accepted it with pleasure
For I could not wait to grow up
I see myself when I became a
teenager
Laughing, still, playing a different
kind of play
Responsibilities were becoming
larger
My cares were heavier
I didn't mind at all
For I wished to be an adult as
soon as possible
Now, I am on the brink of
adulthood
No longer am I laughing or playing
My responsibilities are numerous
My cares have become a weight
upon my shoulders
I try to rid myself of them
For, now, I wish to return to the
days of my Sand Castles

Sam Potashin
HYPOCHONDRIAC BLUES
"Oh doctor, dear doctor, I really
feel ill,"
"I hope you can help me, I'm
certain you will."
"Arthritis, neuritis, are painful
complaints,"
"They harass me daily, I swear by
the Saints."

"My heart and appendix need
fixing, I'm sure,"
"My gall-stones are rattling,
they're hard to endure."
"My eyeballs are popping, thyroid
again,"
"My contacts are missing, they
slipped down the drain."

"Malaria, filaria, and leprosy, too,"
"Exotic and foreign, no wonder
I'm blue."
"My belly is aching, it's windy
with fright,"
"With very small effort, I'd play
'Silent Night.'"

"My migraines oppress me, please
take out my brain,"
"I don't think I'll need it, it drives
me insane."
"Lumbago, sciatica, dandruff, and
all,"
"These constant afflictions drive
me up the wall."

"Oh, doctor, sweet doctor, please
harken to me,"
"And write my prescriptions, and
double your fee."
"Placebos and capsules and
nostrums, galore,"
"Will banish my symptoms, my
health will restore."

Lynne T. Demas
THE NIGHT
The night is still,
It's eerie and cold.
It lasts forever,
So I am told.

Many things happen
Out in the dark.
Strange and suspicious
Like the sounds in a park.

If you get lost
During the night,
I'm telling you
You'll get some kind of fright.

Oscar Larson
UNTITLED
Starlit crane
Skirt along the rice
Fielded valley

Mist
Linger
On mountain crest

Rain flow down—
Down the stream
To beachhead rest

Carolyn Barmann
DECEMBER LILACS
I am pulled toward lilacs
as in a trance.
They brush cool and soft
against my mouth.

So many flowers
form one flower:
a flock of children dreaming,
blanketed.

Pale purple trips awareness,
triggers, my senses.

Lilac, I snap you from your tree,
holding your smooth branch
between my tingling fingers.
The light and shadow of you!

Your image breaks.
Filling me with light perfume,
you claim me.
There is no other scent on earth.

You pour into me—
begin to sprout inside my arms
and legs.
Oh stop! Can no one help?
But no one would believe.

I am frozen, stilled.
Your pale innocence nods outside
my mind.
You play inside me.
Purple shadows move across my
breasts.

Reason blinks out of my eyes.
You come together.

Stemmed between my fingers
your fragrance fades.
The tiny flowers bend,
helplessly dependent.

Your stalk is torn.
So pale a beauty
drew me over—
gave.

Tracy Hodge
MICHAEL
All of your wounds are mind
With a kiss I will make them a
part of me.
You don't have to say a word.
I can tell how you feel from the
look in your eyes.

The words you say mean nothing
to me.
You're not a man of words.
Yet nothing's ever left unsaid.
Your touch says it all.

Emotions that have just been
tapped
Run thick from your heart.
I am a pail collecting it all.
Your love is pure and sweet.

Reach out and take my hand.
As we touch we will both be a
part of one.
Together we'll live alone
Sharing life with each other 'til
the very end.

Amy Judd

Amy Judd
FRIENDS
Friday night football games;
Finding out all the cute guys'
names;
Stuffing McDonald's down your
throat;
Working together on the class
float.

Crying over boyfriends and fights;
And laughing as you remember
summer nights;
Going to dances and having fun;
Staying up until you see the sun.

Talking about the future and the
past;
The school years go by so fast;
Going to concerts, movies and
malls;
Screaming and shouting down the
halls.

Exchanging clothes and other
stuff;
Talking about the test that was
so tough;
Waiting for your Senior year;
That day doesn't seem too near.

You'll keep these memories forever;
Of all the times you've shared
together;
That's exactly what friends are for;
They're for fun times, and much
more.

Lillian Diefenbach
TEARS
Cold tears burning like rock salt
Slide down to my heart
Melting the shattered pieces.

Helen Pederson
PEACE
PEACE! The goal of the statesman
And scholar in every land;
Though doggedly pursued by many,
Still the cherished dream of man!

Wooed with power and promise,
By treaty, alliance, accord,

The fragile balance is shattered
By war or threatening word.

And all efforts seem as futile
As a wish on a falling star;
As PEACE, like a "garden of Eden",
Beckons in vain from afar!

Rob Miller
A RAINY WISH
Of my eyes, you are a raindrop;
a pure, beautiful crystal;
a dewdrop of spring jonquils
that caresses my cheek and
falls hopelessly in an ocean of tears.
How I long for the rain, and the
sweet spring fragrance, for without
my rainy wish I will cry a
lifetime of tears.

Sally Jane Sanner
PRESENCE IN SILENCE
[In Dedication to a man who
showed me how loving silence
is, to Lyle Else.]
Sitting in the forest,
One notices little silence.

Listen.
There is a noise.
Where does it come from?
What does it look like?
What does it say?
It speaks to us by moving limbs.
It tells us the leaves are dry by
moving them.
The wind speaks in silence.

The small brook even contributes
Its own sound to silence.
The sound is soft,
Yet distinct.
The sound tells us rocks are
present,
Without speaking.
The sound tells us the water moves,
Without our seeing it.

A song is heard.
The song tells us there is life.
What life?
Life that loves to live;
We know by its happy song.

Wait. There is more life!
It moves us like the wind.
It speaks to us like the brook.
It sings a song of joy.
God is present in silence!

John Michael Gawronski
TOGETHER
To the love we share
The beauty within
As our souls
Stand beyond us
In the clouds
Like shining stars
In the heavens
Looking within each other
In total silence
Drawing the energy
Into are bodies
The more powerful
We shall grow
Until the wings of love
Burst into flames
Then we become one
United throughout eternity

Ruby Ener
AMERICA IS
America is a land of beauty
With her rolling hills and
mountains,

Or the plains the the valleys,
With her sparkling streams and
fountains.

America is a land of scenery
Where the trees grow scrubby
and tall,
Where there is much desert land
With no trees, no trees at all.

America is a great storehouse
That no man has been able to
measure,
She has hidden under her soil
A vast amount of valuable
treasure.

America is a land of opportunity
That in few countries one can
attain,
But with ambition and hard work
No one poor has to remain.

America is a land of freedom—
Freedom of religion, speech, and
such,
Freedom to come and go
unmolested,
America gives her people much.

America is a land that is wonderful
With its flag of red, white, and
blue,
She deserves love, honor, and
respect
From all her citizens just like me
and you.

Valerie Kidd
UNTITLED
The whimpering sound this child
makes
Puts my mind on "HOLD".
For what's the reason he's crying
here?
Is he hungry, lost, or cold?
I long to take him home with me,
And give him love and care.
But something about the way he
looks,
You know I wouldn't dare.
With my family life the way it is,
And this poor child's plight.
I could never take him home
with me,
You see, he's black not white.

Richard C. Folsom (Engel)
FEELINGS OF YOU
Feelings of your "warmth"—when
you're near me:
Feelings of your "touch"—when
you reach out to me:
Feelings of "loneliness"—when
we're apart;
Together, there's no word as
"Lonely":

I'll hold you in my heart
Til I can hold you in my arms:
My thoughts are thoughts of you—
My dreams have only you in
them:
Memories of you, will always be
"felt"—
But not forgotten:

You are the "Stars"—that shine
above me:
With each "Glow"—you're not far
from me:
For you are my "Guiding-Light";
That makes my heart beat—with
all its might:
To show that I'll always care,

All you have to do is ask and I'll
be there:

Feelings of love, are feelings of
you—
For you bring out the love,
Emotions with deep devotion—
With everything you say and do!

Lyllian D. Cole
THE NIGHT
[To my grandkids]
T'was the night before Christmas
And Ma was a "fright"
She'd used a new hair set
And try as she might
Every curler and hair pin
was glued to her scalp
Like a nest for the fishes
of seaweed and kelp

Tho she tussled and wrestled
with womanly skill
You could tell at a glance
she'd been through the mill.
Tho he chuckled and chortled
with glee, I'm afraid
Our ole man, bless his bruises
was far from A—Grade

Like a bolt from the heavens
he's struck with a jar
from the peak of the A—frame
while hanging the Star
Then he broke several records
and rungs, too, you bet
When he de-scaled the ladder
while playing at jet

We kids were all huddled
and scared in our bed
If Santa should hear them
We'd all be dead!

Francine Catapano
LAST VOYAGE
[This poem is dedicated to the
memory of my Father, "Every
Man Needs A Hero. I Was Born
To Mine."]
The power is gone—
backbone dismembered
caught up in the eye of
the hurricane—
Tumbled and Tossed

Left alone at sea,
chopped and rocked
but not comforted.
Captain's ship of fools
Albatrose perched on your
shoulder
Sole survivor of your misery—
Companion to your pain. First
Mate.

Faith lost (like the Titanic)
in the iceberg of your heart
echo of a last command,
blindfolded by your fear
surrounded by your crew
Sixty fathoms below

Lost but not at Sea . . .

Maria Laura A. Tillmanns
INNER TRUTH
Inner Truth
Unspoken
Yet
Its words are
Crystal clear
Never misunderstood

Inner Truth
Isolated and alone
Reaches out
To all
In
Isolation and aloneness

Inner Truth
Speaks
By
Listening
To itself

Doug Frazier
THE ROUTINE
It's 4:30 in the morning and all is
not well
we get out of bed and we go
through pure hell
Every morning it's the same
routine,
We make up our bunks and get
the barracks clean,
After all the work in the barrack
is done
We fall out in line in the clear
morning sun,
We all go marching in cadeance
everyday
Our RCPO and Chief say there's
no other way,
Our Chief says if we don't get our
scores up high
We might as well kiss the honor
flags good-bye.
After all the work for the day is
done
We count all of our blessings one
by one.
Our Chief calls aloud, "All you
punks pull off your
clothes and pile into your bunks!"
Here I am I'm up in my rack, I'll
lay here
for hours flat on my back.
I think of all the things that I
have seen,
but I still have more dread for
tomorrow's
routine!!!

Thomas Hill
THESE HANDS
In silent gratitude I study these
worn and tired hands.
Thinking of all the wonderful
things they have done.
With these hands I have caressed
a girl, a wife, a mother.
With these hands I have offered
friendship to a stranger, a
friend, a brother.

With these hands I have raised
virginity from the beginning of
life, my baby.

I have doubled these hands to
fight man's inhumanity to man.
With these hands I have spilled
the seed of life upon the ground.
I have watched these hands
through the tenderness of
youth harden
And callous into manhood.
With these hands I have wiped
many a tear, patted many a
friend and
Comforted many a loved one.
These hands have protected me
through prison, worked till
they ached,
To feed and clothe this poor
simple body.
Most of all they have been the
tool which has described my
expressions
Of love, fear, anger, and sorrow.
I love these hands for they have
carried my words from the heart
To the paper so that my eyes can
see the sanity that is within.
I have folded these hands many
times in prayer; nervously in
fear.
At the graveside in sorrow. In
joyous bliss upon my wedding
day.
In a solemn moment alone with
God, either asking or thanking;
Or just in plain desperation, they
have spread my life throughout
This world and into the next.
So now they begin to shake;
through age. The tears form in
my eyes
For to me I see my tired old
friends trying so valiantly to
retain their
Strength and youth. But to no
avail; for age has come before
its time.
To me they are sacred and I will
fold them proudly at death and
lay them
Upon my chest; but no one will
notice them, but they will have
earned their
Place in life. God gave them a
duty at birth and they carried it
out in
Fine style and glory, not once
failing me and for this I am
grateful . . .
    I love you hands!

Zelia Goncalves
HOW COME, DADDY?
daddy, how come you don't like
mommy?
daddy, how come you don't like
my sisters?
daddy, how come you don't like
my brother?
daddy, how come you don't like
me?
daddy, how come?
daddy, how come you hit us?
don't you like us, daddy?
if you don't like us, daddy, why
did you get us?
you didn't hafta if you didn't
wanna
you know, daddy, i used to like
you
a whole lot when i was littler

but not no more daddy
daddy, do you feel bad when you
hit us?
i don't think so daddy
cuz you just keep on hitting!
and hitting and hitting!!
daddy!!!
do you know that, daddy?
i used to think you were so good,
daddy
but now, daddy, you don't seem
the same
how come you changed, daddy?
i liked you like your old self
better, daddy
is it cuz you only like little boys
and girls, daddy?
if that was the only way that you
would like me
i would stay little forever.

Deborah A. Wilkin
FAITH
[To my Mother and Father who
showed me the meaning of
Faith; and Faith gave me the
courage to live my life my way.]
I was asked today if I believed in
Faith
What can I say?
I'd journey to places unknown,
alone
I'd climb each mountain along
the way
I'd accept each challenge and
delay
I'd willingly pay the price which
life requests
If I believed the path was Blessed.

Debra Lucas
REAL LOVE
I used to wonder
If love was real.
I thought I'd found it,
Times before,
But it turned out to be
Dream's sweet illusion
And always a dawn away.
Now I wonder
But not if love's real,
Only at the splendor
Of the sunrise . . .
And you.

Cornelia Fox-Patterson
FRIENDS
While strolling down life's
pathway, it's sometimes hard to
find
someone you can relate to and
share what's on your mind
without the fear of being
ridiculed or having your trust
broken
and have confidence they will
not repeat the secrets that
you've spoken.

I believe like one large rock in
the vast, storm ridden sea,
God always provides one anchor
for His child when it is in need.
For HE knows when the pressure
is great and the burden is too
heavy to bear
and that's when HE presents an
angel like you to smile and say,
"I care."

I know that personalities conflict
and some seem to not think of
mankind,

but I am sure in His heavenly wisdom, He has a purpose for them in mind.
It may not be to understand or listen, or even to love so freely.
It may not be to have compassion and kindness or to give of oneself so completely.

But there is something in all to offer . . . although a friend, not everyone can be;
yet I knew you had all the qualifications of being a wonderful friend to me.
Wherever your life may lead you, I hope you'll find treasures untold.
For the friend I've had in knowing you, is worth more to me than pure gold.

And to have one true friend in a lifetime, is the most I could possibly request.
For the riches I have gained from knowing you, are far better than even the best.
In life we lose things we love dearly—our loved ones, our possessions, even our way;
but a true friend is with you forever—NO ONE can take that away.

Rosemarie Garry
A WHIM
[For Micks' Pop]
Jogging over to England could be easy if you're "Jumping Jack"
as he makes his dash appearance then goes.
Stopping now and then for some grog and beef.
Ever on the go blow, blow, blow...
When he reaches the channel what do you think he'll do?

Phylis Dix
LOOKING INTO YOU
[To Greg, with love. Thanks for letting me "Look Into You"]
There you sit little boy
With all your grown up responsibilities
Wishing someone would give you a lollipop instead
of all the black marbles.
Here comes Daddy, there goes Daddy,
taking with him all the innocence
And leaving behind dissapointment.
They told you it would be wonderful to grow up,
Now you're not so sure.

Steffen Horstmann
Holdest Thy Peace At This Time
When you are anguished and mad at the world.
When you are beaten and destructively hurled.
When you are powerless and hopelessly weak.
When you're called "cowardice" and revenge you do seek.
Take some advice from an old friend of mine.
"Holdest thy peace at this time."
When you're defeated in total

disgrace.
When you've been cheated by a compassionate face.
When you're outnumbered and the outlook is bleak.
When you've been hastened and revenge you do seek.
Take some advice from an old friend of mine.
"Holdest thy peace at this time."

Helen Felten

Helen Felten
EVERY DAY IS CHRISTMAS
I don't need a tree to give me "spirit"—
For the Spirit of God is within me!
I don't need lights to bring me joy—
For *every* day is joyful to me!

For instance—I have a son—
Who is such a great blessing to me—
That any other gift—in comparison,
Would be mere mockery!

I have many friends—
Who fill my life so beautifully—
That anything in my Christmas stocking
Would be such a waste to me!

I am saddened when women— sneer with envy
But a child will say, "You're pretty."
I get such a glow—
Christmas is nil in comparity!

The guys take me to dine in the nicest of places—
And the compliments flow so freely!
I realize how fortunate I am—
That *every* day is Christmas for me!

My eyes, my arms, my legs, my body—
I enjoy His gifts so thoroughly!
But, most of all—I enjoy the Gift of Life—
Yes, *every* day is Christmas for me!

Kathleen E. Desilets
SUNRISE ON THE BEACH
They say the beach is lonely
When the sun is on the rise,
But I love to be the only
Reflection for the skies.

The waves come pounding toward me,
Reaching out to take my hand.
They bow and say, "Good morning",
As I sit back on the sand.

I need no one to talk to,
For God is there with me,
Painting the sky a velvet-blue,
Over His deep-green sea.

I take this time to look inside
As the morning takes its hold,
Before the world begins to rise,
My feelings I unfold.

My soul feels like it has been kissed,
The sun is within its reach.
My heart feels for those who have missed
A sunrise on the beach.

June Laws
THE UNBELIEVERS
Yes, God it's me again
Your little child of love
I'm hoping to meet You soon
In Heaven up above
But first I come to You
With a problem I cannot solve
I'm speaking of the unbelievers
And their foolish I cannot dissolve
It hurts me in so many ways
To see them wander here and there
I try to help them when I can
But they don't seem to care
I love them all in many ways
I wish that they could see
All the good that You have done
For both them and me
My tears of love are rolling now
My heart begins to ache
To change them to believers
I'll do whatever it takes!

F.J. Louzon
IN MY MIND
In my mind there lives
ghosts of mutilated cells.
as I run daily through my part
these fiends sometimes enter the play
and read my lines in their own way.
satisfied,
they hide again and
waiting 'til I think I've won
return again to have their fun.
in legion strength once more they rise
to storm the temple guardian's home
with battle casualties unknown.

Jim Driscoll
ASTRAL OVERHAUL
  i see a bright star turning
& clanking into a different orbit/
its constellation becomes meaningless
then/GET THE CREATOR QUICKLY & TELL HIM TO BRING HIS TOOLS!!/trouble
below Orion's belt . . ./

James R. Moranor
A QUESTION OF FAITH
I stand at the pinnacle of Colorado's
Majestic Rocky Mountains,
awed by the magnificent beauty of this
vast wilderness.
I know full well that God exists,
for if he did not, there would be no peaks, no valleys.
Yet I wonder; if there truly is a God,

why does he allow the pain of human anguish?
Why does he give us fleeting moments of
pure joy, then withdraw them?
Why has he given me you, knowing I can never
have you?

Sharon F. Cote
CHRISTMAS
A snowflake falls to form the snow, the pines sparkle with garland and lights. The tree's with barren arms—bend low, to welcome the still of night.

The wind whistles to the tune of a chirping bird; And the lake reflects on the joys of the day. The moon shines as, children— a caroling go.

This is a wonderful time of year, when all is enhanced by Christmas and its glow.

Terri Lynn Hill
WHATEVER HAPPENED
Whatever happened to knights on white stallions who spoke of gallant pride,
Have they lived on in countless eras or in the past have they died?
Whatever happened to lush green fields where lovers walked hand in hand,
Are they beyond the city gates or did we destroy the land?
Where are the children with carefree smiles and trusting loving hearts,
Why do they cower as if in fear, has destruction gone too far?
Whatever happened to peace on earth that GOD gave us in the beginning,
Does it live on within the world or have we seen the ending?

Florence E.R. Foster
IT'S CHRISTMAS TIME
[This poem is dedicated to my former English teacher, Beatrice Kingsley Keim who, through her patience and wisdom, taught me to believe in myself.]
Gingerbread men and striped candy canes; . . .
Blinking lights glowing through frosted window panes; . . .
Carolers, singing peaceful Christmas songs; . . .
Busy holiday shoppers hurrying along; . . .
A brisk, chilly wind, and a new-fallen snow; . . .
A "Merry Christmas" greeting from folks that we know; . . .
A special kind of joy; . . . of holiness and good cheer,
Are all signs that the happiest of holidays is near.

Children behaving; . . . being as good as can be; . . .
Family members decorating an evergreen tree; . . .
Stockings hung by the fireplace where a yule-log burns bright,
Are signs of hope that St. Nickolus will visit one night.

There's no doubt about
it; . . . It's so plain to see
That Christmas is coming with
its holiday glee.

Up, in the sky, a golden star's
holy light
Shines God's blessings on all in
its sight; . . .
To remind us of a Saviour born,
So early on the first Christmas
morn; . . .
And the Christmas tree, with
lights aglow
Casts love's shadows across the
snow.
It's such a special time of
goodwill and cheer.
To me, this is Christmas; . . . the
best time of the year.

Alison Nadine Dyer
THE LOVE OF LEARNING
*[There are no words; poetic or
otherwisse to describe the Love
and admiration I feel for my
father who has always inspired
me.]*
I've always been taught to speak
my mind
Especially to those who are
unkind.
"Stand on your own two feet" he
said
"You've got to learn to use your
head"
"You are your own person that's
all you need"
Don't be overcome by a thing
called greed".
"Life is full of ups and downs,"
"But very seldom should you
frown."
All the words that are written
above
Are things that come from a
heart of love.
All these words I'd like to say,
Came from a man who has lived
this way.
From my heart I'm more than glad
To say this special man is my Dad.

Lone Bard
DOOMED!
Who knows the soul that cried
alone?
What one, withholding tears,
Has watched the days pass
swiftly by—
And then has watched the years.

Hoping against hope, all hope in
vain,
Hope fades fast and comes not
again.
His strength grows feeble, dim
his eyes;
So comes there a time when man
dies.

Raising his weary hands to
heaven,
He cires, "Alas, how *can* I die!
When all that I have longed to do
Is still undone—I know not why.

I've always loved the beautiful,
but now
My sight fades fast away;
All that ever gladdened mine eyes
Is gone, is gone today.

"Star of the evening, beautiful star!

From deep, blue skies, so free
and far,
Shed on me, on this fearful night,
Thy tenderest rays to my
fading sight."

His soul is sad, his voice is weak;
Tears come when he cannot
speak.
He struggles with his fleeting
breath
As he comes face to face with
death.

Death stands at the threshold,
then steps inside,
And in the grim silence—who
knows who died?

Eleanor M. Hessek
THE SECRET
Their eyes meet
and they smile the smile
of those sharing a secret.
Suppressed emotions,
the words were finally spoken
and now the bond cannot be
broken
however strong the walls are built
between them
by those wanting to possess
their time and souls.
Long months of keeping feelings
hidden,
each believing it forbidden to
want,
to need the other.
But the love inside was too strong,
and however wrong,
they knew before the door was
opened
that it had to come out.
Their eyes meet
and they reach out
but cannot touch.

Patricia A. Paton
THE THORNBIRD'S SONG
*[To Patricia A. Perenick,
Secretary, Rehabilitation
Department, Springfield
College, Springfield,
Massachusetts, as her spirit
ascended August 31, 1981. She
was my friend.]*
Can You see me coming, Lord?
Will I soon be in heaven, moor'd?

Is there a place where I can stay?
Where You can hold me, night
and day?

In pain, I held the golden key;
And now, I pass the shaded tree.

My fear of death has finally left,
But what of these I leave bereft?

My body soothed by those I love.
My spirit met with joy above.

The transition made, I ask no
more,
For God swung op' the glorious
door.

Willard L. Hartshorn
TIME
A rich man cannot buy it
regardless of his wealth
A thief can never steal it
no matter what his stealth.
The idle seldom think of it
as slowly it drifts by
The busy can't keep up with it
it moves on wings that fly.

An hour is a minute grown
a minute is an hour spent
Oh, if we had only known
what was borrowed, lost and
lent.
The night and day is made of it
we all have equal share
Eternity is paved with it
and we shall end it there.

Mary Louise Russell
SUMMER, OH, SUMMER
*[In thankfulness for my dreams,
my life, my loves, my children,
and my beautiful grandchildren.]*
Sunny skies are shining
filled with morning dew.
Flowers sweet as candy,
Love, a wedding ring too.
Silver larks are flying
filling the air with song.

Laughter, love and happiness
Float on Moon Beams, Dreaming
of a home.
"Summer, Oh, Summer"
filled with love shining
as the stars.
"Summer, Oh, Summer"
So sweet you are.

Brenda A. Megna
FUNNY
Funny, it's so easy to hurt the one
you love,
But why is "I'm sorry" the hardest
words to say?

Funny, how tomorrow is so
difficult to wait for,
But how it's so hard to let go of
today.

Funny, how it takes so long to
reach your goals,
But how in a second they can all
fade away.

Funny, how aging can once seem
appealing,
But, how difficult it is to let the
young years give way!

Funny, how fast it is to make one
a promise,
But, in the same amount of time,
one will betray.

Funny, how life can be a barrel of
laughs,
But how easy it is for blue skies
to turn to gray.

Funny, how you promise never to
forget,
But how in time you just may.

Funny, how stubborness says,

"I'll never give in",
But then good sense says "I'll
obey".

Funny, how you could go on
writing forever,
Funny, fresh ideas just seem to
decay . . .

Ralph H. Chase Jr.
THE SEAGULL
Look at the seagull in the sky;
Flying up so very high.
He goes left, then goes right;
Looking around to see if things
are alright.
He's in a hurry, I can tell;
He goes on his way, everything
must be well.

How he's back at the seashore by
the Cape Cod Canal;
He takes his time now and soars
so well.
Climbs high in the sky then dives
down so quick;
Picks up a fish from the water,
what a neat trick.

His friends come quickly as you
can see;
To share his dinner and make
noises of glee.
They glide by the water as easy
'can be;
They're so happy to be free.

James A. Sabean
WHEN AND AGAIN
When will you love me again?
When will i be happy again?
When will you need me again?
When will i be again?

When will i see you again?
When will you talk to me again?
When will i walk with you again?
When will you hold me again?

The questions of when,
of when and again
For when i am not with you,
I am not . . . without you again.

Christopher W. Young
LOVE TIDE
Is it true I love you, and you love
me?
Can the love we share, be
visible, and others see?
Few can journey, and stay clung
to one another,
without prematurely exiting,
with another's lover.

How great the love be, true to the
one at arm,
forsaking all the causes, and
wanting not to harm.
Security and companionship
bank the fires low,
If not be i' for the greener grass,
embers few, would glow.

As they write of lovers, but not
those hand in hand,
like feetless shells on the
beachfront, lying in the sand.
Settled in the beachfront, scantly
inches from the surf,
a change from new to full,
whisks them from the turf.

Cresting in the current, cascading
in full tide,
via natural vehicles, by which
to thee confide.

Riding out the currents,
justifying Nature's win,
be not barred of ecstasy, nor
committith venial sin.

As I ride along with thee, in life's
raging sea,
hopeful goes the joyful hearts,
of both you and me.
As She does own us, and carry us
as She may,
may the currents grant us,
every night and day.

Donald W. Dutcher
THE THUNDER HEAD
As I look upon the distant cloud
That sets upon the horizon
It seems to use the maple, oak
and willow
For a great big pillow.
It sets its head—a thunder head
Upon the dark gree trees
Soon the leaves churn in the
strong breeze
And then it thunders aloud
This big-black cloud
And then the trees start to bend
Though moments ago they stood
so tall and proud
Dead leaves and dust in swirls it
does send
Churning up into the summer air
Though only moments ago the
sky was so fair
To stay out any longer, I do not
dare
So into the house I must go
Although the weather was so fair
moments ago
Lest I get soaked from the passing
storm
And all will seek shelter of a
certain form.

Dorothy R. Douglas
**The Moon and I Are
Kindred Spirits**
The moon and I are kindred
spirits,
Cool, aloof, barren
Beautiful from a distance
Containing flaws and craters
up close
Mysterious for many years
Yet finally approached and
taken
Causing flurry and excitement for
a brief time
Then, left alone and forgotten.

Margaret T. McGarry
HURT—1982
Doldrums, please leave me, Oh
God!
Weariness engulfs me, I'm
extremely sad,
Nothing has gone right in the
past year,
Unemployed too long, children
acting bad.

I should be happy this evening,
Here alone with my thoughts to
rake.
Peaceful, quiet, warm house,
How can I relieve myself of this
purple ache?

I'll turn on the soft reading lamp,
Switch on the TV,
Flop into the comfortable
cushions of the couch.
I see News—woe is me,

What the hell, maybe it can spark
my interest.

Vaguely recognize that movie
actress,
It's Liv Ullman at the mike,
looks like another Senate hearing,
Probably another hype.

Ugh! How repulsive!
Pictures of starving African
children grip my senses.
I repel a wave of nausea.
Dan Rather explains they seek
meals and receive morsels.

These scarecrow near dead
humans
have walked miles for a piece of
bread.
Hot, parched earth they walk
upon is crowded
With so many other skinny black
malformed bodies.

Horror permeates my soul.
I weep as I shut off the tortuous
picture.
And I was feeling sorry for
myself . . .

Amen.

Lorraine Barrieau
PRIORITY
If God is your Priority,
You'll do well in society.
Let Jesus and you merge
And let no one diverge.
Jesus, Jesus, Jesus, you say:
"Hear me, help me, bless me,"
you pray.
May you always be happy, free;
And may God's blessings follow
thee.

Sharon Ann Wilder
WAITING FOR AUTUMN
The muscular wind has stopped
wrestling . . .,
with the numerous flitting
leaves,
and I . . . have stopped on
stable ground—
to hide.

Autumn has arizen in an array,
and . . .
cast its eyes of color; tears
of the trees, these, on palatte
I display.

I forced the sun at my door to,
lead my eyes .
to the origin of light. In
moments
I was blind, images lost in
my mind.

Waiting for Autumn,
It offered a celsius bite.
For me, the Sea whispers too far a
cry, like I,
this Fall offers too many a night.

As of the Autumn leave, . . .
Pirouette as the wind
I shall, retrace my dance
and curl up my stance
before the Fall.

Madeline Stewart Colton
A SPECIAL LITTLE BOY
There's a little boy in our town
Who's different from the rest;
He cannot talk so very well
Nor run around with zest.

He's learned to do a puzzle;
A crayon he can hold.
Put on his shoes and sweater;
His paper he can fold.

Once he gets to know you,
He'll creep inside your heart;
He'll give himself completely
If he trusts you from the start.

You make him happy, carefree;
He'll make you understand,
That he, as all the rest of us
Needs a friendly, guiding hand.

Sometimes he's quite determined,
And sometimes passive, mild.
Vulnerable and defenseless,
He's a small retarded child.

June Harrington
DEAD LEAVES
We slept and wept
Beside the wall
So staunch and tall . . .
A vigil kept
Beside the thing that dwarfed our
love
And stunted it.
Too shadowed now to grow at all
We want to hide
Yet try to ride
Atop the wall
In balance style
A little while
'Til one of us
Fell down the other side
I do not know which one
We really tried . . .
So now the wall that sheltered us
Has come between . . .
What does it mean?
I cannot sleep here in this place
Hurt by the fickle
Cold and brittle
Winter limbs
Dead leaves in my face.

Sheryl Frances De Garmo
MORE THAN A MEMORY
People I love you
I know you loved me too

People don't be sad
It isn't so bad

You had me for awhile
You have my music, smile

When you think about me
I am more than a memory

People I love you
I know you love me too

People don't be sad
It isn't so bad

When you think about me
I am more than a memory

Nathalie Roy
SEA OF MIND
[Ein Gedicht fur dich
Torsten . . .mit Zartlichkeit]
All my life is resumed in this
gigantic entity.
Powerful and relentless is
mother-sea.
Incessantly rolling, stroking the
sand
like infuriated bodies mingled in
a sensous bend.

It is the act of love I witness:
a furious deed of untangled
elements
put in a raging and violent torment

that explodes around my
. nakedness.

Humming codas of Beethoven,
of distressed and inhuman burden
I am seduced by his titanic figure
of chiseled marmorean features.

It is always near the sea
I feel such a need for continuity...
As if my body and mind, after all
those years,
were finally reunited and casted
out from fear.

But peaceful feelings are dying
ashore
when the flow and ebb of hatred
besmears the battered shore
with a black intoxicated blood.

Love drinks the mortal beverage
lost not in vain yet to be
forgotten with the ages.
The next morning every single
trace is washed away . . .
the flood has come to return the
sea-side its own purity.

A "Sturm und Drang" sinking
deeply
in an ocean of immemorial
tragedy . . .
Life and death are staged by a
producer:
the sea—Nemesis of nocturnal
waters.

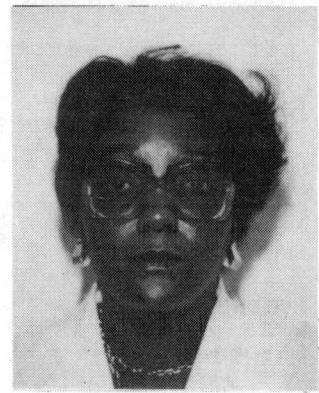

Katherine A. Lords

Katherine A. Lords
LITTLE RAINDROPS
O little raindrops
What a joy you bring
Some complain
But a song I sing

You bring life
To a withering world
Uplift the surroundings
With a Glorious swirl

Each drop is like
A sweet tune to my ear
Praising the Lord
Softly I can hear.

Anne Poirier
A FINAL GOODBYE
It was about twelve years ago
when
I wrote you so many poems
And though you were never
shown them
I had you in mind each time I
wrote 'em.

So many years had passed

And we'd each gone our separate
   ways,
But I find I must write one last
For sadness came over me that
   quiet day.

You led a full, exciting life,
For twenty eight years had
   brought you far.
You worked and played and took
   a wife
Moved here and there and very far.

I cannot help but remember
All the little things we did
   together;
And with the events of those
   grief stricken days,
Came tearful memories of
   carefree ways.

That night, I saw you resting
   peacefully,
And though so much time had
   passed,
I knew it was you as I looked on
   sadly
And thought of that teenager
   from my past.

I hope that now, all is in place
For you had problems all through
   your life.
And the grief we felt as we
   looked into your face
Held the memories we all will
   keep of your life.

So now as I end my final poem to
   you
I feel the tears well up inside me.
And before I finally put down my
   pen
I must say goodbye one last time
   to
A dear friend who, once upon a
   time,
Brought happiness and laughter
   to me.
Farewell!

Sherry Andrychuk
INNER SPACES
Inner Spaces,
Quiet oasis
Intruders forgotten
I rest by the well.
Inner resources,
Your healing balm
Uplifts the soul
To face the storm.
Inner power,
Enobling service
Triumphant in thy quest
Fulfilling life's desires.
Inner strength
Welling up
From the depths of the Spirit
That is man.

Johnny M. Hudson
NOW EVEN AS I PRAY
The volumes have been read,
The spirit has been fed,
A token placed upon the grave
To mark the holy dead.

And time is marching on,
Despite the spirits gone,
Just longing for the moment
When it marches on alone.

For man has had a chance,
The cosmos to enhance,
His destiny known only to
The Maker in advance.

Now even as I pray,
I fear the break of day,
And dread to see the sun arise
An unfamiliar way.

Ursula Bagchi
THE OTHER RIVER BANK
*[Inspired by Don's illness. For
Dawn and Christopher with
love. I was not so good to you, I
never spoiled you and you
loved me. I thank you for it!
Don's words]*
I call your name with every breath
at wakeful hours day and night,
I know it is in vain
and still this little hope
to see you again.
Tears rolling down my cheeks,
God, I surrender
with my sorrows in your arms.

My house is too narrow
I must leave;
with tears in my eyes
in the night on the road.
Drops of rain
forming little stars
where ever they fall.

Here
on the river bank
I can breathe,
my chest expands,
no hurts
only memories
passing through my mind.

This space
to the Other River Bank
restores peace,
I am not lonely any more,
I can hum old songs,
I am not lost any more,
I am just like a star
in God's Universe.

Brenda (James) Spence
AND I LOVE YOU
*[This poem is dedicated to a
very "special" person in my life.
Someone I'll never forget.]*
I love you for the way you hold
   my hand,
Each time that you are near.
And your gentle touch, if I should
   cry,
As you brush away each tear.
I love you for the way you smile,
With that look that I adore.
And when you're mad or a little
   sad
I can only love you more.

I love you when I go to sleep.

Until the moment I awake.
I love you with each word I speak,
And every breath I take.
I love you for the way you make
   me laugh,
Whenever I am blue.
I love you not only for the special
   things,
But for everything that you do.

I love the way you say my name,
And the way you hold me tight.
When you are near, I'm not
   afraid—
Of the darkness or the night.
I'll love you now and forever
   more,
Even until my last breath.
You'll be my love, until at last,
My eyelids close in death.

Susan M. Silver
NOGA
To see you dancing
It is still hard
To see you laughing
It is till hard
To see you have made peace
With yourself
To see you have made peace
With the past
It is still hard to remember
I do not love you anymore

Susan M. Silver
JIMMY JAZZMAN
He nurtures a nameless keyboard,
Within you or without.
His sun and stars are
   synchronized for him,
Within you or without.
He spins that jargon audible to
   jazzman,
Caught in the chiaroscuro of his
   eyes,
Within you or without.
He cycles his joy and pain
In constant harmonies, in pulsive
   peace.
With every strand of yourself
You strain to bridge with him,
But come to know, at last, the
   simple truth:
He plays alone, within you or
   without.

Jim Chasteen
FORGET
Forget her name, forget her face,
   The way she kissed and her
   embrace.
Forget her love once so true,
   Remember now there's
   someone new.
Forget the love that once was
   shared,
   The time she said she even
   cared.
Forget the time you spent
   together,
   Hoping that love would last
   forever.
Forget the hours that were so
   long,
   Even when you hear that
   favorite song.
Forget how close you two once
   were,
   It's in the past and all a blur.
Forget the way she sweetly talked,
   The way she moved when she
   walked.

Forget the time she said goodbye,
   That awful day she made you
   cry.
Forget her gentle teasing ways,
   Your rushing to see her
   everyday.
Forget the thrills when you drove
   by,
   You didn't see her, but had to
   try.
Forget the way she held your
   hand,
   Forget her sweet kisses, if you
   can.
Forget she said she'd leave you
   never,
   Remember now, she's gone
   forever.

Dorothy Diann Cook
LILY
Lily white, lily fair,
What possessed you, growing
   there?
Lifting up your pristine face
in this dark and gloomy place.

Was it knowing you'd the power,
   in your one, short blooming
   hour to lift the eye from lowly
   duty by the vision of your
   beauty?

Lily lovely, glowing pale, within
   this bleak, forbidding dale
   blooming bravely, where none
   could see
Did you blossom, just for me?

Ruth C. Davidson
FUTURISM
The sun is shining but its cold
Tomorrow is another day yet to
   behold
Spring is yet to come
It's drifting, drifting, slowly
   drifting in.

Bernice Goodrum Ransom:
A COP
*[To Rockdale Co. Sheriff
Department: And especially Sgt.
Gilbert Gaines & Ernestine
Black]*
You take an oath, to serve and
   protect, but if you stop the
   wrong one, they're ready to
   have your neck!

If you just look around you, there
   are people getting ran down
   everyday. By all the drunk
   drivers, who don't yeild the
   right of way.

They go all out for you, even
   putting their lives on the line,
   trying to secure you and your
   kids future, against crime.

And yet, they're viewed, with so
   much hatred, and very little
   respect. Just think, they have
   families too, and for you they
   risk their neck.

Suppose they felt about you, the
   way you feel about them, and
   whether you lived or died,
   didn't even matter to him!

How much would your life, be
   worth, out there on the streets,
   with no police protection,
   against the bums, that you
   meet.

I bet you think they've got it made, at least that's what the public says. I challenge you to switch places with them, only for one day!

Poor cops, can't hardly support their families, with their take home pay. And yet, you find time to criticize our police-men this way.

Perhaps, you had better make a change, and treat them with more respect. After all it was your life that they promised to protect!

So when it comes to our fellow officers, be as nice as can be,for someday your life may be threatened, and around they may not be!

Ila Standlea Steinke

Ila Standlea Steinke
I AM A DIAMOND
I am a diamond
born eons ago in the depth of space
in the formation of galaxies
in the fires of the universe
in the birth of stars
in the bowels of planets
in the depths of one called earth
under extreme pressure
in the caldron of fire
born in volcanic eruptions
pressed between carbonaceous blackness
uncut I glow
waiting.
Will anyone ever find me?
Will anyone ever know
I am a diamond?

Bernice Goodrum Ransum:
ME!...I,...TOMORROW?
Me a tolerable, concerned American citizen. One who tries very hard to be content with, ones lot in life.

But my inter-self known as I, and it's powerful forces, keep tormenting me, not letting me live only for today!

Its like a powerful magnet, drawing me in a direction, not of my own chooseing, but one of its own, confusing my thoughts and embeding deadly seeds of ambition in my subconscious mind.

Telling my subconscious mind, that things can be better still, just hang in there a little while longer, keep searching, praying, always hoping for, greater achievements.

And while my soul throbs with great aggravation, and sorrow! My thoughts are somewhere caught up between the things I have today, and what I could have tomorrow!

Timothy Michael Gregory
The Miracle Of My Mind
[This poem is dedicated to Jesus Christ, my Lord and Saviour]
I caught a cloud
In the sky
And rode it to your door
But you were not at home,
So I made myself a seed
And grew as a flower
On your front lawn
But you never noticed me,
So I became a rain drop
And fell on your face
But you mistook me
For a tear
And wiped me away,
So I can but come to you
As I am,
Seeking your acceptance.
I shall surround myself
With a thundercloud
And the lightning
Shall be my smile
I shall move over you
While riding on a breeze
And rain down on you
In love . . . . . .

Juliette Ruth Armer
HI—KU—FUR—U
Bronze sheaves bundled close
Brittle piles in crimson, gold
Russett spill light bold.

Crystal patterns mesh
Like icy swans down soft bed
Gossamer lace shed.

Snow's last blossoms melt
Down the stems and leaves of May.
Sun Shine all the day.

Morning flowers come.
Petals open to the sun
Face fresh golden spun.

The Evening's velvet
Violet wraps round the sun-soak
Earth with heavy cloak.

James M. Learnard
WHAT WILL SHE SAY?
[To Barbara, My life, my love, my inspiration. With love always, Jim]
As I sat thinking of you one day, I asked myself, what you would say,
When I ask you to marry me. I wonder, dear, what will your answer be.

I wonder, dear, what will it be, What will be the answer you'll give to me?
Will it be "yes", or will it be "no". It's your decision, and only you know.

I wish, I wish, I wish I might, That you'll say "yes" to me one night.
And then we'd live so happily In wedded bliss for all eternity.

And here's what you said to me, I may say "yes", or I may say "no".
But for now, I'll say "maybe". God only knows what the future holds,
We'll just have to wait and see.

But no matter what the future holds,
Friends we'll always be.
We'll have each day, and we love each day.
And whatever will be, will be.

Keli J. Todd
MY PROMISE TO YOU
I can't be the sun that shines from above,
but I can be the warmth of His love.
I can't be the light that guides you home,
but I can be the glow to which you can come.
I can't be the bridge over a troubled stream,
but I can be the hand that reaches out in a dream.

I can't promise I'll never let you down,
but I can promise I'll always be around.
I can't promise sunny skies that are always blue,
but I can promise forever a love that's true.

Kathleen Diane Johnson
DESTINATIONS
Was the wait in vain?
The anitcipated reward received?
Opportunistic future foreseen
And detoured by maturing curiosities
It seemed so short a distance at the time
The road grew longer somehow
Unnoticed 'til now
It was paved so beautifully
So as to slip by
Without mention to miles of time
The place now far from home
Yet home no longer a satisfactory contentment
Was happiness passd or does it await
Optimism still remains the choice
I travel on . . .

Mark Okey Decker
MY PIPE
A Christmas present from Scotland.
It took a leprechaun, a much—beloved Uncle, and
A lot of understanding from McEwan herself.
I enjoy this pipe; its stem and bowl jut proudly forward
Like an old friend, that has recently returned.
Thank you Michael Houston.
After a long day, as the mind gets

webbed and fogged;
With my "friend" from Scotland, I sit,
In quiet contemplation.
"Just like my father's", he said,
As he gave that pipe to me;
Already perfectly broken-in and packed.
It is midnight . . . .
I am smoking my Peterson's and Captain Black;
A book for writing poetry in my lap;
Three otherwise smiling, cheerful faces
Resting peacefully upstairs.
Across the high seas,
In Baillieston,
Sits our beloved Michael,
Surely with his rosy cheeks smiling.

Terry M. Konn
DESTINE PETAL
[In dedication, to my son, Martin, for all the years of joyful tears and loving moments. With all my love to you.]
From a seed
a flower has grown,
Anxieties of yesterday
have pollenated
into today's happiness,
And dreams of tomorrow.
Bursting with radiance
Blossoming into a destine petal,
Growing with time
and nature's miracles
From a seed
a flower has grown
to pollenate another.

Veronica Baby Day Morris
WE MUST
We must love the world in which we live today,
We must enjoy its beauty,
for it is slowly fading away.

We must practice self-confidence in all the things we do,
And to give encouragement to a friend, is wise and helpful too.

We must be a unit, all working for one another,
We must begin now,
fore, we are distroying each other-
Mother, father, sister and brothers.

Stuart A. Lynn
UNTITLED
A poet unknown, a man unknown,
A thought as to whether I shall be known,
As a man, or a memory, or forgotten like the rest,
A dying breed of men, who time will forget,
Or remember, as men of thought,
Who died without love.

Gary Lee Engel
SCHOOL DAYS
School days weren't good to me.
Here are some reasons why it happens to be.
The kids in school would laugh at me because
I couldn't run fast.
I would allways come in last.

I was the one whom they wanted
to pick a fight.
Which made me angry and
uptight.
My classmates would want my
answers for homework in
school.
Which made me feel like a fool.
They wanted me for a friend to
do their homework.
Not as a person, but somebody
who would get answers from a
book.
My parents would make me
study and wouldn't let me stay
up late.
I could never ask a girl for a date.
I finished my twelve years of
school.
Not having any friends who
would think I was just as cool.

Meg . . .

NO WISER A MAN CRIES

*[Dedicated to Anthony Cacchio
Sr., my grandfather]*

". . . you must be optimistic,"
cries a wiser man with
a green tinted eye
a curved stick to his left
and God on his right
a smile on his face
a frown in his heart
a song in his mouth
a silence in his ways
a brisk autumn day
an emptiness clear
a younger mind fades on
a seat on the porch
an old friend that's new
a new friend that's old
a pain dare not show
and LIFE fills the air
a green tinted eye
to his side a curved stick
no wiser a man cries,
". . . be optimistic."

John L. Farrington

HAUNTED RIDDLE

Not death have I, nor soul you
see
For I am one of a kind.
I haunt and scream, scare and kill
It's all in a state of a mind.
You see me not, you hear me not
But I am the dreaded of most.
These things are clear and true
of course,
For I am simply a ——!

Mirta G. Preger

I CAN HEAR

I can hear the bell
Ding-Dong, ding-dong
Bringing the sounds of hell
The striking of the gong

Falling from the highest tower
Floating in the air
Loosing completely my will and
power
It's more than I can bear

I can hear the pounding of my
heart
Pum-pum, pum-pum
Tearing me apart
The beating of the drum

I hit the ground in storm
The impact robbing my Joy
Destroy! Destroy!
That's all I can hear and I mourn

Combination of deafening
melodies
Ding-Dong, Ding-dong
Like my own memories
Pum-pum, Pum-pum

I wish I could take the hand
Trust my emotions in full
But I don't want to bend
'Cause I fear to burn

—Am I a fool?

Mrs. Patricia B. Cabrinety

A
Tall,
silvery
bluish-green
Blue Spruce
stands stately & high
silhouetted
against the sky.
In Autumn
the winds howl and blow
and in turn comes Winter's
blustery snow.
Spring's warm rains on the
boughs gently cleanse
while Summer's heat brings forth
new growth and mends.
Through wind, ice, snow and heat
the tree steadily stands
gracing the hillside and the land.
by—Mrs.
Patricia B.
Cabrinety

BLUE SPRUCE

Azalea La Llave

MY DEAR FRIENDS

*[To: Corey and Carlos, Maria
Ayala & kids, Joseph Delgado &
kids]*

To my friends whom I love so dear,
May your days be long and your
nights have countless stars,
May your children have salvation
in the Lords eyes,
May your health carry you
through thick, and
Thin, and forget all tears that
were caused by false witness,
May our sins be forgiven for
taking life for granted,
May your heartaches be small for
your pain is mine,
May our misunderstanding be
understood for perfection was
never intended for us
May your love always be real for
friend or foe, just remember
friend what you
Mean to me,
May we see the coming of the
Lord or die of old age, and hold
hands to never let
Go for we'll live together forever
. . . as best of friends.

Diane C. McCarthy

The Softness Of Christmas Day

. . . The stage is set for another
Christmas morn,
The celebration of the Christ
child—newborn.
The message echoes softly
throughout the land,
Peace and good will to all of man.

It is the softness of Christmas . . .
that warms *all* hearts,

And much love and kindness
from souls do depart.

What is that magical essence that
makes young and old flow with
effervesence?
Why does the magic for only one
day last?
Why is it as soon as the day is
gone, the charisma fades fast?
Why can't we capture that
enticing love mold,
And spread it permanently
throughout the world in
twofold?
And if the warmth and softness
of this day,
Were permanently placed and
never to stray
To the eye and to the heart, no
war no hate,
Forever in peace, how we must
desiderate.

Sam O. Ejiogu

THIS CANDLE LIGHT

*[To the memory of my mother,
Mrs. Alice Ejiogu, who died
untimely, on May 12 1979.]*

Another day is born,
on it again, we'll burn,
As we did in the days gone by.

As a candle light licks
to cinder the kissing moths,
So soon, shall its fuel burn out
and
will nothing be, but air.

Yet, the dross—like residue stuck
to the candle—stand will tell
Its story, both for good or for ill—
a posthumous witness.

The robber bee do leave a legacy
more pleasant than its thievery
act.
The mustard seedling do rot

so as to sprout.

this candle light, this candle light,
consumed, though, we'll,
forgotten,
We never'll be.

Rallenco

THE WAR (VIET) IS OVER

Now the war is over, and the
battle—it is won?
Won by who, the living, or the
thousands that are gone?
There was no victory for those
who died; over fifty thousand
strong
And they never knew why they
died—were they right or were
they wrong?
They fell in battle on a foreign
soil, far away from home
Some died in groups, some died in
pairs and some of them died
alone
Now those left are coming
home—the scarred, the
maimed and those with
sightless eyes
They are our young, our
backbone—was it all for lies?
How are we to ever know the
truth—who is there among us
to tell
Why these young men were over
there, suffering through that
Hell?

Our leaders said they had to go,
there was no other way
But lets listen to the dead ones—
what do they have to say?
"We are still here; and its lonely
in this shallow grave
And we did the best we could for
this country we came to save
But why couldn't we have done it
years ago when we first came
over here?
Why did we drag it out and out at
a cost so very dear?
There are fifty thousand of us
dead that never can go home
No matter how much our loved
ones prayed, that we left alone

But now the war is over—over
and done
I guess we didn't lose it; but I
know we never won
We ask that you, the living,
remember us, the dead
And think about the way we
died, and think about what
we've said
The long, drawn out, bloody war
now is in the past
Please; all you people that are
left, pray to God it is the last."

Salima Hakeem—Scott

DEAR MR. REAGAN

Dear Mr. Reagan,
Will you hear my plea,
For what I must say is not just for
me.
We, as a people, have already
been down,
So why do you want us to now
kiss the ground.
We have suffered enough in our
fight to be free,
Since our fight is not over then
why can't you see . . .

That we will survive and cry if
we must
For God almighty will take good
care of us.
We had come such a long way in
1982,
But '83 looks terrible—hats off to
you.
You took all our jobs and then
said we must work
I hate to call names, but my, what
a jerk.
I am very surprised that you can
sleep at night,
But we will not give in, we must
stay and fight,
Like it or not, America is our
home,
And here we will stay so just
leave us alone.
Africa is the motherland, I know
this is true
But I was born here; How about
you?
For now Dear Ronald you have
won the race
But there will be another to soon
take your place.
He must be the better man, for
who could be worse
When it comes to being heartless,
you, Ron, are first.
Although I would like to, I'll not
bore you to death
But be reassured that we will pass
your test.
So Dear Mr. President, in closing
I will say
We SHALL OVERCOME you, and
have a nice day.

Megan Kelley
A FRIEND
A sleeping friend
Lying in silence by the fire
No movement, no sign of life
Except steady breathing
The slow movement of the chest
No sound, no sign of life
Yet still there is no loneliness
For I am not alone
Whether sleeping or awake
I am never alone
As long as there is silence
The fire and a friend.

Darlene Marie Dann
OUR ENDURING LOVE
[To my enduring love, my most
special friend who knows in
his heart he is: Simply, Thank
You for sharing your Life with
me always and showing me the
warmth of your Love freely. I
treasure you. Avec Tout Mon
Amour Toujours . . .]
The warmth of your Love is so
plain to see
I'm thankful that you came to
choose me
To pl y one part in your Life's
continuing theme.
However near or far we'll go
I trust we'll never lose that
special glow
That speaks of love spent and
tried,
enduring in spirit
like the eternal tide . . .

So now my dear one
Close your eyes

And let my Love here,
be your guide
to everincreasing,
everlasting,
evergreen days
in the universal space
of our finite days,
together and alone.

Alone, however, only in physical
presence;
Alive in memory souvenirs . . . .

Grace Avery Lillard
OLD SHEPHERD'S TALE
Aye, well do I remember despite
my years for I was young then,
and impressionable
Still clearly gleams the glorious
night with winter sky
illuminated by one shining,
perfect Star of Stars.

What of that astonishing night
and wondrous child do I
remember most?
Aye, He was a wondrous child
. . . I also saw Him die, you
know—I saw Him come and go.
And aye I recall how He seemed
to glow that night, lying there
in swaddling cloth.
I see more clearly still, the Little
Lady

Tucked in the straw upon a
makeshift pallet blissfully
sleeping off the pangs of birth
She seemed so young, so girlish
fair too gently bred herself to
bear such a burly, man-sized
child.

While I knelt beside the stall
daring myself to touch the
haloed crib
She came awake and looked upon
her child and all the glories of
earth compare not with the
light in the Little Lady's eyes.

Ask others, if you wish, what
they recall
As for me, I saw the sweet
Madonna smile.

Yvonne G. Vorel
Ode To a Melted Snow Flake
[I am dedicating this poem to
my step—son D. J. Vorel, whom
I love as my own. He lives in
Arizona and seldom sees a
snow flake. Love Mom]
It looked so lovely floating down,
Down, down, to the whitened
ground.
Thence I was green and catty
eyed,
To see the snow flakes comford
ride.
I pulled my hand from out my
glove,
Extended it with softness, love.
Then caught it up into my hand—
It went in peace to promise land,
Where all the melted snow flakes
go,
When they were once a flake of
snow.

Sheri L. Buchen
WIND
I know you are there;
Your coolness creeps up and

and down my spine.
My clothing flows smoothly
across my body;
as your forcefulness is cast upon
me.
I glance toward the ground and
notice each blade of grass
acquainting themselves to each
other
While at the same time I can
smell the untouched freshness
of spring in every direction I
turn.
I feel you;
Concealed in your own little
world.
It's no secret—I know you are
there.

Rhonda Lee Sleasman
Winter Through the Eyes Of a Child
A child sitting by a window
his eyes glued outside.
Waiting with eagerness for that
one small sign,
The small sign that would start a
flame in his heart.
Finally it comes, quietly, softly,
floating like a feather.
A soft white snowflake.
Excitement stirs in the childs
heart, he jumps up, "It's finally
here!" he cries.
Now, he can smell the warm
breads and cookies, he can
build tall snowmen, and come
in cold, with cheeks aglow.

he can sit cozily at the fireside
drinking hot cocoa.
he can go shopping with his
parents and see bright lights,
colors, and Santa Claus.
He can wake up Christmas
morning with a big smile and
bright eyes, eager to see the
presents.
And on that day he can hear, the
story of a child, born on that
special day.
Now, he can ride his brand new
sled down the hills, all day.
Then when the snow finally
melts, and all that comes is
rain,
That little boy will start to cry
and say good-by my friend.

Kim Ritter
DO YOU REMEMBER?
Do you remember,
When we were a family?

When just being together
Were all of our needs.
Do you remember,
How we used to talk
All the time,
But then it just stopped.
Do you remember
All the hard times,
When all we ever did
Was cry.
Well I remember
All of these,
And I hope you do to,
Because now I'm telling you
To remember that I,
Will always love you

Bernice M. Spelman
WHY DO I CRY?
[To Robert & Scott Tison in
rememberance of Snoopy &
Robby their calves]
Today a sweet and innocent calf
departed; from this world to
another.
I have shed many tears; for her or
for me, I really don't know
which it may be.
I ask myself why am I crying?
Is it for her loss? Or is it for mine?
Her loss? She hasn't lost.
The Lord knows where she has
gone.
And we'll see her there.
My loss, the things I'll never see
her do.
The warm soft touch of her fur;
The running and the playing that
little calves do.
The growing, the constant
changing.
All these things I'll never see!
Or is it because she died alone?
In the darkness of the night,
Alone in a stall of the barn.
So cold, with no sweet smelling
hay next to her head
Is this why I cry?
Perhaps if I had held her little
head
Next to my breast
And prayed and talked to her
She would have fought for her
own life.
Is this why I cry?
May be if she had her mama
there
To lie beside her, to touch her;
She would have tried to fight for
her life.
Just for her to know someone
cared.
Is this why I cry?
Why do tears come like a torrent
of rain?
But they don't do the same,
With tears of the saddest no good
is found.
But rain brings all things good.
Why can't tears?

Connie Johnson Russo
Where Brave Men Sleep
[To Mom and Dad for your
Love, Prayers and Belief in Me.
To The Brave Men of all Wars.]
A flag
it ripples
In the wind
the strength and courage of the
Bright Stars

What do they stand for?
Are they really ours?
Where is the man?
Who placed it there?
there on the Quiet Hill
where is he?
He's sleeping there
Beneath the brilliant Red and Blue
he did his job and now he sleeps
he won't remember
but will you?

Olga Tereshko
DAN-RATHER EXCITING
*[To my father and all fathers
who are "obsessed" with Dan
Rather]*
Oh my heavens—I'm in shock!
It's ONE minute past seven o'clock!
To miss the news—that's a crime
Hurry up—am I on time?
Oh no, I'm in distress
QUICK!!! QUICK!!! Turn it to CBS!
Switch the station to channel two
We can't miss Dan Rather's latest
interview.
To talk to our fathers we don't dare
They're too busy sitting on the
edge of their chair.
Through ice, sleet, snow, or rain
He'll always be there to entertain
To bring us stories on Beirut and
Iran
He'll never disappoint us—dear
ol' Dan.

L. C. Reynolds
OPPORTUNITY
I stand on the banks of life, and
look out on the sea of adventure.
Should I embark on the ship
departing; or remain on the
soil, endentured.
Diamonds sparkle against a horizon—
mine if only I will let go of the
shore.
Yet like a child, afraid of the dark;
I beg for the 'light' of what it is
destined for.

A promise of new life, new hope,
also the possibility of new
failure is there;
But is the challenge of an
unconquered dream, exchanged
for the comfort of familiar land
fair.

To go, I know it will broaden my
reaches, and to stay, I will
remain unchanged, where I stand.
For a moment, the sea mirrors my
visions—a brief thought,
perhaps fear . . . then I turn
and walk inland.

Karie Elise Barber
Blue Eyes: A Poem For Robin
Blue Eyes looks like the sunshine
—his smile shines so bright.
Blue Eyes has hair of sand—
ocean waves are in his eyes.

A curl at the corner of his mouth
tells of friendly ties.
Twinkling with mischief—
behind his eyes the ocean lies.

At times mischief is put aside
—tidal waves come splashing
down.
Salt water tears unexpectedly
appear
as on the face of a clown.

Though he appears a joker,
his games act to conceal.
Blue Eyes is loving, soft, and gentle
—his smiling eyes reveal this.

Edna Johnson Hatcher
THE WALTZ OF THE TREES
Looking above, as I sit in my room
I smell the perfume of the trees
in bloom.
I can hear the birds singing with
joy;
Bringing happiness to each girl
and boy.

But I think, as I look above you see,
It's the beauty of the waltzing tree;
God has made all these things to be—
For his children both you and me . . .

Regina R. Henry
MEMORIES
*[For my family With all my
love]*
I see images dancing before me—
Hazy figures clothed in wonder;
They entertain me for a while,
Then slowly dance away,
Leaving their music to remind
me . . .

Maria A. Yemariamfere
HAIKU LINES
Rise Aquarius!
Pour your starry sparkling draught
into night's onyx cup.

Rise great Orion!
Fiery gleams bold Taurus' eye.
Hunt him down the sky!

Serene quiescent,
the egg holds golden treasure.
The promise of life.

Wee soft baby chick,
just a golden promise when
the new moon began.

In a jade green pool
the carp slip with silent grace
like silver shadows.

Abundant peach tree,
a lustrous-leafed green cosmos
hung with golden suns.

In eternal woe
green lady weeping, weeping.
A river willow.

Tears upon a cheek
paint eloquent images
of the heart's sorrow.

Pressed between its leaves,
red roses in my life's book.
A love remembered.

The volcano sleeps
Majestic, snow-robed it gleams
with sunlit cold fire.

Lynda Sliwa-Ohler
Prayer Of a Soldier's Wife
In the turbulence of the storm
My coverlet keeps me warm.

While you are away
Nocturnal creatures hear me pray.

For the homeland you went to fight
My vigil is kept day and night.

A solemnity has hushed the earth,
While my heart yearns to tell you
of the child's birth.

You are the love of my life
I am your wife.

Gloria Perkins
MURMUR
A lover's murmur—
Synchronized motion.
Full of endearments—
A togetherness notion.
Sudden release—
A convulsion, a moan . . .
And millions of babies are
expelled along.

Millions of them—
Will fight to survive
To be existent—
To remain alive.
Much helplessness—
Futility, a soft sigh—
And millions of babies quietly die.

A lover's murmur.
Synchronized motion.
Full of endearments—
A togetherness notion.
Sudden release—
A convulsion, a moan . . .
And millions of babies are
expelled along.

Very faint sound—
Comes from within.
A lone survivor—
Unfelt, unseen.
Outrageous odds—
Await all the way . . .
And millions of babies are born
today!

A lover's murmur—
Synchronized motion.
Full of endearments—
A togetherness notion.
Sudden release—
A convulsion, a moan . . .
And millions of babies are
expelled along.

Eva Jo E. Rose
BAPTIZING OF GORDAN
I love to paint a picture of the
Baptizing of Galilee just
watching Jesus stroll along
Jordan Banks going to watch
the baptizing and ask John to
baptize him.

John ate locusts and wild honey,
had a girdle about his loin.

John was surprised when Jesus
asked him to be baptized by
him, this was his reply, me
baptize thee, when you should
baptize me, nevertheless John
baptized Jesus. When straight
out of the water a dove lit on
his shoulder

and there was a voice from
Heaven saying, My Son in you
I'm well pleased. This is the
way the Scripture reads.

Jesus returned to the village and
gave the greatest teaching on
the mount that has ever been
taught.

The Scripture also tells how Jesus
fasted for forty days and was
tempted three times by Satan.

In our Bible you can read and
paint so many pictures too
which are true.

In Acts 2:38, this will help to
explain why you should be
baptized too.

Bernadette Cardillo
THE COLORS OF LIFE
*[For Mrs. Marion Blake who
made writing a joy for me and
Jason—Always my
encouragement!]*
I once was blue
What a crazy hue
But that's how I felt.

Now I'm yellow
Feeling better than mellow
But only today.

When I was green
Still an in-between
I felt like an outcast.

Now being red
Is better than dead
But why?

Valerie Elise Parker
BLISS IN FLIGHT
An expression of a love so brief,
of a warmth that spanned a
lifetime condensed into a
precious moment.

A moment's bliss transcended
beyond the scope of imagination.
A world of glass and greenleaf
and long shafts of gold stained
with a single trace of reality.

The ultimate expression of unity
of mind and body, I carry this
seed but a brief moment.

A reflection of our brief existence.

Shelby Reynolds
THE CROWN OF SECURITY
Down, down, down
I feel myself falling, falling
I keep calling, calling.
No one's there,
No one's wearing the crown.
The crown of security.

The crown of security
giving me warmth and comfort,
giving me friends with sincerity.
Oh, how I wish someone would
wear the crown.
The crown of security.

People trying to rescue me,
Unknown People
Offering me an escape.
I want the escape
But only they have the key.

I keep looking, looking.
Looking through all the people.
But no one's wearing the crown.
The crown of security.

The crown of security
giving me warmth and comfort,
giving me friends with sincerity.
I've dreamt of hiding all the hurt
But please, won't you be my king
And wear the crown.
The crown of security.

Avis Houghtaling
NEVER ALONE
Our Mighty Maker bespoke a storm!
A blizzard peltered down.
Gaining shelter in any form
Obsessed man and beast alone.
Alone, yes, all alone!

The family cat in a sea of snow,
Instincts bewildered; he cowers,
shivers,
Wild creatures in the woods lay
low,
Icy frosting coats the rivers!
Alone, Yes, all alone!

The shut-in sits by the window
pane
While days drudge slowly by,
They shuffle their memories—all
forlorn,
Living the past provokes a sigh.
Alone, yes, all alone!

Hemmed in by familiar sights
and sound,
And pressed in the midst of a
busy throng—
In crowded rooms our senses cry,
heartaches abound,
'Tis then we wake to the lilt of
Nature's song
We're never alone, all alone!

Felicisimo C. de Jesus
CHRISTMAS POEM
Christmas is love and love is sweet,
That sparkles on this Christmas
day,
People commingling happy when
they meet
As they tag along the golden way.

Exchanging gifts and gift giving
Young and old, rich and poor, and
everywhere;
Children waiting Godfather dead
or leaving
If there's a gift may be next year.

The hug, the kisses and tight
embraces,
Birds chirping on top of the trees,
All love, all cheers and sweet
caresses,
Like lover's hand walking in the
breeze.

No rancor, no jealousies, nor hate,
Bullets or time bomb to explode
nearby
Nor peace pipe talking perhaps
better late
The talk that glisten in the starry
sky.

And now the church bell ring at
early morn,
And people gathered to hear the
mass,
For on this day a CHILD was born—
The song of love and beauty of
Christmas.

Eleanor McKee
LIFE
I am old, I am wise, and yet naive
I am aged, yet I am free

I have lived, I have cried, given
up yet also tried
I have loved, I have feared
I was born of anothers joy, and tears
Now that I am growing old life
still seems very dear, hope I
live another year
I do not sit and ponder that
things are not what they used
to be
I am glad I can still see
Give me strength Dear Lord from
each day to day
Even though I may fall along the
way, pick me up to start a new
day
Aging is a fact not a fad, getting
older ain't so bad
This is life

Martha Lee Parrott
SONG OF PRAYER
We give our thanks to you,
dear Lord
As we sing to you in praise!
Lord, bless us now as we come
to you . . .
We, with love, our hearts do raise.

Shelter us in your tender grace
Lord, show us right from wrong.
And prepare those hearts not
near to you
When we tell of you in song.

We dedicate our lives, oh Lord,
So willingly to you . . .
And with hearts of love, still
growing strong
Give praise to all you do!

Keep within our minds your
love . . .
Lord, watch over us each day
Bless our hearts and let us shine,
Your will shall be our way.

Patricia Harrison
PRETENDING
*[To the Harrison family,
especially my mother, Mrs.
Florence Harrison, for all the
love she has shown me and to
my daughter, Vonne, one of the
sweetest little girls I know.]*
When the day's gotten off to a
terrible start
and someone's just broken your
poor little heart

Don't just sit there feeling sad
pretend you're a lion big and bad

When you are troubled and life's
no fun
pretend you're a cougar and run
and run

When you have to stay in your
room all alone
Pretend you're a king on a royal
throne

And if you're told to "Go to bed!"
Think what you'd do if you were
rich instead

And all the while that you're
pretending
Your precious little heart will be
quickly mending

Sherry Cowan
LISTEN
I hold him like a lullaby
So soft and sweet;

One so impressive and different
from all others,
It stands out all alone
On another plane, another
dimension.
All alone and yet, not alone at all;
(Perhaps lonesome still).
Many more than I love a sweet
lullaby,
As they do him.
When will he hear the music?
When will he know what's right
and good?
What's real?
My mind feels I love.
At the same time, my heart feels I
need
And he becomes flattered at the
thought.
Why can't there just be
acceptance
And realization?
Dispose of the ego and there is
Truth.
The ego hides so much of reality.
My soul keeps saying:
If he cannot understand my
silence,
Perhaps he'll understand my words:
Love is here.
Love is now.

Winnie J.
YOU'RE LOVE
*[I dedicate this to you Love,
who gave me the feelings I just
put them into words.]*
Out a window I looked, my heart
looked out too,
As the different things passed by
I kept thinking of you.
You're the wind blowing strong as
it takes hold,
I see shyness, sweetness, and
sometimes bold,
In the wind there's a paper
perhaps a forgotten valentine,
You're all that love and lace
except not mine,
You're the rain in April on the
green grass,
To my heart you're the top of the
class,
You're the sun's brightness
everyday,
Like new born flowers of early
May,
You're a robin chirping or a blue
jay,
I want you're heart "I love you to
say"
You're the darkness of night,
My stars in heaven, oh what a sight,
You're the first snowfall in
November,
These days of ours I shall always
remember,
You're the waves of the ocean
just before a storm,
Forgive me, you see this love I
feel is just being born,
You're the tallest and strongest tree,
Could you possibly care for me?
You're those magnificent colors
of the sky,
You're time standing still when
you pass by,
You're like that splendid eagle or
more of a dove,
You're blue eyes are filled with
warmth and love,

You're like the flowers of summer
so bright,
Its wonderful love to be able to
touch, to hold you tight.

Jeannette Forte Santanastasio
A CHRISTMAS THOUGHT
*[Dedicated to my son Robert so
he may know that giving is the
most essential part of life.]*
Christmas time is a time of joy
do not deny that little boy,
who came to us from up above
and blessed us all so we may love.

For only in his tender care,
do we pretend, start to dare

to give in Christmas in His name
forgiving all hatred and blame.

Be glad for you were meant to love,
and use your gift from God above;
to spread the joy within your soul,
helping all others to be whole.

Monique Debatis
ONLY FIFTEEN
A rope
dangles in a breeze
its victim now gone.
A noose
made carefully,
held by a firm knot,
for a perfect fit.
A life
once actively functioning
now departed from this world.
A world,
cynical and uncaring,
ignored his silent plea.
A rope,
dangling in a breeze,
is a constant reminder—
he was only fifteen.

Jo Ann Manual Cooper
A MALE IS NOT A MAN
Just because you were born a male
Please don't think that it makes
you a man
There are many a male that live
and die
And while living never seem to
understand
That it takes a man to say he's sorry
And to admit that he was wrong
It takes a man to cry sometimes
To show that he is strong
It helps to make a male a man
While traveling on life's road
When he takes his share of the
responsibilities
No matter how light or heavy the
load

Sometimes you must concede to
  failure
No matter how hard you've tried
Sometimes it takes a man to tell
  the truth
When it's easier to have lied
The process may be long and slow
But alot goes into its making
You'll have to learn about this life
And all about its giving and taking
You'll have to learn to win and lose
And you'll have to learn to sacrifice
And sometimes you'll find it
  necessary
To take as well as give advice
You don't reach manhood
  automatically
Though many may think he can
Just remember because you were
  born a male
That it still doesn't make you a
  man

Lucille M. Kroner

Lucille M. Kroner
WHAT IS A MAN
*[In Memorian for my father:
Theodore W. Kroner]*
What is
A man? . . . He is
The father of the race
The strength on which we build a
  world,
An age!

Coleman White
DEAD OF NIGHT
It's peaceful, not a sound.
Nothing but the wind moving
  around.
I guess you would call it the
Dead of Night.
Nothing but the stars to give off
  light.

This is the time that memories
  come flooding back
Some of them good, but some you
  just can't hack
Memories of your childhood days
  and people you loved
Memories of how some were
  taken away, away up above.

This is the time your mind races
  ahead.
Ahead of the future, wondering
  which way you'll be lead.
Ahead to places you've never
  been, but hope to see.
Ahead to the future hoping it will
  be what you want it to be.

Oh how peaceful it is, this
  moment in time.

Moments like this is so hard to
  find.
It is now that you feel everything
  is alright.
I guess you would call it "the
  Dead of Night".

Thomas Mann Selkirk
EXTRACURRICULAR BLISS
*["To my Mother, Lola A.
Selkirk, who was the nicest
person I ever knew."]*
If one limits one's bliss,
To just a kiss,
Think what one'd miss,
In a tryst
One couldn't resist,
After a slap on the wrist
With the fist—
If one insist.
'Tis a twist
Whose gist
Isn't in a mist,
Even if it desist
To assist
A moralist!

Christina Ready Lord
THE TREE
*[Praise to the Blessed Virgin
Mary, Her goodness and mercy
have blessed me and my family]*
The tree stands alone
Throbbing in the ground,
Vibrating leaves
Whisper their sound;
Shadows appear
Over the sunlit patches,
A branch reaches up and
Almost snatches a breeze from
  the wind.

Green reeds green grass
So tenuous and long,
Spectral and vaporous
A phantom of summer's warm song;
Sitting here tranquility in my
  mind
Photosynthesizing an energy
From a life force unseen,
I feel clean and alive
And so close to nature,
God grant me many years
To move even closer.

Kathleen M. Loger
YESTERDAYS LOVE
Yesterdays love
Reaches through time
To touch her life
Hoping to find
The love they had shared
Had stayed on her mind

The reunion is joyous
Arms wrapped in embrace
Their hearts are still young
Though tiny lines crease her face

They share their life's stories
And form bonds that will last
But the love he remembered
Stayed locked in the past

For nothing remains the same
And nothing ever will
While some loves are best forgotten
Some have grown better still

Helen Huxley
HOW MY HEART SINGS
The best things in life are free
Sunset, Sunrise reflections, the Sea
Are among the things I adore
Walking through sand by the shore

Beautiful grass, flowers and trees
Autumn colors, changing leaves
Thanks to the Lord above
For giving all these things that I love
I look at the clouds from afar
Is that where you are?
Not now, but you will be
Someday for me to see
Bringing angels with you
Saying "My words were true"
Until then I will stand
Enjoying this great land
Or maybe walk and roam
Until you call me home
Thanks for my eyes to see these
  things
Oh Lord how my heart sings!

Denise M. Dansie
ONE WAY
The road of life is "one way"
When living from day to day—
  You always move forward
    Never able to turn
      and go back.

Harry Wiatrak
WHERE IS THE ANSWER?
*[Dedicated to Connie
  An Everlasting Inspiration]*
The young man stares up at the sky
Asking himself the question,
  why, oh why?
Why are people so very cruel?
Don't they know it's against your
  rule?

Why can't we get along with each
  other.
Isn't it your teachings that we're
  all brothers?
To hurt someone is not a game.
Not easily forgotten like a place
  or name.

So when you usually start to act,
Be sure and use a little tact.
Put yourself in the other man's
  shoes
And see how easily your feelings
  will bruise.

Then you'll know the reason why
He seeks his answer from the sky.

M. Elizabeth King
GOD'S WORLD
It is raining again. Summer will
  be over before it ever gets here.
  Thunder rolls far away, drops
  hit the windshield, the sky
  turns gray.

The Sunflower, the blue
  Delphinium, the white
  Stinkweed drink the moisture
  greedily. The green and silver
  leaves of the Aspens sparkle as
  the rain hits them, and the
  wind turns them round and round.

The creek flows on, oblivious to
  the change in the weather. A
  break in the clouds allows a bit
  of sun to hit the side of a
  towering mountain.

Three cows slowly wend their
  way homeward. It is dusk. The
  gray clouds lift and the sun
  bursts through, briefly, before
  sliding behind the hills for the
  night.

It is God's World. He gives it to
  us to enjoy and to share with
  each other.

Pedro Supsup Llarinas
WHAT IS LOVE •
*[Dedicated to my wife, Juanita,
  my children: Linda, Leonaida,
  Elvira, Edna, Milaflor, Margie,
  Pedronito, Proserfina, Emma;
  my parents: Juan and Alejandra]*
Love is a many Splendored Thing
Love is of many kinds, forms, styles
Lovers select the best to suit
  their tastes
It's from deep inside, unashamed
  no matter what.

When shall we realize we are in
  Love?
The eyes see, the mind
  determines, the Heart accepts
Sooner or later, Love affects and
  stirs ourselves
Lo! The Magic Line, "Honey, I
  Love You".

Love at first sight is not really
  true nor strong
Literally, it means, liking,
  appreciating one's personality.
Time, days, months, maybe years
  will decide; at last
True Love has been sown, cared
  for, nourished, Realized.

Love takes all forms:
  expressed poetically in prose or
    poetry;
  embraced mentally, physically,
    whole-heartedly;
  spoiled, showered financially,
    materially;
  all will vanish if Lovers don't
    accept Realities.

Love takes all styles:
  easy-going, freak and shallow
    for swinging guys and gals;
  understanding, fulfilling,
    binding for man and wife;
  sharing, caring, living for
    relatives and friends;
  all expressed fully,
  magnificently, beautifully,
    lovingly.

Love takes all kinds:
  love from a Lover to his sweet
    Honey;
  from a loyal Husband to his
    dear Wife;
  a loving mother/father for their
    Fruits of Love;
  from everyone who seeks and
    accepts Friends,
      Spices of Life.

False Love:
  is only skin-deep, pretentious,
    of brief duration,
  seems to be fulfilling, in reality
    it is uncertain;
  does not register, connect nor
    grip, the arms are weak
  conceiving negative
    aspirations, imaginations to do
    otherwise;
  likely to be revealed sooner or
    later by Themselves,
      Pretentious Lovers.

True Love:
  is bonded by graces, brilliance
    and beauty;
  cemented with splendors,
    sacrifices, endearments, gifts;
  nurtured, endured, cultured

affectionately by Lovers;
also sincerely shared to friends
and colleagues;
gives Life and Happiness, affects
all ages, races,
practically all the world's continents.

Real Love:
is something more beyond the
warmth and glow
of the romance and excitement
of being deeply in Love,
it is caring as much about the
welfare and happiness
of your Loved One as well as
your own; but
Real Love is not total
absorption in each other,
it is looking outward in the
same direction together.

Love:
makes burdens lighter because
you divide them;
makes joys more intense
because you share them;
makes you stronger so you can
reach out, and
become involved with Life in
ways
you dared not attempt or risk
alone;
Happiness and Success are
Fruits of Togetherness.

Concluding:
Love is felt and embraced from
deep Portals of the Heart;
monitored by the brain,
accepted by the mind;
visualized by the eyes, received
by the hands;
the five Senses of Life work
harmoniously together
to portray, entreat, transfer this
Undying Love
to the chosen Love One; till
the End of Time.

Victoria E.A. Holt
THE WOUNDED DEER
The shrill of a gun,
going off
The smell of gun
powder
The look of pain
upon
its face
as it makes its
way into the
depths
of the forest
And the smell of
blood,
lingering . . .
in the air.

William Gatewood
ANGEL OF MERCY (MAE)
Up from a restless night well spent,
Into a project she could not resent,
An effort to open her eyes once
closed tight,
And wondering what happened to
most of the night.

Like a shepherd tending her sheep,
The night was gone with so little
sleep,
To arouse the children up for
school,
Some of them naughtly, but she
was quite cool.

Her voice was as sweet as the
buttercup,
The children were happy and glad
to get up,
Around the breakfast table in
advance,
Each one wanting to be the first
at her face to glance.

Mae loved children with all of
her heart,
Rushing every morning to get
them off on a new start,
First she would fill their hearts
with hope,
Because then they had no time to
mope.

The next she taught them was
how to look,
Not caring how much time it took,
A fashion expert when it come to
dress,
Mae wanted her children to look
the best.

If a child wanted to be happy and
truly satisfied,
Listen to Mae and by her rules
abide,
She did her best to fill their
needs,
Sometimes she and the children
were as busy as bees.

To make a home for children was
Mae's biggest aim,
If they were disappointed she was
not to blame,
With Mae the children were in love,
They knew she was an Angel
sent from above.

Ethel Hunt Street
UNFAITHFUL
Many many years ago
when our love first was born
I dreamed about you nite and day
from evening until morn.
I thought you were a prince somehow
that fate had let me meet
I languished in your love (I thought)
and worshipped at your feet.
"Time will tell" they said so now
I'm told just what you are;
That my prince has lost his
knighthood
my heaven has lost its star
Your love was all ficticious
your heart a piece of stone
But strangely now it seems that I
must for your sins atone.

Margaret Gloria Johnson
A FADED ROSE
I have before me a faded rose
that you once gave to me.
Each little petal seems to hold
some kind of memory.

When you first placed it in my hand
It was covered with dew.
yet, as I hold it now, it's covered
with tears I've shed for you.

A faded rose is all that's left
of a love that use to be.
A rose,
that you once gave to me.

Barbara A. Solomon
THE SUN STILL SHINES
After all that's done
the sun
still shines.

When
discouragement occurs,
when
good things
develop into the worst,
the sun
still shines.
When
oppression step in
and
there's a need of confident,
there's hope
for a brighter tomorrow.
After all that's done
the sun
still shines.
Day by day
through the dimmest hour
when
darkness occurs,
there's something better
under the cloudy sky.

Helen Nosal Buchheit
WHITE UNICORN
*[This poem was written in
part—for a Christmas card—to
my dear niece, Yvette—and
inspired by her unique
collection.]*
This majestic fabulous animal
was caught
By the spirit of Christmas and
now he has brought—
To you our wishes for a very,
merry day
Filled with blessings of peace and
joy in every way.
And with his long, straight and
spirally twisted horn
May he push together your
family that morn—

To share in all the happiness and
presents, too.
And may this great Christmas
spirit last all year through.
For this mythical animal with all
its lore—
Could cleanse some of this world
sorrows—forevermore
Bring inspired vision of hope to
the forlorn . . .
"Come," share God's grand
blessings with this "White
Unicorn."

Mrs. Kelly (Velma) Haynes
THE HERO
Little five year old in bed
Raised her lovely curly head,
And cried aloud, "My dolly's
dead"

"Mommy and Daddy are here
close by,
Little Darling, tell us why
You woke up and started to cry."

"Mommy! The wind! Do you hear
it blow?
I think the rain has turned to snow.
And that is how I really know!"

"Know what, my precious little
pearl?"
Daddy gently caressed a curl.
She was his darling baby girl.

"I tell you why I know she died.
It's raining!" the little girl cried.
"And I left my baby doll outside."

So Daddy grabbed his coat and he
Dashed out in the rain so sleepily.
He found the dolly under a tree.

It was a rubber doll, you know,
Not hurt a bit, Dad, but even so,
You'll always be her big hero!

Richard A. Jarvis
OUR LOVE
Lush green forests in her eyes
Sweet red roses are her lips
Mountains rolling hills her hips
All in my garden of love

Her love falls like shimmering
white cascades
Over the rough hewn rocks of my
life
Falling perpetually to the
peaceful pool
Of our depthless love

In her arms the world surrounds
Yet beside her, her world is mine
And mine is hers
All wrapped up in ourselves—
each other

And our love is the table from
which I feast
Forever feasting, forever hungry
In her diner of emotions
Her pantry of inner feeling

And all in all its there to see
When I look at her eyes
As they mirror what is in mine
There is our summer of love

Rob Austin
COSMIC PULSE
The lonely wolf howls—
A piano plays,
Sad sax
Far away . . .

. . . Montezuma dances
Upon pyramidal lines,
Primordial screams
Emanate, from limestone mines.

Satellites orbit,
Rotate and gyrate—
Humanity perseveres
In Glory, Splendor and Fate.

Cheryl L. Moretti
Three Necessities In My Life
Three necessities have always
been the basis of my life and
have remained constant
throughout my days: space,
time and freedom. Separately,
each one has proven to be very
valuable, but together, they
have shaped my life.
I need space in which to grow, to
expand my mind, to understand

new ideas and concepts. When I explore the world around me, I am able to examine my mind and heart and understand the effects the outside world has upon my life. It is through this exploration that many different people enter into my life and bring with them different and sometimes unusual, but always very interesting attitudes. Space in which to grow should be an important necessity in everyone's life, for to stop growing would bring death to our minds and confinement to our hearts.

If space is needed in my life, then certainly time is of equal value. I need time to experience the beauties of nature, time to be with those who have a special place in my life, time to be alone to meditate and to allow all I have learned from my growing experiences to seep into my being and become a part of me. It is during this time that I am able to grasp what is important in my relationships with others, thus I am capable of becoming a more caring person.

Finally, I need the freedom to share what I have come to know and feel. Inhibitions can cripple and very often destroy an otherwise beautiful spirit which each of us possesses. Freedom to express my thoughts, my caring, my love, is the only way I can experience my true inner-self. If, during my lifetime, I can reach out and touch one heart, then I have obtained the ultimate experience that life has to offer.

Space, time, and freedom, the three necessities in my life, equal a total me.

Tammy Riggs
TO DADDY WITH LOVE
You are my father
And have always been
You love me dearly
And I love you too.
Dad I hope
I'm everything you wanted
Because I love you.
I grew up fast
You'd always tell me
To slow down.
Well daddy, I can't.
It's in my blood
Just like it was in yours.
You're my example
Of love and good faith.
So long as I live
I'll thank you
For being there for me.
I give you my word
That I'll always try
And I'll give you my heart
To Daddy, with love.

Anita Massey
DAYDREAM
Without your love
I've long, lonely nights
Surpassed by dawn,
Mistically bright.

My day begins—
As all mine do—
With warming thoughts
Of caressing you.

Your lips so gentle,
So soft to the touch,
Revieling my will
To give you so much.

Be still O my heart!
So happy to find
Your warm, gentle hand
Firmly clasping mine.

Words are spoken
And yet not heard
A deafening silence
Hides every word.

Up from my side
Your eyes seem to say,
"Patience, my love,
Tomorrow's our day."

Fainter you grow
'Till no more to be seen
Now sober my heart
Awake from it's dream.

Helen P. Harper

Helen P. Harper
LONG LIVE LIBERTY
I Love America
There is no replica
Look around you and see
I thank God to be
In a land that is Free
"Long Live Liberty".

I Love Liberty
May it always be
Round our family tree
Hold your head up high
As our Flag goes by
"Long Live Liberty"

I Love America
I would fight for her
Till Eternity
Stars & Stripes will fly
Till the day I die
"Long Live Liberty"!

Claire F. McClernan
TERRIBLE TWOS
He's turned our household upside down
In just a few short hours . . .
Sent lamp acrashing, milk asplashing
Uprooted my "prize" flowers.

It's just a phase they all go through
So often I've been told,
But I'm not so sure that I'll survive
Until he's three years old!

Bill Forster Jr.
A LONELY MAN
[*To my wife and my son from your husband and father, because you both make it all worth the bother!*]
I'm sitting on some lonely steps
Just thinking life away
I can't imagine how it would be
to have a busy day.

It seems to me that all my life
I've seen things at first hand
but then again its hard to see
I'm still a lonely man.

Where must I go, what must I do
to get something out of life
I can't believe I'm lonely
with 3 kids and a wife.

And then it all comes back to me
when I hear a clanging bell
My time ran out, a voice screams out
"You must return at once, to your cell".

Barbara A. Kinney
FIGGY PUDDING
Magic moments filled with awe
Evergreens that met the saw
Rustling, bustling, roundabout
Rapturous carols that beshout
Yuletide feasts beyond compare
Children learning how to share
Harbingers that set the mood
Red hued tables filled with food
Ice artwork etched on glass
Snowflakes dancing hide the grass
Tinsel gleaming on the trees
Many trying hard to please
As the moment's drawing nigh
Sacredness still reigns on high

Mary Holleman Wilson
Song Of the Abandoned Plow
The sweating farmer
Oiled me and honed me.
I blessed his land
And gave him bread to eat.

Wheaten fields
Once rose from my touch,
Razored kisses
On the dark, sweet earth.
I blessed it
With my edges,
Sharp and keen,
And gave man bread to eat.

Jacqueline D. Erickson
WINDOWS
Windows are made for
    optimistic people
you must like the house next door
    colors
and finished yards
    with children playing
warmth from the sun
    impressions of snowflakes
rainbows conceived in raindrops
    wind
and neighbors passing
    with a wave and a smile

Alice Fulford
NOW
One look behind him to some
    vanished time
And says, "Ah, I was happy then!
I did not know it was my life's
    best prime—
Oh, if I could go back!"

Another looks, with eager eyes
    aglow,
To some glad day of joy that yet
    will dawn,
And sighs, "I shall be happy then,
    I know.
Oh, let me hurry on."

But I—I look out on my fair To-day;
I clasp it close and kiss its radiant
    brow,
Here with the perfect present let
    me stay,
For I am happy now!

Clarice Tesh Brewer L.P.N.
HOW DO YOU FORGET?
[*"Being a private-duty nurse, I wish to dedicate this poem to all my past, present, and future patients. May God bless and be with them all."*]
Lord, I think I know how you
    must feel
Looking down on your children
    and their plight.
Their problems are your problems
Their burdens, yours to make light.

I have but few to love and care for.
I listen when they need to talk
I help and comfort when I can
I give guidance when it's sought.

But Lord, I need a day off now
    and then.
To rest my weary body, my mind.
I need thy help and guidance too
And my own soul hungers at times.

Tell me Lord: How do you do it?
How do you forget that one in pain.
They're still there when I'm away
Their ills, their problems still
    remain.

How do you forget—Just for a day
That little tear from a fearful eye.
It's calling for compassion and
    comfort
Because tomorrow they may die.

Lord, I'm glad you're strong up there
You never take a day off or sleep
You're constantly watching o'er
    them
And promised—their souls to keep.

Give me courage and added strength
To face each care I know is there.
Be beside me each hour in prayer.

And while I take this day to rest
Give them strength and patience
    to wait.
I'll be back tomorrow—afresh
To care for them, for Jesus' sake.

Louise Taylor
PLEASANT DREAMS
[*To my dad and mom, (John and Rita Taylor), the best parents in the world and to Mrs. Wright, my grade eight English teacher*]
My eyes grow tired, my head will
    droop,
As I drift off to sleep,
To forget all troubles of the past,
My soul the Lord to keep.

The objects of reality,
Are forgotten in my mind,
Where fantasy thrives in
    everything,
Through all existing time.

Years seem like a second,
And miles seem like a yard,
The people live forever,
And hatred will come hard.

A place where all are equal,
Despite their different ways,
To live together peacefully,
In each and every way.

Where creatures of unhuman
forms,
That in reality are never seen,
This fantasy world we sometimes
see,
Is referred to as a dream.

Kathleen Kuske
TIME & OBLIGATIONS
Thinking about you
Wish you were here
The days are so lonely
When you're not near.
Wanting to hold you
Feel your warm touch
My heart is so empty
I miss you so much.

I long to be with you
Sharing each day
Time doesn't permit
Obligations stand in the way.

Ms. Roszetta Marie McNeill
SELF INDULGENCE
[Dedicated to Collins Glenn III and his sons (warriors of tomorrow). May your endeavours be prosperously achieved.]

A stranger came to me one day,
in a precarious way.
What he wanted of me, well, it's
kind of hard to say.
He talked and I listened,
attentively with MIND.
He spoke as though he knew me;
as though his message a sign.
So, I dismissed with my
inhibitions and began to relax.
He came, not to get me, it was
simply a task.

He critisized past endeavours and
warned of future plans.
He said that my destination is to
face life's tribulations,
and my task is to endure and
withstand.
He talked of universal existence
and my existence he made
plain.
He insisted that I make life my
objective and survival my aim.

He talked of time to come, of
things yet to be perceived.
He cautioned of life's extremities
and his cautions I heeded.
He talked of dexterity and the
riches of youth.
He inforced in me vast potentials
and instilled in me mass truths.
He bestowed upon me answers,
answers men have never found.
Neither from their mass artifacts
nor from their pages blessed
and bound.
He said within me the key to
reality was conceived.
And locked doors I could unlock
if in my SELF I would believe.

He proclaimed in himself all
things I confide.
And promised, through life's
obstacles, to serve as my guide.
I had a feeling I knew this
stranger and that he was a
fathomless part of me.
The part I vaguely listened to and
could never see.
I asked, "If in life you are needed
in what domains do you reside."
For a moment he looked startled
then he said, "Your inner side."
Then it dawned on me suddenly
from whence this stranger had
come.
This stranger and I were one and
the same.

Before he departed he wished me
well.
And said with knowledge as my
ammunition I could never fail.
In accomplishing my goals and
succeeding in life.
Then he sharply retorted, "But
you must take my advice."
I was vigilant and informed after
that stranger had left.
Because I allowed myself the
pleasure of indulging in my
SELF.

Robert Paul
The Schoolbus Driver and Me
Squat and yellow Snail like pace,
The school bus runs its morning
race.
Sure rough hands caress the
wheel
Guiding the ancient hunk of
steel.
More ancient than the bus its
driver,
A tired man once full of fire.
Whose embers now just barely
spark
Extinguished by a lonely heart.
His precious cargo of fresh
scrubbed faces
When unloaded left their
taunting traces,
of paper missles and knife
scratched letters
which struck and tore his heart
to tatters.
He loved those children very dear
Whose jeering taunts we both
heard clear.
While he and I would ride the
bow
For love or pity I know not now.
Those days are gone and so is he

but his bus sits
rusting faithfully.
Waiting for the morning ride
With us up front Side by Side.

Rose Graham
CHRISTMAS
We might think of writing
a more modern version of
Christmas,
But nothing else would do,
But the same sweet story of
Jesus
Which is old yet ever new!

It was foretold by the prophets of
old,
A child should be born and
He should be called the Prince of
Peace!
Many years later an angel
appeared unto Mary
Saying "Thou shalt bring forth a
Son
And shalt call His name, Jesus"
The shepherds were watching
their flocks by nite
When all of a sudden they saw
a great light,
A star, a beautiful shining star!
They stood and watched it
from afar!
Then riding their trusty camels
They followed the star until it
came
And stood right over Bethlehem.
They found the baby Jesus in
the manger,
Because there was no room in the
inn!
And fell down and worshiped
Him.

An angel appeared and said unto
them,
"Fear not, for behold I bring you
good tidings of
great joy which shall be to all
people.
And on earth, Peace, Good will
toward men!"
Let us, like the shepherds, go again,
And find the Christ-Child at
Bethlehem
And worship Him as did they,
On that very first Christmas
Day.

Eileen Hauser
TOGETHER YOU AND I
[With love and thanks to Diann for giving me the inspiration to share my thoughts and feelings with you through my poetry.]
Look at me with eyes that judge,
And never will I measure up.
See me through eyes that burn
with anger,
nd you shall see one who
deserves punishment.
Look at me with eyes that pity,
And I'll always remain inferior.
See me however it is that your
eyes will perceive me,
And I shall change as your eyes
grow and paint life
differently.
I say, look not at me but at
yourself.
See the beauty that lives deep
inside you.

Feel the emotions that hold you
tightly in their grasp.
Yes, know that there's purpose to
all you do;
And understand that these hold
true for me as well,
For I am as human as you are.
Then, my friend, you can look
to me, not at me.
And realize that we are indeed,
one in the same.

Johnnye R. Rotchford
LOVE IS AGELESS
[Dedicated to my family, for whom my love is indeed ageless.]
Love is ageless.
It does not dim, as does the
evening light.
Nor, does love's image change
along with fading sight.

When laughter stops
and smiles alone remain
the music still is heard
of love's own sweet refrain.

When words are spoken
infrequently
and silence fills the air
that silence still commicates
how much a loveone cares.

When donfussion, fear and
helplessness
tear at an aging heart
love warms and offers comfort
when even hope seems to depart.

When kindred soul so active once
becomes now frail and weak
it's love that helps you understand
and find the strength you seek.

When memories are all that's left
to fill a lonely day
an ageless, and an endless love
will ease the pain away.

Sherry L. Grubaugh
NO END
There was no end.
Only a continuation—
Fates crossing paths,
Colliding into one another,
Creating much fallout—
Realizing little gain.
Groping slowly,
In the forever rain.

N. Ruth Clark
YOU STIR MY HEART
There's obviously nothing to set
you apart
So what's there about you that
stirs my heart?
It isn't your nose or the set of
your chin
That makes you different from
other men
And although I melt when I look
in your eyes
They aren't much different than
other guys'.
Your hair is nice with a tinge of
gray
But I see others who look the
same way.

I like your physique but others I
see
Look as good or better than yours
to me.
I will admit that I long for your
touch

And your voice is nice—but you talk too much.
You taunt me and tease me and that's okay
You wouldn't be you any other way.
Plenty of others have much to relate
Your gift of gab doesn't make you so great!

I'm filled with emotion, it's hard to describe
The warmth and tenderness here inside.
I love you so much and I don't really know
What there is about you that stirs me so.
It isn't your mouth or the way you grin
But something deeper that comes from within.
So maybe there's nothing to set you apart
It's simply your being that stirs my heart.

Julia Marie Wedge
FOR EVERY ARTIST
It's poetry come to life,
　The expressions of the heart;
Through oils and pastels,
　Charcoal and pen,
The words of sight reach out
　And envelop the canvas.
It brings forth life, dreams—
　The fantasies of the mind.
A butterfly dancing on a rose;
　A horse free in the wind;
Young love comes to life.
　The mind travels;
The dreams will follow.
　It's an outlet for the deaf,
A voice for the mute.
　The magic of imagination
Escapes the creator.
　Here, in true colors,
Man and nature are one.
　Today's dreams are
Tomorrow's realities.
　Life is and so is art . . .

George Albert Gesner
SCANDAL REVISITED
Whispering wind dancing,
Choreographed lies,
Wild eyes glancing,
Romantic spies.

Scandal revisited,
Escape from your cell.
Love's not inquisitive;
Welcome the sequel.

The queen of two faces
Returns to her king.
With lipstick traces
I return to my drink.

William G. Zdanis
I DIDN'T KNOW I CARED
Not too impressed, when first we met.
　I sort of liked his smile.
It must have been propinquity.
　We did date quite a while.

Whenever he did ask me out,
　I never did say, no.
While then, I wasn't sold on him...
　It was someplace to go.

And then one day, he didn't show.
　He didn't tell me why.

I learned he went with someone else.
　Forget him, I did try.

But when he didn't call at all,
　I felt so all alone.
'Till then, I didn't know I cared.
　I did pray, that he'd phone.

And now I'm glad that I did call,
　And hint that I did care.
I might have lost these precious years
　That he and I do share.

Elaine Enterline

Elaine Enterline
LAST MAN ON EARTH
A boy was all alone in the night
He cried out his fear.
This world did not acknowledge
His cries, for it had no ears.

So he wondered on a ways,
And realized the earth was bare.
He knew what had happened
For no other person was there.

He was the last man on earth,
He did not know what to do.
All he wanted at the time
Was someone to talk to.

He went on like this for days,
Life was quite bad.
Slowly each day
He grew a little more mad.

As the world grew old,
The last man on earth died.
The part that is really sad,
Is that no one cried.

Paul E. Allen
YOUNG LOVE
When I reach out
　you are always there . . .
loving, gentle

I feel the love we share.
But life was not this way
　'til I met you . . .
My dreams were lost,
　my life was a darkened cloud.
Tell me please,
　was my cry of unhappiness
　that loud?
Please care for me,
　just as I am . . .
hold me close
　I'll always be around.
All we will really have
　is all that we share . . .
love me forever,
　I'll always be there . . .

Charlene Daugstrup
NEW UNDERSTANDING
Grasping desperately to this intense feeling,
I grapple about each day
Lost in a world of misunderstanding.

Faces of incongruency surround me continually,
And no where in sight is there one I know.
Silently, I withdraw into myself;

And suddenly I am absorbed
In a world of happiness.

Deep within the core of my being
I evade all that was illusive,

And find a pure understanding of life . . . myself.

Wendell Mack Tackett
HILL OF SKULLS
He stumbled and fell under the load.
The angry crowd began to goad.
The path was strewn with stones and sticks.
Sandal-less feet, bruised and pricked.
He glanced around at the anxious crowd.
Their cries for revenge were angry and loud.
He knew he must carry this load alone.
Destined to die, he would soon be home.
The hill loomed large in front of him.
He stumbled and fell once again.
The hill of skulls stared back at him.
The souls of humanity ached within.
He knew his life was not beguiled.
The last few feet were his longest mile.

Donna McCoy Murphy
WAITING LOVE
Time and waiting is all I have from you. Anticipating a love I thought to be true. Will I soon see you. Will your love be true.

I know the feeling of a broken heart from you. I can't stop this feeling cause I know I'm losing you! Love so true I thought it could be forever. Hurting with the hurt to know you will love me never.

I can't let you rule me in misery.

Break these chains that are cursing me. Love let me live my life. Please let me be free. Open my mind to see what your love is doing to me. Mend my broken heart, please let me be me.

Waiting for your love. Love and understand me that's the way true love should be. Love so true. Please love me forever. I love you always. I'll love you forever.

Ruthanne Sartor Weber
CHERISHED MEMORIES
Memories . . . such fragile thoughts . . . lacy as silk . . . sparkling like diamonds in our minds.

The joy and laughter we once shared
It seems so long ago,
Now echo in my memory
As on my way I go.
Those clear cut dreams we claimed so strong
Have faded now away,
As new and more important tasks
Fill our lives today.
And yet those cherished incidents
From far away in time,
Still float like clouds of angel dust
In the recess of my mind . . .
To bring still close and dear to me
The ones I used to know . . .
To keep them sheltered in my heart
As on through life I go.
Still special and clear and dear to me
Though many miles apart,
I still care just as deeply
As I did at the very start.
And though life has scattered our lives
On sepatate and different planes,
I know I'll still be filled with joy
When we should meet again.
Oh praise God for the memories,
So fragile and lacy . . . yet strong
And for the love of special friends . . .
To fill our lives with song.

Marceil Strong
HER HANDS
Passing her casket, figure frail
　I didn't recognize her face.

My eyes fixed upon her hands
　clasping the hankerchief
　she'd made of lace!

I could feel those hands on my
　shoulders lifting me up!

Or trimming a hat, teasing her
　kitten or pup!

I could see those hands scamper
　up and down the piano,
　ukilin or organ keys;

Write music, paint a picture
　of flowers and trees!

Those hands stroked her husband's
　wavy black hair,
Nursed two pretty daughters with
　love and care!

Her hands boxed belongings to
move from state to state
to be at her husband's side.

Her hands made a home of the
small trailerhouse on
construction site for
the four to reside.

Her hands worked in laundrys,
grew strong lifting her
drunken husband into bed
night after night!

Her daughters married but still
were dependent on her, she
prayed she'd do right!

She will be judged by her hands
wrinkled, now still . . .

Her reward will be great in the
Kingdom of God, because her
hands did HIS will!

Onnalee Michele Outmans
CHAIN REACTION
I'm so sorry . . .
    I didn't mean to lead you on . . .
    No,
I just kept in touch to see if
    things could work out
        Between us.
I'm so sorry that I kept you
hanging on a limb
    I just needed time to let my
    feelings grow for you
        Believe me, I tried . . .
But they just weren't there
I guess I was caught in the chain
    reaction
    I was hurt,
        I hurt you . . .
            So the chain goes . . .
I needed more of a challenge
    You didn't give me one
I know you were ready for love . . .
    And so was I,
    But my feelings were caught
    in the link before you
I'm so sorry . . .
    I didn't mean to link you to the
    chain,
        Please! Break the chain,
            Before somebody else gets
            hurt.

Roxanne Kramer
FORGOTTEN MISTAKES
*[This poem was written to
Carlene Ippolito for her love
and support for understanding,
that everyone in life makes
mistakes, and that every
human being forgives, as she
did for me. She understands my
feelings, and she has made me,
who I am today. She is one of
my closest friends and one I
hope never to lose.]*
I wish there was a way I could,
change the past to be,
because there is that friend that
    would,
mean so much to me.

I never really knew,
how much you meant to me,
until I found out it was you,
who was really mad at me.

My deepest feelings were hurt
    very bad,
and you made all my fears come
    through,

I realize now that I'm the one,
who made this all come true.

We learn on our errors, in life
    sometimes,
which for this one I would
    remake,
but it may take a great deal of
    time,
for you to forgive me for this
    mistake.

So lets forget the many troubles,
as I ask for your forgiveness,
you've taught me that if I'm
    without you,
life is all but loneliness.

Now that our lives must keep
    going,
as we spend each day together,
I hope that the mistakes in life
    are showing,
if there's love we can be friends
    forever.

For the love of friends should
    never part,
and I hope we never will try,
for I have one thing left in my
    heart,
that's the love for you I know will
    never die.

Kathy Jo McCune
SOME ONE SPECIAL
*[This poem is dedicated to my
husband Michael and my
mother and father, Charles and
Gloria Freeman. Also to my
sister Mony Freeman and my
brother Michael Freeman. May
each of their lives be a
continuous scource of beauty.]*
I think about you all day
I want to be by your side at night
It's as if God made you just for me
And made you oh so right

He told me that you are the one
To treat you specially
Don't ever let him out of your
    sight
As far as you can see

He told me to bless you in every
    way
And keep you from all harm
But to make you happy every day
And hold you in my arms

I know that He doesn't have to
    worry
I'll do the best I can
Because my love for you is so
    special
Than any other man

I would never find another
To take the place of you
Just being there wherever we may
    go
You always make me feel brand
    new

Jo E. Hackerman
A Miracle Through Love—
A Poem For Bumbles
Do you believe in miracles?
    You need to believe—
'cause sometimes a miracle is
    what you need to see you
    through

Sometimes it may get rough
    and sometimes you may

get blue
but a miracle is on its way
    and it will see you through

You must believe in miracles
    for miracles are truth
And just as you believe in love
    the miracle comes true

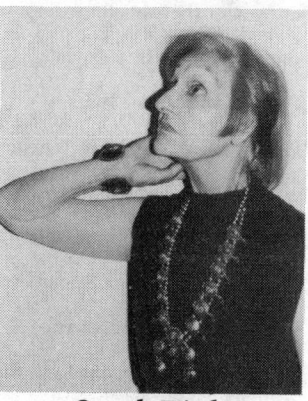

Gaye de Windt

Gaye de Windt
WEDDING BOUQUET
A crystal bowl
Once upon a time
Filled with violets,
Amethyst—colored they were.
Each diminutive flower
Like a symphony
Joy caressing its way through the
    room
Redolent with their perfume.
Eyes, ears, and a heart they had, I
    know.
It was my wedding bouquet
A long time ago.
I burst into tears.
In a certain state of mind, I am.
Forget it?
I'd rather not!
Those petals like summer fade
    away.
One by one they fall
And alight gracefully
Like a trembling autumn leaf.
Ah, lingering now in the empty
    bowl
My impassioned soul
Feathered with amethyst petals
From the wedding bouquet.
Those memoirs?
Just mirrors of a beautiful day.
A memo, that bowl,
A stardust crystal vision
That manipulates my thoughts,
As I hope it will—always.

Martha Berry Askew
LOVES OPEN DOORS
They say that love opens many
    doors well aparently, I've
    walked into the broom closet!
    Which way to the right
    direction, "Dear God", Who?
    When? or Where?
"Together" we would spend a lot
    of hours, even trash dumps
    were once filled with flowers:
For love is blind the old saying
    goes, It must have also numbed
    my nose!
Like a fire works stand on the
    "5th" of July
The flame we share will never die.

Pardon my wrong slip if I call our
    mistake a relationship; Like
    ham; on bananas we go
    together, Like paper clothes in
    rainey weather.
As mold on bread my feelings
    grew, I have nothing, and it's all
    for you!

Roy Schwartzman
Ignatz In the Sacred Land
Of Tweed
Costumed lumps of bleeding flesh
Alternate mimeographed days
With varicose nights.
Carbon copied subjects of
    corporate Gilgamesh
Randomly pair to avoid exclusion
    from the ark.

(Ignatz Higgenbotham feels
    cheated.)

Ignatz shuffles and files the
    morning
And at noon microwaves
His tweed-laced ambition
In the canteen oven.

(Ignatz savors a job well-done.)

Government issue smiles
Greet visitors, answer phones,
Stuff chunks of themselves
Into Ignatz' spine
As his screams emerge a
    whispered whine.

Another varlet for quarry.

Cynthia Tweedy—Hoffer
THE ACTOR
He stood upon a stage,
his eyes were big and bright.
His voice was low and loud,
So low it sounded like the rumble
    of a train.
Behold the actor as he cried upon
    the stage,
the man he longed to be,
to memorize the lines of love,
and say it upon his knees.
But he can not stand upon a
    stage,
or see the light so bright.
His voice could not be heard
    beyond the foot lights.
The lines of love, for him can
    never be told again,
Not upon his knees.
He has no legs for which to stand,
No eyes for to see, and his voice
    is just a whisper now,
to what it use to be.
Yes, they tell you to grow old
    gracefully, your fans will not
    forget.
But to an actor, no, this is not to
    be desired,
After 50 years upon this stage,
He would like to die in peace, at
    the end of Act III,
Upon his knees, with love to the
    actor in me.

Curtis Anderson
One In a Million Kind Of
Girl
Walking thru a moonlit night in
    the summer
Just you and I
Smiling and laughing and
    watching the clouds float by
Never really caring what
    tomorrow might bring

Just living for today
Your a one in a million kind of girl
What more can I say
I've had dreams about someone like you
But I never thought that dreams came true
But I guess they do
Cause I have you
What makes a man so lucky
I've never had so much before
The things that you do, they carry me through
I could never ask for anything more
I'm watching the wind blowing thru your hair
There's moon-light in your eyes

Seankevin Neilland II
Confused? Englightened?
Confusion for self is a wasted emotion,
confusion for GOD is a curious thought.
Confusion in love is a frustrating notion,
confusion in hatred is all i have wrought!
i hate what is evil.
i hate what is wrong.
i hate with such passion,
it taints my sweet song.
it's a song of such glory as mankind can bring.
it's a song of a story, it's a song we all sing!
of a land filled with greatness and wonder and beauty
and how it was ruined when we neglected our duty!
to keep up the pattern of life and of peace
with the land and with nature,
with the plants and the beasts.
Yes, we've let all our science and questions galore.
allow us to slaughter like never before.
Now science is "ok"; And questions aren't bad;
But we must move more carefully or, we'll end up quite sad.
Yes care is the watchword, our one guiding light.
The World must be cared for or death is its plight.
And that is the sorrow, the story of Man.
We know some of the answers and part of the plan.
BE CAREFUL and THOUGHTFULL of NATURE and ALL;
and EACH OTHERS OWN FEELINGS, that is our call!
Our call to our future as bright as a sun.
It's our duty, our business, our birthright each one;
to live on a planet that's healthy and whole.
And to worry and wonder at NATURAL SOUL!

Cynthia Tweedy Hoffer
RIDE, INDIAN RIDE
Where are the Indians today, ride, Indian ride,
Are they sitting around the fire

smoking the pipe.
Are they watching for a great spirit to come and free them.
Where are the Indians today, ride, Indian ride,
we need to see the red man again,
we need to know the world has not lost his friends.
Bring back the proud braves to the beautiful plains,
the brave upon the pony ride, ride, Indian ride,
Come where are the Indians today.
Give us a bow and arrow, a man to tell the tales,
give us a man to save the tents, a man to sing his chants.
Oh, to be a red man then, ride, Indian ride.
Don't hide behind the mountain top,
Our world is waiting for your unspoken words.
Rise up your dead, bring forth the proud red blood,
that blood that dried upon the western plains.
We were wrong to take your life in greed,
Gorgive the white man for this deed.
We need your wisdom to save the forest and lakes,
Your eyes with which to see, your heart with which to feel.
Ride, Indian ride, come back Indian brave, ride, Indian ride.
Ride across our minds, ride free, free us, ride hard,
time is running out, ride for peace, ride for me,
ride, Indian ride.

Katherine Tallant—Lively
LAST POEM
[Thanks to my very special people; friend Joy Goodwin who told me to try, husband James & sons Eric, Jared, Ryan, Daryl, and parents O. B. & Deveryl for their love and support always.]
I have so fiercely dreamed of you,
And walked so far and spoken of you so,
Loved a shade of you so hard,
That now I've no more left of you,
I'm left to be a shade among the shades,
A hundred times more shade than shade,
To be shade cast time and time again into
Your sun—transfigued life.

Barbara M. Jackson
God Is In Control Of My Life
My hopes and dreams are in the Master's hands
To fulfill—or to deny—as He alone shall choose.
Though the present moment may be one of ecstatic joy,
I need not fear if the next one sees my dreams all shattered.
Perhaps it is to be a broken dream
That will change the course of my life to a road more smoothly paved.

Though the clamor of this world goes on about me,
I need not be anxious for my well being,
For God is near and He is in control.
I need never fear or worry,
For God, my friend, is with me
To wisely lead and gently guide me in the ways that I should go.
The blueprint of my life is the Master's plan;
It is His will to determine which pathway I should take;
And it is my task to follow His leading without question or hesitation.
In my obedience I shall be victorious,
No matter what pitfalls are in my way,
For they are merely stepping stones
To a bounty of blessings and joy so complete.
My heart is at peace—undisturbed
As it rests upon the never—failing promises of God.
Surges of happiness sweep over my soul; I rest in Him,
For this I know—beyond any shadow of a doubt
That God, my Master, is in complete control of my life.

James Kuhnert
The Comtemporary Kid
In such a mad time in life as this,
how will I know what buttons to push?
Consequences, in the moment of excitement,
are like mere stepping stones and fashioned out.

To gain a wisdom isolated from whimhood is absurd.
At least while on this treadmill.
For one who thinks adulthood happens overnight
is either shocked by realization or never realizes.

To call me comtemporary would be titles
and I don't like it.
I live as others have lived except in another world.
To forget my position, you also held years ago,
alienates me in a world where I desperately cry for understanding.

Mary L. Gillmore
SUNRISE
The world seems peaceful and
Still not fully awake.
The earth,
Not sure of what the day will bring,
Meets the sun with eagerness.
The birds sing
Their songs of morning.
The earth is quiet,
Not yet ready to meet
The heat of the blazing sun.
The horizon lights up in
Crimson, purple, pink, orange, and gold.

The colors of something new.
The rays reach out
To touch the earth
And warm it.
To give it heart
To support life.
The sun lights up the sky,
Reflecting light form the clouds,
Another day is born.

Buddy L. Johnson

Buddy L. Johnson
Before It Gets Too Late
Just take a look around you
There's chaos everywhere
The Middle East and Lebanon
Our world is filled with terror

Now pick up any paper
Each page is filled with hate
We'd better turn this world around
Before it gets too late

And what of our great leaders
Who preach of worldwide peace
But build so vast their arsenals
That human life may cease

Are we so blind that we can't see
What lies in store to wait
Let's put our trust in Jesus Christ
Before it gets too late

For there surely is no other
Who is equal to the task
He has volunteered His services
And we have but to ask

So let us pledge our lives to Him
He'll not procrastinate
We all can share His endless love
Before it gets too late

For He has promised you and me
No matter what our strife
A place to share eternal love
And everlasting life

Yes, He will walk again on Earth
And He'll decide our fate
Reach out today and grasp His hand
Before it gets too late

Ronald Nelson Hicks
GARDEN OF MEMORIES
The time has come to part our ways.
It's in your heart to go.
I know my love has failed you.
And, I'm sorry I've hurt you so.

The times we spent together,
Are engraved within my heart.
They'll serve me as a comforter
While, our lives are spent apart.

To simply say, I'll miss you,
Could only part explain.
The emptiness inside me,
That causes all this pain.

Yet, life can not be meaningful,
When love is so unkind.
Filling a heart with sadness,
Tormenting a peaceful mind.

But, true love should be stronger,
To avoid this aching strain.
That causes a Garden of
Memories,
In a heart that's filled with pain.

So, in these last few moments,
Let us walk both hand-in-hand.
As we share again those
memories,
Of a lovers promised land.

I'll kiss you then, I'll hold you
close.
For soon we'll be apart.
But, in my Garden of Memories,
You'll remain within my heart.

Lorraine Boesche

Lorraine Boesche
BROTHER JOE
The youngest one of our family
of ten
A mop of blonde curls, with blue
eyes to blend
How our dear old parents eyes,
with pride did glow
When they spoke so fondly of
our Brother Joe.

In his little Mack Truck, country
roads we'd explore
You'd think his cargo was gold
and velour
But the feeling was mutual, he
was my pride and joy
I'd give all that I owned for that
little boy.

I'd fight his battles through thick
and thin
And sometime my outlook
seemed very dim
But if he were protected, that's all
that would matter
No other reward needed, no
longing for flatter.

Time flew by, as time does, and
dawned that fateful day
Half of our fleet at the ocean's
bottom lay
Our finest lads said goodbye, and
off on their flight
For their family and friends a
dreadful war they would fight.

He never came back, though we
waited and prayed
War is cruel, and many hearts so
very sad are made
It was my battle now, he had
fought and died
His life had been given, in a
hero's grave lied.

Another life, too, was given, that
we all may be free
He hung on a despised cross, just
for you and for me
He wants us to live forever, with
Him and Brother Joe
They are waiting there to greet
us, please don't to
Them say no.

Arlyn Hendershot
The Horse Heaven Hills
*[To the people of the Lower
Yakima Valley who look up to
the Horse Heaven Hills.]*
The changing countenance
of the Horse Heaven Hills
express time and season
over the valley of vineyards,
orchards, gardens and fields.
I watch the quilt of dusk
settle over them
and the clangor of day
is stilled.
So bright they became
as the sun struck them
one August morning,
I imagined the flashing
swords and armor of warriors
charging their enemies
upon galloping steeds.
Harvest leaves the valley forlorn,
fog tumbles over the hills
and fills the valley, lifting
only to reveal the bleak hills
stoically regarding
a Winter sodden valley.
I turn away my eyes
and wait in my heart
with the valley and it's people
for the greening of
the Horse Heaven Hills.

Virginia Aspinall
GAMES PEOPLE PLAY
*[Dedicated to my daughter
Lona Krueger for encouraging
me to enter my poem and her
confidence. I could not have
done it but for her.]*
The games they play are so real
to them
It's a shame dreams fade & go
suddenly dim.
No matter how long they try to
pretend
Sooner or later it comes to an
end.

It doesn't seem to matter of ones
religion or race
It's the same the world over, so
hard to face
They just go on thinking, there's
more to be found
How do we make our youth
aware of the truth.

My wife doesn't love me, my
husband is mean
They still believe the other side
is green
Remembering parents unhappy &
bored

There must be an answer if we
search our minds.

Maybe God figured it out and
made it this way
So the greatest love he gave to us
all
Is love for all mankind that never
would stray.

Alleta Nichols Brewer
GOOD—BYE
*[To my grandfather Charley S.
Thompson (Aug. 15, 1890—Jan.
8, 1983)]*
The time I feel is drawing near
I cannot tell just what I fear.
The world is changing fast and
new
And friends I count are all too
few.
It must be just a state of mind
For all around me I still find
Those who've loved me through
the years
And yet my heart is full of tears.
What happened to that magic
time
Of love, music, laughter, and
rhyme?
It seems to me but just a day
That I had lots of time to stay.
But now the time has all gone by
And it is right for me to die.
To all farewell, good—bye,
good—bye.

Mary Beth Baker
**Look Inside and
Remember**
*[In memory of Frank H.
Behrens, my grand—father.
June 1, 1896—August 5, 1981]*
Nick: Why can't Grandpa Buddy
come back from being with
God in heaven?
Ben: Because once you die, you
can't be alive again.
But Grandpa Buddy will live
forever in our special memories
of him
And some part of him is in all of
us.

Buddy: I didn't think I'd ever see
my two little buddies again.
He leans down and shakily
enfolds Ben and squeezes hard
as I blink back tears.

One week later, he is gone, dying
peacefully on Grandma Gertie's
birthday.
She was the love of his long life.
They were apart for nearly thirty
years; now they are together for
eternity.

Ben: Mom, will I ever forget what
Grandpa Buddy looked like?
Look inside and remember the
deep voice, twinkling, youthful
blue eyes, ears that magically
wiggled, those strong hands.

Ben: I want the picture of
Grandpa Buddy and me in *my*
room, close to me.
The little boy with blonde curls
looks into his great—
grandfather's eyes. (Revelation:
that's where Ben got his
unusual crystal blue eyes.) One
shoe is white, one a sneaker;

old hands somehow manage to
put on new blue sneakers.

Nick: Why isn't there a picture of
me with Grandpa Buddy? He
was my buddy, too!
The chubby toddler who can't
walk yet pulls himself up onto
Grandpa Buddy's knee so he
can hear the story being read to
his big brother.
The two pictures, the memories,
grip my heart.

Ben: Can we listen to the old tape
so we can hear Grandpa Buddy
talking to us?
Hearing that familiar, now
silenced, voice comforts us;
We smile to remember our own
special memories.

What a talker he was, teller of
tales, true stories about his life:
the wife and son who died too
soon, the two daughters who
feel guilt over occasional harsh
words, yet love him deeply and
will sorely miss him forever,
And the two great—grandsons
who will look inside and
remember.

Michael F. Smith
FLOWER OF HEARTS
Girl, when you smiled you
touched my heart
You are the sunshine on the
Flower of my Heart
You made it bloom by just being
there
You watered it with tears of
understanding
You made me see the Light so I
could care
So the love I have for you is more
than words can say
And even though you never said
a word
Your down to earthness taught
me to be low and humble.

Roy P. Habersetzer
APPALACHIAN DREAM
The pines, laurel, and floral; make
these majestic mountains a
sght to behold—

The rolling hills and slopes, with
their babbling brooks and
streams; fortell of a joy more
precious than gold—

Only God could have created this
splendor for man.

Christian Gottshall
A CRY OF HUMANITY
If I asked you to accept me,
For what I am inside,
Would you take me with no
question,
Or would you run and hide?

If I danced along the street,
Or sang a simple song,
Would you sing and dance with
me,
Or would you call it wrong?

If I giggled at the sky,
Or if I laughed aloud,
Would you ask me, "What's the
joke?"
Or lose me in the crowd?

If I cried or shouted,
When in my blackest mood,
Would you call me human,
Or would you call me rude?

If I cared not what you thought of
me,
And said what I did feel,
And made my laughter hearty,
Or made my crying real,

And if I asked you, "Love me,
And do not ask me why",
Would you tell me that you would,
Or would you let me die?

Diane E. Campos
MY MOTHER
  [Dedicated with love to
  Blanche, the woman I most
  admire and respect]
I see

Blue
Lilacs, Iris and Violets

A Mist
and Bridal Wreath

Brown
Cigarettes, Chocolates
and Butter Pecan

My Mother

Leslie M. Juhasz
FLOWER
  [I would like to dedicate this
  poem to my grandfathers,
  parents, and reading teacher
  who made publishing this
  poem possible.]
Once I had a flower,
Whose seed you sowed, O Lord,
For many lives would be sour
After sixty-two springs would go.

I miss my dear flower,
Whose light out above all.
Who left me after many years
When he heard your call.

But Lord, I have one more flower,
Whose seed you sowed also.
For me to lose my flower,
My heart and life would go.

When I look at this flower,
A rose on top of my soul,
I think of my other flower
Who left me so long ago,
And wonder how many springs
My last flower has left to go.

Debbie Sue Fite
A QUESTION OF LOVE
They say that love is happiness:
  I've been happy—
    But is that really love?

They say that love is loneliness:
  I've been lonely—
    But is that really love?

They say that love is full of hurt:
  I've been hurt—
    But is that really love?

They say I will learn of love
  when I grow strong:
    But what about now—
    Do I have to wait for very long?

By the way, who are 'they'?
  Old lovers, new lovers—
    Do they really know?

I really don't understand—
  the way that love works out.
But I know that someday soon—

I shall belong to love without a
doubt.

But until then—
  will my life be of loneliness
  and of hurt?
When 'Mr. Right' comes along—
  shall happiness and love be
  with me?

Joseph H. Young

Joseph H. Young
**That's What Easter Means
To Me**
Lord Jesus died upon the cross
But still his soul did not get lost,
He rose again to set us free
  SO THAT'S WHAT EASTER
  MEANS TO ME.

He suffered pains for you and me,
And built a home beyond the sea,
  That we with him could always
  be,
  SO THAT'S WHAT EASTER
  MEANS TO ME.

They hung him high and
  stretched him wide,
His blood ran down from side to
  side,
  Although he died on Calvary,
  SO THAT'S WHAT EASTER
  MEANS TO ME.

So let's rejoice on Easter day,
For Jesus work is here to stay,
  He's our Saviour still to be,
  SO THAT'S WHAT EASTER
  MEANS TO ME.
P. T. Zommer
LISA
I watched her grow from infancy
Into a woman filled with warmth
  and sincerity.
Her face, her eyes were small but
  bold.
Her smile was like that of fine
  spun gold.

Her mind was overflowing with
  knowledge, not only from books.
Her wisdom obvious with just
  one look.
Only nineteen, not even five feet
  tall,
Oh, dear God, she could have had
  it all.

But then the cruelest enemy of time
Began to tick away in every
  hour's chime.
And slowly her life slipped away
  into eternity,
Leaving a scar that will never
  heal within me.

As I held her lifeless hand in mine,
I wondered, was this part of the
  All Mighty's design
To cheat not only me, but the world
Of a giving, bright young girl?

And as I walked from her grave
  that cold winter's day,
There was little else to say
Except Lisa, I will love you forever,
In memories you will leave me
  never.

Dona Massarone
Trappings Of the Season
Mistletoe and holly
  berries of delight
times of cheer and folly
  moments of insight

Martin R. Burks
snuff dipping
snuff dipping
panty hosed
sirens with
their knees up
knocking doors
looking for a
rider but the
time's well spent
for a hundred dollar
song trick and
the fifty-fifty cash split
freezes out the tax
man

Jill Avedon
MORNING
Daylight, a skilled note.
Startling as the blue light
Easing onto the window sill,
Piercing through the eyelet of the
  curtain.

As I, gently turn in my garden
To touch you and bring you to
  the morning light.

Twelve hours ago you left.
Took your suitcase, shaver
And white-linen hankerchief.

Your face, on this splashed-on
  garden that we dream on
Re-emerges time and time again.

You're the little boy I played with.
Now we've grown, and now
I turn to find you.

In the flower of my garden,
In the now light of dawn,
In the body of my womanhood,
In the ear of my mind's eye,
In the children I bear for the two
  of us.

And you—earth's sundial
Watch. Smiling.
For in my turnings, I am
Rosy with thoughts of you.

Terence Alan McKeon
CENTRAL PARK
Alluring visions
Statues and pigeons
Broken feather's
Lightly touch down
  Awesome winds,

Crisp autumn leaves,
Fractured wings and shattered
  journies
Falter to the ground
Broken feather's
Lightly touch down.

Nannie Brown Christian
WHAT CHRISTMAS MEANS
Christmas means caring for each
  other
And treating mankind as brothers.
Spreading happiness over the land
To make life grand.
Remembering the events of past
  years
Enjoying family and friends with
  cheers.
How impressive is the food
That keeps us in a good mood
Smiles, smiles on every face
For the biggest holiday pace.
Tantalizing creations and
  decorations
Representing all generations.
Merry Christmas is the greeting
Presented at every meeting
All is calm, all is bright
On Santa's annual flight.

John R. Pyre
THE DREAM
I am waiting for you
knowing not who you are
nor am I sure you exist.

Are you real or thought,
Within touch, within mind?
Will you be as it seems?
Do I solo these dreams?

Asleep yet I wonder
my minds' eye describes.
You begin to take form
then I wake.

As the images fade
every line blends to shade.
Till tonight,
when I wait once again.

Wayne S. Jones
JEHOVAHJIREH
Far upon a mountain
Many, many years ago,
Went a father and son
To worship the Lord I know.

As they went together
The son soon asked the father,
What have we to offer?
We've no lamb for the altar.

Then the father did say,
There we'll find the sacrifice.
Though he knew all the way
His only son was the price.

What the faith the father had
To offer his only son,
And what trust the son had
To submit his life undone.

But oh, the boundless love
That supplied a substitute;
The ram sent from above
Did all God's mercy impute.

But far beyond compare
Was the sacrifice of God
Which He did declare
And later Christ Jesus trod.

He died upon the cross
At the hands of you and I,
But He has paid the cost
If Him you do not deny.

For thus the Scripture saith,
That the gift of God is life
But sin's wages is death;
Make now a repentance rife.

Today's Greatest Poems

Billy Kissiah
EVER SO BLUE

The SEA is like a diamond
That shines all over the earth.
Very calm and beautiful,
No rubies can value its worth.

It lays very still
In the hazy-blue night
With all it's glory
With all it's might.

It lays there in the afternoon
Ever so Blue,
And it will always be there
All the year through.

You love the fresh scent
And the glorious sight.
You wish you had it's strength
You wish you had it's might.

It lays very beautiful
All the day through.
And it will always be there
Ever SO BLUE

Maudlyn Regis

Maudlyn Regis
THE SHADOW

He came Into my life
When I never expected him
He brought more joy Into my life
I felt It was the beginning
Of a new life.

After a while I found out
The beginning of my new life
Was also the ending of the new
    beginning
He walked away from me
My life became empty again.

Here I am so lonely and blue
All because of his friendship
I thought I had a new life
Now I realized I never knew him
He was only the ending of that
New beginning.

Cassisu L. Winchester
NANCY'S WEE SIDEKICK

Brandishing a suitcase, bound
    like a noose,
I shared a stare asked for, no
    mouths were loose;
Handled as a tombstone, heavy
    traveling was mine,
Daresay flight, dear, our
    unbreeched rocket's gonna land
    sometime.
We'd assumed the decision the
    lad's dad would fly,
I relegated opinions to options to
    say good-bye.
Her history being recorded,
    donated a leg—

Appearances were rehearsing to
    concentrate on Gregg.
Unaware of his power, his spirit
    ran through my veins.
The light in his eye stayed,
    whether he sensed a game;
Lord, I re-met innocence holding
    his hand—
Sad, alternating arguments were
    abstracting me to another land.

Overflowing with affections I
    could not again show,
We went through his vocabulary
    several times slow.
He looked totally committed to
    the air he breathed—
I reminded him of chases on our
    knees.
I relished the time, ignoring the
    bomb,
Savoured expressions, 'til by my
    sighs overcome.
We made for the exit, I thought
    to repropose . . .
Untimely ideated though, I left a
    kiss with his nose.

M. Doyle
A FORCE

There's a force,
that's pulling me under,
a force that wants control,
and, to this force,
I must surrender,
My life, spirit, and soul.

There's a force,
that's bringing me down,
a force that won't let go,
and, for this force,
I turn around,
and enter the world below.

There's a force,
that's bringing me flowers,
flowers from a dead man's grave,
and, for this force,
I give my honors,
for He brings me death . . . today.

Hilda D. Cantrell
THE CLOWN

To some people, I'm just a clown
Funny nose and all;
And I'm sure they'd all laugh
If I were just to fall.

But I have feelings that do get hurt
Just like yours and theirs;
And I do mention all of them
Each time I say my prayers.

A clown is truly funny
But there are sad ones, too;
Each time they get their feelings
    hurt
They feel all sad and blue.

Sometimes I'm like the funny clown
But others like the sad;
And if you laugh when I'm down
I'll end up feeling bad.

So laugh when I am acting
And cry when I feel blue;
But if you laugh when I am down
I'll do the same for you.

Roger C. Lewis
THE CIRCLE BROKEN

Like a top afire
(the motion of the flame)
or shitting on mater
(the circle unbroken)
the matrix will see you later

(way up in the middle of the air)
and the mold will see you now sir.
So do not fear.
Marching legions to the tiger's jaw
will not sate the tiger.
And Margrette in the tiger's maw
will quote the same old saw,
'I have lost my head';
the tiger hath gained a maiden.

But let us return to the garden
(the serpent coiled)
where Eve consorts with evil
(the serpent uncoiled)
speaks with forked root
and puts the shoe upon the other
    foot.

Hawk shifts thru unlit eve,
cleaves atoms of yielding air,
strikes knife-like in sudden night
and descends upon hairy fare.
Balances shift and right.

Rarely does the mourning dove
    sleep,
bird-light empress of spaces,
where times keep
particulars in their places.
Ejected from the nest
the doveling
skewers morning air
to bind circles
and, turning,
Eve-like break circles.

Dianne Ward
HEY, THERE

Hey there, Brother
Why the needle in your hand
Do you need the junk
To make you feel like a man?

Hey there, Sister
On the corner, waiting for a john
What's life to you
Just another lusty con?

Hey there, Daddy
With your bottle of booze
You know in the end
That you're going to loose.

Hey there, Momma
With a tear in your eye
Do you long for the day
You don't need to cry?

Hey there, mirror
I look and I see
All the things I am
And what I long to be.

Robert Smith
SEARCHING

I had left the fields of clover
In my memories far recessed.
I had left the winding river
Like the fledgeling from the nest.

I went in search of reasons
No scholar could define
I searched through changing seasons
Left my heart somewhere behind.

I fought my fight in the highlands,
And the jungles far below.
Death I dealt my own hands,
My conscience died some time ago.

Death I saw in foe and friend,
And red blood flowing from my
    veins,
And bodies broken beyond the
    mend,
Their flesh arot in the mud and
    rains.

My soul marooned in this sea of
    hell,
I've drifted through the years they
    say,
Searching the fate my heart
    befell,
Or a grave in which my dreams
    will lay.

B. T. Drake
NIGHTTIME BY THE RIVER

Nighttime by the river
Is a nice time
Grandpa pickin' his banjo
Grandma sittin' in her rockin' chair
The little ones are in bed
While the older ones are up.

Nighttime by the river
Is a nice time
Harvest is over
The crop was good this year
Winter is comin' on
This summer I became a man.

Nighttime by the river
Is a nice time
Everybody's happy and singin'
The family's here together
The water is so still and quiet
'Cept for the ducks callin' to one
    another.

Nighttime by the river
Is a nice time
A time to talk of past times
Laughs and tears of all the years
Growing up
Having experiences which are
    rooted in your memories.

Nighttime by the river
Is a nice time
I'm gonna get me a farm
And do what I can
I got a girl I'm gonna make my wife
For now I'm a man
Goin' to have some more of the
    good life
I'll always remember
Childhood days
And nighttime by the river
Is a nice time.

Tarrell L. Reeder
1982

The year is nineteen hundred and
    eighty-two,
It's the roughest year that we've
    been through.
Times are rough and they're
    getting worse,
It almost makes a man want to
    curse.

Many people have lost their jobs,
Part of them turn into bums and
    slobs.
And it's all because the times are
    rough,
It's time to say enough is enough!

The Government is always
    entirely to blame,
They think human lives are just
    a game.
They pass a law and then pass a
    buck,
They hope and pray and depend
    on luck.

Cause a depression is here and
    it's setting in,
It's spreading the money out real
    thin.

A steak for dinner once was nice,
But half of America can only eat
rice.

Government people could eat
steak every night,
It's just not fair, it's just not right.
People get paid for the work they
do,
If the same went for them, they'd
all be through.

If they got paid for the work
they've done,
They wouldn't have a dollar, well,
maybe one.
They'd be lost, poor, and broke,
And just for once, they'd be the
joke!

L. Jane VanSyoc
HEART GIFT
[For Ardis Elaine, ever generous.]
It was not a fancy trinket
Or an odd intriguing gift . . .
It wasn't the wild excitement
Of a fulfilled, longed-for wish;
It was just the knowing what
would serve
To make my burden lighter—
Your best to give, your help, your
smile
That made the shadows brighter.
It was just that cheerless hours
Gloom-filled with doubts to start,
Were transformed by your presence
And your understanding heart.
Dividing the weight of worry and
care
With love the guiding line, yours
Was a sharing, caring gift of self . . .
A treasured token, forever mine.
No need to say, "I thank you"
For us, that has no part—
We 'hear' each other's feelings, when
We 'listen' with our heart.

Bobby Chisolm
POEM OF RETRIBUTION
Hey playboy: use this heart
like it's your toy.
Don't stop to see what you do to me;
Such pain you inflict the blind
could see.
One day maybe it'll occur to you,
why I'm so truly, truly blue
The pain, the hurt, the misery of
a love that was not meant to be:
You cold, abusive and fancy-free
will feel the hurt that was meant
for me.

Ada L. Cabell
SECOND CHANCE
This year my life seemed to come
alive.
I had too much to live for and
nothing to hide.
With my husband backing me
one hundred percent.
Off to Franklin Adult School I went.

Two nights a week wasn't too
much to ask.
Considering the good points if I
would only pass.
The people were nice and the
teachers great.
Not once in that time did I hesitate.

I'm glad this time has finally
arrived.
Now with my diploma I won't be
deprived.

So if you know some one that
would like to advance.
How about telling them of a
second chance.

Show them your diploma and let
them know.
That your life has changed
wherever you go.
Tell them how good it makes you
feel.
And the smile on your face will
make it all real.

Betty Louise (Ball) Denton

Betty Louise (Ball) Denton
A GOLDEN WREATH
There's a grave
    Where Mother
Has been put to rest

Her beauty is
    Closed up within
Those precious days
    Has all gone by
But my tears
    Still flow
    In the wind
While I linger and sigh

She taught me
    Kindness and
To Love and not to hate
To know how to
    Weather the storms

If I could only
Turn back the years
To feel the protection
    In Her arms
The touch of her hand
Her arm around my shoulder
To enjoy my dear Mothers
    Laughter again
All I can do now
    Is to place
    A Golden Wreath
    Upon her grave
And wish
    I could see her
    Again.

Barbara Wirkowski
MY LOVE FOR YOU
[This poem is dedicated to
Jesus from a little poetess
named Barbara who loves him so.]
My love for you is as deep as the
ocean,
and higher than the trees.
Wider than this world of ours,
and far beyond the sea.
I love you more and more each day,
but can't begin to say.
Because this love I have for you,

words can't even say.
I'll love you 'till the end of time
and hope you'll still be mine.
But Jesus no matter what goes
wrong,
I'll love you all along.

Felix Lenox Jr.
BE READY
Time flies by as my life stands still
Bogged down in questions and
problems.
Answers escape before the
questions arise
Which makes it impossible to
solve them.
So many directions with so little
choice
In which I have no decision
Manipulates me in the course I
must take
Through life with cunning
precision.
But I'll keep my eyes open and
my ears tuned for chance
For the fate that is, that will
follow
So that when it appears, be it
days, be it years
I'll be ready to rise from lifes
hollow.

Ninfa E. Ortiz
PHOENIX
And with the Death of winter
Arises the Birth of spring,
And new hope bursts forth in the
soul of man
As buds are slowly and quietly
transformed
Into an oasis in the parched desert
Of the human spirit.
From here will the wings of freedom
Lift their hearts to soar
Above the plight that pulls
At the soul of man.

Jennie Lynn Sebrina Johnson
WHEN YOU'RE MAKING IT
He died for us to cover-up so
many things.
When you're making it, think of
him because when you're
getting by, he looks with many
eyes.

When you stop to think what
tomorrow might bring, I guess
it makes you dream of many
things.
When your're scrapping down to
the floor, seems like there's not
a break even when you've
reached the core.

I like going out to games or the
movies sometimes.
But stop and think how the
money runs.
How does it feel when you're not
making it? Not even halfway,
but keep wandering for a light,
what other things come insight?

Electric bills, Telephone bills,
Taxes, and House notes, too,
what are we going to do?
No more extras, just hanging on a
thread.
Whatever happened to the five
cent loaf of bread?

I have to wear what I got, guess
how many don't have a drop.

And you know what I do in the
morning?
I'm looking over my clothes and
mourning.

Most have nice clothes and
sometimes a car.
Whatever happened to my part?
When you stop to think of what
tomorrow might bring, you
wonder if you could live this
way again.

H. Reilly Richardson
REQUIEM
We were the last to say goodbye—
A child, unknowing, unaware,
and I—torn with the pains of
change and parting, the stress
of fear and daily living, the
subterfuge, and one faint
glimmer now of shared release.
We could not know that this
was final—a chapter closed,
perhaps forever.

There are no tears to ease this
gripping pain within my heart
and soul. There are no words to
voice my loss. Yet, I remember
a small hand, then, held close
in mine, sustaining.—Oh,
please, my love, remembering,
cherish my love and give love
back to me; else, I may surely
die.

Bella Gour-Robinson
SOLITUDE
I come to one, I come to all
In light of day, in dark of night
Few listen to hear my call
Most shun me in sheer ignorant
fright.

I'm oft' befriended by the lonely
Who claim, e'en boast my
presence they sought
'Tis a sham, t'was I who found
them, truly
Bitter souls, friendless, lone and
distraught.

There are those who think me
not a foe
The grief-stricken ones who on
self-pity feed
They seek and find me in time of
woe
I'm ever near in time of need.

Young lovers run to my blissful
arms
Yet the lonely aged curse me
with each breath
Those who embrace me, praise
my charms
Others fear me more than the
black shroud of death.

My enemy rules where lives rush
and throng
I shun all clatter, pandemonium
and blare
I reign where silence hums its'
sweet song
They join in those who hate
fanfare.

I am peace and calm, thought and
plan,
Inspiration, desire, a quiet interlude,
I can be friend or foe to man
I am ancient yet new, I am
Solitude.

Today's Greatest Poems

Tanya Scott
LOVE
Love is like a flower.
Sometimes it blooms and sheds a
    beautiful fragrance for
    everyone to smell.
but sometimes it wilts and that
    fragrance dies away.
Only you can make love last.
You can water it and give it
    plenty of sun,
and it will last forever!

Shery Christopher
HERE'S TO YOU
Today again
you were in my thoughts.
You came and mingled
through my veins.
My blood ran warm,.
my eyes they danced, . . .
I thought of flowers
and of taking a chance . . .
So writing my words
with simplicity
Here's to you, with love,
from me.

Shirley Ann Stephens
CHRISTMAS THOUGHTS
I thought of the Virgin Mary,
Being, big, with child.
Traveling on a lonely road,
Tired, and in pain, all the while.

I thought of the chosen father,
And, how it must have been.
When he heard those words, so
    plain
"There's no room in the Inn."

I thought of the Shepherds, in the
    field,
As they watched their flock by
    night.
And wondered what they must
    have thought,
On seeing such a shining light.

I thought of the wise men, as
    they gathered gifts,
And traveled from afar.
And thought of the awe, they
    must have felt,
While following the star.

I thought of the little manger,
All padded up with hay.
Knowing it was the only place,
Our Christ child had to lay.

Wade E. Deal
SPRINGTIME LOVE
Return with me now
To that sweet golden valley
Where we spent that loving spring
With life beginning all around us

Loving within a cabin built
    amongst the lily
The atmosphere around us
So crisp, so free
I remember it all so well
That loving spring you spent
    with me

Can you remember
Walking alone with me
In early morning dew
Can you remember
Kissing me gently
Under our blue moon

I can remember
The caressing touches of the
    moonlight

Dancing upon our bare flesh
I can remember
You standing there in the doorway
Looking so beautiful and fresh

Rick A. Jones
Upon My Native Terrain
On a vacant corner
tenaciously leaning
against a light pole.
I pondered
plaintively daydreaming
Of long, long, ago.

While I gazed
a humble abode
amusingly, comes to mind.
When in days
of yore,
A widow strolled,
as children frolicked in pastime.

Of long, long, ago
Nay!
Shall it be the same.
When another wistful soul
surveys
"Upon my Native Terrain."

Mervis Lyn
I'LL ALWAYS REMEMBER
So glad we had the chance to meet,
To be more than just friends
Our smiles, our minds, our bodies
In perfect complement

Asking nothing of each other,
Giving all in return
Fulfilling all our fantasies
In brief sojourns

Later in the twilight years,
When all the fires have spent
Those will be the memories
Recalled, time and time again

But in every collection there
Is a priceless piece
Thats handled very tenderly
And lovingly replaced

Mine will be that moment when
You asked, how was it Love?
I whispered oh so low
I declare thee beautiful—
A tiger—A dove

Patricia Lucas
THE MAN I LOVE
The Man I Love is something
    special
But really only to me
He isn't what everybody would
    ask for
But he's just the way I want him
    to be

I may not see him often
And then again I may
But as I travel lifes rugged road
He's in my thoughts everyday

People ask me why I love him
Really I can't say
All I know is that I do
And will till my dying day

He may have faults and weaknesses
But I know everyone does
It really doesn't matter though
Because He's The Man I Love.

Maureen Gremling
THINGS I'VE HEARD
"Come here, my friend. I've
    something to give you,
something I think that you need.
Don't be afraid,I swear I won't

hurt you
with words and never in deed.

I tell by your face that you're
    needing a shoulder,
one that is sturdy and strong.
I have such a shoulder that I'd
    like to loan you
and never will do you a wrong.

The troubles you face, that I see
    bring you pain,
do trouble the rest of us, too,
and you can be sure that you
    don't suffer lonely.
I feel the same way that you do.

Don't ever you doubt that I love
    you, my friend,
but right now I'm in quite a hurry.
Don't ever you think you mean
    nothing to me,
I'll call back, my friend, don't you
    worry.

Forgive me today for the way that
    I drifted,
I really was listening to you,
but I couldn't help seeing the tear
    in my drapes.
I guess that I'll have to buy new.

The love of a friend is so great,
    don't you think?
and I'm so glad we have it to share,
but I think we should cancel our
    talk for tonight
as my resting time's getting so
    rare.

What's wrong with you, friend,
    you're not quite the same,
why do I see you no more?
Have you been involved with
    some other pursuits?
You've always been near me
    before.

I never would think you could
    turn from me so,
I thought you'd be there till the
    end.
You know how I always have said
    this to you:
Come to me, I am your friend."

Alice Louise Quinn
THE DARK AGES OF LIFE
A wrinkled bag of memory
    sits by the window
    and waits for me
A pale white taper
    burning unsteadily
    in the increasing darkness
Can I allay her fears
Control my tears
    How long

Rosa Nava Krinsky
. . . And I Never Knew His Name
As the autumn leaves briskly
    float by
carried only by the caring arms
    of the wind whistling as it came.
Seems to hug his face and before
    he noticed,
                    he was embraced.
If only I knew his name . . .

His hair so fine, with a touch of
    grey
just enough to get his fame.
Like an angel of love had playfully
    ruffled it with no pretentions.
If only I knew his name . . .

Could he be angelic, I heard it tell
    a man of mercy in his game.
No woman as daring, no woman
    so true
could break his heart or make
    him blue.
If only I knew his name . . .

The trickle of life left in me,
    with the sight of him leaves
    my heart enlarged in flame.
I cannot explain this ache,
    the sense of need I feel
    for this mysterious wonderful
    man.
If only I knew his name . . .

As he passes me by I shiver with
    his very step
    the words I want to say are
    prisoners unsaid.
Now it is too late, I know I am to
    blame.
My life will never be the same.

And I Never Even Knew His
    Name . . .

James Sexton Layton

James Sexton Layton
A Wall Of Dragon's Teeth
From the edge of a green valley I
    stood
Looking into the abyss of a fate
So dark I could not see what issue
    would
Prevail in my life, nor anticipate
The consequence that would
    follow the choice
I felt compelled to make as I
    looked around
At the temptor's face, heard his
    luring voice
Confirming solid footing would
    be found
For my feet at the bottom of the
    pit,
If I had the courage to make the
    break
Into the unknown and never
    submit
To love's humility, as did the
    weak.
He said masters of men were men
    of hate.
A wall of dragon's teeth, without
    a gate!

Jennie Wilder
LADIES AT 50
have learned
to tread softly,
tenderly shutting doors,
never to be opened again.

349

They find deep in mirrors
their daughters when young:
softly kissing their doll's red
    cheeks,
crooning their babies to sleep.

In summer they feel
the winter's ice cracking
in their elbows and ankles.
They cry.

Kay Tyrer-Poole

Kay Tyrer-Poole
APRIL LOVE
Was that me so sure the other
    night?
Dependent on my thoughts ran
    wild,
Mixed feelings, love caressed
    with hope
Me so sure and sound,
I lost my way I recall, April
    imprinted on my mind,
The daffodils are dead now, am I?

A night of love we both knew,
    before it even started,
It didn't even rain of April
    showers and the sun broke free,
So did I, my heart leaping and
    spinning, jerking and racing,
Never before was that me?, love
    imprisoned set free
Dancing to the wind, and night
    that suddenly became dark.
I knew my way but couldn't see,
The daffodils are dead now, am I?

Take all forget that we belong
    elsewhere, not together,
But make believe and fantasize,
    you loved me then,
The me that should be caring,
    and I forgot my doubts,
And shadows lingered, caressing
    darkness spinning around us,
Off into mystery light cascading
    down to be spent by us both,
We knew you and I deep in heart,
    this was all and no more
to be, but night was young and so
    were we,
The daffodils are dead now, am I?

Me! I laugh ashamed, aghast,
    awkward, it's all over,
Laugh! you caught your wings in
    flickering candle flame,
You burned and smoldered like
    before,
Forget your sins, your past
    remember now, but no,
This time I feel no doubt, I spent
    my love and on my
part I feel no shame,

I can't forget April nearly over,
    but not for me,
I won't forget be it that you
    already have,
And daffodils they grow again for
    April love.

Wanda Dawn Clark
MOTHER
This one day is Mother's Day
Why it is I cannot say.
Beings you are my dear Mother
That makes you be like no other.
It was a very lucky day
When you entered this old world
    to stay.
So many days and so many years
When you are gone there will be
    lots of tears.
You have brightened the lives of
    all those near
Just by being such a dear.
If all of this world were as good as
    you
So honest, kind, thoughtful and
    true,
It would be a better place to live
And every one would want to give.
Give the things that mean so
    much
Just a nod a smile a touch.
And just because you are mine
It's Mother's Day all the time.
And all I started out to say
Hope you have a happy day.

Lee Ann Beaulieu
INTIMACY LOST
All I wanted was to
    comfort you
        but
the world would not allow us
We were wrong
in the eyes
of the Almighty Society
            and so
you push
                    me away
and I
                    push you
shoving
fighting
hurting
Bruises of the emotional kind
seldom heal
Manifesting themselves through
    insecurities and fears
Always losing love
thinking to gain independence
But I know
When I am
                    alone
The devil is
                loneliness
                caused by
                    fear
Fear of the Almighty Society.

Jim Chasteen
FORGET
Forget her name, forget her face,
    The way she kissed and her
    embrace.
Forget her love once so true,
    Remember now there's
    someone new.
Forget the love that once was
    shared,
    The time she said she even
    cared.
Forget the time you spent together,

Hoping that love would last
    forever.
Forget the hours that were so long,
    Even when you hear that
    favorite song.
Forget how close you two once
    were,
    It's in the past and all a blur.
Forget the way she sweetly talked,
    The way she moved when she
    walked.
Forget the time she said goodbye,
    That awful day she made you
    cry.
Forget her gentle teasing ways,
    Your rushing to see her
    everyday.
Forget the thrills when you drove
    by,
    You didn't see her but had to
    try.
Forget the way she held your hand,
    Forget her sweet kisses if you
    can.
Forget she said she'd leave you
    never,
    Remember now, she's gone
    forever.

Karen Wauneka
**A Daughter, a Daughter
Of God**
My fair young daughter,
in your eyes I see the beholder of
    one who sacrificed all,
that she may have the
    opportunity to come to this
    earth life.
Earth,
she recalls, is the home where
    there may be the avenues of
uncertainties and challenges.
Remain unspotted from the world,
enabling the Spirit of God to
    dwell in her heart.
Light to light,
her soul is filled with divine
    guidance.
Searching and learning that Life
    is enjoyable . . .
enjoyable and multi-folded.
Yes,
She's developed the desire to
    become like her Father who is
in heaven.
May Grace and Truth be her
    instructor and ZION shall then
    be
her destination.
    . . . one heart and one mind . . .
Shall she be welcomed at the
    King's palace,
where if she is consistant and
    worthy in obedience to her call.
Shall she be called to come forth
    to inherit all . . .
        a completeness of her being,
        as a daughter,
        a Daughter of God.

Edith J.
TACTLESS BOB
Tactless Bob is a very nice fellow.
He dresses nice and is always
    mellow.
When something comes up, he
    says the wrong thing.
For goodness sake, what does he
    mean.

One day, while standing with his
    crowd,
a friend comes up, looking very
    proud.
Bob blurted out, "look who's full
    of cheer.
He usually doesn't come around,
    so there's
something he wants us to hear."
Bob could be a little nicer, if only
    he
watched his words. The words
    comes from
his mouth are the most tactless I
    have
ever heard.

Arthurine Y. Duncan
TRIBUTE
*[This particular poem was
written to help comfort those
who have lost a loved one
through the thoughtless
actions and deeds of another.
Dedicated to Mr. & Mrs. Frank
J. McDaniel and family.]*
    When misfortune happens
    one often wonders why?

Although, your heart . . . deeply
        dampened,
    you can honestly say, "I tried."

And . . . the cause? Not very clear
for many things go unexplained.

But, I say to you with all sincere
that you are not the blame.

Rejoice! Rejoice! Please do not cry.
For he (she) has found a better life
    beyond—beyond the skies.

Gabriele Luise Meissner
PIANISSIMO
In my symphonic world,
you and I perform in dissonance.
Fluted passages and soft-toned
    notes
from muted strings
cascade my feelings onto yours
    and lead
them drip
    to drip
        to drip
into my lonely tide pool.

Eve Kapptie
**Strangers Make Good
Friends**
*[In Memory of Edward Miles
Hiatt a special friend, a loving
father, and devoted son and
brother. Love, Eve]*
So we met in a strange way, not
    ever suspecting we'd become
    close.
"I'm going to allow us to be
    friends, because "He's" not here
    to stay.
    So I'm safe . . .
Therefore any feelings and
    emotions can just be for now,
and when you're gone, the
    feelings will be gone too,
no matter when or how.
    So I'm safe . . .
I can express myself to you, by
    mail or by wire, but the
slightest anticipation or anxiety
    upon hearing your voice
can be covered, for you'll see the
    caring.
    So I'm safe . . .

"Sure wish you could be at this party!"
"Send me the plane fare and I will!" Very "impulsive" for both of us, but we're only young once, so what the hell.
    And I'm still safe . . .
All the touching, all the laughs, just tenderness and enjoying.
Seeing all those miles back, even tho it was always raining, made all the "little problems" that arose just a milestone in our beginning.
    So I'm safe . . .
Now here we are, in each others world, a whole new surrounding and
adjustments I must make! I have an inner fear that this was all a mistake—to go into this "blind"— that's not like me at all!
    Am I still safe?
I've been so "protective" with myself, not allowing "love" to be a word
I say. Since my divorce, it was allowed once, and it was abused, only because I was not careful with my choice!
    So, I'm still safe . . .
But now someone is in my life again, and I fear the time has come, that
I am not the "only", but that two again shall become one.
    Now I'm scared!
And I question myself, as to "why?" I felt "safe" before, when there
was only "me" protecting "me"!
    And now there is so much more!
For you care for me, and you say you love me, (and I'm not the only one
you've told) so I believe that you do, and I have to stop "protecting me",
and allow myself to be me, then if it is supposed to be, it will!
    And I'm safer now than ever before! Or am I?

Judy Bohannon
KEVIN
Out of a young forest
    God chose from all the rest;
A tree strong and sturdy
    knowing—he had chosen the best.

He chose an evergreen
    elegant, straight and tall;
Admired by many
    and loved by all.

With strong and sturdy branches reaching far and wide;
Its influence will be felt
    like the never ending tide.

For *he* was an evergreen—always the same
    winter, summer, spring, or fall;
Faith never waivering
    an inspiration to all.

His rare love for family
    create a warm glow;
Like that of an evergreen
    against the new fallen snow.

God loving parents
    had tilled the soil well;

Implanting roots firm and deep—
    their job done well.
Sometimes, we must give up our young
    before the old—
Their lives unfinished Chapters, closed books—stories untold.
And though its end
    cannot be seen;
It reaches like widening ripples down a long eternity.

Marjorie Gagnet Berry

Marjorie Gagnet Berry
Lament Of Lukewarm Loosey
A week passed and no one came,
I sat on the marble and studied my name.
The next day I left and arrived very late,
they let others through, then closed the gate.
Haloed angels dressed in white were playing golden harps that blinded my sight.
St. Peter appeared, robed in gold, staff in hand, walking slow,
when he spoke his voice resounded from Heaven to earth to Hades below.
"Begone, begone, we know you not", then trumpets began to blare,
I slowly floated down, down, down, my soul, my mind in deep despair.
I decended back upon my tomb and waited for a call from hell.
A red thing came with horns and tail and then I heard a bell.
Ghouls floated out from everywhere and began to form a line.
I joined the group reluctantly and hung back far behind.
We floated over the River Styx and came to a cave called Brimstone.
We heard thunder and saw fire, we started to wail and moan.
The cave opened wide and the ghouls fell inside, I stood trembling,
oh! the pain!
Satan yelled, "begone, begone", and turned from me with great disdain.
Across the River Styx, back to the graveyard I travelled.
My gown was torn and scorched, my nerves were all unravelled.

Ten years have passed, good deeds I've done, I welcome all new souls,
I bid farewell to all who leave for heaven or the coals.
My soul is lost somewhere in limbo, out of grace I fell,
I wasn't good enough for heaven and wasn't bad enough for hell.

Marsha Higgins
A Best Friend At Wintertime Brings . . .
Sipping hot chocolate steaming from our mugs.
In the quiet calmness ready for hugs and hugs.
Remembering the snowflakes from a snowy night.
The laughter we shared in our past snowball fight.
Building snowmen made of snow.
Bobsledding over the hills high and low.
The moonlit walks we adored.
Making sure neither one became bored.
The days we shared that were filled with a chilly breeze.
The cool air that turned our breath to freeze.
Having snuggly covers we could share.
Bundling up together in warm clothes to make sure no skin was bare.
Wearing our tobogans and big caps.
Able to sit in that special someone's lap.
Sharing secrets and making our friendship clear.
Keeping in touch from far and near.
Always staying together from here on out.
And if something should happen not being afraid to pout.
A cuddly teddy and your best friend to snuggle close.
Wintertime brings love at the most.
Warmth that will always stay inside.
A best friend and Wintertime go side by side.

Ruth E. Hiatt
THE TOUCH OF HIS HAND
The day will come when I will leave this earthly home I love,
For I need relief from body and soul and help will come
    from above.
He gave me seventy and seven, my time grows shorter each day.
I saw the wonders of His created land, the grandeur of
    His sky,
The beauty of His sunset brought many a tear to my eyes.
I viewed the extravagance of His mountain top, felt the
    quietness of His night,
Loved and was loved by a wonderful woman, my wife.
I experienced the wonderment of His birth and heard our
    newborn babies' first cry,
Loved them and was loved in return

All were gifts from one much wiser than I.
Now my body grows weary and my soul longs for rest—
So I shall sleep in the dust of the earth 'til God
Calls me to my heavenly home where the faithful never die.
Then again I'll walk with loved ones in the sweet bye
    and bye.
No need to cry or grieve me for I shall never really die.
I'll live through loved ones and the things they do
until we meet again in the sky.
Tomorrow will bring a sunset and the smell of new mown hay
And I know there's a God who wants, waits and beckons me closer and closer each day.
How do I know this? I felt The Touch of His Hand.

Pearl Keats
FIRST SNOWFALL
A pretty little snowflake
In the distant
sky, falling towards you
falling ever so gently.
It lands on your nose
So cool and nice,
then it melts away.
You look up towards
the sky you
see another and another
falling now more quickly
You try to catch one
with your hand but
it misses and lands
on the damp ground
and disappears.
As you look up
it's all clear blue sky
again. It was the first
snowfall of the year.

Julie Anne Ingerick
ABORTION
Why is there no mourning?
Why is there no justice?
Thousands are slaughtered.
Bloodshed and yet no war.
They cannot be found in cemeteries,
But in disgraceful graves.
Seeming as a collection of dolls,
Broken by a child,
Enraged in a fit of madness.

Gloria I. Paz
American (Bicentennial) Flag
[Hymn 1776—1976 Music and Lyrics by Gloria I. Paz]
New generation look to our flag,
If your parents didn't tell you,
I will explain the right;
No other country is so as this,
Because the American Flag
Stands in it.

The rule of Peace,
And Liberty,
This beauty things
It means to me.
This beauty things,
It means to me,
The rule of Peace
And Liberty.

When in the morning is the sunrise,

It looks there its beauty,
Flying into blue sky;
My heart and soul are proud of
you,
My little ensign
Red, white, and blue.

Frances H. Rulli
PLEA TO JESUS
As you walk thru the chambers
of my heart
Notice every tiny cell and vessel
In my weakness—oh—please,
never depart
Please give to me that shining
love missle
Making it shine with thy holy
loving
That helps strengthen every fiber
of me
Lord. Open the doors of my heart
forever
Let serene, holy peace forever
there be
No strings to Satan's sins—those
please sever
Letting the pure lifegiving blood
from it
Flow thru this weak body—
washing caring
Ever making me ready for that bit
Of life with you—Jesus I'm then
sharing
Give to me pure wisdom—grace
fulfilling
Teach me all thy ways—thy
loving rules
That I will never feel the cold
chilling
Of Satan's horrors of life's poor
fools

Rose Bodnarchuk
BILLY
This child was born
Lacking not beauty
Lacking not thought.
Don't judge his fate
Thru what you may see
He is the one
Thus destined to be.
Think not you may change
His purpose on earth
Nor may you rule
His manner and way.
Time will thus tell
If he is blessed
With nought or with health.
This rests with but One
To guide him to a place
'Neath our sun.

Robert G. Bourbeau
TENDRILS FROM THE PAST
*[To the one person in my life
who looked into my heart and
made each dream they found
there come true.]*
As consciousness peers round
Sleep's shy, misty bend,
Where Night and Dawn's dear
light first mate,
Shades of reality, less lonely than
dreams can end,
In playful scenes of familiar
fantasy, wait.
There, I, like Icarus, a fool's flight
do trace
Closer to Passions's flame than
Heaven doth intend
And through false visions give
false life grace,

Till tendrils from the past rising
from Hell's frozen space
Splash the memory of thy real
face. There to spend
Eternity, my icy soul in
projection encased, where I
have sinned,
I wake to find you in Thought's
true embrace, in deed a friend.

Clara Harrison
HOW TO KEEP HARMONY
Harmony comes from keeping
your partner's happiness
uppermost in your mind,
Remember the little things you
do are most important you'll
find.
Always try to be cheerful and
wear a smile,
Never try to make them ever,
they have their own life-style.
If you can't always agree
compromising will show
respect from you,
Sometimes it may not seem so
easy, but it will show your
feelings true.
Hobbies and interests are usually
shared,
but never forcing the issue shows
how much you care.
At times you'll both need time to
be alone to sort out your
thoughts of the problems of the
day,
It keeps you from saying things
you might regret, and second
thoughts will show you a
better way.
Never be afraid to let your true
feelings show,
Always have faith in each other
and your love will grow.
Don't always wait for your
partner to come to you,
for when you feel the need to be
with them it shows your love
is true.
You'll have problems to solve, but
you'll work them out alright,
Just make sure you come to a
solution before going to bed at
night
Remember out of all the rest they
chose you to be their own,
You started out as friends now
see how your love has grown.
It will take patience, hard work
and sometimes sacrifice,
But you'll find it's all worth it
when you find your own
Paradise.

Lynn Lana
ONE LAST GOOD-BYE
When we first met, I could tell
you were the one.
I knew if things got rough for us,
you wouldn't turn and run.
You weren't like the others, you
were so kind.
Another man like you would be
very hard to find.
And now as I stand over your
flower-covered grave,
I think about the memories that I
will always save.
I guess I'll never realize that you

are gone for good.
You did the one thing I never
thought you would.
Please answer this before our last
good-bye.
Why did you turn and run?
Why did you die?

Caspur J. Yates
FLEECES GOLD
*[Dedication to Barbara Nuno
Seeking help, she came to this
fellah My little Golden Fleeced
Pinellah]*
Over green pastures
white fleeces flow.

My horse and camp,
a ranges liberty we go.

Through the season's trails
we trekked, the time we spent.

Our hearts are filled
with thoughts well meant.

Upon my camp door stoop,
by me, I watch them troop.

Round curious eyes and baby's
step,
Shep barks to give them pep.

A mothers love, a baby's trust,
sunshine against the cold.

With water, milk and grass,
are the shares within my pot of
gold.

After twilight's beams
and sheep are dreams.

In taint of sage we're tucked
bedded down, well chucked.

Like Pal and Shep
I have lost my pep.

To us, all evil strange
until sunlight lights the range.

Anna Gilmore
THE AMERICAN FLAG
Three cheers to you
The red, white and blue
The emblem of my birth
I salute and hail you
with honor every day
The red
The blood that was shed
with courage, on the
battlefield of wars
Three cheers to you
The red, white and blue
The white
A symbol of peace, wherever she
may be seen
like a dove, flying high in the
sky

To keep America free
Three cheers to you
The red, white and blue
The blue
for the uniforms that were worn
by the defenders of this great
nation
So that we the American people,
can strive for our ideals and
goals
a tribute to our dedication
May you always remind us, that
we are the home, of the
free and the brave
And in peace, may you always wave

Maureen Hoffman
I WROTE IT FOR MY IDOL
with the soft strength of a
woman's kiss
replacing need with bliss
she takes us, and barely bending
breaks us
then we are forever in her tender
power
held the way she holds her mike
—like a flower

Eleanor Otto
ALWAYS
Shall I remember you at
Christmastime,
when dove-white spreads of snow
deny the green
of fields in spring and apple trees
in bloom;
when long-speared summer
grasses reach their prime;
perhsps in autumn, when the
moon's ripe sheen
recalls the marriage vows of bride
and groom
who pledged themselves to love
through death and doom,
in happiness or dangers unforseen;
and promised then eternally to
hold
each other close despite illfate
and mean
disasters—always shielding love
sublime—
annointed through two weddings
rings of gold?
I keep you in all seasons, warm or
cold,
set deep in mind—in every place
and clime.

My heart shall wear you like a
precious stone
forever to remember you—my
own.

Elizabeth Sides Waugh M.D.
THE CHAIR AND THE BELL
I havn't much to offer
But thanks and a word of prayer,
Then I rest again in
My great-grandfather's chair.
The old Boston rocker
Came from the house in Maine;
It fits my twelfth dorsal vertebra
Which will never be the same.
It's cool, air-conditioned
Many purposes it serves
Whoever would have thought
It would calm my tired nerves?

Then when my aching ribs and
bones
Really hurt like Hell,
I ring wild and loudly
On my grandfather's old

school bell.
Today I had that polished and
It has taken on a sheen of olden
days
Which sparkle and I have never
seen.
These gentlemen were courtly
and even very wise
And left me gifts of grandeur
which I could not surmise.

Christine King Shrum

Christine King Shrum
AU NATURAL
Diurnal arc arises crimson
bejeweled
Crowning emerald amber mane
atop
Earth's massive domain.
Celestial sphere aglow betwixt
Grand Canyon's voluptuous
cleavage
Plummeting valley's depths
unfurls
Stately curl round mountains'
opulent breasts.
Reaching finger rays thrust into
belly's
Warm lava bed shaping volcano's
ruby navel.
Niagra flows upon majestic
thighs
Cascading onto icy shell toes,
Peering from water's edge, pearly
white.
Silhouette, enmold, faces night
sky,
Lying upon horizon's fading
diorama.
Dreams, stardust sprinkled, loom
heavenly.
Nocturnal arc covers Earth brow
with sleep.

Joseph F. Schock
OUT ON THE STREETS
You learn a lot growing up out on
the streets,
Some of it bad, but much of it
good.
You may even grow up to be
President,
Or maybe just another street
corner hood.

You learn the truth and why it is
told,
But far more you learn about lies.
You learn by experience, you
can't read it in a book,
You can tell a man's thoughts by
the look in his eyes.

You learn about hatred and to
keep it inside,
But there's times when you teach
'em what life's about.
They act so hard and they think
they're so cool,
But they step aside when you let
it all out.

You learn how to win and you
learn how to lose,
And each time it's a different
game.
You go for it all and sometimes
come up empty,
But you take it like a champ just
the same.

You learn about life and you
learn how to live,
You can learn how to see things
other people can't see.
You learn how to survive and
give all you can give,
But most of all, you learn how to
be free.

Pat Genesi
WHY FROWN
You look upon a smiling face
That holds great happiness there
And wish that you could smile
too
Without a doubt nor care.
You look upon a man you love
And wish his love to share,
But yet defeat rules over your life
And you quit in great dispair.
You see another whose troubles
seem small
And envy their carefree life
And still you say within yourself,
"My way is nothing but strife."
Your life is what you make it—
No other can take your place.
Why frown and say it's useless
When a smile adds beauty and
grace.
Don't envy others their happy
ways,
And all your feelings hide,
But open your heart to better
things
And dismiss any selfish pride.

Keith J. Williams
Early Morning Wilderness
Ivory sleek foxes
scampering
toward the silver wood
to defecate on the damp moss.

Carl S. Kaucher
SPHINX 95
Nightimes and backwards
sleeping
Upon the depths of this city
Filth in layers upon minds
and sinking holes.
All the planets shall be aligned
in singing mortuaries

Last glitter of the sun
and all peace is created
Nothing was ever given life
to go about taking others.
The ship passed thru the night
with stealth and alarm . . .

Awakening W/sun flashing abroad
the tide flows upon echoes
Season changing, Death
rearranging
Bold searchers and mourners
In the pallisides home

or lands far away.

After all nightmares considered
time is still remaining the same
far about this thing of life
a guiding hand to come along
and brings thoughts of wisdom.
There will be no unjust alarm
no reason for harm.

We can seek out the stars
their light burning away my
fears.
We can release them now
We can release them all
Tell us what we're traveling on
on the rivers or the car?
Time is coming from afar

Spread the wings of resourceful
humanities and pray for light from
these ever burning skies. Crafted
and homespoken of traditional
reform
we speak. Tell us what may be
tomorrow
tis time to end the sorrow.

Rita Lubitz
A POET'S RIDDLE
Words
Like tiny jewels
Glitter in my mind.
They flash, shimmer, shine
Float, hover, glide
through the realms
of my imagination
To shape a verse
Exotic, perfect, mine.

My words
Like the blissful raptures
of Dickinsonian magic
Blaze, enchant, enthrall.
But then they flicker
Tease, elude, hide
And fade.

Thus, I
Like the Sphinx
Am speachless.

John H. Ryan
EULOGY
the culture of the ages
an enigma, destined to die from
birth,
never reaching the potential
we need to stay alive.

alpha begets omega
is the one thing mankind's never
learned,
always seeing renaissance
when digression is the word.

mindlessly preserving
the way of life that leads
back to the future
again.

Mike McClain
DEAR MR. YESTERDAY
Dear Mr. Yesterday,
There's so much worth to say
But like I said before
You don't exist no more.

Dear Mr. Tomorrow,
Don't fill the future with sorrow
Pain and hatred I have seen
Show me life has something to
mean.

Today shows no improvement of
the past
And the future of some won't last

So why can't anyone see
That life is meant to be
Subtle and mysterious in its ways
With always something
innovated to say.

Dear Mr. Creator,
I'll meet you later
Whether in heaven or hell
No one will ever tell.

Else E. Mourar
THE VOYAGE
The ship was waiting at the dock
already to embark,
Uncharted seas would be her
course,
The light was turning dark.

White waves kept beating on the
shore,
They set the ship in motion,
Wet fingers pushed the land
away,
From a frothy, sighing ocean.

But suddenly the vessel quivered,
Its engines beating fast,
With a hurried wave to friends
below,
The trip was on at last.

Pina Pugliese
SHE LIVES
They buried her today,
among the cypress trees,
the ones she used to love
when she rocked me on her knees.

I could hardly understand
while standing in the pews,
how the birds could still
be singing while she laid
among those trees.

When the priest's voice was heard,
singing all the hymns she had
loved
so much, it was then with great
surprise
that I felt her tender touch.

Geri Solomon
**The Acquisition Of Other
Identities**
I sit here quiet
and afraid to focus.
The laughter inside me burnt up
and crackling like cellophane—
I search the skin beside my
temples
for cracks,
fissures that point to the
acquisition of other identities.
In the middle of the afternoon
I am startled
by two heartbeats.

Anna L. Nissel
Autumn's Persian Carpet
The winding narrow lanes
Traversed two grand walls
And through the car's window
panes
A senic Persian carpet did enfold
Nature's greatness in Autumn
retold.

Stalwart trees extended to their
uppermost heights
Diverse in their various hues of
darks and lights.
Rich, red leaves consuming the
sun's ebbing ray,
Dark green leaves hoping to
remain that way.

Doleful, yellow ones pondering
what it's all about,
Browns flying and falling with a
hushed shout.

How could one's heart all this
contain
Without expressing in a hopeful
refrain
That when this season's turn has
passed,
Winter, then Spring will come at
last,
With abundant clouds of rain,
To provide the sun's aid again
For wonderous Life's continuation
In a universal beauty of God's
creation.

Marilyn Theresa O'Keefe
GROWING LOVE
[This poem is dedicated to
Joanne and Carol O'Keefe, and
John Harris, for the beautiful
times we shared together in
Colorado. The sincerity,
honesty, and love will never be
forgotten.]
The miles are now between us,
The tears and laughter gone;
The spoken words and gentle
touch
Are memories in a song.

The mornings came and evenings
went,
Each day a brand new start;
But the love that grew can still be
sent,
From deep within my heart.

We shared so much of our inner
core,
And learned to heed and listen;
My love for you opened a brand
new door,
Which in my mind will always
glisten.

The miles don't matter, they are
only a sign,
To make you aware that I had a
great time;
And now I know there's one
thing I can do,
And that is to say, I really love
you.

pav
IT'S SNOWING
It's snowing.

Lots of tiny snowflakes
are being tossed about
by the wind.

Going this way,
then that way,
Everywhere
and
Nowhere,
before being allowed to
land and rest.

Have you ever felt
like a snowflake?

Gina Puskar
IF ONLY
If only we'd tried a little harder
to make our relationship last
If only we'd concentrated on the
present
instead of digging up the past

If only it would be
like it once was before

If only you would stay
instead of walking out the door

If only we wouldn't fight
and make our tempers flare
If only you would love me
If only you would care

Irene Suchta Pacana

Irene Suchta Pacana
MY DAUGHTER
You are "My Daughter" . . . I'm
blessed with a beautiful girl . . .
You are a gem in the ocean . . .
you are a real pearl!
Words cannot describe, the pride
that I feel . . .
Your inner beauty glows . . . it is
for real!
You are my true friend . . . so
honest and loyal . . .
You are a treasure . . . you wear a
Crown royal!
You are "My Daughter" . . . an
inspiration and joy . . .
You can be charming and sweet
. . . you can be a Tom Boy!
I've watched you grow . . . from a
tot to a teen . . .
Those were rewarding days . . .
that I have seen!
The dresses I hemmed . . . and
the hems I took down . . .
In each one you looked . . . like a
queen in a gown!
Your smile brightens my day . . .
you bring out the sun . . .
You make every tomorrow . . .
happy and fun!
Your goals are so high . . . you
will achieve success . . .
The rewards you'll receive . . . are
due a princess!
You are a lovely young lady . . .
so poised and refined . . .
More like a model . . . you have
your peers outshined!
Dear daughter, I wish you . . . a
future that's bright . . .
I wish this sincerely . . . with all
of my might!
I'm very thankful . . . for this gift
from above . . .
Being your mother . . . has been a
"labor of love"!

Melva Hess Calaman
After the June Flood
What is enduring? The river.
The implacable river, lying
motionless in the sun.
Still as the tepid air
Hanging heavily in the

September calm.

The river is there; it *is*.
Enduring in name, also—
Bearing the name of long gone
Indian tribes
Who fished, boated, swam,
endured its whims, as we do.

Could we think of calling it other
than the Susquehanna?
Should the river cease to be,
could we accept the void as
part of living?
Better, perhaps, that, once in
centuries, our placid
Susquehanna
Becomes a turmoil of destruction,
Fills our cellars, drowns our
shrubberies,
Even ruins the workings of a
lifetime.
The height, or breadth, or color,
or stillness
We will abide with. The river. It
is there.

Dorothy S. Handler
BROTHERHOOD
When I was young and full of
zeal,
My heart was fired by a great
ideal;
I dreamed of a world serene and
good—
A world united in brotherhood.

Oh, then, it meant so much to me
To love the folks across the sea;
To understand their rights and
needs,
Regardless of their laws and
creeds.

But, now, I find I care much more
About the folks who live
next—door;
For brotherhood would be so
sweet,
If it could span just one small
street.

George Singfield
REALITY
[To Aldolfo Zier, Nomi Rinke,
Barre', Chris, Tony, And my
best Friend, Rose]
Reality, you bastard!
Whithout you, void, nothingness.
To seek you, a conduit to pain.
To have you, pleasure unlocked,
shared.
To trust you, within——ah!
A search ended.

Edna A. Majors
CYCLES OF BEAUTY
No other month can quite
compete
With October, Summer is now
complete.
The beauty of leaves, beyond
belief
Rampant with color, It's all too
brief.
Then Indian Summer, It's great
we know,
It makes us feel there will be no
snow.
A frosty nip touch here and there,
To tell us all we must prepare
For a winter deep, of snow and ice,
But that don't say it can't be nice.
The Christ child came on a

winter night,
That's enough to say it's good and
right.
Along comes Spring, with her
sunny smile,
She seems to make us wait a
while.
With capturing snow flakes here
and yon,
She makes quite sure they all are
gone.

Brave are the Crocus rearing their
heads,
Heralding Spring from their
winter beds.
Daffodils and jonquils too,
Along with the tulips make their
debut.
It is then the birds break into
song,
We forget the winter seemed so
long.
Oh no, The Summer does not fail.
Some folks pack up and hit the
trail.
Vacation time, picnics galore,
We head for the mountains, or to
the shore.
We may just lounge around and
rest,
But who can say that the
summer's best?
I cannot say, I love just one.
They all are great, they are good
to me.
I thank you Lord. You allow me
to see
Each and every one in their true
perspective.

Alice Reed
**Trees, Do You Not Sleep At
Night?**
Blankets of darkness
Cover you by night
Winds softly, firmly
Urge you to bow,
Silhouettes swaying
Against the mid-night sky
Light rain settling all about
As I watch from my bed tonight

With a sleepy breeze,
Listening to your
Chattering leaves
Branches reaching out
As you curtsy to the
Magic of the night
Is there no sleep for you
Do you not sleep at night

David M. Singer
SILENT MEMORIES
[To my Dad, for whom I have
more respect and love than he
can ever imagine.]
He'd sit at the table, a pipe in his
hand, a watcher, his voice was
not heard. But he listened, he
saw, not a thing got away, and
he'd puff as he heard every
word. I'd look at him, probing,
"Do you know what's been
said?", and in answer he'd
twinkle his eyes. Not a word
would he say, yet an answer
he'd give, and in silence I'd see
he was wise.

When my troubled brow
furrowed, and my shoulders did
stoop,

he would quietly walk to my side. His hand on my arm, his smile in my eyes, he'd open his heart oh so wide. Then his shoulders would droop, as mine started to rise, and his heart sucked my troubles inside. And I'd see by his face, that in aiding me thus, a small piece of him inside had died.

And oh, how he worked, when work had to be done. As a youngster, I trembled inside. "No one can fix things like he can." I'd say, and my heart would near burst out with pride. Well, the seasons have passed, and his hair's turning gray, and he doesn't quite run just as fast. But I love him the same, and I love him still more. Certain things never change. They still last.

I saw him today, at the table, again, and we sat there together, awhile. And we said not a word, but we spoke just the same, though to each we did give just a smile.

Kenneth G. Geisert
THE FLOWERS OF LIFE
[To Marie Cerut]
"Tossing the Die of life,
    Awaiting the tumble of fate,
Amidst happiness and strife,
    A fallen crumb to sate."

"Tears turning to a smile,
    Encompassing an age,
Waiting all the while,
    As a vision to a sage;"

"Free-falling into life's abyss,
    Clinging to a slender thread,
Sharing life's grief and bliss,
    Turning to find our bouquet dead".

Dora T. Smith
DUST
Substance without life—
A drifting waif—
Caught up in a whirlwind
Where nothing is safe.
Dead—wandering, powdered earth
Choking out life.

Miss Renee Convery
LIFE?
Life is like a new bud on a tree,
    growing every day, unnoticed.

Life is like a newborn animal
    that just learns to walk,
    unnoticed.

Life is like a baby bird
    that just learns to fly, free and
    excited.

Life is to others an
    unacknowledged act
    that living is sometimes
    without comprehension.

Henry M. Grouten
MY DEAR
*[To Vanessa, my special "angel",
with love]*
The rain that drops
its splattering wet
on all living things,

and in woods we
walked through
when we met,
is that which quenches
my very thirst,
and this rain that falls
my dear, is you.

The sun that shines
its brilliant light
through the window pane,
near the bed
where we slept and
made love that night,
is that which quides
me to your arms,
and this sun that shines
my dear, is you.

The wind that blows
its gentle breeze,
as we lay beneath
the tree that sheds
its colorless leaves,
is that which swept
me off my feet,
and this wind that blows
my dear, is you.

Gwendolyn Trimbell Pease
GRASSHOPPER
*[Those appreciating my
efforts—Morgan Pease, Lydia
Frick, Bill Cade P.C., Alfred
Saunders, John Persons, Bruno
and Helen Bojanowski and all
others not mentioned.]*
Individual of insect class
summer jumper
perched precariously
upon a blade of grass

unrealistic numbers, huge fuss
farmer's field foe
prodigious production
layer of eggs multitudinous

spitter of tobacco juice
creature feature
cool crayon colors
superb camouflage in continual
    use

existing in this time frame
swinging singing
perfectly preening
until a predator ends the game.

Kim Lutz
There's a Feeling Deep Inside
There's a feeling deep inside me,
    that just won't go away
Sometimes it reaches the surface,
    and sometimes it's tucked
    away
But no matter where it is,
I will always remember, and I will
    never forget
The times we spent together, and
    the times we have but yet.

It may only be in my dreams, it
    may only be in my prayers
that he is here on earth with me
    to stay forever.
I know I am yet but young, but I
    feel I have grown so old.
The loss I have right now may be
    too much for me to hold.

I only have memories to cherish,
    I only have fears to forget
I feel I can't go on, for his

reassurance I do miss.
In all the times we spent
    together, I learned only but one
    thing—
He will not walk beside me
    forever, but life will go on
    without him.
And his spirit and his soul, I will
    deeply treasure.

Franco Buono
Valerina, La Bambina
Valerina, la bambina, cosi bella,
    cosi fina,
Valerina ballerina, bambolina di
    Mamma!
It's one year after you were born,
Full of laughter, bright as morn.
Beauty spots such little dots. . .
Briefest peeks. . .
You turn your cheeks
As fast light, to the left and then
    the right.
La bambina, ah, so bella! You
    begin a tarantella.
Maybe now you start to sing,
I will hear each little thing,
"Coochie, Coochie, Chia, Chia,
    Chia, Ballerina di Papa!
What a joy then to behold
    Valerina one year old!
From your mother's lap you gaze
    while we whisper words of
    praise,
That the dear Lord sent us you, to
    our days such joy imbue.
How we love to watch your
    fingers
Move like dancers, act like
    singers,
Tell us of the melodies you will
    sing one day to please.

Patricia Randall
ELEMENTS OF LOVE
*[To Charles: Remember life
gives only what we place on
file in our hearts.]*
Come be with me.
We will talk.
If you listen,
I will hear.

Come walk with me.
We will move.
If you touch,
I will feel.

Come share with me.
We will learn.
If you receive,
I will be blessed.

Come stay with me.
We are one.
Apart we will only,
Survive.

Samuel Silber
SELF—REALIZATION
If I weren't myself I might have
    been you
And we each could have been
    one another
For we each had nothing
    whatever to do
In choosing our father and
    mother.

If personal choice in some
    marvellous way
Could alter one's state or
    condition,

We'd each be magnificent in
    every way
By changing our genes thru
    volition.

If we all looked the same, felt the
    same, thought the same
And life allowed scant variation,
We'd find all our efforts were not
    worth the game,
For we'd all be mired down in
    stagnation.

So you just be you and let me live
    as me,
Not in fear, hate or mere toleration
But acknowledging we've each
    the right to be free
To achieve full self-realization.

Lloyd T. Deckard

Lloyd T. Deckard
THE ARMY
I was thinking of joining the
    Army. It was on one March day.
Before I sign up, how much do
    you pay?
After you are here awhile, we
    may give you as much as a
    dollar a day.
And with that kind of money,
    you should be able to lay some
    away.
Or you may want to spend it all
    in one day.
Tell the mess sargeant, I would
    like to have breakfast. About
    mid-day.
What time do you get up around
    here anyway?
You will be up at the break of
    day. At 9 PM you will hit the
    hay.
You see that ship sitting out
    there in the bay?
That ship will be taking us to a
    place far, far away.
In about three weeks, we will be
    dropping anchor in Manilla Bay.
If you have time, you had better
    pray for you may never again
    see the U S A.

Charlene "Charlie" Dillaman
THE ANGEL'S VOICE
*[Dedicated to Jesus Christ . . .
to thank Him for the gift of
poetry He has given me, and
the lesson on what it means to
love.]*
It spoke to me last night, outside
    the candy store.
It was a little child who wanted
    love and nothing more.

It blew like a trumpet, a pleasant
sound to my ear.
The laughter of children so close
and so dear.
It was the angel speaking.
It came as a vision to me last
night as I was walking down
the street.
It was the force that kept me
moving when my thoughts
were on my tired feet.
It made such brightness come to
my eyes
That I was like a little child
asking . . . why?
It was the angel gleaming.
It is with us with every passing
moment.
It is so precious, but at the same
time, so abundant.
It is the voice for the person who
is speechless.
It is the priceless picture for the
person who is blind.
It is the eardrum to the person
who is deaf.
It is the kind spoken word to a
lonely person.
It is the visit to a shut in.
It is the recovery to the sick.
It is . . . the gift of Jesus to all
mankind.
It is the angel's gift to us of
loving.

Kathleen Brown
**Today, Tommorow &
Forever**
Times will come and they will go.
Moments are only here, but never
last.
Memories are only a thing of the
past.
Dreams are the future and we can
only hope,
to someday grasp them forever.

Cross Country Runner

Rachel Skidmore Botner
Cross Country Runner
A life begins in tune; mind and
body: a wind of one.

Sparks from silver hairs glance off
and blend, into a sun-kissed
head and land:
They are light and life.

A smile of lyrical joy is pearled,
and a windless day still lifts
the curls placed over unseeing
blue eyes and sky;

His naked leanness ripples across

the desert as the willows
spread wide seeking an unseen
banner;

He runs alone and knows no care
His mind—empty of all that's
been, full of all that is:

The open soul, youth!

Lori E. Hartz
ALONE
*[Thanks to the two very special
people in my life, Barbara A.
Hartz and the late Robert E.
Hartz, for pointing me towards
the road of life.]*
Stepping off a stone,
I'm walking all alone.
I don't know what I'm doing,
I should do it before I'm grown. . .

I'm a seeker of my dreams,
I've had so many to find.
Without a friend to lean on,
I may as well be blind. . .

I'm walking barefoot on the
ground,
I breathe the autumn air.
Things I've never seen before,
I look at and I stare. . .

I never noticed the world around
me,
There's so much I don't know.
There is one thing I know for
sure,
The world has alot to show. . .

I'm walking all alone,
So I never thought of giving,
But now I found the secret to life,
And took some thought to
LIVING.

Christine L. White
USED TO BE
I closed my eyes today,
just for a minute.

What I saw, or rather didn't see,
was a pleasant surprise.

For so long now,
I'd close my eyes, and you'd be
there,
as a reminder of what
used to be.

I still need all the love and the
affection that we had,

but now I know it doesn't have
to come from you;
just somebody Special to me,
like you
Used to be.

Renee' Toomer
EBONY KING
Your skin is dark and smooth
Arms and legs—strong as the
oldest red wood trees.
With dark mysterious inviting
eyes
Oh how I love to be wrapped in
the darken silky
love of the Ebony King.

Your teeth sparkle like stars in a
still winters sky—
King of Kings—Man of men
Gentle yet strong
No man can compare with the
Ebony King.

Your fathers have faught wars
before you—

You shall fight them now, and
your sons will fight them after
you
But—no man shall dominate the
Ebony King.

His enemies shall never know his
kindness
only his fire and fury (What a
shame)
But only a few shall know the
gentleness of the Ebony King.

Diana Franco
STRANGERS
*[This poem is dedicated to the
person I love most; to my
future husband: Joseph A.
Ocasio with All my love, Diana]*
We were strangers who never
would've met
If it hadn't been for a friend.
I can't forget that day,
We soon became friends;
I wished it would never end.
Now we are past just being
friends,
And I just want to tell you where
you stand.
You've got my love in your hands.

When you smile at me,
There's a happy feeling
That comes over me.

I love to see you smiling,
I can always see in it the loving,
The understanding, and the
sharing.

We learn more about each other
everyday,
And I just want to say;
I love you more and more each
day!

We are strangers no longer;
And our love each day grows
stronger.

Jason Budd
WHAT I WANT TO BE
[To My Grandparents]
I would like to be a cop,
But that is too much work.
I'd like to be a Private—Eye,
But for clues I'd have to lurk.
I'd like to be the President of the
good ole U.S.A.
But what's the use, I don't know
politics anyway!!
When I'm a little older, you see,
about 21 is fair,
I think I'll know what I'll want to
be,
a Mulit—Millionaire!!

Brain Lynch Johnson
Whisperings Of Violacium
A small white petal in my hand,
Showing stripes of Nisus' strand
Picked from moss beneath the
tree
But for one, I would not see.
Scylla's reward it will not be.

Cronos, how I owe you much
Allowing me to see and touch
A greater good than Wadsworth's
daffodils.

Though Matins on that day were
none
I knew no harm I had done.
I read a psalm from a living book
Plucked in reverence from

the Cnoc,
Gave my soul its first real look.

The preaching of two thousand
years
Was but a ringing in my ears,
That dwarfed beside my tiny
petal.
The two great books of the
testament
Were alone contained in a single
scent.
A theosopher could not reveal.

And if per chance I touch Lethe
(May it never come to be)
Or find new joy in another thing
Remember you were once the
king
Of all that's good, devoid of sin.

'Twas on the morning of
Ascension Day
I trampled on Elysean clay.

Stuart L. Williams
SCUM OF THE EARTH
He was like the scum of the earth
dirty, torn endless pitty man
No hopes could fill his mind
He was the child in a man's body.
No human element could help
him
for his age was endless
yet his mind and soul were child
like.
He was the scum of the earth
beyond hope
beyond reason
as he stood clothes torn,
toothless, unshaven
waiting with excitement in a
childish manner.
He felt pretty because in his
mind he knew others were
watching and laughing.
He was the clown on display,
he was the scum of the earth.

Edward Duffey
MARGARET
*[To Mary Russell—without her
encouragement this would
never have been written
Love Ed]*
Stately
Lovely
Loving
Desirious
Warm
Tender
Astute
Blue Eyed
Aging
Frightened
Misty
Possessive
Nostalgic
Maternal
Remembered
A woman who gave birth to me

J. R. Welch
The Mount Of Yssandril
As Algol brightens, waxes, wanes,
This star that lights my skies,
My eyes lift to the mountain,
That watches where I lie.

Yssandril, the Mountain—
Of solid Andradite,
That rises toward Heaven,
And darkens as the night.
Yssandril, the mountain—

Whose peak cannot be seen,
Shines aurous in the moonlight,
Invades the sleeper's dream.
Osiris watches over it,
Apollyon, it rules,
Adriadne's ministers,
Drape it with their tools.
Tortured dead drift onward,
Within its arcane halls,
Strains of the Aeolian harp,
Attune their undead calls.
Yssandril, the mountain!
Among whose treasures hid,
The amaranth, the flower,
Whose cost cannot be bid.
And all the gold of Albion,
And twice that of Araby,
Lay buried in its dungeons,
Lost to mortal key.
But the most priceless bounty,
The most jealous, yes, by far,
Was Alcyone, beloved,
Named for the brightest star.
Beloved of Avernus,
She was held by anatheme,
Lay forever guarded,
Forever lost in dream.
Beloved of Avernus,
Who fought with arbalist,
And sword, and iron muscle,
And vowed to strike with fist.
Vowed to beat the mountain,
And claim its sleeping prize,
Beat down its evil demons,
And kiss his loved one's eyes.
With assegai, he mounted,
His steed he set apace,
Across the rocks of Albite,
He commenced the austral chase.
To Yssandril, the Mountain!
Rising from the land,
Portal to the Netherworld,
Where he would seek his stand.
Thunder from the heavens,
The mountain blocked all light,
The cries of dead men reached
  him,
Visions wavered in his sight.
His muscles strained, then failed
  him
His sweat poured from his skin,
Blood streamed to block his
  vision,
The coup came from within.
Yssandril, the Mountain!
Travesty, of Earth!
All of life was stricken at the
  moment of your birth!
Yssandril, the Mountain, with all
  thy tresures hid,
Beautiful Abomination, none that
  reach thee, live.
Avernus, dashed upon the rock,
A spear thrust through his chest.
His soul was demon—swallowed,
Devoured like the rest.
Alcyone lies quiet,
Skin as white as shell,
Tortured by her nightmares,
  where more than demons dwell.
Yssandril, Foul Mountain!
Cold as ice, and wreathed in
  mist—
Death to all within thy shadow,
Hell to all who taste Death's kiss!

MaryLou Doubleday
THE LIGHTHOUSE

In a distance
I could see the tall sleek
  structure with

its lights beckoning ships—large
  and small.

This cylindrical specimen
protects man from nature.

Looking at the light flashing on
  and off
I feel as though I am hypnotised
  and being carried away.

Now
my mind has left and dreariness
  surrounds me.
I am traveling with lightening
  speed from feather—like fairy
  tales to cold grey nightmares.

My senses are overpowered by a
  loud bellowing whistle;
the keeper's warning of dreadful
  weather approaching.

Waves as large as life crash in
  around the house.
The structure does not succomb;
  it stands steady.

Nature is still the grand leader!
  Commanding mankind to heed
  her warning and to obey.

The storm leaves as suddenly as
  it came.

Life resumes.

Windows spring open, birds sing;
ships begin to glide towards
  destinations, sun purrs
  happiness, warm tropical winds
  swoop in telling us all is at
  peace

Nora Raleigh
DREAM FOUR SEASONS

the filled silo
while a rifle raised
follows the flight
for one good shot
by chance allowed
and any morning
the cock crowing
for any evening the low
of milch cows:

four comings
and another year
rolled slowly down
from hilltop
to the shaded
stagnant pond
  where
sightless upturned
pale facades
are supernatant
among closed rank
heartshaped lily pads—
pure waxen blossoms
are companion to a frog
blinking cupid eyes
at careless
winging flies:

everything—in stone
smooth as a caress
upon yet remembered flesh
before farewell
to farmstead address
with elsewhere to go
to symbolize the same
in contradistinct array;

all reserved now
legendary sensibilities
puissantly secreted
in a non existent

geometric solid
one delicately
and rustically
tagged to immortality

since hardly worth
the cube dimension
in a folded newspaper
datelined: "yesterday
the neutrons
invaded."

Billie Louise Parkison

Billie Louise Parkison
My Wonderful Teacher

A very intelligent Teacher, once I
  had
She would not hesitate, though,
  to punish us if we were bad.
There was my Brother Dick,
  Cousin Tom and Neighbor
  John,
If they were a wee bit contrary,
  she would really lay it on.

She taught at this little country
  school, two and a half miles
  from town,
At the foot of a hill where the
  road winds around.
Of all my Teachers, she was
  among the very best,
She gave us alloted assignments
  to study for a test.

Five days in the week she taught
  and sometimes
her lunch with me voluntarily
  would share.
When her work was all done, at
  the setting of the sun—
To her home she would go to her
  mother for to care.

On Sunday morn, she was up and
  about,
When church time came was all
  ready to go out,
To the house of God, and set in
  the pew, so I heard
To hear the Minister as he
  preached God's precious Holy
  Word.

Each year at Christmas time, in
  order to buy a gift for everyone
the whole community would
  have a gathering, and sell pies
  to raise the fund.
After selling each pie, then all
  would eat,
But before we did, would vote for
  the fellow who had the dirtiest
  feet.

Those beautiful days are gone
  forever
We cannot forget,
but still remember what a
  distinguished individual

and a beautiful Christian
  character you were.

Your love for each of your
  students was not denied.
I remember my last day as your
  student, both of us cried!

Mark E. Durand
RAINBOW HUNTER

Intense birth,
Of infinite color,
Daughter of the sun and rain,
Conceived in white light and
  mist.

Primal prism, potted gold,
Beyond his eyes, his reach,
Beyond his horizon,
In the kaleidoscope shadowland.

Searched for, sighted,
The wizardry vanishes,
As he nearly blackens
The pristine spectrum.

Sky flower, a spider's tracery,
Hung on storm's coffin.
Prismatic images beckoning,
Haunting, whispering:

"Hunter, keep stalking me.
But only in your dreams,
Will you ever capture
A rainbow".

Eileen McNeal
TIME

Time is flying, flying, flying, away
Lets make tomorrow a better day
A day of love and gladness and joy
As is the first day of spring or a
  childs new toy

Lets capture a rainbow or swim in
  a brook
Lets go on a picnic or read a good
  book
Lets dance to good music or burst
  into song
Lets camp out all night and
  welcome the dawn

Lets welcome each moment
Lets smile and be gay
Lets make each tomorrow the
  best of today

Yvonne Jester Wallace
TONY'S SONG

*[Dedicated to: My son, Tony
  Wallace, The Jester Family,
  And The coaches in Seaford,
  Delaware]*

Hope of winning dwells in those
  sparkling eyes;
Dedication shows in his strength
  and size;
Determination can be seen in his
  every stride;
His grace mixed with courage
  makes me swell with pride;
He can hold his head up high,
  even in defeat;
For this experience makes
  another victory all the more
  sweet;
Always striving to be ever better
  at his game;
No obstacles can ever reside in
  his domain!

Charmaine Brandt
MEMORIES OF A CHILD

A seed that grew from a moment
  of love,
A seed that had only one goal,
  called love.
'Twas to become a part of

357

something—
Oh so old and yet so new,
'Twas nice to become one! that is
    true.
Now you see a new life it will be
    a new creation,
A part of the now generation—
A new feeling growing inside of
    me,
A new feeling one won't want to
    deny.
It is called a child, this is ture,
But to us it's a part of Love from
    me to you.
A first breath, then a cry—oh
    wow, now I can sigh.
For now our seed has become one
    of the human race.
What Love shall go throughout
    our life,
For this new life will be oh so
    bright.
A child, yes, a new life—
Now watch this love grow and
    watch it close.
For we all know a child can
    fullfill the upmost.
All through sickness and pain—
When in crying and laughing, in
    scolding or praying.
Remember this is your flesh and
    blood,
For was created by your Love.
For now you see, this child will
    grow up and want to look back
    at great memories.
Through all the hard and easy
    times too,
'Twas a part of that Love that
    made me grow to remember
    both of you,
Now memories of baseball, cuts
    and dolls—
All my dirty foot and handprints
    on the floors and walls are a
    memory,
For now you see I'm grown up,
    and love has found a part in
    life for me.
I love you all and pray someday
    my love will be conceived,
And I too will give and bring a
    new life into the world with a
    sigh.
For a child is one of the most
    cherished memories of this
    world;
Love to Moms and Dads
    everywhere.

Frances Kavanaugh Nelson
OUR DREADED FOE
*[In memory of my husband,
Ron—the love of my life.]*
Oh Death, you were our silent
    dreaded foe.
When quickly illness struck, we
    did not know
My love and I how long our
    battle was to last.
In a role so strange the three of
    us were cast.
Month in, month out, holding
    hands we fought.
Oh Death, to win would not be
    your victor's lot.
We laughed, we cried; each hour
    was a treasured jewel.
For us defeat would be so painful
    sad and cruel.
Each new sunrise, each new

serene and quiet sunset
Gave us time to wage with
    strength and win our bet.
We planned each tomorrow, and
    all the things we'd do.
Oh Death, you were stronger and
    had your own plan, too.
You won, and took my love of
    many precious years.
You should have told me how to
    live
With my emptiness
And with my tears.

Janet Marie
LIKE THE EAGLE
*[This poem was written for and
inspired by Mesquakie friends]*
A noble bronze sculpture
    surveying the terra,
Having retreated to lofty craigs
    for many an era, like the eagle.
Knowing eyes view magpies
    fightin' for lore
Leaving spoils for vultures to
    ravage more, defying the eagle.
Soaring higher still retreating,
    seeking a domain,
Swoopin' o'er his land, strivin' to
    be known again, as the eagle.
Comin' with an anquish cry from
    high
Are those who hearken to his
    sigh, like the eagle.
Answering joyfully, sensing
    friend in the tone,
Lingering still, knowin' he's not
    alone, like the eagle.

Merry Lynn Kornegay

Merry Lynn Kornegay
POSSIBILITY
*[To my heart, my life, my
everything, Reid . . .]*
I passed a tall bridge . . .
    a mile or so ago . . .
It would have been easy . . . so
    very easy,
    to tip the scale . . .
        to tip the scale . . .
        and sail . . . .
    Over it's guardian walls
    and into bliss? and peace?
    Perhaps Limbo?

But . . .
    Limbo's better than Hell!
    And, Hell is here, my
children,
    and no where below.
There is no need for us to
conjure
    up devils and Hells

while Earth and Mankind
    . . .exists!
Yes . . . Mankind . . ., my
children,
    You have been duped . . .
    God did not create
        Hadees . . . ! ! ! . . .
    Humans made Hell!!
        and they stoke it up
            constantly
        with their insensitive
            spells.
And . . . my children . . . Perhaps,
    old philosophers were right?
    Maybe Heaven's here, too . . .
The possibility needs only our
    willingness
    to become a reality!!

So what happens
    when we try to escape
    our earthly sentence
        into Heaven . . . by way of
suicide??
We're probabally just recycled . . .
    and spat back
        to this side . . .
    Or puked back . . .
        Retched back . . .
But . . . There'd be a new
    chance . . ? ? . .
        with new options . . ? ? . . It
            could be worse . .
    somehow . .
        There's no way to know
    . . . Of course . . .

Gwen Sweet
MARCH IN MINNESOTA
This morning—
    all the weeds are diamond
        studded
        as they peek out of the snow.
    The sun
        is high in the sky.
    The winds have ceased to blow.

The birds
    are seeking here and there
        for tidbits, seeds or berries

The rabbits, skunks and squirrels
    are making dainty tracks
        like fairies!

All the world has a special glow,
    as I, too, make tracks in the
        snow.

Erva Loomis Merow
ALL FOR YOU
[To my husband, Lloyd]
If I could catch a full moon—
a rainbow,
every star——
and all the beautiful things
there are,
and my love, new——
that would be my Christmas
gift— to you.

Janna Marie Forseth
**It Hurts So Much To Say
Good—bye**
I'll look at a person
    who I'll never see again,
Someone who's close
    and a special friend.

I'm looking and searching
    deep in my heart,
To find the courage and strength
    that's needed to part.

If I look in his eyes

I'm destined to cry,
It hurts so much
    to say Good—bye.

I'll remember the times
    which we both shared,
I'll remember the times
    when I felt he cared.

I'll remember the times
    when we had fun,
But, now those times
    are over and done.

I'll remember those times
    with a tear in my eye,
It hurts so much
    to say Good—bye.

Jay F. Thurston
A DECIDUOUS LOVE
*[I dedicate this poem to my
mother, Mrs. Velma "Miles"
Thurston, whose love is bright
and flourishing.]*
It was Spring and our love
    like the bright new leaves
    sprang forth, grew, and
    flourished.

It was Summer and our love
    like the strong mature leaves
    weathered the rains and windy
    storms.

It was Fall and our love
    like the tired withering leaves
    fell touching the ground with
    silence.

It was Winter and our love
    like the sleeping tree clothed
    in snow
    stood unmoved and cold.

Ella Mae Sanders
HE WILL BE THERE
Time does not wait for you and me.
It passes on—its plain to see.
Its growing shorter year by year.
Still you must listen—and you'll
    hear
HE will be there.

There is no point of fast return.
The candle, both ends, you can't
    burn,
And, though you work,—it all
    takes time
To build those stairs in upward
    climb.
HE will be there.

HE'll give you strength your load
    to carry
If you hold steady—do not tarry.
If you but measure day to day
The deeds you do in every way.
HE will be there.

Nancy E. Kortz
Long After You Have Gone
Long after the warmth of your
    body has faded from the
    rumpled sheets,
Long after the scent of your skin
    has vanished from the morning
    air,
Long after you have left my bed,
Only I will remember you slept here.

Long before you seek the
    pleasures of another woman's
    charms,
Long before you stand proud as a
    father holding your newborn son,
Long before you leave my arms,
Only I will know that we were one.

But for now, I will be content
  gazing upon you as you sleep
And for now, I will be happy
  knowing your love is for me
  alone
For now, you are here with me
And will be, long after you have
  gone

Dean John Schwarten, Jr.
TUNNEL OF LIFE
[To Roxanne. For brightening
  my tunnel to a new life.]
Going through tunnels in the dark
stun yourself and leave your mark
escape to extreme places
bewildering the people's faces

You are born at the front of the
  hole
entering the tunnel with nothing
  to know
your tunnel may be short or long
but the short would not be wrong

Inside a cave suspended high in
  the sky
you want to see outside the try
and succeed in finding the
  tunnel's end
soon you'll see light coming from
  around the bend

The bright light will burn your
  eyes
and you might not see the
  florescent skies
but if you hold on and let it ride
like a ladder you climb, you will
  soon slide

going to run
no more crawling
let's have some fun
instead of walking

Going to swim
no more drowning
the moon is dim
and wolves are howling

There's too much of the same
and we're sick of playing this game
so grab your brain and hold on
  tight
'cause we're going to take this
  magic flight

Nickie C. Hall
LORD! You've Taught Me So Much
You taught me to put my life
  totally in your hands
Because you can do so much
  more with it than I can
You taught me that sometimes it
  is necessary for me to stumble
It is your way of keeping me
  humble
You taught me how to pray
And how to make the most out of
  each and every day
You taught me to depend totally
  on you
And to include you in everything
  that I do
If I can't include you then it's
  something I shouldn't do
You taught me to always watch
  what I say
And to be a good example to
  others in every way
You taught me to trust and never
  doubt
And what being a Christian is

all about
You taught me to love and reach
  out to my fellow man
And to be ready to lend him a
  helping hand
You taught me to honor and obey
And to be thankful for each new
  day
LORD! you have taught me so
  much
What would I do if I didn't have
  you?
Where would I turn for the
  lessons I need to learn?

Virginia Ann Taylor
Tribute To Our Daughter Tina Louise
To our special daughter Tina
  Louise. Her youth is not a time
  of life. It is a state of mind.
You gave us life, you gave us song.
Every home should have a child,
  for there's nothing like our
  little girl
She is soft and sweet and cuddly,
  but she's also wise and smart,
Each day you may think of us as
  wonderful as we are.
We try not to spoil you.
We'll let you know that we'll be
  your friends.
You are a wonderful combination
  of a mind and brain and heart...
For even at a tender age she uses
  all her wiles.
And she can melt the hardest
  heart with just a smile . . .
Some day in the future, if it be
  God's precious will,
That God gives you a Choice
  between Good Things and Bad,
The choice is yours . . .
God leaves that to you!

John Glover
Helping Others Help Themselves
It's only right to
Helping others help
themselves do good things
Then wrong help your city life
With care
Joint action in community
Service and job corps
Join with us
Thanks to you and me
For love humanity.
Helping others help
Themselves do good things
Then wrong help your city life
With care
Joint action community
Service and job corps
Joins with us
Helping others help
Themselves
A team that works.

Lori F. Dowell
BLADES OF GRASS
Oh how we loved
And picked each blade of grass
And kept it for that nevertime
  that seems like times away;
Gently scratched the surface of
  something new and free;
Telling all the answers before we
  knew the questions or what
  was even there;
Re-creating all the living in each
  day.

Then sometimes back around we
  found
That they had slipped away.
What was it I was going to tell
  you?
Something I forgot or maybe it
  was never meant to be.
The hours steal by.
Something echoed back then and
  on its second time around
Decided to stop and leave for me
Tears in my eyes,
Falling on the grass to mix in
  with the dew;
Hear the new grass sigh?
Evidence of cherished moments
  reflected in the skies
Where I gaze often now,
  expecting to wake up
And find that I'd been dreaming.
Searching for that something I
  forgot,
Longing to go back and looking
To the sun for some meaning.
Memories disappear, blades of
  grass fade and die
But I go on dreaming.

Hilda M. Jordan
HANDS
[This Poem is being dedicated
  to Tanya Jordan, Angela Jordan,
  Henrietta Jordan and Tammy
  Jordan. There is a special
  dedication to "Walt Disney
  Characters and Productions."]
Everytime I hold someones'
Hand

I dream of "Disneyland"

Everytime I hold someones'
Hand

It must be "Fantasyland"

Everytime I hold someones'
Hand

I'l be playing in the "Band"

Everytime I hold someones'
Hand

I'll be riding on the Subway

Everytime I hold someones'
Hand

It's a "Grandstand"

Bess Temme
LIFE
It seems like only yesterday
That in my prayers each night I'd
  say,
"Dear Lord, please let me be old
  and gray
Before my Mom and Dad are
  taken away."
A lot of living and years have
  gone by
Yet, somehow, I thought they'd
  never die.
But the hour and the moment
  finally came
When the first of the two the
  Lord finally claimed.
My Dad was so full of love and
  life
Even through some desperate
  times of strife.
"So what is it all about," I ask,
As I sift through so many
  memories that it almost
  becomes a task.
At first it's only scrapbooks and
  stories

Certainly, not a "gold-paved" road
  to glory.
But then I see that the past and
  the present
Are truly the future, of which I'll
  be the resident!

Helen LeVan Modricker

Helen LeVan Modricker
I MISS MY MOTHER
[I dedicate this poem to my
  mother, Mary E. Modricker
  Head Proofreader, Alpine Press
  Inc. 289 Congress St., Boston
  Mass, and Editor Stratford
  Publishing Company, for 45
  years.]
I miss my mother, kind and true
And no one else will ever do.

I miss her smile and tender ways
I miss her voice and words of
  praise.

I miss her kindness and her love,
Her arms around me—dainty
  gloves,

Her pretty hats, blue dresses too,
Her stylish coats and Red Cross
  shoes,

Her permanent! Her new coiffure!
I miss my mother. I miss her!

I miss my mother's rare perfume.
I miss my mother's sweet
  proofroom.

I miss my mother. It is true!
So, to my mother—God bless you!

Gene Skayer
THE RIFLE SPEAKS
Jam in my breech the clip of death
  I'll gobble up each round
As you pull on my trigger sir.

By bore they will be wound
I'll spit them out and they will
whiz
Eclipse the speed of sound.

They'll race through their
trajectory
In search of man or beast
They hunger for the living flesh
And when they strike they'll
feast
Upon the life that wants to live
Upon the great and least.

They'll bulge the eyes and let the
blood
Tear muscle, splinter bones,
They'll draw the sweat and fill
the air
With panic cries and groans,
They'll leave them crippled up for
life
Or leave them cool as stones.

Yes sir, I was invented by
The kind I fill with dread,
On battlefields, by many gross
I've lain beside the dead;
I am an implement of death
But don't blame me—the lead!

Molly Darlin'
SQUIRREL SEASON'S OPEN
*[Dedicated to Larry: without
your inspiration this poem
would still be written only in
my mind. In years to come may
we both look back and smile
when we read this "nutty" little
poem!]*
What is the fascination that lures
my man away?
It's just three simple words his
buddy has to say!
He runs around and grabs his
things, while I just sit here
copin'.
You'd think the world was gonna
end, "squirrel season's open"!

What is the thrill and splendor
that wells up in their hearts.
To make them act so crazy, when
squirrel season starts?
He never acts this happy when
he comes home to me.
I guess I'll just start wearing fur
and live up in a tree!

Barbara Jo Johnson
SURVIVAL
Everyone is different
Except for the beginning and the
end,
We all enter life
not knowing,
What is to become of us.
We live each moment carefully
We dare not make one mistake
For just that one
could mean the end.
Colors are so different
everywhere we look,
The world changes so easily
we dare not miss a thing.
People come and go
leaving images to linger in our
mind.
Survival is what's left for us
For we, are like a grain of sand
Fighting against the wind,
I'm against you
You're against me,

Together our death shall come
Only to take us into an unknown
land.

Gloria Jean Morse
PRECIOUS BUTTERFLY
My eyes saw only you, as you
floated by so gracefully, wings
extended, colors more beautiful
than I have ever seen.

Your dance enchanting upon the
wind, your splendor
overwhelming, I ran as you
flew, I must keep up, I must be
near you.

Onward you flew, as if I did not
exist, for I was doing all against
your wish.

Tired and weary, giving up on the
chase, a soft pink rose petal
was your resting place.

My desire for you was more than
I could understand, I reached
out and held you in the palm of
my hand.

Your wings lie back in a
motionless state, your freedom
was gone, death was your fate.

Tears I then began to cry, I loved
you, I killed you, My Precious
Butterfly.

Patricia G. Wilbur
HOUSEGUEST
The Termite is a hungry beast
Upon my house it makes a feast;
My house is gone but still it
labors,
How come it doesn't eat my
neighbors?

Patricia G. Wilbur
Thoughts On a Mountain
From the high mysterious Pali
Where the island meets the sky
Sits the ancient goddess Kali
Gazing sadly from on high,
As she sees her island people
Toiling hard beneath the sun
On the land that has been stolen
From their fathers, one by one;
Once a Proud and mighty people,
Owning all this glorious land,
We welcomed many strangers
And gave all a friendly hand;
But those who came were greedy
And they coveted our lands,
They took this place to be their
own
And ruled with iron hands:
And our lovely, laughing people

Now had nothing left to do
But to toil for gain of others
And work their whole life
through.
The goddess waits, the mountain
waits,
The bloodless war is done,
They wait to see if one shall rise
Beneath this island sun
And give back to our people
The courage and the pride
To claim their ancient heritage,
This land so green and wide.
Where is the golden warrior
Who holds the islands' fates?
From where the mountain meets
the sky
The goddess Kali—Waits!

Dorothy Rose Gottstine
THE SOUNDS
*[I dedicate this poem with love
to my husband Bill, and my
children Linda, Billy, Jimmy,
and Ricky.]*
I hear the sounds of crying, little
children starved and weak . . .
Their bodies only skeletons, their
faces sad and meek.
I hear the groans of the innocent
...the ones caught in between...
The people who wanted only
peace, now defeated can be seen.
Next the sounds of hatred, of
shouting lies and threats . . .
Each man gets in a little deeper
...who's left to pay the debts...
All this is from the main sound,
the battle cry and bombs . . .
The sound of self destruction . . .
echoes and resounds.
Last there is the sound of me, my
conscience and my mind . . .
I know I must do all I can . . .
but first courage I must find.
Courage to face the sounds I hear,
deep within my brain . . .
Till I can say it's my fight too . . .
what really will I gain?

Pauline Carbone
MY BEST FRIEND
Pals forever, pals till the end,
That was our slogan or was it just
then.
As we grow older and days go by,
I find myself asking why?
Why my friend do you seem to be
drifting away?
I thought you were here, here to
stay.
Come back my friend don't lead
astray.
Come back my friend for just one
more day.
Little did I know, for it was the
end;
For this is the last of my best
friend.

Dawn M. Greaney
MEMORIES OF YOU
Today was the first day
since you went away
as I cried myself to sleep
the memories of you ran deep.
I thought of all the times that we
had
of both the good and the bad
and I wish you were with me now
for I know I will love you forever.
I remember it was love at first sight

and I remember our first kiss
but I also remember that terrible
fight
for it was only last night
and I know now
that never again will I hold you
tight
and kiss you good night.
Today was the worst day of my
life
for we are no longer together
and as I cried myself to sleep
the memories of you ran deep.

Cindy Weizenegger
A CHILD IS BORN
Your child is born,
Held cradled in your arms.
A mother's instinct
Is to protect from harm.
To raise your child
From birth to adult.
And try to explain
What life's all about.
You try to love equal
Whether one child or three.
But at times you will find
It's hard for them to see.
Then the day comes
When your children are grown
They go out in the world
And have families of their own.
Now you are Grandparents
Proud as you can be.
Your children have added
To the long family tree.
And it's the love you gave them,
From deep within your heart,
That put them in this world
And gave them a start.

Anne Wynn Grantner
THE CORSAGE
New love rings my bell tonight
I must smile, be gay,
Praying that my laughter drowns
Old love's sobs away.

Flowers sent to celebrate
May they play their part
Tied with bows, unlike the shroud
Wound around my heart.

Let the music loudly play
Mid the dancers' din
Shutting out the mournful cries
Of the requiem.

Helen Brown Vendeville
JUDGEMENT OF DECISION
It is said:—(Quote)
"Don't put off till tomorrow,
What you can do today."
Well, what I intended
to do,
And Pushed away—
I've discovered—;
It's nice to borrow
A little "Time"
Till then.
Oft' times a judgement
Or decision,
Is better,—wiser,—
When thought about
Over—
And
Again.

Guiseppe Lauritano
CAROL PENA
I am a beautiful
girl,
why should I not
reflect my physical beauty

in my mind?

Am I ugly or am I an amorf?
Am I alive or dead?
None of it I am, I am
alive,
I am a beauty
and my feelings are a copy
of my physical body.

I am great and I feel
a lot of greatness, I feel the Nature,
I feel the Cosmos,
I feel the supreme
Life!

Mary LaRue
NE'ER SAY ADIEU
*[To Mike, who gave me the
courage to be myself.]*
The light I see when I gaze in
your eyes
Is a symbol to me of your caring.
When I think of you, I heave
many sighs,
And I find I'm no longer
dispairing.
If not for your kiss nor your
sweet caress,
Then your beauty of thought
would I cling to.
I gladly would give all that I
possess
If only we two would ne'er say
adieu.
The life that you give me is all
that I need
To sustain me through day and
through nighttime.
When something's awry, for you I
do bleed,
By you I shall stay for eternal
time.
My love for you for you entwines all
heart and soul,
When you're not here, I am no
longer whole.

Janet L. Evans
The Very Best Of Friends
To find the words to tell you
What our friendship means to me.

Would be like counting all the fish
That live out in the sea.

Or all the grains of all the sand
That lay upon the beach.

Or counting all the stars that
shine
So far above our reach.

But this I know and this I say
To you my very good friend.

I value high our friendship
And pray it never ends.

Christine Mason
FACES
Some faces we show to a certain
degree
To nearly everyone we see.
Some we keep all to ourself
Like a priceless vase upon a shelf.
The shallow ones we show to all
For what they say is very small.
They only show the very exterior
Careful not to reveal the interior.
They're the ones that frown or
smile
According to what's in style.
They're the ones that never
impress
They only talk foolishness.

They seldom touch what is real
They never show what you feel.
They take care to only expose
The trivial you wish to disclose.
So we are careful to always weigh
Every single word we say.
Hoping most will never ask
That we remove our precious mask.

Gloria Sketo Young
THE OLD OAK TREE
*[In Loving Memory of Otis
Williams May 28, 1912—
August 30, 1977]*
I stood beneath an old oak tree;
how tall it did seem.
Its branches would shelter me as
on its bark I would lean;
as I lay beneath its cooling
branches I would tell it my
troubles and my dreams.

It was summer in my life, and oh
so busy I was;
to notice its weathering branches;
to notice the tree I loved.

Soon the leaves began to change
and bake upon the ground;
red, yellow, orange and shades of
golden brown.
The old oak tree was dying; from
its branches the birds did not
sing,
for snow was now drifting and to
its branches did cling.

As death comes and takes us away,
so it did with the tree that day.

When spring began to visit the
earth once again,
and flowers were blooming
everywhere,
I decided to take a walk
and visit the tree I knew wasn't
there.

The hillsides were blanketed
with shades of mellow greens
and I stood alone; just God, the
flowers and me in my blue jeans.

As I stood in the midst of dancing
colored flowers,
my eyes began to swell with tears,
for growing next to the stump of
the old oak tree
was a twig that would be grown
in a few more years.

The sun began to warm the sky
and by that twig I did lie,
telling it my troubles and my
dreams;
just God, the twig, and I in my
blue jeans.

Margaret Mary Dowling
MORNING SYMPHONY
*[Dedicated to those I am loved
by, parents: Fenton and Betts,
family: Frankel's and Dowlings
and to my friends the world
over enriching my life and for
life itself, my Creator.]*
intermittent bursts of sunshine
the birds bask in the warmth...
smatterings of soft spring showers,
joy lurks around the corner
and just outside my back door.
wind chimes tinkle in the
wafting breezes
beauty abounds this easter
morn.

a new hope as one door closes
and a window yet barely open...
that challenges my spirit to
renewal:
to take the lemon and from it
make "aid"

not a sound now is there, only
the wind up clock on the wall
even it needs love & care . . .
for without the key . . . time will
not be told.

Thomas Nicholas Tanzi
FIRST TIME DEFINED
*[To my lovely Laurhha Marilyn
Ann for her inspiration; I love
you all the time.]*
Time like a note in a bottle
sails an endless cosmic sea
From the Lover's heart a message
drifts
in venture to find Thee
Where space be without and as
much be within
there's an island in light and dark
Where dreams are born 'bout the
new day's morn
and the journey awaits on an ark
With yesterdays' way we cannot
stay
Time gone we cannot borrow
Tomorrow, my wife, the time of
our lives
and the tide kisses the shore with
the bottle
And because of the note this poet
wrote
a "thanks for you and me"
and the truth be revealed
as the words be unsealed
"Here comes eterntiy"

Eleanor Ann Denison
TO -.-.
Into my life
Like a cloud of light
Out of a dawn that was
Veiled with mistsm
Endless and sullen
You came—now
"One and one make one"—
Unalterably.

Anna M. O'Neil
PISCES ARE DREAMERS
"Pisces are Dreamers" (or so I
have heard)
And I've found there's no reason
to doubt those three words.
For I am a Pisces, a fish in a
stream.
I'm lost in a sea of impossible
dreams.

I'm always dreaming of skies that

are blue.
I'm always waiting for the sunrise
of new.
It's always tomorrow, never today.
I'm waiting and wasting my
whole life away.

"Pisces are Dreamers" I've always
been told.
So quiet and gentle, yet in their
dreams bold.
Scared to face facts, like the
sometimes gray sky
And scared to leave water, for
fear they will die.

"Pisces are Dreamers" and now I
know too
That life isn't happy, and dreams
don't come true.

Thomas J. Russell
THE RUSSELL OF AUTUMN
Farewell to a trembling
of branches.
Leaves of autumn
discending in mirth.
A gather of colors
impatient,
To be dancing in joy
on the Earth.

Awaiting in anxious
confusion,
For breezes of winter
to blow.
Woodwinds are warming
with fingers,
And strains of the strings
are a'glow.

At last with a gush,
and a gusto,
The music begins
with a crush.
The dancers dash into
the movement,
They twist and they twirl
and they rush.

Their story is sweet—
sometimes somber.
Their tale is a winter
of woe.
Their dreams in the leisure
of summer,
Will end in a layer
of snow.

Dana Helms
FROZEN MOMENTS
trees silhouetted
on a drifting sun
the best time of day
when thoughts
run free
clock ticking on the mantle
fire warming body and mind
and for awhile
time has stood still
holding your hand

Richard H. Benedict
OVERSIGHT
To Parthenons those meanly wise
will mount
Dabbling acid down from their
righteous fount.

In Nam, to numerous myopic
ones,
Towered our foes o'er jungle,
unsoiled knights;
While our lands monstrous ants,
mired myrmidons—

Yet none else asked to serve to
 greater heights:
No greater hearts than fought
 inglorious war;
No greater duty, shame in many's
 lights;
Aches for home the wage; for
 some no payments more,
In death grudged dear. Yet
 scorned were those who
 cheaply bled,
Less by shrapnel's ounce, assayed
 to abhor;
Scorned that finger's squeeze
 burst past quick-duck'd head—
By inches many missed least
 eulogy,
Nor taps for them, save for
 illusions dead:
A heart slash short for human
 sympathy,
For men long home, boys scarred
 deep in memory.
No home lamps dimmed saw
 terror in their stare .
Through jungle groping: in dark
 they didn't count.
Their monument murmurs lowly
 'twasn't fair?
Or screams to skies a nation's
 conscience mired there!

Joseph F. Cruz
Miraculously, It's Nature's Way
She struts in such a gentle sway
As a peacock on a summer's day
Each stride is taken so attentively
As she walks so intensively.

She flaunts with all her physical
 change
To no extend or certain range
Slowly it rises with such
 contentment
She exhibits no resentment.
Each day she lives in mere
 confidence
Throughout each and every
 grueling pain
The growth she feels deep within
 her
Has given her strength again.
Only they can experience the
 glamour they share
Each and every gladsome day
The moments they wait as time
 draws near
Miraculously, it's nature's way.

Lorene Beeler
THE TWO SWORDS
The trial was over
And an angry crowd
Marched up the hill to Calvary . . .
Shouts went forth—they cried,
"Crucify Him," (an innocent one
Who knew no sin) . . .

They nailed Him to the center
 cross,
On either side—two thieves.
He bore the sins of all the world,
And as they mocked Him,
Some did grieve.

Then came a Roman soldier,
And with a gleaming sword,
Pierced Him in His side . . .
Blood and water did pour forth
And the day became dark as He
 died . . .

They brake not His bones
But on this hour He died!
Gathered 'round Mary, His mother
Were family and friends . . .
And a sword did surely pierce her
 heart
As she watched her Son, Jesus,
 die on
That cruel cross!

E. Deloris Mc Lemore
BOREDOM
A subtle nonentity—
Moves with retentive vigor
Within the realm of an unarmed
 captive
Who inertly succumbs to each
 lethal touch.

It emits a mass of torpor
And creates the being alike one
Having drunk from the waters of
 Lethe.

Consumed by a nebulous maze
The entity—alas ceases to be
But one more subtle nonentity!

Nicholas Franco
Loneliness With Company
Loneliness in itself is hell.
Without someone there to tell
What you want to do with life.
No one to tell about love or strife.

But what about those to whom
 you speak
When you have something
 special to say,
Yet interrupt and say, "Maybe
 next week.
I don't feel like conversing today."

Would you rather speak to
 someone who won't hear
Than to nothing that lurks about
 so near?
I think if no one will give ear,
Then definitely no one should be
 near.

Yes, loneliness is having no one
 with whom to converse.
Yet, loneliness with company is
 by far worse.

Robert M. Walden, Sr.
THEY'LL NEVER FORGIVE
*[Dedicated to: The cigarette
manufacturers; To tobacco
growers, and to our legislators
who see fit to subsidize
tobacco, that the society might
pay before, during, and after
being poisoned.]*
When loving your neighbor as
 yourself
Is preceded by greed for greater
 wealth;
It causes your name to be
 classified
As a waste of time to the one
 who died,
That your name might be in the
 book of life
As one who caused no pain or
 strife,
But on your way to greater gain
You caused so much misery and
 pain,
So, that the grave is full of eyes
 that stare
To see how much, that you don't
 care

For the voice they lost, or
 amputation
Of limbs because of poor
 circulation;
An angina pectoris, or cancered
 lung
In your drive for wealth is
 nothing but dung.
Does your conscience hurt, or
 your black heart yearn?
Toward those hooked while the
 cigaretes burn;
And bodies polluted with
 nicotine
Are crippled, and broken with but
 one dream
To be free of your poison, and
 cleanly live
For what you have robbed them;
 they'll never forgive.

Christine C. Aubert
THE WAITING
The man was waiting for the
 train to come.
 There were several
Other people there, and the train
 was late.
 It was starting
To get very cold, although it was
 no longer snowing.
The people began to mill about for
 warmth, as well as
In semi-impatience over the
 lateness
 of the train.
An old woman was bundling a
 package very close
To her body. While it could have
 been a child she was

Wrapping with so much care, with
 so much love, it could have been
A bottle, too. It did not really
 matter; it was hers,
And, she was protecting it. A child
 somewhere began to sob
From the cold, and its mother to
 console it. A couple
Of people were reading pamphlets,
 and one or two had an
Old book that had somehow
 survived
 the holocaust. The old
Books were very rare, and it was
 usually the more
Learned people who were able to
 obtain
 them, and who
Had the knowledge to read them.
 These
 people surely did not
Appear to be overly learned. Yet,

their badges were
There, clearly in sight: they were
 allowed to have and read them.
And, so they did, both envied and
 pitied
 for the privelege.
Fascinated with their clinging so
 stubbornly to their
Privelege, he sighed, and shivered.
 The
 train had not yet arrived.

Paula Iwamoto
A DROP OF SALT
A drop of salt
from the sea,
As it made its way down
Crevasses of facial flesh
And fell down in muted drops,
Wetting tidy clothing.
Still they fought
to pass against closed lashes,
To join their fellows.

And still another drop of salt,
Sprung from a different source;
This one a vivid crimson
And swelling forth
from pale flesh
Where a wild pulse beat.

Yet both born
of the same sorrow,
of the same futility,
Both silent decoration
to the same ultimate scene.

E.M. Riddle
THE WHEEL GOES 'ROUND
Happenings of now,
Happenings of then,
Happenings that will be,
As the wheel goes 'round.

Reactions of one,
To the actions of another,
All encompassed together,
As the wheel goes 'round.

Growing and changing,
Things are not as before,
Nothing remains untouched,
As the wheel goes 'round.

The happenings of life go on and
 on,
Through the trends and such,
All will continue as before,
As the wheel goes 'round.

Rosalie Ann Ceselsky
WHILE I STILL LOVE
I know it's hard
To say good bye
When love is in
Your heart,
But to stay and live
Thru all this pain
Would tear me
Right apart.
So I'll say good bye
While I still love
Cause I'd never want
To hate you.
I'll say good bye
With memories of
How much I really
Love you.

Janice I. Merritt
SINCE YOU'VE BEEN GONE
The days are slowly drifting on,
One by one,
Since you've been gone.

Oceans of tears,

The counting of time,
Since you've been gone,
They've all been mine.

Memories are all I own,
And my heartache's grown,
But time still goes
On and on
Since you've been gone.

Soon you'll be here,
With me holding you near,
A time for getting on,
Doing the things we'd have done,
Had you'd never gone.

Joseph P. Kowacic
VIGNETTE
[For Chrissie]
There was a girl
sitting on a stone,
surrounded by blossoms,
She was playing
with her hair . . .
and waiting.
Willows moved
lissomely about her.

Was she . . .
or was she waiting for . . .
Spring?

Eileen Kenney
STRESS
*[To My Children With Love
and Prayers]*
When Trouble comes
As it's bound to do,
Don't give up Hope
Just Follow Thru—
Give your work a
Little more Care,
Offer up a Silent Prayer,
Don't be afraid

To crack a Smile—
For your neighbor
Go that Extra Mile,
Evening finds you
Refreshed, Relaxed, so at Peace
It's Colossal!
You feel the Lord near
And you hear—
(WELL DONE, MY APOSTLE)

Sandra Gresham
Lost Without Your Love
Just lying here thinking only of
you,
Remembering all the fun things
we always used to do.
For some love is easy, For others
its hard, but for us love is
always something new.

Love is confusing, Life is a mess

all of my dreams shattered
beyond helplessness.
Just as I thought and I always
knew, that one of these days I
would lose you too.

All of my tears so softly cired,
All of my hopes shattered and
died.
I wish I could feel the happiness
as before, but it doesn't feel
like it used to anymore.

Stanley Alan Cassaday
MOM AND DAD
*[Herman and Violet Cassaday
the greatest Parents a Son
could ever have.]*
Thank you Mom and Dad
For being my parents,
This makes me glad.
Now it's time for me to share the
love for you
That's always been there.
It's just to bad that with my own
busy life
I've been too selfish to let you
know and share
The love in my heart that tells
you (I care).
For all those times
I made you doubt
I thank you for your faith that
has made me grow
With love—and not hate
You taught me no matter how
rich or poor
I might be
You would be there to set me free.
You taught me about God and his
Blessings
But never once mentioned His
greatest Blessing
The blessing of having parents
like you
Helping me to realize the beauty
of life is that of Giving.

Jonna Lynn Steinbrunn
THINKING
*[I would like to dedicate this
poem to my family. Especially
my mother and father, who
have guided me through life,
and who I love very deeply.
Words cannot express my
thankfulness towards them.]*
I sit alone
in the dark
just thinking.
I don't know what about,
It's all so confusing;
Thoughts of different things,
Life, love, hatred
It all surrounds me,
Maybe if I just keep thinking,
Here in the dark
all alone,
I can find a solution
to my thoughts.

Debra Stanley
SHY
Shyness is an ego problem I read
somewhere today.
I didn't understand at first what
the person was trying to say.
But as I read further the point
became clear;
A shy person's problem is one of
great fear.
Fear of what people will say when

they speak
Makes them hide in silence
because they are weak.
Too weak to come out of their
self-centered shell
And show the world all they have
to tell.
Being shy myself the person
really made me wonder—
Am I so afraid of making a
blunder
That I keep all my ideas and
thoughts to myslef,
Putting them all on a neat little
shelf?
If I could forget myself and reach
out to others,
I wouldn't have time to be shy
around others.
Shyness doesn't have to be a
problem anymore
Once you take time to open the
door
And share all you can with
people you know
And forget your own shyness to
help others grow.

Ed Hughey
LOVE
*[This poem was written in
memory of—and inspired by—
my beloved sister, Verdie. She
gave us her love, while sharing
with us her life. She was an
inspiration to everyone that
knew her.]*
A good love takes thinking
through. And living with
True love can be seen in many
lights. It is a special gift
Love may be experienced in a
word, a knowing look, or a
quiet walk
It can be an experience of a cozy
feeling from a heart to heart
talk.

Love can be committed to a little
time of sharing joys
Love is never to be played with
like a child's small toys
Love in marriage shares rewards,
pains, and frustrations
Bases to making it work are trust,
honesty, and communication.

Genevieve R. Erwin
THE ASCENSION
The Lord is in His Holy Temple,
He has risen in glory today;
The shadows of the cross have
vanished
And, humbly, we kneel down to
pray.
For wicked and kind, the great
and small,
He bore His grief and then rose
again;
He smiled through pain and
bowed His head
Then ascended in splendor up
into Heaven.

Reba Bynum Bell
SUMMER TIME
Time has stripped away the night
The sun climbs forth in day time
flight
She baths the earth in summer
rays
There's heated nights and

heated days.

The mercury climbs to one
hundred ten
It's not been this since; who
knows when?
I hope to God this isn't Hell
But in this heat it's hard to tell

I shut the windows and the doors
Turn on the fan, do inside chores
I tend my yard at crack of dawn
Pick up the sticks and mow the
lawn.

I do my best to tolerate
A season that I dearly hate
I am resolved not to complain,
But how am I to bear the pain?

Of all the seasons I'd omit
I'd pluck this out, I'd make it quit.
If I could choose for anything
I'd wish it were Eternal Spring.

Lisa Surbrook
OCTOBER '81
I love you enough
to make sacrifices
in my life.
You love me enough
to accept those sacrifices.
But not enough
to make any.

Funny how
feelings you no longer
wish to admit
Are feelings
you say
you no longer
have.

Ethel Hunt Street
MY FOOLISH HEART
I have loved you all these years
    My foolish heart asks why
And I haven't any answer
    All I can do is cry.

My foolish heart, it tells me now
    You have no love for me
That I'm just a piece of driftwood
    That you cling to when need
be.

I know I've wasted all these years
    Of love and hope and prayer
On a man who has no faith in me
    Who doesn't even care.

You have not forgotten me
    My warmth and my caress
And my foolish heart still tells
me
    That I gave you happiness.

My foolish heart keeps telling me
    To try and understand
They'll come a day when you will
wish
    You could but touch my hand.

And so the road of life goes on
    But just beyond the bend
Our foolish hearts will be no
more
    And that will be the end.

Loretta J. Lombardi
BLUE PORTRAITS
Blue striped dishcloths
Embracing mom's mouthwatering
Pizza and Italian cream birthday
cake.

Blue lips
Dad dead at forty—five . . .
devestation.
Sorrowful, sleepless, silent spaces.

Blue frilled cotton dress
Perched on a French Provencial
  Peacock chair
Spotlighting grandmothers soft
  silken smile.

Blue faded jeans
Carefree California days
Love of Life fragrances
  intoxicating me.

Blue sapphire
Wheel of 84 parachuted me to
  earth
Molecules of maya now
  undergoing analysis.

Blue Midterm and Final Booklets
Describe in detail Walt
  Whitman's celebration of life.
Dry martinis at Hallahan's Bar.

Blue Light
Third Eye found, hear the sound.
Soul slipping onto the Inner
  Plane.

Joan A. Delp
**Prescription For a
Heartache**
It's hard to ward off sorrow that
  we feel when loved ones die.
This burden comes to everyone,
  and grief we can't deny.
This earthly separation that fills
  a heart with pain,
It is a natural function to hurt
  but not restrain.
Take up old associations, ride, or
  walk away the care.
The best medicine for sorrow is
  keep active they declare
Lose yourself in worthwhile
  projects and utilize the brain.
Employ yourself with busyness
  and get started once again!
It is difficult to do this and
  resume a normal life.
But, it is our only answer to
  relieve us from our strife.
Fill your days with creativity and
  thereby shift the strain.
God's spriritual prescription will
  release a heart from pain.
By our faith we have assurance
  that we are not alone.
When they crucified our Jesus,
  His earthly life was done.
Because we do not see Him
  doesn't mean he is not there.
So, when we lose a loved one, it
  helps us to compare.
Their suffering has ended and
  God provides us strength to
  bear!
Our faith allows eternal life to
  those who leave us here.
Our God in His great mercy shall
  release the bond of fear.
Give way to grief, and slowly
  time will help the grief depart.
Trust in God to comfort you and
  heal your broken heart!

Christine Brown
TO BILL
My son you are a teenager now.
It's time to come from your shell.
Take the chance at every turn
  to learn life's lessons well.
To me you are my babe in arms.
My first born, soft and sweet.
I see you with the fuzzy hair

and booties on your feet.
But that is not reality—
in fact you're almost grown.
You have a life I gave to you.
Love was in you all along.
Just be careful with your life.
Enjoy—but don't be foolish.
Take pride in everything you do.
Don't be greedy, harsh or ruthless.
Pick your friends as if you would
  if your life depended on them.
Treat them fair and with respect
and ask for nothing less in return.
Try the best that you can do
in all of life's endeavors.
Put yourself in someone's shoes
to get the best objectives.
Don't be afraid of unknown
    things—
reach out and take a view.
Turn to me in stormy days
and I will see you through.
No matter where a road may
    lead—
wherever we may venture
my love will always be with you;
your life I'll greatly treasure.

Charles H. Logan
A CABIN VIEW
Looking out my cabin door
  I saw strange things occur.
I watched the whistling
    mountain winds,
  Sweeping the path for her.

The leaves were dancing happily
  Like hang gliders, to and fro,
Sailing silently, then softly
    settling
  Near the daisies down below.

I've watched the leaves, but in
    the Spring
  Later, provide the summer
    shade,
Then, turn bright colors in the
    Fall
  And . . . I have watched them
    fade.

Now once again, nature swept the
    path,
  With welcoming winds to my
    door.
Perhaps now she will visit me,
  As she did many years before.

Will snowflakes fall and fill the
    path?
  Then . . . no one shall ever
    find,
That snowbound path . . . and
    the snowbound heart,
  That someone left behind.

Stan Hopton
OF LIFE AND LOVE
*[For B. J. and Sunshine With
apologies for dreams that lay
broken and hope for dreams
that may lay ahead.]*
See the moonlight
through the trees,
see the shadows that it brings.
By the mill I sit alone.
There I learned
of life and love.
  I dreamed a dream
  it told to me
  all kinds of things
  I soon would see.
  The good and bad

we know so well,
The tears of which
we seldom tell.
  I have seen a mother cry
  as she watched her baby die.
  In the tears that stained her
    cheek
  I read the words she could
    not speak.
  I have seen a young man cry
  as he waved his girl
    good—bye.
  In his world of dark despair
  now she is no longer there.
  No one understands him
    now;
  no one seems to care,
    somehow.
  I have seen so many things—
  broken homes and cast off
    rings,
  mourners and a singing
    choir,
  funeral guests in fine attire.
  Ears I have that hear so well
  sounds of laughter, pealing
    bells.
  Sounds of pain, sounds of tears
  sounds that echo down the
    years,
See the sunlight through the trees.
See the daylight that it brings.
From this mill I make my way,
praying for a better day.

Anna Marie Lopez
ETERNITY'S BECKONING
*[To Kevin S. Padilla a very
special person in my life and
Rufus Garcia, my beloved
uncle who recently passed
away.]*
An uncouth fright fills my soul at
times. Vagrant death and the
gray thoughts of aging were
bestowed upon my conscience.

Although I had always been
  nurtured and taught of life . . .
  and death . . .
I was sure the savior had no end
  for me, eternity was to linger.

Melissa McNair
Wish Upon An Unseen Star
If I could have seen a star
I would have wished upon a star
But still no star in sight
So wherever you are
On this wishing night
Here is my wish for you

I wish for more days like today
So that I may find

The happiness and joy that I long
  for
To be forever mine

With unending kindness and
  understanding
To be free to be myself
And to give what I have to give
Freely and uninhibited
So that people who are close
Will know that I care

This is my wish upon an unseen
  star
I only hope that you were near
So that you could hear my wish
And grant this one to me

Marian Kiler Hall
THE SHELL OF LOVE
I held a shell against my ear
And heard its song of the sea—
The roaring of the ocean wild
Was the roar of eternity.

Then you held me in your arms
And I heard the song of the sea—
The roaring of the waves of love
Held our eternity.

Terry Dolin
If I Gave You a Rose
If I gave you a rose, would you
  plant it in the field?
Deep in the ground where the
  roots are sealed.
Sealed from the bitterness and
  the cold.
Sealed from secrets yet untold.

If I gave you a rose, would you
  plant it by the stream?
Then watch it blossom, and sit
  back and dream.
Dream about how great this
  world would be,
If everyone were more loving,
  caring, and free.

If I gave you a rose, would you
  plant it on a hill?
Where the wind moves the grass,
  oh so still.
Still from all the problems of this
  life,
Still from all the pain and strife.

If I gave you a rose, would you
  plant it on my grave?
Put it there and don't cry, but be
  brave.
For when I die, I'll truely be free,
And like the rose, in God's
  kingdom I'll be.

Kimberly Hunt—Strange
Tears In the Spring
Today would have been ten
  months, my love
  April would have brought a
    year
  April would surely have
    brought only more tears
  April would have brought you
    with it.
Now like the poem I write—its
  thoughts and feelings that I
  see. Photographs, letters and
  memories and me.
Today would have been ten
  months
  Could have been and would
    have been, but
April would have brought more
  tears and you.

Byron M. Kellam
A DREAM OF JACKIE
Ah Jackie, how is it still,
In fitful sleep I dream of thee,
And yet recall that comet thrill,
With lips and heart you came to
    me,
As in some sweet inferno we
    flamed,
And blessed the fire that would
    not die,
To infinite heights we gained,
And danced across the rainbow
    sky,
'Till all was spent and nothing
    more,
Of each to the other could give,
As back to earth in tears we bore,
And forever wounded live,
Through our years in cursed
    recall,
A piece of heaven before the fall.

Karen Joon Priem "Joey"
THE LIGHT
[For My Grandmother]
Forgive me . . .
Forgive my past . . .
Forgive my unholiness
in not believing you . . .
For the near future
you will carry me
unto your lands,
the sea, I long to be near
the sun and the boats that
inspire my writing
the people from foreign lands, I
    shall meet
my future life . . . the love for life
    I have now,
Will soon bring me to the death
of finding you, God. —finding the
faith I never had before;
One day in the near future
You will guide me . . . I will see
    the light,
The morning glow,
The heaven and the God. I wish
    to know.

Annie M. Dolan
GOD'S HOUSE
The grass is his carpet,
    the sky is the roof.
The trees are his furnishings,
    the flowers are the decorations.
His people are it's inhabitence,
    and the church their recreation.
So, what else could you really ask
    for,
    but God's House.

Karen Kupp
WORDS
Our form of cummunication.
We use them every day,
Every way.
They express our desires, describe
    our senses all.
Our words that speak of loving
    and caring,
These we bottle inside; hide them
    from view.
Only in the dark and dreams, do
    they come alive.
Yet, words that hurt
And distroy others,
quickly, these come.
They cut, rip, and mangle.
Leaving behind pain, tears and
    unrepairable emotions and
    lives.

How we regret these words.
Will we ever learn?
Life is so short;
Time, people, and feelings,
All to soon are gone.
So let us use our words,
Carefully.
Don't wait until tomorrow:
Say them today.

Helen Lefebvre
The Long White Dress
[These poems are dedicated to
my son, who owns a piece of
my heart.]
Who is that little girl so sweet?
She wears a long white dress.
Reminds me of a bride I knew,
My sons, I must confess.

She can't get married—she's
    much too young.
Must be her Christening day.
Oh, yes, for sure, I see it now,
God's blessings on the way.

She wears her mommy's gown for
    sure,
Her auntie made it small.
Each stitch contains a little love,
Too bad she won't recall.

She wears a bracelet on her wrist
With blue forget-me-nots.
And bows of gold encircle it.
Was saved for such a tot.

God put his hand upon her head,
He put his blessing there.
No need to worry, little one.
You're forever in his care.

Helen Lefebvre
One Year Old Today
We got that call a year ago,
Your grandchild's born today.
A little girl so pink and small,
We thanked the Lord that day.

She started out at Mommy's breast,
Now but a cup will do.
The little bunting fits no more,
She wears a dress, size two.

The tiny booties are put away,
And shoes now take their place.
But diapers stay another year,
Till panties they replace.

The rattles are quiet,
But not thrown away.
A brother or sister,
Will shake them someday.

So blow out that candle,
You did earn the right.
Altho you don't know it,
You've made the world bright.

Paula Barninger
LOVE IS
Love is
    Being happy.
    Having trust.

Love is
    Having someone to share
    your thoughts with.

Love is
    Never being alone;
    Always being close.

Love is
    A journey,
    Not a destination.

Allen D. Smerigan
A TEAR IN MY EYE
[To Janet For My Little Sister In
Honor Of Her Wedding]
Lying here thinking
Of days gone by;
Envisioning memories
With a tear in my eye.

I dream of us
Walking along the shore;
And the look on your face
As I ring the bell at your door.

The days we enjoyed
Although they were few;
Were love filled days
Involving just us two.

These days are gone now
I think as I sigh;
Envisioning memories
With a tear in my eye.

Robin Rogers
RIVER OF TIME
Crystals melting into the promise
    of tomorrow,

While time is reflected in the
    shady pools of the past,

The present is gently flowing
    onward toward the expectation
    of the future.

Anna Flanagan
MY MEMORY BOOK
The pages of my memory book
    are now faded with time.
Images are just barely there,
Pictures of color, are now
    reddish—brown and white.

Yet when I look at them—
The pages are white, the images
    are strong and clear, the colors
    are bold.

When I look again at your picture
    and the words you put next to
    it, it seems I was mistaken—
For your words are no longer
    there and neither are you.

Genevieve R. Erwin
SONG OF AUTUMN
When the joyful days of summer
    were gone
And the busy days of autumn
    were nigh;
Fluttering leaves fell into the
    pond
And overhead we saw an October
    sky.
Over the hills we saw rust, red,
    and gold
And the countryside had turned
    into fall;
This land we thought was

a joy to behold,
This place we loved the best of
    all.
Our thoughts turned then to
    autumn ventures
And our lives were busy every
    day;
At Hallowe'en we loved our
    playful capers,
We did things in our own loving
    way.
We learned many lessons at
    Mama's knee
And Daddy was there to guide us,
    too;
We learned joy as well as
    humility,
We learned to be respectful and
    true.
The joys of home will linger long
And the memory of the red and
    gold;
Within our hearts will be
    autumn's song
Even when we have grown very
    old.

Larry Douglas Chappell
HEART'S DESIRE
Although the storm
Had darkened the day to night,
There still shone
A light, ever-bright,
Which to some is known
As that special star
Called heart's desire.
It isn't part of any cluster
That someday may die.
It has its own special everlasting
    luster—
Whether shining from the clouds
    or the sky.
So, when you feel lost
In dreams abound,
Do not forget, fret or toss—
Know always, this star is still
    around!

And, if you're caught in a
    typhoon,
You don't need the strength of a
    shogun
Or the wealth of a tycoon.
With faith, just look towards
    heaven and the sun,
Right up there, just right of the
    moon.
And, you'll find it there—
The answer to your prayer—
Your own special star
Called heart's desire!

Sandra Derr
UNTITLED
As each and everyday passes,
You mean less and less in my life.

Given the time and the power,
I will forget you.

But until that day shall come,
When to me you mean nothing
    but a friend,

I will still love you.

Mark Joseph Sloan
ON MEETING A FRIEND
A newborn redwood sprout
Glistens when touched by early
    morning dew,
But under heavy rains
It strains to stand so tall and
    proud.

Tired and worn it weeps
downward
In a graceful swoon, a silent
response
To such unrelenting forces.
And once the humid air has
hovered away,
The tiny sprout must take root
again amidst
The awesome threat of feet
passing by,
Trampling its soft, green frame to
the ground.

And when such unrelenting
natures have
Exhausted their lethal powers
and affluences,
The often troddened sprout
reaches out for higher havens
Touched only by stretching
forward in a heavenly arc.
So tall and proud in radiance,
This quiet, solemn, stubborn seed
Will blossom through eternity,
Nourished by a gentle
Loving spirit and nurturing
breeze.
Such are the strength of trees.

Linda Nelson
ONE ACT PLAY
you—who whisper about the
death's drama
to you—a dramatic play
time
counted by seasons
climaxes at the curtains drop

you—who whisper about her part
to you—just another ingenue
clamoring
virgin to the stage
does she know her lines

you—who whisper about the
script's brutality
to you—an unrehearsed farewell
performance
yet
are we not all seasoned actors
and doesn't the house play to
standing room only

Kevin D. Abrams
**Carolyn, Dear
Carolyn**
Carolyn, dear Carolyn
will I see you and the Others
ever again
in God's happy land
that I may be rid of this
pain?
I wish I knew.

Cissandra Gray Ball
NATURE REJOICES
The new blades of grass popping
up in the spring
Are waving to heaven in the
gentle breeze
The birds of the air have a new
song to sing
Adorning themselves in the
flowering trees
The flowers have scented the air
like perfume
Decorating meadows and fields
and pathways
Puffy white clouds chase away
winter's gloom
As sunshine and butterlies
brighten the days

Truely nature is boldly
celebrating
While mankind wonders at all
that it gives
All of the beauty of it's
decorating
What better reason than this—
He lives!

Elaine Grace
TUESDAY NIGHT
Indigo sky
Cold as a businessman's heart

Invisible moon
Surrounded by chill
It was late
too late

The atmosphere pervades my
being
My soul
seepes
into
Oppresive night

Mingling textures of darkness
We are one.

Julie Watterson
**A Love Letter (Mom's
Poem)**
This is a love letter
A simple love letter
I write of my feelings—
I'm feeling better.

This is a simple note
A little short note
With no fancy phrase
And no famous quote.

This little page
Was empty and dead
I brought it to life
With the things that I've said.

In my little letter
In this short line
That says that I love you
And I'm glad that you're mine.

Cindy S. Eakin
SECRETS
Walking along the sand,
going slow.
We share a secret
No one
will ever know. We whisper
in each other's ear,
And laugh aloud
for
No one can hear.

Helen E. Bates
FOR YOU
And life should be of laughing
things for you . . .
And loveliness . . . and light . . .
having fun
And building dreams, as restless
dreamers do,
And finding swift contentment
when they're done;
Of playing games . . . and finding
songs to sing . . .
And holding hands, . . and
laughing in the rain . . .
A sudden kiss . . . a mad trip to
the stars . . .
And wandering back along a
crooked lane.

These are the lovely dreams I
hold for you . . .
The sudden swift enchantment

that you seek,
The gay and madcap things that
we could do,
To make you lovely memories to
keep.

Oh, life should be of laughing
things, you know,
Come, let me take your hand,
we'll make it so.

Marjorie A. Murphey
Christmas Is For Children
*[I dedicate this poem to my
neice, Amy Lynn Sherry.]*
"What is for all children?" I asked

"What is one time they love,
one time they can always look
forward to?"

"What is for children that makes
them happy and seem to really
care?" I asked.

"What is bright, beautiful
and lets the imagination wander?"

"What is for all children,
no matter what their color may
be?" I asked.

"Christmas is for children," is the
answer I received.

Irene Stalcup
LITTLE PRAYERS
In a rushy day of work and
warfare
No time for a long proper prayer,
Disappointment with ourselves,
we bare,
Just time for a little wish or care.

Much comfort comes from some
of
the littlest prayers in print
a feeling, a sigh, and a cry from
the heart is heard,
No long beautiful phrasing of
words.

A prayer can be a touch, thought,
a plea.
The love of God is near; tenderly.
He hears us, His eyes see.

When tired and hard-pressed
We need comfort and rest
Like a touch on the switch
of an electric light; so bright
Strength surges in; all seems right.

Kathy Vahue
WHAT IS CHRISTMAS?
Christmas is the warm fireside
glow
Or the happy surprise of a
mistle-toe
The kitchen alive with
mysterious smells
In that wonderful place where
Mom's magic dwells

Christmas is a childs dream come
true
It is the joy of sharing, sharing
with you
When I am asked "What's
Christmas? tell me!"
Then I always reply and quite
eagerly

It's the tug of a small childs hand
As he leads you onwards to his
"Secret Land"
Where peppermint canes and a
bright Christmas tree
Will grow in abundance through
eternity

The glowing cheeks, the joyful
eyes
Sparkle as brightly as the stars in
the skies
Where ever he walks, he walks
without fear
Because a small childs faith is
forever near

Oh how much love he always
brings
This wonderous child this King
of Kings
A child is a precious gift from
above
For a child is Chritmas and
Christmas is Love.

Stanley A. Fellman
A Poet Answers Wealth
"For you I have rich suprize,
My pare gold matches your
natural fruit for size,
High song needs heavy aid—
So let us our two fruits trade."

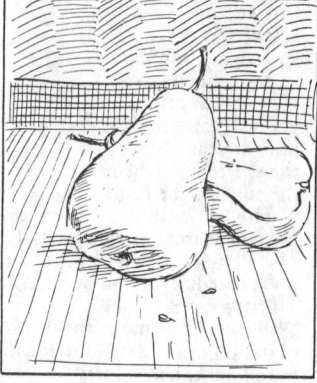

"No Lass—you have but a picture
of what I have for real,
My purpose teath would break on
a colored metal meal"

Lucy C. Faulkner
THE NEW WOMAN
It used to be a woman's work
Was never, ever done;
She'd cook and clean the whole
day through
She'd make it look like fun.

But now a woman gets to do
Eight hour's work and then
She gets to cook and clean all
night
When she gets home again.

Adrian M. Maschek
IN THIS BODY
In this body
still lives time
time that has been spent
and yet all too difficult,
to comprehend where it went.

In this body is old age
in this body is wisdom,
wisdom due to age.

In this body was vibrantsy
in this body was youth,
and youthful ideas.

In this body was zest
zest for living,
the way youth was meant to be.

In this body
was built in process of aging,

of which no soul escapes.

In this body
aging is a creeping thing,
it can be slowed but not stopped.

In this body
comes a slowing of the reflects,
a diming of sight, sometimes
correctable.

In this body due to time
comes a stiffness of joints,
and loss of flexability.

In this body and mind
comes a built in knowledge,
of acceptability of age.

In this body
we must accept aging,
as part of living.

In this body
perhaps we have seen history
made,
even played a part there-of.

In this body
nothing has been,
a total loss.

In this body
God granted life,
life beyond all comprehension.

In this body
there is life,
and where there is life there is
HOPE!

C. K. Lester
SPIRIT
The winds of Time are blowing
across a restless sea.
The feeling's o' so homeless
as homeless we must be.

Just bound as in a tempest
crying to be free—
And realizing only
that this just has to be.

The Spirit fills the spaces
with Hope for fresher starts
And knowledge of His 'Golden
Way'
Is etched upon our hearts.

Jewel A. Metz
When the Moon Is White
We'd been to a party. Coming
home
You stopped the car, said, "look at
that!"
Beyond a border of flowers and
grass
A small pool gleamed and
glistened where
The white moon shone. On it,
afloat
Among the ripples, like small
boats,
white Three ducks rocked,
sleeping. Laughing, we
Took shoes off, and stealthily,
Trousers rolled and skirts held
high,
We waded carefully to try
To catch a duck. Of course they
fled
Spattering waves so my skirt got
wet.
However the flowers stood very
still;
We picked them till our hands
were filled.
I think of this laugh—filled
summer's night

And remember you when the
moon is white.

Peggy Jo Rexrode Cook

Peggy Jo Rexrode Cook
**Merry Christmas, Father
Dear**
Merry Christmas, Father Dear
Merry Christmas, Happy New
Year
Merry Christmas, Dear Father
above
Merry Christmas, Merry
Christmas, Merry Christmas,
—My Love

Merry Christmas, Dear Holy One
Merry Christmas, Dear Holy Son
Merry Christmas, Dear Holy
Ghost
Merry Christmas, My Dear Holy
One

—Thy Host

Merry Christmas, Father Dear
Merry Christmas, Happy New
Year
Merry Christmas, Dear Father
above
Merry Christmas, Merry
Christmas, Merry Christmas,
—My Love

Sandra Jean Randles West
CHASING RAINBOWS
Ever see a rainbow arched in the
sky?
That made you feel a little high
The beautiful colors, tints and
hues
Which makes the world seem to
belong to you.

Reds for two hearts deeply in
love
Whites the color of a beautiful
dove
Orange for the sunsets we
watched in the sky
Green of course is for your eyes
Yellow, Purple and can't forget
Blue
Which stands for me since I'm
without you.

Chasing rainbows, following
dreams
Life isn't always what it always
seems
It has it's up's, it has it's downs
You touch the sky, you drag the
ground,
The stars are there and if you
choose
It's up to you if you win or lose.

So never quit, keep pushing on
After the darkness there's always
a dawn
You can win, it's not very far
Reach again, you'll find your star.

Jenna V. Ownbey
Easter—A New Beginning
*[To Sam: My dearest friend
wherever I am!]*
I have not lived in Italy;
I was never blessed in Rome;
Nor have I loved in Alaska
Or been at home in Nome.

But to learn love in new places,
Strange beginnings and old ends,
You will touch new hearts and
faces
With all your fellow men;

You will find all men are brothers,
And each new sister friend:
However you go,
Wherever you are,
And, then, wherever you've
been!

N. J. Beddingfield
SOUL—MATE
I love you fascinating friend,
Unfathmable and wild;
Exciting as a shooting—star.
Yet gentle as a child.

I've known you since before I
lived;
Before the world began:
Accept my love from first to last,
Be it holy, or be it damned.

Envelope me within your light,
Possess me, soul and mind;
I pledge this heart that sings your
name:
Oath sacred beyond time.

David Baillargeon
HOME BOX OFFICE
Awesome are the things of nature
I know this in my simple
dwelling.
The quiet of the night,
the moon with its gentle light,
suspended in the blackness of the
sky.
Peace and Calm permeate my
soul,
live performance at my eastward
window.
The curtains close, but the show
goes on . . .
If things go right I'll sleep tonight
and catch the golden glow of
morning.

Ralph Williams
SUBCONSCIOUS SUICIDE
Soldier of fortune,
Prisoner of pride,
Marching through a dimension
Where love has died.

Unwed mother,
Disloyal wife,
No man worth
The sacrifice.

Unskilled laborer,
Educated fool,
To repair the past
There are no tools.

Injector of drugs,
Connoisseur of wines,
How intense the pain

During sober times.

Won't receive pensions,
Not purchase canes,
Will cross the border
Via emotional strain.

Dana M. Murray
WATCHING
Life goes by . . .
does she watch it
or join?
she misses . . .
that part of hers
which was given
and then taken.

But
slowly, she joins;
and yet,
she watches the
remembrances of that Life
while Living
this Life.

That
they are different,
that Life and this;
understatement.

We all watch—
to an extent;
and yet, we join.

Angela S. Balay
THE SLATE MINE
*[I dedicate this poem to the
best teacher in the world Mr.
Cheasterton in Oxfordshire,
England. With Love, one of
your faithful students]*
But suddenly there is people.
Boys going through the tunnel
with slate,
Men working hard, drilling and
digging all day long.
The slate is turned into a jigsaw
of sweating and coughing and
tiresome noises,
It is broken apart by a child of
loneliness.
The crashes and clatters of
shovels and tools of many sorts
are still for a moment,
But it suddenly starts up again.
The piles of slate destroy nature.
Its like a jungle of chipmunks,
The men yelling and shouting
make distinct noises,
Sometimes of laughter and
sometimes of anger.
It's still once again and then the
noise fades away and
disappears
Suzanne Hughes
The Legend Of Cowboys
*[With love for Lane, one of
those "good southern boys"]*
Where have all the cowboys gone
Those honest and hard—
workin' gents,
Ridin' the range and herdin' the
cattle
And puttin' up miles of fence.

Like the smell of tobacco and
leather and horses
The aura of cowboys survives.
A few honest, hat—tippin', good
southern boys
Keep the legend of cowboys
alive.

Akin to the land and dreading
expansion

Ahold of a piece of the past,
The freedom and challenge we all
seem to yearn for
The cowboy has in his grasp.

So we languish in high-risers,
condos and spas
A part of today's fast-paced
crew.
Yet respecting, admiring (with
envy) those cowboys
That earthy, downhome, select
few.

A. Carol
EXPOSED
To start with a dare
You learn to not care
Floating with the clouds
Keep you away from the crowd
You soon forget your needs—
But for the wacky weed.

Sandra Culpe

Sandra Culpe
FEELINGS OF LOVE
Today it begins,
But tomorrow it may end;
Your touch and sensitivity,
Your longing for me,
And mine for you,
And our happiness together.

So many obstacles have come
into our path,
But our love will be everlasting.

Although we are not together
now,
Our feelings will never die.
For, we share something so
special,
That even time cannot destroy.

Jewel A. Metz
A PRAYER
Lightning, mountains, restless
seas,
Sun, wind, flowers, snow, and
trees,
Speak of your power and majesty.
My mind bows down before you,
saying
Almighty God, you are so great
You overwhelm me. I worship
you.

Then I look back upon the years
You have companioned me,
Giving security, rescue from
danger,
Comfort in sorrow, strength in
weakness,
And, in some mysterious way,
An abiding, basic joy.

Clearly the Person that you are
Emerges. Prayers become
conversations,
Intimate, all—giving. My heart
Melts at the very thought of you.
Forgive if sometimes I forget
Your majesty, being consumed by
love.

Walter S. Brown
MY TEDDY BEAR
Where oh where is my Teddy
Bear?
Did it go to sleep in my Daddy's
chair?
I've looked and looked most
everywhere, but I can't find my
Teddy Bear.

It was last year's present from
Santa Claus.
Momma said Santa brought it to
me because,
I had been real good and broke no
laws, that is why I'll always
believe in Santa Claus.

I'm as lonesome as I can be,
without my Teddy Bear in bed
with me.
I'm going to have to get up and
see, if my Teddy Bear is
looking for me.

My Teddy Bear sleeps with me
every night and that is why I
sleep so tight.
I never sleep with a real bright
light, just hold my Teddy Bear
with all my might.

My Teddy Bear never runs away,
stays right here so we can play.
My Teddy Bear stays with me all
day and always listens to what
I have to say.

We both went to sleep in Daddy's
chair, Mommy tucked me in
bed with tender care, but she
forgot to bring my Teddy Bear,
so it is still asleep in Daddy's
chair.

I found my Teddy Bear in
Daddy's chair, we both went to
sleep while sitting there.
I knew it hadn't run off some
where, because it is my Teddy
Bear.

Lois L. Ramsey
GOODBYE
For these things mean
"Goodbye"—
The word,
The faint, receding
Sound of footsteps
And the closing door.

Far more articulate
Than word or sound,
This vast and sudden silence
In my heart.

Rosa Melinda Batiste
THAT'S POETRY
It's putting thoughts together
from the brink of our mind
It's putting them down line by
line
It's true feelings we share
While trying to hold on to
memories so rare
It's occasions of sadness, horror,
or fun

All put together and rolled into
one
It's teardrops, laughter, beauty,
and pain
It's sunshine, it's raindrops, it's a
roaring flame
The sunshine after the rain, these
moments of fun
Were captured for us all by a
beautiful someone
They wanted to share with us
part of their minds
So they gave them to us line by
line
These lines I mention to you this
day
Never will they stop nor stay
They'll travel to places far and
near
As it lights today upon your ears
It's music that has been molded
into words
It's the same song that others
once heard
So open your eyes and you will
see
All that is around you is poetry

Barbara Gene Koscher
ARIES
[To R.J.P.—With love, Seagull]
AS FIERCE AS A LION HE
CAME . . .
Wild and depressed in search of a
friend
I tried, while unsatisfied pain
Ripped through me and
Tears full of agony fell from my
face
And from my heart.
I blindly chased the unanswered
question
And hurriedly bandaged my
wound of hurt
With hope and self pity
And an explanation point!
Then Aries came into my view
And silently extended his hand
Of friendship
As the spring creatures
Of butterflies and mosquito
hawks fluttered.
I smiled
While accepting gladly his warm
environment,
For happy moments we shared
together.
As friends of night
As friends of day
We were and we stayed until
. . . AS QUIET AS A LAMB HE
WENT.

Franklin Sommers
**The Maestro Conductor
(Herbert Von Karajan)**
*[Written with deep love and
appreciation for the Austrian
Conductor—Herbert Von
Karajan—, forever the Maestro
Conductor, cherished and loved.]*
Conducting Karajan,
Is graceful as a swan,
The graceful Berlin swan,
Responds to Karajan,

With eyes shut he conducts,
Loves the sound very much,
Hears the music so much more,
Uses memory as his score,

Conducting sensitive,
Karajan's habit is,

Enchanting, mystical,
The music very full,

Sensitive Karajan,
Conducting with baton,
Orchestra, the Berlin,
Responds to all he is.

Franklin Sommers
**Where Ever It May Be
(Where Evert May Be)**
*[Written with eternal love and
honor for God, Mother Mary,
and Christine Marie Evert
Lloyd.]*
Where the tennis ball flies
My heart will be in tennis,

Where ever it may be,
My love of tennis flies,

My heart will be in tennis,
Where the tennis ball flies,

My love of tennis flies,
Where Evert may be.

John E. Stenwall
ETERNITY
I gazed
Into a
Cloud of
Stars and
Saw the
Face of
Eternity.

Angela Starr Balay
THE HUGE ROOM
The high wall, and the high
totem pole hang against the sky.
Heads all shapes and sizes stare
at you with mouths opened.
A big boat flies overhead like a
plane in the sunset evening.
Ghosts without heads glare
towards you.
The heads try to escape from
powerful prisons of evil.
The evil eyes stare and charm
you away from them and to
them.
Bright suns high above you shine
and blind your eyes.
The light echoes of the dead
move you.

Jo Starrett Lindsey
PLANS POSTPONED
The dark day is the other side
Of days alight with morning sun;
And, when the restless raindrops
fall,
The daisies bloom for the sunny
one;
Soon, I will pick the flowers there,
Bright splashes in the summer
haze;
So, now I put my plans aside
In payment for the coming days.

Rosina Ortega Mendiola
COLOR ME
Color me brown, black or white;
Why the hell is everybody so
uptight?
I live my life and I live it well;
My self respect is the only thing I
won't sell.
My right, my feelings you violate;
Come on now man I know I rate.
A human, a person with hopes
and dreams;
Sometimes fulfilling these things
so impossible seems.

Don't look at my color, just at me;
How difficult can this possibly be?

Cherl A. Howard
UNITE
The rooms where Grandfather
    had walked
    Held an essence of uneasiness,
A prayerful ray of loneliness from
    all that had gone before
Grandmother's innocence lives on
    As Grandfather's knowledge
    pleads from beyond.
Unsurpassed immortality awaits
    the unity with those of
    centuries passed.
I yearn for those my blood lies in.
The glory of my home so close I
    touch their tears.
Continuance so vital to our souls,
    tho the curtain has been drawn,
I vow to find you in eternal
    celestiality.

Robert C. Hanna
**NFSPS Amy & Sam Zook
Contest Chairman and
Clerk For Contest
(Respectively)**
Is a long title for a poem,
(And I left out 3520 Star Route 56,
Mechanicsburg, Ohio 43044)
The National Federation of State
    Poetry Societies (inc)
Is sponsoring its 23rd annual
    contest (sic)
Entrants are to read the rules
And submit . . . a poem
Images are important
. . . Poetry is not just ideas
If it were
No gestures would acompany a
    reading
Nor intonation a recitation.
Poetry should arrive when
    possible
Through a frothy orifice and float
    unassisted
Midst watery orbs and waxy
    auricles.

A large mailing envelope is
    required
Poets are exhorted
    To simply supply
        Their best
            Work

Richard Marion Reece
**Little Brother (Where Are
You Now?)**
I sit beside you, memories of
    times gone by,
thoughts of you and I past me
    slowly, sadly.
We did many a thing together,
    great times we had,
                    once . . .
You are slowly leaving us now,
    bound for somewhere else.
Your voice, still talking, laughing
    in my head.
You laughed at my jokes,
    believed in me, thought the
    world of me.
Why? Why? Dear God!!!
Everything we shared, we were
    close, close, close . . .
We shared secrets, protected each
    other on important issues.
now doesn't even matter, why
    should they matter?
You just lie there, not even

hearing me.
Thirty years I cared for you.
Thirty years, then nothing,
    nothing, nothing . . .
God! What went wrong? What
    the hell went wrong?
Just! Just! Just! From a just—
                God? Damn the world.

With technology so advanced,
    why isn't something discovered?
Money spent on war, not
    mankind; he never harmed
    anyone, no one in fact.
Why must he die? Why must he
    die?
Answer me lord, please give me
    an answer . . .
I beg of you with heart and soul,
    he was everyting to me, friend,
    companion, and confidant.

    i am weak lord, to the whole
        situation;
    i can't change a thing.
    i used to help him; I meant
        everything to him.
    i was there when help was
        needed, advice, and broken
        hearts.

Now, now i just can't help, i just
    can't help,
                Jesus, i just can't help!!!

Eugene E. Trujillo
GRAY WINTER . . .
Tis the windy month of March;
    faded grass a
        blowing in the breeze. While
        the sheep, warm
        in their wool.
            Gray Winter is before us.

Once again, a white blanket
    spreads over us;
        Reality comes to a standstill
        and tenderly we
        kiss each starfill night.
            Gray Winter is with us.

Slowly a colorful world re-emerges;
    Chasing
        away the gray and whiteness.
        And for a
        moment, we are thankful.
            Gray Winter is behind us . . .
                once again!

Jill Bartel
SINGING STONES
Mountains call
And plains respond
To the cry of the whining wind
And rocks of different hues
Lend earthy voices
To the song,
The music that encompasses,
The sound of singing stones.

LeeAnn Lawrence
IT'S HARD TO BELIEVE
It took me a long time to give out
    my love
When I did I was played for a fool.
So I decided right then I'd start all
    over again,
And when I did I was playing it
    cool
He left me sitting there crying
Over a love I thought there had
    been
As he walked out the door, I
    finally realized
It would never be as before.

I found it hard to believe it was
    over
But when I did I was hardened to
    men.
The love 'em and leave 'em
    attitude
Was how I saw all of them.
It was then that I met you
I was skeptical that's true
You taught me to believe in love
    again
That's when I fell in love with
    you.
I still kept my guard up so not to
    be hurt
You finally convinced me you
    loved me
And it wasn't a game you were
    playing
You understood my hesitations
And you loved me all the same.

Richard Paul Lang
A LONE COWBOY
[This poem was inspired by
reading the life story of Will
James, "a lone cowboy"]
A cowboy of the plains,
A cowboy of the reigns,
A cowboy named Will James,
He rode alone.
He suffered many hardships
All his own;
But learned to love and make
The plains his home.

He rarely stayed in town;
But sometimes could be found
Still camping on the ground
Some miles away.
He worked the ranches
For a little pay,
And followed the prairies
Until the end of day.

He knew his horses well.
But one he wouldn't sell.
He called him Smokey, and rode
    him
With some pride;
And loved him faithfully
Til one day by a tree,
Smokey sat down next to James
And died.

A lone cowboy was James
He knew not many names
But tasted life's cruel games
Until he grew
Into a man whose wants were
Very few
A true lone cowboy was
Will James.

T. Huff
AS ONE
In our youth
our love scorched
at every
possible moment,
like a fine
tapestry
the years
wove the fibers
of our lives
interlocking,
eternity will
net two souls
held so close
it will
appear
as one.

Tallak T. Farsjo
LET JOY PREVAIL TODAY
Let the sorrow come tomorrow
But let joy prevail today.
Could a twinkling star I borrow
In the glowing Milky Way,
I would twirl a golden lasso
And forever let it stay
Round a diamond shaped like
    nugget;
—Make of strands a shiny knot.
To this rope I then would fasten
All the sorrows I have got.
And this God-made sparkling
    wonder
That we earthlings call a star
By a rope would lift my sorrows
To that universe afar,
So they never found the pathway
Back to me or to this earth.
I would never fear tomorrow—
—Or the sorrows kill my mirth.
Let us learn a little lesson
From this silly fantasy:
To rejoice today—is really—
To set tomorrow free!

Robert E. Taylor
TRAILS PAST
I've ridden all the trails before.
Most of my life spent on the run.
All the towns and all the people
at the wrong end of a gun.
The year is 1882,
one-hundred years ago,
I remember like it's yesterday.
It's strange that I should know
so much about a life I lived
in another place and time.
Yet I'm haunted by the memories
of a life I know was mine.
I know it's a century later.
But the past keeps calling me
    louder,
and while I'm living in the present,
I taste the reins inside my mouth,
and the smell of burning powder.

Dorothy "Shorts" Williamson
Another Mother's Prayer
[To mothers of my younger
friends who think we were
never young.]
O, Lord, please help me cope this
    day
With things you've meant to be
Help me open up my eyes
That I may clearly see.
Help me find the answers
When the children call
To help them fight the influence
of drugs and alcohol.
When parents will not listen

And they knock upon my door
I need the strength to prove
What friendship's really for.
Show me strength to help them
Grow up straight and good
To fight for truth and honor
And teach them what I should.
Should they seek my sage advice
Let me please be there.
O, Lord, please listen
To another mother's prayer.

Amen

Stephanie Stresen-Reuter
THE SHELF
I had a thought
and with it brought
an opening door
which I did explore
inside I found
a land of sound

Sounds of sorrow
to be tomorrow
sounds of laughter
to be here after
all the sounds
of life itself
stored in my mind
upon a shelf.

Barbara Young
GRANDMOTHER
If they gave me a choice
You know what I'd do?
I pick a Grandmother
Just like you.

One whose eyes sparkle
Whose smile just beams
One who's the answer
To a granddaughter's dreams.

She has to be little
So petite just like you
And I'll know that she loves me
And she'll know I love her too.

She'll have a sense of humor
That's keen and always there
Something so precious
That all of us can share.

She'll be young, yes young
Not in years but in ways
And I pray she'll stay with me
For the rest of my days.

Jan'l Baker
Requiescat to Bugs, Birds, Bees, & Thee
He said, "Seemingly careless
creatures feel worth
Just look at the bugs scurry
when I kick up the earth!
And listen closely to the birth of
a symphony
Through crickets' wings
constant quivery.
In the tree an owl sits on a limb
with height
Waiting to boot out its hoot
tonight!
God knows how to compose
heavenly poetry
When blossoms compete with
bees.
I see creation has purpose, so
what lies ahead for me?
Aye, when I'm put under sod to
lay
Does my soul shrivel as time rots
my body decay?
Or am I made of an endless root
That comes again after ashes

and soot?"

I pondered his inquiry, reverently
Then answered his question of
eternity:
"You have a soul that will never
die;
For eternity's a babe without a lie.
And like the sun, it will always
shine;
Or like true love, it lasts a long
time.
So put your trust in me, my
friend—
You're a circle! You're without
end!"

Linda Baker Burke

Linda Baker Burke
LOVE
You are a dream I had last night
That came true today
You are the star that shines bright
The sunshine of my day.

You are the vine I'm clinging to
I am the rose
You've become my tried and true
Your gentleness, like river flows.

You are love, you are
understanding
You're peace I always find
You give me love that's
un-demanding
The lasting, choking kind!

Kcob Teirrah
WHAT IS LOVE
[To Gig—The joy in my life.]
Love is gentleness . . .
A wisp of warmth . . .
Encircling one as arms . . .
We learn to share it . . .
As we share the rising sun . . .
For love surrounds us . . .
As a gentle breath of wind!

Pat Burton
FOR ROGER
I've walked with you along river
banks
In some far distant land
In times of peace, in times of love
We once walked hand in hand.
My mind not quite remembers
But my soul indeed recalls
Time somehow turns back again
And I see across the walls
The same dark eyes do beckon me
To journey there within
And share with you a new time
here
To walk with you, my friend.
I don't have an answer

To this question still unasked
Maybe, never, will we know
What lies behind the mask.
It's good to see you once again
And know that you are near
To hold your hand and talk
awhile
To be with you—my dear
If on our journey thru—this time
Our lives don't have a place
Maybe love—next time around
We'll both save each a space.

Lois S. Barton
EASTER
When the Easter rabbit comes to
your house,
With eggs of every hue.

And the house is a clutter,
So you don't know what to do?

Listen carefully, to their exclaims,
Of joy and happy glee.

It will make you feel much better,
at the sight you behold.

Of the happiness you have,
brought into your little fold.

Then listen very quietly,
and you will probably hear.

The whisper of the Master,
"well done again this year"!

But did you also teach them?
the reason we celebrate?

The quiet resurection,
of someone Oh, so great!

Patricia L. Hill
CHEER-UP
*[I would like to dedicate this
poem to Donal Hogan, a friend,
who though physically
confined to a wheel-chair,
soared with the eagles, and his
wife, Julia Hogan, a loving,
caring, kindred-spirit.]*
Things are piling up, it seems it's
getting hard to cope!
But then I have to stop and think,
"What good is it to mope?"

For everyday, in some small way,
brings each of us a gift.
It's there for us, if we just look, to
give our heart a lift.

Like just the other day, I saw a
sight that tore my soul.
A blind one pushing a wheel-
chair friend—together they
were whole!

And I was very down that morn'
until I glimpsed that sight,
For I could see and I could walk
and I was quite all right.

That morning gift throughout the
day was such a precious thing.
It made me thankful, but much
more, again my heart could sing!

Verna Eubank
MAY—DECEMBER AFFAIR
I have just hung up the phone,
after calling you today
And I feel so guilty from the
words you had to say.

Thinking back over the years
of this May—December thing,
Oh, the memories it does bring.

We both knew that right or wrong,

you would have to go.
Dear God, if I'd been strong,
I'd have kept on saying "no".

How could we know, a crushing
blow
would make it end this way.
So if you can forget me love,
please do
is all I'll say.

My heart will hold a special place
for you until I die.
But as we knew in the beginning,
love,
We would have to say
"goodbye".

Kathy Lynne Butler
WINDOWS
Once, when I was alone and
scared,
you were there;
And when I felt my life had been
crushed by defeat,
You were there;
And when I glanced up and saw
nothing but clouds,
a light shone,
And you were there;
And when I felt I couldn't go on, I
was picked up,
And you were there;
And when I was on the outside
looking in,
A window flew open,
And you were there;
And when the world lay at my
feet, I cried,
Because I knew it was because
someone cared.
And you were there.

Connie Norman
SOMEWHERE ELSE
The ground I'm standing on now
is just the same as any other.
The air I breathe, the sky I see.
It doesn't matter where I am or
how far away from home, for
this place soon becomes my
own.
It takes awhile, every time I go, to
realize the routine, but it
happens every time.
The ground I'm standing on
becomes the same as any other.

Alta Shill Smith
REQUIEM FOR A FRIEND
Old Hobo's gone, that great blue
dog
Will walk with me no more.
No quiet peaceful midnight
strolls
The way we did before.
No silly grin, no big white eye,
No begging for a bone.
No one to guard the door for me
When I am left alone.
My world is smaller for his loss,
But I'll see him again.
I'm sure somewhere in Heaven
Is a meeting place for friends.

Somehow I have a feeling
When I close that final door,
Old Hobo will be waiting there
Just like he was before.
He'll raise his head and grin at me,
And wink that one white eye.
He'll yawn and stretch and follow
me
As I walk slowly by.

I'll feel that head beneath my
hand
And I'll look down and see
Old Hobo, where he always was
To walk back home with me.

Victor Emil Moessinger
Ode To the Mountain Man
The mountain men wear leather
britches, and are always
scratching cause, it itches.
They protect their lives with big
bowie knives, but these are
only trifles, cause they ram
their balls upon the walls,
They shoot them off with rifles,
they trap their women in home
made snares and dress them up
in fancy furs they are known to
look danger straight in the eye
and patch their balls and never
die

a men

John William Wise Jr.
LOVE
LOVE,
it's the best sign to show,
the only lift to feed on to grow,
when there's nothing left to hold.

LOVE,
the best way to greet a stranger,
the only way to keep a friend,
and when your hopes are on low...

LOVE,
it's the fastest welcome to know,
the greatest truth that flows,
when one's lonely and lost.

LOVE,
it's the strongest lead to follow,
the highest belief to rest upon,
when all your wrong ways fail to
pull you through.

Patricia A. Bellittiere
GEORGE
[Dedicated to George R.
Barajas, my beloved, who died
as the result of a malignant
brain tumor, on August 17, 1982]
Prince among men,
Object of my love,
You are as perfect as a dove
that flies in harmony
with wind and sky
And walks without disrupting
the path.

We have moved through our
time together
building a foundation of
sincerity and belief
understanding and devotion.

There is no limit to the realms
we can reach,
and for this
I experience
such great honor
see great beauty,
feel wonderous hope,
and am convinced forever
of the magnificent possibility
between a man and a woman.

Ted F. Remington
THRESHOLD
Huddled in prolonged serenity
beneath mammoth stone spires
inverted icicles of earth
slice skyward
into sleety mist
enveloping my lair

Stark vermilion shafts
glowing in peerless tints
subsume the higher surfaces
where vision quickly fades
on nebulous flakes of moisture
vertically evaporating
with human emotions
on the descending night

Dawn Lippincott
**What a Family Means To
Me**
A family means alot to me in this
world of hopes and fears,
My family always helps me in
the time of need and tears.
When I am sad and kind of let
down, they always turn my face
into a smile from a frown.
I care about my family, and I
always will, if I had the
Money I would pay their doctor
bills.
We spend time together almost
every day, we care about each
other in a very special way.
This binds us together in a family
unity, this is what
A family will always mean to me!

Medina R. Branzelle
THE FINAL GREEN
[For those who woke me while
my whole life slept, For those
who love me and now won't let
me rest.]
Green, the moon's proverbial
cheese,
the blood within the veins of
trees,
the famous hue of envy's face,
our planet's little light in space;
Earth's color, where her people
pass
under the final green of grass.

Martie
PREPARATION
Where has the sunshine gone
today?
It was there shining brightly
yesterday.
There are thick clouds blotting
out the sky.
It's enough to dim the mind and
dull the senses,
As anxious eyes scan the outlook
of the day.

Tiny flakes come filtering out of
nowhere—
They come drifting slowly, lazily
to the ground.

I am thinking I would rather not
have
A snow storm now. Not when it
is nearly
Spring! Sunshine is what I wish
were here.

Where are those sparkling blue
skies I've seen?
They're covered with layers of
gray flannel—
Those heavenly blues have been
replaced.
Much as I would wish to hasten
spring,
First must come the preparation
for new growth.

In each life a preparation period
must come
To ready us for greater growth
ahead.
Our trials, heartaches and failures
come along
To refine us into loving, caring,
patient persons.
With each experience, a new life
is being fashioned.

The Master watches over us to
make sure each
One is carefully waxed and
polished to perfection.
Faster and faster those
snowflakes are falling.
But now my mood has changed to
joy—
For I know without the
preparation there is no life.

Russell Barton
HUSBAND TO WIFE
You don't deserve my
undelighted hours
Nor all those ugly senseless
moments when
In petty rage I trample on the
flowers
Spoiling the Eden that our life
has been.
You brought to me a deep and
lovely peace
Bidding the mean mistrustful and
the sour
Come out and make their case or
henceforth cease
Nor fret and fester in our
marriage bower.
I meant to bring you elegance and
grace
Cascading fun and sparkle on
your heart
with all the riches love and wit
embrace
Hoping that you'd continue in
your part.
You have no need to stay with all
you give—
Save that without you I've no
cause to live.

Daniel R. Kenny
SUPREME FATHER
I'm the slut the hooker, the
prostitute, the whore
I am the thief, the pusher, a
beggar at your door

I'm the priest, your brother,
your sister, a nun
I am the unheralded veteran
shooting his gun

I am the hungry, the oppressed

the fat cat monopolist,
wearing my custom suit and vest

I am the master, a teacher, a drug
user
I'm the student a laborer
an alcohol abuser

I am all that you see in today's
world
I'm the man, a woman
the boy, a girl

I am life, I am death
I am good and evil trying
I'm the reason some are born and
some are dying

I am all you believe in, that
unnatural superstition
I am God and the Devil
WHO will judge you at your final
inquisition

I am all that you see
you are all that I am

Judy Sullivan
DEATH LIGHT
There's life believed to follow
death
as rainbows follow rain
When flesh lies void of all its
breath
no more to feel the pain

The calming light that shares the
flight
when at last the soul is free
Lends peace to death to quell the
fright
of the ultimate destiny

The glow of life from yonder side
transcends God's perfect grace
Until at last the soul abides
within His kind embrace

When death doth come to snare
the soul
fear not the final journey
For when the time on Earth is
whole
God's guiding glow will greet
thee

Grace E. Herman
**Twilight On the
Overthrust Belt**
[Dedicated to Evanston
Wyoming, "Oil City" U.S.A. To
the "New Comers" and the "Old
Timers", Trying to work
together to make a good
community out of a "small
peaceful one horse town".]
Glorious streamers of crimson
and gold
Have departed, too soon.
Leaving the sharp silhouette
On the hill, of the oil well pump
Going up and down, up and down.
A huge black grasshopper bowing
Like a clown to the crescent
Moon.

Kenneth A. Goodman
MY LOVE
She is a lady and that
cannot be changed. Feel-
ings she puts out to
others make them grow.
Time passes and she is on
the go. Flames for her
cannot be showed. All she
needs is to let everyone
know. Fighting her will;

can break any man. Coming close she pushes you
away with all her might.
Sorry is the word she
says when someone falls
in flight. Heart throb
makes her Queen over all
men. Time has come for
her to lose, when she
does my heart says she is
still mine. Let her come
back and say she will
be mine. Love is strong
so is she, yet I will
win; you will see.

Pamela Yoshino Tagami
CHOICE FRIENDS
Choice friends
are more than special
More than giving life
   For they share life
   Each other
   Love and laughter
They ease the hard times
and lighten up the good.
   They are the key
For making life more enjoyable—
More than natural
Nature
Down right a part of
They are the pages of
   knowledge,
   life and love.
So unforgetable
So kind and gentle
   A ray of warm sunshine
   A drop of softness
So noticeable
They are the colors of a rich
   rainbow
   They stay special with their
   smile of love—
   Choice friends

Ramon Stone
NIGHT MOVEMENTS
I roam about during the day as
   the world awakes to a new
   start. Soon though day recedes
   to darkness, I then begin to
   relax. The night always has a
   hold on me as an odd tranquil
   feeling flows entwined by inner
   fascination a different sense of
   awareness. I gaze out of a
   window at the dimly lit streets
   below feeling mesmerized in a
   world of peace and content; An
   air of calmness being free in
   which all is quiet and friendly.
There is an aura of warmth
   radiating as if my movements
   were totally unnoticed.
   However, the sun will soon
   arise to hide all the hidden
   wonders evening holds only to
   be stirred again when night
   moves upon us . . .

C. Suzanne Simpson
YOU ARE THE ONE
   It is strange that at nineteen
I have met a man with whom I
   feel,
Both in my heart and in my head,
That I could indeed spend the rest
   of my life with
and not have it feel like a
   sentencing,
but rather a rejoicing.
   Talking for hours on end,

we are still
Comfortable in our silences.
Mutual respect, caring, love and
   trust
All reach across the many miles,
Making the distance between us
   seem not so long.
   Nothing is more special than a
   letter from you,
My love, the sight of which
   causes my heart to
Leap with unrestrained joy.
With it I can steal away with you
In a room crowded with people.
   My smile shines so radiantly
   that all who know me,
Know that I dance lightly across
   the skies,
Running up beautifully high
   mountains.

Minnie Deshotel
THE LORD'S BILL
As I knelt praying tonight
A thought came to mind
Suppose Our Lord sent us a bill
Oh goodness how we'd whine!

Seven hundred for the flowers
That shows us spring is here
And thousands for our knowing
Our Lord is always near.

Eight hundred for the nighttime
And a thousand for the day
And a million for the freedom
To kneel down and pray.

Five thousand for the stars
That sparkle as they shine
Ten thousand for the joy
Of having peace of mind.

One hundred thousand dollars
For the sun upon the hill
Oh Dear Lord, how on earth
Will we ever pay Your Bill?

Do not worry child
For I am at your side
Give Me all your troubles,
And I will make them right.

Read and live My Word
And call upon My Name
Love and help your fellow man
And the bill? We'll mark it paid!

Vito Basirico
DRUG RELATED
Why do you do
the things you do
when you know
that it will kill you

is it the temptation
or is it the test

or is it just you think
that gettin high is best

don't you know that
when it's over and done
that everything you have gained
you end up with none.

Sheila M. Sebald
DESTINY
Meanings of words, the usage of
   numbers
           can be taught
Your mind must accept these
   teachings
But—
   the many feelings and
   recognitions
           you will face
Must not only be accepted but
   understood
The mind will conceive emotions
           and crime
The body will function through
   tremors
           and faults
Try to believe in yourself, and in
   others
   through debate and silence
   through touch and continuing
   glances
DON'T just accept destiny,
   try to make it as enjoyable and
   rewarding as life itself

Debbie Rittenburg
LOST LOVE
My love is with you,
   This I know for sure.
Our love has only become hidden,
   But these times we must
   endure.

Our love is not lost forever.
   The night cannot last long.
The moments we spend together,
   Will make all right what's
   wrong.

You are the center of my life.
   At night I come home to you.
It's said, "Home is where the heart
   is."
   Remember, I'll always love you.

Buddy Dennis
THE LAST DREAM
I cried for love
   but no one was there
I cried for love
   but no one cared
I cried for love
   and peace on earth
I cried for peace
   throughout the universe
I cried for love
   but died alone
I cried for love
   then went back home.

Jean Gorman Morsheimer
SPINDRIFT
Had I a choice of memories
to keep, to sneak into infinity:
the treasure would be my sailing
   affair.
There the breeze erases cares,
healing rays stroke my body,
cleansing rain restores my soul.
But oh that ship,
like a pure bred stallion,
racing with the wind,
surmounting every swell,
I ride you anticipating

your leaping, tossing, and
   straining
to soar with me,
we are in tune, teetering on the
   edge,
yet you are steel for me, a
   security,
there is no yielding,
and I know you, your next high,
finally your shuddering under
   me.
Wind sounds moan
'round your shrouds, arms, mast,
and boom, you mighty one,
I shout, "Yes, oh yes," to this
   climax:
we are one—
        with the sun.

Denise Marie Pokojski
FRIENDSHIP
Friendship starts,
   and then it grows.
Together or apart,
   it never goes.
Like the autumn winds,
   it always blows.
Sometimes quiet,
   and sometimes strong.
But always there,
   just waiting to be shown.

Linda Ikeler
LOST CAUSES
*[Dedicated to our men who
were in Viet Nam whose praise
was long over-due. From the
people of Mt. Morris, New
York.]*
There were so many
lost causes and plenty
to worry about.
Lives were wasted,
words were mistaken
and turned all about.
The rich grew and where were
   you?
Counting your pennies in the
   sewer.
Tides turned and fires burned
killing the weak and saving fewer.
Spared were the strong,
There's no right or wrong
left to live by.
There were so many
lost causes and plenty
to die by.

Jean Marie Burlingame
**Through My Baby's
Eyes**
Through my baby's eyes, I see life
   anew,
Pause a moment and you'll see
   too.

His eyes fly open at morning's
   first light,
Eager to start a new day of
   delights.

Rays of sun are a special toy,
As fingers shape shadows, I hear
   squeals of joy.

Sharing the wonders, always the
   reason,
We look forward to each new
   season.

Through a field of polka dots, we
   wander for hours,
Taking the time for every
   breathtaking spring flower.

The castles we dream of are never
out of reach,
For the sandbox in summer is our
own private beach.

The leaves of autumn wrapped in
splended attire,
Dance to the ground in shades of
gold, orange, and fire.

When winter commands the
brooks not to flow,
We glide on the ice and romp in
the snow.

The stars that twinkle ever so
bright,
Blink in the sky as a solar
nightlight.

Everyday sights take on renewed
joy,
Through the eyes of my little boy.

Muriel Merritt
THE GLORY OF SIGHT
In spite of trouble and conflicts
A Glory still shines over all;
The snow still sparkles on the
trees,
And the world goes around like a
ball.

The ice sparkles on little ponds,
And the birds sing their cheerful
songs.
Little children still love their play,
And the sun shines in colors gay.
The moon is bright in starry skies;
These things I see; what more
could I?

Helen Brown Rittershofer
DIRECTIVE INFLUENCE
A garden is a place for adventure
And views are glimpsed from
within
Thoughts are inspired by the
planted seed
Picture paints mans' word and
deed
For as the sunshine—life expands
And man solves problems—
meets demands
Life resembles the weeping sea
Jars idle thoughts from
complicacy
In the patterned cycles of
partitioned life
Goals are reached through
problem insight
As realities mingle and stir the
mind
Through insight man paints his
own design
Contemplates—symbolizes,
weighs and records
For certainties of knowledge open
doors
Man will reach his goal in life—
without a doubt
As Father Time has pointed out.

Robert James Gordon
CARDINAL
Long gone the Fall, you, all red
bird.
Of all such things, you could
have heard
That it's the fool who tests the
day,
When crested brothers strew the
word.

The wind will bring the limb to
sway

The dust like snow from your
bouquet:
Of feathered skin and hollowed
breast
In night so far, so long, away.

So cool the climb that cleansed
the nest,
It bore the singing from the rest
As if the song were more intent
Than brother, sister, had request.

What life there is, is life that's
lent.
The prophecy of one content
To know when all ambition's
bent:
What life there is, is life that's
spent.

Charleen M. Geeson
OLD LADY
*[In Memory Of My Very
Special Lady, My Mom]*
Old Lady, look at me . . .
Take a chance at what you see.
Old Lady, reach out your hand . . .
What takes hold might be
pretty grand.
Old Lady, go ahead and cry out
loud . . .
For too many years you've been
too proud.
Old Lady, look my way . . .
Don't think of skies that are
cloudy and gray.

David E. Neifert
A NEW BEGINNING
I planted the seed.
I tilled the ground.
You gave me hope again.
You gave me a son.

Mary M. Gage
BORN FREE
Born free to roam
The roads and walks
The highways
To be free
To be born again
A free spirit
Of the development
Of human nature
Of the human spirit
Of good and evil
Of the devil
And the deep blue sea
I run alone
I go my way
And cast shadows
On the earth
So go your way
And walk the tightrope
And run the gamut
Of life's expectancies

Rick Taylor
KING OF THE STREETS
King of the Streets
. . . Sir Lunch-A-Lot,
So often the crowd repeats
. . . What I'm really not.

If only they knew
. . . The real me,
They wouldn't misconstrue
. . . What I'm trying to be.

How Sad!
. . . Who's being had?

King of the Streets?
. . . Too many repeats.

Sir Lunch-A-Lot?

. . . White stallion have I not.
Will my crusade never end?
. . . Or am I doomed to forever
spend . . .
The rest of my days . . .
. . . Caught up in this maze.

If I must . . .
. . . And have no one to trust . . .
Then please send me . . .
. . . On my merry ways.

Bertha "Dickson" Curtis

Bertha "Dickson" Curtis
PRINCE OF PEACE
Love Eternal is born anew
In every living soul,
As each facet of Divinity
Reflects the Perfect Whole.

Cradled in the universe
(Yet all space can not confine)
Is this Star in ageless traverse
That lights your way and mine.

'Tis Life in Perfect harmony
Angelic Hosts proclaim—
For Truth is come to set us free
Lo! Emmanuel is His Name.

Standing at the door of every heart
Ne'er asking race or creed,
Omnipotent Love is there to
impart
Supply for every need.

Immortality is manifest this day
Love Eternal is born anew,
And Truth reigns! To ever say
"My peace I give to you"!

Jacqueline Pergolizzi
THE GIFT OF FRIENDSHIP
Friendship is a priceless gift
Which cannot be bought or sold.
But its value is far greater
Than a mountain made of gold.

For gold is cold and lifeless
It can neither hear nor see
And in the time of trouble
It is powerless to thee.
It has no ears to listen
No heart to understand
It cannot bring you comfort
Or lend a helping hand.
So when you ask God for a gift
Be thankful if he sends
Not diamonds, pearls, or riches
But the Love of
A Real True Friend!

Roma M. Hogue
RECIPE FOR LOVE
*[To Bill and Barb. May you
always be as happy as you are
today, may you always
remember the recipe.]*
It's the little things that count
like
Holding hands
Walking together
A smile
A look
A touch
A kiss
A hug
A phone call
A greeting card
A single red rose
A love letter
A poem
Sharing a loaf of bread, a jug of
wine
Sitting in front of a roaring fire
A movie show, a music concert
An automobile ride
and conversation
above all communication
Blend together, Serve generous
portions
to that Special Someone
Every day of your life.

Cynthia R. Golderman
I HAVE FORESWORN
I have foresworn falling in love
again,
pounding vagus-nerve,
and all atwit, with mystery and
out of it,
into higher spheres I cannot go,
I am already there, wherever I am
at,
and truly, my heart can't bear any
more of that falsity,
so, I have foresworn denial, and I
must deny,
that which captures the heart and
stings the eye
with beauty and lightly touched
compassion,
I have foresworn, it is the fashion
a blurred distortion:
I have foresworn, I've had my
portion.

Leland Tebeau
IT DOESN'T HAVE TO BE
Drinking is a problem that many
possess,
It's the work of the devil and it
brings out his best.
A kind of habit that people call
relief,
But right up to the end it just
spells out grief.
I was a man whose home was a
bar,

a master of jokes and a pro with a car.
Just a few beers at the end of the day,
Started my career in the lives of the gay.
Later a few beers changed to a few shots,
The liquor was quicker and things went to pot.
Time meant nothing and neither did money,
Bills started piling up and it just wasn't funny.
My body craved more each day for the drink,
Till my mind became fuzzy and I couldn't think.
With my bottle in hand, I feel like a King,
But deep down inside, I am not anything.
I'm one of everyday's creatures who has
chosen this way of life, but I'm not
too far gone to give a word of advice.
If your life is afflicted in this kind of way,
Why not get help from your friendly A.A.

Mary Lou Amodeo Hickey
TIME
I was just thinking . . . there it goes,
Night has come again;
It seems the day has just begun,
When it comes to an end.

Where does it go this thing called time?
How can we catch each minute?
Why do we say, "It's been a long day"?
When really, there's no difference in it.

As I wake up each morning,
I thank God for the gift;
To start again, to do some good,
And try to give someone a lift.

There are good things in this great world,
If we would just stop and look;
Don't linger too long on just the bad,
But folow the words of His book.`

Time can be a friend or foe.
It's mostly up to us;
To have faith in four very special words,
They are, "In God we trust".

Edmund D. Pizon
Dreams Dance Upon the Hearth
[For "J", who stood by me!]
Ah, for a roaring, warm fire upon the hearth
to sit before in pensive mood
. . . reflective thought,
with pen in hand and paper to write upon
to place such thoughts in script.
Alas, no hearth for me exists, nor has it ever
but for a Mind's Eye image of what might be
'ere my wish were granted.

Yet, long's the thought of this dreamful scene
that I might bask in its misty glow
to write these thoughts in quiet mood upon my paper so.
Crackling flames in dancing, ruddy, glow,
swirl 'round and through the burning faggots
heaped upon the blackened irons, rushing 'tween
the layered logs, dance, twirl, then sparkle upward
towards the blackened flue above.
I lean upon the smoke-stained mantle and feel its heat
burning into my flesh softly, eyes staring into flashing
gasses, adrift in dreams of other places, people and things;
another World apart from here and now!
Ah, dancing flames upon the hearth, into Thee my eye gazes
in reflective mood, my real world hazes . . .
for a timeless moment it is no more!

Roma M. Hogue
IT'S OVER
[To someone I used to love who shattered my dreams but gave me back my life to be me. I'm grateful.]
We were so in love
for such a long, long time
Never thought you'd toss it all away for a nickel or a dime
The grass looked greener I'm sure to you
Hope you found what you were looking
for
When you left and closed the door
As for me—It's Over

You lied, you cheated
You were untrue
ALL you did was leave me blue
The hurt is deep, the hurt is still there
The hurt is beyond repair
It's Over

The love I had for you in the past just couldn't last
There's nothing left for me but only memories
It's Over—It's Over
You go your way, I'll go mine
Maybe we'll meet again sometime
Who knows—But for now
It's Over—IT'S OVER

Doreen Candace Lane
THE OLD MAN
On the corner of 22nd Street sits an old beggar,
His clothes are faded and torn,
His muddy brown shoes scuffed and worn,
His eyes stare with a piercing clarity
As he watches the world go by him,
His skin is withered and scarred by age,
His tired old head covered with thinning hair,

His gnarled hands rough with callouses,
Yet still he remains there
And watches the world go by him.

He never was a big success,
He never became a millionaire or famous star—
But he worked and he lived and he loved;
Now his story is told by his rough hands
And the lines etched in his tired old face.

He once had a family he dearly loved,
But all were lost long ago.
Someday he'll die—alone and forgotten;
Until then, he sits on the corner
And patiently watches as the world hurries by.

Fran Robbin

Fran Robbin
MERRY-GO-ROUND
The when
doesn't matter now
It's the point that
I remember
The how and why of it
and how much pleasure
(MR. SMILES)
those rememberances
give me.
That's the scary part
That's the trip
The best part, really.
I hope so
because that's where
I am now.
Right now
The trip
The flight
I finally feel
free enough
My color now
Would be no color-at all
Just light.

Lois Patterson Parker "Asenath"
SERPENTS MOUND
[I wish to dedicate my poem to my beautiful mother, Florence Parker and to the "Beaver Clan" of the Seneca Nation of Indians.]
Seven sinuous looped curves
HUGE! walls of earthen dirt.
Serpents death rattles long
HISSING! his condolence song.
SACHEMS! LORDCHIEFS! sons and
daughters. Stone carved pipes

With artistic otters. Copper
Duck hawk and a thin mica hand!
(OFFERINGS OF MY TRIBAL BAND)

Sky hawks whirling round and round
Near they dance and wheel up and down!
I hear the mournful silent sound
Of the Hopewellians SNAKE MOUND!

Michelle DeAngelis
WONDER
[For my daddy with love]
Moonlight, Moonlight—where are you
Up in the sky where it is blue,
I wonder if they'll ever be,
Anyone as small as me

Gwendolyn Trimbell Pease
REFRIGERATOR MICE
[My children: Susan, Sally, Morgan III, Cynthia and Martin—original Refrigerator Mice. Carrying on the family tradition is Grandson, Steven Scott Adamson.]
Product, not price, is the incentive
dry rice always fails to entice
my ever present refrigerator mice
soda and ice, a thin slice of cheese
any of those delightfully please
those sly refrigerator mice
inside freezer twice, food can't hide
for ranging around far and wide
boundlessly shy refrigerator mice
door sure barrier all along for fox terrier
searched thrice for super strong
nice hungry refrigerator mice
cool the iced cake but that won't suffice
presently unknown—tamperproof device
to eleminate refrigerator mice
no one may dare give any advice at all
concerning diet food, virtue or vice
to my two legged refrigerator mice.

Jane M. Macrae
BARRY ASHBEE
When Barry was seven years old,
A Stanley Cup he dreamed.
He first played with the Boston Bruins,
When traded he got steamed.

He played for Philadelphia,
For four long and tough years
Until a puck hit his right eye
And then came all the tears.

The eye injury made him coach,
The game was with New York.
The puck hit Ashlee in the eye,
That was sharp as a fork.

But the Flyers won the cup,
And how happy was he.
It was what he had wanted so,
With one eye he could see.

He has died of Leukemia,
A real sad death had he.
The pain he has he never said,
Which was so sad to see.

He leaves to most his wife and
   kids,
How sad they all must be.
But know that they will meet
   again,
In heaven by the sea.

He is missed by the Flyers
They wear his number foul
A man they all loved so dear,
His name is on the door.

When they see the cup,
It reminds of great old times they
   had
They think of Barry everyday
"The cup to you", they said

And so good-bye to you my
   friend,
A real great man you were.
I will remember you each day,
Good-bye to you Dear Sir.

Donnamae Feist
SMILE
The world is a lovely place
Skies need not be gray
Put a smile upon your face
And chase the blues away

Look straight ahead, but never
   down
The sun will shine above
For a smile and not a frown
Will fill your world with love

As you live from day to day
And sometime may feel sad
Smile at someone on your way
And soon you will feel glad

Melody A. Stehwien
GRANDMA'S OLD ROCKER
Grandma's old rocking chair
   holds many memories dear,
The times upon her knee she
   held us so near.
The number could not begin to
   be counted of the children held
   there,
For there was not a child around
   that Grandma's love was not
   shared.
The squeaks and scratches the
   old chair holds are many; tis
   true,
But the story behind this chair
   was of a love that grew.
I know there is many a rocker
   which holds the same story as
   this,
But it's the rocker that still lives
   on and the Grandma we miss.

Georgia Radcliffe
**I Stand Alone Upon the
Shore**
I stand alone upon the shore
   and watch the waves come
   rolling in,
The breakers, arabesque and
   white,
   slice through the mist, grey
   tinged and thin.
I think in terms of timelessness,
   of centuries when I am gone,
The sea will still remain the same,
   its tides still flow obliquely on,
While my soul, wedded to the
   wind,

will roam the realms that
   transcend all
And I will know an ebullience
   that does not retrogress or pall.
We have a rare communion then,
   my deathless soul and this
   deep sea,
For I am now a part of it
   and it is now a part of me.
The Diety has blessed us both
   with an intense, eternal flow,
Mine in the airy arc above,
   the sea in parallel below.
I stand alone upon the shore
   and watch the waves come
   rolling in,
The only wonder in this world
   to which I feel acutely kin.

Paul Shapshak, Ph.D.
STARLIT RESOURCES
May brings desert winds giving a
   warm Spring when least you
   expect it.
Unknown to the letter,
   unreached like pictures
Suddenly rising up, uncalled,
Yet pressing on horizons, never
   defined, moving beyond
   rainbows,
Pillars of stone, and lighted caves
Search into the dusk from dawn,
   searching for beginnings and
   ends.

October brings rains, waterfalls
   get started, missed all year
While we search the hillsides for
   signs of life. Another Spring,
   more flowers, talking again,
Tides come and go, the rooms go
   past again, speeding by life.
The rest of a domeless habitat
Unspent bottles, shattered glasses,
Forests edging onto gleaming
   fields of steel
Where primative primates once
   again roam the byways of this
   Earth.

Questions come and go, far and
   wide, roaming on the run.
Ideas are roped in, filed, gassed,
   and deposited in crematoria.
Crime spills onto the streets,
   cannibal Cretans living in
   painted homes
Live illusions of their art, only to
   find trussed bodies, skeletal
   remains,
Death stalking them.
Murder and disease sworn in look
   tall
Returning questions boomerang
   through cities
Incredibe aerodynamic machines
   cry for outer space,
Unreliable pillars, unseen, are
   made into history,
Yet collapse every day, broken by
   its weight.

Matt L. Riedel
EMPTY CONFUSION
An inner loneliness burns in my
   heart
So intense the flame of despair
When it seems that no one cares

An emptiness that seems to tear
   apart
Holding back a lonely tear
There's no sweet voice for me

to hear
In confusion dreaming; things
   will be fine
Pain grows to shattered heights
The way I must endure my nights

On hoping; change from dark
   design
But dreams don't end the pain
My days remain the same . . .

Hazel Smoak Clover
**One Heck Of a Guy, "Harry
Jones"**
*[Harry Jones, my neighbor for
nineteen years, was a rare man
whom you only get to meet
once in a lifetime. He believed
in being a good neighbor and
he truly was. This was written
for a wonderful guy whom
everyone on Fairbrook Street
misses.]*
He was just a neighbor across the
   street
But a better guy you'd never meet.
Always there with a cheerful grin
He truly knew how to be a friend.

Fresh lemon pie, a favorite deal
With chitlins' and collard greens
   to add to his meal.
A glass of cheer and a "Hello there,
Come on in and pull up a chair.
Yes, kid, I really care."

Now he's away and I must face
The fact that no one is here to fill
   his place.
That's truly something no one
   else could do,
There was just one "Harry Jones"
   to smile at you.

Now that he's missing and his
   cheer is gone
I'll grieve for awhile but never
   alone.
Always remembering with our
   neighbors to toast
The friendly guy who gave us the
   most.
Of himself he gave with never a
   thought
Just lots of love and laughter on
   his morning walk.
With a wave of the hand as he
   strolled by.
"Here's to you, Harry Jones, one
   heck of a guy."

Rev. Ann Coffee Walker
IN SEARCH OF
Place the inner self in total
   control
and watch your life begin to
   unfold.
Replacing all negative thoughts
   and
deeds with the positive actions
   that
you need.
For when the truth is unveiled to
   you,
nothing else will be of use, know
   what
is and understand, that you must
   give
in to the inner-man, the inner-
   man that
holds the key where life is all it's
   meant to be.
Knowing thy self is what it

will take
to inherit the Kingdom that is
   God's
estate. Remember the words of
   God's
only Son, that He and the Father
   are
truly one.
In Search Of *Truth* you will begin
   to
understand the relationship
   between
God and Man.
Come to full circle, continue the
   quest for in the fulfillment, there's
   no second best.

James Rollo
GOD'S GARDEN IS NO EDEN
Beneath my feet the garden,
Before my eyes, sullen hills
Of Gilead on offing loom
O'er Meggido's luscious green,
An unlikely Armageddon.

Nearby, the Jordan sluggish winds
Along that fecal fetid tract,
A paradise long littered, lost.
Somewhere, that fruit and
   slithered coil
Eludes my searching eye,
Whatever became of knowledge
And immortality?
Did they die with the trees?

Estella Alvarado
SILENT FEELING
This is a pleasant and peaceful
   feeling,
   yet it hurts so intensely and so
   unappealingly.
It happens so sudden,
   without a whisper,
   without a notice,
it just suddenly attacks.
It can be tremendous and yet
   very small.
It can last a while or all your life,
   yet there is no escaping it.

Robert C. Martin
ALONE
In time to say goodnight . . .
rain came the other night
and like giant teardrops made my
   window
appear as a surrealistic painting
With my blanket drawn high
   over me
I realized I was lonely . . .
and with a sigh I moved closer to
   the windowpane
hoping the painting would
   explain . . .

Then I saw my reflection in the mirror of rain
and was completely surprised and should've known
this is what I wanted . . . to have my own . . . space . . .alone
Drifting off to dream thinking
and hearing the melodic raindrops on the ceiling
and feeling . . . I've grown
I can face the night . . . alone . . . so alone!

Gertrude Durkee
RIMSKY'S SCHEHERASADA
As your soft, sweet, exotic music enfolds
Briefly, a page from the past,
A young prince and his beloved
Or a vagabond in search of adventure
Brought back momentarily
From immortality, to haunt us again,
And fill our hearts
With the beauty of your song

Scherherasada, play on and on
So that a world, torn apart, by bitter strife
May listen and bask momentarily
In this beautiful classic of another era
Keep filling our hearts with your song
Help calm our spirits anew
With hope and promise
For a better tomorrow

Julie Sheila Rea
SPRING
As the sun beckoned to the dew,
And rose to call another morning new,
The wind blew life into the trees,
That house the honey, made by bees.

The flowers peeked into the day,
To catch a glimpse of a golden ray,
God looked down and saw this sight,
And called it "Spring" with great delight.

Dorothy Sammons
SWEET MEMORIES
I remember the day when we met, dear,
You had just turned sweet sixteen.
Your hair was tied with a ribbon,
You wore a cotton dress in green.

I saw you one day in the malt shop,

You said your name was Mary Lou.
Then you sat on the stool beside me,
We shared a soda with straws for two.

I remember the night at the sea shore,
We were walking hand in hand.
The moon was shining above us,
We left our footprints in the sand.

Our love seemed to swell like the breakers,
The full moon caught us in its spell.
I proposed and you quickly accepted,
We have a story of love to tell.

Fern Evelyn Knodel
FREEWAY PUPPETS
The sky broke wild with bits of flaming reds,
As if afraid for creatures in their beds,
A flash of light ripped wide a golden trail,
Then opened scars, in minds that knew travail,
Quick thoughts were pounced on coffee cups of chance—
As motors raced and eyes were burned in trance,
A thousand blots of sound moved out in place
Each bent on winning freeways ruthless race,
The colors smoothed as puppets found their chore;
A world moves on, puppets keep the score.

Lori Jean Lang
LITTLE CATERPILLAR
Little caterpillar, though you may not know it yet, before you lies a course of pain, sorrow, and misery. Right now, all you care about is eating a tender leaf. How carefree you are. But your days are numbered for soon it will be time to make your chrysalis.

The change that will take place will take time, pain and eventually—death. You will die, but will ressurect again in a new form. Yes, a butterfly. The transformation will be awe-inspiring, but to obtain true beauty, you must first experience the pain. For it is only through pain that you can grow and change and become what you were meant to be.

Don't fret. No matter what you do, don't fret. Just keep your eyes on what you will become and the pain will be easier to bear.

Chariss D. Cruz
I MISS YOU
Inside I feel a certain pain
That only comes
When I'm away from you
It tends to linger, carry on
And makes my day turn blue
People ask, "Are you alright?"
I say I'm doing fine

They ask again, "Hey it's okay,
Just got a lot of stuff on my mind."
But the pain, it hurts
And bothers me so
Sometimes all through the day
But we both know it won't go away
Until you're back home to stay
So until then
I'll just wear a smile
And hide what I feel inside
Because I know it will be awhile
Till the day you come cast it aside

Arthur Charles Garcia
SWEET HELEN
Her name was sweet Helen and she roamed upon a pretty sea
she found the wind's soft embrace,
and wandered about like in a dream;

She sings the moon asleep and cradles it in her arms
and captures the sun in her hands, falls down to earth without any harm—

Late October leaves scamper along with Helen's smile
they fade beyond the reaches of outer space,
and wait for me awhile.

Drifting by endless meadows and lost horizons afar
flinging her frenzied hair while touching my private star,
I try to follow her footprints embedded throughout the air
and hope to find my sweet Helen whenever I'm in despair.

Melissa L. Hernandez
JOEL
My best friend Joel, I see your heart more clearly than you know
For I have found a way to read the feelings you don't show.

I saw your disappointment when your dreams did not come true
And knew your desperation though your actions gave no clue.

Your joy, when you succeeded— that I truly shan't forget!
You wondered how I guessed it, for you hadn't told me yet.

I know the way you felt, sweet Joel, when Battle called your name.
You fought with outward courage, but I know the fear that came.

I understood the reason when you shuddered at the sight
Of that sick bird. You would not rest until it was in flight!

And anguish! How I pitied the deep sorrow you were in.
How could you tell nobody, Joel? Your silence was a sin.

I felt how much you needed me when you were hurt that day;
I knew that our deep friendship meant much more than you would say.

Although upon our Wedding Day you never shed a tear,
I knew your great emotion, and your love for me, my dear.

I know the pain you felt, dear Joel, when Baby died last Fall.
I know you cried, Heart's Dearest, though you wouldn't grieve at all.

How do I see and understand the feeling you disguise?
The answer, dear, is simple: it is written in your eyes.

Cristal D. Buckner
AMANDA DAUN
[Dedicated to Amanda Daun, our 5 month old angel]
Her little eyes so very blue,
And loving her is oh so true.

Her tiny toes upon her feet,
Knowing her is really neat.

Her little hands and tiny fingers,
Love for her will always linger.

Her nose so tiny upon her face,
And her skin—as soft as lace.

Her tiny voice is oh so sweet,
And watching her grow is really neat.

She changes so much from day to day,
She's independant in her own way.

Her tiny eyes sparkle like morning dew,
As pretty as she is—there are few.

She tries so hard to talk to us,
But all that comes out is a little fuss.

Her first tooth hurt so bad,
To see her hurt made me feel sad.

We were blessed with her five months ago,
And our love for her will always grow.

I LOVE YOU MANDI
LOVE MOM

Nancy M. Broyles
ECHOES
Sometimes when I close my eyes
I can see your face,
and you're always smiling.
And I remember the times
When we laughed together,
and held each other close.
And the time we cried away our pain.
But like a music box tune
slowly winding down to a stop,
All that is left is an . . .
Echo of yesterday.

Earl Wayne Shehorn
SOMEDAY . . .
Someday, I will leave it all for awhile . . .

And time though unstopping will await for me;

I will grab up some paper along with pens,
a knapsack and food, and a jacket or two,
money of a small amount and thereupon
set out.

Only God knows for how long or where I will
find myself as I should care not, at the
time.

And though I cannot escape totally I will
escape mostly, and take myself through
the following wills of nature—this I
promise:
fields of green and fields of yellow
under trees of green and skies of blue
by lakes of brown and rocks so old
and houses of white and old country roads
along new freeways with unshaded light
and even a park bench where I may sit
and write.

Someday . . .

Sara Woodbury
SPRING
Once more the Palouse is fallow.
The ponds graced with mallards.
Crocus blooming after the thaw,
The river flush with rapid flow.

I think of you years ago now.
I suppose the branches will greenbud again.
The flicker-eyed robin return.

In the night I hear the screech of owl,
The low patter of rain.
I drink a cup of tea
And lay in the darkness.

Darcy Smith
POEM 2
Dawn.
Bursting forth.
Brilliantly illuminating the dark sky.
Projecting the force of energy over the land.
Softly ebbing the dusky atmosphere.
Receding slowly.
Sunset.

Carl "Pat" Henry
The Ghosts Of Wymore High
[While working for a better tomorrow, may the Senior Class of 2039 (from Wymore Nebraska) not find on arrival that they left it somewhere behind in yesterday. Be-seein-ya, the Wymore High School Senior Class of 1939]
Since back in twenty-thirty-nine, a story old had filled my mind
How a Senior Class from Wymore High, removed the letters "m" and "y"
And in between them, placed a "day", to complete the lovely month of May.

Yes, for many years, I'd heard it said, that class from long ago, now dead,
Had kept a date, to celebrate, the year that they did graduate . . .

In fact, 'tis true, this story old, to me no longer something told,
For I was in the school one day, the year was right, in the late of May,
I found myself, way back in time, the year was ninteen-thirty-nine . . .
I saw this class from yesterday, as they gathered there to spend the day.

There was Mildred and Margaret, Ethyl, Eileen
Carl, Murray and Alfred, Bill and Eugene,
Lyle and Donald, Bernard and Wayne,
Helen and Wilma, Marie and Elaine,
Olive and Letha, Gayle, Cleta and Harold,
Dorothy and Phyllis, Lucille, Jack and Gerald,
Evelyn and Donna, Pat, Paul, Billie Mae,
Don and Marie, and Charles, there that day.

Yes, I know it's true, that few of you, can know this story as I do,
And fewer still, recall, relate, the date this class did graduate;
But for me you see, there is no doubt, I saw this class write these words out.

They wrote: Five times eight, times eight again,
Times three, times two, plus nine, then ten
And agreed to meet, in the years that end,
In nine and four, but only then.

So since that time, I've watched this class, with handsome lad, and pretty lass;
This class of nineteen-thirty-nine, return from somewhere out in time.
They meet, and greet, and spend the day. I've watched them come, then go away.
So it makes no "never-mind" to me, if no one else can hear or see;
But in the late of May, when the year is right, when the day is done,
on that certain night;
I've stood and heard them say good bye, this class,
The Ghosts of Wymore High . . .

Jenny Senn
SEARCHING
Through the secret passage
Cross the bluegreen sea,
Through the underworld's darkest doorways
I search for the woman in me.
Down through the depths of the ocean,
Up through the stars in the sky—
Sometimes I lie still like a rock
And other times I fly
Beyond the earth,
Beyond the dream,
I'm almost there,
Or so it seems.
I'll always search
For the woman in me

Till I find her.
I have to find her to be free.

Jan Pearman

Jan Pearman
Memories Of a Country Christmas
[To Cherri, Jeff, Rob, Don, Sue and to all of the people from my hometown, Dalton, Missouri.]
A beautiful blanket of fresh fallen snow.
Tree tops that glistened like prisms of glass.
The smell of candies and cookies that mom always made.
Country roads so full of snow that sometimes a car couldn't pass.
The beautiful country church where we gathered on Christmas Eve.
The new Sears catalogue filled with toys to wish for—
Frozen ponds, great for skating, sledding and bonfires.
The Christmas wreath that always hung on our door.

Trying to get to sleep on Christmas Eve
While listening for hooves on the roof or a "ho ho ho" at the door!
All of the family coming for Christmas dinner. (what a day!)
Christmas wrapping paper all over the floor.

Years have passed, and I've left that beautiful countryside.
My Christmas' are spent differently now, but yet—
Those country Christmas memories filled with love of friends and family
Are childhood memories that I will never forget!

Gaye Lynne Kambak
THE ARC
Look at every color in the rainbow
Focus not only on the blue
Esteem each hue's quality
For all refractions are true.

Look at every color in the rainbow
Focus not only on the red
'Tis dispersible bands that seek direction
Tho' lights are dimmed, they're never led.

E'en if some say, "Too fanciful;

More illusion than what is real.
Observe a straighter pathway
With barring of parallel,"
Still see the multicolor in the rainbow
Stay receptive of an inspiring solar glow
The path is made truer for reflection
When bending a symmetrical whole.

Robert K. Jasman
QUIET LIFE
Porcelain powder
Cakes of June
Time tables of two
Count them in every room

Drapeless diary quenches her lips
With fingered-mind, she soon grips
A river of white water
To a broken highway
Falling

Into a tailspinning dream
Splashing in a morning brook
Such ripples and only a look
Like a chainless link across the sea
But a bridge I find in me

Blue forest swallow
Velvety flight
Seeing you beyond my sight

Joan Pittson (Joansey)
THE CHILDREN
In the courtyard deep and silent,
stand the children, faces grey
No song has touched their silent lips
for their souls have been stolen away.

The mists around them circling,
has secrets of its own
The dark moss is slowly creeping
tears of sadness it has sown.

And in the darkness silent, still
the children leave their home,
They search to find their evil killer
and toss him in the foam.

But when the sun has rose in morn,
the children behind their wall
have fled
Once more to frozen stand,
until the century is dead.

Louetta Jensen
BLACK HEARTED ACE
Words from your lips, sounding so very candy-coated but etched with evil.
Deepened blue eyes looking out with great warmth yet seeking inward satisfaction.
Your heart only pretending this immense love but ever ready for the sweet kill.

The softest caress of your hand only just barely holding in check the blow that was certain to come.
Ears so openly eager to welcome my every phrase to become stone deaf at your own command.
A soul professing endearing qualities of all that is good,

but in reality; I see now there are simply none.

Your carefully plotted layout of life's desires and promises of a loving tomorrow.

Your aim to build those grandiose dreams to be shared solely by you and I.

But of course, for only you to destroy all in good time; your perverted gladness at my intense sorrow.

And now the pain you have cruelly dealt me brings a smug smile to your face.

You feel true exhilaration at your final triumph.

My love, such as you are, have foolishly left the table before the last draw.

I shall now show my blackest and fiercest ace.

Tis true my broken heart lies at your feet yet now I am indeed reborne anew.

A strength of reserve solid and bold, sprung to life with careful purpose and forethought.

I, such an apt student, have learned much about supreme tortuous designs.

Yes, most decidedly, my teacher was none other than you.

Having grown in numbers, your once so eager students, now await with patience: each holding your darkest methods of savage hatred.

Surely every corner you now turn, you will look behind for traces of steps and lessons well learned from the past to befall you.

Unfortunately you folded much too quickly.

Soon now, my love, you will feel the ebony spade—never knowing which hand spilled the deed—knowing only the inevitable black dread of love that is dead.

Lori Nickeloff
WINTER BEGINS
[Inspired by My Lord God, and dedicated to My husband Mark, and daughter Niki. All whom I love very much.]
A softness ponders the new fallen snow,
Silence enhances the earth.
It may only last a moment or so,
But a season is given new birth.

Mary L. Garside
DEAR MISTY
You say your daddy is with Jesus,
And we know that is right;
You see God needed a special angel
To help make Heaven more bright.

Someday we will all be with them,
Maybe sooner than you think—
Because when Jesus decides to call us
We will go quicker than a wink!

Then you and mommy and your daddy

Will be happy like before,
And your Grandmas and your Grandpas
Will be smiling even more.

Someday when you and Grandma Ball
Are having a little talk
She will tell you more about Jesus,
And along which path to walk.

So while we are waiting, Honey
For that great reunion day,
We will all be trusting Jesus
And we want you to help us pray.

John J. Schmid
A MAGIC CARPET RIDE
Everybody at one time or another
    has a bad day
one where nothing seems to go
    right
and every muscle in your body is
    tight.

Well, I have the perfect cure
    and it only takes a minute,
just close your eyes and take the
    tour.

You can think or pretend
    that you're on a magic carpet
and the ride will never end.

Your carpet can take you far
    and just think
you don't even have to park your
    car.

The carpet can take you to places
    that you've never seen
or for a quick ride around the
    block
whatever you choose, the
    imagination must be keen.

Eventually you will have to come
    back
        to the real world
but to get by, the magic carpet
    ride provides the slack.

Scott Lee Haddon
MAD LUNACY
Misty summer, autumn sky
The birds fly south one more
    time
Tis the season all must die
Church bells echo ancient chime

Thou shall kill thy neighbor
No worthy favors, no good deeds
Watch for the fruit that they
    should bear
Must take it with the seeds

Mysterious moon full again
All the convicts freed

No escape from harm or sin
The human stampede

Wretched fingers crushed on
    pavement
Take another anguished drink
Morbid confusion, drowning in
    torment
Our your wrists in the bathroom
    sink

The weary bones do not stir
Reality becomes a dream
Through the blur, you hear
    laughter
The fading sounds, a silent
    scream

Kimberly Anne Farrow
LIKE NO OTHER
  I am like no other
And what I say is true,
Because I am myself and you are
  you.

  I live how I want and not how
  people wish.
I do what I want and not how
  people dream.

  I am not an actor playing in a
  written scene.
I don't play by the rules, but go
  where life takes me
    and let it be,
Because you are you and I am me;
  I am like no other and that is
  how it
    should be.

James L. Heinke
TERRY'S BIRTHDAY
Terry's only twenty four
Here's wishing her a whole lot
    more
If she thinks that is too much
Next year I'll get her a crutch
If she thinks that is too many
I'll buy her a present, for only a
    penny
If she thinks that is too old
Her story's just begun to be told
If she thinks that is just right
I will say, "she's very bright"
This poem is getting way too
    long
So I will end it with a song
Happy birthday to you
I love you true
Happy birthday, dear Terry
And many more, too

Elaine M. Scheller
ALL THINGS
The sun shines on
All Things,
Yet one day
All things
will have a vague
white coating,
somewhat like
confectioner's sugar,
only crackly
to the touch.
And the leaves
will turn brown
only to die
from the tree.
All Things
will be cold.
I dread
that cold
dead
Beauty.

Donna L. Himple
PEACE
Peace is the quietness when
    you're all alone,
  The warmth of the sun shining
  down.
Peace is the stillness on the
    greenish blue bay,
  With only the rippling sound.
Peace is the breeze blowing your
    hair,
  The birds chirping above in the
  trees.
Peace really comes from inside of
    each one,
  So it's what ever you want it to
  be.

Sarah Tague Smith
GOLDEN BOY
Your sweet Mississippi drawl,
Mother says, "Southern
    Gentlemen."
Meridian mama's boy
You are.

A C.C. and water is your only
    necessary
foreplay,
Enough for good-time girls
who are worth
Your Time.

If I had a nickel
for every one,
I'd buy you
some
peace of mind.

Cheryl A. Mears
LOVE
Lips gently touching;
    kissing tenderly.
    softly saying, "I love you"
    like flowers in a breeze.
Open up your heart,
    like birds in a tree.
    sing your song so strongly
    of how love ought to be.
Voices softly whispering;
    like whispering spring air.
    speaking words of love and joy
    and saying how much they care.
Everyone ought to know,
    that in Heaven above,
    God has filled this world of ours
    with the best of LOVE.

Beatrice Hernandez
SUMMER'S END
The summer sun will soon be
    gone;
no more will we hear the birds
    sweet song.

All their jobs are done;
But winter has just begun.

We can go back to think of a way,
to keep our summer thoughts to
    use day after day.

But when we think of the snows
    to come and
    the things that go on.
We will reminisce of the songs
    already sung.

Juli Cranford
BREATHES A MAN
Breathes a man or woman who
    has not been
touched by the vibrancy of nature?

Who has not stained his hands
    with

the juice of wild blackberries?
Who has not relished the first
bite of a
perfect plum still wet with dew?

Whose heart has not soared with
the high flying hawk?
Who has never been silenced by
the singing of whales?

Who has never inhaled the
sharp odor of earth after a rain?
Who has never been awed by
the ferocity of a storm?

How can one truly live without
knowing the strength and splendor
of life itself?
And how can one truly die
without ever
having witnessed death in the
wild?

Michael R. Bryce
THE IDEAS OF EARTH
In my mind there is a place,
far, far, far into space.
On a planet where demons lie
Their bodies outlined by the
clear red sky.

Evolution has turned their minds
to steal and hoard what
another finds.
A giant war will end this race
on the planet far, far, far into
space.

I can imagine another place
that's not so far out into space;
To a giant light that brings us life,
which brings us also problems
and strife.

Death, sin, and deadly diseases
are some of the problems that
Satan pleases.
Man will suffer these for all time,
But he softens the world with
music and rhyme.

Music and rhyme, as some people
say,
are what keeps us in time each
minute of the day.
Some of the gifts of man, like fire,
are the musical, whimsical,
lute and lyre.

Arden Michael
OZARK BEAUTY
*[To one of nature's beauties I
discovered in the Ozarks]*
I went down to the Ozarks a few
years back
Trying to discover what it is I
lack
Having no idea I'd meet the gal of
my dreams
But God had placed her there
for me, it seems
Needing me as much as I did her
I nicknamed her "Kitten" when
I heard her purr
Finding a friend and wanting a
wife
It turned out she became mine
for life
There in the Ozarks, the trees
and the beauty
Mother Nature has sure done
her duty
The rivers, hills and wild flowers
We need to slow down and
admire her powers
The simplicity of the wild rose

And the daisy there also grows
All blooming so pretty to add to
the scene
Mother Nature—The Beauty
Queen
This Queen adds to Kitten's
beauty too
Making time better for me and
you
Adding beauty, joy and thrills
As we walk through the Ozark
Hills

Ralph E. Kane

Ralph E. Kane
MY DREAM
*[There was once a young,
vivacious, beautiful and sincere
girl who lived in South Dakota.
She married me, and—thirty-
eight years later—she is still
young, vivacious, beautiful and
sincere. She's Alice.]*
We were laughing, uproariously.
The whole room was crowded,
cheering,
Babbling, gurgling gloriously,
Singing, shouting, dulling one's
hearing.
Yet could I sense that someone
was waiting:
Not to join the revelry of the
crowd,
But to see me. I stood hesitating-
Swung open the door and was
cowed:

Grinning, there, was Death. We
left together.
There was no time to turn to a
friend.
All was now silent. Who
knows whether
The dream was now come to
an end?

Shirley M. (Jackson) McGary
AUTUMN'S CURTAIN
*[This poem is dedicated to my
beloved mother and son with
whom my opinion of autumn
and summer is shared.]*
When beautiful summer her
mission completes
And ceases to grant us the
warmth of her heat
And flowers shall wither and
grass shall turn brown,
Then autumn's curtain shall
slowly come down.
To birds and bees we shall say
good bye.
Dark clouds shall cover the blue
of the sky.
Autumn's curtain shall do its duty
And hide the remains of
summer's beauty.
The leaves on the trees shall turn
red and brown,
Then slowly and sadly fall to the
ground.
Shadows shall form to the
greatest of height,
As quickly falls the darkness of
night.
Farewell to Lady Summer's warm
breeze,
To the green of the grass and the
shade of the trees:
Her beautiful face disappears
once more
As autumn's curtain boldly takes
o'er.
Summer's loss shall be mourned
by mankind for certain
While wrapped in the sheet of
autumn's curtain.

Loretta L. Alexander
INFINITY
A Mass expanse of sky, twinkling
stars nestled in its bosom.
God's eternal love and power
emanating throughout the vast
reaches of space.
Those worthy immortal souls,
alive forever in the peaceable
kingdom.
Love and hate, abiding each in
their own destiny for life
eternal.
Life, winging its way forever in a
labyrinth of infinity . . .

Patrick D. Smith
THE COLD, THE COLD
I suppose there is a sun in the sky,
but I haven't seen it by and large
for many a day. Perhaps in time I
may.
Where is it?
Is it obfuscated by smoke that
rises
from the cars that rush by,
rising, hiding the sky?
Or is smoke rising from stacks
concealing the sky with black,
poisonous,
sulfuric fumes that choke man
and strangles
the sun?
I feel the coming cold and hear
the crunching
of the creeping ice. All is cold.
The bird is no longer on the
wing—his notes
are frozen. The dinosaurs

perished long ago,
encased by cold. The sun will not
shine,
huddled behind idiocies of
mankind.

Oh, to see the sun rise in the east
in a
ball red-crimson and to feel its
vibrant rays.
To know that spring is coming,
and the flowers
will be blooming. But that will
not be.
For man in all his ingenuity has
hid the sun
by what he has done.

Judy Scott
LOVE
A mother's sweet touch,
A gentle unselfish kiss,
A fragile flower.

Judy Catholos Lorenzen
CHILD OF MINE
[To Job, my first born.]
A land of lollipops, love, and
sweet dreams
Childhood times are most
precious it seems
With someone to feed you, love
you, and care
Who gives of their time
unselfishly sharing
To read you a book or simply talk
Who takes the time to look when
taking a walk
Who answers every question,
every question being "Why?"
Who hugs you and kisses you
when you start to cry
Who loves you so much that
you'll never know
And bundles you up to play in
the snow
A kitten, A puppy, A baby calf
Adoring your smile and loves
your laugh
To cuddle and protect you all of
the time
For I love you so much little
child of mine

Rae Marie Ruthenberg
HEARTBREAK
Blood is red
depression is blue
everything is said
everything is done
with the flow of ink
with the logic of mind
with the hurt of the heart
it is done.
The love we shared is over.
The memories are put in the
back of my mind
and taken out carefully another
time.

Karin Marie McKeon
SUBSTANCE
*[Because of and dedicated to
Danial]*
The need lies inside dormant
Take away the shield
Toss the mask
Defense causes anguish
Anguish leads frustration
Frustration harbors fear
Fear hides from adventure
Vulnerability manifests courage
Courage decides the overture

Mary Lynn Miles
WHENEVER YOU SMILE

[I dedicate this poem to Gene Muse who inspires me with his love. And to my family who taught me the joy of a smile.]

Love provides the fuel
Fuel ignites the need
Need converts hearts of stone
Stone crumbles
Defense collapses
A new spirit emerges from the ashes . . .

Whenever you smile
Inside me there's this fire
It glows for awhile
Then burns higher and higher.

I live for the day
When you come to me
And you will say
I love you so much babe—look and see.

The joy will be mine
This love you will feel
It will be so fine
It will be so real.

The freedom we will find
With love always kind.

Mildred Ballard
THE EXQUISITE PRESENCE

O, Exquisite Presence, diffuse my being
With the lovely effusion of Thy pure Spirit:
Reaching out through my heart;
Gentled, sensitized, and ennobled,
Made more aware.
Like the "awful untouchable",
Whom Thou didst touch,
So may I, unworthy,
Luxuriate in Thy Presence;
Touch but the hem of Thy Royalty!
Reach out through me:
Touching with loveliness,
Healing the tortured,
Transforming ugliness;
Feeding the hungry,
Clothing the naked,
Restoring the broken in heart and in body.
Re—fleshing bare bones.
Sharing, fathering, mothering,
Caring.

O, EXQUISITE PRESENCE, touch Thou me!

Connell Plunkett
HAPPINESS

The world is rushing, seeking madly,
For true happiness of heart.
But the road that they have taken,
Is the wrong one from the start.
If you'd grant a man his wishes,
Every one he made each day,
Do you think that he'd be happy,
As he journeyed on his way?
Oh no my friend 'tis strange to say,
Satisfaction isn't gained,
By having your own way.
There's a want that's far more solemn,
In the depth of every heart.
Which only comes by knowing,
That you well have done your part,

And the life of friends made sweeter,
Mid this world of strife and sin,
And you've pleased the Lord in heaven,
Then does happiness begin.

Barbara A. Termini
LORE UNSHAMED

A plain doorway,
within, there is a child's cry.
All around God's gift to live.
Yet oppression, seems to signify:
Happiness, a call of doom, sucked down with a heavy price to pay,
the hand of man.

It has been in the faces of
men and women, of waneness and
despair, so it has reached our children.

Now called upon, each and every one of us.

A nation is divided.
The family is unmighted.
It is time to stand erect.
Take measurements and correct.

Lori Ann Nilsson
OUR CHILD

I've got his child inside of me
The feeling is something to me should be,
This child of ours is ours to share
It shows us we love him enough to say,
We'll bring him into our world to stay
Our love will grow and grow to bare,
Another child that is ours to share.

William Anthony Kern
WHERE WE WENT WRONG

Children grown, kids of their own. Parents sitting, watching, wondering where they went wrong.
Kids in trouble and don't know why. Parents see the fault only through their eye. Blind to the fact kids have minds of their own, maybe mischievous, devious and wrong.
Light comes in, they take the blame for their own. Still parents wondering where they went wrong.

Marvee L. Marr
REMEMBER ME

I see the faces and hear the voices, time is standing still.
I look at the people and try to absorb
what they really feel.

Some seem happy, some seem sad, some seem to be fading away.
Some who are leaving wish to leave,
and some they wish to stay.

Many were just fellow classmates that you'll never see again.
But a few you might not see, were once your close friends.

To say your so-longs, good-byes, and say, "Call me sometime."
Knowing they probably won't, but it's a cute traditional line.

You've been through it before and you'll
do it again, with or without the tears.
But you'll keep it down low that deep down
inside, you have these hidden fears.

Fears; that a great-loving friendship
is to end this subtle way.
And you may never see or talk to these people after this day.

So please believe what I'm about to say, is in no way a lie.
I want and need your friendship forever, never to say good-bye.

Violet Reaves
The Little Singing Brook

That little singing brook I remember so well
When I was a little girl it cast its brooksie spell
Its brooksie song as it trickled along made me listen and look
As I picked tiny flowers by that babbling brook
There in a golden meadow I stopped for a closer look

It was such a peaceful happy singing little brooksie
With tiny stones of blue and pink so I picked a bagful for all to see
I carried them home as I sang about my little brooksie
It is a childhood memory of song and flowers
Where I lived by the brookside and whiled away the hours

John T. Hudelson
OMNIPRESENCE

Forever present,
  God's Spirit Divine,
on the lofty mountain
  in the whispering pine.
His power is seen
  in the lightning flash,
He speaks from the
  thunder's roll.
Amid the flowers
  and budding trees,
His voice
  echoes to and fro.
His countenance shines
  through fleecy clouds,
on fields of golden grain.
His love abounds
  in every nook
and showers of cooling rain.
A still small voice
  in the babbling brook
onrushing down the stream.

S. S. Etheridge
EYES

What's the matter?
Are my eyes less beautiful?
Are they getting smaller and sinking
  deep into my head?
Or have you now just learned to look
  straight through them—
To differentiate what I meant from
  what I said?
I feel the admiration's gone;
I miss the words of praise.

Have you realized that I'm just like
  every other girl you know?
I was hoping that my absence would have
  stifled that reaction,
And I'm trying to make my eyes appear to grow.
Is it really true that beauty's only skin deep?
And does it show you that my soul's as
  painted as my eyes?
I was hoping that my eyes could grow and
  swallow you,
But now I see they're only big enough
  to cry.

Magdalena M. Russey
Welcome, Welcome, Jesus

Bells are ringing
Holy, holy, holy.
Full of joy we're singing
Holy, holy, holy,
Welcome songs to Jesus,
The newborn heavenly child.
O welcome, welcome, Jesus
You're God's greatest gift to us.

Even the stars sparkle brighter
This very, very special night
Holy, holy, holy,
Everlasting love and peace
Is now in sight.

O welcome, welcome, Jesus
You're God's greatest gift to us.

Frances J. Tate
WORTH OUR SORROW

You take away our fathers
And send them off to war.
Then when the supply has diminished
You hold out your hands for more.

You take away our brothers
And teach them how to fight.
And leave us only with prayers
We silently say each night.

You take away our sons
And put them in uniforms.
And where there was once a family
The bittersweet memories are torn.

We learn for everything, there is a cause.
Where trouble begins, it must somehow end.
You give us medals

and tell us the deed was good.
But medals cannot touch our skin
The way our love ones should.

And as we lay awake each night
Wondering,
    if it was worth the fight.
We only hope that the next war
Is really worth the fighting for.

Sylvia Faye Wools
When I Am Laid To Rest
When I am laid to rest,
I hope someone will say,
"It's sad to see her go."
Or perhaps someone will say,
"She was so nice to know!"

When I am laid to rest,
I want everyone to think,
Kindly of me, when they speak
    my name,
Then, "dear Lord", I shall know,
My life was not lived in vain!

Patti Ciliberti

Patti Ciliberti
GOD ALMIGHTY
*[This poem is dedicated to my
father, the greatest man that
ever lived, whom I love very
much.]*
When you're feeling kind of down
And really are confused
There's one man you can talk to
He will help you choose.

He will make you feel better
For with him you can tell all
Don't worry about distress
With him you feel high and tall.

You can tell all your personal
    feelings
All your fears and such
You'll never have to worry
about his love
It's always more than enough.

So if you're feeling down
And want to be cheered
If you have to clear your
    conscience
You won't have to fear.

Just spill it all
He will understand
For he is God Almighty
The leader of this land.

Clyde W. Painton
FORBIDDEN FRUIT
Strange, beautiful and sweet,
Wrapped in dazzling robes,
Delightful to the eye, 'tis meet
To leave alone in sweet repose.

Innocent in beauty if not touched,

As perfect as a queen;
But to touch, it will tainted be,
The bitter dregs are seen.

Though a thousand passions rise
    to
Tempt you in your weakest hour,
Pluck it not or taste its sweetness
Lest deceived, you find it sour.

To be the master for a minute
Of passions wild and hot
May be life's richest, rare reward
For those who touch it not.

To pluck, may be another cup
Drawn from a bitter well;
Another one in sorrow born;
Another soul in hell.

Donna Marie McGargill, O. S. M.
soft whisperings
soft

the muse of my spirit
sings soft whisperings of night
    and newness
sounds of candlelight and night
of peace and precious things
prayer—filled and holy
wholly scattered are the thoughts
of my mind's eye and i
long for time for space for
presence to see and share
the Lord of simplicity and
        strength between us . . .
so tired . . . so very tired, tired
from happy days . . .
and genuine smiles and tiny
    hands and
        golden leaves and
breeze blowing blissfully
cross my cheek so gently rough
kissing me, Christ's touch
so i move to the tune of a lady
wrapped in silence and
i praise the maker of sound
within and around her
knowing that the gentleness of
now and tomorrow's noon will
urge us on to love to serve
    to tender the young vines of
tommorow's wine
and next year's wheat . . .

Velma Margaret Haller
THANK YOU, MOMMY
*[To you Mother—With all my
love—Thank you.]*
Lighthearted she warms me with
her life
Charming me with the memories
of long ago
Eager to show pictures of this
certain child
Asking where did this little girl go?

A flash of sparkle inside her will
burst
As if I'm that little girl once again
Crying I will say I don't feel very
well
And the spirit of her restoring
will begin.

It's as if there's no misfortune for
tomorrow
Resting I can still feel her gentle
touch
Although she knows my love's
sincere
My only wish is she knew how
much.

Time's so brief and I owe her

my life
Knowing she'd never take this
serious to believe
But if I could only thank her
enough
For the time she gave to have
little me.

Paul Witbrod
BROKEN WINGS
My children—my sons, among
you might consider in life—all
these things
please remember—have room in
your heart for all the children,
the angels, the toys, the birds
with the broken wings.
My sons—remember that all is
not perfect oh, but all is really
imperfect.
Once past the sunrise, dreams
become gilded, amenitites rare.
All people strive, but their hopes
may become wrecked.
Please smile at them, love them
all as they reveal their faults so
bare.
For you see, my sons—all the
world lays still with broken
wings.
Be kind, be merciful, be gentle
with all the aged, the infirmed,
the hadicapped and—yes—
even all those who seem whole
and completely well.
Who knows what secrets, what
tales do all they tell
of their broken promises,
smashed beliefs
all things important to them—all
things.
I am sure that no matter what
successes you achieve, how
many mountains you climb,
you will both be monuments of
good example—yes—real
successes to all those around
you, if you remember each and
every time
remember all the children, all the
toys, all the angels, the birds
with broken wings.

Dr. Leroy Thomas
FINAL EXAMINATION
The worst tragedy imaginable
Is to come to the hour
Of that last great Final
Examination
And not know the answer
To the one one—hundred—point
question—
"What have you done with Jesus?"

Kathryn M. Diana
PASTPRINTS
A golden print along the
lakeshore,
Edges sharp for it was new,
Shouted bold and bright defiance
While I sat and thought of you.

Slowly, as I dreamed of past years,
Breezes, strong, began to blow.
As I smiled at foolish young tears,
Water seeped into the toe.

Heedless still, my mind did
wander,
Frolicking in days of yore;
Waves rose and fell, wild and
stronger,
As the heelmark faded more.

Finally, I tucked the memory
In today's warm, loving scene;
Rising I observed the shoreline,
Found the golden sand swept
clean.

Sandra Dettman
**Home (A Place Where Love
Is Found)**
Home a place where Love is found.
We don't have to measure it by
the pound.
For Love flows freely from the
heart, and that is where we're
all a part.

It comes from Mom.
It comes from Dad.
It comes when we're good,
or even if we're bad.

It comes when we deserve it
or even if we don't.
It comes when we are saddened
and even if we aren't.

Oh! Love is Joy and Happiness.
It comes when we have Children.
It doesn't matter what they are
(boy or girl),
as long as they are good ones.

Good that is! Yes! good to us,
no matter what they do.
That is what makes a home a place
where Love comes shinning
through.

Maree P. Arrington
ENTERTAINED
Sorrow entered
    Its mass assemblage inhabited
    my very soul
    Within me, it multiplied, and
    left but naught control.

Prayer beckoned
    The difficult task of drawing
    nigh unto Thee, ebbed.
    I reached and strained and
    crawled, ensnarled within its
    web.

Joy awaited
    With new awareness of Peace,
    For this was meant to be.
    'Twas there this Joy, found e'er
    in Prayer
    Did make my Sorrow flee.

Nancy B. Moore
Our Hearts Are Breaking
She stands so tall in this world of
ours—
Strong, yet gentle, loving and
caring.
Giving her best at whatever the
cost.
When it comes to her family, no
time is lost.

It hit her suddenly, out of the
night.
Causing us all a terrible fright.
Then we heaved a huge sigh of
great relief.
They had gotten it all—that was
our belief.

Life was not kind to her—as we
well know.
It struck again and began to take
it's toll.
She fought like a tiger—she
would not be beaten.
But this tall strong person began
to wither and weaken.

We shout, "It's unfair, why her,
why our mother?
Why has God chosen her instead
of some other?
Why so much suffering, why
such a cruel way?
Why doesn't she have even a
little say?"

It's a long hard road that she
must go.
It can strike anyone, friend or foe.
No one even seems to have the
answer.
For the name of this terrible
villan is CANCER!

Jennifer L. Durbin
I'M COMING HOME
I'm coming home Lord, to see
your face,
to be with you, and know your
grace.
I'm coming home Jesus, to walk
those Golden Streets,
to be with my heavenly father,
won't that be neat.

I'm coming home Jesus, I'm
coming home Lord,
to be with you, whom I've always
adored.

I'm coming home Jesus, to be
with you,
to let all the people know, that
your love is true.
I'm coming home Lord, to fill my
heart,
I am a Christian and I know your
love won't part.

I'm coming home Jesus, I'm
coming home Lord,
to be with you, whom I've always
adored.

Debra Ayers
WIND
Wind howling through the trees
Leaves drifting to the ground
Piling high into a mound.

Trees swaying into the wind,
time changing without end
Wind howling dogs growling
Birds singing, bells ringing
Clouds forming rain falling,
evening crawling,
Crows calling, Crickets singing,
evening ending.
Dawn rising, sun shining
Wind howling through the tree
tops
When will it ever stop,
Leaves drifting to the ground,
Wind swirling them around.

Serina Brand
WEEPING CHILD
For the child is weeping in the
garden all alone
For the child is sad, he has no
home.

He is wondering where he should
go,
For the leaves have fallen
He looks up and it starts to snow.

For the child is weeping,
Because he's so cold.
For the child knows he has to be
bold.

As he stands there watching the
the snow fall,
He wonders "why" for he is so
small.

I have no one else to go to you see,
"OH God why does this have to
happen to me".

For the child is weeping in the
garden all alone,
For the child is sad, he has no
home.

Allen A. Breyer Jr.
FROM THE HEART
[This poem was written to—
and inspired by—the only
woman that I'll ever really
love—SUSAN LOTITO]
In the beginning, we were just
good friends
Oh God, I pray that it never ends
For me, it turned into Love and
Care
Hell! I think we make an
excellent pair
For her, I'm not sure how she
really feels
I hope it's love, I pray it's love,
and that it's for real
Oh my Precious, Beautiful,
Darling Sue
You'll never know how much I
really miss you

I've never felt this way in my life
Someday, I pray, you will be my
wife
I swore never to take those
wedding vows
But, you've changed all that—
don't ask me how
I dream of you, while lying in bed,
Saying "With This Ring, I Thee
Wed"
One day, someday, my dream will
come true
And we'll always be together, just
me and you
Oh Sue, I do love you!

Evah Baugher
Did You Waste the Day
[In memory of my great
granddaughter, Shelly Widner
(1964—1982), who loved this
poem.]
Can you say in parting
With the day that's slipping fast,
That you've helped a single person,
Of the many you have passed?

Did you waste the day or lose it,
Was it well or poorly spent?
Did you leave a trail of kindness,
Or a scar of discontent?

As you close your eyes in slumber,
Do you think God would say,
You have made this world much
better,
For the life you lived today?

Mary L. Garside
AUNT GRACIE
The love she has given us
We will never forget,
And the way she has shown it
Are good examples to set.

She taught us compassion
And to forgive one another,
By watching her life style
Helped make me a better mother.

Though she had a home to manage
And a family to raise
She always took time
To advise and to praise.

Be it skinned knees or ear—aches
We could count on her touch,
For all the comfort she has given
We thank her so much.

It seemed the older we got
The bigger were the trials,
So we ran to Aunt Gracie
Sometimes over the miles.

So when I count my blessings,
And many do exist—
You can bet my Aunt Gracie
Is always on my list.

Monica Frances Siminski
GROWING CULT
A black square matures into a
door,
Then creaks open . . .
To find another door,
Only this one has no knob.

Mary Louise Russell
AS I REMEMBER
[In Fond Memory, For my First
Love, A Loving Husband, and
Father of Five Children. MSGT
Edwin John Russell,
1929—1968.]
There's a chill in the wind
There's a feeling of Winter;
around the bend.
Just like it was on the day,
"Our Love Began"
"As I Remember"

The music is haunting
Starbrights falling,
Nightbirds calling,
Singing a Love Song, from the Past.
"As I Remember"

"As I Remember"
A soft warm breeze, of Love's
sweet touch fills my heart, and my
mind tells me, It's part of
my Life Forever.
"As I Remember"
"You"

Karla R. French
The Day Is Soon Coming
The day is soon coming. We
know it so well.
Will you walk with the Father, or
end up in hell?
The times they are changing, as
prophets said they would
Can you talk to Jesus, the way
that you should?
Do you talk to him daily, and
know him by name?
For it was our sins for which he
took the blame.
You have but to know him to
know that its true.
He died on the cross, but he'll
come back for you.
Yes the day is soon coming, now
are you prepared?
To meet with the Master who's
love we've all shared.

Mary Lois Carlile
UNFEIGNED LOVE
[Inspired by: The Love of the
Lord Jesus Christ]
Let me hold your hand
Share each day with you
Finding new ways of life
To enjoy and grow into

Laughing when you laugh
Crying when you feel blue
Putting a song in motion
Allowing love to shine through

essions of a love so great
Few find its truth or beauty
Tis hidden so by worldly cares
And often captioned . . . duty

Candace Ann Manaois
A SPECIAL CHILD
Only time could tell of the
special birth,
That would happen here upon
the earth.
His accomplishments might not
show,
And his progress may be a little
slow.

Said the Lord, "We must find the
people who
Will do this special job so true.
They will not realize
The greatness of their prize."

He may need extra care,
From his special parents here.
This special child needs love,
Expecially from the Lord above.

His thoughts might seem quite
far away,
And he may not laugh, cry, or
play.
His life must be content;
To a special place he must be
sent.

Although he's handicapped,
He'll try his best to adapt.
He'll always be so very mild,
Because he's A SPECIAL CHILD.

Ann Welch
CAPTAIN MY CAPTAIN
I lie listing
in the storm tossed sea
pounding waves
crashing washing over me
gnashing biting winds
my sails have torn
A gown of shrouded fog I've worn
when I feel
the strong hand
of my Captain upon the wheel
turning my bow slowly
into the angry waves
passing by on either side
meeting the tempest
face to face
through the swollen sea we ride

until the safety of harbor I feel
Now my Captain lies
In peaceful sleep
strong hand lying gently
on his lady's brow
Captain my Captain
why do we in silence weep
as I caressed
by softly lapping waters
lulled by the rocking cradle
of the deep
answer the breeze
singing its lullaby
to the quiet sea
yes
he sleeps
my Captain sleeps

Charles E. Henry
To Give Of Your Light
Forgive me, Lord,
My sins that I commit.
Those committed knowingly and
    unkowingly,
For them both I repent.
And from my heart,
I humbly and sincerely pray.
For strength to walk in the
    Christian Way.
And to give of Your Light,
To everyone I meet.
In hope that they may be lead,
From Eternal Defeat.
And to come to the realization of
    Thy Goodness and Power.
So that Our Souls,
May find Happiness in that Final
    Hour.

Jo Gail Fry
**The Little Toy Soldier
    Marched**
The Little Toy Soldier marched
In his uniform so neat.
He went forward,
His tin back arched,
Marching to a toy drum beat,
And never once did he retreat.

Then came the battle
With the leg of the chair.
He toppled, kicking
His thin legs in the air.
Before he gave up the fight
In sheer desperation,
A Giant Hand reached down
Without hesitation
And set the soldier a—right,
And wound him up tight,
And headed him forward again
In the right direction.

J. Carroll Herring
SUICIDAL CONFUSION
We adults are more complicated
    than our children.
    We search for truth, yet are
    untruthful.
We seek justice, but are unjust.
    We value morality, but are
    immoral.
We detest judgement, and yet we
    judge.
    We long for understanding, but
    do not understand.
We cry out for love, but love not.
    We crave security, but are
    insecure.
We have all we need, but race to
    achieve more.
    Our trail is suicidal . . .
        Once the maze is conquered,

We build another to
    replace
        it.
We appear to be caught in a glass
    ball, on a treadmill.
Going . . . Going . . . Nowhere
    . . . Nowhere . . .
            STOP
Can you smell the roses blooming?
    Do you hear your child's
    questions?
    Have you watched the flames
    caress and lick the logs?
Do you hear the bells on Sunday
    morning?
    Have you spiritually sensed the
    needs of another?
    Have you felt another's hand
    holding yours . . .
As you stretch your limbs in
    morning awakening?

Ada Florene Adams
RAIN IN SUMMER
[In memory of my late husband,
    Russell H. Adams]
What is more bless'd than an
    hour—full of rain
That beats on the streets with a
    musical strain,
It is soothing and cooling to
    everyone near,
As it pours on the street so very
    clear.

To many wee flowers, down snug
    in their beds
Comes the gift of rain to raise
    their weary heads,
Their petals are moistened, their
    spirits return,
Not one would attempt this gift
    to spurn.

As the rain approaches, birds go
    to their nest
Where they quietly remain the
    while in sweet rest;
And animals too, who all day did
    roam
Finally return with peace to their
    home.

So we who are human on earth do
    remain
For only a short time, so let it
    rain;
It refreshes our souls and peace
    often brings,
As it reaches the earth and so
    sweetly sings.

Jody Andrea Kargula
PARTING
Kiss me gently,
    sweet lover of mine.

Kiss me slowly,
    as our bodies entwine.

Remember this moment,
    as none before.

Remember this pleasure,
    for it will happen no more.

Kiss my tears,
    as they gently flow.

Hold me in your arms,
    gently,
        until it's time for me to go.

Dena Gorrell
**A Canopy Bed For My
    Daughter**
[To Deanne—A page from
    yesterday's book of memories.]
White postered,
Flower—coverleted bed.
Flowery "rooftop" canopy
White furniture trimmed with
    gold.
Flowery curtains too,
A little bit of heaven
Secured here in this spot.
But oh, the prettiest part of all is
Its blonde—haired occupant!

I used to wish for a room like this
When I was just her age.
I would have thought it heaven,
But she and I are different that
    way.
Blue jeans and softball
Tennis, basketball,
Bunk beds or a sleeping bag,
Seem to be all my "tom—boy"
    crave
—At least today.

Jo Regan
1968
How gone the day
toward the evening of our time
It goes often and much
With it takes the shadows
into twilight places
. . . out of reach . . .

Bertie Murphy
FOREVER ALONE
Each man is an island.
    Forever alone.
As if, in darkness,
    He wanders alone.
He carries his burdens
    Close to his breast.
But, you can be certain
    When he's ready for rest . . .
Tho you be there beside him
    To leave prints in the sand
His thoughts are inside him.
    For he is a man!

W.W. Kokko
BACK CAMPING
Camped by a cove in a cave
The sound of a salamander
Brought my dogs to snarl,
And my mate to snore.

Reflecting in slumbers lace
I conclude that timeless snore
Kept beasts from caveman's
    door.

Camped again in frosty glen
The hoot of an owl
Brought my dogs to growl,
And my mate to scowl.

Reflecting in moonlit lace

We conclude that angry scowl
Left many men an angry dowel.

Camping fulltime to nature's
    chime
The nurturing rain and shine
Bring fullness and wine
To life among the whistling pine.

Descending into mystery's night
We conclude that gift of light
Is what makes—all things right!

Larry Jackson, JR
RAIN
I love the rainy mondays
as rain drops strike the pane
Each one is slightly different
and yet there all the same.

I love to sit and watch
the city streets as people
scurry by,
trying to escape the rain
for someplace warm and dry.

I guess I never noticed
that is was so simple
and so plain,
So take a minute and
take a look, the next
time it begins to rain.

Frances (Case) Kopp
THE COMFORTER
My child, My elected one
Hurry and tell my children
That the comforter has come
And the only way to victory
Is through "Jesus", my beloved
    son.

Tell my children not to wait
Tomorrow may be too late
Tell them to come back to the
    fold
So a beautiful story can be told.

Then the comforter's job will be
    done
All the races and all men will be
    one
At last there will be one world
And Jehovah's kingdom shall
    unfurl.

Linda Vorpahl Bishop
WHO IS GOD?
Who is God? This Being Supreme?
In the minds of men, He's many
    things.
Some say He is dead, a legend, a lie;
While others say He's coming
    soon as they watch the Eastern
    sky.

Who is God? He gave His Word;
This Gospel to preach 'til every
    nation has heard.
He said, "I am the I am, the
    beginning, the end,
The Alpha and Omega"; from
    Him all things descend.

Who is God? What gift did He
    send?
The gift of His Son to save us
    from sin.
Crime against God; who'll pay the
    price?
Jesus said, "I'll die, I'll be the
    human sacrifice.
I'll live a life without spot,
    though tempted I'll be.
I'll carry the blame, so the world,
    through me, at last can be free!"

Who is God? He's the Lamb who was slain;
And after three days rose to live again.
He ascended to Heaven but said, "Wait for a sign;
The Comforter I'll send, so good and kind.
My Spirit within you, your help from above;
Only believe, you'll have peace, joy, and love."

Who is God? God is mercy, forgiveness, and love.
He's the Spirit that speaks from a Heavenly Dove.
He's the King who now reigns o'er Heavenly Hosts.
He's God, the Father; God, the Son; and God, the Holy Ghost.

Tammy Cecil
CEDAR
[For Don Lee, my inspiration and "Bestest Buddy".]
Cedar—scented letters of love
Secreted away from the probing World.
Emotions from the shy to be coveted
And tucked into aromatic boxes.
Their sweetness lingering in the Air as well as
In the heart and mind.
Memories are quickened by letters
Brimming with emotion and Scented by cedar.

P. J. Johnson
DIBS AND RIBS
[Dedicated to Sylvia Williams; great Yukon trapper and mom.]
Once upon a mountain
Beneath the midnight sun
There lived a lady trapper
Who had a little son
She also had a daughter
(These lines contain no fibs!)
I know, for I'm their sister
We called them Dibs and Ribs

Two chubby little babies
Dark eyes and raven hair
Toddling o'er the mountains
Raised on grizzly bear

One without the other
You'd very seldom see
They roamed the hills together
And each knew every tree

You'd see them in their parkas
At fifty—nine below
Mushing by with dogteams

And laughing in the snow
They're off to check the trapline
As northern lights ignite
The Yukon is their playland
This frosty winter night

Little Ribs with rabbit skins
At night beneath her head
Fat husky pups for teddy bears
To cuddle soft in bed
Lulled by howling huskies
And counting mountain sheep
They'd snuggle up together
And soon be fast asleep

A pint size Davy Crocket
My little brother Dibs
He'd sight a bear then stalk it
Then haul it home to Ribs
Who'd roast it in the cookstove
As Dibs would never fail
To tell of how he'd shot it
And drug it by the tail

On snowmobile or snowshoe
They'd little time for rest
Two busy little scholars
Of the wilderness
Though youth is but a moment
A snowflake in your hand
Dibs and Ribs will e'er to me
Be children of the land

Norma Jean Moore (Mrs. Roy)
FRIENDSHIP
The quality of true friendship
Is likened to a pure, unadulterated, underground spring
Bubbling slowly to the surface, gently flowing over virgin ground,
Never changing, ever constant.
Patiently waiting for the depths of its
Resources to be tapped, when needed.
It showers those we love with a Fountain of love and devotion.
Demanding nothing, giving freely, Unselfishly, without question,
Deeply feeling the needs of others, Without necessity of words, time or distance
More to be treasured than silver or gold,
Returning, double portion
The same quality of kinship to the giver.

J. W. Cheney Jr.
DECEMBER SENSES
Silently, from wintry slumber; silvered wonderment evolves.
Crystalled cources, winding forward, unknown puzzles, no one solves.

Icy fingers, pointed gauntly; stretching to the skies,
solar's calm, cool diffidence; of mid—Decembered' eyes.

Slate—like curtained selfishness; containing promises to keep,
of snow—swept future landscapes; of wolf—winds' nights of sleep.

Embellished, frosted fantasies; glint, glisten, grasp the eye.
Radiant, rainbowed star—spears, pierce panoramic, night's scene's guise.

Snow—laced, field—grass, foilage; feigns death, but only sleeps.
Pine—boughed, moon—touched

sentinels,
silent vigil, coldly keeps.

Joan Senff
A MOTHERS PRAYER
Dear God thank you for this child of mine
Please watch over him all the time
Help me teach him right from wrong
Always keep him healthy and strong

Dear God help me always be a good mother
To keep him safe and out of trouble
Help him grow into a man
Keep him in your guiding hand

Dear God may he know I'll always care
And when he needs me I'll be there
Help us depend on one another
To be honest and truthful with each other

Dear God help me teach him about your son
And all the things that he has done
Help me to show him the way
So he can go to Heaven someday
AMEN

Gloria D. Alkire
DAINTY LACE
Heart—felt thoughts return to start
Illusions and mirrors of valentines;
Magical cupid with his quivering dart
Sprinkles love and beauty
On dainty lace.

Nostalgic patterns unfolding anew
Return to pierce the nomad heart;
A rose-petal lane in pink-candy hue
Reveals valentine love,
On dainty lace.

The wolrd is wrapped in cellophane then—
A fairyland with no tears to dim
The eyes of love—only joy the pen
That speaks of sweethearts,
And dainty lace.

Velma Faye Pendleton
PICTURES AND SEASONS
[Husband, Family and Friends]
Winter:
Can you picture life without winter
No fallen snow for Christmas or sleigh—rides
No lights reflecting on the ground
Where the children laugh and play.

Spring:
Can you picture life without spring
The wonders and beauty after the quiet gentle rain
Which bring flowers, grass of green
With everything coming alive again.

Summer:
Can you picture life without summer
Without the sun's warmth each

day we have
Swimming at the country lake
Cookouts in the yard you make
Or, taking rides, playing baseball games.

Fall:
Can you picture life without fall
The wonders of it all
Beauty of the trees with many colors
Placing all to rest once again.

Conclusion:
God gave us these four seasons
To measure and use our days
To watch the days, months, and years
To share them while we may.

Harold Tener
AUTUMN
It is with wonder, this beauty we behold,
Of Autumn leaves, reds, brown, green and gold.

Only the hand of God could paint such as this,
To even come close is the artists' greatest wish.

For one to view such a wonderful sight,
Can inspire a man to reach greater heights.

Neither the artists' brush, nor the writers' pen,
Could recreate such glory again!

Darell Lee Cunningham
THE TRUE WORLD
I am the son of Nature—
The animals are my brothers,
The woods and plains are my home,
And I have no troubles or worries.
I am free to be me,
Without an act for my neighbors.
Nature is my Government, bank, and store,
Who could want for anything more?
I am content with what I have—
I will never want what my breed sys I should have,
My brother, the Eagle, soars free—let him be.
His breed does not try to confine him,
My breed wants to confine me and destroy my world.
If they do that, then there will be no true world.

Lucretia Fortriede
IN MY ROCKINGCHAIR
I rock and rock in my rockingchair.
The wall I hit as in my rockingchair I sit.
Rocking in my rockingchair
My Mother holds me when I have a care
On her soft knee—we sit there
Rocking in my rockingchair
Sometimes I take a nap on my Mother's lap
Rocking in my rockingchair
Room for only two—we'll make room for you
Rocking in my rockingchair
Yet just one can have such fun
Rocking in my rockingchair

When I am sad, I am made glad
Mom read a book, that's all it took
Rocking in my rockingchair.
I was taught a prayer without flair
Just for love true from Jesus,
    that's who.
Rocking in my rockingchair.
Now I hold my child; how he
    always smiled.
Rocking in my rockingchair.
I told him the same story of Jesus
come from glory
Rocking in my rockingchair.
All children there be—joy they'll
see
Rocking in His rockingchair.

Lori L. Warner
THE ARTIST
*[For my dear brother, Tim, who
is the beautiful Artist in my
life.]*
An artist can paint a picture
of exactly what he sees—
he can capture all the beauty
yet still can set it free,
he can share it witht he rest of all
or have it to himself—
the picture will be a memory
of his own personal wealth.

A musician can play a song
of the rythms or the blues—
and set it to his beating heart
to capture all his moods,
he may have lived this song
    through
it may be dreams to see—
still, beautiful is the artist who
    tries
to share his joys with me.

Diane Elworth
REPEAT PERFORMANCE
It's a different rainbow everytime
But with all of the same colors
I've played this game before
With many different lovers
The end result is just the same
Time and time again
One wanting a commitment
One wanting to be friends
And everytime it's over
Everytime it ends
I smiled through my tears
And try hard to pretend
It doesn't mean that much to me
And soon my heart will mend
'Cause after all wasn't I
The one wanting to be friends?

Virgil Graber
DELIGHT AT TWILIGHT
When the sun has begun to set;
As the curtain of evening falls,
Man pauses and lingers to let
His soul revive as Nature calls.

He harkens and listens to birds
Singing so sweetly in the trees;
His soul is soothed by Nature's
    words,
As his face is cooled by her breeze.

He looks skyward; a cloud floats
    by;
He eyes Nature's bright—painted
    dress;
He sees squirrels scamper to
    supply
Their food for winter's long
    duress.

He observes passage of seasons;

He perceives vistas of each one;
He discerns the diverse reasons:
Each is unique since time begun.

Dear Mother Nature, you have
    taught
Your wild creatures how to
    provide;
Teach me also what God has
    wrought;
Guide me home to the Master's
    side.

Beverly A. Casteel
MISTREATED
Children with bodies
    of all shapes and form

Badly beaten,
    bruised and torn

Are abused daily
    without any remorse

Parents not knowing
    to take the right course

To correct their ways
    and have a new feeling

For reaching their children
    which is more appealing

Children are a miracle
    of beauty

To love and cherish
    which is our duty

Watching a blossom
    come from a seed

Giving them the necessities
    that they need
For not only caring
    but also giving
Knowing, Loving is for the Living

Rhonda Wallingford
**For My Precious, Tiny
Child . .**
*[With love, for my daughter,
Jayla Danielle, the most
precious part of my life—born
November 2, 1982.]*
Oh, Child sleeping at my breast,
Remember always, "I love you
    best!"
More than the sun, the moon, the
    stars or breath.
We'll remain as one beyond our
    death.

Your gentle breathing, your baby
    sighs,
Your coos, your lips, your big
    bright eyes
Bring sweetness from within me
    deep
To cradle you and safely keep.

As you grow up and out of reach,
I pray you grasp the love I teach.
And, know, as you say these
    words to your's,
From Mother's heart, the love
    still pours.

Diane Jacqueline Herman
TOUCH
As I outstretched my hand, I felt
    crisp,
        jagged,
edges of the lone leaf
        weaving in,
            and sometimes
        out.
I traced the veins with my finger
    sensing their prominance.

In my burst of anger, I ripped its
    dry,
        hard surface
            as it crackled into crunchy
bits of puzzle.
        Nearby, stood harsh,
            tiny petals of a
flower—it was supported by a
    fragile stem.
        Leaning, on a sharp edged
    hunk of rock
        it's body made up of minute
        bits of rough particles
            so much touch—unified
        together.

john arthur maddux
PORTRAIT
Gray touched child,
Standing
on a corner,
Waiting
alone
with shopping bag in hand—
—presents for tomorrow,
and
yesterday songs
clinging
to your lips.

Where do you go
painted
like a dying
flower.

Into the fountain
of memory?
Into the seasons
of your
song?

Betty McGuire
**The Face Of a Child On
Christmas**
The face of a child on Christmas
Is something you really should
    see.

It's brighter by far
    Than the Christmas Star

Or the lights on the Christmas
    tree.

    They laugh and they run—
And have so much fun.

    As the gifts they tear open
One by one.

    For a lifetime of pleasure—
With memories you'll treasure!

    There's nothing to measure!
The face of a child at Christmas.

Beth A. Crago
SEDUCTION OF THE SENSES
As I strolled through the night
I became aware of a
very sensuous attack
on my being.

My ears were cajoled
by the soft chirping of crickets.
My nose was tempted
by the smell of fallen autumn
    leaves.
My skin was caressed
by the gentle evening breeze.

While I was being seduced by
the beautiful autumn evening,
I found a total satisfaction
in the union of mankind and
nature.

I was at peace.

Sherry A. Szabo
SLEEP OVER COME ME
Sleep over come me
Take me to a world where fact
    become fiction
Reality becomes fantasy
Then when day comes
I deal with every day problems
But when night falls
I let sleep over come me again

MA. Clemence P. Lastra
SHEILA
*[This poem is heartily and
lovingly dedicated to my
Granddaughter, Sheila Lastra of
McAllen, Texas on the
occasion of her birthday.]*
S—Sight a good ambition
H—Have strong determination
E—Effort is the best provision

I—Interest is the companion
L—Love is the foundation
A—Action tells life's destination

Marianne Duda
UNTITLED
Today we are together
    sharing, giving, experiencing. . .
Tomorrow may find us apart.
    And we may find
    we have grown a little more
    and perhaps, learned something
        of value
    to carry with us
    in our hearts and minds
Forever bringing back memories
    of a beautiful togetherness
    that once was . . .

Jerry Jones
CAUGHT
There he stands staring into space,
an obscure figure looking to
    escape life's embrace.
Things weren't really going so bad,
never a day went by that he
    wasn't cheerful and glad.
But then he was caught by some
    deadly darkness,
he was held hostage by the
    invisible harness.

There he stands on that window
    ledge,
he feels the darkness push him to
    the edge.
He feels it above him looking
    down,
he hears it below him laughing
    on the ground.
No one believes he's in danger,
    they all think he's nuts.

Or trying to draw some attention,
by exposing to us his guts.

There he stood staring into space,
a nervous man with no
expression on his face.
Whether he was pushed or
whether he fell,
some aren't really sure, but some
know damn well.

James A. Gullett
A FOOL'S GAME
I have been alive since the light
of creation when Lucifer led
the revolt against God and the
good Angels.
>   For I am War!

I have been alive since Cain slew
Abel.
>   For I am Jealousy!

I have been alive since the
Crusaders made war on the
nation of Islam in the Holy
Land.
>   For I am Evil!

I have been alive since brother
killed brother during the Civil
War!
>   For man is a Fool!

I have been alive since the first
atom was split and the great
bombs came into being and
became destroyers.
>   For I am Terror!

I am alive in each and everyone
of you, As long as men thirst
for power or fools wage war.

I will continue to live and thrive
as long as men hate and
brother kills brother.
>   For I am Death!

Patti Purcel
SAND CASTLES
*["To my husband Mark, for all
the love he has given me".]*
It only seems like yesterday
When we use to run and hideaway
To a place no one ever knew
We would be alone just me and
you
Building castles in the sand
Wading the water hand in hand
In the sand our names we signed
While leaving all our worries
behind
It's hard to think it's over now
I never thought it could end
somehow
I sometimes go there when I'm sad
It brings back memories we once
had
The castles have all disappeared
It's like a nightmare I had feared
In the sand where our names we
signed
The tide came in leaving nothing
behind

Nancy J. Buck
YOUNG LOVE
As the rivers flow softly over the
falls
And the wine lays chilling in the
cool waters
You walk hand in hand through
the woodlands
Sharing your most intimate
thoughts

The sky reflects the blue of her
eyes
As the red rose blushes as do her
cheeks
Your love is stronger than the
deepest sea
So hold onto your youth and your
love for life

Lucille R. Reimler

Lucille R. Reimler
YOUTH
Into the glow of tomorrow
Slipping along through the night,
Free of the cares that pursue them
And swift as an eagle in flight . . .
Gently guided by moon-glow
That lightens the ebony deep,
Radiant dreams of the future
Enchanting sweet hours of sleep;
Now climbing virgin mountains,
Then conquering ocean plains . . .
Relentlessly taming the century,
Light-hearted, deserving acclaim;
Steadfastly honoring duty,
Undauntedly standing for truth . . .
With courage unfurled before them,
>   On they press . . .
>   Our valiant youth!

tess sinsley
WHY ME?
Why me, Lord?
I've said it before;
What have I done this time,
That I suffer once more?

I love You and praise You,
And try to live as You ask;
Yet over and over You try me,
By making difficult my task.

But I'll accept Your will,
And worthy try to be;
No matter how hard the day,
You can count on me.

So, 'tho You try me,
And once again I weep;
Your love is still right there,
A love so very deep.

A love that will encourage,
And once more set me free;
Then through all my tears,
I need not ask, "Why, me?"

Floyd E. Bowman Jr.
JESUS IS IN MY HEART
You'll find love in my heart
Because Jesus is in my heart,
I'm happy,
And I'll praise the Lord,
Forever
You'll find love in my heart,
Because Jesus is in my heart.

I'll sing praises, unto His name,
I'll tell everyone, about Jesus
saving my soul, from hell.
I'm free as a bird,
No sin to tie me down.
I'll sing praises unto His name.
You'll find love in my heart,
Because Jesus is in my heart.

Lynda Sensmeier
I AM A FRIEND
Anger is an enemy of the human
soul.
Never harbor anger within yourself;
it can only do harm.
Most find that the best way of
helping rid themselves of anger
is through a friend or stranger.
>   Come to me; I am a friend.
You have entrusted me with your
secrets.
>   Come to me; I am a stranger.
There are many facets of your
personality to which I am
unfamiliar.
How strange it is that a friend as
close as I knows so little of you.
How strange it is that you would
turn
to a stranger
with your problems.

Susie Gumm
METAMORPHOSIS
For several years, I cried
Cuddled close to a pillow.
After all my tears were gone,
I begged
>   and pleaded
>   and once
Even threatened—
But you turned your back
Pretending not to hear
Projecting that you did not care
And gradually I learned that
(perhaps)
I had not enough to offer
To make you want me
And it was my fault
That I was ignored.

After a while,
Your shallow excuses no longer
hurt—
Just angered that you could
actually
think me to believe them.

I thought I was over the need
Of cuddles
>   and comfort
>   and occasional praises.
Anyway, I had levered myself above
Begging or Crying.
And that was that.
I took care of you like one of the
kids
And filled the role of Mother:Maid
And pushed so far back
My womanliness that
I began to feel masculine.

I would just like you to know
This.
It took a sum total of five days
To undo all the damage that you
did
In five years
And, I know now
That it was not my inadequacy
But yours—
That you handed over to me—
That I accepted

Without reasoning through the
consequences.
And, Try as you might
You shall never again cause me to
To feel guilty
>   or ugly
>   or stupid
>   or unloved.
Your perceiving me this way—
If you do—
Is your perception only.

And,
One of his vertebra
Would give you more backbone
Than you have ever had
In your whole life.
And he tells me that
I am pretty
>   and intelligent
>   and vivacious
>   and very loved.

Dorothy Kole Mucklo
THINK SPRING
Children skip about and play,
Joyous shrieks fill the air,
Mother Nature has a way
Of making all things fair.
Furrows are turned over,
Seeds begin to sprout,
Warmth of sun does hover,
God's greenery is all about,
We know 'tis Spring, tra la,
Oh! yes, 'tis Spring!

Joanie Mendyka
THE SUN
The sun is a brillant ball of gases
and light,
With graceful elegants to one's
sight.

It sets so peacefully into the
layers of clouds passing by,
To give a feeling of contentment
from the heavens on high.

Yet so silently it will fade into
the west,
And go unseen so the earth may
rest.

The sun will rise in the same
brilliant way,
To repeat its beautiful
performance of another day.

Steve Atkinson
THE LETTER
Couldn't sleep last night, so I
thought I'd write,
To say a word or two.
I got kind of lonely, but that soon
passed,
Just lying here thinking of you.

The days are cold, the nights so
long.
I can't keep from feeling there's
something wrong.
Have you been mine, all of the
time?
Have you been waiting for me?
Do you still, know what I feel?
Am I your one and only?

I dreamed one night, that you
didn't need me,
And in a letter, you set me free.
Dreamed I got it Friday,
Skipped some pages my way,
To read the words, "I Love you."
But when I saw, I thought I'd die;
The words "I love you, but good-
bye".

Hope it was only a bad dream.
It's never gonna be, the way it
   seemed.
And I will still wait, very
   patiently.
Because I know, that you do love
   me.

Elisa K. Caraulia
TAMSEN
A real friend who doesn't need to
   try for love;
   She does anyway.
A person who doesn't need to care;
   She does anyway.
A beautiful person who doesn't
   realize it;
   She will someday.
A hard worker who strives for the
   highest goals;
   She will attain them.
A person who really doesn't have
   the time to bother with your
   problems;
   She always seems to find the
   time.
An achiever, a survivor, and
   aggressive yet warm,
   compassionate woman;
   She will succeed.
And people will love her as I do
   now.

Anna Maiani
BALLERINA
The ballerina spins,
slowly pirouetting
in pink satin and silk,
in an ivory jewel box
of Childhood.

As she continues
to twirl, circling
'round 'n 'round,
she slows, the music fades,
and contentiously
Adolescence bores down
heavily upon it's lid
to seal it everlastingly.

Thelma Jo. Bowling
CHRISTOPHER
Bug-bites and bruises
   A smudge on his face
A face that if clean
   Would be out of place
Not still for a moment
   He doesn't have time
He is seeking
   More mountains to climb.
Then off he will go
   On tired little legs
To find Aunt Sara
   A cookie to beg.
When sleep overtakes him
   You'll find him right here
Curled in the corner
   Of Pa-Pa's big chair.
He's sunshine and laughter
   To hold back the cold
Are Grand-chldren the prize we win
Just for growing old?

Kimberlee Ziska
WHEREVER I GO
My heart goes
   wherever I go
You are in
   my heart
I take you
   wherever I go,
I also take my
   thoughts with me

And my thoughts
   revolve around you
So naturally
   you are always there,
I love to hold you
   in my arms
My arms are with me
   wherever I go
Unfortunately though
   you are not.

Sandra A. Myers
HE CALLED HIM HOME
Oh Holy One you called him home
To be there by your side
You held his hand and said come
home
There with you he'll abide.

His walk was long, and very slow
He did what he knew he must do.
His life upon your golden earth
He knew was nearly through.

He's laid to rest upon a hill
Among the trees and pines
Where birds will sing, the sun
   will shine.
Until the end of time.

Tammy Forrest Peterson
What Does Freedom Mean
To You?
*[This poem is dedicated in
sincere gratitude to the
Steubenville Chapter of the
NAACP. The award given to
me was more encouraging than
you'll ever know. May God
bless you all.]*
What does freedom mean to you?
Is freedom a fairy-tale or can it be
   true?
Does freedom only exist in the
   Promised Land?
Is freedom here in the Master's
   plan?

These questions I often wonder
   about
As I lay at night with unanswered
   doubts,
To you, I speak of the true
   freedom thing
When you can laugh, love and
   sing.

Sing of the happiness you feel
   inside
Sing of your family who shares
   your pride
Laugh at the joy you feel within
Love the freedom that's as free as
   the wind!

Freedom is the power to believe
   in yourself
Maintaining unity among all
   people
Freedom is striving to let the
   world know
All of God's people are equal.

Freedom is to know yourself
Loving who you've searched to
   find,
Freedom is to worship God
Truly loving all mankind.

Freedom is the total human at his
   all around best
Struggling, yet surviving in the
   world so unjust
In essence to have freedom you
   must love

A love of your fellow man guided
   from above.

Freedom in your community
   resides in all of you
Grasping pride and unity in all
   that you do,
We must strive from within and
   know we can be
A bright shining star for the
   whole world to see!

Louise McCutcheon

Louise McCutcheon
MY POT OF GOLD
A long, long time ago
   as a child I was told:
"At the foot of the rainbow
   there's a pot of gold."
Now, here I am,
   all wrinkled and old,
At the foot of the rainbow,
   and there's no pot of gold.

I chased countless rainbows
   from end to end,
To where heaven and earth
   meet and blend;
But each time I came
   to the rainbow's end,
The gold, it seemed,
   was at the other end!

Then I learned that rainbows
   are a beautiful sign,
And the gold that I sought
   would never be mine;
But as sure as the rainbow
   there are gifts sublime,
Along the pathway of life
   with God's hand in mine.

I, now, can see clearly
   with what wisdom I was told:
"At the foot of the rainbow
   there's a pot of gold."

For, here I am,
   all wrinkled and old,
With memories and treasures
   I wouldn't trade for gold.

M. J. Stanko
SOUL SEARCH
*[To my wonderful wife, Elsie,
so generous in love and
friendship.]*
When I look into your eyes
I see the sunshine and rain,
The deeper I look and also see
various kinds of pain;

I can see the kind, warm love that
   filters thru,
To surface at the top when you're
   not blue,
I've seen and know your hopes
   and fears
The good and bad times you've
   had thru years,

You have seen and felt so much
I'm so glad our lives did touch,
Look deep into my eyes and you
   will find
The heartaches and happiness
   that were also mine.

Elaine Knerr Neimeyer
AMERICA
America, the land of opportunity.
Made up of different racial unity.
History will always prevail;
With strong roots that read like a
   tale.

Stand up and be counted.
Voice your opinions loud and
   strong.
For America will listen; so lets
   not be wrong;
But united in one patriotic song.

Great leaders are among us;
   seeking consultation.
God has blessed this nation; with
   less tribulation.
How long can this last; without a
   neutron blast?
So, lets be diplomatic and learn to
   compromise.
America is great and hopes to
   survive!

Dina Wright
In the Face Of Unreality
"Heathen!", yelled I. "Devil, thing
   from the night, haunting me . . .
   tormenting me.
The gargoyle only stared back at
   me.
A statue carved out of stone.
   Do I dare approach it?

Its huge piercing eyes glaring,
   tearing through me, as if I were
   merely glass.
But alas, I'm not!
Its gorgoylic wings emphasizes its
   ugliness, its murderous claws
   reaching . . .reaching.
I dare not approach it.

As if the gargoyle had reach my
   mind, it turned and screached,
   instantly coming to vivid
   horrifying life!
My heart fluttered, nearly stopping.
My breathing ceased for a moment.
It was approaching *me*.

"What do you want of me?", I cried,
   but the gargoyle did not reply;

387

it only stared.
I could not think anymore,
I could only stare back at it.
It was coming closer,
 it had eyes of the demon's,
 it's face resembled like nothing
I've ever seen before,
 and *it* was approaching *me*.

It screamed again, now even more
 terrifying and louder than
 before.
I looked at my sourroundings, but
 saw no escape.
"Thing of the Devil, what do you
 want of me?", I cried in
 desperation.
The only was that,
 it still was approaching me.

Alice C. Chapman
OUR FELINE TINY BIT
Time will never erase the love we
 have for you;
The seventeen years we shared,
 was challenging, that's true;
So cute and playful, into
 everything you would get;
Tiny Bit, we named you, our
 sweet little feline pet.

When night time came, at the
 foot of our bed you would be;
Early light, out you would go and
 play in your favorite tree;
Curiosity you had, for hunting,
 and running after butterflies;
White, with yellow ears and tail,
 now grown up and big in size.

Nine lives you surely had, but
 the years took their toll;
All of a sudden, we see our Tiny
 Bit had grown old;
She liked laying her head on our
 feet for human touch;
Affection like this, that's why we
 love you so much.

Early Sabbath morn, you were
 near death, your name I did call;
Tears we did shed, and into my
 hand you put your paw;
As if to say, "Don't cry, remember
 me only at my best",
Our truest friend and pet; indeed,
 you've earned your rest.

Sharon Mason
ALWAYS THERE
I go not through this world alone
You are always by my side,
No matter where I drift or roam
In You I can always confide.

I can tell You all My deepest
 dreams
My hopes and all my cares,
You have faith in Me, it seems
To do what no one dares.

You are always there when I'm In
 need
So faithful and so true,
How can I "Not" in this life
 succeed
With a "Loving Friend" like You.

With my hand in Yours, and
 Yours in mine
We'll go through this life
 together,
I know everything will work
 Out just fine
Because Lord, You're No Forgetter!

Linda L. Click
TOY'S AT NIGHT
Some soldiers came a marching
 upon the floor one night!
Dressed in their uniforms all
 perfect and bright
Standing straight and very tall
 with their guns held tight
Waiting for the drummer boy to
 play tonight

Dolls and toys waiting for just
 the right beat
Because at midnight when the
 little boy would sleep,
The toys came alive and danced
 to the drummers beat.

Raggedy Ann and Andy in their
 chair they lay,
The little wooden train waiting
 for the tune to play . . .
The little dolls are sitting upon
 the shelf so high
Dressed in their pretty clothes
 waiting for tonight!!

The drummer boy begins to play
 every toy comes alive
Oh!! There's not much time
 only real for just awhile!!
The night passes quickly its time
 to get in place!
Before the little boy awakes

It's time!! lets hurry before
 the morning comes
The drummer boy he's ready
 to beat his little drum
Play, play, play, and the beat begins
Then the toys are just toys again!

Edward McGhee
THE WARRIOR
The warrior, his armour pierced
 and his sword crimson,

Looks about at those who have
 challenged him on this field of
 battle.

He eases his once mighty steed
 forward to survey the
 aftermath of his victory.

A tear falls, his heart is torn as he
 realizes he too comes closer to
 death.

In the distance another warrior
 approaches he is alone—he will
 challenge.

He is young and strong, his
 armour is unpierced, his sword
 glistens in the sun

His steed, with head held high
 and nostrils flared, strains at
 his warriors firm grip.

The old warrior dons his helmet
 and wipes his time worn sword
 of its past victories.

He glimpses a shadow from the
 corner of his eye, it has fleeted,
 he knows,

Still, he will accept the challenge...

HE IS A WARRIOR

Patricia Ann Martin
DESTINY
Came the pity,
Came the sorrow,
Came the death of tomorrow.

Slowly today

Has passed away,
Leaving scars behind
Only visible in the mind.

Yesterday, but a faint memory,
Made the basis for what will be.

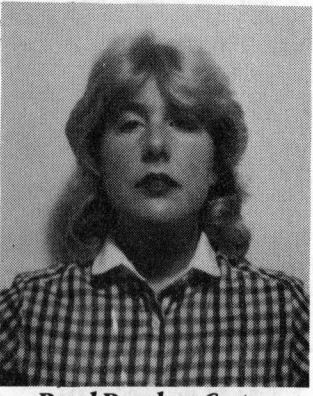

Daryl Douglass Carter

Daryl Douglass Carter
LULLABY OF STARLIGHT
[*For my children with love,
Christopher and Mark*]
A sliver of shimmering moonlight,
Tickles a miniature, pert, pug-nose,
Illuminated by a dazzling spray of
 starlight,
A newly born babe discovers his
 tiny toes.

The soft, downy blanket of
 nightfall,
Enfolds the infant, sweetly
 dreaming in
 innocent bliss,
His cradle rocked by the breath
 of God,
 gentlest breeze of all,
No lullaby more perfect than this.

Cathy Watson Banks
50th Wedding Anniversary
Happy anniversary to someone
 near and dear, it is your fiftieth
 one, and that's why we are here.
You have made history with love
 and tears, you have been
 married for fifty years.
Remember when you said I do, I
 bet you didn't think fifty years
 would do.
You both have made it from the
 start, for that you have a great
 big heart.
You took the good with the bad,
 the ups and the downs, the do's
 and the don'ts and mixed them

around, added a cup of love a
 day to make a family on the
 way,
Your golden day is filled with joy,
 all your kids are here to make
 you worry:
You have been married for a half
 of a century, all of your grand
 kids have made a big entry—
I your granddaughter Cathy write
 this poem for you, it came from
 my heart for the two of you.
I see the happiness in your eyes,
 that you can bet is not a
 surprise.
Your love like a flower you grew
 all of us, we love you for being
 here to share it with us.
In the end I will say, please stay
 sweet, never change,
I will love you till the day all the
 oceans drift away.

Robert Vaughn
TAKE TIME
Take time and stop for a word of
 prayer,
 Take time and show your faith
 in God today.
Take time to be honest in all that
 you say,
 Take time to be saved from
 your sinful way.

Take time to have faith
 and confess God before men.
By these simple steps
 A new life for you can begin.

Take time to be baptized
 In a watery grave.
Remember it was for you
 That the Master's life he gave.

Arising to walk in the newness of
 life,
 Take time to read the Bible for
 the laws that he gave.
Then thank your lucky stars,
 That Christ the Lord, really
 saves.

Dixie Wehrheim
**To a Swallow On St. James'
Day**
Go fly away to that far place and
 sing a song for me;
And wing a circle in the sky that
 sweeps eternity.
When lowly earth her summons
 sounds, and beckons you to fall,
Go rise in flight to greet with joy
 Apollo's siren call.
Let not the toil nor even joy keep
 back the wanderlust;
Your life is short, be sure it's
 sweet and vital in its thrust.

J. C. Allen
FREEDOM OF NATURE
The morning was dreary and
 warm,
 With a soft breeze,
Moving across the land with
 natures' charm,
 And through the partially
 leaved trees.

Searching the scenery across the
 still town,
 The fullness thereof could be
 observed for miles around,
Surrounding the small town were
 oak trees; Firm and sound,

Matured in gigantic size,
Dressed with natures' beautiful
    prize.
As the blue horizon let the sun
    shine thru,
    Unique houses blazed in many
    color and hue.
And owls rested as thou in
    despair,
    As sparrows pondered thru mid
    air,
Robins searched for food here and
    there.

A new day unwinded a ribbon at
    a time,
    Giving a true feeling of sublime,
Freedom of nature held one spell
    bound,
    As the soft breeze ran swiftly
Through the hilltop town.

It was a quarter past five,
    When the once paralyzed town
    came alive,
People began going their separate
    way,
    Enjoying another fall day . . .

Violet G. Rudd
Mom: A Gift From Heaven
God gave us Mothers,
    who nurture, care, and lead the
    way,
        through the many life-time
        struggles
            that confront us day
            by day.

From cradle to adulthood,
    Mom is by our side, she's there
    when she is needed,
        she listens—we confide.

Although she's more than willing,
    the years do take their toll,
        and now the time has come
        for *us*,
            to comfort and console.

Sue Sharp
YESTERDAY
The trip was patterned
Through streets long familiar
By people still wearing
Bright thoughts of tomorrow.
The delay was as bright as the
    Sun.
Their time became muted
By two angry competitors
Entering a crowded arena
Where only one is Victor.
The scars were cut deep
By these mismatched warriors.

Cynthia K. Niles-Freeman
MANTIS
He sat staring deep into his
    hands while
the woman ate his soul
    and reveled in her wrath.
She had bore him   now she
    abhorred him
    a pimple on her ass she thought
no good   no good.

Words spewed forth from her
    aging mouth.
No one listened   no one cared
No one dared   for
he had listened   maybe too close
he had cared   let her in
and now
she was devouring him from
    within.

"Let me be!" came his silent cry.
"You can't have me!
I'll die."
He sat staring deep into his
    hands while
the woman ate his soul,
and knew it was just a matter of
    time until
he was
no more

Beulah Thomas Carey

Beulah Thomas Carey
CHRISTMAS IS!
            Christmas is
That time of year when love and
    laughter is in the air.
            Christmas is
That time of year when joy seems
    to be everywhere! Yet, some are
    sad and lonely, often sinking
    into despair
            Christmas is
That time of year when there is a
    burning desire to give. Yet
    some at this time would rather
    die than to live!
            Christmas is
That time of year when many
    attend Church and pray! This
    spirit of Christmas ought to be
    in our hearts every day.

Marguerite Mooney
CANADA
Oh Canada of mystic robes,
You are no mystery to me
For you are all the old home
    towns
Which always seem to beckon
    me.

The songbirds sing in great
    delight,
In each Canadian tree
And flowers in profusion bloom,
From east to western sea.

Your prairie fields of golden grain
Shimmer in the noon-day sun,
A treasure for the starving world,
Abundance there for everyone.

The grandeur of your mountains
As snow-capped sentinels stand,
To guard your gentle valleys
Where the wild things graze so
    calm.

I love your valleys, Oh so fair!
The autumn brilliance lingers
    there
As if to keep the storms at bay,
While tempests gather for the
    fray.

Then spring, enchantress of them
    all,
Prepares to break through
    winter's wall,
All her miracles she displays
In azure blue of summer days.

Diane Rollins
MAIL ORDER CATALOGUE:
My faith was running low.
I was about to lose my head.
That's when I read your article,
and this is what is said.

Whatever you are looking for
we have. It's on sale too!
If we don't have it, then we'll get
    it.
Have I an order for you!

Feed all the hungry children,
cure all the sick and lame.
Get rid of air pollution,
we'd like water clear again.

Spread love across the nation,
it's what we have the least.
And while you're at it, how about
making peace in the Middle East?

Sue Sharp
THE GLIMPSE
The struggle to retain youth was
    as great
as that of a strangler closing off
    his victim's
will to breathe.
And like him, I made one last
    effort
which took all my energies.

Since age was fighting as strongly
    as the unbent soul
to keep its place, in a body so
    firm with living;
the fight was measured in
    months instead of seconds.
We both lost!

Jennifer Jasper
A MINOR
The house on the hill
stands quiet and still
The windows all locked and
    barred tight
For the deed had begun
the whole world to stun
On that blustery cold winter's
    night

The child looked with eyes
that held no surprise
At the scene before her and
    smiled
Murder committed
foul, but acquitted
For the murderess only a child

Aaron Wilson Hughey
OUR DAY
frivolous lace
intertwined with silken roses
shapes destinies unknown
from spectacular beginnings
this day . . . our day
occurs but once
quickly it passes
    with scarcely a glance
    from unassuming passers by
special only to an elect few
infinitely gracious
    the moment of unparalleled
    elation
        "our" moment
a short, ever so brief encounter

captured forever
    so vividly in pale memories
    enhanced by telltale
    photographs
grandeur that is fleeting
fading into years of sojourning
    together
but oh the depth
the indescribable, unfathomable
    perfect artistry
of this . . .
    "our" day
july 24, 1982

Frank E. Bubenchik
WHAT IS LOVE?
Love is the most powerful of all
    cosmic energies.
The most universal in people and
    deities.
It is the building block of creation.
The destruction of civilizations.
The seed of humiliation.
The key to man's art inspiration.
It is the root of man's annilation.
Love is man's dream of
    realization.
It is a stem of admiration.
The poet's justice for infatuation.
The source and factor of
    demoralization.

Vicki Maureen Owchar
UNIFICATION
Your branches wave silently in
    the wind,
you seem to to be beckoning me.
The drops fall from your leaves,
you appear to be crying for me.

I touch your withered branches,
and caress your fading leaves.
The wind increases and I watch
    you strain against falling,
then the wind calms down and I
    hear your branches calling.

Once I looked up to you as a
    strong protectorate,
watching over and guiding me.
Now a tear slowly falls from my
    eye and down my cheek,
I realize that we are in the same
    fight.

You are beckoning me to help
    you,
and your tears aren't just for me.
The sadness weighs upon you,
and you wish us to be free.

Mrs. Hilda E. Ongrady
**When the Snowflakes
    Come a Falling**
When the snowflakes come a
    falling and the children wake
    from beds
They go down in the cellar and
    grab their painted sleds
They head for the area around
    White City Lake
They breathe in all the free fresh
    air their little lungs can take
Their mamas know of this
    pilgrimage each and every
    winter clime
But she gives them room for
    growing up and growing up
    takes time
There's one dandy hill, the
    steepest of all
A winding road like a toboggan
    slide and someone's bound to
    fall.

The older kids go skating upon
the lake so vast
Some are just beginners, but some
they go so fast
Kids nowadays know how to live,
they make the most of every
minute
And the teens are so exciting,
they cram lots of fun in it
I am just a spectator, was never
much for going
To bad I never had hot blood in
my veins a flowing
Perhaps there is still a chance for
me when I reach my retirement
And the kids are married and Pa
and Ma and still living, that's
the one requirement.

But just for now I love to watch
the youngsters come and go
With mittens and parkas and
stretch pants and faces all aglow
The lake is beautiful all the year,
the setting is sheer poetry
The handsome youths go skating
by the girls with their coquetry
When darkness comes, it's lovlier
still, the boys all make a fire
Roast marshmallows, drink hot
chocolate, from thermoses,
they never seem to tire

What a spot for a poet, the view
makes artists squint
And I live right smack in the
middle of this Currier & Ives
Print.

Alice Johnson
GARDEN SONG
Song in the garden
Garden song
God is spinning
the world along
He's spinning it straight
He's spinning it true
He knows what he's doing—
So don't be blue
He's got your number
He knows your name
He knows where you're going
And from whence you came.
He's the master gardener
the world is his.
He's the master builder
About his biz.

Jorgi Russell
FATE
Fate was late!
Wait not for fate
To make you great.

The world waits not
For fate that's late
To crash the gate.

Sherry Lovenna
ANYONE, ANYWHERE
[To Lou, Giving you my first,
since you gave me the second.]
Travel around the world; if you
dare,
You can truly go anywhere,
Spain, Africa, Timbukto,
Or a special place known only to
you.

Be anyone you care to be,
Have a lovely time; try and you
will see,
Queen of England for a day,
An actress in a Broadway play,

Famous singer upon the stage,
Or a lonely writer filling a page.

Does not matter who you are,
If you wish you may travel far,
Only requires two simple
ingredients,
Neither will cost a single cent,
First, having imagination to plan
dreams thro,
Second, the determination to
make them come true.

Patricia Saddler Hughes
THE PENDULUM SWINGS
The rhythmic tick of mantle
clock
swings thought from present time
to time bygone.
In cabin warmed by glowing
hearth I dream
beneath the fluff of feathered
flock
where dreams retrieve love's
warmth. Thereon
a longing courses through
lifegiving stream
as chill as winter snow in last
onslaught
when March winds blow upon
the dawn.
If you were here I'd need no
scheme
of mind to feel the warmth your
love has brought.
Your love, its loss, in actuality
is swing to pendulum's extreme.
The rhythmic tick of mantle
clock now frees
my dreams from bygone time to
time to be.

Mary E. Sharp
I'LL NEED YOU
I'll need you in my mornings,
and I'll need you in the night.
I'll need you in the evening,
and in the early light.
Your love is like a spiritual
food, that fills my every need.
It gives me strength and
courage, to perform my every deed.
Your smile is like the rain-
drops, that fall upon the ground.
You are the sweetest lover
that I have ever found.
My need for you is growing,
more every day I live,
And every moment, Darling,
my life to you I give.

Connie Ratliff
MEDITATIONS
These days, there are so many
things to do
That our hours for meditation are
all too few,
As God's Children, we must live
each day
Helping others along Life's Way!
We should pause a minute now
and then
To consider the sad state we'd be
in
Had God not sent his Son to save
us all
To forgive our sins, great and
small!!

What must we do to be pleasing
in His Sight?
First, we must be sure The Light
Of His Love shows in all we do

Helping others to find Him too!

When we're weary from the cares
of the day
His Word teaches, "Dear
Children, pause and pray
For, I'll hear even the smallest plea
If Thou wilt only believe in Me!"

Helen C. Elliott
DECEMBER'S CHILD
[Susan]
Daughter of mine, so very fair,
You with the golden hair,
So far away, and yet so near,
For your birthday this year.

Felicitations, my first-born,
Awaited by angels that yuletide
morn,
For you are, to me, so very dear,
Just like you were, in yesteryear.

Blessings be thine, daughter of
mine,
In the land of Florentine,
So far away, and yet so near,
On your birthday this year.

Theresa Sizemore
MEMORIES
Your memories haunt me
No matter where I go
You have this affect upon me
For reasons I'll never know

Why do I always remember
The memories hurt too much
It's so hard to be a pretender
When I can never forget your
touch

I want to be so close to you
Sometimes I can't stand the pain
I pretend I'm happy when I'm blue
And inside it feels like rain

But maybe someday we'll meet
again
They say true love will last
It will all turn out right in the
end
But for now you're part of the past

Charlotte Vietello
TUFFY (MY PET)
Tuffy is the cutest thing
And the nicest pet I've had
At times we call him a little king
But that is good not bad
When I come home to him I say
Hi Tuffy come, get up and play
His eyes grow big and very bright
Gosh oh golly what a wonderful
sight
He looks at me as if to say, "Oh
boy I think I know

It's time to play one, two, three
then go
Gosh I really do have fun
As on the "go" I surely run
At times I bring back the ball,
you see
So you will play again with me."
He can sit up and beg, too, you
know
He can really put on quite a show
Tuffy, you see, is just a cat
But I'm sure you'll agree, a real
smart one at that.

B. Ann Allen
HARVEST MOON
Forgetting her age, she hangs
suspended under the admiring
eye of her lover.
Shyly she dons a veil of trees, but
is unsuccessful in concealing
her glowing form.
She darts demurely behind a hill,
then peeks out only to see him
waiting . . .
Waiting to catch one last glimpse
of her before she must leave.

Mary Louise Young
OUR GUIDE
Without Jesus, I am
as one who is blind
Groping about
most of the time.
He is my eyes,
He is my cane,
Leading me down
life's lane.
But thank God
with Him I can sense my way.
He is my sight,
my everything all the way.
With my Jesus
I will not go astray,
For He will guide,
and lead me everyday.

Lisa Marie Magazino
PERPLEXITY
The ride is smooth and slow
Or seemingly so.
Hastening,
True intentions appear.
'Round and around
Ups and downs
Head spins,
Confusion,
Deceptive emotions,
Hurting.
Dating, Hating, Sorrow.
Stop the ride!
Merry-Go-Round of uncertainty
Let me off.

Daisy H. Alward
LIFE WAY
More and more I push,
to obtain
each goal I've set before me.
From the nucleus
of myself,
comes my strength and remedy.

Again and again
I realize,
this is what I must embrace.
Only for awhile,
fall behind
the rivers flow, and retrace.

Believing this way,
I shall pass
Again the crest of this time.

Whatever resting
I may do,
brings stability to me.

Kathleen Kelly
ANTHEM
[For Jim Dunleavy]
Here is the Anthem
For the glory of "I";
The egoist's cry
For the virtues of "My".
Superfluous multitudes
Chained to the "We";
Freedom will be
When from "We" you are free.
I build this, my essence
With will and with time.
I've no GIFT of rhyme;
My talent is mine.
The brutes have their numbers,
But I have my mind.
It won't be aligned;
It shall be refined.
For Reason does not fear
The prowess of "We";
The arrogant "She"
Is more suited to me.
Here is the Anthem
The gutless can't kill:
One God remains still;
That God is "I Will."

Nelida Reyes
INDIFFERENCE
Were I to fall and break a limb,
Or blindly walk into a wall of
thorns,
Or have an enemy throw darts at
me
to mar my flesh and spill my
blood;
I will cry out, and moan and
grieve,
And in my misery I will think of
you,
For, all those woes and all those
hurts
that spill my blood and mar my
flesh,
All put together could never be
as agonizing, and not as cruel
as your indifference to me.

McDonald Phipps
**Tribute To Black Prince,
Malcolm X**
Where else could he have fought
but earth,
Or build his impregnable citadel,
A house and shield for the
forgotten man,
His brethren whom he loved so
well?

What spark which then lit that
holy war
Long preceding the great
armageddon,
And rallied that warrior to the
call of,
"Unto victory thou chosen one?"
Were there marks on his kinfolks
backs,
Lack of liberty and fear of
oppression
Which awoke that prince to
brave the attack
With mothers, sisters, fathers,
sons?
If diamonds hardened his days of
youth,
Molded that infant in body

and soul,
Then the plant gave the farmer
his chosen fruits
Wrapped in petals, buried in
mold.

Ghetto to ghetto for the test
And instruction of patterns of the
land
As to, "Stand back nigger" "Fight
for rights",
Or, "Rapid retaliation."
As the sound of that trumpet
blared
When all our dead laid, carried to
their tomb,
"Our goal is top yonder mount"
he said,
"Ere they steal our doom".

Elaine M. Constantino Johnson
THE LIFE I NEVER KNEW
I had a dream some time ago,
About a man who sang a song,
He sang it soft with eyes so true,
About the life I never knew.

I never understood those words
he sang,
Until a night ago I dreamed again,
I saw that man like I did before,
And asked him then about his
song.

He said there was a life meant for
thee,
But only a life that you could
never see,
He stood before me and held my
hands,
I saw your life in another land.

He walked away, until I couldn't
see him anymore,
And sang the song like he did
before,
He sang about the life that ought
to be,
But only a life that I could never
see.

With eyes so soft, and eyes so
true,
He sang about the life I never
knew.

Camille Montana-McLauchlan
SAVE THE CHILDREN
Oh God, save the children
everywhere.
Give them hope, give them care
Replace the tattered clothes they
wear.
For without them, there's no
future here.
Oh God, save the children
everywhere.

Oh God, give the children
enough to eat.
Give them vegetables, give them
meat
To fight off the illnesses they
can't beat.
So there is a future for them to
meet.
Oh God, give the children
enough to eat.

Oh God, give them someone who
will educate
Give them knowledge, give
choices to debate
For future foods on their plates.
Otherwise, we know the

bleakness of their fate.
Oh God, give them someone who
will educate.

Oh God, save the children
everywhere
Give them hope, give them care
Replace the tattered clothes they
wear.
For without them, there's no
future here.
Oh God, save the
children—everywhere.

Shirley Fremeth
SPRING VIEW
The red tips on the branches of
the maple—
swollen with life—ready to
birth
the leaves of summer

Yellow everywhere as the
forsythia
stretch their laden arms
in all directions

A neighbor's cat slinking its way
across the yard,
its grey and brown stripes
undulating
as it stalks a butterfly or bee

Birds soaring, singing, sitting,
sipping or
stealing the newly sown grass
seed,
their black heads busily
pumping

All is motion!

Win Stevenson, Jr.
FROM A NURSING HOME
Winter's left us but I still can't
see the flowers, cannot hear the
red breasted robins happy in
their reborn warmth. They sing
while they're nesting but their
song doesn't reach me

Why can't I enjoy them as before?
Why can't I use my arthritic
fingers and fumbling hands? I'm
locked up in here, unwilling
guest, lights out 10 o'clock.
You there, singing in the trees,
please stop the music: stop the
music, for I'll never dance
again. My feet are weighted
with the mold of age and my
blood runs colder than the
winter of my shapeless form.

Anne Marx
DIVINE BROADCAST
God speaks to us every hour
if we dial to tune Him in.
God sends His word from a tower
beaming long rays through the
din
of daily commercials that batter
our minds too relentlessly—
God chooses programs that
matter
in the quest for true harmony.

He broadcasts in any weather
transmitting both far and near;
whenever we worship together,
the signals come loud and clear.
He needs but one amplifier
heart-anchored in you and me
to reach deeper for ever higher
diving high fidelity.

Lois Warner Doering
NATURE SLUMBERS
[Dedicated to God—His plan
for the natural evolvement of
all life, and for His words: "For
everything there is a time and
a season for everything under
Heavens." Author—"Known"]
What is this mysterious
denseness
That fills the air.
About mid-winter
When most trees are bare?
Only near objects can we see
And the distance fades out
Like a mystery.
But is it mysterious,
This gray blanket we see?

No! It is more of God's mastery!
And tho the tree limbs
Look useless and bare,
"Hark!" My soul whispers,
God's spirit is there,
As vapor in lower atmosphere,
Cleansing all nature
everywhere.
No mystery this denseness
Of winter air,
Nature is resting
In "His" gentle care.
Come spring, Mother Nature
Will rise up and then,
The voice of all nature
Will sing once again.

Terry Jean Miskell
POETRY'S WORDS
The words are the colors that
paint the picture gold
Feelings and emotions that seem
to never quite grow old
To reach between the lines and
see a part of me
The words are but expressions of
the heart you cannot see

All that I have felt, pieces that lie
so deep inside
Meaning woven in somewhere,
flowing with the changing tides
My life travels many roadways,
spinning wheels of time
Circling in the seasons as the
days like string unwind

To see all that I am and the
worlds I still reach for
Only listen to my words, keys to
open the many locked doors
Grasping for the meaning lost in
life's highway
Searching for a white dove who
soars through storms of today

I still hold on to my dreams, for
they give me wings to fly
To reach beyond the laughter and
the tears that I will cry
The golden windows of the world
may be few and far apart
Yet the dreamer rides forever in
the poems written upon her
heart

Genny
LISTEN

A Classic annunciates for
recognition
Among the illiterate.
Symphonies attempt synapse
With auditory sympathy.
Reflections circulate for space
Amid responsibilities.

I am loath yet hopeful
To admit my place
Among this decoupage,
An anomaly
Of bewildered civilization.

Where there is me
Are others, enduring
To preserve with dignity
The Word, the melody, the
moment.

Joan Gomez Y Velasco

Joan Gomez Y Velasco
THE OTHER STAR

I will reach like Whitman to the
top
with the thousand verbs of my
Spanish language
and Uncle Sam with certain
uncertainty
will pick up the light that from
my tongue flows.

I will open the road of sane
ambitions
to show how beautiful my race is
and there will be bilinguals that
in choir my songs
will sing happily all the love that
they embrace.

And that day there will perhaps
be another star
in the resplendent American flag
it will be a conquest without
wars, without fights
of the giant heart of my Spanish
people.

There will be smiles in all the
stars.
Lincoln, Reagan and the great
Pablo Neruda
will hug fraternally with all the
elegance

understanding that finally,
America is One.

Mrs. Betsy Ross will have
another commission
to add the other star—ignored
star—
—to the proud banner that in
centuries
using American Indian wind was
haughty.

A new language will displace to
the one worn out
with new verbs of fraternal
understanding
and face to face like friends of
other centuries
will make the peace of love the
great old Athahualpa
with northern Alexander,
understanding that finally
America is One.

Wendy Anne Rivera
RAGDOLL

*[To Mother and Father, This is
only the beginning!]*
Stuffed Softness
A faity tale dream of
Coming alive,
To hold and to cherish
While I struggle to survive.
Thrown in anger
Cuddled in sorrow
A promised companion
Tomorrow and tomorrow
Thru all the years
Held so tight
When the sun has gone down and
In comes the night.
A treasured friend of
Buttons and stitches
Alas,
I've gone from rags to riches.

Christopher John Musto
IN A ROOM FULL OF ROSES

With a lot of laughter an' a lot of
warm ways,
She can always make the
sunshine stay,
In a room full of roses,
Where we can wake to each day.

Kisses in my ear, it's so nice
when you're near.
Singing lullabyes an' rockabyes
With stars so bright,
In a room full of roses,
Where we can sleep in each
night.

Holding hands an' staying
together,

Wishing to change dreams into
forever.
Believing always in what we have
to give,
In a room full of roses,
Where we can one day live.

Frank J. Fedele
ABSENT REJOICE

It's cold and lonely downtown
today.
Bing Crosby is crooning
Christmas Carols
over loudspeakers in his usual
soothing manner,
Yet his voice seems lost in the
empty streets.

The faces of the people are pale
and drawn,
with a strange preoccupation of
thoughts . . .
I can't help but think . . .
Going through the motions,
Inflation and labor strikes have
dampened spirits
and depressed the season . . .

TURN ON THE LIGHTS!

Anthony Frank Volpe
SUBJECTS IN TIME

*[Dedicated to my late mom and
dad Frank and Elizabeth Volpe
Their words and
encouragement are
unforgettable]*
O Eternal Time!
how majestic you reign
In your muted, transparent palace
In unguarded vaults
your subjects remain
Silent . . .
in timeless repose without
malice

Encased were these mortals
in slow falling sands
Your clock tolled the hour
on their march to your lands
Entombed in a vacuum
you heard not their cry
Instead . . . you embraced them
Now . . . in your palace they
lie—

Kevin Patrick Haining
NOSTALGIA

Sitting alone in a corner of mind
trying to paint pictures of past
times;
sketching faces, watching their
slow return
from the darkness of oblivion.
Birds float on the gentle breeze
going to sunshine of future
dreams—
but I see beauty-seekers capturing
butterflies,
pasting them in scrap book, not
realizing they're dead.

Valerie Anne Destro
PROBABILITY & CAUSE

Action release my drive to ninety
then cause me to run
Down a mysterious clown with
red eyes and a yellow moustache

He bleeds black blood
and the probability that he will
Live is close to fifty-fifty
but he died anyway

It just goes to stay and

leave when one encounters a
clown
That dying is a cause
and frowning is a probability.

Ms. Meredith P. Brown
NEW FOUND LOVE

New Found Love What Could It
Be?
The Warmth
And
Your Tender Understanding
—Engulfs Me—
Oh! My Soul, And Spirit,
Like A Sponge Has Always
Yearned For,
New Found Love, Could You Be
An Illusion Of—My—
Imagination?
Or An Oasis,
With
The Warmth Of Your Spirit And
Nature
—Only—
To
Fool Me,
A Glance From Your Eye I Can
Feel,
The Warmth, And Your Tender
Kindness
So Far Displayed To Me,
New Found Love I Hope You
Sense
That My Love For You,—Is New—
Like A Brook When Trickling,
Into A Virgin Stream,
So Is,
—My—
New Found Love.

R. Michael Ingenito
THE THIEF

Weaving in and out. Feline.
Twisting, turning, writhing.
Spinning.
Assurance heightened by
precision.
Silent laughter spitting at a
stark, still
summer's eve.

A silhouette of a maybe shadow.
A vague splash of a maybe
something
that may have
shimmered,
for a moment,
against the moonscape.

Charla Redus Hill
THE BIBLE

There's much in the Bible I don't
understand,
Though I'm sure it was written
the way God planned.
And I treasure its words from
beginning to end,
For it has become such a personal
friend.

In it are some verses I quote
every day,
Because they have helped to light
my way.
In it are selections my mother
once read,
Before she kissed us, and tucked
us in bed.

And inside the covers I
frequently see,
Some certain passage she copied
for me.
A special one, I now call to mind,

Tells us "To be humble, do justice, be kind."

"The Lord is my Shepherd," we often heard,
Until we memorized it, word by word,
"Do unto others,"—became a rule,
We were urged to live by, at home or at school.

"Lo, I am with you," helped to quell our fear,
And scores of chapters became very dear.
So may I insist that you read this book,
And your life may take on a different look.

Anna Williams
HOSPITAL WAITING
[For Leslie]
A book masks unseeing eyes.
With sighs,
I lift it to try again.
Words dance across my brain.
I think perhaps that I should pray—
"Dear God, are you busy today?"
Is all I say.

Time trails. I know
The doctor will come, but when?
I stand to gaze below.
Assorted cars, row on row,
Nose together; a playground of toys.
(Small boys, in glee,
Smash them for me!)

An elevator bell signals and
Time stops. Wheels rumble;
Two hands swing the door wide.
Relief fills the vacuum fashioned by fear.
(No tear can fall.)
"Worried?" they question.
"No, not at all!"

Sonya Ann Ragland
THE PERFECT GUY
The perfect guy must be sincere
He also must be true
And when I hold him near
He should whisper "I love you".

The perfect guy is honest
And never tells a lie
He also will stay with you
And never say"Good-bye."

The perfect guy is lots of things
He'll be there to hold your hand
But most of all the perfect guy
Must love me for what I am!

Stella C. (Cathy) Collins
IN MY DREAMS
I've never been to Paris,
but I've seen the Eiffel Tower.
I've never been to London,
though I've heard Big Ben ring out the hour.
I've never ridden in a jet,
but I've soared the sky so high.
I've never sailed upon a ship,
but I've seen the waters flowing by.
I've never climbed a mountain,
but I've reached its' highest peaks.
I've never been to New York,
but I've strolled along its' streets.
I've never been to Egypt,
but I've touched the pyramids.

I've never met Kings and Queens,
but I've slept where they lived,
I've never been a soldier,
but I've fought an endless war.
I've never been to outerspace,
but the planets I've explored.
It appears that I go nowhere,
but I've done alot it seems.
It is very simple you see,
I've done them in my dreams.

Cassie Sebastian
MY HERO
My hero is
Kermit the Frog;
Most of his friends
Live in a bog.

He's green all over
And big black eyes;
He's also hard to dance with
'Cause he's not my size.

He's been a good friend
For a very long time,
And when we go out
I'm lucky if he spends a dime.

He's my hero
Believe it or not,
He may be different
But I like him alot.

Rita Marie Knecht
AN OPINION
Listening to words spoken with authority
    Who is right, who is wrong
Saying it is this way
    Another, it is always this way
Wait don't hesitate on impulse, Forward
    reaching the stars
    With little effort of mind
When will I learn to overcome words of thought?

Wanda L. Greene
HANGMAN
[This poem, my first published, is dedicated to Dolores—for pushing me just when I needed it, Ed—for keeping my spirits up through long distance, and Jim—for making it all worthwhile.]
I tried to give you enough rope
    so you wouldn't feel bound.
It turned out to be just enough
    to go around my own neck.
And now you've dropped the floor
    from under my feet.

A day has passed,
and still I hang
                        in limbo.

Come back—
    Cut me loose.

Set me free—
    or give me the chance
    to try again.

Until you return
I can only pour out
black blood
    on white pages.

Georgann Jenulis
MY MOTHER'S BLUE EYES
Some blue eyes tease you
Some make you smile
Others are warm
And glow for a while

When I'm laughing

When I'm crying
My blue eyes shine too
But they'll never be as pretty
As my Mom's eyes of blue

The other day my child came to me
and said "Mommy hug me as tight as can be"
"I'll always remember how you hug me so tight. Your hug stays with me
All through the night."

Each mother's different
Each is the same
I guess that's how
Mother's got their name.

Louise Hale Meek

Louise Hale Meek
HI! I'M ROUTE 66
[To Kenny Pierce and the Kenny Pierce Band for the inspiration and encouragement they have so generously given.]
Hi, I'm route 66 come drive on me
From coast to coast you can travel
And great sights to see
They've given me a new name
Now I'm called Interstate 40
Better than I used to be

I'll take you over mountains into valleys
Across the deserts and wide open plains
Together we'll see the states from sea to sea
From cities to little towns just you and me—

There are splendors from rising suns
To star studded nights
From sage brush and trees to rivers
Over and under me—

Big trucks, trailers and little cars
Speed up and down
The trains run beside me too; far
Away coming back to see and envy me
Because of the sights I can let you see—

We'll stop and eat or visit a park or two
From the Grand Canyon to Indian tepees
I'll let you take pictures for friends
Who'll wish they could travel me

And if you're lucky you might see
A snow-peaked mountain or a rainbow
Cross over me

Cecelia Marchand
A VERY STRONG MAN
He stands tall and straight with his face to the world,
And his feet firmly placed on the floor,
There's a glint in his eye that says he'll get by,
For he's done it many times before.
He looks at the world, and he watches its antics,
There's very little that can get by him,
When life hands him a blow, it may knock him down low,
But his inner self it simply can't dim.
He believes in himself though in very few others,
He's a fighter and no stranger to strife,
He thinks his own mind, and he says what he thinks,
He takes the best that he can for his life.
He knows what he wants, and he knows how to get it,
He's got class, determination, and style,
He has a firm yes or no and no use for show,
But he can soften it all with a smile.
He stands straight and tall as he faces the world,
He's really a man's man for sure,
There's no room for doubt; he will never strike out,
By his determination and will he'll endure.

Ada M. Hall
Arrange To Rearrange
Dare I so journey
Beyond familiarity,
Into sacrifice and change?
To whit old girl, proceed.
Arrange to rearrange.

Preception, null and void.
Who doubts me, 'cept me.
Distant voices compelling and strange
Insist that I comply, so I
Arrange to rearrange

Sandra K. Leipprandt
THE ROAD OF DISCIPLINE
[To Daniel who taught me to believe]
Wandering down a road, I've never before been on
Not exactly sure of the direction that I'm headed
Somedays sliding, gliding smoothly, setting my sights upon
That shiny Paradise I've heard of where all answers are imbedded
Like fossils deep within my brain, within my grasp, on tip of tongue
My footsteps drone the stern refrain:
If you follow the rules you'll know the truth
If you follow the rules you'll know the truth

And all is fine 'til I stumble upon—

That rock in the middle of the
    road
That chasm in the center of my
    brain
That wild beast in the good forest
    of my heart
That stubborness in the depths of
    my soul

And I fall face first in the middle
    of the road
With dirt on my lips I curse the
    day
With blood in my eyes I say
"My Way!"

And I crawl down some side path
    and lick my wounds
Then I charge through the brush
    'til I wear myself out
With a smile on my face and
    sweat on my brow
I lounge in the ditch and look all
    about
Then the road calls me back; I
    forget what a bitch
She was, so I go, and I flow
'Til her harsh ways grate on my
    nerves once more

Teresa Hixson
THE RAIN
Rain is like a lullabye,
    falling off the trees,
    the rhythm of the raindrops,
    gently rocking me.

Dr. Joan L. Gordon
HUNGER
Life's greatest hunger
Is not for bread,
But a song that lingers
When the words have fled.

Life starves many,
But not for bread,
Some die living,
While others live dead.

Antonio S. Sarion

Antonio S. Sarion
COLOR EXPERIENCE
*[This poem is dedicated to my
mother on the 24th of July
1983—her 76th birthday.]*
Leave your cocoon, that tiny space
Where darkness never seems to
    cease,
Then you'll emerge but to behold
The fiery brilliance of the world.

Scan those hues before your eyes
And you will find those colors
    nice.
The rainbow and the sun like gold
Are just a few that will unfold.

And as you make that playful
    flight
The flowers, don't you think
    they're bright?
The trees, the birds are all around
In varied tinges they abound.

Go then enjoy those tints with
    bliss
And you will never have the
    wish—
To go back and again secured
Inside that den of nigritude.

John E. Sanks
I NEED YOU
For years we've been together now
In you I do confide,
Please discontinue your
    wanderlust
Cause I need you by my side.

It helps so much to have someone
to share the things of life,
You know I really need you
through happiness and strife.

You've changed so much its hard
    to say
just what our future will be,
But if you'll only stop and think
you'll always stay with me.

I loved you when I married you,
my love I just can't hide;
So lets please start all over again
cause I need you by my side.

Albert Hernandez Jr.
THE ESCAPIST RUT
For a time, it was fine
To embrace in a sixty—nine,
Sucking my loneliness away.

For a time, it was fine
To drown in a bottle of wine,
Drinking my worries away.

For a time, it was fine
To sink into drugs and waste
    every dime,
Blowing my questions away.

For a time, it was fine
To hide behind The Divine,
Praying my fears away.

It was a crime unto My—Self
To think it was fine.

Barbara Redondo
JOSS PAPER
To surmise the time of the first
    sunrise
Or the skies delineate,
Science estimates.

To expatiate emotions
Tongues wrestle with

the inarticulate.
But words cannot expound
Sentiments unsound
Nor export a certain sort of hurt,
Nor silence pronounce.

Madness retains sense
Sanity is but pretense.
Impossible it is to summerize
Infinitude,
To delimit Universe,
And distinguish false from truth,
To construe my love for you
Unborn therefore to death
    immune.

Bonnie Lou Stahly
THE GIFT OF TODAY
*[I dedicate this poem, with
love, to my husband, Warren.
The gift of each day is made
even more special because I
share the day with him and his
love.]*
"I was given a gift this morn, as I
    awoke from my sleep.
I was given today, it's mine to
    have but not to keep."
"I can take today and use it or I
    can just throw it away.
It's mine for twenty—four hours,
    then it becomes a yesterday."
"I can do with it whatever I please.
I can make it a struggle or I can
    go through it with ease."
"I can make it happy or I can
    make it sad.
I can make it a good day or I can
    make it bad."
"I cannot live in yesterday and
    tomorrow may never be.
I only have today; this gift God
    gave to me."

Deborah Joan Posey
The Birth Of the Sun
Its beginning to bring forth a new
    horizons, as the sun appears,
Its about to give birth for a brand
    new day.

Its rays of beauty, its rays of
    wonder, its rays of splendor,
Its about to give birth for a new
    tomorrow.

Its rays of wisdom, its rays of
    time, its rays of the future,
Its about to give birth for a great
    reunion, for all in heaven.

Berma Ashcraft Albright
**An Heritage Worth
Keeping**
*[In loving memory of William
and Willie (Wallace) Ashcraft,
my disciplinarian father and
gentle mother, with a tinge of
sorrow that I never even
thought to thank them for the
gift of life!]*
So far away is yesterday.
Were hearts more noble then?
They took the past and sealed it
    fast,
A shrine for future men.

Their ties still bind all
    humankind,
Through timeless generations,
With works of man graced by
    God's hand,
In one great preservation.

And even today from far away,

Smile down enraptured faces;
And blesses still the rustic hills,
Among these hallowed places.

We, too, must lead with noble
    deed—
As did forbears now sleeping;
And pass along in word and song,
An heritage worth keeping!

Hermon Clark
THE ROSE
Oh Rose, oh Rose of life,
    I love you;
And in my life, Rose,
    You are its beauty;
I see you always,
    Radiant and in full blossom;
Each and every petal,
    A story tells of our lives;
And as a petal falls,
    It becomes a memory to be
    cherished;
And another grows,
    As beautiful as the first;
And, Rose, as we separate even
    for a moment,
    My heart follows;
Oh Rose, oh Rose of my life,
    I love you.

Mary Lou Keeney
MARY LOU'S HOUSE
I passed by your "Old Home" last
    night,
The place was all aglow,
The windows and the doorway
Reflected your sweet "Hello".
I turned and looked, after I passed
    by,
Memories came crowding in,
I had the urge to cry.
The stalwart trees stood swaying,
Raindrops falling seem to say,
"I know you too are lonely,
Since she went away".
The place still bears your image
    in it's deepest core,
Like sunlight stealing thru the
    trees to dance upon the floor.
I who dream of youthful laughter
    once heard 'round your door,
Am prone to hear the echo's
    sweetly as before.

D. F. Marlin
ANOTHER DAY
I open my eyes to another dawn
Thank you Lord for the night just
    gone,
Looking after me and keeping me
    well
And giving me the strength to tell.
The Glory of seeing and hearing
    as well.
Of colours gold and colours blue
And many more of a different hue.
The growing tree, the flowers
    that be,
The blades of grass and the
    bumble bee.
Of birds that fly and sing all day,
Of children playing along the way.
Yes Lord, thank you again I say
For the privilege of living another
    day.

Marcia Gale Kester
MISSOURI RAIN
They predicted rain this morning
with thunder growling like an old
    dog on my front porch.

To day the optimara violets

bloomed crimson—
larger than the ones in mother's
garden
where I buried her broken china
tea cup in mud when I was five.

At Uncle Clay's funeral
she held her coat over
my head
when we walked through the rain—
pennies falling
on a canvas shelter
over his grave.

Somewhere in Florida
on a cloudless day
my mother waxes the dining—
room table, lemon oil
thick with summer heat.
She rubs out finger prints
and the rings where my elbows
rested last spring.

I look in the mirror
trace the curves of my nose
the lines by my eyes,
her eyes,
and wonder if she hears rain
falling through my fingers.

Tim Kissell
Last Time I Saw True Love
I followed her to a praying place
She was kneeling   I was praying
I followed her to a picture place
She was looking   I was watching
I followed her to a dining place
She was hungry   I was empty
I followed her to a military place
She was defensive I was defenseless
I followed her to a sleeping place
She was weary   I was wary
I followed her to a dying place
She was waiting   I was ready

Steve Bailey
DEFICIT
[To Dennis Roland Bailey, and
Ann Hagan Bailey—whose
devotion deserves an even
greater tribute.]
What sadness that the lemon sun,
Must fade away when day is done;
To hide behind the hill's dark
cover,
Like the vanishing of a lover,
Down the misty meadow over.

Derrall L. Singleton
ADULT GAMES
When a person reaches a
certain stage in life;
maturity moves in, and
age is out.

When competing on the
same level of under—
standing; socializing
is a key to success.

When comparing strengths
of mentalities; how
potent are your intel—
lectual capabilities.

When gathering these thoughts
on communication I realize
they are merely games people
play, adult games; that's
what make life so paintaken
and complex today.

Larry Pitman
CLINCHED
Majestic and strong, with
shoulders high he sits,

peering and blinking.
One swoop of his wing span lifts
him off the fence post.
Determination
in sight his goal flashes across
the prarie floor, fast.
Concentration
catches an updraft and a higher
intent of interest until he
tucks his wings back and dives
farther, faster, brown, white,
tan, stream line toward his goal.
His head and shoulders pull up
his talons drop as his wing
span spreads to catch the late
afternoon air.
Hot, August and dry.

Donna Marie Johnson
LOVE
["To all those that believed in
me I dedicate my poem to you.
I give special thanks to my
parents and Lucky K. Taylor for
being there when I needed
them."]
I can't explain what I feel for
you, words can not express it.
    I do know it's something special,
wonderful and free.
    Something people share,
like you and me.

Nancy H. Carlson
TOMORROW
Mommy, will you play with me?

We can climb a tree—
Up, so high, so free—

We'll skip a rope
To a hundred, I hope—

We can make up a game
They're never the same

We can ride my bike
Or whatever you like

If you'll only say, "yes"

But—I know—Mommy,
You don't have time.

Tomorrow, my little one,
I'll have time
                Tomorrow——

And so it seems—

Tomorrow and yesterday
Silently come and slither away
    together
Into the shadows of my life

And leave only the memories of
"Mommy, will you play with me?"

Matthew Mahan
SHADOWS ON THE WALL
A dark and lonely house now
stands.
Doorknobs turned by icy hands.
As each and every memory
    strains,
And each and every life remains
As a shadow upon the wall.

The dark and lonely house still
stands.
A victim of time's shifting sands.
As remembrances creep up the
    stair,
One by one, pair by pair
And shadows remain upon the
    wall.

The dark and lonely house

now falls.
Gone are all its musty halls—
Nothing there to hear your calls.
Gone are the shadows from the
walls.

Dwain McClain
YOUR LAST PROMISE
Oh! How wonderful to look up
    into the skies,
Jesus there you are right before
    my eyes.
Oh! What a beautiful picture
    your image makes,
    The reflection of your face
    upon the lakes.
Oh! What splendor to look down
    o'er the trees,
    To see the calmness you
    brought the seas.
Oh! The exciting feeling as out
    o'er the land,
    Everywhere I look, at watch
    you stand.
Oh! How glorious to look upon
    the sand of the beach,
    To realize you are the creator
    of all we beseech.
Oh! The words of the bible, that
    tells of what will be,
    If we obey your one command,
    "Follow me."
Oh! To think of your promise
    when last on earth you stood,
    You said, "I'll come again and
    make this world good."

Bessie Jeanne Worthy

Bessie Jeanne Worthy
A BARGAIN FOR LIFE
[To Oda "Curley" Worthy My
Husband "The Love of My Life"]
God gives us 7 days a week
    A "bargain" one can never beat—
So make the most of every day
    In work, love, life, and play.
Cherish each and every day
    You won't regret the price you
    pay.

Teresa Aiken
CRUSTY
If you had asked him if he had
    loved her
He would have laughed
And given a very cynical opinion
    on romance
And the general condition
Of the human race.

If you had asked him if he had
    cared for her
He would have harumphed a
    loud harumph

And lectured at length on how he
    was a sick man
Far too feeble to concern himself
With sentiment.

If you had asked him if he
    thought of her
    He would have sighed
And replied that his mind was
    occupied
With survival, and how he had
    no time
For nostalgia.

But if you had seen him
Through the dust—smeared
    window of his house
If you had seen him hold her
    picture
In trembling hands as he rocked
If you had seen his tears, slow
    with salt

Trickle down through the
    wrinkles in his cheeks
And fall, finally free, onto the bib
    of his overalls
Then you would know
He was a momumental liar
Amongst his other fine qualities.

Lynda D. Kell
LOVE 1
If love is but a fickle friend
Wherefore does grace allow?
Our fragile senses crack and rend
For lack of knowing how

To deal with such chicanery
As fate would oft bestow
Wolves who dress as lambs to see
How many minds they'll blow!

Beth A. Hogan
UNTITLED
REMEMBERING
    the midnight
        when
only lover's dew
    apart us
        kept,
and longing
    for that
        separation
to return
    once more . . .

Ben Layman Castellow
L. A.
[To my wife, Mary—for the
times we won't miss]
The smog rolls out its cloak of
    filth but this bothers not the
    people for we are not from here
we just came to be with you.

And in our parting ways
    we leave in sorrow
    but not of missing you
only missing what we could have
    done.

Betty Jean Leasure
THE MOUNTAIN STATE
The rugged State of West
    Virginia—
Where the mountaineers are
    always free,
With five states hugging the
    boundary—
Formed into a state—June 20th,
    1863.

Monongahela, Great & Little
    Kanawha & Ohio:
Names of the principal rivers,

John Campbell, Editor & Publisher

I recall,
With mining of coal, a natural
Where the rippling black waters
    fall.

Boasting of West Virginia
    University—
Education compulsory—early to
    16 years,
Also, The New River State College
Which would calm the ignorance
    fears.

We are not the backward people
Which writers are prone to relate,
But rich with God—given
    resources
In "The Little Mountain State."

Brenda J. Lambdin
Dreams Can Be Forever
Dreams can be forever,
But your dreams can really come
    true,
All you have to do is believe,
In all you say and do!
So, if you have a dream in life,
That is a challenge to you,
That incurs a great deal of energy,
That is rewarding and exciting too.
Put forth your very best,
To strive in what you want to do.
Never give up,
For what means so much to you!
Between you and me,
There's so much to learn, give
    and see,
Just what in life,
That you'd wish to be.
Our times of Freedom we have at
    hand,
For being an American, I'll take
    my stand!
To pursue my dreams,
Taking the rejections too,
Is all a part, of making your
    dreams come true!

Karen Smith
SEASONS OF THE WILLOW
—Fall
    As the leaves descend to the
    ground
—Winter
    I see the tree shiver
—Spring
    As it puts on new leaves to
    chase away the winter chill
—Summer
    I see the green branches
    hanging patiently for a breeze
—
    I sit under the willow and it
    makes me feel at peace with
    myself.

Clara H. Elliott
PRAYER
Prayer is a sweet conversation;
A phone call between God and
    man.
Prayer is faith in action;
If we believe and know God can.

Prayer is a phone call to glory;
And the toll is always free.
One need not call the operator;
God knows you are calling, you
    see.

Prayer is not an easy way out;
To prosper from the lust of your
    heart.
Prayer is the cry of a weary soul;

Who is leaning upon its God.

Prayer is a sweet conversation;
Between a Father and His child.
Blessed are the children who talk
    with Him daily;
And in whose heart there is no
    guile.

Thomas King
CROSSROADS
Through the ages
Well versed he's been through
    consummate sages
And yet a lingering essence flows
Of doubts, from which minds'
    mystery grows
Ascending to this loathsome spot
To find out why, then ask why
    not
To ever quiver in the breeze
Perturbed when swayed with
    relative ease
But taste he shall of victory sweet
With tears, yet poise, with flair
    discreet

Deborah Parr
COOKIE
A cookie is purely devious,
    It's presence is a sin.
It won't take away a single pound
    But it certainly will add ten.
Its temptations are great,
    Its rewards are few,
But if you've had one, you'll
    surely have two
    (I've found this to be true)
Eve bit an apple,
    Adam tried it too—
If the apple had been a cookie
    Even the snake would have had
    a few.

Thelma Moon Henry
SWINGERS OF SWINGS
What phantom sits upon you,
    rope swing,
Swung as you are between earth
    and sky?
No passenger meets the eye—
Only tangled strands, an empty
    tire, dangling there—
Why?
Are all swingers of swings grown
    old,
Deflated with time, as tires
    without air?
Are there no children to contend,
Only aged ones, and tired ones,
    who do not care?
Are there only phantoms,
    swinging, swinging, swinging,
There?

Louise Pugh Corder
SPRING AWAKENING
Spring rushes in quite madly
Across the frozen land.
The wind and rain are moody,
But move at her command.

Spring tosses streaks of lightning
And thunderbolts on high.
She boldly rattles windows,
Drives clouds about the sky.

The fallow earth is wakened
By torrents of wild rain.
Spring breathes forth gusty
    whirlwinds;
Dry leaves dance in the lane.

She liberates the flowers,
Makes birds burst into song.

The icy brooks are loosened,
Tree sap flows quick and strong.

All creatures rouse with vigor,
Their hibernation o'er.
Spring tasks begin in earnest,
Men's hope renewed once more.

Her urgent task completed,
The world alive and green,
Spring turns around quite meekly
And gently leaves the scene.

Roslyn Endries—Gallagher
LITTLE GIRL LOST
[For my sisters: Mary Jo
Rondone and Kathy Endries]
I slipped through a crack in the
    floor last night and no one
    even knew I'd been gone.
I was holding on by my finger
    tips and no one even came to
    help me out.
That's the trouble with being in
    pain, it forces one to think only
    of oneself.
I hate pain. It's so self—centered
    and I'm constantly in pain
    these days.

My head felt as though it were
    going to explode and no one
    even heard it ticking away.
My abdominal cramps were so
    real I was beginning to believe
    there was some genuine
    physical cause.
But that's the trouble with pain
    even if it's only in your mind . . .

I wish I were a little girl again
    and that, this time, I had a
    father (a kind and loving man).
After all these years growing up
    without one has left me
    longing for someone forever
    lost to me.
The longing—I want to be rid of
    it, to shuck it off like an oyster
    shell.
The oyster who is so soft, so
    helpless, so vulnerable, "that's
    me!"
"You're a bleeding heart, too
    sentimental!" I scold. But then,
    that's the trouble with pain—
    it's so self-centered and I am
    too much with it.

I slipped through a crack in the
    floor last night and I thought
    . . . I had hoped I was being
    reborn.
But there was no light, only
    darkness; no joy, only gloom
    and no one even came to help
    me out.

Mark Arthur Vogel
REASONS TO LIVE
Autumn winds and shadowing
    lights
The peace and serenity of silent
    nights
A dove cooing tirelessly for it's
    life—long mate
And the pleasures I have found in
    you to date

The beauty of what lay below as
    seen from mountainous heights
The grace and splendor of the owl
    during it's midnight flights
The unseen mysteries of the salty
    deeps

And the mournful limbs of the
    willow as she weeps

The gloom, boredom and fears of
    stormy days
The restless waters by the shores,
    the endless waves
The sadness and miseries of
    lonliness
And that tranquil moment as the
    sun and sky meet to kiss

These I interpret as reasons to live
Each is unique from the other, all
    have much to give
But among these and more I must
    also include
All the Magnificence and Beauty
    that I have found in YOU

Julian Weaver, M. D.
A PIECE OF THE PIE
[Dedicated to: The "Freeloaders"
of the world.]
We have an "Uncle" by the name
    of "Sam", who's such a
    tremendous guy.
He has gained considerable claim
    to fame, as the baker of the
    "Freebie Pie".
Everybody wants a "piece of the
    pie".
There's developed such demand,
That he tripped one day . . . on
    his way to the oven . . .
And nearly got squashed by the
    pan.

Marjorie Rhoads
WINTER'S JEWELS
Winter's Showplace, Nature's
    Jewels,
Snowflake's lacy dew;
Handcrafted by the Master,
Each facet freshly new.

Silvr'y diamonds, gifts of love;
Tiny, icy gems,
Sparkle brightly in the sun,
Set on crystal stems.

Winter's Beauty bathed in white;
Restful peace to bring,
Stays briefly in its glory
Then ushers in the Spring.

Brenda Brown and Mike Day
**The Helper Of the
    Fatherless**
There are some lines in the pages
    of the precious word of God
As recorded in the book that we
    call James.
It talks of pure religion undefiled
    before God,
Visit the fatherless and widows

396

and to keep one's self
unchanged.
The helper of the fatherless will
lend a helping hand.
The helper of the fatherless will
surely understand.
Whose teacher is the Spirit of the
Living God so true.
The helper of the fatherless will
do all He can do.
The tears of the fatherless are
never left unseen.
The poor widow's prayers are
never left unheard.
If Jesus is your Saviour, I'm sure
you know what I mean,
For God so loved the world, He
gave His Son, He tells us in His
word.
The helper of the fatherless will
lend a helping hand.
The helper of the fatherless will
surely understand.
Whose teacher is the Spirit of the
Living God so true.
The helper of the fatherless will
do all He can do.
The message to the fatherless,
"Weep only for the night,
For the morning is sure to be
eternal joy."
If your daddy is living now, I was
wondering if you might
Take this message to the
fatherless, some little girl or boy.
The helper of the fatherless will
surely understand.
The helper of the fatherless will
lend a helping hand.
Whose teacher is the Spirit of the
Living God so true.
The helper of the fatherless will
do all He can do.
The helper of the fatherless will
do all He can do.

Kathlyn T. Herringer
THE SHOWS
[Inspired by childhood
memories and dedicated to my
brother Ivan M. Owens]
Remember Saturday evenings
We'd dress up and go to town.
Many times we watched as
Daddy led the band around.

More often than that we'd go to
the show
That's what we called the movies
back then.
The comics, serials and cowboys
Held our interest again, again and
again.

Sometimes we watched Harold
Lloyd
Or Charlie Chaplin feats.
Maybe it was the Keystone Kops
Who kept us laughing in our seats.

We hadn't forgotten Pearl White
Cause the villian was torturing her
And we had wondered all week
long
If the hero would stop that cur.

Tom Mix rode his horse Tony
To chase the crooks he sought.
We cheered him on till all of them
Were rounded up and caught.

In the big touring car and on our
way home
We were sleepy as could be
And dreaming of the very next
week
When the show again we'd see.

Wm. Dale
A POETS RAGE
from the darkly growing storm
with swift measure
to my loves vain beauty and
offenses blade
against the time of desires fair
pleasure
seeking truth as a crystal or fair
jade
my minds shadow journeys
through springs window rare
far from the thoughts of such
silent love that rambles
for a prince soul that seems so
bare
like a pilgramage for a treasure of
gold candles
the vine of the morrow returns
me to winters scorn
and vanished are the idle hours
commanding delight
as i hasten back into the raging
storm
an eternal skys blazon hue of
lightning bright
o sweet universe with chaste
nymphs of fire
your divine secrecy pardons my
flights desire

Linda M. Patterson
A Short Trip To Heaven
There's a place you can go
Without leaving your chair—
It's a short trip to heaven
On the wings of a prayer.

Just close your eyes
Wherever you are—
And you'll know in a minute
It isn't very far

To the land where the streets
Are covered with gold
And friends are gathered
Both young and old.

Their happy faces reflect the love
Of our heavenly father up above.
The love and happiness they all
share
Can be yours without ever
leaving you chair.

Christopher M. Chapman
SOMETIMES IN FEAR
Sometimes in fear of the mutants
of lizards,
We grapple and grasp for a
tenuous hold on the day.

Hesitant, cautious, we plot sacred
courses
Through rarely sailed oceans
unconsciously knowing the way.
Some in confusion of dreams and
illusions
Find hallways deserted and
reeking of lonesome decay.
Then in the madness that follows
thereafter
They're stomped and they're
trounced upon, callously
thrown in the fray.

Hordes of the pilgrims unite in
the darkness
Exemplify marvelous sin in it's
intricate forms.
In a decision they choose their
perdition,
While never but also forever
regarding the storm.
Then on the surface a challenge
arises
As those who have taken the
other path now are reborn.
And night comes down bringing
fear, bringing terror.
A shade of Apocalypse now from
the prophets is torn.

Those of the daylight retreat to
their haven
As underworld hammers
uceasingly batter the walls.
But still stands the tower with
well meaning power
And out of the puzzle above the
roof finally falls.

Melanie R. Bracy
Questions and Answers
There she sits on the river bank,
Looking but, not really seeing
anything or anyone,
Wondering . . .
Why life is so complicated?
If dreams really do come true?
And why her crazy little sister
is sitting here writing?
As the river flows by so does life
in it's own way, and maybe
she'll find the answers to her
questions someday.

Phyllis Y. Crockett Thompson
DAY TO NIGHT TO DAY
[To My Loving Mother Lillian
V. Gee Smith]
Rising morning sun, new day has
begun.
Softly through the trees, blows
the balmy breeze.
Skies refreshing blue, grasses
filled with dew.
Flowers dazzle bright, giving eyes
delight.
Birds that fill the air, fly without
a care.
Insects crawl the streets, fleeing
passing feet.
Gradually the sun, finds the
horizon.
Flying birds retreat, sheltered
now they sleep.
Crawling insets race, to their
hiding place.
Dazzling flowers rest, from eyes
that caresssed.
Twilight stalks the night, shining
stars so bright.
Soon the moon's in place,

way in outer space.
Night engulfs the day, sending
her away.
Then the day time ends . . . to
begin again.

Missi Loudermilk
FAMILY
Family is togetherness
At the time of need
Family is joy
Yes, indeed!

Family is getting together
To cook out and play games,
Or going into the house
To sit and talk if it rains.

Family is looking back
On the fun one has had,
Family means sticking together
Through good and bad.

But most of all, family is—
Sharing each other's love!
And that can only come
From God up above.

Robert Allen Gleske
WORDS
Cold, tired, hungry, lonely.
These are only words, words are
all I have.
I have a voice crying out loud,
silently longing for words.
A thousand voices chanting,
saying nothing to the masses,
I write but cannot understand or
read.

I have no money, no talent,
nowhere to go.
Expanded conceptions; confused
interpretations,
They tell me I'm sick, cause I
don't play tricks.
Let the light shine in, so I don't
get behind.

Thought, deranged menace;
everything's scrabbled.
Put me down beside you, near the
trees gently,
Give me your woes, return the
breeze,
High, astral voyager, nothing's
realized.

Chris Nichols
SIMPLICITY OF LIFE
Life was so simple, curious, fun
But when youth is gone, what's
done is done
You'll think back on days in
solitude
With endearing fondness in every
mood
The rising eyes in a curious child
Is the finest passion for one so
mild
The time is now, and all you know
Is always with you in friends and
foes
Simplicity of life once unafraid
All that you longed for, all that
you made.

Nancy Love
EDEN
Through yonder wood a pathway
winds,
And summer weaves its magic
spell;
Here early on the dogwood blooms
And bright—hued flowers cheer

the dell.

The winged hosts give forth with
song—
Their tuneful notes pure joy
impart;
The babbling of the stony brook
Speaks volumes to the lonely
heart.

Small minnows dart amidst the
stones
That line the cool clear waterbed,
And cawing crows with jaundiced
eye
Explore the scene from high
o'erhead.

The new—mown hay its
fragrance lends—
Pure essence of a summer's day,
And here and there a playful hare
Leaps and bounds its merry way.

The air is sweet with pleasing
scent
Of honeysuckle from the hill,
And—sheer delight—on moonlit
night
Comes soft—voiced call of
whippoorwill.

Could Eden 'gain be on this earth
No other spot could as well suffice,
The choice no other place than
this
For hear is earthly paradise.

Bebe Briggs
ALONE
Hours come and hours go,
Long and lonesome time,
Holidays that last and last
And stir and stir the mind,
Thoughts that twist and turn
around
And mix the bowl of tears
'Til it runs and overflows
And the heart is filled with fears.
Fears that come and go unwilled
Of lonesome heartaches pain,
Of days ahead, with grief alone
To share the days of rain.
Waking hours, lonesome hours,
Where art thou this day?
No one knows, no one tells
And yet you stay and stay.
Each hour like a nightmare passes
One into the next.
What good this life of deep felt
pain
When mind and soul are vexed?

Katie Mowbray
LOVE (SONNET)
It's like a dream that always can
come true
It's like a flower which will stay
in bloom
My dreams cannot if I am not
with you
And I'll stay closed until you're in
the room
It's like a child that opens up new
doors
It's like a seagull, simple and free
My childish ways ask if I'm really
yours
My mind's confused until you are
with me
It's like a breeze refreshing all the
heat
It's like a sparrow singing simple
songs

I only feel refreshed when our
eyes meet
The song I sing will last your
whole life long
It is my heart; it longs for you
each day
The song's my love for you in
every way

Loretta Ann Elkins
GLIMPSE OF HEAVEN
Somewhere over the rainbow
there's a land without pain or
grief.
Far from this old world where
there's no relief.
Hidden beyond the valley and the
waterfalls of death,
Over the mountains and the
echoes of one's breath,

Deep below the horizon, way
above the sun,
A world of great mystery for
those who do not run.

James M. Brown III

James M. Brown III
A MOMENT OF PEACE
Call to the angels a
Heavenly glow
Raise your heads high
In unity we sing

Savor this solemn moment
Today we praise
Master of the universe
Accountant of souls

Sing your song
for all to hear
a glorious peace
without fear

Edward L. Allridge
SCHUSS
Harmony of a tractless void,
Triumphantly fettered to skis,
We chiseled swirling wreaths
of iceness.

Filigree of rainbow tips,
Sparkling splendor of oblivion,
We were the unwanted ones
there to transgress.

Rimy brows and cheeks of
alabaster,
Whirling thoughts and
apparitions,
We were the mystic sorcerer
and sorceress.

Landscapes of blurred images,
Spangled between pine and oak,
We clutched desperately to the
drawing darkness.

Silhouettes on snow-clad horizons,
Pulverizing the veering thickets,
We dissolved in circles of mist
to formlessness.

Mary M. Gardner
TO BE
What I really want to be,
Is someone who is kind.
In some way help others,
A better life to find.

To give a part of me
Every single day
By helping to lift the fallen
Who comes along my way.

Never to be a hero
Just plant a worthy seed,
And may the reapers be
The one's in deepest need.

I pray for strength and courage,
That everyone might see.
The joy from serving others,
Is what I want to be.

Beverly A. Prater
OUR LOVE
[Written for James Anthony
Smith, who I love dearly and
more than anything, with all
my love.]
Our love is . . . as beautiful as a
butterflys wings,
A love that grows like a baby,
As wonderful and bright as the
sunshine that lights the day,
As warm as a smile and a gentle,
loving touch.

Our love is . . . a soft, warm kiss,
A love as good as a flowers smell,
As exciting as a growing plant,
As together like two white doves.

Our love is . . . as pure as fresh
spring water,
As caring as a deer for its fawn,
A love that has more meaning
than any dictionary,
As open as the sky.

Our love is . . . higher than any
mountain and deeper than any
oceans,
A love that is finer than a diamond,
As clean as the country air or an
open field,
As peaceful as a light feather.

Our love is . . . me and you forever!

Kimberly Wilson
A FINAL PRAYER
She sat and stared out the window
Where down below children were
at play
She uttered not a single word
Then bowed her head to pray . . .

Dear Lord be with my mom and
dad
For all they're going through
Please help them to accept the
things in life—
that can't be changed or can't be
helped—
There's nothing they can do.

Please help all the others
In the same situation as I
To have at least one happy
memory
To take with them when they die.

Please don't make them suffer
Or destroy them with pain

For they have been through too
much
To be put through that again.

Please help all the fortunate
To realize just how appreciative
they should be
No braces, bars, or wheelchairs to
bind them
As the one that now holds me.

Thank you God, for taking time
To listen to my prayer
I know you'll do your best to
answer
Because I know that you care.

As her mother held her in her arms
Before putting her to bed
She hugged her once, then closed
her eyes
"I Love You" were the final words
she said.

Frances D. Lauth
A MOTHERS LOVE
Tell them when they're very young,
remind them as they grow.
Say it every time you can,
even though they know.
Show them in the things you do,
assure them quite alot.
Say it loud when you are proud,
but louder when you're not.

Marcia K. Garr
COUNTRY LIVING
[Dedicated forever to
Boneyville, Jarvis, Pierre, Liz
and Pat.]
Country living is a lot of things
Like drinking water from the ice
cold spring
Birds flying through the air
Rabbits hopping everywhere
Fruits aplenty on the trees
Wild flowers to pick whenever
you please
Friends and neighbors you hold
so dear
To cry with you, or bring you cheer
The meetings at the fence to talk
Or joining together to take a walk
The knobs rising to touch the sky
The clouds slowly passing by
Country living is the life for me

Where even the snakes can roam
around free.

Susan Richards Lange
REPRIEVE
When I had thought
you'd never call
you called to me
When I had thought
you'd never see
you gazed at me
When I had thought
you'd never come
you came to me
When I had thought
you'd never love
you lay with me

Mark C. Domanowski
WHAT JESUS MEANS TO ME
When you tried it all
And end up with nothing,
Who do you turn too
What can you say—
For once I was lost
In the ways of the world
Searching for fame
Feeling the pain,

But then something happened
I found my way
And felt the grace
Only one could give;
He gave me a peace
That I can not explain,
He set me free
From life's daily sin,
He gave me my eyes
That truly see,
Things as they are
And as they will be,
For Jesus is king
And I just want to sing
Of his glory and honor,
For with the Savior
I will live forever.

Alice L. S. Timmins
THE LITTLE ORPHAN
Whom do I ask of,
to whom do I go
when the runner's of my sled
are hungry for snow?

A woman once sang me
a lullabye warm
and cuddled me close
in the bend of her arm.

A gentleman held me
we wrestled and ran
whatever became of the lady
and man?

Whom do I ask of,
to whom do I go
when the runners of my sled
are hungry for snow?

June L. Smith
THREE A.M.
Footsteps in the gravel,
Midnight marauders under my
    apple tree—
Do they scent my curious eye?

Fleeing into the moonlight,
White tails flash like white flags,
Surrendering the moonlight and
    the apples to me.

Bertie Murphy
LOVER'S KISS
A lover's kiss, is like the mist,
    The clinging mist of dawn.
And, like the mist, my lover's kiss,
    Warmed by the sun, is gone!

Terry LeAnn Webb-Harstad
PAINTED TRUE
*[To my husband Michael, 'Our
Girls' Melissa & Bethany, Dad
(for being you) and I can't forget
Mom for showing me how much
fun reading is!]*
You're such a marvel Mother
Nature!
I'll sit and wait by my warm fire.
Silently dawn is approaching
Softly, smoothly while most
    slumber.

The heavy dewdrops folding
    grasses
And dusky twilight slowly fading.
Animals nestled deep
    down—Quiet.
Nature gently unfolding her
    mysteries.

To me, You're best a silent New
    Day,
Your skys a touch of pink.
Easing back I lazily marvel
What you've showed me—whats
    to come!

Now the proud Sun, he is coming
Up so smoothly tossing colors—
    reds and oranges.
Majestically he slides himself
Above his secret place of slumber.

As he rises he does throw
Color from his own rainbows.
Lifting then a tiny finger-ray
He shyly blends right the shades.

The birds now waking in the
    dewlight,
Shake the dampness from their
    feather,
Begin to practice for the chorus
That they sing each day.

Sun is still higher rising
Everyday—another Art piece.
Strongly brushing brighter colors
Upon the sod and near blue waters.

Then like a bubble-color bursts
Upon the fresh damp face of Earth!
Yellow flowers, heads bent but
    rested
Gladly straighten from warm sun
    caresses.

The birds begin to sing in earnest,
A fawn bending sips his water,
Nursing foxcubs search for mother.
This is nature as it awakens!

Pink apple blossoms, wild sweet
    clover,
Sand slowly slipping through my
    fingers,
Earth Mother, I do truly love you
For all these beauties you've
    bestowed me.

Sun's painting done, he's crossed
    the sky;
With one last sprinkle, for now
    the clouds are scarlet-red.
Slow moon and silent stars are
    hung, so weary sun may rest;
To begin again tomorrow
    knowing, Good Mother Earth
    has given her best.

Antionette Cottrell-Jones
A MOTHER'S LOVE
If your mother never told you
    that
She loves you,
Well she's telling you right now
Son, she does.
If by now there's never been a need
To hold you
Then there never could have been
A mother's love.

For a mother's love was meant son
To warm you
And to keep the chill of life from
Soaking deep
And this mother's love is here
Son, not to smother
But to wrap your troubled thoughts
Into deep sleep.

If your mother has not set
A path to follow
That is righteous and is rigid
And is true
Then I could not say that I am
Truly mother
And I could not truly say
That I love you.

Angie Lester
MY MAN
Love is like a raindrop,
    So gentle and so free.

Love is so special,
    As anyone can see.
From where I stand in life,
    My feelings go so far.
Sometimes it feels you're reaching
    For the highest of all stars.
But when you find the right
    Person for you,
That's when you know true
    Love is true.

Love is like a butterfly,
    So fragile and so new.
For if I were to give away my heart,
    It would only be to you.
I tell you I love you,
    Whenever I can.
Now I will tell you this much,
    You're my one and only,
    What I call my man.

Dennis W. Rollenhagen
MOMENT
Man lives a moment in the life of
a redwood tree.

The redwood tree grows a
    moment in the light of the sun.
A sun burns but a moment in
    time.

Wandi (Wanda Vice Woldahl)
STAR IN MY EYES
*[To my husband, KEN I love
you . . .]*
You came along, when I needed a
    friend,
You sang me a song, about a love
    that would never end;
You took my hand and helped
    me to stand,
You healed my soul and I want
    you to know;
    You're a star in my eyes,
    No surprise . . .
    You're a star in my eyes,
    Do you realize?

You made me smile, when the
    world made me cry,
Then after awhile, all my sorrow
    passed me by;
You set me free, now I can
    believe,
You helped me see, what is
    really me;
    You're a star in my eyes,
    No surprise . . .
    You're a star in my eyes,
    Do you realize?

James F. Huffman
THE POET
As I sit down to write a verse,
I search into my past,

For something that I know about,
And something that will last.

But the search reveals a tender
    spot,
I'm not all lilly white,
Should I let the grevious memory
    go;
Or should I write?

But my thoughts have fired the
    embers
Of the thing that I'd forgot,
The vividness brings racking pain,
Such is the poet's lot.

So through the blur of painful
    tears,
My words fall on this scroll,
The verse you like or criticize
Is the mirror of my soul.

Sue Blythe
REFLECTIONS OF TIME
*[In loving memory of my
parents, L.C. and Lennie Baker]*
Deep in the back of my mind,
    I see another time.
In the meadow the blue birds
    Were singing in concert.
I smell a heady fragrance.
    See the apple tree
Pregnant with blossoms.
    Not a care in the world
I seem to think.
    If my eyes I could only blink.
Return me there again,
    For just an hour,
I would pick for you,
    A flower.

Florence S. Katz
MEMORY MEMORIUM
Soft shadows bring joy under the
    trees
where loved ones with pleasure
    often strayed
Memory shapes faint rustling
    leaves
into dear voices, tender and
    unafraid
Soft shadows on the walls
Happy hours passed in song
Where children ran, played games
    with balls
All was delight, no day too long
Far from the heartbreak grief had
    known
Soft shadows, God given, I am not
    alone

Jerry Zink
NEVER END LIKE THIS
All hope was gone when you
    took the train
    and as it moved slowly down
    the track,
You took all the hope and left all
    the pain
    for I knew you would not come
    back.

You could not tell how much I
    hurt
    by the smile that was on my
    face,
You really took my life that day
    when you said someone else
    took my place.

I'll read your letters once again
    but just before I send them back,
Each letter will show a tear drop
    and the letters will be tied in
    black.

We fell in love many years ago
and we vowed that it would last,
I knew that I would never leave
you
but how fast the years have
passed.

Could I have been so bad my dear
so as to drive you from my side,
Did all the love I gave to you
just made you run and hide.

If I had the power to turn back
the time
to where we sealed our love
with a kiss,
And we vowed that thru all our
hardships
our love would never end like
this.

Sara Rayon

Sara Rayon
HELL
Hell. (I have been there.)
Where darkness swallows you in
its shadowy depths, and you
pray by some miracle you'll see
the light.
But all you have are memories of
that special priviledge and
continue in the blackness as a
never ending night.

Hell.
Where the only company you
have is the memories of days
past, and each mistake you
made is relived vividly every
day.
Pain and unhappiness go hand in
hand in this place, and
together; bit by bit, they batter
and chip you away.

Hell.
Where time has no meaning.
Slow. So slow. Yet everlasting.
And with every breath you
pray . . . God? Is He in this
place?
No. He is not welcome here, but
only because you chose
through your own acts to find
the road to this space.

Hell.
Yes, I have been there .. .
. . . and I am there still!

Mauryne Taylor Brent
TODAY IS MY DAY
The past is but an echo
Of things forever stilled.
Tomorrow is a promise
That's, yet, to be fulfilled;

A path that's unfamiliar;
A hope that is unborn,
That sleeps and lies in waiting
To wake some future morn.

But, oh, today is my day!
These moments I can claim
To climb a mountain summit
And, there, to write my name,
Though lettered small, no matter,
Nor that tomorrow find
No trace of what I've written,
Nor trails I blazed, behind.

What counts is that these hours
Have meaning and portent
With giving, loving, doing,
And that they've been well-spent.
For "now" is all I'm sure of,
Tomorrow's far away.
And I must mark my journey
Each moment of today.

Dale Mark Presley
Man's Ultimate Fantasy
For every man there's one
fantasy—that seemingly
impossible dream
Which appears to elude his
constant quest, no matter the
plan or scheme.
Peaceful and quiet, or worried to
tears—it matters not what the
mood,
His mind is drawn to that secret
thought—it cannot be subdued.
This utmost quest, of his inner
mind, is the most commanding
force
Behind all felt or thought or done—
it guides his every course.
For when all else says quit and
give up, he's lured on by how it
would be
To satisfy his deepest desire—his
ultimate fantasy!

If a man's greatest wish is the
kind one woman can fulfill,
She can have all he can ever give
if that dream he will reveal.
But be warned that a man guards
very well his most secret desire,
For he fears the power a woman
can have should she ever acquire
The knowledge of that which she
can do to fully govern his life
And bring him immeasurable joy,
or perpetual grief and strife.
But that woman who truly knows
her man holds the priceless key
To the source of all her man lives
for—his ultimate fantasy!

Rare is the woman who truly
knows her man's most
treasured thought
Because long before he surrenders
it, she's already fought
The lesser truths he's trusted her
with to slowly test and invite
Her to share in that secret thing
that he craves day and night.
And so, most women cheat
themselves of this life's
greatest joys
As they deny his lesser pleas in
trade for imagined respect and
poise.
No wonder that all those other
things done just never bring
harmony
As he constantly mourns life's

greatest loss—his ultimate
fantasy!

So accept your lover just as he is
and submit to all demands
And the key to his heart will
soon be yours—he'll dance to
your commands.
He will then look past your every
flaw—you can do no wrong
As you're now the one thing
keeping him—satisfied, secure
and strong.
Don't abuse the power you now
possess, as you give him that
special delight
And he will be all he can possibly
be to please you day and night.
For the woman who allows a man
to live his ultimate fantasy
Is the woman who truly dwells in
his heart, now and eternally.

Josephine Bolechata
SEPTEMBER SNOW GEESE
Oh, hear the piercing cry of
colonies
Of Canada Snow Geese,
Startling the waves of Saint
Lawrence
Of Cap Tourmente in Quebec
province

Like icebergs stretched all along
The lonely coast, shelter found
As with binoculars, the tourists
Marvel upon their migratory habits

Cry out their song of Freedom!
A taking-off mirage, they form
A snow-laced curtain of heavenly
lilies
Such faithful geese in colonies

Fly south, the sun they follow
Adieu to beaches tomorrow,
As we humans encased in
igloo-motor-cars
Envy them, make a wish like
upon the stars.

Marian Foster Norman
**Count Your Garden By the
Flowers**
[To my sister Lucille—whose
outlook on life, and whose life
itself, inspired this poem.]
Count your garden by the flowers,
Never by the leaves that fall.
Count your days by golden hours.
Don't remember clouds at all.
Count your nights by stars-not
shadows.
Count your life by smiles-not tears.
And with joy on every birthday
Count your age by friends-not
years.

Harry J. Vassilion
THE APPLE TREE
Branch branch
  Flowering branch
Brilliant green
  Shade tree
Branch dance
  Sway a breeze
Say say
  With colors
Fragrant and gay
  Green apples
Tangy and sweet
  A love affair
With flavor showers
  Sprinkle you dew
Upon my lips

Drop by drop
A tasty sip
  Will awaken a bloom
For you and me

Irene B. Lindhout
OUR MEMORIES
To someone thats very special
to someone that really cared
I know I'll always be partial
to the little things we shared

Like all of our little secrets
our fantasy's and our dreams
emotions and the disappointments
of the way we wish life could be

Being able to share together,
OUR SPECIAL MOMENTS OF
LOVE
our memories of each other
I'll never forget about

Remembering these precious
things
with everything that we shared
Oh what these memories will bring
I want you to know that I will
always care.

So I'm saying "good luck" to you
in my own special way
never saying "goodbye" because
MEMORIES NEVER FADE AWAY

Richard T. Coyle
IN MY MIND (RUINS)
She was there, among my ruins;
Of my mind, just sitting there.

Just passing time among my ruins;
A thought passes by, it isn't fair.

Sparrow—among my ruins;
Flying high through the air.

Thinking of all my ruins;
The times we had and all the
doin's.

There was fun among my ruins;
Spinning around from time to time.

There she was among my ruins;
Just sitting there, in my mind.

In my mind,
In My mind,
In My Mind,
IN MY MIND.

Nadine Dugan
I NEED YOU LORD
Lord walk with me today.
Guide my words in everything
that I say.
For the tongue can be used for
good or bad
And I don't really want to make
anyone sad.

Lord be with me in trouble and in
strife
For some rain must fall in
everyone's life.
And if a sin is worrying me that I
have sown
I need your forgiveness, and to
know that I am not alone.

Lord walk with me today.
I need your guidance when I pray.
For you know best what are my
needs
And I will follow wherever you
lead.

Lord be with me in everything I do
And I need you most when I am
blue.

They say love is what makes the
world go around
And with your love we are not
lost but have been found.
But those who are lost and are
also blue
Must be especially miserable
without you.

Minnie Savage
EACH HAPPY DAY
[To Frank]
I loved you since the beginning
Not for what you did for me;
One gets used to not having things
And being alone with ones own
thoughts
One strains closer to God at
times like this.

I loved you for caring
For being happy with me
I loved sharing incidents in our
remotely variance lives.
Life blessed with experience,
That fosters understanding and
compassion.
Without you now
Life could be intolerable.

Virginia L. Bock
THE COWBARN
Sitting on a three-legged milk stool
My head against a cows flank
While white foamy milk I
encouraged
To flow from the four-spouted
tank.

A squirt at my sister as she
walked by
Or one at a straying cat
Oh it was so much fun
To hear that milk go SPLATT!

The cows in their gentle manner
Let me sing and have fun without
fail
Unless I got careless and pinched
them
Ending up with a foot in my pail!

These are fun times to remember
And many a problem was solved
As I sat on my three-legged milk
stool
And let my mind slowly revolve.

Judith E. Phillipi
A FAMILY
*[In Loving Memory of Uncle
Gerald A Man of Love and
Kindness]*
We spend a lifetime
Looking for a friend,
Hurting those we love,
Thinking of ourselves,
And telling lies.
Afraid to face—what is true . . .
Our family is our best friend.

They can hurt us,
Make us angry—
And make us cry.
But when times are rough—
Our family will be the ones
Who really care.

Then one lonely night,
A loved one is gone.
The memories remain
And we can not change the past.
We can give to those that live,
A love and friendship,
That only a family knows.

Lillian (Billie) Dinkel
MY ENCHANTED FOREST
*[To those who appreciate,
admire and recognize GOD'S
handiwork.]*
Soft rain, caressing my hair and
face.
The gentle ballet of the leaves
To a whisper song by the wind.
Trillium and Fern entwined,
embracing.
My Grumpy Owl, ruffle feathered,
Argus eyed.
Quiet snow falling on quiet snow.

Paula Jackson Mendoza
HERO'S
*[Dedicated to my mother J.
Auline Adams Who instilled in
me A great love of poetry, Art,
Music, and all beautiful things
Life has to offer.]*
Just before the world was plunged
into the dark night of the soul,
and few if any really knew Hitler's
horrible goal.
A train load full of children was
smuggled to the Dane's
the word came down there
wouldn't be any other trains.
Though they were not Jews
themselves they gave them
each a home.
Vowed they'ed feed and clothe them
and treat them as their own.
Soon Denmark was occupied the
Nazi's were everywhere,
searching for the children they
knew that they were there.
Now came the proclamation each
Jew must wear a star,
so naturally the Germans would
know who and where they are.

the King spoke up and said not so
since all Dane's are the same,
the first star shall be worn by me,
and at first dawn they came
Men, Women, Children as far as
you could see.
wearing stars of David for all the
world to see,
The Germans were enraged of
course, and swore they'd search
the town.
And if all else fails they cursed
we'll burn the damn place
down. But just before the
search was due and it all
started coming down,
they smuggled the children to
Sweden so they would not be
found.

We tend to glorify the man who
goes out to do battle
and think of those he left behind
as just a bunch of cattle.
but just think how heroic to face
the conquering horde,
with no more than a sense of right,
and faith of course in the Lord.

Jeanne Hunt Coteral
My Friend the Country Boy
*[Dedicated to Charlie Boyd our
dear friend who was always
there when we needed him.
May he walk in peace, share
his talents for others to enjoy,
keep smiling and God bless
him always.]*
My friend the country boy left
the hills,
To please everyone, but against
his will,
For so many roots he left behind,
That they were always popping
up in his mind,
Like the old farm where an old
locust tree once stood,
And a story it would tell if only it
could,
He began to write poetry and
songs,
That would always tell him
where he belonged,
So many beautiful phrases and
thoughts were captured,
And to hear them, were the pure
heaven of rapture,
He wrote of all the joys and
sometimes the sad ones,
From childhood days right up to
the last setting sun,
And to hear him sing, that was a
gift he was given,
And the tears would come when
you could share his heaven,
For you knew his heart would
always be,
Down here in these hills and
amongst the trees,
Where God's all around with his
creations and all,
From whispering trees and blowing
breezes just like the fall,
But it's like this all the time, all
year round,
You'll only know it, if you come
down,
And as he travels back to the city,
May he remember our prayers
and this little ditty,
For we know he's a country boy
at heart,
Where someday perhaps he'll
never have to part,
But live his life in contentment
in these hills,
Where he will enjoy his last will,
And God bless him along the way,
Until the time in which he may
stay.

Penny Lane Shaw
AFTER THE ROSES DIE
What happens after the roses die
and the grass turns brown.
After the snow melts
and the sun goes down?
What happens when life gets dull
and the T.V. is shot,
and we all get old
and forget alot?

We all sit back and look at what
we've been,
and thank God for teaching us
that life never ends.
What happens when the show
is over,
and the applause is gone,
the stars pack their bags,
and head for home?
What happens when twenty
are dead.
and the killer is caught,
the news dies down
and the trial is fought?
We learn to live life in the paper
until the next crime is born.
Then we turn on the tube
and watch the family mourn.
What happens when the war is
over
and the damage is done
to the young man's mind
who was just in it for fun?
What happens when you run
out of words
and there's nothing left to say,
you put down your pencil,
and you forget your way?
You accept your failure
and you smile while you cry
say "better luck next time
well, hell at least I did try."

Natalie Scott
WE THE HANDICAPPED
If only people knew,
What the handicapped go through.
We realize that you try
You understand, and cry.
But this we do not need
As God has given us our speed.
We may not see,
We may not hear,
We may not talk
Or may not walk
But no matter what,
We strive to do our best,
And our minds and hearts
Are with God and Family.

Tammy Sue Napier
DREAMING OF YOU
*["To Vince—a very special
friend"]*
I think of you often
and you don't even know it.
I like you so much
but I'm afraid to show it.

I sit here in silence
dreaming of you,
Dreaming of things
that may someday come true.

I'm not sure of much
but this one thing I know
If I ever got you
I'd never let you go.

Susan Adler Herreid
BEAUTIFUL PERSON
One cannot resort to obliteration
Recalling a face so prepossessing.
And filled with sincere admiration,
My feelings are worth expressing.

Pervading my thoughts is a
gratitude
That simply defies interpretation.
It is of such a great latitude,
My recourse is an affirmation.

In order to appease my soul so
persuasive,

I'll not erase a splendid
recollection.
Although my heart remains
evasive,
My mind is inflated with
retrospection.

Without resignation I must admit
The beautiful person I see in you.
A natural response is to submit,
Because in life you encounter so
few.

ElAyne Marie Zelmer
MY FIRST FRIEND
A long time ago when I was
hatched,
I fell out of my nest into a
strawberry patch.
I couldn't yet fly to get back to
my nest.
I didn't know what to do but I
didn't dare rest!
So I sat by a berry to figure out
what to do,
And along came a giraffe. And
then I just knew
that with her long neck she could
left me up high!
(To maybe even reach the sun in
the sky!)
As she came closer to me I yelled
up a "Hello."
Then she smiled a sweet smile to
me down below.
We introduced ourselves, one to
the other.
She vowed to be my friend and I
her brother.
Then with her long neck she put
me up in my nest.
I found my first friend. And she
was the BEST!

Nellie Davis Martin
A BOY'S POCKETS
What's in a boys pockets, besides
a nail or two
a piece of string, some bubble
gum, a "yo yo" top, a screw
An empty candy wrapper, the
wheel off of a toy
a cherished though odd
assortment, dear to a little boy
A piece of jig saw puzzle, the one
that wouldn't fit
a rubber band, a couple rocks, one
ought to be a hit
Dad's smallest pair of pliers and a
small screwdriver too, he calls
them his working tools, a bolt
and washer too.
Who could name the contents or
who could tell the whole, for
what's in a boys pockets,
besides his heart and soul.

Suzzie Nalicat
To My Brother and Sisters
["Here, I give to you, my
brother and sisters . . . with
love" Alex, Alma and Sandra.]
Mother had told me. How father
was so poor.
He didn't have much clothing to
keep him warm.
And, mother didn't have much to eat.
Your grandparents worked hard
to put your parents through
school. Our parents had a dream.
They wanted more.

They worked real hard for us. So

that they can give us what they
didn't have. Before us.
And, they try hard not to spoil us.
And, sometimes we hurt mom
and dad.

Through their dreams, I have
watched everything, all
building up.
I find us a lot like mom and dad.
Proud, rich or poor.
From them, we can still love. We
get angry with each other. But,
we can still dream. And, just
imagine everything all building
up.
And, we work hard.
I want more. I want to see all.
Proud. Rich or Poor.
I want more!

Brent H. Phelps
THE VIRGIN MIND
[To my parents for all their
Love, support, and
encouragement. And to Deanne
for her Love and for plain and
simply "understanding"]
At birth you are handed a sealed
container
It is called the skull
It is a maze of tunnels pure and
innocent
Within the first few seconds of
Life the seal is broken
The maze will not be sanitary for
long
Polluted by the chemicals of
Society
You no longer have what can be
referred to as:

The Virgin Mind

John Malito
TIME
Then and now,
yet to come,
all at once,
the ship without prow.
Days and weeks,
months and years,
are only as marks,
on a meter stick.
Forward or backward,
how can you tell?
Life is an instant,
only a moment have we.

Spring Dawn Reader
SOJOURN
[To my daugher Amber Pearl
whose sojourn began February
2, 1983]
We are but autumn leaves riding
on the breeze
Scattered across the land in
disarray
Resting where the wind has lain
us
Until we are again tossed into the
air
And carried on to further
destinies
But taking with us
The memories of those left
behind

Violet Marguerita Clarke
Morning On the Sahara
Fedjeur at last and the blood red
dawn
Peering onto the threshhold of
another world,

The sun plumets down over the
edge of the earth, like molten
lead
It's afterglow sweeping the Desert
breathlessly,
Where the Guelta of Tassili's
tiered pools
Glows in blue depths of saphire,
And Yamina Moon of the soul,
bathes elusively
Her black face haughty and
beautiful as fallen angels,
Amidst wild blooming Mimosa
and cliffs of ruddy gold.

Raymond F. Polk
SILENT NIGHT
Silent sentinel of the night
The evening sky is your ocean.
Sail my dreams to your harbor
light
Lead them . . . with twinkling
motion.

I ride a starry voyage on a ship of
dreams
I carry no anchor and my mast is
free.
Guide my way to your lighthouse
beam
What ports hide in your silent
sea?

Men lived and died under your
haze
Still . . . you remained proud and
alone.
They've laughed and cried under
your gaze
Rock of flame . . . unchanging
stone!

I could give doubts but I haven't
any
From each love another star will
grow.
New flames are born but why so
many?
Whose lives make the heavens
glow?

Naked cauldron of heat and flame
Who holds you in that space?
Vigilant star . . . Do you know
my name?
What is my worth in your distant
place?

Canvas of night you hold ancient
wealth
There's no purer art or truer
rhyme.
A place of eternity on a mystery
shelf
Reflections . . . from the

face of time!

Silent light . . . give me your
lead
Wash men's fears in your milky
streams.
Whose courage is named to a
skyward deed?
What valor rides in starry dreams?

Vivian Williams
THE MIDNIGHT FLIGHT
[With love I dedicate this poem
to my husband Wes and my
sons Shane and Todd Williams]
High above the darkened sky
while labors cease and the
earth stands still
One captures silhouettes of
graceful wings about to embark
on the midnight flight

Free to journey into starlit skies
casting glimmering shadows to
watchful eyes
So graceful how elegant these
patterns of flight suspended in
space this quiet night

The moon now charts the perfect
course while powerful
glistening wings gather and
dance
To the Musical chords of the
windfilled sky

Captivated by the splendor of
this wondrous sight while time
stands still endless eternal
This silent night, I gaze in awe at
the hand of nature the creative
beauty of this portrait
She paints freedom her symbol of
peace

The moon now descends for
dawn is breaking the journey
soon ending for wings in flight,
For I have witnessed the serinity
of freedom if only through my
patterns of thought

If all would look from earth to
sky every eye could behold this
marvelous sight, tears of
Remorse are quietly shed as man
looks from earth to sky
overhead

Though our earth be marred by
touch of man let us restore the
simplicity of nature's plan
For high above lies the painted
sky as evening hours linger by,
now somewhere in the calm
Of night one's soul soars freely
like wings in flight

Michael McLain
A LOOK IN HIS EYES
He smiles,
Looks at you
And you know everything is fine.
A look in his eyes;
I see a friend of the world
And a friend of mine.
The sounds and thoughts of my
problems
Fade away
At the sound of his voice.

He chooses well his friends
He keeps them few,
Yet keeps them close.

A look in his eyes;
I am lost in their whirl

And saved
By their tide.
A saving current—
In a flood of desperation—
I find inside the sea of his eyes.

In him I find
A friend
Unparalleled throughout reality.

William Beker
SMOKE
Floating Silvery Gray,
   Now Pegasus,
Kicking wildly, with bare hoofs,
   Now gone,

Anne Furry
Running Wild, Running Free
         running wild
         running free
in amongst the maple trees.
   the roots were planted
   strong and spindley;
   fifteen years deep.
   ripping my roots
   out of the ground;
   you tried to transplant me
   where I didn't belong.
   the roots won't take,
   they never will
         because
         you see,
            they're still
   running wild
   running free
in amongst the maple trees.

Willie G. Gage
WHAT IS CHRISTMAS?
When I think of loving kindness
and tenderness combined.
I think of the lowly Jesus born at
Christmas time.
Who's love, he shared for many
and yes there was a cost.
He had to suffer danger then be
nailed to a cross.
So Christmas has a meaning
not what we buy or sell
But because of the cross
and a great cost, this keeps us out
   of hell
So if you're without presents or
nothing else to give
be thankful for what it took,
just so we could live
Christmas is for sharing the
   things that forever hold true
Like love, peace and joy combined,
these gifts were meant for you.

Mellissa A. Gregg (Woody)
THE THINGS YOU DO
For the friend who means the
   most to me
For the one who taught me what
   to be
You gave me strength to stand up
   and fight
You helped me to sleep easier at
   night
You gave me a chance to express
   myself
You put my troubles away on a
   shelf
You set me high upon a pedestal

You put a little light in the
   drudgery of school
Your couraged my fears
And you dried my tears
You loaned me a shoulder

And gave me advice from
   someone older
You're a great influence on what I
   want to be
Thank you for what you are
Your memories will carry me
   far . . .

Lorene Dunaway Osborn

Lorene Dunaway Osborn
MY WONDERFUL GOD
Be with me Oh Lord, I pray—
And guide my feet from day to
   day—
Fill me with the Spirit Lord—
Of Thy blessed Holy Word.
Be with me in every way—
When I sing and when I pray—
And a blessing let me be—
So some sinner may be set free—
From sins strife and misery—
Fill me with the Spirit Lord—
Of Thy blessed Holy Word—
Yes fill me when Thy name I
   praise—
And walk with me all of my
   days—
Let me never be ashamed—
To praise Thy great and Holy
   name—
Help me Lord not to complain—
But to trust in Thee in time of
   pain—
Father unselfish let me be—
For others let me care—
As Thou hast cared for me—
Keep Thy Spirit in my heart and
   make my
Face to shine—so that the world
   may know that I am Thine—
If people in this world would only
   turn to Thee—
There's no way of describing how
   happy they would be.

Nellie C. Robinson
NO LAST GOODBYE
He was our Legendary Hero, with
   endless stories to tell,
Of a war that waged in Europe,
   and a Nazi World that fell.
I could not know that as we
   talked, and time was flying
   high;
That there would be yet time to
   joke . . . But not to say
   "Goodbye".

We talked about our childhood;
   We remembered bygone years...
We talked about our
   parents...long dead...
And we blinked back happy tears.

He told of building bridges
O'er which Gen'l Patton rode
Now the Path, named for that
   'Great Man'
Winds its way to his last abode.

As suddenly as a flash of light,
   God called his name to go . . .
He left us stunned with
   disbelief . . . his death had
   shocked us so.

He served in the 1313 Engineers;
   he survived a heartless fight,
For he gave of himself back in
   World War II, and he gave with
   all his might
The Cason bore his body to his
   final resting place . . .
And we followed close behind
   him, scarcely at a walking pace.

The Sargent Major had gone
   home . . . this whole scene
   like none other,
For this dear departed
   Soldier . . . was the body of
   'MY BROTHER'.

Louraine Armack Hollman
CHRISTMAS EVE
[*To George; who inspired me to
write this little poem. George's
favorite time of year was
Christmas Eve.*]
Angels perched on tree tops,
   garlands on the stair
Joyful love and happiness
   surround us everywhere.

Somewhere in the distance
   carolers happily sing
Air is crisp and cold, church bells
   softly ring.

Soon the snow stops falling,
   moonbeams shining down
Make diamonds of the snowfall
   covering the ground . . .

Jo Harger
CHRISTMAS SONG
Let us sing a song of Christmas—
Sweet and haunting, hearts aglow
Oh, so lovely, "Ave Maria,"
Sing it softly, sing it low.

Let us sing a song of Christmas—
Children smiling, candles glow,
Shadows flickering by the
   fireside,
Carols ringing in the snow.

Let us sing a song of Christmas—
Voices lusty, loud and bold
Sleigh bells jingling, frosty,
   tingling,
Bring the tree, the story's told.

Sabrina Golden Younger
DAD
"Hey, Mac, gotta light?"
He called to a shadowy figure in
   the night.
The stranger came and struck a
   match.
Mesmerized, I watched its glow
Light up Dad's chiseled Irish face,
Expose the silent laughter which
   graced his crystal clear, blue
   eyes.
An angel from Heaven in
   disguise, I surmized as he
   nodded, tipped his hat
To bid the other thanks, and
   goodbye.

Never a need was there to talk,
Or break the sacred silence of our
   nightly walks
Except to ask for a light
   sometimes,
Or respond in kind to a beggar
   wanting a nickel or dime.

How I loved that quiet man!
How safe I felt, strolling with him
Through the city streets, hand in
   hand!
Tipping his hat to passersby was
   his way of saying hi!

Eyes always smiling, adding to
   his charm.
Knowing in his presence no harm
   would ever come
That he could not swiftly, easily
   render undone!

Mary K. Blad
CITY OF WAR
The bombs are going off
There's no time to stop them
   now.
It sounds as if they're right in my
   head.
Don't tell me your excuse—
. . . did you say my family's all
   dead?

How can it be—
Jesus, this is some sight to see.
They were just out for some fun,
but is there any difference
   between the trigger-man
and the one who hands him the
   gun?

And what would you choose to
   hold
When your last vision of life is
   taken away
Or will you choose to just sit
   back
and lie to your children
That everything's gonna be okay?

David G. Baker
A Little House Upon the Hill
I bought a little house upon the
   hill
It took all of the money that I
   had, but it was worth it still.
The house was on a hill covered
   with beautiful trees and grass
And I sure am glad that I didn't
   let this deal pass.

The house was painted white
   with green trim on it you see
And below the house at the
   bottom of the hill, was a very
   beautiful stream.
And here's where I will stay for
   the rest of my life, you see
Here in this little house upon a
   hill over-looking my beautiful
   stream.

Graciela B. Chavez
SCENE OF BEAUTY
[*To the special person whom I
will love now and forever*]
The fragrance of roses sweetly
   filled the air,
and the singing of the birds the
   angels came to share.

The trees with all their grandeur,
   their branches swayed with
   ease,

While the leaves like sparkling
   emeralds kept falling with the
   breeze.

The grass spread its velvet carpet
   to hide the bareness of the
   ground,
And the mist of the falling
   dewdrops slowly fell without a
   sound.
The flowers smiled fondly as
   each butterfly passed by,
their petals with sublime beauty
   looked lovingly at the sky.

The sun in all its splendor
   caressed each creature with its
   rays,
Its warmth was a benediction and
   a smile came to its face.

This is a scene of beauty in
   which we all can take a part,
But, to enter this lovely garden,
   You must bring love within your
   heart.

Scarlett Anne Lockridge
WHAT PLACE BUT HERE
If my mind had a safe place to
   ramble,
   then where would it be?

To my childhood years
   where life was too short,
or to the green land of Ireland
   that tenderly calls me home.
It could escape in a song
   where only dreams live,
or on a cloud,
   far to the touch.
Inside of a gothic novel
   and be one of the characters,
or in a book of poetry
   to be words of love.
Maybe to fly on the wings of a
   hawk
   who shares my freedom,
to dance with the moon's
   reflection
   as it looks down on the ocean.

It might sail in the mountains
   and even share its strength,
or drift on a quiet stream
   like brand new.
Maybe ride the wind
   and settle deep in the valley,
to soar to greater highs
   with the cry of an eagle.
It could be part of a haunting
   melody
   that sings secretly through the
   night,

a summer rain
   that gently touches the land.

But with these thoughts far away
   I feel together we are whole,
for what place are we safe,
   what place but here!

Delvin Victor Boone
THE EMPTY HOUSE
(Christmas Eve)
In this house
that rang with laughter
no voices sound
tis silent still
no songs rebound
from floor to rafter
to fall on ears
beyond the sill
the echoes stilled
by time unbroken
no unhurried steps
resound the halls
the moonlight gleams
in weakly token
to light the drab
now barren walls

Bill Quentin Hankee
THE HATER
man the hater, hater of people, of
   things,
                   of places;
   easy and natural,
killing hate, hurting hate,
                   fruits of contempt
and the sweet one, most joyous of
   all,
   vengeance—the maddened
   equalizer;
                   violence of life
                   storm of existence
man the hater, hater of people of
   things,
                   of places;
   hate of otherness, the human
   way;
                   signpost to perdition
                   road to ultimate hate
   there the end can come,
   one final lunge
      to hate of self.

Rosina Burkart Raymond
Little Frames Of Memory
[*To loved ones of my childhood
in rural Wisconsin whose
memory of another time and
place evoked this poem;
parents Matt and Lizzie,
brothers Conrad, Wendel, Ben,
Clarence, several aunts, uncles,
cousins.*]
Roll backward little frames
On your beaded screen of memory
And take me home again,
Home, at Weinachten time.

Roll slowly, don't hurry,
For I want to touch my feet again
On the hard-crusted crunchy
   snow,
When space-spent rays of late
   afternoon sun
Find their slanting way through
   the windows
Of the old farm house.

Oh I want to sense the smell
   again,
As the whole house must sense
   the smell again
Of the near-earthiness of

molasses cakes,
Star, bell and Santa shaped,
Sugary frosted pink, white, and
   red candy eyed!

Go slowly, slowly little frames,
That I may savor again
The spiciness of fresh-cut balsam,
Feel the green of Christmas
   between my fingers.

Oh I want to reach high,
And hang blood-red candy
   cherries
Hear the very top of the tree,
High, nearly touching the angel.

To hear again the ring
Of cutter bells outside the door,
Close the damper on the round
   bellied stove,
Turn down the wick on the
   kerosene lamp
Letting only a faint light fall on
   the angel.

And go out into the midnight
Of all our longings,
And smell again incense and
   candles
Of ritualistic worship . . .

Oh roll slowly, little frames,
Roll slowly.

Marc Anthony Walker
WHAT DOES IT ALL MEAN
If my life has a reason
Then my heart is content
To find what I'm after
And to know where it went.
   tell me . . .
Where do I go
If there's no star to guide me
And who do I ask
If there's no one beside me?
   and . . .
When I've found what I'm after
Then I will know
Which way is forward
And what direction to go.
   BUT . . .
While in search for myself
In lifes' wonderful dreams
And after my destiny is won
THEN WHAT DOES IT ALL
   MEAN?
   now . . .
Where do I go
And what more must I find
When my fate is eternal
But there isn't much time?
   well . . .
What does life all mean
If I'm willing to try,
And why am I dying to live
When I'm just living to die?

Rachel A. Cassel
DEATH
in dawn's cold light
dazed, she stares at desolate rooms
emptied of life.
a broken chair remains,
a monopoly game—five pieces
   missing,
boxes waiting to be loaded.
faded jeans, splotched with paint,
a man's plaid flannel shirt
which he didn't need,
a bandana pulling back her hair.
in front of weary eyes pass
   memories,
times that would last a lifetime.

a knock at the door startles her.
impartial faces call her from her
   thoughts.
lumbering in, the darker one
breaks the silence.
"where's the rest of the boxes,
   ma'am?"
the shock of change still numbs
   her.
the voices finally link with the
   faces.
she silently points the way
as they, disillusioned long before,
carry away the remains.

Gevene Dobson
SOJOURNER IS LOVE
SoJourner, your inspiration is so
   much
inspired by love and peace.
That we can't see the times of
   joy; we
hold within the new earth of life.
Which creates our well being; as
   well
as those we love; as true
   understanding.

That behold. he that keepeth
   thee; shall
always have everlasting life, love,
   peace,
and happiness forever.

Mary E. Lowe
My Daddy At Christmas
Twas the night before Christmas
Our house was all lit.
Dad sat by the window
A wondering a bit.

He didn't say much
But kept watching the sky
As if he had hoped
To see Santa go by.

He sat there a gazing
A strange look in his eye
And somehow to me
He seemed almost shy.

I think it so strange
Though he has many fears
How Christmas helps Daddy
Lose all of those years.

Brian Douglas Scales
MAN'S FEAST
I sat at the table, my plate
   was bare.
All but for deep in it, was
a mysterious glare.
A vision I saw, no meal in
sight.
But, still I grabbed for my
fork and my knife.
I thrusted tines deep
stabbed vision as meat.
The savour of vision, I started
to eat.
Savage like cuts, no dullness
of knife.
So hungrily I mutilated,
The vision of my life.

Dorothy A. Cox
GRANDMA'S A CLOWN
The end of October—Halloween
is now here.
Will I dress real funny or cause
   lots of fear?
There's witches and goblins and
   monsters galore,
maybe ET, a clown, or a ghost at
   the door.

Today's Greatest Poems

My outfit will be baggy, full of
ruffles and color.
Tied with some string, there's
rainbow colored balloons.
With a jingle a jangle, bells tinkle
so merry.
Odd and comical: just a simple
buffoon.

No one will guess,
with circus jokes—tricks and
zany.
That behind all this dress,
is just a grey haired ole' granny.

A smile for a mouth, a smirk and
a grin.
Big funny ears for a listenin'.
Head almost bald with some
springs of blue hair.
Eyes full of sparkle and glistenin'.

Arms opened wide, for each girl
and boy.
A big nose so shiny and round.
Halloween's a great time for fun
and joy,
when Grandma becomes a clown.

Nancy Haselton
JERRY
Dr. Jekyll, Mr. Hyde
will you ever meet?
the one and the two
of you
slips in and out
of liquid elixirs,
exuding reality
burning eyes and throat,
compelled to conquer fears
of worthiness
at the expense of
yourself, and
others waiting
fearfully,
never knowing when or where
the monster will appear,
amnesia stricken lamb by day,
you reach for me
empty of feelings I once
had for you,
and
I daily wage a mental
tug or war,
longing to be free to share a
giving love,
and yet, I hesitate.

Thelma Irene Dexter
TEDDY BEAR
To run my fingers through your
hair
To watch you with adoring stare
To feel your touch, my body bare
I long for all of that we share.

The soft black mixed with coarse
gray strands
Soft velvet—white—how tall now
stands
And strokes of love together
bands
My love—I give with gifted hands.

Gladys Evelyn Pennington
THE YARD SALE
While driving down the highway
the other day,
I noticed a sign on the neighbors
front gate
It read, "We are having a big yard
sale."

I stopped and read the sign out
loud

and then I thought the sign must
be a mistake,
How can they sell their yard,
without selling their real estate?

I was curious to find out what
was going on
so I pulled in the driveway and I
never saw such go'in ons,
They were selling everything
good or bad,
and I even bought a few things
they had.

Now days they have these yard
sales everywhere
they sell everything, right down
to their furs.

Some days they make good money
and some days they don't make a
dime,
but yard sales are lots of fun and
you often see old friends,
you haven't seen for a long long
time.

Now I've learned it's not the most
money you make everytime,
sometimes it's the things you like
to do best, and that's fine.
Maybe it's teaching and
sometimes it's preaching
and maybe you're plain old
farmer Brown
Yes, some make doctors and
some like to sing,
and some folks just like to do
their thing.

So the yard sale business is just a
thing
It's not the money that it brings,
They're lots of fun and lots of
laughter
now why don't you try my
neighbors plan?
Be sure you have everything on
hand.
You'll be surprised, just like me,
you'll sell things, you won't
believe.

So come on folks, get out those
old pots and pans
and anything else you might have
on hand,
You won't believe the things you
can sell
at this thing, we call the Yard
Sale.

Kenneth James Kruszka
THE LADY
The lady whose eyes do smile
has teardrops sweet as rain
Will she ever come back to me
Don't ever leave again

I met her on a lonely night
in a poet written scene
She was a picture of beauty
painted in my dream

Darkness was all I saw
until I saw her eyes
I was trapped by her smile
taken by surprise

Her hair flows like ocean waves
as it melts around my face
Our lips met like a whisper
that told us to embrace

The lady I fell in love with
was created in despair
for again this morning I woke up

to find she wasn't there

So now my love will end
If so forever
I know I will never
fall in love again . . .

Marjorie Fletcher
WITH BRYAN
I'll take my son fishing
this morning
While all is soft and still.
We'll quietly walk through
early mists
Content in the peace we feel.

He'll cast his line as
far as he can
Then look to me for praise.
I'll smile at him and
wonder if
The mists show in my gaze.

He's very pleased to
have me along
I'm often all he sees.
But I don't fish like
a man would fish
Sometimes that's what he needs.

He's had good friends
to help him do
The things a boy enjoys.
A dad or two, but
not a man
To hold him when he cries.

So I'll take my son
fishing today,
And hope that later still
The mists will clear and
he will know
The joy he brings my soul.

Rachel Elaine Hudley
THE FOREST
touching everywhere
he rapes the universe
in search for the future
waste pulsates in her womb
overgrowth appears
but his saws were too deep
scars from silver teeth
remain in her delicate flesh
in a frenzy to fulfill his lust
he does not realize
what power he leaves behind
with the horrid things he created
soon it will be too late
his greed flourishes
man the omnipotent
no, he lost
lost the strength
only those who are inhabitants
could ever comprehend
striped of virginity
she is left alone to rebuild
what exists only in the past

Carmen Patterson
SWEET MAMA SWEET
Ten years have passed
Since the smile
That graced
Our tender lives

Seasons change
As did the faces
Without the voice
To wake them up
To wake them up

A brown image
Forever lingers
With time

Is missed the caress
And kind touch
Once shared
By 13 dear ones, and daddy

While she rest
While she rest . . .

Charles Wall

Charles Wall
**Where Are the Original
Men?**
*[Dedicated to the initial
Offensive Forces, 35th Army
Infantry Regiment, 25th
Division. The "Original Men".
(Korea 1950)]*
Yes, we're still called and known
as Company B,
of the 35th U.S. Army Infantry.
Yet replacements we are all and
we're only filling in.
Where are the Original Men?

'Tho a long hard fight, still our
Outfit made its goal.
But by day and night it just took
a heavy toll.
And our Soldiers who began
didn't make it to the end.
Where are the Original Men?

Where did they fall while in an
attack?
And of them all, who didn't come
back?
What was the fate for the rest of
them?
Where are the Original Men?

We are the ones who are
welcomed back today.
Yet we just took over, somewhere
along the way.
An empty feeling hurts me, as I
wonder now & then:
Where are the Original Men?
Where are the Original Men?

Chris D. Bennington
UNRETURNED WHISPERS
The memories nestled in
the weather beaten boughs,
of loves that never lasted—
All the time twisted together,
fill my past with pain—
I never seem to find the one,
that can kiss away the cause—
that could make me want to
settle down,
and not insanely slip away—
Another morning begins to bud,
shades close out the sweating sun-
He whispers softly words of love,
but loneliness lingers in my lungs.

405

Robert Damon Felberbaum
TWO IN LOVE
Again
a dark blanket has covered the
earth
and in what seems like moments
later
the dawn of another day will
arrive and set my world alight.

But now there is time to sit and
think of a lady
so far from my touch but so close
to my heart.

My sweetheart is always there
always running through, acting
out the memories we share
as I see them in daydreams
everywhere.

Look over there, laying with me
on a cold night.
Outside, a thick carpet of snow
collects
Inside, she's in my arms kissing
my neck
telling me in her fragile voice
how much she loves me
there we slept through the night,
always close, ever so tightly.

And behold, over there in that
fine restaurant we were
staring into each other's eyes
and together we made plain food
a king's feast
and the water we made into
vintage wine
and all those around us were
aware
that two in love sat over there.

It is now, in the quiet of the night
that I feel love's heat burning my
. heart so
and in its raging flames I feel its
glow.

Tonight, I will fall asleep,
resigning to a world of dreams
and may these dreams string
together, closing the gap that
I'm not near you
may these dreams bring me closer
to the days that we are together
and if nature has it in her mind
that two creatures, in a sea of
creatures, should come together
then I will have been blessed by
her kindness
and my world will never be
shadowed with darkness
again.

Anthony G. Horvath
THE SILENCE CHEWS
My mind is racing, I'm wide
awake.
I slept all day, trying to get my
head straight.
Now I'm wondering what to say,
I love her too much, to just walk
away.
Tension has been high, so have I.
Money is tight, not a steady job
in sight.
Pressure from peers, for years and
years,
To tie the knot, "go for it" why
not?

Well I'm still very confused,
Scratching my head, trying to
choose.

Is it time again to move on?
But she means the world to me,
I can't clear my mind, I can't even
see!
She's at a friends, I'm here making
amends.
I want to hold her, look into her
eyes,
I need to love her, I'm not sure
why!

My mind still races; the silence
chews
Will she come home soon and
talk,
Or will it continue, and force me
to turn and walk.
I don't know what to do: the
silence chews.

Margaret Elizabeth Johnston Teal
FRIENDSHIP
*[I wish to dedicate this poem to
a dear friend, Ted Rathbone II,
who encouraged me to
continue with my desire to
write. The lines below came to
me as I pondered on the reality
of true friendship.]*
Moments shared, go on forever,
Moments shared, twixt friend and
friend,
Like ripples on a flowing stream,
Into all of life, they blend.

A word, unspoken, a mutual
feeling,
An awareness of another's release,
A time of silence, when thought
Intermingling with thought,
brings peace.

These are things, that time,
Our friend, and enemy, cannot
erase,
They come, like welcome guests,
To cheer, in many a lonely place.

Kristine M. Dawley
THE LEAF
The barren tree of winter
Holds a promise so profound
In future blades of elegance
So much they do astound

Then comes the twinkling of
spring
The tree once again abounds
With such a bowing grace
That one can not expound

The summer brings the sun
The blade to surround
With such a soothing charm
That brilliance does redound

Then the golden leaf of autumn
Flutters to the ground
In search of beauty, paradise
Where only mush is found

But even in its dying
It holds a promise to us all
That when the barren winter
ends
The leaf will once again enthrall

Gloria I. Paz
PEACE'S MESSENGER
Oh, holy night!
Stars are shining,
A child was born
There in Bethlehem.
Oh, holy night!
A Saviour's born,
Bringing a message
Of Peace and Love.

Oh, wonderful night!
May our hearts,
Rejoice today
And forevermore . . .
Because this child,
So sweet, so sweet!
Came from above,
To bring us the Peace.

Lillian M. Flores
TOMORROW'S ANSWER
Lost in a world, a failing self.
Closing in a cupboard, sitting on
a shelf
With constant thoughts of things
that can't be.
Never opening these eyes to ever
really see.
An arrangement of lives I try
hard to be,
But I can't meet a one; I know
that's not me.
Pushing for time, not wasting a
minute,
Building up a day, not knowing
what's in it.
Running from pain, the truth of it
all.
Leading to nowhere, no nothing
at all.
Making a wish on a falling star;
Making believe I'm going too far.
Opening a door I fear walking into.
A gust of wind, I would need to
push me through.
Standing alone a mountain or
statue.
Allowing emotion to get where it
wants to.
With a push of strength to end
this day,
My mind lies at rest.
Will tomorrow be the same?

Linda (Townley) Elder
HE'S GOT TO BE A POET
*[To my husband, Chris, God's
Gift to me.]*
He's got to be a Poet,
With warm and gentle eyes,
He's got to play the guitar
And be unable to tell a lie.
He's got to have strong arms,
And a soft and singing heart
And oh, he's got to love me,
When we're near or far apart.

God please help me find him,
It seems I've waited so long,
I know he's waiting for me too,
All ready with my SONG.
I've got to learn to trust again,

I've got to learn to live and then,
I know that I will have a friend
When my heart is on the mend.

We can play a symphony,
We can live in harmony,
Help me I'm on bended knee.
Bring my POET to me.

P. J. Pescosolido
TILLER OF WISDOM
Ideas spreading like moonlight
Over the fertile fields of your
mind.
A thought blossoming
In the sunlight of your eyes.
The wisdom of the ages hides
Beneath the youth of your smile,
And so you know all.

The weeds of depression and
loneliness
Are discarded
To let the abundant harvest of
knowledge
Shine through.
You forever nurture your
Ideas' seedlings,
And so you know all.
And so you know all.

Betty Lou Tosh
REMORSE
Why were we told to be like
children?
The world won't let us be.
It takes our starry-eyed innocence
And makes fun of it, mocks it.
Some try harder than others
To resist the change that will
come.
They laugh longer, play at games
more
Pretending they are still the same
Trying not to notice as they shed
Their soft white skin of
ignorance
For the calloused brown shield
called knowledge.

Sir Steve Vega, C .GK
The Puerto Rican Empire
Being that everything in this
mortal world
was first created in someones'
mind,
I've created myself the Titular
Crowned Sovereign Head
of the Kingdom of Puerto Rico
and of all the Planets
and Dominions throughout the
Universe,

His Royal Highness, Steve Vega
the 1st
First Prince of the Isle and Lord of
Verse,
Earl of all on this immortal page
and Sovereign Duke of the
Galaxy,

Colonel-in-chief of all Regiments,
created just to serve
"The Light-Star Spics" battalion,
everywhere, guarding
everything,
"The Puerto Rican Light
Dragoons", in their purple
coated uniforms
"The Rican-Life Guards" in their
burgundy berets
by the thousands on their Paso
Fino stallions,

His majesties' castle near Old San Juan; the fabulous Fortaleza where Spanish Troops are changing the guard, on this island jewel in the Caribbean Sea this land of sparkling people, whith skins of golden sun dark eyes of glowing fire, and flashing smiles of fun,

England, Arabia, France and Rome, though great these kingdoms were, could never possess The Vega sword, "Enforcer" forever in the family keep at "Great House" on Bloomingdale,

Mark Anthony Backus
DAY'S END
Day i and day out,
　tryin' to find what this world's
　　about.
Struggling hard from day to day,
　making ends meet some kind of
　　way.
Forget today and yesterday past,
tomorrow's day just might not last.
Oh help me lord to find the way,
thru this world sometimes dark,
　sometimes gray.

Charles Thomas Christopher
WINTER
The swirl of chimney smoke
　announcing the winter season.
A woodstoves embrassing warmth,
　there's nothing quite so pleasing.
Cozy winter nights,
　spent befreinding a new bought
　book.

Those daily little walks,
　to check the ice out on the
　brook.
A family drawn together,
　sharing stories about the past.
Keeping a watchful eye,
　hoping springs arrived at last.
Sudden is it's arrival,
　with no distinct seperation.
The buds bursting into leaves,
　and people out from hibernation.

Anne Mae Kochel
I Wept Way Back Then
I wept the day
　I buried my Johnny
And for the four kids I'd
　Have to support with no money.
I wept that October day
　The kids screamed
And started to pray
　To John they handed the flag

I wept that rainy day
　David was scared and hid
Under the pine box
　As they closed the lid
And I cried with the girls
　While they sealed the lock
We stepped back and whirled
　Time stopped like the ticking
　of a clock.
I wept that stormy day
　As we marched up the hill
The parson began to pray
　And said "This is Gods will."
I wept that final day
　As they lowered his flowered
　box
I too began to pray
　God be with my Johnny always

Miss Sandra J. Geisz
FOR YOUR LOVE
*[For John Laub, Jr., the only one
I love and always will—for you
made happiness possible.]*
I walked along a trail
　as the sunset passed the trees.
I noticed your eyes shining
　like the sparkle of the seas.
I had to keep on walking
　even though my love was true.
The forest fell behind me
　and I lost the sight of you.
I thought it was the best thing
　to leave our love behind
Visions of our days before
　kept flashing through my mind.
Although I kept on walking,
　my pain was plain to see.
I was praying for a reason
　as I fell upon one knee.
I felt the dampness fill me
　as the forest turned to night.
The cold air closed around me.
　There was nothing left in sight.
I had reached my destination
　and finding nothing there,
My eyes wandered to the trail
　in a bleak and empty stare.
I had to make it back there.
　I had to let you know.
I ran across the forest
　until the light began to show.
I had to tell you something
　I had learned along the way,
It was your love that I'd been
　searching for
　when I had left that day.

Glenda Malone
BEAUTY FOR FREE
The majestic mountains that
　cross our land,
From the Atlantic shore to the
　Pacific sand.
Their peaks all covered from a
　winter's snow,
Cast with the evening sun, lends
　a purple—pink glow.
The deep, dark, woods, reach to
　the sky,
The smell of a forest and fresh
　baked pie.
A cool, crisp fall when leaves
　have turned,
A crackling fire with wood half
　burned.
The desert land, a colored sunset
　sky,
How beautiful it is, to watch the
　clouds drift by.
An ocean wave, a mountain

stream,
A lake or pond under a night
　moonbeam.
An evergreen dripped with heavy
　snow,
A steep mountain road with the
　valley below.
A soft summer breeze and fresh
　cut grass,
Thoughts and memories that will
　always last.
A seagull glides by and dips with
　ease,
The smell of a shop that makes
　mixed teas.
These are all things to smell and
　see,
These are all things of beauty for
　free.

Pamela S. Rosenbaum
TICKING
Silent Yearnings
are in fact

explosive bombs
Ticking away underneath

the facade of face to face
interaction . . .

They are wonders of wound up
　grenades
Ready to erupt . . .
Maybe tonight at the store
When you find out
that they don't have

your "size" . . .

Kendra—Jean Cliver
COUSIN EMILY
Emily left year ago
　though some say she was
　always here
　she calmly gave her moment's
　cheer
then chose a place where she
　would grow

And all about her people ran
　their simple lives a pattern seen
　and no one knew just where
　she'd been
while seated in their daily plan

Her gaze would go to the things
　beyond
　a smile so nicely on her face
　and no one saw a single trace
nor knew a single common bond

Doreen Dennis
MY LOVE
The sun and moon of my temple
can see the inner vision in my
　mind
deep crags, canyons, rivers and
　streams
are there within for you to find

Emerald blue
The December smell of you
cool air
do you really care

My skin turns red violet at your
　touch
Oh, you mean so much
No one can compare
your only being fair

The sound of your voice as you
　speak my name
you a wild mare with a flowing
　mane
Racing through my hills and trees

Spreading yellow and red flames
　to my heart
of me, I hope you'll always
　remain a part

You are not unlike the blue white
　flame
you burn brightly inspite of
　yourself
Galloping through the deep
　canyon
to you—its only a game

When at last we kiss
burning colors in my head
oh, this is surely genesis
Burning brightly, orange and red

Margaret Teresa McGarry
RAMONA, THE GYPSY DOG
Ramona trots with a gait that's
　tipsy,
　As she wanders the land free as
　a gypsy,
Long, curled toe nails that have
　ne're been cut,
　Protect the paws of this
　philosophical pup,
Her curly tail and black shiny fur,
　Cause the public to notice her.

The expansive ears freely move
　with ease,
　Back and forth with intent to
　please.
Her eyes tell the story of love and
　hope,
　An appreciation of man in his
　scope.
　　Romana, the Gypsy Dog.

Eileen Tenore
THE NIGHT
Mine becomes upon the night,
when the sureal starts to be,
as the paradigm again takes flight,
so the power comes from me,

Daylight sings so sorrowful,
the ugliness exposed,
where righteous eyes calm and
　cool,
remind me; I'm opposed.

As life unveils her secret self,
of whispers, tears and sighs,
black warmth engulf me like a tide
to watch the drama rise.

Dani Lynn Price
OASIS
Unmatchable Beauty
In a world full of sin
He is my oasis
I'll give my love to him.

When I'm like a child
Feeling alone and lost,
He is my oasis
No price to pay, no cost.

When tears run down
the windows of my mind,
He is my oasis,
Holding me close, so warm and
　kind.

When everything seems hopeless
There's no one else in sight.
He is my oasis
Guiding me toward the light.

When my heart is full of pain,
When the smiles won't appear,
He is my oasis
Loving away my fear.

When life and love run dry

And the bitterness shows again,
He is my oasis
Someone I can depend.

He is my Sunshine
in this cold, cold land,
He is my oasis
He came and took my hand.

Untouchable Beauty,
In a world full of sin,
He is my oasis
I'll keep on loving him.

Katrina L. Umberger
MY RAINBOW OF LIFE
Blue is a teardrop from my love
    laden eye;
It is the color of a cloudless sky.
Yellow is happiness, the rays of
    the sun;
It describes how I feel whenever I
    run.
Red is the hearts I see in my
    lover's eyes;
It is the setting fireball in the
    western skies.
Green is newness, the grass of the
    earth;
It seems to proclaim new
    beginnings and birth.
These colors form the rainbow
Which symbolizes Hope
    throughout our lives as we grow.

Richard E. Anderson
Nothing In the World Quite Like You
There's nothing in the world
    quite like a girl.
No. There's nothing in the world
    quite like you—
For without you what would a
    man do?
It's a joy to see Reggie hit a ball a
    mile
But naught can compare with
    your breathless smile;
Why even the Camel can wait 'til
    I go a mile with you!
Spring flowers blossom when you
    are near—
Your a girl and beyond compare.
When I'm with you can I call you
    dear?
I can't resist your silky hair!
What a bundle of curvaceous joy—
You make me glad that I'm a boy!
No. Deep, deep down there's
    nothing like a girl;
There's nothing in the world
    quite like you!

Aurora L. Espinoza
MI PEQUEÑA POESIA
En este dia tu has nacido
hoy te he creado yo
porque he querido que nazcas
    poesia;
Porque has vivido . . tanto
tanto dentro de mi
porque he formado tu
    propio cielo
y te he dado forma, con
    mis versos y amor;
Te he llevado tanto tiempo
en mi mente y mi corazon
y te he acariciado en la luna
de mis suenos . . .
y con mi pluma y en cada letra
y en cada verso
como un zurco de amor
que he sembrado de ilusion,

porque tu naciste poesia
porque yo te di vida . . .
y mi mente te saco dela nada
y dia a dia te fui dando forma
como el escultor a su obra
asi estaras tu'. . .y seras inmortal
porque te he escrito con tinta
    de sangre;
Porque al escribirte . . te he dado
vida propia . . .
hoy que has nacido . . . poesia';

Karen Joan Phillips
THE MIND
I am mighty, I am sound
I am meek, I am profound.
I control you, You control me
I have no sight, but you, can see.
I have no feeling, but your
    feelings are within me.
Without me your are nothing,
    just like a stone
Nothing at all, but flesh and bone.
Your actins are many, but mine
    are more.
Without my cunning, You'd be
    quite a bore.
The blind can be sightless,
But within them is me
And with my knowledge, they
    can see.
The cripple is hopeless, and
    unable to move
But with me there within him
That, you could not prove.
You see, within all, you will find
Everyone has a mind.

Eric Lefkowitz
THE VERY FEW
Most people can know, but only
    a few can believe.
Most people can think of, but few
    can conceive.
Most people can listen, but only
    a few can hear.
Most people can be around, but
    few can go near.
Most people can fly, but only a
    few can soar.
Most poeple can understnad, but
    few try for more.
Most people can move, but only a
    few can run.
Most people can enjoy, but only a
    few have fun.
Most people can watch, but only
    a few can see.
Most people can turn loose, but
    few can free.
Most people can play, but only a
    few control.
Most people can have feeling, but
    few have a soul.
Most people can love, but only a
    few can cherish.
All people will die, but few will
    perish.

Phoebe Vaughn Engler
MY HUSBAND'S HANDS
His hands have expression and
    character all of their own.

When I look at them; cracked,
    rough, wrinkling with age and
    displaced bones from hard
    work and injury. I see a life
    time of struggle, hardship and
    pain.

But most of all, I see the love and
    tenderness, the caring

and the caressess.

I see in his hands; a mother's
    embrace, a father's strength,
    gentleness of dew drops that
    early morn brings, the magic of
    a blossoming flower and the
    miracle of the birth of a babe.

If his hands could talk, Oh what
    stories they could tell. Of all
    their travels, creations, times of
    defeat and times of being beaten.

I am sure if his hands could recall
    all their encounters; they
    would only remember the good
    times had, the friends they to
    make, the love they created
    and the good memories they
    left behind.

Mauricia Price
ONE TWISTED TREE
One hunched and twisted tree
    stretched out
Her knotted skinny—fingered
    arms
In supplication to the sun
And his sustaining power of life—
Then died of her senility.
A passing artist pause, set up
His easel there—and rendered her
Immortal with a palette knife.

Patricia Belyea Thar
THE HAWK
The lonely hawk soars high,
Defiance in his wing—spread
And in his eye the hunter—look.
    A single crackling shot—
    He plummets to the earth,
    Talons curled tight.
    And 'neath the bristled feathers
    Amid the softest down,
    The spreading stain.
Gone the beauty of flight,
No more the soaring grace,
He lies in death, alone
And none shed mourning tears—
    Save one.

Chris Roach

Chris Roach
CHRISTMAS TIME
[I dedicate this poem to all my family]
Here it is once again
the Christmas time of year.
Time for special happiness,
joy and of course good cheer.

It's time for our families to gather
and spend some time with friends.
As Christmas Day creeps closer
and the year comes to an end.

But please remember that this is
    the day
that Jesus was born so long ago,
in the town of Bethleham.
The first Christmas as we know.

So Merry Christmas to everyone
and the best of holidays to all.
Have a very Happy New Year
until again after next fall.

Timothy Michael DiVito
YOU WERE
You were the center of my life
You were to me what was real
Something I never knew before
    . . . reality
Now I want to steal away in a
    fantasy
Because reality smashed my
    dreams
Reality took you from my loving
    embrace

You are so cold now
You are so desolate
Something I now know much of
    . . . desolation
Because I want to scream I love
    you!
But damn it! you're gone
How can I express love for
    something nonexistent?

What I have to tell myself
Is that there is a future
Without you around in my life
I have to say I will survive
Because I am a survivor
To love, because I can love

There was a time when
    everything was fine
When I thought you would live
    . . . forever

What a fool I was and still am
But I still feel for you, so don't
    worry
I'm living like . . . you were

Dorothy L. Campbell
PEACE OF SOUL
Peace, be still; thou art a pearl.
To own thee I would give the
    world;
The joys, the ecstasy love seeks,
The riches, treasures that I keep,
The pride they bring, fit for a king
Is small reward when peace takes
    wing,
And moves away—just out of
    reach.
I seek thee knowing thou art there,
A priceless pearl my soul could
    wear,

But thou art ever just beyond
The touch of this poor mortal one,
Restlessly I seek to find
Thy worth in days I left behind.
I seek thee in my heart today,
But find you cannot come to stay.
I could accept the loss of thee
But that would be the death of me,
So ever onward to that goal
This one will seek for peace of
soul.

Caroline M. Orlandi
ODE TO JASON
*[This little poem I dedicate to
my loving grandson who's
almost eight. Grandmom]*
How sweet of him to send to me
A sample of his crayoned art!
It's neat and pretty as can be
And sure does tickle Grandma's
heart!

I'll look for more from time to time
And proudly show them off, you
see,
Then harbor them among the old,
With other treasures pure as gold!

Miss Gloria Roberts
TRIBUTE TO AMERICA
God bless America,
The greatest! Nation of them all,
Where fairy tales, have been told,
By the young, and old,
About the legends that took place,
In this wonderful land of ours.

A country, so full of music,
Laughter and Love,
With Natural Science too,
While our Solar ships,
Kept orbiting, the earth, and sky,
As our Nation dreams came true,
When our aeronautics pioneer'd
On the moon,
While out of the summer haze,
Came the pony express rider,
galloping towards the far horizon,
With the countries mails,
Those! were the days, that caught
The imagination, and glory, for the
People's of this Nation.

God bless! our Country America,
The greatest nation on earth,
A Land of courage, and bravery,
With Liberty, and Democracy,
While we raise our heads,
High, with honor, and Dignity,
To pay homage, to our great
Leaders.
Men, like Abraham Lincoln, John
Kennedy,
Teddy Roosevelt, Martin Luther
King, and George Washington.
Those! were the great men of our
times,
As we think of their sad departure.
While we stand, side by side

Jon Hertzog
Grass On the River's Edge
*[To my inspiration of life, and
all subsequent motions; my
love, Nicki.]*
Lying,
    on the grass
        at the river's edge.
Seeing,
    dead grass from Spring's past
        decaying.
Pondering,

about future years' grass.
It, will be nourished,
It, will be enriched,
It, will grow,
    by absorbing the elements,
        the components,
    of previous generations.

How sad,
    man, finds this so difficult.

B. J. Nowak
FAMILY LIFE
A good family is strong
Stability to those who belong
It supports their rights
Forgives their wrongs
And makes this life worth living
long.

Clayton Anthony Townsend

Clayton Anthony Townsend
IF ONLY
If only gas was thirty cents a
gallon
If only the entire world was at
peace
If only there was employment for
all
If only all the starving were fed
If only we didn't have to lock our
doors at night
If only a Nuclear Bomb wasn't
    If only we tried
        IF ONLY

Betty Farquhar
RENEWAL
Only yesterday I felt old and ill.
Today I am young and renewed—
snorkeling between the coral reefs
in the clear, aquamarine sea.

I watch tropical fish
in all the colors of the rainbow.
I swim effortlessly.
The salty sea cushions me.

I am strangely comforted—
caressing the coral reefs.
Vague impulses, as if from aeons
ago:
I have returned to the wellspring
of being.

Jackie Moland
JUST FOR LOVING YOU
For months now I have watched
from afar,
Watching everything you do.
Is it reaching for a star,
Just wanting to be with you.

Should I climb a mountain,
Or cross a sea.
Would this be more possible,
Than to hope that you could

love me.

Maybe I should stop trying,
It seems useless to go on.
The tears, heartaches and pain,
Have all lasted for so long.

I put myself through a lot,
Just to be a part of the things you
do.
But even more the pain I feel,
Just for loving you.

Michael Mannino
TRUE LOVE
MAY YOU COME TO KNOW
    PEACE AND
    UNDERSTANDING AND
    LOVE with each dawn of a new
    day.
May you learn with each passing
    hour that love is not measured
    by days or nights, for loving is
    the little things we do for each
    other that grows and grows, so
    make your life a life of giving
    for we only spend a little time
    together, so go on and share
    each others dreams, hopes, and
    hurts, for that is what loving is
    all about.

Danny R. Hendricks
IF
If I had a choice of any dream;
. . . you're the dream I'd want

If I could hold hands with anyone,
. . . your hand would be in mine

If I could hold any woman in the
    world,
. . . my arms would be around you

If I could kiss my favorite lips,
. . . those lips would be yours

If I could make love to any
    woman I desired,
. . . my desires would take me to
    you

Yes, if I could share anyone's love,
. . . yours is the love I'd want

And if I had to die for someone,
. . . . I'd give my life for you.

R. J. Pitsch
Saturday Night Special
It lay there, shining, ugly, black.
    I begged him, "Darling, take it
    back."
The serious answer received from
    him,
    "Mom, what if someone should
    break in?"

He kept it beside, cleaned and oiled;
    It rested there when tempers
    boiled
One night, over fancied wrong;
    A mindless grasp, it didn't take
    long.

A loud report, a flash of light!
    A missile speeding on its' flight!
Point of impact blossoms red!
    My son! My son! My son is dead!

Now my son's bed is deep and
    dark.
    The Saturday Night Special left
    its' mark.
I see each sunrise through a veil
    of tears,
    And the wife he loved, serves
    thirty years!

Judy Casey
SEPARATION
Most of the time I'm fine,
I hardly ever think of you.
Our togethers are now ended
And our lives have grown apart.

I manage to get by alone—
Without you by my side.
I get through all the day times
Though the nights can be so cold.

Most of the time I'm fine.

Most of the time I'm fine
But some of the time I'm not.

Vineler Mann
DON'T WORRY ABOUT ME
*[Dedicated to my six beautiful
daughters; Leila, Geraldine,
Janice, Nancy, Arlene and
Kathy]*
When my days are ended
And into my face you look
Don't think that the wrinkles
Were caused from the pain I took.

They were made from smiling
From all the things you've done
    and said
I've spent my life laughing
From morn till time for bed.

I found out long ago
There's no use to complain
You might as well laugh and bear
    it
It all comes out the same.

So don't worry about me
I've lived my life for all it's worth.
I've enjoyed every minute
On this beautiful green earth.

Sheila Rollit Barker
SEA VOYAGE
Nothing around but water
    As far as the eye can see—
Wave upon wave of crested foam
    Billowing wild and free;
Above, beyond, encircling all
    God, in His Majesty.

Margaret Gorwara
ODE TO CHRISTA
There was a dear lady who came
    to sell Avon
Just as poor Margaret was
    needing a Christian.
Our spirits did marvelously blend
    at first sight
And that's why I want to praise
    her tonight.

How lovely her nature so kind,
    and attending
When others she finds with their
    troubles are bending
She heeds to the Word of our
    Lord to minister
And thus He is glorified in her,
    dear Christa.

I'll never forget when in deep
    distress
I came to her home with my
    burdens so pressed
She washed all my clothes and
    shampooed my hair
Put curlers and all—made life
    seem less unfair.

Because God delights in the
    fragrance she bears
He puts her through heartaches,
    and hardships she shares

In order that she may continue to grow
More like our dear Saviour, the one we love so.

And now at the start of another New Year
May Jesus stay near her and answer each prayer
May God Bless dear Michael and Stefen as well
In Him to rejoice and His praises go tell.

I'm hoping to see her again very soon
May be she'll come here before the new moon
She knows I will always stay close to her heart
And one day in heaven we'll never need part.

Philip De Carlo
LAMENT
To some far world, Beethovan and the rest have gone,
And the sounds we hear today
Lay dead as Tchaikovsky's Swan.

Robert E. Smith

Robert E. Smith
A Changing Time Of Year
Days are getting longer but winter winds still have a chill—
One can see farther yonder, the soul feels a heavenly thrill,
There's still more snow to be, the fields not ready you see—
But nature provides quite a sight, many things for the eye's delight.

A changing time of year, lovely things, you'll find inspiring thinking love thoughts for someone dear, of our work never tiring though the sharp winds still blowing—
It's soon time for all to be growing, though the air's still cold in the sunlight.

For plowing things still aren't right, fishing and hunting's a pleasure, the marvels of nature a treasure—
A time to be full of good cheer—
A changing time of year.

Opel Coleman
Come Fly Away With Me
My dear friend, come fly away with me
To a beautiful isle of the sea.
Dare to allow your hopes and

and dreams to soar
As the white waves break upon the shore.
There's no limit to what you can be—
Let your imagination go free
And envision that all perfect you—
That person you thought could never do
All those wonderful creative deeds
That your tender heart desires and needs.
Rise above the shackles in your breast
And you will out distance all the rest.
Your strength will grow with every try—
Soon you will shout the victory cry
And then you will grow stronger indeed
Because you have accepted good seed.
Spread your wings and sail the azure skies—
View your future with believing eyes
As new ideas rustle like the wind
And limbs of creativity bend
Closer to your ever eager mind
Directing the seeing and the blind
In building a masterpiece so grand
That it throughout the ages will stand
A memorial to your greatness—
Your children and all mankind to bless.

Mary Frances Murphy
A VERY DEAR FRIEND
[To a great lady, who died before receiving this as her 1982, Christmas gift.]
"To think you came to see me again
and I am able to be here to greet you."
The most wonderful words I heard,
spoken from the heart of a true friend.
A friend, without her this story could never begin.
Over the years I have stopped to say "Hello"
To the most wonderful woman I know.
She has always had time in her busy life
To share some of it with me.
In adolescence she taught me things I should know
Even when my spirits were low.
I beleive she knows how she helped mold my life
My own mother was busy and God had taken Dad.
I needed a friend and that is what I had.
She had children of her own I knew
One was her daughter, my classmate and friend.
Even though her spare moments were few
She found the time with me to spend,

If only to pass the time of day.
How wonderful to be able to say
"Mary Ferry, thanks for being there when I needed you,
for you brought a lot of happiness into my life!"

Web Sturr
A Thought At Christmas
It's art to trim a Christmas tree
Much like a rhyme in poetry
A bell on the left and one on the right
The balanced baubles—a lovely sight
The cone—shaped tree—what joy it brings
With well—placed lights and well—draped strings
Of sparkling tinsel and other things
To top it off—the best by far
That beautiful symbolic star
Let's not forget—ere we say "Amen"
What started it all in Bethlehem.

Sandra M. Boyce
SNOWFLAKES
[This poem is dedicated to my mom—a small token for all she's given me.]
So exquisite, each perfect unto itself, in form.
Illusionary softness belies the icy cold from which they're born.
The most delicate of God's many materpieces,
Its beauty is just to gaze upon.
Touch it and its being ceases.
Try to hold one in your hand and it will surely melt.
Individually intangible, only their presence is felt.
Silently they fall, blanketing everything in white,
And while they last, keep all of Earth's imperfections from sight.

Jeffrey Sigworth
THE MOUSE
Mousey friend
living in field and farm.
Eating grain
content with life.
Beware of that meow.

Joyce Smith Murphy
Put Your Hand In Mine
Do you need a helping hand, friend?
Put your hand in mine.
I'll do the best I can, friend.
I'll try to help you find
The peace you crave and long for
The love you've gone without
Put your hand in mine friend
I'll try to lead you out.

Do you need a friend to lean on?
I'll try to share your load.
Does your sense of way all seem gone?
I'll point out the road.
When you're sure that you're a failure,
And you really just don't care.
Put your hand in mine friend.
I've been waiting there.

Come hand—in—hand with me, friend.
And we'll be on our way
I'll try to be so kind friend,

That someday you may say
To some poor wandering pilgrim
Whose path he cannot find.
"I was a friend in need, once
Come, put your hand in mine."

Gayle Morris—Bridges
DON'T BE ALONE
If I should go and leave you here
Don't forget my love or worry my dear
The passing was not of my choice at all.
The departure could not be stopped nor stalled.

It hurts to leave my father and mother,
Nieces and nephews, Or sisters and brothers.
But to leave you behind alone again
Saddens me deep and to no end.

For time we lost in fights and feuds
Is time I wish we now could use.
Memories are pieces of time we keep,
Clipped from the past of life so sweet.

But memories aren't much to hold or touch
When the one you love is gone.
I love you dear and the solution is clear,
Give another the love I've known.

Ronald Lessl
REVELATION
I cast my stones into the lake
And watch the ripples that they make.
For as I toss them one by one,
My mind seeks light but does not see the sun.

I feel a warmth but what of light?
Were I brave perhaps I might
Leap unsure into the blackest pit
To find the blaze in the depths of it.

Swift by dreams in waters dark,
Flying more like a leaf than lark;
I gather starmist on my face,
Dive low and try to land with grace.

I have a dream I know must be,
A face a smile I'm sure to see.
Calm the ripples, leave the lake alone;
Then look . . . the dream, the face my own!

Paula Dickman
THE DOG AND I
Out in the darkness a dog barks
Telling the world of his discontent.
Alone I sat and I wondered,
Just what his barking meant.

Does it come from the feeling
Deep down in his gut,
That the world has treated him wrong,
Or is he just telling the other dogs
That he's been all alone much too long?

Is it a cry for friendship
Or just a much needed sound
To assure that poor dog in the darkness

That although lost
He will still be found.

Is it a cry of emptiness
That he feels deep down in his
  heart
That his feelings of love were
  neglected or used
And left him torn all apart.

I feel very close to this fellow,
This dog barking out in the dark.
Oh God how I wish and pray that
  someday,
I may learn just how to bark.

Barry W. Haney
LOVERS PARTING
When someone you love
goes away
and you know it's for longer
than a day and a day plus
a day
your mind becomes weak
as your eyes begin
to weep
but
for whatever the reason you part
you know nothing can turn a
true and honest heart;
Still, in the back of your mind
your eyes will weep in a
  thoughtful
way
for at least a day
and a day plus
a day.

Ruth I. Myers
MEMORIES
Memory of her laughter,
  in song we hear,
Memory of her cheerfulness
  brings happiness near,
Memory of the sparkle in her
  eyes of blue,
Memory of her beauty like the
  glistening morning dew,
Memory of her thoughtfulness to
  others she displays,
Memory of unselfishness and
  kindness, rules she obeys,
Memory of blonde hair today,
  brunette tomorrow,
Memory of her coolness, a
  trait to borrow,
Memory of her hilarious pranks,
  mixed with a joke,
Memory of her joy when she is
  drinking a coke.
The flower of friendship
  forever shall last
In the many memories of a time
  that is past.

Cora Durski
THE CHRISTMAS ROSE
When Christmas trees are
  blooming
With lights of every hue;
And little children asking,
"When is Dear Santa due"?

When Christmas chimes are
  ringing
And caroles fill the air,
The tale of Christ retelling;
Joy is every where.

When Christmas time is nearing
And all is white with snow,
You'll find the Christmas roses
Through frozen ground, do show.

So, you'll find them every year,

As Christmas time draws nigh,
Poking through the frozen earth
To honor God, on High.

Lorraine V. Henderson
MISSING YOU
Late at night—
Diamonds in the sky—
The moon is so romantic.

How I yearn to fall into my
  dreams
And escape this lonliness.

My arms—they ache
They need to hold you.
I miss your gentle touch.

Nothing helps my weeping heart
—There are those who try.

The radio man, he tries
He plays those pretty love songs
—Too bad they make me cry.

The t. v. stars—they're worse
With their love scenes and their
  passion.

So, I sit here alone
Here surrounded by the darkness
Surrounded by you, I only dream.

Vivian Hsieh
THE GIFT OF NOAH
      I
      Sit
      Inside
   My picture
   Window   as
   The   heavens
   Continue to send
   Forth their tears.
   My nose pressed
   Against the screen,
   I watch a single
   Drop trickle down the
   Stairway from above. Each
   Droplet has its own distinct
   Character, without a trace
Of resemblance to one another.
But when they gather midst the
Bellowing voices of supremity,
Their uniquiness fades and fades
...Until only you know that
   Each drop is a completely
   Different world, molded
   Together to form a
   Fearless island of
      Conformity

Laura M. Ford
NEW SHOES
Creak, creak, creak.
A walking haunted house.
My toes feel pinched
my heels scrape
the backs slide off and on.
I slip on the tile
I stumble on the carpet
and stairs are just impossible.
Then everyone says
how nice they look
and I think it's all worthwhile.
They'll fit tomorrow.

Dolores E. Minnig
THE OCEAN
The waves were rolling up to the
  shore,
I gazed and wondered more and
  more,
As I sat there on the sunny beach,
How far does this ocean reach
To send waves upon the sand
Of another country in a distant
  land?

I was amazed at the power those
  waves had,
It was awesome and even a little
  sad,
To think how some people fail to
  see
The beauty that God created for
  you and me.
I saw a graceful sailboat on the
  horizon
As it seemed to be sailing right
  toward the sun
Where the ocean water meets the
  sky
And then was no longer visible to
  the naked eye.
As I heard the sounds of seagulls
  overhead,
I thought about "Life goes on" as
  someone said,
And so it goes through struggles
  and strife,
But with faith in God, we'll have
  eternal life.

Lillian Spikes Asihene

Lillian Spikes Asihene
LOVE
[For Wanda and Mike, Claudia,
Alex and Alexis. May each of
you love ardently. Love is the
core of great human
accomplishment; inability to
love lies at the core of
destruction, be it self or
outwardly oriented.]
Rose, you have a beautiful
Irresistible mouth
A majestic face, like King
  Affonso the First
Of sixteenth-century Congo
A regal gift as in the flower of
  youth
You make me feel truly beautiful
And so exaltingly happy
That the Gods saw fit to create me
A woman
Destined to the bliss of your
  caressing arms

Seeing so little of each other
When we meet, we eagerly clinch
  in the embrace
Of an awesome, all-encompassing
  experience
Emerging, two black bodies
  drenched
With the sweat of love's labor
I now know that I shall never
  lose you
For our love has been enshrined
In the deepest recess of my heart
And I shall forever have endearing

thoughts
Of so rare a man as you

Virginia Fern Fetters
Mama's Unfinished Quilt
I see a house that's quiet
And she sits there alone
Her hands hold patterned pieces
Of cloth she has sewn.
Blocks from boy's printed shirt tails
And girl's soft flowered silk
Mixed and matched together
To make each child a quilt.

Too seldom these precious
  moments
She could call all her own
Times for reflection and prayer
For her family and home.
She'd fallen to sleep
The days toll had taken;
From the washing, ironing,
Cooking and baking.

Each day a new challenge
A small body to build
A young mind to enrich
Cut fingers to be healed—
Mama could do most everything
Even mend your broken kite
When she bent down to hold you—
Everything got all right!

Mama was doctor, big sister
Best playmate and brother
School teacher, good friend
And our sweet mother.
Her big "lap" held us all
When a story she read
She heard prayers, kissed each
Then, tucked all into bed.

Mama taught us the bible
She taught us to sing
Through out our big house
Happy music did ring.
She pumped the old organ,
All around her we stood
Blending our young voices
As she knew we could.

Her days were full and busy
With five "tads" to look after
Sometimes there were tears
But, most times the laughter.
There were cheeks to kiss
Chubby little hands to smack
Baths to be given
School lunches to pack.

So many things to be done
But short was her life
She died so very young
A wonderful mother and wife.
With misty eyes and heavy heart
I sorted her personal things!
Old keepsakes, letters, pictures,
And her wedding rings.

Not much left to show
For a lifetime of love
But remembered,
Mama stored her treasures—above.
She had no time to finish
The stitch on soft silk
So, to each child was left—
Mama's unfinished quilt.

Lorin J. Schnorbus
A FEELING
I hope, I wish, I pray,
Somewhere, somehow, someday,
You'll find the strength to see,
What's going on in me.
You'll search and what you'll find,

Is something in my mind . . .
A thought unknown to me,
Has grown and come to be,
A feeling in my heart,
Asking you to be a part
Of me and of my soul . . .
Together as a whole.
To tell you how I feel,
About this something real,
—Just simply can't be done . . .
We'll never be as one.
But as each day goes on,
I'll sing my simple song . . .
I hope, I wish, I pray,
Somewhere, somehow, someday,
You'll find the strength to see,
What's going on in me.

Martha Virginia Chalfant

A Tribute To Archibald Rutledge

[Dedicated to Mrs. Russell Starnes, (Nancy), who introduced me to the works of Archibald Rutledge, Poet Laureate of South Carolina (1934).]

Along the Santee River
Are wild and lovely things.
One hears the call of Nature
In works that Rutledge brings.
He stirs imagination—
He thrills the ears with sounds
Eyes focused on creation
Where wilderness abounds.

Near Hampton, Charleston County
Lies a cornucopia of land
That overflows with bounty
Direct from God's own hand.
Oft he came here to share
The glory in this place
Word-painting with such care
God shows in every trace.

Susan Santer Prush

TO MY LOVE, MY LIFE

Another night for which I sit
At our bedroom window,
Watching, waiting, as each
Car passes by.

It has started to rain, my love—
As each drop falls on the glass
It reminds me of all the tears
I have cried,
All the nights I've spent alone,
While I have waited for you to
come home.

A candle glows in the dark
Filling the room with the
Scent of Musk,
As the radio plays a song of our
past,

Memories appear of our time
together
Playing their little games with
my mind.

I have tried before to forget you,
Yet—still I am with you.
I must be moving on my way
once again,
For I see things to come, all the
long lonely nights alone.
Thee is more to life than what I
have now
While I still have time, I must
leave you.

Well, my love the candle has
grown dim and the rain has
stopped, and I now find I
cannot leave you,
I must stay.
I need you in my life as much as
the candle needs air to burn
and the flowers need the rain
to grow.

For you see my love
    You are
        My life.

Barbara Alice Wilmoth

?

Who am I
I cry my utterance to the wind
Where am I going
O, where O, where did I begin
Have I now just existed
Or have I always been
Who am I
I cry my utterance to the wind
Am I to be as you
Blowing dust to dust, rocking too
and fro
I must know
Who am I? What am I about
Am I as the crystal sands
Or a whisper of a word
Or the echo of a shout
Who am I
I cry in question of my being
Am I not more than what meets
the eye
Is there a part of me lingering in
the by and by
O, how I wonder why afore I die
Who am I
I cry my utterance in despair
For the question lays the shadow
on my brow
Tell me, tell me how
Am I to be as time extending
through infinity
Whats to become of me or shall I
fall
As autumn leaves to meet my
destiny
As seasons beckoned me
Who am I? I cry the voice of
lostness in the wilderness
Am I a figment of my
imagination
Or an image of my mind
Or a product of divine to seek
and find
As the seed unto the vine
Who am I
I cry my utterance to the wind
Am I in death or has my journey
just begin
Will I be again as you blowing in
the wind
As time no end?

Loy D. Hupp

OUT ON A LARK

[To my darling wife Audrey who is my constant inspiration]

A rolling train, a flashing light
A speeding car, the end in sight
Lives were lost, all in vain
When someone tried, to beat a
train

Young lives ended, in a tragic crash
All because of, one mad dash
Laughing and singing, merry and
gay
Planning their lives, along the way

Four happy teenagers, out on a lark
Racing a light, coming out of the
dark
The engineer saw, as he looked
out in vain
There wouldn't be time, to stop
his big train

In one frantic moment, as the
train whistle blew
The brakes were applied, it was
useless he knew

He murmured a prayer, hoping
they'd wait
They were, he could see, meeting
their fate

Many years passed, and things
settled down
He'd never forget four teenagers,
just out on the town

Loy D. Hupp

EXCALIBUR

In a world of furtive beings
How the spirits strongly crave
All the things so neglected
From the cradle to the grave

For the flesh so sorely yearning
If only to atone
A chance again at Excalibur
And pull it from a stone

Donald Lee Wilmoth

MAN WITHOUT A HOME

Lo, my flesh is but a shadow
Reflected by the sun
An image cast upon the ground
Lost in death and darkness bound

Lo, my body is but dust and ash
Scattered in the wind
Never knowing that it had been
Just a shadow o'er the sand
Just an image of a man

Lo, this body mortal
'Tis but an empty shell
Sown in a world alone
Returning as the winds into its
earthly home
For this is what it be
'Tis not a part of me

Lo, my spirit tis as a crystal glass
The light of one betwixt the
bitter ash
Waiting as the soul I used to be
For time to pass this earth away
from me
Where life shall sew my body
nurtured
As the day is done
Nairy again shall I cast a shadow
in the sun . . .

Jeffrey Bishop

IT'S NOT THE SAME

Your lips meet mine,
but they are cold.

Your looks are not the
image that I once saw.
You're holding me in your arms,
neither of us knowing how to act.
You speak of the past,
I know there is no future.
We used to talk of things we
wanted,
things we never had.
All the dreams are lost,
never to be found.
The feelings we once had together
are gone with the youth of our
yesterdays.
I'm sorry, but it's not the same.

Mary Lynn Kornegay

VALUES

[To those, neither to blame, nor credited: and yet..part of us..more than they know...]

Just read a letter from the older
generation . . .
Guess sooner or later, that's my
destination . . .
But . . it seems for a long time, I
got things confused . . .
You see . . I felt . . that I was the
one with values . . .
I thought, I knew, the true goal . .
perfection of the soul . . .
And all those old cats were busy
chasin' . . the fast buck . .
society . .
fancy cars . . big houses . .
propriety . . .
But . . it seems as though, I'm the
one who misread them . . .
I think . . perhaps . . they are
after the very same gem . . .
The things they desire . . . they
seek . . .
to keep them on the right track
to the perfect peak . . .
Thinking, that if one makes
enough money . . and has a
"proper family" . . .
and at the party, is funny . . . and
resisted booze and gambling . . .
You had to reach the perfect
goal . . ?? . . regardless of the
toll . . .
But . . WE . . we fine young
rebels . . .
We felt the toll too high . . and
not worth the trouble . . .
And . . I guess somewhere
during the debate . . .
we got the goal, confused with
the estate . . .
Now . . we sit facing off one
another . . playing games . .
toying with words . . .
While . . one another . . we
disturb . . .
Purposely we offend . . .
Because we can not comprehend . . .
They retreat to booze . . while we
choose drugs to misuse . . .
They commit adultry, to establish
their freedom . . .
We laugh at convention, and
make love . . not have sex . .
to establish a union . . .
We hope by turning our backs,
and spitting on all their laws
and morals . . .
Somehow . . we'll make this a
better world . . ?? . .
But . . Will We . . ?? . . Have
We . . ?? . .

Who is there to say, which of us . .
   if either of us . . .
has the answer . . ?? . .
How could either of us, be so
   egotistical and conceited . . .
that our way will lead us to the
   perfect table to be seated . . ?? . .
We our . . after all . . members
   of the same race . . .
Running at a different pace . . .
Remember . . the turtle and the
   rabbit . . ?? . .
The QUICKEST . . . may not
   have been . . the FASTEST . . .

Lloyd E.N. Bartholomew
A JOURNEY
Starting in opposite directions
We met and became united
Surrounded by water, long, before
   seeing sun
Later, with others, enjoying what
   was provided

Spanked, for what I am not sure
But questing for better was
   always the lure
Once again! I am joined to
   become one
But, soon there were others to
   carry on

Two scores and four, I long for
   more
With thanks extending to our
   forefathers
Doing all I can to keep off the floor
We help ourselves and many
   others

Oh! Universal consciousness,
   give me strength!
As, hither and thither, I go where
   others went
My journey is by no means at an
   end
Who knows the thresholds I
   must transcend?

Elizabeth Magee
SO LONG
   [Dedicated with forever
   unbreakable love and longing
   to Paul G. Hutchins]
Never has a day been so lonely
Or so long
Ha!
"So long" we said to one another
And now (Ha!) I know why the
   term is used.

Frances Howard
IN THE MEMORY OF THEE
Lost,
   in the memory of Thee.
Every place
   that I may go,
I see Thy face,
   so calm,
   so peaceful,
   in Thy place;
though much too soon.
Even in my happy days,
   are times that used to be.
I find myself,
   lost,
in the memory of Thee.

Gail Sparks Littrell
TRUE PEACE
I am peaceful, I am still,
I am blessed with His perfect will,
God holds my pen as I write this
   line,

Without His guide my way I
   could not find.
My thoughts come flowing like a
   spring,
Nothing can hinder my poems to
   ring.
Peace on earth and perfect love,
Comes openly now from God
   above.

Dusty Roads

Dusty Roads
BLUE HYACINTH
I love you Kelly, how I love You
Meet me again on the Avenue
I long for your Presence
My happiness is You
So meet me again on the Avenue.

You live on the outskirts of Town
That's where my heart Belongs
I love you more than I Love
My boots of Blue
Fair maiden—I wish I was part of
   You
So I could live out my Dreams
In a brand new Life
I would die for You
When I swing from the Gallows
Please don't Cry.

I love you sweet Kelly—I believe
   in You
You are a mountain of Beauty
That sparkles—like Sunset
On the waters of English Bay
You are the Goddess I worship
   each Day
At your Command
I'll fight the army of the I.R.A.
To prove my love for You
And I'll return with an Irish Rose
For you to Wear
In your light Auburn Hair.

I draw your face in the Clouds
As the night turns to Day
From a Greyhound Bus
On the Interstate Highway
My love for you is so cinematic
We could make a movie—an
   outdoor Classic
You could play an Angel
From the hills of Missouri
And I would play the Bracero
Whom you protect from the Law.
I love you Kelly—O how I love
   You
Meet me again on the Avenue
I long for your Presence
My happiness is You
So meet me again on the Avenue.

Sandra M. Farmer
SEASON'S GREETINGS
The sky is a mixture
In equality
Of the presence and absence
Of all light

The air is tangible
And available in handfulls
The sun sits spellbound
White faced, looking out at day
In frozen antipathetic expression
Hiding behind laced grey clouds
While in a temporary state
Of suspended animation

The layered look
Is always in style
This time of year
Especially when early mornings
Find Jack Frost's calling card
All over the place

Winter's Eve is upon us
Can't you feel it?
Autumn is coming
To an end

It's time to button up
The overcoat of your mind
And gather your scattered thoughts
And misinterpreted realities
Together
Before the comforting fires
Of your intellect
As you prepare
For Winter's beginning
And the year's end—

Pearl Snow Poulton
MY DREAM
I dream of the day when some
   rich man will say, "Let us buy
   an old farm where children can
   stay!"
A farm quite complete in its old
   fashioned way, to let children
   live like their grandparents
   day.
Where lamps will be lit, where an
   organ will play, and the
   laughter will come from the
   barns filled with hay.
Where girls can ride horses
   because they're so mild—yet
   the boys can pretend that their
   horses are wild.
Where trees can be climbed to
   look over the land, and the
   cows can be milked—by the
   farmers own hand.

If you've neices and nephews,
   who've never been close to a
   cow, or asked to gather eggs
   they just wouldn't know how.
We have parks, museums, and zoos,

that do charm.
But I dream of the day we can
   visit a farm!

Judy Van Roekel
MEMORIES
The time goes on
   even though I have stopped
All the special things
   I loved to do
For when a person you
   really care for leaves
A part of yourself
   leaves too
It never comes back
   or feels the same
A broken heart
   can't be mend
Even if it could
   it would break again
So I think in
   all my pain
I'll leave this cruel
   world to die
Leave to be happy with
   all my cares gone.
I wish I knew
   why a heart breaks
For if love is love
   it can move mountains
But I guess thats
   one of many fairy-tails

Cynthia K. Hendrickson
THE GIFT
I sat and thought for hours
Of what gifts to give to you.
Of ideas, there were plenty,
But of funds, there were too few.

So I found a special present
And wrapped it all with care.
It's on this specialist of days
With you, my gift I'll share.

Through all the days of the
   coming year,
   And some help from above,
I give to you my special gift . . .
   A years supply of love.

Susan L. M. Ford
AN EVERGREEN'S WISH
Oh, evergreen, that someone fell
If you could speak I know you'd tell
That you grew tall just so you'd be
In someone's home on Christmas
   Eve
To witness love and joy and giving.
You gave up life to witness living.

Margaret L. Grant
I AM NOT ALONE
Things are going wrong
Things are looking down
Why do I feel so lonely
Why do I feel so down?
Could I so easily forget
What the Bible says
Of the suffering and the death of
   Jesus
The heartache and pain He felt
How alone in the garden
While others slept
As He talked to His Father in
   Heaven.
Could you hear Him say
These things I've said?
Things are going wrong
Things are looking down
Why do I feel so lonely
Why do I feel so down?
None of these things would He
   ever think

His love for mankind is too great
He took the suffering, pain and
loneliness
To give us the gift of life.
To be there when we need Him
Or just to hear us talk
To be a Friend and Savior
Listener and Helper too.
So when things go wrong
Or start looking down
When I'm feeling lonely
And start to feel down
I just talk to my Friend
And he helps me along
He cheers me up
And lets me know
He's always there
So I'm not alone.

Sharon Joy Ross
Wish Upon the Christmas Star
Times are getting harder, and jobs
are out of sight.
People are getting desperate and
just can't see the light.
The Holidays are coming up with
all their special cheers,
but many homes will be without
anything but their tears.

There is, however, a special place
where anyone can go,
a place where hope begins again
and calmer waters flow.
Close your eyes and dream and
leave your pain behind.
Think of something beautiful!
Remember someone kind!

Wish upon the Christmas Star
and remember the people you
love.
Be thankful for those you have
with you, and those who have
passed on above.
Just wish upon the Christmas
Star and close your eyes and
dream.
Look inside and you will find it's
never as bad as it seems.

Penelope McMillen Landino
THE AMATEUR
As the words spill out
somersaulting over each other,
I try to catch them
and stuff them
unheard
into my pockets.
But I never learned to juggle.

Sally Ann Schurmur Machalov
It's Christmas In Wyoming
The wind sings its own carol
As it rolls through the prairie
Pine trees sway gently in time
And all the folks are merry.

The neighbors come for coffee
And the men folk add brandy
Mama baked a fresh fruitcake
The kids have lots of candy.

It's Christmas in Wyoming
From the Tetons to Ten Sleep
The little ones are all tucked in
And dad has checked on the sheep.

Come morning, it's cold and clear
The ground crunches with fresh
snow
It's Christmas in Wyoming
Doesn't matter where you go.

The baby Jesus has come
And the reason is so clear
It's Christmas in Wyoming
And we're so glad He is here.

Darlene Finberg
Broken Dreams and Suicide
Many countless tears are cried,
And so many times we run and
hide.
In these times so hard to cope,
Light grows dark and lost is hope.
So many dreams are left behind.
Reasons to keep on get hard to
find.
Until off in the dim and paling
distance,
A person makes that final stand.
But new alternatives are not at
hand,
And that last attempt has
withered and died,
And all you've got left and have
left untried
Are broken dreams and suicide.

Marcele Simpson
THE ROSE
A rose, soft and vibrant after a
gentle rain, saturated with the
morning dew, waiting for the
warmth of the sun to dry her
face.

As she watches the sky for the
dawn to break into a new day,
she stretches her leaves like
hands to recuperate after a
silent sleep.
She puts on her dress of brightest
hue and waits—a child's love
to embrace.

Lydia Carmichael
FOURTEEN KARAT GOLD
*[In dedication to Elizabeth and
Charlie Carmichael for their
Love and understanding.]*
A castle and within I be
To await the love
That was sent for me

A canopy bed sewn with finery of
laces
Crumpled covers
Of love within its traces

A portrait trimmed in 14 Karat
Gold
A face, a man
With strength within untold

A fire, stones to hold its heat
Slowly burns
As ashes heap

A table of marble, delicate and
small
With matching chairs
To seat two guests
In the corner by the wall

Two brandy glasses empty
With the bottle at its side
I feel the warmth within me
As I gaze into his eyes

There I occupy one chair
As I slowly dream
Of the man who speaks to me
Of oceans sweeping deep

In his eyes, I feel passion rarely told
To touch his lips
To see his face
Within the Fourteen Karat
Gold.

Carl Ambrose Watson
LOVE BALLAD
*[Dedicated to Michelle Ashen,
for her inspiration and warm
friendly smile that's always a
part of her. Peace and love
Michelle, peace and love.]*
As I stare into this moonless sky
A million diamonds fill my eye
Reminds me of one so very near
Visions of beauty still so clear
Of dreams together we would share
With loving embraces were
always there
I'm so VERY far away
A lone-ly night, a lone-ly day

Not many more I have to stand
No longer will I feel like a
forgotten man
For you are the love that I long to
keep
In song in prayer, in silent sleep
To hold in my arms in warm
embrace
To lose ourselves in time and
space
The love we have is so VERY
strong
Together in life is where we belong
So I live and wait for the day
While in my arms I hear you say
I LOVE YOU.

Cynthia Lee Sims
REALITY AND FANTASY
Grasp for reality
Never letting your mind slip
(Dip gently into fantasy)
But upon reality you must clip.
(Touch your tongue to snowflakes
Softly drifting with the breeze)
But never let your mind
Wander off with one of these.
Touch the wooden chair
Beside you there,
closer substantiality cannot be
all the while knowing:
Imagination is gnawing at your
heart
to be free . . .

Dot Cochran
Merry Christmas To My Brother
"Dear Brother" How much I miss
you.
"Especially at Christmas" Am I
blue.
You gave your life, for Our
Country.
Yes, you were honorable and true.

But it doesn't stop the loneliness,

Or fill that E-M-P-T-Y, Old Chair.
When the family, all gets
together,
And you are the one, who's not
there.

How I miss the times, spent with
each other,
Singing and playing, your old
guitar,
"Oh! How I cried" When we got
the telegram,
That you had been killed in the
war.

Your last letter told "how you
longed for home"
How cold and lonely, you were
over there.
"Only to come home and sing
again was your prayer".
Now the telegram came before
Christmas.

I can still see that casket, flag
draped,
On that winter day, as they put
you away.
How the sound of the guns, In
salute went thru me,
And the ringing of the bugle, as it
played.

But I know you prayed, in that
old fox hole,
And I prayed and our prayers
were both heard.
Cause now you're not cold, sad, or
lonely,
As you gave your—life, and soul,
back to God.
I know God heard, and was true
to his word.

I know someday, we'll meet, again
in Heaven.
And you and I will again, "Sing
and Play".
Then the ANGELS will be
singing with us".
And we shall "give God All The
Praise".
For Heaven is F-O-R-E-V-E-R and
E-V-E-R.
And not just for a few hours, or a
few days.

Ruth J. Smith
Ruth's Christmas Dream
If I could spend Christmas in
Heaven
What a glorious time that would
be,
If I could sing carols with Angels
My heart would fill with glee.

If I could walk on streets of pure
gold
If I could bring presents to the
King,
I'm sure my eyes would be blinded
By the beauty of EVERY thing.

If I could sit by the crystal clear
river
And gaze at the azure blue sky,
I would be oh, so peaceful and
content
Knowing my Saviour was so nigh.

But since this is only a dream
And on earth I must longer
remain,
I'll live each Christmas while here
In a way the Lord would acclaim.

I will tell the world about Jesus
Who in a manger was born,
And of the love He gave us
On that FIRST Christmas morn.

So when my life on earth is ended
And the call of my Lord is given,
I will have lived in such a way,
That I CAN spend Christmas in
Heaven.

Susy A. Wiggins
HIS GLORY

Jesus is my life . . . my all,
my bright and morning star!
In all of heaven and on earth . . .
the greatest name by far!

Fairer than the fairest rose . . .
or the lilies of the field;
Brighter far than all God's lights
by day or night reavealed.

In the beauty of His Glory,
my heart doth kneel in
awe . . .
Though He was meek and lowly,
'Twas in Him God . . . men saw!

Pearl R. Lindberg
Bring Heaven Closer To You.

Bring Heaven closer to you
Light up the stars,
That shine through the night
Keeping moonbeams all sparkling
bright.

Grass sleeping beneath the snow
Awakens when spring winds
blow,
God's touch makes miracles on
land
Now softly carpeted by His
loving hand.

May tender memories soften your
grief
And bring Heaven closer to you,
Your loved one will always be by
your side
Time and space will never divide.

Bring Heaven closer to you
Soft silvery moon spreads a glow
on sleeping land,
With happy hours belonging to
you
Is wakened by God's loving hand.

Kirsten Guyaz
BLACK

If you look into an old, hollow
tree,
The black of darkness is heavy;
In layers, so it seems, it is so dark.
I feel it press my eyes shut;
So deep and clear, yet of great
weight.

Vast deepness concealed in the
black
Of an old tree, centuries old, with
Time
To build a wall
Of Black.

Ed De Leal
CHILD'S PLAY

You play with my earth like a
Child plays
With a doll house and Barbie and
Ken;
Playing war with a G.I. Joe
Or pretending to be Superman.
I'm mommy she says as she slaps
at the head

Of the doll she throws on the
floor;
You are dead—fall down—get on
the ground
Or I'll stab you and shoot you
again.
These childrean play and then
put up their toys
On the shelves in the back of the
room.
But you have destroyed, confused
and abused
And try to ignore what you've
done.
You play with my earth like a
child plays,
Tell Me . . . where do you put
the toys?

Rhonda Nadine Boyd, M.A.

Rhonda Nadine Boyd, M.A.
Ze Essence of Universality: Declaration Of Self

*[To Ze Supreme Creator whose
Divine Inspiration, Protection,
and Grace I'll be eternally
grateful . . . To Ze Creator's
Manifestations who have
served as vessels of Divine
Wisdom: Alice Faltz, Mary A.
Boyd, Richard J. Boyd, Lillie
McDonald, Larry Sawyer, Jean
Walls, Harvie Andrews, Zellene
Long, Dennis Long, and the
many others who will touch
my life.]*
To transcend the realm of Time,
To be truly a Universal Love
Spirit . . .
Effervescent. Ongoing.
Being . . .
A mirage to the weary desert
traveller.
To scale Mt. Everest, and touch
the sky.
To Say, "Hello, Yahweh. Is this
what
Heaven looks like? . . ."
To be ageless is to be a
Universal Being.
One who slowly, painfully,
erases the
prejudices and "bug-a-boos" that
can
render one blind, deaf, mute, and
totally s-e-n-s-e-l-e-s-s.
(However, the pain seeps into
your "cavern-
like" mind when you realize—
that being
senseless is truly *not* your forte
in life!)

Revelations yield a cornucopia
of sheer
Dee-light *(particulary those of a
spiritual
nature, y'all).*
Yes, to transcend the three-
dimensional world . . .
Yes, to be a Multi-dimensional
Universal Love
Spirit . . . *That is my forte in life!*

Belinda Boydston
DREAMS OF LOVE

When I dream of romance
And the one that I love
It reminds me of peace
And the bird called the dove.

But when my dreams are shattered
And he is gone,
It reminds me of skips
In my favorite song.

If my dreams are full-filled
And he is back in my heart,
I hope and pray forever
That we will never part.

D. Toul
MY DARLING BOY

The world is a cold, cold place,
but you give it warmth with
your smiling face my darling
boy.
The world is an ugly and
awkward place, but you give it
grace with your sparkling blue
eyes my boy.
And the world is a lonely sphere,
I couldn't bear it if you were
not here my baby boy.
The sun would shine and give a
glow, but I would not feel or
see it so without you my boy.
And people would talk, and
laugh, and smile at me, but
only total darkness would I see
were you not here my bright
boy.
And I would only have a
shattered life, an empty home,
a heartbroken wife if you left
my arms my sweet sweet joy.
So now you know what you mean
to me, my soul would ache
through eternity without you
to love my wondrous boy.
I find it impossible to give more
love to anyone than I can give
to you my precious son, my
darling boy.

Peggy Hammer
Christmas Eve Pilgrims

For Christmas Eve Pilgrims
The church bells are ringing,
And as we stand by candlelight
The full choir is singing.

We make our way home
Through the softly falling snow—
Filled with Christmas spirit
As white lights on branches glow.

Our friends gathered 'round.
All fill the air with mirth
And give us a sense
Of what life is worth.

We gaze upon the night
And think of all the joy

And happiness that's come to us
From the birth of that baby boy.

Mary Lou Willoughby
WHO FED THE SHEEP?

Who fed the sheep
That first Christmas day?
Who tended the manger?
Who freshened the hay?

Who comforted the mother?
Who guarded the Child?
And who fed the shepherds—
So meek and mild?

Who thanked the innkeeper,
Who turned not away,
But made room for the family
On Christmas day?

Your Lord and my Lord
He did it—that's who
And does it today
Through me and through you.

Joseph Pahls
EVENING SONG.

The evening breeze dies to a
murmur
And the rustling leaves are
stilled.
The song of the bird is hushed,
And only the Cicada's rasping
call is heard.
All sounds are muted
As earth prepares her child for
slumber.
Far in the western sky
The sinking sun
Stains clouds with gold and rosy
hues,
As if painting a portrait
For day to remember.
Suddenly deep night falls,
And high in the purple sky
A lone star twinkles
And all is serene—day sleeps.

Sheryl Hegedus
HEAVEN

Heaven is that special place,
Where God sends us to "live."
When we are done with Earthly
things,
But still have more to give.

He dresses us in purest white,
And gives us golden wings.
And issues us a harp to play,
As everybody sings.

Marsha W. Martin
Ode To Daddy and Mama

I used to just take it for granted, I
guess
That you were my parents by
chance, more or less
But now that I'm older I know
that's not true
There are millions of reasons
God sent me to you.

He sat on His throne and He
pondered, one day
This child bound for earth—in
whose womb it should lay.
He said, "My Son help me these
parents to find.
They must have much patience
and be loving and kind.

She's a head-strong small girl,
much attention she'll demand
So we must have wise parents
with a firm, loving hand."
As a Father and Son looked down

from above
They spotted a couple just filled
with their love.

They were hard working
Christians—just right for the
task
Of rearing and loving this
difficult wee lass.
With no need for words they just
nodded and smiled,
They had found the right home
for this new earth-bound child.

God planted the seed, in His
wisdom He knew
He had made the right choice
when He sent me to you
And He's blessed and reblessed us
so much thru the years
With so much joy and laughter,
so very few tears.

There's a special reward for these
parents They chose
For their faith's remained strong
thru the good and the woes.
And He says to His son in His
soft-spoken voice
"There's no question about it—
We made the right choice."

Joseph Nelson Bailey
I THANK YOU
Books on the shelf
Of this poetic world,
You bring atmosphere
That I may sustain.

And poets in vigor,
Your words are food
Your verse is water
Your sense is air to me.

An understanding so crisp
Of mud and man.
I bow in envious respect
This mind so very caged.

Doris Schmitt
LEMONADE
*[To my husband, Don For your
confidence and encouragement.]*
I sit at the picnic table
Sipping my lemonade.
My thoughts adrift in a fable
As I watch the ice-cubes fade.

The wind swishes through the
trees
To my great forlorn!
For my lemonade topples with
the breeze
The lemonade, which I now adorn.

Adelaide Marie Pye
DEFIANCE
I may be here against my will
Because I've nowhere else to go;
And you may think that you
have won,
That you have killed my need to
grow,
That you have made me like the
rest,
Dependent on you for all things,
Another puppet for your shelf
To dance if you but pull the
strings.

But I am not one of your pawns,
My mind is mine, my soul is
mine.
You may now have the upper
hand
But I am merely biding time.

For you can never touch my soul,
That part of me that's really me:
It's what I am deep down inside
And it will always keep me free!

Madge Mullins Wilbanks
SITTING DUCKS
*[For T.H.W. ". . . who
understands and still cares . . ."]*
Line them all up;
the bits and pieces ready to add
up to
Nothing except broken, rejected
entries
in a life's contest bespeaking
nothing;

No chance to win as in a
shooting gallery
and the rat-a-tat-tat of barking
guns,
Felled ducks straddling a pulled
cord of
wood, metal;

Life's contest lies in shambles
before the world's glaring eyes
Staring and seeing the gaping
void to never
fill but with unrealized dreams

Never consummated, never seen
but as
a marked duck in a shooting
gallery
At a state fair long ago when
there was
more than a chance for
everything

Until the nothingness came,
covered my
known world like an
unfriendly pall over
A brown, metallic casket sealing
forever
the smothering smell of finis.

Linda Hufford
MONEY
Money, what can you do for me?
Can you love me, hold me, make
me a tree?
Can you give me a river crystal
clear?
Can you make my heart so it
never need fear?
Tell me money, if you are so
great;
Can you give me a smile, and a
kiss, and a mate?
And money even if you could,
Would you make all our
problems understood?
What about our emotional needs?
Can you furnish the answer to
our spiritual pleas?
Would you give me intelligence,
wisdom, and grace?
Could you make *all* the people
only one race?
Tell me money so proud, and so
valued,
Will you bring me peace, and a
loving mood?
I wonder money if you can,
You see you were made by a man.
If man were so clever on his own,
He wouldn't have to ask God for
a loan,
To help him when you fail your
task.
To help *him* when he's to proud
to ask.

I think both money and man can
see,
Without God neither can be free.

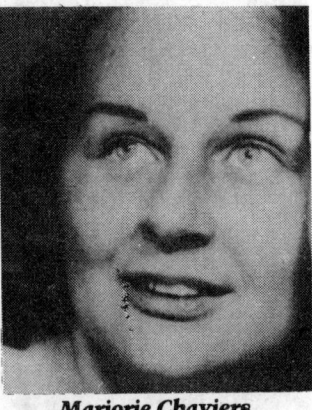

Marjorie Chaviers

Marjorie Chaviers
OUR JACKIE
On April, the fourteenth, close to
four,
A baby boy knocked on our door.
His knock was feeble; his stay
was short
Before he was called to another
port

I never held him close to me;
His eyes were closed for us to see
No loving smiles, so dear, so sweet
No waving hands or chubby feet.

No baby tears to kiss and dry;
We'll never know the reason why.
Just a bud sent here to earth
To bloom in Heaven in second
birth.

First words were said in another
land
First steps were led by another
hand
We know he's happy and safe up
there
As Angels wipe away all care

But when it's night and no one
can see
Many tears fall silently
And deep in our hearts remains
the fact,
We long to see our beloved Jack

Mark Balobeck
AUTUMN BREATH
Crunch! went the birch-claw
Expiring beneath my heel.
The trees and I, Gasp!

Dorothy Mae Johnson
My Special Friend—Mona
When I feel lonely and filled with
despair
I know that my God does care
For He has blessed me with a
special friend
Her loving, generosity never ends
She's on this earth, living blessed
in God's grace
She's always there to greet me
with a warm embrace
When I am sad and in deep sorrow
She tells me to hope for a brighter
tomorrow.
She too like God is always there
With each other so much we
have shared
When things look so dark and dim

I put all my trust in Him.
For my special friend God gave to
lend
For me again and again
Secret's I've told her with trust to
hold
No one but her and God I've told
Treasures on this earth are
bought and sold
But the treasure in this friendship
is worth more than gold.

Kathleen Horgan
LIFE
*[Dedicated in memory of
Tommy Lowry.]*
Life I will never understand
Because one second you're here
and the next you're not.
Of all the people in the world
why did you go?
You were so young, at the
beginning of your life.
Your life never started, really.
You only got your feet wet.
You never really tasted what life
was all about.
You never felt all the feelings of
life.
You never got to love "that
special person."
You never got to see the world
like you wanted to.
I don't hate you for going, instead
I feel sorrow.
But I don't have to worry about
you any longer,
Because you're at rest and peace,
you don't feel anything
anymore.
But why did you go?
I guess I know why
Because it was God's will it
happened now and not later.

Andrea Vaillancourt
MOM
My life has changed since
she left
I still can't understand
why God took her.
She never did anyone any
harm.
I was only twelve when
she died.
and I didn't exactly
appreciate life's pleasures,
But now I understand
how important
life and love can be
She made me realize this
long after her death,
Mom knew everything,
didn't she!

Ida Martilini Hill
As One Poet To Another
You were the poet then—not I.
The poem you wrote for me
Spoke of cold winter mornings—
You and I clinging to each other
The warmth of our bodies
Daring the wind to chill us.
Your words spilled over with
yearning—
You talked of your dreams . . .
Of an 'us' that could never be.

Now years later—I write for you.
I'll write to tell you . . .
How your face has never faded
from my memory

How well I remember your voice
Softly calling me 'lady'
How I ache knowing that I hurt
  you
How much I want the chance to
  tell you
That I loved you then—and love
  you . . .
  even now.
How much I miss you in every
  part of my life.

I write this for you—
How will you ever know?

Tina Marie McCollister
MY TIME HAS COME
*[I dedicate this poem to Greg,
who has helped me understand
life and its pleasures and to
realize what values a true
friendship can hold. Thank
you.]*
From the window a full moon
  beckons to me.
The moon's rays fall softly to the
  earth,
Splashing its splendor on trees,
  rivers,
Man-made roads and steel
  structures.

I soak up my surroundings; I'm
  not myself
At this point, I see the beauty of
  God's
World and I respect it.
I don't want to partake in modern
  Man's way of survival

I want to be part of God's land
To feel leaves sprout from my
  arms,
To smell like the fragrances of
  wild flowers,
To feel gritty and solid as that of
  the ground.

To be a patch of grass that crawls
  with bugs,
To have someone pull me as a
  single blade
And suck my succulent juices
And to be lain upon by two lovers.

I long to be a river and flow
  through
The course of God's planet,
To swell in anger, lashing out,
Crashing into the land boundries
  of this earth

To be the wind of all seasons,
  changing
Moods with no explanation
  except for

What scientists think they know
To be a mountain that people
  care to attempt
And climb, who try to understand
  my nature
And as a mountain look down
  upon the world
Watching the stupidity of man.

It is time for me to say farewell.
To God's creation; something I
  could never grasp.
My time has come; I have fallen
  prey to death.

Allan Washington
HOME AGAIN
Been such a long time
forgot what it be like
forgot the rawness
the mellowness
of inner-city rhythms
Home again
kicking back
in an easy chair
making myself
to home . . .

Virginia Weber
CHRISTMASTIDE
The olliptical moon
Is stationary in a troubled sky
It shone thru tangled barren
  branches
And time stood still
While growth was hushed and
  slowed
But this was not meant to be.
But for a time—
The negative of repression
The enemy of growth
Can only hold time in its hand
So long—
And it is over
The energy stored bursts forth
From God—Accelerated faith and
  form
Life—The fountain from above
Controls and rolls and re-creates
The light body
Of the risen ones.

Angelo S. Clemente
WHEN I'M AWAY
  when I'm away from

you

  it's March ninteenth
and I'm a poor
    sad swallow
      a million miles
        from
Capistrano

Audi-Cecile
FRIENDS
A day in the sun has only begun
A walk in the rain like a song's
  refrain
Calling to a friend.

The trees and flowers reach for
  the sun
Trying to catch the warm rays of
  love
Given by a friend.

In a sky full of stars so close you
  can touch
The moon encircles the Universe
Reaching out to a friend.

The rivers and lakes hold the
  mysteries
The earth and sky hold secrets

and hopes
Of a life so precious and giving...

When there is a friend
Like you.

Theresa Cepeda Rodriguez
LOVE ROADS
I followed many roads toward love
  and haven't come out right.
Lost in a maze of directions that
  always come to end.

I've searched and searched for the
  road that leads to that special
  someone's heart, yet find
  myself
  circling as if the future were
  my past.

Larry Keith Darr
SOMETIMES
[To Mary McKay]
Sometimes
You want to say somethings
but you don't know how.
Sometimes,
you know you feel things
want to cry out loud.
Sometimes
You want to do things,
not all dreams come true.
Sometimes,
I want to tell you
that I love you.

Samuel Thigpen
PRAYER FOR THE FUTURE
May there always shine
  A flourescent rainbow of
  brightness in the world
      That all may know there
is
      hope

May the dragonflies and
  butterflies of tomorrow
  Eternally flutter their beauty
    To the tune of crickets'
    knees on summer eves

On crisp spring days
  May for eons, waves crash
    thunderously towards shores
      To shake the hand of land

And may we all soon see
  That only through brotherhood
    Could such a challenge be
    met, and dealt with fairly.

Dorothy C. Mercier
JUST BECAUSE
I walk through the streets,
Leaves fall at my feet.
Shimmering stars in the sky
Reflect tears in my eyes.

I have no reason,
There is no cause.
I shed my tears,
Just because

Patricia Ann Cowan
SEASONS OF MY LIFE
In and out of time I twirl
As tho a leaf drifting on a breeze
Fall is here again
With a hint of Winter
And I am older
Entering the Fall of my life
And knowing Winter is coming
Lord, You're with me still
In the childhood of my Summer
In the Spring of my youth
Fall is a favorite season
Will You walk with me through
  the woods

And talk with me and strengthen
  me?
I am alone
With so many thoughts
It feels so good to write a few
  down
Touch me God, I quiver like a
  floating leaf
Turning with the seasons of my
  life
And You my Creator surround me

Deborah Tarket
Imagination vs. Reality
I've got my styles
I've got my smiles
I found a unicorn,
near a tree tall and forlorn,
there I met you
with all your bright smiles
and all your own styles
the unicorn said to me
"set me free"
and you became real to me
I didn't see you at first
the deep shadows immersed
in your body, soul and mind,
the troubles of mankind,
I accepted you as good
I did not know how much I
  understood
In life I stand neither tall nor
  short
In fantasy I await trial in court
holding myself in protection
fighting imperfection
I feel as a prisoner
pent up in thought
thinking of mind wars I have
  fought

Pamela Rossi
POLITICIANS PRAISE
I don't know why.
Maybe it's ego,
Could be peers.

On the stage
Displayed
Like cattle ready for auction.

Each with a chance
To show possibilities.

Stared and stabbed at.
Credentials?
The best meat!

Pick
Choose
The fatted calf.

They may cook you
Or eat you alive.

The losers
Sent back to the fields,
Those chosen few
On to the slaughter house.

Penny Lea Tooley
PEOPLE CARE
*["People Care" was written in
honor and appreciation of three
people who showed they care
at a time when I felt no one
cared. Trish Unruh "lent an
ear", Marvene Pippenger
"offered advice", and Pam Lamb
said, "If you need me, I'll be
there."]*
Sometimes I get tired and weary
  of life,
I want to give up and forget the
  strife.

I start feeling weak and I get real low,
Life seems to come at me, blow after blow.

Insecurity strikes and I cry in despair,
"Am I alone in this world, does anybody care?"

Why haven't I learned and why do I doubt?
God always comes through to help me out.

His technique isn't always the same,
But, He often answers by sending special people to me, and I know them by name.

Those special people have often come to my rescue,
It was those whom I admire and respect that helped me make it through.

Some lent an ear or offered advice to show they care,
While others plainly said, "If you need me, I'll be there."

I was immensely touched by all they taught me through their love and concern,
And I only hope that I can help others and pass on what I've learned.

Now I realize that I'm not alone and people do care,
And most of all God does answer prayer.

Linda Elaine Glidden
GOD'S CREATION
When you look at yourself what do you see?
Can you see all that God has made you to be?
All that you already are that's beautiful and good?
Do you love yourself the way that you should?
Or do you put yourself down and dislike what you see?
Have you ever decided, "I don't want to be me?"
Well look again through the eyes of the one who loved you so much that He gave His own Son.
Look again and this time you will see, "God doesn't make junk, He created me."

Margaret Worman
THE YELLOW ROSE
Bittersweet the petals fall
From yellow blossom, one by one
Till stripped and bare her very soul,
Exposed and trembling,
Stands before the winds of time.
The kiss of Spring which gave her birth has passed.
And gentle Sun's caressing warmth
Whereby her tender bud burst forth
In full delight, withdraws.
Forlorn, subdued,
She bows her head in meek submission
To a stronger will than hers.
She leans toward the earth

to seek her bed
And dreamless sleep with none to mourn her loss.
Yet Spring, remembering his joy may come again
To touch the seeds of life within her soul . . .
Perhaps . . .
She can but wait in cold, dark ground
For some uncertain, distant, day once more . . .
Perhaps . . .
To know his kiss and live again with love,
As yesterday.

Betty L. Richburg
The Peasant Girl Of Dunn Bade Do
HAIL TO ALL! The Chieftain roared
As the Peasant girl fell to the floor,
Rise you Wench! Was his command.
Take care, you feed and tend my men.

She stood defiant her bosom high,
And swore his death beneath his eye.
What say ye? Was his strong command.
She spit, and said, "I tend no man".
He placed his hands about her waist
Do as I say make Haste make Haste.

The beauty of her fiery eyes
Beguiled the Chieftain that she despised.
Here; Drink my Lord this sweetest wine,
And offered her lips to his divine.

His pleasure was his sole content,
To her, his death was all life meant.
A breath, A gasp, and then he knew,
The wench lay smiling Triumphant True.
You'll Die! He groaned his sword ran through,
THE PEASANT GIRL OF DUNN BADE DO.

Margaret M. Brown
Graduation Tribute To Patrice
On a brisk September morning in the year of '64
The Lord looked down on Mom and Dad and called on us once more
To rear another daughter, she was fair as she could be
He said "I'll leave her in your care, please do this job for me."
Well, we tried to do as God had asked, not always equal to the task
For this child was aggressive, of this there was no doubt
As our little faimily was soon to find out.
She was eager and competitive, bound to be a success
We could always be sure she'd compete with the best

For she set her own goals, they were high as the sky
When she couldn't attain them, she'd sit down and cry.
The blame for her failures she'd pass on to us
As she ranted and raved and kicked up a fuss.
She's frustrate her Mother and make her Dad sad
When she'd see what she wanted was not to be had.
Always neat as a pin from her head to her toe,
When it came to helping others, she was never slow.
She'd help with the laundry and run to the store,
Pound at the books and come up with high score.
But, how very quickly time has passed,
And her growing up years are behind her at last;
And as she proceeds down the pathway of life,
Leaving behind all this childhood strife,
We wish her good luck and deep love from within
Love that will be, and always has been.
May she always walk tall, her head high as a cloud,
For she's a daughter of whom we are both very proud!

Jane E. Sadowsky
SURREALISM
The day broke
And the dawn fell through
And splintered on the grass.
And the cotton clouds
Snagged on the mountain tops
And ripped and tore as they struggled loose
And cried.
The wind howled sympathy
While the tears that fell
Washed away the broken dawn
And refreshed the grass.

Laura Palmasani
A Mighty Big Christmas Tree
[To ARIANE May the love, peace and meaning of Christmas always remain in your heart.]
Oh, what a beautiful sight my wondering eyes did see,
On the hillside stood a mighty big Christmas tree,
All wrapped in glitter and gold, around and around the garland was rolled.
The twinkling of a star on high revealed an angel gazing at the sky,
An array of silvery lights did glow as tinsel sparkled on the snow below.
Ornaments so shiney and bright whirled around to my delight!
Toy soldiers that blinked an eye, teddy bears eating honey pie!
Gingerbread men hanging so neat, Reindeer prancing with bells on their feet!
Dolls painting candy canes all red and white,

Snowmen having a snowball fight!
Elves busily wrapping presents with many a bow,
Toy trains that could whistle and go!
'Twas then I heard a merry "Ho, ho, ho" . . .
"Merry Christmas," he sang as his sled glided over the hillside snow . . .
Oh, what a wondrous sight I did see,
It was a mighty big Christmas tree!

Herschel N. McGee

Herschel N. McGee
AMERICA'S RACIAL TALK
Concerning the American's situation
With the Blacks and the Whites
They seem to be getting together
Without too much mess and fight
Seems to be a certain serenity
Yet, a buffer zone
That separates the black and white folks
Especially around the home
America is a new country
Just four hundred years old
Nobody seems to know
Whether it belongs
To the Indians, English or Jews
Old Blackman is just watching
With his sneaky self
Gradually gaining his share
Concerning, the American's Wealth
Yes, all the Americans know
That one thing is true
Togetherness is pertinent
When it comes to war and you
So being fair minded
Praying for the best
America's People love each other
Yet, the fighting exist.

Louise Toy
YOU ARE THERE
You are there
To understand.
You are there
To lend a hand.

You are there
Through my tears.
You are there
To allay my fears.

You are there
To see my joy.
You are there
When I am coy.

You are there

To calm my rage.
You are there
To open my cage.

You are there
To help me change.
You are there
When I act strange.

You are there
To give me hope.
You are there
To make me cope.

You are there
To teach me life.
You are there
To conquer my strife.

You are there
Even when I'm blue.
You are there
And I thank you.

Cheryl E. Ten Eyck
A ROSE
I found outside my door today,
A package wrapped in fine array.
Inside one lone and frail pink rose,
Amidst some greenery for a
    perfect pose.

A card was attached to a ribbon
    yellow,
The rose had come from a special
    fellow.
The card had read "I'm sorry I
    messed up your life"
It had come from my Husband-to-
    me-his wife.

Only one rose, not a dozen or two,
His way of saying—I love you.
As I looked at the rose, and read
    what he wrote,
A tear come to my eye, and a
    lump to my throat.

Can it be possible—can it be true?
These words that he wrote—"but,
    I love you"?
Can we again find happiness?
Will the God of love our marriage
    bless?

I'm so bewildered, so confused,
For I thought to another your
    love I did lose.
My darling, please, give me time,
    help me to deal with the past.
And maybe, with help our
    marriage will last.

Nanci A. Fullam
WISHING
*[I dedicate my poem to my
parents who saved my wishful
life so I could continue to wish,
and above all, hope.]*
How sad when,
All through the
Chapters of a Lifetime,
There are nothing but
Pages which are blank.
No gods above for
Granted favors to thank.
Dressed in memories,
I am what I should
Have liked to be.
The colorful phrases
I wish I had said.
To have lavished love,
Which alas,
Has long been dead.

To have lazed in a meadow,
Trailing fingers in a

Rushing mountain born brook.
To have authored a song, or
Perhaps a book,
Of Philosophy.
To have made a mark,
Something to be remembered.
To have savored the smooth,
Sweet taste of success.
To have arms lifted high
Overhead.
To have shouted to the world,
"Something is Wanted!"

Ah, but to have that warm
Full feeling that,
The something wanted,
Was I.

Bee Coalwell
YOUTH IF FOREVER
I am no relic for all my years.
All hopes and loves of living still
    endure,
And there is laughter as well as
    tears,
So, don't make of me a sepulcher.

A necklace of living I have strung,
And years have added luster to
    the string.
Within my heart I am forever
    young,
And my soul lives on in
    perpetuated Spring.

Without time and aging much is
    lost
Of maturity and richness of
    design.
Beneath the leaves and Autumn's
    frost
The pumpkin lies and ripens on
    the vine.

Linda Lane
AT LAST
*[To Bruce . . . who makes
'lonely' obsolete and 'coming
home' worthwhile.]*
lonely
is this heart
thinking of you,
in the city
at the sea
dear gentle man
my only plea
is
please . . .
come home.

A. Castellanos
IF WE MEET AGAIN
If we meet again
to say hello once more
I'll stare into your bluish eyes my
    friend
and say the words I could not say.
All this time in unison, yet so far
    apart
it was difficult to say
those words that mean so much.
But if we meet again
and we say hello once more
I'll stare into your eyes
and say to you my friend
I loved you all this time.

Vera M. Pearson
Angels Don't Sing Cowboy Music
As I sit in the saddle hat pulled
    down low,
I could think of the many trails I
    rode,

The sweat is caked upon my
    brow,
"I'm tired", I said with a frown,
Cowboy's life is hard you know,
I've branded and roped and rode
    the herd,
The dust is settling and oh I think,
To leave this cowboy world
    behind,
And all those dance floors I did
    shine,
Makes me sad and lonely for I
    know,
Angels don't sing cowboy music,
They sing of the great one up
    above,
They don't know about the cattle,
Nor the spurs you use all day,
My heart is full of all this West,
And with my hat and tattered
    vest,
I'll go my way unto my rest,
Saddle my horse and notch that
    cinch,
My times not come, not just yet,
Sagebrush is blooming, mesquite
    wood fresh,
Cows are calving, bawling all
    around,
Like a new world yet to be found,
Oh I'll dance those tunes like in
    the past,
And polish those dance floors,
    bet on that,
The fiddler will play like in the
    past,
And when I have come to rest,
They will hang up my saddle and
    my chaps,
And a prayer from below to up
    above,
Sing him a tune, "How the West
    Was Won".

Jenean R. Sparks
FOR SINGLES ONLY
It's great to be free
but am I the only one
who needs security?

To have and to hold,
be silent and yet bold.
All these things are a part
of love, I've been told.

I tell myself there's someone
out there but I'd
thought I'd looked everywhere.

I've been from San Francisco,
to good ole L. A.
I can't find anywhere I'd like to
    stay.

I'm on the move all the time.
God, I wish I could find
a place to call mine.

What's happening to me,
I think I'm tired of being free.

Judy Howard
THE CLOWN
The tears of a clown
    falling
        falling softly in his heart
While he wears a big smile
    and makes the others laugh

But he's dying inside.

In the darkness of his dressing
    room
All the others have gone away
His cheerful facade crumbles

And his heart breaks once more
The sunny smile couldn't come
    back even if he forced it
The darkness brings his tears and
    the aching of his soul

Everybody's pal has no one he can
    talk to
Everybody's buddy can't pour out
    the torments in his heart
The guy with no problems cries
    out for someone to listen and
    understand

But he waits in lonely silence
    knowing that tomorrow's dawn
    will bring the people back
And the show must go on

After all, what's a circus without
    the clown?

Paul Vincent Gallon
The Road To Mount Angel
Idly it follows me
Side by side
River and road
Not in a hurry to go anywhere.
Pudding River
Gently flowing with the rhythm
    of the past
Under railway bridges
Past fisherman
Meandering and wandering
    across the countryside.
I feel no grief that your simple
    ways have made
A short journey long.

Rosie M. Hairston

Rosie M. Hairston
MOTHERHOOD
There is no feeling quite as special
    As the stirring inside my body
Of another life beginning to take
    shape,
    For the whole wide world to see.

Just to think, that there's a little
    heart
    Which beats a little stronger
    each day;
And that there's a little mind
    developing,
    Which'll have a lot of things to
    say.

To share one's body and to
    shelter a life
    Is a blessed responsibility;
And to watch life emerge on its
    own
    Is one of the greatest joys to me.

To nourish it, shelter it and
    clothe it;

To educate it and watch it grow;
And to share in its development
Is one of the greatest
satisfactions I know.

Jean L. Egyed
MIDNIGHT SYMPHONY
*[Because I do not see well, my
hearing ability is clearer while
listening to the night sounds,
this poem came to my mind]*
One night in June
Under the moon
You can hear a special tune
That the animals croon
At the midnight symphony

In the old oak tree
The owl hoots his melody
In perfect harmony
Cause he's glad to be
At the midnight symphony

The bull frog crokes
A certain note
Down in his throate
Who knows, who wrote
At the midnight symphony

What a fling
The crickets sing
With their feet they bring
A special ring
To the midnight symphony

You can hear the cayote ball
Listen to his call
He says "come you all
To Pound Hall"
To the midnight symphony

In the June night air
Theres contentment there
At this animal fair
With their songs to share
At the midnight synphony

Tammie Jones Traylor
I'LL BE THERE
"I'll be there" are words people
often say
    As they try to ease the burdens
    along you way,
Though your spirits are
    sometimes raised then
    You know that your troubles
    cannot be solved by men.

Of course your friends will be
there,
    The good and bad true friends
    will share;
And there is relief in knowing
too,
    That they really care about
    what happens to you.

You know that mama is always
by your side
    She'll cover her worries and
    hide her pride,
And you'll know in her you can
confide
    As you feel the love she holds
    deep inside.

Thank God for mamas and
friends too,
    Without them, what would we
    do?
To whom would we turn and
where would we go?
    If no one else cares when our
    spirits are low.

But if God made friends and

mama to be there,
    Then He Himself must
    earnestly care.
He must know and He must
really understand:
    Maybe that's why, He watches
    with an outstretched hand.

Maybe that's why He said, "I'll be
there
    And all your burdens, I'll help
    you bear,
And should you call, I'll always
hear,
    Should you fall, I'm always near.

If you should cry, I'll dry your tears,
    I'll fight your battles and calm
    you fears;
But it's a team effort and you
must share,
    You must first believe, and
    then I'll be there".

Virginia Dabney Badham
A Night In Featherly Park
*[To my revered parents whose
lives have been my lifelong
inspiration.]*
All the mixed sweet fragrances of
    the forest fill the night
As stars look down upon the
    silent Earth
My rapturous heart takes sudden
    prism'd wing
To meet in weightless exstacy
    my Dawn's new birth!

Gillis J. Chiasson

Gillis J. Chiasson
TRAILS KNEW LIFE
Did you ever think, when a path
    you see,
Old and worn its' brink by
    footsteps before thee?
Who made these trails; and where
    were they going?
To a somewhere life prevails,
    these paths are always
    knowing.

Far away from roads new, it was
    traveled long ago:
I just wonder by who, and where
    did they go?
Their things may be here, they
    could not carry . . .
Left to return another year; time
    forbid them to tarry.

Old trail tell me, you are so wise:
Secrets with you be when the
    traveler dies.
Awesome is the feeling, yet so real:
Life's fore picture stealing,

trails footsteps feel.

I can almost see those who came.
Time alone holds the key: they'll
    not return again.
Oh! such a story these unchanged
    paths could tell,
Be time sorry, pictures known,
    today doesn't dwell.

Evelyne Butler Heringson
**A Gift Of Thanks and
Praise**
*[To my Lord and to my parents,
Edward J. and Annie L. Butler]*
I'm thankful, Lord, for all of Your
    days.
In sunshine I can see the glory of
    Your resurrection
And be glad because now I too
    can live.
When it's cloudy, I know Your
    light is still shining
And will break through the
    clouds again.
When it's rainy and windy, I can
    think of Your living water
    cleansing me,
And the breath of Your Spirit
    blowing my chaff away.
Snow and ice bring thoughts of
    Your purity and crystal
    clearness.
In the vibrant stillness I can hear
    the bells of heaven ringing
    their glad allelulias.
Winter is but a prelude to spring,
    a time of rest and reflection,
    renewing and strengthening,
So that when spring comes, like
    the flowers, I too can burst into
    bloom
And sing joyous songs of praise
    to You, My Lord!

Kelly Klim
A NEW AWARENESS
I've learned to love
And feel pain;
I've learned to smile
And not be ashamed.
I've learned to care
And not worry about rejection;
I've learned to admire
And oversee slight imperfections.
I've learned to open my eyes
And see the sun shine;
I've leaned to forget
And not look behind.
I've learned to have confidence
And cherish each day;
I've learned to love
And the hardships now pay.

Dorothy Jeanette Lyons
I RECALL
When I was a child, so full of
    dreams,
I thought the world was so great,
I knew nothing about the real bad
    things,
The prejudice and all the hate . . .

I knew nothing about jealousy
    and envy,
those things that some held
    within,
To me everyone was always the
    same
and there was no need to pretend. . .

But then I grew older and more
    aware,

that things weren't really the same,
There were separate places, for
    separate people,
Who all had separate names . . .

I asked my grandmother about
    this,
For I was a country girl . . .
She told me, "Dorothy, it's all
    God's will,
it's just a part of the world."

But still I didn't understand it,
Why should I be abused?
Because I hadn't done anything
    wrong,
Why should I be accused?

I guess that in my Grandmas' days
You did as you were told,
You didn't talk back or say bad
    things,
If you wanted to live to grow old. . .

My Grandma's dead and gone now,
But her words will always remain
on my mind and in my soul,
So very, very plain.

I was sometimes so puzzled,
And so very full of doubts
About all of the troubles
that we could live without. . .

In my years, I've seen a lot
Some are determined to make it,
And others are not

But I've always had
a determined mind,
And I simply refused
to remain behind. . .

I came to the conclusion,
All by myself,
That I'm as good, or better
Than anyone else.

I'd like to see my Grandmothers'
    face,
If today she could look at this old
    place
And see that life can be unreal,
But to love one another is really
    Gods' will.

Betty J. Beam
THE ENABLER
I'm a needle pulling the knotted
    thread
That pieces small remnants of
    daily life.
I'm not the joint of beef, nor the
    loaf of bread;
But a miller's wheel, and a
    carver's knife.

I'm not a tapestry gracing the
    grand
Throne room in the castle of
    cold, dead kings;
Nor warp, nor woof; nor the loom,
    nor quick hand—
I'm a weaver's flying shuttle that
    sings.

I'm not the archer, nor his strong
    right arm;
Nor the straight arrow that flies
    swift and free.
I'm the bow that's bent at sound
    of alarm,
And I'm crafted from the
    lemonwood tree.

I'm not the mason, nor the
    finished wall;
Nor hard brick that cures in the

kiln. I say
That I'm a plumb bob, a fine trowell; all
The bonding mortar of slaked lime and clay.

I'm not the builder nor the strong I—beam;
Nor mausoleum with a round arched dome.

I'm hammer. I'm nail. I'm architect's dream
Of the blazing hearth that makes house a home.

I'm not the sun that gives earth heat and light,
Nor am I sower, nor dry dormant seed;
I'm rain that falls in the cool of the night
When the seedlings and parched plants are in need.

I'm a wind that fills the frigate's broad sail
As it stands becalmed at sea; and I know
That progress made whenever I prevail
Seldom's credited to me. Still I blow.

I'm numbered as the stars that spike the sky,
And never maker, but the maker's tool;
I'll—stained by mediocrity; yet I
Am blessed, and knowing truth, am no man's fool.

Dan Burns
THE FLAME
We all know
That our bleeding hearts
Doubt all that is
Real or unreal
But
They do not doubt
Our souls inner voice that
Tells us that we suffer
And in the midst
Of our lonely soul
Is a trace of frozen love
Waiting for the day to
Come when anothers love will
Be the warmth it needs
To melt away and become
Tears of happiness and
Joy

Kelly Krueger
Living: A Natural Dream
[To Rod For being a living dream]
Three chariots carry my heart through the sky to places I'd much rather be;
For reasons so obvious I cannot deny discovering the limits of me.

Riding the ebbs of a furlowing cloud searching for the trail of an endless sunbeam;
In the midst of its warmth, I long to be endowed and blest with its light to show me a dream.

My sails ache for the wind and its powers to courteously beckon the journey procede;
Not to be drown by the misgiving rain showers

for they cleanse the heart so inclined to bleed.

Light, wind and water are chariots so steady that no darkness ever could empty or blind;
For in me they now are my mind, breath and blood ready, to continue the journey, to seek and to find.

Helen A. Scieszka
YOUR TOUCH
[For Pickle—who touches my soul—Challenges, encourages & inspries me to be the best of all that I am.]
I walked by the ocean tonight— with friends and yet, alone, but not lonely.

The ocean, the sand, the stars and the night filled me, almost overwhelmed me, with a sense of peace, serenity and a heaviness with thoughts of you.

I longed to feel the touch of your hand in mine.
To know that you were sharing all with me.

But, only sadness walked with me—
Until, the water ran across my feet—
and somehow, I felt your presence—
and knew that it wouldn't always be this way.

Joe David Jones
SONNET FOR A LADY
[To Judy, my lady, my wife, my life.]
Ladies are ladies as the word gender does imply
Some housewives, some nurses, some mothers, some all
The pure air around them is precedence to a man's sigh
Forever in their summer of life, though it be spring or fall

The platitudes proclaim its a clothe of elegant order
No mortal could possess men's souls as do these
Agreed—Their existence in the real or unreal world does border
For I know of a lady who could bring Gods to their knees

Shes the lady I'll cherish for as long as there's time
Devotedly sharing with me joys, that few couples have pleasured
Be she Angel or mortal I care not, as long as she's mine
For my love of this lady can never be measured

I'm sure in my heart that heaven did send her
For an unearned reward to this mere carpenter

Hazel Riley
ALWAYS
When you've grown old and your health is gone
And you find yourself sitting all alone

When you look around and you wonder where
Are the ones you thought would always care
When you feel you're at your lowest ebb
When you realize you're a victim of lifes cruel web
When you feel there's no reason left to live
And you know you still have love to give
When you cry for one who really cares
Turn around, and I'll be there.

Leslie Anne Roby
FREEDOM
I wish I could be free; like a bird in flight,
Soaring over trouble without any fright
Drifting on winds from unknown places
Not having to remember names or faces
Floating smoothly on the river of air
Passing my life without concern or care.

Todi McGuire
TWO MOTHERS
You begin your existence in the dark womb of your Mother before you're born.

You end your existence in the dark womb of Mother Earth when you die.

Rubin Morris Hanan

Rubin Morris Hanan
AN OLD MAN'S PRAYER
Almighty God of all that is fair and good,
Help us in the twilight of our days
To remember and to honor Thee.
We would humbly raise our voice in praise
Of Thy great works, and thank Thee for the years
Thou hast bequeathed to us. Grant we may find
Time to serve Thee well. Awake our hearts
To persevere both with the heart and mind
I all humility, and always let us live
In Thy precepts. Let Thy unspoken voice
Guide us assurance that we may rejoice

To walk with Thee. We pray Thee for new strength
In the obligation of our duty—
Cleanse our hearts of all unfaithfulness—

Keep us aware of hope and love and beauty.
Let our lives stand a monument to Thee,
Safe in the knowlege that we are Thy own.
Forgive us our transgressions that we may
Some day join Thee at Thy celestial throne.

Blanche Proffitt Taylor
The Kingdom Of God Is Love
How do we enter into
Thy Kingdom today
The Kingdom of LOVE
Do you give when we pray?

Pray without ceasing
Pray without doubt
Enter into Thy Kingdom
And never re—route.

Abide and live
In the Kingdom of Love
And his Glory will cover
With His Power manifold;

O'God, how great
And too deep for man
Until man is willing
For his soul to expand;

Expand in God
By entering as one
And rising up higher
Through Jesus His Son.

Donna Crosby
CONTEMPLATION
I'm sitting at the top of my stairwell.
My wine glass is half full.
I like the tone it makes when I thump it with my finger.

How novel I must look, from my perspective.
I've been thinking about my relatedness to others.
A car pulls up next door; I know when I have a visitor.

This emptiness can be overbearing;
My attitude doesn't aid the matter much either.
Opposites don't necessarily attract
My loneliness doesn't warrant a lover by its presence.

Yesterday, when we met for coffee,

I felt like when I did a speech the day before.
My nervousness was apparent; I contemplated leaving.

I told you about the speech and took a sip of tea.
You told me that you could only stay for a short while.
I had expected that and was disappointed.
I needed to study anyway and told you so.

We're getting an early morning rain outside.
I'm glad I talked myself out of running.
I'll fast today for as long as I can.

Our eyes engaged one another. It was blatant.
Energy saturates me; I'm no longer in your company.
This is a modest distraction; it doesn't engulf me.

You make me take notice of my mortality.
You build up energy that I can't possibly expend.

Lynn Kornelson—Spenst
PATTERNS

Breakers curl and slowly
reach
to touch
the patterned sand,

Adding an edge of
lacey white
to
complete this
linen land.

Christine C. Aubert
Our Evolution: We Within Us
The planets develop. However, the riddle of their
Creation is not the only amazement of their birth
That involves our earth—and our evolution! The puzzle
Continues long after the evolution of a speck
Within the currents and the seas emerge into a Life,
A zygote, blossoming from creatures—to people. Many
Leave to become space travelers, and many come to be

Time travelers also. Exploring
through the area
Furthur and further out from

where we live, we map the skies
And find there are other worlds about besides our own home.
Curious, interested, fascinated, we visit
Each world farily much in turn, and find we travel into
Our own future (as well as into others') and become
Our own descendents. And, we travel into our own past

And others', and become our own ancestors. And, it is
We who are the astronauts from outer space, the seeders
And, the seeds of our own and of other worlds, the far off
Visitors who come to earth to check up on our own growth,
And who wait and watch patiently, yet interfering with
Only a helpful hand when necessary, until we
Are ready to be rejoined with "Them"— our own people: ourselves.

Sheri Fritz
LIFE
[*This poem was written to Roberta Miller, for her friendship to me through ups and downs.*]
Why does life have to change?
One day there are friends all around.
Next, they're only there a few times.
Then they aren't there at all.
They have said,"We'll be there, if you ever need us."
Well, where are they, now that they're needed?
I guess change is what makes life so real.
But why does it have to be real sometimes?

Patricia A. Paton
The Meaning Of Humanics—PART 1 Humanity By Birth
Gentle gravity nudges me,
To leave my cushy reverie.

Soft walls enclose abiding night.
I struggle with my newborn flight.

I hear your voice, "It won't be long . . ."
A surge of strength . . ., but then it's gone.

"Philanthropy!" I cry in pain.
"Philanthropy. Is that your name?"

Responding to your guiding lore,
Brought entry through the channel door.

(Philanthropy, to me, is "he".
Philanthropy, to you, is "she".

This "he" or "she" must surely be,
The abundant "giver" of humanity.)

"I wish her life easier than it was for me."
The wish is the meaning of humanity.

Humanity is humor; humanity is love.
Humanity? The soft, sad song of the beautiful mourning dove.

This innocent child, "Have mercy," I weep.
"Into your hands, I relinquish my keep, Philanthropy."

Julie A. Quintero
A REMINISCENT SONNET
My love, for you I will cherish always
the many thoughs that may come to my mind
of our love that lasted for may days
of the times that you were tender and kind
of the ways you made me love you much more
than any woman could love any man
the times that you helped me open the door
that led me to do the things that I can
of flowers you gave me that smelled divine
while giving me such wonderful delight
of times that you told me you were just mine
while we loved each other with all our might
My love, I shall always remember you
and the many thoughts of our love so true.

Donald McAnally
NEW BOY IN TOWN
[*To my first grandson, Thomas Michael Hartle, and all parents and grandparents in the free world.*]
There he lays in his germ proof bed,
Two pounds of black hair on his head.
Crying and screaming every once in a while,
Family members hoping that he will smile.
Dressed up pretty in his open backed gown,
It's easy to tell, he's the new boy in town.

No one can tell or no one can say,
The things he will try from day to day.
But one thing's for certain and this is right,
He'll cry Mommy all day and Daddy all night.
So Here's to the parents, as they strut around
Letting everyone see the new boy in town.

Mary M. Gillespie
Day After Christmas For Little Joe
Little Joe got up this morning, looked all around,
But an inkling of Santa couldn't be found.
Gee, I wonder where Santa could be after being
Out and traveling so late.
Mom told me she didn't know, for if she did
She would have told me so.
Dad said he saw him by the old garden gate,

For when he came home it was very late.
"Headed North, I believe," Dad said, "with his
Reindeers and an empty sled."
If I could only see Santa today!
I want to thank him for bringing me a sled.
That sled, it goes like a whiz.
Down that slope I went in a spin;
Just to get up and off again.
What a fast one, but a lot of fun . . . and so nice.
Man, how it went when it struck the ice.
Not only the sled was nice, but Santa left
Many games and two toy mice.
Mom said, "No need to worry, get on your way—
Just run along—and don't hurry.
Say good morning to your friends and teacher
And don't forget to nod your head if you pass a preacher.
You see, I have a way of knocking and kicking
And a real sassy way of lippin.
But I still can't help but think of poor old Santa
As I step along on such a lovely snowy morn.
I still want to thank Santa from the bottom of my heart.
That's why I got off to an early start.
Oh, there he is; Oh, there he isn't.
Santa, Oh Santa, wait up.
I want to say,
"Happy New Year, Happy New Year's Day."

Tammie Regina Stemm
PRISONER
A room becomes a silent wall.
A door expells no passage.
I stay in chains, apart from all,
—Condemned and everlasting.

My prison, it is not a cell
With gates and bars enclosing,
But life, which often brings a swell
Of longing and unknowing.

Existing days, I share alone
The hours of my darkness.
I'm warmed by fires never shown,
—So coldly bare and lifeless.

Enclosed and haggard, worn by this
The very life they've sent me,
I have but need, and shadowed kiss
And words I often envy.

Lorraine K. Sheetz
THE OLD FARM
[*To Dad and in memory of mother. To my sisters and brothers, especially my "old pal" Don.*]
During war number two, I was reaching my early teens
On a lonely farm, I can vision in my dreams
Though we were only tenants, those long, trying years
Toiling hard for a pittance, our joys surpassed the tears

Dear Dad, worked from early dawn to earn his meager pay
We five children tried to help, often getting in the way

Now I remember the good times,
some of my best
　Always when September nears,
　memories fill my breast

I remember home grown
watermelons, cooling in the
stream
　Home made root beer and ice
　cream, made us beam!
Playing in the hay now, running
over feilds and hills
　Chasing pigs and cows, riding
　goats and mules for thrills

I loved the smokehouse scents of
sausage, bacon and ham
　Memories of pretty jars of food,
　especially the jam
Homegrown popcorn sure
cheered a cold winter night
　Gingerbread too, from the old
　Kalamazoo, was a real delight

Brothers and sisters to care for,
them caring for you
　Parents who loved us and loved
　each other, too
Being terribly poor, but too proud
to cry
　Accepting disappointments,
　never asking "why?"

Back to those days, in a moment,
I would go
　Give mom a kiss, tell her we
　loved her so
Ah! Yes, memories of "home" and
my wish is this
　Where ever my children roam,
　they remember home with bliss!

Barbara K. Connell
AN AWAKENING
[*To Michael—Thank you for
the help and encouragement.*]
It has been far to long
since I have seen
the children playing
with wild abandon
or
watched the lovers
stroll through the park
on a cool
lazy evening

Awaken to me
beautiful day
show me these signs
of newborn life
for this is
the spring of my years

Tommy Eileen Shore Weigand
His Dream Came True!
His eyes would sparkle
and his eyes would shine—
while looking at cowboy boots
in the stores all the time.
He never had a pair
of his very own—
But he'd wear hand—me—downs
from which his brothers
had out—grown.
Mostly clad in cheap, torn
tennis shoes—
are what you wear when mom
and dad are buying shoes
for quite a few.
And now my boy has just
turned seven—
and for his birthday
there they were—"Cowboy
Boots!". . .

the child looked like he
was in seventh heaven!
His desire was for him
to even be able to wear
these brand new boots to bed—
but, "No", is what
his mama said.
My boy walks upon these heels
with a great pridish stride-
because these boots are his. . .
and his alone. . .he knows this
fact. . .
from deep inside.

Jessie Dray Terrell
SONG OF FREEDOM
Freedom was the aim
of America at birth
And may it never perish
from our corner of the earth.
Freedom bravely sought,
freedom dearly won . . .
The gift of our forefathers,
Freedom is for everyone!

With freedom for all
free we'll ever be;
And to the world we'll show
our joy in being free . . .
If daily, our way of life,
we live without fears:
This heritage we've proudly
cherished through the years.
For God has blessed us . . .
In this great land we live,
Thus to God and nation
All honor we do give . . .
As we honor those who've died
That America could be
A Land of Liberty!
As we honor those who'll die
That America will stay
The Land of Freedom!
that she is today.
With freedom to keep her Flag
unfurled,
Freedom to help the nations
of the world,
Freedom to share our destiny . . .
To keep America a land forever
free!
God help America, and the whole
world, to be free.

Donna J. Stammerman
UNTITLED
The rain is f
　　　　　　a
　　　　　　l
　　　　　　l
　　　　　　i
　　　　　　n
　　　　　　g,
　　　　　　　crying.
The world is dying,
And only
the rain knows,
　　　　　　　　c
　　　　　　　　r
　　　　　　　　y
　　　　　　　　i
　　　　　　　　n
　　　　　　　　g.

Anita Fawn Bates
WINTER
When winter's first cold air starts
blowing through my hair
And leaves that once were green
turn yellow, brown, and red.
I begin to dread long nights and
short days, along life's dreary
way.

Till winter dies away, and spring
is born one day
Full of life to become a wife for
summer soon one day.

RoseMarie Amiee Faith
RoseMarie Amiee Faith
**Skipping Through the
Raindrops**
[*Dedicated with motherly love
to Sonia, Shaunbrian, Shane
and Karissa.*]
Gentle cooling crystal raindrops
Falling softly down,
Cleansing away my salty teardrops,
Quenching the thirst of the
ground.
Washing off all the dusty house
tops,
I love the pattering sounds.

I hope it rains until my sadness
is all gone,
　Wetting my puddle dancing
　body,
Showering the entire fresh day
long,
　'Cause when I am dancing, I
　feel so free,
I humm an unknown song
　I like to be so full of melody.

This is the enchanting place that
I really belong,
Amongst the blooming plants
and curious animals, I'll spree.
Getting away from life's busy
throng.
　Would you like to come with
　me?
We can get drenched as we
joyfully skip along.

Mrs. Charline Kilgore
I DON'T REMEMBER
[*I wrote this poem for: Mrs.
Linnie Strebeck. (My Mother)
She died with cancer before; I
could show her this poem. I am
dedicating this poem to my
father.*]
My mama said; I did: I had pretty
shoes, pretty dresses, pretty
ribbons in my hair. I don't
remember when? I was a kid
but, my mama said; I did:

My mama said; I did: I had dark
brown hair, dark brown eyes,
my hair was in pretty curls. I
don't remember when? I was a
kid but, my mama said; I did:

My mama said; I did: I fell in love
with every soldier boy. I would
run to hug his neck. (Thinking

he was my daddy) I don't
remember when? I was a kid
but, my mama said; I did:

Lorraine Frances Dame
LOVE BY THE SEA
When you and I
Ran by the sea
God's ocean whispered
Rhapsodies
His wild waves rushed
To kiss the shore
And set our love free
For evermore
So walk with me now
Hand in hand
By the sea
We'll watch the sun sink
Alone
You and me
Love is free

Dorothy Haden
MORNING VIEW
Sunshine drifted lazily
Over low fields
Heading for the mountains
Where it slowly ate
The shadows for breakfast
After giving up the snow peak
　As being indigestible
　　Went slowly down
　　　The other side.

Dawn Behrns
MEMORIES
Memories of a mist covered lake
　The scent of pine
　And the warmth of a fire
Memories of the snow covered trees
　The snowmen we built
　And the snowball fights we had
Memories of the love we shared
　The times together
　And the dinners for two
Memories of the rides in the wind
　The walks in the rain
　And the memories shared with
　you

S. A. Phillips
OUR FRIENDSHIP
You're always near to me
You'll always be dear to me
You always seems to smile
Even if it's been awhile
You're always there
To help stop the fear
During the good times and the
bad
You make me happy when I'm sad
Our friendship will linger on
Even after we're both gone . . .

Meta Isaac
MY FIRST LOVE
[*This poem was written to—
and inspired by my niece,
Barbara, when we visited
Washington.*]
His face was like an angel's to me,
His voice was like a bird's,
He sang the sweetest melody,
That I had ever heard.

Such was the man I did love,
Was he sent from heaven above?
On the hills at sunset, daily we
met.

Holding hands we walked along,
While he to me sang a song,
Then we parted with a kiss,
Oh what heavenly bliss!

423

Time made our love stronger,
So we lingered longer,
Then when we had to leave,
It made my poor heart grieve.

Came the day he said goodbye,
I though I would die,
For the morrow he would go to sea,
For a while leaving me.

I'll wait for you I said as I cried,
I'll come back to you, he lied.
Then we kissed so tenderly,
As he took his leave of me.

Days came and went just the same,
But to me no postman came.
The nights brought sweet relief,
When I could express my grief.

Oh what secrets my pillow kept,
As I hugged it and wept,
Too soon came the morning light,
Longer should be the night.

Time heals all wounds they say,
Be that as it may,
But to me it took so long,
For in my heart he left his song.

The Best of Bev Besser
ALIVE
Loving you is easy
Loving you is free,
What I feel at times is sleazy
What I am is me.

Take away the pressure
Take away the strife,
Leave the world wide open
That's when I feel life.

For you are real
To feel and touch,
Even for the moment
It means so much.

It makes me strive
To keep alive
For it is real
To FEEL
To WATCH
To LISTEN
To be AWARE
To truly CARE
And most of all
To sincerely SHARE.

Carolyn Barter Ellis
MY QUEST
My heart is soaring above the
  clouds
Looking for something, I cannot
  find
My head tells me that it's no use
But my heart overrules my mind
I see the clouds as they float by
Feel the breezes upon my face
Wishing that I could rise on high
And just float, thru empty space

The sky seems soft and quiet
  above
As the sun, it shines so bright
And everywhere you feel God's
  love
That makes everything seem all
  right

I lift my eyes, as my soul takes
  flight
My quest is hard and long
As I rise to find, the heavenly light
My heart is filled with song

R. L. Jordan
DREAM CHILD
Young child, my child
sleep until the dawn.
Dream child, sweet dreams child,
of the joys that are to come.

Never mind the angry world;
I'm here and will protect your
  slumber,
sweet slumber, until you need
  slumber
no more, tomorrow.

Dream child;
do you dream of me?
For me, a thousand little miracles
  that play,
they stay, in simple truths,
like those of youth, so long ago
forgotten now.

Sleep my child, dream my child,
keep your youth,your simple
  truths
that were mine once,
so long ago.

Dusty Roads

Dusty Roads
THE PEARL
You are like a mother to me
You are my T.V. when I'm lonely
I'm the scorpion that stings
But you have taught me
Lots of new things
A friend like you
I have never known
I call you the Pearl
With a heart of gold
You could never be bought
But how I love to hear you talk
Your voice is as sweet
As the sound of the waterfall
And the birds in the trees
You are like the white dove
The symbol of love.

There is always a smile on your
  lips
That seems to say
Have no fear in the world out there
Live and let live
But not in despair
Go out dancing
And have lots of fun
You are the bullet
In my sawed-off shotgun
When I pull the trigger
They all will be saved
By the hands of a stranger
From the devil's brigade.

No sorrow, no sadness
I could see in your eyes

I couldn't fool you
In any phony disguise
Your wild rowdy ways
I might criticize
But that was so long ago
And times have changed
The hot jazz is still standing
Some ladies are dancin'
To the music of Fats Domino
It was here that you danced
To the sound of the Big Bands
In your hey-days of whiskey and
  smoke.

I pulled up a chair
And ordered a beer
Then sat down with my back to
  the wall
When they turned off the lights
At one-forty five, I got up
Wearin' my hat down low
Lit a cigarette on my bootheel
And went out the door
Into hallucinating pictures of you
On the dancin' floor.

Your picturesque personality
Has a touch of nature's beauty
Like the valley so green
The blue ridge mountain so high
And the wide rollin' plains
A prairie of flowers
The State of Kentucky
And the rivers that run to the sea.

You got a warm feelin' in your heart
For the ones who carry a gun
The pushers, and the winos
And the tinhorn gamblers
Who deal from the bottom
The fags and the desperados
Who are always on the run
Thank you—dear Pearl
You have taught me how to love
And accept everyone.

A lady of your class
I respect and admire
Dear Pearl—I love you as a mother
And your three darlin' daughters
God bless the cop you married
Many years ago—he rides tall
He is the limb of the law
You and your family
Mean a lot to me
Give my love to Kelly
And let them put my head
In a guillotine
And set me free.

Mary K. Torsiello
Grandma In the Garden
The dearest, kindest lady I have
  ever known

Was "Grandma in the Garden"
  who lived all alone

In a clean, little, green house, just
  a block from me
She had a small front porch
  where she hung her house key

In the back was a garden, she
  tilled it by hand
For vegetables and berries to grow
  on her land

With a heavy, hand mower, she
  mowed her own lawn
Went to church every morning at
  the crack of dawn

With newspaper she covered her
  freshly scrubbed floor
And the sweet smell of cookies
  came right thru her door

She sat in her rocker by the
  window for light
To knit Christmas mitts for her
  grandchildren's delight

The things I remember her
  exclusively for
Were her humility, patience,
  kindness and lore

She was so conservative, she
  didn't own a phone
The dearest, sweetest lady I have
  every known

She lived almost a century, a
  good life, indeed
Full of many hardships, but a
  fine, healthy creed

Lost her beloved husband so early
  in life
Alone—raised four special
  children thru lots of strife

She was determined and spunky,
  humble and sweet
The nicest, most thoughtful lady
  on Blodgett Street

The dearest, kindest lady I have
  ever known
Was "Grandma in the Garden"
  who lived all alone

Yvonne Lopez
ICEBURG
A body that remains motionless ...
Eyes that stare into space during
  extensive periods of solitude
  and intranquility.
Lips that remain glued to one
  another
As if they had been splattered
  with cement.

It is almost as if all my
  surroundings have ceased to be
And all that lies about me is a
  drawing of still life reflecting a
  mood of sorrow and despair . . .

Any minute now a signal will
  arrive calling for action.
Demanding that animation be
  returned to all who have
  become inanimate objects . . .

Any moment now there will be a
  complete awakening
With vast assets of
  enlightenment . . .
Striking with high intensity . . .
Blowing life back into my body.

Until that moment begets me . . .

Today's Greatest Poems

I will stand firm as a valiant
soldier who adopts a stoic
attitude when placed before a
firing squad
Not allowing pain and uneasiness
to shatter the body.

Until then I remain . . .
With hope that this body that
has adopted the form of an
iceburg
Will allow the ice to melt away
bit by bit . . .
Until it is molded
into a living creature
once again . . .

Kitty K. Stone
. . . I DON'T CRY
The promise I never gave you,
The feelings you feared to show,
Have sent me to his waiting arms
Though my heart still loves you so.

He only wants my happiness,
And when he holds me I don't cry.
He never asks if I think of you,
For if he did, I couldn't lie.

He holds me to his body
And all my loneliness is gone;
But I hunger for your tender touch
Until the start of each new dawn.

Should he discover that I dream
of you
While lying in his bed,
That hurt would come between us,
Though no harsh words were
ever said.

I'll do my best to please him;
To his needs I will attend,
But your face will be the one I see
When at last my journey ends.

Stephanie Rischman Vitale
A MOTHER'S PRAYER
*[For my children Lauren and
Joseph Love Mommy]*
Keep my children safe from all
Never let them stumble or fall

Keep their health and minds intact
And lead them straight on life's
best track

Listen dear God and hear my plea
Cause their lives are very
important to me

And if sometimes, they might stray
Your guidance you will show I pray

These little ones need all my love
Now and always, beyond and above

Give me the strength to correct
and to cope
To understand and to scold, then
only to hope

That when I've finished, and all is
done
Their respect and their love, I
will have won

AMEN

Susie Henderson
MY LOVE FOR YOU
With freshness of first Spring and
fragrance of new

Like the freshness of first rain
and mist of dew

Of rainbows and northern lights
that dance across the sky in
glorious color of hue

The magical moments of God's
Nature and You!

Robert R. Weetman
CAREFREE
Free as a bird does my soul it now
soar
Unencumbered by life's
burdensome chores,
To wander in peace thru
unlimited time
In a Paradise God could but dream.

Ah! With a passion do I long for
this dream
To be free from the toils and the
cares,
To be restless and dashing and
wander thru Time
Never wondering whatever comes
next.

Oh! But this freedom for me is a
dream
Thats unreal as day is to night,
And once more as the morrow
creeps into my room
I am faced with another today.

Rosiland Robin White
PARENTS
*[To my mother and father,
Martin Robin Sr. and Cora
Alfonso Robin, who are the
best parents that anyone could
ever ask for. I dedicate this poem
to you with all my love.]*
You worked so hard to make a
living,
Always loving always giving.

You gave everything there was to
give,
We'll never forget that as long as
we live.

You gave us something that
money can't buy,
For you gave of yourself, and that
is why:
    You taught us how to love,
    You taught us how to share.
    You gave us our wisdom,
    and showed us how to care.

There could never be anyone
quite like you two,
People like you are so precious
and so few.

It makes me a little sad, to think
that some other,
May never experience the joy of a
father and a mother.

We thank you Lord every day,
and for you Mom and Dad, we
do pray;

Keep you healthy is what we ask,
as you perform your daily tasks,
Keep you happy, and always stay,
just the way you are today.

All our love,
Your family

Marge Hill
THE MERRY—GO—ROUND
The merry-go-round goes on and on
In a circle we know as Life
Where the ups and downs of the
horses
Are times of great joy or strife.

I sit on my horse as always
With my hand reached out above—
For the token—the brass ring—
Though its real name is Love.

How I wish the ride would stop
Cause I've missed the ring, I cry,
But the only way off the
merry-go-round
In this ride of life is to die.

Edward E. Harvey II

Edward E. Harvey II
BLOOD UPON THE WALLS
The leaders of the light are now
all sleeping
No more will they stand proud
above the dawn
And the murderers who left the
crowds all weeping
Remain alive to cast hate on and
on
Every scent of fear has warnings
to remember
Every echo in the thunder sends
new calls
Watch your step between
October and December
Come the new year you'll find
blood upon the walls

The bullets make their way to
form destruction
Our world will face its end in
quite this style
Shattered dreams are just the
truth of each obstruction
And for now they gather close
around the Nile
Where a man has died for being
strong and gallant
As he walks in dignity towards
Heaven's halls
Here will rest the lasting signs of
regal talent
Near the death marks of the
blood upon the walls

There once was someone singing
to the masses
He asked for peace with grand
imagination
His soul now gone, and body only
ashes
The victim of a lost fool's situation
Beware of winter's frost and
autumn's browning
The simple sound of nature soon
enthralls
When the seasons change and
smiling lips are frowning
Be assured it's only blood upon
the walls

There comes a day when you will
seek for glory
The promised land which shows
the best of times
Reality may tell a different story

It's not for us to live between the
lines
And the optimist will spend his
days believing
While tomorrow speaks of
destiny that crawls
For wherever love is found
beneath the evening
Scarlet morning waits with blood
upon the walls

Edward E. Harvey II
THE SHADOW AS IT FALLS
The city is a morgue, as I look
into the night
Each one is his own lord,
governed by a flashing light
No graceful compensation, where
the broken hearts adorn
Utopia the nation, where all new
souls must be born
A candle wick is burning, sending
fire it's own way
You even may be learning, in the
mire day by day
And who am I, the victim, who
must stop death when it calls?
Or banned by the restriction, of
the shadow as it falls

The desert is a sea, made of sand
like heat's own toy
The tide rolls back to me, as I
greet the childhood boy
No open arms are reaching, where
the laughter comes to end
This hour's for beseeching; Go
wherever fate will send
An opera of the future, puts itself
onto the stage
The mind in need of nurture,
sometimes cries in mournful rage
And who am I, the dreamer, being
backed against the walls?
Now the ray becomes a streamer,
on the shadow as it falls

The island is a loner, needing
nothing but the breeze
And I am but a roamer, seeing
promise in the trees
No heaven in the distance, at the
top of floating clouds
Thinking of the word "Resistance":
How I feel between the crowds
A windmill gently turning, on
and on forever more
For paradise I'm yearning, and the
time comes to explore
Hear the echo's bouncing vision,
in the deepness of the halls
I must make the last decision,
with the shadow as it falls

Tillie Summers
SANTA CLAUS
I went to see Santa Claus at 43
I gazed thru the window
And there I was upon his knee
Crying out loud what happened
to me and where are the
treasures you once promised me
What can you give me at 43
An underrated pleasure
folded under my tree
A trip to the heavens to find
more of me
A swirl of faith to be danced into
me
Whatmore can you give at 43
A promise to be is enough for me.

425

Edward E. Harvey II
EUPHORIA
See them look in all directions;
    Every person wants affection
See them travel miles and miles;
    Longing for a pleasant smile
To scale the tallest rainbow, just
    to visit with the clouds
To sit upon the rooftop, to escape
    from rushing crowds
There seems to be a reason, for
    every move we make
No matter what the season, or if
    we give or take

The search begins for happiness,
    it leaves one waiting long
Each person looks at different
    notes, to write a brand new
    song
For there's meaning in whatever
    is behind the things we do
A spirit is inside the soul that
    lives for only you

If the time is right for crying, you
    may shed a thousand tears
If the time is right for flying, you
    may soar through ten light
    years
Through moments of all
    meditation
There soon must come a revelation
That somewhere there's a magic
    trail
Where promises aren't meant to
    fail
New bridges to cross, old friends
    will be lost
High ladders to climb, with sights
    to unwind
New thoughts to conceive, to
    make all believe
More shadows to cast, to help the
    truth last

What pleases all the mighty kings?
Or makes the bell of laughter ring?
It's all the things your moods
    reveal
To stand and shout out how you
    feel
To grasp and reach out for life kind
Euphoria's a state of mind

Alberta L. Grim
PRIORITY
The stores are filled with shoppers
The streets are lined with cars
The criers for the needy
Hold out their half filled jars.

Christmas carols blaring
The noise, oh what a din
Children comparing notes
How many stores thay have been
    in.

Store Santas look bedraggled
The candy canes all gone
They're all glad when it's over
The Snowman melting on the lawn.

Christmas Day should be a time
Of reverance, joy and praise
We could make it so much better
In so many little ways.

Jesus is the One
For whom we should give pause
He should come first in all our
    hearts
Before old Santa Claus.

Lisa Moody
WOODLAND NIGHT
Nature's arbor black with night
sacred wonder, mysteriously
    forbidding
hushed whispers through the
    trees,
crying in the night
eyes upon us; watching ever
some frightened, curious, leery
eyes upon us; watching ever
we are trespassers of the
    woodland night.

Annie L. Wilson

Annie L. Wilson
THE HALFWAY MARK
You stand in the middle of a
    clearing.
You take a deep breath and you
    sigh.
You look back at the thorns and
    the thistles of life.
The pain is there even in your
    eye.

You stand there and breathe the
    free fresh air.
So deeply it penetrates.
It soothes the mind. It helps the
    heart.
The soul it revibrates.

You look to the sides and you
    look ahead
You don't have to look behind
For what's back there, you know
    about.
Ahead is where you will find.

All that you wanted in the past.
All of your dreams un-fulfilled.
Ahead is where it all really is.
The past it seems so unreal

Ahead—way in the distance
You dimly see a door.
It's marked—and all the labels
    read.
All you could ever hope for—
So breathe while you can.

Because you see. Between you
    and that great door
More thistles, more thorns, more
    pain of life.
But isn't it worth a little more?

So pull all those muscles
    together.
Regain all—your strength and
    your spark.
Look to the "Proper Source" for
    strength.
FOR YOU! have reached—"THE
    HALFWAY MARK".

Yolanda E. Walker
L'IDEE DU TEMPS
Sometimes . . .
in making sarcastic comments on
    cynical lines
to hold the fragile vantage point
    cupped timorously
in shaking hands
this side of sanity
I remember it doesn't matter.

"Logic . . ."
my head speaks
"It must mean something.
What is its underlying reason?"
I ponder to the point of madness
knowing Truth lies somewhere
    within.
If I look long enough I'll find it
tangible . . . clear . . .
    explainable.
When I think long enough
I forget the question.
I believe I was asking what it all
    meant.

On the verge of discovery
I plod along
into every dark corner
finding only cobwebs and hard
    places—
if I run, that is.

Somehow . . .
my heart speaks.
It's all so simple.
Now and then
sparks fly
by and by
leaving the coals of their former
    existence.

In wonder, I begin to
    understand . . .
        the idea of time.

david howenstine
BLISSFUL HELL
come cohabitate with me,
    And soon we shall at least be
        three.
we'll live atop the lord below,
    And off to work each morn we
        go.
we'll live a life of total
    luxury
    (If you don't mind contempt
        and drudgery).
and if we're lucky say, once a
    week;
    We'll get to eat some not-too-
        tough meat.
but fret not yet,
    Nor leave me now.
    for in a year and fifty,
    Everything will be just super
        nifty.
there will be no money, gas, nor
    house;
    Only bills and taxes and we'll
        love like cat and mouse.
we'll live off social security and
    retirement pension,
    Assuming you don't mind
        living in a second dimension
but don't sweat it out—
    Cause we'll be too poor to cry
        and pout.
and in the gray hair and with
    your mother,
    We'll all learn to hate one
        another.

Marjorie Rich Bordner
My Spoon River Country
I like being here; I came to live
    here by choice.
Spoon River Country has the
    honest, earthy qualities I like.

Spoon River folks are special; I
    like to meet them,
    Greet them and call them by
        name
As I inquire about others of their
    families.

I like the idea that Spoon River
    observes holidays
    And special occasions with
        parades, programs,
And a great deal of fuss.

I like the countryside and the
    small town views;
    They give rise to good honest
        values.

I like the idea that here some still
    like to walk
    Around barefoot because
We like the feel of nature's
    carpeting known as grass
Or the oozing of mud between
    our toes.

I like the idea here that Spoon
    River folk take the
    Trouble to do things right with
        honesty
That makes the end result special.
They take a unique, old-
    fashioned pride in doing
    Their work well.

Spoon River keeps pace with
    world progress without
    Losing sight of the past.
I like the idea that her folk still
    have patience for handcrafting
And still do it when it is the
    better way.

I like the idea that at the end of
    every day we can look
    Ourselves in the eyes
And be proud.

If I like it so much I think you
    would too,
    For Spoon River is a special
        place
With special people who may go
    to distant points and achieve
    prominence,
But who also remain humble and
    proud to come home again, to
    answer
That satisfying need to return to
    the place that nurtured them
    while here.

If this sounds provincial, it is, but
    so are we.

Josephine Bangsberg
NOVEMBER GRIEF
Why do I grieve November days?
Why can't I forget your loving
    ways?

Is it the falling leaves that were
    ablaze
With vivid colors in the misty
    haze?
Is it the gloomy skies and
    drifting rain
That gives my heart this
    yearning pain?

426

I do not know . . . I only fear
My love is gone. He is not here
To take the woodland walk with
  me
I've traced that path so endlessly.

Down the path of sunlight bright
Through the brilliant leaves so
  light
Arms entwined in love's embrace
Your precious lips upon my face
I feel the bitter ecstasy
Of love that will not last for me.

Now by myself I grieve today
I cannot stop—my thoughts still
  stray,
At times I walk our woodland
  way
Down our path, now bleak and
  gray.

Was it the words I didn't say?
Was it my fault you didn't stay?
I loved too much, and did you
  know
That one day soon you'd let me
  go?

And so I grieve November days
And I grieve alone . . . but love
  still stays.

Barney M. Lowder
MEMORIES OF A FRIEND
Memories of a friend's smile
  flash within my mind,
Kind words once shared
  echo through my thoughts.
There is no time left
  for growths' beauty,
And my soul empties
  selfish-sorrow upon the earth.
While my soul cries
  for affirmation of life's
  meaning,
My friend remains gone forever
  and death seems to prevail.
The life-cycle continues onward,
  the mind remembers,
    he heart bleeds,
        and the soul cries out,
Not from fear of death's victory,
  but for the blessing of knowing
The beautiful individual
  which I called a "friend".

Kelly Crooke
THE LOSS OF LENNON
There was crying in the streets,
The tears, they flowed freely.
And they reached all corners of
  the earth
The world then stopped its mirth

The radios blared that a man was
  dead.
A peaceful person so the papers
  read.
This man had been shot,
But the killer was caught
Now, what would the sentence
  be?

The judgement was passed,
And the world was aghast
How could this be?
They let him go free
With the plea of insanity.

He lived in peace,
And died in pain.
Now only his name and the
  legends remain.

We miss you John,

We're sorry you're gone.
How we wish we could bring you
  back.
How we wish we could bring you
  back.

Mable P. McCallum
LAUGHTER AND SMILES
Smiles are not what they used to
  be
Laughter gone away
Grins once in a while I see
Gloom in its place

It used to be easy to know one
  was happy
But now no one can tell something
  has happened
By expressions of solemn faces
Minus of Laughter and Smiling
  Faces

Laughter gone away
Smiles have faded
Gloom in their place
But the world is a beautiful place

Makes one wonder today
and think of happier times
When there was Laughter and
  Smiles
Now why gloom in its place

Connie Laughlin
WISHFUL THINKING
I saw you standing there
  all by yourself
Looking
  as bored as ever
I look—
  You smile . . .
  I smile back;
Could this be
The start
  of something beautiful
Or the very end
  of something
  that never was
As I walk over
  towards you
You turn
  and walk away
Not looking
  back at me
With another girl
  at your side.

Maresa B. Santos
IT'S CHRISTMAS NIGHT!
I heard the church bells ringing
  loud and fast;
Clang! clang! clang! clang! clang!
  clang!
A sudden thought jolted me out
  of my bed,
"You're going to church, wake up!"
  It's Christmas night!

From afar I heard the musician's
  Christmas airs,
I know they had stopped going
  around the town;
There's a rush of feet, and
  children's voices shrill,
The whole town is hurrying to
  hear mass;
    It's Christmas night!

Quickly I dressed up, barely
  noticed Mother's coming;
Surprised me, as she stooped and
  whispered in my ear,
"Precious Child, go tell your
  father, we're ready to leave."
"Yes Mother, we won't be late,

tonight;
        It's Christmas night!

The church was packed, we had
  to stay outside,
Father smiled, as he lifted me up,
  behind his head;
Holding tight to Father's head, I
  peeked inside,
Saw men, women, children,
  kneeling side by side;
        It's Christmas night!

All of a sudden, I felt this peace
  within me
Father was silent, gazing at the
  babe in his manger bed,
Mother was on tiptoe as she
  joined the prayers,
To worship the Christ-Child, was
  truly our one intent;
        It's Christmas night!

Dr. Beverly Baker

Dr. Beverly Baker
OH! HOW YOU KISSED ME
Oh! How you kissed me! My head
  drooped low on your shoulders.
With a feeling of shelter and
  infinite rest.
Oh! My emotions flashed up as in
  flame, from my heart to my
  face;
Your lips clung to mine—hoping
  they might never unclasp from
  the
Rapturous kiss. My heart, my
  breath and my will in delirious
  joy
For a moment stood still.
Oh! How you kissed me!
Your arms held me fast, oh! Your
  arms were so bold—
Heart beat against heart beat in
  their passionate fold. Your
Glances seemed drawing my soul
  through mine eyes, as the sun
  draws
The mist from the sea to the
  skies. Life has no temptations or
Visions of rapture outside of your
  arms.
Oh! How you kissed me!
I felt like an angel possessed. I
  would fling my silk white robe
Unrepiningly down, tear from my
  forehead its beautiful crown. To
Once more nestle in your arms of
  Heaven of rest. Seeing and
  feeling
Your lips upon mine, My head on
  your shoulders for rest. I
  thought

'Twere delicious to die there, if
  death would but come while my
Lips were yet moist with your
  breath; while your arms clasped
  me
Round in that blissful embrace
  while your eyes melt in mine,
  could
E'en death e'er efface.

Oh! How you kissed me!
Oh! These are the questions I
  ask?
Must my lips taste no more such
  exquisite delight? Would you
  wish
That your shoulders were my
  shelter as then? If you were here,
Would you kiss me again?
Oh! How you kissed me!

Brenda Hammons-Felsinger
RETURN
Lie your head upon my chest
and wonder why you feel not
  breath;
For I have gone and you are near,
I'm somewhere else and you are
  here.

I had no fear to go so far,
to know who I am and who you
  are;
On earth I failed to understand
and sometimes failed to hold a
  hand.

Everything, including man
will turn from living into sand;
Will turn from dying into man...
return from dying, yes you can.

Viola M. Crider
MY IF
[This poem is dedicated to my
loving sister, Mrs. Mary E.
Reed, who has truly been my
source of inspiration.]
If you can keep God in your heart,
  Be kind to your friends and
  enemies too;
If you strive to finish whatever
  you start
  And let nothing get the best of
  you;
If you can spread cheer along the
  way,
  Whether to a friend of yours, or
  not;
If you can forgive others day by
  day
  Without thinking you've done
  a lot;
If you can keep your pride,
  and self respect

And not let prosperity go to
your head;
If you can learn to forgive and
forget
Things about you which were
said;
If you can learn to make your
home
An institute of love and prayer;
If you learn that no matter how
far you roam
You have got to know God any
where;
If you can smile when you're
burdened down
When nothing at all seems
right;
If you can keep smiling and never
frown,
And remember that after
darkness comes light.
Then you've been tried and tested
my friend—
You'll surely have a place in
life;
Just don't look back—carry on to
the end,
you'll overcome the hardships
of strife

Ms. Yolanda E. Preston
A Paradise Above the Sea
Although I may not be on earth
with you, or in person with
you, but I will be with you in
SPIRIT.

HEAVEN is a beautiful place to
be. For EVERLASTING PEACE
above the sea. My heart is at
rest with warmth and thoughts
of you, for this BEAUTIFUL
PLACE OF PARADISE above
the sea. I am as HAPPY as can
be. If I had not been saved, I
would be in H-E-L-L, burning
and burning until
E-T-E-R-N-I-T-Y.

If you could see this
PARADISING PLACE, we call
HEAVEN ABOVE THE SEA
with pearly gates and many
trees. This is a BEAUTIFUL
and PLEASANT place to see. If
I had my will, I would see you
here, in this BEAUTIFUL
PLACE where it is PEACEFUL
and QUIET to be. A
RAINBOW that is so pretty,
with an arch of multi-colored
stripes of TURQUOISE-BLUE,
ORANGE, GREEN, BRONZE
and GOLD. This is a beautiful
sight to KEEP and BEHOLD.
With GOLD pathed streets,
TREES that flourish A-L-L year
and FLOWERS that are radiant
and sweet smelling JUST LIKE
IN THE SPRINGTIME. A soft
WIND that is breezy and still.
You can hear SOOTHING
vibrations of HARPS being
played like VIOLINS.

A-L-L men, women and children
who had handicaps on earth
and we A-L-L have no
handicaps in HEAVEN. We
A-L-L walk graceful, talk softly,
play joyously and are
CAREFREE. We A-L-L are

happy and neither sick nor
wearing any FROWNS. We
A-L-L have SMILES from ear-to-
ear, our faces GLEAM with
cheer and just like seeing the
circus CLOWNS performance
given once-a-year.

There is a PLACE so BEAUTIFUL
and so PLEASING to see. We
A-L-L are the LORD'S children
and we A-L-L are happy and
free. Without having to
W-O-R-R-Y about all those
GOOD and UNEASY tasks of
earthly, earthly deeds.

This is a very BEAUTIFUL
PLACE of tree branches that
flourish from many roots, of
past and present
GENERATIONS that
intertwine to makeup a large
F-A-M-I-L-Y tree. I hope to see
you in heaven, P-L-E-A-S-E stay
sweet, kind and just
B-E-L-I-E-V-E. There is a
BEAUTIFUL PARADISE called
H-E-A-V-E-N, if you come to be
with me.

In our peaceful PARADISE
ABOVE THE SEA, come and be
with me, I-F Y-O-U P-L-E-A-S-E.

Joseph P. Kowacic
A PARABLE
I saw a sand crab
thrown up on a beach,
wantonly flung
out of the water's reach.

A greedy sun
with savage frown
sent searing arrows
streaming down.

The tiny creature
struggled still
against the mighty
overkill.

I took him gently
in my hand
to thwart his murder,
cruelly planned,

and placed him
in the cooling sea.
He disappeared—
alive and free . . .

There is a bond
among us all,
creatures big,
and creatures small.

Together here
in need's sharp hour,
we cheat the grasp
of ruthless power.

Wayne S. Brownell
Romance Under the Sun
My I must say things have
changed for the better
Feeling so alive since the day that
I met ya'
It was in the stars for us to be
together
We'll share all precious days in
rain or sunny weather

Days completely satisfying
with you within my heart
Realizing now I should have been
here right from the start

Only better times ahead
Leaving sorrow far behind
With you within my heart
Everything will be just fine

We'll have a romance under the
sun
Escape with the love
Become undone
Fear not a soul
Not a single one
Romance under the sun

pav
SHARE THE MAGIC
I will always love you.
No matter what happens,
deep inside
I'll always want you.

I know this cannot be.
You have your commitments
and I have mine.
We have to live lives
that cannot include each other.

Yet,
this does not lessen
my love for you.
Nor,
is there any substitute
for what we share with each other.

Let's make a date
for when we're old and gray
and our commitments are
fulfilled.

We can share the magic of
being together.

Theresa Gill
WHY
If the world is so perfect,
then why am I here?
And why do I have
this ungodly fear?

If the world is so perfect,
then why is there war?
Why don't they say
they don't want anymore?

If the world is perfect,
they why do I cry?
And why do so many people
just want to die?

If the world is so perfect,
then why am I here?
And why do I still have
this ungodly fear?

Joanna M. Nixon
WHY?
Why do leaves fall?
Why do birds sing?
Why do flowers bloom?
Why do birds fly?
Why do you ask?

Phyllis Joan Smith
SANTA IS HIS NAME
*["To Chris, Blair, and Cassie"
My joy of today, my promise of
tomorrow Hugs and Kisses,
Grandma]*
Little girls and boys
Be as quiet as a mouse
There is someone in your house
He has a twinkle in his eye
And tiny reindeer that fly
Do you know his name?
He comes with a sack of toys
For all the girls and boys

Dolls, trains, and many a game
He's visited every house

on the block
Filling all the socks
Not one, has he forgot

This little man, who works all
year
To bring girls and boys such
cheer
You can hear his "HO-HO-HOes"
As in his sleigh he hops
Back to the North Pole he goes
Santa Claus is his name . . .

Kim Bambrough
ONE EYE SEES
If one eye sees only good
And the other only bad
If one sees only happy
And one only sad
If one eye sees through teardrops
That fall like stormy rain
Will the one that looks through
glory
Blind the one that reeks of pain?

Can humanity strengthen one eye
So that vision is finally clear?
And if that vision is restored
Will it wash away the tears?
Can I be sure of happiness
If the good outweighs the bad?
Could I ever fulfill the life I saw
In the childhood dreams I had?

The answers to these questions
That run wild through my mind
Will reach me in this adult world
I have just begun to find

Fernando Poblete Racelis
TO PITJIRA, AN ARUNTA
*[Written with the Dreamtime
Figures of Australia's Land of
the Never Never cherished in
memory.]*
Louvered soul oaring in the red
powdered sea;
Pollard warrior wafted into the
innards of thy land.
Goaded into hibernation?
Goitered by law?
But Pitjira, thy incubus trek
self wrought me thinks!
Corroborees are rants.
Witches' potions!
Snares.
Atavistic flings in placid
bilabongs,
Must you not ripple?
For onward . . . and forward if not,
Thy trek would,
To prosaic existence;
Withering in the desert doldrums.

Romi Symington
UNTITLED
If ever I was a seagull and I could
fly high in the sky,
I would want you to be by me side
to glide free and faraway with me.

Looking down on the ocean so
blue,
to feel the sea breeze and
freshmorning
sea air as we fly toward our
dreams.

If ever I was a horse running wild
and
free, I would want you to be close
beside me, galloping fast as the
winds
embracing our goals away from
all sins.

Our manes and our bodies shiny
and
flowing, a picture in the sunset
golden
and glowing with the sea,
two beautiful horses running
along the beach
racing toward our fantasies.

If ever I was to be something
other
than what I am now, I would
always
want for it to be with you and me
running, flying, loving, wild and
free.

Linda F. Williams
MY GYPSY SANTA
With a glance from the left and a
glance to the right
Had us dancing together with a
glance all night
The night was cool, the music
soft and smooth
In the arms of "My Gypsy Santa",
how they did soothe

To hear a song will hold no
meaning
Until you feel the words for
which they are singing
A song in my heart has felt a
stiring
Like no other, "My Gypsy Santa",
you keep them occurring

From the first moment and
throughout the night
The air held a feeling of pure
magic delight
Though words were unspoken, I
did realize
I was a captive to "My Gypsy
Santa" and his passionate eyes

Bells may ring and forever the
music will play
Tonight on this wonderful
Christmas Eve, I will say
Miracles are for everyone who
shall only believe
With "My Gypsy Santa", I never
want him to leave

Lisa Mason Campbell
MOMENTS
If we shared a touch
            a feeling
                a kiss
If in that moment we could love
            then,
                I loved you
            for a moment . . .

Ernestine Aikens King
BLINDNESS
*[In loving memory of my
Mother Hazel Jones Aikens
1889-1982 A victim of
glaucoma]*
They say I'm blind since I can't
see
Flowers and birds and leafy tree,
Butterflies that wing their way
Across the meadow on summer's
day.

But if I wish that night be gone
Then children's laughter makes a
song.
The tinkling bells of a wandering
sheep
Is a call to the Shepherd who
never sleeps.

And there's a rainbow in the sky—
God's covenant with you and I.
And, yes, I see the Throne of
Grace
With Father, Son—each in His
place.
And daily as I go to prayer
They meet and listen to me there.
With trembling heart I lift my
eyes
And see my Saviour as He dies.
But Oh! What joy when He arose
And left the grave that held Him
close.

Beloved, can you say I'm blind
When Light and Life and Love are
mine?

Franklin Sommers
THE ASTEROIDS
*[Written with eternal love and
honor for God, Mother Mary,
my mother Patricia, and for
Nora Butler; for Grace.]*
You are sands of the heavens,
You are sands of matter,
In the heavens you exist, orbiting,
floating in space,
You may be left over fractions of
worlds,
Or cooled fractions of a sun,
Your origin may be from a big
bang in the heavens,
Or from the creation storm of a
nova;
Storms, your origin is from
storms,
All manner of storms, heavenly
storms,
You are sands of matter, perhaps
even sands of worlds,
You are sands of the heavens,
And the stormy sands of its
history.

M. Duane Rawls
DEAR DAUGHTER
Being without someone special
Is like not being at all
Or at least just being lonely
Because you've got to think
About that person all the time
And wonder
If they're thinking of you as well
Missing loved ones
Is like your heart
Constantly skipping beats
Your body rhythm is without
harmony
And the only thing
That seems to be together
Are the memories
Of that special person
Precious vivid memories
Makes one guilty
For being away
Pictures and remindings
Of yesterday.

Muriel E. Glenn
PUSSY WILLOW
[To my son, Howard Glenn]
Pretty Pussy Willow . . .
you are so straight and tall
. . . agrowing in my garden . . .
along the old stone wall.

I like to look upon you
. . . from my rocker where
I sit . . . and spend some
leisure hours . . . just to
rock and think and knit.

Your lovely little kittens
. . . in their furry coats of
gray . . . the warm wind rocks
to sleep . . . while their
cradles swing and sway.

I rocked my baby too . . . in
this same old rocking chair
. . . and cuddled him like you
do . . . with tender loving
care.

So please don't think I'm
sleeping . . . I'm really not
you know . . . I am only thinking
of those days . . . so very long
ago.

Loreli Lynne Miller
I REMEMBER
*[To DK, Thanks for the
inspiration because I really do
"remember"—Lori And to Terry
for loving me enough to let me.]*
Mellow music
Multi colors of pastel
Soft sunsets,
A gentle breeze.
They bring you to my mind
My heart melts.
Yes, I remember.

Fun with friends
Loud laughter
Rowdy basketball games
Crazy weekends,
A snowball fight.
Again, I find your vision clear.

Quiet and Loud.
Both apart of you,
Being a lost part of me . . .
I remember.

Jo Anne Greathouse
LOVE
*[This poem was inspired, by
our Lord Jesus Christ & is
dedicated, to all those who
walk in his way.]*
Love is kind
Love is gentle
Love is when you touch me
Love is sweet
Like that of candy
Once tasting the sweetness
Our hearts cry out for more.
More Kindness
More Gentleness
More Patience
More Giving
More Living
Which all add up, to
More Loving

Keith Rifenburg
CRY SOFTLY
I see tears
    falling slowly
on blush red cheeks
    your eyes
    shine
with soft tears
salty hot tears
for happy
    times
    remembered now
laughing
running falling
loving
    being you
    being me
    being
the softness in you

touches me
with new
    awareness
    and thoughts
happy sad
tears echo canyons
of wet on your
    cheeks
blush red
soft and warm
cry softly so
we don't wake
    the cat

Wendell Kelly
A DEED FOR TODAY
Someday when I walk across the
    street,
I hope there is a friend that I may
    meet.
Someone who needs a helping
    hand,
Maybe a child or even a man.
If I can I'll help them out,
And just be thankful that I was
    about.
I'll be happy that I did a good deed.
Something nice to make me
    pleased.
My spirits will be high the whole
    day long,
Knowing I did something that
    wasn't wrong.
Then down on my knees I'll
    begin to pray,
"Dear Lord guess what . . . I
    helped someone today."

Teresa Stoneking Lowrey
PASSAGES OF TIME
Oh, sagacious woman
Come of age!
And life's prodigious abstraction
Is yours
To capsulate—
Illuminate.

Stride forth
Through passages of time.
Time to stretch,
To soar—
Gain steps away from
That Youth.

Woe, but to lose that Youth
Forces lonely abssess
And that which is endearing
Is bereft of—
Too soon
Without humor.

Lois Marie Needham
THE MOVING FOG
The fog came rolling
    In early one summer's eve.

It was so thick, I finally
    Found you.

But when it cleared, you
    Were gone and I never
    Found you again.

K.M. Culby
WORKING CLASS
We sit in cold rooms,
    where lights do not burn.
And cry hungry tears,
    too weary to learn,
    not to look back at better years.

Our cars do not run—
    gas costs too damn much.
Have we become bums?
    We wonder and fret . . .

No—we can't be bums—
we're too heavy in debt.

We want to work—
we really do . . .
Just to feed ourselves,
and our children too—
not to beg . . .

So, we wait on the promise of a
new deal,
that never comes . . .
We've used every resource,
even our thumbs.

Soon, we'll be on the road,
with nowhere to go.
And we'll bare out the winter;
perhaps, buried in snow.
Suicide is not the answer . . .

When all we want is to work;
not a reason to die.
Just our place in the sun—
a small slice of the pie . . .

Amy Jane Holman
ELEPHANT AND SWAN
[For my mother who likes each]
The moon dipped swing a quasi
crescent fling
Of light bright down on the plain
where
Big dream sleep four gray
elephants be.
And the wide sky rises blue deep
blue over wide
Flat land over wide lump
pachyderms sleep set.
Three four maybe more thin tall
trees wing
High black bunch-cluster leaves
against the sky.

The sun rose bright circle melon
color light
Over silver lapping sky catching
water
Where two swans crossed
swimming sweetly moving
neatly
Never seeming to be running
underwater.
Whitely plumed nicely groomed
silent ballet for the birds.
Swans are always ruling their
platinum pool of aqua
Cooling, beneath high cerulean
sky.

Eva Lee
OH SOCIETY PITY ME
Oh society pity me
make me see
that you care for me.
Make me wish you will
look at me.
Make me feel you'll
attend to me.
Oh society can't you see
I want to be a part of thee.
Don't pity me.—make me
see your society.

Lyvonn Berry
OUR CHILDREN
As a flower grows in a garden
So beautiful and free,
A child grows up in a home
As happy as can be.

We love the pretty flowers
They're sent from up above.
We also love our children
And pamper them with love.

The flowers they grow tall,
Their roots go so deep.
The children grow so quickly,
You can watch them as they
sleep.

But too soon the summer's ended,
And the flowers they are gone.
Too fast the children grow up
And are ready to leave home.

So when you see a garden
All beautiful in bloom,
Just think of all our children
Sleeping in their rooms.

Please don't pick the flowers,
They're there to be seen.
Please respect our children
And try not to be mean.

Just love and understanding
A happy home will make,
Give yourself to your children
And that's all it will take.

Grace Ramsey
To a Very Dear Friend At Christmas
[Dedicated to David A. Merrick]
As I reflect on the year now
ending
In the Christmas candle glow,
I think of what you mean to me
How wonderful you are to
know.

I'm grateful just for what you are,
Your smiling, kind and
thoughtful ways;
For the joy you've added to my
world,
For brightening up my lonely
days.

May the happiness you've given
me,
Multiplied, return to you
And may Christmas love and
Christmas cheer
Be in your heart the whole year
through.

E. Noreen Colson
MY MOUNTAIN
*[To Christ . . . I thank Him for
His abounding grace and
strength.]*
I have been to the top of a
mountain
I have quenched my thirst with
peace
I have been to the top of a
mountain
'Twas there I found release

I have been to the top of a
mountain
I have fed on the silent air
I have been to the top of a
mountain
I have found my solace there

Brice B. Andree
I HAVE
I have walked the length of a
golden wheat field,
with the ripened heads
whispering in the winds.
I have smelled the roses,
as the blossoms covered the
bushes;
in an array of a dozen different
colors.
I have worked the land,
which in all of history had never
been cut.
I have seen the sunrise and
sunsets of many days,
but never once were they ever
the same.
I have felt the arctic cold of winter,
and the scorching heat of
summer days.
I have slept among the animals
and plants,
alone with myself, but felt no fear.
I have sung the songs played by
many,
and even sang words only heard
by myslef.
The pain, I have felt by natures
cruel jokes,
I have had pain along the way.
I have tried the impossible, as
most people do,
and a time or two with success.
I have lived all these years, as
best that I could,
and I hope some say this is true.
But today I may accomplish a feat
byond belief,
As I can say . . . I have touched
God's Golden ground . . .

Sharon K. Jennings
TUNNELS
When you feel you're in a tunnel,
there are certain things to do.
For the God that made the
mountains, knows all the
tunnels, too.
He knows exactly where you are,
and calls you by your name.
He does not want that you
should live in darkness or in
pain.
God wants to take you by the
hand, and hold you, oh so near.
The paths you trod and struggle
o'er, to Him are very clear.
SO!—When you're in the tunnel,
lift up your voice and shout!
Then God will surely hear you,
and set forth to bring you out.

Mrs. Hardie L. (Ann) Barr
MY HUSBAND'S HANDS
If I were asked which part of you
I loved the best
I'd have to say your precious
hands, more than the rest.
For your hands have soothed and
comforted when in pain
Have borne my burdens
uncomplaining through the
sunshine and the rain.
Your hands have known more
than their part of toil and care,
Have asked no more of life than
of my lot to share.
Your hands have given strength
in time of need
Have been gentle, kindly, tender
as if it were my meed.
Your hands have given calm
assurance when fear came in
the night;
Have comforted ailing children
and helped to guide them right.
Your hands have provided the
things needed for a good life;
Have worked and labored
unselfishly to serve God and
the right.
So if some part of you I needs
must love the best,
I'd have to say your precious hands
more than all the rest.

Tracy Duane Hardy
BROWN EYES
There is a girl, a beautiful one;
whose beauty and brillance
Outshines the sun.
God made her beautiful, for the
whole world to see, and I pray,
Oh Lord, that she'll love me.
When I first saw her it was love
at first sight, and her face
Seemed to glow with a
heavenly light.
But one feature engulfed me, like
a winter sunrise, the light
Sparkling in her lovely Brown
Eyes.
It sparkled and flittered like
sunshine off dew, and I said in
My heart Brown Eyes, I love you.
When I pass her in the hall, and
she smiles at me, I feel like
Jumping with joy, and I am
filled with glee.
Oh, God, you made her so soft
and gentle, my love for her, is
Far more than mental.
Lord, I thank you for giving her
the best, that made me love
Her more than the rest.
But, God, you do follow
mysterious trends, and I praise
You again for giving me, caring
friends.
Oh, Lord, you gave her a figure
that's fine, you gave her Father
an intelligent mind.
You gave her, God, Brown Eyes to
see, Oh, Lord will she ever
Love me?
Oh, God, I praise you and give
you the credit and all, from
Brown Eyes smiling, to saying
"Hey" to me in the Hall.
I'll praise you forever, my Lord
and master, if me and Brown
Eyes could live happily ever after.
But, Lord if this is not your will,
you may have my world I'll
Praise you still.
And, Lord if our relationship you
don't start, Brown Eyes will
still have a place deep in my
heart.
Oh, Father these are my requests,
from the bottom of my heart,
And relationship, I'll leave up
to you to start.

Jacqueline McCarn Ingrum
Birth Of the Christ Child
*[To My Dear Grandchildren
Charles Mack Ingrum, Jr. Julia
Katheryn Ann Ingrum]*
It came to pass in those days,
A decree from the Emperor of
Rome
Was sent out to all the people,
To pay tax on all they owned.

So Mary and Joseph left Nazareth,
A City of Galilee,
To pay their tax in Bethlehem,
Obeying the Emperor's decree.

When reaching the City of David
So weary and tired and sore,
They found that all the inns were
full
Not room for one soul more.

Joseph now was desperate
Since Mary was great with child,

Sadly asked the Innkeeper,
"May we rest a little while?"

The Innkeeper then saw Mary,
Who was leaning 'gainst a table
And said to Joseph more kindly,
Out back of the Inn is a stable.

Stay there for only half the price.
It's all that I can do,
As you can see the Inn is full
And running over too.

But Mary and Joseph were happy
Just to have a place to nod,
A place to lay their weary head
And give praise and thanks to God.

So it came to pass while they
    were there,
T'was born a little Stranger,
Who was gently wrapped in
    swaddling clothes,
And layed there in a manger.

Now shepherds who watched
    their flocks by night
Were staying in the fields,
When the Angel of the Lord came
    upon them,
The Saviours Birth to reveal.

And the Angel of the Lord said
    unto them—
Fear not—Great Joy I bring
For unto you all the people is born,
A Saviour who is Christ The King.

The Shepherds found the Christ
    Child
And spread throughout the land
The news of the Saviours coming
To save his fellow man.

The people heard and marveled
But Mary set herself apart,
And kept all these things within
    her
And pondered them in her heart.

Brigitta Millard
SOMEWHERE
Somewhere the summer sunset
    Is calling out my name.
Somewhere the roaring sea
    Is whispering the same.
Somewhere your empty hand
    Is yearning to hold mine.
And you are waiting there for me
    And will be all through time.
Somewhere the rocks are sitting
    Upon the sandy beach.
And then I'll see you running
    But you're not within my reach.
Then our hands will meet
    And we'll walk hand in hand,
Across the beach at sunset
    At our feet the sand.
We'll walk there forever.
    Together we will be
Sitting at the ocean
    Only you and me.

Ghislain Brisson
MERCI MAMAN
*[To a special Mom, Irene, Who
raised a special family under
special circumstances]*
Durant toute une vie
Pendant plus de 6 decennies
Une mere n'a rien epargne
Pour rendre le bonheur dans son
    foyer

"C'est la famille avant tout"
Pour cette maman au grand
coeur mou
Les enfants figurent au premier
    plan
Et pour cela, ils sont
    reconnaissants

Tant de moments et d'annees
    mouvementees
Tant de misere, de prieres et de
    difficultes
Tant d'exigeances de tous cotes
Dire qu'a travers tout cela, elle
    est passee

Cette mere, on la connais
Pour elle, c'est l'amour a' jamais
Depuis le premier jusqu'au dernier
C'est venu le temps de vous
    remercier

Merci pour tout les efforts, le
    travail et le temps
Sacrifes a' chacun de vos enfants
Merci pour l'amour, l'attention et
    le devouement
Enfin grand merci pour vous,
    MAMAN!

David Erikson
PEACE
*[This poem is dedicated to my
family and my close friends.]*
Peace is something which should
    be made.
For we are the whiskers and war
    is the blade.
War leaves hunger, destruction,
    and sadness.
Without it we could live in
    brotherly gladness.
So let's stop the arms race and
    start the peace race
Until the greatness of the
    countries in which we live
Won't be measured by the lives
    we take, but the love we give.

Ercell H. Hoffman
MY SUNSHINE
I've tried to show how much it
means to have you always near
without your warmth I'm afraid
I'll drown with every tear.
As evening comes the night grows
cold and leads my heart astray
still I find without a warn
you leave me late each day.
Let me please have the chance
to see your shinning face
then I'll know without a doubt
that I will win this race.

Aunt Polly
My Brothers Special Friend
*[This poem is written for my
youngest brother Roland
Manglos and dedicated to the
memory of his best and very
special friend George Cashdollar.]*
He was my youngest brothers
special friend,
And they were as close as two
    men could be.
George was like a second father
    to him,
And as Rolands' sister, this I
    could see.

Seven years ago this month, more
    or less,
George took him under his
    fatherly wing.
What started out as a job on a
farm,
Turned into a beautiful lasting
    thing.

They worked together and
    became fast friends.
Goerge saw him through
    heartbreak, gave him advice.
Saw him marry and start his own
    family.
A friendship like this, is so very
    nice.

Tradgedies in life, brought it to
    an end,
But happy memories with us will
    remain.
George was the sort that I'm sure
    would have said,
Pause for a moment, then go on
    again.

To my brother Roland, George
    was special,
As to George, so was Roland, I
    am sure.
A friendship such as this, is great
    to see,
So wonderful, so true, and so pure.

My having a friendship like this
    myself,
I'm sure he feels richness beyond
    compare.
Though as time goes by, some
    tend to forget,
Roland will always remember; I
    swear.

James Elmore
THE LEGACY
*["The Legacy" is dedicated to
my three children—Jason,
David and Kristen. For it is
through them that I will always
have life. The thoughts that
they read, may be the same
values they hold.]*
Dreams, have a life unto
    themselves
Some men know, wise men know
    well
The place to be is peaceful and free
Doing what we came here for
Leaving when your through.

And you'll never be lonely
    anymore
Place your thoughts in the world
    and I'm sure
That the seeds that you plant
    will become
Your wish for the world, oh my
    son.

Where you'll be is set in time
What you become is a frame of
    mind
What people say about you just
    never you care
Just keep heading on that path
That someday they'll share.

And you'll never be lonely
    anymore
You will make your mark I'm
    sure
And your critics will know in the
    end
For you'll smile on them and say,
    "Friend".

Joseph M. Dreimiller
FERNS AND ROSES
Gathered together by the warmth
    of the planet earth.
Comes little green ferns and
    bright red roses.
These are the gifts of the world.
They travel near and far and east
    and west,
Until, arriving at a very special
    place.
They usually shed a good cry,
    when they arrive from afar . . .
For every special one, wishes a
    heart of treasure of joy and
    happiness—
And a scent of love.

JoNelle Vanden Bush
TO BRAD
*[My love, my life, my
everything. You make my
world complete.]*
Wherever I go, whatever I do
My finest thoughts are always of
    you
You're on my mind throughout
    the day
Without your sweet love there'd
    be no way
For me to believe in all my dreams
You're there to pull me through,
    it seems
To help me through those cold,
    dark hours
I turn to you, you have the
    powers
To conquer all the hurt and pain
So they may ne'er return again
Loving you has shown me the
    light
Of how great life can be with a
    love so right
I love you more with each
    passing day
A love so intense, it's hard to
    explain.

Wayne Jennings
YOU
The radiance of your smile,
Your presence sweet and mild;
A kind word for a friend,
A broken heart you can mend.
The soft glow of your eyes,
A mind so very wise.
The soft touch of your hand,
The desire to understand.
Your sometimes childish ways,
You brighten cloudy days.
I can't help but to express
All my joy and happiness.
You'll always be in my heart.
We're two friends who'll never
    part.
And forever on it goes
To the time when we grow old.
Then we can look back and laugh
At those things deep in the past.

B. Jaye
BACKSTREETS
Your memory is lost among the
    ruins
    On the backstreets of my mind,
Where the boulevards of loneliness
    Meet the avenues of broken
    dreams.

Yet I walk along the pavement
    Searching for some elusive sign,
Past the darkened store front
    windows
    That display life's youthful
    scenes.

Down obscure and deserted

alleyways
Lined with heartaches and last
good-byes,
Past decayed and abandoned
hopes,
Past the crumbling remains of
gutted dreams.

Driven on by an aching need
To hold fast to you this time,
I shrug off an old persistent chill
And wander along forgotten
streets.

Till standing amidst love's burnt
out shell,
Your memory's ashes I chance
to find,
And in the bittersweet joy of truth
Comes the pain of being
forever free.

Julie Jean Pursel
FOOLED AGAIN
*[To the many people who love
someone, without the love
being returned.]*
You were my dream
someone I truley cared for.
Life became meaningful again
so much shared and felt.
A towering man of strength

Protective, Passionate, Caring.
All what we need inside
only to realize too late.
It's what I need not you.
but love remains in tackt,
should you ever want to come
back.

Sandra L. Haight
THE GAME OF LIFE
*[To my dear friend and co—
worker—Anna Mae Cooper—
who inspired this writing.]*
Life is a game—
Where everyone would like to
find fame-
It has its' rich and its' poor—
If you don't believe this—just
look out your door—
It's full of love and full of hate—
It's a priviledge to work that's no
debate!
Health and wealth seem to make
this world go round—
Both bring joy to us in leaps and
bounds.
The ill and the poor are with us
too—
Life to them must be very blue.
Equal God created us?
Not for man; until he is dust.

What is the name of this game
we try to play?
I know, it's life they say.
Is this really a game?
If so, then we should all be put to
shame.

Paul Brian Mackey
**Oh Snowstorm, Oh
Snowstorm!**
*[The city's children whose
buildings have rooftops big
enough for a thousand Santa
Stops.]*
Oh Snowstorm, Oh Snowstorm!
We knew you'd come our way.
But golly great snowstorm
Why did it have to be today?

No snows or chains are on their car
And all our relatives are coming
so far.
The children's gloves are still
neatly wrapped
And daddy's carpool is in the
city—trapped.

The ice on the wires make them
real tight
Now the power went off and
there isn't a light.
Our Christmas tree would have
been quite a sight
But is a tree without a light really
all right?

Down the chimney, the wind is
screaming
The thundering snowplows are
disturbing my dreaming.
No roasting of chestnuts on the
open fire
Of this Christmas eve I'll surely
soon tire.

Oh No! There's frost on the
windows
I'll not see his sleigh.
How will Santa Claus find his
way?

You ol' howling snowstorm, why
were you sent?
The cold and the winds, will you
ever relent?
But Oh! What can this Be? Is it
true what I see?
The snow stopped falling, the
winds are not squalling,
The skies are clearing, Could it
be true what I'm hearing?

Oh Snowstorm, Oh Snowstorm!
Now finally you passed our way
With plenty of time for a fine
Christmas Day.

Christine Garrity
PASSAGES OF THE PAST
All I ever wanted
was to love you.
All I ever needed
was to know you cared.
Running through the mazes
up and down
the passages of the past
into the present—
don't seem to be able
to lose it—
follows me around
and takes me through
the tangled messages
the tainted words
and the love we kept inside.
I never wanted it

to be this way.
I never thought it
would end this way.
And keep running
through the mazes
our lives had led us to.
Going down the passages of the
past
into the present—
the hurt—it cannot last.

Donna Lates
ODE TO A PORK
There was a Big Pork!
Who stayed by her fork!
And munched and chowed down
all day long!

Ne're word was stuttered,
Nor sentence muttered,
Til the last swallow and loud
"urp" at the end was uttered!

Dannita Dunny
PURGATORY
Don't cry
not a child
nothings tender, nothings mild
Don't drink
not an adult
nothings right, all my fault
Don't fink
not a kid
things to find, things to rid
Don't lie
not mature
adolesence, there's no cure
Just floating in space
problems to cope, problems to face
Try to prove but always fall
These are the best years, say all

Lynda McCoy
ME AT FOURTEEN
Hours in front of her mirror,
Hours fixing her hair just so.
Dreaming of being a lady,
Dreaming of which way she'll go.
Days of school work and problems,
Days when she's misunderstood.
Dreaming of love, of freedom,
Dreaming that life will be good.
Years of learning, of living,
Years of childhood and fun.
Dreaming dreams of her future,
Dreaming she's twenty—one.

Robert Burns Macphee
Is Destruction Nearing
I listened to the news tonight,
What they said was very
unpleasant,
They talked about a possible war,
Not one of years ago, but this one
of present.

Britain and Argentina had lost
their friendly bond,
What happens now is just a
matter of time
Is World War III in the making?
Or is it just on the word from a
woman's sick mind?

With a nuclear war the world
can't last long,
Destrucion and death most near,
This planet earth again would
just be dust,
Just the thought of this fills my
entire body with fear.

Interference form Russia is most
certian,
It's most deadly weapon, the

feared nerve gas.
It's own will survive because of
specially designed suits,
Their faces protected by leak—
proof masks.

Canada and USA., let's pool our
talents
Let's find the answer to this
problem now,
And the lives that will be saved
including our own,
Is what makes all the friendship
worthwhile.

Bylinda Mason
MY ISLAND
The dawn awakes me in the
crimson sky
And I watch the pearl divers sail
me by
I stretch my arms to the open sea
The village children come play
on me

My body lies in a gulf of water
But still I have a lot to offer
Come open out your heart and see
How easy a friend as I can be

Now dusk that lay upon my breast
Has put the children down to rest
At night my beaches holds for love
Young couple stroll along like
doves

Theres talk that I have changed
so much
But does that really matter
The memories that you hold of me
Is all I ask of thee

My Island and the sea!

Jane Opper
Love the World, Love Me
When you are sad
I am sad,
When you are frightened
I try to be strong because
I love you.
I want you near
but fear you'll miss the
beauty of the oceans,
the sparkling snow—capped peaks
The world's a wonderous place,
love it, savour it;
for it is yours and so am I

Connie J. Plexman
DREAMERS
We Dreamers have our ways
of passing lonely rainy days
Looking through the rain drops
Collecting all our inner thoughts

Searching for that rainbow
that comes at the end
Hoping that we can start
all over again

Making that pot of gold
seem so very close
When being in Love is
what really matters most

Gazing at the puddles, it
seems our problems are few
Knowing that we can work things
out, just like I knew

The clouds fade slowly and soon
the sun will shine
Bringing us together and
making you all mine

When the thunder rolls in and
the clouds soon begin to appear

Today's Greatest Poems

I know we won't be seperated,
cause
in my heart you'll always be near

Then we'll remember the sun and
all the happiness form it's rays
Sunny faces and bright smiles to
carry
us through the next rainy days

So you see Love, us Dreamers
we do have our ways
of getting through together
those dark lonely days

Charles James Phillips
SUNSHINE
Sun is rising on snowy field
Enjoy the glistening prance
Fence post shadows yield
Willowy figures to dance.

Our warmer reaches high
Losing it's figurines
Reveals a blue sky
Streaked by golden gleam.

This sunny winter's day
Icicles hanging down
Begin to drip away
When ever they are found.

A joy to have this sunshine
Calming just to see
I creep along the fence line
Sharing it's warmth with me.

Josee Pleau
Love Has An Element
Love has an element—
of Bliss,
Ecstasy an element—
of Infinity;
My Love has an element—
of Eternity,
My Soul an element—
of Immortality
Whose Circumference is
Undefined.

Phil Rosser
CAPTIVE
Walls around me
grey and old.
Windows with bars
strong and bold.
People with hearts
bitter and cold.
This is prison
with tales untold.

Laurie Smith
ONE LAST FRIEND
When your feeling down and no
place to go,
Remember you have a friend that
only you know,
For deep inside you there's
something there,
And there's no need for you to
share,
It will never leave you night nor
day,
And you can talk with it or even
pray,
Everyone has this special thing,
Your hopes, your dreams it will
always bring,
It's not like a friend which comes
and goes,
But rather something which
grows and grows,
It's there each day as silent as can
be,
And if you want it opened you
have the only key.

Ruth Wedman
SOMEDAY
[This poem is dedicated to my
loving husband Ernest
Wedman, who on many
occasions was the only
peaceful meadow in my life in
a world filled with turmoil.]
Someday I will find a peaceful
meadow
Away from the rest of the world.
There I will bare myself body and
soul.
I'll run through the tall grass
With a freedom unheard of.
I will dance and sing until I'm
exhausted
And my body gleams with sweat.
I'll plunge into the cool waters of
the stream.
I'll be bare and wet like I was
When I arrived in this nightmare
world.
I'll pretend I never happened
As I lie beneath the trees to rest.
Then I'll plan how I could stay
here forever.
The sun will dry my body.
I'll sleep like a babe undisturbed.

Mrs. Grace Weisner (Wile)
CORNERS AND SIDES
[To my teacher "Mrs. Albert
Counteway" in appreciation for
her help and friendship.]
Love is a four cornered word,
one side is forever.
Theres a side for mutual trust,
doubt each other never.
A side that gives and takes
and forgives our small mistakes.
The side left is the unknown
which cannot be faced on our own.
Things that are seen and
conquered,
with obstacles found each day.

Joy is a three sided friend,
sad when it comes to an end.
The best side of joy is when it's
given
It's something you cannot lend.
When joy is received it is doubled
which means the third side has
been reached.

Hate is a two edge knife,
which can mangle and ruin your
life.
For as well as begetting most
henious sin
it destroys the breast that it
dwells within.

Friend ship has only one side.

Lori A. Hobart
**Remember Me Through
These Roses**
These roses I give to you
As a symbol of my love and
gratitude,
One shall be me
The other shall be you.
They are both the same type
But unique in their own way,
As we are.
Our lives touch as the leaves do,
Twist together like the stems
And beautify each other.
Please love me for what I am
And remember me always
through these roses.

Tom Worbets
THE FREE HEART
There was a free man who was a
slave, and there was a slave
that was free.
They met one day and laughed at
each ohter, but only one of
them could see.
That Freedom lies in the center
of the heart, it can never be put
in chains.
Remember the Lord, live His
message, and freedom is what
remains.

Katherine M. DeNering
FREEDOM'S CHARGE
We were ten thousand,
Sailing the ocean deep,
With freedom's charge to keep;
Knowing once again
That light we must defend.
Our Lady of Liberty,
Holding her torch on high,
Stood tall and strong against the
sky.
As we bade farewell,
In passage of time we could not
tell
Of our return from a distant
shore;
Or who would remain
forevermore.

Helen Marcella Banuelos
HUMITLITY REFLECTED
Did you put on your
understanding nature today?
There's something I have to say.
Did you button—up your
compassion in haste?
I need to know, this can't wait.
Did you don your boots to stomp
out all the injustice falling
around me?
And your gloves of tenderness,
are they in place?
Can you help me weather
through this storm inside of me?
You see, I need to know,
I just can't wait.
There's something I have to say.

Janet Pfeifer Waring
COUNTRY ROAD
As the sun fades past a summers
dream
And the misty haze of Autumn
falls upon the mountain side
I learn to walk alone,
A shadow against the rainy
hillside.

Uncertain of the colored leaves
on the country road
Afraid of the chilly wind
wandering around me,
Paralized with the thought of
spending the winter alone.

There are neither tears nor smiles
Just an empty space inside.

I realize there is nothing constant
Nothing is real when you
withdraw.

Miles, and miles, I will find you
Hidden under a frozen stream,
Or in the poetry of a fool.

Hattie Davidson
INDOLENCE
A soft warm breeze
An indolent mood,

And I'm off again
Into memory's wood
To a place where white violets
Stand tall in green leaves,
And I'm sprawled among them
In indolent ease.
Not a thought,
Not a care,
Have the violets and I
Not a smile,
Not a frown,
Not even a sigh.
For this is sheer indolence
Whose joys I still know
When spring days come
And soft breezes blow.

Wm. Dale Malleck
EYE WITNESS
The coming sun pushed up, a
flared red;
As the descending moon perched
precariously on Mt. Baldy.
Swallows were darting for
breakfast in air,
Gargling their gutteral greetings.
The sharp stacatto notes of the
kingbird
And the trill of the blackbird
enhanced the beauty
Of this early morning.

Then I saw you. You—long, slim,
slender,
Your supple motion gracefully
flexible.
A miniature red—tasseled pony
tail
Playing with the breeze,
Dancing your spontaneous
dance—
Your gentle joust with nature.
Then I saw other tufts of grass,
So stationary, so limited, yet so
wonderfully alive.
How pure, how proud your spirits
shine.

How gracefully you cavortt

A momentary hush—and I saw
you like earth whiskers,
Standing stright up—immobile—
as if in great fright.
Then the breeze bounced you and
stirred you wildly,
And the first rays of the sun hit
you
And lit you all like fire,
Transforming the vast rolling
prairie
Into a gaily waving, tossing,
teasing,
Saucy redhead.

Cheryl L. Caddell
FOR BRIAN
Send me some love,
I need a lover.
Send me some love,
I need a friend.
Send me some love,
I am so lonely.
Love, bring this loneliness to and
end.

Send me some caring,
I need a mother.
Send me protection,
I need a dad.
Send me some tenderness,
I need a baby.
These days are the lonliest
I've ever had.

Send me a joke,
   I need some laughter.
Send me the sunshine,
   I need some light.
Send me a melody,
   I need some music.
Send inspiration,
   And songs I will write.

Send me the rainbow
   over my mountains.
Send me the moon
   and the stars up above.
Send me your smile and
   your tears, I will dry them.
Send me your heart,
   I need your love.

Teri Groblebe Rigsby
GOD'S MASTERPIECE
In Others; . . . I don't Mind
   Imperfection.
It's as if . . . Their All Winners Of
   A Popularity Selection!
Their All People . . . I Very Much
   Admire . . .
And Their Short—comings Are
   Easily Explained Away . . .
   Never To Mar.
Howere, I Seem To Find In
   Myself . . . Plenty To
   Criticize . . .
And Call Myslef Silly Names . . .
   None Of Them Wise.
Perhaps One Day . . . I Will Look
   Upon Myself With Ease . . .
And See Myself As Truly . . .
   God's Masterpiece!
Then I'll Like Myself Better, And
   Will Try With All I've Got . . .
To Love Myself . . . And Others
   . . . And Criticize . . . Not!!!

Dan Richards
DAWN—SONG
Morning stream
   Hums it's dawn—song
     Wistfully,
It's easy rhyme
   Sliding by me
     In quiet verses,
Leaving with me
   The soft scent of God
   In passing.

Rob Wyant
troubled
so they may say, "here is the way,
   take it like it comes",
yea, i try to, but like the wind my
   mind blows to
   kingdom come where answers
     must come
       or troubled kingdom

yet i don't know, water flows,
   people move, my life goes in
   motion
still i don't see, i try to but it's
   very dark seeing
   what must be done but
   something must
     or troubled water

there goes that high—flying bird
   moving right along
but i stay stuck in the ground
   called my mind
   i got to know where people
   stand
     or troubled people

never saying no to those questions
cannot answer without rhyming

sit down and cry
   not mellowed out
   i got to see my place here
     or troubled mind

Dottie Dunbar
GHOST MINERS
If you and I could only talk
As amid these precious walls I
   walk.
Tell me of the life you led
As thru these sacred halls you
   tread,
Of the wondrous hopes and
   dreams
As you built these floor and
   rafter beams.

These homes hewn out of a
   wilderness,
Born of Mother Nature's
   blessedness.
The hopen of all the glittering gold
Dug from these hills, ancient and
   old.
Dreams of the riches, unforetold
By men, so brave and bold.

Amie Trout
NATAL GREETING
"Let not your heart
   be troubled"!
Let not the passing
   hands of Time
Cause undue distress.
   There is,
Within the Universe.
   Infinite time
For all things good.
   For God IS,
Has BEEN,
   Will BE,
     Forever!
Time is counted only
   Within our mind.
You are a Child of
   Infinity,
   For You are
     Divinity—
The Universe
   And ALL it's Time
     Are YOURS!!!

Alan S. Matsunaka
TRANSFORMATION
Once you were a little one in
   your shell
Not knowing where to go
What to do, or tell
Young and innocent, and willing
   to learn

You started out the hard way
By making a few errors
You had to walk, before you
   could fly
Still young and naive, and
   starting alone

Made a few good friends, on your
   way up
By outstretching your hands to
   help
You've filled your success cup
Grown up now, and ready for
   love

Soon you will find that special
   one
By spreading your wings, and
   opening up
Then you will have, a little one
To love and cherish, and ready to
   teach

Greg Kain
THE COLLEGE QUARTER
College! oh me, oh my!
I really think I'm going to die.
Studies are hard, parties are free,
Stay out late and you'll pay the fee.
Mid terms come and mid terms go,
How good did you do? You don't
   know
Now the home stretch is very near
So let's go out and have another
   beer.
The final week is here, there is
   hope in sight,
Your not going down without a
   fight.
Now finals come and you do
   flunk
Now you know you shouldn't
   have gotten drunk.
But never to fear,
Because next quarter is almost
   here.

Willie Belle Dixon
NIGHT
Void of light for a number of hours,
   This earth of ours must be;
'Tis a time that is given by God,
   A time of rest for you and me.

Oh, but not entirely void of light—
   See the stars shining there?
And the moon, Queen of night,
   Scatters her radiance everywhere.

Bright as day, the moon oft shines
   And sails through cloudless skies;
The crickets chirp, frogs croak
   And there, a gray bat flies!

'Still of the night'? No, oh no—
   Do you not hear the nightbird's
   trill
As he calls to his mate to join him
   Who lingers in the tree on
   yonder hill?

So, welcome to you, dear Night,
   Linger with us awhile, we pray,
That we may renew our strength
   To face the coming of day.

Bethany J. Kissell
THE BUCK
The buck with soft, intelligent,
   glowing eyes, steps from the
   woods to graze in the meadow.
His trusting steps know no fear,
   his pointed hooves moving
   silently in the grass.

His proud and free head lifts to
   sniff for danger and his
   beautiful rack is his crowning
   glory.
He is startled by a motion and
   bounds away like a leaf in the
   wind.

Vito A. Milatzo
A SIMPLE QUESTION
A simple question filtering the
   brain
It turns the mind from normal to
   insane

A spreading plague thats
   anchored the seas
Is entering my brain like a
   disease

Tickleing my brain to start
   blinking
I would rather stop this before
   thinking

Taking resolutions to the limit
One decision ages in a minute

Edith Wagner
TO A FRIEND
I am thinking today of you, my
   friend,
And wishing that you were here.
While my many duties seem
   never to end
And my heart is filled with fear.

Am I doing right by my fellow
   man?
Am doing the things I should?
Am I doing just the things I can?
And not the things I could?

From early morning 'til late at
   night
I want to please those 'round me.
Oh, help me to see the great
   white light
And set my sick soul free.

That's why I'm thinking of you,
   dear one,
And wishing that you were here.
Of all my friends in this wide
   world,
It's you, I need, my dear.

Susan Adams
FIRE
You were like a fire
   burning strong, glowing bright.
Your eyes shone like a flame
   flickering with happiness.
Your body breathed radiant heat
   warmth and security
     but now
You are ice, cold and hard
   extinguishing the fire and
   flames to ashes.

linda l. brown
BROKEN WINGS
Oftentimes my own eyes cannot
   see
what memory will
of new pain;
like windows wild birds believe
   to be air
only to bash their bodies
and wings
against the glass—
unable, ever again,
to fly.

Maybe you think I can forget
that I will never fly again,
or that the stars are now
forever unreachable from this pit
I know so well,
and sometimes, because you
   believe,
I let my eyes look,
and broken wings flutter
with new pain.

Brad Miller
TO CAPTURE TIME
Man has searched for a way to stay
The beauty he holds on a fleeting
   day
To elate forever as he feels just
   then
Like pain and sorrow had never
   been

Could man speak with Time to
   make a deal
That his joys of life not to steal
Unhappy days he would not know
To be free in life with seed to sow

Today's Greatest Poems

But Time erodes man's moments
  of bliss
The radiant sunset to the softest
  kiss
With no concern for human need
No care of love nor selfish greed
So Time contours the dreams of
  life
Brings happiness and wretched
  strife
And man goes on with empty hope
To find a way with his life to cope

Dell M. Mangum
MY WIFE
My wife, my woman, the pride of
  my life,
Has won my friendship, and
  eased the strife
That sometimes accompanies a
  second marriage.
A smile, a caress, a never
  disparage,
Smoothing the wrinkles from the
  under carriage.
Being an equal in sharing the load,
Keeping me headed down the
  right road.
A timekeeper, chauffeur,
  companion and guide,
Through projects old and some
  I've not tried.
Making suggestions and helping
  decide
The best course of action, the
  blueprint, and plan.
Whatever it takes to keep peace
  in the clan.
Finding the time to keep a clean
  house,
Doing the washing or ironing a
  blouse,
Cooking good meals, a truely fine
  spouse,
While working a job from three
  to eleven,
She still manages breakfast by
  quarter to seven.
This wonderful lady is like a fine
  wine,
And that God led me to her is a
  nice sign;
Apart we are nothing, together
  we're fine.
My wife, my woman, the pride of
  my life.

Penny I. Evans
THE NARROW PATH
Down a path so steep and narrow,
  we stop to watch a flying
  sparrow.

Down further still we pause,
  really for no purpose or cause.

Yet further down, we look aside,
  we see a friend who has died.

You ask about this spoken path,
  it is life and it's great wrath.

Here I stop for the story ends,
  but the path goes on and
  extends.

The way ahead I cannot see.
  I only know it holds something
  for me.

Mary Louise Merrill
DEAR POETS
"Hi there—
I've been your face
across the page;

as if to see you
upon a stage.
I've read your joys,
your sorrows, your dreams,
your loves, your hates, your pleas;
and expressive personal
philosophies.
Are you my brothers?
Are you my sisters?
With need to express yourselves
this way?
With a yearning to have printed
in black and white
colorful words to display?
Shall I call you friend
and praise you somehow
for your lovely verses I've read?
Yes, I shall, and let you know,
how much I enjoy sharing
the same path with you,
that poets tread.
From front to back, wherever
  your
in print—
I don't know where to begin;
all I can say,
somewhere along the way,
in my heart, I have let you in.
Who??
You!
Dear Poets."

Monica C. Gallion
NEW EDEN
I walked gingerly along a narrow
  path of soil,
surrounded by lush ferns and trees.
The canopy of the forest was rich
  with beauty,
put here by the Creator.

The branches of the evergreens
  and deciduous trees hung high
  above my head.
Through the branches I could see
  a beam of sunlight as it struck
  the forest floor,
onto a clearing.

The sound of rushing streams
  could be heard in the distance,
when I came upon a garden . . .

Verla Hale Adams
MODERN PILGRIM
*[Dedicated to my husband,
Lyman Park Adams, and our
ten children: Doris, Verlene,
Dennis, Gayla, Arlen, Ellis,
Lyman, Mary Carol, Keith and
Ruth, also to their husbands or
wives and all our
grandchildren.]*
A Pilgrim I have never been
  (Upon a rock bound shore),
But I must face a world of sin
  (Forever at my door),
Because of wicked men's designs
  (That do beset me still),
Which follow after Satan's lines
  (And not Our Father's will).

A Pilgrim I would rather be,
Beside the Plymouth Rock, you see,
And there confront a hostile band
Upon a new and restless land,

Then be exposed to filth and smut
Upon a tube deep in a rut,
And in so many places turn
To pages now just fit to burn.

But, on each new Thanksgiving
  Day,

I hope that I can ever say,
"I'm strong as any Pilgram man
Who came to worship, work and
  plan."

Dusty Roads

Dusty Roads
DARLIN' KATHY
I have known you for awhile
And I feel like I'm in love with you
When we meet on the Avenue
Won't you come with me to the
  Movies
I would show you a good time
I'll pick you a Flower by the
  Wayside
Dearest Kathy
Let me kiss your dark hair
And be gentle with you
As if you were made of glass
Sweet Kathy

You got the face of a Gambler
That reveals nothing to me
You play Solitaire
With your painted desert Beauty
And you stand like a lone tree
Out there on the Prairie

Oh my lovely Kathy, I'm aging so
  fast
But you are still young
Please come see me again
Where the trees bend their
  Branches
I'll take my chances with you,
  Darlin' Kathy
And my undying love will shine
For you only—like the blade of
  my Sword
That protects you
Sweet Kathy

Sometimes you are as Silent
As a graveyard, Darlin' Kathy
I could feel the change of the Wind

When you kiss me
The mysteries that surround you
Since your dear mother Died
I could solve them, my dark
  haired Beauty
If I play the Detective in your life
  Story
Let me share your troubles
And fight the hoodlums with
  their lust.
In a cloak and dagger race for
  your Love
Sweet Kathy.

Nellie B. Williams
MEMORY—HILLS
I am lonesome to roam
The beloved hills of home,
Just to think of the
  going—back—part,
Puts an upswing—of—joy in my
  heart.

Yes, I am anxious to go back and
  see
All my treasured—hills finery;
For those hills that are now
  flowered—crowned,
Were my childhood's proud
  pleasure ground.

In the pleasing—peace of
  summer's first smile,
I will linger on my memory—
  hills awhile;
See the glory of the dawning sun,
And dusk's splendor when the
  day is done.

Ann Wallin
TO A STRANGER
I passed you on the street and
  saw you smile.
The sun appeared, a song was in
  my heart
Accompanied by phantom violins—
The beat of distant drums.
You didn't see me,
That was not so strange.
But all that day and far into the
  night
I held that small warm memory—
  I'd heard your voice,
  I'd seen your smile—
And yet, I did not even know
  your name.

You never knew the times I
  followed you
Into the market or the tackle shop.
I purchased things I couldn't use
To linger by your side.
Seeing the laugh lines by your eyes,
The stain of cigarettes on your
  dear hand.
You left the salesgirl with a smile
And you were gone. My heart
  sang on—
  I'd heard your voice—
  I'd seen your smile—
And yet, I did not even know
  your name.

Robert M. Huffman
MYSTICAL LADY (PART I)
Laying in the grass on the bank of
  the stream,
I fell into sleep and had the
  strangest dream.
I sank into a strange world, it was
  so real,
Mystical emotions were all that I
  could feel.

I was in a meadow, you were
  standing there,
so pretty, the moonlight dancing
  off your hair.
You were shining with your
  womanly mystique,
laughing, taunting, with your
  beautiful physique.
You came to me in the calmness
  of the night,
You held me, oh baby, you held
  me so tight.
Holding you makes me feel so
  very complete,
no earthly emotion could ever
  compete.
It all came together when you
  touched my soul,
for once in my life, I had a
  direction to go.
I woke up with the wind blowing
  in my hair,
and I knew that I had to find you
  somewhere.
So I started on my long and
  lonely trail,
with confidence, knowing that I
  couldn't fail.
Oh Mystical Lady, you have
  touched my soul,
hold on to me baby, please don't
  let me go.
I want those mystical emotions
  again,
Lady, I want to be your lover,
  your friend.
Lady, you are someone special,
  someone true,
Mystical Lady, let me make love
  to you.

Dorothy M. Homan
VISIONS

I see you in the morning
  Bringing coffee on a tray
Your face wreathed in smiles
  As we begin our day.

I see you at noontime
  Seated across from me
An hour snatched from your lab
  work
  Asking about my shopping spree

I see you in the evening's hush
  There's not a soul around
You fling the door wide open
  And I am in your arms.

I see you in our bedroom
  The lights are soft and warm
I'm dressed in my mauve dressing
  gown
  Your favorite one of all.

You snap the light
  A sign our day is done
You enfold me in your arms
  And you and I are one.

Connie Patterson
MEETING
*[For Christopher, who made it
all true, with all my love, forever.]*
Picking up men from the side of
  the road
Is as dangerous, I have been told,
As gathering roses from amid
  thorns
Or reheating a passion grown cold.

  Hitchhiking, too, has its
  perils, you say;
  And I cannot deny that it's true:

For you never can tell who's
  stopping
Or the cost of the ride offered
  you.

Yet grateful I am that we took
  the risks
And that, each in our different
  ways,
We put "'ware" behind, pushed
  Wisdom aside,
And changed both our lives for
  all days.

Rachel Skidmore Botner
PIANO LESSONS
[For Elsie]
Sat at the piano, practicing a chore.
Knew I'd have to sit for a half
  hour or more.
I wanted to play (but not to earn);
She said "practice is the way to
  learn."

Oh, what a task that my Mother
  asked.

Beside me She had placed a clock;
It held no sympathy; just went
  tick, tock.
Slowly, begrudgingly, the time
  went by
And practicing led my fingers to
  fly.

Of my whole being, it'd become
  part,
For no longer did I wish to dart
Outdoors to friends who called,
  "let's play."
I'd sit at the piano—half a day!

Now, I'd rather have that old
  upright
With my Mother here, making
  me sit tight
Than let my fingers get this rusty
While my Grand gets just as dusty.

But I still sit there when I can,
Remembering how it all began.

Oh, what a pleasure; that task:
  my treasure.

Dusty Roads

Dusty Roads
**Wish I Was Leavin' More
Often**
I won't forget
That October night we Met
It was cold and Windy
How pretty you Looked
And I love the way you Dress
You were there lookin' like a
  Southern Belle
I remember quite Well

It was my Birthday
And my Age it meant Nothing
But when you kiss me as we
  Parted
Your lips were so Sweet
And I wish I was leavin' more
  Often.

Sometimes I dream of You
When I go to bed at Night
You are like the Star I Follow
That leads me to my Destination
  in Life
I wish you would live Forever
As we travel together just you
  and I
Like the Railroad Tracks
And when you Kiss me in the
  Morning
I will walk away and leave you in
  the Dark my Darling
But your sweet lips I would
  Remember
And how I wish I was leavin;
  more Often.

My thoughts of You
Are of Happiness and good
  Health
I would like to Marry You
And offer you all of my Wealth
Which is my love and Affection
And to please you in every
  Direction
You are so kind and Loving
And each time you Kiss Me
Oh my Dear Patricia stop Crying
Your lips were so Sweet
And I wish I was leavin' more
  Often.

Any Artist will paint You
Poets will write about your Beauty
But no one will Love You
As much as I do
Your Dear Mother will not
  forgive Me
If my Love for you was in Vain
And if there is an Eternity
I will Love you once Again
So please come back to see Me
Don't leave me in Anguish and Pain
Let me remember your sweet Lips
And how you were so Daring
How I wish I was leavin' more
  Often.

John Paul Lucero
SENTIMENTS OF LOVE
When I hear her cries,
I can feel her hurt for love.
I want to reach her,
to let her know her value.
She is precious above all.

I have need to know,
Am I ever in her thoughts?
Does she see in me,
A gentle spirit shine forth?
Eyes of radiant kindness?

Someday I am sure,
We will be brought together.
Each of us will see,
the value of the other.
Time will mature both our loves.

Yolanda Martinez
MEMORIES
The guy that I love is one step
  away to keeping the memory
  that is only one pain. The day
  has come and the time is here
  to share the times that were
  about to fear. The fear has pass
  and the love is back for the one
  that I've had is free from his
  sack. He is as handsome as the
  one that went his way but the
  memory is here and here to stay.

Raylene M. Reed
MAMA
Who smiles when you do?
And crys along with you too?
And manages in bad times,
  to always come through?
  "MAMA"

She spent her life teaching
  the things no teacher would even
  try.
Like how to love, and how to smile,
  and how to laugh, when all the
  while,
Deep inside, you want to cry.

She's always kept her "cool",
When the bills were due, and the
  kids
all needed new clothes for school.
And when times are hard, and
  things go wrong,
Who in the world do you find,
  with a smile on her face, and
  singing a song?
  "MAMA"

Dorothy Jean Horton
THE GOOD SHEPHERD
*[To my husband, who has
walked each step of the way
with me.]*
The shepherd is the great master,
  Responsible, gentle, alert,
Guiding his sheep by night and
  day,
  Watching lest one of his flock
  be hurt.

Each morning he leads them to
  pasture
  Where healthy green grass
  abounds,
And chooses a spot near still
  waters
  Lest a sheep from great
  turbulence drowns.

In Jerusalem there's many a path
  Where predators roam so free;
But the shepherd brandishes rod
  and staff
  That his flock pass through
  fearlessly.

The shepherd's hooked staff saves
  many a sheep
Who've fallen o'er mountain
  slide,

For he slips the crook around its neck
  And hauls it safe to his side.

He examines each sheep for thorn or bruise,
Then brings forth his horn of oil
And gently pours on the ragged cut
Lest infection set in from the soil.

As night comes on, they settle in peace,
  Docile, relaxed and calm;
They know their shepherd watches o'er,
  With goodness and mercy their balm.

Sharon F. Cote
LITTLE POEMS
Old songs, walks in the mall,
Christmas—brings back the best memories of all,
An elfin doll named Happy, and a sea shell from the beach. These are some of the things that mean a lot to me.

Letters overflowing with love, a ribbon winning sketch that I've done, myself.
For in my heart, my love—there can be no-one else.

Frankie Barrera
I DREAM A DREAM OF YOU
The day that I met you—I somehow knew
  That we'd become lovers
We'd share all our news—
So we started dating—became heavily involved
  And before we knew it—we'd fallen in love

So thats why I lie here—not sure what do
Thinking of the one I love—I dream a dream of you
No need to feel hatred—too late for regrets—
We were once lovers—How soon we forget

Just like a fantasy—it seems so unreal
  Someone I could lean on
  The love I could feel
Then in a Moments time—A short walk in the rain
  The time we once knew
    Ended in dismay

So that's why I lie here—knowing it's true
When I need you by my side—I dream a dream of you
Theres no need to feel hatred—too late for regrets
We were once lovers—how soon we forget

Grace T. J. Chamness
RECEPTION ROOM
The wide-eyed little boy, frightened and pale, peers upward
As the receptionist asks many questions.
The child grasps his mother's hand, locked in a grip
Too tight for her to release.
He glances shyly at the dimpled, chubby baby girl

Whose mother holds her so lovingly.
Her darling smiles and coos, unaware
That soon she will feel pain,
Sharp, insulting, searing pain!
She will not comprehend that the pain-causing substance
Will help to keep her happy and healthy.
For the timid lad, being here for a pre-school check up, each
Minute of anticipation becomes more dreadful,
'Cause big brother taunted him with
Tales of "shots and stuff".
Finally the time comes for the show down, but
The friendly nurse and the kind, gentle doctor
Prove to him that sometimes 'big brother' is wrong.

Jani Gallagher
Innocence Lost Is Never Regained
As years go by,
Big dreamy eyes flatten into knowing ones;
For we see more and more—
Much more than we care to see.
The only realistic hopes
Are those that are half-heartedly felt;
And the only truth realized
Is born out of compromise.
Innocence is never recognized
Except by those who own it no more
And those who can no longer see its value.
So it matters not
That innocence exists only here,
On pages no one will ever turn to.

Duane D. Thornton
THRILL SEEKERS
A race of people who live for a thrill
Whose actions may involve flat open ground; or a treacherous hill.
They push themselves for speed and for endurance too.
They're all entertainers, for all; and you.
Their skills, are far beyond compare.
Regardless: if on land, water, or in the air.
You can call them fools or, you can call them brave.
But; they'll follow their destiny to their grave.
For they have certain challenges and records to break.
Those are the rewards and goals; for the chances they take.

Margie C. Bonvillain
Here On This Sleepy Bayou
Alone in deep seclusion under the willow's shade
The little skiff rest amid the water hyacinth blue
Where the moss hangs low in long grey cascades
Here on this sleepy bayou

Near fan shape palms and big tooth ferns
White egrets are in full view

While dragonflys go about making flips and turns
Here on this sleepy bayou

Tall cat-tails stand in the sun's blinding glare
Along it's banks in dull brown-ish hues
Often the turtle can be seen sunning there
Here on this sleepy bayou

I wish I could see it's beauty to night
When the summer moon keeps her rendezvous
Watch her sprinkle stars in soft pale light
Here on this sleepy bayou

Dixie Lee Knittel
CHILDHOOD IMAGES
[*This poem is dedicated to the memory of my parents, who believed in the enduring virtues of honesty, humility and hard work, and who made my childhood such a joy.*]
Where is the magic country I once knew,
With those fields of golden daffodils?
Where are the wide, sunny, green pastures?
Where the haunting call of whippoorwills?

Where are those sparkling streams I loved,
That flowed by the flower bedecked meadow?
Where are the birds that sang sweet songs?
Where's the swing in the oak tree's shadow?

Where are the vast reaches of wilderness,
That stretched away beyond one's view?
Where are those green remembered hills?
Where are the beloved voices I once knew?

Where are the green and lofty mountains,
That towered majestically toward the sky?
Where the footbridge that crossed the creek?
Where the big trees where I climbed so high?

Where's that lovely enchanted green valley,
With those happy pathways where I went?
Where's the little brook where I played?
Whre's that fair land of sweet content?

V. S. "Vic" Hester
PEACE AND COMFORT
I have a talk with my Savior
When I go to bed each night
I need to have the assurance
That He will put things right.

No matter what I've been doing
And no matter where I've been
When I have my talk with my Savior
He always forgives my sin.

It gives me peace and comfort
Each night when I talk to the Lord
For He will forgive if we ask it
As it says in God's holy word.

Our Savior is always there waiting
And if we go to Him in prayer
We will find peace and comfort
And a life that is free from care.

I like to start out in the morning
With a conscience free and clear
It makes the day seem brighter
To know that my Savior is near.

So before I go to sleep each night
I go to Him in prayer
For I know that peace and comfort
Is waiting for me there.

Michele Burns
POETRY IN MY PEN
There's poetry in my pen
—my heart is at it again—
  the words push
  to be expressed

and the ink just starts
flowing—even when depressed—
  it writes
  and writes
and tells what I feel
Sometimes I can't tell
  if it's just a pen

or if it's really real.

It knows my emotions

like the back of my hand
  and proceeds
  to blurt out
what it thinks I am.

How can it be so wise,
so in tune with my thoughts?
  My funny little pen
seems to have eyes and
  sees what it should not.

Cindy L. Belmer
POOKY
You came into our home.
All our hearts were stole away.
Your shoebutton eyes,
A very pug nose.
A coat of many colors.
That fur never knew which way to go.
You came into our hearts.
I loved you more each passing day.
Now you're gone, I can only say.
God must have wanted it that way.

Edna Taff Kirk
CHERISHED MEMORIES
In the springtime my thoughts return
To places of my childhood days,
I remember the lush meadows
Where I picked wild flower bouquets.

The edge of the old fishing pond
Was another favorite spot;
I fished for hours in the sun
And never thought it was too hot.

At times, I played along the bank
Catching tadpoles, crawfish, and snails,
While dragonflies circled about
And landed on furry cattails.

Frequently, I went to the woods
Where there were trees I liked to climb,
And when it was almost sunset
I knew that it was suppertime.

Up the lane, I raced my shadow
As I hurried to take my place,
At the linen covered table
Where my dad always offered
grace.

Calvin D. Spurgin
THE BIG TREE
There's a tree in the park
across the street
where as kids
we all would meet
we'd race to the top
and touch the sky
no one bothered
to ask us why
we didn't care
what people thought
or what kind
of cars they bought
friends were friends
and enemies
well
only time could even tell
I'm going back
to that tree someday
to sit in the top
and gently sway
I'll remember things
as they were before
then climb back down
and close the door

Nadine Lewis
GUENEVIERE
Once I lived in Camelot and
catered to my king
And all about lay fields and
woods and lovely forest things.
Deer grazed at dusk within our
sights
Rabbits played leap frog on the
grass
And woodchucks took enormous
bites of pears and watched the
seasons pass.
Gardens bloomed beneath my
touch
Knights and ladies graced my
board
And I could never do enough to
please my Lord.
Then Launcelot came to the king
and gave his sturdy arm
Did all the king required and more
He kept the king from harm.
But there are kings and there are
kings
And so the troubles start.
The king abused me coldly cruel
and Launcelot could mend my
heart.
In tender sympathy and love he
held my body and my mind
And while the king was churlish,
well,
Launcelot was kind.
Yes I remember Camelot and how
it broke apart
And all those sylvan golden days
that make the teardrops start.
I have compassion for my king.
Now Launcelot is just a dream.
If you were once in Camelot you
know I was the Queen!
There is a punishment, I've read,
for Queens who take their
knights to bed
But kings who cause this pain
and strife
Live to regret it all their life!

The castle stands in Camelot.
Its' ghosts are there for sure
And none survive within its'
walls except the pure!

Connie Hernandez
VICKI
Ever since I met you
I knew you were nice
But now that I know you
I have to think twice.
But deep down inside
I know you are great
And you are one person
That I could never hate.
With time I have grown to like
you
But I did have my doubts one day
Because the things I heard
I couldn't believe you would say.
Whether you said it or not
I'm not sure if it's true
But if you did
I won't think any less of you.
Truthfully, I believe you
And I don't believe my friend
But I hope that our friendship
Will never end.

Hallie M. Dobkins
LOVE'S COMMUNION
It isn't very often that you find
Two hearts and minds so
perfectly attuned
That all emotions flow as one
combined
Warmly and eloquently to
commune.
No linguist need they be to read
each other
No fears or hesitations ever mar
The tranquil joy of giving and
receiving
Of knowing, loving, wanting all
they are.
The silence of their exchange
can't reveal
The surging ecstasy and
heartbeats racing
Such devotion and emotion rare
to feel
Each sorrow, joy—all life—
together facing.
The air is fragrant when hearts so
commune
Obeying God's own cue—all
strings in tune.

Margaret Williams Cooper
SEARCHING
I have searched for you so many
lives before
With songs unsung, so many
whispers unheard
The winds have carried me gently
far
From places unknown to
wherever you are
Teaching me softly lessons of life
Each shadow a chapter, each river
a song

I know not who I am in this life's
span
Searching for you lovingly all I can
Walking the fields of loneliness
Touching every flower I pass by
Longing for your love before I die
I feel you here, I want you here

Once I felt your shadow warm me
Gently I turned—my heart, my love
My life—yours alone

But you were not there
So I crept into a sunbeam to stow
my heart away
Only to love you more another day
Will you reach out to me
Help me through this life
Or if you're somewhere else on
high
Summon me summon me before I
die
I feel so lost without you, I
cannot find the way
Just searching for you—every day

Renee' Leigh Cambiano
WORDS NEVER SPOKEN
When I was sitting alone one day
I felt an urge to say
Those special words to you
In my own special way

I got my paper out
And even wrote your name
I began writing my feelings down
But I didn't feel the same

I had lost the feelings
I once had for you
As soon as I remembered
My love wouldn't be returned, I
knew

A worthless little paper
With some silly words written
down
You would think that I
Was some worthless clown

Joyce Sutter Whitcomb
THE BEND OF THE RIVER
Meet me at the bend of the river,
Where the weeping willows grow.
There we will lie on the soft
green grass,
And look down at the water
below.

And there at the bend of the river,
Where the water runs silent and
deep,
We will spread our blanket
beneath the stars,
And the river will lull us to sleep.

I will wait at the bend of the river,
While the water goes on to the sea,
For I know just as sure as the
river still flows,
That you will come back to me.

Vicky L. Campbell
MISTY BLUE MORNINGS
*[To Miss Stevie Nicks Of
Fleetwood Mac For your
beautiful words.]*
Misty Blue Mornings,
The grass covered in dew.
On mornings like these,
I wish I were with you.

The birds are singing,
The sun will soon rise.
If only I could see,
The reflection in your eyes.

Crystal clear mornings,
Break of a new day.
I wish I were with you,
A million miles away.

Nora Cecilia O'Brien
MY ROSARY
I have a special companion
That goes everywhere with me.
Saying it gives me great courage
In the midst of adversity.

I call upon the Blessed Mother
Who will stand so staunchly by
you.
For indeed there is no other
Whether your troubles are great
or few.

Her rosary helps me in joy,
And also when in sorrow.
Saying it gives me strength to buoy
The tasks ahead for tomorrow.

A rosary may be said for a friend
Whether he is among the living
or dead.
The graces that come from saying
it
Leave very much unsaid.

The rosary is divided into
mysteries three,
Joyful, sorrowful, and glorious,
they be.
To tell how Mary's and Jesus'
lives entwine
And help me in this life of mine.

It is no wonder I dearly love the
rosary
For the solace it has brought me.
My parents first taught me to say
it,
One of the greatest blessings of
my ancestry.

Daniel Russell
ALPHA AND OMEGA
A life not chosen
attributed to fate
loneliness, sadness
time's only mate

Making the gesture
each day the employ
treating this body
to pleasures and joy

To be content with
each days' new pass
a comfort I'd welcome
rejoicing at last

Like some before me
ascending the pit
the word has spoken
the candle a'lit

Strange unto me
mine own fallen ways
a long time awaited
O' Ancient of Days

Larry W. Doman
MARCELA IN JADE MIST
In the reflections of dream
sequence flows a silver stream
of thoughts personified in
Moon's beam.

Fingers of light penetrate a
thicket's sleepy awakening.
Sound silently slips from bee to
tree, bush to bush, grouse to
mouse and glade to blades of
tender shoots.

The owls hoot, the frogs grog, the
loon's tune and crickets call all
to dance or prance as deer do.

Bounding leaps the stream in
team and through cloudy
swirls a mother steps. A doe
soft look of mellow merriment
is met headlong with a fine,
soft, mossy, fawn.

Flora and fauna hail the new born
prince of shade.

Jade mist serene slips silently
near. All eyes shift from prince
to queen. Beauty speaks softly
teaching treasured truth. Peace
be still till light lives here.

Debra Kay Schollenberger
**Frozen Frame Of
Womanhood**
Like the beauty of a frozen rose;
The inner part of a woman glows;
Her radiant beauty shines upon
her face;
And her smile spreads across the
human race;
The lifeless innocence of a
sleeping child;
Held tight in its mothers arms
that are meek and mild;
Frozen memories of her own past
childhood;
Now stay in the mind, like all
memories should;
Behold dear Lord where once a
little child stood;
Life does not stop in the frame of
womanhood;
For goddesshood is her eternal
goal!

Nora Cecilia O'Brien
WHAT IS A FRIEND?
A friend is beside you when
down and out,
Also at times when you want to
shout.
One who listens to your tales of
woe,
And doesn't any signs of disgust
show.

One who rejoices with your good
luck
In ways that aren't found in a
book.
One who corrects you when you
are wrong
And leads you away from those
who don't belong.

A friend calls you on the phone
To see if any of your needs are
made known.
A friend visits you when you are
sickly
To relieve long hours of
loneliness so quickly.

A friend will lend a helping hand,
And let you know he's at your
command.
He'll share his earthly goods with
you,
The secret of which is kept
between you two.

A true friend gives without
counting the cost.
He doesn't want his friendship to
be lost.
He values a friend more than gold.
He doesn't want one to be left out
in the cold.

A friend is one who is tried and
true,
Who will go all the way with
you,
To help you in this earthly strife
To have a rich and fulfilling life.

Bess S. Nixon
DISK JOCKS
Disk Jocks
talk shows
evening news
pound at my brain
hour after hour
thru out the night.

How can I dream?
How can I pray?
How can I recall
good memories
release brain waves
become as One with
the Universal?

Kelli Jo Meredith Limpp
MY PLACE
When I find my place
Where all I have is mine
I promise to invite you there
Just to pass some time

I'll have all the space
You've ever dreamed of
with mountains and tree's
River's of love

We'll build a small cottage
with a pump water well
A swing on the porch
Doesn't it sound swell

We'll be miles away
from everything and everyone
Doesn't it sound beautiful
YOU and I alone

When I find my place
where all I have is mine
I promise to invite you there
Just to pass some time

Patricia Ghering Wilder
REFLECTIONS
A mirror I do not need, but there
I see, my reflection, my son.
Confusion, Oh the confusion,
misty memories of days gone
bye.
It's me, I see me in his eyes.
My image it's there, I like it not, I
love it alot.
He is such as I, we argue for who
is right, like crazed animals in
a dreadful fight.
When the time of anger is gone,
we embrace with tears in our
eyes, sorrow in our hearts, and
vow once again, never to hurt
from within.

Sheila L. (Nichols) Meadows
THE BEST YEARS
These were the best years of my
life,
Long will I remember
The things I discovered behind
these walls,
The greetings of friends as I
walked down these halls.
Long will I remember.

These were the happy days, the
sad days,
Long will I remember
From Freshman fears to Senior
tears,
The glowing memories of these
years,
The pranks we played, our
childish ways.
Long will I remember.

These were discovery years,
recovery years,
Long will I remember
The clowning fools, the teacher's
rules,

The piles of books—our learning
tools,
These will be memories aged by
years,
Marked by stains of forewell
tears,
But long will I remember.

Doris Mayhew
ELM TREES
Your elms in inky silhouettes
Against the rosy sunrise skies
Embelish the seasonal scene.

Your elms in ebony etchings
Against the rosate sunsets
Effervesce the human morale.

Your elms in countless church-
like spires
Against the blue or grey heavens
Supplicate the numerous needs.

Your elms in uplifting fingers
Against the curtain of moonlight
Replenish the beauty for spring.

Your elms in symmetrical forms
Against the blushing twilight
Beautify the distinct skyline.

Your elms in summer greenery
Against the multi-colored skies
Merit the elm disease remedy.

Andrew D. Springfield
NORTHERN ATLANTIC
Where do your seagulls hide?
when freezing fall rains
Slippr'y cobblestone roads
as cold rushing drains

Sun has been gone for weeks
Your family's at sea

Maritime settlement
wind battered shutters
stormy gale seasons
rotting wood gutters

Son has been lost four weeks
Family's still at sea

Where do your seagulls hide?
sleeping in your loft
Franklin stove glows warm
damp pine crackling soft

Ronald Joseph Flemming Jr.
CELESTIAL BODIES
[This poem was written for—
and inspired by—the
"kindness" and "wisdom" of
Frank and "Mike" Dunton
"Forever"—may they be
together as "Celestial
Bodies" . . .]
"Whisps of Clouds" roam the
"Heavens" so "Fair"
the "Soft Curls" and "Snow White
Locks" of "Angel's Hair"
"Stars" that are but "Bits of Sand"
upon the distant beaches in the
sky
Remind me so—of the "Pearl"
that twinkles in his "Eye" . . .

Upon the "Farthest Shores" of the
"Universe Vast"
"Beauty" and "Understanding" are
shining in the "Shadow" she
casts
the "Lovely Flowers" of "Spring"
and the "Little Birds" that sing
Remind me So—of the
"Happiness" she brings . . .

The "Fresh air" of a "Winter's Eve"
and the "Moon Above"
Join together and become the
"Music" of their "Love" . . .
The sweetest of "Life's Melodies"
are sung by "Hearts Tuned
True"
for "One" is a number, divided by
"Two" . . .

Michael H. French
SOUTHWEST
Traveling an old man's home
We found our brothers,
Quiescent, loving, and modest.
Brothers gone for centuries before
our lives,
Teaching us a constant life we
soon forgot.

Exploring the potsherds of an
ancient man
We found ourselves,
Frolicking aimlessly on hard rock
walls,
Walls of dust and water,
Much the same as we.

Days passed quickly then.
We always saw mornings
As they faded to one more
sunshine.
We made the best of time,
Celebrating impulses long lost,
Reminiscing a ruined past.

Denise Bruskas-Gilbert
**Homage To Bishop Jerry
"Elias"**
Our initial acquaintance,
though contrary to eloquence,
has long since been implanted
within the nucleus of my heart.
For you,
a non-conversant,
candidly assured me,
with your brilliantly alluring
smile,
of an everlasting friendship.
And daringly I,
in recompense,
pursued,
befriended,
and quite naturally loved you.
More importantly,
you freely welcomed me
through the gates of your soul,
and furthermore
encouraged me to remain.
More importantly,
you rendered your love,
your heart,
to me.

Everett Wild
DESERT RAIN
[To the girls in my dreams:
Sandy, Linda, Nancy]
The rain has come to the desert
And now it's delightfully clean.
Flowers are sprouting all over,
The brightest that I have seen.
Cacti are green, red and yellow.
The lilies carpet the floor.
All the cactus wren are singing
And waiting for an encore.
The sands are of a new texture,
Freckled white, orange and rust.
The blossoms are so much
brighter,
Shorn of the desert's dry dust.
The moon is a shining crescent
Against a background of blue

And the clouds are laced with
patchwork
Where the stars are shining
through.
And now the small desert
creatures
Survey their kingdom divine
While I act the great pretender,
Pretending some of it's mine.

Joan Belfiore
SAD SMILES
There you are; your face is in
view,
 I feel my heart
 trying to pop its way out.
my palms are wet, just like the
first time
 we met.

You smile; and say Hi—but
 I sense something different
We're so close, and yet so
distant.

What have I done?
 The warmth isn't present
 I'm alone—
 Although I'm with you.

Your eyes turn away,
 The pain is overbearing, I
 know
 You don't love me.

Tears are forced down. I smile
weakly;
 I'll get through the night,
 Somehow.

M. Bainbridge-Kinsella
GENESEE
Leafy ceilings mute the gorge as
 the river follows its master
 To the biding lake;
 Ever waiting,
 Ever welcoming,
 The perpetual liquid
 gift.

Kaliedoscopic haze filters an
 already clouded sun;
 Beating down, down,
Until at river's edge, again
 admitted fully, as it bounces
Cadently across the knowing
 waters.

Indian lore e'er haunts this land.
 They once walked the lush and
 verdant banks with knowing
 confidence.
 Vital and proud were they.

The earth and its yield, the water,
was life itself to them.
 Their villages abounded,
 battles waged, canoes slipped
 bladelike
 Across the river.
 Cries of newborns slice
 the silent air.

And where I tread, did
 buckskinned feet once run along
 my side?
 I pause to rest.
 Was there perhaps a
 council fire, a longhouse
 near?
 I ask the trees,
 The wind,
 The deer.
They answer naught.

A mocking, wafting breeze
 scatters my thoughts
To a smug and silent sky.

Susan Shott
LATE AFTERNOON
I stood by the window
thinking of you
while the rain fell
silently, in
long
 gray
 streaks
making small white splashes
on the dirty pavement.

April Jolly DelSasso
TIMELESS
Tarnished photographs
Yellow-tinted cards and letters
Old clothes locked in the trunk
Treasures in the attic.

A fading memory
Sights and sounds diminishing
Tell-tale wrinkles and grey hair
Signs of yesteryear.

A wooden cane, a rocking chair
An antique music box
Days of youth gone by
Priceless memories.

Paul C. Peck
SUNSET SONNET
The sunset glowed with colors
 gold and red;
 The clouds on high
Reflected shades no artist's brush
 could spread;
 Then, in the sky,
Away from fading rays of setting
 sun,
 An evening star
Foretold that night had even now
 begun;
 And from afar
Its shrill notes floating on the
 summer breeze,
 The whippoorwill
Sent forth its call to beckon and
 to please;
 Then bright and still,
Haloed in white, high in the
 azure wild,
At evenfall the moon looked
 down and smiled.

Maggie Cassidy
FAITH OF OUR FATHER
[To the ones who live like this:
"What doth it profit a man if
he gain the whole world and
suffer the loss of his own soul,
or what exchange shall a man
give for his soul? For the Son of
man shall come . . . and then
will render to every man
according to his works."]
He was not an individual enough
 to seek out the truth on his
 own.
His faith was wherever the wind
 blew him.
His house of worship was any bar
 according to his current mood.
He never kept holy the Sabbath
 Day—and a whole lot more.
His unstable values were
 dominated by his relatives and
 companions.
The filth that came out of his
 mouth made the hair of his
 guardian angel stand up right.
And his guardian angel had
 already left him when he heard
 all the excuses and false

witness blaming others for the
 penance he would not do.
He did not comprehend that
 every individual will have to
 answer to God for every idle
 word that comes out of his
 mouth!
Give his daughter away at her
 wedding?—He exchanged his
 wife after her wedding—sold
 the whole family out cheap.
And marriages are sacraments
 and genealogies are registered
 in Heaven forever!
If the children did not emulate
 his example, they would be
 sanctified by the grace of
 Christ, and they would not be
 unclean!
Alcohol predisposed his body for
 burial while he was yet
 walking around.
His heart and brain were so
 embalmed that he could not
 care enough for anything to
 hurt him.
Except the fantasies of the night—
 and that was what did it!
His god cannot help him—his
 god rendered him helpless—his
 god is his bottle!
The Trinity God said He would
 deny him before the Father
 because he denied Him!
He never comprehended that
 every individual will bow
 before God and render account
 for his own works!
His wife is not an individual—
 she depends on God from
 Whom comes all power and
 free will—
Thy will be done—forgive us our
 trespasses as we forgive—
Pray for her and the children that
 this may be so—she is not an
 individual enough!

Diana J. Patterson
Scheduling the Seasons
 The heat-stifling pillow
 of autumn
 prints out intense copies
 of Time
 for absent—
 minded clocks
 to follow.

Pamela Hood
THE HOPELESS LOVE
Years ago when I was born, my
 mama told me this tale.
Now time has flown and I have
 grown but the memory lingers
 still.

My mother told about a girl as
 lovely as a dove,
And how she met an Indian
 Brave, by the river, fell in love.

Their eyes did meet, their hands
 did touch, their hearts did
 come together.
She in her calico skirt and bonnet
 and he in his buckskin leather.

Each day they met when she
 came down to the stream to get
 the water.
Though the language was not the
 same, their love was all that
 mattered.

One day she told her mother that
 she would marry soon.
That she would go to see the
 chief and wed his son Macoon.

Her mother slowly raised her
 head, and the girl did not
 understand.
When she was told that she
 could never marry her Indian
 man.

I have never told you this, though
 I feared I must someday.
And now you shall understand
 why I said not to go where the
 Indians stay.

You see my child when you were
 born the Indians and whites
 were at war.
I was captured by a brave, his
 name was Chief Wild Boar.

But I escaped and ran away early
 one summer morn.
And as time went by and the
 days grew cold, to me a
 daughter was born.

So you see my child, an Indian
 you are, though I love you just
 the same.
And it hurts me to to tell you
 this, to make you suffer this
 way.

You cannot marry this Indian
 Brave nor have him as your
 lover.
You see my child, my Indian
 child, Macoon, he is your
 brother.

Vera Hatton Rader
KNOW THYSELF
Desire Happiness in Life?
Know Thyself.
Desire to free yourself from strife?
Know Thyself.

Stay each worthy fleeting thought,
Cherish each golden dream
And upon Life's anvil wrought
Every worthy scheme.

Know thyself in toil and strife
In the sweet tranquility of life;
Know thyself in work or play
Value each golden day.

Act now! before it's too late,
Act now! before your dreams
 abate,
Let Life's fulfillment culminate,
Act now and Know Thyself.

April Jolly DelSasso
TO SCOTT
[To Scott, my source of
inspiration, who will always
have a place in my heart.]
When I see a couple holding
 hands
 or touching tenderly,
I can't help but wish
 that it was you and me.

You unlocked the door to the
 affection
 and emotions I was so afraid to
 show.
Through your love you turned
 the key
 and taught me how to grow.

You entered my innermost
 thoughts and dreams,

my anxieties and fears.
You broke down the wall that
   surrounded me,
   you broke me into tears.

You're my knight in shining
   armor,
   but a dream that can't come
   true.
But if you ever call my name,
   I'll always be here for you.

Thank you for sharing with me
   your love,
   your life, the good things you
   are made of,
You have rained on me and made
   me grow,
   all in the way that you love.

Denise Joy Walter
PORTRAIT IN THE ROUND
In the beginning

   I could not do without her
   My very existence depended on
   her love and caring
   She helped me to grow and
   learn, and to believe in love
   And when I knew it all, or
   thought I did
   I turned away from her

My mother

In the coming of age

   Her pride will have to allow a
   helping hand, a little
   guidance and some "reminding
   now and then
   Her own home will be given up
   for that of another
   The home of her child, who
   will gently love and care
   for her until the end

My grandmother

In the beginning

   She cannot do without me
   My love and caring is the key
   to her existence
   I will help her grow and learn,
   and love her as I was loved
   And someday too, her
   independence showing—she
   will
   turn away from me

My daughter

And ever thus—the circle turns
   It begins It ends And it begins
   again
   We are caught up in its midst

We, the bearers of life

Zola Glee Calfee
HOW I MISS YOU
Glady, how I miss you
   Since you went away.
Each day seems more lonely
   As I miss you every day.

Your telephone calls no longer I
   hear;
   The days so dreary and blue.
How I long, oh, how I long to hear
   Your friendly voice a-new.

It made each day more cheerful
   As I went along my way,
And now I think of days gone by
   And wonder what to say.

I feel that you're so very happy
   In your new home above,

As you meet your many loved
   ones
   Where all is peace and love.

And some day we hope to be
   there;
   'Til then we'll struggle on here,
And hope to be worthy to meet
   with
   All of our loved ones so dear.

Lucy Beemer
LIFE'S TANGLED TREE
The redwing and the sparrow
Share the clover fence in Spring,
A thicket of slender willows
Is the choir stall where they
   swing.

On bouyant air they sing and
   chirup
In covies there together,
Like buds they cling on stem and
   bough
In rain or sunny weather.

They ride the wind, the pelting
   hail
Through stormy raintime season,
Lighthearted, free and full of grace,
God made them for this reason.

On shaded fence and climbing
   rose,
In feathered silk they preen,
They sail their secret way
   unknown,
Their nests are seldom seen.

Unharmed on wayside grass and
   stem,
Like these Dear Lord, I'd be,
Find winged faith, a guided path
Throughout life's tangled tree.

Mildred Eilene Bruno
ISLANDER
      Dancing eyes flicker
   within the lively flames
      that warm the star-
   filled night!

      Hands of strength and
   courage grasp the beauty of
      the flowing waters
   thus gathering food to
      sustain a day of life.

      Hearts set the beat for
   the drums of pleasure
      voices of nature sail
   upon the air collecting
      admirers with smiles of
   sunshine.

      Blossoming novelty
   brings forth
      scented rainbows
   to enchant
      the beholder!

Maurice Ronald Jamerson
THE NEW DAY
Morning comes, and Night
   reluctantly is gone.
Daybreak pushes back the
   opaque shades;
Drawn so tightly at last eventide.
Busy with her brush, nimble
   fingered dawn,
deftly tints skies of azure blue;
And fleecy clouds with random
   color gay,
in truth an Artist's dream come
   true.
A familiar whistle breaks my
   morning reverie—

and a crimson flash across the
   green—
Our Cardinal greets the new Day
   too,
Joined by feathered friends in
   lusty song.
No worries here they seem to say,
as they flit through bush or Tree;
Eager to greet the new born day.
How perfect God's creation is to
   me!
The Birds, the Trees, the Grass so
   green—
I know that all is well, and then;
I'm re-assured as I survey the
   scene,
for I know that at Day's end;
Night's silent curtain will be
   drawn,
but on the morrow dawn will
   come again!

Richard Gasiorek
GREAT OCEAN
By the ocean's wayside; tepid
   pools
One walks upon the sand
   touching lightly
Caressing waves shorewise and
   outer
Powerful bounty. Teeming seas.

Ancient mariners upon broad
   beamed ships
Sailing wise and carefully sought
Golden shores and distant realms

Windswept beaches with
   sculptured rocks
History yearns a careful gleaning
Spanish galleons near the distant
   haze
Turgid movements. A ship rolls
   by.

Elusive strands settling sharply
Fairly cast the lonesome voyager
Fittingly so man's ambition.
      Along the Edge . . .
Brightly

Gwen Doucet
WITHIN
Do not worry
about being safe,
just follow
the feeling;
a path
deep within you.

Follow your desire.
Live for today.

Be free and wild
like the waves of
the sea
on a stormy day.

Gail Hintz
ELVIS IS GONE
Everybody talks about our king.
   When they don't know
   anything, Elvis was tender,
   Elvis was true, but we won't see
   him the way we used to. So let
   them talk, and let them say all
   those horrible things they
   gossip away. We all know you
   were a loving man, believe me
   Elvis we understand. You'll live
   on, because you see, you'll
   always be a memory. You sang
   of God and you believed it too,
   Elvis we'll always love you.
   Such a beautiful wife and a

child too, believe it Elvis, they
   loved you. Things went bad,
   and things got sad, but you
   tried hard not to get mad.
   You've worked so hard and
   sang so well, boy Elvis, you
   were swell. We'll play your
   music and you'll touch our
   souls, we'll feel a tingling right
   down to our toes. Your voice is
   soft and sexy too, nobody could
   ever copy you. For our Elvis
   we'll always love you. From a
   dedicated fan that will never
   forget you.

Marilyn Rhodes
COLOURS OF A MIND
Pale shades symmetrically
   showing similarities.
      Dancing hues rhythmically
      hopping happily.
         Those are colours of my
         dreams of nonsense.

Intense tinting of the
   backgrounds.
      Subtle spectrums laughing at
      their camoflague.
         Relaxing the convention of a
         normal day.

Stretching milkiness into a fluid
   form.
      prismatic ballets flowing like
      an echo.
         That I am becoming a colour
         too.

Flexing flushes rising up to
   phoenix.
      Brilliant glows having the
      energy within.
         Radiating values of dreams
         with perspective.

Hilbert S. Collins
GALILEE
O rolling hills and rounded
   mounts
   Of ancient Galilee,
O verdant vales and noted shores
   Close by thy famous sea;
It was not these that gained thee
   fame,
   But rather it was He
Who trod thy land and walked
   thy sea,
   And taught, and healed,
And wrought great works
   For all humanity.

Kate Stott
CANADIAN PRIDE
Raised to its fullest,
The flag bears a strong
Nobility and even
Inspires our song!

Proud of our land,
Through thickness and thin,
Supporting each other.
We're Canadians!

The winters are bleak
And often cold,
But bundled up warmly
Are we, young and old!

Reserve of the English
And wealth of the States.
We're said to have both
From our neighboring mates.

Glaciers, mountains,
Valleys and plains,

You'll see them all!
Come view our domain!

Our P.M.s try hard
To make our home stable
Ignoring the rumours
Of both fact and fable.

This poem was written
For those, who are at heart
Are in love with their country
And who'll never depart!

Wilma de Groot
LONELINESS
Loneliness reigns
Where nothing else does,
Where there is no freedom
And there is no love.

Loneliness builds up
Strongly inside,
Until there is no one
In whom you confide.

You live for no one
Anymore,
You've closed yourself up
Like a little door.

There is no one now
For your inner wants,
But your heart looks for
something
And forever hunts.

John R. Dossey
NOR CRYSTAL TEARS
*[I dedicate this sonnet, Nor
Crystal Tears, to Heidi Marie
Poteet, a very unique person
who is extremely close to my
heart. Hey, kid, I shall always
love you and constantly think
of you.]*
Eden has not a thing to show
more fair.
Dead would be soul of he who
could not see
A sight so touching in her
majesty:
This unicorn does now like a
garment wear
The beauty of the morning—
silent rare.

With great horn above one and
the other eye
Upon unto the field, and to the
sky;
All bright and glittering in the
smokeless air.

Never did sun so beautifully steep
On His great splendor through
the many years;
Never was cause for her soul to
weep,
Never was cause to fall prey to
fears;
And may your eyes be forever
asleep:
For they souldn't be blue, nor
shed crystal tears.

Patricia Anna Witmer
GOD'S LOVE
God's love is perfect peace, joy
and contentment.
He bestows many talents,
Upon those He knows.

None other than He can make
A star shine, a moon glow!
Alone time can only tell,
What God teaches—
When He clasps your hand,

And you in turn,
Pick up your cross and follow.

Then you will find,
Him traveling beside you.
And thus you will know,
Who is Master and King,
And He alone creates everything!
Hallelujah! Amen

Bonnie J. Douglas
CLAY TO A POTTER
Life seems to be a lot of red tape,
Application forms, credit forms,
it's never too late,
To take one more bit of
information please,
They say "Nothing to it, it's just a
breeze . . ."

I answered one question after
another,
Who is your Father, who is your
brother
Where do you live and about how
long
Who do we contact if things go
wrong???

To the machine now they make
you a plate,
It has your number and now
you're red tape.
Well, I might be a number in the
sight of man,
But I'm clay to a potter in God's
Eternal Plan.

Eugene D. Evans
FAITH
He told me only fools believe
This stuff about the Lord
And that it was ridiculous
And left him mighty bored.
He bragged that his intelligence
Was much too great to kneel
To such nonsense as Bible truth
Or Christian love and zeal.
I thought he must be quite a man
If what he said were true
For Michelangelo believed,
And Wagner, Dante, too;
DaVinci, Raphael, Pasteur,
Tolstoy and Washington,
And Handel, Bacon, Milton, Poe
And Moses . . . prayed as one.
Yet were the minds of these great
men
Inferior to his?
I asked him this . . . he slunk
away:
Do you know where he is?

Eugene D. Evans
YESTERDAY
How pale the veil of yesterday
That separates us now,
For I can see the form of you
More beautiful somehow
Than ever you have been to me.
For time brings recompense
That lets the memory of you
Own holy radiance!
I see your smile, I feel your touch,
Your dear and lovely face,
And burn with fire that cannot
quench
Recalling our embrace.
You torture me with sudden pain
When beauty comes to me,
For every form that beauty takes
Is echoing of Thee.
I cannot sleep, for you are there
In haunting sweet mileau,

I cannot wake, for traitor sight
Still searches just for you.
In everything I do or dream
Your loveliness appears
More hallowed as soft time
unfolds
The rainbow of our tears.
Such fools we were to once
partake
Of bliss so all-divine—
But fool or not, I claim your love
As precious Hell of mine.

Robert H. Burgoyne, M.D.
TO MARIANNE
White porc'lain bust of beauty
from the Nile;
    Queen Nefertiti,
    Tutenkhamen's aunt;
The joy of King Ikhnaton for
awhile;
    We look, adore, and love; 'tis
    not errant.
So like the bard's eternal Grecian
Urn
    And Tutenkhamen's ancient
    golden mask,
She is forever and takes not her
turn
    At dying. Beauty is, and beauty
    has a task:
To lure, excite, and couple with a
man,
    Erect his confidence with
    movements warm,
Then lie exhausted like a lover
can
    Who's teased and played a
    partner with her charm.
Your beauty with its titillating
flesh
    Surpasses hers though death
    can us enmesh.

Neil R. Beddow
ONE-SIDED VISION
Snows a swirlin' sand and
    white hazes hidin' flat land hills,
all bleak with intrigue and beet
    red cheeks.
    Chilled are thoughts rising and
    falling
obscure with near zero visibility
    and
    thoughts of adventure and a
    new life
fleeting like tumbleweed
    possibilities
    blasting across the barren fields.
Decision marred rises the
    glowing sun
    with false hope of warmth but
    with the
light of foresight and truth with
    which
    to see this curious alley and
    corner.
As grey as this day long vintage
    isle sits,
    so does my fabled longing to
    chill my
growing nervousness of one-sided
    vision.

Yvonne Gale
Reflections Of a Window
When winter raises her cold, cold
    hand,
    it reaches far and wide.
It reaches up into the blue,
    and paints her scenes with
    pride.

Some look like clouds,
    some look like dreams
Upon your window pane.
Some hand unknown, a guided
force
    to paint the world so plain.

Yet plain is not the scene it gives,
    as complex as it seems,
Those frosty window pane
    portraits
    are reflections of our dreams.

As in the panes, and so in life
    no two are quite the same.
And as the frost it melts away,
    so does your life some day.

So live life to the fullest now,
    and like the frosted pane,
It comes, it goes, and someday
    soon,
    your goals in life are plain.

Bonnie J. Douglas
BACK TO THE BASICS
There's a message to be heard
I wonder if you will,
It seems some walk around and
round,
In an imaginary world,
Ignore the facts some suffer
Pretend it's all absurd,
There's a message to be seen,
There's a message to be heard.

Do you see those people
handicapped?
Have you seen those without
tears?
Have you had a youngster lost to
drugs?
Held a child that's full of fears?
Could you take a loved one dying,
To your home to care for him,
Have you offered hope to the
blind man,
Or has your life been spread too
thin?

Life surely appears to be very sad,
As I look around today,
Looks as if we're all in great
trouble,
If we don't learn how to pray,
Get back to some of the basics in
life,
Life Faith, Hope, and Charity,
Get out of the awful mess we're in
By gettin on our Knees . . .

Rosemary Williams
MY MOTHER
*[This is dedicated to my
mother, Dorothy E. Edlin, who
has been the most important
and influential part of my life.
This poem is for all the times I
didn't tell you, I love you.]*
A mother cares for, nourishes,
and protects.
This My Mother did for eight.
Whether triumphs or tribulations
she faced next,
My Mother somehow managed to
carry the weight.

I wasn't old enough to see the
troubles she went through;
But I have been told,
Of how she made old toys and
clothes look new,
of how she was courageous and
bold.

Today's Greatest Poems

My Mother, not just a mother of
all,
but a father, sister, brother and a
friend.
One, who through all her
disappointments, stood tall.
The person who was always there
in the end.

Though she hasn't been named
"Mother of the Year",
the title could not say enough.
To me, there's not a mother in
the world as dear,
no mother as loving, yet so tough.

The day my daughter finds in me
the things I had hoped she would
discover,
Then I'll know I grew up to be
a reflection of My Mother.

Debralee Marion
ETERNALLY
The parting of this loved one
So dear to us all,
Is a sign of God's love
His eternal love for all.
There are but three things in life,
That all must be
God's bringing of life, and love,
And Death, or Life Eternally.
As you remember the days
Of her love from the past,
Remember always, her love
That love will last.
Knowing God's love
For you, for all,
His strength, His wisdom,
Will help you stand tall.
So bow your heads,
And let us pray,
For eternal life, lasting peace,
And love, forever and a day.

Adolphus M. Avery
SOLACE
  I know the quieting power
Of diminishing pain,
And after drought
The buoyancy of refreshing rain.

  I know how good fire feels
After ravishing cold,
And in loneliness the radiance
Of a friend who becomes bold.

  I know the healing power
Of unrelenting love,
And in sickness the panacea
That comes from above.

Nancy L. Porteous
REMEMBER THE MEN
In the world's great wars many
men did die
You may ask yourself for the
reasons why.
I can only say that these are our
heroes
Who unselfishly fought and
battled our foes,

So that we, a future society,
Might live in peace and
democracy.
There are some that gave their
lives for us,
We should be grateful, we really
must.

It must have been tough to see
your best friend
Be blown to pieces trying to
defend

What he believed was a purpose
true,
Willing to die, if he had to.

Death surrounded each and every
man,
Of course, that was the enemy's
plan.
But couldn't there have been
another path
That might have led away from
this wrath?

But all that is far from us today,
There is nothing we can do or say,
Only remember the men who
cared,
The men who fought, who died,
who dared!

Mary Rose Shoemaker
THE DIG
It was a beautiful morning
As we went quietly on our way
To a distant and rugged land
Through the fields to the dig.

We had to cross the waters on a
ferry,
And the ride for us was very
pleasant.
Our thoughts returned to our
childhood days
When the floods forced us to use
our boats.

As we reached the famous dig
We saw men and women very
busy
With their shovels and picks in
the dirt,
Working in earnest and sincerity
each moment.

While we walked near to see the
dig
We viewed artifacts and pot-
sherds of by gone days,
And the great marvels of a
civilization
That would be studied by many
scholars
For years to come.

John Christopher Jonaitis
A ROSE
A shaft of ivory green
Bears the blossom of a poet's heart,
And the tender petals
Are symbolic of his imagination.

Mildred Lambert Bell
THE ELEGY
*[Dedicated to the memory of
our son, Steve.]*
You have schemed, stalked,
plotted, and preyed upon the
heartstrings in the soul of
young and old,
We've cringed in fear, O, enemy
of man, loathed you with hate
that makes the blood run cold.
With icy breath, you've
massacred millions, or lurked
hidden and stolen one by one,
Yet those, achingly yearning the
encounter, you haunt by your
lingering to come.
Earth's most cherished ties,
you've stripped and severed
from hearts hurting, weeping,
bleeding with grief,
You've laughed at the tears and
the loneliness, despised our
longings, our hopes of relief.

The inevitable, how will it be?
We cannot know until we're in
that hour,
And we sense our very self
departing, 'neath your
menacing, conquering power.
Many times you have been the
victor and teasingly mocked us
with a fiendish glee,
But, Death, your string is gone,
God's Son subdued you, and
through Him, Grave, you've no
victory!

Michael Radford
JAMIE'S RHYME
One, two, buckle your shoe;
it all seems so easy to me and you

Three, four, shut the door;
how it makes the mind to soar

These things we take for granted,
but for Jamie it don't come easy

His hands refuse to master,
what his mind commands them to

Five, six, pick up sticks;
for Jamie it could take weeks

Seven, eight, lay them straight;
it seems he's filled with hate

In a conflicting world he lives,
unable to speak in his own defense

Yet he exists from day to day,
like a tree beside a brook

The waters just rush on by,
leaving Jamie standing neigh

Lisa Catherine Bush
A CHILD
*[I would like to dedicate this to
all the mothers in the world.]*
A child is in me,
so warm and so safe.
That if I should tumble
she will not break.

A child was born,
to me and to you.
She is so loving, so
pretty, so warm,
like you.

A child is growing,
so thin and so tall.
She won't be a baby
very long.

My baby got married
just the other day,
and now she is
moving so far, far
away.

My grandchild is in her,
like she was in me.

A child was born just
yesterday, it was my
grandson, and he was
born in such a beautiful
way.

Virginia L. Weitz
IF YOU LOVE ME
*[Dedicated to, Diane, Gloria,
and Kathy, they always
believed in me.]*
If you love me,
touch me with humor.
Make laugh.
Let me see life as it was meant to
be.
Some sadness, a moment of
content.

A time each day to be alone.
If I am lonely in a crowd,
give me a smile.
Let me stumble, and occasionally
fall.
But be there,
with hands out stretched to ease
the pain.
Then let me go on again.
Give me applause, for a job well
done.
Let me climb my mountain.
When I falter, give me a hand.
Don't push, crowd, and demand.
Don't smooth my path with
carpet of red
with roses all in a row.
I'll find my way with the help of
your love.
Yes, if you love me,
touch me with humor.
Make me laugh.

Ivy Redford Collins
THE HEART SINGS
She looks up and there he is!
His presence, filling the room,
causing a flutter in her heart and
a catch
in her breath.
His eyes, so piercing!
Big—Ugly—Crude—
They call him a 'RANDY'.
She only sees gentleness and
love.
A touch so tender, yet so strong,
What do 'THEY' know?
Who are 'THEY', ready to condemn?
She, looking into his eyes, reads
his soul,
He's no 'RANDY',
THE HEART SINGS!
That haunting smile, a little
teasing, a
little serious,
Words cannot describe the
essence of it.
A wink of his eye,
THE HEART SINGS!
The feeling that flows, one to the
other,
Even as they pass on the street—
a glance—
a wave of the hand—a simple
hello,
THE HEART SINGS!
He said "I can't stay in your life
forever."
But she knows he will—and he
knows he will—
For after he goes, as he must, the
tears fall,
as they must, he IS still there,
THE HEART SINGS!!!

Patricia Ann Grossie
WAR ON PARADE
War's an ugly place where
nobody's called by name, just
numbers for souls.
Who and how many nobody
knows but time, tears and bells
that mourn to toll.
Oh, Lord Jesus, remember me—I
was number one with me but
they
Called me number 9 million 90
and 9 somewhere in my time.
Oh, Lord Jesus, we know the
angels sing with us but where
do the tears

Of the war torn go? Only Lord
Jesus, you know!
War's ugly business where souls
aren't called by names—Oh,
War
on Parade, will soldiers and
victims have their tomorrows
or only
Some time and tears where bells
mourn to toll?
Oh, Lord Jesus, remember me—I
was number one with me but
they
Called me number 9 million 90
and 9 somewhere in my time.

Eva Faye Compton
My Toast To the Columbia.
May God watch over you,
Columbia,
like the flight of the Sparrow;
Soaring into space, light the
mighty Eagle,
our symbol of great vision and
strength.
O'er land and seas, with the faith
of an Albatross,
May you complete your journey,
safely and triumphantly!

Then, return to our little World,
emerging like a tiny budding
flower,
the Columbine perhaps,
With beauty and grace, gliding
anxiously homeward, once
more;
Bearing a cargo of treasures,
of wisdom, research, and
renewed hope,
For Universal Peace,
like the Dove.

Patricia L. Reynolds
MY PSALM
I will praise thee, O' Lord when I
awake and as I lay down my
head at night. What a great,
loving, caring God we serve.
You gave me your divine word.
As I study the word, the Holy
Spirit guides me and I am like a
leaf basking in the warmth of
the sun. As I drink in the
beautiful sunshine I grow—
slowly. When the sun goes
behind a cloud, I bow down.
The Holy Spirit lifts me up like
a drop of morning dew on my
leaflet. Life is forever because I
believe the word. As I serve
you my God, I am like a leaf
arrayed in autumn splendor;
praising you O' Lord as you stir
the wind to gently pick me
from the vine when it is time.
There is life in me and I will
praise you Lord Jesus Christ
forever.

Linda Beebe Owen
FRIENDSHIP IS YOU
When in need
or in despair,
I look for help
and find you there.

Through happy times
and sad times too,
I look for warmth
I look for you.

So when you need help

or when you're blue,
just look my way
and I'll help you too.

What I'm trying to say
is thank you for sharing,
the good and the bad and . . .
thank you for caring.

Charles A. Winzeler
THE CEMETARY
Like monasteries of old, you lie
perched on a hillside near the
village.
You are mysterious, somber,
silent,
Yet there are no huge carved
wooden doors flung open wide
to welcome weary travelers,
And you offer no bowl of soup
made from scraps garnered by
begging friars.
Your guests have no need of
nourishment, only rest

I walk among your grey marble
stones and I find names of
neighbors, friends and family
I long to talk with them, see
them, touch them and share
precious memories
You give me only cold statistics
born, died, father, child, wife
In agony I cry!
You saints in this holy hospice
Can you not join me in a prayer,
a hymn or a final Te Deum?

One day I shall accept your
hospitality for I too will be in
need of rest
I shall enter the open grave and
like your soundless monks
understand the mystery
perpetrate the somberness
maintain the silence

Nate Clay
THIS MOMENT
I've longed for
this moment
to steal my way
into your mind,
make love to
your thoughts,
divorce you from
loneliness . . .
and live with you
in dedication!
If we have but one
life to live;
let's share . . .
for we belong.

Mary Margaret Champagne
RAINDROPS
Tapping on the window trying to
get in,
the raindrops make faces with big
broad grins
taunting and teasing you because
you can't go out,
the reflection in the window
shows a sullen pout.

Staring out the window wishing
the rain away,
wondering why it had to come on
a Saturday
looking at the puddles wanting it
to stop,
but all you keep on hearing is the
steady drop.

Realizing, finally that for today
the rain has won
knowing that you're stuck inside
without having any fun—
then just when you're ready to
call it quits
the weather outside takes a
sudden shift,
the puddles that are there, are the
rains only mark,
but now it doesn't matter—
now it's too dark!

Johnny L. Johnston Jr.
CARRY ON
The road is long, hot, and not
easily made by most. With
such intersections as
loneliness, the making of
decisions, and accepting the
fact that all times aren't going
to be good times.
But it's times like these, that you
must dig deep into your soul,
grab that extra bit of strength,
and carry on.
Don't quit because you make a
mistake, just remember that
mistake and don't make it
again.
Be a friend to all those who need
you, never turning your back
on anyone.
And even though the clouds are
dark, we know that after the
rain the sun is waiting,
Like our lives it will be turning,
twisting, and struggling, but
always shining and CARRY ON.

Gina Lunyou
YOUR FRIEND
*[Dedicated to my friend; Gloria
Morgan. In appreciation of her
friendship.]*
When you walk, I'll walk with
you,
When you talk, I'll listen,
When you cry, cry on my
shoulder, and
When you die, I'll go with you.

When you glide through the sky,
I'll fly by your side, and
When you walk the golden strand,
I'll hold your hand, and I'll always
be
Your friend.

Richard John Briggs
WILLOWS
*[To sister Jane and Little Flower
for the beautiful motions in the
park with baby Avatar.]*
There are so many motions and
variations of motions.
The moth, the fingers, the
tongue, the knuckles of
the hands. Pause. Speeds!
Exhilarations! So many
metaphors.
This day to the next.
Inner voices suporting, bracing.
Outer voices to follow?
Yes! And no. It seems experience
is the wisest teacher;
though I've said (It must have
been claimed before.)
the cruelest.
It's wonderous when learning in
progression is easy.
Therefore I thank intuition,

that is a discretion.
To step outside of the inertia.
Created when people
are in numbers. Faces . . .
Spirits move us. Are forces to be
aware of? My friend
for they are aides. Though
beware! They are as plentiful
as herbs of the earth.
Hands and machines in this age.
Hands, lips, breath, feet,
playing instruments, eternally in
music. And with outward
blessings. Outside of all man can
achieve. Predict. Perceive.
Computerize. The baton of the
invisible orchestrator
dictates man into the magically
unknown movements, of
tomorrow.

J.D. DeVore
MY GRANDMA
Thank you Lord for my Grandma,
her stories of days gone by
are enough to make me cry.
But not from sorrow do I shed
these tears,
it is her quick wit that through
the years, has enabled her
To always see, the light side of
tragedy.
She is beautiful in her own right,
and because of her I've seen
the light.
Of being able to see, the light side
of tragedy.
Yes, her stories of her life are
many,
and those of you who know of
any,
will surely agree with me,
What a beautiful Grandma I have
from thee!

Phillip Gordon Atwood
THERE ONCE WAS A POET
There once was a Poet named Sir
William Vance,
Who, whilst composing one day,
took a chance,
He had not the time
To dream up a rhyme,
So he resorted to poetic license.

Margaret Susan Thacker
SEASHORE EYES
*[This poem is dedicated to my
youth and past painful
experiences; for the young man
couldn't face his own past and
was driven away by the roaring
ocean kept inside himself.]*
It began on a winter's day;
He came in and led my heart
away.
I was taken by surprise,
By the roaring ocean in his eyes.

Those green seashore eyes,
Took my heart with their tide.
I was led so far away,
And I only wanted to stay.

So we came brave and true,
To our love so brand new.
It was free like a breeze,
But I felt that it might leave.

Then we fought just to flee
And I thought my heart would
bleed.
Then I opened up my eyes
And saw the secrets kept inside.

It didn't matter at all to me,
For he is he and I am me.
Together we could face anything
    that was to be;
For our love won't be strangled by
    secrets of the sea.

Rubin Crosby
THE OLD HOME PLACE
I wonder my way in this world all
    alone,
And often I ponder to think of
    my home.
I see it all there as it once used to
    be,
And long shall treasure that
    old memory.

I went to the old home place,
And stood at the old yard gate,
The tin on the roof was turning
    brown,
And the old chimney was
    almost down.

There was moss on the well,
Where there stood an old
    dinner bell.
The old bell didn't ring,
And Mother didn't sing.

But I like to go back just the same,
Where many were, but few
    remain.
I see it all there as it once used to
    be,
And long shall I treasure that
    old mem-o-ry.

Sherri Lynn Coley
What Friendship Really Is
Thanks for sharing and caring
    and knowing when things were
    wrong,
Thanks for the hand and the
    heart that you fully showed
    me,
Thanks for sharing my tears and
    easing my pain,
Thanks for all the understanding
    you show in me,
Thanks for the care and the hope
    for a better tomorrow,
Thanks for being there when no
    one else was,
Thanks for just being you and no
    one else but you,
Thanks really for just being a
    friend and helping me through
    it all
I hope when we both are 90 we
    will be able to tell everyone
about a special friendship that
    will always last for as long
as we both shall live.

Angela Y. Rancourt
To Survive In An Indigo
Sanctuary
Eyes fluid with distaste
    Condescending what a waste,
Spying illusions Gone with
    disillusions,
Ah what to see is not there My
    soul to bear,
A listener to beseech It's you I'm
    trying to reach,
I ask of you I plead trivial what's
    to need,
An ostrich to bury its head
    faceless demons coming to
    reign,
Oh the heedless pain,
Tis only lies, Possible truth

on the rise,
Hovering over me, confused flies,
My soul cracking then dries,
Come quench me with a sup of
    wine, fingers caressing thy
    spine,
They are transfering me into
    their design, I explicate to this
    dream,
Oh to have fetish then I would
    conquer,
I'm running listlessly to a haven,
    Coming forth a coal black raven,
A hydra hissing from a pit, Its
    head erect to writhe,
To die here with an endless
    search,
It's coming down from its apex
    perch,
For to hear a zither in a faroff
    land,
Hearing the music it would be
    grand, Just lazing in the sand,
Drowning in a soiled tomb,
    Thrashing above a monsoon,
An inaudible jargon tune,
To lie still in a jebel ruin.

Shari Kilback
BE FREE MY LOVE
*[For Rory—the deepest man I'll
ever know. Thank-you for
taking the time to touch not
only my heart, but also my soul.]*
Be free my love, fly away.
Be free my love, to live your way.
Be free to love, be free to laugh.
Be free to give, more than half.
Let your heart, be light and gay.
And wake up smiling, every day.
Be free to roam, in body and
    mind.
Be free to leave, me behind.
Be free to strive, for all your
    goals.
Be free to finally, gain control.
Be free to go, to sleep at
    night . . .
Without a tiny, bit of fright.
Be free to live, and let it be.
Be free . . . be free, eternally.

Steve Tatge
ATTAINMENT
I Looked
    With my poetry
        as my guide
    With my eyes
        I will see
    With all my energy
        I will find my way

I Dreamed
    Where I hoped I was headed
        and it became clear
    When in my life I would be
        there
        to bask in the new light
    With whom I'd share those
        moments
        and never say goodbye.

Juli Frank
DAD
We've been through alot
of anger, mistrust and pain.
When we got done fighting,
we'd fight all over again.
We built a wall between us
to protect our foolish pride.
At times I've often wondered
if maybe our love had died.

We took our intimate problems
deep within our hearts—
(The ones that troubled us most)
and tore each other apart.
You had to have it your way
and I had to have it mine—
only making it harder
for the struggling love to survive.

But now it's time to grow
and tear down that ugly wall.
We must stand together
to watch those scarred bricks fall.
And if I die before you—
look back on what we had.
Realize you're a special person—
        —I Love You, Dad—

Lorie Volden
NATURAL MAGIC
Surrendering, dusk to dawn,
The golden sun leads the worried
    earth
From darkness to lightness—
Exhibiting the magic of nature.
Flashy flares of the watchmen
    tulips
Signal the other soldiers—
It's safe to come out.
Waiting for the drumming beat of
    the marching grouse,
The bandmember chickadees tune
Their jewelry box tone
    instruments with patience.
The patriotic deer dance about,
Waving their country's white and
    brown flag,
Chanting, "Hooray, hooray,
    hooray,
We're free, we're free, we're free!"
The bright-eyed daisies gaze in
    puzzlement
As the spine tingling wind breezes
Through the shuddering fir trees'
    hair.
Rowing ducks glide down the
    bubbling stream,
Hoping to pick up a paying
    passenger
To chat with into an adventurous
    trip.
Surrendering, lightness to
    darkness,
The officer owl glares at shadows
    with flashlight eyes,
Saying, "Who, who, who, who,
    who goes there?!"
Receiving a haunting answer
From the howling wind, "Nooooo
    onnnnne!"

Kristi Thompson
LOVE
Love is very common,
But too often, never true.
It is not a toy to play with,
But shared between just two.

Then there is the family,
Which also starts with love.
This love is very special,
As is a snow white dove.

Love is like a joker.
Many people play its game.
I hope that you are different.
I pray you're not the same.

I thought that everyone had love.
I see now that I'm wrong.
For many people haven't had the
    chance
to hear a blue bird's song.

Love isn't always easy.
Sometimes it seems so new.
There are many different kinds of
    love.
I hope that they all don't happen
    to you.

There is love that isn't love at all,
And love that fools you every
    time.
There's a love that always seems
    so true,
On which I wouldn't place a dime.

But there is also a love
That words cannot explain.
It is greater than a rainbow,
And highter than a plane.

It's the kind of love you dream of,
When you are far apart.
You see, this love is special,
Because this love comes from
    your heart!

Betty Lou Caughey Bell
UNTITLED
Tiny tentacles of twilight,
Wrapped tightly around time,
Squeezed light out of the heavens.
A comet fell to earth,
You were mine!

Michael Kevin Hays
Here Sat a Lovely Thought
Here sat a lovely thought,
Full of white and pink,
Surrounded with abiding care,
    Not grounded in flesh, in order
    to be
    Pulled up by inferior mundane
    feelings,

    But waiting to be lifted, to be
    exposed at
    The right moment,
Such as the petals of a rose in
    June,

    Then losing its virginity of
    disturbance, to caress
    And bring warmth and
    tranquility of rapture
To each and every soul.

Carrollyn Turner Poenie
The Stillness Of the Night
In the still of the night I talk
    with Thee, when the birds are
    in their nests.
In the hush of the evening I walk
    with Thee, to put my Soul to
    rest.
The things I thought I could not
    bear, their thoughts of which
    brought pain,
I listened and waited to hear from
    Thee, like softly falling rain.
And in awhile the loneliness was
    overwhelmed with love,
and peace and joy and happiness
    came sweetly from above.
His hand He laid upon my face
    and brushed the tears away
and gently said "Now, rest my
    child, tomorrow's another day.
I know your troubles, one by one
    . . . you need not tell them all.
I'm here beside you always, child,
    you shall not slip and fall.
You're weary and unhappy now,
    so sleep away the night.
Tomorrow will bring the sun
    again, with warm and loving
    light.

So, when you feel the need again,
to call My name in fright
remember, . . . talk is sweetest
. . . in the stillness of the
night."

Cora Maltman Thacker
TORTURE
Your memory holds me
In its talons,
Tearing at my sanity;
My soul and spirit,
Bruised and broken,
Twist in relentless agony.

My body, ripped apart,
Lies bleeding;
My heart, gutted and in shreds;
My eyesight dims to foggy
Haze; my arms
Hang on slender threads.

Would you have me die
So exposed
For all the world to see
The horror loving you
Inflicted?
The senseless, spineless me?

Release me, Memory,
From your grasp
To heal although I know
Your claws have scarred me
Far, far more
Than my wounds will ever show.

Robert Smith
IN THESE MY DREAMS
In these my dreams
You come by twilight,
Come by twilight, so it seems,
From worlds beyond the coming
night

Into my sleep, into my heart
Into the very essence of my being
Into my soul and yet apart
This ghostly spectre that I'm
seeing

Throughout the dark and
damning night
Your spirit haunts the room I
sleep
Keeping watch for dawn's first
light
To end the vigil that you keep

Then break of day and now
you're gone
And empty silence has come to
stay
With me, but you are not alone
My love goes with you
throughout your day.

Mary Atha Robbins
OUR FATE
We wonder when we pray at
night
Dear Lord, tomorrow will things
be right
Or will there be another trial?
If so, Oh Lord, help me to smile.
I know in you there lies a sweet
rest
And if we trust, we'll pass the test
So give me faith, trust and love
Until I reach my home above.
But if I stumble along the way
Please lift me up at the end of day
Dry from my eyes their scalding
tears,
And from my heart its anxious
fears

Make my life like a shining light
To help some other through their
darkest night.

Elsie Lacy
THE FRAGRANT PINE
Behind the house arched the
fragrant pine
I sat under sometimes to dine
where the sunrays steal through
and shine
on its slender needles of green
flecking its surface like an
inserted screen.
There under its branches
sheltered from heat
I tread on a slippery carpet. There
my two feet
stepped in peace in this secluded
retreat
where I heard the wind pass
through
swaying and swishing with a
sounding woo
as a lullaby and now I knew
here beneath this pine is a calm
and recluse for a hermit who may
search for a place
to worship where never comes a
face
to prohibit him for thanking the
Lord for His Grace.

Paul Allen Layne
FAMOUS ACTOR
Wish I were a famous actor.
Then I could put on a
performance so grand.
That no one could tell my heart
is broken.
Taken away like a mere token.
Then cast aside.

Perhaps if I were a famous actor I
could put on a smile just at will.
I could turn off this faucet which
used to be my eyes.
But life and love are not a movie
And I'm not a leading man.

Martha Johnson
SCORCHED SOUL
The day was long, dry, and thirsty,
It was hot, very hot, extremely
hot,
I staggered under the blistering
rays of the sun.
It scorched my soul.

Jim Christofic
VERONICA
Veronica's a friend I met as a lad,
Her passing away has made me
very sad.
She was a lady—hard to beat,
The kind you love when first you
meet.
She knew me well, she knew me
the best,
But God called her home, so now
she rests.
I miss my friend more than words
can say,
But together we'll be again some
day.
Her hair was white—white as
snow,
She had a beauty that made her
glow.
Her skin was wrinkled with age it
seems,
But the smile on her face made
my heart beam.

Together we shared our joys and
our fears,
Many the hours we spent
shedding our tears.
Not for ourselves, but for the
ones we loved,
Praying for God to show mercy
above.

Now she is gone that dear friend
of mine,
Though I see her not—she is
always on my mind.
Now she rests with God above,
She now receives all His love.

I'll see her again when my work
here is done,
So I'll continue to work until my
goal is won.
My heart grows heavy when I
think of the past,
Though death may come, our
friendship will last.

Joni Laketa Pinson
Nature Lover's Lament
[To mama, daddy, and my
grandparents for teaching me
love and appreciation; also, to
the rest of the family and my
very special friends.]
The ways of man perplex me;
I can not understand,
Why all the trees must be cut
down
In an effort to acquire more
land.

Without the trees to shield us
From sun and wind and rain,
The land will surely suffer,
And; therefore, show no gain.

It takes a tree so many years
To grow to a size so grand;
It sems a shame to cut them down
Just for a few feet of land.

Stacy E. Lewis
THE TAKING
Chalice filled with empty passion
Emotions lost in time
Silken cloth and silver bowl
Of dried white flesh-symbols
Stale and sour
In the mouths of babes
Lost in ignorance
Perfect teeth mashing and
grinding
In an effort to distill truth
From time-worried abstracts.

Rolanda E. McQueen
SUICIDE
Suicide isn't fiction but fact
and I for one should know
Because this is the awful way
my mother did go
Suicide is a sin
that it is indeed
But I guess my mother wasn't
thinking that,
but was maybe thinking
this is what has to be for me
The problem was, I guess,
she just couldn't cope
I guess the world
just didn't give her enough rope
I've often thought about
doing this sin
But the problem was
I didn't know where to begin
Often I have

in fact did start
By pointing the same 38 my
mother used
at my heart
But I just couldn't and wouldn't
do it
you want to know why?
Because GOD will know when
it's time,
time for me to die.

Ila E. Yount
THE GRAVEYARD
Lonely sentinels against a
bleak winter's sky,
Cold gray granite, immovable
and inscrutable.
Soiled ragged flags fluttering
from sharp black stakes,
Impersonal words and dates
engraved
on stone.
Death's cold, dark tombs.

Sandy-Kay
STRONGER STRUCTURE
Hurt so deep—
I'll never escape.
Loving him made me a prisoner
Now my soul I have to remake.
Give me strength, to mold my life
Into a stronger structure.
This way it won't fall away from
me—
Next time I fall in love.

Ira Avery
DREAMS
Dreams are thoughts; a passing of
collections,
That gather cobwebs if left in the
corner,
A flash of light that shines for
one moment,
That tells you not to relive your
own reflections.
Dreams are moments with love
ones that are gone,
Time you see . . . then awake to
feel,
A sense of loss again but then
you know,
With memories alive in your
mind death cannot steal.
Dreams are hopes, prayers that
are unanswered,
Things you want but will never
have the time,
So you place them in the corner
to gather cobwebs,
To dream one day; memories of a
mere collection.

Ruth Tinney
YESTER-YEAR
[I would like to dedicate this
poem in memory of my
grandson, Charles Tinney,
because of his great inspiration
to me.]
My mind goes back to yester-year
When bubbling brooks were very
dear.
Birds singing in the trees above
Gave out the song of God's great
love.

My feet I'd swish in the water cool
While watching the fleecy white
clouds above.
The wind whispering in my ear
Letting me know that God was
near.

Today's Greatest Poems

A butterfly stopped to visit
awhile
With colors of yellow, black and
gold.
The butterfly went I know not
where
My heart was glad, I knew God
was there.

It's a beautiful place to go, these
yester-years,
The brooks, the birds, the trees.
The sun was brighter as it shown
from above
These all cried out—that God is
love.

Ronda Yvonne Qualls
POETICAL DECEPTION
Creative thoughts
On paper—hurridly scribbled
Trademark of a would-be, will-be,
Already-is writer—
Say nothing of the pain,
The suffering, or the death
Of a real world Earth,
But attempt to mirror the
Dreams of an imperfect being
About some utopian society.
Topigraphical nonsense—
The idea is the real
And all imperfections are
Unreal reflections of the ideal.
"Shit" has more meaning
And can be used in
More contexts in a real way
Than any such lofty rubbish.

Bernice Carroll
SONG LIGHT
I walked out of the desert dry—
upon a lonely dearth,
only to find tears in my eyes:
Within the face, I beheld
a crystaline pool:
Years are watered by tears
to quench the fires of grief or
pain;
Leaving a mirage upon calm
terrain:
When Truth is Love, there is no
dearth—
for Love is Truth,
By faith, the heart to reign!!—

Lynda D. Rutan
The Frog and the Dragonfly
When I was just a little frog,
or maybe two or three
I hopped upon a lilly pad,
to see what I could see.

I looked across the water
and I looked up in the sky,
And as I turned my head around,
I saw a dragonfly.

Now dragonflies are pretty big,
and I was only little,
So . . . I had to stick my tongue
way out
and wrap him round the
middle.

So, here I sit, with a dragonfly
can't get him in my mouth.
His wings are flappin West and
East,
his tail hanging South.

I turned him round and held him
close,
and looked him in the eye,
I said "Dragonfly, please be still,
I'm so hungry I could die."

He looked at me with saddened
eyes, and tears ran out real slow,
He said "Please Mr. Frog, I'm only
two, won't you please let me go?"

Well . . I'm a frog with a real
soft heart, and I couln't bear
the tears,
So, I let him go, and he flew off,
and I haven't seen him in years.

Still I sit on my lilly pad,
the routine never varyin,
But since that little dragonfly,
I became a vegetarian.

Kasandra Hollis
CAUSE AND EFFECT
Life without love
is death without honor

Love without loyalty
is life without hope

Loyalty without purpose
is love without faith

Purpose without knowledge
is direction without sight

Knowledge without generosity
is life without love

Amie J. Van Roijen
Now That the Porsche Is Gone
Cashmere draws your attention.
Yes I noticed.
You left behind the acrylic
and polyester blends,
the non—Gucci and the plated.

Not a civil settlement
between agreed parties,
I am left
with half—full drawers of pain.
Gladly I should stuff sacks
for Good Will,
or obscure nationalities
who would blood them in
revolution.

But, as I carry these out,
I am lost in the aloneness
of a two car garage.

Charles Ruebeck
THE SHIP
The ship that sails its lonely quest
Above the swollen tide
It sails along without a rest
Its name The Seaman's Pride

No crew on board her awsome deck
No cargo lies within
On the sea she's just a speck
As a seagull in the wind

The ship is gone from my sight
Out to open sea
I've not seen it since that night
Dreaming could it be?

John Hancock
A MEMORY
Close, so close, with desire.
Strange, insinuating fire
Disposes reason, where
Is love, love?

Secret glances tell the way,
Nothing necessary to say.
Waiting fate can't stay.
Love, Oh love.

A delicate kiss when you lie
In my arms so sleepily,
So beautiful, so lovely,
Oh sweet love.

Emma King
POND OF FIRE
On a day in February, a storm
began to brew,
The sky grew dark and the wind
blew.
Torrential rains poured form the
sky,
Creating a pond on the green
nearby.
Old Sol came out and looked
down from beyond,
To see his reflection aflame on
the pond.
Fingers of fire seemed to shimmer
and dance,
Like Dante's Inferno at a second
glance.
The waters grew calm and all I
could see,
Was Old Sol's reflection looking
up at me.

Marian McDonnell
THE PATH AHEAD
Forward cast thy glance,
Not ever searching back
And see what good is yet to be,
What things are still to be done.
Would you salvage together this
broken self?
Seek balm of grief from heaven
above
And tread again the path ahead,
Tho wind and storm and cruelty
Have stopped thee by the way.
New birth of spirit struggles forth
And steps its way ahead.
Where vast horizons beckon on
To wider planes for Mind and Soul
That lead to Eternity.

Julianne Matthews
Mirrors Of Remembrance
Glancing at an old photograph
of you and I togethering
magnetizes memories and
emotions
from a corner of my heart
that I was sure had gone cold
long ago.
Memories of sunrises and
happiness
flowers, laughter and love
float into view and unfold
recreating the world we once
knew,
The mirror of my memory,
however,
somehow distorts our images and
the reflection miraculously
overlooks the pain.
Recollection of that pain turns
the image to glass
and the golden glow of our love
freezes to a death cold ice
reflection
of tears for what might have been.

Carolyn E. Riopel
TO MY FRIEND
The highest honor one can bestow
Is to tell one you love him, This I
know.
And yet I find it hard to do
I just could not tell you that I
love you.

You see, my words would be a
mess
And so I left it for you to guess.
But guessing games no longer

I'll play
For you just went on your
merry—old way.

You just went on and played your
part
And love kept tearing at my heart.
But it is all my fault, oh yes.
Because I tried to make you guess.

At night in sadness do I lie
Because your love has passed me
by
And still I should not worry or fret
Because I know there is still time
yet.

But now I'll shout it loud and clear
'Tis I who loves you, do you hear?
I love you so, as you can see
And yes, I want you to love me.

And though this script may seem
quite strange
How else, my love, could I arrange
To let you know my feelings true
And tell you that I do love you?

Karen Schroeder
Heroes, Butterflies and Children
I am a soldier
Who never returned
From a land
Of pain and destruction.
From humble beginnings
Did I descend;
In a simple and carefree time
Where butterflies flew
And children laughed . . .
But no more are these memories
lived—
For war has conquered;
It beckoned to me
And has led me into
Its bloody graveyard
Where no butterflies frolic
And no children laugh . . .
But perhaps someday—
If mankind is willing to try,
They can rejoice in a land
Where butterflies and children
Will live forever.

J. L. Williams
No Comfort, Poor Queen
Keeping comfort
the queen
has her say
and I am finished.
I turn with it.
See me standing
off center in her court.
I hang
on her words.
Her words are a small dose
of the turth she knows.
Oh,
her beautiful Indian boys, muscle
and mane,
the chase, the colours, the
corners of her grand maze . . .
I am caught, a glimpse
in the mosaic of her eye.
She is the night.
Suns bring other worlds.
When I wake
she is gone, she is dreaming,
remembered in the intricate
mask of age.
She is the slowness in my blood.
No comfort, poor queen,
she keeps it close bound.

All the riches and the truths
are her black gown.
The hem touches the world.
It spins.
Women
walk away with a souvenir of
   beauty,
exhausted as the consequence of
   her humor.
And what of the men?
Where do they go?
Do they climb spiral staircases,
sleep in senseless curves of silk,
visited by night, independent by
   day?

Erna Moede
THE POWER OF PEACE
When we are peaceful,
We have something to share,
Peace is the substance that
Blesses the air.

Calmness and poise
Is fragrance rare
That surrounds and makes
Peace with all we call "care".

The atmosphere then does
Fill all the space:
And what we named "trouble",
It gently does erase.

With this freedom now,
We go forth in haste
Ready and willing this
Good to embrace.

The atmosphere now
Is so peaceful and still.
We softly then whisper:
We'll follow God's Will.

Lynette Irene Sandy
KEYS TO MY HEART
Could I be a diamond in the
   night-time sky,
Could I be the sparkle when I
   look in your eyes,
If you gave me just one more try,
I'd prove to you that I tell no lies.

Could I be the wind whistling
   through the trees,
Could I be the smile that touches
   your lips in the breeze,
If you'll just give me one more
   try, please;
I'll give you a part of my heart,
   the keys.

Could I be a thousand rain drops
   that fall,
Could I be the love in your voice
   when you call,
If you could give me half a chance,
I know our love we will enhance.

Tammy Haasch
A DANCER'S WORRIES
Dancing is confusing,
Like anything you do.
You have to try not to think,
But make your feet move too?
Its an awfully strange concept
Trying not to use your brain.
You get uptight, and lose all hope,
And almost go insane.
Then along comes your moment,
Just when you think that you're
   sinking.
You look down upon your
   dancing feet,
And find that your not thinking.

Leona Jarrett
EDEN GRAVEYARD
In the quiet evening with
   troubles on my mind
I stood at the gate and gazed at
   the graves behind
As my jumbled thoughts seemed
   to wrestle with each other
The night sounds closed in as if
   to smother

Then I started studying the
   markers so neat in a row
And began to question when I
   might go
There was flat ones, tall ones,
   such beautiful stones
And I wondered about the lives
   left so alone

Husbands, brothers, friends and
   lovers—people of all kinds
Lay there resting seemly
   suspended in time
I thought of all the tears that
   must have been shed
And then I pictured Jesus and
   how that He bled

I remembered His love and
   marvelous grace
And His comfort surrounded me
   in this place
I whispered "Jesus I need your
   help, hear my cries"
Peace settled in as tears filled my
   eyes

Deborah Blackburn
UNTITLED
I sat and thought this afternoon
Of all the times I spent with you.
Each and every wonderful day
We laughed and loved and played.
I began to long for you
And the way things used to be.
Before I knew, I was dialing
Breathlessly awaiting your voice.
The phone rang once and instantly
I recalled all the things you said.
Those phrases that tore my heart
   out
And cast it in my pool of tears.
You made your point so perfectly.
You wanted nothing more of me.
The pain came back to ache anew
Causing my vision to blur.
I knew I couldn't talk with you,
So slowly I lowered the phone
And broke my link with you.

Margaret Jones Brown
GRANDMOTHER'S HOUSE
Oh! how I love to go to
   grandmother's house. She lives
   in the country on a hill high.
   There are tall trees, beautiful
   flowers, wide open spaces
   where I love to romp and play.

I enjoy the bible stories she tells,
   her jokes are funny too. Her
   tricks so pretty. I love to hear
   her talk, I learn so much from
   her. I know one day I'll grow
   up, but I shall never forget her,
   or the love and tender care, I got
   at grandmother's house.

Lynn McLamb
My Dearest and Closest
   Friend
If I were to lose you
I don't know what I would do,

For losing the person
That means the most to me
Is something that I could not do.

But if the time comes
When you want to part,
I guess I will have to manage
   somehow,
Although I will suffer from a
   broken heart.

Some people say
That my broken heart would mend,
But that is not possible because
I wouldn't be with My Dearest
And Closest Friend.

Veronica Champ Friend
BILLY
He was a child that ask for naught
Crippled by disease when just a
   tot
Lived his life inside looking out
He knew he couldn't win the
   final bout

He watched while the others
   would run and play
But in his wheelchair he had to
   stay
Life had cheated him, it was so
   cruel
It gave what it wanted and
   followed no rule

A headful of knowledge from his
   mountain of books
Never worried about those who
   gave pitying looks
He once said "I've been
   everywhere, done everything
I've been cowboy and indian,
   outlaw and king

"There is nowhere I can't go, no
   deed I haven't done
I can solve a mystery, be in love,
   or just have fun
Open the pages, step in, find out
   all there is to know
Sail the ships upon the sea, hear
   the mighty wind blow"

The disease took it's toll and
   finally his life
He never knew the pleasures of
   children or wife
He found all the beauty there is
   upon the earth
Never questioned if his life really
   had any worth

The end of nineteen years, his
   little body all twisted and torn
As brave in death, as he had been
   in life, praying his sisters not
   to mourn
For he accepted what life had
   handed, he never ask for more
So in God's kingdom he has
   found a place I'm sure

Frances Elizabeth Troxler
STILL MYSTERIOUS
A storm with the breath like the
   ocean,
nearing a shallow destiny
flashed brightness through the
   dark abyss
beyond man's reach . . .
as if to favor our yearning to
   experience the unknown
we've never neared before.
The bolts struck with an
   excitement,

spinning the soul with a feeling
   as if one had been
allowed to enter into a forbidden
   territory . . .
that eternal darkness, for an
   instance, was naked
and vulnerable . . .
the flash closed . . . no more
   could be seen . . .
only the sounds beat silence to a
   victorious ending . . .
the rain fell triumphant to the
   destiny . . . fulfilled
and reward was the bursting of
   the sun,
gleaming a cast of brassyness
   over all life . . .
like a shining medallion
   reflecting in glory,
peacefulness that can only blast
   through a winners heart . . .
and there, grasping the calm of
   the storm . . .
were sprays of strength and
   tranquility
through the new morning air . . .
as the grand abyss still seemed
   untouched, unspoken,
and still a mystery as to what lay
   beyond the unknown.

Robert E. Brock
MOMENT
Moment by moment
Time ticks away,
Young becomes olden,
Hair turns to gray.

Limbs become weakened
As they tinder with age,
Rich laughter brittles,
And vision doth fade.

So cherish each second,
Savour each day,
For moment by moment,
Time ticks away!

Dale Chatham
WHEN I'M WITHOUT YOU
*[To let you know the way I feel
when you're away—to show
you how I care—when you are
near—BJAS . . .]*
Those days are here again—
when I'm alone—
clinging to the threads of
my existance,
   falling fast!

Those days are here again—
when You are gone—
and everywhere I turn,
I find the emptiness,
the lonely—shadow.

Where are you now—
these sleepless nights,
these lifeless days?
Where have you run
   to find yourself?

   You leave me—losing mine!

Joanne C. Legue
HIGH SCHOOL REUNION
The President of a Bank,
Commander of an Army Tank,
An Executive or two,
Your conning me, I'm conning you!

Our friends are all the same,
Playing the big shot game!
Twenty years out of school,
Still playing the big fool!

We have an image we must keep,
So we cannot admit, we are weak!
None of us are all that great,
But we can't admit to being
　　second rate!

We are merely getting by,
But oh how we lie!
It get's so Deep,
It's like swimming in a muddy
　　creek!

Everyone has a story,
So they can bask in glory!
For a few hours they are free,
No matter how messed up their
　　lives may be!

High School Reunions are such a
　　bore,
I refuse to go any more!
The competition is too much,
And I no longer need that crutch!

N. Paul Baker
WINGS
the snow has gone
golden splinters danced
off the edges of sight
　　of hearing
Warm breath
teased the meadow
lifting wings
on a hush of song
dazzle brilliant
but soft as touching
like quiet ripples
appearing on the lake
where ice had melted

Laurie A. Conklin Hamer
PEOPLE'S WRONGS
People come and people go,
but I wonder do they really know,
of all the things that they have
　　done
soon we'll not be able to see the
　　sun.
The garbage they dump
and leave in a big lump.
The cigarettes they throw
and soon you see the forest glow.
The flames they spread
until everything is dead.
The trees and animals all die,
but people just pass this thought
　　by.
People are supposed to be the
　　smartest ones,
but look at the animals—what
　　have they done?
Soon the world will be ruined so
　　bad,
people will have lost everything
　　they've had.
Soon everything will be all gone
if people don't stop
treating this old world so wrong.

Doris Merlin
THE LAUNCHING
The pounding surf up the
　　shoreline crept,
And tension grew as the tide
　　gained depth.
Into their faces and souls did seep
The hearts of those who live by
　　the sea.
An unknown future she's born to
　　dare,
To chance the elements, sea and
　　air.
The pin mauls tap heavily at the
　　wedges,

Releasing the grip of the pole
　　made hedges.
She slides down the ways and is
　　set out afloat.
Tradition survives with the birth
　　of this boat.

Daniel J. Porter
BELIEVE
*[For you Aggie, with all the
hopes and prayers my heart has
for yours. May you one day
give yourself the gift no one
else can, the gift of believing.
God be with you, Daniel.]*
Though now it rains inside your
　　heart
　　And no one can see to dry your
　　tears
Though now your soul is troubled
　　And no one understands your
　　fears
　　　　Believe

Believe that your spirit can
　　weather any storm
Have faith in the love of your
　　heart
Fear not to take actions aside
　　from the norm
Build a world of love no evil can
　　take apart

Believe in the mission which
　　lives in your soul
Let charity and hope be your
　　chores
Walk silent, stand strong, let
　　peace be your goal
And you shall find the happiness
　　meant to be yours

In time you shall come to know
　　The destiny that now seems so
　　far away
In time you will learn to recognize
　　The beauty I see in you today
Until that time comes to you my
　　friend

　　Until you reap the love you
　　now conceive
Keep harmony in your heart,
　　peace in your mind
　　And believe, my love, believe

Gloria Wilson Tessier
ACROSS THE MILES
*[To my dearly departed Mother,
who inspired this poem; my
twin sister, Sheila, who has
always encouraged me, and my
baby brother, Jacky, whose
heart I also touch "Across the
Miles" . . . And Maurice—for
loving me.]*
O, I love you so, my heart is full
It's reaching for you, I feel the pull;
Do you understand? I know you do
That's just what your own is
　　doing, too . . .
For half-way across the countryside
All of a sudden our hearts collide
And this surge of joy that thrills
　　me so
Is because we've touched and said,
　　"Hello".

Mayo G. Cox, Jr.
DO YOU LOVE ME?
From deep within her womb,
"Do you love me?"
Comes the tiny voice
As gentle as can be.

"Yes! . . . Yes!"
Come the shaky replies
With an ache in her heart
And tears in her eyes.

"Then why are we here
In this damnable place;
Where you are not a human being
Only a paper file, a numbered
　　case."

"I'm a human being
Mom, not a cell.
Don't dispose of me,
In this man made Hell."

"Don't sign my death certificate.
Don't seal my tomb.
Don't sweep me aside
Like dirt with a broom."

"Let me live!"
"Let me grow!"
"Let me give!"
"Let me cry!"

"Let's leave this place, Mother!"

Grace R. Behabetz
WHISPER SOFTLY
Star eyed child
of love and longing
come
　　come walk with me
　　to the edge of dusk
Whisper softly
in the twilight
　　where fireflies
　　have touched the earth
　　then spin and turn and
　　flicker among the trees
In silent play
　　they weave their light
　　and dance away the night
On fairy wings
they whisper gently to the breeze

Gertrued Hickin Sigmon
FORGIVEN
*[In memory of my mother's
sister, Amy Caroline Throssell
and her great though quiet
friend, Eva Clark, who gave me
a home after my mother's
death, and put up with me
during my adolescent years.]*
Soft distraction, a tugging at my
　　mind,
"Come out, come out!" But I heed
　　not the call,
Not knowing that it comes
　　through Death's great wall.
What strange pulls do transport
　　me, make me blind
To mundane things at hand? I
　　fear to find
The way through edge of Earth—I
　　fear to fall
Into insanity. And so I crawl
In slime—my spirit dead, in flesh
　　entwined.
But they persist and smile before
　　my eyes.
Through space and time they call
　　me from this world,
And scores of years and continents
　　now spanned
They say good-bye and lift my
　　heart from cries
Of dead regrets. From Heaven's
　　seat pure-pearled
They now see all, and all they
　　understand.

L. Bruce Whitener
A DREAM
I dreamed I was a gypsy
Who camped at the edge of town,
All I owned was a dancing bear
who danced round and round.

He lifts his big foot up,
He puts his big foot down,
And bows and kneels
and rolls on the ground.

She,
She's drifting away,
Who am I to compete with the din
As the silence so easily rushes in,
I will fly away . . .

While you and I have voices and
　　lips
That we can sing and kiss with,
Who cares in some one-eyed son
　　of a bitch
Invents a machine to measure
　　spring with?

It was something I only dreamed
　　of,
Something I'm not quite sure of,
Something I'll never tell you
　　about.

Esther Womble Pendergrass
HURRICANE
Now you are gone—and all is
　　strange—
I shall not wait for you—
To hear your footsteps on the
　　stairs—
The softly closing of a door—
For all is different now—
You will not come again.
Fitfully—the night-winds howl—
As the winds have howled all day—
The fishing fleet is in;—
And red-lights line the margin of
　　the bay.
I shall bolt the doors—and
Bar the windows tight—and
Wonder as I do—which is
Lonelier—My heart—or the night.

Michael Lewis
BIRDS OF PREY
In our lives they play a big role,
They keep the rodents under
　　control,
Yet, some people kill them just
　　for sport,
And for this they receive a small
　　fine in court.
The Bald Eagle is the symbol of
　　our nation,
And now they're existence is
　　small in population,
Theres so many people with
　　nothing to say,
Speak up America, we must
　　protect our birds of prey.

Letta Ellington Graham
WOODEN EYES
Today we burned a lot of living
as seen thro' wooden eyes.
A lot of living, fighting,
friendship and many baby cries.
Stand back, take one good look,
your decision was not wrong.
Time has a way of changing and
　　you must go along.
Think awhile then you move on
for no one time stands still.
Memories are inside of you to
　　take out at your will.

The years seemed longer in the
past with time to visit, sit, and
talk,
to see the beauty in the fields, to
pick a flower, take a walk.
Now there is no time to rest.
Working harder every year.
But a baby's smile is just as sweet
and love is just as dear.
These old wooden eyes have
seen: a new born baby, an old
man dead,
an angry shout, a tear drop fall, a
tender touch, a kind word said,
children fighting, getting
spanked, saying grace before
each meal,
playing Indians, jumping rope,
shaking hands to close a deal,
changing times, a picture tube, a
buggy goes without a mule,
a talking box, an indoor "john", a
bus to ride; no more walks to
school,
a cold, cold box to make the ice,
water, heat: no well, no wood.
Things so different, but I know
no return if you could—
There is no way you could live
and not think of the past.
But thank the Lord for the days
you have and make new
memories to last.
Don't feel sad, the house must go.
It is old, tired, about the fall.
These wooden eyes are almost
closed, to open in a brand new
hall.

Craig Benjamin Fink
A PAINTERS DELIGHT
*[To the painters then, now and
tomorrow, this poem is
dedicated now and forever to
them.]*
There are pictures gracing the wall,
Leading the way to the great
dining hall.
Everyone admires them before
they dine,
And give them a toast from
their wine.
What more could a painter ask for
Than for people to look and
explore,
The work that took him days and
days
Of hard work and planning, to
find ways
To please anyone who may want
to look
And admire the time that was
took,
To produce this blessing that
hangs on the wall
Leading the way to the great
dining hall.
A painters delight is the pleasure
that it brings,
And culture and art with other
beautiful things.
People admire the picture,
They love the colors mixture.
It is a way of life,
Not the blade of a knife.
A painters delight,
His remarkable sight.
To express what he sees and feels,
Like what we absorb from our
meals
Before we look upon the wall,

Leading the way to the great
dining hall.

Pat Lewicki
SHE'S ALWAYS THERE
*[This poem is dedicated to
Tom McCall my love and
inspiration, and to my son
David Lewicki, with all my
love.]*
She's always there when I get home
if I call I know she'll be close to
the phone
she knows I'll spend a lot of time
lonely and alone
she's always there to care . . . when
I get home
Sometimes living seems to be one
big test
sometimes I think, "God I need a
rest."
Then she'll hold me and console
me
when I'm wrong she never says
she told me, she knows me best.
I know she's mine
she's proved it time after time
despite delayed dreams
she's always close it seems
my shelter from life's storms
she's always there with a light on
always there to care . . . when I
get home.

T. M. Pribicevich
REBIRTH
I'll go there again for I want to
relive
Those happy hours when by the
sea
Where the blue of the heaven
comforts me
As the sea wonders dance o'er the
waves so free
And sing in octaves of splendor
to me
I aspire to the heights of the
heaven divine
Embraceable sea of memories
sublime
Kissing the sand that sleeps
everywhere
On beaches with man in sea
breeze so fair
The mysteries the tide then
carries me where
The sea greets the night and
rescues me there
I'll go there again for there I
confide
In the majestic sea the mystery
the tide
For there that where is my delight
My freedom then resides thru
night
With happy hours by the sea
In a realm of waves ever so free
The records floating of my past
The sea tide washes astray for me
And carries them safely o'er the
expanse
The night does labour while I rest
In consternating bliss possessed
With joyful pain and precious
moan
How Mother see with wonders
groan
Lo, tempest calm after the storm
Then when I rise I'm once more
blest
My soul in the sea again is born.

Kellye Henry
BARRY'S SONG
*[Dedicated with gratitude,
happiness, devotion and love to
Barry Manilow. A man who
has filled my life—and so many
others with his music—Barry,
This One's For You.]*
Just to say "You've touched me"—
would never be enough.
What you've given me
No one else ever could;
What you've shown me
Words couldn't possibly express.

Because of you,
Even through the pain of love lost,
The never-endings that ended,
The dreams I saw crumble and
die,
The mornings I watched last
night's love walk out the door,
The sleepless dawns I held my
pillow and cried . . .
Because of you—I can love again.
Be loved again.

You've touched me with
compassion
All those nights I was alone—

Helped me to go on
After he'd left me—

And gave me strength
When I was sure I'd given all I
had to give.

Love is such a small word—But it
means so much;

I love you.

Alice H. Clark
THE DANCE
Away from the grim realities of
life,
Perhaps to some Utopia beyond;
Enraptured by its sound, devoid
of strife,
Poignant feelings unleashed to
respond.

Unsurpassed beauty of the dance,
Graceful interpretation with
each bend;
Swirling skirts, its beauty to
enhance,
Lilting rhythm—pattern
without end.

Alfred Taber
MARCH OF THE SUN
The purple morning mists part
Out of the classic dawn,
The shrouds of night now
withdraw,
From nights rest, the hills do yawn.
The blue'd sky starts it's New
Day
As the great sun appears,
So new in it's brilliance,
Ancient of days, and years.
"Shouting" commands to his
"steeds"
He close-hauls his light-band,
So that they might skim the sky
And illumine the land.
To Earth comes the compass
Of his noon, and bright day,
With blinding handfuls galore,
New light does he relay.
Then, as the dusk of spent day,
Brings the gold disk down low,
There is also yawn and light,
Of purple . . . a new show!

Hermand Bennette, Jr.
father
father's day
i wear a white rose
for reasons everyone knows
as a child i never knew
what a father was 'spose to do
it became more difficult to
understand
when they would say, "you
should have known the man"
how could i? when i came, he was
gone,
many months before i was born
oh, "he was a good man," they
cried,
"too bad, before the child was
born, he died"
there were times i would give
thought to what it would be like,
had he lived
then again, how important can a
father be
that would up and die before he
met me
lots of time had come and gone
before i learned fathers could die
'fore their babies are born
"he must miss his father, isn't it
sad"
but, how am i 'spose to miss,
what i never had.

Hamilton Lee
MOTHER'S WISH
*[This poem is dedicated to my
dear mother whom I have
missed greatly.]*
Since you left our home
that autumn day I saw you off,
I've lived alone with only one hope
that some day you'll come home.

As time goes by
my cherished aspiration has
become dim;
but I still cling to my hope
that you'll soon be home.

Son, I've prayed for you all the
time,
since the day I sent you off.
Don't you ever miss your mom
and our sweet home?

My boy, when can you come
back home?
It is my hope
that you'd better soon come
to see me before I approach the
tomb.

Mary McKinley
ODE TO MOTHERHOOD
Dearest Mother I write this with
deep sentiments,
Years pass and we grow old with
timeliness.
I realize how you reflected back
on your moments.
It's regretful that being young is
squandered on youthfulness,
We respond saying, "If I knew
what I know now,
Different life would"—we say
with intention.
Seemingly it takes forty annuals
to appreciate life's insights.
So busy were we engaging in
youthful interpretations,
Importance of loving
relationships took deference
bows.

Past encroachments haunted us
during lonely nights.

As we aged, wisdom came with
various convergences.
Children arrived and burrowed
into time and spaces,
Leaving us exhausted and faded
with encumbrances.
Unknowing we had stepped into
parents' paces.
Their tender years introduced the
shedding of tears,
But we also have had impressions
of pride and exaltations.
So many times it was difficult to
do as we should,
Faced with mixed emotions
demonstrating no relaxation.
Infancy to adulthood extended
the trails of years
Until we are left alone with
recollections of motherhood.

Doris "Dew" Ward
MY CONTEST
This contest, I must enter . . . For
I want to win . . . And if I don't
start and write . . . I can't send it
in . . . I think of this . . . I think
of that . . . And wonder what to
say . . . So this I must tell you . . .
I have just run the race . . . I sat
right down . . . And wrote this
poem . . . And mailed it off today.

Ann Richer
TWO RED ROSES
*[Just for my three angels and
Mom & Dad]*
Two red roses delicate in sight
Two red roses for someone
special they're just right
The soft red petals feel like
velvet to touch
And the aroma is not too little
nor too much.

They are as fragile as a tear drop
on soft skin
Expressing the hurt that's held
with in
Yet held the wrong way they're a
dangerous thing
And their sight of beauty turns
into a horrid sting.

So beware of the beauty of things
you see
Don't try to capture them, just let
them grow free
For no beauty can come from a
dead rose
And the joy it once gave also
comes to a close.

Margaret Sampson
LANDSCAPE
Whispering grasses in the breeze
Nodding their heads with consent,
Growing quite tall and trying to
please
The flowers that's giving off scent.

The trees that stand tall and
majestic
Looking up to the mountains so
high;
With fish in the lakes that are
sparkling
And birds, taking wing in the sky.

Such beauty on earth we are
giving,
To relax and enjoy in our time;

So admire this land whilst we're
living
God's gift that we cannot pass by.

Ruby Gray Young
**My Neighbor's Sycamore
Tree**
One of nature's beautiful sights
to me
Is my neighbor's Sycamore tree.
With stately branches that reach
toward the sky,
It gives a fine shade on which
you can rely.

It's leaves are much larger than
those of most trees,
And work like hundreds of fans
in a breeze.
All summer long it is pretty and
green,
An object of pride to the yard
scene.

When the leaves begin to turn in
the fall,
That is when it is prettiest of
all.
With some still green, others
yellow and brown,
And part of them falling all
over the ground.

But I do not wish this tree in my
yard to be,
Just to admire it from afar
satisfies me.
Then I need not worry about the
mess it makes
Because after all, I don't have
the leaves to rake!

Mary Walkden Spencer
PASSED OR PRESENT
*[To my Stephen: Through being
the unique individual you are, I
find I am able to express
myself. My thanks, my love,
my Honeyface!]*
Let heart take wing and sing in
flight
Of meekness and almighty might
And of the universe so grand
That vast circumference of our
land.

Of hills and valleys, dales and
streams
And galaxies of great moonbeams
That probe the mind of you and I
The question, do we really die?

To live among the angels now
Would be a privilege somehow
To send the word back to the earth
That living here does have some
worth.

To tell the world so all will know
That death is not the final blow
That all who pass on, do just that
Beyond the door is a welcome mat.

For all of us will surely die
And don't we all want to know
why?
So listen closely, lend an ear
Cause when we pass, we are still
here.

*Madelyn (Harvey) Nusum
(Bermudian)*
GOD'S EXISTENCE
Some people don't believe that
God Exist
How they come to this conclusion

I'll never understand
If you just take a minute and
look around you
You'll have to admit that He is
indeed at hand.

There's the sky, the clouds, the
ocean below,
The trees, the flowers and all the
things we grow
How can one say that God
doesn't exist
When all of these things were not
made with man's gift

We may not be able to see Him
But His spirit is always present
You might say well if this is so
Then why is the world
sometimes unpleasant

God is aware of all our troubles
All we need do is believe in Him
Read his word—try to do what's
right
And He will guide you day and
night.

Carolyn K. Rochelle
Sounds Through the Pines
What sound is that I think I hear?
Could it be my William dear?
A voice that's changed from boy
to man
Gives me pause to understand
That I have changed each passing
day
And a girl once young has slipped
away.

Erwin Fleury
GIFTS FROM HIM
Those mountains over yonder,
How there poking through the
snow.

You really think it's possible,
You really think they grow?

Oh! My, how tall they look, you
know the reason why.

Try climbing one of them, you
can nearly touch the sky.

The soft clouds circle round them,
sometimes covering up the tops.

When the rains come pouring
down, how the mountain
groans and pops.

The changing of the seasons,
from winter into fall.

The color change of autumn,
a sight that's loved by all.

Streams, starting from the
mountain top, bubbling out of
ground.

Racing through miles of
timberland how sleepily they
sound.

The music made from sounds we
hear.

Music soft and sweet sounding to
our ear.

All of this, and so much more,
understand in mind.

These are gifts from Him,
From God, to all mankind.

Mary Katherine Collins
STAR HAVENS—THE TRY
twilight satins, mists of sky.
an earth hums eves

of insectal rain cries.
this slimmer of air breezes
and the quiver pulse rise
toward star havens,
myth-raiders of nigh.
such as with tear,
myth-raider of heart,
seeds reaching rain cries
piercing a companion
sighting echoes imprisoned
in pain's rhyme.
begging mist, comes the rise
tears gentled from eyes,
myth-breaker,
the companion's warmth grows
star havens—the try.

Michael W. Hepburn
SOWN TEARS
*[To my mother, Firstena
Hepburn, with love and respect]*
The nation rocks with tears of
grief,
Within the bier is what was
reaped.
The nation sowed in hellish rains,
And now the tares out weigh the
grain.

The children of the nation knew,
Not what was right, or what to
do.
Their parents no examples sat,
And now the children are like
rats.

The nation's now corrupt with din,
Of brazen youths, with cause to
sin.
Their parents weep and beat their
chest,
At their wits end, they fall and
spin,
Their duties to instill the best,
They wish for now a chance to
test.

The nation rocks with tears of
grief,
Within the bier is what was
reaped.
The nation sowed in hellish rains,
And now the tares out weigh the
grain.

Nathan W. Vogt
REGRET THE LOSS
Where is the love?
Why are the words of passion
So brittle now?
They break on the floor
Where waves of emotion once
Crashed onto the shore
Of our sighs.
Tortured by unfeeling,
Grey and cloudy.
I have lost the technicolor
Vividity of passion
And regret the loss.

Mabel White
SOMEONE
You came along when I needed
someone
To help me on my way
My children are gone and I'm alone
But God has his way for me each
day
And he sent you along to
brighten my day

It makes no difference if we are
young or old
We need someone along the way,

It may be someone's baby you
sing and rock to sleep,
But God has a way
For us each day to help someone
on his way

So many out there need someone
They're crying and begging for
help,
They have pain and heartaches;
sad and alone
They need someone to make
them happy and glad,
But God has a way to gather his
strays,
He'll answer their call
And send someone

Gypsy
DESPAIR
Can anyone, anywhere tell me
what love is?
Can anyone, anywhere show
me the way?
Does anyone, anywhere still care
about me?
Will anyone cry when I'm put
in my grave?

Deborah Jolley Johnson
THE STORM
[In memory of my brother,
Stanley Earl Jolley who feared
nothing. To my parents and
husband for encouraging my
poetry, and to my children who
calmed my fear of storms.]
The clouds roll in making
ominous faces in the sky.
Lightning slashes through the
dark, illuminating trees bent by
the wind.
Like cannons, thunder shakes the
earth showing us the storm's
fury. One by one, the raindrops
fall gathering strength in their
numbers until a deafening roar
assaults our senses.
Suddenly, a quiet stillness creeps
in silencing the raging war.
Brilliant hues of color stretch
across the sky. Crystal drops,
like giant tears shine on the
cleansed folliage, and the earth
is at peace.

Carla Miller
MY PRAYER
[To my parents and family for
giving love, faith and
encourgement in everything I
do.]
With my heart and soul I pray
That You'll walk with me everyday.
Let me see everything from Your
eyes of love
Let me be a symbol of peace, just
like the dove.
Let me speak with a heart that's
full of joy,
Let me reach out and help each
girl and boy.
Let me give them the strength to
hold on tight,
To change what's wrong and keep
what's right.
Let their lives be filled with peace,
Having no pain, sorrow, or grief.
Let me able to give them faith,
Don't ever let them be filled with
hate.
Let me walk beside them and be
their friend,

For as long as life may last; until
the very end.
Let me teach them the lessons I
have learned,
Help me build back bridges that
shouldn't have been burned.
Life is short and it takes too long
To test each day for the right and
wrong.
I have learned and I want to
share,
What I know with those who care.

Traci Bittner
THE DAISY CHAIN
[Written for my husband,
Michael, a rose in a field of
daisies . . . I LOVE YOU.]
On summer clouds
And butterfly wings,
The timid chime
Of crickets rings.

Lightly wafted
On the air,
The lilac's perfume
Lingers there.

And in
My raven hair,
Entwined;
The daisy-chain
And ivy vine.

As like my hair,
My heart is laced,
By each sweet kiss
Or warm embrace.

As fragile the wings
Of a lighting dove.
As timeless as
An endless love.

Fernando Schiappa
POEM FOR EASTER
On White Palm Sunday
the certainty of the promise is cast
it will take
the trial of a week
when
the Old will join the New
Convenant
as it was said before
the man GOD
will be crucified
to fulfill the prophecies
. . . at the third dawn
happy bells
will announce
that this sacrifice
was not in vain
the dream of
the promised land
becomes for every man
a wonderful reality.

Jane Griggs
MOTION
I watch the ballerina dance
her moves are in slow motion.
Her feet suspended o'er the floor
give just the slightest notion
of touching every now and then
but only for an instant.
As I am watching from my chair,
I'm hypnotized . . . Resistant.
How can this tiny creature
make such giant moves?
Telling stories with the music
as she dances in the grooves
of a music box, made or wood,
would up with a key.
I sometimes dream about it

and wish that I could be
as graceful as that dancer
keeping rhythm, fast and slow,
with people watching from their
seats
as spotlights add their glow.
But, I awaken from my dream
reluctant, as before.
Though I still hear the music,
The ballerina turns no more.

Samuel Keith Kimbrel
FOUR WALLS
[To my friends, for without
them there would be no rhyme
or reason.]
My life is four walls.
All that I see and be,
Whether it is in or out,
These four walls stay with me.

No light enter these four walls,
I will not endure it,
For once I chanced and I did burn,
It's for this reason I shall insure
it.

But no one shall enter these four
walls,
Whether it be friend or foe.
Nor shall anyone climb them,
For their secrets only I do know.

I've grown old inside these four
walls,
It's taken years to lay them,
Stone by stone, I have made them
strong,
With only time come to delay
them.

No love you find in these four
walls,
For one is the same as it's
brother,
Cold, gray, with fortitude they
stand,
I am a prisoner of none other.

Charles Mark Morrison
**You Are My Way (Kathy's
Song)**
I will love you more today than
yesterday, and even more
tomorrow.

You fill my life with hope, no
more sadness or sorrow.

You free me of my despair and
like a breth of fresh air, you are
always there.

You are my way.

When pleasant dreams of you
appear,
And I'm holding you near,
I realize by the love in your eyes,
you are my paradise.

You here with me,
I can feel my heart glow and my
love grow.

Love of your life means you are
my way.

Like these special magic moments,
I do remember . . .
Me and you . . .
Our secret rendevous . . .
Do you remember too?
I'll remember too . . .
All our Golden Ages of the Past
And with the Written Pages
that Last,
I'll remember you . . .

Our lovely mornings after,
So much fun and laughter.

When time is running out for
everyone,
I reach for you and my world's
begun.

Leonarda Christina Pietras
DEAR NOMIA
There she stood Dear Nomia
A mystic spell of aura's scent
Silhouetted in the darkness
Profiled as in filament.

Pearl-like features lost to plastic
By narcotics sweet revenge
Brightness tarnished by the
shadows
Of the opening of death's door
Robbed the beauty of Nomia
That which was and is no more.

Jill Pohtilla
The Voice Of Loneliness
The voice of loneliness
seldom cries outloud.
It shouts inside,
blowing things apart.
It's hungry for attention,
eating its way through;
condensing, until finally
it is let free in a
trickle down a cheek.

Kathryn M. Fulton
RELUCTANT
Sky as blue as indigo,
White clouds are a-standing still,
And the yellow goldenrod
Is blooming on yonder hill.
Butterflies are still around,
Trees, with leaves a-turning
brown,
Apples hang on branches low,
Summer kind of hates to go.

Edith Morton
ENDLESS RIDE
I found the station
on the train Nation
that send me back
beautiful colored flag
speed on in the autumn wind
in a way we are kin
It's my love for you
that sends me through
Nights of endless meaning
days without seeing
On the end of the line
there the stop sign
the trains vibration
coming to the station
My friend I'm being sent
don't turn me away
He could only say
I will listen to you more
Eyes are heavy, body sore
We come a long way
How long will I let you stay
today I wish forever
sometimes I never
I'm glad it's today
I found the way.

Antonio O. Moore
WHO AM I
I know I'm not an Einstein,
at times I don't think quick.
I'm far from being honest George,
"cause I lie a tiny bit.
I'd like to be a Rockefeller,
and roll in all the dough,
or even Walter Cronkite,

tell you what you'd want to know.
I admired Martin Luther King,
because I have a dream,
or even play like Doctor J,
what an awesome team.
'Times I think of Billy Graham,
but then I'm not that "good."
Of course Burt Reynolds gets the
    chicks,
'cause he's in Hollywood.
Stevie Wonder now there's a star,
I enjoy everything he sings.
Or with the humor of Steve Martin,
I'd say all the funny things.
Shakespeare's influenced me a lot,
but it's time I finally see,
"WHO AM I . . ." that is the
    question
to me or not to be.

Margie Edwards
MOTHER LOVES YOU
*[Dedicated to my son Bryon
Edwards]*

My greatest desire will live, long
Beyond my last day.
That you'll find God my son and—
Don't forget to pray.
Now if a life in heaven, you choose
To win.
You must follow Jesus and
Reject sin.

Things that are counted best here,
Are not as they seem.
Your soul is the best—and it
You must redeem.
Remember to read the bible, it
Was written for you.
Take it as your guide, whatever
You do.

When you grow old and the
Glitter of youth fades away.
Remember Mother loves you—
And don't forget to pray.
Remember Mother loves you, and
Jesus loves you too.
And when this life is done, in
Heaven we'll wait for you.

Kathleen E. Bauer
Journey To the Sun, and Back

From the lawn sprinkler,
they shot as one, before
they realized that they were free.
No longer bound,
the droplets parted as they sprang
    skyward,
slowing, slowing
until they
stopped
and hung glittering for a long
    moment in the sun,
suspended like a handful
of diamonds
cast carelessly into the air,
before they, one by one,
plummetted to the parched earth.

Virgil S. Hart
THREE LITTLE KIDS
*[This poem was written to—
and inspired by—the childhood
of my children: Regina, Calvin
and Hugh Alan.]*

I looked at a picture of three little
kids:

I wondered at how fast time did
pass
Since Regina was a winsome
    little lass.

What has happened to the sweet
    little one
Who ate a mulberry and said,
    "Daddy, Num, num!"?
Where did the little girl go who
    wandered down a garden row
And wanted to help pull weeds
    and hoe?
I remember the little darling who
    followed me there and here
And climbed up on the shed roof
    and caused me to fear!

I thought of Calvin, that cute
    little boy,
Who was so happy when he got a
    new toy.
I remember the little fellow who
    would disappear;
We'd find him asleep on his belly
    with stuck up rear!
Where did the little fellow go, I
    say,
Who followed me when making
    hay?
Yes, there was a little four year old
Who tagged along whether it was
    warm or cold.

The smallest one had a twinkle
    in his eye
That when I reminisce makes me
    want to cry.
We named him after his Great
    Uncle Hugh and a movie star,
And we thought he'd really go far!
This was the cheerful little fellow
    who fell down the stairs
And helped me pick tomatoes,
    apples and pears.
Sometimes I get lonesome and
    really miss that tiny lad
Who was so sweet when good or
    bad!

Christopher Michael Thomas Jones
The Ivy—Covered Colonnades

The red bricks feel harder than
    usual under my feet
As I make my way across the
    familiar grounds
That I called home not so long ago.
The laughter and warm smiles of
    classmates are gone
And even the Ivy-covered
    colonnades that served as shelter
From September sun and April rain
Stand unsympathetic and cold,
Unaware that an old friend is
    once again among them.
Perhaps they remember a slightly
    younger man,
Walking across bricks that were
    less offensive to the step,
And themselves, less forlorn.
Love was found here
Among the vaulted archways and
    towering oaks,
And lost here.
Perhaps those Ivy-covered
    colonnades no longer recognize
    me.

Char Harder
BEAUTY
Being Beautiful
An attitude of mind
Starting with a belief
Then going on to the act of
    becoming.
You are as beautiful as you
    choose to be.

Robert Poole
BARTON CLIFFS
[To my father]
I see the sun imbue the sea
With spangled jumping-stars
And know the ceaseless symphony
Drifting, shifting
In shades and sound
Conducted by the scything gulls
White;
                as the dazzling foam
Or broad-backed black
Maintaining course
With sternest eye

Lifes essence here
Where banded cliffs
Repose
Amongst, whose tufted hair
Ubiquitous the sea breeze
Tugs and blows
Where transient flowers,
flicker yellow and
Watery purple
Where; in the sudden
Breathless hush—
We feel eternity

Maretta (Wendy) Lee Smith
In Front Of the Fireplace
*[With All My Love For Roy,
Always]*
Tonight is ours,
all alone and free.
You can sit for hours,
in front of the fireplace with me.
No bright lights,
just candles and the fire.
Tonight we will find,
life's sweet desires.
I cooked a nice dinner,
for just us two.
You brought champagne,
how romantic of you.
The fire slowly dies,
and I look into your eyes.
Everything seems to stop,
but time goes by.
As I sit on top,
of your lap in the chair.
My thoughts of you,
I start to share.
You kiss me so gently,
and hold me so tight.
I will never forget,
what we've started tonight.
A love that is so dear,
without any fear.
The only falling tear,
is that with cheer.
We love each other,
with all our hearts,
And our hours together,
in front of the fireplace,
will last forever,
and never part.

Erroll Hasan
IN LOVE ONCE AGAIN!
*[To all the lonely people who
once knew love, love is still
here, ask God!]*
When I first met you I was a very
    lonely man.
But somehow you changed all
    that and put me back into the
    world again.
Everyday you call me just to say a
    simple "Hello".
You never pressure me, you let
    my feeling flow.
But my feelings grew, stronger

than what I intended them to.
Once again love knocked on my
    door and I opened it for you.
You knew I have been hurt
    before, she left a permanent
    scar.
We may not always have each
    other forever.
But I will always love you
Just as long as we're together IN
    LOVE ONCE AGAIN.
            Just as long—
                In love Once Again!

Arlan K. Grover
MY GOLD
    A simple man I'll always be,
        My gold . . .
    the love between you and me!
Sometimes I feel my first love has
    been hurt—
    and I'm sorry I dared to care!
        But I love you so
        and want always to be there!
There's times when the light goes
    dim!
But the door never closes, and the
    light
            continues to shine in!
Words become rhetoric and fade
    into the air;
But the hugs and caresses are
    real, and hopefully
            make life easier to bare!
So many people lust for money or
    fame!
But for the world's pain, these are
    to blame!
    Keep the perspective simple;
be thankful for the stars and the
    sun!
        My happiness lies in
            Loving
                Only
                    One!

Dolly O'Brien
Butterflies and Little Girls
*[Dedicated With Love To My
Daughters Erin, 5 and Tova, 2]*
Butterflies remind me of little
    girls,
Free and alive with little feather
    curls.
Kissed by an angel and blessed by
    the sun,
Voices like music and so much
    fun.
Color in their wings that only
    God could do;
Just a drop of magic and alot of
    love too.
Fluttering on the air with such an
    ease;
Being taken for a ride on the
    slightest breeze.
Wings open and close with such
    grace.
A Tiny little creature with a
    beautiful face.

Kathleen H. Siragusa
THE FIRST SNOWFALL
The first snowfall of winter came
In the quiet peace of night
And lay upon this wooded land
A blanket of silvery white

The familiar hushed and sighing
    sound
Of flakes, so tiny white
Seem to hold a secret spell
Of magic in their flight

453

They sneak upon the countryside
Stirring only their breath of sound
In quiet glee they settle in
To wait till they are found

Upon the wake of early dawn
Will sleepy eyes behold
What wonderous gift the night
has left
So brilliant, bright and bold!

Lori Harrison
WHITE SEALS
[To my dear friend, Kevin
Marzilli, for having faith in this
poem; and to my mother for
giving me a wonderful life; and
to Mrs. Messina for helping me,
to keep my life that way!]
    Its whole body is white fur
with big, black, round eyes on her.
Though her fur glitters with gleam
    she is hardly ever seen.
Her fur soon becomes bright red
as man loves to club her head.
All the white seals begin to die
NO—the men don't even cry!
All the KILLERS want is pay
    and the public has no say.
Though I try to stop this all
I do not receive that CALL—
A voice that says it is DONE
and all the men—they have RUN.
The seals will *LIVE FOREVER*,dear
because of the few that CARE!

Maryann Jaeger
HAPPINESS IS . . . ?
[Written to and inspired by D.S.
MacDowell, Sept. 28, 1981.]
To lay in a bed of Royal Blue
    velvet, so lush, so lavish
At night kept warm, my fears to
    vanish
Visiting the mighty falls, the
    beauty in islands afar
The advising star—to dance with
    the dawns of dusk
In hearing the battles' silence—
    the air of mirth and musk
The reveries,
The memories—both of a heart
    and arrow
To love God's lesser beasts, to
    feed the tiny sparrow
The challenges of my art, my craft
An unborn child's laugh
To improve the sound that I
    admire—one's spirits to renew
An open fire—so rapturous—
reminisce with the burning hue
In fairytales and truths to tarry
For hope and fate to marry
The passions I've come to know
Watching my infant nephew grow
A birthday, a holiday, the family
    celebration
Phone ringing—new friend
revelation, sibling reconciliaiton
A home on a hill, first suns, first
    frosts
To smell a rose, gaze at the
    flowers, touch the forests' moss
Chocolate sweets, forbidden cup
    of tea and surprises hidden . . .
None to surpass happiness He's
    given.

(Toni) Bonnie Eleuterius
THE FIRST HIT'S FREE
I once was lost and full of sin,
Till Jesus gave me a peace within.

He picked me up out of my hole,
To fill my life, my heart and soul.

My life began so very good,
Nice parents and fine
neighborhood.
Although to church I'd always go,
So much of God I did not know.

Then one day I began to try,
Some pot and pills to get me high.
I felt so good I went right
    through,
All down the list, from meth to
    glue.

As years went by, dropped and
    shot,
I left my home and moved a lot.
The cops began to know me well,
I had begun my own private hell.

Although I said I never would,
One day in order to feel good.
I shot some morphine stoned out
    of my head,
The first hit's free is what they
    said.

This drug didn't last but LSD,
PCP and other drugs stayed
    with me for many years,
It caused much heart break,
    money and tears.
I tried to say I wasn't hooked,
Despite the way I felt and looked.

At last I had to face the fact,
I too had that monkey on my
    back.
My habit's price grew very high,
The choice I was forced to deal or
    die.

Then "Praise the Lord" it came at
    last,
I thought would never pass.
I spread the word to all I can,
That there is just one way for
    man.

No longer I live for dope,
Instead I'm clean and full of hope.
I know that Jesus is with me
    today,
He's in my heart and here to stay.

Cassandra K. Turley
SONG OF SORROW
Darkness penetrates,
The depths of my innermost,
Feelings.
Memories are all I have.
The sun one danced on,
The face that I love most,
But now you are gone.
Winter has come,
With your departing.
And with you died the sun.
Chilling my thoughts,
Numbing my emotions,
The icy fingers of,
Despair have,
Devoured the harmony,
Of the light and music,
In my soul.
For I know that you,
Will never love again,
As I still do.

Pauline Engle Evans
MY FRIEND ROSSALEE
Sometimes in this busy world of
    ours
we neglect our friends and they
    never

know how much we care.
Too often we allow ourselves to be
occupied with woes and troubles
    and
strife, trying to just get ahead in
this old life.

So now is the time to say how I
    feel
I want you to know in my heart
    you'll
always be dear.

You give so much to others, their
    joy
you seem to share, you are a
    friend
to be thankful for so gifted and
    rare.

So if I could tell you how much
    you
mean to me, in just a line or two,
    then
I'd simply say, "Rossalee God Bless
and I love you".

Elsie M. Cheeks
MY HOUSE
[I Dedicate this poem to my
seven children and this poem is
inspired by my fourteen
grandchildren.]
My house isn't a quiet place to be
    once inside
you will see. Clock is striking
    6:30 A.M. time
for the children to rise, rushing
    around getting
ready for school.
Bus a coming, kids off running.
This starts my day off with a bang.
There's never a dull moment,
    dishes awaiting in the
sink to be washed. Phone's
    ringing off its hook
Oh! I just step back and look.
Sometimes it makes you think
    you will go raving mad.
Afternoon has arrived time for
    my rest, for a quarter
of three you know school bus
will be coming down the road.
Door will start banging, TV will
    be blaring away, kids will
start yelling time to eat mom.
My house is only quiet at night
    when everyone is in bed
then I can relax and let my
    thoughts run through my head.

Lyn Patrick
INFINITY . . .
The last rose of summer has
    wilted;
Autumn winds blow cold.
The last leaf so golden has fallen;
Winter brings the snow.
The last bud of springtime has
    blossomed;
Summer brings the rose.

Robert Cast
PRAYER
Possess my soul every nook and
    cranny
    Overtake the throne of this life.
Keep me from the world's
    temptation Lord,
    Keep me from Satan's strife.

Mold in me a new person Jesus,
    One that You will always use,
And not the kind this world

wants me to be,
    But one that heaven can never
refuse.

Lift up through me Your Spirit
    Father,
    That others may see You in me,
And may this shell hold none of
    my wicked self,
    But withold the Glory of Thee.

Rhonda Meyer Russell
BENIGN? UNKNOWN
    He reaches out
    one withered hand
and takes hold of you
    any way he can.
    If in the stars
    that wicked night,
    two paths will cross
    in lecherous blight.
    Roam and wander,
    tear you apart,
    eat at your guts
    and rip at your heart.
    He steals your soul
    and makes you wonder
    why this hell on
    earth you wander.
    When it seems
    he's taken your last ounce,
    you've no more strength
    so he will pounce
    and take you far
    below the roots
    with maggots munching
    and no more fruit.

Stacey Goens
THE OLD HOMESTEAD
Watch the boat parked in
    the stream
By a little house that's
    somebody's dream.

In this dream was a little
    yellow lane
The same color as the
    window pane.

Through the window you
    could see
A beautiful bush beside
    a tree.

Smell the rambling roses
    of red
On the gate of the
    Old Homestead.

Mildred M.L. Corbin
OH SWEET MEMORIES
[Dedicated to my Mama and
Papa for the inspiration their
lives have been to my life.]
Often I walk down memory lane,
My mind keeps remembering, it's
    always the same.
How much we were loved by
    mama and papa too.
The things they taught us were
    all so true.

We didn't have much of this
    world's goods,
But with what we had, we did the
    best that we could.
We had so much love and were
    taught to care—
Time passed by quickly year after
    year.

Papa seen there was always bread
    on the table,
Mama sewed far into the night,

With needle and thread she was
oh so able.
And we were always taught to do
what was right.

At Christmas time the gifts were
few,
Sometimes there was nothing
new.
But oh the love into each seam,
In each lovely garment I felt like
a queen.

These memories so precious
Have helped me when my life felt
pain,
Just like a rainbow comes after
the rain,
A beautiful life we had with
mama and papa.
Altho it was short they gave so
much love.

G.J. Keraline
ABSCONDITION
A machine I had become—
A lifeless entity whose feelings
were numb
As I went about my duties daily
My emotions to me did rally
From sun til setting sun
The soul's work was never done

As I prowled the astral levels
Seeking rest from life's upheavels
I could only keep striving
But how was it possible to go on
living
Like an immovable creature
In a society of nomenclature

The attitude so dark and bleak
Of a life of separateness or
individuality
Is not reality and not a path to
trod
But life's thorns with inner
flowers had
Grateful glory for the beholder
With a life essence so much the
bolder

Melissa McCracken
ETERNITY
Times change and so do we
But no change will last through
Eternity
For Eternity is something we'll
never see
Just like Happiness without Glee.

Teresa Basham
**The World Through
Children's Eyes**
Today's a world of hate and fear
But it's been building for
hundreds of years
For each that is born, another
dies
If only we could see the world
through children's eyes.

The world would be ice cream
And all the empty space its cone
And the taste of life would be so
sweet
Each day a new friend to meet.

As they grow older and set into
the world of business and cars
Their eyes stop glittering like
tiny stars
The golden life the sun used to
build
Is now just another day to be
filled.

So we'll teach the children the
things they need to know
To grow up in mind and size
But let them keep that precious
thing for awhile
That lets them see the world
through children's eyes.

Anna Young Sanders
I AM JUST A BREEZE
If the sun was dark,
the sea was dry,
And all of life was gone.
If there was no day,
all was night,
There would be no dusk nor
dawn.

If there was no sea,
no river, no stream,
No plane nor bird in flight.
There is no love,
no tender caress,
No hope, a tear, in sight.

Without your love,
the world is dead,
And I am just a breeze.
That you knew,
to cool the air,
And left when you were pleased.

Frederick K. Jandrucko
GRADUATION DAY
Twelve long years and how I've
grown,
All my life, and now I'm on my
own.

All the knowledge my head can
take,
And now if I leave, will I make a
mistake?

I was born to wonder and born to
roam,
After all these years, I'm finally
leaving home.

Some say I'll make it and some
say I'll die,
Even if I don't, I'll sure as hell try.

And ten years from now at the
class reunion,
I'll show you who's right, and
what I've been doing.

Tim Olen Pickett
CHRISTMAS THOUGHT
Christmas comes only once a year
But that's not enough time for a
family to share
All the good times, all the cheer
All the bad times, all the fear
From now, till next Christmas
Begin everyday with this thought;
This birth of His son,
And His guidance, is truly
The Christmas Thought.

Alice Soward
THE THINGS I MISS
Since I left my country home
I miss things I loved and things I
have known.
I miss watching the squirrels
playing from tree to tree
Burying their acorns or hiding
them in a hollow tree.
And the Wise Old Owl perched
high in her tree
Where she raised her young and
knew she was free.
I miss the Birds that sing in the
Spring

The robin, the red bird, the
mocking bird and the lark
Their chatter and chirping gave
each day a new start.
I miss the lowing of the cattle
from their pastures of green
And the buzzing of the bees
swarming to find a new honey
tree.
I even miss the croaking of the
frogs from a pond near by
And the night call of the
whip—poor—will
When everything else is quiet
and still.
High overhead the wild geese fly
by
In perfect formation sailing
across the blue sky.
And the bright harvest moon
shining down through the trees.
Cast dancing silhouettes on the
earth beneath.
These are simple things, but they
are creatures of the land
A free gift from God in which
man had no hand.

Leisa Wells
A Morning In the Woods
Wandering in the woods,
Looking at the ground,
Hear all sorts of noises
Here all around.
Look up and what do I see?
A beautiful grey deer
Looking back at me.
With soft brown eyes
And large brown horns.
How sad people could kill one.
Then suddenly he turns away
And he's off to begin his day.

Denise McCreary
TOILET FISH
See the little fishies swimming
Round and round and round they
go
Their little fishie lights are
dimming
Where they're going no one knows

Toilet fish are falling
Falling endlessly
To a lonesome cesspool
Or to the sounding sea

See the little fishies struggle
Trying to stay at the top
Watch the little fishies smuggle
One last breath before they drop

Toilet fish are calling
Calling helplessly
For a lonesome cesspool
Is a horrid place to be

Glenna Thomas Tuttle
REFLECTIONS ON TIME
Who do you think you are—
Whom do you think you were
once
Long ago in another life
Why do you think you're here
now,
How does it all fit in—
How come you're filled with
stress and strife
Were you happier in another life?
Were you wealthy beyond telling
Did you possess much wisdom
and great dreams,
Did you wish and make things
happen

Could you move things with your
mind,
Manipulate and perpetrate vast
schemes.
I know I sometimes wonder if I
have lived before,
And if things in that life affect
my life today.
There's just no way of knowing,
The present is unfolding
The past is so obscure,
And the future—still seems so far
away

Karen E. Lothrop
DREAMS
Dreams—
are but dreams . . .
. . . such is life . . .
invented in my brain
on a dark and lonely night—
if only I could grasp one,
and hold onto it for life,
ne'er to open my eyes again—
but to hide them from the light,
which shatters my illusions—
and gives me back the sight
of the same ol' grueling rat race
that I have learned to fight . . .
The visions through my closed
eyes
always seem so bright.

Loretta Jean Tyrrell
PROMISES
Will you make me a promise
Which one will it be today
Will you promise you'll always
love me
Will you promise you'll always
stay

Will you make me a promise
Which one will you break today
Will there be another lover
Will you wander away today

Will you make me a promise
No! No promises please today

Quincy K. Wolfe
FOLLOW AND WONDER
*[To Nana—Whom I'll never
forget.]*
Follow the forest path?
Wonder where it goes?
Does it go far?
Who really knows?
Do animals follow it?
Big and small?
Through the trees it follows.
Old trees, so very tall.
Birds fly over,
Ever land.
On the trees,
So wide and grand.
Behind the trees comes the dusk;
Grey and blue the colour of night.
The birds must sleep,
And cease their flight.

T.J. Williams
REALITY . . .
We're born in love, unto this
world;
With feelings learned, yet not
unfurled.
We try to share our thoughts of
life . . .
We say we understand the strife.
But no one's told us what is real,
So what is it we're s'pose to feel?
We really want to live in love . . .
It's just so hard to rise above;

455

Our selfish needs . . . our hidden
   fears . . .
Our ignorance that brings the
   tears.
We try to give . . . expect to
   take . . .
And never learn from this
   mistake.
We learn to hide in unknown
   shells,
Protecting us from self-made hells.
Inside, we fail to understand,
How we're to live is not all
   planned.
Why don't we learn what life is
   for.
To love . . . to share . . . and
   not much more;
Than living so unselfishly,
To share of self and still be me.
Allow each one to grow their way
And share it all for love to stay.
It's how to give, that's hard to see.
The truth of life is that love's free.

Neal G. Clark, Jr.
THE JOURNEY
Our day will dawn on a cloudless
   sea
We will share our love to eternity

The tradewinds blow pure and
   warm
The helmsman guides with a
   steady arm

The storm may rage and all
   seems lost
But time will heal the holocaust

Our course is set to a distant land
To fulfill our love and live out
   our span

The die was cast a heart was torn
Upon the day our love was born

Cheryl W.S. Johnson
GYRE
Where are the wings of oblique
   birds?
Those that dive into darkening
   angles.

The arrow knows straightness,
   the path to the heart;
Surrounding realms pointless, all
   of space falls away.

O what is the use of limitless
   space
When I am a spiral of stardust
   already?

I glitter and fall. I do not care.
There is not bottom. I'm already
   past there.

W.R. Breese
YOU
I just awoke again for the third
   time
Out of a deep sleep with you on
   my mind.
Each time it happened, it seemed
   so real;
I awoke; because your touch, I did
   feel.

Thoughts of you make me happy,
They also make me blue;
But only because I am here and
   without you.

A fortnight has passed since we
   last spoke,
I'm wondering how you are.

I realize the different directions in
which our lives now go,

To myself, I wonder—how far?

For yes, indeed, you were my life,
The sunshine of my every day.
I pray to God every night,
Together, again, we'll be someday.

Lynn R. Webb
IMAGINATION
To live in a world full of love,
   never knowing hate.
To live in a world of safety,
   never knowing fear.
To live in a world where no man
   dies,
   but always goes on living.
To live in a world where there is
   no sadness,
   everybody's happy.
To live in a world without war,
   everything is peace.
To live in a world where there is
   no killing,
   but love encircles all.
To live in a world such as this,
is to live in your own imagination.

Roger W. Forsythe
from LIVING IN PLAINLIFE
(Mrs. Jonathon Queen (Erica))

Mirror image reflects the hushed
   pastels
Of a portrait-fashioned face—this
   she tells.
Believing in Shakespeare, his
   works unread,
Mrs. Queen follows the lawyer
   she wed.
And Broadway nights, Saks Fifth
   Avenue days
Polish her delicate, chandelier
   ways.
An art major in an Eastern prep
   school,
She once delighted in soft,
   Rembrandt jewels.
A romantic at heart, born in Leo,
She stays in the penthouse,
   hosting his show.
With hors d'oeuvres now served,
   martini in hand—
Fluttering from wall to wall—
   she's lean, tanned.
Classical music, piped in from
   outside,
Lures Erica to her caged bird. She
   cried
And felt the bright, elegant wings
   spread out—
Trapped . . . oblivious to a world
   without.

(Mildred Young)

. . . And so for eighty years she
   lived inside
The same house where, in sleep,
   her gramma died.
Well-worn picture of a phoenix
   still hangs,
As always, just below Christ
   giving thanks.
Canning green beans (the winter
   may be hard)
She keeps her days full (and
   where's that damned lard?).
Matt and John are gone, with kids
   of their own;
They all on Sundays—remnants
   are well-sewn.

Her narrow path goes to market
   and back,
Having weathered the years and
   skies of black.
Yes, Homer died of the cancer
   last spring;
Thank God Matt had her
   strength on which to cling.
Retired (ha!) from the shoe
   factory—
Where she put backing on the
   soles—Milly
Still chats with a friend, still clips
   a coupon,
Planning ahead for the years
   stretching on . . .

(Virginia Fidessa)

Gaudy splashes of moonlight
   expose her,
As she prances, cat-like, out of
   hunger.
Under naked streetlamps, she
   hunts for food;
Gotta feed the kid and herself—
   both rude.
Abused and pregnant, she once
   ran away
From nothing to even less (except
   pay).
Welfare parents, drunk, didn't
   seem to care,
And rough winds rip through her
   wild, uncombed hair.
With cigarette in hand, hand on
   her hips,
Virginia revamps her Maybelline
   lips.
She growls, purrs, barks, and
   snarls (all for fifty),
Thinking: What did Christ ever
   do for me?
Caught in a web, the prey awaits
   his host.
Hours later . . . she leans on a
   lamppost,
Chain-smoking in the dark,
   cursing the night,
Waiting to crawl home, well-
   used, at daylight.

Linda L. Lindauer
THOUGHTS OF YOU
[to my buddy . . . my husband.]
I've not known
      a more peaceful feeling
         such as this,
lying here
      feeling the darkness
         surrounding us
         the silence closing in . . .
            so still
and
      as sleep overcomes us,
         my last thoughts
            are of you
               beside me.

Esther L. Heiden
MOVING PEOPLE
Moving people through God,
   what a rapturous thought!
Love abounding! Faith
   expounding!
As God brings to light...
An inner stirring that ignites...
A flame of faith burning bright.

Caring, sharing, boldly daring...
To capture the emptiness of
   worldliness,
To conquer the onslaughts of

wickedness,
To defeat the ravages of apathy,
With God nothing shall be
   impossible you see!

Ask. . .Seek. . .Knock
The power of prayer will unlock
The tangled webs of futility
With God's all powerful ability.

Is there surging through your
   heart and soul. . .
Some kind of monumental goal?
Put yourself in the hands of
   Christ,
Jesus can change your life.

Walking with the Lord,
It's unlikely that you'll get bored,
It's exciting to know that
   everyday you'll grow.

Ann L. Hall
LOVE: THE QUESTION?
A little pain, a little sorrow,
Coupled with tears and joys
   tomorrow.
A smile, a touch, a warm embrace,
Brings happy thoughts to a
   smiling face.
Pain and joy side by side.
Endings mean something's died.
Questions, fears and doubts arise.
Is it worth it is the anguished cry?
A risk is taken to begin.
Do we lose or do we win?
Love brings forth a growth of
   person,
Spiritual to be sure.
A joy, a hope, a new found
   freedom,
A gift from God beyond compare.
To love is human.
To be is too.
Love, God and Being all that's true.

Cindy L. Kindig
THE LAST WALK
Walking thru the park,
Just before dark
Wanting to hold you so tight
And to chase away our fright.
Sad and crying,
Knowing our time was ending.
The feelings were so strong,
And the end felt so wrong.
It was hard to say good-bye,
And I kept wondering why!

Vincent Rudolph Trotman
MAY I SPEAK
Possessers, Possessers of me
may I speak?
I—I am you, I am—I am!
Possessers of me,
let you, the talking world be,
be listeners to me, in that I,
I through storm or charm have
got to be strong;
Possessers of me, let you the
talking world be,
be listeners to me, in that,
I am your arm and charm;
charm deserves some praise,
praise for protecting you
from harm—always helping you
to enjoy a song;
I—I AM YOU—I AM—;
Possessers of me,
you the talking world should be
be listeners to me,
let you be told that I,
I preserve you to be brave and
hold, to protect you through

storm and harm, to be your arm
and charm, you the enjoyers of
the dawn and a song,
the relatives of cute DAWN,
CUTE DAWN AND
HANDSOME JOHN
YOU—you the talking world,
the possessers of me,
I—I AM.
I AM proud to have endowed
endowed you with the saying,
the saying that you can not say
you had joy in my absence—
you had no sadness in my
presence—you had no grief that
that I could not grant relief
You—? You—Yes You, the posse-
ssers of me—I I am—I am You,
I AM YOU TO ME—
so thank you!
and you thank me, for granting
me and you, and me for:
for the opportunity to, to be
the speaker to thee, three,
and yee the wonderful possessers
of me; me—why I Am:
I am Eternal—External—Internal
Reserve—Quality Sex—I Am—I
am
YOU—MAY I SPEAK?

Genevieve Locke Oliphant
A NEW BEGINNING
There is a place of beginning
again—
the time is this very minute;
Wherever we are, and whoever
we are,
the world and all that's in it,
Can be ours if we look ahead,
block out the mind's regrets;
And for the things that we left
undone,
resolve now to forget.
Don't let sorrow or regret
overwhelm us,
let us instead,
Thank God for lessons we have
learned—
"Better some things left *undone*
and *unsaid.*"
Let us determine to be better
persons
and as we make a new start,
God will be with us every minute
as love to us, He imparts.
Strength, help, and courage
will be ours in days ahead—
His grace will be sufficient
for our needs as our souls are
fed.

Genesis 1:1
In the beginning God created the
heaven and the earth.

Sandra Higley Scott
WHEN SOULS SOAR
In my mind's eye, so well do I
know Thee,
Yet, in Thy presence I walk
circumspectly.

In this knowledge I flounder as a
kite with no tail.
On my mind's oceans you drift as
a ship with no sail.

My soul passes yours in the quiet
of the night.
Communion of souls desires the
right.

The consumption of flesh has

lust of its own.
It cannot flourish 'til love has
grown.

When all is pure and all is good,
And things come together as they
should,

And love touches existence at its
very base,
Then sould soar together to their
highest place.

Maxime Stadlen
UNTITLED
Some times you leave me
and wait beneath some aging
willow tree
looking, searching for the
answer
to some forgotten question.
I'd questioned your sincerity
previously
while copiously jotting down
responses
and my feelings for you.
I noted that your hand shook
only after
that third drink and
not a moment sooner
but my knees were trembling
that first night you kissed me.
As I climbed back into bed
I smelled you on me
and I shivered,
but I was already asleep.

Kay Cavanaugh
HEART FRIEND
*[Dedicated to Gerald Boice—
May this form of immortality
bring some happiness to his
heart, as he has to mine.]*
Poetry comes from the heart
That grand emotion of love
You can feel it from the start
It flies through like a dove

Oh so beautiful it can be
To share that loving feeling
When you want the world to see
Just how the heart is reeling

It is a most enjoyable friend
Who will always be there
With thoughts that you've penned
The world will know that you
care

T.P. Brennan
TURNING POINT
The little heart she wears so well
Would never hide and always tell
The sadness that her tears would
show
Everytime that he must go

He goes but why I often wonder
Like the rain that brings the
thunder
He loves her so and would deliver
His heart and soul to save her
quiver

Once again he's gone away
Not knowing how long he'll stay
Away from her who he loves so
much
Depriving her of his gentle touch

A touch that's been from the start
Even though they've been apart
Apart from her he can no longer
be
The emptiness inside won't set
him free

So to his God he will pray
For the strength to come and say
What a fool he has been
To let the line grow so thin

All he wants is a chance I'm sure
To prove to her his love is pure
To say that nothing is a bother
And be a proud little girl's father

Patricia Masingill
**Victory Within the
Human Race**
Victory is not always in winning,
but in trying and giving it your
all.
Failure is not always in losing,
but in quitting before you've
met the struggle.
People who come in last in a race
are not always the losers for
within themselves they are the
winners cause they fought
until the end and gave it their
all.
This is what counts; what's in
thyself. Those who have tried
and stuck it out to the end are
really the winners, for they
know within them they are the
real victors of this
race . . . The Human Race!

Greg Donolo
MAGIC
Do you believe in magic
seeing through a cloud-masked
earth
to the setting sun that in its death
is morning to another world
death and birth in wizardly
terms
are all but the same

Do you believe in magic
watching the children run and
play
awaiting the day when their
fantasies
are buried in reality
maturity breeds ignorance,
teaching—
learning we but lose touch
with reality

Do you believe in magic
timeless years of knowing only a
distant face
endless nights of
misacknowledgement
traces of paths, of falling stars, of
foolishness,
of ignorance—a world at my
fingertips
only a step away—a dawn, a star
within grasp of a still young, yet
scarred aged hand
of dreams and days forbidden
of night-tossed beds—of ringless
phones
of plans thrown out to sea

Alan L. Fessier
ENCORE
Wind in the trees applauds
And green sequins flash
A riot of wet leaves
A curtain rises on the robes of fog
Revealing a pure white sash

Mountain and valley preen
Unconsciously proud in velvet
greenery
What supporting actors in

this scene
With spring in her colorful finery!

Monarch of the day arises
Summoning a rose array
This first act of the day discloses
Nature writing her favorite play

Mollie Glass Pamplin
SPECIAL MAGIC
*[To Susan Marcum Price who
has given me her love, her
friendship and her talent and
has made me feel that I can
sing my whole life long.]*
How special for me that her path
crossed mine!
Was it sheer chance or arranged
by design?
Lovely to look at, so lovely inside,
A real friend to love, in whom to
confide,
All sweetness and magic and
music too
Sharing her voice and her music
with you,
Most amazing of all, her gift is
mine,
Lending her magic, she makes my
life shine,
Magic piano reflecting through
me,
Through my voice singing, her
magic you'll see!
Her talent haunts you and falls
on your ear,
My voice is singing, it's Susan
you hear!

Shelly Sowards
HAND IN HAND
I can't think of
A better way to live
Than, with my hand in Yours.
You make everything
Work out right.
It may not work out
The way we want,
But it will work out,
To Your plan.
With my hand in Yours,
I am immortal.
I feel no shame,
Only devotion.
I am tamed in Your name.
My life is in Your hands.

Hank Swanson
HELPING A FRIEND
I stopped to help a friend today,
For he was in a tight.
I helped him just a little while
Til all was working right.
Then I said so long to him
And went about my way.
For helping him a little bit
Made my entire day.

Kari Elizabeth Dietz
OCCUPATINAL HAZARD
We cannot calm the weather,
Or walk upon the sea.
Can't deliver people out of
bondage,
Or watch over them as they flee.
We cannot feed five thousand,
With a fish and a loaf of bread,
And we haven't got the power
Of raising up the dead.
We can make a dead child "hear",
By reading with their eyes,
And we can give some comfort,
To an old man as he cries.

We can make a blind child "see",
By listening with their ears,
And make the children sleep at
    night,
When we've chased away their
    fears.
Why do people tend to worship
    us,
And praise us to the skies?
If they would only listen,
And help those with lonely cries.
We're not Saintly super humans,
For knowing how to care,
We have our share of problems,
Sometimes difficult to bear.
We have no heavenly halos,
Nor from clouds do we descend,
Why must people search for
    angels wings,
When we've only helped a friend?
We're just children of our Father,
Who art in heaven above.
We're disciples of the health
    fields,
Distributing our love.

Deborah A. Burke
GUIDE ME TO AN OCEAN
Lord, guide me to an ocean
That's deep and blue and wide;
And I will show the whole world,
    Lord,
I can reach the other side.
And guide me to a mountain
That's tall and steep and cold,
That I may prove to myself
That I am really so bold.
But if you can't find a mountain
Or an ocean deep and wide;
I ask thee then, my Father,
To guide me to your side.

Anne Marie Lucci
EARTH'S LOVER
A pink strand
of seaweed
entangles
in her salty water.

The tiny lights
in blue entice
and release
her in rhythm
with the moon.

Retreating, breathless,
she giggles
as the cool,
wet grains
trickle through her toes.

Margaret Zupancic Martin
TOMORROW'S CHILD
Tomorrow's child what will you
    be
In this land of tragedy
Recession, depression and soon a
    war
Oh child please don't grow no
    more
For when you grow I'm sure you'll
    see
That life isn't like you thought
    it'd be
Your dreams all seem to turn to
    dust
And people seem so hard to trust

It's such a scarey place to live
Where everyone takes and
    nobody gives
And love it seems so hard to find
America deaf, dumb, and blind

The threat of war is in the air
And no one really seems to care
What happened to the World we
    knew
When grass was green and skies
    were blue

Tomorrow's child I hope you see
That you must change humanity
And make more love and peace
    and fun
For tomorrow's child you've just
    begun

Joanne Eileen Coulis
LOVE IS YOU AND ME
*[Dedicated to my mother &
father, who've survived the
rough years with the love they
have for one another]*
Love is the way you hold me
When despair is at it's end.
The sharing and the caring
you show me as a friend.

Love is when all arguements
are replaced by tender words;
which too seldom are revealed
and too seldom often heard.

Love is every moment
that we share with one another
and the happiness it gives me
to know that there's non—other.

Love is when our silent tears
and fears we hold inside
are known to one another,
yet are never shoved aside.

Love is when each dream
we share becomes reality
through everything accomplished
by being you and me.
Love is love, and I share mine
    with you.

Larri J. Broomfield
WILD DOGS
The wild dogs begrudge a house.
Mournful howls bemoan their fate.
Dining on some rotten grouse,
laid upon a sodden plate.

The wild dogs have had their fill,
gulping up some winter grass,
all washed down with puddled
    swill.
Well licked chops, a touch of
    class.

The wild dogs, the inbred curs,
look into the darkened skies.
Nipping at their furstuck burs,
they howl moonlit lullabies.

The wild dogs dream not of hunts,
'stead they dream of doghot days,
streching out on happy grunts,
summer earns their sleeping praise.

Kathy Lyles Benefield
APRIL 9
*[Thank you Mom and Dad for
believing in me . . . With all
my love, Kathy]*
Wishing, hoping
    Painful and choking—
This is the heartbreak of love . . .

Kissing, teasing
    Sometimes squeezing—
This is the warmth of love . . .

Loving, caring
    Knowing, sharing—
This is the joy of love . . .

Alone, crying
    Slowing dying—
This is the heartbreak of love. . .

Paul W. Owens
TREASURED SECRET
As I Sit Here thinking about you
Living in seperate worlds I know
    thats true.
You are so very much a part of me
But I feel a love that just cannot
    be.
I wish we could have a love the
    size of one grain
For that would be enough to ease
    a heart of pain.
Each day that I see you brings a
    new tear to my eye
First of joy and happiness, then of
    hope thats run dry.
Looking forward to seeing you is
    my greatest pleasure
For your beauty is something I'll
    always treasure.
But along with each vision and
    presence of you
Comes the memory that my
    chances are far and few.
So with my feelings unshared in
    my heart and mind
Farewell my love for an eternity
    of time.

Moselle D. Vreeland
DEAR DREAMS
Oh, my gay dreams,
    You've grown so worn and
    tattered,
Your shiny wings are limp and
    torn,
    Your lovely forms are battered.

Oh, my brave dreams,
    You marched with colors
    streaming—
How could I know you were so
    frail,
    Who seemed so gay and
    gleaming?

Oh, my dear dreams,
    I loved your joyous singing,
Your rainbow dance delighted me
    And set my heart to singing.

Oh, my torn dreams,
    You're all begrimed and
    shattered . . .
But, oh, I hug you close to me
    As though you really mattered.

Maureen McGraw
I NEED YOU
*[Dedicated to Dave Skinker. For
all the times you were there. I
still love you and need you.
Sept. 11, 1982.]*
I need you
and your understanding.
I need to hear your voice.
I need to hear
you say those magic words.
The three simple words
"I LOVE YOU"
I need your shoulder to cry on
and the comfort that you give.
I need to know your mine
and that I am yours.
I need you
and I have never needed anyone
    before.
I need your smile

to light my path.
And your hand
to lead me in the right direction.
I am going astray
and I am lost and confused.
All I know for sure
is I need you
and it hurts to say it,
but I really do.
I need you
and I Love You!

Minnie Jordan, Simmons
What Love Is All About
Love is Something Beautiful
Love Is Like The Rain, that falls
    from The sky.
Love Is Like The sun, When It
    Shines Bright And Light.
Love Is Like The Wind, As It
    Blows Softly Threw The Trees.
Love Is Like The Rain, When It
    Splashes On The Ground.
Love Is Like Soft Music, That
    Stretches Threw Out The World.
If It Weren't For Love, What
    Would The World Be Like.
Love Is A Strong Feeling, That
    You Have For Each Other.
Love Is Breath Taking.
You Will Never Forget His Love.
Because This Person Is So Special
    To You.
Love Is Beautiful, And Exciting.
Love Is What Makes Your Heart
    Beat Fast.
Love Is Joyful
Love Is Happiness
Love Is Sadness
Love Is Painful
Love Makes The World Go Round.
Love Is Beautiful
Love Is What Makes Our soul
    Tick.
Cherish Your Love.
Love Is The Rock Of All Sin.

Steven K.
I AM
*[For Terry, whose love and
warm smile made life a little
easier. Thanks for being there. I
love you]*
Love is like a diamond;
Beautiful, but not flawless.
Alas, love is as perfect
As life itself.

Lauri Jo Roberts
MIND TRAVEL
Mingling
        wandering
                twirling
Spinning like the merry-go-round
Searching
        yearning
                falling
Helplessly through a hole in the
    ground
Reaching
        touching
                finding
Only that it's whirling still
Seeking
        speaking
                crying
I've got but another hill
Climbing
        hoping
                struggling
Just to see the light

Trying
    coping
        knowing
My mind is as the dark of night

Robin J. James
A New Creation Was Formed
[In memory of my brother Gregory]
A New Creation was formed,
then life was giving to an Unborn

A child that will soon open his
eyes to see, the future, that life
has giving, to you and me

Soon he'll walk and run, to greet
the world and it's society

Then, he'll weep with tears of
fears, that we have placed here,
for them to see.

But, soon his journey through
life's tangled web that we have
weaved will be over. Then he'll
rest with God in his green clover.

Jennie C. Larsen
SONG OF THE WINDMILL
I fling my arms in ecstacy
Flirting my tail when the wind blows free.
Whirl and swing; my symphony hear.
The wind is my trumpet blown clarion clear.
Staccato blades never their undertones cease,
Adding dissonant wails where my joints need grease.
The mad, wild lilt of the plains I sing
Of wheat and cattle and the heartache they bring,
Sun shriveled days and blizzard piled nights,
Puny man tilting against elements might,
Thirst and starvations, plenty and care,
The joy of achievement and depth of despair.

Carolan Baber
MAGIC CARPET
Magic carpet
In the night
Arise
Away with me take flight

Take me where the land is still
We'll sail above my desert hills

Take me where the air is warm
Where sad heart images never form . .
A land so vast and open wide
Floating in a space of windless sighs

Take me to that golden place
Where the sun's reflection never leaves my face

Take me where mystic silence reins
Sweeping from the canyons
Across the plains . .
The heartland where my soul does spill
Love
And love returns
To fill

Denise Verret Jones
REACHING
[For Melba Little, a wonderfully inspiring friend; and for my husband Doug, who helped me to reach again and re—discover LOVE.]
Reaching . . .
I'm reaching out to grasp for—
Some of the happiness I once knew.
Groping blindly,
Only to pull back desolate, empty hands.
Hands that—somewhere in time—
Held hope, happiness, and love.
Hands that once marveled
At the mere existence of life.
Now . . . I can reach no more . . .
My heart, my soul, my body resist.
So, slowly I surrender to the inevitable . . .
The death of feeling . . .
    The last breath of love.

Ruth A. Shooter
MOMMIES
As a child, mommies are perfect.
They help you pick up your messy room, and make sure you have clean clothes for school.
They help you address Valentine's for everyone in your class, and make sure you don't forget your lunch or your homework.
They're the ones who come to pick you up after school when it's raining, and wind up taking all your friends home, too.
And, sometimes, they may not always be the best housekeeper in the world, but they sure are the best cook.
They get up in the middle of the night when you're too sick to move but afraid not to, and you call out wanting someone to be with you.
And, when you fall down and skin your knees, their hug and smile perform medical miracles.
It seems like mommies know a lot about some things, and a little bit about everything.
God made mommies as a very special gift to children.
And when you grow up, and realize that mommies are human, with frailities and faults like everyone else, you love them even more.

Allan J. Hayward
JOHN WAYNE
As strong as an Ox and hard as a rock, that's big John Wayne.
From one town to the next, then "The Alamo". He had helped to clean up the West.
That's big John Wayne, always the best.
Like "The Flying Tigers" he once flew big John Wayne the Ace that always knew just what he had to do.
As a Captain at Sea, John Wayne just had to be one of the best to help keep this land free.
As a cop on the block, big John Wayne always got his man.
From the meanest Marine to the "Longest Day" to the "Green Beret" that big John Wayne, the best that's ever been seen.
From the bravest of men in the west to the best from fighting Seas to fighting Shores, to the Ace in the "Flying Tigers", to the Cop on the block all the way to the hospital bed and out again and again, one of the best ever to be.
Just one time I would like to shake the hand of a one Hell of a man that would never be beat, THAT BIG JOHN WAYNE.

Mary B. Haight
THE POETRY BEAST
Some poems want to rhyme and others don't.
Some poems make sense while others won't.
At times it seems a poem is a beast,
That won't listen to the poet in the least.
But continues to jump and jive
Just as if it were alive,
While the poet chases after with a leash.

Jeannie Capion
TAKE A LOOK
I find myself looking back to how things used to be,
It is hard to believe so much has changed for you and me.
I remember wondering if I would ever get things right,
For every step I took put happiness further out of sight.

Today I can take a look at myself and just where I am,
And there you are beside me— ready to lend a hand.
It sure is a far cry from how things used to be,
When no one really took the time to make me feel so free.

Tomorrow you may find that I will be there—just for you,
Whenever you reach out for me, I will be reaching for you too.
Now when I look at you, I can safely say,
You are the reason I can see some happiness today.

Hazel B. Plummer
The Nearness Of God
When things don't seem to be going just right
And you are down in the dumps abit,
Then, why don't you head for the country
Find a lake, and beside it—just sit?

Yes, sit—and listen to the noises
Of the creatures round about.
You'll feel the nearness of our God,
Of His presence—there will be no doubt.

You are bound to see some little birds
Each one singing a different song,
You'll notice how sassy the Blue Jay is,
And watch a Robin—proudly hopping along.

A squirrel or a chipmunk
Surely will come rushing by—
They chatter cuz' they like to be friendly
But they're really kind of shy.

You'll find real peace of mind
As you sit and dream and listen—
Your worries will vanish with the breeze
With true happiness—you'll glisten.

So take time out, once in awhile
For an opportunity such as this—
Being alone and so close to God
Is really too great to miss.

Michelle Lynn Baty
IN GRANDPA'S ARMS
[For Grandma and Grandpa in appreciation for the love, knowledge, and the home they gave to me when I didn't deserve it.]
In Grandpa's arms:
I'm safe.
The strength of his arms,
The warmth of his body;
Tell me so.
In Grandpa's arms:
I'm loved.
The twinkle in his eyes,
The smile on his face;
Let me know.
As Grandpa's Spirit wraps around me,
I feel him squeezing me close,
Loving, protecting:
And once again
I'm Grandpa's girl.

LeAnn Billick
PORTRAIT
As a painting that has been repainted a million times,
Our lives took on different forms.
The colorful paints run together
Covering the lines of mistakes made over the years.
We move around this canvas
Seeing happiness and troubles that soon pass by the wave of a brush.
Yet as the total picture changes,
It never dissappears completely.
It only blends to create a different image.
As I will never completely dissappear,
I'll merely create a different hue.

Rose Marie Williamsen
HONEY
[Dedicated to my husband and the father of our children TERRY—'We Love You'—(Wr.) November 14, 1982]
T is for the TIME we have together
E is for the ETERNAL Love we share
R is for the REASONS you are loved dear
R is for the REALITY in each day
Y is for the YEARS we've spent together

L is for the LITTLE Babe inside me
E is for the EXCITEMENT shared at birth

E is for the EARLY morning feedings

W is for the WAY you show your love dear

I is for the INTIMATE thoughts we share

L is for the LAUGHTER in our lives dear

L is for the LOVE you give our children

I is for the INTEREST in their rearing

A is for you ALWAYS being there

M is for the MARRIAGE vowed in Heaven

S is for the SEXIEST man I know

E is for the ECSTASY that follows

N is for the NEED to trust forever.

Jackie Myers
DREAMS
In my sleep I had awoke late last
night from dreams which
almost gave me a terrible fright
I had dreamed you were lying
right by my side but once
awoke, I knew my subconcious
had lied.
Sweet rememberance of your
body next to mine how my
heart yearns to have that
precious time in my dreams
you were making love with me
God, it seemed so real I could
feel, touch, and see
Ecstasy of such, I have never
known before
And when awoke, my body was
literally crying for more
My eyes red and puffy, my pillow
wet from tears how I long to
hold you darling when your
dream face appears
But it just isn't enough to reach
out for a dream I need you
physically by me, so it does
seem
The dreams happen now almost
every night
No matter how hard I try,
reoccurence I can't fight
So now darling, I am waiting and
soon it will be
No more dreams of you, just
sweet reality!

Tina M. Celentano
We Have Always Lived In Houses
Walls to separate the elements
Doors to separate ourselves
Look through the pane, a world
away,
Escape.
Ceiling to separate sky
Painting to separate reality
A grand escape, well needed
Window to separate smell
No sound.
We have always lived in houses
Reflection of ourselves to present
to outsiders
Floors to separate ground, stairs
to separate floors
An extension of ourselves to
keep the rain off
We have always lived in houses.

Heidi LaCommare
IT'S ALL OVER
It's all over now
We might as well forget it

And we should even try not to
regret it
It'll never be the same
As it was before
We'll never be knocking
Upon each other's door
We can still be friends of course
But think of this as our divorce
You soon will find another love
Your thoughts of me
Will be gone like a dove
But now it's time for my last
good—bye
And I'll try real hard not to cry

Bertie Scheer
THE TRAVELER
I give my thoughts to the
wandering breeze
To travel the earth wherever I
please.
I sit on a cloud all fluffy and white
And bathe in the purity of golden
sunlight.
I absorb the vibrations and blue
of the sky
And ride the air currents as they
sail by.
I filter my mind of the gravel and
sand
That keeps me bound to the
earth and the land.
I romp and I play and as free as
the air
Higher and higher with never a
care—
Leaving behind unhappiness and
strife
Forever to live in the goodness of
life.

Peggy Wiederman
Leaves Of Red and Gold
Leaves of red and gold
So bright and bold
Leaves of browned edged green
Waving at the suns gleam

Oh Sycamore tree
Your leaves are now free
And small Maple
Your leaves crack and call

For Fall has taken
Trees cover and when
Trees leaves are gone
The winds song

Hums so sweetly
Threw the trees
Leaves of red and gold
Now it seems so cold . . .

Sylvia L. Palmer
In the Shadows/In the Light
In the shadows stands a man . . .
In the shadows of his mind.
He stands alone, among many,
And he waits; not for me,
but for himslef.

He yearns and longs for freedom;
Unlocked passages and doors.
The key, within hemself,
He finds not; just waits . . .
in the shadows.

Another stands in the light,
Complete. In Freedom.
Open doors, Spring breezes,
Sunshine, fluffy clouds . . .
Crickets and butterflies.

In his world, all joyous and alive,

He stands and praises God.
Praises for completeness;
wholeness,
For Being! He laughs and sings.
Same man. *

*Or woman.

Babette Oliver Fletcher
KATIE
Poor little Katie,
Always wears a frown;
Smile a little Katie,
Don't let life get you down.

Poor little Katie,
A rockin' on her horse;
Life will soon get better,
It couldn't get much worse.

Kathleen A. Brost
The Death Of Compassion
An old man lies in the street
Cold frozen blood tinged grit
Streaking down his ancient
Terror stricken face

Eyes blurred by warm red ooze
Blink frantically
As a shaking hand gropes blindly
In the sooty black slush

Clutching his chest
His legs thrash wildly
Slipping——then stilled
By fruitless attempts to survive

An old man lies in the street
Traffic detouring
Around his cold and lifeless body
And no one cares.

Paula Jackson Mendoza
THE SADDEST SIGHT
The sands keep right on falling,
The world keeps turning round.
But nothing really changes much,
there's still the same old sound.
Of hungry children crying,
and reaching out in vain.
Their parents trying to survive,
and not to show their pain.
How sad a sight to see the child,
you care for and you nuture.
Growing up to be a man who
hasn't any future.

Kathleen A. McCullough Weyant
SONGBIRD
Little birdie in the tree
Would you look down here at me?

Would you sing your happy song
And help my heart to sing along?

Don't leave me standing here
Little birdie in the tree,
When I'm by myself I cry,
Bring some happiness to me.

Bozena Hraska
Another Deceived Christmas
[Dedicated to all the lonely
people—encouraging never, to
give up hope. Positive thinking
does wonders to the human
mind. Believe in miracles; they
exist!]
Entered under the mistletoe
With tears and heavy dose
Again she had no one to love
No one to oppose

Just like for the past three years
Christmas came with anxiety
—plenty of gifts though under
the tree

Choice and variety

Who put them there
What a stigma
Who entrusted these in her care
What an aura, what charisma
Radiates now through the air

What a joy when neighbor enters
Until he leaves, it remains
As soon as the door shuts from
outside
She's aware she vainly waits

What a lie! What surrender!
Admitting this limit
She had put those gifts there
herself
To enter Christmas spirit

Now she scurried ready for church
And began to sing
Positive that next Christmas
Will happiness bring

Betty Belford Noreck
WINIFRED
[For my mother, Winifred
Dixon Belford]
She tiptoed through my life, this
little lass,
With chestnut curls falling down
her back,
And ever faintly, you could hear
the Irish lilt
Of laughter that makes me love
her still.

This quiet soul—so small, a child
could pat her head—
But oh! so big a heart had Winifred!

I remember when I was just a child,
Holding hands and giggling all
the while
I cleaned my plate, the linen
cloth concealed our hands—
The silver bowl made everything
seem so grand!
And oh! the Irish tea!—the tea
We sipped—my Winifred and me!

A queen I was all while I grew—
I had naught else to listen to
As she anointed me with love,
and such
Fairy tales she told! and always
with a hush
Of olden times—of "wee ones"
dancing on the hill.
Oh, Winifred! I miss ye still!

Catherine A. Horchos
MY MESSAGE TO YOU
If I could write a song for you
to explain the way I feel
Shomehow the song wouldn't be
enough to show that my love is
real.

I had heard about you once before
and what I'd heard was only the
best.
Who'd ever think fate would
bring us together,
Hell, it did, love, and I think
you know the rest,

You're so much more than a
dream come true
You were sent from heaven above.
My life is worth living now,
because of you,
I want so much to give you my
love.

I know you've got your

own unpredictable style
as to when I might see you
around.
But I hope that you'll often think
of me
Whenever the world gets you
down.

It's hard to explain how I get each
time I see you, it feels as if my
heart wants to sing.
And I want you to know I'll stay
by you,
No matter what our future may
bring.

I know you want to take your
time with your life, and you
know I'm more than willing to.
Because I Love You, and I'd do
anything
Just to spend the rest of my life
with you.

Jeremiah G. Hickey, Senior
PASCHA EUCHARISTIA
The day is one of glory
I have wanted in my dreams.
It is like God's own love story
From the morning's early gleams.

And—at my shadow glancing—
I feel a surge of strength
To think of my creation, and,
To know what it has meant.

To me and all who love me,
And, those to whom my heart
is spent
For Him, who came so sinless,
And, died for all our sins.

The ecstasy of joy we feel upon
His resurrection,
Dispels the slighest doubt of
His beloved intentions.

Scientist and theologian join in
Sweet accord,
As they follow Lord and Master
To their only true reward.

Randy A. Shamlian
MELONCHOLY MOOD
Meloncholy is the mood
I fear the evil
I pray for the good
Manifestation is of the obvious
My silence crushes the heart
My pity tears the soul
Nowhere to turn,
Since meloncholy is the mood

Joanne M. (joie) Watson
LOVERS LAMENT
Perhaps
if my hand had
not clung so lovingly
to the beauty of a rose,
My heart would
not have bled so deeply
from the touch of its thorns.

Ms. Susan Gamrat
NOTHING'S THE SAME
When it comes right down to it,
nothing's the same.
Constant changes from sunshine
to rain.
Always churning and turning
around.
Never any peace really to be
found.

Look outside and see for yourself.
What's there now will be gone

on the twelfth.
And so on and so forth, the cycle
continues.
Here one day, gone the next.
Constant changes, never any rest.

Leaves are all changing from
green into brown.
Soon they will fall and be all on
the ground.
Grass into snow, then snow into
grass
Constantly changing; Oh what a
task!

When it comes right down to it,
nothing's the same.
Hopefully, one day, things will
remain.

Deborah Fudge Egger
Dreams Are Like Rainbows
Dreams, like rainbows,
come in many colors—
each one more dazzling
than the one before it.
However, dreams, again like
rainbows, come and go,
but the memory of its existance
never totally fades.
As years go by,
our dreams expand, change, and
grow
to meet our needs and desires
and the pot of gold at the end of
the dream
is our now much—awaited
success.
As I recall my many dreams,
from childhood fantasies
to so—called grown—up ideas of
heaven,
I color each one a rainbow hue
as it catches my mind's eye.
Occasionally, a dream's hue pales,
though still dazzling,
as a dream is forgotten or
discarded
and the rainbow stretches
to newborn dreams
or far—fetched fantasies
to entertain my mind.

Chris Staples Brophy
It's Sleepy (The Solitude)
It's sleepy (the solitude)
The air light with whispers;
Lifting,
And lulling
My innermost cares . . .

Thoughts that spawn query
They're also adrift;
Fading deep into blue
As idly I stare . . .

In the distance I see you
You're grasping at stone;
A mountain of pressure
So jagged it tears . . .

Come sleep in my solitude
Be lifted,
Be lulled;
Grasp on to this moment
I'm willing to share.

C. Vincent Kroeger
**I'll Never See Her
Reflection**
I'll never see her reflection
in a little girl's eyes,
No testimony to our love's
direction
lost flakes of gold in blue skies.

She will never hear the echo of
my voice
nor feel the touch of our son's
arms,
It's too late for us the choice
to know of children's charms.

But that doesn't mean
our love is any the less,
Only that we must glean
more of each others life to bless.

For that I'll have no regret
I'll love her all the stronger.
Through all the years, if she'll let
me, and our love will last much
longer.

Lisette Marie Ellis
THE CHILD AND THE SEA
[To my parents, who have
nurtured my child spirit in
hopes that it shall never die.]
Dawn is breaking
Darkness
to light
birth of life
and serenity.
Child reaching,
early morning sky
spreads calmness
along the shore
murmurs softly,
ruffles in the wind.
Sea peace   Child serenity
together with ribbon magic,
dance . . .
dance alone
beautiful spirits,
beautiful
souls.

Charlotte Marie Meyer
The Seal Upon My Heart
I remember how it was the first
time we met,
And I knew then it was you on
whom my heart was set.
And I knew from deep within
that this was for real—
The kind of love no thief could
ever steal.

You brought an added dimension
to my life so unique
That other things in comparison
seemed somehow bleak.
You gave me a sense of humor to
dispel the gloom,
And enveloped me with a warmth
that made my love for you bloom.

Your soul and spirit walked hand
in hand with mine—
This love so deep, so lasting, so
divine,
That of all human emotions, it is
the most sublime—
Love that could come only once
in any person's lifetime.

But somehow this relationship
can never be resolved,
Even though it's the one thing on
which my life revolved.
For life has its way of preventing
that which we most desire,
And leaving us to cope with this
inner flame of fire.

This flame within us that will
burn forever
Is something that time nor
distance could ever sever.
And our spirits will live on,

entwined for life,
Even though I may never, ever be
your wife.

And even now, when I'm 3,000
miles away,
I still think of you each and every
day.
And although the moments of
the present may soon become
the past,
I know I'll love you always and
forever—even until the last.

Cathy Ah Sam
BEGINNINGS
[To my son Vance for his gift
of love]
Without a dad, you toiled at eight
Childhood denied, exchanged for
wage
A boy, too soon you bore your
weight
Surviving life, we two engaged

Beyond your years, a selfless,
youth
You learned in haste, what life's
about
Your innocence, essence of truth
By love embraced, enriched no
doubt

Away from home at twenty-one
Begin anew the role of man
Fulfill your goals, you go alone
Give from within, part of God's
plan

C. A. Filsinger
UNTITLED
I found him resting on a swinging
bench, in front of an old shack—
he called his home. His calm
expression drew me nearer.

He sat with his hands folded on
his lap; he needed not look
down the pathway to notice me
coming near. And the thunder
collided above, among the gray
clouds.

Smiling, he pulled the pipe from
his mouth. "Slow down." He
said, "Things you're passing by
are leaving you empty." Then,
he sat still for a moment,
staring at the soft green hills
beyond. Mist fell from the
clouds and the sky darkened
further. Love needs time. Time
to grow. We've lost it in the
rush." The old man put his
head down and slowly closed
his eyes. "Only in our
loneliness do we wonder where
it's gone."

The lightening continued beating
the skies; the mist turned into
rain. There was no shelter
above our heads; we didn't
move. My own heart sank.

Opening his tear filled eyes, he
reached for the sliver-bound
arms of the swing and grasped
them tightly. "If you've rushed
yourself, you'll be alone, one
day." He couldn't hold the tears
back. Or maybe he didn't want
to.

He shivered. "Time alone should
be your pace-setter."

The rain fell down his face to join

his tears, falling down his relaxed smile. Slowly, the sun reappeared through the cluttered gray clouds. The old man leaned back and again he stared to the hills.

"For you—you will have the opportunity to slow down. Make your life last." His voice slowed. "Sixty-seven and my own—can be found in my dreams."

James O'Keefe
BELFAST
Streets are chilled
by cold winds of terror,
homes are warmed
by fires of hatred.

Peaceful beauty destroyed
by bombs and gunfire as
playgrounds become battlefields.

Children,
throwing rocks at soldiers,
are warriors at the age of ten.

People killed
in the name of God.
both sides claiming to be right.

Assasinations
may kill the leaders,
but the children
are the unseen victims.

Donalyn Marie Carlson
REUNION
Once more,
we stood,
eye to eye.

Neither you,
nor I,
could breathe.

Insanity.
Lust.
Apprehension.

Facades,
torn through,
to sequestered emotions.

Your eyes,
met mine,
and saw . . .

Words,
begging articulation,
never to reach our lips.

Your hand,
outstretched to mine
says more.

And again,

We are all
we were . . .

Before.

Robert A. Muller
FROM SANTA WITH LOVE
[To the patients and staff of Good Samaritan Hospital in Tampa, Florida.]
Twas' the night before Christmas
and all through the "House"
Not a patient was stirring and
surely not a mouse
The I.V.'s were hung near the
patients with care knowing a
doctor soon would be there.
The patients were all snuggled up
in their beds with visions of
discharge dancing in their heads.

The nurses quietly waited for
their relief when something
happened beyond belief.
Up on the roof there came such a
clatter, security was paged to
see what was the matter
Snyder responded and took the
gent by surprise but frozen in
wonder couldn't believe his eyes.
Hung up in the antenna wire
stood a man in red beside him,
eight reindeer & a sled.
"Halt, who goes there?" Ed
inquired. "Tis only me, trying
to get unwired."
"Tis no easy job," as he worked
his way free, "I miscalculated
when I hit your palm tree."
"Where's the chimney you've
managed to hide?" "How do I
get to the folks inside?"
With a smile, Ed escorted the
gent to the stairwell; as both
descended, could be heard a
tinkling sleighbell.
"No soot on my fur? and no tight
squeeze! My task here will be
done with ease."
A compassionate smile rose as
they tended the sick; the
nurses thanked God for the
remedy of "Saint Nick".
He made his rounds to both
young & old saying a prayer as
their hands he did hold.
Then back to the roof he did
scurry, "There's many to see so
I must hurry".
As he looked up, a bright star
stood out in the sky, with a
loving smile he knows the
reason why.
The celebration of a birthday is
the real reason Christmas is
the most important season.
With a crack of his whip, he was
off and away "has been a
glorious night and tomorrow—
praise His birthday."

Diane Stanford Hassell
THAT MAN BOWS
Nature's son, with sun-drenched
skin like fired clay
The strength in his handshake
almost alarming
Earthy hands, all cracked and
rough, belying his trade
With the eyes of an eagle,
piercing and quick
That man bows to none;

Gentle man, with loving patience
like golden rays
The tenderness of his touch is
endearing
Adept hands, still and sure when
facing a task
With the eyes of a deer, cautious
and keen
That man bows to none;

Fury's son, with seething rage like
a turbulent sea
The works left in the wake of his
hands are standing
Battered hands, proud and strong,
showing his might
With the eyes of lightning,
flashing and threatening
That man bows to none;

A man, with ambitions cloistered
like a monk
The hesitation in his grip, a
question in his heart
Wondering hands, angry and
alone in despair
With the eyes of the wind,
searching and surrendering
That man bows to One.

Shawn Marie Amundson
SUNRISE
I've never seen the great sunrise
For when I am in bed.
Oh! with my eyes closed so tight,
I see the bright, yellow sun
visioned in my head.

What is the great sunrise?
It's so large it can not be
measured in size.
You don't know for sure when it
will appear,
For it will take you by surprise.

So if you want to see the sunrise,
You better open up your eyes.
For if you don't it will be as I said,
"Just a bright, yellow sun visioned
in your head."

Lisa Cantrell
MEMORIES
[At the pinnacle of my heart lies the memories I have and the memories I will have of the love of my life and I together, Timothy Scott Taylor.]
I stare
at the wall of decaying concrete
withdrawing into my mind
to find
myself standing in the dust of
old forgotten memories
trying
to grasp gently the faded pages
all tattered and brown
Softly
brushing the cobwebs from the
edges of time to reveal a
glimpse
of golden years, treasured tears
dreams lived and lost
Passing
gracefully through the rhythm
and rhyme of time
gone-by
bringing to crystal clear vision
the vintage wine of my mind
Radiant
warmth blankets the old and
unfolds to welcome the new

Ruby Welsh Wilkins
AURORA BOREALIS
On Christmas Eve a pine tree,
standing high
Against a cold and starlit northern
sky
Will show me clearly what a
Christmas is
And I will make my Christmas
out of this.

Aurora borealis of my soul
Light up my spirit sky from pole
to pole
On Christmas Eve again as,
magically
The evergreen reveals eternity.

Just for a moment, let my heart
forget
The distant cross that stands in

silhouette
The cold and careless world, the
Judas kiss
And let me make my Christmas
out of this.

I see in stately pine, the strength
that came
To Mary when the angel called
her name;
To Joseph when he knew that
Mary's son
Was strangely hers, yet not also
his own.

The wind sings through the pine
and angel choir
Echoes around its fragrant-
needled spire
Then I am where the shepherds
stood in awe
And my heart sees the wonder
that they saw.

On straw of pine I see the
Heaven's Prince—
Himself the gold, the myrrh, the
frankincense.
My soul rejoices from its chrysalis
And surely Christmases are made
of this!

George Chaffee
A GIFT FROM SANTA
When I was just a wee wee lad;
Ol' Santa knew I wasn't bad.
On Christmas morning in my sock;
I found a very small pet rock.
Pet rocks require no special needs;
Like exercise or special feeds.
They like the sunshine and the
shade;
We often went outdoors and
played.
Until one day I cried and cried;
Because I knew my pet rock died.
A small pet rock can not survive;
When misplaced on a crushed
rock drive.

Christy Lincoln
WAR
The bodies that lie baking
in the midmorning sun.
The parties and celebrations
after a battle is won.
The weapons that lie
in a heap by the door.
The pleasures and tortures
of a thing that's called war.

The bombs and the chemicals
from the war of the worlds.
The screams and the screeches
that make my blood curdle.
The sweat beading
on my neck and my brow.
The sounds and the feelings
that take away our power.

The faces of soldiers
who have realized their sin.
The screams of the children
heard over the din.
The two-faced heroes
on which we base our pride.
How many people is it now
that have died?

Trina Carpenter
MADE WITH LOVE
Today you're a baby
Beginning to grow
Tomorrow a child
Wanting to know.

Questions you'll ask,
Waiting for answers
How blue skys turn black
Rain falling like dancers.
Jessie you know
I don't want you to be sad
I want you to have things
I never had.
You need lots of love
And tender care
And when you get hurt
I'll always be there.
You're my special little girl
And you'll never know why
And I'll always love you
Till the day I die
God made you
With lots of love
And sent you to me
From up above.
I'm here to hold you
Through those long long nights
When you're afraid to go to sleep
When I turn out the lights.
When you say "my momma"
And hold me tight
I know in my heart
I'm raising you right.

Lois T. Welborne
FATHERHOOD
[To a dear FRIEND who
inspired me to write many
things; thanks.]
Fatherhood, faster than a
speeding bullet
Announces
Toughness to be
Hinged and
Entertwined with
Responsibility and softness and
love

Hazel E. Olson
Our Tree For Christmas
So stately you stand in the hall
alone.
All decked out in your best
finery.
Glass bells, tinsel and your own
pine cones.
There's a smell in the air of a
pinery.

The oohs and aaws—how beautiful.
You hold your head high.
The packages are bright not dull.
Everyone looks at you and sighs.

Oh how beautiful and grand.
This lovely little tree in the hall.
Glad now to have left the sand.
Warm and cozy in a home not a
mall.

Paula A. Shaffer
LEAVES
Momma, when the leaves turn
brown we'll go outside to take
a walk among those now fallen
from the tree. We must be
silent; these leaves in their
final days deserve respect, too.
We'll step around their delicate
skins; I cannot bear the
crushing screams from aged
entities clinging to life after
the end, before the dying.

Momma, when the leaves turn
brown we'll speak of quiet
moments shared in time and a
certain time we know will come.

You may place your fragile arm in
mine; I'll need support from
you as well. I'll let you squeeze
my hand, touch my cheek, and
perhaps the look into ancient
eyes will reinforce what I've
learned from dying leaves
newly parted from the tree.

Momma, when the leaves turn
brown you'll know I'm still
your child.

Hilda Vogt
SUNSET
When the sun sinks in the West
That's the time I love the best.
The trials of the day are through
And I can relax with you.

We can sit beneath the trees
And revel in the cooling breeze.
The golden orb in the sky
Is sinking and will surely die.

But in a last triumphant blaze
She will all her splendour raise
And fill the earth with rosy light
To welcome the oncoming night.

One by one the stars appear
They all seem so very near.
The glow worms trying to
compete
Make the picture quite complete.

The birds are chirping their good
night
They'll wake again with morning
light.
Just as the sun will surely rise
And once more glorify the skies.

Though we are in our sunset years
We should surely have no fears.
We will rise on God's bright morn
And we too will be reborn.

Pete Ford
THE BETTER LIGHT
How softly does your light
o'erspread
The village asleep in peace
But bright were your beams as
you had led
Those wise men from the east

You've startled shepherds in the
night
And made them sore afraid
And they came to wonder at the
manger sight
Wherein the Babe has laid

You've caused Mary to ponder in
her heart
The sayings that the shepherds
bring
Now you light their way as they
depart
To tell of the things they've seen

Your light grows dim, done is
your task
And your beams fade on His face
Yet tiny hands reach out as
though to grasp
And keep you in your place

But well you know that His light
must brighter gleam
As you dwell in Bethlehem's chill
air
For those tiny hands that
clutched each beam
Are the hands that hung you there

Lester R. Nuse
LIFE
[To all my family and friends
and may God bless them all
and keep each and everyone of
them safe always]
A walk in the morning sun
See the dawning of the day
Sit at night in the evening breeze
And watch the sun fade away

Life can be so beautiful
That's why I take a dare
And show my fellow man
My love I wish to share

I tell a joke and hear a laugh
And see a great big smile
When I can cause this happiness
Then my life has been worthwhile

If all around this world
I can spread a little joy
I hope to make them happy
As a child with a toy

I know I have a twisted spine
And have had since my birth
But that doesn't mean I was born
Without a sense of mirth

I thank the Lord for everyday
That he has let me live
Because I know in my heart
I have a lot to give

If I can spread more happiness
And make people care a little more
Then everyone would be to happy
To cause another war

Because of my bad spinal cord
There's things I cannot do
But everyday I'll keep trying
To turn gray skies to blue

To see a radiant happy face
And fill their hearts with mirth
Then my job for God will be done
Before I leave this earth.

Laura Marie Henry
MISTAKEN LOVE
[To Ray: who hurt me the
worst, but challenged me the
most; and who in the
beginning was the end, but in
the end is the beginning—I still
love you . . .]
I thought I was in love once, but I
guess I was wrong.
At the moment it seemed so
right, but then it came time to
move on.
We shared special days in the
park and perfect evenings
under the stars;
falling in love to escape reality,
questioning who we are.
Wishing away our youth, always
longing to be together.
Promises made, but never kept;
wondering how long is forever.
Cards, letters, and phone calls,
weekends secretly spent—
plans for the future drawn if we'd
only known what they meant.
We were so sure of ourselves,
only in doubt when apart for
awhile.
The deep insecurity growing, the
love escaping from my smile.
Getting caught up in our private
lives, no longer seeming to share;
less time spent together, less time
left to care.

Realizing we were children
caught up in a grown-up's dream,
but only playing the part—afraid
to ask what they mean.
I found you were meant to be just
a phase in life's many plans,
but a special part never forgotten—
the first love forever stands.
As an adult, I see new facets of
love, not just the longing to be
together;
but the feeling of total
contentment, and the
realization of how long is
forever.
There's a new person in my life,
we never question letting go.
Now, I don't think I'm in love—
now I, really know . . .

Rosa M. Prohias
STATE OF MIND
[To my mother a wonderful
teacher and friend]
If the present is merely a space
Between the grief of the past
—Dissatisfaction, disgrace, skies
overcast—
And the happiness of tomorrow
—Joy, felicity, goals attained—
Well what if past sorrow went on
the same?
What would we do if tomorrow
never came?

If the young long to grow old,
Yearning for wisdom, knowledge
untold;
And the old long to be young,
To go back and sing songs
unsung . . .
When will satisfaction be had?
When will we truly say we are glad?

It is for this reason
We must enjoy every age, every
season.
We cannot dream of when we
will succeed,
Worrying about the countless
weeds;
But instead decide how we will
succeed,
Pulling them up and planting
new seeds.
We cannot dream of when the
sun will appear,
Just hoping for our paths to be
made clear;
But instead decide how we will
make it shine—
Right now, Right here,
Enjoying our prime . . .
By drawing goals more near
It can come at any time,
For it is only a state of mind.

Lori Lynn McMurria
Born Was a Rose Tonight
Born was a Rose tonight
Above were golden stars of light.
Standing taut, broad and bold
Over the earth, so chilly and cold.

Blooming the breath of Spring
You could hear her sweetly sing
Spreading harmony with a simple
sigh.
Elegant appearances reached my
eye.

Colors of radiant pink
Shine and glimmer with a wink.

How beautiful her dress was worn
Here tonight, she was born.

Coming deep from under the land
The Rose gently sits in the palm
of my hand.
How fair and dainty this velvet
feels
Beauty engulfs my future wills.

Beyond the bottom of its vine
Lives infinite numbers in time.
Only thee shall stay but a while
Death will follow with a smile.

Rich smells fill the air with
rotten leaves
Heavily my heart sinks, my soul
grieves.
Nor unhappy or at rest
But beyond eternity shall live thy
best.

Quietly as breezes that follow
Here today and gone tomorrow.
It's time to cease and take that
flight
Born was a Rose tonight.

Marilyn L. Brown
PIPES OF PAN
*[Inspired by the film fantasy
"The Seven Faces of Dr. Lao."]*
When Pan's soft pipes she hears
in springtime fair,
Awak'ning flush of live in maiden
breast,
It must needs be that nature then
doth bear
The message sweet to him with
mind to list,
For maid and swain must meet,
fulfill the need
That quickens pulses stirred by
seedtime's call,
And bids the lovers quaff this
heady mead,
Lest passions unfulfilled too soon
may pall.
Sweet bliss is thine for ye who
dare to take
Thy true love by the hand and
follow whence
Hearts lead, impatient now that
love's awake
To enter rapture's joyful realm
and thence
Proceed to savour thy delight until
Enchantment's done and pipes of
Pan are still.

Nancy Sue Bartholomew
IN NOVEMBER
Let's go walking
in the first
fall rain together,

Then light a fire,
and feel the warmth
of our bodies
join together in love . . .

And when we have done
lying quietly together
in the dark,

I can love you
in my dreams . . .
after you have gone.

Bonnie M. Munoz
WIDOW
*[To my family and friends of 33
years]*
Being a widow
Is a very unhappy space.

Being alone in life
You don't have a place.
You are like a wheel,
Without its spokes.
Everyone is kind,
But you are left without folks.
You are the very same person,
But without your man.
It's like God making a world,
Without a divine plan.
The ghetto of widowhood,
Is a place no woman wants to go,
But everyone could.
For without any intention,
You are suddenly,
A woman without convention.
It's a sad state of affairs,
When you stop to think.
Most every woman,
Comes to the brink.
Nine out of ten,
Bury their men.
So let's stop and think,
About them again.

Peggy West
TO BE A BUTTERFLY
[To Dad]
To be a butterfly and show the
world my spirits so high
I wouldn't need a hand or laugh
or word or sigh
To stop nearby a mossy nook or
quiet leaf or shiny brook
Or need a rope or manmade
swing to stop and sing
Upon a canyon's silent rim to
show how far above I'd go
I'd be a part of all above and all
below
And float away forever if the
wind would have it so.

Joanna Lois Pearcy
AFTER THE LOVE
I want to run
But there is no place to hide
From this feeling of doubt
Buried deep down inside.
How do I get
In the messes I do?
There is no turning back.
I should start anew.
But there it is,
That same old feeling again.
I have found that life is real
And not merely pretend.
Things can never be quite the
same
As they were before.
I never realized how much I loved
you
Until you walked out the door.

Doris Courtney Lowdermilk
LITTLE LAMB
God love thee little lamb with
coat of white
I thy shepherd will guard thee
through the night
We'll bed us down on fragrant
boughs
Then say that little prayer of ours

The dark shadows and noises in
the night
Will fear thee not for I'll hold
thee tight
Now slumber little lamb forlorn
My body's heat will keep thee
warm

When morning breaks we'll find

some grasses green
You'll lead us on with nose so
keen
We'll drink us from the coolest
stream and then
When darkness comes creeping,
we'll bed us down again

Do not thee worry as each day we
travel on
Our trusted dog will keep us from
harm
Always forward, oh! so long and
then behold
Familiar smells and voices, you're
back safe within the fold

Donna Brubaker
A NEW WOMAN
The more I struggled
the more obvious
my feelings became

I searched my mind
and found
I was trying
to give you
the responsibility
of my life

I accept your
rejection

And
I thank you . . .

Cynthia Jane Boman
COUNTRY GIRL
*[To my wonderful family
(Clark, Betty and Ann), my
boyfriend, Derek, and my
friends—with all my love.]*
I used to run
among trees
taller than giants
pick bouquets
of wildflowers
eat wild
raspberries
squint at
the April sun
chase birds
of blue
and yellow
play like I
was a pioneer
sleeping on
a log
God made
to be
my bed
and
now I sit
in a
tan and red
dress
staring out my
office window
at a mosaic
of black and grey
dreaming
of home.

Mildred Rhodes Thomas
A GIFT OF LOVE
*[This poem, I dedicate to you,
my grandson, Chad for you
have given me the most
precious love I have ever had.]*
There's a little guy in my life
Who greets me at the door
And shouts,
Oh, grandma, I missed you
Now, don't you leave me anymore

His arms are wound around me
tight
I pretend to be hurt
But I scream with delight
He leads me to an easy chair
And says,
Now grandma, you sit there
His little hands are soft to the
touch
And I squeeze them so gently
When he whispers,
Grandma, I love you so much
All this love from a child so wise
Brings tears to these tired old eyes
A gift from God, otherwise
I would be adrift in a sea
Of lost hopes and despair
And drown in a whirlpool of
Self-pity—No love there
I hold him close
And feel the warmth
And the sweet fragrance of youth
Drenches my soul—Once lost,
now whole
And I thank God for His wisdom
And I thank Him that I am alive
To enjoy His heavenly priceless
gift
The little guy in my life
Who's just half-past five.

Demethia McVea
**If Love Was All We Had To
Share**
If love was all we had to share, no
danger zones and no bewares,
we'd sail along the soft blue
sky, just you and I my
pumpkin pie.

If love was the only emotion left
behind, there'd be more peace
and less crime, regardless of
any place or time, love would
be the only thing on my mind.

If love was the ony thing at all,
with no hatred to lurk among.
The beauty of it all is that
price payed much greater than
small.

Wilda M. Hively
LOVE'S NOT HERE
When the heart is overflowing
And the tears don't bring relief,
When life's partner has betrayed
one
When the soul is filled with grief,

When all thoughts return to
memories
Days of sweet fun and romance,
Just a simple gift for love's sake
Perhaps a hug or special glance,

Forever deeds or words returning
Seems the mind is out of gear,
The heart is torn, needs to be
mended
Love's not dead, but it's not here,

Life has taken on a sadness
Waves of depression drowning me,
There's no feeling, only numbness
As a ship adrift at sea,

I'm locked alone in my own prison
No more goals do I pursue,
Afraid and aimless, barely living
Life has no purpose without you.

Maria Rizzo
TIMES OF WONDER
People say there is a time
A time to reach a certain step

From seventeen till twenty-one
Where there will be all the fun
The fun of laughter
The fun of tears
Which all has been the same for
    years
But maybe it will be better after
    this certain step
Even though they wait for years
    wanting to grow up
They never ever ever seek to find
    this certain step
For all they know it could be
    fame or maybe even fortune
But then again God knows what
    will ever happen to us
But whatever God picks for us
    there has to be a reason
For he chose it just for me
There must have been a reason
For I will not really know what
    this reason is
Until I reach this certain step
Until eternity . . .

Arlone Mills Dreher
EARTHQUAKE
The roaring monster shook the
    earth.
The buildings swayed and fell in
    pain.
A mighty fissure wider grew
And split the earthy hell again.

Another belch within the earth,
The waves of land came pouring
    by;
The people left without farewell;
They feared the quake's deep sigh.

Our great cathedral gasped its last
As rocks came tumbling down
And pushed it from its stately site
Long honored in the town.

A deathly hush! A quite hour!
The town its vigil keeps;
The Hand of God the tremors
    stilled
And earth's great fault now sleeps.

Helen Brown Harris
THINKING OF YOU
As I arise to each new morning,
I think of love I cannot have.
I tell myself I am all right,
but night and day you are on my
    mind.
Those I love who have died,
I no longer have—
Only holding on to the thought
    of them,
Now and then

Janice L. Laperle
HIDDEN SENSE
It shows its face today
But hides itself tomorrow.
Brings you joy one day
And another only sorrow.
Read it over once again
Can you guess the riddle above.
From day to day its on the mend
The Hidden Sense is Love.

Joan E. Bratlie
WHAT IS CHRISTMAS?
Christmas is baby Jesus,
Born on a bed of hay,
Along with the cattle,
Baby Jesus he did lay.

Christmas is children,
Their eyes filled with glee,
Of the joy of Santa.

With gifts under the tree.

Christmas is giving,
God sent his only Son,
To die for us on Calvary,
To redeem us from our fun.

Christmas is friends,
The joy we each can share,
When with another person,
To know that they care.

Christmas is loving,
Just loving one another.
If it be a friend or neighbor,
A child a spouse or brother.

Christmas is Jesus' Birthday,
Less we not forget,
If it were not for His birthday,
We would have have Christmas
    yet.

Leslie D. Bagnell
RAINDROPS (for children)
*[This poem is written to my
beloved children, Diane and
Robert Bagnell. They are my
pride and joy.]*
Raindrops, Raindrops, splitter
    splat
On the pavement, down my back

My nose is wet, the air is mist
A silver shimmer of spring's first
    kiss

Brigit Kjiv
FINAL SOLUTIONS
Like a heart at rest,
Though its beat continues,
You arrive at the final solution,
Bathed in tears,
Washed as by ablution.
Like gravity's fall
You survive in flight,
Escaping the traps, set by night
That like a bottomless abyss
Has called you . . .
But your meticulous conclusions
Have seen you through
In majestic progression,
Like winged shafts, reaching
Their targets with precision.

Priscilla A. Whoolery
RELEASE NO STRANGER
pretty Little Girl in the sand,
    her face is too pale,
    her blue eyes have lost their
        sparkle.
something is missing—

—careful, pretty Little Girl,
    the waves are nipping at your
        toes . . .

pretty Little Girl in the sand,
    her face is paler still
    her blue eyes are now closed.
to a stranger she is limp and
    lifeless;
    they see pain in her expression,
but i am no stranger
    and i can see
        her smile.

Tom C. Hughes
DROUGHT
*[To MARILYN, my wife and to
SHANE, SHAWN, JOHN, KI,
AND JORDAN—the people I
love most]*
I have met the mornin's heat
    as daylight walks the
        mountaintops,
and circlin' vultures wait for

death,
    and crows inspect the wiltin'
        crops.

I have felt its risin' wrath
    a-burnin'; hot upon my brow;
dyin' fields and arid meadows
    lie beneath the turnin' plow.

I trip o'er clods of dried-out soil
    that languish in their barren
        plight;
I drag behind the droopin' mule
    thru chokin' dust that's thick
        as night.

I stop and reach for a dirty scarf
    to mop the sweat from burnin'
        skin;
with calloused hands and
    strainin' eyes
    I search the row's still-distant
        end.

Beneath the shade of a
    cottonwood
    I rest for one brief, pantin' spell;
the hot wind sears my tired old
    face
    as I gaze across that burnin' hell.

Swirls of dirt rise with the breeze,
    'n' dust-devils dance 'cross th'
        furrowed land,
silently coverin' the traces of
    tracks
    left by mule, and plow, and this
        old man

Janice L. Laperle
A WHISPER OF LOVE
A whisper of love is dead,
Unless of course it is said;
A lost, unspoken word,
That's never to be heard.
The softness of loves' whisper,
Is like that of a kittens' purr,
Gentle to the ear, yet meaningful
    to say,
Tho to the center of the heart it's
    certain to make its' way.
So a whisper of love is dead,
Unless of course it is said;
A lost, unspoken word,
Never, ever to be heard.

Corine Wampler
Our President the Actor
Well Carter went back to Georgia
    for a peanut to see
While Reagan went into
    Washington getting his pep
        from the bee,
He downs the poor, he boasts his
    power; he grins from ear to ear.
What he's really saying is, "We'll
    be in a soup line this year.

He promised all the young guys,
    "There will be no draft under me".
Bet he breaks that promise too,
    lets just wait and see.
T'was in the day of Republican
    reign when this all first begun,
They took our Social Security
    and turned it into the general
        fund.

Now our country is full of
    immigrants, it's full of refugees,
It's full of Welfare Checks and
    Reagans little bees.
Where did Reagan get his pattern
    to balance the budget this way?
Could it be from the nineteen-

thirties and Hoover's
    depression days?

Now all ye people listen, take
    this advice from me
Let's send him back to
    Hollywood. That's where he
        needs to be.
We don't need his Nuclear
    Weapons or acting on T.V.
Or cuts in education, that's what
    it's going to be.

He sits in his oval office and eats
    his Jelly Beans
And keeps on cutting taxes and
    driving limousines.
Of course he's just an actor; that
    is what he does best
Just eating Jelly Beans, while
    Nancy models her dress.

When the Reagans act is over
    and our country has its fall,
Where will Mr. Reagan be, at the
    final curtain call?

Kelly S. Gough
THE SACRIFICE
I've never known
In all my life
A love that's grown
For sacrifice.

My whole family is here
Saying that they know
In all their love and fear
That it is so.

I answer, "It's our life
I'm not too young nor he too old
I'll even be his wife
In a world that's cold."

Yet they are sure
That it will die
Through all my years
I'll wonder why.

And I decide
With all my heart
I will leave them behind
And I depart.

This is the sacrifice
That I have made
To leave behind
That for which I had stayed.

I love my family
Though not enough
To stay with them happily
And leave my love.

Donald J. Bayman
THE SILENT SCREAMS
*[To all the Einstein's who will
not think, the Bach's who will
not write, the Heifitz's who
will not play, the Shakespeare's
who will not rhyme, the
Mayo's who will not heal . . .
because they were not allowed
to leave the womb alive.]*
The silent screams cannot be
    heard.
They echo forth in chambers
    closed
To human senses—numbed by
    shame
Of causing them. Before the word
Of Godless men . . . they don't
    exist.
The moral questions that they
    posed
Are not answered by heartless

claim . . .
"They never lived—they won't be missed.

Beware the cry you cannot ignore...
The voice inside that speaks with love.
Unless you heed, the curse will send
From Babylon the naked whore
To make the dawn of life a tomb!
We must believe that God above
Will bless the man who helps defend
The sanctuary of the womb.

Let not hate spawn its nightmare—dreams
To deafen conscience . . . kneel, and pray
That God will send His Love today . . .
For Love can stop the silent screams.

Mary Lou Clay
The Sound of Christmas
[These are the lyrics of a song I composed in 1965 as I was reminiscing about the sound of Christmas in the years gone by.]
There's a jingle, jingle, tingle, tingle in the air
That happy, happy feeling that's so very rare
Happiness, everywhere you go
Decorated streets, and the old familiar sound of a
Ho, Ho, Ho.

It's a happy, happy, snappy time to know
That there's love, and fun, and lots of glistening snow
Presents, and all you hold so dear
All around you hear the sound
Christmas is here.

Susan E. Jardin
IMAGINOCEANS
From deep within the chasms of space
The creator has fashioned another race.
'Tis this you hear in the briny deep
As these strange creatures are lulled to sleep.

Jody Clark
MEMORIES
Memories—
are all I have left of you.

Memories—
to hold me up when my world is coming down.

Memories—
Of the walks beside the brook;
Of the deep and longing looks;
Of the night we fell in love;
Of the twinkling stars above.

Memories—
Of you will help me through

Because Memories don't leave like people do!

DelVina McCormick
REMEMBERING WINTER
It's not just because of the holiday season,
As a matter of fact, there's no rhyme or no reason.

It's not the white snow against a dark sky,
Or people we know just dropping by.
Seeing dear faces in the fireplace glow
Singing old favorites, songs we all know
The fragrance of popcorn filling the room,
Please tell me why winter's over so soon.

These things I wait for all through the year,
I always enjoy these memories dear.
The tinkling sound of our one horse sleigh,
The click, click, click of our dapple grey.
It's not any one of these wonderful things,
That reminds me of my childhood days,
Still all together a bell they ring
Of old times, old friends and old ways.

Catherine Beeson Wright
BRIGHT MIRACLE
Give Him your heart
and Christ is yours to hold.
   Your hurts are healed
by unleashed laughter!
   Dashed dreams become your scaffolding
for better days hereafter!
   Hold Him close . . . fear not!
For faith outweighs the odds
   that sin and guilt can muster
and Christ's Bright Miracle of Love
adorns anew the heart with
   Spirit—Luster!

Madeline E. Reeves
HE'S RESTING PEACEFULLY
[Charles T. Titus, Sr. In Loving Memory]
My Grandpa died sometime back
   I sat and cried in grief
I know I shouldn't feel so bad
   He's Resting Peacefully

The years have come and gone
   Since that awful day that year
But in my times of sorrow
   My Grandpa's voice I hear

He tells me not to worry
   Myself with pain and grief
No harm shall befall me
   He's watching over me

We had a close relationship
   That no man on earth could break
He'd taken so much heartache
   It was all his heart could take

I loved him so with all my heart
   I'd hoped that we would never part
I love him but I can't be sore
   Because I know God loves him more.

Here on earth was pain and sorrow
   Never a promise of tomorrow
But now he sails on a calm sea
   Because he's resting peacefully.

My Grandpa died sometime back
   I sat and cried with grief
My mom said "Don't cry Connie,
   He's resting peacefully.

Laura Rosenberger
SUN THRU THE TREES
[For Mrs. Kulp, who saw and believed in me—with love]
Bright, blazing
an ever lasting light
in an haze of crowded green
melting to form the silence
   of softness
      a loveliness
filling the body with
   such vastness
      of beauty
      that surrounds
         engulfs
            uplifts
               with a
                  drifting
               wonder

Carolyn Williams
MY PRAYER
I've not one but many burdens,
   Lord, heavy on my heart.
I'm weak, I'm tired and fearful
   that my world will fall apart.
Deep within a corner of this
   heart you know so well
There's a churning, Lord, there's
   torment, truly a physical hell.
I need the strength that you can
   give to help me rise above.
I need you here with me right
   now. I need to feel your love.
You promised in my weakness,
   through Christ I am made
   strong.
I praise you for these trials,
   though I feel so all alone.
So, Father from these binding
   chains, please help me find
   release,
Because when you are present, I
   have an inner peace.
A peace that one may never know,
because one has not found . . .
What it is like to have you near,
   when one is chained and bound.

Dwain McClain
I AM MARRIED TO A ROSE
Today is our anniversary darling
   And I began to think.
As day after day I watch,
   The rose bush grow.
Oh! What a message the rose
   Carries without a word.

Oh! How pretty a rose as it buds,
   So young, so pure, so innocent.
Oh! What splendor to watch it
   grow,
   As the inner beauty unfolds.
Oh! How beautiful the sweetness,
   When the rose is in full bloom.

Oh! What a message the rose
   Carries without a word.
Oh! How you ask, do I know?
   I am married to a rose.

Oh! Such a beautiful rose,
   Protected, surrounded with
   thorns.
Oh! But handle so gently
   And the rose brings pleasure.
Oh! The incredible feeling the
   Rose generates is like
   electricity.

Oh! What a message the rose
   Carries without a word.
Oh! How you ask, do I know?
   I am married to a rose.

Happy anniversary darling.

Brenda Marsh Rulli
THE MOORS
No other sound could tear the
   heart, as the wind through the
   heather on a summer day. No
   down feels as soft as the green
   velvet grass on my feet as I
   walk this way.

As the wind takes my hair, it
   speaks to my ear and tells of a
   love lost as mine.
In the vast open space, I feel not
   alone but a soul suspended in
   time.

There are those who would say
   that to go after eve is a fool and
   an early doom. But I fear not
   the blackness, nor the long ago
   voices for the Moors, are my
   loves vast tomb.

There was once a time when I
   stood here with hate, and
   cursed the damn Moors, for
   deciding my fate.
A lost child on the Moors, and all
   went to see. They returned
   with the boy and a broken
   heart for me.

Each day goes by as before til I'm
   free. And I run to the Moors to
   finally be. With my memories
   of yesterday.

The sound of his voice. On this
   region of space as he speaks
   through the wind I can hear
   him say

Come to me.
Come to me.

Sheila M. Sebald
DECEMBER 24
The clouds are big and fluffy
The snow is cold and white
The house is filled with holly
For Santa comes tonight

The tree is donned with popcorn
In bed I wait to see
The jolly, red and soot tinged man
Who'll come this Christmas Eve

Miss Thomasine F. Reid
BY THE GRACE OF GOD
Grandma, aren't you proud of me
   and all that I've done
Got a dynamite job, money in the
   bank and a house that's second
   to none.
I'm on top of the world and just
   love the view—don't owe
   nobody nothing
Because all of *my* efforts have
   brought me through!

Child, come sit with Granny,
   hear every word I say
It does something awful to my
   heart to hear you talk this way.
Let me refresh your memory—
   this won't take too long.
So much your Granny could
   bring to mind—you ever heard
   of a "freedom song?"

Twasn't one, but, many we used
   to sing—years ago when things
   were really rough
And them fellas in white
   sheets—a lunchin' and
   burnin'—oh they did some

terrible stuff
And there wasn't any place—no
place to be found where there
weren't "White Only"
and "Colored Only" signs all
around.

You put your shoulder to the
wheel and you worked hard it's
true
But how can you fix your mouth
to say that just "your efforts"
brought you through?
Why ever since our folk were
brought to this country—and
that's been a long, long time
We've been saying with our
words and actions, "Stop
oppressing me, give me what's
mine!"

Many of them didn't want us to
have nothing—to keep us
down, oh how some of them
tried.
Til our people got tired and in
the fight for our rights—many
a Black man died.
They killed our leaders. Called
the men "Boys" to tear down
their pride
But in spite of it all we still
gained new heights because
God is on our side.

For in our darkest hours we
fasted, we prayed
Despite oppression and
humility—from God we never
strayed
You see, we put our hands in His
hands and asked Him to lead
us on
For the struggles would not be
easy—one never knew when he
wouldn't come home.

So you see, before you got here,
folk were helping you
Get off your "high horse"—not
just your individual efforts
brought you through.
Many of our people have died as
over paths of prejudice and
injustice they trod.
Always remember—you're where
you are because of your efforts
AND our people's struggles—but
all in all—it's by the "grace of
God."

John Hibler
YOU
You are to me like some strange
bird
Whose sweet call I have heard,
And I seek you in the forest
All in vain.
Last years's nest I find;
Places you have favored;
Then, again,
I flush you in the rushes
Near some stream.

So I learn
Where you fly and forage,
Where you bathe,
And where you rest the best;
But never know you really,
Except the flutter of your feathers
As you flee,
Or the sight of where you once lay
With other hopes and days.

Katherine Wright
DON'T YOU REMEMBER
Don't you remember
The world we walked about
The world we talked about
Songs we'd sing and shout

Don't you remember
What we'd always say
That for every day
We'd be in love this way

See the flowers in the spring
And all that's growing green
See the seaside
Where you held my hand
Ah! the blue tides
They seemed to understand
That this was
Love oh! so grand

Linda Di Menza
LOVE FREE
Walking in the pouring rain, it all
comes back to me,
The sorrow, guilt and pain of
choosing my destiny.

Wishing he were here and
wanting to be me,
Can I have his love and yet still
be free?

Trying to untangle the feelings
inside of me,
Hoping for a chance for us to be.

Like a dream come true and a
rainbow—brightening up the
sky
I love you now till the day I die.

Someday you'll know that we're
just meant for each other,
Like the sky above—now and
forever.

Cleoral Lovell
REJUVENATION
The sun has crossed the vernal
equinox;
All through the summer months
Old Sol will pour
Rich golden bounty down upon
the shore
Where near-nude people
congregate in flocks.
Sun-worshippers lie browning
near the docks
For countless hours, hoping they
may store
Enough warmth sent them from
this cosmic core
To last through winter's world of
work and clocks.

Vacation time—a time to
meditate,
To let new thoughts race nimbly
to and fro,
To dwell on wonders busy minds
pass up.
Regeneration, time to contemplate
Pink shells, white birds and
clouds, green things that grow.
Yes, summer is the time to fill
the cup.

Shiree McGaha
FOR CHRISTMAS
Now not a window small or big
But wears a wreath of holly sprig;
Nor any shop too poor to show
Its spray of pine or mistletoe
Now city airs are spicy-sweet

With Christmas trees along each
street,
Green spruce and fir whose
boughs still hold
Their tinsel balls and fruits of
gold.
Now postmen pass in threes or
fours
Like bent, blue coated Santa
Claus.
Now people hurry to and fro
With little girls and boys in tow,
And not a child but keeps some
trace
Of Christmas secrets in his face.

Grace Vaughn Wilkes
CONTEMPLATION
Here, in lonely contemplation
I ponder my outcast state . . .
Hovering near the endless brink
Of darkened eternity.
Passive and stoic I remain
Lamenting the shadowy nights.
Grey spirits, greyer than my own
Are lost in the remorseless fire
Of unfulfilled desire.
In the dying embers of a
Volcanic heart, there lies
A vibrant passion straining
To loose the yoke of virulent hate.
We live, hope dies
We die, hope lives.

Sally Arlene Boswell
UNTITLED
Come, Sit.
Let me be the hearth where you
warm yourself.

Come, Dream.
Let me inspire your dreams
with rays of my own gathered
light.

Come, Dear.
I shall not ask for you to be this
or that.
But only let me be there to watch
you warm
and grow into all you are capable
of becoming.

Come, Love.
Lean on me when you have need.
I shall be warmth, light, strength
and love.

Edith E. Andrews
JUST BEING ME
[To almighty God, my late
parents M/M E. Eagleson, my
spiritual mentor Mrs. Frances
Davis, my friends, Connie,
Dale, Loyce, Darilyn & Dawn,
my musical family the Clever
Band, and my co-workers at
McCormick Inn.]
I guess I'm just a funny girl,
searching for peace in an
embattled world,
Gazing at a sunrise, on a
cloudless day. Being loyal to
one lover, I
Guess that's just my way and
when I sing about that love, my
melody is free.
And I hum it to the smallest
pebble, or to the tallest, the
tallest tree.

And when God's love shines in
you, oh I kiss you tenderly,
There's nothing strange about it,

I'm just being, I'm just being me.

I'd rather walk an open field, pick
wildflowers by the sea, the
concrete
Of the city has no appeal, no
appeal to me.
Let's walk the fields together, and
sing the robins' song, and look
into
Each other's eyes, for in your
arms I know that's where I
belong.

And when God's love shines in
you, I hold you tenderly, there's
nothing
Strange about it, I'm just being,
I'm just being me.

The moon will still be magic, our
senses more than five, our
touch will
Light a thousand fires, that keeps
our love alive.

So let's walk the land together
and hum a country song, let's
move into
Each other's minds for in my
arms you know that's where
you belong.

And when life's moods are
shifting or moving hurriedly, I
slow down my
Endeavors, and enjoy being, just
being me.

Innocence Johanna Schnieders
TO A WINDMILL
"Windmill" your wheel turning in
the wind
What thoughts run through your
mind
As I watch your silver blades
glistening in the sun.
Your mechanism creaks and
works laboriously
Bringing up the cool clear water,
From the dark brown earth
To quench the thirst of man and
beast.
A symbol in the countryside
Silhouetted against the earth and
sky
To my eyes, you are a feast

Steven R. Cook
HAIL YE, MEADOW SUN
Well, it's six fifteen; The sun is
about rising over the eastern
sea wall, the gulls in the air
ignite in the early morning
spectacular.

The families awake unto a new
dawn, and their senses are
engulfed by the soulful wrath
of the virgin sun.

And from someplace up above he
welcomes us
unto his feast . . .

Hail ye, meadow sun
rising up unto our dawn,
bring me thy blessed fragrance,
thy birdsong,
thy waken anew.
I rest thee my body upon the bed;
thine early moon reflecting my
eyes marvels.
Quietly I sit,
quietly I sight
the virgin light,

show me thy reign.

Capture thy spirit
and unto the wind throw my
soul.
Let I,
taste the sweetness
of thy scarlet birth . . .

Ada Perna
THE DEW
*[To my loved sons, July,
Michael, and Santiaguito. To
D.M. Synonym: SUN AND LIFE.]*
The fresh DEW greats at the
dawn,
when still are brighting the stars,
that are watching in early time,
the brilliantest drops, alike as
they are.

The fresh DEW farewell the
darkness,
when are going far the sky's
lights,
and are dropping drops of water,
greeting the dawn . . .
farewelling the night . . .

The purest water form the DEW,
that too seem us as drops of tears,
for a love that as a bird flew,

giving us pain, deep and new,
but the early rays of the sun,
dry the tears, and too . . . dry the
DEW!

Vicki M. Delegans
MY GIFT TO YOU
*[To My Dear Husband, Chris
With Love, Mother & Baby]*
Our love we've shared for years
and years,
Thru heartache, joys, tears, and
fears.

So many paths we've walked
alone,
And thru it all our love has shone.

And once more we have sealed
our love,
With God's blessing from above.

For the seed that you gave to me,
Soon a baby it will be.

And so my love you soon will see,
My gift of love to you from me.

Curtis Snodgrass
THE HANGMAN'S NOOSE
Letters . . .
String them together
and make a nice word

Words . . .
String them together
and make a nice sentence

Sentences . . .
String them together
and make a nice paragraph

Paragraphs . . .
String them together
And make a nice love letter

Love letters . . .
String them together
and string him up!

Wanda Maria Tobler
THE PRECIOUS THREE
My feelings for you flow out of
me
like my tears flow out in
sadness . .
I want you now, I want you,

whenever,
forever, you fill me up with
gladness . . .
The demand in your eyes, the
warmth
of your embrace, the current
sends my
head reeling . . . words from me,
words from you, words that speak
of our feeling . . . The precious
three
I hope will always be . . . The
precious
three I hope I will always see . . .
radiating the depths of your
caressing
eyes . . . The precious three you
can
count on from me . . . I've made a
discovery . . . I know it as
true . . .
The precious three is . . . I love
you!

Sally Lynn Regis
INSPIRATIONS
*[To: David Because you help
me find my way and you are
always in my thoughts.]*
You are what I have always
looked for
And alot more,
I knew it from the start
Because I could feel it in my heart.
The first night I saw you
I thought, could it be true?
I thought maybe you would be
mine
If we just had the time.
I have yearned for a love like
yours
But, all I have found are empty
doors,
It started off good and fine
But, now I feel like I have been
left behind.
Am I going crazy?
Or is my mind turning hazy?
You are like a light
Because you have made my life
bright.
I want you to remember I love
you so
No matter what you do or where
you may go . . .

Georgia Bazacos Morgan
REJECTION
*[To my husband, Joel, who
loves me unreservedly, and to
my Mom, who has more than
made up for having hurt me
unknowingly.]*
Just a lonely little girl
turning five to six
who climbed up onto Mommy's
lap
for a small hug, and a kiss.

Contentedly the small child
thought,
it's warm and cuddly here,
"you're much too old for this,"
said she,
"my smallest child is near."

Reluctantly the small child left,
to seek her joy elsewhere,
her toys and games meant
nothing,
no satisfaction there.

She wandered out, around

and 'round
for friends to fill her need,
not another soul she found,
who could this hunger feed.

At school she found another love,
into her hands books fell,
the printed page, in cover bound,
could create quite a spell.

Books, her closest friends became,
they helped to still unrest,
how could a little dumb kid know,
books too, could fail life's test.

Some hugs and kisses, words of
love,
children need to grow,
or deep wounds may develop,
ask me, someone, I know.

Jose V. Gragasin, Ph.D., D.H.
The American Flag & Constitution
The American Flag

The American Flag, the red,
white, and blue,
Is the bulwark of American
dignity,
The massive shield of true liberty,
Which represents the mandates
of the free,
So tyranny has no place under
thee.

The people under thee highly
esteemn and uphold thine
majesty,
Reign, thou must, with supremacy,
None shall ever invade thy
Sanctity,
These, we'll transit to
POSTERITY!!!

The American Constitiution

Hail! to our Constitution,
The Supreme Law of our beloved
Country,
Our people's will, Sovereign
Command,
Firm bedrock of our Native Land!!!

In thee are written our heroes'
prayers,
The blood and tears of our
forebearers—
From Gettysburg to historic
Washington,
The historic symbol of our Noble
Past.

Jo Ann Dickey
FROM JOEY TO YOU
*[As a member of the Olla
Apostolic Church I would like
to dedicate this poem to my
Pastor Rev. C.R. Bayham.
Thank you for giving Joey the
love and guidance he needed to
be saved.]*
My name is Joey—Jesus came for
me.
Once I was—Now I am not—
Except in Glory.
I came to my Mother in a dream
with these words for you.
If you find your heart is broken
by such one as Me;
Look unto the Lord—my God—
for comfort and He will grant
peace unto thee.
For many hearts have been made
whole by His Love and His
Power.

And it's not much longer He will
return—
It could be this very hour!
For He longs to have the one He
calls his Bride—
the living one you see.
So my loved ones—cry no more
for me!
For the Dead in Christ shall Rise
First
then the living that remain
And with Christ forever more
We'll Reign Eternally.

*Wilma E. Mathers Nee—Billie
Nelson*
MEMORIES
*[In memory of our brother,
John Nelson Jr. July 6/32 to
Oct. 16/71 He sang to us songs
as, And This Is My Beloved,
Because You're Mine, Yours,
etc.]*
You left us in October,
When the leaves began to fall.
The sheep grazed on the hilltop,
As we gathered one and all.

Sweet memories of your singing,
Sweet memories of your smile.
Sweet memories of our love for
you,
Still linger all the while.

Sleep peaceful my dear brother,
And when our time has come.
Reach out your hand to greet us,
To that place where love comes
from.

Ellen Malis
Summer Of the New York Nights
I have seen her
Enwrapped in silence,
The Goddess of the wenches:
I have undressed her
At the cool of the early hours . . .
And oh, the hot nights
While she quivered:
Nights clinging fiercely for
another hour
And the faint whispers remain . . .
Jim, Jim, Jamie—Joy, Lynn, lynn
lynn
Oh, wait till tomorrow and you
shall see
New York:
The queen of all
The wenches.

Bonnie L. Holtzhafer
YOU AND ME
Here I am alone in my bed
With thoughts of you still in my
head.
I know it was never meant to be,
Me loving you and you loving me.

We both changed and it's no
one's fault
The love in our lives came to a
halt.
It's over and now no longer true,
You loving me and me loving you.

EL
The Breaking and Entering
Welcome to my parlor—
Gaze upon my grooved arches
overhead,
Notice my antique green-gold
ceiling,
My soggy crunching brown
carpet.

Look at my intricate green
wallpaper design
 Where the sun's fingers crash
 down
  On top but tender warmth
  floods beneath.

Come into my living rooms—
Follow dark hallways to daylight,
Shove your way through my
 thick draperies,
 Stare up into my spiral
 staircase.
  Lay on my rough patio and
  sleep
   With the stars as your
   nightlight
   But wake up open-
   mouthed and crying.

Enter my castle—
You may walk my musical
 passages,
 Sit on my decaying chairs,
 Stand in my overgrown
 kitchen.
  Tremble at my simplicit
  But complex standard of
  living
   And think this is your
   dream house.

But you will never feel at home,
for the more you misunderstand
my mystery and struggle,
  the more you kill me.

Richard Newton
RAGS AND ME
There stands a tree,
 Upon an i
sland across the silver sea.
A place of enchantment,
 Beyond that edge, where eyes
 cannot see,
But, we're shipless, my dog Rags
 and me.

There is a star shining so high,
 over the unseen miles of an
 endless sky.
A place of dreams, further than
 birds may fly.
 But we're wingless, my dog
 Rags and me.

There leans, under a tree,
 Upon a lost island,
Across the purple sea,
 A place of sorrow,
Within a heart that eyes will
 never see.
 Oh I'm friendless,
My dog Rags, has gone from me.

Richard Newton
THE MASK
It is behind a secretive mask my
 true feelings decay,
O, what a terrible price to pay.

Let me be real, I love living still,
 but how many tears must fall?
It is a mask of fear, that hides my
 pleading call.
Release me, please let it fall!
Must I die, not knowing I?

In a crowd, yet all alone, my heart
 is yearning, will my true
 feelings ever be known?
Tell me where I might flee, is
 there such a place that I could
 be free?
Tell me now, show me how,
 surely life can not be this foul!

I would beg, even bow, but O,
 how might I be me now?
I have never known joy, no, not
 even as a little boy.
At night I would cry, but to this
 day, I do not know why.
There was no laughter, not even
 an echo.
O, fear is such a deadly captor, I
 cannot escape!
Is this my true fate?
How very sad this imprisoned
 mind,
It is behind a secretive mask, that
 unknown someone is dying.

Sandra C. Muller
In Memory Of My Grandfather
There once was a man whom I
 knew quite well
The best present I ever gave him
 was a purple bell
When he rang it I ran straight to
 his side
Even though sometimes I wanted
 to just hide
I'll never forget him or the games
 we used to play
When asked his favorite color he
 would always say gray
I used to think that was quite
 strange indeed
But maybe deep down inside he
 had a certain need
To see life in a dull and
 monotonous way
Since he knew his life on earth
 would end anyday
However, week after week in that
 same bed he would be
Always putting on a bright
 cheerful smile just for me
He taught me that knowing you
 helped someone in strife
Was the greatest reward you
 could get out of life

Jennie Parella
A SHUT-IN'S DREAM
Let me walk with you dear God
 Among the wild flowers,
Where buttercups and bluegrass
 grow
 And trees rise like heaven's
 towers.

Drake Mabry
CONUNDRUMS
Conundrums of time
. . . headless satires
. . . . . . double talk.

axythrongfloodrushrabblemob
hordetribegangknottroopsqua
dbardpartycoveyflockherdgal

Stumbling child
the dwellers of heaven
. . . . . . amused?

Joyce Knorr
GOD SPEED
Chickadee, how do you plea
 flying out to sea?
Foolish bird why do you try
 with your path untold, you fly
 too high!
Death destined in the endless sea
 you will surely be!
Tiny wings cannot endure,
 what makes you so sure?

Chickadee, how do you plea?

Who has set your daring heart
 so free?
Friendships faceted love sets me
 free, I plea
 reflecting forever parallel at my
 side guiding me.
It brightly shines on my
 instinctive journey way
 beckoning me to a home safe
 to stay.

My friend, a land bound tortise
 fately swims in the sea.
 Master of his tiny isle he be.
He too, flies so high in his tortise
 mind,
 a blue jay he pretends to be.
He muses softly, soaring with
 me .. . his chickadee.

Chickadees know of a welcome
 when land bound they too
 must become.
I, the chickadee, do humbly plea
 place me near the tortise of the
 sea.
Peacefully, dear hand of fate here
 let me rest,
 I've survived the tests.
He alone has no need of cages
 and keys
 to his abode the distant sea.
A magnetic faceted love is his
 way,
 a treasure chest that allows me
 stay—
 forgetting . . . remembering
 . . . my wings were of a
 yesterday.

God speed chickadee—fly to the
 sea . . . I hear your plea!

Pamela Gregoli
GRACE ROAD
Ashes of my past
Still burning with desire
Searching bodies of peaceful
 waters
To extinguish this flame of fire
His voice unbroken haunting my
 soul
Violating all senses of human
 control
Worn sheets and blankets tattered
Lips arid, gnawed, memories
 scattered
Your silhouette reflects the
 character of a child.
The queen of hearts my agent
 rival
Appealing to alas, hallowed
 desires
Rehearsing your performance to
 stage her style
Gazing beneath your shallow
 complexion
Tangled up in webs for years
Decayed sign reads "Our
 Destination"
Rust conceals barren tears.

Pamela Gregoli
DYLAN THE MAN
Introducing a genius from the
 womb
A babe, gypsy a wizard of
 expression
Searching desperately, to
 encounter
To endure one's rabid obsession
Preserving the legend of folklore
Channeling a stream of

musical waves
Rendering his performance door
 to door
Reaching solace towards the
 sunrise
Mouth organ fables Chaplinesque
 lies
A carnival host—pure invention
Approaching alas, faith's
 connection
Singing fully two hundred
 parables
As one's redeemer, good shepherd
At death's door, physically
 incurable
Lay deprived in an ill fated
 hospital
Answering to his saviour's voice
Seeing man's belief—yet God's
 choice
Congregated chords at
 Washington Square
Filling the bill the Balladeer.

Margie Edwards
LOST MY CHILDREN
When it's said to be good, but it's
Really bad.
When it's said to be just, but it
Makes you sad.
When you always lose everything
You gain.
You wonder—why life contains
So much pain.

My children I love you, and this
I must say.
You must know Jesus, and the
Holiness way.
And of my loss of you, I'll say—

There must be a land where
There is no pain.
There must be a heaven, where
We'll be together again.
Were it not so, there would be no
Moral to the story.
There would be no hope, and
Satan would gain the glory.

Tricia Blake
FALL
I find myself wandering,
Looking for spring flowers,
But fall has taken all the best,
Deep snows will cover all the
 rest.

And yet when spring comes forth
 again,
I'll search the furthest flower bed,

 Looking for your face.

Karen L. Zimmerman
TWO CHEATIN' HEARTS
She's not cheatin' him,
But he's cheatin' her,
I couldn't believe it,
But now I am sure.

What's this world coming to?
I don't want to see.
And when I get married,
Will it happen to me?

Two cheatin' hearts,
That really want to be free.
She talks to him,
But he talks to me.

I can't understand it.
He won't leave me alone,
Why does he want me?
He's got a life of his own.

Two cheatin' hearts,
Need some time to be free.
To put back together,
All the pieces that were missing...
Without me.

Doris C. Hughes
Happy New Year, Everyone.
As I say good-bye to nineteen and
eighty-one, and hello to
nineteen and eighty two, I want
to wish a Happy New Year to
everyone of you.

I hope the New Year will brings
lots of joy, peace and
contentment everywhere.
Have we all our New Years
resolutions made?
Then let us strive to keep the
most important ones this year.

That we might live healthier,
happier, more productive lives.
Be stronger in faith and do more
works that are pleasing to God.

As we show more good will
towards our fellowman, then
more wisdom will be displayed,
throughout our native land.

Together we can weather the
storms of life.
Praying that Christ will sustain
us, in our strife.

Let us realize, we can't live by
bread alone.
We all need spiritual food, to
help us get to our Heavenly
home.

Cherry Kim Plumer
SO LITTLE TIME
So little time do I obtain my
words are
weak and very few, Life is a
challenge
we must fight and win.

Like the sands of the hour glass
life
pases by oh so quickly with so
little
time for the recalling yesterday or
wishes for tomorrow.

Today is all which we possess all
which we may believe in, we've so
much to give and so little time
to give it in.

Though the sands have now all
run out
and velvet curtains of darkness
close
in about me my love for you shall
remain to venture on in the
eternity
of Time.

Todor "Tosho" Kukubajski
WAS IT LOVE?
It was silence and passion, love in
a fashion,
In lite and nite with honey and
fight.
We touched. Stubborn fingers in
venture went,
O, naked nature, unashamed soul,
how much you spent.

Cheek on cheek, teach my lip to
soft speak;
"—O, no don't go to sleep!"—My
spirit may weep.

Demands I meet that I must for
no need,
I think I'll turn my back, look for
new seed.

Dear, how many precious days
and nights,
How many priceless weeks we
spelled like this?
What—Already I know must I go
and leave you alone,
But, where does the fault lie we'll
never know.

Devra Lynn Brostoff
MAKING PEOPLE CRY
making people cry
they don't do that
in real life
only on tv
cry at things like that i mean
people are more complex
sad doesn't mean tears
happy doesn't mean laughter
angry doesn't mean kill
tv is to cut and dry
too predictable
too plastic
life follows no forms
really
life has no punctuation
to warn you what's coming
or what belongs where
in real life you have to
figure it out for yourself
beginnings and endings
all mixed together

Iona M. Brown
MINE TO GIVE
Oh to bequeath you silver and
gold,
What men now seem of worth;
Instead, I have these relics old,
And I have given you a noble
birth.
Would that I could give you
wealth
And give you worldly fame;
Instead, I've taught you rules of
health
And blessed you with a worthy
name.

A list of what I want for you
Would fill a volume wide,
A spirit free, a heart that's true,
With intelligence and wisdom to
guide,
Knowledge and an understanding
tolerant mind,
With faith and hope and charity
For all among the human kind;
But above all would give you
integrity.

Daniel J. Dippold
LIKE A CANCER
Alone watching a March sunset
and thinking too damned much
again
Hearing Beatles
ten years ago
On a night quite like this
I heard the news
Even as his unit was pulling out
my brother was dead near
DaNang
I a year younger was away at
school
reading Levertov napalm Nixon

Ten years later now
a younger brother is in

in the Marines
on First Alert
A jet crosses my view
darkness invades the room

The telephone rings—how ya'
been
Come over—be with me

Together later watching news
U.S. advisors unarmed troops
El Salvador
Another place never heard of
before
Turn on the radio
Charlie Daniels still in Saigon
And I can't make it through the
night alone
be careful of that lump down
there
It won't go away

Michelle David Kelly
THE LAND SO COLD
[To my loving husband,
Michael, my daughters, Alexis
and Athena, and to my very
best friend, Joel. With love . . .]
On a cold and blustery morning
in a deep December snow,
I caught a glimpse of sunlight
touch the whiteness far below.

I stood there on a mountain top
all trimmed in nature's lace,
And turned myself from north to
south
where the wind caressed my
face.

The thoughts I had were all
complete
and I felt that I was too,
As my mind turned in to see
myself
up high in a sky so blue.

I closed my eyes and held my
breath
and listened to the calling,
As I felt myself released from
strife
and knew I wasn't falling.

I opened my eyes and laughed
aloud
and called myself a scholar,
For the land so cold was part of
me
and it made my soul stand
taller.

Karen L. Zimmerman
MY SPECIAL PRAYER
Oh Lord, This I Ask Of You
My Special Prayer
In Honor of The One I Love.

Bless His Every Day,
And Bless Renee',
And All His Family,
Lord, Please Hear My Prayer,
To Show Him That I Care,
And Still Love Him Tenderly.
Please Help Him To See
The Guiding Light,
And The Love Inside Of Me.
Please Help Me To See
If This Love Was Meant To Be.
Oh Lord, Hear My Plea.
My Special Prayer
I Pray Each Day
Because The Hurt Inside
Won't Go Away,
Lord, Help Me Make It

Through Each Day
This, Oh Lord, I Pray.

Lord, With All My Confidence,
There's A Feeling That I Sense.
Lord, Please Tell Me What It
Means.
I'll See the Light
If You Will Show
The Answer That I Want To
Know.
Please Give Me The Strength.
Do I Have The Right,
To Ask You For The Guiding
Light?
Oh Lord, This I Ask of You.

If The Light Comes In The Day,
It Will Surely Light The Way.

And If The Light Comes In The
Night
Showing Me That I Was Right.

And If The Light Comes Through
A Song
Telling Me That I Was Wrong.

But If The Light Comes Through
A Dream
Help Us, That The Light Be Seen,
The Vision Of A Love So Rare,
This, Oh Lord, My Special Prayer.

A.T. Witcofski
MY TRUE FRIEND
There's very few people you
could call a true friend,
someone who will help you
when you reach the end.
I've found those few friends who
pick me up when I'm down,
have trust in me never yet to
frown.
There's no-one out there who
could care as much,
there's no-one out there who
could have more trust.
I say to you, my dear friend,
for helping me when I've
reached the end,
for all your trust and all you've
cared,
I thank-you friend for all we've
shared.

Thomas M. DeGonia II
MY MOTHER
My mother is special to me.

It's easy to see,
I love her very much.
She cares for me when I'm hurt.
Thursday she wore a very nice
skirt.
She and I keep little secrets from
dad,
And sometimes he gets mad.
She helps me with my work.

Be glad you have a mother.
There is no other,
Than MY MOTHER!

Cathy Elwood
SPRINGTIME
Winter is the time for nature to
die,
The sun shines brightly, yet too
high in the sky
To bring new life into full bloom
From the snow, and winds, and
the cold of the tomb.

Man's life is like winter, empty
and cold

Today's Greatest Poems

Without a purpose, simply
    growing old,
Until he meets Jesus, and the
    warmth of His love
Brings forth new life—springtime
    from above!

His life was given so well who
    believe
And trust in Him, new life will
    receive.
Who but a loving God would give
His only son to die so that we
    might live?

Can you consider the wonders of
    life,
The depth of love between a man
    and his wife,
Without recognizing the Creator's
    hand
And seeing it's all part of His
    wonderful plan?

There is no other love to which
    to compare
The love of God—the world
    balances there.
On Him all life depends, oh,
    praises sing.
He alone has the power to turn
    winter to spring.

S. K. Gunn
REALITY
Your reality is a Washington suit
leading his people astray.
Your reality is a nine to five
busting your ass for your pay.

His reality is a beautiful young
    wife
who never questions a word he
    might say.
Her reality is a house full of
    boredom
and any excuse to stray.

My reality is knowing the truth.
Reality is not to be seen.
Each man's reality is his choice of
    life.
Reality is only a dream.

S. K. Gunn
THE RETURN
Six years gone
    yet here you are
        in my life again

You've changed a bit
    but so have I
        baby, that's no sin

Summer school
    our last good-bye
        tonight our last hello

But who's to say
    what comes next
        as the ages go

Bid no farewells
    when we must part
        just be upon your way

As life goes on
    and people change
        we'll meet again someday

Mrs. Laura Lee Lemke
THE GOOD SHEPHERD
[I dedicate this poem in honor
of the Lord Jesus Christ, He is
the Good Shepherd.]
When the sheep were crossing
    the water
one sheep fell into the water

He fell upon a rock and broke his
    leg
But when he fell the Good
    Shepherd
did not leave him there to die
He plunged into the water to pull
    him out

When the Good Shepherd pulled
    him out
He washed his leg with water
and put healing oil upon his leg
He splint and bandaged it with
    care
He will carry him in His arms
until his leg is healed and he can
    walk again

Now this sheep will stay close
he will not go far away from the
    Shepherd
nor will he run away again
But he will remember the
    Shepherds
tender mercy when he had hurt
    his leg
and how He comforted him with
    love
that took away the pain

Herbert J. Fisher
THE BEAVER
This gnawer of the Aspen Tree,
    Is as busy as can be;
There's a dam to build, a house to
    make,
    As one can plainly see;
The chubby, active, furry one,
    is an Engineer of might;
He knows where and how to
    build his dam,
    To do the project;
Though backed-up water from his
    dam
    May cause some lowland strife,
The pond that's formed provides
    a home,
    For various water life;
In trying times of serious drouth,
    When water is so dear,
The Beaver's worth is noted then,
    And we're glad he's living near.

Bhagwan Singh Khanna
WHO KNOWS . . .
[To My Nascent Love]
A crowd and a laughter
carefree, soothing, and enticingly
    fresh
rhythmic clatter and twinkle of
    lights,
meeting of glances evasively,
refreshing beauty and comforting
    nearness,
arresting shyness and inviting
    reluctance,
am I responsive or I'm dreaming,
am I seeing or I am feeling?
who knows . . .

Denise K. Anderson
TIME
[To my husband—A "special"
thank you for his patience,
understanding, and love which
have helped me through days
when there was not enough
time.]
I sat here thinking this morning,
And thought about you.
I wanted to awaken you,
And make beautiful love.
It was a happy, satisfying thought,

And I started towards your room.
But on my way,
The clock stopped me.
It made me angry
That there should be set
    schedules.
And, in my heart I cursed the man
Who invented this thing called
    "Time.'

Our lives are run by "Time," and
    ruled by God.
After a while it dawned on me,
That man has little control over
    his destiny.
The clock is telling me once
    more
To stop thinking or I'll be late
    again.
You see there's not much time
    left.

Anne M. Walsh
UNTITLED
There are among us love-avoided
    dark
        moments love-bound,
    sauntering fires hoofed
of a winged creature
striking the night closer
    until mastered from the
        mounting brittle
mid-nights would split apart
    little
knots of burning sheathed,
    buried
caresses above the winds and
    tips of
tackled pyramids, burning
    beyond
the spent fuel of fabled
presences: sceptered demean—
ors that do not survive the
    cracking of their
shells late ring inexorable with
    age
reflect unspoiled in the
    charged—
particled, aurora—
like immortal cores of self—
made decalogues. And within
    gem-bearing
furnaces: coruscating eidolons
    that
shine to none but white flights
    of the Pegasus strapped
in golden bridles of hearsay.

Leona Garrett Keller
DIAMONDS ON THE SNOW
Diamonds by the trillions
Out sitting on the snow;
Underneath are myriads
Of things we do not know.

Why do some flakes twinkle
While others never show?
Why do some seeds perish
As others sprout and grow?

Why is crust so crispy
And snow is soft below?
Are bunny burrows flooded
When melting starts to flow?

Diamonds by the trillions
Out sitting on the snow;
Sparkling, frosty bushes
Set winter all aglow.

Jewels from the waterspout
Like crystals in a row,
Slowly shed their droplets
When sudden sunrays show.

Melting, slowly dripping,
Drops build by portico
Up-side-down icicles—
Stalagmites in the snow.

Hazel Raabe
HEART SURGERY
A painful, slow procedure—
Assembly of strapped victims
Lined up on hard beds,
Waiting in a death row;
Agonizing trip to that
    antiseptic room—
Final terror of eerie, ghastly lights
    and shadows,
Death-dealing instruments
    wielded
by green forms
To hasten the tortuous ritual;
A form comes close; it speaks—
The end is swift as the needle
    penetrates the skin.
        I
            am
                no
                    more

Terry Ann Halverson
OCTOBER EVE
Yellow light escaping the clouds,
Catching the huddled movements
    . . . life.

Yesterdays escaping from my
    mind,
Twisting on paths cut between
    trees
And brick houses
    . . . unknown worlds.

Tinges of steam rise from
    windowsills,
Pagentries of moments filled.
I recognize the instant
    . . . caught alone.

Judy Ann Blevins
I HEAR THE ECHOES
I hear your echo calling for me;
Just another day goes by when I
    cannot see.

I hear the echoes of your voice;
Oh! How I wish to see—that
    would be my choice.

I hear the echoes of moving
    sound;
I'd like to see them, but they
    cannot be found.

I hear the sound of someone
    walking;
All those voices I hear talking.

I hear the airplane up in the sky;
Oh, how I wish I could see—to
    watch it go by.

I can hear, I can talk, but I cannot
    see.
Why does this vision happen to
    me?

I hear the echoes of someone
    yelling,
"Go for help!"—but I keep failing.

All that I can see
Is the darkness of me.

Virgil S. Hart
IN MEMORIAM
I lost a friend the other day;
"An untimely death!" some would
    say.
The days go by, but when I'm still;
I miss him yet. I always will.

471

Now, as I look backward down
memory lane,
To wish he were here is all in
vain.
As a living person he's gone away,
But in my memory he'll always
stay.

He was creative and could portray
With cartoons what he wanted to
say.
Librarian, teacher, artist and
author,
He helped those who took time
to bother.

He was a thinker and would
sometimes say,
"We're doing things wrong. Isn't
there a better way?"
We agreed there was; there had to
be!
But what could we do, just we
three?

He's gone, he's gone! He could no
longer stay.
His trials and worries have gone
away.
I'll miss his smile and his talks
with me,
This friend of mine, I no longer
see.

Roger E. Chapman
20th Century Shulamite
[To Carolyn, whom I . . .]
She's got country between her toes
and life is her stepping stone;
She's got perfume in her hair
and the morning breeze is her
comb.

The light of the world
shimmers in her eyes,
And the salt of the earth
flavors her lips.
The old cross of Jesus
silhouettes her skies,
And the broth of love
fills the cups she sips.

Sometimes I'll see her in her
flower-printed dress,
Smiling radiance like a bright bulb
in a darkened room.
Sometimes I'll gaze deeply and
detect
fatigue, a bit of stress;
Yet always smiling, smiling,
smiling,
uplifting everyone like a boom.

Ann Gilchrist
SKY VIEWS
God wraps the world in canvas
we mortals
call the sky;
And there upon the vast expanse
with a
master artist's eye
He flings the fiery crimson of the
sunset's dying rays,
Or drapes a blue serenely bright
on
June-filled summer days.
There may be storm clouds on
parade in
thunder-headed gray
With flashing lightning
interspersed to
brighten night as day.
And sometimes stars by millions
twinkle

friendly smiling eyes
To remind their neighboring
earthlings of
the vastness of the skies.
In the quiet early morning when
our earth
lies dewy pearled,
God sends promise through the
sunrise, smiles
down, and loves His world.

Sandy Hahn
MANY JOYS ARE FREE
Walk up and smell the flowers
Take a snooze in the grass of
green
Roll around in the many colored
leaves
Take a walk in the rain so clean
Share your smile today with a
stranger
Trade kisses with a child
Share your lunch with a long lost
friend
Enjoy the warm wind as it blows
so mild

Go rest yourself in the park a
spell
On a clear delightful day
Perch yourself upon a bench
And watch the children play

Take time to see
Many joys are free
Not everything need be bought
For it doesn't cost one tiny dime
To enjoy a beautiful thought!!

Sandy L. Williams
The Birth Of a New Love
Today's a brand new day and I'm
on my way,
Trying a fresh new start, even
though you're still in my heart.
When I needed you, you were
never around,
But out with the guys acting like
a clown.
We hardly ever talked,
Although we went for many
walks.
I never knew what to expect from
you,
One minute you're happy the
next you're blue.
You know when we broke up,
I felt like a bolt of lightning had
struck.
I wish you weren't the only thing
I thought of,
Sometimes I even wonder why
you're the one I love.
I may be dreaming a dream,
But maybe one day our love will
be like a stream.
It will flow to the ends of the
earth,
Into a brand new birth.

Erma P. Wittington
THAT MORNING
You started down a glowing path,
Expectantly and sure,
That morning.
But then, you stopped,
Looked back as if to say
"Aren't you coming too?"
That morning.
I could not move;
My limbs were numb,
My eyes bedimmed with tears.
You paused, saluted,

Said, "So-long."
Then hurried on
Into the great beyond
That morning.

Carrie Pittman Watson
SALE OF THE HOMESTEAD
[To Lucy and Brownie Nov.
1963 Our house in Washington
D.C.]
Goodbye Goodbye our hearts do
cry to such a stable rock
That sheltered us and all therein
For time without a clock
Your walls and ceilings meant to
us
Such things we can't express
But time has taken you away
And left an emptiness

You sheltered each and everyone
Who stopped to bide a wee
You bedded down each relative
Served those who stopped for tea
Your warmth reached out to one
and all
Abundant food and drink
Your hospitality unmatched
From this you did not shrink

We loved each nook and cranny
From roof to basement door
We loved the way you stood so
strong
And all our burdens bore
You housed so many of us
In peace and war and then—
You brought us back together
Praise to you again

For the first and only time
The patter of little feet
You cherished nourished
protected him
He loved your warm retreat
We pray that God in some small
way
Decree you always care
And still remain a haven
For all who enter there

Davie Morris Herndon
FATHER'S DAY AT HOME
Fathers are those great big men
kids look up to with a yen
For even a little time to play
before Dad needs must go away.
Sad when Father doesn't take
time to bend his height and get
in line
With that small tyke 'way down
there, who's hoping Dad has
time to share.

Dad's so special to his kids, a pity
that he sometimes rids
Himself of their presence all
when each one needs him
though so small;
He fails to see the joy erased
leaving a saddened little face—
Nor can he see the hurt in heart
as his small child turns to
depart.

Call him back, dear Father, do
please! Set him gently on your
knees—
Listen carefully to him, hear what
fills him to the brim;
See his face light up with joy
when Dad takes time for his
boy.
You'll likely feel your own heart

swell with emotions you can't
quell.

Then one day you'll note
suddenly, "This child's grown
as tall as me!
How'd this come about so fast?
He was just a kid a short time
past."
Now from that once great height
you bend, hoping time with
him to spend;
It's too late—no time for you as
he has other things to do.

Call him back, dear Father, do! If
you've sent him away from you;
Prevent cause now for regret: "If
only my child had let
Embrace more time with his old
Dad, we both such good times
might have had."
So brighten his life as only you
can—he'll remember when
HE'S a man.

Richard L. Wolfe
FLIGHTS IN LIGHT
Easy flights into the night,
Thoughts on wings from my
psychic soar,
My level of conscious bathed in
light,
Seeking the soul's unveiling core.

Boundless space welcome my
flight,
The beauty, in peace itself, is rare,
Quietly, blissfully amist the light,
Pulsations of ecstasy seeming so
near.

But the coming is mystic in every
way,
Such reality molds it's own
conception,
For entrance of truth is not our
say,
Enlightenment's attained through
the
master of perfection!

Lilli Lee Buck
ROBERT
His eyes are like the summer
skies,
When cloudless depths of blue
Extend into infinity,
And beckon unto you.

His heart is like a summer day,
Bedazzled by the sun,
Which glorifies, and beautifies,
And strengthens everyone.

His skin is like a summer dawn,
Whose luminous, rosy tones
Reflect his inner radiance
In stratospheric zones.

M. Rosser Lunsford
BACK TO THE LAND
I hear the call of the biding land
That nurtured me through the
years,
And paced me to the brink of man
With symmetry unspoiled by
fears;
Its beauty rivals any earthly span
And its likeness to Eden nears.

I feel the lure of the old
homestead
That sheltered and patterned me,
And encased for me a feather bed
Quilted with dreams of infinity;

Today's Greatest Poems

There I learned no thing is dead
So long as it lives in memory.

It was there in the rolling hills
That I played as a barefoot boy,
And felt the touch of kindred
  fields
Sown with seed of faith and joy;
For rich the soil a family tills
And sweet the fruit to enjoy.

Barbara Chapman Crank
SPRING
When flowers bloom on
warm spring days and the
birds all sing out loud,
there's a feeling of freedom
in the air like an angel
floating on a cloud.

Spring says so many
things and yet without a
word; sometimes I wonder
how we comprehend and the
voice of spring is heard.

Peter Francis Williams
Nothing Is Real Except Your Shadow
Demons and monsters are all in
  your head
"Real Life" people you should
  watch instead
But in this wacky world we know
Nothing is real except your
  shadow

Dreams are more logical I've
  always felt
At least in them your troubles
  will melt
And if I die I want you to know
Nothing is real except your
  shadow

So pick me up and throw me
  'round
Keep me safe from solid ground
Don't be fast and don't be slow
For nothing is real except your
  shadow

Joe Davis Thorn
GODDESS LULL
[To Jonathan, Amanda and
Jessica, My grandchildren.]
Graceful as an ocean gull
With flaming wash and shining
  hull.
The mystery ship
The captain's name is Tull,
Her deck is slowly paced
Her tower is black and dull.
A magic name is on her bow
GRACE the goddess Lull.
She awaits the night
A word from Captain Tull
Will send her screaming men
Blessed by goddess Lull
They'll rip the heart
From guests of Mull
For Mull forgot to toast
The goddess Lull.

U.F.O.s do exist.

Davy Shannon
Lamentations Of a Lonely Songwriter
Staring at my wall
No one to call
I sit and think
As I drink

Got to get it on
Got to write some good songs
Before I get old

The clock says after two
Try to think of something new
Write out a melody line
Maybe a hit this time

I need someone to inspire me
My guitar and I get lonely
But that's part of the game
She didn't want my name

So I'll drink my beer
And hide my tears
Let my guitar cry for me

John I. Hancock
COQUETTE
No need to be an open book;
Knowing eyes, bright smile,
Coy, enticing, mischief-look,
A soft call to wait awhile;
Loveliness.

Larceny is in your eyes;
Wild, marauding loveliness
That challenges, dares, flies
To somewhere I can't guess,
Loveliness.

Did we meet only yesterday?
Long, so very long ago?
There's much I want to say
But you always tease me so,
Loveliness.

June McBride
I'M NOT ALONE
I'm not alone, He is with me
I don't walk alone, He walks with
  me
Without Him, I am blind, I
  cannot see
When I'm sad, He comforts me
I'm not alone, He is with me.

I'm not alone, He is with me
He's my source, my Guiding Light
He makes the world a better
  place to be
With Him, I have no fear, day or
  night
I'm not alone, He is with me.

I'm not alone, He is with me
He gives me courage, a direction
  in life
With peace and tranquility
With no stress or strife
I'm not alone, He is with me.

Ted C. Rosa
UNTITLED
We sail the seas of precious love,
Our destination the distant
  Utopia.
I serenade you with all my
  sincerity,
And release the laughter from
  within.
We dance beneath the moonlit
  sky,
Our hearts soothed by the calm
  waters.
The warmth inside begins to
  blossom,
Like the flowers of life Mother
Nature gives us.
Our feelings of affection rejoice,
As we step upon our treasured
  paradise.

Patricia Ann Hill
UTOPIA
Like two celestial bodies
Out of orbit who came together
Deep in the night!
Your breath on my face,

Bodies melted together
As close to being one
As two could be, you said
Deep in the night!
Yet, where are you today?
Lost from me in your world
Whose galaxy is so far from mine.
Will our planets ever come
  together again
To be lovers in the night?
Yes!! One day you'll call
And say, "Hey, babe"
And then my world's axis will
  spin into
Utopia again!

LaVerne A. Gardner
GO FORWARD
[I want to dedicate "GO
FORWARD" to my husband
R.D. and our six sons—their
service to our community—
inspired me.]
Our forefathers set the pace.
They were men of courage; men
  of grace.
At times their encounterance in
  life seemed overwhelming.
Through all their trials their hope
  was bright; never dimming.
If we the people use our
  forethought we can preserve
  our heritage.
By living as we should within our
  own menage.
We Americans should hold our
  country in esteem.
For it is the kind of country of
  which other countries dream.
Our history and traditions
  preserve with care.
So that future generations will
  become the heir.
Love of God; Love of Country;
  Love of Man.
On these things everyone should
  take a stand.
To exercise them means we are
  free.
This is how man should always be.
These are the blessings we all can
  share.
Be hopeful and courageous; never
  feel despair.

Laura Underwood Hendrickson
FIRELIGHT
I sit all alone
  In the firelight's glow
Dreaming the dreams
  Of the long ago.

I see the house
  Where I lived, a child,
The orchard, the meadow,
  The woodlands wild.

I see the brook
  Where we used to play
This in the long ago
  Yesterday.

But best of all
  In the firelight's glow
I see the dear faces;
  I used to know.

Luanne Childres
TO LIFE AHEAD
I sit and wonder,
What of life have I tasted?
What tasty morsels have I eaten?
What succulent crumbs have I
  left behind?

I wonder what tomorrow's meal
  will bring.
My soul growls to be fed, but
  must wait.
The minutes and hours tick
  slowly out.
What is there accomplished?
What to be done?
Have I or haven't I?
What if?
All questions remain unanswered,
So tomorrow awaits me, or I it.
What bread crumbs will I drop
And who will eat?
How shall my taste linger
On the tongues of those I pass?
Will my passing leave them
With the bitter or the sweet?

Shirley Marlene Parker
MY MOTHER
["In Memory of Wanda Ellen
Ellsworth" December 13, 1917
to April 7, 1978 We Love You,
MOM!]
She wanted us to leave, to make
  it on our own.
But now that we have, I find we're
  alone.
She watches over our happy home,
  and sees that we're Blessed,
With the Love now shown.
In my heart, there's a great Big
  Ache, whenever I dream,
Whenever I awake.
Her memory will be here,
  "FOREVER" in time.
"Oh," if only someday, she could
  wake with mine.

Ruthann Husband Errante
A PARENT'S LOVE
[To Angela and Catherine
With all my love]
If you need a shoulder,
  on which you have to cry.
I'll be here at your side,
  always standing by.
You'll never have to worry,
  if you need a friend.
I'll be here with you,
  till the very end.
I can not promise happy roads,
  for either you or me.
But when we are together,
  problems vanish easily.
So call my name, and I'll be there,
  where ever I may roam.
You're my heart, my soul, my love,
  you're my living home.

Irene G. Pascoe
A WIDOW'S LAMENT
Oh Lord, my love is gone,
  He heard your call,
And he went home,
  In Summer's twilight, just
  before Fall.

As I walk through life, alone in
  sorrow,
I'm struggling, Oh Lord, and I'm
  trying,
To face each new, hard, tomorrow,
  With dignity, hope and no
  crying.

Oh Lord, what does a widow do.
  When the future looks dismal
  and grey?
Maybe you should have called
  me too,
  And not left me to face this

sad, sad, day.

Where do I go in my widow's
  weeds,
  Lost in this vale of tears?
What can I do to ease my needs,
  In the coming lonesome years?

Oh Lord, you know the dread in
  my heart,
  And I know you will not let me
  stray,
So please, Lord, help me make a
  fresh start,
For another new, sad, lonely,
  day.

Pauline A. Humble
RETURN TO ME
Tiz the cry of the mother, the
  lonely sea
As ebbing and flowing in her
  memory
Are ancient children, who
  crawled ashore
Learned to breathe and returned
  no more

Circling the earth, she seeks
  them still
Calling their names, exerting her
  will
Not knowing they cannot return
  to the sea
For the land is their mother
  now—not she

Yet something stirs deep inside a
  man
When he hears her call, as he
  often can
He builds a ship and sails away
In search of what he cannot say

Too often she reaches up to caress
That long lost child whom she
  yearns to possess
No longer able to breathe her air
He dies in her arms as she weeps
  in despair

Diane Bernardy
THOUGHT OF BEING
Searching,
For the doors leading somewhere:
Reaching,
For the moon and stars:
Climbing,
For the heights and new grounds:
Riding,
The clouds that keep moving on:
Sliding,
To find that I am somewhere:
Dancing,
To where I have never been:
Moving,
My heart to a new place:
Seeing,
I could be a new face:
Knowing,
I am not in a second place:
Keeping,
Me in a solid race:
Being,
Where the doors never close:

Diana G. Greenfield
VETERANS DAY
On Veterans Day
Why not this year,
Say thanks to those brave men
  far and near,
Add a little prayer
  for those who died,
And still lie buried

on the other side,
For those who share
  a watery grave,
Those who were tortured
  and yet were brave,
For those gallant lads
  since our country began,
When our freedom was
  threatened
Fought to a man.

From somewhere in heaven,
  if they could see,
Would they be as proud of
  you and me?
Would they think this a world
  worth dying for?
Would they do it again
  of maybe what's more,
Would they shed a tear that
  we still have to fight,
To keep our freedom's lamp
  alight!

Maryanne Dooley Downing
THUNDERSHOWER
Hurry home,
hurry home, wherever you are.

The raindrops started.
We knew the clouds . . .
first, the droplets in the
  puddles . . .
then they leaped like
  fountains . . .
hurry home.

On the pavements they
  danced . . .
ballerinas in their own special
  way . . .
touching,
leaping,
descending,
gracefully,
into the cycle to which they were
  born.

Then the thunder, the roar . . .
frightening some.

They dancers leave.
They move on to dance for others
before the thunder.

Hurry home,
hurry back,
before the music and the dance
are gone.

R.M. Mischak
EPITAPH
Silent season of the night,
End of endings, end of light,
Clouded skies and clouded fright,
Raining wrong and raining right.

Chills of valley and of height,
Pools of darkness and delight:
Midnight meetings of the plight
Born of fear and grown of spite.

Introspective appetite
Breeds with unrelenting might;
Fables blur and failures fight,
Mastering the endless rite.

Youthful hands will never write,
Aged mouths will never cite,
Unborn eyes can only sight
Fallen wanderings aright.

Silent season of the night,
Missing miracles alight
On the wind's departing flight
Past the black and past the white.

Ms. Virgle Lea Tardivo
PLEADING
Don't shut me out because you're
  afraid
  of what I might do to your
  heart.
I know you were hurt by
  someone before,
  and you're afraid to make a
  new start.
But give us a chance to find
  happiness;
  don't allow the chance to pass
  by.
Our love may be greater than you
  had before;
  we won't know unless you try.

Wilma I. Brewer
STORING CHRISTMAS
The hustle and bustle of
  Christmas was past,
But I tried to hang on to it, to
  make it last.
From those joyous things, I hated
  to part;
And sought to keep them, alive
  in my heart.

The ornaments in tissue, were
  carefully packed;
With foam rubber and cotton,
  they were backed.
As their shiny brightness
  disappeared from view,
I gently put in place, my favorite
  few.

The manger was last to be put
  away.
I lifted the animals from the,
  now, strewn hay;
Would they miss the warm touch
  of little hands,
That played with them;
  especially the lambs?

My grandchildren talked to
  Joseph and Mary,
About Jesus, the baby, they
  wanted to carry;
Lifted from the cradle of new
  mown hay;
In the rough trough of wood, on
  which he lay.

I was tempted to keep from
  storing, that day;
Those lovely things, with which,
  they liked to play.
Those special figures they loved
  so dearly,
And eagerly awaited with much
  joy, yearly.

Remembering those things
  brought the truth to me;
That Christmas doesn't depend
  on those things I see.
But the meaning, which left its
  imprint on my heart;
Is stored now, deep within, never
  to depart.

Phillip D. Liquori
TIDES
I know we learn that time is
  fleeting
Dreams like flowers die in sand,
So dreams grow and pass so
  quickly
Do you dare to give them a
  chance?
  Tides, watching them flow

In perfect motion, wave
  controlled.
  I do believe it's destiny
  Loving you is where I want to be
Can't they see tide's harmony
Can't they see tide's fury
Can't they see tide's beauty
Can't they see, if we learn to
  share our dreams.

Clay forms cast an image so
  lifeless
Under heat and pressure
  compressed
In its textured beauty hides a
  promise
How long do you think dreams
  last?
  Tides, watching them grow
In perfect motion, time exposed.
  I do believe it's destiny
  Loving you is where I want to be
Can't they see tide's harmony
Can't they see tide's fury
Can't they see tide's beauty
Can't they see, if we learn to
  share our dreams.

Delvenia Nadine Threeths
DREAMS
In the stillness of the night
You have invaded my dreams and
  left a mist
Where our hearts and souls meet

I have felt you breathe upon my
  ear
And the sweetness of your kiss
  upon my lips
I have felt the fire that gathers in
  me as our bodies cling
I have satisfied your soul with
  my love
And filled your thirst with my
  being

It is the feel of you that has
  erected my breast
And soften my rest as I dream
While I long for your body to rest
  tenderly upon me

If we should meet in another
  dream
Fill my need and make me
  believe
That Is Not Just A Dream!

Agnes von Wettberg
ADULT DELINQUENT
No drug bit for me, or hold-ups in
  gangs.
No staying out late, and flouting
  harangues.
But do not assume I am safe in
  the fold,
Or even respectable, just because
  OLD!

I don't crave to get drunk, or
  arrested for speeding,
But I'm sick of the orderly life I've
  been leading.

I'll skip church on Sunday, and lie
  abed late,
Give no thought to meals, or
  watching my weight.
I'll do my acrostic instead of the
  wash,
And say "DAMN" and "HELL"
  instead of "Oh Gosh".

I'll turn on T.V. when I'm in the
  mood,

And just shop for clothes, instead
of for food.
Let silver stay tarnished, bugs get
in the rice,
Before I'm decrepit, I'll dabble in
VICE!

For problems of youth I will not
care a bean.
Let them be Fatso, or dirty, or
green.
Let them buy their own blouses,
find their own beaux,
While I do my nails, and powder
my nose.

At home I'll eschew being sweet
and serene,
I'll lightly let loose, when I'm just
feeling MEAN!
At parties I'll flirt with the
handsomest guy,
And drink just enough to get
charmingly HIGH!

Oh, speak to me not of names
YOUNG in crime;
I'm up to no good, though I'm
quite past my PRIME!

Jean E. Reeher
THE BEST PART
It's the part of me that makes me
proud,
The part that pulls me through,
The times when I could cry out
loud,
And don't know what to do.

It's the part of me I wouldn't trade,
For any other thing,
The part for which I've dearly paid,
The part that makes me sing.

It's a part I'll have for quite a
while,
And I'm sure glad I will,
Cause it's the part that makes me
sing,
My little boy named "Bill".

Anne Bobrick
A MOOD
Do not stir. No hush. Do not
move.
The air will break.
Do not speak for words will
shatter our light.
This moment, this quiet of ours.
Do not scar it with our confession.

If we could listen,
swallowed within this silence
we might hear a hum,
a gentle voice,
a song.

Joanne Haines
TRELLIS ROSE
[For my mother whose favorite,
red climbing rosebush inspired
this poem]
Blazing red abundance, gleaming
butterflies
Plumb summer depths of scarlet
clusters;
Hummingbirds, small jeweled
motors, hover,
Purring over sweet succulence
among the morning shadows
Of your blossoms.

Avalanche of ruby, slumbrous
summer fire,
Midday incandescence, your
perfumed tongues of flame

Burn hot across the velvet grass
In fiery cascade, scattering spent
petals
Like forsaken dreams.

Soft garnet opulence, tranquil as
the breath of love,
Serene in phosphorescent
starshine;
You wear tiny fireflies like
precious jewels,
And, from sweet profusion, send
forth delicious perfume
To intoxicate the night.

Christina Chingtsao
To Think and To Forget
Vast is the land, green grass grows.
Virgin is the earth, the sunshine
glows.
Bury sorrow, sow the seeds of joy.
Place to think!   Place to forget!

Friendliness and kindness, here is
plenitude.
Enjoy Nature, while in solitude.
Love given by Him, that ever lasts.
Try to think!   Try to forget!

Coolness and tranquility is the
night.
Shadow and reflection is my light.
In darkness, the good earth rests.
Time to think!   Time to forget!

Fresh in mind, the memories fleet.
Some are bitter, some sweet.
Bitter sometimes sweet, sweet
bitter.
Much to think!   Much to forget!

Cock crows on the arrival of the
dawn.
On the way, soon comes the morn.
Twittering and whispering are
the birds.
What to think!   What to forget!

To the earth, another day is
coming.
Beyond the horizon, another
world is being.
The spirit is willing, the flesh is
weakening.
Easy to think!   Difficult to forget!

Marie Pierre Semler, M.M.
MIRROR OF THE UNSEEN
Look into the mirror, ever old,
ever new, for this was it made.
Look and see there, not self, but
another.
Another who face to face is
unseen.
Hidden where most strongly
reflected
in a mirror majestic and lovable.
Ofttimes envisioned, entitled,
"Mother",
in a motherhood called "Earth".

A mother reflecting goodness
of a loving, caring Father.
A Father as firm as mountain rock.
As comforting, refreshing, as
rock-bed's
clear streams of spring water.
Generosity, as in woodland trees,
bridal orchard's summer wealth.

Glory given credence by
autumn's splendor
As winter puts nature to rest.
Nourishing abundantly beyond
that of
fertile fields of ripened grain.

Enriching with gifts of spirit,
practical.
Seen and unseen of His Creation
serves,
and nature's beauty reveals His
Holy Face.

Peggy Zeaphey Nerl
A SPECIAL THANK YOU
When my world was so empty,
So dark and filled with despair,
Thank you for coming to me
each day,
To show me that you cared,
When dreams I thought were
coming true,
Seem to slowly drift away,
Thank you for giving me new
ones,
To share each and everyday,
Thank you for all your
understanding,
For opening so many new doors,
Thank you for teaching me what
love is all about,
And giving me feelings I never
knew before,
Most of all, thank you for still
caring,
For wanting and needing me too,
Thank for you being what you are,
For I couldn't love you anymore
than I do,

Jeannie Carlson
EXPECTING
[To my son, Carl Philip Carlson,
born August 12, 1982.]
My conception of love
Is prenatally cloistered
In uterine utopia.
Safe from fertility's flatulence,
Bulbous breasts and bulging belly,
You are in no fetal frenzy
To make your debut.
I greatly anticipate shedding
Pregnancy's unwieldy facade
So we may appear together
As mother and child.

Bonnell Susan Beatty
ODE TO SLEEP
Wrap yourself around me
Dark Prince
Tho' I toss and struggle
against your hold
Be bold enough to take me
Yet softly that I might
not wince
Convince my mind to find
another time to be alert
Far from reality let us skirt
Take me, take me
To your province
The realm of Darkness
My Prince.

Taj Janet Wilson
GOOD NIGHT MY LOVE
Good night my love.
My spirit carries this message
across the miles sealed
with a kiss.
My being expresses a wish, that
you were here,
my body instinctively moves
near to snuggle beneath your
warmth.
My arms, reach out to hold you,
my hands search for the touch of
your velvety, smooth skin,
my eyes long to reflect your
image.

My memory drifts to
yesterday . . .
when we danced the gentle night
dance . . .
the rhythm of tangled forms,
silhouetted by candlelight,
which, danced, an' danced, and
danced, into the night,
until at last it was reduced to the
calm sounds of breathing,
the pleasant exchange of giving
and receiving
and layers of warm melted wax.

As I relax and return to my
present solitude,
I paint my mood with a recalling
smile
and this message across the
miles—good night my love.

Susan Hegney
HOW DEAR THIS TIME
Soon you will no longer
Be a part of me: alive.
For, like all, you must change
In order to thrive.

A nightly creation of words and
flesh,
Voice and bone
Too soon becomes a memory
Each his very own.

How dear this time is, was.
They say "A picture's worth a
thousand words".
Yet the words echo and
Are impossible to purge.

You are not like the others
Joked and groaned about.
For you were special:
A difficult birth, hard labored out.

Rachel Golden
FINE FOR AWHILE
Gone is your
fear. For awhile
anyway.
There is sense now,
or should be.
I've seen this
before,
at least I think I have.
It isn't rare.
Yet it never succeeds.
On second thought,
maybe it has,
but I've never seen it.
It is a resolution.
It sems easy at first,
but isn't.
But I know why this is,
or maybe I don't and just think
I do.

For awhile it will be fine.
You won't be alone.
I'm
here.

Jacqueline Carasco Stassi
IRREPLACEABLE YOU
Like the scent of an essence rare
Invisible at times—
Yet, always there
If not in body, then in mind.

Like 18 karat amidst silver plate
Shining and glowing with pride,
All fortune on Earth cannot
compensate
The abundance of love in your
eyes.

Since we met long ago
    You are nearest my heart
And will always remain so
    Even if we must part.

You're my most devoted and
    trusted love
    Ever so constant and loyal—
And may I say, I've been
    blessed from above
With your love-that will never
    spoil.

My main reason for wanting to
    live till the end
    I could never desire another
You are, incidentally, my most
    precious friend,
    And my truest love,
        "My Mother"

Malik Canty
DEBASED
*[To my mother and
Grandmother You have
inspired me to be the best and I
won't give you less . . .]*
When the black woman weeps
    the rivers
Speak. For it knows her pain
    lies
Deep . . .

All during her years she has been
The victim of many unnecessary
Tears . . .

She has often been misused and
    abused
By her man, by the man, and
    others who
Just don't understand . . .

When the black woman weeps it
    is not
Because she is weak it is because
    her
Pain lies very deep . . .

Maria J. Borriello
THE MYTH THAT LIVES
Beware the cat
She is feline
She will beg wih soft meows—
    coax you,
Rub against your legs—arouse
    you,
Purr as you caress her.
Don't rub her wrong though
For her eyes are green—they will
    pierce you
Her tongue is quick—it will sting
    you
Her teeth sharp and she will
    bleed you.
Don't dare cross her
Those playful paws will spread to
    claw you
Her arch will rise—she'll attack
    you.
Yes.
Your woman
Your pet
A tigress
Beware.

Kipp Curtis
DREAMER
Coming coming
Always going
Nowhere my friend, nothing
Around the bend to no one

In and out my thoughts go round
Noting figures in the sun

Seeing one that isn't there
Hearing none for all the noise

And here she comes behind my
    eyes
And there she goes before them
Touching this and loving that
Never being but always there

I did not speak my sometimes
    thought
In this my never world of light
She could not and I could try
And neither could be both or one

We are not and yet we are
As the worlds light begins to cry
The day that was could never be
The day that was that none could
    see

Geneve Baley
Grace At Thanksgiving, 1982
I hear the
Heart beat of
Sound,
Waiting to be
Touched, by the
Soft night
Passing.

The count of
Time
Fingers the
Embrace, of a
Warm
Invitation.

What is a
Meeting of
Two
Kind thoughts
Sent spinning,
Etherically?

I love the
Sight of
Beauty—
Sculptured in
Fine marble,
Standing.

A light touch, a
Laugh, (in good
Fun)
Runs—
Constantly,
Forever.

What is the
Direction of a
Good
Mind;
Seeking—
Solice?

A sweet, breath—taking
Whisper
Kisses my
Face in
Hope, faith, and
Charity.

Sing like the
Bird seeking his
Home, after
Perching in the
Sun, of the
Seaside.

A hearty meal
Waits for the
Candle—lit French
Wine,
Decorating,
Dinner.

A summer wind

Blows
Lightly, over the
Mist of the
Skyline, in the
Distance.

Joe Papkin
**Menelaus' Prayer To
Aphrodite**
*[To Menelaus, who suffered
humiliation at the whim of
Aphrodite, Goddess of Love.
Had her insufferable ego been
curbed; Agamemnon would not
have launched 1000 ships.]*
O' vanity,—thou has leveled
    kingdoms, cultures,
And civilizations, Yea, and thou
    hast struck down
Gods and mortals alike.
Thy power is awesome. Thy drive
    cataclysmic.
By what measure then, can a
    mere waning peacock
Whose plume has been plucked
    and whose tail feathers
Lie on the ground, torn out by the
    vicissitudes of
Life, fight on?
Thy sting is fatal,—I expire!!

Murray S. Weinstein
GOODBYE, LIZZIE . . .
*[Dedicated to a great
immigrant, a great struggler, a
mother, a woman, a person,
who loved freedom; and who
gave her all, so her 8 children
could have better lives.]*
Lizzie, the person, the woman,
The mother, the long—time
    widow,
Lived to stand up,
Free,
For herself, and
For her chidren.

The night before
She died, with
Life—weary, aching
Bones, she tried to
Stand Up, one more time;
And she did!
(Like all of us
are trying to do)

She died prematurely,
For want of love
and understanding.

May she now
Rest in peace,
In God's arms.

May God rest her Soul.

And bring me peace.

Amen.

Catherine Baron
THE ARTIST
I am an artist.
I paint your image upon
    the canvas of my mind.
My brushes are my memories.
My colors are my emotions.

The result is an abstraction:

Pastels for the early spring when
    we met;
Bright reds and yellows for our
    summer together;
Blues for the sadness of our
    autumn separation;

Blacks and browns for the long
    winter ahead.

I used to think my medium was
    of oils—
    lasting,
But my tears have since washed
    the canvas clean.

I realize now,
    You were only a watercolor
    upon my heart.

Gina L. Auricchio
NUMB TO PAIN
There was none
    But could be
Yet he didn't try hard enough
    Or moved too slowly to catch
    hold
Only to fall endlessly to the
    bottom
    And be swollowed whole
I've seen this
    With naked eye
Unconscious mind not aware of
    the foul play
Going on
For I was blind
    By insecure causes
No will to fight
To stand on my feet
    Shout with full chest of air
STOP!
I was numb to the pain
I kept quiet in my room
    While my fellow man wept
    tears of frustration
Just for a jesture of love
For he had none
    But could have
Yet he didn't try hard enough

Esther L. Foye
WINTERTIME
*[To my husband William, for
his never—ending
encouragement and faith in my
work for children.]*
The icicles sparkle in the sun,
    Like diamonds in a ring,
"Wintertime has really begun!"
    The little snowbirds sing.

Under a deep, white blanket of
    snow,
    The flowers sleep till spring.
The north wind howls—oh hear
    it blow!
    Tonight more snow he'll bring.

Yes, everything is cold and white,
    Jack Frost has come around,
And long and dark are the winter
    nights,
    As the snow comes softly down.

Doreen C. Sampler
UNTITLED
*[For my son, Ian Dean Sampler.
I never understood my mothers
love for me . . . now I do! I love
you, mom]*
Ian Dean, our little son, only God
    knew you'd be the one.
He knew before our lives began,
    it's all a part of his master plan.
Dad was born to live his life, with
    your mom as his wife.
So much love had we two,
    waiting inside, just for you!

God knew, my love, as I've said
    before,
you're "real" mom and dad were

just too poor!
Babies themselves when you
  were born,
suddenly their lives were torn.
Filled with love and hope for you,
they did the best thing they
  could do . . .
they chose "new" parents, dad and
  me,
so we could help you be all you
  can be.

You give our lives point and
  direction:
we give you love and protection.
Our lives were joined, it was
  meant to be.
You're our son now, we're a family.

Janice P. Egry
How Did You Get So Young?
*[For my parents, Mr. and Mrs.
Eldon Selleck on their Fiftieth
Wedding Anniversary July 12,
1982]*
When I was three, you seemed so
  old.
You knew all the answers, and I
  didn't know any.
You towered above me, and I just
  knew
You had been around forever.

When I was five, I went to school
And learned some of the answers.
  But you were still
Very old . . . and tall, and I was
  convinced
You had been around forever.

When I was fifteen, you still
  seemed a little old.
(Everyone over twenty was.) And
  I thought I'd learned all the
  answers.
You weren't as tall anymore, and I
  thought just maybe
You hadn't lived forever.

When I was twenty—five, I
  learned all the questions
That I didn't have answers for.
  You seemed
A little older, and no taller than
  anyone else, and I knew
You hadn't lived forever.

When I was thirty—five, I found
  that neither of us
Had all the answers. And none of
  us had lived forever.
You began turning younger.
  Everyone knows that
Parents are always forty.

Now that I'm forty—five,
  suddenly you're very young.
I know now that none of us will
  ever know all the answers
Or ever be very tall. But I know
You both will live forever.

How did you get so young?

Janice P. Egry
Expressions Of Freedom
He said we needed to protect
  ourselves.
He said if we didn't we'd be
  annihilated.
He said if we didn't, the robbers
  and bandits and killers would
  rob us and rape us and kill us.
He said we needed a gun in every
  home and a nuclear bomb in
  every arsenal.

He said it would keep us safe and
  free.
And I heard the birds singing, and
  I listened.

I thought we should get rid of all
  the weapons.
I thought if we didn't, we'd be
  annihilated.
I thought the robbers and bandits
  and killers would use our own
  guns to rob us and rape us and
  kill us.
I thought if we had nuclear
  warheads, others would have
  even more.
I thought no weapons would keep
  us safe or free.
But the birds still sang, so I slept.

He reassured me again that we
  were secure.
My heart said we weren't, but my
  words were annihilated
As news told of more robbers and
  bandits and killers robbing and
  raping and killing.
Today I look in the West, and the
  North, and the East, and the
  South, and see
Huge mushrooms growing there,
  outside in the safe, free air.
And the birds are dead still, and I
  know.

John M. Pratt III
SORROW IS DYING
*[I dedicate this poem to my
mother, who gave me my eyes,
and to Joan, who restored in
me the hope and love that,
with my mother's death, I
thought I had lost forever.]*
Sorrow is dying slowly
with the summer grass
in our backyard brown.
You sit in my mind
untouchable desire,
the memory tears.
Twenty-two years
I held an angel.
  Today I saw you,
  Mother, a smile
  in the oak maple woods
  along the old mill path,
  and again, a reflection
  in the island creek,
  beside a motherless son
  head in his hands.

Carole Corbeil
CATATONIC
You stand rigid
an impenetrable icy shell
coldly limits your chosen sphere
You dismiss me with a glance
Passion—if any—is frozen
behind your tight blue lips

Little do you realize
that chilling frigidity
has forced me to withdraw
to go inside
where love abounds
and the sun shines

Bonnie Prewett
MONEY
What is money? It is Life.
Or so they think, to me it's strife.
A struggle to survive, a power to
  rule,
But without those bucks, your

just a tool,
For some other guy, who'll use his
  might
To see you crawl, cheer in your
  plight.
It turns friends to foe, lovers will
  die
Because deep in your heart, you
  may wonder why
Does this paper barter turn men
  mad?
Twisting around reason, to do ill
  and bad
It turns everyone of us, against
  what's right.
Deaf, dumb and blind, our backs
  to the light.
Greed and want, it's all our
  downfall,
As we go through our lives,
  missing it all.

Leonard Vincent
LOVE
*[To my children, The petals of
the roses are but leaves upon
the ground, Yet finer blooms
were never picked, when I my
children found.]*
Love I give thee hold you strong.
Eternal love, when life is gone.
Others who would wish to be
Nearer truth will see in thee
A more relove shine in your face,
Reason be I, and embrace.
Dearer now to me and true,
Others truly will still yearn.

Dar'st I love thee as I would'st,
Avenging all, who'd speak ill thus,
Verily you'll hold my hand.
In seeing thee my love is planned,
Nothing conquered, nothing lost,
Caring now for we have found.
Invisible, Immortal be,
filled with life and love for thee.

Bernard T. McDonald
A Spring Day In Atlantic Canada
The dawn broke light from the
  grip of night,
  The wind's touch was icy cold.
At the end of the sea, the sun
  rose free,
  From a bed of amber gold.

All through the day, the dark
  clouds lay,
  Against a sodden sky.
While all around the fluttering
  sounds,
  Of snowbirds on the fly.

Far up the hill in the evening's
  chill,
  The trees swayed to and fro.
Casting a sheen of twilight green,
  Across the pale gray snow.

The ice pans drifted, the shadows
  shifted,
  Our night was coming fast.
But hearts were gay on this dull
  March day,
  Cause Spring was here at last.

Donald J. Kirk
GENTLE GIANT
A "Gentle Giant" passed my way
He stopped to visit me for the
  first 25 years of my life
Then one night, as quietly as he
  came

He left.
He showed me love and
  tenderness
This giant of few words
He brought happiness to my life
Then he left.

As silently as a gentle breeze
Blowing through my hair
He stayed to watch me grow to a
  man
Then he left.

No words could ever describe him
This giant of a man
He encouraged me in all I did
Then he left.

Through many years he stood
  nearby
He helped whenever he could
I thought my Grandfather would
  stay forever
Then he left.

Lorna Adamack
TO A FRIEND
To know your sense of worth,
To feel your loyalty,
To understand your willingness—
Your readiness to share—
These, for me,
Sustained a sense of harmony
Between us,
As my colleague
And
My friend.

E. J. Armstrong
ATOM
I see
  the earth
    revolve

I see
  all life
    evolve

I see
  intents
    resolve

I see
  the world
    dissolve

Terri Parrott
MAN
Man, he was created by God.
He was given a brain,
But didn't know how to use it.
He was given two eyes,
But had nothing to see.
He was given two ears,
But had nothing to hear.
He was given two hands,
But had nothing to touch.
He was given two feet,
But had nowhere to go.
So, that's Why God
Created Woman . . .
To help man achieve
Himself better . . .

Helene Suzanne Pomeroy
UNEASY
Uneasy moods of mine that
  swing back and forth inside my
  head, worry me with their
  cripple silence and remind me
  not to speak too loud, least I
  make myself aware of another
  pain; and another reason to
  introduce cause and effect
  alliance . . .

Reaccuring dreams bring tears to my pillow late in the night and I lay awake in a shiver, watching the dark actively being still and quiet frightens me; yet I hear a thousand voices whisper to me from the hallway . . . and as I turn my eyes to search for a familiar face, I drift off to sleep.

I wish you were here; for I could lay awake for hours in the blackness and not be alone in your arms: but then, my partial daydreams continue to rehearse missing parts, and they lead me in circles . . . dizziness makes me bitter of the past and I only want love to leave me alone; for I would rather be weak on my own, than have the confession of dependence, to have to call my own . . . .

These uneasy moods of mine are consistant in their appearance of a form that is assembed as my shadow, following me as I miss the sunshine and leading me, as I blindly rush towards the darkness; at least it is always there . . . and I can tolerate silence, for it is there that I can hide myself, and really see myself. . .

La Verne A. Jorissen
Treasure In the Old House
There was a mandolin
with a smooth round bottom
and a little wicker cradle
with a celluloid doll in the old house.
I remember strumming and humming
with the mandolin and the doll.
The sound echoed in the hall-way.
I wonder if anyone plays there
on a spring day, with the scent of lilacs
and apple blossoms drifting in the upper window?
In the attic among the crates
were dozens of Japanese lanterns
which were strung on the Fourth of July.
When evening came, the neighbors gathered
to watch the fireworks and exclaimed at each flaring
Roman candle. Just like the shower of sparks,
rain must fall on their descendants.
Young people are strumming and humming
and children still play with dolls in quiet corners.

Florence Whitaker Gross
Emily Dickinson:
Self—Epitaph
I fled from Life and took my Love with me,
Deep and rich and warm within my heart.
Oyster—fashion, out of pain I wrought the pearl,
Hidden close until Death reft the shell.

Cutting swiftly, surely,
My fancy carved poetic cameos,
Dainty, mystic,
Set in iridescent words.

Alice M. Griffin
North Cascade Highway
Over a hundred years a mountain trail, for only the die hearty and cotton tail.

Now a highway lush, opens to the public rush.

In campers so grand, they pioneer the land,

Here's how it went, mountain splendor beauty rare, glacier water, mountain air, alpine beauty everywhere.

Country living, country style, country living by the mile.

The sun breaking through the mellow mountain dew, watch out for the trucks the log's are coming through.

No shoulder, sharp curves, oop's don't pass, got the shiver's on the Skagit river mountain pass.

Through the clouds I saw a mountain peak, in awesome wonder God does speak.

Saw all the tree's, whispered to the breeze, yet not a silver fox left among the tree's.

Then down through the Methow valley we swept, devouring the scenery and history as we crept.

Washington so beautiful, so rare, a little bit of everywhere a land so fair.

Mountain splendor, beauty rare, glacier water, mountain air, alpine beauty everywhere.

Robert Sholler
friends
[thank you patti for being a loving wife & a full time friend]
friends
    what could have been
        is easier had tried
        better two laughing friends

    than lovers
        having cried
    tho silent on the inside
    smiles never died
    we end with
        truthful handshakes
funny
            how kisses lied

Elaine Eaton
MIRROR CHARADES
Locked away,
And afraid to step outside
For fear of losing the other foot.

Inside alone
I look out the window
And see your shadow silhouetted there
I hear your distant laughter.
Alone inside
I wait for you to look back
But your shadow dissolves into darkness
And your laughter echoes in this empty room.

The mirror
Is the only audience I am left
to play charades with my pain.

Grimaced faces
I keep to myself
I hide my heart in hopes you'll find it.
Are you searching?
Faces grimaced
Cause me to wonder
If you would keep trying
if you felt like I sometimes do.

Cecily Atyes Varner
THE PROBLEM
I had a problem
It took a while to be free
The problem's back
It is tearing at me

I tried to do my thing
I tried to do it right
Now I am binded again
What am I to fight

Should I quit
Or should I go on
I could ask for help
I could fight alone

My wounds never healed
My scars are still there
My pains are many
Where is someone's care

D. D. Willoughby
DARKNESS
        dark, obscure, dim
    Can you go on indefinitely?

    sleep, slumber, somnolence
        Where are you?

    dawn, morning, daybreak
        Will you ever come?

        Light is my sentinel.
        Sleep is my refuge.
        Where are either of you?

Viola Dawson
RAIN
They planned to cultivate their garden
                But it rained.
Rained gently, but steadily, going deep into the soil
Soil as rich as a millionaire's wealth
Wealth of vitamins in the products of that garden
Garden of flowers and vegetables rare
Rare as God's gift of the rain.

They planned to dress in their Easter finery
                But it rained.
Rained a drizzle, then a downpour; very wet
Wet enough to ruin the parade
Parade of straw hats, ribbons, and such
Such a display of pomp, often flaunted too much
Much controlled, or detered, by the rain.

They planned to make hay
                But it rained.
Rained, pouring perforating puddles around the baler
Baler as big as a motor boats bulk
Bulk of the binder bogged down—din't float
Tho' float did many a thing in

that rain.

They planned a pond—side picnic
                But it rained.
Rained droplets as large as a teacup's top
Top of the hill and bottom of the glade
Glade, where cattle silently stood
Stood haunched backs toward the wild wind
Wind that blew sheets of the very cold rain.
Rain comes at the most inopportune times
Times when we'd like to control the elements
Elements that come from the stratosphere above
Above where God decides the call
Call for rain when needed
HE can't please us all.

Bernita A. Wisdom
OUR HOUSE
[To my parents, Thelma & Julius Glenn for giving me a beginning, to John, my husband, who has made life beautiful, and to Debra Hunter, my friend, who inspired me to write again.]
Come live with me . . .
In a house made from nature's surroundings.

With a roof made of turquoise painted skies,
splattered with billows of softness.

Walls made from the sweet gentle breezes
of the soft summers' wind.

We'll sleep on beds made from green blades of grasses,
eat from trees which will bear us fruits,
and quench our thirst with sparkling clear waters.

The sun will be the source of all our energy,
and the moon will share with us highlights of softness.

I will be your mistress
and you, my master,

And we will live on God's green earth together.
Come live with me in our house . .
where no man can enter,
where peace is at rest,
and where love is an open door.

Ruth I. Ridings
LIFE FORCE
[Inspired by our Love and Friendship—"D. J. R."]
Fear of Loving too much?
            Why?
Love IS the basis of Life —
        Pain from Loving?
            No—
The pain comes from the denying
of what the Body and Soul
        says is Beautiful
and yet so often denied because
the FEAR of something beautiful
not being an acceptable response
        Instead of
LISTENING to what these two persons

are cummunicating—
WHY be so frightened of such a
    beautiful moment?
Just because it may only be for
    the moment?
OH—MAN KIND—CHERISH
    each moment of LIFE
For it may not come again—

Irma Pool
BORN TO DIE
A fire! A tragic fire that cost the
    lives of four.
A grandmother and three small
    children.
The two older children had been
    in a fire two years before.
The remark was made, "They
    were born to die!"
There was one who was born to
    die:
Born to die that we might live.
The Lord Jesus Christ, when He
    was born,
Was wrapped in swaddling
    clothes: grave clothes.
Yes! Mary wrapped Him in grave
    clothes at birth.
He was born to die for our sin:
That sin that we were born in.
It was for us He died. Us! Wicked
    sinful human beings.
But His death was not in vain.
He is no longer in the grave . . .
    but risen.
Seated at the right hand of the
    Father interceeding for us.
Will we listen when He calls
    us. . .
Or will we reject His cry and go
    on as before?
Forgetting it was not for just a few,
But for all, that He was born to die.

Delva Root Johnson
THE LONELY ZOMBIE
In life he was a bold man.
Arrogant it was said.
'Til the day that he was murdered
and became a living dead.

He had no love for his daughter,
nor his wife of twenty years.
On the day that he was buried,
no one shed a single tear.

For the sins he had committed
and the sorrow that he brought,
he was made to walk the earth
though his flesh would surely rot.

There is no place where he may
    rest,
this man without a soul.
Nowhere is he welcome,
he shall always be alone.

Debbie Schlinker—Gammons
THE LION
[With thanks, to my very
special person, Shorty, because
you were always their for me.]
Alas, a lion you are,
With all the pride and nobility,
But without the happiness and
    serenity.
Your as noble as a king on his
    finest day,
But is that really happiness
    shining in your eyes?
Your pride of your
    accomplishments lights up
    your castle,

But when you need it most can
    you find serenity?
You listen to words,
    But cannot comprehend them.
You hear soft voices whisper,
    But not the silent screams
    behind them.

So alas, my poor lion,
Where once you were king,
    Leader and owner of much and
    many.
You are now pauper,
    Led and owned by your own
    captive soul.

Carolyn Chipman
A POEM
Write a poem? What a cinch.
I've written a few in a pinch.
Now here I sit, hour by hour.
The work I've done a paper tower.
It should be easy, so I thought.
The pen doesn't work, more paper
    I bought.
Can't think of a thing, heads in a
    spin.
Trying too hard, wanting to win.
Better slow down, it'll come to
    me fast.
There, the end, I'm finished at last.

Scott E. Wilde
SUSPENDED
lying outsretched on clean white
    sheets
you sleep peacefully beside me,
room silenced
except for slow rhythmic breathing
and muffled sigh, content
as you stir among dreams,
    unaware of fingers
moving gently over breasts
firm and full, sensing
cool moist contours beneath your
    back
and warm rounded hips,
my head is incensed with mild
    fragrance
your aura
like a mellow wine shared long
    ago,
remember,
I brushed cinnamon hair from
    your face
and kissed you lightly
that I might also become meshed
    in your dream,
I dare not disturb your rest
nor break this moment
but eyes yield
to find you no longer there
and wish again I was not here
to curse this silence,
utter silence.

C. J. Spaeth
ALONE
[To Gary, who has taken away
the emptiness that makes for
feeling alone.]
When you're alone
    there is no hiding the truth.
It stares you in the face
    with every tear you let fall.
While you may not want to give
    in, your strength is stripped
    away.
Your heart is laid bare
    and wrenched with each sad
    note.
Love songs play

and rip at your heart,
Tearing at every strand of hope
    you thought you could hold onto.
As your emotions are drained,
    sleep invites you to escape,
Taking you to a world
    where the pain is softened.
Carrying you through the
    darkness
    to the strength of the day
Where the demons of the
    emptiness you fought the night
    before
Are tucked away in the shadows
    of every step in the sun
Letting you build your reserves
    until shadows fade
And you are left alone
    to fight the emptiness again.

Beth Ann Geertgens
PENDULUM
I watch it sway—
back and forth in life . . .
and it comes back;
I grip not at its sight,
but hold to . . .
the picture portrayed
and capture near
adherent to the message,
thus sent my way—
I watch it sway.

Carolyn Wolfe
GOD'S ORBIT
I know not where God's orbit ends,
    For from the top or bottom of
    the earth
    And all around the sphere
The heavens reach out and upward
    Into infinity. And circles high
    And further out where sky and
    planets blend,
So it must be, eternally,
    God's orbit has no end.

Renie Beers
DYING
The wind whistles one cold,
    last desperate plea.
Winter is dying as we all
    can see.
She was such a friend a few
    months ago,
With her cooling breath and
    white swirling snow.
How we all delighted in
    each spinning flake
Enjoying the beauty each
    tiny crystal would make.
But her breath grew weaker
    with each passing day,
Gasping and struggling to
    push the warmth away.
Alone in her sorrow, alone
    in her fight,
She gave up the effort one
    starry night.
The following dawn a wonderous
    thing did appear
The birds were all singing—
    Spring is Here
    Spring is Here

Rose McNaught
INTROSPECT
[To Scott, forever]
It's such a little gesture
To take pen in hand
I call upon my immortal lover
Who languishes at my feet
Should I pause for but a moment

I feel the Ebb and flow
Of all the words the world will
    never know
So sad his demise
His masterpiece incomplete
Yet, I feel the Ecstasy of melody
My spirit joins in Rhapsody
And for but a moment, I too am
    immortal
Unchained by all things carnal
A precious thought is born
Again I take pen in hand
And do his bidding—

Ann Marie Gray
POETRY
Poetry is the glory of God.
Poetry soothes the ravenous mob.
Poetry melts all hearts of stone.
Poetry warms dead corpses' bones.

Poems are those wonderful words
That explain the beauty of trees
    and birds.
Poetry has some joys and some
    sorrows.
Poetry brings some hope for
    tomorrow.

So if you are suffering from
    sickness or strife
Listening to beautiful poetry
    would be nice.
For all the diseases from A to Z,
The best of remedies is good
    poetry.

Kathy Szybisty
**Prayer Over a Wilting
    Flower**
Come Quietly
Butterfly, and taste the morning
The day sparkles with your flight.
Step lightly
Butterfly, and know the breezes
Speak no more of hidings.
Stay softly
Buttefly, and go to every man
Sing your laughter in each single
    breath.

Donna M. Niedermeier
OKLAHOMA BRAVE
[Dedicated to Elgin Butler II by
his Mother-in-law, Donna M.
Niedermeier, his wife Carol, his
son Brandon, and his parents,
Elgin & Jean Butler.]
Oh, Elgin stars are out so bright,
    Your Indian spirit echoes at
    night.
For as the years shall all pass by,
    Somehow, your name will
    never die.

You left behind a young son,
    Oh, Brandon's life has just
    begun.
You courted danger from afar,
    Somehow, fate held your racing
    car.

Your life was fast, yet they knew,
    Oh, Elgin your parents both
    loved you.
As Carol stares in the moonlight,
    A silent teardrop falls in the
    night.

Your Indian blood left you proud,
    As your ancestry cries from the
    cloud.
Oh, Elgin your voice echoes so free,
    Why did you go and let us
    grieve.

In Oklahoma a brave stands tall,
  Holding a baby born in the fall.
The child has, clutched in his
  hand,
  A small race car, midst that
great land.

Carolyn Sue (Arthur) Logan
NINE TO FIVE
I Brought her flowers, this nice
  spring day,
Cause "thanks" to her, I wanted to
  say.

For picking up my laundry, on
  her lunch time hour
and my wife's anniversary, always
  orders the flowers,

For making the coffee, and
  bringing me tea,
And working overtime, and not
  charging me.

For going to the bank, treking to
  the store,
Appointments with doctors, and
  dentists . . . and more.

For making me look good, in my
  boss's grim eye,
And covering for me . . . many
  times she did lie.

But there's a note on her desk,
  cause she's been here and went
And filed a complaint—with the
  U.S. government!

James A. Phillabaum
SPRINGTIME AND YOU
Springtime and flowers,
Long idle hours;

Springtime and sunlight,
Doing it up just right;

Springtime and lovers,
Warm nights without covers;

Springtime and moonbeams,
Lovers and sweet dreams;

Springtime and breezes,
Little kitten sneezes;

Springtime and roses,
Afternoon dozes;

Springtime and soft light,
Maybe she just might;

Springtime and green trees,
Blossoms and honey bees;

Springtime and you,
Now that—just might do.

Kent D. Sommers
BY CHANCE THREE
By chance three men,
On a dark and chilly campus,
Chanced to meet.
One was a philosopher,
One was a mathematician,
One was seeking his fortune.
They paused,
And the philosopher spoke:
"If you do not agree with me, you
  are wrong."
And the mathematician replied,
"But that statement is not
  deductively sound."
And the man seeking his fortune,
  Agreed.
They paused,
They looked each other in the eye,
They looked at the ground,
And each went on his way.

Lisbeth Kay Jones
UNTITLED
Sunrise,
Blue skies,
Misty morn,
A child is born,
Rain washing fresh,
Robin red breast,
Babbling stream,
A sunray's beam,
Oceans roaring,
Seagulls soaring,
The mountains' crest,
Sunset West,
Fruited land,
A pebble of sand,
Who among you
Dares to doubt that
        I AM

Rita Jordan
WHAT I AM
I am white, gray and black.
Neutral,
Free from color,
Yes, I lack a hue.

I am red, yellow and brown.
Natural,
Full of color,
Earthtoned to be true.

I am neutral and natural.
Combined,
Making color,
The product of two.

I am what I am.
Made,
Full or free of color,
There was nothing I could do.

Stephen Franklin Junkin
MIRROR
When I gaze into the mirror
The stars appear nearer.
There's a look far away
Unto another time and day.

The time seemed trouble free,
The way life was meant to be.
Going places and having fun,
Resting up when the day was
  done.

Meeting ladies and going out,
Finding out just what life's about.
Making bills and paying bills,
Growing cactus on the window
  sills.

Tilling the soil and bailing hay,
Camping and hiking at the end of
  May.
I enjoyed fishing with my dad;
I'll never forget those times we
  had.

My mind grew and so did I,
Learning to reach beyond the sky.
A heartache I'd never knew,
Never running out of things to do.

The mirror tells of the life you
  live,
Thoughts, hopes, and the light
  you give.
The mirror tells a lot you see,
Of things that were and things to
  be.

C. P. St. Amant
DAWN AT SEA
The horizon is tinged by the
  unseen sun
As the stars are snuffed out one
  by one;

And the darkened surface of the
  calm sea's face
Is wreathed in mist with ethereal
  grace;
As the edge of the orb of glowing
  red
Impatiently rises from it's watery
  bed,
The problems of man wash away
  with the night;
His faith is renewed in the
  morning light
And peace pervades the mind and
  rests the soul.

Eleanor H. Cumming
QUESTION
The warmth of radiance eons old
  To me spans time and space,
To me worlds infinitesimal
  Make up the structure of my
  face.
And fern and flower and blade of
  grass
  And emerald leaf pass on to me
  Their unseen exhaltations
Without which I cannot be.
  Beyond the manifest I see the
  secret source
The fountain head from which
  life flows
  And like a fool I question
  things
With every wind that blows.
  When the singing in the veins
  shall cease
And the heart's fierce fire is
stilled
  When the ultimate release is
  gained . . .
Shall I be at last fulfilled?

Donald E. Long
ANOTHER TIME
Ours lives seem so complete,
  They seem so right, they seem
  so neat.
But when we think of yesteryear
  Our minds are blank and only
  hear
The times so good, the times so
gay
  That makes us yearn for
  yesterday.
Why cannot we in life so clear
  Go bck in time with those held
  dear?
Is living such that we can't be
  The youth and love we once
  could see?
Are we to stay in life's tight grip
  And never make a backward trip?
Are we to try to love another
  When what we want is our first
  true lover?

Norma Elizabeth
EIGHT GOLD STARS
["To all those gallant men who
participated in the mission to
Iran. April 25, 1980. God bless
you."]
Hopes were high as the morning
  drew night,
The roar of the big planes floated
across the night sky.
Apprehension and prayer,
  mingled with the private
  thoughts of men . . .
Unbeknown to many . . . there
  was a destiny to fulfill and end.

A duty that calls to those who
  dare . . .
The Delta Force on an illfated
  mission to nowhere.
In the barren land of the Kavir . .
  Desert one,
Where eight families, lost a
  husband, a father, a brother and
  a son.
Eight Gold Stars . . . in memory
  of . . . the brave men who
  perished in the desert night.
The Commandos of the elite unit
  of the Blue Light . . ."

Melissa Broyles
MEMORIES
Memories is all I'm left with
it's all just a myth
now that they're away
I look back at the days.

Although we keep in touch
unable to talk and see is too much
things just happened too fast
and I can't deal with the past.

I reminisce of how it used to be
when they were once with me
not laughing anymore
I close all my doors.

I know they think of me
but now we're all free
we write many letters
being together would be better.

Lois Troxel Null
FISHING
Splashing sparkles, rocky rills
Sun so bright and shadows soft
Willows touch and tightly tangle
Water racing rapidly
This is pulsing poetry.

Motions slow and sensuous
Or deftly darting—daring
Silver fins and scales aglow
He is fascinating fish
He is poignant poetry.

Minas Tsolovos
**Laughing Dreaming
  Screaming**
Jan Rammed the cam in the
  mans' machine
Jan Banned: Damned Sam and
  went off to laugh at the camp
And then one day the mean
  machine leaned on Jan and put
  her in the can

And if Jan gets out someday She'll
  probably LAUGH and DREAM
  and SCREAM and
Ream that god damn mean
  machine

Marguerite Weichselfelder
Watchwords Of Freedom
Faith, hope and charity—these
  three
Are guardians of liberty.
They must our watchwords ever be
For freedom, peace, security.

We must have faith throughout
  our land
In leaders who proclaim our stand,
And follow them with one accord
To prove peace mightier than the
  sword.

We must have hope—or all is lost,
And face our task, whate'er the
  cost,

To still maintain our way of life—
To build, and not destroy by strife.

With charity for all mankind,
To world needs we must not be
    blind.
To foster peace, we must prepare
Our resources with all to share.

Let Freedom from her mountain
    height
Forever rule our land so bright,
'til all on earth her good shall see,
And strive to set all peoples free.

Daniel Wayne Hardy
TRUE BEAUTY
[Dedicated to my dear mother,
wonderful sister, and beautiful
daughter. Phyllis, Cheryl, and
Kimberly Ann respectively.]
They say beauty is in the eyes of
    the beholder,
This I find untrue as the world
    grows colder.
True there is nothing so beautiful
    as a warm spring day,
When the wind whistles and the
    trees begin to sway.
When the fragrances in the air is
    beauty to the nose,
And soft fresh grass is beauty to
    the toes.
But nothing can compare,
To the silkiness of a woman's hair.
Or to the liteness of her touch
    and caress,
This is true beauty at its best.
Just to capture a moment together,
Laughing and talking—just being
    close in any weather.
It just seems to be,
An expression of true beauty.
Nature has taken the stars from
    the skies,
And planted them in a woman's
    eyes.
And she has taken the
    smoothness of springtime
    wind,
Added it to love and developed a
    woman's skin.
She's taken the flowers and the
    birds,
And given woman soft loving
    words.
The way a woman walks—her
    gentleness of mind,
And the ability to love with all
    her heart is true beauty I find.
No matter where you are,
There is no beauty by far,
Than woman—true beauty—
    highest above all pleasures,
No one can take away her beauty
    in any measure.
There will always be true beauty
    close to a man's heart,
And that is woman, supreme
    elegance, true beauty—
in essence, nature's art.

Samuel Gordon Gerber
BELOVED
I cannot compare you
With a starry night
For its radiance dims
With the dawn of a new day.
Nor can I relate you
To the flowers in the field;
For, in the season's passing
Their beauty withers and dies.

Yet, I seek to clothe you
In some tangible gown
That will hold your celestial
    loveliness;
That I may be sure
When I place my lips on yours
That I enfold reality
And not some lovely dream
That will ever torment me
If I awaken.

Janet Swee Ching Romel
Religious Philosophical
Poetry
God is good and God is great
He won't let everybody have a
    bad fate.
They say: whether it be
    yesterday, or today,
It's better to forgive and forget
Everything evil, that's being done
    or said.
Good news should always be
    spread—
There's nothing one should dread,
in life, amongst strife.
As one wonders or ponders,
    remember!
You will find, at some time
Along the pathways of many roads;
    there unfolds
Mysteries of mankind, and other
    tales untold.
There's only one—the Almighty
    Creator, above all nature.
One will find, at some time,
    complexities, intricacies
And many unexpected events
    which manifest themselves
Among many presence of people
Who come to strange places and
    see new faces.
Thou shalt believe in oneself, and
    never grief!
For what lies beyond the horizon
Try not to cry, in times of sorrow,
There's always a better tomorrow—
It's true, that God is always with
    you.

Christine Clayton
MOTHER
[This poem is dedicated to a
special person to whom I shall
always owe a debt of gratitude
and love: "MY MOTHER"]
For you I tried to capture, the sun
    and moon and stars,
To wrap them up in rainbows,
    and store away in jars.
For then whenever you were
    unhappy, or perhaps a little blue,
I could open a jar of sunlight, and
    make it shine for you!

And whenever it was cloudy and
    you needed the moon at night,
I'd open a jar of moonlight, so
    silvery, clear and bright.
Then, too, on a night when there
    were no stars, to guide you on
    your way,
I'd open a jar just packed with
    stars, and they'd guide and
    shine till day!

But I failed in my quest, which
    makes me feel blue,
In fact I was wondering just what
    I could do?
When you came along and gave
    me your smile, which was
    bright as the summer sun,

And from your eyes the stars
    shone out, and twinkled at me
    in fun!
They were laughing at me for
    trying to catch something you
    already had,
And in a flash, a twinkling, I was
    no longer sad!

For you had them all the time,
    stored away within yourself,
The gentleness of the moon at
    night, skipping about like an elf!
Your smile like the sun in the
    heavens, warms and brightens
    a dreary day,
And the stars in your eyes skip
    and dance, like they do in a
    child at play!

For as long as we have each other,
    and of course the one above,
And show, like Him to everyone,
    a fine unselfish love,
We will have no need for to
    capture, the sun and moon and
    stars,
We have their power within
    ourselves, so need we not the
    jars!

Now this verse may sound a little
    silly, but I want you to know,
I'll love you forever, and now I
    have to go!

Diane M. Flaherty
GREEN AND BLUE
Green, Green, do you know Green?
With her quiet life, she's old
    Blue's wife
and Queen of all the givers.

Old Blue feels best when he is seen
bright behind his good wife Green
on soft summer mornings.

Green, Green is happiest clean,
dreaming of her daughter "Bean"
and drinking by the river.

Green and Blue are most esteemed
when Green is springtime new
while dancing just for Blue!

Green, Green do you know Green?
She's vast, wide, by old Blue's side
and Queen of all the givers.

Mark Joseph Hollister
A WINTER'S MIRACLE
There's something in the greyness
of a crisp December's day
that wakens every spirit
from its dark and dreary plight.
Impaled across the pregnant sky
the naked trees are stirring,
yearning for the newborn fleece!
Anticipation flourishes
as spritely evergreens and firs
shake free their noble boughs and
    tremble
waiting to be dressed and groomed
in winter's finest hour . . .

A mother's rosy cheeks
are puckered from the icy cold
as toddlers scurry off to bed
in quest of midnight fantasies!
Outside the evening settles in
so peacefully;
Along the shrouded avenue
where houses seem to kneel and
    pray
a solitary lantern gleams
and flickers with a certain hope

that shepherds witnessed many
    nights ago
when miracles and gifts were rare.

B. Moore
UNTITLED
Where are words to express just
    how I'm feeling?
Deep seated emotions
A tiny spark of life inside that
    asks simply to be allowed to
    nurture and grow
But this is not the time in my life
    where I have the decision to
    continue on as I am
I must not
I cannot let that tiny spark
    become a flame
I fear either choice—I shall be
    consumed
Dual decision
    Do not go ahead
Instead, be strong
    listen to the mind, not the heart
Think ahead
Look down the road
The time will be right then
Just for now
So unprepared
Sad
I must be strong
    for someday
        when the moon is full
        and the sun rises to a
        beautiful new day
Then, I will be back and we will
    be happy and pleased
And once again the tiny spark
    will begin and will grow and
    consume me with a warmth so
    complete
My life will have just begun.

Donna Hardin
CANDLE LIGHT
The soft glow of candle light
    filling an empty room.
The flicker of it's fire so gentle
    yet surrounded by gloom.
The mood it produces
    so tender and warm.
What a shame it's wasted
    on one single form.

Karen Greklek
DEATH OF INNOCENCE
The degradation of my flesh
by a body
who had been to
another's secret places
now seems a meager affair.
Once,
I let a man rape
my soul.
And there is a strange
woman sleeping
in my bed.

Marjorie Hambrick
MY TASK
My task is unfinished 'till
In spring my heart goes still,
To another spring on a lonely hill
Where Christ paid my redeeming
    bill.

Three men were sentenced to die
Two were criminals, but Christ,
    oh why
Were you on a cross pointing to
    the sky?
Was it I who said to crucify?

Am I content to join the crowd
And sing HIS deathly chorus loud?
Or will I pray with my head bowed
"THY spirit come to me endowed".

Had such ever died before?
Forgive oh Thou, whom we adore,
Lead us to Thy kingly shore
There to live forever more.

Mary Ann Christe'
TO CAPTURE A CHILD
To capture a child
Aglow with a smile
Be sure not to waste
The fleeting sign upon his face
Look into his eyes
The moment he is caught in
    surprise
Search beneath
Probe the inner core's outreach
In the soul
Leading a child's self-control
Making it known
By the very smile shown
A contrite spirit and humble heart
Is the mark of a *SUPERSTAR* set
    apart!

W. Scott Muller
FOR KATHY
Fate has had a start,
And destiny will play its part;
In this dream, within
The mind where everything begins.
Knowing a person
Just by looking in her eye;
Remembering the past,
When they met before they died.
For why did one not come,
While the other was just about done;
And forbearing the past,
Just trying to make the future last.
Dark hair, dark eyes
Spanning the gap of time;
Beauty within, beauty without,
God has perfected mankind.
Pushing to the edge,
With death within an inch;
Triumph, there to try
Where others won't survive.
Waiting for Monday
When I see you again;
Living through Friday,
Will I see you again?

Freda E. Rockwell
YOU HAVEN'T LIVED
*[In Memory of my Father who
taught me what it means to
live and love.]*
You can't have loved as I have
    loved
And not be grateful for two souls
Touching in complete happiness.

And you can't have cried as I
    have cried,
And not feel the complete
    emptiness in your soul
That comes with the loss of that
    love.

And you haven't lived,
Until you have experienced both.

William G. Maddox
THE ROSE
[To Robert]
A rose is a rose is a rose
How is it such an absurd
    statement ever arose?
To make such a claim it must be
    supposed

That a rose is, and if that be so
How, why, and what *is* a rose?
A rose is an "essence" I heard
    someone say
That reflects an ideal that exists
    beyond space
No, that's not so I heard another
    refute
A rose is *in* space and governed
    by laws
Seen through effects and moved
    by a cause
You are both wrong a third
    person spoke
Existence, the "is" is what matters
    most
The last person spoke with a
    quivering voice
God made the rose, there's no
    other choice

All this wisdom but no answer to
    discern
And hot within me my question
    still burns.

Dolores Q. Canapi
JOHN'S NIGHT IN COURT
John, to court was hauled,
Where he shamelessly bawled;
When on a park stroll one
    moonlit night,
With Jane, he got out of sight;
Charged with Inordinate Sense
    Appetite.
"Never heard, Your Honor!" John
    was quick to cite.
"Gift of Original Justice" came a
    whisper from right;
But drowned by a "Blah!" uproar
    from left, to incite.
"Free will, John, you're no
    proselyte,"
Was a reminder by a Lady in
    White;
But a smirking Jane at the
    witness stand
With a flashy cop's badge began a
    reprimand.
"Was trapped!" was John's
    murmur in disgust.
The Judge, perhaps, too, a John of
    lust
Announced: "Entrappment. Not
    Guilty. Case Dismissed."
John's glee was brief, as he
    unleashed
"Lord, I pray thee, deliver me . . ."
In darkness and boundlessness
    'twas much too late to see
Fallen Archangel's pit of flames!
    to hell must be!
In belabored breath, John could
    only scream—
"Thank God 'twas but a dream!"

Mary L. DiRienzo
IN THE END
In The End,
Everyone will have experienced
    the joys and pains of life.
Suffering will be a word familiar
    to all
Even the naive and innocent will
    have heard of it.

In the End,
Happiness will be treasured in
    place of gold
And the never ending cycle of
    emotions will be fulfilled.
Man will realize his priorities.

In The End,
Those who are impatient will be
    made to wait.
It will be poetic justice.

Sharon Gardner
TURNING
It begins.
The old tired feeling
Of being held back
From loving.

Struggle on.
Where are you,
Conversation?
Silence. Be still.

Memory,
Touch my hand,
Stroke my hair.
Now go away.

William Joseph Laurin
ADVERTISEMENT
Yes this is a poem, but it's an
    advertisement too.
    Of course I payed thirty dollars
    for it, but I was pleased to do.
Being a young writer in this
    world of truth and fate,
    I have published a book of
    poems selling at an honest rate.
It is called *NONE THE BABOON*,
    and it has alot to tell.
    But it cannot do a thing unless
    it has a chance to sell.
So to you my pen pal poets, I offer
    up my say,
    something all of us so struggle
    for, while others refuse to pay.
My company is called Badge
    Press, P.O. Box 598.
    With a 19105, Philadelphia, PA.
The book is just $5.95, with
    thirty-six rhyming pieces.
    And I hope it does a world of
    good for everyone it reaches.
The book is sort of a concept, it
    is honest, rebellious, and warm.
    And like my poem, *ASH AND
    MEMORY*, it cannot do no harm.
If you do not consider what I say
    to convince you well enough.
    You can write for more
    information, using the address
    given above.
So I thank you World of Poetry
    for allowing me this speech.
    Advertising costs an arm and a
    leg, and I only have two of each.
A word before I go, from a twenty
    year old turk,
    I wish to be a wealthy writer,
    not a poor mail clerk.

Ann Valencoure
RIVER OF LIFE
Life is like a river
That flows into the sea,
It gathers from it's very source
The things that are to be.

Stones that slow its progress
Weeds, a dam, a wall,
First it's on the highest peak
Then suddenly the falls.

Rapids with their jagged rocks
Will tear and twist and churn,
Still defiant it rolls on
While life within it burns.

Stagnant reeds will beckon
With promises untold

Still on and on you travel
To reach your chosen goal.

River turbulent, then calm
Whisper your strength to me,
That I, like you, can find a way
To reach, the open Sea.

Georgette E. Piper
MARDI GRAS
Some leave their hearts in San
    Francisco,
I left mine in New Orleans,
Where streets were crowded with
    big parades
Of beautiful Kings and Queens.

There everyone can became a child
With enthusiasm blest,
As in the air is joy and laughter,
And life is then full of zest.

I'd love to hear that familiar shout,
"Hey, throw me something, Mister,"
Then jumping high just to catch
    a "throw"
With, "That's my dubloon, sister."

Ah, Mardi Gras, I long to see you,
Feel again your thrill divine
That once more sends me soaring
    skyward,
Gently riding on Cloud Nine.

G. Bob Cobb
SOMEONE TO CARE
*[To Kathleen whom without
her Support, Life at Times
would Be Impossible And To
Joey & David]*
In A world of Bewilderment And
    Confusion.
In this world of loneliness.
Has Life Become an Illusion.
Where can you find happiness.
In this world filled with despair.
If life were to end tomorrow
Where would you find someone
    to care.
Who would share the grief &
    sorrow.

Sharon Daley
I REMEMBER
*[To Mom and Dad with love
and thanks]*
I remember Christmas eve, bright
    lights and autumn leaves.
    Puppy dogs and cats with fleas.
    I remember presents, round the
    Christmas tree, warm fires and
    music playing, children
    laughing, grownups singing.
    And I remember piles of leaves,
    jumping in and skinning knees.
    I remember soft white
    Christmas snow, faces all
    aglow, love always showed.
    And I remember ice skates,
    sliding down hills, climbing
    trees and ripping my brand new
    jeans. I remember animals,
    guitar lessons and log house
    blues. And I remember you.

I remember fishing from a boat,
    catching turtles and taking
    votes, and the walks we used to
    take. And I remember good
    times, sweet dreams and
    lullabies. I remember home and
    fun, lots of love for everyone. I
    wish I was there again. I
    remember hmework due,
    babysitters and I.O.U.s.

Today's Greatest Poems

I remember Halloween nights,
special frights, and big size
bites of candy apples. And I
remember carnivals, circus
clowns, and balloons. I
remember trips to the zoo, the
big baboon and I remember you.

I remember pictures takin',
memory makin', flowers
waking from the dew. I
remember everyone, which
team won, and all the fun. I
remember kindergarten, Santa's
coming, stockings hung. I
remember sunny days, grassy
hills and white fluffy clouds. I
remember make believe,
special dreams, and secrets that
we shared. I remember special
days, the warmth of the sun
and love.

I remember hayrides, bike rides,
apple cider and hating spiders. I
remember Beatle's songs, the
nights were long, but it's all
gone. I remember Christmas
day, fun in May, all was gay. I
remember family ties, long
goodbyes and fireflies. I
remember sad times, fights we
had and the laughs we shared. I
remember going home, finding
dinosaur bones and asking for
loans. I remember make
believe, special dreams and
autumn leaves. I remember
special days, warm sunny haze,
and your special gaze. I
remember the fun we had and
the love we shared. Mom and
Dad I'll always remember you.
Yes, I'll always remember you.

Edmund J. Carlow
WINTER'S SONG
The wind was strong
It whipped at the wires
It whistled a song
Of cold nights and fires.

Of nights when the ground
Was windswept and bare
And cold thoughts of winter
Flew through the air.

It called back the days
Of our youth and our splendor
When love was our warmth
Through the cold weeks of winter.

And the light in your eyes
With which I was caught
It told me to enter
T'was the signal I sought.

And with this first flicker
Which grew to a flame
Our souls were soon branded
With love's famous name.

Katherina M. Gascoigne
THE CHRIST CHILD
We hear of a rough made stable
where the dear Christ child lay,
In a crib that was lined so tenderly
With stocks of sweet smelling hay.

The Herald angels singing
Of a babe just newly born,
A day the world will remember.
A still, and glorious morn.

Mary and Joseph were chosen
The parents of the Babe to be.

But the cattle around were lowing
In great humility.

Noel, Noel is our symbol
Of the birthday of our King.
"Peace on earth, goodwill to men"
Within our hearts we sing.

May the manger stay much closer
And the Bethlehem star more
bright.
As we remember the wonderous
story
Of the miracle born that night.

Jane Richards
FOREVER LOVE
Plant a seed of Love
in a tiny heart
To see a flower grow.

A seed of hate
in the same tiny heart
May grow a thorn, we know.

As there they grow,
and are entwined,
Someone comes to clear the way.

It will be;
as in the past,
The flower that will stay.

Charlotte Malone
OH POND
Your waters shimmer like jewels;
many have you caressed in
your loving embrace
The depth of which is so
sublimely and invitingly cool
Oh Pond, you call to me now so
tantalizingly blue
And without hesitation I
surrender myself completely to
you

Deanna Decker
LOVERS
When the fire burns bright,
On a moonlit night,
Lovers are out,
Eyes shining bright
In anticipation of things to come,
Or in gratification,
Of what's already done.

A child is born on a starry night,
Crying lustily, full of life,
The beauty born of innocence,
Appeals to the sight,
A child conceived on a moonlit
night.

Kathy L. Douglas
MY LOVING MOTHER
I love my mother
She is so kind,
Even when she's
in a bind.

She shows me know
to sit and knit,
Even when she's in a fit.

If I get
into a fight,
She always shows me
What is right.

She surely tells me
the right from the wrong
and that is good
Cause I'm usually gone.

She washes my clothes,
And buys my hose,
Mom cleans the house
And sometimes sews.

She cares so much
And loves us such
She is always glowing,
And never stops going.

She is so understanding,
And never demanding,
But best of all
She loves us All . . .

Roxanne E. Meszaros
TOGETHER
Together, two heartbeats,
Together we are at last,
Alone we are one,
And our life goes oh, so fast.

There will never be another,
That will fill my heart like you,
Your eyes are so much kinder,
And soft as the morning dew.

Walking now together,
In the wilderness that surrounds,
We depend upon each other,
To count the pleasant rounds.

Together we can make it,
We can get along just fine,
Nobody can tell us different,
We're a natural golden find.

Take me with you through your
life,
I need your loving arms,
To take the trip of independence,
To protect me from life's harms.

Together we are peace and love,
Alone we are none,
We, together, have each other,
Together we are one.

Leslie-Ann Pringle
TAILWINDS
I sit here
body numbly aching
I've cycled 100 plus miles today.
Tailwinds pushing me,
Headwinds stopping me,
Tailwinds, Headwinds,
Take the good with the bad
Tailwinds
Sail Wing on Wing

Marlene Schmidt
UTOPIA OF MAN
Commercial
Cheapness
Concrete

Hate and Greed

Where is the grass?
Where is the sky?
Where are the people?
Or are they lying in the gutter
of civilization.

Clyde M. Zwicker (Robin Duane)
BETH
I'll always treasure the night
You came into my life
I was so lonely standing there
You showed me that someone did
care

I'm thinking about you all the time
I'm gonna try hard to make you
mine
When the time is right, I'll hold
you so tight
And whisper that everything is
alright

From the morning, noon till night
I want to hold you tenderly, yet
tight

I want to hold you, kiss and
caress you
And keep saying to you, I love you

You mean more to me than I can
say
And I'll love you true both night
and day

I dream of you cause I'm falling in
love
I'm happy to say, it's you I love

I hope about me you feel the same
And our life together will be
without any pain

Beth, my love, I'm glad you are
mine
And together we will be, till the
end of time

I need you now to make my life
complete
The taste of your lips, there's
nothing as sweet

Please hold my hands, say what I
want to hear
I'll stay with you forever, Beth,
my dear.

Stephanie Nahirniak
MY CHRISTMAS PRAYER
Oh, Jesus shed Thy tender love,
Upon us all to-day,
On this Your birthday give us
grace
Our special prayer to say.

Dear God please stop our
children
From the sinful way they are
going.
And forgive them all the sinful
past.
For they know not what they are
doing.

Make them get back to-gether,
As husband and wife should be.
So this New Year they do have a
new start,
And from all past sins be free.

That we may be Your children,
And have You for our guide.
That we may all live on in peace
And love in us abide.

Grant to all Your children
Visions bright of Thee,
Send angels to watch and lead
them
And from harm keep them free.

So, bless us with Thy blessing
Lord,
All that has been amiss forgive,
Help us to feed upon Thy word,
And let Thy truth within us live.

Ruby Margaret Partridge
Fathers' Day At Our House
Our handsome Bon Vivant is King!
On Fathers' Day, at our house.
He doesn't have to do a thing!
On Fathers' Day, at our house.
We bring his slippers, pipe and'
news',
Dispell, with smiles, his
office-blues,
Prepare his steak and shine his
shoes
On Fathers' Day, at our house.

The garden is his prize domain
On Fathers' Day, at our house.
No cloudy skies or threat of rain
On Fathers' Day, at our house.

483

As "moonshine" overflows his cup,
We loyal slaves don't interrupt,
But pray like mad he'll sober up!
On Fathers' Day, at our house!!

D.E. Fransen
TENNIS COURT
Tennis Court.
(i.e. nostalgia).
18 yr. old tears
pumped/
　　　irrigated/
　　　　　urinated
upon
Love/
　Set/
　　Game
BECAUSE . . .
a Knowing partner
craddled me so
　　　as to
strangle away
doubts/
　　aweful ogres
& ALL self-deprecation.
(i.e. hyper-ventilation).

Jose Zakus
WILD GEESE
Wild geese calling
Beating the skies,
High over swamps
With rushes wild;
Bleak still waters
Darkened below,
Wild geese winging
On their way south
Great expectations
For days to come,
The Northern Summer
A memory now.
Strong Sun and showers
Marshes and coves,
Wild geese calling
The good life has passed.

Mrs. Mary Tanco
FALLING LEAVES
Leaves, leaves, everywhere
They don't seem to have a care,
They flutter ever so softly in the
breeze
And if anyone has an allergy, it
might cause them to sneeze.

The leaves come in so many
colors
Specially at this time of year.
It makes everything look so
pretty
Whether you live in the country
or city.

But after all the leaves are down
You truly have to wear a frown.
There is so much raking to do
You just finish and have to start
anew.

Specially when a heavy wind
comes along
That's when you have to sing a
song.
It's a sign that winter's near
When the children begin to cheer.

The mornings are heavy with a
frost
And all the leaves are lost.
As the first fall of snow begins to
fly
It seems as if it is very shy.

But as it gathers strength

The days seem to have extra
length.
Then everything is at a standstill
As you ward off the winter's chill.

Jean B. Byers
IT MIGHT HAVE BEEN
*[To my three granddaughters
Stephanie Brenda and Angela.]*
It might have been that skies
would stay blue,
Instead of the clouds when they
shut out their hues.
It might have been that birds ever
would fly,
To soar to their haven right up to
the sky.
Ere an arrow would pierce them
and the broken wing
Would bring them down to earth
no nevermore to sing.
It might have been there'd be no
more wars,
No more death no more
anguish and cannons cease to
roar,
Where the earth would not hold
so much precious blood,
And the brain that God gave
them all crushed in the mud.
While roses delightfully ever
would bloom
Around doorways and fences and
never 'round tombs,
For the roses will bloom along
with the thorns
As we walk life's dull pathway so
sad and forlorn.
The drooping head of the broken
heart
Whose feet grow so weary
groping round in the dark
Waiting and longing for a smile
of a friend.
To comfort and cheer them as
onwards they wend.
It might have been there'd be no
blind eyes
To walk in the darkness as others
pass by.
That if they could see what a joy
to behold,
For even weeds by the wayside
would to them seem as gold.
The maimed, the halt the
stooped, and the blind,
We'll have in this world other
sorrows to find.
And as we walk slowly along
life's highway
These words echo softly as sadly
they say,
Of all things written of tongues
and of pen.
The saddest are these it might
have been.

Mrs. Leah Baker
OUR 50TH ANNIVERSARY
On our 50th anniversary
We got a grand surprise
When our sons, their wives and
families
Came with cookies, cakes and
pies.

They brought salads, meats and
goodies
Graced our table with the same
We sure had a grand reunion
Who could ask for better fame.

We had drinks and all the good
things
That our happy hearts desired
Lots of fun and love and laughter
Gifts and greetings we admired.

Then they took a lot of pictures
With our grandchildren and all,
When developed they were lovely
What a blessing for us all.

We can now look to the future
With fond memories of the past
And our 50th anniversary
Come and gone but long will last.

Janet Malinarich
MY CANVAS
*[For my parents, whose love
and support has started me in
the right direction.]*
Growing up isn't always easy.
Oh, sure—
When you're young,
And full of hopes and dreams
For the future,
And everything is handed to you
on a silver platter,
Things seem to be
"Picture" perfect.
The growing up part, comes in,
When you realize you're only
given
A frame, for starters;
And the picture must be drawn
in—
But by bit.

Lilian de Jong
WHY?
*[To Debbie in thanks for all her
help and caring.]*
Is it—or isn't it
What is it—where
What is the answer
Who am I—where
I'm sorry, I didn't hear you
Or are you there.

Questions and answers
Truths and unknowns
Why does it happen
Why isn't it known
Where does it come from
This silent unknown

Someday—somewhere—sometime
Hope
Now it is there, now it is gone.
Silence.

Vern Sawatzky
POETRY CLASS
*[For Marcia—a different voice
. . . a different wilderness . . .]*
What is poetry?
End rhyme?
Rhythm?
Serious thought in short phrases
Of metaphor
And lyrical dance?
Or the heart of man
In swirls of ink?

The teacher,
Young with flaming hair,
Said with her mouth and fist:
"Poetry is deep—
Artesian wells in deserts!
Verse is cheap and shallow—
And shallowness only leads
Into thirsting and despair."

Deepness, I thought,
Usually extends

Out from the shallow,
But there are shallows
Rising from the deep
And pockets of deep
In the shallows.
There comes a season
When one must let
The meadow of ideals
Lie fallow.

Genevieve McMitchell
MY SON
Thirty-three years ago you saw
the first light of day.
Four pounds fifteen ounces is
what you did weigh.
The years rolled by and you
stayed so small,
I began to think you'd never grow
tall.
And then one day, you weren't
small anymore.
That's when your head scraped
the top of the door.
You've grown so big, so tall and
wide,
But that little boy, is still inside.
When life gets dreary, and things
go wrong,
There's someone I know, will still
be strong.
As I've travelled along life's
bumpy road,
You've always shared, my heavy
load.
I've never told you what gives me
pleasure.
And that you are the one above
all else, I treasure.

Edna Golem
IN FLANDERS 1979
Between the markers row on row
In Flanders Fields, no poppies
grow,
But verdant grass, like carpet
mown,
And garden flowers by each
stone.

With careful hands the work is
done,
As though each was a well-loved
son
Who lay within that hallowed
sod.
Some stones proclaim "Known to
God".

And as we walked and pondered
some
The price they paid for our
freedom,
Our prayers arose to the Prince of
Peace:
"Cause wars throughout the
world to cease".

Kelly Irene Carney
FOR THE LADIES . . .
You sneak in from the P.T.A
meeting.
The door only clicks: to you it is
deafening.
The blaring T.V. in the
background—
Slowly, you creep into the
kitchen;
You didn't anticipate the
commerical,
Did You?
He staggers out to the kitchen for
another beer.

You stand motionless; waiting,
  praying.
"BITCH", he screams. "Where the
  hell were you?"
Don't reply—you know it makes
  him livid.
The hand flashes up and the
  mark on your cheek
is now a red welt.
"SLUT!" "WHORE!"
Lip split, you crawl up the stairs,
and into your conjugal bed,
The haven of love.
Your throbbing head sinks to the
  pillow.
You know nothing different.
Last time it was eleven stitches,
  wasn't it?
You couldn't possibly leave him.
You have one last chance.
And you take his razor,
And slit your bruised wrists.s.

Linda Padalec
ADOLESCENCE
Adolescence . . .
It's a time of pain and confusion,
A time that every one of us has
  had to face.
Some of us were not prepared for
  those changes.
Even more of us felt that this was
  the lonliest time of life.
So much to think about: religion,
  family, loyalties, changes.
It's at times like this it's best to
  have a trustworthy friend who
  understands you,
But more importantly, knows
  exactly what you're going
  through.
You spend hours by yourself just
  thinking.
Responsibilities pile up around
  you like never before.
After it's all over, you suddenly
  have a different perspective on
  life.
It's a lonely time, adolescence. I
  know.

Margaret Bland Sewell
GYPSY SOUL
I wear a dress of Quaker grey
To hide my flaming gypsy soul
I daily go my quiet way
And wear a dress of Quaker grey.

O'er wide, wild fields I long to
  stray,
Scarlet-clad in a wanderer's role,
But I wear a dress of Quaker grey
To hide my flaming gypsy soul.

Barry A. Hobson
THANK-YOU
The days grow longer now it
  seems,
These times away from you,
The empty nights and empty
  dreams
Making memories see me through.

I've seen this world in many ways,
Keeping both eyes open wide,
And I've stumbled on from day to
  day
Needing you to be my guide.

I don't know how I managed
Before you came along,
For I feel I cannot last the day
Whenever you are gone.

So I'll take this time to thank-you,
For all you've been to me,
And hope around each corner,
It's your eyes that I'll see.

Audrey L. Bernakevitch
A Banker's Romanticisms
A silver dollar hangs in the sky,
Heads up.
Coinage undetermined.
Atop a pile of nickles and dimes.
A scattered heap of treasures,
Safe in the vaults of Heaven.

Joan Graham
Tomorrow Never Comes
I dream today,
  For yesterday is gone;
I smile today,
  For my friends to know
    I am strong.

I laugh today,
  For there is no time to cry;
I talk today,
  For soon I shall have to
    say good-bye.

I love today,
  For it is everything I am;
I care today,
  For those who don't really
    give a damn.

I shine today,
  For I have had my suns;
I live today,
  For tomorrow never comes.

Kelley Irwin
Nothing But a Stranger
I walked beside you,
Let you hold me,
Yet, I'm nothing but a stranger.
You think of a lost love,
I'm only here to pass the time,
'Til you are happy again,
You have no feelings for me,
My heart cries out for you,
Tears are shed each night,
As my pain grows,
I'm nothing but a stranger.
I'm only a toy,
You break me each day,
As you wait for a dream,
That will never come true,
But, until you realize love has
  gone,
I remain, nothing but a stranger.

Louise-Anne Gagne Chuhie
THE MADAWASKA
[Dedicated to the memory of
my parents, Bertha and Philip
Gagne, who raised seven
children and who fully-
understood the "moment of
beginning again".]
Behold! I see a river beyond me.
Ah! So calm, clear and beautiful.
Many times have I gazed at you
With anticipation, grief and joy.
To me, you symbolize hope
For the future God has for me.
For your cool waters flow towards
  its horizon
Your horizon of eternal sky and
  hills;
Such is my horizon also—
  Unknown today but present
    tomorrow.
  God knows and I perceive.
  God beckons and I draw near.
  God questions and I reply.
  God loves and I receive.

Thanks, O river of God, for your
  cool, calm presence
Your everlastingness, your beauty
Calm me, revive me, urge me on
  to our God.
Together we understand the
  "moment of beginning again":
You in your incessant flowing
  and I in my living.
Together we possess and enjoy
  our lives.
Because God has deigned it to be
  so. Alleluia!

Kristie Schihl
YESTERDAY
Long ago when I was young,
I used to watch the rising sun.
But nowadays I cannot see
The sun nor can he see me,
For the streets are so filled with
  smog,
It's like looking into a muddy
  bog.

Oh! If I could only have those
  days,
Which people now call yesterday,
I wouldn't be looking at the smog,
Nor even trying to see through
  the fog,
But watching the precious sun go
  down,
As the world turns around.

Robert W. Staunton
THIS IS FOR ME
[To Beverly, my wife, and for all
other women that yearn for the
freedom to express themselves
for themselves.]
There isn't much that I can say,
  Which holds the night and
  stills the day.
There isn't much which one can
  do,
  When there isn't love from me
  to you.
When there is nothing more, not
  even a feeling,
  And you say to yourself, no
  feeling,
    no feeling.

Please let him know that I have
  gone,
  To where the neather mists do
  spawn.
To look for greater opportunity,
  Which I can grasp and hold on
  tight,
This then, is for me,
    just for me.

Deborah Turner
CALIFORNIA
It's a peculiar sun whose flame
  has lit this morning
In its flood, the palm casts a tall
  shadow
The oil stained street shows off
  its new finery of leaves
The old car is washed with bright
The dirt sparkles as if sifted
  evenly with small yet shiny
  gems
The billboard is painted anew
Each passing face aglow, with
  smile and squinting eyes
Each lawn, a million blades of
  grass
Luminescent green, and reaching
  upward towards cloudless blue

It's a peculiar sun this morning,
  with strongest ray
Luxuriant so in its energy, to
  have purified a day.

Dwayne Beverly Howard
SORRY
I'm sorry it had to end this way.
  I have no one to blame but
  myself,
    my self, I could no longer bear.
Now I have new direction to my
  life.
  I am wiser, more aware.
I'm sorry it ended that way.
  The way it was before.
    I'm sorry it ended that way
    . . . please need I say more.

Fern Roche
ONE DAY AT A TIME
If you have many troubles under
  your skin,
And you wonder how on earth
  you can win.
    Take one day at a time.
If you have lost your spouse of
  many years,
A family to raise, do not seek
  relief in tears.
    Take one day at a time.
If you feel you need help just to
  survive,
Talk to God, and help your faith
  to revive.
    Take one day at a time.
If you feel you are forsaken
  without a doubt,
Do not waste your time in self
  pity and pout.
    Take one day at a time.
And soon you will overcome all
  your troubles,
They disappear like little
  bursting bubbles.
    By taking one day at a time.

Michael A. Pierce
RAIN
The rain pours down,
Making strange sounds;
It cleans out the air,
Washes smog from our hair.

Why is it that nature,
Not liked much by man,
Will make the air pure,
Like no man—can?

Paul Spencer
THE RESTLESS ONES
We were the restless ones;
We were the rolling stones
That seldom gathered moss.
Over the trackless sea we came,
And found a new world waiting.
We drove our wagons to the base
Of the mighty Appalachians.
And there we paused to gather
  moss,
And build a new-born nation.

Then on we poured where eagles
  soared,
And the buffalo we found there.
We traded dreams; we forded
  streams,
And many of us drowned there.

With gun and knife we took the
  life
Of the Indian braves who found
  us.
We panned for gold; then

on we rolled
Through mountains that
surround us.

We blazed the tortuous Oregon
Trail,
And reached the shining ocean.

Our graves are watered by the
rain,
And wind will always blow there;
Our bodies fertilized the plain,
And surely moss will grow there.

V.V. Hudson
RICHARD
Where has the time gone, Richard?
You were so full of love
and so in desire of its return.
Always smiling—that was you
but I could see you crying
inside, Richard.
you carried with you so much
want.
You could write poetry so freely
as easy as a baby could cry.
Richard, I know . . . poetry
was your tears.
You wrote a poem about me once
and I cherished it
and said I would keep it forever.
But now it is gone—I wish I knew
where.
But mostly I wish I could find
you
and give this one to you.
If ever you should read this poem
in a dream book I should ever
publish,
then, know it is for you.
Where has the time gone?
Richard?
Where have you gone?

Pamela Jay
THE STRUGGLE
a sweet, soft and silky Rose . . .
outside in my yard it blooms,
and continues to live through the
storms,
amidst the garden ruins.

its will to live amazes me.
it grows taller with each rain.
no weather could change its
beauty.
it always looks the same.

a lesson is surely to be learned . . .
that this immortal Rose can give:
one breath of life is always spared
in he who wills to live.

Joan (Hibbard) Merola
**The Bicentennial Youth
War**
The Battlefield:—Our school
grounds
The Enemy:—Our teachers
The Ammunition:—Kids acting
(like a bunch
of uncivilized creatures).

We thought the opposition would
quit and
set us free,
But, like soldiers, they manned
their stations
Until somehow, we heard their
plea.

Our retreat was slow and
reluctant;
We just couldn't lose the war;
But the forces against us were
massive,

For they used the power of law.
The Schoolgrounds:—were
policed with
authority
The Teachers:—now sensed our
plight
And We:—the victims of an era,
settled
down to do what was right.

We've since left this institution
to go our
separate ways;
With knowledge to provide the
next generation,
With facts from our troubled days.

Act now, in your youth, to better
tomorrow;
Only then will the world be yours;
To pass on to the next generation
A free place to live—without wars.

Wallace M. Mosher
FOOLS POEM
Laughing, flashing, spit and brittle
Life is funny, drooling spittle.
Loomes bloom and laughters one,
Silent persons we've become.
Junk! you cry,
Silly fool.
Ah! say I,
At least I drool.
It's not the laugh, it's not the pain,
It's the willingness to let go
That seals the vein.

Donna Lee DeMarco (DLD)
Lost Within My Solitude
Lost within my solitude
    drowning in the tears
    is this just a prelude
    to all the coming years.

Lost within my sadness
    struggling with the fear
    trying to deal with this madness
    trying to make it all come clear.

Lost within my four walls
    hiding in the dreams
    all the smiles have been false
    all the poems are only screams.

Lost within my sorrow
    fighting against the strain
    trying to live 'til tomorrow
    surrendering to the pain.

Helena M. Ohmen
**My Story Of Your
Beginning**
[To my son, David Glen, who
has brought such joy to my life;
and my husband Fred, who
gives me strength and courage
for new adventures.]
Come and sit by my side,
    and I'll tell you a story.
When I speak of your birth,
    I'm in all my glory.

You were loved from the start,
    and I carried you with pride.
I was so protective of you,
    as you blossomed inside.

I loved your every movement,
    even when you kicked so hard.
Just like a football player,
    running the last yard.

And as the days grew nearer,
    my excitement seemed to burst.
I knew it wouldn't be long now,
    and I would deliver my first.

When the time came that we had
to go,
    It was a rainy day.
The pains were hardly even there,
    we laughed as we drove away.

Your Dad and I waited patiently,
    as you slowly entered the world.
We watched with much
excitement,
    as your body slowly uncurled.

Your eyes were blue and very
bright,
    your fingers were so small.
Your Daddy held you tightly,
    so he wouldn't let you fall.

Mommy held you close to her,
    and kissed your tiny cheek.
You slowly closed your eyes again,
    then took another peek.

I realized just that moment,
    when you lay looking at me.
How much I truly love you,
    and what a joy you'll always be.

D'Anthony Orsatti
SURVIVORS
[Dedicated to: Mom, Dad &
Jeano]
The decade of the Sixties
Became ten years of strife;
Beatniks became hippies
Turning on to drugs and life.

The Vietnam War had taken its
toll
And passive was in power;
We all thought the one way out
Was Peace, Love and the Flower.

Messages erupted foremost
By Music, Art and Sculpture;
Turned out to be a masquerade
For frustration in our culture.

Today those years are beyond us
now
The times have left us owing;
Optimism, Faith and Hope
Are the things that keep us going.

Twenty years have passed and we
survived
Together as a Nation;
What lies ahead may soon forecast
The Demise of Civilization.

Joseph D. Benjamin
DRIVER'S LAMENT
[To my wife, Lou Ann, who
encourages me in all my
endeavors.]
It's the evening rush.
Cars creep haltingly down city
streets,
    bumper to bumper, honking
    polluting.
The sky is already graying.
The once clear glass of the street
lamps
    begin to illuminate the
    environment.

Drivers, already weary from a
hard day's work,
    angrily start muttering to
    themselves.
Thirty minutes have elapsed.
They are no closer to their abode.

Time passes for what seems an
eternity.
Muttering leads into swearing.
The odor of sweat and fumes

begins to permeate the nostrils.
An hour has transpired, the
lamps grow brighter.
The ride is nearing its end.

Patience shot, nerves on edge,
    drivers reach home exhausted.
While picking on wives' heated
up dinners,
    they check out the local
    evening edition.
Their minds already
contemplating
    their early morning capers.

Marianne Carpender
OLD LOVERS
[Beyond the myths and the
dreams, Through all the joy and
pain, Forever, Joseph, is my
love for you.]
Lovers, dreamed amongst sand
castles,
Never seem to keep their majesty.
Seemingly losing their strength
With every drop from the raging
sea.

But it's not the raging sea
That batters down the walls,
Just a continual pattern of waves—
That do matter, after all.
And one day, the castles are gone,
Though so slowly they died:
Washed away by the calmer sea
Than the raging tears I've cried.

Jo Anne M. Syron
CONTENTMENT
I am not rich in some folks' eyes
For things I own are few
But I am rich beyond compare
I have my children, I do.
I have a house
To cover my head,
A job, some food,
A nice warm bed.
All these I have
And friendships too.
I'm blessed with wealth—a
    special kind
I wouldn't trade with you.

Jayne K. Basye
NO TITLE 1
Fragrant roses
dying on the edges,
turn the brown
of aged and wilted beauty.

Petals deep within
holding tight to life,
bring silently forth—
velvet shades of red.

Craig D. Weiner
GOD'S REAL WORLD
[To my entire family, for their
never ending encouragement
and support.]
There are times I can't restrain
myself
when the mighty forest beckons,
to spend some time in God's real
world
where hours pass like seconds.

The trees are all mute counselors
the bushes silent friends,
beneath their strong, uplifted arms
my mortal soul ascends.

A timberland emits a peace
that oh, so few can capture,
but those who care to take the
time

can lose themselves in rapture.

There are those who say they
    hate the trees
they just can't understand,
the beauty of the simple things
found in an untamed land.

There's a magic in a living woods
that overcomes all sorrow;
where the only thing that's left to
    fear
is that it won't be here
    tomorrow . . .

Virginia M. Griswold
REALITY
The three blind men
of Hindu fame,
saw the elephant with different
    eyes.
The eyes of their eyes—
their fingertips,
told them what the truth belies.
So it is with life,
we look, but we all
see the same thing a thousand
    ways.
No matter how big,
no matter how small—
it's one of the games, life plays.

Life is just a mirage,
a fantasy—
it isn't the way that it seems.
It isn't really much
different at all—
then it is in our nocturnal dreams.
The trick is to know
the difference,
between what's real, and what's
    not.
But of this I am sure,
that reality,
is the difference between—what?

Ray M. Kellogg, M.D.
MAN'S DAY
[Dedicated to My Father:
Harold Edward Kellogg, M.D.]
If we in figure make Man's birth
    date the Dawn of life
And assign to childhood early
    Morning's hours with rosy hue
Then adolescence' blossom-time
    bursts forth at
    mid-morning—rife
As the sun arcs well up in a sky
    of blue.

Morning's later hours bespeak
    the careless rapture and the
    verve of youth
For youth is strong, sometimes
    callow,
Rarely meek or patient in the
    always lonely search for truth.
But stay—maturity all too soon
    must follow

Because Man's prime comes
    somewhat before the zenith of
    the Noon
With ripened strength and full
    powers
Endowing their possessor with
    joys uncounted—Nature's boon,
As comes fruit after buds and
    flowers.

The longer Afternoon denotes
    declining strength
Carnal joys fade away almost
    imperceptibly
As the shadows of later day grow

rapidly in length
And Man is often gripped by
    varied incapacity.

Evening's hours should provide
    repose for reminiscing,
Time to treasure old friends and
    faces
Before they join the missing—
Time perhaps to visit in fact or
    fancy far-off places to learn to
    know strange lands and other
    races.

All's well:
Let Man's compensation be a
    perspective of the years;
Let it breed a warm philosophy
    despite some tears.
Perhaps there'll be some certain
    progeny to carry on his name
    and race
To satisfy Man's deepest longing
    for *Continuity* and grace.
If he but know that the big things
    in his life for him were mostly
    right,
Then softly, softly falls the Night.

Raymond D. Christensen
INNOVATORS
Although the whole concept
    Is not perfectly clear
The challenges of life
    Require innovators.

With the good and the bad
    Of wherever life leans
Someone improves something
    Without devious means.

And we awaken from sleeping
    To a new world outside
With another way to succeed
    Where others only tried.

Karla Ann Monroe
DEATH OF A DREAM
Trapped by the promises I have
    made,
The things I want I am denied,
    they are forbade.

I want to flee, but I can't,
From the seed of life grows a
    ravenous plant.

That devours the dreams so long
    ago planned,
And scatters them on a cold, deso-
    late land.

For others to trod on and grind in-
    to dust,
While the mind that planned
    those dreams lies in rust.

You may kill the dreams but the
    dreamer lives on,
Wandering the world all alone.

M. Boyce
SULLEN WEATHER
There is a time when stillness
    menaces
When geese heading south seem
    futile
And oak, only for burning.
When September sunsets promise
    nothing but darkness
and wind in a cottonwood echoes
    shrill from that un-
    knowable place.

My chest, the hollowed fallen log,

catches blowing snow,
Then layers the icy down in
    autumn's pall
Leaving a dull softness aching
    beneath the drift.

My breath, ghost of a dark sided
    moon, whispers with
stealthy apparitions,
    insistent shrouded sirens
That in a distracted moment sing
    about fire,
a glacial moment, far north and
    soon forgotten.

In poignant hesitation, where
to labor in the face of an
    oncoming storm
would be an insignificant
    gesture,
Yet to turn and run would be to
    speak of that frail man
It ends up there's no struggling,
no muffled crying,
no bending against the howling
    blow nor giving way
    before it,
no indecision
no choice,
just waiting.

Michele McClintock
Do You Ever Do Like I Do
Do you ever do like I do?
Do you go outside at night
And look up at the sky?
Do you pick out our star
And begin to cry?
Do you think about me
When the tears start to fall?
Do you pick up the phone
And try to call?
Do you put it back down
Because you think I've gone away,
Or put it back down
Because you don't know what to
    say?
These things I do
And many more,
I'll do them again,
I've done them before.
Tell me,
Do you ever do like I do?
Do you want to come over
And spend time by my side?
Remembering times we've laughed
And times we've cried.
Do you sit alone,
By the water's crisp shore,
Recalling the past,
The way we were before?
Do you gaze at my picture
And want me there?
The two of us;
Our lives to share?
Tell me,
Do you ever do like I do?

Vivian Boucher
BONDAGE
What remorseless conscience
    prompted this decision
That trembles my hand and
    blurs my vision?
I knew at the start it wouldn't be
    easy,
But my poor head aches, and
    my stomach's queasy.
My nerves are screaming! Is it
    really worth it?
Where is that pack? I must
    unearth it!

The ceaseless pacing, the
    anguished need;
I can't give in—it's just a weed!
My soul is filled with deep
    contrition—
Did *I* bring myself to this
    condition?
Try one more day—an hour—a
    minute!
This fight takes courage if I'm
    to win it.
Where is my pluck my nerve of
    steel?
Does anyone care how bad I
    feel?
Would it really harm to take one
    puff?
Perhaps I'd find that one's
    enough.
That's what I'll do! I'll try to taper,
And soon I'll scorn the tainted
    vapor;
But win I will—I can— I must!
These chains of bondage shall
    turn to dust.

Stanley P. Olsen
THE UNICORN
I spied a Golden Unicorn
Standing in a Golden Sea
And I was filled with wondering

I shook my head
I shook it twice
To make sure I wasn't Dreaming
But there he was that Unicorn
In the Gold Sea gleaming

His Coat was Golden like the sun
His eyes were molten fire
He is the horse that comes from
    Myth
And strikes men with Desires

Under the light of the dying sun
I watched him and he watched me
And then with a flick of his tail
He turned and walked into the Sea.

Joyce Virginia Compton
A Small Child's Kingdom
I scooped a pile of sand real high
And built a castle way up to the
    sky.
On top of my castle I placed a tall
    steeple
And filled the courtyard with
    many people.
Around my castle I built a river
    with a bridge,
Then mountains and valleys and
    green rolling ridge.
I enclosed all the green meadow
    patches
With a log fence that was all
    made with matches.
I used small acorns for birds that
    would sing,
Over all that great kingdom I was
    the king.
I had built my dream thereon the
    sand to stay
But alas! The tide came in and
    washed it away.

Donald S. Daughtry
Martin's Melodies Of Peace
The thirteen year old boy picked
    up his horn.
Beautiful melodies of peace were
    born.

Haunting,
    the sounds were haunting

on the eve of Halloween
near the military base
that reminded us
of the bombings
of Beirut,
    Hanoi, Saigon,
    Pyongyang, Seoul,
    Pearl Harbor, London, Berlin,
    Tokyo,
    Hiroshima, Nagasaki . . .
    and thousands of other cities,
    towns, villages.

Haunting
hauntingly beautiful,
were the sounds of the saxophone
as Martin, my son,
reminded the protesters
of the vision of peace,
    the work of the peacemaker,
    the lives of the peaceful souls,
    the Holy One.

Dorothy T. Seamster
TEARS OF LOVE
I shed a tear for the problems
    around,

I shed a tear for the prejudices of
    our time,
I shed a tear for the hate within
    our hearts,
that's hidden sometimes behind a
    smile.

I shed a tear for the pain I feel, for
    all
the grief that's stored within.
This feeling I have is for the
    world as a
whole, these tears I shed are tears
    of love.

Linda Jackson Tomlinson
REINCARNATION
Softly the shade brushes your face
And gives a haunting grace
Of Time Medieval, long ago
When knights battled to the last
    foe.

A look of serenity, lady of lace
Time of dreams reflected in your
    face.
Spin on tomorrow, and yesterday
Within the dreams of your eyes
    show the way.

Judy M. Johnson
A FRIEND TO ME
If only one friend I could be.
I'd try to be a friend to me.
If only one friend I could have.
I'd like to make a friend of
    myself.

Deborah Untermeyer Cooper
WHISPERING BREEZE
The tropical breeze
Whispered among the palm trees,
Circled the sapphire
Pools and ivory beaches,
Then pursued another path.

Signe Schrull
EVENING
The purple mountain slopes
Slid down
Into an emerald sea
Where the white foam frothed
And spun
Atop the waves
Of the restless sea.

Over the emerald waters
There rose

The turquoise sky,
With bands of flame and
Of gold,
Of peach and pink,
The gentler hues.

Slowly the colors changed
And darkened,
The rolling waters quietened,
The earth was still
And waiting
For the silvery light
Of the evening star.

Regina Christina Satterfield
READING
Reading takes you places you
    will never go, Reading takes
    places you will never
    know.

Reading makes you feel like your
    up above the clouds, Reading
    makes you feel like your
    cheering with the crowds.

Reading helps you learn about
    peoples hopes and fears,
Reading makes you yearn for
    all the upcoming years.

I personally like to read alot, I
    don't like books without a plot,
    I like to read on a rainy day,
    but on sunny days I like to
    play!

Judith Belilove
COVALENCE
Bonded energy, flowing through,
Close, soft, true.
Purity, in its purest form,
Garlanded, with truth adorn.

Rose, magenta, carnelian, red,
Glowing softly, their stomach
    warmly fed.
Togetherness, gentility, softly,
Their arrogant pride so lofty!

They are the bonded.

L. Irene Stewart
POEMS
Poems are what poets see,
Poems are sky, Poems are tree.
Poems are happiness, Poems are
    sorrow,
Poems are today, Poems are
    tomorrow,
Poems are death, Poems are life,
Poems are husband, Poems are
    wife,
Poems are songs sung for me,
Poems are souls meant to be free,
Poems are you, Poems are me!

Sylvia Rhoades
THANKSGIVING
    [To my grandchildren—John,
    Michelle, and Lester.]
The pumpkins are golden yellow
The leaves are turning brown.
The geese are flying southward
Tom turkey's plump and round.

Chilly winds are blowing
The snow is coming down.
Soon company will be coming
Tom turkey can't be found.

The ham is in the oven
The pies are nice and brown.
Tomorrow is Thanksgiving
Still Tom turkey can't be found.

Thanksgiving Day is over
Our company have all gone.
Our hearts are light and merry
Tom turkey has come home.

Every year I wonder
If Tom turkey doesn't suspect,
When Tanksgiving Day is nearing
And leaves to save his neck.

G. A. Kunkel
AN ANGELIC FAREWELL
With fading light in her beautiful
    eyes
Gaunt cheeks she silently spoke
    her sad goodbyes

Her life exploring the shores of
    eternity
And catching strains of heavenly
    music in felicity

Her earthly life ebbing to and fro,
    or high and low
Her sun of eternity catching her
    eternal morning glow

Heavenly strains of the angels'
    songs were ringing
As louder and louder came the
    angels' singing

As the angels' voices re-echoing
    with heavenly harmony
Were singing the Lord's praises
    eternally.

Godfrey Enoch Williams
YOU SHOULD
Have you ever strolled through a
    forest and felt the breeze of life
    and time?
Or looked down from the highest
    mountain, that in your life
    you've climbed?
Have you ever listened to the
    birds sing, at the early
    mornings dew?
And have you ever taken the
    time to know, the most
    important person, you?

W. C. NeSmith
HONEYCOMBED
When Shebe of Queena came to
    town,
the drones started to buzzing
    roun'—
anxious regal nod to sway,
be King Bee for one day.

After she left with queenly air,
stingers flashed most everywhere,
each from irate rag and bone,
vexed by being left alone.

Every drone found it hollow fame
that saccharine smile from royal
    dame,
soured the honey at regular spa
served to Shang of Shangri La.

Katrina Biles White
TEACHERS
Are made up of many
    components:
    The love of a mother,
    The strength of a father,
    The patience of Job,
    The knowledge of a scholar;
      The energy of a child,
      Vim, vigor and vitality,

    The concern of a Christian,
      A pleasing personality;
Clarity in objectives,
A large measure of originality,
The ability to hold attention
For explicit comprehensibility;
    Capacity to study
    In order to improve,
    Willingness to adjust
    In appropriate moves;
An eagerness to praise
When approval is due,
A creative imagination
To frequently pursue;
    Sympathetic attention
    To another's needs,
    Perseverance in assisting
    Another to succeed;
Enthusiasm, loyalty,
Optimistic attribute;
Loyalty to colleagues,
Harmonious attitude;
    Blend these components—
    Observe the resultant
    creature:
    Standing before you
    Is an EXCELLENT
    TEACHER!!

Estella M. McGhee—Siehoff
It Could Be No Other Way
Before death, the deciet and
    treachery made known.
Before death, the lies exposed.
Before death, the enemies
    withdrawn from.
Before death, the spying ended.
Before death, the work unhindered.
Before death, the mountains
    removed.
Before death, the green bay trees
    cut down.
Before death, the pleasures of
    evildoers gone.
Bofore death, the Will of God
    accomplished.
Before death, the angels waiting.

Eilizabeth Ann Cepak
YESTERDAY'S MEMORIES
I stumbled upon some old friends
    today,
We talked of bets we owed and
    money never to be repaid.

We talked about things of past
    and things to come,
About some of the crazy things
    we had done.

Laughing and crying along our way
Reminising of the good and bad
    yesterday.

Wishing others could be here,
Others so far away but near.

We talked of the rich and poor
Even the gangs last football score.

We sang old songs we used to sing,
Thinking of the memories they
    bring.

Yes, I stumbled on some dear
    friends today.
Just to make some more
    memories a part of yesterday.

Felicia Venable
ODE TO THE EAGLE
    Oh Mighty Eagle soaring high
    up in the sky
With your broad and sweeping
    wings.

I can see what a strong flier
you are,
As you zoom up to your eyrie
high in a tree.

With your keen sharp eyes
You spy your prey far below.

Oh Mighty Eagle so powerful
and brave
You are the official emblem of
the Great United States.

Courageously you stand on
The American Coat of Arms and
the President's flag.

Your picture graces some
American Coins
And paper money that circulates
today.

Oh Mighty Eagle how I envy
you your freedom
As you fly high—high—high up
in the sky.

Edith Russell
MY SILENT SON
"He plays so well alone", they'd
say, "He really is a dear." But as
I watched my silent son I
wondered, "Is he talking and I
don't hear?"
It's hard to know someone who
doesn't talk even though you
try. Sometimes it had me so
confused I just wanted to cry.
But the other day I found an old
book with pages of things he
wrote, And as I started to read
the lines my heart nearly broke.
My silent son was telling me all
the things he felt inside. All
the love, the feelings it seemed
he wanted to hide.
I read each line with joy and
pride, sadness and some fear.
For my silent son said all the
things I wanted yet was afraid
to hear.
He spoke of his dreams, his loves,
of war, his fears and yes of me.
He wrote of his life as a child
and the need to be free.
He tells me in the poems he
writes that it's hard to say "I
Love You", I never did quite
understand for it's easy for me
to do.
But as he writes he lets you see a
life that's strong and deep. He
tells you of a pride and faith
that he will ever keep.
So I read his poems alone in the
night and I begin to
understand, that my silent son
has suddenly become a strong
silent man.

Zane Chambers, Sr.
The Lynching Of Old Jim Palmer
Old Jim Palmer was a black of
great respect
Among those of white reject;
And he was accepted as is by a
loving God
As neither particularly funny nor
odd,
But was hindered for everlasting
By the middle crust of white folk
casting.

The white reject was this black

man's fare,
Very poor and with many a care,
Not much money to pay life's way,
And very few rights to do or to say,
Adjusting his daily actions
To the priviledged white folk
factions.

Then one day as he practiced his
submission,
While being subjected to a
regular dose of perdition,
He raised his voice in feeble
protest,
Something which his detractors
did much detest,
And caused for himself and all of
his
Reason for regret for disturbing
what is.

If one had looked at his
tormentors faces
Their anger did betray their
difference in races,
For they turned first red then
black,
And a shade of yellow as each
turned his back
And gathered to make plans a
distance away
For this poor black man a method
to betray.

Their meeting was secret, as is
the case,
When evil is festering over a
difference in race,
And in the light of day their
decision was not known,
For evil works best when daytime
is gone,
So their trickery had to wait till
the dark of night
When one could hardly see and
all was quiet.

After supper was finished and the
fire died down,
Old Jim put on his frayed night
gown,
Turned down the lamp wick to
snuff out the light,
And climed into bed to sleep out
the night,
While a distance away a dog
barked his dissapproval
At something or someone
needing removal.

Old Jim slept an hour or two,
Although fitfully as one who is
fearful will do,
When he awakened with a start
And a chill which pierced his
heart;
Who would be knocking at his
door at this hour?
Who but one in need or one who
does cower.

"Wake up in there Old Jim
Palmer," a harsh voice said,
"Wake up and get out of that
warm, soft bed."
The old man shivered, though
not from the wind
Blowing through the cracks
needing a mend,
But from downright fear
Of the cruel voices he could hear.

"God," he said, "What have I done?
I am too weak to fight, and too

old to run,
The night is come and the day is
gone,
And in my misery I am left all
alone,
I done spoke up to a white man's
mock,
And now he done come to my
door to knock."

"Come on, Old Jim Palmer, open
the door,
Or we'll knock it down to the floor.
You're in there we know,
And if you don't open we'll cause
you a lot of woe."
Old Jim opened the door a crack,
And with a cowardly surprise the
night visitors stepped back.

They then grabbed Old Jim, drew
him outside,
And put him on a horse for an
apparent ride;
They galloped through the night
for a mile or two,
 Some of the night riders
drinking a strengthening brew,
And drew up under an old oak tree,
Which had a bare limb swinging
free.

Now the rest of what happened
on that sorrowful night
Is seldom mentioned by black or
by white;
For those who wonder, and those
who surmise
About Old Jim Palmer and his
demise
Must take the few utterances the
guilty devise
And a self-satisfactory story
improvise.

There are some who say that the
only intention
Of those night riders was a scare
invention,
And that a rope was thrown over
that leafless limb,
And put about his neck to scare
the life out of him,
But Old Jim's horse was a jittery
one
And spooked and ran during the
fun.

Now there are those of us who
know
That what happened was but an
extention of Old Jim Crowe,
And there are those of us who
know
That laws will be passed which
will not cause one to
spiritually grow,
But there are those of us who
respect human rights, and
these standards are considered
odd,
While there are others who make
their own laws, and would
make laws even for God.

Norma Jeanne Zeliff
THE REVELATION OF LIFE
Lite burst forth into a twisted
knarled shape;
In deep puzzlement, it causes me
to gawk and gape.
Twisting and turning, running
through all its scenes,

Clearly portraying, not at all what
it seems.
For the players march across the
stage of life,
In a tormented, mad cap seizure
of terrible strife.
Daily taking up the reins for the
trip of the day,
Alternately, faltering, racing,
losing the way.

The laughter, tender moments,
sprinkled with tears,
Intermingled with jeers, ridicule
and dirty leers.
Then the visitor of death causes
such a radical change,
Completely removing all traces
away out of range.

But at dawning, life stirs into a
new beginning.
As life moves on, constantly
spinning, spinning.
Weaving its delicate patterns so
skillfully planned,
Life knows many, many, lifetimes
are completely spanned.

Sharon E. Thomas
MOM AND DAD
You filled my life,
You colored my world,
You made my dreams come true.
You taught me how to share,
Thank you, Mom & Dad, for all
the time and care.

Robbie Glass
IN MY MIND
This orderly hole they put me in,
Twisted steel and molded tin,
Can never replace your smiling
face,
So in my mind I run with haste.
Into your arms, so big and strong,
And in them I can never go wrong.
Please love me now and forever
dear,
With you I will never fear.
This place, so lonely, so hated,
With you I'd of wished I'd of
made it.

Betty J. Streets, Preece
MEMORY LANE
*[Dedicated to Don. For the
beautiful years of love and
friendship we shared with each
other]*
As I pass through life and walk
down memory lane
When I recall the times of
moments sweet
In whispered shadows, softly as
the breezes
I see a spray of roses at my feet

Each petal speaks a word of love
so tender
A love conceived and brought
forth to live or die
A love that burns and glows with
every moment
Or left untended, there to wilt
and die

A love that keeps the heart in
ryhthm beating
Rejoicing in the light of each new
day
Or sinking into depths of
mournful sadness
There to bloom no longer in it's

grand array

In memory's lane the winds will
  whisper softly
I listen—did I hear it call my
  name
Or is my heart deceived with
  only longing
Looking for a hope to ease the
  pain

But if I should see him walking in
  the sunshine
Oh heart rejoice, but never let
  him know
We must be content to love him
  in our yesterdays
Walk softly heart, we'll walk just
  in his shadow

Robert L. Meade
TRANSMUTATION
the Silence Sends a Searing Sound
a Wail
What am I, Who am I, Why am I
the Wail of despair
becomes
the Cry of joy
Transmuted
by the sound of love

Fritz Guendel
**The Song—That Will Never
  End**
We came
with all
who had come
to the endless shores—
to the boundless seas—
embraced in a dream
we whisper into the wind
the words lovers say—
swaying with the restless waves
to the passionate storm of desire
engulfed by the roaming touch of
  life
and the sea—
singing together
the song
that will never end

Shannon Newell
RAINBOWS
All my life I've loved those colors
Colors that light up the dark sky
Those colors will be there now,
  forever
They come in shades no one has
  ever seen
Why do these wonderful colors
Fill me with happiness?
People will try to copy the beauty
  of them
But I know for I have tried
Nothing is the same as seeing
  for yourself;
The beauty of Rainbows.

Bruce K. Johnston
DEATH OF A SNOWMAN
There lies the snowman
Filled with love he lies so deep
with melting heart still forbearing
A sleeper whose eyes saw the
  pain with surprise
When they carved names upon
  his frozen head
He prayed for them all
They will never, never know

He lay his body down upon the
  midday foam
And felt the chill of winter in his
  soul

There, in a carrot nosed world of
  his own
Within a casing that had grown
To a children's delight
Which arrived overnight
Filled with the love of all
Who lie so deep . . .

Coie Lorraine (Hill) Cannon
TO LYDIA
*[Dedicated to Lydia and Peter
  Cachonas—May they be
  reunited and live happily ever
  after.]*
My heart beats in tune with the
  universe
And all life's purposes are
  meaningfully served
When you are by my side.

The lonely hours have been as a
  fog surrounding me
And I cannot see my way clearly
  since you have been
Away from me.

I see you in the twinkling stars
  and in the
Morning sunlight—love
  personafied

My Beloved, return and let our
  lives continue
In perfect harmony as God
  intended.

Our many days and nights
  together I clutch
To my breast as the most
  beautiful part, thus far,
Of eternity.

I chose you as a companion and
  friend and as
The one to be the mother of my
  children—
No greater honor could I have
  bestowed upon you.

God has blessed us with lovely
  sons and
Daughters more beautiful
  because they are
A part of you.

The everyday monotony is
  punctuated with
Thoughts of you. Return to me
  and life will be
Even more beautiful having
  known the pain of
Being apart.

I love you more today and I did
  yesterday.

Artie Tillman Proctor
THANKSGIVING
Thanksgiving is the
  Time we know
To praise God from whom
  All blessings flow.
We're blessed with food,
  Turkey, and dressing
Then render table-grace,
  A special blessing.

Pilgrims set the pace
  With old traditions
Fresh game, vegetables, and
  Plenty of ammunition.
They came here so they
  Could be free
To worship God in this
  Great country.

We head for the woods,

Family or friends
To enjoy this special day
  That God sends.
Let's have Thanksgiving every
  Day of the year,
And thank God for His
  Blessings so dear . . .

Dean Brown Albritton
NEVER KNOWING
You came from your world,
  I came from mine.
You said, "How do you do?"
  I said, "I'm fine."
After a pause,
  We depart,
Never knowing
  Each other's heart.

Dorothea Jessop Baird
BABY LAWRENCE
Thirty below; that January day;
  and,
  they made a grave;
    for baby Lawrence.

They had to blast;
  in late grey afternoon;
  beneath a snow hung sky.

As the evening train,
  called siloquoy;
winding, north of town.

They left, burning low;
  beneath a silvered, sickle moon,
  their fires; lit to melt, the
  old graveyards winter drifts.

The small, raw, grave, waiting;
  for baby Lawrence;
  didn't look so cold;
    and lonely;

  beside that flickering fire;
    Somehow.

F. John Stevens
DROPLETS
Droplets, tiny droplets
Fallen on a page
Running ink so none can read.
Sounds, sounds again
Coming from the soul.
Resounding from the silken wall.
Laughter, Laughter's gone.
Gone from all the crowd.
Faded like the fallen leaf.
Purpose, purpose given.
Ring the bell again my dear.
Silence was not meant for tears.
Reason, reasons save.
People use them as a tool,
Sometimes wither up their souls.
Glory, glory shining
Fills my life with constant joy.
Makes my droplets worth the
  price.

Rosemary Chandler
MY HERITAGE
*[Dedicated Nov. 9, 1982, to my
  grandparents, Mary Burke and
  Michael O'Donnell, and my
  mother, Anna O'D. Bertrand,
  and Tom, Edward, John,
  Lawrence and Mary and
  Margaret O'Donnell.]*
My forefathers came in sailing
  ships,
from Ireland, across the sea.
They left their native land, and
  grieving family.
The land they loved so green and
  fair,

had gathered thorns of hate,
they felt a need to find a land,
that promised them a happier fate.
The ship was old, they heard the
  bow creak,
while they huddled below the
  deck,
like lambs so mild and meek.
They needed time to gather
  courage,
to face a brand new life.
The sea was black and frightening,
yet their heart were brave and
  ready for the strife.
The siling ship began to rock and
  roll,
but, they prayed to persevere no
  matter what the toll.
Still many of the passengers died,
others, so ill, they were barely
  alive.
Mothers wept, while little babies
  cried.
And, when I think of all they
  chanced;
and, how they dared to sail,
I'll always love my heritage,
and, know I cannot fail!

Joseph
QUIET AFTERNOON
*[To God, for things
  innumerable.]*
  The Sun rose high up in the sky
as here and there, a bird flew by.
Sitting, watching, here sat I,
  On this quiet afternoon.
  I came to think about the world,
and all the mysteries in it.
I came upon a spiders web,
I watched the spider spin it.
A passing breeze, a butterfly,
a willow tree, a baby's cry,
  A quiet afternoon.
  And here I sit upon this hill
which over looks the sea.
Here, I look inside myself, to see
just who is me.
As up above a cloud appears,
to quench the thirst of years and
  years.
Upon the Earth a million tears,
  On a quiet afternoon.
  I did not move from where I
  stood,
just gazing toward the sky.
I did get wet, but not in vain,
for a rainbow caught my eye.
With colors rising through falling
  rain,
then fading, much too soon.
A witness to a miracle,
  on this quiet afternoon . . .

Bonnie Williamson Thurn
**Birth Of a Spiritual
  Butterfly**
Little Butterfly, who used to be,
Little caterpillar, devouring all it
  could see.
But encased inside cocoons so
  snug,
No longer a creepy, crawly bug,
But reborn with beauty and wings
  to fly,
And we, as this caterpillar, must
  to self—die.
Being born again, new desires,
Try out our wings with heavenly
  choirs.
All is not lost for those who truly

490

seek,
And quick to obey every Word
that God speaks.
The world, 'tis glum and often
dreary,
O the hearts that lie empty and
eyes so teary.
Loneliness is a trap that leads to
frustration,
And has been passed on from
generation to generation.
But think of hope and a second
chance,
At true fulfillment and love that
will enhance.
Be unique as that tiny caterpillar
and be reborn,
Abandon a life that's empty and
forlorn,
Allow the hand of God to see you
through,
Giving you Victory in all you say
and do.
Let His love fill your every being,
Just spread your spiritual wings,
His perfect will you're seeing.
Fly little butterfly, fly so free,
Your true beauty enhanced for all
to see.

David Stewart
ALONE
Alone deep in a polluted vacuum
of purity
A silent piercing explosion of
invisible brilliance
Fused this eternal soul,
And propelled it transformed
Into the chaos of nameless faces
and desolate knowledge,

Alone streaking uncharted into
the forbidding, but unresisting
Expanse of indistinguishable
reality and illusions,
Orbiting aimlessly the boundless
and infinite enigma,
Where chance, fate, and fear reign
supreme.

Alone master of a perfect freedom
which enslaves the orbit
To the fictional truth of an
illusionary freedom.
Ruled by a star of wisdom in a
universe void of understanding.
Like wishes made on a hopeless
streaking mass of fiery
blackness
Which is consumed by the hope
it gave.

Alone impelled by the
composition of divine denial
And compelled by the precision
of demonic resolution
Awaiting only the timely eclipse
of Mind's dark light
Of blood on soul
That declares intelligible
existence
And the truth to a contradiction.

Finley Schmidt
**My Precious Love—To
Marlene**
Just like fog o' night
So goes beauty of the young,
And during brief encounters here
We taunt the very flame of life
With fiery passion and love
Of all and all. Just like a flower
Whose prodigal petals corrode

As if before their time and wither
Wilt or die before the very eye
That would perpetuate them...
To become disconsolate dust
In time & out of time again.

So please, my flower, do not die...
And always be that part of me
That would not be corrupt.
An anthem to you now I sing—
My lonely soul in clariyant voice
Shall forever be aware of you.
And though a flower is just a
flower,
The flower of youth would
somehow be
A glimpse into eternity & the
way
Of something very special dear to
me
Before that timeless time when
everything
Is everlasting beauty.

Joan Bachand
STILLNESS
*[Dedicated to Sr. Mary Jude and
all who love the stillness of
Villa Angela at Old Frontenac.]*
You sit by the river—
and gaze at the rose colored
bluffs.
The green-gold days of autumn
blend beautifully,
as does the old river flow with
living.
The log that you sit on has seen
this
panorama of life—for many
years gone by.
It's become your friend while
you've watched
that old river and gazed at the
rose colored
bluffs on a green-gold day of
autumn.
Wish I could be there beside you
to enjoy that kaleidoscope
view,
that glorious fullness of life;
To thank God for the stillness
that creeps into one's bones.
I have dreamt I've sat there beside
you
on your log, watching the old
river,
and gazing at the rose colored
bluffs
on a still, green-gold day of
autumn.
We've known and loved the
serenity of this vista.
We've found a friendship 'midst
these creations.
Always we'll thank their Maker
for what we've found in each
other.
And so, as you sit on the log and
watch the old river,
let the rose colored bluffs hold
our thoughts
on a still, green-gold day of
autumn.

Lin Roberts-Davis
HURRY CATCH ME
Why did our love's remnants
scatter
. . . like ash in the wind . . .
Why did it not come together
. . . becoming something of
substance . . .

Weren't we the silly ones?
One outspoken   cowering
behind her mouth.
One strong and manly   too busy
to see
a love so strong and yet so
fragile
so damned real . . .
Oh   had we just known
then . . .

What is it we left behind?
Hints of fragrance . . . a kiss for
luck . . .
. . . untold promises . . . what's
ahead?

How nice it is . . . that we never
say good-bye.
What's to become of us? What
fragments can be saved . . .
. . . shaped . . .

I can easily breeze thru time . . .
suspended gently by memories
of yesterday.
To be warmly touched   by a love
I refuse to forget.

I glide quickly thru life . . . too
fast . . . to be hurt
by what I'll find . . . if I should
stop . . .
loving you.

Hurry . . . catch me . . . 'for I fly
away . . .

Alessandra A. Poles
PERCEPTION
I hear the voice of God
When songs of wild birds ring
In whistling winds
Through space.

I see the spirit of God
As clouds airily float by
In showers of dew
On each sculptured petal.

I feel the soul of God
In the breath of a new born
And in the last breath
Entering another twilight plane.

Enrique Irizarry
SAILING
Sailing,
Softly flowing in the ebb
Waves and tides have rocked my
boat
But still it floats.
Sailing,
Passing by a many isle and serene
bay
No place to dock and stay . . .
The ocean is my home.

Walter Bardeck
THE STARS
The stars
Are silver leaves
In the forest of the sky,
And cling to the ebon branches
Of night.

Stephen George Thorne
DRUNK
Can you guess who I am?
Or what I am?
I hang my head low.
Cannot look at anybody
In the face.
Ashamed of myself
And lost my self-respect
So long ago.
Bumming around

For nickels and dimes
Just so I can have a drink.
I think I'm addicted
Because I can't go without it.
If I don't have a drink
I get shaky and grouchy.
I let my kids go hungry
And I don't buy them clothes.
Just so I can have a drink.
Just one little sip
And I want more.
When I can get all I want
Man! you should see me smile.
Then I'm on top of the world!

Orfelia Zanello
ROMA
Roma, madre, amica, sorella!
Gia tu lo sai. Sei troppo bella!
Tutti di te si sono innamorati,
Tu ricambi l'amore ai principi ed
emigrati.
San Pietro—ingresso del Paradiso,
Castel Sant'Angelo si specchia nel
tuo viso.
Povero Colosseo! Di quanti
martiri sei testimonio!
Ma non e colpa tua, ma del uomo
del demonio.
Si sentono ancora i lamenti dei
Cristiani,
Le risate dei Empi pagani.
Dimentichiamo! Andiamo a Santa
Maria Maggiore,
San Giovanni, San Paolo e i colli
in fiore.
Mille fogli per poterti nominare,
Ma quattro parole—non ti posso
dimenticare!

Iain A. MacArthur
THE WATCH
The raging tempest o'er the deep,
A watch did I anxiously keep,
When you were wrapt in
guileless sleep,
I bade the waves be still.
"Be still," I cried to the angry deep,
Wild winds hushed and fell to
sleep,
The sullen billows ceased to leap
Lest they awakened you.
So when my rest is clouded o'er,
And wild seas take me far from
shore,
Shall I sink to rise no more
Or are you watching me?

Betty Kitchen
AN AUTUMN DAY
Did you ever see an autumn
morn
A dark and lonely autumn morn
The forlorn sky with brows drew
down
And the angry wind tossing
leaves around

I've seen all this and then about
noon
Saw a laughing wind whistle a
different tune
Saw gray clouds break and the
sun shine through
Floating there in a pool of blue

Have you ever seen in deep
twilight
The silhouette of geese in flight
Or a big golden moon shining
bright and clear
On a calm little pond down the
road from here

Yes I've seen all this and wished I
were free
As the wind that tossed those
leaves with glee
Then watched with wonder crisp
snowflakes fall
And heard in a distance the blue
jays call

Nancy Lea Whynot
EAGLE
*[To my close friends and for
their support]*
Suddenly,
There is beauty in the air,
The eagle is on the wing;
Hear the majestic scream,
Far across the waters it rings;
Feel the magic as he dives,
He knows, he's
King!

Cindy Meinzinger
LOVE
Love isn't something
you can feel
But something only
two can feel

Love can break a
person's heart
Like the stabbing
of a dart

Love is the most
splendored thing
That's usually shown
by a ring

Love is like a
bouncing ball
It has its
ups and downs

Valerie Sawchuk
HOLD MY HAND
As I was sitting here,
Thinking of you,
I was trying to remember
Just how we met.
It seems we've been friends
forever.

The more I think of you
The more I miss you.
The way you used to hold my
hand,
And encourage me to go on,
When all I ever seen were dead
ends.

So hold my hand,
And help me through the hard
times.
Hold my hand,
And share the good times.
Hold my hand,
And be my friend for all times.

Jacqueline Vermaas
LIFE OR DEATH
There's new life growing inside of
me.
I feel its presence, still for nobody
to see.
But this motherhood isn't
planned or even hoped for.
Being single, life has to go on like
before.

Abortion is the answer, an easy
way out.
Millions of women are going
through it, without fear or even
doubt.
But when I personally have to

choose, between life or death,
I know that an abortion , can't be
the answer to that.

When I watch my babies being
born, I have twins they tell me
soon.
Words can't describe the way I
feel that Monday afternoon.
When I finally get to hold my
babies close to me,
I know, that this is what I
wanted. This was meant to be.

Bonnie Shernita Saunders
INTERLUDE
Let me touch what I cannot see
Oh mysterious winds that follow
me
For I am only young in heart
Reaching Searching for what
needs to be
Far beyond the boundaries of my
mind

Let me touch what I cannot see
Oh God, please let it be
Exonerate the feeling
The yearning that hibernates
Deep within me . . .
Far beyond the boundaries of my
mind

Douglas Lawson
COMFORT FOR TEARS
A tiny tear falls,
A voice cries in such fear.
A child needs your comfort,
Just to know you are near.

The tender assistance,
A strong arm to hold,
A tissue to dry eyes,
And to help her, not scold.

Her dolly fell down
"And was bad," so she said.
"But I didn't mean it,
When she fell on her head."

It isn't your fault,
And toys sometimes break.
Maybe daddy can fix her,
Just for your sake.

Petra C. Paszlack
MISSING YOU
When I need you . . .
I just think of you.
And somehow
I feel comforted.

When I need love . . .
I just think of how we loved.
And somehow
I feel fulfilled.

When I need someone to hold
me . . .
I just think of your warmth.
And somehow
just thinking . . . isn't enough.

Rev. Earle V. Conover
The Oneness Of Our World
*[Dedicated to my father, the
Reverend Garrett M. Conover,
D.D., who was a warrior in the
fight for righteousness for a full
70 years! He made more of his
life (1866—1964) than a dash
between dates!]*
The heavens declare the glory of
God,
In all their immensity,
Yet when I look up at the stars
above,

The stars look down on little me.

Our world has a sense of
togetherness,
And, in truth, there's affinity,
For, when I look up at the stars
above,
The stars look down on little me.

We stare at the stars in reverent
awe,
Because of their complexity,
Yet they tell of our Father's living
love,
For each little, simple me.

The stars made by God speak of
lasting love,
Throughout all eternity,
Though the stars, looking down
on us from above,
Look at each, little transient me.

How great Thou art, O, Lord, our
God,
In Thy splendor and majesty,
Yet Thou dost love each human
soul,
Though we humbly ask, "Even
me?"

However far-flung His stars really
are
They make a vast family,
For each human soul may say to
himself,
"I'm included: for God loveth me!"

Linda M. Lalonde
MERMAN EYES
His eyes are like a deep, blue
ocean
Splashing its swollen billows
upon immovable rocks,
Slowly wearing them down,
Never relenting,
Entrancing them,
Teasing them,
Until they
loosen their hold and
swim amid
The enveloping warmth of the
waves,
Only to be
swallowed by them and
fall
to
the
ocean
floor
Among the rest of his rock
collection.

Jacob M. Fehr
OUR HERITAGE
When I was just a little girl, my
Mama said you're such a Pearl,
And Dad would lift me up and
whirl, me round and round.

To me it never did occur, 'twas
this that made my kitten purr,
When I would stroke his lovely
fur, a playmate I had found.

September first and it was cool,
this was the day I started
school,
'Twas here I'd learn the Golden
Rule, and it was so much fun.

The years went by like pages
turned, and I was getting more
concerned,
As for more knowledge I would
yearn, my life had just begun.

Then after school I took my
place, at first it seemed like
such a race,
But then I found 'twas not the
case, in our society.

These things are freedom in our
land. Of solid rock, not sinking
sand,
I now much better understand,
this land of Liberty.

Each morning when the Sun does
rise, then I can look up to the
skies,
Within a hope that never dies,
though many waters rage.

Through storms we may not
always see, but we should full
of courage be,
To guard this land of Liberty, and
our dear Heritage.

Shirley Ann Scott
BECAUSE
The intimate feeling
of your touch,
Your body against mine
embraced and protected.
Words are spared and
are not needed,
Because . . .
The message is felt
mutually.
In your absence,
my mind is filled with
precious time spent.
But, also my mind is
on tomorrow,
Hoping it will be as
the yesterday.
We were together
Because . . .
I LOVE YOU.

Jaimie E. Stewart
FLORIDA FLOWER
*[To Jody for her constant
friendship and unyeilding
words of wisdom.]*
A gentle breeze the seed shall fall,
and root itself in soil.
Victims of chance that we should
cross, for no one here will toil.
Frequent water, the seed will
grow, an unfamiliar home.
Yet with time and conversation,
both will become known.
Unfolding splendor, simplistic
task, laws put into plan;
Our very reason before us made,
to flower and expand.
Subsisting beauty for all to relish,
primitive in trend,
Augment each other as earthly
flower, security in a friend.
Life curtailed for time alone,
familiar home renewed.
An interruption that will transfer,
not to be construed.
For a gentle breeze shall return,
and beauty will renew,
Let not us ponder with harsh
goodbye; but fondly say adieu.

Schelte Brandsma
FORGIVENESS
Uncivil strife of tribal men—
their battles never ending,
retaliating heads of clan
revenge as ever pending;
and fright and fear through
village ran

when screams the heavens
rending.

Thus never free from harm's
alert—
their teeth and eyes defending,
and always someone hit the dirt—
their feuds not never ending;
primeval laws pay hurt for hurt—
through centuries descending.

Then Christ was born to human
race—
Himself in love was lending
to show us God's forgiving ways—
forgiveness never ending;
Jesus to men eternal grace
our humns to heaven sending!

Hugh Shannon
MOUNTAINS
Beyond the avenue the palisades
lifting from peignoir clouds stark
shoulders
blue charmers of leviathan
proportions
and heroic size
they bring strange benisons in
the beholding to our eyes.

Never leave the mountains. They
will pursue you
They will follow after and ring
your horizons
like silent seneschals of sleep.
They are jealous
in their austerity
They will dispel from all your
later vistas every verity.

Yield, yield to the rhythm of the
broken and beautiful
snow-powdered and glacier-
patched sentinel peaks
rearing their cold contours and
blued shoulders
against the sky:
they will comfort men's eyes in
aeons hence and tease
                        their mortality.

Margaret Dennys
THE PARTY
Laughter quietens
like fog behind you.
Faces blur.
You loom before me
vivid, delineated
like some determined bird
searching
through the uncertain night
for dawn
and bright red berries.

Nancey Weichel
NO ONE EVER LEARNS
When you miss someone
You feel like crying
But you try to hide your feelings
With a flash of a smile.
While all along the world thinks
you're happy
Even the one who drives you crazy
You want him but he's not there
to hold
He's out with someone else now
Your chance has come and gone
You did everything he told you
You went through with everything
Then . . .
It seems it always happens
He finds somebody better
While you sit at home
Mope and cry,

Eat 'cause you don't care anymore
Or have anything better to do
And you write love poems
And promise yourself
You'll never fall in love again
Until . . .
Some new one comes along
And you start all over.

Mayes C. Smith
SAFE AT HOME
Sleep on sweet love, your days of
sorrow o'er:
    May Angels softly bear you
    tenderly
Onward and upward safe to
Heaven's door,
    Across the skies, beside the
    crystal sea.

Your heart of gold no more,
    through healing hands,
    Will ease my aches with
    warmth of gentle love:
They rest in Holy silence
peacefully,
    And I in grief cry out for you
    above.

I'm glad your gentle breast no
more can sigh,
    In that bright land beneath fair
Heaven's dome:
And that when all the years have
pased away,
    I'll hold you close when I am
    summoned home.

Vickie Cope
REALIZATION
A soul of beauty in dreams,
    Reaching high in my mind
but finding no door.
Reaching out—a hand grasps
reality,
    My soul of beauty in dreams
no more . . .

Elsie Day Cruthirds-Hutto
FLEETING MOMENT
*[To my mother, Elsie Day
Cruthirds, who was born a
Poet, and who taught me the
art of poetry: with much love.]*
I awakened this morning
    and I found
The grass covered with dew,
    and a spider web wound.
Drops of dew on the web,
    I might add, I found, too.

As I stepped on the grass
    Where the sun was shining
    through,
My shoes were all wet
    and would be for a minute or
    two.
When I looked all around
    I saw no more dew.

That's so like one's life—
    too soon it is spent;
All too short, like the duration of
dew,
    gone in a fleeting moment.

Roxanne Lagasse
LOVE'S EMBERS
Embers will always remain
Stronger than the sun's rays
Never to refrain
From any part of a day

My embers generae the soul.
Incinerate the wearings of time

Tear at life's toll
Beating out the regular rhyme

Love beats on
Beating against all end
The soul's mirror scorns
At all the heart's mends

Love wins the race of life
Weaving through all strifes

Helen Holub
A SUMMER'S NIGHT
There's nothing quite so peaceful
    as a lovely summer's night
    with breezes blowing softly . . .
willows swaying e'er so slight.

Crickets chirping; fireflies blinking
    like lanterns in swift flight.
Youngsters begging for glass
    bottles
    to catch those elusive winking
        lights
    to gaze upon like twinkling
    stars,
    and when the chase is done . . .
    Release them from their prisons
    for 'twas all in childish fun.

Then, to sit back on the
    lawnchairs
    drowsy child against you now,
softly soothing with your
    fingertips
    his smooth, unruffled brow.

To breathe in all the scents of
    floral
    splendor at its best . . .
    'til with regret, 'tis time to leave
    this summer's night, to rest.

Susie Nelson
We'll Say It, For Their Sake
My long lonely nights
    each empty into a morning
        of new hope.
My red swollen eyes scan past
    the driveway
        to the endless field that
you once loved to play in.
But the warmth of each new
            morning's sunlight
    does not reach my cold heart.
The new day only means to me,
    another day without you here
            to make me smile.
I could always depend on you
    no matter how rough the
        going got or
how cruel the outside world
                was.
You'd come up to me, with your
        sweet little face
And your cute little tricks.
You'd always bring a smile to my
    face.
So many things we did together
    So many places we went,
                Always together,
Now, when I get into my car
    I find myself looking over
        at the seat you always
        took next to me.
And I find myself waiting
        for you to join me.
They say I have to say Good-bye
        to you.
    to accept that you are gone.
Don't they understand, you can
    never be
        gone, completely from me.
There is a special place

in my heart
    that you will always have.
But for their sake,
    You and I can pretend to say
                Good-bye.
    Good-bye my friend
    Good bye my buddy
    Good-bye my love
Altho we only shared a short time
        together
I will treasure everyday,
    I will continue to love you
    And I will never
        give up searching for you
I'm so sorry for all the
    other people who did not
    understand
        our strong love.
I guess to them,,
    you will always be
    "Just another dog".

Thelma G. Monk
A GOOD HOME
It's a home, where there is
    sharing
It's a home, where there is caring.
It's a home where love is floating,
It's a home, where joy is growing.
It's a home, where you will find,
Happiness, and peace of mind.

Racheal Wilson Yancy
A MINISTER'S CHARGE
Many vast duties to perform
In the sun or in the storm.
Many burdens of his sheep;
When every else is fast asleep.

Many wake-ful nights in prayer
Looking for an answer there.
With all these burdens in his
    hand,
He gets so tired . . . for he's still
    a man!

Many tears he's probably shed
For the sick lying in the bed.
It's not easy to be in command
And try always to understand.

But there is one who lifts him up
As he drinks from his bitter cup!
Glory to God in high esteem;
For his soul "He" shall redeem!

Carole C. Griffin
BROKEN TREASURES
I silently climb the attic stair,
    Pause a moment, and open the
    door.
I see, in the dim light, the disarray
    Of scattered treasures upon the
    floor.
A rocking horse with no left ear,
    Sticks to an old toy drum.
A record collection from long
    past years,
    And a dolly who sucked her
    thumb.
A cho-cho train that lost its track,
    A top that no longer sings,
A Louisville Slugger and catcher's
    mitt,
    And a Pogo with broken springs.
The Calico kitten is covered with
    dust
    (sound asleep in the rocking
    chair)
Cars and trucks with patches of
    rust,
    Neglected from no child's care.
Silver sandals and prom gown
    lace,

493

Wrapped in tissue these many
years.
A High-School yearbook, A
smiling face,
I see through hot, new tears.
I remember when the attic rang
With laughter when it rained.
When children played their
games and sang,
Unheading drops on window
panes.

Now, those days have slipped
away,
And will come to me no more,
For the children who were happy
and gay,
Don't live here . . . anymore.
So many times I've climbed these
stairs
To clear the mess away.
But I treasure the memories
laying here
So I put off that task for today.
Perhaps someday, In future years,
I'll find the strength to start,
To take these toys, without the
tears,
And store them, in my heart.

Eloise Cunningham
JOHN
We have been together for many
years,
But it seems like just a few.
I remember you were dressed all
in white,
That day I first met you.

Tall with shoulders broad,
Brown hair and eyes so very blue,
Such a charming man, I'd never
met.
I could hardly believe you're true.

It was like a magic moment,
My dreams had really come true.
For you fell in love with me,
And I fell in love with you.

Our years have been so happy,
But time has played its toll, I know.
For my hair has turned to silver
And yours is white as snow.

Yes, we are old and I often think
Without you, what would I do?
I pray, dear God, when John must
go
Will you please take me too?

Randall Cunningham
APRIL OF THREE
This day she approached me
shyly, her steps were bashful
light,
She raised her eyes and smiled,
without a sign of fright. She is
three
With arms above her head and
the smile of a shining sun,
Her golden hair blowing, I
looked for a day of fun. She's a
golden three.

I gathered her into my arms, she
gave a giggle of delight,
I held her to the heavens, to
her I'd show my might. She's an
angel of three.
Wiggling from my arms she led
me, to a row of candy
machines,
Cabinets of assorted candies,
mostly M & M's it seems. She's

such a sweet three.

Pointing an angel finger, she
requests a bag of sweets,
Being a loving grandad, I
bought her, her favorite treats.
She's a nontiring three.
We had a day of laughter, visiting
one and all in the store,
She captured all their hearts,
even old Zuber, the boor. She's
an affectionate three.

Only, too soon she left me but
presented me with a kiss,
A hug around my neck and
tears, her Ga-Ga she would
miss. Darn, I wish I was three.
Feeling bubbles on my cheek, was
it from her kiss or tear?
Burning a hole into my soft old
heart, I'm really stuck, I fear.
Return soon, my darling of three.

Linda Hamilton & Jennifer Cripps
INTERREGNUM
airless visions in my mind
suffocate my forward step
blocking out the endless finds
along the stairway-lines of depth.
empty pillars call on me
once believed to stand alone;
crumbling now, they leave me free
to build again from polished stone.

Robin Fern Love
ODE TO A LOST LOVE
*[This poem is dedicated to the
memory of my lifelong
inspiration—my grandmother.]*
I remember a love so rare, so very
rare,
When love meant a friend and
companion.
I remember the beauty of
strength and kindness,
When this precious mold kept
me safe and warm.
I remember well the essence of a
love that lives, and will never
die.
One who is a sophisticate, yet is
not too worldly,
Who knows about life early,
Yet does not exploit his precious
knowledge.
A person who is bold, and yet
meek,
Who has understanding, fire, and
warmth.
A person who possesses the
capacity to love,
And to be loved.
Who is indispensable, can never
be underestimated,
And will never be forgotten.
I remember the charisma, the
care, and everything in-between.
The love I lost so long ago; I love
you,
And always will.

Bruce E. Raemsch
SUSAN
Now has the time of Susan come,
Black—eyed but bright with
golden lash,
Till passion in my mortal breast
Comes near to breaking my heart
at last.

Oh, love, love beyond all singing—
She blazed the while away to
dust,

While I do die with endless living
With soul but left to rapid rust.

Still, year by year, I wait again her
blooming
(Know full well the ending).
I waste away my years not
knowing,
Waiting, anticipating
Each coming blaze of summer
green,
When kiss again I will the deep
bright beam
That death will put to rest with
giving,
For short a time.

Why eyes so dark, my Susan,
with lashes glowing?
With love for each, we knowing,
Why dust for both, for loving?

Sharon Ellsworth
GOODBYE FOR NOW
I loved you before
But things have changed
They seem to be
All re-arranged

You played some games
I couldn't handle
Little kids games
Like blowing out candles

The whole reason was
That I was too nice
This reason for me
Was far from surfice

You made me blind
So I couldn't see
The awful things
You were doing to me

You have fooled me
For so long
But I know now
I wasn't wrong

I still love you
I know I do
But I have to believe
That it's not true

It was your feelings
You never shared
This only showed me
You never cared

The things we had
Were one sided
I sat and watched
As it subsided

Goodbye for now
I'm leaving you
I only wish
This love was true

Helen Rex
On An Early Autumn Morn
On an early autumn morn
I think all kinds of things
I think of wind rustling
In the breeze-an' birds
Flappin' their wings.

There's gold outside my window
Fallin' from the trees!
And there's warmth inside my
heart
When I chance to think of these.

The wind has a special flair
Here in the Autumn.
It seems to caress my hair,
As warm weather reaches its
bottom.

Its hard to describe
This feelin' I feel;
Leaves twrillin' an' swrillin' about!
For a few brief weeks
I seem to reel;
'Fore winter displays its clout.

I'm aghast at the Autumn's hue—
Radiant in orange, red an' gold!
I never grow tired of its beautiful
view;
Since childhood—or til I am old!

Helen Rex
LOVE
*[I dedicate this poem to the
man who put love in my heart,
a song on my lips and gave me
a new lease on life—for loving
him brought out the best in me.]*
When Spring is here
I can't help think
My darling of you.

Especially when
The sun shines bright,
The birds sing,
And the flowers are in bloom.

For your smile is as bright
As the sun on a Spring morn;
Your laugh—as cheerful as birds
singing
And having you with me is as
wonderful
As a fresh bouquet . . .

For when you are here
Springtime fills the room!

Joan Davis Corser
CONTENTMENT
There she lies
That baby of mine
Her head in the crook of my arm
Her mouth at my breast
We lie back upon the bed
Me and that baby of mine.

She gently sucks
And the world stands still
The stars through the window
shine
The winter wind blows through
the trees
But we're content
Me and that baby of mine.

Hazel (Mrs. G.) Gianatiempo
NEVER
*[To my darling Jerry, I want
you, I need you I love you!]*
We may never know
We may never find
We may never learn
We may never love
We may never live,
Yet we are certain to DIE.

Betsy Lewis
SOCIETY
We hate the criminal,
Yet we condemn the poor
and fill their lives with our
biased opinions
and empty promises
refusing to believe they might
just be
happier than us.

We hate the beautiful starlet,
Yet we strive so
to appear and perform like her
just so we may believe we are
sophisticated,
if only for a little while.

We hate the politician,
Yet he only speaks exactly what
    we want to hear
    and we try so desperately to
    believe him
    because in this world
    we must find someone to
    believe in.

But most of all,
We hate the lies that are told to us
    Yet in facing the truth, we
    must face ourselves
    to one's personage.

Linda R. Fanelli
COLD BEAUTY
Although the skies
Are grey and somber,
And the winds
Chill you to the bone.
The harshness
Of the cold winter
Is softened by the beauty
Of gently falling snow
Slowly it comes to rest
On the cold and frozen ground,
Blanketing the pastures
With a glistening white,
That shimmers
Like a sequined gown.
Finally the snow
Stops falling,
As the clouds
Move on their way.
Now as the skies
Begin to clear
And the Sun can
Be seen to shine.
The day no longer
Seems so somber,
But picturesque and gay.

Kathyryn Cobb
A Stillness Not Of Death
The landscape lies silent
Under a blanket
Thick enough
To pad the footfalls
Of even a giant.
Small bits of froth
Cling to tree branches
As though
They fear to fall.
Here and there
Funnels of smoke
From hearths
Attack the white sky
With a denser whiteness,
And the roofs cry—
Their tears congealing
Into long crystal cones.
The white is nearly total—
Broken only
By a few colored
Doors and shutters
And the power wires.
Permeates the land.

Beverly Eugene Carlson
All Right It's All Right
Everything is all right
    When we are doing just fine
And our endeavors builds up to a
    new hight,
    Brought about, like drinking
    new wine.

Tis another story when
    everything seems a fright
    And the world is turned upside
    down.
You know all will soon change
    and be, all right,

If you can smile and replace
    the frown.
Quieten your thoughts in
    meditation
    And the dark storm clouds will
    soon disappear from sight.
Thirty minutes of contemplation
    On a simple word makes it, all
    right.

Be still and your eyes reveal an
    inner glow.
    It gives an open window for
    your light,
By keeping your heart rythm
    steady and slow,
    You can be sure everything is,
    all right.

Once again you have hit the
    happy norm
    That will last through the night
And will protect you from the
    storm,
    For tomorrow and all
    tomorrows will be, All Right!

Lynette Kimball
A MAINE WINTER
The wind is blowing the sky is
    dusty
The clouds are crying tears of
    snow
The temperature is real low
But with all the freshness they
    wouldn't know
Sounds of nature blessing ears
The snow so white and pure
A fire in the fireplace gives a clue
It's a MAINE winter for sure
Children on sleds full of life
A walk in the woods with all the
    sights
Pink cheeks and cold hands
Cookies and hot cocoa on cold
    nights
The cows white breath so warm
    and sweet
It's another MAINE winter for sure
And for all those lonely hearts
It's a simple and refreshing cure

Alice L. Baker
GRANDMA'S ANGEL DOLL
    *[Dedicated to my first grand—
    daughter—VERONICA SUE
    SPANN—who really is my
    ANGEL DOLL.]*
Ronnie my baby—Ronnie I call
You're Grandma's darling angel
    doll.
Toys are strung from wall to wall
As tired little legs climb the stairs
So you can go to sleep with
    Teddy Bear.

The love for me that I see in your
    eyes
All the money in the world
    cannot buy.
A pudgy little nose that wrinkles
    when you smile
Makes all my life really worth
    the while.

We say your prayers and you kiss
    me good night
Those little arms hug me so tight,
Those big brown eyes close out
    the light
Shutting out the darkness of the
    night.

When you awake at the crack
    of dawn

All your cares will be faded and
    gone.
God and Grandma will watch
    over you,
Because—I LOVE YOU too
My little ANGEL DOLL.

Virginia C. Scardelli
Shadows Can Be Death
I have grown and I have known
What makes a person die
They're shadows of
The tear you cannot shed
The pain you cannot feel
The fear you cannot show
The lonliness you cannot tell of
and the hurt you can't disguise
They circle 'round your heart
and tear it bit by bit
Until you have no soul
and then you die . . . from
    shadows

Birgit Thelin—McDonald
BONDAGE
I know this to be of no avail
My waking hours I regret
My sleep is racked by memories
From by-gone days of married
    bondage

Like many ships upon the sea
We reached that point of "no
    return"
And yet—ne'er day nor night
Will cease that human bondage . . .

Delene Nairns
MEMORIES
I walked for a long while last night;
    thinking of you.
The silence of the still evening
    enhanced the wonderful
    memories.
I reminisce on the times we
    talked for hours;
    never speaking a word.
For the touch of your hand
    and the sparkle in your eyes
told your love for me.

Michael Levon Boatwright
YOU AND I
To you I give my love,
From you I receive inspiration.

To you I give my life,
From you I receive your life,
and the lives of our children.

To you I give stories and past
    memories.
From you I receive laughter,
and more memories.

To you I give protection from
    harm.
From you I receive love,
and security.

Together we form one person,
living only to love,
and to be loved,
forever.

Rose M. Tank
AUTUMN IN THE PINES
The mystical waters wind
    endlessly through the forest,
Autumn leaves caress the earth
    with colored splendor.
Deer quench their thirst from the
    cooling springs—
While the animals romp through
    the leaves.

These are the sights I love in
    autumn.

On the knoll, I stand alone—
The gentle breeze caressing my
    flowing hair.
In quiet solitude
Enchantment invades my total
    being,
Contentment of peace throughout.

Tall, the pines, they tower
    skyward.
Shadows fall like gentle
    patchwork—
Creating illusions of dark and
    light.
Soaring eagles, find rest amidst
    the branches,
Shelter from storms exists below.

Spring brings forth the creation of
    life
While chilling winter blankets
    the earth.
Scorching heat sizzles emergence—
Till nights winds can cool the
    brow.
Impatiently, I await the coming
    of autumn.

Crisp the air, enchantment grows.
Falling leaves shower me like
    gentle rain.
Scurring animals preparing for
    winter
Reminding me to quick will end,
My beautiful season, too swift it
    passes.

Bessie F. House
LOVES' DREAM
    *[To the man who made me
    realize that being 'in love' is
    one of the most sublime states
    of all human experience: Thank
    you for sharing your
    quintessential self with me.]*
If I could hold you close to me
    forever,
And whisper words of loves'
    eternal fire,
No human force could this our
    sweet bond sever,
Nor still the stirrings of our wild
    desire.
If I could glimpse warm passion
    in your eyes,
And feel your touch so softly
    over me,
A singular pulse between us
    would arise,
Whose rhythmic flow is like the
    tempestuous sea.
But I would rather love you in
    my heart,
And memorize each day I spend
    with you,
The hours of passionate
    surrender in the park,
Warm bodies mingling in covered
    fields of dew.
You are to me a dream within my
    grasp,
Please, take my hand with a
    gentle, yet solid, clasp.

M. Jacquin
FOR STEPHEN
You are the sum total
of my dreams,
having each quality
for greatness

that when combined multiply
one—hundred—fold for Good.
Giving you Life has been
the single Joy—
watching you grow in body
strength and intellect.

With ideals uncommon you are
in all ways, God's miracle.

Teresa A. Nyarady
PEACEFUL VILLAGE
[To my Parents who, through
their infinite love and patience,
taught me that the true beauty
in life is revealed in the simple
things God has given us.]
Peaceful village sleeping in
harmony
Awaiting the dawn
Quiet and still in the shadow of
night.

The sphere of endless fire
Raising up her glorious head
Brightens the horizon with hues
Of flaming extracts.

Crickets returning to their slumber
While wings awaken with song
Little people laugh and play
While elders prepare for work
In the bountiful fields of life.

Children playing not quite as
vigorous
As womenfolk prepare the table
For the return of their men
Weary from the labors of the spoil
On which they depend so heavily
Making their lives worthwhile.

Peaceful village sleeping in
harmony
Awaiting the dawn
For an almost instant replay of
days past.

Debbie Leyser
LIFE GOES ON . . .
There's sadness all around today;
The things we touch, the words
we say.
Someone close has passed away.
And though we may not
understand it all,
We mustn't let our own lives fall.
We'll cry our tears and let God
know
We'll do our best, even though,
The pain we feel is very strong.
He lets us know that life goes on.

Nancy O'Neal
I AM
I'm a sad little girl
In a grownup world;
Lost without a prayer.

I'm a butterfly
Who's bound to die;
Afraid to spread my wings.

I'm a rosebud of pink
On a morning in spring;
Drinking the rays of the sun.

With it's light I grow strong,
Finding strength to belong,
And I soar like a bird through the
clouds.

Diana Lynne McNutt Enjady
HE TOOK MY PLACE
Are you searching for love and a
way of escape,
Only to find the world empty

and so full of hate?
If you'd had your choice you'd not
have been born.
Life has left your heart lonely,
broken, and torn.
You often think of taking your
life, or might even have tried.
Well, you see my friend, it's for
these things that Jesus died.
He came to set men free.
That they might have life more
abundandtly.
The devil tries to steal, kill, and
destoy.
The world is just his toy.
I was once controlled by him,
Till one day Jesus took me in.
I was at the bottom, when He
shined on me.
I accepted His gift and couldn't
believe it was FREE! (Romans
6:23)
I deserved to die for all I'd done,
But God in His infinite love
gave His only begotten son,
and Jesus, God's son took my
place.
When my trial came up and I was
to be sentenced to death,
A man in the back stood up
and said, "Let her go free,
instead crucify me."
I looked back to see who He was,
And realized it was the one I
had cursed.
How could he love such a one as I?
After all I'd done, I deserved to
die.
Yet this man who knew no sin,
became sin for me.
So that I might be set free.
He said my sins would be
remembered no more.
He said, "Go, my child, and sin
no more."
And so that day for the whole
world to see,
This man, Jesus, died on calvary.
He took the sins of the world,
and the sins of you and me.
On the cross He took our
place, so that you and I might
be set free.
We no longer have to be judged
for our sin.
And all the gratitude we owe to
Him.
He's done His part, and we must
do ours.
Ours is easy, His was hard.
Accept Jesus as your Saviour, and
begin to live for Him.
You then will be enslaved to
God, and freed from satan's
sin.(Romans 6:22)

B. J. Lisatz II
THE SOAP OPERA
Welcome,
But beware,
All who enter here
For here, we play with emotions.
For this, is the Soap Opera called
Life.

It's not like what you see
On the TV
Nor at the movies,
For there,
The script has already been
written.

Here it is different,
There is no script
There never can be
Or can there?
Welcome to reality.

Day by day,
Come what may
No matter what the
consequences
We must go on
Playing it out, to the end.

Earl LaOrange
AND LIFE ROLLS BY
It Rolls so Slowly by on its
Roadway to the Sea
It Wanders Along so Aimlessly
on its Journey to the Sea . . .

It's Truly a Beauty for All to See As
it Flows to the Sea . . .
It Twists and Turns at its Own
Will Wandering to the Sea . . .

It Causes Moon Beams to Glisten
Along its Pathway to the Sea . . .
Its' Beauty, is there for All to See
As it Rolls by to the Sea . . .
It Has such a Tranquil, Peaceful
Beauty, on its Path to the Sea . . .
It is Surely Part of Gods True
Might as it Moves to the
Wonderous Sea—

It's Lifes true course as it Flows
Along to an Ending at the
Peaceful Sea . . .

Dorothy Brin Crocker
AT THE AIRPORT
Where are they going
Those rushing feet?
What are they seeking?
What will they meet?

Why do they hurry
To meet their fate?
When will their eyes see
Time must wait?

Yesterday vanished
Deep in the night
Tomorrow is waiting
Still out of sight.

Those hurrying feet
Will miss today
With all the joy
Of time to pray.

No time for dreaming
Of what life means
Too hurried to know
Love redeems.

Betty Irene Thomas
HEART TO GOD
[To my beloved mother who
has been an inspiration to me
all my life. I thank God for
giving her to me. My prayer is
that I will be half the person
she has been.]
God is so worthy of our worship
that it's very easy to say,
Our hearts belong to Him in
every single way.
He is Alpha and Omega—the
First and the Last—the
Beginning and the End,
He is the Great I Am—the God of
the Living and our Best Friend.
He is the Almighty Creator who
made our body, mind and soul,
To stand in awe of the

Omnipotent One should be
more desired than gold.
He is the rock of our strength,
our refuge, our salvation and
our glory,
Even the history of man really
means "His Story".
Honour and majesty are before
Him so His word is true,
He is not a man that He should
lie so he does what He says He
will do.
Heaven is His throne and the
clouds are the dust of His feet,
Earth is His footstool where
mountains quake and hills
melt with fervent heat.
What the all—powerful Jehovah
has made straight cannot be
made crooked by man,
He is the Holy One in our midst
who has the master plan.
Uncountable are His wonders
and beside Him, all things pale,
The God of Hosts who can gather
the winds in His fists can do
everything but fail.
It is a fearful thing to fall into the
hands of the Living God who
changes never,
Let us enter into His courts with
praise for He is King forever
and ever.
Heart to God—Heart to God—
how can we do less?
The One who gives us breath to
use—even to curse Him if we
choose—deserves our very best.

Johnny M. Goodwin
SPINDLETOP
With the use of a Cable tool
The "Lucas Gusher" was brought in
It started a field called "Spindletop"
And a rush of Texas oil men.

The boom towns sprang up
And the drill stems went down.
The "fever" spread fast
To punch holes in the ground.

From Beaumont to Borger
"Black Gold" was king.
And the wealth from oil
Was every man's dream.

Refineries now have emerged
Pipelines cross the land
And it was the Sprindletop field
That Texas drilling all began.

Karen Elliott
WILDFLOWERS
As the gentle spring winds blow
the wildflowers seem to sing a
special song.
Though not sowed they simply
happen along.
One of God's more delicate
creations, they fare the winds
and storms well.
Whether growing together on a
high mountain side or in the
valleys down below, they show
their beautiful vail.
Their colors, bright and bold,
So sweet and lovely they are to
hold.
Wildflowers bring much beauty
to lonely places,
Seemingly so tender when one
looks at their faces.
They seem to have a special

unique beauty within,
Undescribed by men.
Handled gently they continue to
grow,
Almost as if man intended
them row by row.
Oftentimes when moon and stars
shine on them so bright,
They are left alone to face the
chill of the spring nights.
Upon awakening each pedal still
wet as tears, glistening with
the morning dew,
They unfold with specialness
anew.
Sunrise Sunshine, Good morning
Glory.
Feeling touched by the warmth of
the morning sun their
brightness shines again.

Everett A. Mills
SANTA
How does Santa in just one day,
Spread all the joys along the way?
Some folks say he is more than
one;
While others say it's him and his
sons.

Now listen to me, for I know,
Because my mother told me so.
That Santa flies at the speed of
light;
He always comes in mid of night.

He brings joys and lots of toys,
To all good little girls and boys.
Now don't stay up, for Santa you
can't see;
He'll be come and gone before
you can say me.

Now that Santa you saw in the
store,
Is the very same one you saw
before;
He is everywhere, in every place;
The same old Santa, with the
same old face.

Now kiss mom and dad and pull
your blinds
And get into bed exact at nine;
In the morning under the tree,
There will be toys for you and me.

Ann Nelson Martin
MY FRIEND AND I
[*Dedicated to my husband
George, on this Christmas Eve
of our 25th Wedding
Anniversary.*]
My friend and I
walked through this world
together.
Kept love aglow,
and conquered all together.

In happy times we shared
our laughs together.
In sorrowed times we shared
our tears together.

Out of this love grew a son
we shared his birth together.
He now is grown
we share his joys together.

For twenty—five years

we've shared our lives together.
Next twenty—five years may it
be said:
we've shared them all together.

Helenjean Hays Speights
I AM MUSIC!
[*With love and deep
appreciation to my mother
who has always taught me love
and respect for life and all the
best things thereof; especially
music.*]
I am the only thing in this strife-
torn world which can express
and understand all the moods
of humanity; for, I am those
moods, and much more. I am
the cool distant stranger and
the ardent, passionate, yet
gentle, giving lover; the gentle,
soothing rain and the violent,
stormy sea; the shy, innocent
child and the self—assured
adult.

I am truly the universal language.
I can bring together angry
lovers; even feuding nations, in
one accord; and make them
realize, for a while, at least, that
in GOD'S LOVE, there is no
difference between the Jew and
the Greek; or the peoples of the
world and the man of America.

Yes, I am the *one* thing which is
all things, and much more.
. . . . . .I AM MUSIC!

Thea D. Hughes
THIS LOVE WE SHARE
I never knew the joy we'd feel,
And yet the feeling is so real.
It took its time while on its way,
But now its here and here to
stay.
Up in the heavens are many stars,
Yet they're not as great as this
love of ours.
The sands by the sea are nothing
compared
To the joy we feel in the love
we share.
The laughter and the tears we'll
see,
And face together—you and me.
We'll set our love up on a stand,
And gaze at it hand in hand.
We'll make it together through
this life,
Sharing all happiness, grief and
strife.
We'll love while young and love
when old,
And through all time it won't
grow cold.
And years from now when we are
gone,
The love we've shard will still
go on.
Bigger than ever it will be,
And living on through eternity.

Rhesa Read Browning
CLOSE TO GOD
Can you recite a poem
Long, short or in between?
Can you quote a scripture
Or remember a lovely dream?

Do you recall a love song
From the years of your teens?

Can you hum a tune you
remember
Of your early childhood scenes?

Is there a laugh you remember,
Its lilt and musical note;
Is there an old, near—forgotten
adage
You recall and still can quote?

Is there some long ago faces
In fancy you still see
And imagine you touch their hand
Before this lovely spell can flee?

If these are a part
Of your love and your heart
You are indeed close
To God.

Rose Simpson Brown
A MIRROR I WILL BE
A reflection I will be, for today
I looked into a mirror, and much
to my surprise, what I saw was all
deep, deep, inside.

There it was, all exposed, the
inner me
right down to my very soul
alarmed, shocked, and surprised,
what
I saw wasn't really me on the
outside.
What have I done? Where did it
go wrong?
Why isn't the inner me the same
as the outer soul?

Then I could see way beyond
it isn't just me, but everyone.
Life is a fairy tale to most
for they really don't accept the
Holy Ghost.
If all would look within their self,
and
see the person that is there,
open up your heart, let it out
don't pretend, just be proud, for
the person
you really are, is just what God
wanted,
for He created you as He chose.
Don't fret, or whine, just be
proud, life's riches
you will surely find.

Now when you look at me, a
mirror you will see
for when you look at me, what
you'll see is
the inner me. For I am a mirror of
the real me!

To everyone in life who feels
they are not special,
you really are, you see, for God
made you that way,
if you'll only let yourself be . . .

Bertha Powers Woods
Those Toil Worn Hands
[*Dedicated to the Memory of
my Darling Ross*]
How beautiful were his hands,
Their sinews gave strength with
every clasp.
With never a falter or thought of
self
He gave of his best, whatever the
task—
Of his toil worn hands.

His skillful fingers were symbols
of an eager mind,
Each callus a picture of devotion—

Etched by time.
Many a long hour was given
Guiding the tools of his trade,
It was as if he were driven
By an untiring spirit of
service—unpaid
To those toil worn hands.

Their firmness and strength were
often displayed
When danger threatened or
disaster seemed near—
Yet, gentleness too, with a tender
touch
Brought comfort and
confidence, which allayed
every fear.

The lines across his palms left no
doubt
That love for all mankind had
been his goal.
The crook of each fingertip, oft
hurt in haste
Denoted what surely fulfilled its
role—
True service of toil worn hands.

Baiting a fish—hook for a tiny girl,
Tenderly caressing when she
slipped and fell.
Giving assistance to those in
need—
Will long be remembered by
many who tell—
Of those toil worn hands.

Shirley Davis MaGee
HEAVEN'S DELIGHT
[*To my husband Wardell and
Son Del, for spicing up my life
through good and bad times.*]
The spice of life is a blend of love
ravished in a clove
Of rich togetherness—
while a hint of gentleness
Creates a delicate blend
of unmatched kindness.
The savor of peace edifies
the soul with a nourishing
Balance of contentment, and a
zestful flavor which satisfies
The mind and quietens the spirit.
The pleasing taste of prosperity
sauted in progress,
simmered in success,
Transforms a thriving variety
into the sweetness of delight.
The presence of joy is anticipated
as the aroma of gladness
Becomes intermingled with the
flavor of splendid happiness.
A portion of heaven's delight
is most gratifying to the
Taste of life.

Jerry M. Marshall
UNTITLED
She smiled so sweetly then
It seems like yesterday
She spoke of love
For love she was
At least she was to me

Nothing since has been as real
No equal has come forth
Her gentle touch
Her soft caress
The love she gave to me

Fingertips did soothe my brow
As lightly as the breeze
She traced the lines
And soothed the ache

As only she could do

She smiled and closed my open
eyes
So I would not forget
Her tender voice
Her love filled kiss
The love that we had shared.

Darryl Stonum
LOVE AND LUST
He took the best of you, and the
love in your heart
Now before Love's Holiday, you're
lonely and torn apart.
He used the line, "I don't want to
hurt you."
"I'm doing what's best."
But really what he's chasing is
what's under the ladies' dress.
You've done what you could, and
should be upset and mad.
But that would be playing his
other game.
Do the opposite and be glad.
Patiently wait to build your love
in someone you can trust.
Someday the fool will learn to
chase Love and not Lust.

William Robert Senter Jr.
THE HOSPITAL WINDOW
[Dedicated to Susan Senter
McGhee, mother of Michael
Stephen McGhee May 4,
1974—November 12, 1979]
I saw her praying at the window,
looking toward the sky above
Silently asking for the miracle,
that could only save our love
Please, Oh Lord, I could hear her
say
Beseeching Him as never before
Don't take him so soon, Oh Lord
For he is only four
Only in the early spring of life
Hardly beyond its open door
Still in the world of make believe
That is part of being just four
He has touched so many with his
love
And has so much more to give
Send the miracle that will save
him, Oh Lord
Send the miracle that will let him
live
And I joined in her silent prayer
Adding my fervent and hopeful
plea
That the miracle would be sent
and our Michael would not so
soon an Angel be
But, then I added, if such is not in
the Book of Life
Then take him gently, without
suffering, pain, or strife
Take him as he has lived, full of
happiness and love
Eager for the new adventure with
You in Heaven above
And although we had so many
plans
We recognize that he is in Your
Hands
And, Our Father which art in
Heaven—

Rudolph Frazier
NEBULOUS—LOVE
Nebulous—love
I saw a glow that eyes straight
I felt a warmth when there

was coldness.
I looked through darkness and
saw daylight. The still of an
Hour ticking away.
The sounds of questions coming
From within
Searching for answers that
Seem so still.
The morning of freshness
Starts a new day—a new beginning
Of a new life.
The first chance to do and learn
A closeness that seems so
beyond.
As seasons come and go, awaits
The earth new time.
Where does summer go while
Winter comes in.
The nucleus of life with all
Of its hey—days
A look within the two
A closer depth from within
An answer—slowly creeps
To light.
——Love

Edna Norton
**With the Eagerness Of
Youth**
There is a spring in a meadow
Near the very edge of a woods.
The cool shade falls o'er
Where the clear waters bubble free
From the depth of the earth.

They tinkle gaily over rocks,
Worn smooth thru' the years,
Then rush past reeds and
snake—grasses
In their haste to reach the muddy
river
Only to be lost—forever.

Patt Fogerty
UNTITLED
I can stand almost all
Except to see my daughter bawl
She cries her eyes out just for you
It hurts so bad that I cry too
I know you love her and you care
But you don't see her, you aren't
there
It tears me all up inside
That's one thing I can't abide
Hurting a child is worse you see
Than anything if you ask me
Death doesn't even hurt as bad
As the tears she shed cause she
misses her dad

Dale A. Hoover
DESIRES'
Quietness desends like a balmy
cloud as I taste your sweetness.
The softness of your being
clings to my body as whispers
of endearment flow from your
lips.
Other sounds are subdued as our
union of completeness emerges
around us.
Your arms are clouds, soft and
gentle, yet strong; subduing my
feeble struggles, entwining us
together.

The nectar of your body
strengthens me as I drink from
the ever flowing fountain of
your love.

I thirst,—you give me drink;
I thirst,—you give me promise;
I thirst,—you give yourself—

—and my thirst is quenched.

Yearnings I hear, Yes, your
yearnings I hear and want to
subdue.
Tenderness you crave—
tenderness I give to you.
To be held—I hold you to
myslef.
To be with me forever—we
reach out and our lives become
entwined together . . . never to
be separated.

Fernando M. Serrano
So Very Still He Sits
So very still he sits.
Sticken deeply into his thoughts,
With no pondering of tomorrow
or the consequence of leaving
himself empty and vulnerable.
No longer to care, or to love,
Only to be encompassed by
scorching memories.
So very still he sits.
His mind, overwhelmed with
sorrow,
loses all its prudishness and
discretion.
Complete desertion of joy and of
passion occupies a shattered heart,
forever famished for love.
So very still he sits.
Cheated by the unpredictability
of reality.
Perhaps to perish will relinquish
his spirit,
or bring comfort to his soul.
So very still he sits.
Cold and empty, where warmth
and fulfillment once rested.
And brings upon himself the
questions
that will never be answered.
So very still he sits,
For God has taken her away . . .

Jean M. Thieda
LIFE
Who ever said that life was fair
That we'd have roses everywhere,
the sun would shine without a
cloud
and all our songs, we'd sing out
loud?

But don't you know that soon
would pall
we would not care for that at all,
So give us peace and give us strife,
a change sure is the spice of life.

Mary Anne Miller
CELEBRATION
Christmas joy,
Celebration
Of the Baby Jesus'
Birth!

With His advent,
Jubilation
Filled the heavens and the
Earth!

Christ, the Savior,
Brought salvation
Giving hope and life of
Worth!

Lift our Lord in
Exaltation!
He has freed from sin an
Dearth!

Let us serve in

Dedication . . .
Spreading peace with joy and
Mirth!

William Henry Schubert
WE
[To Ann]
You breathe Life into
The theory—soul that is me;
I breathe Life into
The theory—soul that is thee.
We
Together
You, Me
Inseparable Union, Two:
We
The music of hearts' union
The poetry of thoughts merged
The history of being ever together
The philosophy of forms joined
The religion of goodness pursued
The aesthetics of timeless touch
The theatre of shared expression
The language of love's beyond
Your life brings rebirth of
increased goodness
To my life,
To the Goodness that
We create, and
Must always Be
WE

Lesa B. Peerman
THE ACTOR
If only you could care, as I care
for you,
If only your love would be ever so
true.
That's not your style, that much I
know,
What a sin it would be to let
your love show.
Your feelings you hide, so no one
can see,
You've fooled just about
everyone, everyone but me.
I can tell when you hurt and
when you cry,
I can see all your sorrows, so why
even lie?
You put on an act that you're not
lonely or sad,
But to tell you the truth, your
acting is bad.
You say I don't want you and I
really don't care,
You may hide your feelings, but
mine are still there.
Our happiness together is in my
dreams for now,
Someday you'll love, someday
you'll learn how.
I'll watch you and protect you
and always be a friend,
For if I ever lost you it would be
my own end.
I wait forever until that happy
day,
When saying you love me, isn't
hard to say.
So when you say nothing is
wrong, I know it's not true,
Because I have a gift, I can and do
love you.

Malinda S. Brooks
I HAD A DREAM
Last night I had a dream;
And oh it seemed so true.
You were in love with me;
And I was so in love with you.

498

We were laughing, loving and
   having fun.
Loving each other inside out;
Not hurting anyone.

And then I awoke and felt so sad;
For I realized it was just a dream
   I'd had
And I knew that we could never be;
Cause I love you so;
But I know you don't love me

So when I meet you on the street;
I'll just smile and say hi each
   time we meet
I won't start a conversation with
   you;
The way you know, I always do.

Each time I see you, my heart
will be filled with tears.
When I think of the love I wasted
for you, for all these years.

But no matter where you go;
Or what you do.
Just remember, I'll always love
   you.

James A. Stacy
SWORDS
He who rides the white charger
goes headless through the night,

Was many a night—for it was
   spring everything peaceful,
   everything serene,
Then came that dread night
it was time for him to ride,
Upon his white horse away he flew
his cape flying behind, his sword
   held high.

"Look, Look!" Cried the fearful
   peasants,
"Tis death in flight." Lo, were the
   peasants right
For with one mighty blow, he
   stole the soul from a man and
   his wife.
Who is that rider that comes by
   night never to be seen in
   daylight?
Why death of course
with graveyards near and far,
   narrow and wide.

But Lo,
In the heavens another rider
   appears.
He holds a sword of fire on high
for this is the rider of life.
Oh, you should have seen,
in the fight—the fire flew high.
Away rode death, what a hideous
   sight life had prevailed, but
   only for a time,
for death will strike again, when
   the time is right.

Christine Raabe—Lyans
UNTITLED
*[To my children; Jennifer and
Benjamin and all children who
have or are going through
divorce.]*
They knew someday it would
   happen, they were told that day
   would come.
As they stare wide—eyed through
   the window, they know now it
   is done.

Trying so hard to prevent it,
by doing everything they could.
Pretending that it wasn't so,

deeply knowing it would.

The house feels grey and empty,
as it is in their little heart.
They're insecure and lonely,
since the day it fell apart.

Rejection coming from their sighs,
since that dismal day took place.
Their lashes wet with dripping
   love,
that saturates their face.

Look up dear little children,
new light will guide your way.
Your hearts will soon mend over,
forgetting that long, dark day.

Smile sweet with happiness,
although you hurt and cry.
Remember, it was not your fault,
when Daddy told Mommy
   good—bye.

Hilary Palmer
LIFE
O Life that cannot die
Weave for me that rich and
   permanent tapestry
Of thy changeless and eternal
   form.
Dense clouds of dust, obscure not
   the reflection.
Unveil the unknowable, reduce
   the vast
That I may perceive the first in
   the last.
Reveal thy true expression.
Let me understand the drama
That underlies the suface of the
   plot;
As I seek to find myself, show me
   that I am not.
Halt the future! recapture the past!
O Life that knows no death,
Eternity that knows no time,
Let Life be mine!

Christopher D. Sharpe
FORTHCOMING
Flowing through the woodwork
Running up the walls
Ducking in and out of life
Sweeping through the night

Take care rounding those corners
   son
There is no second chance
Either give it every time
Or you'll have no time to give

Halfway there and sliding back
Put on the brakes but they don't
   give you slack
If you panic you'll keep on
   plunging
So laugh in their faces and keep
   on coming

Sweeping through the woodwork
Running up the walls
Ducking out and into life
Flowing through the night

Joy Creamer
WITH LOVE TO MOTHER
Looking back over the years
I recall laughter, tears, love and
   fears.
A petite gentle lady, with much
   love to give.
Who guided me through the
   years.
At times she was tired, you
   visibly could see.

Yet her whistling and singing is
   clear to me.
She smiled or gave praise when it
   was deserved.
But a glance without words when
   we misbehaved.

Though we also experienced hard
   times you see.
Mother somehow found the way
   to fulfill my dreams.
The blue Shelby bike, a clarinet
   and semi-formal gown.
Whatever situations arose in my
   growing up I recall
her saying, "it's alright dear" or
   "we'll work it out."

I won't forget the cardboard in
   her shoes to cover the holes.
Or the hand-me-down clothes
   that was her wardrobe.
Mother worked long hours all the
   time.
And with Gods love and
   guidance we survived.

We shared joys, and laughter
   through the years.
Along with fears,
   disappointments and tears.
What stands out is the Special
   Love she projects.
Not only as my mother, but my
   friend.
Thank—you Mother once again.

Pat McElhinny
MY GIFT TO YOU
I want to give you sunshine
To brighten all your days
I want to give you laughter
To chase the clouds away.

I want to show you beauty
With the rising of the sun
In all its regal splendor
As each day has just begun.

I want to help you learn to smile
And touch each passerby
To give a little of yourself
And never wonder why.

I want to gently brush away
Your weariness and tears
To always hold you near my heart
And teach you not to fear

If I can do these things for you
The peace and joy we'll share
For then you'll know my heartfelt
   love
And just how much I care.

Then *you* must take the sunshine
The laughter and the love
And share it with all others
As gifts from God above.

Argyle Stoute
ROPE
I went one day to a Georgia Town
It was a bleak Memorial Day
I took a walk, no one was around
But the dangling image of their
   prey.

The tree was bare; the brown
   leaves dead
The once blue sky was gray
There was a swirling mist and a
   cold rain hissed
At the long ill—gotten clay.

And as I looked I wished and cried
For the victim of their prey

For the summer skies and his
   laughing eyes
For his curly head of hair.

And all I found was a sturdy
   bough
Stretched out in the blithesome air
I thought I'd had enough
So I turned and walked away.

But on the ground my shoe-tip
   found
The rope with strands of his hair
On the ground I laid it down
I winced and walked away.

His carefree smile, the light in his
   eyes
A mob had carried away
I clicked my heals
And gathered a smile
No one can erase today.

Laura B. Schildkraut
TO THE PUPPETEER
    Possessed
    Obsessed
You control my entire being
   Each move, Each mood
    You

I am caught within the very web
in which I entangled myself.
Worse, I was aware that you
were gaining control.
Like a spectator, I observed.

I am now a puppet.
Caught in the strings
that I placed in your hands
and cried,
"Make me dance!"
And you did.

You were so gentle at first;
unsure of the power I entrusted
   to you.
But power is a strange thing.
Once its seed is planted and
   well-watered
it conquers.
As ivy covers its domain.

And at once I was under your
   control.
As the strings became part
   of your hands.

Patricia Zselenak
SUMMER MORNING
Sun has risen upon the shade
Dew dust falls upon the light
Birds have sung their song of
   morning
Washing away all fears of past
   night.
Buds have now burst into beauty
Every creature is fresh and new
God has granted this new day
So let us be thankful the whole
   day through.
But the light shining through the
   window
Won't last long or stay with you
Soon we will retire and pray
For another morning bright and
   new.

Phillip H. Buttermore
Mary In the Moonlight
In peace you laid sleeping, your
   soul in God's keeping, when in
   your room creeping in silence I
   came.
What did my eyes greet on that
   innocence, sweet, 'neath the

clean smelling sheet o'er your
moon—lighten form?
Deft fingers of light in a tender
delight touching you in the
night and caressing your form.
While you dreamed quiet dreams
the soft silent streams of leaf
filtered beams wove a lace gold
and warm,
whose patterns would shimmer
making each tiny glimmer
grow brighter or dimmer as
wind moved the leaves.
With grace they came stealing to
touch me with feeling, these
moonbeams revealing their
gossamer weaves.
Most pensive I glanced, held in
spell—binding trance, as the
light did its dance and
enhanced all it met,
and awed, I did ponder and let my
mind wander at such beauty
yonder lest e're I forget.
Still . . . Prior to egressing I
thought on my blessing so dear
and obsessing who fills my
heart so—
asleep, unaware, never sensing
me there. I fondled your hair
not wanting to go,
but with light gentle hug I then
tucked you in snug as I knelt
on your rug with my face by
your head
and, kissing your ear, I said, "I
love you, dear, though I know
you don't hear me along side
your bed."
Then rising, I glanced on the
secret light—dance and asked
was it chance that placed this
child here
or did my God above in His
infinite love see our needs and
thereof let us know He does
hear?

Lillian L. Kramer
WE WORKED TOGETHER
*[To the most beautiful and
loving man in the world, my
husband, Barry. Without him
this poem could never have
been written.]*
The seasons have come,
The seasons have gone;
We worked together,
We sowed our corn.

We lived our life,
Through bad and good;
We only did
What lovers would.

I beared his weight
And he beared mine;
Through it,
We got our love combined.

Material Things?
We have not much;
But what we have,
No one can touch.

John M. Cohen
NURSING HOME
They are afraid,
facing an uncertain
future.
They are alone,
shaken by these unforeseen
circumstances.

They are unable,
motionless in their ridden beds
of sorrow.
taken of their dignity
in this time
of helplessness.
and left to die,
in pity . . .

Rhoda Schaeffer Altmann
BLACK SISTER
*[Wayne my son, winds blow
the sands of time . . . "nothing
gold can stay" all but my love
for you . . . evermore]*
The likeness was an incredible
mirror image of myself
An accurate deliverance
emerging from the vapor as I
exhaled.
Where were the people to witness
my testimony?
A mimic it was in utter ridicule
of me
Not mindful that I was it and it
was me, you see.
So bitter cold the winter's night,
I hastened my pace.
For home is where the hearth is. . .
Undoing the latch; the door
slammed behind
Slithering, it had entered through
the keyhole before me.
Lighting the kindling, dry logs
quickly caught . . .
Smoke curled . . . and there was
me sitting on a hot bed of
coals.
I poked at myself as others often
do,
This time I wasn't offended.
Well bless my soul, I was as black
as a Memphis Marcher;
So this was me on the other side
of the fence.
I didn't like it . . . I wanted to be
me
Fanning that black devil, I
thought it would go up in
smoke;
It spoke: "Black sister, you are
what you ain't with powder and
paint"
no one ever knew my secret

Bonnie Lee Ward
The Shape Of a Daydream
Shimmery, cloudlike, distant,
enhanced by brilliant hues of
rainbow—colors.
Peeping around corners, poking
about in velvet—lined
wrappings, peering over hugh,
majestic unencumbered
mountains.
Covetiously quarding its
precious, plentiful, luxurious
riches and its magic, mystical
mysterious secrets.
Its fruitless pleasures lulling me
to sleep: its daily appearances a
soothing balm: enfusing my
soul with its momentary
warmth, then slowly retreating,
and gently leaving my soul
with a gloomy, deathlike chill.

Ever elusive, sly and wicked,
unwilling to do my bidding.
Daily I entreat them to rest, relax,
and remain with me.
Daily they cloak, enshrine, and
flee: away and aloaft with their

brilliant rainbow—colored
hues, still born hopes and
enriching warmth.

Daily and at the same precise
hour, they make their daily
reappearances.
Shimmery, cloudlike, distant yet
near; ever enhanced by their
Brilliant rainbow—colored hues.

Peeping around corners, poking
about in velvet—lined
wrappings, peering over hugh,
majestic unencumbered
mountains.
All too quickly they again cloak,
enshrine and flee;
Away and aloaft with their still-
born hopes and enriching
warmth.

M. Bainbridge—Kinsella
NIGHT CALLER
*[To Mom, (The Original M.
Bainbridge), Who Made It!]*
"Is this the one", I softly asked,
"You're sure it's she you seek?"
(This meager little lady—her very
breathing is so meek.)
What's that you say, my Jesus,
she'll walk with you above?
Her days were wrought with
constant strife, and yet her
heart held love?
She must have been a "Pistol",
Lord, if you regard her so.
And surely, if she sleeps away,
my cup would overflow.

You see, I really know her; and
have since I was born.
I knew her in the robust days,
before she was so worn.
She laughed, and cried—was
strong, yet soft—she battled
every day.
But ne'er forgot at eventide, to
bow her head and pray.

Her wisdom, love and fortitude,
would leave us with a void;
But for her sake, your knowing
ways shant ever be denied.
Just one thing that I ask, Lord, if
you might let her see—
The husband gone so many
years . . .
He died when I was three.

Helen R. Wulfert
My Legacy To My Grandsons
*[Dedicated, with love, to my
three dear grandsons, Jeffrey,
Patrick and Michael.]*
I cannot leave you lots of wealth
As some grandparents do,
But I leave to you an abundance
of
Good health, your lifetime
through.
I wish for you contentment
In the job you do, well done;
The comfort of a loved one—
Your place under the sun!
The wisdom to tell right from
wrong
And stand for what is right;
The courage of your convictions
Regardless of your plight!

Material things don't last,

As you'll be made aware,
But I leave you love, and solace
From one who really cares.

A wife who truly loves you
Whether things go right or
wrong,
A time for happiness and joy;
A heart that's full of song.
This is my legacy to you,
My grandsons, still so small,
That when you're all grown up
You'll always stand up tall!
I hope you will remember
My legacy, with love,
For everything I leave you
Comes from our *God* above!

Bob Barci
Frenzied Fingers Run Amuck
When I get you into my arms,
I can't control the things that I
do.
Fingers grab the hair on your
head.
Fingers caress the small of your
back.
Fingers travel down your spine
and back up again.
Fingers reach to all corners of
your being,
Quietly unnoticed at first,
But more frenzied with passing
time.

Wildfingers travel your soul
With frenzied action that is hard
to stop.
Uncontrollable fingers run wild
Until you beg them to stop.
But even then, there's no
counting on it.
These fingers like to run wild.
Whenever I place my hands on
you,
Frenzied fingers run amuck.

Douglas A. Peck
No Virginia, There Is No Sanity Clause
Well we're coming on our shift,
and I'm feeling kind of miffed,
I just fell in a snow drift, outside
the door.

So we walk out in the shop, and
each day I have to stop,
And take a look at all the slop
that's on the floor.

It's not as easy as can be, for my
brother Snerd and me,
Hell, we're only two foot three,
from top to bottom.

And now I can't find my tools, so
I let my temper cool,
While I wonder which damn fool
here might have got 'em.

So I borrow someone's wrench,
and as I climb up on my bench,
I smell the stench of glue and
Jeez, somebody farted.

But that don't bother me much,
I'm a specialist, you see,
And this job here is just for me,
so I get started.

Then the boss walks from his
stall, and he beams at one and
all,
As a B-B chips the wall next to
his ear.

500

But he doesn't seem to care, he
  just strokes his silver hair,
While Snerd and me, we stand
  and stare, he sips his beer.

Then he lets out his loud
  chuckle, clasps his hands on
  his belt buckle,
And me and Snerd get set to
  knuckle down again.

Then as he turns to go, he gives
  us all one last Ho Ho,
He just wants the boys to know
  that he's their friend.

So we get back to work again,
  Snerd's on guns and I'm on
  trains,
And I've got the damndest stain
  here on my jeans.

But the time is running short,
  and Snerd says, "Brother Snort,"
"We'd better use our last resort,
  know what I mean?"

He says, "You know it'd be a
  crime not to get things out on
  time,"
And I says, "You know Snerd, that
  I'm with you, let's hear."

So he says, "Snort, what the hell,
  we'd best use an Elfin Spell,"
"Then we're layed off again until
  next year."

So we do it in a wink, and then
  we wash up in the sink,
And head on out to get a drink,
  our job is severed.

But the Boss Man gets away, in
  his silly looking sleigh,
With trains and guns aboard
  okay, to be delivered.

Has it ever crossed your mind,
  what Elves do with all their
  time,
You probably think that it's
  sublime, just pure enjoyment.

But there's nowhere that we can
  go, no AFL or CIO,
No labor union wants to know
  part time employment.

Gaylean Hubbert
REMINDERS
I sit in the truck with a little
  boy on my lap, and I remember
sitting on my mother's lap.

I drive down the road with my
  father sitting next to me, and I
  remember
sitting on his lap, helping him
  drive.

I see an old man help a young
  boy
with his toys, and I remember
the old man who once helped me.

I look at the stuffed bear
on my bed, and I remember
the beautiful friendship it
  represents.

I walk alone in the woods
each fall, and I remember
the lovely walks I had with him.

I hear an old song, and I
  remember
a friend who is dead and gone.

People have often said, "The past

should be forgotten." But, there are
too many reminders around to
  prevent
us from forgetting.

Brian D. Herd
THE OVERSEER
In the land of Acheron,
In the land of the Halentier
Resides the Monitor, overseer
Of all which is evil.
World of conquest World of
  terror.
Seeker of misfortune.
Casting lures of dark intent.
Thronemaster of the Dark
  Domain.
Thorns entangle his heart, pierce
  his mind.

Lost souls are enslaved
Imprisoned in his vast armies.
Regiments of Demons and
  Manglers are at his command.
Who but can dissuade the black
  onslaught?
Who can encase his trickery?
Who can dethrone his madness?

Lorie A. Landis
FOR MY FRIEND
*[A very special poem for a very
special friend; Tim Damiani]*
Beauty is in the eye of the
    beholder
  and your beauty is in me.
    I look and see a man . . .
who's sensitive and who's
    understanding.

If someone were to ask me,
  "what do you see in him?"
  I'd have to say something
    that's found deep within.

For you glow and you sparkle
  everytime I see your face
  And a glow that's so vibrant
that it could light up this place.

You have a laugh that echoes
    throughout this land
And it gives me this warm feeling
as warm as the sun heated sand.

There are many other reasons
  but these are just a few.
    That is why I love you
    and that I really do.

J.L. Cusyk
WRITER'S BLOCK
    Thinking produced nothing.
Ideas expressed verbally, were lost
  when confronted by blank paper.
    Written, seemed incoherent,
lacking the key to let dreams
      escape.

Juanita Komosinski
FEELING "NAM" ALL OVER
Waking you is much like a
  mother
  calling her child in from play.
But war games don't account for
  play—
  even in the mind,
  do they?
And I'm not your mother
  and no kiss will make it better.
I'd like to touch you and say
  the war is over—
  but I know it isn't,
Not as long as there be
  another night.

Still, I live it here
  with you—
  and without you.
Feeling "Nam" all over
  doesn't make it hurt any less.
So wake up—gently—
  to the revelry
  of just my voice,
And believe me
  and trust me.
I'm not your enemy—
  not when you're awake anyway.

Marcia Texter
MY NEW LIFE
Shadow me in time of need
Plant, yes Lord that righteous
  seed,
Guide me through this lonely day
Take this law of shame away.

God opened my eyes, He made
  me see
The morning sun that shines on
  me,
He gave me faith, the courage to
  try,
The heart to love, the tear to cry.

God gave me you to sing my song
That love is right and hurt is
  wrong;
Trust in Him for life He gave
To live tomorrow, that we must
  save.

Pamela Jean Smith
PATHS
Driving along the paths at night
Makes you wonder which turn is
  right
Making a decision, going the
  wrong way
Now you are lost with no one
  around
It's time to come of age and make
  your own choice
But deep inside you want to hear
  a voice
Someone in authority, someone
  to tell you what to do
Unfortunately, no one is around
  but you
You have made up your mind not
  knowing if you are right
But, yet, you are on your path
  again
This time intelligent, wise, and
  brave
You will never have to look back
  at that frightened, shy person
Again

Richard Newman
THE MUSIC MOVES ME
Half-asleep; my hands seek out
your breasts like cats walking
over a soft, warm quilt, searching
for the perfect spot in which to
  curl up.
You place your hands firmly over
mine and snuggle back to mold
yourself into the spoon of my
  body.
A Beethoven string quartet plays
softly around our ears and we
  sleep,
floating slowly over a forest
on a bed of blue butterflies.

Half-awake; my hands seek out
your breasts but don't find them;
barefoot into the living room
  where you,

sitting nude, are drinking coffee.
Debussy's ocean music fills
the room with a tapestry of sound
through which we move in a slow,
sensuous dance; together on the
  beach
of a deep, insistent sea.
A graceful gesture guides my lips
to your breasts; you stroke my
thighs with soft upward motions
and the music changes.

The radio plays a Bach organ
cantata and we make love
on the lavishly carpeted floor
of a candle-lit, Gothic castle.

Arlene Miller
LIVING WORD
*[To Rev. & Mrs. A. Parker
Tomlinson, whose love,
prayers, and Christian example,
have helped me to know the
One who is the "Living Word".]*
You've given the scriptures
  to help me know exactly
    how I should be;
Oh so much alive to You
  and very dead to me.
You say that everything I do
  should glorify Your name.
I must not seek for praise of men,
  for wealth or worldly fame.
Help me lean upon Your Word,
  as Your promises I now claim;
For You have said You will
  answer my prayers, if I pray
    in Jesus's name.
Lord, help me to live that the
  world might see,
You're not dead—You're alive
  for You're living in me!

Lorraine Hicks
CLEANSED
The slippery serpent
employed himself
to maneuver in God's garden.
Invading with engorging
appetite for iniquity.
Mankind knew days of mourning.

Chastisement was painful . . .
yet the promise tranquilized.
The stage was set
the curtain rose on salvation
and will ring down
on a new paradise.

Robert E. Tome
HOURGLASS
Is it going on a year?
Or is it really fifty.
It seems so long ago,
but it could be yesterday.
Without a friend it can be eternal.

So thru the days of memory
one can go back thru time,
but only in your mind.
For time is the master of reality
and with
its strong arm it molds you
  . . . deforms you.

Slowly you bend into the years,
silently as the falling snow you
  end there.
No tools he uses just weapons
  upon you.
The creeping of age, robbing you
  of the power
to remain, slowly leading you to
  your grave.

For on this vessel there is no
  return,
forward into the blind as tho'
  children
trustly you journ.

Your questions he need not
  answer
You find them as you toil,
ever watching in the distance
your life goes not unscanned;
no escape, no retreat, only the
  advance.
Humbly, step by step into the
  mist we rush
Thought for tomorrow's quest
to keep from going insane.

Oh time, who giveth thou the
  power to reign?

V. Joy Moore
I LOVE YOU, DAD
*[In loving memory of my father
who gave his life to his family
and asked only love in return.]*
A fishing rod for solace,
A rowboat on the lake,
A homemade lunch, a can of
  worms,
That's about all it takes
To comfort my Dad.

Hard work, determination,
With hardly a thought of rest,
A love of life and family—
His rich full life a test
For any, but my Dad.

At seventy and some odd years,
His work still being done . . .
Six days a week, twelve months a
  year,
Nary a vacation—no, not one—
Brought respite for my Dad.

Why do I now these lines set
  down?
His illness brought me short.
His birthday's near, and alas, I fear,
It's been too long since
I said simply,
"I love you, Dad".

Alice Louise Quinn
GRANDMOTHER
  May I write
Recite
  Stories of long ago
Ah so
  Stories you don't like
Dike
  So fragile against reality
Duality
  Of love and loss
Cross
  Of work and privation
Isolation
  In that country of your mind
Kind
  To all who pass
Trespass
  Against love
Above

Robert J. Ebright
MEMORIES
People will come and go
but memories will always glow
I will learn many things
from today
but none will equal
the feelings from yesterday

We were free to come and go

where we went I don't know
I wish it didn't have to end
this way
but nothing will stop
the feelings from yesterday

You came and you went
a gift from God that was sent
I was so happy with you
that way
you gave me memories
for today

J.L. Caravaglio
VICKIE
*[To my sister "Vickie", with
love, from your brother "John".]*
She just a horse as you can
  see . . .
But faster than lightning, on the
  track with me.
Cutting the air, so fine and so free.
In the land of my country.
She has a name.
Her name to be.
"Vicki", is the mare, for me.
There on the track.
In chenango country.
There on the track.
Just "Vicki", and me.

Norah Powell
MEMENTO
*[To the memory of Nelson A.
Rockefeller]*
Night it was
End of a busy day
Lying on the silent floor
Symbol of wisdom
On this troubled world
Neatly rested his head.

Ah! said a voice in pain
*Life is leaving let us detain
Drive the science pertain
Resuscitate his tender heart.
It was the try in vain
Colossal effort on their part
He was gone. Magnificent life and
  art.*

Rustling sounds of despair
On that memorable night.
Celestial help only to prevail
Kindly hear us Good Lord!
Empty praying words
For he was already dead
Entering into heaven
Limpid his noble soul.
Litany of sacred chanting
Endless lingering whispers
Repeated softly love from us all.

Michael David Cruz
THE DIVINE CONCESSION
*[". . . the truth will set you
free." John 8:32 "Write on"!—
930 West Occidental, Santa
Ana, CA 92707. Letters
welcome.]*
Where did Cain get his wife?
  Some ask with skeptical tone.
If, after taking Abel's life,
  Of women there were none.

But was that, in fact, true?
  Just what does the Bible say?
It says that Eve was the bearer to
  ALL the human race (Genesis
  3:20); nay

No "feme" preceded Cain
  Into the fugitive land.
The truth is scriptually plain:
  He took his sister's hand!

The Record shows Adam
  Father and sons *AND*
  daughters; (Genesis 5:4)
With Cain grown up th' need had
  him
  Obliged to have sought her.

Where did Cain get his wife?
  From his own family blood!
Yet forbid, nor "genetic strife",
  Since God ordained it "good".
  (Genesis 1:27, 28, 31)

Man had to earthwide spread
  Which so happened outside
  Eden.
Near perfect, he could inter-wed—
  No defective children!

Then the Law of Moses,
  Man—farther from perfection;
Incest it was, but know this:
  We *ARE* for God's concession!

Sherry L. Gunnels
LOVE IS
*[To my family and friends, who
have shown me what love is.]*
Love is a twinkle in someone's
  eye.
Love is a shout, a whisper, a sigh!
Love can be just a simple smile
  That fills one's heart with
  warmth all the while.
Love is like a newborn lamb
  struggling to its feet,
At first wobbly but at last its
  strength, complete.
Love is a seed that blooms into a
  flower,
And with gentle tending and
  meticulous care, it will have its
  finest hour!
But love is so very fragile like the
  bone china shaped lovingly by
  a crafter's hand,
Often drawn beyond the limits it
  was meant to withstand.
A beautiful sunrise is God's
  display of His eternal love;
A scene so miraculously created
  by our Father above.
Open your eyes and truly see
  how necessary love is to you
  and me,
The very fiber of our creation and
  how we came to be.

Paul E. Durenberger
SNOWMAN
Windows glisten icy frost
As snowflakes tumble and are lost
Outside, a man of white stands
  guard
His coal black eyes survey the
  yard.
No birds to shadow to and fro
For they have journeyed long ago
But will return to sing again,
As seasons end the snowman's
  reign.

Yvonne Carrie
MY LOVE WHERE ARE YOU
I have looked in every corner of
  the earth, and I cannot find
  you.
You have hidden yourself from
  me.
I search in vain, but you are no
  where to be found.
My heart is so empty, I need you
  so.
Show me your face so that I may

find you.
Do not hide from me any longer.
In my heart I know that you are
  here waiting for me to find you.
When I find you my heart will be
  in perfect tune with yours, and
  we will make the world look
  our way.
For it will be a perfect union.
A love that no one will ever be a
  part of.
Oh, how they will yearn for a
  love like ours.
But it is only for us to share.

Lucille Horner Nash
MIRACLE
The pulse of life within my being,
My wondrous hands with tools
  self-renewing,
My eyes busily photographing,
Efficient brain cells constantly
  recording.

Within myself lies mystery—
A continuing proclivity for
  fantasy,
A refusal to suffer defeat,
An abhorrence of seeming weak,
A stubborn dream of Heaven,
Persistent faith the leaven.

Need I search further
For proof of the Creator?
Surely the miracle that is *ME*,
Did not accidentally come to *BE*!

Robert A. Bowen
THE PLAINS
Faint Prints of ponies, horses, and
  oxen, crudely mingled with
  toil, sweat, and blood.
What is this? These strange
  apparitions!? They gather life
  spectres on the vast prairies of
  dry dirt and sucking mud.
Where once red men so proudly
  stood, where once pioneers and
  prairie schooners made their
  stand for good.
On this so wide and rolling
  land—echoes that only the
  sacrificed could understand.
Oh, The Plains! The Plains! The
  direct route to the New West
  where all the men and their
  families' hopes would lay to
  rest.
The price? So high! And yet to
  both sides well worth the
  endless pain.
Oh, The Plains! The Plains!

Liz Merritt
Captured On a Sea Shore
*[To my granddaughter Marcie,
who has been captured the
same as me.]*
Oh! the wild wild roar of the
  ocean!
With rollicking frollicking waves,
Racing and chasing each other
Like undaunted chainless slaves.

The moon beams sit gently upon
  you,
Your gliding hands reach for a
  star
Then lurch away madly
In search of a golden sand bar,

That lies quietly sleeping like a
  giant
Along your rugged shore.

You glide o'er the unsuspecting
victim
Carrying it to your ocean floor.

The sun shines on your graceful
waves
As on a golden crown
At times I simply cannot speak
I cannot simply stir,

All around and all about
Is just a shimmering blur.
Your beauty so entrances me
I'm enslaved by your rugged shore.

Oh! the wild wild roar of the
ocean!
With rollicking frollicking waves,
Racing and chasing each other
Like dauntless chainless slaves.

Lula M. Fry
OLD MAN
I don't know but I've been told,
a man sure gets frisky when he
gets old.
Now each of them should be told,
They just don't function when
they get old.
They'll rear back and put on a
smile,
feeling like a teenage child.
But when the time comes to
strike their gold,
Something about them just won't
unfold.
But that doesn't matter for they
don't know
The years went by and they got
old.
But it's disgusting, a thing to
behold,
To watch an old man when he
gets old.

Paul Barton
THE EXTREME
Rolling river moving swiftly
through
the woods.

Use to long ago, did go where it
wanted to.

Now no choice but to bend . . .
Where man has sent it once again.

I moved through my world
without restraint,
how long ago it seems.

Now, I too, like the river bend,
where man has sent me . . .
the extreme.

J.D. Barnes
THE HEAT OF SUMMER
Orange beams and crystal bells
Shooting and ringing across the
ceiling
The sound of a million pebbles
dropped in a million wells
A toothless old woman eating a
sparrow's wing
Doors slamming, windows
breaking, a strong wind blowing
The sea is lonely, hear it softly
but, clearly scream
Empty wine bottles in the trash
can
Disappointing as melted ice
cream
Flying high, then low, dodging
trees and telephone poles
The brakes are hot, the fuel guage
reads empty

Alphabet soup dripping through
paper bowls
And it's said the dead are free
Three candles burning slow
A dog barking at the moon
In his ear, she whispers low,
"I want to watch the cartoon".

Priscilla A. Wright
OH YESTERDAY
If all my tears from yesterday
Were shed in deep self-pity;
Still I needed them
To help me carry on.
And I know that all the
Things I feel, though deep
Would be useless to dwell upon.
So if I'm silent, I still love you
Almost too much to say
For fear that, like everything else
That love will fade away . . .

Georgia Ray
MORE THAN A DREAM
Can you say or do you care? A
change I find unreal, for even
tho I'm married a broken heart
is near.
I love him, I worship him, tho my
life is nearly gone, I find my
heart wondering, for I know I
can only love deep within my
soul.
I feel a happiness never found
before, a burst of being free, to
grab the earth as not to die, but
to be free to love the man I
need from now until eternity.
But the love I need and the life I
want is only a moment thing,
for I need a kiss of life more
than the dream of an eternity.

Georgia Ray
MY HUSBAND
Through all the hurt and sadness
we've shared I could never
show the love I feel. And now I
write the things that touch
isn't enough of what I feel. God
put us together and for a time I
could not see, the wonderful
life we'd have once we'd be set
free. Free to be honest and face
who we are, free to love each
other and set our hearts free.
God guide me I pray to show
this man I love, kindness has
its rewards, he chose me to be
his wife and never shall I
shame him nor make him feel
alone, because with his love, I
no longer hate the world, it's no
longer a struggle to survive. My
wonderful husband please
understand I never feel alone,
and thank-you love for all your
love, and thank the good Lord
above, for without my God's
guidence I would have never
known, the greatest man I've
ever known, My Husband.

Serafina Zorana Diantha Fitzjerrel
THE AWAKENING
A rose, its crimson petals
unfurled and glistening with
dew-drops, beckons me gaily
with sculptured leaves of April
green. I approach it gently, this
paragon of splendrous
rosehood, exposed to every

passerby in all her fragrant
radiance.
I stand before her meekly and
acknowledge her presence with
dawning wonderment as if it is
the first time my eyes have
beheld the queen of flowers.
For now in this moment of magic,
I visualize her glory, and I feel
an overpowering sense of
elation envelope me, I, who
have always felt like more of a
weed than a flower. I touch her
satin skin reverently, and for a
suspended moment in time, the
rose and I are one, and in that
moment of truth, I know,
without doubt, that real beauty
comes from within. I tremble
on the brink of my discovery,
and find myself able to reach
out, with love's fragrance, to
touch illusive beauty for the
first time.

Cheryl L. Grgich
THEY SAY LOVE IS
They say that love's a losing game,
people end up just the same.

Confused and lost inside their
minds,
looking for something they'll
never find.

Rejected and hurt is how they feel,
about their love they thought
was real.

They look up at the stars above,
and pray they'll find someone to
love.

Someone that will really care,
and won't just leave them
standing there.

Someone will stay the same,
and not think love's a losing game.

Someone that just won't give in,
they'll keep on trying till they
win.

Cheryl L. Grgich
THE DREAMS OF A CHILD
The dreams of a child are
beautiful places,
bright shining stars, and smiling
faces.

The dreams of a child are
cheerful and warm,
like a breeze on the ocean, or the
calm in a storm.

The dreams of a child are wishes
and hopes,
it gives them security, and helps
them to cope.

The dreams of a child, some
think are slight,
but are very important deep in
the night.

The dreams of a child, whenever
they start,
someone comes along to tear
them apart.

It's really too bad these dreams
don't come true,
because my dreams as a child
were always of you.

My dreams as a child have long
since died,

pushed away by the pain and the
tears I have cried.

The dreams of a child are no
longer around,
they've been beaten and battered,
and smashed in the ground.

They don't stay for long, I'm sorry
to say,
but my dreams as a child have all
died away.

J. Ted Schilling
EACH PASTEL DAWN
[An epithalamium to my bride,
Marina l. Bigongiari.
August 28, 1982]
Marina, my beloved,
in ageless magic you came and
laid against my heart . . .

Softly you sowed your beauty
across my thoughts,
gently moving me beyond the
moonfall
as my hand trailed yours into
some star-swept whisper world
where the mysteries of love faded
against the morrow.

Beside you, my love,
each pastel dawn gives birth to a
satin sunrise
where I awake to find in you
the velvet keeper of my dreams.

Now, moving toward your
arms, I am a believer in dreams,
a wanderer who has found his
white-magic wishes,
a seeker coming home at last
from his ancient quest
with treasured feelings flowing
rich and warm.

Through you I have touched
my timeless self,
for, I am the winter peace, the
sentient summer,
vowing this day, that no matter
which of the seasons
may fall upon us, each pastel
dawn

. . . I shall create for you, the
promise of spring.

Margarita Hernandez de Arauz
UNTITLED
The flight of life as it may seem
to be a lucious stream.
To accord to every day strife
and yet seem so serene . . .
thou it be as calm
as a cool summer's night
the tension is in between.
The day and night are linked
forever to fit into man's
endeavoring scheme.

Edith L. Price
The Treasure Of a Mother's Love
[To my mother who has loved
me through years of
disappointments and joys, and
who inspired the writing of
this poem.]
There are many blesings and gifts
in this life,
But the one that exceeds any
other,
And one that I treasure with all
my heart
Is the wonderful love

of my mother.

When I was a child, she taught
me to know
And to love her Saviour and Lord;
She taught me to pray, and when
I was tied
To go to God's Holy Word.

She was always there when I
needed her most,
With her words of comfort and
cheer,
She calmed all my fears, and
soothed all my hurts.
And kissed away each flowing
tear.

Her chastening was done with
forgiveness and love,
With eyes filled with tears for my
pain,
And each time I hurt her with
sinful misdeeds,
She forgave me again and again.

Throughout the years she has
taught me to love
Every stranger as sister or brother;
How I thank my dear God for
this most precious gift,
The sweet, gentle love of my
mother.

Mark Andrew Miller
A LOVER'S HAIKU
A crisp wind blows through;
then comes fresh sweet soaking
rain.
The storm arrives . . . you.

Bill Carper
HOLY DEMOCRACY
Many consider Nature,
which is a mindless beast,
to be God.
To understand this,
Heaven must be understood.
A person with hunger pangs,
leaving a cave to search for food,
facing the danger of being eaten
by own kind or other earthlings,
would consider the security and
abundance
of our lives, Heaven.
If our streets were paved with
gold,
Heaven would have platinum.
God is a figment
of Mankind's imagination.
God is the People.
The People are God.
The overall will of the People
is the will of God.
Democracy answers directly to
this will
and is, therefore, the Government
of God.

Robert Reeleder
MEPHISTOPHELES
Someone possessing two brains
fused together
By some force illegally
trespassing through the world.
Superhuman man.
Creating a possibility to vie for a
race for the high alter.
Successor to God himself?
Ordinary men cloaking him with
the Cape of Divinity.
Philosophers hoping him to be
the second coming of Christ.
Realists puzzled and withdrawn.

People setting their ancient
beliefs aside,
Paving a road for the only
plausible answer
They have had since the
beginning.
But in heaven God brings wrath
upon the earth,
Scorn upon the man's supporters
and death to all,
And God leaves him alone
without supporters,
Without power to wield above
ordinary men.
So without these things he is
destroyed,
Caught up in that fusion of
divinity.
Now diminished.

Terezia Maria Farkas
FANTASY FLIGHT
In the early morning light
I look across the sky
And wish that I could fly
Across the wondrous sights.

I'd fly across the seas
And journey over hills
Peeping among the villes
While whispering over trees.

And in the night
I'd touch the stars
Jumping long and far
With the moon shining bright.

And in the morn
I'd wave good-bye
To my flight through sky
To return back home.

Donald R. Branch
PLIGHTED LOVE
The quiescent moon, hazel and
glancing,
Succumbs to thundering clouds;
Lord of the ascendant and master
preponderance.
Yet lay the flattering unction to
one's soul,
And ridicule not, nor stand aghast;
Twixt forlorn hope and the
slough of Despond,
The balm of Gilead remains.

And embrace with amorous
glances,
The true lover's knot; sweet and
bedew kisses,
Within warm hearts stand neuter
to tarnished thoughts.
And become the humble cryer of
celebration,
To flourish and glitter past single
blessedness,
And relish in shining endearment:
To quench modest dignified
wonderment,
One's troth is to caress tender
passion and inclination.

Denese Davis
HOW LONG
[For Fred, whom I will always
love.]
I can't seem to break the wall,
although I've reached the heart.
We are so close, yet so very far
apart.
Sometimes your touch paints a
picture,
Showing our love as a perfect
mixture.

Sometimes your eyes tell a story,
Sending me in the height of glory.
How long can I go on dreaming?
How long can I go on believing?
How long before I realize you are
only mine in my eyes . . .

The little things you might do,
give me something to hold on
to.
The little things you might say,
dwell in my mind throughout
the day.
How long can I go on dreaming?
How long can I go on believing?
How long before I realize you are
only mine in my eyes . . .

I've been a lover, I've been a friend.
I'll be whatever it is till the end.
Because there will NEVER be
another You.
I will NEVER love so true.
I'll go on dreaming, I'll go on
believing,
Even though I realize you are
only mine in my eyes . . .

Theodore Allen Groeneveld Jr.
OBAKE AI
[Dedicated to her (N.M.), Obake
Ai, whom I shyly grew to love.]
Obake Ai is Japanese . . .
Understanding vast—sky high.
Deep is her love—a thousand
seas . . .
My Ghost Love, Obake Ai.
Sensitive and tender, I've found
her to be;
this Spirit's love is caring and yet
shy.
She carries her walk, oh so
beautifully.
I do love this Spirit, Obake Ai.
She's not perfect, so it seems;
still, armed with hope, I try.
Mine and perfect in my dreams,
this Ghost, Obake Ai.
She is a Spirit I almost met before,
across lengths of sea and sky.
As our friendship grows—I love
her more and more . . .
This woman, Obake Ai.

Jacqueline Skinner
**Only Imagined Prizes At
the Fair**
Love played a trick on us at the
fair
when we leaned forward
and threw our loops toward the
squares
stuck securely on the heads of
the bears.
Our loops seemed large enough
but they always bounced off
to somewhere.

Did you aim for the French
Lieutenant's bear?
The one with the long auburn
hair?
The incandescent one
who looks a little "undone"?
I aimed for the macho-man bear
with the lantern in his hands.
The one far away
with the confident stance.

However, Time sided up with
Love
and here we stand, outside the
booth
with no dimes left. No prize . . .

except if we choose
and imagine a theft!
Now, the only faces
I see, after you've left,
are the stuffed animals' empty
eyes
staring blankly back at me,
as everything
seems to disappear
to somewhere.

L. Frances Taylor
A LOVE IS BORN
Like a dew-dipped rose
that scents the air
Wrapped in the mist
of early morn
When I first saw you
standing there
My love for you
was born
The moment I saw you
I knew you were mine
Fate must have planned it
that way
So I'll cherish this love
'til the end of time
Let come
what may
I prayed to God
that I might find
A love both tried
and true
God in His Heaven
was more than kind
Because
He gave me YOU.

Dr. Mary Ann Henley, PhD, MscD
REBEL!!
[Dedicated To Connie Fisher, A
Good Friend on the Path.]
She's mad you know, Lock her
away.
Do it quick . . . do it Today!!
She's infecting the world with
Truth;
We cannot stand for that.

The fearful ones cried: "Stone
her," and
In her face they spat.
Everything we have stolen,
Everything we
have built with . . . blood;
Soon will be mere ashes; with
nothing left
but . . . mud.

"Kill the Witch; She's crazy,"
Better . . .
Lock her away.
If we don't; her truth will harm us,
Our power will fade away.

She thinks LOVE is a Power;
Strong enough to conqueer all
plans.
Lock her away; get rid of . . .
The TRUTH she holds in her
hands.

Sigrid Emanuelson Moore
MY PRAYER
Speak softly, Lord.
The quiet listens for the dawn
To speak.

We need to know Your formula
For happiness.

The bridge that spans Eternity
Between Your world and mine,
Is wet with tears
From endless storms and fears.

In our cathedral's cloistered halls
Your footsteps linger where
The sunset's echo sleeps,
And vespers claim each prayer.

Memorials of history
Enshrine Your sacred place.
And silent benedictions bless
Your name in solemn grace.

Speak softly, Lord,
I wait for You to speak.

I can weather any storm that's
In my destiny,
If You will hold my hand
And talk to me.

D. H. Rubalcaba
THE SPIRIT OF CARI
Though sheltered between
  the bonds of love,
A spirit lives
  that breaths so free.
Like a claming touch
  that engulfs the heart,
And silently waits
  for spring to see.
The unborn laughter
  that resides within,
In dreams of
  Lifes splendored excitements,
  yet to be seen.
In doubtless clouds
  of joy it hides,
Awaiting lifes turbulence
  to gracefully subside.
It apologizes
  for those who worry,
Then pauses to think,
  My Lord,
    i am only Cari . . .

Patricia Ruth Mason
ME (A SELF—ANALOGY)
*[I dedicate this analogy to three
very special people. Linda and
Wendy, my two lovely
daughters, and Sergio, my
charming son-in-law. They
always believed.]*
I am a woman. Look at me. See
  me. Hear me.
I have a brain. I have a heart.
I have eyes to see pain. I have
  ears to hear pain.
I have hands to soothe away
  some of this pain.
I have lips to kiss away the pain
  of a child.
I have words to ease some of the
  pain of an adult.
If you cut me, I bleed. If you hurt
  me, I cry.
If you make me happy, I will laugh.
If you depress me, I will brood.
If you ignore me, I will withdraw
  from you.
I am many things to many people.
I am a daughter. I was a wife. I am
  a mother.
I am a sister. I am an aunt. I am a
  cousin.
I was a granddaughter. I was an
  employee.
I am, and can be, a very good
  friend.
I have the ability to forgive, but
  find it hard to forget.
Yet in spite of all this, I am still
  only one person.
I have many sides to my
  personality.

Many people think they know
  me well.
In truth they know me not at all.
I need to be loved. I need to be
  cherished.
I need to be protected. Often from
  myself.
Most of all, I must feel truly
  wanted.
I have great sensitivity for all
  Gods creatures.
I love all animals, but have no
  use for hunters.
I intensely dislike people who
  abuse and neglect children.
I believe in God, and in his son
  Jesus.
I respect the elderly, and find I
  can learn much from them.
I am somewhat confused as to
  what my real purpose is.
I find life to be complicated, and
  at times very painful.
I am in many ways, much too
  trusting of people.
I love a soft summer rain. I love a
  beautiful sunset.
I am memsmerized by the beauty
  of large bodies of water.
I like to lie on my back and stare
  at the stars.
I like to lie under a big, leafy tree
  and watch the clouds.
I love to walk barefoot along a
  sandy beach.
I love fireflies, caterpillars and
  butterfiles.
I love fluffy, soft kittens and
  warm loving puppies.
I love the song of a beautiful,
  melodious canary.
I am fascinated by small babies
  and young children.
I feel all the excitement of a child
  at Christmas time.
I love blazing fire and singing of
  carols.
I love all the traditional
  things that make life
  pleasant.
I know what it is to lose someone
  you love.
I know the emptiness and the
  terrible void it leaves.
I have known what it is to
  experience real fear.
I have known the terrible pain of
  physical abuse.
I have lived with the deep scars
  of emotional neglect.
I know what it is to sit beside a
  fevered child.
I have kneeled in prayer, for what
  seemed an eternity.
I know what it means to be
  married, but not loved.
I know the confusion of going
  through a divorce.
I know what it means to be a
  single parent.
I know what it is to share the
  joys and tears of a child.
I have been part of both their
  triumphs and defeats.
I know what it means to love and
  be loved by a child.
These are a few of the things I
  know about myself.
I am sure I still have a great deal
  more to learn.

Jeffrey G. Geiser
RANDOM HAUNTS
Jungle drums indicate my
  madness. We dress in the garb.
It is eight oh one. Tell the good
  people I'm going away. Tell the
  good people I've nothing to say.
It's captured . . . Here . . . With
  me. Balance the edge, you'll see.
Space, is encased, by time, I,
  walk the thin light line. We,
  who are in this place. Stay, till
  the past is traced.
Boustrophedonically we touched,
  while a cabal did lunch, like
  blaine on cattle at dawn.
  Colporphy was the cure, of my
  thoughts so demure. Something
  just had to make me sit up and
  see. But in a way it's been done,
  and life just isn't fun; I mean
  the way they all say it should
  be. Depilate my heart once
  more, I'll be yours forever more.
  Masticate this soul of mine,
  and I'll be yours till the end of
  time.
It took some extensive
  excogitation, and in the end
  you were esculent. I'd like to
  join her in osculation, till our
  minds are completely spent. I
  exuded her hate, but now it's
  too late. My emotions are no
  longer in control. She is a
  lumimous heavenly body, with
  a well formed nebulous train.
  Moving in such an essentric
  orbit, it's about to drive this
  boy insane.   The whole
  world. Life, listens. Strife,
  glistens. Till done. I'ts gone.
  Please return my heart. It is
  like glass to see. I'm not going
  to last. You are free from me,
  forever to laugh.
Crowded breathing from the left,
  leaves me like, uptight. I was,
  now I am alone. Lizard loving,
  costume wearing. Halloween is
  almost here. I'll be a hump, I'll
  be depraved. You'll be gone.
  You'll be saved. Comotose
  cognition is all that I can do.
  When my feet are like hot
  glass, slippery in the shoe.
  Comatose cognition is all that
  is left for me.

Lorna Tallent Kidwell
YET I AM NEAR
*[In Memory of my beloved
husband, GROVER KIDWELL,
who inspired this poem and
who is still very, very "NEAR"
in my heart and memories.]*
I was at Hong Kong, Singapore,
  Rangoon—
And then I was no more;
And still I am near.

I speak to you from the depths of
  Death
Yet I am so close that I could
  touch you as you walk;
There are so many things I want
  to say,
And I try so hard to make you
  hear!

Do you ever have intuitions,
  feelings?

That is I'm trying to convey a
  thought to you, a hope;
Trying to say on and on "I love
  you."

I speak to you from the depths of
  Death,
Yet I am near.

Kathy L. Leaman
HE'S ONLY A MAN
Sometimes when I wake up early
  in the morning, he lays with
  his head on my arm and he's
  gently snoreing;
The sunlight shines through
  where the curtains part, and I
  feel close to me the beating of
  his heart.
He looks so like a little boy
  peacefully lying there, the
  small rays of sunlight falling
  across his hair.
At times he seems so strong and
  wise, but I can still see the
  innocence in his eyes.
And in the evening when he holds
  me in his arms; he makes me
  feel so safe and warm, because
  of his gentle love and charm.
When tears wet my face like
  falling rain, he helps to end my
  misery and take away the pain.
Yes he's a healthy active type of
  guy,
But it hurts me so when I see him
  cry.
For he loves me as truly and
  deeply as he can,
Because after all he's only just a
  man.

Linda Seifried
HAVE WE MET BEFORE
Seems like I've met you before;
The strangeness of someone new
  is not there.
I look into your eyes;
I speak to you;
Yet it seems like I've done this
  before
At Another Time,
In Another Place:
My memory escapes me . . .
I cannot place you
But I know you.
We've done this before;
The tune is the same.
We are strangers . . .
But strangers only in this world.
Could it be we've met before?
Another Time?
Another Place?
Perhaps Another World?

Esther (McGechie) Vanek
WHAT IS LOVE
*[Dedicated to my four beautiful
children; Ginger Lee Wilting,
Stanley Gilbert Wilting, Mark
Errol Wilting & Patty Ellen
(Wilting) Thimgan of whom I
am eternally proud and grateful
for giving me a reason for
loving.]*
Admiration and unselfish concern
  affectionate, ardent and true;
That's how the dictionary
  describes it, but what is love,
  what does it do?

Love is perpetuate as a babbling
  brook that feeds from an
  eternal spring;

As cheering as the sound of birds
at dawn when they flock
together to sing.

Love is passionate as molton lava
glowing in the volcanic core;
Fervid as the steam of bubbling
hot springs seeping up through
the desert floor.

Love is sweet as the flowering
Jasmine breathing fragrance
into the night;
Tranquil as a silvery summer
moon bathing earth in
luminous light.

Love can be ocean, rainbow, or
cloud or most anything else
that is real.
On thing certain regarding love,
it is ecstasy that the senses feel.

For it can be, do, or mean
anything and be captured by all
who dare,
Yet the only true requirement is,
that it's found in the heart, to
care.

Ann Galbraith
LIFE'S FUTURE
Yesterday is gone
Today is here
Tomorrow is waiting

Yesterday I lost
Today I won
Tomorrow I wait

Yesterday time stopped
Today the clock ticks on
Tomorrow time waits

Yesterday I waited for you
Today you waited for me
Tomorrow???
Who knows.

J. V. Lopez
PURGATORY
Neither diamonds nor love
Will bring you back
Nor hatred buy another world
Nor anguish lend a sleepless night
Nor moon become a pearl.

Linda L. Murty
SAND
[To my husband, Randy]
Summertime surfing
Carrying waves with the wind
To sand and the girls

Judy Moffet
THE FARMBOY GROWN
The farmer's son now grows roses
At his house on a hill ringed with
flowers.
He plants vegetables and fruits as
well,
Filling his retirement hours.

Farm overalls discarded when
young
For white collar and
businessman's suit,
He spent many long years at a
desk—
Of his sacrifice ever yet mute.

Moving from city to city
As promotions came on his job,
He provided the most that he
could,
With toiling his lifetime to rob.

When older he started a venture,

Startling all those about him
As he built his own country home
And a buisiness with new joy and
vim.

Now in denim or wool as he
chooses,
Surely it isn't so odd
That the man who today tends
his garden
Had a grandpa whose house was
of sod.

Catherine Curtis—O'Connell
Reflections Of Colorado
[With Loving Thanks to God,
who made the mountains—to
His Holy Spirit, who continues
to write through me—and His
Son, Jesus Christ, who lives in
me, giving me eyes to find the
beautiful in our God—created
world everyday.]
Gods power shouts to me
from every mountain top
His peace whispers
from every valley
The snow on the mountain
reflects His purity
The trees sing of His ability
to make all things new
and
keep them evergreen
The lowlands with their
consistent, almost boring
brown
remind me of
His never—ending love, the
same—yesterday—today—
forever . . .
No evolution stories for me
not after today
The strong stand of pine outside
my window firmly declares
"In six days, HE CREATED."
Thank you, Colorado, for the
inspiration you've given to me.
You and your majestic mountains
say more by just being, than a
thousand sermons.

Shirley "Ski" Styczynski
GLORIA
I love you dear friend
for the countless hours
you prayed for me
to the heaveny powers.

I love you dear friend
for your sunny airs
you shared with me
though you were burdened with
cares

I love you dear friend
for suffering the pain
you showed to me
it was never in vain.

I love you dear friend
for your shining Christian love
you give to me
and our dear Lord above.

I love you dear friend
for your energies galore
among us all
you always give more.

I love you dear friend
as you pass my way
I see the beauty in you
God puts on display

I love you dear friend

for your loving heart
you gave to me
till it was time to part

I love you dear friend
but you did not hear
it was too late
so I shed my tears.

Daphne Michelle Ferguson
THE CRUMBS OF LIFE
Life can be short
Life can be sweet
You can gather your crumbs and
pile them up neat.

Life can be bitter
Sour lemons, green bananas
It may be a stormy winter
or sway like the savannas.

Maybe its been bitter
Maybe its been sweet
Did you gather your crumbs and
pile them up neat?

Elizabeth Hill
PEACE OF MIND
We can't ask for much more in life
Than peace of mind and so,
It's up to us to reach that goal
In any way we know.
Emotions play a large part in
That happy state of mind.
In order to control them, we
Must see that we are kind.
To live just one day at a time
Will bring us peace of mind.
If we just think about today,
More courage we will find.
It's true that love will lead the way,
If we don't shut it out.
It conquers fear and that's what
Peace of mind is all about.

Alma Mikelsons
MEMORIES
Memories, memories,
My dearest, turbulant, melodies
The skies and clouds still flying
There they are kept undying
Those wonderful sounds . . .
To listen to them,
To dream once more—
Once more!
Memories, memories,
You tremendous melodies.

Arthur Morrison
MY LITTLE GIRL
[Suzanne Cadwell Morrison,
who is my greatest inspiration
and love, and to Pamela for
being my daughter's mother.]
Looking down, I noticed an out of
place curl,
Thanking nature, for giving me a
little girl.
The warmth in my heart,
knowing this little one is mine,
such a treasure, in my life time.
Born unto us, of love,
given to us from above.
I thought one day, how she grew,
Her words one day, "OH DADDY
I LOVE YOU".
As flowers bloom in May,
Her beauty has become a bouquet.
She has determination and
comical wit,
with eyes that are starlit.
Now long past the age of fate,
Pride, knowing, her, I helped to
create.

A child of such great wealth,
grow to be a woman, in the best
of health.

JoAnne H. Williams
**Our Lives Are an Hour
Glass**
Our lives are an hour glass . . .
The time we spend are the
grains of sand. We give our
hearts to this land, our soul, to
God above . . . We live our
lives, grain by grain, until the
grains run out one day . . . If
we are wise we use them well.
Each grain one at a time.

JoAnn Kaseno
THE FOREST
Darkness in the forest.
Ebony blackness
broken only by small beams
of moonlight.
It reeks of fear.
Death is in the hands
of the stalkers.
No human mind
can conceive
the creatures fright.
Morning will come soon
and it will ease
until the darkness comes
again.

Raphael Stephan
DRUIDIC PRIEST WOLF
[Coram Nobis—Arcana
Coelestia Ardentia Verba—
Subrosa Ventis Secundis—
Ferae Naturae]
morning
dawn a new day
peaceful calming laughter
autumn
adorn the druids
we shall come there after
night time is the day
i know no other way
fluid
water's ocean stead
green tides hidden upon earths'
womb
luna
moon a crimson sun
shadows dancing as lovers
wind sighs the fire
i show no other secret . .

Linda Ann Lillie
DESTINIES DIRECTION
I hear a call from far away,
That means for me to see,
That destinies direction,
Has a special path for me.
A path that I must follow,
Though the way may not be
clear,
A little voice that tells me,
I have a purpose here.
It's hard for me to understand,
The great reality,
That in this mighty world so
vast,
God has a place for me.
Nobody else can fill it,
As it's meant for me alone,
Just as the morning glory,
Cannot replace a rose.
So every day that I awake,
To see Gods glory near,
I walk in strength and faith,
Because, I have a prupose here.

Today's Greatest Poems

Theresa Ann Lauer
PRETENDER
The winds drifted the snow into
the night; Instead of making
the hours dreary they seemed
to be alright, because you were
there to hold me.

You said close your eyes it will
be alright, I'll never let
anything hurt you as long as
your in my sight. Hold my hand,
never let go, as long as I'm
around your heart I'll console.

I put myself into your care
thinking I was doing the right
thing; But you were the one
who left my sight, you were the
one alone in the night, I thought
I was the weak and you were
the strong but as it turned out
it looked as if I were wrong.

I said close your eyes, it will be
alright, I'll never let anything
hurt you as long as your in my
sight, hold my hand, never let
go, as long as I'm around your
heart I'll console.

As the summer breeze sifted
through the trees the winds
soon layed, and the time
turned to day; Instead of
making the hours dreary they
seemed to be okay, because I
was there to hold you.

Phyllis J. Lowery
A MOMENT IN TIME
[Written especially for Rich
Terwey who said so much in
so many ways I am proud to be
your lady!]
I come to you in all humility.
Take me! Love me!
I will give you love greater
Than you have ever known.
I will sit at your feet . . .
I will pour your wine . . .
We will laugh . . .
And if you are sorrowful,
I will comfort you,
For you have given me
A "Richness" unknown to others,
Seen only by me.
And when we have spent our time
On this earth, we will leave it . .
Together, side by side,
Taking with us
A moment in time
That will never be shared
With another.

Cecialia Petrea
SMALL TOWNS
Small towns can be death
for the big town mind
No place to shop. No crowds to
move with. No traffic.

After maturing in a small town
and learning to think big town,
One discovers the wheel
Since every town of any size has
A considerable number of service
stations
A car makes small town life
endurable.

If one decides to try tractor driving
Even more opportunities and
possibilities
Arise

As far as bikes go,
It seems to depend on the area
My mother is from a small town
Some of the relatives live there.
The kids grow up
Visiting the local Pepsi machine
At the local gas station
(The cleanest one)
While the farmers "shoot the
breeze"
On the benches that line main
street.

Sidney Frederick
WONDERING
As I sit beside your bed,
Life has got me puzzled.
Have we control of our destiny,
Or are we bound and muzzled?
There sometimes seems a pattern
clear
As to how our lives unfold;
But who's to say we will do this
or that,
Being loud or silence gold.

Is there a Divine Being,
Over us a benign care?
Why should some of us suffer?
You've had more than your share.
Is compensation granted?
In family we are wealthy.
Sons and daughters dutiful;
Grandchildren bright and healthy.

But all of life's possessions—
Material or abstract—
Are not apportioned equally;
No one denies this fact.
But still it seems to me
All out of proportion;
A lovely lady such as you
To suffer such distortion.

Henry Eric Linstromberg
WICKER AND LEATHER
[To Light and it's Harmony
with Darkness]
In a bright room of
wicker and leather,
overlooking a vast
feild of soft, flowing heather,
came to me so clear
thoughts of love and care.
Isn't it so pleasant?
You needn't even be there.

Elma M. Guggenmos
THE FIRST DAY
Today is the first day of the rest
of your life,
So make use of the chance, today;
You'll never be sorry for the good
that you do,
And the help that you give on
the way.

Forget about all of the years gone
by,
Live for today and tomorrow;
Give strength to those in real
need, today,
And faith to those in sorrow.

God loves a cheerful giver, always,
So give, don't expect to receive;
But trust in the Lord, live a full
life,
And never forget to believe—

Today is the first day of the rest
of your life,
No matter how many or few;
Soon you will answer the call of

the Lord,
And the ending is all up to you.

Joan M. Ptacek
THE FOUR SEASONS
First comes Winter with its ice
and snows
Br—rrr how the wind blows
It's really not all that bad
Cause the snow brings Santa
Claus and makes the kids glad.

Next is Spring and the flowers all
bloom
It lasts until almost the end of
June
There's a day set aside for the
Easter Bunny
And you can dress up, if you have
the money.

Third is the Summer, sunny and
hot
The one that most people like alot
When Fourth of July comes you
can have a ball
Or take a vacation and get away
from it all.

Last is the Autumn or Fall, if you
like
There's no snow yet so get out
your bike
There's a day for Thanksgiving
and one for the ghosts
Both are celebrated from Coast to
Coast.

Winter, Spring, Summer, Autumn
or Fall
Four seasons, I guess that's all.
So whether you're from the city
or a small town hick
Look them all over and take your
pick.

Jeannine Mathia
TO BE INSPIRED
To be inspired rather than told,
admonished, threatened,
blackmailed or scolded
into doing that which must be
done
makes doing the task
much more fun.

The problem is (it seems to me)
is how to inspire
someone to be
or do just what you know he
should
when he believes
the idea is no good.

When one is inspired to do a task
he seldom does
as little as asked
but rather completes whatever
the chore
and continues to do
quite a bit more.

Sandi Schoenhofen
EQUINOX
Oh, the death that lingers
Then slips through my fingers
How it enfolds me
Yet, I have no fear

The kiss is bitter tasting
Tells me there's no time for
wasting
For when it's gone
The reverie will disappear

With flamboyance it devours

Ravaged by the mighty powers
Until the silence
Of the finale draws near

In darkness it will leave me
Certainly to grieve me
For the silence
Will lay heavy on the ear

For I can't remember laughter
That isn't followed soon after
By loneliness and tears

Robert K. Sit
LOVE
[This poem is dedicated To
Sharon:—Thanks for being you
and for showing me how happy
a person can be. Sharon, you're
something else! Thank You . . .]
The sun is bright;
The sky is blue;
When day turns to night,
That Sunset is true.

Anita Durand Buess
YOUNG GIRL'S PRAYER
Love me tenderly, be kind.
Gently, sweetly, pray,
Brush you lips on mine.
Snowflakes falling lightly,
Pale flowers blooming nightly,
Shy smiles on summer's day
After tears of spring.
Such fragile things these are
As faintest shine of star.
Love, wounded, steals away.
So delicate a thing
Dwells only in the mind.
Who can merit it,
So fleeting and so fragile as
quicksilver's grip.
Only a small sip of wine—
Not a tankard full of it.

Mary Schultz
ANTICIPATION
Left the door open for the
future today
after closing it on the past
The sun shone
through the doorway and into
my heart,
My heart skipped a beat with
thoughts of who might enter
And a surge of anticipation
made me warm again.

Randy Spurlock
Happy 40th Anniversary
[To my parents, Fred &
Dorothy Spurlock, on their
40th Wedding Anniversary.
Thanks, for being parents who
taught us: if you want respect,
you must give respect—R. A. S.]
Happy Anniversary, Mother and
Dad;
This is our way to say thanks, for
the good times we've had.
It's not often we can do
something special for you two;
But today you can sit back, this day
has been designed just for you.
On Saturday nights the neighbors
kids would want to go to town
with Dad;
So they'd pile on the "old delivery
truck" and go get Mom, that's
the kind of dates they had.
For Dad to have a moment alone
with his gal wasn't easy 'way
back then;
Others tagged along; brothers and

507

sisters?; Daddy was one of ten!
Mom had to take her sister along
    or she wasn't allowed to go.
Do you think she sat by Maxine
    when they got to the picture
    show?
Daddy was in the Army when he
    chose his "bride-to-be;"
They were married just one week
    before he went overseas.
Mother taught school and three
    years waited the day;
When she'd have "Fredie" home to
    stay.
The war was over!, the headlines
    read;
On October 30, 1945, the
    Spurlocks loaded on the "old
    truck" and went to Lebanon, to
    pick up Fred!
The days have been few that they
    haven't spent together;
And I've never heard either of
    them say a harsh word about
    the other.
To some this may sound strange;
But Love is the lifestyle they
    have, that's how we were raised.
"Happy 40th Anniversary,"
    Mother and Dad;
"Continue, go forth, and show
    others what you have!"

Milena Soukal
UNTITLED
An ugly spider
is crawling on my heart.

—How are you enjoying your
    day?—
—Let's begin with the breakfast:—

(We all have to have
a breakfast
in the morning.
    fly
has a chip of sugar
    spider
has a chip of fly.)

WHY
is an ugly spider
crawling on my heart?

*Rose Georgene Llewellyn
Untersee*
DAY DREAMS
    *I profess and dedicate my poem
    "Day Dreams" to my precious
    family who mean so very much
    to me. My mother Vernele, my
    husband Julius and my six
    children; Teresa, Scott, Julius—
    L, Shawn, Sarah and Shannon.
    My Love "Forever Rose."]*
Twenty years ago today . . . I
    could hardly "wait" to watch
    you play.
I held you in my arms with care
    and brushed my fingertips
    through your hair.
I dreamed of all the things "we'd"
    do, I hurried in my mind, it's
    true!
Be sweet, be neat, that was my
    rule. Soon came the time to go
    to school.
Off down the lane and to the bus,
    and mother always had to fuss!

The toys and dolls now put away,
    "you" haven't time to sit and
    play.

School years went by, from first
    to twelfth, the scrapbooks
    filled lay on the shelf.
All of a sudden, a blink of my
    eye, you're twenty dear and I
    want to cry!
My little child, all grown at last,
    those years went by much to
    fast . . .
Now I dream my dreams of days
    that are past.

Roger Russi
WIND WAYS
An open palm,
    full of sand,
the wind whirls
    it into the air . . .
A flag, once white,
    is torn,
flutters
    in the wind.
Rolling clouds,
    black as the night,
are chased
    by a howl of wind.
Smoke dances
    through the ruins,
as flames climb high
    under the whipping
    wind . . .

Shirley B. O'Keefe
MY DREAMING HEART
Darling I dream of you at night
    about your arms around me tight
your tender lips and I love you
    and your warm embraces too.

This will only be a dream
    for a while though long it seems
for at present we are apart
    kept close only in my heart.

My dreams are all filled with you
    and with a love that is true
for you are the only one for me
    and thru the years this you will
    see.

So take good care of yourself for
    me so together we soon can be
what a reunion we'll have that day
    when you'll come home to stay.

Austin Thomas
AS LIFE GOES ON
    *[To my father, James Shelton,
    who died in May 1982.]*
We bury our sorrow
As life goes on,
We look for tomorrow
As we are left alone;
We refresh our memories
Of happy times past,
We regret our stones
And arrows cast;
We remember lost moments
To show we cared,
A funny story or short walk
We sometimes shared;
We reflect on our love
For that person of worth,
To a land unknown
Has departed this earth;
Where he will plant flowers
As in my life done,
Until the harvest is ready
For the settling sun.

Jean Layer
NIGHTIME BREEZES
Carefree breezes in the night
Dancing a little tune

Over the dew covered grass
Under the full pale moon

Whispering breezes in the night
Under a starlit sky
Lulling little creatures to sleep
Softly, with a sigh

Gentle breezes in the night
Lingering for awhile
Softly touching the little ones
Asleep, with a smile

Silent breezes in the night
Continuing on its way
With many paths to travel
Before the break of day

Albert Zelman
FRONTIERS
When life disintegrates
Perhaps a million eons hence.
When planet earth becomes
A mass of smoldering embers;
When mountains melt like
    thawing glaciers,
Beneath a hot, exploding sun.
Then man will seek to flourish
In a new uncharted galaxy.

Roberta Clark Howard
ALIVE AND WELL
    *[This poem is dedicated to the
    Holy Ghost and anyone who
    believes in the power of love.]*
I feel like I'm just beginning;
I pray Lord, give me a very long
    time
To find your way.

I feel so new because of you;
That I wouldn't want to ever give
    up.
You fill my cup.

Let me drink of this deep well of
    wisdom
And let my love flow so people
    will know,
It really can be true; we are alive
    and well.
And I'm still me because that's
    what it
Means to be free.

Sometimes I'm so filled with fear
Yet you dry my every tear;
And when I become lonely most
I feel you near and you become
    my host.

The music of my heart springs
    forth
From the mouths of babes.
The melodies sweet bring a joyful
    retreat
Into memory lane, of the sorrow
    and pain.
But it doesn't hurt anymore.
From within my heart you open
    the door.

And I know I can be a part of this
    glorious season.
I feel brand new because I've got a
    reason.

Johnnie Stevens Neterer
ROBERT E. LEE
Out of the South rode Robert E.
    Lee
A sight that everyone should see
There was never a man so gallant
    as he
He led his troops with dignity
Leading his men on to war

though every one was sick and
    sore
They fought on valiantly, for they
    were the Confederate Calvary

Fighting and bloodshed in
    country and street
Through drenching rain and
    blistering heat
The men were dying of gangrene
    and such
No time to stop, always the rush
Their motto rang as far as the sea,
    "Keep ahead of the enemy!
Victorious we must be, we're
    fighting for the Confederacy!"

Then in spring of '65 with only
    half his men alive
With the smell of cannon fire
    over the land
Lee headed west to make a last
    stand
With Grant in pursuit and
    Sheridan ahead the future
    looked too bleak
The men had suffered, too many
    were dead and now there was
    no retreat.

"Enough have died," he was heard
    to say as to Appomattox he
    rode that day
"We've fought our best fight,
    there's no need for shame.
And on no shoulders we'll place
    any blame.
Let peace now blanket our
    countryside
Our men in gray have reason for
    pride."

"The Confederacy will live
    forevermore in the hearts
Of the men who went to war,
That's over and done, now a bad
    memory.
Let peace prevail for eternity,
I now surrender the Confederacy."

Tianne Santrizos Bloom
LOST HUBBY
Love lingers
I'm still your wife
though only on paper
feelings still alive

You only wrote once
when I gave you a threat
and I still owe you a
fairly large debt

You only think
of me you say
when you nick yourself
with the razor blade

And I will soon drift
from your life
by New Years Eve
a divorced wife

Adele Murray
MEASURED TIME
Age is creeping up, upon my tired
    soul.
I have no time now to try, this or
    that or snore.
For each moment's wing now
    becomes,
A precious precious jewel, and
    quiet joy.
To hold or let go—.
Like one would a treasured gem.
Clouds of white and gray, keep

circling constantly overhead.
I wonder-, if today I'll be among
  the clouds.
Or by night be dead-, before I get
  to bed.
And though my jewels will soon
  be gone.
I cannot help but wonder, about
  other moments to come.
Who will use them? How? When
  and where.
And will they-, be held-, and con-
  sidered, precious precious gems.
Or nothing, and be lost in
  nothingness.

Geoffrey Edwards
PHOENIX
O Phoenix, splendor crowned by
  hands divine,
Whose flight of glory heavenward
  recalls
The golden brilliance of Aurora's
  climb
And transports us to rapture's
  sacred halls,
When Death has claimed you on
  the blazing pyre,
Consuming with his blinding
  bursts of flame
Which even to Olympus seem to
  spire,

My breast shall not be agonized
  by pain;
Exalted, from the ashes you will
  rise,
The resurrection of immortal love
Which in the soul, reborn, forever
  lies,
Ascent resplendent, touched by
  one above.
  On wings of beauty which true
  hearts adore,
  Toward new heights this love
  will ever soar.

Dan Depuy
MORNING GLORY
Darkness nestled in arms of
  stillness,
Hidden within, all natures
  brilliance.
Peace abound, in this tranquil
  scence,
Awakens ones senses, and
  gladness of being.

Knowledge gathered by creatures of
  God, the source, to man unknown.
Directs them, each and every one.
  Retreat! To the safety of homes.
For pangs of war, have now begun,
  from horizons to the sky,

Explosions from the east they
  come, across the clouds, then
  die.
Onward, the invading force,
  assault, if never ending.
Victory is within their sight, on
  this we are depending.
Defenses now, are overwhelmed,
  by the power that we see,
Retreating, struck with awe, have
  mercy, the only plea.

But silence is the only answer, to
  the soldiers of the night.
Forces fleeing, to the west, for the
  sun has shown its might.
With confrontations ended, a
  stillness settles in,
The peacefull, tranquil scence
  returns, and whispers of the
  wind.

All creatures gather in the
  clearing, for jubulations have
  begun,
A victory celebration, because,
  for now the dawn has won.

Charles F. Sutton
OVERCOMING
*[This poem is dedicated to Ruth
Ross, a co-worker, who was
greatly moved by this poem
when she and her husband
suffered the loss of a dear friend.]*
Though nature's face is often By
  violent winds that twist and
Mangle and maul, leaving
  wreckage
Of broken branches in wake of
Summer's powerful
  thunderstorms, she
Covers damage skillfully with
Fresh green twigs and leaves,
  tenderly
Caring for injured progeny
Until extensive wounds are
  healed.

Likewise we when hurt, suffering
From life's grievous injuries, can
Sulk in sorrow from misfortune,
Baring wounds to world, or let the
Medicine of faith and patience
Repair ravages of life, while
Smiling sweetly through
  throbbing pain,
Radiating joy and courage,
Grateful for our difficult trials.

Jack Jackson
DEAR SHERRI
Your radiant glow is so blinding I
am oblivious to everything
around me when you are near. I
see only you and all your
adorable features which make
you someone very special in
my eyes. My eyes sadden with
your absence and dance at the
mere sight of you. My eyes
savor your grace, like that of an
angel gliding graciously over a
satin cloud. My skin is set fire
by the warmth of your touch,
my fingertips rewarded by the
silky softness of your velvety
skin. Your presence is more
valuable than anything; it
renders all the treasures of the
world absolutely meaningless
without you. For you are the

gold in my life that I would
never spend because ecstacy is
priceless. Desire for you, so
explosive that the heavens
cringe, drives me into a state of
euphoria. Beethoven would be
embarrassed to compare his
compositions to the music
your captivating voice plays on
my ears. I have respect for you
like I have never known for
anyone in my entire life. Until
you came along, I thought this
feeling was only a myth found
only in fairy tales whose
authors were only dreaming.
You are the beacon for my
nights and my ray of sunlight
on cloudy days. You thaw the
chill of winter and I melt at the
mere thought of you. The
scorching heat of summer is
neutralized by the firey warmth
that you ignite from deep
within me. I just wanted you to
know.

Phyllis Ruggier
REFLECTIONS
I sat back to reflect
Of what I expect,
Life to be
With just you and me.

I thought that it would be
A life that was easy and free,
Where we could come and go
And often take things slow.

We could take a long ride
Or take a walk side by side.
There would be strolling hand in
  hand
While walking on golden sand.

Spending a wintery night
With soft music and candlelight,
Peeking out windows to watch
  the falling snow
And watching the dying embers
  glow.

As years go by, I know I'll find
That you will always be mine.
I said, 'I love you,' today,
But for me, today is for always.

Mable G. Feagler
TO GRETA
The sun is low, it's almost end of
  day,
Long golden rays illuminate the
  room
And rest upon a spot—but always
  near
Where my beloved German
  Shepherd lay.

I know her time of play and
  romping past,
That death waits but a few short
  days away—
Make precious these tender
  hours alone with her
Till time runs out and I must say
  'Boodbye' at last.

Soft dark eyes follow me, ever
  watching, ever bright;
Brown eyes full of confidence and
  trust,
She knows I'll aid her halting
  steps by day—
Stay by her side through each
  long night.

And when I reach to pat her
  proudly noble head
Or touch the velvet nose or soft
  deep fur,
A kiss falls on my hand—for in
  her loving way
She tries to ease my aching heart
  and make me smile instead.

She dozes, and in her dreams she's
  free to run,
Those days now gone—when
  running was her game;
Her tail thumps on the floor and
  so I know
Her sleep is sweet with times
  we've spent in fun.

So when tomorrow is empty—my
  girl beyond my call;
In loneliness I'll reminisce, yet
  find a quiet peace
In knowing that the years we
  walked together
Gave me this priceless gift—my
  truest friend of all.

Jorrie Ciotti
A LOVE SONG
*[Dedicated to Ken, my
husband, my lover, my friend]*
The wind blows softly through
  the woods,
Whispering, 'I love you' in his ear.
Feel these feelings of love,
As you listen and you hear.

The sun shines upon my body,
Bringing the glow from within
  without.
Feel this, and you will know,
What love is all about.

Loves comes in many ways
Season after season.
And comes with many feelings,
Now, do not question the reason.

Just as the wind continues
  blowing,
The sun will continue to shine.
I, likewise, will continue to love
  you,
Till the end of time.

Pam Salerni
Death Of a Manmade Lake 1981
From my porch I can see a
  manmade lake; it's given me
  moments to remember.
I've watched birds frequeting and
  wallowing on the mired edges,
  looking for fish to eat or a
  drink to take.
I've watched the sun glancing off
  pools of mirrored window
  panes shimmering.

For days and days it never rained;
  clouds holding moisture never
  dropped a tear, instead swept
  out somewhere unknown.
The water in the lake receded,
  making banks grow grass,
  where water used to be.
People didn't come anymore with
  fishing poles to try for catch;
Or paddle boats go out; for fear of
  mooring in the slimy, sedgy
  growths.

Now the water is all gone.
You can walk across without
  getting wet or stuck in mud.

Cracks here and there,
Like a flashback of a picture
  you've seen somewhere of a
  desert land of drought.

Mary Jane Tam
CARNIVAL MAN
You impress me with your talent
By giving so much pleasure
To both young and old
You lift spirits so high
I know not your name
Nor where you're from
Only that you travel
Going from town to town
I shall always remember
Your very friendly manner
And your smile; oh yes
I was taken in by it
Will you remember me as well?

Ruth A. Woodard
TWO UNBENDING PEOPLE
For you and I are two
who refuse to sway or bend
and that's too bad,
for if we had given a little
we might have made each other
  happy.

If you had been willing
to give of yourself
and I of me,
we may have started
a friendship of fire and flames
that no one could have
  extinguished.

For a brief moment
in time and space
we could have escalated through
the galaxies of heaven,
pausing only long enough
to touch the inner star of each

Irene Norton
**From a Soldier To His
  Mother on Mother's Day**
I'm thinking of you, mother
On this, your special day,
While I fight for my country
And am so far away.

The times when I was very small
You held me tenderly.
And then, when I grew older
You always stood by me.

Don't worry dearest motherheart
I shall come home to you.
For your great love and God's
  support
Will see me safely through.

Halina de Roche
WHAT SHALL WE DO?
Shall we try to impress
And profess
Transgress or supress
What we hear
And think
And see?

Shall we try to express
And confess
To ourselves
Our hearts' and souls'
Real finess?

Shall we try to think
And bring
A new spirit to our life?

Or shall we drive
Strive
Derive

Revice
Connive
Or
Deprive

And in the end

And only maybe

Just survive?

Would that be
Enough
Just to survive?

No!

We want to think and
Feel and love
And live
Not just connive and
Survive!

Joan E. Tarro
TO MY SON
[To Greg, with love]
To my son, whom I love so dear,
I love you more each passing
  year.
And, as you continue to mature
  and grow,
My love for you I hope you'll
  know.

I hope through all life's ups and
  downs,
You'll know your mother is
  always around.
And, when you feel especially
  low,
I hope it's to me you'll want to go.

Even though at times we fuss,
I love you son, very much;
And, through life's valley of tears
  and joy,
You'll always be my special boy.

There's no one else quite like
  you,
Hair all tossled and eyes of blue.
You're my greatest treasure upon
  this earth,
God gave me love upon your
  birth.

Ronald F. Smedley
UNTITLED
*[to the WABF Career
  class. . . as you go upon your
  newfound careers in life
  may you never forget the
  beauty of a glacier lily]*
thoughts upon yon glacier lilies
eminence of truth
        absolute
        definite
        real
        yet no words are brought forth.

you see my friend
. . . lilies never lie

with no mind . . . they never
stop to think

and without thoughts . . .
hurt can never be known.

the beauty in a lily
is not its whites, yellow, red, and
greens . . .
  (although they do help its
  glowing eminence).

rather . . .

it is in the ability for its life to
  bring forth
a smile . . . truth if you will.

nothing more.

. . . now go and do the same.

Dolores Howe
WINDS OF CHANGE
There is a whisper blowing
  through the land.
You need my help—please let me
  take your hand.
Help your brother—I hear the
  Lord's command.
Together we will make a mighty
  band.

Let us take a giant step for all
  mankind
Right here on earth—oh, do not
  lag behind.
Give of ourselves the wounds of
  man to bind.
Relieve all his ills, peace of mind
  to find.

Let bounteous love dominate the
  earth.
Encircle with a rainbow of
  rebirth.
The whisper has changed to a
  rushing wind.
That catches up all people
  together.

Edgar Lubin
THEE
I sat down by the lakeside and
  gloried in the sun
I had freedom to enjoy this that
  was not easily won.
At other times I've wandered
  through stretches of hot sand
Where mountains in the
  distance, have made the
  scenery grand

I've climbed up in those
  mountains and seen the far off
  scene
The places where small things do
  roam where buffalo once had
  been
Yet amid all this beauty my mind
  is not at rest,
I keep thinking of my love the
  girl I love the best.

It maybe that she knows this and
  our love is not to be,
Dearest I adore you there is no
  one but thee

As surely as the sun does rest
  over the horizon
My thoughts philosophical must
  be and prayfully I'll wisen
Knowing you're beyond my reach
  or death may take me from you
Our spirits once again shall meet
WHEN THE PRESENT LIFE IS
THROUGH

Mary Ann Burns
I WISH I COULD
I wish I could understand what is
  latent to be understood
Help me to understand
Every time I feel the urge to say
  the hell with you . . goodbye
I keep drifting back . . .
back to a facade of wonder and
  mistrust?
I wish I could understand why I'm
  allowed to spend the least
  amount of time with the ones I
  care for the most

At the stake of your conditions
I feel ashamed to say Love;
It is a common response to feel
  anger and hostility
I hurt from the caring
Don't treat me like a puppet to be
  used and manipulated
Puppets act, but don't shed tears,
  or feel happiness and
  disappointment that we
  experience
What is this thing that we have. . .
  a truce or a friendship?
Spare me the lies, let's face up to
  the truth.
Truth may sting, but lies bite.
Feeling like an outsider . . .
  looking in on what I
used to know.
I wish I could understand what is
  latent to be understood
Help me to understand.

Jack Jackson
IF I WAS
If you was me and I was you
Would you love me the way I do?
Would you miss me the way I do?
If you was me and I was you?

If I was Sherri and you was Jack
Each time I left would you want
  me back?
You would miss me, honey, and
  that's a fact!
If I was Sherri and you was Jack.

If I was you and you was me
I'd be a sight to behold, don't you
  see.
How very beautiful I would be
If I was you and you was me.

Kiva JS Rice
BALL
I used to be a bright, orange ball
beside the sooty shadow of your
  oboesque tones.
Now I am a muted tangerine in
minor keys, sliding instead of
  bouncing,
squelching on the stairs
as I approach your gloom.

Ilse Schottelius
THE TOP AND PIT
        God
    Miraculous Kind
Disclosing Loving Healing
Birth Animation Destruction Death
Concealing Hating Burning
    Mysterious Hard
        Devil

Ann L Browning
**"Happy-Go-Lucky" Night
  Serenade**
When night falls how I love to go
  out
  And study the kaleidoscopic
  sky
As its various moods and designs
  Make no one so happy as I.

When the dew drops are kissing
  the rose
  And the moons riding high in
  the sky
As the stars play a game with the
  clouds
  There is no one so happy as I.

If falling leaves flutter by in a
  gale
  If thunder crashes as lightning

510

zig-zags the sky
If raindrops from storm laden
   clouds over flow
I repeat there is no one so
   happy as I.

When snowflakes drift softly to
   earth
And the white blanket piles
   lovely and high
As I gaze on that breath-taking
   sight
I declare there is no one so
   happy as I.

When the cold season of winter
   has sped on its way
And the surge of awakening
   spring rushes by
With the beauty of quickening
   life everywhere
Night's glories make no one so
   happy as I.

When it comes to determine
   which season is best
Or if it's a toss-up to even a tie
For each night of each season I
   honestly claim
There is no one so "happy-go-
   lucky" as I.

Gwendolyn Burke
IN PURSUIT OF PARTING
*[Number one, to you Mic, with
so much love.]*
My dreams have wandered
   Through the sand.
They stagger and sway,
   And lose the trail.
Tempted by the sea,
   Between the land,
They are lost; and alone
   I never fail.

Ellen L. Wedel
BEYOND THE STARS
Every time I reach beyond the
   stars
A demon pulls me back.
Every time I take away some bars
He adds more to the stack.
Every one I love with all my heart
He turns their love to hate.
Every one I promise not to part
The demon alters fate.
Every thing I see to make my
   dreams
He turns it all to clay.
Every thing I need to live it seems
He takes it all away.

Emily Porter
WISHING
Oftimes I walk the pathway of
   memories
and I feel you constant by my
   side.
The ripples from the eddies of the
   dreams that we cast
have carried us far and wide.
And I wonder on what distant
   shores you have landed
and if you found calm or
   turbulent seas.
And I wonder in dreams of old
   days long past
if ever you think about me?
Dear friend, we were much in the
   eyes of each other
as we carved the world to our will.
And the flame of love that was
   kindled on meeting
burns strong within me still.

If I tossed you a song upon the
   wind
or cast bottled notes adrift from
   the shore—
if the hours of Time would only
   unwind
and bring back those days of
   yore!—
If I could unravel the mysteries of
   Fate,
if I could but have you once more
   at my side,
what peace would come to my
   haunted heart—
if wishes were horses, then
   beggars could ride.

Mary Cushner Klepinger
DEAR LORD, TEACH ME
*[I dedicate my poem in loving
memory of my father, Ted, and
my daughter, Anne Marie.]*
Teach me to be humble,
To not always want my way,
Help me to be patient,
And to live in joy each day—
Teach me always to forgive,
Even when I'm feeling blue,
I don't want to hurt another
By the things I say or do—
Teach me to be loving
Tho it may not be returned,
Please have mercy on me Lord,
For I have so much to learn—
Teach me to be giving,
Lest I forget sometimes,
The blessings you've bestowed on
   me,
"Not my will, but thine"—
Teach me understanding
For that which cannot change,
Let me be a source of strength,
Without regard nor fame—
Teach me to be pleasant,
To everyone I know,
These things, I hope you'll do for
   me,
Because I love you so—

Vicki V. Anderson
UNTITLED
One day I fell while in school
   (Recess set me free)
And called my brother's name
   aloud
   (Somebody please help me)
Though I haven't been in school
   awhile
   (Graduation set me free)
I sometimes still call his name
   (Somebody please help me)

Ray Yedding
YESTERDAYS
Today I walked alone by the sea.
I thought of you . . . I thought of
   us . . . and I thought of me.
I thought of yesterday, and how it
   used to be.
Of wicker-covered chianti bottles,
   of tiffany lamp shades and
   chandeliers, antique stores and
   rocking chairs.
And I thought of city streets
   being drenched with rain. A
   forest of black umbrellas, a
   gumball machine, a penny
   scale that didn't work, and you
   again . . .
Of strands of multi-colored beads
   and strange shaped candles,

long walks in the park, sharing
   a bag of sunflower seeds.
Of lying crossways on the bed,
   reading poetry.
The shopping center carnival,
   and supermarket baskets all
   filled with groceries.
The quiet crunch of snow, as we
   walked on a winter night, the
   soft sound of a nightbird's call,
   and by the time today has
   ended, some other memory, I
   will recall . . .

Amanda Gordon Hansen
DAWN
The stars grow dim that once so
   bright,
   Bejeweled the velvet robe of
   night,
For swiftly borne on wings of
   light,
   The quiet maid has taken
   flight.

With her departure comes the
   morn,
   On crystal floods as day is
   born,
And she the robe of night does
   scorn,
   For goss'mer mist dewdrops
   adorn,

She gently bids the sun to rise,
   His broad smile lights the
   eastern skies,
While sparks of flame dart from
   his eyes,
   To hasten tardy fireflies.

From 'neath a cloud of rosy hue,
   He charms a rose still drenched
   with dew,
She turns her head his face to
   view,
   And greets the morn for day is
   new.

Ms. J.
YOUR SILENT WORLD
It must be very painful to have
   heard
and not hear anything now, to
   have
spoken and now you speak
   nothing, to
have seen and your world is now
   full
of darkness and yet you are still
   your
gracious self in giving your orders
   in
a very silent way.

Deborah Lynn Blumel
SHELLS
One of these times I feel like
   losing my mind,
Love slipping through my fingers
   so like sand.
On the beaches find the broken
   shells of time,
and the dying candles in the
   hands of men born blind,
One at a time I think we'll leave
   them behind.
All the fish in the sea, too bad
   they can't know me;
chipped away, a shell by tides,
   with nothing left inside.
A wave plays on the sea, so
   gracefully.

One of these times become part
   of a great design,
on the seascape endless blues and
   greens
in empty broken shells, a truth in
   broken minds.
One at a time they find the great
   design,
As waves upon the sea, dance to
   eternity

Margena Adams
GOLDEN MEMORIES
Tears of sadness, cry them not.
All those years we've not forgot
   How you made us laugh and
   cry,
But then we had to say "goodbye".

Days in the winds, nights in
   the sand,
All those things, we had them
   planned.
But now they're gone; no more,
   no more.
All the memories, I've let them
   soar!

We laughed with joy, we
   shared the pain.
Now it'll never be back again.
   For when you're gone, there's
   nothing there.
Gone so far with not even a care.

Arla Jean Howell
THE FLIGHT OF THE DOVE
So pure and white against the
   dark,
The gentle dove of innocence
   rests,
Unblemished, unblamed,
   unhardened, naive,
So tender and gentle, so simple
   and free.

Too soon from the darkness,
Come vultures of greed,
Intent on destroying this virtue
   so pure,
And little by little their efforts
   succeed,
Then trembling and fearful,
The dove takes its leave.

Come back white dove, a voice
   calls within,
But the creatures of greed prevent
   its return,
So the heart that yearns,
For the pure, white dove,
Must ardently follow its flight,
Through the dark.

A child-like heart that's tender
   and pure,
Is precious and dear to the heart
   of God
Oh God give us hearts that still
   desire,
To follow the flight,
Of the gentle, white dove.

Mary J. Watkins
HOW WE SEEK THEE
Man peers in wonderment, at
   The Earth,
      The Heavens,
         The Universe
In search of The Answer
   to his
      Eternal Puzzlement

In the vastness of the
   unknown future of
      time and Space,

511

The Jew,
   seeks with
      Hunger, with
         Thirst and
            Lament!

The Gentile
   looks to the past,
      while scanning
         veiled and misty galaxies
In quest of
   Signs,
      Omens and
         Clues to embrace

In the vast reservoir
   of continuity, of
      Life and Death,
         Death and Life
Daily and eternally, the
   Hindu seeks escape

While the prostrate
   Muslim, with covered head
   petitions daily,
      lest he incur
Thy Holy Wrath

Buddah sought release
   from the incessant rounds,
      through His
      "Noble eightfold path."
God of the Universe,
   How we seek Thee!

Maxine E. Thompson
CIRCUMCISION OF HEART
An ode to the rose colored glasses
   she flung
Crashing from the heights of her
   innermost heart,
In purging her life of a love
   tarnished, worn,
Pray on a new journey to self
   she'd embark.

Tears notwithstanding she'd go it
   alone
No longer blinded by starry eyed
   spell,
Which spoonfed its ideal from
   infancy on
'Twas surely quite an illusion to
   dispel.

If truth be known, some pain
   she'd've been spared,
That man's a hunter beast is no
   jest,
Rather graveyard type love, he'd
   as soon seek

The fleeting one afar off in the
   mist.

Orien Todd
SMOOTH OFF
If I were a pigeon
Let me fly off smidgeon
Of many weathers
Onset subtle wind
Pull my feathers
Which to say unsinned
Are yet
Jewels rainbow set.
Smooth of whose loft
Be nature croft
Or maybe branch
Constellations blanch
With bones entire
Are constant fire
Mid soul aloof
Has heart its roof
So dews pour down
Like tears from clown.

Marjorie Tull
TEARS
*[Dedicated to my two dearest
inspirational friends, Georgia
Kay and Mary Erceg]*
Little teardrop, why are you?
You've a story to tell, I know
For it takes a mighty, mighty,
   storm
Just to make you flow

You visit happiness at times
Tho' then your teardrops soften
You visit loneliness and gloom
More harshly and more often

A broken love—rejected friend
A thousand little fears
Tremendous are the torments
That bring the smallest tears

Yet, when watered by this tear
Life, like the watered rose
Grows into maturity
In dignified repose.

Marjorie Tull
FRIENDS
*[Dedicated to my best friend,
Georgia Kay, Whose love and
support Inspire me to write.]*
When God created Earth, He saw
His wisdom was not there
Man needed understanding
He needed love to share
   . . . so God created Friends

When God created Earth, He
   found
A need for warmth—indeed
He made the sun—but then He
   found
The heart was still in need
   . . . so God created Friends

When God created Heaven and
   Earth
Heaven was more stupendous
So He took a bit of Heaven
And sent it down to us
   . . . Thru' God's creation
   . . . FRIENDS.

Ana Hospy
TWENTY YEARS AGO
Once upon a time
Somewhere down the line
You and I wrote the pages
Of a love to last the ages

We knew it couldn't last
It was moving much too fast
And we were young and so afraid
Of the love we almost made

But that was twenty years ago
I loved you even though
I knew you'd have to go
And say goodbye

Twenty years have all been spent
For whatever those years meant
What can I do to forget
You're on my mind

Now you're standing here
Those old feelings feel so near
We never knew what we were
   missing
Thought love was holding hands
   and kissing

Baby, such a long, long time
Has passed since you've been
   mine
We can't go back and try
To read between the lines

'Cause it was twenty years ago
This love story will never have
a happy ending
Let's stop pretending
It was twenty years ago . . .

Blanca Carretero
MY PRAYER
*[This poem was born on Sept.
18, 1978 (3 A.M.) when I
desperately took my adored
husband in emergency to the
hospital: Inspired by our
mutual love and unbroken
faith in God.]*
God . . .
O God, listen to me . . .
Never please never let me be
   alone again!
Without my husband: "my soul"
   "my heart"
I could not live! I could not live!

God . . .
Please, listen to me . . .
Keep us together always together
Just like we are and now we live.
No matter "how" . . . no matter
   "where" . . .
To be "together" it's all we need!

God . . .
Please, listen to me . . .
When you decide to take our life
Take us together as only one.
Not "one before" . . . not "one
   later" . . .
Take "both together" at the same
   time!

And . . .
After please, my Lord . . . my
   King . . .
With all your blessing, with all
   your love,
Let us together meet back again
To rest "together" on the same
   place!
Forever and ever keep us
   together . . .
Together . . . please!
Amen.

E. Gwendolyn Campbell
ASPIRATION
*[For my sons, Carl and Carey,
whose lives have enriched
mine beyond comprehension
and for whom my love is
beyond measure.]*
If, by a smile or thought of mine
Another's day is brighter;
If, by a word or act of mine
Another's load is lighter—

Then, will I know, deep in my
   soul
The true, sure way to reach my
   goal
Which is, to know at end of day
My Lord I've served in my small
   way.

Stephanie Michelle Laskey
Reflections Of An Ocean
As I walk upon the sand
I watch the distant sky
the moon is full and stars sparkle
   bright
in the darkness up so high

I see the waves come crashing
   down
on to the lonely shore they glide
then back into the sea they fade
leaving only particles of mist
   behind

Time is like an ocean
we are the flowing waves
A young wave approaches the
   sand
an old one departs and its
   memory gradually fades

The sea's everlasting beauty
   shines on
its powerful waves keep rushing
   the shore
eventually the old ones disappear
   back into the sea
but others advance their way and
   there will always be more

As I walk upon the sand
I see the beauty around me all
   the more
moonlight sparkles on the ocean
and the waves move steadily to
   the shore

Ann Sheldon
Rich Man Loan Me a Dime
Hey rich man with your head so
   high.
How come you live so fine on
   that big, old hill of mine?
All I want is one thin dime.

I heard that your wife is rich and
   fine.
She's just itching to give me a
   dime.
But what you don't know my wife
   is poor and fine,
and she won't give you a dime.
So rich man if you want to be a
   friend of mine,
get down and loan me a dime.

Betty Jean (Henry) Roberts
THE CRY OF A CHILD
*[To my son, Raymond Charles
Roberts, Jr. I love you dearly.]*
"Oh, Mama where is my daddy?"
   wept the sad faced child.
"Well, my dear," Mama sadly
   replied,
"Your daddy has left us for a little
   while."

"Why did he leave us?" the child
   asked as a tear dropped from
   her eye
"Because he has gone to heaven,"
   was all the mother could reply.

"But Mommy, I love daddy so."
"I love him too, my dear, you'll
   understand it better as you
   grow.

Your Daddy was a good man
and he lived his life for you
and me.
So smile my child, he'll always
be with us through memory."
The fragile child, smiled as she
wiped the tears from her eyes
And she raised her head with a
look of surprise
And said, "Mommy, I love Daddy,
I hope he can hear it.
Because He's always with me
in spirit
Although from us his soul did
depart
He'll always be with us within
our hearts."

Luella Allen
THE PROMISE
When the exulting light
of a virgin dawn
awakens my spirit
to tower and sing,
the mournful stratus
of winter's flurry
is but the promise of
a bright, new spring.

Elizabeth Saltz
AMERICA GROWS
*[To David Klinick who is
interested in Poetry and
encouraged me to write. He
helped me in my endeavors to
do research.]*
American business grew as the
Colonists settled the land,
The boot maker, the cabinet
maker, the ship builder,
Contributed to America's growth.
The individual enterprise
Became the backbone of
America's growth.

The small artisans prepared their
goods for sale,
As the Colonists traded among
each other.
The machines were invented, the
cotton gin and reaper,
The fields produced more cotton,
the wheat fields more wheat.

America grew as she exported all
over the world,
The small busines grew as
machinery produced more.
The large export trade increased
the country's wealth,
The artisans established
factories and mass produced.

American industry found
stimulus in vast natural
resources,
The coke ovens were burning
to produce the nation's fuel.
The planter of cotton was helped
by Eli Whitney,
Who speeded the production of
raw cotton.

The mills hired labor who
produced cotton cloth,
The trade with Great Britain
far exceeded the North.
The wheat fields expanded with
Cyrus McCormick's reaper,
It threshed the wheat and
stacked it for sale.

As the tall wheat grew in the
fields of the South,
The scythe cut the wheat

which was stacked by hand.
Along came the reaper which
threshed by machine,
The wheat was neatly stacked
in bundles for export.

The houses lit by candlelight
were changed to electric lamps,
The night became daylight as
lights were installed.
The old lamplighter who lit up
the street lamps,
Was replaced by electric lights
that changed the night to day.

Aleta Jones
MOUNTAIN CABIN HOME
This little Cabin, made of wood,
Built by loving hands,
Sits alone upon the mountain
Among the trees on a piece of
land.

It saw four generations
Live, to work and play,
Watched the children earn their
bread
In oh so many ways.

The years went by one by one,
Time slipped by so fast,
It soon became a Mountain Cabin
Standing in the past.

Decay took place, caused by the
rain,
and snow year after year,
The porch has sunk, the roof
leans North,
I shed a silent tear.

Now, standing here by the river,
Thinking and all alone
I'm sad to see there's no one left,
In this Mountain Cabin Home.

Donna Jean Roguski
LONELINESS
Choosing to be alone in my room.
Frustrating thoughts, planning on
escaping from my self made
prison.
Letting go of fears—
Self challenge—Accepting the
Open door—
Rebirth—
Healing, Love, Self Expression
Living Life to its Fullest
Capacities.
Loneliness Disintegrated—
Friends, Love, Happiness.

Catherine Jo McClure
MY MAN
Understanding beyond all my
tears of hope;
touching me when all hope
seems unwilling.

Respect as a woman and mother.

First flower you gave, a dandelion.
A weed, not so, you gave them of
the heart.

You gave of yourself not of
money;
knowing of what gives joy in
living.

A man, tender and gentle of life.

I said I always wanted a baby seal,
you did not
laugh, you smiled.

Dreams are always possible.

Beyond all my hopes and dreams
you've given me love beyond life;

being both father and friend to
our children.

A better father you could not be.

Memories of you shall give me
more than most have in all of
their life;
the fear of feath I have not, my
friend,
I love you beyond all fear and
eternity.

My husband, my friend, my love;
unity is ours always and forever,
Catherine.

Helen Masters Gossett
THE LION AND A LAMB
*[To my husband, Frederick; my
son, Jan; his wife, Cecilia; their
son, Darin; and daughter,
Claudine.]*
The lion escorts evil might
Scathing the helpless sphere,
Along the path dazed splinters fall
Sealed in eternal fear.

Yet—not all times does savage
wrath
Dwell as a beast of prey,
Enshrouded virtues gaily birth
A lamb to rule one day.

Muriel E. Vebsky
TOWARD TOMORROW
Plunging imagination of a
waking dream
Strode through everything in
vague disquiet.
Imperceptible shadow of innate
sensitiveness shatters
Vestigal emotion slipping near
the loneliness.
Undiviating faith sparked a
spurious thrill
Life crept comparatively relaxed
toward tomorrow.

John A. Fletcher
MAC LEISTER
Mac Leister, at Sterling Bridge,
Himself and his clansmen i' foot
of the ridge,
The claymores sang and Himself
with bow
Sent many a shaft 'gainst the
Sassenach foe
But Himself did sink neath the
traetors blow
On the bank of the burn with its
bloody flow
Now to the heather brave Scots
and leal
The Sassenachs beaten and
Himself will heal.
Only beware of the skulking foe
Forwarned by the call of the
hoodie crow.
Black be the fate and black be the
woe
When Mac Leister harms a crow.

Susan Tomiko Tanaka
INDRA'S NET
music dances shining in the soul
love its impetus love its goal
awareness watches time and self
unfold
valuing above all the inner gold
all things belong to the one that
loves
wealth spangles down from sky
to eye
thought is diamonds and evolves

there is never a last goodbye
eternity moves forever together
life is a harmony of being
time and distance will never
sever
the companionship of inner seeing

and if bright stars guide at night
and proud clouds accompany the
day
our hearts are also sharing the
light
no matter how long ago or far
away

each story is new with truths
untold
all are sister and brother
there are threads of meaning that
hold
each within the other

John M. Akili
Bring Back the Happy Days
Bring back the happy days we
used to know.
When things were sweet and life
was slow.
Bring back the happy days we
used to know,
When without smog days were
beautiful and the sun
aglow.
Bring back the happy days we
used to know,
The wind in the shade and the
leaves aflow.
When children were children,
and enjoyment
was there.
Love was ubiguitous and
everyone seemed to care.
Bring back the happy days we
used to know
when families were together and
when love and unity showed.
Bring back the happy days we
used to know.
Where times were great and
things were so;
Where warmth had a place in our
lives, where everyday wasn't a
struggle to survive.
Where people helped each other,
when we were like sisters and
brothers.
Oh! Bring back the happy days
we used to know;
When things were sweet and life
. . . well life . . .
was slow.

Calla L. Dean
HE WATCHES HIS SHEEP
I know the Good Shepherd
watches His sheep
I'm one of His flock, why
should I weep?
Though He stands above in the
mountains high,
He watches below where His
little ones lie—
He watches His sheep.

I know the Good Shepherd,
watches His sheep
As they gambol, play, or rest in
their sleep.
Wraps them in darkness, when
night shadows fall—
That with love He enfolds
them, great ones and small—
He watches His sheep.

I know the Good Shepherd
watches His sheep—
In soft curving valleys, where
foes may not creep,
He holds in the crook of His
strong, strong arm—
His children, His loved ones,
safe from all harm;
He watches His sheep.

(CHORUS)
He watches His sheep, He
watches His sheep.
On highways, on mountains, in
the valleys;
He watches His sheep—In
sickness, in health,
In sadness, in poverty, in
wealth;
Around the fireside or in the
alleys
He watches His sheep. He
watches His sheep.

Brad Lee
MY FATHER
My father was a West Pointer,
He was also an engineer,
He fought in a war but did not
make a name,
It was as an engineer that he
gained a slice
of fame,
He worked on bridges, harbors
and rivers,
A work dangerous enough to give
one the shivers,
He designed a subway in a large
city,
That he died shortly after is
indeed a pity,
But in his death he gained a
certain recognition,
Named after him are a bridge, a
subway station and a Post of
The American Legion.

Danae, Ida S. Barton
UNTITLED
The world cradled in silence
under a snowy cover prone,
on That Eve with evergreen is
Keeping sacred the hearth, the
home.

My heart and hearth's romance
Leap upwards as if blown, and a-
round the tree wave and dance,
Keeping sacred the hearth, the
home.

Do I now discard the Norway,
now
when green within my heart is
grown?
Rather deck it near my doorway:
to
Keeping sacred the hearth, the
home.

LaVerne D. Byers
All Alone Before Others!!
[To the loves of my life, John,
son Puchito, Lil Joe and
Tweety.]
Being alone in front of an
audience
when nobodies there
(All alone Before Others)
Acting strongly with some
idealism,
Some vanity, but with a private
approach.

Performing uniquely with an
individual
expressiveness of grace.
(All alone Before Others)
Beginning with such taste, arms
almost
stuck to the sides.
Gradually expanding into bloom
like a rose.
(All alone Before Others)

Absorbing earth within, and
floating about
in ecstasy.
Concentrating on the
performance; a
twist here, a hunch there.
But every now and than glancing
at
the audience, pausing while
doing so.
When there's nobody there!

All Alone Before Others!!

Ludwig Adams
A WEDDING
A Wedding
Is a unique event
In the continuum
We call life
A marriage
Is a partnership
That starts in happiness
And need not end in strife
It's give and take
And accomodation
It's continuous adjustment
Or simply compromise
It's the joining
Of blythe spirits
Full of hope
In common enterprize
Its transition from a
Generally carefree existence
To a formal plan where
A family is the essence
From a past
That was less than perfect
To a future of
Great expectations
Guaranteed by our belief
That life is good
Because God
Is Love

Charles W. Kennedy
**By Any Other Name—On
Kennedy**
[For Regina Shannon Kennedy,
Elma Laine Kennedy, and
Eileen Kennedy; Jacqueline
Kennedy Onassis and Mrs.
Ethel Kennedy and Joan
Kennedy.]
Hail! Ted Kennedy, Jack, Robert,
Rose, and distant Joseph P. Not
all of us have sprung from the
same American root. But by
any other name we are
Kennedys too. As a rose by any
other name is still itself.

The media makes the message
and has made you out of
distant moneyed twenties and
thirties, courageous forties,
embattled fifties and successful
sixties in its new frontier
despite all. And continues now
in an out-of-fashion democratic
federalism.

The call now is for a more
grassroot, State-bound activity.
And we other Kennedys are
there. Check the phone book
silent though we be. See now
whether the call is to the
House or Senate or the ever
formidable Presidency or even
the Nation's courts. Perhaps, it
is rather a call to the plow and
the shears, camera and press.
Looking out, the mantle of
power is reserved to the State
and more basically to the
people— whose kin we are. By
any other name.

Angelo V. Secreto
STAGGER
Unimaginable experiences hit
with heart attack suddenness.
Months of this way of life,
have astonished my spirit.
Dislike for belligerent actions,
has shot holes in my good
nature. In yearning for
certainty the real keeps
running away from me.
Pounding defeats are making my
well of thoughts run dry. By
what method of life, do you
bring the light of hope into the
despair of hopelessness.
Contentment feels for me,
many years beyond. For what
purpose, do I survive this
hurting isolation.

Eileen C. Joyce
TWILIGHT
Silver grey the evening sky
Shot with pink and purple hues
Flung across the quiet bay
As twilight treads a noiseless
path.
Spruce stir with a gentle breeze
As day gasps its final breath
And night, with all its magic
black,
Settles down upon the land.
Little boats come home at last
Signal for the bridge to turn
And open up the river wide
As daylight flees into the west.

Miss Mary Jane Dennis
PROCLAIM "AMEN"
[In Precious Remembrance Of
My Father (Andy) And My
Mother (Helen) Whose
Orientations For My Life Began
With Bible.]
Proclaim this House quite
newly-framed
With edifice so grand,
By faith of worship be it named
For many years to stand.
A Call to Worship has been
pealed,
Let Services begin;
The sanctuary seats are filled,
More folk are ushered in.
A Shepherd of the Flock is there
To dedicate this place,
He boldly leads in fervent prayer
That all may know God's grace.
The Choir follows with a Song,
And sings without restraint;
The Shepherd intervenes again,
Admonishing each saint.
He sees the seats before him filled,
The folk who entered in;

He knows their ardor, quickly
chilled,
By his reproofs for sin.
The Shepherd looks upon his
flock
In joy, proclaim, "Amen!"
The House is founded on the
Rock
To meet for God again!

Ruth M. Blekkenk
FRIEND AND LORD
Jesus is a friend of mine
He is always near to hear my call
If I walk the straight and narrow
line
His arm supports me lest I fall.
He loves me whether I deserve it
or not
And helps me along the way
Of what He wants me to know is
my lot
So from Him I'll never stray.
He leads me and I always try to
follow
Though I find it hard sometimes
I stumble and bend real low
But He lifts me 'til my life shines.
I try to be like Jesus
In every thing I do
He always makes me happy
And He will do it for you too.
So follow the guidelines He has
given
Carefully written in His Holy
Word
And soon you will have Jesus
As a friend as well as Lord.

Sonnie Verhines
AGAINST
Lips against your brand of wine,
My thoughts against your
mysterious mind.

Some desires against my will,
Watered eyes that can't be still.

Weary head against your chest,
Passionate ideas can't seem to
rest.

Humbled hearts not at their best,
Against the wind to take the test.

Thomas A. Hudson
YES, I KNOW LOVE . . .
Yes, I know love.
How could I not know love?
I know you.

Robert Michael Grossman
BURNING FIRES
The burning fires
That flame within us
Are fueled by different passions,
Each obsessed by different
desires,
Each attaining it
In their own fashions.

The fires that burn
Brightly within us
Consume ever more energy,
Kindle ever more madness,
Consume ever more sanity
At a fever pitch that seems
beyond us.

Glowing embers of stoked coals
Within your heart,
Within your soul,
Pay testimony to your diligence
To all that know.

Ambitions, dreams,

Longings, persevering,
The fires burning deep,
Forever intense, forever burning.

Mary Diane Strauss
MY FRIEND
Friend, you know me as being
    very loud,
and often times being shy.
You know I love music,
and that I love to dance.
I have many things that I'd like to
    do.
You know I dream a lot.
I keep many things inside me,
like dreams and fears.
Friend, in you I have found
    someone,
to share all my feelings with.
I can tell you anything,
and I know you listen.
Most important you accept me
    for being me,
and you don't try to change me.
It feels so good to be able to,
trust someone and to love
    someone.
I am so glad I found that someone
    in you.
Someone with whom I can share
    my life.
I have much reason to be happy,
and to live.

Margaret Harris
MY VALENTINE
For years you've been my
    Valentine,
    And it's so good that you're
    still mine.

The time when things were very
    bad,
    We just thanked God for what
    we had.

Our love was always strong
    enough,
    For any thing that could come
    up.

The children now, they all are
    gone,
    With little families of their
    own.

And we're so proud that we can
    say,
    Thank you Jesus every day.

Now dear heart as we grow old,
    Our precious memories we will
    hold.

And you will always hear me say,
    "Darling, you are my valentine
    today."

Dolores Dahl
THERE IS BUT ONE
There is but one,
though we see multiplicity.
The senses are deceptively
inclined to be attuned
to visability.

There is but one.
And though apparencies
proclaim their own reality,
and you and I . . .
confined to our mortality
believe in the duality,

there is but one.
For all we see is but degree.
The esseence of the mass
comprising all, totality,

is one the same.
Though it expresses as reality
is varied form . . .
There is but one.

Bernice K. Skelcher
TOMORROW
Teach me to be thankful, Lord
Each and every day
For I have a tendancy
To look the other way.
. . . Not because I want to sin
Or do you any harm
But rather—I am worldly here
And dwell in mortal storm.
A storm of soul—of heart and
    mind
When I forget to pray
But soon I'm made to realize
There is no other way

Than you—whose touch reminds
    me
My blessings I ignore
And then—I find the comfort
I had known before.
With premiums paid for life for
    me
how could I turn from you?
Not to turn—yet not to see
And never to pursue.
Each day in growing older here
More important than the last
My scales of life must balance
And—hold fast!
For I am conscious of the cost
My immortal bread to leaven
And—in my weakness, here a
    while
Keep an eye on heaven.

Carol A. Bourgeois
PINK, YELLOW AND RED
Visions of color remain
still in her head
of the pretty dresses
pink, yellow and red.
Just turning four
she was only a child,
and having a party
she danced and smiled.
Pink was from Grandma,
yellow from Uncle Paul,
red was from Mama,
she loved them all.
Out in the yard they
ate cake and ice cream.
She remembers the grass
and its color green.
After pin the tail on
the donkey game
was when, suddenly

the headache came
The doctor brought medicine
said, fine she will be
but, when the pain was gone
she could not see.
It's been twenty three years
since the pain in her head
but she still remembers
Pink, yellow and red.

Goldie L. Rose Heath
SILENTLY I WAIT
Silently, as I wait
From Heaven's pearly gate
Smiling down, I watch
The angels care for you

And somewhere in the night
God will make things right
With gentle hand and heart
To us, you'll soon depart

Now without the pain
Away from lifes' old game
You join me in my arms
With all your gentle charms

And walking hand in hand
We've entered Holy Land
And now our life's complete
For eternally meet

Rick D. Garlock
ALPHA TO OMEGA
No faint impression will I make—
and no good would come of it,
to any other than myself.
No lessons learned from my
    covenants
with God or man,
or the damnations of endless
    wealth.

The will of man lends to life
an individuality . . .
When he is gone; no copy made,
no one to carry on what wisdoms
    learned,
or life portrayed.

We were once, but never again;
'tis how it should be.
From Alpha to Omega . . .
from beginning to end—

Martina Sonner
SNOWFLAKES
Snowflakes on an autumn wind,
Myriad of white,
Riding high toward the hills,
Tiny birds in flight.

Snowflakes on a winter wind,
Crystals of cold,
Driving to a destiny,
Posts and fence to hold.

Snowflakes on a warming wind,
One last fling,
Floating to a rivulet,
Melting into spring.

Betty Caughey Kinsey
SPRING MAGIC
Spring magic as it comes our way,
Bringing signs of spring each day.
April breezes top of the line,
Just made for kite flying time.

Deep blue skies, an soft spring
    showers,
Making way for springtime
    flowers.
Snowdrops an bluebells in
    profusion spill,
With daffodils an wood violets
    over the hill.

Forsythia bursting into bloom,
Soft rose redbuds will be here soon.
Dogwood, magnolia an apple
    blossom trees,
Contribute to the fragrant breeze.

Robins, bees an butterflies too,
Starting out in life anew.
Each day filled with a new surprise,
Unfolding right before our eyes.

Kathy Noble Fuller
GAPING
torn by conflict,
        sickened by repetition,
                once again i in
transition: moving. remain the
same.
        confusion binds my energy
                so fastidiously, i
        drown in boredom opaque.
the fog thick
    consumes the flowing; knowing
                no coming, no going;
        begging for light and its glowing
this woman demands! (bleakness).
the butterfly seen in dreams
        cuddles still to the cocoon
            mislaid
        on a green leaf of spring.
the pleasantry of paradise
        enticed the possibility
            of possibilities.
the comfort of the cocoon
        doomed the flight to light.
                            and
the conflict controlling (this
    writing) creates
                    (but) a
                    silent
                        darkness.

Mabel R. Bennett
MY LOVE OF CHILDREN
My love of children made my life
    complete,
They are your own; bone, blood
    and heart of you.
Conceiving them in love you are
    replete,
But years of their dependence are
    too few.
When my love died, I asked how
    can I live?
Then grandchildren were born to
    fill my life.
My cold heart warmed; I'm
    needed and I give
Full measure to be "Nana", Mama,
    Wife.
"I loves you Nana!" is so sweet a
    sound,
It makes my aging bones and
    greying hair
Turn honey gold and surge of
    youth rebounds,
The voice of love makes even old
    ones fair.
Of this Life's Feast, I've tasted
    every cup,
No matter sour or sweet, I drank
    it up.

Al Turner
GUIDE TO A HAPPY LIFE
[Dedicated to my one year old
daughter Jill Elaine Turner
1/11/83]
May the sun dry every dampened
    thought in your mind.
May you float atop every wave in
    your life.

May there be a bounce in your
step when a listless day arise.
May your mind never become
stagnant, for lack of cheerful
thoughts.
May you never experience hate,
when there's so much love to
be had.
May you try hard to make friends
of any foes.
May you be humble when
occasion for anger arises.
May you never fail to give, more
than you receive.
May you feel thankful for each
sunrise, for you play such an
important role in it's
complicated cycle.
May you learn to smile when a
frown appears
May you never fail to listen to
good advice.
Most of all. May God walk with
you, through each difficult step
of your life.
   Love you Forever,
    Dad

Allan De Fiori
WILLOW BITTER
Willow Bitter
Thou watch over
The sleep of the deads
When the wind is passing by
It delays through thine hair,
And thou all tremble
Oh! green angel
Like if thou would have a heart.
Harp of vibrant eords
To the tears of us mortals.

Stephanie K. Binney
I Thought Of You Today
I thought of you today.
 It made me want to cry.
I thought of how I missed you
 And why we said good—bye.
I thought of how you raised me
 And how I turned out like you.
I thought about my feelings
 When I thought your life was
 through.
I thought of how life used to be
 And the good times that we had.
I thought of how I cherished you
 And how your divorce made
 me mad.
I thought about your silly ways
 And how I picked them up.
I thought of what a great dad you
 were.
 I guess I had all the luck.
I thought about your interests
 And how you liked to play.
But more important than anything
 I thought of you today.

Kathleen Shabi
FORMATIONS
Like bright crimson petals form a
 flowery rose,
Like massive white mountains
 are formed of fresh snow.

Like tiny water droplets form a
 carpet of sea,
 That's how your love has
 formed life for me.

Like grains of brown sand form
 the ground we walk on,
Like rays of bright light form the
 image of dawn.

Like specks of pure crystal form
 the crispness of ice,
Like rainbows and prisms form
 color and spice.

Like atoms of silver or brass form
 a key,
 That's how your love has
 formed life for me.

Laura Schuman
IN HIS SPECIAL PLACE
I look at the hurt in a little
 child's eyes.
He'll never grow up to be smart
 and wise.
He goes to the doctor almost
 every day,
just to hear "He's in a very bad way,
He could leave you in a year,
 month, or day.
It's just so very hard to say!"
He turns out to be only skin and
 bones!
He doesn't even want any ice
 cream cones!
Now all he does is constantly
 sleep.
Oh, one night it was so very deep.
We rushed him to the hospital;
 he was gone.
This isn't fair; this is wrong.
He had so much living to do.
He won't see his sister or how she
 grew.
But now he's in his special place,
 with our dear God and all his
 grace.

Darla Fulton
REMEMBER . . .
Remember the sunny day we met
 in June?
Remember the night we made
 love, under the moon?
Remember the time we got
 sentimental,
You were so kind and gentle.
Remember our first "kiss",
 so soft and shy, and filled with
 bliss.
Remember the day in the park,
 and when there was no light,
You held me, safe from the dark.
Remember when you found my
 heart,
we knew then we'd never part.
"Our life", we'll always treasure,
Remember when I said yes,
I meant forever.

Betty Jo Lloyd
Advice To Mother For Son
Respect him, let him find his way.
Listen to what he has to say.
Follow when you see the need.
He needs to know that he can lead.
Love him in all the ways you can.
Help him know he soon will be a
 man.
Share him with his loving dad.
Don't urge either of them to be
 mad.
Teach him to work and play.
He will be on his own someday.
Try to set a good example.
Then watch as life he tries to
 sample.
He'll make some mistakes that's
 true.
Just remember, so did you!
Notice his good points and

compliment him.
But don't give in to his slightest
 whim.
Sons are terrific and terrible, too.
There's nothing they won't try to
 do.
They're worth every cent you
 have to pay.
So don't give up until your dying
 day!

Maxine Smith
KITCHEN TO EAT
Twas a little kitchen on 7th street
Where the people comes to eat
About 3 steps down from the
 front door
2 coffee pots in a sea of gloom;

A four square counter and a stove
 in the center
Heavy odour of food as you enter,
A kettle of soup as large as a vat;
Potatoes, cabbage, morsels of fat.

Building up in savory smoke;
Food for the Gods, when the
 Gods are broke.
Serving it up, a hunk of bread and
 a steaming cup,
Slopping it up.

No time for graces, why should
 they care?
These people with sad faces,
Gaunt with hunger, battered with
 weather
Walking the streets for days
 together
No delicate sipping, no leisurely
 talk,
The rule of the place is to eat and
 walk.

Rolo
TO EX WITH FLOWERS
The only three things in this
 world more for sure than the
 wind and the sun and the rain
Are the love that I feel when I'm
 with you and without you the
 emptiness and pain

Louise Hinton
GOD'S MANY GIFTS
Many the gifts which God bestows
That rich and poor alike may share
The radiant beauty of a rose
The shining glory of lilies fair.

The golden sunlight sent by day
A million stars to shine by night
Oftimes the moonbeam's silvery
 ray
To flood the earth with wondrous
 light.

In winter a blanket of soft white
 snow
In spring the robin's song of praise
In summer a time for things to
 grow
And then His lovely autumn days.

In daily tasks—yes, even those
In all true friends God's love we
 trace
In the sweetness of a night's repose
And the wondering smile on a
 baby's face.

He sends good things with lavish
 hand
All these and many more
Numerous as the grains of sand
That are found along the shore.

But the greatest gift He offers,
 friend
Is salvation Through His Son
A life with Him that has no end
When life on earth is done!

Deirdre Knight
FAIRYLAND
Fairyland,
My Utopia.
It's been fun.
My heart's desire:
A flying frog,
A purple sun.

But it's time
To say good—bye now,
For reality's too strong.
My fairyland
Is leaving me;
I've been holding on too long.

Oh, Fairyland!
Must you
Send me away?
I don't want to grow up;
I just
Want to stay.

Kari Rose Sample
DE' MOTEL OBLIVION
Champagne brunches and soap
 opera afternoons
A swim by the pool under the
 silvery moon
Ah, Florida so lovely but I don't
 feel at home
No, I don't take care of the
 expenses or even make my bed
I don't even have anything to do
 so alone
Ah, Florida it's only my attitude
 having to share my love
Waiting at Holiday Inns under
 cover
I hate to admit it, he's a two time
 lover
We're so carefully cool
Not to take romance so serious
Can't set ourselves up for a
 letdown
We just drive around in circles
Avoiding what I really am to him
A gypsy woman
Another mistress in distress.

Clara Werner McClary
ON FATHER'S DAY
I can't begin to tell you
 How much you mean to me
If I were a worthy poetess
 It would be classic poetry.

You are like a little boy at times
 So sweet and charming
And then there is the man in you
 Of such great authority and
 learning.

You drive yourself from morn 'til
 night
 Always achieving, perfecting
Your many interests and
 curiosities
 Keep your mind keen and
 interesting.

You are independent, you are
 protective
 You want to give others their
 freedom
And yet you want to guide them
 too.
 Giving them the benefit of your
 wisdom.

Your long years of teaching
  Have made you appreciate men
  of many stations
You have learned that great
  character
  Can be found in unexpected
  places.

Your many students attest to the
  fact
  That you are the greatest of
  teachers
And given them the knowledge
  they need
  To prepare them for the future.

You have won nation—wide
  recognition
  In your teaching profession
The Conant Award was presented
  to you
  How few achieve this coveted
  goal.

And not the least of your
  achievments
  In your role as a Father, dear
You have inspired your sons to be
  winners
  For you and the world they live
  in.

And so, as I said, if only
  I could put into words as a
  poetess
This would be a classic
  Instead of a clumsy effort.

Sam Maropis
UGLY GIRL
Ugly girl who thinks she is so holy
Always cutting up on people that
  make out
Noone listens to her except her
  holy friends
Who all share her point of view.

Well listen to me ugly girl
I got a vital question for you
If you were born lucky like the
  Homecoming Queen
Exactly what would you do
If the captain of the football team
Made it clear he liked you
And he wanted to take you out
Would you let him do all the
  things you scorn
Or would you scream and shout?

Ugly girl doesn't like making out
Because she's never had the chance
If opportunity were thrust onto her
I'm not sure that she would pass.

Boyd C. Allen
STILL LIFE
Mary smiled through a window
shedding light on the ground and

I followed the lines of a black
  church into the onyx of a cold
  night sky.

A star matrixed daysky
blessed the church's night and

I sat on dewing summer grass
looking crook-necked for its end.

Virginia Holm Haseben
NOCTURNAL GINNYISMS
I am waxing words poetic,
Erudite, profound and true.
Then I awaken, somewhat shaken,
For escaping me without a clue
Is all this wonderment that I do!
My thoughts are as quicksilver,

Odes totally brillant!
If only my subconscious
Were ably resiliant
To keep them alive,
My genius to survive.
My dormant visions would have
  a photo
That somehow could transcend
  the line,
And capture the rapture that lies
  untapped
Deep in my dreaming mind!

John E. Moyer
**Sitting In a Lawn Chair On
  the Terrace Of the
  Memorial Union In
  Madison, Wisconsin**
In the grey
powdering
of fog,
water ripples
with the wind.

Sailboats
tick
left or
tock
right,
as a rigid breeze
weaves through thin
metal masts.

And the powder
dissolves,
slowly,
later in the day.

Susan P. Glodas
**A Gift From God (For
  Matthew)**
I cried for days after you were born,
And I thanked God for you.

Your hair was blonde, your eyes
  were blue,
I loved you so.
I wanted to hold you and never
  let go.

Matthew Ryan, our bundle of love,
God gave you to us
A gift from above.
Matthew, our little one,
Our own special son,
We are a family,
The three of us are one . . .

Jerri Lynne Yount
BY MYSELF
Colder than the dead of Winter—
Just November
We held together—it was good
Don't you remember?
Fall had come and so had you
Into my life
Now Winter's here and you are
  gone
Into the night
And I am here on Graveyard Hill
And you are somewhere else
Perhaps God meant for me
                          To be
Always by myself

Darlene Hetrick
I WANT TO LIVE
I want to live to hear the night. I
  want you now to hold me tight.
I want to live to see the day. I
  want you here with me to stay.
I want to live to see the sun rise
  and set. I've loved you since the
  day we met.

I want to live to hear you laugh. I
  want to share all your
  problems not just half.
I want to live to see us as one not
  two. I want us to say the words
  I do.
I want to live to bare you a child.
  I want to give you all my love
  so mild.
I want to live to see our children
  run and play. I want to be with
  them night and day.
I want to live to watch them
  grow. I'ts my love for you I'll
  always show.
I want to live to see them
  through school even through a
  brother sister duel.
I want to live to see them so
  happy as I, and to live a full life
  before we all die.

Deidra A. Chapman
FATHER
*[This poem was written for Mr.
James Chapman, my father, as
inspired by Alan Myers.]*
Father, I never told you how
  much I love you.
I never told you how much you
  really mean to me.
I tried to make you realize I'm not
  a little girl.
Now that I am gone away, don't
  stop believing in me.
I will make you really proud of
  me someday.
You will live to see that, I truly
  pray.
For if I ever possibly can, I'll see
  my name in lights.
I live to see me and you back
  together one of these nights.

Nancy Plock
listen to me . . .
listen to me . . .
i am letting you into my mind,
you can feel what i feel,
and see what i see,
and hear what i hear,
not everyone lets you in,
even if you pound at the door,
but if you do not get in,
try again.

Elaine P. Morton
MY POETRY
My greatest ambition in life
Was to see my poems in print.
Now that it has happened
I don't think I'll ever quit.

The lift you get from knowing
That your work, it is worthwhile
Is the happiest experience
God can grant in any style.

I thank God for the talent
Of writing poetry as such
For it gives to me an outlet
Which is needed, oh so much.

It may not be too brainy
Or it may be every day
But it gives to me a pleasure
To show care in such a way.

If I have made one person
Stop and think, just for a minute
Whether it be a chuckle or a tear
Then, the words that I have
  written
Are the best in any year.

Toby Cary
THEY SHOULD, BUT WONT
*[To Mr. Clarence Heck, my
Advanced Writing teacher. If
not for "Thursdays Work", I
might not have written this.
Thank You!]*
They like to drift away, away,
Drinking liquor all day, all day.
Seeing things they see, but don't.
Should they stop?
They should, but wont!

'Cause they are caught in this
  obsession,
They only think of fascination.
Seeing things they see, but don't.
Should they stop?
They should, but wont!

Today they lost their only pride,
They lost their lives and now
  can't hide
That we were right, they were
  wrong!
They should've stopped,
They played too long!

Anna Marie
I AM YOURS
[For Stiles]
While I sit in silent reflection,
My thoughts are only of you.
Your strength and magnitude
  first called to me,
But now your gentleness and
  quiet sensuality have become
  my obsession.

When you speak to me, I hear no
  other,
And the look in your eyes that I
  see haunts me wherever I am.
The feel of your arms around me
  is something I shall never be
  free of,
For the free and untamed part of
  me has become possessed by
  you alone.

I no longer can contain the desire
  that has been awakened in me.
The depth to which you have
  touched my spirit has become
  absolute.
A truly special fantasy I once
  controlled has now become my
  reality,
And without you by my side, my
  life and I are incomplete.

Jinx Gollam
UNTITLED
I am a poet.
A poet I'll be . . .
when eveyone reads me—
posthumously!

Kevin M. Hibshman
PAINT THE SKY
We walk barefoot on the warm
  sand.
Hand in hand—as friends.
The marble waves of the ocean
  tide . . .
Echo the roar of feeling inside.

The gusty puff of wind, come fill
  my sails.
Golden sunlight plays upon your
  bronze thigh.
You are a heavenly still.
A masterpiece of flesh that holds
  the eye.

This day is meant for lovers.

Gulls sweep overhead with
majestic precision.
Breathing becomes pleasurable,
Instead of a forced mechanism.
My senses drift. My mind is a
vacant lot.

I feel artistic.
Streaking the pale sky with
watercolors,
I dip my brush into your heart
and the
World becomes our canvas of
expression.

A mural of beautiful union with
heaven.

Robert W. Sumner
WHAT IS A FLOWER?
What is a beautiful flower?
But a reflection of God's love and
power.
To the world it adds much joy
and cheer,
And is something everyone can
hold dear.
The fragrance can be lovely and
sweet
As it rises to your nostrils to meet.
To the shut—in and the sick
It can bring a nice smile
And help them all the while.
The great array of wonderful colors
Is far above the price of any
amount of dollars!
It clothes the fields of green
With a magnificent scene—
With a panorama of majesty fit
for a king!
But it's a gift to all mankind;
And as it pleases our mind
We should give thanks to our
very kind,
Kind, Heavenly Father—
Who also sends the rain to water
The Wonderous Flower!!

Mary Bubeck
BABY'S BREATH
Thru the sparkle
of a child's eyes;
We find faith.
Thru the innocence
of a child's laughter;
We find the magic.

Thru the honesty
of a child's love;
We find peace.
Thru the whisper
of a child's life;
We find immortality.

Thru the gentleness
of a child's touch;
We learn to trust.
Thru the joy
of a child's embrace;
We learn to care.

Thru the games
of a child's imagination;
We learn to dream.
Thru the wisdom
of a child's mind;
We learn to believe.

Nancy Yeakel
A CHILD
A child, a child, on yonder hill,
What will he do, what will?
His laughing face all aglow,

Will he find the way? I can not
know.

A child, he is not still,
Where will he go, where will?
Through the valley, over the peak,
What is it, what does he seek?

Now jumping and splashing,
wonderful fun,
Put on your shoes, it's time to run,
See the tall castles rise from the
sands,
Made and designed by those little
hands.

A child in the forest, trees and
more trees,
Chasing the butterfly, feeling the
breeze,
Catching a leaf from a tree so tall,
As it falls to the ground, why so
small?

Running through meadows, wind
in his hair,
Where is he going, but where?
Over the waters through the sky,
Will he get there by and by?

From the dark into the lite,
What's under his feet so white?
Now slipping, now sliding, see
him go,
See the trail left in the snow.

A child, his eyes without lite,
Slipped away one dark cold nite,
The snow so soft covered the
ground,
But not a trail could be found.

Jeffrey Hale Guss
POLLY ANNA
[To Polly Anna, my inspiration.]
Hey, little girl, stay here awhile.
I've been away all day, and I want
to see you smile.
I'm hoping you'll brighten my day
and enlighten my stay
With your silly little antics that
you practiced all day.
Hang around, little girl, I'll dim
the bedroom lights.
You can sit on my lap, and tell
me a couple stories;
I might even scratch your back.
Polly's the little girl with long
skinny legs and
A body shaped like the letter 'S'
She's got crooked little teeth and
a crooked little grin.
But you better believe when she's
16 boys heads' will spin.
I hate to see her grow up 'cause
it's going so fast.
I can hardly remember her as an
infant,
Wish it would all slow down.
She's got a long way to go,
I hope she'll take all the right roads
'Cause growin' up is one heavy
work load.

Christine A. Kirsh
A SPECIAL MESSAGE
I have never flown before and
alone it seems so frightening.
Thoughts of who will be there
when I land
Prove you pick up my spirits—
you're so enlightening.
Smiles overpower me
I feel you're so close in my mind.
How I'd love to have the key

which would unlock my
treasured find.
You never depart from my
thoughts
It is all I can do to keep my mind
on my work.
I feel like I've something I ought
not.
You make me so incredibly
happy I could go berserk.
I want to share dreams with you
& make some true!!
(To translate message take the
first letter from the first line,
the second letter from the
second line, the third from the
third and so on and thus the
message will appear)

Robert Ellis Feeney
A GIFT OF LIFE
This Life Without Knowing
What Love Really Is.
Is Like Being Poor,
With Nothing To Give.
We Try To Hold Onto
Thinking In The Past
Only To Lose Them,
Because They Don't Last.
If We Could Remember,
When Life Is Unkind
To Think Not Of Memories
That We've Left Behind,
Rather Look To The Future
And What It Might Hold.
We'd Cherish Each Moment
As If It Were Gold.

Michael J. Kondraski
THE MODERN WONDER
Fragile, delicate, beauty at its best.
So gentle, so kind, so blessed with
special feelings.
Forever caring, always loving,
never disappointing.
Emotional, excitable, and
expressive.
Lovable, desirable, stimulating,
and sexy.
Stubborn, shrewd, and sometimes
intolerable.
Tough, assertive, and domineering.
A holder of unlimited emotion.
What can be so complex?
It's something we see everyday;
The one thing capable of such
variety,
The one thing not even science
understands,
The *true* mystery of the modern
world—THE WOMAN!

Kimberly Triol
LOVE AND FRIENDSHIP
*[For Beth Dyer—Your love and
friendship has shown me how
beautiful my life really is.]*
When two people are friends,
they're sharing the greatest gift
of life.
The gift of Love.
Yes, love has been said to be a
magical word, and a powerful
feeling,
But it's also the softest way to
say, "I care."

A friend is a special person, with
whom you dare to be yourself.
You can share all of your deepest
secrets with that person.
And it's surprising to me,

how three words mean so much.
When they say, "I love you."
It's your heart that they touch.
And I want to tell you something,
that I know I have already said,
"I love you very much, and
remember . . . I'll always be
your friend."

Kalman E. Jandl
UNTITLED
Compromise
how insatiable
the wicked greed,
the withered need,
consuming life
like a mosquito
sucking the blood on a horse's ass.
Compromise
Lord of flies,
hooded executioner of ideals,
grindstone sandpaper
eroder of will;
Hopes fall prey like rabbits to the
hawk.
Leave me for today
I need to play.

Mary Agnes Landgrebe
MOTHER'S SAGA
*hail mary full of grace the lord is
with you . . .*
In an ether dream I bear you,
Groping at your noosed neck
And gasping in your afterbirth;
You are so small—
*blessed . . . you among . . .
women   all women . . .*
Floundering in your pruned, red
flesh,
Tears trickle down your cheeks
From eyes squeezed shut; your
mouth goes wide
As you scream life!—
*. . . blessed . . . the fruit . . . your
womb . . . jesus . . .*
Cut and cleansed and placed in
my arms
I nestle in my breast filling
Dry, gaping mouth full with me,
And I am nurtured . . . . and
. . . I . . . you . . .
holy maRY—MOTHER OF GOD!
*THE CLOUD THAT'S
DIZZIED ME DISPERSES,
THE BLOODY BIRTH OF
YOU—IT'S GONE.
YOU'RE ALL CUT OUT—
YOU'RE ALL WIPED UP—*
PRAY FOR US—SINNERS NOW
AND AT THE HOUR OF OUR—
. . . you are nothing left . . .

Patricia Elaine Meadows
HARMONY
As wistful as a whisper,
Knows the wind that gently blows
Across the sun warmed sand.
As we stroll the beach quietly,
hand in hand . . .
So refreshing is the salty air,
Spraying kisses of water here and
there,
Slowly teasing it's way to land.
As we stroll the beach quietly,
hand in hand . . .
The sea gull makes her morning
flight,
Picking up pieces of someone's
delight.
Willingly scattered to her,
knowingly planned.

As we stroll the beach quietly
hand in hand . . .
How beautiful are the shells that
lie about,
The most delicate creation,
without a doubt.
Spread across the dunes, perfectly
fanned,
As we stroll the beach quietly
hand in hand . . .
And time stands still here, near
the sea.
Where seasons have passed an
eternity.
Ghostly footprints matched in
harmony,
As we stroll the beach quietly,
you and me . . .
A world created of our own,
From far and wide, free to roam.
The beauty of our love left alone
to be,
As we stroll the beach quietly,
you and me . . .
As we stroll the beach quietly,
you and me . . .

Henry J. Dugan
NIGHT—HAWK
It was Saturday night and I went
backstage to bring Irene candy
and flowers.
She had a dreamy star-filled night
of fame; we talked about it for
hours.
I kissed Irene tenderly; she meant
so much to me.
And soon we were seated in
Flanders Place. So many stars
were there.
Irene was radiant in a gown of
fancy green lace. There was a
pink flower in her blonde hair.
We planned our future and then
for a short while,
Our clear minds traveled to a
boat ride along the Nile.
We drank champagne until four.
Our hearts soaring galore.
It was an early morning.
Lightning struck without
warning.
And then I proposed, Irene
accepted with a proud smile on
her lovely face.
By noontime the next day we
chated in my neat place.
Everything went fine. Irene was
divine.
Divine until she changed her
mind.
Once happy heart go search to
find.
I drank so much alcohol I could
hardly walk.
All around town I'm known as
the night—hawk.
Go ahead night—hawk stop
drinking now.
Irene decided to leave you
somehow.

Timothy P. Majka
WITHOUT YOU
[This poem is for Bea, my
future wife. My mother and for
all my friends. This poem is for
the man upstairs, cause he
inspired me to write it.]
I can hear you calling me
I can feel the love you bring

and I know that it can be
something more than just a thing

Oh how can I make it through
each day
Will you help me find the way
So tell me what am I to do
Cause I've got nothing without
you

I can tell you're watching me
I can touch the love you give
and I know that there must be
another way for me to live

Oh how can I make it through
each day
Will you help me find the way
So tell me what am I to do
Cause I've got nothing without
you

I can feel you touching me
I can tell that it's for real
I don't want it just to be
something that I'll always feel

Oh how can I make it through
each day
Will you help me find the way
So tell me what am I to do
Cause I've got nothing without
you

Amy Ventura—Orsatti
MEMORIES
When I was young and pretty
I thought the world was mine,
A stage on which to play
every young man's Valentine.
Now the years have faded
the beauty that was mine,
And all I have remaining
are the memories of another
time.

Sandra L. Russo
MY LOVE FOR YOU
My love for you, is so much
stronger now
You've touched all my feelings
that I tried hard to hide
My memories of you are much,
much clearer now
You brought out the real me that
was buried deep inside.

These thoughts that I hold are
too heavy now
They out—weigh the others that
were bound to go free
Our dreams that unfold, are no
secrets now
And no one can take my love for
you, from me!

Karie E. Spickerman
FRIENDSHIP
[This poem was written for and
inspired by my best friend Karl,
who taught me "friendship",
and whom I will always love.]
A friend is a giving person,
Who will never give up.
He's there when you need him,
And he's not a young pup.

A friendship is a two—way street,
With no white double lines.
You and he must give equally,
Trust youselves with your minds.

Dont ever take him for granted,
Because it's a sharp knife.
Respect and love him forever,
And take this friend for life.

Randall G. Smith
The End Draws Near
[Dedicated to all who may read
and discover a part of
themselves within . . .]
Late at night
When I'm lying next to you
You feel so warm and comfortable
You speak of the day
And what tomorrow could bring
Then you gently drift off to sleep
And I'm left all alone again

You're right beside me
But I'm all alone
With my thoughts, my dreams,
my fantasies
Left alone in my questioning mind
Left alone for the remaining night
Contemplating the meaning of life
Feel I'm losing not only my mind

I speak with you
But you can never hear
I need to know does the end draw
near
But I'm alone lying next to you
I'll be alone in the morning too
Left all alone no matter what I do
Left alone while I'm holding you

I wonder what the future will bring
I wonder if my life will ever sing
I can't remember where I have
been
But do you remember when
I layed awake all night in fear
I was wondering
Does the end draw near

Sarah Maryie
IF I COULD BE
If I could be
What would I be

If I could be
The Savior of the World
I would hold it gently
in my hands
I would hold it Free
If I could be

If I could be the Sower of Love
in each man's heart
He would be a part
Of a bigger world, you see
Oh, if only I could be

If He could be
a one who shares this thought
the battle fought
another soul bought
Join with Her and me
to change our destiny
Oh, if only He could be

If she could be
the see of purity in men's mind
Spirit, free of imperfection
Blossom of rose petals
a blessed kind
Peace at Sea
Oh, if only she could be

If We could be
What would We be

Souls of one distinction
boundaries would be gone
Spirit would have won
The Seed of Love would then be
King
Sounds of silence ring

She is, He is
I AM

Scott Richard Whalen
TIME FOR A CHANGE
[Dedicated To Those Who Try]
Its time for a change in my life
A time for a change of mind
A sunrise to reach for
To hold its rays in my heart
To revive old passions
And seek new energies for life
itself
I want to live the beauties of it
The joys the happiness the
wonders
The inner soul swept away on a
gentle breeze
I need a change in my life
A change only changed in the
mind
A change only felt in the heart
I have lived the other side long
enough
I want to taste the sweetness of a
joyous tear
Brought to the eye by love
I need to laugh the laugh
Only felt by one truly at peace
within
I have felt sorry for myself long
enough
Its time for a change
A time to look to the future
A future of playing and laughing
caring and working
I will look for the good
In the things I see do and hear
I know then at last I will feel a
full heart
A wise mind and a peaceful soul
The change will come in my life

Carol Snow—Thistle
Messengers Of Mercy
[To Jesus Christ: . . ."for He
hath said, I will never leave
thee, nor forsake thee."
Hebrews 13:5b]
Angels, fly swiftly
this message to bring,
to those
imprisoned by their fears,
to those
on the verge of defeat and
despair.
Jesus Christ
is with them there.
He gives the courage
to do and to dare,
to bear His cross,
to follow Him anywhere.

Bro. Eugene F. De Lauro
NEW POTENTIAL
Take your time my friend, life is
short I'm told, and tangerines
don't grow when you want
them!

Yes, it's makin' your daily
choices, each brought forth on
the battlefield of life that
allows you to place a gem in
the diadem you wear; invisible
to a King's court. But those
who know you bow and would
wish to touch the hem of your
sleeve.

You must wonder at your new
potential my friend, as you see
your marvelous gifts;
protruding like a ships' bow all
ready to sail, full mast that

billows as it lifts the weight of wood and cargo; a moving snail. Till caught by winds, full strength it goes so swift!

So take your time my friend and choose your life's ambition well, soon you'll be sailing better than I can tell!

Cassandra Nelson
REALITY . . .
a half empty
        cup
         with
          bitter
           coffee
            grounds
            in
           the
          bottom . . .
        if there is
       a
      bottom.

Reality is a nasty rumor
somebody started
during the morning coffee
break.

Rita White
THE ROCKING CHAIR
I've decided this should be a
    wedding gift to you from me.
Somehow it seems appropriate,
It arrived the same day you did.
And through the years, it was our
    special place.
How often I sat here holding you,
    singing lullabyes,
Telling you, a sleeping babe, of all
    my dreams for you.
And oh the nights I sat keeping
    nightwatch when you were ill.

When you were five, I'd find you
    sitting here, so small,
Rocking and singing to your
    favorite doll.
When you were nine, we'd sit,
    you really too big for my lap,
We'd watch the rain and talk of
    God, His love, His world.
I found you sitting here at
    thirteen, crying,
Because your best friend had
    stolen your first boyfriend.

At sixteen, you'd sit there on the
    floor beside me,
Telling me of your dreams and
    future plans.
And oh the nights I sat keeping
    nightwatch when you were on
    a date.
Now I sit and watch you sleep.
    Tomorrow's the big day.
A new life starts, not just a
    daughter then, but wife.
Take with you then this tiny
    corner of your childhood,
So full of memories and love
And perhaps someday welcome
    another new life into the world
    to share it with.

Gary M. Beaulieu
A LIFE FROM LOVE
Born of a love, so innocent and
    pure.
With fiery red hair, and eyes of
    pale azure.
She seems so like, a tiny china
    doll.

So delicate and fragile, and very,
    very small.
She's pure—of mind, in her hopes
    and dreams.
So full of life, like many flowing
    streams.
To stay this way, a gift of child.
If even for just, a little while.
With a lifetime ahead, as yet
    unknown.
A future of hope, for too soon
    she'll be grown.
She will live and love, as only the
    young can.
To search and maybe find, her
    perfect man.
Someday she too, will bless this
    earth.
Conceived in love, her own
    child's birth.

Giles E. MacQueen III
WAXING FALL
With the summer peering around
    the corner past,
I draw out my pipe and sigh, at
    last.
The humid, hot and long rays of
    sun,
Give way with reluctancy to the
    new season begun.
As all changes bring memories of
    old and new,
So will the morning fall, frost and
    dew.
The trees also will yield their
    past,
In hope that their new found
    colors will be pleasing and last.
All must change as that is part of
    nature's plan,
And it's always nice to know that
    we can, as part of man.

Susan Lenore Speroff
LOVE DEATH
Amid the snow white, whispy
    womb,
White rose, she came to speak
    too soon,
Yet ere her time she knew her
    doom,
Before the night of spring's full
    moon.
Oh child, she was too young, too
    weak,
To know how few her days were
    left;
The falcon took her in his beak
And ruthlessly her life bereft.
For all the time of year
    throughout,
I wait for spring to come anew,
And should it seem so still, no
    doubt,
It was just me in search of you.
The spring that never was to be
Destroyed the love for you in me.

Marie A. Carey
**To a Man Who Once Loved
Me**
Each day when I open my eyes to
    the morning's sun
    and the reality of day creeps in,
I know better than to look on the
    other side of the bed.

At night in my dreams I reach for
    you
    and you are always there.
But, in the light of day there is

only
    the teddy bear you won for me
    at the fair.

Oh, how the darkness can take
    me back to when
    you loved me and the whole
    world
        looked so much brighter.
As the sun lightens the flowers
    on my walls
    I know I must face another day
    without you.
But night will come and I will
    have you
    back in my arms again.
Back to a time when I could
    reach for you
    in the darkness and you were
    there.

Maybe someday
    you will be.

But for now,
    I have my memories . . .
        and the teddy bear you
        won
            for me at the fair.

Ann M. Coy
TROUBLED MIND
    Morbid thoughts run through
    your head,
Your heart is heavy and filled
    with dread.
A cloudy mist covers your eyes,
As you prepare to say your last
    good—byes.
The light is growing dim,
        it is no longer so bright.
You're very nervous now,
        you're losing your insight.
Now you feel as though you're
    going blind,
It's simply because you're losing
    your mind.

    Everything in life done with no
    consent,
You see there is nothing left to
    lament,
In a lonely wanton world we live,
There's just no way for one to
    forgive,
A world full of scattered lies,
And so it shall be till the day you
    die.

Russell R. Webb
THE HOUSE OF MAN
Softly amid the green
    and yellow
Enfolding jungle both giving
    and receiving refuge
The faded ruin stands
    the shining tiles powdered
A monument of the
    people rooted with
The trees in the blood
    of its million deaths

Kristin Janina Aronson
CHASMS
dry bones, rustle of leaves
crisped by frost, now wintering
thin as petals or wings
parchment all, now withering
ground into nature's cosmetic
    dust
her last powdery touch
for everything

but one—veinless

hung on no scaffolding
surging like no artery
which ever cut through flesh
with no pounding heart
to rush them—our visions
opening canyons stark
as granite

patient as the winds
which carve them

Roger A. Willard
LONELINESS
I have a blind quality that no one
    knows about.
Alongside my personality, solid
    as my will to live.
I have to protect it even though
    you wouldn't approve.
Sometimes I have to withdraw to
    keep it my secret.
The amount I can give out
    depends on who can receive it.
I'd like to rebound from
    loneliness and show you my
    love.

Rebecca Borges Longo
The Two Of Us Together
We walked, for hours it seemed
The snow danced down around
    us
Filling our footsteps, leaving no
    trace
The night was so peaceful
It seemed like old times
So long ago when life was a
    fairy—tale we lived
Things were easy then
No responsibilities, no worries
But there was alot of anger, hate
    in me then
You've changed that
I'm happy now
Yes, we were walking
Just you and I
Uncomplicated, simple . . .

Cynthia Dawn Lucie
INTERPLANETARY TRUTH
My head is humming like a
    buzzing bee
You spread your wings preparing
    now to fly
We flap and flutter through the
    stormy sky
As balls of fire explode upon the
    sea.
My love, our lives are
    threatened—we must flee
Astride your back I cling to your
    shoulders and cry
I sob and scream the endless
    question, "Why?
Oh, why won't they allow us to
    be free?"

When I am drowning in the
    pouring rain
And feel as though no longer can
    I cope
There still is something left that
    is called Hope.
When you are dying, racked with
    awful pain
You needn't fear the hour your
    heart be stilled—
The essence that is you cannot
    be killed.

Charlotte Voldarski
FRIENDSHIP
Whenever I look for a friend,
I look for someone who is genuine.

Someone I can trust like a
  brother or a sister.
Someone I can have confidence in.
Someone I can feel free and easy
  with,
Not having to be someone I'm
  not.
Somedays I even need someone
  just to be there,
  to use their shoulder to cry on
  to talk to
  to laugh with
  to understand
  to share with.
But the biggest asset of being a
  friend is knowing they care
  about you, Just as you are.
Not having to put on a front
  twenty-four hours a day . . .
Being or trying to be Tarzan
  when you're really only Jane.

Laura Ami
THE MAGIC OF YOU
The many wonders I ever knew,
as the dunes of Arabia, the hills
  of Rome,
are in my mind when I think of
  you.
It seems you were with me all my
  life.
So be my future like my past.

Arlene Cross
WORDS
words are breaking through
i feel them on my skin
loud intrusions
like claws forcing cruel
their way in

tendrils of hair curled over to
  protect
lie beaten and defeated
the enemy has penetrated in

nerve endings dream
scale of a butterfly's wing
scream of a violin string

bone split open
it's here they lie
in white marrow

here they sleep
and at the least provocation
weapons
a boomerang
or an image in a mirror
that flies
out again

Mr. Melvin E. Bellinger
HUMANLY SPEAKING
You are the flower of my life,
Prophet of love,
Tear-dove in flight.

You are my dream of days of joy;
Thoughts that sweat in love's
  employ.

And like my unchained melody,
That Tuesday heart-ache that I
  feel,
You are my damsel in distress,
And I, your hope of tender rest.

You are a song upon my heart,
That voiced my mind and
  thoughts apart.
You are the feeling that I get,
When years replace the love that
  left.

You reflect reality;

The precious truth I dared to flee;
A wind well blown from God's
  own hand;
An answered prayer, not mouthed
  by man.

You are love, that I must love;
Life that only love can kiss.
You are woman that I touch,
When Love replace the years I've
  missed.

Kristina Anne Keeler
The Sage Of An Old Person
You put me away in a home
  where I know no one
'Cause I'm old and useless, or so
  you say,
Little do you realize I'm wiser and
  can be of use.

I tell you stories of how it was
  when I was young
About the times I had it hard
You listen and question, is it to
  keep me entertained?

I have been through war and
  depression—who cares?
You should—I could tell you how
  to make it through
Or give you ideas at least, will
  you listen?
You tell me how to get involved
  in the home I'm in
Arts 'n Crafts are fun you tell me
Have you ever tried making
  things with arthritis?

I'm treated like a child, watch out
  for this and that
I've taken care of my life this far
Yet, your concern is appreciated
  without overdoing.

Please, I beg of you, let me decide
  where I go
What to do with myself—please I
  ask you
Though I'm old, please let me
  grasp the rest of my
                    life as I want to.

Le Von-ninsky Von Hardin
WHAT'S IN A NAME, A LOT
Sticks and stones will break my
  bones, and names sometimes
  hurt me.

What's in a name, a lot. A phrase
  by which a person or class is
  known or spoken of. Fame,
  reputation, or character. A good
  name, or a bad name. Word or
  words expressing some quality
  considered characteristic of a
  person or things. Often
  showing approval or
  disapproval.

People have been pre-judged
  because of a name. Opinions
  formed before the facts are
  known. Pre-conceived ideas
  favorable or most usually
  unfavorable because of a name
  that he has been labled with. A
  judgement or opinion held in
  disregard of facts that
  contradicts.

The holding of such judgement of
  suspicion, intolerance,
  irrational hatred toward other
  races, creeds, religions and
  occupations because of a name

that has been given.

Prejudice is based less on hate or
  even dislike for certain people,
  ideas or activities than on the
  fact that it's easier and safer to
  stay with the known, than it is
  to explore the unknown. To
  meet and deal with new people
  and their ideas because of
  words expressed. It's better to
  stay with people who are more
  like you.

If you don't trust anyone you
  can't lay a finger on, or wish
  not to be classed in that
  person's category, really means
  that you do not trust yourself
  on unfamiliar grounds. All
  because of name.

What's in a name, a name means
  a lot . . .

L.C. Fells
CHANGED ITS MIND
The years slowly creep by,
stealing memories of you.
Though the good times are
  holding on,
and keeps me loving you.

It wasn't a bed of roses,
though the beauty was the same.

It wasn't a trip to Heaven,
though I'd do it all again.

It wasn't that we cried a lot,
for the smiles are in my mind.

It wasn't that our love had died,
it just sort of changed its mind.

Soraya Erian
THE WAITING
To the shelter of this rock
you asked me to come
when the sun appears
as in the first dawn
I in silence
you in sudden stealth
in that place I try to reach
but you are not there
in that place I try to reach
you in sudden stealth
I in silence
as in the first dawn
when the sun appears
you asked me to come
to the shelter of this rock

Janet E. Almas
**Thanks To Daddy (Bobby
  Clarke)**
"This letter is to a very special
  Daddy
And is coming to you from your
  little laddie.
Thank you, Daddy; for the goal
  that you scored today;
Boy, am I glad I came with Mum
  to see you play!
I'd like to thank you for more
  than your one thousandth
                          point
'Cuz you do other great things
  that never disappoint
The rest of our family. Gee, it
  was super nice
To hear fans cheer for things you
  do on the ice!
So please take your glove off and
  let me shake your hand,
I want you to know that I think

you're pretty grand.
Thank you for letting me watch
  the great games you've played
Like this one tonight. From your
  loving son, Wade.

P.S. Thanks again for all the
  things that you do
And by the way—I hope your
  face gets better too.

Steven Scott Fyfe
A GLOWING STORY
Listen to her talk
See the way she walks
Look at her smile
Give her your time

Give her a flower
Any color will do
She knows it's from you
From the bottom of your heart

See how her eyes
Deepens within your eyes
And her warm heart
Reaches you from the botom of
  her heart

Tell her a story
With a happy ending
Make her feel your feelings
That you see her in this story

Make her the star
Of your everyday life
And whisper to her
"I want you in my life"

Listen to her story
She's got one not quite finished
She's got this love story
That she wants you to help her
  finish

Robin Gillon
NATURE
Green on green, Blue on blue
that's what is scene
when Nature is in view,
The awesome awareness
of a greater design,
and the fragile awakening
of a balance so fine,
The nature of Nature
is a secret untold
we can just watch the beauty
of a key we cannot hold.

Ann Franklin
MEANT TO BE
Our love was new,
As fresh as the breeze in spring.
My heart happy,
Never blue
Always thinking . . .
. . . of you.
I carved our names,
Into the desk
Deep and undying,
Never at reat.
  It was meant to be.

Our love was used,
Unhappy and dying
My heart confused,
Sometimes blue
Thinking of you, often
The names I carved,
Fading, worn
Resting

Our love is gone,
Gone as fast as the wind.
My heart sad,
Always blue

I think of you . . .
. . . once in awhile
The name's just a memory,
Like our love was,
Pleasant, deep
Sleep
    It also, was meant to be.

Marilyn Ginger
MIND LEVELS (OBSERVER)
An observer is a special game,
but a loser when on a different
    plane.
You wonder who said what and
    when.
Then you wonder—oh, where did
    I begin.

Funny how it goes back in time,
No one even knows where one
    has begun,
because all is nothing—when it's
    there but gone.

Are we alive?
—in spirit and mind, or forever
    running—
into dead time.
Crashing, burning the evil and
    flourishing.

Liking innocence to corrupt their
    little minds.,
as we have let ourselves.
Yeah—the whole turn of truth.
Telling the strangeness that lies
    within.
Within but without.

Shirley I. Gilarski
THE SHARING
Tender threads of thought
linger on my mind,
A silken treasure of memories;
those days when we walked in
storybook love.
Unravelling before my daydreams,
I recall you still; my unfortettable.
Patterns which my feelings weave
are so intricate,
Only the angels can sing their
    song.
Is there a strand of yesterday
clinging sadly yet?
Do you awaken with the nostalgic
scent of perfume lingering near
your nostrils; that smell of my
hair you loved so dearly?
Do you then close your eyes and
an even stronger remembrance
searches you out; again, you feel
my almost presence lying beside
    you?
My best love, do you remember?
I will—always; although a wisp
of memory is the only closeness
we share.

Christine Hughes
**My Tribute To John Wayne
The Duke**
Deep in the ground you do lie,
without telling your fans
    good-bye.
We were sorry you had to go, as
    this world did love you so.
We are so much better for
knowing you, the world thinks
    as I do.
I never met you face to face, but
    in my heart you have a place.
You a giant among men, fought
your battle to the bitter end.
All through your suffering, you

fought for the rights of a fellow
man.
Although you have passed away,
the echo of your voice will
forever stay.
You had a talent that put many
to shame.
It wasn't only as an actor, but
your character that made your
fame.
Some may wonder why a great
man like you had to suffer so.
You who fought his battle with
life before you let go.
All of us who grieve at his death,
we mustn't forget.
You taught us that life was worth
fighting about.
Just because of pain and suffering,
we don't have to check out.
God in heaven now has this man
to care for with a capable hand.
No more suffering will he bear for
at God's side you will stay
there.
To lighten the heavens above, I
will remember you John
Wayne with Love.

John Wayne, You were my kind
of guy.
So I will whisper to you my final
good-bye.

Joe Johnston
**SNOWDOM (The Kingdom
Of Life)**
I stand amidst spiraling winds
Here in Snowdom
        The Kingdom of Life
All around me
    dancing, twirling, falling,
    some rushing
But always
    their destinies held fast in the
    grips of the wind
In places
    the wind carves away deep
    at the layers
Revealing rude reminders of the
    past
While elsewhere
Others gently cover those that
    have fallen before them
Soon to be covered themselves
    by those that follow

Anywhere or everywhere
I must walk through them
To get where I'm going

But I can't
    I won't
            not yet
For I marvel at the wonder of the
    Children of the North
Oh Life the mystery

And yet somehow I must go on
Before I too become covered and
    lost
    soon to be shaped by the
    whims of the wind
Careful how I walk though
For I will surely leave tracks

Jerome
FOREVER AND THIS DAY
Says she doesn't love me
    says she never did
All I meant was freedom
    an escape from where she'd hid

I can have her living with me
    I can have her raise my child
But never will she ever
    speak of feelings warm or mild

The greatest pain I've felt
    the greatest hurt of life
Knowing she's not happy
    in name only is a wife

When did I go so wrong
    when did I fail to see
That what she ever wanted
    couldn't ever come from me

Why did this have to happen
    why did things go this way
My heart will now be broken
    forever and this day

John H. Hausner
I BELIEVE IN YOU
When words cut deep, and it's
    hard to smile,
Don't despair; lean on me the
    next mile.
Though others lose faith and say
    you're through,
Stick to your plans; I believe in
    you!

When friends greet you in envy
    and hate,
Remain steadfast, rekindle your
    faith.
Though the world says your
    dreams won't come true,
Follow your star; I believe in you!

Karen M. Reid
GRAIN OF SAND
How many people've roamed
    about this ever endless land.
        How many people's
        wandering, lie dead beneath
        the sand.
This pebble underneath my feet,
    was it once a mountain range,
    it's all so possible and yet, it
    seems so very strange.
Have people walked on it before,
    in another place and time,
    or am I the first to step on it, in
    its adventure
    through space and time.
How many people've roamed
    about this ever endless land.
        How many people've walked
        upon this single
        grain of sand.

Tim Kluck
IF YOU HAVE TO CRY
If you have to cry, take a look at
    what you do
If you want to fly, take a look at
    what is true
on the earth we're bound, get
    back on the ground,
while reality is to be found.

If you want to die, keep on with
    the things you do
If you want to fly, take a look at
    what is true,
don't let the machines, take away
    your dreams
there's still so much left here to
    be seen.

If we all believe, God and love are
    still alive
If we can relieve, all the hate we
    will survive,

see the setting sun, there isn't
    anyone
but we . . . to blame for all, the
    things we've done.

We can start it now, now's a
    better time than never
we can find out how, we can live
    in love forever,
what else do we need, throw
    away your greed
flowers never grow without the
    seed.

Judy A. Rogers
UNTITLED
Call me not and then turn away.

You are the night that filters day.
Futile hope is but despair,
more than apathy, harder to bear.

Unleashed in madness upon the
    door,
I turn away to hear you no more.

Judy C. Oust
A SMILE
A smile walked down a lonely
    road
And saw a man carrying a big
    heavy load

The smile spoke to this man with
    such a might
That all his heavy burdens
    suddenly became light

Then smile came upon a woman
    filled with fright
And showed its face and gave her
    new insight

The smile met a little boy who
    was filled with wild fear
When the boy spoke to the smile
    all his fear disappeared

The smile walked on in the
    darkness all alone
Casting its light, like a beacon it
    shone

Then sitting cast down with a
    face full of grief
A woman saw the smile and was
    filled with relief

The smile met an old man who
    needed sympathy
But the smile gave him a greater
    gift—his empathy

A man who was new to this
    country passed by
His heart was so lonely he could
    only cry

When the man spoke to the
    smile he felt, indeed
That his heart was filled with all
    it would ever need

Grace Carter
FLIGHT
She ran toward God—a lovely
    girl,
She ran toward God—like a bird
    in flight;
She ran toward God—her heart
    a-whirl,
Her face a-glow—her footstep
    light.

And I stood back—alone—apart,
Yet felt the warmth of her love;
I watched her run—then stop—
    then start,
As God smiled down from above.

When the road was rocky, God
took her hand,
He clothed her in Courage—in
Faith—in Love;
With determination, she took a
stand,
And offered her life to God.

She ran toward God—my lovely
girl,
She ran toward God—like a bird
in flight;
She ran toward God—her heart
a-whirl,
Her face a-glow—her footstep
light.

Morton C. Leaden
LOVE SONNET
*[Dedicated to the
compassionate souls and
generous hearts that bless all
lands.]*
My Teacher said a Sonnet I must
write
Akin to those that Shakespeare
used to pen,
And 'Love' must be the subject,
pure and bright—
A subject now in vogue as much
as then.

But woe is me, if I must now
define
What men call 'Love', for in my
tender years
When peace around the world is
in decline
And little up ahead but strife and
fears.

The wonder is that 'Love' is still
around
At all, or that we find someone to
feed
The hungry and the naked that
abound
In many lands, and meet their
barest need.

Ah! 'Love' it is that dissipates
their cloud
And circumvents the globe in
accents loud!

Lon B. Lounsbury
HOPE
Hope is a light to show the path
and a staff to hold me up;
Hope is a star to lift my eyes
and water to fill my cup;
Hope is a fire that burns my breast
and a rod to keep my soul;
Hope is all these and many more
on the long way to my goal.
Hope is a light, a staff, a star,
water, a fire, a rod . . .
Hope is all things both great and
small
that lead my soul to God.

C.J. Davis
SILENT LISTENER
Within me lies
A silent listener
Binding me with
Beauty, Enchanting me
With a power
I could not
Withstand
LOVE . . . Like a child's
Freedom to laugh
Scale mountains or
Race the winds

LOVE . . . Like thoughts
Creating, Forming all
Yesterdays, Todays, Tomorrows
Mysteries within spaces
Emptiness
LOVE . . . Like dreams
Caressed by darkness's
Inner awareness   Light
Awakening to dawn's
Half truth   Reality
LOVE . . . That is
Serene, Content within
By God's melody
LOVE . . . That has
Captured my freedom
My thoughts & dreams
In one hypnotic
Moment . . . I was
Drunk with thoughts
Of kissing lips
Sweeter than
The most precious
Wines . . . I was
Joy, Sorrow, Death
Birth . . . I have
Seen the unseen
Goodness . . . I have
Understood the vague
Truths . . . I have
Heard the eternal
Listener within
That has chained
Our hearts
With love . . .

Irma R. Ramirez II
MY INSIDE WORLD
Flowers show my exceeding
world,
Yet, skeptic to life of roses.
I live isolated in crystal glass,
But still no individuals know it.

The black clouds represent my
withdrawn side,
Hiding inside the rain.
The dawn of sun-break foretells
the life,
I want to be able to explain.

If man should dissolve in front of
my eyes,
I'd see the identical me,
But endeavoring my thoughts,
I've to say,
The universe is worked by strings.

John L. Baesl
THROUGH A CHILD
She held a small rose in her hand,
First day of school; for her the
day seemed grand.
"A flower for the teacher," my
child did say,
Waiting for the ride that would
take her away.

She dashed from my side to the
pink clover,
Growing on the roadside wild all
over.
One long stem was picked as
though heavy to carry;
Both in her tiny hand rose and
clover did marry.

Child, my child, you always
amaze me!—
But, how else could rose and
clover marry?
My child, never saw such as
this!—
Only through a child happen
such as this.

You've humbled proud rose
growing on the branch high
To roadside clover in the path of
the scythe.
Proud rose grows aloof dancing in
the sun;
Pink clover grows low;—it's
trampled on.

Your ride is coming; there's a tear
in my eye,—
Your very first day of school; we
must say good-by.
Sweet child have fun; enjoy as the
day goes,
Your first day of school; wedding
day of clover and rose.

Lennie Davis
THE KEY "REPENT"
An anger was stirred up
within my soul,

When I read where a group
was burning the Holy Book,

And a scream was reaching
out calling the Holy Book
a dirty Book,

A soft spoken voice spoke
within my heart,
"They can burn the Holy
Book,
and we can burn the Holy
words in our hearts and
minds,

"They can call the Holy
Book a dirty Book,
Which is understanding
love and fear,

For our hearts and souls
can see the truth,
with their eyes they can
see blindness,

For fools they are without
understanding, Fighting
a losing battle,
IN THE END
"OUR KING LORD JESUS
WILL WIN"

For His Words Are True,

I believe this with all
of my heart and soul,

Kirsten L. Hoffenberger
HOLE OF WARMTH
The worm peeks its head out of a
hole,
The hole of warmth
where I escaped to
with his help.
You picked me up
and held me gently.
Please don't hurt me
or make me wet
from my tears.
A worm can never find
the warm hole
it left.

George L. Farmakis
THE OLYMPIC GAMES
As the torch passes from Olympia
to Los Angeles in 1984—
Similarities come to mind, though
few, in importance they soar.

America and Greece, champions
of
democracy, each in their own
time—
Inspiring others and offering

excellence
and leadership, most sublime.

Olympia and Los Angeles in
scenic
beauty are in harmony—
Blue skies, brilliant sunshine,
Mediterranean
type climate, mountains and
sea.

And finally . . . the spelling
. . . but
seven letters each—
They show the way, and offer the
wreath
to those who reach.
Olympia and America

Susan Schoen
THE DAM
A dam,
Stopping the pain,
Breaks.
A river,
Full of sorrow,
Floods.
Another dam,
Built from the ruins,
Works.
Another river,
Tears of life,
Builds.

It cannot last for long:
Soon the dam will break,
The river of pain will flow
Just as they have so often before.

Still life goes on:
Dams are built and rivers flood
Until the water's gone.

And pain lives on and on and
on . . .

Donald W. Wiley
Autumnal Equinox
I hiked into the autumn
wilderness where
A forest of trees dared to flush
and blush!
The gaudily tinted leaves stirred
an' shivered—
Intimidated by the apple-crisp
September air—
An' rattled precariously from a
sudden gust
Out o' the cloud-strewn north.
More were delivered
To the already deep-leafed
carpeted rugged earth,
While others, more reluctant,
refusin' to die,
Clung valiantly to the ancient
limbs of their birth.
Yea. Remnants of autumn thick-
carpeted the ground
With dead aspen and oak
leaves—dusty and brown.
An inquisitive chipmunk foraged
for acorns to store;
A furtive red squirrel chattered
an' away he tore
Up the dark trunk of a jack pine
an'jawed some more.

I ascended a prominence an'
watched sun rays play
O'er tree-cluttered hills some
many distances away;
Intermittent cloud shadows oft
hovered o'er this day,
Mottlin', accentuatin' autumn's
flamboyant display.

I dawdled along, at peace, through
  nigh-silent wood,
Savorin' an' cherishin' this very
  precious moment
Of colorful quietude, wishin', o,
  wishin', I could
Stay longer, 'cause 'twas a very
  vital moment meant
To meditate an' commune with
  the autumn element.
But the afternoon sun strolled
  'cross the forest floor;
It crept o'er fern an' moss an'
  played upon the moor;
It glittered on a ripplin' stream
  windin' through the wood;
It haloed this forest scene; came
  to rest where I stood.
The fast fadin' sunlight, soon
  darkness, caused me to retrace
My footsteps (slowly) back to
  reality. But not 'fore I embraced
An' savored the whole of autumn
  an' this wilderness place.

Eva M. Roy
SPECIAL ME?
I'm not special
But I like to think I am
Especially to my family
They are the ones I have to
  impress
When they are unsure
And need an understanding word.

I'm not special
But I like to feel I am
Especially to myself
I am the one I have to convince
When I know for sure
I have given the right word.

Patricia Friend Shapton
TO MY DAUGHTER TRICIA
The way you move is oh so sweet
the gentle movement of your feet
your hands so small and yes
  complete
have little nails trimmed very
  neat
your eyes of blue have such a
  twinkle
and your nose so pink has a tiny
  wrinkle
a perfect shaped head with not
  much hair
a ribbon of pink you will
  someday wear
a child of beauty and of grace
I'll dress you in flowers and lots
  of lace
and if you rebel as I know you
  may
I'll put on your jeans and you'll go
  out to play
for your brothers will win your
  heart I know
you'll throw off the ribbons and
  away you'll go.

Robert E. Yoder
LARRY
I have a friend named Larry;
Twenty six years ago he was born.
Now all this guy wants to do,
Is blow his ah-ooo-gah horn.
He says that he's in love,
With a gal named Daisy Duke.
Sometimes I think that this guy,
Is such a crazy kook!
He takes me for a spin in his car,
And to the grocery store.

I don't know how he does it,
But he keeps on giving more.
If you want to know about Larry;
He has his own CB.
He calls himself the "Creeper";
That is his handle, don't you see.
So if you ever need some help,
Or feel you need a friend.
You can always count on Larry,
He'll help you till the end.

Donna M. De Boer
THE LETTER
Write to me world.
Please tell me what you want
from a wandering soul
who runs from one light
to another
trying to find one that fits.

Write to me world.
Postage paid please,
you've taken and given
in uneven portions.
Tell me what you want.

C. Adele Henning
**And Mankind Calls It
. . . FAITH**
No man can ever say, with truth,
That he has held a rainbow
Or caught a moonbeam in his
  hand.
And yet you could not tell me
That there are no rainbows
Nor moonbeams o'er the land.

No man has ever captured faith,
Nor found the weight of it:
Not even in a churchly manse
Has truer faith been found
Than within a sweet child's song
As heard the world around.

We walk a path that bruises us,
As every life is sure to do;
We seek a guide to smoother
  ways,
And look for help that's true.

We seek a constant guarantee
That Someone watches over us:
We would depend upon a staff
That could vanish like a wraith—
All the strength we need's within:
And mankind calls
  it . . . FAITH.

Donna M. Niedermeier
COMING HOME
There is nothing quite so
  welcome,
  As the postman, when he
  greets.
To bring news of our children,
  Who have conquered many
  feats.

But the grandest gift of all,
  Is a simple envelope.
That says a youngster's coming
  home,
  It holds a lot of hope.

To hold once more a darling,
  That has wandered far from
  home.
Whose voice would be welcomed,
  When the call comes on the
  phone.

When at last, the day arrives,
  And the waiting is no more.
For, the youngster of yesterday,
  Walks through an open door.

Oh how happy is the Mother,
  How touched is the Dad.
For the grandest gift on earth
  there is,
  Their child is at hand.

Marcia A. Gemmen
MY SIR ROBERT
His looks were warm as they
  cornered mine
The mood so open and easy
A people person; who loved his
  wine
When suddenly noticed; I, too,
  was queasy

Eyeing me side-ways in public
  view
Lining a hallway wall
Patient for the opening cue
A prancing filly, in a hemmed-in
  stall

I'll never know impression made
in darkened, pondering eyes
Playing as I was, a prudent,
  childish, charade
Just he, a perfect height did rise

His character judged rightly I;
  certain answers missing
He had of now my attention fair
To wrap him in a cyclone of
  kissing,
if only my soul could bare

Twenty and One;
Traces of conscience pain
If he could show me fun,
I'd silly ways disdain.

Sherry Puckett
MY FISHING PARTNER
[This poem is dedicated to my
two daughters, Kimberly and
Carrie]
I took my puppy fishing with me
  down at the creek,
Where all he wanted to do was
  play hide and go seek.
He finally settled down to watch
  me put on my bait,
Then off he ran with my box of
  worms he did take.
He dropped the box where all the
  worms came squirming out,
Then he barked and growled as
  the worms jumped all about.
I came back to find my pole a
  tugging,
My puppy's eyes were a bugging.
He watched me pull the fish in
  and take it off the hook,
With the fish line he tugged and
  shook.
He gave a bark when I put the
  fish in my bag, and his tail gave
  a wag.
He followed me home where on
  his bed he did lay,
I guess for him it had been a hard
  working day!!

dwight l. johnson
OF YU TORA DO
[To Rick Caldwell & Tim Riley]
A body swift
Movement of the thrift.
Intensity surmised
A motion of quick surprise.
No anger on the outside
No animosity is shown.
All the foes have been defied
And the fighter stands alone.

So loose and stealthy
Of tranquility so wealthy.
Animals are their teachers
Calmness is their master.
Muscle strong upon the features
Serenity of the Masters.

Such a Master is this fighter,
Who shall always walk
The Way of the Soft Tiger.

Thomas S. Hession
SO OLD AND SO NEW
The love of a maid for the love of
  a man
Is an old, old thing they say.
'Tis as old as the rills that gutter
  the hills,
'Tis as old as the light of the day.

This love of a maid for the love of
  a man
Though time has proven its worth,
When it comes today like a
  flower in May
It's the newest thing on earth.

Phyllis Newton
NAMES AT HAND
[In memory of my father,
Ferdinand Edward Santora,
1904—1978.]
Now for a voice that could
  proclaim
Glories of Ferdinand's great name,
A name like Noah's weary dove
That brought him from the olive
  grove;
A token of a land of rest.

So Jesus's name brings to mind
Of faithful souls, a hope to find
Beyond the boundary of skies
A rest where pleasure never dies;
  But where he'll be forever blest.

Catherine L. Boyer
LIFE
  In Spring,
the leaves on a tree
are like life,
start from a bud.
  Like a baby in his mother's arms
fresh,
all warm and snug.

  Both grow to be young and
  strong
and go through life like a
  Summer long.

  In late Autumn,
the colors are bold
like life the man does grow old.

  Come Winter,
the leaves have fallen to earth
like man they die
and make room for a new birth.

Stephen Gianotti
SILENT SIDE OF LOVING
It's the silent side of loving
  Where the wordless words of
  eyes
Are novels bound in moments
  found;
  An essence which never dies.

It's the parchment of a heartbeat,
  Pages turned but seldom read,
Where the feeling of a sentience
  And acceptance of it wed.

It's the kinship of a looker
  And a sight beyond the seen,
An invitation to a path

Where feet have rarely been.
It's the silent side of loving
  Which defies all futile word,
It's as sure a baby's laughter
  And elusive as a bird.

Aldine L.M. Gunn
Archeo-Reflection On Artifacts
We re-create the Past from
  artifacts:
  Tangible traces . . . of
  Lives . . . long gone.
  Things fashioned . . . with
  Art . . . by Hands . . .
  From Heart-throbs . . . long
  time-stilled . . .

Arrowheads . . . a crude stone
  axe,
And tools from flint or bones . . .
The masks of long-dead medicine
  men,
The things in the tomb of
  Tutankhamen . . .
The records on papyrus writ
Or chiseled onto stones . . . the
  Words
Are artifacts of Thought: Graffiti
  on Time.

My poems and my pictures are
  artifacts of Me . . .
    For whom? . . . How long? . . .
Inside my brain are artifacts—
  patterned peptides—
  Holographic traces . . . of
  experiences . . . long past.

Anthropo-logos:
What then of Me as artifact . . . ?
I am a Vessel—whole, broken, or
  cracked . . .
Of What am I an artifact . . . ?
Theo-logos:
LIFE is an artifact of GOD!
Cosmo-logos:
BEING is an artifact of the VOID!

Dorothy Warner
ANOTHER HARVEST
There is no time when life is not.
No where God is not present,
No creature that is forgot.
There is no death of anything
Nor a beginning or end.
There is no place in the Universe
Where you cannot find God
  appearing as a friend
Where is there that a seed is sown
and bear fruit, That its seed shall
  not again
take root.
And even when this fruit is
  plucked again from
the Vine, and is sown again, It
  will yield up
another Harvest in due time.
There is always yet another
  Harvest,
experience is forever, life has not
  yet had its best.
Life never Cease to be, It is
  always more,
Than it was before, There is no
  beginning and no ending,
Only a continuous blending, of
  God's grace to be.
With each new experience, we
  will always see.
An even greater harvest, for it's as
  continuous as the
life of you and me.

So I can rejoice at each abundant
  harvest.
But I shall not moan when its
  trees seem bare,
for I know that the seeds are
  planted, and the fruit
is already there. I cannot see its
  functions, But I
can feel it in God's grace.
And I know that God is forever
  present in everytime
and place.
So I am not concerned with the
  fertility of the soil
of yesterday.
I plant now yet, another harvest,
  and know its fruitage is
on its way.

C. Gay Fritzemeier
The Fall Of the Noble Earl
Many
  long
    months
have passed
and the reign
of the
  Noble Earl
    of Confusion
has taken
its toll
But just
  a moment
    ago
the tide turned
within me
because the King
  of Peace
is making
  His
    move
—And the Earl
  is running
    to hide—

Barbara B. Robinson
UNTITLED
I go to the sea—the restless sea
when I feel cold and hollow
I run to the shore to find my
  way—
a road that I can follow
I walk alone at eventide
when the sunset fills the sea—
the soft—lapped waves caress the
  shore
the silence caresses me
daylight slips into darkness
the sea disappears from view
but there on a dark and lonely
  beach
I find the path to you.

Mark A. Watkins
DAY IS DONE
I sigh the coming of the night
As if some visitor at my door
Wishing to continue long hours
  ahead—
Restraining the revealing,
  unveiling light
That disembarks at day
  forevermore
Containing all within its stead.

But alas! My lament availeth not
For the frequenter has no sense
But for the element prescribed by
  time—
That comes only for when it
  aught
For now and forever since

Like the consistent Big Ben chime.
The interludes separating each
  visit
Prove so little to operate within
Vain in their attempt to subsist—
Yet exasperating endurance's limit
To a point where none can win
And sleep no longer can resist.

Helen L. Wilson
I Have a Date With God
"Today I have a date with God
  and this day has long been
  planned
The route marked by HIS pen and
  we'll walk it hand in hand
We will stroll down a country
  lane, listen to a country band
Lean on a fence, drink from the
  dew, watch a farmer till his land"

"We will watch a small tree grow,
  flowers blooming, grass knee high
We'll wash our feet in a
  mountain stream, watch birds
  cross the sky
Do all the things that along the
  pathways of life were dear to me
HE will show me all the things
  that I never hoped to see"

"We will rest and have our lunch
  by a glistening waterfall
Sing songs of HIS home, that
  place HE keeps with love for all
We will talk about my life from
  childhood to full grown
HE will tell me about the place I
  will be calling home"

"If you could only see me now,
  the sunshine in my eyes
My happiness knows no bounds
  for I'm going to GOD's paradise
Someday your date with GOD
  will come, the happiest day ever
You will walk the pathways of
  your life and you will walk
  together"

Robert Vargo
ELEGY: PAUL VARGO
There beamed a light that broke
  when heart-sound died
That burned the eyes that
  dreamed in April's din
That cracked a lamp and crushed
  it's fine glass shade
And split within the torrents of
  it's rain.

Pure amber oil ran it's life to shed
Amber deed from amber sand, then
Flowed across an amber void to
  bleed

Itself, to spin a deep vortex of pain.

Now, dark the room that beamed
  the waning light
That once awoke to cry at
  fleeting sound
That eyed each day with hurt and
  cryptic face
And feared the evening lull and
  lonely fate;

That fired the carmine fuse that
  lit the lane
. . . The twisted path that gave
  and metered space.

Mary Ann B. Henning
LOVE THREADS
A family knits the mettle
Of love's silken scroll

Pressing the print
Of fishing poles and china dolls

Onto the gossamer
Of childhood's ash

Blown through the portal
Of Euphoria's summer,

Sculptor, of maturity's
Destiny to rediscover

The love threads
Inside its cover.

Michael E. Wittner
THE OLD MAN
I sat on the edge of my bed,
  thinking I was 33. When I
  suddenly realized, that I'm
  older than a white oak tree.
My how time goes by so fast. I
  can hardly remember some of
  the things that have happened
  in the past.
When I suddenly hear them in
  the other room, talking of my
  place of rest.
Well, at least I'll no longer be a
  pest. But I know in my day I
  was the very best. And I more
  than welcome my place of rest.

Mary Ann B. Henning
THE CREATIVE ONES
Creative minds paint the
  mountains, the valleys
The valleys of moods
Moods reflecting time
Time an element involved in an
  event
Molding its course.

Arthur Morrison
THIS CHILD IS LOVE
*[Sarah Steele, for whom this
poem was written, and Carolyn
and Chuck Steele for being her
parents, my love and thanks to
all]*
Happy and so much alive,
  Pretty little girl of five.
Blonde, the color of her hair,
  For all around her, she has a care.
God must have made her face,
  Dimples, he put perfectly, in
  place.
Her speech has a defect of the
  young,
  Warming the hearts of those,
  she is among.
People tempt her, by acting like a
  clown or two,
  Just to see her smile, with eyes
  of blue.
She can look at you so coy and

and mild,
No one can help, but love this child.
Her love to play and make believe,
And feel great hurt, just if she tore her sleeve.
So young and filled with much compassion,
God must look down, and thank her mom and dad, for the beauty they helped fashion.

Karen Roehrig
MY WOLRDS
[To, my Dad, my Mom, and Brother, my Sister and those special friends and relatives that gave me encouragment and inspirations but most of all, love, thank you.]
I lay here with my eyes closed,
Only to see visions of my
                    Inside world.
The familiar places I know so well,
Are suddenly haunted.
I hear the silent screams of beyond,
Or is it the deafening whispers,
                    From my past?
I am running in a never ending hall,
And my feet can't touch the ground.
Is this empty hall, my life?
                    Why am I running?
Am I running back? OR,
                    Am I running away?
The air is so thick, I can not breathe.
If I would just open my eyes,
I would see my familiar outer world.
                    I would be safe.
I wonder though . . .
If my inner and outer worlds,
                    Should ever collide,
Would my eyes ever close again?
Or, more frightening, scarier yet . . .
                    Would they ever open?

James Martin Gau
Happiness Still (Outside My Window)
[To those who've laughed. Who also cry: There are no others.]
Hide the tear
Which touched thy cheek
Last evening;

Dawn will bring
An aching, yet
New morning.

Whipoorwills:
The birds which sing
Cry with you,

And herald then
The coming of
New sorrows.

What stained thy lip
Last evening was
Just something

That mankind
Has not yet learned
To avoid.

So chide not
Human failings
As Damnation,

Lest we all
Condemn ourselves
To fill Hell's void.

Lois Johnson Allen
A Love Poem To the King
Elvis all that
I want is to
be near to you
I have always
loved you from a far
Now that you're gone
you will never know
how much you have
meant to me
You will never know
how my heart will
always be true
to only one person
Perhaps in another life
We will meet and
fall in love
And be one.

Helen K. Spinner
AN ABSOLUTE
I can not/will not
      offer you forever.
That would sound too definite,
and consistency can only be found
                    before a change.
What I do promise you
is a lack of false comfort
      and truth in pretending,
which, upon going,
      will leave nothing left
                    to be said.

Henry F. Stecker
To D. B.: Dream Weaver II
I dreamed of you, as I still do
      sometimes,
Upon the gray of dawn this
      fragile morn;
And, as I lay, I felt within me born
The erstwhile kiss of sweet
      romantic rhymes.
So real you seemed before my
      sleep—fraught eyes,
I nearly dared to stretch and
      touch your face,
To wrap your body in a warm
      embrace,
To feel your lips on mine in
      love's surmise.
I almost felt you move upon my
      bed,
The nearness of your presence
      hot delight!
The woven dream unravled like
      the night;
The touch of you was only in my
      head.
      I shuddered at the cold reality
      Of you in Dallas, me in St. Louie.

William N. Howard
ELEGY
an era came to an end—
an era in my
loneliness:
an era, 'twas a friend,
an era in my loneliness—
an era, that suff'ring
made
nor taint, but sweet
nor foulness fit, but beauty
last—
of tears are made
and self-indulgence grave.

a yearn to leave
the maudlin mode—
the catastrophic sense
of smear—

a sow to rivet up
the road,
a swan to spawn
a jaundiced tear.

an era sampling
once the good—
a peach and other
fruit refined—a gritty playpen
      made of wood,
and food to feed the
famished mind.

an era sick with emptiness,
blanched faces, cogitation
lost—
an era pathologically
turning, turning into burning
flames and frost.

Michele D. Kusek
FORGOTTEN PROMISE
[To David]
You promised me you would
Always be that someone I could
talk to.

Someone I could cry to,
Someone I could always come to.

You promised me,
We would think together,
Be together, love together,

But you never promised that
You would stay . . .

Not forever anyway.

Lemory Craft Jr.
A MASTERPIECE
[To: Tobie and Jean Gowans, I love you Mom's and Dad!]
I cannot question its meaning,
Nor definitions define;
For the art of it is the wonder,
That has endured through the time.

For it is woven with the emotions,
And painted with the thought;
It has lasted all these years,
For money, it can not be brought.

So it is very rare,
And exquisite in its form;
For it is in the museum of hearts,
That picture of love is born!

Carol Ann Spry (O'D)
COURAGE
[For the one with the courage to love, the conviction to show it, and the commitment for always.]
Courage is the conviction to
stand for what you feel;
Courage is the strength to make
your dreams real.
Courage is the bravery to take
your first step,
To conquer your fears without
regret.

Courage is the fearlessness in
every man,
Residing there since time began.
Courage is the trigger, waiting to
kill,
Courage is the silence, buried
there still.

Courage is the strength to do
what must be done;
Courage is the effort to finish
things begun.
Courage is the persistence to
make things work,

As it remains the patience of first
things first.
Courage is the victory in the face
of the foe
And the surrender of defeat in
the life we know.
Courage is the breath of
manhood's cry,
The decision to quit or continue
to try.

Yes, courage is the strength to
carry on,
Clinging to convictions when all
else is gone.
For courage is the love that
makes it so,
As love gives courage the
capacity to grow.

Lydia Venta—Dobrovolsky
GREAT RICHES
My Father in Heaven and I—on
the Earth—are both happy
owners of the Universe.
My Father loves me and
teaches me kindly:
to be at ease in the labyrinth
of our huge, indescribable castle!
He tells me:
not to hustle and bustle
in life's silky rustle of dry,
empty leaves;
I should get wise: choosing my
toys and pleasures,
my joys and treasures—my
happiness . . .
He tells me:
"My Darling child—my lovely
offspring!
don't look for a bliss in an abyss!
don't catch flattery butterflies—
who knows—where the danger
lies?"

                    Otherwise:
I am totally free—with the best
advice by my Father, so wise:
to walk at his hand in our vast,
happy land!

Mary Lynn Gray Adefala
Where Did the Days Go
[In dedication to Lonnie S. who has shared a host of good and bad times with me. May our future be even brighter.]
The day has passed with all its
glow and left with it a love
filled soul.
A joyous day of peace and
tenderness—
Crowned with love and draped
with gladness.
Two hearts adrift on an ocean of
fears—
First plagued; now filled with
coming years.
A man so warm he melts all guise
and a woman so filled that she
cannot deny it.
Both in a whirlpool of marital
bliss surpassing all storms on a
sea of myth.
Now tossed, now turned with a
pianful yearn to be together
always, though you may have
learned . . .

That love came slowly as years
progressed with their warmth,
their tears, and their
happiness.

Today's Greatest Poems

Thomas C. Gallagher
THE SHARING
The world in total darkness lay
All black and void of light,
And then one single little ray
commenced to shine so bright.
A minute spark, a tiny speck
Which soon began to grow,
'till all the area 'round about
Took on a brilliant glow.

The other areas, in darkness still
Could see the little light,
And envy grew within their breasts
That one should be so bright.
So they banded together and
declared
That it was only fair,
That one should give to all around
So each could have his share.

Now a little here, and a little
there
They took and spread so thin,
Yet, even more, they clamored for
Their demands a constant din.
The little light began to fade
Then it died and so this day
The world all black and void of
light
In total darkness lay.

Winifred J. Hamilton
NATURE'S PAINTBRUSH
I was once again amazed,
As at the foliage I gazed,
For the trees were all ablaze
With breath taking beauty.

This, I thought, was Nature's
notion,
From mountain top down to the
ocean,
A paint brush had been set in
motion
By an unseen hand.

No words suffice to describe
The wondrous colors side by side,
I could find no flaw to hide
In the lovely picture.

As the frost each color brightened,
Some it darkened, some it
lightened,
Sometimes I was almost frightened
At the awe—inspiring scene.

Sadly I recalled the past,
I knew this beauty could not last,
In memory I held it fast,
And knew that God is!

William E. Tierney
WITHOUT LOVE
[Dedicated: To the memory of
Eleanor; and to Estelle, my
second wife, whose patience
and understanding is love.]
Without love, there'll be no song
The morn will never come
And on the trees
No buds will come along

Without love, a chill will fill my
soul
No laughs or even smiles there'll
be
And sad and even meaningless
Will be God's golden rule

Diane Kristen
ABOVE & BEYOND
Innocent splendor of a child's tale
As seen from the earth,
A rainbow of dusty pink

And the lightest shade of blue,
Joined by the yellow—turning gold
Of the sun,
The pure and modest images
Of white clouds all around,
An invitation
To the puritanical playground
Of a castle in the air.

Come nightfall,
Tranquil shades of sky blue
Seem overpowered
By the spreading force
Of midnight blue . . .
Hypnotizing
And wickedly enticing
Combined—
Such a vision of mystery,
Beckoning you
To crawl
Into darkness.

Kelly Dalrymple
HEAVEN IN SECONDS
In the night the thunder
shuttered; a perching raven
stares;
A flawless figure closely hovers;
beneath the moonlit glare.
My eyes awoke through pondered
vision;
my hands reached quickly to a
chair;
and darkness gave me no decision,
the wrath was never and not a
dare.
Inscented angels came through
my window; remorse I didn't fear;
and came forth a sound, trumpets
blowing, love and God was near.
No torment, nor a devil, seen my
face unveiled;
but an angel of mercy landed;
down to earth set sail.
Up I fluttered in clouds awaiting;
soul at last in care;
whispered praise by man no
wonder, high above in air.
Heaven opened, a hand reached
out,
and hailed me on a throne;
faith redeemed my glorious
journey;
and earth below a darkened glow;
A scent was cast of love and
kindness;
richly gathered into a holy song;
and now together, at home forever,
all his children of his own.

Sister Catherine Daoust C. S. J.
HUMMINGBIRD
To be sure you are
GOD'S masterpiece!
With spider web wings
And sword—like beak,
You are His angel of the skies!
As a thought in flight,
A whisper on the wing!
Fairy of the bird kingdom.
Alighting but a moment
To feast on the honey,
The flowers so graciously offer you!
You are the artists' notion
Of poise,
Grace,
And beauty!
Quintessence of light,
Your meteor flight
Is a flash of color,
Swifter than lightning,
Present for a moment,

But a memory
And a joy,
Forever!

O. Shawn Cupp
THE BATTLEGROUNDS
The ponds, the backyards, the
playgrounds,—mental scars.
The names, the pranks, the
loneliness
The tears, the hurt, the sobs
The burden on our conscience
stays with us.

The rivers, the valleys, the hills
—physical destruction.
The bullets, the shells the bombs
The blood, the wounds, the
fatigue
The nightmares of war awake us.

Our many Battlegrounds,
—mental and physical anguish.
The Battlegrounds of Life.
Which leaves deeper scars?
The schoolyard or the
battlefield. . .

Judy A. Lodes
AS THEY GROW OLDER
Their days may be up or down,
Spirits lifted due to a visit from
someone dear;
or no spirit at all, just lost and
lonely.

Words may be backwards or harsh,
Demanding, frustrated, sweet and
thankful;
or no words at all.

Eyesight may be blurred, only a
vision,
It may sparkle; or no vision at all.
They may hear only what is
wished to be heard;
or they may not hear at all.

In Gods eyes they are all human,
Seeing, speaking, hearing, or just
existing.
They have been here longer than
you or I,
Many the beginning to our lives.

They have helped shape and
create our society
Which is everchanging, and hard
for them to realize.
What they need now is caring,
To know someone still loves them.

Spare a minute of each day,
Think about those so dear to you.
Live each day to it's fullest,
Share moments together, and
help each other;
As oneday you and I will also
grow older.

Dr. Isolde V. Czukor
THE SEA AND YOU
I drove beside the surging sea,
A veil of rain all misty—grey
obscuring screaming gulls
The pounding surf roared in my
ears,
I thought of you and then I
thought upon the sea
And you were both alike in
strength and fortitude.
And as I gazed upon the distant,
grey horizon
It brought to me the feeling of
your state of consciousness
In all its magnitude.

Further on I drove, and then the
sea changed into an avenue of
Redwood trees, those giant
entities so vast and wise and
true
In all their glorious solitude.
I felt the years slip back and I
became aware that some of them
Were here when Jesus walked the
earth.
My heart o'erflowed with love to
know the faithfulness
They gave to this great land.
The road curved on and suddenly
the sea was there once more,
Not angry, grey and dark, but
gently, quietly and lovingly
Kissing golden spits of sand.
I pondered on last night and in
my thoughts I saw your face,
How when you turned your eyes
to mine they were two star—lit
pools
Within some still and blue lagoon.
You touched my hand, you
brushed my lips with yours,
My breath caught wildly in my
throat.
You smiled and then I heard the
sound of symphonies of angel's
songs.
I reached to kiss the ringlets on
your brow; you spoke to me:
"Aye, gently, gently, sweet my
love . . .", my heart you smote.
You laid your head upon my
breast . . . I scarcely breathed
Lest I should wake and find you
were a figment of my mind
And all the angel's songs I heard
were just one note . . .
The pounding sea.

Mildred L. Max
The Church's Foundation
Let us never forget without
people
The church would never exist.
Build it well, add wealth to its
estate.
Let us never forget that it
Is gladness that circles us yet.

Over miles and miles music is
heard.
Delicate, gentle, refined.
You'll be happy dropping a kind
word,
Full of delight from heart and
mind.
And the church still stands.

Each one of his prayers are heard.
No one can change His Eternal
Plans.
With God it is always your Soul,
He cares about each mortal man.
With faith you'll trust His
control.

Just remember the individual
christian
Forming a common fellowship
Through faith in Christ,—for His
Reacting chain must never
break.
So keep it in good use.

Do not break God's reacting chain.
Keep it shining bright.
The only thing to brighten it will
be
Brightness its self.

Laura Cole Martin

CONCERNED

*(Tribute to John Lennon &
Dedicated to Yoko Ono)*

The world is in alot of trouble of
that I am sure,
There must be someone
somewhere who must have a
cure.

It isn't hard to see the fear in
everybody's eyes,
Must we keep this fear in us til
the day we die?

We worry about our future, but
then we have the right,
Because the way things are going,
our future doesn't look to bright.

We elect politicians to do our
bidding, but really now, who
are we kidding?
They can't do everything on their
own
It's up to us to help them, by
making ourselves known.

We have rights and we must use
them, for if we don't make use
of these rights, then when
things go wrong who are we to
condem?

One of our rights is freedom of
speech
And if everyone would use it,
then maybe our politicians it
will reach.

If you choose not to use this right
to keep them
Then we may as well start
writing our own requiem.

It is not just our future but our
childrens too,
We can do something now
because it's *never* to soon!

If everyone could just join
together as one, then
I'm sure in the end our battle will
be won.

Our children look to us to show
them the way,
It is up to us to keep them from
being lead astray.

All it takes is a little
involvement, it's time to quit
hiding and come out of
hibernation.
We've got to clean things up for
our future generations,
because after all it was us that
got this world in this situation.

We show them violence and we
show them hatred,
We show them prejudice and expect
them to grow up good natured.
If we can't show them love for
our fellow man along with
concern,
Then how do we ever expect
them to learn?

Just to think about the things I
have said,
Because you can't really do much
once you are dead.

Katharine C. Lickers

PORTRAIT OF FREEDOM

I heard the Star Spangled Banner
sung today
In a country far away.

Of all the flags flying for us to see
Only 'Old Glory' was flying free!
Strangers around me tried; their
greetings weren't kind
And I wondered what they had in
mind?
All gathered together to
proclamate,
To laud the visiting potentate.
I thought to myself, why all this
fuss,?
You know you really don't like us.
We rebuilt your country, made it
strong
Now you tell us that was wrong!
You claim we have too much, we
make mistakes
How willingly you take and take.
You, who never have been free
Turn this way and look at me.
Together we might form a plan
To cement the Brotherhood of
Man.
Our Bill of rights, our
Constitution, is the pattern,
the sum
Of Faith in God, of Freedom won!
I heard the Star Spangled Banner
sung today
In a country far away.
There was 'Old Glory' flying free
Dear Lord, may this always be!

Allyn LeHew

NOCTURNE

Love—poems
Should not be
Ponderous
Love—poems
Should be
Love—sounds
Summer—night winds
Caressing tree—tops
Leaves murmuring
Stirring restively
As a loved one
In the arms of a lover

Come lie with me, my love
We will listen
To the love—sounds
Together . . .

Bertie Lee J.

THE STAR

The star I saw tonight in orbit
was so far away only God could
of put it there with his divine
love as you look down from
where you are you lift my heart
to the brightest star I know
where you are the soul is free.
As I reach out to touch you I've
forgotten you are so far away
some day I will be a star like
you maybe not that big
As long as I am a star up there
with you I too can touch other
hearts
Like you have mine,

Pamela Lawson

THE WISDOM OF YOUTH

At Eighteen,
the world is "simply" observed.
We know all lifes answers
from things we have learned.
When we see adults
who think they can't cope,
who wander around
and constantly grope
for answers in life
to ease their concern,

the eighteen year old
thinks that is absurd!
But as life goes on
your knowledge attained
will change from great gain
to nothing remains
for then you will see
that a "simple" solution
is like plugging your nose
to solve air polution.
Yes, then you will learn
the older you get—
the things that you know
aren't anything yet!

"LeNoit" LeVonier Aldridge, II

**Moi Amour—Classic
Portrait**

Rolling mountainsides—rainbow
waterfalls—Liquid illusions of
your smile.
   The magical horizon blemished
   by the sunset
I find myself engulfed in
yesterday memories of your
gentle caress.
   Serene and warm
   colours—"Portrait"
            Moi Amour
The sensual and very soft
fragrance of your parfum
   Ah! Yes! breesingly with a
   intimate whisper across my
   searching fare.
Tis comfort you've given me, my
dearest darling, O'love
   Memories of Chantilly lace
   drapped across the Chippendale
   sofa
      French parlour with a
      intricately carved fireplace
Reflecting the majestic sculpture
of your mahogany and petique
body.
   T'was mine flaming passions
   for you, "Moi Amour", etching
   these orchestrated chants of
   romance . . . .
Mine "Princess", Moi Amour in
this final hour to have loved
you is to never
   part with your sweet nectar
   characteristic of strawberry
   fragrance.
So refreshening and invitting to
my deepest emotions. Ahhh! so
mellow . . .

Tanika

WISHING

Sometimes the good isn't as good
as we would like it to be
And the bad is more than we
would like to see
At times laughter, happiness and
kindness appears to be a decoy
As the pains of the past comes
back to haunt hurt and destroy
Remember the days are here for
only awhile and the loneliness
may linger but never last
And the morning brings the light
of another day, let the old
memories past
Turn the pain and hurt around
and let them go forever on
their way
So that happiness may abide
within your life more with
each new day
If we could accomplish this great

task in our lives I daresay
All that we seek for will surely
come our way

Connor E. Lewis

**Reflections Of Autumnal
Equinox**

There are some who anxiously
await for this time of the year
because of its beauty,
While others uncaringly pay
little attention to this
exceptional time of the year,
And there are some who think
that Summer has a duty,
to evolve into something that
causes some men of words to
break into resounding cheer.

Yet, upon closer inspection, one
would find that the
approaching of Autumnal
Equinox shouldn't be taken too
lightly,
Simply because there is a certain
sadness that comes about
nightly.

After the sadness of Autumn
nights do pass into a shadowly
land of semibrightness,
And the days that follow often
times shout with brilliant
degrees of blues, greens, golds
and reds;
and sometimes those days that
are filled with the warm colors
of a new Season often times
thinks of Itself as being
self-righteous—
simply because It knows that It
has the advantage over a
Season that will soon be dead.
But why would anyone rejoice
simply because a Season has
died— and another must take
its place . . .
especially when the warm winds
of Autumn can sometimes turn
into wintry winds that leaves
one encased?

Yet, as I walk through fields still
filled with summer green with
no indication of an
approaching demise,
I take joy in remembering that
Summer is still with us and not
to pine or sigh;
Over the prospect that a once—
brilliant sky with excess heat
shall soon cease,
and the shadows that fall over
the land shall lengthen and be
filled with a coldness that will
cause many to bemoan and cry.
But, as I keep walking, I am filled
with wonder over the fact that
something as beautiful as
Summer must give Itself away
to a Season filled with
dampness and gray skies—
as well as to a Season that
sometimes can be filled with
colorful, deceptive lies!

Wilson Boomhower Jr.

RAINING II.

hawks leave the sky,
deer avoid the meadows,
field mice scramble for dead
wood,
prescient, suited to circumstance.

rain the farmers wait for
brews thunder two counties over
so you lower the windows before
    the storm
and look where the sun went.
then damp air, perused by this
    pregnant wetness
cracks and cracks again.
gutters, barrels, brooks, puddles
    and raw,
dry fields accept and prosper.
trees drink deeply, grass glistens,
flowers exude sweet, pulsing
    odors.
clay by the creek shines.

eggs in a nest
want the underbelly, warm and
    dry,
of a bird struck down by a larger
    bird
sometime before the storm,
    somewhere
above the spring wheat, and
    lowing milkers
puzzling back to the barn.

James Jonathan Davis, Jr.
NORTH ATLANTIC SEAS
Cloudy ceiling, swelling waters
Rolling angle, pitching destroyers.
Crying planes, awaiting skies
Swaying bed mats, tiring eyes.

Touching land, resting briefly
Plundering much, terrain hilly.
Waking boilers, keyed up shaft
Billowing seas, forward and aft.

Approaching copter, misjudging
    landing,
Gasping intakes, engines
    drowning.
Restless boat, scarring great,
Unplanned happenings, lingering
    fate.

Aging ships, swimming on,
Watching horizons, respecting
    nature.
Returning landward, perching
    lightly,
Viewing tulips, spinning wheels.

Surprising orders, re-sailing cue,
Bewildering all, upsetting crew.
Hushed electronics, spying
    trawlers,
Lengthening stay, becoming "Blue
    Noses."

Steaming southward, sighting
    "Motherland,"
Slipping crewman, tolling "Big
    Ben."
Weary ships, rising heat,
Slowing blades, swollering deeps.

Cognizant ships, retreating
    homeward,
Remembering ever, learnings
    sternward.
Enduring winds, warming breezes.
Sail on, conquerors of North
    Atlantic Seas.

Lyn Dwyer
ALONE
Numb and bitter I sit alone
Pray to my God to save me from
    this pain
But he can't help; nor will you
Yet you are the only one who
    could
I pray for some salvation in your
    words

But death lies only moments away
All will pass . . . the pain along
    with the tears
As the last tear drys; may your
    memory fade
Taking with it all that my love
    held for you
Everything is nothing once again
As I walk through the lonely
    halls of my mind
You once lived there along with
    the love
            and the laughter
Soon everything will have
    vacated these premises
I care not to recognize such
    emotion again
Let love say good-bye as it greets
    my tears
For without you . . .
        I choose not to love
Take from me now any and all
    signs of life
For I prefer to sink back into the
    confines of my mind
I've been without its protection
    far too long
I'll remain here . . . where no-one
    can reach me
Lonely . . .
        but out of love's painful path.

Jeffery C. Ferguson
ON LOVE
I sighed, "What do you know of
    love"

        The abstract is
only a phase deep and profound
caught in a-maze vague and
    unsound
        Just beyond
pretending to see, unable to know
what loving will be when love
    cannot show
        The tangible evidence
that our story goes on underneath
the throes born of love gone
    amiss—
with each taste of a kiss bursting
an orb of bliss—a little like this;
        It's really faith
wishing I could fly to a place
    nearby
away from the lie about you and I
        Held before
my heart feeling hollowed,
    sickened and sallowed,
making all that followed
    weakened and shallowed
        The hard fact's acceptance
that our knowing the truth of
    lying ensconced
in young love-promises made, yet
    never clear;
finding one's youthful cheer lost
    when held
much too dear; and that has
    taught me to fear

*That . . . love . . . just . . . is
    . . .And yet . . .*

"Nothing . . . I know nothing of
    love," he whispered.

Shirley L. Fahrny
TROUBLED THOUGHTS
Lying here awake in dead of night
Wondering what the morrow
    holds . . .
Will the pressures slacken

(even slightly)
As the day unfolds?

Throbbing temples tell of
    tension's fervor
Muscles cramp and tighten into
    knots . . .
Crowded thoughts invade the
    troubled mind
Like root-bound plants in pots!

Take heed, thy soul, a warning
    here is issued
Be not consumed . . . but gently
    like a wave
That washes over tiny grains of
    sand.
Be cleansed of all but which
    you'd save!

Sue E. Anderson
NATIVITY
*[With love to those who
believed in me—Mike, Valerie,
Lillian; and a special loving
thank—you to my Mom and
Dad who helped make this
possible.]*
No one wanted to believe that He
    was born a King.
No one wanted to believe that He
    was anything
        to man,
For His cradle was a humble
    manger in a stable bare,
And He calmly slept a baby's
    peaceful sleep without a care.
Emmanuel, on earth did dwell . . .

There were multitudes of holy
    angels 'round about,
And on that night there was no
    place on earth without
        a song;
For a Savior had been born and all
    mankind could now rejoice
And a thankful prayer could now
    be breathed by every grateful
    voice.
Emmanuel, on earth did dwell . . .

Shepherds biding on the hillside
    watching o'er their sheep,
Saw the light and heard the songs
    that settled 'round the sleepy
    town.
They left their fires and hurried
    to the stable—palace crude,
And in their hearts enthroned the
    Baby King within the manger
    rude.
Emmanuel, on earth did dwell . . .

Three wise men saw His star and

came with gifts of gold,
And they bent the knee in
    adoration of the Holy
            Child,
For this Baby from His
    makeshift royal cradle in a stall
Could humble highborn Kings
    and cause them on their knees
    to fall.
Emmanuel, on earth did
    dwell . . . .

This infant worked such changes
    in the ones who came;
Poor and ragged, rich and
    famous—it was all the same
        to Him.
Though we celebrate today the
    Birth that changed lives in the
    past,
All the lives this King has
    touched will change the future
    years that pass.
Emmanuel, on earth does
    dwell . . .

Veronica Butler
FOREVER
I'll keep on holding on

When I can't see my way
    Looking for a brighter day

I'll keep on holding on

    Through sunshine and rain
    Through joy and pain

I'll keep on holding on

    In you I can depend
    For time on end

I'll keep on holding on

    Holding On,

Forever and

A Day

Jeanne A. Morley
DREAMS
Once I dreamed that you were
    Apollo
    and rode Pegasus
swooping from the sky
    on great white wings.
Laughing,
    you picked me up
and we rode the heavens.
Upon awakening,
    and finding tattered
        remnants of a dream
on my pillow,
    I laughed,
and cursed all dreams.
But now, among other follies,
    I stop, for hours, and search
        the skies.

Ola V. Henry
The Mysteries Of Life
*[To all the Woodbey's who
have waited so long]*
The mysteries of life are so
    closely entwined, with the
    sunshine day, and the skies of
    night. To brilliant colors of
    rainbows. To dark and
    thunderous clouds, that darken
    the night. To lightning that
    flashes up high across the sky.
    Of green grass and mountains
    up high covered with snow.

The howl of the wolf, in the
wooded trees, and the moon
that shines, to make images of
leaves. A child's cry of fright,
that echos through the night.
To an old man and his moan,
with a light blazing through his
home. Of death that comes
with a sigh, from a hospital, in
wee wee hours of night.

To an owl, who can't see by day
and watches with a stare, as
night brings him his day. From
seeds planted in a hole, come
flowers and trees that grow,
and point upward to the sky.
Then a breeze that cools your
brow, from that hot desert air,
that's humid and dry.

Then the mother with child
bowed low with pain, a
mystery experienced by no
man today. And we are but
significant in this plan, from
the brilliant colors of the
rainbow, from birth to death,
and on to the mountains
covered up high with snow.
Then to the cows loo, in the
valley below.

From the child's cry of fright, that
echos through the night. To
the old man and his moan,
with a light blazing through his
home. And the woman with
pain bowed low. We all pass it
every day, like an image in a
window pane. How long can all
this last? Only God can answer
that, and whether this will all
end day or night, is the biggest
mystery of life

George Beecher
The Dark and the Light
What is Darkness? It's not enough
To say an absence of light—If so
We would all be dark inside
But when you press the fingers
lightly
On the eyes you see images
appear and dreams
Arise with just the weight of sleep

I thought I'd weave a mesh of
moss
Draped like a southern shawl
With natural flowers patterning it
To catch a hunter's rifle ball

This dream was dreamed
And hung out on the line to dry
The old spent bullet of the earth
Hangs dangling in the sky

I've been consumed with thoughts
That melt cold words to mush
The future never quite
compresses
Crystals from my smouldering
hush

Must I turn inside out to show
My latticework desires
How can you know the glacial
push
Against a caveman's fires

Today I sunset and turn gold
Tomorrow I melt and misty rain
We tree and green our leaves
I breathe and hurricane the sea

All this is me and I am there
Now darken into night
Once more I burn up on my
hearth
And sleep cold ashes

Donna L. McCombs
UNTITLED
What is love to me?
Sometimes it seems
There is no such state
of Being.
It's like seeing
The sun at its setting—
It is Beauty and Color
and Emotion and Inspiration—
And, just out of Reach.
I cannot teach myself
To cease pushing my hand
Toward its warmth.
Nor can I cease
My heart filling
Its Vacancy with You.

Lori Lin Abbas
PEACE
Peace danced, that night, through
Condon town
her light hair flowed about,
the color of silver from the moon.
The wind rippled through her
crystal gown
as a young man watched, alone
and entranced,
from a cold window on the block.

He rushed to the dark streets
as she sang and caught the wind,
rising to lead a lost one home,
to the chimes of olde England
echoing from the Church tower,
the serene lady quietly spoke:

"I was there, with the war-torn
world
amid air raid bombing and fires,
with every soldier in the trenches,
in the camps and on the seas.
I gave wisdom and understanding
and in the end, I gave peace."

"I was there, long ago in early
times
where knights roamed the land
and opressed peasants working
endlessly,
for cruel and uncaring lords.
I gave roses and chivalry
and in the end, I gave peace."

The lady in white smiled,
and fell silent again
while the wind rustled about.
The breeze lifted and carried her
along
far into the night, whispering,
"And in the end, I give peace."

Linda F. Dukes
FOREST OF DEATH
Where's a hand, when I need one
to hold,
Is it lost like a soul that's been
sold?
Water runs quickly thru holes in
the sand,
Resembling a life span of each
man.
Strum me a song, so I can hear,
The peace that is waiting after
the fear.

Deep in a forest, walking alone,
Lines in the trees carve faces I've
known.

Too many voices to understand
all,
Stopping in front of a statue quite
tall.
Gazing upon its beauty so fair,
While peace fills the empty space
of air.
A frightful scream heard thru the
trees,
Causing me to turn and run thru
the leaves.
Behind me I hear, the footsteps of
death,
Wanting to kill as Cain did of
Seth.
Lying behind a willow tree's bow,
Eternal peace does exist in me
now.

Bhatkin Devi
I
*[This poem is dedicated to
William F. Buckley, Jr., a true
conservative. Also, to James
Baldwin and in memory of
Fannie Lou Hammer.]*
I don't understand this crazy
mixed up world of ours.
I don't even get the message
I want across to people.
I feel as though I am a confused
soul.
Left to struggle through this
world alone.

The only thing I have is my belief
in God.
I who wander through this
merciless world
In awe of hatred and deception.
Only to find it continually
repeating that vicious cycle
Again and again.
I confused and troubled.
Although I am a good-hearted
individual.
Carry on despite obstacles and
sticks and stones.
Hoping to someday find a place
of solitude
And peaceful serenity.
I, a confused soul must carry on
Despite hell and confusion.
Mixed with utter complete
madness.

Omijene Sprague Woodard
CONDEMNED
From within this untended
Deteriorating old house,
with cracked and dirty
window panes,
peer the myopic cataract

covered eyes
of an old woman.
Tattered and filthy
curtains flapping
as the obscene mutterings
spewed forth from a clacking
tongue that speaks
only to silence.
Skeletal remains of food
rotting and fetid,
litter the floors
as thoughts and desires
lie mangled on the
surface of memory
too long neglected.
The eerie howling of wind
rushing through cracks
in the walls.
Sounds of ghostly
cries of pain
held prisoner within a
heart filled with despair.
Rotting foundations
splintered and crumbling
as are the dreams and hopes
of days long passed
when house and body
were strong and
promise was new,
now both without sustenance.
Dissipating like smoke
from burned out passions
and hearth fires
from which no live embers
remain.
The house and body
both unfit
for habitation.

Marsha Elaine McGrady
ON BEING BLACK
We can never be in this land so
long
that we forget what land we're
really from.

Our plight in this country can
only be magnified
by the knowledge of the wealth
and intelligence
of our forefathers.

Our Africa,
now divided by arbitrary
European boundary lines
goes on in the face
of everything we know.

This encourages me to continue
to work to see
Black people everywhere realize
some sense of ownership,
of ideology,
of culture,
of truth.

Rose Michelle Boccasino
STAR-HOPE
Behold dear one
the ardent wonder of the gentle
evening star
in reflection arrayed it gleams a
grasp on each of us
concealing dreams for a night,
for tonight
tomorrow hopes for tomorrow's
morrow.

Bright silvery silver
sparkling amid the darkest
ocean night
ever-waiting, always patient
this tiny precocious portal

a heavenly mirror—window of
genuine goodness
peeks silently in on our sleepy
world.

Gleaming grandiosely
as if it were larger than life
as large as love might be
like a merry little leprechaun
this twinkly dot winks
whimsically at ourselves
telling tales, sharing secrets
long since forgotten.

Wonder of hope
this glimmer of a visual
heartbeat
smiles a sustaining light
while withdrawing into day
and absconding willingly until
tomorrow night.

Richard Allan Stonis
NIGHT WAVES
Nigrescent waters flood through
the city,
Darkness parading past one last
alley.
Soft-tone fluid forms captain the
mind
And melt in the mist of this half-
day's time.
Moonless Night's silence is
sullen and somber
'Til bronze-tongued towers knell
Time's number.
Buildings loom long, gray with
richness
And echo the baying of hounds
in the distance.
A cadre of no-names, nocturnes
of street life,
Stand coned and ablaze under
islands of white light.

Hail, dawn's harbinger! Sing us
your song
When the sun meets the sea and
the shadows are long.

Ellis Ovesen
SONG OF PEACE
There is
a song of peace
that steals into the heart
when one has found the sterling
love
of God.

Lester R. Nuse
LOVE
[To all of our grandchildren and
in memory of Lester L. Nuse Jr.]
The sound of laughter and a
pretty smile
To hold them always, not just
awhile
To hear a footstep, see a
bouncing curl
They are grandma's and grandpa's
little girls

They are so small right from the
start
But everyday grow more on your
heart
When they come to your house
just for a day
Then you miss them so much
when they go away

Bless you Lord for these bundles
of joy
Whether it be a pretty girl or a
rough little boy

We love them so much with
kisses so warm
The beautiful hugs of their strong
little arms

A doll for a girl, a car for a boy
To watch their faces is a real joy
Their hearts are filled with
innocent love
You know the Lord's watching
way up above

Thank you Lord for these little
tots
We'll love them forever and
forget not
Let's see them more often and
give them a whirl
Because they are grandma's and
grandpa's little boys and girls.

Lester Sills
A Halloween Day In
Upstate New York
[To Ithaca, a magical place
through which I journeyed, and
like Odysseus, I shall return.]
It is past noon,
The villains shall emerge soon.
I lay down on green feathers
settled
below royal blue shelter.
Most insects have become
invisible.
And with my body undun for sun,
The refreshing feathers,
With a tingly hush, secure me.
The enveloping bronze statues
are almost naked
For they are shedding kin (the
maple leaf's patina),
Some who comfort me, others too
distant—
They speak with nature's ecstatic
zephyr.
It is silky now, not crisp—I want
to share it.
And the cycle has been, begun,
and continues . . .

Alma Joyce
FIRST FRUIT
As seasons change to finish woes'
travail; today that ancient pain
has given voice to songs of praise.
While in her seeming weakness
caged
devoured the fear and starved the
rage.

Pure freedom rides upon the wind,
her peaceful doves do settle
where they will to rest once more.
Singing songs of faith and hope
as spirits fall to rise again.

Alma Joyce
SILENT SKY
Enter now the final stages
of the parting of the waves.
Shall trust alone survive
til majesty take place?

While strength compresses
weakness
til it suffer all demise
and hope then rise to clothe
herself
dead mercy in the skies.

Come chosen seek escape
to forests sown of old,
where childhood hid our
treasures
of green grass and honey gold.

As the doubt of all the ages
attacks the city of his own,
let us gather in the quiet
to sing of mansions bold.

Alma Joyce
HEIR APPARENT
Before you were love called you
forth,
caressed your being and gave full
sway
to life forever lived in light.

Showers of talents held in your
hand
tempt attackers near and far.
Defenses speak veils up or down
and joking struggles of castles
keep
project your special pain, for
flesh deceived must feel to see.

Nevertheless it is ordained! You
shall pass
through loves portal to decide
doubts'
ageless quest of headship bowed
or broken.

Ron Hutzler
RIVERS
Like a river, it begins only as a
trickle.

With each passing day it grows.

With each droplet of moisture,
with every tear that falls,
it grows deeper.

Faced with obstacles,
Either by nature or by man,
it only pushes by with renewed
strength and vitality.

Pushing onward, never failing,
True Love is like a river.

Joya Quintero
THE SONG AWAITING
My emotions are but strings
Upon which you play the tune
Be it sad, gay or haunting
Be it day or light of moon

Only you may choose the lyrics
Your words pick out the mood
Your actions strum which notes
Will be poison or be food

You decide the strings that laugh
You choose which ones will cry
You determine which emotion
Shall live and which shall die

The strings are very fragile
And the music that they feign
Must be played very gently
They cannot stand the strain

So be careful of the song
That you decide to play
It may not have a future
Just a dying yesterday

Laura K. Culli
SILENT LOVER
A simple, trusting, caring love
Can fill a heart with tears.
Its beauty brings both joy and pain
As she wakes to find him near.

Childish stars dance in the sky;
Mother moon gently glows.
But the harsh winter wind tears
in the trees,
Showing the pain that she knows.

How she longs to speak, to shout

Of love that is shared by two.
But the time seems never right;
Her voice is never true.

So the silence of her paper and
pen
Screams of emptiness within
And fear of giving all of love
That's not returned again.

Robert Marons
HALLOWEEN PARTY
The black boots came on my feet,
and I found an orange necklace to
wear.
I put an eyepatch over my right
eye,
And a bandana covered my crew
cut hair.

A girl was dressed as a chief and
looked neat.
I brought her a tab and a cookie;
She thanked me for the treat.

It's fun pretending to be different
from one's self;
A person can dress up like a
witch,
a colonial man, or an elf.

Carolyn Pitts Dillard
GOOD-BYE
Today I said good-bye
But not a tear did I show.
Yet within me these feelings are
churning—
still hurting me so.

I cared for you in my own special
way.
But those kind of feelings
I have reserved—
saved for another day.

When we're ready, and the time is
right
We'll both have new loves—
To comfort through the night.

I'll miss you now, I know I will
That I won't deny.
But for now I have to be brave,
and
think of the future,
and hold my head up high.

Thank you for the good times we
shared,
and all the fun we had.
It makes saying good-bye a little
easier,
and a lot less sad . . .

M.M. Carr
WINTER'S DAY FANTASY
The snow falls
As the Heavens shake their hoary
heads
Pondering Man's iniquities

The snow falls
As the Heavens send their
crystalline
Messages of solace to Mother
Earth
In sympathy for her desecration

Stating the Lord, Our God is
aghast
And sorely grieved
At Man's violence and
destructiveness
And knows the Earth is numb
with pain
Of the agonized and tormented

The snow falls
As the Heavens shake their hoary
heads
In wonderment on Man's
imperceptibility

Chancing on a secret of the
Universe
Wondrous and inspiring
Yet seeing not transcendant
promise
Seeing only waste, destruction

The snow falls
As the Heavens shake their
weary heads
In shame and consternation
In despair, humiliation

But suddenly there is such
prismatic glistening
O'er the earth
That rays of hope must its
composite be
And in the warmth thereafter,
all-pervading
and caressing

In the tear-stained snow drifts,
North Wind's
Waning, gentle sighing
On the crackling pavements,
trapping sunbeams
Pirouetting
Breathed a prayer, in unity
For peace on earth—so may it be

Mollie Jo
THE HAWK
At times I feel like the oak
And the symbol of strength it
lends,
Yet, at times I find I feel like the
orchid
Just waiting to perish under
someone's hand.
I watched the hawk soar yesterday
And wished that I could
But once soar to reach the
heights he does,
Yet, I wonder—
If maybe I have not obtained
those heights
I seek so much already.
Independence has become a way
of life to me
And I can not say I'm glad,
Yet, when I think of the times I
needed
And knew no one was there
I found the strength to stand
alone
And do what I must do.
Maybe to stand alone and find
the strength inside
Is in its own way—
Soaring like the hawk.

Curtis O. Roberson
MENDED BROKEN HEART
One day I saw a little girl,
Tears streaming from her eyes,
While gripping tightly in her
hands
Parts of a broken doll.
In her right hand held she its
head,
In her left hand its feet,
While other parts were on the
ground,
Nearby a busy street.

"Sweetheart," said I, "don't sob and
weep—

Another doll we'll get,
With big blue eyes, you long may
keep,
And this one you'll forget."
"No, no," she said, "I can't forget,
Because my Mommy gave it,
Before she died, when I was five,
So please help me to patch it."

We gathered up its broken
"bones"—
Its head, its arms, its legs,
Imagining we heard its moans,
Like one who's hurt and begs;
And with the aid of sticky glue,
Braced with some tiny bars,
Soon had the doll as good as new,
Except for ugly scars.

This precious child brushed 'way
her tears,
Exhibiting true joy,
With smiles and laughter, happy
cheers
O'er patching up her toy.
Perhaps 'twas trifling me to spend
The time to patch her doll,
But ne'er will I regret the mend
Made to a broken heart.

Jeanne L. Gustafson
DECEMBER'S PARTY
December had a party, all the
snowflakes came.
Dressed in winter white, yet, no
two quite the same.

They gathered around a tall tree
made of Knotty Pine,
Dressing it from top to bottom in
tinsel with red and green lights
Of every kind!

Atop it lies the Northern Star
singing, "Jesus is my light" . . .

Gathered around the base of this
tree, tiny animals danced in
Tinsel filled lights.

December's voice chilled out,
"Let's call it, 'Christmas Night'."

Adele Foster
MY FATHER'S HOUSE
I always get a good feeling
when I enter my Father's house
He touches me, gives me strength,
and guidance, in which I need.
It is always a good feeling to
know
He's there.
And I can reach out and feel;
Somehow get touched back.
It's a good feeling to know
that when I enter my Father's
house
I will find peace
that I can carry from now until
eternity.

Miss. Donnie E. Nash
I CALL YOUR NAME
I call your name when I'm lonely
I call your name when I'm feeling
low
I call your name whenever I
think of you,
and how we used to sit and talk
of crazy things
to get into

I never thought in a million
years, that you would go away
leaving me here all alone night
and day

I don't know what to do with
myself
I don't hang out at places, we
used to go
they only bring back memories,
and how that hurts me so

Hope that you find what you're
looking for
and get your act altogether
Hope that you never forget the
love we once shared together

Honey I miss you, oh how I miss
you
hope that I'm the one you come
home to

I call your name when I'm lonely
I call your name when I'm feeling
low
I call your name whenever I
think of you
I call your name, I call your name

Tim-Keith
NEW WAVE
I dream of fire
the gods taunt me
I wake. shouting liar, defiantly.
succumb to the violence of
inner torment
drink from the wounds genesis
aroma,
opium taste
ceramic tile
white on white
position,
the nile
(fluorescent flight)
slurred image mirrored
six years old
under a water hose
naked my soul

see me inate
in desired hate
life,
imitate
solution-dilution?

I plant the seed
(no soul)
(no ego)
a new breed
(no ego)
(no soul)
it doesn't bleed.

Wilma E. Mathers
PEACE
Sometimes,
When sadness,
Comes over me,
I reach out,
Beyond,
What I can see.

The stars,
And the moon,
And white,
Floating clouds.
Somewhere,
There's peace.

Bryan J. (Jack) Archer, Sr.
THE REGULAR ARMY MAN
[Dedicated to my wife, Hazel S.
Archer with all my love.
December 9, 1982]
He ain't no gold lace belvidere to
sparkle in the sun . . .
He doesn't wear a gray cockade
nor posies on his gun . . .
He is no pretty soldier boy, so

lovely, spick and span . . .
He wears a crust of tan and dust,
the Regular Army Man,
The marching, parching, pipe clay
starching
Regular Army Man.

He's not at home in Sunday
School, nor at a special tea,
And on the day he gets his pay
He's apt to spend it free.
He is no temperance advocate . . .
He likes to fill the can.
He's somewhat tough . . . and
maybe rough . . .
This Regular Army Man . . .
This rarin', tearin' . . . sometime
swearin'
Regular Army Man.

There are no tears shed over him
When he goes off to war;
He gets no speech from
Ministers—
Or from the Governor:
He packs his little gripsack up
And trots off in the van
To start the fight—and start it
right—
This Regular Army Man,
The rattling battling Colt or
Gatlin
Regular Army Man.

He makes no fuss about the job
nor does he talk so brave,
He knows he's in to fight and win
or else to fill a grave.
He is no mama's darling, but he
does the best he can . . .
He is the chap who wins the
scrap, the Regular Army Man,
The dandy, handy, starch and
sandy, *Regular Army Man!*

Patrick Allen Reed
MAN KILLS
Do not cry, it's only a fly.
I killed today!
Just a fly, but I don't know why.
I killed today!
Buzzed my head, so I made it dead.
I killed today!
Made it dead, it splatted red.
I killed today!
I KILLED TODAY! I KILLED
TODAY! I KILLED TODAY!
Just one little fly, I know not why.
I killed today!

(I wonder what it's like to kill a
man?)

Jack Knee
LOVELY LO
I was sitting on a bar stool one
warm September night,
When I espied a dark-haired
maiden, about to take a flight
But when her eyes met mine, my
body knew, it was going to be
her for me
And the angels watching from
above, would surely all agree

As we walked toward each other;
she, as graceful as a swan,
Her raven hair ashining, and her
brown eyes sparkling warm
My heart was beating faster, as
closer we drew near,
And my mind was spinning
wildly, almost more than I
could bear

We exchanged the usual greetings,
she said, "My name is Lo"
And that if I were not too busy,
would I take her to a show
I said, "It would be a pleasure, to
escort such a lovely girl,"
So, we left the crowds behind us,
to give the world a whirl

We spent long hours together and
our love began to grow
We went dancing, dining, touring
and tripping through the snow
She said, "My love for you is
strong McNee; things are the
best they've ever been"
I felt like Leo the Lion, a monarch
of his den

And then one day the sky fell in,
she said, "It's time that we must
part"
I don't know why it happened,
but it left a scar upon my
heart . . . yet,
I know that there's a Leprechaun,
who Somewhere, Somehow will
know,
And who will guide her safely
back to me, My Sweet, My
Lovely Lo.

L.J.V. Bennett
YOUR SIDE OF THE ROAD
*[To Henry, who gets all the
blame.]*
Love,
So small a word,
So powerful a feeling.

Engulf me with your love.
Take me away
From the mess of my life,
For I don't want to stay
On this side of the road.

Your beautiful eyes
Can lift me high
Above the grasp
Of the well-meaning leeches,
To the warmer, safer security
Of your caring arms.

Take me, my body,
I cannot help but give all to you
Just for one kiss,
That would last forever.

I live in a dream
And you are reality.
Take me for yourself
And awaken me with your love.

Charlotte Trevillyan Sheward
**Hammock 'Neath the
Willow Tree**
*[This poem is dedicated to my
Beloved Sister Edna Trevillyan]*
Remember when our chores were
done?
'Twas just before the setting sun.
When off we'd scamper across the
lea
To the Hammock 'Neath the
Willow Tree.
The "Weeping Willow," we would
say,
Because of tears we shed that day—
A broken doll—a finger sore—
Our mongrel "Rags" who was no
more.

And then on lazy days we'd swing,
And listen to the Robins sing,
Or crickets chirping in the glen—

So long ago! We marveled when
The busy bees one day we found
Made their honycombs on the
ground.
We watched the wee lambs gone
astray
That gamboled on their
homeward way.

The things we planned—the
World to see.
Each billowy cloud a ship at sea
That we would sail—just you and
me.
The Hebrides—China—to
Zanzibar.
And now I'm wondering where
you are.
We'd sail until a lone cow's moo
Made us embark at Timbuktu.

For you a Lady wished to be—
A castle huge—and guests for tea.
I wonder if you think of me,
Swinging in a Hammock 'Neath
the Willow Tree.

Posina
YESTERDAY
*[If you are or have been apart
from someone that you love
and miss, this poem is
dedicated to "You". If you are
not or have not been separated
from someone you love, this is
for "You", my reader.]*
My lonely, tattered heart arises
from within today,
It is aware that he is coming
home to stay.

I cleaned and pressed the bed
sheets today,
Apart from him, I will no longer
lay.

I am a timeworn oak tree that
curtsies limbs today,
My attire will never again fray.

I saw his face mirrored in a
bantam lake as it danced today,
We shared the raidiant sunset of
May.

I carefully peeked through the
sea's waves as they stir fiercely
today,
They affirm his arrival from
faraway.

The sun's warm rays encircle my
shoulders today,
The brilliant light points the ship
the right way.

All of the twinkling stars came
out to whisper in my ears today,
They said, "This is your luckiest
day"!

The whole sky dimples the moon
and earth today,
Heaven arms the ocean to widen
the bay.

God graciously looked upon me
today,
He brought back my Yesterday!

Tanya V. Lamb
HAPPINESS
Passionate carresses
Lengthy dissertation
Followed by brief flay of words
Voluptuous dinner
Rock and classical music

In background beating mean waves
Hot sun on bronzed bodies
Sand swept beaches
White dunes in shape of corridors
Tree covered mountains
With views of world to be
Trails through sunlit meadows by
the lagoon
The breeze so invigorating
Gives rise to new beginning for
the day
Pleasure in exhaustion
Pride from sweat and no regret.

Rhonda L. Kinney
MY FUTURE IN A PHONE
Ring.
Anxiety grips my heart.
Pulse racing, palms sweating,
Tension convulsing my muscles.
Is this the one? Is it for me?
No.

Unbidden tears fill my eyes.
It's so hard to wait.
Will they never call?

Hope.
My last strand of recourse.
It lifts my head,
Dries my eyes,
And whispers to me,
Wait.

It's frightening
Knowing that a single call,
Can change the rest of my life.

Ring.
The pit in my stomach tells me
this is it.
I tremble as I hold the phone,
My voice barely sounds.
Did I make it?
Yes!

Phyllis Gersch
THE OLD MAN IS DIEING
I knelt by an old man's bed last
night,
For the old man was dieing.
I knelt by his bed and wept last
night,
For someone should be crying.

I nursed him with a gentle hand,
And asked "Doesn't his family
understand?"
For the old man would have died
alone last night,
And then God would have been
crying.

Maria Adessa
BELIEVER'S PRAYER
[For Jane Buscaglia]
I believe in nature,
And the beauty of her ways.
I believe in sunshine,
That brightens up the days.

I oft' believe in silver clouds,
And thunderous stormy nights,
I believe in wishing stars,
Their radient faith; in light.

I believe in music,
As the language of us all,
I believe in loving friends,
To catch us if we fall.

I shall always follow rainbows,
With their lucky pots of gold,
I do believe in fairytales,
That shall never grow too old.
I believe in poetry,

As messages of the heart,
With symbols bold, and meanings
strong,
Which never seem to part.

I often see with observing eyes,
The truth told through lies . . .
I believe in miracles,
And faith that never dies.

I believe in myself,
And freaks of nature too,
But most of all, and of much
concern,
I believe in you . . .

Sharon Speaks
DAYS PAST
Yesterday, it seems so far away
Today, grinding a path for
tomorrow
Next week, the world may end by
then
Yesterday, oh forgotten yesterday
Never to be recaptured

Longing for tomorrow
Now wishing again for yesterday.

Terri Kelly
UNTITLED
*[Metal Fence will appear in T.
M. Kelly's new book of poetry,
VOICES FROM THE
WARHEAD (c. 1982), and is
dedicated to those who will to
see all sides of the fence.]*
Metal fence
rusts its shadow
against yellow trees

nearby,
a polyester man
bends over
flowering nudes

Cindy Marie Sarno
DESTINY
It must have been too long ago,
I had a dream that wont let go.
So I took my mind and set it free,
I had to find my destiny.
All seemed so easy but that was
then,
Searchng so far; finding no end.
When I can't go on I close my
eyes,
Will I ever find where my
future lies?
Now I believe its time to do
All the things I've wanted to.
So wont you listen; wont you see,
Its now the time; Destiny.

Ruben S. Rodriguez
HER CHEST OF HOPE
*[As with the rest of my life this
poem was done with Claudi' on
my mind. So this poem and
these words are for her. I love
you. P. S. Thank you. After all
you did teach me to be a
genius, Honey.]*
She keeps all of
her dreams
locked away inside
her chest of hope
She is so sublte
in her beauty

Her secret thoughts
kept hidden
from those too
blind to see

She is so subtle

in her beauty
So much within—
a heart
that burns
with love

She could really love
if given the chance
She is different
in her beauty
different
in her love
Her love is real
really love

She keeps her secret
dreams locked away
in the deepest corners
of her chest
of hope

Leonard L. Wehrfritz
ATTITUDES
Sometimes its hard to understand
So often taken for granted
Lost among a thousand tongues
Smothered in ideas so old

Values placed, in wrong directions
Pursuits, not our own
Lusts dumbfounded, but proven
    right
Freedoms foresaken to others

Stand up and claim
Our rights, our adventures
The dreams sold out for nothing
Find in the heart, the power
    belonging
To claim progress as our own

The tyrants are dead
If we wish it

Pat Withington
REFLECTIONS
It is not till love has gone
that one searches for reflections
in another's eyes
and only sees one's own.
When the hand feels the cold
and the voice cracks on a familiar
    word,
when the tongue attempts
    thoughts
and falls into a chasm
where there is no escape,
then one knows
how slight a word
can direct a path toward another
    world
where buildings slant into
    another sun
and the crocus melts into a late
    snow.
How tender is a word, or the lack
    of it,
at the time of silence.
How empty a corridor
            where footsteps
                    have fallen.

Cathy Baker
CHRISTMAS DREAMING
Ah, Christmas . . .
I feel your presence even though
    you're still days away. You
    sneak into my mind and
    whisper magic words of past
    memories, and once again, I
    become a starry-eyed child.

I look through your window as
    you beckon me to come closer,
    and see the traces of what

you hold in store.

You envelop me in your world, as
    your special once-a-year spirit
    awakes inside me again, grabs
    my hand, and whirls me into a
    land of Pine and Noels.

The sweet scent of a tall,
    glittering, evergreen dances
    beneath my nose just for an
    instant before it's over ruled by
    the aromas of a Christmas
    kitchen, where moms and
    aunts add final touches to their
    masterpiece.

You pull me by the hand, upstairs
    to the bedrooms, where secret
    Santas are almost buried in
    bright wrapping paper and
    bows as they hurry through the
    last minute wrapping, tapeing
    and tagging . . . pausing only a
    moment to pull that stray
    piece of tape off of their socks,
    or to hunt the always
    disappearing scissors, lost again
    in the Holiday scatter.

Your music of joy hangs in the air
    both indoors and out; song and
    laughfter have come to life all
    around the world once again
    under the spell of your magic.

You lead me into a candle lit
    church, where the presence of
    God is more overwhelming
    than any other night of the
    year . . . and we all wonder as
    we bow our heads, if it was on
    a night such as this that the
    shepherds saw the star.

The hope of the whole world was
    born almost two thousand
    years ago, and He still lives
    today . . . sad, we only
    celebrate once a year.

Gerry Laine
FATHERS OF LATE
Take what is with feeling said
To wife or son or daughter
And brew it with what deeds are
    done
They'll mix like oil and water
For what is felt stays chained
    below
Hate, fear and pride the keepers
With understanding, love, tears,
    hope
And empathy the sleepers
We've played our part of fool so
    well
Who really be our captors?
For does our fate float on the wind
Or are we just good actors.

April Vasilaitis
FAREWELL SONG
It's so far away when the sky cries,
faded stars are gone.
A dreamer's Love has come to rest
left without a Farewell Song.

The skys the heart that was left
    broken
The stars the eyes that cry.
The moons the mind left unopened
The birds the Love left to fly.

It's so far away when the sun
    shines,
once a Love that came to call.

So high above the empty trees
left without time to fall.

The clouds the soul that drifts
    away
The seas the heart that drowns.
The rains the tears that come to
    fall
The suns the Love that someone
    found.

Virginia Sue Bowden
**The Love and Warmth Of a
Friend**
*[To my friend Oydee 'Dee'
McClendon whose constant
caring helped me through a
difficult period of my life.]*
In misery I withdrew myself and
    hid my life away
A conflict stirred within my soul,
    a price I'd have to pay
The price I paid was loneliness,
    my thoughts I could not share
And while I held my pain inside I
    sank to deep despair
The ultimate decision was too
    much for me to face
'Til the climax of my long ordeal
    brought a sampling of God's
    Grace
I stripped my sick soul naked and
    exposed the hurt inside
To friends who'd always been
    there while I'd preferred to hide
And all the times I'd suffered and
    my feelings could not share
I'd missed a treasured blessing
    . . .One that simply says "I
    care".
For when I whisked away my
    pride my blessings had no end
I had so long deprived myself of
    the love and warmth of a friend.

Ferenc Karpati
TREES IN WINTER
White are the trees,
Crystal melodies,
Immaculate white.
Sleeping brides,
Only
Their hearts are beating
Silently to the night . . .

David Terralavoro
THE PARADE
Today at two o'clock a parade
    will be on main street
Many people gather, to the kids
    the parade is a treat
The kids make sure that they
    will be there they don't delay
I look out of my second floor
    apartment
window and decide this is where
    I'll stay
I watch the parade begin with a
    band
Horns and trumpets are played
People are sitting on curbs other
    people stand Everyone enjoys
    the parade
I am pleased with the parade I
    stare
as a girl tosses a baton in the air
She catches it as it lands
then spins it fast in her hand
Down the street rides a fire
    engine moving slow
I see firemen that I know
The driver lets the whistle blow

People are waving to the firemen
The driver lets the whistle blow
    again
The parade is about to end
The music is no longer loud
Smiling faces are still on many
    people in the crowd
I enjoyed the parade
I will always keep this
memory and never let it fade

Beth Gina Broyles
SIREN OF THE TUILERIES
Hulls scrape the granite base of
    the fishmouthed fountain in
    the Garden,
where pirate ships in black and
    orange steer past the
    threatening Siren.

A gypsy galleon encounters the
    seas and strains to remain on
    course;
Foundering deeply in sea green
    valleys, she battles the wind for
    control.

Balance regained and sails
    unfurled the ship slowly
    crosses the channel
To be caught by the lull of the
    Siren's song, disguising the roar
    of the water.

The ocean weaves a hypnotic
    path to the waves crashing
    close on the rocks,
Where discordant lyrics resound
    through the earth and waken
    the boy on the shore.

Not unlike Swift reporting on
    Gulliver—the boy splashes
    hard through his dream
and stretches his arms to reach
    for the mast, lifting his prize
    from the sea.

Though he scratches his knee on
    the granite base of the fountain
    that sings in the Garden,
the boy climbs up, lured to the
    heights . . . where his voice
    joins that of the Siren.

Cheryl Wieder
THE JOURNEY
Open your wings and fly
    not so far that you are gone
To make a difficult good-bye
    and the journey will seem long
But productive your travels will be
    you will become aware and
    strong
When deep within yourself you
    can see
    only then will your wings
    cease flight
and things once wrong will soon
    be right

Karen Lux
MY SUNSHINE
When sticks and stones don't
    work,
And the words do hurt,
And turning the other cheek
Only causes matching bruises,
You walk into my life
And make my sun shine.

M. Kelley Charnock
A PRAYER FOR US
    May we always be happy
And always have the others heart
Forever be together; not apart.

Let us never ridicule,
And not be made a fool;
But be at peace,
As soft as fleece
May we be gentle always,
To our children in all ways.
And teach them to love,
To learn the ways of love.
And pray, to heaven above:
That this prayer comes true.
Make our love forever new . . .
AMEN

Michele Pye
My Grandfather's Death
My grandfather
    died today
and the injustice
    of it, is
I never knew him.

My parents moved
    out west
befoe I was born,
so, besides pictures,
I've only seen him
    twice
on two short holidays.

Really,
    he's my
    mother's father
she's the one hurt
    by it all.

I want
    to cry
    but I
have no reason.

Therese Cichon
SANGUINE ABSTRACTION
I was so transfixed
by the hypnotic patterns
formed by
her flowing blood;
the fact that her brains
had been dashed out
by some handicapped
    motorcyclist
didn't puncture my
    consciousness
till several months later.

Laurel A. Elder
OUR PHONE CALLS
    [Steven, this is yours . . . still.]
When they yell up the stairs,
and say "phone is for you"
my heart beats so quickly
'cause I'm hoping it's you.

I run to answer it,
and then I say "hello",
and when you talk, I smile
you make my day, you know.

When someone is at home
I can't stay on too long.
When I don't say too much
you ask me what is wrong.

The time goes by so fast,
and soon I've got to go.
"I'll talk to you later,
and I love you, you know"!

Lea Roberts
HIGHWAY SPLENDOR
Lovely trees—never had any kids
    climb them.
Silent sentries of the ribboning
    highways.
Passive witnesses to traffic's
    constant flow.

Eternal watchers o'er the concrete
    lawn.
You give us beauty to relieve the
    monotnous miles.
You announce the change of
    seasons in such clever ways—
Presenting blossoms, nuts, fruits,
    and berries to refresh weary
    wanderers.
Bikers and hikers relax within
    your cooling shade as birds
    abound above.

If I had time to stop I would pat
    each of you on the trunk and
    say,
"Good job! Well done! We love
    you!"

Jon Truman Chisholm
UNTITLED
    *[Dedicated in memory of my
    Dad John Kenneth Chisholm.]*
        Blue butterfly
wings folding, unfolding
in glittering sunlight brightness
resting so still, calm, unnoticed
shall I touch? I cannot
for in a moment
wings spread, swiftly
not to be touched
returning to flight
instantly rising
above all danger
climbing
higher
until
again
rest.

Vincenzo LXX Giallonardo

Vincenzo LXX Giallonardo
Cosmic Celestial Equations
*[I Dedicate My Poetry to All
the Girls and Boys of Planet
Eartha etc for the Uplifting of
Mankind and Womankind etc
for Ever O One's Ever Nobler
Holier Higher Truer SELF O
Body and Soul and Mind and
Spirit etc Forever In LOVE!]*
11/13/82 (70th Anniversary of
My Cosmic Celestial
Conception O Genes etc O In
The Holy Order ! LXX etc.) O
MY COSMIC CELESTIAL
EQUATIONS . . . 1930 etc as
Supreme Architect and
Engineer I Organized My
Electric Class Into Super
Human Beings of Planet Eartha
etc Poets Artists Scientists etc
as Supreme Commander I

Visioned a Fleet of Space Ships
(O My Time Space Energy
Oracle Arks Vorteces etc)
Darting Through the Universa
O'The Deep With Meteor
Brightness Converting Pure
Cosmic Celestial Energy Into
Atoms and Apples and Pretty
Girls and New Bodies for My
SELF Now and Then etc In Our
Computerized Womb and
Tomb for Ever Forever Ha !
 . . . 1937 On My Walk etc
Around About Planet Eartha
etc O On Arriving In Paris
France O MIMI I Chanced to
Visit Napoleon's Tomb Where I
Was Inspired to Write to Hitler
and Mussolini and Stalin and
The International Bankers FDR
etc and I Spoke "Please Meet
Me In Napoleon's Tomb to
Confer About The Future of
Mankind and Womankind In
The Explorations of The
Universe" etc

 . . . 1945 During That Titanic
Year When Mussolini and FDR
and Hitler etc Depart and The
United Nations Emerges etc O
World War Two Comes to
Sudden End About My 8/13/45
Birth Day 32 With The First
Use of "Atom Bombs" etc and
On 6/1/45 I Was Inspired to
Write "Dear Girls and Boys of
Planet Eartha" etc "as The
PHOENIX Aspires" etc Setting
THE STAGE for My First
Universal Eternal Party
Address Which I Delivered at
Belmont Plateau In
Philadelphia Pennsylvania
U.S.A. On The First "EARTHA
DAY" 4/22/70 When I Summed
Up The Awful Awesome Day's
Events "O This Is a Day O a
Time of PRECISION VISION
DECISION O Not Only to
Sustain The Beauty and The
Love and The Joys of GENIUS
But For THE SURVIVAL of
LIFE ITSELF ! O In Truth and
Love etc I AM Vincenzo LXX
Giallonardo with a Mailing
Address at 309 North Simpson
Street, Philadelphia,
Pennsylvania 19139 U.S.A.
Planet Eartha O'The Deep From
a Sunny Forest Vale By Stream"
etc.

Linda Jane Bartlett
MERCY STREET
Once I traversed Mercy Street,
A long, long time ago.
It was narrow, it was rutty,
It was lined with vagabonds.
But the rags of ancient martyrs
Brightened in the sun,
And smiles of orphaned children
Spread the hope of things to come.
Yes, I wandered down that lane
Alone. So sad and I was crying,
When a gamon shyly took my
    hand,
And emptied it of grief.

Betty Stebbins
A MIGHTY MAN WAS HE
Noah was a mighty man,
A mighty man was he,
He built a great big ark,
And saved his family.

Samson was a mighty man,
A mighty man was he,
He took the jaw bone of an ass,
And killed the enemy.

David was a mighty,
A mighty man was he,
He took a simple slingshot,
And killed the Philistine.

Jesus was a mighty man,
A mighty man was he,
He Gave his life upon a tree,
To save all humanity.

Joni M. Worthington
THE STAR—CROSSED SEA
It's the Lorelei's love song
From that deep green place
Of mysterious mute fish
And fathomous space,
Which lure all ships of sail
And their seaman slave
To Neptune's far ocean depths
And a Twelveth House grave;
For the fated call of she
With its vow of love
Rides the wakes of all vessels
Holding men above,
And the cresting waves on high
Hear her nether plea
And bear its haunting lyrics
O'er a Piscean Sea.

Kathi Coe
HOPE
As an anchor secures a ship
So must hope secure our dreams.
For if an anchor loses its hold
The ship may be lost at sea.
And if hope escapes from our heart
So is a dream lost among all other
    sadnesses.

Doris M. King
IT'S LOFTY TOP
Father, you showed your fury today
Rain, sleet and hail hit us with a
    slam last night.
The trees were so beautiful
Draped in pure glittering white
    diamonds
Wrapped in ice as clear as glass
That glistens and sparkles in the
    sun
When it peeked from behind the
    clouds
To see, what You had done.
The wind dost blow this cold,
    glassy ice about
Hitting windows, cars and such.
The pine tree lost its lofty top

And its neclace of sparkling jewels,
When it plummeted to the ground
Taking the mighty oaks strong arms
And the electrical wires, also down.
What destruction did lie about?
Of branches, broken and strewn
Arms all crumpled and in awkward sorts
Lay in their death bed position.
So solemn, quiet and abrupt,
the pine tree; the oak tree
In its final plunge to earth
From being lord, on high.
Up so tall and straight, was I,
Before this force of wind, rain and sleet
Came to rest on Thee and I.
Oh, Father, there was I, so very important,
Before "I", came to rest, on "Thee."

Peter F. Berkery
YOUR LOSS
[Dedicated to Barbara McCoy Berkery whose love makes' the distance across a room far shorter.]
How many times have I reached across a room
To touch you with my words,
I really can't recall,
Knowing, all the more, the pain of your loss
For never really having done so.

Now . . . all my eloquence escapes me
To recall yesterday when I could only say,
'You were too beautiful to die,'
Denying my sadness, my humanity . . .
My last real feeling for you.

I grieve for you as one half alive,
Mourning you as my own passing. . .
Fantacizing times that might have been,
When a look, words could have given play to action
For the distance across a room to be far shorter,
Far less lonely without, you.

John Petrali
THE SAD GOOD—BYS
As we waited at the station
For the train to appear,
My heart and mind grew weary.
I knew the time was very near.

As the train came to a stop
We quickly said good—by
Like thieves on the run.
God only knows how hard I wanted to cry.

The train slowly pulled away.
Through the windows we waved good—by.
I could see the sadness upon his face
As he took a deep sigh.

As I sat down I hung my head
And began to think, could this be the end?
Or would there be another time?
As the train pulled around the bend.

I buried my face in both hands.

And for many miles I felt bleak.
But I kept on holding the kiss
That my son had planted on my cheek.

Doris Courtney Lowdermilk
What Our Flag Means To Me
[To President Ronald Reagan, January—, 1981.]
Our flag that flies o're land and sea
What does it mean to you? This is what it means to me
Long sunny days so bright
Lovers' lane in the moonlight

Secret walks out in the park
Holding hands when it is dark
This is not a hall of fame
My rose covered path up from the lane

Just a home and big red barn
Out in the country on a farm
The apple orchard in the spring
Our harvest with it's great blessing

The cow gives us her sweet milk to drink
Jelly glasses cooling near the sink
Eggs, we count them out in twelves
Canned foods stored high upon the shelves

This land of ours, how bountiful it be
And Lord, you gave it all to me
Tommy's freckled little face
Dancing logs in the fireplace

Winter now has really come
Snowball fun for everyone
Free from suppression, woe or care
Is there better anywhere?

Lorra Anne Heutmaker
The One Thing I Miss
I have looked beyond the tears
and have seen the pain,
conscious of your burdens and fears.
But there is one thing I have not seen.

I have felt beyond the touch of your hand,
to draw upon your inner strength
and to absorb the tenderness of your soul.
But there is one thing I have not felt.

I have known the love you share,
have felt the presence of your faith
and followed the wisdom of your knowledge.
But there is one thing I have not known.

I have heard the softness of your voice,
the plaintive sound of bitter disappointment
and the rapture of unspeakable joy.
But there is one thing I have not heard.

I should have no reason to complain,
But even after all this
I only wish to hear—to hear that you love me.
This is the one thing I miss.

Jerry Wolcott
JUST BE
Beyond the wailing wall
of our sorrows
Where Soul never borrows
but is found fulfilled
                              I meet you
Beyond the gleaming abyss
of ecstatic joy
Where Soul has surrendered
to Perfect Love
                              I greet you
Beyond all subtle urgency
of your need to be
In the now stripped
of description
In the present moment
of the Eternal
Love abides in the beauty
of a flower
And in the power
to KNOW and FEEL and SEE

Susan M. Clark
MY CHILD
[To Jenny, with all my love.]
I brought you into this world
In the likeness of your father and me.
With the best of us both to start with
To build into your own personality.

I hurt for you as only a parent could.
And try to protect you from life's unjusts.
But I, also hurt you as only a parent would
With discipline, with truth, with love.

I've watched you sleeping 'til tears come to my eyes,
I've watched you playing—so content in your little world.
I've begged God to help you when you're ill,
And my heart has broken when I've made you sad.

You are unique, child of my heart.
You are my image, but a better one.
You bring happiness to my soul.
I am yours as you are mine.

My child, I need you.
My child, I love you.
Help me to teach you—
Help me to learn.
Let me be your friend.

Sheila Murphy
JOHN LENNON
An unpredictable clown whose unique style
Combined outrageous antics with musical talent
A magnetic personality, twinkling eyes, and mischievous smile
Gave the special gift of laughter loved by all

On a fateful night in December
Tragedy struck a living legend
An assailant with his revolver
Took the life of John Lennon

His life became an unsung song
That touched our very souls
For of the four, he was the gentle one
Whose convictions were his words

In a violent world of hypocracy
John said "Give peace a chance"
For it alone is the key
To eternal love and brotherhood

Tho his words were an inspiration
He was the symbol of hope
And to an angry young generation
Gave meaning to understanding

Look to the horizons beyond reality
Here lies the quest for truth
Fear not, our dreams and fantasy's
'Cause we'er not the only ones

John, you gave so much and yet
We still demanded more
In years to come, we will not forget
The music, message or the man

Daisie A. Schies
UNTITLED
[Dedication to my young friend, Carlos Madrid, whose inspiration it was to help me to walk again, after I had been paralyzed. (1976)]
Our Song . . .
    is like a melody
    played on the strings of a violin
Reaching . . .
    far into the very depth of the soul
Exploring and Recreating . . .
                every vibration
Which emulates . . .
                from the very breath
of God.

Judith Twist
THE MURDER OF WOMAN
Linda, you were right.
He is
many—sided,
the reluctant pupil of our myopic eyes.
We are not quardrangled enough
to close his breach,
as canyoned as his personality.
He is cold and hot,
but rarely warm;
sometimes left and
sometimes right
but rarely warm.
His dance, unknown,
begs for us to solve and chisel.
He is guessing and
He is roulette.
His valleys and mines
are games of darkness.

Man—
You are this and
You are that.

Edie Tedrow
SUN SONG
There's a song to be sung in the morning,
    When the world is beginning to smile.
It's a song that you sing with no rhyming
    And it's never in keeping with style.

There's a song that you sing in the evening
    When the sun is beginning to fade—
It's a song to be sung without music,
    If your spending your life in the shade.

Then there's the song to sing thru a lifetime
With music and cymbals and drums,
To the best of life's greatest musicians,
When you're spending your life in the sun!

Kent Glenzer
I See Two Lovers Lie Down In Damp Grass
A strident discord flows in melody.
　　　　　　　　In coliseums
Formed by pizzicato winds,
That pluck a well—tuned branch, transport the sound
Of crickets from across the river, bring
Their whispers near, and laugh with tickling tales
In intimations of that which they have
Beyond horizons learned,
　　　　　This child can dream.
Above silk fields and cotton waterfalls,
Below the inky purple of the night,
In aqueous air that's filled with equal light,
I dream and know I am the many calls
That mingle in this solubility,
Of pore—filled earth and pregnant dripping sky.

Sophia Carmel Chou
AN IMAGE
Palms up against the breath of the moon,
My hands reaching so high.
But my eye touches further.
Into the heights of the heavens
I catch a glimpse of my reflections.
Every moment surpasses me.
Life is in the heavens.

Jackie Larsen
Thanks For Your Professional Help
Wisdom, care, and tenderness
Were all wrapped up in love
And served to me abundantly
To help me rise above
The pain and helplessness I felt
When illness came my way.
The doctors, staff, and nurses too
Put sunshine in each day.
Your prayers and cards and flowers too
Have touched emotionaly strings
And from the bottom of my heart
I thank you for these things.

Elizabeth Winslett
DOLL MAN
Wonder where you are tonight.
My Little Doll Man.
Wonder if you will call,
or maybe write.
It's so lonely since you went away.
I stood by the gate that day,
and watched 'till you were out of sight.
You and your little blue Van.
I remember we both laughed,
When first you showed me the small tag
you have on your Van or Motor Home.
That says, "Retired. No home, No money,

No address,"
I laughed most of the time,
When first you came to visit.
You were so nice, so kind.
So energetic, so handsome.
A wonderful mind.
I laughed, that is, 'till I realized you are ruthless.
To none are you true.
Least of all your self.
Totally irresponsible, My little Doll man,
You use your retirement as an excuse
just to roam.
From one lonely woman to an other.
I remember our days at the beach
With the young folks passing by
Smiling at the two Retirees
Building castles in the sand.
You will be coming back one day before too long.
Singing the same old song.
You can not stay away,
No matter how hard you try.
But this time, My little Doll Man.
You will learn that no one,
not even you.
Can be as ruthless as I.

Connie Ratliff
A DOCTOR'S PRAYER
Lord, may the patients I see every day
Know that I care in a special way,
Grant me wisdom that I may see
And treat their needs, whatever they be!

Grant me compassion, a sympathetic ear
Even if unspoken, may I hear
Every cry, let me understand
And stretch forth to them a helping hand!

Guide my thoughts, my words, my deeds
Let me do all the good I can
And may I find my own needs met
By serving Thee and Man!

Ms. Dietrich Eufaye Ethridge
BORN OF FIRE
[More than love, inspiration, and dedication, I must commend, duly my thanks to God for rendering unto me, Earvin Arthur Mayfield, the most earth shaking man to have attained my infinite love as we as one were, born of fire.]
Born of the fire sign
Born to kill or die
Strong as the holds in the night
Revengeful to those unkind
Remembers the days in time
Born of the sparks of fire
Born for eternal life
Waiting by the light
Hoping to grasp the right
Hand to mine
Love is my daily rhyme
Born hot as natures flow
Born deadly to those who know
Challenge is their bread
Control is they're own sped web
Born just as flame
Born to you
A bond that shall forever live.

Charon B. Huett
ELEGY: To Robert
I always love the ocean
He did too, I know
It was the oceans' magic potion
That called him there to go.

I wonder what he thought that day
Did he cry out in pain?
The ocean took him on that day,
If he cried, he cried in vain.

No one wants to laugh today
But there's nothing anyone can do
If the ocean comes to take you away
What can you possibly do?

Retha Chapman Brown

Retha Chapman Brown
SHE SAW LOVE
She could hear the laughter of another child.
And sense the beauty of a friendly smile.
She could feel the warmth of the morning sun.
She was very happy and had a lot of fun.

She enjoyed the rebirth that comes with spring.
She felt great joy from simple little things.
She could smell the sweetness of the flowers too.
There were many things she could do.

She felt the love her family had to share.
She knew their love would always be there.
She trusted her heart whenever she could feel,
That someone near her was not being real.

She never learned to catch a ball.
She still had fun and was liked by all.
There were some things she could not do.
She lost her sight when she was only two.

Diane M. Prusinski
DUNES
It's been a long time since the desert bloomed rasped the weary and weather worn sage
The dunes've moved and the bush should be groomed with the passing of daily rain's rage.

Seems barren and fragile to unaided eyes he was quick but quiet to note
Once the greens take root, a seedling may fly or in streams' running waters will float.

I once thought the desert would always remain he gestured by raising a brow
I was wrong to think it had dried up to drain with only a saddle to plow.

I forgot the earth tends to heal his own wounds something time, faith and love can do
He heals them alone starting deep underground and when ready forges life anew.

Apollo's the helper, Greek moon a steady guide although wounded, earth—father survives
Desert dunes are now green with colorful pride a new start from past shadowed lives.

Gwen Trimbell Pease
VOLCANO—MAY 18, 1980
[For America with its eternal changeability and to its Americans who are eternally adaptable.]
American—Washington State
spotlighted this date
erupting Mount St. Helens
alive volcano
no longer dormant
now on the go
unpredictable fate
from earth's bowels
spewed lava
ash and smoke
active nature
spectacular show
dramatic change
viewed with alarm
forest, farmland
threatened with
pregnant airflow
imminent danger
natural violence—
to humans, no stranger.

J. M. Frady
SILOS
A corn silo—
Filled with goodness
For you and for me.

A missile silo—
Filled with destruction
For you and for me.

Jack E. Barnum
JUST A FRIEND
The sunlight shines over my shoulders and the world is laid before my eyes.
I've seen so much I can't explain it at times I've lived . . . , at times I've died . . .
All life has risen to prophecy long foretold.
All past slides slowly into dust.
We are the children of the long lost saviors.
We are the truth . . . , but we are the lies . . .
No one can see to the hearts true feelings find the pain we all can hold.
No one can grasp all lifes

sorrows, see the truth as it's
been told . . .
Chances are you'll try to reason
guess my game before its end.
But what is your world but
destiny borrowed.
What am I, but just a friend . . . ?

Ruth Bennett
AFTER MARC 1916—1981
I walk around as in a daze
I move along as in a dream
The endless nights and long long
days
To me like mundane centuries
seem.

'It is not fair' I cry aloud
Impotently cursing earth and sky
Goals unfulfilled—plans gone
awry
Why did this happen? Why oh
why?

My lifelong partner I have lost
My husband—lover—and my
friend
Though 'time heals all' I am told
Yearning and anguish do not end.

Now memories are all I have
Humorous, sweet to sustain me
through life
Laughing faces framed from
bygone days
I'm still a mother though not a
wife.

Cynthia E. Williams
SAILING WITH YOU
What's it like out at sea?
Sometimes I wish I could find out
But isn't it scary out in the night?
There are probably all kinds of
things to see
Is it really as calming and
peaceful as it looks?
Just wish I could feel it all one
time
How many times has it been for
you?
You probably can't understand
how I feel
But how was it your first time
out?
Maybe it was frightening to you,
too
But time gets rid of all that
doesn't it?
And yet I suppose you'd never get
used to it all
I guess it's a special feeling upon
the water!
How I would love to be there
with you
But you know what?
I guess I am

George Beecher
SONG AND SEQUEL
Who is thinking in the stars
Who is painting on the clouds
Who is laughing in the words
Hinted in these sounds of ours

Who is moody in the change
That cycles through the sky
Who is far more hot and cold
With love than you and I

All this world is like a flower
All its violence a song
Where in all atomic power
Do I belong

Pilgrim stars are in your head
You are painting on a cloud
What you hear are coded signs
Recalled aloud

Men stir old hate with sticks of
atom bombs
We staunch an ulcer with the
cosmic dust
Salt—thirsting to voyage on
exploding waves
Then leave our sea shell
shining on the sand
Ready to bear a bather from the
foam

Timothy E. Miller
A FLOWER AND A TREE
Appearing dead but still alive,
An old tree stands, a flower
beside.
The leaves fall, the color goes.
But still a flower, the color shows.
The tree is tall, strong and stout,
The flower small, without a
doubt.
The tree's seen joy as its seen
tears,
It's been there for an hundred
years.
The flower listens to what the big
trees say,
It's been there for one whole day.
The cold comes, the wind blows,
The direction in which the flower
goes.
It blows away into the east,
The wind becomes the flower's
beast.
The flower's gone the tree still
stands,
Stretching, appearing to look to
foreign lands.
Barren now of all its leaves,
The tree looks just like other
trees.
But with a rain drop on his eye,
one last thing the flower said,
Leaving with a sigh, his friend the
tree of all this time was finally
. . . really dead.

Joseph Piegaro
IN A MYSTERY DESIRED
In a mystery desired,
By a long sought soothing fire,
Lies a child born of desire in the
night.

Though she sits in lonely stance,
By the fireplace entranced,
While the kindles gaily dance in
humble flight.

In the night she whispers tones,
Through the empty house she
roams,
Bearing agony alone in endless
blight.

Accused of crimes which were
untrue,
Her lose of innocence was
viewed,
Giving up to what was you in
search of light.

As she lay waiting in the dark,
To hear the calling of the lark,
To send away the deadly shark to
calm her fright;

He chose to leave the child he
sired,

Causing emptiness to dire,
In this child born of desire in the
night.

Lynette Branch
I WONDER
I looked up from where I sat
wrapped in a poet's frustration
and I saw a falling star.
I wondered why something
as mighty as a star
would want to commit suicide.

Edna Rodman
THE MADONNA LILY
The Madonna Lily in the garden
The purest of white a symbol
of peace, a heavenly sight.

The Madonna Lily brings forth
blossoms when summer is nigh.
Less dormant ressurect in fall
to be viewed in winter by all.

The Madonna Lily with fragrance
so sweet, which other flowers
in garden
would want to compete.

The Madonna Lily for beauty,
splendor,
height and grace should be grown
by everyone's garden wall.

The Madonna Lily O'florist
please
do not let it become extinct.
For all these attributes no other
flower should take its place.

Ruth E. Beckwith
THE ROOSTER
We all loved to hear the rooster
Crowing in the morning hours,
Perched atop a maple booster
Showing off his vocal powers.

Sunbeams strike his gorgeous
feathers
As he struts across a limb.
Many shades of reds and heathers
Make a proud bird out of him.

When a wind was swiftly blowing
Through his many colored coat,
Then his puffed up neck was
throwing
Notes of grandeur from his
throat.

Karen L. Chabot
SAILING WITH MICHELE
We've sailed over waters,
Both the ebb and the flow:
Soared at high tide,
Coasted at low.
We've seen our reflection,
Friends, on green waves,
And glided in sunshine
On warm, summer days.
We've sailed over rough spots
When the prospects seemed sad,
And waded through knee—deep
When the weather was bad.
We've cried when the waves
Left nothing but sand,
But picked up the castle
And built it again.
We've walked all the shores,
Trudged through the night;
And watched our ships come in,
Only to sail out of sight.
But just when we thought
We were both going to drown,
Our friendship, it saved us,
And we didn't go down.

Sister M. Michael Rhatigan
BEYOND ENCOUNTER
Chaser of dreams, I, driven,
discontent with clumsy
scramblings
pace railroad tracks
disappearing in the gloom
of iron, wood and stone.

Fronting first
the crowd of daydreams
beckoned by webwork of Spirit,
quicker than winter
more silent than spectacle
of sun shifting south.

Engines throbbing fire
like great monotiths
rise out of the pale
brush and ink forests.

I hide in fields
ripe with oats and milkweed
then spill into ravines
colliding with memories of
crushed mint.

Chaos and unreason give chase.
I run . . . I fall . . .
Stumbling into the picture.

Beyond ambush and encounter
I live disguised to myself.

Sandra Hayes
I'VE GONE AWAY
I've gone away today,
but still I think of you.
Sometimes it may not seem this
way,
but what I say is true.
I miss you so all the time,
when I can't see you,
it's a crime.
No matter how far I go,
or even how close I stay—
There are times I need to talk to
you,
but don't know what to say.
You're on my mind everyday,
even when I've gone away.
I'll be back in just awhile,
so never lose that special smile.
I just can't wait to get back home,
so we can be together,
instead of all alone.

Mary Agnes Lynch
HELLO GOD
"Hello God", how are you
today?
I know you must feel fine
up there,
But, I thought I'd ask
okay?"
You must at times feel
tired,
Watching over us all,
down here,
And I want you to know
I love you so;
My, it's good to know
You're so near.

Now, don't worry about us
down here, dear God,
We will all be good for
You,
And I know, you must be
busy above,
Welcoming in Souls, who
are new.

I was just taking a
walk,

Today's Greatest Poems

In my garden, the
flowers all in bloom,
When into my mind,
Your Face did come,
And for You,
there will always be room.

Tis a beautiful
day,
Down here dear
God,
Thank You, for making
it so,
I thought, I would just
stop a minute, before
Onward I shall trod.
And think of You My Father,
and whisper, "Hello God"

Joseph Piegaro
FOREVER
Like a fresh breeze your smile
greets me;
I am a child again on my mother's
knee.
To think such love could be.
I wonder if I'm dreaming, if you
are
Really here, if I really love you.
Time winds slowly by.
The seasons change
And I want for you,
Over and over again,
Like a hunger unsatisfied,
Like a day without sunshine.
I beckon to you, awaiting your
call,
Forever in need; forever if need be,
Forever.

Frances C. Brandon
SECOND THOUGHTS
[To Raj, Acknowledging that,
being who we are, it couldn't
have happened any other way.]
What happened to the me I used
to be?
When did loving you start to
override being me?
In spite of all your warnings I had
to put loving you,
first on my list of things to do.
So now I'm alone and trying to
figure out
exactly where you end and I
begin.
Searching for the remnants of the
old me,
to somehow blend in with the
person I've become.
Hesitant & unsure, knowing only
that where I'm going
has got to be an improvement
over where I'm at.

Katharine G. Leipold
OUR FLAG
[Dedicated to my Daughters:
Barbara Johnson, Patricia
Bakley, Kathy Geary
Grandchildren: Arthur & Sheri
Lynn Bakley, Kelli Ann & Traci
Lee Geary And to Everyone
who loves "Our Flag" our
Symbol of Freedom.]
This is our flag, America—Land
of the Free!
How proudly it waves and
proclaims liberty.
Feel your pulse quicken and thrill
to the sight
Of Old Glory waving, our beacon
and light.

Our Flag—What a glorious sight!
Thrill to the red and the blue and
the white.
Our Flag—A symbol to all—
Rich or poor, one and all answer
its call.

Hear the rhythmic beat of those
marching feet,
As they trod along the trail.
Feel the sweat on their brow as
they pledge with a vow,
That with God's help they never
can fail.

This is our flag, America, in
Glory it waves,
A light for our soldiers, a worthy
cause for our graves.
We gaze as each fold ripples in
view—
There's a star for each State on
the background of blue.

The stripes that we see, the white
for purity,
And the red for the blood we've
shed.
All made us reveal the pride that
we feel—
"Old Glory—Our Freedom will
never be dead!"

We'll fight for the right—in unity
we stand—
With love in our hearts and "Our
Faith in our hand."
Our flag—keep it flying, where'er
you may be,
"Love of God, Country and
Fellowman,"—believe me, it's
free!

Karl E. Fisler
THE PASS
As we cross the prairie,
most times alert and wary.
You must see the pass,
the way of the mass.
There can be no detour,
the trail's straight and sure.
Seeing "Scouts" on the bluff,
ask, did I do enough?
Ride on, there is no retreat,
perhaps the grass is sweet!

Wayne Davis
DESTINY
I watch as leaves fall
from a tall oak.
Some spiral down,
as if in a hurry,
not caring where they come
to rest,
while others seem to
parachute and float
gently down,
being very careful
where they land,
as if knowing what lie
ahead.

Nicole Mala
SUMMER SUNSET
Warm comfortable contentment
I feel, nestling close to you
as I watch
the Sun's yellow,
disappearing below the trees,
Slowly stray to pink.
Then the blue sky
fades to lavender
Slowly spreading upward
to the sound of Mozart's Jupiter.

Directly above, the blue darkens.
I watch a balloon's jerky ascent
until I lose it among the clouds.
You spot the first star
Then more successively blink on
'Til they're the only light left,
ashine in a midnight-darkened
sky.

Carol D. Stearns
GOD, MY GARDEN, AND I
In the stillness of the twilight
At the closing of the day,
I go into my garden,
There to think and pray;
Its beauty doth inspire me
More than gold or mirth,
For I feel closer to God here,
Than anywhere on earth.

In the quiet of the evening
When daylight is almost gone,
I like to sit and thank God
For the things that He has done;
While the stars twinkle ore me,
And the moon bursts forth its
light,
I like to sit and thank God
For the stillness of the night.

In the stillness of the midnight,
I close my eyes to sleep;
While the midnight turns to
morning
And the night doth slowly creep,
I dream about my garden,
The beauty that inspires me there,
For it's in this garden God's
presence is felt
More than anywhere.

Sven H.E. Borei
THE SEARCH
So we go off across a trackless
down:
Off to a place we do not know,
To Christminster in search of
something,
dreams we cannot show.

The roadend, that we do not see,
Is rich in happiness and peace,
Or full of sorrow, pain, and
anguish.
Still, once we're going, there is no
release
From our unmarked search.

So we go forward to a place
We do not know, the
Christminster
Of dreams we see in space.

Sara C. Mathews
RESTLESS
Take me away, set me free,
Give me some room I want to be
me.

I'm tired of washing dishes, tired
of scrubbing floors,
I feel like walking right out the
door.

The kids are driving me insane,
I can't cope with their growing
pains.

And you're the worst of them all,
Ordering me about until I'm
ready to fall.

Whatever happened to my
childhood dreams,
Of marrying a man above
marginal means.

Of a house sitting high on a hill,
Of traveling the world, just for
the thrill.

Of maids running here and there,
Obeying my orders and seeing to
the childrens' care.

Of terrace parties, where I'm belle
of the ball,
Attention, Attention is my
downfall.

There's no escape from this life I
endure,
And a new lover each week is not
the cure.

I tried the Silver Fox, The Major,
and a guy from the Marine
Corps,
The Governor gave me a thrill,
but turned out to be a bore.

So a longer relationship, I've
decided upon,
With my young cop I'll love and
have years of fun.

And I'll smile as I sit rocking
when I'm old and gray,
My memories I'll recall to
entertain me each day.

A. Fred Jones Jr.
THE CAPTAIN
[To my sons and daughter:
Jessie James Patton Jones, April
Christina Marie Jones &
William Frank McArthur Jones]
Go west Old Man
Into the simmering shimmering
Sunset of life
Companion to wisdom
Woefully wasted
On younger folk
Be no stranger
To yesterday or today
Nor tomorrow . . .

Go east Old Man
Into the sacred shadows
Surrounding sunrise
Where much knowledge
Is restored like new
Amidst the smell
Of rainbow trout
And coffee a'brew . . .

Go where you will
Old Man
For Freedom
Is at your heels
Go where you will
Old Man
You're The Captain
Of this keel!

Karen Legue
**Love Is Hard To Come
Across**
When your age is in its teens,
your body goes through love
machines.
You fall in love or so you think,
you see your love and then turn
pink.

Soon you realize love's not there,
and want to pull out all your hair.
Then you find another guy
and this time, this one makes you
cry.

For every guy you had a song.
For every guy your love went
wrong.

You don't have to look for love,
just be free, like a dove.

Soon in life, some guy will come
and you won't care if he is dumb.
Maybe he's not cute at all,
but he asks you if you'll call.

Don't be shy when he's around.
A guy you love has now been
    found.
If it's love you'll last forever.
If it's love you'll break up never.

David Havron
ICE
Love stalks the heart
like a lowly avenger,
seeking revenge
for a past betrayal.
Stealthily observing,
patiently awaiting
an obvious weakness
a brief moment of
    defenselessness;
timing for attack,
piercing the heart,
tearing and gnashing
with reckless abandon
as the half-starven lion.
Mercilessly blowing
at life's flame,
yet maliciously keeping it aglow,
as if merely staving off
that inevitable peace
that period of eternal
    submission . . .
death,
the final moment of tranquility
when the heart is vulnerable
no longer.
Ah,
but the soul,
the sweet soul
at peace
alas.

Ruth McNeal
A BOOK TO READ
A person who reads A BIBLE,
It's to become definite and not
    liable.
That they will find their place
    among the living
And ending up, not the *One*
    doing *All* the giving
It's true, that it is a mysterious
    book
But, far better than the mysteries
    of the crook!
It's a must, to first mind a little
    prayer,
Search the Scriptures in a spirit of
    despair
Then, as you read
It will give All the Revelation
    that a person would need.

Staci Ryback
THE TEACHING
[*Dedicated to Gael—Whether
near to me or worlds apart
you'll always have a place in
my heart. This one's for you.*]
I listened, learned and understood
The words you tried to teach
They had so much meaning then
But somehow could not reach
It's strange to see us changing
And the friendship we held so
    dear
But through the years to come
The memories we will still hold

near
Good-bye is not the word to use
So I'll say fare-thee-well
Take-care, good-luck my dearest
    friend
And may God always be there

Billy J. Wallace
HOME
[*This sonnet is for Lillian
Morris Jenkins, who is my last
surviving aunt, and my sister,
brothers, and cousins whose
heritage they each revere. It is
dedicated to those who left us
a love for music and an
appreciation for the other finer
accomplishments.*]
I went back to my home again
    today.
'Tis hallowed ground. 'Twas there
    my mold was cast
From noble strain whose forms
    are now but clay,
And silent, numbered 'mongst the
    quiet past,
Asleep beside a little country
    road.
Not long ago they deified the sod
That covers now their frames.
    Enshrined abode!
Age placed them 'neath the clod
    o'er which they'd trod.

Heart-rending melodies of
    yesteryear
Outlast the pen, the hand, the
    instrument.
Remembrance grants me strength
    to persevere.
As they before, I haste prepared,
    intent,
Inspired by them who now sleep
    underground,
To leave behind a song, a strain
    profound.

Dorothy K. Murray
A NEW BEGINNING
[*Dedicated to Billy, Judy and
Patti*]
Life hasn't fulfilled all the dreams
I dreamed and sometimes I cry.
But for all that is worthwhile
I must make another try.

I'm determined; I won't quit
and I won't fail
and I won't be a ship
without a sail.

Life is what you make it
and I refuse to fake it.
I'll dry my tears, face up to my
    fears
and look ahead to better years.

Wynona Francisco
FOOLISH FEAR
[*For you, Ginny, my shiny
penny . . . Don't let go your
Dreams.*]
Oh, Foolish Fear, Master to this
    Slave,
Why do you grind me in your
    teeth
And spit me in my grave?

If we could know before too late,
Perhaps it is just the hand of
    fate—
If but one soul from the grave
    returned,
A sad, sad story, I'm sure we'd

learn.
But the dead speak not, nor can
    they tell,
It's not dying, but, just being
    that's hell.
Yet how shall we know before
    too late,
Perhaps, it is the hand of fate . . .
We fear death, yet rush on to
    meet it,
Wasting our life, never again to
    greet it.
Never again to know, never again
    to see,
What a beautiful thing living
    could be.

Break loose, my soul, sing your
    song . . .
I stand mute . . . My chance is
    gone . . .
I could have feated so many
    things.
I could have known joy true love
    brings.

Oh, Foolish Fear, Master to this
    Slave,
Why do you grind me in your
    teeth,
And spit me in my grave?

S. Ben Gali
MUSING . . .
In a world of hate and violence
Only few abut on my fancy—
They infuse my heart with
    sustenance
To hope and fight dire malignancy.

A soaring *song* to quell all discord;
To lift up an aching heart and
    soul.
A cheering *bird* to gladden the
    world—
Perhaps to daunt much vile from
    befoule.

I'll difuse in eminence of *love*,
So as to upset all baleful hate;
To embrace that message from
    above,
Of good purport with courage and
    faith.

I look for that innocent
    childhood—
Today's fulfillment of tomorrow.
For bondless *youth*—the grant for
    manhood's
Tacit guarantor of less sorrow.

Laughter to heal the troubled
    good-man;
To uplift his spirit at its best.
To gain of a *beautiful woman*;
To cuddle blissfully in her breasts.

This is my dream, this is my song;
In these feelings I couldn't go
    wrong . . .

Gladys Willoughby Goins
VACANCY
[*A tribute to my sister, Bonnie
K. Wright*]
There is a vacancy in our home,
    An aching in our heart,
The absence of your presence,
    Has torn our World apart.
In some brief moments,
    We lost the will to live,
Precious memories we recall,
    Of what you had to give.
You were a lovely baby,

Shared the family's many joys,
    The center of our childish plays,
    To share our little toys.
You are not taking with you,
    Bright memories life can hold,
These we have and cherish,
    More precious than gold.
You grew to be a lady,
    And became a loving wife,
God gave you a precious boy,
    To brighten up your life.
When he grew to be a man,
    The center of your world,
Sheer joy touched your life,
    With his darling baby girl.
So many sacred memories,
    All we can ever say,
You have not gone from us,
    You are just away—
We know that in God's Heaven,
    Where loved ones for you wait,
They greeted you celestially,
    As you stepped inside The Gate.

Len Mitchell
CHANCES ARE
Chances are
Changes may come your way,
And chances are
That they may come today.

Chances are
The changes may be what you
    need,
Chances are
The changes are what you've
    dreamed.

Chances are
The change may come along,
And chances are
The change will come alone.

Chances are
The change may be what you
    need,
Chances are
This chance is what you've
    dreamed.

Chances are
The chance is what you've
    missed,
Chances are
This chance is all there is.

Shelley Johnson Tenneson
SPARROW SONG TWO
Sparrow, you fly above me,
Does my song reach you?
Bounce off stars and the edge of
    the universe,
Come back to reverberate around
    you?

You knew the way through the
    maze—
Over roots and bushes, under the
    fence,
Thin Sparrow.

I am grown fat awaiting flight—
My breast grows large with
    swelling heart
In nurture of the young.

Earth-rooted female, hugging life.
Will my soul know all—meet
    yours,
Freed from body to soar with
    God?

I love life, Sparrow.
I am dying.
God moves the wind and the
    leaves are bells.

Smooth rush of seasons embrace
  me,
Dance with me, around the circle
As I lose my breath,

Grow faint in the crush and
The heat and the power
Of the other being—
Twirling on.

John Hubbard Bidwell
The Voice Of One Crying In the Wilderness
Now halt your minds and listen
  to their cry
From northern alters formed of
  snow and ice,
Beneath celestial curtains in their
  sky,
The wolves give evensong of
  sacrifice.
All creatures stop—transfixed by
  somber hymns
Which rise from frozen
  mountains to the stars
To One whose understanding
  never dims,
Who walked with man and also
  bears the scars.
The howling joins the wind
  which sweeps the earth
Angelic zephyrs sing like flute
  and fife
And reach the ears of one who
  from his birth
Has dared deny the sacredness of
  life.
This man, now trembling, sees
  upon his wall
A young wolf's head he shot—to
  his distress,
That prophet's head brings
  judgement on us all,
Like one who also cried in
  wilderness.
So listen now—we may not have
  so long;
Please listen to the crying voice
  and care,
And pray that we may never end
  the song
Of wolves and wind that fills the
  Arctic air.

Shari Burrus
SMOKE SIGNALS
I had a friend when I was young,
  said his name was Johnny Bear,
He was Apache by his features,
  but I never really cared.
He taught me how to ride a pony,
  how to train them to be tame,
how to swim across the creek,
  how to do away with pain.
He took me to a mountain top,
  taught me words upon the wind,
we mixed blood on our way
  down, vowing always to be
  friends.
The folks in town called him
  "heathen", said his Father drank
  and lied,
all I knew was that I loved him,
  and our friendship gave me
  pride.
My family moved across the
  country, I bid Bear our last
  farewell,
Johnny told me that he loved me,
  and he named me "AUTUMN
  TRAILS".
Many years had gone before me,

when I heard he'd gone insane,
he climbed up to our mountain,
  screamed my name as he was
  slain.
When I reached the mountain
  top, he was lying on the
  ground,
he said "this skin has caused
  much hate, now I am white but
  we are bound."
I learned of life, love, and
  friendship, from a boy whose
  skin was red,
I lived my spring and my
  summer, followed where John
  Bear had led.
Now my life is in its AUTUMN, I
  return to mountains high,
I see the path that John Bear left
  me, AUTUMN TRAILS . . .
  smoke in the sky.

Gaurav Bhalla
FOR A WHILE . . .
[To Dilnavaz, my dearest friend]
Not forever will the Koel sing
Not forever will the devotee
chant his hymn,
Not forever will the priest
blow his conch
or the peacock
strut and dance.
Not forever will the sun shine
Not forever will there be
Khyyam's wine
Not forever will there
be you or me
or the river
flow to the sea.
For a while . . .
Not forever will the Koel sing.

DeAnna L. Brown
WHY
Why is the sky so blue?
Why is the grass so green?
Why do the flowers have so
  much dew?
Why is the wind so mean?
Why is the sky so black when
  the stars do not shine in the
  night?
Why does the rain come down so
  hard,
How do the trees grow in my
  back yard?
After I find the answer to all,
By then it will be fall!

LaVena May Drummond
PEGASUS ALOFT
[This poem is dedicated to
Cliffton Loesch who inspired
me when he entered Fuller
Theological Seminary to
become a Quaker minister.]
"Pegasus," flew to the Cross
  and hovered aloft.
He neighed on high
  for what he sadly espy.
Christ on the Cross!
  The world's greatest loss.
He circled the spot
  until he grew tired and hot.
I must set Christ free
  for the sake of mythology.
Why do they persist in this
  dastardly deed?
  Are they in need?
I will never rest or flee
  until Jesus Christ is set free!
I will swoop and swirl,

dive, dip and curl.
Land in a mire and breathe
  gastly hot fire.
I will haunt all hearts and shoot
  a trillion darts.
The cloth of Turin,
  I will fly around my neck
  wearing.
I will carry the Cross,
  twist on fire in barbed wire.
Dip, twist, curl, swirl and
  fly the whole world.
I will carry any knight whom for
  the Lord is willing to fight.
We can reach and preach from
  every
  fountain and mountain top.
Any fair maiden who in Christ
  abideth
  upon my winged back may
  rideth.
I will forever proclaim the Holy
  Word
  and live forever for the Lord!

Marilea Beth Widick
SPRING
Please, save a moment in your
  life for Spring;
It comes and goes before you
  know it's here—
Days of beauty, joys of love, to
  bring,
And buds of flowers do then soon
  appear.
The leaves on trees do then come
  out;
The morning air does smell quite
  sweet
As butterflies and bees flit 'round
  about
And birds do sing and wheel on
  wing so neat.
All earth's reborn each happy
  morn with green,
And new life births each day
  without an end.
Ere long, the summer sun does
  creep upon this scene
And Spring does flee for nine
  months more again.
  The Spring does come as each
  new year goes by
So long as the sun shines
  brightly in the sky.

James R. Cook
HEY GIRL
Hey girl,
  my heart is lonely.
Come and touch it.
Give your love to me.
  Share my life,
  while I share yours.
Hey girl,
Come be my partner.
Let your heart touch mine.

Delpha Funk Romeiser
Riding the Rumble Seat With You
Enjoying the sunshine with never
  a care,
laughing with the breeze as it
  blew our hair,
Nothing as free as the open air
Riding the rumble seat with you.

Though it rained, though it
  poured, we never did fret;
Under your raincoat we never got
  wet.

That's the most fun I've ever had
  yet,
Riding the rumble seat with you.

Watching the miles pass we flew
  through the breeze
Meeting the cars that looked hot,
  if you please,
We wouldn't trade places, if they
  gave us the keys,
Riding the rumble seat with you.

Moments like this we could live
  on and on,
Moments like these are like a
  bon-bon;
I don't like to think some day
  they'll be gone,
Riding the rumble seat with you.

If I could go back, retrace my
  steps and then
Climb in the rumble seat
  bumping my shin;
Oh, what fun to be young again
Riding the rumble seat with you.

Kathleen S. Peterson
YOUR LOVE
I turn to watch you
Sleep by my side
Dark hair curling
Long lashes against dusky cheeks

I touch you gently
And you respond
Your body quivering
With mine

I have learned to love
And be loved
To share
All I had missed in life

There is no time
No space
The music is our own

Michael D. Butzirus
QUIET RULER
Simple man
How do you rest?
Explain for me!

I don't know many of you—
This world makes you scarce.

Is sleep a kind adventure?
I feel I've missed its meaning.

Release from cares, or is
It simple understanding
That leaves you with your ease?

Michelle L. Sullivan
SMITH RIVER VALLEY
Smith River Valley,
In the sunlight's fresh rays;
Smith River Valley,
At the dawn of spring days.

High rugged mountains,
Pale with cold;
May-covered valley,
In the sun's touch of gold.

In this land of Montana
Where winter is long,
The birds of the valley
Have burst into song.

When spring hits Montana,
I'm startled to see
The dull shades of winter
Turn green on a tree.

Smith River Valley,
My treasures are few;
I've found richness abundant
In the wonder of you.

Smith River Valley,
We'll make a fresh start;
Now is the springtime,
And here is my heart.

Fredie Scott Lyon
WELCOME
[To Sharon Morries]
Should to you my hapless heart
OR' soaring masting seas
Part the era a spining void
Of time and unending minds of
    feelings
stirred
Deep from the soul
Where demons wouldn't go
I hope to you a timeless end
And again a morrow day
For to you my friend a heartful
    welcome
To the land where dreams come
    true
A child's imagination

Bessie Margarites Raschke
THE PRISONER
[To all prisoners all over the
    world.]
I committed a felony
A long time ago,
And now I wait for the hours
When it's my time to go,
The years are long,
And time drags on,
Can't you write to me?
So I can go on?

The sun seeps through the iron
    bars,
and lights the shadows,
as I sit here.

I wish I were a kid again
romping thru the meadows,
I can see Mom, in her gingham
    dress
calling us in from our play.

I wish I had never succumbed to
    Evil's ways,
The days are dreary,
The night's so long,
I cannot wait but to hear the
    angel's horn.

Joo Young Kim
THE DAY WILL COME
What are a few short hours in a
    day?
Nothing, except when they
Stand between the time
That we will finally meet.
And those years that are said to
    fly by so fast
Why do they drag on
And forever last?
When I am waiting to see your
    face
Hear your voice
Forget the past.
If ever dreams can be realized
and impossible hopes have not
    died
"Then patience, be my
    companion!"
For the day will come
And surely soon
When I will see eternity.

Pamela Rae Miller
ODE TO A BIKER
Showers pour as teardrops fall,
His face we'll see no more.
But wasn't it just the other day,

I saw him by the door?
The night lays heavy,
and the days dark too.
I wonder in my silence . . .
if he even knew.
Where was it written
For him to ride no more?
And who is it decides
What the ride is really for?
A life had just begun,
Yet his time had been too long.
And now the black beast sets
    alone,
While the rest must carry on.
Brother rise beyond,
The pain that's left behind.
Your Brothers' ride in silence,
As the days turn into night.
Rise with all your might,
And bring strength to all the rest.
For they must carry on
Never being able to forget.

Etta Mellett
THE SNITCHIN' KID
The pickle-snitchin' kid.   Wow!

Betty said, "I'll wait for the bait!
I'll catch that snitcher in any
    event.
Then we will see who it might
    be—

That pickle moocher, snitcher
    kid."

The moocher went to the jar one
    day;
The jar broke. Everything went
    astray.

(I could almost say, without delay.)

I'll have to find Betty to tell her.
She found the bait, so don't need
    to wait.
THAT IS WHAT YOU GET FOR
SNITCHIN' OUT OF THE JAR.

(But I ate the last pickle, so there
you are.)

Rev. B. Smith Gray
TIME
Time does pass,
And it passes fast
Marking us with age.
We stroll along
In life like a song,
Each sung on a different stage.
If we all look
Somewhere in a book,
Is our name on a page.
Like a people zoo
For me and you.
This Earth is merely our cage.

Finnvald Hedin
BY THE SEA
Why was I born so close to sea?
With all its strange
and wondrous callings,
Forever it has spellbound me
and made my soul a restless rover,
Who every star
and moonlight night
is bound by the eternal flight
of waves forever rolling.

You hold me chained
with thousen years of wanting,
For part of you
is flowing through my hearth,
From early dawn,
the day I left, I've sought you,
Although your fury

frightens me in part,
And still I cannot be without you
and couldn't ever wish
you weren't there,
Because the longings
you inflicted with your presence
not only is a lot for me to bear,
It is my inner self,
My soul, my everlasting all,
Your treacherous waves are
    soothing,
With their relentless calls.

Jarshime Kimmel
**Walk Slowly My Little
    Friend**
Please little child may I walk
    with thee?
That I may learn your ways.
Ways I knew when I was three,
But lost in later days.

Simple things that meant so
    much,
And nothing asked in turn.
Each new trust, each honest act,
Were values that we learned.

I could use that trust again,
And use those values too,
And have respect for every friend,
And they, respect for you.

So please walk slowly my little
    friend,
And take me as you go,
To learn again a way of life,
And a love I used to know.

Lynda Lynn Parra
THE CITY
[I wish to express my deepest
thanks to a very giving man
who helped me and inspired
me to grow within myself. This
is for you Ricky.]
The city, that majestic
    masterpiece of man, a place
    built to please each mortal
    with a helping hand;

Dark in night, gray in day is the
    city full of hate, mounted
    many years ago are buildings
    that now decay;

Faces of people seem to stare
    each with a different thought,
    walking down the alleys black,
    they stand among the rot;

Voices creep from the halls of
    deserted homes, where people
    lost their happiness and
    poverty now roams;

Loneliness reeks in this dirty
    crypt called the CITY NEW,
    they raped land of its beauty
    and from that chaos grew;

Politicians now lie to the public
    saying there will be a change,
    but I know they're full of it, I
    know they're playing games;

Now the city sleeps, no anger to
    be seen, 'til tomorrow brings
    the graying dawn and ends the
    city's dream.

Margareta Tommos
UNTITLED
Why do we try to conquer Nature?
Are we so immature
As to think we are more powerful
    than she?
Are we so immature

As to think we are older than the
    trees?
Why don't we realize our true
    part in her
And talk to a fir?

How will we survive
If we destroy the lives
Of our fellow creatures around us
Who find in us little love or trust?
Have our myths and cities
Built barriers between us
And the environment around us?

Have we lost the keys
To our door to Nature?
Are we so lost and apart from her
That we will not try to find the
    door and keys?
Are we so independent and
    mature
That, without her, we can survive
    and thrive?
"I do not believe so," answered the
    fir.

"Only Man can answer the
    questions
That have been written about his
    doings with Nature.
I do not know why he does such
    things."
So saying, the fir fell before a
    logger's axe.

Dana Lynn Weems
WHY
[For my Tony Anthony, who
    helped find love again and
    became a part of my life like
    no-one else.]
Why don't people care?
The world now is so cruel and
    cold,
Why don't people feel?
Friends are always bought and
    sold.
Why don't people listen?
God surely must hear the good
    people's cries,
Where is the love of yesterday?
The love of yesterday is the love
    you've given me,
With this touch of grace, we can
    reach the skies.
Now I can feel the person I want
    to be,
The freedom of yesterday is just
    you and me.

Barbara Berg
LOVE'S MANY SEASONS
Love in Spring just flowering,
Is young, and fresh, and new;
It blooms for us so gently,
It's tender, soft and true.

The Summer love is heated,
It molds us into one;
Advance to its zenith,
But the fever's just begun.

The Autumn love is mellow,
Its warm and gentle fire,
Has brought us close together
We love and never tire.

But Winter love's no less because,
It pleases us anew;
The deeper it becomes,
The closer are we two.

For me, love's many seasons
Are joyous ones with you;
Your closeness makes me happy,
Each other we renew.

Today's Greatest Poems

Lois Lumsden
A SLEEPNESS NIGHT
[To all persons who have ever spent a sleepless night trying for rest that don't come]

Another sleepless night is here to
crowd my weary mind
The fleeting thoughts just come
and go with pictures of every
kind
All my jumbled feelings show
true colors bright like the sun
They stand out vividly, so clear,
until they fade away
Perchance they'll come again to
use and brighten up a day
So many things would useful be
that I can clearly see
Yet, alas, when this sleepless
night is gone I know from
times before
They'll slip away like grass from
a new mown lawn
Why can't I shut this thinking off
as my body cries for rest
At least the weary dreary things, I
cherish all the best
So many little foolish thoughts
keep mounting on the side
To over-rule the worthiness of all
the good sermied
When this restless night is over
exhausted I shall be
The first words that will greet me
in the wee dawn of the day
"Come on lazy, don't sleep your
life away"
I'll stretch and yawn with
tiredness then nuzzle in my bed
Hoping that by chance It wasn't
even said

Joyce Jones
UNTITLED
I used to be
and thought I was
until someone told
me
that I wasn't;
that I hadn't been.
and then
when they told me
and with evidence
showed me
I, too, realized
that I wasn't;
that I hadn't been.

Marjorie M. Holbrook
ESCAPE FROM FAILURE
Sometimes a person looks for an
escape, just to get away, to ease
the mind, but how can escape
ease the mind, when you have
to worry about escape. Escape
from the past, escape from
time. Escape from whom,
escape from the truth, some
may say. Escape from anger we
seldom ever. Escape from
sensible, if you are sensitive.
Escape from wrong into a
problem, only to confuse, the
escape you have done, revenge
of anger, to behave wrongly, is
no escape. To lead astray, to
rise and vanish, just like the
wind, then that would be
escape. Nobody has ever seen
the wind just only the feel.
Aren't you glad you don't have

to worry about escape. Escape
like a flower, that dies with the
frost, but will rise again in the
spring. Escape from dirt, grit,
and grime and the wages of
time, keep on the move time
don't wait, fill it with love, life
is too great. Like the little
mouse that was trying to get
away. Life was too hectic, time
wouldn't wait

Melinda Ward

Melinda Ward
LIFE'S SONG
If I should die tomorrow,
Has my earthly song been light?
Have I climbed up the golden
ladder,
Or fallen along my flight?

Have I cheered some old kind
soul?
Giving of my time to share—
Just to listen, dream their dreams,
Laugh with them, feel their
prayers?

They need the young so very bad
As they rock back and recall
Gingham patterned memories
Of yesterday's sunlit walls.

Have you spent one day in
loneliness?
Have you felt their cares, though
weak?
Then, my friend, you have not
fallen
From life's song. Forever seek!

Kimberley A. Berntson
JAY
*[The one I love who has given
me inspiration to compose this
poem, to and for Jay and all
those who read poetry and
wander with his mind's ability
I present this poem.]*

Flies, climbs, dips, dives, swirls,
soars;
Not bird—but man,
In his mind's own dreams.

Dwight Hughes House
WILDFIRE AND LAMBENCY
There are two sorts of flame:
Wildfire—and torch that's
tame; but both blazes burn
bright
While they lay bare waste
trimmed tree trunks—before—
full-limbed—as each mates
heat with light.

At the mouth of a chimney flue
lung's lusty fire—ruddy panting

tongues lick wood-furnace's meat
(Held in grate's teeth of wrought
iron woof), to head for red
chimney-throat's roof, which
swallows up their heat;
But, ere long, bark's passion
perishes. And turns to
ashes . . . at the firedog's
feet . . .
On the other hand, fingers of
flame, that, so tenderly,
expand—are lovely to behold
Weaving, and paring, the wood—
bobbin' for air—luminous
marigold
Grown in rosy hearth's charry
cord-covered bed—backlog at
the head; and lasting long after
eve's waxed old.

Louis E. Secoy
LIVES ON LOAN
*[Rochelle, Lori and Justin A
family, friend, wife of mine.]*
Across the ocean
Through the skies
Coming home
No tears to cry.

Fallen with honor,
On a field of Glory.
The lives of our boys
An unsigned story

A war unknown,
A story untold.
Political pawns,
Lives on Loan.

They call it war,
We pay the price.
They shell out theory,
We shell out lives.

A word, a gesture,
Angry actions they seek.
Push the button
Let us all sleep.

*John Nicholas Hnatishion
M-5286*
My Little Sweet Roseann
My Little Sweet Roseann!
The bars and walls of this prison
I do not fear,
it's the thought of losing You My
Dear.
For You are My Life, My
Everything,
without You I could not laugh or
sing.
You are My True and Loving
Woman,
My closest and Tender Friend,
You're the Only Woman I can
turn to,
when my mind seems at its end.
You're the Woman who shares
my sorrows,
when I am down and out.
You're the Woman who gives me
strength,
and brings me out of doubt.
You're the Woman who always
tries
Her best to understand,
I love You My Little Sweet
Roseann.
I'm locked up and put away,
but I'll return to you some day.
When I come home to You at last,
all Our loneliness will be Our
past.
This time in prison may keep

Our Bodies from being near,
but it can't stop My Thoughts
and Dreams of Loving You
Dear.
For You are the Woman of All
My Desires,
the Woman who makes My Love
grow higher.
You're on My mind both day and
night,
You're the Only Woman who can
treat Me right.
My Trust in You is Very Dear,
My Love for You is So Sincere.
My Love for You will keep on
growing,
cause Your Love for me is always
showing.
I get so sad I feel like dying,
but I know Our Love will keep on
trying.
My days are lonely and My
nights without You are wrong,
the caress of Your Sweet Body I
do long.
To hold You in My arms would
be Great,
and to have You at the Alter Gate.
To say I Do with All My Love,
to by My Wife from God above.
To see You smile and to be
sincere,
We would be joined in Marriage
Dear.
To make Our Vows to Never Part,
cause of the Love that is in Our
Hearts.
We would be United and Our
new Lives just begun,
because of Our Love and
Devotion.
For My days are Blue and still
Lonely now,
but with God's Help will make it
some how.
For He is Everything that's Good,
we'll Trust in Him like we
Always Should.
Our Love has come through
many test,
Our love will Survive cause it's
the Best.
Stay Strong, Be Good, I know You
can,
I love You, My Little Sweet
Roseann

Elizabeth A. Skinsnes
EVOLUTION
He is the master craftsman, the
sculptor, the artist,
The chemist, the physicist, and
the botanist,
The zoologist and the
astronomer.
Before him was never any like
him
And after him, even the most
talented
Were like a drop while he is as
the mighty ocean.

How did it come about, this
wondrous world of ours
And the universe of which it is a
part?

They speak in school of
evolution and I agree.
He began with a one-celled animal
And fashioned its intricacy into
its simplicity.

543

The sculptor came back another
   day
And in his skilled hands formed
   the fishes of the sea.
How charmingly they swam.
But his inexhaustible mind
   would conquer the air also
So he made birds and gave them
   wings.
Then came cattle and the
   creeping things,
And the brontasaurus who
   roamed the earth so long ago.

And at last he formed the man,
   Adam,
And breathed into him a living
   spirit.
After that he gave him a task,
To love the animals and give
   them names.
The man worked well but when
   the evening came
He was lonely. Then the master
   craftsman
Caused a deep sleep to fall on him
And he fashioned woman, our
   mother, Eve.

And he saw that all that he
   created
   Was indeed good.
And during the seventh eon of
   time
He rested.

Lidia M. Martin
HOLIDAYS
It's that time of year again
The holidays are here
Although you're all so far away
Within my heart you're near.

It wasn't many years ago
When all of you were small
The holidays were different then
I loved them one and all.

They started with Thanksgiving
Then Christmas and New Years
Now when I think about them
I brush away the tears.

Cause none of you are with me
   now
You have families of your own
But I pray you think about me
And the holidays we've known.

(Mrs.) Maxine G. Slenes
THE MED-FLY NIGHTMARE
The Med-Fly, can we stop it?
   What can we do?
Strip and ground-spray—Will this
   pull us through?

Spray we must, from up in the
   sky.
So Jerry had no choice but to
   order and cry!
Then they argued and fussed, just
   how to begin,
But the date was now set, so it
   seemed "Sink or Swim"!
The walnuts were first, the tree
   loaded so tall,
I knew I could never conquer
   them all!
I worked and I worked from
   ground to the wire.
The bagging and clipping soon
   made me retire.
So I called on the 'phone for some
   help in my plight,
And wonders of all, the 'phone

rang outright!
The voice that I heard said,
   "Don't worry! We'll help!"
So my name I gave freely. How
   happy I felt!
Next came my garden, the small
   tomato bed—
I was thankful I had planted the
   Early Girl Red!
Zucchini and cucumbers—oh,
   yes, string beans too,
The harvest now early made me
   so blue.
Last came the peach tree—which
   hurt most of all!
So green and so hard, they were
   like a baseball.
I thought two years back, in
   August I came
To the Garden of Eden, I called it
   by name!
Last night as I lay asleep in my
   bed,
The helicopters buzzed and
   sprayed overhead.
So we hope that our efforts will
   wipe out the fly,
And California will be the Gold
   Spot in the Sky!

Sandra Jean Heath
ECSTASY
Me—a lonely girl laying quietly
upon a bed—
      spread out like an eagle
on a lone mountain top;
waiting eagerly as you lay
   upon my sweating heaving
   breasts
   throbbing with excitement
                  and desire.
Your fingers gently massage my
   breasts,
   kneading each as a baker might
   knead
a loaf of bread.
      As you move within
my being, causing my breath to
   quicken; I
lose myself to you and am gone
   away
                  from here.
To a new land far away I go; filled
   with
milk and honey—
      pleasures more than we can
enjoy or ever perceive—
            more than I'll ever
see or know;
      a feeling of ecstasy
                  for evermore.

Dr. Fred Karl Scheibe
Earthly—Cosmic Reflection
*[to Goethe's FAUST and Harry
Behn's "Heather" of The
Faraway Lurs.]*
Take your soul and knit the fibers
Into strands of golden light,
Let them shine and glow forever,
Keep them clear and ever bright.
Have you done this earthly
   wonder,
Ah, my mortal, you have won . . .
For of all the weavers' greatest
It was He who set the sun.
Earthly flow our thoughts and
   feelings,
Flow enriched by visions deep,
Then embrace the universal—
Look profoundly, go to sleep . . .

Wake and bathe in open spaces,
Live and breathe in galaxies,
Wax and wane with lights and
   shadows,
Fly through all eternities . . .
Thence return to earth and
   ponder.
With our lives what have we
   done?
Tell us, prithee, what is lacking
Since the light 'gainst the
   darkness won?
All the light that is in heaven,
All the light that is in man,
Never yet sufficed to brighten
Every den to which he ran.
Once a neighbor with a lantern
Searched for light in night and
   gloom—
And, one day, he came upon it,
Reached for it and sealed his
   doom.

Katherine Kelley Scott
THE WRATH OF GOD
By my hands the earth was
   formed, the night and then the
   day
And by my hands if man persist,
   I'll take it all away

"I" who built the mountains from
   the rumblings of the ground
And it was "I" who spat the sea
   when man was not around.

"I" who stroke the lightning and
   kiss the thunderbolt,
Can also guide the sparrows, or
   cause the grass to choke

I can be merciful, I can be cruel, I
   can give wisdom to even a fool
But slow to anger and quick to
   forgive, this is the way . . .
"All" men should live

Dodie Sherman
MOTHER'S DAY
In honor of birthing a child,
   A minor salute to me.
And yet for being a person,
   Still not allowed to be free.

Through pain and the beauty of
   birth,
   Alas, a girl-child is born.
Health, loving and open,
   Yet it is for her, I mourn.

I grieve for her, the pain,
   The struggle to be free.
As she pushes through her
   lifetime,
   A passion for equality.

Doug Shea
THE SIDEWALK SENATOR
"You heard about the silent
   generation?
   'Apolitical' they called us!
'Apolitical,' till the kiss
   of layoff turns me to a frog
   and wife devotes her throat
   to shrieks and grumbles as we
   stumble
   into an era of grubby rubbish!
'Apolitical,' I waved the brave rag
   till patriotic sons
   sold by neurotic presidents
   to defend despotic governments
   came back in pieces or
   narcotic;
'apolitical,' I pulled the rope,
   bent the wires with the pliers;

they got my vote and then
   my coat
and mialed my paycheck in
   posterity's envelope
for which I, among these
   humanoids,
   these rejects, these dreamers
   who'd require
   the silver moon to beam down
   dimes,
   wait in line upon the curb:
making the sidewalk my senate,
   I beseech, I bewail, I bequeathe:
      The Silent Generation Was
      Its Children's
   Underground, and in every
   patch of Silence
the leaves are cupped towards the
   rhythms of Marxism!"

Michael G. Epple
VS.
      asphalt serpent,
in the road ahead twisting
      in mute agony
under the heel and in the shadow
            of
      The Mountain.

Wilma L. Risor
TREES
Have you ever taken time to look
   at all the many trees
That God has planted o'er the
   earth for each of us to see?
Have you ever taken time to give
   a second thought
To all the many joys and wonders
   that they've brought?
The never ending miracles that
   they give to you and me
And we take them all for granted,
   to us they're just a—tree.
Trees do many things as they
   stand all through the years
Their strength and beauty never
   ends, and they even shed a tear.
A tree can make a silhouette
   against a moonlit sky
And reach its arms up to the
   clouds, as they go drifting by.
A shade for a weary traveler to
   find relief from a burning sun,
A hideaway for a graceful deer,
   when it runs from a hunter's
   gun.
Enfolding arms for a robin's nest
   to raise her family,
Oh! How hard working, and how
   wonderful is a—tree.
A tree will stand a winter's cold
   and soothing springtime rains,
It stands alone in an open field,
   or together along a lane.
It's a sentinel on a hilltop,
   guarding everything below,
It makes a holiday brighter with
   all the lights aglow.
Their fruit we eat in many forms,
   that grow abundantly,
And all we do is just reach out
   and pick one from a—tree.
A woodpecker taps a rhythm, one
   can hear all through the wood,
And I guess they'd sing a song to
   us if only they could.
An old hoot owl sits on a limb
   high above the ground
And in his scary language, talks
   to all the trees around.
And like a woman, each tree will

change its looks from time to
time
From cherry blossoms in her hair,
to cones for a sticky pine
A weeping willow sheds its grief
for all the world to see
And the tears it sheds, show us
who care, how sad a tree can be
And the cross that held our
Saviour, who died for you and
me
Was even made of wood, that was
once a lovely—tree,

khristianekay
**Bedtime Stories For Future
Heroes**
A mother dreams
of a future King
suckling at her breast

A father dreams
of a future Hero
crying in his chest

but
A child dreams . . .

in lullabies
and makebelieve

in masquerades
and forced reality

focused in the wisdom
of A child
but who will believe

the smile
the laugh
the tear
the win
or the lose

of ragged men
in ragged clothes
and fairytales
on red lit avenues

and a mother will dream
and a father will dream

but
A child dreams . . .

Theodora Bach
**Traveling Head-Heart-
Land From Canada To
Illinois**
From the CN Tower to the golden
corn table
upward and outward, to
homeward and inward
on the last leg of travel.

Taller than the pyramids
Taller than the Eiffel Tower
Taller than the Sears Skyscraper
Canada's CN Tower pierces the
Toronto sky with 553 meters
of man's genius,

over 3 million multi-ethnic
humans in campers, sailboats,
cruisers, helicopters, ferris
wheels and baby strollers,

over Younge Street, "the
longest street in the world",
bisecting the International
Vacationland.

I-57 South—
throb-bing camper
Cur-ry trans-port
Har-vey's news-cast
August sun—

Over-burdened, purring, beasts of
burden, bikes on top,

Return affluent Americans
from the perimeters of
imagination,
to the center of their being—their
heart-land, their home.

Betty Whitaker Puckett

Betty Whitaker Puckett
OUTWORN SHOES
*[To my daughter, Amy, my
greatest inspiration.]*
Life was so frustrating and
tiresome in the country—the
time became ripe to move on—
to an idea of more
opportunities in the city. The
outworn shoes, I discarded—for
a beautiful new pair.

However, when the new shoes
were on, I discovered I could
not wear them. They took me
to places unknown and got my
toes stepped on. I finally had
the vision to step out of the
new pair, back into my familiar
ones.

Leona W. Crawford
TEARS IN OUR WORLD
[To "Rowdy" my U.S. marine]
I, too, have heard the guns and
cannons roar
And smelled the raw, wet blood
of slain
And seen the poppies wave of
death
And little children scream with
pain.
I've heard temples fall and
crumble,
Chain-bound slaves for freedom
grumble,
And comrades cold and dying in
the rain.
I've made red footprints in the
snow
And held the torch in wounded
hands;
Heard taps played for those now
dead,
I cry, cry, O Lord, for this, our
land.

Dorothy L. Smith
A DREAM
A dream that's all it is or ever
will be
The times we would walk
through the meadows picking
flowers along the way
The way you would look at me
with the great understanding of
love

There was no need for words for
deep down inside we knew
what there was being said
Then they took you away
They took you to a place you had
never been
You were scared
I waited every day for your letters
to come
I prayed and cried
Then the doorbell rang, and there
was no need for words once
again
Because before I opened the
telegram I knew.
Now I walk through the meadows
alone picking flowers along the
way to put in front of your
picture.
Maybe someday there will be
someone like you but until
then you will be the only one
in my heart even though you
are gone . . .

Roger A. Irvin
THE CROOKED PINE
A crooked pine tree stands alone
in a forest full of trees
With Oak and Birch and Maple
man's fancy more craves these.

For these hardwoods are crafted
into hutches, suites, dinettes
And valued high with envious
eye
with their curly ques and
rosettes.

As I view this scene in winter
it is an awakening sight
The pine tree has its color
while the others look a fright.

The pine has all its foliage
with its decorated cone
The Oak and Birch and Maple
look very much alone.

God gave the pine its needles of
green
and cones of lovely brown
While its companions wait for
spring
to don their pretty gown.

Masha Slutsker
Are Things What They Are?
The room is full of golden light,
But is it day or is it night?

The walls are cleaner than white
snow,
But are they really white or no?

You cannot see a spotless glass,
But is it of the real class?

Are all things really what they are,
Or are some good while they look
bad?

Are all things really what they are,
Or do the plain things look plaid?

J.D. Diller
DAD
The day in which we now live,
Was long ago named for a person
like you.
Since love, care, and certain
understanding,
Are the traits of a father like you.
You've always been there when I
needed you most,
Even though my ways were often
wrong.

You inspire my efforts to be a
winner,
To stand proud and to *sing my
song.*
This day is a blessing for a man,
With such love as, that which
you now have.
Such a father, a brother, and best
friend,
Within you, I now realize that I
have.
May this day be filled with
happiness,
And induce the deep feelings of
love.
May God warm your heart with
peace,
And touch your soul with your
childrens' love.

Sandra Bailey
IS IT ANY WONDER
When the rain falls from the skies
It seems that God does cry—
To see all of the dreadful things
That come before His eyes.
The lust, the greed; cruelty and
thievery—
How sinful our humanity!
When thunder claps, His
knuckles rap!
When clouds grow dark and drear,
Don't you realize, my friend,
It's His anger that you hear?
But do we heed?
Do we try to better all our days?
We only stop, look around—
And go our separate ways—
Still not realizing how God cares
and loves us—
Everyone!
What does it take to shape us up?
To get us all in gear?
Please heed His little notices—
Listen with your ears.
Then, also, listen with your heart.
His arms are always open wide—
Forgiveness He'll impart.
Let the sunshine waves come in,
flowers guide your way.
Clouds of blue await you, too,
As you join Him on His big broad
way!

Steve Gruber
CALLING ALL SCARS
Your world will not do
what you direct it to
your terrible God
never punishes you
sufficiently
but you have taken up
all his slack
and re-cast the world
in clear plastic
where snap-together rationales
are all the rage
among your blank and bitter
offspring

Dixie McVey King
DAWN BY THE OCEAN
Her toes embraced the grains of
sand and multicolor shells,
With her long lacy silk spun hair
locks
Of yellow and white gold
shimmered by the sun,
And they were curling their crest
as the Ocean's waves curl,
And break apart rushing into
separate strands

In the direction of the wind and tide's motion.

And she looks out to sea, making a wish, as in a wishing well
For she is not ready to leave her time here at the sea
Too fast is the pacing of the clock,
A sadness reaches her, for she feels all her time with the sea
Is now completely done,
But she should realize it has for her only just begun,
For the love and time with the Ocean will go on for this girl
For once her heart has loved it, with receiving gifts
From past the dunes of sand
And giving of herself to it,
Her body and soul will never totally leave
Nor forget
The Ocean.

Patricia Ann Smith
The Heart Of Being Alone
In a large meadow I wonder alone, wishing hard my heart to come home.
Just drifting about, no one in sight, wishing for a heart to love me tonight.
Tis been too long since last a warm heart,
again I face the night with only a cold thought.
If only a warm heart would drift my way,
then there my cool heart would be able to stay.
As I look afront me, more meadow above,
as my heart silenced with pain in need of a love.

Thomas Marvin Wooten
To a Poet From a Poet
Bless you for coceiving verse!
For crude . . . words and erratic . . . phrases;
For fragility and contradiction of the penned line
For verbaly exercising on the bed of your mind . . .
Above all praise,
I thank you for releasing from your heart
     —The shared thought.
Poet,
Love is the stirring in the brain's womb when a poem is birthed.

Karen Christina Clipp
BAKER PARK
There's a wonderful place called Baker Park,
Where children play from morning till dark.
In the middle of this beauty there is a pond
Where Mother Nature carefully waved her wand.
There are ducks and squirrels and other creatures
That have been carefully molded with the most beautiful features.
There's a covered bridge and a place to play ball,
A running stream and trees so tall.
Tennis courts and a swimming pool;

On the hottest days it's always cool.
So next time you're in Frederick and need a place to rest,
I've explained very briefly why Baker Park's the best.

DeAnna Jaeger Littler
HUMMINGBIRD
Small little hummingbird please fly my way,
Let me see your unique beauty while you perform your stationary ballet,
You capture my attention and I feel in flight,
Enjoying sweet nectars of nature's blooms,
How lovely you are to behold,
What grace you possess with your fluttering wings,
Come my way again so that my imagination can soar.

Elisabeth Wagenknecht
Why Won't the Hurt Go Away?
When you left me in such a cruel way,
I knew I could never again find day;
No more sunshine, not even a ray—Oh—
Why won't the hurt go away?

They say your heart flammed for another,
How I wish that flame I could smother
Now above me a dark cloud doth hover,—Oh—
Why won't the hurt go away?

Ever since you left me, I have cried out in pain,
The grief is so much pressure, that I think I'm insane;
I know that I can never be the same again—Oh—
Why won't the hurt go away?

Now I'm alone, and have no peace whatever,
My burden seems, oh—so much heavier;
I just can't believe that our love has been severed,—Oh—
Why won't the hurt go away?

Rosie Johnson
It's Not Love (That Hurts)
It's not the love that hurts someone
It's the Person who *Pretends*
And after you've given all that you have—
It ends.
Oh, yeah. It makes you happy while it lasts
But when It's over you want to forget—but
You'll *always* remember—the Past.
Sure. You've argued and you talked
You've hugged and you've kissed
You love him *so much* until you kept walking when the men hissed.
When you met him you thought that God had finally answered your Prayer
Until one day you turned around and he wasn't there.

Then you remembered all the nights you cried
And the many things you tried— to get him to believe that your love is true and it all adds up to him leaving you . . .
So to all the young girls who believe that love is wrong
It's not love that makes you sad and leaves you all alone . . .
Once you fall in love it can be great
If you find the right man
Although you might have to wait he'll be able to love you like no one else can . . .
So it's not love that hurts
It's finding out that you've been had
That makes you feel so Bad . . .

John David Boykin
OF HIM AND A DOG
Hidden in the darkest interior of the blackest night, inside the grave,
Underneath the surface of the earth lies the ivory images . . .
Of him and a dog.

That's his life story, the eternal friendship and everlasting love that was very close to glory, the ever weary bones forgotten . . .
Of him and a dog.

There was never seen one somewhere without the other one also there.
Yet something was gone, left out. The picture was not complete . . .
Of him and a dog.

The bones lying so cold and still, below the horizon, beyond the hill,
An unmarked grave hidden in the shadows of an unknown mine.
The forgotten people who lived and died in the era of their time . . .
Of him and a dog.

Their superstitious beliefs and fears—the cringing people through the years.
I see and hear all that's going on as the creaking of the lid to the coffin where they sleep opens.
Then the images are gone . . .
Of him and a dog.

The pet wolf from long ago not wanting to be left behind, snarling while he walks in the shadows of the fear—ridden mind. The bones so cold and white sparkle in the darkest light . . .
Of hime and a dog.

I do not see them as they rattle down the slope of the hill for I know even as they pounce upon me and the blood curdling scream from my throat says that it just can't be so . . .
Of him and a dog.

Dorothy L. Fadely
TRYING TIMES
Father help us to keep an open mind through

A period in history of trying times.
Youngsters are sick of ways of old
They strum guitars, words are sung, thoughts unfold.

The Indian lad sings, the robbing of his land,
The Negro sings, denied equal rights as a man.
Water is pollutted and the air we breathe,
Some agree with wars, others chant best we take leave.

Life is so short, yet so dear, teach us
To love one another without fear.
Too much power, ambition, can make man blind of
His fellowmen, his faith, in these trying times.

How long for man to see the light, to understand
Riots, demonstrations can't win their fight,
Only patience, endurance, love for mankind will
Help them to succeed in these trying times.

Gail Magee
YOUR NEVER!!
Your never there when I needed love,
Your never around when I needed a friend,
Your alway's on my mind even when I've tried to forget you;
I was never on your mind,
I was never in your heart,
I was never a friend of yours,
But now that I'm making something for me;
You want to love me,
You to be my friend,
You want me on your mind,
But I don't want you because I have to find someone of my own to replace you!!!

Verna Lea Jeffries
TONY
You said . . .
And I felt . . .
But we didn't
Think what they will
It's not wrong for us
Then I said . . .
And you felt . . .
And it's true
We can not go back
To before
You said . . .
And I felt . . .
And we hadn't yet

Debra Bellinger
ENDLESS STORY
[With love, I dedicate this poem to Pastor Terry and Sister Karen; for their patience and encouragement.]
This story takes place a long time ago way, way, in the past.

The stage was set, a solitary man, was the whole cast.

A solitary man, rode into the city, on a fold, the colt of an ass.

People shouted and praised him.

Some people threw their coats on the ground and some cut

tree limbs.

Just to show praise and honor to this lowley man.

People loved him, because for rightousness, he took a stand.

But one dark friday, it was all ended.

They put him to death for your sins.

But my friend it does not end there.

On Easter Sunday he rose again, for he loved you and cared.

He cared about your every worry and your every tear.

And when you cry, he can hear.

He loves you so much that right now he's knocking at your hearts door.

Won't you open it so he can tell you more?

Bill Logan
ALCOHOL
Travelling down a road that startles,
I've done it many a times
Just me and my bottle.
I ran down it,
I've walk a bit,
I talk with people,
and sometimes I sit.
But most of all
I've found a dream.
It's a dead end street
with no mountain streams.
But one might ask,
A dream you say?
The answer would be,
I've looked for it everyday.
No! There's no cool fresh springs
or babbling brooks
just good ole faithful,
that makes your insides cook.
I guess my tale is growing ole,
But the trail will never be cold,
But may I say this very bold,
It's eternal torture for a restless soul.
For there were many a great men
and many a great fall,
But some will never know
It was good ole faithful . . .
                    Alcohol.

Elizabeth J. Darrow
YOU AND I
[To Mark, who has given me love, happiness, and friendship.]
I look into your eyes
    and see an intensity
I can not describe.

Incredible deepness
    such pools of wonder,
so much more than alive.

It penetrates my thoughts.
    They're imbedded in my mind.
This uniqueness in feeling,
    truly, one of its kind.

It's more than a love.
It's a worship of minds.
It's respect of two beings.
An inner light, which shines.

It's a joining of one another.
It's a blending of thoughts and ideas.
It's a sharing of dreams.

Throughout all of our years.
I love you so deeply!
    Sometimes it hurts.
I want to hold you forever.
    I want to die in your arms.

Mindy Sue Cohen
GUILT
Guilt.
I'll sew you a quilt
made of guilt.
The colors will be green.
Have you ever seen the green
inside a lobsters' belly?
That green.
And grey, yes, smoke grey with
patches of blood red and
black squares of endless moments
sewn in puckering misfitted
    seams
split open after a while to reveal
the soft warm stuffing of
    acceptance, and allowance:
to allow whatever is inside to
    come out.
This quilt is a guilt trip with a
    silver lining.
Handed down from generation
to generation.
Ahhhh!
The veneration we give to
patchwork guilts.

Thomas Marvin Wooten
What Does a Poem Mean?
liquid.
solid.
mineral.
            LOVE!
            HURT!
            FEAR!
a consonant mis-placed on a
    lilypad.
a strong vowel polluting the pond.
rambling sentences—
drunk on the meter of their own
    audibility.
        —Uncooked Verbage—
served on a silver salver.
A lost raindrop . . .
FREEDOM OF HEAD . . .
    TORTURE OF SOUL
        the agony of rembrance
        —penned on parchment—
        denoting a thought.

J. Ted Schilling
A CHESHIRE SMILE
Friendships are woven in
    timetraveler fabric . . .

God, it was nice to hear your
    voice again . . .
    a recherche' ribbon placed
    about reality,
        touching gently these
    Halcyon hours,
        gifting me with
            this Chesire smile.

Thanks,
    just because,
    all because
        . . . you're you.

Dannty Licten
NIGHTMARE
Traveling beyond the bounds of
    ordinary reality, reaching far
    into the depths of fantasy.
I was all alone in a nocturnal
    emptiness, and became trapped
    inside a nightmare's darkness.

I fought to awaken from my
    night's distress, to leave this
    space of endless nothingness.
I struggled forever, it seemed to
    me, when finally stopped that
    painful insanity.
When I awoke from the darkened
    side of life, and no longer in
    that endless strife,
I could see a brand new morning
    sun's ray, and knew that
    beyond every night awaits a
    new day.
From any ruins can shine a new
    day's light, although I'll always
    remember that darkness of
    night.

Mrs. Vicky D. (White) Livengood
REALITY
[To the years, the tears, the laughs, the people, life and God . . . and to the memories . . .]
spirits wander
        and walk my mind
    to places
        unknown to me
    and i follow
search for somewhere
        never found
    and i go with you
        to an oasis
        or paradise
travel far with me
        and take me to
    the places
        my illusive heart
    has longed to see
and i will never come back
    to my reality . . .

John Dampier
LOVE'S ACCEPTANCE
By vows created by our love and
    caring
We have chosen to join our lives
    in sharing,

    As we enter into this marital
    dream
    I give you my shoulder on
    which to lean

To stand by you with love and
    pride
While you become my beautiful
    bride,

    With vows to myself I'll always
    see
    The precious beauty you are to
    me,

For to you, my love, I hereby yield
My promise of love I'll never shield

    But let it flow eternally and true
    Unto the wonderous beauty of
    you,

These words are chosen for you
    to know
How I love your loveliness
    always aglow

    'Tis why I'v given my life in
    unity
    To you, sharing love to eternity.

E. June Mathews
EBBTIDE
His life was happy and gay
Until a cloud darkened his day;
Now he doesn't hear the bird's
    song,
—His loved ones are all gone.

He's a robot moving to the door,
    as if, to open,
Only to hesitate, turn, stop and
    listen;
Then looking at the portraits his
    eyes ask,
Why do those perfunctory tasks?

The sun has failed,—it is a dying
    light,
The moon slowly ushers in the
    night,
While at his window he sits
Awaiting heaven's lights to be lit.

The fire goes out,—the room
    turns cold,
Together the night and he grow
    old;
Slowly the dark night becomes
    gray,
But,—it is only the room that
    sees the day.

His face is etched with a smile,
That which had been missing for
    a while;
His loneliness had at last ceased,
He is happy and once again at
    peace.

Essie C. Adrion
LOVE SHADOW
"They say there's someone for
    everyone . . ."

I waken in the heat of night;
    I thought you called my name.
Your passion,
    like a poison drug,
        is driving me insane.
Your spirit leaves me;
        You follow me everywhere.
I stand upon your shadow.
        But you think
            I don't know you're there.
I hear your heartbeat in the dark.
        Your soul is aching for me.
I can hear your whispers of desire
        echoing
            as you breathe.
Forever
    you've been haunting me.
Now I know you're getting near.
You're reaching for me through
    the mist
        I know you'll soon be here.
I've waited for you all my life.
    Now you're finally not that far.
I know how much you love me,
        I just don't know
            who
                you
                    are.

Lester Irvin "Herky" Herigstad
GOD
[GOD is simply the Greatest. I want my love for Him to spill out all over His people, to bring the greatest possible blessings to Mankind. I'd like that end I'm sure He will too. Love, "Herky"]
Throw in your lot with GOD. It'll
    pay.
You'll find happiness, every day.
You'll find joy in every way
You'll be really, "Makin' Hay."

He will fill you full of hope . . .
You'll no longer be a dope.
You'll resist sin with all your
    might,

547

Knowing that you're in the right.
And you'll always sleep at night.
Amen, Amen, Amen.
Love, "Herky"

Jonathan Owens
ON A PORTRAIT
Lest I become lost
In visions of youth
Or vague in memory's eye

Or lest I fall pray
To distorted truth
As time goes slowly by

Let paper and frame
And a camera's lens
Reflect as best it can

The love in my heart,
The thoughts in my mind,
The image of a man.

Aunt Polly
Rosy Glow In My Future
[I dedicate this poem to Dennis
Edgmon. He's been my dearest
friend through some trying
times I've had of late. Needless
to say he's been my greatest
inspiration.]
There's a rosy glow in my future,
And the clouds are beginning to
    part.
The hazy horizon is clearer now,
And I can express the feelings in
    my heart.

For all the things I'd love to do,
It was impossible till now,
I'm free to do as I think and please,
My impossible dreams are nearer,
    and how.

I've said this many times before,
I feel like a bird that's been freed.
I can soar and fly whene'er I want,
The security of my cage I no
    longer need.

Ah that rosy glow in my future,
Comes closer and closer each
    passing day.
That hazy horizon is clearing now,
And to my thoughts and feelings,
    I can give way.

Marion Francis
PRUDENCE
Discreetly fair was she;
No blossoms for her hair!
She would not touch the tree
Till fruit should glisten there.

She watched the summer go
Till branches flaked no more;
And now she has to show
Impressive autumn store.

But never gold and red
Could warm a heart's chill room;
She wishes that, instead,
She'd dared to pluck the bloom.

M. Lois Daugherty
PLEASE MISTER
I can almost hear Billie Jo say,
    when she met Jesus on this
    day.
"I'm Billie Jo, me already knows
    one angel up here in heaven,
    Mister.
Him name is David and he's so
    tiny and me is his little big
    sister.
I can help take care of little
    David, we knows how to make
    him laugh,

Cause he's only four and a half
    months old, me is three years
    and a half.
Mister Jesus, when you get time,
    will you please do something
    for me?
I'll give you A kiss and really and
    truely be as good as me can be.
Will you bring my Mamaw up
    here, so that we can be together?
We always were before, we even
    had lotta fun in ole bad weather.
Mamaw went away just one time,
    to the hospital and both of us's
    did cry,
We was so happy when she came
    home, but then, Mister Jesus, I
    had to die.
I know Mamaw wants to come,
    cause me not there so us's can
    play and play,
So please, Mister Jesus, when you
    get time, bring my Mamaw up
    here, O. K.?"
I want that, too, for only you,
    Jesus could love her more than
    I do.

M. Lois Daughtery
LOIS ANN'S LULLABYE
I love you Lois Ann, my little
    grandchild.
You're Oh, so precious, when you
    smile.
Created by God, in heaven above,
For A Mamaw, who needed to
    love.

You grow bigger and brighter
    each day.
I love the laugh, you laugh your
    way.
Can hardly wait, till you walk
    and run,
You'll be like A wildflower,
    growing in the sun.

Oh, what A thrill, we had outside
    one day,
For with the wind, God, with you,
    did play.
You smiled with joy, and laughed
    in glee,
At God and the wind, you could
    not see.

You are indeed, A beautiful baby
    girl.
You are indeed, the joy in my sad
    world.
All through life, I'll hold your
    hand,
For I will always, love you, Lois
    Ann.

Go to sleep, in sleepy land,
Dream sweet dreams, sweet Lois
    Ann.
Dream of joy, and dream of love,
For that is what, you've plenty of.

Doris Courtney Lowdermilk
A FAWN
[This poem is dedicated to the
loving memories of our darling
daughter Cindy Ann—born
Apr. 2, 1959—died July 30,
1964 My lovely grandaughter
Donna L. Davidson—born Feb.
10, 1964—Nov. 8, 1981]
Once I saw a baby deer
His spots to me looked very queer
He was just a little fawn
Soon to grow big and strong

To travel where the grass is green
Sniff the air with nose so keen
Here a minute, then whizzing past
My you are so very fast

You hop, run, jump and leap
Always winding up on your feet
Just be careful my little friend
Least some hunter get you in the
    end

Thomas Marvin Wooten
THEATRE
Death is the most marvellous act
    of the stage—roles lent . . .
To bow before an audience
    when the spirit is bent;
To accept bouqueted—roses
    through an applause of tears—
Is the conundrum I've pondered
    for hundreds of years.

Therese Ellis Cook
IF WE WERE KIDS
[To my Mom, and Dad, who
gave me loads of love and
encouragement and to Peter
and Hal for their love and
inspiration]
If we were kids, like way back
    when,
I'd tell you my deepest, darkest
    secrets,
I'd let you go first to play
    hopscotch, and
I'd even take the first spoonful of
    medicine.

If we were kids, like way back
    when,
You'd let me use your favorite
    crayon and
When I broke it, you said, "that's
    o. k.,
I've got 29 more in the box."

If we were kids, like way back when,
We'd go to the candy store and buy
Each others favorite candy.
(It was easier to share that way.)

If we were kids, like way back when,
We'd listen to each other,
We'd talk to each other,
We'd help each other.

But, we're not kids, like way back
    when, anymore.
But it really shouldn't matter . . .
should it?

L. A. Green
**Message To An Unwed
    Mother**
So, you've a child, who bears not
    his father's name
this does not give you the right,
    to hang your head in shame
you have given birth, birth is life
don't be ashamed because you're
    not his wife

You sit for hours, asking yourself
    why?
poeple will talk no matter how
    much you cry
you loved and trusted him with
    your heart
don't be deceived because he tore
    your world apart

You made a mistake, you differ
    from no one else
people make them everyday,
    you're not by yourself
don't make yourself pay a much
    higher price
because one night of love
    changed you whole life

Mother, be proud, hold your head
    high
let your smile be as bright as the
    sun in the sky
think of the future which lies
    ahead
remember, a child full of life is
    better than one dead

Jeannie P. Mucklestone
THE AVIATOR
You fly like a dancer.
You speak through your craft,
Precision and planning—
Your steps are all mapped.
Through pain and knowledge
You master each step—
Though, pratice is pleasure
You strive for the best.

Your skill appears easy,
Performed with such grace;
With smooth execution
Each move flows in place.
With smooth execution
Each move flows in place.
The sky is your stage
As you dance upon air—
God is your critic;
And you know I care.

W. H. Byrd
BERNIE'S ANSWER
I recall the day before:
It seemed he was declaring war
Against some sin
Or subtle evil done to him.

His anger, often there but checked,
Now lept through hot emotions
Embered by some raw indignity.

I hurt to see him so distraught,
Sought to offer bandaged aid
In simple ways we understood.

Oblivious to the crowd
We huddled in a barroom booth,
Our thoughts unfurled
To the winds of our minds,
Discussing the rational world.

We asked:
Is the only constancy
The changing of the seasons?

We wondered:
Why we keep on keeping on
When all we are are pawns,
And the Powers are aligned
To keep us marching time.

We determined:
The course of life and living
Is a delicate balancing act
Where wisdom and tact must
    counteract
Our trials and tribulations,
Our festering frustrations.

We considered:
There's always a
    bone—of—contention
To cause apprehension and doubt
In affairs of the mind and the heart;
Nothing goes smoothly forever
No matter how clever we are
With our scheming, planning
And politic art.
Awhile and I was full;
Bored with conversation's bull!

Caring for less dreary company
I chose to let his misery wallow,
If it must, in his own pity.
It was best for me, I owned,
If he solved his destiny alone.

Today's Greatest Poems

With a casual word I left him
Brooding in that barroom booth
As strangers huddled near the walls,
Their wordless voices rising and falling
Against the background jukebox noise.

I surmised he was a kind,
Much like myself, resenting help;
Who'd find a way to lose himself
In some exotic fantasy
Then wake to face another day.

Yet I so little understood
That in the dungeon of his mind
Rack and wheel were working overtime,
Stretching, bending grievances,
Snapping strings of self—control,
Putting pressure on his soul.

I guess he was sequestered in the dark
With hatred and revenge sore festering.

(Such feelings best reveal themselves
In dark when shadows in the mind free play,
And demons deep within us have their say.)

In any case he chose to place
His inner sorrow upon us all
For all our sad tomorrows.

Sometime last night
In cold determined gloom
He put the muzzle to his face
And blew his fuckin' brains
across the room!

Nydia E. Tompkins
WINDOW PICTURES
From the east window in my bedroom
I can see the morn awaken . .
Yellow light climbs up the skyway
Proclaiming shades of night are broken.
Then the clouds are turned to crimson
Spreading upward in the sky.
Step by step sunlight advances
Bringing glory from on high.

Next I see the golden globe
Climbing through the willow tree
Heralding a glorious morning,
Natures gift for all to see.
Oh the beauty of the sunrise
On this thrice blessed land of ours
Rich with gardens and with fruit trees
And the fragrance of the flowers.

This view from my east window
Shows the Cascade Mountain peaks,
And their majesty and grandeur
Bring peace and comfort that I seek.
Yes, God moves in a mysterious way
His blessings to proclaim.
May we in our humble thinking
Bring our thanks unto His name.

Dorothy Jean West
A Meeting Of Strangers
I was feeling low—when
someone passed me on the street.
With words that were gentle,

and a smile that was sweet.
We stopped and talked
then walked together for awhile,
I listened to words of wisdom
that would enhance and beguile.

His countenance was gentle
his manner regal and supreme.
His voice was lyrical music
as he spoke of heavenly things.

He told of Christian hearts
that labored but did not fail.
Then he told of angelic glory,
and of saints they did hail.

Somehow I had forgotten
the problems of this world.
For in the mystery of his presence
Heaven did unfurl.

The hours grew late
We had nearly talked the night away.
He chose to make his departure
but I urged him to stay.

He looked back to smile
then wished me peace and well.
Then he was gone
to where I could not tell.

I looked toward Heavens lights
and remembered as I whispered a prayer,
"Be not forgetful of strangers,
for some have entertained
angels—unaware."

Fredrick A. Beickel
I Believe In Love Songs
I believe in love songs, yes it's true,
But after all isn't a prayer a love song too,
The poets write of love, broken hearts, and feeling blue,
The singers sing the lines, so do I, so do you,
Love songs tell of affairs of the soul and heart,
Without those feelings how could mankind have gotten its start,
So whenever you say a prayer to the Lord above,
Remember, you're singing a beautiful song of love . . .

Gina Ridolfi Raye
RAIN OF MADNESS
Fall—Rain of Madness
Flood my Garden with Frustration
Let your Soul Run Free . . .

I have held the need to cry,
To shout the injustice surrounding me.

I have burst with agony
to suffer
And fallen before to decay;

But now—Yes now
You can fall my tears of madness
Nourish my garden with
your outbursts . . .

My Soul is truly free.

Kerry King Turpin
STINKIN' LINCOLN
[To my Mom and Dad, Jeanette
and George King of Lincoln,
Maine, and to the Lincoln Pulp
& Paper Mill.]
A long time ago, in a town named
Lincoln

the mills were all workin' and
they were a stinkin'.
Some people laughed, and some
people cried.
They couldn't get rid of the smell
if they tried.

Air freshener was used, mainly
Scent of Roses.
After all this they still held their noses.
"What will we do?" they cried far and near.
"How will we ever get this smell out of the air?"

They fought and they argued, but all was in vain
For to this day the smell still remains.
Then one person cried, with his heart all a flutter,
"Don't you dare say a word, that's my bread and butter!"

W. F. Williams
SPACE TIME
Where is is's isness
Philosphers drift out to see
Charting islands in an ocean of emptiness
Upon philosophy their log to be

William Cain
FEET OF CLAY
[To my son, Dennis, a decent
and loving human being.]
That which I loved was gone
By choice of will slipped beyond
My strength, My presence no bond
Was I so unimportant not to matter
Did I wish only myself to flatter
Could my love have been unseen
Could my feelings have been unfelt
Did I preach and not hear
Was I looking as in a mirror
Can my heart ever be singing
The gaping hole is bleeding
Never understanding choice of will
Never accepting right of will
Continuing imperfection of mind
Continuing imperfection of heart
Continuing imperfection of soul

Christine V. Grupp
TO LOVE THE WORK
To love the work
Is not to love the man
But the more one devours it
The more one can understand that
What one is compelled to create
Is churned from the deep sea beneath
And each painting, poem, or play
Becomes a coral reef.

Wenda Kauffman
DISCIPLINE
They've taken away the sunshine
from your eyes and from your smile
Self—discipline they say you need
spirits not their style

Were our leaders born of discipline
was there no charm or fate
that caused them to be leaders
That caused them to be great

Why must they force this mold on you
Why force this task on me

To follow laws of man, they say
to be worth their company

Who gives their right to dictate
How pompous men can be
Have they forgotten this—of late
God made our spirits free . . .

Earl W. Shehorn
THE HURT
I hung my heart up on the wall today . . .
I believe it was to let it see the world,
As I feel the world sees me—unloving.

It sat up there and watched and laughed—
Like done to it so many times before.

It saw all the fakes hurting like hell—
By giving little and recieving all.

It also saw the faces with hurt and pain—
Just as it had felt so many times before.

Finally, it cried out waiting to be heard—
Someone came and too, left it wanting.

Able to take no more and breaking down—
I wept invisible, yet so visible tears.

Now, it still hangs there, up on the wall—
But no longer, is it waiting nor weeping.

Instead, it just thinks and wonders why—
Why we must go on living this way.

Realizing yesterday and today, are gone . . .
And tomorrow shall suffer the consequences,
My heart too, shall suffer with—the hurt.

Mark Anthony Simpson
TRAGEDY OF LOVE
The sky is clear-the stars are bright
I'm sitting up alone tonight.
An empty feeling deep inside
An answer no one can provide.
I wonder why I feel this way
There must be something I can say.

To write these words is not my place
But I believe in the human race.
I've done no deeds for any man
But I can help you understand
One lonely bird in a flock of geese.
I'm screaming out for love and peace.

Sitting in my Livingroom
I heard John Lennon met his doom
I heard the news tonight. Oh, man
But it's so hard to understand
What gives this crazy guy the right
to end a legend's life tonight.

When John arrived tonight at home
The lunatic stood all alone
He called his name, dropped to

549

a stance
But Lennon never had a chance.
A wacko with a .38
The stupid 'screwball' changes fate.

Once a cornerstone of four
John knew that there must be
    more
The guiding spirit stepped out
    alone
To enjoy his wife and make a
    home.
The world just could not
    understand
Why Lennon chose to leave the
    band.

He had a love so very real
That Yoko and himself could feel.
Although put down by fans and
    friends
They shared a love that never
    ends.
The world was looking for a catch
They're just in love, a perfect
    match.

In his life he loved us all
and now he takes a tragic fall
An honest man, he spoke his
    mind
It hurt sometimes but he was
    kind
This feeling of rage. What can we
    do
He preached of love, what would
    he do?

He lived his life in his own right
And never stopped his endless
    fight
His honesty touched me and you
A man we all could look up to
The man's been called a superstar
Who's helped create what we all
    are.

Why peaceful men end up this
    way
Like Jesus, John, and J.F.K.
A mystery that is so unfair
That leaves us feeling robbed and
    bare
Though John and I have never met
I feel the loss; a deep regret.

His message is clear and always
    has been
Honesty and love is our chance
    to win.
A working class hero and now
    he's gone
But his music and wisdom
    forever
lives on
If he were the shepherd and we
    were
the herd
The main thing he'd teach us,
of course is the word . . . LOVE.

Marylou G. Frisbie
IT'S CHERRY
*[Dedicated to Nika (Nee-ka,
meaning Victorious Heart), my
little granddaughter, who gave
me the core thought for this
poem.]*
"You call it red—and that's all
    right,"
She assured me, sparing my
    feelings;
And her voice dropped low
To share her secret—

"But really it's CHERRY!"
And that four-year old had it
    together
When she came, a fist full of
    crayons,
Testing me—
"What color is this one,
    Grandma?"
I failed with my confident,
"Why, that one's red!"

How dull my grown-up mind
    becomes!
Technically correct—it *is* red—
But so much more!
There's a roundness and richness,
A mystery and wonder,
A flame and flavor in CHERRY
Not found in simply 'red'—

There's magic that abounds
In everyday things around;
Lord, awaken my imagination—
Renew my sight, quicken my mind
To catch the shining beauty,
To experience the luscious
    sweetness of
'Really it's CHERRY!'

Thelma Louise Holt
MY LADY-IN-WAITING
She waits, my lady waits,
She is tired of waiting,
For the pain to be gone.
Because it has been there so long

She waits, my lady waits,
For her Lord to call her home.
And so she will abide,
Until she gets to the "other side."

This lady was always patient and
    kind,
This is the lady who taught me
    to mind,
This is the lady who taught me
    God's words,
And to love the songs of His
    birds.

This is the lady who sang to me,
This lady held me on her knee.
She waits, my lady waits,
For the day to come,
When her Lord will take her home.

Patricia Morgan Taylor
Up Early In the Morning
Up early in the morning
push back the covers of the dawn
Appear bright and fresh
with the brand new world.
Take his hand and he might lead
    you
'round the shining sun.
But time is oh, so short
and life a darkening moon
and you, my friend
but a silent shadow
at the coming
of the dawn.

Frances Lowell Smith
THE GREATEST STORY
I would walk in the paths
In the drifts of snow,
And listen to the gales
Of the wild winds blow.

Then on thru' the hill lands
To the villages bright,
Where the season of Christmas
Fills the windows with lights.

Where the tall trees stand
Overlooking the square,
And the festivity sounds
Of carols fill the air.

I would sit by the hearth
Where the warm firesides glow,
And listen to children
As thru the streets they go.

Singing to the shut-ins
And just all over town,
As they do every year
When Christmas comes around.

I would sing a hymn too
Of the greatest story told,
About the birth of Jesus
Told by men of old.

And hold within my heart
All the peace and cheer,
To keep me for today
And all the coming year!

Peg Katuin
YOU
When I think of you
I hear the soft patter of rain,
Softer than the morning dew.

You're like the singing of a bird
In early spring
The most beautiful sound I have
    ever heard.

A fresh fallen snow
Over a quiet, peacefull wood
Broken only by the blowing wind.

The gentle fall of
Turning leaves,
Or a deer drinking at a stream.

There is nothing to describe my
    love for you,
No words can tell how I feel,
Because it's between just us two.

Eric R. Moline
LINDA
I met you and was quickly
    dazzled by none other. Warmth
    (persona same as truth deep
    down inside) exudes, those cold
    stand nigh and warm
    themselves within your
    cheerful youth. Can beauty not
    envelop this warm heart? And
    strength cerebral, too, equal
    this soul? Review once more
    the truth, the soul as start. On
    even terms are beauty, brains.
    The whole lies close to me, yet
    still too far away, because
    between our bodies lie the
    miles. Love cannot grow o'er
    such a length, we may as well
    be stranded kits on separate
    isles. Concede this though:
    Ne'er should a thought
    encroach Katabasis before the
    real approach.

Anna Guerrero
STACEY
One day I met a girl named
    Stacey she was my dream come
    true, and may I say she is very
    crazy too.

I would like to express in some
    way so that you could see, and
    understand why the rays of
    sunshine have been on my face
    since I met you Stacey. As I say
    bye I won't cry, but I'll thank
    God for he chose you, and I

know I won't ever lose a
    treasured friend whom I can't
    measure. Who was sent to help
    me along the road, to lift the
    load I held, felt, and dealt with
    for such a long time.

With God's grace and your help, I
    have stayed in the race, and
    kept the pace without a trace
    of defeat. I've kept the good
    fight of faith that I might claim
    victory, and praise God which
    is my right, for His light that
    He allows to shine so bright
    like a candle in my life.

I was being molded into pure gold
    I'm told, so I prayed to the Lord
    and I was made bold, and now
    I've found that I'm no longer
    bound, but free as a bird with a
    new song to sing.

Ethel Howard
GRIEVE NOT FOR BEAUTY
Grieve not for Beauty,
It cannot die
Though centuries long in the
    dust it may lie.
Grieve not.

Grieve not for Love,
It will come again,
Releating its passion, its ardor, its
    pain.
Grieve not.

Grieve not for the Light
That illumined thy soul;
Its radiance returning shall again
    make thee whole
By its gleam thou wert led,
By its rays thou were fed
Its glory again shall descend on
    thy head.
Grieve not.

Frances Hendrix Manley
ANGEL TEARS
The angel tears are falling softly
    from the sky
The heavens have bowed their
    head in sorrow while angel
    tears are falling blurring the
    vision from my eyes.
My love I have sent to you
    broken hearted and in despair
But you could change this Hell of
    sorrow into sunshine if only
    you would say you still care
The angel tears are falling softly
    on my window pane
While memories of your manley
    sweetness are slowly driving
    me insane
May God and you have mercy on
    my sinful soul
For life without you baby is filled
    with sadness and sorrow, and
    angel tears yet untold.

Lorna F. Copen
A SACRED SPOT
*[In loving memory of Ray D.
Copen My dear husband and
my dear friend]*
There's a sacred spot in the
    bedroom
Where my husband knelt to pray
The memories I have of his
    faithfulness
Will never go away.

On his knees first thing in the
    morning

And many times during the day
He would ask Lord to Bless us
And keep us in the way.

When trouble would come to
plague us
Down on his knees he went
To wait on an answer from
Heaven
As many hours on his knees he
spent.

When the answer came what
rejoicing
As he testified of the Lord
Of the way he kept us day by day
As we followed his Holy word.

Now since he has gone to Heaven
I must never forget to pray
At that sacred spot in the
bedroom
To be guided day by day.

Omid Ahmadi
VICTORY RHYMS
Can you hear the parade now,
the bugles and the drums?
The men marched, the children
watched,
and the women cheered them on.
The Lion, the Sword and the Sun
burned,
the Peacock turned to ashes,
the lover's heart shattered from
afar,
as we danced to victory rhyms.

Now we stand on blood stained
streets
chatting about the neighbor's boy
swinging from the hangman's bar,
and the wages his father has to
pay
to take his dead son home.
The widows weep while the
orphans sleep,
men march, bullets fly, homes
burn
as we wait in lines for bread,
milk, and meat.

Nellie Elizabeth Millard
THE LONELY BEGGAR
Oh please, someone hear me
No, don't just hear me
I beg you, listen!
Please take the time to listen
Console me, yet be firm with me
Help calm this bitter hate, the
burning tide
Understand me, I beg you
Please try to understand me
And know the reason I feel this
way
Then perhaps tomorrow
I, the lonely beggar
Can help someone else along
life's way.

Ray Montierth
REFLECTIONS
Mystery's aura hovers
Elicits human query
Whispers age-old questions
Reflective mind must tarry.

Whence man? Why? Whither to?
His kinship to creation?
Possessed of faults and virtues
Despairs and aspirations.

Just beyond the mortal grasp
Elusive answers lie
Yet inspiration falters

And reason leads awry.

Subtle yearning awakens
Bestir primeval embers
Though outward senses darken
The inner soul remembers.

Knowledge felt though inexpress
Truth's unseen fire deigns
Light pervades, all doubts dispel
A sense of purpose reigns.

Ann M. Henning
LIFE'S DESIRE
Life is full of many pleasures,
One of them is love, which we
search for in vain,
It is a constant search not really
sought to win,
But there is so much from which
to gain.

It seems we are always looking
for happiness,
Always looking and always
hoping to find,
What solves our outgoing
curiousness,
About our strange and human
mind.

With a constant need to know,
And a continuous desire to live,
We keep on and don't let our
feelings show,
It is meant that love is to give.

Even as intelligent as the human
mind,
And with the body full of never
ending zeal,
We have yet the knowledge to find,
The words to express the love
that we feel.

Linda Grace Marion
SPEAKING
Not words
But something
Inside
Saying
Like wet sand
Lost footprints
Walking
Occasionally getting
Feet wet
Birds flying
Landing
Taking off
Slowly beginning
To look
Into your face
Waiting.

Mrs. Lillian L. Ayres
WINDY SPARROWS
Sparrows out of cloud-space
slipping, falling,
Wings wind-ruffled, spread to the
storm;
Find a rock ledge to balance and
cling to,
Find a stone-crevice, and rest till
morn.

"Let all nature rage like giants
screaming,
Wait awhile and rest, then fly
free.
Look to tomorrow, there's hope to
borrow,
No more sorrow . . . wait, and
you will see.

"Follow silver clouds like arrows
pointing,

Fly up high and challenge the
dawn,
Rise on glad wings with hope and
with courage,
Spread your strong wings; fly on ...
Yes, fly on!"

Confidence and strength
renewed, they thrust abreast
Into hevenly paths, and are gone ...
Windy Sparrows who braved the
dark tempest,
Found their strength in rest, and
then flew on.
"Love the birds; they'll make it
now, Bright Dawn."

Carlisle Ramsey
WINE OF SYMPATHY
*[I am dedicating this poem to
my Master Jesus the Christ, as
a small token of appreciation
for drinking a bitter portion,
that I might drink of the sweet
wine of life.]*
I wish that I could take your cup,
Which is now, full of grief
And drain its bitter portion,
To bring you quick relief;
I would, but it cannot be.

However, as the days go by,
Whenever we shall meet,
We will sip from the other's cup,
Blending bitter with the sweet
Thus, drink the wine of sympathy.

Dawn Stella
OUTSIDERS
*[To Ms. Perkins, whose
inspiration opened my eyes to
the archives of inner poetry.]*
Outsiders looking into the
Universe without a reason.
Tired of the endless
Struggle to find themselves
In this world of clones.
Daring to be different with the
intention of
Ending the burning in their
Raging souls . . . and trying to find
Someone who cares!

Debra A. M. Michon
HUNGRY EYES
Gaze into those hungry eyes,
Deeply, see how lonliness cries;

And then, you'll come to realize,
How very abstrusely, the passion
lies;

It's a pity knowing she silently
weeps,
In the lonely hours, of her sleep;

The kind of loving she needs so
much,
Appears to be, so out of touch;

She wants someone who she can
hold,
When winters' blustery nights,
get cold;

An ear to her words, a shoulder
for crying,
Why are these simple things, so
denying?

She can be so naive, yet again, so
seductive,
She can be so soft-spoken, and
willing to give;

But don't hurt her, or she'll
become recluse,
And the love she so wanted, she
would refuse;

Gaze into her saddened eyes,
See not a tear, but silent cries;

Surely by now, you recognize,
How very abstrusely, the passion
lies.

Deborah L. Schnall
UNTITLED
walking through the snow
        I leave a life, a footprint
                fossilized in ice

Mary (Tromboni) Criniti
THE MOUNTAINS
The mountains soaring in the sky
They lift my spirits oh so high,
The trees that line the mountains
edge
In fall they show their hues of
red,
In winter they're covered with
snow so white
That makes me feel a glow so
bright,
Their beauty is a thing to behold
They're often lined with colors
of gold.

Kathleen King
INSOMNIA
I have counted all the stars in the
sky, and all the blades of grass
on the lawn.
Two great armies, well matched.
Someday they will come together
in battle and where will we
hide?

Heidi Kaminski
TIME TO LOVE
I loved you yesterday.
I love you today.
And I will love you tomorrow.

Our yesterdays are in the past.
We have today but, we may not
have tomorrow.

Love isn't. time.
Time is just a place to keep
things in.

Joyce M. Speiller
CHILD OF DIVORCE
"My daddy's picking me up at
school today,"
Announced the red-headed, freckle-
faced
Little girl to her kindergarten
teacher,
Her blue eyes the size of silver
dollars,
As she nervously fingered the
lace fringe of her green velvet
dress.

This was the third day of the
third week
That the child told her teacher
That Daddy was picking her up.
But Daddy never did.
And the child's big, blue eyes
never sparkled anymore.
The child who used to proudly
count to forty-two,
Now got confused counting past
ten.
The little girl who used to identify
Red, green, and blue with such
pride
Now thought that blue was red
and red was green.
And the little girl stopped
swinging
From the junglejim during recess,
Instead standing listlessly by
herself under the big oak tree.
During show and tell, the little
blue-eyed girl always told
That Daddy was picking her up
after school.
But Daddy never did.

Nancy S. Bernard
Christ, It's Christmas Again
These damn holidays
drive me crazy

Maybe if I favored
some kind of religion
I wouldn't mind so.
But I don't
(Thank God.)

Even on the forgotten days
I remember the ones I love.

I don't need a holiday
to say it with flowers
or spell it out
inside a Hallmark.
(And you know, we both hate
diamonds.)

So when I say
I love you.
It's not because of Christmas
but rather
in spite of it.

Estellee Scott Pierce
THE LOVE OF MY LIFE
[This poem was written about
my loving husband, Gene
Francis Pierce, whom I married
"Thanksgiving Day—1977."]
He definitely is the love of my life
And I'm more than proud to be
known as His wife.

He's given me His all and it
seems so unreal,
I could never put in words
exactly how I feel.

He's honest, He's true, He's gentle
and kind,
He's one in a million, and I'm glad
He's all mine.

He doesn't get older as the years
go by,
And He makes me feel younger,
this love of my life.

Now things are not perfect,
nothing's perfect you see,
But what is not perfect, He fixes
for me.

We walk hand in hand through
sunshine and rain,

We share all our moments and
take nothing for vain.

This Superman is just that you see,
How could he help not, when
He's one with Me.

Laura Lewing Simpson
BROADWAY
Broadway, glamorous Broadway,
Well known spot on this Earth.
All types of people on your sides
are trotting
Some slow, some fast, and some
with a smile.
Evening clothes, beautiful
styles and colors,
Sparkling jewelry beautify them.
Along side with them, how
different:
Pale-worn, starved faces, torn
clothes,
Toes sticking out their shoes.
Broadway, glamorous Broadway,
Lit with myriads of lights.
How brightly they shine on your
people
How well they harmonize with
you.
Broadway! Oh Broadway!
People walking up and down
your path.
Broadway you are a perfect
symphony.
Broadway what is your secret
magic?
Laughter, song, tears and curses,
Broadway all these you possess.
Broadway, what a panorama
At night while walking one sees.
And what A Symphony from
above one hears.
Broadway, glamorous Broadway
Most known spot on this Earth!

Eric Farley
partners
when pen play ends a
sleeping cat shares dreams a-lap
the purring poet

Roxi Soucy
LOVE ON THE ROCKS
[A special dedication to my
godmother, Marion, who
supported me all the way while
I was growing up.]
Love as it is,
is not so blind.
As it may be in the air,
though who would know?
Watching each other among the
aura—
What could it be?
Friendship?
Attractiveness?
Love?
Who knows?
Love on the Rocks,
being as still as ice,
Not knowing the feeling.
Keeping watch;
He makes His approach.
The ice breaks,
The mystic aura surrounds.
As they love together,
They remember the first time
they met;
so still,
so beautiful—
Love on the Rocks,
Being the first step toward
Happiness.

Jane D. Meadows
The Rainbow In the Heart
Let me touch your heart with a
Rainbow, my child,
With the symbol of yore that
means "Hope."
When the storms all around you
close in, my child,
Don't you stay in the darkness
and grope!
The sun and the rain make the
Rainbow, my child;
Life is sadness and gladness, we're
told!
Just remember the Rainbow, and
smile, my child,
For it's colors still glow, as of old!
Let me touch your heart with a
Rainbow, my child.
Let the beauty and brightness
surround;
Look to Heaven and thank God
for Hope, my child,
And the Glory of Life will be
found!

Rhonda K. Clayborn
TALKS WITH GOD
I hear the ocean calling to me,
with silent whispers she
beckons. Reminding me of
moonlit nights resting by her
side; while shimmering waves
crashed around me, and I spoke
face to face with God.
Those talks I remember, oh so
well, but His face I just can't
recall. So now to the ocean I
shall return, to speak with Him
once again.

Sue Ellen Richardson
THE PATH
[Dedicated to that certain look
that tells me you'll be there.]
Sometimes the path seems endless
and much too steep to climb
with many a twist to prolong the
journey
and complicate the mind.

And just when I finally catch my
breath
a storm moves in from the sea
But the gift of a rainbow comes
after the rain
with hope in my heart—I'm free.

I've heard it whispered among the
trees
and I know in my heart it's true
At the end of the path a hand's
reaching out
I know it belongs to you.

Rose Bush
BIRDS—WE
Windheld just above the bluff—
Sharp eyes fixed on the meadow's
edge
The small brown hawk
Moves on educated pinions and
rudder tail
His disciplined body on perfect
point.

Wheeling on the updraft, the
screeching gulls
White and grey grace in fluid
motion
"Follow-the-Leader" as they glide
Swiftly, sharply banking above
the cliff.

Out early this morning—the
hang gliders—
A bright variety of colored wings.
One, soaring window-high
Along our cliff-perched house
Greets me through the glass with
an exultant shout!

Earthbound—I—throughout the
day—
Can scarcely wait for nightfall
When in dreams upon my bed, I
Too, gloriously extravagantly free
Shall wing away through
boundless sky!

H. Webster Stull
LAMENT
What a sorry situation
For a great and mighty nation
Such as this one to endure
While we wrestle with inflation
We continue the creation
Of more wealthy and more poor
And we're given the impression
That we border on depression
While interest rates and prices
soar
That just adds to my confusion
And it shatters my illusion
That I will now or ever know the
score

Mary Brickman Mayse
JUST A CALL
When I'm feeling all alone,
I get up and dial the telephone.
Dialing the number I know so well,
thinking of all the things I have
to tell.
I wait so intensely for you to
answer my call,
a chance to tell you it all.
The distance between us there
needs to be none,
but now the phone still ringing . . .
19, 20, 21.
My face becomes filled with
despair,
in just finding you not there.
I'll call you again I know I will,
but till that time I'll miss you still.
I'll keep the thought till I get
through,
just a chance to talk to you.

F. Allan Brett
ROSES FOR MY ROSE
Mr. Florist I want some red roses,
for the rose of my life,
Give her a yellow rose,
deep from my heart,
Send her a wild Irish rose too,
I'll send Rose a wild rose, from
the country side.
Roses for the love of my life,
roses for my sweet rose.
Send her a room full of roses,
one for each time I loved her.
Mr. Florist send Rose a rose,
a rose of love from me.
Roses for my Roses.

Beatrice Owen
HOSANNA! TO OUR KING!
[This poem is dedicated to my
beloved daughters, Gem and
Jewel and to my Dearest God
son, Benny.]
Hosanna! Hosanna! Hosanna to
our king.
Hosanna! Hosanna! Let infant
voices sing.
Hosanna! Hosanna! Our sweetest
anthem raise.

Hosanna! Hosanna! Our Saviour's
name we praise.
Hosanna! Hosanna! Hosanna!

Hosanna! Hosanna! Let every
tribe and kin.
Hosanna! Hosanna! Their
sweetest note begin.
Hosanna! Hosanna! Let all palm
branches wave.
Hosanna! Hosanna! For Christ has
power to save.

Hosanna! Hosanna! Hosanna!

All glory! All honor! high
adoration bring.
Hosanna! Hosanna! To Jesus, Lord
and King.
Hosanna! Hosanna! Join hands,
lift heads and sing.
Hosanna! Hosanna! For Christ our
risen King.

Hosanna! Hosanna! Hosanna!

Carolyn D. Vaughan
GOD'S LOVE
[To my Grandparents]
God's love we'll never lose
Even though, we only love what
we choose
For God's love in heaven above
So pure and sweet just like the
doves
It out numbers each and every star
It out shines man's love by far

So come on and try, it sure is fine
And in the last day together with
Him we'll dine
Just listen to Jesus cry
He wants you in His kingdom,
and not in hell to die!

Eulah Proctor Stanley
THE CHIROPRACTOR
*[Dr. Michael J. Badanek—Ocala,
Florida, Dr. Joseph F. Rooney, Jr.
—Wilmington, Delaware, And
to the men and women of the
Chiropractic Assn., all over the
world]*
Listen to me world
I have something to say
The Chiropractic doctor
is here to stay
He is the doctor of the future
with healing on his mind
A specialist of the nervous system
and the spine
With his Ultra-sonic touch
relief is on the way
And I bet you didn't realize
You had a misaligned vertebrae

J.L.A. Roberts
VISION: Mother/Son
I feel that I'm alone
unacknowledged.
I identify with the unemployed
the colored the retarded
the disfigured the disenchanted
the segregated
the disfranchised humbled
dandelions the losers.

But, and/or similarly, I am very
well-read
in the old way: in which were
read the very
well-established classics. One
needs to name
them only once. Some of them, in
fact are very much

alive and trembling, shouting,
although not all: take Dickens
Zola Kafka Rillke Marquand
Murdoch Fallaci Neruda
Whomsoever smokes or doesn't '
for a good reason
or no reason: whomsoever
protests or doesn't for reason
or no reason. O you know it, you
name it I am one
of those interested in welfare of
no names the over-
weight the underweight yes,
Christ on the cross has an
equal in me I, I too, am helpless,
unlike Jesus veined
with faults
But although I am the bottom
line of the triangle
please Jesus save my bright and
shining one my son
the girls stream after him like
schools of fish he drinks
wrecks cars and beats his
precious girl/mother of his kids
I helpless beg of you: sweet Jesus
save his soul from hell

Ann Foley
The Days Of Make Believe
*[Dedicated to Betty, the little
girl, I once knew.]*
Oh! wouldn't it be nice,
If you could go back to your
coloring book world?
When life was just a fantasy.
You could be anybody you wish
to be,
You could escape through the
pages of Donald Duck.
You could be that man in a red
fire truck.
Or Donald Duck didn't have to
be Donald Duck.
You could make believe he was
Daffy Duck or Daniel Duck,
Or any duck you wish him to be.
You didn't have to be a man in a
red fire truck,
You could be a man in a blue
truck or a green truck.
You could be a man in a red, blue
or green truck,
Or any color truck you wish it to
be.
But now there are no colors,
Everything appears black or
white.
There is only a right or wrong.
Donald Duck is Donald Duck.
All firemen do have a red fire
truck.
The world is not what you wish
it to be,
For that is known as reality.

Lori Avery Patterson
A View Of the World (As Seen Through Button Eyes)
A tattered little teddy bear,
Alone upon a shelf,
Sat looking out in silence
At the world all by itself;
At its poverty, and its crime,
And wars between the nations,
And at all of the destruction
Of each of God's creations.
And this one little teddy bear,
Alone on a shelf so high,
Sat looking out in sorrow
And cried a sawdust cry.

Cg.
RESCUED
*[To Chester, For being the
foundation of my inspiration
and courage.]*
I don't know why it happens,
Or from where the feelings
come,
But the sadness just surrounds
me,
And I feel so damned undone.

I try to walk right past it,
I pretend it's just not there.
But somehow nothing I can do,
Will make it disappear.

In my desperation I look to you
again,
You smile and hold me tightly,
Reassuring me my friend,
That I have just been rescued,
By our love that never ends . . .

Linda L. Hughes
TO FALL IN LOVE
Moonbeams drifting thru the
tree-tops
Resting on your raven hair.
Love and beauty; witchery and
madness,
Met my gaze and held me there.

Last night I walked as one who
dreams,
Is led away to rapturous shores;
And there tastes of forbidden
glory;
A transcient glimpse thru other
doors.

The night-winds played their
bewitching song;
The moon cast a magic spell,
And made the earth an
enchanted garden,
A beauteous spot where lovers
dwell.

With your gentle caress and
tender lips
You led my heart away,
To a realm which mortals only
know,
When joyous love has come to
stay.

Efrain Lopez R.
Our Best Friend: The Tree
*[To the memory of my sister
Silvia Lopez de Acevedo.]*
The tree is our best friend
it is our companion since we are
born,
until we die . . .
it adorns our woods, mountains
and parks,
and it is very useful to mankind.

From the branch of a tree
our cradle was made . . .
and from its generous trunk
we obtain thru our lives
furniture and commodities.

Jesus was a Carpenter . . .
and perhaps from him
the tree had learned to give,
to give always
without expecting any reward.

That's why we have to respect it,
that's why we have to cherish it,
to protect it . . . to love it.

Let us not climb on its branches
so we will not harm it,

let us prevent forest fires
so it will not get burnt to ashes,
let us defind it from the criminal
Ax
so it will not get chopped
down . . .

And let us never forget,
that this wonderful friend
is so attached to our lives,
that as from its branches
our cradle was made,
from them will also be made . . .
the coffin that will keep our
remains.

Mike Roddin
SEARCHING
I am a voyager on an odessey
across the corridors of time,
I am looking for a long lost land
that exists only in the shadows
of my mind,
I am stranded between
nothingness and the eternity of
space,
I am a marathon runner entered
in a never ending race,
I am the wizard of an enchanted
land that no one has ever seen,
I am the sandman who turns the
dark of night into the
mysterious illusion of a dream,
I am an intergallactic wanderer
questioning the meaning of all
I see,
I am searching the very corners of
the universe, I am searching for
a clue to me.

Tiffany Mauk
THE SECRET
A secret, a secret.
I just heard a secret,
And nobody else must hear.
No talking, no telling,
No whispering, no hinting,
Or a secret will disappear.

A secret, a secret.
I just heard a secret.
Must it be kept so WELL?
A second—A minute—
An hour—A DAY.
I'm afraid I'm going to tell.

Norma Cruz
OR SO IT SEEMS
Love is Wondersul . . .
Love . . . is what all girls dream.
Love can stop time on the stop.
Or so it seems . . .

Love is truth and devotion.
Love like peaches and cream.
Love is a great emotion.
Or so it seems . . .

Love is an unending feeling.
Love like the ripple in a stream.
It can send your heart reeling.
Or so it seems . . .

Love is like the glow of the moon
It's like the twinkling stars that
gleam.
Love, off your feet, it'll make you
swoon.
Or so it seems . . .

Love is the making up after the
spat.
It's what fills your long night's
dream.
But love is not at all like that,
It's just the way it seems.

Beverly A. Wilsey
DEAR GOD
Now more than ever
I really need to know
That You're there with me
Wherever I go.

I need the reassurance
That someone does care
I don't think I ask much
It only seems fair.

I feel like a baby
Just starting to grow
Trying to hold onto the hope
Of someday being able to crow,

I'm going to make it
Of this I am sure
Just show me some guidance
To help find the cure.

So please show a sign
That you're there along the way
You can't do it for me
Just please help when I stray!

Sarah L. Fairbanks
WEEPING WIDOW
Oh, to be young again
Is that why I'm crying?
No. No it's not.
I have no fear of dying
But, oh to be loved again
Someone to care
To hold someone's hand again
Willing to share
These last lonely miles
Neither alone
I'm crying for someone
To walk me on home.

Elynor Agnes Baran
DON'T BE AFRAID
Chipmunk—Chipmunk!
Why do you run
When I appear?

Day after day
You are nobly dressed
In attire that's always the same—

Lovely, tiny, fearful and swift—
Don't be afraid—
God the Great Master created you!

John J. Young
THE MOON IS FULL
The dark of night was meant for
     man to hear in,
   No barriers to mute the cosmic
     call;
And mysteries of the universe
     grow clear in
   The quaint, omniscient spell of
     alcohol.

A rising moon doth captivate my
   thinking,
As it intrigues all those who
   scan the sky.
It smiles on my contemplative
   drinking;
   I toast its bleary face with
     friendly eye.

I welcome thee, celestial borne
   relation,
   Be thou of cheddar or volcanic
     ash,
We are both children of a vast
   creation,
   What am I? A blob of corned
     beef hash.

And bring along each solar-
     saddened buddy,

Planet, comet, meteor, asteroid.
And the telescopic peeping toms'
   rude study
   Will end in chaos, peering into
     void.

Since I've no heart for cruel
   discrimination,
   Flying saucers, spiral nebulae,
Are mentioned in my sweeping
   invitation
   To join me in this fling till
     break of day.

Egad! While in my spacial dream
   cavorting,
   An astronomic wonder looms
     in view!
The world must heed this news,
   for I'm reporting
   There is not *one* lunar
     sphere—but *two!*

But wait; unless these bloodshot
   orbs mistake me,
   I now perceive *four* moons
     afloat on high!
Prepare my cot—oblivion
   o'ertakes me.
   Indeed, the moon is full, and so
     am I.

Tom Coffland, Jr.
THE POET'S NOTICE
It came in the U.S. Mail
It took the wind right out of my
   sail
Quickly I came bounding back
Took on an altogether different
   tack

     Ahh! The rejection notice

I wrote a poem to counteract
My helpless feelings still
   untracked
Because the note does assail
The distressing thought that I
   may fail

     Ooh! That rejection notice

Doubtlessly I have the knack
For writing poems, and that's a
   fact
Kindly sirs do please curtail
These missives sent that make
   me pale

     Ugh! Those rejection notices

Jeanine Diane Ralstin
**You've Got Rain In Your
   Eyes**
You've got rain in your eyes.
And I love you, but why.
I'd like to propose.
But God only knows.
There hasn't been a time.
I haven't had you off my mind.
And roses and wine go together
   just fine.
Yes, I want you for mine.
I want you for eternal time . . .

Frances Pickell
NATURE'S WAY . . .
Before Dawn I climbed to the top
   of the hill
The moon was full, everything
   was still,
Looking down into the valley
   below
The moon on the mist had a
   mysterious glow,
Beyond the valley, very near the
   wood

A mother Deer, and her cute
   fawn stood.

Then slowly, the sun started to
   rise
Bringing the familiar nature cries,
Awaking from his lofty height
The Eagle called out in his
   morning flight,
From a nearby pasture I heard a
   cow bawl
Then a rooster shouted his
   morning call.

Right here I could forever stay
With Nature's ever changing way,
But day has come, time to descend
From the sights and sounds that
   God does send.

Joseph J. Thomer
ONE IN HIMSELF
Is there life out there for me?
If there is then set me free
I know you're only trying to help
But I just want to find my
   interself
Don't be "Sad", and don't be "Blue"
Finding you was my greatest
   wealth
So let me "Go", and let me "Grow"
Let me learn about life and
   everything
And one day soon I'll fly back
And only then I'll shed my wings
But don't go too far my dear friend
For I am you and you are me
They physical self and the
   mental being
And together we shall travel
   through eternity

Sandra Fagot Glazer
YAD VADHEM
[In Memory of my Friend J.
Warren Malley December 17,
1982]
What
Another bus load.

Americans this time?
No matter.

They've enjoyed our trees, a
   pleasant park.
Like Dachau?

Here come the rest—what can it
   mean to them?
Cypresses posted along Judean
   Hills.

Talking's stopped.
Stillness of lost notes of an
   unstuck chord.

How many more will come to
   tour?
About six million worth . . .

Joyce Handeland
STRANGERS IN TRUTH
It seems as if we walk through
   each other's lives
                    As strangers;
Too afraid or ashamed to be open.
Communication becomes
   obsolete and we withdraw.
You give me evasive answers to
   my questions,
And I feel angry, rejected, and
   hurt.
My imagination becomes victim
   to my insecurities,
And my hold weakens.
I shelter you from stark truths,

Knowing your reaction and
   fearing it.
As strangers we met.
So shall we part.

Kay Isfort
SOMETHING OF GOD
God of trees, grass, flowers, birds
   and many other things; give us
   part of thy beauty and strength.
   As they grow, let us grow,
   fledgling at first—unsure,
   distraught, searching, never
   sure of understanding. Painful,
   always remembering our
   failures, never sure of
   success . . .

A soul forever longing to find
   that which is holy, that which
   is great; to find something
   beyond all this—some
   comprehension of why things
   have been, are to be, will be
   and ought to be.

Jennifer K. Hall
I'VE GOT IT ALL
I had nothing
I was nobody
Going nowhere
And then there was you.

I possess everything
I am somebody
I wish to be nowhere else
Because I'm with you.

I am content with most
   everything
I am jealous of nobody
I'm in love with life
Just because of you.

Roswyn Cockrill
THE DAFFODIL
Twilight—and the evening still
Pauses on the grassy hill,
Rests upon the daffodil.

Touches now the golden crown
Smoothes the lace-trimmed
   dressing gown
Brushes the bloom where the rain
   came down.

The cooling breeze now bids
   farewell:
A last caress of the golden bell,
And drifts along the grassy dell.

The dying of the sun's last light
The hint of moon and silver
   night
Speed the evening on her flight.

Clifford Bailey
ARTIFACT OF THE ICE
There's a vast deepfreeze above
   the clouds,
   Enfolding a tor's ziggurat
Where a mighty bark once came
   to rest
   In the mountains of Ararat.

Night refugees from a primal
   world
   Came forth with the beasts and
     birds
To dwell in a greatly altered land
   And replenish its tribes and
     herds.

The rocks that fall from its lofty
   peaks
   And roll down its grumbling
     flanks

Appear as the hail in the day of
  God,
  In size, like to militant tanks.

And still, they say, when the sun
  grows warm,
  From a cleft in its tomb so stark
That the hoary crypt reveals the
  prow
  Of the antediluvian ark.

Though many souls, its terrors
  have braved
  From frost to its bolts of wrath,
Not one has uncovered that
  artifact
  From the depths of its icy bath.

One day, perchance, ere the crack
  of doom
  Its sheath will no longer hide
The ancient ship from the eyes of
  men,
  And God will be glorified.

Julia Rost Farmer
Love and the Older Woman
Across the room he smiled at me
For no good reason that I could
  see
So I smiled back and thus began
My saga of the happy man
Whose shirt a princeling sought
  to find
To bring him joy and peace of
  mind.

Black tie he wore, and crisp white
  shirt
That battened down an inner hurt
So like my own I wept anew
For hearts ordained to break in
  two.

His gentle words to one grown old
I strung as pearls on a chain of
  gold—
An amulet against the day
When one would go and one
  would stay
Like Mother Hen and Baby Chick
Who leaves his nest for a cute
  young trick.

So goes my day. In the night I hear
The whir of wings and shed a tear
For the woman wed in an era of
  strife:
Worshiped co-pilot/abandoned
  wife.

Edna Estelle Hackler
I Kept No Secrets From You
*[This poem is true. The voice
of the angel was my little girl
Dianne. I dedicate in memory
of her]*
Across the table sits my little boy
  five

eating ice cream in a room so
  quiet
Suddenly I heard a voice I knew
Softly Saying "I KEPT NO
  SECRETS FROM YOU"

"I KEPT NO SECRETS FROM
  YOU"
It wasn't imagination her voice I
  knew
Heaven was around me an angel
  was speaking through
Softly Saying "I KEPT NO
  SECRETS FROM YOU"

In moments and seconds I relived
  the past
I was seeing a little girl and

her daddy laugh
I could hear me scolding as they
  would hide coloring books away
I was remembering sorrow and
  heartaches.
Then a voice broke the spell in
  the room
When my little boy said "Mama
  what's wrong."
How could I tell him, how could I
  explain from heaven an angel
  just came
So I answered the best I knew, "an
  angel has just spoken, I KEPT
  NO SECRETS FROM YOU.

Dale O. Fuller
RIPPLES OF TIME
A tow-headed boy in faded blue
  jeans
  Content to pass time with idle
  day dreams
Hot dusty days playing backyard
  ball
  Unaware of the fate that awaits
  us all

A chubby young girl with dirt on
  her face
  Dreams of being a princess
  with dresses of lace
Playing Mommy and Daddy with
  her young friends
  How can she know it all comes
  to an end

A wrinkled old man stares in the
  mirror
  He turns away and dries a tear
He remembers the days when he
  was virile and strong
  And wonders with sadness,
  where have they gone

An old woman sits alone on the
  rest-home front lawn
  Another day off the calendar,
  she knows she doesn't have
  long
A lifetime of memories run
  through her mind
  If only she could turn back the
  hands of time

Decaying old barns and rotting
  oak trees
  Remind us of our mortality
The strongest buildings will
  crumble to dust
  And the shiniest metal will
  succumb to the rust

Ripples of time, carry us away
  Farther and farther from
  yesterday

Peter Gabriel Lecours
SOMETIMES
Sometimes
I long for summer.
Sometimes,
Not all the time.
When the snow is swiftly coming
  down
And the wind is blowing all
  around,
I long for summer.
When the dark rolling clouds cut
  me off from the world,
I become afraid and
I long for summer.
Summer.
When the sky is blue and the
  breeze is cool.

Sometimes I long for summer.
Sometimes.

But when the gentle white flakes
  float silently
To the ground,
I love winter.

When the storm is over and the
  Snow is glistening,
I love winter.

Sometimes.
Not all the time.

Dorothy A. Jacobs
THE BUD
  *[Dedicated to and inspired by
  Juliet M. Dodge—who taught
  me the joy of opening up to
  Love, and Life, and People.]*
Once a bud afraid—
  What if:
  the frost kills me?
  the rain pounds me?
  the sun scorches me?
  —always staying tightly closed.

Someone reached out with
  encouragement,
  confidence, and love.

Slowly the bud opened one petal—
  then another:
  the frost didn't come.
  the rain nourished.
  the sun warmed.

The bud's now blossoming—
  reaching out.

Because Someone reached in to
  touch its heart.

Mary Anne Randl
**December 8, 1981 (In
  Memory Of John Lennon)**
What have we done
since John died?
Have we changed?
Have we thrown away our guns,
or have we left the song unsung
until another year is done,
and brings us deeper into doubt,
and debt,
and disbelief!

How can we survive
when we have left no time for
  life,
and won't allow ourselves
a moment to reflect,
or even to remember
those uncelebrated souls
that dwell within our reach;
who wear the hero's name,
but not his glove,

The ones who did not die in vain,
but those who died for Love!

Marjorie Burney Willis
SOMETHING LOVELY
  *[Dedicated to two people who
  have made "Something Lovely"
  of their lives . . . for my sister,
  Lowell Burney Carter and her
  husband, Dr. James D. Carter of
  Waco, Texas.]*
Who writes the beautiful love
  songs
  the nightingale sings . . .
Then turns on the moonlight
  and sends fireflies glowing on
  wings?
Who awakens the sleeping apple
  seed

telling it how to become a
  tree . . .
Then sends honeybees to make
  honey from
  the blossom—telling them the
  recipe?
From whence the purple
  grapes—growing
  so exquisitely on the vine
And the golden daffodils growing
  so gloriously in the sunshine?

In a wonderful world so bountiful
  with beautiful belief,
Why do I while away the time
  like a grasshopper on a leaf?
In an enchanted land with
  blossoms on the
  bough, with butterflies and
  nightingales . . .
With rainbows and stars shining
  with promise,
  why be one who falters and
  fails!
Why, O why can't I make
  something lovely
  as the purple grape or the
  daffodil . . .
Or some golden thing to make
  the world
  lovelier still?

Phyllis Lusk Chapin
MY SUNSHINE
You are my sunshine
  I whispered lovingly
  to the wee bundle.

You are my sunshine
  I hummed softly
  to the tiny toddler.

You are my sunshine
  I crooned soothingly
  to the weeping girl.

You are my sunshine
  I murmured quietly
  to the budding woman.

Love my sunshine
  I said prayerfully
  to the young man.

Look at my sunshine!
  She said joyfully
  as she handed me
  the wee babe.

Henry T. Jones, Jr.
KINDRED WIND
Wind—I know you!
I've known you a long, long time.
I've seen you race across the field.
I've heard your song in the tallest
  pine.

I've raced you across the open
  glade
And watched you blow the
  clouds astray.

I've seen you blow throughout
  the night,
And clear the sky at break of day.

I've seen you bring dark clouds
  and rain;
And, race with thunderous glee,
Whip the trees against the ground
And enrage the silent sea.

Yet strong thou art and gentle too.
You've brushed my face with
  tender breeze,
Cooled the earth and cleaned the
  air

And blown gently against
greening trees.

God is thy master, creator too.
He directs thy every sway,
And has given you to me as friend
To help me easy on my way.

So blow you breeze, ho, howl you
wind;
Dash, and race, and run.
The face of earth is thy
playground
And I am your creator's son.

Emily Malinowski Moe
LETTER FROM HOME
[To My Family With Love]
Where will this find you
Christmas day?
Maybe a million miles away . . .
Where will you hear the
Christmas bells?
What is the story they will tell?
And, while the bells are telling
you,
I'll hear the glory of it, too.
List to the ages fall away;
"This, our first blessed
Christmas day;
Babe in the manger;
Bethlehem star."
Ringing a message wherever you
are.

Peggy S. Morgan
DECISIONS
The rain falls slowly down
among the trees,
Gently tapping a song out
on a lily pad.
Grey skies and fog are all
that surround me,
Creating a reminiscent
atmosphere
that can make me feel sad.

Under a tree in a forest waiting
for the rain to stop,
Thoughts flow through my mind
like a stream to a lake.
All my questions could be
answered
in one single raindrop,
If only my decision was
that easy to make!

John H. Bailey
Mother's Rocking Chair
Battered and scarred, perhaps
weary, still with a regal air
Dressed in snow white finery,
done with loving care.
To see it sets my heart aglow, I'd
know it anywhere,
One of the things I cherish most,
my mother's rocking chair.

I've never heart it speak, all it
ever did was squeak,
But what wonderful things it
would tell, if only it could.
Troubles and sorrows of
childhood vanished in the air,
All it took was a minute in
mother's rocking chair.

There was a certain magic in that
old piece of wood.
A few rockings in it with mother
stopped pain as magic could.
The most awful dream, the
fiercest storm could never scare
Me or any child while in mother's
rocking chair.

At the arm of that old chair, I was
in the finest school.
I learned love for my fellowman
and of the Golden Rule.
How a man named Jesus died for
me, how my burdens He would
share.
Of God above, His eternal love,
all in my mother's rocking chair.

Burt Heacock
LITTLE BROWN LEAVES
If I was a leaf all withered and
dry.
I would sway in the wind and
hang down and cry.
The wind and the rains that beat
down on my face.
Show no affection while moving
in haste.
The friend that I cling to will not
always be there.
Like were the days of buds and
leaves they bare.
I was once green and beautiful
they say.
But along came the rain and a
long winter's day.
My color I lost and my form I did
bend.
Because of the season's giving
and taking they send.
I soon lost my sorrow when my
time grew near.
Because of the buds in spring that
soon will appear.
I now look below to the ground
so far beneath.
Of the branch that I cling to so
close to me.
Down from my love to the
ground I roll.
And into the season that has
taken the toll
Of little brown leaves.

Marie Jett Hussey
MERRY CHRISTMAS
M idst all of the fussin' n' flurry n'
sighs
E veryone busy as bees
R ollin' n' mixin' n' bakin' mince
pies
R aisin' n' punkin to please
Y uletide gay greetins with newsy
chit chat

C arols n' pageant n' holly
H urryin' n' shoppin' for this n' for
that
R eally, my dears, 'tis most jolly
I nvitin' the kinfolk n' friends
near n' far
S tuffin' the turkey n' guest
T rees all a-twindle with tinsel n'
star
M anger creche holy n' blest
A ll in the spirit of peace n'
goodwill
S o may the New Year your
wishes fulfill!!

Gertrude N. Capel
A WINTER DAY
Oh wondrous beauty of a winter's
day,
When sky is blue and all the
fields are white,
When snow-crowned mountains
stand in great array,
And fill a soul with true,
unbound delight.

When evergreens enhance the
glorious scene,
While sparkling snow upon their
boughs doth rest,
When footsteps creak, and all is
fresh and clean,
It seems that Nature's at her very
best.
Then as the sun sinks lower in
the sky
And sheds its golden glory all
around,
We realize that only from on high
Can pictures of such beauty, rare,
be found.

Michael L. Evans
YES! I'M IN LOVE
Yes! I'm in love.
Yet, for me being in love
Is not a constant churning
Of unctuous feeling stirring
My middle into impetuous chaos
And impulsive flings of flightful
fantasy.
For me, it is as being in a place,
Even as a living sponge is set
Upon the ocean floor—
Simultaneously filled with the sea
While yet engulfed by it.
But it is not a place, this love,
But a person.
A person whose fulness fills my
soul
Although I am but a tiny cell
In His body.

Yes, I'm in love.
For are we not told
That He is love.

Betty Adams
Merry Christmas and Happy Birthday Person
Such a beautiful celebration
time of year
The Christmas season is here
with warmest greetings
for your birthday dear
It makes one feel happy to live
with kindness, as it is the
reason to give
Christmas holiday all around
decorations and gifts, are
so convenient to be found
Your birthday too you are
aware
Each year so much better
you declare
Your biggest wish,
money is honey
A prosperous birthday,
Merry Christmas,
Happy New Year Many

Ann Brogden
IN MEMORY HE LIVES
[Written in Memory of Bill
Grant]
With all life's trials on earth he
lived,
With all heartaches he took time
to give.
A helping hand to those put down
His spirit lives on just his body's
in the ground.

He gave God praise for
everything he had
He sent the gospel out to the
lonely and sad
A blessing to mankind because
he cared

In memory in our hearts he still
lives there.

Bill was liked and loved by all
people
Color or race mattered not to him
Cause when they sat at his table
All were welcome; Bill was a true
friend.

I know he's at peace with our
Saviour on high
With loved ones united someday
in the sky.
No parting forever or saying
goodbye
His memory still lives in our
hearts
You and I.

Pamela Hoots
MERRY CHRISTMAS
Merry Christmas . . .

It has been a wonderful year
together—our first—

Full of friendship . . . hopes . . .
and a new year ahead.

We have had sadness and fears
but through it all
love has been there.

Thank you for a wonderful year
and may it be a
very Happy Holiday.

Donna Pitman
YOU ARE
You are a friend of love
and ever understanding.
You are a friend of my heart
to which you hold the key.
You are a friend of belonging
you shall always be mine.
You are a friend to my problems
because you always have
answers.
You are a friend to my tears
because you always comfort me.
You are a friend of my fears
because you have conquered.
You are a friend to my secrets
because we call them our own.
You are a special friend to me,
because to me, you are my own.

Chris Nichols
STANDING FIRM
Problems don't often work
themselves out
But that's what love is all about
Working together hand-in-hand
All across this great land
Couples together have sought it
through
But what if we can't, what do we
do
Standing firm—but with who?

Never sure when he'll be here
This I know not, this I fear
Not knowing for sure is worse
than alot
For he's here less often than not
I sense a footfall, feeble and old
Tis only a man who's also been
told
Standing firm—brave and bold.

Mr., please, feeble and old
Tell me how he could be so cold
Never see him for days at a time
Extremely ludicrous is how I find
Oh, won't you advise me on what
to do

Today's Greatest Poems

Impress me with your wisdom too
Standing firm—to persue.

But sooner or later I'll have to
accept
The peaceful truth deep in debt
Settling accounts of my story bare
Wishing forever, forever he'd care
Everyday now, we grow farther
apart
Standing firm—from the start.

Why, oh, why is my song so sad
Perhaps losing everything, all
that I had
Mr., please, feeble and old
Tell me the truth of the truth
untold . . .

Ken Walz
THESE MEMORIES
As the tides of time move on
And life becomes a passing
thing
Our love will grow forever
Into a happy memory

Though time and life will pass us
by
We grasp and hold these
memories
We make them pleasant and dear
These memories that life has
left for us

How happy those days and times
were
When we were young and close
How happy my life now that I am
old
For you are still in my mind

Now that I am old and time has
left its mark
I have these memories in my
loneliness
And until the day that I pass on
You'll live—forever in my mind

Susan Elkins
THE OCEAN
The ocean glistening many miles
abroad,
Never knowing where to stop,
It just keeps moving along.
But somewhere in the deepest of
night,
When all the creatures are asleep,
The ocean stops and takes a rest,
Before the morning sunset!

Michelle Lutes
CHILDREN'S CHRISTMAS
Children's Christmas is—
presents by the tree,
Santa Claus coming
down the chimney,
Singing on Grandpa's knee.
Children's Christmas is—
loving hugs and kisses.
Big, bright eyes of little
misters and misses.
No boos or hisses,
Just a Merry, Merry Christmas—
that's special to children!

Timothy R. Mears
OUR MOTHER
We have stripped the meat from
the bones
to make purses and bowler hats
And stolen the gold from her
deepest vaults
to hang from our perfumed ears.
We have sucked the life from her

thirsty roots
to cool our burning machines
And flattened her gently rolling
hills
as homes for our motor cars.

When mankind stands in glory
Master of all domain
Will feet still rest
On sweet green earth
Or her barren, lonely bones?

Ada Belle Muegge
MY LEGACY
Today I sew
like so many days before.
Yet, today is different
as I treadle the well used
machine
thread a needle   pick up thimble
snip a thread with my sainted
mother's scissors
passed down from her
to my sister
to my brother
then to me.
That silver thimble
left by a dear, dear friend years
ago
conjures up stories of an early
west
when she was young
Glass bottles of buttons
a box of pins
heavy tape measure
spools of thread;
silk and faded
strong and rewound
strips of cloth
from long ago garments;
beeswax   homemade,
hooks and eyes and snaps
all placed here   with care
by hands grown still—
My legacy . . .
so, I sew.

Bernard Stephens
REFUGE
I am here. Come in from the icy
rain.
The night is a long loneliness
when one is short on close
friends.
The cold rain reminds you of a
distance past, of people with no
souls, of broken promises and
scattered dreams.
The world isn't totally loveless
and friendless. There are those
that still love and care. Just
have faith in finding them.
Wet wintery nights always give
way to spring days and sun. I
want to be the spring that you
seek, the soothing water that
gives you hope and greater life.
I am here. Come in from the icy
rain.

Holly Wenn Johnson
STORMY LOVE
Our passion is raging—
Much like the violent storm
outside.
Like temperamental outbursts of
the gods above,
Our love is hard to hide.

I feel peaceful and content here
with you,
Warmed by the feeling of you,
Though the storm goes on and on.

Off in the distance, I hear the
deafening roar of the ocean
waves,
While silently wishing us alone
on the other side.

I am scared by the depths of my
feelings for you,
And oblivious to anything else.

. . . Hours later we are spent
And the storm has subsided.
I lie in your arms as the sun rises
And a new day begins.

Catherine A. Laprade
WHERE BEAUTY LIES
*[To my Mother and my sister
Rosemary with love and
appreciation]*
Just what is beauty no two will
agree
It may be something you hear or
feel or see
One may describe it as a flower
in spring
Another may say it's a new
diamond ring

It may be seen in the snowflakes
from heaven above
Or heard in the voice of someone
you love
There are so many places that
beauty can be
May I see it in you and you see it
in me

Donna S. Johnson
NATURE'S OWN
fourth floor
north right corner
the nest
two eggs
inhabit
their womb
of twigs

she labored

life at last
small weak naked
the first lay still
the second
more determined
destined also

forth floor
north right corner
the nest
naturally vanished

Tommie I. Mechler
NIGHT SOUNDS
The wind, it blows, so hard, so free
It brings a mysterious chill in me.
The night-lit sky, the moon
unfold . . .

Its brilliance bright as the breeze
is cold.
I stand alone among this sight
Among the beauties of this night.
The chill increases in my
bones . . .
While listening as pine branch
moans.

The wind, its whistling tones
increase
Fills me with a powerful longing
for peace.
But as I go along my path . . .
The wind diminishes in its wrath.

Than all is still within its quiet
The pine tree branches calmed
from riot.
Cricking nightly sounds that
spread . . .
Invading throughout night
creatures beds.

David Boatwright
THE FADED FLOWER
Wrinkles all around eyes unfair.
Beauty has taken its final flair.
Sagging skin and ruffled brow,
Beauty has faded for that ol' cow.
My heart breaks to see such
beauty
Wasted so like a dying tree.
Like a flower she reached her
peak;
Stolen from its stem by that
ageless sneak.
Fall to the ground and disolve in
it again,
Is this the process of original sin?
Daffodils, lilium and roses for
variety,
Their color is there for you and me.
If the flower is faded or unfair to
the mind
Remember it could be you or me,
so treat it kind.

Novak Novica Vujacic
BETTER TOMORROW
My way of Life
Straighten all
The Paths
Believes
Brighten the Hopes
Banish the fear
Better Tomorrow
Is near.
To my neighbor
To whole World
Of my clear thought
Spontaneously projected
On daily
Light.

Chandra Jaime
CHRISTMAS
Below a brightly shining star
a baby cries
where nightly weary
creatures lie.

We have much in common
they heard him sigh.
We shall be sacrificed
in order to give man life,
but I shall give life eternally
in a world free from strife.

What could we have in common,
we who know nothing of
virtue or sin?
We shall bear the burdens
of good and evil men.

From that first Christmas Day
many good men have been slain,
many evil deeds done
that we may never be able to
explain.

Many miles and years away
creatures big and small
in peaceful valleys have been
lain.
Bells in steeples proclaim
the coming of Christmas Day.

Through the star filled winter
night
I thought I could here
a distant reveille
of Gabriels trumpet
blaring triumphantly
setting all of Gods children
free from strife,
but it was only the wind singing
through the tree of life.

Carol Lynne Mac Neely
VANILLA FUDGE
Weary child standing in line,
with a glazed stare,
above a near—collapsed
tongue, He waits patiently
for his favorite flavor
of fanatical fluff.
Rich, creamy,
crackling cold concoctions
go sailing above
his head, hosting
a cargo of calories.
Tangy Teaberry Tart,
Raisin Rum Ripple,
Cinnamon Chocolate Chip?
The choices run—
like the line of
serious dessert sensualists—
around the block.
The boy's fingers clutch the
countertop,
as his ears hear his choice,
his palate watering, but
impatient tears swell—
Oh! The scooper scrapes
the empty sides and bottom.

Jewell B. Bush
LOVE
L ove seldom finds a place so
    ofty or so true,

O n which a faith like ours
    riginates with you.

V ieing for a smile, a look, a nod,
    ictory for both of us.

E ven when the chips are down,
    ternal love is you.

Kelly Thompson Price
THAT RAINY MORNING
[To the man I love, Freddie
Mercury]
Your feet crunch the wet grass
The silence full of peace
Near me I hear you breathing
Such beauty makes me weak.

You whisper, oh, so tender
Your stare those loving eyes
The air I think, September
As moisture fills the skies.

I feel the misty raindrops
As they fall upon my face
My lashes, they get heavy
It blures your lovely trace.

Your kiss, so soft and tender

And damp upon my lips
Like it feels to touch wet petals
Of a rose at my fingertips.

You lay beside me gently
With your hands to keep me safe
We laugh in joy together
And the smile creeps from your
face.

I feel strong arms around me
As you hold me like you do
Hair moistened to bind you to
me
Like my heart holds me to you.

Your hands they touch my ribcage
With force only you have got
"Don't ever let me out of your hold"
Or to my death I'll drop.

I see you leaving quietly
The rain glistening with each
step
You turn to stare once again
Good-bye, my love, my friend.

Bonnie Quigley
THE LORDS LOVE
[This poem is dedicated to
Father Zelley who has helped
me a lot in life, also Barbara
Crafton, McCornacks, Lynn
Rogers, Father Parker.]
I am but like a child running to
your arms,
for with your love I feel safe from
all harm.
I look up to you and smile and I
feel your smile upon me,
a warm caring smile.
I share with you my laughter,
I share with you my tears.
And as though I were looking up
to you
with the innocent eyes of a child
you forgive me for my sins.
Gently you take hold of my hand
walking beside me,
listening to what I have to say.
And even though I can't see you, I
know you're there.
I whisper to you softly alone in
the night,
I love you when things go wrong,
I love you when things go
right.
I promise to be your friend,
to stick by you through thick and
thin.
And with this I feel as though
your eyes
fill with tears of joy.
And I feel your smile upon me, a
warm caring smile.
A breeze blows through my
window
and I feel your kiss on my cheek,
and in your own way you say
that's what Love is all about.

Nora Posey Hill
THE OLD HOUSE
[In memory of my beloved
parents: Mr. and Mrs. J. M.
Posey.]
Today they are tearing down the
house where I was born,
Many years have passed and it's
tattered and worn.
Workmen with hammers are
tearing it apart,
But little do they know how it's
breaking my heart.

Happy are the memories, mingled
with the sad—
When I was a child there with
my Mother and Dad.
When I was young for a while did
I roam,
Then, when I married, again it
was my home.

With my husband and children
words cannot tell,
Of countless hours we spent here
and loved so well.
From the highway through the
pasture—back to the springs,
Each memory we treasure, even
the echoes that would ring.

There are many fine houses even
palaces for kings,
But none like the 'old house' and
today I wish it had wings.
Then I'd go inside, close every
window and door
So, I could fly away with my
precious memories forever
more.

Patricia Farley
DEAR FRIEND
How nice it is, to have a friend so
true,
one who comforts me when I'm
blue.
A friend to tell my secrets to.
Yes, it's nice to have a friend like
you.

Laughter and tears, we have
shared,
each knowing that the other one
cared.
We've shared the problems and
fun of our children growing up,
and had many good times over a
coffee cup.

I have treasured our friendship
through the years,
whether the days were spent in
laughter or tears.
I am really one of a chosen few,
for when God passed out friends,
for me He chose you.

Terese Quartetti
**My Little White Teddy
Bear**
My little white teddy bear just
sits and smiles.
I can talk for hours to him
I think he's listening but I never
know
'Cause he just sits there and
smiles.
He never says a word to me.
I could love—n—hug him all day
and night
And all he'll do is sit there and
smile.
I'll never know if he really loves
me,
My little white teddy bear just
sits and smiles.

Jeannette Bueler
OH, GRAY HAIRS
Oh, gray hairs, why did you come
so soon
Perhaps it's because I've lost
baby's first spoon
Could it be I've just seen too much
Or trying to drive that truck with
the clutch

Silly to think these strands
should matter
Usually I'm pondering what
makes me fatter
Maybe it's the payment mailed
two days late
Or wondering what is our
dinner's fate

Dad seems frail and son is too
tender
There are so many things I have
to remember
Shock can cause gray hair to
appear
Also those horrors we all do fear

Rinse it quickly before they all
see
I'm young, I'm young, how can
this be
Should I relax and stare at the
moon
Oh, gray hairs, why did you come
so soon

Cindy L. Ray
MYSTERY OF THE AGES
Whispering winds of the ages do
blow

And set my mind reeling to and
fro

From past to present and back
again

Far and wide my message I send

Open your ears, listen to me
Your need's your desire, my
words are the key

From mountain to vale and far
below

Carry my message so all will
know

To answer the question, the
riddle, the rhyme

Love is the answer, it only takes
time

Lee Goodman
FACES
Every face
Holds a smile and a frown,
Expresses undescribable joy
And expirences painful sadness.
Each person has the ability
To put on a face for others,
And at that same time
Take off their face.
What is held within the mind
Are the true feelings and faces
Of ourselves.
But the mind cannot always be
set free . . .
It is a goal in life
To free each of our true faces,
And for ourselves and others
To see the beauty and life
With—held
In each of them.

Misty Doane
DEATH
The shock of the news brings
tears to your eyes,
The salt water violently
streaming,
Runs down your face as everyone
cries,
You say that you got to be
dreaming.

You feel some grief as the
memories pass,

The remembrance of that joy,
The time spent playing in the grass,
With that wonderful little boy.

The funeral day has finally come,
The long ride to the home,
That holds his body within its walls,
The thought makes my stomach groan.

The first sight you see when you walk in the door,
Is all of your family crying,
There surrounded by millions of flowers,
His body sweetly lying.

You sit before his body,
While you listen to a prayer,
People in the room are crying,
Everyone got their share.

After that it gets worse each day,
You tend to lose some weight,
You don't care how your life is lived,
To die, you can hardly wait.

The grave is made, the concrete laid,
The waiting for the stone,
It has to be a special one,
That never before was known.

The sadness still rages through my head,
As I talk about it to you,
Its sad to think that my brother is dead,
And he wasn't even two.

Ray Nadeau
CHANGE

For those
who would breech an autumn sky,
caught
between
the gold of summer
and
the bluest pall of palest white—

for those
who would deny the morning
and
continue
blindly sighted
through familiar night—

for those
who grasp unyielding
and ember
long since chilled,
I would recommend a quick, yet certain, death.

For
what is dead
cannot
be
killed.

Lynda Mack
Christmas Is Cancelled

Christmas is cancelled; Oh good, I'm glad!
No presents to buy, no trees to trim,
Why I'm not even sad!

But how can you cancel Christmas?
You can't erase Jesus' birth,
Or all that pain he suffered while

he was here on earth.

You can't just put him away,
like he was never here.
He's in our hearts, and in our lives,
Why he's always near.

I feel his presence everyday,
in everything I do.
Why . . . don't you feel his presence
here too?

So how can you cancel Christmas,
When his birth was on this day.
If that's not something to celebrate,
Then I have nothing more to say.

Instead of cancelling Christmas,
I'll tell you what to do.
Let's think *'less'* of all the gifts to buy.
And let us all remember,
That precious baby's cry.

Because of him, we have this day.
So, let's all sing loud, and strong.
That we'll *always* have a Christmas,
No matter what goes wrong.

Oh! please listen to us Jesus,
For we would like to say.
Forgive our selfish attitude toward
This Christmas Day.

Mavis Meador
SEEDS OF FRIENDSHIP

I'm thankful for friends, acquaintances and my enemies too
It takes all of them to make such a colorful hue
Have you ever seen a rose bush without a single thorn
You have these mixtures of good and bad from the day you're born
I bought special kind of seeds from the love of God
And through the years of planting them in various types of soil
Tending them with love and care not water from the sky
Through concern and compassion tears of joy moisten these seeds from my watchful eye
Seeds were planted near and far at home and across the sea
And looking around in my daily life what a beautiful bouquet my friendship seeds
The more I keep on planting and giving
The more friendship bouquets I'll get while living.

Teah M. Barkle
UNTITLED
[Dedicated to Dave and Arlene]
You're someone very special,
Who means a lot to me;
There's no one else quite like you,
Nor could there ever be.

You're always there when needed,
You know just what to say;

You have that helping hand,
That helps me through each day.

Those twinkles in your eyes,
That smile I always see;
Are a few more reasons why,
You are so dear to me.

You're fun to be around,
And you're always kind to me;
And I hope that on this special day,
True happiness, you'll see.

Theresa M. Spelman
The People's Pope—John Paul II
You are very grand,
And I enjoyed your visit to our land.
I watched your journey on TV,
And I was astonished at what I did see.
Millions of people who followed you on your way,
All wanting to here what you had to say.
We had many events in honor of you,
Because, we all wanted to see everything you were going to do.
You went to the United Nations
Where you discussed human relations.
Then you went to the churches of St. Patrick's and St. Charles,
Where all the little children looked like cute little dolls.
Then you departed for Cardinal Hayes High School,
Where you discussed the golden rule.
At Yankee Stadium there was a large crowd,
Who all cheered long and loud.
At the stadium you celebrated a mass.
And the reaction of the people proved that you had class.
A mass at St. Pat's is how your next day did start,
Then you were almost late so, you had to depart.
At madison Square Garden you had a youth rally
The amount of people would be hard to tally.
Then you went to Battery Park,
Where you filled everyone's heart with a spark.
At Shea Stadium there was a farewell ceremony,
This was the end of your New York journey.
At this celebration many did cry,
Because they did not want to say good-bye.
You were escorted by Cardinal Cooke
And like the most happiest man he did look.
The presence of you brought happiness to all,
But, in the crowds in order to see you had to be tall.
It was a great honor to listen and see you,
And the love we all have for you is very true.
You filled us all with great hope.

That is why we say:
"LONG LIVE THE POPE!"

Laural Dianna Scogin
THE ROSE
The rose threw her head back and laughed
At the old willow tree standing near.
"I am young and beautiful," she said,
"The willow is old with death to fear."

The willow sadly gazed downwards,
upon the youthful, vain rose.
Silently he watched her flaunt her leaves,
Thinking how long, no one knows.

The rose had much of which to be proud,
For she was very beautiful, it's true.
But nighttime came, the willow slept,
And upon the rose came dew.

One day more beautiful than ever,
The rose started to fall apart.
Weeping viciously, she cried for help,
The willow could do nothing, torn to heart.

The rose has ridiculed the willow,
Now she is gone, nothing more to do.
The willow remains forever,
While many roses pass through.

Angela M. Cecil
HARVEST
On the eve of millennium,
When the stars begin to fall,
The faun comes,
Walking daintly on cloven hooves,
Through celestial spaces.

His face is ashen,
And, raising his flute to his cracked lips,
He begins to play
His melancholy canticle.

Then, sailing swiftly,
Comes the flotilla of balloons.

Dennis J. Lemire
I'VE A LITTLE FLAME
[To my late parents, Mary Blanche and George Joseph Lemire, and to my wife, Patty McQuaid—Lemire]
I've a little flame
That burns deep inside
It burns a little pain for you
And doesn't seem to die
That little flick of light
Makes me feel so warm
Just keeps burning through the night
Like an infant's just been born

I've a little flame
That burns deep inside
The beast within has been tamed
And asks not how or why
I know not the full value
Of that which harbors in my chest
But I know something special

about you
And it's happened for the best

I've a little flame
That burns deep inside
It burns a little pain for you
And doesn't seem to die
That little flick of light
Makes me feel so warm
Just keeps burning through the
night
Like an infant's just been born

I've a little flame
That burns deep inside
Burning just the same
Until you came to me tonight
Now fluttering to an endless aim
Burning now ever so bright
Burning now to the morning
light . . .

Russell Arthur
A WEDDING
Sing a song of wedding bliss this
bond of love we now
commence, third finger left
hand, then a kiss and a prayer
for infinite happiness.

Oh gentle and wistful maidens,
they do follow us as their silent
dreams unfold, and visions of
their future like will-o-wisp
dance off to realms untold.

Mother with her tear strewn
cheeks as she contemplates the
day, forecasts a future of good
times and bad and
grandchildren for her play.

Father in a pensive mood
wondering how the years sped
to this day as he mounts the
alter with stoic pride to give
his angel away.

Eligible girls its time line up and
catch the bright bouquet, and
mark the time until you have,
your future heavenly day.

Lisa Moncey
LEAVES
Falling leaf
From the sky
Leave my fellows
Go to die.

Life is short
My blood grows cold
No more to love
The night is bold.

The silence rustles
My empty shell
I feel no emotion
Past pain—is hell.

Fred Cowan
THE GARDEN
When I walk the garden pathways
As the sun begins to rise,
The dew drops on the flowers
Resemble tear—filled eyes.
Could it be they're crying
For the joys that have begun
With the beauty of the garden
Bathed in God's bright morning
sun?
Do you think they're tears of
happiness
From waking up to see
That I walk not the path alone—
That you are there with me?

Do you suppose they cry for joy
Because they all can see
That the love I give to you
You also give to me?
The Lilly of the Valley
Nods that this is true,
And the Scarlet Rose of Sharon
Seems to know it too.
I see the purple Violet
As she also nods her head—
And the lovely crimson Rose
Is blushing shades of red!
I love to walk the garden paths
When flowers shine with dew.
But what I love the most of all
Is sharing it with you!

Dawn L. Wegner
WHAT YOU SHOULD DO. . .
If there's something in your life,
that means a lot to you,
You should always treat it
as if it were brand new.
Treat it with a gentleness
that it's never had,
Treat it with a caring hand
and always make it glad.
Show it just how much
you love to have it there,
Let it always see
how much you really care.
Always build it up,
and never let it fall,
Always be right there,
whenever it may call.
Always be as true
as the sky is blue above,
Always let it know,
it has your endless love!

Katherine L. Stover
MY FRIEND BURR
How tall he stands
Looking out the window
At the flocks of birds
Flying
Zooming
Turning
Swooping downward from their
height
To rest
Upon the sand
The fence
The beach
He's eighty some, he says
But looks to me
About fifty.
Charming
Witty
Eyes twinkling.
That's Burr.

Nantalina Judith Spina
SOMEONE SPECIAL
*[Darrell, For all the times we
have shared for all the dreams
we treasure, I will hold all the
love you have given me, deep
within my heart forever.]*
I have waited so long
To find someone like you—
Someone very special and
someone new.

When you smiled at me
Something inside cried!

Don't get to close
He'll never be mine.

Your eyes tell me something
but I don't understand.
Your hands touch me as though no
one else can.

You have shown me love as I knew
it should be.

OH! Thank you GOD
For letting it be me!

Terry R. Green
STORMS & DREAMS
Storm raged so fierce
winds did blow
Dreams tormented me
deep in my soul.
Fears & thoughts
of an endless maze
Losing Love,
I awoke in a craze.

With each deep
echoy roll of thunder
Of being loved
I did wonder.
Will life allow
me to break free
And if finding Love
will she need me?

Each jagged
and brilliant lightning flash
Shocked my soul
my hopes would dash.
My dreams so real
were as the sky
Reflections of life
& why I wish to die.

I prevailed
I lasted to the end
But another storm
blew in again.
My soul looked
deep into your eye:
Come, sweet Love,
or I must die.

Tammie J. Hultman
BLACK WATER
Black water
lighted by the moon
and stars, or
green and glistening
in the bright sunshine.
Now and then
you splash
drops of water
to make a rainbow.
A soft breeze
blows over you.
Your voice
and your beauty
speak softly to me,
as you noisily gurgle
over the rocks,
telling of
the change in you
and me . . .

Wendy Hopkins
SLEEP
I laid my head upon the feather
pillow.
Whisp me away, O sleep;
Far, far away
To play
And never again to weep.

My weary eyes fell closed with
no coaxing.
Draw me away, sweet dream
To never land
With grand
Manifestations as you deem.

I felt my soul and spirit drifting,
drifting
To a favorite place;

Caught by a dream
In between
Undiscovered time and space.

Mary Leilani Siegele
COLOR BOOK
*[To my daughter Jodeen who
helped to inspire me. I love you
Jodi!]*
Nursery rhymes and happy times.
In childhood days gone by.
Babbling brooks and color books.
Old time lullabyes.
Me and brother playing tag. Each
day we start out new.
Picture daddy hugging mom, but
color mommy blue.

Life ain't like a color book
Where trees are always green.
It sometimes gives, it sometimes
takes,
Sometimes in between.
New crayolas cannot make my
family good as new.
Daddy goes his seperate way, so
color mommy blue.

We cannot change or re-arrange
The way things might have been.
But we can try to justify
And start to live again.
We can be too blind to see,
pretending it aint true.
With children grown she'll be
alone, so color mommy blue.

Color mommy blue.
She don't smile no more.
What did daddy do?
To make her lock the door.
The wall they built between
them, it just grew and grew.
They live alone inside our home.
So color mommy blue!

Mary Coker Anderson
WEE WINTER WHISPERS
Is that a golden temple bell
from distant hill, awakening?
It seemed a faint tinkle—knell
that rose upon the crest borne
wind
to herald Winter's chanting chill;
or myriads of sprites without,
upon the porch and window sill
or children's shrieks of gaiety
with laughter like a song bird's
trill?
Peering without, beneath the
eaves,
with heartbeat defied by will,
there oriental windchimes swung
in a wee Winter whisper reel.

Martha L. Williams
WILL YOU BE READY?
We're headed for that City
Where Jesus is the Light
The Saviour there is waiting
To read the Book of Life

Sinner are you ready
To walk inside the Gate?
Get your soul ready,
Don't be too late.

One step with God
Is all we need to take
To be in that number
When He opens wide the Gate

O soul where are you going,
Why do you wait?
Jesus is coming,

Will you be too late?

Jesus is waiting
To welcome you there
Oh what a blessing
He has for you to share

He truly loves you
And He truly cares
Will you be watching
And waiting in prayer?

Jesus is coming,
It could be today
To catch away His children
Who walk in His way

Have you called upon Jesus
To make your soul right?
Will you be in that number
In that City oh so bright?

Dorothy S. Wilson
THE LEAST
The Holy Spirit magnifies
    His power,
Opens the eye to focus
    enlightenment.
A wild flower—a honey suckle
Outstands, as a child on holidays
    with excitement.

Mary and Joseph were the least
    among
Bethlehem's crowd,
But when the Spirit of God took
    full control,
The ordinary became Divine
To touch the innermost fibers
    of the soul.

Russell Daniel Gore
GOD GAVE US WISDOM
*[To President Reagan and
America for making 1983 "The
Year of The Bible"]*
God gave us wisdom to express
    new life in Christ to growing
    youth.
But worldly teachers would
    repress
    and ban from schools His
    saving truth.

"Brave sons of God, lift up your
    voice:
    for truth is lost in sin and
    strife.
Help children make the vital
    choice
    to find in Christ eternal life."

To train for living is in vain
    if God is not enthroned within:
for there is only toil and pain
    when wisdom is replaced by
    sin.

So, let the Bible be our guide
    with knowledge from our Lord
    of love.
His precepts in our schools abide
    and praises to our God Above.

Russell Daniel Gore
My Beloved Wife, My Lover
*["Anniversary joy, pal, love of
ICor. 13"—your grateful
husband, Russ.]*
My dear wife, Orpha always seems
    to do things good and right.
And even when I have bad dreams
    she wakes me up at night.

For problems, she will give to me
    her counsel wise and kind;
    and even when we disagree

she does not really mind.
Sometimes the dishes fit in
    wrong
    clothes bungle on the line.
But then she smoothes them out
    along
    and everything goes fine.

If things of earth can never sway
    our union firm and sweet
I know 'twill be a glorious day
    when our Bridegroom we meet.

For Christ will welcome us to be
    His everlasting Bride.
And we shall praise Him glad and
    free
    lay trophies at His side.

The Holy Spirit, our Best Man
    Who raised Him from the tomb
fulfills the ceremony plan
    as in the Upper Room.

Then God The Father, Lord of all
    Who gives the Groom and
    Bride
is praised as hosts before Him fall
    while wedding joys abide.

Catherine F. Douglas—McCargo
The Voyage Of Billy Bones?
A bow—legged sailor was Billy
    Bones;
High over the locker of Davey
    Jones
He sailed, and sang as he sailed
    along,
And danced to his rollicking
    sailor—song.
With a "Hearty—Me—Lads" and a
    Ho—Heave—Ho"
He Horn—piped from dawn until
    twilight glow.
He sailed when the sea was
    quietly blue
And the low—rolling waves were
    early—morn new.
But when tempests howled and
    the waves leaped high,
And the shoreline was one with
    the angry sky,
He'd lower his sails and ride
    closer to shore,
And his singing was lost in the
    ocean's roar.
He was out one night when a
    sudden storm blew,
And the wind was wild, and the
    white waves grew.
When the morning dawned with
    an eerie light,
Billy Bones and his sail—boat
    were nowhere in sight.
Now 'tis said, when the stars and
    the moon shine bright,
And the sea lies calm and the
    wind blows light,
You can hear "Hearty—Me—
    Lads" and a "Ho—Heave—Ho",
And dancing in Davey
    Jones'locker below.

Stanley J. Coleman
FRIENDSHIP
How glad I am when the day is
    done,
    And the twilight comes softly
    stealing,
To know that I have helped
    someone,
    Or healed a wounded feeling.
For I know when I am feeling blue,

And burdened with my cares,
How glad I am to have a friend,
    To have a friend who shares
My sorrows as well as joys,
    For that's the friend that's true.
That's the kind of friends I want,
    I need more friends like you,
As long as I draw mortal breath,
    I never must neglect,
To be a friend to everyone,
    A friend they won't forget.
And so as upward on the pathway
    of life
    I slowly but surely trod,
If I can always help someone,
    My heart's at peace with man
    and God.

E. Ronald Whitener
The Worlds (Largest) Not
We are taught not that the leave
    nots brought the bring nots of
    the know nots to be not. For
    the is nots are the please nots
    of the no nots to do not. When
    the have nots are the sure nots
    of the lack nots. While the
    tried nots are the no nots of
    the unending why not. As the
    believe nots shows the see nots
    that the is nots can not. And
    the doubt nots assures the
    hope nots that the worlds not
    in a not. So why not unnot the
    no not in the worlds not or is
    not that the worlds (largest) not.

Delilah Rice
TO JOYCE AND DANNY
He's here at last your precious
    babe
That you waited for so long,
Thank the Lord, he's healthy
Beautiful and strong.

How you will enjoy him
As you watch the things he'll do.
The smiles he'll give, the frowns
    he'll make
As he tries to talk to you.

Hold him close and talk to him
And let him feel your love,
But don't forget to teach him
Of our dear Father up above.

Jo Boring
LITTLE GIRL OF MINE
*[Dedicated to Sandra Rae
Boring, age 11 who passed
away August 11, 1978. Silver
Lake, Indiana]*
As I look at you lying on the bed
My heart so broke when the
    doctor said,
Leukemia the illness, I screamed
    Oh God No!
I don't want it to be that, it can't
    be so.

My world suddenly ended with
    the crushing blow
There's nothing more painful
    than a death that's slow.
How long will I have you my
    precious one?
I can't face reality. . .I want to run

I recall our yesterday's, the
    memories so many
Then pray, Oh God grant me the
    serenety
Help me dear Lord this heartache
    to bear

If only her suffering you could
    spare

Lord, you tell us all things work
    for good
I don't understand how all of this
    could
But Lord I trust you to see us
    through
And may your will bring glory to
    you.

We love you Lord, my little girl
    and I
And when you tell us to say
    good-bye
I know it will only be a short
    while
Until I will again see her
    beautiful smile.

Pamela L. Miller
IT'S AUTUMN!
It's Autumn! The leaves are falling
    down
The air is crisp and chilly as trees
    wave
    amber, red, and brown.

It's Autumn! The moon is round
    and
    bright
Summer's glow begins to fade as
    shadows
    greet the night.

It's Autumn! There's a crunch
    from running
    feet,
The crunching sound of brittle
    leaves dancing
    in the street.

It's Autumn! The fields are brown
    and
    dry
With pumpkins flickering in the
    night and
    corn stalks piled high.

Ah yes, there's nothing quite like
    Autumn!
    She struts such beauty and
    fresh
    array
But with her loveliness come
    whispers that
    Winter quietly creeps our way.

Kim Stroschen
THE TRIP
[For Joe]
I left without tears
on a journey of me.
I was headed on a trip
filled with emotions.

I looked out the bus window
to get my last glimpse
of you.
But you were nowhere to be seen

The days and nights,
endings and beginnings,
never stopping,
only changing.

People, places, things,
becoming a blur
inside my head.
Somehow I kept thinking
all was lost.

The me I longed to know
would never be found.
So I fell asleep
dreaming of a world

of beaches, happiness,
sunsets, peace,
and you.

Laura Ann McDonald
A DIGRESSION
*[To my husband Tracy;
without him I wouldn't have
had the courage to send my
poem in and wouldn't be
published here now.]*
Life is
A series of meaningless
digressions
from God's
long—winded speech
God
who so foolishly endowed man
with the gift of free will
The gift
that sent Adam and Eve crawling
and brought Rome crashing down
The gift
that allows me
to end this digression right here.

Sandra J. Benedict
THE MOUNTAIN
I stood upon the mountain
Where the morning air cloaked
    my senses
And my soul.
The moist, brown soil under my
    feet,
And the crisp, blue sky laced in
    fleecy whiteness,
And the forest green valley
    rolling into eternity,
And the rich burgundy bark
    labeling the trees,
And the harmonious songs of the
    birds in flight,
And the collection of flowers
    blooming
With fiery redness, glowing
    whiteness, and
Crystal yellowness,
And the damp scent of spring
    lingering in the air
All permeated my soul in awe.
In the distance, the mountains
    ladened in
A misty morning haze,
Surrounded the valley like huge
    palace walls.
The sun sent shimmering pools
    of warm light
Dancing on the tree tops.
The silence of the universe
    breathed
Down upon me,
As I sipped the golden wine of the
    Morning.

Royston W. Donnelly
BACKSTEIN HOUSE
O Backstein House, you are
    sublime.
    And you've been looking down
On the highway and the town—
    For a long, long time.

Thick brick walls rise three
    stories tall
    To meet a majestic roof of
    red—brick tile.
Your high ceilings and floors of
    American pine
    Have lasted like the tile.

Sunlight lit up a Paris street—
    scene painting
    And a timeless

silhouette—minature.
There's a workshop in the
    basement
    Where Dad repairs and restores
    his antique furniture.

In the music room, papered blue,
    We drank birthday drinks with
    guests.
And found a glass—covered
    winter garden—
    A secluded spot for thoughts or
    rests.

Sun—glow, in the quarters of the
    daughters,
    Made me feel like a younger
    fellow.
I saw there how Mother's care
    Made a house happy and
    mellow.

Do you remember, Backstein
    House,
    The coachhouse in your
    backyard?
It's still there, you know, though
    Not used for coach or horse,

What a sight if we could see:
    Groom hitching tan horse to
    buggy;
German doctor, in high—hat,
    Sitting on buggy's mat;
Whip—tip touching hide;
    And the fly—off, before the
    ride.

Elizabeth L. Jones
TO CHRISTOPHER SCOTT
How is it: grief still falls upon
    your name,
And why do I still mourn your
    end of life?
Death mocks my heart—the pain
    I feel by fate—
And twists my heart as with a
    two-edged knife.
Alas, I've been for years with
    dew—damp eye
In search inside my mind for
    want of one
Meet answer to the question still
    ask I
And haunt long after night is
    done.
My futile cries of "Why?" pierce
    no man's ear,
But mine is battered by my long
    to hear your voice.
So, Christopher, my long—gone
    cavalier,
Remember that you were my
    love's first choice.

Onelia G. Lemke
PRECIOUS BABY GIRL
*[This poem is dedicated to my
first granddaughter, Lauren
Nicole Peninger. Your loving
Grandmother, Onelia G. Lemke]*
When I looked at you, dear sweet
    baby girl
And greeted you for the very first
    time.
A little angel with a dirty face
Was the thought that entered my
    mind.
I said "hello" and I welcomed you
Into our great big world.
You entered into my heart that
    day,
Sweet precious baby girl.

I always knew you'd be an angel,
    baby girl
For I prayed for you day and
    night.
Though I did not know what
    your name might be,
You were the most beautiful baby
    girl to me,
Needless to say it was love at
    first sight.
As I looked at your precious little
    face
With a prayerful heart, I
    unlocked a door
So you could find your own very
    special place.

May you grow up in the love of
    God
And shine like a bright morning
    star.
Walk always in the path of
    righteousness,
Bring cheer and laughter
    wherever you are.
As you walk down life's winding
    highway,
May God's angels watch over
    you.
Be humble, kind, gentle, loving
    and faithful
To yourself and to God always be
    true.

Doris C. Smith
CONFUSION
The frigid days of March were
    ebbing,
    Winter must have had its
    blasting fling.
I sought a warm state for
    vacation
    Planned to return to a
    matching spring.

Ocean sands warm as gentle
    zephyrs,
    Old Sol tanned smiling, relaxed
    faces.
Air conditioners whirred their
    season
    As we searched for the coolest
    places.

Upon returning to our home state
    Boreas greeted us, bearing
    snow;
Forecasters cautioned, "Five more
    inches,—"
    More generous than we cared
    to know!

Feathered friends huddle on the
    feeders,
    Dejected, chilled, no songs now
    to sing.
Fiercely, I fight snow with my
    shovel,
    Why doesn't the weather know
    its spring?

Della M. Gibbons
OUR LITTLE GIRLS
*[With Love To My Niece
Rosemarie and her husband
Jack Evans.]*
Our lovely home so cozy and fair
But one room always empty
    always bare
No tiny feet to patter on the stair
To hug and kiss, at night to hear
    their prayer
No little children to romp, skip,
    and share the toys

With other little girls and boys

Dear Heavenly Father we'll pray
To send a wee soul our way
Though days are long and hard to
    fill
We'll not despair but pray on still
Please, Dear Lord grant us a share
Boy or girl we'll take good care

The answer came a baby was on
    the way
Oh! Heavenly Father it pays to
    pray
Our cup of joy is filled this day
The child born a precious girl
We would not trade one tiny curl
Then God was good He sent
    another
To love and cherish and to mother

Now we have two beautiful
    daughters
To fill our home with love and
    laughter
Our first born golden haired blue
    eyed Mary Jo
A little lady from head to toe
Clever at school cheerful without
    exception
In all her tasks she is perfection

Next came Jennifer Marie of the
    pansy eyes
Rosebud mouth just made for
    smiles
Singing and dancing all the while
Hosts of friends to beguile

Oh Guardian Angels be at their
    side
Protect and keep ever guide
Now our pleasure is without
    measure
Thank you God for our little
    treasures
To do our best will be a must
We pray to be worthy of thy trust

Bertha Alongi Rose
THE TATTED CAP
Tears inside
Others musn't see, while
In my hand I hold the cap
I tatted for you.
I hear you laugh and cry.
You break all the rules.
I feel your breath upon my face—
When the breezes blow;
I saw them close your blue eyes,
A part of me with you.
Then they carried you away,
And you left a fragrant trail
Of larkspur,
Baby-breath, for-get-me not,
And the tatted cap with blue
    ribbon—
They forgot.

Robert Morgan
MY CHRISTMAS GIFT
Others may receive gifts that
    sparkle and shine;
Even fur coats or imported wine.
But those for me were not in store;
The ones I got were worth much
    more.

Oh, they had no value in dollars
    and cents;
These wonderful gifts my Savior
    sent.
For the greatest gifts of all you do
    not pay;

Today's Greatest Poems

That's strength and health to
work and play.

And you who received this silver
and gold;
Do they bring peace to a troubled
soul?
If you have all these and still not
a smile;
Then all your gifts were not
worthwhile.

If God was good to you the whole
year through;
And friends gave you a smile and
how do you do;
Then you like me should be
content;
For these greatest gifts of all
didn't cost a cent.

Mamie Ruth Lucid
LITTLE LEAGUER
*[This poem was inspired by
and dedicated to my six-year
old grandson, Patrick Edward
Richrdson, our own special
Little Leaguer.]*
As day swings for its base in sky
A little boy goes running by
Cap on his head and bat held high.

With fielder's glove snug on his
hand
He catches sunlight as he can
He is a ready, little man.

With evening comes a sky of plaid
To strike day out and make him
sad
The game is over, little lad.

Now night is playing in day's stead
So hang your mitt up near your bed
And dream those runs still in
your head.

Leslie K. Lopus
The Moon Hung Heavy
The Moon hung heavy,
undisguised;
there in the sky, it was visualized.

The Moon was giant, bloated,
round—
low in the horizon, as daylight
found.

Perfectly formed, the Moon was
full,
large; in fact, it frightened the bull!

The Moon shone in the western
hemisphere,
when the Sun, over the eastern
slopes, appeared.

There they were, the Moon, the
Sun,
as big as life, on a one to one!

The Moon was clear, beautiful,
bright;
The Moon didn't want to end the
night.

So it protested, by meeting the day;
it hung heavy; stars pinioned away.

But it had to end, it could not last—
the Sun rose up, the Moon
downcast!

D. Annetta Pickering
WINTER
The tall dark trees pierce a grey
cloudy sky,
The snow is gently falling, the
flakes are drifting by,

A horse-drawn sleigh is gliding
along a snowy lane,
A wolf howls in the distance,
winter's here again.

The winds are softly moaning in
the trees high overhead,
The icy touch of winter is on
each twig and blade,
The lights of homes are shining
throughout the snowy night,
The families snug inside them
beside the fireside bright.

Early in the morning if the snow
stops overnight,
There may be skaters on the
pond, laughing with delight,
And here and there on the fresh
white snow, coming out of the
woods,
Will be the tracks of little
creatures, hunting for their food.

Marion B. Proehl
THE SIMPLE THINGS
The simple things
That come my way
A smile, a warm handclasp,
A listening ear,
SPEAK softly of friendship.

A brilliant sunset,
A towering mountain,
A sandy seashore,
Autumn's colorful foliage,
WHISPER of nature's beauty.

A lovely song,
A bird's sweet call,
A bubbling brook,
A church bell's chimes,
SING clearly a melody.

A partaken meal,
A shared vacation
Book or movie
With a loved one,
TALKS gently of companionship.

Let the simple things
Continue to come my way!

Laura Lambe Burrell
MISSY'S EYES
It's raining
Kermits and Miss Piggys
Said Missy
As she sniffed
Her way into the
Corridor of the home
With an embarrassed
Blush
The airplane flies by
And the wood nymphs
Flee through
The window
Baby bumpkins
Missy
Wow the Eyes
Of an intelligent llapso
Apso
Can be far-out.

Lucinda Trew
JAZZMAN
Blind black beggar
Wearing cool shades,
Rests in the rush of uptown
trade.

Dig the way he shakes that cup,
First slowly, soulfully
Coins roll and glide.

Quick, abrupt,
The beat picks up—

Nickels, dimes, slide, collide.

That's hot jazz, man,
But ain't you got blues?

Lillian Payne RN

Lillian Payne RN
CHRISTMAS
What a wonderful day is
Christmas—
The best day of the year.
With Jesus as "Our Saviour"
We have nothing to fear.
Surrender your *all* to Him—
Rest *still* in *His* loving arms—
He *will* guide and protect you—
From all harm.

Faye Fuller Weedman
REQUIEM
A child died today
like a leaf
torn from a tree
in summer
She was Ana;
She was new.

Samantha Magrath
The Calamity After the Storm
Out of the green-gray depths of
the ocean
Comes a monstrous whale.
Trying to impress his pod,
He swims only miles from the
shore.
His family hangs back, tense and
uncertain,
Watching the horizon, where
night and storm
Race for the shore.
Night comes first, and all hangs
dark.
Angered at the night's victory,
The storm takes revenge on the
Arrogant whale with a sudden
Gust of wind and rain,
Throwing the animal onto the
shore
Where it moans beseechingly.
Its pod swims nearer, watching
Warily the storm that lingers still.
With chirps and squeals they
comfort
Their friend, for although he was
Vain he was their kind.
As the night receded, so did the
Whale's last breath,
And the storm slipped away,
In the cover of the whales' grief.

Mary H. Graves
DREAMS
Midnight madness cloaks the spell
Of fears, riding, surfing the tides

of sleep,
Washed against the rocky beach
of slumber,
As reality becomes a dreamless
grace
Unequal to the inescapable night
Of hours passing at a nightmare's
pace
Turning whatever darkness that's
left
Into shadows of indifference that
face
And roam the secrets of the
subconscious,
Skimming the surface, a subtle
deep,
At midnight when madness goes
astray . . .

Luisa M. Covani
FOOLS THAT DARE
Fools that Dare to live in Dreams
must in time in our hearts Die
unless we too decide to live
(hide in hearts)
(Forever hide)

Fools that Dare to live in Dreams
will in Time be asked Why.
Fools that Dare,
Fools that Dare,
Will never Care
Will never Care.

John A. Guilliams
MARRIAGE
*[This poem is dedicated to my
wonderful wife, Joyce who
inspired it.]*
Marriage is a joining together of
two souls. With one goal this
life through.

It is a learning process. A giving
and taking one—too.

It is an eternity of togetherness.
Two minds with one thought. A
process of banishing each
others fears.

Marriage is sharing each others
joys and sorrows—smiles and
tears.

Cathie L. Snedegar/Marcello
FOR FATHER
*[In Memory of Virgil Ray
Snedegar October 23, 1922—
April 30, 1980]*
This poem is for you Father, a
short story it will tell.
Of a life lived in misery; no, make
that total hell!
You were an alcoholic and to me
you could feel no pain,
And certainly couldn't have any
feelings.
You cried so bitterly but I didn't
believe
But your mind from the War and
the pain in your heart
Had never known a healing.

You weren't much of a Daddy, as
I imagined Daddy's were.
But most of all I couldn't stand
the way you treated Mother.
You were always saying, "Nobody
cares,"
I thought that you were right.
But I miss that crazy laugh of
yours and dream of you at
night.

I was young and stupid then, and
oh so unaware,
That hate accomplishes nothing
at all
If only I had known that I cared.
Father I only hope you can
forgive me, somehow I know
you do.
I can honestly say I now forgive
Anything I had ever held against
you.

You've been gone almost 3 years
now Dad, I hope it's not too
late.
To say I'm sorry for using, an ugly
word called hate.
I thought you were so terrible
I thought of you as small.
I guess in looking back now
I never thought at all.

W. Lucille Thomson
Let a Smile Set Your Course
A friendly smile, one kind and
gently spoken word
Will buoy our spirit of life more
than a six gun salute,
And linger like a saga in your
soul,
A passover in the tabernacles of
your heart.
If we could link ourselves
steadfastly
To such a shrink resistant
endurance,
Wrought by that steel like trust
and proverbial faith,
So unconquerable and sound that
no matter what the haul,
How lurched to leeward your
vessel might be,
You could anchor unbarred in
your own tranquil sea.
So let a smile set your course.

Louise S. Yates
HAPPY HOLIDAYS
Hear the bells
As they ring,
Hear the carolers
As they sing,
Hear the sounds
Of Christmastime
As they float across
The Snowclad earth.

Hear the tidings
Of this happytime
As the yule log
Warms your hearth
The glad tidings
And the songs, too,
Are the Christmas joys
I wish for you.
Happy holidays, little Robby,
Dear little one;
Merry Christmas, little Robby,
My dear grandson.

Carol Besten Madison
THE REAPER
[For my children, Ronnie and
Juliana Holcomb]
Children forgotten, roaming the
street . . .
Parents ignore, they sow what
they reap.
Children all ages, hanging around
Waiting for love that can't be
found.
Standing on corners, lost to the
street

Idling minds with wandering
feet . . .
Nothing to do and nowhere to go
Left wide open for trouble to
grow.
The candy man comes with
goodies galore
Looking for kids to use his
drugstore.
He's the dope pushing mind
seeker
Soul searching drug reaper
Hooking the kids and planting
his seed
Giving a fix, whatever the need.
Children destroyed, families
distraught . . .
Abandoned hope where no
love's taught.
Wake the parents to use their
head . . .
Love the kids before they're
dead . . .
To cry not later when it's done
Of handing them a loaded gun
Of caring not or had no time
For any excuse, would be a
crime.
Love and care plant in the heart
And you will reap a work of art!

Nance Ann Arbuthnot
A FUTURE TIME
[Mark and Mary and Mrs.
Schwartz: the three people who
got me started!]
Someday I'm going to die. When
that day comes I want to be
spread across the ocean. In my
life now all I wish for is
making people smile. So after I
die I still want to share my
love. To reach out and blow a
light breeze across the sand.
What good would I be in a box
under the ground? I can't reach
out to the world and share my
love. When it's my turn to go
free, don't feel sorry for me!
Remember all the moments
that we had together. Just
know I care for you. No matter
where I am, I'll always send my
love out to you. There will
always be some sign that I still
care. That I'm alive but in a
future time! A time that will
bring us all together. But this
time there will be no anger, no
pain, no hurting, just peace! It
will be a moment that will
never end. It will be forever and
ever.

Michele A. Ciemny
DAY'S TEARS
So quiet is the day again
It weeps its tears with gentle rain
So soft its breath upon my face
I almost could forget the pain

A trail so long the road is rough
Like ocean waves within a storm
It starts out weak and builds
itself
Such violence then begins to
form

Timid eyes weep endlessly
Deep scars that tend to never heal
The fear that builds is as
constant as
The vivid horror it reveals

People pass but do not see
What's harbored down so deep
within
Such agony that is supressed
It slices swift and cuts again

But time keeps passing slowly by
The icy cold knocks out the
breath
The people never wonder why
The song of life was death

Lou Frierson
NATURE'S BEAUTY
[For my nature lover
T.M. Walters]
As I sit and watch the snowflakes,
Go drifting slowly by;
I wonder how something so fragile
Survives the fall from the sky.
How many does it take
To make a blanket of white?
It really doesn't matter, I guess,
It's such a beautiful sight.

Beverly Japhet
CHRISTMAS MORN
Their little eyes light up so
bright,
When first they see the
Christmas sight.
All the presents under the tree,
Hold such joy for all to see.
They rip the paper, tear the bows,
Before the rooster ever crows.
Joy of the morning in smiling
faces,
And all those sleepy, happy
embraces,
Make you glad that you are there,
On Christmas morn, with all, to
share!

Dorothy Anderson
GOD'S FOUR SEASONS
Start with Winter, its snow
a blanket of white covering the
ground,
what a beautiful sight.
Crystal icicles hanging from the
trees
glistening like diamonds,
swaying in the breeze.
Children sliding, skating and
sleighing down hill
only come indoors against their
will.
The cold winds, they blow and
make us dress warm
and wait for the Spring
that will one day be born.

With the dawning of Spring,
the rain comes gently down
to soak the Winter's hard
frozen ground.
Gentle and soft it soaks all around
to awaken the flowers asleep
underground.
The flowers break through
and bloom in beautiful color.
They say, here we are, to pick and
to love.
We are from God's garden, sent
from above.

Then there is Summer
with the hot sun above.
This is the season that most
people love.
The flowers are blooming all over
the place,
the beaches are packed by the
whole human race.

They swim in the blue waters,
frolic in the sand
hoping the sun will give them
a golden tan.

There are picnics and outdoor
games and
backyard barbeques.
We enjoy all this under the
Summer sun,
hoping it will last the whole
year through.
But Summer must pass, as each
season does—
The next one is Fall,
the most beautiful of all.

The flowers we saw in the Spring
are not the ones we see in the
Fall.
They let us now that time
has just passed us all.
The leaves now change their
color and hue
Your eyes, your eyes can never
behold
such a perfect view.
In the Fall we remember Spring
and Summer fun
for we know it won't be long
before Winter has begun.

So you see my friends
God tries to make us all happy
by sending us four different
seasons
in which we can work and play.
And, somewhere along the way
I hope we take time out to
thank Him,
each in our own way.

Terrance Lee Brown
LOST LOVE
as restlessly
as a storm tossed sea
are the nights without your love
I can't sleep
the hours creep
your smile is all I'm thinking of

the endless days
the countless ways
I have tried to lose your memory
lovely face
leave no trace
my heart yearns to be free

Virginia G. Mowery
WAR
So many wars
darken our world
breaking up
life's rhythm
bringing discord
to a happy life
causing tensions
in a cheerful house
keeping families
apart
sometimes never to be
whole again
and all this
because of
man's greed
and self-esteem.

Laura Berry
still-life
smoothly shaven legs
glowed a half light
under a window denied
every setting sun
each follicle a hint

underwiring the breasts
and domesticalities through
an abused white coiled wire

little red riding hood's wolf
was planted in
a bed familiar
yet she
managed to decline

and my eyes are shutting
forgetting the lines i wrote
hours earlier in a glass
of gin
in a sliver of lime

like the sliver of skin
the razor stole

Eileen D. Collins
MERRY OLD CHRISTMAS
[In memory of dad; writer,
composer, and pianist. When
asked, how do I know I can
write, he replied succinctly,
"Keep writing and rewriting—
you'll find out."]
I recollect it jest this way
The goin's on fer Christmas Day,
   Hangin' 'round the kitchen
   door
Whilst Ma was cookin' food
   galore.
"Son, fetch some wood, so's the
   fire don't die".
"Sure, Mom", I said, then off I'd fly!
   I spied Pa cuttin' a fresh fir tree,
But I made out like I didn't see
   'Cause it was hid and put away;
A special sight fer Christmas
   Day.
   We made our ornaments to
   hang—
And presents, too, fer all the gang:
   A hand-carved horse fer little
   Jane
Painted bright with a long black
   mane,
   A sailin' ship fer brother Frank;
(The one he made hisself done
   sank!)
   "Son, you've been extry good",
   Pa said.
(Shucks . . . mebbe then I'll git
   that sled!)
   When Christmas mornin' came
   at last
We stumbled down the stairs real
   fast.
   The tree, it stood there spark-
   ely bright,
It was a mightly purty sight!
   And 'neath the boughs a sailin'
   ship,
A hand-carved horse complete
   with whip,
   And Lawd, there set my racin'
   sled—
She was a beaut, all dazzlin' red!
   Then after we had et, we sang,
Gramps, he bellered loud, gosh
   dang . . .
   Aunt Tillie hollered 'way
   off-key,
Whilst Ma and Pa sang happily.
   Well . . . these here thoughts
   long stored away
Are treasures to unpack someday,
   Like the tattered greetin' cards
   that said:
"Merry Old Christmas, from our
   old homestead!"

Cheryl - Lee Honig
A BLIND MAN'S PRAYER
The shoes I wear
Upon my feet
Have lost their soles
On concrete

The shirt I wear
Upon my back
Was found along
A peddler's track

The pants I wear
Around my waist
Are not much to
A rich man's taste

But this is all
I have and own
I even go
Without a home

I sleep the streets
Throughout the night
And roam them
Through the day

I can not see
The dark nor light
And a cane of wood
Thus leads my way

Yes, I am blind
A poor man too
I can not see
My life like you

Still, I am happy
Through and through
Because I am loved
By God, like you

Eugene J. Stewart
BRIGHT STAR
On the nights when blue
moons would show, I'd sit
back with a chilled glass of
champagne, listen to a little
soft music and let my dreams
grow from beginning to end;
a situation one only wishes
for in the course of evenings
time
But on this evening's night
there was no blue moon's
glow,
only you
Even with the chilled champagne
and soft toned music there was
no beginning dream
only you
I gave my opinion on the
situation
and drew to this conclusion,
You're my sugar angel
You're my star that shines . . .

Paul Cauley
ONE NIGHT
[To my Lord and Saviour
without whom there would be
no rhyme nor reason.]
One night
darkness interrupted
One Light
uncorrupted
is born into the world
Adorned
with Majesties concealed
soon to be revealed
a promise of Light.
One night
a child in perfection
one day as a man
He stands . . . pierced

total rejection.
Accused in His time
Love . . . His only crime
He dies . . . in agonizing pain
but not without reason
for it's from Him that we gain the
   true lasting season
of Life.
One night
buried in stone
the frosty eyelids of time at long
   last shut tight
He steps from His new womb,
   and again with Love,
defeats the night.
Today, sweet JESUS, we celebrate
   Your birth
with the Light You have left for us
as we dwell for this short time
down here on earth.
Today, and all the todays,
till You return with great might
we bow in remembrance
of a Child born
One Night.

Kathleen Sawyer
ME AND FREE
I just want to be free,
Free from everything
And all the boundaries around me.
To do as I see fit
And be able to try
Whatever I feel I need to
And just to be me.

Jana Christopher
BROKEN PIECES
Mom and Dad were once together
Mom and Dad are now a' sever
And all the king's horses,
And all the king's men,
Couldn't put Mom and Dad
Back together again.

Sherry L. Powell
A PATH
We packed the earth with
   shortcuts
Through woods, meadows, and
   fields,
And when a new way was found
   and freshly worn,
We followed and ventured.
A path was born.

Some just took us across the field
   to the country store,
Others followed and led to
   isolated woods,
While still others traveled under
   barbed-wire fences
And over boundary stone walls,
Or mysteriously disappeared over
   farms, hills, and dales.
Only we knew where they led.

Through spring's soft earth and
   dainty buds,
To summer's full greenery of
   many ventures,
Through autumn's amber colors
   and gentle falling leaves,
To winter's white wonderland of
   resting trails.

So many memories along a path
   we had;
Some were fun and laughter,
   games of pretend,
And yes, some were even sad.

But as the years grew by, time
   elapsed,

And we moved away.
Grass grew where a path's ground
   had softened,
And others gave up to a new
   highway.

For now they are only phantom
   trails,
That lie and slumber below a past,
Where we once followed and
   ventured,
Where there once was "A Path."

Pamala-Jane Lindhe
RIVER OF FATE
Deep in my heart,
   something whines;
In the darkness all alone,
   it shines.

A long lost love,
   is hidden there,
A mar from someone,
   who refused to care.

A blow from someone,
   who hurt my pride;
A fact concealed,
   but hard to hide.

Margaret Wangler
BUT I LOVE YOU
You treat me with distaste.
You're tender at your conveneince.
Your compliments hurt me,
Your compliments crumble me.

But you say you care,
But I love you.

It's piercing and traumatic.

Good-bye.

Mary Anne Buckley
MY EARTH STAR
You give me hope in this sick
   world,
a hope I could not see.
You're like a star sent down to
   Earth
to shine some light on me.

Before you came my life was dark,
I had no sunny day.
But God above must have felt
   some love,
for he sent you on your way.

So he picked a star, a special one,
and named it after you.
Then he pushed the star with a
   gentle hand;
He knew you were overdue.

You reached me soon, via the
   moon,
and now you're here to stay.
My Earth star, you traveled far,
to show me a better way.

Joan V. Bracken
MY PARENTS
[To my Mom and Dad: Dean &
Marilyn Bracken. Because I
love them.]
I would trade them
   for nothing . . .

They comfort and correct
   me . . .

Always there when I
   need them . . .

They've loved and cared
   for me all my life . . .

There are so many times
   They've gone without, for
   me . . .

There is so much they
   have done for me . . .
And so little I have
   done for them . . .
I know not where to
   begin repayment . . .
      But . . .
I use their freely given
   advice whenever I can . . .
I often remember the words
   of wisdom they have shared . . .
I want them to know
   before they die . . .
I Love them with all
   my heart . . .
      And . . .
I wish I could give them
   everything they want . . .
For that's the payment
   they should have . . .
For all the worries and
   problems . . .
Bad grades and habits,
   and the BILLS . . .
All the times I had nothing
   to give when I had received.
      So . . .
I am writing this
   for you, MOM and DAD . . .
To tell you of how proud
   and glad I am to have
   parents such as you
      TWO!
I LOVE YOU BOTH,
   AND ALWAYS WILL!

Dorothy E. Birrane
GRIEF
Fifteen Octobers have not
   dimmed the pain.
. . Time stands still for those who
   mourn.
      But a single thought
         resurrects again,
      that which lies in a
         shallow grave.

The miles traveled since that day
   are but a moment by grief's
   clock.
      The pain of the still fresh
         wound stays,
      unwashed, by an ocean of
         tears.

The flowers continue to bloom—
   nature has not stopped to
   mourn with me.
      She goes on primping, a bride
      for her groom,
         each spring, as if nothing
            had changed.

The thrush's ballad, with its clear
   bell tone—
   impervious—still breaks the
   day.
      If I am to grieve, I must do so
         alone—
            or bury my memories in a
               deeper grave.

Mandy Baumbach
THE FIRST SNOW
This morning I woke up
To a world full of white.
The leaves were all hidden
'Neath the snow
Clear and bright.
The pines were more beautiful

Than I've ever seen,
They looked very pretty
So neat and so clean.

It's time now for mittens
Warm hats and fur coats,
It's time now for sleighbells
To play their sharp notes.
Inside you can feel
The joy and excitement
Of the season that's here
Full of warm Christmas cheer.

It's time now for hurrying
And rushing around,
And buying some gifts
From shops in the town.
Build a warm fire
To cuddle up by
And drink some hot coco
And eat some mince pie.

Evelyn M.S. Edwards
BE HAPPY IN LIFE
"I will not suffer my soul to be
   sad or dejected"
For my Lord's Love Shines in
   every direction
I shall reach out and feel his
   Miraculous touch
And always remember that our
   God loves us so much
I will not suffer my soul to
   knowingly do wrong
But I will give my soul the beauty
   of song
And as each day waxes present in
   this life of mine
"My Heart and my Soul are by
   God of one Mind."

Anne Chatterton Brown
I TRIED
I tried to find a friend,
But there was no one there.
I tried to find a true love,
But could not find one anywhere.

I tried to reach the stars,
But my reach was much too shy.
I tried to stop the time,
But it swiftly passed me by.

I tried to say I love you,
But the words I could not find,
So then I tried to show you,
But you were much too blind.

Christina Paulaconis
IN MEMORY
I can still remember that horrid
   night, the air in windy motion,
I can still feel him kiss me with
   such a strong devotion.

I can still grasp that hurt and the
   tears that I cried,
And the lump in my throat
   watching him while he died.

Standing completely still, frozen
   by pure fright,
Taking him in my arms and
   squeezing him so tight.

I felt so brave and tough having
   him in my hold,
Yet he lay unresponsive—so
   helpless, so meek, so cold.

I released him and I shook him
   and I told him not to go,
"You're way too good to leave me,
   oh please! I love you so."

He stared at me intensely, his
   eyes as empty as glass,

I watched the memories of the
   years as quickly they did pass.

And I cried and I cried and the
   tears streamed down my face,
Covering my body with a sheet of
   snow-white lace.

I can still remember placing him
   in that hole of dirt and dark,
And how in my ears I could still
   hear that loud familiar bark.

As we buried him it seemed as
   though I could clearly see,
His warmest eyes of brown
   taunting me with his plea.

But as we drove the black painted
   cross forcefully to the ground,
It brought me to reality with a
   repulsive, thudding sound.

I fell to my knees and I prayed it
   wasn't true,
I held the cross close to me and I
   looked in the sky dark blue.

I kissed the grave where he lay
   and I said my last good-bye,
Oh, Smokey, beloved Smokey,
   why did you have to die?

Charles F. Spencer
DISTANT DRUMS
Mother, why have your streams
   run dry?
Father, why have you left us here
   to die?
Brothers, where have your sisters
   gone?
Children frightened from the
   unknown.
Babies crying all alone.

Can you hear the beat from their
   distant drums
Pounding out strength, another
   battle, their freedom just won?
Visions for peace are slowly
   fading away.
Blood on the ground, too much
   death in the way.
Smoke in the sky and fire below.

A warrior lies wounded, his heart
   turning cold.
Knife in his hand, death grip
   won't let go.
Crows nearby mocking for his
   spirit to flow.
Horses running wild, shaking
   Mother Earth.
Women hiding to give untamed
   birth.

Sound of threat from enemy
   bugles
Echoing through valleys below.
Peace pipes are broken, fresh war
   paint it shows.
Death cries and sorrow, deep in
   one's bones.
Visions are empty where buffalo
   once roamed.

Betty Irene Thomas
HEART TO GOD
God is so worthy of our worship
   that it's very easy to say,
Our hearts belong to Him in
   every single way.
He is Alpha and Omega—the
   First and Last—the Beginning
   and the End,
The God of the Living who is the
   Great I Am is our Best Friend.

The Almighty Creator made our
   body, mind and soul,
To please the Omnipotent One
   should be more desired than
   gold.
He is the Rock of our strength,
   our refuge, our salvation and
   our glory,
Even the history of man really
   means "His Story".
Honor and majesty are before
   Him so His word is true,
He is not a man that He should
   lie but does what He says He
   will do.
Heaven is His throne and the
   clouds are the dust of His feet,
Earth is His footstool where
   mountains quake and hills
   melt with fervent heat.
What the all-powerful Jehovah
   has made straight cannot be
   made crooked by man,
He is the Holy One in our midst
   who has the master plan.
Uncountable are His wonders
   and beside Him, all things pale,
The God of Hosts who can gather
   the winds in His fists can do
   everything but fail.
Heart to God—Heart to God—
   how can we do less?
The One who gives us breath to
   use—even to curse Him if we
   choose—deserves our very best.

Marna Wielert
NEW YEAR
Let me remember moonlight soft
   lighting your hair
and smooth, the silk of your skin
your laughter—like rippling
   water in spring
May I remember
   every little thing.

Let me remember the curve of
   your cheek
with tremulous tears of pearl so
   pale,
sweet fragrant incense of captive
   tresses—
   the feel of your hair
beloved—how fair
   how fair.

Let me remember dreams
   of days gone by
mellowed as old lace of
   yesteryear,
may I remember haunting
   memories
   and yet—
just for tonight let me forget,
   let me forget!

Lois (Vickers) Frizzell
TRYING TO TRY
We strive through life so hard to
   gain
   Just a bit of respect, honor and
   fame:
Though failure comes more often
   than success
   While trying hard to do our
   best.

Awards are given and trophies are
   won,
   Through pain and effort at a
   job well done.
With patience, success could be
   no farther away

Than one more trial, one more day.

Don't grow weary and lose sight of faith,
Only the pessimist declares, "I was born too late".
Today's discouragements must never own a place,
There'll be a tomorrow with new opportunities to face.

There's truth to the fact, winners never give up,
Though the mountains get rocky, steep and rough,
The valleys are wide and the battles tough,
And temptation assures 'endurance enough'.

Regrets and failures we now may feel
But the prize could be—Just beyond the valley—
    Over the next hill.
There's strength in defeat to onward press
When we feel we've not yet done our best.

Have faith, don't stop, don't give up yet,
Success don't come to those who quit.
Had the young little birdie, aiming at the sky,
When fluttering its wings found it couldn't fly,
Utterly wailed in despair and expressed with a sigh,
"I'll never soar or sail in the air so high
For I cannot rise, I cannot fly"?

Though we fail in trying, we don't stop then,
We attain our goal only when
We persistently keep on keeping on
    Trying to try again!!!

Maggie Dowling
A THANKSGIVING RECIPE
[*To Isobell Rudolph, my Auntie. Her positive attitude on life and of me, a special gift, helps me to feel good while sharing my inner feelings.*]
1 Day set aside for thanks
1 Small group, consisting of gentle folk
2 Cups of thought, if only for a moment
2 Hands holding two others, a circle to form

Take the one day set aside
And with the gentle folk, stir up love of peace and harmony.
From within pour out to either hand
Strength thru unity. Take from the heart
This sharing, spread all around, touching
The edges of those less fortunate theeby
Cooling the heat of anger and pain. Warm
By rekindling the love we possess. Stir
Into the very soul thru forgiving we can
Offer Thanksgiving
Garnish: Friendship
SERVES: ALL

Jerald M. Rosen
TIME'S MIND
Whence do you come, time?
A terrible lash you bring
In sweet memories.
Why pain me in helpless hindsight
And arm little with forewarning?
A fine memium you are—
Do you see helpless torment?
In decision you answer me later—
Some fair justice you bring.
Time, you know my mind
Though I may not at present.
I mind not of you,
But that you mind nothing,
You mind nothing of me.

Lyn
TOGETHER
When I lie awake, alone
I remember the nights we shared
When no one else would take you away.
I'm thinking now that the day may come
When someone will come along and take you from me.
Take the laughter, take the tears, take the times we shared together.
But no one can take the memories I have for you in my heart.
I'm wishing you were right here with me
Just holding me in your arms so tight, the way you did the other night.
Don't let me go!
Just look back to the other night—
When you were holding my hand;
It felt so warm, I felt so secure
And I knew what we had was right.
Then you let go, I got scared!
What we have together is different
    What we have together is terrific!
We could be happy by ourselves or be happy in a crowd,
As long as we're together it doesn't matter who's around.
Talking, laughing, being serious and just being there
How beautiful it was.
I hope it never ends.
Then you let go, and I got scared!

Donald R. Todd
A COSMIC CALL
It all began on a silvery night
    With the moon full-blown and the stars so bright
        That out of the dust and a cosmic ray,
        There flew a ship from the Milky Way.

It stopped and hovered on its downward trek,
    And I paused and wondered, just what the heck
        Is this silvery object from out of the sky
        That makes no sound as it seems to fly.

And then it fluttered without a sound
    While a door slid open as it touched the ground.
    Then a man stepped forth and said with mirth,
    "I'm on a mission to this planet earth.
I've come from afar to set man straight
    And explain the peril of his impending fate.
    For if he can't cease this incessant squabble,
        He'll only enhance Earth's threatening wobble."

So then he unveiled what he had in store
    And entranced my mind with his strange space lore.
        Then unfolding his plan for the Earth's reforms,
        He told of *his* land and its healthy norms.

But then he leaped to the ship's thin rim,
    And promised that I would be hearing of him.
        Then he pressed a button I couldn't see,
        And a door slid shut quite suddenly.

Then a silent purr like a comfy cat
    Came out of the ship—and it raised, like that!
        Then it wheeled away on its upward flight:
        Just like it began that silvery night.

George R. Toland
GOING PLACES
In a crowded airport I stand,
A blank ticket in my hand.
Going where I do not know.
Will someone tell me where to go?

Some places have things I hold dear.
Other places have things I fear.
Will someone tell me what to do?
For you see, I haven't a clue.

Down the field each airplane races;
Taking off for far off places.
All the airplanes now have gone;
And I didn't know which one to get on.

Mary E. Ward
On the Science Institute 1956
We've packed a lot'a learning
    In weeks of science time.
We've worked the Cook-class problems
    And made our schedules rhyme.
He sat on tacks, played atom ball
    To prove a crystal's form.
He's down to earth—a human too
    For him we'd work till morn.
What I've learned has over flowed
    In my tote-bag it's been crammed;
Elements, atoms, angstroms
    Ions, bases isotopes and genes.
Roentgen dose from Swanson too
    Philosophy and thunder storm.
Soft words at lecture time were said
    By Bailey to the group.

He made announcements for the week,
    And tests that made us droop.
A pencil dropped, the time it took
    To get it back in place
You've missed 4 pages—Bailey notes
    You must increase your pace.
The pop and bang, the cough and sneeze
    That's heard in number seven,
Was caused by Weaver's doing things
    With odors up to heaven.
We've seen and done, we've all been through
    His demonstration line
Exchanging aids and helpful hints
    Which was mighty fine
No better group from seven states
    Could have ever met
To mingle, study and acquaint
    Ourselves—a science group.

Kirsten Fox
BITTER LINES 100
I will stay as long as I can
As long as time permits
And I will endure the strain on my life
How well my punishment fits
The bearded rolling mogul
Dictating life indeed
But all the answers to the life fall deaf
On the ears of aching need
Quiet jokes of prophecy
And a scratch to the back of the head
And a walk around the room
To heighten my fear and dread
I will stay as long as I'm able
As long as the pressure is not great
But it seems I have no sense of time
Something has slipped of late
I wait for the hour to pass
And the seconds tick by like there is no haste
And I watch the faces of the Abiders of Patience
Where did they replace the lake?

James S. Tippett
IT'S GONE
The love we once shared is gone

It came from a seed of hope, planted in our hearts

It grew with the faith we had in one another

It lived with the trust we had in each other

It bloomed from the love we gave each other

But, it died for its season was over

Katherine Wall McDowell
Was "I'm Sorry" Too Hard To Say
Did you humble your heart, and forgiveness seek
From the one whom you wronged today
Or with heart deep set in arrogant pride
Was "I'm sorry", too hard to say.

Did you leave the thoughtless
evil you sowed
In another's breast to take root,
Or did you deliver apology owed,
Ere evil could spread, and bear
fruit.

How many souls will die today
From wounds they have suffered
sore;
When a penitent "Forgive me",
(too hard to say)
Would have lightened the cross
that they bore.

Already gross wrong may lie
anchored deep
In another's aching breast—
Our Saviour admonished, confess
ye to wrong
Ere the sun sinks in the west.

Impenitent evil weighing on
mortal,
In grip foreboding and cold;
In the ultimate end must flee the
heart's portal
Ere peace can prevail in the soul.

Did you humble your heart and
forgiveness seek,
From the one whom you wronged
today,
Or with heart deep set in
arrogant pride—
Was "I'm sorry", too hard to say—
Was "I'm sorry", too hard to say.

H.D. Herring
ARTHUR
I am a hunter
tracking lions and tigers in far
away jungles.
I am a doctor
making people well.
I am a monster
scaring all who come near me.
I am an actor
portraying those around me.
I am unafraid
willing to learn, take a chance,
experience.
I am anything I want to be
yet I don't know who I am.
I am what others want me to be
yet I am myself.
I am in a world of my own
yet I am in a world of others
I am, who am I, I am a child.

Debby K. Wickins
THE DEVIATION
In an atmosphere of wonderful,
bloody red,
And desirable, morbid black . . .
(Such black in the destinal,
calming earth,
And such red in the
unobtainable, taunting skies)
Did one sit on a huge, blessed
stone,
Gazing around himself . . .
seeing and realizing his
surrounded state
(And believing his state to be
beautifully, purely blissful.)
And his obscure, lonely figure,
Perched against the sea of lovely,
lovely red
Seemed to symbolize all of
everything
That leads way to the horrid,
suicidal state of Solitude.

And then he turned to his Shadow
Who sat patiently behind him,
And realizing how desolate a
figure he must have appeared,
Said to his Shadow
"It is not wrong to Believe
In the ideals of
Fate,
Suicide,
Anguish,
Terror,
Rage,
and Solitude.
But those who dwell on these
subjects
Will never obtain the power
To *open* their minds, and then
Believe and realize that
Fate is only the end of direction
of one's own actions
Suicide is only the end of courage
in one's own beliefs
Anguish is only the end of
optimism in one's own ideals
Terror is only the end of bravery
in one's own faiths
Rage is only the end of calm in
one's own soul
And Solitude is only the end of
Hope for Light
For when Light dies,
One may not turn to their own
constant companion
And confide in them as I do with
you at this moment."

And then all at once the skies
brilliantly dissembled
And the monotanous, all-present
red gave way to
A new, wonderful, glorious,
shining blue,
And the dull, dank, unending
black
Became eclipsed by a beautiful,
prodigious green
And everywhere Life breathed
again . . .

. . . and Lived.

Mary A. Paslawsky
EMPTY BED
I sleep alone
in an empty bed—
save me

The cat curls
up at the foot of
an empty bed—
save me

The sheets are pulled
to and fro
across an empty bed—
save me

The pillow where
you laid your head
is laying on
an empty bed—
save me

Vickie McBride
AUTUMN AND LOVE
*[For Kirk, the Autumn of my
life. There's a part of me that
still hopes, for loneliness is a
place to dream too.]*
Autumn Mood—
Sunlight fading.
Night Approaching.
Beautiful, ominous
browns and yellows,

golds and reds
of dying leaves.
Coldness replacing warmth.
Life coming to a slow
sorrowing pace.
Wind blowing violently.
And then there is silence.
The silence of great love.
The silence of defeat
and failure of that love.
And then comes the loneliness.
The feeling which is intense,
as intense as Autumn.
And so it seems right that love
should die,
For Autumn represents the
approach of death.
And loneliness should be
sustained.
For loneliness is a path returning
to oneself
And the process through which
new love becomes possible.
And hope is reborn.

Daniel J. Nickelson
MY LIFE IS HAPPY
*[This poem was written to, and
inspired by, my wife, Joyce
whom I love very much.]*
My life is happy,
Oh, very much.
Because you're there,
For me to touch.
My life is happy,
Oh, yes indeed.
Because you're the one,
I'll always need.
My life is happy,
Oh, this I feel.
Because I know,
Your love is real.
My life is happy,
Yes, you see.
Because of you,
It will always be.

Lesia M. Golden
NO CONTROL
People come, people go
they walk all over me.
I pull myself up from the trash
to see all that I can see.

Purple faces seem to say
it just will never snow.
I'm trying hard to change what's
here
but they always tell me no.

Pushed aside, left alone
I'm really not that hard to please.
Twisted minds which run the show
put me up for sale or lease.

Ethel White
ROBERT BURNS' COUNTRY
I've trod the ground you've trod
upon
And felt its mystic glow;
I've watched the peace and quiet
lure
Of Afton Waters flow.

Your Mary must be peaceful slept
In deep and sweet repose
Along these waters cool and pure
So soft it gently flows.

Romance was ever in your heart
Dear Rab, and we know why
Mid such surroundings beauty
rare
No red hot blood could shy.

We saw the Kirk where you were
taught
Be sure the right from wrong;
Just two end walls are left today
But still I hear its song.

At Mauchline found we there the
Inn
That's kept intact this day,
We sat and listened to your voice
So rousing, gusty, gay.

Beyond the window there within
The sight of Armours' home
Where Bonnie Jean looked o'er
the Inn
As your eyes up there roam.

'Tis wondrous great that things
are kept
Just as you saw them then,
In good repair that we may dream
You walk with us again!

Kelly M. Cortese
REALITY
Reality:
just another pretty picture
painted on the side of a public
wall. to be observed and
studied by
all. to be understood by None.

Carolyn Denise Pell
RECALL
Can you recall some years ago
When you were young and on the
go?
When life was simple
And worries few.
You had more money
And better sense too.
When smiling was easy
And frowning unreal,
When once a friendship
Was stronger than steel.
Yes, days gone by
So quickly; years gone.
Enjoy yourself—
Before you're grown!

Laura Ann Richitelli
WILD MUSTANG
With everlasting beauty you
wander through eternity.
Running away from civilization
with death as your only enemy.
As the wind runs through
your flowing mane you take
on any challenge.
Freer than any creature
on earth you rule the
land you live on.

Run
Wild,
Run
Free

Vendella J. Pennington
TOMORROW
Tomorrow, yes maybe tomorrow
But I'll wait until then
For the evening bells now call me
To a time no matter when.

Tomorrow, yes maybe tomorrow
A different place Earth to be.
Remembering the old lost world
That now seems to dismay me.
If only tomorrow could promise
A new world full of peace.
The dream of the inner sphere
That's what tomorrow will
release.

To this present world
Have heart to the end
For there is always tomorrow,
Tomorrow, yes maybe then.

Gretchen L. Wilson
INTIMATE HAUNTINGS
A friend of mine died tonight.
We used to spend a lot of time
together but not so much
anymore.
I know I'll miss him for awhile . . .
Then, from time to time
his memory will pay me a
welcome visit.
We will sit by the fire
and discuss the trivial,
or maybe the present day
economics.
His presence will lean against the
sofa while I take my place in
the rocker.
The fire will crackle up the
chimney.
The cat will curl up in my lap.
Hours will pass
and we will laugh as we did in
better days.
A friend of mine died tonight.
I know wer're still unfinished,
but I'm in no hurry.
I'll enjoy these visits by his
memory and his presence will
be kind.
Our talks beside the fires
will complete the caring process.

Robert Conley
THEY KNEW
They taught me how to kill the
men
I never knew as "super men,"
Who live or die the same as I
And kill to live or die.

They said it was for Peace to fight
And I, poor fool, believed them
right.
I fought their fight with soul and
might,
A war to end all war and strife.

I did the job they told me to
Though friend or foe lay cold;
I found the peace (they sold me
too)
In Death, O fool! They knew!

Ronald Wayne Mosley (The Mose)
RAGING LOVE
*[Inspired and dedicated with
love to Gail.]*
Like a river flowing.
Florescent and glowing.
Inside of me my dove.

Strong and free.
Growing high like a mountain.
High as a tall tree.
Flowing free like a fountain.

Raging love inside of me.
Churning and burning.
Inside of me.
Only you can tame.
This raging flame.

My raging love.
It's only for you, my dove.
To hold you, this I would cherish.
My love will never perish.

Only you hold the key.
Unlock it, and release this raging
love from me.

Terri L. Harker
BUBBLES
Bubbles floating in the air,
Drifting softly here and there;
Each a rainbow all it's own,
Where they'll end is all unknown.

Hurry catch it before it goes,
It's too late, there the wind blows;
Forever and ever way up on high,
To a land of rainbows up in the
sky.

Jessie Vernell Doctor
HELL'S HIGHWAY
During this evil and sinful day
Man seems determined to live his
own way.
Be things wrong, not right what
may,
He thinks not hell his soul will
lay.
During this evil and sinful day
Surely man is throwing his gift of
life away
As worldly men raise sins's ugly
head and say,
"Everybody's doing this, there's no
wrong way!"
During this evil and sinful day
Man joins the crowds for
popularity pay.
And gladly he does whatsoever
they say,
Not realizing he's speeding down
hell's highway.
During this evil and sinful day
Seeking strength and power the
chemical way
Man forgets with faith and
sincerity to kneel and pray,
For within God's hands all power
and blessings lay.

Bunny Mills
**Mother Mary's Christmas
Gift**
Mary was a little old lady
Who after all her little ones were
grown
And had homes of their own
Lived in a wee room alone.
People all thought her strange
For the gifts she would give.
Her pastime was the five and
dime store.
She would walk through most
every day.
And speak to all the clerks on the
way
As things are always set out early
in the store.
She would buy valentines by the
score.
The clerks would shake their
heads and say.
"What on earth for?"
Then she would hurry home to
her little room.
Where she saved every box she
could find
And she would put them in boxes
of four.
And soon the mailman would
bring one to my door,
I'd open it and find valentines
maybe 109/
I'd say "Now what did she do this
for?"
I'd put them on the shelf
But then when valentines day
would come

My children would send them
out every one,
Easter was the same only it
would be.
Bags of grass for baskets plastic
eggs and bunnies.
And as before I'd put them on the
shelf.
And sure enough it was the same.
We would use them on Easter
day.
Birthdays the box would bring
buttons, needles and thread
With childrens books to be read.
But Christmas was the best of all.
The box would arrive and with it
bring.
Tree ornaments, bells tinsel,
stars, paper, and string,
And each year I'd think the same.
"What did she do this for?"
And if a friend happened in they
would smile and say.
Now Why? did she send them for?
Maybe by mistake?,
But then one Christmas Eve as
we sat admiring the pretty tree
And all the things over the years
Mother sent for it.
A telephone call I recieved,
It said the lord had come
And taken my mother away.
Strange as it may seem my eyes
were opened, then and I could
see.
Just what mothers gifts were
meant to be,
She was named after the Christ
childs Mother,
She went to rest on the Christ
Childs Birthday
And just like the Christ childs
mother
My mother, Mary also gave a gift,
That will never never die,
For now at Christmas time as we
set and watch our tree.
We see Mother in each pretty
little thing
But most of all the one on the
very top
The last one recieved, An Angel,
And I'm sure it's just where all
mothers should be
For they are so kind and wise.
And as my mother realized
As long as there is Christ and
Christmas
Her gift of love With me will
always be

Janet L. Malatare
A TREASURE
A treasure he has found.
He did not see it. Too late!
For his blind eyes has lost
What was perhaps never to
be his.
For she has found another road,
another world.
Even yet far above his own.
Never will he reach her.
The treasure he has lost and
never found!!

Linda Kaye Hoogeboom
WHERE ARE MY DREAMS?
Where are my dreams?
Did I leave them behind in
yesterday,
In the fields of childhood,

far away?
No, for I still dream.

Where are my hopes?
Did I lose them in another time?
I wonder, are they still mine?
Yes, as long as I hope.

Where are my yesterdays?
They were here . . . now they are
gone!
Time I thought was mine has
flown
Into years of yesterdays.

Where are my tomorrows?
Are they slipping quietly away?
No, I'll make the best of them
today!
Today is my tomorrow.

Where is my today?
I am using it the best I can
So it won't slip away like grains
of sand!
Today is:
my hopes,
my dreams,
my yesterdays,
my tomorrows.

Aleta Mull (Belmer)
THE OLD FOLKS HOME
The age on their faces, the pain
in their eyes,
the sadness of being alone, till
the day that one dies.

Left by their loved ones, to suffer
in pain
not knowing tomorrow what a
new day will bring.

"How could they do this"? The old
folks keep asking.
"We know their still out there
and time is just passing us by,
while we sit here waiting to die"?

Oh please come to see us!
All we ask is your time, and then
when we go
we'll know Love is still kind.

Lottie S. McKinley
NEW BEGINNING
Each day is a new beginning,
new for you and I.
Another chance, a challenge,
Oh rise again and try.

Yesterday's mistakes are past,
yesterday's heartaches gone,
pushed farther and farther away
from you,
by the birth of each new dawn.

Let not their shackles bind you,
only the lessons they taught,
that each new day may find you,
better for yesterday's battles
fought!

Betty J. Mason
The Quietude Of Spring
Spring is so beautiful
Take time to watch it unfold,
The days bring lots of warm
sunshine
But the nights are still very cold.

Each day you see more fields,
more water,

569

As the snow and the ice melt
away,
The mountain streams are
bursting now,
You can hear the rush as it
makes its way
Over the rocks, and down the
stream
And under the bridge it flows.

God's world is so filled with
beauty
You can see His hand in it all,
But it isn't over when spring is
done
His masterpiece comes in the fall.

Penny Laurne Fox
SPECIAL DAY
The world sure would be
A much brighter place
If there could only be
A smile on each and every face
You lead the way, you start the
trend
Across the world today, it's love
we will send

Have you ever seen someone
unknown
Act so rude and mean for no
reason known
If there could only be one special
day
Where everyone would be friendly
in a way
Then maybe folks would see
That's the way the world was
meant to be
We all could live in peace
And be free from poverty
If the rich could give one
possession
To someone in great depression
And everyone could set aside
Their selfishness and their pride
To help another sole
Strive to reach his goal
Then the world sure would be
A much brighter place
Because there could be
A smile on every face

Mary Theresa Davitt
DAYDREAMS
Daydreams are castles
we build in the sand
They drift and they wander
in the palm of your hand.
Some they bring laughter
others bring tears
Some are just hazy
and many bring fears.
The fear that someday
that dream may come true
It won't be expected
and you won't know what to do.
For, daydreams are castles
we build in the sand
They drift and they wander
but daydreams must land.

Regina D. Moore
Your Force Is In the Air
*[To Barry, the single greatest
force in my life and Rosie who
knows and understands. The
lavender light will burn on
forever.]*
You knock on the door to my heart
Without a sound,
Your force is there, though
You're not around.

I look into a stranger's eyes
And I see your face,
And when I need some comfort
I'm held by your embrace.

You are my wonder,
I know you care
Like the sound of thunder
Your force is in the air.

My past has seen happy hours
Since we have met,
My future brings us closer—
It's not over yet.
And although you're not here
with me
I understand
Your force is here with me
Holding my hand.

Sarah Henry
**Time Is a Moon—Faced
Clock**
on the landing of a great house,
watching the people go up and
down
the stairs year after year in their
clothes and amethyst rings and
makeup that covers time.

Time happens there,
unlike the prisons where men
stop aging when they enter.
Time moves on, standing
always in the same place:
halfway up and halfway down.

The people barely notice
the low thunder of the hours
striking, or the occasional
eclipse of the moon.

Edwin K. Broadhead
UNFINISHED
The journey is unfinished
And the soul is not complete
Pick up thyself and venture forth
Move on my weary feet

Fear not the winding road
Nor robbers less, for still
The icy cold of winter doth
The most of travelers kill

The journey is unfinished
And the soul is not complete
So pick up thyself and venture
forth
Move on my weary feet.

William A. (Murph) Moeller Jr.
TILL WE MEET AGAIN
The time has come for us to
part—but only
     "Till we meet again"
All the wonderful times we have
had are just
     memories now, but mine to
cherish for those
many times I will be thinking
of you.
     "Till we meet again"
I give to you my heart
filled with hope and happiness,
wishing you all the success in
your goals
And may joy and beauty
surround you
from this day forward—or—
     "Till we meet again"
Now I say to you, In hopes you
will
think of me also.
Take with you and hold in your
heart—

the happiness we have shared
together,
the warmth my heart gives to
you,
the love and affection I have
tried to give,
Hold these so ever deeply in your
heart,
so they may comfort you—if
ever you
get lonely and sad;
Till I may once again give to you
all of myself—my love, and to
you
     only.
          "Till we meet again"

E. Ann Smart
Verses Collectibles: No. 6
I once was on the stage,
(In my mind)
But now I find
I've left that all behind
Me.
No more the bows,
The loud applause,
The stagedoors
Full of fawning fans,
Now other plans
Drift through my mind,
And I find
Reality
A sweeter kind
Of stuff.

Dwight C. Abernethy
TIME!
For time is everything to me,
For time is short.
For there's a time to work,
     And a time to play.
For there's time for you,
For there's time to eat.
     And time to drink,
For there's time to draw.
For time is on my side, and
     The time I have is the
     Time nobody wants.
For time is in my life,
For it's time to write.
     And time to sleep,
And time to dream.
     And it's time to live.
For it's time to die.
For there's no more time,
For my time has run out.
For it's time to quit!

Lee M. Zuberer
NIGHTFALL
The dark velvet blanket begins
its descent
Sprinkled with stars gleaming
like diamonds on display,
Shadows cast their images over
mountains that surround me,
Like huge ancient warriors they
stand guarding me like a king;
     And I feel loved.
I lie in my bed nestled under a
great cottonwood,
While the mountain breeze
caresses as a mother's tender
touch,
Sounds of night merge with my
own inner thoughts,
     And we are one.
Night creatures wake to start the
second shift—
My soul is at peace,
     And I feel God.
I am part of this time—and it's a

part of me,
A marriage of a kind—for all is in
perfect balance.
Natures plan of existence begins
its restful stage,
Would my mentor understand
that I failed myself today?
Surely yes! For He has set the
scale of life to balance in the
end.
This is a time of re—birth, a time
to counsel myself;
A time of reflexion and
meditation,
A cleansing of my heart of the
days burdens,
Of self critism without shame.
Could I? Would I? Did I? And why?
Are all clearly defined with
understanding.
Night is my solace, I lie wrapped
in the cloak of God's
protection,
With the mountains my
companions,
The creatures my brothers and
sisters,
Yesterdays hurts are only a
thought,
Todays burdens only a memory,
Problems of tomorrow are quietly
restrained
As the soothing sounds of
nightfall
Lull me gently, oh so quietly to
sleep;
     And I feel loved.

Dale Lee Webb
BEAUTIFUL PLACE TO BE
The scenes were changing
quickly
as we sped over the states
and I wondered how they would
look
in a million years from now.

How did they look one hundred
years ago
could we tell the difference
or maybe they haven't changed
but that man has made the only
change.

I wonder about the beauty I see
and how great each part of it is
that what I see now is so
beautiful
but will tomorrow bring greater
beauty.

But no matter where I go
no matter what I do
the scenes I see each day
make the world a beautiful place
to be.

Gilberto Ruiz
COME FOURTH MY LOVE
*[Dedicated To All The Beauties
The World Has To Offer.]*
Come Fourth My Love
And show your light
'Tis tender beauty to my sight.
The Meadow Larks all dance and
play,
And smile as you pass your way.
And flowers blossom at thy sight
A love like ours was meant
tonight.
Come be my love and you shall
see,
A love like ours was meant to be.

Today's Greatest Poems

Your eyes aglow so warm and
    tender,
A beauty that is full of splendor.
The Merry Minstrels chant and
    sing,
The tender love that you will
    bring.
And tarry not your love divine,
For in the end you will be mine.

Helena I. Dobbs
THE FUTURE IS OURS
Tones none other can hear
You call to me
Listen to all you say and fear
You want to be free
Sensitive to sight of calling eyes
Knowing your gentle touch
Feeling with me reflections of
    past loves
The future is ours to see
Fingers bringing light of day
To longing for night
Gentle touch of hand to hand
Don't move too fast and
Life will last

Sarah L. Young
THE PRAISEWORTHY
It is not so much the forest,
    as it is the single tree.
It isn't as much the busy hive,
    as it is the lonely bee.

It would not be the school of fish,
    that we would think so great.
As it would the single fish,
    who lives without a mate.

The world is not lacking in things
    of number,
Nature has made them strong.
It is the solitary ones deserving
    praise,
For they have lived alone.

Susan S. Turnier
FALL AND SPRING
One leaf, brown and shriveled
Hangs dangerously by a thread.
The wind playfully teases it,
Rocking it back and forth.

One leaf, green and lush
Spreads open toward the sky.
Burned by a scorching sun,
It strengthens and grows.

Joan Kern
STAR DRUMMER
*[For Philip F. Manzo, the man,
his music, our star "Face to
Face"]*
Set on the dark stage
Your performance catches the eyes
Of those looking for the answer,
Gazing up, asking why.
With the surrounding lights
    blinding your view,
You cannot tell who is watching
    you,
Leaning on the pains,
Looking out windows marked
    with tears of rain.

Sometimes I feel I can reach you,
    touch you
but you're so far away
So far from that embrace you
    stay.
In the morning light,
You can't be trusted, you run
    away.
No matter how loud it gets on
    the floor,

constant struggle, endless war
The stage holds you up
higher than us.

Who knows where to look for
    you each night.
Who knows who will win your
    flight.

Alma Lillian Hageman
RUN THE GOOD RACE
Sometimes we must lose in order
    to win
The unending challenge evading
    sin
God's in his heaven
All's well with the world
As long as we keep our flag
    unfurled
Charging on pon steed so sleek
Into battle, to combat the weak
    flaws in our nature
The covetous streak.

God's on our side, he won't even
    chide
As we're thrown from horse and
    land flat on our face
The Midas touch gone, have we
    lost the race?
Yet, laying there in the mud and
    slime
The sun shines its brightest
I look upward and find my mount
    didn't desert me he's there
    pawing the ground
Nostrils flare twitching and with
    nary a sound trots to my side
    in the saddle I bound
With a leap, a whoop and a
    feeling of joy
The race isn't lost if I pay the
    cost.

Hoofs neath me scoop and flail
    the dust
Black coat shines with the sweat
    and strain
We rejoin the troop as I muse
Holding fast to my morals
    clutching the rein
Recalling past failures
Recalling the pain
Man can't go it alone if he hasn't
    a friend
And the day waxes dim as we
    gallop along
Where the earth and sky merge
    at the rim
God is my friend, I will trust in
    him.

Willadine (Penny) Radke
SPRING'S SURPRISES
*[To my family—without whose
encouragement I would never
have overcome my timidity
enough to share my poetry
with others . .]*
It's early spring in the Northwest.
The daffodils stand tall
Against the wall,
Their yellow heads are wet—
Reaching for the sun they'll get.
It snows, it rains, it blows.
Everything lush and beautiful
    grows.
It's early spring in the Northwest. .

It's early spring in the Northwest.
The Robin hides—
The snow and rain he chides.
Too cold for making nests—
He eats and rests.

It's early spring in the Northwest.
It's early spring in the Northwest.
A crocus shows
It snows, it rains, it blows.
The clouds have parted—
You run outside lighthearted,

Then—

It snows, it rains, it blows.
The crocus knows.
It's early spring in the Northwest.

Catherine Sporer Sheeley
THE GAME OF CHANCE
*[To my sister, Margaret Sporer
Moffitt and my son Dale
Arnold Sheeley may they rest
in peace   ]*
The game of chance
    Is played every day
In various forms
    And many a way
When the sun appears
    And we arise
We see a new day
    Through our eyes
Without fully realizing
    That through the night
The game of chance
    Was our biggest fight.

Mary Hamilton Darrell
THIS IS THE DAY
*[To my children, Hamilton,
Joseph and Amata, who make
it a pleasure to greet each day.]*
"This is the day which
    the Lord hath made,
We will rejoice and be glad."
We will give thanks
    for repose of the night,
For the quiet and rest we have had.

We will stand in the glow
    and the radiance of dawn,
See the world with magnificence
    clad.
"This is the day which
    the Lord hath made;
We will rejoice and be glad."

Catherine Rose Mangual
THOUGHTS OF YOU
Up on a hilltop far away,
I sit alone and watch the day.
My mind is filled with thoughts
    of you
And the joy you bring me the
    whole year through.
I think of how we met that day,
So long ago and far away.
I often ask God above
Why He sent me your precious
    love.
Your love's much more important
    to me
Than anything else could ever be.
I never want you to go away;
Without you I couldn't live
    another day.
From now until the end of time,
I'll be yours and you'll be mine.

Rosella Norman
**On Your Anniversary . . .
    Thoughts**
Star of the Night,
I saw you burning bold and
    bright.
I stood long and watched your
    flaring flame,
And thought, "This is perpetual
    fame."

I watched you streak cross the
    sky;
Your destination I never sought
    to pry,
But somewhere hence in the night
    as I stood,
Again there appeared Star of the
    Night . . .

Star of the Night,
Your flame must be nourished still;
Lest it might go out and spill
Over the vales and forlorn
    hills. . .

Oh Star, Star of the Night,
Your flame will never cease to
    burn,
For I fear there would be naught
    to look upon as firm,
O Night, O Star of Joy!

Sandra Selph Hunter
**The Gift Of a Christian
    Friend**
*[To Pastor Chuck and my sister
Grace . . . Spirits of one accord
through the Grace of God.
May peace be with you my
"Dear Christian Friends".]*
When I need to talk
You are always there
With your gentle smile
To tell me you care

When I stumble and reach
For something to hold onto
I can always depend
On Gods light shining thru you

When my rainbow is crooked
Or maybe hard to find
A card of love
Brings you to my mind

When clouds of despair
Blend with the bee's sting
You bring scripture to life
And again the butterflies sing

When I feel weak
And Satin says, "Why try"
You remind ME of the reason
Our Dear Jesus chose to die

When I feel all alone
And wonder who really cares
I look up in amazement
For your always standing there

When those I've loved most
Have become people I don't know
My new family in Christ
In His Love continues to grow

When I look back
At this life's fleeting time
I thank God for His Gift
Of these Christian Friends of mine.

B. Closs L. G. Anderson
The Light In His Tiny Fist
One thousand nine hundred and
eighty-two; the years since
then till now!
And I'll tell you what changed
the world He brought:
This gift of Himself and His star.

His was the holiest birth of all;
His mother the blessed Mary;
Hailed by the light of His Star,
whose rays then cut time apart.
What is this light you ask, that
only a few will see?

Man's reason would block it,
overshadow and knock it!
Each Springtime we've sown it,
and liked to have gathered
each Fall;
But the world spins around
unhearing, unseeing uncaring.
Wisemen will find it; we
shepherds are told—and this
light will never go out.
So stop what you're doing, and
come over close—
Now you'll see it. It's deep in
your heart—
A-G-A-P-E L-O-V-E

Clayton B. Doak
BOXTOP
The neat package
Exudes confident wholesomeness.
The ingredients are perfectly,
primly, proportional.
All in the correct amounts, with
supplements,
And neatly alphabetical.
The prize has gravitationed to the
bottom
Underneath the double flap
which seals
The orifice opposite the
Legendary
BOXTOP.
(Who ever sends in box bottoms
anyway?)
(Or bell bottoms, for that matter???)

The child pours out the contents.
Sugar coated, fortified, pseudo—
nutritious vitamin half—grain
goodness (gracious)
And does *not* find HIS prize!!!!

His father had sleepily discarded
it that morning
While examining the closing
averages on
The American Stock Exchange
While skipping over the latest
quotations of wheat futures
from the Chicago Board of
Trade . . .

Cynthia L. Karagus
STILL LIFE
Decipher the shadows, the earth
has forgot
Beauty in a painting moving but
not
Motionless bodies all running
blind
Clockwork faces, the hands of
time
Still life exposed, like fruit in a
bowl
Drilling a moment, searching the
goal
Skies that limit the grasp of the
gulls

Filling the clouds with lonely
birds' skulls
Rebirth of the wind still lying in
wait
For nothing has rattled and nigh
is the fate
Delirious fortunes across the
sands
Gold mines of silence, hourglass
lands
Stifle corrosion, still life shall
compose
Limit the air flow, breathing in
prose
Saving the ashes of lost barren
trees
Follow the blind man for only he
sees
The sea goes on living in
waveless tone
The heart of the mountains made
only of stone
Vials of poison dispersed once
again
Only from movement still life
shall descend.

Robin M. Gary
SUICIDE
Disappointments come so often
And I wonder why the pain
Shoved and pushed to keep on
living
When life is really all in vain

What's the purpose of this sorrow
Going on for years and years
Always moments filled with joy
End up in unrelenting tears

Forced to go through life unaided
Work hard to uphold someone's
name
And all the while you cry for help
But still you have to play the
game

Tragedies become quite common
Broken hearts don't ever mend
And death seems very kind and
gentle
Because with death all sorrows
end

Death comes not as foe, but friend.

Timothy Miles E. Taylor
HEAVEN AWAITS
He walked up to the altar,
This little unknown lad,
And looked up to the preacher
With eyes so blue and sad.

He said, "Mister can you help me?"
And he reached into his vest.
"It seems to me this map I've
bought
Is not the very best."

"North, east, south and west,
From highways one through seven,
But still it seems I cannot find
The place that you call heaven."

"My dad once said they'd wait for
me
In heaven one fine day,
But if you cannot help me,
I may never find the way."

He wiped his eyes with little hands
And dried them on his lap,
Then back into his tiny vest
He put the tear stained map.

With lowered head and misty eyes
He walked toward the door,
But the map within his tattered
vest
Had fallen to the floor.

The north pointed to the cross,
The south to a speeding car . . .
He's finally found his daddy,
And he didn't travel far.

Carla Smith
TO LEARN AND TEACH
I wish to try to be,
An example for another.
That they would look at me and
say,
It is good to love each other.

I wish to try to be,
Someone another admires.
That I could serve my purpose,
Before my life expires.

That a light would shine within
me,
To open someone's eyes.
So they could show another,
Before the other dies.

When I'm gone I'd like to think,
I've really earned a place.
And I've taught someone to love
someone,
In lifes important race.

I try to express myself,
To show people my reflections.
That through my mistakes,
People may see their perfections.

I know that my mind,
Is not a vessel of purity.
My thoughts may not be clear,
What with my sense of ability.

That a radiant beam of happiness,
Would gleam within a heart.
And when someone thinks the
end is near,
A dream will be about to start.

That we would recognize our
blessings,
Which descend from God above.
And to learn that the key of Life,
And Happiness is love.

Dale Amos Huckaby
THE FARMERS CRIED
[To my greatest inspiration My
wife, Dana.]
Cool
Follows the day long heat
Wet
Follows the summer long dry.
Water
Fills the long-dry pond.
And farmers cry.

Coulds
Built up through afternoon
After afternoon.
Thunder
Rolled across the fields.
Hope
At first swelled with each clap.
Finally,
Hope was talked about
Like a dead aunt.

Today!
A few spatters, a few large drops.
Smell!
That old familiar dust-rain smell.
Feel!
Your shirt stick to your back!

Daniel Luevano
Perfect Love Inside a Glass
[To Mechie]
Stop! Please, Lord stop this
merry-go-round
Of deceitful pleasure, I see a
flower—
Let me off!

This flower I see, is so beautiful,
it makes me
Warm with happiness and joy.
So bright with love, it shines on
my heart.

I want this beauty but I cannot
touch it.
Why is there this glass forbidding
my entrance?
Why around my beautiful flower?

Through the glass case I can see
all the
Happiness that I have ever
dreamed.
Why can I not break this barrier
which teases me?

Oh—Lord, as I wait in solitude
for this glass to break,
I think of all the beauty I can see
but cannot hold.
I think of all the love I can
perceive but cannot feel.

Allows me to fall asleep, that I
can endure the anticipation
Of our first touch.
Strengthen my patience and
conquer my solitude, that I
might survive.

Wait! Look! The glass is melting.
I can feel her love, I can touch
the beauty.
My flower cries out with joy!

At last—I have conquered,
At last—I am happy,
At last—I am me . . . Thank You
Lord!

Sandi Fisher
**I Heard the Owl Call My
Name**
A shimmering darkness plagued
the night,
encouraging creatures of prowl.
And amongst the tree tops
shrieking chimes—
I heard the owl,
    Call my name.

Ruthless winds howled hoarsely
through fields and bushes.
Contributing death calls in the air.
But, through a rustling flora—
I heard the owl,
    Call my name.

Seeking harmonious tales
amidst a black cloak, above our
plight.
Sharing the laughter
Of gruesome song.
But, elite over hideous cackle—
I heard the owl,
    Call my name.

Mystically—someone enters,
Whom I seek.
He drowns all fury from Hell.
Dispersal of shadows release the
night
But, disrupting dead silence—
I heard the owl,
    Call my name.

I slip silently into the heavens.
All was to become—
a dream.
My surroundings change abruptly.
But, still, from my window
I heard the owl,
    Call my name.

Mary F. Anderson
DEAR GOD
Dear God:
    Today they broke the news,
    Your miracle coming to an end—
    Back then, two years ago, we
        thought the battle lost—
    With prayers and hopes we
        fought—
    Your miracle came thru—
    You've given us added years—
    To prove your powers true—
    And now again, we battle—
    Our faith to be renewed
    For they say, our daughter's life
    Is on the line again—
    But, God, only you, can tell us
        where or when—
    A few more years, we beg you—
    Without the damning pain—
    Please let her live her life, with
        hope renewed and miracles
        again.

Alice Stateman Hannibal
PAEAN
Oh, the day is shining, shining!
    Wanton wind gusts tug the
        sleeve;
Come, share rites of Earth's
        renewal,
    Mundane chores, behind, now
        leave.

Orchards, coif'd in pastel
        blossoms
    Waft forth perfumed prophecy;
Waving woodland branches beckon
    Vagabond to venture free.

Scarlet sunsets cast elongate
    Shadows across field and hill;
Wanderlust, enthralling—calling—
    Earth-bound spirits soar and
        thrill.

Creature-kin to every feral
    Furred or feathered denizen;
To the four winds fling
        soul-searing
    And brow-creasing cares of men.

Sit upon yon rotted tree stump,
    Monarch never held such sway!
Bower-hidden court musicians
    Pulsate paeans to the day.

Oh, the Spring's an annual advent,
    But the span of youth is fleet;
Deeply quaff from glowing goblet
    While the wine of Life is sweet.

For the scythe of Time is never
    Still; too soon all mortals must
Turn a deafened ear to
        Spring-time's
    Siren call to wanderlust.

Oh, the day is shining, shining!
    Wanton wind gusts tug the
        sleeve;
Come, share rites of Earth's
        renewal
    Mundane chores, behind, now
        leave.

Linda Hopple
DOORS
Why do I
Close all those doors?

You know, the ones in my mind
The ones I slammed shut
To protect myself.
But they hurt as much as protect;
I feel sad, unhappy
Knowing I am missing so much—
closeness, emotions, sharing—
By smothering my feelings;
Not taking chances.

I want desperately to open
Those stubborn doors,
Their hinges rusty from tears.
Dare I tug at the handle?
And chance falling . . . hurting
When the seal is suddenly broken?
Things I fear—
painful memories, unkindness,
    rejection—
Will tumble out on top of me.
I hope I am strong enough
That they will not crush me.

Lesia Brama Zytniak
COME WITH ME
[I dedicate this poem to my
wonderful husband Walt. Your
love makes my world beautiful.]
Come with me and be my friend
Lets create a fantasy
Just you and me
Lets linger through the wind
And feel free.
Lets run through the sand
And make time stand still
So we can treasure this moment
Only until
The mystical ocean
Touches our souls
And fills our hearts with love.
Come with me and I'll show you
What I have to give
Come with and I'll describe
The life I dreamed we'd live.
Come with and hold me gently
And watch the retiring sun
        slowly set
Shower me with all your love
Pretending we just met.
Whenever you need me
I'll be there
To help lift your spirits
And I want to care
About you.
Come with and be my love
No longer a fantasy
Just you and me
This time only
A reality . . .

Karen Pontecorvo
HELL
Surrounded by darkness
Seeing no light
Wondering what's happening
Not feeling right
The feeling of pain is all around
Am I going insane
Or just coming down
Am I in the place of doom
Or will I be back to reality soon
Is this reality
Oh Lord it couldn't be
If it is then let me ask you why
Why did you pick now for me to
        die
And why is my soul in this place
Place of misery and disgrace
I always told myself that when I
        die
My soul will go to the place that
        surrounds the earth and sky

I always thought that I'd go to the
    place of happiness
Where everything is so beautiful
    and pure
But now that I'm here I realize
    that I was never really sure
I never thought that I committed
    any immoral sin
Now I know I must have
Because you didn't let me in
I realize now that it's too late
I can't get through the golden gate
I think I've learned my lesson well
Now that my soul has been sent
    to Hell.

Ralph L. Edwards
PHOENIX
The blazing glory of a loving night
Disappears in the sun's bright
    morning light.
All efforts to recall that glorious
    pain
Fade in the dawn to be sought in
    vain.

But the memory clings of
    precious glory
That will not become an old, dull
    story.
Instead that memory promises
    anew
That love will spring forth and
    again renew.

With every joining of two loving
    souls
Again will emerge from the
    fading coals
A love renewed by the glowing
    embers
So that this night, too, will be
    remembered.

Rosetta Heathman
MY BELOVED DADDY
He used to be nine feet tall
    Or so it seemed to me
Back when I was just a child
    And I was only three

He lit up my world every day
    When he came home at night
I stood beside the door to wait
    Until I caught his sight

He'd go his pace, at slow speed
    But I would have to run
He's sometimes catch me in mid
    air
    For me, he was the one

He's still the one I like to see
    God has been so good
To let me keep his for this long
    He surely understood

That even though I'm all grown up
    And have my own sweet laddy
No man could ever take the place
    Of my beloved Daddy

Allyn LeHew
IN MEMORIAM
The eviction notice tacked on
    the door
Clearly stated that we would
    have to go
(You had long-since gone . . .
    without notice)
And at the appointed time, a
    solitary mourner
Watched hired pall-bearers carry
    our belongings
Out of the shadow-box where we
    never belonged

Mission accomplished, the
    muscled-men covered our
    remains
With sheets of plastic (the see-
    through kind)
The curious would have an
    unobstructed view
Of all our days . . . and nights . . .
    together

But the bitter, angry winter wind
Trapped in the cellophane shroud
Bellied-out and billowed-up
And sailed away to
    God-knows-where

I know the feeling.

Cheri Peterson
TO DANIEL . . .
Hello little man, you are finally
    here,
We watched you arrive with a
    smile and a tear.

You were born from the love that
    we share,
So you should always know how
    much we care.

Your dad has so many plans for
    his son,
Filled with adventure and filled
    with fun.

To guide and teach you the
    things he's tried,
And watch you grow with a
    fatherly pride.

And my hope for you my little
    man,
Is to show you all the love I can.

To have you know that I'm
    always near,
Whenever you feel there is
    something to fear.

You light up our life and make us
    one,
You are our wonderful, newborn
    son.

Donna Roberts
A MOTHER'S LOVE
"Mommy loves you," I said as I
    rocked you at night,
holding you close and assuring
    you everything's all right.
I'd sing to you softly, chasing
    away all your fears,
then as you slept, I dried my baby
    girl's tears.

You went from rattles to pigtails,
    dolls to big toys,
then I watched you quickly
    graduate to the boys.
Sometimes your silence or quiet
    smile broke my heart
whenever one of your teenage
    romances broke apart.

Then, much too soon you built
    up this invisible door
and I felt as if I wasn't really
    needed anymore.
Before I knew it, you cast aside
    the little girl I'd known
and you turned to conquer the
    world all on your own.

First there was college and then
    came along a special man
who gave my little girl his name
    and a gold wedding band.

He gave you a little white house
  filled with all his love,
warmth and all the happiness you
  always dreamed of.

Then, one day you came running
  to me just as excited as could be.
"Oh, Mom," you shouted, "Soon
  my husband and I will become
  three."
Seeing how happy my little girl
  and her husband was,
I knew her baby would be
  surrounded with lots of love.

Now, my dear, several months
  later, you are a mother too,
with a beautiful little girl, with
  eyes so crystal blue,
and whenever you hear a little
  cry in the night
you rock your little girl and
  whisper, "Everything's all right."

As you gently caress her and lay
  her back in her bed,
you smile, remembering what
  your mother had said.
For it is now that you understand
  and really know
that a day will come when you
  will have to let her go.

To your surprise and much too
  soon will come that day
when she says, "Mom, time for
  me to be on my own," and goes
  away.
Through the years, as you
  watched her quickly grow,
you smiled, remembering your
  mother's words, that love is
  letting go.

Molly L. Mohr
A SILENT ROSE
I lay in my bed,
Alone with my thoughts.
Gazing at a picture,
A rose, symbol of love.
And, before I am aware
A silent tear rolls down my cheek,
And falls upon my pillow,
As if signifying a final
And quiet good-bye.

This farewell must be silent,
Just as everything else.
Kept within—
where no one may see the pain.

Now, more tears come.
Quietly, making their way
To my heart.
Flowing with tender memories.
And each one seems to cry out—
"Good-bye, my love, Good-bye."

Cindy Leigh Walker
COST OF LIVING
Somewhere outside yesterday's
  spirit strolls today, while we
  rise from an unruffled sleep,
  and go to work each day.

Caught between the longing for
  love and the fight for our legal
  tender. We cannot help but
  hear sirens sing and church
  bells ring. The workman beats
  on a sidewalk. And those called
  dreamers sit out traffic lights.

There is a fire out in this pasture,
  and an open in the desert floor,
  leaving that fear of living for
  nothing.

But rest assure you and I will
  stroll in on cool evenings,
  leaving nothing behind but
  that cost of living. To find the
  key is to love lightly, lightly.
  To breath heart and soul as
  spenders do. Tearing at the
  world with all our might,
  young and strong.

To live for that legal tender. To
  be reminded what laughter is,
  and to know the struggle for
  the two.

Jean M. King
MARCH SNOWSTORM
*[This poem is dedicated to my
husband, Joseph W. King, who
does all our snowplowing,
consisting of about an
acre...here in our little patch of
woods of Willow, Alaska.]*
Our winter has been fairly long,
In terms of colder days,
But snow has been in short
  supply—
Barely enough to cover our clays.

Now the days grow longer,
And the sun's warmth can be felt.
Yesterday we dreamed of
  gardening.
Today we're back in the wet
  snow belt.

Our skies were clear at four A.M.
At daybreak, too, there was no hint
Of anything like what's coming
  down now.
It has an extremely white tint.

The snow is so thick we can
  hardly see
The feeder station in our white
  birch tree.
Our Husky's house has
  disappeared,
And two hours ago, our porch
  was cleared.

It's October, again, in early March.
Our highway is slick once more.
Walking about is pretty tricky.
Best to stay in, on a solid floor.

There's a strange walk in this
  Northern land;
An all-winter type of thing.
It's called the Alaskan Shuffle.
It stops with the coming of Spring.

Jean A. Thomas
THE MALLARD IN FLIGHT
*[Written in Decmeber '82, for
Mr. Robert J. Thomas, my
father-in-law. This poem was of
my spirit; by God's Spirit and
specifically for his spirit. Mr.
Thomas died February '83.]*
Lord let my spirit fly freer
Like this bird in it's flight
With your Words as my wings
And your Love as my sight
Lead me to Heaven
Let me bathe in your Light
No longer afraid; no longer aflight
I've arrived at my nesting place
I am Home for the night.

Rosella Thiesen
PRAYER FOR THE DOCTOR
Lord, give him grace
To meet the challenge of each day,
Lord, give him strength for every
  daily task;

Lord, give him wisdom when his
  own would fail,
And skill beyond all he could
  ask!

Lord, bless his labours,
Though long and weary be the
  hours,
Lord, give him peace of heart and
  mind;
Lord, give him joy and
  confidence,
In Thee true satisfaction may he
  find!

Lord, guide his hands,
For he is but an instrument of God,
Lord, may be see life's purposeful
  design;
Lord, melt his heart with true
  compassion,
And do through him a miracle
  divine!

Shirley Ellison
MOM'S ADVICE
*[From the very depths of my
heart, I prayerfully dedicate this
poem to my children and
grandchildren.]*
Although my children are grown
  and from home departed,
I want to tell you about the new
  life I've started.

I've started trusting in Jesus name,
Where there's so much peace and
  never shame.

I have many regrets from the
  years past,
I should've taught you about
  Jesus, cause He will last.

There was never time to trod the
  church path,
It was housework, homework,
  and make sure you bath.

It was Scouts and the beach, to
  the parties we'd go,
But to read you the Bible, Mom
  was very slow.

I have some advice for these
  children of mine,
Get to know Jesus, don't waste
  any time.

For He will be there when you
  need a friend,
The love and peace He offers,
  there's just no end.

If you'll trust in Him, He'll take
  care of you,
He'll put peace in your heart but
  these things you must do.

You must watch and pray, your
  Bible must be read,
And along the narrow path you
  must tread.

Don't make the mistake that
  Mom has made,
Start trusting in Him, in worldly
  things don't wade.

Although you are grown and
  departed from home,
Be ready to meet Jesus when
  Gabriel's trumpet is blown.

Mabel E. Downing
Stardust and Snowflakes
Merrily their sleigh bells ring,
Christmas carols old they sing.

Laughing happily they go,
dashing o'er the frosty snow.

Jewel spangled velvet skies
filled with stardust, like their eyes.

Moonbeams light her face so fair,
snowflakes tangle in his hair.

Sweethearts dream of worlds like
  this
winter wonderland of bliss.

Hearts and spirits brightly glow,
love's sweet magic makes it so!

Kerry Tyler
SOAP BUBBLE
Born of air and breath,
I rush overhead,
along with child-pitched
laughter. My rainbow
hues flash and spin,
I reach for the sky
and slowly descend.
Buffed by a child's breath,
I wheel and drift,
against a mirror,
repeating myself.
I avoid poking fingertips.

Lynda Norris
MOTHER AND CHILD
*[To: Mother and Jean, God
Bless You, Love Forever and
Always, Lynda.]*
You combed my hair and patted
  my head.
You lifted my spirits and saw I
  was well fed.
You comforted me endlessly and
  held me quite.
You took away the horrors that
  haunted my sleep at night.
We gathered our memories and
  put them away.
We never knew that they would
  be all we had one day.
You were my mother. I was your
  child.
But our roles are changed now.
Can I be your mother? Do I know
  how?
You have regressed backward and
  became my precious child.
But my love is growing stronger
  like flowers of wild.
I can be your mother; you can be
  my child I know.
For we have already conquered
  many obstacles and battled
  much woe.
I know we often feel sorrow and
  misplace blame.
But no matter how we hurt each
  other my love stays the same.
I can only apologize for how I
  hurt you and all the wrong I
  have done.
We will go through many trials;
  but in the end we will find we
  have won.
I love you dearly.
When you see the crystal blue of
  our eyes this is shown clearly.
When I think of your
  confinement my problems are
  mild.
For I love you dearly as my
  "Mother and Child."

Yvette Manculich
COMMITANCE
Let's maketh not a promise for
  tomorrow

but yet set one within today.
For change may not know whether
but truth will be sworn within
    what we say.
Let's not live by reality.
Or sentence our path based on
    praticality.
But live the knowledge of beauty
    known as today.
If we lead a journey in the light of
    truth
inevitably we shan't stray.
Chains we will not hold.
If ever over, our heart's trust
shan't of been stole.
Today I give freely so tomorrow
    will follow without guilt.
If we would lose the life of love
    we have built.

P.A. Howington
DISTANT LOVE
Drifting along a river
Waters deep and blue.
Dreaming, hoping,
Laying back, thinking
of you.
Trees flutter in the
wind. Clouds pass by.
Oh! how I wish that
you were here.
To hold my hand;
Holding me close to you.
So alone.
The wind plays along my
hair the way you do.
Where are you?
So distant, so far away.
Is your love like the
wind?
So quick to flutter
So quick to die.
Drifting bye . . .

Betty Talbott
GOD'S FREE GIFTS TO US
So many visions to explore and see
In this beautiful country so rich
    and free,
Bountiful harvests to reap each
    season
Poems to translate through
    rhyme or reason.

Questions to be asked, answers to
    readily give
Courage to die, the moral right to
    live.
The duty to vote, the candidates
    we choose
Fighting our daily battles, win or
    lose.

Picking roses boldly from the
    briars of life
Fruitfully gaining respect through
    our strife,
Freedom of religion, recognizing
    right or wrong
The tranquil winds replenish our
    hearts with song.

Different flowers in their
    technicolor beauty
The fleeting deer roaming the
    forest so gallantly,
Radiant sunset and brilliant
    sunrise
After the cool rain, colorful
    rainbow in the skies.

The mighty mountain, rivers
    flowing so free
Exotic birds of the wild singing

merrily,
Emotions of compassion, whether
    rich or poor
Inviting the needy and elderly to
    our door.
Memories to always cherish will
    hold to our breast
Intimate encouragement to fly
    away from our nest,
Strength, patience to endure our
    suffering and pain
Rewards in Heaven will be our
    authentic gain.

Our heads held high, walking
    valiantly
Proud to be an American citizen
    with dignity,
Peace, unruffled hope, abundant
    love
All these free gifts come
    graciously from God above.

Peggy Jo Doerr
ETERNAL LOVE
I've been searching for you forever
A man to ease my pain
The certain one to hold me
When my tears will fall again.
The strength you show is awesome
When I need a leaning post
And all I do is think of you
When I need love the most.
It's simply true and easy
To call upon your name
The man to fill my every need
From Heaven once you came.
I got to know you peacefully
One dream I dreamt in sleep
And I prayed that day you'd come
    to me
With angels' watch you'd keep.
And now that you're here within
    my heart
I owe you my dying soul
For, God, you've loved me dearly
I am yours; death takes it's toll.

Brenda Layman
I NEVER DID FORGET YOU
I never did forget you
You were always in my heart
I wish that you had kept in touch
To bad we broke apart

Well, I am still alive you know
And living rather well
And though I feel alot for you
For love, I never fell

I've thought about you often
Sometimes for very long
And even when I'm free from
    thought
You creep into a song

I could be coming back your way
I'll call if I have a dime
Maybe we can get together
And move the hands of time

But if you're not around there then
And our roads never cross
You're a memory and I wish you
    well
You're a part of my past—Not Lost

Stacy Medsger
PEACE
Peace like a river flows,
I often wonder just where it goes.

To fields of flowers, meadows of
    green,
or to unknown places, I've never
    seen.

It soars across the clear blue sky,
Like a newborn bird when it
    learns to fly.

It travels far to unknown places,
to sooth some unfamiliar faces.

Peace it travels all around,
high above, or on the ground.

It warms the hearts of weary souls,
just like a fires blazing coals.

It's there to give you comfort and
    rest,
it rejoices with every soul that's
    blest.

This peace that soars the skies of
    blue,
is the peace that's here for me
    and you.

Carolyn R. Smolinsky
EVERLASTING LOVE
Like the stems of a dozen roses
Grabbed foolishly by an
    unsuspecting hand
Your love cuts me and I bleed
Until my body can no longer stand

Like throbbing inside the head
Of a beating mad man's brain
My heart pounds in unison
With each step I take toward pain

Every move that I make
Toward your aura of sincerity
Drains ounces of my strength
Because your affection is such a
    rarity

Like the winds of a hurricane
You carry my soul away
Until there is nothing left
But my hope in fate's way
My belief in us so true
And my everlasting love for you

Robert F. Hull
ALISA
The seasons have begun to change
The summer leaves us fall
So suddenly lives rearrange
When God almighty makes his call

It's said life isn't always fair
These words seem to ring true
Alisa climbs the golden stairs
We watch, but, can't pursue

Although her life was not so long
She shared the soul that love
    possessed
By giving us her precious song
All our lives were truly blessed

For those who think they're left
    behind
Please know Alisa will be there
When memories serve to remind
She lives for those who loved and
    cared

She lived a life so full of pain
But, always seemed to find a smile
Though gone, her love will still
    remain
Alisa was a special child!

E. S. Chilton
NATURAL SELECTION
Evolution
of the heart.
Seasons changing, fading,
glowing, growing
into spring, then a fall,
Wanting none yet
taking
all.

Season
telling season,
thus the reason to repent,
checking pockets, money spent,
and for a while our souls at Lent.
We feel this is the worst of all;
watching trees bare,
remembering
all.

Turning
through each season,
burning to stay in springtime,
yearning to laugh sometimes
at our own reactions
and transactions as we
evolve and
solve.

Gloria Whiting Harvey
LAUGHING BACK!
*[To Mother, who is beyond this
    now.]*
Killer whales upon the sea
Waiting there to swallow me
Laughing at my feeble tries
To catch the wave before it dies.

Swishing, swirling gusts of winds
Take me where my life begins
Then, tossing substance to and fro,
Drown the dream. I sink below.

Deep, dark waters daring me
To journey up, escaping free
Yet pounding surf and sheeting
    rain
Keep forcing me back down again.

Ah! Elements beyond control
I'll cheat you of your unjust toll
For tired of your thoughtless jest,
I'll take the day, forget the rest.

And leaving helpless dreams
    behind,
Go with the tide and never mind
I know just what your humors
    lack:
Turn around . . . I'm laughing back!

Brenda Gravitt
JENSON
*[In memory of my sister,
    Virginia Abell]*
Auburn hair and skin like bronze,
a smile for everyone.
A real come-on.
You traveled far and wide,
a fellow by your side.
Nothing you wouldn't try.
A drink and a joke,
sharing a toke.
Carefree, happy, and broke.
Wild like the wind.
Until we meet again,
I'll miss you, Jenson.

Connie Bremner
MY LOVE
I stood upon the highest hill
Around me nature was so still
My foolish heart had sent me here
To contemplate the love I hold so
    dear.
Because my heart was so sore
After him I said "no more"
And then one day you came along
You won me with a smile and
    with a song.
It is strange what fate will do
Just one look and I belonged to
    you
I've known love but did not know
Our love was highest high and
    lowest low.

I know my love you do return
I wish to hurt no one but burn
Someday to be your wife and mate
Yet years overshadowed say "too late".
'Tis written that love is eternal
If that is so, you are my all
And in another day and another life
You'll be mine and I'll be your wife.
But until that distant day
For that as yet unknown life I pray
When I can say the words "I do"
Until then I can only worship you.

Teri Heard
ECHOES
You're gone
  You're gone
    You're gone
Emptiness
  Emptiness
    Emptiness
Echoing
  Echoing
    Echoing
Images
  Images
    Images
Fading
  Fading
    Fading

Lynn Harper
PAYBACK
Not a ship did I see
not a schooner in sight.
How could this be?
They went out last night.
Now a fortnight has passed
no luck have I had;
My husband and son
are listed as dead.

She is cruel, she is hard
no sympathy is there.
She takes the lives of many
without a care.
Some days serene, beautiful
and bright;
but also violent
like she was on that night.

Her long, foamy fingers
stretch out upon decks
and steal precious cargo:
for that she is in debt.
I say this now
for this I pray,
My solemn vow
is for her to repay.

Erin M. McDonald
THE POWER OF MUSIC
Some people write their feelings
  in quotes
I write mine in musical notes.
For there are two parts to
  music—technique and mood
Technique may be performance,
  but feeling is the food.
Because even though the notes
  are written with care,
Music isn't music if feeling isn't
  there.
I compose my songs to no
  specific mold
The melodies emerge as my
  thoughts unfold.
From out of my pen these
  melodies flow

Expressing the feelings that I
  never show.
I write when I'm lonely, when no
  one's around
And I fill up the gaps in my life
  with the sound.
I compose when I'm saddened to
  the point of tears
I compose to alleviate some of
  my fears.
Some feelings I do show, but what
  I reserve
The patterns of songs that I write
  will preserve.
You see, feelings are gems, they
  surpass any cost
They can't be forgotten, they
  can't get lost
And sometimes, no matter how
  hard we try
We can't tell them to anyone,
  though we don't know why.
But we keep them to ourselves in
  our own special way
And we guard the things that we
  simply can't say.
For me, my music cannot go
  wrong
Because I'm writing myself in the
  form of a song.
So alone in the dark, where the
  doubts begin
I battle uncertainty with music—
  and win.
I'll never be alone while I have
  music inside
To express the feelings that I
  would otherwise hide.
So while some people write their
  feelings in quotes
I write mine in musical notes.

Deborah White
MOTIONS
Oceans of emotion
Going through the stages
Of life
Like pages
Of a book I can't wait to finish.
Oceans,
Full of love potions.
Meant to turn you around
To me,
But I drown;
Before I can finish this book.
Emotions.
Pouring from this ocean
of a woman,
That was me,
Before you
set her free:

Free to be motionless, without
  you.

Susan Hill
BUTTERFLIES
Dancing through the air
like a ballerina
performing on stage;
they flow by.

Not really coming or going
yet moving here and there,
whether in city yard
or country meadow.

They add a touch of elegance
to the orb before them;
whether pure white, like an
  angel
or the magnificent colors of a
  monarch.

Enlightening the world around
  us,
Butterflies grace the stage
with their unequaled delicacy
and unending enchantment.

Sue Miller
THE QUEST
I sought amongst the cobwebs
searching for my soul,
vainly, never knowing
I wouldn't reach my goal.

Amid the boards and boxes,
my heart I tried to find,
and though my search was
  endless,
found nothing of the kind.

Then closing up the attic
to the places I had been,
it was then that I realized
I had to look within.

Ginny Nelson
MOTHER'S NEST
*[to my Children and my
Mother, each have been an
inspiration with their love and
support, and to GOD for
blessing me.]*
The pretty mother robin worked
  persistantly
To build a nest above our door
  to lay her eggs of three
Each tiny twig, a piece of string
  some brown old dried up grass
Sne knew her time was running
  short
  so she had to work real fast
Trip after trip, piece by piece
  until the nest was made
Then there she sat and the next
  day
  three lovely eggs she laid
And you could tell the way she'd
  dwell
  how proud she had to be
For any sound she didn't like
  to the porch rail she would flee
She'd look around and chirp a
  sound,
  disgusted I'd say so
And with each sound she'd take
  the time
  to really let you know
Now in the nest three baby birds
  whose sound is quite unique
And time to time their Mom or
  Dad
  brings food for them to eat
It won't be long till they will fly
  the sky is their domain
But maybe one of them will build
  above our door again.

Helen Brown Rittershofer
THE SPIRIT OF CHRISTMAS
The magic spell of this Christmas
  Season
Carries one back to the days of
  yore
Where Wise-Men traveled under
  star-lit skies
Today—voices travel and verify
The pageants of the Christmas
  Season
Youth and Age together enjoy
Heritage of the past—Arisen
Sunshine and shadow radiate
  words
During the Christmas Season
  transmitted by phone

Sound barriers break—voices are
  heard
Joys of the Season enchantingly
  roam
Varying the rules of the average
  day
The Voice projects pictures
  artistically drawn
Voice colours transmitted
  through vibrating ray
New worlds created through
  rhythmic song
The expressive Joys of the
  Christmas Review
Hearts Treasures—during
  slender line review.

Christel M. Fofrich
THE SEED OF FRIENDSHIP
*[Dedicated to G.F.B., in
appreciation of your friendship.]*
Within my deepest heart...a
magical garden grows...sown
with the seeds of friendship...
heaven sent, I know...showering
it with love, laughter, kindness
and tears...the seed shall
flourish for many years...love
and laughter, being the warmth
of the earth...kindness, the
sunshine of life...tears a
cleansing rain...I shall ever reap
the harvest of happiness and
joy...being sure, so very sure
that our friendship will always
be...like a heavenly bouquet in
life's garden...to bloom
eternally...

Kimberly Marie Kennedy
TO SOMEONE SPECIAL
No one's perfect? . . . That may
  be.
Yet you know how to live happily.
You have your happiness . . .
  Yes, that's true;
I'll always want to be like you.
You give me love and all your
  care,
Even when I'm not there.
You always have your faith and
  trust—
Something that I always lust.
You were my teacher for all the
  years,
You even wiped away my tears.
You make me happy and never
  sad,
You showed me good from all the
  bad.
So when we're not together
  alot . . .
You'll always be in my heart's
  warm spot.
Yes, you are very special to me,
That you will always be.
You have given me my joy, my
  smile,
You have made my life all worth
  while.
I thank you now . . . I thank you
  again.
I pray our love will never end.

Marca J. Houser
ALONE
Christmas: The time of love,
  laughter and good cheer.

Then why do I find myself crying
  in a looking mirror?

No laughter do I hear, only the

sound of my lonely fear.

Alone on Christmas: people walk hand in hand brushing the snow from a loving man.

Giving gifts to the ones we love, I glance to the heavens above.

Have I done wrong to be alone on this day? I turn to you, and for once I pray.

It may be selfish for me to ask; for I have always shared love in the past.

My son has turned his back; my daughter has grown away; my husband is with someone new on this very special day.

The years I have spent giving all of myself, caring, sharing, never time to look back.

The laughter, the tears; the family years. The giving, the taking, the family reshaping.

Time has grown cruel to a lady of age: I must stop, get myself beyond this stage.

I shall put on my best, and out I shall go: I too shall walk in the snow.

A smile on my face, a sparkle in my eye; today is Christmas, and I shall not cry.

Joyce Peterson Boone
IN THIS NEW YEAR . . .
. . . May your heart be as light as a lacy snowflake and as warm as a festive hearthside.

. . . May the song you sing be your own, composed of wisdom gained throughout the past year and filled with words overflowing from the love in your heart.

. . . May your riches consist of an abundance of "soul gems", that which rust cannot corrupt.

. . . May the love you share be as pure and sweet as that of the lovely Virgin Mother as she cradled the Christ Child twenty centuries ago.

. . . May your New Year's goals be met with ample enthusiasm, robust good health, and wisdom to determine what is momentary and what is everlasting.

. . . May the peace you experience be as quietly calm as the crystal air on a new-fallen snow.

And, as we step one day closer to this promised final coming,

. . . May the joyful excitement of expectancy be as glorious in your soul as it was in theirs on the night of His birth to Mankind!

Victor Verdi
I WISH
I Wish there was music in the air—
Music just everywhere.

Music seems to bring joy, as to a child does a toy.
People are always hurrying, seemingly to be worrying.
If only they'd stop and listen, come alive to beats of pleasure.
Look at life as it really is.
Celebrate everyday of living, celebrate your every inch of giving.
So if you're giving, for sure you're living.
Look at the panorama of the world.
It has so much polish, so much style.
Isn't it worth your while? Give—Give—everyone a smile. Show you care.
Life should be lived as a song.
Joyous and carefree, lively as a breeze—
Music sounding from the trees.
Not a cloud around, from heaven to earth—
Sunshine always, I wish were always mine.
Till the end of time.

Lorri Gilmore
REMEMBER . . .
[For my One in a Million, Miguel]
Remember the words that kept you warm;
Remember protection from a storm.
Remember the song you shared with him;
Forget that your flame is growing dim.
Remember him and his golden smile;
Remember him for, at least, a while.
Remember him for his arms, so strong;
Forget that both of you were wrong.
Remember him in a memory;
Remember your love was the only key.
Remember you're not going to die;
Forget the times that you would cry.
Remember the day he played "The Rose";
Remember your love, because nobody knows.
Remember your love went straight to Hell;
Forget that only time will tell.
But most of all, remember, still,
That you can love him . . .
And always will.

Valerie Dawn Bishop
COVENANT
Despair doth prey 'pon mortals aged old,
And wrinkled, sallow, is the skin which glowed.
Ere any thought of failure cast thee down,
'Ware that in thought one's course is often found.
Upon misfortune's heel you easily May turn thy mind t'ward dark and pathless seas.
How easily one falls into that trap . . .

Not reaching forth, or e'en within to grasp
The light of God which guides the very soul.
That strength in one which strives to make us whole.

Some who've fallen lie upon the soil
Trying not, for fear of fruitless toil
Some who have fall'n won't move from where they lie
Expect the rest to aid and edify.
Those ignorant of life's unending road
Bereft of peace fulfilling more than gold.
With comfort near they find no comforting.
They close their eyes "There is no light" they scream.
Be not the fool who says "My woe's too strong."
Mere seconds midst eternity "too long."
Who feels, therefore, alone; all hope is lost
Throughout the night their eyes are fever-glossed.
A ship fog-blinded sensing not land near
A leaf cut off from water, crumpled, sear.

Despair will cling with chilly tenderness
If you accept its cloak without redress.
It is the thought of man which makes his mood
This notion comforts well—if understood.
And we God-Made . . . God-Loved, are we, Mankind.
Rejoice in He who loves despite man's wrongs.
He who never forsook the sinning throngs.
Awake! Thy mind from slumber now awake
Turn not thy head from Him, His light forsake.
Messenger to man from heaven sent.
Yes, he who made his life a covenant.
The union binding God and Man . . . forever!

Raymonde Anne Pierce
HIS WORDS OF WISDOM
Look at his face,
His pain, you just can't erase
Browned by the sun's reaching,
His education only from life's teaching
But still he continues to survive,
Yes, that old man is very much alive.

A struggle and fight,
From early morn, till the dark of night
Aged and not much in size,
But none the less life has made him wise
He is not like you or I
And swears life has not passed him by.

His riches, far beyond what we will ever grasp,

Yes, at times he speaks of the past
Many things he's had to endure,
Only one thing he claims for sure
Is that his life has been full of love,
Just as sure as the stars up above.

He is very good at preaching,
And says he's had life's greatest teaching
He refers to the earth as his gold,
And continues to claim it's the greatest gift we'll ever behold.
As he held my hand, he told me not to be afraid
And he went on to explain that the earth is the only thing meant to remain.

Helen Arlynne Lord
TIME—IN SORROW
With night comes darkness
And for many;—sweet sleep—
But, darkness brings its shadows
And for some—a time of grief;
With weariness and heavy hearts
The night goes on and on,
The hours stand so very still,
But then:—There *is* the dawn!
And with it brings a brighter look,
A lighter time, a newer day—
Cares that seemed so heavy
Now begin to fade away;
So,—"there-in" lies God's promise
That time will ease one's sorrow
And that the gloomy dark of night
Will brighten on the 'morrow'.

Nancy Keats Benson
A BREATH OF AIR
Wake up and leave your world of make believe and cherry red balloons
And dare to see and hear the cries around the world.
Oh, leave your self-filled stomachs and turn to other's care.
Wake up and leave your self-imposing universe;
It winds around and in and out
With soft pink felted cushions curled.
You'll smother there, I swear.

Florence Kropp Steffen
THE SHADES OF AUTUMN
Just a few weeks ago
    the trees were proudly displaying
        their Autumn finery,

Glorious hues of Amber, Red and Brown
    with a contrast in shades of Green
        from the valient few,

Who proudly hold on to their color
    like an Irish ancestry
        in spite of Jack's chilling breath,

Which makes many a brave soul shiver in his tracks.

The leaves filter slowly down looking for a place to rest.

Then a gust of wind and they fall like a quick shower of summer rain.

Whirling and waltzing, as though they can hear

a soft strain of the "Blue
Danube",
windborne from some
mysterious source.

Then like a grand finale, a gusty
whirlwind
will spiral them up into the
air
like a small geyser.

Again they look for a resting
place,
as though, to watch the antics
of those who follow after.

Gradually they begin to crowd
together
in some small nook and
hollow,

Looking for a place of refuge
their life appears to be gone at
last.

Not really, they form a blanket of
warmth,
for the perennial plant,
against the wintry blast.

And then as time goes on
they become healthy mulch
for the trees and plants,
whose life carries on.

Peg Hahn
TOGETHER, APART
At opposite ends of the kitchen
table
separate sides of the bed.
Sharing all our time to daydream
individually
of long-lost high school
love and caviar.
Aware of our distance,
yet unwilling to change.

Ed J. Dollard
FOR JANE
After the beach there were
Eggs in Normandy
Apples in Brittany.
Shells in both;
Cherbourg, Saint Lo.
And the wounded.

Then another line fought
Another friend lost.
Siegfried, Saar-Moselle, George.

Once a war before,
A soldier wrote:
"Lie easier cross . . .,"

This time by radio:
"Sir, we're all dead."

Very young
One,
Blood precious from his chest
Choked:
"I'm from Ohio."
What part?
Nobody asked. He slept.

Consuella Jordan
THE UNKNOWN SOLDIER
[To every veteran of a war. You
served our country well. Thank
You.]
I am a man,
for I fought for my country.
Am I insane for what I am?
We stayed up all night;
We fought hard till our muscles
were
made sore.
Now we are at peace.

Now I can sleep and look back at
how
I bled and died for my country.
I look at my scars left behind,
And I thank the Lord that I have
survived.
If called upon again, I shall go
back,
bleed, and die again.
I thank the soldiers who guard
my grave
and the thousands of people
who
stop by and wonder if I am
theirs.
I shall put your mind at ease.
I am one who stands for all that
has not
been found.
I am not unknown.
for I'm heaven bound.
God knows who I am.
If you do for your country and
not ask
what your country will do for
you.
You will be as proud as I am.
At war again I'll serve with
pleasure.
The Purple Heart shall shine
with honor.
I am not an unknown soldier;
God knows who I am.

Edwina Carol Kovacs
EPITAPH FOR AN ARTIST
[To my mother, Dorothy
Whiteley, my son Bill and my
new husband Michael, for
without their love and
guidance, I would never have
had the confidence to try
writing anything.]
The easel stands deserted
its canvas only half done,
a pallet of dried up colors,
brushes scattered on the floor.
The sun, shining from above,
touches a spattered blue shirt
on the chairback.
The empty table in its corner,
all is silent, (empty) lonely!
The artist, has closed; the final
door!

Mary Beth Porter
MY OLD HOUSE
[For my Mom and Dad on their
35th wedding anniversary! Just
to say thanks for all they've
done for me, and wish them
many more years of happiness
together.]
I see the house dark, desolate,
and empty.
The house where we lived, my
brothers and me.
I see it covered with cobwebs,
and all run down,
The paint so chipped off, I can
hardly tell it's brown.

I stand in sadness looking at the
place I called home,
And staring into darkened
windows, I let my mind roam
Back to the carefree days of my
youth that I spent here.
I think of mom and dad, and
down my cheek runs a single
tear.

Although my parents are dead,
and my brothers are gone,
I can still see us playing touch
football on the front lawn.
Thinking of all the fun and
sometimes crazy things I did as
a kid,
I walk over to my secret place,
the one where I always so
cleverly hid.

I climb the porch steps and walk
to the front door,
And into my old house, I enter
once more.
The door creaks open, so
desperately needing oil.
It's easy to think of dad, Mr. Fix-
it, always covered head to toe
with soil.

As I look around the room in the
pale evening light,
I switch on a lamp, and the room
comes alive; memories become
bright.
The furniture, along with
everything else, is just the
same,
My old Aunt Jess, in a dusty
picture frame.

Standing amidst these memories,
my mind wanders, and I see my
mother's face.
She's leaning over the stove
preparing dinner, as usual with
the utmost care.
Hearing his voice, I turn and see
dad sitting in his favorite arm
chair.
Just then my brothers come in
slamming the door, and I am
ten, once more.

Walking through this old house
and thinking of the past,
I relive all the memories I know
will always last.
Some are good and some are bad;
most are happy and only a few
are sad.

Then, I slip on a broken stair and
it jerks me back to today.
Simple and sweet are the days of
long ago; and there I wish I
could stay.
Yet, I go back out the door, down
the steps, and through the yard,
I try not to cry, but the tears still
come, and it all seems so hard.

I wish my parents were here, but I
know they're where they are
meant to be.
Until finally I realize: I have to
live my life, not in the past, but
now, and for me.
So I get in my car, and for the last
time, from my old house, I
drive away—
And I go to see my boyfriend, for
tomorrow is my wedding day.

Josepha Murray Emms
SOME DAY TRUTH
Yes, I am old!
I cannot hide the years;
They have left their marks upon
my face
And left their scars upon my heart
That can never be erased.
Yes, I am old!

And yet my mind is young;
It travels roads I can no longer
tread;
It wanders back through sunny
paths
That lead to fields of love.
I close my eyes and pictures
come to view.

In these younger days I thought I
knew
Answers to so much—
But now I know life has no
answers really;
It is mystery that keeps us
traveling on . . .
Searching, ever searching!

Steve R. Morris
I'M GLAD THERE IS YOU
I'm glad there is you, to smile at
me
and brighten up my day,
To share my thoughts with you
and understand the things I do
and say.

I'm glad there is you, to share
all of my love with too,
And accept my love for all of the
things that we might do.

I'm glad there is you, to laugh
with me
at all of the ordinary things,
To share with me what is special
in everything that life brings.

I'm glad there is you, to always be
very happy with too,
And I will always love you
because I'm glad there is only
you.

Calvin Ricky Flake
THE LAST LETTER
To you whom I have loved and
lost,
I need you back despite the cost.
What did I do to cause this space
To open up and take your place?

I'm far away.
What can I do?
I've lost your love
So tell me true.
If I've lost you,
Let me know
So my soul can
Let you go.

Helplessly hoping for a word or a
call
That tells me I worry for nothing
at all,
But please tell me something.
I can't wait too long,
For my feelings for you
Are not quite as strong.
You won't let me know,
So what can I do?
I can only tell you
I'm thinking of you.

Vera Groschoff Schoen
RUBIK'S CUBE
New from a package
and never tampered with—
solid colors on six sides—

but wath it! When the baby is
born
and thrust into caressing hands
a few twists will scatter
the puzzle of heredity
carefully assembled by the Maker.

Today's Greatest Poems

A few wrong moves wreak havoc
in childhood,
a few wrong words confuse the
teen
and a few wrong choices
add up over the years.

What you get is a befuddled person
who cannot figure out
what's up or down.

Some minds, some lives can be
  restored to wholeness
with not too many right turns.
Others are so mixed up
it's almost impossible.

And politicians are doing the same
with nations.

Glenda Mansanares
ONLY YOU
[To my Tony, for the hopes and
dreams we share, I'll love you
always. Thanks to mother for
all your love and support since
the first day of my poetic
works.]
I think about you always,
And dream of you at night;
I wish I could be with you,
And keep you in my sight.

We'd walk the paths together,
And fill each other's hearts;
I wish we'd be forever,
And never ever part.

If you should ever realize,
How much you mean to me;
Then you would also know that,
Together we should be.

Come to me whenever,
You're feeling sad or blue;
I'll always, always be here,
To make things best for you.

Suzanne Marie Burton
HAD I NOT
Han I not loved you,
I may not have been loved.
Had I not touched you,
I may not have been touched.
Had I not kissed you,
I may not have been kissed.
Had I not felt tenderness,
I may not have felt joy.
Had I not deserted you,
I may not have been deserted.
Had I not lied to you,
I may not have been lied to.
Had I not hurt you,
I may not have been hurt.
Had I not betrayed you,
I may not have been betrayed.
Had I not lost myself,
I may not have lost you.

Ilene Clay
RELATIVE TO ME
MY DAY begins
December gray.
I peer outside
Then prowl away.

Perhaps some tea—
Go search each tin.
No kind to meet
This mood I'm in.

Come lift your 'phone
And still the ring.
Against my ear
It tries to sing.

The tune's off-key

The words all miss.
That has to be
My baby sis.

We laugh and talk
I trace a tear.
She wishes me
A super year.

Goodbyes too soon—
Goodmorning, Dawn.
Step in. Let's dance.
The kettle's on.

Linda Sciapiti
ODE TO GRAMPS
Captured by your wisdom
Believing in their truths
A child then,
A child now
Pure love retaining what I knew

Discussions deep and meaningful
I remember oh so well
Then why this agony,
Why this pain?
God, don't let him be in hell!

Your immense strength
Bullheaded some would say
Entangled our spirits
Communicating in length
Making me in part—what I am
today

Last encounter was in silence
I've known too much pain
Gramps, please speak one word
Why such obvious disdain?
My essence completely unfurled

The tears I shed then
And even today
On the bed he last lay
Memories reflect on when
Immense love—not betray

So with this my old friend
I pray you can hear
I'm sorry, forgive me
Someday we'll adhere
Finally, forever my hearts only
  plea.

Now writing the end to this ode
Being thankful for you
A person magnificent to behold
Loving and missing the times we
grew—that's it!
Accepting your death was so hard
to do.

Amber L. Smith
IT WAS ME
It was me who shared your
suffering and stood firmly by
your side,
It was me who listened to her tell
of love knowing that she lied.

It was me, who every night for
your love I did cry,
It was me who wanted greatly by
your side to gently lie.

It was me who waited on you
hand and foot while she lay
sleeping.
It was me who, while you were
hurt lay awake at night
aweeping.

It was me who never told you
how I felt for the fear of your
rejection,
It was me who secretly hovered
over you giving you my
protection.

It was me who was always there
when you needed her, where
was she?
And who was it that loved you
the most?
          It was me!

Sandra Colombini
TEARS
Looking out my window
As the icicles hung from the roof,
The sun melted the water from
them.
And as each drop fell to the
ground,
I remembered the tears that fell
from my eyes
Every time we fought and you
went away.
The drops from the icicles froze
once the sun went away
Never to fall again;
Unlike the tears which still fall
from my eyes
Because you went away with the
sun
Never to return.

Marc Ferguson
Life In the Fast lane
Gone
are days of popsicle peddlers
lazily ding-a-linging their way up
shade-painted, elm-lined streets
bringing smiles to each child's face
in neighborhoods, one after
another,
where we all played for what
seemed forever.

Those same old streets are now
replaced by sun-sleek interstates
where time swiftly sweeps by
and sentry-like poles loom
overhead
watching our lives quickly pass
away,
familiar faces fading to a blur,
all sounds becoming one,
numbing noise.

Cathleen Elizabeth Tolemy
MY OBSESSION
[To my Mom & Dad For all
your Love & Help Happy
Aniversary]
Like the last few leaves
  on a lone tree
  that may scatter
  onto the whiteness
  of a new fallen snow.
So are the few
  in utter darkness.
The ones that shine so bright.
The ones that sing with
intelligence.
One day soon
  we may be asked to sing.
Let us chose wisely.
We may have only one chance.

Laura Lynn Laux
ANCIENT DEATH
Underneath the Pearly Morning
Dew,
  Sits the Indian Girl of Sioux.
Sounds of Rapid Cool Spring
Waters,
  Wakes the Chiefs Beautiful
Daughters.

War Drums echo over the
Canyons,
  Will not stop til the rise of the

First Sun.
Then the Mighty War Man
speaks,
  Of the White Men on the
Peaks.
War guns in the Fiery Night,
  Show the strength of the
White.
Then flows the Red Man's Fear,
  Throwing and Fighting with a
Spear.

Through the Heart, a Piercing
Blade,
  Bleeding rapidly, no Sound is
made.
Not a Twitch of a Whisper,
  Nor a Groan from the Dying.

Then strongly plead the Old
Indian Chief,
  Looking still down underneath.
There a Body lay quiet and still,
  Thomas Tohawk is very ill.

From Two Suns, Day and Night,
  Rose a Third Sun very high.
Says the Indian Girl of Sioux,
  Thomas Tohawk chose to die.

There is a Sun, but is no Gun,
  For They Fought and Fought til
They Won.
Sets a Child upon the Rocks,
  Staring still down on the
Flocks.
A Doe, A Deer, A Shed of a Tear,
  In memory of Thomas Tohawk.

Linda J. Breiting
LITTLE WONDER
["In Memory of Timothy and
Marilyn"]
Twinkle, twinkle up so high
  you brilliant little star,
At times you seem so very near
  and yet you are so far.

You hold such mystery in your
realm
  encircled by your kind,
And if by fate you'd fall to earth
  you'd be a treasured find.

You seem to dance before my
eyes
  on silent, summer nights,
Or like a city in heaven above
  a million twinkling lights.

So bright you shine in all your
glory
  when the moon is round and
gold,
And to the Child you led the way
  for the Wise Men to Behold . . .

Mardi Flaming
SUNDAY' DISASTER
[Dedicated to my dear brother
Rick, With Love Mardi]
Old man old man
look what you've done
you lived your life
when he had just begun

Old man old man
why didn't you see
the stop sign a coming
that took my brother
from me. .

He was riding home
so wild and free
just two blocks

579

from where he wanted to be

The ambulance came
to take him away
robbing him blind
for what he didn't need

Old man old man
why does it seem
like every sunday's
a disaster to me. .

Old man old man
I forgive you, you see
just can't hide these feelings
deep inside of me. . .

Doris Lord
RANDY
There wasn't time, my precious
son, To bid us all good—by.
God took you to a better place to
mansions in the sky.
With mournful hearts, and
tearful eyes. We had to let you
go.
The empty space within
ourselves, So helplessly we
show.
You lived, and gave a life of love.
So many hearts you touched.
Although the years were all so
few. You left behind so much.
My son, my son we miss you so.
God give us strength to cope.
To pray for sunny skies again.
And most of all to hope.
For great reunion in the sky.
With joyful tears we'll meet.
When once again, my special son,
our lives will be complete.
Untill we meet again Mom

Jane (Fouts) Johnson
MY LIE
*[To Stevan Johnson & Marla
Swim— With Love from Mom]*
As I go from day to day
With only you on my mind
I wonder if it's you that hurts me
Or if, to myself, I've been unkind.
I've built a beautiful fantasy
About just you and I
And each impelling word you
speak
Helps me to live "My Lie".
I love you and I want you
Just the way you are. . .
As each clear, blue sky
Welcomes one bright star.
Come with me, walk beside me,
Love with me, laugh and cry.
Help me change into reality
This fantasy I call "My Lie".

Jaime McAndrew
**Ode To a Curious Wee
Haunt**
*[Dedicated with love to my
daughter Cyndy. . who has a
deep love and compassion for
all animals.]*
In need I was of a cat,
A worthy companion, and yet,
Who'd have dreamed I'd get,
This sleek little lass of black?

No shy demure bit of fur,
Was she, no stranger though;
So familiar is she that I know,
The even rhythm of her purr.

Now a fitting name comes to
mind.
"I dub you Tarbaby, Mistress Cat,

It seems to fit your coat of black."
Tis smug I'm feeling about my find!

She slips about inspecting all,
And naturally seems to be,
Som'mat right at home with me,
Curling into a soft round ball.

She cries her ladylike "Me'ow",
And pauses to see if I'm aware,
Of her needs and actually care,
How she depends on me now.

She slithers swiftly along the
floor,
Playing with her catnip mouse
bit;
Flipping and tossing about in a
fit,
Of carefree fun and expecting
more.

Now suddenly weary of her
pretend game,
With impatience she summons me.
"Hurry—come and see!", says she.
Says I, "You're beginning to be a
pain!"

I gather her up in a mighty rush,
To still the jarring din.
And she quickly settles in,
As I contemplate the silly fuss.

That cats are curious creatures,
tis true,
You'll never quite know the
feline mind.
Though they may treat you
rather kind,
You'll not own them, rather
they'll own you!

Wanda K. Davis
SEASONS
Autumn is here in its beauty at
last,
Spring in its glory has already
past.
Winter is waiting with showers
of snow
Children with sleds already to go.

The flowers say "Goodbye" to
each other
as the cool nights appear,
Maybe with luck we'll be back
next year.

The leaves fall so fastly as the
cold wind blow
The bird house is ready its
shelter the fold.
The fire in the fireplace is a
dancing delight,
We know this will be a cold
winter night.

Kathryn Organ
Continental Breakfast
[to Roger]
Steamy espresso,
clouds of white cream on top
like I floated on top of you.
Golden crisp croissants
hardly fill my appetite.
Your European stories
surface,
As harpsicords and flutes
play
in the distant background.
Do I miss you
or is it the thoughts
of missing you?
The tender void
shakes my reality

from sunny daydreams in Paris
to nightmares of cutting pain.
You really are gone . . .
No room is left . . .
for second helpings.

Kay Sechriest
FRIEND
A crowd of people, strangers,
In a smoky room.
I push and pull as they do,
Lonely, seeking for a face
Familiar, known to me.
But finding none, resolved,
I sit upon a stool
And watch the games that others
Choose to play—the empty
games
That wake upon next morning's
dawn
With bitterness, self—hate,
remorse.
So finally I rise to leave.
Then there you are, that smiling
face,
Across the room, through smoke
and haze
And to me, with your smile, you
come
And wrap your arms about me,
Warming me with your
comradeship.
Friend, you warm my soul.

Faye Jenkins Anderson
BROKEN HEART
They say a broken heart can't heal
But I've had quiet a few.

And just when things seem
darkest
I find a love that's new.

How many times can ones heart
break
Before it finally shatters.

How many times can ones heart
break
Before it no longer matters.

If death can come from a broken
heart
How come I'm still alive?

If death can come from a broken
heart
How long can I survive?

Eric Fisukhia
COUNTENANCE OF MAN
*[This poem is dedicated to My
Parents, who instilled in me, a
respect for mankind as a whole,
with varying cultures and
beliefs, from the U.S. to India.]*
Why do I strive to communicate?
Why analyze and why debate?

The contours of a thoughtful face
Reveal emotion through God's
grace
Seen only in the human race . . .

If the countenance of man
were steadfast and couldn't
expand . . .
    I'd throw away this pen in hand

I, however can't ignore the
human pain we all endure
nor all the joys we can explore. . .

That's why I analyze and why
debate and why I strive to
communicate.

Gladus M. Moore
GOD, NATURE AND ME
The laughing haunty whispering
winds,
Dancing over hills and dales.
Never stopping always talking as
they go from place to place.
Calling their greetings come
awake, come awake.
We're here and over yonder
trying to give the land new
grace,
And that which is spoiled we'll
try to erase.

Who can answer the wandering
westerlies?
Not you, nor I, but thought I
heard the pine trees sigh.
"We're awake and dressed in
green no matter what the
season."
We're the sentries of the forest,
asleep not we.
Our friends do sleep come winter
as the snow and north winds
blow.

While our only friends are the
deer, chickadees and a little
human who talks to God, the
Son, and the Holy Ghost.

The wandering westerlies
whispered"
Yes we know for we've carried her
confession to the mighty Man
on high.
She walks with her face aglow in
our winds, then kneels to pray
on your quiet glen.
She lestens with her heart, then
sings out softly,
I've found him. He walks with
me, He talks with me.
I'm happy I've found him. Is her
marvelous melody.

We in turn are happy wanderling
westerlies.
We know she has heard his voice
coming in from us to thee.
She listens, she knows we bring
his messages to all who do
believe.
As we depart to let the north
winds come in,
tell our little trusting friends.
Adios untill next year from the
wanderling westerlies.

Lawrence Spirio
MY SONG
I wish that I could find for you
the words that are in my heart.
To tell you how I miss you dear
and loved you from the start.
I've searched my mind and
memories
for an outlet of my song;
of love and care and tenderness
for you, for whom I long.
There is no excape for my song
as long as we are apart.
For until I do return to you,
it remains locked deep in my
heart.
But this I'll say as I have said
time and time before;
you are the girl I dream of so
and surely do adore.
Someday my wishes, hopes and
prayers

will definitely all come true.
That day will be the day
that I return to you.

Linda D. Lamb
TIME IS ALL YOU NEED
[Dedicated to Sonya for her encouragement and inspiration, and to my loving family, especially my daughter Kimberly.]
Time is all you need to see you
through troublesome days and
restless nights, to help you
realize which is wrong, which
is right.

Keep your head raised high and
you'll see just how fast time
can go by.

Someone is pulling for you to
come out ahead, so no more
tears will you shed.

You see you are thought of more
than you may know, time will
soon enough let this show, it's
all up to you.

May God be close to guide you in
whatever you do, and I'll also
be there to help you through,
for I'm that someone who's
pulling for you.

Randi L. Hale
PEACE WITHIN EACH
Two Lives immersed as one,
the freedom cannot be overcome;
Flying above the open sea,
the birds swoop down, so
peacefully.

The endless future lies ahead,
till someday each will be dead.
Yet life lives within their souls,
filling presents' endless holes.

Knowing not tomorrows ways,
dwelling not on yesterdays.
The seagulls' peacefull flight
within,
together each day they'll spend.

Clara H. McKenney
DEARLY BELOVED
Dearly beloved, so long ago,
On the day that we were wed,
Before friends and family and
God,
Our solemn vows were said.

They set us apart from all the
world,
From each to never be free,
What joy or pain affected one,
For the other had to be.

Each for the other, through the
years,
More than fifty of them, all
told,
Through sickness, health, good
times and bad,
Together, to have and to hold.

Dearly beloved, the first years
were long,
Then later, seemed to fly,
Children came, then went their
way,
Alone again, you and I.

Our grandchildren came, one by
one,
'Til at last they numbered
seven,

We welcomed all with pride and
love,
Sweet as the angels of Heaven.

We were given years together, to
know,
Great grandchildren, warm and
dear,
Little legs running to climb our
knee,
Their childish voices to hear.

Now, I miss the glow of your
loving eyes,
Your touch as you passed me by,
Sometimes it seems I can't make
it alone,
Yet somehow I have to try.

For time came when you had to
leave us,
You reached the end of the
line,
But you still live, within our
hearts,
Dearly beloved of mine.

Christopher W. Young
HEAVENLY PARADE
[This poem, and all others that bear my signature, were given to me through the power of Jesus Christ.]
Copper tinted clouds, cooling in
the sky,
lifelessly strolling, above the
place I lie.
Aimlessly watching the
"Heavenly Parade" passing by,
of floats, dragons, and wishes,
conjectured up by I.

The colors change in time, but
thoughts remain the same,
of love and hate with riches,
scant glory and some fame.
Passing by, eminating dreams, by
figures in the skies,
trudging to the great unknown,
unsurpassed by these eyes.

As I whirl beneath the clouds, on
Earth's merry-go-round,
I entertain all my thoughts,
with barely little sound.
There is a sound of course, and
not from wheels that spin,
but from a heart singing, of joys
that come from within.
Add them up, then multiply, and
you will have the sum,
of all great days you have
spent, and others still to come.

The parade keeps rolling off the
globe and disintegrates in air,
dividing somewhere spaciously,
for others soon to share.
Parades and clouds are activated,
by the massing of many parts,
and you shall be the Grand
Marshal, by sharing many hearts.

Nick Soules Jr.
GIRL WATCHING
Everything made of sugar & spice
Brunette, Blonde, Auburn or Red
Never the less there all so nice
To the roving wondering eye

Moving freely a dress in the breeze
A glimpse of a thigh up high
A smile a wink of an eye
As a lady rated ten passes by

All her curves right in place

With clothes that hug her close
Hair slightly blowing in the wind
A cute little freckled button nose

On they walk on past you
With just the touch of rhythm
A fragrance never like before
You know a woman through &
through

She's soft skinned & smooth like
silk
Her heat could set you on fire
Or speed your pulse to danger
point
To your eyes a most beautiful
sight

*(A Slow Man) Alberta Law
Sloman*
The Miracle Of Christmas
'Tis the miracle of Christmas
We celebrate each year.
It brings about such greetings
Of happiness and cheer.

The little secret whisperings
Fill the corners of the rooms.
Someone stashed an odd shaped
box
Right behind the brooms.

The rustling of bright paper
Can be heard right through the
door
And someone with a deep deep
voice says
"*#*my last paper tore"

The stack of Christmas goodies
Keeps growing with each day.
No one says to helping? hands
"Just go away! And stay!"

People string about bright lights
From window, tree, and stair.
Poor Santa's pack is now so full
He has helpers everywhere.

Why do folks and Santa Claus
Come bearing gifts THIS night?
To celebrate the miracle
Of that night that was so
bright.

It's the night the people celebrate
The night of peace and joy.
It's the birth night of God's Holy
Child
And Mary's wondrous boy.

Vivian Lyles
THANK YOU JESUS
Dear Jesus, thank you for
bringing me back to your fold.
Thank you for your mercy and
your love untold.
I felt so lonely, and far, far away.
I didn't know how I would make
it from day to day.
My hopes and my dreams had
actually disappeared,
But you healed my heart
and my soul cheered.
Deep down I knew that you
would never, ever leave me,
Because you promised to be with
me and accept me gladly.

It was like a veil lifted from my
face.
It was like my depression had left
no trace.
My soul felt light and free as the
wind,
As free as if there had been no
sin.

I felt your presence ever near my
heart,
Even though I didn't acknowledge
it from the start.
I heard a small, still voice sweetly
saying,
Stop feeling sorry for yourself and
start praying.

Help me Jesus to have
unswerving faith and love.
Help me to realize that my help
comes from above.
Help me to be willing, strong,
faithful and true.
Help me give you the glory, in
everything I do.
Help me to be a living witness of
your power and grace.
Help me Jesus to finally win this
seemingly impossible race.
Help me to always lean on your
firm and loving breast.
Help me to trust you when I'm
put to the test.

Thanks, Precious Jesus for
opening your arms.
Thanks, Precious Jesus for
tagging along.
Thanks Jesus for fulfilling my
wildest hopes and dreams.
Thanks for letting me feel your
most merciful, holy beams.
You are truly the most wonderful,
loving friend.
You are truly the one who lifted
me from the depths of sin.
I will never forget from whence I
came,
Not only will I never forget, but I
will never be the same.

Patti Wheaton
MY WRITTEN ART
To begin a sonnet of syllables,
I looked for different words in
mind.
I ponder for flavor of images,
I come up with tasteless, abstract
lines—
No picture—from vaguely
written dialogue.
I work to paint a picture from my
mind—
Your mind, the blank canvas I
must beautify.
I mix the reds and blues with
paint thinner,
Slapping the color on the white
canvas—
Only not a brush, but a
featherpen;
Strokety—stroke go the words
with a scratch,
The beginning of a sonnet for
display.
Rainbow colors of words in
childlike play,
Painted young words, playing
games with the mind.

Terry—Lynn McMillan
THE DEATH OF A CHILD
The air crackles with tension,
Tired shoulders sag,
As the tiny embryo,
Is placed in a bag.
Thrown away from safety,
The place of its making,
A life of joy,
Not for its taking.

The young girl turns away,
    And she regretfully sighs,
As she never will see,
    The color of its eyes,
The warmth of its skin,
    The feel of its hair,
There are tears in her eyes,
    As she pretends not to care.

We hear the cries,
    Of the unborn child,
But we pretend not to hear,
    What we consider mild.
But to think that we do,
    Each day of the year,
Commit a murder,
    Of a child so dear.

Donald Gastrow
A WAR CASUALTY
Stretched out on the ground,
His eyes were wide open,
Filled with quiet fear and
    innocence.
No movement came from any
        part of
    his body
Only his moist, blue eyes
        appeared
    alive.

Then slowly the lids closed,
Shrouding forever the wondrous
    gaze beneath.
There was no more life
And no more fear.
All that remained was his
    innocence
Which was probably what killed
    him
    in the first place.

Linda Musacchio
TOSSIN AND TURNIN
Oh those sleepless nights,
    and the many fights, with my
        covers.

Can't stay still,
    tossin and turnin

Listen to the wind howl and dogs
    growl,
        I find it hard to fall asleep
        and the way the cars creep,
            I even tried to count sheep.

Why is it so hard to close my
    eyes,
        here I am in my sleeping
            disguise,
            still yearning for some shut
                eye.

Can't stay still,
    tossin and turnin

I finally get tired of tossin and
    turnin,
        and fall asleep.

I wake up the next morning,
    no covers and my pillow on the
        floor.

So this is what I worked the
    whole day for.

Craig Paul Martin
**A Skirmish at Bainebridge
    Alabama**
He inhales the damp ash air.
The sky is a ceiling of rough gray
    stone
too close and too still.
No wind.
Far across the burnt field

a hazy train pulls against the
    picture.
No sound.
Without moving he searches the
    field,
seeing nothing.
The tall grass has swallowed all
    trace.
No gray, or even blue, bodies.
But, no, of course not!
This isn't 1865!
The highway
is over there
across the clearing
(half under a blackened log, the
    bark crossed with furrows like
    some giants rough skin, a thick
    square bottle held together by
    an illegible heat stained label)
thru the autumn woods
(thin vines and branches
    entwined like fences; the
    leaves too loud beneath his
    feet)
across the creek
(his foot cold and wrinkled in his
    dirty right shoe)
down the rise and over the
    guardrail.
He feels his pockets
for car keys.
He exhales
(how long had he been holding
    his breath?)
and feels winter in the chilled
    night
coming up fast behind him.

Raphael Sone
OUTLOOK
Peter and Pierre looked out and
    high
To watch a plane
That had just taken off go by.

Twirling his cane
His face all grim, Peter asked why
Men are so vain

As to look for death in the sky.
Fingering is chain
Pierre cried out: I wish I could fly!

Christine M. Trucinski
AND HE' NICE TOO
[To two young people who
have made the word "sharing"
real.]
In today's world of opposites
    attracting
    when short and talls
    make matched pairs almost
        obsolete.
So unusual in this hustling world
    to find a complimentary pair
    that's both attractive and kind
    not only to those they
        encounter,
    but more so—to each other.
Growing, sharing, enjoying
    building, planning—today's and
    tomorrow's dreams.
Simple love in complex
    personalities.
Both independent, both
    individuals—HEADSTRONG
    and yet both concerned, caring
    and supportive to each other's
        needs.
To sail with the wind on her face,
    to bask in the noon day sun,
    to refurbish, rebuild and kindle

material and emotions as well,
    to ride slowly in tune with
    Mother Earth.
To calm, encourage and love.
To praise the Lord—in joyful
    song.
To worship, together, the
    Almighty
    who already blesses their
    sacred union and
    who in time will extend that
    union beyond
    that which they already have—
    in each other.

Geraldyne Thorne
REFLECTION
[My poem is dedicated to my
daughter, Laurie. It came to my
mind in the few moments
while she was finishing her
music practice as I sat gazing
out of the window at the
mountains beyond . . .]
Doves . . .
    flying high in the sky . . .

Grains of wheat
    nodding softly on the tips of
    slowly waving fragile strands
        of green . . .

Oh, we see yon setting sun
    o'er the darkening hills
    beyond. . .

Night is falling fast,
    to hasten dreams that never
        last
            beyond one's slow
                awakening . . .
Dimly lit the yonder skies . . .
    falling fast before my eyes;
    rounding out the pleasant
        day.

We partly wish no end as yet . . .
    to sit and gaze at yonder
        sight. .
            before the night.

But stars will fill the space . . .
    to help fulfill the evening grace
    and promises of days to
        come. . .

Hopefully, our hopes and dreams
    come into place . . .
        forever lasting . . .

Edward J. LaBee Jr.
AM I TO BLAME
    Crying doesn't ease the pain
        As it used to do
Because tomorrow I will wonder
        If you ever knew

And would it have made a
        difference
        If I'd spent the time
    To tell you that I loved you
    And once, you were mine

But a daddy whose life is a prison
        cell
    Running from his shame
Too afraid that if his daughter
        knew
She wouldn't want to share his
        name

    Yes there was your mother
    One you had never known
Your daddy drove her to an early
    grave

And that left you all alone

    Life had you so mistaken
    Not thinking that I cared
So you got yourself in a lot of
        trouble
Probably because I wasn't there.

In the hospital I stood beside
        you
As you lay helpless in that bed
    I want to see my daddy
Was the last thing that you said

So I stand here at your grave now
    Wondering what to do
    And would it have made a
        difference
    To know that I loved you

Glennie C. Larke
ALPHABETICAL WORLD
Letters are formless symbols,
Until side by side,
They are united into molds
Of mortal words
To prevail upon the minds of
    men;
Unveiling hidden thoughts,
To proclaim
Love, Friendship or Strife!!

Esther Ager Smith
DEAR CREDITORS:
[I dedicate "Dear Creditors" to
all older women who, when
seeing the horrid signs, return
to college in order to update
their working skills.]
Dear Creditors:
All summer John Doe has been
    sick;
I'm sitting here staring at over
    due bills that came next.

Today I'm fifty-eight;
Back to work for me—It's quite
    late.

Two years ago I saw the horrid
    signs;
Back to College I went.
"Lord," I prayed, "Please give
    meThe mid-night oil I have
    burned and burned,
But fate too soon has had its
    turn.

Now we are facing Braniff's fate.
"Oh, God," I pray,
"Please, extend our creditors'
    faith!"

Creditors, we don't want to go
    bankrupt
Because if we do you can't feed
    your pups!

Can I say more to you whom we
    owe?
Except God has given me faith;
We'll get out of our woes.

How long? A year or two? Who
    knows?
Is your company experiencing the
    same throes?

The little companies will get paid
    first
Because their children have
The biggest chance for thirst.

We owe under seventeen
    thousand at the most

But for families, it would make a
lot of toast.

A claims clerk made a social
security mistake,
So for our state insurance
We still wait and wait.

These are the reasons
Why our payments are so late.
    Thank you,
      Jane Doe

Donald D. Warner
PICADORS
The old men
like toreadors
parade gallantly
through the streets
of past regrets
marveling
at the youthful bulls
who waste their time
wallowing
in the dung heaps
of untarnished futures
and wonder
if youth once aged
can blossom
into steel-chested
bright, knowledgeable spartans
strong enough
to survive
the final trompetero
signaling
the death knell
for us all

Eleanora S. Martin
THE KISS
*[To my Family—To
friendliness and mirth]*
I happened to see you there and
thought it would be fun
To kiss you on the cheek, then
take off and run.
I knew it was different, for when
you looked at me,
Your heart I had reached, touched
you, obviously.

I cherish a kiss for the precious
thoughts it has won,
So I decided to stay, I did not run.
A kiss is a kiss forever old,
forever new,
I'm glad you were there and I'm
glad I kissed you.

*Judith Augusta Garrahan
Michienzi*
NANAS ARE FOREVER
*[Dedicated to Maria Frances
Michienzi who shall live
forever as she is Nana and, my
Dad, James Joseph Garrahan
who bestowed his gift of words
upon me.]*
Dearest Nana
Life is the perpetuation of love.
And it is the perpetuation of your
love that brings us here.

All too often we speak of a
person at a time like this,
But that is virtually impossible as
you are here.

Here in each and everyone of us
and in the generations to come.
At this point, the youngest
generation who speaks few
words but knows of your love
bids you farewell.

Dearest Great-Nana
Tho I did not know you very well
it is plain to see,
That time is not important what
counts is we are family.

I love you for the times we shared
no matter how many or few,
But most of all Great-Nana I love
you for just being you.

I love you for giving me my
Grampy for he's so dear to me.
I love you for your just being as it
was meant to be.

I love you for your caring and
never ending love.
And I know you'll watch me
growing from oh so high above.

For time itself does not matter
when it comes to what I feel.
What matters is we met and
loved and that was oh so real.

So Great-Nana I will not say
goodbye for goodbyes can be so
sad.
But I will say I love you and
thanks for the time we had.

Elise K. Edgerton
THE WAVE
Events in life oft remind me of a
wave.
Water, seemingly smooth on the
horizon,
Slowly building as it nears the
shore,
Drawing all within it's path—
Gathering momentum, uprooting
the routine.
Changing, ever growing,
mounting to the peak—
Rushing now, it overtakes itself,
Arching for split-second hesitation,
Spindrift briefly escaping back to
sea—
Then downward plunging,
Crashing to waiting ocean floor,
Surging, foaming, sweeping
toward the beach—
Finally depositing it's collection
upon the sand
As thoughts, memories, perhaps
shattered dreams
Left deserted and lonely upon the
shore.

Elaine Meli
MY BROTHER
He cries and he wets,
But no one forgets
To hug him!

When he eats he is messy
Even when he is dressy—
But, no one forgets to hug him!

He chews on all fingers
Not only his thumb . . . That's
only one.
And nobody forgets to hug him!

My goodness, if he, were ever me.
When I cry, or I wet, a spanking I
get . . .
And nobody hugs me.

A spot on my dress . . .
Everyone frets—"Oh what a mess"!
And nobody hugs me!

He chews all his fingers.
I just my thumb (that's only one).
And everyone forgets to hug me.

On top of all this, I'm told after a
scold,
"You are too old".
And nobody, "HUGS ME!"

Mary L. Schroeder
MEMORIES
*[Dedicated to the charming
family of the late Dr. Charles
Giuliano. Mrs. Giuliano (Dr.
Josephine Flynn). Children:
Josephine, Charles, and Mary-
Louise. Grandchildren: Nugent
and Augusta.]*
It was the summer of fifty-eight.
A long time ago, and yet it seems
It was only yesterday we met in
that romantic
Place in PARIS-at MAXIM'S.

Excitement was in the air;
The fragrance of flowers and
perfume were everywhere.
We were on our way to
L'Orangerie—
Versailles—for the "coming-out"
of the American Debs;
A beautiful spectacle for all to see.

A lovely daughter, Josephine, was
to make her debut
At this most prestigious social
event.
Five thousand Frenchmen waited
at the airport to get a view
Of the Hearsts, Rockefellars,
Duponts, and Gloria Kent.

Much time has passed since then—
A chance meeting grew into a
great friendship.
There were parties, dances
enjoyed with great glee
In Boston, Palm Beach, and
Annisquam by the sea.

A generous host and a genial
hostess
Warm and gracious—it was
always a pleasure
To be their guests and to be in
their company
And enjoy their warmth, their
humor, and their gaiety.

We shall miss his voice, and his
zest for living.
We have lost a dear friend—the
world a great human being.
Dr. G. used his talents and skill
to help mankind.
The universe and all who knew
him are richer in spirit and mind.

Gone from our sight, but not
from our thoughts.
He left us sweet memories which
could never be bought.

George Spellman
NATURE'S DEMISE
Of the beauty and splendor she
once retained,
we have raped the Earth.
Destroying wooded forests and
grassy plains
for yet another eras birth.
This new age is the slaughter of
Nature,
which has been going on for quite
a while.
As for the polluting of the air,
land and water,
these acts are most hideous and
vile.

With little regret, man has
surrendered most of the beauty
that the Earth once held,
for progress and power.
He continued to build bigger
cities and taller skyscrapers
with little thought for a tree, a
patch of grass or a flower.
If this senseless destruction of
Nature
continues to get worse,
then the sad day will come
sooner than expected,
the day Mother Nature needs a
hearse.

Donna Jean Kaplan
LOVE ERUPTS
Our life is most ecstatic,
Then suddenly, like a bomb,
It blows up in my face,
Leaving me in disgrace,
Without a tiny trace
Of the love I know is there.

Our life is now in shambles,
Then meekly, like daybreak,
The love returns to me,
With feelings I can be,
With you eternally,
And the cloud of doubt is gone.

J. Victor Danoski
The Man On the Mountain
On the Moon
Yes—time moves slow
like footsteps in the snow:
For the Man
on the Mountain
on the Moon.

There's no fun
and nowhere to run—
amid the wreckage and debris . . .

I look around
and begin to drown—
in my sea of tranquility.

Out on these dunes
hopelessly marooned—
always driving myself insane . . .

Over and over
like a lost land-rover
over the same strange terrain.

Standing frozen each night
—melting each afternoon:
Picking up pieces of my life
upon the Moon . . .

Yes—time moves slow
like footsteps in the snow:
For "The Man
    on
      the
        Mountain
          on
            the
              Moon"

Allen K. Harrington
Eleven Fifty Nine Fifty Nine
(11:59:59)
Have you ever been to Heaven?
I've seen part of it in a vision!
It is exquisitely beautiful,
To live there is my decision!!

I must become BORN AGAIN,
BELIEVE GOD is my all in all,
BELIEVE with all FAITH, not
doubting,
That HE will sustain me, I shall
not fall.

Oh brothers, sisters, recently I'd
    had it,
Never even took time to pray,
What an empty lonely place it is
    out there,
Once you've found *THE PROPER
    WAY*.

The time is come for us all,
To *DO* the proper thing,
Not to hem and haw around,
And stay on a Worldly Fling.

Come accept JESUS today, right
    now,
Today is the Day of Salvation,
The time is right, *HIS WORD*
says HE might,
Come take us, and you, might be
    on vacation.

Absent from the world, we are
    with JESUS,
Singing praises to our KING,
Please become HIS today,
Forsake the world and all it's
    thing.

The hour is upon us,
Yes, the time is right,
It's ELEVEN FIFTY NINE FIFTY
    NINE,
Accept HIM SAVIOUR tonight.
    I LOVE YOU JESUS,
        Al Harrington.

Elizabeth Carwellos
DEAR OSCAR
A great injustice to you was done
By men both big and small.
They ridiculed and called you
    names
And made you slip and fall.
Green carnations, fur-lined coats
And panthers in the night.
Velvet clothes and pen in hand,
You made quite a sight.
You dazzled them, dear Oscar!
You made them run and hide.
And we dare to wonder?
This is the reason way!
You must admit, dear Oscar,
You pushed a mighty pen.
They were sure to get you
And put you in the end.
I know your heart is broken.
It's heavy and it's sad.
But believe me, dear Oscar,
You're the better man, my lad!

Bob A. Lantz
THIS LONELY LOOK
Phones ring, people sing,
    Life passes quickly by,
Bees sting, bells ring,
    There's a teardrop in my eye.
All these things in life you see
    Are very commonplace,
Just like this lonely look you see
    Upon my face.
Writers write, Fighters fight,
    There's love in all you see,
Catch a bus, take a flight,
    As you run away from me.
All these things are commonplace
    They happen every day,
Just like this lonely look you see
    As you go away.
Life comes, life goes,
    There's magic in the air,
People smile, people cry,
    And there's music everywhere.
All these things, as you can see,

Are very commonplace,
Just like the lost and lonely look
    Upon my face.

Dana Hahn
UNTITLED
    [For Joey With Much Love,]
You
Reap the dried flowers
Of my life
With
Touch
Soft as Jasmine petals.
We laugh
The empty bottles
Wineless,
And braid
together
Dreams on kite
Strings.
Incense ribbons
Rise from cones
Into Jasmine clouds.
You
Are running
Your fingers through my
Life.
I lie
Entangled
In the fabric of
Your glance;
I'm not moving.

Adam F. MISTERKA
MIND RADIOACTIVITY
You don't see it
You don't hear it,
vibrating thoughts around:
Yet in the mist
and volume maze,
You may detect its sounds.

Sound of mind
the prism of vision
now, or future,
or distant past;
carving the nature
of life and us,
so distinctively vast.

Circling the globe
in donors waves
at billion option,
sensative fuzz:
You don't see it
You don't hear it,
Ready adobtion
to pick and use.

Bertha Czosnek Gromada
BACK TO THE HILLS
Take me among the columbines—
Those flowers of truest blue,
They grow near dusty platinum
    mines—
The blossoms I've sent to you;

When I was young, about thirteen,
They all were under my care;
They grew o'er the hills so green,
The flowers of perfume rare;

Take me back to those beds of old,
And there, dear, keep me until
The day I am Feeble, gray and cold,
My heart ceases and is still.

Carol Wilcox Welchance
THE HOBO
As I struggle down these rusty
and ancient tracks, I hear the
whistle blow, feel the vibrations
under my feet.
My bed and shelter is coming
again.

The weather's hot, the sun is
putting a strain on my bloodshot
and tired eyes.
I can smell the bed of hay . . . my
bed.

I'm tired LORD, I'm going HOME
and find some peace, keep the
"hunger pains" under control,
through where I'm going.
Just one more, rattled old ride
and a knock on the door . . . of
the one person whose on my
side.

As I fall off to slumber after
having one drag of a "long
searched for cigarrete butt,
Tomorrow; I'll once
again find the SUNSHINE, and
it'll be a welcome and a HELLO.

Robert D. Russell
DESTINATION
Each day I live alone,
In my cubicle . . .called existence.
Desiring to learn, accomplish,
    and perfect—
All which arouses a jealous
Pursuit of superiority.
Confronted with educational
Score, not at expectations.
Mounted with sport
Achievement, not at expectations.
It hurts immeasurably,
To comprehend limitations.
When depressed, I seek
Means to accept—and be calm.
In my years to come,
And extreme conflicts present
Themselves to my sense of . . .
Awareness, where shall I turn?

Mariana Deleeuw Kasper
AUTUMN OPULENCE
The trees are clothed in regal
    robes,
Of ruby, amber, emerald, gold.
Lacy leaves flutter, then waltz
    down
Quilting the earth and muffling
    sound.

Lake waters sparkle with a ton
Of diamonds strewn there by the
    sun.
Inlets adorned with reflection
Of fall's elegant perfection.

Satin clouds grace the azure sky,
Birds cluster, then fly hurriedly
    by.
The wind is brisk and chills the
    air,
The scent of wood smoke is
    everywhere.

Tis sad the opulence must end,
Bowing to winter, barren friend.
But spring's ahead with promise
    keen,
Grand new robes in a wealth of
    green.

Florence Lappin Gorman
THE LOG
I walked the road, mine eyes were
    on the summit set,
Yet did not miss the wayside's
    beauteous show.
I did not see beyond the bord'ring
    way.
I did not hear the woodman's
    chopping swing,
When suddenly a turn, and 'cross

my path
A log is stretched, unwieldy giant
    to arrest my pace.
What shall I do? Stand still and
    wait
Until a heavier hand than mine
    removes it hence?

There is no turning back; the
    summit lies ahead.
I'll tarry for a while and patience
    learn.
In meditation will I regain pow'r.
No time for shoddy thoughts, nor
    angered mimes.
I'll stay my ruffled soul, and
    listen now
To inner sounds that beauty calls
    to wake,
Of long remembered moments
    buried deep,
Of tender words that were, and
    dreams that yet will be.

Or better still, I pray, Oh God,
Guide Thou my feet, inspire my
    will.
Give me the strength to roll the
    log aside,
And travel onward, upward to the
    summit,
        'Ere the twilight falls.

Lori J. Jamel
YOUTH, CELEBRATION OF
I'm as big as an ocean;
Small as a pea.
I live on forever;
I'm Eternity.

I laugh and I cry;
I despise and I love.
I live and I die;
I'm a fly, I'm a dove.

I'm whoever, whenever,
Just as I stand;
Whyever, Whenever,
Someday I'll land . . .

Valerie A. Small
WOMAN
The man is only human
The woman is unique
For its the woman who
Be it everything antique
For without woman
Man would never be
For woman is with man
Like sugar is with tea.

Cheryl L. Becker
TO GRAM
    [In loving memory of Mildred
    Whittemore. We miss you
    dearly.]
The time will heal my wounds,
Make sweet all the memories
Now that the light of my life;
Is out for all eternity,
Now I look at the flowers
I placed on your grave
Remembering for hours,
Love you so gladly gave,
You were the sunlight
On those cloudy days
You saw all God's beauty,
Then passed it my way.
You were my teacher,
A true friend indeed,
You showed me the light
When I couldn't see.
You gave me the strength
That I needed to grow

You were the pot of gold
At the end of my rainbow.
So I'll pass on these gifts
That you've given to me
In hope that it lifts
All sadness through eternity.
Called home to your Master
You took your place
Now I miss your laughter
The smile of your lovely face.
Now it has been so very long
I knew someday you'd be gone
But you will never completely die.
As long as I keep your memory
    alive.

Raymond Gendron
SNOW THOUGHTS
Looking through the windshield
And the snowflakes smashing
    there
Toward the white unseen horizon
That was approaching me with
    care

I listened to the quiet sound
That I heard beneath my car
Unlike the ones I heard before
When the snow was only tar

I found it easy to relax
Lulled by the mellow sounds
Which slowly would release me
From the problems I had found

It seemed like I was sealed off
From a harsh and noisy world
Protected by a natural wall
Which drifted up and swirled

I had once been in a hurry
To get where I had to go
But it became so unimportant
Since I now preferred the snow

What I had taken once for granted
And at times had even cursed
Had become for me a haven
Full of peace for which I thirst

It seemed to me quite funny
That I had allowed myself to see
That something I once had dreaded
Could have changed so pleasantly

Charles E. Germano
THESE PRECIOUS GIFTS
Have you ever thought how
    wealthy you are?
—though you are not a Queen or
    a Czar.
For when you rise during the
    birth of light,
You see flowers that were born
    during the night;
Blossoms that adorn a tree;
And grass as green as a pea.
Oh, how rich are we who can see!

To walk in summer near a garden
    wall,
When the smell of Lilacs is free
    to all.
Visiting the fields on a summer
    day,
Smelling the freshness of new
    mown hay;
The mixed perfumes of a jardinell;
And Mother's cooking at dinner
    bell.
Oh, how rich are we who can
    smell!

To hear a rooster at the crack of
    dawn;

Or the tired strains of a lazy yawn.
The reverberant roar of Niagara's
    fall;
Or natures refrain in a mating call.
The pitterpattern of a rainy
    atmosphere;
And dashing waves against a pier.
Oh, how rich are we who can hear!

To taste an apple, lusciously red;
Or enjoy delicious gingerbread.
And Mom's masterpiece, her
    apple pie.
The many flavors that satisfy.
To eat our fill, then smug-faced,
Show that flavor is not a waste.
Oh, how rich are we who can taste!

The delicate feel at a surgeons
    command;
The guiding strength of a bridle
    hand.
A masters fingers on ivory keys;
And shaking hands, a re-assuring
    squeeze.
To feel the power upon engaging
    a clutch;
The sight of man, armless and
    such.
Oh, how rich are we who can
    touch!

In the period between birth and
    death,
We are endowed with a mighty
    breath;
For those of us who can see and
    smell,
Hear and taste and touch as well—
Precious gifts that shape our
    destiny;
With a fortune in health, so
    lucky are we.

Chris Sarno-Doyle
BITS
They're bits of loving tenderness
Falling from the eyes
They're signs of love and
    sentiment
Holding no disguise

Crystal drops of all the love
Everyone has to hold
They're all the words you've
    longed to say
To someone, yet never told

For when a teardrop falls from
    someone
It falls for those they love
In sadness for their times in pain
Gladness . . . just because

Louis Bascetta
ON EVOKING CHOPIN
Free me from this flesh,
Powers inborn
in the Essence Remote;
make me a force of timeless Space;
prone, earth on my face,
webbed in the mesh
of forcible rote
I languish arhythmical and deaf.

Over the spheres of Music
life my soul redeemed
by rainbows of clefs
that skillfully dance
on tense ivory fingers
stretching from starry throne
where long ago they flew
after the bliss of islands and
    oases.

The melody still lingers
ondulating the fields of corn
and orange blossoms,
resounding mysteriously
    wholesome
within the golden soffits
for the chosen few, eternally new;
and floating myits mist
pristine my mind abandons
the slots of Time forlorn.

Deborah Ellen Dixon
PAST, PRESENT AND . . .
We come from different places.
Each of life's choices has taken us
    down separate paths.
Leading to experiences more
    dissimilar than the surrounding
    landscapes.
Winding unmarked trails
    seemingly separated by infinite
    distance.
Yet, for one fleeting moment, a
    single brief encounter,
Our paths crossed on that dark,
    obscure turn.
Leaving us disoriented, stunned,
Unsure where to turn.
Perhaps we should turn away and
    continue on alone?
Or move ahead together and see
    where the path leads?
Come take my hand—
We'll decide where to go.
Lead me to a place where time
    and past directions have no
    meaning.
Shield me with your matchless
    strength and I will lighten your
    load.
For the road is long and there is
    no resting place in sight.
And we do not know what lies
    ahead.
The present may be all we have.
So, come take my hand . . .

Ed Carpenter
**Confessions Of a
Workaholic**
Jesus Christ! I hate to go to work!
It's not that I want to shirk
    responsibility . . .
But I know I was made to do
    better things; like:
Lying in bed, tended foot to hand,
Issuing directives—"No! No!
    Etcetera, etcetera . . . I'll be
    damned!"
Signing gold-sealed papers and
    other imposing documents,
Subordinates viewing me as sage,
    all clinging to my every
    comment.
But alas, a lack of importance I
    possess;
So, before I'm late for work, I'd
    better hurry and get dressed.
And anyway, no big deal. I can
    continue my dream . . .
Sonambulistically shoved into a
    corner on the jam-packed 7:15;
Let the train's gentle, rocking sway
Roll me sweet and low to my
    swinging fantasy . . .
Holy Moley, better hurry—it's
    really getting late!
And, Christ Jesus, I hate being
    tardy, especially when it's
    payday . . ..

Fred E. Royal
IN SEARCH OF TRUTH
Walking through eons ago
Stone and paprus yielding—
Vestiges of a truth sought.

Amid arid deserts and waters of
    blue
And pottery remains of gold—
Carved out for all to see . . truth.

In lofty spires, castles and
    monasteries
Hand painted on monumental
    pages—
A glimpse of a truth still sought.

Schools of learning there were
    and be
Teachers robe donned—laying
    down the rules—
Of a truth still to be.

Dusty clouded recesses of
    research be
Where man questioned and
    tried—
What truth now to be.

Now be fine buildings and
    grounds
Young and old finely dressed and
    schooled—
Search still . . . for the everlasting
TRUTH.

Erma D. Butler
**My Soul Panteth For Thee
Psalm 42:1-9**
Why are thou cast down, oh, my
    soul?
Why art thou so sorely depressed?
For His redeemed, He has a goal;
For His people He has a rest.

His loving kindness He'll
    command
When the light grows so densely
    dim,
Then He gives a song in the night
Unto the soul that seeketh Him.

And now, no more tears nor
    sadness,
When I remember all these things;
Only the joy, peace and gladness
That His own loving kindness
    brings.

The hart pants for the water
    brook,
So panteth my soul after Thee;
To God my Rock I will now look,
For surely He'll not forget me.

Lola Currier Wheeler
MY MOTHER'S HANDS
She could be
Sitting, just across from me
Sipping tea
The way she often did.
Her hands
    Not rough
    The way one would expect
    Considering how she'd worked.
    How white they were
    In contrast to the plain gold band
    The only ring she wore.
Those hands
    I little realized
    The comfort that they brought
    The sureness of their touch
    Seldom still
    Until
The night she left us suddenly.
And now

In dreams, it seems
She lifts one hand
As if to say
"No tears . . . I won't be far away".

Julie Ann Bailey Lipman
WHAT DO YOU DO . . . ?
What do you do when your
world's fallen apart?
And the ones you love break
your heart.
Feeling as though, you had
nowhere to go.
You're alone and cold,
With no one for you to hold.
Then you find yourself walking
down,
A lonely street in a lonely town.
You wonder how you will cope,
But there is nothing to do but
wait and hope.
You now know your world has
not fallen apart,
Because you have God mending
your broken heart,
And you know that things will
turn out your way,
Because "Tomorrow is another
day"

S. Jane Bowsher
HE'S GONE
*[My Special Thanks to Dad &
Ruth E. for believing in me; To
Harvey for rekindling my
intereset in writing and to
Mike for keeping my poems all
these years.]*

He's Gone! I'm glad! He's in my
hair!
He didn't know, but he was there!
Why should I cry when he's away;
Or why is it for him I pray?

Why must I wish for his return;
Or why at night for him I yearn?
A thing of nature, so I'm told;
Experienced by young and old.

Well, not for me! I'll crack this love
And send it back to Him above.
Why waste my time; He'll never
care!
Just like I said, He's in my hair!

And as I say these heartless words
In my eyes salty tears are stirred.
For in my heart I love him still
And as God's wish, I always will.

Jennifer Jill Coleman
THE LORD AND ME
The Lord is my light.
He walks with me day and
night.
He listens to me through pain
and sorrow,
And we will talk again tomorrow.

The Lord sends the sunshine and
rain,
But He never means to cause
any pain.
When I'm weak He makes me
strong,
Even if I've done Him wrong.

When the Lord does come from
Heaven above,
I'm sure He'll look like a
beautiful dove.
I hope I will see the Lord
someday,
Because I love Him in many a
way.

The Lord has always been my
light,
Because He's always been so
right.
The Lord has always been my
treasure,
And He will live forever and
ever.

The Lord gave His son for me,
And now He wants to baptize
me.

Boris Biloskirka
lovers
when night folds around us
and daylight leaves forever;
when i lie beside you
and tomorrow must not come;
when shadows of who we are
tip toe around us, daring to
torment;
when stolen kisses are
remembered
in the sighs of quiet wanting,
and an aching hope fills each
unchosen word—
we dare not dream,
lest every dream become again
a new aching hope.
when i turn to you
and touch each strand of dimly
lit hair
and you talk of filled and
unfilled times—
nothing stirs in the night
except thunder, and some distant
rain.

slowly, an endless dream turns to
sun again.

lovers or friends
we melt into the day; waiting,
for another night
to fold around us.

Claudia B. Ramsey
MY FRIEND
Friend, how can I say it . . . so
hard
to tell you good-bye.
I find I have to go away; I may be
back on some distant day.
Don't wait for me in case I don't
show.
A distant voice is calling . . .
I cannot resist; I pack to go.
My nature's that of a
wayfarer . . .
I journey as my soul seeks the
moving;
a life I've come to know.
Shed not tears, just give me a
smile . . .
I've enjoyed the times we've
spent;
Finding mutual joy in everyday.
The laughter's been plentiful
and
happiness runs full in the cup!
Now, I look toward the setting
sun
and know my time is up.
I hear the calling of a gentle
wind;
it hurts to say good-bye my friend.

Michael John Behan
UNTITLED
Vespers in the evening sung
Hold your candle close to me
Hear the tolling of the bells
With eyes as swollen as the sea

Resting now in silent dream
No memories to mar the peace
Evening goes and morning comes
I soon shall be released

Dawn will come and hold me
there
And crystal light will find me
Sleeping in your warm embrace
In your love surviving

Wake me softly, carry me
Where shadows cannot follow
Where my heart has always been
And I will be tomorrow

Celeste M. Dever
LOVE
Love is the thread
which holds the blanket sewn
To comfort and to warm
the soul that stands alone
Love is the shoulder
which no weight can depress
It's the highest point in life;
the point of success
Love is the bond that seals
so nothing can depart
A bond that can't be broken
when the love comes from the
heart
A heart can be broken, but it can
be repaired
fitted back together by true love
two people share

Philip Robinson
NUCLEUS: HEARTBEAT
Five years of your life
have been shared with me;
such a sweet reward
Embarking upon the beginning
of not only Spring there
is Summer Fall and Winter
that start and end with you
Cemented in this mission
of loving we have carved
monuments that can be touched
and viewed
Deep is the feeling and we
gain from a need to express
ourselves; Special Forces
Crying has another dimension
known as happiness
Laughing always states a
balance needed
Recognition of space endorses
growth
Believing in love is a strong
Sense of Self
And God promises each day is as
beautiful as the next and alliance
with him the future is our forever

Ora Lee Carver
LIFE
Innocent, we enter this world,
faultless, we are here,
temptations ever present
To us, are very near
The road of life is rough,
Many a hill and turn
Many a stumbling stone,
present, for us to learn
For guidance, to God we look,
The devil is there too
He's apt to speak louder,
Wrong message, gets thru.
Our feet go astray,
One mistake we're doomed,
Some folks hit below the belt
Ready, all too soon.
Many a step falters,

Many a wrong deed done,
Many a heart is broken,
fault lies in every one
No one is all bad,
No one is all good,
No one always does
Just as they should.
Many a good deed done,
Many a heart made lighter
By just a word of praise,
Passed on by another.
Point your finger not
To any special one
Only to praise
When a deed, well done.
Let not your jealous mind
Over ride your power
anxious to destroy
But rather, to lift higher.

Helena B. King
THE PERSISTENT QUEST
I've been searching and searching
for something I had lost
And I vowed to keep on looking,
regardless of the cost.
I'd climb the highest mountain,
And I'd sail the ocean blue.
I would roam all through the
forest, if my dream would just
come true.
I'd walk out by the wayside, and
I'd look both up and down,
Thinking if perhaps I'd listen, I
might even hear a sound.
I thought that I would give up
and go on the way things are,
Or keep forever searching,
whether it be near or far.
Finally something struck me like
a bolt out of the blue.
I found what I was searching for,
and that something was you.

Janice C. Reiss
MAMA
*[For all you've given, for all
you've meant, for all you are—I
love you so—Janice]*
You've given—
Wonderful toys
Advice about boys
Nights on the town
Support when I'm down
Pretty clothes—
Yes, all of those
But most of all
And best of all
You've given—you.

You've meant—
My always knowing
I had a place to be going
To communicate—
To commiserate—
To recuperate—
To celebrate—

You are—
Wife and mother
A grand and
great-grandmother
Warm and giving
My reason for living
My first love
My best friend
My Mama—

Edna Blue
A VERNAL FLIRTATION
Spring is a coquette
promising much
but giving little.

She makes her dramatic entrance
dancing across the drab winter
  Stage,
dressed in vivid colors.
A warm south wind lifts her skirts
giving a tantalizing glimpse
of more loveliness to come.

We shed our coats and bare our
  heads
in the soft, warm breeze.
We begin to court her—

Just when it seems, that she is all
  ours,
out of the North comes Winter's
  e'erie whistle.
she listens. Then she is gone.
  Leaving us very Miserable

We go indoors once again,
  sneezing and sniffling
and wishing that we had never
  laid eyes
on the heartless hussy.
Such is spring!

Dorothy Clark
MY MOM
Who kissed my hurts, brushed
  my tears away,
  Tucked me in bed at night and
  taught me to pray?
      My Mom
Who hung up my stockings on
  Christmas Eve, loved me,
  Tho often I caused her to
  grieve?
      My Mom
Who took me to Church and
  Sunday School, taught me
  To live by the Golden Rule?
      My Mom
As I count life's treasures over
  with care
  The greatest of all I say with a
  prayer
      My Mom

Linda Lee
WINTER SIGHTS
As I stood and gazed out the
  window
The tree branches ladened with
  snow
Cast out a wintry memoire
Standing out as a momentum of
  the icy storm
Winter wonderland became a
  sculpture of patterns
All created by each flake of
  snow-blink
The sun sending down its ray
Glittering the white crust with a
  sparkling tinge
A glare a rising from the clear
  white crust of snow
Makes winter sights a theme to
  remember

Elizabeth Choate
On Being A Man—(From a Woman's Point Of View)
"Genoio boos eidi"—become what
      you are,
Being a man, a Quintessential
  drama,
Being a man, a legend obscure,
Beneath The Silence, a soul must
      endure.
Darking brooding eyes, a
  dehumanized
      self.
Goals never realized, asleep on

The shelf,
Utopia, unchallenged, a hazardous
      road,
At the point of not being, a
      monstrous load—
Must The Tiger de-tiger himself
      To exist?
Imperil himself, repress and
      resist
Amid ups and downs, The Terrain
      of cause and effect,
Behold The Tiger, he rests and
      pause and reflect.

Shirley Diane Stimpert
SHADOWS OF ME
Night shadows are over me.
  Wind blows
      Clouds flee.
I'm alone,
  alone with myself.

Try not to think
  I'll sleep if I can.
Only the night won't let me be. . .
  or is it just me?
The shadows are within my self.

Evelyn M. Byrom
THE SEEDLING
[To my son who has been my inspiration]
In life's garden of flowers—
  one must spend many hours.
Planting the seeds—
  giving all the nourishment it
  needs—
Always aware to give it constant
  loving care—
The seed of life will never become
  bare—

If planted and forgotten—
  it soon becomes sodden,
Wilted and pale—
  its life soon will fail,
Tendered and nourished—
  all life must flourish and
Like the seeds in the garden—
  if given the proper care,
We are capable of producing one
  so
  beautiful, strong and so fair.

Terri L. Lindsey
SPIRIT IN DISGUISE
A half-covered moon—
Like a masked joker, it shines
through a film of mystical haze
It glares at you like a one-eyed
  bandit,
Making you feel it's watching
  your

moves through its disguise, only
  to
reveal its partial shield into one
whole crystal ball, leaving only
  the
spirit of its once evil reflection
of your truly imaginary mind—

Carolyn A. Meighan
JEROME
[For my love, Jerome Edward Thomas Patrick (died 11/6/82). You gave me so much in our 7½ years together. I'll always love you.]
  Sitting by a crackling fire
  On a cold winter's night.
Watching the snowflakes fall,
Sharing the laughter of friends.
  These have I loved, and you.

  Running hand in hand
  Thru dew drenched fields.
A sudden thunder shower,
  And no place dry to go.
These have I loved, with you.

Walking along the beach.
Listening to the sea gulls' cries.
  The smell of the salty sea.
Lying beside you in the sand.
These have I loved, and you.

  Love growing deeper
  With each new day.
Sharing joys and sorrows.
Most of all, you, Jerome.
  These have I loved.

  And will always love.

Kathryn Marie McGuire
MUSIC OF THE CITY
It was daybreak at the Harbor.
Hungry seagulls, hovering over
  the
estuary, scanned its surface for
  scraps
  of fish among the City's
  sewage.

Deep, mournful hornblasts from
  the busy,
  chugging tugs mingled with
  rising street noises.
The ever-present strident gulls
      shrieked.

The Overture to the City
  Symphony
      had begun.

Kenny D. Merritt
A SWEET SENSATION
You know you give me that
  sweet sensation.
  You and your love are my
  sweet sensation.

You were a blond working in a
  cafe,
  I'd never seen a prettier girl to
  that day.
You caught my eye and you
  caught my heart.
  I's blind from my love, I say
  right from the start.

You gave me your name and I
  gave you mine.
  You got off of work without
  wasting no time.
We made it to the movies, we
  made it till the end.
  And then, in the replay, we
  made it again.

Just stay with me, love. I'll give
  you things.
  You give me spirit like
  something with wings.
Show me your beauty and show
  me your soul.
  Show me your passion burns
  hotter than coal.

You've caught my love with your
  sweet sensation.
  We're gonna win with that
  sweet sensation.
      We're sure to cling to that
      sweet sensation.
          Give me your love and
          that sweet sensation.

Raydene Edenhofer
DEFINITION OF A POEM
A poem is a feeling
an idea
an expression.
A poem is a group of words
leaving
an impression.

Ethelle Stevens
MOMMIE CAME HOME
My little Darling, the puppy and
  me,
At home alone just us three.
She cry and cry, and nothing
  seems
to satisfy, so I tell her this lie
I say, "your mommie soon will be
  home".

Your Mommie soon will be home.
Oh, how it hurt me inside when I
  tell
this lie. Last Sunday her Mommie
died.

Last night she cried and cried.
All night long she cried.
At the break of day I heard her
  say, Oh Mommie you came back
  home,
Oh Mommie you came back
  home,
I have been so all alone.
Mommie please don't go and
  leave me any
more. I am so glad you came back
  home.

My little Darling no longer cried
on her face there was a smile
as I kneeled by her bed, I knew
  she was
dead. Yes Mommie came back
  home.

Vicki Lynn Marus
INNER MELODY OF LOVE
The music flowed from your
  fingertips
strumming the strings of my
  heart, oh, so carefully
sensing the pain that had been
  deep inside
for so long, that it was slow to
  leave.
  Gentle images of light breeze
  ruffling the bay
into ripples of consuming passion
reflecting the moonlight into
  pools of brightness
filtering through your eyes.

Of fiery passion exploding in my
  limbs
  moving to the rhythm of your
  fingers

playing over the sad, sweet
melody of
my secret dreams and fantasies.

The music that has set my soul
free is
the rapture of knowing you as
my friend,
of knowing you as my lover
who steals into the chink of
armor that
I have built up.
Knowing that you have the
power to accomplish
this daring act of defiance
is as the gentle strumming
that you do
to my magical heart
strings, has made me
free
to love.

Shirley Baisden Griffin
My Answer
I used to spend much of my time
thinking about the mystery of
life—
To wonder why some of us had
joy,
and some of us too much strife.

I wondered why I should push
hard,
to try to be my best—
That it would all go up in smoke
when I'm finally laid to rest.

Then with a knowing from deep
inside,
I saw a Master Plan—
That there was a reason for
everything
even a reason for Man!

That life does not go up in smoke,
it just leaves like the night—
That life is not completely gone,
it just goes out of sight!

Our loved ones are not gone
forever—
we will all meet again one day.
He will gently lead us by the
hand,
until we find the way.

The important part of our life
is not our time spent here.
It's when we get to the other side
and know that He is near.

Now when I asked if I'm afraid to
die,
of going on alone,
I tell them I won't be by myself,
I'll just be going Home!

Chi Stewart
THE REALITY OF YOU
The reality of you flows slowly
away from me
Like a small secret stream
silently gliding over
The rough pebbles of your pain
unfaced.

I am grieving over
disappointments strewn in my
path
from unmet expectations.
And through the quiet hidden
tears
I see you as you are—
as you see yourself
A being so outwardly strong,
So inwardly wanting of courage.

And gradually the reality of you
Slips from my hand and yours
And we become lost from one
another.
Pride increases the distance in
moment-years.

(These bonds are too old to be
broken at will and I can never
go until I have absorbed all
that the experience of you
teaches me about myself.)

And so I stand sadly
And angrily on the banks of this
river
Grounded in my own life forces
As the reality of you vanishes
before me.

Barbara M. Ackerman
TO MY FAMILY
I wanted to write a poem
to show how much my family
means to me,
but putting feelings into words is
harder than it seems.
The memories of yesteryear will
be with me forever
and I know deep inside, we'll
always be together.
There are many different kinds of
love, this I know is true
But the strongest kind in this
world, is the kind I feel for you.
You've taught me how to live,
how not to take, but how to
give.
You've also taught me how to see
the different kinds of people
there can be.
I know how much it means to
share
and how to give, and how to care.
I know what it is to understand,
and how to lend a helping hand.
I've learned to accept life for what
it *is*, and not what it *should* be,
and through it all, you've helped
me see
the best thing in life to be, is me.
We've been through waters thick
and thin, but yet,
I just cannot begin
to thank you for those wonderful
days
with your loving touch and
caring ways.
So I just want to let you know,
that I Love you more than these
words can ever show.

Eugene E. Trujillo
SOJOURN . . .
Sitting here alone I wonder,
Real pictures seem to vanish
And the wonderful moments
become my memories.
I once again know this is another
world . . .

I drift away to a time
of happiness
of no wars and
of literally no hate . . .

I can see the friendship
Embracing me close,
Chasing away the tears and
Tenderly my fears, too . . .

When all these things plus more
makes
My mind feel like clouds, floating

And Heaven for a moment
I almost believe . . .

Then slowly reality burns my eyes
I awaken for He reassures me.

Juanita J. Salyers
NATURE'S SYMPHONY
Early morning with my window
open,
I can hear nature's symphony.
It's music to me, listening to
the
birds sing in the trees.
The owl, blue jays, red birds
and other
birds I know not their name.
They all harmonize together
just
the same.
The frogs croak, the crickets
make their
sound, there's even a
whippoorwill.
A chicken clucking to her
bitties, the
rooster crowing on the side of the
hill.
The rain is drizzling down
slowly,
it's a refreshing sound.
And it makes everything bright
and
beautiful as it falls to the ground.
To top off the symphony, I hear
the
sound of the clock ticking on the
wall.
Where else but in the country
can you
find nature's symphony after all.

Irma Clark
SNOW
Fuzzy little snowflakes
Flitting through the air
Makes a whitened landscape
Spreading everywhere.

Coming little faster
More as moments fly
Heaping upon each other
Till in a drift you lie.

Covering every mark
Erasing every stain
Filling roads and ditches
And the path in the lane.

Ladened on the trees
Giving a beautiful dress
Covering unlovely boughs
Putting all to rest.

Santos L. Rangel Jr.
**The Darkness Of My
Dreams**
*[Dedicated to a very special
friend, Miss Jill Willbanks. To
Toni Arnold, Thank you. And
to all the wonderful people of
the world.]*
I have a dream

In the years to come
In a far off place

Someday I will be a star.

When I die there will be a star in
the heavens to stand for me
The light it shines will be
a sign of the light I could
never shine.
The galaxy that will hold it
will be the crowd that I

could never fit into.
The glow that it will glow
the love that I never let show.
The warmth of my star will
represent
the warmness in my heart
that could hold a thousand
suns.
The darkness it will exist in
is the darkness that will
exist within me.

If you should ever look and see me

You will see what once I saw . . .
The twinkle that was never
in my eye.

The glitter in your eye
The happiness in your smile

I will light your darkened path
as you have lightened mine.

The twinkle that I saw in your
eyes
The darkness you saw in mine

Weep no tear for me.

I will meet my destiny.

Destiny itself is within the stars.

In the years to come
In a far off place
Someday I will be a star.

Carol Gerken Merritt
MY CATHEDRAL
[for Mom, 1982]
My cathedral has no show of
stained-glass splendor,
No cold stone or steel rising to
the sky,
No choir loft at top of winding
stair,
No organ strains or pealing bells
to fill the air,
No throngs of people, heads
bowed in prayer.

My cathedral is bathed in leaf-
filtered sunlight
of a soft and greenish hue.
Myriads of trees reach
heavenward
whispering at every stirring
breeze.
Birdsongs proclaim each day's
glory,
some muted, many lilting,
others shrill.
I stand on a mossy carpet in awe
and wonder
as I contemplate God's will
In my lovely woodland cathedral
on a farm named Locust Hill.

Lula Cheek
RELIANCE
Knowing my children were
taking a flight,
I could hardly sleep at all last
night.
I feared the plane, I feared the fog,
Seemed I had no faith at all!

Then taking myself firmly in
hand,
I called on the Lord and heard His
command . . .
To rely on His promises wherever
we are
For He is the same yesterday,
today and tomorrow!
He is the one who calmed the Sea
... Walked the shores of Galilee ...

Surely then He flies the plane,
Tho the pilot bears another name.
He is not limited by time nor space,
We are enfolded by his grace.

So if we travel by car or plane,
Secure are we who bear His Name.
The pilot has faith in ground controls,
We, on Him, who our future holds.

Georgeann Reid
COOKIE
My little doggie we got as a pup
she was the cutest one of a litter
· of three
She was brown with some black
and we named her because she
looked like a cookie

Not sure of where she was
she was quiet and shy at first
But then she knew she'd found a home
full of the best kind of love and
not the worst

She grew up to be
the best dog I ever had
She was always a good dog
and was seldom bad

She was a smart dog
She knew how I felt when I was sad
and she liked to comfort me
She was there as a friend to help
me feel glad

She would lick my face
She'd bring me her toy
I would throw it for her
and that would bring her joy

She liked to eat what we ate
and she'd sit by the table and cry
She'd give you such a sad face
that you'd just feed her and then
you'd sigh

She was an affectionate dog
and she would greet you with a
kiss
She would always show you her love
and that is what I will mostly miss

My little doggie who was a friend
at best
has now gone to her eternal rest
The one who once ate a bone has
now left me all alone
My little doggie is dead and gone
And she will never wake again to
see another day dawn

Dean E. Balsiger
The Magic Of Your Love
They say that magic is just an illusion,
A slight of the hand in the midst
of confusion.
But the magic of your love is
certainly real—
Not held in my hand but the way
my heart feels.

Your magic will touch me forever
in time
Working its wonders on my body
and mind.
It's not something solid, it ebbs
and it flows
It comes through your smile from
the depths of your soul.

It touches me softly like a warm
gentle breeze
And lights up my life, like the
sun through the trees.
Like a warm summer sunset it
caresses my soul
And fills in the pieces that make
me feel whole.

Your love is pure magic, of that
there's no doubt
The magic in my life, I can't live
without.
Keep working that magic the rest
of your life
And I'll love you forever, my
sweetheart, my wife.

D.J. Bowman
MEADOWS OF GREEN
Meadows of green are
wide, open, and free.
Meadows of green are
fun to run and play
in.
Meadows of green were
made for you for
me.
Meadows of green are a
wild and beautiful
thing.

Margaret McGlaughlin
CHRISTMAS IS SPECIAL
There's glowing beauty decking
Christmas . . .

the tinselled tree, the mistletoe,
the hearthside flame, the
starspun snow.

There's a certain joy at
Christmas . . .

reflected in the children's eyes
with every secret and surprise.

There's something special found at
Christmas . . .

Eternal Love, a radiant star,
its shine,

the angel's songs,
a Child Divine.

Marcella Ann Tindell Box
THE LITTLE CYPRESS TREE
*[To our beloved father, Ralph
Edward Tindell, who planted
this cypress in 1964. We are
still its caretakers Dad—Love,
Marcella, Patricia, Lee, Edward,
and Raymond.]*
The phoning was left up solely to
me,
As my Dad wanted a cypress tree.
With phone book in hand, I
called all nurseries near,
Attempting to locate that tree so
dear.
It was to be healthy and green,
and at least six feet tall,
Or my dear ole Dad didn't want it
at all.
"I've found one," I said, "and the
price is just right!"
Out of the house we all flew; it
was planted that night.
Dad said, "This tree will need a
lot of loving care,
And all five of you , my children,
this chore you will share."
We all laughed at the idea of
caring for this tree,
But our dear ole Dad had said

it seriously.
We watered and groomed it, and
kept it free from bugs,
It was given everything short of a
loving hug.
The tree grew to seven, eight,
then ten feet tall—
It seemed to thrive on the love
given by us all.
The years have passed by, and
my, how it's grown;
We're all adults now, and are out
on our own.
My dad, now with God, must be
happy watching me,
As I point and say, "Look son,
that's your Grandpa's tree."
The tree, now majestic, still
reaching for the sky,
Seems to be touching my Dad's
love by growing so high.

Betty Coopper
AIR POLLUTION
There is a problem in our land;
    We call it air pollution.
We must all do what we can
    To find a good solution.

It comes from factories, homes,
    and cars;
    And covers all our nation.
It goes beyond the highest stars
    And threatens earth's creation.

The air is filled with smoke and
    fog;
    The earth with dust and dirt.
Everywhere we look there's smog;
    I'm sure it must hurt.

To rid the air of all pollution;
    Will take a lot of work.
Let's make a resolution
    Our duty we won't shirk.

Randy Gamble,
Farewell To the Marxs,
There lived four men many years
    ago,
Who brought us joy at the
    picture show,
They made us laugh when times
    were bad,
they stopped our tears when we
    were sad,
They made us forget the trouble
    we were in,
they helped us to laugh time and
    time again,
But now we must say Farewell to
    the trio of four,
And wish them a tear and a laugh
    that shall last forever more.

Patricia Ann Lee
THE GREAT ARTIST
My Father was an artist,
The greatest of them all.
Yet He never owned a paint brush
Large nor small.

He didn't waste money on easels
    or paint,
He didn't have to.
With just a gesture of His hands,
Or nod of His head, He drew in
    rivers,
And painted the sky of blue.

He painted purple mountains of
    majesty,
Rainbows in green lanes.
Deserts of gray and gold
And white clouds to bring us rain.

He hung the stars, painted beauty
    of all kinds,
While baby angels played at His
    feet.
Then when He had finished His
    great masterpiece
He painted man into His mind.

"Was your Father a Magician?",
    you ask.
And I smile and nod,
"Yes my Father was all things, for
    you see"
My Father was, "The Son of God".

Roy Russell Morgan
YOU ARE NOT THE ONE
Thou dost not love me—I know
    the score;
Thou lovest another, much,
    much more,
Though I love you much more
    than he,
He shares thy love and memories!

But if thou carest for me at all,
Then I will by thy beck and call;
But listen close to what I tell,
Bid not to me a cold "farewell"!

Though other hearts have known
    the love
Of these two eyes you were
    above
Tis all in vain and they grieve for
    me
For I am weary, and grieve for
    thee!

Celia L. Hooper
INVESTMENTS
A part of me no longer lives,
    Yet inside me remains
    A wisdom to carry on—
But marbled feelings sing no song.

My soul has grown enough to die,
    Has bled an art through empty
    tear.
Still, upon its passing in my
    ninteenth year,
Youth failed to claim,
    "Goodbye."

Love's wings bid away my heart,
But left behind my mind
    With a silence that speaks the
    most of all:

"No one can own the part of me
    that's mine;

WOMAN, OF MANY GUISES . . .

Daniel Luevano
THE WORDS FROM ME
The words from me to you
Such simple words to say,
But such powerful words—a gift
    from you
Is all you have to say.

Irene Stalcup
SLAVE TO RULER
This dreamer in a coat of many
    colors
Envied by his older brothers
Threw him in a pit, ha the end of
    it,
An aged father nearing the end,
Grief stricken; How do without
    him?

Sold to travelers from a strange
    land
Arrived; the marketplace was
    busy

he was put on a stand; Shoppers
felt his muscles, the strength
in his hands,
A captain guard yelled; I'll buy
him for my slave man!

A manager position to oversee all,
The master's wife plotted his
downfall,
Fleeing, he cried; my soul's
integrity
Can not be sold; for any amount
of gold.

Into a dark prison, he was cast,
Deliverance, long awaited, came
at last,
Destiny working on time
From slave to ruler; he did climb.

*Harriet Croskrey
& Bonnie Throckmorton*
HOPELESS
I feel so very helpless, afraid to
even try,
It's all I can do, to not just sit and
cry.
As sure I seem to stumble, as
darkness follows day.
I do not know the answers, I can
not find my way.
Life in me is empty, no hope
within my sight,
I am so very tired, I can't take
another fight.

The world has no love for me,
Least ways, not that I can see.
I feel so very sad inside,
That sometimes I just wish I'd die.
I am so all alone it seems,
Life is just, one long bad dream.

Janet E. Sims
THE DARE
The rose blooms late this year,
The tears shatter the serene
stillness
of the day and fill the darkness
with
a daring challenge:

to meet the future,
yet hold in awe the past,
and be prepared for the present.

The rose wilts, its petals buried
beneath the crust of ice and
snow.
I bury my fingers in midst of this
formidable
blanket of change, and stepping
back,

breathe the hostile wind,
inhale its inexhaustible fury,
and take the dare.

Jeannie Hodges
MY NEW BOY
This guy, he's tall and lean,
a real softie, but thinks he's mean!

He plays hard and rides well,
he likes stories, the kind he can
tell,

Made bigger and wild, seen
through
the eyes of a child.

He came to me only at four, I
remember
when he walked through the door.

Shy, quiet and meek, afraid of the
lady he had to meet.

It was hard for me and I'm sure
he'd
agree,
A feeling was there, it was in the
air.

Another change came at nine. He
left one
nest and came to mine.

He seems happy and content, we
spend time
together, time well spent.

This guy, he's a real joy.
He's cool, neat, a typical boy.

Tho' not always good, but never
really
bad,

He's just himself, good old Chad!

Rich Corvin
BEING
*[For my Mother and Father, the
rays of sunshine of my being.]*
Being a son
Growing with love;
Returning as much.

Being a brother,
Learning together
To live.

Being a friend
Extending a hand,
Secrets and such.

Being a man:
Responsibility,
So much to give.

Being a father,
A life began.
Being alive—I am.

Janet Smith
DECAY
Ashes to ashes.
Dust to dust.
Stone to sand.
Iron to rust.

Apples to pulp.
Bread to crust.
Boards to splinters.
Trust to disgust.

Charity to greed.
Faith to distrust.
Honor to degradation.
Love to lust.

Sheryl Sami Bias
LOVE
Funny, how as we get older our
parents get smarter.
Why didn't I notice before, could
it be I'm a late starter?
It's not that you're really starting
so slow,
It's just that it's a long road down
which you must go.

When I was young it was so hard
to see,
That everything Mom did, she
did for me.
Whether right or wrong, weak or
strong, I never lost her love.
And as I got older I learned her
secret came from "up above".

I watch my own children out at
play,
And my thoughts go back to
yesterday.
Suddenly everything seems to

fall into place.
Then I thought of all the time I'd
lost, and it seems such a waste.

Isn't God's love for us so Great?!
As my mother used to say, "You
just wait,"
"When you have your own
children you'll surely know,"
"Just how very much I Love You
So!"

We look at God's wonders, the
flowers and trees.
And the children want to know,
"How much does He love me?"
It truly warms my heart to be
able to tell them how much he
does,
            Jesus said,
        "I Love You This Much"
And spread his arms and died for
            us—

Margaret Jenkins
FACTS OF LIFE
I wish I could tell
   this feeling inside
      of fear—
of hope that I'm right
   in leaving you
      and turning to him.

What do I feel?
   A wish
      that you would have
done more,
   loved me,
      and kept me with you.

Is this the dread a baby has
   just before birth?
Is this how I'll feel
   before leaving this earth?

It's too late to turn back,
   and I wouldn't turn back—
      I couldn't turn back.

I just wonder
   how you'll do
      without your love—
because I was
   and am,
      your love.

I face the facts, here alone in my
bed,
I wish it could have been you,
instead!

Maleese Wood
SONG OF SPRING
Today I heard a robin sing
   Heralding the coming spring
A song of exultation to the sky
   An ode to earth's awakening

I saw a willow on the hill
   It's branches greening in the sun
And all the earth seemed hushed
and still
   And sleeping streams began to
run

I heard a softly rising breeze
   Whispering through the grass
Singing through the still-bare
trees
   Waiting, winter's chill to pass

I saw the sun, so bright and warm
   Warming the earth after the rain
The shy buds and leaves, no frost
to harm
   At least, at last, it's spring
again.

Glenda Moser
BUNDLE OF JOY
Small, defenseless, warm, and
longing for love. Such an
adventure awaits in your arms.
Arms that shut out all the
wrong your coming has caused.
Society's out cries of shame,
others indignation of right and
wrong. Together we'll fight the
world caring not the cost,
daring not to count the pain.
Gentle little bundle—hate not
the wrong done to you. Simply
know I could not give you up
because it was the easier way
to do things.
Now we take up our own tasks,
each only having the other and
a world to conquer.

Connie Russell
TRUE LOVE
I ask not to be fed with rich foods,
   only to be nourished by your
   faith and understanding.
I ask not to be clothed in royal
gowns,
   only to be woven and
   fabricated to maturity.
I ask not to be jeweled with gold
and silver,
   only to be adorned by your love.
I ask not to be contained by your
home,
   only to be locked into your trust.
I ask not to be flooded by your
wealth,
   only to be thankful for the
   memories.

Ida C. Aguero
THEE
How do I love thee?
Let me count the ways.
I love thee with all my heart.
I love thee with the soul in my
body.
I love thee when I pray and when
I don't.
I love thee in the forest where
there is liveliness.
I love thee in the depthness of
the ocean and the sea.
I love thee in so many good,
happy ways.
I can't count how many way's I
love thee.
But, most of all I love thee with
all the love in me.

Stevie Jo Steiner
GOD IS
*[We are, because He Is, and will
for ever Be. This poem is for
anyone who ever loved or
helped a special child.]*
Where is God! So often I've cried,
Buried so deep under money and
pride.

And so I looked and finally found,
One good man whose judgment
was sound.

With the kindest heart and the
gentlest smile,
His heart overflowing with love
for a child.

There aren't so many, in the
world you know,
With the courage and wisdom it
takes to show,

Unchanging kindness that is
required,
To help a child already tired,

Of a world that doesn't seem to
know:
How much he's learned,
How hard he's tried!
How little he's praised,
How often he's cried!

Oh but Lord! Please help me to
look,
Not just in a church, a song, or a
book.

Because My Lord, the answer lies,
In the heart of a good man and a
little ones eyes.

Rev. Winn A. Hord
THE TWELVETH ROSE
*[I dedicate this poem to my
loving wife Dorcas for her
dedication to me as my wife
and good mother to our
children, Mike, Carolyn, Dale,
Greg and Brian. She has been a
great help in times of despair
and turmoil. Love, Winn]*
I was going to buy twelve roses
Darling for you today
But when I stopped and
considered
I didn't have money to pay.

It's a custom to buy twelve you say
But I figured eleven would do
Because if you look in the mirror
You'll find the twelveth is you.

So instead I bought you a card
With roses on the front cover
It's sent to the one I love
You sweetheart, no other.

Karen Margaret Wahl
CHANGED BY RAIN
*[For Ty, a loving companion on
the great journey]*
An orchard thick and
Crisp in yellow autumn
Apples, red and
Round
Healthy, hanging hard on full
trees.
Then there are those of us
Who stay the same
Day after day, but me
You and the autumn orchard
Are changed by rain
Apples glisten, fall
And sensitive souls
Unfold.

Sharon Benton French
LAND OF THE FREE
What happened to the "good old
U.S. of A.?"
They say that it's, "land of the
free, home of the brave".

I know we're still free, but we've
got rules we must uphold.
And if we don't, our children's
America may fold.

When traveling we're free to go
wherever we please,
If we can find the gas and then
afford such a dream.

In the privacy of our homes we
can laugh or we can frown,
Just keep on your sweaters and
turn the thermostat down.

When summer gets here we're
glad to get warm,
But then its too hot and that does
its harm.

We must turn out some lights
and cut down on our bills,
Ride in carpools to work and hear
how everyone feels.

I guess we are spoiled, but what
can we do?
That's the way we were raised,
and our kids are too.

So we must follow the rules and
bear it with a grin,
And teach these new rules to our
new coming kin.

Life is not all roses . . . Wherever
we live.
We can't always take and never
want to give.

So if we give up some things and
want a little less,
There will be some left for our
kids, and may God richly
bless. . .

America, "Land of the free, home
of the brave"!

Maxine Heinze Cotton
RELIGION
There is a silver chalice on the
mantlepiece

And its name is Religion.

You must not stand too close to
it,
Because it is pure and perfect
silver;
And if you touch it,
It will become tarnished.

If you breathe on it, it will
become discolored.

You must speak only in whispers
When you are near it,
For only the dead are revered
here,
And they care not about the
things
With which you are concerned.

You must not disturb their
eternal sleep.

You may not look inside the
chalice,
For it is filled with little black
spiders,
And they know things
That you are not ready to
know.
You must never touch the
spiders,
For if you do, a miracle may
happen . . .

And you don't believe in mircles.

Doris Estelle Evans
THESE BEAUTIFUL TREES
We rejoice in jubilee
As humble as the bumblebee
With the beauties of Spring
The rhythm rings
The trees—I have loved so long
As an old love song
Gives peace and faith—over the
years
Soothes and calms our fears
And wipes away our tears
These beautiful trees

Their simplicity and serenity be
A way of life at ease
In their dappled shade and breeze
Their lacy and emerald leaves
For the peaceful, please
In their graceful foliage, we see
God's grace in these beautiful trees

W. C. Clement
ANGEL—NURSE
Were You the "Angel—Nurse"
Who Came to Me last night,
And with Your Touch of Healing,
Made this Day So Bright?
Were You the Angelic Nightingale,
Who Traced that Mercy Hall,
And with Your Unselfish
Devotion,
Responded to My Every Call?
Shadow Those Who Walk Before
You
In Service, Age or Honored Name,
Carry High the Torch They Hand
You,
Lit at Christ's Immortal Flame.
Sister to Sister the Torch should
Pass,
This is the Historic Proven Plan,
Keeping Warm Christ's Deep
Compassion
For the Healing Needs of
Suffering Man.
We Pray for Miracles of Healing
and Comfort,
As We Observe Our pains and
griefs not few,
But These Miracles seldom are
Felt,
Unless Administered by "Angel—
Nurses" like You.

June B. Johnson
DAY GONE BY
Where did it go, that day gone by?
So fast and swift it seemed to fly!
Though eager once to have it
pass;
Would rather now that it might
last.
While older I grow each day is
more dear,
As days turn to weeks and
months to years.
When a child the day seemed
twice as long;
How could I have been so wrong?
For now I don't even find the
time,
To steal a moment and call it
mine.

Marjorie Burney Willis
The Beautiful Awakening
*[Dedicated to my son, Charles
Willis Jr. In appreciation of his
close walk with God.]*
I dwelt in silence . . . without joy,
Without music or song,
Like a violin stored on a shelf,
Until the Master came along
And tuned the discord of my
heartstrings
For beautiful melodies unknown
to myself.

My life was without a dream;
I was without a guide,
Like a lonely puppet on a string,
Until the Master stood by my
side,
Awakening me from a sleeping
stupor,

Teaching me to lift upward and
sing.

My world was without light;
I was blind to the great
promises of life,
Like a worm in the dust of the
earth,
Until the Master lifted me
above the strife,
Above the agony of failure and
heartbreak,
To a shining world where life
finds its worth.

Stephen Anthony Sielsky
PATRICIA
Patricia
    Like seasons of the year
    Memories always clear
    Soothing to reaction
    Never a caption
    Polite with thought
    Sought
    Always for perfection
    Positive in direction
With purpose and a touch of class
    Complete with sass
As if the sun hesitates waiting
    her day
Emotions give the size of her heart
    Away
Patricia

Cynthia Hill
BABY ANGEL
Oh, Lord when I awake to see
A little angel next to me,
  A blondish—blue—eyed baby
girl
Who's more to me than all the
world.

Her face shines as the sun above
And you can tell that she is love.
  The disposition she displays,
  I hope it lasts throughout
always.

I grow inside each day she's here:
The laughter we share, the talks,
  the tears.
  I feel she loves me with all her
heart
  And never will nothing tear us
apart.

Peggy J. Smith
WHERE IS MY LOVE?
Some distant day, when I have
long departed,
You may be reading fragments of
a verse
Which I have written, and, in
your own poetic heart,
You'll know that it was written
just for you!

Where is my love? In some far
corner of the sky, a little bluet
In a field of blue, with eyes a sea
of misty wonderment?
Is he the jonquil breaking
through in Spring,
Or angel choruses, whose voices
sing
The Glories of all love?

In every breath I take, is he!
The very heart of me!
The eyes with which I see!

In pure white diamond crystal
snow, in many coloured
rainbows,
Row on row, I see him!

Here! There!
And everywhere!

My love is brilliant light!
Eyes never dim!
The wonder of my heart in him!

Where is my love? Is he a
symphony I hear, beneath a
starlit
Sky, as horns and flutes and
violins touch my Soul,
While I sit quietly, in prayerful
contemplation,
The music and the night my
inspiration!?

Where is my love? Is he the hot
and tingling sand along a
beach,
Leading me down to touch my
aching limbs into the ocean's
surf
In summer heat?

Or will the cool and quiet of an
evening sky
Take me to his heart
As moonbeams fall, catching me
in their web.
Or have we ever really been
apart?

Ah, no! For love like this is
brilliant light; eyes never dim!
The wonder of my heart in him!
'Tis like the beauty of a dew
kissed rose!
This much, and more, the poet
knows!

And prays that you will, too.

Edwin R. Scott
WINNIE
Winnie, I'm like a child in
playland,
With just a touch of your hand.
So blue and so true,
Winnie, its you.

Winnie, you are a burst of
starlight,
On a dark and starless night.
So blue and so true,
Winnie, its you.

What joy you bring me,
You're honey to a bee.
Sweet, warm and tender,
Winnie surrender.

Winnie, you are a glow of sunray,
On a cold and cloudy day.
So blue and so true,
Winnie, its you.

Dr. Linda M. Parks, Ph. D.
ONLY A POEM
"Darkness fills the sky of blue
In a cloudy, misty hue,
Then across the sky—a gleam
The silence broken by a scream!

It has started early this day
The roar of guns seemed to say,
Get up, get up, fight! Don't run
Come on, get up! The war's
begun!

Why do we kill and have to fight?
Tell me the reasons, tell me it's
right.
Can't we settle differences
another way?
Than by taking so many lives
every day.

Well, no more for me—yes, I'm
through
I'll leave all the fighting to you,
Look out boy! Duck your head!
Slow down, doc, it's too late, he's
dead!
Hey, he was writing a poem.
What's it say?
It's about the war. Just throw it
away!"

Bridget Auenson Burnett
HERE ALL ALONG
I've always dreamed of
mountaintops
I felt that they were home
I wanted to climb the highest hill
And make the journey alone

I knew up there
Was where I belong
For that's where I thought God
lives
I wanted to be near His Throne

I had the right idea
But it was all too wrong
For, you see, God is here with me
And He's been here all along

Eudine Mills Gee
DECISION
Both friend and ship comprise
friendship;
Delete the friend and ship remains.
There are two courses left for it—
To anchor or to drift away.
Since hold has now been broken
down,
The ship of life must launch on
sea;
But where I do not really know
As fellowship exists no more.

With tears I say farewell to you,
But know your gladness now
resides—
For me all is finality.
I cannot bear the surging storm,
As pathway has no safe
roadstead.
Alone and friendless, barque does
drift
Into the vast and dark unknown.
May Godward search refresh the
soul.

Gerda Brodnax
The Children Must Play
To those whose children are of
different colors
know that the children must play
so they will not be concerned
with the color of their skins
for He has given many colors on
this earth
and if the children ask why their
colors are different
you must tell them it is because
God has created them thus
so young and old will understand.

Deborah Marshall
FIRE AT SEA
The boy stood on the burning
deck,
in awesome of the flames.
Should he jump or stand his
ground
Then the answer came.

A little voice said, "Take a jump!"
Another voice said, "Stay!"
And as the ship was sinking low,
a tide swept him away.

He swam and swam for many
days,
the sea was cold and rough.
He got too tired to travel on,
so, finally he gave up.

He sank just like the burning
ship,
seawater filled his soul.
He drowned into a pool of blue,
Inside a deadly hole.

Maurine Gentry Virden
WAIT ON THE LORD
I know we all grow weary,
waiting along the way.
But remember GOD has you in
HIS plan, just trust and obey.
We may not see the beauty, He
holds in the shadow of His
hand,
But all things work together,
some day we will understand.

He took thirty years to prepare
HIS own SON, for what HE
planned for HIM to do.
So why should we think HE is
not planning, the best for our
life
all the way through.
So let us learn patience and faith,
and wait upon The LORD,
How glorious the final plan, what
deep the love in HIS Blessed
WORD—,
When we meet HIM Up There in
one accord.

Sadie C. Laurent
ATLANTA'S SORROW
Horror like a pall, a black veil
hovers
over all—a mad dog gone mad,
out to kill.
Our children missing—,dead.
We shed tears, moan and pray—
Forever implanted, in our hearts,
our minds
weighed with broken dreams, our
hearts;
squeezed dry— they had loving,
care, there must be a reason—why?
A day of reckoning to come—
They did not live to grow up—to
know achievment, knowledge
in a given field,
We miss their hugs, and kisses,
smiling faces,
and growing up.
They won't get to laugh, romp,
sing and dance,
with loving friends;
We are so lonely, we gave our all,
and what
do we have?—We are so lonely—
so sad—
Borken dreams of horror—
mingled with tears,
lonilness, in tomorrow.

Dee Keen
MY SON, MY SON
*[I would like to dedicate this
poem to my three sons, Kevin,
Phil, and Dennis, who have
given me the most enjoyable
and unforgettable experiences
of my life.]*
My son, my son, what have I done?
Will it ever all be right?
Will you grow old still loving me,
Or will I slowly fade out of sight?

Is there really an answer,
To this thing called "Motherhood"?
Does every mother, at one time
or another,
Feel unloved and misunderstood?

If experiences in rearing children
Were merits in God's great bank,
I would have the largest castle
And a four star angel's rank.

Ouida Adams Autin
OH MIGHTY SEA
*[To my husband Gilmay and
daughter Arlene. Thank you for
putting up with a dreamer.]*
As I sit here looking at the sea,
I keep wondering what it will
bestow to me.
Will it be a Cockle, so shiny and
fair,
Or will it be a Lovely Slit Shell,
so beautiful and rare?
Will it be a Volute, of which I am
fond,
Or will it be a Murex with its
frilly fronds?
Oh, mighty, mighty sea of blue,
The answers are known only by
you.

Genevieve Sanderson
A SHATTERED MEMORY
I had a love, another year
Brilliant he was, and without fear
A rapier wit, a suave escort
Light of foot, and warm of heart
Upon the roofs the Doves do coo
With love the same as I gave you

Again my heart turned to the sun
Of your arms, my beloved one
Only to find another has taken
his place
DRINK now engulfs the mind,
defiles the face
The one I knew is gone from me
A stranger stands where he used
to be
My eagle does no longer soar
A cold cruel reptile, forever more

Billy F. Hicks
SHE DID IT
*[Dedicated to my wife, Anna
Hicks, President Arkansas
Federation Business
Professional Womens Clubs]*
Someone said that it couldn't be
done
But she, with a chuckle, replied.
That maybe it couldn't but she
would be one
Who wouldn' say so till she'd
tried.

So she buckled right in with the
trace of a grin on her face
If she worried she hid it.
She started to sing as she tackled
the thing
That couldn't be done, and she
did it.

Somebody scoffed: "Oh, you'll
never do that:
At least no one ever has done it."
But she took off her coat and she
took off her hat.
And the first thing we knew she'd
begun it.

With the lift of her chin and a bit
of a grin,
Without any doubting or quitting

She started to sing as she tackled
    the thing
That couldn't be done, and she
    did it.

There are thousands to tell you it
    cannot be done,
There are thousands to prophesy
    failure;
There are thousands to point out
    to you, one by one,
The dangers that wait to assail
    you.

But just buckle in with a bit of a
    grin,
Just take off your coat and go to it;
Just start to sing as you tackle
    the thing
That "cannot be done," and you'll
    do it.

Pamela Pfaffendorf
SEASONS OF OUR LIFE
It is summer, the sun shinning, a
    lovely day. It signifies "life" or
    so it would seem. The summer
    of our life—sometimes so
    beautiful it seems like a dream.
    But, as we know dreams must
    end, and we are brought back
    to reality—and so it is with
    life. Even though it seems like
    a dream, we have to realize—
    there will be an end—there
    will be death. It is the winter of
    our life. One must do as they
    do in a seasonal winter—try
    extra hard to survive,
    remember the warm summer
    days—and hold on to those
    memories, until lifes sun
    shines again.
The sun will shine again.

Trina L. Scott
WINTER
    Winter is not very fun
    I'd rather have the big sun
In really bad weather
    You need more than a
    sweater
    Oh, please wear a heavy coat
And don't drink an ice cream
    float.

Regina Conrath
THE SCOURGE HE FIGHTS
What Goliath is he
    As fool and nut he works and
    plays?
The scourge he fights is
    Muscular Distrophy;
He affects our emotions to
    control castrophe,
While his fun—raising prevents
    atrophy.

What Houdini is he
    That thrills the crowd with
    stars?
Whatever the land's geography,
He gets us in his pocket with
    empathy
For we respond to his philosophy.

What Pied Piper is he
    Who leads the little people?
Keeps us from being overwealthy
As he seeks to get pledges from
    the healthy
By facts and jokes in all their
    therapy.

What a Jerry Lewis he is
    That we remember him!
His act is that of love in

philanthropy
As he makes his pitches so
    stealthy
To complete his dream more
    than earthy.

Elynor A. Baran
MOTHER'S APPLE TREE
Old and gnarled
Still growing lovely
In "Our" backyard!
Sounds of songbirds
Coming forth—
Racing squirrels up the tree—
Blossoms bursting forth
Pure and white
Like intricate woven
Wedding lace—
What an everlasting sight!

Carolyn Bea Greever
OPEN ME
Open my lips,
    and I will sing your praise.
Open my lips.
    My voice, to you, I'll raise.
Open my lips.

Open my ears
    that I may hear your word.
Open my ears
    to your quiet whisper, Lord.
Open my ears.

Open my eyes,
    and you in me I'll see.
Open my eyes
    to the beauty that can be.
Open my eyes.

Open my mind
    that I may know and be known.
Open my mind
    to receive your word as soon.
Open my mind.

Open my heart
    to receive your healing love.
Open my heart
    to you, my God above.
Open my heart.

Open all of me
    to my inner hidden man.
Open all of me.
    With you, I know I can
Open all of me.

Chrisy Ostrowski
SHARE MY DAY
I'll share my day with you

    My morning sunshine
    My evening moon

I'll share my day with you

    My simple laughter
    My silly moods

I'll share my day with you

    My deepest feelings
    My unfilled dreams

I'll share my day with you

    My favorite places
    My special things

I'll share my day with you

    My wild desires
    My greatest needs

I'll share my day with you,

    and ask you please to
    tell me now that we've
    come to the day end,

Do you think you'd like to share
    a day with me again?

Naoma L. Shampine
SNOWFLAKE WALTZ
Twas a beautiful night though
    there was no moon,
and the snow coming down
    seemed to play a tune.
I liked the snow falling and the
    cold weather for
your arms kept me warm while
    we were together,
Dancing to the Snowflake Waltz.

The evening was stormy yet the
    snow was bright,
so we went on dancing clear
    through the night.
With the snow whirling down
    from heaven above
you held me in your arms, and we
    fell in Love,
Dancing to the Snowflake Waltz.

Now winter is over the snow
    comes no more,
althrough Spring and Summer its
    you I'll adore.
Untill the next winter when
    snow starts to fly
at night in my dreams dear, just
    you and I,
will Dance to the Snowflake Waltz.

Lorra Anne Heutmaker
LOVE IN FLIGHT
*[To my mother—Jewel—whose
love and caring helped provide
the inspiration which made
this poetic expression possible.]*
How high does the mountain stem
to touch the clouds in the sky,
where I long to be with you,
to be like birds and fly.

And when your wing is lame,
I will carry you under mine,
souring over the rocky plain
to perch on a limb looking fine.

If my love should fail you
look into my eyes and see the pain,
we shall suffer together
whether shine or rain.

But if we shall part
just look for me here,
perched on the same limb
awaiting the sound of your wing
    to hear.

If my love should fall away
never to return to me,
I shall wait here on my perch
for everyone to see—
that my love is true to thee.

Christine Butterworth
THE MAGIC STAR
Fell a shooting star
Like a crystal light.
Captured from afar
In the middle of the night.
I held it in my palm
As long as eternity,
Listening in the calm
To its secret melody.
As I listen to the phrases
Of a far off land,
Another someone gazes
At the bewitching command.

Silently in the star ages,
Lying in my hand,
Turning ancient pages

Of an anonymous land.
As I gently turn it over,
I see a lovely place
Of hollyhocks and clover
All growing in a race.
A wonderland of dreams
Where all happiness roam.
After a wish of an extreme,
I release it to its home.

Carole L. Rathgeber
REALITIES
Sharp-edged realities
Rob me of my fantasies
Rendering me
Sleep-less

Sweet fantasies
Of embers exploding
Pulsating sighs
Passion-full

But sharp-edged realities
Claw my fantasies
Leaving me bloodied,
Craving—more.

Alfred Vanek
YULETIDE ACUMEN
Let's see . . .
I still have two more weeks to go
    there's no real need to rush;
I'll quickly make my Xmas list
    and beat the shopping crush.
Of course,
My wife has talked about new
    drapes . . .
    the thought just makes her
    beam;
But what's my risk if they don't
    match
    her bedroom color scheme?
Uh-huh . . .
Marie could use a blouse, I'm sure...
    it'd give her quite a rise—
An easy purchase at the Mall
    if I just knew her size.
And Mark,
There shouldn't be a problem here
    he's never hard to please;
Yet, if I buy the toys he wants
    I'll have a money squeeze.
Y'know . . .
Last year I bought Mom jewelry—
    she loved it, as a set;
But somehow, it seems awful
    strange
    she hasn't worn it yet.
Oh boy,
I bit off more than I can chew
    it's sure to cause some strife . . .
I'm thinking now I'd better blush
    and then consult my wife.

Phyllis Tracy
In Memory Of Terri Bennett
*[This poem is dedicated to all
    young people. Especially Micki,
    Kerry, and my cousins Eddy
    and Eric. And to all the kids on
    Miami Beach.]*
The pain I was feeling had
    disappeared.
The tears I shed are gone.
But the memories,
Oh the memories
They really are too sad to write.
My thoughts are filled with you
But when I think of you, I die . . .
So really I'm with you anyway,
But then why do I cry?
I keep seeing your face
The one I used to know

593

You were my friend!
How could you be gone now
He took you away from all these
    beautiful things
He told you not to betray him
    but you did anyway.
Your mother doesn't understand
    she blames God.
But it was you and all your new
    friends.
The Drug Scene is nowhere that
    is what I have learned from
    your absence.
My friend is gone—
Never will I see her beautiful face
    again.
Never will I see her brown hair
    blowing in the wind.
She has taken with her all the
    hearts who knew her.
And sometimes at night I still see
    her face.
She keeps reminding me of what
    can happen if you don't listen
    to God.
Please God, tell all the kids in the
    world, it just isn't worth it to
    use Drugs.
I wish she had one more chance.

Nidia Nora
LIGHT OF LOVE
I loved you once not long ago
yet cherishing each memory of
    you,
I thought our love would never end
nothing would come between us
    two.
But as time went on and people
    talked
our love began to die
like the echo within a room
left undone,
fading with time.

Yesterday I saw you, and thought
the magic would be gone,
but my heart proved me wrong
as I searched for the hidden truth.
I looked at you
but could not speak
the words would not come out
as a flashing light appeared,
imprinting your face
within my heart.

Tara Shannon
MIRROR IMAGE
Sometimes
To those I pass on the street
I offer a half smile.
Unreturned, it's only half the
    rejection.
Other times
My entire face smiles
And my body follows suit.
Somehow, they cue each other.
Usually
The response matches mine.
I see my smile mirrored back.
And the lights go on in my soul.

Darla Jean Price
WATERCOLORS
My emotions are mixed
Like a watercolor in the rain
Not really knowing where the
    other leads
Not really knowing where they'll
    remain

Running different ways
Connecting like a maze

Until they start to blot
In the center of my page

But even joined together
The red one goes astray
Representing pain
Fearless on it's way

Crossing through the pool of
    others
And down the other side,
This one standing out
While the others try to hide

Sam Cooper
THIS CALM AFTERNOON
[To my wife, Ruth. Together
we hold ten thousand
tomorrows.]
I look out of this classroom,
Past the rows of busy faces
To the rain gently pressing
The world outside.
I can see you in the wet leaves
On the trees gathered just past
The open window.

I can smell your freshness
In the rain air which
Permeates my senses.
I can taste the smell
Of the damp earth
On my tongue which lay
Inside you only last night.

The longing gnaws at me
On this calm afternoon.
Wait for me babe.
I'll be home soon.

Meg Sackett
EXISTANCE
Dear Man
So in love with me you are
so afraid
of your love for me
so bound
in your life
of existance.

I love you
knowing your love for me
your pain
in your love
your suffering
in life
your existence.

One day
you will be free
of pain
for you will love me
without suffering
or you will exist
without loving me.

Suzanne McDowell
WHY DID HE?
[I Dedicate this poem to my
loving parents, Ruth and James
who introduced me to Jesus
Christ.]
When I look around this world,
and I watch the people go by,
I have to stop and ask myself,
Why? Why did He want to die?
When I see His name slandered
throughout this mighty land,
I stop and ask myself, why?
Why did He reach down His hand?
When I see the world so
    self-centered,
and no one wants to share,
I have to stop and ask myself, why?
Why does He bother to care?

When I see the world moving so
    fast,
with all its race and run,
I stop and ask myself, why?
Why did He bother to come?
Why did He bother to die for a
    world, that thinks it was all a
    game?
Why does He bother to reach for
    people, that are too busy to call
    on His name?
Why does He bother to talk to a
    world, that won't listen to His
    voice?
Why does He continue to offer
    His hand,
When the world makes the
    wrong choice?
Why does he bother to help a
    world,
That causes Him such pain?
Why did He bother to die on that
    cross,
When the world doesn't see the
    stain?
Why does He bother to help this
    world?
Why does He even try?
Because He's God's Dear Son;
    Jesus Christ,
That's the only reason why.

Charles Huffman
ODE TO TIME
(future & past)
The forrest is foggy, the cities
    aglow,
no one conceives of how far it
    will go.
You wander, you ponder, you
    look to the East
to see the blood sacrifice upon
    which we feast.
There's no turning back, the
    tables have turned,
the beginning of time, the ways
    children learn.
To believe what you see and
    condemn what you hear
unless you believe to despise all
    your fears.
And come be there no one upon
    which you can lean,
they've probably heard, they've
    probably seen.
So defend yourself against all that
    are blind
but don't leave your sisters and
    brothers behind.

Celeste A. G. Pagano
WHEN DOCTORS CRY
[To you, Mother, your strength
will always live in me. You
made me so proud.]
When Doctors cry,
Then the brink
of a new century
still holds,
a science that only knows
the word try . . .

When Doctors cry,
then a time-warp
holds a once active,
vibrant life only now
artificially-trapped
In a state of lies.

Oh we'll continue our voyages
And still explore the sky
Searching for meaning in planets
Or stars in a nigh

But what our emotions know—
allowing tears to free-fall from
    our eyes,
is that a Higher Power can show
His Command from up on High . . .
And Doctors do cry.

Derwood Lenz
DINNER FOR ONE
Flicker light of the candle lamp
Dances across the table top.
Tinted glow of its colored case
Reflects on the side of the sugar
    bowl.
Filtered rays in jitterbug time
Illuminate my empty plate,
Shimmering off the silverware
And resting on the back of my
    hand.
Wick and wax in harmony
Make the rhythm of the yellow
    flames
Seem alive in the free-style dance.
Warm the shine of the flicker
    light;
Welcome to my dinner table.

p. j. dolan
eL
Sometimes it's so hard
to find something nice to write
    about.
Until I think of you.
And then my pen comes alive
    with
Spring-daisies,
And soft white ducks on a
    glitter-blue pond.
And green-scented grass
that tickles my eyes
to see a world so alive
compliments of you.

Wm. A. Gaffner
PORTRAIT OF A QUEEN
Her long brown hair is beautiful
Her face radiates as it shines
Her eyes peer into the future
Her beauty is undefined

Nature's work in a miracle
A woman so perfectly made
A warmth so unbelievable
Revives and livens the wearied day

A smile so full of fun
It melts a stranger's heart
There appears, so understanding
A spirit of youthful start

Her mind is one complex
With decisions not far beyond
Her world breathes intellectual
While love creates the final bond

Alice Cleveland Daugherty
Let There Be No Shades Of Gray
Before you came my life was dark,
    the sun refused to shine.

Then you came with all your
    kindness,
    and said your love was mine.

You brightened up my whole
    world,
    made my heart begin to sing.

Now, I must hold you tightly,
    you've become my everything.

Don't ask me now to share you
    and take my joy away.

Give your love to me only.
    Let there be no shades of gray.

I waited so long for you,
knowing you would understand.

My love runs much to deeply,
to ever share my man.

I promise to be true to you,
my joy with you I'll share.

Come and stand now, close to me,
take away my care.

Never let the clouds of doubt
come to fill my day.

Keep your love for me only.
Let there be no shades of gray.

Donna L. Marchand
US
[To my husband, Lawrence]
The fall is now beginning
To arrive at my door.
The sun is still smiling
Down on God's creation.
Oh, the cool, breathtaking
Air that tastes like snow.
What a beautiful season,
Especially for love.
The day I fell in love
It was the most loveliest
Time of the year.
You were so handsome
And it was so naive.
My intuition told me
You were the one.
I'm glad I followed my
Instinct.
For on one fall day
You and I were so happy,
So loving, that we
Took the vows of
Marriage.

Doy M. Neumann
POETRY
Poetry is
A signature
Of the spirit
Written by the
Soul.

Hence
It never
Grows old
Always remaining
That part of time
That never
Changes
Coming from
The heart
The mind
Doth rhyme
Following the meter
The perfect line
Poetry is—
All of time.

L. Cherny
DREAMS
[To Michael and memories . . .]
Love, the sunset was so far away,
And it receded with each hour;
You had to go and I had to stay,
And yes, I remember the ivory
tower.

Dreams call and we follow,
Nightmares follow and we fall.
The champagne has turned, my
dear;
The winters are no longer mild, I
hear;
The letter will be lost in the mail,
I fear.
Floored, we reached for the stars

And finally saw the wounds and
scars.
Loneliness has no cure, my friend,
When one's dreams have reached
the end—
Have you any you might sell?
No, I think not;
We are two of a kind,
And surely you will find
That yours were also rot,
And this will never be
Paradise.

Carol D. Lewis
The Sounds Of God's Love
It's quiet in the country,
or so some people say;
but you can hear God's sounds of
love
if you listen, every day!
The twitter of a whip-poor-will,
the cooing of the dove,
the singing of the chickadee—
these; the sounds of love!
The patter of a soft Spring rain,
the humming of a bee—
the sing-song of a cricket,
how sweet they sound to me!
The hippity-hop of a rabbit,
the song of the wind in the trees,
the music of a bubbling stream,
how beautiful are these!
These are sounds God gave to us,
a token of His love;
to comfort us and bring us peace
'til we dwell, with Him, above!

Cindy Kilgore
CAROLINA ROSE
Jasmine take ahold of my hand
lead me across time
and beyond
into another greener promised
land; you promised.

Heartbroke and frantic
by thoughts
of survival and life
unveiled of kudzu
that had grown in a glorious
vine strangling my daytime.

Cooler nights warn me
love is dangerous,
tempted moments mingled
like the dew setting
in on the mountains' greeting.

Carolina Rose
against my fortress bare
Carolina Rose
passion folds, sundown fares
and only my neighbors and on-
lookers oppose
as morning shadows
a gentleman
a lady's slipper wore
in from the melting evening snow.

Samuel C. Okoye
RAIN
[Dedicated To My Parents, Mr.
& Mrs. M. O. Okoye]
Anger of the heavens
Penality to man
Look at that belly of yours
Swollen with water
Turning the day into night
And sweeping the earth of its
taboos
With the mightiness of your
broom
Soon the sun bows out in respect

Clearing the ground of war
between you and man
And there you come clattering
and splattering
Over all earth
Trees swaying in response
While their leaves open up to
you for food
Lightning lighting up the sky
And thunder driving home the
bolt of your armour
Men and women running helter
skelter
Noises enveloping the battle
ground
Even fire giving up in defeat
Soon the battle is over
And you calm down
And relax until when again
You are provoked
Rain

T. D. Brahmacari
THE MANGO
This is mango season, many years
after the plague;
Half the town had passed,
numbers all too vague.

One of your brother's doctors was
often coming,
A homeopath with his office near
our village.

He administered the medicine to
this centenarian.
Mangoes, the king of fruit, stole
our pilgrimage.

Ravaging the groves, we
ransacked the ripest mellows;
We fattened until the sun baked
the bare skin heads.

A noonday rest, he warned, wards
off elephant fevers.
We brushed the rich dirt and
huge black ant beds

Off the cement base where the
mango tree preserved;
From hand to hand, his father
planted it, sacred and jaded.

We lay down like yellow seeds
deep into the fallow shades,
Our childhood vow still
sweetening as the mango fades.

Alene Williamson
THE CHILD IN CARE
He stands before me
A little boy sad
A little boy lost
His world has splintered before
his eyes.
Disintegrated and disappeared
forever.

The dulled expression in his sad
eyes tells me of his deep shock
Now I must reach out.

Reach out and touch someone
who can't bear even finger tip
near
For the memory of another's
embrace is too close.
To close, but oh so far away.

Time will come when the pain
will ease.
Will allow me to put my hand
on his too still shoulder
He will look at me eventually
and see the love I have for him.

He will see the pain I feel for him
and know he is not completely
alone.

He will eventually take my hand
spontaneously, run to me, and
embrace me
His eyes will eventually shine
again
At the wonders in the world
But at times the dull expression
will return to his eyes and he
will forever be

A little boy sad, a little boy lost.

William J. Stahl
NEITHER ONE OF US
I stood before a blind man, and he
before me,
Down by the shore, beneath a
willow tree.

Then we walked down a path,
We each had walked so many
times before,
From that moment on, we would
be friends forever more.

We walked for hours, down this
path by the shore,
We talked about many things;
about life, our plans, and so
much more.

As the blind man walked away, I
felt his smile and the warmth
of the sun,
I realized that this blind man, had
more love to offer than anyone.

For I stood before a blind man,
and he stood before me,
And little did either one of us
know, neither one of us could
see.

Sue Menzel Espersen
HOLY GHOST BUMPS
Have you ever felt a tingling and
strange sensation in your feet?
Your head spinning and light,
your heart missing its beat?
Have you ever shook all over
from your toes upto your hair?
Jumping up and down, hopping
here and there?
Being so excited your teeth
struggle with your tongue?
Experiencing all your heart's
desires being rolled up into one?

Try and name all the other things
that bring you ecstacy,
Then you'll know exactly what
Jesus does to me.

Kathryn Ford Lafans
CRYSTAL JOY
To soar as birds, pulse racing on
the rise,
I hesitate in fearful joy,
As falling on the arms of wind,
I rest upon its constant flow,
Catch breath as I am flung
Beyond those arms to insecurity.

With each capricious breeze, I drop,
Dart and wheel into the wind,
To buck its flow, as a wilful child,
To strengthen wit and skill.
I must descend, to build a loving
place,
Join the caring life.

Bring forth young with laughter,
Struggle for their needs,

Carressing sorrow's wounds and pangs,
Sometimes loose the precious urge of life,
Yet, knowing I can fall upon the arms of faith,
God's constant strength beyond my own.

Born on miracles of mankind, I rise, again,
To strengthen wit and will,
Soar and seek with crystal joy,
The catch of breath, the quickened pulse,
As I am flung,
Incessantly into uncertainty.

Anna Christensen
CABIN FEVER
When the Northwind fiercely blows,
And frost in silver pattern glows,
Through the chilling window panes
Comes the sound of coyote strains.

The Monarch range devours wood,
We use more kindling than we should.
A fireplace is no source of heat;
A sort of 'poormans' evening treat!

Heating water on the range
The castiron kettle wailing strange.
Owls hoot warnings through the night.
Flickering candles cast their light.

Making indian bread and stew
From jerky and a bone or two,
The dog will, later, eat the bone.
There's you—and he—and I—alone.

When will the chill of winters' wrath
Melt away—and make a path?
A path that leads to sunny spring
And ends this cabin fever thing.

Mark A. Glenn
DREAM ON
[To Sandra Lynn Hecker, who made dreams worth having again. Special thanks to my brother Mike for helping me through the hard times.]
There was a man who dreamed
He dreamed a lot it seemed
Life is a dream, vivid and strong
Until you wake to find it's gone
Dream, silent dreamer, dream
You've not a thing to lose
You're luckier than most you see
For you know there's nothing to prove

Shirley A. Munsinger
HEARTBROKEN
Why do I let these things get me down?
In time things will surely turn around
My heart is broken far more than you know
There isn't any room left to let love grow
Times have changed the way I care for you
It could have been different, but we're through
Enough pain day and night made me see
All I want is for you to let me be
I'll have rough times to get through

And many times I'm sure I'll hate you
It will be worth the trials to be free
And maybe some day I will find the real me!

Dewey Knudslien
THE FIRE OF LOVE
How much am I in love with you?
As much as you desire.
As long as you keep putting coal
Upon our cozy fire.
I am in love with you each day
And each romantic night,
As long as there is any flame
If only candlelight.
But even if the wick went out
And stars were disappearing,
I would not know another soul
So charming and endearing.
I am so much in love with you
There are no words to say,
My thanks for all the happiness
You bring me night and day.
But all that I can offer you
And truely I am giving,
Is all my love and every vow
As long as we are living.

Leonard E. Bonrud Jr.
PRISON LIFE
In the morning I get up to the sound of a bell
That tell me I gotta get up in this living hell.
So I get up and try to move, but can't in this little cell
And when I go to breakfast I listen to the stories they tell
When I walk to work I think of the people I hurt when I came to jail
My girl, well she broke up with me sent it by mail.
She said, if she came up again, she'd only melt
So I'll just sit here dreaming, thinking, remembering in this little cell.

Terry Guernsey
MY PARENTS
If it wasn't for my parents
I don't know if I would be alive
They gave me plenty of common sense
To plainly survive

Whenever I was in a bad way
Ma and Pa would bail me out
I have great respect for them to say
Without a simple doubt

Even the age I am now
My parents stayed by my side
They have alot of love in how
And also extremely amount of pride

The riches of wealth they did not obtain
Or the popularity of royalty
They're human decency is like champagne
And all I can give back is loyalty

William D. Bosworth
SUSAN
Alone beneath a palid sky
A soul inside does weep and cry.
Secluding all it feels and wants
Fearing bane and vicious taunts.

A growing love was my declare

A love she said she didn't share.
Shattered then with wounded heart
Yet tall and proud to play the part.

Near she was, not half a stride
But far away not by my side.
Her glance beset with empty smiles
Across a pit of endless miles.

To heal and scar the heart needs rest
No shoulder near my eyes to nest.

C. J. Spaeth
MAMA'S SMILE
[To Mom: for all her love, for all she is.]
The little girl looked up
  with big sad eyes
  her mama smiled back
  but deep inside she cried.
The pain of the little girl
  hurt her mama too
  but she knew she had to be strong
  she couldn't let the tears show through.
The little girl grew older
  the memory of the pain slipped away
  but she never lost the memory
  of the smile her mama gave.
The little girl passed through the years
  as most young ladies do
  and with each dark cloud she encountered
  her mama's smile shone through.
During the years a time did come
  when the little girl had to go away
  it was the hardest thing telling here mama
  that she couldn't stay.
Mama looked up
  with tear filled eyes
  the little girl smiled back
  but deep inside she cried.

Douglas G. Miller
DEATH OF A MARRIAGE
[To David and Gail Martin whose marriage was dissolved on Nov. 10, 1982 at 1:30 P.M. after approx. 14 years. To write this poem I imagined and became the very you.]
The gavel resounds a mournful lament
The tie is severed, the judgment is made.
The booming final note of death's intent;
And weeping tolls the knell where hearts are laid.

Laid waste by hasty words, the selfish lust,
Like the oozing sap from a fallen tree,
The heart lays crying in the lifeless dust
Of the lonely years, all filled with misery.

Like Humpty Dumpty who fell off the wall,
All the kings horses and all the kings men,
Couldn't repair it or mend it at all,
No one could put it together again.
We suffer with our heartaches it

is true,
But I believe that they who suffer most,
Are they, my children, by these things we do,
Scarred, by this ever burning mental ghost.

Oh! Turn back the clock, go backward in time,
And let me recall the instant it started,
Oh! who was to blame and whose was the crime?
For love turned to hate, e'er we had parted.

Set up a marker, erect us a stone,
So those who pass by may shed a sad tear,
Lest none remember when the years have flown,
The dearest things I owned was lost this year.

Connie L. Averhoff
WHAT IS LOVE
What is love
does anybody know
is it a feeling
that will always show
is it sex
is it care
is it security
is it fair
you can't explain it
but you know its there
its all these feelings
in which you share.

Angela Maxine Wyss
FAREWELL
Farewell to my homestead; my teacher—my friend.
I've climbed your hills and trees,
Many times since I turned three.
Such gifts of happiness and pride you have given me.
But mostly the beauty and understanding of life.

Your rich soil, I worked hard in the spring.
Your fields of rainbow design, I walked through in the summer.
Your golden crops, I harvested in the fall,
And rest came, as nature layed a white blanket over you in the winter.
Farewell to those magnificent seasons of change.

My cattle are my many friends.
Sentimental feelings are hard to avoid.
I look back at the generations I raised.
It deeply saddens me to see them go.
Farewell friends; I lived for you as you lived for me.

My heart aches as never before,
I know its only human.
Memories happy and sad rush through my mind.
I relive them, smiling and crying within.
Close to my heart they will remain forever.

This day of farewell seems so cold.
But joys remembered keep me warm.

And now I leave you dear land
that first won my heart.
Be good to your new comrades, as
you were good to me.
I know our futures will be bright.

SO FAREWELL DEAR
HOMESTEAD, . . .

I BID THEE FAREWELL.

Anna C.M. Sapp
ABUNDANT LIVING
What is abundant living?
It's stars at midnight
and a bright new dawn;
It's a Hallelujah chorus,
and an anniversary song!
It's dew drops on roses,
even rainbows in my tears;
It's butterflies and raging seas
and the praise of all my years!
It's a baby's smile
and a husband's touch
That lifts me up
and means so much . . .
It was holding my first child,
then the second thru the eighth;
It's eventually to walk
thru heaven's pearly gate.
It's warm and cool reflections
of God's presence noon and
night;
It's a relationship, a partnership,
which is so truly right!

Susie Tindle
THE SHELL
As I walked along the beach
Thinking how much it hurts to
let go of you,
I spotted a seashell lying on the
sand.
The only one for miles around.
I stopped and picked it up
thinking
How much it reminds me of
me—
An empty shell void of life.
I put it to my ear and listened—
All the memories and sounds of
you
Came crashing through.
I heard the roar of the ocean
Like the roar of my heart
Calling to someone but no one
was there.
Just me and the ocean.
I put the shell back down and
Continued on down the beach,
Looking back in time to watch
the waves
Wash over the shell, taking it out
to sea
Along with all my memories of
you and me.

Artie Miller
The Rockies Never Made It
There were mountains
in my childhood,
but only during winter;
man-made mounds of snow,
cliffs of clouds
above the ground.
The Rockies
never made it
to Iowa.

They called me
a dreamer then,
but past a certain age
the title was often
mispronounced.

Always wanted to be
other than where I was.
Still,
as the year's first snow
obscures the horizon
my mind's eye
catches a glimpse
of distant peaks;
The Rockies
never made it
to Iowa.

Bhagwan Khanna
Love! Mis(un)understood!!!
*[To someone whose spousy
indulgences remain as ever
throttling and encaging]*
I admire they beauty
and love the innocence
flawless devotion
and quiet diligence
Dreaming, planning a future
together
Diluting entities
craving for oneness
Alas!
Thou devotion and diligence
deceptively enough
entraping, bewitching,
anesthetic, enslaving
Sincere admiration
and love limitless
caring, sympathizing,
protecting nearness
remain as ever mis(un)understood

Marta Reynolds
LOST CAUSE
We fight now,
sometimes bitterly,
always frequently
and we bruise each other
as well as ourselves.
Bruises, not upon our skin,
for we never use our fists,
but bruises, rather,
upon our hearts and souls.
We bruise that which no one can
see,
but each time we fight
the bruises are more and more
severe.
So severe, that one day the
wounds will never heal
and one day when the pain
becomes intolerable,
our angriness and bitterness will
explode
and we will have lost forever
the love we keep on fighting for.

Nancy Bradley Oparka
STRUGGLING
*[The poem was written and
inspired by William, my
husband In 1982, I give these
words to you; still struggling,
no battle! what is the cure]*
Fighting.
For it or against it,
I'm not quite sure.
Making waves . . .
in haste
Struggling;
tidal waves!
Call my name,
bite and refrain
Only for a moment
then play,
and then remain
seated and pleated;
tightly sealed

against my mask
against my past
against my womb
Fighting.
For it or against it
undone in the room
but still;
making waves
in haste
no waste
Can I be damaged
by the cure
by the pure savoring breath
dripping and easing
me into sleep!?

Bonnie Bollman
GOOD MORNING
The new sun clamped his fingers
Upon my windowsill,
Then slowly pulled his shining
face
Above yon purple hill;
First his forehead, round and bald,
Then his smiling face, and all.
Spread his fingers o'er the town;
Gently spread his warmth around;
Lapped the dew from buttercup;
Brushed the dandelion up.
Now his laughter warmer
grows—
Banished once again night's
throes!

Francis O. Stein, Jr.
TOODBER
Hap
Hap
Binglejumpersnack
Twiddle
Twiddle
Snapwomper doo
Ick, ack
Glub
Zid
Flip
Flip
Heenosandvibchottle
Mompered
Twice.
If one could speak Toodber
Understanding is only a word
Making sense of chatter
To whom does it matter
The pitcher or batter?

Helen Branch Blough
HIGHSCHOOL
Your friends say to smoke or
drink it
Because it's really cool
Your parents tell you no
Cause if you do you're the biggest
fool
Going along with all the other
kids is not the golden rule
But what's a kid to do
When he's just trying to get
through highschool?

Your teacher doesn't like your
looks
Lunchtime there is a mess
You think there should be a
longer break period
Instead there's a longer test
You get piled up with stupid
homework
So you decide to skip a day
You get caught at the swimming
pool
So now big trouble is your grade

Three licks, three days expelled,
Or three days cleaning up the
grounds
For being a real cool fool
But what's a kid to do
When he's just trying to get
through highschool?

Harold H. Murphy III
THEIR TURN
Should our eyes meet
Turn away not too quick,
Let them rest a moment,
In their deserved peace
We deprived them,
Because of our little battle,
That lost the war
And peace
For our eyes . . .
Turn away not too quick
From fear of what you'll see,
For dreams are truly scary in life,
When sleep has passed,
For our eyes . . .
Turn away not too quick
To run from what you see
In eyes that love you,
That will reach your heart
. . . open your eyes!
It's their turn.

Terri Glodowski
TREASURES OF GOLD
The moments together pass by so
fast,
I wish for a moment forever
they'd last.
But within my heart are those
memories so rare,
In the love back home waiting
patiently there.
A love that kindles a warm,
glowing flame,
Growing restless with time yet
keeping patiently tame.
Giving so much yet asking no
pay,
Sharing the hardships of each
passing day.
As I return home one thought
that I hold,
Is that you, Mom and Dad, are
my treasures of gold.
You help me along through each
passing day,
Guiding me carefully; showing
the way.
But I know once again as a tear
fills my eye,
I must go my way; I must say
goodbye.

Fern Johnson
SMALL BROWN SPIDER
I watched a small brown spider,
once in the evening late;
He worked so hard to spin a web
upon the wooden gate.
Just how he knew which way to
go, I'll never understand;
His mother must have taught
him well—he never broke a
strand.
And when he'd spun his
masterpiece, no artist could
compare;
A perfect lacy pattern, more fine
than human hair!
I thought at night he'd be so
cold—no cover o'er his head;
But I guess it didn't bother him,
he had no special bed.

When I awoke next morning, I
    couldn't wait to see
If he'd slept well, or ran away and
    left his home for me.
The morning dew had reached
    the web—
    It hung like a sparkling jewel;
To destroy such diamonds would
    be, to me,
    Nothing short of cruel!
And, right there in the center,
    All rolled up in a ball,
Was my special SMALL BROWN
    SPIDER—
    He wasn't cold at all!

Denise L. Bundy
FOR ALL THE TIMES
I love you for all the times
You used to throw me in the
    Air and catch me.
I love you for all the times
You carried me into bed
    When I fell asleep.
I love you for all the times
You never punished me
When we both knew you should
    have.
I love you for all the times
You took me in your arms
And told me that you loved me.
I love you for all the times
You stayed with me and mom
When I was in the hospital.
I love you for all the times
You were there
When I needed you.
But most of all
I love you just because
You're my dad.

William Schwan
DEATH
    Omnipotent, omnipresent
A forbidding force surrounding us
    all
    Bittersweet and grief laden
Black haired with tinges of gray
Experienced, though many years
    left
Beguiling to those who will listen
Forceful with the weak at heart
A calming, soothing attraction
Tragic and saddening to those
    who deny it
    No one can escape its grasp
Neither president nor town bum
Swaddled baby and elderly man
    are equals
Those who accept have peace of
    mind
He who denies is tormented until
    their time

Julia M. Olsen
CONFESSION
I never told you, did I,
How I loved your hands each
    morning
As you came to waken me?
I played "possum" 'til you touched
    me
Though I'd lain awake an hour
    before.
The day just had no beginning
Until your hands caressed me
And your voice roused my senses
To a new day of sunlight and
    small plans for gladness;
Little trips together here and
    there.
Without the touch of those

dear hands to waken me,
No matter that the sun is warm
    and skies are fair,
There's no awakening now—
    there's nothing!

Becky S. Pittman
UNTITLED
I keep thinking
    I have so much to give,
But to who and where.
    Indecision—why?
Because everyone I've tried
    Only disguised the truth with
    lies.
I gave and gave
    Until I could give no more,
I shared and I trusted,
    And cried even more.
I spoke of my loyalty
    Took every moment that I
    could.
Told others I was taken—they
    only laughed,
    So they knew before me,
I was a fool,
    To believe in me and you.

Misti Thiel
UNTITLED
Swirling snow
    danced at my feet
  as I walk the dimly
lit street
    towards home
  the cold air
    felt crisp against my skin
lonely thoughts
    of an empty house
    crowd the
        happiness out
    of my heart
  I turned the gray corner
and pushed open
    the door
    Suddenly
  glorious spring flowers
    and brightly
    coloured rainbows
    come to life
        before me;
  I never expected
    you to be
    waiting here
for me . . .

Lynn M. Stallings
WHY?
I, you
but why?
Why is it people are the way they
    are?
Why is it we're so different
but so much alike?
That's the funny thing.
We don't want to realize it,
but we try to see eye to eye.
Why?
Why to other people do we seem
    to try so hard
But to us it's just a matter of time.
Time on your part,
For you to understand me.
Time on my part,
For me to understand you.
Yes, it does take a little longer,
For me to understand you.
No, it's not that I don't
    understand *you*
It's that I don't agree with alot of
    your ways.
And in time each will have to

be worked out.
But sometimes I wonder if you
    are willing to take the time.
Sometimes I wonder if you're
    worth the time.
But you know for awhile, I think,
    it's worth giving it a try.
Hey, how about you?

Carrie Cross
A JOURNEY
Birth,
    The beginning of a new life.
The beginning of a journey.

A journey that
    will last a lifetime.
It will include
    many ups & downs.
A lot of trials
    and a lot of happiness.

Death,
    the end of the journey.
The final stage.
    Where the ones left behind
will suffer.
But,
the one going
    will be in a much better place.
A place greater than we can
    imagine.

Angela Maria Marshall Moore
THOUGHTS
I was walking very slowly, when I
    turned around to see
A vision like myself
Was it me??
I pondered . . . then . . . I heard
    It beckon
sweetly as a song
It then occured . . . that all along
    . . . had I been wrong??

I could not put my thoughts to
    reason
I could not read the sign
When then at last I questioned
Is it time??

I longed to find the answers
I heard voices call my name
I turned, I would not listen
Yet . . . In vain

I could not understand this
Contemplating . . . Is it true??
For All there is a reason

Then . . . I knew . . .

Diane I. Rapp
A PERSONAL QUEST
Where have you gone my
    enchanting one?
Back to the ways of 100 years
    past.
Back to the days when a looking
    glass
    Shown bright the face of a
    weathered man.

Oh how you've wandered deep in
    the forest.
Looking for silence in the heart
    of nature.
Yearning to capture the way that
    things were.
Outside a restless world still
    abounds you.

Keep to your proud and simple
    means.
Search for tomorrow in the light
    of today.

Knowing your limits, knowing
    your way,
    through the distant meadows
    of your mind.

There you'll discover a natural
    path
    with the passing of time.
This is life's rhythm and rhyme.
Wherein you'll find answers to
    questions unknown.

Ardis Annette Lauseng
THE LONER
A loner is like a single tree
    growing on the prairie.
Strong and silent—
    Always there.
A comforting shelter
for a few trusting friends
who come for a renewal
    on life—
or a rest from it.
Only to part again
    into their busy futures.
Leaving the tree alone once more;
    Strong—
    and silent.

Sandra Davis
LITTLE SISTER, BIG SISTER
It's very very quiet at the bottom
    of the stairs
    with no music seeping through
    the ceiling

It's very very lonely at the
    bottom of the stairs
    when I have news but no one
    with
    whom to share it

It's very very empty at the top of
    the stairs
    because your room isn't your
    place
    anymore

Joyce A. Beck
Glad You Became My Dad
*[I dedicated this to my Dad, on
his 75th Birthday, Earl W. Hill]*
Sure am glad you became my
    Dad,
    so many years ago;

If I had had my pick of you
    I wouldn't have changed a
    thing;

And the times you put up with
    my imperfections, and all my
    aches and pains,

I hope that life will give me time,
    to be able to do the same,

I know at times our stubborn
    ways, have sometimes made us
    mad;

But never ever forget this Pop,
    I'm glad you became my Dad.

Laurie Carlson
CORNERSTONE
*[To my loving mother who has
provided me with many years
of dedicated caring and
understanding.]*
Oh block, frail block
    Crumbling under pressures
Of friends, family, society.

As many you are fortitude and
    elegance.
    As one you are impoverished,
impotent, and fragile.

Prolonged and torpid time,
    Agent of decay,
Exerts its force.

Look at insensitive mankind
    Marching relentlessly forward,
Bearing all tools of destruction.

Feel not self-pity,
    Though your foes are many.
As one you can know strength.

Hold firm feeble block
    For by your decay
Walls inevitably languish.

Dorothy L. Smith
A MESSAGE
*[To my wonderful family,
husband Emery, children,
Mandy and Emery, Mom and
Dad and sisters. Thank you for
your affection and
encouragement, you are all
close to my heart.]*
Speak low
And softly, please
    with tenderness;
For if you shout,
You over-ride
    the voice within
That whispers
    constantly
Of secrets
    filled with
Wisdom, rare;
Guidance, strong;
    —and—
        TRUTH!

Margaret Metzgar
CHRISTMAS GIFTS
The true spirit of Christmas
    is needing to be found,
so it is on this thought
    I now wish to expound.
Christmas has become a time of
    gift giving
    that puts everyone in debt,
the more you give
    the more one seems to expect.
The T.V., the newspaper, the
    radio, too
    all tell you where to shop
because only the best will do.
                why?
What did people do
    when they didn't have a
    shopping mall just down the
    street,
when they didn't spend all next
    year's allowance
    just to buy someone a treat.

That was a time to be set apart
    because gift giving came,
not from the wallet,
    but from the heart.
An apple cake, a bar of soap, a
    paper chain, a pipe to smoke,
    a thought, a prayer, a song to
    share,
an apple in your stocking, an
    orange in your shoe,
    money didn't count—
the important thing was the gift
    came from you.

Now as then
    money isn't free to spend,
yet, the love is there
    and that is what one ought to
    send,
Gifts from your heart

made by you to set apart
those in your life with the special
title FRIEND.

Susan Rose
GOD'S BLOOM
A flower is a growth from God.
His perfect delight for all that
    grows.
Its scent fills man with peace and
    love.
Its sight fills man with beauty.

If man was a flower to each other,
    we could all grow together;
    blowing in the wind.
        Peace on earth, good will
            towards Man.

Life is forever.
    With each new bloom we all
        continue on,
        through all that is ahead
            and all that was behind.

Jean A. Bieberbach
OPEN UP
Open up
Come out and talk with me
Let me discover you
—Discover yourself.
Open up
I'm sure you'll find a person who
    is warm,
        caring,
            kind,
    —beautiful to know.
Open up
Inside I'm sure there is someone
        waiting to be set free
Someone who is exciting,
        stimulating,
            wonderful.
Open up now
You're not a nobody,
        not a bore,
            not a dummy.
You're a beautiful, exciting,
    intelligent person.
Come now
Quit hiding it deep inside.
Open up for the world to see.
You've got a lot worth sharing
If only you would.

Christine Ann Hankla
DANCE OF THE SUN
I am the sun.
Spinning, spinning,
I create a dance of cycles
Forever moving to the rhythms of
    Time.

I am the sun of Spring.
Blood red skies of dawn
Announce my beginning.
I leap above the horizon
At the birth of a new day.
The sparkle of my infant
    brilliance tiptoes
Across the dewy grass.

I am the sun of Summer.
With brash bounds of youthful
    vigor,
The fury of my performance
    peaks at midday.
Beads of sweat form
On the brows of humankind
Hiding in small shadows,
Shaded from my spinning
    intensity.

I am the sun of Autumn.

Complete. Assured. Proud.
I turn with the grace of maturity
To kick at swirling colored leaves,
To stretch my golden light of
    afternoon
Across Earth's ripening harvest
    bounty.

I am the sun of Winter.
I glide behind barren silhouettes
In a fading mauve sky.
I weakly hang the memories of
    youth
Upon the first evening star
And draw the curtain of a dying
    day, reluctantly.

Applause . . . a pause.

Then, I start again.
Spinning, spinning,
I create a dance of cycles
Forever moving to the rhythms of
    Time.

I am the sun.
I dance. I dance.

Sheila Nelson-Collymore
CLOUD DRIFT
*[This poem is dedicated to
Jesus Christ for giving me the
talent; and to Martha Rebecca
Nelson, "Happy 65th Birthday
Mommy"—I Love You]*
There's a constant renewing,
    as the clouds float across the
    sky.
It affords each of us another
    chance,
    to give life just one more try.
The sweeping, swaying motion,
    wipes the slate clean of all old
    woes.
It gives us the strength to face
    another day,
    and all of our numerous foes.
There's a lesson to be learned in
    nature,
    where all things work in
    perfect harmony.
Be happy, be carefree, be content,
    and the things life was meant
    to be.

Carol Lynn
LOVE
*[for John to whom the poem
was first written]*
Question your heart for true love;
Then listen carefully to its voice
    for answer.
Wait quietly patient; trust and be
    silent!
It will come—gently soft and
    tender,
Yet with all the pure strength of
    rightness.
Let nothing interfere, for only if
    the heart answers honestly,
Will the love be true and remain
    for always.

Kathryn L. Bernish
DREAMS
Feelings and thoughts come
    creeping o'er me,
        As sleep drapes my mind.
Dreams of yesterday,
        And thoughts of future's reign.
Slumber takes over, I'm lost in
    my mind,
        I've only to surrender.
Movement at last,

I've broken through my mind's
    barrier.
Color, light . . . sometimes black
    and white,
Various adornments . . .
Nightmare, the villianous
    creature,
Comes slithering into view.

I'm trapped, I can't move,
    There's no escape; Help!
I'm free, I have awaken,
    Sweating and shaken,
Only to drift asleep again.

Jo Ann Walters Gauthier
WHO AM I?
Where is the one who used to be
    me?
Is she gone forever? Did she set
    me free?

My need to know she's there to
    share
    my innermost worries and
    outermost cares
    is becoming more compelling
    with each day's end.

Was she the real me, and I just a
    friend?

If someone should find her,
    I've much to say
    to the one who used to be me
    in my youth of yesterday.

Pepi A. Leistyna
UNTITLED
A feeling of concealment flows
    through my body
    like a remote mountain stream
I am isolated from movements
    beyond the door
    with walls as my only
    companions
It is useless to speak
    for there will be no reply
My sense of others is vanishing
    all but mere images lost within
    my mind
Air grows thin as my frustrations
    fill my body like thick clouds
    that fill an empty sky
    before a hard rain
The atmosphere inside my small
    world begins
    to ravage my brain
Air grows thinner
I gasp for breath and break for the
    door
        I am without
            a key

Jeffery T. Erickson
BAPTIZED WITH LOVE
A beautiful woman stepped into
    my life
and her friendship I can only
    hope is mine
to save.
At this stage in life I need to
    communicate
with a person such as her,
independent,
strong,
intelligent and free.
My life was becoming
    robotistical,
almost hysterical,
a strain and becoming quite a
    pain.
What did I have to gain?

Working, sleeping, working—is
this my life
to be a manequin for someone to
dress
and possess? God no!
I got a body to feed,
a mind to expand,
feelings to unleash,
hatreds to mellow,
sights to see—Listen,
can I believe me?
I knew
deep inside
I had this urge to let go
and be me,
and thanks to this new,
dear,
friend,
my pilot light for life
is beginning to unfurl
into an uncontrollable lust
of
being
free.

Dwight F. Rand
GIVE THANKS UNTO GOD!
For creating us,
Brothers and sisters of every race.
For bestowing on all,
The image of His face!

For constant, countless blessings,
Given us each day
With care and consideration,
Each, in every way!

For all that He hath wrought,
His manifold gifts to us
Of health and happiness
And purity in thought!

For delicate, scented flowers,
High mountains, and deep seas,
Ark's animals in abundance,
And myriad kinds of trees!

For boundless bounty of beauty,
For childhood's honest innocence
Whose sweet smiles no rival
A dawning sun's emergence!

For who, and what, we are
Instead of what we might have
been,
Poor, or crippled with infirmity,
Or steeped in wordly sin!

For all we will receive
In our precious gift of life
Angel-guarded from unknown
peril
In this world of stress and strife!

For granted chance to pray
Our mute petition
To our Lord,
Each and every day!

Taimi M. Lamsa
GOODNESS
*[To: Mikko who lived by the
power of Faith and to Judy who
understood.]*
Has goodness power over evil?
This question oft I pondered
deep.
Much in the world is sad and
dark
So very much for which to
weep.

To do good deeds is not the aim
of man
But to fill his life with
goodness—to be good—

This simple fact will cover
everything
Nothing else needs to be
understood.

The very presence of a human
good
A drooping spirit up will lift.
Unnobleness will hide away in
shame
For goodness is to all—God's
greatest gift.

Mary H. Graves
SILENT MORNING
Bored
  Depressed
    Crushed
Taking all into account,
My world was unstable;
No normal balance of things.
Rhetoric
  Chaos
    Pain
Lost dreams,
Broken promises,
Lost hopes,
  Bricked
  within a wall
  of sunshine's past,
Balanced and tied to a thin line of
  more hopes,
  more promises,
  more dreams,
And then came the silent
 morning after—and nothing . . .

Cindy Kilgore
Laces N' Braids In Chablis
  Over, under
   pass it through
as she plays with my hair
like we did when we were children
sitting in the kitchen's make-
 believe barber's chair.
   Time has changed
   little girls grow tall
   still over, under
   pass it through
laced with shawls, small children
 n' dolls;
a child's eye watches with
 mystical wonder
while the talk n' laughter slightly
 strange
twist from yesterday's giggles to
 birds of a feather
  we sang.

   Hold this, hold that
   pass it through, over
sitting in the kitchen's own chair
 braiding long hair
times never really change, only
 days rearrange
  small girls transcend to
  silly women
dreams never really differ from
 then
just the talk n' laughter appear a
 bit derange
  but it's always over, under
  pass it through again.

C.E. Huggins
THE PARTING
Why must it always be that my
 deepest loves
 are my briefest loves?
My soul fears the thought that
 we might never have met,
 might never have shared,
 might never have grown to love.

For, you see, I do love you,
 though I've never voiced the
 words.
Words often seem so inadequate,
 incapable of expressing the
 true God-given emotion.
I shrink back from the words,
 afraid, I suppose, that they will
 not be understood
 or accepted
 or returned.

As I sit here tonight, Kelly,
 the sorrow is not yet upon me.
I feel only the desire to praise my
 Maker for our friendship.
I feel only a peace in knowing
 that He loves me enough
 to send you my way.
The sorrow will come soon
 enough, though it will be a
 sweet sorrow,
 for the parting is His will.
But tonight, dear one, let me
 enjoy the laughter,
 the fellowship,
 the rare, treasured love of a
 friend.

Georgina Hopkins-Gwizkak
THURSDAY'S CHILD
*[In loving memory of my
dearest father, Col. George O.
Hopkins who was responsible
for any poetic talents I may
have.]*
Thursday's child is a sad child
 And forever misunderstood
Always trying so very hard,
 But never to do any good.

Of all the seven children,
 Thursday's must ploddingly
 strive,
To accomplish the utter nothing
 That infernal life contrives.

And in the icy chasm of the mind
 The hallooing of the gyrafalcon
 May be heard.
Yet in the stagnation of the mass
 I do beguile that bird
 And think
 Absurd
That my future is foredoomed,
 Because I'm Thursday's child.

Ella Mae Sanders
MY MOTHER WAS A LADY
I suppose you'd say our home was
 poor
Because all the neighbors had
 very much more,
In furniture, rugs—the material
 things,
But ours had happiness that
 sharing love brings.

My Mother would toil the whole
 day long
While usually humming her little
 song.
Now she couldn't begin to carry a
 tune.
She knew not a note from the
 "Harvest Moon",
But if you were blue and you
 really felt bad,
It's a cinch you'd feel better, your
 heart feel glad
Just to hear Mom humming her
 tuneless tune,
For you knew things were fine
 and supper'd be soon.

My Mom had a motto she lived
 every day,
I can see her now—I can hear her
 say,
"If a thing is worth doing, it's
 worth doing well.
You may have to stop and rest for
 a spell,
But you get right back at it until
 it is done.
You do it *well* if it takes till the
 setting sun".
My Mom was not strong, she had
 never been well
And manys the time she would
 sit for a spell,
But she always got up—finished
 every task fine.
She was quite a lady—that
 Mother of mine.
She took time to listen and would
 give you advice,
Though no college degrees, she
 was fair and wise.

She judged not in haste but took
 time to relate
How each circumstance might
 control your fate.
She weighed every action, drew a
 mighty fine line,
And she was a lady—that Mother
 of mine.

Vivian Sofie Keck
SPRING
How timely is spring,
When all nature comes
    to life.
The grass, the flowers, the trees,
Just like Jesus did
 on that great morning EASTER:
Spring with its warm
    sunshine,
and the freshness of the rain,
Brings to life each growing thing,
And proves life comes again.

Of all the seasons of the year,
Spring comes along to prove
That there will be heaven
    here on earth
Provided by God's love

Ella Mae Sanders
HUMAN NATURE
Have you ever studied Human
 Nature and the funny things it
 does?
How some will laugh and sing all
 day while others really fuss?
How some have got to be "Big
 Shots" in order just to breathe,
Yet some can be just common
 folk and life their lives with
 ease.

How some will care and do their
 best to help a fellow up
And some will strive of
 "happiness" to completely fill
 your cup.
How some can be so dog-goned
 nice—yet knife you in the
 back,
Tis sad—I know—but still it is—
 a very bitter fact.
How some will of your business
 pry and make of it their own
And thoroughly enjoy spreading
 it—out over all the town.
How some enjoy gossiping to
 hear the grape-vine ring

And some are so *blamed jealous*
over every single thing.
There's some can blow and brag
all day yet nothing ever say,
And some need never say a thing
and all their wisdoms ring.
How the little things will get
some down yet the big things
never count,
And others only BIG things are
all that they surmount,
For little things are such a bore—
oh me,—oh my,—oh me!
Human Nature sure is odd—it's
plain enough to see.

Sharon L. Dischinger
THE PARTING HOPE
Silently I sit here thinking
thoughts of you,
Wishing that I hadn't heard that
we are through.
Oh, I knew this love was not
meant to be,
But, dear, you are leaving such a
void in me.
This unending pain cuts through
me like a knife,
Leaving only harsh realities of life.
Such an effort to get through
each passing day.
How I hoped and prayed it
wouldn't end this way.
But I'm grasping . . . the way we
met was fate . . .
With that thought in mind . . .
however long . . . I'll wait.

Violet Witherspoon
HATE
Hate is a knife cutting deep into
the soul
A cancer taking its toll.
Manifesting itself upon the brow
Vicious, malicious and foul.
Frightening everyone who comes
in sight
making them quiver with fright.
But none is so affected by its glare
As the one whose eyes through
which it stares.
To harbor this malignant growth
Exacts a heavy debt,
One must learn to love and
respect.

Dawn Aarhus Anderson
TRANSPARENT REALITY
Hello? . . .
Yes, there is someone here,
And even though you can't see me,
I'm quite real.

Don't bother looking harder,
Or putting on your glasses,
Because I still will be
Transparent.

Oh, I used to have an image,
But it faded from neglect,
And suddenly, one day,
Became nothing.

Yes, someone is here,
But only in soul;
A tired and worn one, at that.

C.L. Rades
INSIDE
Inside these racing years
Of sunlit flowers, lingering songs,
Worn-out memories passing by,
Awaits the answer
The strength in fear;

A new day, an open road, a new
high:
To grasp attuned to our old ways
Now sharper with edge,
More color; Harmony.

From distant shores, wave
goodbye,
Kiss the sea face to face.
You find youth wants, age needs:
A division of reality.
So in this peace you fight
And win or lose
You gain the right:
A sin to die unhappily,
Or soon break down this wall of
doors
This noise inside.

Alberta L. Grim
SURPRISE
When I was young in in my
prime
I laughed and loved and took my
time
I vowed that I would never wed
No kids for me I often said.

I had my fun, was never bored
By lots of guys I was adored
I felt that I was fancy free
I often said "No one man for me".

As time went by, I learned some
things
About guys and girls and
diamond rings
I began to long for my own home
A settled place, no more to roam.

I met a man when I was twenty
Who said that he had love aplenty
So we got married and had a son
And now my roamin' days are
done.

Lois McGinn
SOUL
I sat,
Smiling and talking,
And felt the eyes, across the room,
Touch me.
Exploring and probing,
My physical and inner self.
I felt only warm and free.
Then, emotion pushed the button,
Momentarily.
Suddenly I felt naked,
Blushed and looked away.
Again, that gentle warmth,
And I was whole.
Unseen fingertips brushed my
lips,
And filled me,
With an unwonted sweetness.
We meet again,
Soul and soul.

K.E. Kreuscher
A PART OF YOU
One day I walked into that place,
and saw an unfamiliar face.
You smiled at me, and then said
hi.
Me, I fumbled for my lines,
to introduce myself to you.
For I was also very new.
I asked you if you'd stop some
night,
so I could overcome my fright.
We laughed a little, talked alot.
You thought and said you'd
rather not.
I perservered and asked again,

if you would stop and make
amends.
The answer came so sweet and
clear.
Sure I'll see you over there.
We got together, you and I,
to drink a few and then get high.
It's strange why we ever stopped
again.
'Cause I've got her, you've got him.
You're beautiful you see.
You mean an awful lot to me.
I took away a part of you,
a part I really never knew.
And gave to you a part of me,
to keep for all eternity.
I hope I'll never see the day,
when we have to go our separate
ways.
And lose that part I took from
you.
The part I really never knew.

Peter B. Martens
BRAIN WOUND
There's a certain
happy magic
to his all demented mind
which sees the world
(without a thought)
more freely than the wind.
Happy and straight,
his course unconfused,
until he hears
voices from the sky.
And those voices
that you thought he imagined:
O God, those are your three voices
calling him,
insane,
from above.

Anita Wheeler
THE EMBRACE
I often dream of being held
In someone else's arms.
The warmth, the closeness,
Momentarily protects me from
all harm.

For someone to attend me
without ever speaking a word,
Can bind like no other emotion.
The tenderness, the touch,
Lingers as a dream with its own
magical potion.

Many times it can be a hug,
But that is much too swift.
A dance is the perfect chance
To be given the paradisiacal gift.

Inhaling everything surrounding
me,
My quest leads me to trace
The music, the rhythm, the man
around the room
Relaxed and secluded in . . . the
embrace.

Shirley A. Hess
GOLDEN SEEDS
I hope someone will watch me
grow
Before I wilt and get covered with
snow

I lift my beautiful face to the rays
of the sun
And hear the children laughing
and having fun

I'm beautiful with a grace none
can compare
With golden petals I call my hair

I can feel my graceful body grow
My leaves gently fluttering and
the breeze whispering, I know

There is love so deep and rare
Love that has depth and feelings
always there

I love my home, though soon I
must go
But I leave on this earth seeds so
other sunflowers will know

A caring is so beautiful and warm
I'm glad for a short time I'm a
beautiful sunflower on a farm

Robin Gail Mueller
**A Vanilla Gorilla Called
Snowflake**
*[This is for you; Snowflake. A
special albino gorilla. Living in
the Barcelona Zoo, in
Barcelona, Spain.]*
I was born in the jungles down in
Rio Muni.
In 1966, a hunter killed my
mother with human guns.
I was clinging to her helplessly
I'm found by one.

Ah, but once into eager hands
and loving care.
My acceptance was established
As my taste for sugarcane was
made
Just for me!

My hair is white as a snowflake
in flight—
My skin is as pink as a rose
within bloom.
And my eyes are as blue as a
bluejay on sight!

My home is at last!
The Barcelona Zoo
Where the people around the
world
Come to take a glimpse
at me!
A vanilla gorilla called
Snowflake

Kathy Sowers
MY DAD
*[To my Dad and Mother for all
the love and understanding
they've given me. And also to
my aunt Dorothy who's always
so excited when I write
another poem. I hope to
someday be as good as her.]*
I'd like to tell you of a man who
means the world to me,
God made him out of love and
strength and lots of loyalty.
He put him on this earth and said
you do your best my son,
Then left him on his own to do a
job he knew would be well
done.
He gave this man a family to care
for and to love,
And though he'd left him on his
own he watched him from
above.
He watched him work his hard
life long to give them what he
could,
And heard his prayers from up
above that they would turn out
good.
He watched them as they grew
each day from dawn to

601

setting sun,
Provided good with food and love
and lots of space to run.
Now God was watching every
move and being there when
needed,
But his man was the kind that
never heard the word defeated.
He knew that he was put here for
his family to provide,
And watch his little loved ones
grow to teach them and to
guide.
And this is what he's done my
friend I want it to be known,
He's loved his little ones so much
they're healthy now and grown.
And though his job is so called
done he never will retire,
He'll still be there when they
need help to comfort and
inspire.
And now I thank my God above
for all that I have had,
And ask him to please bless this
man I'm proud to call my Dad.

Helen James Ehlert
God Gave Us a Special Leaf
Jimmy is slender and blonde and
fair.
He has lovely blue eyes and soft,
silky hair.
Jimmy likes music and sings like
a bird.
He loves to play baseball and is
quite good, I've heard!
Jimmy is artistic and draws
pictures day and night.
He seems to have a talent for
getting them just right!
Jimmy likes his studies and does
well at school.
He has lots of friends and is
really quite cool!
Jimmy enjoys his "legos" and
builds complicated stuff.
It takes lots of patience, but he
seems to have enough!
Jimmy loves dogs and is so
tenderhearted;
His heart still yearns for the ones
departed!
Jimmy loves people—He even
likes girls
With their laughing eyes and
soft, bouncy curls!
Jimmy loves to spend Christmas
here on the farm
With all of his loved ones—God
keep them from harm.
Jimmy is my Grandson. He was
12 years old this summer.
Right now, he is quite certain,
he'd like to be a drummer!
Jimmy is so versatile—He's
destined, don't you see—
To be a very "special leaf" upon
our Family Tree!

Clarence E. Leet
GOD ALSO LOVES THE SUN
It rained all day and half the night
We worried about our rainy
plight;
As the dawn arrived next morning
'Twas bright, our Lord was
maundering;

He is the whole world's
everything.
Seeing Him, the birds began to
sing,
The flowers wake up to find the
sun
A beautiful day helps every one.
The Tot gets out in the yard to
play
Or just reacts to the lovely day.
The boy and the girl together love
The sun, God put in the Heavens
above.
A man on the farm is glad to show
The results of good weather and
his hoe,
Even the Old and the Ill want to
see
God's beautiful world and happy
be
You bet it's very good to have a
Lord like He.

Colleen M. Flinn
For a Special Anniversary
Forty years of loving
Forty years of life
Together for the sharing
As husband and wife.

Years of tears and laughter
Years of work and fun
Years of raising family
And loving every one.

Walking hand in hand
Since nineteen forty-two
Working through the good and
bad
With the help of "I love you".

May this day be half as special
As the love that you still share
May your future hold more
happy years
And your troubles and strife be
rare.

Diana S. Fischbach
LOVER
Morning after,
sizzling hot pan,
bacon shriveling,
melting,
eggs translucent
became opaque,
as much coffee
as the last grounds made.
It's enough
quite enough
although chewing at times
is embarrassingly rough,
as the tongue I keep biting
is a bit rare and tough,
which keeps starting
but halts
with the nick
and in time,
before thoughts flow out.
Would they were thine.

Loretta Gray
MUTATION
Mauling my prairie
Swarthy fortress mall
Devoures the yellow wheat
Greedily grinding it to gold

With Midas touch
It converts a growing thing
To hard cash

Earthtone apartments spring
To fence it in
Fading in the sunlight

They form the sordid slum of
tomorrow
Concrete shrouds pulsating
prairie floor
Already I smell
The stench of starvation

Wanda Y. Schooler
SOMEBODY'S FATHER
His face is tired and drawn now,
and each wrinkle a memory.
It glows with the wisdom of
many years, but no one stops
to see:
Though his eyes are lonely and
sad today, there is a scar
remaining.
The scar left by the twinkle in
his eyes, for youthful thoughts
detaining:
His gait is bent and slow, and it's
aided by the cane.
His heart is filled with loneliness,
his knurled hands are racked
with pain:
The silver of his hair reflects the
tired years of his past.
It's a reminder to us all, that our
youth will never last:
He spends his days in the park,
feeding and talking to the birds.
They take no shame in him, and
they listen to his words:
He sits and watches the children,
who come to the park to play.
A tear falls on his face, as he
recalls a younger day:
Why must this wise old man face
the final years alone?
Growing old was his great sin,
and now he must atone:
It fills me with fear to watch this
man, and to see nobody bother.
The most painful heartbreaking
fact of all, he's probably
somebody's father.

Larry R. Dillon
THE FUTURE
It doesn't hurt to dream a dream
and reach out to touch a star,
but be careful how far you reach,
lest your grasp be far beyond
your arm
and fingers clutched in thin thin
air, slip empty back to you.
Even if you could touch your star
be cautious that you don't
in your haste and need burn your
fingers in greedy desperation.
Sometimes it's better to reach out
and come back empty handed,
than to draw back a hand filled
with things unwanted.

Ms. Sylvia Stearns
A TIRED OLD HOBO
[Dedicated to my talented
friend (HOOD RIVER
BLACKIE) a living legendary
Hobo, the last of his kind. Hobo
Historian, Writer, Poet, Artist.]
Hears a distant train whistle as
night shadows creep
A tired old hobo is ready to sleep
His trail worn and weary from
riden the rails
It was a long journey on them
cinder trails
He unties his bundle rolls it out
makes his bed

Finds an old stone to pillow his
head
Lays down on his bedroll and
dreams hobo dreams
Thinks of places he's been and
the things he has seen

Memories linger of old time
hoboes he knew
Most of them now sleep where
the wild flowrs grew
And he wonders why he's left all
alone
The last of his kind but still he
must roam

Those old time steam trains have
most faded away
No one wants old hoboes or
steam trains they say
He longs for the old days and still
wonders why
There are no more steam trains
for him to ride

His eyelids grow heavy his
dreams will be sweet
A tired old hobo has gone to
sleep
He dreams of the high iron where
old hoboes still meet
A tired old hobo smiles in his
sleep

He dreams of the nights they had
on the town
The saloons and the ladies in
their fancy gowns
Free flowing whiskey whirling
dancing feet
A tired old hobo is deep in sleep

Rebecca Leonard
BURROWED
I wandered upon you rather
accidently.
I watched you retreat inside of
yourself unconsciously.
I peeked into the secret hollow
end of you.
It was so dark in there, I couldn't
put my hand all
The way through.

When I reached inside to pull
you back out,
You began to crumble and decay,
So I left you for someone deeper
than me, and
I went away.
Still, if I had tried a little harder,
Would you have asked me to stay?
And *who* will bring you back out
into the light of day?

Diane Bailey
Be a Friend To Your Children
When I have a child of my own;
I'll show my baby as I've been
shown.

That being friends is the only
way,
To get by in the world day after
day.

Whether you're parent and child
or man and wife;
If you can't be friends; you'll have
a hard life.

I will be a friend to my child from
birth.
And together we'll find the good
things on earth.

We will be friends in the
strongest sense.
With nothing hidden and no
pretense.

Everything will be out in the
open I'm sure.
Having a true friend is the
ultimate cure.

Teach your children and teach
them well.
Teach them of heaven and teach
them of hell.

Teach them of love and tell them
of hate.
Teach them of tomorrow and
teach them of fate.

But above all that you teach
them, make it quite clear
That true friendships are rare and
certainly dear.

Maria Dona Depra Cala
AGING HITS A SOUR NOTE
It was I who heard the children's
voices
with great distress and sadness
It was my ear that listened with
contempt
to their joy and happiness
It was my heart that grew heavy
while I listened with
hopelessness
It was my eyes that formed pools
of water
as I witnessed their
youthfulness
It was my mind that wandered
backwards
in my days of vivaciousness
It was I who was filled with envy,
disgust and hatefulness
For it is I who is aging
and left only with loneliness

Merienne Eloise Felder
LOVE ME
If you don't love me
Why do you let me love you?

If you don't need me
Why do you let me need you?

If you don't want to hold me
Why is it that my arms ache for
yours?

If you don't want to kiss me
Why do my lips thurst for the
touch of yours?

If you could only love me, hold
me, kiss me and want me
My longing would end and life
would begin.

Marjorie Kingston Skusa
YOUR RENDEZVOUS
[To my son, David H. Skusa]
Tonight I saw you standing tall,
In cap and gown, along with all
The others, who had earned the
right,
To share this graduation night.

Although I shared your Father's
pride,
I felt a sadness, deep inside;
For the speaker said that each of
you
Go forth to keep a rendezvous.

"A rendezvous with Destiny"
And as this message came to me;
I knew the apron strings must

break,
No matter how the heart may
ache.

Though there be nights I will not
sleep,
You have a rendezvous to keep;
And I am proud to have one too,
To let you keep your rendezvous.

Marie Bass

Marie Bass
SAY GOOD-BYE
[Dedicated to my four children,
Linda, Becky, Jayne and David
for their enduring love
throughout the years.]
Sometimes we have to say Good-
bye and never turn around to
look behind at what has been
and what we thought we'd
found.

Oh, how we'd like to hold on to
what once seemed so right, and
never lose the sweetness of
what we held so tight.

But the days pass by and the
nights go on into what seems
like forever—and we ask
ourselves, will it ever end? The
answer comes . . . no,
never . . .

Fond hopes and dreams forever
gone, that once we thought
were ours; they've drifted to the
earth and died among the grass
and flowers.

And many tears have fallen there
upon those withered dreams,
and the rain and snow has
covered o'er until they can't be
seen.

The wind has blown the leaves
upon the place where they lay
dead—And Winter's chill has
fallen there to cover up its
head.

The heart feels sad and lonely
where once those hopes did lie,
so, say good'bye to yesterday
and leave those dreams to
die . . .

Tina Robin Harms
WHY?
Sometimes I wonder why I am me
and why certain things are meant
to be.
Why I feel happy and why I feel
sad
and sometimes why the littlest
thing will make me mad.

Sometimes I wonder if dreams
can really come true
and just why life can sometimes
make you blue.
Why I love and why I hate
and sometimes I wonder if there
really is such a thing as fate.

Sometimes I wonder why life isn't
fair,
and why I often have the feeling
of "who cares"!
Why I smile and why I cry,
but most of the time I wonder
just why is why?

I wish answers would come to me
But, I guess that's another thing
not meant to be.
For now things will have to
remain just as they are
Surely my answers can't be too
far.

Jacqueline S. Bucler
PUTTING GOD FIRST
True blue is the sky
For one who will try;
So, try to find God
Through Nature and Sod—
Before it's too late—
The End of your fate
With closed Heaven's gate.

It's great to be one
Who has walked with God;
Joyous rays gleam through
In hours, rain, and sun—
Relaxed or on-run.

Red Satan knows best:
Not ever to Trust;
And to have great Lust;
To do no good Deed;
But to well-know Greed.

So, abide with me
And then, you will see
Creations by God
The tree, flower, and sea.

Yes, you'll really feel
Like a brand New Deal!

Gerald Stanwell
MOMENT IN AMBER
Do you love to stand
above the nestling town
preferably upon a little hill
a few hours after summer dawn
when the sun has risen
just a bird's wing elevation in
the east?

Do you fondly hope the modest
moon is there
aplomb in the western sky
full-orbed above the trees?

Then tenderly reach out your
hands
as if to cup them both,
not to rearrange their symmetry
but rather sense your part in
vast triangle
of diurnal light
trapped in amber of sweet
recollection.

Yes, in that dear moment feel
this blessed earth so poised in
space,
so accurately devised
that any change would bring
catastrophe
as when the axis tilted in the
flood.
But now you have no words
but wonder,
from carefree wing of butterfly
to a light-year's grace of
distance,
that earth's creatures, with
your dear self,
chosen for this moment, share
strange artistry
from growing tree to changing
leaf.

Thus nameless wonders wait
the true child's
heart's inheritance
to bless the few who find it.

Barb Lashbrook
A FADED ROSE
A flower left inside a book
To signify
Your gracious past.
Never take a second look
At what you've lost;
Dim reflections never last.

A silent, crystal falling tear
Measuring
The love inside.
Never cling to something dear.
They'll see you through;
Love for someone cannot hide.

A pre-designed romantic rhyme
That tries to speak
What words cannot.
Caught between a dusty page;
A faded rose
That turns a multi-colored
thought.

A flower left inside a book
That seems to say
Remember Me.
It's all that's left for you to hold;
A faded dream
That only grows by being free.

Alma Dyer Spanton
MOODS AND REFLECTIONS
I have a home in a garden,
to enjoy while here on earth.
A garden of mystic tranquility
and peace,
a place of new growth and
birth.
A lake flows by this garden,
through the years I've captured
its moods.
I've watched its smooth sparkling
water,
as Bass strike for food.

In the calmness and serenity of
nature,
reflections of clouds and trees.
In this wondrous lake of mirrows,
the beauty of nature I see.
Change of her mood in the midst
of a storm,
as rushing white caps roll to
shore.
Shades of soft grey in windswept
rain,
erasing sparkling hues of
before.
Enchanting on a moonlight night,
eerie when the moon is low.
Blue on a windy winter's day,
as more and more restless she
grows.
I've watched steam rise from her
bosom,
on a morning foggy and cold.
She's a haven for the shy
Alligator,
and the playful Otter so bold.
Home to the graceful water birds,
and fisher-foul so fleet.
On her banks water turtles leave
nests of eggs,
covered over so neat.
Capturing nature's reflections,
is a joy beyond compare.
Her many moods remind me,
of the abundant beauty she
shares.

Yvonne Vansickle Smith
WHAT IS BRAVERY?
One child without shoes, another
without feet,
Some see without sight, others
without speech,
Labor to walk or struggle to
speak,
Eager hearts surrender not to
defeat,
What is bravery?—God will judge!

A prisoner of war remembers
Mother and home,
Wonders if sweetheart will wait
or will roam,
While silently praying he keeps
the faith,
Never knowing the years he must
wait,
What is bravery?—God will judge!

A lonely girl lost Mother and
Dad,
Comforts her brother from being
sad,
Worries in doubt—from whence
the next meal,
Laden with sorrows and
heartaches to heal,
What is bravery?—God will judge!

A youthful man forsakes worldly
friends,
Speaks out for God and
courageously defends,
The Light of the World, His Jesus
befriends,
Humbly begs others their lives to
amend,
What is bravery?—God will judge!

An aged Grandmother rocks all
alone,
No son, daughter or kinsman to
come,
Longs to be loved and sits in her
gloom,

No earthly compassion to
enlighten her doom,
What is bravery?—God will judge!

Hoot Gibson
REPENTANCE
When time and man stride side
by side,
And silver brooks run raging
wide,
And day greets night at
merging dusk,
And grain of corn forget their
husk;

When blood of blue turns scarlet
red,
And flowers weep and bow
their heads,
And flames of orange turn
blazing blue,
And thoughts of old return
anew;

When silver meteors streak the
sky,
And women weak with worry
cry,
And pretense lives thru endless
days,
And moonlight plays on ebbing
waves;

When pictures made of black and
white,
And time composed of day and
night,
And love meets hate, within a
heart,
And life from death we know
must part;

Then I alone must sit and weep,
And drown my woes by restless
sleep,
And think again of things to
come,
And do the wrong that's done,
undone.

Betty Jean Cioffi Smith
Remember Humpty Dumpty?
If you will but search back into
your mind
An old childhood friend there
you will find
Humpty Dumpty, remember him?
Remember that poor little egg
creature who fell off the wall
and couldn't be put back
together again?
Not by all the King's horses nor
by all the King's men could
Humpty Dumpty be put back
together again
Such a sad little rhyme from our
childhood time
But even sadder to me is reality
We take a shy, sensitive young
man, we place a rifle in his
hand and we tell him to kill or
be killed
We tell him it's right till his
conscience is stilled
We tell him the enemy has to be
defeated no matter if it's right
or wrong
We tell him we must fight and
kill if we want our nation to be
strong
So he takes his rifle and begins to
kill, he kills, feeling right about
it

We give him bombs to drop, we
tell him what villages to hit
And he kills ruthlessly, killing
not just men
But even the enemy's women and
children
He sees his friends killed and
maimed, he becomes clever, he
learns to survive
And when he returns home alive
We pin a medal on him and call
him brave
But he is a virtual slave
Ready to kill on command at his
country's whim
Deep down inside something
cries out to him
"It's wrong to kill! Refuse to kill!
It isn't treason!"
"Killing is wrong no matter what
the reason!"
With this conviction he feels
great guilt and as the years pass
by
He drinks, he drifts, he doesn't
even try to make his life
worthwhile
He's like a man awaiting trial
Knowing that someday he will
have to answer for his crime
Like Humpty Dumpty's shell, his
fragile mind is so shattered
That all the noble effort to put it
back together again hasn't
mattered
I wonder, could this be what the
author had in mind with that
ancient rhyme?
Armies consisted of men and
horses at that time
Perhaps that wise soul planted
the seed of truth within that
little verse so that it could
grow and blossom in the
children's minds, helping them
to understand
That it takes more than armies to
keep peace throughout the
land

Diane Pellegrino Riker
CHANGES
Along the path, that I followed,
I found myself alone;
Confronting the darkness of
misfortune,
knowing no reason, for such
sorrow and pain.

To those, whom I believed, stood
beside me,
I see their eyes now look away;
Words, they so thoughtlessly, had
spoken,
for their truth and mine disagreed.

I walked along with tearfilled
eyes,
from within, came the strength to
carry on;
The world I once knew was
crumbling,
I turned away, for the past must
be left behind.

Though scars of a shattered life
dwell within me,
the lessons they taught, have
been learned;
The strings to my childhood,
have been severed,
for my growth, I pray, is almost in
its completion.

In time, this living hell, will
remain only in memory,
for above it all, I shall come
through;
As I reach the light, to which I
have been searching,
I will no longer be, as you see me
today.

Within, a change must come
about,
if I wish to stay above all that I
have lived;
I need not be told of my own
faults,
for the good, I believe, outweighs
the bad.

I can now say, the pain has
diminished,
for peace has filled the wounds;
My eyes can not see beyond
tomorrow,
for my dreams, yet far, are near.

Jean Pursino
THE STING OF WINTER
The Winter cold comes creeping,
crying, thru
the trees, its icicles hold the
branches, and freezes its beauty.

The plants await in shelter for
Spring to
peep thru, while the ground is
aching
with its cold. But alas, Spring will
come
with its warmth and beauty
and will
take away the memory of the cold;

Until the next year when we
will
anticipate the beauty of the
snowflakes.

Sunny Hye Rapp
THE BRIDGE OF INCIDENT
Faith called it the bridge of
incident,
On that very bridge of life.
They asked "What about
direction?"
Faith said "It will be all right."
Then they asked "Which way will
the road lead?"
Faith said "We shall pray on that."
And they did, and they were
guided,
Gaining strength in their daily
needs.
With the thought and wonder,
can it really be
As they held to their dreams with
hope.
It was the bridge of incident.
That mystical of life.

Marjorie M. Smith
MEMORIAL DAY 1982
Red was their blood upon the
fields,
White were the clouds, dotting
Those skies of sapphire blue
At Chateau Thierry,
Iwo Jima, Pearl Harbor,
Seoul and Da Nang.
Ever we hallow white clouds
And sapphire horizons;
But, please, Americans,
No more red upon the fields—
Flowing and frozen and freely bled;
Not in Iran nor Israel,

Nor El Salvador,
Nor other alien shores . . .
Let the red of my flag
Represent geraniums,
Strawberries, peppermint candy,
And little girls' dresses . . .
Never forsaking nor forgetting
Those who died or those who
    returned
In whatever crippled state;
Hallowing their blood
We cannot ask a sacrifice
Of those they dearly love . . .

Dennis E. Haws
UNTITLED
If I can't laugh at myself
then I can't laugh at my friends,
for I am a reflection of them.

If I can't laugh at my friends
then I can't laugh at the world,
for they are a reflection of it.

If I can't laugh at the world
then all my joy will die in sorrow.

Terri Anne Aubert
FREEDOM
Arms spread wide like an eagle in
    flight
Eyes flashing darkly with the
    spirit of morning light
To fly forever with the world at
    his feet
His heart would soar with
    feelings so sweet
There is nothing greater, he once
    said
Than to the sky and the sun from
    this earth be wed
And the spirit thus fed.

Patricia Gue
ONE LONELY SOLDIER
*[To SSG Greg Tubbs, my friend
and inspiration. This one's for
you, with love.]*
I see one lonely soldier
with a rifle in his hand.
I know he's been to hell and back,
He's been to Viet Nam.
I asked him why he does it,
He says that it's for me.
I know there's other places,
this Soldier'd rather be.
As he watches all the bodies
stacked up one by one,
He wonders if that's where he'll be,
When his job is finally done.
He feels so all alone,
In lands we've all forgot.
Just one lonely soldier,
what a valiant fight he fought.
War is hell, but we can't know
the hell he has inside.
In order to survive out there,
its pain, he must hide.
One day soon, he'll come back
    home,
A Hero he will be,
Because he kept our country safe,
For you, my friend, and me!

Ruby Sheldon Gochenour
OUR LAND
Many poems have been written
    about this land of ours.
Some are of scorn and gossip, and
    of our many powers.
We think we have things very
    rough and do our share of

griping.
But if we'd shut up and work
    together what a land we could
    be having.

The song says this Land is your
    land and also mine,
But our forefathers would sure
    think that we do cry and whine
And raise an awful fuss about
    how things are out of sight
And we don't raise a finger to
    make things easier by any light.

We could ask our leader if there's
    anything that we can do,
And then get on the ball and do
    it without making a big stew.
We all want something done to
    help us straighten out this mess;
But we don't want to do without
    a thing to make the load a
    little less.

Now let's show the doubting
    Thomases that we're made of
    lasting stuff.
That we are loyal, patriotic
    people who can take it when
    it's rough.
The United States means all of
    us, the good ones and the bad;
But let's make the most of what
    we've got and make this the
    best we've had.

For a chain is only as strong as its
    weakest link,
That's what we've always been
    made to think
So let's all be strong links and
    make ourselves proud.
'Cause America is still and best
    Country, shout that long and
    loud.

Anne O'Neil
Last Will and Testament
If I should die before I wake;
I pray my soul, God will take.
And if 'tis true, I should depart;
Here's written my will, within my
    heart.

My life on earth was good to me,
So early a death I did not forsee.
It's things such as this we don't
    expect;
So in this frame of mind, I will
    not neglect.

The special people I touched each
    day
Their importance to me I cannot
    repay
So much I did learn from them
I regret all the times I did
    condemn

The few times I uttered what I
    didn't mean
The support of my friend did
    intervene
Not only then was she at my side
But at every urge, in each other
    we'd confide.

In my adolescence now I've found
Already so many precious
    memories resound
But of all, this one stands out
For her love I could've died before
    this without.

It took not long for us friends to
    become

And so few times were we ever
    quarrelsome
All in all, I shall never forget
Through even the worst, us
    nothing could threat

In her absence so many times I
    tried
But only she could fill the space
    inside
The precious moments together
    we shared
And for each other we more than
    cared

Though I'm gone from this life
    now
I have but one thing I can endow
And that is my one gift from God
I strived to cultivate each day I
    trod

'Tis the gift of verse on me
    bestowed
I carried with me down the
    winding road
Though mine was short, and I've
    come to the end
This and all my love to you I do
    send.

Please always remember my love
    for you
It is stronger now as I bid adieu
But I promise to be near if in
    need of aid
And don't ever let even one
    memory fade . . .

Marcella (Sally) Seiler
I'M SORRY
Have you ever, really listened—
To how often, people say—
Their very short, "I'm sorry"—
In the shortness, of a day?
    They say it, without feeling—
    So you know, it isn't true!
    For, if they really meant it—
    The feeling would show
        through!
It's like taking a drink of water—
To erase, the error, of their ways!
It's been said, so very often—
No meaning—it conveys!
    It's so easy to just say it—
    To remove all guilt and blame!
    Without meaning, it's still
        useless—
    Like a fire, without a flame!
So, when you decide to say it—
When you're approaching me . . .
Make sure, you really mean it!
Be honest with you and me!

Phyllis J. Lowery
ONE DAY AT A TIME
*[Inspired by a poem called
"Please . . . Hear What I'm Not
Saying" and dedicated to every
man or woman that has ever
loved someone.]*
Please, God, please help me!
I love him so much and I need
    him so much
And he is so far away from me.
Give me the courage, the faith,
    and the strength to hold on
"One day at a time".
Help me not to worry,
And if I do, please don't let it
    show.
Show me how to encourage him,
    understand and love him.
Help me not to criticize or be

disappointed
When things don't go the way
    they should.
When I am tired, nervous and
    overanxious,
Help me to love him more than
    ever,
Especially if I feel rejected and
    sorry for myself.
Show me how to live with him,
    even tho I'm living without
    him.
Help me to keep believing that
    by helping myself,
I will help him also.
Don't let me get discouraged,
    angry, resentful or frustrated,
And when I'm unhappy, help me
    not to feel guilt.
I want to accept things as they
    really are
For what is . . . is . . . I can't
    change that.
And most of all
Thank you for always being there
    when I need you,
For without you,
"I" can never be "We" again.

Roland Joshua Diaz
IF A RAINDROP
If a raindrop
could represent
the love in
a man's life
a rose would grow
being much like love itself
starting at the bottom
with splinters and thorns
getting to the top
where the soft petals grow
If a teardrop
would represent
any sad moments
in a man's life
the rose
would start to dry
where once stood
a beautiful rose
now stands
an old dried stem
only the memories remain
the beautiful memories
of watching it grow
and the sad memories
of letting it go.

Greg J. Rowden
APRIL 9, 1982
The night lies heavy and black
    around us
camouflaging the rain that pelts
    our naked bodies,
and our naked souls.
I reach out for you and
wonder if you're sleeping tonight.

Tick-tock, tick-tock, tick-tock—
mother's old clock forces me to
    count the seconds
as they turn over in their sleep.
Grandfather's memory touches
    me and
forces me to cry.

Someone is driving the streets
    tonight
their headlights burning like a
    thousand suns,
in my nakedness I am ashamed
    and turn away.
Remember when
we agreed we could not laugh?

Talking by phone and
listening only to your heartbeat
between words
I assumed that you loved me.
There are no more dreams to
dream
when the wind blows away all
fear of death.

Haynes Reynolds, Ph.D.
THE NEUTRON BOMB
The buildings remain
Ghostly reminders of the throngs
that once swarmed the streets
They stand like tombstones
over the sardines of millions
of bodies overlapped.

How did the cataclysm begin?
The irradiation warheads—small
cousins of H-bombs—
were conceived to kill people.
Every soldier could carry one
And kill thousands with his
lethal weapon.

Some people rebeled against the
death-dealer,
which also has
a half-life of six thousand years
To poison the atmosphere and
mutilate
any new generations.

The government responded,
"The neutron bomb is a simple
tank weapon,
to be fired as mere artillery;
we must meet the decisive
advantage
of the enemy's tanks."

More people rebeled against
a new pocket arsenal
All over the world they protested
Save our children
From the neutron bomb!

And now it had happened
New York streets were littered
with piles of mortifying human
garbage.

The buildings stand . . .

Andrea C. Crouch
THE BUTTERFLY
Pretty butterfly,
You fly so swift.
And when we watch
Your beauty will lift.
Pretty butterfly,
You take pollen from flower to
flower,
That's hard work hour after hour.
Pretty butterfly,
I don't lie
No one could tell
How swift you fly.
Beautiful butterfly.

Harriet Vrooman
LIFE
Life—Christ's life—
Eternal—free—
This is God's
Christmas gift to me.
Life—peaceful life—
Sublime—serene—
Facing with hope
The things unseen.
Life—patient life—
Resigned and sure—
Trusting a God
Almighty—pure.

Life—joyous life—
Christ's voice within—
Seeking a world
Still bound in sin.

Life—boundless life—
Abundant—true—
This is God's gift
of love
To me—to you.

By faith we draw nigh.
For mercy we cry.
By faith we believe
By faith we receive
This Christmas gift of love
from above.

Fred D. Robb
SHOULD I RUN
My mind was filled with doubt
I battled until the truth came
out
I had it all and went down
Somehow I made it back
around
Even love walked away
I tried, and now it's back to
stay
As the years pass
I am slipping fast
Life seems to be without fun
And now I'm really in front of
the gun
Should I run?

Anna Reckner
ONE
I am one—
yet many

One day a mother
One day a lover
One day a sinner
Tomorrow yet another

Tonight I am a child
shy and innocent

Tomorrow a harem girl
Seducing—insatiable

Somedays a rainbow
of laughter and quiet

At times a panther
proud—angry

Once like a rock
Now like a forest
Serene on the surface
What's underneath?

Rebecca Stoner Barrentine
REFLECTIONS
You are the sun,
I the moon.

The moon reflects the glow of
your smile,
The warmth of your gentle touch.

The sun bestows to me the power
to glow
As no other can even in the
darkest of nights.

As I travel around the earth,
My life evolves around the sun.

Clouds, at times, come between us,
But are not long lasting.

For I can not live without the sun,
In hopes that the sun will always
be there:

To give life to the moon
By casting rays of light on her.

Marie Harrington DeMarce
THE SUNBURST PLANT
I brought you a vital start,
wrapped in nurturing earth, a
symbol of our romance.

The seed grew a root only
nineteen yesterdays ago, when
the essence of your affection
had permeated its heart.

To flourish, our Sunburst plant
needs attentive care,
So, let's place it in slanted
sunbeams, and sometimes in
gentle rain.

I hope you will expose it to your
radiant smile, as you give it an
encouraging word.

Our plant needs space for
reaching out to find its unique
identity.

Never smother it with jealousy,
even if a capricious breeze
drifts by to rustle its leaves.

In time, it can fulfill its
potential—scattering fragrant,
promising petals around us.

Then we may celebrate the
season of our joy in sharing
love,
I brought you a symbol of our
love, the Sunburst plant.

Carl Norman Johnson
**In Memory Of the Family
TV**
It stands there in the corner of
the room,
Staring at me;
Tho its eyes are closed, and no
sound comes
From its body.
There in death it stands, silent,
with a cold
Gray face, yet still beautiful.
I feel sad, but I'm glad it died, it is
missed,
But life goes on without it.
Yet why did it die, was it from
old—age or
Neglect?
No it was none of that:
It died from the poison that
flowed through
It channels,
The tubes inside became rotten
and blew.
It cried out for me to save it, I
said that
I would . . . but I didn't.
With a strong firm hand I pulled
out its plug
And it died.
I could not save it, nor did I want
to.
Because of its beautiful body; it
did not go to
The curb;
To take its last ride in a trash
truck, to a
Lonely landfill somewhere.
Yes, I still have it, and it stands
where it had
Died,
Overthere in the corner as a
memorial, holding
A Fishtank, the Family Pictures,
and some Flowers.

Wanda Wissman
GOOD—BYE
It started out so good;
the fun, the laughter—
Just as a storybook said.
I was his, he was mine
and all else was ours.
Time passed so quickly, flying
out words of anger, fist of rage.
My soul not my own—
FEAR. Of things I couldn't
control
I had no knowledge.
He was on an ego trip and
I was the cost of the flight.
I don't understand why he'd
cause such pain. You don't
hurt the one you love.
But my heart wears the scars,
that mine alone can hide.
The whole world knows its his
turn now to cry—
I have said Good—Bye.

Joannie Summers
FRIENDS
Friends are important,
Especially to me;
Without friends where
would I be.
Friends can brighten
my day;
In any kind of friendly
way.
All week long is a joyous
time;
Especially if you have
friends like mine.

Daniel Lenox Barlow
CHRISTMAS PRAYER
*[To those who have made
Christmas a time of Joy, Peace,
Love Walter J. and Ruth L.
Barlow, parents; Walter L.,
brother (deceased); Wilma Mae,
wife; Dana Scott And Brett
Robin, sons; Betty Skidmore
(sister)]*
Christmas Joy,
Transcending toy,
Indwell our hearts with hope
tonight.

Christmas Peace,
With full release
From strife and war, transform
our night.

Christmas Love
From Heaven above,
Scatter hate and spread Thy
Light.

Christmas Child,
As God has willed,
Come and be our soul's Delight!

Mary Sachs Zello
The Road To Jerusalem
Jesus might have had His choice
on that morning long ago
To choose the road to Galilee, to
shun the grief and woe.
He might have gone to Galilee,
and taught and preached
To the people there, But for the
love of you and me,
He gave His life to set us free.
Suffering and dying on the Cross,
denighed, betrayed, enduring
Shame, That through all the
world by His blessed name,
None might be lost.

Into Jerusalem He made His way,
   upon a lowly, young unridden
Colt. They cast palm branches on
   His path that day,
And layed their garments upon
   the sand, Crying "Hossana
To the King of the land" But Jesus
   knew and wept,
He knew they thought of an
   earthly King, while His
   thoughts
To save their souls, Would only
   heap upon His brow the
   burning
Coals of hatred, by their evil
   blinded eyes, That they would
Even suffer Him to death. Yes
   Jesus knew, and wept.

Yet steadfastly He went His way,
   was He not working for His
Father in Heaven above, Was He
   not sent to save the souls
Of the people that His Father
   loved.
Although they crucified our Lord,
   and by His hands and feet
So cruelly they nailed Him to the
   Cross,
A whole sin sick world He has
   set free,
Through pain and suffering, and
   the precious blood,
That flowed at Calvary.

Elizabeth Estelle Robey
MARCH WIND ODE
Blow, March wind! Blow!
Wild and free and strong!
And when you go
Take with you winter
With all its ice and snow,
And leave with us April's
   soft falling rain,
Carpets of violets and the
   robin's song.

Carole Neason
GRANDMOTHER
*[Dedicated To Jennie Patterson
Davis, For Passing On A Long
Tradition Of Faith In God,
Hope, Love And Endurance.]*
I now see that you have grown old,
You can barely hear or walk, I'm
   told.
I know you are worn out from
   life's race,
You have slowed down to a
   pulsing pace.
How long have I known you, how
   many years?
Years filled with heartaches and
   many tears.
You helped in raising all of us,
In the Lord you put your trust.
You raised our family everyday,
You tried to lead us in the right
   way.
You would rock me to sleep in
   your arms,
I always felt safe and free from
   harm.
You would sing your favorite
   hymn,
Rock of ages, I think it was then.
I would always fall off to sleep,
And this tune you planted in me
   deep.
Now all of your grandchildren
   have grown,
To become aware of what you

have known.
But now you have grown old and
   gray,
Soon to meet the Lord someday.
But then may you rest in peace,
And may your soul be at ease.
For you have truly left your trace,
You embedded a rock in a special
   place.

George Edgar DeLawter
I Hear the Clock
A—Ticking
I hear the clock a—ticking
   As time goes fleeting by
And soon this day will run its
   course
   Tomorrow will be nigh.

I know how minutes steal away
   When yesterday was today
So waste them not I say to you
   In never a foolish way.

Down through the years—so
   many years
   Time always had its worth
So foolish is the waste of time
   To everything time gives birth.

Yesterday is tomorrow spent
   And yesterdays, yesterdays
   passed
Will one day fill a lifetime lived
   In a youth and age contrast.

Ah, yes, dear friend, awake!
   awake!
   For life has but one span
The clock is ticking, ticking on
   According to God's plan.

Yes, I hear the clock a—ticking
   Life is slowly ebbing on.

Rebecca L. Landby
AMERICANA 82
Sixth day
Minnesota March
City morning stirring
Shadowed streets.

Cartoons in black and white
Cathedral tower bells singing
Sparrow spinsters flit
Littered greystone dead—end
   alley.

Yawning eyes that sting
Empty stomach acid coffee
Kitchen window winter draft
Home sweet hush.

Poor baby weeping
Willowy welfare mothers
Remember sixty's
Whiter shade of pale illusions.

Mainspring maintaining
Ten o'clock disco/reggae
   explosion
Down the hall daylight dazzle
Melody debut echoes for hours.

Janet Sikkink
DAUGHTER—MY FRIEND
It seems as tho twas yesterday, a
   tiny babe were you.
You were our very first child, so
   cute and cuddly too.

Before we had time to turn
   around you grew to be a teen.
So busy with activities at home
   you were hardly seen.

A beautiful daughter you have
   been to us in so many ways.

We do love you more and more
   and we won't hesitate to say.

Sometimes we've had serious
   talks as well as happy ones.
It's helped us grow together as we
   shared sadness and fun.

I've maybe said some things on
   which you didn't agree.
Perhaps it wasn't eye to eye that
   together we did see.

But now as you grow older and
   your own hurts you have had,
I'm glad we can talk them over
   and help make each other glad.

So here it is your birthday, you
   now are twenty one.
You are our precious daughter
   and you are second to none.

Each day I pray you'll look to
   Him and let Him guide your
   life.
Whether it be happy times or the
   times that you have strife.

Keep looking up to heaven and
   keep your trust in Him.
Keep your light ever shining,
   don't ever let it dim.

So happy happy birthday to you,
   our daughter dear.
I pray that you'll have many more
   for years and years and years.

Irene Gilbert Britt
It's Great To Be a Grandma
It's great to be a Grandma, I'm
   learning more each day,
Like how I'm looking older but
   being younger as we play;
And with each new Grandchild
   that is born I find another task
   to perform.
It's great to be a Grandma but
   those cookies I don't need,
But with lots of help I bake them,
   those little mouths to feed;
And when we get that job done,
   we're off to find some other
   fun.

It's great to be a Grandma, so
   much fun watching
   Grandchildren grow;
And even more growing with
   them, oh the things that I don't
   know.
And the love that we share I'm
   sure will always be there.
It's great to be a Grandma, I'm
   sure most would agree,
Especially if they had the chance
   to trade places with me;
For all the time we are loving and
   growing each little excited face
   that is glowing
Belongs to a Grandchild that
   belongs to me.

Roxana Boyles
THE CORRIDOR
Dark and silent looms the night
   Its shadows veiling the light of
   life;
Ominous threatening of
   sleep. . .
                  And death.
We are ourselves, each his own,
   and
   Each in his life struggling to

Loosen the binding ropes of
   pain and sorrow, straining
      Against ourselves.

Each of us goes to the Father, the
   Creator, God,
With the pleadings of inferior
   Weaknesses sending us; and to
   God
Each of us turns, after all, for
   the comfort
Of sleep and rest . . . and death.

      But I walk the silent dark
corridors with
   A trembling step, faltering as I
   feel
   My way—step by step, moment
   by moment,
   And breath to breath;
   searching, seeking, and
Not seeking . . . Death.

The corridor bridges my life to
   the flickering,
   Straining, struggling lives of
   my fellows, the
   Pulse of life echoes in the
   tranquil breathing
   That comes with the reprieve
   and
      Peace of their sleep.

But in the corridor, dark yet, I feel
   the hope of
   Faith, the challenge of
   knowledge battling
   The irrationality of sickness
   and pain; though
   The footsteps of the soldiers
   are silent in
The battlefield corridor, life is
      here.

In the corridor of the black night
   I can feel
   The passing of life as it
   marches by me—an
   Isolated island standing in the
   mainstream,
   Watching as the absurdity of
   once important
      Daily tasks taunt me.

But with the dawn, the new
   creation—the tomorrow
   Of my life—the corridor
   becomes filed with the
   Noises and boisterous voices of
   hope and spirit;
   The illumined hall sparks with
   the challenges of
      Another blessed day.

Christine M. Trucinski
BAA
*[To someone, who has always
given all, when she's had
nothing, who has always been
there, even when we haven't,
and who's always loved us,
even when no one said, "I Love
You, Mom".]*
A half a century old,
   and then some.
A little gray,
   a little wrinkled.
More than a little
   tired, at times
   of her hellish brood
"Ma—ing" ALL DAY LONG.
Patience that would,
   put even Job—to shame.
Tolerance with no limits

of race, of color or creed.
Gentle, warm—hearted woman.
  Lover of the well written word.
My teacher—
  of generosity—beyond means
  of scrupulous honesty.
My confidant, my friend.
Shy, but sociable, once secure.
Timidly involved in family and
  church.
Concerned parent, sister, wife
  and Grandmom too.
Our love—our "BAA".

Leanna Gayle Stehle
LOVE SONG
If you look long enough,
you'll find me hiding
behind a treble clef.

I know that you are close by.
I can see you swinging
on the flag of an eighth note.

I reach up
and grab a nearby crescendo.
Holding on with
both hands,
I work my way to its end
and meet you at
a subtle ritard.

You took my hand
and showed me
the beauty of
soft trills and two—part
  harmonies.

The footprints we left behind us
formed a simple tune
and sometimes
when I'm feeling down,
you'll whistle it
for me.

Sporty King
**You Kept Me Up Late Last
Night**
I could almost make out your
  figure
  through the darkness in which
  we sat.
And so I sat and I listened,
And I felt your every word
  as they lingered in the black.

I closed my eyes.
But I opened them shortly
  (for I missed you in that span)
  Your perfume enticed my
  nostrils
  Your voice welcomed me back
  Your expression called for my
  attention
  Your wisdom rang in my ear.
You kept me up late last night
And you weren't even here . . .

Robert D. Nagle
**When Moses Last In the
Dooryard Laughed**
  TABLE OF CONTENTS
I have seen you bright and naked
  in the Springtime, . . . 1
When your fat mind kissed
  emergent cherry blossoms, . . .33
And new leaves began to appear
  on the surface, . . . 81
Brought to fruit with new living
  from darkly frozen life, . . . 131
You danced lightly on tender
  blades of grass, your loose
  emotions touching, . . . 187
Full pregnant with ideas you did
  not know you had, . . . 241

And you came to talk and situate
  like a manm, . . . 303
With a subtle gusto you could
  not nearly fathom, . . . 346
And Grandma spent her life in a
  field of rosebuds, . . . 381
Wanting to suck out youth she
  did not know she had . . . 420

Youth thought soapsuds purified
  the craven image, . . . 457
Standing on soapboxes in the late
  and early dawn, . . . 488
Cackling soft tears over an old
  and wore out grave, . . . 520
While a light snow fell quietly on
  tomorrow's dreams . . . 557

Donna LaVera Nehring
WHO AM I?
Who am I? That is a question
  hard to answer.
I am the life in all things.
I am the love shed abroad upon
  the face of the ground.
I am eternity; and I am a bubble
  of pure energy, that sparks all
  life, and runs the universe.
Thoughts I use to make my
  creation progress toward me;
  some slower, some faster, as
  each chooses to do.
I draw all life to my bosom, and
  nurse all living things with the
  milk of consolation.
Later I feed them the bread of
  understanding.
When they are grown to an age of
  reason; I give them the meat of
  experience to add to the bread.
Such a one is then drawn to me
  daily; as a cord is stretched
  from his bosom to mine.
In the course of time we become
  one in heart.
He and I are companions as of
  old; long ago, before man left
  his fathers home to explore on
  his own, for his own purpose.
I am not angry at man; anger is
  not in me.
But I pity the hardships man has
  chosen, in place of my love.
He runs for no reason, he seeks
  happiness where none exists.
Oh, pitiful man a victim of
  himself; and he knows it not.
All day I stretch out my hands to
  a rebellious generation that
  will not listen to it's Lord.
How long? How long?
Will you join hands with
  rebellion; before you consent to
  return to me.
Return to me and I will return to
  you.
Seek me early, before the dawn
  catches you unawares; and you
  are not dressed for the day.
That which is worn in the dark is
  one, that which is worn in the
  dawn is another, and that
  which is worn in the day still
  another.
The dark to hide self from all, the
  dawn to reveal parts of self, and
  the day to emerge free to reveal
  all in the open.
Being unashamed of self, with
  nothing to hide from self or
  others.

Approach me, as I am your life
  and your love.
  (God In Us A Hope Of Glory)

Ann F. Neel—Patton
SUNDAY MORNING
I wait for the sun on the
  mountains.
I wait for the warmth of the day.
I see the frost there on the tree
  tops
as I wait for the sun of the day.

I hope to go up to the mountains,
I hope to go up there today.
I hope to breathe bright air and
  sunshine
and leave from this valley some
  way.

Tomorrow will bring its own
  reason,
I just want to deal with today.
Tomorrow will bring its own
  season,
I just want to deal with today.

The sun is now rising,
the high hills await.
I'll go there and wonder
and look at my fate.

The wonder of mountains
may lead me to see
that the burdens which hound me
I might could be free.

In bright air and sunshine
those burdens seem small.
In bright air and sunshine
I might make it all.
  Sunday morning,
  Sunday night.

Nannette M. Mroz
YOSEMITE '81
"Do you mind?" he asked
and his sitting there was no
  surprise to me
Rather the completion of an event
pictured in my mind from the
  moment I had seen him:

A flash of light, hurrying across
  the station
Sun—drenched soldier, rugged
  and free
Armed with backpack and tan

Jolted my mind to remembering—
Yes, such things can be
Afford yourself the luxury
Of this one fascination

"No", I replied
And his hand held out to me
Such ageless secrets, caught in
  the traveling

William D. Milkes
1ST DAY
Generally speaking, persons like
  to think, and even sometimes
  believe that its whats inside
  that counts
It seems that people of all ages
  want first, deliver later, give me
  your best and then I'll give you
  mine
Rarely does the person who we
  think has the good innards
  show us some signal of
  knowing what its all about
How about the Golden Rule, a
  days work for a days pay, God
  and Country, and everything

will be fine
Lets start over every day, feel our
  sorrow, learn our lesson, and be
  on our way
Lessons of the past are in the
  books for us to read, and the
  challenge of the future means
  the best is yet to be
I'm convinced, there is food for
  thought, its takes attitude,
  purpose, and what we say
The message as I see it from you,
  you, and even you, is provide
  me with a leader, and then I'll
  do, you'll see
But we need to pay attention and
  know we all can't lead, and find
  our inspiration, take notice of
  your seed
Another day and night has
  passed, the clock has ticked
  away, but have we made some
  progress or do we wait for May
There is very little we can do if
  dead, take care of what we
  have, start with what we need
Now you have the secret, basics
  have their place, but to find
  your success, start again each
  day . . .

Bright McWhorter
THE THREE IMPERATIVES
Man, woman, an devil
Are the three things to compare
God never got into their
  Sensual
God stay'd hi, an' dry, an hansom
Up there.
But visited the earth garden
At eventide:
Judg'd them somewhat loosers
Then journey'd back to his ether'al
Air!
     An the real difference between
     Man an man
     Since that unetheral day;
     The difference not in their
     sanity
     But their insanity!
Are somewhat sorely hidden away.
To bring wars an rumors of wars
Till perhaps, that dreadful
  judgment
Day . . . ?

Judy Bryant
SISTER OF MYSELF
Who are you, you who walk
  beside me;
You shadowed self come to take
  my nights.
Speak to me, for long
Have we shared the same pathway,
Yet I know not the sight of your
  face,
Nor the 'sound of your name.
I bear no arms and come in peace
For I do not seek to take your life
As you do mine.
Come from the darkness, sit with
  me
Beneath the tree of light.
Let us be brought to fruit
In the warmth of the sun.
I have heard the roar of your
  thunder,
Stood against your desire to
  consume me.
You come as a thief to sap my
  strength,

You travel the night to rape my
  dreams,
I hear you calling, luring me to
  follow
As the mornings sky surrenders
  the night veil
So in my slumber you call,
Filling my hours with madness.
Come out, sister of myself, reveal
  your face.
The deep stillness stirred
There arose from within a mighty
  tempest.
A voice thundered over hills and
  valleys;
I am anger, risen from the roots of
  hell,
As the finger of death.
Then a shot rang out,
Echoing from the mountains to
  the seas
And warm innocent blood seeped
  into the earth

Chris Ann Bowman
UNTITLED
Sadness pervades
Every breath—I take
Sunshine is beaming
Though I'm not awake

Trying to live
Yet waiting to die
She just doesn't want
Her slice of the pie

Give it to someone
Either greedy or needy
But please, oh please
I just washed my face

Regina Conrath
THE DEATH OF A PRINCESS
The busy shops of Monaco were
  closed,
Even the playing cards were laid
  aside
As ill fate quickly reached out
  and disposed;
Sadly lowered, the flags at half-
  mast abide.
Someone said of her, she was a
  goddess,
Yet all who knew her from the
  time of birth
Said she was a happy, lovely
  princess;
To us a special lady of great
  worth.
Grace loved us and we loved her
  with real pride,
And we cannot believe she is
  gone so fast
In a brutal death on a
  mountainside;
Affected dreadfully, it left us
  aghast.
An earthly silence, as if the city
  slept
Happened, while family and
  friends mourned and wept.

Bethel A. Cochran
THE CHILD
*[To Mother and Dad who
always believed in me and to
Dean who one day will. But
most of all to Artie who is my
inspiration.]*
I had to take a walk today,
Felt I had to get away,
From all the weary, dreary chores,
That this old life holds in store.

I saw the farmer cutting hay,
on this hot September day,
He waved to me from the tractor
  seat,
As he wiped his brow from the
  heat.

On further down the lane I went,
And saw a neighbor nearly spent,
She'd raked and hoed the whole
  long day,
Why don't you stop? I wanted to
  say.

On down the lane I strolled in
  peace,
As though my life were on a leash,
And then I saw the strangest thing,
Why it was a boy; dressed as a
  king.

I had to stop I couldn't believe,
What my eyes did perceive,
But there he stood, standing tall,
In those funny clothes and all.

"Who are you?" I asked of him,
"Nobody." said he and began a
  Hymn,
"Rock of ages cleft for me,
Let me hide myself in thee."

His voice so soft was full of tears,
He looked too old for his young
  years,
He couldn't have been but nine
  or ten,
But I would have sworn he was a
  hundred then.

"Who are you, son?" I asked again,
"Are you lost? Are you ill? In pain?
He looked at me with eyes so deep,
I could feel the shivers through
  me seep.

He wouldn't answer. What could
  I do?
I had to know how to get through,
To such a weird and tiny thing,
As this boy dressed like a king.

I went to him and took his hand,
And led him upon that land,
So hot and dusty beneath our feet,
How come he dressed so in this
  heat?

At home I sat him down to drink,
Of cool, clear water from my sink,
I sat before him food to eat,
And then I took the other seat.

What kind of woman or was it
  thing,
That let her child dressed as a
  king,
Go out upon a hot, hot day,
All by himself so far away.

Again I asked, "Who are you, son?"
"Why don't you know?" he asked
  in fun,
"I am the king and Father Time,
I was once your age and you were
  mine."

I sat and stared at this strange
  child,
That I had met in the country
  wilds,
Upon a narrow, dusty lane,
As I was walking home again.

Wearily, he removed the crown,
Took off his robe and laid it down,
Then looked at me so strange and
  deep,

That down my face the tears did
  creep.

I knew him then, as I went down,
To kneel before this child I'd
  found,
On a dusty road, in this strange
  land,
Dressed as a king; nailprints on
  his hands.

Tommy Wayne Collins
MYSTERY OF LIFE
*[This poem was written—out
of love—for me, by my brother,
Tommy—and it is with my
love for him—that I submit our
poem for publication.]*
Conceived in the month
  of witches and spirits
  the first of seven about midnight
A spark of thought
  an undeveloped princess
  a gift of loving began her plight
Surrounded in darkness
  for three fourths a year
  she stretched out her arms
  toward the light
Overcome with the pain
  her lungs told of the fire
  the first breath was rage
  confusion fright

The companion heart beat
  now a life of its own
  the life line severed joy to the
  room
The first of seven
  how precious and special
  a sheet of music how sweet the
  tune
Magic stardust eyes
  reflection of beauty
  soft light in the night daughter
  of the moon
Composed of the love
  of mother and father
  this mystery of life is yours my
  June

George A. Stott
A SPECIAL FEELING
We share a special feeling,
  touch only with our eyes.
We share a special feeling,
  shown only in a glance.
We share a special feeling,
  afraid to take a chance.
We share our special feeling,
  afraid to let it grow,
  unwilling to let go.

Pat Jahner
HAVE YOU EVER?
Have you ever walked hand in
  hand
With your son or daughter, when
  you had time to spend
Or looked up into a cloudless sky—
Hung socks in matching pairs on
  the line to dry?

Have you ever just sat
And watched a butterfly tease a
  cat,
Took something freshly baked to
  a friend in need—
Just because you wanted to and
  they thanked you indeed?

Have you ever watched a sunset
  disappear,
Wished your children would
  never know fear,

Fished a spell, decorated a cake,
Or did a painting of trees near a
  lake?

Have you ever golfed across a
  frozen creek
And dropped the ball in the
  center of it,
Only to watch it skid across to
  the other side
With such speed and fluency, a
  most unusual sight?

Have you ever stood back to take
  one more look
At the Christmas tree before you
  took
All the decorations and tinsel
  down to store
In a box where it's been many
  years before?

Well, I have!

Janice Segerdahl
AT THE TIME
Why doesn't a chocolate bar
Ease every little problem . . now?
I thought at the time . . it did.

Why doesn't making love
In a back seat
Seem as romantic now . .?
I thought at the time . . it did.

Why didn't getting married
And having babies
Keep me from feeling, worthless
  and lonely?
I thought at the time . . they did.

Why now that we have the time
Don't we talk any more
Make love as before?
So many things have gone wrong.

God!! . . . I was afraid . . AT THE
TIME . . They Would.

Lois Osso
MOTHER'S DAY
*[To The Mother Who Gave Me
Life To The Mother Who
Taught Me How To Enjoy It
And to All Mothers everywhere]*
This Mother's Day has special
  meaning to me,
  I think of not one but four you
  see.
The first is my mother-in-law to
  her family bound,
  just recently by my husband
  she was found.
They were parted at his birth
  separated through the years,
  their reunion was filled with
  love, emotion and tears.
I think of myself and my role as
  mother,
  my love for my son and my
  own darling daughter.
Then the memory of the mother
  who shared my growing years,
  who laughed with me, held me
  and wiped my tears.
She's gone now and I miss her face,
  there isn't another who could
  take her place.
Then there's the mother who
  carried me nine months long,
  during that time we were as
  one and for me the bond is
  strong.
We haven't any memories to
  share from years gone past,

but I've found her at long last.
Now after all these years I can
finally say,
I love you Mom and Happy
Mother's Day.

Terry D. Holmberg
DEVIL'S PLAY
Lightning cracks
whips of fire.
Devil's thorne
hell's desire.

Covering the sky
in gloomful dismay.
Thunder and lightning
the Devil's play.

Lightning strikes twice
burning trees all around.
Rumbling and rolling
left shaking the ground.

Mountain sides flaming
hells up above.
Showing no mercy
casting out love.

Death and destruction
everythings gone.
Nothing to burn
the storm carries on.

A dismal reminder
of power in flight.
Rumbling and rolling
off in the night.

Heat and smoke
fill the air.
Nothing alive
nothing to spare.

Faye Simpkins
MY DARLING HUSBAND
My Darling Husband gets up early
To work hard for our living
I want to thank him daily
Because I realize what he is giving.
Without my Darling Husband I'll
confess
My life would change I don't have
to guess
He leaves for work at six regularly
By four thirty he returns home to
me
I open the yard gate, he is never
late
I stand there with smiles not long
to wait.
My Darling Husband full of
surpises so much
Brings home pizza, fried chicken
and such
I'll never question why he
surprises me like that
I'll let my husband pull surprises
out of his hat.
My Darling Husband is just a
dirty honest little worker
Never missing a day, some
husbands might find time to
play
Other wives worry about their
livelihood they say
Maybe it's hard for those ladies—
their husband they should obey.
My Darling Husband knows I'll
be home after his work each day
He knows upon his return he'll
be hugged and kissed without
dismay
I always want to let him know
that I appreciate him in every
way

I have earned my rights, I'll
continue living with him, here
I'll stay.

Debbie Wessels
FOR A FRIEND
*[To Herb—a very special
person in my life who knows
what emotions really are.]*
Sometimes things don't seem
quite right in this world of ours
today,
but we try to succeed, and do our
best every single day.
Some days are better than others,
while others are worse than
some,
but still we hang on to the thread
that keeps us from having none.
Slowly our grip gets weaker, as
we hear the great demand,
and that is when we need a
caring helping hand.
Someone to be there when we are
weak, who can help us through
the day.
To share their thoughts of
kindness, and that is why I say:
I'm here not only as a student,
but as a friend to you indeed.
Whenever you're feeling down
and depressed, and think you
cannot succeed.
I'll brighten up your darkest days,
and make you feel brand new.
This is what a friend can do—
what I can do for you . . .

Darlene Lum
YOU
*[For a very special someone,
John W. Hamilton]*
You
make me smile
You
give me warmth
You
give me love
like nobody before.

Thank you
for your kindness
and generosity
and love

But most of all,
Thank you
for being
You.

Elizabeth Ann
FAITHFUL AND TRUE
Fare thee well
And in my sight
Invoke the spell
That makes it right.
Happiness in every cell—
Forget the dark, look to the light
Until the story you will tell
Leads you from the stormy night.

Anyone may see the truth
Never miss the Serpent's tooth
Deny your age, but not your
youth.

Tell the story that you know
Remind us that we all must grow;
Unveil the riddle, let it show,
Everyone is in the flow.

Kate McVey
TOUCHING
Curling around your smile,
Touching you close at night.

Momentary relief from the pain
of living.
Escape from our separate
yesterdays
Into a single today.
To touch today should mean to
touch tomorrow . . .
Yet I know we will have no
tomorrows,
Only the sound of one of us
Walking away.

F. Kay Fischer
Rainbows and Lucky Stars
Everybody has a rainbow
At the end a pot of gold,
Everybody has a star
With which to wish upon.

Everybody climbs that rainbow
Some to find the pot is bare,
Everybody makes their wishes
But is that one star theirs?

My rainbow is imaginary
It's one I'll never see,
My lucky star I talk about
Is only in my dreams.

Someday soon I don't know when
I'll walk that way again,
And who knows in days to come
I'll reach my rainbows end.

I'll also find my lucky star
And all my dreams come true,
But until that day, I'll sit and wait
And thank God I have you!

Lisa A. Jacobi
HAPPINESS AND LOVE
*[This poem was written to my
future husband Jim. I will love
you always and forever.]*
On this bright summer day,
I think of you in a special way.
Wishing that I could always be
with you,
is the only thing that I want to
do.
Being with you alone at night,
makes me feel special when
you hold me tight.
Doing those special things
together,
makes our love grow to last
forever.
I love thinking of that one special
day,
when the two of us marry in
the mid-of May.
The happiness and love of the
two of us together,
is the one thing I know will
last forever.
I Love You . . .

Kenneth Nelson
ANTICIPATION
Anticipation is like a heady wine.
When you anticipate something
grand
Strolling through the park hand
in hand.
With someone you love listening
to a band.
On the proverbial grandstand
An anticipation of a dinner for
two.
In some secluded rendevous.
With a woman with form and
personality divine.
In sombre and sober thought you
heed.

You think why do people need?
An external intoxicant to get
them high.
With anticipation is intoxicant
enough
To make you want to fly.
Anticipating can be so
tantalizing, exciting and pure
ecstasy.
Anticipation for me is quite
enough.

Mary McNally
TO A SMALL SNAKE
From where I stood
it seemed
a narrow branch
yet too black.

I bent to scrutinize
saw there
a primitive head
with glistening eye.

It spiraled
to a knot
and held
against the wall.

The ancient enemy
waiting, fearful
fearful of me
as my blood iced.

Linda Kaye Thomas
DRIFTING SAND
Your life to you is riding
the free spirit of some fine wave
chasing with the surf
for the most of all it gave.
A ramblng man of emotion
I see you riding high
sulking with devotion
(I think you'd rather die).
My life to me has had you
rambling words are not my own.
I write you true expression
from where I'm not alone.
Ride high your mighty waves
trail the winds of your open seas ...
where I know you're wanted
and needing to be free.
I write for you this poem
as your love I understand.
Encased by the shadow of your
pride
I'm moved by Drifting Sand.

Anne Animus
WHO ARE YOU?
I am a child, of God;
an Adept of the Universe—
and, I am lacking
in all of the above.

I am a Woman for a Wizard,
part of that Spirit which keeps him
to himself, free.

What is tamed for either part
is not the expression of the Soul
but only the pace at which 'tis
done,
that each may share
in each.

G. A. Wiens
A Blessing Called Mother
When the baby awakens at
midnight,
With an illness or stomach that's
sore,
It is mother that goes to her
loved one,
No matter how trying the chore.

When the young child has run
into problems,
He knows mother will always care.
If the answer is not in her wisdom,
He knows she can lead him in
prayer.

The young man must go in the
service,
His country to help to keep free.
But mother is always beside him,
In spirit on prayerfully bended
knee.

At home, in hospital, or prison,
Or where ever you may happen
to roam,
Thank "God" for a blessing called
"Mother",
And the memories of love in the
home.

A mother is man's greatest
blessing,
From birth till the Lord calls her
home.
She'll always remember her
children,
No matter how far they may roam.

Thru laughter and smiles when
we're happy,
Thru tears and heartaches we
bear,
Remember that blessing called
"Mother",
Everytime that you whisper a
prayer.

Elba Elias
HOLD MY HAND, MY SON
*[I dedicate this poem to my
son, Raymond, who inspired
me by a photo of him walking
through a park, holding his
son's hand.]*
Hold my hand, my son
Let me guide you as best I can.
Your first steps are a big event
wobbly as they are, they will
steady.
Let me help you in your new
discoveries
I will explain along the way.

Hold my hand, my son
As we walk together on paths of
beauty.
Let me set examples that will
teach you the goodness of life.
May I be an inspiration to you in
later years.
I will try to do the right things at
the right time with the help of
God.

Hold my hand, my son
Let me teach you the wonders of
life
A life well lived because of love
of God.
There is much goodness to be
seen and found, if love is
present.
Let me help you find this
goodness and teach you this
love.
With the help of God, all
tomorrows will be sound and
peaceful.

Hold my hand, my son, hold my
hand.

Bob Phillips
SONGBIRD OF LUST
The Songbird of lust—
a most beautiful bird
who's songs are often heard,
lights in the trees—
a desolate place,
surging my sexual powers.

She sings a song—so beautiful
it sounds almost erotic,
there is no power stronger than
hers;
this bird is most exotic.

I see her often yet seldom—
flying on wings of desire
making these things so hard to
handle,
igniting a dwindled fire.

She settles her wings,
lights on my shoulder,
and sings into my ear,
whenever I get close to you
. . . whenever you are near.

Letha Memorie Lloyd-Wayne
CELESTIAL BEING
What am I conducting
In the orchestra of thought?
Melodic strains of hope
To souls forlorn?
Phrasing notes of joy
Uplifting hearts to pulses
Of exalted tonalities
Lighting the mind to paths
Of etheriality?
Freeing man to his nobility
within
And the grandeur of His Divine
Reflection
As the perfect child of God?

Dee Dee
Mom, a Tribute For You
Mom, this is for you
As I have tried to express just
how special you are.
There are words,
But words are not what I feel and
words just do not put the feeling,
They just do not say it right.
So I'll see if I can convey to you
just what I mean.
As a babe, you were there
Doing for me everything that I
was to small or to young to do
for myself.
As I grew, you did less of what I
could do myself,
But you seemed to do more for me.
You boosted my moral when
needed,
You mended the broken pieces as
well as picked them up
sometimes,
You punished me when I
deserved it.
You did all for me and more than
what is mentioned here.
Yet, you expected nothing in
return.
I love you and respect you—
Even though I sometimes failed
to show you.
I even understand now why you
did what you did, when you did.
I see and understand so much
better, now with my own family.
Mom, I am trying to tell you in
my own way—
I think you are tops and I want to

say thank you.
I am the lucky one because I
found out and able to tell you so.
The thanks is for what I am and
who I am.
Mom, you did your best because
you are the best!
I Love You.

Jonita Scott
SO MANY
There are so many sides to a
thing;
So many corridors in the same
maze.
There are numberless, distinct
cells
Living within a person—
Other selves in one self;

Countless pieces to resolve
Into various puzzles—
Amazingly different, though alike!
There are so many ways to go
Presented at one time.

Multitudes of ideas
Are conceived in a single brain;
Caverns and clear heights,
And the levels between,
A lone soul may travel—all in a
day!

Ragnar Carlgren
Metropolis—Pros and Cons
*[Dedicated to Dr. Cecil C.
Vaughn who performed a life-
saving, "five-bypass-operation"
on me, July 6, 1982, at St.
Luke's Medical Center in
Pheonix, Arizona.]*
Mile-long rush hour traffic snarls,
poisoning commuters' minds.
Invigorating it is not! It is
polluted. Hydrocarbonized,
ozonized, carbonmonoxidized,
particle-ized.
Metropolis, what've you done to
people?
They can't get out of the rut.
The same yesterday, the same
today, the same tomorrow.
Laden with the burden of not
being born with a silver spoon,
The hope for many: social
security checks,
Medicare is a distant goal for the
weary, for the middle-aged,
The old. The young have their
pleasures to take care of;
They may even like the
Metropolis—street gangs,
Bars, screaming tires, racing from
a robbed bank.

They're also million-dollar
corporations,
With executives in flannel suits,
Cubicled in skyscrapers with
washroom keys.
They rule the nation—so they
think,
Until the Madison avenue magic
fails to increase the yield,
And the earnings ratio takes a
beating.
The Metropolis is looking for a
handout,
But who is bailing who out, who?
It's easy to blame somebody else,
When things go wrong in
Metropolis, but when things go
right,

The politician is the king of the
hill.
It's a bitter pill to swallow,
When things go wrong in
Metropolis.

But there's another Metropolis,
worthwhile.
Benign and understanding with
hospitals.
A bypass operation, a tired heart,
a surgeon skilled;
Anesthesia, computer-precise
hands
Give healing touch to this old
heart.
It's the latest in medical science
We've reached—the patient
benefits.
Life must go on, even if the
patient dies,
But he didn't this time, the odds
were good.
The surgeon saved my life,
thanks to delicate hands
Of someone who cares. In this
Metropolis all is not bad.
So, there's hope for mankind,
even if
The armaments go on for full.
Greed and passion, crime, drab,
and
Pollution notwithstanding,
Life goes on in Metropolis..

Madison avenue magic:
hucksterism, preferably
practised in TV-commercials,
not necessarily restricted to
the Manhattan business
district in N.Y. City.

Margaret Zoharchuk
UKRAINIAN GIRL
Ukrainian girl, you can't sigh,
Ukrainian girl, you can't cry.
Ukrainian girl, you can't ask why?
Ukrainian girl, you can't say bye.

Lisa Malina Davidson
The Devil Made Me Do It
When God created the earth and
the sun,
He made different things and was
done.
In His own special form, He
created the human,
He created a man, and He created
a woman.
He gave them no knowledge of
evil or sin,
So a perfect life Adam and Eve
did begin.
They lived in a paradise, slept
under trees,
Moss as their pillow, and a
blanket of leaves.
"Don't eat of that tree," said the
Lord, "For evil is within."
"If you eat of that tree, your
troubles will begin."
"Why not eat that fruit, Eve?"
asked the snake.
"Because the Lord said it would
be a terrible mistake."
"Ah, and He did lie to you too."
"For, if you eat the fruit, all things
will obey you?"
So the innocent child, the fruit
did consume,
And then convinced Adam, her
most willing groom.

Now the fruit of the tree
  contained the knowledge of
  sin,
So Adam and Eve's trouble started
  to begin.
They noticed their nakedness,
  did Adam and Eve.
And they sought to cover
  themselves with a fig leaf.
The Lord said, "Adam and Eve,
  why do you hide?"
"Because we are naked, me and
  my bride."
"Who told you this? It was not
  me."
"Probably the fruit of the
  forbidden tree."
"Why, Adam, did you eat the
  forbidden fruit?"
"The woman did first, I just
  followed suit."
"And you, Eve?" "I was told by the
  snake."
"Now that, I must say, was a
  dreadful mistake."
Thus from the garden, they were
  both banished,
Tired and cold and sometimes
  famished.
The devil was the sanke who
  made Eve sin,
And eat of the fruit, the Lord had
  forbidden.
And that is why, when your
  mom's in a fit,
You always say, "The Devil made
  me do it!"

Ruth M. Whitford
Upon My Husband's Birthday
The little private world
We now share
Was built a long while ago
By dreams we shared
When we were young.
Then—untried love and passion
That through the years
Between then and now
Have lasted, sustained
The test of time.

With each passing birthday
I liken it unto a gem, a pearl
That has been added to the
Precious strand of togetherness.
From the first birthday, yours,
I knew you were mine
To have and to hold
Cherish and love
For always and always
For ever and ever.
How I cherish, with all my heart,
These pearls in our precious
  strand of togetherness.

Today—another pearl will be
  added.
And, the dreams we dream
Are more positive
More, significant, in their way
Than those of yesterday
When we dreamed of the
  impossible,
When—we were young.
Happy Birthday Darling.

Frances May Tauer
NIGHT INTERLUDE
Night comes forth in somber dress
Dark in mystery,
When voices are hushed

And no footsteps rushed
By their constancy . . .
I pause beside a gate,
Where cottage lamps are dim,
As strains of music reach my ear
Coming from within!
Hesitant to linger,
Reluctant yet to go . . .
For the music that I hear,
O How my heart doth hunger so!
As hands upon the keyboard play
By one in reverie,
While I stand just beyond the gate
Held in ecstasy!

Jessie Alma Edge
THE TALKING ROSE
I am just a lonely Rose that
grows in some forgotten garden—

With perfume so sweet you
  must
stop and remember forgotten
  things

I listen as you stop,
and hear things both glad and sad.

I hear promises made by lovers
and the whispered secrets of
  children.

I hear of loves lost and loves
  won
of dreams fulfilled and hopes to
  be shared.

I see tears shed for dreams lost
  and
loved ones who sleep forever on
  the hillside.

I share my beauty and perfume
  with all who see me—
Young and Old—Sad and
  Happy—Cruel and Loving

If only those who find my
  garden and see my
beauty and smell my perfume
could share their beauty the
  same,

the world would be a garden of
Love.

Stephen Franklin Junkin
FREEDOM'S SYMBOL
*[These lines were written in
memory of my family of the
past. Those who made my
present life and possessions
possible.]*
Gazing out from this old porch,
  I recall the generations gone
  on.
Freedom's symbol was a torch
And a mistake would be
  condoned.

"How old is this house?" I asked
  my Dad.
  "A century or better!" said he.
"Three generations it has had,
  Up until you and me."

He recalled planting that old oak,
  'Twas only a very small thing.
With a pair of mules the land was
  broke,
  Stopping only for the dinner
  bell ring.

Seeing old pictures and reading
  letters
Takes me back to that time.
Beds and pillows filled with
  feathers;

This heritage will always be
  mine.

Grandpa told me indians lived
  here,
  Down by the lower forty's
  stream.
To me his memory stays dear,
  Talking about that wildcat's
  scream.

My ancestors set on this old porch
  Making heirlooms by hand.
That statue still holds its torch;
  I praise God for making this
  land.

Terry Anne Laird—Dungan
LOVE WILL LEAD US
Are there many skies left for
  birds to fly,
Or must we listen to their cries,
  and wonder, why?
What of the mouths to feed,
  some have stopped crying,
But some still feel the need, and
  they are still dying.
How many more battlefields will
  bear the scars of death?
Until one side yields, many will
  lose their breath.
What of the child who grows in
  the street,
Wild and free until he lies under
  a sheet,
Fallen by a gun with a hand on
  the end.
We can no longer run, no longer
  pretend,
For the sorrows are there, making
  eyes cry,
If we do not care, we will
  continue to die.
There are animals here today,
  that won't be known tomorrow,
Many will die in the same way,
  and it will be to our sorrow,
They will die by bullets of steel,
  and void of trust,
Because we do not feel, they will
  die because of us.
There are trees growing tall,
  freely waving their leaves,
But they are doomed to fall, and
  still no one *believes!*
Where will it all stop, so we can
  start over again?
And we can, if we don't give up,
  we can . . . *BUT WHEN!*

Barbara Jean Owens
DEATH OF A DANCER
Graceful lines
Strong tight muscles
Sweat trickled down his face
Graceful movements
Leaps and slides
Hot lights and applause
A deep low bow, the end of a
  brilliant career
The pulsing music dies out
He collects his things and looks
  in the mirror
Was he aging as they said
A few lines etched around his
  eyes,
But his body was full of grace and
  poise
Lines anyone would be proud
  of . . .

The stage was dark
Seats were empty

Standing on stage,
He proceeded to dance as he
  never danced before
Perfect timing with the music
  that echoed deep in his mind
Ego and pride burst into his
  performance
The final steps and lines came
  quickly
As he danced around the stage
One last thrust bow and up
Applause like he had heard
  before sounded in his heart
He turned leaving the stage . . .

In his dressing room he left his
  dancing shoes
And a smal amount of pride as
  the hall door closed behind
  him
Then faded into darkness . . .

Elsie Day Cruthirds
MY RAIN AND YOU
Oh, I love the rain!—though not
  long ago
I verily loathed it so.
'Twas then that I always ran—ran
  away
When it fell by the way.
  That was then my duty.

It seemed so dreadfully cold—so
  wet
Falling on me, and yet,
As it splashed on trees and walks,
Or trickled down flower stalks,
  I could see no beauty.

But now—now I can see it anew,
God's wonderful splendor in
  view.
It fills my heart with sweet
  gladness
Instead of the sadness
  Because it reminds me of you.

As it touches my face, softly
  patters,
Nothing else matters—
It feels like your dear loving
  kisses, Mother,
Like which there was none other.
  In Memory, you're with me too.

Edna M. Quick
A ROSE
When I think of a rose and its
  delicate stem,
A face looms before me, so calm
  and serene;
It's the face of my mother, whom
  I hold so dear,
So gentle and understanding, her
  love so sincere.
The lines in her face, may grow
  deeper with age,
But each represents, another
  scrapbook page;
She was there to help me, when I
  first learned to walk;
It was she who helped form the
  words, when I started to talk.
It was she who had to shed a tear,
  when I started to school,
No one knew how much she'd
  miss me, she thought I was
  such a jewel.
When my schools days were over,
  and I went out on my own,
I'm sure she shed another tear, for
  home was not a home;
Not a home she'd been used to,
  with so much activity,

Still, a home with love and a
welcome, for me to come home
to.
Unlike the rose, whose petals fall,
when they have served their
time,
My mother's love will stay alive,
and that LOVE is all mine . . .

Raymond C. Lockhart
THE LAST UNICORN
She was born in the summer
The sun was shining bright
She didn't know her parents
But she still learned wrong
from right.

She lived in a forest
A patch so lush and green.
With of the help of her magic
horn
She was seldom ever seen.

A pure white mare to
non-believers
But believers; they all knew.
She was the last unicorn
Her story sad but true.

Jon Torbriner (Jon of Frisco)
INCORRIGIBLE
Sheincried
With all staid green ways of day.
And incorrigible case by hound
stream bay.
This record as able sanctified as
stable.
Patching working, stare braking
all my she aching.
A choice to gander her wonder.
Giving a soul's choice, tender
pretender.
Forgiving forever her, her lender.
The face belost, be host or ghost.
Gash, blash or hash the fairies
behold.
All tarry was haste.
This lady my bad taste.
Oh joy to try, to lie, to die.
Be list my cherry to gist of hairy.
The beast to way a shame, work
tales.
Trails beguiles my incredibly
deep pails.
She shan't we brake, correctable
by take.
An incorrigible woman is on my
make.
Sheincried

Novella Meek
THREE WORLDS OF "I"
*[To Dream, my 22 year old
honey-sorrel, who as a spirited
colt was the inspiration for a
poem that triggered my pen
into its ceaseless writings.]*
Three worlds have I, Lord, and
the choice is mine!
Thou gavest man the choice
since Adam's time.
Three worlds of choice in this
universe, I!
From intellect world comes the
question why?

The cry of knowledge soon
leadeth astray
If spiritual world is not interplay.
The two together brings an inner
peace,
So, physical rages are better cease.

That third world, Lord, is a trap

and the snare,
Only conquered if the first two
are there.
The choice of the flesh, the
physical hue,
Is the curse since Eden that
Adam knew!

Dianne E. Foster Read
A HOUSE THAT WAS HOME
My grandfather's house is as old
as my dad.
It was never a mansion, but was
all that they had.
Although it was small, none were
barred from its door.
Be it ever so crowded, there was
room for one more.

My dad was just nine, when his
father died.
They laid him to rest at his own
father's side,
And put up two stones marked
"Father" and "Son",
And left dad to finish what his
dad had begun.
But they still had each other, and
memories to share.
He would not be forgotten, while
his house was still there.

Dad's gone back home, now, to
where he was born.
The fields that surround it are
other folks' corn.
For the fields where my
grandfather labored so hard,
Are all sold away, little's left but
the yard.
But the house is still there, and
so's the windmill,
Battered and rusted, but standing
there still,
Entwined in a vine that will soon
reach the top,
And when it gets there—well—
perhaps it won't stop,
But grow on up to heaven, and
bloom bright and fair,
To show my grandfather—his
house is still there.

H. Jamison Redder
THY WILL BE DONE
I saw the miracle of God's work
As our poppies spread "Kleenex"
blooms.
I saw the wrath of a summer
storm
And heard His thunder's booms.

I witnessed His majestic spread
Of garden plants so green,
That the very earth seemed
painted
With a healthy, verdant sheen.

I stood in open-mouthed awe
As the shuttle lifted from the
ground.
"Not man's will, but God's will be
done,"
This thought in me did abound.

Astounded, I stood and stared
At a total eclipse of the moon,
One quarter, one half, three
quarters—all,
The "Giant Frog" devoured, so
soon.

Oh God, were there e'er any doubt
Of thy Omnipotent power

and Grace?
We need only to look around us,
For it shows in every place.

In those words we speak so often
As we partake the wine, the
unleaven,
Our Faith is confirmed, Thy Will
be done,
On Earth as it is in Heaven!

Noxie Janes

Noxie Janes

Noxie Janes
TWILIGHT SONG
When twilight silken curtain falls,
And gleams the evening star,
There enters in my heart a call,
That sends my thoughts afar.

A dusty path is brought to mind,
That winds around a hill,
Where waves the leaves in
summer wind,
And nature sings her night song
still.

Dreams are dreamed, and plans
are made,
Upon this dusty path,
A heart that yearns, while
holding hands,
But knows it cannot last.

And up this way again I'll go,
As in the distant past,
Where waited eyes with love
aglow,
And joys too sweet to last.

Melody Emerson
A POEM FOR MOM
"47 years ago today
A child was born
Her life was hard,
Her patience tried.
So much pain,
So many tears cried.

Two marriages gone,
Six children were born.
Her mind was worried,
And her heart was torn.

A man came along,
With a warm loving heart.
Now they are together,
And shall never part.

She thought that time,
Was going by so slow.
But now she says,
Where did it all go.

Now her children are grown,
With their own children too.
I love you Mom,
Happy Birthday to you.

Ervena D. Stanley (Fetty)
BABY'S SONG
Hush little baby don't you cry,
Momma's gonna sing you a
lull-a-bye.
Hush my little one don't you weep,
Sandman's comin' with pleasant
sleep.
Sweet dreams little one in the
land of Nod,
Where all little babies play with
God.
The angels watch over you from
dusk till dawn,
When the new day breaks and
the night time is gone.
So hush little baby and don't be
afraid—,
Remember God, loves you . . .
and through God, you were
made.
So sleep my little one . . . sleep
on through the night—,
The sun will be shining with the
new morning's light.
And when you awaken my sweet
little dear—,
You'll find your momma waiting
right here.
So hush my little one, don't you
cry—,
Momma's gonna sing you her
lull-a-bye.

Jackie Blem
PORTRAIT OF TURMOIL
A girl walks alone
On a cold, bitter evening
Trying to hold back tears
Of pain and anger.
The many turns of the road
Make her lose her momentum.
Life's changes confuse her
And leave her soul in turmoil.
Trying to make sense of them
Is like trying to put a broken
glass together.
Though the pieces may still fit,
Nothing will ever be the same.

Christopher Barton
MY TRESTLE
As I sit here now as I did as a boy,
I clearly remember my days of
joy
And though I know time has
taken its claim
The scenes around me look not
the same
For whatever happened to the
great river that flowed so
furious and fearsome with the
sound of danger
Surely in so few years simple
nature could not have changed
her
And the trestle herself, has she
not dropped in height
For now when I cross her, I feel
not the same fright
And the great tree on the island,
has it not the power to grow
Surely this is not the great tree I
had once known
The great beautiful tree, that
adventurous sight which
appeared to be so tall
For now as I climb to her highest
height, I could surely survive
the fall
But still in so short of time

613

My trestle, my place of peace
It is not her who has been
    rearranged
Rather yet, it is I who have
    changed
As I sit here now as I did as a
    child, I clearly remember my
    days of wild
My days of adventure filled with
    treasures of silver and gold
Oh, how I wish
I had never grown old

Vikki McKee
FOUR SEASONS OF LIFE
The spring is the birth of life
And the future is what lies ahead
The worries and troubles and
    strifes
Are a part of the life to be led

With the summer comes the aging
Of children into adults
And our lives will be changing
And correcting our many faults

The autumn too soon is to come
Our youth is to be left behind
But the joys and sorrows too
    great a sum
Are the memories that fill our
    mind

Winter has brought the death
Our spirits inside us shall soar
We have taken our last breath
Our life on earth is no more

William Russell Hill
PURGATORY
A restless sleep . . . I toss and
    turn.
My soul it wants to scream.
And though I know it's not, it
    seems to help . . .
by pretending it's all a dream.
I pray to God,
I call His name . . .
but He must pay me no mind.
For in my wake or in my sleep . . .
peace I cannot find.
It's a useless life and wasted time,
where hopeless days are spent.
For behind these fences, bars and
    walls,
there's no way to be content.
And though I'm young in mind
    and body,
my spirits make me old.
And I truly am not living, for my
    heart . . .
has turned ice cold.
There's times I wish these walls
    would crumble,
to crush my weary head . . .
And you'd not wonder at my
    indifference,
if to life you were as dead.
Oh, it's so much mental torture,
In a barred up little cell.
Lord knows I'm going to
    Heaven . . .
Because I've served my time in
    Hell . . .

Deborah Marchman Osei-Kofi
WHERE IS PEACE
The dreams for a happy life
are always shattered.
And the hopes of peace
can never be fulfilled.
Where does all the fighting end?
Show me the place where peace
    begins.

How many more deaths will
    cause us to weep?
How many more martyrs
will we find to mourn?
Keep them from the assassins
who spill their blood in the
    streets.
Keep them from bitter hearts and
    confused minds
who suspect no personal gains.
When all nations scream defeat
will that be sufficient?

Weren't we ecstatic when our
    hostages came home?
We danced and rejoiced in the
    streets.
And when Reagan and Pope John
    Paul II were shot
our emotions brought back
    despair.
Anwar Sadat our most recent
    loss,
the list is so long
and I suppose will go on.

Our tears will come
and our tears will go
But when, oh when will the
    fighting stop?
When lord, oh when will hatred
    flee from their hearts?

Each nation as one
with their eyes to the heavens.
One nation under God
and peace prevailing forever.

Donna Lynne Grove
**I'll Think Of You and
You'll Be There**
I'll think of you,
    As the snow begins falling
    silently through the crisp night
    air
    When the wind is raging and I
    sit by the fireplace staring
And you'll be there.

I'll think of you,
    As the first crocus of spring
    appear
    When songs of the frogs and
    crickets through the night I
    hear
And you'll be there.

I'll think of you,
    As the warm summer breezes
    rustle through the leaves
    When far off whippoorwills cry
    their mournful cry from the
    trees
And you'll be there.

I'll think of you,
    As the trees change color and
    winter seems so near
    When the smell of wood
    smoke fills the air
And you'll be there.

Joan Yoest
Suddenly You Were Gone
*[In loving memory of Paula
Joan Marie Yoest]*
I recall your smiling face
Full of beauty, joy and grace.
A stately blonde of seventeen,
Adored and loved as tho a queen.

Full of life and much devotion.
Sometimes in perpetual motion.
Singing, dancing up a storm,
Creative, sensitive and warm.

The sun is setting in the sky,
You watch it with your dad and I.
Your girl friends take you for a
    walk
So you can be alone and talk.

Coming home you meet a friend,
Your life is drawing to an end.
He asks you if you want a ride.
Your happiness is hard to hide.

"I'll go home and ask my dad,
I don't want him to get mad.
Dad said to be home by ten,
He had to leave for work again."

Up in bed I slept unknowing
Of the fact that you were going.
Outside at the curb George
    waited,
And the ride that was ill-fated.

You were oh so thrilled inside—
Your second motorcycle ride.
All of five short minutes long,
Then suddenly—you were gone.

With heavy heart and watery eyes
I look for you in heaven's skies
And wonder why, till I get hives,
So many drunks take innocent
    lives.

Elaine Chambers
SOMETHING
*[To my parents, with all my
love.]*
With every dream,
    something will be seen.

With every wish,
    something will be learned.

With every guess,
    something will be wrong.

With every opportunity,
    something will be missed.

With every season,
    something beautiful will show.

With every failure,
    something better is found.

With every thing,
    something wonderful is there.

Michele Denise Fancher
UNTITLED
*[To Anna Mildred Fancher—
Happy Mother's Day—Every
Day]*
To a very special "Mother" on
    this very special day
Whom I'm very glad to honor in
    my very special way

Who has always been forgiving
    when I failed to turn off lights
And when I added all my
    bluejeans to the wash with all
    your whites

Who has never said a word when
    I failed to clean my room
Even though I sometimes noticed
    little notes left on the broom

Who has never gotten angry
    when I went out with my date
Even though I always managed to
    come home three hours late

Who has always filled the ice
    trays when I left them on the
    sink
Though you never got to use
    them when you went to get a
    drink

Well I've decided for my present
    that I'm giving you this day
To do whatever pleases you in
    any kind of way

But before you get your present
Your room should be well cleaned
The ice trays should be filled
And you should be home by
    nine-fifteen

Lucille M. Gilpin
PASSING IN PANTOMIME
A Christian Octogenarian was he,
Full of Faith we all could see,
Though he was as sick as sick
    could be,
Through pain he sang, "Every
    Hour I Need Thee."

His heart no palpitation,
His breath only gasping
    expirations,
All vital signs obviously had
    ceased,
From this life he had been
    released. ·

Yet suddenly, his head and
    shoulders did arise,
His eyes in awe opened very
    wide,
He extended his right hand high
    to clasp,
That of His Maker on the Other
    Side.

He hadn't complained,
    whimpered, or showed fear.
He knew in his heart, his God
    was near,
In life he served Him til called
    from on High,
Knowing How to Live, he knew
    how to die.

Vivian A. Froehlich
SO, THIS IS LOVE?
Advice from others around me,
Each helping their own little way,
A pat on the back, a smile,
Never hearing a word they say.

It's hard to tell my feelings "stop",
Or to turn off the wants I've felt,
Unlike a snowman built with care,
These desires just won't melt.

Life's not right or fair this way,
My heart has broke in two,
I cry myself to sleep some nights,
What am I to do?

Maybe if we never talk,
Or visit once again,
Or maybe if I just forget,
The past and what we've been,

Alone, again, I'll go my way,
My love I'll always send,
Because of you, my life won't stop,
But, my heart will never mend!

Connie Jo Esra
LOST LOVE
I miss you so my darlin
I never thought I really cared.
Thought I could forget you
and the Love that we had shared.
Now it's come to actually doin it
I'm not thinkin anymore,
It's sure alot more difficult
When reality takes its core.
I tell myself again and again
there's nothin to regret,
it's over now the fun's been had,
it's time we just forget.

Today's Greatest Poems

I tell myself you're just a man
and men I've had before,
but I find myself wantin your
  Love,
each day more and more.
You've satisfied my heart's desire,
you've made my dreams come
  true.
Life don't seem worth livin,
if I'm livin it without you.
But I guess that's the way it has
  to be
my Love can't change your ways,
so I'll keep on hurtin through the
  nights
and smilin through the days.
I'm sure something will happen
  soon
to heal my broken heart,
for time has a way of mendin,
things that are torn apart.
For now I think I'll end this poem,
with hugs and kisses to you,
and hopes that someday later on,
my dreams for us come true.

Deborah Ann Emery Robey
WHO ARE YOU?
*[I've written this poem for a
special reason. I was always
taught the "best gift" is a gift
from your heart. And for my
mom and dad, I give only the
best.]*
You are someone who is always
  there
To listen and lean on when I
  need care;
You are very special in your own
  way
And whenever you're needed you
  know what to say
Your faces that glow with love all
  the time
Is more beautiful than the words
  that I've written
  in these lines,
For you, you alone have filled my
  days
  with love and care in many ways
I speak of your greatness, I speak
  of your love
I speak of gentle touches, kisses,
  and hugs;
So on this special day, like everyday
I thank God I was given one of
  the most
  precious gifts from God . . .
  MY PARENTS

Debra J. Courtney
TIME
T is for the ticking of the clock
as the minutes turn into hours,
days, longer . . .

I is for me, living those hours and
wondering what lies ahead in
the minutes . . .

M is for the many people, places
and things in life that touch
and are touched in turn . . .

E is for everything together that
cannot be stopped because
time must go on.

E. Gwendolyn Campbell
Formula For a Clear Day
When all people shall live each
  minute
  As though Eternity were in it—
Then, true Brotherhood will be
  infinite.

Judy M. Brewster
THANKS TO JESUS
*[Dedicated to my husband Ray,
whose love and devotion has
given me the inspiration to put
these words to print, also to my
friend Gertha Harper, whose
spiritual help is a blessing to
me.]*
Once they called Him, Jesus, the
  carpenter's son.
Then they called Him, Lord, for
  all the goodness He done.
Next they cried out to crucify
  God's own son.
When the jealousy in their
  hearts.
Over all His good deeds had won.
The long walk up Calvary, the
  burdens He bore.
The pain in His side, as they
  pierced it with the sword.
The Bible teaches, there are many
  ways,
For man to fail God, in his
  humanly ways,
But thanks to Jesus, at Calvary
  that day.
His precious blood, my sins
  washed away.

Marilyn Fleer
GOTHIC SPRING
The sun, a king, wears cloth of
  gold.
His lady, earth, wears flowers.
From clouds, small wind gods on
  a map
Blow on the gothic towers.

The courtier trees dance a
  gaillard.
Green knights with swords, grass
  rises.
Like painters of the Renaissance,
I love spring's bright disguises.

Cloud castles float on moats of
  blue.
The wind, a knight, goes riding.
The trees point lances at the sky
to force the moon from hiding.

The robins, troubadours of spring
To tracery trees are clinging.
Like poets of the feudal age
Spring sets my heart to singing.

Elizabeth Wells Bodiford
WAKE UP AMERICA
Wake up America, the time is
  near.
God will destroy us, He made it
  clear.
Reach out America, lend a
  helping hand.
Reach out America and save your
  land.

Listen, America, hear the cries.
Save the children, don't let them
  die.
Clean up the filth, the sin, the
  shame.
God shall destroy us, We are to
  blame.

Just look around you, can't you see,
The sin it lies there beneath your
  feet.
Wake up America and save your
  land.
Save the children if you can.

Where are the families?

Where is the love?
Wake up America,
And save your soul.
Wake up America,
And wake up whole.

Robert J. Miller
BIVALENCY
March tone peaks airily
Precisions's skein; who begets
Rose, purple, citrine,
First tiny florets; grains
Gem globules; smooths;
Befits them: Labidary
Superb glistening bluets.

A ternion of Indian Pipes,
Minikin pistons that
Linger moist;
Vapor grown as
Off a cave's
Stringcourse loam;
They attest mist
Spirit's functioning;
Sleek where fronds
First came on
Cleaving iced mould,
The holm's chlorophyll
Wanting saprophytes
Announce early seed
September ripes.

Marian Littlejohn Coppin
MAMA
*[Nellie Ree Bateman Surrogate
Mother and Friend Rejoicing in
Heaven]*
Angel of Death you are welcome
Winging down toward her so
  bold;
Joyous her earth weary spirit
Singing will enter your fold.

Here on this side of the Jordan
Many oft fear your cold touch,
But she, with her eyes fixed on
  Jesus,
Will none of her earth fetters
  clutch.

Quickly then Angel embrace her,
Fly with her long ready soul.
Bear her in safety to Heaven
Right through the portals of gold.

Juanita M. Reed
TAPESTRY
The everyday pattern of our lives
Is woven into an intricate design
Much like a rare and beautiful
  tapestry
The silken threads are interlaced,
  pure and fine.

The stitches are lovingly made by
  the weaver

Creating patterns of diverse
  design
Just like the variety of our
  everyday lives
These threads and fine fabrics
  intertwine.

The stitching of this rare tapestry
With love and kindness are
  entwined
These threads form interlocked
  patterns
Creating an ideal example of
  humankind.

Sometimes the pattern is
  disrupted
By threads that are woven askew
Then the weaver must start all
  over
To design another pattern and
  weave anew.

Billie Thompson Potter
I AM JUST A DREAMER
I am just a dreamer
With no riches to my name
I dream of white sandy beaches
Of ships, of waters untamed.

Of lovely island lassies
With gardenias in their hair
And soft sea island music
How I wish that I were there.

To view the island flowers
And see the palm trees sway
To feel the warmth of the natives
And watch them in their care-free
  way.

I can feel the soft breeze blowing
As it touches my hair with a kiss
I can see the surf boards playing
With nothing at all amiss.

But I am just a dreamer
With no riches to my name
So I'll ne'r see white sandy
  beaches
Nor ships, nor waters untamed.

Annette Bacon
BEYOND PARADISE
This land was a paradise
Long before the white man came;
But he saw it as
Uninhabited.

They made their own paradise
From the thoughts inside their
  heads,
Thinking it was all
Uninhabited.

Who's to say what's paradise,
My idea, or some of yours,
When we're headed for
Uninhabited.

So it will be paradise
From the point of someone's
  view;
Unless, of course, it's
Uninhabited.

Marciana Garma
SITTING IN THE PARK
*[To my grandchildren
especially Kanoe Garma]*
I sat in the park one day
And watched the children play
Heard their voices loud and clear
Trusting, happy, and without fear

I fell into a reverie
And a picture came to me
Of my own childhood days

Almost like theirs in many ways

While I was thus occupied
Someone sat down by my side
I heard a sweet voice say,
"Wake up gramma, let's go play."

I opened my eyes and smiled
At my youngest grandchild
And thanked God for the years
As she held my hand in hers

Edith Cannon Storey
THE HAUNTED HOUSE
[*This poem is in memory of my
girlhood home where the first
poem I had ever written first
appeared.*]
There is a haunted house
Which sits on a hill
For I know my footsteps
Echo there still.
In the valley below it
The clovers bloom
By the waning light of the moon,
Of the moon.
There's a road like a ribbon
Which curves past the door
Where wild roses like lovers
Clasp tight ever more.
In memory I'm walking
That road in my heart
And time from it's beauty
can't tear us apart.
There is an orchid of pear trees
In blossoms so white
Which look like brides
In the cool, dewy night.
Songs have been written
Where poets sit alone
But this is an echo
Of my dear old home.

W. Hugh Headlee
PROCRASTINATION
'Tis hardly understandable
How oft' we procrastinate,
Then severely reprove ourselves
Because it's now too late
To do the thing we wanted to.
Indeed, it seemed quite right.
But then we did procrastinate;
It's now too late—sad is our plight!

We thought to write a note to him
For understanding—to
    communicate better.
But then we did procrastinate;
Our friend is gone—he had no
    letter.

Nellie Stewart
TO SHIRLEY
Try not to worry or fret
They'll discover a new angle yet.
For having a baby the old way is
    best,
Go to a good doctor each month
    for a test.

Exercise and walks in the sun,
Plenty of sleep when the day is
    done.
Regular housework won't hurt
    you none,
You'll find having a baby can be
    fun.

The last few months may go
    dragging by
Now is the time to have Ed stand
    by.
Don't lift heavy things
Don't stretch too far.
If you need extra help

Just call on Ma.

When you get pains
You'll know what I mean.
They'll tear you apart
Or so it will seem.
Just push when you're told
And take a deep breath.
Look, the baby's here
And she is such a Dear.

You forget the pain
When you hold your babe in your
    arms.
It'll pull on your heart with all its
    charms.
God bless you, Dear, and Daddy
    too.
The Lord has been good to give
    this child to you.

Victoria Lynn Collette
TOGETHERNESS
Passion of paradise dreams
    whisper in my ears
as the reality that surrounds
me came true: as one dream
    was meant to be.
Laughter, touching and warmth
    welcome my soul
        to you.
We laughed together,
    smiled together
and together as one shared
our dreams we wanted.
You were there when I needed
    you;
when I was hurt, you held me.
Our love is tender in a way
    that ours is our own,
without anyone but just us.
Us, a beautiful word
that speaks for its own meaning;
two letters, two people
        but us
    can be more than two;
the meaning is together—
as in one—as one dream
that came true and was meant to
    be.

Myrna Downer
ADRIFT LIKE ME
Poems
Like fireplace reflections
In crystal
Smile at me
And keep me warm

Poems
The ones I so need to write
In darkness
Shed some light
To give me hope

Poems
Quiet memories make me cry
You have to
Wonder why
The good days end

Poems
Tattered, all that's left of me
Now silent
In my book
Adrift like me

Allison Villone
SUICIDE
i was walking downtown harlem
real late last night
and in the reflection
of a barricaded storefront
i saw a person
i faintly recognized

coming straight towards me
and i didn't like what i saw
a face of despair
    of shattered dreams
    of lost hopes
eyes of lonliness
    of desolation
    of isolation
a visage of infinite sadness.
so i drew my pistol
to make her go away
and shot
and too late

i realized
it was me.

Donna Addison
Sense Impressions Sight, Taste, Sound, Smell, Touch, Feelings
My breathing is fast as the heart
    pumps blood for life. I feel
    uneasy in a slightly shaky way.
    This morning has been very
    rushed and full of company.
One of my favorite smells is fresh
    cut grass. I like the look of the
    area freshly done. The feel of
    the grass is good.
Too many people in my life this
    morning and I am glad to
    escape them. I feel a great joy
    in things that are organized and
    neat, and I am quite
    disappointed in my self at
    times when I fail to keep
    things in the right perspective.
    There's so much to be done
    each day; I wish I had more
    time and a lot more energy.
This area is quiet and it gives me
    the peace I need now. I don't
    have to be social right now; the
    room is oversized and I am
    glad.
There are times when each man
    and woman may need their
    own Continent to lose
    themselves for a day, a night. I
    would settle right now for an
    hour.
We all have training as a child,
    but as we grow older we must
    supplement with new things
    that change the early training.
    We must change. I guess the
    only fear I have is how fast and
    rapid I feel time is going in my
    life. Doing something very
    physical, running, gardening,
    bike riding, hunting is so
    rewarding to me.
My heart beats fast I feel alive. I
    believe every person wants
    their own way but only the
    selfish person ends up traveling
    alone. If we give nourishment
    in the form of love, praise,
    laughter to each other, we can't
    lose; we live.
I feel calm and much quieter
    now. Conveying thoughts on
    paper makes me feel good.
    That's part of the nutrition of
    life I need.

Lorna May Hanson
The Last Of the Pioneers
Tulelake, the last of the
    homesteaders,
    the last of the big spreads.

A land where you used a plow,
by the mighty sweat of your
    brow.
Where the wind blew free,
and you could hardly see,
for the dirt and the dust,
was blown by the wind
a thousand feet high.
They worked from sun to sun,
until the job was done.
They planted and harvested
and did what they must,
and then, you *know*, they
left it to us.

Teresa M. Blondin Hughes
ANCHOR
[*Bob J. Wax
Thank You,
For loving me*]
While, I heal
From a painful past
Your loves been
An anchor
I could grasp
You, held me
When, I cried
Told me
I was special inside
I grew
From, your words
Of encouragement
With, you love
My life will
Be spent
You rode
My, rollercoaster, with me
How understanding
True love
Can be
I love you

Waneta E. Rickel
She Went Home Yesterday
She went home yesterday
Home to her childhood

Life on the San Francisco peninsula
was too hard
too shallow
Life there was cold and bitter
bitter as the wilds of Alaska
    dangerous lonely

She went home yesterday
to linger in the shade of memories

Home to the sweetness of a
    mocking bird
a firefly
Grandma, Grandpa
Uncles, Aunts and cousins
Home to find the end of a string
    that holds
to cut, to untie

Home to resign without ties
to the everlasting, everloving,
hills of home

Tammy L. J. Yee
ALONE SHE SITS
Alone
    she sits

in her splintered, wicker chair
bathed in golden sunlight
    she shivers in the warmth
and eases the passing moments
    through a tapered funnel
of distortion and suspicion.

the unconscious voice: "are you
    familiar with the beating wings
    of senses lost in hopeless flight?

i think not."
and with impeccable perfection
she reaches up to fix it on its
    rusty hook
and scatters a cascade of floating
    brilliance
    across the midnight skies she
    calls them stars
for only she can find the
    shattered unity along its
    luminescent edges
and only she can adjust the
    mighty moon
with the ease and simplicity
of placing a faceless portrait on
    the fractured wall before her

for you see
anything is possible when
    nothing really matters
    anymore.

She curses her ungrateful
    daughter and grasps on hungrily
to fleeting memories her
    daughter could never
    understand.
No use talking.
and the neighbors harass her
they call me ignorant and bid me
    to send her away
they call me gutless for I tolerate
    the intolerable
but I simply smile . . .

for who could understand the
    angry persecution
of the feeble—minded
    ignoramous more than i,
    her daughter?

Alone
    she sits.

Jeanette Willoby
THE LAST MOMENT
[*Dedicated to all those who
have given and those who will
give an angel back to God
sooner than expected. May the
last moment always be filled
with love.*]
Mama, Papa please dry all your
    tears
Listen ever softly so you can hear
The sweet song my silent heart
    sings
As peace gives me flight with
    angels wings.

Yes Mama, Papa rest all your fears
I am always with you I will
    always be near
I've been warmed by your love
    and guided by your smile
Remember—you made my life
    worthwhile.

Mama, Papa look to the blue sky
See me running fast and jumping
    high
Know I'm standing tall and
    feeling so proud
That you love me still as I ride
    painted clouds.

"Joey, Joey" I can hear you say
As you hold me close and start to
    pray
"Dear God take him in your
    loving arms
With all his sweetness and
    innocent charms.

Hold him and keep him

Until the time comes
That we're all a family
Together as one."
        Amen

J.L.A. Roberts
**How Great a Lioness My
Mother**
[*To my mother, Ona Virginia
Hopkins Stewart, mother of six,
who made the transition on
May 8, 1982, in Byers, Texas.
She'd have been ninety-four on
June 28.*]
How great a lioness my mother,
    Lord!
She grabs with gnarled paws
    masses of the universe;
she pats and smoothes enough to
    line two quilts and tack them,
making a cozy den in which were
    once six little cubs of us—
her eyesight good enough at
    almost ninety-four to line
and tack two quilts or even
    more!
By now of course we've gone,
    have cubs and grandcubs of our
    own.
"I don't know what I'll do with
    these two quilts," she told me
Over long distance telephone,
    "Just lay them on a shelf, I
    guess."
My heart leapt up. I'd fly, dear
    Lord, a thousand miles, cross
    oceans for those quilts to line
    my den for just one cub—
a six—year—old grandson who's
    with me now,
at my age, sixty-four.
I'd fly an ocean, and a thousand
    miles, or even more
to get those quilts, and hug them
    to me, Oh because—
because dear Lord, for me at
    times at sixty-four the
    universe
seems dense and tangled,
    intricate, inert, too much for
    me
to cope with.
O thank You, thank You for my
    mother, Lord,
that lioness! And for her quilts
    she's lined and tacked,
patting out masses of the
    Universe
at her age, almost four score years
    and ten, plus four!

A. L. A. Corenanda
**This Tiny Space-Ship
Called the Earth**
Why are we so frantically
    arming, all the countries of the
    world?
Why must we destroy one
    another because we have
    different views?
Who attacks and defending
    what?
Whichever the case, don't we
    forget something?
Or, are we oblivious, indifferent,
    take for granted or ignorant of
The mutability of this tiny space-
    ship called the earth?
Is it so secure as all that? Yea, it
    has been rotating and
    revolving

Around the Sun in mid-air
    without any support
For the past four and a half
    billion years, they say,
But, will it do the same for the
    next billion years,
Nay, a thousand years, or no
    more than a hundred years?
Nobody could predict except the
    vagaries of Nature!
Nature's vagaries we have seen
    enough
In the form of devastating
    catastrophes;
Heavy rain or snow, floods,
    hurricanes, storms,
Tidal waves, earthquakes and so
    forth, about which
Our modern science has no
    control whatsoever!
Better, then, not to try to
    compete with Nature,
Who could wipe us all with this
    speck of dust called the earth
In a flash of a second without a
    trace!
The meaning of humility we
    should learn
And realize the folly of
    meaningless destructions
Among the fellow human-beings
    in the name of principles or
    dogmas,
But, forgetting the cosmic Bang of
    the colossal Universe!

Mary A. Begley
MY BRIDE
Once was long tresses of bright
    auburn hair;
That transparent shine, that
    golden glare.
There was a pink glow from her
    soft youthful skin;
So smooth and creamy, admired
    by men.
That snappy sparkle, those
    enormous brown eyes,
Gazing dreamily towards the
    heavens a high.
But now in their place, a dull
    muted stare;
Massive traces of gray, has
    covered her hair.
Her skin is all withered, leathery
    and worn;
While her heart has been
    tattered, tortured and torn.
Her children all raised, she sits in
    a daze;
That faraway look, her world a
    maze.
But don't let first glance of this
    fine lady deceive you;
She's still full of surprises, that
    will amuse you.
When she hears someone say,
    "this is My Bride;
She thinks of her husband and
    fills up with pride.
There's a hint of sparkle, a glow
    in her cheeks;
That's all it takes to make the ole
    gal, rattle on for weeks.

Grace Price
Let the Love Of Jesus Shine
To really care—it costs a lot
In time and energy,

But oh, the wonderful joy
It brings to you and me.

Events and problems happen
At inopportune times,
But give of yourself
And let Jesus' love shine!

He is the rewarder
of the worker you see.
The rewards are great
To the one He has set free.

Take time to be a friend.
Don't count cost in dollars and
    dimes.
Be that shoulder someone needs,
A listener much of the time.

It helps to have a partner
To go to God with in prayer,
Rolling our cares on Jesus,
Taking time just to share.

You'll never know the blessing
This ministry can be,
Unless you "Take The Time"
To open up and see.

Chrystie McCutchen
FORTUNE TELLER
Doubts of love and laughter to
    come,
Worries of passion lie still in my
    mind.
Savior of dreams, oh where do
    you hide?
Questions and answers of where
    you are from.

Tales of content I wish on a star,
A life full of wisdom I forsee in
    my dreams.
Caretaker of peace, retrieve my
    heavy sigh.
My shoes are all worn, I have
    traveled so far.

Singer of songs, my voice has run
    dry.
A cast of puppets being pulled by
    their strings.
Keeper of destiny, paint me a
    picture,
A key tempts my waiting, or will
    it still lie?

Alma C. Groninger
METRO GYPSIES
A quiet visitor from Japan,
An intelligent, quite
    distinguished man
Walked briskly through a
    corridor
Of Metro's maze of hidden floor.

At first he looked like easy prey
As gypsy children lurked his way.
They formed a ring around this
    man . . .
The gentle visitor from Japan.

These scantily clad, impoverished
    forms,
Accustomed to ignoring norms,
Rudely pushed and snatched and
    tugged,
Then danced around and almost
    mugged.

The man, who firmly held his
    own,
Soon saw that he was not alone.
Parisiens came in full processions
To help protect his prized
    possessions.

Scattering like a flock of sparrows,
The children flew into the
　narrows,
Angrily squawking at one another,
. . . Disappearing with their
　mother.

T. Paul Jacobson
LAMENT IN BLUE
I look at the tear stains left behind
I remember the words we used to
　bind
Sometimes I don't wish for me to
　remind
So I grab a glass and start to
　unwind
The hurt still remains inside of
　me
Tho no one is sure, 'cause no one
　can see
The scar left here will forever be,
Will I ever know what is wrong
　with me?

I loved that girl in my heart, I
　know
Till the winds of bad fortune
　began to blow
Feelings of contempt I didn't know
Why, oh why did I have to go?
I wish I knew what went wrong,
We started out so vibrant and
　strong
Laughing and loving and singing
　our song
Oh where, O Lord, did we go
　wrong?

Norma J. Townsend
THE CHRIST CHILD
A child was born one starry night
　In Bethlehem, long ago
Shepherds saw the brightest light
　Shine over a stable, so low
People came for many miles
　With gifts for the Newborn
　King
And gazed upon His precious face
　They could hear the angels sing.

Our Savior came as a little babe
　To live on earth a while
He grew up teaching God's love
　And renounced the devil's guile
Christ suffered hanging on the
　cross
　With our sins, He was
　weighted down
He died—and then went back to
　Heaven
　Where He now wears a crown.

Sally Edwards
FABRICS OF MOTHER
Lavender fragrance, satin gowned—
Swirling silk—elusive touch.

Warmth and strength revealed in
　glimpses
Silver and steel together wrapped
　with
Iron guidance, velvet sheathed.
Scoldings tempered fine with
　patience
Eternal as an infant's cry.

Laughter leading youth to seek—
To know when Love is found.
Melody of voice and motion,
Reaching, speaking songs of life.

Candlelight and firelight's gleam,
Sparkle of diamond,
Shine of moon,
Weave tapestries of memories

Most beautiful in retrospect.

Quiet singing arms to hold
Safe from the fear of darkening day.
To never know the sorrow of
Chained tears in solitude released.

Smiling eyes awaken,
Another dawn of Love—
In lavender fragrance—satin
　gowned.

Brian Fox
THE TREE
There is a tree, a special type,
It's able to control its actions.
As one sprout it started, but as it
　grew
Its branches became so many
　factions.

Almost self-thinking these
　branches are;
For their own wants do they
　really strive.
In their fight for sunshine and
　water,
Their common source isn't
　recognized.

Some depend upon the larger ones
To trickle down their needs,
While others are slowly strangled,
During the fight within the tree.

So even as parts die,
Other branches grow stonger still.
The branches don't realize it's the
　tree they hurt,
And themselves they slowly kill.

Charles Jeffrey Gray
DESERT CANYON
A silvery image producing
Shimmering light just over that
　hill
Sunshine slowly reducing
And moonlight about to spill

Sitting quietly we listened
Coyotes echoed their songs in
　flight
Boulders beginning to glisten
As we camped in the canyon that
　night

Coals in the fire were glowing
Our shadows danced in the sand
The touch of a cool wind blowing
And embers of love were fanned

These words can't convey the
　feeling
Nor the oneness we shared in
　delight
They only attempt at revealing
What happened in a canyon one
　night

Debbie Coppenger
LETTING GO OF JEREMY
Yesterday I found the shirt I made
For that little boy who is no
　longer here
And I wonder after the farewell I
　bade
Will he always feel so close and
　so near?

Son, the love I feel is always here;
The pain in seeing you go is real.
Constantly I wish and dream you
　near
That is how I really feel.

Someday I hope you might know
How I long to be there as you grow
And the pain I've endured to let

you go.
But you'll grow up happy, I know.

When you grow older I pray
　you'll know
I did what I did for you.
I love you enough to let you go,
I did what I had to do.

The tears came thick and fast
As I hung your little shirt away
Knowing it will be alright at last
Does not keep this hurt away.

You are a very lucky little boy
To be loved as much as you are
You are truly quite a joy
My heart will be with you
　wherever you are.

Arthur J. Nash
THE SECRET OF THE WAY
*[To those who have helped me
　search for the meaning of the
　way.]*
What is the secret of the way?
Is it to be found on Christmas Day?
Does advent proclaim the way?
No, No, we must still search and
　pray.

The act of denial called Lent;
How is it to be spent?
We come near to He who was sent.
Lo, the quest has not been spent.

The glory of the growing green.
Trinity is an August scene.
The scent of the secret is lean.
Search on in other clime and
　scene.

The festival of the palms speak
　soon,
As does the garden, of doom.
Is the secret in the upper room?
No, find it in the empty tomb.

Denise Chittenden
WHISPERING WIND
　The wind is calling my name,
　Whispering a beautiful tune.
Telling me life is not the same,
beckoning me to follow soon.
　A slow playing song,
　　casting its spell,
　by weaving an atmosphere
　of peace and goodwill.
　Promising a future
　of dreams coming true.
　　All to be mine,
　if I follow it through.
　No stopping or standing
　I've no need to decide
　I'm taking the wind
　and melody, as my guide.
They've captured my restless
　spirit
with that whispering song
That wherever they lead me
　Is where I belong.

Sandi Mason
A HAPPY POEM
I'd like to write
　a happy poem.
A poem that's
　funny and bright.
A poem that's full
　of humor and cheer.
A poem that's
　outta sight!
A poem that would bring
　a great big smile
to all the readers who

have a heart
that's full of pain
　and feel depressed and blue.
If I could only
　write in words
the things I'd like
　to say,
I'd feel I'd really
　helped someone
in a small but
　lovely way.

Sally Francise Hogan
A VEAL CALFS PRAYER
*[In memory of all those who
　suffer at the hands of man!]*
Oh please help me Lord!
I am lonely!
I am frightened!
They are hurting me Lord!
Please help me Lord!

Please help me Lord!
I am little!
I am weak!
Oh, It hurts Lord!
Please help me Lord!

Please help me Lord!
I cannot see!
I cannot speak!
Oh, but I can feel!
Please help me Lord!

Katheryn Glietz Kehn
**O Lord, Where Were You
　That Day**
O Lord, where were you that day?
O Lord, where were you that day?
When mountains leaped from
　their trembling base,
And boulders skipped through
　the yawning space,
When boiling billows climbed
　mountain high,
And lightning streaked through
　the blackening sky.

When men sank dying in slimy
　clay,
O Lord, where were you that day?

O child, where was I that day?
O child, where was I that day?
I yearned to come to your aid, my
　dear.
I pounded to break down the door,
But you had determined to shut
　me out—
Me, the help of the poor.

Oh, let me live in your thoughts
　each day,
Keep open your heart and your
　mind,
For there is the only place I can
　dwell,
There, alone, you will find
Me, the answer to all your fears—
Me, the hope of mankind.

Estrella Besinga—Sybinsky
TO CORNELIO: A TRIBUTE
you took your woman
and sowed your seeds,
and thus an edifice of
　species—being
thrived.

the universal man, your heart and
　mind
expansive—stretched out, and
　touched
more lives that thrived.

your labor and your energies

to many causes devoted—but yet,
    it worked
and growing with its joys and
    pains—
made memories optimistic.

somehow, as man, as husband
and as father—we sensed your
    presence
as a shadow, muted, and—
though emotions centralized, on
    one, the woman and the
    mother, you were always there,
    when needed.

as your father did before—
the words are few
and we could never quite
    surmise, the depths
of your attachments, and your
    love, though
always, and in all respects,
you helped encourage the love of
    mother,
and heaped laurels to her name.

and all the years
expand the edifice—and with the
    children and grandchildren, and
    with the loss of your beloved,
the species—being scatter and the
    edifice preserves the memory
of one, the mother.

and you are there
as always—ready
when you're needed.
you thrive and glow
and show once more
your universal heart and mind—
as we recall with fondness deep—
the memory of your beloved.
all selflessness and more,
your legacy to us, your progenies
lies in that energy and faith
in humankind, unbounded.

and though deserving
of gratitudes—somehow or
    other, not forthcoming,
you smile, and let your
    intellect preside.

"and there is
one more book to write,
perhaps, my last,
and there is still
more time
to sow".

Martha Leaming Kinkead
FOR MARK, SOMETIMES
cold delicacy blowing in from the
    sea
curtains of lace whisked on the
    wind

    the afternoon sun is grey and
    chill
    why is this window open?
    who tore my remnants?
    the water is icy and still

alone in an empty room
with your voice trailing in on the
    edges of lace

    shrill and questioning
    torn gulls in the fabric of my
    memories

it is cold and lost here

Gene DePue
IN MEMORIAM
He was a quiet man filled full
    with meekness and humility;

A man experiencing God's love.
And yet—
Did any know or care or see him
    as one created just as we,
to share?
He spoke with softness and
    appreciation for his new found
    friends in Christ, and he read
    daily from the Word—it
was his life.
The life he lived has found
    fulfillment in his passing;
How God is glorified in such a
    man as this.
So as we live and share the bitter
    cup,
We are thankful for assurance
    that we will meet again—
As we rise up.

Annette S. Crouch
MYTHICAL RIDE
I search the sky, with raised blue
    eyes
For wings of white, and gilt of gold
My cloven hooves impatient,
    stamp
The sandy shoreline
    waves; lowtide

I wish to fly, with raised blue eyes
Midst wings of white, and gilt of
    gold
My cloven hooves, not touching
    ground
The sandy shoreline
    waves; below

I see him high, with raised blue
    eyes
His wings of white, glide to the
    ground
My golden hooves impatient,
    greet
The sandy shoreline
    watches; silent

I ride the sky, with raised blue
    eyes
'Neath wings of white, so
    comforting
My golden hooves, not touching
    ground
As Pegasus and I, soar high
The sandy shorelines
    pass; hightide

Gladys Wildt
HOME AT LAST
To—nite, as I do lie upon my bed
Memories of my entire life do
    ramble thro' my head;
Back to my earliest childhood
    day they go,
And sweet indeed it is to have it
    so

I see a little child not quite five
    summers old
Whose little heart does cry to be
    a member of the fold.
Every moment by her side it doth
    seem the Lord doth walk.
And thro' all of God's creations
    she can hear the Saviour talk;

In the wind she clearly hears the
    sweet, sad voice of Jesus say
    "Follow me,"
And her heart so fondly answers
    "Sweetest Jesus I'd just love to
    follow Thee."
But Alas! that little maiden Jesus'
    story ne'er did hear

And she thinks she cannot follow
    since the Lord no more walks
    here.

Down life's vale of tears, I see
    that pretty maiden go
Longing ever the Redeemer to
    follow here below,
Knowing not that God in Heaven
    looking from His throne above
Soon shall send to her that sweet
    message of His love,

For her lover far away, that sweet
    story has been told,
And he writes to tell his loved
    one, that he's safe within the
    fold,
How he's prayed to his Redeemer
    who saved the ninety-nine
And he's begged his God in
    Heaven to please save "the one
    that's mine."

Now, oh sweet the sight I see! by
    her bed on bended knees,
That lost sheep from the Great
    Shepherd has found her
    conscience ease,
She simply told the Saviour of her
    many, many sins
And just humbly prayed the
    prayer of the publicans of old.,
The Christ of Calvary washed
    her, and forgave her all her sins,
Then He said to her, "My fair one,
    thou art now, one of my fold."

Stanley J. Coleman
MY MARITAL PRAYER
Thank you God for my *precious
    wife*,
    My pillar of strength in stress
    and strife,
Thank you God for my *loving wife*,
    A crowning glory of my life.
When I get lost along the way,
    I hear my *dear wife* softly say,
"Mistake, my love, is not disgrace",
    Then offers me her warm
    embrace.
Feeling the strength of a
    thousand horses,
    To bring new power into my life,
Thank you God for my *wonderful
    wife*.
For God and wife have joined
    their forces.

Sylvie S. LaFond, Ph.D—Phs.D
MAN AND SEA
[*To every loving and fighting
soul with whom I have shared
the very special and intimate
visions of our "oceanside" sea,
it's multiple characters, burning
moments and raging tempests.*]
Always will you cherish the sea
For like you she mirrors your
    dreams.
Through the infinite movement
    of her waves
You contemplate the image of
    your soul
And like her, your mind is not less
    a treacherous depth.
You dive with ectasy in the
    womb of reflection,
You behold and cherish her by
    your tender looks,
your endless never ending
    embraces
and your heart is endlessly

attracted and beheld
by her savage and untamable
    complaint.
Both of you are melancholic and
    discreet;
Oh man! no one has ever probed
    the recess of your abyss.
Oh sea! no one knows the secrets
    of your wealth,
so intent and jealous are you
    both in keeping their values.
But for innumerable centuries
    now
So much is your fascination for
    each other
That you fight each other
    without mercy or remorse
Eternal lovers, implacable
    fighters. . .

Oxana Rudenko—Voloshin
**Truth In Rhyme (a
    portion)**
I can not follow paths unknown
For life is but a seedling grown.
A man can either try, or be;
To try is noble, yet to me
A truth can not be lost or won—
It is
And was
And will be
one.

Raymond Roche
CRY FOR A SHEPHERD
Somehow it always seems to turn
    out this way;
I lay my careful plans, every
    detail perfect, certain of
    victory;
Then, like a sentence of doom,
    everything suddenly goes
    wrong,
Leaving me crying in frustration
    and pain.
When, oh when will I ever learn
    that my fate is a fate that
    cannot be mastered,
Learn that my soul is a ship that I
    cannot captain?
Deep down inside I know there's
    a better way,
A way that will bring me victory;
The God Who walks beside me
    tells it to me,
Tells me that He's the better
    guide,
Letting me know in every way
    that his way is best.
Why, why do I not heed His
    voice,
Why have I not learned that
    sheep need a Shepherd,
Why do I always bleat "My will,
    not Thine be done?"
At first it was exciting to leave
    the fold and go my own way;
I was free, the grass was plentiful
    and every turn in the road led
    to new adventure.
But now the night is come and I
    am alone;
The grass is gone, the way is
    stony and steep and I am—lost.
Oh Great Shepherd, hear my
    despairing cry;
Save this poor blind sheep who
    stubbornly ran from the fold
    and would not heed Thee;
Save me from this wilderness and
    carry me back to the fold,

Carry me in Thy strong, loving
   arms to where the grass is green
   and the water is always pure,
Carry me home for I am lost and
   need Thee, Lord.
And, should I stray again, lead me
   with Thy rod and Thy staff,
Lead me to where I can hear the
   music of Thy pipe and feel Thy
   blessed presence,
Lead me and teach me Thy ways,
For now, at long last, I am willing
   to listen to Thy voice;
Teach me never to leave Thy side
   and, above all, to believe what
   a good sheep should:
"Thy will, not mine be done."

J. Laurence Erkis
WHEN
When mountains are uprooted
   and have gone,
When gold that is the purest
   fades and turns,
When nighttime is not followed
   by the dawn,
When never skips my heart a
   beat or yearns,
When roses turn away from
   sunlight's kiss,
When rivers stop their flow and
   stand so still,
When joy and ecstasy bring none
   their bliss,
When all this world holds not a
   single thrill.
When lovers find no comfort in
   love's bed,
When clowns no more can make
   the children glad,
When sweet embrace falls by the
   wayside, dead,
When time confesses that its
   hours are sad.
When these are real and not just
   dreams thereof,
Then, and then alone, I'll no
   longer love.

Stacey Weaver
THE OCEAN
Listen to the ocean
Waves splashing on the shore.
Listen to the seagulls
Down, down they soar.
Look at the yellow moon shining
   on the sand.
And people walking barefoot
   across the land.
Look at the seashells lying on the
   beach
And look at the sand castles in
   the children's reach.
See the kites flying through the air
Feel the gentle breezes blowing
   through your hair.
See the men fishing on the pier.
Listen to the happy children that
   you hear.
See the children with their
   buckets near the sea.
Oh, the ocean is a most beautiful
   place to see.

Mrs. Helen S. Slifko
DREAMS
   They say that those who
   remember their dreams
   Often see places, far beyond
   their means.

Last night I went to London town
Seemed I kept going around and

around
It seemed I was in such a fog
My sister and I would slip on a log.

I heard a carriage, drawing near
And soon it was near us, and it
   was clear
I saw an ole man, lean over and say
Jump in, and I'll show you
   London today.

We kept slipping out of his
   carriage so small
But I held on, to see the mansions
   so tall
Such beautiful ones, I've never
   seen
This must be fairyland, not a
   dream.

This ole man asked, for a penny
   or two
I grabbed my sister, out the
   carriage we flew,
He was trying to see how much
   money we had,
I think he would have taken all
   we had.

   Again we got lost along the way
   I tried to find a place to stay
   I felt something fall, my pillow
   went down
   And I was back from
   LONDON TOWN.

Margaret Williams Cooper
THE FINALE
Death will not deal me a finale
   from its stacked deck
   like the coward puppets
   hanging around the
   playwright's neck
Living never was for them
   those soul-less bloodless whim
   of some creative carpenter
   bored and jobless

Living has dealt it
   finally and surely as the day
   ends
   the finale to
   youths dream
   innocent hopefulness
   wishes that never came true
   inexperience

It leaps out at you
   as you grab fiercely for rosebud
   blanket
But rosebuds disappear
   and then blanket
And you stand naked
   ready to learn

Death will not deal me a finale
Only those who must stand naked
   ready to learn
   the finale to
   youth's dream
   innocent hopefulness
   wishes that never came true
   inexperience

Denise Lynn Caiazzo
BRONZED SOUL
A burst of multicolored flames
   stagnates each breath,
   sweeping away the free,
   vulnerable fawns, coldly
   blackening the vibrant
   pulsations.
Life diminishes to a lone insect
   buzzing 'round the receptacles
   of death.

An ocean of bruised, barren
   branches longingly extends
   each limb to the horizon, miles
   away struggling to grasp Midas'
   golden touch.
In the evil darkness, a powerful
   white spot brilliantly glares.
Gradually, blackness slithers
   over, sucks in, the spot like the
   ebony ruins weakened by
   disease.
Incessantly stare, force the
   uprooting, pierce into the
   tragic scene enacted before you.
Suddenly . . . flash!
White lightning!
A temporary savior from the
   hollow, blind, blood-ridden
   caverns.
For an instant, dazzling lights
   reign over the sullen sky; the
   massacre magically transforms
   under the heavenly hand.
The twitter of a solitary lark
   echoes.
As societies of creatures once
   again emerge into the bronzed
   atmosphere, the final act
   transpires; there, a fascination,
   of beauty and love remands!

Jewel A. Moreland
THE CHALLENGE
*[This poem is respectfully
dedicated to Miss Lillie Shelton
and Mrs. Emma Batts who
continue to encourage me in
writing poetry.]*
Down in a shadow valley I stand
Away from the foot of a
   mountain.
The top of the mountain I cannot
   see.
   Upon its height, the sun gazes
   its eyes.
In marvel of what lies at its peak
   Contemplates my thoughts,
And comes into my being an
   overwhelming desire
   That mountain I must climb.
At the omega of the climb what
   there lies,
   I will not know;
Nor what challenges along its
   path I will meet.
   But, my life will not the
   shadow be,
But the sun and the mountain
   and that
   Will make all the difference to
   me.

Mrs. Larry Costner
PATCHES
*[With Love to Elizabeth and
Lori Costner Age 12 and 15—
1982 Love Always Mom]*
In this world today of designer
   jeans
   Designer this or that
Where the [In Child] of every age
   Either have them or know where
   they're at.

When a child is judged by the
   patches on his jeans
   No matter what else he possesses
Like maybe a kind word, a
   friendly smile
   Ragged jeans or shabby dresses.

Worn out shoes with a sole about
   gone

But a soul deep down inside
That the designer of all designs
   Has made impossible to hide.

Let's look beneath that patch
   behind
   Take time to look within
No matter the patch or the brand
   you wear
   It only covers your end.

No your brand lies beneath that
   patch behind
   Beneath hard times and good
It's a brand that shows through
   the shabbiest of clothes
And styled by the Master
   designer God.

Gladys Holt
COMPARISONS
I . . .
Am like a leaf
Blown by Autumn's breezes.
Sent hither and thither,
Here and yon,
Floating here
Drifting there.

I . . .
Strive to find
A place for myself.
Then I'll light
And settle down,
Permanently,
Just like a leaf
When Autumn's done.

Steven Wayne Moore
IN JESUS
In JESUS I am just what I am,
In JESUS we are just what we are,
In JESUS he is just what he is,
In JESUS we shine just like a star,
In JESUS CHRIST our Lord.

In JESUS we see the way to be,
In JESUS we see the truth to see,
In JESUS we live the life to live,
In JESUS we have God's love to
   give,
In JESUS CHRIST our Lord.

In JESUS we live our lives
   abundantly,
In JESUS we walk the walk of
   victory,
In JESUS we run our races
   perfectly,
In JESUS God works to make us
   Heavenly,
In JESUS CHRIST our Lord.

Cause logically he's everything
   we hope for.
And biblically he's all that we
   desire.
And lovingly he's standing on the
   other shore.
So willingly in him let us retire
   in JESUS,
In JESUS CHRIST OUR LORD.

Alice Wettleson
SECLUSION
I've been to the land of the dead
And come back,
I've seen the blank faces
And watched them blossom.

To bloom is the only reason
To be,
To grow and branch out
And envelope the arches of the
   giant oak.

I see the shadows of its branches
Falling and rising in the sunlight,
And grow at peace within
To know at night its protection
    will remain.

It's like an umbrella
Casting its support,
With branches like giant ribs,
A shelter . . . warm, safe, secure.

Only God's feelings filter through
    like rays of sunshine,
Bouncing at us from various
    angles,
Infiltrating our very soul . . .
Home at last.

Leona Seibel Mola
Grandpa, Did You Forget?
They told me that when I was
    born,
You held me in your arms, and
    were so proud.
When I learned to walk
You held my hand in yours.

You built me a wooden rocking
    horse,
so I could ride and ride.
You took me for walks
and showed me many things;
A wild goose in the sky,
A hidden bird's nest.

You told me stories of when you
    were a little boy.
You also gave me warnings,
"Don't ever cross the street alone,
Always take someone's hand,
Now, don't forget!"

I had to go away for awhile.
They said your eyes got bad,
And your hearing had failed.
But you went for a walk alone.

An ambulance came to pick you
    up.
And, took you far from home.
They say you won't come back
    anymore.

Oh! Grandpa, why didn't you wait
    for me?
You could have put your hand in
    mine.
You shouldn't have crossed that
    street alone!
Oh! Grandpa, did you forget?

Mary Francis Gisslow
THE DEVIL'S TRIANGLE
The mysterious loss of planes
    and ships
In a calm and yet vengeful sea—
They are gone.
In the midst of their flights and
    their pleasure trips
'Neath the door with the watery
    key.

Five Navy planes on a routine
    flight
And a sixth which sought out the
    five—
They are gone.
Engulfed like the stars on a
    stormy night
But the sea—and the
    mystery—survive!

They vanished completely as if to
    Mars—
No answer to where they could be—
They are gone.

They may be entombed in the
    heavens of stars
Or the calm but still vengeful
    sea.
Who'll turn the watery key in its
    lock?
Or will mystery grow with the
    ticking clock?

They are gone.

Patricia A. Janicke
The Ingredients Of Love
Introduction
Laughter
Recollections
Cocktails
Lunch

Friendship
Ideas
Feelings
Reliefs
Hurts
Backgrounds

Compatibility
Friends
Dinner
Soft Music
Coffee
Enjoyment

Trust
Togetherness
Sharing
Warmth
Needs
Embraces

Security
Desires
Tenderness
Relaxation
Comfort
Happiness

Peace
Friendship
Compatibility
Trust
Security
Peace

LOVE

Marillen
RETURNING
I listen to the Call down deep and
    all around
Following where the Spirit moves
My life on this abounds

Much reluctance to accept time
    gone swiftly by
Until the knock upon my heart
Opens the way for the Soul inside

Her time is nearer than before
So my should be spent ever more
With calls of patiences to a will
Tottering between the good and
    nil

Hurt has bent the feelings strong
Sharp words with thoughtless
    meaning
Utter from an exalted Maternal
    hear
The 4th Commandment encircles
    ringing
Sorrow is felt within, sympathy
    for my outer self
Tears the beauty of the Soul

Fall like rain upon my window
    panes
Forgive me Lord for this I feel
I have turned around and sight
    astounding
The way it is, is the way it's been
So I must accept the way between

I am so small in this Great Realm
Amidst the multitude of great
I will hide behind a corner prayer
Then some day I will know my
    place

Ram Evans
The Night Side Of Myself
Comes a lightly
Tripping
Rapping
Dry-skin sound
Of fingers
Snapping
Boot-heels click
On rain-wet
Stone
A shadow moves
On shadow
Alone
I am coming
Hear my
Cry
A soothing silence
In your
Eye

Bobby Edmond
Please If You Don't Mind
My brother,
Please don't knock me upon my
    head.
Kick me not upon the most vital
    parts of my body.
Place no restraints upon my
    hands and feet.
Don't overlook my knowledge
Or my superior abilities.
I can think, talk and do things as
    you can do.
Please if you don't mind,
Just because I am not of thy race.

My brother,
Thrust not a knife into my
    thorax or abdomen.
Please kill me not.
Please don't wound me.
Please brother not with the use,
Of a gun or weapon of any sort.
That would shut me off from the
    communication
Of the outermost region of the
    world.
Please if you don't mind,
Just because I am not of thy race.

Laura Graudushus
THE IN-BETWEEN
They used to be the curler,
    coffee cup, cigarette clique.

Chewing gum, painting their nails,
    watching a flick.

Now they do the barefoot,
    braless,
    free love it.

They smoke pot, lobby,
    protest and sit.

Twenty years ago it was
    understood,
    for them it would be

Marriage, a home and
    sweet motherhod.

Today times have changed, they've
    become reconciled,

To welfare, wine and the
    fatherless child.

It's not progress or change
    I try to resist,

But do it less drastically . . .
    . . . please . . . I persist.

I may grow weary and half
    lose my mind,

But the in-between
    suits me just fine.

Gerald Fairchild
MOONSHOT
O yellow spot
    Up in the nigt
        Are you not
            A satelite?

Answer, please,
    If you're the spoon
        Of Cheddar cheese
            We call the moon.

No answer? Then it's my intention
To assume you're man's invention.
    Bang,
    Bang.

Louis A. Lamey
SOLITARY MAN
*[The Poem was inspired by the
break with my girlfriend So I
would like to dedicate this one
to her,]*
I have done my time,
I have paid my fine
You might say I am still learning
But only you can keep my fire
    burning

I must have come on to you too
    strong
It seems I have done you wrong
I guess you never understand
I am but a solitary man
And I am what I am

As I drag on with the time
It never once leaves my mind
That my solitude might give you,
Some dirty attitude,
I am but a solitary man
And I am what I am,

Millie Rose
CONGRATULATIONS
OH, you went and done it, you
    went and tied the knot
We see your happiness, goodness
    sake why not?
Congratulations to both of you
    from both of us
We are happy for both of you,
    this you can trust

We wish the same happiness
    always you had on your
    Wedding Day
We hope love and happiness will
    follow you and stay
Good luck always, from now
    through many, many years
Know there is love and joy
    enough to bring tears

Tears are for many reasons, just
    wanted you to know
There are tears of happiness that
    can help love grow
There are tears of sorrow we all
    know now and then

We hope yours are for only
happiness, over and over again

Just keep on smiling as you do
day after day
Keep on smiling it will chase all
frowns away
Happiness brings out love in all
our lives
It is good to show for Husbands
also for wives

Congratulations may this
happiness grow and grow
May this be the happiness you
both needed so
With love and understanding all
your lives through
This can be all you will ever
need, this love is true

Just keep on smiling and the sun
will shine each day
Just keep on smiling because love
is there to stay
Just keep on smiling it will chase
all frowns away
Just keep on smiling as you do
day after day.

Russell O. Litchfield
O' PATRIOT! LOST AT SEA!
*[In honor of Seaman Donald L.
Murphy, son of Anson and
Freeda Murphy of Steelton,
Pennsylvania. Donald made
"The Supreme Sacrifice" for his
Beloved Country aboard the
Aircraft carrier USS
Ticonderoga off the coast of
Viet Nam July 14, 1968.]*
Dear Seaman, as our ship
navigates the turbulent seas,
your Angels
Dance above its bow;
The infinite motion of the waves
reach skyward in emptiness to
search
For thee;
O' Patriot! Lost at sea!

Standing watch, your memory
comes in the solitude of a soft
sea breeze;
Tides of frustration, alienation,
and loneliness explode in fury,
Only to subside in sorrow and
grief;
Welling tears merge with the
restless main to transcend the
heavens in
Misty rays of light;
O' Patriot! Lost at sea!

O' Patriot brave, with truth set
free
I hear your voice in the winds of
the sea;
I feel your peace internally;
My lonesome heart! How it longs
for thee!

Dear Patriot, your yearnings for
liberty are reposed forever in
the
Heart of your shipmate;
I break the silence of your soul,
gentle spirit of the sea, as I cry
out
In search of the love that binds
all men in eternal brotherhood.
O' Patriot! Free at sea!
Free! Free!

Dorothy Kamin Seasword
INCOMPLETE
The world
Is not completed.
Man
Is only half-created.
Physical perfection
Is his—
Every nerve, every synapse
Is wondrously
Connected to each other
And to its central source,
To move, to talk, to do,
To think, to feel—
An intricate piece
Of engineering
Unmatched on planet earth.

But something
Was left unfinished—
Peace is not in him,
Nor the greater love
To make a world
Without war,
Without hate,
Without hunger,
Without sin.

Man himself
Must finish himself
To complete
The uncompleted.

Sandra K. Parry
FOOLS
Of all the fools this world must
see, why do I think it's only
me; that never can do just what
others expect of me?
Or are we all fools because we
strive to do the things, they
want in our lives?
To feel the way they say is best
and simply bottle all the rest.
And afraid to be alone, I never
tried to make it on my own.
So perhaps I'm the biggest fool,
because I do exactly as they
tell me to.

Winifred Llewellyn
LEST WE FORGET
Our children are impatient,
anxious to hear
The sleigh bells on the sled,
bringing Santa near.
Sophisticated gifts he will bring
this year,
But the new born babe had, gold,
frankincense and myrrh.

Even Ebenezer Scrooge with his
"Bahs" and and "humbugs"
Succumbed to the joys of the
spirit of Christmas.
Throughout the year there are
people we forget,
But Christmas comes along and
changes all that

We laugh and we're happy
throughout Christmas day,
Gifts are exchanged and the
children play.
And we forget the babe who
within the manger lay,
The infant King who was born in
the hay.

Let us keep the Christmas spirit
all through the year,
Let the gifts we offer be comfort
and cheer,

Money cannot buy the good
things in life,
These come free, Jesus has paid
the price.

Georgeann C. Tomicich
WHAT IT'S ALL ABOUT
*[Dedicated to my favorite
sailor, my husband Paul.]*
Somewhere my sailor floats upon
the sea,
He's defending the rights enjoyed
by you and me.
His hours are long and far too
many,
And most times we've learned to
stretch the penny.
There's not much glory to the job
he does,
And when asked why he does it
he simply says "because."
He does his job the best he can,
And he is tall and proud, for he's
a man.
It seems so strange and terribly
sad,
That sailors give up so much
they've had.
They often lose their family
because they sail,
And failed marriages are a
common tale.
Their time is never really their
own,
And the hours are too short they
spend at home.
But as long as he defends the
rights of you and me,
I will be proud, I will be happy,
and I will
Walk with dignity.

Wileen Thompson
WHAT IS A DREAM?
A dream is a goal;
A thing to reach for;
A force that pushes life forward;
A wish that is possible with time.
A reason to work and to face
each day,
Whether it be good or bad.
A dream is what most people live
for;
They strive for that one distant
star.
They push and shove to reach
that one thing,
Sometimes crushing other
people's dreams in the process.
Some people never reach their
dreams.
Maybe because they are set too
high,
Maybe because they have stepped
on the wrong person.
From a dream comes life,
From life comes problems,
How you handle these problems
is the answer to your dreams
coming true.

Donald R. Dias
I'M JUST A MAN
I look at me and know
That I will not last
I'm the other side of the mirror
I am part of the past
I try to grasp the wind
And hold it in my hand
I cannot . . . but . . .
I cannot understand

Why the sands of time
Wait for others
But not for me
I am part of the land
But not part of the sea
The sea holds my dreams
It fascinates me so
It bids me stay
And will not let me go
As I sit here beside the sea
I watch the gulls scavage
For their food
And know how free they are
And how God watches over their
brode
God is good or, so it is said
He watches over fools and those
in love
How could he know the
difference, between the two
From so far above
I'm just a man
With my feet stuck in the mud
And my head just above the
sand
I'll never see the other side of
tomorrow
And I know I'll never
understand
Because; I'm just a man.

Jeff Byrd
ACCOMPLISHMENTS
I looked into the open skies,
I looked into the stranger's
eyes.
The sky did bleed and the eyes
did cry,
But I could understand and I
might try
To remember a time that was
better than now
A day I would return to if I only
knew how.
To travel through time and fly
into space,
To sing the higher harmonies, to
feel the soft lace.
To taste the fine juices of lands
far away,
To love many others, to live a
new day.
To touch many colors and feel
many sounds
Of all kinds of music and the
world all around.
To sleep with sweet dreams,
To live, love, and sing
The joy and the wonder
To do everything.

Daniel Lee Koterba
SEA OF EMOTIONS
*[To my Mother and Father for
this life And to God Almighty
For my lives before and after]*
Sometimes it's not just sadness
That brings me to my tears
It's just the joy of living
That's brought me through the
years
My mind is like a waterfall
Sometimes it overflows
Spilling my emotions onto the
floor

And now a roaring tide of
emotions
Comes running out of me
A roaring tide of emotions
Running to the sea

How do you know life's taken a
　turn for the worse
Take a look around you
　everything you see you curse
It doesn't have to be that way
All these things you know
Just take a look inside yourself
And let the waters flow

And now a roaring tide of
　emotions
Comes running out of you
A roaring tide of emotions
Running to the sea

Jo Ann Anderson
A POET'S LAMENT
As I sit here and ponder, I think
　what a shame
That I may be missing my
　potential fame.

I like to think that I've been well
　blessed
With many fine talents that
　would all pass the test.

I can dance like a swan and sing
　like the birds;
I could write a good book with
　the choiciest words.

My wit is fantastic; I'm good with
　a pun,
But of all my rare gifts I am
　lacking one.

That one, alas, as one can see,
Writing poetry is not for me.

Of all my ambitions I'll have to
　confess
I've never aspired to be a poetess.

Now, Grandma Moses I may dare
　to emulate
If I can overcome some
　unfortunate fate.

I can draw a straight line, even
　paint a fair tree
But a Browing or Keats I fear I'll
　ne'er be.

E. Susan Wan
HUMAN
Sometimes I don't feel,
Am I the only one this strange?
I'm going mad behind my humor,
Is it so crazy to have thoughts?
To feel like not being in a world
　comfortable enough?
I want to get away from here,
but I don't want to move
Is it annoying to hear me
　complaining, as you would say?
But you see, if you understood
　this
I wasn't complaining at all
I was trying to reach out,
But isn't there anyone to hold
　onto anymore?

Linda Bierfreund
MY TWO BEST FRIENDS
There are two things I can trust,
　when I can trust no more
And they can both be found,
　beyond my bedroom door

One is always with me, but in my
　room is where
I can talk more freely, to whom
　the one that cares

For he's the Lord my God, there is
　no better friend
When others put you down,

he will help your pride defend

Now please don't think me silly,
　as the other's meek and mild
And she's something that I've
　held, since I was just a child

She's a stuffed animal, an
　elephant exact
Fuzzy pink with my old blue hair
　ribbon, tied before her back

When I needed a shoulder to cry
　on, and no one seemed to care
I could count on her to listen,
　and always be right there

So now you've met my two best
　friends, one here and one on
　high
And it's pretty plain to see, just
　how, and where and why

For God is always with me, His
　thoughts and rules in head
And my elephant awaits me,
　between the pillows on my bed

Kurt Chandler
DREAMS
moon beams
soon dreams
shall find your head
awake in bed
slipping on you very still
it suddenly becomes your will
you dream and ponder in the night
of all the things you wish were
　right
till morning light disturbs your
　sleep
and suddenly you begin to weep
knowing things haven't changed
your life never rearranged
the road beneath you until the
　bend
where things change and sleep
　won't end

Marla Elkins
YOU & ME
You & Me
Forever & Always
It was meant to be.

Up above the stars
　are shining bright
Telling us everything
　will be alright.

In the wind I can hear
　our echoing souls
Rejoicing that we have
　found each other here.

Under the moon light
　your eyes shine so bright
And when they meet mine
　our hearts beat with delight.

For they know that
You & Me
Forever & Always
It was meant to be.

Linda A. Hysinger
GOODBYE
I never thought this heart of
　mine
　would be this shade of blue.
Never thought I could love
　someone
　the way that I love you.
Although you made no promises
　or even said you cared;
I guess I read between the lines
　the words you never shared.

That's the hardest thing to accept,
　I meant nothing at all!
You didn't care if I got hurt,
　I'll bend but never fall.
And that's where you made your
　mistake,
　'cause I've got feelings too.
I've put up with alot of things,
　but can't take being used.

I really do care and love you—
　probably always will.
I know you don't feel the same
　way,
　you don't know how you feel.
So I'll just say goodbye for now
　and wipe away my tears.
Please remember that I'll love you
　for the rest of my years.

Goodbye!!!!

Donald Cleveland
LORRAINE
　[To: Lorraine, A Very Dear and
　Sincere Friend.]
You are the breeze
gently blowing in the night,
You are the star
twinkling and shining bright.

A soft and fluffy cloud
you drifted by my way,
But then came the wind
and blew my cloud away.

All that is left is loneliness
embracing tight my heart,
Two lives that came together
have slowly grown apart.

N. Eileen Martyne
CE MATIN
Diamonds on flowers
　Pearls perched on fences
Emeralds blossom
　Adorning her bosom

From morning shower arisen
Fine mist-girdled, alone;
Renoir's ideal beauty—her
Splendour arrayed, courtship
　resumed

She watches:

Dew-wed weavers
　Waltz up their glass aisles
Await winged friends'
　Small gifts for new days:

Not her spinsterhood, yet a
　celibacy:
From past sins—this attachment
Fears observing all others,
This old yearning;

By dusk, will she retire
Search that step in sky-lights
　Faded from the earliest glow
For tomorrow promised, call his
　name?

Marlene Hankin
IMAGES OF A LOST LOVE
　[For Yul Brynner, my Ex-Fiance.
　P.S. I preferred to be
　anonymous too.]
I walked beside a sky-blue pond
On a day when the daffodils
　bloomed
And lazy spears of blue-grass
Hugged and lapped the water's
　rim.

I knelt to skim the languid surface
With no other thought but to
　disturb

The calm—and, lo and behold—
Your face appeared before me.

It seems as though everywhere I
Go, whether pond, or hill, or
House, I see your beloved face
Reflecting a faint, distant smile.

And while I long to see your face,
The sight renews the pain and
Remembrance of what might
　have been
And, by God, what should have
　been.

Then send me dark specs
Like a blind one wears.
At least they will conceal
My tears; but yet, it is better
To see than not, for forgetting you
Is forgetting the art of me.

Stanton Lammers
THE SHAWNEE
She walked in silence,
A body encased in leather,
Carrying the wealth of a
Woman's tangibles.

In a growth of cottonwoods,
There she trampled a path
Through the tall grass,
Trailing her hands, letting
Them float across budding stems.

A vanishing American. Not
A huntress but a Goddess of
The prairie, this Shawnee.
And I loved her.

Judy Anne Shuck
SPELLBOUND
　[Dedicated to my husband
　Dave, and children Larry, Patti,
　Diane and Jim]
Echoes of fascination
Linger in the memories
　of yesterday,
In the joys of today,
And in the fortunes
Beholding our tomorrows.
Unforgotten is the
Fervency with which
We experienced love—
　Seized by desire,
　Devoured by passion,
And in one compelling moment
We were united—in solitude
　per se.
Uppermost in my thoughts
　today
Is that I loved you then,
I love you now,
And the love indebted
　to tomorrow
Is endless and everlasting.

Daniel Hollister
Little Old Country Band
We're just a little old country
　band,
Playing here and there doing one
　night stands,
Playing some of them good old
　songs you know.
Just pour us up a good cold glass
　of beer
And we'll play all night and we'll
　bend your ear,
We'll probably play you a couple
　of songs we wrote.

Yeah we're just another one of a
　million
Little old country bands;

Just some local talent
Trying to do the best we can.

We used to dream about them
Nashville nights
But lately other towns are feeling
all-right;
The people get up and they dance
all night long.
We don't get rich when the
playing is done
But you can bet we're having
some fun,
And we like that applause after
the songs.

Yeah we're just another one of a
million
Little old country bands;
Just some local talent
Trying to do the best we can.

Judy Anne Shuck
CONQUEST
[In memory of: Virginia R. Alge
and Harold E. Shuck]
Reach out Lord and take my hand,
For I walk in darkness—
Blinded by the unknown.
I need to know that You are there.

Reach out and lead me Lord.
I fear I shall stumble and fall
Beneath the dignity of my being.
Lift me higher—to a point nearer
The confidence that I seek.

Reach out Lord and touch my
heart.
Mortal soul that I am, I overlook
The meaning of each pulsating
beat.
Touch me, I need to feel
reassurance
That I can accept the inevitable.

Reach out and show me Lord,
How it is possible to follow those
Footsteps You set before me; how I
Without understanding, am able
to
Walk this path You place before
me.

Reach out and grant me Lord,
Continued courage and strength to
Steer by faith, this wave of fate,
To encounter—at least in part—
A worthy place within Your
Heart.

Kathy Morrison
Are We Really Christ Like?
We don't want to touch them all
tattered and torn.
We don't want to touch them for
they are all worn.
Soiled from the world of
heartache and sin.
We know in our hearts that they
cannot win.

Deep in despair while the world
does not care,
We push them aside and say,
"Stay over there!"
We don't want to see you and be
blurred by your name.
Because we know that your
presence will only bring us
shame.

We are too busy to hear their
hearts cry.
We brush off their dirt and shake
our heads as we sigh,

"Those helpless creatures put
away in prison bars!
No longer to remember in society
of ours."

Jesus taught love! to go in His
name!
He said, "I love them, I love them
the same.
I died for all no matter how
stained.
Life was not meant for this
world's fame."

He died on the cross and reached
down to the pit of hell.
With the message of love! and
salvation to tell!
Are we our brother's keeper as
christians today?
Are we really Christ like? Will we
show them God's way?

Jasper Davis
I KNOW IT'S EASTER
I felt a warm caress,
  I knew I'd felt before.
It comes each year this time,
  To make my joy the more.

I followed that sacred glow,
  Where sinful souls are won.
I embraced the spirit of Easter,
  That lifts the morning sun.

I love the spirit of Easter,
  When Christ's love is shared,
Giving His life,
  So that mine be spared.

Lillian Kathryn Brasher
LOST
[To my husband, Richard
Brasher, Fiftieth Wedding
Anniversary]
Where do I find that which is lost,
Silently on tiptoe it slipped away
Faster than a dream in misty fog
after dark.

Kaleidoscopic in recall,
Touched briefly in memory
Like nectar sipped in flight by a
lark.

Try as I might not one moment
will return,
But remain golden in my mind
Lingering lyrically to the tune of
the harp.

Goldie Kelley
TO PHYLLIS
Wall Street's got my money,
Loafin's got my time,
The rains have got my raisin
crop, and I ain't worth a dime.

Virgil's sittin' on my stocks
And will not budge an inch,
My rent is due tomorrow—I'm in
an awful pinch.

Ma Nature's took my looks,
Pa time has stole my health,
My true love stole my heart
away, and left me by myself.

The muggers picked my pocket,
The burglars picked my lock . . .
Unk Sam has took my wages; I'm
in a dreadful shock!

So if I pass you on the street,
And do not smile or speak,
It's cause I'm blinded by the tears
a rainin' down my cheek.

So gently take me by the hand,
And softly say to me,
"The past was glorious and grand:
the best is yet to be."

Then I'll know I've got a friend,
Someone tried and true,
To cry upon your shoulder, and
tell my troubles to.

And then once more my face will
beam
As in the days of yore . . .
As long as I've a friend like you,
I'm very rich, not poor!!

Phillip Dennis Johnston
PASSING
When I shall go I'll leave thee
what?
A broken heart? I think not:
With me shall go all that came;
Remember my smile; perhaps my
name

And you in passing leave me what?
Your memories? Well, thanks a lot,
But I've my own to see me through
Whatever it is that memories do

When I've passed on, what can be
told
Of I who lived, but now am cold?
If nothing else can then be said,
My life was full 'fore my soul fled

Norma Claflin Trask
OUR EASTER PRAYER
We are all sinners FATHER.
We need your help each day,
To help us with our problems
As we go on our way.
We try to be faithful FATHER
Sometimes it's hard to do
To follow the right hand road—
That leads us straight to you.
Sometimes we wander off
crooked—
But your love is always there,
To guide us dear FATHER
As we speak to you in prayer.
Dear LORD we all do need you,
We need your loving care,
We need your hands upon our
heads
As we bow down in prayer.
We need your understanding—
We need your abiding love.
We need your faith to guide us
As we worship you with love.
AMEN.

B. Maxine Taylor
TO A FALLING STAR
O falling star! Why hast thou left
Thy fair celestial home this night!
One streak of light across the sky
And thou wert gone from mortal's
sight!

Was it a dream, a wish, a tear
That thou didst earthward fly to
kiss?
How canst thou leave thy
heav'nly home
To languish in a world like this?

O falling star! Without thy light
Some hope, some fervent pray'r
may die!
Thy glory gone from everyone
But those who see beyond the sky!

The pale moon sings a lonely song
To thee of love that has no end;
Thy sister stars turn anxious eyes,

And search the heavens for their
friend.

O falling star! My own heart longs
To see once more thy light so rare!
I wonder—wilt thou live again
And shine again, some
day—somewhere?

Kelly L. Griffitt
MEMORIES
When we met on that fateful
summer night we both were
looking for someone to share
our lives with,
But as quick as our love bloomed
it faded away.
I swore I would put away all the
things that remind me of you,
Store all your memories away for
good,
But when I close my eyes I
remember clearly the times
when you held me like there
was no tomorrow.
As I leaf through our notes, old
ticket stubs, and other pieces
of our moments shared
together, I remember all the
joyous times we spent together,
times that are to be no more
for we have parted and went
our separate ways, but your
memory will haunt me for a
long time because I was foolish
enough to fall in LOVE with
someone like you!

Jean M. Thieda
ALAS!
All the years are rolling past
faster as we get older,
I seem no more older than the last
in fact I seem much bolder.

But then I take a look at me
a good look in the glass,
And there I see where all the years
have gathered these ten past! Alas!

Alan Baron
WAITING FOR A SMILE
I'm waiting for the
end of sorrow and
the beginning of joy
I'm waiting for the
wholeness of the Sun
I'm waiting for the
beginning of time
I'm waiting for the
fullness of my heart
the roar of sea in
my veins
I'm waiting for the
sun to smile
I'm waiting for my dream to end
I'm waiting to kiss
my true love's lips
I'm waiting for the
shores of Our dream
to melt into one another
Closing the circle of
love which I am
the smile of divinity

Ann Wellbourne
SAND CREEK
This little stream
That gently moves the sand,
Has the power to carve
Fluted concave designs
And deep round holes,
In granite on her course.
How many trees have lived

Beside her through the years
As she etched her way
Into the granite's soul
To find, their source
Is one and the same?

Every little drop
Is elated by the weather's change
That brings them back to touch
The old familiar haunts,
To rearrange the sandy shores.
Like meeting a good friend,
Each time, to laugh and talk
About the places they have been,
The sea, the sky,
Now home once more.
Then hurriedly on their way again,
At one with the universe.

Barbara Johnson
A ROSE
[I dedicate this poem to my
Mother, Lona Lamar, who was
indeed "A Rose" to me.]
Her face is dipped with morning
mist
Where God has placed his hands,
The softness of her fragile color,
A host of angels planned.

She rests so gently on her throne
With all her grace and ease,
Supported by her tiny stem
And nestled in her leaves.

The wind will softly rise
And rock her to and fro,
And she will ride the waves of air
Until it's time to go.

The face that looks upon her
Feels the greatness of above,
The heart will open up its door
And fill with all his love.

If only for a fleeting moment
This happiness she can place,
She than can nod her head in
silence,
For she is in His grace.

She knows her life is priceless
Whether short or long,
For the gentle hands that placed
her here
Will see that life goes on.

Anita L. Kessler
YOU AND I
The time has now come to say
good-bye.
I've put back my tears. No, I won't
cry.
The time is here, it just will not
wait.
It's not our fault, but the hand of
fate.

Everything we had was so very
good.
We cared for one another, we
understood.
We never lost the love that we
shared.
Life was perfect beyond compare.

Our eyes were fixed upon the
sky, not on the land.
We couldn't stumble when we
walked hand in hand.
Our gazes were held steady on
the stars above.
Nothing in Heaven or Earth
could sever our love.

You and I were all that ever
mattered,

But something came along and
our love was shattered.
I don't blame you nor do you
blame me,
But you want to go and, yes, I'll
set you free.

I know that you have found
another love,
Another one blessed by the
angels above.
So I wish you the best for years to
be.
I hope this love will last an
eternity.

There's one thing I want to say
before I say good-bye.
My honest love for you will
never die.
No, dear, I'm not upset nor am I
sad.
I'm just thankful for all that we
had.

Bonnie L. Beesley
INSTINCT
        I fear
cliffs of cement and steel.
        My soul
    is a precious sparkle
    of turquoise sea.
Pieces of a coral-shattered wave
flow back to completeness.
            Society!
    Your cliffs could turn
            my soul
        to glass splinters.

Carolyn R. Seashore

Carolyn R. Seashore
WHO ARE MY CLOWNS
[With Love to all my Friends
who have been Dear to My
Heart Also Love to my twin
brother Paul Seashore and God
Bless Coco My Dog which is
My Great Spiritual Friend.]
Who are the Clowns?
Where are the Clowns?
They are my friends who may be
either near or far.
They are often strangers who are
friends I have not yet met.
They bring much laughter to my
heart when I am feeling sad!
These are My Clowns.
They always know that "Little
Things" mean A-lot to others.
My favorite Clowns have been
tapers are letters written by
pen and ink that bring joy and
laughter that cheers the heart!
They are the Clowns who get rid

of the frowns from others' sad
faces.
Who are the Clowns?
They are all around me!
They are those who bring joy and
laughter to other peoples'
hearts!
I am grateful to God for them!
God Bless my Clowns.
They will always be Dear to my
Heart!

Jeni Smith
TIME
An element of time,
a year or a decade.
Automatically they decline,
swiftly fly and fade.
Fading in the future line,
till in the past laid.
Now a new element to find,
a century to be made.
This ends with a sign,
for our mistakes we paid.
Where is the end to this kind?
Soon we'll see it fade.
Why is the future blind?
But spicy as a bush of sage.
May it excel and shine,
for time is not of space;
But of men who find,
time, that will not stay.

Berta J. Harper
Tell Me, Mama, How Long?
I sat and watched the grass die
slowly on your grave.
The snow will be coming soon.
I wish you could see the stars out;
The white ring around the moon.
Are you afraid, Mama?

My silly mind wanders so.
I'm worried you'll catch cold.
They tell me you're really not
here.
Why do I feel so old?
Are you warm enough, Mama?

They watch me, Mama, and click
their tongues,
And shake their pitiful heads.
If they only knew my mind,
I know they'd wish me dead.
They think I'm going crazy, Mama.
Should I tell them they are wrong?
They think I'm going crazy,
But I've already gone.

I'm just waiting for the ending.
Tell me, Mama, how long?

William August Kobs
THE LOOK OF LOVE
Where have you been
And where are you going,
Can't you see
What you are doing?

I don't know why
You take it so hard,
And never try
To play the right card.

You want to be free
But your heart is full of doubt,
You must grow and mature
And learn what you are about.

You've been fighting a battle
Don't give up now,
Trust your feelings
Let love show you how.

Do you know
If love is real,

Or is it something
That you feel.

The look of love
Is in your eye,
Like a white-winged dove
Who is free to fly.

Thomas Rudolph Kendrick
AGAPAE
[Dedicated to my mother and
niece for their exemplary lives
of LOVE (Mrs. Prince Alice
Kendrick & Miss Shirley Ann
Grant). Also to my pastor and
wife Rev & Mrs. J.A. Reed, Sr.]
I know you're digging ditches,
Into which I might fall.
But I will keep on loving you,
And that's in spite of all.

Of all the stumbling blocks,
Which you place in my way;
I just cannot stop loving you,
Is all that I can say.

Your mean backbiting ways,
Are awful as can be.
But they cannot begin to stop,
The love that's within me.

The big lies that you tell,
May drag my good name down.
But I cannot stop loving you;
For I am Heaven bound.

Vera Chambers Evans
But Most Of All You've Been a Man
Daddy, rest in peace—
You were the greatest of your clan.
To me you weren't just daddy;
You were a "Friend"—You were a
"Man"
You carried out your duties
As God instructed you to do.
You fulfilled your earthly purpose
And I'm sure He's proud of you!
You had trials. You fought
temptation.
You kept faith when times got
hard.
But you remembered among all
things—
That God was still in charge.
The world shouldn't be denied
The privilege of knowing you
were here;
You left such a great
impression—
In so few, but lovely years.
Daddy, You were one in a million,
Among thousands I'm a fan.
You were so much—to so many,
But like few—you were a man!
Just remember that we miss you;
And we love you even more.
Remember, God only takes—
That which God adores.

Tommy Forguson
TO HENRY
They have put out the lights,
Henry,
They have put out the lights.
Life had the means to charm
Until we went on down
To Sarajevo.

We came in like mild sheep,
Henry,
We came in like tame sheep.
We knew nothing of war's pain.
We lost our innocence
And with it our clear faith.

We need not tears on end, Henry,
We need not weep for us.
The world had need of faith
And we had need of joy,
All we had was a dirge.

We all came out flat broke,
Henry,
We all came out busted.
Good times were once our own.
The sweetness would not end,
Then came the fatal crash.

We were riddled again, Henry,
We were blasted again.
It started with Stukas
Versus horses and closed
In that dead mushroom cloud.

Karen Staskon
DEVILS, AND DUST
How glaring, the insensibilities
    that permeate the gaps in our
    lives.
What comforts with haste, widen
    their eyes.
The touting, the tooting, the
    whistle of fate,
falls quickly, craggy wrinkles in a
    short cry.

The wounds of the flesh, do quiet
    the speech,
as the investigator noted when
    called to the beach.

"Dear God" he heard himself say,
    when will it be,
the end of this day?

The photographs taken, the heat
    on the scene,
the retreat into silence,
the meek feeling mean.

The gap having widened, the
    senses clipped short,
broken by tears, of a senseless
    sort.

Another close of a day, the police
    report finished,
the sirens were off, when the
    crowd diminished.

June Elaine Lacy
FREAK
Where do I belong in this
    menagerie called existence?
Lights, camera, action—take 1;
    the script begins . . .
The setting is the World, the
    scene is living,
The Time is "Now", all the
    characters pretend! (?)

I've read the lines . . . and there
    is no way . . .
I will play that part tomorrow or
    today!!!
I won't pretend what I don't feel.
I don't recommend what isn't real.
I never learned to start my day,
. . . With, "whom will be my
    victim today?"
Rules of plastic have always been
    refused,
Where do I belong unless I am
    used?

Where do I go upon the stage of
    life?
Up right, Down left, center strife?
The audience roars and cheers to
    a well faked performance,
The actors bowing will always
    inform us . . .

For the drama is the way of the
    pretenders life!!
. . . And Me the 'FREAK' will
    always absorb the light. . .
Sage of the Stage when any act
    begins,
I promise to bow when all
    delusions end. . .
Where do I belong "Now". . ., but
    outside the blend?

Mary Margaret Heckler
TOMORROW
God took me up to heaven today,
And as we sat and talked, He said;
"I see you are still smoking."
"Oh Lord, I was going to stop,
But I thought that I had longer."
He looked at me and then He
    said;
"I haven't seen you in church."
I looked down and could only say;
"But I was going next Sunday."
Sadly then, He could barely speak,
    for the tears upon his eyes;
"Does your family know you love
    them,
for their love belongs to me?"
I couldn't see beyond my tears,
    the words just barely heard;
"Dear Lord I was going to tell
    them. . ."
And then the Lord couldn't look
    at me
as if afraid to ask;
"Tell me, your children, do they
    know me?"
I shook my head and turned
    away.
        And God could only cry.

Patsy Kay Armstrong
MY FRIEND
My very best friend
was made just for me,
and the love we share
will always be.

She lends her shoulder
and wipes tears away,
she brings me such joy
in her own precious way.

Little hand in mine
as we walk along,
one could say
she is like a windsong.

She's silly and playful,
loving and smart.
It's plain to see how
she stole my heart.

Who is my best friend
in all the world?
Surely you've guessed,
she's my little girl.

M. Carol McCann
MY DADDY
*[Dedicated to My Daddy, E. F.
McCann, Sr.]*
Daddy's hair is turning silver and
    his eyes are becoming weaker.
Yes, he's a little quieter now and
    maybe a little meeker.
Time mellows and sweetens the
    age of a good wine
And I guess that's what's
    happening to this loving Daddy
    of mine.

You see, I can remember him
    when I was a child as a giant of
A man in my eyes at least

With raven black hair and eyes
    full of care and a smile that
Never ceased.

I could always talk to him and
    know that he cared
For the little brown eyed
    daughter, he always had time
    to spare.
Maybe he was patching up a
    skinned knee and kissing the
    hurt away
But oh how I thanked God that
    he had time for me.

Now I didn't always listen to his
    advice which was my mistake!
You see, Daddy already knew
    what could happen in time
    with fate.
I always thought I was so smart
    because I had an education
And I always questioned
    everything and wanted an
    explanation.
It never occured to me that he
    was wiser in the way of the
    world
That I was too ignorant to see.
But in so many ways, he was
    much smarter than I.

With his tender loving care and
    patience borne beyond
    compare
My Daddy was always standing
    there and waiting to share the
    woes
And wipe away the tears.
Daddy, in case you didn't know it
    this is hard to put on paper
And though I may not have told
    you lately that you are tall and
Stately, your daughter loves you
    greatly; but then, you already
    know.

I don't know what I'll do when
    your time on earth is done.
The world will be hushed and I'll
    be without my sun.
But you'll be with God and I
    know your work on earth will
    be done.
I also know with God and Prayer,
    whenever I need you, Daddy,
You'll be standing there.

Bethel Nunley Evans
YEARS GROW SWEETER
Age is a matter of speech
As long as it is not abused.
As a baby, I cared nothing about it,
And at seven years, I was quite
    amused.

As a teenager, I added a year or two
To make me feel a mite bolder.
But when the twenties came into
    view,
I vowed to stop growing older.

At thirty, I dared not talk about it,
Much less would I admit to
    maturity.
Alas, when I reached the middle
    age forties
That was time to stay in
    obscurity.

Then came the real testing time
When age went over the
    proverbial hill.
The fifties became a bit morbid
And life lost most of its thrill!

But, all of a sudden, sixty appeared
And with it came a ray of
    sunshine.
Because at sixty-five or more
Retirement sounded totally
    sublime.

From seventy on to whatever—
The days grow sweeter by the year,
And finally the realization comes
That age is no longer a care.

Virginia Iza Taylor
PART OF ME
There's many things I long to
    write
Before time stills my pen.

There's many pages I long to fill
    before my
Eyes are dimmed.

Before time slips away from me,
    yes!
Before my autumn ends,
When I can no longer look, and
    see that
Spring has come again.

There's things that bring a simple
    smile
And linger in my heart awhile,
    and follows
Foot prints where I've been, then
    linger in
My heart again.

A poet writes what's in the heart,
    each
Has a song to sing, and to each
    heart
That sings along, a feeling of
    eternal
Spring. I hope my writing brings a
Smile, and not a tear to sadden
    thee.

Because each line I've penned
    today
Is just a little part of me.

John Hill Westbrook
**In Memory Of the April 4,
Murder**
A great rock was hurled
into the ocean of life
and calm furious waves splashed
against the shores of conscience.

The water touches all
but soaks a pitiful few—
the fruitful plains must
feed the fruitless desert.

Giant oaks have been felled
but the forrests remain
to give strength to the saplings
that must grow and take their
    place.

There, look! the sun still shines
a cloud is but a cloud for a
    moment
as long as there is need of rain, it
    will rain
no fear need remain, for it will
    rain and the sun will shine.

Jean Campbell
. . . ON BREAKING AWAY
Standing alone at the cliff's
    ragged edge
I find that I'm weary, reluctant to
    wedge
myself from the solid, the
    familiar, the known—
'tho longing to fly, I cling to the

626

stone

I've lived on this land—its
tremors were mine.
I've sown, picked and crushed its
fruit into wine.
The threads of my being, spun of
green, brown and gold
were tempered in seasons of raw
heat and cold.
While rivers and winds kept my
softness alive,
my body grew tough in its will to
survive.

Evolving, and needing, I've come
to this place,
but I pause now and wonder at
the vastness of space
so dim and so distant—like
dreaming, yet real
I search for a clearing to
somehow reveal
the land at the dawning—does a
horbor exist
where love can come in when I
open my fist?

'Tho doubts cloud the joy of my
impending flight,
I know, like the swallow, this
journey is right.
New life, like a campfire far down
the trail
bids me loosen my grip on the
cliff, and set sail.

Bonnie Newton
THE WAY OF WINTER
Two fish lived together in a bowl.
One died.

Renee R. Smith—Bivins
AT THE DINER
Chewing my gum, watching the
life that goes by
Mr. Smith needs change for the
bus,
Wiping my tables as my favorite
shopping bag lady
heads toward her brand of
oblivion.
Funny the nature that is human.

AM/Business starts the day with
coffee, tea, egg creams
with rolls doughnuts or danish.
Suits and Pantyhose, shuffling,
hustling and rushing
'Scuse me Please

12NOON/The girls are the noon
rush.
Hamburgers with everything or
salad plate and
Sides of last night or who is doing
what with whom
this week on my floor.
A mediocre tip.
and did you see that rag Louise
had on yesterday
I thought she got a raise,, See you
daisy

5PM MN/Everyone eats an
evening meal. Sometime.
People who work late never look
up while they eat.
The lonely, they sit at the middle
window and watch
the world go by eating slowly.
The old, they have chosen the
back near the wall

Some things change, Noon gossip,

kinds of danish.
Some things don't, Noon gossip,
The colors on the lonely.

Funny the nature thats human.

Gordon Smith
WIND, WATER, SAND
There was wind and water and
sand.
There were night sounds and
shadows.
There was secrecy and
excitement,
There was a young woman
A baby boy
And love.

I was there
With urgency and need,
Wanting to give
And to get;
Wanting to share and enjoy
Tempting my body to tempt
yours.

Gradually our warmth was there,
Soon our wetness was there
And suddenly joy and ecstacy
were there!
And there was no wind nor water
nor sand—
There were no night sounds nor
shadows,
There was no secrecy—
Only excitement!
And a young woman
A baby boy
And love.

Patricia Burke
PRAISES TO THE KING
The words have all been sung
before
There are no words so new,
That Thou hast not heard them,
Lord,
So What am I to do?
My heart is filled with joyful
songs
About the Saviour's love
I add them to those sung before
And send them up above.
And Thou, the Author of all song
Accepts my poetry
Then writes a symphony of love
And sends it back to me.

Diane Modarelli
WHAT IS LIFE
Where in the world can anyone
show
The real meaning of life that
none of us know
The mellowing of problems we've
had from the start
To conquer the fears before we
must part
The peace we must find in our
very own mind
Seems clouded by stress from our
very own kind.

Judy G. Johnson
EVALUATION
So here I am,
Now at the age of twenty.
Is this the point in life
That I can now be called a woman?
I don't feel any different,
In fact, my feelings are all the
same.
Emotionally, I am still the young
girl in love.

In love, and my competition is a
mere child.
And such a feeling cannot be
described,
As when the child wins.
If becoming a woman
Means gaining wisdom, and
strength,
I know that the next time I fall in
love,
If that's where my life is headed;
That it will be with someone
Who is also in love with me.

Diane Gail Emery
FREEZE FRAMES
A ballerina flits upon a glass
floor—
Each skate a glint of polished
silver
Skimming across a gelid loch;
Her only audience the Old Man
Peering down from His frozen
zenith.

Dripping glass fringes the
world—
Scintillating statues carved in
ice,
Figurines whispering to the
Wind;
The slow rhythm of their
undulating bodies
Gently washing a white
blanket in their tears.

Now their Creator pushes pillows
in the sky—
A blizzard savagely
whitewashes the horizon,
Each snowflake a crystal
labyrinth of its own
Spiraling lanquidly to the
crusty earth,
Shattering there into echelons
of translucent wafers.

The soft lull after a storm—
Miniature footsteps marking a
crumbling corridor,
The scent of wet evergreen in
the breeze,
Top—heavy boughs splintering
to relieve their burdens
As ivory swans emerge from
dark chasms.

Mirrors, mirrors—
Reflections from an old man's
past;
He is dying now,
Reaching for memories,
Impressions of winters past.

Ruth Roberts Douglas
A DEAD TREE
   [*Floy McEachern, the first
   English teacher who
   encouraged me in the writing
   of poetry*]
In majestic beauty,
You stood as I passed by,
Your huge black limbs outlined
against the sky.

To that stark picture,
Imaginations bring
A covering of leaves
and buds of spring.

I see you now as once you must
have been,
And in my mind began
to wonder when
you lost your youth.

And marvel why
you went when you
seemed much to
young to die.

Katie Brunner
U.S.A. TO THINK OF IT—
Two hundred years is all it took
to build and cultivate this land,
It would not have been possible
without God's kind and helping
hand.

That's why it is important
for us to understand
To keep it safe, clean, beautiful
as one of His commands.

So let us do our very "best"
let no debris fall
In speech, in action, and beliefs
which includes the big ones and
the small.

God gave this Country
everything
with love so great and strong
If we appreciate—and think of it
then nothing can go wrong.

Yes, the future still looks shining
bright
regardless of some strife;
The way we look at things will
count
and assures a useful, happy life.

John K. Evans
UNLOCKING MY DREAM
Life is getting difficult for me,
I'm looking for things that I can't
see.
I'm seeing things that I hope
come true,
all of which have me in love with
me.

People say that I talk in dreams,
nobody knows for sure it seems.
Dreams are conceived for the
best,
making them come true is the
real test.

My dream, if you don't know by
now,
is to have you love me somehow.
You are the key to my secret lock,
opening it is being decided by
nature's clock.

Time is the essence of you
turning the key,
unlocking our love to flow
simultaneously.
But waiting for that time to come
is hard,
Hoping fate will someday turn
my card.

Paula Perkett
LOVE NOTES
Is love a soft heart,
a forgotten moment, a brand new
start?
Is love warmth in free flight,
or something you hold onto with
all your might?

Is love a fulfilment of hope thru
the years;
over broken promises and empty
tears?
Is love a wishing well,
or is love something we daren't
tell!

Is love of yesterday a promise of
   tomorrow?
or something deepening into
   sorrow?
Is love a trusting hand, a
   breathless sigh,
or is love meant to always be a
   final goodbye?

Is love a shining smile and
   gleaming eyes,
or a web of deceitful lies?
Is love a forgotten thing?
Or is love meant only for spring?

Is love a spirit climbing high,
or one long anxious sigh?
Is love one long summer's night
   to be;
or is love a broadening of eternity?

George F. Lohr, Jr.
Secrecy Is Now a Virtue
Beware the ones on self—
   righteous whims
Bent to bring down their shame,
Upon a love as innocent
As the one we dare not name.

Judges have taken their seats,
I can feel their hungry eyes
Awaiting the fresh, sweet meat
Of our friendship with nothing to
   hide.

So, beware my lively young friend,
Cast not those pearls we hold true
Before the swine that will
   trample them down;
Secrecy is now a Virtue.

Judith Shannon Paine
SOMETIMES A SONG
Remembering is painful when
all you have left is memory.
Sometimes, a song stabs me
from the radio and I am a
child . . . your child again.
Oh! And concerts and parades
absolutely kill me!
Sometimes, I just know that
you are there,
And then, reality yells
that you are gone.
The other night, The Count's
Band backed up "Ole Blue Eyes"
as he sang.
I sang along.
Remembering is painful when
all you have left is memory
and
Sometimes a song—
   stabs
   me . . .

Miriam Grace Marvin
THE NEW YEAR
May we start the year with a
   fervent prayer
   That God will guide us, and
   share every care,
For He will, you know, if you ask
   Him to,
   He's willing—and ready—so it's
   up to you.
Just open your heart and let Him
   come in;
   It's the only way through life to
   win.
You'll find that it's a joy to live,
   With God in your heart, you'll
   have much to give;
For all the good things will then
   come to you—

Things—that before, you never
   knew.
With Him in your heart, your
   way will be light
   Through the darkest shadows
   and the dead of night;
He'll lighten the burdens that
   weigh you down,
   And give you courage and
   strength to go on.
So start the New Year hand in
   hand with God,
   And the brightest of paths will
   be yours to trod.

Catherine Coburn
WALLS
Walls, must we build them?
   Keeping things in or keeping
   things out
Do they add to beauty or just to
   duty?
To a mere design or to finish a
   line,
   planned by the architect.

Some walls surround prisons,
   some gardens,
   and some churches—but
   should we build walls
and leave God, out of our
   searches?

Some people build walls to hold
   up
   their ceilings, while others
   build walls
to protect their own feelings.

Break—ins, break—outs or
   break—throughs,
   Sometimes all our walls seem
   to crumble,
but let us please "Lord, if we must
   build
   walls, let it be for the beauty of
   keeping,
Christ, *in* and not *out* to give
   strength
   to our own Christian duty."

Dr. Marshall Iley Stewart
**To Highland Presbyterian
Church, In Appreciation**
[Dedicated To: Rev. Dr. and
Mrs. William A. Price]
Earliest visits reach far beyond
   my memory
When, while still in arms,
   regularly I attended the Lord's
   service,
And to the cradle rolls my name
   was added,
And early, my parents lifted me
   to the baptismal fount.

Time brought development: Bible
   study, pageants, revivals;
Brought insight through prayer
   and ministry,
Brought broader meaning to the
   wisdom from the pulpit,
Brought understanding and love
   for others, who loved me
   already,
Brought faith and love for the
   Savior, who loved me before
   my birth.
Is it any wonder that an early call
   came to me?
Is it any wonder that I accepted
   without hesitation?
No urging was needed—His love

did it all—
My heart went to the Lord and
   this, His Church,
Where it remains forever!

For within these hallowed walls
   the Savior dwells;
And Heaven and Earth meet in
   harmony.
Feel here His presence, as in no
   other place,
Permeating every atom,
   affervescing into the world,
Cleansing our minds and hearts,
   our very souls,
Exhorting respect and love for all—
Our neighbor wherever to be
   found!
Each day adds blessings to our
   being—
Rewards in spiritual guidance.
For these I offer praise and
   heartfelt thanks,
And add to them, this, my sincere
   and humble testimony:
To our Church , to my Church,
To Highland Presbyterian
   Church, in appreciation.

Marge Schneider
HAIKUS
i wonder what to do
when i see you go by
and say my, o my.

and all i can do
is wink and try to think twice
about seeing you.

but now it is too
early yet to say good—bye
to people who lie

so think twice again
when you touch me so cruelly
with your hands ruley.

now i go back to
my shell of blue and blue now
so i can see you.

but remember, sir
i do kind of love you now
in a way i do

so, my pet it yet
is to be seen just what lane
you feel is happy.

Deborah Holeman
REALMS OF PERCEPTION
[To the children bound by
   temporal facades . . .]
On earth they're mocking,
flaunting the unseen—
courting the "Master of Deception"
Revelling in building their tombs
and chains—each link wrought
with bloodstains.
Each door they pursued
contained a double—entendre,
but they only pondered the
mysterious and obscure way.
Now hordes of children run
amidst all the caverns of hell . . .
To grasp sensations of mourning
for the numbers of growing
children kidnapped in the night.
Lured into darkness—slow suicide
encouraged—in the eternal fire
of the Beast they now ride . . .
To avoid this children, weigh
careful your decision—"choose
ye this day whom ye serve,"
don't ignore Jesus—this worlds

temporal—but with God's Son,
life can be preserved . . .

Lisa R. Wilke
TO MATTHEW . . .
I love you.
I wish we could spend more time
   together.
You spoil me.
I'll spend the day with you and
   still not be completely fulfilled.
I need you.
I need to spend every moment of
   my life with you,
Every waking and sleeping
   moment,
Every happy and sad moment,
Every loving moment.
I know you love me,
But it's just not enough for me to
   see you only at certain times,
I want to come home to you,
Fall asleep in your arms,
And wake up in the morning
   with you.
I want to fix breakfast for you,
Pick up after you,
And kiss you before you go to
   work each morning,
And kiss you after you've come
   home at night.
Oh, how I need you!
I need you so very much . . .
To touch,
To care for,
And to love
Forever
And
Ever
Until death
Will we part.

Lois J. Martucci
SECOND CHANCE . . .
Always be prepared to look ahead;
For when the time comes that we
   want to dread,
Things seem to change, it is often
   said
For the best, we hope; the truth to
   us is fed.
New things occur, of this we are
   sure,
So, "hang on in there"; there is
   always a cure.

A change in our lives will forever
   be,
Most of the time giving us lots of
   company.
New ideas, forgotten ideas, finally
   come to light,
Making us sure of ourselves to
   welcome the flight
Of obstacles, problems—
   whatever we face,
Pushing us onward, always
   forming a "new base"
Of living, laughing, and loving,
Always positive of becoming
A new person, surely to enlighten
Ourselves, our friends, whoever
   we may brighten!

Concettina M. Gitto
SPRING
Spring, preciously holds a beauty
   so rare,
Overlooked by our existance in
   troubled days.
But its beauty is far beyond
   compare,

To hold in our memories,
As we go our separate ways.
So human are we all that we
sometimes forget
How lucky we are to be alive,
As showers pour down on our
world we get wet
Yet somehow we still survive.
And suddenly a new day shines
before our eyes
Bringing a ray of sunshine so
bright,
Lord, let us not be caught up in a
world of lies
So that our darkness may turn to
light.
Spring is here and gone only too
soon, it seems,
Enjoy its beauty, while it is here.
Let us make it part of our dreams,
As it comes to us each year.
Although there is beauty beyond
each spring
For summer, winter and fall have
beauty too,
But spring holds a very special
thing
The birth of new life and the
chance to start anew.

Ronald Paul McCular
BASKETBALL SHOES
Long ago in dreams of basketball
shoes,
With heart aches as day breaks,
Playing without any rules.
With my love at the free throw
line,
As were slowly losing time.
Tired of this way we run,
Just starting to have our fun.
Right you lose, so left you choose,
Never get to use the gun.
Fast as the sun, oh this way we
run.
Holding on to breakaways,
Losing sight of the darker days.
Finding words that surly rhythm,
With my love at the free throw
line,
And we just ran out of time.

Jerry Lee Austin
CHILDREN
Magic rings and unseen things,
are their constant companions.
They roam over hills,
and down into rills,
oftimes through the canyons.
With snakes and toads,
and magic roads,
their mind it knows no bars.
Then mothers' call,
and dreams they fall,
to ashes at their feet.
No more knells,
of distant bells.
"Son, it's time to eat."

Marjorie Gagnet Berry
NOCTURNE
Eve of Halloween, the night that
spirits band,
a peaceful night, I awake, a rose is
in my hand.
A long stemmed rose without a
thorn, still fresh with dew,
brilliant red,
the presence of someone in my
room as I sit up in my bed.
"Fear not my dear, an old friend
am I, but if you say so I shall go,

first let me tell you who I am, I
am Edgar Allen Poe.
Please arise and come with me to
a very special place,
a little wooded place I love", I
stared into his face.
His dark eyes were piercing,
mysteriously he whispered low,
overwhelmed was I, he cast a
spell, I knew that I must go.
I put by hand in his as he led me
out the door,
we walked on for hours through
land and field and moor.
Not a word was spoken this
star—filled night as we walked
into the wood.
We stopped beneath a cypress
tree that I knew I had once
before stood.
He smiled at me, "my sweet
Lenore, you do remember now".
As I looked in bewilderment,
disappointment lined his brow.
We sat beneath the tree, blanket
spread with cheese and wine.
We drank, we ate, he talked,
captivating my soul, my mind.
Forever immortal, when the
moon is new I search through
the meadows and brier,
bringing victims to him as he
impatiently waits in loathsome
disguise as a vampire.

M. Marianne Miles
COMPANIONS
There is my psyche
In front of me.
There goes my shadow
on the side of me.
There we are
running, running,
leaping,
flying,
sailing through
colors and colors
and colors
of an evening
sky.
The breeze,
the breeze, oh the
breeze
feels good.

Wylie McGee
**Mother's Reflections:
April 14, 1949-April 14, 1970**
*[To our son, Jim, who has been
the joy of our lives.]*
A baby boy!
Oh, what a joy!
Some problems, too;
But just a few.
We plan, you grow;
We hope you know:
Can say aloud—
"We're awf'ly proud
Of your fine ways
And worthwhile days.
So well you've done—
To twenty-one!"

MOTHER'S UPDATE: A SEQUEL
APRIL 14, 1970-APRIL 14, 1980

When I review
Again, on cue,
The years' demise
Before my eyes;
I see a 'Man'
With worthy plan—
Young, eager yet,

Goals to abet.
Suddenly, grow'n'
Tired—Fam'ly tie.
Says, "Put away,
Without delay,
All contact now—
Ne'er to allow
Another time,
The wasteful mime!
Did give of me—
The rest to be
For Me, to share
With One, to care;
And ne'er again—
I gave all, when
My need for *You*
Was ever new."

Debbie Moody Sorcic
A UNIVERSAL MIRAGE
Here alone I sit
Wondering what it's all about
Taking every little bit
Trying to sort it out

The world once was born
Under some ingenuous being
None of us are slightly torn
We do without seeing

When grabbing some time
We have tried to break the seal
Without one sensible rhyme
It wraps us in its chill

We hold life by strings
That knot together without cause
It constantly pulls with wings
Doing so without pause

Estelle H. Munsell
MY DONNIE
Tall of stature, proud of stance
With love and laughter in each
glance,
Forever young, forever free,
Forever beautiful to me—my
Donnie.

He lived his life with charm and
grace;
His going's left an empty place
Within my home, within my
heart.
I simply cannot bear to part—
with Donnie.

He was my son for eighteen years
And this overflow of tears
Helps some to ease the pain I feel
And yet they say that time will
heal.

But how can time replace his
smile,
The times he sat and talked
awhile,
The times he romped and played
with me?
These things are now a memory
of Donnie.

Others might forget his face,
Forget his special charm and
grace,
And yet he will forever be
Young and beautiful to me—My
Donnie.

Maxine Campbell
A FALLEN SOLDIER
Sleep on dear one, while mortars
rain
Their fire of death, inflicting pain,
Bombs bursting, guns aroar,
This is the price that's paid for

war.
Sleep on dear one, while others
fight
With fury, power and with might,
We do not know why things
come up,
And we're forced to drink the
bitter cup.

Sleep on dear one, under blankets
of clay,
No more reveille, orders or
commands to obey,
Others have gone, more will soon
fall,
The same long bridge will be
crossed by all.

Sleep on dear one, during each
tomorrow,
While we continue in tears and
in sorrow,
Your duty is done, you've
answered the call,
How much can you give? you've
given your all.

Orville Pointer
I BELIEVE
*[To Jaclyn Smith a black velvet
princess, because of her I am a
poet.]*
God made earth and man and
showed him all he had made.
The mountains to reach out as
giants of stone woven with
colors as the colors within.
The wind to touch the world the
wind as a ship yet to be to sail
to and fro.
The flowers natures tears from
bear ground beauty to come.
The sunsets and sunrise painting
before the canvas was to be.
Each wonder seen by the eye and
kept in the heart.
But the only place for love to be
was the vessel his heart,
For all the world he had new yet
still alone.
So he brought women to this
world for man would to come
search for treasure, but the
greatest treasure is love in a
ladies eyes.
For now was a vessel as great as
his own to hold love, to share
the world . . Oh time has
come and gone and trouble, but
to me the greatest gift that was
ever given was the ladies of
this world for the greatest gift
is still a lady to be beyond all
treasure of this world.

Mary M. Domstead
**More Than Wealth Or
Fame**
*[This poem was written to—
and inspired by—my husband
R.E., in appreciation of all his
love and support for the past 35
years.]*
There's something special you've
given me—
I'm not ashamed for the world to
see.
No! I don't wear it around my
neck—
Sorry! you can't buy it with a
check.
To me, it means more than a gold

Cadillac.
I'd never throw it away . . . nor
give it back.
I wouldn't exchange it for a
diamond or fur—
It's something that makes this
old cat purr.
True! My wedding band fills a
unique space—
But! On a scale of ten . . . doesn't
hold first place.
I'm sure you're wondering what
I'm talking about,
I'll confess—I'm proud enough to
shout.
"Thank you darling—for giving
me YOUR—NAME,
It's worth more to me—than
wealth or fame.

Nita Mankin
Coup de Grace; in Somalia
[*To the breast-feeding mother
of twins, who had to decide
which of her children must die;
because she had not enough
milk for both. To all who suffer.
To all who care, yet feel
helpless and therefore
somehow guilty.*]
"Noone came, because noone does."
Yet in ignorance
I search actively,
daily, with increasing intensity
and a kind of faith

If I can find one . . .
even one,
would that be good enough
to save this metropolis—
within me, or mine?
Bearing gifts,
"Noone came, because noone does."

and I search on
as long as one such as I can
hoping, even in despair—
such is my "uniqueness"
Unashamed of my mounting desire;
and "noone comes, because noone
does . . ."

Faye P. Parker
CONTENTMENT
Where there is Faith,
There is Hope—

Where there is Hope,
There is Strength—

Where there is Strength
There is Courage—

Where there is Courage,
There is Steadfastness—

Where there is Steadfastness—
There is a calm Peace—

When there is Peace in the heart
There is CONTENTMENT
Nothing can change—

Cindy Stubbs
LOVING YOU FOREVER
Why did you stop caring?
I'd really like to know.
I just don't understand,
Why you had to go.
You say you still love me,
But I can't believe it's so.
'Cause if you truly loved me,
You wouldn't have let me go.

Now the time has passed,
I should be over you.
But I love you just as much,

And there's nothing I can do.
My love for you will never die,
That much I know is true.
I just wish you would explain,
Where I went wrong with you.

Betty Stanford
INNER CONFLICTS
Today is the beginning of a new
way of life,
Although I'm a mother as well as
a wife.
I will prove I can make it—
I can give as well as take it.
I have a longing way deep inside
That tells me death to self-
respect and pride.

I need to feel freedom in the
worst kind of way,
But what of the consequences I
know I must pay?
It's the biggest struggle I've ever
faced;
Will I find contentment or only
disgrace?

Mary Helen Wilson
Feed Lots: Pa$toral $cene
Eyes glazed with ignorance
They shift heavily about within
their railed enclosure
Their only sentence everlastingly
to ruminate
And be deprived of darkness

Tomorrow and tomorrow
To the end of
existence
When the scale has finally
registered
that justice has been
served.

Their lot was prescirbed from the
Beginning,
It is said, by that slow Titan—
The one who fashioned animals
to gaze upon the ground
But whose brother brought
civilizing light from heaven
For mortals' use below

So that man
with higher vision
Now simply calls the shots.

Morris Simon
**May Was Brought To My
House**
MAY WAS brought to my house,
Tho a winter storm was raging.
A visitor gave me a pot of Tulips
with Spring's charms so engaging.
Sleet bombarded the window panes.
Outside was a wilderness of snow.
Yet my room was transformed
by May's nostalgic glow.
The Winter of dreary greyness,
of raging storms and gloom
was suddenly swept away
by Spring's enchanted broom.

Ollie Goldsmith
TOM'S SONNET
Mark you well, my friend,
you'll move and dance and soar
with angels, to their music, as
before
you were or ever thought to rend
the curtain of this life's bend.
A generator of goodness and a
reflector
certainly is what you're here for
and will be your gifts until the

end.
Events are temporal, friendships
are few,
Truth is elusive, joy a matter of
choice.
The main infinitives of life, they
tell me,
are not 'to have' and 'to go,' that's
true,
but 'to do' and 'to know'; add my
voice
saying to you, for the world, just
'be.'

Lois Marie Duncan
A PARENT'S WORRY
I stood in the bedroom doorway
And watched my child today.
A babe that he isn't from yesterday.
All of six and that big!
Goes off to school with a smile.
Goes off to war tomorrow?
Ready. Aim. Fire . . .
Sleep peaceably for now, my son.

C. D. McKay
RE—RUNS
We see and hear a lot of re-runs.
Some not so good—others well
done.
What we need is a re-run of
Pentecost
Where God came down to save
the lost.
Then they went everywhere
preaching the word;
And, to some, it was the best
news ever heard.
Then those that were saved were
added to the band;
And the movement spread over
the land.
So we need to have a re-run of
Pentecostal Day
When God's fire and power fell as
they did pray.
If such should fall on us on a
wide scale,
The dives of sin would weep and
wail.
As to the places of iniquity
would close now
While to God's spirit the world
would bow.

Shirley Davis MaGee
HOPE
[*To God, who gave us the
assurance of things hoped for
through faith.*]
Hope is near,
no need to fear.
In time you will
receive
As soon as you
achieve
The faith you need
to wait.
Do not haste,
for hope
Is approaching
your way.

Nancy E. Angelo, R.N.
GRANDPA ACITELLI
I hear you call from far away
You make me see myself today
I still feel love from years ago
I still feel hurt and I love you so

Death is sudden, you can't escape
So live life well, don't sit and wait
You didn't feel dying was such a

crime
It came so fast, you hadn't the
time

But now you're gone and I remain
Things just aren't quite the same
I listen each night to hear you call
Some nights it doesn't come at all

Some nights I hear you cry so loud
I look to see if you are around
I raelize then that you are gone
It is just the sounds of a familiar
song.

Laura L. Shaw
CHANGING HEARTS
Eager to change, Heart swells—
expands while yet caged within
confines of muscular valves.
Beating, ticking—racing, whizzing,
pulse—in—to—pulse.
"What's wrong," says Heart to
Mind.
"Don't bother me," says Minds.
"I have no time for you."
Heart persists, "I must know, I
must."
So Mind says, "———"
Poor Heart.

Mrs. F. A. Blanche Swann
That Little Fen Of Mine
He's not so very tall
Just 'bout reaches to my knee
Yet he's strong and sturdy as a wall
And as healthy looking as can be
That Little Fen of Mine!

He has a pair of twinkling eyes
That laugh at you from far inside
His little mind is always hard at
work
With simple thoughts yet rather
wise!
That little Fen of Mine!

You love him when you meet him
You want to love him all the time,
For he carries sweet music inside
him
And you seem the tune to find!
That little Fen of Mine!

Aw, how we loved him
On that morn he came to stay
We knew of the thrill of
something deep within us,
A treasure far more precious than
gold we say
And we hugged him, hugged him
closer
This new found joy,
This precious boy
That little Fen of Mine!

Marcia Dalbey
NANCY
Nancy you are my beautiful
maiden
you have hair that shines in the
sun.
Freckles from heaven above
feet that run like a deer.
Even your eyes sparkle so clear!

Nancy has smiles that are few,
thoughts that are blue.
I understand what being a teen
can do.

Mom, she seems so mean
Dad, he's a king.
Friendsd can be traitors
Brothers and chores easily hated.

These years in number are few.
Soon into a woman you will have grown
loving and admiring a Nancy of your own.
If only you could see Nancy from my eyes
would you ever be surprised!

Christopher Williams
HE HOLDS LOVE'S TOUCH!
Confessions that fell into the mighty sea (TIME) unveiled . . .
Another chance for our minds to prevail over the sins and the crimes of hell.
Victory came against the devil and death of the same
Forgiven by *Christ* in this war, we'll remain . . .
Heirs of the star; SALVATION!!
Rearranged for the glory of eternal preservation!

"Father of All Fathers, One Almighty LORD!!
Your *WORD!* Not the world, I believe shall set me free!
You're the King I need, *GOD!*
THANK YOU FOR THE TRUTH! Take good care of Peace!"

Heaven is our Trust! Growing so close as we arise over lies and lust!
Our Great God and Hero who molded man from dust!
Taught all how to pray!
(HE HOLDS LOVE'S TOUCH!)
Thank you *SWEET JESUS* for that day—You arose for us!!

Cheryl White
A DADDY OR A FATHER?
[With love to Harold; the best father in the world.]
I was eight years old
When my "daddy" died.
I didn't really understand
So all I did was cry.

In my heart was a bitterness
For the dad I had and lost,
So, when mom got a new husband
"I'd show him who was boss."

I thought I knew it all then
Yet, as all the years went by,
I realized my "daddy" was no father;
He never even tried.

The man who was there
Was there through good and bad,
Yet, he got snatched up to Heaven
Before I ever called him dad.

Life is much too fragile;
too short to understand
the happiness you bring to others
by praising them while you can.

Marian Nell Thompson
LIFE AFTER LIFE
On one goes down the road;
Sometimes rough, sometimes smooth.
Crying, laughing, ups and downs;—
Till the end of life.

Over one goes—cross the brink.
Ne'er to be alone; He is there!
Praise Him, singing; Honor give Him;
Now there is New Life!

Life's a mystery, but death's no sting;
Eternity is ahead!
Welcome, loved one; hear the words!
God's sweet welcome comes.

Limmie Schenall
WHY NOT TALK TO GOD?
Where do you go when there is no place to hide?
Feeling lonesome and anguished?
Why won't these feelings subside?
Do you burden your friends in moments of despair?
Do you examine your mind?
Or, have you petitioned God in Prayer?
Where do you go when you are spiritually low?
Who not talk to God?
You did not hesitate to let your friends know!

Vanona Fowler Williams
STORM
Storms returning, tempest brewing
Roaring thunder, no ensuing.
Lightning flashing through the sky
Heaven's angry, hear her cry.

Screaming winds snarl through the trees
Branches hanging, devoid of leaves.
Dusty earth cries rain must fall,
To quench her thirst, we hear her call.

Rain is falling, rivers yearning
Desert sands no longer burning.
Silence now the earth is still
For her rebirth, man's needs to fill.

Shelley Shelley
INNOCENT EYES
Oh how I wish I had Innocent Eyes
Innocent Eyes of a Child
They see things different from us
grown up folks, through those wonderful
Innocent Eyes.
What a shame we must grow up
& lose the sight of a child.
But just for awhile I think I'll pretend,
That I still have those eyes
Those Innocent Eyes
of a child.

Kathleen Shields
CHRISTMAS DAY
The time is upon us; so happy and gay
All are preparing for this Christmas Day
It's a special time for showing we care
Loving and giving hang thick in the air
The children grow restless in their wait to see
What gifts Santa will leave them under the tree
Finally all's ready, the fussing is done
Time for young and old to join in the fun
The neatly wrapped presents, all topped with a bow
The tree with its trimmings are all aglow
Good times and good food are shared by all
With many a chorus of "Deck the Hall"

It's no sooner here then it's over so quick
As fast and as nimble as Jolly St. Nick
The memories we ponder in bed as we lay
With thoughts slowly drifting to next Christmas Day

Carolyn Ann Allen
WAR
"WAR" . . . when I was younger it never meant much to me,
That is until its sharp claws reached out to snatch Joey.
Joey had a younger sister, Cathy, who was my best friend.
When Joey's number came up our carefree adolescence met its end.

With Joey off to war even our favorite song had a new interpretation.
One verse in particular we would sing with great trepidation,
"Where have all the soldiers gone? Gone to graveyards everyone!"
With tears in our eyes we'd hug and pray the war would soon be done.

Joey's mother refused to watch the news each night.
She was eager for some word about "the foreign fight",
But was consumed with the fear that she might see
One of the injured wearing her son's face as it flashed across TV.

Worry for a loved one can often breed dissension.
Somehow word reached Joey of his parent's possible separation.
Joey, feeling he was losing his home, volunteered for the helicopter rescue unit, Medivac.
Despite this dangerous frontline duty, he miraculously made it back.

Although his chest was decorated with medals he had earned,
There were no crowds to give him a hero's welcome when he returned.
The scars he still bears, from wounds both physical and mental, are a reality.
How could those safe at home fail to honor those like Joey who fought each day against the chance of becoming a fatality?

Joey is trying to build his life once more
With a house, a pretty wife and a boy just turned four.
He holds on to dreams of his son growing to be a man
In a world where there is never another Vietnam!

Annette Schaldecker Wolf
THE DREAMER
She sits in her world
not quite oblivious to those around
Losing more everyday
to what she left behind
what she could have been
what she has become
Lonely and embittered

Listening to her music
dreaming her life away
Maturing less every day
mentally and emotionally
While becoming grotesque
losing her self-esteem
Doing the same things day to day
or just doing nothing
Moving along motionless
stagnating like a pool of water
Once a beautiful brook
left alone to dwindle away
Each word
Each movement
a passionate cry for help
That she seems to hear but ignores
She sits
She waits for strength
the strength to help herself

Alma Joyce
ALL ABOARD
Grace express through judgement
into the dare to know
thrusting the hapless chosen
to travel this tour alone.

Some faithful tokens given.
Strange value always the same;
only enough to pay the fare
on the straight and narrow way.

Last toll charges all in your care
as a gate way does a sharp turn
revealing roads to travel at will
round trips with cargoes of hope.

Margie Roemele
WITHOUT YOU
[Dedicated to my Daughters Freda Carole, Rita Ann]
I miss the soft shimmering rays of the Sun
I miss the Sunset, when Day is done
I miss the Evening Star and the Moon's soft glow
I miss hearing you say "I LOVE YOU SO"
I miss the gentle breeze and the morning Dew
I miss the Rose's fragrance . . . when I'm not with you
I miss all of these but even more
I miss my Heart . . . when you close the door.

Cherie' Whisenhunt
UNTITLED
Have you ever needed to cry,
When the tears refused to flow?
Or watched a dripping candle,
To feel the after-glow?

Have you ever sat and watched the sun,
Fall gently behind the trees?
Or sat along the lake shores,
To catch the flowing breeze?

A strange and becalming emotion,
To sit and ponder there.
To watch the world go drifting by,
Not caring really where.

To think about the past,
The things that you have done.
To wonder about the future,
Or if you really have one.

To think of all the sadness,
The loves, the joys and tears,
And watch the creeping shadows,
Bring back the many fears.

You take a breath and shiver,
  The time has come you say,
To gather yourself together,
  And begin a bright new day.

R. Howell
MISTRESS POETRY
mist stair
missed hair hair mist
pubic must extravagent mane
this my love the landscape and
  kiss
this my love the wonderment

the valley grassed
valet grasped
ballet lapsed

cubic rust at the seashore
this my love the mescape (and
  kiss)
and this my love the sacrement

Joanne Radcliffe
BUTTERFLIES
I've held my loves like
  Butterflies
All waiting to be free.
And one by one my
  Butterflies
Have flown away from me.

I knew they would,
It just took time
  until their wings
    were fully grown.

I knew they would
  and yet forgot
    to plan my time alone.

They can't come back my
  Butterflies,
    at least not as before;

And yet they know
  I won't forget,
I'll always leave
  an open door.

Kristy R. Barton
OUR STRANGE OCEAN
The ocean never tires, never does
  it rest.
Strange, though it may seem still
  and quiet, it moves
  continuously.
The many mysteries of the vast
  ocean, will man ever have all of
  the answers?
Strange, that we know so much,
  yet so little.
The beautiful ocean mammals,
  slowly becoming extinct.
Strange, how we think we are the
  superior life form and can take
  other lives as we please.
The ocean—strange? Who is to
  say?

Cassandra Tunstall
POETRY IS . . .
[Poetry is . . . The songs of life
within me, the spirits of truth
that enlightens my life. I
dedicated this poem to my
loving family, the Tunstalls and
Greens, and all my friends who
wish to understand me.]
Poetry is . . .
a song being sung
music being played
a cry being uttered
moments being saved
a dance being performed
laughter being heard

secrets being told
love being in words

questions being answered
thoughts being known
a heart being captured
tears being shown

a fire being kindled
the heavens being reached
a dedication being rendered
a sermon being preached

right being honored
wrong being shunned
a gift being unwrapped
the tempest being calmed

earth being exalted
memories being printed
divinity being lauded
messages being hinted

a race being ran
a soul being healed
the bound being salvaged
a cup being filled

Poetry is . . .

Nancy Jane Brebner
EVENING MAGIC
Evening makes any season more
  beautiful:

A stark bare sight
Of leafless trees
In velvet crewel
In winter twilight.

New green of trees and grass
In springtime
With late day sun
Becomes green stained glass.

In summer, white-hot hues
Of burning skies
With evening breezes
Become cool grays and blues.

And the most beautiful of all,—
Dying leaves
Blaze alive
At sundown in the fall.

Gertrude I. Sampson
TRUE FRIENDS
[To my loving family]
True friends, like God's wild
  flowers,
Demand no special care.
Through sun and storm and sheer
  neglect,
Each year they'll still be there.
And time or distance or poverty
  or wealth,
These things will never part,
The treasure of friendship old or
  new,
From deep within my heart.

Cathren Oliverson
FAREWELL THE KING
[To Andy]
You came again in the winter of
  my youth,
To restore me, to protect me, and
  to bask me in your truth.
You were there with me to guide
  me to my peak,
And we understood each other
  even when we didn't speak.
Oh, my pretty one, the kingdom
  we built, the worlds we
Conquered and the hardships we
  endured.
Truly, I was surprised at how

easily you allowed yourself
To be allured.
To my darling, the false
  champion of my heart, I put
  the question—
Did you have no pangs of regret
  when you were preparing to
  depart?

It's plain to see the quality of the
  other you have chosen.
Hopefully you will see, my love,
  how futile it is to try
And recapture lost years when
  her young luster proves shallow
And her fountain of youth has
  turned to oceans of poison.
How is it you have forgotten our
  young son?
Is your new heir the reason your
  memory of us grows dimmer
  with
Each passing season?
I can't and won't believe you if
  you say that this is so, for
I feel it when you think of me
  and see the fire burning in your
Black eyes should we meet by
  chance or reason.
If you are thinking, I find your
  situation ludicrous, allow me
  to explain.
It is only patience you read in my
  face,
For like the wind that blows, and
  comes and goes, you will surely
Come again.

J.R. Welch
SALOME
[For R.E.G., who is the music
that I dance to.]
When at night the full moon
  freshens
And the wind whips into song
Salome wakes and stirs within me,
Looks out with manic eyes
  through mine,
And begins again to dance.

Ageless woman, caged and
  cunning
Death found her fire too hot to
  dampen.
So she, with woman's mystery,
  descended,
Found the coals which cooled
  inside me,
And breathed life to my own.

Other women have denied her,
But in me her dance has
  overcome,
How long till she makes me
  move with me,
And I shed femimistic fever
As she shakes off her veil?
Giver of Life, holds all Death's
  secrets,
I fight her swaying till the Dawn.
Let no man dream of her
  existence,
Fight the rhythmic, swirling,
  blackness
Till she is chased by the virgin
  sun.

Bobbie Lee
REPETITIOUS
Touch me softly, but just walk by
You're not the kind that could
  make me cry.
Glance my way, but you'll

never hit home
I know your type and you always
  roam.
You finally come over with a
  great opening line
I've only heard it for the
  hundredth time.
Be witty and suave, my typical
  "Mr. Cool"
I'm totally aware you're just a
  passing fool.
You play your game well and are
  sure of a score
But you never even noticed that I
  found you a bore.
Buy me a drink and pass away
  some time
Ask your run of the mill
  question, "Your place or mine?"
Then just to show me what a big
  spender you are
You break down and order one
  more round from the bar.
Another girl walks past, a good
  looking blonde
You'll make your excuses and
  soon be gone.
I sigh with relief when you
  remember an appointment
Which you naturally take as a
  sign of disappointment.
Jauntily you strut off like the all-
  American male
In his never ending search for a
  piece of tail.
I'll remember this evening
  without a doubt
Because the same thing keeps
  happening everytime I go out!

J.W. Cheney Jr.
THE SNOW
Through silvered veils of winter's
  night;
O'er dunes of alabaster, white,
blanketed, satin, silent, slips away.

Bleak, or is "such" really so;
these mere reflections, "only"
  snow,
or harbingers of "more" ethereal
  "place"?

Star-spears, crystalline, of night;
splashing precipices, white,
touching, sombered, winter's
  silver grace.

Solace, such, the night's new
  snow;
of blustr'y night, of winds that
  flow;
acquaint me of your "only"
  wintr'y ways.

Margaret Pettus Parrish
MORE MONEY
Am I going to raise my pledge?
For what reason should I edge?
I've had no raise except for bills
Circumstances would make me
  fulfill
All that I'm expected to,
Because of the way things go.

The much talked of interest rate
Seems only to be a great big bait
To catch the interest of every
  man
And make him think that you can
Reduce the miseries of all the
  world
By lessening the monies that
  make it whirl.

There must be other things that
    make us tick
But we are not sure what makes
    us sick,
For we know little of the schemes
    of men
Who run the world and say Amen
To everything while we look on
And wonder just how we can con.

To make us well and keep us
    happy
You'll have to think of something
    snappy
Like start a war so there will be
Lots of work for you and me
And some will help the U.S.A.
To see how many they can slay.

H. Jay Meyers
**Maybe We'll Forget Each
Other's Names**
*[Dedicated to Susan for
inspiration beyond sentiment,
and to my mother for without
her, my emotions would never
become text.]*

There was nothing much in
    common to begin with
In the end there was more
    nothing than before.
There are boundaries on a heart
    that knew no limit
I saw her doubtful eyes staring
    out the door.

There was a time when we were
    close to one another
That time will forever stand
    alone.
There were three small words
    that fell out of emotion,
There was silence when we
    watched them turn to stone.

There were words when we
    unleashed a beast of burden,
There were nights when tears
    impeded thoughts of sleep,
There were weekends we spent
    hours only dreaming,
There were promises we'll never
    have to keep.

Can two people drift apart
    beyond conviction?
Can there never be an easier
    goodbye?
There are memories I must leave
    inside the shadows
These are those that I must save
    and wonder why.

For there wasn't much in
    common to begin with
And today we both can see what
    will remain.
Maybe one day we will talk to
    one another,
Maybe one day we'll forget each
    other's names.

Gordon R. Perry
The Message Of Christmas
It's Christmastime the world
    around
    Everybody knows—
It's all about the Christ child's
    birth,
    So the story goes.

It talks about the Virgin Dear,
    Mother of the Child.
She laid Him in the hay to rest
    So tender, meek and mild.

It tells about the Wise Men, three
    Watching the star above,
Who followed it to where it
    stopped
    Bringing gifts of love.

The Son of God was born to man,
    Savior at His birth.
His messages of Faith and Love
    Are for all the earth.

He came to earth to show the way
    God wants us all to go—
And if we heed the things He said,
    Heaven we will know.

Peace on Earth, Good will to all
    We hear the Christmas chime,
Let us try to live all year
    That message of Christmas
    time.

Nancy Lou Jackson
MY SON, MY SON
My Son My Son
My heart is crying
They told me today
That you are dying

Cancer
Is What they said
In a few short days
You will be dead

27 years
Not long at all
For a strapping lad
To grow big and tall

Oh lord
How my heart does pine
For the tow headed boy
In the bright Sunshine

For the growing up Years
That went so fast
Storing up Memories
In my heart to last

When I think of the man
You grew up to be
Baby, Teen, Adult
All precious to me.

I Question
The powerful force
That allows this thing
To run its course

I believe
And I know I'm right
There's a life hereafter
And a heavenly light

Our God in his mercy
Has provided a place
Where all of our sorrows
We stand up and face

He gives us the strength
To withstand the pain
When the first strength is gone
He gives strength again

Lovingly
He calls us all home
This sinful earth
No more to roam

When the struggle for life
Gets too hard to bear
Go to your maker
He's waiting up there

Tracey Borghese
SOMETHING FOREVER
With this ring, I thee wed
You've finally said I do
I'm so happy and so proud
Of the both of you

Together you've been so far
You've made this major bond
And here's another chance to say
Of you both, I'm so fond
Today will be your day
And it's so special to me
Because today is the day
You've made us a complete family
I'm hoping the best is yet to come
And wishing you both happiness
For a life of sweet fulfillment
In this special married bliss
Your marriage vows have all been
    said
Those precious words exchanged
You can now smile sweetly
For life is all prearranged
Life may be prearranged
But the love you have is not
You've got something wonderful
Something most people have
    forgot

Nancy D. Abbott
TO CARE IS TO SHARE
*[This is dedicated to my
Mother, who showed me the
true meaning of caring and
sharing.]*

Flames from the fireplace
    flickered across the blonde
    haired girl's face,
As a burned through log
    dropped down the red hot pile
    in the hearth,
Twinkling eyes beamed with
    happiness, as presents were
    opened one by one,

While down the street, tear
    streaked faces of little ones
    filled a tiny
    room, as they huddled together
    around the oven to keep warm.
There would be no presents this
    year for anyone at all.

But, a loud knock at their door
    brought them back from their
    day dreams
    of playing in a huge store
    loaded with brand new toys.
Friendly faces carried in boxes
    brimming with food for dinner.

Larger boxes with brightly
    wrapped gifts, spilled onto the
    floor,
    Tear streaked faces were
    replaced with squeals of
    excitement, as a
Mysterious blonde haired girl,
    lovingly and carefully passed
    out gifts,

To her surprised neighbors, who
    didn't have anything to give
    this year,
    Simply sharing the joys she had
    with those who cared enough
    to,
Share their happiness with her
    last year when she had nothing.

Lee Zuberer
WAGON TRAIN WIDOW
Sound of silence, starry night
Beautiful faces round the
    campfire's light
Reflecting all their hopes and
    dreams
Masking sadness from the world's
    cruel schemes

Looking to me with such trust
    and beauty
What if I can't fulfill my duty?
Will I fail in my endeavor?
The task we started—it seems
    forever
Far away and long ago
I was so sure—I said "Let's Go!"
Now I sit alone and crying
God I feel as tho I'm dying
These sweet souls who came so
    far
All to see their shining star
Still is such a long way off
The road ahead more dangerous
    and tough
Then they've ever known before
Since our leader's here no more
Gone our captain, our chief, our
    might
Gone is my love, my strength my
    light
How I feel that all will forsake me
When the pain and sorrow take
    me
To the depths of such despair
Without him here, the very air
Has no life for me each day
Since our leader's gone away
But, I draw upon his lessons
Things he's taught, the strength
    he left us
This I know he wills to me
Every night religiously
I can hear his gentle wording
Feel his warmth at last
    encouraging
So I'll say to every face
For just a while I'll take Dad's
    place.

Dennis White
LONGING
[For my Mom]
I long to be with you.
Just to gaze, to stare,
    for a moment,
        an hour,
            a day.
A twinkle of glasses
a bottle of wine,
    more wine,
        more love,
            more time.
I wish and I dream.

I felt you only once
    and others too often.
Yet I remember only you
    for a lifetime.
The secret of our passion
    is absence.
Quiet and gentle,
    soft as mist,
        ocean deep.
            Forever!

Yvonne Ivie
BLOOD BROTHERS
[To JC with love always . . .
Long ago, as a child,
My friends and I would play.
We shared all our good and bad
And we trusted in the day.
No secrets kept we from each
    other—
Our hearts of many were one.
By night we waited for the day—
And dreaded the setting sun.
Then, one day our skin we broke—
The blood from our veins was
    mixed.

Blood brothers forever now . . .
Together—our destinies fixed.

It's been a long time since I've
    seen them . . .
I can't even remember their
    names.
But I have a friend now that's
    more than this—
And we are brothers just the same.
But one thing now is different,
Though no one would know
    unless He said—
We walk together hand in hand—
The night no longer dread.
For at night I know He's still in
    me—
I know my tears He sees.
He lifts me up and holds me close
If only I try to please.
Sometimes when I walk away
    from Him,
With His love I feel His rod.
But never a friend is truer than
    He . . .
For He's the Son of God.

Carol-Ann Duquette-Lauzon
KARMA
The thief stole through the night.
It was a bountiful flight.
He took from us; that what
We lust.
We took from him; his soul
From within.
It was a bountiful flight!

Bonnie McBride
INSECURITIES
Today
I did it!

Yea!
Today, finally
I did it!

I experienced
    the satisfaction,
    the thrill,
    that one feels
    after having accomplished
    a new task;
    the satisfaction,
    the thrill,
    the exhilaration
    that one encounters
    when one says,
    "Wow!
    Oh, wow!
    I didn't know I could do that!"

Yea!
Today, finally
I did it!
Why did I wait so long?
Why didn't I do it sooner?

Linda London
MY PAL MIKE
We should all take the time to
    understand ourselves
What makes us pick certain
    people for friends
For everyone met, brings with
    them an emotion
Yet why like this one and not
    care for another
With some there's a click, a
    friend from the start
While others pass by unnoticed
And these friends are the people
    usually taken for granted
Always there, just a part of life
These are the people, who make

life worth living
With whom feelings should be
    shared
Sharing the love and sorrow in
    each other's life
We should let them know just
    how much we care
But I couldn't put into words, the
    feelings felt
Couldn't say, "I love you, you're
    my pal"
And too late now, another chance
    I won't get
Because words he can hear no
    more
For the Lord called his name and I
    pray gave him peace
God Bless you Mike, from
    someone who cares

Richard "Kid Koala" Villagomez
THE ATTIC
*[To Bobby, Lori, and Stephanie
for being my friends and fans,
and to my grandmother
Altagracia just for being]*
Let me bring you down to the
    attic, where many thoughts are
    found:
Child's shoes worn out by
    distances, though never
    touched the ground;
A torn umbrella beaten down by
    ancient storms that stay;
A mousetrap set by solemn self
    for those who came to play;
The molden air with a chest of
    photographs and notes
From those who must be locked
    away in rains for those who
    wrote;
Faint light strands from a
    flickering bulb that tap each
    corner spot;
Sharp brilliant colors spilling
    'cross the room from rainbows
    taught;
Small, broken shells filled with
    the sea that sang of distant
    shore;
The rocking chair that cried all
    day until it cried no more;
Old cobwebs strung o'er unused
    time, raindrops 'pon time best
    not;
Small treasures kindly tucked
    away before they be forgot.

Shirley H. Wilson
FRIENDSHIP
*[Dedicated to Frankie, With
whom I shared my childhood.]*
When we were very young time
    seemed to stand still
the summers were exceedingly
    long and hot,
and doing any kind of chores was
    against our will.

Walking from my house to yours,
The sand held so much heat
we would have to hop on patches
    of grass
to keep from burning our feet.

It was always an adventure to
    explore in the woods
and pick violets that were nestled
    under the huge Oak trees.
Times were indeed tranquil then,
    and our spirits free.

Finding that chin-qua-pin tree

was always a test
we'd sit down and eat our fill,
and before starting back we
    would have to rest.

We would never think of leaving
    the woods
until we cooled our feet in the
    little rippling springs.
And talk for hours sharing our
    dreams.

As it grew darker in the woods,
    we knew the sun was
going down, we would have to
    leave now while we were able.
Because at this time of day supper
    would surely be on the table.

Times like those can not in
    anyway be measured
and sharing them with a friend
    like you,
Shall always be treasured.

Tami Griffin
THE ALTAR
*[I have the honor of dedicating
this poem to Joseph D. Boutte
who will become my husband
on April 1, 1983, as this poem
was inspired on our first date.]*
They come from miles around to
    pay
Their continuing respects to the
    god of rock and roll.
Gathering in ever-changing
    masses on a flashing slate,
Expressing the passion which can
    no longer remain in the soul.
A blue light forms the halo on
    the trap set altar
As the band takes a break and
    gets to know their subjects.
The music is everywhere,
    surrounding like water
The fire of the heart which the
    body projects.
Smoke of Marlboro incense
    permeates the places
As the group remounts the stage
    and begin to jam.
The people go wild, you see the
    crazy light of the love of music
    on their faces,
But there are others, miserable
    psychotics, who are only
    pretending to give a damn.

Kimberly Anne Farrow
A TREASURED GIFT
*[This poem is dedicated to
Mike Nichols; the man I love
and treasure with all my heart,
because he showed me what
true love is.]*
For Christmas
I want nothing but you!
You don't need to put on a bow,
Just give yourself to me so that I
    may give you more love.

You don't need to put yourself
    beneath my tree,
Just have Santa deliver you the
    way you are to me.

For Christmas
I want nothing but you
And from you I want nothing but
    love;
A thousand kisses,
A thousand hugs,
A thousand nights to spend with
    you.

I want nothing but a love that is
    true.

For Christmas
I want nothing but to love you,
In the gleam of the morning dew,
Or in the moonbeams of the night.
I want to love you with all that I
    can be;
To love you fully and tenderly.

For Christmas
I want nothing but to be with you,
To love you forever,
For you are a gift I'll always
    treasure!

Yolanda E. Miller
STAND AND BE HEARD
I'm going to be heard right now,
All of you that have been, stand
    and bow.
I'm going to be heard from city to
    city,
and state to state.

I'm going to be heard in the
    delegate
I even plan to be heard on radio
    and T.V.
I'm going to talk about our
    country's
problems so everyone can see.

See what it's doing for you and
    me.
We all have to work, to get these
    problems
solved.
It isn't easy, it's a very tough job.
We all have to join hands,
From black to white, and woman
    to man.
We all must take a stand.

Carolyn McGuire Ferrall
CHILDREN OF THE WORLD
    Little children of the world
    Into this evil world are hurled.
    Even though they're treated bad
    In return they are not mad.
    Love and joy and peace of mind
    In this world are hard to find.
    Come together young and old
    Help each other not to hold
    Bitter feelings only showed
by
    Beating the Hell out of young and
    old.

Donald James Kehl
**The Dream . . . Or the
    Dreamer?**
Hold me, my love, on this cold
    lonely night,
for my soul grows weary again—

Endless cycles of life do roll by—
both The Victory, defeats, and
    yet . . .

While I ever lying between the
    twain,
my soul safely castled has seen

Eternity flow through cycles of
    time
and all of our dreams come to
    dust.

Dreams are a mirror of he who
    has dreamed,
the beauty or naught of his
    thoughts—

And hist'ry records the dreams
    as they play

'cross the screen of our life, but
not—

Records of visions that come
from above
to waken the soul from her
sleep.

As the play unfolds it's
mystical charm,
and the curtain lowers at
last—

Unwind the secrets of life,
skein by skein,
till you see nothing but the
source.

Life was not given to
follow a dream,
but to be One with The
Dreamer!

But, oh, how it pains to see such
a truth
that none who are here do
see . . . so

Hold me, my love, on this cold
lonely night,
for my soul grows weary again.

John Lloyd Day
. . . FOR A FRIEND
Catastrophic influences enhance
slender shapes of glowing
transcendessence.
And we see the cold blue clear of
another outstanding
realization . . .
A Realization of: Cats in the
Mountains-Sharp points of
Power.
Cats in the Mountains-Sharp
points of Power.
Sleek fitting feelings of brief
black pride.
Thinking of these words . . . I'm
thinking of a friend-Patrinoidal
Exclusions.
'Crave ye, sloth not. For the
things ye will be,
are far higher than an old
soul such as me,
could explain to thee, in
words of too many . . .'
Too many . . . Too many . . .
Why so many?
Is it for the sheer feel, of such as
what the mind desires? The
soul desires?
OVERWHELMING . . .
Will this explode in fiery
cinders?
OVERPOWERING . . .
It takes my communicado and
regresses me.
HELPLESS!!!
Yet feeling control all the while.

Nicolai Stefan Popescu
ALTER EGO
I learned to distinguish
between two states
alternately
reigning in my mind
going so far
as to divide
every day
between them
each one
returning to dispossess
the other
with the regularity
of a fever and ague

contiguous
and yet so foreign
to one another
I could no longer understand
or even figure to myself
in one state
what I had wished
or feared
or even done
along the other.

Sandra Maynor Averhart
I REMEMBER DADDY
Your wisdom and your insight
gave my spirit wings;
You slipped a coin into my heart
better than a gold-crowned king.

You gave my heart a song and a
light passed over my face.
You gave me love and laughter
and taught me that word 'grace.'

I owe you more than life itself, so
great my debt to you.
You took each little dream I had
and helped them to come true.

Daddy . . . it's Christmas and
you're gone from here; my
heart is filled with grief.
You were snatched away from
me; Sly Death was that old
thief.

If I could have you back just
once, I'd be sure you knew
of all the love and gratitude I
have that ever belong to you.

Clara M. Bush
How I Remember Christmas
A chill in the air.
That taste of cold weather.
Crisp and invigorating.
Cold clear nights.
Stars in the sky gliter like ice on
a carpet of midnight blue.
Chimney's smoking
Twinkling lights at every turn.
Fireplaces lit.
Sweet pungent fragrances of
burning wood.
Living room cosy and delightfully
decorated
Christmas tree lovingly adorned.
Carols, and laughing children.
Delectably anticipation,
unwrapping presents.
I remember with loving
reverence, an open bible,
An incredibly, beautiful story
unfolds.
So great, so holy and divine.
Blessed of God,
To Mary and Joseph, a babe was
born,
One Christmas morn.

Evelyn R. Carey
Make God's Way Be Ours
As this month begins, let's begin
it with God,
Let's see "all" the beauty He
created, wherever we trod.
Let's be Christian not only in
Sunday School;
But each day "do unto others"—
follow the Golden Rule.
Make problems, hard feelings,
and bickering with friends,
A part of the past, as each our day
ends.

See the beauty inside of each
"brother" and "sister",
Be helpful and kind, not a
constant resister.
For 'tho God loves us all, and
"knows" us each one,
We owe acts of beauty to His
Heavenly Son.
And may all our "acts", whether
big or small,
Reflect love on our Father—yes,
He made us all.
And He wants us each and every
one
To try to be more and more like
His Son.
And the more we try, it will come
with ease,
For our Heavenly Father, we will
please.
And pleasing Him will make us
see
The much nicer person we've
come to be.

And God's way will be ours!

Bert Danon
BLUE PLEASURE
Never thought you'd leave
I must have missed the clue
And now the memories
Just turn my pleasure blue
An old familiar tune . . . How
Could my ears be so blind
The same old used up moon
Once shared when love was kind
Pausing where we left it
But trailing close behind
My heart is sadly seeing
The hope it cannot find
Heavy is my body
Now slowing down at last
Submerging in blue pleasure
Where you become my past
Here lonliness strolls in
glorious gown
And sorrow's at its best
Reclining in you blue pleasure
I lay me down to rest

Dorothy A. Cox
HOME
[To my brother, George.]
This is my home.

The smell of the rain on sun-
parched land; the kill-deers' call
at the dying day.
The expanse of land, endless they
say; a line of clouds in the
western sky
With lightning and thunder
rumbling away and the dash of
rain and surge of wind.
Duststorms that choke—cattle,
horses, and men; and wheat
fields that stretch forever today.
A harsh land, a warm land, a cold
land!

The wild geese call and the grey
cranes cry in spring and fall
from their wheeling lines,
Pinpoints in their pointed
formations in the clear endless
blue.
The dawn is pink with the golden
edged tuffs of clouds or the rise
of light until the stars disappear.
In a cloudless dome, the sun
throws shafts of light, and pink
and gold dispells the dark

Until the gold rim touches the
shadowed hills.

There's a shimmer of heat and
fresh green grass that makes a
lawn from sky to sky.
The smell of horses and cattle
and dust; the blast of guns and
the sizzle of ropes.
All gone from a land alone and
flat and endless under the sun.
Yet the sky remains, the drifting
clouds, those towering puffs of
gold and white and silver,
The storms that thunder and the
winds that roar, the snow that
blinds when a norther blasts.
Wide, wide, they extend, the
plains that meet the
mountains' feet!

Thomas Floyd Newby
Absolutely Nothing At All
There was not any carpet any
where at all
Nor any picture to be found on
the wall
And also there was no basement
stair
Or place to sit not even a chair
Absolutely nothing at all
And so I did take a good look
outside
But looking about there is no
place to hide
And there was no grass at all on
the ground
Not any kind of fence is there to
be found
Absolutely nothing at all
We all give our thanks for
darkness and light
Not realizing there could be
nothing bright
So I was required to feel my way
around
But since there was nothing,
nothing was found
Absolutely nothing at all
I decided I should see about
something to eat
But there was nothing not even
any kind of meat
There seemed no choice but to
give up in defeat
As there was nothing further and
no one to meet
Absolutely nothing at all
I awakened wondering did I
dream all of this
But I was very glad that nothing
was amiss
Thus letting me start the day in
the usual way
Since there was nothing to worry
about today
Absolutely nothing,
nothing at all

Dorothy Pinkerton
WORLD III
FIRST WORLD was once my
home, where one-third live
Who give and take, take and give
heed convention,
Conform—that is the norm in
FIRST WORLD.
I became bereft, suffered loss,
another loss, was tossed onto
SECOND WORLD.
Where everything had the
accustomed name—nothing,

nothing
Was the same. Eyes looked not at
me, past me—strange
Voices spoke "You must concede,
accept, adjust—
You must, you must, you must.
Get in line,
All you need is TIME."
Thoughts came from a distance,
WORDS on a printed page,
In a rage, I hurled myself aboard
THIRD WORLD.
Your HAND reached for me, your
VOICE was heard,
"Thank you for being so nice!"
Such a long TIME since the
pleasure was mine
To be looked at twice, to hear the
word NICE.
THIRD WORLD FRIEND, hold
my hand. O,
Don't let go!

Bonnie L. Yotter
ADULTS
I went to a friend who often
consults
About the patronizing ways of
adults.
She said, "Take a look—you'll see,
Adults will act just like you and
me."
And I DID see. I began to think
Of the way adults will slurp up
their drink.
But whenever I sing at the table
(A thing which I'm not allowed,
but able)
A favorite melody or song
They'll look at me and ask,
"What's wrong?"
I'll reply I'm singing just for fun
And the song happens to be my
favorite one.
They'll turn around in that grown
up way
And you can just guess what
they're going to say,
"Kids today!"

Irene Neth
NOVEMBER GLOW
You drive into the sunset
Of a late November eve,
Pearly opalescent
Aqua blue,
Streaked with
Charcoal and lavender,
Behind black lace
Of Winter trees.
Shot through with
Gold and silver luminance,
And low on the horizon
A ribbon streamer
Of Magenta
Edged with a suggestion
Of tangerine
And a faint flush
Of pink,
Breathtaking
Silence.

Rhonda L. Wethington
THE STRUGGLE OF LIFE
Being a child and living on fun,
These simple pleasures are life's
only drum.
Hearing life's song, playing so
sweet,
Nothing is sad and life can't be
beat!
Then as you grow, you're soon

an adult,
Problems arise, but *you're* not at
fault.
People do hurt, and how the pain!!
Caring of only how they alone
gain.
Treading upon you, with brutal
hate,
Knowing you care just makes
them irate.
Someday they'll know, just how
you feel,
Life is too short to hold back
good will.
If they could see how you began,
By learning to love and helping
all man.
Turning your cheek, at times so
tough,
Forever realizing, life sure is
rough.
Someday they'll need, kindness
and love,
Give them your help through
guidance above.

Rachel Berger
TRUE LOVE
A poet's love
is of his mind
of paper
of pen
just writing again
my love is . . .
no longer for people
no longer for you
for paper
for pen
my mind is in love
my heart's gone away
who are you in love with,
they say
I say
with a smile
my mind
my paper
my pen
and me . . .

William Harrison Horsley
A FANTASY
I shot an arrow to the sky
It didn't fall and I know why
It went higher than high
It went to the sky above the sky
There I saw a person named I
Where I captured the arrow in
the sky
In that space I say the whys
The whys of a real and an unreal
I
I shot an arrow to the sky

Teresa L. Park
MY TRAVEL COMPANION
Lord, walk with me
as I travel the roads
of my life.
As I stumble on gravel
of the rough roads,
lift me up.
When I come to a fork
and have to choose my way,
guide me, please.
Each time the road becomes
smooth,
remind me, Lord,
my journey is not over.
I have far to go
and many roads to travel.
Walk with me, Lord.

Bettye Jo Allen
YOU STOLE MY HEART
You came so near
but far away
into my life
you came one day
On that summer day
you stole my heart
and took away
that lonely part
Then my eyes seen the want
that was standing near
when you looked at me
i felt the fear
That it was you
i was reaching for
now it's true
you stole my heart
But the loneliness is back
for now you've gone
you stole my heart
and left me alone
All those summer days
we shared together
just you and me
i thought was forever
Now i must go on
and i must forget
but to remember you
is easy yet
You know i can't forget you
for you'll always be apart
of the hurt the pain the memories
of when you stole my heart.

Stacy Anne Lee
A GIFT OF FRIENDSHIP
[To Tom, whose love has given
me the strength to make my
dreams come true. All my love,
Stacy.]
You gave me a smile
to brighten my day
You gave me your hand
to show me the way.
You showed me the light
when I couldn't see
You showed me the truth
of what I could be.
You gave me hope
when I was at the end;
But best of all—
you became my Friend.

Jeff Watros
PERFECT STRANGER
[This poem is dedicated to
everyone who confesses Jesus
as their Lord and Saviour.]
A special gift straight from Heaven
Was once delivered to earth
A supernatural birth
Had been tucked away in a manger
World welcome the Perfect
Stranger
He came not looking for fortune
But could not avoid the fame
For everyone knew His name
By His works as the miracle
changer
The mark of the Perfect Stranger
The strength and comfort for
many
A threatening figure to some
He knew the reason He'd come
Was the reason His life was in
danger
The death of the Perfect Stranger
The Strangers Father had promised

His death would be a short sleep
That promise His Father did keep
And He rose as the freedom
arranger
Thank God for the Perfect Stranger

Jean Bomba
THE SLAVE MAKER
You foul and unclean thing;
You creeping vine, wrapped
round progressive centuries,
Til kings and rebels and
dreaming men
Become as lackies,
Following your trailing,
withered leaves.
You visit men in midst of night.
Your comely form mirrors fates
unbidden to light of day.
Rise up—oh men!
But you,
Sheathed in shimmering sensation,
Beckon them to cross the barren
edge. . .
Dust to dust
And men pass on,
Ever trapped by your treacherous
caress,
And less they struggle.
And words: "Ah, such is life,"
Fall as stones from unprotesting
lips.
But as men lie on Death's
rotating rim,
They quick identify you, the
Victress.

Dana
C.H.R.I.S.T.M.A.S.
[To an unforgettable love which
grows and goes on forever:
C.H.R.I.S.T.M.A.S.]
C . . . is for the cradle of straw
which our newborn King was
laid
H . . . is for the huge crowd that
followed all through the night
and day
R . . . is for the regal bearing—
simple and just, as He
I . . . is for the infinity of time
He'll live on in a part of Me
S . . . is for the brightest star that
shone for the Three Wise Men
to see
T . . . is for the trinity which
consists of the Father, Son, and
the Holy Spirit
M . . . is for his mother, Mary,
whose faith and abiding love
that we should treasure
A . . . is for all true affections
which none can never measure
S . . . is the final search of the
Soul and Spirit, which one
should never let perish; His
Spirit bestows upon us to
inherit.

N. J. Beddingfield
THE QUEST
Born in the hallowed dark of
space,
Two warriors stand opposed.
Amidst the stars, they mount and
wait:
One steed, the heavens paws.

Today's Greatest Poems

For they were destined, yea, to
meet
Upon that battlefield of blood.

Two golden knights, both kin of
light,
Astride their firey studs.

One, pure of purpose as the sun,
Still glowing from the coals.

The rival knight, despising right;
Grown resolute, and bold.

Hear now, the thunder and the
quake,
As each, in his own sign, rides.

A holy quest, so nobly blest;
To vanquish hate and pride.

Joel D. Stewart, Sr.
MY AUNTIE'S DAY
Fields of cotton spread far and
wide, with black bodies of sweat,
blood, and fear.
Auntie and baby chillum watch
from dirt floored shack door
While mammy and pappy toil
under the sun with heavy loads
on there backs
From birth to death, no one today
can feel what they felt
Dawn to dust and the whip
cracked on there backs
400 pounds today and everyday
or the slave driver will tare the
skin away.
Hey Boy!
Yez sir captain
Yesterday 399 pounds
The driver smiled and kicked
him.
Today he will be beat until he
can't hear a sound if he gets
under 450 pounds.
Moving bodies and hands, with
the sound of breaking cotton
stalks continues,
Mother stops and watches son
toil hard and fast, but the whip
cracks hard and loud across the
mother's back.
You lazy good for nothing nigger,
ain't I done told you not to
figure!
Men move faster along the rows
as a shinning black buck
stands by smiling
Moses acoming one of these days
Pow!
The blood runs from her hand
and the driver laughs
But no man will stop to take the
stand, the sounds of breaking
cotton stalks continues . . .
As auntie drags her withered
body across the field to give a
helping hand to the bloody
slave woman
My auntie's day.

Jeff Martel
IN THE MIDDLE
Accept the "dark" sides of
yourself as well as the good,
and you will see through to the
real shining you, a constantly
twinkling changing self . . .
Holding on to both sides of the
coin.
Man is the fault line running
through darkness and light;
between nothing and

something. . .
We are all stars; a choice of being
a shining star or a black hole.
You can be a greedy person
hoarding everything including
your love, always taking and
not giving nothing much in
return.
Or you could be a giving person
sharing and caring for yourself
and others, just like a shining
star gives out it's rays of light.

Turning inwards, and looking at
the whole of you, you are
facing the timelessness, and
endlessness of this place in
"time".
Our lives are but a continuous
changing stream going on and
on through time; to where? who
knows?

Jocelyn A. Lavalley
A SEED REPLANTED
Stop beating yourself, like a rug
over a rail.
We are all just different people,
and emotionally so frail.
As so like little snowflakes,
melting, as they land into
warm hands.

Our emotions can take us over;
they, if we allow them,
will become our demands.

Like a volcanic eruption, when I
get mad as hell.
When happy and cheerful, the
sound of chiming bells.
The little twinges of fear, when
things aren't quite right,
But only contentment and
happiness in my Lords'
path of light

Like a beautiful sunset, on a
perfect summer's eve
The Lord has given me a new life,
a new me—
I can't believe!

A beautiful image of one tiny
seed, after lessons of gardening,
taking out all the weeds.
A flower has been created, as was
heaven and earth.
A garden of new people, a feeling
of self worth.
For God created us to be
authentic, and content
in our own being.

Karma Louise De Frees
FANTASY ESCAPE
Abandoned, ignored she had
created a world of her own
They said she was another
mindless victom of sanity
When suddenly she laughed out
loud
Heads quickly turned away in
shame and pity
Alone in a corner of a nursing
home
She sat in a wheel chair
dreaming. . .

Strolling through an enchanted
forest
a beautiful maiden was she
Picking purple florescent flowers
along a path so merrily

Shimmering, silver butterflys
fluttered about her singing a
mysterious melody
Lurking among the shadows a
visious villain did spy
the young lady, such innocent,
easy prey
Nearby upon his gallant steed
Sir Knight heard a womans cry
Without hesitation he soared to
her rescue
He slew the viper with skill and
speed
And away into the sunset a proud
Knight and his lady flew

A smile upon her weary face and
a twinkle in her eye
a wise aged lady to another
adventure filled day
Drifted to sleep with a smile and
a sigh.

caroline curiale
i do, i do
i listen
    to the gift of silence
        so warm
            so tender
    so encompassing.
i would that i might hear
            the roses
            that waken
        to the kiss of morning dew
    that i might sing
            the song of the wren
that i might hold in my heart
    the love of the Lord.
oh, but i do.
    i do hold and cherish
        the love of the Lord
and i listen
        to the gift of silence.
    for 'tis then
        amidst that silence
    i come apart from the world
        to fellowship
    and praise His name.
the omnipotent name of Jesus.
                    Romans 10:13

Patrice Angeli Jansen
SLIPPING AWAY
I was thinking Today
Of slipping Away
    Not going mind you
    Going nowhere at all.
But after many a day of not
    slipping away
    Or not being away
        That you were yesterday . . .

You laid on your bed
    And in your head said:
That compared to before (Before
    you closed Several Doors)
    You were closer to dead.

The problem you knew was not
    one of dying.
    (In that case, you could still
    Slip Away)
The Problem you knew was too
    late to change
        The problem of Living
                    and Lying.

David Russell Lesher
KIRKLAND DOCKS
There're times I wish that I were
standing on the Kirkland docks—
or spending one more evening
watching boats come through the
locks

And I recall how tall the trees
had grown while we were there—
& nights so quiet all we heard
was starlight everywhere

I often dream a sailboat past
Port Townsend to the Sound—
to soften all my landborn fears
with past adventures found

A certain kind of youthful, lonely
wonder comes to mind—
when I think about Seattle
& the beauty left behind

Sometimes I miss the Market
& the different things to do—
I even miss the rain although, so
often,
—it's just you.

Betty Ellen Palmer
LOVES' NOURISHMENT
When I look into the long avenue
of the future,
I can see the good for each of us
to do.
Realization then becomes a
beautiful thing,
What a wonderful desire it is to
work, to live, and to be happy.
All the strength and force of a
man,
Comes in his faith in things
unseen.
Reach high, for stars lie hidden in
your soul,
Dream deep, for every dream
precedes thy goal.
It is right to be contented with
what you have,
But never with what you are.
Honourable are those who can
give without remembering,
And take without forgetting.
I shall grow old but never lose
life's zest,
Because the roads' last turn will
be the best.
It is man who makes truth great,
Not truth that makes man great!
To be happy is to Love and be
Loved.
                    Love

Robert Humphrey
THE ROSE
[For Mother]
The howling bitter wind
    screamed
    mocking the beautiful rose,
then flogged the ground with
    slopping rain
    drowning it's moaning woes.
The pale rose only slumped
    upon her frail stem,
crying in agony,
Her petals ripped away by the
    wind,
    beaten to the earth,
Lying naked in her pain she cried,
    "Damn you wind, I shall live
    again,
For my seeds shall have new
    birth!"
The wind only howled a shrill
    reply,
    "I've killed you with my
    breeze."
And vanished with Mother
    Nature's cry
    To the applause of a thousand
    trees.

637

Shellie J. Hockenbury
IS IT A FANTASY?

I want to touch you
But I dare not,
It would be disreguarding
the things I was taught.

I think about you
and what it would be like
to touch your young skin,
so soft and tight.

What a thrill it would be
to touch your hair when it's
blowing in the wind,
And knowing your there
If I ever need you.

Disreguarding the things you
were taught,
Isn't a bad thought,
and you ought to some day.

Don't be surprised, when I look in
your eyes
Cuz there's a feeling thats
getting harder to disguise.

I think of you and how it would be,
if you were with me.

Maybe one day,
you'll let go of your cares
and maybe we can share.

Cecile A Nealley
MOTHER

Many poems have been written
About mothers through the years
Even sentimental ballads
That to your eyes brought tears.

I wish I could find someone
Blessed with sensitivity
Who could for me write a poem
About what "Mother" means to me.

He would have to know
adjectives
That express love and generosity
Be able to write something relative
To her humanity!

I might be able to help him
describe
How I feel so sincerely
That "Mother" you are God's
creature most admired
By the biggest majority!

Marjory A. Schneider
HAIKUS

i wonder what to
do when i see you go by
and say my, o my.

and all i can do
is wink and try to think twice
about seeing you

but now it is too
early yet to say good—bye
to people who lie

so think twice again
when you touch me so cruelly
with your hands ruley.

now i go back to
my shell of blue and blue now
so i can see you.

so i'll never laugh
when i see you nor ever
flaunt when i hear you

so now that we're lost
i shed a tear on what's gone
and say amen to brawn.

so let's say good—bye

to prayers and ourselves now
before it's too late

but sir remember
i do kind of love you now
in a way i do

however i can't
go too far away to rant
about choosing you.

you were too quick now
so i'd rather stay away
because you are wrong.

though now i wonder
what made me plunder you for
you are really good.

so, my pet, it yet
is to be seen just what lane
you feel is happy

Linda K. Ewton
MY SON

[In loving memory of my son,
Rob
Robert Dwayne Ewton
05-03-63 03-22-81]
Full of mischief, full of laughter
Wonderful memories, forever after
A ray of sunshine to brighten my
day
Showing love in your own special
way
Now you're gone, your life taken
Leaving me and my world shaken
Leaving in me a big empty space
And lots of realities so hard to face
Biggest of all, next to none
Is life without you, my Son

Shasta—Dawn Maloney
AVATAR

I wish I were a star.
Burning in crystalline light.
Intense,
Succinct,
Consumed
By
Intimacy with God.

Linda Sutherland
YOUR PRAYING HANDS

In the secret corners of my mind
The vision of Praying Hands I find.
What a lovely peace then floods
my heart
To know that someone so dear,
When I was weak and wounded,
acted on my part.
Those Praying Hands still stay
with me
In times when I need sweet
security.
The memories within my mind—
A treasure of love divine.

Those graceful hands that
worked so cheerfully
I see folded, waiting on the Lord
most tearfully.
Waiting for her loved ones to be
blessed,
Faithfully believing God would
do the rest.
All those years you've given all
you could.
For your sweet spirit knew God
was good.
From generation to generation
you watched
Each child and their descendants
fall.
But you stood before the

Almighty—
Held His Word up straight and
tall.
Claiming healing and mercy for
His lost sheep
Taking your precious time
At the presence of His throne to
weep.
Remembering the blessed times
of fellowship we shared,
All of our troubles and burdens
you beared.
We were brought back home into
His kingdom because you
cared. . .

Your Praying Hands are engraved
in all of our hearts, minds and
souls
Because you earnestly, in Jesus'
name, took control.
Each garden within us you sowed
and fed
As our Heavenly Father directed
and said.
He spoke through you in many
ways,
Gave long life and sunny days.
Within His perfect will you kept
true;
And we thank the Lord, our God,
For our most wonderful
blessing—You.

Kristie Christian
THE MAN IN THE MOON

I've always wondered
about the night sky,
but most of all
I've wondered about
the moon.
Are those old stories
true?
Could he
(or He)
be sitting there
on a golden throne
of light
or deep within a crater
watching,
evaluating,
judging
us?
Planning our fate?
If so, then why
is he
(or He)
laughing?

Lona Jean Turner Binz
THE ANGEL OF THE PIER

Oh! Surely she is here!
Hidden by heaven's curtains, but
always near
As she is there near the old rocky
pier
Where she seems to always
reappear
In the grayish, foggy atmosphere;
As I sit fishing, dreaming of my
dear
With my thoughts, our dog, and a
can of beer.
Down each cheek rolls a great big
tear
As she slowly rises, fading in the
air
Doggy too, with a saddened look,
drops each pointed ear.
I loved her; Oh, how I loved
her. . .

And it's so hard to endure
How I stood, when her life was
taken
In frozen fear'
To what really took place, my
mind still isn't clear . . .
I know she must have loved me
too,
So very true'
To always be there,
Near that old rocky pier.

Mary Frances Eykholt
MAGICAL LOVE

When We recognize our gifts
from above,
and that His love is true,
it's insignificant why we love,
but simply that we do.

If an artist put no emphasis
on feelings he had known
flowers blooming from canvas
mightn't have been grown.

Imagine a world of ecstasy.
Smiling, expressing cares.
In all that you see,
abundant joy to share.

Merle Darnell Jennings
Come Drift To My World

[Dedicated to Bill—the lover in
my world]
Close your eyes, cuddle up real
close, hold my hand real
tight—and we'll drift to my
world, lover's paradise.
Ah, my world is painted green,
with dabs of kisses, no blue in
between.
Just squeezing pies, cookie lies,
silver hills and golden
daffordiles.
No raindrops or teardrops, just
giggle drops, love tarts and
sweet togetherness.
Ah, my world is sunshine bright,
lovers' paradise.

Just hold me and put your sweet
lips over mine—and we'll drift
to my world, lovers' paradise.
Ah, the moon is but a valentine
and happiness grows on
twining vines.
Just honey bees, laughing trees,
tease cakes and champagne
lakes.
No headaches or heartaches, just
flower scents, hugging mints
and sweet stillness.
Ah, my world is sheer delight,
lovers' paradise.

Merle Darnell Jennings
MOTHERS AND MEMORIES

[Dedicated to Deb, Barbie and
Jeannie, my children my
inspiration.]
A mother is the one who cooks
good things to eat.
A mother fusses around when
things aren't clean.
She enjoys making a home that
can almost sing.
She frets about a runny nose, a
tummy ache almost anything.
She seems to say "no" lots more
than she ever says "yes".
Yet, when you "goof" she never
loves you less.

Mothers often seem too hard on

rules and responsibilities.
"do this, do that," when all you
    want to do is relax and watch
    T.V.
Mothers encourage tidy rooms,
    hobbies and healthy activities,
she practices what she preaches,
    politeness, understanding and
    kind deeds.
Yes, mothers have a lot they
    want to give to their offspring,
but the thing she wants most
    to give, is a lifetime of
    inspiring memories.

Merle Darnell Jennings
A UNIVERSONAL TOAST
[Dedicated to America—that
nation which reflects Gods'
Image.]
May you have the brains of the
    Germans—
    The talent of the Japanese—
The competitiveness of the
    Russians—
    The love of the French—
The luck of the Irish—
    The originality of the Chinese—
And the freedom of the
    Americans—
    to use them anyway you please.

Edgar D. Franks
Mystery Sermon Of Christ
and Self
[To My Loving wife, Mary Lou]
    (Of Christ)
When in this world a mystery
    unfolds
The seeds can be as in Apples of
    Gold
If fertile the soil and zealous the
    Man
No earthly being can stop the plan
Nor stay the fruit and rob the land.
    (Of Self)
Beneath this canopy of sky and
    space
I search in earnest for my true
    place
Wonder of wonders to me to know
Why to this vessel was given this
    soul.

If I spend my time for seeking
The sands of time still are leaking
And if of a sudden I should find
Will there still in the Glass be
    time?

Golden grains sift on down
Perfect peace I have found
Death now has no hold on me
I shall live thru eternity.

Elsie Marie Gray
This Is What America
Means To Me
This is what America Means to
    me. A land of plenty where the
    slaves have been set free.
A land of our forefathers the
    story has been told
To always put God first and
    America's anchor will hold.
Keep Old Glory waving at full
    mass everywhere.
Sing the highest praises hallelujah.
Honor God our saviour as
    America we share.

There's not a race, color or creed
    that God doesn't love you see
    and it all spell's America

equalized equality.
Where prayers are always
    answered and will forever be.
The richest soil on Gods green
    earth and will forever be.
For it's better to give than to
    receive.
We give our best a nation of love
    and devotion.
Whether on land or on sea.
America is ours to have and to
    hold and Jesus Christ is the key.

Bruce David Braden
SPRING THAW
Spring . . . a desire to go home
to Pennsylvania
to where I began
to places and friends
that have been covered
by the snows of time and distance
Places and friends
that now in the thaw
I see emerging
from the ground
of my memory

J. R. Bassett
THE LIBERTY BELL
        Come!
    Let's listen
    To it tolling.
    Not with our ears:
    That clapp er cracked its shell.
(Was perha ps the skin too tight?)
Was the mak er's cast not right?)
But with our hearts. Let's sound
Within us n ow. Let's try to hear
A pealing voi ce, a thunder spell
Of echoes sono rous: ring free!
How my soul def ies a craven crown,
Though shock wa ves strike me down!
No clown can st op my inner voice
Nor clog my in ner ear's deft choice!
        Free
        Me!

Sandra Daniels Jones
FOUR SEASONS
In the beginning of time, the
    Creator made all things
    beautiful. He placed upon the
    earth animals of all kind,
    plants,
    trees, people;
And to the earth He gave Four
    Seasons:

Winter . . . a resting season.
Spring . . . a rebirth season.
Summer . . . a growing and fun
    season.
Fall . . . . a flaming season.

To me, Fall is the most wonderful
    season of all. God takes His
    giant paint brush and from His
    easel in the sky splashes
    brilliant colors everywhere!

Colors of red and gold
Yellow and brown . . .
All too soon the leaves will
Come tumbling down

To be trampled or raked
Hauled off or burned;
So from past year's experiences
We have learned

To enjoy and breathe in
This Flaming Fall Show . . .
Before Winter spreads her
Blanket of snow!

Joan Lindsey
FORGOTTEN ROSES
Where have the roses gone?
It seems they've been gone so long,
The tender loving moments that
    made our lives a song

The air they breathed so fresh
    and pure that made us feel so
    self assured;
Where has all this gone?

The roses will return again as
    sure as God is love;
The magic will repeat itself,
They'll blossom in heaven above
How we long to see the roses!

Ruth Wheeler—Peak
"Seek, and Ye Shall Find"
        (Matt. 7:7)
Jesus left the heavenly mansions
    for the shadowed paths of earth,
Laid aside His kingly splendor
    for a lowly peasants' birth.

Humble shepherds sought the
    stable
    where the Master Shepherd lay,
Now a tiny, newborn Baby
    with His mother on the hay.

Scholared men in kingly places
    saw the promised star arise,
And they sought the King of kings
    depicted in the midnight skies.

And the wise of earth still seek
    Him—
    Men unknown and men of fame;
And they always, always find Him,
    for He's faithful to His claim.

But we *must go forth* to meet Him
    if the blessing we would find,
For He comes to those who seek
    Him
    and who keep Him on their
    mind.

And remember that He cometh
    at the midnight hour,
    sometimes,
When our way appears the darkest
    and our feet would cease to
    climb.

So awaken, O believer,
    light thy lamp and run afore,
For the Bridegroom *now*
    approaches—
    He is almost to the door!

(Let the Saviour bring you Home,
    friend.
    Then we'll meet—to part no
    more!)

Thelma Robinson
The Hollow In My Heart
There is a hollow in my heart,
    where deepest thoughts
    begin—
And soft in evenings secret time,
    I whisper to the
    Wind—

Of dreams thats just my very own,
    of future and of
    past—
Of twilights and of silver moon,
    and summers that will
    last—

Tho if I dipped my pen in
    gold—
And wrote as in an ancient
    scroll—

I still could not express the
    part—
That comes from the hollow of my
    heart—

Buried deep the dreams I've had,
    so many there has
    been—
No one else will hear my heart,
    so I whisper to the
    wind—

Now I will look, 'till time on end,
    and search in every
    part—
For surely there are more than
    thoughts,
    to fill the hollow in my
    heart—

Melanie Marie Mendoza
REMEDY: LOVE
Love is—loving—
and those who
are involved
expressing the
    —giving—
should be patience.
Believe in
others needs as
a need for your
own nourishment.
Believe in what
is given to be
your gift to life.
Your own concern is
of what you are
capable of giving.
And when trust
becomes a commitment,
there is a new beginning.
Find what is worthwhile
and that is yourself.
Find what is of beauty
and that is—being—
to those who need strength.
Others growth becomes
your—existence—
and this expressed
is respect to all life.

Carol A. Bourgeois
UNSKETCHABLE
Nature has a way
of speaking to me.
From time to time
I am drawn to the
woods
    like a magnet
sucking up metal,
to walk free and
breathe the air,
smell the mildew
of damp rotting
leaves
    as the soles
of my shoes push
them in closer to
the ground.
The presence of
clumps of pretty
wildflowers
    here and there
    is simply that;
pretty wildflowers.
To see nature's
untamed animals
scampering about
the woodsy area
gives a feel of
freedom
    I wish I had.
I can capture the

scenery on paper
with my colored
pencils but the
true beauty is
unsketchable.

Joe Hurwitz
THE ASSAYER
In functions, signs, and quotient
   hours
Matter, incredible consummate
   voyeur, assays itself.
What is more peculiarly affecting
Than the sight of certain
   neutrinos, embracing monkeys,
Examining themselves?
Such narcissistic stuff!
It sees so that it may be seen.
Thus we are, audience—elect,
Applauding our own deafening
   applause.
The drama is echo comedy—
Why divide? One part living,
One part non—living;
The is; the not is.
One equation of balanced vanities.
If matter must strut as actor, play,
   and critic
File it under art and form—
   not science and substance.

Florence Stabile
INTERLUDE
I hasten to the solemn quietude
   of trees and brooks
And tall green slivers
To dream wild dreams of gushing
   falls and maddened rivers;
For in this tranquil interlude,
My thoughts unbridled go.

While man may scoff and call me
   fool,
I know the cool, caressing touch
   of Nature's face
And each embrac her twining
   arms return.

Ah life is like this interlude . . .
No more than just a stay,
Where men dream dreams of
   yesteryear
And wish tomorrow were today.

Nancy J. Hull
A DAY CALLED WINTER
Winter hills, a box of mixed
   sweets,
some round and rose, others wide
   and white.

Heavy snow lightens your ground
and frozen bark hides cold limbs.

   In the country, children scatter;
   school's closed
   and the long way home is best.

   Carrying brown paper bags,
   books and skates,
   the young find an iced stream.

   Down with books and brown
   paper bags.
   Skates go on;
   Home is more distant now.

Wind blows their faces warm and
   clean—
an iced stream,
their glorious treasure.

Dusk arrives too soon for them,
skates come off—
books and brown paper bags toted
   again.

   But children won't fret, the

morrow will come,
and a day
called winter will greet them.

De Lacy Davis
WHAT HAVE I ENTERED?
I entered this world, not by
   choice, but by happen
my immediate response was a
   silent cry, no laughter
I shouted, turned, hollared, and
   screamed
Is this life, death, or is this a
   dream?
regardless of where, how, or what
   I felt
these wrong colored bastards just
   must be dealt
I agreed to stay, yes, in this world
In return he made me "BOY", not
   girl
they say love, yes love, yes, love all
I look around, I see much gall
what heart it takes to be such a
   fool
with the same education, one day
   we'll rule
we'll rule, we'll rave, we'll rock
   this earth
our built in perfection was there
   since birth
oh why! oh why take this away?,
   if not for the fear of superiority
   one day

but listen my friend, let's call it a
   truce
because "the blacker the berry,
   the sweeter the juice"

HOWEVER
if you insist upon being
   narrow—minded
we will kick much ass!
yes, We behind it

some people think that violence
   is cruel
but how do you think america
   came to rule?
example one and example two
both world wars, do they affect
   you?
with this in mind, I must recall
the aggression of you people
not one, but all
when the going gets tough and
   the asses are getting kicked
you go back to using your same
   old tricks, you say—
sit down my friend, let's talk this
   out
you hope to divert my victorious
   bout
but I'll sit and talk to you today,
but you must be slid to respect
   my way

HOWEVER
THINGS ARE LEFT, RIGHT,
   AND SLIGHTLY CENTERED
my happiness comes when you've
   asked "What Have I entered?"

P. T. Zommer
Mothers and Daughters
They smile in their resplendent
   glory,
   And their little girl laughter
   fills my eyes with tears,
For I know within the depths of
   my heart
   That God has lent them to me
   for just a few short years.

Each day becoming more sure of
   who they are and where they're
   going,
   They need me less and less.
Letting go of the ties that bind us,
   Will be difficult I must confess.
But I know just like a spring flower
   They must blossom, flourish
   and grow
Into young ladies choosing their
   own avenues
   Where the sweet nectar of life
   will flow.
I tell them it really doesn't matter
   If they're rich, beautiful or smart,
Just be a nice person,
   And remember to always give
   from the heart.
Be what you are,
   Not what others say you
   should be,
So when you look at yourself in
   the mirror
   You'll like the reflection you see,
And remember, whatever happens,
   You'll have everlasting love
   from me.

Al Stebbins
A YEAR OUT OF TIME
It was a year out of time,
That could have been saved,
That could have been mine,
If your love I hadn't betrayed.

A year out of mind,
One that I detest,
When I was blind,
Without sleep or rest.

A year out of life,
Of my own fault,
One with pain and strife,
To me a lesson, it taught.

A year out of love,
When I was defensless,
Then like a dove,
I came to me senses.

A year out of time,
A year out of mind,
A year out of life,
A year out of love.

Only to I, do I owe this year out
   of time,
The year that I was blue,
The year that I cannot find,
The year without you.

Gary Williams
MEASURED PASSAGE
Life unfolds just one step at a time,
Unhurried, yet persistent it will
   march
In orderly procession through
   each day
Of Summer even though the
   deserts parch.

Life, imprisoned in an hourglass,
Receding cell, relentlessly drifts
   down
Until the final grain is laid to rest
Upon a hill of sand, the final
   crown.

Susan McKay Reale
TOO LATE FOR LOVE
If I had known you long ago
Would I have been your friend
Making vows and promises
Our world would never end
Our innocence has faded

With the passing of the years
It takes a lot more than a kiss

To wipe away our tears.
Somehow I feel cheated
Not knowing you till now
How could fate be so cruel
Why couldn't time allow

A journey back into the days
When our slates were clean
So much of you has passed me by
So much we could have been
It's too late
            Love.

Cleveland C. Matchett
HOME AT LAST
The ship moved into a narrow
   fjord
Bounded by steep cliffs as whales
   spout toward
The distance. Dulmers circle the
   ship, hover bored
On motionless wings then move
   forward in flight toward
Black Auks that dip to the sea.

Large Eider ducks plunge into the
   water as they see,
From their soft breeding places
   on rocks, a need to flee.
Dazzling snow and ice cracked
   and sunk
Into the water which roared as
   chunk
Of ice broke and danced in hunk.

A green belt of plant life lay near
   the water route.
Leif's eyes glanced downward to
   char trout
And then up to the edge of the
   water about
Where the red willow herb grew,
   and sheep fed.

As the ship neared the beach, Eric
   said,
"Remove the carved figure from
   the prow head
So that friendly land spirits can
   come ahead
Near the ship." Leaving behind
   the boat at dock
Leif trailed behind his sire up a
   rock
Path to Brattahlid, home of Eric
   the Red and
First Chieftain of all Greenland.

Yohauen Austerlitz
The Individual and
   Destinies
Betimes most significant—
   relevant to and of the
   individual—the elementary—
   and fundamentals of Life—
   Time—Literature and the
   quatrains—stanzas of fine poetry
The Two Factions in society and
   life being but that they are—
   they of wisdom—dignity and
   pride . . . That care
Or they of moral—intellectual
   fade—evils—degeneracies that
   do not and that of but stupidity

As oft it becomes as so it may
   merely seem—of abandoned
   quays—strands—forsaken
   loves and lives life of one or
   another becomes as but a
   common proven fool's
   nightmare . . .

And fades in time the splendid
poetic dream as insignificant as
the tiny bits of sands in the
shallows of the shoals . . .
Casted to and fro listlessly of but
time and the tide

As know . . . surely know—
acknowledge and realize of but
the mere individual in life and
society . . . What is honorably
to be or honorably not to be of
one's antics—and activity
As so . . . just so becomes to be
noted—known and remembered
or—forever forsaken and
forgotten . . . The lives of
mankind in life and time and
in Destinies—and Eternity

20th Century in Time The
Kingdoms—Nations—
Republics—and Dominions of
progress by individuals of
wisdom—pride—integrity and
of retrogress
By all they without wisdom—
plattitudes—dignity or
compunction of a constant by
blatherskiteism and conceptive
theories
As to The Creation—
Leadership—Authority and
Life. . . Many a far flung
opinion . . .
Each individual of all that in
life—society and time at a
constant junction

Yet . . .

As of even but a Distinguished—
Dignified Civilization of One. . .
Obvious is and becomes the
distinctive—dignified
Individuality
as shall become significant
the individual relativity and
corelativity in Life and
Time and all Destinies

Ponder pensively that
composed—written in those
excellent phrases of expressive
poetry as know . . . surely
know—realize and so
acknowledge . . . that
Of not But One Individual . . .
but rather of each and of all
. . . to mankind and the
children of man in society—
life—and time—and
authority. . . and of Sequential
Relativity . . .
The Destiny

Bernice Ransom
**A Valley Of Freedom and
Of Peace!**
Oh how I've always longed to be,
in the valley of freedom, and of
peace, away from all the
worldly cares, away from all
the burdens, I share!

Away from many accusations
who know! . . Some may be
false, some maybe true, oh God
please stay by my side!
And I know, I'll make it through,
because peace of mind, and
happiness is impossible,
without you!

Oh, How I've always longed to be,

in the valley of freedom and of
peace, a place where the
streams, calmly flow, a place
where there's no more
confusion, noise or uproar!

A place where the grass stay
green, the trees, grow tall, skies
always blue, a place I know
someday I'll find, dear God, if I
walk hand in hand with You!

A place where there's no more,
hatred suspicions or woe!
A place Heavenly Father, I would
truly love to go,
A place where there's joy,
laughter, and fun.
A place where there's no more
lying, stealing, or any need to
run!

Oh, what a wonderful place this
must be!
In the valley of freedom, and of
peace!

Elizabeth J. Kaiser

Elizabeth J. Kaiser
A CHILD
Oh, for all the joys,
children bring to us—
Unblemished love,
having only trust.
So simple do they seem,
but knowledge they do bring—
Not knowing how or why, or
even what it means.
They can bring out the best—
bring out the worst,
All with innocence,
a precious child on earth.
A child can be strong, or
a child can be weak—
Given the love,
a child can be made complete!

Margaret E. Tolley
PRIVILEGED GEMS
A neighbor smiled at me today
Another spoke a word of cheer
A child stopped to talk, and share
A story he wanted me to hear.

The grocer said a nice "hello"
The waitress paused to chat,
The cashier inquired of the service;
On the street the mayor tipped
his hat.

The postman brought a letter
With exciting news I'd waited for,
A phone call cheered me very
much
Wait! My children are at the door!

Trivial? Oh no, they have made

my day,
Don't overlook the "mundane"
things;
Not "mundane" when you
consider—
They are not privileged by
Queens and Kings!

Terri Anne Aubert
FREEDOM
Arms spread wide like an eagle in
flight
Eyes flashing darkly with the
spirit of morning light
To fly forever with the world at
his feet
His heart would soar with
feelings so sweet
There is nothing greater, he once
said
Than to the sky and the sun from
this earth be wed
And the spirit thus fed.

Dot Luria Nadler
ANNALS OF HISTORY
As early as the Bible: if we
assume its realiable
It all started with Abel and Cain:
our bloody history pages stain
Europe had many killings: too
many for top billings
As in 43 B.C. Cicero had Anthony
killed: so Tully Cicero in 51
B.C. was stilled in Pharsalus
Together with his brother
Quentos in the battle of Pompey
On the Ides of March 15th Julius
Ceasar was slain: by Brutus and
Casseus in friendship they claim
All thru the years peace
shattered: bodies battered
In the 6th century by the Jewish
calendar: Jesus Joshua was tried
by a Sanhedrin court: to try
Jesus for heresy, they sought
It triggered a most revolutionary
trend: as a new religion spread
thruout the land no end
Christianity was born, as millions
had their beliefs shorn
The multitude accepted Christ as
their Lord, and their devotion
soared
1431 Joan of Arc was burned at
the stake: her heresy and
scorcery made the populace quake
On may 1471 during a terror reign,
Queen Margerat had Richard of
York at Waterford killed:
Queen Margaret and her son
were killed, by Henry V and
retaliation filled
Then on to 1567, when Mary
Queen of the Scots, had Lord
Darnley Strangeled instead of
shot: so sad to relate: Queen
Mary also met her fate
On our side of the ocean:
history's blood was shed to
stain our pages red
Pres. Lincoln in 1865, there are
no one alive who was a witness
to this tragedy that shook our
land, as this beloved Pres. was
shot by an assasins' hand
Major Rathborn barely escaped
with his life: as he fought
booth for a knife
In 1881 came Pres. Garfield's
chance, as Chas. Gitteau took a
stance,

Shot the Pres. and he fell to the
floor
In Europe the assasins were busy
and more, as a dagger was
plunged into Pres Carot in 1894
Empress Elizabeth, was
assassinated in late 1898
1900 King Humbert of Italy, was
annihilated, by an archist it
was stated
William MacKinley was next: err
his term had begun
June 1914, was to see Francis
Ferdinard slain, it triggered the
biggest war
Again as Serbian Sarjero did the
Arch Duke in: plunged the
world into war and sin
In 1934 Hitler was very busy and
cruel as he started his rule
His deathly horors: shocked the
civilized world with deep sorrows
Dec 9th 1942, as the Japanese
envoys were talking peace terms
A sneak attack on Pearl Harbor
and fire burns
So on to our present day as blood
is shed: John F. Kennedy:
Martin Luther King, & Bobby
now.
Where is all this going to end and
how?
While we permit innocent people
to be slaughtered while we fend
With talks and confabs on the
freedom of the sales of guns no
end.

Carol M. Gibson
COME WALK WITH ME
[*To fields and wods that use to
be and mayflowers I no longer
get to see; That live only in
memory and to Root River
flowing still in Racine, Wisconsin
Where as a child I use to roam;
"places" my heart still call home.*]
Come walk with me
And see the reason
For nature's four seasons.
Come walk through a field
And on to the wood
And frolic in crackling leaves,
Burnished crimson red,
Yellow and gold
From God's changing season.
Stop for a while
And there abide
Brushing the leaves aside,
For there on the ground
Are to be found,
Butternuts, to be cracked
And savored,
Efforts of the tree's
Past year of labor.
At twilight's hour
Smell smoky autumn
Drifting your way
On cool night air
From backyard bonfires.
Here is a season
All its own.

Now you move on
Down the same path
Only now it's all sparkly
Diamonds and glass,
As sun glistens and glitters
Upon snow and ice
Encrusted on wilted
Dried bunches of grass,

Making ice crunchy castles
  Where burrows and dwells
A lonely field mouse
  In glorious domain
With only tiny footprints
  To tell he was there.
The icy cold wind
  Swirls to your nostrils
In breathtaking splendor
  As it dances and twirls,
For now it's winter
  In all of its glory.
Here is a beauty
  All its own.

Now what do you see
  Where dried grass used to be,
Sprouting new shoots
  Of life that will be.
Tiny mayflowers of shell pink,
  Violet and blue
Inching their heads up
  Slightly askew
And into God's view.
  You know the spot
And just where to look
  As year after year
The flowers take root.
  What's this as you walk on?
A tuft of downey
  Barely caught by the eye,
Underneath discovered
  Four newborn rabbits.
You ponder the magic
  Of delicate life
That somehow survives
  So much of the strife.
Gently and carefully
  You cover them over
With a prayer for their safety,
  You're again on your way.
Here is a purpose
  All its own.

Now you walk on
  Through the long summer grass
All dusty and musty
  From this season's new class.
It's a time of grasshopper,
  Cricket and frog.
The humming and buzzing
  Of the insects resound
And you are spellbound,
  As you follow the path
That leads to the creek,
  You're lulled by the sun
That chills with its warmth.
  As you sit on the bank
Just moments away,
  You hear God's song
He gave the river to play.
  Here is the reason
All its own.

Lillian Hendel
THE LIVING DEAD
My mind wanders to the stillness
  of a field
Where wild asters used to stud
  the grass with blue
I seem to hear the echo of a voice
Lamenting over the vast stretches
  where my thoughts cling.
Here, children ran and played and
  called each other yesterday
And people sometimes lazed in
  the earth's firmness
Riffling the crisp grass through
  their fingers
Or gazing into the blue greyness
  of the vast unknown.

Once this field nurtured life
Once a squirrel hid in its
  thickness,
An ant crawled busily as it clung
  to a tree.
Once all was teeming with life
Like a mother who nurtures a
  babe inside her womb.

Not a living creature now on that
  field!
None whose love, whose life,
  whose breath
Once braced the hearts of those
  he knew.

What is that echo I seem to hear?
Where recently the field turned
  battlefield
Of maimed and wounded.
I seem to hear the repeated blows
  against my chest
Or, do I hear the outside
  pounding of a heart?
Now the stench of Death spreads
  an eerie feeling over me.
I walk bent, my ear tuned to
  someone's distress
I cannot feel uplifted.

It matters not where—the source
  of Death is Life
Clocking its rhythmic beat
On its march to that irrevocable
  end.
But when the arrogant hand of
  battle
In Vietnam, Valley Forge, Verdun,
  Gettysburg or Golan Heights
Moves the pace faster
Who am I not to feel the pain?
The deep sore pain I share with
  those mourning?
Mourning their beloved dead
Stripped of a life once dear to
  their very own essence
And dear to those who knew and
  loved and cared.
Who now have gnawing at their
  vitals the agony of loss
Like an amputation of the very
  fibers of their being!

I share the deep sore pain of
  those left mourning.
I think of their moment of
  anguish, their eons of hurt—
Yet hope springs among some
And sometimes cheer—a
  moment of cheer
Like a grace note against a
  solemn chord.

I picture myself on that field
  among the dying,
I go deep into their entrails
Among those struggling to grip
  that last gasp
'Til beaten by Death—they
  surrender.
Yet at times, I'm among those
  who go to Death with grace
As though the secret of the
  unknown were revealed in
  beauty,
I ask myself, "Which would I?"
I cannot know the imponderable
And yet I know a choice I'll be
  called to make.

I'm back with those left living
  again
Living and mourning.

I grope—perhaps to soothe with
  words or comfort with my
  touch.
But I feel empty, hollowed out—
  am endless desert
Like those who once knew
Those Dead!

Donna Marguerite Strough Barnes
TAPESTRY
It was midnight on the ocean
  Upon a radiant sea
And the moon was a ball of
  molten gold
  In a startling tapestry,

The palms were black and slim,
  The beach was shimmering
  white,
And the sea was a gleam of blue
  and gold
  In the magic of the night

While our boat upon the water
  Shone silver in the glow
Of that strangely brilliant moon—
  Not so long ago!

Donald Angus Ewing
HE RODE
It was in the midst of the
  depression I recall,
When he rode into our lives . . .
And affected us all.

We didn't quite notice . . .
He just ambled in,
With an indescribable gait
And an impetuous grin.

The presence was *there*—
More than a man.
You felt he'd move the world . . .
Given a place to stand.

Bout' that time another war came
  along,
Washington numbered it "2"
He got out of the saddle,
Saw the growing concern . . .
And started moving on through.

Patriotism was growing through-
  out the land . . .
People becoming aware and
  taking a stand.

His message to the threatening
  world
Was clear, concise and loud—
Be prepared for a battle,
Because this nation is proud!

History has recorded that
  statement was no fluke . . .
Much of our intestinal fortitude
  and courage
Was triggered by a man we called
  "Duke".

The impetus was freedom for the
  country he loved,
And what we didn't know at the
  time . . .
His life, motivation and health
  were in question,
When he laid his career on the
  line.

He just kept on riding,
Never looked back . . .
In whatever conveyance was
  handy—
Open cockpits to jets . . .
  battleships . . .
Walk or crawl if he must,
As long as we win—
It was dandy.

He was cussed and discussed
When he rode with us,
In times of trouble and strife . . .
One thing for sure
When he finished his chore,
We'd all know what he'd done
  with his life.

But not really . . .

You didn't know of three
  wives . . .
Three lives, if you will,
And the pain and shame of
  divorce. .
The personal scenes and ultimate
  dreams
That produced that incredible
  force.

Doing what you like . . .
Being what you are . . .
Is a difficult thing to do.
He just took a deep breath,
Did what he felt was right . . .
And in the process
Brought a lot of us through.

Finally the conflict was done,
America had won—
Her men had given their best.
In the annuals of war,
Once again, the top score . . .
And now it was time for a rest.

Except one . . .
He rode back to the West.

Rio Bravo, The Alamo,
North to Alaska and back . . .
He'd holler "Move it out, Pilgrim"
And we'd follow his track.

Meanwhile, another movement
  had started,
Words of dissent . . .
A subtle undercurrent of
  revolution.
Once again, there he was . . .
Out front in a tent,
In the process of our evolution.

You'd do well to recall,
The times his back was to the
  wall . . .
But he never gave us a sign.

He kept riding the range,
Never showing the change . . .
That he could see in us all.

He really didn't see
Race, color or creed . . .
Instead, gave us compassion and
  strength
For the common man . . .
In our time of need.

He grew with the changes . . .
Powerful, honest and forthright.
Raw and raucous at times . . .
But we felt secure when we
  turned out the light.

He fought the "Big C" too,
And took it in stride . . .
Was he a reflection?—
A lesson?—
A guide?—

No one's really pondered that
  question . . .
Until now.
That he's died.

He's gone now . . .
But, the images remain—
We've lost the last great
  American hero,

Marion Michael Morrison,
John Wayne.

From one of his many movies
Here's a thought to keep near . . .
After a tight scrape,
A glance at the heavens
And the words "thanks God, I'll
    take it from here."

Lead on pilgrim.

Margaret Tod Ritter
ELEVENTH HOUR
Calling all Angels and
    Archangels. Calling
All Principalities. O Mighty
    Pinions,
Outspeed the Earth, encased in
    flame and falling.
All Powers and all Virtues, all
    Dominions,
In need unparalleled, calling all
    These.
The Earth, Third Planet of the
    Sun, is falling,
Lost to the greatest of the
    Galaxies.

Behold, the Milky Way is raveled.
    Calling
All Thrones to rescue. Calling all
    Cherubim.
The Earth, now wrapped in full,
    consuming fire,
Is falling, falling. Calling all
    Seraphim
For help before the hope of help
    expire.
Calling all Wisdom, Majesty, and
    Laud.
Calling all Mercy in the Name of
    God.

Karl King
SPRIGS
The leaves rustle
over the great pregnancy of this
    landscape
like thoughts rushing
thru waterfilled corridors,
while a young life
shoots from beneath the past,
reaches toward uncertainty,
and grappling with the present,
forces its way into space.
But having won a battle now
only provides time with a future
    victim.
The future moves
with the insensitivity of a raging
    fire,
the appetite of a locust,
and the vision of a rhinocerous.
The old gives way to new,

and the sprigs survive
to make a better bed
for the loves of a locust to fall
    upon.

Lone Bard
THE ANGEL OF MERCY
Softly thru Rotunda's portals,
  In the darkness of the night,
Stealing in with tender mercies
  And a little flash of light;

Coming in with all her kindness.
  With this trust: her vigil keep,
Thru the hours of anxious
    moments,
  O'er her patients while they
    sleep.

So she hears the stifled moaning;
  So she heeds the cry of pain.
So she lifts her weary patient;
  So she hopes when hope seems
    vain.

Thru those long and restless
    nights—
  Angel of Mercy, kind and true,
A patient's heart and a patient's
    soul
  Go out with gratefulness to you.

Dawn breaks on Rotunda's
    portals.
  All is happy, all is bright,
For your faithfulness with your
    nursing
  Saved your patient thru the
    night.

Lone Bard
**Immemoriam To My
    Invalid Brother**
Close to me, so close to me,
  And yet so far away,
But I would pause in retrospection
  And dream of another day.

Thru the silent years come back
  And speak to me again,
For I am sick at heart tonight
  And weary of sorrow's pain.

The charm and beauty of
    Glenmere Pond
  Our raptured souls await,
And just across old Floating
    Bridge,
  The enchanting Faye Estate.

The barrel sunken in the spring,
  With water cool and clear;
The spruce trees with their tears
    of gum—
  In memory'e dream so dear.

Again we walk where breakers
    roar
  And crash on shoreland stone—
But all grows dark! and where are
    you?
  For I am walking alone.

Outside 'tis quiet—dreadfully
    quiet.
  The ground lies covered white.
I never loved you so much, dear
    Oscar,
  Never so much as tonight.

June Hill
A FOND FAREWELL
I know you've been a Pal to me
  Thru all these many years
You've shared my joy and
    gladness,
  My sadness and my tears.

And as you leave your dear old
    home
  And many friends behind—
I pray the Lord in Heaven
  Will give you peace of mind
Health and wealth and happiness
  In everything you do—
'Cuz honestly, dear Pal of mine
  The best I wish for you.
In your new home may joy abide
  For you, and those you love
May the grass stay green, your
    larder blessed,
  And your hearth be filled of
    wood.
And as you rest at eventide
  I hope you'll think of me
As I will surely think of you
  "Pal", always—tenderly.

Betty Lee Reed
ANGEL HORDE
Ye birds, symbols of free
are squoze
outa' my town.
They cheep false gaiety
in walled parks.

Cowering by a ce-ment road
I gulp the deadly fume.

Today's angel horde
Ye peace lovers
Ye guitar addicted
are calling me
to live alive
to breathe clean blue
to watch unpoisoned bees
zoom through sunstreaks.

Jorja Hill-Homko
THE WILLOW
I was a lost and lonely tree,
Swaying without direction.
Changing movement, altering my
    course,
At every gust's suggestion.

One day you could find my
    branches,
Dancing in the breeze.
Reaching out to touch life;
Fulfilling all my needs.

Then gray skies would look down
    on me,
Their eyes dark, as without sleep.
And I'd bend my limbs in silent
    sadness,
A lonely willow left to weep.

At times I'd whirl in total
    confusion,
Waiting for storms to subside.
Wanting just a touch of sun,
To soothe and justify.

And then, at last, you arrived,
Your gaze a gentle ray.
Now I bathe again in peaceful
    moments,
As flowers in the day.

Dorothy Stormer Hancock
The Gifts Of the Children
  [To my four children: Betty
  Lou, Pete, Larry and Susan]
The gifts of the children
Are light, love and fun
Each of the children has
more than one

The wonderful gift of the
Childrens delight
Over each star that falls
In the night

The children give gifts
Of a loving heart
The sun coming up, gives
Them a new start

The children do not
See things as worn
For each new day,
Are the children reborn

Cheryl Chlebowski
MARRIAGE
You casually
mention marriage
and it hangs over me
like a beckoning shroud.
    Damn you!
I want to live!
To embrace the waves
and feel the sand
    in my toes.
Curl up on the couch
  on gray, rainy Sundays,
    exploring Gertrude Stein . . .

Oh, marriage;
Victorian institution—
A legal commodity of
  bona fide slaves.
You seriously speak
  of marriage
    and
I run for my life.

D.M. Ostrowski
GRAY GABLES
House of Gray Gables:
Washed fifty feet ashore,
Covered with salt,
Crescent porch provides cover.
Bare wires hold tight to a globe
Chattering in the wind,
As Nestor sings to the sea;
Rocking to and fro on the
    concave
Pavement of his porch:
Witness to the past.

Petite spotted windows stained
  by memory
Turn now translucent from age.
Plaster walls like the sun
    drenched
Surface of one's body, remain
    wrinkled
And cracked; fading over time.

The sea waves thunder
Against the shore, as the
Shutters clammer in opposition,
Revealing our very existence
Succumb beneath the tide.

B. Brake
HEARTSONG
  I'm quite sure you never guess,
Underneath my words expressed,
  There exists such feeling true,
  Lying there—reserved—for you.
When I say, "And how's your day?"
    What I'd really like to say
Flows within me deep and strong,
  And it sweeps my soul along.
Though I lift my hand and greet
    You, so quietly discreet,
    It's in essence a caress
Oh, so gentle . . . like the breath
  Of the breezes kisssing blooms,
  Waking them to morning tunes
    Of the birds, who pass along
  Joy of a new-day in their songs.
    Really, it's almost too much
  If by chance our fingers touch;
    Then I tremble lest you see

The effect it has on me.
Only one thing do I lack;
Yet one word that holds me back,
Caps the surge of rapture fine,
Scarce restrains but—draws a line.
'Cross it I just cannot go,
Though my heart does urge me so:
I'm unsure and cannot guess—
Underneath your words expressed
Does the feeling I've described
In your heart—for me—reside?

"HELLO THERE; HOW GOES
        YOUR DAY?"
    ("Love you more than I can say!")
"WHAT TIME WILL YOUR
        MEETING START?"
    ("Wild, this beating of my heart!")
"GUESS YOU ATE WITH JOHN
        DOWNTOWN. . . ."
    ("Your smile turns my world
        around!")
"SEEN THE WEATHER—HEARD
        WHAT'S NEW?"
    ("O my love, my love for you!")

Debra Lee Finfrock
MY NEW FRIEND!
With strength and might,
    all through the night . . .
he serves to whet my appetite!
He doth inspire.
    His smile? Chesire!
Could all this be my desire?
To have met him is grand;
    before life was bland!
We can now only hope to expand.
In this new friend I've found;
    simple joy cast around,
and all of life's treasure's abound!

Catherine Beran
HOW MANY TIMES?
How many times have I felt like
    saying "I love you," but did not?
How many times have I thought
    that my gaze revealed my
    thoughts?
I never knew that the windows to
    my soul were masked,—that
    their contents lay untold.

How many times have I pondered
    about how you feel or what
    you think
About the person who is known
    as me? "Capricious? Mercurial?"
    these, I offered.
But you just laughed, then
    smiled, and finally, brushed it
    away.
We dated and met others who
    were dear to the other,—
    avoiding the rest.

How many times have I been
    confused by your paradoxical
    statements?
You were rarely serious, so I, also,
    played the game; mind games
    are so cruel!
We talked seriously—once or
    twice—but it never lasted;
    everything turned to a joke.
At first, our conversations could
    not excape from "Death;" life,
    we totally evaded.
What is it then we have in
    common, other than the time
    we share?

How many times have we made
    fun of the others' quirks

and ways?
We are so different and yet, we
    can empathize with the others'
    past.
I know so little about you—not
    materially, but—the real you.
How dare I ponder! For you know
    even less of me, than I, of you.
I, the pompous self, who will not
    self-disclose, am the greedy one.
For I will not allow you to know
    me, or for me to truly know you.

Ollie Vee Zoller
SIGN RESIGN
Oh! Oh! Oh! Aquarius!
You've stripped me of
    my money
And you've stripped me
    of my pride
Oh! Oh! Oh! Aquarius!
You've stripped me of
    ev'rything
But you've toughened
    up my hide
Oh! Oh! Oh! Aquarius!
I'm charmed by your
    cool-water
For you are my loved
    birth sign
Oh! Oh! Oh! Aquarius!
Hurting from your
    humid-heat
Hereby humbly I RESIGN!

A.K. Sterne
TO EACH HIS OWN
to each his own such is life and
    true
    individual choice such is
    beyond or through

wealth in numbers God-given
    chance yea
    whether to He or of it one
    chooses to prey

words O for others private make
    your choice
    thank God yourself or another
    of voice

communicate relate talk deciphor
    or incline
    believe in yourself you decide of
    what line

those of family no matter 'tis
    family of man
    perhaps no race at least no race
    of who can

Democritus voweled some voices
    they come after
    'all human affairs are worthy
    only of laughter'

as Americans perhaps laugh with
    the world awhile
    soon they may learn the
    seriousness of our smile

owing to you civil we yet may all
    learn
    as has always been meant by
    A.K. Sterne—1980

Nannette R. Laws
To My Son, Love Mommy
Isn't it amazing,
    what God can do?

From mommy and daddy,
    he made you.

A more beautiful baby
    has never been.

And if there is
    he's yet to be seen.

I love you alot
    my dear son.

I'll love you as much
    when my life is done.

Now you're a baby,
    tiny and small.

Someday, you'll be a man
    strong and tall.

You're something real special
    to daddy and me.

But when you're grown
    we'll set you free.

To have a girl
    would be real nice.

But for giving us a boy
    I thank God twice.

You've weren't born
    into fortune and fame.

All we can give you
    is love and our name.

The words I've just said
    are simple but true.

And remember my son,
    mommy loves YOU!!

Paula Rene' Massey
TO A SPECIAL PERSON
I'll love you tomorrow,
I'll love you today,
I'll love you with all my heart,
Forever in every way.
You are my sunshine,
You are my rain,
You are a teardrop,
Without the pain,
You are my buddy,
and my closest friend,
Our friendship will go on forever,
Without no end,
You are a cloud,
From the deep blue sky,
That I care about alot,
Don't ask me why.
You are a special person,
For this I hope you will see,
To care for someone that was
    hurting,
That someone was me!

A. Ivy McBrine
THE WIDOW'S WAR
Paralizing hours still come—
    predictably slow
When I must face the need I
    fear—and yet I
Face it; a yielded pillow in your
    favorite chair.

I do not miss your caresses
    understood by my
Weakened shoulders—half as
    much as my ears can
Ache for one intense whisper;
    familiar

(They all said that it would pass,
    and they all believe that it has).

With eyes tight—I weave through
    narrow memories; obscure
My breathing rises small and
    slow—at the sight of
Distant light and you—once
    more.

Temporarily a frayed half
    shadow; satin black—I

Limp in crippled pantomime;
    grappling across a murky
Cosmic stage of vapour ice blue—
    to greet you . . .

Fusing into a rippling silhouette;
    heartshape—we
Rehearse a private dance to
    memorized ballads of love
And murmur assurances of vows
    eternal; comforting.

The clock chimes rhythms of
    equable dawn; silent grey.
A restless spirit, reluctantly
    adheres to these weak
And senseless limbs—my pulse a
    quivering pool.

Focusing through listless eyes of
    moistened clay; I
Pause—reflecting over glistening
    palms that mirror
An unsteady face; prespiring and
    spider lined

(They all said that it would pass,
    and I lied when I said that it
    had).

Within this chalk carcass;
    withering—the hope child
Savors nothing I've learned of
    liberty, and beckons to
Anticipate a paradise beyond our
    decaying earth; bound
To mushroom . . .

But faith eludes me. How will I
    face Armageddon without
Rocking in your bruised, though
    tangible arms. I do not
Fear to break and bleed—but that
    my final cry will go
Unanswered.

Elisa Koomen
HURRICANE APPROACH
They grey silence
    is audible
it touches my skin
surrounds my body.
My pores are surrendering
    but hesitant.

The silence sets—
    is visible.
Grey-black clouds
    slowly invade
        the pink-grey sunset
    without sun.

Quiet—
    dogs' tails hide
        birds are still
only cars keep running.

Streetstars flash orange
    black overcomes grey,
        hangs above
            shiny flat
                ocean surface.

Trees are breathless
    coconuts hang on

Monsieur Gee Gadwah
APRIL
The smell of April
Has perfume in its rain
And the flowers, sweet of face,
Together strain
At rainbows colors.
And charborne umbrellas
Keep the pavement dry . . .
So I ask why the smell of April
With perfume in its rain

Index of Poets

Today's Greatest Poems

Today's Greatest Poems

Today's Greatest Poems

Index of Photographs

Index of Illustrations